PERFORMANCE EVALUATION REVIEW
Special Issue
Volume 42, No. 1
JUNE 2014

Association for Computing Machinery

Advancing Computing as a Science & Profession

SIGMETRICS 2014

Proceedings of the 2014 ACM SIGMETRICS International Conference on Measurement and Modeling of Computer Systems

June 16–20, 2014, Austin, Texas, USA

Sponsored by:

ACM SIGMETRICS

Supported by:

Akamai, Facebook, Hewlett-Packard, IBM, Intel and WNCG

Association for
Computing Machinery

Advancing Computing as a Science & Profession

The Association for Computing Machinery
2 Penn Plaza, Suite 701
New York, New York 10121-0701

ISBN: 978-1-4503-2789-3 (Digital)

ISBN: 978-1-4503-3088-6 (Print)

Additional copies may be ordered prepaid from:

ACM Order Department
PO Box 30777
New York, NY 10087-0777, USA

Phone: 1-800-342-6626 (USA and Canada)
+1-212-626-0500 (Global)
Fax: +1-212-944-1318
E-mail: acmhelp@acm.org
Hours of Operation: 8:30 am – 4:30 pm ET

Printed in the USA

SIGMETRICS 2014 General Chairs' Welcome

We would like to welcome you to the 2014 SIGMETRICS Conference on Measurement and Modeling of Computer Systems, held in Austin, TX, USA from June 16–20, 2014. SIGMETRICS is the leading research venue in the area of performance analysis of computer systems, and the development and innovative applications of tools towards this end.

SIGMETRICS 2014 is located on The University of Texas at Austin campus. The conference is from Monday, June 16 to Friday, June 20, with the presentations on Monday and Friday focusing on Workshops and Tutorials. The main conference occurs over three days, and consists of 40 regular papers, 29 posters, three hour-long presentations, and an industry mixer. The three hour-long talks are the Sigmetrics Achievement Award lecture (Prof. Francois Baccelli), the Keynote lecture (Prof. Ion Stoica) and the Sigmetrics Rising Star Award lecture (Dr. Florian Simatos). There are three workshops associated with Sigmetrics – GreenMetrics, MAMA and (W-PIN+NetEcon) – each with a great program. We also have three tutorials on Friday – one on Algorithm design for MapReduce and other such environments, another on Bandit games, and the third on Big Data and Privacy.

SIGMETRICS 2014 is brought to you by a great team of organizers, and we would like to thank all of them for their time and dedication. This starts with the TPC Chairs, Bianca Schroeder and Marc Lelarge, who undertook the herculean task of putting together a great program committee, and selecting from the huge number of submissions. Moez Draief put together a great set of workshops and tutorials. Our Registrations Chair – Sewoong Oh – handled participants' registration. Varun Gupta, the student activities chair, coordinated the student travel grants. Our finance chair was Lei Ying, who helped with budget issues. Sara Alouf and Minghua Chen ensured publicity for the conference. Linda Xie helped smooth the many issues with getting papers to publication. Subhashini Krishnasamy set up and kept up-to-date the conference webpage. We would especially like to thank our industry supporters Akamai, Facebook, HP, IBM and Intel for their generosity and continuing engagement with SIGMETRICS. Finally, thanks to everyone at ACM for helping guide us through this process.

Welcome to SIGMETRICS 2014 and Austin, TX!

Sujay Sanghavi and Sanjay Shakkottai
SIGMETRICS 2014 General Chairs
University of Texas, Austin

Program Chairs' Welcome

It is our pleasure to welcome you to SIGMETRICS 2014. SIGMETRICS is the flagship conference of the ACM special interest group for the computer systems performance evaluation community.

This year's conference continues the long-standing SIGMETRICS tradition to publish the highest-quality research on the development and application of state-of-the-art, broadly applicable analytic, simulation, and measurement-based performance evaluation techniques. We are pleased to present a diverse set of papers in areas such as sensor, mobile and wireless networks, queuing and scheduling, social networks, memory technologies, large-scale measurement studies, system tracing and monitoring, data center resource provisioning and energy management. Our authors hail from 13 countries on 4 continents and represent both academia and industry.

SIGMETRICS 2014 received 237 submissions, the second highest number since the founding of this SIG. Of these, we accepted 40 papers, the largest in the history of the conference, while still maintaining a highly competitive acceptance rate of 16.8%. During the review process, the Program Committee provided 4-6 reviews for each paper and made extensive use of HotCRP's Comment feature for online discussions. The Program Committee then met in person in a 1.5-day meeting on February 7-8, 2014, in Toronto, Canada, and selected 40 papers to be included as full papers in the technical program. In addition, 31 papers were invited as 2-page posters, and the authors of 30 of these papers accepted our invitation. As an experiment, we invited for the first time also all authors of full papers to present a poster version of their paper during one of the breaks at the conference to foster interaction between authors and attendees. We used Eddie Kohler's excellent HotCRP software to manage all stages of the review process, from submission to author notification.

We wish to thank the many people who contributed to this conference. First and foremost, we are grateful to all the authors who submitted the results of their research to SIGMETRICS 2014. We had a wide range of high-quality work from which to choose our program. We would also like to thank the attendees of SIGMETRICS 2014 and future readers of these papers. Together with the authors, you form the SIGMETRICS community and make this research area vibrant and fun. We also wish to thank all conference organizers for their work, in particular our Webmaster, Subhashini Krishnasamy, and the general chairs, Sanjay Shakkottai and Sujay Sanghavi, who have been a great pleasure to collaborate with. We also extend our thanks to the members of the SIGMETRICS board, who provided invaluable advice and feedback. Thanks!

Finally, we wish to thank our Program Committee for their many hours of hard work in reviewing and discussing the submissions. We were privileged to work with this knowledgeable and dedicated group of researchers. Together with our external reviewers, they wrote nearly 1,000 thoughtful and meticulous reviews. Their reviews, and their thorough and conscientious deliberations at the PC meeting, contributed significantly to the quality of our decisions.

It has been an honor and a pleasure to serve as this year's program co-chairs. We look forward to an interesting and enjoyable conference!

Marc Lelarge
SIGMETRICS'14 Program Co-chair
INRIA

Bianca Schroeder
SIGMETRICS'14 Program Co-chair
University of Toronto

Table of Contents

Keynote Address

Session 4

Session 5

Session 6

Session 7

Session 8

Session 9

Poster Session 1

Poster Session 2

SIGMETRICS 2014 Conference Organization

General Chairs: Sujay Sanghavi *(The University of Texas at Austin)*
Sanjay Shakkottai *(The University of Texas at Austin)*

Program Chairs: Marc Lelarge *(INRIA, France)*
Bianca Schroeder (*University of Toronto*)

Publicity Chairs: Sara Alouf *(INRIA, France)*
Minghua Chen (*The Chinese University of Hong Kong*)

Workshop Chair: Moez Draief *(Imperial College London)*

Finance Chair: Lei Ying *(Arizona State University)*

Publications Chair: Jiang (Linda) Xie *(University of North Carolina at Charlotte)*

Registration Chair: Sewoong Oh *(University of Illinois at Urbana-Champaign)*

Webmaster: Subhashini Krishnasamy *(The University of Texas at Austin)*

Student Activities Chair: Varun Gupta (*The University of Chicago*)

Steering Committee Chair: John C. S. Lui *(The Chinese University of Hong Kong)*

Program Committee: Samuli Aalto *(Aalto University)*
Animashree Anandkumar *(University of California Irvine)*
Ricardo Bianchini *(Rutgers University and Microsoft)*
Thomas Bonald *(Telecom ParisTech)*
Sem Borst *(Alcatel-Lucent Bell Labs & Eindhoven University of Technology)*
Giuliano Casale *(Imperial College London)*
Claudio E. Casetti *(Politecnico di Torino)*
Ranveer Chandra *(Microsoft Research)*
Minghua Chen *(The Chinese University of Hong Kong)*
Yuan Chen *(HP Labs)*
Florin Ciucu *(University of Warwick)*
Ton Dieker *(Georgia Institute of Technology)*
Moez Draief *(Imperial College London)*
Tudor Dumitras *(University of Maryland at College Park)*
Ayalvadi Ganesh *(University of Bristol)*
Bruno Gaujal *(INRIA)*
Anshul Gandhi *(IBM Research/Stony Brook University)*
Brighten Godfrey *(University of Illinois at Urbana-Champaign)*
David A. Goldberg *(Georgia Institute of Technology)*
Roch Guerin *(Washington University in Saint Louis)*

Program Committee (continued):

Bruce Hajek *(University of Illinois at Urbana-Champaign)*
Mor Harchol-Balter *(Carnegie Mellon University)*
Benny Van Houdt *(University of Antwerp)*
Stratis Ioannidis *(Technicolor)*
Matthieu Jonckheere *(Universidad de Buenos Aires)*
Kim Keeton *(HP Labs)*
Orran Krieger *(Boston University)*
Richard La *(University of Maryland at College Park)*
Benjamin Lee *(Duke University)*
Marc Lelarge *(INRIA-ENS)*
Minghong Lin *(Facebook)*
Patrick Loiseau *(EURECOM)*
John C.S. Lui *(The Chinese University of Hong Kong)*
Richard Ma *(National University of Singapore)*
Peter Marbach *(University of Toronto)*
Laurent Massoulie *(INRIA-MSR)*
David Meisner *(Facebook)*
Sean Meyn *(University of Florida)*
Masakiyo Miyazawa *(Tokyo University of Science)*
Erich Nahum *(IBM Research)*
Thu Nguyen *(Rutgers University)*
Jason Nieh *(Columbia University)*
Sewoong Oh *(University of Illinois at Urbana-Champaign*
Alina Oprea *(RSA Laboratories)*
Shankar Pasupathy *(NetApp)*
Alexandre Proutiere *(KTH)*
Gaurav Raina *(Indian Institute of Technology (IIT) Madras)*
Kavita Ramanan *(Brown University)*
Philippe Robert *(INRIA)*
Stefan Saroiu *(Microsoft Research)*
Bianca Schroeder *(University of Toronto)*
Abhishek Sharma *(NEC Labs)*
Evgenia Smirni *(The College of William & Mary)*
Christopher Stewart *(Ohio State University)*
Alexander (Sasha) Stolyar *(Bell Labs)*
Vijay Subramanian *(Northwestern University)*
Patrick Thiran *(EPFL)*
Bhuvan Urgaonkar *(Pennsylvania State University)*
Maaike Verloop *(IRIT-CNRS)*
Milan Vojnovic *(Microsoft Research)*
Jean Walrand *(UC Berkeley)*
Haifeng Yu *(National University of Singapore)*
Ding Yuan *(University of Toronto)*
Xiaodong Zhang *(Ohio State University)*
Xia Zhou *(Dartmouth College)*

Sponsor:

Supporters:

Rumor Source Detection with Multiple Observations: Fundamental Limits and Algorithms

Zhaoxu Wang
Dept. of EEIS
University of Science and Technology of China
Hefei, China
wzxboa@mail.ustc.edu.cn

Wenxiang Dong
Dept. of EEIS
University of Science and Technology of China
Hefei, China
javin@mail.ustc.edu.cn

Wenyi Zhang
Dept. of EEIS
University of Science and Technology of China
Hefei, China
wenyizha@ustc.edu.cn

Chee Wei Tan
College of Science and Engineering
City University of Hong Kong
Hong Kong SAR, China
cheewtan@cityu.edu.hk

ABSTRACT

This paper addresses the problem of a single rumor source detection with multiple observations, from a statistical point of view of a spreading over a network, based on the susceptible-infectious model. For tree networks, multiple sequential observations for one single instance of rumor spreading cannot improve over the initial snapshot observation. The situation dramatically improves for multiple independent observations. We propose a unified inference framework based on the union rumor centrality, and provide explicit detection performance for degree-regular tree networks. Surprisingly, even with merely two observations, the detection probability at least doubles that of a single observation, and further approaches one, i.e., reliable detection, with increasing degree. This indicates that a richer diversity enhances detectability. For general graphs, a detection algorithm using a breadth-first search strategy is also proposed and evaluated. Besides rumor source detection, our results can be used in network forensics to combat recurring epidemic-like information spreading such as online anomaly and fraudulent email spams.

Categories and Subject Descriptors

G.2.2 [**Graph Theory**]: Graph algorithms, Network problems

General Terms

Analytical modeling, Anomaly detection, Social networks

SIGMETRICS'14, June 16-20, 2014, Austin, Texas, USA.

ACM 978-1-4503-2789-3/14/06 ...$15.00.
http://dx.doi.org/10.1145/2591971.2591993.

Keywords

Graph networks, inference algorithms, maximum likelihood detection, multiple observations, rumor spreading

1. INTRODUCTION

Identification of malicious information sources in a network, be it in the case of an online spam spreading in the Internet or a misinformation or rumor propagating in an online social network, allows timely quarantine of the epidemic-like spreading to limit the damage caused. For example, law enforcement agencies may be interested in identifying the perpetrators of false information used to manipulate the market prices of certain stocks. It is challenging to understand how the source of the spreading can be identified in a reliable manner from a number of snapshot observations of the spread conditions, e.g., infected nodes in virus propagation or users possessing the rumor, and the underlying connectivity of the network. This can lead to a fundamental understanding of the role of network in aiding or constraining epidemic-like spreading [1, 2].

In this paper, we consider the issue of reliably detecting a single rumor source with multiple observations from a statistical point of view of a spreading. Our goal is to find the rumor source in order to control and prevent network risks based on limited information about the network structure and multiple snapshot observations.

1.1 Related Works

This network inference problem is a combinatorial problem that is generally hard to solve, and has remained surprisingly unexplored until late. In the seminal work [3, 4], Shah and Zaman studied the rumor source detection problem, and conducted asymptotic performance analysis of the Maximum Likelihood (ML) detector for a single rumor source using the susceptible-infectious (SI) model. Then, this work was extended in [5] for random graphs. The authors in [6] studied the Maximum A Posteriori (MAP) detection based on various suspect set characteristics. In [7], the authors investigated the detection of multiple rumor sources in the SI model. In

[8], the authors considered the case where nodes randomly report their infection state in SI spreading, which means we only get an incomplete picture of the infection state. Besides, other types of models have also been considered in [9]-[11]. In [9], the authors analyzed the detection under susceptible-infected-recovered (SIR) spreading, and proposed a probabilistic method based on sample path estimation. In [10], the authors proposed an approach based on message passing algorithms to detect a single rumor source in the SIR model. The authors in [11] studied the detection in susceptible-infected-susceptible (SIS) spreading of regular tree networks.

1.2 Our Contributions

One key question in rumor source detection is to determine the right number of observations or adaptive measurements such that the source can be correctly detected. The existing works, however, rely critically on the assumption that only a single snapshot observation is made in the detection. In practice, there can possibly be multiple observations of a *recurrent* online anomaly, e.g., fraudulent email spams and recurring malcode, which are usually originated from a common culprit. *Dependent* and *independent* multiple observations, respectively, refer to snapshot observations made on different spreading instances (from the same single source) that are dependent and independent from one another. Obviously, the interdependency between observations and network structure affect detectability. Single observation detection does not leverage all degrees of freedom and can perform poorly. Indeed, the multiple observations add an interesting dimension to detecting the source reliably. Can we do more with less by having as few observations as possible and yet enough to provide detectability guarantees? This paper answers this question. To the best of our knowledge, there has been no work done on rumor source detection with multiple observations.

In summary, the contributions of the paper are as follows:

(1) We show that, in SI spreading over a tree network, multiple *dependent* observations, i.e., sequential observations for a single instance of rumor spreading, cannot improve detectability over the initial snapshot observation. On the other hand, we show that multiple *independent* observations lead to dramatic improvement in detectability.

(2) For multiple *independent* observations in a tree network, we propose a unified detection framework based on a graph topological quantity called union rumor centrality and design an efficient algorithm to identify the union rumor center. For degree-regular trees, we characterize and evaluate the exact and asymptotic detection probability.

(3) For general graphs, we extend our detection framework by applying a breadth-first search (BFS) strategy to obtain induced trees from multiple observations. Our numerical results show that the algorithm performs more effectively than that for a single observation in small-world and scale-free networks.

1.3 Organization

The structure of this paper is as follows. We introduce the system model in Section 2. In Section 3, we study the problem with multiple sequential observations. In Section 4, we study the problem with multiple independent observations, and propose a detection framework for tree networks. We analytically characterize the detection performance for regular tree networks. In Section 5, for tree-type networks, we propose algorithms to calculate the exact correct detection probability and identify the union rumor center under multiple independent observations. We extend our framework to the general network case in Section 6. In Section 7, we numerically evaluate the performance of our algorithms. Section 8 provides proofs of the analytical results. We conclude the paper in Section 9.

2. MODEL AND PRELIMINARIES

In this section, we introduce the SI rumor spreading model, and describe the ML detector for the rumor source in regular trees, general trees and graphs, respectively. We list the key parameters used in the paper in Table 1.

Table 1: Key Terms and Symbols

Symbol	Definition
δ	node degree
s^*	original rumor source
$\widehat{s}$	detected rumor source
$T_u^{s^*}$	subtree rooted at node u, with node s^* as source
G_{n_j} $(1 \leq j \leq k)$	a snapshot observation of n_j infected nodes for the jth rumor spreading
$\{\cap G_{1\to k}\}$	the intersection of observations, i.e., $\{G_{n_1} \cap \ldots \cap G_{n_k}\}$
$\{\cup G_{1\to k}\}$	the union of observations, i.e., $\{G_{n_1} \cup \ldots \cup G_{n_k}\}$
$R(u, G_n)$	rumor centrality of node u in G_n
$R_k(u, G_{n_1} \ldots G_{n_k})$	union rumor centrality of node u in $\{\cap G_{1\to k}\}$
$\mathbf{P}_G(\cdot)$	probability distribution of an infection sample in a rumor spreading process, or of an infection sample equivalently constructed using the Pólya's urn model
$P_c(\cdot)$	correct detection probability
$P_e(\cdot)$	error detection probability

2.1 Rumor Spreading Model

We consider a network of nodes modeled as an undirected graph $G=(V, E)$, where the set of vertices V represents the nodes in the network, and the set of edges E represents the links between the network nodes. We assume V is countably infinite in order to avoid boundary effects and consider the case where initially only one node $s^* \in V$ is the rumor source.

We use a variant of the SIR model for the rumor spreading known as the SI model, where a node that is infected with the rumor retains it forever. A rumor is spread from node i to node j if and only if there is an edge between them, i.e., if $(i, j) \in E$. Let τ_{ij} be the spreading time from i to j for all $(i, j) \in E$, which are mutually independent and have exponential distribution with parameter λ. Without loss of generality, take $\lambda=1$.

2.2 ML Rumor Source Detector

(1) ML Detector

Suppose that a rumor originates from a node $s^* \in V$. We observe the network G at some time and find n infected nodes, which are collectively denoted by G_n. Our goal is to construct a detector to detect a node $\hat{s}$ as the rumor source s^*. The ML detector of s^* given G_n maximizes the correct detection

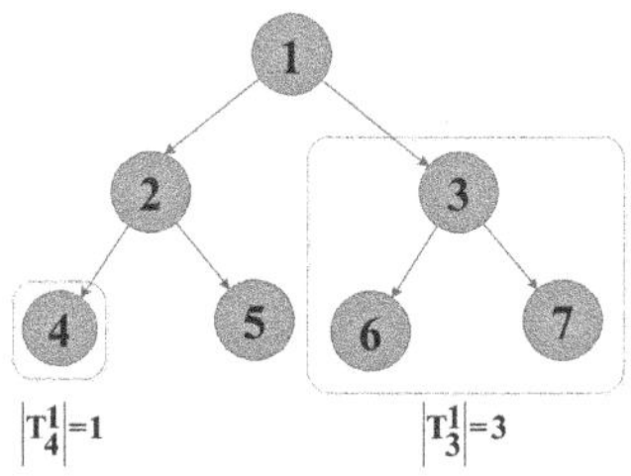

Figure 1: Illustration of subtree $T_u^{s^*}$

probability and is given by

$$\widehat{s} \in \arg\max_{s^*\in G_n} \mathbf{P}_G\left(G_n \mid s^*\right), \tag{1}$$

where $\mathbf{P}_G\left(G_n|s^*\right)$ is the probability of observing G_n assuming s^* to be the rumor source.

(2) Exact ML detector for regular trees

In general, the evaluation of $\mathbf{P}_G\left(G_n|s^*\right)$ is computationally prohibitive since it is related to counting the number of linear extensions of a partially ordered set. By leveraging the concept of rumor centrality, first introduced in [4], the exact ML detector for a regular tree is given by

$$\widehat{s} \in \arg\max_{s^*\in G_n} \mathbf{P}_G\left(G_n \mid s^*\right) = \arg\max_{s^*\in G_n} R(s^*, G_n), \tag{2}$$

where $R(s^*, G_n)$ is the rumor centrality of node s^* in G_n and can be evaluated by

$$R(s^*, G_n) = (n-1)! \prod_{u\in \text{child}(s^*)} \frac{R(s^*, T_u^{s^*})}{|T_u^{s^*}|!}, \tag{3}$$

where $T_u^{s^*}$ denotes the subtree rooted at node u, with node s^* as the source, and $|T_u^{s^*}|$ denotes the number of nodes in the subtree $T_u^{s^*}$; e.g., see Fig. 1.

In the following analysis, we will abuse notation and use $T_u^{s^*}$ to refer to both a subtree and the number of nodes in the subtree.

(3) Approximate detector

For general cases, intuitively, a rumor tends to travel from the source to each infected node along a minimum-distance path [4], and this serves, along with the rumor centrality, as a reasonable and useful heuristic for constructing approximate detectors. For general trees, an approximate detector is thus given by [4]

$$\widehat{s} \in \arg\max_{s^*\in G_n} P(\sigma_s^* \mid s^*)\cdot R(s^*, G_n), \tag{4}$$

where σ_s^* represents the breadth-first search (BFS) ordering of nodes in the tree.

For general graphs, we approximate the diffusion tree by a BFS tree; that is, we assume that if node s^* was the source, then the rumor spreads along a BFS tree rooted at s^*, denoted by $T_b(s^*)$. So an approximate detector is given by

$$\widehat{s} \in \arg\max_{s^*\in G_n} P(\sigma_s^* \mid s^*)\cdot R(s^*, T_b(s^*)), \tag{5}$$

where σ_s^* represents the BFS ordering of nodes in the BFS tree $T_b(s^*)$.

Besides, a message-passing algorithm has been proposed in [4] to compute the rumor centralities for all the nodes in a general tree with n nodes using only $O(n)$ computation steps.

3. SEQUENTIAL OBSERVATIONS

In this section, we first define the ML rumor source detector under multiple sequential observations for one single instance of rumor spreading for general trees. Then, we analyze the performance of the ML detector and show that sequential observations cannot help improve the correct detection probability for any general tree.

3.1 ML Detection

Suppose that a rumor originates from a node $s^*\in V$. We observe the network at k different times. In the jth $(1\leq j\leq k)$ observation, we find n_j infected nodes carrying the rumor, which are collectively denoted by G_{n_j}. Without loss of generality, assume observation is in turn according to the time order. Due to the SI spreading, G_{n_j} $(1\leq j\leq k)$ must form a connected subgraph and contain at least a node, which is the rumor source, i.e., $s^* \in G_{n_1} \subseteq G_{n_2} \ldots \subseteq G_{n_k}$. Note that we assume a uniform prior probability of the source node among all the nodes in the network. Our goal is to construct a detector under k sequential observations to detect a node $\hat{s}$ as the rumor source s^*.

For clarity, in the following analysis, we denote the sets $\{G_{n_1} \cap \ldots \cap G_{n_k}\}$ and $\{G_{n_1} \cup \ldots \cup G_{n_k}\}$ by $\{\cap G_{1\to k}\}$ and $\{\cup G_{1\to k}\}$, respectively. Then, the ML detector under multiple sequential observations maximizes the correct detection probability and is given by

$$\begin{aligned}\widehat{s} \in& \arg\max_{s^*\in\{\cap G_{1\to k}\}} \mathbf{P}_G(G_{n_1}, G_{n_2}, \ldots G_{n_k} \mid s^*)\\ =&\arg\max_{s^*\in\{\cap G_{1\to k}\}} \mathbf{P}_G(G_{n_1}|s^*)\cdot\mathbf{P}_G(G_{n_2}|s^*,G_{n_1})\cdot\\ &\mathbf{P}_G(G_{n_3}|s^*,G_{n_1},G_{n_2})\cdots\mathbf{P}_G(G_{n_k}|s^*,G_{n_1},\ldots,G_{n_{k-1}}).\end{aligned} \tag{6}$$

3.2 Impossibility Result

For ML detector under multiple sequential observations for general trees, it is intuitively apparent that only the first observation is useful in detecting the rumor source. This intuition is made formal in the following proposition.

PROPOSITION 1. *Suppose the rumor spreads on a general tree-type graph as per the SI model, multiple sequential observations for one single instance of rumor spreading cannot improve detectability over the first snapshot observation.*

Remark: The impossibility of performance improvement demonstrates the need for early detection.

The argument of Proposition 1 basically follows from the fact that any $\mathbf{P}_G(G_{n_j}|s^*,G_{n_1},G_{r_2}\ldots G_{n_{j-1}})$ $(2\leq j\leq k)$ is conditionally independent of the source s^*. Hence, from (6), the ML detector of s^* under arbitrary k sequential observations becomes

$$\begin{aligned}\widehat{s} \in& \arg\max_{s^*\in\{G_{n_1}\cap G_{n_2}\ldots\cap G_{n_k}\}} \mathbf{P}_G(G_{n_1}, G_{n_2}, \ldots, G_{n_k} \mid s^*)\\ =& \arg\max_{s^*\in\{G_{n_1}\cap G_{n_2}\ldots\cap G_{n_k}\}} \mathbf{P}_G(G_{n_1} \mid s^*).\end{aligned} \tag{7}$$

Therefore, for general tree graphs, the ML detector under sequential observations $(G_{n_1}, \ldots G_{n_k})$ is nothing but the ML detector based on the first observation G_{n_1}. This means that multiple sequential observations cannot help improve the correct detection probability.

4. INDEPENDENT OBSERVATIONS

In this section, we describe the ML rumor source detector under multiple independent observations, which will be shown to be equivalent to a topological quantity that we call the union rumor centrality, for regular tree graphs. Then we leverage the concept of union rumor centrality to develop analytical performance results of the ML detector for regular tree-type networks.

4.1 ML Detection

Suppose k different rumors originate from a common node in the network, regarded as k times independent rumor spreading with the same rumor source. For the jth $(1 \le j \le k)$ rumor spreading, at some time, we observe a snapshot of n_j infected nodes carrying the rumor, which are collectively denoted by G_{n_j}. For arbitrary k independent observations, due to the SI model, each G_{n_j} $(1 \le j \le k)$ must form a connected subgraph and the rumor source must belong to $\{G_{n_1} \cap \ldots G_{n_k}\}$. We assume a uniform prior probability of the source node among all the nodes in the network. The ML detector under multiple independent observations $G_{n_1},\ldots,G_{n_k}$ maximizes the correct detection probability, as given by

$$\begin{aligned}\hat{s} \in & \underset{s^* \in \{G_{n_1} \cap G_{n_2} \ldots \cap G_{n_k}\}}{\arg\max} \mathbf{P}_G(G_{n_1}, G_{n_2}, \ldots, G_{n_k} \mid s^*) \\ = & \underset{s^* \in \{G_{n_1} \cap G_{n_2} \ldots \cap G_{n_k}\}}{\arg\max} \mathbf{P}_G(G_{n_1}|s^*) \cdots \mathbf{P}_G(G_{n_k}|s^*). \quad (8)\end{aligned}$$

For a δ-regular tree, since all nodes have the same degree, every permitted permutation has the same probability that is independent of the source [4]. Hence, we have

$$\mathbf{P}_G(G_n \mid s^*) = \sum_{\sigma \in \Omega(s^*, G_n)} P(\sigma|s^*) = R(s^*, G_n) P(\sigma|s^*), \quad (9)$$

where $\Omega(s^*, G_n)$ is the set of all permitted permutations starting with s^* and resulting in G_n, and $P(\sigma|s^*) = \prod_{i=1}^{n-1} \frac{1}{di-2(i-1)} \equiv P(d, n)$.

Then, by substituting (9) into (8), the ML detector under arbitrary k observations for a regular tree becomes

$$\begin{aligned}\hat{s} &= \underset{s^* \in \{G_{n_1} \cap \ldots G_{n_k}\}}{\arg\max} \Big(R(s^*, G_{n_1}) \cdots R(s^*, G_{n_k})\Big) \Big(P(d, n_1) \cdots P(d, n_k)\Big) \\ &= \underset{s^* \in \{G_{n_1} \cap \ldots G_{n_k}\}}{\arg\max} R(s^*, G_{n_1}) \cdots R(s^*, G_{n_k}). \quad (10)\end{aligned}$$

Note that in the model we do not require that all the rumors originate simultaneously from the original source, or that all the snapshots are observed simultaneously. In fact these k rumor spreadings can be completely asynchronous, as long as they are independent.

4.2 Union Rumor Centrality for Regular Trees

We need to evaluate $R(s^*, G_{n_1}) \cdots R(s^*, G_{n_k})$ in (10) for multiple independent observations in a regular tree network. We call this quantity the union rumor centrality, denoted by $R_k(s^*, G_{n_1} \ldots G_{n_k})$, which enables efficient implementation of the ML detector. Note that the rumor source $s^* \in \{\cap G_{1 \to k}\}$. If $R_k(s^*, G_{n_1} \ldots G_{n_k}) \ge R_k(u, G_{n_1} \ldots G_{n_k})$ for all $u \in \{\cap G_{1 \to k}\}$, then s^* is called a union rumor center. For the union rumor center, we have the following proposition.

PROPOSITION 2. *For a rumor source s^* with m $(0 \le m \le \delta)$ neighbors in $\{\cap G_{1 \to k}\}$, given multiple independent observations $G_{n_1}, \ldots, G_{n_k}$ of $n_1, \ldots, n_k$ nodes respectively, then:*
(1) When $m = 0$, there is only one node in $\{\cap G_{1 \to k}\}$, which is the rumor source s^*; when $1 \le m \le \delta$, node s^* is a union rumor center, if and only if for any $u \in \{\cap G_{1 \to k} \setminus s^*\}$, we have

$$\frac{T^{s^*}_{u,G_{n_1}} \cdots T^{s^*}_{u,G_{n_k}}}{(n_1 - T^{s^*}_{u,G_{n_1}}) \cdots (n_k - T^{s^*}_{u,G_{n_k}})} \le 1, \quad (11)$$

where $T^{s^*}_{u,G_{n_i}}$ denotes the number of nodes in $T^{s^*}_{u,G_{n_i}}$ of the observation G_{n_i} $(1 \le i \le k)$.
(2) If there is a node s^* such that s^* has the maximum union rumor centrality among all its neighbors in $\{\cap G_{1 \to k} \setminus s^*\}$, then s^* is a union rumor center.
(3) Furthermore, the intersection $\{\cap G_{1 \to k}\}$ under multiple independent observations has two union rumor centers, say, s^* and s', if and only if

$$T^{s^*}_{s',G_{n_1}} \cdots T^{s^*}_{s',G_{n_k}} = (n_1 - T^{s^*}_{s',G_{n_1}}) \cdots (n_k - T^{s^*}_{s',G_{n_k}}), \quad (12)$$

and these two nodes are neighbors. In addition, there can be at most two union rumor centers in $\{\cap G_{1 \to k}\}$.

Remark: The union rumor center generalizes the rumor center introduced in [4]. Notably, the union rumor center is a graph topological quantity that has a more restricted range $\{\cap G_{1 \to k}\}$ than each observation G_{n_j} $(1 \le j \le k)$. Due to space limit, we only present a part of the proof of Proposition 2(3).

Proof of Proposition 2(3)

Here, rewriting the assumptions, we will prove that neighboring nodes s^* and s' with equal union rumor centrality are two union rumor centers. For this purpose we need the following lemma, which indicates that the error detection events are all disjoint.

LEMMA 1. *For any node s^* with m $(0 \le m \le \delta)$ neighbors in $\{\cap G_{1 \to k}\}$, i.e., $s^*_1, \ldots, s^*_m$, let random variable X_{i,n_j} be the number of nodes in subtree $T^{s^*}_{s^*_i,G_{n_j}}$ of a snapshot observation G_{n_j} $(1 \le i \le m, 1 \le j \le k)$. Then, there is at most a neighbor of the node s^* satisfying*

$$\prod_{j=1}^{k} \left(\frac{x_{i,n_j}}{n_j}\right) \ge \prod_{j=1}^{k} \left(1 - \frac{x_{i,n_j}}{n_j}\right), \ i \in [1, m]. \quad (13)$$

Based on Lemma 1, since s' and s^* are neighbors that have the same union rumor centrality, while s' is the only neighbor of s^* with a larger union rumor centrality than all other neighbors, s^* also has a larger union rumor centrality than its neighbors, thus leading to Proposition 2(3).

4.3 Detection Performance for Regular Trees

This section examines the performance of the ML detector leveraging the union rumor center. We characterize analytically the performance for finite and asymptotically large number of nodes, for regular trees with an arbitrary degree δ. We present the proofs in Section 8.

The following two theorems study the special cases of node degree $\delta = 2$ and 3.

THEOREM 1. *Suppose the rumor spreads on a regular tree with degree $\delta=2$, i.e., a linear network, given two independent observations G_{n_1} and G_{n_2}, then:*
(1) When $n_2=n_1=n\geq 1$, the correct detection probability P_c is given by

$$P_c = \binom{2n}{n} 2^{-2n+1}, \qquad n \geq 1. \tag{14}$$

As $n_1=n_2=n\to\infty$, P_c asymptotically scales like $\frac{2}{\sqrt{\pi n}}$.
(2) When $n_1 = 2$, $n_2 > n_1$, P_c is given by

$$P_c = \left\{ \sum_{m=0}^{\lfloor \frac{n_2}{n_1} \rfloor} \binom{n_2-1}{m} - \mathbb{I}\Big(\frac{n_2}{n_1}\Big) \binom{n_2-1}{\lfloor \frac{n_2}{n_1} \rfloor} \right\} \cdot 2^{-n_2+1},$$

where

$$\mathbb{I}(\frac{n_2}{n_1}) = \begin{cases} 1 & \frac{n_2}{n_1} \in Z \\ 0 & others. \end{cases} \tag{15}$$

(3) When $n_2 > n_1 \geq 3$, P_c is given by

$$P_c = \left\{ \sum_{m=0}^{n_1-1} \left[\binom{n_2-1}{\lfloor m\frac{n_2}{n_1} \rfloor} \binom{n_1}{m} + S_{n_2-1}(m) \binom{n_1-1}{m} \right] -2\binom{n_2-1}{\lfloor \frac{n_2}{n_1} \rfloor} - \mathbb{I}\Big(\frac{n_2}{n_1}\Big) \binom{n_2-1}{\lfloor \frac{n_2}{n_1} \rfloor} \right\} \cdot 2^{-(n_1+n_2)+2},$$

where $S_{n_2-1}(m) = \sum_{i=\lfloor m\frac{n_2}{n_1} \rfloor+1}^{\lfloor (m+1)\frac{n_2}{n_1} \rfloor-1} \binom{n_2-1}{i}$.

Remark: For linear networks, the above results provide exact correct detection probability under two independent observations. The performance does not improve much compared with that of a single observation in [4] and [6]; also see Fig. 4(a).

In the following, we see that when the degree is greater than two, multiple independent observations dramatically boost the performance.

THEOREM 2. *Suppose the rumor spreads on a regular tree with degree $\delta=3$, given two independent observations G_{n_1} and G_{n_2}, then:*
(1) When $n_1 = n, n_2 = qn$ ($q\in Z^+$), P_c is given by

$$P_c = \frac{qn+q+2}{2(qn+1)}. \tag{16}$$

(2) When $n_1 = n, n_2 = qn+1$ ($q\in Z^+$), (16) still holds.
(3) When $n_1 = n, n_2 = qn + t$ ($q \in Z^+$), $t < n$, we have

$$P_c = \frac{qn+q+2}{2(qn+1)} + \Delta P_c, \tag{17}$$

with $\Delta P_c < \frac{1}{2(qn+1)}$. This demonstrates that as $n \to \infty$, the asymptotic correct detection probability $\lim_{n\to\infty} P_c = 1/2$.

Remark: Note that in [4], as $\delta \to \infty$, P_c asymptotically approaches 0.307 under a single observation, while here even with only two independent observations, we achieve $\lim_{n\to\infty} P_c = 1/2$ for $\delta = 3$.

For general k, the following theorem describes certain basic properties of the correct detection probability pertaining to its monotonicity.

THEOREM 3. *Suppose the rumor spreads on a δ-regular tree, for k independent observations $G_{n_1}, \ldots, G_{n_k}$, then:*
(1) The correct detection probability P_c is increasing with δ. As δ grows sufficiently large, P_c approaches 1.
(2) When fixing $n_1, \ldots, n_{k-1}$, P_c is non-increasing with the number of nodes of the kth observation G_{n_k}, i.e., n_k.

Remark: Theorem 3 reveals that, detection under multiple observations exhibits definite monotonicity behaviors with node degree and snapshot sizes. Such properties shed insights into understanding how the network structure and observations affect the ML detector. In addition, the following corollary is a consequence of Theorem 3.

COROLLARY 1. *Suppose the rumor spreads on a δ-regular tree. For two independent observations G_{n_1} and G_{n_2}, given the number of nodes of G_{n_1}, i.e., n_1, and considering $n_2=qn_1$ and $n_2=qn_1+1$, $q\in Z^+$, these two cases have the same correct detection probability, i.e.,*

$$P_c(n_2 = qn_1) = P_c(n_2 = qn_1 + 1).$$

For any finite $n_1, \ldots, n_k$, we can use Algorithm 1 in Section 5.1 to calculate the exact value of the correct detection probability P_c. Furthermore, the following theorem precisely quantifies the asymptotic behaviors of P_c, for large snapshot sizes, degree δ, and number of observations k.

THEOREM 4. *Suppose the rumor spreads on a δ-regular tree, given k independent observations $G_{n_1},\ldots,G_{n_k}$, then:*
(1) When $\delta \geq 3$, we have

$$\lim_{n_1,\ldots,n_k\to\infty} P_c = \phi_k(\delta) := 1 - \delta\left(1 - \varphi_k\left(\frac{1}{\delta-2}, \frac{\delta-1}{\delta-2}\right)\right), \tag{18}$$

where
$$\varphi_k(\alpha,\beta) = \int\!\cdots\!\int_{\prod_{j=1}^{k} \frac{x_j}{1-x_j} \leq 1} \frac{\Gamma(\alpha+\beta)^k}{\Gamma(\alpha)^k \Gamma(\beta)^k} \prod_{j=1}^{k} \left(x_j^{\alpha-1} (1-x_j)^{\beta-1} \right) dx_1 \ldots dx_k,$$
$\alpha = \frac{1}{\delta-2}$, $\beta = \frac{\delta-1}{\delta-2}$.

As δ grows sufficiently large, $\phi_k(\delta) \to 1$; also, as k grows sufficiently large, $\phi_k(\delta) \to 1$.
(2) In particular, when $\delta = 3$, $\phi_k(3)$ can be written as

$$\phi_k(3) = 1 - 3 \cdot 2^{k-2} \int_0^1 \!\!\cdots\! \int_0^1 \frac{\prod_{j=1}^{k-1} (x_j(1-x_j))}{\prod_{j=1}^{k-1} x_j + \prod_{j=1}^{k-1} (1-x_j)} dx_1 \ldots dx_{k-1}, \tag{19}$$

which is increasing with k and is bounded as follows:

$$1 - \frac{3}{4}\left(\frac{\pi}{4}\right)^{k-1} < \lim_{n_1,\ldots,n_k\to\infty} P_c < 1, k \in Z^+; \tag{20}$$

that is, as k grows sufficiently large, $\lim_{n_1,\ldots,n_k\to\infty} P_c \to 1$ exponentially.

Remark: For general k observations, we mainly provide the results in the asymptotic regime as $n \to \infty$. The lower bound in case of $\delta = 3$ provides an intuitive insight that $\phi_k(3)$ increases with the number of observations k, and further indicates the convergence to be exponentially fast; see Fig. 2(c). According to Theorem 3 that P_c increases with δ and decreases with n, we have as $\delta > 2$, $k > 1$, $P_c \geq P_c(\delta = 3) > \phi_k(3) \geq \phi_2(3) = 1/2$. Indeed P_c may by far exceed $1/2$, if $\delta > 2$, $k > 1$; and as any of k and δ grows sufficiently large, P_c converges to 1. Therefore, Theorem 4 reveals that multiple independent observations significantly improve the detection performance.

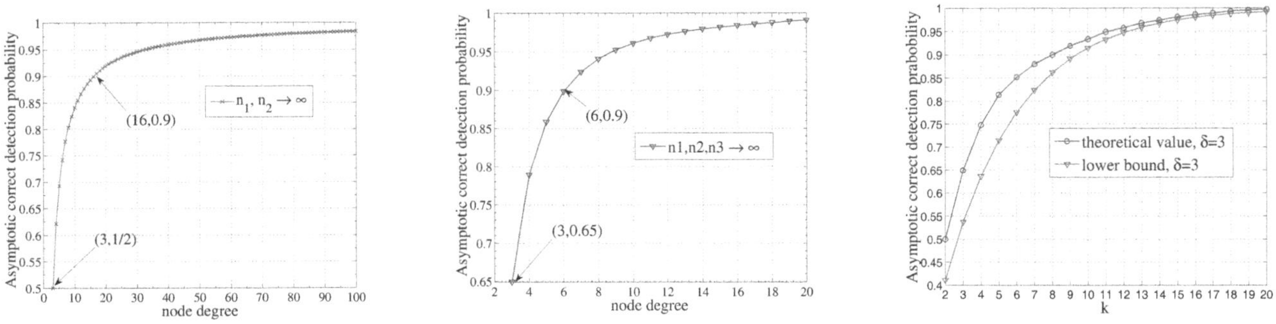

(a) Two independent observations (b) Three independent observations (c) $\phi_k(\delta)$ vs k, $\delta = 3$

Figure 2: Asymptotic correct detection probability under multiple independent observations

COROLLARY 2. *Suppose the rumor spreads on a δ-regular tree, given two independent observations G_{n_1} and G_{n_2}, then: (1) When $\delta \geq 3$, we have*

$$\lim_{n_1,n_2\to\infty} P_c = \phi_2(\delta) = 1-\delta\left(1-\varphi_2\left(\frac{1}{\delta-2},\frac{\delta-1}{\delta-2}\right)\right),$$

where
$\varphi_2(\alpha,\beta) = \iint_{x_1+x_2\leq 1} \frac{\Gamma(\alpha+\beta)^2}{\Gamma(\alpha)^2\Gamma(\beta)^2} x_1^{\alpha-1}x_2^{\alpha-1}(1-x_1)^{\beta-1}(1-x_2)^{\beta-1}\mathrm{d}x_1\mathrm{d}x_2$,
$\alpha = \frac{1}{\delta-2}$, $\beta = \frac{\delta-1}{\delta-2}$. *As δ grows sufficiently large, $\phi_2(\delta) \to 1$.*
(2) In particular, when $\delta = 3$, the asymptotic correct detection probability equals to $1/2$, i.e.,

$$\lim_{n_1\to\infty,n_2\to\infty} P_c = \frac{1}{2}; \tag{21}$$

when $\delta = 4$, the asymptotic correct detection probability is

$$\lim_{n_1\to\infty,n_2\to\infty} P_c = \frac{16}{\pi^2} - 1 \approx 0.621. \tag{22}$$

Remark: Corollary 2 is a special case of Theorem 4 for $k = 2$, illustrating that the asymptotic correct detection probability under merely two independent observations already significantly exceeds $1/2$; see Fig. 2(a). Besides, Fig. 2(b) displays an example of Theorem 4 in the case of three independent observations. As observed, when $\delta = 3$ or 6, the asymptotic correct detection probability equals to 0.65 or 0.9, in sharp contrast to that of 0.25 or 0.307 for $\delta = 3$ or $\delta \to \infty$ under a single observation in [4] and [6].

5. ALGORITHMS FOR TREES

5.1 Detection Probability for Regular Trees

In this section, we present Algorithm 1 to calculate the exact correct detection probability under multiple independent observations $G_{n_1}, \ldots, G_{n_k}$ in the finite regime for regular trees, based on the theoretical results established in Section 8.

5.2 Union Rumor Centrality Calculation

To find the union rumor center from k different independent observations $G_{n_1}, \ldots, G_{n_k}$, we need to evaluate the maximum union rumor centrality in $\{\cap G_{1\to k}\}$. In [4], a message-passing algorithm is proposed to compute the rumor centralities for

Algorithm 1 Correct Detection Probability Calculation

Input: δ, k, G_{n_j} $(j = 1, \ldots, k)$
Initialize $P_e = 0$
for $x_{1,n_k} = 1 \to n_k - 1$ **do**
 ......
 for $x_{1,n_1} = 1 \to n_1 - 1$ **do**
  if $\prod_{j=1}^{k} x_{1,n_j} > \prod_{j=1}^{k}(n_j - x_{1,n_j})$ **then**
   $P_e = P_e + \prod_{j=1}^{k} \mathbf{P}_{G_{n_j}}\left(X_{1,n_j} = x_{1,n_j}\right)$
  end if
  if $\prod_{j=1}^{k} x_{1,n_j} = \prod_{j=1}^{k}(n_j - x_{1,n_j})$ **then**
   $P_e = P_e + \frac{1}{2} \cdot \prod_{j=1}^{k} \mathbf{P}_{G_{n_j}}\left(X_{1,n_j} = x_{1,n_j}\right)$
  end if
 end for
end for
Output: $P_c = 1 - \delta \cdot P_e$

one time observation in a general tree G_n with n nodes, using $\mathcal{O}(n)$ computations. In this section, we propose an algorithm for calculating the union rumor centralities among all infected nodes based on message-passing, using $\mathcal{O}(|G_{n_1} \cup \ldots G_{n_k}|)$ computation steps. A baseline algorithm for comparison is to naively execute k instances of the single observation message-passing algorithm in [4] to find the union rumor center, using $\mathcal{O}(\sum_{j=1}^{k} n_j)$ computations. Since $|G_{n_1} \cup \ldots G_{n_k}| < \sum_{j=1}^{k} n_j$, our algorithm is more computationally efficient.

According to (3) and (10), the union rumor centrality of node s ($s \in \{\cap G_{1\to k}\}$) can be written as

$$R_k(s,G_{n_1}\ldots G_{n_k}) = R_k(s^*,G_{n_1}\cdots G_{n_k})\prod_{i\in\mathbb{P}(s^*,s)} \frac{T^{s^*}_{i,G_{n_1}}\cdots T^{s^*}_{i,G_{n_k}}}{(n_1-T^{s^*}_{i,G_{n_1}})\cdots(n_k-T^{s^*}_{i,G_{n_k}})}$$
$$= \frac{(n_1-1)!\cdots(n_k-1)!}{\prod_{u\in\{G_{n_1}\backslash s\}} T^s_{u,G_{n_1}} \cdots \prod_{u\in\{G_{n_k}\backslash s\}} T^s_{u,G_{n_k}}}, \tag{23}$$

where $\mathbb{P}(s^*,s)$ is the set of nodes in the path between the source s^* and s, not including s^*. This is the key to our algorithm for calculating the union rumor centralities for all the nodes in $\{\cap G_{1\to k}\}$. Let us briefly describe the idea of our algorithm. We consider the extended infected tree-type graph formed by the k observations, $\{\cup G_{1\to k}\}$. We first select an arbitrary node $v \in \{\cap G_{1\to k}\}$ as the rumor source and calculate the size of all of its subtrees and its union rumor centrality. This is accomplished by having each node u pass three messages up to its parent in $\cup G_{1\to k}$. The first message, denoted by $t^{\mathrm{up}}_{u\to \mathrm{parent}(u,\cup G_{1\to k})}$, contains up to k variables, each of which is denoted by $t^{\mathrm{up}}_{u,G_{n_j}\to \mathrm{parent}(u,G_{n_j})}$, representing the number of nodes in u's subtree of the observation G_{n_j}, as u and its parent both belong to G_{n_j}. The second message contains two variables, one of which is the cumulative product of the variables in the first message, which we call $t^{\mathrm{up}*}_{u\to \mathrm{parent}(u,\cup G_{1\to k})}$, and the other of which is an optional variable, denoted by $t^{\mathrm{up}'}_{u\to \mathrm{parent}(u,\cup G_{1\to k})}$, when both $u, v \in \cap G_{1\to k}$, thus assisting in calculating the union rumor centralities of neighboring nodes. The third message is the cumulative product of the sizes of the subtrees of all nodes in u's subtree of each G_{n_j}, which we call $p^{\mathrm{up}}_{u\to \mathrm{parent}(u,\cup G_{1\to k})}$. These messages are passed upward until the source node receives its messages. By multiplying the cumulative subtree products of the children of the source v, we obtain the union rumor centrality $R_k(v, G_{n_1}\ldots G_{n_k})$.

Algorithm 2 Union Rumor Centrality Calculation

Input: Graphs $G_{n_j}, j \in [1,k]$

Choose an arbitrary node $v \in \cap G_{1\to k}$ as a root.
for each $u \in \cup G_{1\to k}$ **do**
  if u is a leaf **then**
    $t^{\mathrm{up}}_{u\to \mathrm{parent}(u,\cup G_{1\to k})}$: $t^{\mathrm{up}}_{u,G_{n_j}\to \mathrm{parent}(u,G_{n_j})} = 1$, $j \in \{j : u, \mathrm{parent}(u) \in G_{n_j}, j \in [1,k]\}$
    $t^{\mathrm{up}*}_{u\to \mathrm{parent}(u,\cup G_{1\to k})} = 1$, $p^{\mathrm{up}}_{u\to \mathrm{parent}(u,\cup G_{1\to k})} = 1$
  else if u is root v **then**
    $v', v\in\cap G_{1\to k}, \forall v' \in \mathrm{child}(v, \cap G_{1\to k}), r^{\mathrm{down}}_{v\to v'} = \frac{\prod_{j=1}^{k}(n_j-1)!}{\prod_{i\in \mathrm{child}(v,\cup G_{1\to k})} p^{\mathrm{up}}_{i\to v}}$
  else
    $t^{\mathrm{up}}_{u\to \mathrm{parent}(u,\cup G_{1\to k})}$: $t^{\mathrm{up}}_{u\to \mathrm{parent}(u,G_{n_j})} = \sum_{i\in \mathrm{child}(u,G_{n_j})} t^{\mathrm{up}}_{i\to u} + 1$, $j \in \{j : u, \mathrm{parent}(u) \in G_{n_j}, j \in [1,k]\}$
    $t^{\mathrm{up}*}_{u\to \mathrm{parent}(u,\cup G_{1\to k})} = \prod_{\{j:u,\mathrm{parent}(u)\in G_{n_j}, j\in[1,k]\}} t^{\mathrm{up}}_{u\to \mathrm{parent}(u,G_{n_j})}$
    if $u \in \cap G_{1\to k}$ **then**
      $t^{\mathrm{up}'}_{u\to \mathrm{parent}(u,\cup G_{1\to k})} = \prod_{\{j:u,\mathrm{parent}(u)\in G_{n_j}, j\in[1,k]\}} \left(n_j - t^{\mathrm{up}}_{u\to \mathrm{parent}(u,G_{n_j})}\right)$
      $\forall u' \in \mathrm{child}(u, \cap G_{1\to k})$, $r^{\mathrm{down}}_{u\to u'} = r^{\mathrm{down}}_{\mathrm{parent}(u,\cup G_{1\to k})\to u} \cdot \frac{t^{\mathrm{up}*}_{u\to \mathrm{parent}(u,\cup G_{1\to k})}}{t^{\mathrm{up}'}_{u\to \mathrm{parent}(u,\cup G_{1\to k})}}$
    end if
    $p^{\mathrm{up}}_{u\to \mathrm{parent}(u,\cup G_{1\to k})} = t^{\mathrm{up}*}_{u\to \mathrm{parent}(u,\cup G_{1\to k})} \cdot \prod_{i\in \mathrm{child}(u,\cup G_{1\to k})} p^{\mathrm{up}}_{i\to u}$
  end if
end for

Output: Union rumor centralities of all the nodes in $\{\cap G_{1\to k}\}$.

Based on the union rumor centrality of node v, we evaluate the union rumor centralities of the children of v using (23). Each node in $\cap G_{1\to k}$ passes its union rumor centrality to its children in a message which we denote by $r^{\mathrm{down}}_{u\to u'}$, for $\forall u' \in \mathrm{child}(u, \cap G_{1\to k})$. Each node calculates its union rumor centrality using its parent's union rumor centrality and its messages $t^{\mathrm{up}*}_{u\to \mathrm{parent}(u,\cup G_{1\to k})}$ and $t^{\mathrm{up}'}_{u\to \mathrm{parent}(u,\cup G_{1\to k})}$. Therefore, our union rumor centrality calculation algorithm calculates the union rumor centralities of all infected nodes by message-passing, using $\mathcal{O}(|G_{n_1}\cup\ldots G_{n_k}|)$ computation steps.

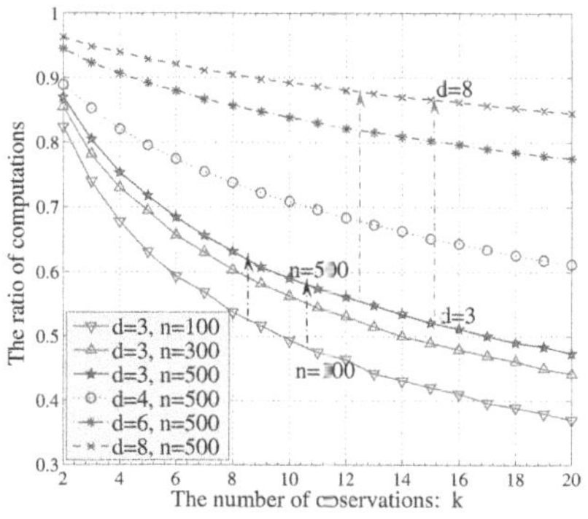

Figure 3: Ratio of computations between Algorithm 2 and the direct implementation of multiple instances of single observation message-passing algorithm.

We perform simulations with different node degrees and infected set sizes to empirically evaluate the computational efficiency. We define r_a as the ratio of computations between Algorithm 2 and the direct execution of multiple instances of single observation message-passing algorithm in [4]. For each simulation experiment we conduct the Monte-Carlo simulation 10000 times. As shown in Fig. 3, r_a decreases with the number of observations, and increases with the infected set size and node degree. These imply that Algorithm 2 is advantageous in cases with small node degrees and large number of observations. For example, when the node degree is 3, the number of observations is 20, and 500 infected nodes are observed in each observation, Algorithm 2 almost reduces half of the computations as compared to running multiple single observation message-passing algorithms.

6. DETECTOR FOR GENERAL GRAPHS

For general graphs, owing to the lack of knowledge of the spanning tree, we use the BFS heuristic to obtain an induced tree network from each observation. We assume that if node $s\in G_{n_j}$ $(1\le j\le k)$ is the source, then the rumor spreads along a BFS tree rooted at s, denoted by $T_b(s, G_{n_j})$. Therefore, based on Section 2.2(3), we obtain the following rumor source detector:

$$\hat{s} = \arg\max_{s^*\in\{\cap G_{1\to k}\}} \prod_{j=1}^{k} P(\sigma_s^* \mid s, G_{n_j}) \cdot R_k(s^*, G_{n_1}\ldots G_{n_k}), \quad (24)$$

where σ_s^* represents the BFS ordering of nodes in $T_b(s, G_{n_j})$. In the next section, we will show with simulations the performance of this detector for different networks.

7. NUMERICAL SIMULATIONS

In this section, we evaluate the performance of the proposed rumor source detector on different networks.

7.1 Tree Networks

Here we provide simulation results for regular trees in order to corroborate the analysis in Section 4. For each configuration, we conduct the Monte-Carlo simulation 10000 times to assess the correct detection probability.

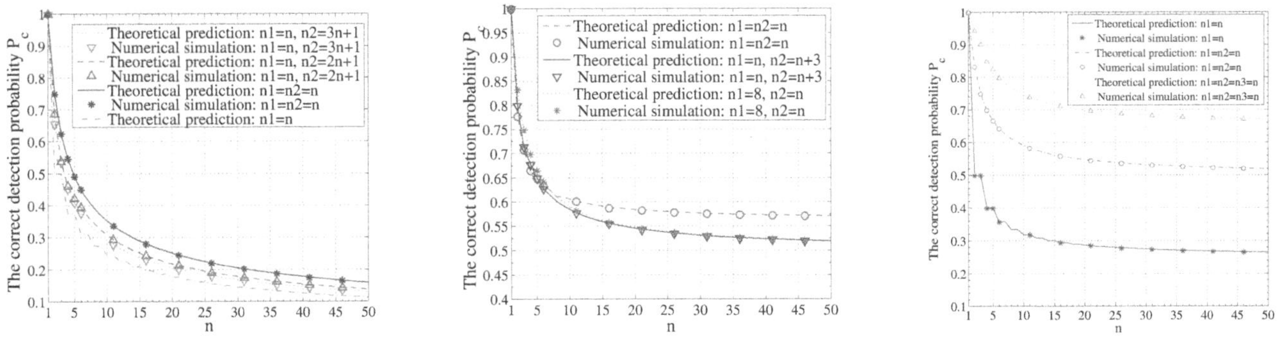

(a) $\delta = 2$ (b) $\delta = 3$ (c) P_c vs n, $\delta = 3$

Figure 4: Simulation results for regular trees

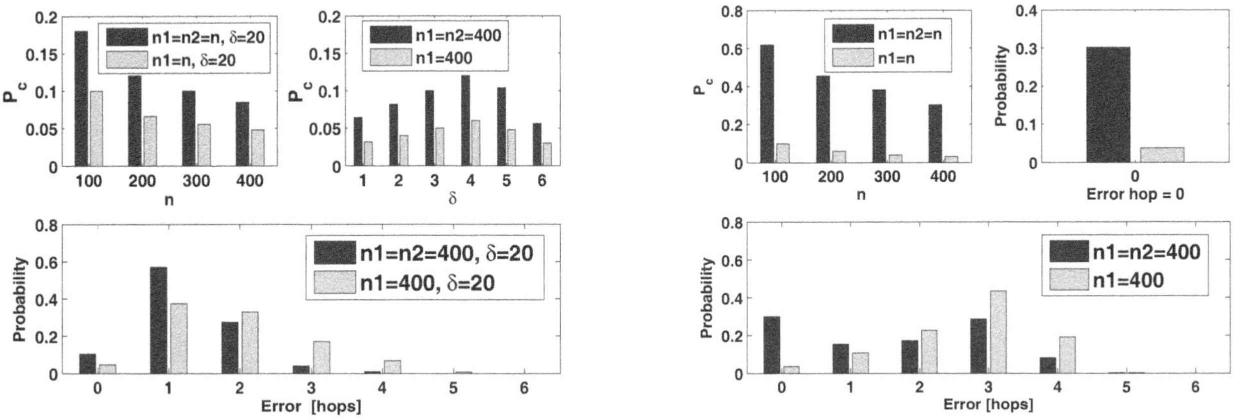

(a) Small-world network (b) Scale-free network

Figure 5: Simulation results for general graph networks

In Fig. 4(a), for $\delta = 2$, the simulation results under two independent observations coincide with the theoretical values as predicted by Theorem 1. Similarly, in Fig. 4(b), for $\delta = 3$, we observe the consistency between the simulation results and the theoretical prediction in Theorem 2. When n becomes large, P_c is close to $1/2$, as predicted by Theorem 2.

In Fig. 4(c), we show that when $\delta = 3$, P_c increases with the number of observations and decreases with the number of infected nodes. As shown, multiple independent observations significantly improve the performance, compared with a single observation.

7.2 General Graph Networks

We perform simulations on small-world networks [12] and scale-free networks [13]. For both topologies, each underlying graph contains 5000 nodes and we let the rumor spread to infect up to 400 nodes in each observation.

For both Fig. 5(a) and Fig. 5(b), in the top left subplots, we study the correct detection probability with the number of infected nodes. For both networks, we have a larger correct detection probability with two independent observations compared with a single observation, and the correct detection probability decreases as the number of infected nodes increases. Then for small-world networks, we change the average degree δ to investigate its effect as displayed in the top right subplot of Fig. 5(a). We observe that even when δ is large, two observations still enhance the detectability considerably.

In the bottom subplots of Fig. 5(a) and Fig. 5(b), we investigate the error (i.e., the number of hops between the detected source and the actual source) on the two networks, respectively. Comparing two independent observations with a single observation, we have a better performance in both networks, especially the scale-free network (see the top right subplot of Fig. 5(b)). The reason for this may be that scale-free networks have a highly heterogeneous degree distribution and thus contain many high-degree hubs.

8. PROOFS

8.1 Lemmas

We need the following technical lemmas, whose proofs (along with that of Lemma 1) are in the appendix. For a rumor source s^* with m $(1 \leq m \leq \delta)$ neighbors in $\{\cap G_{1\to k}\}$, i.e., $s_1^*, \ldots, s_m^*$, let random variable X_{i,n_j} be the number of nodes in subtree $T^{s^*}_{s_i^*,G_{n_j}}$ of observation G_{n_j} $(1 \le i \le m, 1 \le j \le k)$.

LEMMA 2. *For the source s^* and the inferred $\hat{s}$, introduce*

$$\begin{cases} P_1 := P\left(\hat{s}=s^* \middle| \forall i, 1\le i\le m, \prod_{j=1}^k x_{i,n_j} < \prod_{j=1}^k (n_j - x_{i,n_j})\right) = 1, \\ P_{\frac{1}{2}} := P\left(\hat{s}=s^* \middle| \exists i, 1\le i\le m, \prod_{j=1}^k x_{i,n_j} = \prod_{j=1}^k (n_j - x_{i,n_j})\right) = \frac{1}{2}, \\ P_0 := P\left(\hat{s}=s^* \middle| \exists i, 1\le i\le m, \prod_{j=1}^k x_{i,n_j} > \prod_{j=1}^k (n_j - x_{i,n_j})\right) = 0. \end{cases}$$

The correct detection probability P_c is given by

$$P_c = P_{\frac{1}{2}} \cdot \sum_{\prod_{j=1}^k x_{i,n_j} = \prod_{j=1}^k (n_j - x_{i,n_j})} \prod_{j=1}^k \mathbf{P}_{G_{n_j}}\left(\bigcap_{i=1}^{\delta}\{X_{i,n_j} = x_{i,n_j}\}\right)$$
$$+ P_1 \cdot \sum_{\prod_{j=1}^k x_{i,n_j} < \prod_{j=1}^k (n_j - x_{i,n_j})} \prod_{j=1}^k \mathbf{P}_{G_{n_j}}\left(\bigcap_{i=1}^{\delta}\{X_{i,n_j} = x_{i,n_j}\}\right). \quad (25)$$

LEMMA 3. *The correct detection probability P_c in Lemma 2 can be rewritten as*

$$P_c = 1 - \delta \left\{ \frac{1}{2} \sum_{\prod_{j=1}^k x_{i,n_j} = \prod_{j=1}^k (n_j - x_{i,n_j})} \prod_{j=1}^k \mathbf{P}_{G_{n_j}}\left(\bigcap_{i=1}^{\delta}\{X_{i,n_j} = x_{i,n_j}\}\right)\right.$$
$$\left. + \sum_{\prod_{j=1}^k x_{i,n_j} > \prod_{j=1}^k (n_j - x_{i,n_j})} \prod_{j=1}^k \mathbf{P}_{G_{n_j}}\left(\bigcap_{i=1}^{\delta}\{X_{i,n_j} = x_{i,n_j}\}\right) \right\}. \quad (26)$$

Remark: Algorithm 1 in Section 5.1 is based on Lemma 3.

LEMMA 4. *Suppose a rumor source s^* spreads on a δ-regular tree, resulting in an observation G_n. As $n \to \infty$, the probability that a subtree $T^{s^*}_{s_i^*,G_n}$ $(1 \le i \le \delta)$ is empty asymptotically vanishes:*

$$\lim_{n\to\infty} \mathbf{P}_{G_n}(X_i = 0) = 0, \qquad 1 \le i \le \delta\ . \quad (27)$$

LEMMA 5. *Suppose a rumor source s^* spreads on a δ-regular tree, with multiple independent observations $G_{n_1}, \ldots, G_{n_k}$. For $1 \le i \le \delta$, define*

$$E_i = \left\{ \tfrac{x_{i,n_1}}{n_1} \cdots \tfrac{x_{i,n_k}}{n_k} < (1 - \tfrac{x_{i,n_1}}{n_1}) \cdots (1 - \tfrac{x_{i,n_k}}{n_k}) \right\},$$
$$D_i = \left\{ \tfrac{x_{i,n_1}}{n_1} \cdots \tfrac{x_{i,n_k}}{n_k} = (1 - \tfrac{x_{i,n_1}}{n_1}) \cdots (1 - \tfrac{x_{i,n_k}}{n_k}) \right\},$$
$$F_i = \left\{ \tfrac{x_{i,n_1}}{n_1} \cdots \tfrac{x_{i,n_k}}{n_k} \le (1 - \tfrac{x_{i,n_1}}{n_1}) \cdots (1 - \tfrac{x_{i,n_k}}{n_k}) \right\}.$$

As $n_1, \ldots, n_k \to \infty$, we have

$$\lim_{n_1,\ldots,n_k\to\infty} P_c = 1 - \delta \cdot \lim_{n_1,\ldots,n_k\to\infty} \mathbf{P}_G(E_1^c) = 1 - \delta \cdot \lim_{n_1,\ldots,n_k\to\infty} \mathbf{P}_G(F_1^c). \quad (28)$$

8.2 Theorem 1

Here we only present the proof of Theorem 1(1) for $n_1 = n_2 = n$; the other cases can be deduced similarly.

Since the rumor source s^* has m neighbors $(0 \le m \le \delta)$, we have $\delta+1$ cases depending on m. For clarity, we abbreviate x_{i,n_1} and x_{i,n_2} by x_i and y_i $(1 \le i \le \delta)$, respectively. Our proof proceeds in two steps. First, for each of the $\delta+1$ cases, we calculate P_c using Lemma 2. Second, we sum up all the cases.

When $\delta=2$, the joint distributions of $\{X_i, 1 \le i \le 2\}$ and $\{Y_i, 1 \le i \le 2\}$ are respectively (see [6])

$$\mathbf{P}_{G_{n_1}}\left(\bigcap_{i=1}^{2}\{X_i = x_i\}\right) = \frac{(n-1)!}{x_1!x_2!}\frac{1}{2^{n-1}}, \quad \mathbf{P}_{G_{n_2}}\left(\bigcap_{i=1}^{2}\{Y_i = y_i\}\right) = \frac{(n-1)!}{y_1!y_2!}\frac{1}{2^{n-1}}. \quad (29)$$

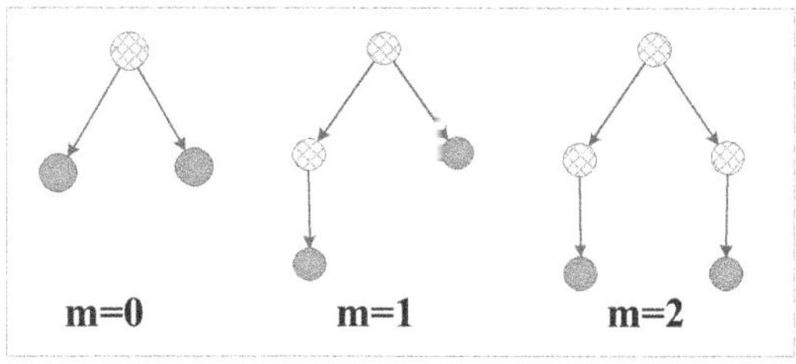

Figure 6: Illustration of a rumor source s^* with m neighbors $(0 \le m \le \delta)$ in $\{\cap G_{1\to k}\}$, $\delta = 2$. Latticed circles represent infected nodes in $\{\cap G_{1\to k}\}$.

Consider the case of $m=2$; see Fig. 6. According to Proposition 2, (x_1, x_2) and (y_1, y_2) should satisfy

$$\begin{cases} x_1 + y_1 \le n, \\ x_2 + y_2 \le n, \\ x_1 + x_2 = n - 1, \quad x_1 \ge 1, x_2 \ge 1, \\ y_1 + y_2 = n - 1, \quad y_1 \ge 1, y_2 \ge 1. \end{cases} \quad (30)$$

Then when multiplied by the joint distributions $P_G(X)$ and $P_G(Y)$, from Lemma 2, the contribution to P_c is given by

$$P_{c,2} = \left\{ \binom{n-1}{1}\left(\binom{n-1}{1} + \frac{1}{2}\binom{n-1}{2}\right) + \sum_{x_1=2}^{n-3}\binom{n-1}{x_1}\left(\frac{1}{2}\binom{n-1}{x_1-1} + \binom{n-1}{x_1} + \frac{1}{2}\binom{n-1}{x_1+1}\right) + \binom{n-1}{n-2}\left(\binom{n-1}{n-2} + \frac{1}{2}\binom{n-1}{n-3}\right)\right\} \cdot 2^{-2(n-1)}$$
$$= \left(\frac{1}{2}\binom{2n}{n} - 2n\right) \cdot 2^{-2(n-1)}. \quad (31)$$

Likewise, the contributions to P_c in the case of $m=1$ and $m=0$ are $P_{c,1} = 2(n-1) \cdot 2^{-2(n-1)}$ and $P_{c,0} = 2 \cdot 2^{-2(n-1)}$, respectively. Summing up all the cases from $m=0$ to 2, Theorem 1(1) is proved.

As $n \to \infty$, by Stirling's formula, from (14), we have

$$P_c = \frac{1}{2^{2n-1}} \cdot \frac{(2n)!}{n!n!} \approx \frac{1}{2^{2n-1}} \frac{\sqrt{2\pi n}(\frac{2n}{e})^{2n}}{(\sqrt{2\pi n}(\frac{2n}{e})^n)^2} = \frac{2}{\sqrt{\pi n}}. \quad (32)$$

8.3 Theorem 2

Here we only present the proof of Theorem 2(1); the other cases can be deduced similarly.

Our proof proceeds in two steps. First, we identify error detection events from Proposition 2 and Lemma 1. Second, we calculate P_c by Lemma 3.

Since $\delta=3$, the joint distributions of $\{X_i, 1 \le i \le 3\}$ and $\{Y_i, 1 \le i \le 3\}$ are $\mathbf{P}_{G_{n_1}}(\bigcap_{i=1}^3\{X_i = x_i\}) = \frac{2}{n(n+1)}$, $\mathbf{P}_{G_{n_2}}(\bigcap_{i=1}^3\{Y_i = y_i\}) = \frac{2}{qn(qn+1)}$, respectively. Hence, the marginal distributions of X_1

and Y_1 are

$$\mathbf{P}_{G_{n_1}}(X_1{=}x_1){=}\frac{2(n{-}x_1)}{n(n{+}1)},\quad \mathbf{P}_{G_{n_2}}(Y_1{=}y_1){=}\frac{2(n{-}y_1)}{qn(qn{+}1)},\quad (33)$$

respectively.

From Proposition 2 and Lemma 1, when X_1 and Y_1 satisfy

$$\frac{x_1 y_1}{(n-x_1)(qn-y_1)} \geq 1, \quad (34)$$

the error detection events happen.

Applying Lemma 3, when enumerating the error detection events, we have

$$P_e{=}\sum_{x_1=1}^{n-1}\frac{2(n{-}x_1)}{n(n{+}1)}\Bigg(\sum_{y_1=qn-qx_1+1}^{qn-1}\frac{2(n{-}y_1)}{qn(qn{+}1)} + \frac{1}{2}\sum_{y_1=qn-qx_1}\frac{2(n{-}y_1)}{qn(qn{+}1)}\Bigg) = \frac{qn-q}{6(qn+1)}. \quad (35)$$

So P_c is

$$P_c{=}1-3\cdot\frac{qn{-}q}{6(qn{+}1)}=\frac{qn{+}q{+}2}{2(qn{+}1)}. \quad (36)$$

Theorem 2(1) is thus proved.

8.4 Theorem 3

a. Theorem 3(1)

From Lemma 3, in order to prove that P_c is increasing with δ, we just need to demonstrate that for any $(x_{1,n_1},\ldots,x_{1,n_k})$ satisfying $\prod_{j=1}^k x_{1,n_j} \geq \prod_{j=1}^k (n_j - x_{1,n_j})$, $\delta\prod_{j=1}^k \mathbf{P}_{G_{n_j}}(X_{1,n_j}{=}x_{1,n_j})$ is decreasing with δ. Note that the marginal distribution of X_1 is given by

$$\mathbf{P}_G(X_1{=}x_1) = \binom{n-1}{x_1}\frac{\prod_{i=1}^2 b_i(b_i{+}\delta{-}2)\cdots(b_i{+}(x_i{-}1)(\delta{-}2))}{\delta(\delta{+}\delta{-}2)\cdots(\delta{+}(n{-}2)(\delta{-}2))}, \quad (37)$$

where $x_2 = n-1-x_1$, $b_1 = 1$ and $b_2 = \delta - 1$. By defining $f(a,b) = \frac{\frac{1}{\delta-2}+a}{\frac{\delta}{\delta-2}+b}$ and $F(\delta) = \delta\prod_{j=1}^k \mathbf{P}_{G_{n_j}}(X_{1,n_j} = x_{1,n_j})$, we have

$$F(\delta){=}\delta\prod_{j=1}^k\binom{n_j{-}1}{x_{1,n_j}}\frac{\prod_{z_1=0}^{x_{1,n_j}-1}(1{+}z_1(\delta{-}2))\prod_{z_2=0}^{n_j-x_{1,n_j}-1}(\delta{-}1{+}z_2(\delta{-}2))}{\delta(\delta{+}\delta{-}2)\cdots(\delta{+}(n{-}2)(\delta{-}2))}$$
$$={\delta^{-(k-1)}}\prod_{j=1}^k\Big(f(1,1)f(2,2)\cdots f(x_{1,n_j}{-}1,x_{1,n_j}{-}1)\cdot f(1,x_{1,n_j})\cdots f(n_j-2-x_{1,n_j},n_j-2)\Big). \quad (38)$$

Rearranging $f(a,b)$, we have

$$f(a,b) = \frac{a\delta - a + 1}{(1+b)\delta - b} = \frac{b+1}{a} + \frac{\frac{b+1-a}{a}}{(1+b)\delta - b}.$$

Hence if $b \geq a$, $f(a,b)$ is decreasing with δ. So all factors of (38) are decreasing with δ, and so is $F(\delta)$. As δ grows large, $\lim_{\delta\to\infty} f(a,b) = \frac{b+1}{a}$ is a finite number. By applying (38), $\lim_{\delta\to\infty} F(\delta) = \lim_{\delta\to\infty}\delta^{-(k-1)}\cdot C = 0$, where C is a bounded number. Due to the fact that the total number of the error detection events is finite, as δ grows without bound, the correct detection probability P_c approaches 1 asymptotically.

b. Theorem 3(2)

Here, we will prove that P_c is non-increasing as n_k increases to $n_k{+}1$, with given $G_{n_1},\ldots,G_{n_{k-1}}$ (i.e., fixing $n_1,\ldots,n_{k-1}$). We define events $D(\cdot)$ and $E(\cdot)$ as follows:

$$D(n_k){=}\left\{\frac{x_{1,n_k}}{n_k} = \frac{\prod_{j=1}^{k-1}(n_j - x_{1,n_j})}{\prod_{j=1}^{k-1}(n_j - x_{1,n_j}) + \prod_{j=1}^{k-1}x_{1,n_j}}\right\}, \quad (39)$$

$$E(n_k){=}\left\{\frac{x_{1,n_k}}{n_k} > \frac{\prod_{j=1}^{k-1}(n_j - x_{1,n_j})}{\prod_{j=1}^{k-1}(n_j - x_{1,n_j}) + \prod_{j=1}^{k-1}x_{1,n_j}}\right\}. \quad (40)$$

Thus $D(n_k)\cup E(n_k)$ is

$$D(n_k)\cup E(n_k) = \left\{\frac{\prod_{j=1}^k x_{1,n_j}}{\prod_{j=1}^k (n_j - x_{1,n_j})} \geq 1\right\}. \quad (41)$$

It can then be shown that the correct detection probability in Lemma 3 is equivalent to

$$P_c{=}1{-}\delta\Bigg\{\frac{1}{2}\sum_{x_{1,n_k}=1}^{n_k-1}\mathbf{P}_{G_{n_k}}(X_{1,n_k}{=}x_{1,n_k})\sum_{D(n_k)}\prod_{j=1}^{k-1}\mathbf{P}_{G_{n_j}}(X_{1,n_j}{=}x_{1,n_j}) + \sum_{x_{1,n_k}=1}^{n_k-1}\mathbf{P}_{G_{n_k}}(X_{1,n_k}{=}x_{1,n_k})\sum_{E(n_k)}\prod_{j=1}^{k-1}\mathbf{P}_{G_{n_j}}(X_{1,n_j}{=}x_{1,n_j})\Bigg\}. \quad (42)$$

We assume $|G_{n_j}|{=}n_j$ $(1{\leq}j{\leq}k)$ and $|G_{n_k}|{=}n_k'{=}n_k{+}1$, and evaluate the change of P_c as $|G_{n_k}|$ changes from n_k to n_k'.

Here we outline a sketch of the subsequent proof procedure. For any fixed $(x_{1,n_1},\ldots,x_{1,n_{k-1}})$, we can determine the solution set of x_{1,n_k} as well as that of $x_{1,n_k'}$, through (41). For the fixed $(x_{1,n_1},\ldots,x_{1,n_{k-1}})$, we can then evaluate the change in the correct detection probability. Therein, several possible cases need to be considered. Finally, based on (42), we conclude the proof by observing that for each fixed $(x_{1,n_1},\ldots,x_{1,n_{k-1}})$, the change of P_c from n_k to n_k' is bounded by zero from above.

In the following, we use X_j $(1 \leq j \leq k-1)$, Y_k and Y_k' to denote X_{1,n_j} $(1 \leq j \leq k-1)$, X_{1,n_k} and $X_{1,n_k'}$, respectively; furthermore, define

$$\bar{y}_k = \min\Big\{y_k{:}(x_1,\ldots,x_{k-1},y_k){\in}\{D(n_k){\cup}E(n_k)\}\Big\}, \quad (43)$$

$$\bar{y}_k' = \min\Big\{y_k'{:}(x_1,\ldots,x_{k-1},y_k'){\in}\{D(n_k'){\cup}E(n_k')\}\Big\}. \quad (44)$$

For arbitrary $(x_1^*,x_2^*,\ldots,x_{k-1}^*)$, take $x_k^* = \bar{y}_k$. If $x_k^* \in E(n_k)$, due to the fact that $\frac{x_k^*+1}{n_k+1} > \frac{x_k^*}{n_k} > \frac{x_k^*}{n_k+1}$, we have $x_k^*+1 \in E(n_k')$; but x_k^* may not belong to either $E(n_k')$ or $D(n_k')$. Besides, note that x_k^*-1 cannot belong to $E(n_k')$ or $D(n_k')$, because x_k^*-1 does not belong to $E(n_k)$ and $\frac{x_k^*}{n_k} > \frac{x_k^*-1}{n_k} > \frac{x_k^*-1}{n_k+1}$. Hence, for given $(x_1^*,x_2^*,\ldots,x_{k-1}^*)$, when $x_k^* = \bar{y}_k \in E(n_k)$, we have $\bar{y}_k' = x_k^*{+}1 \in E(n_k')$ or $\bar{y}_k' = x_k^* \in E(n_k'){\cup}D(n_k')$. Similarly, if $x_k^* = \bar{y}_k \in D(n_k)$, according to the definition of $D(n_k)$, we have $\bar{y}_k' = x_k^*+1 \in E(n_k')$. In summary, for arbitrary $(x_1^*,x_2^*,\ldots,x_{k-1}^*)$, we have four possible cases:

(1) $\bar{y}_k = x_k^* \in E(n_k)$, $\bar{y}_k' = x_k^* + 1 \in E(n_k')$ and $\bar{y}_k' = \bar{y}_k + 1$;
(2) $\bar{y}_k = x_k^* \in E(n_k)$, $\bar{y}_k' = x_k^* \in E(n_k')$ and $\bar{y}_k' = \bar{y}_k$;
(3) $\bar{y}_k = x_k^* \in E(n_k)$, $\bar{y}_k' = x_k^* \in D(n_k')$ and $\bar{y}_k' = \bar{y}_k$;
(4) $\bar{y}_k = x_k^* \in D(n_k)$, $\bar{y}_k' = x_k^* + 1 \in E(n_k')$ and $\bar{y}_k' = \bar{y}_k + 1$.

To proceed, we need the following fact from [6]:

$$\sum_{y_k'=x_k^*+1}^{n_k} \mathbf{P}_{G_{n_k+1}}(Y_k' = y_k') = \frac{1+x_k^*(\delta-2)}{2+n_k(\delta-2)}\mathbf{P}_{G_{n_k}}(Y_k = x_k^*) + \sum_{y_k=x_k^*+1}^{n_k-1} \mathbf{P}_{G_{n_k}}(Y_k = y_k). \quad (45)$$

We also notice a complementary relationship that, if some $\overrightarrow{x^*} = (x_1^*, \ldots, x_{k-1}^*)$ satisfies Case 1, then $\overleftarrow{x^*} = ((n_1 - x_1^*), (n_2 - x_2^*), \ldots, (n_{k-1} - x_{k-1}^*))$ has to satisfy Case 2. Hence, in the following we combine Case 1 and Case 2 to evaluate the change of P_c.

In Case 1, for $\overrightarrow{x^*}$, we have $\bar{y}_k = x_k^* \in E(n_k)$, $\bar{y}_k' = x_k^* + 1 \in E(n_k')$ and $\bar{y}_k' = \bar{y}_k + 1$. Let $y_0 = n_k + 1 - x_k^*$. From (45), by letting
$P_d(\overrightarrow{x^*}) = (\sum_{y_k'=y_0}^{n_k} \mathbf{P}_{G_{n_k+1}}(Y_k' = y_k') - \sum_{y_k=y_0}^{n_k-1} \mathbf{P}_{G_{n_k}}(Y_k = y_k)) \cdot \prod_{j=1}^{k-1} \mathbf{P}_{G_{n_j}}(X_j = x_j^*)$, we have

$$P_d(\overrightarrow{x^*}) = (\frac{1+x_k^*(\delta-2)}{2+n_k(\delta-2)} - 1)\mathbf{P}_{G_{n_k}}(Y_k = x_k^*)\prod_{j=1}^{k-1}\mathbf{P}_{G_{n_j}}(X_j = x_j^*). \quad (46)$$

Correspondingly, in Case 2, by letting
$P_d(\overleftarrow{x^*}) = (\sum_{y_k'=y_0}^{n_k} \mathbf{P}_{G_{n_k+1}}(Y_k' = y_k') - \sum_{y_k=y_0}^{n_k-1} \mathbf{P}_{G_{n_k}}(Y_k = y_k)) \cdot \prod_{j=1}^{k-1} \mathbf{P}_{G_{n_j}}(X_j = x_j^*)$, we have

$$P_d(\overleftarrow{x^*}) = \frac{1+(n_k - x_k^*)(\delta-2)}{2+n_k(\delta-2)}\mathbf{P}_{G_{n_k}}(Y_k = n_k - x_k^*)\prod_{j=1}^{k-1}\mathbf{P}_{G_{n_j}}(X_j = n_j - x_j^*). \quad (47)$$

By adding up (46) and (47), we can show that the total change in Case 1 and Case 2 as n_k increases by one is positive, i.e.,

$$P_d(\overrightarrow{x^*}) + P_d(\overleftarrow{x^*}) > 0,$$

in which we use the fact that $\frac{\mathbf{P}_{G_n}(X=n-x)}{\mathbf{P}_{G_n}(X=x)} = \frac{x}{n-x}$, which can be verified by (37).

Following similar way, for all the four cases we have that for any fixed $n_1, \ldots, n_{k-1}$, the change in the error detection probability, as n_k changes to $n_k + 1$, is lower bounded by zero, i.e., that the correct detection probability is monotonically non-increasing with n_k.

8.5 Theorem 4

a. Theorem 4(1)

For the rumor source s^* with m $(1 \le m \le \delta)$ neighbors, i.e., s_1^*, s_2^*, ..., s_m^*, let random variable X_{i,n_j} be the number of nodes in subtree $T_{s_i^*,G_{n_j}}^{s^*}$ of observation G_{n_j} $(1 \le i \le m, 1 \le j \le k)$. Note that as $n_j \to \infty$, the limiting marginal distribution of the ratio $X_{1,n_j}/n_j$ converges to a Beta distribution with a density function given by

$$\frac{\Gamma(\alpha+\beta)}{\Gamma(\alpha)\Gamma(\beta)}x^{\alpha-1}(1-x)^{\beta-1}, \quad (48)$$

where $\alpha = \frac{1}{\delta-2}$, $\beta = \frac{\delta-1}{\delta-2}$. So for k independent observations, $\mathbf{P}_G(E_1)$ is regarded as the cumulative distribution function of the ratios $\frac{X_{1,n_1}}{n_1}, \ldots, \frac{X_{1,n_k}}{n_k}$, given by

$$\lim_{n_1,\ldots n_k \to \infty} \mathbf{P}_G(E_1) = \int\cdot\cdot\int_{\prod_{j=1}^k \frac{x_j}{1-x_j} \le 1} \frac{\Gamma(\alpha+\beta)^k}{\Gamma(\alpha)^k\Gamma(\beta)^k}\prod_{j=1}^k\left(x_j^{\alpha-1}(1-x_j)^{\beta-1}\right)\overline{d_k}, \quad (49)$$

where $\overline{d_k} = dx_1 \cdots dx_k$. From Lemma 5, we obtain (18). From Theorem 3, $\phi_k(3) \le \phi_k(\delta) < 1$ $(\delta \ge 3)$. Combining with the property that as $k \to \infty$, $\phi_k(3)$ goes to 1, which we will prove next, we have that as k grows without bound, $\phi_k(\delta)$ approaches one for any $\delta \ge 3$.

b. Theorem 4(2)

According to (18), when $\delta = 3$, as $n_1, \ldots n_k \to \infty$,

$$\lim_{n_1,\ldots n_k \to \infty} P_c = 1 - 3 \cdot (1 - \varphi_k(1,2)), \quad (50)$$

where

$$\begin{aligned}
&1-\varphi_k(1,2)\\
&= 1 - \int\cdot\cdot\int_{\prod_{j=1}^k \frac{x_j}{1-x_j} \le 1} 2^k \prod_{j=1}^k (1-x_j)\,\overline{d_k}\\
&= 2^k \int_0^1\cdot\cdot\int_0^1 \left(\int_{\frac{\prod_{j=1}^{k-1}(1-x_j)}{\prod_{j=1}^{k-1}x_j + \prod_{j=1}^{k-1}(1-x_j)}}^1 \prod_{j=1}^k (1-x_j)dx_k\right)\overline{d_{k-1}}\\
&= 2^k \int_0^1\cdot\cdot\int_0^1 \frac{\prod_{j=1}^{k-1} x_j^2 \prod_{j=1}^{k-1}(1-x_j)}{2\left(\prod_{j=1}^{k-1}(1-x_j) + \prod_{j=1}^{k-1} x_j\right)^2}\overline{d_{k-1}}\\
&\overset{(a)}{=} 2^{k-2}\int_0^1\cdot\cdot\int_0^1 \frac{\prod_{j=1}^{k-1}x_j^2(1-x_j) + \prod_{j=1}^{k-1}(1-x_j)^2 x_j}{\left(\prod_{j=1}^{k-1}(1-x_j) + \prod_{j=1}^{k-1} x_j\right)^2}\overline{d_{k-1}}\\
&= 2^{k-2}\int_0^1\cdot\cdot\int_0^1 \frac{\prod_{j=1}^{k-1} x_j(1-x_j)}{\prod_{j=1}^{k-1}(1-x_j) + \prod_{j=1}^{k-1} x_j}\overline{d_{k-1}}, \quad (51)
\end{aligned}$$

where (a) follows from substituting $x_j = 1 - x_j'$, $1 \le j \le k-1$. By applying (51) into (50), we get (19). By rearranging (19),

$$\begin{aligned}
&\lim_{n_1,\ldots n_k \to \infty} P_c\\
&= 1 - 3\cdot 2^{k-2}\int_0^1\cdot\cdot\int_0^1 \frac{\prod_{j=1}^{k-1}(x_j\cdot(1-x_j))}{\prod_{j=1}^{k-1} x_j + \prod_{j=1}^{k-1}(1-x_j)}\overline{d_{k-1}}\\
&\overset{(b)}{\ge} 1 - 3\cdot 2^{k-2}\int_0^1\cdot\cdot\int_0^1 \frac{\prod_{j=1}^{k-1}(x_j\cdot(1-x_j))}{2\sqrt{\prod_{j=1}^{k-1}(x_j\cdot(1-x_j))}}\overline{d_{k-1}}\\
&\overset{(c)}{=} 1 - 3\cdot 2^{k-3}\cdot(\frac{\pi}{8})^{k-1} = 1 - \frac{3}{4}\cdot(\frac{\pi}{4})^{k-1}, \quad (52)
\end{aligned}$$

where (b) follows from the inequality of arithmetic and geometric means, and (c) follows from $\int_0^1 \sqrt{x(1-x)}dx = \pi/8$. This leads to the desired result.

9. CONCLUSION

We studied the rumor source detection problem for the SI model with multiple observations. By providing characterization through the interdependency of observations and network topology, we established a number of explicit analytical results for regular tree-type networks. We showed that having multiple independent observations dramatically enhances detectability: even two observations can more than double the detection probability of a single observation. We may thus find the right number of observations needed to provide detectability guarantees. We also showed that for degrees greater than two, the detection probability increases with the number of observations and decreases with the number of infected nodes. The detection probability increases with the degree as well as the number of observations, i.e., richer connectivity and diversity both enhance detection. We provided a unified inference framework based on message passing for tree networks and leveraged it as an effective heuristic for general graphs. In the next step of work, it would be interesting to explore exact detectability results on general graphs. Other future topics also include developing efficient network forensics protocols, and addressing practical issues, e.g., non-unique initial sources, complicated spreading models, and outliers.

10. ACKNOWLEDGMENTS

The research has been supported by the Doctoral Program of Higher Education (SRFDP) and Research Grants Council Earmarked Research Grants (RGC ERG) Joint Research Scheme through Specialized Research Fund 20133402140001, National Natural Science Foundation of China through Grant 61379003, and the Research Grants Council of Hong Kong under Project M-CityU107/13.

11. REFERENCES

[1] A. Ganesh, L. Massoulie, and D. Towsley, "The effect of network topology on the spread of epidemics," in *Proc. of IEEE INFOCOM*, 2005, pp. 1455–1466.

[2] D. Easley and J. Kleinberg, *Networks, Crowds, and Markets: Reasoning About a Highly Connected World.* Cambridge University Press, 2010.

[3] D. Shah and T. Zaman, "Detecting sources of computer viruses in networks: theory and experiment," in *Proc. of ACM SIGMETRICS*, vol. 38, no. 1, 2010, pp. 203–214.

[4] ——, "Rumors in a network: Who's the culprit?" *IEEE Transactions on Information Theory*, vol. 57, no. 8, pp. 5163–5181, 2011.

[5] ——, "Rumor centrality: a universal source detector," in *Proc. of ACM SIGMETRICS*, vol. 40, no. 1, 2012, pp. 199–210.

[6] W. Dong, W. Zhang, and C. W. Tan, "Rooting out the rumor culprit from suspects," in *Proc. of IEEE ISIT*, 2013, pp. 2671–2675.

[7] W. Luo, W. P. Tay, and M. Leng, "Identifying infection sources and regions in large networks," *IEEE Transactions on Signal Processing*, vol. 61, no. 11, pp. 2850–2865, 2013.

[8] N. Karamchandani and M. Franceschetti, "Rumor source detection under probabilistic sample," in *Proc. of IEEE ISIT*, 2013, pp. 2184–2188.

[9] K. Zhu and L. Ying, "Information source detection in the SIR model: A sample path based approach," in *Proc. of IEEE ITA*, 2013, pp. 1–9.

[10] A. Y. Lokhov, M. Mezard, H. Ohta, and L. Zdeborova, "Inferring the origin of an epidemy with dynamics message-passing algorithm," *arXiv-v1303.5315*, 2013.

[11] W. Luo and W. P. Tay, "Finding an infection source under SIS model," in *Proc. of IEEE ICASSP*, 2013, pp. 2930–2934.

[12] D. J. Watts and S. H. Strogatz, "Collective dynamics of ąősmall-worldąŕnetworks," *Nature*, vol. 393, no. 6684, pp. 440–442, 1998.

[13] A.-L. Barabási and R. Albert, "Emergence of scaling in random networks," *Science*, vol. 286, no. 5439, pp. 509–512, 1999.

APPENDIX

Proof of Lemma 1

We illustrate the proof for ruling out the hypothetic case where node v has two neighbors satisfying the condition in Lemma 1. Denote the two neighbors by v_1 and v_2, which satisfy $x_{1,n_1}x_{1,n_2}\cdots x_{1,n_k} \geq (n_1-x_{1,n_1})(n_2-x_{1,n_2})\cdots(n_k-x_{1,n_k})$ and $x_{2,n_1}x_{2,n_2}\cdots x_{2,n_k} \geq (n_1-x_{2,n_1})(n_2-x_{2,n_2})\cdots(n_k-x_{2,n_k})$, respectively. Summing up the two inequalities, we have

$$\prod_{j=1}^{k}x_{1,n_j}+\prod_{j=1}^{k}x_{2,n_j} \geq \prod_{j=1}^{k}(n_j-x_{1,n_j})+\prod_{j=1}^{k}(n_j-x_{2,n_j}). \quad (53)$$

Noting that v_1 and v_2 are neighbors of node v, we have $x_{1,n_j}+x_{2,n_j} \leq n_j-1$, $\forall j \in [1,k]$. It follows that $x_{1,n_j} < n_j - x_{2,n_j}$ and $x_{2,n_j} < n_j - x_{1,n_j}$, $\forall j \in [1,k]$. Adopting into the left hand side of (53), we obtain

$$\prod_{j=1}^{k}x_{1,n_j}+\prod_{j=1}^{k}x_{2,n_j} < \prod_{j=1}^{k}(n_j-x_{1,n_j})+\prod_{j=1}^{k}(n_j-x_{2,n_j}),$$

which contradicts (53). Hence it is impossible to have two neighbors of node v satisfying the condition in Lemma 1. Similarly, the possibility of having more than two neighbors can be ruled out, and hence there can be at most a neighbor of node v that satisfies the condition in Lemma 1.

Proof of Lemma 2

If for all $i \in [1,m]$, $\prod_{j=1}^{k} x_{i,n_j} < \prod_{j=1}^{k}(n_j - x_{i,n_j})$, according to Proposition 2, s^* is the unique union rumor center. Therefore, we can make sure to correctly detect s^* as the rumor source. If for some $1 \leq i \leq m$, $\prod_{j=1}^{k} x_{i,n_j} = \prod_{j=1}^{k}(n_j - x_{i,n_j})$, according to Proposition 2 and Lemma 1, there are two union rumor centers. Therefore, the probability to correctly detect s^* as the rumor source is 1/2. If for some $1 \leq i \leq m$, $\prod_{j=1}^{k} x_{i,n_j} > \prod_{j=1}^{k}(n_j - x_{i,n_j})$, then s^* does not have the maximum union rumor centrality. Therefore s^* is not a union rumor center, and we cannot detect it as the rumor source. Then Lemma 2 follows from summarizing all the correct detection events.

Proof of Lemma 3

Denote $P_e = 1 - P_c$ as the error detection probability. Define $D_j = \left\{\prod_{i=1}^{k} x_{j,n_i} = \prod_{i=1}^{k}(n_i - x_{j,n_i})\right\}$, and $F_j = \left\{\prod_{i=1}^{k} x_{j,n_i} > \prod_{i=1}^{k}(n_i - x_{j,n_i})\right\}$, $(1 \leq j \leq \delta)$. According to Lemma 1, $D_j, F_j, 1 \leq j \leq \delta$ are all disjoint. Hence, based on

Proposition 2, P_e can be evaluated by

$$P_e=\frac{1}{2}\mathbf{P}_G\Big(\bigcap_{j=1}^{\delta} D_j\Big)+\mathbf{P}_G\Big(\bigcap_{j=1}^{\delta} F_j\Big)=\delta\Big(\frac{1}{2}\mathbf{P}_G(D_1)+\mathbf{P}_G(F_1)\Big),$$

where the second equality follows from symmetry.

Proof of Lemma 4

Note that the marginal distribution of X_1 is given by

$$\begin{aligned}&\mathbf{P}_G(X_1=x_1)\\&=\frac{(n-1)!}{x_1!x_2!}\cdot\frac{\prod_{i=1}^{2}b_i(b_i+\delta-2)\cdots(b_i+(x_i-1)(\delta-2))}{\delta(\delta+\delta-2)\cdots(\delta+(n-2)(\delta-2))},\end{aligned} \quad (54)$$

where $x_2=n-1-x_1$, $b_1=1$, $b_2=\delta-1$. As $n\to\infty$, we have

$$\begin{aligned}&\mathbf{P}_G(X_1=0)\\&=\frac{(n-1)!}{(n-1)!}\frac{(\delta-1)\cdot(\delta-1+(\delta-2))\cdots(\delta-1+(n-2)(\delta-2))}{\delta\cdot(\delta+(\delta-2))\cdot(\delta+2(\delta-2))\cdots(\delta+(n-2)(\delta-2))}\\&=\frac{\Gamma(\frac{\delta}{\delta-2})}{\Gamma(\frac{\delta-1}{\delta-2})}\cdot\frac{\Gamma(n+\frac{1}{\delta-2})}{\Gamma(n+\frac{2}{\delta-2})}\overset{(a)}{\sim}\frac{\Gamma(\frac{\delta}{\delta-2})}{\Gamma(\frac{\delta-1}{\delta-2})}\cdot\frac{\Gamma(n)n^{\frac{1}{\delta-2}}}{\Gamma(n)n^{\frac{2}{\delta-2}}}\to 0,\end{aligned}$$

where (a) follows from $\lim_{n\to\infty}\frac{\Gamma(n+\alpha)}{\Gamma(n)n^{\alpha}}=1$, $\alpha\in\mathbb{R}$.

Proof of Lemma 5

First, according to Lemma 4, as $n_1,\ldots,n_k\to\infty$, the probability for the rumor source to have less than δ infected neighbors (i.e., empty subtrees) asymptotically vanishes. So we only need to consider the case where the rumor source has $m=\delta$ infected neighbors, and denote by $P_{c,m=\delta}$ the correct detection probability in that case.

According to Proposition 2 and Lemma 2,

$$\begin{aligned}P_{c,m=\delta}&\geq\mathbf{P}_G\Big(\bigcap_{j=1}^{\delta}E_j\Big)=1-\mathbf{P}_G\Big(\bigcup_{j=1}^{\delta}E_j^c\Big)\\&\overset{(a)}{\geq}1-\sum_{j=1}^{\delta}\mathbf{P}_G(E_j^c)\overset{(b)}{=}1-\delta\cdot\mathbf{P}_G(E_1^c),\end{aligned}\quad (55)$$

where (a) is the union bound, and (b) follows from symmetry.

Again using Proposition 2 and Lemma 2, we have

$$\begin{aligned}P_{c,m=\delta}&\leq\mathbf{P}_G\Big(\bigcap_{j=1}^{\delta}F_j\Big)=1-\mathbf{P}_G\Big(\bigcup_{j=1}^{\delta}F_j^c\Big)\\&\overset{(c)}{=}1-\sum_{j=1}^{\delta}\mathbf{P}_G(F_j^c)\overset{(d)}{=}1-\delta\cdot\mathbf{P}_G(F_1^c),\end{aligned}\quad (56)$$

where (c) follows from that $F_1^c,\ldots,F_\delta^c$ are disjoint (Lemma 1), and (d) follows from symmetry.

Therefore, we have

$$\begin{aligned}&\lim_{n_1,\ldots,n_k\to\infty}P_c=\lim_{n_1,\ldots,n_k\to\infty}P_{c,m=\delta}\\&=1-\delta\cdot\lim_{n_1,\ldots,n_k\to\infty}\mathbf{P}_G(E_1^c)=1-\delta\cdot\lim_{n_1,\ldots,n_k\to\infty}\mathbf{P}_G(F_1^c).\end{aligned}$$

Collecting, Organizing, and Sharing Pins in Pinterest: Interest-driven or Social-driven?

Jinyoung Han*
Seoul National University
Seoul, Korea
jyhan@mmlab.snu.ac.kr

Daejin Choi
Seoul National University
Seoul, Korea
djchoi@mmlab.snu.ac.kr

Byung-Gon Chun
Seoul National University
Seoul, Korea
bgchun@snu.ac.kr

Ted "Taekyoung" Kwon
Seoul National University
Seoul, Korea
tkkwon@snu.ac.kr

Hyun-chul Kim
Sangmyung University
Cheonan, Korea
hkim@smu.ac.kr

Yanghee Choi
Seoul National University
Seoul, Korea
yhchoi@snu.ac.kr

ABSTRACT

Pinterest, a popular *social curating service* where people collect, organize, and share content (pins in Pinterest), has gained great attention in recent years. Despite the increasing interest in Pinterest, little research has paid attention to how people collect, manage, and share pins in Pinterest. In this paper, to shed insight on such issues, we study the following questions. How do people collect and manage pins by their tastes in Pinterest? What factors do mainly drive people to share their pins in Pinterest? How do the characteristics of users (e.g., gender, popularity, country) or properties of pins (e.g., category, topic) play roles in propagating pins in Pinterest? To answer these questions, we have conducted a measurement study on patterns of pin curating and sharing in Pinterest. By keeping track of all the newly posted and shared pins in each category (e.g., animal, kids, women's fashion) from June 5 to July 18, 2013, we built 350 K pin propagation trees for 3 M users. With the dataset, we investigate: (1) how users collect and curate pins, (2) how users share their pins and why, and (3) how users are related by shared pins of interest. Our key finding is that pin propagation in Pinterest is mostly driven by pin's properties like its topic, not by user's characteristics like her number of followers. We further show that users in the same community in the interest graph (i.e., representing the relations among users) of Pinterest share pins (i) in the same category with 94% probability and (ii) of the same URL where pins come from with 89% probability. Finally, we explore the implications of our findings for predicting how pins are shared in Pinterest.

*Jinyoung Han is currently a post-doctoral researcher at University of California-Davis.

SIGMETRICS'14, June 16–20, 2014, Austin, Texas, USA.

http://dx.doi.org/10.1145/2591971.2591996.

Categories and Subject Descriptors

H.3.5 [**Online Information Services**]: Web-based services; J.4 [**Computer Applications**]: Social and behavioral sciences

General Terms

Human Factors, Measurement

Keywords

Pinterest; Online Social Network; Social Curating; Content Propagation; Repin

1. INTRODUCTION

Pinterest[1] provides a social curating service where people can collect, organize, and share content[2]. Pew Research Center reported that 15% of online adults use Pinterest as of Dec. 2012 [3]. Pinterest has also been marked as the fastest growing web site to reach 10 million unique visitors [5]. According to the marketing service Experian, Pinterest has become the third most popular social network in the United States (as of Mar. 2012), behind Facebook and Twitter [6]. Currently, Pinterest is the 26th and 12th most popular web site in the world and Unite States (as of Nov. 2013), respectively [1].

The huge upsurge and popularity of Pinterest are attributed to its unique and attractive properties. First, Pinterest allows users to collect, organize, and share content (i.e., pins in Pinterest) by their tastes or interests [2, 4, 7, 15]. Second, about 80% of Pinterest's users are female [2, 7, 15, 25], which contrasts with male-centric services like *Quora.com* that mostly relies on early adopters of technology.

The popularity of Pinterest has attracted the research community to investigate user behaviors. Recent studies have revealed valuable insights into Pinterest internals [8, 15, 16, 19, 25, 32, 33]. However, most of these studies paid little attention to how pins are collected, organized, and propagated over Pinterest, which is the key to understanding Pinterest-like social networks.

[1]http://www.pinterest.com
[2]Pinterest serves two types of content: image and video. Since image content is dominant in Pinterest, we focus on analyzing image content in this paper.

In this paper, we seek to demystify Pinterest by answering the following questions. How do people collect and manage pins by their tastes? How many interests do people usually have? How do pins propagate in Pinterest? What factors drive people to share their pins in Pinterest? How do the characteristics of users (e.g., gender, popularity, country) or properties of pins (e.g., topic, content) play roles in propagating pins in Pinterest? Are there any differences in the way of sharing pins between Pinterest and other social networks?

We answer the questions from the perspective of pin curating and sharing with the dataset (350 K pins and 3 M users) we collected by crawling pages from Pinterest. That is, we investigate pin (or content) propagation patterns in Pinterest by keeping track of a propagation path of each pin. For example, if user A shares user B's pin, we can learn that B's pin is shared by A, which indicates the pin is propagated (or *repinned*) from B to A. Note that a pin can be propagated over multiple hops (e.g., from user A to user B to user C) by *repinning* in Pinterest. By keeping track of all the newly-posted and shared pins in each category (e.g., animal, kids, women's fashion) of Pinterest from June 5 to July 18, 2013, we construct pin propagation trees, each of which is built for a pin. With the dataset, we have analyzed: (1) how users collect and curate pins, (2) how users share their pins and why, and (3) how users are related to one another by shared interests.

We highlight the main contributions and key findings of our work as follows:

- **Measurement:** To our knowledge, this is the first measurement study to comprehensively investigate how people collect, manage, and share pins in Pinterest. We make our anonymized dataset online at: `http://mmlab.snu.ac.kr/traces/pinterest`.
- **Key Findings:** We reveal that pin propagation in Pinterest is mostly driven by its properties like its topic or content, not by user's characteristics like her number of followers. We also find that users in the same community in the interest graph (i.e., representing the relations among users) of Pinterest share pins (i) in the same category with 94% probability and (ii) of the same URL where pins come from with 89% probability, which implies that Pinterest users are highly related if they share interests.
- **Implications - Predictions on Pin Consumptions:** We explore the implications of our findings for predicting how pins are shared in Pinterest. We demonstrate that our proposed predicting method considering properties of pins exhibits higher precision (about 4.5 times) than other methods. Our trace-driven study for predicting pin consumption patterns in Pinterest suggests that properties of pins are much more important factors than those of users.

The rest of this paper is organized as follows. We introduce Pinterest and review related work in Section 2. We present the measurement methodology in Section 3. We start our analysis by investigating how users collect and organize their pins in Section 4. In Section 5, we analyze how and why pins propagate in Pinterest. We then analyze how users are related to one another by their shared interests in Section 6. Finally, we explore how to apply our findings to methods for predicting how pins are shared among users in Section 7.

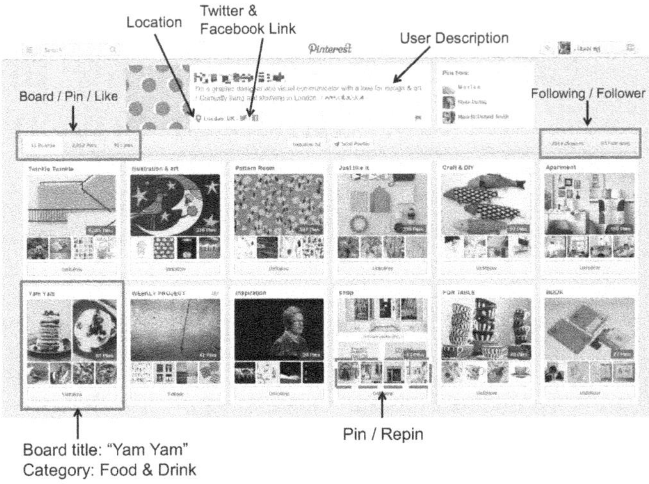

Figure 1: An illustration of a user's profile page in Pinterest.

2. BACKGROUND

2.1 Pinterest Overview

Pinterest [2, 7, 15, 25] is a pinboard-style content sharing platform that allows users to exhibit collections of images or videos. The main idea of Pinterest is to collect, organize, and share content (mostly images since image content is dominant in Pinterest) that users find interesting; Pinterest focuses on collecting and sharing content (i.e., pins in Pinterest). That is, Pinterest's basic function is to let users collect, organize, and share pins by their tastes or interests. Direct communications (e.g., private messages in Facebook or Twitter) between users are not available in Pinterest. Instead, user interactions mostly occur at the time they write feedbacks on or share pins (e.g., a user can *like* or *comment* on someone's pin). Figure 1 illustrates a user's profile page in Pinterest. We describe key terminologies in Pinterest below.

- Pin/Repin: Each image/video is called as a pin, and the act of posting a pin is referred to as pinning. If a posted pin is shared by someone, the shared pin is called as a repin, which is similar to *retweet* in Twitter. The act of sharing other user's pin is called repinning. Users who posts and shares (i.e., repins) a pin are the (original) pinner and repinner, respectively.
- Source: A user can directly upload a pin or fetch a pin from other websites like *Tumblr.com.* In the latter case, the URL of the pin is referred to as a source.
- Like/Comment: Similar to Facebook, a user can push a like button for a pin that she likes and leave a comment on a pin.
- Board/Category: A board is a collection of pins organized by a user. Each board belongs to one of the categories in Pinterest. At the moment there are 32 categories in Pinterest, varying from "animals" to "history" to "women's fashion".

- Following/Follower: Like Twitter, the relation between two users in Pinterest is not symmetric. The fact that user A follows user B does not necessarily mean B follows A. If A follows B, A can see the updated news (e.g., the act of posting a new pin) of B.

2.2 Related Work

Pinterest: Despite its young age (only 3 years old), Pinterest has attracted much attention since its launching. This in turn has spurred research into its gender differences [15, 25], repository perspectives [16,32], and applications [19,33]. Ottoni *et al.* showed that females are more active, make more use of lightweight interactions, and invest more effort in reciprocating social links than males in Pinterest [25]. Gilbert *et al.* found that being females means doing more repins but having fewer followers [15]. Some studies considered Pinterest as a repository like a digital library [16,32]. Zarro *et al.* found that Pinterest serves as an infrastructure for a repository that supports the following activities: discovery, collecting, collaborating, and publishing [16]. Zarro and Hall further discussed about how digital libraries could take advantage of Pinterest, allowing users to create personalized collections incorporating their content [32]. As an application on Pinterest, Kamath *et al.* introduced a supervised model for board recommendation [19]. They found that using social signals (e.g., repins, likes) can achieve higher recommendation quality. Zoghbi *et al.* suggested and evaluated information retrieval models for linking the texts of pins to web pages in Amazon [33]. While these studies mostly focus on user behaviors in Pinterest, we focus on pin propagation patterns with empirically-grounded evidences.

Information/Content Propagation in Online Social Networks: As online social networks are becoming the norm to spread information of interest, there have been studies to investigate patterns of information propagation in online social networks such as Twitter [11,12,20,26,27,31], Flickr [13], Facebook [9], and Digg [21]. Kwak *et al.* observed that retweets in Twitter reach a large audience and spread fast. Rodrigues *et al.* analyzed the word-of-mouth exchange of URLs among Twitter users and showed that users who are geographically close together are more likely to share the same URL [27]. Park *et al.* investigated how bad news about a company spreads in Twitter [26]. Ye and Wu analyzed the propagation patterns of messages in Twitter and showed how a breaking news (i.e., Michael Jackson's death) spreads in Twitter [31].

Some of the studies have focused on what drives information propagation in Twitter. Cha *et al.* analyzed how users play different roles in spreading popular and unpopular news in Twitter [11]. Cha *et al.* also showed that the most influential users (in terms of spawning retweets) are not necessarily the most followed ones [12]. Wang *et al.* found that information spreading is dependent on social context and the individuals' characteristics [30].

Flickr, Facebook, and Digg have also been analyzed as media to spread content or news. Cha *et al.* analyzed image-content propagation patterns in the Flickr social network; they showed that even popular photos do not spread widely and quickly in Flickr [13]. Bakshy *et al.* examined the patterns of information diffusion in Facebook, and found that weak ties play a more important role in dissemination of information in Facebook [9]. Lermn and Ghosh *et al.* tracked how interest in news stories spread on Digg, a popular social news service, and showed that social networks play a crucial role in the spread of interests [21]

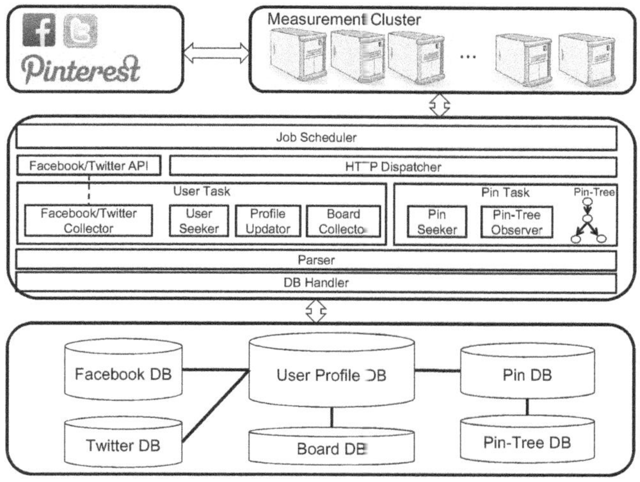

Figure 2: The architecture of our Pinterest crawling and analysis system.

While these studies have revealed valuable insights into the information propagation in Twitter, Flickr, Facebook, and Digg, there has been little research on how content is collected, organized, and propagated in Pinterest, which is a unique social curating service. We believe Pinterest is an ideal platform to investigate content propagation patterns since we can easily keep track of the propagation path of each pin in Pinterest. To our knowledge, this is the first comprehensive measurement study on how people collect, manage, and share pins in a social curating service.

3. METHODOLOGY

In this section, we illustrate our measurement methodology for data collection, and describe the dataset that is used in this paper.

3.1 Data Collection

Since Pinterest does not provide an official API for data collection, we developed our measurement system by crawling Pinterest pages as shown in Figure 2. We fetch web pages in Pinterest, from which the relevant information is extracted; the data about each pin or board can be extracted from a web page. This is challenging since we need to crawl a large number of web pages from Pinterest. For example, if a user has 1,000 boards, we need make 1,000 HTTP requests to collect the data about her board. To address this problem, we designed a distributed crawling system. Our measurement cluster consists of 25 PCs, which continuously send HTTP requests assigned by the job scheduler. The HTTP dispatcher processes the HTTP requests and responses according to the tasks explained below.

There are two main tasks in our system: *pin task* and *user task*. Unlike prior measurement studies (e.g., [15, 25]), we focus on pin propagation patterns. To this end, we periodically (every five minutes) monitor all the newly-posted pins in the menu of each category (e.g., animal, kids, women's fashion). Since Pinterest shows all the recent activities including posting a pin, repinning, and leaving a comment in the menu of each category in the chronological order, our pin seeker fetches 10 recent web pages not to miss newly-posted pins. The pin-tree observer keeps track of each pin and its associated repins to build a pin propagation tree, which is called a *pin-tree*. If a user repins the original pin, Pinterest provides a link to the board that includes the re-pinned one; we can find and fetch the associated web page of the repinned one among other pin pages in the board, so that we can keep track of the chain of the pin-tree. The collected information of each pin-tree are stored in the pin-tree database. The pin (and repin) dataset consists of the number of likes, number of comments, its category, its source, and its description, which is stored in the pin database.

In the user task, we collect the information (e.g., number of pins, number of followers, number of boards, gender, country, etc.) of each user. In addition to the 1 M users found in pin-trees, the user seeker additionally finds 2 M users using a breath first search (BFS) in Pinterest. For the discovered 3 M users, we collect the information of each user, including her name, her description, gender, number of followers, number of followings, number of boards, number of pins, number of likes, her external website, location, and Facebook/Twitter links, which are stored in the user profile database. Along with the user profiles, the board collector collects the information of each board including its category, and number of pins, which are stored in the board database. To identify the gender and country of users, we use external links to Facebook and Twitter, which can be found in the profile pages of users. The Facebook/Twitter collector sends queries to Facebook and Twitter through their APIs and fetches the gender and country information of each user if available. We finally decide the gender and country of each user by collectively combining information from Pinterest, Facebook, and Twitter.

3.2 Dataset

Our dataset had been collected from June 5 to July 18, 2013. We kept track of 346,329 pin-trees, which contain 346,329 (original) pins and their 1,215,045 repins, which are shared by 1,561,374 users. In addition to the users found in pin-tress, we further discovered 1,412,754 users using a breath first search (BFS) through Pinterest. Finally, our dataset includes 2,974,128 users (i.e., 1,561,374 users found in pin-trees + 1,412,754 users discovered through BFS). The dataset collectively contains 40,800,940 boards, 3,362,100,884 pins, 656,123,740 followers, 302,363,300 followings, 1,392,394 Facebook links, and 183,900 Twitter links. We also obtained the country and gender information of 1,354,132 and 1,392,394 users, respectively. We found that 85% of Pinterest users are female in our dataset, which is congruent with prior reports (e.g., [2, 7, 15, 25]). Top five countries in terms of the number of users in our dataset are United States (85%), United Kingdom (6%), Brazil (1%), Netherlands (0.6%), and Spain (0.6%). The ratios of female to male users in these five countries are 87:13, 80:20, 68:32, 75:25, and 67:33, respectively.

4. SOCIAL CURATING

In this section, we investigate social curating behaviors in terms of the number of pins, boards, categories, and followings/followers. Here, social curating indicates the act of collecting and organizing content by tastes or interests, with social functionalities such as liking, commenting, and following [15, 16, 25].

4.1 Pin and Follower Distributions

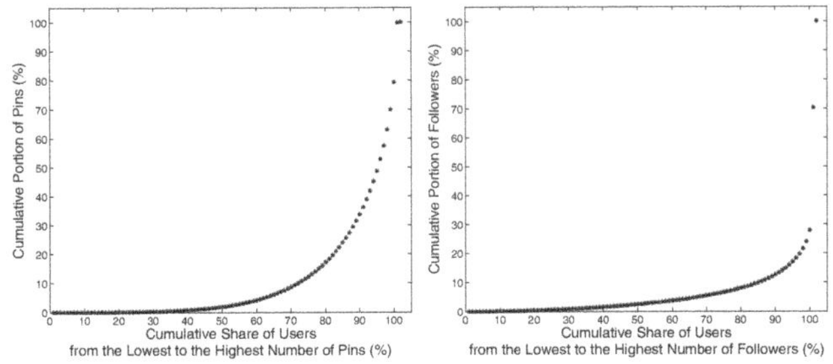

(a) Pin distribution (b) Follower distribution

Figure 3: Gini Triangles of (a) pins and (b) followers. A small portion of Pinterest users own a large portion of pins and followers.

We first analyze the distribution of pins and followers in Pinterest by calculating the *Gini coefficient*, a well-known estimator to evaluate the disparity of a distribution in Economics [14]. The Gini coefficient is always within the range of [0, 1], where 0 and 1 indicate a perfect uniform distribution and an extremely skewed distribution, respectively [14]. Figure 3(a) shows the Lorenz curve [23] of the pins where the x-axis is the cumulative share of users from the lowest to the highest number of pins, while the y-axis is the cumulative portion of the number of pins. Figure 3(b) is the Lorenz curve of the followers. Obviously, a small portion of users own a large portion of pins and followers. For example, top 20% of users in terms of the number of pins own 82% pins of Pinterest and top 20% of users in terms of number of followers have 90% of followers. Note that the Gini coefficients of pins and followers are 0.78 and 0.90, respectively, which exhibits high skewness. Interestingly, only 8% of top 1% users in terms of the number of pins are males, while 18% of top 1% users in terms of the number of followers are males. This implies that males are more interested in social networking than pinning in Pinterest.

4.2 Curating behavior

We next investigate the curating behaviors of users in terms of the numbers of pins, boards, categories, and followings/followers in Figure 4. As shown in Figure 4(a), 45% of users have fewer than 100 pins while top 20% of users have more than 1000 pins; the average, median, and maximum numbers of pins are 1130, 106, and 194,515, respectively. 32 categories are Pinterest-defined topics while a board can be interpreted as a user-defined topic. For example, if a user has a basketball board and a baseball board, both of which may belong to *sports* category, but she may have two topics personally. Figure 4(b) shows around 55% of users have fewer than 10 boards, while top 1% of users have more than 100 boards. The average and median numbers of boards are 14 and 7, respectively. Figure 4(c) shows the number of categories on which the user has posted pins. While 23% of users have only one category, top 10% of users are interested in more than 10 categories. The average and median numbers of categories are 4 and 3, respectively, meaning that an average user of Pinterest manages a few Pinterest-defined topics. We next examine the number of followings and followers in Figure 4(d). Interestingly, most of users have more followings than followers, but a small portion of users have a

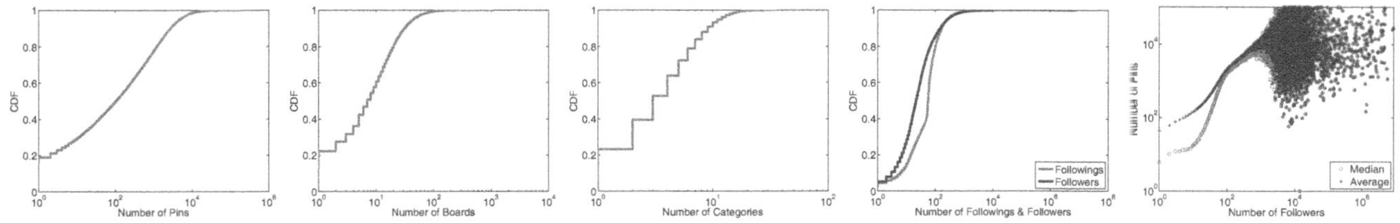

(a) Pins (b) Boards (c) Categories (d) Social Ties (e) Pin vs. Followers

Figure 4: Distributions of the number of (a) pins, (b) boards, (c) categories, and (d) followings/followers. The numbers of followers and pins for each user are further illustrated in (e) to investigate their correlation.

very large number of followers, hence the average number of followers (221) is about two times greater than that of followings (102). As to the number of followers, 25% of users have fewer than 10 followers while top 15% of users have more than 100 followers. Note that the maximum number of followers is 8,430,910. Finally, to investigate the correlation between the number of followers and that of pins for each user, we plot the number of followers (x-axis) against the number of posted pins (y-axis) in Figure 4(e). The average is mostly above the median until the number of followers reaches 1,000, indicating that there are outliers who pin far more than ordinary users with the same number of followers. There is a positive correlation between the number of followers and that of pins up to $x = 1{,}000$. However, there is a weak correlation beyond $x = 1{,}000$, which signifies that a user who has a large number of followers does not necessarily post a large number of pins.

We next investigate whether and how user's efforts on pinning are evenly distributed across different boards by calculating the Shannon's entropy [29] defined by:

$$H_{board} = -\sum_{i=1}^{B} p_i \ln p_i \qquad (1)$$

where B is the number of boards and p_i is the relative portion of the pins in the ith board of a user. We can easily calculate $H_{category}$ similarly. Figure 5 shows the correlations between the number of interested topics (boards and categories) and its corresponding entropy. Users' interested topics are skewed since all the median and average values are notably below the values of the uniform case in which a user posts pins/repins evenly across different boards or categories. As the numbers of boards and categories increase, the gaps between the values of the uniform cases and the average values becomes wider until the numbers of boards and categories are 200 and 27, respectively, which implies that users who have pins in more boards or categories focus on a small number of interests. However, $H_{category}$ values are increasing somewhat sharply after the number of categories is 28, which needs further investigation.

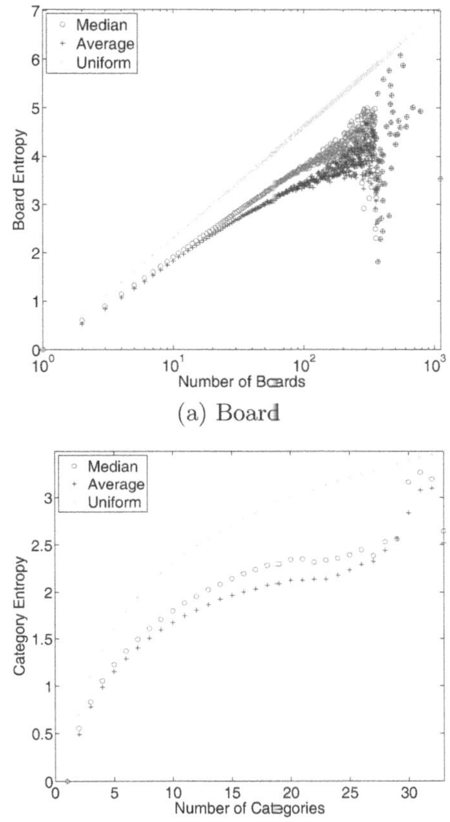

(a) Board

(b) Category

Figure 5: The correlation between the number of interested topics (boards and categories) and its corresponding entropy.

5. PIN TREE ANALYSIS

In this section, we first seek to model how pins propagate in Pinterest. We then characterize the patterns of pin propagation from a graph-theoretical perspective, and investigate what factors affect pin propagation in Pinterest.

5.1 Definition of Pin-Tree

We define a pin-tree as a directed graph, $T = (V, E)$, where V is the set of users and E is the set of repins (i.e., pin propagations), based on the Krackhardt's hierarchical tree model [17]. That is, if user j repins a pin from user i, there exists an edge $E(V_i, V_j)$ from user V_i to user V_j. Note that all nodes in a hierarchical tree (except for the root) have the same ancestor (which is the root). Figure 6 shows an example of a pin-tree. A pinner is a user who posts an original pin and a repinner is a user who fetches the pin from her parent. We define the max depth in a pin-tree as the maximum hop count from the root to any of the leaf nodes. The max width refers to the maximum number of child nodes of a parent node in a given tree. The max depth and max width of a pin-tree in Figure 6 are 2 and 4, respectively.

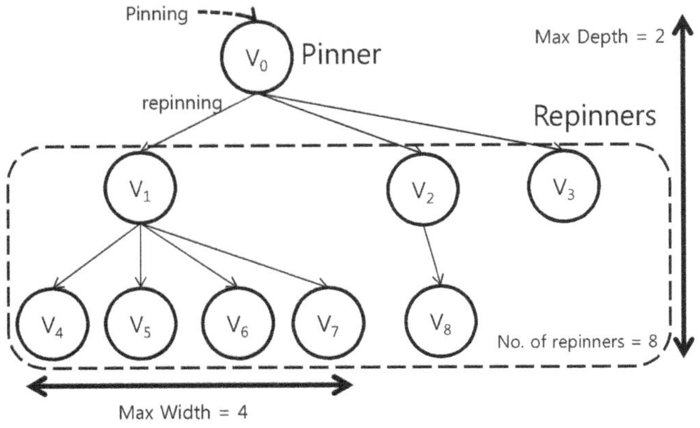

Figure 6: An example of a pin-tree.

5.2 Structure of Pin-Tree

5.2.1 Structural analysis

We first examine the structural patterns of pin propagations (i.e., pin-trees). In this analysis, we consider 144,080 pin-trees which have at least one repinner; 57% of (original) pins are not propagated in our dataset. Figure 7 shows the distributions of the number of repinners, max depth, max width, the number of likes, and the number of comments of a pin-tree, respectively. As shown in Figure 7(a), 77% of pin-trees have fewer than 10 repinners while top 0.5% of pin-trees have more than 100 repinners. The average, median, maximum number of repinners of a pin-tree are 8.26, 4, and 3,400, respectively. When we look at the number of likes and comments in Figures 7(d) and 7(e), a small portion of pins have received great attention; e.g., while the average number of likes of pin-trees is 2.95, the maximum number of likes of pin-trees is 1,303. We also find that 67% of pin-trees have the max depth of 1 in Figure 7(b), which means that the propagation of pins tends to be bounded in one hop for the majority of pin-trees. The median max depth and max width are 1 and 3, which suggests that pin-trees in Pinterest are usually wider than deeper. Note that the maximum max depth and max width are 35 and 1,066; they are two-orders of magnitude different.

5.2.2 Temporal analysis of repinning

We next investigate how fast repins spread in Pinterest. Figure 8(a) plots the distributions of the first-repin times (i.e. time from the original pinning to the first repinning) and the average inter-repin times of pin-trees, respectively. As shown in Figure 8(a), 52%, 90%, and 97% of first-repinnig occur within an hour, 6 hours, and a day, respectively, which means a pin in Pinterest tends to spread rapidly. However, first-repinnings of a few pin-trees occur a month later; the maximum first-repin time in our dataset is about 40 days. The average and median inter-repin times are 1,187 and 377 minutes, respectively, which suggests that repinning usually occurs within 20 hours. In Figure 8(b), we also show the elapsed times of repins from $(n-1)$ hop to n hop on a pin-tree. As shown in Figure 8(b), first-repinnings (i.e., the first hop) only take less than 10 minutes in the 25st percentile, an hour with the median, and 6 hours in the 75st percentile, which signifies the fast interest diffusion in Pinterest since most of pin-trees have a depth of one. Interestingly, the median inter-hop times are around 8 hours from the second hop.

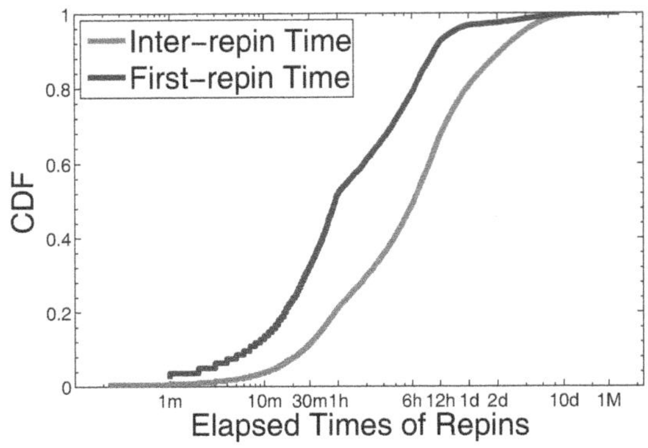

(a) Elapsed times of repins

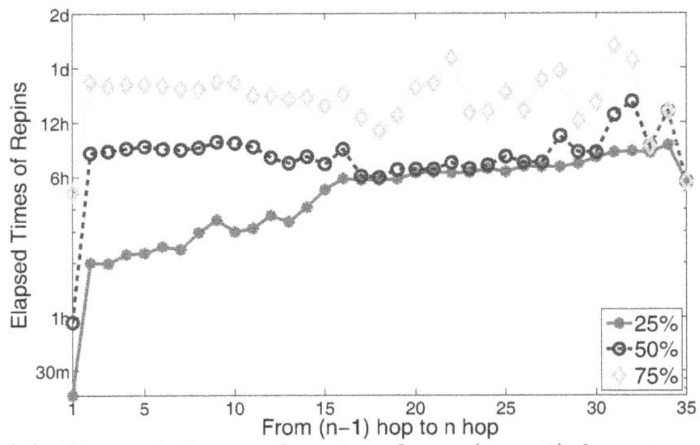

(b) Elapsed times of repins from $(n-1)$ hop to n hop

Figure 8: Elapsed times of repins.

5.3 Pin Propagation Factor Analysis

We now analyze which factors affect the pin propagation in Pinterest: (i) pinner's influence and (ii) pin's influence itself. For the first factor, we investigate two influence metrics of pinners: (a) the number of followers and (b) the number of pins the pinner has. Figure 9 shows the average and median numbers of repinners for each pin-tree against the numbers of followers and pins of the pinner, respectively. As shown in Figure 9, the average number of repinners is not shown to be affected by the number of followers or pins of the pinner. To quantify the correlation between the number of repinners of the pin-tree and the pinner's influence (i.e., number of followers and pins), we calculate the Pearson's correlation coefficient [18], denoted by ρ. The ρ values of the number of followers and the number of pins the pinner has are 0.046 and 0.007, respectively, which indicates that there is little correlation between the number of repinners and the pinner's influence.

To examine the second factor, we examine (i) the number of likes of an original pin and (ii) the total number of likes in a pin-tree against the number of repinners of the pin-tree in Figure 10. As shown in Figure 10, there is a significant positive correlation (Pearson's correlation coefficient $\rho = 0.689$) between the number of likes in a pin-tree and the number of repinners, which means the number of repinners increases as the pin becomes increasingly popular. Likewise, there is also a significant positive correlation ($\rho = 0.423$) between

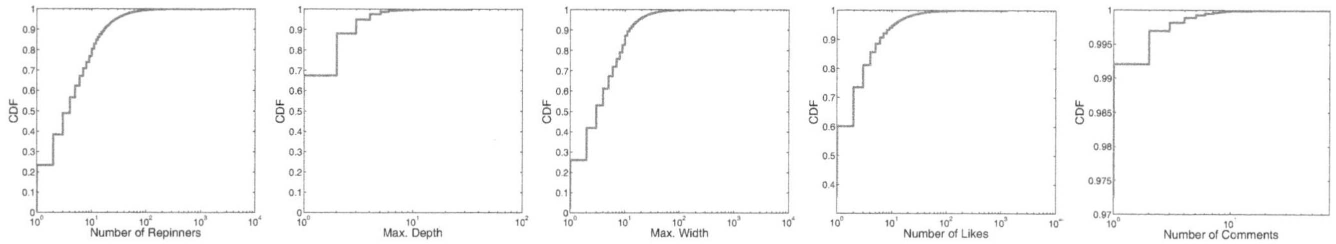

(a) Repinner (b) Max Depth (c) Max Width (d) Like (e) Comment

Figure 7: Distributions of the number of repinners (a), max depth (b), max width (c), the number of likes (d), and the number of comments (e) of a pin-tree.

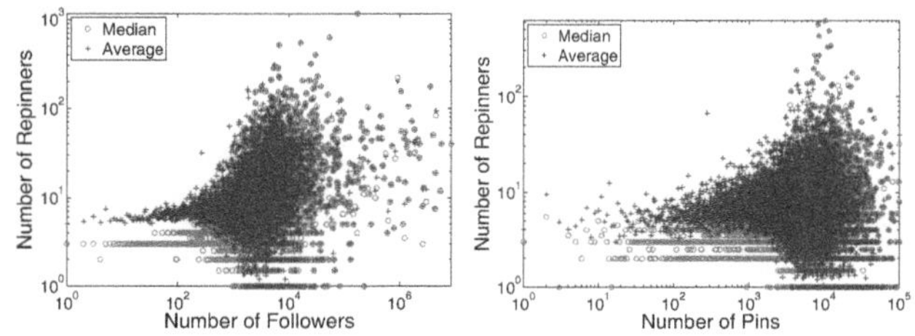

(a) Followers (b) Pins

Figure 9: There is no strong correlation between the number of repinners of the pin-tree and the pinner's influence (i.e., number of followers and pins).

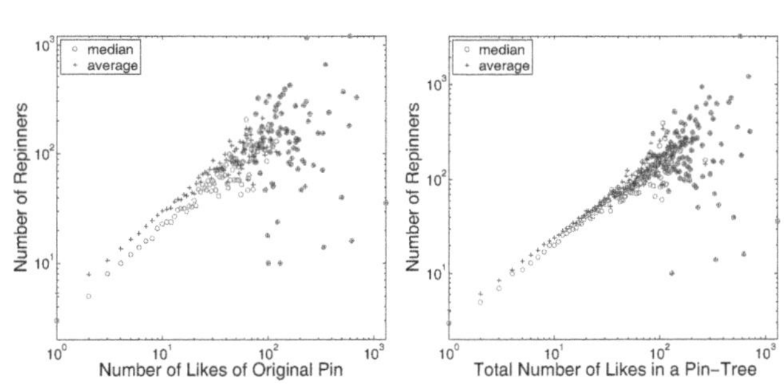

(a) Number of likes of the original pin (b) Total number of likes in a pin-tree

Figure 10: There is a significant correlation between the number of repinners of the pin-tree and the popularity of the pin.

the number of likes of the original pin and the number of repinners; we can predict whether the number of repinners in a pin-tree will be large or not by looking at the number of likes the original pin has received.

In summary, pin propagations in Pinterest are not due to pinner's influence on Pinterest but due to the popularity of the pin. In the following sections, we will further investigate pin propagation patterns (i.e., number of repinners and inter-repin time of a pin-tree) depending on different properties of pins (e.g., categories, sources).

5.4 Category and Source Analysis

This subsection analyzes pin propagation patterns based on the 32 Pinterest-defined categories and the top 20 sources which are sorted in terms of the number of corresponding pins. Overall, there are notable differences in pin propagation patterns across different categories and sources. We observe that even though there are many pin-trees in particular categories or from particular sources, the number of repinners per pin-tree may not be high, and vice versa. We also find that a large portion (65%) of top 20 sources are in the specific categories where their pins are mostly posted. We describe detailed analysis below.

5.4.1 Category analysis

We investigate the pin propagation patterns in Pinterest across different categories as described in Table 1. There were 32 categories in Pinterest during the period of our measurements, which are sorted in terms of the number of pin-trees in Table 1. Figures 11(a), 11(b), and 11(c) show the number of posted pins/repins, the birth rate of pins, and the number of propagated (original) pins in each category, respectively. Here, the birth rate is the number of newly posted pins per minute; the average birth rate of Pinterest during our measurement period is 2.39/min. The number of propagated pins indicates the number of pin-trees, each of which has at least one child. As shown in Figure 11(a), "diy & crafts" (category index (CI) 1) and "food & drink" (CI 7) have the highest and second highest number of pins/repins, respectively. Intuitively, their birth rates should be proportionally high; however, Figure 11(b) reveals that new pins are posted more frequently in the "food & drink" category than the "diy & crafts" category. That is, the pins in "food & drink" tend to be not propagated much. Note that pins are propagated more broadly in the "diy & crafts" than the ones in the "food & drink". Overall, newly-posted pins in the "diy & crafts" tend to be propagated most broadly among all the categories.

Figures 11(d) and 11(e) plot the average number of repinners and the average inter-repin time of each category, respectively. As shown in Figure 11(d), the average numbers of repinners in the categories of "humor" (CI 19), "quotes" (CI 22), "geek" (CI 24), and "tattoos" (CI 31) are higher than the ones in other categories. This is interesting because these categories are usually for particular communities. When we look at the average inter-repin times in each category, we find that the "food & drink" (CI 7) exhibits the shortest inter-repin time, which implies that the "food & drink" category is the most active category since pins are posted and spreading quickly (the birth rate is the highest while the inter-repin time is the shortest). Likewise, the pins in the "health & fitness" (CI 5) are also posted and spreading quickly. The average inter-repin times of the "sports" (CI

1	diy & crafts	2	design	3	education	4	animals	5	health & fitness
6	architecture	7	food & drink	8	products	9	art	10	film, music & books
11	home decor	12	women's fashion	13	gardening	14	cars & motorcycles	15	technology
16	travel	17	weddings	18	hair & beauty	19	humor	20	men's fashion
21	science & nature	22	quotes	23	celebrities	24	geek	25	outdoors
26	illustrations & posters	27	photography	28	kids	29	sports	30	history
31	tattoos	32	holidays & events						

Table 1: Pinterest categories with indexes.

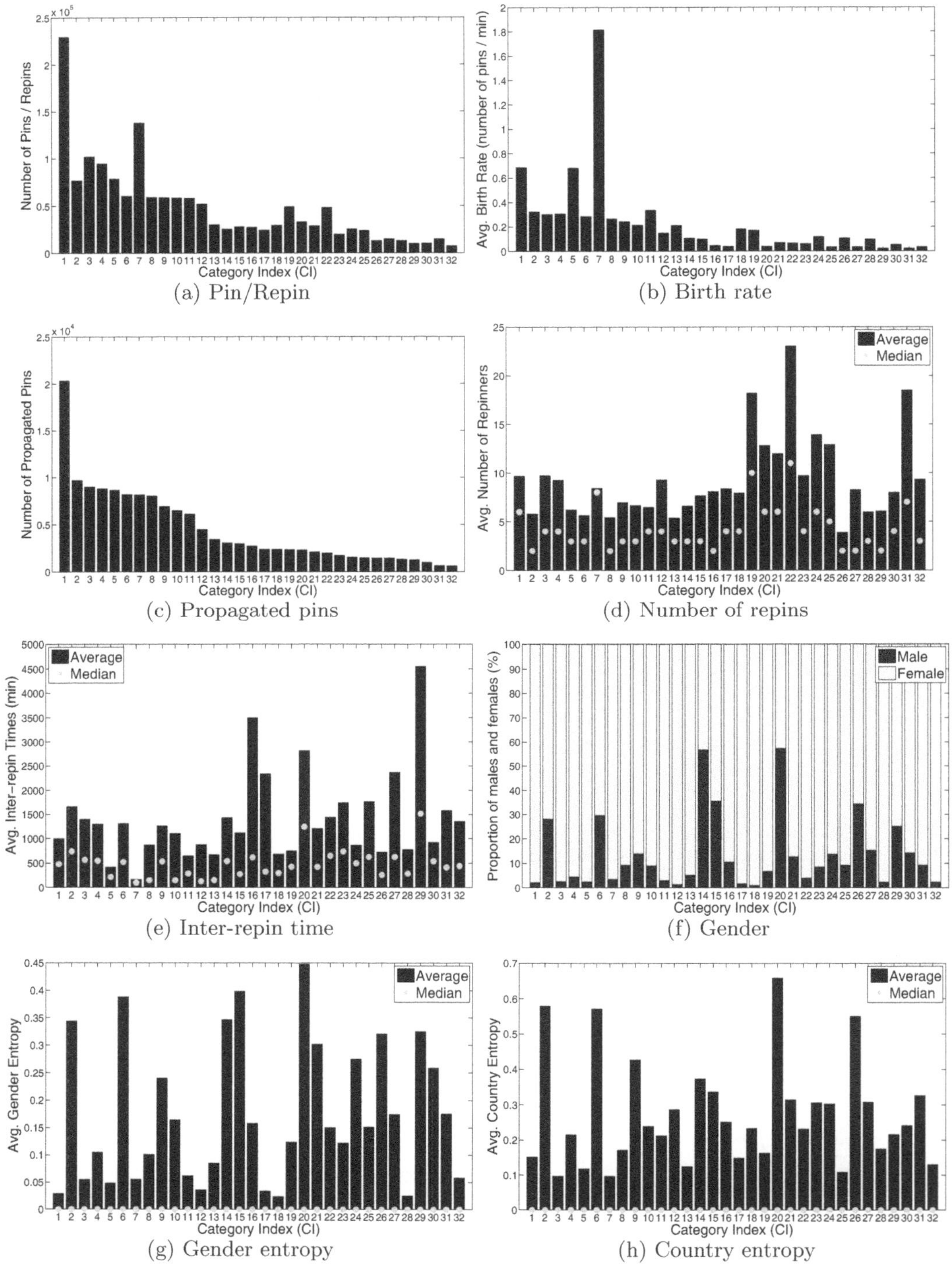

Figure 11: Pin propagation patterns across different categories.

Index	Source URL	Type	Alexa rank
1	blogspot.com	blog	13
2	tumblr.com	microblog	25
3	fitsugar.com	fitness	8,127
4	buzzfeed.com	news	178
5	teacherspayteachers.com	education	5,446
6	imdb.com	movie	48
7	saatchionline.com	art	11,745
8	wordpress.com	blog	15
9	akamaihd.net	CDN (image)	72
10	designspiration.net	design	10,838
11	womenshealthmag.com	fitenss	5,624
12	greatist.com	fitness	3,715
13	archdaily.com	architect	3,277
14	blog.com	blog	1,266
15	google.com	search engine	1
16	ebay.com	shopping	20
17	fitnessmagazine.com	fitness	6,088
18	wikipaintings.org	painting	21,912
19	streetartutopia.com	street art	51,788
20	houzz.com	home deco	586

Table 2: A summary of top 20 sources. We fetch ranking information of each source from Alexa [1] as of Nov. 2013.

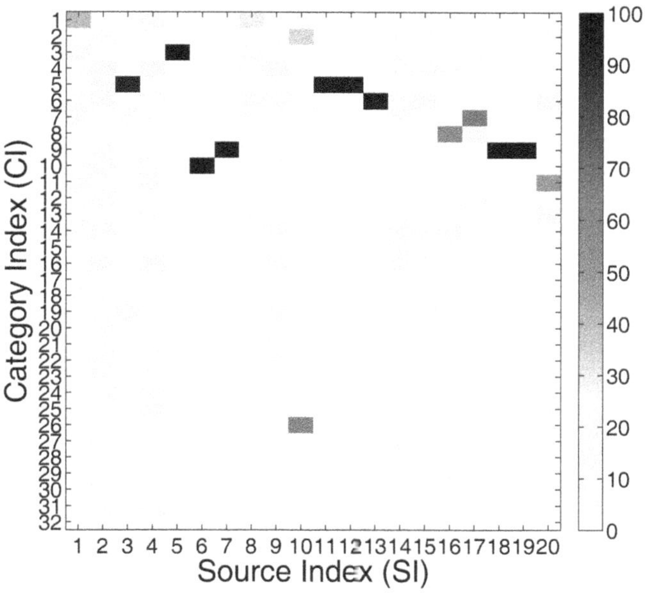

Figure 12: A heatmap of the portion of each source across different categories.

29) and "travel" (CI 16) are longer than those of the other categories, which indicates that pins of these categories tend to spread slowly.

To investigate how the gender and country distributions of pin-trees are skewed in each category, we calculate the entropies for the gender (H_{gender}) and the country ($H_{country}$) as similar to Equation 1 in Section 4.1, respectively. Figure 11(f) shows the ratio of males and females in each category. As shown in Figure 11(f), the ratios of males in the "design" (CI 2), "architecture" (CI 6), "cars & motorcycles" (CI 14), "technology" (CI 15), "men's fashion" (CI 20), and "illustrations & posters" (CI 26) are higher than those in the other categories. Interestingly, the categories of "design" and "illustrations & posters" seem to be not so inclined to females; by the deep analysis, we find that there is a number of male designers in Pinterest. Figure 11(g) shows that the gender entropies of the "architecture" (CI 6), "technology" (CI 15), and "men's fashion" (CI 20) are higher than those of the other categories, which reflects the relatively high interest of males. However, the gender entropies of the most of female-oriented categories like "hair & beauty" (CI 18) and "kids" (CI 28) are low, which means that pin-trees in those categories show a highly skewed distribution in terms of gender. The country entropies of "design" (CI 2), "architecture" (CI 6), "men's fashion" (CI 20), and "illustrations & poster" (CI 26) are higher than the other categories, implying a relatively even distribution of countries. This is interesting since those categories with the higher country entropies often also have the higher gender entropies, which means those categories are relatively less dependent on gender or country. Note that the median values of the gender and country entropies for each category are zero, respectively, which indicates that most of pin-trees are skewed in terms of both gender and country.

5.4.2 *Source analysis*

We next investigate the source information of each pin, which was briefly mentioned in Section 2.1. Here, a source is a URL which the pin comes from. Table 2 summarizes the information of the top 20 sources, which are sorted in terms of the number of corresponding pins. We further manually examine the type and Alexa rank of each source as shown in Table 2. We find that there are various types such as blog, image, news, and fitness; interestingly, the fitness type takes a substantial portion in the top 20 sources (4 of 20). Also, the Alexa ranks of a half of the top 20 sources is greater than 3,000, which means they are not so popular web sites but popular sources in Pinterest.

Figure 12 shows the heatmap of the portion of each source across 32 categories. For example, *imdb.com* (source index (SI) 6) and *saatchionline.com* (SI 7) are mostly consumed (colored black) in the categories of "film, music & books" (CI 10) and "art" (CI 9), respectively. Also, 60% of pins in the category of "illustrations & posters" (CI 26) and 40% of pins in the category of "art" (CI 9) are from the source *designspiration.net*, an image-based website of art galleries. We find that 65% of the top 20 sources are strongly related to specific categories where their pins are mostly posted (over 60% of pins are posted on a specific category). However, pins of some sources like "tumblr.com" (SI 2) or "google.com" (SI 15) are spread across several categories.

Figure 13 analyzes the pin propagation patterns depending on the sources. As shown in Figure 13(a), the numbers of corresponding pins of top 3 sources are about 10,000, 6,000, and 3,000, respectively, which accounts for over 60% of total pins, while those of the other sources are around 1,800. From Figure 13(b), the numbers of repinners are higher in the source indexes 2, 4, 8, and 9; their pins spread across several categories since they are mostly general websites like blogs or news; however, the speeds of spreading of the pins of these sources are mostly slower as shown in Figure 13(c). On the contrary, sources related with "fitness" (SI 3, 11, 12, and 17) have a small number of repinners but their pins spread faster.

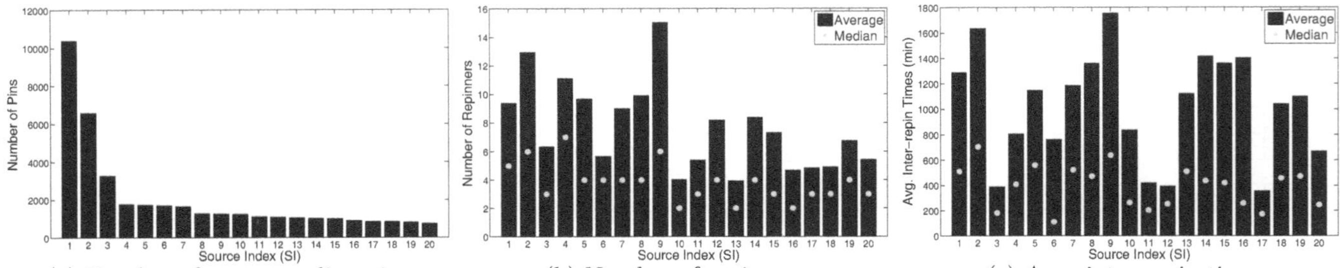

(a) Number of corresponding pins (b) Number of repinners (c) Avg. inter-repin time

Figure 13: Pin propagation patterns depending on different sources.

5.4.3 Analysis on Top 1% Pin-Trees

We finally investigate the top 1% of all the pin-trees in terms of the number of repinners. We observe that the averages of the number of repinners, number of likes, max depth, and max width of top 1% pin-trees are 299, 60, 5, and 68, respectively, which are significantly higher (17 times for the number of repinners, 20 times for the number of likes, 3.3 times for the max depth, and 11.3 times for the max width) than those of all the pin-trees. Figure 14 shows the numbers of the top 1% pin-trees across different categories and sources, respectively. We notice that a large number of the top 1% pin-trees belong to the "humor" (CI 19) and "quotes" (CI 22) even though there are relatively fewer pin-trees in those categories. On the contrary, a small number of the top 1% pin-trees belong to the "design" (CI 2), while it ranks second among 32 categories in terms of the total number of pin-trees (See Figure 11(c)). This implies that the top 1% pin-trees exhibit different patterns compared to all of the pin-trees. When we look at the top 1% pin-trees depending on the top 20 sources in Figure 14(b), we find that most of the top 1% pin-trees belong to *blogspot.com* (SI 1) and *tumblr.com* (SI 2). We further observe that the top 1% pin-trees often belong to *akamaihd.net* (SI 9), an image-hosting content delivery network (CDN) for *Facebook.com*.

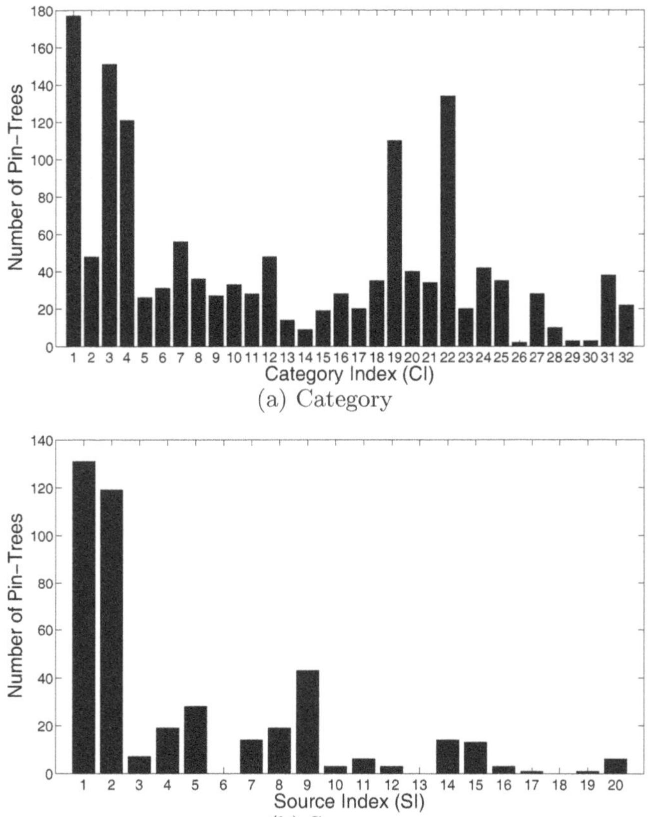

(b) Source

Figure 14: Numbers of the top 1% pin-trees across different categories (a) and sources (b).

6. INTEREST GRAPH ANALYSIS

In this section, we investigate how users are related to one another in terms of shared interests. To this end, we introduce the notion of *"Interest Graph"* to represent the relations among users.

6.1 Definition of Interest Graph

We assume that a directed weighted graph $I = (V, E, W)$ represents an interest graph where V is the set of users and E is the set of (directed) edges between two users. That is, there exists an edge $E(V_i, V_j)$ from user V_i to user V_j if user V_j repins a pin from user V_i. The weight $W(V_i, V_j)$ of an edge $E(V_i, V_j)$ is the total number of propagated pins from V_i and V_j. Overall, the interest graph I in Pinterest is designed to show how users are related to one another by their shared interests. Figure 15 illustrates an interest graph, where three pins A, B, and C are shared among the users. As shown in Figure 15, the interest graph I is constructed by merging the three pin-trees. The weights $W(V_1, V_3)$ and $W(V_6, V_7)$ are two in this example.

The numbers of nodes and edges in the interest graph of Pinterest are 936,795 and 1,170,192, respectively, which means the interest graph of Pinterest is sparse. In particular, the average degrees and weights of I are 2.50 and 1.29, respectively, meaning that most of users are likely to be connected with two or three people and share one or two pins on average. We also calculate that the clustering coefficient [24] of I, which is defined as the probability that two neighbors of a given node are also neighbors. We find that the clustering coefficient of I is much higher than that of a random network (with the same numbers of nodes and edges), by a factor of 207 or larger, which suggests a significant "small-worldness" of I in Pinterest.

6.2 Community Analysis

To investigate how users form a group (or a community) in the interest graph I, we first identify communities of I using

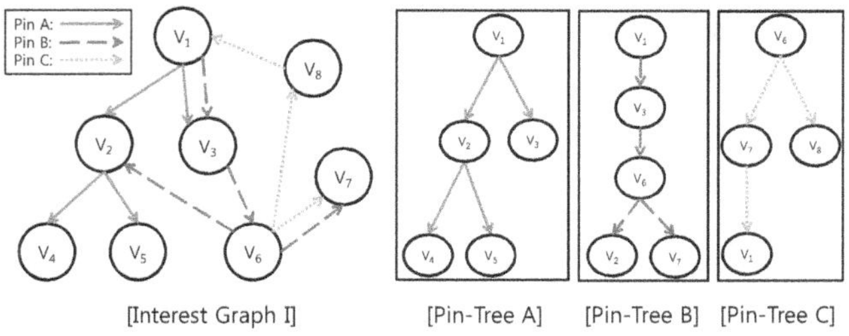

Figure 15: An interest graph with three pins propagated.

Property	Community	Random
Gender	0.81	0.77
Country	0.91	0.82
Major Category	0.21	0.11
Interest Feature	0.34	0.23
Category	**0.94**	**0.03**
Source	**0.89**	**0.01**

Table 3: Uniformities of properties of users or shared interests in the same community.

the Louvain method, a well-known fast community detection algorithm that maximizes the ratio of the number of edges within communities to that of edges across communities [10]. Note that we use the weighted version of Louvain method. The number of identified communities is 15,936 and the average number of members of a community is 58.78. Based on the identified communities, we examine what makes users belong to the same community. To this end, we devise a *uniformity* metric U, which quantifies how much similarity exists among members or among shared interests. That is, U denotes the probability that randomly selected two users in the same community have the same property (e.g., gender or country). The uniformity U is defined as:

$$U = \frac{2}{\sum_{k=1}^{c} n_k (n_k - 1)} \sum_{k=1}^{c} \sum_{i=1}^{n_k - 1} \sum_{j=i+1}^{n_k} \delta \left(P\left(v_i^k\right), P\left(v_j^k\right) \right) \tag{2}$$

where c is the number of communities in the given network, n_k is the number of nodes (or users) in the community k, and v_i^k means node i in the community k. Note that $P(v)$ is the property (e.g., gender or country) of user v and δ is the Kronecker's delta ($\delta(i,j) = 1$ if $i = j$, and $\delta(i,j) = 0$ otherwise).

We conjecture that users may belong to the same community if properties of users or shared interests are similar. To validate this conjecture, we first consider four properties of users: (i) gender, (ii) country, (iii) major category to which the majority of (the user's) pins belong, and (iv) interest feature that characterizes how user's interests are distributed across the 32 categories. The interest feature is defined as a vector with 32 entries [C_1, C_2, ..., C_{32}], each of which is a portion of pins that a user has posted to the corresponding category C_i. For the first three properties (gender, country, major category), each of the uniformity can be calculated by Equation 2. To calculate the uniformity for the interest feature, we use the cosine-similarity function between the interest features of two users instead of using δ in Equation 2. In addition to the properties of users, we further consider two properties of shared interests: (i) category and (ii) source of pins. Since the shared interests are represented by edges (which show pin propagation) in the interest graph, we calculate the uniformities for the category and source by replacing nodes with edges in Equation 2.

Table 3 shows the uniformity of each property. For comparison purposes, we randomly select two nodes (or edges) 10,000 times in the interest graph and calculate its uniformity (denoted by Random). As shown in Table 3, the uniformities of shared interests are significantly higher than those by Random; shared pins in the same community (i) belong to the same category or (ii) come from the same source with high probability. That is, users who have similar tastes or share similar pins tend to form a community in the interest graph. The user properties considering her tastes or interests (i.e., the major category and the interest feature) exhibit relatively higher uniformities compared to Random, which indicates that users with similar interests are likely to belong to the same community. Users in the same community are likely to be the same gender or belong to the same country with somewhat higher probability compared to those by Random.

7. APPLICATION

We have analyzed how and why pins are collected, organized, and propagated in Pinterest. Our empirically-grounded evidences suggest that most of pin propagations in Pinterest are driven by interest. In this section, we seek to answer the following question, which may be important for understanding the patterns of pin consumptions in Pinterest: *What pins will be consumed (pinned or repinned) by each user in the future?* To answer the question, we perform a trace-driven simulation study.

7.1 Trace-driven Simulation

To conduct a trace-driven simulation, we first select 4,667 target users, each of which has at least 10 pins in our dataset. Based on the prediction methods that we describe in Section 7.2, we make a candidate pin list (which consists of 20 pins) to be possibly consumed for each target user (as of Jul. 18, 2013). To validate whether the predicted pins are actually consumed by each target user after 125 days, we check all the pin information that the target user has (as of Nov. 20, 2013). To this end, we have collected additional dataset for 10 days from Nov. 20 to Nov. 30, 2013, which consists of 25 M web pages that contain the pin information of the target users. For evaluation, we measure precision, which is defined as the ratio of the number of pins that the user actually possesses in her boards to the total number of predicted pins.

7.2 Prediction on Pin Consumption

We first present two approaches for predictions: (i) a user-centric approach and (ii) a pin-centric approach. The user-centric approach first finds similar users, and then predicts pins based on the similarity among the users. The rationale behind this approach is that a user may consume pins that her similar users possess. The similarity between two users can be calculated in two ways: (a) $user-property-based$ and (b) $user-interest-based$. The $user-property-based$ considers eight properties of users: the gender, coun-

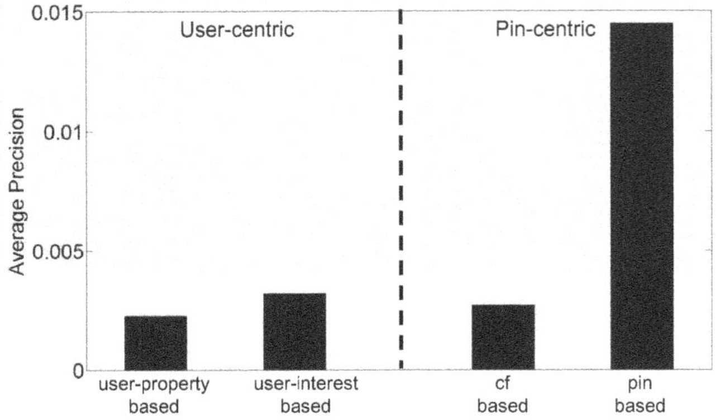

Figure 16: Average precision for each prediction method.

try, major category to which the majority of (the user's) pins belong, number of pins, number of boards, number of categories, number of followers, and number of followings. For the first three properties, the similarity in the $user-property-based$ is calculated by counting the number of matched entries. For the other five entries, we first sort all the users in descending order in each entry, who are divided into five partitions, and check whether the corresponding numbers of two users belong to the same partition. The $user-interest-based$ considers the interest feature (introduced in Section 6) that characterizes how user's interest is distributed across the 32 categories. We use the cosine-similarity between the two interest features of two users in the $user-interest-based$.

The pin-centric approach finds similar pins, not users. This approach assumes that a user may consume similar pins with ones she has. That is, the pin-centric approach finds 4 similar (candidate) pins for each of the five pins recently posted by the target user (20 pins in total). To find similar pins, we first adopt the *(item-to-item) collaborative filtering (CF)* [22, 28] technique. We call this technique $cf-based$, whose basic idea is to find similar pins based on the (collective) opinions of other like-minded users. A key advantage of this technique is that it does not require any knowledge of pins in advance. In the $cf-based$, the similarity between two pins is calculated by the cosine similarity [28]. We further suggest another simple but effective prediction method in this approach: $pin-based$. The $pin-based$ considers both the properties of a pin (i.e., category and source) and collective opinions of other users (i.e., number of likes of the original pin in its pin-tree) to the pin. This method reflects the lessons from the measurements in Section 5, which show that the propagation of a pin is substantially related to pin's popularity (i.e., number of likes), category, and source.

Figure 16 shows the average precision of each method. Our $pin-based$ method outperforms the others (around 4.5 times against the $user-property-based$, 3.3 times against the $user-interest-based$, and 4.5 times against the $cf-based$), which indicates that predicting based on the properties of the pins is more accurate than others. That is, the properties of pins are more important factors than those of users to predict pin consumption patterns in Pinterest; this can be an important implication on designing personalized services in Pinterest-like social networks.

8. CONCLUSIONS

We have conducted a comprehensive measurement study to understand how people collect, manage, and share pins in Pinterest. With the dataset, we analyzed: (1) how users collect and curate pins, (2) how users share their pins and why, and (3) how users are related by shared pins of interests. We found that pin propagation in Pinterest is mostly driven by pin's properties like its topic or content, not by user's characteristics like her number of followers. We also observed that there are notable differences in pin propagation patterns across different categories and sources. We further revealed that users in the same community in the interest graph of Pinterest share pins in the same category and from the same sources with high probability. Our empirically-grounded simulation demonstrated that the properties of pins are more important factors than those of users for accurately predicting pin consumption patterns in Pinterest; we believe this observation has an important implication on designing efficient personalized services in Pinterest-like social networks.

9. ACKNOWLEDGMENTS

We would like to thank the anonymous reviewers for their valuable feedback. This research was supported in part by Basic Science Research Program through the "National Research Foundation of Korea (NRF)" funded by the Ministry of Science, ICT & future Planning (2013R1A2A2A01016562) and in part by the Basic Science Research Program through the National Research Foundation of Korea (NRF), funded by the Ministry of Education (No. 2013-R1A1A2010474). Jinyoung Han is currently a post-doctoral researcher in the RUBINET research group at University of California-Davis, and supported by National Science Foundation CNS-1302691 grant.

10. REFERENCES

[1] Alexa - the web information company. `http://www.alexa.com`.

[2] Can ben silbermann turn pinterest into the world's greatest shopfront? `http://www.fastcodesign.com/1670681/ben-silbermann-pinterest`.

[3] The demographics of social media users - 2012. `http://pewinternet.org/Reports/2013/Social-media-users.aspx`.

[4] Interest, meet pinterest: Site helps users catalog their passions. `http://edition.cnn.com/2012/01/26/tech/web/pinterest-website/index.html`.

[5] Pinterest hits 10 million u.s. monthly uniques faster than any standalone site ever -comscore. `http://techcrunch.com/2012/02/07/pinterest-monthly-uniques`.

[6] Pinterest traffic growth soars to new heights: Experian report. `http://www.huffingtonpost.com/2012/04/06/pinterest-traffic-growth_n_1408088.html`.

[7] Why pinterest is 2012's hottest website. `http://edition.cnn.com/2012/02/06/tech/web/pinterest-website-cashmore`.

[8] Wedding dresses and wanted criminals: Pinterest.com as an infrastructure for repository building. In *ICWSM*, 2013.

[9] E. Bakshy, I. Rosenn, C. Marlow, and L. Adamic. The role of social networks in information diffusion. In *WWW*, 2012.

[10] V. D. Blondel, J.-L. Guillaume, R. Lambiotte, and E. Lefebvre. Fast unfolding of communities in large networks. *Journal of Statistical Mechanics: Theory and Experiment*, 2008(10), 2008.

[11] M. Cha, F. Benevenuto, H. Haddadi, and K. Gummadi. The world of connections and information flow in twitter. *IEEE Transactions on Systems, Man and Cybernetics, Part A: Systems and Humans*, 42(4):991–998, 2012.

[12] M. Cha, H. Haddadi, F. Benevenuto, and K. P. Gummadi. Measuring user influence in twitter: The million follower fallacy. In *ICWSM*, 2010.

[13] M. Cha, A. Mislove, and K. P. Gummadi. A measurement-driven analysis of information propagation in the flickr social network. In *WWW*, 2009.

[14] C. Dagum. The generation and distribution of income, the Lorenz curve and the Gini ratio. *Economie Appliquée*, 33(2), 1980.

[15] E. Gilbert, S. Bakhshi, S. Chang, and L. Terveen. "i need to try this!": A statistical overview of pinterest. In *ACM CHI*, 2013.

[16] C. Hall and M. Zarro. Social curation on the website pinterest.com. *Wiley American Society for Information Science and Technology*, 49(1):1–9, 2012.

[17] R. A. Hanneman and M. Riddle. Introduction to social network methods, 2005. `http://www.faculty.ucr.edu/~hanneman/`.

[18] R. Joseph Lee and N. W. Alan. Thirteen ways to look at the correlation coefficient. *The American Statistician*, 42(1):59–66, 1988.

[19] K. Y. Kamath, A.-M. Popescu, and J. Caverlee. Board recommendation in pinterest. In *Conference on User Modeling, Adaptation and Personalization*, 2013.

[20] H. Kwak, C. Lee, H. Park, and S. Moon. What is twitter, a social network or a news media? In *WWW*, 2010.

[21] K. Lerman and R. Ghosh. Information contagion: An empirical study of the spread of news on digg and twitter social networks. In *ICWSM*, 2010.

[22] G. Linden, B. Smith, and J. York. Amazon.com recommendations: item-to-item collaborative filtering. *IEEE Internet Computing*, 7(1):76–80, 2003.

[23] M. O. Lorenz. Methods of Measuring the Concentration of Wealth. *Publications of the American Statistical Association*, 9(70):209–219, 1905.

[24] M. E. J. Newman. The structure and function of complex networks. *SIAM REVIEW*, 45:167–256, 2003.

[25] R. Ottoni, J. P. Pesce, D. Las Casas, G. Franciscani Jr, W. Meira Jr, P. Kumaraguru, and V. Almeida. Ladies first: Analyzing gender roles and behaviors in pinterest. In *ICWSM*, 2013.

[26] J. Park, M. Cha, H. Kim, and J. Jeong. Managing bad news in social media: A case study on domino's pizza crisis. In *ICWSM*, 2012.

[27] T. Rodrigues, F. Benevenuto M. Cha, K. Gummadi, and V. Almeida. On word-of-mouth based discovery of the web. In *ACM IMC*, 2011.

[28] B. Sarwar, G. Karypis, J. Konstan, and J. Riedl. Item-based collaborative filtering recommendation algorithms. In *WWW*, 2001.

[29] C. E. Shannon. Prediction and entropy of printed english. *Bell system technical journal*, 30(1):50–64, 1951.

[30] D. Wang, Z. Wen, H. Tong, C.-Y. Lin, C. Song, and A.-L. Barabási. Information spreading in context. In *WWW*, 2011.

[31] S. Ye and S. F. Wu. Measuring message propagation and social influence on twitter.com. In *International Conference on Social Informatics*, 2010.

[32] M. Zarro and C. Hall. Pinterest: Social collecting for #linking #using #sharing. In *12th ACM/IEEE-CS Joint Conference on Digital Libraries*, 2012.

[33] S. Zoghbi, I. Vulić, and M.-F Moens. I pinned it. where can i buy one like it?: Automatically linking pinterest pins to online webshops. In *ACM Workshop on Data-driven User Behavioral Modelling and Mining from Social Media*, 2013.

Jointly Clustering Rows and Columns of Binary Matrices: Algorithms and Trade-offs

Jiaming Xu
Electrical and Computer Engineering
University of Illinois at Urbana-Champaign
Urbana,IL,61801
jxu18@illinois.edu

Rui Wu
Electrical and Computer Engineering
University of Illinois at Urbana-Champaign
Urbana,IL,61801
ruiwu1@illinois.edu

Kai Zhu
School of Electrical, Computer and Energy Engineering
Arizona State University
Tempe, AZ 85287
kzhu17@asu.edu

Bruce Hajek
Electrical and Computer Engineering
University of Illinois at Urbana-Champaign
Urbana,IL,61801
b-hajek@illinois.edu

R. Srikant
Electrical and Computer Engineering
University of Illinois at Urbana-Champaign
Urbana,IL,61801
rsrikant@illinois.edu

Lei Ying
School of Electrical, Computer and Energy Engineering
Arizona State University
Tempe, AZ 85287
lei.ying.2@asu.edu

ABSTRACT

In standard clustering problems, data points are represented by vectors, and by stacking them together, one forms a data matrix with row or column cluster structure. In this paper, we consider a class of binary matrices, arising in many applications, which exhibit both row and column cluster structure, and our goal is to exactly recover the underlying row and column clusters by observing only a small fraction of noisy entries. We first derive a lower bound on the minimum number of observations needed for exact cluster recovery. Then, we study three algorithms with different running time and compare the number of observations needed by them for successful cluster recovery. Our analytical results show smooth time-data trade-offs: one can gradually reduce the computational complexity when increasingly more observations are available.

Categories and Subject Descriptors

I.5.3 [**PATTERN RECOGNITION**]: Clustering—*Algorithms*; G.1.6 [**NUMERICAL ANALYSIS**]: Optimization—*Convex programming*; G.3 [**PROBABILITY AND STATISTICS**]: [Statistical computing]

General Terms

Theory, Algorithms, Performance

SIGMETRICS'14, June 16–20, 2014, Austin, Texas, USA.

ACM 978-1-4503-2789-3/14/06 ...$15.00.
http://dx.doi.org/10.1145/2591971.2592005.

Keywords

Clustering; Low-Rank Matrix Recovery; Spectral Method

1. INTRODUCTION

Data matrices exhibiting both row and column cluster structure, arise in many applications, such as collaborative filtering, gene expression analysis, and text mining. For example, in recommender systems, a rating matrix can be formed with rows corresponding to users and columns corresponding to items, and similar users and items form clusters. In DNA microarrays, a gene expression matrix can be formed with rows corresponding to patients and columns corresponding to genes, and similar patients and genes form clusters. Such row and column cluster structure is of great scientific interest and practical importance. For instance, the user and movie cluster structure is crucial for predicting user preferences and making accurate item recommendations [31]. The patient and gene cluster structure reveals functional relations among genes and helps disease detection [33, 26]. In practice, we usually only observe a very small fraction of entries in these data matrices, possibly contaminated with noise, which obscures the intrinsic cluster structure. For example, in Netflix movie dataset, about 99% of movie ratings are missing and the observed ratings are noisy [29].

In this paper, we study the problem of inferring hidden row and column cluster structure in binary data matrices from a few noisy observations. We consider a simple model introduced in [1, 4] for generating binary data matrix from underlying row and column clusters. In the context of movie recommender systems, our model assumes that users and movies each form equal-sized clusters. Users in the same cluster give the same rating to movies in the same cluster, where ratings are either $+1$ or -1 with $+1$ being "like" and -1 being "dislike". Each rating is flipped independently with a fixed flipping probability less than $1/2$, modeling the noisy user behavior and the fact that users (movies) in the same cluster do not necessarily give (receive) identical ratings. Each rating is further erased independently with a erasure probability, modeling the fact that some ratings are not observed. Then, from the observed noisy ratings, we aim to *exactly* recover the underlying user and movie clusters, i.e., jointly cluster the rows and columns of the observed rating matrix.

The binary assumption on data matrices is of practical interest. Firstly, in many real datasets like Netflix dataset and DNA microarrays, estimation of entry values appears to be very unreliable, but the task of determining whether an entry is $+1$ or -1 can be done more reliably [4]. Secondly, in recommender systems like rating music on Pandora or rating posts on sites such as Facebook and MathOverflow, the user ratings are indeed binary [21]. The equal-sized assumption on cluster size is just for ease of presentation and can be relaxed to allow for different cluster sizes.

The hardness of our cluster recovery problem is governed by the erasure probability and cluster size. Intuitively, cluster recovery becomes harder when the erasure probability increases, meaning fewer observations, and the cluster size decreases, meaning that clusters are harder to detect. The first goal of this paper is to understand when exact cluster recovery is possible or fundamentally impossible. Furthermore, our cluster recovery problem poses a computational challenge: An algorithm exhaustively searching over all the possible row and column cluster structures would have a time complexity exponentially increasing with the matrix dimension. The second goal of this paper is to understand how the computational complexity of our cluster recovery problem changes when increasingly more observations are available.

In this paper, our contributions are as follows. We first derive a lower bound on the minimum number of observations needed for exact cluster recovery as a function of matrix dimension and cluster size. Then we propose three algorithms with different running times and compare the number of observations needed by them for successful cluster recovery.

- The first algorithm directly searches for the optimal clustering of rows and columns separately; it is combinatorial in nature and takes exponential-time but achieves the best statistical performance among the three algorithms in the noiseless setting.
- By noticing that the underlying true rating matrix is a specific type of low-rank matrix, the second algorithm recovers the clusters by solving a nuclear norm regularized convex optimization problem, which is a popular heuristic for low rank matrix completion problems; it takes polynomial-time but has less powerful statistical performance than the first algorithm.
- The third algorithm applies spectral clustering to the rows and columns separately and then performs a joint clean-up step; it has lower computational complexity than the previous two algorithms, but less powerful statistical performance. We believe that this is the first such performance guarantee for exact cluster recovery, with a growing number of clusters, using spectral clustering.

These algorithms are then compared with a simple nearest-neighbor clustering algorithm proposed in [4]. Our analytical results show smooth time-data trade-offs: when increasingly more observations are available, one can gradually reduce the computational complexity by applying simpler algorithms while still achieving the desired performance. Such time-data trade-offs is of great practical interest for statistical learning problems involving large datasets [13]. Furthermore, we observed that our exponential-time combinatorial method needs substantially few observations for successful cluster recovery than the other three polynomial-time counterparts, which suggests that a large performance gap might exist between exponential-time algorithms and polynomial-time algorithms. Similar performance gap due to the computational complexity constraint has also been observed recently in many other inference problems such as graph clustering [2, 19], Sparse PCA [6, 5, 30] and sparse submatrix detection [28, 3, 32].

The rest of the paper is organized as follows. In Section 2, we discuss related work. In Section 3, we formally introduce our model and main results. The lower bound is presented in Section 4. The combinatorial method, convex method, spectral method are studied in Section 5, Section 6 and Section 7, respectively. The proofs are given in Section 8. The simulation results are presented in Section 9. Section 10 concludes the paper with remarks.

2. RELATED WORK

In this section, we point out some connections of our model and results to prior work. There is a vast literature on clustering and we only focus on theoretical works with rigorous performance analysis. More detailed comparisons are provided after we present the theorems.

2.1 Graph clustering

Much of the prior work on graph clustering, as surveyed in [22], focuses on graphs with a single node type, where nodes in the same cluster are more likely to have edges among them. A low-rank plus sparse matrix decomposition approach is proved to exactly recover the clusters with the best known performance guarantee in [18]. The same approach is used to recover the clusters from a partially observed graph in [17]. A spectral method for exact cluster recovery is proposed and analyzed in [34] with the number of clusters fixed. More recently, [36] proved an upper bound on the number of nodes "mis-clustered" by a spectral clustering algorithm in the high dimensional setting with a growing number of clusters. An interesting recent work [41] studies the graph clustering problem under both non-adaptive and adaptive sampling strategies of node pairs.

In contrast to the above works, in our model, we have a labeled bipartite graph with two types of nodes (rows and columns). Notice that there are no edges among nodes of the same type and cluster structure is defined for the two types separately. In this sense, our cluster recovery problem can be viewed as a natural generalization of graph clustering problem to labeled bipartite graphs. In fact, our second algorithm via convex programming is inspired by the work [18, 17, 19].

A model similar to ours but with a fixed number of clusters has been considered in [38], where the spectral method plus majority voting is shown to *approximately* predict the rating matrix. However, our third algorithm via spectral method is shown to achieve exact cluster and rating matrix recovery with a growing number of clusters. This is the first theoretical result on spectral method for exact cluster recovery with a growing number of clusters to our knowledge.

2.2 Biclustering

Biclustering [23, 20, 33, 8] tries to find (overlap) sub-matrices with particular patterns in a data matrix. Many of the proposed algorithms are based on heuristic searches without provable performance guarantees. Our cluster recovery problem can be viewed as a special case where the data matrix consists of non-overlapping sub-matrices with constant binary entries, and our paper provides a thorough study of this special biclustering problem. Recently, there is a line of work studying another special case of biclustering problem, which tries to detect a single small submatrix with elevated mean in a large fully observed noisy matrix [28]. Interesting statistical and computational trade-offs are summarized in [3].

2.3 Low-rank matrix completion

Under our model, the underlying true data matrix is a specific type of low-rank matrix. If we recover the true data matrix, we immediately get the user (or movie) clusters by assigning the identical rows (or columns) of the matrix to the same cluster. In the noiseless setting with no flipping, the nuclear norm minimization approach [12, 11, 35] can be directly applied to recover the true data matrix and further recover the row and column clusters. Alternate minimization is another popular and empirically successful approach for low-matrix completion [29]. However, it is harder to analyze and the performance guarantee is weaker than nuclear norm minimization [24]. In the low noise setting with the flipping probability restricting to be a small constant, the low-rank plus sparse matrix decomposition approach [14, 10, 16] can be applied to exactly recover data matrix and further recover the row and column clusters.

The performance guarantee for our convex method is better than these previous approaches and it allows the flipping probability to be any constant less than 1/2. Moreover, our proof turns out to be much simpler. The recovery of our true data matrix from binary observations can also be viewed as a specific type of one-bit matrix completion problem recently studied in [21]. However, [21] focuses on approximately recovering a low rank matrix with real-valued entries.

3. MODEL AND MAIN RESULTS

In this section, we formally state our model and main results.

3.1 Model

Our model is described in the context of movie recommender systems, but it is applicable to other systems with binary data matrices having row and column cluster structure. Consider a movie recommender system with n users and n movies. Let R be the rating matrix of size $n \times n$ where R_{ij} is the rating user i gives to movie j. Assume both users and movies form r clusters of size $K = n/r$. Users in the same cluster give the same rating to movies in the same cluster. The set of ratings corresponding to a user cluster and a movie cluster is called a block. Let B be the *block rating matrix* of size $r \times r$ where B_{kl} is the *block rating* user cluster k gives to movie cluster l. Then the rating $R_{ij} = B_{kl}$ if user i is in user cluster k and movie j is in movie cluster l. Further assume that entries of B are independent random variables which are $+1$ or -1 with equal probability. Thus, we can imagine the rating matrix as a block-constant matrix with all the entries in each block being either $+1$ or -1. Observe that if r is a fixed constant, then users from two different clusters have the same ratings for all movies with some positive probability, in which case it is impossible to differentiate between these two clusters. To avoid such situations, assume r is at least $\Omega(\log n)$.

Suppose each entry of R goes through an independent binary symmetric channel with flipping probability $p < 1/2$, representing noisy user behavior, and an independent erasure channel with erasure probability ϵ, modeling the fact that some entries are not observed. The expected number of observed ratings is $m = n^2(1-\epsilon)$. We assume that p is a constant throughout the paper and ϵ could converge to 1 as $n \to \infty$. Let R' denote the output of the binary symmetric channel and Ω denote the set of non-erased entries. Let $\widehat{R}_{ij} = R'_{ij}$ if $(i,j) \in \Omega$ and $\widehat{R}_{ij} = 0$ otherwise. The goal is to exactly recover the row and column clusters from the observation $\widehat{R}$.

3.2 Main Results

The main results are summarized in Table 1. Note that these results do not explicitly depend on p. In fact, as p is assumed to be a constant strictly less than $1/2$, it affects the results by constant factors.

The parameter regime where exact cluster recovery is fundamentally impossible for any algorithm is proved in Section 4. The combinatorial method, convex method and spectral method are studied in Section 5, Section 6 and Section 7, respectively. We only analyze the combinatorial method in the noiseless case where $p = 0$, but we believe similar result is true for the noisy case as well. The parameter regime in which the convex method succeeds is obtained by assuming that a technical conjecture holds, which is justified through extensive simulation. The parameter regime in which the spectral method succeeds is obtained for the first time for exact cluster recovery with a growing number of clusters. The nearest-neighbor clustering algorithm was proposed in [4]. It clusters the users by finding the $K-1$ most similar neighbors for each user. The similarity between user i and i' is measured by the number of movies with the same observed rating, i.e.,

$$s_{ii'} = \sum_{j=1}^{n} \mathbb{I}_{\{\widehat{R}_{ij} \neq 0\}} \mathbb{I}_{\{\widehat{R}_{i'j} \neq 0\}} \mathbb{I}_{\{\widehat{R}_{ij} = \widehat{R}_{i'j}\}},$$

where $\mathbb{I}_{\{\cdot\}}$ is an indicator function. Movies are clustered similarly. It is shown in [4] that the nearest-neighbor clustering algorithm exactly recovers user and movie clusters when $n(1-\epsilon)^2 > C \log n$ for a constant C.

The number of observations needed for successful cluster recovery can be derived from the corresponding parameter regime using the identity $m = n^2(1-\epsilon)$ as shown in Table 1. For better illustration, we visualize our results in Figure 1. In particular, we take $\log(m/n)$ as x-axis and $\log K$ as y-axis and normalize both axes by $\log n$. Since exact cluster recovery becomes easy when the number of observations m and cluster size K increase, we expect that exact cluster recovery is easy near $(1,1)$ and hard near $(0,0)$.

From Figure 1, we can observe interesting trade-offs between algorithmic running time and statistical performance. In terms of the running time, the combinatorial method is exponential, while the other three algorithms are polynomial. In particular, the convex method can be casted as a semidefinite programming and solved in polynomial-time. For the spectral method, the most computationally expen-

	regime in (K,ϵ)	regime in (K,m)	running time	remark
lower bound	$nK^2(1-\epsilon)^2 = O(1)$	$m = O(\frac{n^{1.5}}{K})$		
combinatorial method	$nK(1-\epsilon)^2 = \Omega(\log n)$	$m = \Omega(\frac{n^{1.5}\sqrt{\log n}}{\sqrt{K}})$	exponential	assuming noiseless
convex method	$K(1-\epsilon) = \Omega(\log n)$	$m = \Omega(\frac{n^2 \log n}{K})$	polynomial	assuming Conjecture 1
spectral method	$K^2(1-\epsilon) = \Omega(n \log^2 n)$	$m = \Omega(\frac{n^3 \log^2 n}{K^2})$	$O(n^3)$	
nearest-neighbor clustering	$n(1-\epsilon)^2 = \Omega(\log n)$	$m = \Omega(n^{1.5}\sqrt{\log n})$	$O(mr)$	

Table 1: Main results: comparison of a lower bound and four clustering algorithms.

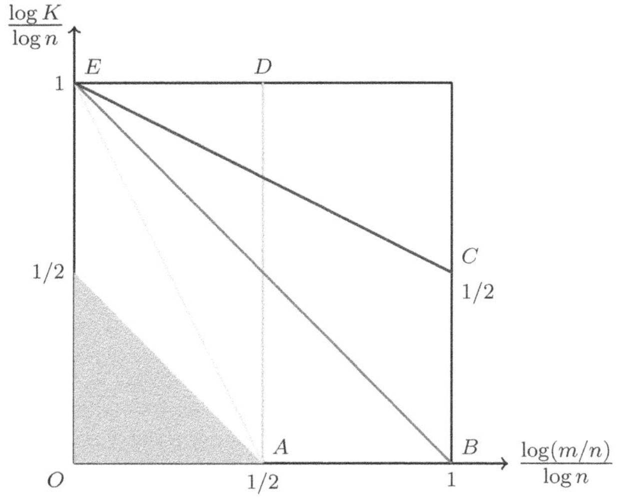

Figure 1: Summary of results in terms of number of observations m and cluster size K. The lower bound states that it is impossible for any algorithm to reliably recover the clusters exactly in the shaded regime (grey). The combinatorial method, the convex method, the spectral method and the nearest-neighbor clustering algorithm succeed in the regime to the right of lines AE (yellow), BE (red), CE (blue) and AD (green), respectively.

sive step is the singular value decomposition of the observed data matrix which can always be done in time $O(n^3)$ and more efficiently when the observed data matrix is sparse. It is not hard to see that the time complexity for the nearest-neighbor clustering algorithm is $O(n^2 r)$ and more careful analysis reveals that its time complexity is $O(mr)$. On the other hand, in terms of statistical performance, the combinatorial method needs strictly fewer observations than the other three algorithms when there is no noise, and the convex method always needs fewer observations than the spectral method. It is somewhat surprising to see that the simple nearest-neighbor clustering algorithm needs fewer observations than the more sophisticated convex method when the cluster size K is $O(\sqrt{n})$.

In summary, we see that when more observations available, one can apply algorithms with less running time while still achieving exact cluster recovery. For example, consider the noiseless case with cluster size $K = n^{0.8}$, the number of observations *per user* required for cluster recovery by the combinatorial method, convex method, spectral method and nearest-neighbor clustering algorithm are $\Omega(n^{0.1})$, $\Omega(n^{0.2})$, $\Omega(n^{0.4})$ and $\Omega(n^{0.5})$, respectively. Therefore, when the number of observations per user increases from $\Omega(n^{0.1})$ to $\Omega(n^{0.5})$, one can gradually reduces the computational complexity from exponential-time to polynomial-time as low as $O(n^{1.7})$.

The main results in this paper can be easily extended to the more general case with n_1 rows and $n_2 = \Theta(n_1)$ columns and r_1 row clusters and $r_2 = \Theta(r_1)$ column clusters. The sizes of different clusters could vary as long as they are of the same order. Likewise, the flipping probability p and the erasure probability ϵ could also vary for different entries of the data matrix as long as they are of the same order. Due to space constraints, such generalizations are omitted in this paper.

3.3 Notations

A variety of norms on matrices will be used. The spectral norm of a matrix X is denoted by $\|X\|$, which is equal to the largest singular value. Let $\langle X, Y \rangle = \mathrm{Tr}(X^\top Y)$ denote the inner product between two matrices. The nuclear norm is denoted by $\|X\|_*$ which is equal to the sum of singular values and is a convex function of X. Let $\|X\|_1 = \sum_{i,j} |X_{ij}|$ denote the l_1 norm and $\|X\|_\infty = \max_{i,j} |X_{ij}|$ denote the l_∞ norm. Let $X = \sum_{t=1}^n \sigma_t u_t v_t^\top$ denotes the singular value decomposition $X \in \mathbb{R}^{n \times n}$ such that $\sigma_1 \geq \cdots \geq \sigma_n$. The best rank r approximation of X is defined as $P_r(X) = \sum_{t=1}^r \sigma_t u_t v_t^\top$. For vectors, let $\langle x, y \rangle$ denote the inner product between two vectors and the only norm that will be used is the usual l_2 norm, denoted as $\|x\|_2$.

Throughout the paper, we say that an event occurs "a.a.s." or "asymptotically almost surely" when it occurs with a probability which tends to one as n goes to infinity.

4. LOWER BOUND

In this section, we derive a lower bound for any algorithm to reliably recover the user and movie clusters. The lower bound is constructed by considering a genie-aided scenario where the set of flipped entries is revealed as side information, which is equivalent to saying that we are in the noiseless setting with $p = 0$. Hence, the true rating matrix R agrees with $\widehat{R}$ on all non-erased entries. We construct another rating matrix $\tilde{R}$ with the same movie cluster structure as R but different user cluster structure by swapping two users in two different user clusters. We show that if $nK^2(1-\epsilon)^2 = O(1)$, then $\tilde{R}$ agrees with $\widehat{R}$ on all non-erased entries with positive probability, which implies that no algorithm can reliably distinguish between R and $\widehat{R}$ and thus recover user clusters.

THEOREM 1. *Fix $0 < \delta < 1$. If $nK^2(1-\epsilon)^2 < \delta$, then with probability at least $1-\delta$, it is impossible for any algorithms to recover the user clusters or movie clusters.*

Intuitively, Theorem 1 says that when the erasure probability is high and the cluster size is small that $nK^2(1-\epsilon)^2 = O(1)$, the observed rating matrix $\widehat{R}$ does not carry enough information to distinguish between different possible cluster structures.

5. COMBINATORIAL METHOD

In this section, we study a combinatorial method which clusters users or movies by searching for a partition with the least total number of "disagreements". We describe the method in Algorithm 1 for clustering users only. Movies are clustered similarly. The number of disagreements $D_{ii'}$ between a pair of users i, i' is defined as the number of movies satisfying that: The two ratings given by users i, i' are both observed and the observed two ratings are different. In particular, if for every movie, the two ratings given by users i, i' are not observed simultaneously, then $D_{ii'} = 0$.

Algorithm 1 Combinatorial Method

1: For each pair of users i, i', compute the number of disagreements $D_{ii'}$ between them.
2: For each partition of users into r clusters of equal size K, compute its total number of disagreements defined as

$$\sum_{i,i' \text{ in the same cluster}} D_{ii'}$$

3: Output a partition which has the least total number of disagreements.

The idea of Algorithm 1 is to reduce the problem of clustering both users and movies to a standard user clustering problem without movie cluster structure. In fact, this algorithm looks for the optimal partition of the users which has the minimum total in-cluster distance, where the distance between two users is measured by the number of disagreements between them. The following theorem shows that such simple reduction does *not* achieve the lower bound given in Theorem 1. The optimal algorithm for our cluster recovery problem might need to explicitly make use of both user and movie cluster structures.

THEOREM 2. *If $nK(1-\epsilon)^2 \le \frac{1}{4}$, then with probability at least 3/4, Algorithm 1 cannot recover user and movie clusters.*

Next we show that the above necessary condition for the combinatorial method is also sufficient up to a logarithmic factor when there is no noise, i.e., $p = 0$. We suspect that the theorem holds for the noisy setting as well, but we have not yet been able to prove this.

THEOREM 3. *If $p = 0$ and $nK(1-\epsilon)^2 > C \log n$ for some constant C, then a.a.s. Algorithm 1 exactly recovers user and movie clusters.*

This theorem is proved by considering a conceptually simpler greedy algorithm that does not need to know K. After computing the number of disagreements for every pair of users, we search for a largest set of users which have no disagreement between each other, and assign them to a new cluster. We then remove these users and repeat the searching process until there is no user left. In the noiseless setting, the K users from the same true cluster have no disagreement between each other. Therefore, it is sufficient to show that, for any set of K users consisting of users from more than one cluster, they have more than one disagreement with high probability under our assumption

6. CONVEX METHOD

In this section, we show that the rating matrix R can be exactly recovered by a convex program, which is a relaxation of the maximum likelihood (ML) estimation. When R is known, we immediately get the user (or movie) clusters by assigning the identical rows (or columns) of R to the same cluster.

Let $\mathcal{Y}$ denote the set of binary block-constant rating matrix with r^2 blocks of equal size. As the flipping probability $p < 1/2$, Maximum Likelihood (ML) estimation of R is equivalent to finding a $Y \in \mathcal{Y}$ which best matches the observation $\widehat{R}$:

$$\max_Y \sum_{i,j} \widehat{R}_{ij} Y_{ij} \quad \text{s.t. } Y \in \mathcal{Y} \tag{1}$$

Since $|\mathcal{Y}| = \Omega(e^n)$, solving (1) via exhaustive search takes exponential-time. Observe that $Y \in \mathcal{Y}$ implies that Y is of rank at most r. Therefore, a natural relaxation of the constraint that $Y \in \mathcal{Y}$ is to replace it with a rank constraint on Y, which gives the following problem:

$$\max_Y \sum_{i,j} \widehat{R}_{ij} Y_{ij} \quad \text{s.t. } \operatorname{rank}(Y) \le r,\ Y_{ij} \in \{1, -1\}.$$

Further by relaxing the integer constraint and replacing the rank constraint with the nuclear norm regularization, which is a standard technique for low-rank matrix completion, we get the desired convex program:

$$\max_Y \sum_{i,j} \widehat{R}_{ij} Y_{ij} - \lambda \|Y\|_* \quad \text{s.t. } Y_{ij} \in [-1, 1]. \tag{2}$$

The clustering algorithm based on the above convex program is given in Algorithm 2

Algorithm 2 Convex Method

1: (Rating matrix estimation) Solve for $\widehat{Y}$ the convex program (2).
2: (Cluster estimation) Assign identical rows (columns) of $\widehat{Y}$ to the same cluster.

The convex program (2) can be casted as a semidefinite program and solved in polynomial-time. Thus, Algorithm 2 takes polynomial-time. Our performance guarantee for Algorithm 2 is stated in terms of the incoherence parameter μ defined below. Since the rating matrix R has rank r, the singular vector decomposition (SVD) is $R = U\Sigma V^\top$, where $U, V \in \mathbb{R}^{n\times r}$ are matrices with orthonormal columns and $\Sigma \in \mathbb{R}^{r\times r}$ is a diagonal matrix with nonnegative entries.

Define incoherence parameter $\mu > 0$ such that $\|UV^\top\|_\infty \leq \mu\sqrt{r}/n$. A small value of μ means that the left and right singular vectors of R are unaligned with each other. Denote the SVD of the block rating matrix B by $B = U_B \Sigma_B V_B^\top$. The next lemma shows that

$$\|UV^\top\|_\infty = \|U_B V_B^\top\|_\infty / K, \tag{3}$$

and thus μ is upper bounded by $\sqrt{r}$.

LEMMA 1. *$\mu \leq \sqrt{r}$.*

Recent studies [12, 11, 35] in low-rank matrix completion have demonstrated that the number of samples needed for exact low-rank matrix recovery depends on the incoherence parameter μ. Not surprisingly, the performance guarantee for Algorithm 2 given by the following theorem also depends on μ.

THEOREM 4. *If $n(1-\epsilon) \geq C' \log^2 n$ for some constant C', and*

$$m > Cnr \max\{\log n, \mu^2\}, \tag{4}$$

where C is a constant and μ is the incoherence parameter for R, then a.a.s. the rating matrix R is the unique maximizer to the convex program (2) with $\lambda = 3\sqrt{(1-\epsilon)n}$.

Our proof shows that with appropriate choices of λ, the nuclear norm regularization is effective in "de-noising" and the effectiveness depends on $\|UV^\top\|_\infty$. This is exactly why our performance guarantee depends on the incoherence parameter μ. Note that Algorithm 2 is easy to implement as λ only depends on the erasure probability ϵ, which can be reliably estimated from $\widehat{R}$. Moreover, the particular choice of λ in the theorem is just to simplify notations. It is straightforward to generalize our proof to show that the above theorem holds with $\lambda = C_1\sqrt{(1-\epsilon)n}$ for any constant $C_1 \geq 3$.

Using Lemma 1, we immediately conclude from the above theorem that the convex program succeeds when $m > Cnr^2$ for some constant C. However, based on extensive simulation in Fig 2, we conjecture that the following result is true.

CONJECTURE 1. *$\mu = \Theta(\sqrt{\log r})$ a.a.s.*

Conjecture 1 is equivalent to $\|U_B V_B^\top\|_\infty = \Theta(\sqrt{\frac{\log r}{r}})$ due to (3). For a fixed r, we simulate 1000 independent trials of B, pick the largest value of $\|U_B V_B^\top\|_\infty$, scale it by dividing $\sqrt{\log r / r}$, and get the plot in Fig 2.

Assuming this conjecture holds, Theorem 4 implies that

$$m > Cnr \log n$$

for some constant C is sufficient to recover the rating matrix, which is better than the previous condition by a factor of r. We do not have a proof for the conjecture at this time.

Comparison to previous work In the noiseless setting with $p = 0$, the nuclear norm minimization approach [12, 11, 35] can be directly applied to recover data matrix and further recover the row and column clusters. It is shown in [35] that the nuclear norm minimization approach exactly recovers the matrix with high probability if $m = \Omega(\mu^2 nr \log^2 n)$. The performance guarantee for Algorithm 2 given in (4) is better by at least a factor of $\log n$. Theorem 3 shows that the combinatorial method exactly recovers the row and column clusters if $m = \Omega(nr^{1/2} \log^{1/2} n)$, which is substantially

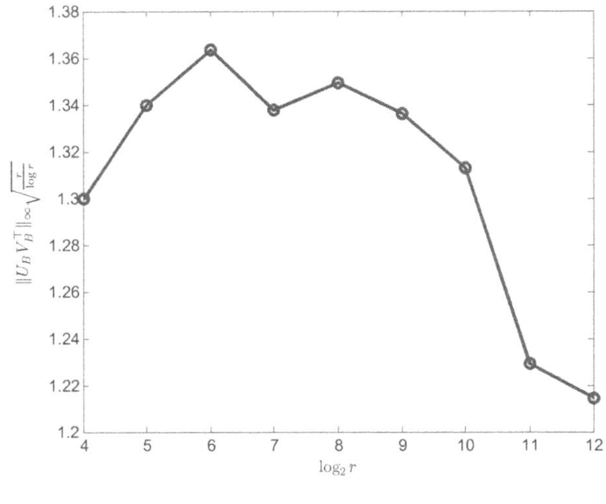

Figure 2: Simulation result supporting Conjecture 1. The conjecture is equivalent to $\|U_B V_B^\top\|_\infty = \Theta(\sqrt{\frac{\log r}{r}})$.

better than the two previous conditions by at least a factor of $r^{1/2}$. This suggests that a large performance gap might exist between exponential-time algorithms and polynomial-time algorithms. Similar performance gap due to the computational complexity constraint has also been observed in other inference problems such as graph clustering [2, 19], Sparse PCA [6, 5, 30] and sparse submatrix detection [28, 3, 32].

In the low noise setting with p restricted to be a small constant, the low-rank plus sparse matrix decomposition approach [14, 10, 16] can be applied to exactly recover data matrix and further recover the row and column clusters. It is shown in [16] that a weighted nuclear norm and l_1 norm minimization succeeds with high probability if $m = \Omega(\rho_r \mu^2 nr \log^6 n)$ and $p \leq \rho_s$ for two constants ρ_r and ρ_s. The performance guarantee for Algorithm 2 given in (4) is better by several $\log n$ factors and we allow the fraction of noisy entries p to be any constant less than 1/2. Moreover, our proof turns out to be much simpler. The recovery of our true data matrix from binary observations can also be viewed as a specific type of one-bit matrix completion problem [21]: Given an unknown low rank-r matrix M, generate a binary matrix $Y \in \{\pm 1\}^{n \times n}$ such that $Y_{ij} = 1$ with probability $f(M_{ij})$ and the task is to recover M from a partial observation of Y. By taking $f(1) = 1-p, f(-1) = p$, our problem reduces to the one-bit matrix completion problem. It is shown in [21] that approximate recovery is possible using the maximum likelihood estimation with nuclear norm constraint. In contrast, as shown in Theorem 4, our convex method yields exact recovery.

7. SPECTRAL METHOD

In this section, we study a polynomial-time clustering algorithm based on the spectral projection of the observed rating matrix $\widehat{R}$. The description is given in Algorithm 3.

Step 1 of the algorithm produces two subsets, Ω_1 and Ω_2, of Ω such that: 1) for $i \in \{1, 2\}$, each rating is observed in Ω_i with probability $\frac{1-\epsilon}{2}$, independently of other elements; and 2) Ω_1 is independent of Ω_2. The purpose of Step 1 is to remove dependency between Step 2 and Steps 3, 4 in our

Algorithm 3 Spectral Method

1: (Producing two subsets, Ω_1 and Ω_2, of Ω via randomly sub-sampling Ω) Let $\delta = \frac{1-\epsilon}{4}$, and independently assign each element of Ω only to Ω_1 with probability $\frac{1}{2}-\delta$, only to Ω_2 with probability $\frac{1}{2}-\delta$, to both Ω_1 and Ω_2 with probability δ, and to neither Ω_1 nor Ω_2 with probability δ. Let $\widehat{R}^{(1)}_{i,j} = \widehat{R}_{i,j}\mathbb{I}_{\{(i,j)\in\Omega_1\}}$ and $\widehat{R}^{(2)}_{i,j} = \widehat{R}_{i,j}\mathbb{I}_{\{(i,j)\in\Omega_2\}}$ for $i,j \in \{1,\dots,n\}$.

2: (Approximate clustering) Let $P_r(\widehat{R}^{(1)})$ denote the rank r approximation of $\widehat{R}^{(1)}$ and let x_i denote the i-th row of $P_r(\widehat{R}^{(1)})$. Construct user clusters $\widehat{C}_1,\dots,\widehat{C}_r$ sequentially as follows. For $1 \le k \le r$, after $\widehat{C}_1,\dots,\widehat{C}_{k-1}$ have been selected, choose an initial user not in the first $k-1$ clusters, uniformly at random, and let $\widehat{C}_k = \{i' : \|x_i - x_{i'}\| \le \tau\}$. (The threshold τ is specified below.) Assign each remaining unclustered user to a cluster arbitrarily. Similarly, construct movie clusters $\widehat{D}_1,\dots,\widehat{D}_r$ based on the columns of $P_r(\widehat{R}^{(1)})$.

3: (Block rating estimation by majority voting) For $k,l \in \{1,\dots,r\}$, let $\widehat{V}_{kl} = \sum_{i\in\widehat{C}_k}\sum_{j\in\widehat{D}_l}\widehat{R}^{(2)}_{ij}$ be the total vote that user cluster $\widehat{C}_k$ gives to movie cluster $\widehat{D}_l$. If $\widehat{V}_{kl} \ge 0$, let $\widehat{B}_{kl} = 1$; otherwise, let $\widehat{B}_{kl} = -1$.

4: (Reclustering by assigning users and movies to nearest centers) Recluster users as follows. For $k \in \{1,\dots,r\}$, define center μ_k for user cluster $\widehat{C}_k$ as $\mu_{kj} = \widehat{B}_{kl}$ if movie $j \in \widehat{D}_l$ for all j. Assign user i to cluster k if $\langle \widehat{R}^{(2)}_{i,\cdot}, \mu_k\rangle \ge \langle \widehat{R}^{(2)}_{i,\cdot}, \mu_{k'}\rangle$ for all $k' \ne k$. Recluster movies similarly.

proof. In particular, to establish our theoretical results, we identify the initial clustering of users and movies using Ω_1, and then majority voting and reclustering are done using Ω_2. In practice, one can simply use the same set of observations, i.e., $\Omega_1 = \Omega_2 = \Omega$.

The following theorem shows that the spectral method exactly recovers the user and movie clusters under a condition stronger than (4). In particular, we show that Step 3 exactly recovers the block rating matrix B and Step 4 cleans up clustering errors made in Step 2.

THEOREM 5. *If*

$$n(1-\epsilon) > Cr^2 \log^2 n, \tag{5}$$

for a positive constant C, then Algorithm 3 with $\tau = 12(1-\epsilon)^{1/2} r \log n$ a.a.s. exactly recovers user and movie clusters, and the rating matrix R.

Algorithm 3 is also easy to implement as τ only depends on parameters ϵ and r. As mentioned before, the erasure probability ϵ can be reliably estimated from $\widehat{R}$ using empirical statistics. The number of clusters r can be reliably estimated by searching for the largest eigen-gap in the spectrum of $\widehat{R}$ (See Algorithm 2 and Theorem 3 in [18] for justification). We further note that the threshold τ used in the theorem can be replaced by $C_1(1-\epsilon)^{1/2} r \log n$ for any constant $C_1 \ge 12$.

Comparison to previous work Variants of spectral method are widely used for clustering nodes in a graph. Step 2 of Algorithm 3 for approximate clustering has been previously proposed and it is analyzed in [27]. In [34], an adaptation of Step 1 is shown to exactly recover a fixed number of clusters under the planted partition model. More recently, [36] proves an upper bound on the number of nodes "misclustered" by spectral method under the stochastic block model with a growing number of clusters.

Compared to previous work, the main novelty of Algorithm 3 is Steps 1, 3, and 4 which allow for exact cluster recovery even with a growing number of clusters. To our knowledge, Theorem 5 provides the first theoretical result on spectral method for exact cluster recovery with a growing number of clusters.

8. PROOFS

8.1 Proof of Theorem 1

Without loss of generality, suppose users $1,3,\dots,2K-1$ are in cluster 1 and users $2,4,\dots,2K$ are in cluster 2. We construct a block-constant matrix with the same movie cluster structure as R but a different user cluster structure. In particular, under $\tilde{R}$, user 1 forms a new cluster with users $2i, i=2,\dots,K$ and user 2 forms a new cluster with users $2i-1, i=2,\dots,K$.

Let i-th row of $\tilde{R}$ be identical to the i-th row of R for all $i > 2K$. Consider all movies j in movie cluster l. If the ratings of user 1 to movies in movie cluster l are all erased, then let $\tilde{R}_{1j} = R_{2j}$ and $\tilde{R}_{ij} = R_{2j}$ for $i = 4,6,\dots,2K$; otherwise let $\tilde{R}_{1j} = R_{1j}$ and $\tilde{R}_{ij} = R_{1j}$ for $i = 4,6,\dots,2K$. If the ratings of user 2 to movies in movie cluster l are all erased, then let $\tilde{R}_{2j} = R_{1j}$ and $\tilde{R}_{ij} = R_{1j}$ for $i = 3,5,\dots,2K-1$; otherwise let $\tilde{R}_{2j} = R_{2j}$ and $\tilde{R}_{ij} = R_{2j}$ for $i = 3,5,\dots,2K-1$. From the above procedure, it follows that the first row of $\tilde{R}$ is identical to the $(2i)$-th row of $\tilde{R}$ for all $i = 2,\dots,K$, and the second row of $\tilde{R}$ is identical the $(2i-1)$-th row of $\tilde{R}$ for all $i = 2,\dots,K$.

We show that $\tilde{R}$ agrees with $\widehat{R}$ on all non-erased entries. We say that movie cluster l is conflicting between user 1 and user cluster 2 if (1) user cluster 1 and 2 have different block rating on movie cluster l; and (2) the ratings of user 1 to movies in movie cluster l are not all erased; and (3) the block corresponding to user cluster 2 and movie cluster l is not totally erased. Therefore, the probability that movie cluster l is conflicting between user 1 and user cluster 2 equals to $\frac{1}{2}(1-\epsilon^{K^2})(1-\epsilon^K)$. By the union bound,

$$\mathbb{P}\{\exists \text{conflicting movie cluster between user 1 and cluster 2}\}$$
$$\le \frac{r}{2}(1-\epsilon^{K^2})(1-\epsilon^K) \le \frac{r}{2}K^3(1-\epsilon)^2 \le \delta/2,$$

where the third inequality follows because $(1-x)^a \ge 1-ax$ for $a \ge 1$ and $x \ge 0$ and the last inequality follows from the assumption. Similarly, the probability that there exists a conflicting movie cluster between user 2 and cluster 1 is also upper bounded by $\delta/2$. Hence, with probability at least $1-\delta$, there is no conflicting movie cluster between user 1 and cluster 2 as well as between user 2 and cluster 1, and thus $\tilde{R}$ agrees with $\widehat{R}$ on all non-erased entries.

8.2 Proof of Theorem 2

Consider a genie-aided scenario where the set of flipped entries is revealed as side information, which is equivalent to saying that we are in the noiseless setting with $p=0$. Then the true partition corresponding to the true user cluster structure has zero disagreement. Suppose that users $1,3,\dots,2K-1$ are in true cluster 1 and users $2,4,\dots,2K$

are in true cluster 2. We construct a new partition different from the true partition by swapping user 1 and user 2. In particular, under the new partition, user 1 forms a new cluster $\widehat{C}_2$ with users $2i, i = 2, \dots, K$, user 2 forms a new cluster $\widehat{C}_1$ with users $2i-1, i = 2, \dots, K$. It suffices to show that for $k = 1, 2$, any two users in $\widehat{C}_k$ has zero disagreement with probability at least 3/4, in which case the new partition has zero agreement and Algorithm 1 cannot distinguish between the true partition and the new one.

For $k = 1, 2$, we lower bound the probability that any two users in $\widehat{C}_k$ has zero disagreement.

$$\begin{aligned}
&\mathbb{P}(\text{Any two users in } \widehat{C}_k \text{ has zero disagreement}) \\
=&1 - \mathbb{P}(\text{total number of disagreements in } \widehat{C}_k \geq 1) \\
\geq&1 - \mathbb{E}[\text{total number of disagreements in } \widehat{C}_k] \\
\geq&1 - \frac{1}{2}nK(1-\epsilon)^2 \geq 7/8.
\end{aligned}$$

By union bound, the probability that for $k = 1, 2$, any two users in $\widehat{C}_k$ has zero disagreement is at least 3/4.

8.3 Proof of Theorem 3

Consider a compatibility graph with n vertices representing users. Two vertices i, i' are connected if users i, i' have zero disagreement, i.e., $D_{ii'} = 0$. In the noiseless setting, each user cluster forms a clique of size K in the compatibility graph. We call a clique of size K in the compatibility graph a bad clique if it is formed by users from more than one cluster. Then to prove the theorem, it suffices to show that there is no bad clique a.a.s. Since the probability that bad cliques exist increases in ϵ, without loss of generality, we assume $K(1-\epsilon) < 1$.

Recall that B_{kl} is $+1$ or -1 with equal probability. Define $S_k = \{l : B_{kl} = +1\}$ for $k = 1, \dots, r$. As $r \to \infty$, by Chernoff bound, we get that a.a.s., for any $k_1 \neq k_2$

$$|S_{k_1} \Delta S_{k_2}| \triangleq |\{l : B_{k_1 l} \neq B_{k_2 l}\}| \geq \frac{r}{4}. \tag{6}$$

Assume this condition holds throughout the proof.

Fix a set of K users that consists of users from t different clusters. Without loss of generality, assume these users are from cluster $1, \dots, t$. Let n_k denote the number of users from the cluster k and define $n_{\max} = \max_k n_k$. By definition, $2 \leq t \leq t_{\max} \triangleq \min\{r, K\}$, $n_{\max} < K$ and $\sum_{k=1}^t n_k = K$. For any movie j in cluster l, among the K ratings given by these users, there are $\sum_{k=1}^t n_k \mathbb{I}_{\{l \in S_k\}}$ ratings being $+1$ and $\sum_{k=1}^t n_k \mathbb{I}_{\{l \notin S_k\}}$ ratings being -1. Let E_j denote the event that the observed ratings for movie j by these K users are the same. Then,

$$\begin{aligned}
\mathbb{P}[E_j] =&1 - \left(1 - \epsilon^{\sum_{k=1}^t n_k \mathbb{I}_{\{l \in S_k\}}}\right)\left(1 - \epsilon^{\sum_{k=1}^t n_k \mathbb{I}_{\{l \notin S_k\}}}\right) \\
\leq&\exp\left(-(1 - \epsilon^{\sum_{k=1}^t n_k \mathbb{I}_{\{l \in S_k\}}})(1 - \epsilon^{\sum_{k=1}^t n_k \mathbb{I}_{\{l \notin S_k\}}})\right) \\
\leq&\exp\Big(-\frac{1}{4}(1-\epsilon)^2 \sum_{k=1}^t n_k \mathbb{I}_{\{l \in S_k\}} \sum_{k=1}^t n_k \mathbb{I}_{\{l \notin S_k\}}\Big).
\end{aligned}$$

Let $p_{n_1 \dots n_t}$ be the probability that K users, out of which n_k are from cluster k, form a bad clique. Because $\{E_j\}$ are independent and there are K movies in each movie cluster,

$$\begin{aligned}
&p_{n_1 \dots n_t} \\
&= \prod_{j=1}^n \mathbb{P}[E_j] \\
&\leq \exp\Big(-\frac{1}{4}K(1-\epsilon)^2 \sum_{l=1}^r \big(\sum_{k=1}^t n_k \mathbb{I}_{\{l \in S_k\}} \sum_{k=1}^t n_k \mathbb{I}_{\{l \notin S_k\}}\big)\Big) \\
&= \exp\Big(-\frac{1}{4}K(1-\epsilon)^2 \sum_{1 \leq k_1 < k_2 \leq t} n_{k_1} n_{k_2} |S_{k_1} \Delta S_{k_2}|\Big) \\
&\leq \exp\Big(-C_1 n(1-\epsilon)^2 \sum_{k=1}^t n_k(K - n_k)\Big)
\end{aligned} \tag{7}$$

for some constant C_1. For a large enough constant C in the assumption in the statement of the theorem, we have

$$K \exp(-C_1 n(1-\epsilon)^2 (K - n_k)) \leq n^{-3}, \quad n_k \leq \frac{K}{2}, \tag{8}$$

$$K \exp(-C_1 n(1-\epsilon)^2 n_k) \leq n^{-3}, \quad n_k > \frac{K}{2}. \tag{9}$$

Below we show that the probability of bad cliques existing goes to zero. By the Markov inequality and linearity of expectation,

$$\begin{aligned}
&\mathbb{P}[\text{Number of bad cliques} \geq 1] \\
&\leq \mathbb{E}[\text{Number of bad cliques}] \\
&= \sum_{t=2}^{t_{\max}} \binom{r}{t} \sum_{n_1 + \dots + n_t = K} \binom{K}{n_1} \cdots \binom{K}{n_t} p_{n_1 \dots n_t} \\
&= \sum_{t=2}^{t_{\max}} \binom{r}{t} \sum_{n_1 + \dots + n_t = K} \binom{K}{n_1} \cdots \binom{K}{n_t} p_{n_1 \dots n_t} \\
&\quad \left[\mathbb{I}_{\{n_{\max} \leq K/2\}} + \mathbb{I}_{\{n_{\max} > K/2\}}\right].
\end{aligned} \tag{10}$$

The first term in (10) is bounded as

$$\begin{aligned}
&\sum_{t=2}^{t_{\max}} \binom{r}{t} \sum_{\substack{n_1 + \dots + n_t = K \\ n_{\max} \leq K/2}} \binom{K}{n_1} \cdots \binom{K}{n_t} p_{n_1 \dots n_t} \\
&\leq \sum_{t=2}^{t_{\max}} r^t \sum_{\substack{n_1 + \dots + n_t = K \\ n_{\max} \leq K/2}} \prod_{k=1}^t (K e^{-C_1(1-\epsilon)^2(K-n_k)})^{n_k} \\
&\leq \sum_{t=2}^{t_{\max}} r^t K^t n^{-3K} = o(1),
\end{aligned} \tag{11}$$

where the first inequality follows from the fact that $\binom{K}{n_k} \leq K^{n_k}$ and (7), and the second inequality follows from (8).

The second term in (10) is bounded as

$$\sum_{t=2}^{t_{\max}} \binom{r}{t} \sum_{\substack{n_1+\cdots+n_t=K \\ n_{\max}>K/2}} \binom{K}{n_1}\cdots\binom{K}{n_t} p_{n_1\ldots n_t}$$

$$\leq \sum_{t=2}^{t_{\max}} r^t \sum_{\substack{n_1+\cdots+n_t=K \\ n_{\max}>K/2}} (Ke^{-C_1 n(1-\epsilon)^2 n_{\max}})^{K-n_{\max}}$$

$$\prod_{k:n_k<n_{\max}} (Ke^{-C_1(1-\epsilon)^2(K-n_k)})^{n_k}$$

$$\leq \sum_{t=2}^{t_{\max}} \mathbb{I}_{\{t\leq K-n_{\max}+1\}} r^t K^t n^{-6(K-n_{\max})} = o(1), \quad (12)$$

where the first inequality follows from the fact that $\binom{K}{n_k} \leq \min\{K^{n_k}, K^{K-n_k}\}$ and (7), and the second inequality follows from (8) and (9) and the fact that $t \leq K - n_{\max} + 1$. Therefore we conclude that $\mathbb{P}[\text{Number of bad cliques} \geq 1] = o(1)$.

8.4 Proof of Theorem 4

We first introduce some notations. Let $u_{C,k}$ be the normalized characteristic vector of user cluster k, i.e., $u_{C,k}(i) = 1/\sqrt{K}$ if user i is in cluster k and $u_{C,k}(i) = 0$ otherwise. Thus, $||u_{C,k}||_2 = 1$. Let $U_C = [u_{C,1}, \ldots, u_{C,r}]$. Similarly, let $v_{C,l}$ be the normalized characteristic vector of movie cluster l and $V_C = [v_{C,1}, \ldots, v_{C,r}]$. It is not hard to see that the rating matrix R can be written as $R = KU_C BV_C^\top$. Denote the SVD of the block rating matrix B by $B = U_B\Sigma_B V_B^\top$, then the SVD of R is simply $R = UK\Sigma_B V^\top$, where $U = U_C U_B$ and $V = V_C V_B$. When $r \to \infty$, B has full rank almost surely [7]. We will assume B is full rank in the following proofs, which implies that $U_B U_B^\top = I$ and $V_B V_B^\top = I$. Note that $UU^\top = U_C U_C^\top, VV^\top = V_C V_C^\top$ and $UV^\top = U_C U_B V_B^\top V_C^\top$.

We now briefly recall the subgradient of the nuclear norm [11]. Define T to be the subspace spanned by all matrices of the form $UA^\top$ or $AV^\top$ for any $A \in \mathbb{R}^{n\times r}$. The orthogonal projection of any matrix $M \in \mathbb{R}^{n\times n}$ onto the space T is given by $\mathcal{P}_T(M) = UU^\top M + MVV^\top - UU^\top MVV^\top$. The projection of M onto the complement space $T^\perp$ is $\mathcal{P}_{T^\perp}(M) = M - \mathcal{P}_T(M)$. Then $M \in \mathbb{R}^{n\times n}$ is a subgradient of $||X||_*$ at $X = R$ if and only if $\mathcal{P}_T(M) = UV^\top$ and $||\mathcal{P}_{T^\perp}(M)|| \leq 1$.

Proof of Lemma 1. Assume user i is from user cluster k and movie j is in movie cluster l, then

$$|(UV^\top)_{ij}| = |(U_B V_B^\top)_{kl}|/K \leq 1/K = r/n,$$

where the inequality follows from the Cauchy-Schwartz inequality. By definition $\mu \leq \sqrt{r}$. □

Next we establish the concentration property of $\widehat{R}$. By definition the conditional expectation of $\widehat{R}$ is given by

$$\mathbb{E}[\widehat{R}|R] = (1-\epsilon)(1-2p)R := \bar{R}.$$

Furthermore, the variance is given by

$$\text{Var}[\widehat{R}_{ij}|R] = (1-\epsilon) - (1-\epsilon)^2(1-2p)^2 := \sigma^2.$$

The following corollary applies Theorem 1.4 in [40] to bound the spectral norm $\|\widehat{R} - \bar{R}\|$.

Corollary 1. *If $\sigma^2 \geq C' \log^4 n/n$ for a constant C', then conditioned on R,*

$$\|\widehat{R} - \bar{R}\| \leq 3\sigma\sqrt{n} \quad a.a.s. \quad (13)$$

Proof. We adopt the trick called dilations [39]. In particular, define A as

$$A = \begin{bmatrix} \mathbf{0} & \widehat{R} - \mathbb{E}[\widehat{R}|R] \\ \widehat{R}^\top - \mathbb{E}[\widehat{R}^\top|R] & \mathbf{0} \end{bmatrix}. \quad (14)$$

Observe that $\|A\| = \|\widehat{R} - \mathbb{E}[\widehat{R}|R]\|$ so it is sufficient to prove the theorem for $\|A\|$. Conditioned on R, A is a random symmetric $2n \times 2n$ matrix with each entry bounded by 1, and a_{ij} $(1 \leq i < j \leq 2n)$ are independent random variables with mean 0 and variance *at most* σ^2. By Theorem 1.4 in [40] , if $\sigma \geq C'n^{-1/2}\log^2 n$, then conditioned on R a.a.s.

$$\|\widehat{R} - \mathbb{E}[\widehat{R}|R]\| = \|A\| \leq 2\sigma\sqrt{2n} + C(2\sigma)^{1/2}(2n)^{1/4}\log(2n)$$
$$\leq 3\sigma\sqrt{n}. \quad (15)$$

□

Proof of Theorem 4. For any feasible Y that $Y \neq R$, we have to show that $\Delta(Y) = \langle\widehat{R}\ R\rangle - \lambda||R||_* - (\langle\widehat{R}, Y\rangle - \lambda||Y||_*) > 0$. Rewrite $\Delta(Y)$ as

$$\Delta(Y) = \langle\bar{R}, R - Y\rangle + \langle\widehat{R} - \bar{R}, R - Y\rangle + \lambda(||Y||_* - ||R||_*). \quad (16)$$

The first term in (16) can be written as

$$\langle\bar{R}, R - Y\rangle = (1-\epsilon)(1-2p)\langle R, R - Y\rangle = (1-\epsilon)(1-2p)||R - Y||_1,$$

where the second equality follows from the fact that $Y_{ij} \in [-1, 1]$ and $R_{ij} = \text{sgn}(R_{ij})$. Define the normalized noise matrix $W = (\widehat{R} - \bar{R})/\lambda$. Note that $||W||_\infty \leq 1/\lambda$ and $\text{Var}(W_{ij}) \leq 1/9n$. The second term in (16) becomes $\langle\widehat{R} - \bar{R}, R - Y\rangle = \lambda\langle W, R - Y\rangle$. By Corollary 1, $||W|| \leq 1$ almost surely. Thus $UV^\top + \mathcal{P}_{T^\perp}(W)$ is a subgradient of $||X||_*$ at $X = R$. Hence, for the third term in (16), $\lambda(||Y||_* - ||R||_*) \geq \lambda\langle UV^\top + \mathcal{P}_{T^\perp}(W), Y - R\rangle$. Therefore,

$$\Delta(Y)$$
$$\geq (1-\epsilon)(1-2p)||R - Y||_1 + \lambda\langle UV^\top - \mathcal{P}_T(W), Y - R\rangle$$
$$\geq [(1-\epsilon)(1-2p) - \lambda(||UV^\top||_\infty + ||\mathcal{P}_T(W)||_\infty)]||R - Y||_1$$
$$\geq [(1-\epsilon)(1-2p) - \lambda(\mu\sqrt{r}/n + |\ \mathcal{P}_T(W)||_\infty)]||R - Y||_1, \quad (17)$$

where the last inequality follows from definition of the incoherence parameter μ. Below we bound the term $||\mathcal{P}_T(W)||_\infty$. From the definition of $\mathcal{P}_T$ and the fact that $U_B U_B^\top = I$ and $V_B V_B^\top = I$,

$$||\mathcal{P}_T(W)||_\infty \leq ||U_C U_C^\top W||_\infty + ||WV_C V_C^\top||_\infty + ||U_C U_C^\top WV_C V_C^\top||_\infty.$$

We bound $||U_C U_C^\top W||_\infty$. To bound the term $(U_C U_C^\top W)_{ij}$, assume user i belongs to user cluster k and let $\mathcal{C}_k$ be the set of users in user cluster k. Recall that $u_{C,k}$ is the normalized characteristic vector of user cluster k. Then

$$(U_C U_C^\top W)_{ij} = (u_{C,k} u_{C,k}^\top W)_{ij} = (1/K)\sum_{i'\in\mathcal{C}_k} W_{i'j},$$

which is the average of K independent random variables. By Bernstein's inequality (stated in the supplementary material), with probability at least $1-n^{-3}$,

$$\left|\sum_{i'\in\mathcal{C}_k} W_{i'j}\right| \le \sqrt{\frac{2}{3r}\log n} + \frac{2\log n}{\lambda}.$$

Then $||U_C U_C^\top W||_\infty \le \frac{1}{K}\left(\sqrt{\frac{2}{3r}\log n} + \frac{2\log n}{\lambda}\right)$ with probability at least $1-n^{-1}$. Similarly we bound $||WV_CV_C^\top||_\infty$ and $||U_CU_C^\top WV_CV_C^\top||_\infty$. Therefore, with probability at least $1-3n^{-1}$,

$$||\mathcal{P}_T(W)||_\infty \le \frac{C_1}{K}\left(\sqrt{\frac{\log n}{r}} + \frac{\log n}{\lambda}\right) \le \frac{C_2}{K}\sqrt{\frac{\log n}{r}}, \quad (18)$$

for some constants C_1 and C_2, where the second inequality follows from assumption (4). Substituting (18) into (17) and by assumption (4) again, we conclude that $\Delta(Y) > 0$ a.a.s. □

8.5 Proof of Theorem 5

The proof is divided into three parts. Recall that x_i denotes the i-th row of $Pr(\widehat{R}^{(1)})$. We first show that, for most users, x_i is close to the expected value conditioned on R. Then we show that the clusters output by Step 2 are close to the true clusters. Finally, we show that Step 3 exactly recovers the block rating matrix B and Step 4 exactly recovers clusters.

Define $\bar{R}^{(1)} = \mathbb{E}[\widehat{R}^{(1)}|R] = \frac{1}{2}(1-\epsilon)(1-2p)R$ and let $\bar{x}_i$ be the i-th row of $\bar{R}^{(1)}$. We call user i a *good* user if $||x_i - \bar{x}_i||_2 \le \tau/2$ where the threshold $\tau = 12(1-\epsilon)^{1/2}\log n$; otherwise it is called a *bad* user. Let $\mathcal{I}$ denote the set of all good users and $\mathcal{I}^c$ denote the set of all bad users. Define good movies in the same way, and let $\mathcal{J}$ denote the set of all good movies and $\mathcal{J}^c$ denote the set of all bad movies. The following lemma shows that the number of bad users (movies) are bounded by $K\log^{-2} n$.

Lemma 2. *If $\sigma^2 \ge C'\log^4 n/n$ for a constant C', then a.a.s., $|\mathcal{I}^c| \le K\log^{-2} n$ and $|\mathcal{J}^c| \le K\log^{-2} n$.*

Proof. Let $(\sigma^{(1)})^2 = \frac{1}{2}(1-\epsilon)$. By Corollary 1, $||\widehat{R}^{(1)} - \bar{R}^{(1)}|| \le 3\sigma^{(1)}\sqrt{n}$. Note that

$$\begin{aligned}||P_r(\widehat{R}^{(1)}) - \bar{R}|| &\le ||P_r(\widehat{R}^{(1)}) - \widehat{R}^{(1)}|| + ||\widehat{R}^{(1)} - \bar{R}||\\ &\le 2||\widehat{R}^{(1)} - \bar{R}||,\end{aligned}$$

where the second inequality follows from the definition of $P_r(\widehat{R}^{(1)})$ and the fact that $\bar{R}$ has rank r. Since both $P_r(\widehat{R}^{(1)})$ and $\bar{R}$ have rank r, the matrix $P_r(\widehat{R}^{(1)}) - \bar{R}$ has rank at most $2r$, which implies that

$$||P_r(\widehat{R}^{(1)}) - \bar{R}||_F^2 \le 8r||\widehat{R}^{(1)} - \bar{R}||^2 \le 72(\sigma^{(1)})^2 nr.$$

As $\sum_{i=1}^n ||x_i - \bar{x}_i||_2^2 = ||P_r(\widehat{R}^{(1)}) - \bar{R}||_F^2$, we conclude that there are at most $K\log^{-2} n$ users with

$$||x_i - \bar{x}_i||_2 > 6\sqrt{2}\sigma^{(1)} r\log n = \tau/2.$$

Similarly we can prove the result for movies. □

The following proposition upper bounds the set difference between the estimated clusters and the true clusters by $K\log^{-2} n$. Let $C_1^*, \ldots, C_r^*$ be the true user clusters and Δ denote the set difference.

Proposition 1. *Assume the assumption of Theorem 5 holds. Step 2 of Algorithm 3 outputs $\{\widehat{C}_k\}_{k=1}^r$ and $\{\widehat{D}_l\}_{l=1}^r$ such that, up to a permutation of cluster indices, a.a.s., $\widehat{C}_k \Delta C_k^* \subset \mathcal{I}^c$ and $\widehat{D}_l \Delta D_l^* \subset \mathcal{J}^c$ for all k, l. It follows that for all k, l,*

$$|\widehat{C}_k \Delta C_k^*| \le \frac{K}{\log^2 n}, \quad |\widehat{D}_l \Delta D_l^*| \le \frac{K}{\log^2 n}. \quad (19)$$

Proof. It suffices to prove the conclusion for the user clusters. Consider two good users $i, i' \in \mathcal{I}$. If they are from the same cluster, we have $\bar{x}_i = \bar{x}_{i'}$ and

$$||x_i - x_{i'}|| \le ||x_i - \bar{x}_i|| + ||x_{i'} - \bar{x}_{i'}|| \le \tau, \quad (20)$$

where the last inequality follows from Lemma 2. If they are from different clusters, by (6), we have a.a.s.

$$\begin{aligned}||\bar{x}_i - \bar{x}_{i'}||_2^2 &= \frac{1}{4}(1-\epsilon)^2(1-2p)^2||R_i - R_{i'}||_2^2\\ &\ge \frac{1}{4}(1-\epsilon)^2(1-2p)^2 n,\end{aligned}$$

where R_i denotes the i-th row of R. Thus,

$$\begin{aligned}||x_i - x_{i'}|| &\ge ||\bar{x}_i - \bar{x}_{i'}|| - ||x_i - \bar{x}_i|| - ||x_{i'} - \bar{x}_{i'}||\\ &\ge \frac{1}{2}(1-\epsilon)(1-2p)\sqrt{n} - \tau > \tau, \quad (21)\end{aligned}$$

where the last inequality follows from the assumption (5). Therefore, in the clustering procedure of Step 2, if we choose a good initial user at some iteration, the corresponding estimated cluster will contain all the good users from the same cluster as the initial user and no good user from other clusters. It is not hard to see that the probability of the event that we choose a good initial user in every iteration is lower bounded by

$$\begin{aligned}&\left(1 - \frac{1}{r\log^2 n}\right)\left(1 - \frac{1}{(r-1)\log^2 n}\right)\cdots\left(1 - \frac{1}{\log^2 n}\right)\\ &\ge 1 - \frac{1}{\log^2 n}\left(\frac{1}{r} + \frac{1}{r-1} + \cdots + 1\right)\\ &\ge 1 - \frac{\log r}{\log^2 n} \ge 1 - \frac{1}{\log n}.\end{aligned}$$

Assume the above event holds. Under proper permutation, the initial good user in the k-th iteration is from cluster C_k^* for all k. By the above argument, the set difference $\widehat{C}_k \Delta C_k^* \subset \mathcal{I}^c$. By Lemma 2, (19) follows. □

Proof of Theorem 5. We first show that Step 3 of Algorithm 3 exactly recovers the block rating matrix B. Let V_{kl} denote the total vote that the true user cluster k gives to the true movie cluster l, i.e.,

$$V_{kl} = \sum_{i\in C_k^*}\sum_{j\in D_l^*} \widehat{R}_{ij}^{(2)}.$$

Then by definition of $\widehat{V}_{kl}$,

$$\begin{aligned}|\widehat{V}_{kl} - V_{kl}| \le &\sum_{i\in C_k^*\Delta\widehat{C}_k}\ \sum_{j\in D_l^*\cup\widehat{D}_l} \mathbb{I}_{\{(i,j)\in\Omega_2\}}\\ &+ \sum_{i\in C_k^*\cup\widehat{C}_k}\ \sum_{j\in D_l^*\Delta\widehat{D}_l} \mathbb{I}_{\{(i,j)\in\Omega_2\}}. \quad (22)\end{aligned}$$

Without loss of generality, assume $B_{kl} = 1$. By Bernstein inequality and assumption (5), $V_{kl} \ge \frac{1}{4}(1-\epsilon)(1-2p)K^2$

a.a.s. On the other hand, as Ω_2 and $\widehat{R}^{(1)}$ are independent, Ω_2 is independent from $\{\widehat{C}_k\}$ and $\{\widehat{D}_l\}$. It follows from (19) and the Chernoff bound that each term on the right hand side of (22) is upper bounded by $(1-\epsilon)K^2 \log^{-2} n$ a.a.s. Hence, when assumption (5) holds for some large enough constant C, we have $\widehat{V}_{kl} > 0$ thus $\widehat{B}_{kl} = B_{kl}$.

Next we prove that Step 4 clusters the users and movies correctly. Without loss of generality, we only prove the correctness for users. Suppose user i is from cluster k. Recall that R_i denotes the i-th row of R. When $\widehat{B} = B$, we have $\mu_{kj} = R_{ij}$ for $j \in \mathcal{J}$ by definition and Proposition 1. Then

$$\begin{aligned}\langle \widehat{R}_i^{(2)}, \mu_k \rangle =& \langle \widehat{R}_i^{(2)}, R_i \rangle + \langle \widehat{R}_i^{(2)}, \mu_k - R_i \rangle \\ \geq & \langle \widehat{R}_i^{(2)}, R_i \rangle - 2 \sum_{j \in \mathcal{J}^c} |\widehat{R}_{ij}^{(2)}|. \end{aligned} \tag{23}$$

Similarly, for some user i' from cluster $k' \neq k$,

$$\begin{aligned}\langle \widehat{R}_i^{(2)}, \mu_{k'} \rangle =& \langle \widehat{R}_i^{(2)}, R_{i'} \rangle + \langle \widehat{R}_i^{(2)}, \mu_{k'} - R_{i'} \rangle \\ \leq & \langle \widehat{R}_i^{(2)}, R_{i'} \rangle + 2 \sum_{j \in \mathcal{J}^c} |\widehat{R}_{ij}^{(2)}| \end{aligned} \tag{24}$$

For ease of notation, let $t := \frac{1}{2}(1-\epsilon)(1-2p)n$ and $(\sigma^{(2)})^2 = \frac{1}{2}(1-\epsilon)$. By (6), $\langle R_i, R_{i'} \rangle \leq n/2$ for all $i \neq i'$. Then conditioned on R, we have $\mathbb{E}[\langle \widehat{R}_i^{(2)}, R_i \rangle] = t$ and $\mathrm{Var}[\langle \widehat{R}_i^{(2)}, R_i \rangle] \leq n(\sigma^{(2)})^2$, and

$$\mathbb{E}[\langle \widehat{R}_i^{(2)}, R_{i'} \rangle] = \frac{1}{2}(1-\epsilon)(1-2p)\langle R_i, R_i' \rangle \leq t/2$$

and $\mathrm{Var}[\langle \widehat{R}_i^{(2)}, R_{i'} \rangle] \leq n(\sigma^{(2)})^2$. Now by the Bernstein inequality and assumption (5), we have that conditioned on R, a.a.s. $\langle \widehat{R}_i^{(2)}, R_i \rangle > 7t/8$ and $\langle \widehat{R}_i^{(2)}, R_{i'} \rangle < 5t/8$ for all $i \neq i'$.

On the other hand, because $\mathcal{J}$ and Ω_2 are independent, by the Chernoff bound, a.a.s. $\sum_{j \in \mathcal{J}^c} |\widehat{R}_{ij}^{(2)}|$ is upper bounded by $(1-\epsilon)K \log^{-2} n < t/16$ for all i, when assumption (5) holds for some large enough constant C.

Therefore, from (23) and (24), $\langle \widehat{R}_i^{(2)}, \mu_k \rangle > \langle \widehat{R}_i^{(2)}, \mu_{k'} \rangle$ for all $k' \neq k$. □

9. NUMERICAL EXPERIMENTS

In this section, we illustrate the performance of the convex method and the spectral method using synthetic data.

9.1 Convex method

The convex program (2) can be formulated as a semidefinite program (SDP) and solved using a general purpose SDP solver. However this method does not scale well for our problem when the matrix dimension n is large. Instead we apply the accelerated gradient descent method proposed in [25, 37] which aims to solve the optimization problem

$$\min_Y f(Y) + \lambda ||Y||_*$$

for some smooth function $f(Y)$. In our case, the smooth function is linear, i.e., $f(Y) = -\langle \hat{R}, Y \rangle$. Define proximal regularization of $f(Y)$ at X as

$$\begin{aligned} P_\mu(X, Y) =& f(X) - \langle Y - X, \hat{R} \rangle + \frac{\mu}{2} ||Y - X||_F^2 \\ =& -\langle Y, \hat{R} \rangle + \frac{\mu}{2} ||Y - X||_F^2. \end{aligned}$$

for some constant $\mu > 0$. Then it is shown in [25] that (2) is solved by the following iterative algorithm:

$$Y_k = \arg \min_{Y_{ij} \in [-1,1]} P_\mu(Y_{k-1}, Y) + \lambda ||Y||_*. \tag{25}$$

We approximate Y_k by first solving the unconstrained optimization problem

$$\min_Y P_\mu(Y_{k-1}, Y) - \lambda ||Y||_*. \tag{26}$$

and then project each entry of the solution to $[-1, 1]$, where we use $P_{[-1,1]}$ to denote the projection operator. The minimizer of (26) can be explicitly written in terms of the soft-thresholding operator D defined as follows. For any $\gamma \geq 0$ and for any matrix X with SVD $X = U \Sigma V^\top$ where $\Sigma = \mathrm{diag}(\{\sigma_i\})$, define

$$D_\gamma(X) = U \mathrm{diag}(\{\max(\sigma_i - \gamma, 0)\}) V^\top.$$

Intuitively, the soft-thresholding operator D shrinks the singular values of X towards zero. Applying Theorem 2.1 in [9], we get

$$D_{\frac{\lambda}{\mu}} \left(X + \frac{\widehat{R}}{\mu} \right) = \arg \min_Y P_\mu(X, Y) + \lambda ||Y||_*.$$

Thus, the update equation (25) of Y_k is approximated by

$$Y_k = P_{[-1,1]} \left(D_{\frac{\lambda}{\mu}} (Y_{k-1} + \frac{\widehat{R}}{\mu}) \right).$$

This iterative algorithm can further be accelerated to achieve the optimal convergence rate of $O(1/k^2)$, which results Algorithm 4 [25]. Note that we do not use a fixed regularization parameter λ. The algorithm has better performance when we start with $\lambda_0 = 3\sqrt{(1-\epsilon)n}$ as in Theorem 4 and decrease it gradually until it reaches $\bar{\lambda} = \sqrt{(1-\epsilon)n}$. In the experiment, we choose $\mu_k = 1$.

Algorithm 4 Accelerated Gradient Descent Algorithm

Input: $\widehat{R}$
Initialization: Set $Y_0 = Y_{-1} = 0$ and $\alpha_0 = \alpha_{-1} = 1$. Pick $\lambda_0 = 3\sqrt{(1-\epsilon)n}$ and $\bar{\lambda} = \sqrt{(1-\epsilon)n}$. Set $\gamma = 0.95$. Set $\mu_k = 1$.
for $k = 0, 1, 2, \ldots$ **do**
  $Z_k = Y_k + \frac{\alpha_{k-1} - 1}{\alpha_k}(Y_k - Y_{k-1})$
  $Y_{k+1} = P_{[-1,1]} \left(D_{\frac{\lambda_k}{\mu_k}} \left(Z_k + \frac{\widehat{R}}{\mu_k} \right) \right)$
  $\alpha_{k+1} = \frac{1 + \sqrt{1 + 4\alpha_k^2}}{2}$
  $\lambda_{k+1} = \max\{\gamma \lambda_k, \bar{\lambda}\}$.
end for

We simulate Algorithm 4 on the synthetic data. Assume K and ϵ take the form given by

$$K = n^\beta, \quad \epsilon = 1 - n^{-\alpha}. \tag{27}$$

Theorem 4 shows that the convex program (4) recovers the rating matrix exactly when $\alpha < \beta$, assuming Conjecture 1 holds.

We generate the observed data matrix with $n = 2048$, $p = 0.05$ and various choices of $\beta, \alpha \in (0, 1)$, and apply Algorithm 4. The solution $\widehat{Y}$ is evaluated by the fraction of entries with correct signs, i.e., $\frac{1}{n^2} |\{(i, j) : \mathrm{sign}(\widehat{Y}_{ij}) = R_{ij}\}|$.

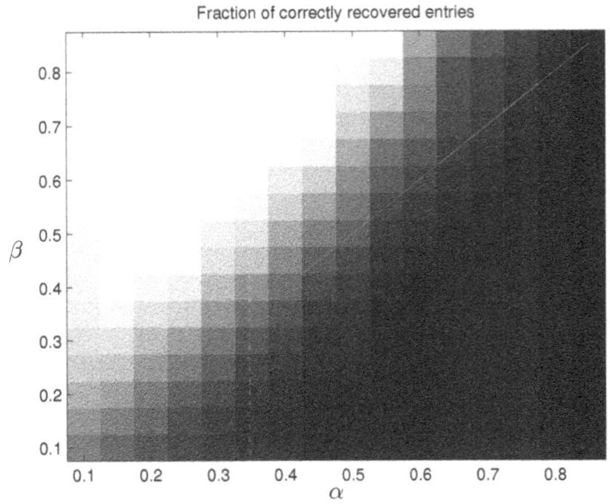

Figure 3: Simulation result of the convex method given in Algorithm 4 with $n = 2048$ and $p = 0.05$. The x-axis corresponds to erasure probability $\epsilon = 1 - n^{-\alpha}$ and y-axis corresponds to cluster size $K = n^{\beta}$. The grey scale of each area represents the fraction of entries with correct signs, with white representing exact recovery and black representing around 50% recovery. The red line shows the performance of the convex method predicted by Theorem 4.

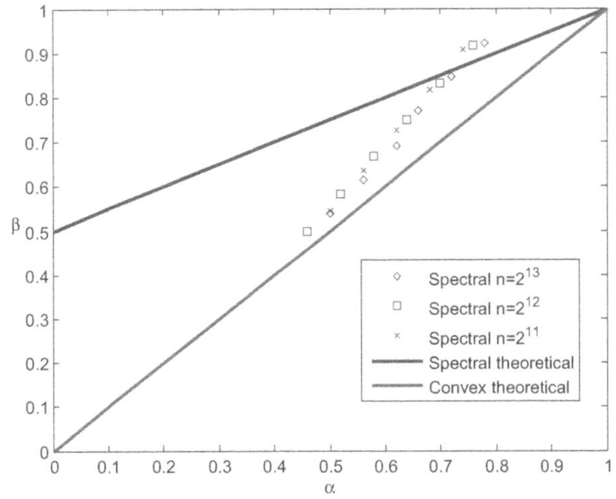

Figure 4: Simulation result of the spectral method given in Algorithm 3 with $n = 2^{11}, 2^{12}, 2^{13}$ and $p = 0.05$. The x-axis corresponds to erasure probability $\epsilon = 1 - n^{-\alpha}$ and y-axis corresponds to cluster size $K = n^{\beta}$. Each data point in the plot indicates the maximum value of α for which the spectral method succeeds with a given β. The blue solid line shows the performance of the spectral method predicted by Theorem 5. The red solid line shows the performance of the convex method predicted by Theorem 4.

The result is plotted in grey scale in Figure 3. In particular, the white area represents exact recovery and the black area represents around 50% recovery, which is equivalent to random guess. The red line represents $\alpha = \beta$, which shows the performance guarantee given by Theorem 4. As we can see, the simulation results roughly match the theoretical performance guarantee.

9.2 Spectral Method

We simulate the spectral method given in Algorithm 3 on synthetic data. Assume K and ϵ take the form of (27). Theorem 5 shows that the spectral method exactly recovers the clusters when $\alpha < \frac{1}{2}(\beta + 1)$.

We generate the observed data matrix according to our model with $n = 2^{11}, 2^{12}, 2^{13}$ and $p = 0.05$, and various choices of $\beta, \alpha \in (0, 1)$. We apply Algorithm 3 with slight modifications. Firstly, we do not split the observation as in Step 1 but use all the observations for the later steps, i.e., $\Omega_1 = \Omega_2 = \Omega$. Secondly, in Step 2 we use the more robust k-means algorithm to cluster users and movies instead of the thresholding based clustering algorithm. The clustering error is measured by the fraction of mis-clustered users and movies. We say the algorithm succeeds if the clustering error is less than 5%.

For each β, we run the algorithm for several values of α and record the largest α for which the algorithm succeeds. The result is depicted in Fig 4. The solid blue line represents $\alpha = \frac{1}{2}(\beta + 1)$, which shows the performance guarantee of the spectral method given by Theorem 5. The solid red line represents $\alpha = \beta$, which shows the performance guarantee of the convex method given by Theorem 4. We can see that the simulation results of the spectral method are better than its theoretical performance guarantee, but worse than the theoretical performance guarantee of the convex method.

10. CONCLUDING REMARKS

This paper studies the problem of inferring hidden row and column clusters of binary matrices from a few noisy observations through theoretical analysis and numerical experiments. More extensive simulation results will be presented in a longer version of the paper. Several future directions are of interest. First, proving Conjecture 1 or removing the dependency on incoherence μ [15] is important to fully understand the performance of the convex method. Second, a tight performance analysis of the ML estimation (1) is needed to achieve the lower bound. Third, it is interesting to extend our analysis to block rating matrices having real-valued entries.

11. ACKNOWLEDGMENTS

Research supported in part by AFOSR MURI FA 9550-10-1-0573 and NSF ECCS 10-28464.

12. REFERENCES

[1] S. T. Aditya, O. Dabeer, and B. Dey. A channel coding perspective of collaborative filtering. *IEEE Transactions on Information Theory*, 57(4):2327–2341, 2011.

[2] E. Arias-Castro and N. Verzelen. Community detection in random networks. *arXiv preprint arXiv:1302.7099*, 2013.

[3] S. Balakrishnan, M. Kolar, A. Rinalso, and A. Singh. Statistical and computational tradeoffs in biclustering. In *NIPS 2011 Workshop on Computational Trade-offs in Statistical Learning*, 2011.

[4] K. Barman and O. Dabeer. Analysis of a collaborative filter based on popularity amongst neighbors. *IEEE*

Transactions on Information Theory, 58(12):7110–7134, 2012.

[5] Q. Berthet and P. Rigollet. Complexity theoretic lower bounds for sparse principal component detection. *J. Mach. Learn. Res.*, 30:1046–1066 (electronic), 2013.

[6] Q. Berthet and P. Rigollet. Optimal detection of sparse principal components in high dimension. *Ann. Statist.*, 41(1):1780–1815, 2013.

[7] J. Bourgain, V. H. Vu, and P. M. Wood. On the singularity probability of discrete random matrices. *Journal of Functional Analysis*, 258(2):559–603, 2010.

[8] S. Busygin, O. Prokopyev, and P. M. Pardalos. Biclustering in data mining. *Computers and Operations Research*, 35(9):2964 – 2987, 2008.

[9] J.-F. Cai, E. J. Candès, and Z. Shen. A singular value thresholding algorithm for matrix completion. *SIAM J. on Optimization*, 20(4):1956–1982, Mar. 2010.

[10] E. J. Candès, X. Li, Y. Ma, and J. Wright. Robust principal component analysis? *J. ACM*, 58(3):11:1–11:37, June 2011.

[11] E. J. Candès and B. Recht. Exact matrix completion via convex optimization. *Found. Comput. Math.*, 9(6):717–772, Dec. 2009.

[12] E. J. Candès and T. Tao. The power of convex relaxation: near-optimal matrix completion. *IEEE Trans. Inf. Theor.*, 56(5):2053–2080, May 2010.

[13] V. Chandrasekaran and M. I. Jordan. Computational and statistical tradeoffs via convex relaxation. *PNAS*, 110(13):E1181–E1190, 2013.

[14] V. Chandrasekaran, S. Sanghavi, P. Parrilo, and A. Willsky. Rank-sparsity incoherence for matrix decomposition. *SIAM Journal on Optimization*, 21(2):572–596, 2011.

[15] Y. Chen. Incoherence-optimal matrix completion. 2013, available at http://arxiv.org/abs/1310.0154.

[16] Y. Chen, A. Jalali, S. Sanghavi, and C. Caramanis. Low-rank matrix recovery from errors and erasures. *IEEE Transactions on Information Theory*, 59(7):4324–4337, 2013.

[17] Y. Chen, A. Jalali, S. Sanghavi, and H. Xu. Clustering partially observed graphs via convex optimization. In *ICML*, 2011, available at: http://arxiv.org/abs/1104.4803.

[18] Y. Chen, S. Sanghavi, and H. Xu. Clustering sparse graphs. In *NIPS*, 2012, available at: http://arxiv.org/abs/1210.3335.

[19] Y. Chen and J. Xu. Statistical-computational tradeoffs in planted problems and submatrix localization with a growing number of clusters and submatrices. 2014, available at http://arxiv.org/abs/1402.1267.

[20] Y. Cheng and G. M. Church. Biclustering of expression data. *Proceedings of International Conference on Intelligent Systems for Molecular Biology (ISMB)*, 8:93–103, 2000.

[21] M. A. Davenport, Y. Plan, E. van den Berg, and M. Wootters. 1-bit matrix completion. Sept. 2012, available at http://arxiv.org/abs/1209.3672.

[22] S. Fortunato. Community detection in graphs. *Physics Reports*, 486(3-5):75 – 174, 2010.

[23] J. A. Hartigan. Direct clustering of a data matrix. *Journal of the American Statistical Association*, 67(337):123–129, 1972.

[24] P. Jain, P. Netrapalli, and S. Sanghavi. Low-rank matrix completion using alternating minimization. In *Proceedings of the 45th Annual ACM Symposium on Symposium on Theory of Computing*, STOC '13, pages 665–674, New York, NY, USA, 2013. ACM.

[25] S. Ji and J. Ye. An accelerated gradient method for trace norm minimization. In *Proceedings of the 26th Annual International Conference on Machine Learning*, ICML '09, pages 457–464, New York, NY, USA, 2009. ACM.

[26] D. Jiang, C. Tang, and A. Zhang. Cluster analysis for gene expression data: A survey. *IEEE Trans. on Knowl. and Data Eng.*, 16(11):1370–1386, Nov. 2004.

[27] R. Kannan and S. Vempala. Spectral algorithms. *Found. Trends Theor. Comput. Sci.*, 4, Mar 2009.

[28] M. Kolar, S. Balakrishnan, A. Rinaldo, and A. Singh. Minimax localization of structural information in large noisy matrices. In *NIPS*, 2011.

[29] Y. Koren, R. Bell, and C. Volinsky. Matrix factorization techniques for recommender systems. *Computer*, 42(8):30–37, 2009.

[30] R. Krauthgamer, B. Nadler, and D. Vilenchik. Do semidefinite relaxations really solve sparse pca? 2013, available at http://arxiv.org/abs/1306.3690.

[31] G. Linden, B. Smith, and J. York. Amazon.com recommendations: item-to-item collaborative filtering. *Internet Computing, IEEE*, 7(1):76–80, 2003.

[32] Z. Ma and Y. Wu. Computational barriers in minimax submatrix detection. 2013, available at http://arxiv.org/abs/1309.5914.

[33] S. C. Madeira and A. L. Oliveira. Biclustering algorithms for biological data analysis: A survey. *IEEE/ACM Trans. Comput. Biol. Bioinformatics*, 1(1):24–45, Jan. 2004.

[34] F. McSherry. Spectral partitioning of random graphs. In *42nd IEEE Symposium on Foundations of Computer Science*, pages 529 – 537, Oct. 2001.

[35] B. Recht. A simpler approach to matrix completion. *J. Mach. Learn. Res.*, 12:3413–3430, Dec 2011.

[36] K. Rohe, S. Chatterjee, and B. Yu. Spectral clustering and the high-dimensional stochastic blockmodel. *The Annals of Statistics*, 39(4):1878–1915, 2011.

[37] K.-C. Toh and S. Yun. An accelerated proximal gradient algorithm for nuclear norm regularized linear least squares problems. *Pacific Journal of Optimization*, 2010.

[38] D.-C. Tomozei and L. Massoulié. Distributed user profiling via spectral methods. *SIGMETRICS Perform. Eval. Rev.*, 38(1):383–384, June 2010.

[39] J. Tropp. User-friendly tail bounds for sums of random matrices. *Foundations of Computational Mathematics*, 12(4):389–434, 2012.

[40] V. H. Vu. Spectral norm of random matrices. *Combinatorica*, 27(6):721–736, 2007.

[41] S.-Y. Yun and A. Proutiere. Community detection via random and adaptive sampling. 2014, available at http://arxiv.org/abs/1402.3072.

Filter & Follow: How Social Media Foster Content Curation

Avner May
Columbia University
New York, NY
avnermay@cs.columbia.edu

Augustin Chaintreau
Columbia University
New York, NY
augustin@cs.columbia.edu

Nitish Korula
Google
New York, NY
nitish@google.com

Silvio Lattanzi
Google
New York, NY
silviol@google.com

"The Internet has turned the news industry upside down, making it more participatory, social, diverse and partisan – as it used to be before the arrival of the mass media."
T. Standage, *The Economist*, July 7th, 2011.

ABSTRACT

The impact of blogs and microblogging on the consumption of news is dramatic, as every day users rely more on these sources to decide what content to pay attention to. In this work, we empirically and theoretically analyze the dynamics of bloggers serving as intermediaries between the mass media and the general public.

Our first contribution is to precisely describe the receiving and posting behaviors of today's social media users. For the first time, we study *jointly* the volume and popularity of URLs received and shared by users. We show that social media platforms exhibit a natural "content curation" process. Users and bloggers in particular obey two *filtering laws*: (1) a user who receives less content typically receives more popular content, and (2) a blogger who is less active typically posts disproportionately popular items. Our observations are remarkably consistent across 11 social media data sets. We find evidence of a variety of posting strategies, which motivates our second contribution: a theoretical understanding of the consequences of strategic posting on the stability of social media, and its ability to satisfy the interests of a diverse audience. We introduce a "blog-positioning game" and show that it can lead to "efficient" equilibria, in which users generally receive the content they are interested in. Interestingly, this model predicts that if users are overly "picky" when choosing who to follow, no pure strategy equilibria exists for the bloggers, and thus the game never converges. However, a bit of leniency by the readers in choosing which bloggers to follow is enough to guarantee convergence.

Keywords

social media; blogs; information diffusion; potential game

SIGMETRICS'14, June 16–20, 2014, Austin, Texas, USA.
ACM 978-1-4503-2789-3/14/06.
http://dx.doi.org/10.1145/2591971.2592010.

1. INTRODUCTION

One of the most transformative forces in media consumption is the recent multiplication of referrers or intermediaries. Most users still ultimately rely on content produced by professional journalists for accuracy and impartiality. But users do *not* depend any longer on traditional media to determine *what* they should see. Increasingly, people use social media to refer them to content of interest. Thus, more and more content is reaching people by traversing a network which was built from previous choices; these choices include what content users decide to post, and whose posts an individual decides to pay attention to.

The main challenge of online content curation is that the interests of users in general do not follow a simple predictable model. Users have a wide range of interests across a large set of topics; even within a topic (*e.g.,* New York sports, U.S. politics, a major geopolitical or societal event, etc.) different users will likely be interested in different subsets of the news about this topic. Social media at its core makes a remarkable promise – that through chains of referrals the torrent of information produced online can be tamed and distilled to deliver to each user the content they are interested in. In other words, the medium formed by users' connections and posting behaviors is efficient from a *communication* standpoint.

Our objective in this paper is to assess the credibility of this promise. Various claims have been made on the power of social networks to diffuse information quickly and efficiently. These typically follow from topological properties and they quote volumes of large viral cascades for content of popular appeal. Most highlight the importance of information intermediaries, such as professional journalists, bloggers, or prominent people who are well-positioned to connect different parts of the network. We wish to go beyond these structural properties and see how social media shape what content is shared: How do today's information intermediaries choose what to post? How are these choices affected by the content's popularity? Can a follower graph emerge from users' decisions that puts the right information in front of them? To address these questions, one needs to combine insight from measurement at a microscopic scale with a macroscopic analysis that predicts the efficiency of the network as a whole.

Our work empirically studies today's online crowd-curation with a new level of detail. We present an intriguing role played by information intermediaries, and analyze theoretically its consequence on the efficiency of social media. More precisely, our work makes the following contributions:

- Based on 11 social media data sets, differing in their source platforms (*e.g.,* Twitter, Facebook, Spinn3r), topics, and time periods, we demonstrate that social curation obeys a "filtering law". This law predicts that the popularity of content received by a user, or posted by an intermediary, is inversely correlated with the amount of content she receives or posts. This relationship is robust to different ways of defining "information intermediaries", and quantifying content popularity. Furthermore, we show that this trend is not simply a statistical consequence of the very skewed content popularity distribution. (Section 3).
- Informed by the above observations, we hypothesize that bloggers are behaving strategically, trying to post a unique, high-quality set of content, in order to attract a large following. Thus, we model the social curation system as a competition between bloggers for user attention, and call this model the "blog-positioning game." But how does a user pick which blogger to follow? We consider two types of factors: 1) how well the content posted by an intermediary matches her interests ("endogenous factors"), and 2) "exogenous factors" such as the reputation of the intermediary and their writing style. Our model considers both types of factors, and is able to reproduce the observed filtering law. (Section 4).
- We analyze whether pure strategy Nash equilibria exist under the above model, and if so, whether these equilibria are "efficient" (in terms of the number of users satisfied with the content they receive, relative to the optimal intermediary configuration). We show that the existence of equilibria depends deeply on the way in which users pick which blogger to follow. If users precisely pick the blogger that gives them maximal utility, no equilibria exist; on the other hand, if they simply pick a blogger that is "good enough", an equilibrium always exists. Moreover, in the resulting social network, at least half of the optimal number of users are satisfied with the content they receive. (Section 5)

Together, our empirical and theoretical findings lay the foundation for better understanding the surprising power of social networks as a communication medium.

2. RELATED WORK

Our work follows the classic hypothesis of a *two-step information flow* [11], where news savvy "opinion leaders" play the key role of intermediaries between the content produced by mass media and the general public. This thesis was revived using empirical evidence from Twitter [13, 20], and more recently identifying mass media and intermediaries as critical to information spread [6]. In fact, our work extends this hypothesis to model how even relatively normal users play the role of information filters for their peers. Much remains to be explored to analyze the intrinsic effectiveness of such information spread. A recent study showed that social networks allow users to be exposed to more diverse viewpoints [2]. On the other hand, study of word-of-mouth propagation showed that this spread is more likely between geographically close friends, hinting at a possible bias effect [16]. Our work is complementary as we explore a new dimension: how intermediaries help manage the *volume* of information by serving as filters and adapting to the interests of the audience. We depart from the purely empirical approach by analyzing the dynamics between bloggers as they compete for user attention.

Since a first version of our work appeared, a recent analysis of Twitter suggested that social media can be efficient at giving users information relevant to their interests [22]. It showed this efficiency is compatible with follower relationships and interests that both derive from the same underlying structure in a Kronecker graph, although this argument currently implies that the graph is undirected. Motivated by the same observation, we offer a very different starting point, by focusing on the behaviors of intermediaries in directed graphs. In our work the structure is not assumed *a priori* but naturally emerges from the interaction of various agents of the curation ecosystem.

As news moves online, how to best serve the various information needs of communities remains an important issue of public concern [18]. Previous works analyzed how to best serve this collective attention, either by analyzing temporal dynamics and treating this as a scheduling problem [19, 4, 14, 21], by adapting personalization tools [7], or by enhancing news navigation. Competition among different news offerings is generally ignored. A recent and notable exception is the debate on the effect of news aggregators. The increase of traffic they generate to news outlet was shown to come at the expense of customer loyalty, leading to a potential loss of advertising revenue for content publishers [3]. Our work is radically different as we consider competition *between* various intermediaries as well. We wish to see if the collective behavior of intermediaries can be harnessed and their incentives aligned to serve every user's interests. Our game theoretic approach resembles recent studies on the efficiency of collective efforts [12], with two important differences: First, the context of content curation is entirely new and it involves two sides (the bloggers choosing *what* to post, and the users choosing *who* to follow). This context allows one to reuse previous bounds on efficiency [17]. Since the first version of our work was presented, a 4-page workshop paper independently derived the same observation and studied best response dynamics in curation systems [1]. Our model differs in its assumptions about how readers select their intermediaries, which has large consequences on the equilibrium properties of the game. Furthermore, in our setting, the existence of a pure strategy equilibrium requires an entirely different proof to show the game is a "potential game."

We are only aware of a few other works analyzing news dissemination with a game theoretic background. Previous work assumed news is equally appealing to all users [9], and showed that local incentives suffice for higher quality news to reach a large audience in a random graph, by a connectivity argument. It also showed that users attempting to avoid spam may be an important limiting factor. In contrast, we are interested in how various blogs emerge to satisfy the information needs of a heterogeneous audience. In [10], a multi-topic model is analyzed to model news aggregators choosing a subset of topics in a sequential game. In contrast, our model allows for a much richer set of posting strategies, in which intermediaries can pick precisely what set of articles to post, across any topics. We assume bloggers compete for user attention through their choice of what to post, and we wish to find the conditions under which such games admit natural equilibria that are also efficient.

3. EVIDENCE OF FILTERING

Our first main result is to empirically validate our hypothesis that users of social media *participate* in, and potentially *benefit* from, an information filtering process. Prior work proved the existence of information intermediaries, while we explore for the first time how these intermediaries affect what information users receive. We wish to answer the following questions: Is the subset of content that people receive today through social media selected in a particular way? If so, can this filtering be understood as a consequence of the way intermediaries post information and how users select who they follow? And do the answers to these questions vary across social media platforms?

3.1 Data-sets

To answer the questions above, we analyze several large traces from social media. This requires (1) records of what users post in various media, (2) a way in which this information can be judged for its quality, and (3) knowledge of the social graph (to know what posts users receive). To the best of our knowledge, no data set available today allows studying all of these factors together, especially without significant subsampling. We hence gathered data from various sources (including Twitter, SPinn3r blogs, and Facebook), and enriched these data sets with complementary crawls, which we now describe.

Collecting information shared on social media.

At a high level, we consider three types of social media: (1) microblogging (Twitter, denoted "TW"), (2) online social networks (Facebook, denoted "FB"), and (3) blogs (Spinn3r, denoted "Blogs"). In all these domains, we focus on posts containing URLs. We gathered a mix of *topical* traces (i.e. relating to an event) and *generic* ones (where all posts are included). We ensure that the data sets are comprehensive, containing users with a wide range of activity levels and follower amounts, and URLs of both wide and narrow appeal.

Data sets	Users (% live today)	URLs (% with bit.ly)
TW NYT	226,512 (92%)	7,504 (99.96%)
TW Bin Laden	700,783 (75.9%)	545,495 (19.7%)
TW Occupy WS	354,117 (88.9%)	316,408 (26.9%)
TW Steve Jobs	719,025 (86.8%)	250,644 (20.0%)
TW iPhone5	81,056 (94.6%)	37,323 (30.7%)
FB iPhone5	330,185 (N/A)	193,024 (14.6%)
Blogs All	67,692 (N/A)	440,933 (30.9%)
Blogs Obama	13,390 (N/A)	84,733 (40.9%)
Blogs Facebook	11,643 (N/A)	69,747 (40.5%)
Blogs Euro	9,659 (N/A)	53,001 (39.9%)
Blogs Mubarak	6,546 (N/A)	42,531 (34.6%)

Table 1: Number of users and URLs for our data sets. For the Twitter (TW) data sets, we report the fraction of users whose accounts are still active. We also report the fraction of URLs with a bit.ly shortener.

- **Microblogging** (TW): Data was gathered using `DiscoverText.com` to harvest tweets from Twitter's unrestricted firehose in two ways. First, during two weeks in Dec. 2012 we collected all tweets with a URL from a particular media source; we report here results from the New York Times (NYT) though we also gathered data from CNN and FoxNews. Second, we collected all URLs associated with a particular event (*e.g.*, the "TW Bin Laden" data set contains tweets with the words "Osama" or "Bin Laden" posted during the 34 hours following his death, from 5/2/2011 at 3:30am EST to 5/3/2011 at 1:30pm EST). We similarly collected tweets on Steve Jobs' death, the Occupy Wall Street movement, and the iPhone 5 launch.
- **Online Social Networks** (FB): We gathered ≈ 1 million Facebook comments, all about the iPhone 5 release, from the GNIP Facebook API.
- **Blogs**: Finally, and in order to validate our results on data sets that are already publicly available, we use the data sets of the ICWSM 2011 data challenge [5]. It contains 386m blog posts collected from Spinn3r during the months of January-February 2011.

Preprocessing and additional crawls.

URL normalization: To avoid duplicates due to formatting variants and URL shorteners, we normalize URLs by (1) recursively following all redirects using HTTP calls, (2) removing protocols (`http/https`) and suffixes (anything following a `#` sign, ".html", or ".htm"), and (3) removing spam.[1]

Twitter Crawls: We performed Twitter crawls to gather additional information about the users in our data sets.[2] First, we gathered general information about these users via the Twitter REST API, as well as a sample of up to 100 "lists" they are part of, to use for classification (see below). Additionally, to find for each user the set of URLs they received via Twitter, we crawled the active users in our NYTimes data set for the set of users they follow (called "friends" in Twitter). To keep the crawl computationally feasible, we stopped the crawl after 50k friends; following more than 50k users is rare (<0.1%) and usually implies that these edges are not relevant for information dissemination. In order to get a sense of the URLs received by users who were not active in our NYTimes dataset ("passive" users), but nonetheless received a link, we crawled users in our data set for their followers (once again capping at 50k); we then crawled a random subset of all these newly discovered passive users (who follow at least one person in our dataset) for their "friend" lists. Thus, for the users in our TW NYTimes data set, as well as for a random subset of their followers, we know who they follow, and thus what NYTimes links they received during this time period.

URL popularity and user posting activity were estimated using 5 different metrics to ensure the universality of our results. First, one can directly *internally* measure

[1]For these data-sets, spam URLs have generally been blacklisted (*e.g.*, spam bit.ly links land on a "warning" page). We removed users posting one or more spam URLs.

[2]Information could be gathered only from accounts that are still live today (between 75% and 95% of accounts, depending on how long before crawl data set was collected)

these in each data set by counting how many times a normalized URL was posted, and how many URLs a user posts. We complement this by measuring *externally* how popular a given URL is in two ways: (1) if this URL was ever shortened using bit.ly, we collected its number of clicks via the bit.ly public REST API.[3] We also collected the number of times each URL was shared on Facebook using the FB API. Finally, to estimate the "external activity" of a user, we calculate the average number of tweets per day by this user, from the time their account was created.

As seen in Table 1, we are successful in gathering a large number and more importantly a large range of URLs and users. The majority of URLs appear only once in our dataset, pointing to a very long tail of obscure or niche content. This set of URLs also contains a tiny minority of blockbusters which spread massively. As a consequence, the average number of posts or clicks is typically much larger than the median, and sometimes even goes above the 95% percentile. This trend is especially skewed for external popularity measures. Similarly, the overwhelming majority of users post only occasionally, while a very active minority of users end up posting most of the content.

Defining information intermediaries in social media is another challenge. We show it is tangential to our work as our trends apply to various definitions of intermediaries. In a "loose" sense, all active users are intermediaries, since anyone who has ever posted a URL has acted as an intermediary to their immediate surrounding. One can argue that this contains too many users reacting spontaneously to news without much of a following. Thus, we consider the stricter definition of only counting users with at least 500 followers (top 30% of active users) as intermediaries; we refer to these users as *Active VIPs* [4]. We finally use a much stricter definition where, among those VIPs, only the ones that appear in a list containing the substring "blog" are considered information intermediaries (among the $\leq$ 100 lists we crawled per user); we refer to these users as *Bloggers*. Figure 1 provides detailed statistics about these different populations for the Twitter NYTimes data set (TW NYT). In all definitions, potential information intermediaries are a very small part of the total audience (<1%) but they are responsible for most of the traffic. They post significantly more tweets per day. They also receive more URLs and follow more users.

3.2 The Filtering Law

We first study the relationship between the volume that one receives on social media, and the popularity of this content. Ideally, depending on how many and which intermediaries a user follows, she may be able to reduce the volume of information she receives while statistically increasing its quality. We now show that this is indeed the case.

[3]For precision, we consider several variants of the URL which could link to the same page, by (1) computing the "core" of the URL (removing the protocol, trailing slashes, and everything after ".htm",".html", "#"), and (2) summing the bit.ly clicks provided by the API for the following URLs: all the ones posted with the same "core" extended by varying the protocol http/https, with and without a trailing slash.

[4]We tried various thresholds here, in addition to 500 followers; however, the choice of threshold did not affect the general trends we observed. For simplicity, we only present the results for the *Active VIP* users defined according to the 500 follower threshold.

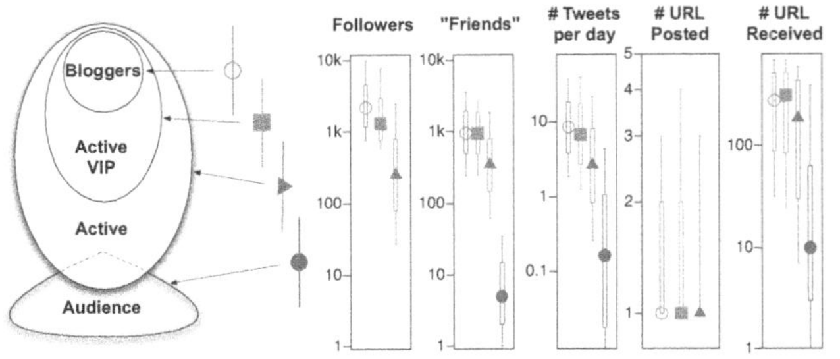

Figure 1: Various types of users (TW NYT): Each group is associated with a symbol. We draw the median value of various parameters, together with the box plot representing the (25%,75%) percentile range, and whiskers for (10%,90%) percentiles.

Our main observation is the following *filtering law*: URLs received by users who receive fewer URLs are disproportionately popular. This is shown in Fig. 2, where we see that the average quality of URLs received by a user decreases as the total number of URLs she receives increases.

What explains this trend? Is it a statistical illusion? Perhaps this is simply due to a replacement effect: as users receive more URLs, they may "run out" of high-quality URLs, causing a decrease in average quality. To show that this is not the case, we contrast the real trend with a random Null Hypothesis (NH) model that is constructed as follows: for each user in our data set receiving n URLs, we reassign the URLs they receive by picking these n URLs randomly from the same URL popularity distribution (*i.e.,* popular URLs appear more often, exactly as in the real data). This popularity distribution is determined by the number of times each URL was received. Importantly, we perform these random draws without replacement, thus not allowing a user to receive the same URL twice. The blue line in the figure denotes the Null Hypothesis, and we observe a very slight (almost flat) decreasing trend. This slight decrease comes from the following effect: Since the distribution is highly skewed, a small set of popular URLs are likely to be chosen first as the set of received URLs is constructed in this random model. For a larger set, since the set of URLs is constructed without replacement, after the first popular URLs are chosen, the random choices will be biased to less popular URLs. Note that regardless of the precise metric (*e.g.,* number of times URL received, number of times URL posted, number of Bit.ly clicks received by URL, etc.) we use to construct the URL popularity distribution for the Null Hypothesis, the resulting trend is flat. On these plots, we show the median popularity of URLs received by users in both the Null Hypothesis model, and in the real data, and we also show the 25th and 75th percentiles of these URL popularity distributions. Note that because we are plotting percentiles, and not confidence intervals, the number of users in each bucket doesn't necessarily shrink the size of the 25%-75% interval.

We observe that real data shows a trend much stronger than the replacement effect of the Null Hypothesis. For any activity level, the difference between the distributions are statistically significant: a standard Student test on the log of popularity always returns statistical difference with $p \leq 10^{-6}$. Moreover, this trend is universal: we observe it for all popularity metrics, as shown in Fig. 2, and when considering URLs received by various subsets of the population (like

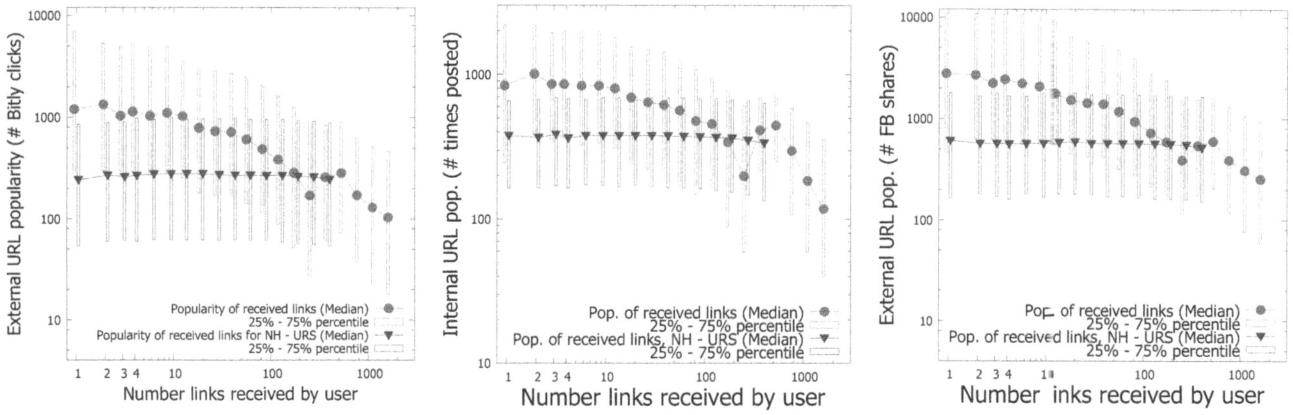

Figure 2: The filtering law. (x-axis) Users grouped by number of URLs received, (y-axis) Popularity distribution of URLs received by these users, shown using median and 25%-75% percentiles. Red circles denote real data, blue triangles denote a random null hypothesis model. The 3 plots correspond to different metrics of URL popularity: (left) number of bit.ly clicks, (middle) number of times this URL was posted, (right) number of FB likes.

Active or Active VIP users, and Bloggers). Our results are encouraging because they suggest that users of social media are effectively navigating the volume/quality trade-off: users who receive less are focusing on the most promising URLs.

These positive results demand further study. The only factors affecting the URLs a user receives are the intermediaries she follows, and the content they post. Are information intermediaries behaving in a way that explains this law? If so, are they naturally encouraged by social media to behave as such? Does this generally lead to an efficient propagation of information? In the rest of this section, we will examine the posting behaviors of information intermediaries, and their consequences.

3.3 Intermediaries posting behavior

We begin our study of the content posted by intermediaries by observing another filtering law: URLs posted by less active intermediaries are disproportionately popular. That is, as intermediaries decrease the number of URLs they post, they are more likely to post the most popular URLs. Fig. 3 illustrates this trend; as before, the trend is much stronger than predicted by a random null hypothesis, where for each user we fix the number of URLs they post, and pick these URLs randomly according to the same overall popularity distribution. With similar tests, we observe statistical significance with $p < 10^{-3}$ (except for users posting exactly 5 URLs where $p = 0.02$). This observation suggests that intermediaries are *filtering* when choosing what content to post (more on that below).

Our trend is remarkably universal. No matter what URL popularity metric is used, or what intermediary definition is used, the trend is statistically significant. We present a few representative results in Fig. 4.

The posting filtering law shows that the network at a macroscopic level filters information to bias small volume towards popular content. However this does not detail how intermediaries select URLs at the microscopic level. It could be that they simply selectively repost a fixed fraction of the content they receive. Intermediaries who receive less, post less; those who follow them receive still less, etc. Figure 5 proves the contrary. We first observe (see top plot) that across activity levels, the popularity of URLs received by users is roughly the same. By comparison, the URLs which users choose to post are significantly more popular than those received; the difference in popularity is even more striking when only considering the subset of received URLs that users choose to repost. These gaps narrow for users posting more than 20 URLs, but this represents less than 1% of intermediaries. Moreover, Fig. 5 (bottom) shows that the average number of URLs received by intermediaries is more or less constant across activity levels. However, users

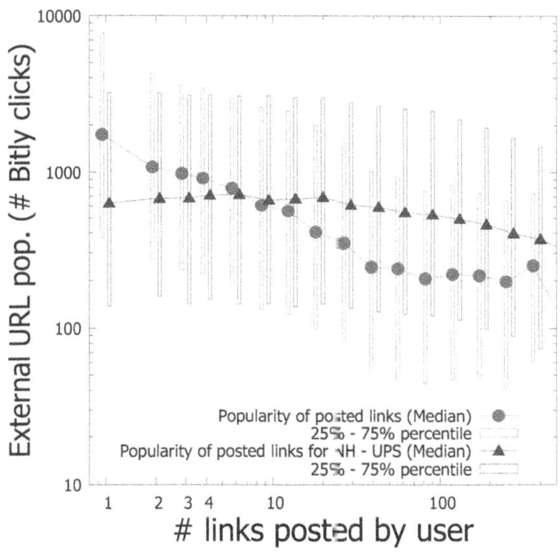

Figure 3: The posting filtering law. (x-axis) Users grouped by number of URLs posted, (y-axis) popularity distribution (by number of bit.ly clicks) of URLs posted by these users; median and 25%-75% percentiles shown. Red circles denote real data, blue triangles denotes a random null hypothesis model.

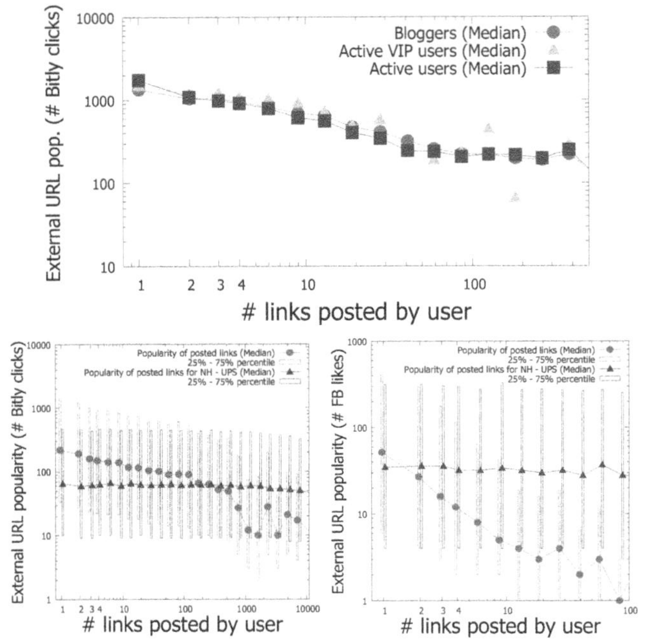

Figure 4: The posting filtering law is universal (same axes as Figure 3): (top) posting filtering law is unchanged when the definition of intermediaries changes, (bottom left) Blogs All data set, (bottom right) FB Iphone5 data set (y-axis denotes FB likes).

with different activity levels differ very much in their reposting frequencies. In other words, intermediaries more or less receive similar URLs (both in number and popularity), but they choose to repost different subsets of it, usually composed of URLs that are more popular. Note that in addition to "reposting" URLs they receive, users can also post URLs which they discover from outside Twitter; however, even these are quite popular on average (as can be seen by the gap between the green-triangle line and the blue-square line in Fig. 5).

Finally, we studied the factors affecting the relative "success" of an information intermediary, defined by her number of followers. We noticed that in general, intermediaries who post more URLs have more followers, though this trend shows diminishing returns. Figure 6 plots the raw measure of success (followers in Twitter, number of likes received by their comments in Facebook) for users of various activity levels. We observe that success correlates with user's activity (roughly in proportion of the square root of activity, also plotted for reference. Note that we do not perform precise trend fitting here). This trend is observed across our data sets. Note that we do not claim causality: it is also possible that popular people tend to become more active. One can also interpret these diminishing returns naturally in light of the filtering law. Posting more often correlates with more occasions to get noticed and gather followers and likes. At the same time, it corresponds to posting less popular URLs, which perhaps contribute to overall success to a smaller degree. For future work, we intend to study what other attributes of intermediaries (*e.g.*, average popularity of URLs they post, earliness) correlate with success.

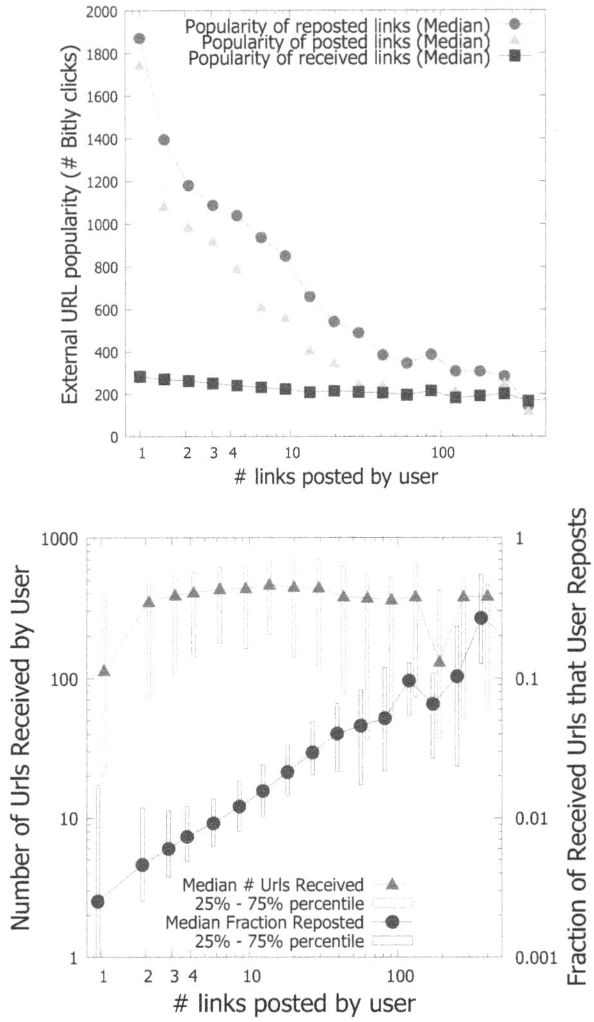

Figure 5: Selection of popular content by intermediaries: (x-axis) User posting activity in number of URLs, (top y-axis) popularity distribution of URLs received by these users, and the popularity distributions of URLs posted or reposted by the users. (bottom left y-axis) distribution of number of URLs received plotted as red triangle, (bottom right y-axis) distribution of reposting fraction plotted as blue circle. (Boxplots show 25%-75% percentiles).

In summary, we have observed two important phenomena about the posting behavior of intermediaries: First, they are selective in what they post, such that the average popularity of URLs posted by an intermediary is inversely proportional to the amount they post. Secondly, this difference in posting behavior is explained not by differences in the sets of URLs *received* by these intermediaries, but rather by their distinct decisions of what to post. In effect, we see that intermediaries differ widely in their posting behaviors. In the next section, we attempt to better understand why such a wide range of posting behaviors might arise.

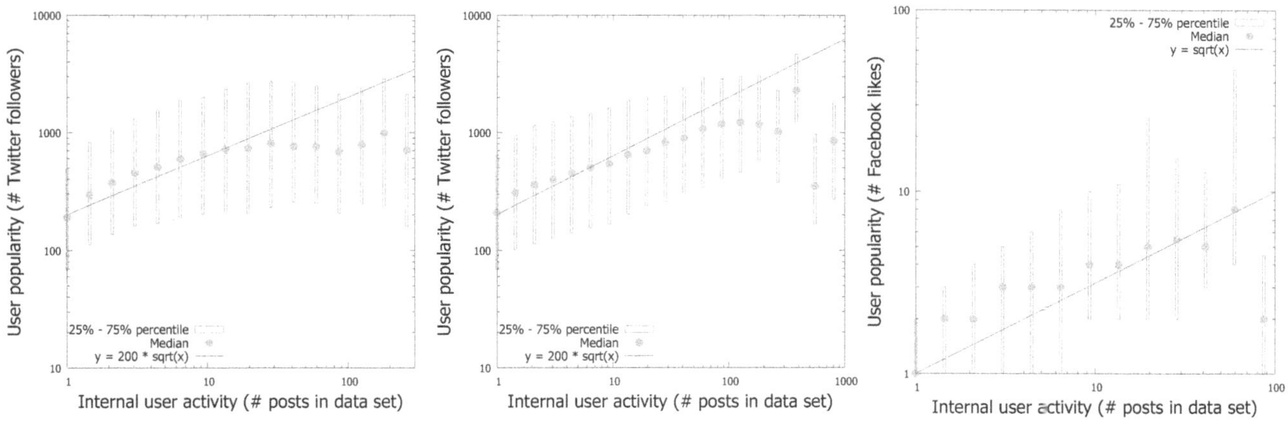

(a) TW Bin Laden

(b) TW Occupy WS

(c) FB iPhone5

Figure 6: The diminishing return of posting activity: (x-axis) user internal activity in number of URLs, (y-axis) user "success" (followers, likes).

4. INFORMATION FILTERING MODEL

The previous section showed that information intermediaries pick different subsets of content to post, the size of which also relates to content popularity. Understanding this behavior in the context of social media efficiency as a whole raises two questions: Can the intermediaries' behavior be understood as the optimization of some natural objective? If so, would this derived model imply that social curation is efficient?

Motivation for Model.

It seems natural to assume that intermediaries wish to increase the attention they receive. The factors that determine which intermediaries a user chooses to pay attention to could be classified into two groups: First, *endogenous* factors related to the content posted by the intermediary, and *exogenous* factors which capture all other variables, such as the identity of the blogger, her writing quality and style, etc. Ideally, a model would allow for both types of factors, reproduce our observations, and remain tractable.

We first note that a model based purely on exogenous factors cannot satisfactorily answer the two questions above. If users choose who to follow independently of the content posted, this could allow for outcomes in which users never receive content they are interested in. Furthermore, in this type of model, bloggers can't optimize their posting behavior to gather a larger audience. This type of model is both unrealistic, and makes it impossible to study the questions we are interested in.

In contrast, a model with endogenous factors immediately provides a natural explanation for the filtering law. Consider the following simple example: All content items belongs to a single topic, and vary only based on their quality. Every user has an "interest threshold" indicating that they are interested in seeing all content above that quality level. In response these user interests, each blogger picks a "posting threshold" and posts all items above that quality level. Each user follows the blogger whose posting threshold is closest to their interest threshold, breaking ties randomly. In this scenario, how would a strategic bloggers behave? Assuming that there was a wide range of user interest thresholds, it would be in the best interest of bloggers to "spread out" their posting thresholds – for some to only post the highest quality content (to satisfy users only interested in the highlights), while others post a larger set (to attract more interested users). If all bloggers posted the same content, any of the bloggers could change their posting strategy and attract a larger set of users who prefer them to the rest of the bloggers.

This simple unidimensional scenario is sufficient to reproduce our main findings: (i) Users who receive less content tend to receive the most popular content. (ii) Intermediaries have very different posting thresholds / frequencies. (iii) Less active intermediaries / bloggers generally post more popular content.

Model Definition: "Blog-Positioning Game".

We now formally describe our model, which we call the "blog-positioning game". This model accounts for arbitrary content spaces, both endogenous and exogenous attributes of bloggers, and different ways in which users may decide which blogger to follow. We define and motivate each component of the game below:

Sets of Agents: We use B to denote the set of all bloggers (these are the strategic agents in our game), and U to denote the set of users in the "audience".

Content Space: We assume that every item of content lives in an arbitrary space Ω. Every day k, a set of news items $X_k \subset \Omega$ are generated from Ω following an arbitrary, possibly probabilistic, but time-invariant process.

Blogger strategies: We assume that each blogger b picks a filtering function $F_b\colon \Omega \to \{0,1\}$, that indicates for each possible news item, whether or not the blogger will post it. We will denote the strategy space of all possible filtering functions $F_b\colon \Omega \to \{0,1\}$ by σ. So, the strategy vectors s in this game live in the space $\sigma^{B} \equiv \Sigma$, where each element of s corresponds to a specific blogger's choice of filtering function. Note that our model can extend to the case where the blogger filtering functions are stochastic. In this setting, $F_b \colon \Omega \to [0,1]$ indicates, for each possible point in the space, the probability that the blogger will post an item at this point. All our results carry over to the case of stochastic filtering functions by replacing the utility of a user with their expected utility, but for ease of notation, we restrict our analysis to the deterministic case.

The set of items a blogger posts on a given day is not always the same since the content generated on a given day is created randomly. However, it seems natural to assume that when the same exact content is produced, then the blogger will select the same exact subset to post. Thus, we are interested in *pure strategies* for bloggers, modeling blogs that apply an invariant filter to content items that are generated randomly every day. This contrasts with a *mixed strategy*, where the blogger initially fixes a set of strategies, and then randomly chooses one of them each day based on a coin toss. Mixed strategies are more general, but seem unnatural: why would a blogger decide to randomly change her behavior from day to day, in a potentially drastic fashion, when her target audience has deterministic tastes? [5]

Blogger objectives: We assume that bloggers are attempting to maximize their number of followers (or expected number of followers). More specifically, they are attempting to maximize the amount of attention they receive from their followers. Each follower is worth 1 "attention unit"; in the case where a user chooses to follow several bloggers, this attention unit is split across these bloggers.

User Utility: How much utility does a user u get from following blogger b with filtering function F_b? We assume a user u gets utility $V_u(F_b, b) \in \mathbb{R}$ from following blogger b with filtering function F_b. Note that we include b as a separate parameter of V_u so that a user's utility from following a blogger can depend on the identity of the blogger (this can capture all exogenous factors), and not simply on the content they post (the endogenous factors). Also, note that this utility could be negative, in which case the user would not choose to follow this blogger. In general, we always allow the option for a user to not follow any blogger and get utility 0 (we assume for simplicity's sake that if a user has the choice between following a blogger who gives them utility 0, and not following any blogger, they will choose to not follow any blogger).

For the sake of illustration, we can specify the following functional form for V_u, even though the specifics of how V_u is defined do not affect our theoretical results. We can assume each user u has an interest function $h_u \colon \Omega \to \mathbb{R}$ that assigns a real number to every item, according to its position in Ω. This value represents how much the user would enjoy seeing this item. If a user receives a set X of content, we assume they receive utility $\sum_{x \quad X} h_u(x)$ (or it could be a function of this sum, with diminishing returns). So, if on day k a user u chooses to follow a blogger b, they will receive utility $\sum_{x \quad F_b(X_k)} h_u(x)$, where $F_b(X_k) = \{x \in X_k : F_b(x) = 1\}$ is the set of items posted by blogger b on day k. The value of this sum may vary by day as content gets randomly produced. Thus, we can define the utility $V_u(F_b, b)$ that this user gets from following b as this sum's expected value. More explicitly, $V_u(F_b, b) = \mathrm{E}\left[\sum_{x \quad F_b(X_k)} h_u(x)\right]$, where this expectation is taken over the probability distribution from which the daily set of news X_k is drawn from Ω (as well as over the stochastic filtering function, when appropriate).

How do users pick what blogger to follow?: We specify 3 separate ways in which a bloggers could pick who to follow. It turns out that the precise way in which a user picks her blogger has an enormous effect on the equilibria of the game. The three models are:

1. **Greedy Model**: In this model, each user u chooses to follow blogger $b = \arg\max_B V_u(F_b, b)$. Note that, in order for a user to behave this way, she must have perfect information about every blogger's posting behavior, a strong assumption to make.

2. **Satisficing Model**: In this model, we assume a user "satisfices", meaning that they randomly pick a blogger to follow amongst the ones that make them "happy enough". More formally, we assume each user u has a utility threshold v_u, and that they pick which blogger to follow randomly from the set of bloggers b such that $V_u(F_b, b) \geq v_u$ [6]. An alternative and equivalent interpretation is that a user splits their attention evenly across these bloggers. If we let $S_u(s) = \{b \mid V_u(F_b, b) \geq v_u\}$ denote the set of bloggers who provide user u with at least the required utility under strategy vector $s \in \Sigma$, then every blogger $b \in S_u$ receives a fraction $\frac{1}{S_u}$ of u's attention (in expectation). This model can be seen as relaxing the assumption that users have perfect information about the blogger behaviors, and could perhaps be seen as more realistic as a result.

3. **Satisficing Model with Blogger Abilities**: In this model, we assume different bloggers have different intrinsic "abilities", which allow us to represent various external factors that can contribute differently to each blog's success (*e.g.*, writing quality, fame, the time since the blog was created). We model bloggers' abilities as follows: We suppose that each blogger has an associated ability $a_b \in [0,1]$, and *if* he provides a user with at least her required utility v_u, the user decides whether to follow him or not based on his ability. In particular, a user flips a biased coin that gives heads with probability a_b; if the coin lands heads, the user follows the blogger, otherwise she does not. As in the previous section, we can assume a user shares her attention equally among all the bloggers for whom the coin comes up heads (or that the user picks uniformly at random from these bloggers). Note that this model is a strictly more general than the previous model. because if all bloggers have ability $a_b = 1$, then these two satisficing models become equivalent. The primary reason we consider this more general model is that it allows us to better explain differences in follower amounts between bloggers that post very similar content.

[5]Note that mixed strategies are fundamentally different from stochastic filtering functions: The latter model minor day-to-day "random" variations in an essentially consistent filtering process, but the former imply that bloggers explicitly make a (perhaps widely) different random choice each day based on the outcomes of a coin toss.

[6]Of course, users need not calculate utility explicitly; they may have a general notion of whether a blog is "good enough" to keep them well-informed.

Formal game definition: Our "blog-positioning game" is a simultaneous game, in which all bloggers need to pick their posting strategy $F_b \in \sigma$, in order to maximize their (expected) number of followers. We assume that all bloggers have perfect knowledge of all users' utility functions V_u, and of which strategy the users are employing to pick their blogger. Given a strategy vector $s \in \Sigma$ containing every blogger's choice of filtering function F_b, each blogger can precisely calculate $V_b(s)$, the number of followers they expect to receive under this strategy vector.

In the section that follows, we analyze the pure strategy Nash equilibria of this game, and in addition study how "efficient" these equilibria are by considering the "price of anarchy" of the game. We perform this analysis for all three variants of the game, corresponding to the 3 different ways users can pick who to follow.

5. OUTCOMES OF BLOG COMPETITION

We now formally analyze the outcomes of the model presented in Section 4. As mentioned, the precise way in which users pick their blogger has unexpectedly important consequences on the nature of the game's equilibria. We are interested in 2 properties of these games: (i) Whether the game has pure strategy Nash equilibria, and (ii) Whether the equilibria of the game are "efficient" relative to the social optimum (we define social welfare to be the number of users who follow at least one blogger. More details below). At a high-level, we will show 3 primary results:

1. Under the greedy user model, there are cases in which no pure strategy Nash equilibrium exists.
2. Under the satisficing user models (with and without blogger abilities), the game is an "exact potential game" and always admits a pure strategy Nash equilibrium.
3. The price of anarchy (ratio of social optimum to the social welfare under the worst possible Nash equilibria) of the game under either satisficing user model is at most 2, and this bound is tight.

5.1 Greedy user model

The first question that we explore is: does the system admit a pure strategy equilibrium in the greedy user model? The answer is negative. In fact, we can prove that there even exist simple cases where only two bloggers are present, in which no such equilibrium exists.

PROPOSITION 1. *Under the greedy user model, there exist cases where no pure strategy Nash equilibrium exists.*

PROOF. We will prove this by showing a specific, relatively simple example of the blog-positioning game, in which no pure strategy Nash equilibrium exists. The example is as follows: Suppose that the generative process of news creation creates one item daily in each of 3 points of Ω: p_1, p_2 and p_3, where p_1 is the most important item, and p_3 the least. Let us assume that we have a population of 66 users, distributed in three groups who value items differently:

Number of users	Value for		
	p_1	p_2	p_3
30	+1	+1	+1
20	+1	+1	−1
16	+1	−1	−1

Then with the *greedy user model*, there is no pure strategy equilibrium in this scenario even with two bloggers.

First note that we can assume without loss of generality that each blogger picks from one of the following 3 strategies: (i) s_1, posting only p_1 (ii) s_2, posting p_1 and p_2, and (iii) s_3, posting all 3 items. In fact, other strategies such as only posting p_3, or posting p_1 and p_3, are dominated. Now, we can construct the 3×3 payoff matrix for this game (where the first number in each pair corresponds to the number of followers the row blogger gets when they play a given strategy, and the second number corresponds to the column blogger's payoff):

	s_1	s_2	s_3
s_1	(33, 33)	(16, **50**)	(**26**, 40)
s_2	(**50**, 16)	(25, 25)	(20, **30**)
s_3	(40, **26**)	(**30**, 20)	(25, 25)

This payoff matrix is computed by considering how many followers each blogger would get, depending on their strategy and their opponent's strategy, under the greedy user model. For example, if both bloggers play strategy s_1, they give all 66 users utility 1, and thus they each in expectation receive 33 users. All other elements of this matrix are computed similarly. For each column, we put in bold the optimal payoff for the row player (indicating their best response), and similarly for each row we put in bold the best response for the column player. The fact that there is no pure strategy Nash equilibrium is immediately evident from the fact that no element of this payoff matrix contains both elements in bold font. This indicates that there is no scenario in which both bloggers are playing optimally, given the behavior of the other. So there is always incentive for at least one blogger to deviate from their strategy, and this proves that no pure strategy Nash equilibrium exists in this game. □

We note that though this proposition applies to a specific news generation process and scoring function, it is in fact possible to come up with many such examples, particularly in continuous content spaces Ω, with continuous user interest functions i_u. The greedy strategy followed by users generally forbids that bloggers that only use a deterministic strategy converge to a stable Nash equilibrium. This seems at odds with the state of the blogosphere. Though chaotic, it seems to be a reasonably stable environment, with blogs following fairly consistent strategies.

Note that the greedy model seems a natural simple first step, but it generally ignores any exogenous factors differentiating bloggers, and the search costs, frictions or lack of perfect information that in practice make it difficult for a user to pick the blogger who is "optimal" for her interest. How is the expected behavior of the game altered if one changes this greedy model to assume that users *satisfice*: that is, they pick a blogger who is "good enough". In such cases, bloggers still compete for attention but, surprisingly, this relaxation of the greedy model is sufficient for the game to always reach a stable state with deterministic filtering.

5.2 Satis cing user models

We now discuss the theoretical results for the satisficing user models. We will prove all our results for the more general model with blogger abilities, and thus all the results hold for the model without blogger abilities as well (recall that the model without blogger abilities is a special case of the model with blogger abilities, where all bloggers have ability 1).

The way we will prove that pure strategy Nash equilibrium exist will be by using results from potential games; in particular, our approach is inspired by the proof of existence of an equilibrium in [12], following a result from [15]. We review the relevant notation, as well as this corollary, below; the notation is adapted from [15]:

We consider games Γ with n players $B = \{1, \ldots, n\}$. Each player i picks a strategy from their set of strategies σ_i. The set of strategy profiles is $\Sigma = \sigma_1 \times \sigma_2 \times \ldots \times \sigma_n$. Player i has payoff function $V_i \colon \Sigma \to \mathbb{R}$. For $A \subseteq B$, we denote the complement of A by $-A$, and we denote the Cartesian product $\times_{i \ A} \sigma_i$ by Σ_A. For sets A with one or 2 elements $\{i\}$ or $\{i,j\}$, we denote $\Sigma_{\ A}$ by $\Sigma_{\ i}$ or $\Sigma_{\ i,j}$. Lastly, for a function $G \colon \Sigma \to \mathbb{R}$, we will sometimes use G as if it were a function $G \colon \sigma_i \times \Sigma_{\ i} \to \mathbb{R}$, or as a function $G \colon \sigma_i \times \sigma_j \times \Sigma_{\ i,j} \to \mathbb{R}$.

DEFINITION 1. *A game Γ is an exact potential game if there exists a function $\Phi \colon \Sigma \to \mathbb{R}$ such that for any player i, any $x_i, z_i \in \sigma_i$, and any $s_{\ i} \in \Sigma_{\ i}$,*

$$V_i(x_i, s_{\ i}) - V_i(z_i, s_{\ i}) = \Phi(x_i, s_{\ i}) - \Phi(z_i, s_{\ i}).$$

DEFINITION 2. *A game Γ is a finite game if it has a finite number of players, each with a finite number of strategies (i.e., both B and Σ are finite).*

Now, we review Corollary 2.9 from [15], which we will use to prove that our game is an exact potential game:

THEOREM 2. *A game Γ is an exact potential game if and only if $\forall i,j \in B$, $\forall a \in \Sigma_{\ i,j}$, $\forall x_i, x_i \in \sigma_i$ and $\forall x_j, x_j \in \sigma_j$, the following holds:*

$$V_i(x_i, x_j, a) - V_i(x_i, x_j, a) + V_i(x_i, x_j, a) - V_i(x_i, x_j, a) +$$
$$V_i(x_i, x_j, a) - V_i(x_i, x_j, a) + V_i(x_i, x_j, a) - V_i(x_i, x_j, a) = 0.$$

Now, we review a (slightly modified) version of Corollary 2.2 from [15], which we will need as well in our proof:

THEOREM 3. *Every finite exact potential game possesses a pure strategy Nash equilibrium.*

Now we can prove our equilibrium result:

THEOREM 4. *The blog-positioning game in the satisficing user model with blogger abilities is an exact potential game, and has a pure strategy Nash equilibrium.*

PROOF. To prove the statement we use Theorem 2, adapting its notation to our setting. Let $\Sigma_{\ i,j}$ denote the strategy space of all bloggers except i and j. According to Theorem 2, we must prove that for any pair of bloggers $i, j \in B$, for any $s_{\ i,j} \in \Sigma_{\ i,j}$, and for any posting strategies $F_i, F_i, F_j, F_j \in \sigma$,

$$V_i(F_i, F_j, s_{\ i,j}) - V_i(F_i, F_j, s_{\ i,j}) + V_j(F_i, F_j, s_{\ i,j}) +$$
$$- V_j(F_i, F_j, s_{\ i,j}) + V_i(F_i, F_j, s_{\ i,j}) - V_i(F_i, F_j, s_{\ i,j}) +$$
$$+ V_j(F_i, F_j, s_{\ i,j}) - V_j(F_i, F_j, s_{\ i,j}) = 0$$

where $V_i(s)$ is blogger i's payoff under strategy profile $s \in \Sigma$ (as above).

First, let us compute the utility of a blogger i when she selects a posting strategy F_i. Recall that $S_u(s)$ denotes the set of bloggers which "satisfy" user u. We abuse notation and write $F_i \in S_u$ if blogger i is in S_u when she plays F_i. We use $U_i = \{u \in U \colon F_i \in S_u\}$ to denote the users to whom a blogger i would provide their required utility if she picked a posting set equal to F_i. Similarly, we let $U_i = \{u \in U \colon F_i \in S_u\}$. U_j, and U_j are defined similarly for blogger j. Let $G(u)_{\ i}$ be the random variable for the number of bloggers followed by u not including i, when these bloggers play $s_{\ i} = (F_j, s_{\ i,j})$. Similarly, let $G(u)_{\ i,j}$ be the random variable for the number of bloggers followed by u not including i, j, when those bloggers play $s_{\ i,j}$:

$$\begin{aligned}
& V_i(F_i, F_j, s_{\ i,j}) \\
&= \sum_{u \ U_i} a_i \,\mathrm{E}\left[\frac{1}{G(u)_{\ i} + 1}\right] \\
&= \sum_{u \ U_i \ U_j} a_i \,\mathrm{E}\left[\frac{1}{G(u)_{\ i} + 1} \,\middle|\, u \notin U_j\right] \\
&+ \sum_{u \ U_i \ U_j} a_i \,\mathrm{E}\left[\frac{1}{G(u)_{\ i} + 1} \,\middle|\, u \in U_j\right] \\
&= \sum_{u \ U_i \ U_j} a_i \,\mathrm{E}\left[\frac{1}{G(u)_{\ i,j} + 1}\right] \\
&+ \sum_{u \ U_i \ U_j} a_i \overline{a_j} \,\mathrm{E}\left[\frac{1}{G(u)_{\ i,j} + 1}\right] \\
&+ \sum_{u \ U_i \ U_j} a_i a_j \,\mathrm{E}\left[\frac{1}{G(u)_{\ i,j} + 2}\right],
\end{aligned}$$

where $\overline{a_j} = 1 - a_j$. Subsequently, we use the following notation:

$$e(u) = \mathrm{E}\left[\frac{1}{G(u)_{-i,j} + 1}\right],$$
$$e\ (u) = \mathrm{E}\left[\frac{1}{G(u)_{-i,j} + 2}\right].$$

Now, we can rewrite the utility of blogger i playing F_i as:

$$\begin{aligned}
a_i \sum_{u \ U_i \ U_j} e(u) \ &+ \ a_i \overline{a_j} \sum_{u \ U_i \ U_j} e(u) + a_i a_j \sum_{u \ U_i \ U_j} e\ (u) \\
= a_i \sum_{u \ U_i} e(u) \ &- \ a_i \sum_{u \ U_i \ U_j} e(u) + a_i(1 - a_j) \sum_{u \ U_i \ U_j} e(u) \\
&+ \ a_i a_j \sum_{u \ U_i \ U_j} e\ (u) \\
= a_i \sum_{u \ U_i} e(u) \ &- \ a_i a_j \sum_{u \ U_i \ U_j} e(u) + a_i a_j \sum_{u \ U_i \ U_j} e\ (u)
\end{aligned}$$

Now we can write the formula of Theorem 2:

$$\begin{aligned}
& V_i(F_i, F_j, s_{\ i,j}) - V_i(F_i, F_j, s_{\ i,j}) + V_j(F_i, F_j, s_{\ i,j}) \\
& - V_j(F_i, F_j, s_{\ i,j}) + V_i(F_i, F_j, s_{\ i,j}) - V_i(F_i, F_j, s_{\ i,j}) \\
& + V_j(F_i, F_j, s_{\ i,j}) - V_j(F_i, F_j, s_{\ i,j}) =
\end{aligned}$$

$$
\begin{array}{llll}
a_i \sum_{u\ U'_i} e(u) & - & a_i a_j \sum_{u\ U'_i\ U_j} e(u) + a_i a_j \sum_{u\ U'_i\ U_j} e\ (u) \\
-(a_i \sum_{u\ U_i} e(u) & - & a_i a_j \sum_{u\ U_i\ U_j} e(u) + a_i a_j \sum_{u\ U_i\ U_j} e\ (u)) \\
+a_j \sum_{u\ U'_j} e(u) & - & a_i a_j \sum_{u\ U'_i\ U'_j} e(u) + a_i a_j \sum_{u\ U'_i\ U'_j} e\ (u) \\
-(a_j \sum_{u\ U_j} e(u) & - & a_i a_j \sum_{u\ U'_i\ U_j} e(u) + a_i a_j \sum_{u\ U'_i\ U_j} e\ (u)) \\
+a_i \sum_{u\ U_i} e(u) & - & a_i a_j \sum_{u\ U_i\ U'_j} e(u) + a_i a_j \sum_{u\ U_i\ U'_j} e\ (u) \\
-(a_i \sum_{u\ U'_i} e(u) & - & a_i a_j \sum_{u\ U'_i\ U'_j} e(u) + a_i a_j \sum_{u\ U'_i\ U'_j} e\ (u)) \\
+a_j \sum_{u\ U_j} e(u) & - & a_i a_j \sum_{u\ U_i\ U_j} e(u) + a_i a_j \sum_{u\ U_i\ U_j} e\ (u) \\
-(a_j \sum_{u\ U'_j} e(u) & - & a_i a_j \sum_{u\ U_i\ U'_j} e(u) + a_i a_j \sum_{u\ U_i\ U'_j} e\ (u))
\end{array}
$$

with one line for each of the 8 terms of the formula. Now, if you look carefully down each of the three columns of the above formula, you will notice that all the terms in each column cancel out. For example, in the first column of terms, the expressions in rows 1 and 6 cancel out. Similarly, in the second and third columns of terms, the expressions in rows 2 and 7 cancel out. Thus, adding these all together, we obtain a sum of 0, which completes the proof that the blog-positioning game is an exact potential game. Now, by simply noticing that this game is a finite game when Ω is finite, and the number of bloggers is finite, we are able to conclude that a pure-strategy Nash equilibrium always exists[7]. □

We now define the *efficiency* of a certain strategy profile $s \in \Sigma$ as the fraction or number of users who end up following at least one blogger under this configuration of the bloggers; note that this is equivalent to the sum of all the bloggers' utilities. We will now analyze the efficiency of the pure strategy Nash equilibrium of this game, by finding a bound on its price of anarchy. We recall the concept of price of anarchy:

DEFINITION 3. *Let $W : \Sigma \to R^+$ be the social welfare function of a game, where Σ is the space of strategy profiles. Let $E \subseteq \Sigma$ be the set of strategy profiles which are equilibria. The price of anarchy is defined as:*

$$
PoA = \frac{\max_{s\ \Sigma} W(s)}{\min_{s\ E} W(s)}
$$

The closer to 1 the price of anarchy of a game is, the more robust it is to its players behaving selfishly. The idea here is that if players behave selfishly, we expect their behavior to converge to an equilibrium; and if the price of anarchy is close to 1, that implies that the social welfare at this equilibrium must be close to the social optimum.

We will now prove that the blog-positioning game is efficient, in the sense that it has a low bound on its price of anarchy.

THEOREM 5. *The blog-positioning game under the model of satisficing users with blogger abilities has price of anarchy at most 2.*

PROOF. From the definition of the Price of Anarchy, let s be the strategy profile in Σ that maximizes $W(s\ )$ and let $s \in E$ be the strategy profile in E that minimizes $W(s)$. For each blogger i, let s_i denote the strategy of i in s , and s_i denote the strategy of i in the equilibrium strategy profile s; similarly, $s\ _i$ denotes the strategy of all bloggers except i under strategy profile s.

Let $Sat_u(s)$ and $Sat_u(s\ )$ denote the set of bloggers which satisfy user u under strategy profiles s and s respectively. Let $B_u = Sat_u(s\ ) - Sat_u(s)$, the set of bloggers who satisfy u under s which didn't satisfy u under s. Let $P_u(s)$ denote the probability that user u follows at least 1 blogger under strategy profile s. Note that $P_u(s) = 1 - \prod_{i\ Sat_u(s)}(1 - a_i)$. Similarly, $P_u(s\ ) = 1 - \prod_{i\ Sat_u(s^*)}(1 - a_i)$. Since the total utility of the system is defined as the number of users who follow at least one blogger, the difference between $P_u(s\ )$ and $P_u(s)$, when summed over all users u, must account for the difference in total welfare between $W(s\ )$ and $W(s)$. Below, we will bound the difference between $P_u(s\ )$ and $P_u(s)$.

We first define the function $P_u(\cdot)$, such that for any subset A of the bloggers B, $P_u(A) = 1 - \prod_{i\ A}(1 - a_i)$ denotes the probability that u follows at least 1 blogger in A, under the assumption that u is satisfied by all bloggers in A. Thus $P_u(s) = P_u(Sat_u(s))$. Now, for any blogger i, user u, and strategy vector s, let $b_{i,u}(s)$ denote the expected attention blogger i receives from user u under strategy vector s. Note that for $i \in Sat_u(s)$, $b_{i\ u}(s) = a_i \mathrm{E}\left[\frac{1}{1+G(u,s)_{-i}}\right]$, where $G(u,s)\ _i$ denotes the random variable for the number of bloggers followed by u, not including blogger i, under strategy vector s. We also use $G(u,s)$ to denote the random variable for the total number of bloggers followed by u under strategy vector s.

To show the claim, we first prove two technical lemmas:

LEMMA 1. *Let $\{x_1, \ldots, x_n\}$ be a set of numbers x_i where $0 \le x_i \le 1$. Then $\sum_{i=1}^n x_i \ge 1 - \prod_{i=1}^n (1 - x_i)$*

PROOF OF LEMMA 1: We use induction to prove the equivalent inequality: $\prod_{i=1}^n (1 - x_i) \ge 1 - \sum_{i=1}^n x_i$. As the base case ($n = 1$), note that $\prod_{i=1}^n (1-x_i) = 1-x_1 = 1-\sum_{i=1}^n x_i$, so the inequality holds. For the inductive case, note the following: $\prod_{i=1}^{n+1}(1 - x_i) = (1 - x_{n+1}) \prod_{i=1}^n (1 - x_i) \ge (1 - x_{n+1})(1-\sum_{i=1}^n x_i) = (1-\sum_{i=1}^n x_i) - x_{n+1} + x_{n+1}\sum_{i=1}^n x_i \ge 1 - \sum_{i=1}^{n+1} x_i$. □

LEMMA 2. *If $\{A_1, A_2\}$ is a partition of a set $A \subseteq B$, then $P_u(A) = P_u(A_1) + (1 - P_u(A_1))P_u(A_2)$.*

PROOF OF LEMMA 2: Recall that $P_u(A) = 1 - \prod_{i\ A}(1 - a_i)$. From this definition we can directly prove the claim:

[7]These results extend to the case of an infinite and/or continuous content space Ω. No matter the nature of the content space, the space σ of posting strategies can always be divided into $2^{\ U}$ discrete areas, where each area corresponds to the set of posting strategies that would result in a subset $Z \subseteq U$ of the users being "satisfied". A blogger's payoff simply depends on which of these areas she chooses her posting strategy from. Thus, regardless of the nature of the content space, or of the user's utility functions, this can be seen as a finite game.

$$
\begin{aligned}
& P_u(A_1) + (1 - P_u(A_1))P_u(A_2) \\
= \; & 1 - \prod_{i \ A_1}(1 - a_i) + (\prod_{i \ A_1}(1 - a_i))(1 - \prod_{i \ A_2}(1 - a_i)) \\
= \; & 1 - \prod_{i \ A_1}(1 - a_i) + \prod_{i \ A_1}(1 - a_i) - \prod_{i \ A_1 \ A_2}(1 - a_i)) \\
= \; & 1 - \prod_{i \ A_1 \ A_2}(1 - a_i)) = P_u(A) \qquad \square
\end{aligned}
$$

Now we will prove that for any user u:

$$P_u(s) + \textstyle\sum_{i \ B_u} b_{i,u}(s_i\ , s \ _i) \geq P_u(s \ ).$$

In fact,

$$
\begin{aligned}
& P_u(s) + \sum_{i \ B_u} b_{i,u}(s_i\ , s \ _i) \\
= \; & P_u(s) + \sum_{i \ B_u} a_i \operatorname{E}\left[\frac{1}{1 + G(u,s) \ _i}\right] \\
\geq \; & P_u(s) + \sum_{i \ B_u} a_i \Pr[G(u,s) \ _i = 0] \\
= \; & P_u(s) + \sum_{i \ B_u} a_i \Pr[G(u,s) = 0] \\
= \; & P_u(s) + \sum_{i \ B_u} a_i(1 - P_u(s)) \\
= \; & P_u(s) + (1 - P_u(s)) \sum_{i \ B_u} a_i \\
\geq \; & P_u(s) + (1 - P_u(s))(1 - \prod_{i \ B_u}(1 - a_i)) \\
= \; & P_u(Sat_u(s)) \\
+ \; & (1 - P_u(Sat_u(s))) \cdot P_u(B_u) \\
\geq \; & P_u(Sat_u(s \ ) \cap Sat_u(s)) \\
+ \; & \Big((1 - P_u(Sat_u(s \ ) \cap Sat_u(s))) \\
* \; & P_u(Sat_u(s \ ) - Sat_u(s))\Big) \\
= \; & P_u(Sat_u(s \ )) \\
= \; & P_u(s \ ),
\end{aligned}
$$

where the third step follows from the fact that user u definitely does not follow blogger i under strategy vector s (because $i \in B_u$, the set of bloggers which satisfy u in s but not s), so $G(u,s) = G(u,s) \ _i$, the sixth follows from Lemma 1, the seventh by the definitions of P_u and P_u, the eighth from the fact that $P_u(Sat_u(s)) \geq P_u(Sat_u(s \ ) \cap Sat_u(s))$, and the ninth from Lemma 2. All the other steps follow from the definitions or direct algebraic manipulations.

Now we are ready to prove the main claim that $2W(s) \geq W(s \ )$. To do this, we take the final inequality, and sum over all users u:

$$
\begin{aligned}
P_u(s \ ) - P_u(s) \; & \leq \; \sum_{i \ B_u} b_{i,u}(s_i\ , s \ _i) \\
\Rightarrow \sum_u (P_u(s \ ) - P_u(s)) \; & \leq \; \sum_u \sum_{i \ B_u} b_{i,u}(s_i\ , s \ _i).
\end{aligned}
$$

Notice, that $\sum_u P_u(s \ ) - \sum_u P_u(s) = W(s \ ) - W(s)$. So:

$$
\begin{aligned}
W(s \ ) - W(s) \; & \leq \; \sum_u \sum_{i \ B_u} b_{i,u}(s_i\ , s \ _i) \\
& = \; \sum_{i \ B} \sum_{u:i \ B_u} b_{i,u}(s_i\ , s \ _i) \\
& \leq \; \sum_{i \ B} \sum_{u \ U} b_{i,u}(s_i\ , s \ _i) \\
& = \; \sum_{i \ B} V_i(s_i\ , s \ _i) \\
& \leq \; \sum_{i \ B} V_i(s_i, s \ _i) \\
& = \; W(s).
\end{aligned}
$$

Note that the last inequality follows from the fact that $V_i(s_i\ , s \ _i) \leq V_i(s_i, s \ _i)$, because s is a Nash equilibrium. This concludes the proof that $2W(s) \geq W(s \ )$. $\square$

We note that one can also use the framework of [17] to prove Theorem 5, but this requires a somewhat laborious demonstration that the blog game is a "valid utility system"; in our setting, it is easier to give a direct bound. Furthermore, this framework cannot be used to prove Theorem 4 and similar results on the existence of pure strategy equilibria.[8]

Next we prove that the theorem above is essentially tight.

PROPOSITION 6. *The price of anarchy of the system in the satisficing user model with blogger abilities is at least* $2 - \epsilon$ *for any* $\epsilon > 0$.

PROOF. We present a simple equilibrium example with the claimed gap. Suppose that in the system there are only n bloggers, each with ability 1, and $2n-1$ users. Furthermore, suppose that n users are interested in the item in position p_1 and give positive score only to it, and each user $n+i$ is interested only in the item in position i and gives positive score only to it.

In this scenario there is a strategy s that covers all users; one blogger covers the first n users and then each other blogger can cover a distinct user. So strategy s has welfare $2n-1$. But now consider the equilibrium in which all the bloggers are covering the first n users; this is an equilibrium because no blogger can increase her share of user attention by moving, and the welfare of this equilibrium is n. The PoA is then equal to $\frac{2n \ 1}{n}$. Thus, $\epsilon > \frac{1}{n}$ yields the claim. $\square$

6. DISCUSSION

Our results demonstrated a new prevalent effect in social media: Users of various activity levels exert different content selection within a topic, varying from broad-interest posts to more niche content. As our empirical results suggest, this phenomenon is present at various scales, for various social media and topics. This observation has important consequences. Most importantly even a population of intermediaries with various abilities can collectively serve efficiently the interests of an arbitrary population of users. A simple reward by audience size, that is naturally implemented today by advertising, is sufficient. However, this result is a non-trivial one as it depends on reader's aggressiveness to react to various news offerings.

Our work relies on a few assumptions that also point to interesting future research. First of all, we deliberately avoided domain specific metrics of quality and success in

[8]The blog positioning game does not satisfy the requirements of a "basic utility system", which would be required to prove the existence of a pure strategy Nash equilibrium. Therefore, Theorem 4 does not follow from previous work of [17] and others.

our empirical study, to study how blogs behave in function of popularity or quality within a topic. This was shown to be fruitful as it applies well to blogs focusing on a single topic of expertise. However, when more domain specific metrics are available, relating filtering to multiple dimensions such as political leaning and diversity of topics can bring additional insight on the ingredient of successful information intermediaries. Second, in our model a two-hop information flow is sufficient to explain how a few selected news reach a very large audience. Indeed, recent results highlighted that viral dissemination generally goes only through a few hops [8]. Nevertheless, a generalization of information filtering through multi-hop dissemination could offer even more insights. As an interesting example, we note that all our results extend to the case where users cannot pick any blog but need to choose one in a given *subset*. Many related topics – such as predicting the success of a post or a user, and understanding information cascades – can be revisited using a game theoretical model of information intermediaries. Our work is a stepping stone to understand these issues as it provides such a tool and shows how it already relates to users' behavior in today's social media.

7. ACKNOWLEDGMENTS

This work is supported by the National Science Foundation, under grant ICES-1139915 and CNS-1254035. We are grateful to `Texifter` for making data-sets collected with `DiscoverText.com` available to us, and especially to Stuart Shulman and Josh Sowalsky for their time and guidance. We also thank participants of the 3rd Workshop on Social Computing and User Generated Content, The New York Computer Science and Economics day, and the first Interdisciplinary Workshop on Information and Decision in Social Networks, for early feedback and discussion.

8. REFERENCES

[1] Z. Abbassi, N. Hegde, and L. Massoulié. Distributed Content Curation on the Web. *Proceedings of ACM WPIN-NETECON Workshop*, 2013.

[2] J. An, M. Cha, K. Gummadi, and J. Crowcroft. Media landscape in Twitter: A world of new conventions and political diversity. *Proceedings of the International Conference Weblogs and Social Media (ICWSM)*, pages 18–25, 2011.

[3] S. Athey and M. Mobius. The impact of news aggregators on internet news consumption: The case of localization. *working paper*, pages 1–36, 2012.

[4] L. Backstrom, J. M. Kleinberg, and R. Kumar. Optimizing web traffic via the media scheduling problem. In *KDD '09: Proceedings of the 15th ACM SIGKDD international conference on Knowledge discovery and data mining*, 2009.

[5] K. Burton, N. Kasch, and I. Soboroff. The ICWSM 2011 spinn3r dataset. *Proceedings of the International Conference Weblogs and Social Media (ICWSM)*, 2011.

[6] M. Cha, F. Benevenuto, H. Haddadi, and K. Gummadi. The World of Connections and Information Flow in Twitter. *Systems, Man and Cybernetics, Part A: Systems and Humans, IEEE Transactions on*, 42(4):991–998, 2012.

[7] A. S. Das, M. Datar, A. Garg, and S. Rajaram. Google news personalization: scalable online collaborative filtering. In *WWW '07: Proceedings of the 16th international conference on World Wide Web*, 2007.

[8] S. Goel, D. J. Watts, and D. G. Goldstein. The structure of online diffusion networks. In *EC '12: Proceedings of the 13th ACM Conference on Electronic Commerce*, 2012.

[9] M. Gupte, M. Hajiaghayi, L. Han, L. Iftode, P. Shankar, and R. Ursu. News posting by strategic users in a social network. *WINE '09: Proceedings of the 5th International Workshop on Internet and Network Economics*, pages 632–639, 2009.

[10] P. R. Jordan, U. Nadav, K. Punera, A. Skrzypacz, and G. Varghese. Lattice games and the economics of aggregators. *WWW '12: Proceedings of the 21st international conference on World Wide Web*, 2012.

[11] E. Katz. The Two-Step Flow of Communication: An Up-To-Date Report on an Hypothesis. *Public Opinion Quarterly*, 21(1):61, 1957.

[12] J. M. Kleinberg and S. Oren. Mechanisms for (mis)allocating scientific credit. In *STOC '11: Proceedings of the 43rd annual ACM symposium on Theory of computing*, 2011.

[13] H. Kwak, C. Lee, H. Park, and S. Moon. What is Twitter, a social network or a news media? In *WWW '10: Proceedings of the 19th international conference on World wide web*, 2010.

[14] J. Leskovec, L. Backstrom, and J. M. Kleinberg. Meme-tracking and the dynamics of the news cycle. In *KDD '09: Proceedings of the 15th ACM SIGKDD international conference on Knowledge discovery and data mining*, 2009.

[15] D. Monderer and L. S. Shapley. Potential games. *Games and Economic Behavior*, 14(1):124–143, 1996.

[16] T. Rodrigues, F. Benevenuto, M. Cha, K. Gummadi, and V. Almeida. On word-of-mouth based discovery of the web. In *IMC '11: Proceedings of the 2011 ACM SIGCOMM conference on Internet measurement conference*, 2011.

[17] A. Vetta. Nash equilibria in competitive societies, with applications to facility location, traffic routing and auctions. In *FOCS: Proceedings of the The 43rd Annual IEEE Symposium on Foundations of Computer Science*, pages 416–425, 2002.

[18] S. Waldman. The Information Need of Communities. *Report to the Federal Communications Commission (FCC)*, pages 1–478, 2011.

[19] F. Wu and B. A. Huberman. Popularity, novelty and attention. *EC '08: Proceedings of the 9th ACM conference on Electronic commerce*, 2008.

[20] S. Wu, J. M. Hofman, W. A Mason, and D. J. Watts. Who says what to whom on twitter. *WWW '11: Proceedings of the 20th international conference on World wide web*, 2011.

[21] J. Yang and J. Leskovec. Patterns of temporal variation in online media. In *WSDM '11: Proceedings of the fourth ACM international conference on Web search and data mining*, 2011.

[22] R. B. Zadeh, A. Goel, K. Munagala, and A. Sharma. On the precision of social and information networks. In *COSN '13: Proceedings of the first ACM conference on Online social networks*, 2013.

Privacy Tradeoffs in Predictive Analytics

Stratis Ioannidis , Andrea Montanari , Udi Weinsberg ,
Smriti Bhagat , Nadia Fawaz , Nina Taft

Technicolor
Palo Alto, CA, USA
stratis.ioannidis,udi.weinsberg,smriti.bhagat,
nadia.fawaz,nina.taft @technicolor.com

Dept. of Electrical Engineering and
Dept. of Statistics
Stanford University, Stanford, CA
montanari@stanford.edu

ABSTRACT

Online services routinely mine user data to predict user preferences, make recommendations, and place targeted ads. Recent research has demonstrated that several private user attributes (such as political affiliation, sexual orientation, and gender) can be inferred from such data. Can a privacy-conscious user benefit from personalization while simultaneously protecting her private attributes? We study this question in the context of a rating prediction service based on matrix factorization. We construct a protocol of interactions between the service and users that has remarkable optimality properties: it is *privacy-preserving*, in that no inference algorithm can succeed in inferring a user's private attribute with a probability better than random guessing; it has *maximal accuracy*, in that no other privacy-preserving protocol improves rating prediction; and, finally, it involves a *minimal disclosure*, as the prediction accuracy strictly decreases when the service reveals less information. We extensively evaluate our protocol using several rating datasets, demonstrating that it successfully blocks the inference of gender, age and political affiliation, while incurring less than 5% decrease in the accuracy of rating prediction.

Categories and Subject Descriptors

C.4 [**Performance of Systems**]: Modeling techniques; K.4.1 [**Computers and Society**]: Privacy

Keywords

Matrix Factorization; Privacy-Preserving Protocols

1. INTRODUCTION

Online users are routinely asked to provide feedback about their preferences and tastes. Often, users give five-star ratings for movies, books, restaurants, or items they purchase, and "like" news articles, blog posts, pictures or other kinds of micro-content. Online services mine such feedback to predict users' future preferences, using techniques such as matrix factorization [9,23–25]. Such prediction can be employed to, e.g., make relevant product recommendations, to display targeted ads, or, more generally, personalize services offered; making accurate predictions is thus of fundamental importance to many online services.

Although users may willingly reveal, e.g., ratings to movies or "likes" to news articles and posts, there is an inherent privacy threat in this revelation. To see this, consider the following general setting. An entity, which we call for concreteness the *analyst*, has a dataset of ratings given by users to a set of items (e.g., movies). A private attribute of some users, such as their gender, age, political affiliation, etc., is also in the dataset. The analyst uses this dataset to offer a *recommendation service*. Specifically, the analyst solicits ratings from new users; using these ratings, it predicts how these users would rate other items in its dataset (e.g., via matrix factorization techniques), and recommends items they are likely to rate highly. New users are *privacy-conscious*: they want to receive relevant recommendations but do not want the analyst to learn their private attribute. However, having access to the above dataset, the analyst can potentially *infer* the private attribute from the ratings they reveal.

The success of such inference clearly depends on how a user's feedback (i.e., her ratings) relates to her private attribute, and whether this correlation is evident in the dataset. Recent studies report many examples where strong correlations have been found: attributes successfully inferred from ratings or "likes" include political affiliation [26,39], sexual orientation [26], age [45], gender [39,45], and even drug use [26]. Yet more privacy threats have been extensively documented in literature (see, e.g., [3,31,32,35,36]). It is therefore natural to ask *how can a privacy-conscious user benefit from relevant recommendations, while preventing the inference of her private information*? Allowing this to happen is clearly desirable from the user's point of view. It also benefits the analyst, as it incentivizes privacy-conscious individuals to use the recommendation service.

A solution proposed by many recent research efforts is to allow a user to distort her ratings before revealing them to the analyst [7,12,22,43]. This leads to a well-known tradeoff between *accuracy* and *privacy* greater distortion yields better privacy but also less accurate prediction (and, hence, poorer recommendations). We introduce for the first time a third dimension to this tradeoff, namely the *information the analyst discloses to the users*.

To understand the importance of this dimension, consider the following hypothetical scenario. The analyst gives the privacy-conscious user an implementation of its rating pre-

SIGMETRICS'14, June 16–20, 2014, Austin, Texas, USA.

http://dx.doi.org/10.1145/2591971.2592011.

diction algorithm, as well as any data it requires–including, potentially, the full dataset at the analyst's disposal. The user can then execute this algorithm locally, identifying, e.g., which movies or news articles are most relevant to her. This would provide perfect privacy (as the user reveals nothing to the analyst) as well as maximal accuracy (since the user's ratings are not distorted). Clearly, this is untenable from the analyst's perspective, both for practical reasons (e.g., efficiency or code maintenance) and for commercial reasons: the analyst may be charging a fee for its services, and exposing such information publicly diminishes any competitive edge it may have.

The above hypothetical scenario illustrates that *both* privacy *and* accuracy can be trivially attained when *no constraints are placed on the information disclosed by the analyst.* On the other hand, such constraints are natural and necessary when the analyst's algorithms and data are proprietary. A natural goal is thus to determine the *minimal* information the analyst needs to disclose to a privacy-conscious user, to enable a recommendation service that is both private and accurate. We make the following contributions:

- We introduce a novel mathematical framework to study issues of privacy, accuracy, and information disclosure when the analyst predicts ratings through matrix factorization (Section 4). In particular, we define a broad class of *learning protocols* determining the interactions between the analyst and a privacy-conscious user. Each protocol specifies what information the analyst reveals, how the user distorts her ratings, and how the analyst uses this obfuscated feedback for rating prediction.
- We propose a simple learning protocol, which we call the *midpoint* protocol (MP), and prove it has remarkable optimality properties (Section 5). First, it provides *perfect privacy* w.r.t. the user's private attribute: no inference algorithm predicts it better than random guessing. Second, it yields *optimal accuracy*: there is no privacy-preserving protocol allowing rating prediction at higher accuracy than MP. Finally, the protocol involves a *minimal disclosure*: any privacy-preserving protocol that discloses less information than MP necessarily has a strictly worse prediction accuracy.
- We extend our solution to handle common situations that occur in practice (Section 6). We deal with the case where the user can only rate a subset of the items for which the analyst solicits feedback: we provide a variant of MP, termed MPSS, and also establish its optimality in this setting. We also discuss how the analyst can select the set of items for which to solicit ratings, and how the user can repeatedly interact with the analyst.
- We evaluate our proposed protocols on three datasets, protecting attributes such as user gender, age and political affiliation (Section 7). We show that MP and MPSS attain excellent privacy: a wide array of inference methods are rendered no better than blind guessing, with an area-under-the-curve (AUC) below 0.55. This privacy is achieved with negligible impact (2-5%) on rating prediction accuracy.

To the best of our knowledge, we are the first to take into account the data disclosed by an analyst in the above privacy-accuracy tradeoff, and to establish the optimality of a combined disclosure, obfuscation, and prediction scheme. Our proofs rely on the modeling assumption that is the cornerstone of matrix factorization techniques and hence validated by vast empirical evidence (namely, that the user-item ratings matrix is approximately low-rank). Moreover, the fact that our algorithms successfully block inference against a barrage of different classifiers, some non-linear, further establishes our assumption's validity over real-world data.

2. RELATED WORK

Threats. Inference threats from user data have been extensively documented by several recent studies. Demographic information has been successfully inferred from blog posts [3], search queries [5], reviews [35], tweets [36], and the profiles of one's Facebook friends [31]. In an extreme case of inference, Narayanan *et al.* [32] show that disclosure of movie ratings can lead to full de-anonymization (through a linkage attack), thus enabling unique identification of users. Closer to our setting, Kosinski *et al.* [26] show that several personality traits, including political views, sexual orientation, and drug use can be accurately predicted from Facebook "likes", while Weinsberg *et al.* [45] show that gender can be inferred from movie ratings with close to 80% accuracy. Salamatian *et al.* [39] also show that political views can be inferred with confidence above 71% by using only a user's ratings to her 5 most-watched TV shows.

Privacy-Preserving Data Mining and Information-Theoretic Models. Distorting data prior to its release to an untrusted analyst has a long history in the context of privacy-preserving data mining (see, e.g., [43, 44]). Distortion vs. estimation accuracy tradeoffs have been studied in the context of several statistical tasks, such as constructing decision trees [1], clustering [2, 34], and parameter estimation [12]. The outcome of such tasks amounts to learning an aggregate property from the distorted data of a user population. In contrast, we focus on estimating accurately a user profile to be used in matrix factorization, while keeping private any attribute she deems sensitive.

Our setting is closely related to the following information-theoretic problem [7, 46]. Consider two dependent random variables X and Y, where X is to be released publicly while Y is to be kept secret. To prevent inference of Y from the release, one can apply a distortion $f(X)$ on X; the goal is then to find the minimal distortion so that the mutual information between $f(X)$ and Y is below a threshold. This problem was originally addressed in the asymptotic regime [40, 46], while a series of recent works study it in a non-asymptotic setting [7,29,37,39]. Broadly speaking, our work can be cast in this framework by treating a user's ratings as X, her private feature as Y, and employing a correlation structure between them as specified by matrix factorization (namely, (7)). Our definition of privacy then corresponds to zero mutual information (i.e., "perfect" privacy), and our protocol involves a minimal rating distortion.

We depart from these studies of privacy vs. accuracy (both in information-theoretic as well as the privacy-preserving data mining settings), by investigating a third axis, namely, the information disclosed by the analyst. To the best of our knowledge, our work is the first to characterize the disclosure extent necessary to achieve an optimal privacy-accuracy trade-off, an aspect absent from the aforementioned works.

Trusted Analyst. A different threat model than the one we study here considers a trusted analyst that aggregates data from multiple users in the clear. The analyst performs a statistical operation over the data, distorts the output of this operation, and releases it publicly. The privacy protection gained by the distortion is therefore towards a third party that accesses the distorted output. The most common approach to quantifying privacy guarantees in this setting is through *ϵ-differential privacy* [13, 15]. The statistical operations studied under this setting are numerous, including social recommendations [28], covariance computation [30], statistical estimation [14,41], classification [10,38], and principal component analysis [11], to name a few. We differ in considering an untrusted analyst, and enabling a privacy-conscious user to interact with an analyst performing matrix factorization, rather than learning aggregate statistics.

3. TECHNICAL BACKGROUND

In this section, we briefly review matrix factorization and the modeling assumptions that underlie it. We also highlight privacy challenges that arise from its application.

3.1 Matrix Factorization (MF)

Matrix factorization [8,23,25] addresses the following prediction problem. A data analyst has access to a dataset in which N users rate subsets of M possible items (e.g., movies, restaurants, news articles, etc.). For $[N] \equiv \{1,\ldots,N\}$ the set of users, and $[M] \equiv \{1,\ldots,M\}$ the set of items, we denote by $\mathcal{E} \subset [N] \times [M]$ the user-item pairs with a rating in the dataset. For $(i,j) \in \mathcal{E}$, let $r_{ij} \in \mathbb{R}$ be user i's rating to item j. Given the dataset $\{(i,j,r_{i,j})\}_{(i,j) \in \mathcal{E}}$, the analyst wishes to predict the ratings for user-item pairs $(i,j) \notin \mathcal{E}$.

Matrix factorization attempts to solve this problem assuming that the $N \times M$ matrix comprising all ratings is *approximately low-rank*. In particular, it is assumed that for some small dimension $d \in \mathbb{N}$ there exist vectors $\mathbf{x}_i, \mathbf{v}_j \in \mathbb{R}^d$, termed the *user* and *item profiles*, respectively, such that

$$r_{ij} = \langle \mathbf{x}_i, \mathbf{v}_j \rangle + \varepsilon_{ij}, \quad \text{for } i \in [N], j \in [M], \tag{1}$$

where the "noise" variables ε_{ij} are zero mean, i.i.d. random variables with finite variance, and $\langle \mathbf{a}, \mathbf{b} \rangle \equiv \sum_{k=1}^{d} a_k b_k$ is the usual inner product in $\mathbb{R}^d$. Given the ratings $\{r_{ij}, (i,j) \in \mathcal{E}\}$, the user and item profiles are typically computed through the following least-squares estimation (LSE) [25]:

$$\min_{\{\mathbf{x}_i\}_{i\in[N]}, \{\mathbf{v}_j\}_{j\in[M]}} \sum_{(i,j) \in \mathcal{E}} (r_{ij} - \langle \mathbf{x}_i, \mathbf{v}_j \rangle)^2. \tag{2}$$

Minimizing this square error is a natural objective. Moreover, when the noise variables in (1) are Gaussian, (2) is equivalent to maximum likelihood estimation of user and item profiles. Note that, having solved (2), the analyst can predict the rating of user i for item j as:

$$\hat{r}_{ij} \equiv \langle \mathbf{x}_i, \mathbf{v}_j \rangle, \quad (i,j) \notin \mathcal{E}. \tag{3}$$

where $\mathbf{x}_i, \mathbf{v}_j$ are the estimated profiles obtained from (2).

Unfortunately, the minimization (2) is *not* a convex optimization problem. Nevertheless, there exist algorithms that provably recover the correct user and item profiles, under appropriate assumptions [8, 9, 23]. Moreover, simple gradient descent or alternating least-squares techniques are known to work very well in practice [25].

3.2 Incorporating Biases

Beyond user ratings, the analyst often has additional "contextual" information about users in the dataset. For example, if users are not privacy-conscious, they may reveal features such as their gender, age or other demographic information along with their ratings. Such information is typically included in MF through *biases* (see, e.g., [24, 25]).

Suppose, for concreteness, that each user i discloses a binary feature $x_{i0} \in \{-1,+1\}$, e.g., their gender or political affiliation. This information can be incorporated in MF by adapting the model (1) as follows:

$$r_{ij} = \langle \mathbf{x}_i, \mathbf{v}_j \rangle + x_{i0}v_{j0} + \varepsilon_{ij} = \langle x_i, v_j \rangle + \varepsilon_{ij} \tag{4}$$

for all $i \in [N], j \in [M]$, where $v_{j0} \in \mathbb{R}$ is a type-dependent bias, and $x_i = (x_{i0}, \mathbf{x}) \in \mathbb{R}^{d+1}$, $i \in [N]$, $v_j = (v_{j0}, \mathbf{v}_j) \in \mathbb{R}^{d+1}$, $j \in [M]$, are *extended* user and item profiles, respectively. Under this modeling assumption, the analyst can estimate profiles and biases jointly by solving:

$$\min_{\{\mathbf{x}_i\}_{i\in[N]}, \{(v_{j0},\mathbf{v}_j)\}_{j\in[M]}} \sum_{(i,j) \in \mathcal{E}} (r_{ij} - \langle x_i, v_j \rangle)^2. \tag{5}$$

Note that this minimization can be seen as a special case of (2), in which extended profiles have dimension $d+1$, and the first coordinate of x_i is fixed to either -1 or $+1$ (depending on the user's binary feature x_{i0}). In other words, the feature x_{i0} can be treated as yet another feature of a user's profile, though it is *explicit* (i.e., a priori known) rather than *latent* (i.e., inferred through MF). Prediction can be performed again through $\hat{r}_{ij} = \langle x_i, v_j \rangle$, for $(i,j) \notin \mathcal{E}$.

Intuitively, the biases v_{j0} gauge the impact of the binary feature x_{i0} on each user's ratings. Indeed, consider sampling a random user from a population, and let $x = (x_0, \mathbf{x})$ be her profile, where $\mathbf{x}$ comprises the features that are independent of x_0. Then, it is easy to check from (4) that her rating r_j for item j will be such that:

$$\mathbf{E}[r_j \mid x_0 = 1] - \mathbf{E}[r_j \mid x_0 = 0] = 2v_{j0},$$

where the expectation is over the noise in (4), as well as the random sampling of the user. Put differently, given access to ratings by users that are not privacy-conscious and have disclosed, e.g., their gender x_0, v_{j0} corresponds to half the distance between the mean ratings for item j among genders.

Additional explicit binary features can be incorporated similarly, by adding one bias per feature in (5) (see, e.g., [25]). Categorical features can also be added through binarization; for simplicity, we focus on a single binary feature, discussing multiple and categorical features in Section 6.4.

3.3 Prediction for Privacy-Conscious Users

Consider a scenario in which the analyst has performed MF over a dataset of users explicitly revealing a binary feature, and has extracted the extended profiles $v_j = (v_{j0}, \mathbf{v}_j) \in \mathbb{R}^{d+1}$ for each item $j \in [M]$. Suppose now a privacy-conscious user joins the system and *does not explicitly reveal her private binary feature x_0 to the analyst.*

In such a "cold-start" situation, the analyst would typically solicit a batch of ratings $\{r_j\}_{j \in \mathcal{S}}$ for some set $\mathcal{S} \subseteq M$. Assume that the new user's ratings also follow the linear model (4) with extended profile $x = (x_0, \mathbf{x}) \in \{-1,+1\} \times \mathbb{R}^d$. Then, the analyst can (a) infer the user's extended profile x, and (b) predict her ratings for items in $[M] \setminus \mathcal{S}$ using the extended item profiles $\{v_j\}_{j \in \mathcal{S}}$ as follows. First, the analyst can infer x using through the LSE:

$$\min_{x_0 \in \{-1,+1\}, \mathbf{x} \in \mathbb{R}^d} \sum_{j \in \mathcal{S}} (r_j - \langle \mathbf{x}, \mathbf{v}_j \rangle - x_0 v_{j0})^2. \tag{6}$$

The minimization (6) can be computed in time linear in $|\mathcal{S}|$, by solving two linear regressions (one for each $x_0 \in \{-1,+1\}$)

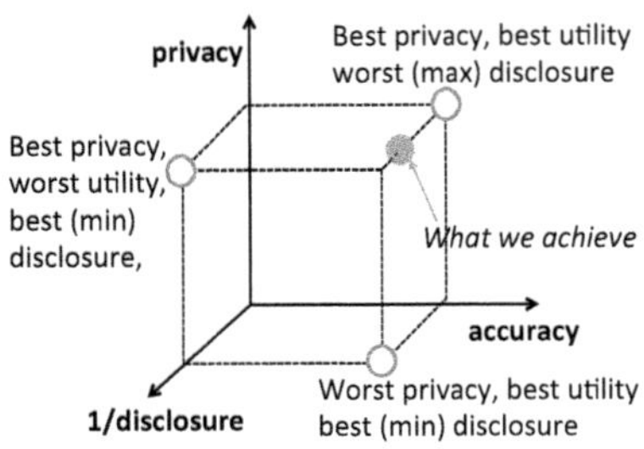

Figure 1: The red circles represent the three extreme protocols (Sec. 4.1) that fail to meet all three properties simultaneously. Our solution (see Sec. 5) lies near the upper front right edge of the cube, as it has perfect privacy and accuracy. We will prove (Thm. 1 in Sec. 5) that the region between our solution and the optimal corner ('zero' disclosure, perfect privacy, maximal accuracy) is unattainable.

and picking the solution $(x_0, \mathbf{x})$ that yields the smallest error (6). Having obtained an estimate of the extended profile x, the analyst can predict ratings as $\hat{r}_j = \langle x, v_j \rangle$, for $j \notin \mathcal{S}$.

Beyond this LSE approach, the analyst can use a different classification algorithm to first infer the private feature x_0, such as logistic regression or support vector machines (SVMs). We refer the reader to, *e.g.*, [45], for the description of several such algorithms and their application over real rating data. Having an estimate of x_0, the analyst can proceed to solve (6) w.r.t. $\mathbf{x}$ alone, which involves a single linear regression.

In both of the above approaches (joint LSE, or separate inference of x_0) the analyst infers the private feature x_0. Indeed, the LSE method (6) is known to predict information such as gender or age with an accuracy between 65–83% over real datasets [4]; separate inference of the private information (through, e.g., logistic regression or SVMs) leads to 84-86% accuracy [45]. As such, by revealing her ratings, the user also reveals x_0, albeit indirectly and unintentionally.

4. MODELING PRIVACY TRADEOFFS

Section 3.3 illustrates that serving a privacy-conscious user is not straightforward: there is a tension between the user's privacy and the utility she receives. Accurate profiling allows correct rating prediction and enables relevant recommendations, at the cost of the inadvertent revelation of the user's private feature. It is thus natural to ask whether the user can benefit from accurate prediction *while preventing the inference of this feature.* We will provide both rigorous and empirical evidence that – perhaps surprisingly – this is possible. Specific features can be obfuscated without harming personalization. One of our main contributions is to identify that, beyond this privacy-utility tradeoff, there is in fact a third aspect to this problem: namely, how much information the analyst discloses to the user. In what follows, we present a framework that addresses these issues.

4.1 Problem Formulation

Motivated by Section 3.3, we consider a setting comprising the two entities we have encountered so far, an *analyst* and a *privacy-conscious user.* The analyst has access to a dataset of ratings collected from users that are not privacy-conscious, and have additionally revealed to the analyst a binary feature. By performing matrix factorization over this dataset, the analyst has extracted extended item profiles $v_j = (v_{j0}, \mathbf{v}_j) \in \mathbb{R}^{d+1}$, $j \in [M]$, for a set of M items.

The analyst solicits the ratings of the privacy-conscious user for a subset of items $\mathcal{S} \in [M]$. We again assume that the user is parametrized by an extended profile $x = (x_0, \mathbf{x}) \in \{-1, +1\} \times \mathbb{R}^d$, and that her ratings follow (4). The analyst's goal is to profile the user and identify items that the user might rate highly in $[M] \setminus \mathcal{S}$. The user is willing to aid the analyst in correctly profiling her; however, she is privacy-conscious w.r.t. her private feature x_0, and wishes to *prevent its inference.* We thus wish to design a *protocol* for exchanging information between the analyst and the user that has three salient properties; we state these here informally, postponing precise definitions until Section 4.3:

(a) At the conclusion of the protocol, the analyst estimates $\mathbf{x}$, the non-private component of x, *as accurately as possible.*
(b) The analyst *learns nothing* about the private feature x_0.
(c) The user learns *as little as possible* about the extended profile v_j of each item j.

To highlight the interplay between these three properties, we discuss here three "non-solutions", i.e., three protocols that fail to satisfy all three properties. First, observe that the "empty" protocol (no information exchange) clearly satisfies (b) and (c), but not (a): the analyst does not learn $\mathbf{x}$. Second, the protocol in which the user discloses her ratings to the analyst "in the clear", as in Section 3.3, satisfies (a) and (c) but not (b): it allows the analyst to estimate *both* $\mathbf{x}$ *and* x_0 through, e.g., the LSE (6).

Finally, consider the following protocol. The analyst discloses all item profiles v_j, $j \in \mathcal{S}$, to the user. Subsequently, the user estimates $\mathbf{x}$ locally, by solving the linear regression (6) over her ratings in $\mathcal{S}$, with her private feature x_0 fixed. The user concludes the protocol by sending the obtained estimate of $\mathbf{x}$ to the analyst. Observe that this protocol satisfies (a) and (b), but not (c). In particular, the user learns the extended profiles of all items in their entirety.

These protocols illustrate that it is simple to satisfy any two of the above properties, but not all three. Each of the three "non-solutions" above are in fact extrema among protocols constrained by (a)-(c): each satisfies two properties in the best way possible, while completely failing on the third. In the conceptual schematic of Figure 1 we illustrate where these three extreme protocols lie.

There is a clear motivation, from a practical perspective, to seek protocols satisfying all three properties. Property (a) ensures that, at the conclusion of the protocol, the analyst learns the non-private component of the user's profile, and can use it to suggest new items–benefiting thusly the user, and motivating the existence of this service. Property (b) ensures that a privacy-conscious user receives this benefit *without revealing her private feature*, thereby incentivizing her participation. Finally, property (c) limits the extent at which the item profiles $\{v_j\}_{j \in \mathcal{S}}$ are made publicly available. Indeed, the item profiles and the dataset from which they were constructed are proprietary information: disclosing them to any privacy-conscious user, as described by the last non-solution, would allow any user to offer the same service. More generally, it is to the analyst's interest to enable properties (a) and (b), thereby attracting privacy-conscious users, while limiting the disclosure of any proprietary information and its exposure to competition.

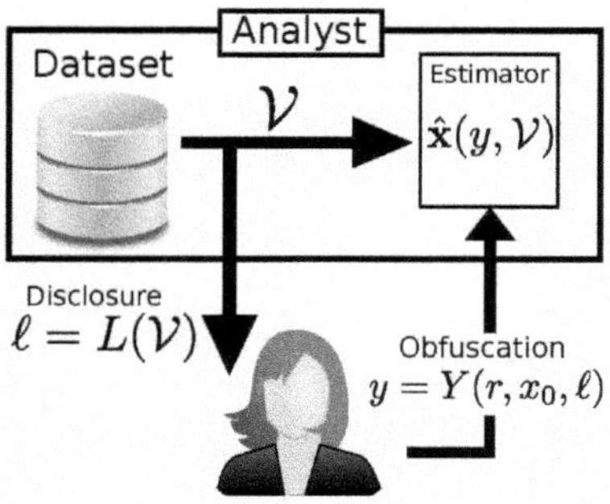

Figure 2: A learning protocol $\mathcal{R} = (L, Y, \hat{\mathbf{x}})$ between an analyst and a privacy-conscious user. The analyst has access to a dataset, from which it extracts the extended profiles $\mathcal{V}$ through MF. It discloses to the user the information $\ell = L(\mathcal{V})$. Using this information, her vector of ratings r, and her private feature x_0, the user computes the obfuscated output $y = Y(r, x_0, \ell)$ and reveals it to the analyst. The latter uses this obfuscated feedback as well as the profiles $\mathcal{V}$ to estimate $\mathbf{x}$, using the estimator $\hat{\mathbf{x}}(y, \mathcal{V})$.

It is natural to ask what is the precise statement of "as accurately as possible", "learns nothing", and "as little as possible" in the above description of (a)-(c). We provide such formal definitions below.

4.2 A Learning Protocol

To formalize the notions introduced in properties (a)-(c) of Section 4.1, we describe in this section the interactions between the privacy-conscious user and the analyst in a more precise fashion. Recall that the user is parametrized by an extended profile $x = (x_0, \mathbf{x}) \in \{-1, +1\} \times \mathbb{R}^d$, and that her ratings follow (4); namely,

$$r_j = \langle \mathbf{x}, \mathbf{v}_j \rangle + x_0 v_{j0} + \varepsilon_j = \langle x, v_j \rangle + \varepsilon_j, \quad j \in [M] \quad (7)$$

where $v_j \in \mathbb{R}^{d+1}$, is the extended profile of item j, extracted through MF, and ε_j are i.i.d. zero mean random variables of variance $\sigma^2 < \infty$. We note that, unless explicitly stated, we *do not* assume that the noise variables ε_j are Gaussian; our results will hold with greater generality.

We assume that the set of items $\mathcal{S} \subseteq [M]$, for which ratings are solicited, is an arbitrary set chosen by the analyst[1]. We restrict our attention to items with extended profiles v_j such that $\mathbf{v}_j \neq \mathbf{0}$. Indeed, given the analyst's purpose of estimating $\mathbf{x}$, the rating of an item for which $\mathbf{v} = \mathbf{0}$ is clearly uninformative in light of (7). We denote by

$$\mathbb{R}^{d+1}_{-\mathbf{0}} \equiv \{(v_0, \mathbf{v}) \in \mathbb{R}^{d+1} : \mathbf{v} \neq \mathbf{0}\}$$

the set of all such vectors, and by $\mathcal{V} \equiv \{v_j, \ j \in \mathcal{S}\} \subseteq \mathbb{R}^{d+1}_{-\mathbf{0}}$ the extended profiles of items in $\mathcal{S}$. Recall that the user does not a priori know $\mathcal{V}$. In addition, the user knows her private variable x_0 and either knows or can easily generate her rating r_j to each item $j \in \mathcal{S}$. Nevertheless, the user *does not a-priori know* the remaining profile $\mathbf{x} \in \mathbb{R}^d$. This is consistent with MF, as the "features" corresponding to each coordinate of $\mathbf{v}_j$ are "latent".

The assumption that the user either knows or can easily generate her ratings in $\mathcal{S}$ is natural when the user can immediately form an opinion (this is the case for items such as blog posts, ads, news articles, tweets, pictures, short videos, etc.); or, when the "rating" is automatically generated from user engagement (e.g., it is the time a user spends at a website, or the reading collected by a skin sensor); or, when the user is obligated to generate a response (because, e.g., she is paid to do so). We discuss the case where the user can readily produce ratings for only a subset of $\mathcal{S}$ in Section 6.1.

Using the above notation, we define a *privacy-preserving learning protocol* as a protocol consisting of the following three components, as illustrated in Figure 2:

Disclosure. The disclosure determines the amount of information that the analyst discloses to the user regarding the profiles in $\mathcal{V}$. Formally, it is a mapping

$$L : \mathbb{R}^{d+1}_{-\mathbf{0}} \to \mathcal{L},$$

with $\mathcal{L}$ a generic set[2]. This is implemented as a program and executed by the analyst, who discloses to the user the information $\ell_j \equiv L(v_j) \in \mathcal{L}$ for each item $j \in \mathcal{S}$. We denote by $L(\mathcal{V})$ the vector $\ell \in \mathcal{L}^{|\mathcal{S}|}$ with coordinates ℓ_j, $i \in \mathcal{S}$. We note that, in practice, $L(\mathcal{V})$ can be made public, as it is needed by all potential privacy-conscious users that wish to interact with the analyst.

Obfuscation Scheme. The obfuscation scheme describes how user ratings are modified (obfuscated) before being revealed to the analyst. Formally, this is a mapping

$$Y : \mathbb{R}^{|\mathcal{S}|} \times \{-1, +1\} \times \mathcal{L}^{|\mathcal{S}|} \to \mathcal{Y},$$

for $\mathcal{Y}$ again a generic set. The mapping is implemented as a program and executed by the user. In particular, the user enters her ratings $r = (r_1, \ldots, r_{|\mathcal{S}|}) \in \mathbb{R}^{|\mathcal{S}|}$, her private variable x_0 *as well as* the disclosure $\ell = L(\mathcal{V}) \in \mathcal{L}^{|\mathcal{S}|}$. The program combines these quantities computing the obfuscated value $y = Y(r, x_0, \ell) \in \mathcal{Y}$, which the user subsequently reveals to the analyst.

Estimator. Finally, using the obfuscated output by the user, and the item profiles, the analyst constructs an estimator of the user's profile $\mathbf{x} \in \mathbb{R}^d$. Formally:

$$\hat{\mathbf{x}} : \mathcal{Y} \times (\mathbb{R}^{(d+1)}_{-\mathbf{0}})^{|\mathcal{S}|} \to \mathbb{R}^d.$$

That is, given the item feature vectors $\mathcal{V} \subset \mathbb{R}^{d+1}_{-\mathbf{0}}$ and the corresponding obfuscated user feedback $y \in \mathcal{Y}$, it yields an estimate $\hat{\mathbf{x}}(y, \mathcal{V})$ of the user's non-private feature vector $\mathbf{x}$. The estimator is a program executed by the analyst.

We refer to a triplet $\mathcal{R} = (L, Y, \hat{\mathbf{x}})$ as a *learning protocol*. Note that the functional forms of all three of these components are known to both parties: *e.g.*, the analyst knows the obfuscation scheme Y. Both parties are *honest but curious*: they follow the protocol, but if at any step they can extract more information than what is intentionally revealed, they do so. All three mappings in protocol $\mathcal{R}$ can be randomized. In the following, we denote by $\mathrm{P}_{x,\mathcal{V}}$, $\mathrm{E}_{x,\mathcal{V}}$ the probability and expectation with respect to the noise in (7) as well as protocol randomization, given x, $\mathcal{V}$.

4.3 Privacy, Accuracy, and Disclosure Extent

Having formally specified a learning protocol $\mathcal{R} = (L, Y, \hat{\mathbf{x}})$, we now define the three quality metrics we wish to attain, corresponding to the properties (a)-(c) of Section 4.1.

Privacy. We begin with our formalization of privacy:

[1]We discuss how the analyst can select the items in $\mathcal{S}$ in Section 6.2.

[2]For technical reasons $\mathcal{L}$, and $\mathcal{Y}$ below, are in fact measurable spaces, which include of course $\mathbb{R}^k$, for some $k \in \mathbb{N}$.

DEFINITION 1. *We say that* $\mathcal{R} = (L, Y, \widehat{\mathbf{x}})$ *is* privacy preserving *if the obfuscated output* Y *is independent of* x_0. *Formally, for all* $\mathbf{x}\ \ \mathbb{R}^d$, $\mathcal{V}\ \ \mathbb{R}_{\mathbf{0}}^{(d+1)}$, *and* $A\ \ \mathcal{Y}$,

$$\mathrm{P}_{(\ 1,\mathbf{x}),\mathcal{V}}\big(Y(r,\ 1,\ell)\ \ A\big) = \mathrm{P}_{(+1,\mathbf{x}),\mathcal{V}}\big(Y(r,+1,\ell)\ \ A\big), \quad (8)$$

where $\ell = L(\mathcal{V})$ *is the information disclosed from* $\mathcal{V}$, *and* $r\ \ \mathbb{R}^{\ \mathcal{S}}$ *is the vector of user ratings.*

Intuitively, a learning protocol is privacy-preserving if its obfuscation scheme reveals nothing about the user's private variable: the distribution of the output Y does not depend statistically on x_0. Put differently, two users that have the same $\mathbf{x}$, but different x_0, output obfuscated values that are *computationally indistinguishable* [17].

Computational indistinguishability is a strong privacy property, as it implies a user's private variable is protected against *any* inference algorithm (and not just, e.g., the LSE (6)): in particular, no inference algorithm can estimate x_0 with probability better than 50% with access to y alone.

Accuracy. Our second definition determines a partial ordering among learning protocols w.r.t. their accuracy, as captured by the ℓ_2 loss of the estimation:

DEFINITION 2. *We say that a learning protocol* $\mathcal{R} = (L, Y, \widehat{\mathbf{x}})$ *is more accurate than* $\mathcal{R}\ = (L\ , Y\ , \widehat{\mathbf{x}}\ )$ *if, for all* $\mathcal{V}\ \ \mathbb{R}_{\mathbf{0}}^{d+1}$,

$$\sup_{\substack{x_0\ \ 0,1 \\ \mathbf{x}\ \ \mathbb{R}^d}} \mathrm{E}_{(x_0,\mathbf{x}),\mathcal{V}}\ \ \widehat{\mathbf{x}}(y,\mathcal{V})\ \ \mathbf{x}\ _2^2 \qquad \sup_{\substack{x_0\ \ 0,1 \\ \mathbf{x}\ \ \mathbb{R}^d}} \mathrm{E}_{(x_0,\mathbf{x}),\mathcal{V}}\ \ \widehat{\mathbf{x}}\ (y,\mathcal{V})\ \ \mathbf{x}\ _2^2,$$

where $y = Y(r, x_0, L(\mathcal{V}))$, $y\ = Y\ (r, x_0, L\ (\mathcal{V}))$. *Further, we say that it is strictly more accurate if the above inequality holds strictly for some* $\mathcal{V}\ \ \mathbb{R}_{\mathbf{0}}^{d+1}$.

Note that the accuracy of $\mathcal{R}$ is determined by the ℓ_2 loss of the estimate $\widehat{\mathbf{x}}$ computed in a *worst-case* scenario, among all possible extended user profiles $x = (x_0, \mathbf{x})$.

This metric is natural. As we discuss in Section 6.2, it relates to the so-called A-optimality criterion [6]. It also has an additional compelling motivation. Recall that $\widehat{\mathbf{x}}$ is used to estimate the rating for a new item through the inner product (3). An estimator $\widehat{\mathbf{x}}$ minimizing the expected ℓ_2 loss also minimizes the mean square prediction error over a new item. This further motivates this accuracy metric, given that the analyst's goal is correct rating prediction.

To see this, assume that the extended user profile is estimated as $\widehat{x} = (\widehat{x}_0, \widehat{\mathbf{x}})$ for some $\mathbf{x}_0$ (for brevity we omit the dependence on $y, \mathcal{V}$). Recall that the analyst uses this profile to predict ratings for $v\ /\ \mathcal{V}$ using $\widehat{r} =\ \ v, \widehat{x}\ $. The quality of such a prediction is often evaluated in terms of the mean square error (MSE):

$$\mathrm{MSE} = \mathrm{E}\ \ (r\ \ \widehat{r})^2 \overset{(7)}{=} \sigma^2 + \mathrm{E}\ \ \ v, (x\ \ \widehat{x})\ ^2\ \ .$$

Assuming a random item vector v with diagonal covariance $\mathrm{E}(v_0^2) = c_0$, $\mathrm{E}(v_0\mathbf{v}) = 0$, $\mathrm{E}(\mathbf{v}\mathbf{v}^{\mathsf{T}}) = cI$, we get

$$\mathrm{MSE} = \sigma^2 + c_0\mathrm{E}\ (x_0\ \ \widehat{x}_0)^2\ \ + c\mathrm{E}\{\ \ x\ \ \ \widehat{x}\ _2^2\}.$$

Observe that the first term is independent of the estimation. Under a privacy-preserving protocol, the value for $\widehat{x}_0$ that minimizes the second term is 0.5, also independent of the estimation. The last term is precisely the ℓ_2 loss. Hence, minimizing the mean square error of the analyst's prediction is equivalent to minimizing the ℓ_2 loss of the estimator $\widehat{x}$. This directly motivates our accuracy definition.

Algorithm 1 MIDPOINT PROTOCOL

Analyst's Parameters
$\mathcal{S} \subseteq [M]$, $\mathcal{V} = \{(v_{j0}, \mathbf{v}_j), j \in \mathcal{S}\} \subseteq \mathbb{R}_{\mathbf{0}}^{d+1}$

User's Parameters
$x_0 \in \{-1, +1\}$, $r = (r_1, \ldots, r_{\ \mathcal{S}}\ ) \in \mathbb{R}^{\ \mathcal{S}}$

DISCLOSURE: $\ell = L(\mathcal{V})$
$\ell_j = v_{j0}$, for all $j \in \mathcal{S}$

OBFUSCATION SCHEME: $y = Y(r, x_0, \ell)$
$y_j = r_j - x_0 \cdot \ell_j$, for all $j \in \mathcal{S}$

ESTIMATOR: $\widehat{\mathbf{x}} = \widehat{\mathbf{x}}(y, \mathcal{V})$
Apply the minimax estimator $\widehat{\mathbf{x}}$ given by (9).

Disclosure Extent. Finally, we define a partial ordering among learning protocols w.r.t. the amount of information revealed by their disclosures.

DEFINITION 3. *We say that* $\mathcal{R} = (L, R, \widehat{\mathbf{x}})$ *discloses at least as much information as* $\mathcal{R}\ = (L\ , Y\ , \widehat{\mathbf{x}}\ )$ *if there exists a measurable mapping* $\varphi : \mathcal{L}\ \ \ \mathcal{L}\ $ *such that*

$$L\ = \varphi\ \ L$$

i.e., $L\ (v) = \varphi(L(v))$ *for each* $v\ \ \mathbb{R}_{\mathbf{0}}^{d+1}$. *We say that* $\mathcal{R}$ *and* $\mathcal{R}\ $ *disclose the same amount of information if* $L = \varphi\ \ \ L\ $ *and* $L\ = \varphi\ \ \ L$ *for some* φ, $\varphi\ $. *Finally, we say that* $\mathcal{R}$ *discloses strictly more information than* $\mathcal{R}\ $ *if* $L\ = \varphi\ \ L$ *for some* φ *but there exists no* $\varphi\ $ *such that* $L = \varphi\ \ \ L\ $.

The above definition is again natural. Intuitively, a disclosure L carries at least as much information as $L\ $ if $L\ $ can be retrieved from L: the existence of the mapping φ implies that the user can recover $L\ $ from L by applying φ to the disclosure $L(\mathcal{V})$. Put differently, having a "black box" that computes L, the user can compute $L\ $ by feeding the output of this box to φ. If this is the case, then L is clearly at least as informative as $L\ $.

5. AN OPTIMAL PROTOCOL

In this section we prove that a simple learning protocol outlined in Algorithm 1, which we refer to as the *midpoint protocol* (MP), has remarkable optimality properties. The three components $(L, Y, \widehat{\mathbf{x}})$ of MP are as follows:

1. The analyst discloses the entry v_0 corresponding to the private user feature x_0, *i.e.*, $L\big((v_0, \mathbf{v})\big)\ \ \ v_0$ for all $(v_0, \mathbf{v})\ \ \mathbb{R}_{\mathbf{0}}^{d+1}$, and $\mathcal{L}\ \ \mathbb{R}$.
2. The user shifts each rating r_j by the contribution of her private feature. More specifically, the user reveals to the analyst the quantities:
$$y_j = r_j\ \ \ x_0\ \ \ell_j = r_j\ \ \ x_0\ \ v_{j0},\ \ \ j\ \ \ \mathcal{S}.$$
The user's obfuscated feedback is thus $Y(r, x_0, \ell)\ \ \ \ y$, where vector y's coordinates are the above quantities, i.e., $y = (y_1, \ldots, y_{\ \mathcal{S}}\ )$, and $\mathcal{Y}\ \ \ \mathbb{R}^{\ \mathcal{S}}$. Note that, by (7), for every $j\ \ \ \mathcal{S}$ the obfuscated feedback satisfies $y_j =\ \ \mathbf{v}_j, \mathbf{x}\ + \varepsilon_j$, with ε_j the i.i.d. zero-mean noise variables.
3. Finally, the analyst applies a *minimax* estimator on the obfuscated feedback. Let $\mathcal{X}$ be the set of all measurable mappings $\widehat{\mathbf{x}}$ estimating $\mathbf{x}$ given y and $\mathcal{V}$ (i.e., of the form $\widehat{\mathbf{x}} : \mathbb{R}^{\ \mathcal{S}}\ \ \ (\mathbb{R}_{\mathbf{0}}^{(d+1)})^{\ \mathcal{S}}\ \ \ \ \mathbb{R}^d$). Estimator $\widehat{\mathbf{x}}\ \ \ \ \mathcal{X}$ is

minimax if it minimizes the worst-case ℓ_2 loss, i.e.:

$$\sup_{x_0 \quad 0,1 \ ,\mathbf{x} \quad \mathbb{R}^d} \mathrm{E}_{(x_0,\mathbf{x}),\mathcal{V}} \quad \widehat{\mathbf{x}} \ (y,\mathcal{V}) \quad \mathbf{x} \ _2^2 =$$
$$\inf_{\widehat{\mathbf{x}} \quad \mathcal{X}_{x_0}} \sup_{0,1 \ ,\mathbf{x} \quad \mathcal{X}} \mathrm{E}_{(x_0,\mathbf{x}),\mathcal{V}} \quad \widehat{\mathbf{x}}(y,\mathcal{V}) \quad \mathbf{x} \ _2^2 \ . \tag{9}$$

The following theorem summarizes the midpoint protocol's remarkable properties:

THEOREM 1. *Under the linear model* (7)*:*
1. *MP is privacy preserving.*
2. *No privacy preserving protocol is strictly more accurate than MP.*
3. *Any privacy preserving protocol that does not disclose at least as much information as MP is strictly less accurate.*

We prove the theorem below. Its second and third statement establish formally the optimality of the midpoint protocol. Intuitively, the second statement implies that the midpoint protocol has *maximal accuracy.* No privacy preserving protocol achieves better accuracy: surprisingly, this is true even among schemes that *disclose strictly more information than the midpoint protocol.* As such, the second statement of the theorem imples there is no reason to disclose more than v_{j0} for each item $j \quad \mathcal{S}$.

The third statement implies that the midpoint protocol engages in a *minimal disclosure*: to achieve maximal accuracy, a learning protocol *must disclose at least* v_{j0}, $j \quad \mathcal{S}$. In fact, our proof shows that the gap between the accuracy of MP and a protocol not disclosing biases is infinite, for certain $\mathcal{V}$. We note that the disclosure in MP is intuitively appealing: an analyst need only disclose the gap between average ratings across the two types (e.g., males and females, conservatives and liberals, etc.) to enable protection of x_0.

In general, the minimax estimator $\widehat{\mathbf{x}}$ depends on the distribution followed by the noise variables in (7). For arbitrary distributions, a minimax estimator that can be computed in a closed form (rather than as the limit of a sequence of estimators) may not be known. General conditions for the existence of such estimators can be found, e.g., in Strasser [42]. In the case of Gaussian noise, the minimax estimator coincides with the least squares estimator (see, e.g., Lehman and Casella [27, Thm. 1.15, Chap. 5]), i.e.,

$$\widehat{\mathbf{x}} \ (y,\mathcal{V}) = \arg\min_{\mathbf{x} \quad \mathbb{R}^d} \Big\{ \textstyle\sum_{j=1}^{\mathcal{S}} (y_j \quad \mathbf{v}_j,\mathbf{x} \ )^2 \Big\}. \tag{10}$$

The minimization in (10) is a linear regression, and $\widehat{\mathbf{x}}$ has the following closed form:

$$\widehat{\mathbf{x}} \ (y,\mathcal{V}) = \big(\textstyle\sum_{j \quad \mathcal{S}} \mathbf{v}_j\mathbf{v}_j^T\big)^{\ 1} \ \big(\textstyle\sum_{j \quad \mathcal{S}} y_j\mathbf{v}_j\big). \tag{11}$$

The accuracy of this estimator can also be computed in a closed form. Using, (7), (11), and the definition of y, it can easily be shown that, for all $\mathbf{x} \quad \mathbb{R}^d$,

$$\mathrm{E}_{(x_0,\mathbf{x}),\mathcal{V}} \quad \widehat{\mathbf{x}} \ (y,\mathcal{V}) \quad \mathbf{x} \ _2^2 = \sigma^2 \mathrm{tr}\big[\big(\textstyle\sum_{j \quad \mathcal{S}} \mathbf{v}_j\mathbf{v}_j^T\big)^{\ 1}\big], \tag{12}$$

where σ^2 the noise variance in (7) and tr( ) the trace.

5.1 Proof of Theorem 1

Privacy. To see that Thm. 1.1 holds, observe that the user releases $y_j = r_j \quad v_{0j}x_0 \overset{(7)}{=} \ \mathbf{v}_j,\mathbf{x} \ + \varepsilon_j$, for each $j \quad \mathcal{S}$. The distribution of y_j thus does not depend on x_0, so the midpoint protocol is clearly privacy preserving.

Maximal Accuracy. We prove Theorem 1.2 by contradiction; in particular, we show that a protocol that is strictly more accurate can be used to construct an estimator that has lower worst-case ℓ_2 loss than the minimax estimator.

Suppose that there exists a privacy preserving protocol $\mathcal{R} \ = (L \ , Y \ , \widehat{\mathbf{x}} \ )$ that is strictly more accurate than the midpoint protocol $\mathcal{R} = (L, Y, \widehat{\mathbf{x}})$. Let $\ell = L(\mathcal{V}), \ell \ = L \ (\mathcal{V})$ be the disclosures under the two protocols, and $y = Y(r, x_0, \ell)$, $y \ = Y \ (r, x_0, \ell \ )$ the obfuscated values. Recall that

$$\ell_j = v_{j0}, \text{ and } y_j = r_j \quad x_0 v_{0j} = \ \mathbf{v}_j, \mathbf{x} \ + \varepsilon_j, \quad j \quad \mathcal{S}.$$

We will use L , Y and $\widehat{\mathbf{x}}$ to construct an estimator $\widehat{\mathbf{x}}$ that has a lower ℓ_2 loss than the least squares estimator $\widehat{\mathbf{x}}$ over y and $\mathcal{V}$. First, apply Y to $y + \ell$, assuming that the private variable is $x_0 = +1$, using the disclosed information ℓ . That is: $y \ = Y \ (y + \ell, +1, \ell \ )$. Second, apply the estimator $\widehat{\mathbf{x}}$ to this newly obfuscated output y , i.e.: $\widehat{\mathbf{x}} \ (y \ , \mathcal{V})$ Combining these two the estimator $\widehat{\mathbf{x}}$ is given by

$$\widehat{\mathbf{x}} \ (y, \mathcal{V}) = \widehat{\mathbf{x}} \ \big(Y \ \big(y + \ell, +1, L \ (\mathcal{V})\big), \mathcal{V}\big)$$

Under this construction, the random variables y , y are identically distributed. This is obvious if $x_0 = +1$; indeed, in this case $y \ = y$. On the other hand, since $\mathcal{R}$ is privacy preserving, by (8):

$$Y \ (y + \ell, +1, \ell \ ) \overset{\mathrm{d}}{=} Y \ (y \quad \ell, \quad 1, \ell \ ), \tag{13}$$

i.e., the two variables are equal in distribution.

This implies that $\widehat{\mathbf{x}} \ (y, \mathcal{V})$ is identically distributed as $\widehat{\mathbf{x}} \ (y \ , \mathcal{V})$. On the other hand, $\mathcal{R}$ is strictly more accurate than $\mathcal{R}$; hence, there exists a $\mathcal{V}$ such that

$$\sup_x \mathrm{E} \quad \widehat{\mathbf{x}}(y,\mathcal{V}) \quad \mathbf{x} \ _2^2 > \sup_x \mathrm{E} \quad \widehat{\mathbf{x}} \ (y \ , \mathcal{V}) \quad \mathbf{x} \ _2^2$$
$$= \sup_x \mathrm{E} \quad \widehat{\mathbf{x}} \ (y, \mathcal{V}) \quad \mathbf{x} \ _2^2 \ ,$$

a contradiction.

Minimal Disclosure. Consider a privacy preserving learning protocol $\mathcal{R} \ = (L \ , Y \ , \widehat{\mathbf{x}} \ )$ that does not disclose at least as much information as the midpoint protocol $\mathcal{R} = (L, Y, \widehat{\mathbf{x}})$. Consider a setup where $\mathcal{S} \ = d$, the dimension of the feature profiles. Assume also that $\mathcal{V}$ is such that the matrix $V = [\mathbf{v}_j]_{j \quad \mathcal{S}} \quad \mathbb{R}^{d \quad d}$ is invertible, and denote by $\ell = L(\mathcal{V}) \quad \mathbb{R}^d$ the vector with coordinates v_{j0}, $j \quad \mathcal{S}$.

For any $x_0 \quad +1, \quad 1 \ , s \quad \mathbb{R}^d$, and $\ell \quad (\mathcal{L} \ )^d$, let $Z_{x_0}(s, \ell \ ) \quad \mathcal{Y}$ be a random variable with distribution given by $Z_{x_0}(s, \ell \ ) \overset{\mathrm{d}}{=} Y \ (s + \varepsilon, x_0, \ell \ )$, where $\varepsilon \quad \mathbb{R}^d$ a vector of *i.i.d.* coordinates sampled from the same distribution as the noise variables ε_j, $j \quad \mathcal{S}$. Put differently, $Z_{x_0}(s, \ell \ )$ is distributed as the output of obfuscation Y when $r \quad \varepsilon = V\mathbf{x} + x_0\ell = s \quad \mathbb{R}^d$, $L \ (\mathcal{V}) = \ell$, and the gender is x_0. The following then holds.

LEMMA 1. *If* $V \quad \mathbb{R}^{d \quad d}$ *is invertible then, for all* $s \quad \mathbb{R}^d$, $\ell = L(\mathcal{V})$, *and* $\ell \ = L \ (\mathcal{V})$, $Z_+(s, \ell \ ) \overset{\mathrm{d}}{=} Z \ (s \quad 2\ell, \ell \ )$.

PROOF. By Eq. (13), for all $\mathbf{x} \quad \mathbb{R}^d$,

$$Y \ (V\mathbf{x} + \ell + \varepsilon, +1, \ell \ ) \overset{\mathrm{d}}{=} Y \ (V\mathbf{x} \quad \ell + \varepsilon, \quad 1, \ell \ ).$$

The claim follows by taking $\mathbf{x} = V^{\ 1}(s \quad \ell)$. □

As $\mathcal{R}$ does not disclose as much information as the midpoint protocol, by definition, there is no map φ such that $L(v) = \varphi(L \ (v))$ for all $v = (v_0, \mathbf{v}) \quad \mathbb{R}^{d+1}_{\mathbf{0}}$. Hence, there exist extended profiles v, v $\mathbb{R}^{d+1}_{\mathbf{0}}$ such that $v_0 = v_0$ and yet $L(v) = L(v)$. As both $v = (v_0, \mathbf{v}), v = (v_0, \mathbf{v})$ belong to $\mathbb{R}^{d+1}_{\mathbf{0}}$, the supports of $\mathbf{v}, \mathbf{v}$ are non-empty. We consider the following two cases:

Case 1. The supports of $\mathbf{v}, \mathbf{v}$ intersect, i.e., there exists a k $[d]$ such that $v_k = 0$ and $v_k = 0$. In this case, consider a scenario in which $\mathcal{V} = v \quad \bigcup_{1 \quad l \quad d, l=k,} e_l$, where e_l $\mathbb{R}^{d+1}_{\mathbf{0}}$ a vector whose l-th coordinate is 1 and all other coordinates are zero. Clearly, $\mathcal{S} = \mathcal{V} = d$, and $V = [\mathbf{v}_i]_{i \quad [d]}$ is invertible. Let $\ell = L(\mathcal{V})$. By Lemma 1, for all s $\mathbb{R}$,

$$Z_+(s + 2v_0\mathbf{e}_1, \ell) \stackrel{\text{d}}{=} Z(s, \ell), \tag{14}$$

where $\mathbf{e}_1$ $\mathbb{R}^d$ is 1 at coordinate 1 and 0 everywhere else. Similarly, in a scenario in which $\mathcal{V} = v \quad \bigcup_{1 \quad l \quad d, l=k,} e_l$, V is again invertible. Crucially $L(\mathcal{V}) = L(\mathcal{V}) = \ell$, so again by Lemma 1:

$$Z_+(s + 2v_0\mathbf{e}_1, \ell) \stackrel{\text{d}}{=} Z(s, \ell), \tag{15}$$

for all s $\mathbb{R}^d$. Equations (14),(15) imply that, for all s $\mathbb{R}^d$:

$$Z_+(s + \xi\mathbf{e}_1, \ell) \stackrel{\text{d}}{=} Z_+(s, \ell) \tag{16}$$

where ξ $2(v_0 \quad v_0)$. In other words, the obfuscation is *periodic* with respect to the direction $\mathbf{e}_1$.

Observe that for any x $1, +1$ $\mathbb{R}^d$ and any M $\mathbb{R}_+$, we can construct a x $1, +1$ $\mathbb{R}^d$ and a K $\mathbb{N}$ such that (a) x,x differ only at coordinate k $1, 2, \ldots, d$, (b) $v, x \quad x = K\xi$, and (c) $\mathbf{x} \quad \mathbf{x} \;_2 \quad M$. To see this, let K be a large enough integer such that $\frac{K\,\xi}{v_k} > M$. Taking, $x_k = x_k + K\xi/v_k$, and $x_l = x_l$ for all other l in $0, 1, \ldots, d$ yields a x that satisfies the desired properties (a) and (b).

Suppose that the learning protocol $\mathcal{R}$ is applied to $\mathcal{V} = v \quad \bigcup_{1 \quad l \quad d,=k} e_l$ for a user with $x_0 = +1$. Fix a large $M > 0$. For each x and x constructed as above, by (16), the obfuscated values generated by Y have an identical distribution. Hence, irrespectively of how the estimator $\widehat{\mathbf{x}}$ is implemented, either $\mathrm{E}_{x,\mathcal{V}} \quad \widehat{\mathbf{x}}(y, \mathcal{V}) \quad \mathbf{x} \;^2_2$ or $\mathrm{E}_{x',\mathcal{V}} \quad \widehat{\mathbf{x}}(y, \mathcal{V}) \quad \mathbf{x} \;^2_2$ must be $\Omega(M^2)$ which, in turn, implies that $\sup_{x \quad 1 \quad \mathbb{R}^d} \mathrm{E}_{x,\mathcal{V}} \quad \widehat{\mathbf{x}}(y, \mathcal{V}) \quad \mathbf{x} \;^2_2 =$.

Note that, since $\mathbf{v}_j, j$ $\mathcal{S}$, are linearly independent, the matrix $\sum_{j \quad \mathcal{S}} \mathbf{v}_j\mathbf{v}_j^T$ is positive definite and thus invertible. Hence, in contrast to the above setting, the loss (12) of MP in the case of Gaussian noise is finite.

Case 2. The supports of $\mathbf{v}, \mathbf{v}$ are disjoint. In this case v, v are linearly independent and, in particular, there exist $1 \quad k, k \quad d, k = k$, such that $v_k = 0$, $v_{k'} = 0$ while $v_k = 0$, $v_{k'} = 0$. Let $\mathcal{V} = v \quad v \bigcup_{1 \quad l \quad d, l=k, l=k'} e_l$. Then, $\mathcal{V} = d$ and the matrix $V = [\mathbf{v}_j]_{j \quad \mathcal{S}}$ is again invertible. By swapping the positions of $\mathbf{v}$ and $\mathbf{v}$ in matrix V we can show using a similar argument as in Case 1 that for all s $\mathbb{R}^d$:

$$Z_+(s + \xi(\mathbf{e}_1 \quad \mathbf{e}_2), \ell) \stackrel{\text{d}}{=} Z_+(s, \ell) \tag{17}$$

where ξ $2(v_0 \quad v_0)$ and $\ell = L(\mathcal{V})$. *I.e.*, Z_+ is periodic in the direction $\mathbf{e}_1$ $\mathbf{e}_2$. Moreover, for any x $1, +1$ $\mathbb{R}^d$ and any M $\mathbb{R}_+$, we can similarly construct a x $1, +1$ $\mathbb{R}^d$ and a K $\mathbb{N}$ such that (a) x,x differ only at coordinates k, k $1, 2, \ldots, d$, and (b) $v, x \quad x = v, x \quad x = K\xi$, and (c) $\mathbf{x} \quad \mathbf{x} \;_2 \quad M$: the construction adds $K\xi/v_k$ at the k-th coordinate and subtracts $K\xi/v_{k'}$ from the k-th coordinate, where $K > M\max(v_k, v_{k'})/\xi$. A similar argument as in Case 1 can be used to show again that the estimator $\widehat{\mathbf{x}}$ cannot disambiguate between x, x over $\mathcal{V}$, yielding the theorem. □

Algorithm 2 Midpoint Protocol with Sub-Sampling

Analyst's Parameters
$\mathcal{S} \subseteq [M]$, $\mathcal{V} = \{(v_{j0}, \mathbf{v}_j),\ j \in \mathcal{S}\} \subseteq \mathbb{R}^{d+1}_{\mathbf{0}}$
$p = \{(p_1^{x_0}, \ldots, p_{\mathcal{S}}^{x_0}), x_0 \in \{-, +\}\} \subseteq ([0,1] \times [0,1))^{\mathcal{S}}$

User's Parameters
$x_0 \in \{-1, +1\}$, $\mathcal{S}_0 \subseteq \mathcal{S}$, $r = \{r_j, j \in \mathcal{S}_0\} \in \mathbb{R}^{\mathcal{S}_0}$

DISCLOSURE: $\ell = L(\mathcal{V}, p)$
$\rho_j = p_j / p_j^+$, for all $j \in \mathcal{S}$
$\ell_j = (v_{j0}, \rho_j)$, for all $j \in \mathcal{S}$

OBFUSCATION SCHEME: $\substack{\mathcal{S}_R = \mathcal{S}_R(\mathcal{S}_0, x_0, \ell)\\ y = Y(r_{\mathcal{S}_R}, x_0, \ell)}$
$\mathcal{S}_R = \emptyset$, $y = \emptyset$
for all $j \in \mathcal{S}$ **do**
  if $j \in \mathcal{S}_0$ **then**
    $b_j \sim \mathrm{Bern}(\min(1, (\rho_j)^{x_0}))$
    if $b_j = 1$ **then**
      $\mathcal{S}_R = \mathcal{S}_R \cup \{j\}$
      $y = y \cup \{r_j - x_0 v_{j0}\}$
    end if
  end if
end for

ESTIMATOR: $\widehat{\mathbf{x}} = \widehat{\mathbf{x}}(y, (\mathcal{S}_R, y), \mathcal{V})$
Solve $\widehat{\mathbf{x}} = \arg\min_{\mathbf{x} \quad \mathbb{R}^d} \left\{\sum_{j \quad \mathcal{S}_R} (y_j - \langle \mathbf{v}_j, \mathbf{x} \rangle)^2\right\}$

---

6. EXTENSIONS

We have up until now assumed that the analyst solicits ratings for a set of items $\mathcal{S}$ $[M]$, determined by the analyst before the user reveals her feedback. In what follows, we discuss how our analysis can be extended in the case where the user only provides ratings for a subset of these items. We also discuss how the analyst should select $\mathcal{S}$, how a user can repeatedly interact with the analyst, and, finally, how to deal with multiple binary and categorical features.

6.1 Partial Feedback

There are cases of interest where a user may not be able to generate a rating for all items in $\mathcal{S}$. This is especially true when the user needs to spend a non-negligible effort to determine her preferences (examples include rating a feature-length movie, a restaurant, or a book). In these cases, it makes sense to assume that a user may readily provide ratings for only a set $\mathcal{S}_0$ $\mathcal{S}$ (e.g., the movies she has already watched, or the restaurants she has already dined in, etc.).

Our analysis up until now applies when the user rates an arbitrary set $\mathcal{S}$ *selected by the analyst*. As such, it does not readily apply to this case: the set of items $\mathcal{S}_0$ a user rates may depend on the private feature x_0 (e.g., some movies may be more likely to be viewed by men or liberals). In this case, x_0 would be be inferable not only from the ratings she gives, but also *from which items she has rated.*

In this section, we describe how to modify the midpoint protocol to deal with this issue. Intuitively, to ensure her privacy, rather than reporting obfuscated ratings for *all* items she rated (i.e., set $\mathcal{S}_0$), the user can reveal ratings *only for a subset* $\mathcal{S}_R$ *of* $\mathcal{S}_0$. This *sub-sampling* of $\mathcal{S}_0$ can be done so that $\mathcal{S}_R$ has a distribution that is *independent of* x_0, even though $\mathcal{S}_0$ does not. Moreover, to ensure a high estimation accuracy, the user ought to ensure $\mathcal{S}_R$ is as large as possible, subject to the constraint $\mathcal{S}_R \quad \mathcal{S}_0$.

Model. Before we present the modified protocol, we describe our assumption on how $\mathcal{S}_0$ is generated. For each $j \quad [M]$, denote by p_j^+, p_j the probabilities that a user with private feature $+1$ or $\ 1$, respectively, has rated item $j \quad \mathcal{M}$. Observe that, just like the extended profiles v_j, this information can be extracted from a dataset comprising ratings by non privacy-conscious users. Let $p = [(p_j^+, p_j\ )]_{j \quad \mathcal{S}}$ $([0,1] \quad [0,1])^{\ \mathcal{S}}$ be the vector of pairs of probabilities.

We assume that the privacy-conscious user the has rated items in the set $\mathcal{S}_0 \quad \mathcal{S}$, whose distribution is given by the product form[3]:

$$\mathrm{P}_{x,\mathcal{V},p}(\mathcal{S}_0 = \mathcal{A}) = \prod_{j \quad \mathcal{S}} p_j^{x_0} \prod_{j \quad \mathcal{S} \quad \mathcal{A}} (1 \quad p_j^{x_0}), \text{ for all } \mathcal{A} \quad \mathcal{S}. \quad (18)$$

Put differently, items $j \quad \mathcal{S}$ are rated independently, each with a probability $p_j^{x_0}$. Conditioned on $\mathcal{S}_0$, we assume that the user's ratings r_j, $j \quad \mathcal{S}_0$, follow the linear model (7) with Gaussian noise. Note that the distribution of $\mathcal{S}_0$ depends on x_0: e.g., items j for which $p_j^+ > p_j$ are more likely to be rated when $x_0 = +1$.

Midpoint Protocol with Sub-Sampling. We now present a modification of the midpoint protocol, which we refer to as the *midpoint protocol with sub-sampling* (MPSS). MPSS is summarized in Algorithm 2. First, along with the disclosure of the biases $v_{j0}, j \quad \mathcal{S}$, the analyst also discloses the ratios $\rho_j \quad p_j\ /p_j^+$, for $j \quad \mathcal{S}$. Having access to this information, the user sub-samples items from $\mathcal{S}_0$; each item $j \quad \mathcal{S}_0$ is included in the revealed set $\mathcal{S}_R$ independently with probability:

$$\mathrm{P}_{x,\mathcal{V},p}(i \quad \mathcal{S}_R \quad j \quad \mathcal{S}_0) = \min\left(1, (\rho_j)^{x_0}\right). \quad (19)$$

Having constructed $\mathcal{S}_R$, the user reveals ratings for $j \quad \mathcal{S}_R$ after subtracting $x_0 v_{j0}$, as in MP. Finally, the analyst estimates $\widehat{\mathbf{x}}$ through a least squares estimation over the obfuscated feedback, as in MP in the case of Gaussian noise.

To gain some intuition behind the selection of the set $\mathcal{S}_R$, observe by (18) and (19) that, for any $j \quad \mathcal{S}$,

$$\mathrm{P}_{x,\mathcal{V},p}(j \quad \mathcal{S}_R) = p_j^{x_0} \min\left(1, (p_j\ /p_j^+)^{x_0}\right) = \min(p_j^+, p_j\ ). \quad (20)$$

This immediately implies that MPSS is privacy preserving: both the distribution of $\mathcal{S}_R$ and of the obfuscated ratings y do not depend on x_0. In fact, it is easy to see that since $\mathcal{S}_R$ $\mathcal{S}_0$ *any privacy preserving protocol must satisfy* $\mathrm{P}_{x,\mathcal{V},p}(j$ $\mathcal{S}_R) \quad \min(p_j^+, p_j\ )$: indeed, if for example $p_j^+ < p_j$, then a user rating j with probability higher than p_j^+ must have $x_0 = \ 1$ (see our technical report [20] for a formal proof of this statement). As such, MPSS reveals ratings for a set $\mathcal{S}_R$ of *maximal size*, in expectation.

This intuition can be used to establish the optimality of MPSS among a wide class of learning protocols, under (7) (with Gaussian noise) and (18). We can again show that it attains optimal accuracy. Moreover, it also involves a minimal disclosure: a protocol that does not reveal the ratios ρ_j, $j \quad \mathcal{S}$, necessarily rates strictly fewer items than MPSS, in expectation. We provide a formal proof of these statements, as well as a definition of the class of protocols we consider, in our technical report [20].

[3]Here, we slightly abuse notation, e.g., denoting with $p_j^{x_0}$ the parameter p_j^+ when $x_0 = +1$.

6.2 Item Set Selection

Theorem 1 implies that the analyst *cannot* improve the prediction of the private variable x_0 through its choice of $\mathcal{S}$, under the midpoint protocol. In fact, the same is true under any privacy-preserving learning protocol: irrespectively of the analyst's choice for $\mathcal{S}$, the obfuscated feedback y will be statistically independent of x_0.

The analyst can however strategically select $\mathcal{S}$ to effect the accuracy of the estimate of the non-private profile $\mathbf{x}$. Indeed, the analyst should attempt to select a set $\mathcal{S}$ that maximizes the accuracy of the estimator $\widehat{\mathbf{x}}$. In settings where least squares estimator is minimax (e.g., when noise is Gaussian), there are well-known techniques for addressing this problem. Eq. (12) implies that it is natural to select $\mathcal{S}$ by solving

$$\begin{aligned} \text{Maximize:} \quad & F(\mathcal{S}) = \quad \mathrm{tr}[\ \textstyle\sum_{j \quad \mathcal{S}} \mathbf{v}_j \mathbf{v}_j^T)^{\ 1}] \\ \text{subject to:} \quad & \mathcal{S} \quad B, \mathcal{S} \quad [M], \end{aligned} \quad (21)$$

where B is the number of items for which the analyst solicits feedback. The optimization problem (21) is NP-hard, and has been extensively studied in the context of experimental design (see, e.g., Section 7.5 of [6]). The objective function F is commonly referred to as the *A-optimality criterion*. Convex relaxations of (21) exist when $\mathcal{S}$ is a multiset, i.e., when items with the same profile can be presented to the user multiple times, each generating an i.i.d. response [6]. When such repetition is not possible, constant approximation algorithms can be constructed based on the fact that F is increasing and submodular (see e.g., [16]). In particular, given any set $\mathcal{S} \quad [M]$ of items whose profiles are linearly independent, there exists a polynomial time algorithm for maximizing $F(\mathcal{S} \quad \mathcal{S}\ ) \quad F(\mathcal{S}\ )$ subject to $\mathcal{S} \quad B$ within a $1 \quad \frac{1}{e}$ approximation factor [33].

6.3 Repeated Interactions

Our analysis (and, in particular, the optimality of our protocols) persists even when the user repeatedly interacts with the analyst. In particular, the user may return to the service multiple times, each time asked to rate a different set of items $\mathcal{S}^{(k)} \quad [M]$, $k \quad 1$. The selection of the set $\mathcal{S}^{(k)}$ could be *adaptive*, i.e., depend on the obfuscated feedback the user has revealed up until the $k \quad 1$-th time. For each k, the analyst again would apply MP (or MPSS), again disclosing the same information for each $\mathcal{S}^{(k)}$, the only difference being that the estimator $\widehat{\mathbf{x}}$ would be applied to *all* revealed obfuscated ratings $y^{(1)}, ..., y^{(k)}$. This repeated interaction is still perfectly private: the joint distribution of the obfuscated outputs $y^{(k)}$ does not depend on x_0. Moreover, each estimation remains maximally accurate at each interaction, while each disclosure is again minimal.

6.4 Categorical Features

We discuss below how to express categorical features as multiple binary features through binarization, and illustrate how to incorporate both cases in our analysis. The standard approach to incorporating a categorical feature x_0 $1, 2, \ldots, K$ in matrix factorization is through category-specific biases (see, e.g., [25]), i.e., (7) is replaced by

$$r = \ \mathbf{x}, \mathbf{v}_j \ + b_j^{x_0} + \varepsilon_j, \quad j \quad [M] \quad (22)$$

where $b_j^k \quad \mathbb{R}$, $k \quad [K]$ are *category-dependent* biases. Consider a representation of $x_0 \quad [K]$ as a binary vector $\mathbf{x}_0 \quad 1, +1 \;^K$ whose x_0-th coordinate is $+1$, and all other coordinates are $\;1$. I.e., the coordinate $\mathbf{x}_{0k}$ at $k \quad [K]$ is given $+1$ if $k = x0$ and $\;1$ o.w. For $k \quad [K]$, let $\mathbf{b}_{jk} \quad b_j^k/2$ and define $\mu_j \quad \sum_{k \; [K]} b_j^k/2$. Then, observe that (22) is equivalent to

$$r = \; \mathbf{x}, \mathbf{v}_j \; + \sum_{k \; [K]} \mathbf{x}_{0k}\mathbf{b}_{jk} + \mu_j + \varepsilon_j,$$

$$= \; \mathbf{x} \;, \mathbf{v}_j \; + \sum_{k \; [K]} \mathbf{x}_{0k}\mathbf{b}_{jk} + \varepsilon_j, \quad j \quad [M], \qquad (23)$$

where $\mathbf{x} \; = (\mathbf{x}, 1) \quad \mathbb{R}^{d+1}$ and $\mathbf{v}_j = (\mathbf{v}_j, \mu_j) \quad \mathbb{R}^{d+1}$.

Hence, a categorical feature can be incorporated in our analysis as follows. First, given a dataset of ratings by non-privacy conscious users that reveal their categorical feature $x_0 \quad [K]$, the analyst first "binarizes" this feature, constructing a vector $\mathbf{x}_0 \quad 1, 1 \;^K$ for each user. It then performs matrix factorization on the ratings using (23), learning vectors $\mathbf{v}_j \quad \mathbb{R}^{d+1}$, and biases $\mathbf{b}_j = (\mathbf{b}_{jk})_{k \; [K]} \quad \mathbb{R}^K$. A privacy-conscious user subsequently interacts with the analyst using the standard scheme as follows. The analyst discloses the biases $\mathbf{b}_j$ for each $j \quad \mathcal{S}$, and the user reveals $y_j = r_j \quad \sum_{k \; [K]} \mathbf{x}_{0k}\mathbf{b}_{jk}$, $j \quad \mathcal{S}$, where $\mathbf{x}_{0k}$ is her binarized categorical feature. Finally, the analyst infers $\mathbf{x}$ through linear regression over the pairs $(y_j, \mathbf{v}_j)$, $j \quad \mathcal{S}$.

7. EVALUATION

In this section we evaluate our protocols on real-world datasets. Our experiments confirm that MP and MPSS are indeed able to protect the privacy of users against inference algorithms, including non-linear algorithms, with little impact on prediction accuracy.

7.1 Experimental Setup

We study two types of datasets, sparse and dense. In sparse datasets, the set of items a user rates is often correlated with the private feature. This does not happen in dense datasets because all users rate all (or nearly all) items.

Datasets. We evaluate our methods on three datasets: Politics-and-TV, Movielens and Flixster. Politics-and-TV (PTV) [39] is a ratings dataset that includes 5-star ratings of users to 50 TV-shows and, in addition, each user's political affiliation (Democrat or Republican) and gender. To make it dense, we consider only users that rate over 40 items, resulting in 365 users; 280 provide ratings to all 50 TV shows. Movielens[4] and Flixster[5] [21] are movie recommender systems in which users rate movies from a catalog of thousands of movies. Both Movielens and Flixster datasets include user gender. Movielens also includes age groups; we categorize users as *young adults* (ages 18–35), or *adults* (ages 35–65). We preprocessed Movielens and Flixster to consider only users with at least 20 ratings, and items that were rated by at least 20 users. Table 3 summarizes the statistics of these three datasets.

Methodology. Throughout the evaluation, we seek to quantify the privacy risk to a user as well as the impact of obfuscation on the prediction accuracy. To this end, we perform 10-fold cross-validation as follows. We split the users in each dataset into 10 folds. We use 9 folds as a *training set* (serving the purpose of a dataset of non privacy-conscious users in Figure 2) and 1 fold as a *test set* (whose users we treat as privacy-conscious).

We use the training set to (a) compute extended profiles for each item by performing matrix factorization, (b) empirically estimate the probabilities p^+, p for each item, and (c) train multiple classifiers, to be used to infer the private features. We describe the details of our MF implementation and the classifiers we use below.

We split the ratings of each user in the test set into two sets by randomly selecting 70% of the ratings as the first set, and the remaining 30% as the second set. We obfuscate the ratings in the first set using MP, MPSS, and several baselines as described in detail below. The obfuscated ratings are given as input to our classifiers to infer the user's private feature. We further estimate a user's extended profile using the LSE method described in Section 3.3, and use this profile (including both $\mathbf{x}$ and the inferred x_0) to predict her ratings on the second set. For each obfuscation scheme and classification method, we measure the *privacy risk* of the inference through these classifiers using the area under the curve (AUC) metric [18, 19]. Moreover, for each obfuscation scheme, we measure the *prediction accuracy* through the root mean square error (RMSE) of the predicted ratings. We cross-validate our results by computing the AUC and RMSE 10 times, each time with a different fold as a test set, and reporting average values. We note that the AUC ranges from 0.5 (perfect privacy) to 1 (no privacy).

Matrix Factorization. We use 20 iterations of stochastic gradient descent [25] to perform MF on each training set. For each item, feature biases v_{j0} were computed as the half distance between the average item ratings per each private feature value. The remaining features $\mathbf{v}_j$ were computed through matrix factorization. We computed optimal regularization parameters and the dimension $d = 20$ through an additional 10-fold cross validation.

Privacy Risk Assessment. We apply several standard classification methods to infer the private feature from the training ratings, namely Multinomial Naïve Bayes [45], Logistic Regression (LR), non-linear Support Vector Machines (SVM) with a Radial Basis Function (RBF) kernel, as well as the LSE (6). The input to the LR, NB and SVM methods comprises the ratings of all items provided by the user as well as zeros for movies not rated, while LSE operates only on the ratings that the user provides. As SVM scales quadraticaly with the number of users, we could not execute it on our largest dataset (Flixster, c.f. Table 3).

Obfuscation Schemes. When using MP, the obfuscated rating may not be an integer value, and may even be outside of the range of rating values which is expected by a recommender system. Therefore, we consider a variation of MP that rounds the rating value to an integer in the range [1, 5]. Given a non-integer obfuscated rating r, which is between two integers $k = \; r \;$ and $k + 1$, we perform rounding by assigning the rating k with probability $r \;\; k$ and the rating $k+1$ with probability $1 \;\; (r \;\; k)$, which on expectation gives the desired rating r. Ratings higher than 5 and those lower than 1 are truncated to 5 and 1, respectively. We refer to this process as *rounding*, and denote the obfuscation scheme

[4]http://www.grouplens.org/node/73
[5]http://www.sfu.ca/~sja25/datasets/

Dataset	Private feature	Users	Items	Ratings
PTV	All	365	50	18K
	Gender (F:M)	2.7:1	-	2.7:1
	Politics (R:D)	1:1.4	-	1:1.4
Movielens	All	6K	3K	1M
	Gender (F:M)	1:2.5	-	1:3
	Age (Y:A)	1:1.3	-	1:1.6
Flixster	All	26K	9921	5.6M
	Gender (F:M)	1.7:1	-	1.5:1

Figure 3: Statistics of the datasets used for evaluation. The ratios represent the class skew Females:Males (F:M) for gender, Young:Adult(Y:A) for age and Republican:Democrats (R:D) for political affiliation.

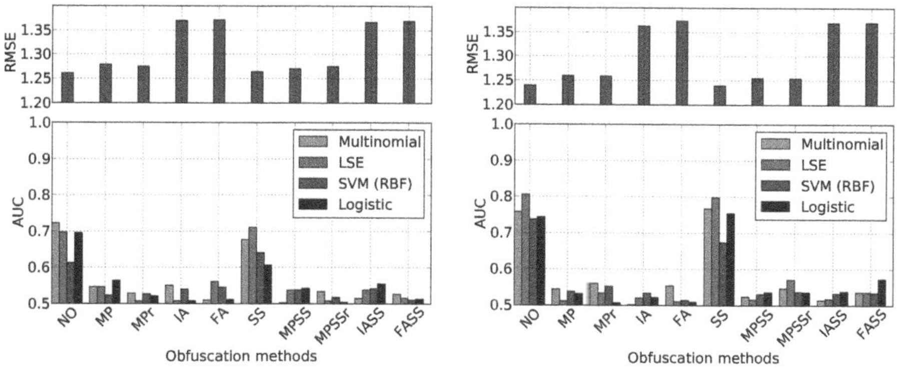

(a) PTV - Gender

(b) PTV - Politics

Figure 4: Privacy risk and prediction accuracy on PTV, obtained using four classifiers and obfuscation schemes (NO-No obfuscation, MP - Midpoint Protocol, r - Rounding, IA - Item Average, FA - Feature Average, SS - Sub-Sampling). The proposed protocol (MP) is robust to privacy attacks with hardly any loss in predictive power.

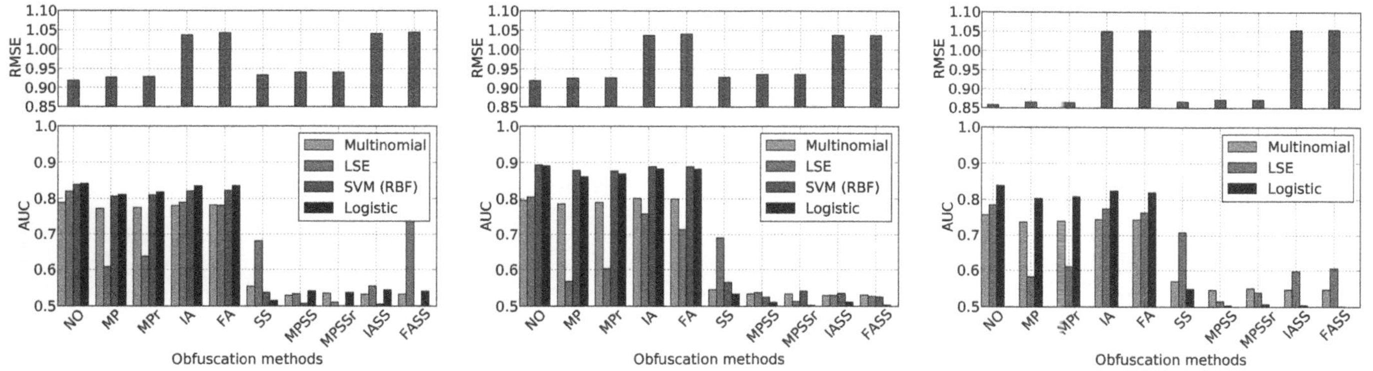

(a) Movielens - Gender

(b) Movielens - Age

(c) Flixster - Gender

Figure 5: Privacy risk and prediction accuracy on Movielens and Flixster (sparse datasets), obtained using four classifiers and obfuscation schemes (NO-No obfuscation, MP - Midpoint Protocol, r - Rounding, IA - Item Average, FA - Feature Average, SS - Sub-Sampling). The proposed protocol (MPSS) is robust to privacy attacks without harming predictive power.

as MPr for midpoint protocol with rounding and MPSSr for midpoint protocol with sub-sampling and rounding.

We also consider two alternative methods for obfuscation. First, the *item average* (IA) scheme replaces a user's rating with the average rating of the item, computed from the training set. Second, the *feature average* (FA) scheme replaces the user's rating with the average rating provided by the feature classes (e.g., males and females), each with probability 0.5.

Finally, we evaluate each of the above obfuscation schemes, i.e., MP, MPr, IA and FA, together with sub-sampling (SS). As a baseline, we also evaluated the privacy risk and the prediction accuracy when *no obfuscation* scheme is used (NO).

7.2 Experimental Results

Dense Dataset. We begin by evaluating the obfuscation schemes on the dense PTV dataset using its two users' features (gender and political affiliation), illustrated in Figures 4a and 4b, respectively. Each figure shows the privacy risk (AUC) computed using the 4 inference methods, and the prediction accuracy (RMSE) on applying different obfuscation schemes.

Both figures clearly show that MP successfully mitigates the privacy risk (AUC is around 0.5) whereas the prediction accuracy is hardly impacted (2% increase in RMSE). This illustrates that MP attains excellent privacy in practice, and that our modeling assumptions are reasonable: there is little correlation to the private feature after the category bias is removed. Indeed, strong correlations not captured by (7) could manifest as failure to block inference after obfuscation, especially through the non-linear SVM classifier. This is clearly not the case, indicating that any dependence on the private feature not captured by (7) is quite weak.

Adding rounding (MPr), which is essential for real-world deployment of MP, has very little effect on both the AUC and RMSE. Though IA and FA are successful in mitigating the privacy risk, they are suboptimal in terms of prediction. They severely impact the prediction accuracy, increasing the RMSE by roughly 9%. Finally, since this is a dense dataset, there is little correlation between the private feature and the

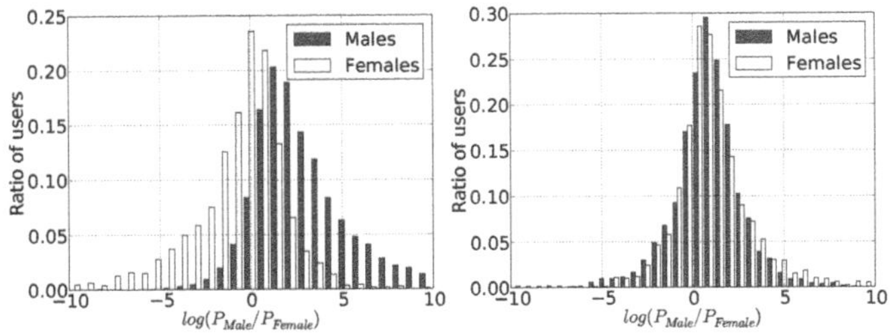

Figure 6: Distribution of inference probabilities for males and females using Movielens dataset and logistic regression (left) before obfuscation and (right) after MPSS obfuscation.

set of items a user rates. Therefore, MP without SS suffices to mitigate the privacy risk.

Sparse Datasets. Next, we investigate the effect of partial feedback by evaluating our obfuscation schemes on the Movielens and Flixster datasets. In these datasets, in addition to the rating value, the set of items rated by a user can be correlated with her private feature. The results for obfuscation on Movielens and Flixster are in Figure 5.

For all three datasets, we observe that MP successfully blocks inference by LSE, but fails against the other three methods. This is expected, as the items rated are correlated to the private feature, and LSE is the only method among the four that is insensitive to this set. For the same reason, SS *alone* defeats all methods *except* LSE, which still detects the feature from the unobfuscated ratings (AUC 0.69–0.71). Finally, MPSS and MPSSr have excellent performance across the board, both in terms of privacy risk (AUC 0.5–0.55) and impact on prediction accuracy (up to 5%). In contrast, IA and FA significantly increase the RMSE (around 15%). We stress that, in these datasets, items are not rated independently as postulated by (18). Nevertheless, the results above indicate that MPSS blocks inference in practice *even when this assumption is relaxed.*

We further quantify the impact of sub-sampling in terms of the number of items that are not reported to the analyst in a partial feedback setting. To this end, we compute the ratio of items excluded in the feedback reported by the user as a result of applying SS. We found that for the dense PTV dataset, 80% of the users include all their ratings in their partial feedback, and the remaining 20% exclude at most 5% of their ratings. For the sparse Flixster and Movielens datasets, 50% of the users do not include 10% and 23% of their ratings, respectively. All users include at least 50% of their ratings, hence the prediction accuracy does not suffer with MPSS obfuscation.

Overall, these results indicate that both MP and MPSS are highly effective in real-world datasets – they mitigate the privacy risk while incurring very small impact on the prediction accuracy. Moreover, these obfuscation schemes work well even when facing non-linear inference methods, such as SVM, indicating that in practice, they eliminate any dependency between the ratings and the private feature.

Privacy Risk. To further illustrate how obfuscation defeats the inference of a private feature, we focus of the effect of obfuscation on logistic regression over the Movielens Gender dataset. Figures 6(a) and 6(b) plot the distribution of $\log(P_{Male}/P_{Female})$ (a) before obfuscation and (b) after obfuscation with MPSS. Here, P_{Male} and P_{Female} are the posterior probabilities for the two classes as obtained through logistic regression. Prior to obfuscation, there is a clear separation between the distributions of males and females, enabling successful gender inference (AUC 0.82 as shown in Figure 5a). However, after obfuscation, the two distributions become indistinguishable (AUC 0.54).

Privacy-Accuracy Tradeoff. Finally, we study the privacy-prediction accuracy tradeoff by applying an obfuscation scheme on an item rating with probability α, and releasing the real rating with probability 1 α. We vary the value of α between 0 and 1 in steps of 0.1, that is, when $\alpha = 0$ no obfuscation is performed, and $\alpha = 1$ means that all ratings are obfuscated. For each α, we measure the RMSE as well as the AUC of LSE.

Figure 7 shows the resulting RMSE-AUC tradeoff curves for MPSS, MPSSr and the two baseline obfuscation schemes with sub-sampling. The figure shows that MPSS and MPSSr provide the best privacy-accuracy tradeoff (the slopes of the curves are almost flat), and consistently obtain better prediction accuracy (lower RMSE) for the same privacy risk (inference AUC) than all other methods.

8. CONCLUSION

We have introduced a framework for reasoning about privacy, accuracy, and dislosure tradeoffs in matrix factorization. This naturally raises the question of how these tradeoffs extend to other statistical or prediction tasks. An orthogonal direction to the one we pursued, when seeking a mininal disclosure, is to investigate schemes that are not perfectly private. It would be interesting to investigate, e.g., privacy-dislosure tradeoffs, rather than the usual privacy-accuracy tradeoffs one encounters in literature. For example, it is not clear whether one can construct protocols in which the distribution of the obfuscated output differs accross users with opposite private attribute by, e.g., an ϵ factor, but leak less information than MP: such protocols could, e.g., disclose a quantized version of the biases for each item.

9. REFERENCES

[1] R. Agrawal and R. Srikant. Privacy-preserving data mining. *ACM Sigmod Record*, 2000.

[2] S. Banerjee, N. Hegde, and L. Massoulié. The price of privacy in untrusted recommendation engines. In *Allerton*, 2012.

[3] S. Bhagat, I. Rozenbaum, and G. Cormode. Applying link-based classification to label blogs. In *WebKDD*, 2007.

[4] S. Bhagat, U. Weinsberg, S. Ioannidis, and N. Taft. Recommending with an agenda: Active learning of private attributes using matrix factorization, 2013. `http://arxiv.org/abs/1311.6802`.

[5] B. Bi, M. Shokouhi, M. Kosinski, and T. Graepel. Inferring the demographics of search users. In *WWW*, 2013.

[6] S. Boyd and L. Vandenberghe. *Convex Optimization.* Cambridge University Press, 2004.

[7] F. Calmon and N. Fawaz. Privacy against statistical inference. In *Allerton*, 2012.

[8] E. Candès and T. Tao. The power of convex relaxation: Near-optimal matrix completion. *Information Theory, IEEE Transactions on*, 2010.

[9] E. J. Candès and B. Recht. Exact matrix completion via convex optimization. *Foundations of Computational mathematics*, 2009.

[10] K. Chaudhuri, C. Monteleoni, and A. D. Sarwate. Differentially private empirical risk minimization. *JMLR*, 2011.

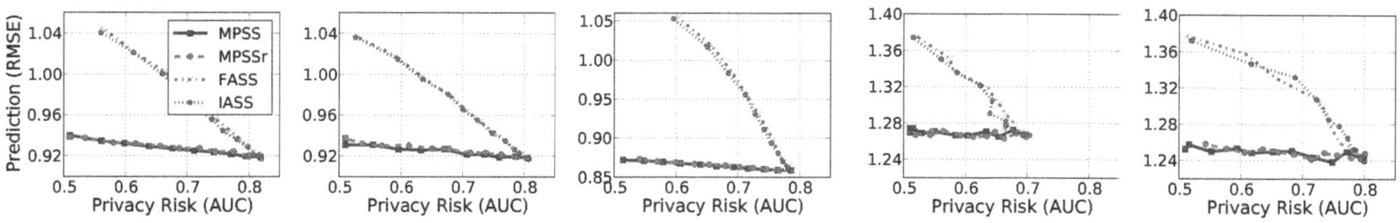

(a) Movielens Gender (b) Movielens Age (c) Flixster Gender (d) PTV Gender (e) PTV Politics

Figure 7: Prediction accuracy (RMSE) vs. privacy risk (LSE AUC) tradeoff for varying levels of obfuscation. Our proposed schemes (MPSS and MPSSr) have little impact on prediction accuracy as privacy is increased, whereas the prediction accuracy worsens dramatically under the baseline schemes.

[11] K. Chaudhuri and A. D. Sarwate. A near-optimal algorithm for differentially-private principal components. *JMLR*, 2013.

[12] J. C. Duchi, M. I. Jordan, and M. J. Wainwright. Local privacy and statistical minimax rates. In *FOCS*, 2013.

[13] C. Dwork. Differential privacy. In *ICALP*. 2006.

[14] C. Dwork and J. Lei. Differential privacy and robust statistics. In *STOC*, 2009.

[15] C. Dwork, F. Mcsherry, K. Nissim, and A. Smith. Calibrating noise to sensitivity in private data analysis. In *TCC*, 2006.

[16] S. Friedland and S. Gaubert. Submodular spectral functions of principal submatrices of a hermitian matrix, extensions and applications. *Linear Algebra and its Applications*, 2013.

[17] S. Goldwasser and M. Bellare. *Lecture Notes on Cryptography*. MIT, 2001.

[18] J. A. Hanley and B. J. McNeil. The meaning and use of the area under a receiver operating characteristic (ROC) curve. *Radiology*, 743:29–36, 1982.

[19] T. Hastie, R. Tibshirani, and J. Friedman. *The Elements of Statistical Learning: Data Mining, Inference, and Prediction*. Springer, 2nd edition, 2009.

[20] S. Ioannidis, A. Montanari, U. Weinsberg, S. Bhagat, N. Fawaz, and N. Taft. Privacy tradeoffs in predictive analytics, 2014. `http://arxiv.org/abs/1403.8084`

[21] M. Jamali and M. Ester. A matrix factorization technique with trust propagation for recommendation in social networks. In *RecSys*, 2010.

[22] S. P. Kasiviswanathan, H. K. Lee, K. Nissim, S. Raskhodnikova, and A. Smith. What can we learn privately? *SIAM Journal on Computing*, 2011.

[23] R. Keshavan, A. Montanari, and S. Oh. Matrix completion from noisy entries. *JMLR*, 2010.

[24] Y. Koren. Factorization meets the neighborhood: a multifaceted collaborative filtering model. In *KDD*, 2008.

[25] Y. Koren, R. Bell, and C. Volinsky. Matrix factorization techniques for recommender systems. *IEEE Computer*, 2009.

[26] M. Kosinski, D. Stillwell, and T. Graepel. Private traits and attributes are predictable from digital records of human behavior. *PNAS*, 2013.

[27] E. L. Lehmann and G. Casella. *Theory of Point Estimation*. Springer, 2nd edition, 1998.

[28] A. Machanavajjhala, A. Korolova, and A. D. Sarma. Personalized social recommendations - accurate or private? *PVLDB*, 2011.

[29] A. Makhdoumi and N. Fawaz. Privacy-utility tradeoff under statistical uncertainty. In *Allerton*, 2013.

[30] F. McSherry and I. Mironov. Differentially private recommender systems: building privacy into the net. In *KDD*, 2009.

[31] A. Mislove, B. Viswanath, K. P. Gummadi, and P. Druschel. You are who you know: Inferring user profiles in Online Social Networks. In *WSDM*, 2010.

[32] A. Narayanan and V. Shmatikov. Robust de-anonymization of large sparse datasets. In *OAKLAND*, 2008.

[33] G. Nemhauser, L. Wolsey, and M. Fisher. An analysis of approximations for maximizing submodular set functions–i. *Mathematical Programming*, 14(1):265–294, 1978.

[34] S. R. Oliveira and O. R. Zaiane. Privacy preserving clustering by data transformation. In *SBBD*, pages 304–318, 2003.

[35] J. Otterbacher. Inferring gender of movie reviewers: exploiting writing style, content and metadata. In *CIKM*, 2010.

[36] D. Rao, D. Yarowsky, A. Shreevats, and M. Gupta. Classifying latent user attributes in twitter. In *SMUC*, 2010.

[37] D. Rebollo-Monedero, J. Forne, and J. Domingo-Ferrer. From t-closeness-like privacy to postrandomization via information theory. *IEEE TKDE*, 2010.

[38] B. I. P. Rubinstein, P. L. Bartlett, L. Huang, , and N. Taft. Learning in a large function space: Privacy-preserving mechanisms for svm learning. *Journal of Privacy and Confidentiality*, 2012.

[39] S. Salamatian, A. Zhang, F. du Pin Calmon, S. Bhamidipati, N. Fawaz, B. Kveton, P. Oliveira, and N. Taft. How to hide the elephant-or the donkey-in the room: Practical privacy against statistical inference for large data. In *GlobalSIP*, 2013.

[40] L. Sankar, S. R. Rajagopalan, and H. V. Poor. Utility-privacy tradeoff in databases: An information-theoretic approach. *IEEE Trans. Information Forensics and Security*, 2013.

[41] A. Smith. Privacy-preserving statistical estimation with optimal convergence rates. In *STOC*, 2011.

[42] H. Strasser. Local asymptotic minimax properties of Pitman estimates. *Zeitschrift für Wahrscheinlichkeitstheorie und Verwandte Gebiete*, 60(2):223–247, 1982.

[43] J. Vaidya, C. W. Clifton, and Y. M. Zhu. *Privacy Preserving Data Mining*. Springer, 2006.

[44] S. L. Warner. Randomized response: A survey technique for eliminating evasive answer bias. *Journal of the American Statistical Association*, 1965.

[45] U. Weinsberg, S. Bhagat, S. Ioannidis, and N. Taft. Blurme: Inferring and obfuscating user gender based on ratings. In *RecSys*, 2012.

[46] H. Yamamoto. A source coding problem for sources with additional outputs to keep secret from the receiver or wiretappers. *IEEE Trans. Inform. Theory*, 1983.

An Online Auction Framework for Dynamic Resource Provisioning in Cloud Computing

Weijie Shi
Dept. of Computer Science
The University of Hong Kong
wjshi@cs.hku.hk

Linquan Zhang
Dept. of Computer Science
University of Calgary
linqzhan@ucalgary.ca

Chuan Wu
Dept. of Computer Science
The University of Hong Kong
cwu@cs.hku.hk

Zongpeng Li
Dept. of Computer Science
University of Calgary
zongpeng@ucalgary.ca

Francis C.M. Lau
Dept. of Computer Science
The University of Hong Kong
fcmlau@cs.hku.hk

ABSTRACT

Auction mechanisms have recently attracted substantial attention as an efficient approach to pricing and resource allocation in cloud computing. This work, to the authors' knowledge, represents the first online combinatorial auction designed in the cloud computing paradigm, which is general and expressive enough to both (a) optimize system efficiency across the temporal domain instead of at an isolated time point, and (b) model dynamic provisioning of heterogeneous Virtual Machine (VM) types in practice. The final result is an online auction framework that is truthful, computationally efficient, and guarantees a competitive ratio $\sim e+\frac{1}{e-1} \simeq 3.30$ in social welfare in typical scenarios. The framework consists of three main steps: (1) a tailored primal-dual algorithm that decomposes the long-term optimization into a series of independent one-shot optimization problems, with an additive loss of $\frac{1}{e-1}$ in competitive ratio, (2) a randomized auction sub-framework that applies primal-dual optimization for translating a centralized cooperative social welfare approximation algorithm into an auction mechanism, retaining a similar approximation ratio while adding truthfulness, and (3) a primal-dual update plus dual fitting algorithm for approximating the one-shot optimization with a ratio λ close to e. The efficacy of the online auction framework is validated through theoretical analysis and trace-driven simulation studies. We are also in the hope that the framework, as well as its three independent modules, can be instructive in auction design for other related problems.

Categories and Subject Descriptors

C.4 [**Performance of Systems**]: Design studies; Modeling techniques; I.1.2 [**Algorithms**]: Analysis of algorithms

SIGMETRICS'14, June 16–20, 2014, Austin, Texas, USA.
Copyright 2014 ACM 978-1-4503-2789-3/14/06 ...$15.00.
http://dx.doi.org/10.1145/2591971.2591980 .

General Terms

Algorithms; Design; Economics

Keywords

Cloud Computing; Combinatorial Auction; Resource Allocation; Pricing; Online Algorithms; Truthful Mechanisms

1. INTRODUCTION

Cloud computing has recently emerged as a new computing paradigm that enables prompt and on-demand access to computing resources. As exemplified in Amazon EC2 [1] and Microsoft Azure [4], cloud providers invest substantially into their datacenter infrastructure, providing a virtually unlimited "sea" of CPU, RAM and storage resources to cloud users, often assisted by virtualization technologies. The elastic and on-demand nature of cloud computing assists cloud users to meet their dynamic and fluctuating demands with minimal management overhead, while the cloud ecosystem as a whole achieves *economies of scale* through cost amortization. Currently, most cloud providers adopt a fixed price policy and charge users a fixed amount per-VM usage. For example, Table 1 shows the available VM types at Amazon EC2, and their hourly prices at different datacenters. Despite their apparent simplicity, fixed-price policies are inherently lack of market agility and efficiency, failing to rapidly adapt to realtime demand-supply relation changes. Consequently, overpricing and underpricing routinely occur, which either dispel or undercharge the users, jeopardizing overall system social welfare as well as the providers' revenue.

Table 1: Amazon EC2 VM Instances

VM Type	CPU*	RAM	Disk	Virginia	Ireland	Tokyo
m1.medium	2	3.75GB	410GB	$0.120	$0.130	$0.175
m1.large	4	7.5GB	840GB	$0.240	$0.260	$0.350
m1.xlarge	8	15GB	1.68TB	$0.480	$0.520	$0.700
c1.medium	5	1.7GB	350GB	$0.145	$0.165	$0.185
c1.xlarge	20	7GB	1.68TB	$0.580	$0.660	$0.740
m2.2xlarge	13	34.2GB	850GB	$0.820	$0.920	$1.101

* EC2 compute units

Towards effectively discovering the market value of VMs, auction-based mechanisms have been at the focal point of recent literature on cloud resource allocation and pricing [9,

28]. For example, Spot Instance [2] is a first-step attempt to apply the auction mechanism on Amazon EC2, which was enhanced by subsequent work [24, 28]. A series of recent work further study auction mechanism design in cloud markets from different perspectives [27, 29, 25]. Unfortunately, all existing cloud auction mechanisms either consider one-round auctions only, or model VMs as type-oblivious commodities and fail to account for the providers' ability to dynamically assemble VMs.

[Cloud auctions should be online.] Real-world cloud resource transactions happen either when customer demands arrive or cloud resources become available, and hence is modelled more naturally by an online auction that incorporates the time dimension. Most cloud computing customers, enterprise or individual, are on a pre-allocated budget for a given time period (*e.g.*, a year or a month like that in an ad-auction [7]). Thus a customer's purchase desire drastically declines over time, which needs to be considered for a practical auction mechanism. However, most existing cloud auctions focus on a single-round auction only, and ignore such temporal correlation in decision making [29].

[Cloud auctions should be combinatorial.] A cloud computing job in practice often demands a bundle of heterogenous VM instances for its successful execution, and hence a cloud auction is naturally a combinatorial auction. For example, a social game application that consists of a front-end web server layer, a load balancing layer and a back-end data storage layer is best served by a combination of VMs that are intended for communication-intensive, computation-intensive and storage-intensive tasks, respectively. Such combinatorial VM auctions represent a dramatic departure of most existing VM auction designs that assume VMs are type-oblivious commodities, in that all VMs are essentially of the same type, and hence are substitutable or substitutable up to a simple multiplicative factor. Embracing heterogeneous VM types in the model further brings about the opportunity of considering *dynamic resource provisioning*: decisions on VM assembling, which organizes the CPU, RAM and Disk resource pools into typed VM instances, are no longer made randomly *a priori* [9], but made dynamically upon receiving user bids. Dynamic resource provisioning enables higher efficiency in cloud resource utilization, higher seller revenue for the provider, and higher social welfare for the entire cloud system.

This work generalizes and subsumes existing literature on cloud auctions by designing the first online combinatorial auction in which VMs of heterogenous types are allocated in multiple consecutive time slots. The final result is an online auction framework that simultaneously guarantees the following properties. (i) Truthfulness, the holy grail of auction mechanism design. It ensures that economically-motivated selfish buyers are automatically elicited to reveal their true valuations of the VMs they demand, in the bids submitted. This simplifies analysis of the resulting auction in theory, and increases the predicability of auction outcomes in practice. (ii) Combinatorial auctions, supporting heterogeneous VM types located at different datacenters. Besides heterogeneity in their types, another dimension of VM diversity may arise due to their geographical locations (assuming multiple datacenters). A combinatorial auction is hence necessary. (iii) Dynamic resource provisioning. The number of instances of each VM type is not predefined, but dynamically adjusted as part of the auction mechanism, tailored to realtime user demand. (iv) Online auction: In commercial cloud platforms, auctions are executed repeatedly and the prices change termly. Each user is subject to a practical budget limitation for a given time period. Our online auction models a long time auction over multiple rounds that are coupled together by customer budgets. A competitive ratio of $e + \frac{1}{1-e} \simeq 3.30$ is guaranteed in typical scenarios, *i.e.*, our online auction achieves a long-term social welfare that is at least a $\frac{1}{3.30}$ fraction of the offline optimum.

Our proposed online auction framework consists of three main modules: (A) translating online optimization into a series of one-round optimization problems, (B) translating an approximation algorithm for one-round optimization into a truthful auction, and (C) designing an effective approximation algorithm for one-round optimization.

First, we formulate a linear integer program that characterizes the long-term social welfare optimization problem in the cloud market for VMs, and formulate the dual LP of its LP relaxation (without the integer constraints). A tailored primal-dual algorithm iteratively adjusts a dual variable corresponding to each customer's budget, acting as a shadow price that signals how "tight" the latter is. A series of one-round combinatorial VM auctions are then executed under a fixed shadow price vector. Such primal-dual decoupling of the auction rounds admits a rather intuitive interpretation: the algorithm strikes to avoid prematurely depleting a user's budget, and gives higher priority to cloud customers with low budget pressures during each auction round. As a result, we prove that the decomposition introduces an additive loss to the competitive ratio bounded by $\frac{1}{e-1}$.

Second, for each one-round combinatorial auction problem, we employ a randomized auction sub-framework, which exploits the underlying packing property of one-round social welfare maximization, and translates any centralized co-operative approximation algorithm into an auction, inheriting the same approximation ratio while adding truthfulness. At the core of this translation is a primal-dual optimization based decomposition technique that decomposes an optimal fractional solution to one-round social welfare maximization into a convex combination of integral solutions, recently developed in the literature of theoretical computer science [13], and successfully applied in the literature of computer networking [30]. We also propose a new technique which can significantly improve the performance of this translation.

Third, we design a specific approximation algorithm for one-round VM allocation, by applying iterative primal-dual solution updates followed by dual fitting. The resulting algorithm is polynomial-time computable, and guarantees an approximation ratio λ that approaches e in practical scenarios. Combining all three modules together, the overall competitive ratio of the resulting online auction framework is bounded by $e + \frac{1}{e-1} \simeq 3.30$ in typical scenarios. We hope that the online auction framework proposed in this work, as well as its three components, may shed light to the design of auction mechanisms in related problem settings.

In the rest of the paper, we discuss related work in Sec. 2, and define the problem model in Sec. 3. Sec. 4 and Sec. 5 present the online algorithm framework, the auction algorithm and the single round allocation algorithm. Simulations are presented in Sec. 6. Sec. 7 concludes the paper.

2. RELATED WORK

Resource allocation in computing and communication systems is a classic problem that has been extensively studied, including from a game theoretical view by analyzing the incentive compatibility of the allocation algorithm [11] [15]. An alternative approach is designing pricing mechanisms with maximized social welfare [19]. Auctions are mechanisms that combine these two approaches and simultaneously target both truthfulness and economic efficiency. Classic applications of auctions are found in a wide range of research areas, such as network bandwidth allocation [26] and wireless spectrum allocation [30].

The celebrated VCG mechanism [23] is a well known type of auctions. It is essentially the only type of auction that simultaneously guarantees both truthfulness and absolute economic efficiency (social welfare maximization), through calculating the optimal allocation and a carefully designed pricing rule. However, when the underlying allocation problem is NP-hard, which is common for combinatorial auctions [20], VCG becomes computationally infeasible. When polynomial-time approximation algorithms are applied to solving the underlying social welfare maximization problem, VCG loses its truthfulness property [17]. One usually needs to custom design a payment rule to work in concert with the approximation algorithm at hand, to achieve truthfulness; for example, this can be done by exploiting the concept of *critical bids* [14]. Another relatively new alternative is to resort to the LP decomposition technique [13], as done in this work, which is universally applicable to problems with a packing or covering structure.

Recently, a series of auction mechanisms are designed for VM allocation in cloud computing. Wang *et al.* [24] apply the critical value method, and derive a mechanism that is collusion-resistant, an important property in practice. Yet their work, like many others, considers only one-round auctions; and their algorithm has a competitive ratio $O(\sqrt{k})$, where k is the number of VM instances. Zaman and Grosu [27] study the modeling of VM provisioning, but their model does not include dynamic VM assembling. Shanmuganathan *et al.* [21] introduce the concept of *computing resources bundles* in VM allocation. Zhang *et al.* [29] is among the first to study dynamic VM provisioning, and designs a truthful single round auction using the LP decomposition method. However, our work is more advanced than theirs in two aspects: (1) We consider the problem over a period of time, instead of just one round, and serve cloud users in an online manner. Our mechanism more closely resembles a real-world cloud market in practice. (2) We not only apply but also propose improvements to the decomposing method, which can improve the performance of the online auction in practice.

Extending single round truthful auctions into online auctions in a straightforward way usually breaks the truthfulness property [18]. The lack of future information brings a key challenge in pursuing truthfulness. For example, the VCG auction does not directly work in the online setting, since the optimal allocation for the future cannot be calculated, even given unlimited computational resources. A known technique for achieving truthfulness in online auctions is based on the concept of of a *supply curve* [12], as applied by Zhang *et al.* [28] in their design of an online cloud auction algorithm. The bidding language and the user characteristic proposed in their work are novel, and capture the heterogeneous demands in cloud market. However, they only consider a single type of VMs, significantly simplifying the underlying social welfare maximization. In absence of multiple VM types, their model naturally ignores the dynamic provisioning problem. Wang *et al.* propose an online auction for cloud markets [25], and their model also focuses on one type of VMs only.

There have been some proposals considering bandwidth allocation in datacenters. Ballani *et al.* [5] propose Oktopus, a system that provides virtual network abstractions to the cloud users. Bansal *et al.* [6] discuss the allocation of VMs while considering network congestion. Meng *et al.* [16] take both intra- and inter-datacenter traffic into consideration in deciding the placement of VMs. Allocating resources including both network bandwidth and computing resources, such as CPU and storage, makes the problem more difficult than focusing on only one of them. We leave the possible discussions on bandwidth auctions as future work.

3. PROBLEM MODEL

3.1 The Cloud System

We consider a cloud spanning Q geographically distributed datacenters, each with a pool of R types of resources including CPU, RAM, and disk storage that can be dynamically assembled into M different types of virtual machines (VMs), for lease to cloud users. Let $[X]$ denote the integer set $\{1, 2, \ldots, X\}$. Each VM of type $m \in [M]$ is constituted by $\alpha_{m,r}$ units of type-r resource, for all $r \in [R]$. There are N users of the cloud system, which request VMs of different types to execute their jobs. The cloud provider acts as the auctioneer and leases VMs to the users through auctions. The system runs in a time-slotted fashion within a span of $1, 2, \ldots, T$, where T is a potentially large number. We suppose the available amounts of resources at each datacenter are time-varying, *i.e.*, there are $A_{q,r}^{(t)}$ units of type-r resource in datacenter q at time $t \in [T]$, whose value may change from one time slot to another.[1] In each time slot, one round of the auctions is carried out, where the cloud provider decides the VM allocation for the current time slot based on user bids. The terms *time slot* and *round* are used interchangeably.

The N cloud users are bidders in the auctions, each submitting a bid containing K optional bundles in each round. A bundle consists of a list of desired quantities of VMs of different types, as well as the bidder's valuation for the bundle. Specifically, let $d_{n,k,m,q}^{(t)}$ denote the number of type-m VMs in datacenter q that user n specifies in its k-th bundle in time slot t, and $b_{n,k}^{(t)}$ be its valuation for this k-th bundle in t. The k-th bundle in the bid of user n in the auction at t is described by a $(M \times Q + 1)$-tuple of elements $d_{n,k,m,q}^{(t)}, \forall m \in [M], \forall q \in [Q]$, and $b_{n,k}^{(t)}$. The cases where a user may join and leave (intermittent bidding) or may bid a smaller number of bundles than K, are all subsumed by our bid model by allowing empty bundles in the bids.

In each auction, upon receiving users' bids, the cloud provider computes its resource allocation and produces the auction results, $y_{n,k}^{(t)} \in \{0, 1\}, \forall n \in [N], \forall k \in [K]$, where $y_{n,k}^{(t)}$ is 1 if user n wins bundle k and 0 otherwise, as well as user n's payment $\Pi_n^{(t)}$, for actually acquiring VMs in its winning

[1]The varying amounts of resources may be caused by removal or addition of servers, due to failure and recovery, or potential reservation or release of resources for special purposes, *e.g.*, as part of a hybrid cloud of an enterprise.

Table 2: Notation

N	# of users	[X]	integer set $\{1, 2, \ldots, X\}$
T	# of time slots	R	# of resource types
M	# of VM types	Q	# of datacenters

K	# of optional bundles in each bid
α_m^r	amount of resource r in each type-m VM
$A_{q,r}^{(t)}$	available resource r at datacenter q at time t
$b_{n,k}^{(t)}$	user n's valuation for its kth bundle at t
$d_{n,k,m,q}^{(t)}$	# of type-m VM at dc q in n's kth bundle at t
$c_{n,k,r,q}^{(t)}$	amount of resource r at dc q in n's kth bundle at t
B_n	user n's total budget
$y_{n,k}^{(t)}$	user n wins its kth bundle at time t or not
$y_{n,k}^{(t)F}$	optimal fractional solution
$y_{n,k}^{(t)l}$	an integer solution to (3)
$\Pi_n^{(t)}$	user n's payment at time t
$\Pi_n^{(t)F}$	user n's payment at time t under fractional VCG
$\Pi_n^{(t)l}$	user n's payment at time t under allocation $\mathbf{y}^{(t)l}$
β_l	probability to choose integer solution $\mathbf{y}^{(t)l}$
$u_n^{(t)}$	user n's utility at time t
ν	the competitive ratio of $\mathcal{A}_{round}$
λ	the approximation ratio of Alg. 2
$w_{n,k}^{(t)}$	the reduced valuation of n's kth bundle at time t
B_{max}	max ratio: a single bundle bid / a user's budget
γ	$(1 + B_{max})^{1/B_{max}}$

bundle. We assume that a user can win at most one bundle among its K optional bundles in each round of the auctions (given that any need for combining two or more bundles can be expressed as a separate bundle already). In addition, the VM demands in each bundle cannot be supplied partially, *i.e.*, the cloud provider either provides all the required VMs in a bundle to the bidder or rejects the bundle.

Let $u_n^{(t)}$ denote the utility function of user n in time slot t, which is decided by its valuations of the bundles and its payment at t. We will present the concrete form of the utility function in Sec. 5. We assume user n has a total budget B_n, which is a bound of its overall payment in the auctions throughout the system span $[T]$ under consideration, *e.g.*, a pre-allocated budget for VM rental over a month or a year, which is assumed to be public information. A user's valuations in its bids are independent from its current budget level, while its current budget level will be taken into consideration at the cloud provider when allocating resources.

We list important notation in this paper in Table 2.

3.2 The Online Auction Problem

We aim to design an online auction mechanism to be carried out by the cloud provider, which guides resource allocation in the cloud system in a round-by-round fashion through multiple consecutive rounds. The auction design targets the following properties. (i) *Truthfulness* (Definition 1): Bidding true valuations is a dominant strategy at the users, and consequently, both bidding strategies and auction design are simplified. (ii) *Individual rationality*: Each bidder obtains a non-negative utility by participating in the auction in any time slot, *i.e.*, $u_n^{(t)} \geq 0$, $\forall n \in [N], \forall t \in [T]$. (iii) *Social welfare maximization*: The social welfare in our system is the sum of the cloud provider's revenue, $\sum_{t\in[T]}\sum_{n\in[N]}\Pi_n^{(t)}$, and all the users' utility gain, $\sum_{t\in[T]}\sum_{n\in[N]}\sum_{k\in[K]} b_{n,k}^{(t)}y_{n,k}^{(t)} - \sum_{t\in[T]}\sum_{n\in[N]}\Pi_n^{(t)}$, which equals aggregated user valuation of the winning bundles (under truthful bidding), $\sum_{t\in[T]}\sum_{n\in[N]}\sum_{k\in[K]} b_{n,k}^{(t)}y_{n,k}^{(t)}$. Payment from the users and revenue received by the cloud provider cancel out each other.

Definition 1. (Truthfulness) The auction mechanism is truthful if for any user n at any time t, declaring a bid that truthfully reveals its requirements of VM quantities, $d_{n,k,m,q}^{(t)}, \forall m, q, k$, and its valuations of bundles $b_{n,k}^{(t)}, \forall k$, always maximizes its expected utility, regardless of other users' bids.

We first formulate below an offline social welfare optimization problem which provides the "ideal" optimal resource allocation strategies for the cloud provider to address users' VM demands in the entire system lifespan $[T]$, assuming truthful bids are known. Let $c_{n,k,r,q}^{(t)} = \sum_m d_{n,k,m,q}^{(t)}\alpha_{m,r}$ be the amount of type-r resource at datacenter q required in user n's k-th bundle.

$$\text{maximize} \sum_{t\in[T]}\sum_{n\in[N]}\sum_{k\in[K]} b_{n,k}^{(t)}y_{n,k}^{(t)} \tag{1}$$

subject to

$$\sum_{k\in[K]} y_{n,k}^{(t)} \leq 1, \quad \forall n \in [N], t \in [T], \tag{1a}$$

$$\sum_{k\in[K]}\sum_{t\in[T]} b_{n,k}^{(t)}y_{n,k}^{(t)} \leq B_n, \quad \forall n \in [N], \tag{1b}$$

$$\sum_{n\in[N]}\sum_{k\in[K]} c_{n,k,r,q}^{(t)}y_{n,k}^{(t)} \leq A_{q,r}^{(t)}, \quad \forall q \in [Q], r \in [R], t \in [T], \tag{1c}$$

$$y_{n,k}^{(t)} \in \{0,1\}, \quad \forall n \in [N], k \in [K], t \in [T]. \tag{1d}$$

Constraint (1a) specifies that each user can win at most one bundle each round. (1b) is the budget constraint at each user. (1c) limits the overall demand for each type of resource in the winning bundles by the amount available.

Introducing dual variable vectors s, x, and z to constraints (1a), (1b) and (1c) respectively, and ignore the binary variable constraint (1d) temporarily, we can formulate the dual of the resulting linear program, to be used in the primal-dual algorithm design in Sec. 4:

$$\min \sum_{n\in[N]} B_n x_n + \sum_{n\in[N]}\sum_{t\in[T]} s_n^{(t)} + \sum_{q\in[Q]}\sum_{r\in[R]}\sum_{t\in[T]} A_{q,r}(t) z_{q,r}^{(t)} \tag{2}$$

subject to

$$b_{n,k}^{(t)}x_n + s_n^{(t)} + \sum_{r\in[R]}\sum_{q\in[Q]} c_{n,k,r,q}^{(t)}z_{q,r}^{(t)} \geq b_{n,k}^{(t)}$$
$$\forall n \in [N], k \in [K], t \in [T], \tag{2a}$$

$$x_n, s_n^{(t)}, z_{q,r}^{(t)} \geq 0, \quad \forall n \in [N], q \in [Q], r \in [R], t \in [T]. \tag{2b}$$

To derive an optimal solution to (1), complete knowledge about the system over its entire lifespan is needed, which is apparently not practical. In a dynamic cloud system, the provider should allocate resources on the fly, based on the current amount of available resources, $A_{q,r}^{(t)}$'s, and users' bidding bundles including resource demands $d_{n,k,m,q}^{(t)}$'s and valuations $b_{n,k}^{(t)}$'s, which are not known *a priori*. We seek to design an online auction mechanism for realtime resource allocation, which also guarantees truthful bidding. We achieve the goals in two steps. First, in Sec.4, we assume that a truthful auction mechanism to be carried out *in each time slot* is known, and guarantees an approximation ratio ν, and propose an online algorithm framework that produces a competitive ratio of $(1+B_{max})(\nu+\frac{1}{\gamma-1})$ as compared to the offline optimum. Second, in Sec. 5, we design a single-round randomized auction, which achieves the approximation ratio of ν as well as individual rationality and truthfulness.

4. AN ONLINE ALGORITHM FRAMEWORK

We design an online algorithm framework $\mathcal{A}_{online}$ as shown in Algorithm 1, which solves the offline optimization problem (1) and its dual (2), using a subroutine $\mathcal{A}_{round}$ running at each time slot. We next discuss the one-round resource allocation problem to be solved by $\mathcal{A}_{round}$, as well as the design rationale of the online algorithm framework.

4.1 One-Round Resource Allocation

Assuming truthful bids are known, the one-round social welfare maximization problem at time t is as follows, which includes the constraints from the offline optimization problem (1) related to the current time slot, and excludes the user budget constraints (dealt with in the online algorithm framework instead). In the optimization below, $w_{n,k}^{(t)}$, a reduced valuation of user n for bundle k from the actual valuation $b_{n,k}^{(t)}$ in its bid according to the level of its remaining budget, is used in the objective function. The rationale will be detailed in Sec. 4.2. Given $w_{n,k}^{(t)}$, the cloud provider's current resource supplies $A_{q,r}^{(t)}$'s, and users' resource demands $c_{n,k,r,q}^{(t)}$'s, $\forall n,k,r,q$, the one-round optimization problem decides the optimal resource allocation $y_{n,k}^{(t)}, \forall n,k$, at t.

$$\text{maximize} \sum_{n\in[N]}\sum_{k\in[K]} w_{n,k}^{(t)} y_{n,k}^{(t)} \tag{3}$$

subject to

$$\sum_{k\in[K]} y_{n,k}^{(t)} \le 1 \quad \forall n\in[N] \tag{3a}$$

$$\sum_{n\in[N]}\sum_{k\in[K]} c_{n,k,r,q}^{(t)} y_{n,k}^{(t)} \le A_{q,r}^{(t)} \quad \forall q\in[Q], r\in[R] \tag{3b}$$

$$y_{n,k}^{(t)} \in \{0,1\} \quad \forall n\in[N], k\in[K] \tag{3c}$$

Adopting the same dural variables as in the dual of (1) and omitting constraint (3c) temporarily, we formulate the dual of LP (3):

$$\text{minimize} \sum_{n\in[N]} s_n^{(t)} + \sum_{q\in[Q]}\sum_{r\in[R]} A_{q,r}^{(t)} z_{q,r}^{(t)} \tag{4}$$

s.t.

$$s_n^{(t)} + \sum_{q\in[Q]}\sum_{r\in[R]} c_{n,k,r,q}^{(t)} z_{q,r}^{(t)} \ge w_{n,k}^{(t)}, \forall n\in[N], k\in[K], \tag{4a}$$

$$s_n^{(t)}, z_{q,r}^{(t)} \ge 0, \quad \forall n\in[N], q\in[Q], r\in[R]. \tag{4b}$$

The primal problem (3) is a special case of the multi-dimensional multiple-choice 0-1 knapsack problem [8], which is both NP-hard and more strongly, has no fully polynomial-time approximation schemes unless P=NP [10]. What we will pursue in $\mathcal{A}_{round}$ is an auction mechanism, which not only guarantees individual rationality and truthfulness, but also employs a primal-dual approximation algorithm that solves problem (3) and (4) to decide resource allocation in polynomial time with a small approximation ratio. We delay the discussion of the auction mechanism to Sec. 5, but first utilize its properties when analyzing our online algorithm framework. We will show that given a competitive ratio ν achieved by the one-round auction mechanism, our online algorithm framework achieves a good competitive ratio.

4.2 The Online Algorithm

When a good approximation algorithm for one-round resource allocation (with budget constraint relaxed) is in place, the difficulty of designing an online algorithm to achieve a good competitive ratio, defined as the maximum ratio between the offline optimal social welfare derived by solving (1) exactly and the social welfare produced by the online algorithm, arises from the budget constraint at each user. The budget limits the bundles a user can acquire over the T rounds of auctions, leading to different amounts of overall social welfare when the budget is spent in different rounds. The intuition we follow in designing the online algorithm is that, inefficiency in social welfare may appear when a user's budget runs out at an early stage, since its future bids become invalid after its budget depletion, narrowing down possible future resource allocation decisions at the cloud provider, prohibiting larger social welfare. The ideal scenario is that each user's budget can last for all the T rounds of auctions, making it possible for the cloud provider to explore the best resource allocation strategies over the entire span, to approach the best overall social welfare.

Under this intuition, we should be cautious when winning a bundle suddenly exhausts a user's remaining budget. Our main idea in the online algorithm in Alg. 1 is to associate the resource allocation in each round with the users' remaining budgets. We introduce an auxiliary variable $x_n^{(t)}$ for each user $n\in[N]$, whose value starts at 0, increases with the decrease of the remaining budget of the user, and reaches 1 when the budget is exhausted. Instead of the actual valuation $b_{n,k}^{(t)}$ of each bundle, $w_{n,k}^{(t)} = b_{n,k}^{(t)}(1-x_n^{(t-1)})$ is used in the one-round resource allocation A_{round} as in (3), such that the bid from a user with a smaller remaining budget will be evaluated less at the cloud provider, leading to a lower chance of acquiring a bundle. A user's budget lasts for a longer period of time as a result. $x_n^{(t)}$ is updated after each round of resource allocation in Lines 7 and 10 of Algorithm 1, where $\gamma=(1+B_{max})^{\frac{1}{B_{max}}}$. $B_{max}=\max_{n\in[N],t\in[T],k\in[K]}\{b_{n,k}^{(t)}/B_n\}$, which is the maximum ratio between the valuation of any bundle and the corresponding user's budget. We consider $B_{max}\ll 1$, given that users typically do not put a large proportion of their total budget on one bundle in one round. $x_n^{(t)}$ is increased if user n wins a new bundle in round t (Line 7) — thus user n's remaining budget decreases, and remains unchanged otherwise (Line 10). The increment in Line 7 is carefully computed (see proof of Thm. 1), such that the budget constraint (1b) is guaranteed over the T rounds of online auctions. We set dual variable x_n in the offline dual problem (2), associated with constraint (1b), to the value of the auxiliary variable $x_n^{(t)}$ after T rounds (Line 13). In this way, the adjustment of $x_n^{(t)}$ in each round can be understood as the adjustment of the dual variable x_n towards an optimal solution to the offline dual problem (2).

Algorithm 1 The Online Algorithm Framework $\mathcal{A}_{online}$

$x_n^{(0)} \leftarrow 0, \forall n \in [N]$
// Loop for each time slot
for all $1 \leq t \leq T$ **do**

$$w_{n,k}^{(t)} = \begin{cases} 0 & \text{if } x_n^{(t-1)} \geq 1 \\ b_{n,k}^{(t)}(1 - x_n^{(t-1)}) & \text{otherwise} \end{cases}, \forall n \in [N], k \in [K].$$

Run $\mathcal{A}_{round}$. Let $\mathcal{N}$ be the set of winning users, and k_n be the index of their corresponding winning bundle, for each winning user $n \in \mathcal{N}$.
for all $n \in \mathcal{N}$ **do**

$$x_n^{(t)} \leftarrow x_n^{(t-1)} \left(1 + \frac{b_{n,k_n}^{(t)}}{B_n}\right) + \frac{b_{n,k_n}^{(t)}}{B_n(\gamma - 1)}$$

end for
for all $n \notin \mathcal{N}$ **do**
$x_n^{(t)} \leftarrow x_n^{(t-1)}$
end for
end for
$x_n \leftarrow x_n^{(T)}, \forall n \in [N]$

The performance of our online algorithm in Alg. 1 is stated in Thm. 1, with a detailed proof in Appendix A.

THEOREM 1. *If we can find an auction mechanism in $\mathcal{A}_{round}$ that carries out resource allocation in each round to produce feasible solutions for (3) and (4), and guarantees $\nu p \geq d$ (hence the competitive ratio of the auction algorithm is also ν), $\mathcal{A}_{online}$ is $(1 + B_{max})(\nu + \frac{1}{\gamma-1})$-competitive for optimization (1). Here $p = \sum_{n\in[N]} \sum_{k\in[K]} w_{n,k}^{(t)} y_{n,k}^{(t)}$ is the objective value of the one-round resource allocation problem in (3), and $d = \sum_{n\in[N]} s_n^{(t)} + \sum_{q\in[Q]} \sum_{r\in[R]} A_{q,r}^{(t)} z_{q,r}^{(t)}$ is the dual objective value in (4).*

We note that when $B_{max} \to 0$, the competitive ratio approaches $\nu + \frac{1}{e-1}$, *i.e.*, the long-term online optimization framework incurs only an additive loss of $\frac{1}{e-1}$ in competitive ratio, as compared to the one-round allocation algorithm.

5. A RANDOMIZED AUCTION MECHANISM

We now present a randomized auction mechanism $\mathcal{A}_{round}$ which efficiently allocates resources according to users' bids in each time slot, and guarantees individual rationality and truthfulness. The auction mechanism in each round allocates resources according to the one-round resource allocation problem in (3) and decides the payments from the winning bidders. The classic VCG (Vickrey-Clarke-Groves) mechanism [23] is a potential candidate for our auction design, which assigns items (VM bundles in our case) to bidders in a socially optimal manner by solving a corresponding resource allocation problem, charges each winner the externality it exerts on other bidders, and ensures that the optimal strategy for a bidder is to bid its true valuations. However, our allocation problem in (3) is NP-hard, and hence a VCG mechanism becomes computationally infeasible. We therefore resort to a fractional version of the VCG auction for achieving both computational efficiency (polynomial time complexity) and economic efficiency (social welfare maximization in (3)), by applying the VCG mechanism to the LP relaxation of the integer program (3). The fractional VCG mechanism produces fractional bundle allocation results, which are not practically applicable. We further employ a primal-dual optimization based decomposition technique that decomposes such an optimal fractional solution into a convex combination of integral solutions, and then design a randomized auction which randomly picks one from the integral solutions as the bundle allocation result in each round and retains the nice properties of a fractional VCG auction. We detail the fractional VCG auction, the decomposition technique, and the randomized auction design in the following three subsections.

5.1 The Fractional VCG Auction

In the fractional VCG auction, the auctioneer solves the LP relaxation of (3) by relaxing constraint (3c) to $0 \leq y_{n,k}^{(t)} \leq 1, \forall n, k$, to decide the bundle allocation in t. Let $\mathbf{y}^{(t)\boldsymbol{F}} = (y_{n,k}^{(t)\boldsymbol{F}})_{\forall n,k}$ denote the resulting optimal fraction allocation, where $y_{n,k}^{(t)\boldsymbol{F}} \in [0, 1]$. To compute the VCG payment from a winner, the auctioneer solves the LP relaxation again with the winner excluded from the allocation. Let $\widetilde{V}_{-n}^{(t)}$ denote the social welfare achieved when winner n is excluded. The payment of winner n, $\Pi_n^{(t)\boldsymbol{F}}$, is: $\Pi_n^{(t)F} = \widetilde{V}_{-n}^{(t)} - \sum_{n'\neq n} \sum_{k\in[K]} y_{n',k}^{(t)F} w_{n',k}^{(t)}$.

The utility function $u_n^{(t)}$ of bidder n in a VCG auction is typically defined as the difference between its valuation and its payment. In our online auction framework, a user's utility in each round should be related not only to its valuation and payment, but also to its remaining budget: intuitively, smaller utility gain is appreciated if a user won a bundle when its remaining budget is small, and larger otherwise. We characterize this property using a utility function:

$$u_n^{(t)} = \sum_{k\in[K]} y_{n,k}^{(t)F} w_{n,k}^{(t)} - \Pi_n^{(t)F}. \quad (5)$$

Such a utility function is consistent with the social welfare calculation in the one-round allocation problem (3). In this way, a user's budget can potentially last longer, enabling its acquirement of a better bundle with the same consumption of budget at a later time, contributing to social welfare efficiency over all T rounds of auctions.

We show in Thm. 2 that under this utility function, bidding true valuations is the best strategy for each user in the fractional VCG auction. A non-negative utility is guaranteed for each bidder, based on VCG auction theory [23]. Due to space limit, most proofs in this section are omitted in this paper and we refer the interested readers to [22] for the details.

THEOREM 2. *The fractional VCG auction which produces fractional allocation $y_{n,k}^{(t)F}, \forall n \in [N], k \in [K]$, and payments $\Pi_n^{(t)F}, \forall n \in [N]$, is truthful and individual rational.*

5.2 Decomposing the Fractional Solution

Since fractional VM bundles are impractical in real-world cloud systems, we next decompose the fractional allocation solution into a convex combination of integer solutions, which will be used by our randomized auction mechanism.

We apply a LP duality based decomposition technique [13]. The goal of the decomposition is to find $\beta_l \in [0,1]$ and a set of integer solutions $\mathbf{y}^{(t)l}, \forall l \in \boldsymbol{L}$ ($\boldsymbol{L}$ is an index set), to the one-round resource allocation problem (3), such that $\sum_{l \in \boldsymbol{L}} \beta_l y_{n,k}^{(t)l} = y_{n,k}^{(t)\boldsymbol{F}}, \forall n \in [N], k \in [K]$, and $\sum_{l \in \boldsymbol{L}} \beta_l = 1$. The randomized auction in each round can choose the lth integer solution $\mathbf{y}^{(t)l}$ with probability β_l, achieving a good competitive ratio in social welfare in expectation, as compared to that achieved by the optimal integer solution to (3). However, there in fact does not exist a convex combination of integer solutions, $\sum_{l \in \boldsymbol{L}} \beta_l y_{n,k}^{(t)l}$, that equals the fraction solution $y_{n,k}^{(t)\boldsymbol{F}}$, because otherwise, the expected social welfare achieved by these integer solutions equals that achieved by the fractional solution, which is apparently a contradiction to the fact that the fractional solution achieves a higher social welfare than any possible integer solution. Therefore, to achieve a feasible decomposition, we need to scale down the optimal fractional solution by a certain factor. According to [13], if there exists an approximation algorithm that solves the one-round allocation problem (3) with an approximation ratio of λ and guarantees $\lambda p \geq d$ (where p and d are the objective function values of the primal problem (3) and dual (4) respectively) , then we can use λ as the scaling factor, and rest assured that a feasible solution to the following decomposition problem exists:

$$\text{minimize} \sum_{l \in \boldsymbol{L}} \beta_l \tag{6}$$

s.t.

$$\sum_{l \in \boldsymbol{L}} \beta_l y_{n,k}^{(t)l} = y_{n,k}^{(t)F} / \lambda, \qquad \forall n \in [N], k \in [K], \tag{6a}$$

$$\sum_{l \in \boldsymbol{L}} \beta_l \geq 1, \tag{6b}$$

$$\beta_l \geq 0, \qquad \forall l \in \boldsymbol{L}. \tag{6c}$$

We next first present a primal-dual algorithm that solves (3) with a good approximation ratio λ, and then discuss how to solve the decomposition problem (6) to obtain β_l and $\mathbf{y}^{(t)l}$, $\forall l \in \boldsymbol{L}$.

5.2.1 A primal-dual algorithm for one-round resource allocation

Alg. 2 is our primal-dual approximation algorithm to the NP-hard allocation problem (3). $C_{q,r}^{(t)} = \max_{n,k}\{c_{n,k,r,q}^{(t)}\}$ is the maximum amount of type-r resource at datacenter q required by any bundle in t. $C_{min}^{(t)} = \min_{r \in [R], q \in [Q]}\{A_{q,r}^{(t)} / C_{q,r}^{(t)}\}$ is the minimum ratio between the total amount of available resource of a type in datacenter and the amount of the resource in the datacenter required by one bundle. In practice, the resource pool is substantially larger than a single user's demand, and hence $C_{min}^{(t)} \gg 1$. The main idea of the algorithm is to introduce an auxiliary variable $z_{q,r}^{(t)}$ for each type of resources (which is the dual variable associated with constraint (3(b)), acting as the unit price in allocation decision. The unit price $z_{q,r}^{(t)}$ is updated according to the remaining amount of this type of resource. The algorithm evaluates each bundle according to the unit prices and the amount of required resources, and always chooses the users with a higher bid on a lower valued bundle as the winner.

THEOREM 3. *Alg. 2 computes feasible primal and dual solutions for (3) and (4), and guarantees $\lambda p \geq d$ (p and d defined in Thm. 1), $\lambda = 1 + \epsilon^{(t)}(e(QR)^{1/(C_{min}^{(t)}-1)} - 1)\frac{C_{min}^{(t)}}{C_{min}^{(t)}-1}$ with $\epsilon^{(t)} = \max_{k_1,k_2 \in [K], r \in [R]}\{c_{n,k_1,r,q}^{(t)} / c_{n,k_2,r,q}^{(t)}\}$. The approximation ratio of Alg. 2 is also λ.*

Here $\epsilon^{(t)}$ is the maximum ratio between the overall demands for any type of resource in any two bundles in a user's bid in t. When Q, R are small constants and the provider's resource pool is relatively large compared with users' resource demands in the bundles, λ tends to $1 + \epsilon^{(t)}(e-1)$. If further $\epsilon^{(t)} \to 1$, or each user bids a single bundle, λ tends to e.

Algorithm 2 A Primal-Dual Algorithm to Solve One-round Allocation Problem (3)

$\mathcal{N} \leftarrow \emptyset, z_{base} \leftarrow QR \cdot exp((C_{min}^{(t)} - 1))$
$y_{n,k}^{(t)} \leftarrow 0, s_n^{(t)} \leftarrow 0, z_{q,r}^{(t)} \leftarrow 1/A_{q,r}^{(t)}, \forall n \in [N], k \in [K], r \in [R], q \in [Q]$
while $\sum_{r \in [R]} \sum_{q \in [Q]} A_{q,r}^{(t)} z_{q,r}^{(t)} < z_{base}$ AND $|\mathcal{N}| \neq N$ **do**
  for all $n \notin \mathcal{N}$ **do**
    $k(n) = \arg\max_{k \in [K]}\{v_{n,k}^{(t)}\}$
  end for
  $n^* = \arg\max_{n \in [N]}\{\frac{w_{n,k(n)}^{(t)}}{\sum_{r \in [R]} \sum_{q \in [Q]} c_{n,k(n),r,q}^{(t)} z_{q,r}^{(t)}}\}$
  $y_{n^*,k(n^*)}^{(t)} \leftarrow 1, s_{n^*}^{(t)} \leftarrow w_{n^*,k(n^*)}^{(t)}, \mathcal{N} \leftarrow \mathcal{N} \cup \{n^*\}$
  for all $r \in [R], q \in [Q]$ **do**

$$z_{q,r}^{(t)} \leftarrow z_{q,r}^{(t)} \cdot z_{base}^{c_{n^*,k(n^*),q,r}^{(t)} / (A_{q,r}^{(t)} - C_{q,r}^{(t)})}$$

  end for
end while

5.2.2 Decomposition with LP duality-based technique

To solve the decomposition problem (6), we can first find all the possible integer solutions $\mathbf{y}^{(t)l}$ to (3) using some exhaustive search method, and then directly solve (6) to derive the decomposition coefficients β_l's. But this method has an exponential-time complexity, since there are an exponential number of possible integer solutions $\mathbf{y}^{(t)l}$, and hence an exponential number of variables in LP (6). We therefore resort to its dual, formulated in (7), where dual variables $v_{n,k}^{(t)}$ and τ associate with primal constraints (6a) and (6b), respectively:

$$\text{maximize } \frac{1}{\lambda} \sum_{n \in [N]} \sum_{k \in [K]} y_{n,k}^{(t)F} v_{n,k}^{(t)} + \tau \tag{7}$$

s.t.

$$\sum_{n \in [N]} \sum_{k \in [K]} y_{n,k}^{(t)l} v_{n,k}^{(t)} + \tau \leq 1, \qquad \forall l \in \boldsymbol{L}, \tag{7a}$$

$$\tau \geq 0. \tag{7b}$$

Even though the dual (7) has an exponential number of constraints, the ellipsoid method can be applied to solve it in polynomial-time. The ellipsoid method obtains an optimal dual solution using a polynomial number of separating hyperplanes. Alg. 2 acts as a key component of a separation oracle for generating these separating hyperplanes, and a feasible integer solution to (3) can be derived each time a separating hyperplane is generated [13]. Hence, a polynomial number of candidate integer solutions $\mathbf{y}^{(t)l}$'s are produced through the process of the ellipsoid method, and the primal problem (6) can be reduced to a linear program with a polynomial number of variables (β_l's) corresponding to these integer solutions. Then we can solve the reduced primal problem in polynomial time. The correctness of the above decomposition method is given in Lemma 1, with detailed proof and the construction of the separation oracle in Appendix B.

LEMMA 1. *The decomposition method correctly obtains a polynomial number of integer solutions $\{\mathbf{y}^{(t)l}\}_{l\in \mathbf{L}}$ to the one-round allocation problem (3), and the probabilities $\beta_l, \forall l \in \mathbf{L}$, which solve (6), in polynomial time.*

5.3 The Randomized Auction

Alg. 3 gives our randomized auction to be carried out in each round of the online algorithm in Alg. 1. It selects an integer bundle allocation solution $\mathbf{y}^{(t)l}$ produced by the decomposition method with probability β_l (Line 8). The payment from a winning bidder n should satisfy two conditions: (1) The expectation of the payment should be equal to the scale-down fractional payment, $\sum_{l\in \mathbf{L}} \Pi_n^{(t)l}\beta_l = \Pi_n^{(t)F}/\lambda$, in order to remain truthfulness. (2) The payment $\Pi_n^{(t)l}$ should be no larger than n's valuation of its winning bundle $\sum_{k\in[K]} w_{n,k}^{(t)} y_{n,k}^{(t)l}$, in order to guarantee individual rationality. We obtain the payment rule in Line 9, which satisfies the two conditions.

The following theorem provides the properties achieved by the randomized auction.

THEOREM 4. *$\mathcal{A}_{round}$ runs in polynomial time and is truthful, individual rational and $\lambda(1+B_{max})$-competitive.*

Our online auction results when we plug in the one-round randomized auction $\mathcal{A}_{round}$ into the online algorithm framework $\mathcal{A}_{online}$ in Alg. 1. The competitive ratio of the online auction can be derived readily from Thm. 1 using $\nu = \lambda(1+B_{max})$, the competitive ratio of the one-round randomized auction given in Thm. 4.

THEOREM 5. *$\mathcal{A}_{online}$ in Alg. 1 combining with $\mathcal{A}_{round}$ in Alg. 3 constitutes a truthful, individual rational, $(1+B_{max})(\lambda(1+B_{max})+\frac{1}{\gamma-1})$- competitive online auction.*

The complete proof of Thm. 5 can be found in Appendix C. We note that when $B_{max}\to 0$, the competitive ratio tends to $\lambda + \frac{1}{e-1}$. Following the discussions on Thm. 3 in Sec. 5.2.1, when λ tends to e, the competitive ratio of the online auction tends to $e + \frac{1}{e-1} \simeq 3.30$.

5.4 Improving the scale-down factor

We have decomposed the fractional allocation solution in Sec. 5.2 after scaling it down by the approximation ratio λ of the one-round allocation Alg. 2, such that a feasible solution to the decomposition problem (6) is guaranteed [13]. According to Thm. 5, λ (as the scale-down factor in the decomposition method) is closely related to the competitive ratio of our online auction, such that a smaller scale-down factor may potentially lead to a better competitive ratio. However, a scale-down factor smaller than λ may not guarantee a feasible decomposition. We therefore design a binary

Algorithm 3 One-Round Randomized Auction $\mathcal{A}_{round}$ in t

1: Solve LP relaxation of (3), with $w_{n,k}^{(t)} = \max\{0,(1-x_n^{(t-1)})b_{n,k}^{(t)}\}$. Denote the fractional solution by $y_{n,k}^{(t)F}, \forall n\in[N], k\in[K]$.
2: **for all** $n\in[N]$ **do**
3: $\quad\forall n'\in[N], k\in[K], w_{n',k}^{'(t)} = max\{0,(1-x_n^{(t-1)})b_{n,k}^{(t)}\}$, if $n'\neq n$. Otherwise $w_{n',k}^{'(t)} = 0$.
4: $\quad$Solve LP relaxation of (3), with $w_{n',k}^{'(t)}$'s. Denote the optimal objective function value by $\widetilde{V}_{-n}^{(t)}$.
5: $\quad\Pi_n^{(t)F} = \widetilde{V}_{-n}^{(t)} - \sum_{n'\neq n}\sum_k y_{n',k}^{(t)F} w_{n',k}^{(t)}$
6: **end for**
7: Solve the pair of primal-dual decomposition LPs in (6) and (7) using the ellipsoid method, using Alg. 2 as a separation oracle, and derive a polynomial number of integer solutions to (3), $\mathbf{y}^{(t)l}$, $\forall l\in \mathbf{L}$, and the corresponding decomposition coefficients, β_l, $\forall l\in \mathbf{L}$.
8: Choose $\mathbf{y}^{(t)l}$ with probability β_l, $\forall l\in \mathbf{L}$
9: $\forall n\in[N], \Pi_n^{(t)l} = \Pi_n^{(t)F}\cdot \frac{\sum_{k\in[K]} w_{n,k}^{(t)} y_{n,k}^{(t)l}}{\sum_{k\in[K]} w_{n,k}^{(t)} y_{n,k}^{(t)F}}$

search-based algorithm in Alg. 4 to compute the smallest scale-down factor that enables feasible decomposition.

The algorithm is designed based on a property of the scale-down factor, as given in Thm. 6 . With its monotonicity, we can find the smallest, feasible scale-down factor using binary search (with arbitrary small error). We should note that this trial-and-error method may improve the performance of our online auction algorithm on average in practice, but does not change the theoretical competitive ratio in Thm. 5 in the worst case. We will investigate the effectiveness of the improved scale-down factor in our trace-driven simulations.

Algorithm 4 Binary searching smallest scale-down factor

Require: allowable error δ
Replace Line 7 of Alg. 3 with the following steps:
$\lambda_l \leftarrow 1$, $\lambda_r \leftarrow \lambda + \delta$
while $\lambda_r - \lambda_l > \delta$ **do**
$\quad\lambda_m \leftarrow (\lambda_l + \lambda_r)/2$
$\quad$Solve (7) with scale-down factor λ_m.
$\quad$**If** Decomposing success **then** $\lambda_r \leftarrow \lambda_m$ **Else** $\lambda_l \leftarrow \lambda_m$
end while
Solve (7) with scale-down factor λ_r.

THEOREM 6. *If the fractional allocation $y_{n,k}^{(t)F}$ can be decomposed under scale-down factor λ_1, then it can also be decomposed under any factor $\lambda_2 > \lambda_1$.*

6. PERFORMANCE EVALUATION

We evaluate our online auction design using trace-driven simulations. We investigate 6 types of VMs distributed in Q (default 3) datacenters, assembled from three types of resources (CPU, RAM, Disk capacity, R = 3), following the configurations in Table 1. Users' resource demands are extracted from Google cluster-usage data [3], which record jobs submitted to the Google cluster with information on their resource demands (CPU, RAM, Disk). We translate each job request in the Google data into a bidding bundle as follows: we calculate the numbers and types of VMs in Table 1 that altogether can make up the resource demands in the job request, and compose a bidding bundle based on the numbers and types of VMs; the valuation in the bidding bundle is calculated as the product of the total cost to acquire these VMs according to the VM charges in Table 1 and a random coefficient in the range of $[0.5, 2]$. In this way, we obtain a pool of bidding bundles from the Google data. In each round of the online auctions, each user randomly picks K (default 3) bundles in the pool, tags each VM in each bundle with a datacenter randomly selected from the Q datacenters, and bids the bundles. A user n's total budget B_n is decided by multiplying the sum of valuations in all the bundles the user may bid in the T rounds of auctions by a random coefficient in the range of $[0.5, 1]$. We also compute the total amount of resource of each type r needed by all the bid bundles of N users in each round, scale it down using a random factor in $[0, 1]$, and distribute the overall amount of type-r resource to Q datacenters evenly, to obtain the amount of available resource, $A_{q,r}^{(t)}$, for each type of resource in each datacenter at each time. Note that we run random bundle selection for each user over T rounds first to estimate users' budgets B_n's and available resources in the datacenters, $A_{q,r}^{(t)}$'s, before running the experiments to evaluate our online auction with the obtained B_n's and $A_{q,r}^{(t)}$'s. We suppose the maximum ratio between the overall demands for any type of resource in any two bundles in a user's bid in each time slot t, *i.e.*, $\epsilon^{(t)}$, is no larger than 2.5, by picking up bundles with similar resource demands for each user in the auctions, which we believe to reflect the reality better.

We compare the performance of three algorithms:

▷ *Alloc*, a pure online resource allocation algorithm, with the one-round resource allocation algorithm Alg. 2 serving in the place of A_{round} in $\mathcal{A}_{online}$ in Alg. 1.

▷ *Auc*, our online auction algorithm presented in Sec. 5.3, *i.e.*, $\mathcal{A}_{online}$ combined with $\mathcal{A}_{round}$ in Alg. 3.

▷ *AucBS*, the online auction algorithm with the improved scale-down factor, *i.e.*, adding the binary search in Algorithm 4 to the auction algorithm $\mathcal{A}_{round}$ in $\mathcal{A}_{online}$.

We compare these algorithms in different settings, based on the ratio between the offline optimal social welfare derived by solving (1) exactly and the overall social welfare produced by each online algorithm over T rounds, which we refer to as the *offline/online ratio*. In each scenario, we repeat each experiment for 10 times to derive the average ratios.

6.1 Different numbers of cloud users

We first compare the algorithms through varying the number of cloud users N from 300 to 3000, while fixing the number of rounds $T = 300$, as illustrated in Figure 1. The offline/online ratio of *Auc* declines when N is large ($N > 2000$), which is consistent with our theoretical analysis in Thm. 3: The larger the scale of the cloud system, the larger the value of $C_{min}^{(t)}$, and consequently the better offline/online ratio results. When users' truthful resource demands and valuations are assumed available for free, the pure online resource allocation algorithm, *Alloc*, achieves an offline/online ratio close to 1, which shows that our online algorithm framework together with the one-round resource allocation algorithm performs closely to the offline optimum in social welfare, if all the cloud users are cooperative. *AucBS* achieves a better offline/online ratio as compared to *Auc*, revealing the usefulness of our improved scale-down factor based on the binary-search Alg. 4 in decomposing the fractional solution into better integer solutions in practical scenarios.

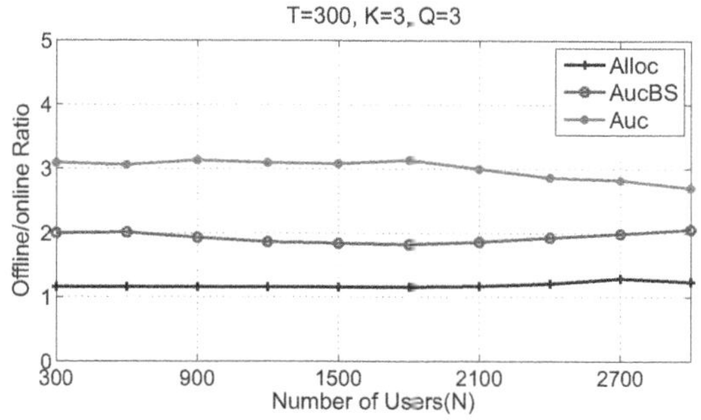

Figure 1: Offline/online ratio under different numbers of users N

6.2 Different numbers of rounds

We next vary the total number of rounds T our system is running for while fixing the number of users to 500. Suppose each round is one hour. A number of rounds in the range of $[300, 3000]$ corresponds to 12.5 days to about 4 months, which represents a reasonable period of time for a user to set a total amount of budget to use in. We observe in Figure 2 that the offline/online ratio of each algorithm always remains at similar levels, demonstrating the stable performance of our online algorithms regardless of the total number of rounds they are applied into.

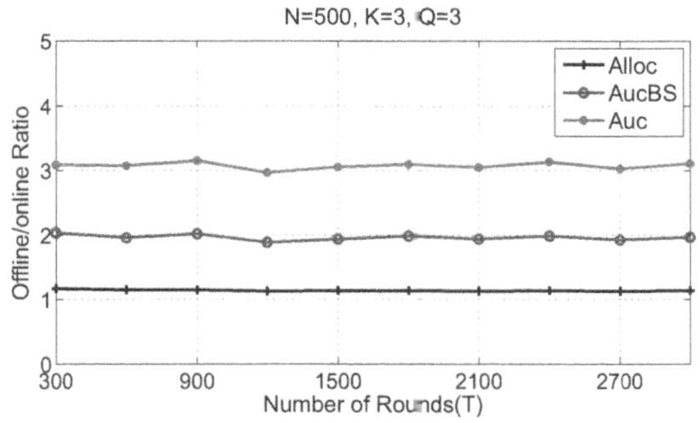

Figure 2: Offline/online ratio under different total numbers of rounds T

6.3 Different numbers of bundles and datacenters

We further evaluate the performance of *AucBS* when the number of bundles each user bids for in each round, K, and the number of datacenters, Q, vary. Fig. 3 shows that in general the performance of the improved online auction is better when the number of bundles is smaller. This can be explained as follows: The competitive ratio of our online auction (given in Thm. 5) is related to λ, the approximation ratio of the one-round resource allocation algorithm in Alg. 2, which is further closely related to $\epsilon^{(t)}$. When K is smaller, $\epsilon^{(t)}$ is potentially smaller (recall $\epsilon^{(t)}$ is the maximum ratio between the overall demands for any type of resource in any two bundles among the K bundles a user bids for in t), and thus λ is smaller, leading to a lower competitive ratio of the online auction. In a practical cloud system, the K bundles that a user bids are typically different representations of the user's same resource demands in a time slot, *e.g.*, different bundles may specify different numbers of different types of VMs requested from different datacenters, which add up to a similar amount of each type of resource across different bundles, to serve the user's need in t. Therefore, we do not expect a large value of $\epsilon^{(t)}$ at any time. When the value of $\epsilon^{(t)}$ is capped (*e.g.*, to 2.5 in our simulation settings), the competitive ratio is bounded even when K takes larger values, as shown by the similar offline/online ratios obtained when $K = 3, 4$, or 5, respectively, in Fig. 3.

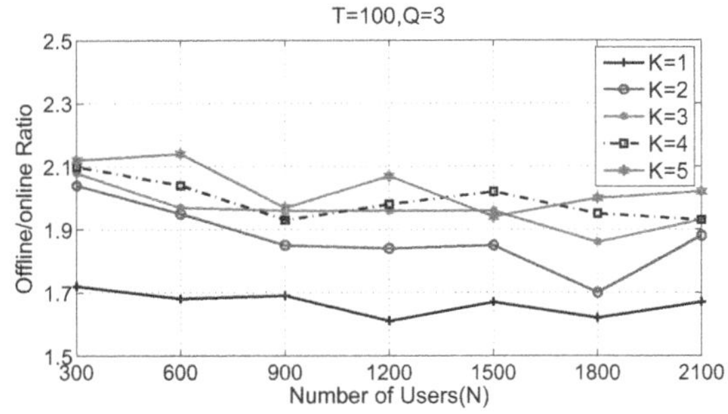

Figure 3: Offline/online ratio of *AucBS* with different numbers of bundles K.

Fig. 4 shows that when the total number of datacenters in the cloud system increases, the performance of our online auction degrades slightly, because the approximation ratio λ of Alg. 2 is larger when Q is larger. Nevertheless, we do not expect more than a few tens of datacenters in a real-world cloud system, and the offline/online ratio is still acceptable around 2.70 when Q is 10.

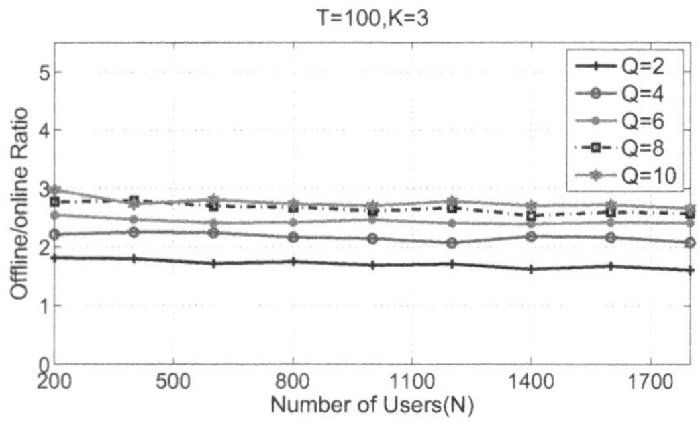

Figure 4: Offline/online ratio of *AucBS* with different numbers of datacenters Q.

We note that the performance ratios obtained in our simulations are much smaller than the theoretical ratios computed based on Thm. 5, in the range of $6-7$ under the same settings as used in our simulations. This promises the good performance of our online auction algorithm in practice.

6.4 User satisfaction

Finally we study the performance of the improved online auction algorithm *AucBS* in terms of user satisfaction, evaluated as the percentage of users who win a bundle in a round, averaged over the number of rounds the online auction runs. We set the total number of rounds to $T = 100$, vary the number of users N, and derive the user satisfaction under different values of K and Q.

Fig. 5 shows that the fewer datacenters, the better user satisfaction results. This can be explained as follows: Once a specific type of resource is used up at one datacenter, bundles requesting resources containing this type of resource in this datacenter cannot obtained, even though other resource is available in other datacenters; a larger number of datacenters leads to more dispersed distribution of resources, resulting in high probability for the above scenario to happen.

Fig. 6 shows that a smaller K leads to better user satisfaction. When K is larger, λ is larger, and hence the performance of the online auction degrads. On the other hand, when a user bids for more bundles, the cloud provider has a larger decision space for resource allocation, which should potentially lead to a higher chance for a user to be allocated one of the requested bundles. Therefore, the results in Fig. 6 reveal that the impact of λ dominates that of the latter.

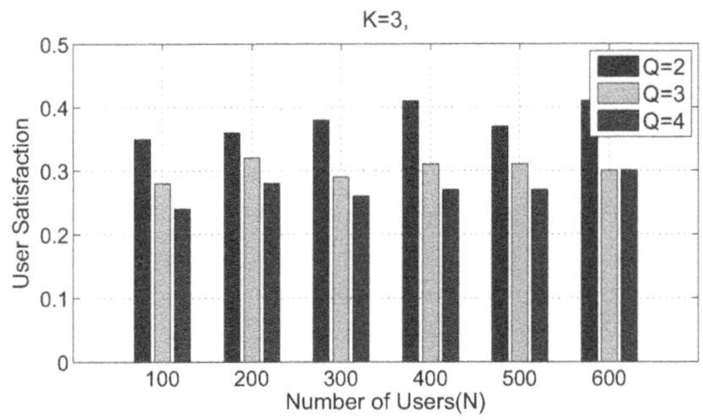

Figure 5: User satisfaction of *AucBS* with different numbers of datacenters Q.

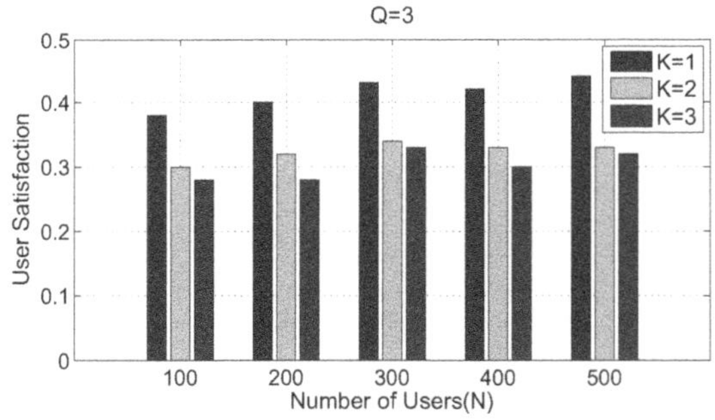

Figure 6: User satisfaction of *AucBS* with different numbers of bundles K.

7. CONCLUDING REMARKS

This work presents the first online combinatorial auction for the VM market in cloud computing. It advances the state-of-the-art of cloud auction design in that all previous VM auction mechanisms are either one-round only, or simplify VMs into type-oblivious good (and hence circumvent the challenge imposed by combinatorial auctions). Our online auction comprises of three components. First, we design an intuition-driven primal-dual algorithm for translating the online social welfare optimization problem into a series of one-round optimizations, incurring only a small additive penalty in competitive ratio. Second, we apply a randomized auction sub-framework that can translate a cooperative approximation algorithm to the one-round optimization into an auction. Third, we apply a greedy primal-dual algorithm that approximates the one-round social welfare optimization. Our overall online VM auction guarantees a theoretical competitive ratio close to 3.30 in typical scenarios, and its design may shed light to similar auction problems in related settings.

8. ACKNOWLEDGMENT

The research was supported in part by a grant from Hong Kong RGC under the contract HKU 718513.

9. REFERENCES

[1] Amazon Elastic Compute Cloud. http://aws.amazon.com/ec2/.

[2] Amazon EC2 Spot Instances. http://aws.amazon.com/ec2/spot-instances/.

[3] *Google Cluster Data*, https://code.google.com/p/googleclusterdata/.

[4] Windows Azure: Microsoft's Cloud Platform. http://www.windowsazure.com/.

[5] H. Ballani, P. Costa, T. Karagiannis, and A. Rowstron. Towards predictable datacenter networks. In *ACM SIGCOMM Computer Communication Review*, volume 41, pages 242–253. ACM, 2011.

[6] N. Bansal, K.-W. Lee, V. Nagarajan, and M. Zafer. Minimum congestion mapping in a cloud. In *Proceedings of the 30th annual ACM SIGACT-SIGOPS symposium on Principles of distributed computing*, pages 267–276. ACM, 2011.

[7] N. Buchbinder, K. Jain, and J. S. Naor. Online primal-dual algorithms for maximizing ad-auctions revenue. In *Proceedings of the 15th Annual European Symposium on Algorithms*, 2007.

[8] N. Cherfi and M. Hifi. A column generation method for the multiple-choice multi-dimensional knapsack problem. *Computational Optimization and Applications*, 46(1):51–73, 2010.

[9] H. Fu, Z. Li, and C. Wu. Core-selecting auction design for dynamically allocating heterogeneous vms in cloud computing. Submitted to INFOCOM 2014.

[10] G. Gens and E. Levner. Complexity of approximation algorithms for combinatorial problems: a survey. *ACM SIGACT News*, 12(3):52–65, 1980.

[11] P. Godfrey, M. Schapira, A. Zohar, and S. Shenker. Incentive compatibility and dynamics of congestion control. In *ACM SIGMETRICS Performance Evaluation Review*, pages 95–106, 2010.

[12] R. Lavi and N. Nisan. Competitive analysis of incentive compatible on-line auctions. In *Proceedings of the 2nd ACM Conference on Electronic Commerce*, pages 233–241. ACM, 2000.

[13] R. Lavi and C. Swamy. Truthful and near-optimal mechanism design via linear programming. In *Proc. of FOCS*, pages 595–604, 2005.

[14] D. Lehmann, L. I. Oćallaghan, and Y. Shoham. Truth revelation in approximately efficient combinatorial auctions. *Journal of the ACM (JACM)*, 49, 2002.

[15] R. T. B. Ma, S. C. M. Lee, J. C. S. Lui, and D. K. Y. Yau. A game theoretic approach to provide incentive and service differentiation in p2p networks. In *ACM SIGMETRICS Performance Evaluation Review*, pages 189–198, 2004.

[16] X. Meng, V. Pappas, and L. Zhang. Improving the scalability of data center networks with traffic-aware virtual machine placement. In *INFOCOM, 2010 Proceedings IEEE*, pages 1–9. IEEE, 2010.

[17] A. Mu'Alem and N. Nisan. Truthful approximation mechanisms for restricted combinatorial auctions. *Games and Economic Behavior*, 64(2):612–631, 2008.

[18] N. Nisan. *Algorithmic game theory*. Cambridge University Press, 2007.

[19] D. Niu, C. Feng, and B. Li. Pricing cloud bandwidth reservations under demand uncertainty. In *ACM SIGMETRICS Performance Evaluation Review*, pages 151–162, 2012.

[20] M. H. Rothkopf, A. Pekeč, and R. M. Harstad. Computationally manageable combinational auctions. *Management science*, 44(8):1131–1147, 1998.

[21] G. Shanmuganathan, A. Gulati, and P. Varman. Defragmenting the cloud using demand-based resource allocation. In *ACM SIGMETRICS Performance Evaluation Review*, pages 67–80, 2013.

[22] W. Shi, L. Zhang, C. Wu, Z. Li, and F. C. M. Lau. An online auction framework for dynamic resource provisioning in cloud computing. Technical report, 2014. `http://i.cs.hku.hk/~cwu/papers/sigmetrics14-techreport.pdf`.

[23] W. Vickrey. Counterspeculation, auctions, and competitive sealed tenders. *The Journal of Finance*, 16(1):8–37, 1961.

[24] Q. Wang, K. Ren, and X. Meng. When cloud meets ebay: Towards effective pricing for cloud computing. In *Proc. of IEEE INFOCOM*, pages 936–944, 2012.

[25] W. Wang, B. Liang, and B. Li. Revenue maximization with dynamic auctions in iaas cloud markets. In *Proc. IEEE ICDCS*, 2013.

[26] C. Wu, Z. Li, X. Qiu, and F. C. M. Lau. Auction-based p2p vod streaming: Incentives and optimal scheduling. *ACM Transactions on Multimedia Computing, Communications and Applications*, 2012.

[27] S. Zaman and D. Grosu. Combinatorial auction-based mechanisms for vm provisioning and allocation in clouds. In *IEEE/ACM CCGrid*, pages 729–734, 2012.

[28] H. Zhang, B. Li, H. Jiang, F. Liu, A. V. Vasilakos, and J. Liu. A framework for truthful online auctions in cloud computing with heterogeneous user demands. In *Proc. of IEEE INFOCOM*, 2013.

[29] L. Zhang, Z. Li, and C. Wu. Dynamic resource provisioning in cloud computing: A randomized auction approach. In *Proc. of IEEE INFOCOM*, 2014.

[30] Y. Zhu, B. Li, and Z. Li. Truthful spectrum auction design for secondary networks. In *Proc. of IEEE INFOCOM*, 2012.

APPENDIX

A. PROOF OF THEOREM 1

PROOF. We prove the correctness and the competitiveness of $\mathcal{A}_{online}$ by proving three claims:

1. At the end of the algorithm, it produces feasible solution for dual (2).

2. Let $P^{(t)}$ be the value of the objective function in (1) after t-th iteration, $\Delta P^{(t)} = P^{(t)} - P^{(t-1)}$, the same for $\Delta D^{(t)}$ in dual (2). Then $\mathcal{A}_{online}$ satisfies $\Delta D^{(t)} \leq \left(\nu + \frac{1}{\gamma-1}\right) \Delta P^{(t)}$, at any round $\forall t \in [T]$.
3. The algorithm produces an almost feasible solution for primal (1). Specifically, its outputs $y_{n,k}^{(t)}$ satisfy (1a), (1c) and (1d). For constraint (1b), we achieve a slightly weaker property : For all user $n \in [N]$,

$$\sum_{t\in[T]} \sum_{k\in[K]} b_{n,k}^{(t)} y_{n,k}^{(t)} \leq B_n(1 + B_{max}) \tag{8}$$

Proof of (1): Since $w_{n,k}^{(t)} \geq b_{n,k}^{(t)}(1 - x_n^{(t-1)})$ no matter whether $x_n^{(t-1)} < 1$ or $x_n^{(t-1)} \geq 1$, constraint (4a) guarantees

$$s_n^{(t)} + \sum_{r\in[R]} \sum_{q\in[Q]} c_{n,k,r}^{(t)} z_{q,r}^{(t)} \geq b_{n,k}^{(t)}(1 - x_n^{(t-1)})$$

Also notice $x_n^{(t)}$ is non-decreasing with t, so (2a) holds.
Proof of (2): At time t, $\Delta P^{(t)} = \sum_{n\in\mathcal{N}} b_{n,k_n}^{(t)}$.

$$\begin{aligned}\Delta D^{(t)} &= \sum_{n\in\mathcal{N}} B_n(x_n^{(t)} - x_n^{(t-1)}) + d \\ &= \sum_{n\in\mathcal{N}} \left(b_{n,k_n}^{(t)} x_n^{(t-1)} + \frac{b_{n,k_n}^{(t)}}{\gamma - 1} \right) + d \\ &\leq \sum_{n\in\mathcal{N}} \left(b_{n,k_n}^{(t)} x_n^{(t-1)} + \frac{b_{n,k_n}^{(t)}}{\gamma - 1} \right) + \nu p\end{aligned}$$

Substitute $\sum_{n\in\mathcal{N}} b_{n,k_n}^{(t)}(1 - x_n^{(t-1)})$ for p, we have:

$$\begin{aligned}\Delta D^{(t)} &\leq \sum_{n\in\mathcal{N}} \left(\nu + \frac{1}{\gamma-1} - (\nu - 1)x_n^{(t-1)}\right) b_{n,k_n}^{(t)} \\ &\leq \left(\nu + \frac{1}{\gamma-1}\right) \Delta P^{(t)}\end{aligned}$$

Proof of (3): Constraints (1a), (1c), (1d) are guaranteed by the constraints in (3). In order to analyze the property about constraint (1b), we prove the following inequality: $\forall n \in [N], t' \in [T]$,

$$x_n^{(t')} \geq \frac{1}{\gamma - 1}\left(\gamma^{\frac{\sum_{t=1}^{t'} \sum_{k\in[K]} b_{n,k}^{(t)} y_{n,k}^{(t)}}{B_n}} - 1\right), 0 \leq t' \leq T \tag{9}$$

We prove (9) by induction. (9) holds for $t' = 0$ apparently. Suppose it holds for $t' - 1$, then for t': If $n \notin \mathcal{N}$, the inequality holds since both sides are still the same value at time $t' - 1$. If $n \in \mathcal{N}$:

$$\begin{aligned}x_n^{(t)} &= x_n^{(t-1)}\left(1 + \frac{b_{n,k_n}^{(t)}}{B_n}\right) + \frac{b_{n,k_n}^{(t)}}{B_n(\gamma - 1)} \\ &= \frac{1}{\gamma - 1}\left(\gamma^{\frac{\sum_{t=1}^{t'-1} \sum_{k\in[K]} b_{n,k}^{(t)} y_{n,k}^{(t)}}{B_n}} \left(1 + \frac{b_{n,k_n}^{(t)}}{B_n}\right) - 1\right)\end{aligned}$$

Comparing this with our target (9), obviously we only need to show: $1 + \frac{b_{n,k_n}^{(t)}}{B_n} \geq \gamma^{\frac{b_{n,k_n}^{(t)}}{B_n}}$. We utilize the inequality:

$$\frac{\ln(1+x)}{x} \geq \frac{\ln(1+y)}{y}, \forall 0 \leq x \leq y \leq 1$$

Since $\frac{b_{n,k_n}^{(t)}}{B_n} \leq B_{max}$, we have:

$$\ln(1 + \frac{b_{n,k_n}^{(t)}}{B_n}) \geq \frac{b_{n,k_n}^{(t)}}{B_n} \cdot \frac{\ln(1 + B_{max})}{B_{max}} = \frac{b_{n,k_n}^{(t)}}{B_n} \ln \gamma$$

Thus, $1 + \frac{b_{n,k_n}^{(t)}}{B_n} \geq \gamma^{\frac{b_{n,k_n}^{(t)}}{B_n}}$, and we prove (9).

Now we utilize the inequality (9) to prove (8). For some user n, suppose t' is the first time $\sum_{t=1}^{t'} \sum_{k\in[K]} b_{n,k}^{(t)} y_{n,k}^{(t)} \geq B_n$. Then by (9), $x_n^{(t')} \geq 1$. The algorithm never gives user n any new bundles once $x_n \geq 1$, since the weight $w_{n,k}^{(t)}$ in $\mathcal{A}_{round}$ will be set to 0. So $\sum_{t=1}^{T} \sum_{k\in[K]} b_{n,k}^{(t)} y_{n,k}^{(t)} = \sum_{t=1}^{t'} \sum_{k\in[K]} b_{n,k}^{(t)} y_{n,k}^{(t)}$. We know t' is the first time user n's total winning bids exceeding its budget B_n. So

$$\sum_{t=1}^{t'-1} \sum_{k\in[K]} b_{n,k}^{(t)} y_{n,k}^{(t)} < B_n, \text{ then:}$$

$$\begin{aligned}\sum_{t=1}^{T} \sum_{k\in[K]} b_{n,k}^{(t)} y_{n,k}^{(t)} &= \sum_{t=1}^{t'-1} \sum_{k\in[K]} b_{n,k}^{(t)} y_{n,k}^{(t)} + \sum_{k\in[K]} b_{n,k}^{(t')} y_{n,k}^{(t')} \\ &\leq B_n + \max_{k\in[K]} b_{n,k}^{(t')} \\ &\leq B_n(1 + B_{max})\end{aligned}$$

Finally we put the above 3 claims together and calculate the actual total social welfare. Since the increment of valuation is the minimum between user's valuation and his remaining budget, total social welfare should be:

$$\begin{aligned}&\sum_{n\in[N]} \min\{B_n, \sum_{k\in[K]} \sum_{t\in[T]} b_{n,k}^{(n)} y_{n,k}^{(n)}\} \\ &\geq \sum_{n\in[N]} \sum_{k\in[K]} \sum_{t\in[T]} b_{n,k}^{(n)} y_{n,k}^{(n)} / (1 + B_{max}) \\ &= P^{(T)}/(1 + B_{max})\end{aligned}$$

By claim 2: $\Delta D^{(t)} \leq \left(\nu + \frac{1}{\gamma-1}\right) \Delta P^{(t)}$, and recall $P^{(0)} = D^{(0)} = 0$, we have $D^{(T)} \leq \left(\nu + \frac{1}{\gamma-1}\right) P^{(T)}$. Thus the social welfare is at least $D^{(T)}/[(1+B_{max})(\nu + \frac{1}{\gamma-1})]$. By duality, the approximation ratio of $\mathcal{A}_{online}$ is $(1 + B_{max})(\nu + \frac{1}{\gamma-1})$. □

B. THE SEPARATION ORACLE AND PROOF OF LEMMA 1

First we describe the construction of the separation oracle. In each iteration of the ellipsoid method, a possible solution of (7) $\{v_{n,k}^{(t)}\}, \tau$ is generated, and is given as the input of the severation oracle. The separation oracle we present in Alg. 5 judges whether this solution is feasible, *i.e.*, not conflict with any constraints in (7a). And if it is not feasible, the separation oracle should return a conflict constraints as the separation plane, *i.e.*, a set of $y_{n,k}^{(t)l}$. So if the input solution has objective value smaller than 1, we use

$$\frac{1}{\lambda}\sum_{n\in[N]}\sum_{k\in[K]} y_{n,k}^{(t)F} v_{n,k}^{(t)} + \tau \geq 1$$

as the separation plane. If the objective value equals to 1, then we find a feasible solution (later we will prove why in this case, it is a feasible solution). If the objective value is larger than 1, we need to find a set of $y_{n,k}^{(t)l}$, satisfies:

$$\sum_{n\in[N]}\sum_{k\in[K]} y_{n,k}^{(t)l} v_{n,k}^{(t)} \geq 1 - \tau$$

Remember the input $v_{n,k}^{(t)}$ and τ makes the objective value larger than 1 :

$$\frac{1}{\lambda}\sum_{n\in[N]}\sum_{k\in[K]} y_{n,k}^{(t)F} v_{n,k}^{(t)} \geq 1 - \tau$$

So we find a conflict constraint if we can find $y_{n,k}^{(t)l}$ satisfies

$$\sum_{n\in[N]}\sum_{k\in[K]} y_{n,k}^{(t)l} v_{n,k}^{(t)} \geq \frac{1}{\lambda}\sum_{n\in[N]}\sum_{k\in[K]} y_{n,k}^{(t)F} v_{n,k}^{(t)}$$

Observe the left side of the inequality. It has exactly the same form with the objective function of (3). Furthermore, the value of $y_{n,k}^{(t)l}$ also should satisfy all the constraints in (3). So we can $\mathcal{A}_{round}$ to get such $y_{n,k}^{(t)l}$. Although there is a little difference here: $v_{n,k}^{(t)}$ can be negative, while $w_{n,k}^{(t)}$ in (3) can only be nonnegative value. In order to handle this problem, we introduce new variables $\widetilde{v}$ and $\widetilde{y}$ in the separation oracle, which is detailed in the proof.

Algorithm 5 Separation Oracle

Require: input $v_{n,k}^{(t)}, \tau$

1: **If** $\frac{1}{\lambda}\sum_n\sum_k y_{n,k}^{(t)F} v_{n,k}^{(t)} + \tau = 1$, **Then** return "YES"

2: **If** $\frac{1}{\lambda}\sum_n\sum_k y_{n,k}^{(t)F} v_{n,k}^{(t)} + \tau < 1$, **Then** return "NO" with separation plane $\frac{1}{\lambda}\sum_n\sum_k y_{n,k}^{(t)F} v_{n,k}^{(t)} + \tau \geq 1$

3: **If** $\frac{1}{\lambda}\sum_n\sum_k y_{n,k}^{(t)F} v_{n,k}^{(t)} + \tau > 1$, **Then**

4: $\quad \widetilde{v}_{n,k}^{(t)} = \max\{0, v_{n,k}^{(t)}\}$

5: $\quad$ Run $\mathcal{A}_{round}$ with input $\widetilde{v}_{n,k}^{(t)}, c_{n,k,r,q}^{(t)}, A_{q,r}^{(t)}$, get output $\widetilde{y}_{n,k}^{(t)l}$. Set $y_{n,k}^{(t)l} = \widetilde{y}_{n,k}^{(t)l}$ if $v_{n,k}^{(t)} \geq 0$, and 0 otherwise.

6: $\quad$ Return "NO" and $\sum_n\sum_k y_{n,k}^{(t)l} v_{n,k}^{(t)} + \tau \leq 1$

7: **EndIf**

The following is the detailed proof of Lemma 1. We first show that for any $\{v_{n,k}^{(t)}\}$, we can find in polynomial time a feasible integer allocation $y_{n,k}^{(t)l}$ such that

$$\sum_{n\in[N]}\sum_{k\in[K]} y_{n,k}^{(t)l} v_{n,k}^{(t)} \geq \frac{1}{\lambda}\sum_{n\in[N]}\sum_{k\in[K]} y_{n,k}^{(t)F} v_{n,k}^{(t)} \qquad (10)$$

Note the $v_{n,k}^{(t)}$ here can be negative value, so we cannot invoke $\mathcal{A}_{round}$ directly. That is the reason we define $\widetilde{v}_{n,k}^{(t)}$. Then we use $\mathcal{A}_{round}$, with input vector $\widetilde{v}_{n,k}^{(t)}$ to get $\widetilde{y}_{n,k}^{(t)l}$ satisfying:

$$\sum_{n\in[N]}\sum_{k\in[K]} \widetilde{y}_{n,k}^{(t)l}\widetilde{v}_{n,k}^{(t)} \geq \frac{1}{\lambda}\sum_{r\in[N]}\sum_{k\in[K]} y_{n,k}^{(t)F}\widetilde{v}_{n,k}^{(t)}$$
$$\geq \frac{1}{\lambda}\sum_{r\in[N]}\sum_{k\in[K]} y_{n,k}^{(t)F} v_{n,k}^{(t)}$$

Also note that $y_{n,k}^{(t)l}$ satisfies $\sum_{n\in[N]}\sum_{k\in[K]} y_{n,k}^{(t)l} v_{n,k}^{(t)} \geq \sum_{n\in[N]}\sum_{k\in[K]} \widetilde{y}_{n,k}^{(t)l}\widetilde{v}_{n,k}^{(t)}$. Thus we find such a integer solution $y_{n,k}^{(t)l}$.

Next we show the optimal value of (7), and hence of (6) is exactly 1. Here is a feasible solution with value 1: $\tau = 1, v_{n,k}^{(t)} = 0, \forall n \in [N], k \in [K]$, so the optimal value is at least 1. Then we claim that it is at most 1: suppose

$$\frac{1}{\lambda}\sum_{n\in[N]}\sum_{k\in[K]} y_{n,k}^{(t)F} v_{n,k}^{(t)} + \tau > 1$$

Then we can find an integer solution using the previous method such that

$$\sum_{n\in[N]}\sum_{k\in[K]} y_{n,k}^{(t)l} v_{n,k}^{(t)} + \tau \geq \frac{1}{\lambda}\sum_{n\in[N]}\sum_{k\in[K]} y_{n,k}^{(t)F} v_{n,k}^{(t)} + \tau \geq 1$$

,which contradicts constraint (7a).

Finally we show the function of our designed oracle is correct. Its correctness under two cases: objective value equals 1 and smaller than 1 is obvious. When it is larger than 1, the oracle generates $\widetilde{v}_{n,k}^{(\cdot)}$ and calls $\mathcal{A}_{round}$. The correctness of this method has been discussed. So this oracle solves (7) as we expect.

C. PROOF OF THEOREM 5

PROOF. The only difference between Thm. 5 and Thm. 1 is we introduce randomness here. Recall the proof of Thm. 1, the only claim affected by randomness is claim (2). We analyze the expectation of the increment on the primal and dual $E[\Delta P]$ and $E[\Delta D]$. At time t,

$$E[\Delta P^{(t)}] = \sum_{n\in[N]}\sum_{k\in K]} E[y_{n,k}^{(t)} b_{n,k}^{(t)}]$$

$$\begin{aligned}E[\Delta D^{(t)}] = &\sum_{n\in[N]} B_n E[x_n^{(t)} - x_n^{(t-1)}] + E[d]\\
\leq&\lambda(1+B_{max})E[p] + \sum_{n\in[N]} E[\sum_{k\in[K]} y_{n,k}^{(t)} b_{n,k}^{(t)}]\cdot\\
&E[x_n^{(t-1)} + \frac{1}{\gamma-1}]\\
\leq&E[\Delta P^{(t)}]\Big(\lambda(1+B_{max})\sum_{n\in[N]} E[1-x_n^{(t-1)}]+\\
&\frac{1}{\gamma-1} + \sum_{n\in[N]} E[x_n^{(t-1)}]\Big)\\
\leq&(\lambda(1+B_{max}) + \frac{1}{\gamma-1})E[\Delta P^{(t)}]\end{aligned}$$

So the final actual competitive ratio is $(1+B_{max})(\lambda(1+B_{max}) + \frac{1}{\gamma-1})$. □

Energy Procurement Strategies in the Presence of Intermittent Sources

Jayakrishnan Nair
Centrum Wiskunde & Informatica

Sachin Adlakha
California Institute of Technology

Adam Wierman
California Institute of Technology

ABSTRACT

The increasing penetration of intermittent, unpredictable renewable energy sources such as wind energy, poses significant challenges for utility companies trying to incorporate renewable energy in their portfolio. In this work, we study the problem of conventional energy procurement in the presence of intermittent renewable resources. We model the problem as a variant of the newsvendor problem, in which the presence of renewable resources induces supply side uncertainty, and in which conventional energy may be procured in three stages to balance supply and demand. We compute closed-form expressions for the optimal energy procurement strategy and study the impact of increasing renewable penetration, and of proposed changes to the structure of electricity markets. We explicitly characterize the impact of a growing renewable penetration on the procurement policy by considering a scaling regime that models the aggregation of unpredictable renewable sources. A key insight from our results is that there is a separation between the impact of the stochastic nature of this aggregation, and the impact of market structure and forecast accuracy. Additionally, we study the impact on procurement of two proposed changes to the market structure: the addition and the placement of an intermediate market. We show that addition of an intermediate market does not necessarily increase the efficiency of utilization of renewable sources. Further, we show that the optimal placement of the intermediate market is insensitive to the level of renewable penetration.

1. INTRODUCTION

Society's insatiable appetite for energy and growing environmental concerns have led many states in the United States to enact renewable portfolio standards. The standards mandate that utility companies must procure a certain percentage of their electricity from renewable sources [38]. For example, California has set the goal that 33% of its electricity should come from renewable sources by 2020. Among possible renewable sources, wind energy is expected to play a major role. There has been an explosive growth in installed wind capacity over the last few years [14] due to the ease of installation and low operational costs.

However, current electricity markets that govern energy procurement were designed for a scenario where there is very little uncertainty. More specifically, until now, supply side uncertainty has been low, arising mainly due to generator failures, which are rare. Furthermore, accurate demand forecasting ensures that the uncertainty in demand is small. However, going forward, the introduction of large volumes of highly intermittent and unpredictable renewable generation will increase supply side uncertainty dramatically. Thus, incorporating wind energy[1] into the energy portfolio of utilities is a challenging task that requires rethinking how electricity is procured [33, 11, 8]. *This paper seeks to provide insights into the impact of increasing supply side uncertainty on the 'efficiency' of procurement.*

Utility companies typically procure electricity via two modes of operation - *bilateral long-term contracts* and *competitive electricity markets* [21, 34, 15]. In the former, utility companies sign long term bilateral contracts with various generators to supply certain amounts of electricity for specified periods. Currently, most utility companies purchase the bulk of their generation through long-term bilateral contracts. This is feasible because the aggregate demand is highly predictable and because most conventional generators have very little uncertainty. To account for daily (or hourly) fluctuations in demand, the utility companies purchase the remainder of their electricity in competitive electricity markets. These markets, in which utility companies are buyers, and generators are sellers, are run by a third party called the independent service operator (ISO). There are typically two markets: a day-ahead or forward market, and a real-time or spot market. A utility company may buy electricity in both markets in order to ensure that it has enough supply to meet the demand.

Integration of wind energy into current electricity markets has attracted considerable attention in recent years; excellent surveys can be found in [9, 33]. Broadly speaking, there are two different approaches to integrating wind into current electricity markets. In one approach, wind power producers participate only in competitive electricity markets e.g., California's participating intermittent resource program (PIRP). Such a scenario has been analyzed, for instance, in [4]. In the second approach, the wind power producers do not participate in electricity markets; instead, they sign long-term multi-year contracts with utility companies. In such contracts, the utility company acquires rights to the energy generated from a certain wind farm installation in return for a predetermined payment. For example, Southern California Edison (SCE), a major utility company serving the greater Los Angeles area, has signed various contracts spanning $2 - 10$ years with various wind farms to procure wind energy ranging from 66.6 MW to 115 MW [29].

[1]For the remainder of the paper, we will use wind energy interchangeably with renewable energy; the models and the insights of our paper apply to any form of intermittent resource.

SIGMETRICS'14, June 16–20, 2014, Austin, Texas, USA.

http://dx.doi.org/10.1145/2591971.2591982.

In this paper, we study the consequences of following the second approach. In particular, we study a setting where utility companies have procured large volumes of intermittent, unpredictable renewable energy via long-term contracts. Because the realized amount of wind energy is variable and unpredictable, the utility company must still procure conventional generation via the electricity markets. Our goal is to study the impact of this long-term commitment to renewable generation on the procurement strategies for conventional generation.

Given the complexity of electricity procurement, we must consider a simplified model to be able to obtain analytical results. To that end, we consider a setting that ignores many complexities of generation and transmission (e.g., ramp constraints and line capacities), but models explicitly the multi-timescale nature of electricity procurement. Moreover, we assume that the utility company is a price-taker in the markets for conventional generation, i.e., it cannot influence the prices in these markets through its actions. These assumptions are standard in the literature and, though arguable, they enable us to derive a closed-form characterization of the optimal energy procurement strategy of the utility company, which leads to several useful, counter-intuitive insights.

Contributions of this paper. The main contributions of this work fall, briefly, into two categories: (i) we characterize the optimal procurement strategy in the presence of long-term contracts for intermittent, unpredictable generation; and (ii) we study the impact of increasing renewable penetration and proposed changes to market structure on the optimal procurement strategy. We describe these each in more detail in the following.

The **first contribution** of this work is to characterize the optimal procurement strategy for a utility company that has a long term contract with an unpredictable generation source, e.g., wind energy (see Section 3). More specifically, we derive closed-form formulas for the optimal procurement that a utility company needs to make in both long-term and day-ahead markets. This result is a generalization of solutions for the classical newsvendor problem [1, 32, 19]. A key feature of our result is that the optimal procurement quantities can be viewed in terms of *reserves*, where these reserve quantities are the additional purchases that the utility needs to make to balance the current uncertainty of the supply and the higher cost of procuring energy in future markets.

The **second contribution** of this work is to study how the optimal procurement strategy changes as the penetration of renewable energy grows (see Section 4). In particular, we consider a scenario where the quantity of renewable generation contracted for grows, and ask how the procurement changes. The scaling for increasing penetration that we consider allows for a wide variety of models for how the unpredictability of renewable generation changes with increased penetration. For example, it includes scaling via additional sources with either independent or highly correlated generation. Our main result from this section yields a simple, informative equation summarizing the impact of renewable generation on the procurement of conventional generation. Specifically, Theorem 2 states that the average total procurement of conventional generation in the presence of a long-term contract for wind is

$$d - \alpha\gamma + \delta\gamma^{\theta}$$

where d is the demand, α is the average generation of a single wind farm, γ is the number of wind farms (i.e., the renewable penetration), θ is a constant capturing the dependence between the generations of different wind farms, and δ is a constant that depends on the details of the market structure.

The way to interpret this equation is as follows. $d - \alpha\gamma$ represents the minimum average procurement, since this is the amount of demand that is not met by the wind. Thus, the 'extra' generation required because of the uncertainty of the wind is $\delta\gamma^{\theta}$. The key point about this term is that γ^{θ} is purely dependent on the degree of renewable penetration and the correlation between renewable sources; thus the impact of market structure is limited to δ.

The **third contribution** of this work is to study the impact of proposed changes to market structure [33, 8] on the optimal procurement strategy. In particular, there are two types of changes to the market structure that are most commonly considered: changing the *placement* of the day-ahead market, e.g., by moving it closer to real time; and *adding markets*, e.g., adding a new market between the day-ahead and real-time markets [28]. The results in Sections 5 and 6 address the impact each of these possibilities.

First, Section 5 studies the impact of the placement of markets on procurement. This is a particularly salient issue because one might expect that as the penetration of renewable energy increases, it is beneficial to shift markets closer to real time, in order to take advantage of the improved prediction accuracy of the renewable generation. Our results highlight that this intuition may not be true. Specifically, we prove that, under very general assumptions, the placement of the day-ahead market that minimizes the average total cost of procurement is independent of the penetration of renewables (Theorem 3).

Next, Section 6 studies the impact of additional markets on procurement. The addition of markets is often suggested as a way to help incorporate renewable generation by providing new markets closer to real time where predictions about renewable availability are more accurate. Our results highlight that one needs to be careful when considering such a change. Specifically, we contrast procurement in a two level market with procurement in a three level market in order to understand the role of adding an intermediate market. Of course, the *cost* of procurement always decreases as additional markets are introduced. However, with environmental concerns in mind, the key question is not about cost but about the *amount* of conventional generation procured. Perhaps surprisingly, additional markets do not always reduce the amount of conventional generation procured. Specifically, if we consider the addition of an intermediate market, then the average amount of conventional generation may drop or grow depending on the quality of the estimates for renewable generation, i.e., δ in Equation (1) may decrease or increase. Informally, if the estimation error is, in a sense, light-tailed (e.g., Gaussian), then the addition of an intermediate market reduces procurement of conventional generation (Theorem 5); but if the error has a heavy-tail (e.g., power-law, heavy-tailed Weibull), then the addition of an intermediate market can have the opposite effect (Theorem 4). Interestingly, it is typical to assume in analytical work that forecast errors are Gaussian [17, 37, 28], whereas empirical work on wind power generation suggests that a Weibull distribution may be a more accurate description [18, 5].

2. MODEL

Our goal in this paper is to understand how the presence of long-term contracts for intermittent, unpredictable renewable generation impacts the procurement of conventional generation. Such long-term contracts are a common, effective way of incorporating renewable energy into a utility's portfolio [29]; however they create challenges for a utility company's procurement of conventional generation. Thus, at the core of the paper, is a model of the electricity markets for conventional generation utility companies participate in, which we describe in this section. The key features we seek to capture are (i) the multi-timescale nature of electricity markets, (ii) price volatility, and (iii) the uncertainty of renewable generation.

Specifically, the procurement of conventional generation typically happens through participation in a multi-tiered set of electricity markets including a 'long-term market' (typically bilateral contracts), which could take place years or months ahead of time; an 'intermediate market', a.k.a. forward market, which could take place a day or several hours ahead of time; and a 'real-time market', a.k.a. spot market. This multi-tiered structure means that when the utility company purchases conventional generation in the long-term or intermediate markets it does not know how much renewable generation will be realized, nor does it know what the price will be in the spot market. So, its decisions must be made using only forecasts of these quantities, and, given the volatility of both renewable generation and prices, this creates a challenging procurement problem for the utility.

2.1 Model overview

To keep the model simple enough to allow analytic study, we ignore issues such as generator ramping constraints and transmission network capacity constraints in our model and further assume that the utility company has no access to large scale energy storage capacity. These assumptions allow us to focus on a single instant of time, which we denote by $t = 0$, and to consider only aggregate supply and demand.

We denote the electricity demand the utility company under consideration faces by d, and assume it is fixed and known ahead of time. This assumption is not restrictive in our setting, since demand uncertainty can be incorporated into the uncertainty of renewable generation. To meet the demand d, the utility company combines long-term contracts for renewable generation (for simplicity we will often refer to this simply as "wind") with participation in a typical three-tier set of electricity markets for conventional generation:

(i) A *long-term market*, in which the purchase commitment is made at time $-T_{lt}$. The price in this market is denoted p_{lt}, and when making its purchase commitment, the utility has a forecast $\hat{w}_{lt}$ of the wind generation that will be realized at $t = 0$.

(ii) An *intermediate market* (forward market), in which the purchase commitment is made at time $-T_{in}$. The price in this market is denoted p_{in}, and when making its purchase commitment, the utility has a forecast $\hat{w}_{in}$ of the wind generation that will be realized at $t = 0$.

(iii) A *real-time market* (spot market), in which the purchase commitment is made at time $t = 0$. The price in this market is denoted p_{rt}, and the utility knows the actual realization of the wind generation w at this time.

Of course, $-T_{lt} < -T_{in} < 0$.

The key feature of this model is the evolution of prices (p_{lt}, p_{in}, p_{rt}) and renewable forecasts $(\hat{w}_{lt}, \hat{w}_{in}, w)$ across markets. We describe our stochastic models for these evolutions in the following.

2.2 Evolution of prices

Prices in electricity markets are typically uncertain and volatile. Thus, for example, when deciding the procurement strategy in the long term market, a utility company does not know what the prices will be in the intermediate or real-time markets. However, in general, conventional energy tends to be more expensive in markets closer to real time. The reason for this is that the marginal costs of production tend to be higher in spot markets than in forward or long term markets because any conventional energy that is demanded closer to real time is provided by generators that have low start up time and these generators typically are more expensive than generators that require several hours to start up.

Our model for the evolution of prices across the markets focuses on the two features described above – price volatility and increasing costs closer to real time.

Specifically, we assume that p_{lt} is the known *fixed* price in the long-term markets. Since long-term purchase commitments are made via bilateral contract where the utility company knows the price, this assumption is very mild and typically true in reality.

Next, let p_{in} be the *random* price in the intermediate market. We make the assumption that $\mathbb{E}[p_{in}] > p_{lt}$. This assumption reflects the fact that the generators used to supply electricity in the intermediate markets tend to have a higher marginal cost of production, and hence on average, the price in the intermediate market is higher than the price in the long-term market [30]. Note that the utility company knows the *exact* realization of the intermediate price at time of procurement in the intermediate market (i.e., at time $-T_{in}$). However, when the utility company is making a purchase commitment in the long-term market, it is uncertain about the price in the intermediate market.

Similarly, let p_{rt} be the *random* price in the real-time (or spot) market. We make the assumption that $\mathbb{E}[p_{rt}|p_{in}] > p_{in}$. This assumption states that given any realization of the intermediate price, the real-time prices are higher on average. This reflects the fact that the electricity generated in the real-time market comes from fast ramp up generators which have a higher marginal cost of production. Note that at $t = 0$, the utility company knows the exact realization of the real-time price, but its value is uncertain at the time of the long-term and intermediate purchase commitments.

Importantly, the assumptions on the price evolution imply that $\mathbb{E}[p_{rt}] > \mathbb{E}[p_{in}] > p_{lt}$. However, any particular realization of the prices may have the price in the real-time market less than the intermediate price, or the price in the intermediate market less than the long-term price.

Additionally, we make the following mild regularity assumptions. Let $[\underline{p}_{in}, \bar{p}_{in}]$ denote the support of the random variable p_{in}, where $\underline{p}_{in} > 0$. We assume that p_{in} is associated with a density function $f_{p_{in}}(\cdot)$ which is continuous over $(\underline{p}_{in}, \bar{p}_{in})$, and $f_{p_{in}}(p) > 0$ for $p \in (\underline{p}_{in}, \bar{p}_{in})$. Also, $\mathbb{E}[p_{rt}|p_{in} = p]$ is continuous with respect to p over $(\underline{p}_{in}, \bar{p}_{in})$. Finally, we assume that $\mathbb{E}[p_{in}], \mathbb{E}[p_{rt}] < \infty$.

Our model is a generalization of the well-known martingale model of forecast evolution [16, 13, 17], which assumes additionally that the random variables $p_{lt} - p_{in}$ and $p_{in} - p_{rt}$ are independent and normally distributed.

Finally, it is important to note that our model for price evolution assumes that the utility company cannot impact the price. This corresponds to assuming that the utility company under consideration is a small participant in the market, and hence is a 'price-taker'. This is a common assumption in literature [4, 20] and is typically true if there is enough competition from the demand side in electricity markets. Of course it would also be interesting to consider a more general model where the prices arrive endogenously from market behavior. However, incorporating multiple forward markets into multi-stage models is notoriously difficult and, as a result, the assumption of perfect foresight (no prediction error) is typically needed to obtain analytic results in these cases, e.g., [26, 6].

2.3 Evolution of wind forecasts

A fundamental challenge of incorporating long-term contracts for renewable energy is the uncertainty about how much renewable energy will be realized in real time and the fact that the utility company must guarantee that it procures enough generation to meet the demand despite this uncertainty. In particular, at the time of each market, the utility company needs to forecast how much wind generation

$$h(r) \triangleq p_{lt} - \int_{p=\underline{p}_{in}}^{\bar{p}_{in}} p\bar{F}_{\mathcal{E}_1}(r - r_{in}(p)) f_{p_{in}}(p)\, dp - \int_{p=\underline{p}_{in}}^{\bar{p}_{in}} \mathbb{E}[p_{rt}|p_{in} = p] P\left(\mathcal{E}_1 + \mathcal{E}_2 > r;\ \mathcal{E}_1 < r - r_{in}(p)\right) f_{p_{in}}(p)\, dp = 0 \quad (6)$$

will be available at time $t = 0$. Note that if the available wind energy was known with certainty, the utility company could purchase its entire remaining demand exactly in the long-term market; however, because the amount of available wind energy at time $t = 0$ is highly uncertain at the time of. the long-term market, the utility company needs to balance its lowest cost purchase in the long-term market with better estimates of wind energy closer to real time.

To capture this, we consider a model where the forecast accuracy of the wind generation improves upon moving closer to real time, i.e., $t = 0$.

Specifically, we assume that the utility company comes to know the value of wind realized at time $t = 0$, denoted by w, only when purchasing generation in the real-time market. During the long-term and intermediate markets the utility only has estimates of w, denoted by $\hat{w}_{lt}$ and $\hat{w}_{in}$ respectively. Clearly, in general, uncertainty about the wind generation w decreases as one moves closer to real time. Formally, we capture this by assuming that

$$\hat{w}_{in} = \hat{w}_{lt} - \mathcal{E}_1, \text{ and } w = \hat{w}_{in} - \mathcal{E}_2, \quad (1)$$

where $\mathcal{E}_1$ and $\mathcal{E}_2$ are zero mean independent random variables, independent of the prices p_{in} and p_{rt}. In other words, we assume that the forecast of w evolves with *independent increments* where the random variables $\mathcal{E}_1$ and $\mathcal{E}_2$ capture these increments. Note that $\hat{w}_{lt}$ is a coarser estimate of w than $\hat{w}_{in}$, since the long-term forecast error $\hat{w}_{lt} - w = \mathcal{E}_1 + \mathcal{E}_2$ is more variable than the intermediate forecast error $\hat{w}_{in} - w = \mathcal{E}_2$. Our model is a generalization of the well-known martingale model of forecast evolution [16, 13, 17], which makes the additional assumption that $\mathcal{E}_1$ and $\mathcal{E}_2$ follow a Gaussian distribution.

Let $[L_1, R_1]$ and $[L_2, R_2]$ denote respectively the supports of the random variables $\mathcal{E}_1$ and $\mathcal{E}_2$, where $L_1, L_2 \in \{-\infty\} \cup \mathbb{R}$ and $R_1, R_2 \in \mathbb{R} \cup \{\infty\}$. We make the following regularity assumptions on the distributions of $\mathcal{E}_1$ and $\mathcal{E}_2$: they are associated with continuously differentiable density functions, denoted by $f_{\mathcal{E}_1}(\cdot)$ and $f_{\mathcal{E}_2}(\cdot)$ respectively, with $f_{\mathcal{E}_i}(x) > 0$ for $x \in (L_i, R_i)$.

This concludes our discussion of the model of this paper. The following notation is used heavily in the remainder of this paper. We use $P(E)$ to denote the probability of an event E, and $\bar{F}_X$ to denote the complementary cumulative distribution function associated with the random variable X, i.e., $\bar{F}_X(x) = P(X > x)$. Finally, $[x]_+ := \max\{x, 0\}$.

3. OPTIMAL PROCUREMENT

In this section, we formalize the utility's procurement problem, and then characterize the optimal procurement strategy. This strategy is the basis for the explorations of the impact of increased penetration of renewables and changes to market structure in subsequent sections.

3.1 The procurement problem

To begin, note that the procurement decision of the utility in each market can depend only on the information available to the utility company at that time. Specifically, in each market, we consider procurement strategies that depend only on (i) the wind estimate available at the time of purchase, (ii) the price of conventional generation in the current market, and (iii) the total conventional generation that has already been procured.[2] Accordingly, let $q_{lt}(\hat{w}_{lt}, p_{lt})$ denote the quantity of conventional generation procured in the long-term market, given the long-term wind estimate $\hat{w}_{lt}$ and long-term price p_{lt}. Similarly, let $q_{in}(\hat{w}_{in}, q_{lt}, p_{in})$ denote the quantity of conventional generation procured in the intermediate market, given the corresponding wind estimate $\hat{w}_{in}$, the realized price p_{in}, and q_{lt} (the quantity procured already). Finally, let $q_{rt}(w, q_{lt} + q_{in}, p_{rt})$ denote the the quantity of conventional generation procured in the real-time market, which depends on the realized wind w, the actual price in the real time market p_{rt}, and the quantity procured already, i.e., $q_{lt} + q_{in}$. For notational convenience, we often drop the arguments from these functions and simply write q_{lt}, q_{in}, q_{rt}. We make the assumption that the utility cannot sell power in any market[3], and thus the quantities procured in all three markets must be non negative.

When determining these procurement quantities, we assume that the utility company is seeking to minimize its expected total cost while ensuring that the total quantity purchased in these three markets satisfies the residual demand (i.e., the demand minus the available wind in real time). Thus, we can express the optimal procurement problem as follows:

$$\min_{q_{lt}, q_{in}, q_{rt}} \quad \mathbb{E}\left[p_{lt}q_{lt} + p_{in}q_{in} + p_{rt}q_{rt}\right] \qquad (P)$$
$$\text{subject to } q_{lt} \geq 0,\ q_{in} \geq 0,\ q_{rt} \geq 0$$
$$q_{lt} + q_{in} + q_{rt} + w \geq d.$$

Recall that q_{lt}, q_{in} and q_{rt} are functions that depend on the corresponding wind estimate, price of conventional generation, and the total procurement so far. Here, the expectation is with respect to the randomness associated with the wind forecast evolution and price volatility.

The optimal procurement problem posed above is mathematically equivalent to a variant of the classical newsvendor problem [19, 27]. In Section 7, we discuss the relationship between our work and the literature on the newsvendor problem.

A final comment about the the optimal procurement problem above is that we have considered a three tiered market structure that models the common current practice. In general, the optimal procurement problem is simply a Markov decision process, and can be studied for arbitrary numbers of tiers, e.g., see [28]. We limit ourselves to a three tiered structure in this paper to keep the analysis simple and the resulting formulas interpretable.

3.2 The optimal procurement strategy

The following theorem is the foundational result for the remainder of the paper. It characterizes the optimal procurement strategy for a utility company in a three tiered market with price volatility.

THEOREM 1. *The optimal procurement strategy for the utility company in the three tiered market scenario of Problem (P) is:*

$$q_{lt}^* = [d - \hat{w}_{lt} + r_{lt}]_+ \quad (2)$$

[2] Given our stochastic model for prices and wind forecast evolution, it is easy to show that there is no loss of optimality in restricting policies to this class.

[3] Our model can be extended to relax this assumption. However, we do not consider this generalization because it adds complexity without providing additional insight.

$$q_{in}^* = [d - \hat{w}_{in} - q_{lt} + r_{in}(p_{in})]_+ \quad (3)$$

$$q_{rt}^* = [d - w - q_{lt} - q_{in}]_+ , \quad (4)$$

where

$$r_{in}(p_{in}) = \bar{F}_{\mathcal{E}_2}^{-1}\left(\frac{p_{in}}{\mathbb{E}[p_{rt}|p_{in}]}\right), \quad (5)$$

and r_{lt} is the unique solution of (6).

The proof of Theorem 1 can be found in [25]. A key feature of this theorem is that the structure of the the optimal procurement strategy gives a natural interpretation to r_{lt} and $r_{in}(p_{in})$ as *reserve levels.* Specifically, at the time of purchase in the long-term market, $d - \hat{w}_{lt}$ can be interpreted as an estimate of the conventional procurement that is required to meet the demand. Then r_{lt} is the additional 'reserve' purchased by the utility to balance the current wind uncertainty and the higher cost of conventional energy in subsequent markets. The reserve $r_{in}(p_{in})$ has a similar interpretation. We note that the intermediate reserve level is a function of the price of conventional generation in the intermediate market. For notational simplicity, we often drop the argument of this function, and simply write r_{in}. We henceforth refer to r_{lt} and r_{in} as the (optimal) long-term and intermediate reserves respectively.

It is important to point out that the reserves r_{lt} and r_{in} may be positive or negative. A negative reserve implies that it is optimal for the utility to maintain a net procurement level that is *less* than the currently anticipated residual demand, and purchase any shortfall in subsequent markets. The values of the optimal reserves depend on the price volatility (via the distribution of intermediate and real-time prices) as well as the accuracy of the wind forecasts $\hat{w}_{lt}$ and $\hat{w}_{in}$ (via the distributions of the random variables $\mathcal{E}_1$ and $\mathcal{E}_2$). Note that the optimal reserves do not depend on the demand d, or on procurements made in prior markets.

As is evident from Equation (5), the optimal reserve in the intermediate market is structurally similar to the critical fractile solution of the classical newsvendor model [1]. This is because, at the time of the intermediate market, the utility company conjectures the average real time price to be $\mathbb{E}[p_{rt}|p_{in}]$, and having already purchased the quantity q_{lt}, it faces a problem similar to the classical newsvendor problem.

Finally, Theorem 1 highlights the need for the following additional assumption in order to avoid trivial solutions.

ASSUMPTION 1. *We assume that the demand is large enough that the utility company procures a positive quantity in the long-term market. That is, $d - \hat{w}_{lt} + r_{lt} > 0$.*

This assumption ensures that the optimal procurement problem in the three market has a non-trivial solution in the following sense: if $d - \hat{w}_{lt} - r_{lt} \leq 0$, then the utility company procures $q_{lt}^* = 0$ in the long term. In this case, the procurement problem effectively reduces to a two-tier market scenario. Intuitively, Assumption 1 will hold as long as the demand d exceeds the peak capacity of the renewable installations, which is of course true in most current practical scenarios. Assumption 1 allows us to rewrite the optimal procurement quantities in three markets as follows:

$$\begin{aligned} q_{lt}^* &= d - \hat{w}_{lt} + r_{lt}, \\ q_{in}^* &= [\mathcal{E}_1 - r_{lt} + r_{in}(p_{in})]_+ , \\ q_{rt}^* &= [\mathcal{E}_2 - r_{lt} + \min\{\mathcal{E}_1, r_{lt} - r_{in}(p_{in})\}]_+ , \end{aligned} \quad (7)$$

where we abuse notation to let q_{lt}^*, q_{in}^* and q_{rt}^* represent the (random) quantities that are purchased in the long-term, the intermediate, and the real-time markets respectively.

4. THE IMPACT OF INCREASING RENEWABLE PENETRATION

The penetration of renewable energy, in particular of wind energy, is poised for major growth over the coming years. A consequence of this is that utility companies will face an ever increasing supply side uncertainty. In this section, we explore the impact of this growth on procurement. Specifically, we ask: *how will the optimal procurement policy change as the volume of intermittent wind resources increases?*

To answer this question, we introduce a scaling regime for wind penetration, which models the effect of aggregating the output of several wind generators. A key feature of our scaling model is that it allows for varying levels of stochastic dependence between the intermittent energy sources being aggregated. For example, our model lets us study the aggregation of independent sources, as well as perfectly correlated sources.

Based on this scaling model, we study how the optimal reserves, the amount of conventional generation procured, as well as the cost of procurement scale with increasing wind penetration. Our analysis yields clean and easy to interpret scaling laws for these quantities. Remarkably, the scaling laws reveal a decoupling between the impact of the level of stochastic dependence between different wind sources and the impact of market structure and wind forecast accuracy.

4.1 A scaling regime

We begin by describing our scaling model for wind penetration. We start with a baseline scenario. Let us denote by α the average output of a single intermittent generator. For concreteness, we refer to this as the baseline wind farm in the following. We let $\tilde{\mathcal{E}}_1$ and $\tilde{\mathcal{E}}_2$ be the error random variables that relate the long-term wind estimate $\hat{w}_{lt}$ to the estimate of the wind in the intermediate market $\hat{w}_{in}$ and the actual wind realization w (see Equation (1)). We assume that in the long term market there is no better estimate of the wind than the long-term average, i.e., $\hat{w}_{lt} = \alpha$. Note that the optimal procurement in the baseline scenario (before scaling) can be computed using Theorem 1. For the remainder of this section, we use $\tilde{r}_{lt}$ and $\tilde{r}_{in}$ to denote respectively the optimal long-term and the intermediate reserve in the baseline scenario. We emphasize that $\tilde{r}_{in}$ is a function of the realization of the intermediate price p_{in}, although we suppress this dependence for notational convenience in this section.

To scale the wind penetration, we introduce a scale parameter γ that is proportional to the capacity of wind generation. The scale parameter γ may be interpreted as the number of (homogeneous) wind farms whose aggregate output is available to the utility company. Thus, the average wind energy available to the utility company is given by $\hat{w}_{lt}(\gamma) = \gamma\alpha$. Clearly, as the capacity of wind generation scales, the error in the wind forecast available at both the long-term and the intermediate markets will also scale, and this scaling will depend on the correlation between the generation at each of the wind farms. We use the following simple, but general scaling model.

$$\begin{aligned} \hat{w}_{lt}(\gamma) &= \gamma\alpha, \\ \mathcal{E}_1(\gamma) &= \gamma^{\theta}\tilde{\mathcal{E}}_1, \\ \mathcal{E}_2(\gamma) &= \gamma^{\theta}\tilde{\mathcal{E}}_2, \end{aligned} \quad (8)$$

where we let $\theta \in [1/2, 1]$. It is important to point out that our scaling regime leaves the prices of conventional generation unchanged; we scale only the volume of intermittent generation.

To interpret this scaling, consider first the case $\theta = 1$. In this case, $\mathcal{E}_1 = \gamma\tilde{\mathcal{E}}_1$ and $\mathcal{E}_2 = \gamma\tilde{\mathcal{E}}_2$, implying that $\hat{w}_{in}(\gamma)$ and $w(\gamma)$ scale proportionately with γ. This scaling corresponds to a scenario where the aggregate wind output with γ wind farms is simply γ times the output of the baseline wind farm. One would expect such a scaling to occur if the wind farms are co-located.

The case of $\theta = 1/2$ (with $\tilde{\mathcal{E}}_1$ and $\tilde{\mathcal{E}}_2$ being normally distributed) corresponds to a central limit theorem scaling, and seeks to capture the scenario where the output of all wind farms are independent. Equation (8) captures this scenario exactly if the forecast evolution distributions for each wind farm follow a Gaussian distribution. If not, Equation (8) can be interpreted as an approximation for large enough γ based on the central limit theorem. Intuitively, one would expect such a scaling if the different wind farms are geographically far apart.

Finally, the case $\theta \in (\frac{1}{2}, 1)$ seeks to capture correlations that are intermediate between independence and perfect correlation (see, for instance [2, 35]).

Note that the forecast error distributions grow slowest when the outputs of different wind farms are independent, and fastest when the outputs are perfectly correlated.

4.2 Scaling results

Given the scaling regime described above, we can characterize the impact of increasing penetration of intermittent resources on the procurement of conventional generation. First, we analyze how the optimal reserve levels scale with increasing wind penetration. Next, we use these results to obtain scaling laws for the procurement quantities in the three markets, and also the total procurement and the total cost of procurement.

The scaling of reserve levels.

The following lemma characterizes the scaling of the optimal reserves under our wind scaling model. It shows the optimal reserve levels in the long-term and intermediate markets follow the same scaling as imposed on the distributions of the forecast errors.

LEMMA 1. *Under the scaling regime defined in Equation (8), the optimal long-term and intermediate reserves scale as:*

$$r_{lt}(\gamma) = \gamma^\theta \tilde{r}_{lt}, \quad r_{in}(\gamma) = \gamma^\theta \tilde{r}_{in}. \tag{9}$$

We emphasize that $\tilde{r}_{in}$ and $r_{in}(\gamma)$ are both functions of the intermediate price. Equation (9) states that the function $r_{in}(\gamma)$ scales proportionately to γ^θ, i.e., $(r_{in}(\gamma))(p_{in}) = \gamma^\theta \tilde{r}_{in}(p_{in})$.

PROOF. From Theorem 1, given any scale parameter γ, the optimal reserve in the intermediate market $r_{in}(\gamma)$ is the unique solution of the equation

$$P\left(\mathcal{E}_2(\gamma) > r_{in}(\gamma)\right) = \frac{p_{in}}{\mathbb{E}[p_{rt}|p_{in}]}. \tag{10}$$

Now, noting that $\mathcal{E}_2(\gamma) = \gamma^\theta \tilde{\mathcal{E}}_2$, and $P\left(\tilde{\mathcal{E}}_2 > \tilde{r}_{in}\right) = \frac{p_{in}}{\mathbb{E}[p_{rt}|p_{in}]}$ (by Theorem 1 applied to the baseline scenario), we conclude that $r_{in}(\gamma) = \gamma^\theta \tilde{r}_{in}$ satisfies Equation (10).

The optimal long-term reserve $r_{lt}(\gamma)$ is the unique solution of Equation (6), with $\mathcal{E}_1$, $\mathcal{E}_2$, and r_{in} substituted by $\mathcal{E}_1(\gamma)$, $\mathcal{E}_2(\gamma)$, and $r_{in}(\gamma)$, respectively. As before, using the characterization of $\tilde{r}_{lt}$ obtained from Equation (6) applied to the baseline scenario, it is easy to verify that $r_{lt}(\gamma) = \gamma^\theta \tilde{r}_{lt}$. □

The scaling of procurement quantities.

Using Lemma 1, we can now characterize the optimal procurement amounts in the three markets. As in Section 3, to avoid the trivial solution with zero long-term procurement, we restrict the range of the scale parameter γ to satisfy

$$d > \gamma\alpha - \gamma^\theta \tilde{r}_{lt}, \tag{11}$$

This ensures that the optimal long-term procurement, given by $q^*_{lt}(\gamma) = [d - \hat{w}_{lt}(\gamma) + r_{lt}(\gamma)]_+$ is strictly positive.[4] For the remainder of this section, we focus on the range of scale parameter γ that satisfies Condition (11). Intuitively speaking, Condition (11) will hold as long as the demand is larger than the peak wind capacity. Under this assumption, using Equation (7) and Lemma 1, we get that the optimal procurement quantities in the long-term, intermediate, and real-time markets is given by

$$\begin{aligned} q^*_{lt}(\gamma) &= d - \gamma\alpha + \gamma^\theta \tilde{r}_{lt}, \\ q^*_{in}(\gamma) &= \gamma^\theta \left[\tilde{\mathcal{E}}_1 - \tilde{r}_{lt} + \tilde{r}_{in}\right]_+, \\ q^*_{rt}(\gamma) &= \gamma^\theta \left[\tilde{\mathcal{E}}_2 - \tilde{r}_{lt} + \min\{\tilde{\mathcal{E}}_1, \tilde{r}_{lt} - \tilde{r}_{in}\}\right]_+. \end{aligned} \tag{12}$$

The above equations reveal that as we increase the penetration of wind, the optimal procurement in the intermediate and the real-time markets increases proportionately to γ^θ. This increasing procurement in markets closer to real time is a consequence of the increasing uncertainty in the renewable forecasts. Indeed, note that the procurements in the intermediate and real-time markets scale in exactly the same manner as the forecast error distributions. Therefore, these procurements scale slowest when outputs of different wind farms are independent, and fastest when the outputs are perfectly correlated. From the standpoint of the system operator, Equation (12) describes how the installed capacity of fast ramp conventional generators that can supply energy in the intermediate and real-time markets needs to scale as the capacity of wind generation scales.

The scaling of the total procurement and the total cost of procurement.

As we scale the wind capacity, we expect that the amount of total conventional energy procured, as well as the cost of procurement must decrease. The following theorem characterizes the scaling laws for these quantities. Let $TP(\gamma)$ and $TC(\gamma)$ denote respectively the total procurement of conventional energy and the total cost of procurement, corresponding to scale parameter γ.

THEOREM 2. *For the range of scale parameter γ satisfying Equation (11), the expected total procurement and the expected total cost are given by*

$$\mathbb{E}[TP(\gamma)] = d - \alpha\gamma + \delta\gamma^\theta, \tag{13}$$

$$\mathbb{E}[TC(\gamma)] = p_{lt}(d - \alpha\gamma) + \delta'\gamma^\theta, \tag{14}$$

where, $\delta \geq 0$ and $\delta' \geq 0$ are defined as

$$\begin{aligned} \delta &\triangleq \tilde{r}_{lt} + \mathbb{E}\left[\tilde{\mathcal{E}}_1 - (\tilde{r}_{lt} - \tilde{r}_{in})\right]_+ \\ &\quad + \mathbb{E}\left[\tilde{\mathcal{E}}_2 - \tilde{r}_{lt} + \min\{\tilde{\mathcal{E}}_1, \tilde{r}_{lt} - \tilde{r}_{in}\}\right]_+, \\ \delta' &\triangleq p_{lt}\tilde{r}_{lt} + \mathbb{E}\left\{p_{in}\left[\tilde{\mathcal{E}}_1 - (\tilde{r}_{lt} - \tilde{r}_{in})\right]_+\right\} \\ &\quad + \mathbb{E}\left\{p_{rt}\left[\tilde{\mathcal{E}}_2 - \tilde{r}_{lt} + \min\{\tilde{\mathcal{E}}_1, \tilde{r}_{lt} - \tilde{r}_{in}\}\right]_+\right\}. \end{aligned}$$

The scaling law (13) has the following interpretation. If there were no uncertainty in the wind generation, i.e., $w(\gamma) = \hat{w}_{lt}(\gamma) = \alpha\gamma$, then it easy to see that the utility would procure the exact residual demand, i.e., $d - \alpha\gamma$ in the long-term market (since the prices of conventional generation increase

[4]One sufficient θ-independent condition that ensures that Condition (11) holds is $\gamma < \frac{d}{\alpha + |\tilde{r}_{lt}|}$. This imposes an upper bound on the degree of penetration that we consider.

on average as we move closer to real time). From (13), we see that on average, the utility has to make an 'additional procurement' equal to $\delta\gamma^\theta$ as a result of the uncertainty in the wind generation. The fact that this additional procurement grows proportionately to γ^θ highlights the benefit of aggregating independent wind sources. Specifically, if $\theta = 1$, i.e., the wind farms are co-located, then the additional procurement is of the same order as the wind capacity. On the other hand, if $\theta = 1/2$, i.e., the wind farms are geographically far apart, then the additional procurement grows much slower than the wind capacity.

The scaling law (14) has a similar interpretation. As before, note that if there were no uncertainty in the wind generation, then $p_{lt}(d-\gamma\alpha)$ equals the (optimal) average cost of conventional procurement. From (14), we see that on average, the utility incurs an 'additional cost' equal to $\delta'\gamma^\theta$ as a result of the uncertainty in the wind generation. Once again, we see the benefit of aggregating independent wind sources. Thus, intuitively speaking, a utility company would benefit from signing long-term contracts with wind generators that are as geographically spread out as possible.[5]

The structure of the scaling laws (13) and (14) also reveals an interesting separation between the impact of the level of stochastic dependence between different wind sources and the impact of market structure and wind forecast accuracy. To see this, consider the 'additional procurement' $\delta\gamma^\theta$ in Equation (13) and the 'additional cost' $\delta'\gamma^\theta$ in Equation (14). The factor γ^θ is purely dependent upon the volume of wind capacity and the stochastic dependence between the outputs of the different wind farms. On the other hand, the factors δ and δ' depend on only the prices of conventional energy in the three markets (and their volatility), and the baseline forecast error distributions. In other words, δ and δ' are invariant with respect to the aggregation of wind sources. As we discuss in the next section, this separation has interesting consequences for market design.

We now present the proof of Theorem 2, which follows from Lemma 1 and Theorem 1.

PROOF OF THEOREM 2. The expected total procurement and the expected total cost follow trivially from Equation (12).

To prove that $\delta \geq 0$, we note that the optimization problem P requires that the total procurement exceed $d - w(\gamma)$ for every realization of wind w. Thus, the expected total procurement must satisfy $\mathbb{E}[TP(\gamma)] \geq d - \gamma\alpha$, which implies, using Equation (13), that $\delta \geq 0$.

To prove that $\delta' \geq 0$, we consider a hypothetical procurement formulation with no wind uncertainty. Specifically, consider a scenario in which the values of $\mathcal{E}_1(\gamma)$ and $\mathcal{E}_2(\gamma)$ are revealed to the utility a priori. This implies that the utility knows the exact realization of the wind generation, and therefore the exact residual demand, before making its procurement decisions for conventional generation. This conventional generation can be procured in the same three-tiered market structure as in our original formulation, with the same price volatility.

The problem of optimal procurement in this hypothetical setting, seeking to minimize the average cost of procurement (and subject to satisfying the demand d), can be formulated as before. Since the prices are ordered on average, it is easy to show that the optimal policy in this case is to buy the entire residual demand (equal to $d - w(\gamma)$) in the long-term market. However, yet another feasible strategy is to make procurements according to Equation (12). Clearly, the average cost for this latter strategy must be at-least the average cost of the optimal policy, i.e.,

$$\mathbb{E}_{p_{in},p_{rt}}\Big(p_{lt}(d-\gamma\alpha+\gamma^\theta\tilde{r}_{lt}) + p_{in}\gamma^\theta\left[\tilde{\mathcal{E}}_1 - \tilde{r}_{lt} + \tilde{r}_{in}\right]_+ + p_{rt}\gamma^\theta\left[\tilde{\mathcal{E}}_2 - \tilde{r}_{lt} + \min\{\tilde{\mathcal{E}}_1, \tilde{r}_{lt} - \tilde{r}_{in}\}\right]_+\Big)$$
$$\geq p_{lt}(d - w(\gamma)).$$

Note that the expectation above is only taken with respect to the prices. Now, taking expectations with respect to $\mathcal{E}_1(\gamma)$ and $\mathcal{E}_2(\gamma)$, we conclude that $\mathbb{E}[TC(\gamma)] \geq p_{lt}(d - \alpha\gamma)$, which implies, using Equation (14), that $\delta' \geq 0$. This completes the proof. □

5. THE OPTIMAL PLACEMENT OF THE INTERMEDIATE MARKET

In current electricity markets, the intermediate market takes place about 14 hours before $t = 0$ (this market is called the day-ahead or forward market) [7]. Because the demand can be predicted reasonably accurately by this time, this allows the utility to procure most of its generation much before the time of use. However, accurate prediction of wind in the current day-ahead markets is not feasible. Thus, it is commonly suggested that as the penetration of wind increases, the system operator may decide to move the intermediate market closer to real time to allow for better prediction of the wind. In this section, we consider the optimal placement of the intermediate market and study how this optimal placement changes as we increase the penetration of wind energy.

Recall that, in our model, the intermediate market takes place T_{in} time units prior to the time of use (i.e. $t = 0$). If the system operator were to move this intermediate market closer to real time, this would imply better estimates of available wind at that time. However, in moving the market closer to real time, the procured conventional generation must come from generators that have faster ramp up times. These generators are typically more expensive and hence we would expect that the price of the conventional generation in the intermediate market would increase (on average) as we move the market closer to real time. We define the optimal placement of the intermediate market as the one that minimizes the average total procurement cost. Note that this optimal placement balances an improving forecast of the wind generation moving closer to real time with an increasing price of conventional energy.

The optimal placement is clearly a function of how the forecast errors $\tilde{\mathcal{E}}_1$ and $\tilde{\mathcal{E}}_2$ change as the function of the intermediate market time T_{in}. It also depends on how the joint distribution of the prices of conventional generation in the intermediate and the real-time market changes as T_{in} changes. Let us denote by T_{in}^* the optimal placement of the intermediate market that minimizes the expected total cost of procuring conventional generation.

Importantly, Theorems 1 and 2 allow the computation of T_{in}^* numerically. However, there is little structural insight for this placement that can be provided. But, an important question that we can provide analytic insight about is the following: *how does the optimal placement of the intermediate market change as we increase the penetration of wind energy?*

The answer to this question has significant implications for future market design. Remarkably, based on the scaling regime developed in the previous section, the following theorem tells us that the optimal placement does not depend upon the scale parameter γ or the aggregation parameter θ.

THEOREM 3. *For the wind scaling satisfying Equation* (11), *over the range of* γ *satisfying Condition* (11) *for all con-*

[5]This above discussion of course assumes implicitly that network capacity is not a bottleneck in the utilization of the available wind energy.

sidered placements of the intermediate market, the optimal placement of the intermediate market is independent of the scale parameter γ and the correlation parameter θ.

PROOF. From Theorem 2, we note that the expected total cost of procurement is given by

$$\mathbb{E}[TC(\gamma)] = p_{lt}(d - \alpha\gamma) + \delta'\gamma^{\theta}.$$

Furthermore, the effect of placement is only on the parameter δ' (via the distributions of $\tilde{\mathcal{E}}_1$, $\tilde{\mathcal{E}}_2$, p_{in}, and the prices p_{in} and p_{rt}) which is independent of γ and θ. Thus, the optimal placement is independent of scale parameter γ and the aggregation parameter θ. □

Theorem 3 has important implications for market design. It says that the optimal intermediate market placement can be decided independently of how many wind farms are there in the system, and how correlated their outputs are. Thus, the system operator can keep the placement of this market fixed as more wind energy is incorporated into the system.

6. THE VALUE OF ADDITIONAL FORWARD MARKETS

One of the key objectives of this paper is to study the impact of increased renewable penetration on the structure of electricity markets. As seen in the previous section, the optimal placement of the intermediate market is independent of the amount of wind present in the system. In this section, we look at another important market design question: *can we facilitate the penetration of renewable energy by providing additional forward markets?* It is commonly suggested that having additional markets would be beneficial, since this allows the utility to better exploit the evolution of the wind forecast. Indeed, the intuition is true in terms of procurement cost – having additional forward markets benefits the utility company (and thus the end consumer) by lowering the average cost of conventional energy procurement.

However, minimizing cost is not the only goal. Another important question is if additional forward markets also lower the *total amount* of conventional energy that a utility company needs to procure. From the environmental viewpoint, this is an extremely relevant question; reducing conventional energy use is one of the key driving factors for the renewable portfolio standards. Indeed, one would desire that the policy decision of adding a forward market for conventional energy increases the efficiency of the available renewable sources by decreasing our consumption of conventional generation.

In order to address the impact of additional markets on total procurement, we study the effect of the addition of a single intermediate (forward) market on the (average) total conventional procurement. Specifically, we compare the average total procurement under the three-tier market scenario with the average total procurement under a scenario where there is no intermediate market. Let us denote the average total procurement under the three-tier market scenario by $TP_{l,i,r}$, and let $TP_{l,r}$ represent the total procurement under the scenario with no intermediate market.

Intuitively, one expects that the addition of an intermediate market helps utility companies exploit the refined wind estimate to better match its residual demand with the overall conventional procurement. This would suggest that

$$\mathbb{E}[TP_{l,i,r}] < \mathbb{E}[TP_{l,r}];$$

in other words, the addition of an intermediate market helps reduce total procurement. However, as the theorem below suggests, this intuition is not always correct. In fact, for some forecast evolution models and price structures, the addition of an intermediate forward market actually increases the average total procurement.

THEOREM 4. *If the distribution of $\mathcal{E}_2$ has infinite support on the left (i.e., $L_2 = -\infty$), and*

$$\lim_{x\to-\infty} \frac{f_{\mathcal{E}_2}(x)}{F_{\mathcal{E}_2}(x)} = 0, \tag{15}$$

then, there exist values of demand d and deterministic prices satisfying $0 < p_{lt} < p_{in} < p_{rt}$ such that $\mathbb{E}[TP_{l,i,r}] > \mathbb{E}[TP_{l,r}]$.

This theorem provides a counter example to the commonly held assumption that adding forward markets is always beneficial both from the cost and procurement viewpoints. Importantly, Theorem 4 highlights that the total procurement with three markets can be larger than with two markets even in situations with *no price volatility*, i.e., deterministic prices. Thus, the counterintuitive behavior does not result from uncertainty in prices, and can be seen as a consequence of uncertainty about wind generation.

Additionally, it is important to note that the condition given in Equation (15) depends on the probability that the random variable $\mathcal{E}_2$ takes large negative values. Recall from Equation (1) that $\mathcal{E}_2 = \hat{w}_{in} - w$; in other words the condition in the theorem looks at the probability that the wind forecast at the intermediate time $\hat{w}_{in}$ severely *underestimates* the actual wind generation.

We can interpret the condition in Equation (15) as a hazard rate condition. Note that if the distribution of $\mathcal{E}_2$ is symmetric, then the condition can be rewritten as $\lim_{x\to\infty} \frac{f_{\mathcal{E}_2}(x)}{\bar{F}_{\mathcal{E}_2}(x)} = 0$. The quantity in the above equation is the conventionally defined hazard rate function. Condition (15) states that the distribution of $\mathcal{E}_2$ is long-tailed to the left [12, 31]. Long-tailed distributions are an important sub-class of the class of heavy-tailed distributions, and are typically used to model phenomenon in which extreme values occur with a non-negligible probability. Examples of long-tailed distributions include distributions with power-law tails. Therefore, Theorem 4 can be interpreted informally as follows. If the wind estimate at the point of additional markets can significantly underestimate the wind generation w with a non-negligible probability, then the average total procurement may increase with the additional market.

Further, note that the assumption of infinite support of $\mathcal{E}_2$ to the left in the statement of Theorem 4 is not restrictive. Indeed, it follows from Theorem 4 that the inequality $\mathbb{E}[TP_{l,i,r}] > \mathbb{E}[TP_{l,r}]$ can also hold with bounded $\mathcal{E}_2$. Starting with a model instance with infinite support $\mathcal{E}_2$ that satisfies the above inequality, it is easy to show that the inequality would continue to hold if the random variable $\mathcal{E}_2$ is truncated at a large enough value.

Theorem 4 highlights the importance of building better wind forecast models and understanding the distributions of wind forecast errors. The theorem also suggests that, if the probability that the wind forecast severely underestimates the actual available wind is small, then adding an intermediate market might reduce the average total procurement. The following theorem formalizes this intuition by giving a sufficient condition for this to occur. In order to provide a clear comparison with Theorem 4, the sufficient condition is also stated in the context of deterministic prices.

THEOREM 5. *Suppose prices are deterministic and satisfy $0 < p_{lt} < p_{in} < p_{rt}$, and that the distribution of $\mathcal{E}_2$ satisfies the following properties:*

(i) $f_{\mathcal{E}_2}(x)$ is non-decreasing for $x < 0$ and non-increasing for $x > 0$,

(ii) $\frac{f_{\mathcal{E}_2}(x)}{F_{\mathcal{E}_2}(x)}$ is strictly decreasing over $x \in (L_2, 0)$,

(iii) $\frac{f'_{\mathcal{E}_2}(x)}{f_{\mathcal{E}_2}(x)}$ is non-increasing over $x \in (L_2, 0)$.

Then, under Assumption 1, $\mathbb{E}[TP_{l,i,r}] < \mathbb{E}[TP_{l,r}]$.

Theorem 5 highlights that there are a broad set of forecast error distributions for which the introduction of an intermediate market will lower the average total procurement. These are defined via three conditions. The first condition simply states that the density function $f_{\mathcal{E}_2}$ is unimodal at $x = 0$, i.e., it has its maximum at $x = 0$, and is monotone over $x < 0$ and $x > 0$. The last two conditions are concerned with the behavior of the distribution of $\mathcal{E}_2$ when $\mathcal{E}_2 \leq 0$, i.e., when $\hat{w}_{in}$ under estimates the actual wind generation w. Condition *(ii)* is in contrast with the condition in Theorem 4; it requires that the hazard rate of the left tail of $\mathcal{E}_2$ be strictly decreasing. This implies that $\mathcal{E}_2$ is light-tailed to the left. The conditions of Theorem 5 are satisfied by many common distributions, such as the zero mean Gaussian distribution and the zero mean uniform distribution.

Interestingly, it is typical to assume in analytical work that forecast errors are Gaussian [17, 37, 28] (leading to the conclusion of Theorem 5), whereas empirical work on wind power generation suggests that a truncated version of a heavy-tailed Weibull distribution may be a more accurate description [18, 5] (potentially leading to the conclusion of Theorem 4).

Theorems 4 and 5 are proven in the appendix.

7. RELATED LITERATURE

There has been significant recent interest in understanding the impact of the integration of renewable sources into electricity markets. Various aspects of this issue have been studied, including energy storage (see, for example, [3, 20]), demand response (see, for example, [22, 23]), and transmission constraints (see, for example, [39, 10]). In this paper, our focus is on the impact of long-term contracts for renewable generation on the efficiency of energy procurement by utility companies.

The problem of energy procurement at the level of the utility company in the presence of renewable generation has been analyzed in recent years by [24, 36, 28, 30], among others. In particular, [24] analyzes a competitive electricity market equilibrium between a generator and a utility company in the presence of wind generation. In contrast, [36, 28, 30] assume that the utility company is a price taker, and pose the procurement problem for the utility company as an optimization with exogenous prices; this is also the approach taken in the present paper. The procurement formulations in [36, 28] assume fixed prices, whereas the formulation in [30] allows for random prices that may be correlated with the wind forecast evolution. Indeed, the procurement formulation (P) in this paper is closely related to the formulations in these papers. However, while the focus of the above mentioned papers is to obtain the optimal procurement strategy for the utility company, the focus of the present paper is to use the optimal strategy as a starting point to investigate the impact of increasing wind penetration and market structure (i.e., placement and inclusion/exclusion of markets).

Another stream of literature that is related to this paper is that related to the classic newsvendor problem [27, 19]. Our optimal procurement formulation (P) is mathematically equivalent to a variant of the newsvendor problem. Indeed, by substituting demand by the residual demand, i.e., demand minus wind (thereby shifting the uncertainty from the supply side to the demand side) and interpreting the real-time price as a shortfall penalty, the optimization (P) reduces to single period newsvendor problem in which procurements can be made at two different lead times. See [32] for a survey of the literature relating to such variations of the classic newsvendor problem. However, in contrast to this body of work, the focus of the current paper is to understand the impact on electricity procurement of the *increasing* supply side uncertainty induced by an increasing penetration of renewable resources. To the best of our knowledge, an effort to understand the effect of "scaling up the uncertainty" has not been attempted in the literature pertaining to the newsvendor problem, and so this paper represents a contribution to the newsvendor literature as well.

8. CONCLUDING REMARKS

Our goal in this paper is to quantify the impact of increasing penetration of intermittent, unpredictable, renewable energy on the procurement of conventional generation by utilities, and to understand the impact of proposed changes to the structure of electricity markets. To accomplish this, we consider a three tiered model of electricity procurement in the presence of uncertain renewable generation and price volatility. Within this context, we derive the optimal strategy for procurement of conventional generation and analyze the changes to this strategy as the penetration of renewable increases. Additionally, we study the impact of the addition and placement of an intermediate electricity market on procurement strategies.

The main messages that follow from our results are the following. First, as is commonly recognized, reducing the dependence between the renewable sources (by locating different renewable sources geographically far apart) is key to ensuring efficient utilization of renewable generation. More surprisingly, it turns out that the optimal placement of the intermediate market does not change as renewable penetration increases. Further, the impact of the intermediate market on the total procurement can be either positive or negative depending on the the distribution of forecast errors. The results in this paper highlight that there are many important, and counterintuitive issues with respect to the incorporation of renewable generation into electricity markets.

This work extends easily along several directions. The model in our work can be easily extended to allow for an arbitrary number of forward markets for conventional energy procurement. Another extension that can be easily incorporated in our model is to allow utility companies to sell excess conventional generation in forward markets (as in [28]). In our model, we assumed that the exact realized wind energy is known at the time of the real-time market. This assumption can also be relaxed by introducing a third distribution that reflects the error between wind forecasts in the real-time market and the actual realized wind (as in [28]). The results presented in this paper can be easily generalized to this setting under the requirement that the utility company maintains a certain loss of load probability at the time of the real-time market.

There are also, however, some non-trivial extensions to this model which are interesting opportunities for future research. One such extension is to understand the role of large volumes of grid energy storage on the optimal procurement policy of utility companies. Another extension of interest is to take into account ramp constraints of various generators, which would couple procurement decisions between different time instants.

More generally, the big question for the area is how and where renewables should be allowed to interact with electricity markets. The setting considered here is one extreme, where renewable energy only interacts through long-term contracts. The other extreme, where renewable energy interacts only in the real-time market, has also been studied in recent work (for example, see [4]). Hopefully, building on these results, we can move toward a unified approach highlighting the most efficient manner for renewable energy to interact with the electricity markets.

Acknowledgements

The authors gratefully acknowledge the support of the NSF through grant CNS 0846025 and NetSE grant CNS 0911041, the ARO through MURI grant W911NF-08-1-0233, and Bell Labs, Alcatel-Lucent. The first author also acknowledges support from an NWO VIDI grant.

9. REFERENCES

[1] K. Arrow, T. Harris, and J. Marschak. Optimal inventory policy. *Econometrica: Journal of the Econometric Society*, pages 250–272, 1951.

[2] F. Baldovin and A. Stella. Central limit theorem for anomalous scaling due to correlations. *Physical Review E*, 75(2), 2007.

[3] J. Barton and D. Infield. Energy storage and its use with intermittent renewable energy. *IEEE Transactions on Energy Conversion*, 19(2):441–448, 2004.

[4] E. Y. Bitar, R. Rajagopal, P. P. Khargonekar, K. Poolla, and P. Varaiya. Bringing wind energy to market. *IEEE Transactions on Power Systems*, 27(3):1225–1235, 2012.

[5] G. Bowden, P. Barker, V. Shestopal, and J. Twidell. The weibull distribution function and wind power statistics. *Wind Engineering*, 7:85–98, 1983.

[6] D. W. Cai and A. Wierman. Inefficiency in forward markets with supply friction. In *IEEE Conference on Decision and Control*, 2013.

[7] California independent service operator market processes. 2011.

[8] J. Cochran, L. Bird, J. Heeter, and D. Arent. Integrating variable renewable energy in electric power markets: Best practices from international experience. Technical Report NREL/TP6A00-53732, National Renewable Energy Laboratory, 2012.

[9] E. A. DeMeo, G. A. Jordan, C. Kalich, J. King, M. R. Milligan, C. Murley, B. Oakleaf, and M. J. Schuerger. "Accommodating wind's natural behavior". *IEEE Power and Energy Magazine*, 5(6):59–67, 2007.

[10] S. Fink, C. Mudd, K. Porter, and B. Morgenstern. Wind energy curtailment case studies, 2009. NREL subcontract report NREL/SR-550-46716.

[11] Western Wind and Solar Integration Study. Technical report, National Renewable Energy Laboratory (NREL), Golden, CO., 2010.

[12] C. M. Goldie and C. Klüppelberg. Subexponential distributions. *A Practical Guide to Heavy Tails: Statistical Techniques and Applications*, pages 435–459, 1998.

[13] S. Graves, H. Meal, S. Dasu, and Y. Qui. *Two-stage production planning in a dynamic environment.* Massachusetts Institute of Technology, Alfred P. Sloan School of Management, 1985.

[14] Global wind 2009 report. *Renewable Energy House, Brussels, Belgium*, 2009.

[15] C. Harris. *Electricity Markets: Pricing, Structures and Economics (The Wiley Finance Series).* Wiley, 2006.

[16] W. Hausman. Sequential decision problems: A model to exploit existing forecasters. *Management Science*, pages 93–111, 1969.

[17] D. Heath and P. Jackson. Modeling the evolution of demand forecasts with application to safety stock analysis in production/distribution systems. *IIE Transactions-Industrial Engineering Research and Development*, 26(3):17–30, 1994.

[18] J. P. Hennessey Jr. Some aspects of wind power statistics. *Journal of Applied Meteorology*, 16(2):119–128, 1977.

[19] M. Khouja. The single-period (news-vendor) problem: literature review and suggestions for future research. *Omega*, 27(5):537–553, 1999.

[20] J. H. Kim and W. B. Powell. Optimal energy commitments with storage and intermittent supply. *Operations Research*, 59(6):1347–1360, 2011.

[21] D. S. Kirschen and G. Strbac. *Fundamentals of Power System Economics.* Wiley, 2004.

[22] N. Li, L. Chen, and S. Low. Optimal demand response based on utility maximization in power networks. In *IEEE Power and Energy Society General Meeting*, 2011.

[23] S. Madaeni and R. Sioshansi. The impacts of stochastic programming and demand response on wind integration. *Energy Systems*, 4(2):109–124, 2013.

[24] S. Meyn, M. Negrete-Pincetic, G. Wang, A. Kowli, and E. Shafieepoorfard. The value of volatile resources in electricity markets. In *IEEE Conference on Decision and Control*, pages 1029–1036, 2010.

[25] J. Nair, S. Adlakha, and A. Wierman. Energy procurement strategies in the presence of intermittent sources. `http://users.cms.caltech.edu/~adamw/papers/Wind-preprint.pdf`, 2014. Full version.

[26] D. M. Newbery. Competition, contracts, and entry in the electricity spot market. *The RAND Journal of Economics*, pages 726–749, 1998.

[27] E. L. Porteus. *Foundations of Stochastic Inventory Theory.* Stanford Business Books, 2002.

[28] R. Rajagopal, E. E. Bitar, P. Varaiya, and F. Wu. Risk-limiting dispatch for integrating renewable power. *International Journal of Electrical Power & Energy Systems*, 44(1):615 – 628, 2013.

[29] Southern california edison renewable energy. 2011.

[30] N. Secomandi and S. Kekre. Optimal energy procurement in spot and forward markets. *Working Paper*, 2012.

[31] K. Sigman. A primer on heavy-tailed distributions. *Queueing Syst. Theory Appl.*, 33(1-3):261–275, 1999.

[32] E. Silver, D. Pyke, R. Peterson, et al. *Inventory management and production planning and scheduling*, volume 3. Wiley New York, 1998.

[33] R. Sioshansi and D. Hurlbut. Market protocols in ERCOT and their effect on wind generation. *Energy Policy*, 38(7):3192–3197, 2010.

[34] S. Stoft. *Power System Economics: Designing Markets for Electricity.* Wiley-IEEE Press, 2002.

[35] S. Umarov, C. Tsallis, and S. Steinberg. On a q-central limit theorem consistent with nonextensive statistical mechanics. *Milan journal of mathematics*, 76(1):307–328, 2008.

[36] P. Varaiya, F. Wu, and J. Bialek. Smart operation of smart grid: Risk-limiting dispatch. *Proceedings of the IEEE*, 99(1):40–57, 2011.

[37] T. Wang, A. Atasu, and M. Kurtulus. A multiordering newsvendor model with dynamic forecast evolution. *Manufacturing & Service Operations Management*, 14(3):472–484, 2012.

[38] R. Wiser. Renewable Portfolio Standards in the United States - A Status Report with Data Through 2007. *Lawrence Berkeley National Laboratory, LBNL Paper LBNL-154E*, 2008.

[39] Y. Zhou, A. Scheller-Wolf, N. Secomandi, and S. Smith. Managing wind-based electricity generation in the presence of storage and transmission capacity, 2012. Under submission.

APPENDIX

In this section, we prove Theorem 4 and Theorem 5. We first characterize the optimal procurement policy with deterministic prices in Section A. We then prove some preliminary lemmas in Section B. In Section C, we prove Theorem 5. Finally, we prove Theorem 4 in Section D. It is important to note that throughout this section, we consider deterministic prices, satisfying $0 < p_{lt} < p_{in} < p_{rt}$.

A. OPTIMAL PROCUREMENT POLICY WITH DETERMINISTIC PRICES

In this section, we first analyze the optimal procurement strategy for the utility company in the three tiered market scenario with deterministic prices.

LEMMA 2. *The optimal procurement strategy for the utility company in the three tiered market scenario with deterministic prices satisfying $0 < p_{lt} < p_{in} < p_{rt}$ is the following.* $q^*_{lt} = [d - \hat{w}_{lt} + r_{lt}]_+$, $q^*_{in} = [d - \hat{w}_{in} - q_{lt} + r_{in}]_+$, *and* $q^*_{rt} = [d - w - (q_{lt} + q_{in})]_+$. *Here,* $r_{in} = \bar{F}^{-1}_{\mathcal{E}_2}\left(\frac{p_{in}}{p_{rt}}\right)$, *and r_{lt} is the unique solution of*

$$p_{lt} - p_{in}\bar{F}_{\mathcal{E}_1}(r - r_{in}) - p_{rt}P\left(\mathcal{E}_1 + \mathcal{E}_2 > r, \mathcal{E}_1 \leq r - r_{in}\right) = 0. \quad (16)$$

Next, in order to understand the effect of the addition of a market, we study the case where there is no intermediate market.

LEMMA 3. *The optimal procurement strategy for the utility company in the two tier market scenario with no intermediate market, and with deterministic prices satisfying $0 < p_{lt} < p_{rt}$ is the following.*

$$q_{lt}^* = [d - \hat{w}_{lt} + \bar{r}_{lt}]_+, \; q_{rt}^* = [d - q_{lt} - w]_+,$$

where $\bar{r}_{lt} := \bar{F}^{-1}_{\mathcal{E}_1+\mathcal{E}_2}\left(\frac{p_{lt}}{p_{rt}}\right)$.

Lemmas 2 and 3 can be proved easily along the same lines as Theorem 1 and the proofs are omitted.

B. PRELIMINARY LEMMAS

In the next two lemmas, we study the sensitivity of the optimal reserves and procurement with respect to the intermediate price p_{in} (recall that the prices are deterministic). For the remainder of this section, we keep the distributions $\mathcal{E}_1$ and $\mathcal{E}_2$, as well as the prices p_{lt} and p_{rt} fixed. Define $\bar{r}_{in} := \bar{F}^{-1}_{\mathcal{E}_2}\left(\frac{p_{lt}}{p_{rt}}\right)$. We can think of $\bar{r}_{in}$ as the optimal reserve in a two market scenario, where the long-term market occurs at time $-T_{in}$.

LEMMA 4. *As p_{in} is varied over (p_{lt}, p_{rt}), the following results hold.*

1. *The intermediate reserve r_{in} is a strictly decreasing function of the intermediate price p_{in} with*

$$\frac{\partial r_{in}}{\partial p_{in}} = -\frac{1}{p_{rt}f_{\mathcal{E}_2}(r_{in})}. \quad (17)$$

Furthermore,

$$\lim_{p_{in}\downarrow p_{lt}} r_{in} = \bar{r}_{in}, \qquad \lim_{p_{in}\uparrow p_{rt}} r_{in} = L_2. \quad (18)$$

2. *The long-term reserve r_{lt} is a non-decreasing function of the intermediate price p_{in} with*

$$\frac{\partial r_{lt}}{\partial p_{in}} = \frac{\bar{F}_{\mathcal{E}_1}(r_{lt} - r_{in})}{p_{rt}\int_{-\infty}^{r_{lt}-r_{in}} f_{\mathcal{E}_1}(y)f_{\mathcal{E}_2}(r_{lt} - y)dy}. \quad (19)$$

Furthermore,

$$\lim_{p_{in}\downarrow p_{lt}} r_{lt} = L_1 + \bar{r}_{in}, \qquad \lim_{p_{in}\uparrow p_{rt}} r_{lt} = \bar{r}_{lt} = \bar{F}^{-1}_{\mathcal{E}_1+\mathcal{E}_2}\left(\frac{p_{lt}}{p_{rt}}\right) \quad (20)$$

We omit the proof of this lemma due to space constraints; the proof can be found in [25]. The next lemma studies how the total procurement changes as a function of the intermediate price p_{in}. Recall that $\mathbb{E}[TP_{l,i,r}]$ and $\mathbb{E}[TP_{l,r}]$ denote, respectively, the expected total procurement under the three-tier market scenario (long-term, intermediate, real-time) and the two-tier market scenario (long-term, real-time).

For the remainder of this section, we introduce some additional notation. Let $q^*_{lt;l,i,r}, q^*_{in;l,i,r}$, and $q^*_{rt;l,i,r}$ denote the *optimal* procurements in the long-term, intermediate, and the real-time market under the scenario that the utility company has three opportunities to procure energy. These optimal quantities are given in Lemma 2. Similarly, we let $q^*_{lt;l,r}$ and $q^*_{rt;l,r}$ to be the optimal procurements in the long-term and in the real-time markets under the scenario where there is no intermediate market. These quantities are given by Lemma 3.

LEMMA 5. *As the intermediate price p_{in} approaches the real-time price p_{rt}, the expected total procurement in the three-tier market scenario converges to the expected total procurement in the two market scenario. That is,*

$$\lim_{p_{in}\uparrow p_{rt}} \mathbb{E}[TP_{l,i,r}] = \mathbb{E}[TP_{l,r}].$$

PROOF. We prove this lemma using a sample path argument. A sample path is defined by the values of $\hat{w}_{lt}$, $\mathcal{E}_1$, and $\mathcal{E}_2$. We will show that as $p_{in} \uparrow p_{rt}$,

$$q^*_{lt;l,i,r} + q^*_{in;l,i,r} + q^*_{rt;l,i,r} \longrightarrow q^*_{lt;l,r} + q^*_{rt;l,r} \quad (21)$$

almost surely. An elementary application of the dominated convergence theorem would then prove the lemma.

From Lemmas 2, 3, and 4, it is easy to show that as $p_{in} \uparrow p_{rt}$, we have

$$q^*_{lt;l,i,r} \longrightarrow q^*_{lt;l,r} \quad (22)$$

almost surely. Thus, to prove (21), it suffices to show that

$$q^*_{in;l,i,r} + q^*_{rt;l,i,r} \longrightarrow q^*_{rt;l,r}, \quad (23)$$

almost surely as $p_{in} \uparrow p_{rt}$. Recall that $q^*_{rt;l,r} = \left[d - w - q^*_{lt;l,r}\right]_+$ From Lemma 4 and Equation (22), we conclude that as $p_{in} \uparrow p_{rt}$. we have

$$\begin{aligned} q^*_{in;l,i,r} &\longrightarrow \left[d - \hat{w}_{in} - q^*_{lt;\,,r} + L_2\right]_+, \\ q^*_{rt;l,i,r} &\longrightarrow \left[d - w - q^*_{lt;l,r} - [d - \hat{w}_{in} + L_2]_+\right]_+. \end{aligned} \quad (24)$$

To see that Equation (24) implies (23), we consider the following two cases. On sample paths satisfying $d < \hat{w}_{in} + q^*_{lt;l,r} - L_2$, we have

$$q^*_{in;l,i,r} \overset{p_{in}\uparrow p_{rt}}{\longrightarrow} 0, \quad q^*_{rt;l,i,r} \overset{p_{in}\uparrow p_{rt}}{\longrightarrow} \left[d - w - q^*_{lt;l,r}\right]_+,$$

which implies Equation (23). On sample paths satisfying $d \geq \hat{w}_{in} + q^*_{lt;l,r} - L_2$, we have

$$q^*_{in;l,i,r} \overset{p_{in}\uparrow p_{rt}}{\longrightarrow} d - \hat{w}_{in} - q^*_{lt;l,r} + L_2, \; q^*_{rt;l,i,r} \overset{p_{in}\uparrow p_{rt}}{\longrightarrow} [\mathcal{E}_2 - L_2]_+.$$

Noting that $\mathcal{E}_2 \geq L_2$ almost surely, we conclude that except possibly on a measure zero set of sample paths, we have

$$\begin{aligned} q^*_{in;l,i,r} + q^*_{rt;l,i,r} &\overset{p_{in}\uparrow p_{rt}}{\longrightarrow} (d - \hat{w}_{in} - q^*_{lt;l,r} + L_2) + (\mathcal{E}_2 - L_2) \\ &= d - w - q^*_{lt;l,r}. \end{aligned}$$

Since the procurements are always non-negative, the above equation implies Equation (23). This completes the proof. □

Next, we prove the following lemma, which is used in the proof of Theorem 5.

LEMMA 6. *Suppose that the distribution of $\mathcal{E}_2$ satisfies the conditions (i), (ii), and (iii) of Theorem 5. Then*

$$\left(\frac{p_{rt} - p_{lt}}{p_{rt} - p_{in}}\right) f_{\mathcal{E}_2}(r_{in}) >$$
$$\int_{-\infty}^{r_{lt}-r_{in}} f_{\mathcal{E}_1}(y)f_{\mathcal{E}_2}(r_{lt} - y)dy + \bar{F}_{\mathcal{E}_1}(r_{lt} - r_{in})f_{\mathcal{E}_2}(r_{in}). \quad (25)$$

PROOF. For this proof, we use the notation $\beta := \bar{F}_{\mathcal{E}_2}(0)$. Let us also denote by $L(p_{in})$ and $R(p_{in})$ the left hand side and the right hand side of the Inequality (25) respectively. To prove the lemma, we need to show that $L(p_{in}) > R(p_{in})$ for all values of $p_{in} \in (p_{lt}, p_{rt})$. Let us consider two separate cases.

Case 1: $p_{lt} < \beta p_{rt}$.

Consider first the case $p_{in} \in (p_{lt}, \beta p_{rt}]$. For this case, we have $p_{in}/p_{rt} \leq \beta$ and hence from Lemma 2, we have that

$r_{in} \geq 0$. Using a change of variables, we can write $R(p_{in})$ as

$$R(p_{in}) = \int_{r_{in}}^{\infty} f_{\mathcal{E}_1}(r_{lt} - y) f_{\mathcal{E}_2}(y)\, dy + \bar{F}_{\mathcal{E}_1}(r_{lt} - r_{in}) f_{\mathcal{E}_2}(r_{in}). \tag{26}$$

Note that $f_{\mathcal{E}_2}(x)$ is non increasing for all $x > 0$. Thus, for all $y \geq r_{in} \geq 0$, we have $f_{\mathcal{E}_2}(r_{in}) \geq f_{\mathcal{E}_2}(y)$. Therefore,

$$\begin{aligned} R(p_{in}) &\leq f_{\mathcal{E}_2}(r_{in}) \int_{r_{in}}^{\infty} f_{\mathcal{E}_1}(r_{lt} - y)\, dy + \bar{F}_{\mathcal{E}_1}(r_{lt} - r_{in}) f_{\mathcal{E}_2}(r_{in}) \\ &= f_{\mathcal{E}_2}(r_{in}) < L(p_{in}), \end{aligned}$$

where the last inequality follows from that fact that $p_{lt} < p_{in}$. Next, consider the case where $p_{in} \in (\beta p_{rt}, p_{rt})$. From Lemma 2, we have that $r_{in} < 0$. Also, from the conditions of the lemma, we have that $f_{\mathcal{E}_2}(y) \leq f_{\mathcal{E}_2}(0)$ for all $y \in \mathbb{R}$. Thus, using the representation (26), we have

$$\begin{aligned} R(p_{in}) &\leq f_{\mathcal{E}_2}(0) \int_{r_{in}}^{\infty} f_{\mathcal{E}_1}(r_{lt} - y)\, dy + \bar{F}_{\mathcal{E}_1}(r_{lt} - r_{in}) f_{\mathcal{E}_2}(0) \\ &= f_{\mathcal{E}_2}(0). \end{aligned} \tag{27}$$

Let us now look at $L(p_{in})$. We will construct a lower bound for $L(p_{in})$ for $p_{in} \in (\beta p_{rt}, p_{rt})$. Note that $\bar{F}_{\mathcal{E}_2}(r_{in}) = p_{in}/p_{rt}$ and hence we can write $L(p_{in})$ as $L(p_{in}) = \left(\frac{p_{rt} - p_{lt}}{p_{rt}}\right) \frac{f_{\mathcal{E}_2}(r_{in})}{F_{\mathcal{E}_2}(r_{in})}$. Recall that for $p_{in} \in (\beta p_{rt}, p_{rt})$, we have $r_{in} < 0$. Furthermore from Lemma 4, r_{in} is strictly decreasing function of p_{in}. From the statement of the lemma, $f_{\mathcal{E}_2}(x)/F_{\mathcal{E}_2}(x)$ is a strictly decreasing function for all $x \leq 0$. Hence, $L(p_{in})$ is strictly increasing over $p_{in} \in (\beta p_{rt}, p_{rt})$. Thus, we have

$$L(p_{in}) > L(\beta p_{rt}) = \left(\frac{p_{rt} - p_{lt}}{p_{rt} - \beta p_{rt}}\right) f_{\mathcal{E}_2}(0) > f_{\mathcal{E}_2}(0),$$

where we have used the fact that $r_{in} = 0$ when $p_{in} = \beta p_{rt}$, and $p_{lt} < \beta p_{rt}$. The above inequality, combined with Condition (27), implies that $L(p_{in}) > R(p_{in})$. This proves Case 1.

Case 2: $p_{lt} \geq \beta p_{rt}$.

In this case, we note that $p_{in}/p_{rt} > \beta$ and hence from Lemma 2, we get that $r_{in} < 0$. Using an argument similar to Case 1, it is easy to verify that $L(p_{in})$ is a strictly increasing function for $p_{in} \in (p_{lt}, p_{rt})$. Therefore,

$$L(p_{in}) > \lim_{p_{in} \downarrow p_{lt}} L(p_{in}) = f_{\mathcal{E}_2}(\bar{r}_{in}),$$

where we use the fact that as $p_{in} \downarrow p_{lt}$, $r_{in} \to \bar{r}_{in}$ (Lemma 4). Thus, to prove the lemma for this case, it suffices to show that $R(p_{in}) \leq f_{\mathcal{E}_2}(\bar{r}_{in})$. From Lemma 4, we note that

$$\lim_{p_{in} \downarrow p_{lt}} r_{lt} - r_{in} = L_1$$

and hence

$$\lim_{p_{in} \downarrow p_{lt}} R(p_{in}) = f_{\mathcal{E}_2}(\bar{r}_{in}).$$

Thus, to prove the lemma, it suffices to show that $R(p_{in})$ is non-increasing over the range $p_{in} \in (p_{lt}, p_{rt})$. To show this, we note that

$$\begin{aligned} &\frac{\partial R(p_{in})}{\partial p_{in}} \\ &= \frac{\partial}{\partial p_{in}} \left(\int_{-\infty}^{r_{lt} - r_{in}} f_{\mathcal{E}_1}(y) f_{\mathcal{E}_2}(r_{lt} - y) dy \right. \\ &\qquad \left. + \bar{F}_{\mathcal{E}_1}(r_{lt} - r_{in}) f_{\mathcal{E}_2}(r_{in}) \right) \\ &= \frac{\partial r_{lt}}{\partial r_{in}} \int_{-\infty}^{r_{lt} - r_{in}} f_{\mathcal{E}_1}(y) f'_{\mathcal{E}_2}(r_{lt} - y) dy \\ &\qquad + \frac{\partial r_{in}}{\partial p_{in}} \bar{F}_{\mathcal{E}_1}(r_{lt} - r_{in}) f'_{\mathcal{E}_2}(r_{in}) \\ &= \frac{\bar{F}_{\mathcal{E}_1}(r_{lt} - r_{in})}{p_{rt}} \left[\frac{\int_{-\infty}^{r_{lt} - r_{in}} f_{\mathcal{E}_1}(y) f'_{\mathcal{E}_2}(r_{lt} - y) dy}{\int_{-\infty}^{r_{lt} - r_{in}} f_{\mathcal{E}_1}(y) f_{\mathcal{E}_2}(r_{lt} - y) dy} - \frac{f'_{\mathcal{E}_2}(r_{in})}{f_{\mathcal{E}_2}(r_{in})} \right] \\ &= \frac{\bar{F}_{\mathcal{E}_1}(r_{lt} - r_{in})}{p_{rt}} \left[\frac{\int_{r_{in}}^{\infty} f_{\mathcal{E}_1}(r_{lt} - y) f'_{\mathcal{E}_2}(y) dy}{\int_{r_{in}}^{\infty} f_{\mathcal{E}_1}(r_{lt} - y) f_{\mathcal{E}_2}(y) dy} - \frac{f'_{\mathcal{E}_2}(r_{in})}{f_{\mathcal{E}_2}(r_{in})} \right]. \end{aligned} \tag{28}$$

Here the third equality follows from Lemma 4 and the last equality follows from a change of variables. We will show that $\frac{\partial R(p_{in})}{\partial p_{in}} \leq 0$ by considering the following two separate cases.

Case 2a: Consider the case $\int_{r_{in}}^{0} f_{\mathcal{E}_1}(r_{lt} - y) f_{\mathcal{E}_2}(y) dy = 0$.

Recall that the density functions $f_{\mathcal{E}_1}(\cdot)$ and $f_{\mathcal{E}_2}(\cdot)$ are assumed to be strictly positive over the interior of the supports of $\mathcal{E}_1$ and $\mathcal{E}_2$ respectively. Therefore, under Case 2a, the intersection of the supports of the functions $f_{\mathcal{E}_2}(y)$ and $f_{\mathcal{E}_1}(r_{lt} - y)$ and $[r_{in}, 0]$ has measure zero. This implies that

$$\int_{r_{in}}^{0} f_{\mathcal{E}_1}(r_{lt} - y) f'_{\mathcal{E}_2}(y) dy = 0. \tag{29}$$

Using the condition defining Case 2a and (29), the expression for $\frac{\partial R(p_{in})}{\partial p_{in}}$ in (28) can be rewritten as

$$\frac{\bar{F}_{\mathcal{E}_1}(r_{lt} - r_{in})}{p_{rt}} \left[\frac{\int_{0}^{\infty} f_{\mathcal{E}_1}(r_{lt} - y) f'_{\mathcal{E}_2}(y) dy}{\int_{0}^{\infty} f_{\mathcal{E}_1}(r_{lt} - y) f_{\mathcal{E}_2}(y) dy} - \frac{f'_{\mathcal{E}_2}(r_{in})}{f_{\mathcal{E}_2}(r_{in})} \right] \leq 0.$$

The inequality above follows from the assumption that $f'_{\mathcal{E}_2}(x) \leq 0$ for $x \geq 0$.

Case 2b: Consider the case $\int_{r_{in}}^{0} f_{\mathcal{E}_1}(r_{lt} - y) f_{\mathcal{E}_2}(y) dy > 0$.

Since $f'_{\mathcal{E}_2}(x) \leq 0$ for $x \geq 0$,

$$\int_{r_{in}}^{\infty} f_{\mathcal{E}_1}(r_{lt} - y) f'_{\mathcal{E}_2}(y) dy \leq \int_{r_{in}}^{0} f_{\mathcal{E}_1}(r_{lt} - y) f'_{\mathcal{E}_2}(y) dy.$$

Therefore, the expression for $\frac{\partial R(p_{in})}{\partial p_{in}}$ in (28) can be bounded by

$$\frac{\bar{F}_{\mathcal{E}_1}(r_{lt} - r_{in})}{p_{rt}} \left[\frac{\int_{r_{in}}^{0} f_{\mathcal{E}_1}(r_{lt} - y) f'_{\mathcal{E}_2}(y) dy}{\int_{r_{in}}^{0} f_{\mathcal{E}_1}(r_{lt} - y) f_{\mathcal{E}_2}(y) dy} - \frac{f'_{\mathcal{E}_2}(r_{in})}{f_{\mathcal{E}_2}(r_{in})} \right].$$

Define

$$p(y) = \frac{f_{\mathcal{E}_1}(r_{lt} - y)}{\int_{r_{in}}^{0} f_{\mathcal{E}_1}(r_{lt} - y)\, dy}, \quad \xi(y) = \frac{f'_{\mathcal{E}_2}(y)}{f_{\mathcal{E}_2}(y)}, \quad \varphi(y) = f_{\mathcal{E}_2}(y).$$

Note that $p(y)$ is a valid probability density function defined over the interval $[r_{in}, 0]$. We can then write

$$\frac{\partial R(p_{in})}{\partial p_{in}} \leq \frac{\bar{F}_{\mathcal{E}_1}(r_{lt} - r_{in})}{p_{rt}} \left[\frac{\int_{r_{in}}^{0} p(y)\xi(y)\varphi(y) dy}{\int_{r_{in}}^{0} p(y)\varphi(y) dy} - \frac{f'_{\mathcal{E}_2}(r_{in})}{f_{\mathcal{E}_2}(r_{in})} \right]$$

Using Lemma 7 below, we get

$$\begin{aligned} \frac{\partial R(p_{in})}{\partial p_{in}} &\leq \frac{\bar{F}_{\mathcal{E}_1}(r_{lt} - r_{in})}{p_{rt}} \left[\int_{r_{in}}^{0} p(y) \frac{f'_{\mathcal{E}_2}(y)}{f_{\mathcal{E}_2}(y)}\, dy - \frac{f'_{\mathcal{E}_2}(r_{in})}{f_{\mathcal{E}_2}(r_{in})} \right] \\ &\leq 0. \end{aligned}$$

The last inequality follows from the fact that $f'_{\mathcal{E}_2}(y)/f_{\mathcal{E}_2}(y)$ is non-increasing over the range $y \in (r_{in}, 0)$. We have now proved that $R(p_{in})$ is non-increasing over $p_{in} \in (p_{lt}, p_{rt})$. This completes the proof of Case 2. □

The above lemma uses the following technical lemma.

LEMMA 7. *Let $[a,b]$ denote an interval on the real line. Suppose that $\xi : [a,b] \to \mathbb{R}$ is non-increasing, and $\varphi : [a,b] \to \mathbb{R}$ is non-decreasing. Also, suppose that $p(\cdot)$ is a probability density function defined over the interval $[a,b]$. Then* $\int_a^b p(y)\xi(y)\varphi(y)\ dy \le \left(\int_a^b p(y)\xi(y)\ dy\right)\left(\int_a^b p(y)\varphi(y)\ dy\right)$.

We omit the proof of this lemma due to space constraints; the proof can be found in [25].

C. PROOF OF THEOREM 5

Let p_{lt}, p_{in} and p_{rt} be the (deterministic) prices in the three markets. Let $\Gamma(p)$ be the expected optimal total procurement in three markets, when the long-term price is p_{lt}, the real-time price is p_{rt}, and the intermediate price is p. In other words, $\Gamma(p)$ gives the expected total procurement for a variable intermediate price (denoted by p). Clearly, we have $\mathbb{E}[TP_{l,i,r}] = \Gamma(p_{in})$. From Lemma 5, we know that $\mathbb{E}[TP_{l,r}] = \lim_{p\uparrow p_{rt}} \Gamma(p)$. Thus, to prove the theorem it suffices to show that $\Gamma(p)$ is a strictly increasing function of p.

From the statement of the theorem, Assumption 1 holds for prices p_{lt}, p_{in} and p_{rt}. From Lemma 4, we know that r_{lt} is a non-decreasing function of intermediate price. Hence for all $p \ge p_{in}$, Assumption 1 holds. Thus, the optimal procurements for all intermediate price $p \ge p_{in}$ are given by Equation (7). Let $q^*_{lt}(p)$, $q^*_{in}(p)$, and $q^*_{rt}(p)$ be the optimal procurements for the intermediate price p. Thus, we have

$$\frac{\partial \mathbb{E}[q^*_{lt}(p)]}{\partial p} = \frac{\partial}{\partial p}(d - \hat{w}_{lt} + r_{lt}) = \frac{\partial r_{lt}}{\partial p}.$$

$$\frac{\partial \mathbb{E}[q^*_{in}(p)]}{\partial p} = \frac{\partial}{\partial p}\mathbb{E}\left[\mathcal{E}_1 - (r_{lt} - r_{in})\right]_+ = \bar{F}_{\mathcal{E}_1}(r_{lt} - r_{in})\left(\frac{\partial r_{in}}{\partial p} - \frac{\partial r_{lt}}{\partial p}\right).$$

$$\begin{aligned}\frac{\partial \mathbb{E}[q^*_{rt}(p)]}{\partial p} &= \frac{\partial}{\partial p}\mathbb{E}\left[\mathcal{E}_2 - r_{lt} + \min\{\mathcal{E}_1, r_{lt} - r_{in}\}\right]_+ \\ &= \frac{\partial}{\partial p}\left(\bar{F}_{\mathcal{E}_1}(r_{lt} - r_{in})\int_{r_{in}}^{\infty}(z - r_{in})f_{\mathcal{E}_2}(z)dz \right.\\ &\quad \left. + \int_{z=r_{lt}}^{\infty}\int_{y=-\infty}^{r_{lt}-r_{in}}(z - r_{lt})f_{\mathcal{E}_1}(y)f_{\mathcal{E}_2}(z-y)dzdy\right) \\ &= -\bar{F}_{\mathcal{E}_1}(r_{lt} - r_{in})\bar{F}_{\mathcal{E}_2}(r_{in})\frac{\partial r_{in}}{\partial p} \\ &\quad - \frac{\partial r_{lt}}{\partial p}\int_{z=r_{lt}}^{\infty}\int_{y=-\infty}^{r_{lt}-r_{in}}(z - r_{lt})f_{\mathcal{E}_1}(y)f_{\mathcal{E}_2}(z-y)dzdy.\end{aligned}$$

The last step above follows from a direct differentiation. Combining the above equations, we have

$$\begin{aligned}\frac{\partial \Gamma(p)}{\partial p} &= \frac{\partial r_{lt}}{\partial p}\left[1 - \bar{F}_{\mathcal{E}_1}(r_{lt} - r_{in}) \right.\\ &\quad \left. - \int_{z=r_{lt}}^{\infty}\int_{y=-\infty}^{r_{lt}-r_{in}}(z - r_{lt})f_{\mathcal{E}_1}(y)f_{\mathcal{E}_2}(z-y)dzdy\right] \\ &\quad + \frac{\partial r_{in}}{\partial p}\left[\bar{F}_{\mathcal{E}_1}(r_{lt} - r_{in}) - \bar{F}_{\mathcal{E}_1}(r_{lt} - r_{in})\bar{F}_{\mathcal{E}_2}(r_{in})\right] \\ &= \frac{\partial r_{lt}}{\partial p}\left[1 - \frac{p_{lt}}{p_{rt}} - \left(1 - \frac{p}{p_{rt}}\right)\bar{F}_{\mathcal{E}_1}(r_{lt} - r_{in})\right] \\ &\quad + \frac{\partial r_{in}}{\partial p}\bar{F}_{\mathcal{E}_1}(r_{lt} - r_{in})\left(1 - \frac{p}{p_{rt}}\right).\end{aligned}$$

The last equality follows from the fact that $h(r_{lt}) = 0$ and that $\bar{F}_{\mathcal{E}_2}(r_{in}) = p/p_{rt}$. Substituting $\partial r_{lt}/\partial p$ and $\partial r_{in}/\partial p$ from Lemma 4 and after some algebraic manipulation, we get that $\partial\Gamma(p)/\partial p > 0$ if and only if

$$\left(\frac{p_{rt} - p_{lt}}{p_{rt} - p}\right) f_{\mathcal{E}_2}(r_{in}) > \int_{-\infty}^{r_{lt}-r_{in}} f_{\mathcal{E}_1}(y) f_{\mathcal{E}_2}(r_{lt} - y)dy + \bar{F}_{\mathcal{E}_1}(r_{lt} - r_{in}) f_{\mathcal{E}_2}(r_{in}).$$

From Lemma 6, we know that this inequality holds for all $p \in [p_{in}, p_{rt})$. This completes the proof.

D. PROOF OF THEOREM 4

Let us fix some long-term and real-time market prices p_{lt} and p_{rt} such that $0 < p_{lt} < p_{rt}$. Let $\Gamma(p)$ be the expected optimal total procurement in a three-tier market scenario with long-term price p_{lt}, real-time price p_{rt}, and the intermediate price p. From Lemma 5, we know that $\lim_{p\uparrow p_{rt}}\Gamma(p) = \mathbb{E}[TP_{l,r}]$. So to prove the lemma, it suffices to show that there exists $p_{in} \in (p_{lt}, p_{rt})$ such that for all intermediate market prices $p \in (p_{in}, p_{rt})$, $\frac{\partial\Gamma(p)}{\partial p} < 0$. Indeed, this would imply that $\Gamma(p_{in}) > \lim_{p\uparrow p_{rt}}\Gamma(p) = \mathbb{E}[TP_{l,r}]$. Since $\Gamma(p_{in}) = \mathbb{E}[TP_{l,i,r}]$, the expected total procurement in the three-tier market scenario under the intermediate price p_{in}, this implies a tuple of prices satisfying the claim of the lemma.

Pick $\bar{p} \in (p_{lt}, p_{rt})$. Now choose demand d large enough such that Assumption 1 holds when the intermediate price $p = \bar{p}$. From Lemma 4, we know that r_{lt} is a non decreasing function of intermediate price p. Thus, Assumption 1 continues to hold for all intermediate price $p \ge \bar{p}$. Following the argument similar to the proof of Theorem 5, we can show that for all $p \in [\bar{p}, p_{rt})$, $\frac{\partial\Gamma(p)}{\partial p} < 0$ if and only if

$$\left(\frac{p_{rt} - p_{lt}}{p_{rt} - p}\right) f_{\mathcal{E}_2}(r_{in}) < \int_{-\infty}^{r_{lt}-r_{in}} f_{\mathcal{E}_1}(y) f_{\mathcal{E}_2}(r_{lt} - y)dy + \bar{F}_{\mathcal{E}_1}(r_{lt} - r_{in}) f_{\mathcal{E}_2}(r_{in}). \tag{30}$$

Let us denote by $L(p)$ and $R(p)$ the left hand side and the right hand side of the above inequality respectively.

From the definition of r_{in} (Lemma 2),

$$L(p) = \left(\frac{p_{rt} - p_{lt}}{p_{rt}}\right)\frac{f_{\mathcal{E}_2}(r_{in})}{\bar{F}_{\mathcal{E}_2}(r_{in})}.$$

Since $\lim_{p\uparrow p_{rt}} r_{in} = -\infty$ (Lemma 4), the conditions of the theorem imply that $\lim_{p\uparrow p_{rt}} L(p) = 0$.

Now let us look at $R(p)$. From Lemma 4, note that

$$\lim_{p\uparrow p_{rt}}(r_{lt} - r_{in}) = \infty, \quad \lim_{p\uparrow p_{rt}} r_{lt} = \bar{r}_{lt}.$$

Thus, using the dominated convergence theorem, we get that

$$\lim_{p\uparrow p_{rt}} R(p) = f_{\mathcal{E}_1+\mathcal{E}_2}(\bar{r}_{lt}) > 0.$$

The above statements imply that there exists $p_{in} \in (\bar{p}, p_{rt})$ such that for all $p \in (p_{in}, p_{rt})$ the inequality in Equation (30) holds. This completes the proof.

Randomized Auction Design for Electricity Markets between Grids and Microgrids

Linquan Zhang
Dept. of Computer Science
University of Calgary
linqzhan@ucalgary.ca

Zongpeng Li
Dept. of Computer Science
University of Calgary
zongpeng@ucalgary.ca

Chuan Wu
Dept. of Computer Science
The University of Hong Kong
cwu@cs.hku.hk

ABSTRACT

This work studies electricity markets between power grids and microgrids, an emerging paradigm of electric power generation and supply. It is among the first that addresses the economic challenges arising from such grid integration, and represents the first power auction mechanism design that explicitly handles the Unit Commitment Problem (UCP), a key challenge in power grid optimization previously investigated only for centralized cooperative algorithms. The proposed solution leverages a recent result in theoretical computer science that can decompose an optimal fractional (infeasible) solution to NP-hard problems into a convex combination of integral (feasible) solutions. The end result includes randomized power auctions that are (approximately) truthful and computationally efficient, and achieve small approximation ratios for grid-wide social welfare under UCP constraints and temporal demand correlations. Both power markets with grid-to-microgrid and microgrid-to-grid energy sales are studied, with an auction designed for each, under the same randomized power auction framework. Trace driven simulations are conducted to verify the efficacy of the two proposed inter-grid power auctions.

Categories and Subject Descriptors

C.4 [**Performance of Systems**]: Design studies; Modeling techniques; I.1.2 [**Algorithms**]: Analysis of algorithms

General Terms

Algorithms, Design, Economics

Keywords

Power Grid; Microgrids; Unit Commitment Problem; Mechanism Design; Approximation Algorithms

1. INTRODUCTION

An electrical power grid is an interconnected network for delivering electricity from generators/suppliers to consumers. In a classic power grid, electrical power is produced at (often remote) generating stations, travels through long-distance high-voltage transmission lines to demand centers, and then through distribution lines to end customers. A *microgrid*, in contrast, is a distributed electric power system, operating autonomously to organize local generation to meet the demand dynamically [19], *e.g.*, a university served by its own power generators, or a hospital supplied mainly by its local generators. An important trend in power grid evolution is characterized by the rapidly increasing percentage of power supplied from microgrids. Such a paradigm shift has been jointly driven by a number of related factors: (a) The *economies of scale* associated with massive central generation starts to fail, as generation units and plants become cheaper to build, and transmission cost catches up with generation cost; (b) Concerns from grid customers on externalized costs of central plant generation and lack of billing control; (c) Environmental concerns, given that classic grids are often driven by non-renewable resources (coal, gas, nuclear), while latest microgrids commonly resort to wind and solar energy that are green and renewable [17]; (d) Reliability concerns, as exemplified by the 2003 Eastern US/Canada major blackout and the largest power outage in history (India, 2012), most power failures nowadays are traced back to the transmission grid instead of generation units [1]; (e) Even with traditional fuel, co-generation in residential microgrids provides both electricity and heat, bringing new opportunities for thermodynamically efficient use of fuel [23].

As a latest example, IKEA acquired a 46 MW wind farm in Alberta, Canada in November 2013, towards its eventual power self-sustainability based on green energy. Prior to that, the furniture giant already owns similar wind farms and solar generation plants in Europe and Eastern Canada, respectively. Microgrids have recently witnessed an impressive growing rate, and are estimated to further grow at a 17% compound annual rate in terms of installed capacity [4]. Global installed capacity is projected to reach 15 GW by 2022, roughly equivalent to the total installed capacity in Portugal in 2008.

For reliability reasons, a microgrid is usually connected to the main power grid in its region (Fig. 1), where the distribution stations reside. Temporary deficits in energy supply can be resolved by purchase from the regional grid; conversely, excess energy generated can be contributed to the regional grid. Such integration of a large number of microgrids to the traditional power grid represents a fundamental revolution in the energy sector, and it is generally agreed that a number of challenges from both technical and economic sides are to be addressed [1]. On the technical side, a plethora of research has been devoted to the study of power quality, voltage stability, harmonics, and grid-wide control and reliability [10, 19, 21, 30], leading to a relatively clear picture for issues and solutions regarding such grid integration. In contrast, the area of

SIGMETRICS'14, June 16–20, 2014, Austin, Texas, USA.
Copyright 2014 ACM 978-1-4503-2789-3/14/06 ...$15.00.
http://dx.doi.org/10.1145/2591971.2591999.

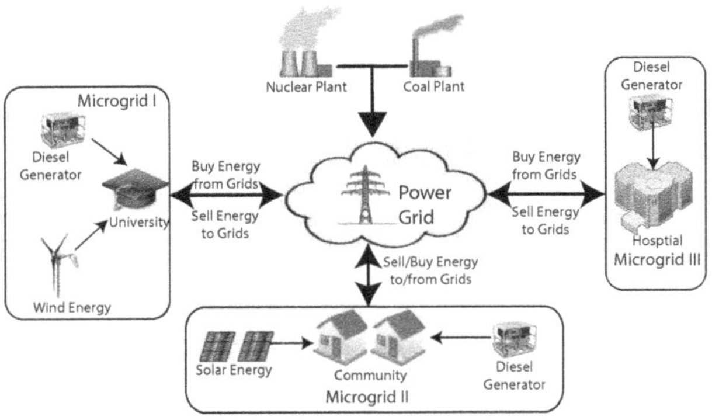

Figure 1: A regional power grid and microgrids.

market analysis and inter-grid energy trading mechanisms have essentially remained blank, witnessing few if any dedicated studies, despite its practical necessity towards smooth flowing of energy between microgrids and the main power grid.

The lack of research activity is partly attributed to the hardness of the problem: any sound economic mechanism design here must appropriately model and handle the Unit Commitment Problem (UCP), engineering constraints of generation units that impose strict limitations on their scheduling and operation. Most generators today, including traditional thermal (coal, gas, petroleum), nuclear, and renewable (wind, solar, hydro, wave-power, geothermal energy), have generator-specific parameters that define (a) minimum and maximum stable output levels, (b) maximum rates of ramping up or down, and (c) minimum time a unit stays ON or OFF. Along with the optimal power flow problem (OPF), UCP is known as one of the two key problems at the core of power grid optimization [28]. A series of studies in the past few decades investigate the modelling and solution of UCP, usually through a mixed linear integer programming model and centralized approximation algorithms [28]. A market mechanism such as an auction has to further consider economic behaviours of the two participating sides, such as individual rationality and truthful bidding. The challenge further escalates considering that a grid's bid for electricity in practice is across multiple consecutive and correlated time slots (*e.g.*, for each of the next 24 hours) [29].

To the authors' knowledge, this work is among the first that designs trading mechanisms for the grid-microgrid electricity market, towards the goal of designing power auctions that explicitly models and handles UCP and temporal demand correlations. Our solution combines (i) two carefully formulated mixed linear integer programming formulations of the social welfare optimization problems in the inter-grid market; (ii) a recent result in theoretical computer science, which decomposes a fractional (infeasible) optimal solution to packing and covering-type NP-hard problems into a convex combination of integral (feasible) solutions, enabling a randomized auction framework that translates centralized co-operative approximation algorithms into (approximately) truthful and computationally efficient auction mechanisms; and (iii) custom-designed approximation algorithms for social welfare optimization in the inter-grid market, which are computationally efficient, have small approximation ratios, and work in concert with the auction framework in (ii).

As a market mechanism, auctions enable market efficiency and agility through resource pricing based directly on realtime supply-demand. Compared with a fixed pricing mechanism such as pre-negotiated contracts (*e.g.*, the FIT program in Ontario, Canada) and flat-rate pricing [2], auctions reduce the chance of over-pricing and under-pricing, better match resources with buyers that value them the most, and hence increase resource utilization efficiency, system-wide social welfare, and seller revenue. Auction based solutions have recently enjoyed success in areas including online advertisement and cloud computing, and are indeed what have been practiced in wholesale electricity markets for decades, although in a much washed down version that avoids technical complexities of UCP [29].

An electricity auction outcome contains information on not only which microgrids win and at what prices, but also a generation schedule in the case microgrids sell power back to the grid, satisfying technical limitations of generators as specified in the UCP constraints. Another key challenge arises from strategic bidders, who are driven by their own commercial interests and may submit falsified bids to maximize their own utilities. Truthfully bidding, as a desirable property in practical auction mechanisms, eliminates such strategic bids from selfish bidders. A well-known truthful auction mechanism is the celebrated Vickrey-Clarke-Groves (VCG) auction, which ensures truthfulness and economical efficiency in terms of social welfare maximization. Unfortunately, the winner determination problem used in the VCG mechanism is proven NP-hard in the two electricity trading problems we study. Hence directly applying the VCG auction becomes computationally infeasible as the system size grows. Approximation algorithms, as an alternative to optimally solving NP-complete problems, have been substantially studied over the past few decades, providing near-optimal solutions within polynomial time. Unfortunately, plugging an approximate algorithm into the VCG framework may result in clearly non-truthful auction mechanisms [26].

The auction mechanism we design in this work follows a randomized auction framework, which translates approximate social welfare maximization algorithms into an approximate-truthful auction and an absolute-truthful auction respectively, with the help of a fractional VCG auction and a convex decomposition technique. The resulting auctions execute in polynomial time, are (approximately) truthful in expectation, and guarantee approximate economic efficiency. At high level, the randomized auction framework consists of three main steps: (i) a fractional VCG auction is first conducted after relaxing integer decision variables; (ii) then a carefully designed convex decomposition technique is utilized to break the fractional solution down into a convex combination of integer solutions; (iii) finally feasible integer solutions are chosen by viewing their corresponding weights as probabilities, and payments are computed for helping the randomized auction inherit truthfulness from the fractional VCG auction.

Specifically, we first study the market where the grid purchases electricity from microgrids. We design an iterative primal-dual algorithm for the winner determination problem (WDP1) by exploiting the underlying structure of WDP1 through Lagrange relaxation and problem decomposition. We then simulate a fractional VCG auction by relaxing the integer decision variables, which is truthful and computationally efficient. Next we utilize a pair of carefully designed primal and dual linear programs to decompose the fractional solution into a convex combination of mixed integer solutions by employing the approximation algorithm as a separation oracle, under UCP constraints. The decomposition process can be completed in polynomial time using the ellipsoid method, providing a series of weights for selected mixed integer solutions. Finally, each candidate mixed integer solution is chosen with probability equal to its corresponding weight. The randomized auction guarantees the same approximation ratio ρ as the plug-in ρ-approximation algorithm does, under truthful bidding. Truthfulness of the randomized auction is not absolutely guaranteed, but is provided in a best-effort fashion. We leave the design of an absolute-truthful, computationally efficient and approximately social welfare maximizing auction for this scenario as future work.

We next study the market where microgrids purchase electricity from the grid for their supply deficiencies. An a-approximation algorithm is first designed for the detailed problem without considering truthfulness, based on greedy primal-dual algorithm design. We then simulate a fractional VCG auction based on the LP relaxation (LPR) of the social welfare maximization, WDP2. Next, we exploit the underlying packing nature of WDP2, and solve a pair of tailored primal-dual linear programs again to decompose the fractional solution to WDP2 into a combination of weighted integer solutions, using the ellipsoid algorithm with the a-approximation algorithm acting as a separation oracle. Finally, we select integer solutions using the calculated weights as corresponding probabilities. Absolute truthfulness is guaranteed by that of the fractional VCG auction. The randomized auction again guarantees the same approximation ratio a in terms of social welfare as the cooperative a-approximation algorithm does.

In the rest of the paper, we review related work in Sec. 2, and present the system model, the randomized auction framework as well as an example approximation algorithm in Sec. 3. In Sec. 4, we design another variant of the randomized auction framework and its corresponding approximation algorithm. Performance evaluation is presented in Sec. 5. Sec. 6 concludes the paper.

2. RELATED WORK

Auctions are extensively employed in traditional power grids, *e.g.*, Nicolaisen *et al.* [27] propose a computational wholesale electricity market operating in a *clearing house* double-auction manner. Similarly, Tesfatsion [29] proposes centrally administered wholesale electricity markets with congestion management using an auction approach. Neither of them takes UCP constraints into consideration. McGuire [24] propose an auction for heuristically minimizing operational cost with substantially simplified unit commitment constraints, by collecting cost bids from each generating unit. No proven guarantee on the performance or computational complexity analysis is provided.

Microgrids, as an emerging paradigm of power generation and supply, have been studied in a series of recent work. Lasseter *et al.* [19] was among the first to propose the concept of microgrids. Barnes *et al.* [6] summarize dozens of existing and undergoing demonstration projects of microgrids across America, Asia and Europe. Lu *et al.* [23] investigate microgrids, considering renewable energy (wind, solar) and co-generation, and propose an online algorithm CHASE with a small competitive ratio in operation cost. With limited prediction into the future, CHASE can be extended to behave more intelligently.

A few studies recently appeared in the literature of auction design for microgrids. For example, Dimeas *et al.* [10] present a distributed control approach for microgrids, using an auction algorithm for the solution of the symmetric assignment problem. Yet they fail to consider the key unit commitment problem in the proposed solution. Tsikalakis *et al.* [30] consider demand side bidding where consumers of the microgrids submit bids to purchase energy from microgrids. Based on such bids, the microgrid central controller chooses either to minimize operational cost or to maximize profit. Their auction is not proven to be truthful.

The celebrated VCG auction mechanism due to Vickrey [31], Clarke [9] and Groves [15], represents a general truthful auction framework, in which no rational buyers have motivation to submit falsified bids. Formally, an auction mechanism is *truthful* if bidding the true valuation is a dominant strategy for each bidder. VCG auctions are proven to be the only type of auctions that can simultaneously guarantee truthfulness and absolute economic efficiency. A VCG auction requires optimally solving the social welfare maximization problem multiple times, for calculating allocation rules as well as payments of winning buyers. Unfortunately, the underlying optimization problem is often NP-hard, making the VCG auction computationally infeasible, especially when facing a large number of bidders. Approximation algorithms are known to be an efficient alternative for solving NP-hard problems, computing sub-optimal solutions in polynomial time. Unfortunately a VCG auction loses its truthfulness when one applies an approximation algorithm instead of an optimal algorithm for social welfare maximization [26].

In a sequence of recent work that initiated from theoretical computer science [8, 20, 25, 32], a polynomial-time convex decomposition technique is designed for converting fractional solution for an NP-hard problem, modelled as a linear integer program, into a weighted combination of integer solutions. Such a decomposition technique enables a randomized auction framework that automatically translates a centralized cooperative approximation algorithm into an auction mechanism, achieving the same social welfare approximation ratio as the plug-in approximation algorithm does, while guaranteeing truthful bidding. A key property exploited in the decomposition is the packing or covering property. A linear program is a *packing* LP if it is of the form: Maximize $\mathbf{b}^T\mathbf{y}$, subject to: $\mathbf{A}^T\mathbf{y} \leq \mathbf{c}, \mathbf{y} \geq \mathbf{0}$, where the matrix $\mathbf{A}$ and vectors $\mathbf{b}$ and $\mathbf{c}$ are non-negative. The dual of a packing LP is a covering LP.

Dughmi and Roughgarden [11] recently proposed another technique that transfers an approximation algorithm into a truthful auction mechanism with the same social welfare approximation ratio. This approach requires that the social welfare maximization problem admits an Full Polynomial-Time Approximation Scheme (FPTAS), which is a stronger requirement than having a polynomial-time constant-ratio approximation algorithm. Many NP-hard optimization problems (including all that are proven APX-hard) do not have FPTAS.

3. THE MICROGRID-TO-GRID ELECTRICITY MARKET

3.1 Generator constraints and social welfare optimization

We consider the microgrid-to-grid market in this section, consisting of a regional power grid and a set $\mathcal{N}$ ($|\mathcal{N}| = n$) of microgrids. Each microgrid has its own generator that produces electrical power. An example microgrid in operation is shown in Fig. 2. Each generator incurs an operational cost in the active generation mode, which depends on the type of generation (*e.g.*, gas or diesel). There is further an amortized infrastructure and maintenance cost. Both costs are private information at the microgrid. The regional power grid (the *auctioneer*) solicits electricity sales from the microgrids (the *bidders*) during periods of under-supply, through a (reversed) auction. If the total amount of energy purchased from the auction falls short to bridge the gap, the grid may further purchase electricity from generation plants based in the near-term markets (which are usually more expensive) [27], or from electricity storage [12]. We consider an operation period $\mathcal{T}$ from $t = 1$ to $t = T$, during which the demand of the grid can be predicted. In practice, auctions in an electricity market are conducted based on forecasts of power demand in an upcoming time period (*e.g.*, the next 24 hours or several days [3]). Correspondingly, near-future demands are assumed to be known in advance.

Figure 2: The Sendai microgrid [1], with an output capacity of 1 MW, remained in full service during and after the March 2011 Great East Japan Earthquake, supplying power and heat to the community around Tohoku Fukushi University.

Let $x_i(t)$ be a binary variable indicating whether microgrid $i \in \mathcal{N}$ is ON or OFF at $t \in \mathcal{T}$. $y_i(t)$ indicates the power output of microgrid $i \in \mathcal{N}$. $z(t)$ is the total energy supplied by plants or batteries rather than microgrids at $t \in \mathcal{T}$. $s_i(t)$ is the amortized infrastructure/maintenance cost of microgrid $i \in \mathcal{N}$ at time t. $u_i(t)$ is a unit cost ($ per MWh) of microgrid $i \in \mathcal{N}$ at $t \in \mathcal{T}$. $p(t)$ is a unit cost ($ per MWh) of the energy supplied by plants or batteries rather than microgrids at $t \in \mathcal{T}$. $D(t)$ is the power demand at $t \in \mathcal{T}$, known by the grid. δ is the maximum output level change between two consecutive time slots. Δ^+ is the maximum output level at the first time slot of a commitment period, known as startup ramp limit. Similarly Δ^- is the maximum output level at the last time slot of a commitment period, known as shutdown ramp limit.

The auction of electricity from the microgrids to the regional power grid is conducted once, at $t = 1$, for the period $\mathcal{T} = [1, T]$, based on predicted information for $\mathcal{T}$. The grid (auctioneer) schedules its power supply for $t \in \mathcal{T}$. Each microgrid (bidder) i submits its bid containing its private costs $s_i(t)$ and $u_i(t)$, and can contribute a maximum output level of P_{max}. At each time t, total supply should cover total demand in the grid:

$$\sum_i y_i(t) + z(t) \geq D(t), \forall t \in \mathcal{T}$$

Then we have the UCP constraints dictating generator schedules. We assume that all microgrids are off at $t = 0$, and all microgrids keep the same status as $t = T$ after the operation period $\mathcal{T}$, *i.e.*, $x_i(T) = x_i(T+1) = x_i(T+2) = \ldots$, for facilitating constraint formulation.

First, a generator, once turned ON, must remain active for at least T_{on} time slots. Similarly it must stay deactive for at least T_{off} time slots once turned OFF:

$$UCP1: \sum_{\tau=t+1}^{t+T_{on}} x_i(\tau) \geq T_{on}(x_i(t+1) - x_i(t)), \forall t \in \mathcal{T}, i \in \mathcal{N}$$
$$\sum_{\tau=t+1}^{t+T_{off}} (1 - x_i(\tau)) \geq T_{off}(x_i(t) - x_i(t+1)), \forall t \in \mathcal{T}, i \in \mathcal{N}$$

The output level of a microgrid cannot exceed its capacity P_{max}, and the minimal output is P_{min} if it is active:

$$UCP2: P_{max}x_i(t) \geq y_i(t), \forall t \in \mathcal{T}, i \in \mathcal{N}$$
$$y_i(t) \geq P_{min}x_i(t), \forall t \in \mathcal{T}, i \in \mathcal{N}$$

Furthermore, the output level of a generator cannot vary abruptly. The *ramping rate* is upper-bounded:

$$UCP3: y_i(t) - y_i(t-1) \leq \delta x_i(t-1) + \Delta^+(1 - x_i(t-1)), \forall t \in \mathcal{T}, i \in \mathcal{N}$$
$$y_i(t-1) - y_i(t) \leq \delta x_i(t) + \Delta^-(1 - x_i(t)), \forall t \in \mathcal{T}, i \in \mathcal{N}$$

There are three types of costs. $\sum_{i,t} s_i(t)x_i(t)$ is the amortized hardware/maintenance cost[1]; $\sum_{i,t} u_i(t)y_i(t)$ is fuel cost; $\sum_t p(t)z(t)$ is the total expense in power purchase from plants/batteries, which is a cost of the regional power grid (auctioneer). A system-wide (grid and microgrids) social welfare maximization translates into the objective of minimizing the aggregated cost, while meeting the grid's demand. The winner determination problem (WDP1) with $x_i(t), y_i(t)$ and $z(t)$ as decision variables is:

$$\text{minimize} \sum_{i,t} s_i(t)x_i(t) + \sum_{i,t} u_i(t)y_i(t) + \sum_t p(t)z(t) \quad (1)$$

subject to:

$$\sum_i y_i(t) + z(t) \geq D(t), \quad \forall t \quad (1a)$$
$$\sum_{\tau=t+1}^{t+T_{on}} x_i(\tau) \geq T_{on}(x_i(t+1) - x_i(t)), \quad \forall t, i \quad (1b)$$
$$\sum_{\tau=t+1}^{t+T_{off}} (1 - x_i(\tau)) \geq T_{off}(x_i(t) - x_i(t+1)), \quad \forall t, i \quad (1c)$$
$$P_{max}x_i(t) \geq y_i(t), \quad \forall t, i \quad (1d)$$
$$y_i(t) \geq P_{min}x_i(t), \quad \forall t, i \quad (1e)$$
$$y_i(t) - y_i(t-1) \leq \delta x_i(t-1) + \Delta^+(1 - x_i(t-1)), \quad \forall t, i \quad (1f)$$
$$y_i(t-1) - y_i(t) \leq \delta x_i(t) + \Delta^-(1 - x_i(t)), \quad \forall t, i \quad (1g)$$
$$x_i(t) \in \{0, 1\}, y_i(t) \geq 0, z(t) \geq 0, \quad \forall t, i \quad (1h)$$

Generator scheduling under UCP is in general NP-hard [16]. This rules out a direct application of the VCG auction mechanism for truthful auction design. We instead exploit the underlying structure of WDP1 for designing a randomized auction that is computationally efficient.

3.2 The randomized auction framework

The electricity auction we design leverages a randomized auction framework that consists of three main steps, as illustrated in Algorithm 1.

Step 1. Simulating the fractional VCG auction. We first simulate the fractional VCG auction with the linear programming relaxation (LPR) of WDP1 as the aggregated cost minimization problem, which is obtained by relaxing the binary variable $x_i(t)$ to $0 \leq x_i(t) \leq 1$. Such a fractional VCG auction is truthful but the solution is fractional and therefore infeasible. Let $(\boldsymbol{x}^*, \boldsymbol{y}^*, \boldsymbol{z}^*)$ be the optimal fractional solution to the LPR of WDP1. Prices charged in the fractional VCG mechanism, $\boldsymbol{\Pi}^f$, are computed as follows:

$$\Pi_k^f = \sum_{i,t} (s_i(t)x_i'(t) + u_i(t)y_i'(t) + p(t)z'(t)) - \sum_{i \neq k, t} (s_i(t)x_i^*(t) + u_i(t)y_i^*(t) + p(t)z^*(t)) \quad (2)$$

[1]There are two types of infrastructure/maintenance costs: amortized hardware cost and running cost. The former is amortized over the generator's lifetime, while the latter is applicable only when the generator is turned on. This work focuses on the latter.

Algorithm 1 A Randomized Microgrid-to-Grid Power Auction

1: **Step 1. Simulating the fractional VCG auction.**
2: — Compute the fractional VCG allocation $\boldsymbol{x}^*$, and payment $\boldsymbol{\Pi}^f$, through solving the LPR of WDP1.
3: **Step 2. Decomposing the optimal fractional solution**
4: — Decompose the fractional solution $(\boldsymbol{x}^*, \boldsymbol{y}^*, \boldsymbol{z}^*)$ to a convex combination of mixed integer solutions, *i.e.*, $\sum_{q\in\mathcal{I}} \lambda^q(\boldsymbol{x}^q, \boldsymbol{y}^q, \boldsymbol{z}^q) \le \rho(\boldsymbol{x}^*, \boldsymbol{y}^*, \boldsymbol{z}^*)$, through solving a pair of primal-dual LPs in (4) and (5) using the ellipsoid method, leveraging a $\rho-$approximation algorithm verifying the integrality gap of ρ as a separation oracle.
5: **Step 3. Randomized winner selection and payment**
6: — Select each $(\boldsymbol{x}^q, \boldsymbol{y}^q, \boldsymbol{z}^q)$ randomly with probability λ^q.
— for each winning microgrid i: charge a payment $\Pi_i = \Pi_i^f \frac{\sum_t (s_i(t)x_i^q(t) + u_i(t)y_i^q(t))}{\sum_t (s_i(t)x_i^*(t) + u_i(t)y_i^*(t))}$, if $\sum_t (s_i(t)x_i^*(t) + u_i(t)y_i^*(t)) \ne 0$; $\Pi_i = 0$ otherwise.

where $(\boldsymbol{x}', \boldsymbol{y}', \boldsymbol{z}')$ is an optimal fractional solution without buying any power from microgrid $k \in \mathcal{N}$.

Step 2. Decomposing the optimal fractional solution.
Applying the recent convex decomposition technique [8, 20, 25], we decompose the optimal fractional solution into a convex combination of integral solutions each with a fractional weight that sums up to 1. This step requires a *separation oracle*, an effective polynomial-time approximation algorithm to WDP1 satisfying:

$$\sum_{i,t} s_i(t)x_i(t) + \sum_{i,t} u_i(t)y_i(t) + \sum_t p(t)z(t) \le \rho OPT_{LPR1} \quad (3)$$

where OPT_{LPR1} is the value of the objective function for the optimal fractional solution $(\boldsymbol{x}^*, \boldsymbol{y}^*, \boldsymbol{z}^*)$ for WDP1.

The goal of the decomposition is to find combination weights $\lambda^q \ge 0$, such that $\sum_{q\in\mathcal{I}} \lambda^q = 1$, $\sum_{q\in\mathcal{I}} \lambda^q \boldsymbol{x}^q \le \rho \boldsymbol{x}^*$, $\sum_{q\in\mathcal{I}} \lambda^q \boldsymbol{y}^q \le \rho \boldsymbol{y}^*$ and $\sum_{q\in\mathcal{I}} \lambda^q \boldsymbol{z}^q \le \rho \boldsymbol{z}^*$, where $\mathcal{I}$ is the index set for all feasible mixed integer solutions to WDP1.

We compute such a weight vector λ through solving the following pair of primal and dual LPs:

$$\textbf{Primal:} \text{ maximize } \sum_{q\in\mathcal{I}} \lambda^q \quad (4)$$

subject to:

$$\sum_{q\in\mathcal{I}} \lambda^q(\boldsymbol{x}^q, \boldsymbol{y}^q, \boldsymbol{z}^q) \le \rho(\boldsymbol{x}^*, \boldsymbol{y}^*, \boldsymbol{z}^*) \quad (4a)$$

$$\sum_{q\in\mathcal{I}} \lambda^q \le 1 \quad (4b)$$

$$\lambda^q \ge 0, \forall q \in \mathcal{I} \quad (4c)$$

$$\textbf{Dual:} \text{ minimize } \rho\Big(\sum_{i,t} \alpha_i(t)x_i^*(t) + \sum_{i,t} \beta_i(t)y_i^*(t) + \sum_t \eta(t)z^*(t)\Big) + \gamma \quad (5)$$

subject to:

$$\sum_{i,t} \alpha_i(t)x_i^q(t) + \sum_{i,t} \beta_i(t)y_i^q(t) + \sum_t \eta(t)z^q(t) \ge 1 - \gamma, \forall q \in \mathcal{I} \quad (5a)$$

$$\boldsymbol{\alpha}, \boldsymbol{\beta}, \boldsymbol{\eta} \succeq 0, \gamma \ge 0 \quad (5b)$$

THEOREM 1. *LPs (4) and (5) can be solved in polynomial time, and the optimal value is* 1.

PROOF. First $(\boldsymbol{\alpha} = 0, \boldsymbol{\beta} = 0, \boldsymbol{r} = 0, \gamma = 1)$ is a feasible solution to the dual, hence the optimal value is at most 1. By way of contradiction, we assume that

$$\rho\Big(\sum_{i,t} \alpha_i(t)x_i^*(t) + \sum_{i,t} \beta_i(t)y_i^*(t) + \sum_t \eta(t)z^*(t)\Big) + \gamma < 1$$

To solve the dual, we need to apply a cooperative approximation algorithm to WDP1:

$$\sum_{i,t} \alpha_i(t)x_i^q(t) + \sum_{i,t} \beta_i(t)y_i^q(t) + \sum_t \eta(t)z(t) \le \rho OPT_{LPR1}(\boldsymbol{\alpha}, \boldsymbol{\beta}, \boldsymbol{\eta})$$

where $(\boldsymbol{x}^q, \boldsymbol{y}^q, \boldsymbol{z}^q)$ and $OPT_{LPR1}(\boldsymbol{\alpha}, \boldsymbol{\beta}, \boldsymbol{\eta})$ are a feasible mixed integer solution and the value of the optimal fractional solution, respectively, to WDP1 with $\boldsymbol{\alpha}$ as bidding prices , $\boldsymbol{\beta}$ as fuel prices and $\boldsymbol{\eta}$ as the unit prices of energy purchased from plants or batteries. Note that:

$$OPT_{LPR1}(\boldsymbol{\alpha},\boldsymbol{\beta}, \boldsymbol{\eta}) \le \sum_{i,t} \alpha_i(t)x_i^*(t) + \sum_{i,t} \beta_i(t)y_i^*(t) + \sum_t \eta(t)z^*(t)$$

which implies

$$\sum_{i,t} \alpha_i(t)x_i^q(t) + \sum_{i,t} \beta_i(t)y_i^q(t) + \sum_t \eta(t)z^q(t) \le \rho(\sum_{i,t} \alpha_i(t)x_i^*(t) + \sum_{i,t} \beta_i(t)y_i^*(t) + \sum_t \eta(t)z^*(t)) < 1 - \gamma$$

The above inequality violates the dual constraints, leading to a contradiction. Therefore the optimal dual objective value is 1. Following strong LP duality, we conclude that the optimal primal objective value is 1 as well.

We observe that the primal LP (4) has an exponential number of variables, which may take exponential time to solve directly. We instead resort to the dual LP (5) that has an exponential number of constraints. The ellipsoid method can solve the problem within polynomial time despite an exponential number of constraints [14]. The cooperative approximation algorithm serves as a separation oracle [8], providing a polynomial number of hyperplanes to cut the ellipsoid, making the dual LP solvable in polynomial time. Each hyperplane corresponds to a constraint in the dual, providing a feasible solution $(\boldsymbol{x}^q, \boldsymbol{y}^q, \boldsymbol{z}^q)$ as well as corresponding primal variable λ^q. The primal LP then can be transformed to an optimization problem with a polynomial number of variables corresponding to these hyperplanes. We hence can solve the primal LP in polynomial time, obtaining weights of the convex decomposition that sum to 1. □

Step 3. Randomized winner selection and payment. Following the decomposition, each possible solution $(\boldsymbol{x}^q, \boldsymbol{y}^q, \boldsymbol{z}^q)$ is selected randomly with a probability equal to its corresponding weight λ^q

computed in the decomposition in the second step. Then microgrid i receives a payment $\Pi_i = \Pi_i^f \frac{\sum_t (s_i(t)x_i^q(t)+u_i(t)y_i^q(t))}{\sum_t (s_i(t)x_i^*(t)+u_i(t)y_i^*(t))}$, if $\sum_t (s_i(t)x_i^*(t) + u_i(t)y_i^*(t)) \neq 0$; $\Pi_i = 0$ otherwise.

Assume truthful bidding, and then the expected social welfare is:

$$\sum_q (\lambda^q \boldsymbol{s}^T \boldsymbol{x}^q + \lambda^q \boldsymbol{u}^T \boldsymbol{y}^q + \lambda^q \boldsymbol{p}^T \boldsymbol{z}) \\ \leq \rho \boldsymbol{s}^T \boldsymbol{x}^* + \rho \boldsymbol{u}^T \boldsymbol{y}^* + \rho \boldsymbol{p}^T \boldsymbol{z}^* \leq \rho OPT_{WDP1}$$

where OPT_{WDP1} is the optimal mixed integer solution. Above inequality implies that the randomized auction framework achieves an approximation ratio of ρ with respect to the aggregated cost if users bid truthfully.

Recall that the auction in Sec. 3 is a reverse auction. Assume truthful bidding again, and then we have the expected utility of microgrid $i \in \mathcal{N}$:

$$E[\Pi_i] - \bar{v}_i(\sum_q \lambda^q(\boldsymbol{x}^q, \boldsymbol{y}^q)) =$$

$$\left(\Pi_i^f - \sum_t (s_i(t)x_i^*(t) + u_i(t)y_i^*(t))\right) \frac{\sum_{t,q} \lambda^q (s_i(t)x_i^q(t) + u_i(t)y_i^q(t))}{\sum_t (s_i(t)x_i^*(t) + u_i(t)y_i^*(t))}$$

Therefore the expected utility of microgrid i is larger than zero since the fractional VCG auction is individual rational, *i.e.*, $\Pi_i^f - \sum_t (s_i(t)x_i^*(t) + u_i(t)y_i^*(t)) \geq 0$.

3.3 The approximation algorithm for WDP1

Plug-in nature of the approximation algorithm. The randomized auction framework in Algorithm 1 requires an efficient approximation algorithm for solving WDP1. We emphasize that any approximation algorithm to WDP1 can be applied as a plug-in module to the auction framework. Such a plug-in approximation algorithm should be computationally efficient, and computes a feasible solution with a cost that is as close as possible to the LPR of WDP1. Below we present an example approximation algorithm design based on primal-dual optimization.

An example primal-dual algorithm. A key observation regarding WDP1 is that $(1a)$ is the only set of constraints that couple schedule variables from different microgrids. Lagrangian relaxation can naturally be applied to relax this set of constraints, such that the relaxed optimization problem is decomposable into a series of independent single-microgird UCP optimization. We introduce a nonnegative Lagrangian multiplier ξ_t corresponding to each coupling constraint $(1a)$, remove constraint $(1a)$, and add a corresponding penalty term into the objective function of WDP1, which becomes:

$$\sum_{i,t} s_i(t)x_i(t) + \sum_{i,t} y_i(t)u_i(t) + \sum_t z(t)p(t) \\ + \sum_t \xi_t(D(t) - \sum_i y_i(t) - z(t)) \\ = \sum_{i,t} s_i(t)x_i(t) + \sum_{i,t} y_i(t)(u_i(t) - \xi_t) \\ + \sum_t z(t)(p(t) - \xi_t) + \sum_t \xi_t D(t)$$

Note that the objective function may be unbounded when $p(t) < \xi_t$, $z(t) \to +\infty$. Hence primal feasibility requires that $p(t) \geq \xi_t, \forall t$. The Lagrangian dual problem to WDP1 is then:

$$\text{maximize } \mathcal{L}(\boldsymbol{\xi}) \quad (6)$$

subject to

$$\xi_t \leq p(t), \quad \forall t \in \mathcal{T} \quad (6a)$$
$$\boldsymbol{\xi} \succeq 0 \quad (6b)$$

where $\mathcal{L}(\boldsymbol{\xi}) = \min_{\boldsymbol{x},\boldsymbol{y} \in \mathcal{P}} \left(\sum_{i,t} s_i(t)x_i(t) + \sum_{i,t} y_i(t)(u_i(t) - \xi_t) + \sum_t \xi_t D(t) \right)$, and $\mathcal{P}$ is the polytope defined by constraints $(1b) - (1g)$.

Next, the Lagrangian dual problem can be separated into a series of single-microgrid optimal schedule problems, solved for each microgrid independently. We can write $\mathcal{L}(\boldsymbol{\xi}) = \sum_i g_i(\boldsymbol{\xi}) + \sum_t \xi_t D(t)$, where $g_i(\boldsymbol{\xi}), \forall i \in \mathcal{N}$ are defined as follows:

$$g_i(\boldsymbol{\xi}) = \min_{\mathcal{P}} \left(\sum_t s_i(t)x_i(t) + \sum_t y_i(t)(u_i(t) - \xi_t) \right)$$

The Lagrange dual problem can be solved by a subgradient algorithm, as shown in Algorithm 2. In each iteration, the sub-problems for each microgrid are first solved, then we update the dual variables by $\xi_t = \xi_t + b_k(D(t) - \sum_i y_i(t) - z(t))$. Due to constraint $(6a)$, the inner optimization $\mathcal{L}(\xi)$ always chooses $z(t) = 0$, and we ignore $z(t)$. Here b_k is a step size sequence that satisfies (i) $\lim_{k\to\infty} b_k = 0$, and (ii) $\sum_{k=0}^{\infty} b_k = \infty$. A typical such sequence is in the form of $3/(2k+1)$.

Algorithm 2 A subgradient algorithm for WDP1

1: **Dual initialization.** Set $\xi_t = p(t), \forall t \in \mathcal{T}$
2: **repeat**
3: — **Primal update.** For each microgrid i, given current $\boldsymbol{\xi}$, compute optimal schedule $x_i(t)$ and $y_i(t)$ by solving $g_i(\boldsymbol{\xi}), \forall i$, through dynamic programming.
4: — **Dual update.** Given current $\boldsymbol{x}$ and $\boldsymbol{y}$, update the dual variables by $\xi_t = \xi_t + b_k(D(t) - \sum_i y_i(t))$.
5: **until** convergence

The single-microgrid optimization is a classic UCP problem with one generator, and can be solved by dynamic programming efficiently [13, 28].

Upon convergence of the subgradient algorithm, the relaxed primal constraint $(1a)$ on grid-wide demand-supply is not always satisfied, although it has been observed that the gaps are rather small [16]. In this study, primal feasibility can be ensured by: (1) purchasing more from power reservoirs (plants or batteries), *i.e.*, increasing $z(t)$ in WDP1 to satisfy the demand; or using existing techniques from the literature, *e.g.*, Frangioni *et al.* [13] use a heuristic strategy to adjust the commitment status of generators to meet the demand; Aoki *et al.* [5] solve least square type problems to find a feasible solution.

The approximation ratio ρ. The auction framework in Algorithm 1 requires the approximation algorithm to compute an integral solution that is within an integrality gap of ρ from the LPR. While the subgradient method can always compute optimal solutions for the dual (and hence the primal) when the original optimization problem is a linear program, it leads to a duality gap when the original problem is a linear integer program. However, fortunately, a series of previous studies have verified that such a duality gap is extremely small for UCP-type problems, often within 1-2% [16]. The overall ratio ρ should be bounded by a constant in most cases, and can be estimated by empirically studies. The auction framework actually allows some flexibility in the value selection of ρ — precisely selecting the smallest upper-bound for the integrality gap serves the best interest of approximate truthfulness and social welfare but is hard; choosing a non-exact upper-bound works in practice with some compromise in truthfulness and social welfare. Our auction in this section is not an absolutely truthful auction. Nonetheless, it strikes to achieve a high level of (approximate) truthfulness, and from the bidder's point of view, it is unclear what strategy other than truthful bidding will lead to a higher utility.

4. THE GRID-TO-MICROGRID ELECTRICITY MARKET

4.1 Market constraints and social welfare maximization

In this section, we consider a regional power grid (auctioneer) who sells electricity to a number of microgrids (bidders) denoted by $\mathcal{M}$. The system runs in a round-by-round fashion from $t = 1$ to $t = T$, for which time period a microgrid $i \in \mathcal{M}$ submits one or more bids. B_i denotes all bids submitted by microgrid $i \in \mathcal{M}$. Each bid $j \in B_i$ of microgrid i, $(b_{i,j}, \boldsymbol{d}_{i,j})$, specifies a willingness to pay, $b_{i,j}$, for a demand curve $\boldsymbol{d}_{i,j}$ that contains entries $d_{i,j}(t)$, which is the amount of electricity demand at each time slot t. In practice, $\boldsymbol{d}_{i,j}$ is derived from a microgrid's prediction of near future power consumption. Similar to the microgrid-to-grid market in Sec. 3, the auction of electricity from the regional power grid to the microgrids is conducted at $t = 1$, when all bids are collected. Moreover, $\chi_{i,j}$ is a binary decision variable indicating whether microgrid i wins bid j or not. Let $\bar{v}_i(\chi)$ denote the true valuation of microgrid i, known by microgrid i only. We assume that $\bar{v}_i(\chi)$ is linear in χ. The available capacity of the regional grid, $C(t)$, varies over time, due to fluctuation in both the output from wind and solar generators and background demand. For example, Fig. 3 illustrates the fluctuation of hourly demand and available capacity within Ontario, Canada [3]. We assume that at each time, a single bid cannot exceed the total available capacity of the grid, *i.e.*, $C(t) > R(t) \triangleq \max_{i,j} d_{i,j}(t)$.

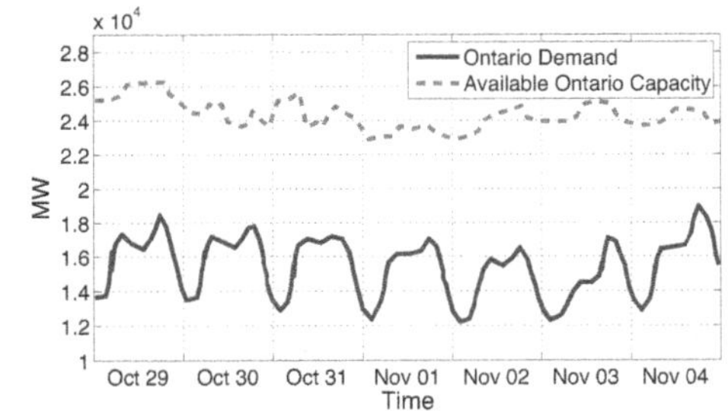

Figure 3: The fluctuation of hourly Electrical power demand and available capacity from October 29 to November 04, 2013 within Ontario, Canada.

We employ the XOR-bidding language [22], such that among all bids submitted by a microgrid, at most one bid can win:

$$\sum_j \chi_{i,j} \le 1, \forall i \in \mathcal{M}$$

Furthermore, the total power demand of all winning bids at each time slot cannot exceed the available capacity of the grid:

$$\sum_{i,j} d_{i,j}(t)\chi_{i,j} \le C(t), \forall t$$

The winner determination problem (WDP2) then maximizes social welfare (total utility of both the grid and the microgrids, with payments from the latter cancelling revenue of the former), under the above two constraints:

$$\text{maximize} \sum_{i,j} b_{i,j}\chi_{i,j} \tag{7}$$

subject to:

$$\sum_j \chi_{i,j} \le 1, \quad \forall i \in \mathcal{M} \quad (7a)$$

$$\sum_{i,j} d_{i,j}(t)\chi_{i,j} \le C(t), \quad \forall t \quad (7b)$$

$$\chi_{i,j} \in \{0,1\}, \quad \forall i \in \mathcal{M}, j \in B_i \quad (7c)$$

A salient feature in the grid-to-microgrid electricity market lies in the temporal dimension constraint that couples demand-supply across different time slots, as evident in (7b). As a result, WDP2 becomes NP-hard (proven below), making it highly non-trivial to design an auction that simultaneously guarantees truthfulness and good social welfare efficiency.

THEOREM 2. *WDP2 in (7) is NP-hard.*

PROOF. We present a polynomial-time reduction from the knapsack problem, a classic NP-hard problem [18] defined as:

$$\max_{\chi}\{\sum_{i=1}^{n} v_i\chi_i \text{ s.t. } \sum_{i=1}^{n} w_i\chi_i \le W, \chi_i \in \{0,1\}\}$$

Let us consider a special case of the WDP2: $|\mathcal{M}| = n$, each bidder submits a single bid and only one time slot is considered. WDP2 degrades into:

$$\max_{\chi}\{\sum_{i}^{n} b_i\chi_i \ s.t. \sum_{i}^{n} d_i\chi_i \le C, \chi_i \in \{0,1\}, \forall i \in \mathcal{M}\}$$

which is exactly a classic knapsack problem. Apparently, the reduction can be done within polynomial time. Therefore, WDP2 in (7) is NP-hard. □

4.2 The randomized auction framework

Theorem 2 suggests that solving WDP2 becomes daunting as the number of microgrids grows, which rules out a direct application of the VCG auction mechanism in the grid-to-microgrid market, since it requires optimally solving multiple WDP2 instances. We resort to the LPR of WDP2 by relaxing constraint (7c) to ($\chi_{i,j} \le 1, \forall i \in \mathcal{M}, j \in B_i$, is redundant and hence ignored):

$$\chi_{i,j} \ge 0, \forall i \in \mathcal{M}, j \in B_i \tag{7c'}$$

Similar to the framework applied in Sec. 3, we design an electricity auction following the randomized auction framework below.

Step 1. Simulate the fractional VCG auction. Compute the optimal fractional solution χ^* to the LPR of WDP2. Compute fractional VCG payments: buyer k pays $\pi_k^f = \sum_{i,j} b_{i,j}\chi'_{i,j} - \sum_{i \ne k,j} b_{i,j}\chi^*_{i,j}$, where χ' is the optimal solution to WDP2's LPR without selling any energy to microgrid k. The fractional (infeasible) solution χ^* is decomposed into integral (feasible) solutions in Step 2.

Step 2. Decompose the fractional solution χ^*. We next decompose χ^* into a combination of a series of feasible integer solutions by finding non-negative multipliers $\{\nu_q\}_{q \in \mathcal{J}}$, such that $\sum_{q \in \mathcal{J}} \nu^q = 1$, $\sum_{q \in \mathcal{J}} \nu^q \chi^q = \chi^*/a$, where $\mathcal{J}$ is the index set for all feasible integer solutions to WDP2.

Similar to the decomposition in Sec. 3, the decomposition step solves a pair of primal-dual LPs through the ellipsoid method, which requires an approximation algorithm to WDP2 that computes an integer solution χ, satisfying:

$$\sum_{i,j} b_{i,j}\chi_{i,j} \geq 1/a \sum_{i,j} b_{i,j}\chi^*_{i,j}$$

Step 3. Randomized winner selection and payment scaling. Select χ^q with probability ν^q, with following defined scale-down payment π_i for guaranteeing truthfulness and individual rationality, as analyzed below.

$$\pi_i = \begin{cases} \pi_i^f \frac{\sum_j b_{i,j}\chi^q_{i,j}}{\sum_j b_{i,j}\chi^*_{i,j}} & \text{if } \sum_j b_{i,j}\chi^*_{i,j} \neq 0 \\ 0 & \text{otherwise} \end{cases}$$

Truthfulness. Since the auction in Sec. 4 is an ordinary (forward) auction, the expected utility of microgrid i is:

$$\bar{v}_i(\sum_q \nu^q \chi^q_j(t)) - E[\pi_i] = (\bar{v}_i(\chi^*) - \pi_i^f)/a.$$

Then truthfulness of the 3-step auction follows from the truthfulness of the fractional VCG auction.

The convex decomposition. We compute values for ν^q, which are weights required in the decomposition of χ^* for solution feasibility, by solving a pair of primal-dual LPs below:

$$\textbf{Primal: } \text{minimize} \sum_{q\in\mathcal{J}} \nu^q \qquad (8)$$

subject to:

$$\sum_{q\in\mathcal{J}} \nu^q \chi^q = \chi^*/a$$

$$\sum_{q\in\mathcal{J}} \nu^q \geq 1$$

$$\nu^q \geq 0, \forall q \in \mathcal{J}$$

$$\textbf{Dual: } \text{maximize} \sum_{i,j} w_{i,j}\chi^*_{i,j}/a + \iota \qquad (9)$$

subject to:

$$\sum_{i,j} w_{i,j}\chi^q_{i,j} + \iota \leq 1, \forall q \in \mathcal{J}$$

$$w_{i,j} \text{ unconstrained}, \iota \geq 0, \forall i,j$$

Our goal is to solve the primal to optimal with $\sum_q \nu^q = 1$. We next prove that $\sum_q \nu^q = 1$ indeed happens at optimum.

THEOREM 3. *Given a polynomial time approximation algorithm to WDP2 that computes an integer solution χ, satisfying $\sum_{i,j} b_{i,j}\chi_{i,j} \geq 1/a \sum_{i,j} b_{i,j}\chi^*_{i,j}$, the primal (8) and the dual (9) can be optimally solved in polynomial time, with optimal objective value of 1.*

PROOF. First note that $w = 0, \iota = 1$ constitutes a feasible solution to the dual, yielding an objective value of 1. Hence the optimal dual objective is at least 1.

By way of contradiction, we assume that $\sum_{i,j} w_{i,j}\chi^*_{i,j}/a + \iota > 1$. The only potential problem is that the dual variable $w_{i,j}$ can be negative, making the approximation algorithm not applicable. Let $w^+_{i,j} = \max\{w_{i,j}, 0\}$. Instead of $w_{i,j}$, we use $w^+_{i,j}$ as input for the approximation algorithm. Assume given $w^+_{i,j}$, we apply the approximation algorithm for verifying the integrality gap of WDP2: $\exists q, \sum_{i,j} w^+_{i,j}\chi^q_{i,j} \geq \sum_{i,j} w^+_{i,j}\chi^{**}_{i,j}/a$, where χ^{**} is the optimal fractional solution given w^+ as input. Let

$$\bar{\chi}_{i,j} = \begin{cases} \chi^q_{i,j} & \text{if } w_{i,j} \geq 0 \\ 0 & \text{otherwise} \end{cases}$$

$\bar{\chi}_{i,j}$ can be verified to be a feasible integer solution to WDP2. We then have

$$\begin{aligned}\sum_{i,j} w_{i,j}\bar{\chi}_{i,j} &= \sum_{i,j} w^+_{i,j}\chi^q_{i,j} \geq \sum_{i,j} w^+_{i,j}\chi^{**}_{i,j}/a \\ &\geq \sum_{i,j} w^+_{i,j}\chi^*_{i,j}/a \geq \sum_{i,j} w_{i,j}\chi^*_{i,j}/a \\ &> 1 - \iota\end{aligned}$$

implying $\sum_{i,j} w_{i,j}\bar{\chi}_{i,j} + \iota > 1$, which violates the first dual constraint. A contradiction occurs. Hence the optimal dual objective is 1. Due to strong LP duality, the optimal primal objective is 1 as well.

Similar to Sec. 3, the primal LP (8) has an exponential number of variables. We resort to the dual LP (9), which has an exponential number of constraints, and can be solved using the ellipsoid method in polynomial time, given a separation oracle (the approximation algorithm in Sec. 4.3). Once the dual LP is solved, by using a polynomial number of hyperplanes found by the separation oracle, we then convert the primal LP to an optimization with a polynomial number of variables corresponding to these hyperplanes, which can be solved in polynomial time as well. The weights then are found as a byproduct of solving the primal LP. □

4.3 The approximation algorithm for WDP2

Dual of WDP2's LPR. We now focus on designing an approximation algorithm to WDP2 that verifies its integrality gap, as required in the ellipsoid method to solve dual (9). Introducing dual variables ϕ and ψ for constraints (7a) and (7b), respectively, we obtain the dual of WDP2's LPR:

$$\text{minimize} \sum_i \phi_i + \sum_t C(t)\psi_t \qquad (10)$$

subject to:

$$\phi_i + \sum_t d_{i,j}(t)\psi_t \geq b_{i,j}, \quad \forall i,j \quad (10a)$$

$$\phi_i, \psi_t \geq 0 \quad \forall i,t \quad (10b)$$

A Greedy Primal-Dual Algorithm. We apply the classic greedy primal-dual framework that is proven effective for approximating NP-hard problems with an IP formulation [7], and design Algorithm 3 for WDP2 in (7). Algorithm 3 first initializes the primal and dual variables (lines 2-6). Then a `while` loop iteratively updates the primal and dual variables by choosing the highest unit-weight bids from microgrids (line 10-13). The `while` loop terminates when all microgrids are satisfied or the generated primal variable χ becomes infeasible, *i.e.*, allocated resources exceed the capacity of the grid. In the following analysis, let ϕ_i^τ, ψ_t^τ be the dual variables, and p_τ be the primal objective at the end of the τ-th iteration of the `while` loop.

Primal feasibility. We study the feasibility of solutions returned by Algorithm 3 first.

THEOREM 4. *Algorithm 3 provides a feasible solution to WDP2,* i.e., *IP (7).*

PROOF. Constraint (7a) will be respected because once Algorithm 3 finds a power supply curve for user i, no more power re-

Algorithm 3 The Greedy Primal-Dual Approximation Algorithm

1: // Initialization
2: $\theta = \min_t C(t)/R(t)$;
3: $p = 0; \mathcal{U} = \emptyset$;
4: $\forall i, j : \chi_{i,j} = 0$;
5: $\forall i : \phi_i = 0$;
6: $\forall t : \psi_t = 1/C(t)$;
7:
8: // Iterative update of primal and dual variables:
9: **while** $\sum_t C(t)\psi_t < T\exp(\theta - 1)$ AND $\mathcal{U} \neq \mathcal{M}$ **do**
10: **for all** $i \in \mathcal{M} \setminus \mathcal{U}$ **do**
11: $j_i = \arg\max_j\{b_{i,j}\}$;
12: **end for**
13: $\mu = \arg\max_{i\in\mathcal{M}\setminus\mathcal{U}}\{\frac{b_{i,j_i}}{\sum_t d_{i,j_i}(t)\psi_t}\}$;
14: $\chi_{\mu,j_\mu} = 1; \phi_\mu = b_{\mu,j_\mu}$;
15: $p = p + b_{\mu,j_\mu}; \mathcal{U} = \mathcal{U} \cup \{\mu\}$;
16: **for all** $1 \le t \le T$ **do**
17: $\psi_t = \psi_t \cdot (T\exp(\theta-1))^{(d_{\mu,j_\mu}(t))/(C(t)-R(t))}$;
18: **end for**
19: **end while**

source will be allocated to i in the future. Values in x are always binary (0 or 1) since they are initialized to 0 (line 4) and updated to 1 only (line 14). Constraint ($7c$) therefore will not be violated.

Let us examine the second constraint ($7b$). Suppose that the solution is feasible so far. Let $\tilde{j} \in B_{\tilde{i}}$ be the first bid that breaks the feasibility when added to the current solution, say, in iteration τ. That is, $\exists t$, such that $\sum_{i,j\in\Gamma} d_{i,j}(t) \le C(t)$ and $d_{\tilde{i},\tilde{j}}(t) + \sum_{i,j\in\Gamma} d_{i,j}(t) > C(t)$, where Γ is the set of bids added to the solution before bid $\tilde{S}$. Since each single bid cannot exceed the capacity constraint, *i.e.*, $C(t) > R(t) \ge \max_{i,j} d_{i,j}(t)$, we have

$$\sum_{i,j\in\Gamma} d_{i,j}(t) > C(t) - R(t) \Rightarrow \sum_{i,j\in\Gamma} d_{i,j}(t)/(C(t) - R(t)) > 1$$

and that leads to:

$$C(t)\psi_t^{\tau-1} = (T\exp(\theta-1))^{\sum_{i,j\in\Gamma} d_{i,j}(t)/(C(t)-R(t))} > T\exp(\theta-1)$$

which satisfies the first stopping condition in line 14. This implies that iteration $\tau - 1$ is the last iteration, and the bid $\tilde{j}$ would not be added to the solution at all. □

Dual feasibility: dual fitting. The primal solution is always feasible during the execution, but the dual is not necessarily so. The following lemma ensures that the dual variables can be made feasible through posterior scaling by a carefully chosen factor (dual fitting).

LEMMA 1. *If $(\phi^{\tau-1}, \psi^{\tau-1})$ is the (possibly infeasible) dual solution at the beginning of the τ-th iteration, then $(\phi^{\tau-1}, \epsilon f(\psi^{\tau-1}, j_i^\tau)\psi^{\tau-1})$ is a feasible solution to the dual (10), where $f(\psi, j_i) \triangleq b_{i,j_i}/(\sum_t d_{i,j_i}(t)\psi_t)$, $\epsilon \triangleq \max_{j',j''\in B_i,i,t} d_{i,j'}(t)/d_{i,j''}(t)$.*

PROOF. According to line 11, we have $\forall i, j, b_{i,j} \le b_{i,j_i}$. Because ϕ_μ is set to b_{μ,j_μ} where $b_{\mu,j_\mu} \ge b_{\mu,j}, \forall\mu \in \mathcal{U}, j \in B_\mu$. That is:

$$\phi_\mu \ge b_{\mu,j}, \forall\mu \in \mathcal{U}, j \in B_\mu$$

which implies that constraint ($10a$) is satisfied $\forall\mu \in \mathcal{U}, \mathcal{S} \in B_\mu$.

Next we examine the bidders $\mu \in \mathcal{M} \setminus \mathcal{U}$. Also note that j_i^τ is decided by a maximization in line 13. Therefore,

$$f(\psi^{\tau-1}, j_i^\tau) \ge \frac{b_{i,j_i}}{\sum_t d_{i,j_i}(t)\psi_t^{\tau-1}}, \quad \forall i \in \mathcal{M}\setminus\mathcal{U} \Leftrightarrow$$
$$f(\psi^{\tau-1}, j_i^\tau)\sum_t d_{i,j_i}(t)\psi_t^{\tau-1} \ge b_{i,j_i}, \quad \forall i \in \mathcal{M}\setminus\mathcal{U} \qquad (11)$$

Note that $\epsilon d_{i,j_1}(t) \ge d_{i,j_2}(t), \forall j_1, j_2 \in B_i, i, t$, Eqn. (11) further suggests that the constraint ($10a$) is respected by the scaled solution, *i.e.*,

$$\epsilon f(\psi^{\tau-1}, j_i^\tau)\sum_t d_{i,j}(t)\psi_t^{\tau-1} \ge b_{i,j_i} \ge b_{i,j}, \forall i \in \mathcal{M}\setminus\mathcal{U}, j \in B_i.$$

This completes the proof. □

Approximation ratio.

THEOREM 5. *Algorithm 3 computes an a-approximate solution to WDP2 in polynomial-time, and also verifies that the integrality gap of WDP2 is bounded by a, where $a = 1 + \epsilon\Lambda(eT^{\Lambda-1} - 1)$, $\Lambda = \frac{\theta}{\theta-1}$.*

PROOF. First we analyze the approximation ratio of Algorithm 3. Let $d_1(\tau) = \sum_{i\in\mathcal{M}} \phi_i^\tau$, $d_2(\tau) = \sum_t C(t)\psi_t^\tau$. Let d be the optimal solution to the dual (10). Let j_μ denote the set selected in the τ-th iteration. ω is denoted the last iteration of the loop.

Case 1: Algorithm 3 stops at ω-th iteration where $\mathcal{U} = \mathcal{M}$ and $\sum_t C(t)\psi_t < t\exp(\theta - 1)$. We know that each cloud user wins one bid. In fact the algorithm produces an optimal solution to IP (7) in this case. Theorem 4 guarantees that p_ω is the value of a feasible solution to IP (7). Meanwhile since $\phi_\mu^\omega = \max_{j\in B_\mu}\{b_{\mu,j}\} \ge b_{\mu,j}, \forall\mu \in \mathcal{U}, j \in B_\mu$, thus constraint ($10a$) is satisfied regardless of ψ, *e.g.*, ($\phi^\omega, \psi = 0$) is a feasible solution, whose value is exactly p_ω as well, to the dual of the LPR. By weak duality for the LP relaxation, any feasible solution to the dual (10) is an upper bound of IP (7). Thus p_ω is the optimal value to IP (7).

Case 2: Algorithm 3 stops at ω-th iteration where

$$d_2(\omega) = \sum_t (C(t)\psi_t^\omega) \ge T\exp(\theta - 1).$$

We analyze the approximation ratio in following two sub-cases.

Sub Case 2.1: If $\exists$ an iteration $\tau \le \omega$, such that $a \ge \frac{d}{d_1(\tau-1)}$, then an a-approximate ratio is found, since (i) $d_1(\tau)$ is a non-decreasing function of τ because it becomes larger when the iteration continues; (ii) $d_1(\tau - 1) = p_{\tau-1}$, which is the value of the primal solution;

Sub Case 2.2: $a < \frac{d}{d_1(\tau-1)}$, for all iterations $\tau \le \omega$. For any iteration $\tau \ge 1$, we have:

$$d_2(\tau) = \sum_t C(t)\psi_t^{\tau-1}(T\exp(\theta-1))^{(d_{\mu,j_\mu}(t))/(C(t)-R(t))}$$
$$= \sum_t C(t)\psi_t^{\tau-1}(1 + \frac{\delta}{\frac{C(t)}{R(t)} - 1})^{(d_{\mu,j_\mu}(t))/R(t))}$$
$$\le \sum_t C(t)\psi_t^{\tau-1}(1 + \frac{\delta}{\frac{C(t)}{R(t)} - 1} d_{\mu,j_\mu}(t)/R(t))$$
$$\le d_2(\tau - 1) + \Delta\sum_t d_{\mu,j_\mu}(t)\psi_t^{\tau-1}$$

where $\delta = (\frac{C(t)}{R(t)} - 1)((T\exp(\theta-1))^{1/(\frac{C(t)}{R(t)}-1)} - 1)$, $\Delta = \max_t \frac{\delta C(t)}{C(t)-R(t)}$. The first inequality is due to $(1+a)^x \le 1 + ax, \forall x \in [0, 1]$.

Note that $\frac{\delta C(t)}{C(t)-R(t)}$ is a non-increasing function of $\frac{C(t)}{R(t)} > 1$, and $\theta = \min_t C(t)/R(t)$, then $\frac{\delta C(t)}{C(t)-R(t)}$ reaches the maximum when $\frac{C(t)}{R(t)} = \theta$, *i.e.*, $\Delta = \theta(eT^{1/(\theta-1)} - 1)$.

Recall the definition of $f(\psi^{\tau-1}, j_\mu)$, then we have:

$$\sum_t d_{\mu,j_\mu}(t)\psi_t^{\tau-1} = b_{\mu,j_\mu}/f(\psi^{\tau-1}, j_\mu)$$

Since p_τ is the value of the primal solution at the end of τ-th iteration, then $p_\tau - p_{\tau-1} = b_{\mu,j_\mu}$, this leads to:

$$d_2(\tau) \leq d_2(\tau-1) + \Delta \frac{p_\tau - p_{\tau-1}}{f(\psi^{\tau-1}, j_\mu)} \tag{12}$$

Following Lemma 1, we covert the dual variables $(\phi^{\tau-1}, \psi^{\tau-1})$ at the τ-th iteration to $(\phi^{\tau-1}, f(\psi^{\tau-1}, j_\mu)\psi^{\tau-1})$, which is a feasible solution to the dual (10). Therefore we have the following inequality to associate d with d_1 and d_2:

$$\begin{aligned} & d \leq d_1(\tau-1) + \epsilon f(\psi^{\tau-1}, j_\mu) d_2(\tau-1) \\ \Rightarrow \quad & f(\psi^{\tau-1}, j_\mu) \geq \tfrac{1}{\epsilon} \tfrac{d - d_1(\tau-1)}{d_2(\tau-1)} \end{aligned}$$

Recall that for all iterations $\tau \leq \omega$, $a < \frac{d}{d_1(\tau-1)}$, implying:

$$\frac{1}{f(\psi^{\tau-1}, j_\mu)} \leq \epsilon \frac{d_2(\tau-1)}{d - d_1(\tau-1)} \leq \epsilon \frac{a}{a-1} \frac{d_2(\tau-1)}{d}$$

Substitute this bound on $1/f(\psi^{\tau-1}, j_\mu)$ in Eqn. (12):

$$\begin{aligned} d_2(\omega) &\leq d_2(\omega-1)(1 + \epsilon \frac{a\Delta}{(a-1)d}(p_\omega - p_{\omega-1})) \\ &\leq d_2(\omega-1)\exp(\epsilon \frac{a\Delta}{(a-1)d}(p_\omega - p_{\omega-1})) \\ &\leq d_2(0)\exp(\epsilon \frac{a\Delta}{(a-1)d} p_\omega) \end{aligned}$$

the second inequality is due to $1 + x \leq e^x, \forall x \geq 0$.

Note that the stopping condition in this sub case is $d_2(\omega) \geq t\exp(\theta - 1)$ and $d_2(0) = t$, as a result, we have:

$$\begin{aligned} & t\exp(\theta-1) \leq t\exp(\epsilon \frac{a\Delta}{(a-1)d} p_\omega) \\ \Leftrightarrow \quad & d/p_\omega \leq \epsilon \frac{a\Delta}{(a-1)(\theta-1)} \end{aligned}$$

Due to the weak duality theorem in linear programming and the relaxation of IP (7), the following inequality holds:

$$OPT_{WDP2}/p_\omega \leq d/p_\omega$$

where $OPT_{WDP2}/$ is the value of the optimal solution to WDP2. This means d/p_ω is an upper bound of the approximation ratio.

We hence obtain the approximation ratio:

$$a = 1 + \epsilon\Lambda(eT^{\Lambda-1} - 1).$$

Recall that the integrality gap of WDP2 is defined as the ratio between OPT_{LPR2} and OPT_{WDP2}, where OPT_{WDP2} is the value of the objective function for the optimal fraction solution χ^*. We notice that $d \geq OPT_{LPR2}$ and $OPT_{WDP2} \geq p_\omega$, which lead to

$$OPT_{LPR2}/OPT_{WDP2} \leq OPT_{LPR2}/p_\omega \leq d/p_\omega = a$$

Thus Algorithm 3 verifies the integrality gap, providing an integer solution of value at least $1/a$ times OPT_{LPR2}.

Finally we examine the computation complexity of Algorithm 3. The termination conditions ensure that the `while` loop in Algorithm 3 iterates at most $|\mathcal{M}|$ times, linear to the input size. Within the loop, lines 10-18 can be finished in polynomial time. Therefore, Algorithm 3 runs in polynomial time overall. □

Exploiting the dual fitting result in Lemma 1 and LP duality, we prove that Algorithm 3 guarantees an a-approximation of social welfare, as well as verifying an integrality gap of WDP2 of a, where $a = 1 + \epsilon\Lambda(eT^{\Lambda-1} - 1)$, $\Lambda = \frac{\theta}{\theta-1}$. In practice, the volume of a grid's power capacity is substantially larger than a single microgrid's demand, *i.e.*, $\theta \gg 1$. The number of predicted time slots T is a relatively small constant. Consequently,

$$\lim_{\theta\to\infty} a = \lim_{\Lambda\to 1}(1 + \epsilon\Lambda(eT^{\Lambda-1} - 1)) = 1 + \epsilon(e-1)$$

which suggests that the approximation ratio a is close to $1 + \epsilon(e - 1)$. When each microgrid only submits one bid, *i.e.*, $\epsilon = 1$, then $a \approx 2.72$.

5. PERFORMANCE EVALUATION

5.1 The microgrid-to-grid market

We adopt the hourly demand curve of the grid in Ontario, Canada from 00:00, Jan. 3, 2013 to 23:59, Jan. 3, 2013 [3] in evaluating the microgrid-to-grid auction. The order of magnitude has been scaled down by 100, under the rationale that microgrids are not expected to fully support the grid, but will act as a supplement supplier. The trend of hourly demand remains the same after such scaling. The maximum and minimum outputs of each microgrid are $P_{max} = 10MW$ and $P_{min} = 0$, respectively. The ramping rate is $\delta = 1MW/h$. Once a generator is turned ON, it must remain active for at least $T_{on} = T_{off} = 2h$. All generators are OFF at the beginning of the simulation.

Performance of the approximation algorithm. We first implement and evaluate Algorithm 2. The results are shown in Fig. 4. Compared with the optimum, the approximation algorithm achieves an impressive performance, approaching the optimum rather closely in most cases. We observe that the cost goes down when the number of microgrids increases. This is because a small number of microgrids means little cheap energy to the grid. In order to satisfy the power demand, the grid has to resort to more expensive alternatives.

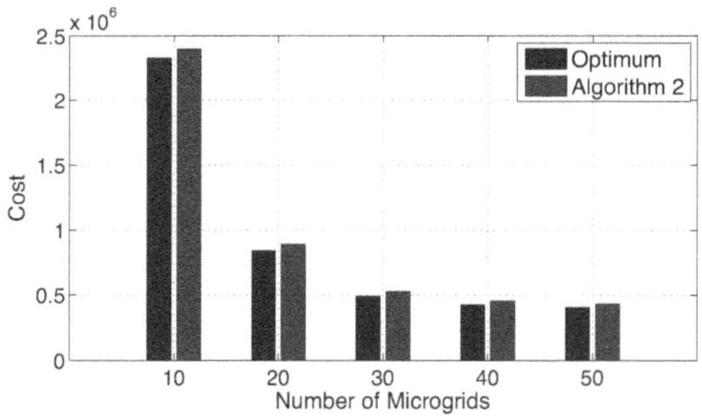

Figure 4: A comparison between optimum and Algorithm 2.

We also compare the energy purchased from plants to supplement the temporary deficits in energy, as illustrated in Fig. 5. We observe that the grid purchases a large amount of energy from plants in the first few hours. This is because all generators are OFF at the beginning. Even if they want to sell energy to the grid, they cannot increase the energy output abruptly due to the UCP3 constraint. In this case, the grid needs to purchase energy from plants or batteries at a relatively high cost. Later a large number of microgrids could help decrease the cost.

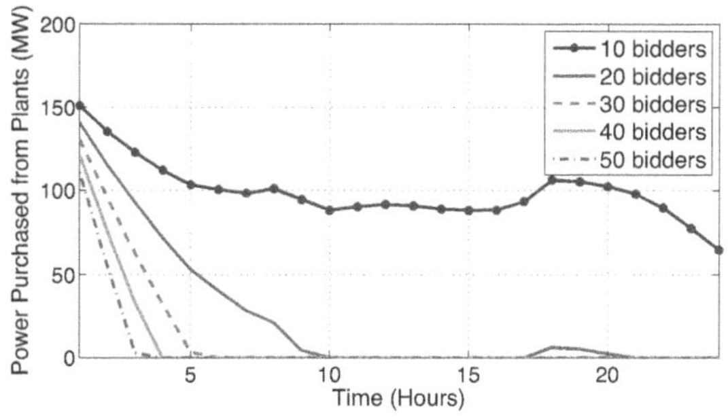

Figure 5: A comparison of energy purchased from plants to supplement the deficits in energy, among different numbers of bidders.

5.2 The grid-to-microgrid market

In this case, microgrids submit bids to purchase energy from the grid for satisfying their own demands. We again use the hourly zonal demands data, shown in Fig. 6, from Ontario, Canada [3] to drive the simulation. These data have been scaled down to meet the reality in practical microgrids, *e.g.*, a community or a university. The trend in demand fluctuation remains the same. We use these data to emulate a number of microgrids, from 10 microgrids to 80 microgrids. The total capacity of the grid is set according to Fig. 3.

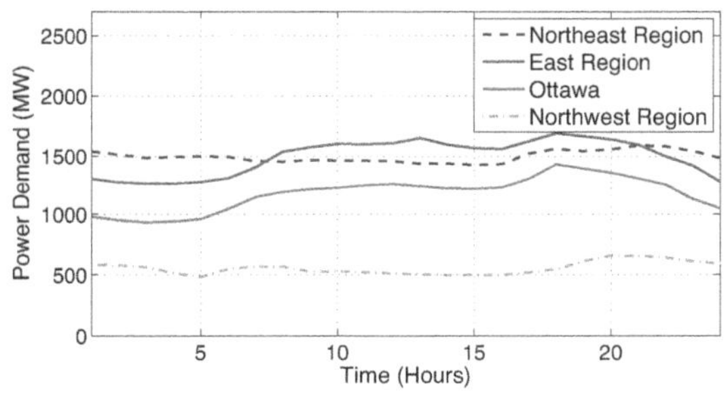

Figure 6: Hourly power demands from 00:00 Jan. 3, 2013 to 23:59 Jan. 3, 2013 in the Northeast, Northwest, East and Ottawa regions in the province of Ontario, Canada [3].

Performance of the Approximation Algorithm. We first investigate the performance of the proposed approximation algorithm, Algorithm 3. The number of microgrids (bidders) varies from 10 to 80. We compare the social welfare of Algorithm 3 with the optimum as well as the theoretical bounds, as illustrated in Fig. 7. We observe that the performance of Algorithm 3 in terms of social welfare, is close to the optimum, and is much better than suggested by the worst-case theoretical guarantee we have been able to prove.

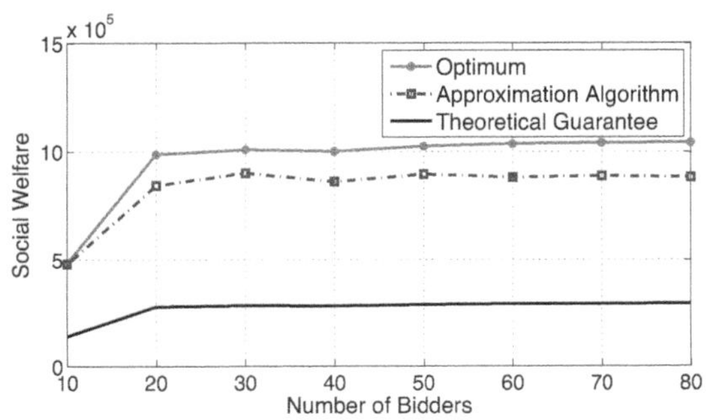

Figure 7: A comparison among the optimum, Algorithm 3 and theoretical bounds.

We further study the performance of the proposed approximation algorithm when demand predictions in $d_{i,j}$ are not perfect, when microgrids underestimate their near future demand by a percentage within 5% and 40%, as shown in Fig. 8. Their bidding prices for unit cost ($ per MWh) remain the same. We observe a close to linear relationship between the achieved social welfare and the prediction error, and the social welfare decreases when the error grows.

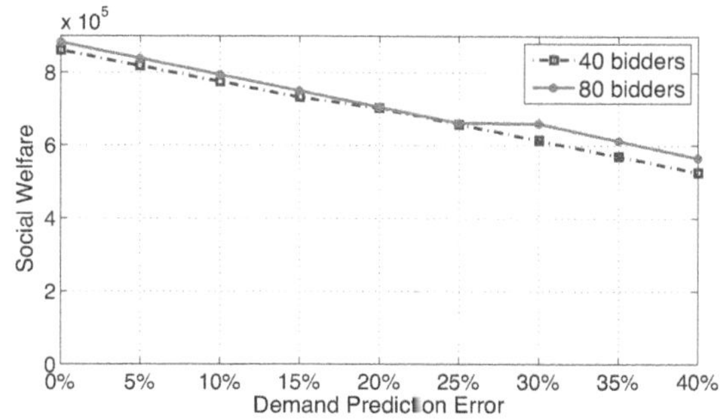

Figure 8: Social welfare achieved by Algorithm 3 under demand prediction errors, when the numbers of bidders are 40 and 80, respectively.

The Randomized Auction. By applying the ellipsoid method and the approximation algorithm, we implement the randomized auction. We obtain the average social welfare by simulating each auction for 20 times, as shown in Fig. 9. The results show that the expected social welfare fluctuates around the theoretical bound. Fig. 10 shows the corresponding total payments. Note that the seemingly high social welfare achieved by the fractional VCG auction is actually infeasible, since the fractional solution to WDP2 cannot be implemented in practice.

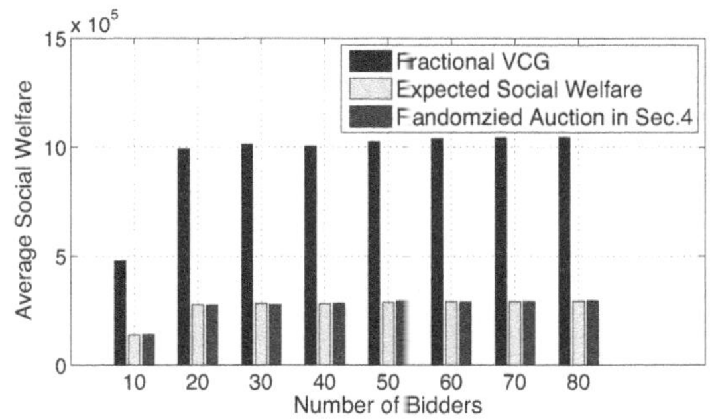

Figure 9: Social welfare of the randomized auction, compared with the fractional VCG auction.

6. CONCLUSION

A fundamental trend in power grid evolution is the proliferation of distributed generation through the microgrid paradigm. The integration of microgrids with traditional power grids requires solutions to both technical and economic challenges. This work is among the first that addresses the latter, through the design of computationally efficient electricity auctions that target good social welfare and truthfulness. The auction designed for the microgrid-to-grid market further represents the first electricity auction mechanism that explicitly models the UCF constraints that are critical in power grid optimization. The proposed auction mechanisms are not completely ready for immediate application in practice, due to its

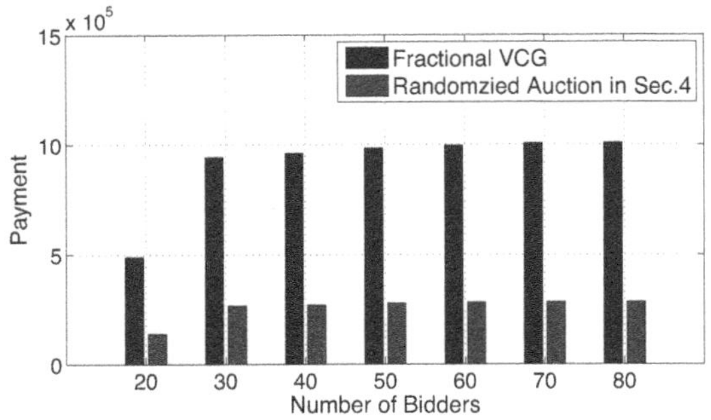

Figure 10: Total payment of the randomized auction, compared with the fractional VCG auction.

limitations in assumptions and computational overhead. We hope the gap will be closed by future work.

7. ACKNOWLEDGEMENTS

The authors would like to thank Minghua Chen for helping motivate the problem studied, and the anonymous referees and our shepherd, Adam Wierman, for their constructive comments that helped improve the paper.

8. REFERENCES

[1] *Distributed generation, Wikipedia*, http://en.wikipedia.org/wiki/Distributed_generation.

[2] *ENMAX Energy Rates*, https://www.enmax.com/Energy/Res/My+Account/Current+EasyMax+Rates.htm.

[3] *Independent Electricity System Operator (IESO)*, https://www.ieso.ca/.

[4] *Microgrid Market - 2013 Report*, http://www.stockhouse.com/News/Press-Releases/2013/09/26/Microgrid-Market-2013-Report.

[5] K. Aoki, M. Itoh, T. Satoh, K. Nara, and M. Kanezashi. Optimal Long-Term Unit Commitment in Large Scale Systems Including Fuel Constrained Thermal and Pumped-Storage Hydro. *IEEE Transactions on Power Systems*, 4(3):1065–1073, 1989.

[6] M. Barnes, J. Kondoh, H. Asano, J. Oyarzabal, G. Ventakaramanan, R. Lasseter, N. Hatziargyriou, and T. Green. Real-World MicroGrids-An Overview. In *Proc. of IEEE SoSE*, 2007.

[7] P. Briest, P. Krysta, and B. Vöcking. Approximation Techniques for Utilitarian Mechanism Design. In *Proc. of ACM STOC*, May 2005.

[8] R. Carr and S. Vempala. Randomized Metarounding. *Random Struct. Algorithms*, 20(3):343–352, May 2002.

[9] E. Clarke. Multipart Pricing of Public Goods. *Public Choice*, 11(1):17–33, 1971.

[10] A. Dimeas and N. Hatziargyriou. Operation of a Multiagent System for Microgrid Control. *IEEE Transactions on Power Systems*, 20(3):1447–1455, 2005.

[11] S. Dughmi and T. Roughgarden. Black-Box Randomized Reductions in Algorithmic Mechanism Design. *SIAM Journal on Computing*, 43(1):312–336, 2014.

[12] B. Dunn, H. Kamath, and J. Tarascon. Electrical Energy Storage for the Grid: A Battery of Choices. *Science*, 334(6058):928–935, 2011.

[13] A. Frangioni, C. Gentile, and F. Lacalandra. Solving Unit Commitment Problems with General Ramp Constraints. *International Journal of Electrical Power & Energy Systems*, 30(5):316–326, 2008.

[14] M. Grötschel, L. Lovász, and A. Schrijver. *Geometric Algorithms and Combinatorial Optimization*. Springer-Verlag, 1988.

[15] T. Groves. Incentives in Teams. *Econometrica: Journal of the Econometric Society*, pages 617–631, 1973.

[16] X. Guan, Q. Zhai, and A. Papalexopoulos. Optimization Based Methods for Unit Commitment: Lagrangian Relaxation Versus General Mixed Integer Programming. In *Proc. of IEEE PES General Meeting*, 2003.

[17] A. Hawkes and M. Leach. Modelling High Level System Design and Unit Commitment for a Microgrid. *Applied Energy*, 86(7-8):1253 - 1265, 2009.

[18] H. Kellerer, U. Pferschy, and D. Pisinger. *Knapsack Problems*. Springer, 2004.

[19] R. Lasseter and P. Paigi. Microgrid: A Conceptual Solution. In *Proc. of IEEE PESC*, 2004.

[20] R. Lavi and C. Swamy. Truthful and Near-Optimal Mechanism Design via Linear Programming. In *Proc. of IEEE FOCS*, Oct. 2005.

[21] X. Li, S. Y.J., and H. S.B. Study on Power Quality Control in Multiple Renewable Energy Hybrid MicroGrid System. In *Proc. of IEEE Power Tech*, July 2007.

[22] Z. Li, B. Li, and Y. Zhu. Designing Truthful Spectrum Auctions for Multi-hop Secondary Networks. *IEEE Transactions on Mobile Computing*, to appear.

[23] L. Lu, J. Tu, C.-K. Chau, M. Chen, and X. Lin. Online Energy Generation Scheduling for Microgrids with Intermittent Energy Sources and Co-generation. In *Proc. of ACM SIGMETRICS*, 2013.

[24] B. McGuire. Power Auctions and Intertemporal Production Costs: Dealing with Unit Commitment. Technical report, 1997.

[25] H. Minooei and C. Swamy. Truthful Mechanism Design for Multidimensional Covering Problems. In *Proc. of ACM WINE*, 2012.

[26] A. Mu'Alem and N. Nisan. Truthful Approximation Mechanisms for Restricted Combinatorial Auctions. *Games and Economic Behavior*, 64(2):612–631, 2008.

[27] J. Nicolaisen, V. Petrov, and L. Tesfatsion. Market Power and Efficiency in a Computational Electricity Market with Discriminatory Double-Auction Pricing. *IEEE Transactions on Evolutionary Computation*, 5(5):504–523, 2001.

[28] N. Padhy. Unit Commitment - A Bibliographical Survey. *IEEE Transactions on Power Systems*, 19(2):1196–1205, 2004.

[29] L. Tesfatsion. Auction Basics for Wholesale Power Markets: Objectives and Pricing Rules. In *Proc. IEEE PES General Meeting*, 2009.

[30] A. Tsikalakis and N. Hatziargyriou. Centralized Control for Optimizing Microgrids Operation. *IEEE Transactions on Energy Conversion*, 23(1):241–248, 2008.

[31] W. Vickrey. Counterspeculation, Auctions, and Competitive Sealed Tenders. *The Journal of finance*, 16(1):8–37, 1961.

[32] L. Zhang, Z. Li, and C. Wu. Dynamic Resource Provisioning in Cloud Computing: A Randomized Auction Approach. In *Proc. of IEEE INFOCOM*, April 2014.

Pricing Data Center Demand Response

Zhenhua Liu, Iris Liu, Steven Low, Adam Wierman
California Institute of Technology
Pasadena, CA, USA
{zliu2,iliu,slow,adamw}@caltech.edu

ABSTRACT

Demand response is crucial for the incorporation of renewable energy into the grid. In this paper, we focus on a particularly promising industry for demand response: data centers. We use simulations to show that, not only are data centers large loads, but they can provide as much (or possibly more) flexibility as large-scale storage if given the proper incentives. However, due to the market power most data centers maintain, it is difficult to design programs that are efficient for data center demand response. To that end, we propose that prediction-based pricing is an appealing market design, and show that it outperforms more traditional supply function bidding mechanisms in situations where market power is an issue. However, prediction-based pricing may be inefficient when predictions are inaccurate, and so we provide analytic, worst-case bounds on the impact of prediction error on the efficiency of prediction-based pricing. These bounds hold even when network constraints are considered, and highlight that prediction-based pricing is surprisingly robust to prediction error.

Categories and Subject Descriptors

J.2 [**Computer Applications**]: Physical sciences and engineering

Keywords

data center, demand response, prediction based pricing, power network

1. INTRODUCTION

Demand response is widely recognized as a crucial tool for incorporating renewables into the grid, e.g., see recent reports from the National Institute of Standards and Technology (NIST) and the Department of Energy (DoE) [13,42]. Demand response programs provide incentives for customers to adapt their electricity demand to supply availability, for example, reducing their consumption in response to a peak load warning signal or request from the utility. Thus, demand response programs can help the grid transition from the paradigm of "generation follows demand" to one where, at least partially, "demand follows generation." Such a transition is fundamental to the integration of renewable energy because generation is becoming more intermittent and less controllable as renewable penetration increases.

SIGMETRICS'14, June 16–20, 2014, Austin, Texas, USA.
ACM 978-1-4503-2789-3/14/06 ...$15.00..

In this paper, we consider a promising demand response resource: data centers. Data centers are particularly well-suited for demand response. First, data centers represent *large loads* for the grid. In 2011, they consumed approximately 1.5% of all electricity worldwide and individual data centers can be 50 MW, or more [1, 20, 43]. Further, the energy consumption of data centers is *growing quickly*, by approximately 10-12% per year [1, 20, 30]. This growth is crucial for keeping pace with the growth of renewable adoption predicted for the coming years. Third, and most importantly, data centers are extremely *flexible loads.* Data centers are highly automated and monitored, e.g., the power load and state of IT equipment and cooling facilities can be continuously monitored and panoramically adjusted. For example, a recent empirical study by LBNL has quantified the flexibility in power usage of four data centers under different management approaches [20]. They find that 5% of the load can typically be shed in 5 minutes and 10% of the load can be shed in 15 minutes; and that these can be achieved *without* changes to how the IT workload is handled, i.e., via temperature adjustment and other building management approaches. Further, if workload management approaches are considered, the degree of flexibility can be larger, without additional time needed to shed the load. Significant research has recently gone into the design of such workload management, e.g., [10, 18, 21, 34, 39, 49, 52, 53].

Data center demand response today. Despite wide recognition of the demand response potential of data centers, the current reality is that data centers perform little, if any, demand response [20, 43].

In particular, the most common demand response program available for data centers is Coincident Peak Pricing (CPP), which is required for medium and large industrial consumers in many regions. These programs work by charging a very high price for usage during the coincident peak hour, often over 200 times higher than the base rate.[1] It is common for the coincident peak charges to account for 23% or more of a customer's electric bill according to Fort Collins Utilities [48]. Hence, a customer has a strong incentive to reduce usage during the peak hour. Although it is impossible to accurately predict exactly when the peak hour will occur, many utilities identify potential peak hours and send warning signals to customers (5-10 per month), which helps customers manage their loads and make decisions about their energy usage. For more details about CPP see [48].

Unfortunately, CPP programs are poorly designed from the perspective of data center demand response. Not providing response may incur a very large charge and providing a response may not actually result in any savings if the coincident peak does not occur during the warning period. As a

[1]The coincident peak hour is defined as the hour when the most electricity is demanded from the load serving entity (LSE).

result, even when they are forced to participate in such programs, data centers tend not to actively respond to signals. Further, even if they do respond, such programs extract very little flexibility from data centers. At best they obtain curtailment of usage a few times per month. This wastes the potential responsiveness of data centers.

Demand response market design. Although researchers have begun to focus on new market designs for data center demand response, e.g., [20, 28, 45, 46, 48], a clear vision remains elusive.

This is also true outside of the domain of data centers. Recently, the design of demand response programs has received considerable attention in a variety of settings, e.g., electric vehicles, pool pumps, and air conditioner cycling. Broadly speaking, the demand response programs that have emerged can be classified into two categories based on the interaction with users: either (i) users bid some degree of flexibility (supply) into the market, usually via a parameterized supply function, or (ii) users respond to a posted price, which was chosen using predictions about the available flexibility (e.g., supply functions). We term these approaches "supply function bidding" and "prediction-based pricing", respectively. Examples of proposed designs that use supply function bidding include [29, 50], and examples of prediction-based pricing designs include [12, 32, 40].

While each of these design approaches has pluses and minuses (as we discuss in Section 3), our focus on data centers motivates us to focus on prediction-based pricing programs.

In particular, a key assumption in the design and analysis of supply function bidding demand response programs is that users are *price takers*, i.e., they do not anticipate their impact on the price. Under this assumption, such designs can minimize the aggregate user cost while achieving the desired curtailment of demand. However, if this assumption is violated, and users act strategically, then inefficiency emerges in the market. Data centers are a canonical example of a user with market power – data centers can make up 50% of the load of the distribution circuits they are on, e.g., Facebook's data center in Crook County, Oregon. Thus, it is dangerous to treat them as price takers.

In contrast, prediction-based pricing is not nearly as impacted by market power issues. It is, however, highly dependent on the accuracy of the predictions of the user response to prices. Thus, there are still significant challenges in the design of such programs, and these issues are the focus of this paper.

Contributions of this paper. This paper makes two main contributions: (i) it quantifies the potential of data center demand response through a comparison with large-scale storage, and (ii) it presents and analyzes a novel design for prediction-based pricing of data center demand response. We discuss each of these in more detail in the following.

The potential of data center demand response: To quantify the potential of data center demand response we perform numerical case studies that compare the value of the flexibility provided by data centers with that provided by large-scale storage. In particular, in Section 2, we ask: *How much (optimally placed) storage can a data center replace?*

Interestingly, our results highlight that the flexibility provided by data centers is as valuable as, and often more valuable than, the flexibility provided by large-scale storage when it comes to ensuring that a distribution network meets its voltage constraints in the presence of a large-scale solar (PV) installation (see Figures 6). For example, the voltage violation frequency that comes from using a 30MW data center, which can provide 20% flexibility, is roughly equivalent to that of 1MWh of optimally-placed storage in the 46 bus distribution network from Southern California Edison that we consider. This is a quite conservative comparison because we assume storage with infinite charging speed (see Figure 5 for the impact of the charging rate). Further, the benefit of data center flexibility is robust to the placement within the distribution network – there are very few locations where the effectiveness of the data center drops considerably (see Figure 7).

Additionally, we look at the impact of a growing dichotomy in how IT companies address the sustainability of their data centers. Some companies, e.g., Apple [24], have invested heavily in on-site renewable generation; while others, e.g., Google [25], have tended to invest in renewable generation that is not co-located with their data centers. Both approaches have merits. Providing renewable generation on-site ensures that it is available where a very large and flexible load is located, but if renewable generation is not placed on site it can be placed in locations with better generation quality and/or cheaper installation costs.

Interestingly, our case studies highlight that co-location of data centers and large-scale PV installations is very efficient. In particular, the voltage violation frequency when the data center is placed at the same bus as the PV in a distribution network is within 4% of optimal. However, it is worth noting that a data center with local PV is not nearly as efficient at helping manage a large-scale PV installation as a data center without local PV. In particular, a 20MW data center with 20% flexibility and a co-located 5MW solar installation provides the same voltage violation frequency as 0.3MWh of optimally-placed storage, i.e., 25% less than a 20MW data center with no local PV. Thus, having PV at the location of the data center is better than having it elsewhere, due to the complementary diurnal patterns of each, but a data center without local renewables is a more valuable resource for grid management than a data center with local renewables.

Prediction-based pricing: Given the potential of data center demand response identified in the first half of the paper, the second half of the paper focuses on designing a demand response program that can extract this flexibility. As we have already discussed, prediction-based pricing is an appealing candidate given the market power data centers maintain. Thus, in Sections 4 and 5 we present and analyze a design for prediction-based pricing. Section 4 introduces the design in a context without the constraints imposed by the distribution network, and then Section 5 incorporates the network constraints into the design and analysis.

The analysis in these sections is focused on three issues. First, we focus on the impact of the accuracy of predictions on the efficiency of the market design. This is, perhaps, the most crucial issue for prediction-based pricing programs. Our results provide an analytic characterization of worst-case efficiency bounds under the assumption of quadratic objective functions (Theorem 2), which is a common assumption in the power system literature. In particular, we derive tight bounds on the competitive ratio of prediction-based pricing that highlight the impact of the variability of the prediction error.

The second issue is the contrast between prediction-based pricing and supply function bidding. As we have mentioned, prediction error hurts the former while market power hurts the latter. Thus, the natural question becomes: Under which settings is prediction-based pricing appropriate? By contrasting our results with those of [50] on the efficiency of supply function bidding, we give an explicit characterization in terms of market power and prediction error of when prediction-based pricing outperforms supply function bidding (Figure 10). Broadly speaking, the comparison highlights that prediction-based pricing is appropriate for data center demand response when prediction errors are moderate and the data center has significant, local market power.

Finally, the third issue our analysis focuses on is the impact of network constraints on the design and efficiency of prediction-based pricing. In our analysis, the network constraints manifest themselves as a chance constraint on the price that ensures that voltage violations in the network are rare. But, despite constraints on the prices, we prove that the efficiency of prediction-based pricing is not impacted by the network constraints, i.e., the competitive ratio remains unchanged (Theorem 5). This represents the first analytic bound on the efficiency of prediction-based pricing in the presence of network constraints.

2. QUANTIFYING THE POTENTIAL OF DATA CENTER DEMAND RESPONSE

Before looking at the design of market programs to extract flexibility from data centers, it is crucial to quantify the potential of such programs. In this section, we accomplish this by contrasting the flexibility provided by data centers with that provided by large-scale storage.

Often, when people think of the challenges for grid management that result from renewable energy, the thought is: "if only we had large-scale storage..." The problem is that large-scale storage is expensive, which leads to the consideration of demand response. But, besides cost, demand response also has other benefits over storage. In particular, storage needs to be pre-charged to be ready for use, while demand response has no such requirement. However, storage has benefits as well. First, the placement of storage is more flexible than that of data centers. Second, apart from pre-charging, storage does not bring with it any electricity demand, whereas data center demand response inherently requires the presence of a large load in the distribution network.

In the experiments that follow, we study the impact of these competing factors in order to understand how the potential of data center demand response compares to large-scale storage. In particular, we ask: *How much (optimally placed) storage can a data center replace?* Since we focus on bounding the potential of data center demand response in this section, we do not model market factors. Rather, we assume that the load serving entity (LSE) can call on the data center and storage as needed. Market design is considered in the second half of the paper.

2.1 Setup

To quantify the potential of data center demand response, we study a situation where a distribution network has a large-scale solar installation and either large-scale storage or a data center to help manage the intermittency of the solar installation.

The performance objective we consider is that of minimizing the frequency of violations of voltage constraints in the distribution network. To measure this frequency we sum the number of buses with voltage violations at each time slot and over time, i.e., the number of buses that result in voltages outside the tolerance bounds given by the network. For instance, a violation frequency 0.1 means on average, each bus experiences voltage violation in 10% of the time. We contrast the frequency of voltage violations when a data center is present and when large-scale storage is present.

Distribution network. We consider two distribution networks in our experiments. Both are distribution networks from the Southern California Edison (SCE) utility company. The first is a 47 bus network (Figure 1) and the second is a 56 bus network (Figure 2). Both are described in detail in [15].

There is no conventional generation on these distribution networks. All power comes from the substation bus, a.k.a., the zero bus, and the solar installation (which we describe later). The demands are taken from SCE load profiles [23], except for the data center, for which the demand is described later.

Given these settings, a significant amount of the solar generation can be transmitted out of the distribution network through the substation bus. However, because we consider a large-scale solar installation, when the installation has near

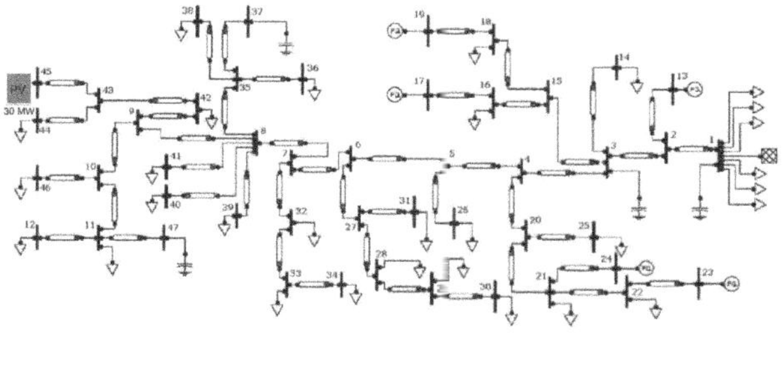

Figure 1: SCE 47 bus network.

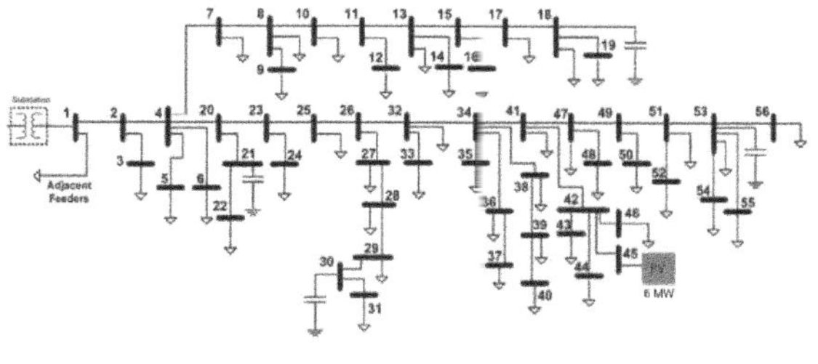

Figure 2: SCE 56 bus network.

peak generation, the network constraints become binding and voltage violations are common. Note that the voltage constraint we consider is taken directly from the network tolerance specifications, and is 3%. The number of violations in our simulations are consistent with previous work on these networks, e.g., [14, 15]. The presence of storage or the data center is used to help avoid such violations.

For our simulations, given the network, the power flow is computed for a sequence of discrete time steps $t = 1, \ldots, T$ using MatPower [54]. Then, we analyze the voltages for each time step and determine the number of buses that have voltage violations. Finally, we sum the voltage violation events from all buses over all time steps, and use it to calculate the violation frequency. The length of the time steps that we consider is one minute.

Renewable energy. To model a solar installation placed within a distribution network, we use solar irradiance data from Los Angeles, CA in February 2012 [26] to alter the power load at the bus where the solar (PV) generation is located. Thus, irradiance data acts like an installed solar capacity. The trace is illustrated in Figure 3(a).

For the experiments reported, the PV is placed at bus 45 and sized at 30MW for the 47 bus network, and also placed at bus 45 but sized at 6MW for the 56 bus network[2]. The results do not qualitatively change when other locations and sizes are considered.

Data center model. To incorporate a data center into the experiments, we need to model two aspects: the power usage of the data center over time and the flexibility in the power usage of the data center.

To model the power usage of a data center, we adopt the model used in [3, 33, 34, 38], which provides a simple but representative characterization. In particular, we model the power demand of the data center as a function of the workload, including interactive (inflexible) and delay-tolerant (flexible) workloads, and the cooling efficiency, as measured by the Power Usage Effectiveness (PUE).

To model the workload we use two traces. The interactive workload trace is from a popular web service application with more than 85 million registered users in 22 countries

[2]We use different size of PV because the capacities of these two networks are different.

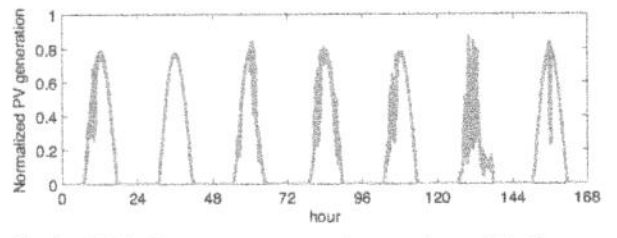

(a) PV generation in February in Los Angeles, CA

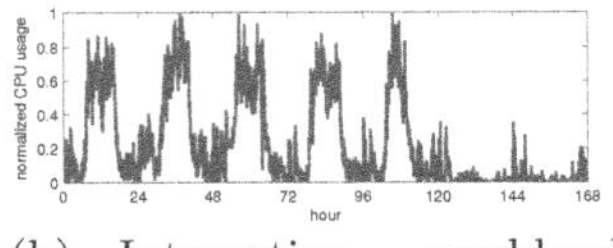

(b) Interactive workload from a photo sharing web service

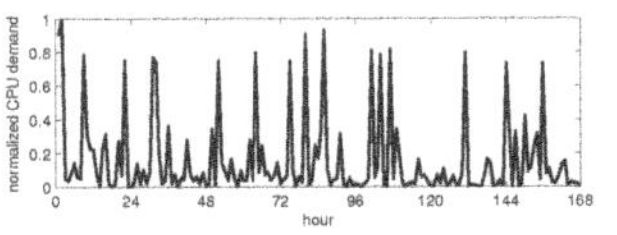

(c) Facebook Hadoop workload

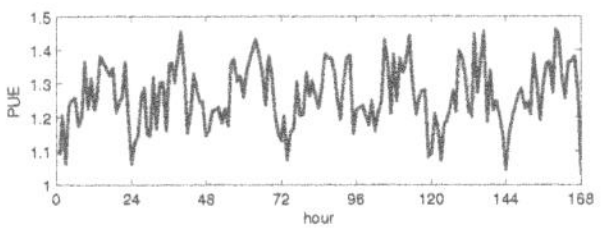

(d) Google data centers PUE

Figure 3: One week traces for (a) PV generation, (b) inflexible workload, (c) flexible workload, and (d) cooling efficiency.

(see Figure 3(b)). The trace contains average CPU utilization and memory usage as recorded every 5 minutes. The peak-to-mean ratio of the interactive workload is about 4. The delay-tolerant workload information comes from a Facebook Hadoop trace (see Figure 3(c)). The total demand ratio between the interactive workload and batch jobs is 1:1. This ratio can vary widely across data centers, but we choose this ratio as representative based on discussions in [35].

To model the data center power efficiency including cooling efficiency, we use a trace of the PUE from Google data centers. As shown in the figure, the PUE varies between 1.05 to 1.45, and has strong diurnal pattern, i.e., higher around noon because outside air temperature is higher.

To combine the workload traces and the PUE to obtain a model of the total power demand of the data center, we use the following relationship.

$$v(t) = PUE(t)(a(t) + b(t)),$$

where $a(t)$ is the power demand from the inflexible workload and $b(t)$ is power demand from the flexible workload demand. Note that the data center power demand has the same average value as the PV generation with the same capacity in the distribution network.

The second aspect of the data center model that we must include is the flexibility of the power demand. For this, our model is informed by the recent empirical study [20], which we have discussed in the introduction.

To model the range of flexibility in our experiments, we denote the demand flexibility of the data center by e and allow the data center to have demand within

$$[(1 - e)v(t), \min\{(1 + e)v(t), C_d\}],$$

where C_d is the capacity of the data center and $v(t)$ is the data center power demand at time t if no demand response is called upon. Thus, $e = 0.10$ could be achieved without workload management, and $e = 0.20$ can be achieved with some workload management, e.g., quality degradation or load deferral. When demand response is required from the data center, the load that minimizes the voltage violation rate is provided by the data center.

Since a downside of data center demand response is that the LSE cannot control the placement of the data center, the placement of the data center is varied during our experiments in order to understand robustness to "bad" data center locations. Note that we assume there is no cost associated with the demand shaping of data center; however the cost of this could be incorporated easily if desired.

Storage model. To incorporate large-scale storage into our model, we adopt a standard model, e.g., from [19,27,31,47]. In order to provide a conservative estimate of the potential of data center demand response we assume perfect storage, i.e., no loss or leakage. This means that, at all times t, the storage level for the next time step is $L(t+1) = L(t)+u(t)$, where $u(t)$ is the energy change in the level at time t. Note that $u(t)$ is positive if we are charging the storage and negative if we are discharging. Of course, $L(t) \in [0, C_s]$ for all t, where C_s is the storage capacity. So, $u(t) \in [-L(t), C_s - L(t)]$, where C_s is the storage capacity. This range quantifies the amount of flexibility that can be called upon by the LSE. As in the case of the data center, the LSE will call upon a feasible $u(t)$ that minimizes the voltage violations. Although more advanced energy storage management policy could be used to further improve the benefit, here we use this simple greedy strategy for both data center and energy storage for comparisons.

For most of the experiments we assume that the storage can completely charge and discharge in one time step. This is, of course, unrealistic, but it allows us to give a conservative estimate of the benefits of data center demand response. We do evaluate the impact of limitations on the charging rate in Figure 5 in order to highlight the degree to which this assumption leads to an underestimate of the value of data center demand response.

As we have already mentioned, a benefit of storage is that it can be placed optimally within a network. The optimal placement of the storage is at bus 44 for the 47 bus network and bus 53 for the 56 bus network. Note that the optimal placement is robust as we adjust the capacity of the storage in our experiments.

2.2 Case studies

Using the setting described above, our focus is on two comparisons that each sheds light on the potential of data center demand response: (i) a comparison between data center demand response and large-scale storage, and (ii) a study of the impact of on-site renewable generation on data center demand response.

Data center demand response versus large-scale storage. To contrast large-scale storage with data center demand response, we first need to quantify the benefits from large-scale storage. This is done in Figures 4 and 5, which show the impacts of the storage capacity and the storage charging rate on the voltage violation rate in the two distribution networks. Figure 4 highlights that, as expected, the voltage violation rate decreases as storage capacity grows. However, it also shows that this relationship is nonlinear and depends strongly on the network structure. Similarly, Figure 5 highlights that, as expected, a smaller charging rate increases the frequency of voltage violations. However, the impact of a smaller charging rate is, perhaps, more significant than expected. Note that for our experiments we conservatively estimate the value of data center demand response by comparing it with storage having a charging rate of 1, i.e., we assume that the storage can completely charge and discharge in one minute. This is unrealistic, but provides a lower bound on the value of data center demand response.

Given the characterization of storage, we can now highlight the value of data center demand response in terms of the "equivalent" storage capacity, i.e., in terms of the capacity of optimally-placed large-scale storage necessary to provide the same voltage violation frequency. The results of this comparison are shown in Figure 6.

Naturally, the amount of storage equivalent to data center demand response grows with the size of the data center. However, the capacity plateaus after the data center size grows beyond 35MW for the SCE 47 bus network and beyond 6MW for the SCE 56 bus network. Note that this is a consequence of two differences between the networks – the structure and the size of the PV installation (30MW vs. 6MW).

But, in both networks, Figure 6 highlights that data center demand response has a significant potential. In particular,

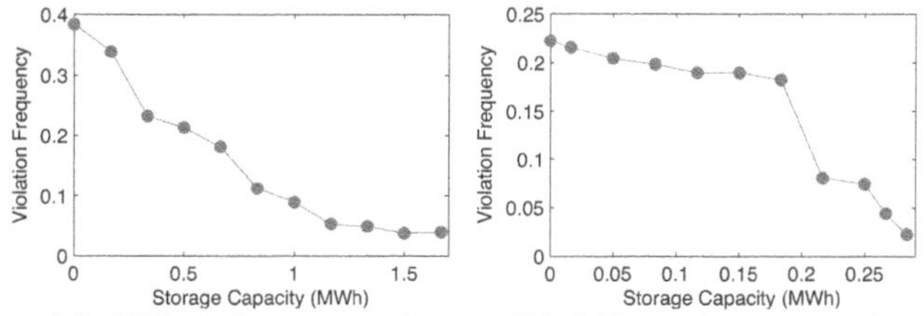

(a) SCE 47 bus network (b) SCE 56 bus network

Figure 4: Impact of energy storage capacity, C_s, on the voltage violation rates.

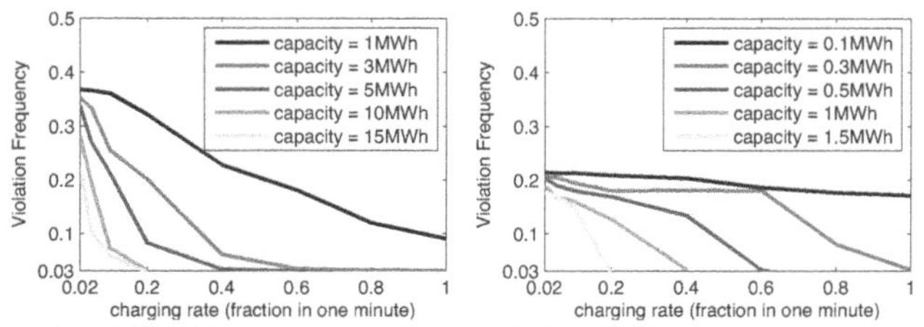

(a) SCE 47 bus network (b) SCE 56 bus network

Figure 5: Impact of energy storage charging rate on the voltage violation rates.

recall that the comparison in this plot assumes storage with infinite charging speed, i.e., a charging rate of 1, and is thus quite conservative (as illustrated in Figure 5). Additionally, the cost of storage is upwards of $500/kWh for lithium-ion batteries (which have small charging rates) and upwards of $5000/kWh for technologies with fast charging rates, such as flywheels. Thus, the flexibility provided by one 30MW data center is worth upwards of $500,000 - $5,000,000. These numbers are conservative estimates, and grow considerably if a slower charging rate is used in the simulations or if the flexibility of the data center, e, is increased.

Figures 7 and 8 delve into the comparison of data center demand response and large-scale storage in more detail for each of the networks. In Figure 7, we fix the capacity of the data center to 20MW, which is a representative size for today's IT companies, and then investigate the impact of the degree of data center flexibility, e, and the placement of the data center. For example, Figures 7(a)-7(c) highlight that the voltage violation rates decrease as data center power demand becomes more flexible. In particular, a 20MW data center with 20% power demand flexibility placed at the PV location is equivalent to 0.67MWh of optimally-placed storage in the 47 bus distribution network. Further, Figure 7(d) shows that the benefit of data center flexibility is robust to the placement of the network in the distribution network, i.e., there are very few locations where the effectiveness of the data center drops considerably and many locations that are near-optimal, e.g., placing the data center at the location of the PV (Figure 7(b)). Figure 7(d) also illustrates that a 20MW data center is better than 0.33MWh of storage pretty much uniformly. The results in a SCE 56 bus network are similar, as shown in Figure 8.

Should data centers invest in co-located renewables?. There is a dichotomy right now in how IT companies address the sustainability of their data centers. Some companies, e.g., Apple [24], have invested heavily in on-site renewable generation; while others, e.g., Google [25], have tended to invest in renewable generation that is not co-located with their data centers.

Both approaches have merits, as we have discussed in the introduction. For the purpose of this paper, the key distinction is how on-site renewable generation impacts data center demand response. This context highlights another benefit of on site renewable generation – it ensures that the data cen-

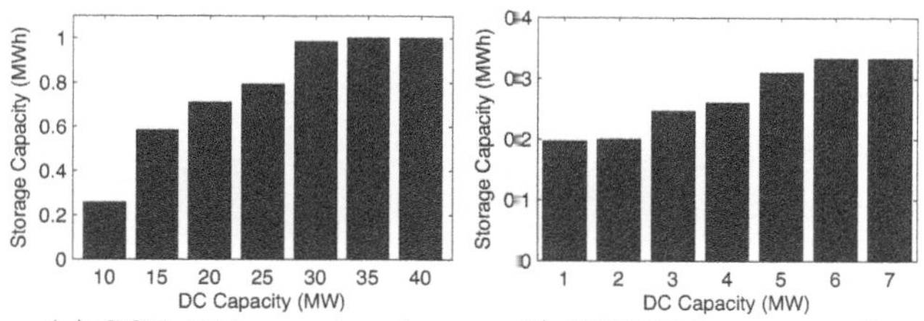

(a) SCE 47 bus network (b) SCE 56 bus network

Figure 6: Diagram of the capacity of storage necessary to achieve the same voltage violation frequency as data centers of varying sizes. The data center has flexibility $e = 0.2$.

ter is placed close to the renewables, which is very often a near-optimal placement for demand response purposes.

First, Figure 7(d) highlights that co-location of data centers and large-scale PV installations is very efficient. In particular, the voltage violation frequency when the data center is placed as the same bus as the PV in a distribution network is within 4% of optimal.

However, it is worth noting that a data center with local PV is not nearly as efficient at helping to manage a large-scale PV installation as a data center without local PV, by comparing Figure 7(c) with 9(a). In particular, a 20MW data center with 20% flexibility and a 5MW solar installation provides the same voltage violation frequency as 0.3MWh of optimally-placed storage when helping to manage 30MW of PV elsewhere on the distribution network, i.e., 25% less than a data center with the same flexibility but no local PV.

Thus, having PV at the location of the data center is better than having it elsewhere, due to the complementary diurnal patterns of each, but a data center without local renewables is a more valuable resource for grid management than a data center with local renewables.

3. MARKET CHALLENGES FOR DATA CENTER DEMAND RESPONSE

The previous section highlights that data centers have the potential to be as useful as, if not more useful than, storage for demand response. However, realizing this potential is challenging. Data centers today tend not to participate in demand response programs and, if they do, they tend to participate passively.

For example, the most common program for data center demand response today is coincident peak pricing and, though many data centers are forced to participate, they typically do not actively respond to the warnings issued by the utility. Further, even if they did, this would mean that the data center provided flexibility only 5-10 times a month, which is far from the amount of available flexibility. Such limited signaling from the LSE to the data center cannot possibly extract the potential flexibility illustrated in Section 2. On the other hand, if the utility company sends too many warning signals, data centers simply will not respond to them.

Thus, realizing the potential of data center demand response requires new market programs. While the design of market programs for data centers is only beginning to receive attention, there has been considerable work on the design of demand response programs in other contexts in recent years, e.g., [2,9,16,17,22,29,37,50]. Much of this work focuses on the design of residential programs for, e.g., electric vehicles, pool pumps, and air conditioner cycling.

Broadly speaking, the demand response programs that have emerged can be classified into two categories based on the interaction with users: either (i) users bid some degree of flexibility (supply) into the market, usually via a parameterized supply function, or (ii) users respond to a posted price, which was chosen using predictions about the avail-

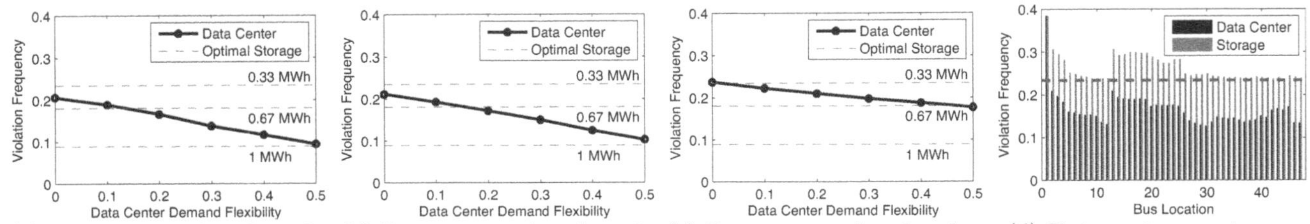

(a) Data center placed at the optimal storage location (b) Data center placed at the PV location (c) Data center placed at bus 2 (d) Data center vs. storage

Figure 7: Comparison of a 20MW data center to large-scale storage in a 47 bus SCE distribution network. (a)-(c) show the violation frequency as a function of the amount of data center flexibility, e, and compare to optimally placed storage, for different locations of the data center. (d) shows the violation frequency resulting from a data center with $e = 0.2$ versus 0.33MWh of storage, for each location.

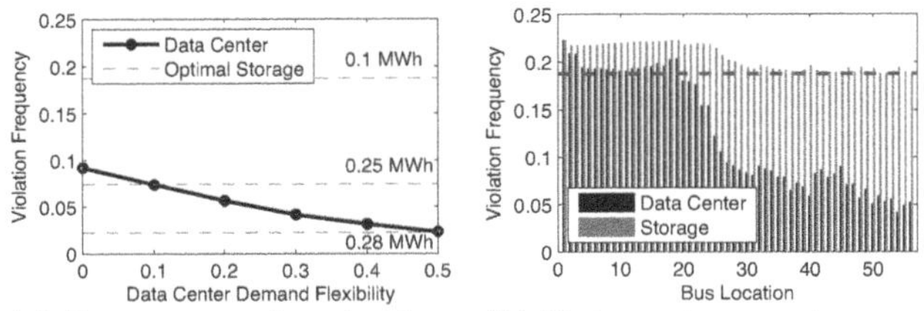

(a) Data center placed at bus 53 (b) Data center vs. storage

Figure 8: Comparison of a 4MW data center to large-scale storage in a 56 bus SCE distribution network. (a) shows the violation frequency as a function of the amount of data center flexibility, e, and compare to optimally placed storage. (b) shows the violation frequency resulting from a data center with $e = 0.2$ compared to 0.07MWh of storage at each location.

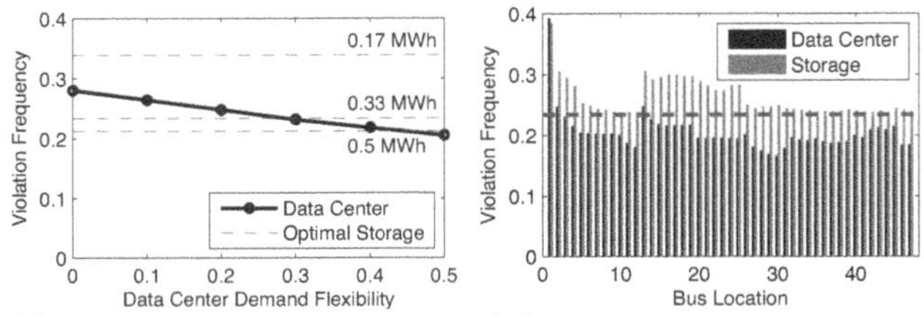

(a) Data center placed at bus 2. (b) Data center vs. storage

Figure 9: Comparison of a 20MW data center with a co-located 5MW PV installation to large-scale storage in a 47 bus SCE distribution network. (a) depicts the data center located at bus 2. (b) shows the violation frequency resulting from a data center with $e = 0.2$ compared to 0.33MWh of storage, for each location.

able flexibility (e.g., supply functions). We discuss each of these approaches below and highlight the challenges of each when it comes to data center demand response.

Supply function bidding. In this approach to market design each user announces a bid to the load serving entity (LSE) that specifies the amount load will be curtailed as a function of the price, a.k.a., a supply function. The form of the supply function is typically fixed to have some parametric form and the bid specifies the parameter. The LSE then chooses a market clearing price that achieves the demand response target. Examples of market designs of this form include [29, 50] and the references therein.

Typically, a key assumption in the design and analysis of such markets is that users are *price takers*, i.e., they do not anticipate their impact on the price. Under this assumption, such designs can minimize the aggregate user cost while achieving the desired curtailment of demand. However, if this assumption is violated, and users act strategically, then inefficiency emerges. Recent work has begun to characterize this inefficiency, and the basic conclusion is that it can be extreme [50].

While the assumption that users are price takers is natural in many demand response settings, e.g., residential pool pump and air conditioner programs; it is quite problematic in the case of data centers. A residential user does not have the power to manipulate prices, i.e., does not have *market power*, but a large data center can make up 50% of the load of the distribution circuits they are on, e.g., Facebook's data center in Crook County, Oregon. Thus, data centers are a canonical example of an agent with market power. This observation motivates the consideration of prediction-based pricing in the current paper.

Prediction-based pricing. In this approach to market design, the LSE presents the user a price that they will pay the user for curtailment, and then the user responds. Examples of designs of this type can be found in [12, 32, 40] and the references therein. The challenge in such a program is how the LSE should determine the price.

If the LSE knew the supply function of the users, then it could easily set a price to extract the desired curtailment. However, the LSE does not have this information, and since it is not provided by the user (as in the supply function bidding approach), the LSE must *predict* the user supply functions. Then, using the predicted supply functions, the LSE can determine an appropriate price to induce the desired curtailment.

Clearly, one should expect prediction-based pricing to only be appropriate if supply functions can be predicted accurately. This is a challenge in the data center environment since the supply functions of the data center may depend on the workloads and weather (among other things), each of which is highly non-stationary.

The key task in the remainder of the paper is to characterize how accurate predictions must be for the prediction-based pricing approaches to be useful. Interestingly, the contrast between the performance of prediction-based pricing and supply function bidding depends on the balance between the market power of data centers and the accuracy of supply function prediction. We discuss this in Section 4.3 by contrasting our results with those in [50].

4. PREDICTION-BASED PRICING FOR DATA CENTER DEMAND RESPONSE

In this section, we develop a market program for extracting flexibility from data centers. Given the discussion in

Section 3, our focus is on prediction-based pricing. In particular, the goal of this section is (i) to optimally design prediction-based pricing programs for data center demand response, (ii) to quantify the efficiency loss created by prediction error in such programs, and (iii) to contrast prediction-based pricing with supply function bidding. We do this in the context of a classic supply function model in this section, and then show how to incorporate distribution network constraints in Section 5.

4.1 Model formulation

The setting we consider here is where an LSE wishes to procure a total amount D of load reduction from a set of users indexed by $1, 2, \ldots, n$. We focus on one time step and ignore the network constraints in this section.

To procure this load reduction, the LSE announces a price p and pays user i the amount ps_i when user i reduces consumption by $s_i \geq 0$. The market design task is to design p so that the LSE achieves the desired amount of curtailment.

To model the user reaction to the price, we assume that each user i incurs a cost $C_i(d_i)$ when she reduces her consumption by an amount $d_i \geq 0$. We assume some parameter(s) of the cost function $C_i(\cdot)$ are random so that for each $d_i \geq 0$, $C_i(d_i)$ is a random variable. This randomness captures the fact that, in practice, the LSE does not know the parameter(s) of $C_i(\cdot)$ exactly. However, the LSE may be able to estimate the parameters from historical consumption data and the effect of estimation error can be modeled through the distribution of the random parameter(s) in $C_i(\cdot)$.

We assume that user i strategically reduces her consumption when faced with a price p in a profit maximizing manner. Let $s_i(p)$ denote the unique cost minimizing curtailment. Specifically, for each realization of $C_i(\cdot)$, denoted by $c_i(\cdot)$, user i solves

$$\min_{d_i \geq 0} \quad c_i(d_i) - pd_i, \tag{1}$$

which gives

$$s_i(p) \;=\; c_i'^{-1}(p). \tag{2}$$

To ensure that a unique solution $s_i(p) \geq 0$ always exists, we impose that each realization $c_i(\cdot)$ of the random cost function $C_i(\cdot)$ is non-negative, increasing, strictly convex, twice continuously differentiable, and has $c(0) = 0$. Additionally, note that we have implicitly assumed that the randomness in $C_i(d_i)$ is independent of the price p. These are standard assumptions in the electricity market literature, e.g., [4,8,41,51].

Given the model above, the total demand response the LSE achieves with price p is the random quantity $\sum_i s_i(p)$. Given the uncertainty about the user costs, this curtailment likely does not exactly match the demand response target D. We assume that the penalty for deviation from the target is captured through a penalty function $h(\cdot)$. In particular, the penalty is $h\left(D - \sum_i s_i(p)\right)$. We assume this penalty function $h(\cdot)$ is convex, non-negative, has a global minimum $h(0) = 0$, and is continuously differentiable with $h'(0) = 0$. These assumptions ensure that the optimal price is well-defined, see Theorem 1.

4.2 The efficiency of prediction-based pricing

Given the setting described above, our task is to first understand how to price, and then to understand the efficiency loss due to prediction error. We start with the case where the LSE has perfect predictions of the data center supply functions, i.e., with perfect foresight. Then, we move to the case where the LSE has only predictions of the data center supply functions. Finally, we quantify the efficiency loss that results from this uncertainty.

Throughout, to evaluate the efficiency of the LSE's choice of p we use a notion of social cost defined as the sum of the penalty of deviation from the demand response target D and the total user costs, i.e.,

$$G(p) \;:=\; h\left(D - \textstyle\sum_i s_i(p)\right) + \textstyle\sum_i C_i(s_i(p)). \tag{3}$$

Note that the social cost $G(p)$ is random from the LSE's perspective for two reasons: both $C_i(d_i)$ and the user responses $s_i(p)$ are random. But, the randomness in both of these originates from the randomness of the user cost functions $C_i(\cdot)$.

Pricing with perfect foresight. Before looking at the design of prediction-based pricing, it is informative to consider how an LSE with perfect foresight would price. In particular, consider an LSE that is clairvoyant, i.e., has perfect knowledge about the cost function, and can choose $p(\omega)$ to minimize $G(p)$ for the realization on instance ω. We use ω here to highlight this price is for each realization ω. In this situation, the price chosen by the LSE is summarized in the following theorem.

Theorem 1. *For each realization ω, there exists a unique minimizer p^* such that*

$$p^*(\omega) \;=\; h'\left(D - \sum_i s_i(p^*(\omega))\right), \tag{4}$$

and $0 \leq p^* < \overline{p}$, where $\overline{p}$ satisfies $\sum_i s_i(\overline{p}) = D$.

An interesting aspect of this theorem is that the optimal price is strictly lower than any price $\overline{p}$ that would exactly satisfy the demand response target.

Of course, using p^* in practice is infeasible. However, it provides an important benchmark for the performance of prediction-based pricing without perfect foresight. Note p^* is random from LSE's perspective, since the cost function realizations are random. Thus, the strategy yields an expected cost which we denote as follows

$$\mathbb{E}\left[G(p^*)\right] \;=\; \mathbb{E}\left[\min_{p\geq 0} G(p)\right]. \tag{5}$$

Prediction-based pricing. In practice, the LSE does not know the exact realization of the user cost function, thus it can only use predictions of the cost functions in order to choose a price $\hat{p}$. Here, we focus on the case where the LSE chooses $\hat{p}$ in order to minimize the expected cost that results, i.e.,

$$\hat{p} \in \operatorname*{argmin}_{p\geq 0} \mathbb{E}\left[G(p)\right]. \tag{6}$$

This yields the following

$$\mathbb{E}\left[G(\hat{p})\right] \;=\; \min_{p\geq 0} \mathbb{E}\left[G(p)\right]. \tag{7}$$

Of course, other objectives that include some form of risk management may also be interesting to consider in future work. Note that we assume that users know their own cost function, and can therefore choose their curtailment amount $s_i(p)$ based on the true cost function $c_i(\cdot)$ (cf. (2)). This means the random events that determine the $C_i(\cdot)$ are revealed only to individual users, but not to the LSE (or other users).

The efficiency of prediction-based pricing. Clearly the cost when pricing with perfect foresight is no larger than the cost when using prediction-based pricing. Here, our goal is to understand how much is lost because of uncertainty about the cost function.

To quantify this efficiency loss, we study the worst-case ratio between the cost of prediction-based pricing and the cost of pricing with perfect foresight. This is a *competitive* *ratio*. In particular, let F be the joint distribution of all random variables in the model, and $\mathcal{F}$ be a set of permissible distributions. Then the competitive ratio we consider is formally defined as $CR = \max_{F\in\mathcal{F}} \frac{\mathbb{E}[G(\hat{p})]}{\mathbb{E}[G(p^*)]}$.

To evaluate the competitive ratio, we need to restrict ourselves to the quadratic penalty function and cost functions, i.e.,

$$h\left(D - \sum_i s_i(p)\right) := \frac{q}{2}\left(D - \sum_i s_i(p)\right)^2 \quad \text{and} \quad (8)$$

$$C_i(d_i) := \frac{1}{2X_i} d_i^2, \quad (9)$$

where $q > 0$ is known, but $X_i > 0$ are random variables to the LSE. Note that this may seem restrictive, but this form is standard within the electricity markets literature, e.g., [4, 8, 41, 51].

Then, for each realization, we can explicitly compute the curtailments of the users. Specifically, from (2):

$$s_i(p) = X_i p \quad \text{and} \quad C_i(s_i(p)) = \frac{1}{2} X_i p^2 \quad (10)$$

Now, we can state the main theorems of this section, which bound the competitive ratio of prediction-based pricing in terms of the variability of prediction errors (Theorem 2) and show that the bound is tight (Theorem 3). Let $X := \sum_i X_i$, denote the variance of X by $\mathbb{V}[X]$, and denote the squared coefficient of variation of X by $\mathbb{C}^2[X] = \mathbb{V}[X]/(\mathbb{E}[X])^2$.

Theorem 2. *Suppose the penalty function and cost functions are given by (8) and (9), respectively. Then the competitive ratio is upper bounded by*

$$\frac{\mathbb{E}[G(\hat{p})]}{\mathbb{E}[G(p^*(\omega))]} \leq 1 + \frac{(q\mathbb{E}[X])^2\mathbb{C}^2[X]}{1 + (q\mathbb{E}[X])(\mathbb{C}^2[X]+1)}. \quad (11)$$

Moreover $\hat{p} \leq \mathbb{E}[p^*]$, *with equality if and only if* $\mathbb{V}[X] = 0$.

Theorem 3. *Under the conditions of Theorem 2 the bound in* (11) *is asymptotically tight, i.e., for all* $\epsilon > 0$, *there exists a probability density function* $f(X)$ *such that*

$$\frac{\mathbb{E}[G(\hat{p})]}{\mathbb{E}[G(p^*(\omega))]} \geq 1 + \frac{(q\mathbb{E}[X])^2\mathbb{C}^2[X]}{1 + (q\mathbb{E}[X])(\mathbb{C}^2[X]+1)} - \epsilon. (12)$$

Before moving on, it is worth making a few remarks about these theorems.

First, the results apply both when the prediction errors from users are independent and when they are correlated.

Second, the competitive ratio decreases as the variability of X decreases. This means that a better prediction can provide better performance. In the extreme case, when there is no randomness in X, i.e., perfect foresight, then Theorem 2 guarantees that the competitive ratio is 1. Moreover $\hat{p} = p^*(\omega)$ and $G(\hat{p}) = G(p^*)$. In contrast, when there is prediction error, the LSE tends to have lower price to prevent over provisioning. This is because the attained curtailment $\sum_i s_i(p)$ is an increasing function of the price p. Specifically, we have

$$\hat{p} = \frac{q\mathbb{E}[X]D}{q\mathbb{E}[X^2] + \mathbb{E}[X]} \text{ and } p^* = \frac{qD}{qX+1}, \quad (13)$$

which both increase with q.

Third, it is interesting to note that the competitive ratio does not depend on the particular distributional form beyond the first and second moments of an aggregated value. This is due to the quadratic nature of both the user cost functions $C_i(\cdot)$ and the penalty function $h(\cdot)$. One should expect that if these functions were polynomials with higher order then higher order moments would show up in the competitive ratio.

Finally, it is important to consider the impact of the number of users, n, on the competitive ratio, i.e., on the efficiency of prediction-based pricing. This does not show up explicitly in Theorem 2, but it is possible to extract the information via a slightly more detailed analysis.

Consider a simple case where all X_i are i.i.d. with mean $\mathbb{E}[X_i] = \alpha$ and variance $\mathbb{V}[X_i] = \sigma^2$. Then, the mean and variance of the random variable $X(n) := \sum_{i=1}^n X_i$ are given by:

$$\mathbb{E}[X(n)] = n\alpha \quad \text{and} \quad \mathbb{V}[X(n)] = n\sigma^2. \quad (14)$$

As n increases, the central limit theorem guarantees that $\frac{X(n)-n\alpha}{\sqrt{n}\sigma}$ tends to a Gaussian random variable with zero mean and unit variance. Hence, informally, $X(n)$ tends to a Gaussian random variable with its mean and variance growing linearly in n as in (14).

Note, however, that (14) only imposes conditions on the first two moments of $X(n)$ and does not require $X(n)$ to be Gaussian nor their distributions to depend on just the first two moments. To highlight the dependence on n, let $G_n, g_n, p^*(n), \hat{p}(n), X(n), \hat{X}(n)$ etc. denote the corresponding quantities when there are n users. Then, we can prove the following corollary of Theorem 2, which shows that the competitive ratio exceeds 1 by an amount upper bounded by the normalized variance $q\sigma^2/\alpha$.

Corollary 4. *Suppose the first two moments of* $X(n)$ *are given by* (14). *Under the conditions of Theorem 2, the bound on the competitive ratio is increasing in* n. *Moreover*

$$\frac{\mathbb{E}[G_n(\hat{p}(n))]}{\mathbb{E}[G_n(p^*(n))]} \leq 1 + \frac{q^2\alpha^2}{\frac{q\alpha^3}{\sigma^2} + \left(\frac{\alpha^2}{\sigma^2} + q\alpha\right)/n}$$

$$\to 1 + \frac{q\sigma^2}{\alpha} \quad \textit{as } n \to \infty.$$

Note that the competitive ratio increases as the number of users increases. That is because the cost $h(\cdot)$ is based on the sum, not mean, of the users' elasticities. A system with a small number of users is identical to a system with a larger number of users in which some are entirely inelastic, which has lower uncertainty than the large system in which all users have random elasticity.

However, the analysis above should be taken with a grain of salt because, in practice, users are correlated. For example, on a hot day, many users will be more reluctant to turn their cooling systems off. We can illustrate the impact of such correlations with the following simple model.

$$X_i = \epsilon X_0 + X_i',$$

where X_i' are i.i.d. and independent of the common random variable X_0. In this case, given $\epsilon > 0$, $\mathbb{E}[X] = \Theta(n)$, $\mathbb{V}[X] = \Theta(n^2)$, so $\mathbb{C}^2[X] = \Theta(1)$, and

$$\frac{\mathbb{E}[G_n(\hat{p}(n))]}{\mathbb{E}[G_n(p^*(n))]} = \Theta(n).$$

This highlights that correlation among users can magnify the impact of prediction errors compared to the uncorrelated case, which has a negative impact on the performance of prediction-based pricing.

Such effects are not too worrying in the case of data center demand response, since it is unlikely for there to be a large number of data centers on any given distribution network. However, we have included the discussion in order to highlight a danger of using prediction-based pricing in other demand response contexts.

4.3 Prediction-based pricing versus supply function bidding

The previous results highlight that if predictions are accurate, then prediction-based pricing can be an effective

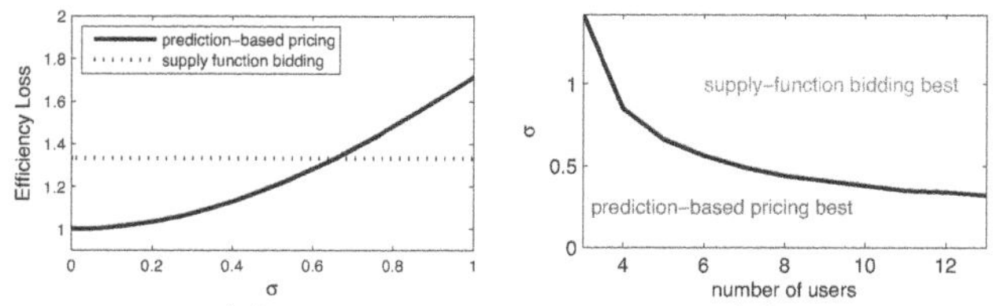

(a) (b)

Figure 10: Comparison of prediction-based pricing and supply function bidding demand response programs. (a) shows the efficiency loss as a function of the prediction error with $n = 5$. (b) shows the prediction error at which prediction-based pricing begins to have worse efficiency than supply function bidding for each n.

market design; however, if predictions are poor the market is highly inefficient. We now contrast the efficiency of prediction-based pricing with the supply function bidding approach discussed in Section 3.

Recall that previous work has concluded that supply function bidding is an efficient market design when agents have limited market power [29, 50]. Thus, which design is appropriate depends on the degree to which participants have market power and the accuracy of the predictions of supply functions made by the LSE.

To concretely illustrate the comparison between these two approaches, we contrast the competitive ratio derived above with the parallel results in [50]. Formally, Theorem 5.1 in [50] bounds the efficiency loss from strategic behavior of customers, i.e., price of anarchy (PoA), by $1+\frac{\min\{D_m,D\}}{-D+\sum_{i\neq m} D_i}$, where D_i is the exogenous limit on consumer iÕs load reduction and D_m is the largest one, i.e., $m \in \mathbf{argmax}\{D_i\}$. This result is tight when the number of customers is no smaller than 2. Therefore, if there is only two large customers such like data centers or one large customer and some small customers considered together, then the efficiency loss can be very high. Generally, the loss decreases when more customers enter the market.[3]

The results of the comparison are shown in Figure 10. Specifically, Figure 10(a) shows the efficiency loss of both prediction-based pricing and supply function bidding. The impact of prediction error (in terms of the standard deviation σ of X_i when fixing $\mathbb{E}[X_i] = 1$) can be seen in the figure, where we assume the prediction errors of customers are independent. In particular, the figure highlights that the efficiency loss increases as the prediction error increase. When the number of users is small (5 in the figure), and thus market power is an issue, even with large prediction error (up to 60%), the prediction-based approach can still provide better performance than supply function bidding.

Figure 10(b) shows how this changes as the number of users grows, and thus market power becomes less of an issue. In particular, the figure shows the standard deviation threshold where prediction-based pricing becomes worse than supply function biding. Naturally, this threshold decreases as the number of users increases. However, even with 10 users, prediction-based pricing tolerates more than 30% prediction error before providing worse efficiency than supply function bidding. This emphasizes that prediction-based pricing is an appealing approach for demand response since it is unlikely to have more than a few data centers on a given distribution circuit.

[3]When this is only one customer, the approach in [50] does apply. Roughly speaking, in this case, the customer is a monopoly, so it can force the utility company to pay as much as possible if meeting the total demand reduction is enforced.

5. INCORPORATING NETWORK CONSTRAINTS

The previous section introduces prediction-based pricing in a context without a power network. In that context, the results highlight that prediction-based pricing is an appealing approach for data center demand response, since the efficiency of the mechanism is robust to errors in prediction as long as there are not a large number of correlated agents. In this section, our goal is to add an additional degree of realism to the model, power network constraints, and to investigate how these constraints impact the performance of prediction-based pricing.

5.1 Modeling the network

The setting we consider in this section is the same as in Section 4, except for the addition of network constraints. Typically, when electricity market issues like demand response are considered, the network constraints are either ignored entirely or a linear approximation, termed the "DC model," is used. See [44] for an introduction. However, due to our focus on reducing voltage violations with data center demand response, the DC model is not appropriate; it assumes the voltages at all buses are fixed at the reference value, which is seldom true in distribution networks.

As a result, we adopt a different model, called the "branch flow" model, which is commonly used for modeling distribution systems, e.g., [5, 11]. This model still uses a linear approximation of the power constraints, but now voltage variations are allowed at all buses except the root bus.

The branch flow model is defined as follows. The power network is represented by a directed, connected tree $\mathcal{G} = (N, E)$, where each node in $N := \{0, 1, ..., n\}$ represent a bus with the root at bus 0, each edge in E represents a line. Denote an edge by (i, j) or $i \to j$ if it points from bus i to bus j. The orientation of edges is fixed to be from the root to the leaves for $\mathcal{G}$.

For each edge $(i, j) \in E$, let $z_{ij} = r_{ij} + \mathbf{i}x_{ij}$ be the complex impedance on the line, and let $S_{ij} := P_{ij} + \mathbf{i}Q_{ij}$ be the sending-end complex power from bus i to bus j. This is the same as the receiving end power since lines are assumed to be lossless.

Let $s_j = P_j + \mathbf{i}Q_j$ be the complex net load (load minus generation) on bus j. Here P_j is the real power consumption, which can be further written as $P_j^0 - s_j(p)$, where P_j^0 is the real power consumption without demand response and $s_j(p)$ is the demand reduction given price p. Under our model, $s_i(p) = X_i p, \forall i$. Q_j is the reactive power consumption on bus j and we assume $Q_j = \beta_j P_j, \forall j$. The branch flow model is defined by the following set of power flow equations.

$$S_{ij} - s_j = \sum_{k: j\to k} S_{jk}, \forall j, \tag{15}$$

$$v_i - v_j = 2\mathbf{Re}(z_{ij}^* S_{ij}), \forall i, j, \tag{16}$$

where $\mathbf{Re}(\cdot)$ is the real part of a given complex number. Here (15) balances the power on each bus, and (16) characterizes the voltages across line (i, j) according to Ohm's law.

The constraint for the voltage on each bus is

$$\underline{v}_i \le v_i \le \overline{v}_i, \forall i. \tag{17}$$

5.2 Prediction-based pricing in networks

The incorporation of the network has a significant consequence for the design of prediction-based pricing. Due to the randomness of the cost functions, it is impossible for the voltage constraints to be always satisfied. This motivates a chance constraint where the goal of the LSE when setting price $\hat{p}$ is now

$$\mathbb{E}[G(\hat{p})] = \min_{p} \quad \mathbb{E}[G(p)] \tag{18}$$
$$\text{s.t.} \quad p \geq 0$$
$$\mathbf{P}\{\text{voltage violation}|p\} \leq \epsilon.$$

To determine more concretely what the set of feasible prices is for the chance constraint above, we first need to transform the power network constraints into constraints on feasible prices. To accomplish this, note that (15) gives that $S_{ij} = \sum_{k \in T_j} s_k$, where T_j is the tree rooted at bus j (including bus j). Then, we can rewrite (16) as

$$\begin{aligned}
v_i - v_j &= 2\mathbf{Re}(z_{ij}^* S_{ij}) \\
&= 2\mathbf{Re}\left((r_{ij} - \mathbf{i}x_{ij}) \sum_{k \in T_j} s_k\right) \\
&= 2\left(r_{ij} \sum_{k \in T_j} P_k + x_{ij} \sum_{k \in T_j} Q_k\right) \\
&= 2\left(r_{ij} \sum_{k \in T_j} (P_k^0 - X_k p) + x_{ij} \sum_{k \in T_j} \beta_k (P_k^0 - X_k p)\right) \\
&= 2 \sum_{k \in T_j} (r_{ij} + x_{ij}\beta_k) P_k^0 - 2 \sum_{k \in T_j} (r_{ij} + x_{ij}\beta_k) X_k p \\
&:= M_{ij} - N_{ij} p.
\end{aligned}$$

Note that M_{ij} is a constant here, while N_{ij} is a random variable due to the uncertainties in X_k.

Next, assuming that E_k is the set of edges from root to bus k, we have (using $v_0 = 1$)

$$\begin{aligned}
v_k &= 1 - \sum_{(i,j) \in E_k} (M_{ij} - N_{ij} p) \\
&= 1 - \sum_{(i,j) \in E_k} M_{ij} + \sum_{(i,j) \in E_k} N_{ij} p.
\end{aligned}$$

Therefore $\underline{v}_k \leq v_k \leq \overline{v}_k$ becomes

$$\underline{v}_k \leq 1 - \sum_{(i,j) \in E_k} M_{ij} + \sum_{(i,j) \in E_k} N_{ij} p \leq \overline{v}_k,$$

which further implies

$$\frac{\underline{v}_k - 1 + \sum_{(i,j) \in E_k} M_{ij}}{\sum_{(i,j) \in E_k} N_{ij}} \leq p \leq \frac{\overline{v}_k - 1 + \sum_{(i,j) \in E_k} M_{ij}}{\sum_{(i,j) \in E_k} N_{ij}}.$$

This condition should hold for all buses, and therefore the feasible set is

$$\max_k \frac{\underline{v}_k - 1 + \sum_{(i,j) \in E_k} M_{ij}}{\sum_{(i,j) \in E_k} N_{ij}} \leq p \leq \min_k \frac{\overline{v}_k - 1 + \sum_{(i,j) \in E_k} M_{ij}}{\sum_{(i,j) \in E_k} N_{ij}}. \tag{19}$$

We can simplify the feasible set further by assuming that the voltage constraints (17) are satisfied when there is no demand response, i.e.,

$$\underline{v}_k \leq 1 - \sum_{(i,j) \in E_k} M_{ij} \leq \overline{v}_k, \forall k. \tag{20}$$

This implies that the feasible range in (19) is nonempty.

Additionally, since we only consider demand reduction with $p \geq 0$,[4] and $\underline{v}_k - 1 + \sum_{(i,j) \in E_k} M_{ij} \leq 0, \forall k$, and we assume $X_k \geq 0$, we can further simplify the feasible set to

$$p \leq \min_k \frac{\overline{v}_k - 1 + \sum_{(i,j) \in E_k} M_{ij}}{\sum_{(i,j) \in E_k} N_{ij}}. \tag{21}$$

Again, recall that N_{ij} is random. Therefore, the constraint above is on realizations. Importantly, for each realization, the constraints are linear, and therefore we can translate the constraints into a bound on the fraction of violation for each bus as follows.

$$\mathbf{P}\left\{\sum_{(i,j) \in E_k} N_{ij} p \geq \overline{v}_k - 1 + \sum_{(i,j) \in E_k} M_{ij}\right\} \leq \epsilon, \forall k. \tag{22}$$

The above equation can be viewed as a concrete specialization of the voltage violation constraint in (18). Note that it has a number of interesting properties. In particular, the violation probability is a strictly increasing function of p that equals 0 when $p = 0$ and approaches $\mathbf{P}\left\{\sum_{(i,j) \in E_k} N_{ij} > 0\right\}$ as $p \to \infty$. Therefore, if $\mathbf{P}\left\{\sum_{(i,j) \in E_k} N_{ij} > 0\right\}$ is smaller than ϵ, the chance constraint is satisfied for all $p \geq 0$[5]. Otherwise there is a threshold p_ϵ at which point the violation probability exceeds ϵ. In this case, the feasible pricing space is $[0, p_\epsilon]$, and the optimizing price becomes the projection of the unconstrained price derived in Section 4 onto this interval.

5.3 The efficiency of prediction-based pricing in networks

The previous analysis highlights that the necessary adjustment in the price used by the LSE due to network constraints can be achieved via a projection onto a feasible space of prices, which we have characterized in (22). The goal of this section is to understand the impact of network constraints, i.e., the projection into the feasible space of prices, have on the efficiency of the resulting price.

The main message of what follows is that network effects do not reduce the efficiency of prediction-based pricing, when efficiency is measured by the competitive ratio.

In particular, let us compare our algorithm with the clairvoyant algorithm that uses the same feasible set $[0, p_\epsilon]$ for each realization. This makes the offline algorithm weaker than the one considered in Section 4, i.e., the performance is strictly worse.

Recall that we denote by $G(\hat{p})$ and $G(p^*(\omega))$ the cost of our algorithm and the clairvoyant algorithm in Section 4 where network constraints are not considered. Let us now denote by $G(\hat{p}_\epsilon)$ and $G(p_\epsilon^*(\omega))$ the cost of our algorithm and the clairvoyant algorithm with the same feasible set $[0, p_\epsilon]$, defined as a function of the network constraints.

Our goal is to compare the competitive ratio without network constraints, i.e., $\frac{\mathbb{E}[G(\hat{p})]}{\mathbb{E}[G(p^*(\omega))]}$, to the competitive ratio under network constraints, i.e., $\frac{\mathbb{E}[G(\hat{p}_\epsilon)]}{\mathbb{E}[G(p_\epsilon^*(\omega))]}$.

The following theorem highlights that constraints on the pricing space actually reduce the efficiency loss from uncertainty, and so the competitive ratio of prediction-based pricing remains unchanged when network constraints are considered. In the statement, we consider the feasible price set $R := [\underline{p}, \overline{p}]$ and denote by $g(\hat{p}_R)$ and $g(p_R^*)$ the cost of our algorithm and the clairvoyant algorithm with the same feasible set for a convex function $g(\cdot)$, e.g., a realization of the random function $G(\cdot)$. Proof is given in the appendix.

Theorem 5. *Consider any positive, convex function $g(\cdot)$ that is a realization of the random function $G(\cdot)$ and any*

[4]Note that all the results here can be easily extended to the case where we allow p to be negative.

[5]This does not happen in our case because we assume X_i's are positive, therefore $\mathbf{P}\left\{\sum_{(i,j) \in E_k} N_{ij} > 0\right\} = 1$

non-empty feasible set $R := [\underline{p}, \overline{p}]$. *Then,*

$$\frac{g(\hat{p})}{g(p^*)} \geq \frac{g(\hat{p}_R)}{g(p^*_R)}, \tag{23}$$

and thus

$$\frac{\mathbb{E}[G(\hat{p})]}{\mathbb{E}[G(p^*(\omega))]} \geq \frac{\mathbb{E}[G(\hat{p}_\epsilon)]}{\mathbb{E}[G(p^*_\epsilon(\omega))]}. \tag{24}$$

A key distinction between this theorem and Theorem 2 is that the feasible price set of both the optimal and the algorithm are fixed to $R := [\underline{p}, \overline{p}]$. This implies that we are not comparing with the "true" offline optimal, which may have different feasible sets for the price for different realizations. Instead, we are comparing with the weaker offline optimal that, because of uncertainty, optimizes over the same feasible price set as our online algorithm, but then has the foresight necessary to choose optimally given these price constraints. This is a common choice for comparison when studying the competitive ratio of online algorithms in situations where clairvoyance yields different feasible action spaces.

6. CONCLUDING REMARKS

In this paper we have highlighted two main points. First, that data center demand response has significant potential and, second, that prediction-based pricing is an appealing mechanism with which to extract this potential.

More concretely, we have illustrated that, not only are data centers large loads to target with demand response programs, they can provide nearly the same degree of flexibility for LSEs as large-scale storage if properly incentivized. However, this last caveat is crucial – it is much harder to extract flexibility from data centers than from storage.

To that end, this paper has argued that prediction-based pricing is a promising market design for this context. While, in general, prediction-based pricing may be less efficient than supply function bidding (due to prediction errors), because data centers typically have significant market power on their distribution networks, supply function bidding can be very inefficient whereas prediction-based pricing is less influenced.

In particular, the analytic results in Sections 4 and 5 highlight that the efficiency of prediction-based pricing is favorable to that of supply function bidding when market power is an issue – even when predictions are error prone. These analytic results are the first, to our knowledge, that provide bounds on the competitive ratio of prediction-based pricing programs, and also the first to provide an analysis of prediction-based pricing programs in a context where network constraints are considered.

However, much work still remains before prediction-based pricing can be used in practice. In particular, in this paper we have adopted quadratic objectives, and it is important to understand the impact of this. For example, in the context of internet congestion management, [36] has studied the impact of convexity of costs on the contrast between time-of-use pricing and fixed-budget rebates. A similar study in the context of predictive pricing and supply function bidding is crucial.

Further, it is important to do an empirical study to understand how predictable the response of data centers will be in demand response programs. Initial pilot studies along these lines are proceeding in some demand response markets, but these have yet to focus on data centers specifically. Depending on the result of such studies, it may be natural to consider hybrid mechanisms that combine predictions and bidding in order to extract supply function information from data centers.

Additionally, many practical aspects of prediction-based pricing programs still require careful thought. For example, what is the appropriate time-scale at which prices should be adjusted? The time-scale chosen allows for a balance between the responsiveness desired by the LSE and the risk-aversion of the data center. Further, in this paper we have assumed a scalar price. One could also investigate location dependent prices in distribution networks, similar to locational marginal prices (LMPs) for transmission networks. While these are not currently used, the extra geographical flexibility they provide could be valuable. Finally, there are interesting exploration-exploitation tradeoffs that come up when setting prices in prediction-based pricing programs. We have not addressed this issue in this paper due to the complexities of the power network, but work in the operations research community has begun to study this in other contexts [6, 7], using "regret" as the performance measure. It would be interesting for future work to incorporate this issue into the demand response context.

Acknowledgment

This work was supported by NSF grants CCF 0830511, CNS 0911041, and CNS 0846025, DoE grant DE-EE0002890, ARO MURI grant W911NF-08-1-0233, Microsoft Research, Bell Labs, the Lee Center for Advanced Networking, and ARC grant FT0991594.

7. REFERENCES

[1] Report to congress on server and data center energy efficiency. 2007.

[2] D. J. Aigner and J. G. Hirschberg. Commercial/industrial customer response to time-of-use electricity prices: Some experimental results. *The RAND Journal of Economics*, 16(3):341–355, 1985.

[3] B. Aksanli, J. Venkatesh, L. Zhang, and T. Rosing. Utilizing green energy prediction to schedule mixed batch and service jobs in data centers. *ACM SIGOPS Operating Systems Review*, 45(3):53–57, 2012.

[4] B. Allaz and J.-L. Vila. Cournot competition, forward markets and efficiency. *Journal of Economic theory*, 59(1):1–16, 1993.

[5] M. Baran and F. F. Wu. Optimal sizing of capacitors placed on a radial distribution system. *IEEE Transactions on Power Delivery*, 4(1):735–743, 1989.

[6] O. Besbes and A. Zeevi. Dynamic pricing without knowing the demand function: Risk bounds and near-optimal algorithms. *Operations Research*, 57(6):1407–1420, 2009.

[7] O. Besbes and A. Zeevi. On the minimax complexity of pricing in a changing environment. *Operations research*, 59(1):66–79, 2011.

[8] D. W. Cai and A. Wierman. Inefficiency in forward markets with supply friction. In *Proc. of CDC*, 2013.

[9] L. Chen, N. Li, S. H. Low, and J. C. Doyle. Two market models for demand response in power networks. In *IEEE SmartGridComm*, pages 397–402, 2010.

[10] Y. Chen, D. Gmach, C. Hyser, Z. Wang, C. Bash, C. Hoover, and S. Singhal. Integrated management of application performance, power and cooling in data centers. In *Proc. of NOMS*, 2010.

[11] H.-D. Chiang and M. E. Baran. On the existence and uniqueness of load flow solution for radial distribution power networks. *IEEE Transactions on Circuits and Systems*, 37(3):410–416, 1990.

[12] A. J. Conejo, J. M. Morales, and L. Baringo. Real-time demand response model. *IEEE Transactions on Smart Grid*, 1(3):236–242, 2010.

[13] Department of Energy. The smart grid: An introduction.

[14] M. Farivar, C. R. Clarke, S. H. Low, and K. M. Chandy. Inverter var control for distribution systems with renewables. In *IEEE SmartGridComm*, pages 457–462, 2011.

[15] M. Farivar, R. Neal, C. Clarke, and S. Low. Optimal inverter var control in distribution systems with high pv penetration. In *IEEE Power and Energy Society General Meeting*, pages 1–7, 2012.

[16] L. Gan, U. Topcu, and S. H. Low. Optimal decentralized protocol for electric vehicle charging. In *IEEE CDC*, pages 5798–5804, 2011.

[17] L. Gan, A. Wierman, U. Topcu, N. Chen, and S. H. Low. Real-time deferrable load control: handling the uncertainties of renewable generation. In *Proc. of ACM eEnergy*, pages 113–124, 2013.

[18] A. Gandhi, Y. Chen, D. Gmach, M. Arlitt, and M. Marwah. Minimizing data center SLA violations and power consumption via hybrid resource provisioning. In *Proc. of IGCC*, 2011.

[19] N. Gast, J.-Y. Le Boudec, A. Proutière, and D.-C. Tomozei. Impact of storage on the efficiency and prices in real-time

electricity markets. In *Proceedings of the fourth international conference on Future energy systems*, pages 15–26. ACM, 2013.
[20] G. Ghatikar, V. Ganti, N. Matson, and M. Piette. Demand response opportunities and enabling technologies for data centers: Findings from field studies. 2012.
[21] J. Heo, P. Jayachandran, I. Shin, D. Wang, T. Abdelzaher, and X. Liu. Optituner: On performance composition and server farm energy minimization application. *Parallel and Distributed Systems, IEEE Transactions on*, 22(11):1871–1878, 2011.
[22] Y.-Y. Hsu and C.-C. Su. Dispatch of direct load control using dynamic programming. *IEEE Transactions on Power Systems*, 6(3):1056–1061, 1991.
[23] https://www.sce.com/wps/portal/home/regulatory/load-profiles.
[24] http://www.apple.com/environment/renewable-energy.
[25] http://www.google.com/green/energy/.
[26] http://www.nrel.gov/midc/lmu/.
[27] L. Huang, J. Walrand, and K. Ramchandran. Optimal demand response with energy storage management. In *IEEE SmartGridComm*, pages 61–66, 2012.
[28] D. Irwin, N. Sharma, and P. Shenoy. Towards continuous policy-driven demand response in data centers. *Computer Communication Review*, 41(4), 2011.
[29] R. Johari and J. N. Tsitsiklis. Parameterized supply function bidding: Equilibrium and efficiency. *Operations research*, 59(5):1079–1089, 2011.
[30] J. Koomey. Growth in data center electricity use 2005 to 2010. *Oakland, CA: Analytics Press. August*, 1:2010, 2011.
[31] J.-Y. Le Boudec and D.-C. Tomozei. A demand-response calculus with perfect batteries. In *Measurement, Modelling, and Evaluation of Computing Systems and Dependability and Fault Tolerance*, pages 273–287. Springer Berlin Heidelberg, 2012.
[32] N. Li, L. Chen, and S. H. Low. Optimal demand response based on utility maximization in power networks. In *IEEE Power and Energy Society General Meeting*, pages 1–8, 2011.
[33] M. Lin, Z. Liu, A. Wierman, and L. Andrew. Online algorithms for geographical load balancing. In *Proc. of IGCC*, 2012.
[34] M. Lin, A. Wierman, L. L. H. Andrew, and E. Thereska. Dynamic right-sizing for power-proportional data centers. In *Proc. of INFOCOM*, 2011.
[35] Z. Liu, Y. Chen, C. Bash, A. Wierman, D. Gmach, Z. Wang, M. Marwah, and C. Hyser. Renewable and cooling aware workload management for sustainable data centers. In *Proc. of ACM Sigmetrics*, 2012.
[36] P. Loiseau, G. Schwartz, J. Musacchio, S. Amin, and S. S. Sastry. Incentive mechanisms for internet congestion management: Fixed-budget rebate versus time-of-day pricing. 2013.
[37] Z. Ma, D. Callaway, and I. Hiskens. Decentralized charging control for large populations of plug-in electric vehicles. In *IEEE CDC*, pages 206–212, 2010.
[38] A. H. Mahmud and S. Ren. Online capacity provisioning for carbon-neutral data center with demand-responsive electricity prices. *ACM SIGMETRICS Performance Evaluation Review*, 41(2):26–37, 2013.
[39] D. Meisner, C. Sadler, L. Barroso, W. Weber, and T. Wenisch. Power management of online data-intensive services. In *Proc. of ISCA*, 2011.
[40] A.-H. Mohsenian-Rad and A. Leon-Garcia. Optimal residential load control with price prediction in real-time electricity pricing environments. *IEEE Transactions on Smart Grid*, 1(2):120–133, 2010.
[41] F. Murphy and Y. Smeers. On the impact of forward markets on investments in oligopolistic markets with reference to electricity. *Operations research*, 58(3):515–528, 2010.
[42] National Institute of Standards and Technology. NIST framework and roadmap for smart grid interoperability standards. NIST Special Publication 1108, 2010.
[43] NY Times. Power, Pollution and the Internet.
[44] N. S. Rau. *Optimization principles: practical applications to the operation and markets of the electric power industry.* John Wiley & Sons, Inc., 2003.
[45] B. Urgaonkar, G. Kesidis, U. V. Shanbhag, and C. Wang. Pricing of service in clouds: Optimal response and strategic interactions. 2013.
[46] R. Urgaonkar, B. Urgaonkar, M. Neely, and A. Sivasubramaniam. Optimal power cost management using stored energy in data centers. In *Proc. of the ACM Sigmetrics*, 2011.
[47] P. Van de Ven, N. Hegde, L. Massoulie, and T. Salonidis. Optimal control of residential energy storage under price fluctuations. In *Proc. of ENERGY*, pages 159–162, 2011.
[48] www.fcgov.com/utilities/business/rates/electric/coincident-peak.
[49] H. Xu and B. Li. Cost efficient datacenter selection for cloud services. In *Proc. of ICCC*, 2012.
[50] Y. Xu, N. Li, and S. Low. Demand response with parameterized supply function bidding.
[51] J. Yao, S. S. Oren, and I. Adler. Two-settlement electricity markets with price caps and cournot generation firms. *European Journal of Operational Research*, 181(3):1279–1296, 2007.
[52] Y. Yao, L. Huang, A. Sharma, L. Golubchik, and M. Neely. Data centers power reduction: A two time scale approach for delay tolerant workloads. In *Proc. of INFOCOM*, pages 1431–1439, 2012.
[53] Q. Zhang, M. Zhani, Q. Zhu, S. Zhang, R. Boutaba, and J. Hellerstein. Dynamic energy-aware capacity provisioning for cloud computing environments. In *ICAC*, 2012.
[54] R. D. Zimmerman, C. E. Murillo-Sánchez, and D. Gan. A matlab power system simulation package, 2005.

APPENDIX

A. APPENDIX: PROOFS

Proof of Theorem 1

To begin, we compute as follows:

$$\begin{aligned} g'(p) &= -h'\left(D-\sum_i s_i(p)\right)\sum_i s_i'(p)+\sum_i c_i'(s_i(p))s_i'(p) \\ &= \sum_i s_i'(p)\left(c_i'(s_i(p))-h'\left(D-\sum_i s_i(p)\right)\right) \\ &= \left(p-h'\left(D-\sum_i s_i(p)\right)\right)\sum_i s_i'(p), \end{aligned}$$

where the last equality follows from $c_i'(s_i(p)) = p$ for all i. Our assumptions imply that $s_i'(p) = (c_i''(s_i(p)))^{-1} > 0$, and hence $g'(p) = 0$ if and only if

$$v(p) \;:=\; p-h'\left(D-\sum_i s_i(p)\right)=0.$$

Now, $v(0) = -h'(D) \leq 0$, $v(\overline{p}) = \overline{p} > 0$, and $v(p)$ is strictly increasing. Hence a unique $0 \leq p^* < \overline{p}$ satisfies $v(p^*) = 0$. Moreover $g'(p) < 0$ for $p < p^*$ and $g'(p) > 0$ for $p > p^*$ implying that p^* is the unique minimizer of $g(p)$. □

Proof of Theorem 2

We first evaluate $\mathbb{E}[G(p^*)]$. From Theorem 1

$$\begin{aligned} p^* &= h'\left(D-\sum_i s_i(p^*)\right) \\ &= q\left(D-p^*\sum_i X_i\right) \\ &= qD-qXp^*. \end{aligned}$$

Hence

$$p^* \;=\; \frac{q}{1+qX}D, \tag{25}$$

which is a random (optimal) price.

Next, from (10) and (25) we have

$$\mathbb{E}[G(p^*)] \;=\; \frac{qD^2}{2}\mathbb{E}\left[\frac{1}{1+qX}\right], \tag{26}$$

where the expectation is taken over X.

To evaluate (7) we have, using (10),

$$\begin{aligned} \mathbb{E}[G(\hat{p})] &= \min_{p\geq 0}\mathbb{E}\left[\frac{q}{2}(D-Xp)^2+\frac{1}{2}Xp^2\right] \\ &= \min_{p\geq 0}\frac{1}{2}\left(\left(q\mathbb{E}\left[X^2\right]+\mathbb{E}[X]\right)p^2-2qD\mathbb{E}[X]\,p+qD^2\right). \end{aligned}$$

Consequently, the unique minimizer $\hat{p}$ and the optimal value of (7) are

$$\hat{p} = \frac{q\mathbb{E}[X]}{q\mathbb{E}[X^2] + \mathbb{E}[X]} D, \tag{27}$$

$$\mathbb{E}[G(\hat{p})] = \frac{qD^2}{2} \frac{\mathbb{E}[X] + q\mathbb{V}[X]}{\mathbb{E}[X] + q\mathbb{E}[X^2]}. \tag{28}$$

We can now quantify the competitive ratio using (26) and (18). Jensen's inequality implies $\mathbb{E}[G(p^*)] \geq \frac{qD^2}{2} \frac{1}{1+q\mathbb{E}[X]}$. Thus,

$$\begin{aligned} \frac{\mathbb{E}[G(\hat{p})]}{\mathbb{E}[G(p^*)]} &\leq \frac{\mathbb{E}[X] + q\mathbb{V}[X]}{\mathbb{E}[X] + q\mathbb{E}[X^2]} (1 + q\mathbb{E}[X]) \\ &= 1 + \frac{q^2\mathbb{E}[X]}{\mathbb{E}[X] + q\mathbb{E}[X^2]} \mathbb{V}[X]. \end{aligned}$$

Rewriting the above in terms of the square coefficient of variation $\mathbb{C}^2[X]$ gives:

$$\frac{\mathbb{E}[G(\hat{p})]}{\mathbb{E}[G(p^*)]} \leq 1 + \frac{(q\mathbb{E}[X])^2\mathbb{C}^2[X]}{1 + (q\mathbb{E}[X])(\mathbb{C}^2[X] + 1)}.$$

Finally, to compare $\hat{p}$ in (27) with p^* in (25) we can rewrite $\hat{p}$ as

$$\hat{p} = \frac{qD}{1 + q\mathbb{E}[X](\mathbb{C}^2[X] + 1)}.$$

Hence

$$\begin{aligned} \mathbb{E}[p^*] &= \mathbb{E}\left[\frac{qD}{1+qX}\right] \\ &\geq \frac{qD}{1 + q\mathbb{E}[X]} \geq \frac{qD}{1 + q\mathbb{E}[X](\mathbb{C}^2[X] + 1)} = \hat{p}, \end{aligned}$$

where the first inequality follows from the Jensen's inequality and the second inequality follows from $\mathbb{C}^2[X] \geq 0$. Both of these are equalities if and only if X has zero variance. □

Proof of Theorem 3

To show tightness we focus on the only inequality used in the proof of Theorem 2, which is

$$\mathbb{E}[G(p^*)] \geq \frac{qD^2}{2(1 + \mathbb{E}[X])}.$$

We need to show that, for any $\epsilon > 0$, there exists a probability distribution $f(X)$ with mean $\mathbb{E}[X]$ and variance $\mathbb{V}[X]$ such that

$$\mathbb{E}[G(p^*)] \leq \frac{qD^2}{2(1 + \mathbb{E}[X])} + \epsilon.$$

We define such a probability distribution as follows. For any $0 < x < 1$, let $d_1 := \mathbb{E}[X] - \sqrt{\mathbb{V}[X](1-x)/x}$ and $d_2 := \mathbb{E}[X] + \sqrt{\mathbb{V}[X]x/(1-x)}$. Then define the following probability density function:

$$f_x(X) = x\delta(\mathbb{E}[X] - d_1) + (1-x)\delta(\mathbb{E}[X] - d_2), \tag{29}$$

where

$$\delta(a) := \begin{cases} \infty & \text{if } a = 0 \\ 0 & \text{otherwise} \end{cases}$$

and $\int \delta(a)da = 1$.

Note that for any $0 < x < 1$, the probability distribution defined in (29) has mean $\mathbb{E}[X]$ and variance $\mathbb{V}[X]$ and

$$\lim_{x \to 1} \mathbb{E}[G(p^*)] = \frac{qD^2}{2(1 + \mathbb{E}[X])}.$$

Thus, the bound is tight. □

Proof of Corollary 4

Given $\mathbb{E}[X(n)] = n\alpha$ and $\mathbb{V}[X(n)] = n\sigma^2$, we have $\mathbb{C}^2[X] = \frac{\sigma^2}{n\alpha^2}$. Thus, we can compute as follows.

$$\begin{aligned} \frac{\mathbb{E}[G(\hat{p})]}{\mathbb{E}[G(p^*)]} &\leq 1 + \frac{(q\mathbb{E}[X])^2\mathbb{C}^2[X]}{1 + (q\mathbb{E}[X])(\mathbb{C}^2[X] + 1)} \\ &= 1 + \frac{q^2n^2\alpha^2\frac{\sigma^2}{n\alpha^2}}{1 + qn\alpha\left(\frac{\sigma^2}{n\alpha^2} + 1\right)} \\ &= 1 + \frac{q^2\alpha^2}{\frac{q\alpha^3}{\sigma^2} + \left(\frac{\alpha^2}{\sigma^2} + q\alpha\right)/n} \\ &\to 1 + \frac{q\sigma^2}{\alpha} \quad \text{as } n \to \infty. \end{aligned}$$

□

Proof of Theorem 5

To prove that the competitive ratio of prediction-based pricing does not become larger when there are constraints on the space of prices, i.e., $p \in [\underline{p}, \overline{p}]$, we consider two cases. The cases are diagramed in Figure 11.

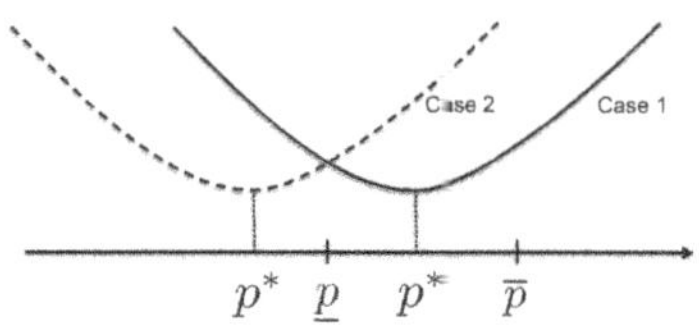

Figure 11: Diagram of cases for proof of Theorem 5.

Case 1: The price p^* picked by the clairvoyant algorithm is within the feasible set $[\underline{p}, \overline{p}]$, i.e., $p^* \in [\underline{p}, \overline{p}]$. We have $p^*_R = p^*$ and therefore $g(p^*_R) = g(p^*)$. If the price picked by our algorithm $\hat{p} \in [\underline{p}, \overline{p}]$, then we have $\hat{p}_R = \hat{p}$ and therefore $g(\hat{p}_R) = g(\hat{p})$. Hence $\frac{g(\hat{p})}{g(p^*)} = \frac{g(\hat{p}_R)}{g(p^*_R)}$.

Otherwise $\hat{p} \notin [\underline{p}, \overline{p}]$. We have $\hat{p}_R = \underline{p}$ if $\hat{p} < \underline{p}$ and $\hat{p}_R = \overline{p}$ if $\hat{p} > \overline{p}$. In either case $g(\hat{p}_R) \leq g(\hat{p})$, and therefore $\frac{g(\hat{p})}{g(p^*)} \geq \frac{g(\hat{p}_R)}{g(p^*_R)}$.

Case 2: The price p^* picked by the clairvoyant algorithm is outside the feasible set $[\underline{p}, \overline{p}]$. Without loss of generality, we assume $p^* < \underline{p}$, as shown in the figure. We have $p^*_R = \underline{p}$ and $g(p^*_R) \geq g(p^*)$. If the price picked by our algorithm $\hat{p} \in [\underline{p}, \overline{p}]$, then we have $\hat{p}_R = \hat{p}$ and therefore $g(\hat{p}_R) = g(\hat{p})$. Hence $\frac{g(\hat{p})}{g(p^*)} \geq \frac{g(\hat{p}_R)}{g(p^*_R)}$.

Otherwise $\hat{p} \notin [\underline{p}, \overline{p}]$. We have $\hat{p}_R = \underline{p}$ if $\hat{p} < \underline{p}$ and $\hat{p}_R = \overline{p}$ if $\hat{p} > \overline{p}$. In the first case we have $\hat{p}_R = p^*_R = \underline{p}$ and therefore $g(\hat{p}_R) = g(p^*_R)$, hence $\frac{g(\hat{p})}{g(p^*)} \geq \frac{g(\hat{p}_R)}{g(p^*_R)} = 1$. In the second case we have $g(\hat{p}_R) \leq g(\hat{p})$, and therefore $\frac{g(\hat{p})}{g(p^*)} \geq \frac{g(\hat{p}_R)}{g(p^*_R)}$. □

Index Policies for a Multi-Class Queue with Convex Holding Cost and Abandonments*

M. Larrañaga[1,2,5], U. Ayesta[2,3,4,5], I.M. Verloop[1,5]
[1]CNRS, IRIT, 2 rue C. Carmichel, F-31071 Toulouse, France.
[2]CNRS, LAAS, 7 avenue du colonel Roche, F-31400 Toulouse, France
[3]IKERBASQUE, Basque Foundation for Science, 48011 Bilbao, Spain
[4]UPV/EHU, University of the Basque Country, 20018 Donostia, Spain
[5]Univ. de Toulouse, INP, LAAS, F-31400 Toulouse, France

ABSTRACT

We investigate a resource allocation problem in a multi-class server with convex holding costs and user impatience under the average cost criterion. In general, the optimal policy has a complex dependency on all the input parameters and state information. Our main contribution is to derive index policies that can serve as heuristics and are shown to give good performance. Our index policy attributes to each class an index, which depends on the number of customers currently present in that class. The index values are obtained by solving a relaxed version of the optimal stochastic control problem and combining results from restless multi-armed bandits and queueing theory. They can be expressed as a function of the steady-state distribution probabilities of a one-dimensional birth-and-death process. For linear holding cost, the index can be calculated in closed-form and turns out to be independent of the arrival rates and the number of customers present. In the case of no abandonments and linear holding cost, our index coincides with the $c\mu$-rule, which is known to be optimal in this simple setting. For general convex holding cost we derive properties of the index value in limiting regimes: we consider the behavior of the index (i) as the number of customers in a class grows large, which allows us to derive the asymptotic structure of the index policies, and (ii) as the abandonment rate vanishes, which allows us to retrieve an index policy proposed for the multi-class M/M/1 queue with convex holding cost and no abandonments. In fact, in a multi-server environment it follows from recent advances that the index policy is asymptotically optimal for linear holding cost. To obtain further insights into the index policy, we consider the fluid version of the relaxed problem and derive a closed-form expression for the fluid index. The latter coincides with the stochastic model in case of linear holding costs. For arbitrary convex holding cost the fluid index can be seen as the $Gc\mu/\theta$-rule, that is, including abandonments into the generalized $c\mu$-rule ($Gc\mu$-rule). Numerical experiments show that our index policies become optimal as the load in the system increases.

*The PhD fellowship of Maialen Larrañaga is funded by a research grant of the Foundation Airbus Group (http://fondation.airbus-group.com/).

SIGMETRICS'14, June 16–20, 2014, Austin, Texas, USA.
Copyright 2014 ACM 978-1-4503-2789-3/14/06 ...$15.00.
http://dx.doi.org/10.1145/2591971.2591983 .

1. INTRODUCTION

In this paper our objective is to develop a unifying framework to obtain well performing control policies in a multi-class single-server queue with convex holding costs and impatient customers. The single-server queue is the canonical model to study resource allocation problems and it can be considered as one of the most classical decision problems. It has been widely studied due to its applicability to any situation where a single-resource is shared by multiple concurrent customers. Abandonment or reneging takes place when customers, unsatisfied of their long waiting time, decide to voluntarily leave the system. It has a huge impact in various real life applications such as the Internet or call centers, where customers may abandon while waiting in the queue, or even while being served. In the presence of abandonments and/or convex holding cost, a characterization of the optimal control is out of reach.

When the holding costs are linear and customers are not impatient, a classical result shows that the celebrated $c\mu$-rule rule is optimal, that is, to serve the classes in decreasing order of priority according to the product $c_k\mu_k$, where c_k is the holding cost per class-k customer, and μ_k^{-1} is the mean service requirement of class-k customers, [13, 18]. The $c\mu$-rule is a so-called *index policy*, that is, the solution to the stochastic control problem is characterized by an *index*, $c_k\mu_k$, which determines which customer is optimal to serve. This simple structure of the optimal policy vanishes however in the presence of convex costs and/or impatient customers. The optimal policy will in general be a complex function of all the input parameters function and the number of customers present in all the classes.

Optimality of index policies has enjoyed a great popularity. The solution to a complex control problem that, a priori, might depend on the entire state space, turns out to have a strikingly simple structure. For instance, in the case of the $c\mu$-rule, the solution does not depend on the number of customers in the various classes. Another classical result that can be seen as an index policy is the optimality of Shortest-Remaining-Processing-Time (SRPT), where the index of each customer is given by its remaining service time. Both examples fit the general context of Multi-Armed Bandit Problems (MABP). A MABP is a particular case of a Markov Decision Process: at every decision epoch the scheduler needs to select one *bandit*, and an associated reward is accrued. The state of this selected bandit evolves stochastically, while the state of all other bandits remain *frozen*. The scheduler knows the state of all bandits, the rewards in every state, and the transition probabilities, and aims at maximizing the total average reward. In a ground-breaking result Gittins showed that the optimal policy that solves a MABP is an index-rule, nowadays commonly referred to as Gittins' index [19]. Thus, for each bandit, one calculates an index that depends only on its own current state and stochastic evolution. The optimal policy activates in each decision epoch the bandit with highest current index.

Despite its generality, in multiple cases of practical interest the problem cannot be cast as a MABP. In a seminal work [35], Whittle introduced the so-called Restless Multi-Armed Bandit Problems (RMABP), a generalization of the standard MABP. In a RMABP all bandits in the system incur a cost. The scheduler selects a number of bandits to be made active. However, all bandits might evolve over time according to a stochastic kernel that depends on whether the bandit is selected for service or not. The objective is to determine a control policy that optimizes the average performance criterion. RMABP provides a more general modeling framework, but its solution has in general a complex structure that might depend on the entire state-space description. Whittle considered a relaxed version of the problem (where the restriction on the number of *active* bandits needs to be respected on average only, and not in every decision epoch), and showed that the solution to the relaxed problem is of index type, referred to as *Whittle's index*. Whittle then defined a heuristic for the original problem where in every decision epoch the bandit with highest Whittle index is selected. It has been shown that the Whittle index policy performs strikingly well, see [28] for a discussion, and can be shown to be asymptotically optimal, see [33, 31]. The latter explains the importance given in the literature to calculate Whittle's index. In order to calculate Whittle's index there are two main difficulties, first one needs to establish a technical property known as *indexability*, and second the calculation of the index might be involved or even infeasible.

In our main contribution of the paper, we verify indexability and calculate Whittle's index for the average cost criterion of the multi-class queue with abandonments and convex cost. In fact, our model can be written as a RMABP where each class is represented by a bandit and the state of a bandit describes the number of customers in that class. The evolution of the number of customers being birth-and-death, the bandit is of birth-and-death type. An important observation we make is that the Whittle index we obtain, which is expressed as a function of the steady-state probabilities, is in fact applicable for any birth-and-death bandit. This is a simple observation that has far reaching consequences since it allows to derive Whittle's index for a general class of control problems, as will be explained in the paper. Note that indexability would be needed to be established on a case-by-case basis. For the abandonment model with convex holding cost, we prove indexability by showing that threshold policies are optimal for the relaxed optimization problem and using properties of the steady-state distributions.

Having characterized Whittle's index in terms of steady-state distributions, we then apply it to various cases. In the case of linear holding cost, we show that the Whittle's index is a constant that is independent of the number of customers in the system and of the arrival rate. In fact, this index policy (with linear holding cost) coincides with the index policies as proposed in [7] and [5], for specific model assumptions, and is asymptotically optimal for a multi-server environment. For general convex holding cost we derive properties of the index value in limiting regimes: we consider the behavior of the index (i) as the number of customers in a class grows large, which allows us to derive the asymptotic structure of the index policies, and (ii) as the abandonment rate vanishes, which allows us to retrieve an index policy proposed for the multi-class M/M/1 queue with convex holding cost and no abandonments.

Our index is expressed as a function of the steady-state probabilities and it can thus efficiently be calculated, but it does not always allow to obtain qualitative insights. We therefore formulate a fluid version of the relaxed optimization problem, where the objective is *bias optimality*, i.e., to determine the policy that minimizes the cost of bringing the fluid to its equilibrium. We show how to derive an index for the fluid model, and we compare it with Whittle's index as obtained for the stochastic model. The advantage of the fluid approach lies in its relatively simple expressions compared to the stochastic one. It shows equivalence with the $Gc\mu/\theta$-rule, that is, including abandonments into the generalized $c\mu$-rule ($Gc\mu$-rule) and provides useful insights on the dependence on the parameters. With linear holding cost the Whittle index and the fluid index are identical.

Numerical experiments show that our index policies work well and become optimal as the load in the system is large.

In summary the main contributions of this paper are:

- Unifying approach to obtain Whittle's index for scheduling problems under average cost criterion.
- For a multi-class queue with convex holding costs and abandonments we prove indexability and obtain Whittle's index as a function of steady-state probabilities.
- For linear holding costs Whittle's index is independent on the arrival rate and state.
- Development of a fluid-based approach to derive a closed-form formula for the indices for general holding cost.

The paper is organized as follows. In Section 2 we give an overview of related work and in Section 3 we describe the model. In Section 4 we present the relaxation of the original problem and show that threshold policies are optimal. We establish indexability and calculate Whittle's index under the average cost criterion. In Section 5 we explain a heuristic index policy, based on Whittle's index, for the original optimization problem. In Section 6 we calculate Whittle's index for linear holding cost and derive properties for general convex holding costs. In Section 7 we calculate the index for an $M/M/1$ queue without abandonments. Section 8 describes the asymptotic optimality result, and in Section 9 we present the fluid model and derive the fluid index. Finally, in Section 10 we numerically evaluate the performance of Whittle's index policy and the fluid index policy.

2. RELATED WORK

There are four main literature bodies that are relevant to our work: literature on (i) index policies for resource allocation problems, (ii) scheduling with convex costs, (iii) scheduling in the presence of impatient customers, and (iv) fluid-based scheduling. We provide below a brief summary of some of the main contributions in each of the domains.

(i) The seminal work on the optimality of index policies for MABP is in the book by Gittins et. al. [19]. The optimality of the $c\mu$-rule, i.e., strict priority is given according to the indices $c\mu$, in a multi-class single server queue for average reward and discounted cost criteria, in the preemptive and non-preemptive cases, is shown in [13, 18]. Index policies for RMABP were introduced in the seminal paper [35]. In [28] the author develops an algorithm that allows to establish whether a problem is indexable, and if yes, to numerically calculate, in an efficient way, Whittle's index. Under the assumption that an ODE has an equilibrium point and that all bandits are symmetric, in [33] it is shown that Whittle's index policy is asymptotically optimal as the number of bandits and the number of bandits that can be made active grow to infinity, while their ratio is kept constant. This result is generalized in [31] to the case in which there are various classes of bandits, and new bandits can arrive over time. In addition to resource allocation problems, Whittle's index has been applied in a wide variety of cases, including opportunistic spectrum access, website morphing, pharmaceutical trials and many others, see for example [19, Chapter 6]. The recent survey paper [21] is a good up-to-date reference on the application of index policies in scheduling.

(ii) A seminal paper on scheduling in the presence of convex costs is [30], where the author introduced the Generalized-$c\mu$-rule ($Gc\mu$) and showed its optimality in heavy-traffic for convex delay cost. The $Gc\mu$-rule associates to each class-i customer with experienced delay d_i the index $C_i'(d_i)\mu_i$, where $C_i(\cdot)$ denotes the class-i delay cost. The optimality of the $Gc\mu$-rule in a heavy-traffic setting with multiple servers was established in [27]. In [1] the authors calculate Whittle's index policy for a multi-class queue with general holding cost functions. In [12], convex holding costs are considered as well and, taking a stochastic approach, the author obtains an index rule that consists on first-order differences of the cost function, rather than on its derivatives.

(iii) The impact of abandonments has attracted considerable interest from the research community, with a surge in recent years. To illustrate the latter, we can mention the recent Special Issue in Queueing Systems on queueing systems with abandonments [23] and the survey paper [15] on abandonments in a many-server setting. Related literature that is more close to our present work consists of papers that deal with optimal scheduling or control aspects of multi-class queueing systems in the presence of abandonments, see for instance [20, 2, 4, 16, 5, 7, 3, 24, 26, 10]. Note that, with the exception of [3], these papers consider linear holding cost. In the case of one server the authors of [16, 10] show that (for exponential distributed service requirements and impatience times) under an additional condition on the ordering of the abandonment rates an index policy is optimal for linear holding cost. In the case of no arrivals and non-preemptive service, the authors of [2] provide partial characterizations of the optimal policy and show that an optimal policy is typically state dependent. It is worthwhile to mention that [2] is inspired by a patient triage problem which illustrates that abandonments are as well an important issue in other areas than information technology. As far as the authors are aware, the above two settings are the only ones for which structural optimality results have been obtained. State-dependent heuristics for the multi-class queue are proposed in [2] for two classes and no arrivals and in [20] for an arbitrary number of classes including new arrivals. In [7] the authors obtain Whittle's index for a multi-class abandonment queue without arrivals, that is, each customer is a bandit and the state of a bandit is either *present* or *departed*. In an overload setting the abandonment queue has been studied under a fluid scaling in [4, 5], where the authors scale the number of servers and the arrival rate and show that an index rule is asymptotically fluid optimal. In our analysis we will show how the indices of [7] and [4, 5] coincide with the Whittle's index rule in the case of linear holding costs and in the presence of arrivals. In [26] the optimal policy is obtained for two classes of customers for a fluid approximation of the stochastic model, which allows to propose a heuristic for the stochastic model for an arbitrary number of classes. We finally mention [3, 24] where the authors derive index policies by studying the Brownian control problem arising in heavy traffic. In [3] general delay costs are considered while in [24] the impatience of customers has a general distribution with increasing failure rate.

(iv) The approach of using the fluid control model to find an approximation for the stochastic optimization problem finds its roots in the pioneering works by Avram et al. [6] and Weiss [34]. It is remarkable that in some cases the optimal control for the fluid model coincides with the optimal solution for the stochastic problem. See for example [6] where this is shown for the $c\mu$-rule in a multi-class single-server queue and [9] where this is shown for Klimov's rule in a multi-class queue with feedback. For other cases, researchers have aimed at establishing that the fluid control is asymptotically optimal, that is, the fluid-based control is optimal for the stochastic optimization problem after a suitable scaling, see for example [8, 17, 32]. We conclude by mentioning that the fluid approach owes its popularity to the groundbreaking result stating that if the fluid model drains in finite time, the stochastic process is stable, see [14].

3. MODEL DESCRIPTION

We consider a multi-class single-server queue with K classes of customers. Class-k customers arrive according to a Poisson process with rate λ_k and have an exponentially distributed service requirement with mean $1/\mu_k$, $k = 1, \dots, K$. We denote by $\rho_k := \lambda_k/\mu_k$ the traffic load of class k, and by $\rho := \sum_{k=1}^{K} \rho_k$ the total load to the system. We model abandonments of customers in the following way:

- Any class-k customer not served abandons after an exponentially distributed amount of time with mean $1/\theta_k$, $k = 1, \dots, K$, with $\theta_k > 0$.
- A class-k customer that is being served abandons after an exponentially distributed amount of time with mean $1/\theta_k'$, $k = 1, \dots, K$, with $\theta_k' \geq 0$.

The server has capacity 1 and can serve at most one customer at a time, where the service can be preemptive. We make the following natural assumption: $\mu_k + \theta_k' \geq \theta_k$, for all k. That is, for a class-k customer its departure rate is higher when being served than when not being served.

At each moment in time, a policy φ decides which class is served. Because of the Markov property, we can focus on policies that only base their decisions on the current number of customers present in the various classes. For a given policy φ, $N_k^\varphi(t)$ denotes the number of class-k customers in the system at time t, (hence, including the one in service), and $\vec{N}^\varphi(t) = (N_1^\varphi(t), \ldots, N_K^\varphi(t))$. Let $S_k^\varphi(\vec{N}^\varphi(t)) \in \{0,1\}$ represent the service capacity devoted to class-k customers at time t under policy φ. The constraint on the service amount devoted to each class is $S_k^\varphi(\vec{n}) = 0$ if $n_k = 0$ and

$$\sum_{k=1}^{K} S_k^\varphi(\vec{n}) \leq 1. \tag{1}$$

The above describes a birth-and-death process with transition rates: $q_k^\varphi(\vec{n}, \vec{n}+\vec{e}_k) = \lambda_k$, and

$$q_k^\varphi(\vec{n}, \vec{n}-\vec{e}_k) = \mu_k S_k^\varphi(\vec{n}) + \theta_k(n_k - S_k^\varphi(\vec{n})) + \theta'_k S_k^\varphi(\vec{n}), \tag{2}$$

for $n_k > 0$, with $\vec{e}_k$ a K-dimensional vector with all zeros except for the k-th component which is equal to 1.

Let $C_k(n,a)$ denote the cost per unit of time when there are n class-k customers in the system and when either class k is not served (if $a = 0$), or when class k is served (if $a = 1$). We assume $C_k(\cdot, 0)$ and $C_k(\cdot, 1)$ are convex and non-decreasing functions and satisfy for all $n \geq 0$,

$$\begin{aligned} C_k(n,0) - C_k((n-1)^+, 0) &\leq C_k(n+1,1) - C_k(n,1) \\ &\leq C_k(n+1,0) - C_k(n,0). \end{aligned} \tag{3}$$

Observe that if $C_k(0,0) \geq C_k(0,1)$, then (3) implies that, for all n, $C_k(n,0) \geq C_k(n,1)$. We also note that (3) is always satisfied when (i) $C_k(n,a) = C_k(n)$, or when (ii) $C_k(n,a) = C_k((n-a)^+)$. Case (i) represents holding costs for customers in the *system*, while (ii) represents holding costs for customers in the *queue*.

We further introduce a cost d_k for every class-k customer that abandoned the system when not being served and a cost d'_k for a class-k customer that abandoned the system while being served.

The objective of the paper is to find the optimal scheduling policy φ under the average-cost criteria, that is,

$$\limsup_{T\to\infty} \sum_{k=1}^{K} \frac{1}{T} \mathbb{E}\Big(\int_0^T C_k(N_k^\varphi(t), S_k^\varphi(\vec{N}^\varphi(t)))\, dt + d_k R_k^\varphi(T) + d'_k R_k'^\varphi(T) \Big), \tag{4}$$

where $R_k^\varphi(T)$ and $R_k'^\varphi(T)$ denote the number of class-k customers that abandoned the queue while waiting and while being served respectively, in the interval $[0,T]$ under policy φ. We have $\mathbb{E}(R_k^\varphi(T)) = \theta_k \mathbb{E}\left(\int_0^T (N_k^\varphi(t) - S_k^\varphi(\vec{N}^\varphi(t)))dt\right)$ and $\mathbb{E}(R_k'^\varphi(T)) = \theta'_k \mathbb{E}\left(\int_0^T S_k^\varphi(\vec{N}^\varphi(t))dt\right)$, by Dynkin's formula. We now introduce the following notation to denote the total cost in state n_k under action $a \in \{0,1\}$:

$$\tilde{C}_k(n_k, a) := C_k(n_k, a) + d_k\theta_k(n_k - a)^+ + d'_k\theta'_k \min(a, n_k), \tag{5}$$

so that the objective (4) can be equivalently written as

$$\limsup_{T\to\infty} \sum_{k=1}^{K} \frac{1}{T} \mathbb{E}\left(\int_0^T \tilde{C}_k(N_k^\varphi(t), S_k^\varphi(\vec{N}^\varphi(t)))\, dt \right). \tag{6}$$

The above described stochastic control problems have proved to be very difficult to solve. Already for the special case of linear holding cost, deriving structural properties of optimal policies is extremely challenging. For example, in [16] optimal dynamic scheduling is studied for two classes of customers (K = 2), $d_k = d'_k$, $\theta_k = \theta'_k$, $\mu_1 = \mu_2 = 1$, and linear holding cost. Define $\tilde{c}_k := c_k + d_k\mu_k$. For the special case where $\tilde{c}_1 \geq \tilde{c}_2$ and $\theta_1 \leq \theta_2$, the authors show that it is optimal to give strict priority to class 1, see [16, Theorem 3.5]. It is intuitively clear that giving priority to class 1 is the optimal thing to do, since serving class 1 myopically minimizes the (holding and abandonment) cost and in addition it is advantageous to keep the maximum number of class-2 customers in the system (without idling), since they have the highest abandonment rate. In [10] optimal dynamic scheduling is studied for $C_k(n,a) = c_k n$, $d_k = d'_k$, and either $\theta_k = \theta'_k$ or $\theta'_k = 0$. For the special case where the classes can be ordered such that $\tilde{c}_1 \geq \cdots \geq \tilde{c}_K$, $\tilde{c}_1(\mu_1 + \theta'_1 - \theta_1) \geq \cdots \geq \tilde{c}_K(\mu_K + \theta_K - \theta'_K)$, and $\tilde{c}_1(\mu_1 + \theta'_1 - \theta_1)/\theta_1 \geq \ldots \geq \tilde{c}_K(\mu_K + \theta'_K - \theta_K)/\theta_K$, the authors show that it is optimal to give strict priority to the class having the highest index.

Outside these special parameter settings, or for convex holding cost, an optimal policy is expected to be state dependent, and as far as the authors are aware, no (structural) results exist for this stochastic optimal control problem.

In order to obtain insights into optimal control for *convex* holding cost, in this paper we will solve a relaxed version of the optimization problem that allows us to propose a heuristic for the original model. This relaxation technique is described in the next section.

4. RELAXATION AND INDEXABILITY

The solution to (6) under constraint (1) cannot be solved in general. Following Whittle [35], we study the relaxed problem in which the constraint on the service devoted to each class must be satisfied on *average*, and not in every decision epoch. The control policy must thus satisfy

$$\limsup_{T\to\infty} \frac{1}{T} \int_0^T \sum_{k=1}^{K} S_k^\varphi(\vec{N}^\varphi(t))dt \leq 1. \tag{7}$$

The objective of the relaxed problem is hence to determine the policy that solves (6) under constraint (7). This can be solved by considering the following unconstrained control problem: find a policy φ that minimizes

$$\limsup_{T\to\infty} \frac{1}{T} \mathbb{E}\left(\int_0^T \left(\sum_{k=1}^{K} \tilde{C}_k(N_k^\varphi(t), S_k^\varphi(\vec{N}^\varphi(t))) - W(1 - \sum_{k=1}^{K} S_k^\varphi(\vec{N}^\varphi(t))) \right) dt \right), \tag{8}$$

where W is the Lagrange multiplier. The key observation made by Whittle is that problem (8) can be decomposed into K subproblems, each corresponding to a different class (or bandit when using terminology from the RMABP literature). Thus, the solution to (8) is obtained by combining the solution to the separate optimization problems.

For the remainder of this section we drop the dependency on the class, and for a given W we consider the individual optimization problem for a given class, that is, minimize

$$\limsup_{T\to\infty} \frac{1}{T} \mathbb{E}\left(\int_0^T \left(\tilde{C}(N^\varphi(t), S^\varphi(N^\varphi(t))) - W(1 - S^\varphi(N^\varphi(t))) \right) dt \right), \tag{9}$$

where now $N^\varphi(t)$ is the state of a given class at time t. Under a stationarity assumption, we can invoke ergodicity to show that (9) is equivalent to minimizing

$$\mathbb{E}(\tilde{C}(N^\varphi, S^\varphi(N^\varphi)) - W\mathbb{E}(\mathbb{1}_{S^\varphi(N^\varphi)=0}), \quad (10)$$

where N^φ denotes the steady-state number of customers in a class under policy φ. We observe that the multiplier W can be interpreted as *subsidy for passivity.*

In summary, the relaxed optimization problem can be written as K independent one-dimensional Markov Decision Problems (9). In the next section we will determine the structure of the optimal control of the relaxed problem (9).

4.1 Threshold policies

In the following proposition we show that an optimal solution of the relaxed problem (9) is of threshold type, i.e., when the number of customers is above a certain threshold n, the class is served, and is not served otherwise. We denote by $\varphi = n$ the threshold policy with threshold n, that is, $S^n(m) = 1$ if $m > n$, and $S^n(m) = 0$ otherwise.

PROPOSITION 1. *There is an n such that the policy $\varphi = n$ is an optimal solution of the relaxed problem (9).*

PROOF. The value function $V(n)$ satisfies

$$\begin{aligned}&(\mu + \theta' + m\theta + \lambda)V(m) + g\\ &= \lambda V(m+1) + \theta(m-1)V((m-1)^+)\\ &+ \min\{\tilde{C}(m,0) - W + (\mu+\theta')V(m) + \theta V((m-1)^+),\\ &\tilde{C}(m,1) + (\mu+\theta')V((m-1)^+) + \theta V(m)\}, \quad (11)\end{aligned}$$

where g is the average cost incurred under an optimal policy. Proving optimality of a threshold policy is hence equivalent to showing that if it is optimal in (11) for state $m+1$, $m \geq 0$ to be passive, then it is also optimal in (11) for state m to be passive, i.e., $\tilde{C}(m+1,0) - W + (\mu+\theta'-\theta)V(m+1) \leq \tilde{C}(m+1,1) + (\mu+\theta'-\theta)V(m)$, implies $\tilde{C}(m,0) - W + (\mu + \theta'-\theta)V(m) \leq \tilde{C}(m,1) + (\mu+\theta'-\theta)V((m-1)^+)$. A sufficient condition for the above to be true is (3) together with the inequality $V(m+1) + V((m-1)^+) \geq 2V(m)$, for $m \geq 0$. The latter condition, convexity of the value function, will be proved below, which concludes the proof.

In case of bounded transition rates, one can uniformize the system and use Value-Iteration in order to prove convexity. However, our transition rates are unbounded. We therefore look to the truncated space, truncated by $L > 1$, and smooth the arrival transition rates as follows: $q_k(m, m+1) = \lambda(1 - m/L)$, $m = 0, \ldots, L$. Denote by $V^L(m)$ the value function of the L-truncated system. By [11, Theorem 3.1] we have that $V^L(m) \to V(m)$ as $L \to \infty$. Hence, convexity of the function V is implied by convexity of V^L for all L, and we are left with proving the latter. The latter is uniformizable, hence we can use the Value-Iteration technique. The proof for convexity of V^L is available in [25]. □

Below we write the steady-state distribution of threshold policy $\varphi = n$. We denote the steady-state probability of being in state i under policy $\varphi = n$ by $\pi^n(i)$, and have

$$\pi^n(i) = \prod_{m=1}^{i} \frac{q^n(m-1,m)}{q^n(m,m-1)} \pi^n(0), \quad i = 1, 2, \ldots, \quad (12)$$

where $\pi^n(0) = \left(1 + \sum_{i=1}^\infty \prod_{m=1}^i \frac{q^n(m-1,m)}{q^n(m,m-1)}\right)^{-1}$.

4.2 Indexability and Whittle's index

Indexability is the property that allows to develop a heuristics for the original problem. This property requires to establish that as the Lagrange multiplier, or equivalently the subsidy for passivity, W, increases, the collection of states in which the optimal action is *passive* increases, i.e., the optimal threshold n increases. It was first introduced by Whittle [35] and we formalize it in the following definition.

DEFINITION 1. *A class is indexable if the set of states in which passive is an optimal action (denoted by $D(w)$) increases in W, that is, $W' < W \Rightarrow D(W') \subseteq D(W)$.*

An optimal solution of problem (9) is a threshold policy, or more specifically, if it is optimal to be passive in state m, $m \geq 1$, then it is also optimal to be passive in state $m-1$, see the proof of Proposition 1. We can therefore equivalently write the following definition for indexability.

DEFINITION 2. *Let $n(W)$ denote the largest value such that the threshold policy $n(W)$ minimizes (9). A class is indexable if $n(W)$ is non-decreasing in W, that is, $W' < W \Rightarrow n(W') \leq n(W)$.*

Provided we can establish indexability, the Whittle index in a state m is defined as the largest value for the subsidy such that the optimal policy is indifferent of the action in state m. Formally:

DEFINITION 3. *When a class is indexable, the Whittle's index in state m is defined by $W(m) := \inf\{W : m \leq n(W)\}$.*

The solution to the relaxed control problem (8) will then be to activate all classes k that are in a state n_k such that their Whittle's index exceeds the subsidy for passivity, i.e., $W_k(n_k) > W$. A standard Lagrangian argument shows that there exists a value of W for which the constraint (7) is binding, i.e., the optimal policy φ that solves Problem (8) will on average activate 1 class.

Obviously, the solution to the relaxed optimization problem is not feasible for the original problem. Following Whittle, we use Whittle's index to construct the following heuristic for the original problem (6) under the constraint (1): select in every decision epoch the class with *largest* Whittle index. We will formally describe this in Section 5.

To conclude this subsection we show that for the model under consideration, the classes are indexable.

PROPOSITION 2. *All classes are indexable.*

PROOF. Since an optimal policy for (9) is of threshold type, for a given subsidy W the optimal average cost under threshold n will be $g(W) := \min_n\{g^{(n)}(W)\}$, where

$$g^{(n)}(W) := \sum_{m=0}^{\infty} \tilde{C}(m, S^n(m))\pi^n(m) - W\sum_{m=0}^{n} \pi^n(m). \quad (13)$$

The function $g(W)$ is a lower envelope of linear non-increasing functions in W (see Figure 1, where we depict the lower-envelope for the case of quadratic cost). It thus follows that $g(W)$ is a concave non-increasing function.

It follows directly that the right-derivative of $g(W)$ in W is given by $-\sum_{m=0}^{n(W)} \pi^{n(W)}(m)$. Moreover, we will prove below that $\sum_{m=0}^{n} \pi^n(m)$ is strictly increasing in n. Since $g(W)$ is concave in W, its second derivative is non-increasing in W. It hence follows that $n(W)$ is non-decreasing in W.

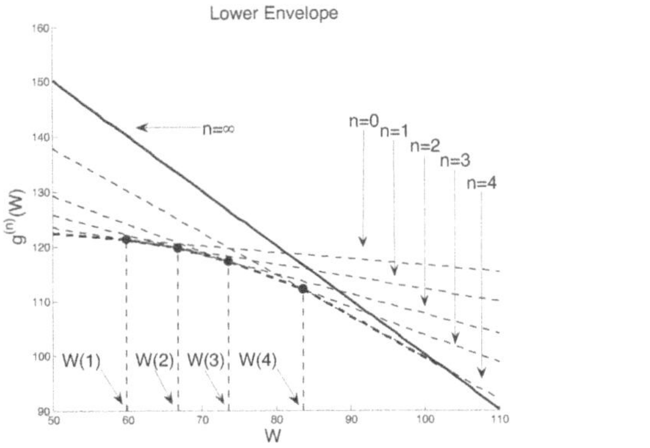

Figure 1: Lower envelop $g = \min_n\{g^{(n)}\}$ when $\tilde{C}(n,a) = (1+2\theta)n + 3n^2$, for $a = 0, 1$, and $\theta = 6, \lambda = 33, \mu = 10$.

We now prove that $\sum_{i=0}^{n} \pi^n(i)$ is strictly increasing, or equivalently, that $1 - \sum_{i=n+1}^{\infty} \pi^n(i)$ is strictly decreasing. Using (12), the latter is equivalent to verifying that

$$\frac{\sum_{m=n+1}^{\infty}\prod_{i=1}^{m}\frac{q^n(i-1,i)}{q^n(i,i-1)}}{\sum_{m=n}^{\infty}\prod_{i=1}^{m}\frac{q^{n-1}(i-1,i)}{q^{n-1}(i,i-1)}} < \frac{1+\sum_{m=1}^{\infty}\prod_{i=1}^{m}\frac{q^n(i-1,i)}{q^n(i,i-1)}}{1+\sum_{m=1}^{\infty}\prod_{i=1}^{m}\frac{q^{n-1}(i-1,i)}{q^{n-1}(i,i-1)}}. \tag{14}$$

holds for all n. Note that $q^n(m-1,m) = q^{n-1}(m-1,m)$ for all m and $q^n(m,m-1) = q^{n-1}(m,m-1)$ for all $m \neq n$. From the assumption $\mu + \theta' \geq \theta$ we have $q^n(n,n-1) \leq q^{n-1}(n,n-1)$. Hence, the left-hand-side of (14) is strictly less than 1, while the right-hand-side is larger than or equal to 1. This proves (14). □

4.3 Derivation of Whittle's index

We are now in position of deriving Whittle's index. An optimal policy is fully characterized by a threshold n such that the passive action is prescribed for states $m \leq n$, and the active action for states $m > n$. Our key observation to derive Whittle's index is that it is not necessary to solve the optimality equation (11), but that it suffices to determine the average cost for threshold policies. In turn, the average reward g can be expressed as a function of the steady-state probabilities, which in the case of birth-and-death processes have a well-known solution. This explains the novelty of our approach with respect to the literature as it gives a unifying framework and determines the Whittle's index for any indexable birth-and-death process. We will come back to this at the end of this section.

We can now state the main result of the paper.

PROPOSITION 3. *If*

$$\frac{\mathbb{E}(\tilde{C}(N^n, S^n(N^n))) - \mathbb{E}(\tilde{C}(N^{n-1}, S^{n-1}(N^{n-1})))}{\sum_{m=0}^{n}\pi^n(m) - \sum_{m=0}^{n-1}\pi^{n-1}(m)}, \tag{15}$$

with $\pi^n(m)$ the steady-state probability of being in state m under policy n, is non-decreasing in n, then Whittle's index $W(n)$ is given by (15).

PROOF. Let $\tilde{W}(n)$ be the value for the subsidy such that the average cost under threshold policy n is equal to that under policy $n-1$. Hence, using (10), we have that for all $n \geq 1$, $\mathbb{E}(\tilde{C}(N^n, S^n(N^n)) - \tilde{W}(n)\mathbb{E}(\mathbb{1}_{S^n(N^n)=0})$ is equal to $\mathbb{E}(\tilde{C}(N^{n-1}, S^{n-1}(N^{n-1})) - \tilde{W}(n)\mathbb{E}(\mathbb{1}_{S^{n-1}(N^{n-1})=0})$. For threshold policy n we have $\mathbb{E}(\mathbb{1}_{S^n(N^n)=0}) = \sum_{m=0}^{n}\pi^n(m)$, hence $\tilde{W}(n)$ is given by (15).

It can be verified that $\tilde{W}(n)$ being non-decreasing, implies that $g(\tilde{W}(n)) = g^{(n)}(\tilde{W}(n)) = g^{(n-1)}(\tilde{W}(n))$. In addition, since $\frac{\mathrm{d}g^{(n)}(W)}{\mathrm{d}W} = -\sum_{m=0}^{n}\pi^n(m)$ is decreasing in n (see proof of Proposition 2), we have $g(W) = g^{(n-1)}(W)$ for $\tilde{W}(n-1) \leq W \leq \tilde{W}(n)$. This implies that Whittle's index is given by $W(n) = \tilde{W}(n)$. □

Equation (15) can be numerically computed, since the cost function and the steady-state probabilities are known. In Section 6 closed-form expressions and limiting properties for Whittle's index will be derived for special cases.

A few comments are in order. The first concerns the form of (15). The numerator in (15) can be interpreted as the increase in cost by deciding to become passive in state n and keeping all other actions unchanged, and similarly the denominator can be understood as the corresponding increase of passivity rate for the process, measured by the additional probability in which a subsidy is received. Thus $W(n)$ can be interpreted as a measure of increased cost per unit of increased passivity, a term coined as Marginal Productivity Index by Niño-Mora [28].

The second comment regards the applicability of Whittle's index (15) in other contexts. Indeed we can outline a general recipe to develop Whittle's indices for bandits whose evolution can be described by general birth-and-death processes:

(i) Establish optimality of monotone policies (as in Proposition 1).
(ii) Establish indexability (as in Proposition 2).
(iii) If (i) and (ii) can be established, then Whittle's index is given by Proposition 3, where the steady-state probabilities are as in (12).

Steps (i) and (ii) are model dependent, but (iii) is immediate and the index will always be given by Proposition 3.

To the best of our knowledge we are the first to observe that for bandits whose evolution can be described by a birth-and-death process, one can get an explicit closed-form expression for Whittle's index. Perhaps a reason for this lies in the difficulty to solve the optimality equation (11), which has two unknowns g and $V(m)$, and this has led researcher to circumvent this difficulty by considering the discounted cost first, equating the total discounted costs as done in Proposition 3 for average cost and then taking the limit in order to retrieve an index for the average cost case. This is for instance the approach taken in [1] to derive an index for convex costs without abandonments or in [19, Section 6.5] for bi-directional bandits in which the *active* and *passive* actions push the process in opposite directions. In [22] the authors develop an algorithm to calculate an index in a multi-class queue with admission control. All these models have in common that after the relaxation, the bandits are birth-and-death, and the obtained Whittle's index is thus equal to (15). We will explain in Section 7 how to derive the index of [1] using this approach. Regarding the bi-directional bandit it can be directly checked that Index (15) is equivalent to the index of [19, Theorem 6.4]. Finally, we note that by adapting the cost structure we obtain that index (15) is equivalent to that of [22, Theorem 2].

Having made this remark on the applicability of (15) in a more wider context, in the remainder of the paper we will discuss the properties of Whittle's index (15) in the context of a queue with convex costs and abandonments.

5. WHITTLE'S INDEX POLICY

In this section we describe how the solution to the relaxed optimization problem is used to obtain a heuristic for the original stochastic model. The optimal control for the relaxed problem is not feasible for the original stochastic model, since in the latter at most one class can be served at a time. Whittle [35] therefore proposed the following heuristic, which is nowadays known as Whittle's index policy:

DEFINITION 4 (WHITTLE'S INDEX POLICY). *Assume at time t we are in state $\vec{N}(t) = \vec{n}$. Whittle's index policy prescribes to serve the class k having currently the highest non-negative Whittle's index $W_k(n_k)$,*

$$W_k(n_k) = \frac{\mathbb{E}(\tilde{C}_k(N_k^{n_k}, S^{n_k}(N_k^{n_k}))) - \mathbb{E}(\tilde{C}_k(N_k^{n_k-1}, S^{n_k-1}(N_k^{n_k-1})))}{\sum_{m=0}^{n_k} \pi_k^{n_k}(m) - \sum_{m=0}^{n_k-1} \pi_k^{n_k-1}(m)}, \tag{16}$$

where $\pi_k^{n_k}(m)$ is the steady-state probability in state m under policy n_k for class k.

Note that in case all classes have a negative index, we define that Whittle's index policy will keep the server idle (until there is a class having a positive value for its index). This follows, since, when the Whittle's index is negative, in the relaxed problem you will keep the class passive even though a negative subsidy is given.

When $\tilde{C}_k(m_k, 0) \geq \tilde{C}_k(m_k, 1)$ for all m_k, the Whittle index $W_k(n_k)$ will always be positive. This can be seen as follows. Recall that $W_k(n_k)$ refers to the value of W such that a threshold policy n_k is an optimal solution of the relaxed problem. Hence, for all $m_k \leq n_k$, it is optimal to keep the class passive, that is, $\tilde{C}_k(m_k, 0) - W_k(n_k) + (\mu_k + \theta'_k - \theta_k)V(m_k) \leq \tilde{C}_k(m_k, 1) + (\mu_k + \theta'_k - \theta_k)V(m_k - 1)$, as we saw in the proof of Proposition 1. Since $\tilde{C}_k(m_k, 0) \geq \tilde{C}_k(m_k, 1)$, $\mu_k + \theta'_k \geq \theta_k$, and $V(\cdot)$ is non-decreasing (see proof of Proposition 1), it follows that $W_k(n_k) \geq 0$.

Instead, when $\tilde{C}(m_k, 0) < \tilde{C}(m_k, 1)$ for an m_k, $W_k(n_k)$ can be negative for certain states n_k. For example, when $\theta'_k = \theta_k$ and $d'_k >> d_k$. Then, even though the total departure rate of class-k customers is highest when serving class k, for certain states n_k it might be better not to serve class k. The latter follows since having a class-k customer abandon while being served, will incur a much higher cost than when it abandons while waiting. The latter is taken care of by the possibility of the Whittle index $W_k(n_k)$ to be negative.

From the practical point of view, the interest of index (16) lies in the fact that the index of class k does not depend on the number of customers present in the other classes j, $j \neq k$. Hence, it provides a systematic way to derive simple implementable policies which we will show perform very well, see Section 10, and which in fact are asymptotically optimal in certain settings, see Section 8.

6. CASE STUDIES

In this section we further investigate properties of the obtained Whittle's index (16). In Section 6.1 we obtain that the index is state-independent for linear holding cost. In Section 6.2 we derive asymptotic properties of the index for general convex holding cost functions.

6.1 Linear holding cost

In this section we consider linear holding cost, that is, $C_k(n_k, a) = c_k(n_k - a)^+ + c'_k \min(n_k, a)$. Hence, under this function, any class-k customer in the queue contributes with c_k to the cost, and a class-k customer in service contributes with c'_k to the cost. In particular if $c'_k = c_k$, then C_k represents the linear holding cost of customers in the *system* and if $c'_k = 0$ then C_k represents the linear holding cost of customers in the *queue*. These two holding cost functions have been considered in the literature in the context of abandonments, for example [7] considers the former, while [4] takes the latter. From our formula (16) we will be able to obtain a full characterization of Whittle's index. Interestingly, we show that the Whittle's index becomes state-independent and does not depend on the arrival rate λ_k.

It will be convenient to define $\tilde{c}_k := c_k + d_k\theta_k$, $k = 1, \dots, K$, which can be interpreted as the total cost per unit of time incurred by a customer who can abandon the system.

We now state the main result of this section. The proof can be found in the technical report [25].

PROPOSITION 4. *Assume linear holding cost $C_k(n_k, a) = c_k(n_k - a)^+ + c'_k \min(n_k, a)$. Then, the Whittle's index for class k is*

$$W_k(n_k) = \frac{\tilde{c}_k(\mu_k + \theta'_k)}{\theta_k} - \tilde{c}'_k, \text{ for all } n_k. \tag{17}$$

An interesting feature of (17) is that it is independent of the arrival rate λ_k and independent on the number of class-k customers present, n_k. In Section 6.2 we will show that this observation only holds for linear holding costs.

The index (17) allows for the following interpretation. Consider there is only one class-k customer in the system and no future arrivals, we then have $\tilde{C}_k(1, 1) = \tilde{c}'_k$, $\tilde{C}(1, 0) = \tilde{c}_k$, $q_k^1(1, 0) = \theta_k$, $q_k^0(1, 0) = \mu_k + \theta'_k$. Index (17) can equivalently be written as $(\mu_k + \theta'_k)\left(\frac{\tilde{c}_k}{\theta_k} - \frac{\tilde{c}'_k}{\mu_k + \theta'_k}\right)$, which is equal to $q_k^0(1, 0)\left(\frac{\tilde{C}(1,0)}{q_k^1(1,0)} - \frac{\tilde{C}_k(1,1)}{q_k^0(1,0)}\right)$. Hence, the index can be interpreted as the reduction in cost when making a class-k bandit active instead of keeping him passive (the term within the brackets) during a time lag equal to the departure time in the active phase.

We now consider some particular cases that have been studied in the literature. For example, let us consider first the case in which all customers can abandon the system, i.e., $\theta'_k = \theta_k$, for $k = 1, \dots, K$, and that the cost for abandonment is the same for both *active* and *passive*, so $d_k = d'_k$. Let us consider two cases: In the first case all customers in the system incur a holding cost. This implies that $c_k = c'_k$, and thus $\tilde{c}_k = \tilde{c}'_k$. Substituting into (17) we get $W_k(n_k) = \frac{\tilde{c}_k\mu_k}{\theta_k}$. In the second case we consider that only customers in the queue incur a holding cost, so we take $c'_k = 0$, which gives $\tilde{c}_k - \tilde{c}'_k = c_k$, and upon substitution in (17) we get the index $W_k(n_k) = \frac{\tilde{c}_k\mu_k}{\theta_k} + c_k$.

We now assume that only customers in the queue can abandon, that is, the customer in service will not abandon, hence $\theta'_k = 0$, for $k = 1, \dots, K$. This is the model assumption of [7] and [4]. We first assume that all customers in the system incur a holding cost, that is, $c_k = c'_k$, and we thus get $\tilde{c}'_k = \tilde{c}_k$. From (17) we get $W_k(n) = \frac{\tilde{c}_k\mu_k}{\theta_k} - c_k$. We can similarly calculate the index in the case in which only customers in the queue incur a holding cost, i.e., $c'_k = 0$, to obtain the index $W_k(n_k) = \frac{\tilde{c}_k\mu_k}{\theta_k}$. These two last indices have been derived in [7] and [4], respectively. More specifically, [7] derives the index $\frac{\tilde{c}_k\mu_k}{\theta_k} - c_k$ when studying one customer and no future arrivals. Interestingly, we observe that the index remains the same in the presence of random arrivals as considered in this paper. When the customer in service does not contribute to the holding cost our model coincides with that analyzed in [4], where it is shown that the index rule $\frac{\tilde{c}_k\mu_k}{\theta_k}$ is asymptotically fluid optimal in a multi-server queue in overload ($\rho > 1$). We therefore conclude that the Whittle's index, $W_k(n_k)$, we have derived, retrieves index policies that had been proposed in the literature when studying the system in special parameter regimes.

To finish this subsection we now provide an intuition to understand the result of Proposition 4 in the case $\theta'_k = \theta_k$ and $c_k = c'_k$. In this setting, at any moment in time, all customers in the system incur a holding cost c_k and can abandon at rate θ_k. Substituting $\mathbb{E}(\tilde{C}_k(N_k^n, S_k^n(N_k^n))) = \tilde{c}_k\mathbb{E}(N_k^n)$ and $W_k(n) = \frac{\tilde{c}_k\mu_k}{\theta_k}$ in (16), we get the relation

$$\theta_k(\mathbb{E}(N_k^{n-1}) - \mathbb{E}(N_k^n)) = \mu_k\left(\sum_{m=n}^{\infty} \pi_k^{n-1}(m) - \sum_{m=n+1}^{\infty} \pi_k^n(m)\right),$$

which can be seen as a rate conservation. Indeed, the term on the left-hand-side represents the difference in the average number of customers that abandons the system per time unit when comparing both policies n and $n-1$. The right-hand-side represents the difference in the average number of customers that is served per time unit when comparing both policies n and $n-1$. The left-hand-side being equal to the right-hand-side is exactly the rate conservation.

6.2 Convex increasing holding cost

In this section we characterize Whittle's index for general convex non-decreasing holding cost functions. We first note that the cost associated to abandonments of customers are linear functions. We can thus use the result of Proposition 4 to rewrite Whittle's index as

$$W_k(n_k) = d_k(\mu_k + \theta'_k) - d'_k\theta'_k + \tag{18}$$
$$\frac{\mathbb{E}(C_k(N_k^{n_k}, S^{n_k}(N_k^{n_k}))) - \mathbb{E}(C_k(N_k^{n_k-1}, S^{n_k-1}(N_k^{n_k-1})))}{\sum_{m=0}^{n_k} \pi_k^{n_k}(m) - \sum_{m=0}^{n_k-1} \pi_k^{n_k-1}(m)}.$$

In the remainder of this section, we will focus on the second term in (18), that is, the term corresponding to the holding cost. We will characterize Whittle's index for large state values and we will observe that for non-linear holding cost the index $W_k(n_k)$ is dependent on n_k, that is, is state-dependent.

We assume that the holding costs $C_k(n_k, 1)$ and $C_k(n_k, 0)$ are upper bounded by polynomials of finite degrees $P_k < \infty$ and $Q_k < \infty$, respectively . Hence, we can write $C_k(n_k, a) = E_k(n_k, a) + o(n_k)$, for large values of n_k, where $E_k(n_k, 1) = \sum_{i=0}^{P_k} C_k^{(P_k,i)} n_k^i$, with

$$C_k^{(P_k,i)} := \lim_{n_k\to\infty} \frac{C_k(n_k,1) - \sum_{j=i+1}^{P_k} C_k^{(P_k,j)} n_k^j}{n_k^i},$$

and $E_k(n_k, 0) = \sum_{i=0}^{P_k} E_k^{(Q_k,i)} n_k^i$, with

$$E_k^{(Q_k,i)} := \lim_{n_k\to\infty} \frac{C_k(n_k,0) - \sum_{j=i+1}^{Q_k} E_k^{(Q_k,j)} n_k^j}{n_k^i}.$$

We assume w.l.o.g. that P_k is such that $C_k^{(P_k,P_k)} > 0$ and Q_k such that $E_k^{(Q_k,Q_k)} > 0$.

In the following proposition we give the expression for Whittle's index for large states. The proof can be found in the technical report [25]:

Proposition 5. *Assume that $C_k(n_k, 1)$ and $C_k(n_k, 0)$ are upper bounded by a polynomial of degree P_k and Q_k respectively. Then, we have $W_k(n_k) = W_k^\infty(n_k) + o(1)$, as $n \to \infty$, where $W_k^\infty(n_k) := d_k(\mu_k + \theta'_k) - d'_k\theta'_k + W_k^c(n_k)$ and*

$$W_k^c(n_k) := (E_k(n_k,0) - E_k(n_k,1)) + (\mu_k + \theta'_k - \theta_k)/\theta_k$$
$$\cdot \left(\frac{E_k(n_k,0)}{n_k} + \sum_{i=2}^{P_k} C_k^{(P_k,i)} \sum_{j=0}^{i-2} n_k^{i-2-j}\left(\frac{\lambda_k}{\theta_k}\right)^{j+1}\right). \tag{19}$$

Assume for example that $P_k = Q_k \geq 2$ and $C_k^{(P_k,P_k)} = E_k^{(Q_k,Q_k)}$, then for states that are large enough, in the case when $C_k(n_k, a) = C_k(n_k)$ or $C_k(n_k, a) = C_k((n_k - a)^+)$, the value of $W_k^\infty(n_k)$ is determined by the highest polynomial. For this example, this is given by

$$\left(E_k^{(P_k,P_k-1)} - C_k^{(P_k,P_k-1)} + \frac{\mu_k + \theta'_k - \theta_k}{\theta_k} E_k^{(P_k,P_k)}\right) n_k^{P_k-1}. \tag{20}$$

The latter is independent of the arrival rate λ_k, and hence, so is W_k^∞ for large enough states. This robust index (20) can serve as an approximation for Whittle's index policy when there are a large number of customers in the system. In particular, it can be of interest in overload settings.

7. M/M/1 MULTI-CLASS QUEUE

The multi-class M/M/1 queue without abandonments has received lot of attention from the research community. In the case of linear holding cost, the $c\mu$-index rule has been proved to be optimal in two main settings: (i) with exponential distributed service times and preemptive scheduling [13], and (ii) general service time distributions and non-preemptive scheduling [18]. A brief explanation of the optimality of an index rule is that having a linear holding cost c_k for a class-k customer per unit of time is equivalent to a problem where a reward c_k is received upon service completion (and no holding cost) [19, Section 4.9]. The latter can be seen as a MABP, for which an index rule (in this case $c\mu$) is optimal[1]. However, this equivalence holds only for linear holding costs, which explains why for general cost functions the structure of the optimal scheduling policy is no longer of index type. In that context, a fruitful approach has been to derive scheduling policies with near-optimal performance or asymptotically optimal performance in a limiting regime, see the references as stated in Section 2.

In this section, we derive an index policy for the multi-class M/M/1 system by considering the limit of our Whittle index as the abandonment rate tends to 0. Note that the Whittle's index $W_k(n_k)$ goes to ∞ as $\theta_k \to 0$, and it turns out that when scaling the index by θ_k we get a non-trivial limit. The proof of the next proposition may be found in the technical report [25].

[1]This is known as the *tax* formulation of a MABP, see [19, Section 4.9].

PROPOSITION 6. *Assume $C_k(n_k, a) = C_k(n_k)$, $a = 0, 1$, $\theta'_k = \theta_k$, and $d_k = d'_k = 0$. Then,*

$$\lim_{\theta_k \to 0} \theta_k W_k(n_k) = \frac{\mu_k(1-\rho_k)}{\rho_k} \cdot \left[\sum_{m=0}^{\infty} \rho_k^m (1-\rho_k) C_k(n_k - 1 + m) - C_k(n_k - 1)\right]. \quad (21)$$

A heuristic for the M/M/1 queue with as objective to minimize the holding cost can now be derived as follows. Set $\theta_k = \theta'_k$ for all k and consider the index multiplied by θ_k as $\theta_k \to 0$. A heuristic is then to give priority according to the index as given in (21).

In case of linear holding costs $C_k(n_k) = c_k n_k$, the index (21) coincides with the $c_k\mu_k$-rule. For general holding cost the index in (21) was also obtained in Glazebrook *et.al* [1] (see also Section [19, Section 6.5]) by carrying out a model-dependent analysis, which consists in considering first the total discounted holding cost criterion, calculating the corresponding Whittle's index, and afterwards taking the limit in the discounting factor. In that case too, indexability needs to be established. Proposition 6 illustrates the versatility of our approach where after having established indexability and obtained the index for the general multi-class model with abandonments, one can apply it to more specific settings such as in the case of no abandonments ($\theta_k = 0$).

As pointed out in [19, Section 6.5] applying directly the average cost criteria to the M/M/1 queue without abandonments gives no meaningful index. Consider an M/M/1 queue with threshold policy n, where the taken action is *passive* for all states below and equal to n, and *active* for all states above n. A classical queueing theory result shows that in the absence of abandonments, under policy n the probability of being in state n will be $1 - \rho$, i.e., independently of where the threshold is set. This result that the subsidy obtained is $W(1 - \rho)$, that is, independent of the policy n, and therefore, the subsidy does not allow to "calibrate" the states. In our approach this is circumvented by obtaining an index for the, well-defined, case with abandonments and then letting $\theta \to 0$, while in [19, Section 6.5] this is circumvented by looking at the discounted problem and scaling the immediate cost.

For large values of n_k, the index (21) is approximately equal to $C'_k(n_k)\mu_k$, which we refer to as the $Gc\mu$-rule. This rule was introduced in [30] for convex delay cost. The equivalence with the $Gc\mu$ rule can be seen as follows. We have for n_k large, $\sum_{m=0}^{\infty} \rho_k^m (1-\rho_k) C_k(n_k - 1 + m) - C_k(n_k - 1) \sum_{m=0}^{\infty} \rho_k^m (1-\rho_k) = (1-\rho_k) \sum_{m=0}^{\infty} \rho_k^m (C(n_k - 1 + m) - C(n_k - 1)) \approx (1-\rho_k) \sum_{m=0}^{\infty} m \rho_k^m C'(n_k - 1) = C'(n_k) \frac{\rho_k}{(1-\rho_k)}$, where we used that for n_k large with respect to m, we have $\frac{C(n_k-1+m)-C(n_k-1)}{m} \approx C'(n_k)$ and that large values of m have a negligible weight on the summation. Hence, we can write $\lim_{\theta_k \to 0} \theta_k W_k(n_k) \approx C'_k(n_k)\mu_k$.

Numerical example. In Table 1 we compare the suboptimality of the $C'(n)\mu$-rule and index-rule (21) in an M/M/1 queue without abandonments. Note that when $\theta_k = 0$, for all k, we need to assume $\sum_{k=1}^{K} \rho_k < 1$ in order to assure stability of the system. Consider 4 classes of customers with the following parameters: $\mu_1 = 16, \mu_2 = 27, \mu_3 = 12$ and $\mu_4 = 21$, $\rho_1 = 3\rho/9, \rho_2 = \rho/9$, $\rho_3 = 5\rho/9$ and $\rho_4 = \rho/9$. The holding cost of each class are cubic, $C_k(n_k) := \alpha_k + \beta_k n_k + \gamma_k n_k^2 + \delta_k n_k^3$, for which (21) simplifies to: $\beta_k\mu_k + \gamma_k\mu_k\left(\frac{3\rho_k - 1}{1-\rho_k} + 2n_k\right) + \delta_k\mu_k\left(3n_k^2 + 3\left(\frac{2\rho_k - 1}{1-\rho_k}\right)n_k + \frac{4\rho_k^2 + \rho_k + 1}{(1-\rho_k)^2}\right)$. We take the particular example: $C_1(n_1) = 6n_1 + 2n_1^2 + 2n_1^3$, $C_2(n_2) = 2n_2 + 2n_2^2 + 2n_2^3$, $C_3(n_3) = n_3 + n_3^2 + 3n_3^3$ and $C_4(n_4) = 8n_4 + 2n_4^3$. We observe that for this example the $C'(n)\mu$-rule is outperformed by the index-rule (21), but both policies give nearly optimal performance.

ρ	0.11	0.21	0.31	0.41
(21)	4.25e-06	1.51e-05	6.07e-06	5.02e-07
$C'(n)\mu$	0.0072	0.0636	0.1002	0.1320
ρ	0.51	0.61	0.71	0.81
(21)	0.008	0.0291	0.0919	1.7129
$C'(n)\mu$	0.1689	0.3616	1.8280	4.9539

Table 1: Suboptimality gap

8. ASYMPTOTIC OPTIMALITY

In this section we will discuss asymptotic optimality of Whittle's index policy.

For linear holding cost, asymptotic optimality can be derived directly from [31]. Assume there are M servers and the arrival rate of class-k customers is $M\lambda_k$. Let W_k be the state-independent index as given in (17). In [31, Proposition 6.2] it is shown that the index policy (W), where at each moment in time a server serves a customers having highest non-negative index W_k, is asymptotically optimal in the following sense: for any policy φ,

$$\lim_{M\to\infty} \lim_{T\to\infty} \frac{1}{T} \sum_{k=1}^{K} \mathbb{E}\left(\int_0^T C(N_k(t), S_k^{(W)}(t))\mathrm{d}t\right) \leq \liminf_{M\to\infty} \lim_{T\to\infty} \frac{1}{T} \sum_{k=1}^{K} \mathbb{E}\left(\int_0^T C(N_k(t), S_k^{\varphi}(t))\mathrm{d}t\right).$$

For general holding cost, we can not derive asymptotic optimality. We do expect however that under certain conditions one would have the following. Assume there are M servers and $x_k M$ queues where class-k customers arrive with rate λ_k, $k = 1, \ldots, K$[2]. A queue can be served by at most one server. In bandit terminology this represents having $x_k M$ class-k bandits whose state (that is, the number of customers in the queue) has values in $\mathcal{S} := \{0, 1, \ldots\}$, and the scheduler needs to decide which M bandits to make active (so which M queues to serve). In case the state space $\mathcal{S}$ would have been finite, the result in [33, 31] implies (under certain conditions) asymptotic optimality of Whittle's index policy as $M \to \infty$. However, for infinite state space, as is the case for our model, no result is known so far.

9. FLUID INDEX

In Section 4 we derived the optimal policy of the relaxed optimization problem (9), which was described by the index value (3). Unfortunately, for non-linear holding cost the index could not be written in closed-form. In this section we will therefore solve the fluid version of the relaxed optimization problem (9), that is, we only take into account the average behavior of the system. This will allow to obtain a

[2]This can represent for example a setting where there are $x_k M$ class-k flows having newly arriving packets (represented by customers).

closed-form expression for the fluid index. In Section 9.1 we describe the fluid control problem we need to solve and in Section 9.2 we obtain the solution and the fluid index. In addition, we compare the fluid index with the index for the stochastic model.

9.1 Fluid model description

We approximate the stochastic model as presented in Section 3 by a deterministic fluid model, where only the mean dynamics are taken into account. Let $m_k(t)$ be the amount of class-k fluid and $s_k(t)$ the control parameter. The dynamics is then given by

$$\begin{aligned}\frac{\mathrm{d}m_k(t)}{\mathrm{d}t} =&\lambda_k - \mu_k s_k(t) - \theta_k(m_k(t) - s_k(t))^+ \\ &- \theta_k' \min(s_k(t), m_k(t)).\end{aligned}$$

and the control $s_k(\cdot)$ needs to satisfy $0 \le s_k(t) \le 1$, $m_k(t) \ge 0$. At time t, the cost for the fluid model is defined as $\tilde{C}(m(t), s(t)) = (1-s(t))\tilde{C}(m(t), 0) + s(t)\tilde{C}(m(t), 1) - W(1-s(t))$, since $s(t)$ can be viewed as the fraction of time the passive action is taken at time t. The cost functions are continuous in both m and s. Note that we have used the same notation as in the stochastic model where the cost functions were discrete in m and s (slight abuse of notation). Assume

$$\frac{\mathrm{d}C(m,1)}{\mathrm{d}m} \le \frac{\mathrm{d}C(m,0)}{\mathrm{d}m}, \tag{22}$$

which is the continuous equivalence of the RHS of (3).

An equilibrium point $(\bar{m}_k, \bar{s}_k)$ of $\frac{\mathrm{d}m_k(t)}{\mathrm{d}t}$ is such that $0 = \lambda_k - \mu_k \bar{s}_k - \theta_k(\bar{m}_k - \bar{s}_k)^+ - \theta_k' \min(\bar{m}_k, \bar{s}_k)$, $\bar{s}_k \in [0,1]$, and $\bar{m}_k \ge 0$. For the remainder of this section we drop the dependence on classes from the notation.

In the stochastic model the aim is to minimize (9), that is, to minimize the time-average cost minus the subsidy obtained. In equilibrium, $\bar{s}$ is the average amount of time the system is passive, hence, the fluid version of (9) will be to find the equilibrium point that minimizes $TC(\bar{s}) := (1-\bar{s})\tilde{C}(\bar{m}, 0) + \bar{s}\tilde{C}(\bar{m}, 1) - W(1-\bar{s})$. We denote by (m^*, s^*) an optimal equilibrium point and define

$$TC^* := (1-s^*)\tilde{C}(m^*, 0) + s^*\tilde{C}(m^*, 1) - W(1-s^*). \tag{23}$$

Since the time-average criteria will be attained by several controls, in the next section we will study controls that are *bias-optimal*. That is, among all controls that reach the optimal equilibrium point, a bias-optimal control is the one that minimizes the cost to get to this point.

9.2 Fluid index for bias optimality

Having characterized the optimal equilibrium point in the previous section, the question is which control minimizes the cost to get to this equilibrium, referred to as *bias-optimality*. Hence, our aim is to find the control that minimizes

$$\int_0^\infty (\tilde{C}(m(t), s(t)) - W(1-s(t)) - TC^*)\mathrm{d}t. \tag{24}$$

That is, minimize the total cost over time minus the optimal cost in equilibrium. The optimal solution to the fluid bias optimal problem is stated below. For the sake of clarity, we will focus on the case $\theta = \theta'$ and we refer to the technical report [25] for the general setting. Full details on the proof can be found in [25].

PROPOSITION 7. *Assume $\theta = \theta'$ and $d = d'$. An optimal control for the relaxed fluid problem (24) is $s^*(t) = 1$ if $W < w(m(t))$ and $s^*(t) = 0$ otherwise, with*

$$\begin{aligned} w(m) &:= C(m,0) - C(m,1) + d\mu \\ &+ \begin{cases} w^{(1)}(m) & \text{if } m < ((\lambda-\mu)/\theta)^+, \\ w^{(2)}(m) & \text{if } ((\lambda-\mu)/\theta)^+ \le m \le \lambda/\theta, \\ w^{(3)}(m) & \text{if } m > \lambda/\theta, \end{cases}\end{aligned}$$

with

$$\begin{aligned} w^{(1)}(m) =& \frac{\mu}{\theta}\frac{C(\frac{\lambda-\mu}{\theta},1) - C(m,1)}{(\lambda-\mu)/\theta - m}, \\ w^{(2)}(m) =& \frac{(\lambda-\theta m)\frac{\mathrm{d}}{\mathrm{d}m}C(m,1) + (\theta m + \mu - \lambda)\frac{\mathrm{d}}{\mathrm{d}m}C(m,0)}{\theta}, \\ w^{(3)}(m) =& \frac{\mu}{\theta}\frac{C(m,0) - C(\lambda/\theta, 0)}{m - \lambda/\theta}. \end{aligned}$$

The fluid index $w(m)$ is non-decreasing and continuous.

PROOF. The holding cost functions $C(m,a)$ are convex and non-decreasing, hence $(C(m,a) - C(m',a))/(m-m')$, $m \ge m'$ is non-decreasing in m and m'. Together with (22) this implies that the functions $w^{(1)}, w^{(2)}$, and $w^{(3)}$ are non-decreasing in m. Continuity of $w^{(1)}, w^{(2)}$ and $w^{(3)}$ follows from the fact that $\lim_{m\uparrow(\lambda-\mu)/\theta} \frac{C(\frac{\lambda-\mu}{\theta},1)-C(m,1)}{(\lambda-\mu)/\theta-m} = \frac{\mathrm{d}C(m,1)}{\mathrm{d}m}$ and $\lim_{m\downarrow\lambda/\theta} \frac{C(m,0)-C(\lambda/\theta,0)}{m-\lambda/\theta} = \frac{\mathrm{d}C(m,0)}{\mathrm{d}m}$.

An optimal control that minimizes (24) is of threshold type, that is, there is an m' such that when $m \le m'$ it is optimal to set $s(t) = 0$ and when $m > m'$ it is optimal to set $s(t) = 1$, see [25]. Recall that the optimal equilibrium point is denoted by (m^*, s^*) and minimizes $TC(\bar{s})$.

First assume $s^* \in (0, \min(\lambda/\mu, 1))$. In that case, the optimal equilibrium point satisfies $((\lambda-\mu)/\theta)^+ < m^* < \lambda/\theta$ and, due to the convexity of $TC(\bar{s})$ in $\bar{s}$, we have $\frac{\mathrm{d}TC(s^*)}{\mathrm{d}\bar{s}} = 0$. Using that $0 = \lambda - \mu s^* - \theta m^*$, $\frac{\mathrm{d}TC(s^*)}{\mathrm{d}\bar{s}} = 0$ can equivalently be written as $W = C(m^*, 0) - C(m^*, 1) + d\mu + w^{(2)}(m^*)$. Hence, for this choice of W, the optimal equilibrium point is given by m^*. Note that $dm(t)/dt$ is strictly negative when $s(t) = 1$ and $m(t) \in (((\lambda-\mu)/\theta)^+, \infty]$, and strictly positive when $s(t) = 0$ and $m(t) \in [0, \lambda/\theta)$. It hence follows directly that the only possible threshold policy that has m^* as equilibrium point, is the threshold policy m^*. Hence, we conclude that for $W = C(m^*, 0) - C(m^*, 1) + d\mu + w^{(2)}(m^*)$, the bias-optimal policy is m^*.

The analysis for the cases $s^* = 0$ or $s^* = \min(\lambda/\mu, 1)$ is more involved. We define the cost-to-go function $K^n(m, W)$ as the cost (24) under the threshold policy n when starting in state m and assuming a subsidy W for passivity. First assume $s^* = 0$, and let $m > \lambda/\theta = m^*$. After some calculations we obtain that for any such m, $K^n(m, W)$ is minimized in $n \ge \lambda/\theta$ when $W = C(n,0) - C(n,1) + d\mu + w^{(3)}(n)$. Hence, we conclude that the threshold policy n, with $n \ge \lambda/\theta$, is bias-optimal for this specific choice of subsidy. Similarly, setting $s^* = \min(\lambda/\mu, 1)$ we obtain that a threshold policy n, with $n \le ((\lambda-\mu)/\theta)^+$, is bias-optimal when $W = C(n,0) - C(n,1) + d\mu + w^{(1)}(n)$.

Hence, we conclude that n is an optimal threshold policy when $W = w(n)$. This, together with the fact that $w(n)$ is non-decreasing in n, proves that if $W < w(m(t))$, then a threshold policy m', with $m' < m(t)$ is bias-optimal, hence $s^*(t) = 1$. Similarly, if $W \ge w(m(t))$, then $s^*(t) = 0$. □

We make the following observations:

- For linear holding cost, the fluid indices are state-independent and coincide with those of the stochastic model as stated in Proposition 4.
- Assume $C(m,a) = C(m)$. In that case,

$$w^{(2)}(m) = \frac{\mu}{\theta}\frac{\mathrm{d}}{\mathrm{d}m}\tilde{C}(m),$$

which corresponds to the $Gc\mu/\theta$-rule. The terms $w^{(1)}(m)$ and $w^{(3)}(m)$ reduce to

$$w^{(1)}(m) = \frac{\mu}{\theta}\frac{\tilde{C}((\lambda-\mu)/\theta) - \tilde{C}(m)}{(\lambda-\mu)/\theta - m},$$

$$w^{(3)}(m) = \frac{\mu}{\theta}\frac{\tilde{C}(m) - \tilde{C}(\lambda/\theta)}{m - \lambda/\theta}.$$

We refer to [12] where index policies based on first-order difference have also been proposed and are shown to empty the system with the lowest cost possible in a single server multi-class queue without abandonments and no future arrivals.
- For large enough values of m, the fluid index $w(m)$ is determined by the value of $C(m,0) - C(m,1) + d\mu + \frac{\mu}{\theta}\frac{C(m,0)}{m}$ (see $w^{(3)}(m)$). In case of polynomial bounded cost functions, as considered in Proposition 5, this coincides with the highest polynomial as determined in (20) for the stochastic model with $P = Q$ and $C^{(P,P)} = E^{(Q,Q)}$.

Having solved the fluid version of the relaxed problem, we can now propose the following heuristic for the stochastic model based on the fluid index $w(m)$.

Definition 5 (Fluid index policy). *Assume at time t we are in state $\vec{N}(t) = \vec{n}$. The fluid index policy prescribes to serve the class k having currently the highest non-negative fluid index $w_k(n_k)$.*

10. NUMERICAL ANALYSIS

The objective of the present section is to show in which regimes the Whittle index policy $W(n)$ (Equation (15)) performs well. We will focus on holding cost functions of the shape $C_k(n_k, a) = C_k(n_k)$, that is, the holding cost is a function of the number of class-k customers in the *system*. Throughout this section we assume $\theta_k = \theta'_k$ and $d'_k = d_k$, so that all class-k customers abandon at the same rate and same cost. Hence, $\tilde{C}_k(n_k, a)$ reduces to $C_k(n_k) + d_k\theta_k n_k$.

In Section 10.1 we compare the structure of Whittle's index policy with the structure of the optimal policy, which is numerically obtained through value iteration [29]. In Section 10.2 we then numerically compare the performance of the index policies with that of the optimal policy.

10.1 Structure of different policies

We compare the structure of the different index policies and the optimal policy for linear and convex holding cost.

10.1.1 Linear holding cost

We performed numerical analysis for a wide range of parameters and observed that for linear holding cost $C_k(n,a) = c_k n$ the optimal policy is of the following structure: when $(N_1, \ldots, N_K)$ is close enough to the origin (and N_i denotes the number of class-i customers in the system), it is optimal to prioritize classes according to the $\tilde{c}\mu$-rule, otherwise to prioritize classes according to the $\tilde{c}\mu/\theta$-rule, where $\tilde{c}_k := c_k + d_k\theta_k$, see Figure 2 (left) with $\epsilon = 0$ as described in the next section. Hence, the Whittle's index (which corresponds to the $\tilde{c}\mu/\theta$-rule in the linear case) captures the optimal action for states that are not too close to the origin.

10.1.2 General holding cost

To discuss the structure of index policies for general holding cost, we focus on two classes of customers ($K = 2$). In a state (N_1, N_2), the action taken by Whittle's index rule is to serve the class having highest value $W_k(N_k)$. Since $W_k(N_k)$ is an non-decreasing function, this implies that there is an increasing switching curve (SC) such that when (N_1, N_2) is below the SC, Whittle's index policy serves class 1 and for any state (N_1, N_2) above the curve the policy serves class 2. Note that for linear holding cost this switching curve collapses either to the vertical or horizontal axis.

By simulations we observed that an optimal policy is as well of switching curve type. For example, in Figure 2 (left) we plot the switching curve of the optimal policy with the following holding cost: $C_1(n) = n + \epsilon n^2$ and $C_2(n) = n$ (parameters $\lambda = [9, 10], \mu = [14, 16], \theta = [2, 0.05], d = [4, 0.3]$). When $\epsilon = 0$, we obtain a decreasing switching curve, which describes the behavior of the optimal policy for linear cost as explained in Section 10.1.1. As ϵ becomes positive, the switching curve becomes increasing. In addition, ϵ becomes larger, and hence the quadratic cost of class 1 increases, and therefore, class 1 gets priority in a larger region.

We now compare the actions taken under Whittle's index policy and the optimal policy. We consider an example with quadratic costs $C_1(n) = (c_{11} + d_1\theta_1)n + c_{21}n^2$ and $C_2(n) = (c_{12}+d_2\theta_2)n + c_{22}n^2$, and set the following parameters $\mu = [15, 18]; \theta = [4, 7]; c_1 = [1, 4]; c_2 = [2, 1]; d = [8, 6.5]$. In Figures 2 (middle and right) we plot the optimal actions (obtained by value iteration) for load $\rho = 0.8$ and $\rho = 2.5$, respectively, and compare it to the actions taken under Whittle's index policy. We observe that the optimal policy can be described by a switching curve. In addition the optimal policy coincides with that of Whittle's index $W(n)$ in almost all the state space as the workload increases. We also plotted the switching curve corresponding to the fluid index $w(n)$ and observe a very good fit.

10.2 Performance evaluation

In this section we evaluate numerically the performance of the index policies. This is carried out by computing the relative sub optimality gap between the average cost of the optimal solution and an index policy. In order to compute this we use the Value Iteration algorithm [29].

We saw in Section 7 that the index policy with index (21) performs very well in an M/M/1 multi-class systems (when there are no abandonments). We considered cubic costs and 4 classes of customers and compared the Generalized index rule ($Gc\mu$) and the index-rule of (21) and we observed there that the latter performs slightly better than the $Gc\mu$-rule.

In this section we will consider scenarios allowing abandonments. We will evaluate the following indices: (i) the Whittle index $W(n)$ (Equation (15)), (ii) the Whittle index for large states $W^{\infty}(n)$ and (iii) the fluid index $w(n)$. We compare these to the two index policies proposed for a multi-class queue without abandonments: the $Gc\mu$-rule, and the

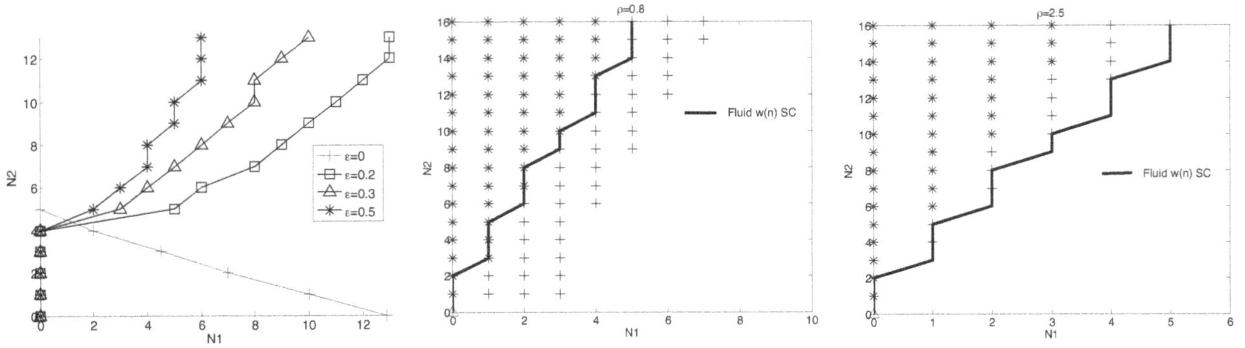

Figure 2: (Left:) Switching curves of the optimal policy for varying holding cost (from linear to quadratic). (Middle and right:) Actions under the optimal policy, the index policy $W(n)$, and the fluid index policy for quadratic holding cost. Area with "+": $W(n)$ serves class 1 while it is optimal to serve class 2, Area with "*": $W(n)$ serves class 2, which is also optimal, and in the white area $W(n)$ serve class 1, which is also optimal.

index-rule corresponding to (21) which is an approximation of $W(n)$ for θ close to zero. We will analyze two different scenarios: (1) varying the workload ρ, and (2) varying the abandonment rates θ_k.

10.2.1 Varying Workload

In this section we aim at observing the behavior of index policies for varying workload.

Example with linear holding cost: We set $C_k(n,a) = c_k n$, $\mu = [15, 25]$, $\theta = [4, 2]$, $c = [1, 1]$, $d = [5, 3.2]$, and let $\rho = \sum_{k=1}^{2} \lambda_k/\mu_k$ vary in the interval $[0, 3.4]$, with $\lambda_1/\mu_1 = \lambda_2/\mu_2$. For linear holding costs, the indices $W(n), W^\infty(n)$ and $w(n)$ reduce to the $\tilde{c}\mu/\theta$-rule and the indices $Gc\mu$ and (21) reduce to the $\tilde{c}\mu$-rule, with $\tilde{c}_k = c_k + d_k\theta_k$.

In Figure 3 (left) we observe that the $\tilde{c}\mu$-rule is optimal in underload, while the $\tilde{c}\mu/\theta$-rule performs optimal in overload. The latter can be explained by the structure of the optimal policy as discussed in Section 10.1.1. In a state far from the origin, the optimal action is to serve according to $\tilde{c}\mu/\theta$, which is the region in which the process will live in overload, explaining why the $\tilde{c}\mu/\theta$-rule performs well in this case. In underload, apparently the effect of abandonments is not that important and the $\tilde{c}\mu$-rule performs very well.

Example with quadratic holding cost: Consider the following parameters: $\mu = [15, 18]$, $\theta = [4, 7]$, $c_1 = [1, 4]$, $c_2 = [2, 1]$, $d = [8, 6.5]$, and we let λ vary, but keeping $\lambda_1/\mu_1 = \lambda_2/\mu_2$. We assume quadratic costs $C_1(n) = (c_{11} + d_1\theta_1)n + c_{21}n^2$ and $C_2(n) = (c_{12} + d_2\theta_2)n + c_{22}n^2$. See Figure 3 (middle) for the sub-optimality gap.

We observe that for low load the $Gc\mu$-rule and the index-rule (21) behave very well. However, as the load grows larger, the sub-optimality gap of these θ-independent policies grows large, while our Whittle index policy $W(n)$, the Whittle index policy for large states $W^\infty(n)$ and the fluid index policy $w(n)$ become near optimal as $\rho > 2$ in this example. Hence, our index policies are very suitable for the overload setting, which are in practice of main importance. Note that the jump around $\rho = 2$ for the index-rule (21) is a result of undefined values around $\lambda_k = \mu_k$.

10.2.2 Varying abandonment rates

In this section we evaluate the performance of the index policies for varying abandonment rates.

Linear holding cost: In this case, the 5 index policies mentioned above reduce to the $\tilde{c}\mu/\theta$-rule and the $\tilde{c}\mu$-rule, as explained in Section 10.2.1. As $\theta_k \to 0$, we observed in simulations that the $\tilde{c}\mu$-rule performs optimal, while the $\tilde{c}\mu/\theta$-rule might perform very bad when the abandonment rates are negligibly small. It is known that for the non-reneging case, the $\tilde{c}\mu$-rule is optimal in underload (the celebrated $c\mu$-rule for a multi-class M/M/1 queue). The $\tilde{c}\mu/\theta = (c + d\theta)\mu/\theta$ index might however give an opposite priority rule when θ's are very small, which explains the non-optimality of the $\tilde{c}\mu/\theta$-rule when θ_k's are very small.

Quadratic holding cost: Consider a system with 2 classes of customers. We assume quadratic holding costs $C_1(n) = \tilde{c}_{11}n + c_{21}n^2$ where, $\tilde{c}_{11} = (c_{11} + d_1\theta_1)$, and $C_2(n) = \tilde{c}_{21}n + c_{22}n^2$, where $\tilde{c}_{21} = (c_{21} + d_2\theta_2)$ and fix the following parameters: $\lambda = [4, 5]$, $\mu = [15, 17]$, $c_1 = [1, 4]$, $c_2 = [5, 1]$, $d = [2, 3]$, $\theta_1 = \epsilon_1 p$ and $\theta_2 = \epsilon_2 p$, where $\epsilon_1 = 0.05$ and $\epsilon_2 = 0.01$, and let p vary. Hence, $\rho = \sum_k \rho_k < 1$ so that the stability of the system is assured as $\theta_k \to 0$.

In Figures 3 (right) we plot the sub-optimality gap as p varies from 0 to 200, hence θ_1 and θ_2 range from $[0, 10]$ and $[0, 2]$, respectively. We observe for the θ-dependent indices a sub-optimality gap of 25% around $p = 0$. As θ grows large, this gap disappears however very fast. Note that the θ-independent indices work well, as we are in an underload scenario.

References

[1] P. S. Ansell, K. D. Glazebrook, J. Niño-Mora, and M. O'Keeffe. Whittle's index policy for a multi-class queueing system with convex holding costs. *Mathematical Methods of Operations Research*, 57(1):21–39, 2003.

[2] N.T. Argon, S. Ziya, and R. Righter. Scheduling impatient jobs in a clearing system with insights on patient triage in mass-casualty incidents. *Prob. Eng. Inf. Sci.*, 22(3):301–332, 2010.

[3] B. Ata and M.H. Tongarlak. On scheduling a multiclass queue with abandonments under general delay costs. *Queueing Systems*, 74:65–104, 2013.

[4] R. Atar, C. Giat, and N. Shimkin. The $c\mu/\theta$ rule for many-server queues with abandonment. *Operation Research*, 58(5):1427–1439, 2010.

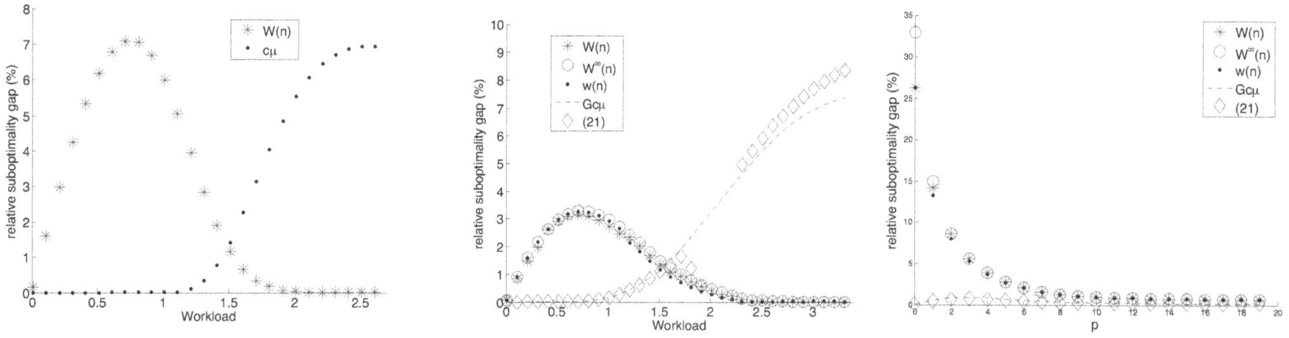

Figure 3: Left: sub optimality for linear holding cost, as ρ increases. Middle: sub optimality for quadratic holding cost as ρ increases. Right: sub optimality for quadratic holding cost as p ($\theta = p\epsilon$) varies.

[5] R. Atar, C. Giat, and N. Shimkin. On the asymptotic optimality of the $c\mu/\theta$ rule under ergodic cost. *Queueing Systems*, 67:127–144, 2011.

[6] F. Avram, D. Bertsimas, and M. Richard. Optimization of multiclass queuing networks: a linear control approach. *Stochastic Networks, eds. F.P. Kelly and R.J. Williams*, pages 199–234, 1995.

[7] U. Ayesta, P. Jacko, and V. Novak. A nearly-optimal index rule for scheduling of users with abandonment. In *IEEE Infocom 2011*, 2011.

[8] N. Bäuerle. Asymptotic optimality of tracking policies in stochastic networks. *Ann. Appl. Probab*, 10:1065–1083, 2000.

[9] N. Bäuerle and U. Rieder. Optimal control of single-server fluid networks. *Queueing Syst.*, 35:185–200, 2000.

[10] S. Bhulai, H. Blok, and F.M. Spieksma. *k* computing queues with customer abandonment: optimality of a generalized $c\mu$-rule by the smoothed rate truncation method. *Work in progress*, 2014.

[11] S. Bhulai, A.C. Brooms, and F.M. Spieksma. On structural properties of the value function for an unbounded jump markov process with an application to a processor sharing retrial queue. *QUESTA*, 76:425–446, 2014.

[12] C.F. Bispo. The single-server scheduling problem with convex costs. *Queueing Systems*, 73:261–294, 2013.

[13] C. Buyukkoc, P. Varaya, and J. Walrand. The $c\mu$ rule revisited. *Adv. Appl. Prob.*, 17:237–238, 1985.

[14] J.G. Dai. On positive harris recurrence of multiclass queueing networks: a unified approach via fluid limit models. *Annals of Applied Probability*, 5:49–77, 1995.

[15] J.G. Dai and S. He. Many-server queues with customer abandonment: A survey of diffusion and fluid approximations. *J. Syst. Sci. Syst. Eng.*, 21:1–36, 2012.

[16] D.G. Down, G. Koole, and M.E. Lewis. Dynamic control of a single server system with abandonments. *Queueing Systems*, 67:63–90, 2011.

[17] A. Gajrat and A. Hordijk. Fluid approximation of a controlled multiclass tandem network. *Queueing Systems*, 35:349–380, 2000.

[18] E. Gelenbe and I. Mitrani. *Analysis and Synthesis of Computer Systems*. London: Academic Press, 1980.

[19] J.C. Gittins, K. Glazebrook, and R. Weber. *Multi-armed Bandit Allocation Indices*. Wiley, 2011.

[20] K.D. Glazebrook, P.S. Ansell, R.T. Dunn, and R.R. Lumley. On the optimal allocation of service to impatient tasks. *J. Appl. Prob.*, 41:51–72, 2004.

[21] K.D. Glazebrook, D.J. Hodge, C. Kirkbride, and R.J. Minty. Stochastic scheduling: A short history of index policies and new approaches to index generation for dynamic resource allocation. *J of Sched.*, 2013.

[22] K.D. Glazebrook, C. Kirkbride, and J. Ouenniche. Index policies for the admission control and routing of impatient customers to heterogeneous servcie stations. *Operations Research*, 57:975–989, 2009.

[23] J. Hasenbein and D. Perry (Eds). Special issue on queueing systems with abandonments. *Queueng Systems*, 75(2–4):111–384, 2013.

[24] J. Kim and A. Ward. Dynamic scheduling of a GI/GI/1+GI queue with multiple customer classes. *Queueing Systems*, 75(2-4):339–384, 2013.

[25] M. Larrañaga, U. Ayesta, and I.M. Verloop. Index policies for a multi-class queue with convex holding cost and abandonments. *LAAS technical report 14098.*

[26] M. Larrañaga, U. Ayesta, and I.M. Verloop. Dynamic fluid-based scheduling in a multi-class abandonment queue. *Performance Evaluation*, 70:841–858, 2013.

[27] A. Mandelbaum and S. Stolyar. Scheduling flexible servers with convex delay costs: Heavy-traffic optimality of the generalized $c\mu$-rule. *Operations Research*, 52(6):836–855, 2004.

[28] J. Niño-Mora. Dynamic priority allocation via restless bandit marginal productivity indices. *TOP*, 15(2):161–198, 2007.

[29] M. L. Puterman. *Markov Decision Processes: Discrete Stochastic Dynamic Programming.* Wiley, 2005.

[30] J. A. van Mieghem. Dynamic scheduling with convex delay costs: The generalized $c\mu$ rule. *The Annals of Applied Probability*, 5(3):808–833, 1995.

[31] I.M. Verloop. Asymptotic optimal control of multi-class restless bandits. CNRS Technical Report, hal-00743781, September 2013.

[32] I.M. Verloop and R. Núñez-Queija. Asymptotically optimal parallel resource assignment with interference. *Queueing Systems*, 65(1):43–92, 2010.

[33] R.R. Weber and G. Weiss. On an index policy for restless bandits. *J. Appl. Prob.*, 27:637–648, 1990.

[34] G. Weiss. On optimal draining of reentrant fluid lines. *Stochastic Networks, eds. F.P. Kelly and R.J. Williams*, pages 91–103, 1995.

[35] P. Whittle. Restless bandits: Activity allocation in a changing world. *J. Appl. Prob.*, 25:287–298, 1988.

Concave Switching in Single and Multihop Networks

Neil Walton*
University of Amsterdam
Science Park 904
1098 XH Amsterdam, NL.
n.s.walton@uva.nl

ABSTRACT

Switched queueing networks model wireless networks, input queued switches and numerous other networked communications systems. For single-hop networks, we consider a (α, g)-switch policy which combines the MaxWeight policies with bandwidth sharing networks – a further well studied model of Internet congestion. We prove the maximum stability property for this class of randomized policies. Thus these policies have the same first order behavior as the MaxWeight policies. However, for multihop networks some of these generalized polices address a number of critical weakness of the MaxWeight/BackPressure policies.

For multihop networks with fixed routing, we consider the Proportional Scheduler (or (1,log)-policy). In this setting, the BackPressure policy is maximum stable, but must maintain a queue for every route-destination, which typically grows rapidly with a network's size. However, this proportionally fair policy only needs to maintain a queue for each outgoing link, which is typically bounded in number. As is common with Internet routing, by maintaining per-link queueing each node only needs to know the next hop for each packet and not its entire route. Further, in contrast to BackPressure, the Proportional Scheduler does not compare downstream queue lengths to determine weights, only local link information is required. This leads to greater potential for decomposed implementations of the policy. Through a reduction argument and an entropy argument, we demonstrate that, whilst maintaining substantially less queueing overhead, the Proportional Scheduler achieves maximum throughput stability.

Categories and Subject Descriptors

C.2.1 [**Network Architecture and Design**]: [Packet-switching networks, Store and forward networks, Distributed networks]; G.3 [**Probability and Statistics**]: [Markov Processes, Queueing Theory]

General Terms

Stochastic Networks, Performance, Theory

Keywords

Proportional Fairness, MaxWeight, BackPressure, Switch Network, Fluid Limit, Maximum Stable, Stability.

*The work of Neil Walton is funded by the VENI research programme, which is financed by the Netherlands Organisation for Scientific Research (NWO).

SIGMETRICS'14, June 16–20, 2014, Austin, Texas, USA.
Copyright 2014 ACM 978-1-4503-2789-3/14/06 ...$15.00.
http://dx.doi.org/10.1145/2591971.2591987 .

1. INTRODUCTION

Switch networks are queueing networks were there are constraints on which queues can be served simultaneously. At each time a policy must chose a schedule that satisfies these constraints. The MaxWeight/BackPressure scheduling policies were first introduced by Tassiulas and Ephremides as a model of wireless communication [36]. Their policy was applicable to the class of switched queueing networks both for single-hop networks – where packets are served once before departing – and for multi-hop networks – where packets are served a multiple queues before departing. For single-hop networks, their policy is called *MaxWeight* and, for multihop networks, it is called *BackPressure*. The MaxWeight and BackPressure scheduling policies have the key properties of having a maximal stability region while not requiring explicit estimation of arrival rates. Subsequently, as a model of Internet Protocol routers, McKeown et al. [24] applied this paradigm to the example of input-queued switches. Extensions of these policies can be found in Stolyar [34]. The MaxWeight and BackPressure policies have proved popular and, accordingly, have been generalized [1, 33, 12, 30, 31, 15, 32]. The defining feature of each generalization of MaxWeight and BackPressure is that it minimizes the drift of a Lyapunov function, which is then used to prove the policies stability.

A further class of maximum stable Internet models are bandwidth sharing networks, first introduced by Roberts and Massoulié [23]. Similar to MaxWeight and BackPressure, these policies are defined by an optimization and are maximum stable; however, unlike BackPressure, they are not constructed from a Lyapunov function. Stability proofs for these systems can be found in Bonald and Massoulié [3] and Massoulié [22]. Further progress on the large deviations and heavy traffic behaviour of proportional fairness can be found in Jonckheere, Lopez [17] and Vlasiou, Zhang, Zwart [37]. To the knowledge of this author, discussions applying these models to switch networks are first made by Shah and

Wischik [31] and Zhong [38] for the weighted α-fair bandwidth allocation policies of Mo and Walrand [25].

This paper merges the MaxWeight and bandwidth allocation policies, proves their stability for single-hop switch networks and, for a proportionally fair case, we extend these results to multihop networks with fixed routing. In essence the paper leverages and generalizes results to switch networks that originate from bandwidth networks [3, 22]. Because of their substantially reduced queueing complexity, there are a number of significant structural advantages which have not previously been observed in switch systems.

1.1 Policies and Results

We now briefly describe the switch policies considered in this paper. A more formal description is given in Section 3. In this paper, we define a switch policy as follows: given parameter $\alpha > 0$ and concave functions $g = (g_j \colon j \in \mathcal{J})$, the (α, g)-switch policy chooses a random schedule which solves

$$\text{maximize} \quad \sum_{j \in \mathcal{J}} g_j(s_j) Q_j^{\alpha} \quad \text{over} \quad s \in <\mathcal{S}>,$$

where $Q = (Q_j : j \in \mathcal{J})$ is the vector of queue sizes and where, allowing for randomization, the maximization is taken over a set of admissible schedules $<\mathcal{S}>$. The interior of the set $<\mathcal{S}>$ also gives the network's *stability region* – the largest set of arrival rates for which a policy can stabilize the network. A policy which is stable for all arrival rates in $<\mathcal{S}>$ is maximum stable. In order to place these policies on a par with the traditional MaxWeight policies, we show that these policies have the same maximum stability property as the MaxWeight. In Theorem 1, we provide a proof which is analogous to the proof of Bonald and Massoulié for weight α-fair bandwidth policies [3]. This is the first contribution of the paper.

Next we consider multihop networks with fixed routing. Here the BackPressure is the canonical maximal stable policy. The BackPressure policy essentially consists of two stages: the first stage, weights are determined for each link j by comparing current and downstream stream queues sizes for each commodity/route and, a second stage, were we optimize these weights over the set of schedules. Notice, for BackPressure to make a scheduling decision it must know the routes of all packets present at each queue. This is not practical when the routes processed a node are large in number and potentially unknown. In contrast, we consider a proportionally fair optimization. This consists of solving an optimization of the form

$$\text{maximize} \quad \sum_{j \in \mathcal{J}} Q_j \log s_j \quad \text{over} \quad s \in <\mathcal{S}> .$$

Here $j = (n, n')$ represents a directed link between two nodes of a communication network and Q_j is the number of packets present at n which currently waiting to pass through link j. A schedule is then chosen whose mean is the solution to this optimization and a job is chosen at random from each scheduled queue.

We consider the fluid model for this fixed route multihop network. We show that the proportional fair fluid model is maximum stable. We give two proofs of this result. The first exploits the structure of our random service discipline and use the properties of the logarithm to reduce our multi-class queueing system with fixed routing to a single-class system with Markovian routing. From this reduction, we can apply the fluid analysis of Massoulié [22] to prove fluid stability. We provide a second and direct proof that emphasized the policies implicit ability to balance the entropy between separate networked components. The fluid stability argument given is compared with the proof of Bramson [4] for head-of-the-line processor sharing networks. The importance of these stability arguments, which originate from bandwidth networks and classical queueing networks, is in their consequences for switched systems.

1.2 Contributions

Let us discuss in more detail a few of the advantages of this Proportional Scheduler for multihop switched networks. Firstly, as we consider increasingly large communication networks, we expect the degree of nodes (routers) to stay bounded but the number of routes or destinations processed by a router to grow substantially. Thus the Proportional Scheduler, which maintains a queue per out-going link, requires a number of queues that is far far smaller than BackPressure, which maintains a queue for each route-destination. Second, to make a scheduling decision with the BackPressure policy, we need to know the entire route or at least the destination in of each packet, while for the Proportional Scheduler knowing the next hop of the packet is sufficient to implement the policy. Third, if we add new nodes to our network then, to implement BackPressure, the newly added node must be aware of the entire topology and route/class structure of the network, whilst the Proportional Scheduler only requires information about neighboring links. So, routing decisions can be determined by packets. Fourth, when different schedules within the network can be implemented independently – here we imagine separate non-interfering network components –, for BackPressure, messages must be shared between the separate components in order to determine the differences in queue sizes. However, for the Proportional Scheduler, the optimization relevant to the policy will decompose into an independent optimization for each component which can then be solved separately. Finally, as a general rule, there are almost no single-hop communication systems. Communication systems consist of a large number of interconnected components. Single-hop switch networks are often considered in performance analysis for reasons of tractability. This statement is particularly true for wireless systems. However, stability in a single-hop system does not in general imply stability in a corresponding multihop system. See Lu and Kumar [21], Rybko and Stolar [27] and Bramson [5] for instability examples which can easily be adapted to switch systems. Notable, recent work of Dieker and Shin [11] considers schemes which extend local/single-hop stability results to global stability results. These allow for multi-class routing. However, like BackPressure, these policies require route information from each packet to make scheduling decisions. To the best of knowledge of this author, this is the first general proof of maximum stability for a multihop switch network where routing information is not required in order to make a scheduling decision.

We now briefly discuss extensions and future consequences of this analysis. The Proportional Scheduler which we consider applies a processor-sharing discipline within each queue, meaning that the scheduled packet from a queue is chosen at random. However, it would be desirable to consider first-in-first-out queueing. In this way, packets will be served by the network in sequence and jitter effects will be reduced. Further, in practice, communication implement FIFO queueing. Surprisingly, the Proportional Scheduler is provably a maximum stable for FIFO queueing disciplines. The proof of this result is substantially more involved than the short proof that we can provide for the processor-sharing case. The FIFO case follows due to underlying connections between proportional fairness and quasi-reversible queueing systems – see [22, 29] for some related discussion. This analysis leads to further structural advantages namely product-form resource-pooling effects and better delay scaling complexity compared to BackPressure. We refer the interested reader to the preprint [6].

In a summary, the contributions of this work are as follows:

- We combine the set of MaxWeight policies and bandwidth allocation policies, to provide a new class of switch policies and we prove maximum stability for these polices.
- Using a random discipline within queues, we consider a Proportional Scheduler for multihop networks with fixed routing. We give two proofs of fluid stability for this system.
- We emphasis several important observations of this last result for switch networks:
    - the policy only needs to maintain a queue for each outgoing link;
    - packets can be routed by only knowing each packets next hop;
    - network nodes do not need to know their network topology;
    - message do not need to be sent to calculate weights and so scheduling decisions can be completely decomposed between independently functioning components.
- We provide the first general proof of maximum stability for a multihop switch network where routing information is not required in order to make a scheduling decision.

Informally speaking, because the Proportional Scheduler does not need to know the route structure of the network to make a scheduling decision, while BackPressure does, the policy's implementation scales better with network size.

1.3 Organization

The remaining sections of the paper are organized as follows. In Section 2, we describe the network and queueing process for both single-hop and multihop networks. In Section 3, we define the (α, g)-switch policies, proportional fairness and we relate these to existing policies, namely, MaxWeight, BackPressure, utility optimizing bandwidth allocation policies, and weight α-fairness. We also define the fluid model associated with each of these systems. In Section 4, we present and discuss the main results of this paper, Theorem 1 and Theorem 2. In Section 5, we provide a proof of Theorem 1. This consists of characterizing the fluid limit of the (α, g)-policy, proving stability of that fluid system and then using this to prove positive recurrence of the prelimit process. In Section 6, we give two proofs of Theorem 2. The first involves a reduction to a proof of Massoulié [22]. The second proof can be argued from the fluid analysis of Bramson [4].

2. SWITCH NETWORK NOTATION

We define single-hop and multihop switch networks. These discrete-time queueing networks have restrictions on which queues can be served simultaneously.

The following notation is used both for single-hop and multihop networks. We assume that time is slotted, that is each time, t, belongs to the positive integers, $\mathbb{Z}_+$. We let the finite set $\mathcal{J}$ index the set of queues or links of a network. We let the finite set $\mathcal{S}$ be the set of schedules. Each schedule $\sigma = (\sigma_j : j \in \mathcal{J}) \in \mathcal{S}$ is a vector in $\mathbb{Z}_+^{\mathcal{J}}$ where σ_j gives the number of jobs that will be served from queue j under schedule σ. We assume the zero vector, $\mathbf{0}$, belongs to $\mathcal{S}$. We let $\sigma_{\max}$ give the maximum value of σ_j for $\sigma \in \mathcal{S}$. We let $<\mathcal{S}>$ be the convex combination of schedules in $\mathcal{S}$. We assume $<\mathcal{S}>$ has a non-empty interior. For real numbers $q, s \in \mathbb{R}$, we define $q \wedge s = \min\{q, s\}$. For vectors $q, s \in \mathbb{R}^{\mathcal{J}}$, we define $q \wedge s = (q_j \wedge s_j : j \in \mathcal{J})$. For a vector of queue sizes $Q \in \mathbb{Z}_+^{\mathcal{J}}$, we define

$$\mathcal{S}_Q = \{\sigma \wedge Q : \sigma \in \mathcal{S}\}.$$

Given that not all jobs can be served from a queue j when $Q_j < \sigma_j$, the set $\mathcal{S}_Q$ gives the set of schedules available given the vector of queue sizes Q. We let $<\mathcal{S}_Q>$ be the convex combination of points in $\mathcal{S}_Q$.

2.1 Single-hop Switched Network

For a *single-hop network*, once a packet has been served at its queue it departs the network.

We let $a(t) = (a_j(t) : j \in \mathcal{J}) \in \mathbb{Z}_+^{\mathcal{J}}$ be the number of arrivals occurring at each queue at time $t \in \mathbb{Z}_+$. We assume $\{a(t)\}_{t=0}^{\infty}$ is a sequence of independent identically distributed random vectors with finite mean $\bar{a} \in (0, \infty)^{\mathcal{J}}$ and finite second moment $\mathbb{E}[a_j(t)^2] \leq K$ for $j \in \mathcal{J}$.[1]

We let $Q(0) = (Q_j(0) : j \in \mathcal{J})$ be the number of jobs in each queue at time $t = 0$. From a sequence of schedules $\{\sigma(t)\}_{t=1}^{\infty}$, we can define the queue size vector $Q(t) = (Q_j(t) : j \in \mathcal{J})$ by

$$Q_j(t+1) = Q_j(t) - \sigma_j(t+1) + a_j(t+1), \qquad (1)$$

for $j \in \mathcal{J}$, and $t \in \mathbb{N}$. For positive queue sizes, we require that $\sigma_j(t+1) \in \mathcal{S}_{Q(t)}$, for all $t \in \mathbb{Z}_+$.[2] It is well known that queue sizes cannot be stabilized when the arrival rates $\bar{a}$ lie outside the set $<\mathcal{S}>$, for instance, see [36]. For this reason, we give the following definition.

Given $\{Q(t)\}_{t=0}^{\infty}$ defines a Markov chain, we say the queue size process is *maximum stable* if it is positive recurrent whenever the vector of arrival rates, $\bar{a}$, belongs to the interior of $<\mathcal{S}>$.

2.2 Multihop Switched Network

In a multihop network we allow packets to visit multiple queues within the network before departing. We will develop

[1]The assumption of finite variance is not essential; however, it allows for bounds more convenient for our proofs.

[2]Observe, this choice of notation is equivalent to defining the queueing process by $Q_j(t+1) = [Q_j(t) - \sigma_j(t+1)]_+ + a_j(t+1)$.

our notation in a similar way to Tassiulas and Ephremides [36].

As in the previous section, we let the finite set $\mathcal{J}$ index the set of queues or links of a network. We let $\mathcal{N}$ define the set of nodes of a network. We consider each link $j \in \mathcal{J}$ to be a directed edge in this network $j = (n, n') \in \mathcal{N} \times \mathcal{N}$. We let $\mathcal{R}$ be a set of routes through the network. Here each $r = (n_1^r, ..., n_{k_r}^r) \in \mathcal{R}$ is an ordered set of nodes such that $j_k^r := (n_k^r, n_{k+1}^r) \in \mathcal{J}$ for $k = 1, ..., k_r - 1$. A route r packet served at node n_k must next visit node n_{k+1} using link j_k^r. We apply the notation $j \in r$ if link j is part of route r. Further, for each $j \in r$, we let j_-^r and j_+^r denote the previous (upstream) and the next (downstream) link on route r.

We let $a(t) = (a_{jr}(t) : j \in \mathcal{J}, r \in \mathcal{R}) \in \mathbb{Z}_+^{\mathcal{J}\times\mathcal{R}}$ be the number of external arrivals occurring at the ingress $j = j_1^r$ of each route r at each time $t \in \mathbb{Z}_+$. Note $a_{jr}(t) = 0$ unless the queue is the first on its route, $j = j_1^r$. We assume $\{a(t)\}_{t=0}^{\infty}$ is a sequence of independent identically distributed random vectors with finite mean $\bar{a} = (\bar{a}_{jr} : r \in \mathcal{R}, j \in \mathcal{J}) \in \mathbb{R}_+^{\mathcal{J}\times\mathcal{R}}$ and finite second moment $\mathbb{E}\big[a_{jr}(t)^2\big] \leq K$ for all $r \in \mathcal{R}$ $j \in \mathcal{J}$. We define the load on queue $j \in \mathcal{J}$ by

$$\bar{a}_j = \sum_{r:j\in r} \bar{a}_{jr}. \tag{2}$$

Also we let $\bar{a}_r := \bar{a}_{j_1^r r}$ be the arrival rate of route r.

We let $Q_j(t)$ denote the number of packets who must next be served along link j. We let $X_{jr}(t)$ be the number of route r packets who will next be served over link j at time t. Thus, it holds that

$$Q_j(t) = \sum_{r:j\in r} X_{jr}(t). \tag{3}$$

We must describe the queueing dynamics for the queue size process $X(t) = (X_{jr}(t) : j \in \mathcal{J}, r \in \mathcal{R})$. In particular – in constrast to single-hop networks which are single-class – because we are considering a multi-class queueing network, once the links have been scheduled we must also decide which routes will be served. For the BackPressure policy, this would involve comparing the queue size for each route at the queue and at the next downstream node. Shortly, we will explain how this decision is made as part of a Proportional Scheduler. In any case, given a schedule $\sigma(t) \in \mathcal{S}_{Q(t)}$ is chosen at time t, we let $\xi(t) = (\xi_{jr}(t) : j \in \mathcal{J}, r \in \mathcal{R})$ denote the number of route r packets served from queue j under schedule $\sigma(t)$. For $\xi(t)$, the following constraints must hold

$$\sum_{r:j\in r} \xi_{jr}(t) = \sigma_j(t), \qquad \xi_{jr}(t) \leq X_{jr}(t).$$

That is the number of jobs served from each class is the number scheduled and we cannot schedule more jobs from each class than there are at the queue. Given this, the queueing dynamics of a multihop switch network are as follows

$$X_{jr}(t+1) = X_{jr}(t) + a_{jr}(t+1) - \xi_{jr}(t+1) + \xi_{j'r}(t+1) \tag{4}$$

where for each $r \in \mathcal{R}$ and each link $j \in r$ its upstream link j'.[3] Notice that once a packet has been served at its queue it joins the next queue on its route. We call this a *multihop network with fixed routing*. It is well known that queue sizes cannot be stabilized when the arrival rates $\bar{a}$ lie outside the set $<\mathcal{S}>$, for instance, see [36]. For this reason, we give the following definition.

[3]If no upsteam link exists for j then we set $\xi_{j'r}(t+1) = 0$.

Given the process $\{X(t)\}_{t=0}^{\infty}$ is a Markov chain, we say the queue size process is *maximum stable* if it is positive recurrent whenever the vector of arrival rates, $(\bar{a}_j : j \in \mathcal{J})$, belongs to the interior of $<\mathcal{S}>$.

3. SWITCH POLICIES

We now define the main switching policies considered in this paper. For single-hop networks, we introduce the (α, g)-switch policies and, for multihop networks, we consider the Proportional Scheduler.

3.1 The $(\alpha$, g)-Switch Policy

We let α be a positive real number and, for each $j \in \mathcal{J}$, we let $g_j : \mathbb{R}_+ \to \mathbb{R}$ be a strictly increasing, differentiable, strictly concave function. Given a queue size vector $Q(t) = (Q_j(t) : j \in \mathcal{J})$ at time t, we define $\bar{\sigma}(t+1) = (\bar{\sigma}_j(t+1) : j \in \mathcal{J})$ to be a solution to the optimization

$$\text{maximize} \quad \sum_{j\in\mathcal{J}} g_j(s_j) Q_j(t)^{\alpha} \tag{5a}$$

$$\text{over} \quad s \in <\mathcal{S}_{Q(t)}> . \tag{5b}$$

In general, $\bar{\sigma}(t+1)$ need not belong to the set of schedules $\mathcal{S}_{Q(t)}$. However, $\bar{\sigma}(t)$ is a convex combination of points in $<\mathcal{S}_{Q(t)}>$. Thus we let $\sigma(t+1)$ be a random variable with support on $\mathcal{S}_{Q(t)}$ and mean $\bar{\sigma}(t+1)$. The (α, g)-switch policy scheduling policy is the policy that chooses schedule $\sigma(t)$ at each time $t \in \mathbb{N}$.

To be concrete, we assume the random variables $\sigma(t)$ are, respectively, a function of $Q(t-1)$ and an independent (uniform) random variable. This ensures that the queue size process $\{Q(t)\}_{t=0}^{\infty}$ associated with the (α, g)-switch policy scheduling policy is a discrete-time Markov chain. Further, the constraints (5b) ensure that a schedule never exceeds the queue it serves.

MaxWeight, Utility optimization and α-fairness

We now briefly compare the class of policies above with the MaxWeight and network utility optimizing allocations. A MaxWeight-α allocation policy would be the special case of the optimization problem (5) when $g_j(s_j) = s_j$,

$$\text{maximize} \quad \sum_{j\in\mathcal{J}} s_j Q_j(t)^{\alpha} \quad \text{over} \quad s \in \mathcal{S}_{Q(t)}. \tag{6}$$

A network utility maximizing allocation in the sense of [18] would correspond to an optimization of the form

$$\text{maximize} \quad \sum_{j\in\mathcal{J}} g_j\left(\frac{s_j}{Q_j(t)}\right) Q_j(t) \quad \text{over} \quad s \in <\mathcal{S}> . \tag{7}$$

Notice in this policy, terms $s_j/Q_j(t)$ are applied to concave g_j, whilst the (α, g)-policy just applies s_j. The $s_j/Q_j(t)$ term is included for bandwidth network because it applies processor-sharing system to each transfer. However, since a switch-network applies its discipline to each component of the switch, we do not divide by Q_j. A further technical point is that, when compared with the (α, g)-policies, it is significantly harder to prove the stability of the above bandwidth network.

A further interesting case is the α-fair family of bandwidth allocation policies, as first introduced by Mo and Walrand

[25]. For $\alpha > 0$ and $\alpha \neq 1$, these are defined as follows

$$\text{maximize} \quad \sum_{j\in\mathcal{J}} \frac{s_j^{1-\alpha}}{1-\alpha} Q_j(t)^\alpha \quad \text{over} \quad s \in <\mathcal{S}> .$$

We remark that the (α, g)-switch policy coincides with the MaxWeight-α policy when $g_j(s_j) = s_j^{1-\alpha}/(1-\alpha)$. For switch-networks, the α-fair policy is first considered by Shah and Wischik [31].

Fluid Model

The fluid model associated with the (α, g)-switch policy is a positive, absolutely continuous process $q(t) = (q_j(t) : j \in \mathcal{J})$, $t \in \mathbb{R}_+$, where, for $j \in \mathcal{J}$ and for almost every[4] time $t \in \mathbb{R}_+$, if $q_j(t) > 0$ then

$$\frac{dq_j}{dt} = \bar{a}_j - \sigma_j^*(q(t)). \tag{8}$$

Here $\sigma^*(q)$ solves the optimization

$$\text{maximize} \quad \sum_{j\in\mathcal{J}} g_j(s_j) q_j^\alpha \quad \text{over} \quad s \in <\mathcal{S}> . \tag{9}$$

Note that we optimize over $<\mathcal{S}>$ rather than $<\mathcal{S}_q>$.

We say that a fluid model is *stable* if there exists a time $T > 0$ such that, for every $\{q(t)\}_{t\in\mathbb{R}_+}$ satisfying (8) and with $||q(0)||_1 = 1$,

$$q_j(t) = 0, \qquad j \in \mathcal{J}, \tag{10}$$

for all $t \geq T$. Here and hereafter, $|| \cdot ||_1$ is the L_1-norm.

3.2 Proportional Scheduler

We now describe a scheduling policy for multihop networks. Given a vector of link queue sizes $(Q_j(t) : j \in \mathcal{J})$, the Proportional Scheduler for multihop networks is defined as follows

PS1. Over set of schedules $<\mathcal{S}_{Q(t)}>$ solve the optimization

$$\text{maximize} \quad \sum_{j\in\mathcal{J}} Q_j(t)\log(s_j) \tag{11a}$$

$$\text{over} \quad s \in <\mathcal{S}_{Q(t)}> . \tag{11b}$$

As previously, let $\sigma(t+1)$ be a random variable on $\mathcal{S}_{Q(t)}$ whose mean solves this optimization.

PS2. From each queue $j \in \mathcal{J}$, serve $\sigma_j(t+1)$ packets selected uniformly at random from $Q_j(t)$ packets at the queue. These then join their next downstream node as determine by their route class.

Notice we do not need to know the routes used by packets in order to define the above policy. We assume that, after service at a queue, packets go to the next hop on their respective routes. The optimization (11) is due to Kelly [18] and is called the proportional fair optimization. We refer to the policy as the *Proportional Scheduler.*[5]

[4]By *almost every*, we mean on all points except for a set of Lebesgue measure zero.

[5]Since fairness is not, as such, an objective in our scheduling discipline, we omit the use of the word fair.

The BackPressure Policy

We now briefly compare the Proportional Scheduler with the BackPressure policy. For multihop networks, the principle maximal stable policy has been the BackPressure policy.

Given the vector of queue sizes $(X_{jr}(t) : j \in \mathcal{J}, r \in \mathcal{R})$, this policy is defined by the following three steps

BP1. For each link $j = (n, n') \in \mathcal{J}$ directed out of each node $n \in \mathcal{N}$, calculate weights by comparing with upstream queue lengths,

$$w_j(X(t)) = \max_{r:j\in r} \left\{ X_{jr}(t) - X_{j_+^r r}(t), 0 \right\},^6 \tag{12}$$

and let $r_j^*(X(t))$ be the solution to this maximization.

BP2. Over set of schedules $\mathcal{S}$, solve the optimization

$$\max_{\sigma\in\mathcal{S}} \sum_{j\in\mathcal{J}} \sigma_j w_j(X(t)), \tag{13}$$

and let $\sigma^*(X(t))$ be the solution to this optimization.

BP3. If $w_j(X(t)) > 0$, at the next time instance schedule $\sigma_j^*(X(t))$ packets from route $r_j^*(X(t))$ from each link $j \in \mathcal{J}$, else, do not schedule any packets on link j.

MaxWeight is the special case of BackPressure when we consider a single-hop network. Notice in the first step above, information must be exchanged along links to make a queue size comparison (12).

In contrast to BackPressure, the Proportional Scheduler does not maintain a queue for each route. It maintains a queue for each link. Further, the Proportional Scheduler does not compare queue sizes with downstream queues. Thus the policy is, in a certain sense, more decentralized. In the Proportional Scheduler packets are selected at random from the queue. In most communications systems packets are served according to a first-in-first-out discipline. We remark that it is possible to prove maximum stability results when the randomized queueing discipline PF2 is replaced by a FIFO queueing discipline. However, the proof is significantly more technical in nature. We refer the read to the forthcoming article for a proof [6]

Tree Network Example

To emphasis the advantages of the queueing structure of our policy. We consider a tree network where each node of degree d and diameter D. See Figure 1 for a tree of degree $d = 3$ and diameter $D = 6$. BackPressure, as described above, requires each node to maintain a queue for each route passing through it. Thus, one can verify, that for this network the central node of a tree must maintain a number of queues given by

$$d(d-1)^{(D-1)}.$$

For this example all routes with the same destination can be merged once they intersect. For this reason, BackPressure can be implemented slightly more efficiently in each node by storing a queue for each destination, however even in this case the number of queue's required grows as

$$d(d-1)^{(D/2-1)}.$$

[6]Here if there is no next link after j on route r then we set $X_{j_+^r r} = 0$.

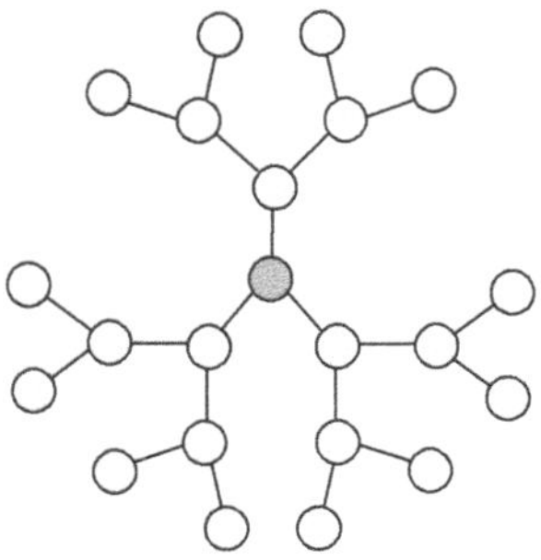

Figure 1: A tree network of depth $d = 3$ and diameter $D = 6$. There are 12 leaf nodes and thus $132 = 12 \cdot 11$ directed routes between leaf nodes.

In otherwords, to implement BackPressure the nodes of this network must maintain a number of queues that grows exponentially with the diameter of the network. In general, one expects the number of queues required to implement BackPressure to grow substantially with the network's size. However, we observe the Proportional Scheduler maintains a queue for each outgoing link from a node. That is for each node n the policy maintains a queue for each $j = (n, n') \in \mathcal{J}$ rather than each link-route pair $(j, r) \in \mathcal{J} \times \mathcal{R}$. Thus, in our example, a Proportional Scheduler would require a number of queues given by d. This is significantly smaller than the number required by BackPressure. In general, for the Proportional Scheduler to be implemented each node requires a queue for each neighboring node, which is smaller than the network size and is often bounded as we increases the size of a network.

Fluid Model

The fluid model associated with the multihop network operating under the Proportional Scheduler, is a positive, absolutely continuous process $x(t) = (x_{jr}(t) : j \in \mathcal{J}, r \in \mathcal{R})$ and $q(t) = (q_j(t) : j \in \mathcal{J})$, $t \in \mathbb{R}_+$, where for almost every[7] time $t \in \mathbb{R}_+$,

$$\frac{dx_{jr}}{dt} = \frac{x_{j^r_- r}(t)}{q_{j^r_-}(t)} \sigma^*_{j^r_-}(q(t)) - \frac{x_{jr}(t)}{q_j(t)} \sigma^*_j(q(t)), \tag{14}$$

where $\sigma^*(q)$ solves the optimization

$$\text{maximize} \qquad \sum_{j \in \mathcal{J}} q_j \log s_j \qquad \text{over} \qquad s \in <\mathcal{S}> . \tag{15}$$

Above, we apply the convention that

$$q_j(t) = \sum_{r : j \in r} x_{jr}(t). \tag{16}$$

Further, in the equation (14), if the queue j is the first queue on route r, i.e. $j = j^r_1$ and $j^r_- = j^r_0$, then we apply the convention that [8]

$$\frac{x_{j^r_0 r}(t)}{q_{j^r_0}(t)} \sigma^*_{j^r_0}(q(t)) = \bar{a}_{jr}. \tag{17}$$

In this way, we account for external arrivals.

4. MAIN RESULTS

The main results of this article is to prove maximum stability for the (α, g)-switch policies in single-hop networks and to prove maximum stability for the Proportional Scheduler in multihop networks with fixed routing. These results are stated as follows

THEOREM 1. *For the (α, g)-switch policy, if the vector of average arrival rates $\bar{a} = (\bar{a}_j : j \in \mathcal{J})$ belongs to the interior of $< \mathcal{S} >$ then the queue size process $\{Q(t)\}_{t=0}^{\infty}$ is positive recurrent.*

THEOREM 2. *For the Proportional Scheduler applied to a multihop switched network, if the vector of average arrival rates $\bar{a} = (\bar{a}_j : j \in \mathcal{J})$ belongs to the interior of $<\mathcal{S}>$ then the fluid model of this system is stable.*

The first result is proven by appropriately modifying the Lyapunov argument of Bonald and Massoulié for weighted α-fair bandwidth networks. For the second result, we give two proofs. The first proof shows how the result can be demonstrated within the framework of Massoulié [22]. Essentially Massoulié's result proves maximum stability of proportional fairness in single-class networks with probabilistic routing (i.e. Jackson type [14]), whilst we wish to prove maximum stability of proportional fairness for multiclass networks with fixed routing (i.e. Kelly type [2, 19]). We note that, due to the structure of the logarithm used to define the Proportional Scheduler, the latter problem can be reduced to the former. The second proof observes the result can be proven within the framework of Bramson [4]. Bramson shows the stability of fluid models of networks of processor sharing queues. We show by the differentiability properties of the proportionally fair objective that the fluid model for the Proportional Scheduler has essentially the same behavior as a network of processor sharing queues. Both these proofs and a number of consequences and conjectures rely on deeper connections with reversible queueing systems. These are described in the forthcoming paper [6].

Theorem 1 shows that the class of (α, g)-switch policies have the same stability properties as the MaxWeight policies. This, like MaxWeight, is proven for single-hop networks; however, for multiclass queueing networks, results that hold for single-hop systems do not naturally extend when directly applied multihop systems. See Chapter 3 of Bramson [5] for various counter examples of this type. This point is particularly poignant for switch networks where there has been a great deal of recent progress on the stability of single-hop switch networks, [16, 28]. Theorem 2 gives the first result where stability of a single-hop switch network implies stability of its multihop counterpart without requiring additional routing information. See Dieker and

[7]By *almost every*, we mean on all points except for a set of Lebesgue measure zero.

[8]This is similar to the proof of Bramson [4] for Head of the line processor sharing networks. Bramson introduces an additional queue for each route as a proof device. Whilst here, the introduction of j^r_0 is purely for notational and conceptual convenience.

Shin [11] for some recent related work. The result relies on the specific properties of the proportional fair optimization. Nonetheless the hope is this initial result will lead to general methods for extending stability results from single-hop to multihop networks.

There are a number of immediate advantages of the proportional fair optimization in comparison to BackPressure. We only need to maintain a queue for each outgoing link, whilst BackPressure requires a vastly more complex data structure. BackPressure must know the route class of each packet within the network to make a routing decision whilst for our policy packets can be routed by only knowing each packets next hop. Messages do not need to be sent to calculate weights and so scheduling decisions can be completely decomposed between independently functioning components. That is, if $\mathcal{S}$ and $\mathcal{J}$ can be split into independent components $\prod_k \mathcal{S}_k$ and $\cup_k \mathcal{J}_k$, then

$$\max_{s\in<\mathcal{S}>} \sum_{j\in\mathcal{J}} Q_j(t)\log s_j = \sum_k \max_{s\in<\mathcal{S}_k>} \sum_{j\in\mathcal{J}_k} Q_j(t)\log s_j.$$

Here we imagine each $\mathcal{S}_k$ corresponds to the constraints of an independent network component, for example, an input queued switch for each k. The above statement shows that, without messaging, we can solve this optimization separately for each component, implement the decision and still guarantee stability.

Informally speaking, for the Proportional Scheduler, does not need to know the route structure of the network to make a scheduling decision, whilst BackPressure does. For this reason, the proportional fair implementation, scales far better with network size.

5. PROOF OF THEOREM 1

The proof of Theorem 1 follows the fluid limit approach of Dai [9]. We prove that a certain fluid model is satisfied by the limit of a sequence Markov chains using (α, g)-switch policy. We prove that the associated fluid model with the (α, g)-policy is stable. We then give a proof of positive recurrence of the original Markov chain.

5.1 Fluid model

In this section, we state fluid model equations and the fluid limit associated with the (α, g)-switch policy.

Let $\{Q^{(c)}\}_{c\in\mathbb{N}}$ be a sequence of versions of our queueing process for the (α, g)-switch policy, where $||Q(0)||_1 = c$. We define

$$\bar{Q}^{(c)}(t) = \frac{Q^{(c)}(\lfloor ct\rfloor)}{c}, \tag{18}$$

for $t \in \mathbb{R}_+$. The following result formalizes a fluid model q, (8), as the limit of $\{\bar{Q}^{(c)}\}_{c\in\mathbb{N}}$. In informal terms, it states that the only possible limit of the sequence $\{\bar{Q}^{(c)}\}_{c\in\mathbb{N}}$ as $c \to \infty$ is a process q satisfying (8).

Proposition 1 (Fluid Limit). *The sequence of stochastic processes $\{\bar{Q}^{(c)}\}_{c\in\mathbb{N}}$ is tight*[9] *with respect to the topology of uniform convergence on compact time intervals. Moreover, any weakly convergent subsequence of $\{\bar{Q}^{(c)}\}_{c\in\mathbb{N}}$ converges to a Lipschitz continuous process satisfying fluid equation (8).*

[9]Recall a sequence of random processes $\{\bar{Q}^{(c)}\}_c$ is tight if every subsequence of $\{\bar{Q}^{(c)}\}_c$ has a weakly convergent subsequence.

The statement of Proposition 1 is somewhat technical. However, the main point is that we can compare the queueing process to a tractable fluid model, q satisfying equations (8). The proof of Proposition 1 is somewhat standard. We refer the reader to Robert [26]. We now analyze the stability of the fluid models.

5.2 Fluid Stability

We consider a process $\{q(t)\}_{t\in\mathbb{R}_+}$, that satisfies the fluid limit equations (8). In the following theorem, we show that these fluid solutions are stable in the sense that they hit the zero state in finite time. This result will be sufficient to prove positive recurrence of the (α, g)-switch policy.

Proposition 2 (Fluid Stability). *Given $(\bar{a}_j : j \in \mathcal{J})$ belongs to the interior of $<\mathcal{S}>$. There exists a time $T > 0$ such that, for every fluid model $\{q(t)\}_{t\in\mathbb{R}_+}$ satisfying (8) and with $||q(0)||_1 = 1$,*

$$q_j(t) = 0, \qquad j \in \mathcal{J}, \tag{19}$$

for all $t \geq T$.

The main idea is to consider the gradient of the tangent line of the (α, g)-switch policy objective between two points: the arrival rate and the optimal solution, see (21) below. Integrating this obtains a Lyapunov function (23). This idea is used by Bonald and Massoulié [3] in their analysis of weighted α-fair bandwidth sharing networks. For switch networks, Proposition 2 follows analogously.

Proof. We define $G_q(s)$ to be the objective of the (α, g)-switch policy optimization,

$$G_q(s) = \sum_{j\in\mathcal{J}} g_j(s_j)q_j^{\alpha}. \tag{20}$$

Recall that in our fluid equations

$$\sigma^*(q(t)) \in \operatorname*{argmax}_{s\in<\mathcal{S}>} G_{q(t)}(s).$$

Any vector ρ belonging to the interior of $<\mathcal{S}>$ is not optimal. Thus $G_{q(t)}(\rho) < G_{q(t)}(\sigma^*(q(t)))$. As $G_{q(t)}(\cdot)$ is strictly concave, $G_{q(t)}(\cdot)$ must be increasing along the line connecting ρ to $\sigma^*(q(t))$. In other words, for all ρ in the interior of $<\mathcal{S}>$ and for $q(t) \neq 0$,

$$\Big(\sigma^*(q(t)) - \rho\Big) \cdot \nabla G_{q(t)}(\rho) > 0. \tag{21}$$

Here $\nabla G_q(\rho) = (g_j'(\rho_j)q_j(t)^{\alpha} : j \in \mathcal{J})$. Since $\bar{a}$ belongs to the interior of $<\mathcal{S}>$, there exists $\epsilon > 0$ such that $(1+\epsilon)\bar{a} \in <\mathcal{S}>$. We define $\rho = (1+\epsilon)\bar{a}$. In this case, we can re-express the inequality (21) as follows

$$\sum_{j\in\mathcal{J}} \Big(\bar{a}_j - \sigma_j^*(q(t))\Big) g_j'(\rho_j)q_j(t)^{\alpha} \leq -\epsilon \sum_{j\in\mathcal{J}} g_j'(\rho_j)q_j(t)^{\alpha}. \tag{22}$$

As $\frac{dq_j}{dt} = \bar{a}_j - \sigma_j^*(q(t))$, we define the Lyapunov function

$$L(q) = \sum_{j\in\mathcal{J}} g'(\rho_j)\frac{q_j^{1+\alpha}}{1+\alpha}, \tag{23}$$

$q \in \mathbb{R}_+^{\mathcal{J}}$. The function $L(q)$ is positive, and $L(q) = 0$ iff $q_j = 0$ for all $j \in \mathcal{J}$. We now observe

$$\frac{dL(q(t))}{dt} = \sum_{j\in\mathcal{J}} \Big(\bar{a}_j - \sigma_j^*(q(t))\Big) g_j'(\rho_j) q_j(t)^\alpha \qquad (24)$$

$$\leq -\epsilon \sum_{j\in\mathcal{J}} g_j'(\rho_j) q_j(t)^\alpha. \qquad (25)$$

The equality holds by the chain rule and the inequality holds by (22).

We define two norms on $\mathbb{R}_+^{\mathcal{J}}$

$$||q||_{1+\alpha} = (L(q))^{\frac{1}{1+\alpha}}, \quad ||q||_\alpha = \Big(\sum_{j\in\mathcal{J}} g_j'(\rho_j) q_j(t)^\alpha\Big)^{\frac{1}{\alpha}}.$$

By the Lipschitz equivalence of norms, there is a constant $\gamma > 0$ such that

$$\gamma ||q||_{1+\alpha} \leq ||q||_\alpha,$$

for all $q \in \mathbb{R}_+^{\mathcal{J}}$.[10] Applying this observation to the inequality (25), we see that

$$\frac{dL(q(t))}{dt} \leq -\epsilon\gamma^\alpha L(q(t))^{\frac{\alpha}{1+\alpha}}. \qquad (26)$$

Observe, by the above inequality, if $L(q(T)) = 0$ for any differentiable point T then $L(q(t)) = 0$ for all $t \geq T$. Now, whilst $L(q(t)) > 0$, we have from (26) that

$$\begin{aligned} &L(q(t))^{\frac{1}{1+\alpha}} - L(q(0))^{\frac{1}{1+\alpha}} \\ &= \int_0^t (1+\alpha)^{-1} L(q(t))^{\frac{-\alpha}{1+\alpha}} \frac{dL(q(t))}{dt} dt \\ &\leq -\epsilon(1+\alpha)^{-1}\gamma^\alpha t. \end{aligned}$$

Rearranging this expression, we see that for all times t

$$L(q(t)) \leq \Big(L(q(0))^{\frac{1}{1+\alpha}} - \epsilon(1+\alpha)^{-1}\gamma^\alpha t\Big)_+^{1+\alpha}. \qquad (27)$$

The function $L(q)$ is continuous and therefore bounded above by a constant, K, for all values of q with $||q||_1 = 1$. Hence, if $||q(0)||_1 = 1$, $L(q(t)) = 0$ for all $t \geq T$ where

$$T = \frac{(1+\alpha)K^{\frac{1}{1+\alpha}}}{\epsilon\gamma^\alpha},$$

and thus, as required, $q_j(t) = 0$, $j \in \mathcal{J}$, for all $t \geq T$. □

The MaxWeight policies are designed to minimize the drift of a Lyapunov function. Notice, if we applied this rationale to L, above, then minimizing (24) would recover a form of MaxWeight-α policy. However, an interesting feature of the approach of Bonald and Massoulie [?] that is applied above is that the policy considered is not designed to minimize drift and thus resources are shared between different schedules rather than prioritized. This is an important feature when extending to multihop networks. Further, because of this feature, solutions to the optimization change continuously with changes in queue size. This could be important from a computation perspective when tracking the current optimal policy.

[10] Note, $||q||_{1+\alpha} \leq (1+\alpha)^{-\frac{1}{1+\alpha}} |\mathcal{J}| \max_j g_j'(\rho_j) q_j$ and also note that $\max_j g_j'(\rho_j) q_j \leq ||q||_\alpha$. So, for instance, we can take $\gamma = (1+\alpha)^{\frac{1}{1+\alpha}} |\mathcal{J}|^{-1}$.

5.3 Positive Recurrence

We are now in a position to combine Propositions 1 and 2 to prove Theorem 1. We can at this point apply the general stability results of Dai [9, 10] and Bramson [5].

PROOF OF THEOREM 1. For every $t \geq 0$, the sequence of queue sizes $\{\bar{Q}^{(c)}(t)\}_{c\in\mathbb{N}}$ is uniformly integrable. This is because the queue size process $\bar{Q}^{(c)}(t)$ is less than the number of arrivals $\bar{A}^{(c)}$, which is L^2 bounded, since we assume its increments have bounded variance. Now, by Proposition 1, for any unbounded sequence in $\mathbb{N}$, there is a subsequence $\{c_k\}_{k\in\mathbb{N}}$ for which $\bar{Q}^{(c_k)}$ converges in distribution to fluid solution q. Let T be the time given in Proposition 2, where $q_j(T) = 0$ for $j \in \mathcal{J}$. Since $\{|\bar{Q}^{(c_k)}(T)|\}_{c_k}$ is uniformly integrable and converges in distribution to $q(T)$, we also have L_1 convergence

$$\lim_{c_k\to\infty} \mathbb{E}||\bar{Q}^{(c_k)}(T)||_1 = \mathbb{E}||q(T)||_1 = 0. \qquad (28)$$

This implies there exists a κ such that for all $c > \kappa$

$$\mathbb{E}||\bar{Q}^{(c)}(T)||_1 < (1-\epsilon). \qquad (29)$$

Note that if (29) did not hold then we could find a subsequence for which (28) did not hold; thus, we would have a contradiction. Expanding this inequality (29), we have as described by Bramson [5], the following *multiplicative Foster's condition*: for $\big|\big|Q(0)\big|\big|_1 > \kappa$

$$\mathbb{E}\Big[\big|\big|Q(T||Q(0)||_1)\big|\big|_1 - \big|\big|Q(0)\big|\big|_1 \Big| Q(0)\Big] < -\epsilon\big|\big|Q(0)\big|\big|_1. \qquad (30)$$

This then implies our process is positive recurrent, see [5, Proposition 4.6]. □

6. PROOF OF THEOREM 2

We give two proofs of Theorem 2. The first proof reduces our multiclass fixed routing structure (Kelly type) to a single-class routing structure (Jackson type). From here we can apply the fluid stability proof of Massoulié [22]. The second proof observes the Lyapunov function arguments of Bramson [4], which apply for head-of-the-line processor sharing queueing networks, can be extended when services rates are proportionally fair instead of fixed.

6.1 First Proof

We state the following result on the fluid model for a single-class proportionally fair system with probabilistic routing. Massoulié [22] considered a process $(q_j(t) : j \in \mathcal{J})$ satisfying, for $q_j(t) > 0$, the following system of fluid equations

$$\frac{dq_j}{dt} = a_j + \sum_{l\in\mathcal{J}} \sigma_l^*(q) p_{lj} - \sigma_j^*(q), \qquad (31)$$

where $\sigma_j^*(q)$ gives the solution to the proportionally fair optimization, (9). The matrix $P = (p_{lj})_{lj}$ gives the probability that a link l job next joins link j. So all packets depart this system, it is assumed that this matrix is substochastic. From this one can calculate from external arrival rates $a = (a_j : j \in \mathcal{J})$ the load induced on each link as

$$\bar{a} = (1 - P^\mathsf{T})^{-1} a. \qquad (32)$$

Massoulié proves the following fluid stability result.

THEOREM 3 (MASSOULIÉ '07). *If $\bar{a}$ belongs to the interior of the set $<\mathcal{S}>$ then the fluid equations (31) are stable.*

Since in Massoulié's model each packet leaving a link must have the same routing behavior, it is not immediately clear that the result extends to multiclass queueing networks where routing depends on a packet's route-class. However, the following lemma makes this possible

LEMMA 1. *For $j \in \mathcal{J}$, take positive vector $x^j = (x_{jr} : r \in \mathcal{R}, j \in r)$ and positive constant σ_j. Let q_j be the sum of the components of x^j. The following holds*

$$q_j \log \sigma_j + \sum_{r:j\in r} x_{jr} \log \frac{x_{jr}}{q_j} \tag{33}$$

$$= \max_{\gamma^j \geq 0} \sum_{r:j\in r} x_{jr} \log \gamma_{jr} \ s.t. \ \sum_{j\in r} \gamma_{jr} = \sigma_j \tag{34}$$

and the above optimization is solved by $\gamma_{jr} = \frac{x_{jr}\sigma_j}{q_j}$.

The lemma is left as an exercise. But what the lemma says is that if packets $x^j = (x_{jr} : r \in \mathcal{R}, j \in r)$ are sharing the resource j then under a proportional fair optimization they share it proportionately and, perhaps more importantly, the equality (33) shows that the form of the logarithm is the optimization remains unchanged after this optimization step. Thus, to solve a proportionally fair optimization given x_{jr}, we can solve the proportionally fair optimization given q_j, i.e. optimizing the $q_j \log \sigma_j$ terms in (33), and then assign rates according to a processor sharing discipline: $\gamma_{jr} = \frac{x_{jr}\sigma_j}{q_j}$. This describes the per-link queueing mechanism, PS2, described in Section 3.2, which possesses significant structural simplification when compared to other policies known to be maximum stable for multi-hop routed switch networks.

PROOF OF THEOREM 2. As a consequence of Lemma 1, we have that the optimization

$$\text{maximize} \quad \sum_{j\in\mathcal{J}} \sum_{r\in\mathcal{R}} x_{jr} \log \gamma_{jr} \tag{35a}$$

$$\text{subject to} \quad \sum_{r:j\in r} \gamma_{jr} = \sigma_j, \ j \in \mathcal{J}, \tag{35b}$$

$$\text{over} \quad \sigma \in <\mathcal{S}>, \tag{35c}$$

is equivalent to solving the optimization

$$\text{maximize} \quad \sum_{j\in\mathcal{J}} q_j \log \sigma_j \tag{36a}$$

$$\text{over} \quad \sigma \in <\mathcal{S}>, \tag{36b}$$

and setting $\gamma^*_{jr}(x) = x_{jr}\sigma^*_j(q)/q_j$ where $\sigma^*_j(q)$ solves the above proportionally fair optimization.

Consider process $x(t) = (x_{jr}(t) : r \in \mathcal{R}, j \in r)$, a Massoulié network of the type (31) where classes are now indexed by (j,r). That is the stations of the network are no longer indexed by j, but by pairs class (j,r). After completeing service at (j,r) packets next join (j^+_r, r) with probability one. This system obeys the fluid equations[11]

$$\frac{dx_{jr}}{dt} = \gamma^*_{j^-_r r}(x(t)) - \gamma^*_{jr}(x(t)). \tag{37}$$

These equations are exactly of the form (31). Thus, by Massoulié [22], this system of fluid equations is stable. However, the equivalence of the optimizations (35) and (36) shows that this fluid system is the the same as our proportionally fair fluid model:

$$\frac{dx_{jr}}{dt} = \frac{x_{j^-_r r}(t)}{q_{j^-_r}(t)}\sigma^*_{j^-_r}(q(t)) - \frac{x_{jr}(t)}{q_j(t)}\sigma^*_j(q(t)).$$

Thus the stability of our fluid model now follows from Massoulié [22]. □

[11]Here $\gamma^*_{j^-_r r}(x(t)) = \bar{a}_r$ when j is the first queue on route r.

The observation of Lemma 1 and its implications to multi-hop switch systems is critical. After observing Lemma 1, the reduction to Massoulié's proof is straightforward. However, to this author at least, it was surprising that the multi-class system can be reduced to a single-class system in this way. For instance, it is not immediately clear that one can reduce stationarity results on BCMP-Kelly networks as a direct reduction from results on Jackson networks. Nonetheless, the fluid stability proof of Massoulié is not so straightforward. A second, direct proof can argued from Bramson [4]. As a brief aside: with Lemma 1 and Lemma 2 (below), the fluid stability result of Bramson for processor-sharing networks [4] and the fluid result of Massoulié for bandwidth networks [22] have some equivalence. However, such equivalences are, perhaps, less striking than their resulting implications for switch systems. We now see that, for the proportionally fair case, stability of a single-hop queueing network also implies stability of its multi-hop routed counterpart. Moreover, the queueing structure of this system is far simpler than Back-Pressure, the canonical class of multi-hop throughput optimal switch policies.

7. SECOND PROOF

Bramson considers the fluid model of a multiclass processor sharing queueing network. Here the service rate at queues $\sigma \in \mathbb{R}^{\mathcal{J}}_+$ is not a function of queue sizes. So, for $x_{jr}(t) > 0$, the fluid model of Bramson is as follows

$$\frac{dx_{jr}}{dt} = \frac{x_{j^-_r r}(t)}{q_{j^-_r}(t)}\sigma_{j^-_r} - \frac{x_{jr}(t)}{q_j(t)}\sigma_j.$$

Bramson considers a Lyapunov function

$$\hat{H}(x) = \sum_{r\in\mathcal{R}} \sum_{j\in r} x_{jr} \log\left(\frac{x_{jr}\sigma_j}{q_j \bar{a}_r}\right). \tag{38}$$

This is large deviations rate function associated with a network of processor sharing queues Informally speaking, his proof relies on the fact that the partial derivatives of this function are, for $x_{jr} > 0$,

$$\frac{\partial \hat{H}}{\partial x_{jr}} = \log\left(\frac{x_{jr}\sigma_j}{c_j \bar{a}_r}\right). \tag{39}$$

If we now replace σ with the proportionally fair solution $\sigma^*(q)$ and consider the following Lyapunov function

$$H(x) = \sum_{r\in\mathcal{R}} \sum_{j\in r} x_{jr} \log\left(\frac{x_{jr}\sigma^*_j(q)}{q_j \bar{a}_r}\right), \tag{40}$$

due to the properties of the proportionally fair optimization, the partial derivatives of this optimization remain the same. This is demonstrated in the following lemma.

LEMMA 2. *For $x_{jr} > 0$*

$$\frac{\partial H}{\partial x_{jr}} = \log\left(\frac{x_{jr}\sigma^*_j(q)}{q_j \bar{a}_r}\right). \tag{41}$$

Proof of Lemma 2. We take the partial derivative of $H(x)$ with respect to x_{jr} from first principles. For $h > 0$, define $x^h_{jr} = x_{jr} + h$ and $x^h_{j'r'} = x_{j'r'}$ for $r' \neq r$ and $j' \neq j$. Then

$$\begin{aligned}
&\frac{H(x^h) - H(x)}{h} \\
=&\frac{1}{h}\Bigg[\sum_{r\in\mathcal{R}}\sum_{j\in r} x^h_{jr} \log\left(\frac{x^h_{jr}\sigma^*_j(q^h)}{q^h_j \bar{a}_r}\right) \\
&\qquad - \sum_{r\in\mathcal{R}}\sum_{j\in r} x_{jr} \log\left(\frac{x_{jr}\sigma^*_j(q)}{q_j \bar{a}_r}\right)\Bigg] \\
\geq&\frac{1}{h}\Bigg[\sum_{r\in\mathcal{R}}\sum_{j\in r} x^h_{jr} \log\left(\frac{x^h_{jr}\sigma^*_j(q)}{q^h_j \bar{a}_r}\right) \\
&\qquad - \sum_{r\in\mathcal{R}}\sum_{j\in r} x_{jr} \log\left(\frac{x_{jr}\sigma^*_j(q)}{q_j \bar{a}_r}\right)\Bigg] \\
=&\log\left(\frac{\sigma^*_j(q)}{\bar{a}_r}\right) + \frac{1}{h}\left(x^h_{jr}\log x^h_{jr} - x_{jr}\log x_{jr}\right) \\
&+ \frac{1}{h}\left(q^h_j \log q^h_j - q_j \log q_j\right).
\end{aligned}$$

In the inequality above, we use the fact $\sigma^*_j(q)$ is suboptimal for proportional fair problem with parameter choice q^h. Applying the same argument but instead observing that $\sigma^*_j(q^h)$ is suboptimal for parameter choice q, we can also derive the bound

$$\begin{aligned}
&\frac{H(x^h) - H(x)}{h} \\
\leq&\log\left(\frac{\sigma^*_j(q^h)}{\bar{a}_r}\right) + \frac{1}{h}\left(x^h_{jr}\log x^h_{jr} - x_{jr}\log x_{jr}\right) \qquad (42)\\
&+ \frac{1}{h}\left(q^h_j \log q^h_j - q_j \log q_j\right). \qquad (43)
\end{aligned}$$

We remark that these same two bounds can also be derived in the case $h < 0$. The function $q \mapsto \sigma_j(q)$ is a continuous function for $q_j > 0$. This is proven in [20, Lemma A.3]. Thus taking the limit as $h \to 0$, both of these bounds together imply

$$\frac{\partial H(x)}{\partial x_{jr}} = \log\left(\frac{\sigma^*_j(q)}{\bar{a}_r}\right) + \log x_{jr} - \log q_j,$$

as required. □

With the addition of a few technical lemmas, we can now give a direct proof of Theorem 2. These additional technical lemmas are stated and proven after the proof of our main result.

Proof of Theorem 2. It is proven in Lemma 4 that $H(x)$ is positive and is minimized when $x = 0$. For $x_{jr} > 0$, it is proven in Lemma 2 that the partial derivatives of $H(x)$ with respect to x_{jr} are

$$\frac{\partial H}{\partial x_{jr}} = \log\left(\frac{x_{jr}\sigma^*_j(q)}{q_j \bar{a}_r}\right). \qquad (44)$$

Thus we can see that the following equalities hold

$$\begin{aligned}
\frac{dH}{dt} &= \sum_{r,j\in r} \frac{dx_{jr}}{dt}\frac{\partial H}{\partial x_{jr}} && (45)\\
&= \sum_{r,j\in r}\left(\frac{x_{j^r_- r}}{q_{j^r_-}}\sigma^*_{j^r_-}(q) - \frac{x_{jr}}{q_j}\sigma^*_j(q)\right)\log\left(\frac{x_{jr}\sigma^*_j(q)}{q_j\bar{a}_r}\right) && (46)\\
&= -\sum_{r\in\mathcal{R}}\bar{a}_r\sum_{j\in r}\frac{x_{jr}\sigma^*_j(q)}{q_j\bar{a}_r}\log\left(\frac{\left[\frac{x_{jr}\sigma^*_j(q)}{q_j\bar{a}_r}\right]}{\left[\frac{x_{j^r_+ r}\sigma^*_{j^r_+}(q)}{q_{j^r_+}\bar{a}_r}\right]}\right). && (47)
\end{aligned}$$

The first we apply chain rule. For (46), we substitute (44) and the definition of our fluid model (14). To derive (47), we increment the first terms of summation (46) so that the coefficients of the logarithms are equal. After multiplying and dividing by $\bar{a}_r$ we gain expression (47). Notice in the first equality, we include the term $j = j^r_0$. Since applying convention (17) we have, $\log((x_{jr}\sigma^*_j(q_j))/(q_j\bar{a}_r)) = \log 1 = 0$.

The following sequence of inequalities hold, for $q \neq 0$

$$\begin{aligned}
\frac{dH}{dt} \leq& -\sum_{r\in\mathcal{R}}\Bigg[\bar{a}_r\left(\sum_{j\in r}\frac{x_{jr}\sigma^*_j(q)}{q_j\bar{a}_r}\right)^{-1} \\
&\qquad\times\sum_{j\in r}\left(\frac{x_{jr}\sigma^*_{j^r}(q)}{q_{j^r}\bar{a}_r} - \frac{x_{j^r_+ r}\sigma^*_{j^r_+}(q)}{q_{j^r_+}\bar{a}_r}\right)^2\Bigg] \\
\leq& -\sum_{r\in\mathcal{R}}\Bigg[\bar{a}_r\left(\frac{\sigma_{max}}{\bar{a}_r}\right)^{-1} \\
&\qquad\times\sum_{j\in r}\left(\frac{x_{jr}\sigma^*_j(q)}{q_j\bar{a}_r} - \frac{x_{j^r_+ r}\sigma^*_{j^r_+}(q)}{q_{j^r_+}\bar{a}_r}\right)^2\Bigg] \\
\leq& -\epsilon.
\end{aligned}$$

In the first inequality, we apply entropy bound Lemma 5 to (47). In the second inequality, we apply the bound

$$\sum_{j\in r}\frac{x_{jr}\sigma^*_j(q)}{q_j\bar{a}_r} \leq \frac{\sigma_{max}}{\bar{a}_r}. \qquad (48)$$

In the third inequality, we apply the Lemma 6. This then shows that our Lyapunov function has strictly negative drift.

By Lemma 4, $H(x) = 0$ only if $x = 0$ and $H(x)$ is bounded when $||x||_1 = 1$. Thus, for all $x(0)$ such that $H(x(0)) \leq h$ for some constant $h > 0$ we have for all $t \geq h\epsilon^{-1}$

$$q(t) = 0. \qquad (49)$$

Thus, fluid stability holds. □

We now prove the lemmas required in the above proof. For two probability distributions p and q defined on the same finite set $\mathcal{X}$, the relative entropy between p and q is defined to be

$$D(p||q) = \sum_{x\in\mathcal{X}} p_x \log\frac{p_x}{q_x}.$$

The following bound on $D(p||q)$ holds

Lemma 3 (Pinsker's Inequality).

$$\sqrt{D(p||q)} \geq \sum_{x\in\mathcal{X}} |p_x - q_x|.$$

A proof of this bound is found in Cover and Thomas [8]. Relative entropy is positive continuous in p and minimized when $p = q$. This gives the following.

LEMMA 4. *The function $H(x)$ is positive, is bounded when $||x||_1 = 1$ and is minimized when $x = 0$.*

PROOF. Observe that, $H(x)$ can be expressed as linear combination of relative entropy terms as follows

$$H(x) = \sum_{j\in\mathcal{J}} q_j D\left(\left(\frac{x_{jr}}{q_j}\right)_{r\ni j}\middle|\middle|\left(\frac{\bar{a}_r}{a_j}\right)_{r\ni j}\right) + \sum_{j\in\mathcal{J}} q_j \log\frac{\sigma_j^*(q)}{a_j}$$
$$\geq \sum_{j\in\mathcal{J}} q_j \log\frac{\sigma_j^*(q)}{a_j} \geq 0. \quad (50)$$

The first inequality follows by the positivity of the relative entropy. The second inequality follows by the optimality of $\sigma_j^*(q)$ and the fact the vector $(a_j : j \in \mathcal{J})$ belongs to the interior of $<\mathcal{S}>$. From the form of the entropy equality above, we see that $H(x)$ is continuous for $||x||_1 = 1$ and so is bounded. Further, we note that the inequalities above hold with equality iff $x = 0$. □

If we now do not assume that p and q are probability distributions but instead we assume that they are positive and sum to the same constant, then $D(p||q)$ is still well defined the following is a consequence of Pinsker's Inequality.

LEMMA 5. *If p and q are two positive vectors components indexed by $\mathcal{X}$ and with*

$$\sum_{x\in\mathcal{X}} p_x = \sum_{x\in\mathcal{X}} q_x \quad (51)$$

then

$$\sum_{x\in\mathcal{X}} p_x \log\frac{p_x}{q_x} \geq \frac{1}{\sum_{x\in\mathcal{X}} p_x}\cdot\sum_{x\in\mathcal{X}}(p_x - q_x)^2. \quad (52)$$

PROOF. Define

$$\tilde{p}_x = \frac{p_x}{\sum_{y\in\mathcal{X}} p_y} \quad\text{and}\quad \tilde{q}_x = \frac{q_x}{\sum_{y\in\mathcal{X}} q_y} \quad (53)$$

Then

$$\sum_{x\in\mathcal{X}} p_x \log\frac{p_x}{q_x} = D(\tilde{p}||\tilde{q})\sum_{x\in\mathcal{X}} p_x$$
$$\geq \left(\sum_{x\in\mathcal{X}} |\tilde{p}_x - \tilde{q}_x|\right)^2 \sum_{x\in\mathcal{X}} p_x$$
$$= \frac{1}{\sum_{x\in\mathcal{X}} p_x}\left(\sum_{x\in\mathcal{X}} |p_x - q_x|\right)^2$$
$$\geq \frac{1}{\sum_{x\in\mathcal{X}} p_x}\sum_{x\in\mathcal{X}}(p_x - q_x)^2.$$

In the first equality above, we apply the definition of $D(\tilde{p}||\tilde{q})$; in the second, we apply Pinsker's Inequality; we then rearrange this term and bound to get the result. □

The follow lemma is used to prove that $H(t)$ has strictly negative drift.

LEMMA 6. *There exists $\epsilon > 0$ such that for $x \in \mathbb{R}_+^{\mathcal{R}\times\mathcal{J}}$*

$$\sum_{r\in\mathcal{R}} \bar{a}_r \left(\frac{\sigma_{max}}{\bar{a}_r}\right)^{-1} \sum_{j\in r}\left(\frac{x_{jr}\sigma_j^*(q)}{q_j\bar{a}_r} - \frac{x_{j_+^r r}\sigma_{j_+^r}^*(q)}{q_{j_+^r}\bar{a}_r}\right)^2 > \epsilon. \quad (54)$$

PROOF. First let's look what is required for the term on the left-hand side of (54) to equal zero – which, by the statement of the lemma, should give a contradiction. We would require that for each route $r \in \mathcal{R}$, for all $j \in r$

$$\frac{x_{jr}\sigma_j^*(q)}{q_j\bar{a}_r} - \frac{x_{j_+^r r}\sigma_{j_-^r}^*(q)}{q_{j_+^r}\bar{a}_r} = 0. \quad (55)$$

So the terms $\frac{x_{jr}\sigma_j^*(q)}{q_j\bar{a}_r}$ are constant over $j \in r$, including j_0. But $\frac{x_{j_0^r r}\sigma_{j_0^r}^*(q)}{q_{j_0^r}\bar{a}_r} = 1$. So we would require that, for all r and $j \in r$

$$\bar{a}_r = \frac{x_{jr}\sigma_j^*(q)}{q_j}.$$

Now summing over $r \in j$ we would require that

$$\bar{a}_j = \sum_{r:j\in r}\bar{a}_r = \sigma_j^*(q). \quad (56)$$

However, we now have a contradiction: by assumption $(\bar{a}_j : j \in \mathcal{J})$ does not belong to the boundary of the capacity set $<\mathcal{S}>$ while $(\sigma_j^*(q) : j \in \mathcal{J})$ does (because it is Pareto optimal). So the above inequality cannot hold. So the left-hand side of (54) cannot equal zero.

Now let's use this last contradiction to extrapolate back and prove the lemma. Since $(\bar{a}_j : j \in \mathcal{J})$ belongs to the interior of $<\mathcal{S}>$ and $\sigma_j^*(q) \in \partial<\mathcal{S}>$, there exist an $\delta > 0$ such that for each vector $q \neq 0$ there is some $j \in \mathcal{J}$ such that

$$\bar{a}_j + \delta < \sigma_j^*(q). \quad (57)$$

Thus, for the above inequality to hold, there exists some r with $j \in r$ such that

$$\bar{a}_r + \frac{\delta}{|r|} < \frac{x_{jr}}{q_j}\sigma_j^*(q) \quad (58)$$

or expressed differently,

$$\frac{x_{j_0^r r}\sigma_{j_0^r}^*(q)}{q_{j_0^r}\bar{a}_r} + \frac{\delta}{|r|\bar{a}_r} < \frac{x_{jr}\sigma_j^*(q)}{q_j\bar{a}_r}. \quad (59)$$

This for this to hold between j_0^r and j on route r there must be two links in the sequence l and l' on route r between j_0^r and j such that

$$\frac{\delta}{|r|^2 a_r} < \frac{x_{lr}\sigma_l^*(q)}{q_l\bar{a}_r} - \frac{x_{l'r}\sigma_{l'}^*(q)}{q_{l'}\bar{a}_r}. \quad (60)$$

Setting $\epsilon = (\frac{\delta}{|r|^2})^2\sigma_{\max}$, we see that (54) must hold. □

8. CONCLUSIONS AND FUTURE WORK

In this paper, we have considered a generalized class of switch policies. We have shown that these share the same maximum stability properties as MaxWeight of policies. For the proportionally fair class of schedulers, we have extended these stability results to multihop networks with fixed routing. This is the first general proof of maximum stability for a multihop switch network where routing information is not required in order to make a scheduling decision. This is also significant given the greatly simplified queueing structure required to define the policy.

Future work might consider the implementation of our policies, which require the solution of a concave optimization problem. Thus, using for instance an interior point method, one can approximate a solution to this optimization in computational time that is polynomial in the number of constraints of the set of feasible schedules $<\mathcal{S}>$. After this one can decompose the mean vector onto the set of schedules $\mathcal{S}$. For instance, in the case of a Input Queued switch one could use a Birkhof von Neumann decomposition. Approaches of this type have been considered previously [29]. Compared to MaxWeight, an advantage of the strict convexity of our optimization is that the solutions of our optimization move continuously with continuous changes in queue size. Thus one could consider an alternative, online convex optimization schema where one continuously adapts the current schedule in order to track the optimum (α, g)-policy. As queue sizes increase the solution of our optimization will change more slowly and thus a tracking policy would expect to converge to the correct scheduling decision [39, 13].

We have emphasized the structural benefits of implementing a Proportional Scheduler but have not thus far discussed the statistical benefits of the policy. As we mentioned in the introduction, there is a close relationship between proportional fairness and the maximum stability of reversible systems. With this, one can begin to show that the randomized queueing discipline considered in the Proportional Scheduler can be replaced by a FIFO service discipline and still maintain its stability properties. This is important from a practical perspective as most communications systems implement FIFO queueing. From a theoretical perspective, the result is far more involved and technical than the relatively straightforward proofs for the randomized service which fit within this paper. However, with this analysis further statistical benefits can be observed. For instance, delay is known to increase quadratically with route length for the BackPressure policy, see [7, 35]. However, one can argue that for the Proportional Scheduler delay will grow linearly with route length.

As mentioned above, we have given a proof where a single-hop maximum stability policy implies stability of its routed multihop counterpart, and, crucially, these scheduling decision are made without discriminating between packet route-classes. It is reasonable to conjecture that this holds more generally than for just the Proportional Scheduler. The hope is that the arguments started here could give a general proof technique. One could then hope to extend recent, notable developments on single-hop networks [24, 33, 16, 28] to multihop networks. Thus we begin to provide performance analysis of switched communication networks where packets are communicated.

9. REFERENCES

[1] M. Andrews, K. Kumaran, K. Ramanan, A. Stolyar, R. Vijayakumar, and P. Whiting. Scheduling in a queuing system with asynchronously varying service rates. *Probability in the Engineering and Informational Sciences*, 18(2):191–217, 2004.

[2] F. Baskett, K. M. Chandy, R. R. Muntz, and F. G. Palacios. Open, closed, and mixed networks of queues with different classes of customers. *J. ACM*, 22(2):248–260, Apr. 1975.

[3] T. Bonald and L. Massoulié. Impact of fairness on internet performance. *Proc. of ACM Sigmetrics*, 29:82–91, 2001.

[4] M. Bramson. Convergence to equilibria for fluid models of head-of-the-line proportional processor sharing queueing networks. *Queueing Systems*, 23(1-4):1–26, 1996.

[5] M. Bramson. Stability of queueing networks. *Probab. Surv.*, 5:169–345, 2008.

[6] M. Bramson, B. D'Auria, and N. Walton. Proportional switching in FIFO networks. *in preparation*, 2014.

[7] L. Bui, R. Srikant, and A. L. Stolyar. A novel architecture for reduction of delay and queueing structure complexity in the back-pressure algorithm. *IEEE/ACM Trans. Netw.*, 19(6):1597–1609, 2011.

[8] T. M. Cover and J. Thomas. *Elements of Information Theory.* Wiley, 1991.

[9] J. Dai. On positive harris recurrence of multiclass queueing networks: a unified approach via fluid limit models. *The Annals of Applied Probability*, 5(1):49–77, 1995.

[10] J. Dai. Stability of open multiclass queueing networks via fluid models. *IMA Volumes in Mathematics and Its Applications*, 71:71–71, 1995.

[11] A. B. Dieker and J. Shin. From local to global stability in stochastic processing networks through quadratic lyapunov functions. *Mathematics of Operations Research*, 38(4):638–664, 2013.

[12] A. Eryilmaz, R. Srikant, and J. Perkins. Stable scheduling policies for fading wireless channels. *Networking, IEEE/ACM Transactions on*, 13(2):411–424, 2005.

[13] E. Hazan, A. Agarwal, and S. Kale. Logarithmic regret algorithms for online convex optimization. *Machine Learning*, 69(2):169–192, 2007.

[14] J. R. Jackson. Jobshop-like queueing systems. *Management Science*, 10(1), 1963.

[15] K. Jagannathan, M. Markakis, E. Modiano, and J. Tsitsiklis. Queue length asymptotics for generalized max-weight scheduling in the presence of heavy-tailed traffic. In *INFOCOM, 2011 Proceedings IEEE*, pages 2318 –2326, april 2011.

[16] L. Jiang and J. Walrand. A distributed csma algorithm for throughput and utility maximization in wireless networks. *IEEE/ACM Transactions on Networking (TON)*, 18(3):960–972, 2010.

[17] M. Jonckheere and S. Lopez. Large deviations for the stationary measure of networks under proportional fair allocations. *Mathematics of Operations Research.*

[18] F. Kelly. Charging and rate control for elastic traffic. *European transactions on Telecommunications*, 8(1):33–37, 1997.

[19] F. P. Kelly. *Reversibility and stochastic networks.* Cambridge University Press, 2011.

[20] F. P. Kelly and R. J. Williams. Fluid model for a network operating under a fair bandwidth-sharing policy. *Ann. Appl. Probab.*, 14(3):1055–1083, 2004.

[21] S. H. Lu and P. Kumar. Distributed scheduling based on due dates and buffer priorities. *Automatic Control, IEEE Transactions on*, 36(12):1406–1416, 1991.

[22] L. Massoulié. Structural properties of proportional fairness: stability and insensitivity. *The Annals of Applied Probability*, 17(3):809–839, 2007.

[23] L. Massoulie and J. Roberts. Bandwidth sharing: objectives and algorithms. *Networking, IEEE/ACM Transactions on*, 10(3):320 –328, jun 2002.

[24] N. McKeown, A. Mekkittikul, V. Anantharam, and J. Walrand. Achieving 100% throughput in an input-queued switch. *Communications, IEEE Transactions on*, 47(8):1260–1267, 1999.

[25] J. Mo and J. Walrand. Fair end-to-end window-based congestion control. *Networking, IEEE/ACM Transactions on*, 8(5):556 –567, oct 2000.

[26] P. Robert. *Stochastic Networks and Queues*. Springer, 2010.

[27] A. Rybko and A. Stolyar. Ergodicity of stochastic processes describing the operation of open queueing networks. *Problemy Peredachi Informatsii*, 28(3):3–26, 1992.

[28] D. Shah and J. Shin. Randomized scheduling algorithm for queueing networks. *The Annals of Applied Probability*, 22(1):128–171, 2012.

[29] D. Shah, N. Walton, and Y. Zhong. Optimal queue-size scaling in switched networks. *SIGMETRICS Perform. Eval. Rev.*, 40(1):17–28, June 2012.

[30] D. Shah and D. Wischik. Optimal scheduling algorithms for input-queued switches. In *INFOCOM 2006. 25th IEEE International Conference on Computer Communications. Proceedings*, pages 1 –11, april 2006.

[31] D. Shah and D. Wischik. Fluid models of congestion collapse in overloaded switched networks. *Queueing Syst.*, 69(2):121–143, 2011.

[32] D. Shah and D. Wischik. Switched networks with maximum weight policies: Fluid approximation and multiplicative state space collapse. *The Annals of Applied Probability*, 22(1):70–127, 2012.

[33] A. Stolyar. Maxweight scheduling in a generalized switch: State space collapse and workload minimization in heavy traffic. *The Annals of Applied Probability*, 14(1):1–53, 2004.

[34] A. L. Stolyar. Maxweight scheduling in a generalized switch: State space collapse and workload minimization in heavy traffic. *The Annals of Applied Probability*, 14(1):1–53, 2004.

[35] A. L. Stolyar. Large number of queues in tandem: Scaling properties under back-pressure algorithm. *Queueing Syst. Theory Appl.*, 67(2):111–126, Feb. 2011.

[36] L. Tassiulas and A. Ephremides. Stability properties of constrained queueing systems and scheduling policies for maximum throughput in multihop radio networks. *Automatic Control, IEEE Transactions on*, 37(12):1936–1948, 1992.

[37] M. Vlasiou, J. Zhang, and B. Zwart. Insensitivity of proportional fairness in critically loaded bandwidth sharing networks. *(preprint)*, 2014.

[38] Y. Zhong. *Resource Allocation in Stochastic Processing Networks: Performance and Scaling*. PhD thesis, MIT, 2012.

[39] M. Zinkevich. Online convex programming and generalized infinitesimal gradient ascent. In *ICML*, pages 928–936, 2003.

The Power of Online Learning in Stochastic Network Optimization

Longbo Huang*, Xin Liu†, Xiaohong Hao*
*{longbohuang haoxh10}@tsinghua.edu.cn, IIIS, Tsinghua University
†liuxin@microsoft.com, Microsoft Research Asia

ABSTRACT

In this paper, we investigate the power of online learning in stochastic network optimization with unknown system statistics *a priori*. We are interested in understanding how information and learning can be efficiently incorporated into system control techniques, and what are the fundamental benefits of doing so. We propose two *Online Learning-Aided Control* techniques, OLAC and OLAC2, that explicitly utilize the past system information in current system control via a learning procedure called *dual learning*. We prove strong performance guarantees of the proposed algorithms: OLAC and OLAC2 achieve the near-optimal $[O(\epsilon), O([\log(1/\epsilon)]^2)]$ utility-delay tradeoff and OLAC2 possesses an $O(\epsilon^{-2/3})$ convergence time. Simulation results also confirm the superior performance of the proposed algorithms in practice. To the best of our knowledge, OLAC and OLAC2 are the first algorithms that simultaneously possess explicit near-optimal delay guarantee and sub-linear convergence time, and our attempt is the first to explicitly incorporate online learning into stochastic network optimization and to demonstrate its power in both theory and practice.

1. INTRODUCTION

Consider the following constrained network optimization problem: We are given a stochastic networked system with dynamic system states that have a stationary state distribution. At each state, an operation is implemented and a corresponding system cost occurs depending on the chosen actions. The objective is to minimize the expected cost given service/demand constraints. Such a constrained optimization framework in stochastic systems is general and models many practical application scenarios, such as in computer networks, smart grids, supply chain management, and transportation networks. Due to this wide applicability, developing efficient control techniques for this framework in stochastic systems has been one central question in network optimization.

SIGMETRICS'14, June 16–20, 2014, Austin, Texas, USA.

http://dx.doi.org/10.1145/2591971.2591984.

However, solving this problem is very challenging and the main difficulty comes from the fact that the state distribution of the system is often unknown *a priori*. Moreover, known algorithms that handle this challenge either do not admit explicit delay guarantee, or suffer from a slow convergence speed. To address such a challenge and to overcome the previous limitations, in this paper, we investigate the value of online learning in optimal stochastic system control. We are interested in understanding how information and learning can be efficiently incorporated into system control techniques, and what are the fundamental benefits of doing so.

Specifically, we propose two *Online Learning-Aided Control* techniques, OLAC and OLAC2. The two new techniques are inspired by the following key aspect of the recently developed Lyapunov technique (also known as Backpressure [1]): the Lyapunov technique converts the problem of finding optimal system control decisions into learning the optimal Lagrange multiplier of an underlying optimization problem in an incremental manner, i.e., at every time, the technique reacts only to the instantaneous system condition. This conversion allows the queues in the system to play the role of Lagrange multipliers, and the incremental nature eliminates the need for knowing the statistical information of the system. Because of this attractive feature, the Lyapunov technique has received much attention in the literature. However, the main limitation of the technique is that under Lyapunov algorithms, the queue size in the system has to build up gradually, which results in a large system delay. Specifically, in order to achieve an $O(\epsilon)$ close-to-optimal performance, the queue size has to be $\Theta(1/\epsilon)$, which is undesirable when ϵ is small.

In comparison, OLAC and OLAC2 explicitly utilize the system information via a learning procedure called *dual learning*, which effectively integrates the past system information into current system control by solving an *empirical* optimal Lagrange multiplier. By doing so, OLAC and OLAC2 convert the problem of optimal control into a combination of stochastic approximation and statistical learning. Note that this is a challenging task, because dual learning introduces another coupling effect in time to stochastic system algorithm performance analysis, which itself is already highly non-trivial due to the complicated interactions among different system components.

To the best of our knowledge, this is the first attempt to explicitly incorporate the power of online learning in stochastic network optimization. We address a general model of stochastic network optimization with unknown system statistics *a priori*. Specifically, we make the following contributions in this paper:

- We propose two Online-Learning-Aided Control algorithms, `OLAC` and `OLAC2`, which explicitly utilize the system information via online learning to integrate the past system information into current system control. `OLAC` and `OLAC2` apply to all scenarios where Backpressure applies. Moreover, they retain all the attractive features of Backpressure, such as having low computational complexities, and assuming zero a priori statistical information. Therefore, they can be applied to large-scale dynamic network systems. Simulation results also demonstrate the empirical effectiveness of our proposed algorithms.
- We prove strong performance guarantees for the proposed algorithms, including near-optimality of the control policies, as well as sub-linear convergence time. Specifically, we show that `OLAC` and `OLAC2` achieve the near-optimal $[O(\epsilon), O([\log(1/\epsilon)]^2)]$ utility-delay tradeoff and `OLAC2` possesses a convergence time of $O(\epsilon^{-2/3})$, which significantly improves upon the $\Theta(1/\epsilon)$ convergence time of the Lyapunov technique. To the best of our knowledge, this is the first result that simultaneously achieves near-optimal utility-delay tradeoffs and sub-linear convergence time, and demonstrates the power of online learning in stochastic network optimization.
- We develop two analytical techniques, *dual learning* and the *augmented problem*, for algorithm design and performance analysis. Dual learning allows us to connect dual subgradient update convergence to statistical convergence of random system states, whereas the augmented problem enables the interplay between Lyapunov drift analysis and duality in analyzing systems that apply time-inhomogeneous control policies. These techniques may be applicable to solving other network control problems.

The rest of the paper is organized as follows. In Section 2, we discuss a few representative examples of stochastic network optimization in diverse application fields and the related works. We then explain how our results advance the state-of-the-art. We set up our notations in Section 3. We present the system model and problem formulation in Section 4, and background information in Section 5. We present `OLAC` and `OLAC2` in Section 6, and prove their optimality in Section 7, and convergence in Section 8. Simulation results are presented in Section 9, followed by conclusions in Section 10.

2. MOTIVATING EXAMPLES

In the following, we present a few representative examples of stochastic network optimization in diverse application fields and the related works, and explain how our main results can be applied.

Wireless Networks Consider the following simplified scheduling problem in cellular networks. A cellular base station (BS) is transmitting data to a mobile user. The channel (i.e., state) between the user and the BS is time varying, and the cost (e.g., energy) and the transmission rate depend on the channel state. The user has a certain arrival rate, and thus the constraint is that the service rate provided by the BS to the user has to be larger than the arrival rate. The objective is to minimize the expected energy consumption, where the expectation is taken over channel distributions, subject to the rate constraint. This example can be generalized in practice, e.g., to include multiple users, multiple hops, multiple transmission rates, various coding/modulation schemes, multiple constraints, and different objectives, e.g., [2], [3].

Smart Grids Consider the following demand response problem with renewable energy sources in a smart grid. The problem is to allocate renewable energy sources (e.g., solar or wind) to flexible consumers (e.g., an EV to be charged or a dishwasher load to be finished). In this case, the renewable energy source provides energy according to a time-varying supply process (state). When the renewable energy source cannot generate enough energy to serve all customer load, it incurs a cost to draw energy from the regular power grid, which has a time-varying price (state). The objective is to minimize the time average cost of using the regular grid (and hence results in the most efficient utilization of the renewable source). The constraint is that the average service rate has to be larger than the arrival rate of the consumer demand. Various related issues can also be considered here, including demand response [4], deferrable load scheduling [5], and energy storage management [6].

Supply Chain Management Consider the following inventory control problem in supply chain management. A manufacturing plant purchases raw materials to assemble products and then sells the final products to customers. There are K types of raw materials, each with a time-varying price (state) and N types of final products, each with a time varying demand (state). At each time instance, the plant needs to decide whether to re-stock each type of raw materials and how to price each final product based on the current and future customer demands and material price. The objective is to maximize profit. In the case of large K and N, approximate dynamic programming solutions [7] and efficient Lyapunov optimization solutions have been proposed [8]. Other issues are studied in general processing networks [9], [10], with applications to semiconductor wafer fabrication facilities and assembly line control.

Transportation Networks Consider the traffic signal control problem in a transportation network. The operator controls each set of traffic signals at traffic intersections to regulate the traffic flow rate in the network. Vehicles enter the network in a random fashion (state), with a constant average rate. They move in the network following pre-specified average turn ratios. The objective is to stabilize the queue and allow vehicles to move as fast as possible. Such a system can be modeled as a "store and forward" queuing network. Feedback policies based on queue measurements have been extensively studied [11], as well as Backpressure based decentralized schemes [12].

Solutions The above examples demonstrate the wide application scenarios of the stochastic optimization problem we consider in this paper. If the distribution of the system state is known or if the system is static, many algorithms have been proposed using flow-based optimization techniques, e.g., [13], [14], and the references therein. However, flow-based schemes typically do not explicitly characterize network delay and algorithm convergence time.

For general stochastic settings, Backpressure algorithms address the challenge of unknown channel state distributions by gradually building up the queues and use them for optimal decision making, e.g., [15], [3]. However, Backpressure is known for its slow convergence and long delay, because the queues have to be large enough for achieving near-optimal performance. Specifically, for achieving an $O(\epsilon)$ near-optimality, an $\Theta(1/\epsilon)$ queue size is required. There have been recent works trying to obtain improved utility-delay tradeoff for stochastic systems. For instance, [16], [17], and [18] propose algorithms that can achieve the $[O(\epsilon), O([\log(1/\epsilon)]^2)]$ tradeoff. However, all the above algorithms require a convergence time of $\Theta(1/\epsilon)$. Moreover, they typically require additional system knowledge, e.g., system slack, for algorithm design, which adds to the complexity of algorithm implementation.

Our learning-based approach overcomes these limitations. In particular, we use an online learning-based approach to take advantage of the historic state information, which is ignored by Backpressure throughout the system control process. Our approach is based on a novel *dual learning* idea, which computes an empirical Lagrange multiplier based on the empirical distribution of the system states. Then, we include the learned Lagrange multiplier to the network queues for decision making. Two advantages manifest themselves in this learning-based approach. First, using the distribution information gradually learned in the system, we can significantly speed up the convergence to the optimal solution. Second, because of the "virtual" value added to the queue, i.e., the empirical Lagrange multiplier, the actual queue size is significantly smaller than that under Backpressure. Specifically, we develop two Online Learning-Aided Control techniques, `OLAC` and `OLAC2`. We show that `OLAC` and `OLAC2` achieve the $[O(\epsilon), O([\log(1/\epsilon)]^2)]$ tradeoff and `OLAC2` possesses a convergence time of $O(\epsilon^{-2/3})$, which significantly outperforms that of Backpressure.

3. NOTATIONS

$\mathbb{R}^n$ denotes the n-dimensional Euclidean space. $\mathbb{R}^n_+$ and $\mathbb{R}^n_-$ denote the non-negative and non-positive orthant. Bold symbols $\boldsymbol{x} = (x_1, ..., x_n)$ denote vectors in $\mathbb{R}^n$. The notion *w.p.1* denotes "with probability 1." $\|\cdot\|$ denotes the Euclidean norm. For a sequence of variables $\{y(t)\}_{t=0}^{\infty}$, we also use $\overline{y} = \lim_{t\to\infty} \frac{1}{t}\sum_{\tau=0}^{t-1}\mathbb{E}\{y(\tau)\}$ to denote its average (when exists). $\boldsymbol{x} \succeq \boldsymbol{y}$ means that $x_j \geq y_j$ for all j.

4. SYSTEM MODEL AND PROBLEM FORMULATION

In this section, we specify the general network model. We consider a network controller that operates a network with the goal of minimizing the time average cost, subject to the queue stability constraint. The network is assumed to operate in slotted time, i.e., $t \in \{0, 1, 2, ...\}$. We assume there are $r \geq 1$ queues in the network (e.g., the amount of data to be transmitted in cellular networks or the amount of flexible jobs to be scheduled in a smart grid).

4.1 Network State

In every slot t, we use $S(t)$ to denote the current network state, which indicates the current network parameters, such as a vector of conditions for each network link, or a collection of other relevant information about the current network channels and arrivals. We assume that $S(t)$ is i.i.d. over time and takes M different random network states denoted as $\mathcal{S} = \{s_1, s_2, \dots, s_M\}$. [1] Let $\pi_{s_i} = \Pr\{S(t) = s_i\}$ denote the probability of being in state s_i at time t and denote $\boldsymbol{\pi} = (\pi_{s_1}, ..., \pi_{s_M})$ the stationary distribution. We assume that the network controller can observe $S(t)$ at the beginning of every slot t, but the π_{s_i} probabilities are unknown.

4.2 The Cost, Traffic, and Service

At each time t, after observing $S(t) = s_i$, the controller chooses an action $x(t)$ from a set $\mathcal{X}^{(s_i)}$, i.e., $x(t) = x^{(s_i)}$ for some $x^{(s_i)} \in \mathcal{X}^{(s_i)}$. The set $\mathcal{X}^{(s_i)}$ is called the feasible action set for network state s_i and is assumed to be time-invariant and compact for all $s_i \in \mathcal{S}$. The cost, traffic, and service generated by the chosen action $x(t) = x^{(s_i)}$ are as follows:

(a) The chosen action has an associated cost given by the cost function $f(t) = f(s_i, x^{(s_i)}) : \mathcal{X}^{(s_i)} \mapsto \mathbb{R}_+$ (or $\mathcal{X}^{(s_i)} \mapsto \mathbb{R}_-$ in reward maximization problems);

(b) The amount of traffic generated by the action to queue j is determined by the traffic function $A_j(t) = A_j(s_i, x^{(s_i)}) : \mathcal{X}^{(s_i)} \mapsto \mathbb{R}_+$, in units of packets;

(c) The amount of service allocated to queue j is given by the rate function $\mu_j(t) = \mu_j(s_i, x^{(s_i)}) : \mathcal{X}^{(s_i)} \mapsto \mathbb{R}_+$, in units of packets.

Note that $A_j(t)$ includes both the exogenous arrivals from outside the network to queue j, and the endogenous arrivals from other queues, i.e., the transmitted packets from other queues, to queue j. We assume the functions $-f(s_i, \cdot)$, $\mu_j(s_i, \cdot)$ and $A_j(s_i, \cdot)$ are concave, time-invariant, their magnitudes are uniformly upper bounded by some constant $\delta_{\max} \in (0, \infty)$ for all s_i, j, and they are known to the network operator.

4.3 Problem Formulation

Let $\boldsymbol{q}(t) = (q_1(t), ..., q_r(t))^T \in \mathbb{R}^r_+$, $t = 0, 1, 2, ...$ be the queue backlog vector process of the network, in units of packets. We assume the following queueing dynamics:

$$q_j(t+1) = \max\left[q_j(t) - \mu_j(t) + A_j(t), 0\right], \quad \forall j, \tag{1}$$

and $\boldsymbol{q}(0) = \boldsymbol{0}$. By using (1), we assume that when a queue does not have enough packets to send, null packets are transmitted, so that the number of packets entering $q_j(t)$ is equal to $A_j(t)$. In this paper, we adopt the following notion of queue stability [1]:

$$\overline{q}_{\text{av}} \triangleq \limsup_{t\to\infty} \frac{1}{t}\sum_{\tau=0}^{t-1}\sum_{j=1}^{r}\mathbb{E}\{q_j(\tau)\} < \infty. \tag{2}$$

We use Π to denote an action-choosing policy. Then, we use f_{av}^{Π} to denote the time average cost induced by Π, i.e.,

$$f_{\text{av}}^{\Pi} \triangleq \limsup_{t\to\infty} \frac{1}{t}\sum_{\tau=0}^{t-1}\mathbb{E}\{f^{\Pi}(\tau)\}, \tag{3}$$

where $f^{\Pi}(\tau)$ is the cost incurred at time τ by policy Π. We call an action-choosing policy *feasible* if at every time slot t it only chooses actions from the feasible action set $\mathcal{X}^{(S(t))}$. We then call a feasible action-choosing policy under which (2) holds a *stable* policy, and use f_{av}^* to denote the optimal time average cost over all stable policies.

In every slot, the network controller observes the current network state and chooses a control action, with the goal of

[1] The results in this paper can likely be generalized to systems with more general Markovian dynamics.

minimizing the time average cost subject to network stability. This goal can be mathematically stated as:

$$\textbf{(P1)}\ \ \textbf{min}:\ f_{\text{av}}^{\Pi},\ \text{s.t.}\ \textbf{(2)}.$$

In the following, we call **(P1)** *the stochastic problem.* It can be seen that the examples in Section 2 can all be modeled with the stochastic problem framework. This is the problem formulation we focus on in this paper.

5. THE DETERMINISTIC PROBLEM AND BACKPRESSURE

In this section, we first define the *deterministic problem* and its dual problem, which will be important for designing our new control techniques and for our later analysis. We then review the Lyapunov technique for solving the stochastic problem **(P1)**. To follow the convention, we will call it the Backpressure algorithm.

5.1 The deterministic problem

The *deterministic problem* is defined as follows [17]:

$$\min : F(\boldsymbol{x}, \boldsymbol{\pi}) \triangleq V \sum_{s_i} \pi_{s_i} f(s_i, x^{(s_i)}) \tag{4}$$

$$\text{s.t. } H_j(\boldsymbol{x}, \boldsymbol{\pi}) \tag{5}$$

$$\triangleq \sum_{s_i} \pi_{s_i} [A_j(s_i, x^{(s_i)}) - \mu_j(s_i, x^{(s_i)})] \leq 0, \ \forall j,$$

$$x^{(s_i)} \in \mathcal{X}^{(s_i)} \quad \forall i = 1, 2, ..., M.$$

Here the minimization is taken over $\boldsymbol{x} \in \prod_i \mathcal{X}^{(s_i)}$, where $\boldsymbol{x} = (x^{(s_1)}, ..., x^{(s_M)})^T$, and $V \geq 1$ is a positive constant introduced for later analysis. The dual problem of (4) can be obtained as follows:

$$\max : \ g(\boldsymbol{\gamma}), \quad \text{s.t. } \boldsymbol{\gamma} \succeq \boldsymbol{0}, \tag{6}$$

where $g(\boldsymbol{\gamma})$ is the dual function and is defined as:

$$g(\boldsymbol{\gamma}) = \inf_{x^{(s_i)} \in \mathcal{X}^{(s_i)}} \sum_{s_i} \pi_{s_i} \bigg\{ V f(s_i, x^{(s_i)}) \tag{7}$$

$$+ \sum_j \gamma_j [A_j(s_i, x^{(s_i)}) - \mu_j(s_i, x^{(s_i)})] \bigg\}.$$

Here $\boldsymbol{\gamma} = (\gamma_1, ..., \gamma_r)^T$ is the *Lagrange multiplier* of (4). It is well known that $g(\boldsymbol{\gamma})$ in (7) is concave in the vector $\boldsymbol{\gamma}$ for all $\boldsymbol{\gamma} \in \mathbb{R}^r$, and hence the problem (6) can usually be solved efficiently, particularly when the cost functions and rate functions are separable over different network components [19].

Below, we use $\boldsymbol{\gamma}^* = (\gamma_1^*, \gamma_2^*, ..., \gamma_r^*)^T$ to denote an optimal solution of the problem (6). For notational convenience, we also use $g_0(\boldsymbol{\gamma})$ and $\boldsymbol{\gamma}_0^*$ to denote the dual function and an optimal dual solution for $V = 1$. It can be seen that:

$$g(\boldsymbol{\gamma}) = V g_0(\boldsymbol{\gamma}/V), \tag{8}$$

which implies that $\boldsymbol{\gamma} = V\boldsymbol{\gamma}_0^*$ is an optimal solution of $g(\boldsymbol{\gamma})$. Note that $g_0(\boldsymbol{\gamma})$ is independent of V. For our later analysis, we also define:

$$g_{s_i}(\boldsymbol{\gamma}) = \inf_{x^{(s_i)} \in \mathcal{X}^{(s_i)}} \bigg\{ V f(s_i, x^{(s_i)}) \tag{9}$$

$$+ \sum_j \gamma_j [A_j(s_i, x^{(s_i)}) - \mu_j(s_i, x^{(s_i)})] \bigg\},$$

to be the dual function when there is only a single state s_i. It is clear from equations (7) and (9) that:

$$g(\boldsymbol{\gamma}) = \sum_{s_i} \pi_{s_i} g_{s_i}(\boldsymbol{\gamma}). \tag{10}$$

5.2 The Backpressure algorithm

Among the many techniques developed for solving the stochastic problem, the Backpressure algorithm has received much attention because (i) it does not require any statistical information of the changing network conditions, (ii) it has low implementation complexity, and (iii) it has provable strong performance guarantees. The Backpressure algorithm works as follows [1]. [2]

Backpressure: At every time slot t, observe the current network state $S(t)$ and the backlog $\boldsymbol{q}(t)$. If $S(t) = s_i$, choose $x^{(s_i)} \in \mathcal{X}^{(s_i)}$ that solves the following:

$$\max : \quad -V f(s_i, x) + \sum_{j=1}^{r} q_j(t) [\mu_j(s_i, x) - A_j(s_i, x)] \tag{11}$$

$$\text{s.t.} \quad x \in \mathcal{X}^{(s_i)}. \quad \diamond$$

In many problems, (11) can usually be decomposed into separate parts that are easier to solve, e.g., [15], [3]. Also, when the network state process $S(t)$ is i.i.d., it has been shown in [1] that,

$$f_{\text{av}}^{\text{BP}} = f_{\text{av}}^* + O(1/V), \quad \overline{q}^{\text{BP}} = O(V), \tag{12}$$

where $f_{\text{av}}^{\text{BP}}$ and $\overline{q}^{\text{BP}}$ are the expected average cost and the expected average network backlog size under Backpressure, respectively. Note that the performance results in (12) hold under Backpressure with *any* queueing discipline for choosing which packets to serve and for any V.

Though being a low-complexity technique that possesses wide applicability, the delay performance and the convergence speed of Backpressure are not satisfactory. Indeed, it is known that when Backpressure achieves a utility that is within $O(\epsilon)$ of the optimal, the average queueing delay is $\Theta(1/\epsilon)$. Although techniques proposed in [17] [18] are able to achieve an $O([\log(1/\epsilon)]^2)$ delay, it has been observed that the convergence time of these algorithms is $\Theta(1/\epsilon)$ (this will also be proven in Section 8).

Moreover, we make the following observation of Backpressure: it discards all past information of the system states, i.e., $\{S(0), ..., S(t-1)\}$, and only reacts to the *instantaneous* state. While such an *incremental* manner is known to be able to accelerate the convergence of the algorithm compared to the ordinary subgradient methods [19], one interesting question to ask is whether such information can be utilized to construct better control techniques? Specifically, we are interested in understanding *how the information can be incorporated into algorithm design and whether this incorporation enables the development of algorithms that possess better delay and convergence performance.*

In our next section, we present two learning-aided control techniques that perform learning through the historic system state information. As we will see, this learning step allows us to achieve a near-optimal system performance and a significant improvement in convergence speed.

[2] A similar definition of Backpressure based on fluid model was also given in Section 4.8 of [20].

6. ONLINE LEARNING-AIDED CONTROL

In this section, we describe our online learning-aided system control idea and two novel control schemes, which we call Online Learning-Aided Control (OLAC) and OLAC2.

6.1 Intuition

Here we provide intuitions behind the two techniques. Both OLAC and OLAC2 are motivated by the fact that, under Backpressure algorithms, the queue vector plays the role of Lagrange multiplier [17]. However, Backpressure's incremental nature ignores the possibility of utilizing the information of the system dynamics for "accelerating" the convergence of the control algorithm, and only relies on taking subgradient-type updates. OLAC and OLAC2 are designed to simultaneously take both subgradient-type updates and statistical learning into consideration.

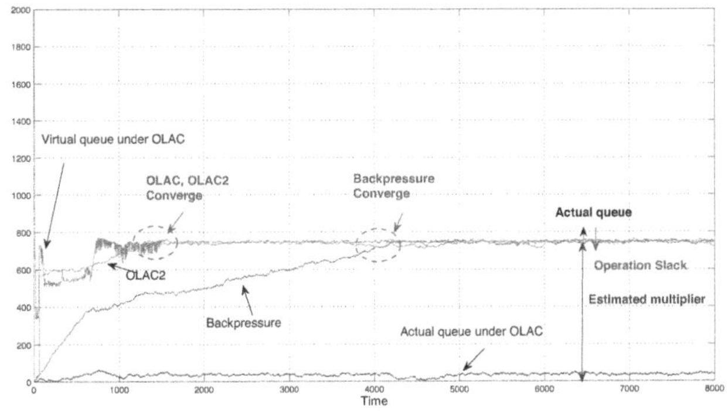

Figure 1: Convergence behavior of queue sizes under three algorithms, Backpressure, OLAC and OLAC2. It can be seen clearly that the virtual queue under OLAC and the actual queue under OLAC2 converge much faster to γ^* compared to the queue size under Backpressure. This clearly demonstrates the power of dual learning.

Fig. 1 best demonstrates our intuition and results. As we can see from the figure, the queue vector under Backpressure is attracted to the fixed point γ^* after some time [17]. However, Backpressure only uses the queue value to track the value γ^*. This results in undesired delay and convergence performance. In OLAC and OLAC2, we instead introduce an auxiliary variable $\beta(t)$ to approach the value of γ^* by solving an "empirical" version of (7) and finding the empirical Lagrange multiplier (called *dual learning*). The reason for performing this dual learning step is motivated by the fact that in many stochastic control problems, the optimal Lagrange multiplier γ^* is the unique key information for finding the optimal control policies. Then, we feed $\beta(t)$ to the Backpressure controller for choosing the actions. Since $\beta(t)$ eventually converges to γ^*, we essentially do not require building up the queues for tracking γ^*. Also, as we will see, at the beginning, dual learning provides a crude but fast learning of γ^*. Hence, by doing so, we can significantly improve the convergence time of the system.

6.2 Dual Learning

The dual learning step is a novel and critical component in our online-learning-aided control mechanisms. Specifically, at every time t, the network operator maintains an empirical distribution of the network states, denoted by $\boldsymbol{\pi}(t) = (\pi_{s_1}(t), ..., \pi_{s_M}(t))$, where $\pi_{s_i}(t) = N_{s_i}(t)/t$ and $N_{s_i}(t)$ is the number of slots where $S(t) = s_i$ in $\{0, 1, ..., t-1\}$. Note that $\lim_{t\to\infty} \pi_{s_i}(t) = \pi_{s_i}$ $w.p.1$.

Although we adopt a simple learning mechanism for $\pi_{s_i}(t)$ here, other approaches for learning the distribution can also be used. In addition, if some prior knowledge of the system exists, it can be incorporated into $\pi_{s_i}(0)$, which further speeds up the learning. Other practical techniques in typical machine learning can also be included, such as using a uniform prior to avoid large fluctuation in the early stage of learning. Depending on the features of the approaches, similar performance and convergence results may also be obtained.

Using the empirical distribution, we then define the following empirical dual problem as follows:

$$\max: \; g(\boldsymbol{\beta}, t) \triangleq \sum_{s_i} \pi_{s_i}(t) g_{s_i}(\boldsymbol{\beta}), \quad \text{s.t. } \boldsymbol{\beta} \succeq \mathbf{0}. \tag{13}$$

We denote $\boldsymbol{\beta}(t) = (\beta_1^*(t), \beta_2^*(t), ..., \beta_r^*(t))^T$ an optimal solution vector of (13), and we call this step of obtaining $\boldsymbol{\beta}(t)$ via (13) *dual learning*. As we will see, $\boldsymbol{\beta}(t)$ plays a critical role in the proposed control schemes to significantly speed up the convergence to the optimal solution. On the other hand, by its definition, $\boldsymbol{\beta}(t)$ is time-varying and error-prone, which introduces significant challenges in the analysis of the proposed algorithms. Thus, novel techniques are developed in Sections 7 and 8 for performance analysis.

In the following, we present two control techniques using the empirical Lagrange multiplier $\boldsymbol{\beta}(t)$ obtained in dual learning for decision making.

6.3 OLAC

In the first technique, we use dual learning in each iteration of decision making. We also use a control parameter $\boldsymbol{\theta} > 0$ to manage the queue deviation (Its function and value will be specified later).

Online Learning-Aided Control (OLAC): At every time slot t, do:

- (Dual learning) Obtain $\boldsymbol{\beta}(t)$ by solving (13),
- (Action selection) Observe the system backlog $\boldsymbol{q}(t)$, and define the *effective* backlog $\boldsymbol{Q}(t)$ with:

$$Q_j(t) = q_j(t) + \beta_j(t) - \theta_j, \quad \forall\, j. \tag{14}$$

  Observe the current network state $S(t)$. If $S(t) = s_i$, choose $x^{(s_i)} \in \mathcal{X}^{(s_i)}$ that solves the following:

$$\max: \; -Vf(s_i, x) + \sum_{j=1}^{r} Q_j(t)\big[\mu_j(s_i, x) - A_j(s_i, x)\big] \tag{15}$$
$$\text{s.t.} \quad x \in \mathcal{X}^{(s_i)}.$$

- (Queueing update) Update all the queues with the arrival and service rates under the chosen actions according to (1). ◇

We see that the OLAC algorithm has both similarities and differences compared to the Backpressure algorithm. On one hand, OLAC retains all the advantages of Backpressure, i.e., it does not require any statistical information of the system and it retains the low-complexity feature. On the other hand, one should note that OLAC has an important component that is not possessed by Backpressure, i.e., dual learning through empirical Lagrange multiplier. This step fundamentally changes the algorithm. In particular, $\boldsymbol{\beta}(t)$

takes advantage of the empirical information to speed up the convergence of $\boldsymbol{Q}(t)$ to the optimal Lagrange multiplier. In addition, it also serves the function of a "virtual" queue vector, and thus reduces the actual queue size of $\boldsymbol{q}(t)$ (See Fig. 1).

As we will see, OLAC achieves a near-optimal utility-delay tradeoff and has a significantly faster learning speed. The dual learning method also connects subgradient-type update analysis to the convergence properties of the system state distribution, allowing us to leverage useful results in the learning literature for performance analysis in stochastic network optimization.

A few comments on the control parameter $\boldsymbol{\theta} > 0$ are in order. As we will see later, the effective backlog $\boldsymbol{Q}(t)$ will eventually converge to $\boldsymbol{\gamma}^*$ (See the right side of Fig. 1). Since $\boldsymbol{\beta}(t)$ also converges to $\boldsymbol{\gamma}^*$, this implies that $\boldsymbol{\beta}(t)+\boldsymbol{q}(t)$ will eventually be larger than $\boldsymbol{\gamma}^*$. Thus, if we were to use only $\boldsymbol{\beta}(t)+\boldsymbol{q}(t)$ as the weight for the Backpressure controller, the system will always "think" that it is in a congested stage and operate at an "over-provisioned" mode, which will lead to utility loss. The introduction of $\boldsymbol{\theta}$ is trying to solve this problem. After subtracting $\boldsymbol{\theta}$, the effective backlog $\boldsymbol{Q}(t)$ can also go below $\boldsymbol{\gamma}^*$, which allows the Backpressure controller to choose "under-provisioned" actions and to achieve the desired performance through time-sharing over-provisioned and under-provisioned actions [21]. We will also show in Section 7 that it suffices to choose $\boldsymbol{\theta} = \Theta([\log(1/\epsilon)]^2)$ to guarantee an $O(\epsilon)$ close-to-optimal utility performance (Here $\epsilon = 1/V$).

6.4 OLAC2

We now present the second algorithm, which we call Online Learning-Aided Control 2 (OLAC2). OLAC2 combines the LIFO-Backpressure algorithm [18] with dual learning, and contains a backlog adjustment step.

Online Learning-Aided Control 2 (OLAC2): Choose a time $T_l = V^c$ for some $c \in [0, 1)$. At every time slot t, do:

- (Action selection) Observe the current network state $S(t)$ and queue backlog $\boldsymbol{q}(t)$. If $S(t) = s_i$, choose $x^{(s_i)} \in \mathcal{X}^{(s_i)}$ that solves the following:

$$\max: \ -Vf(s_i, x) + \sum_{j=1}^{r} q_j(t)\left[\mu_j(s_i, x) - A_j(s_i, x)\right] \quad (16)$$
$$\text{s.t.} \quad x \in \mathcal{X}^{(s_i)}.$$

- (Queueing update) Update all the queues with the arrival and service rates under the chosen actions according to (1) with the Last-In-First-Out (LIFO) discipline.

- (Dual learning and backlog adjustment) Only at $t = T_l$, solve (13) with $\boldsymbol{\pi}(T_l - 1)$ and obtain the empirical Lagrange multiplier $\tilde{\boldsymbol{\beta}}$. Then, make $\boldsymbol{q}(T_l) = \tilde{\boldsymbol{\beta}}$ by dropping packets if $q_j(T_l - 1) > \tilde{\beta}_j$ or adding null packets if $q_j(T_l - 1) < \tilde{\beta}_j$. ◇

Note that although there exists a packet dropping step in dual learning and backlog adjustment, packet dropping rarely happens. The intuition is that at $t = T_l = V^c$, we have with high probability that $\tilde{\beta} = O(V)$. On the other hand, since the queue size increment is always $\Theta(1)$, we only have $\boldsymbol{q}(T_l - 1) = O(V^c)$. The key difference between OLAC2 and the LIFO-Backpressure algorithm developed in [18] is that OLAC2 contains a dual learning phase and adjusts its backlog condition at time $t = T_l$. The intuition here is that $\tilde{\boldsymbol{\beta}}$ computed at $t = T_l$ will give us good enough learning of the system, which provides better estimation of the true optimal Lagrangian multiplier than the queue value obtained via subgradient-type updates under LIFO-Backpressure. As we will see in Section 8 that, these two steps are critical for OLAC2, as they enable the achievement of a superior convergence performance.

Note that the LIFO discipline is important to OLAC2. This is so because if OLAC2 does not utilize any auxiliary process to "substitute" the true backlog. Thus, the queue will eventually build up, and its average value will still be $\boldsymbol{\gamma}^* = \Theta(V)$. Hence, packets can experience large delay. However, LIFO scheduling ensures that most of the packets are not affected by such network congestion and can go through the system with low delay.

6.5 Performance Guarantee

We summarize the proven properties of OLAC and OLAC2 here while leaving the technical details to next two sections.

OLAC: OLAC achieves the $[O(\epsilon), O([\log(1/\epsilon)]^2)]$ utility-delay tradeoff for general stochastic optimization problems. Compared to other Backpressure-based algorithms, OLAC is easier to implement and shows much better convergence performance (see Figure 1). The convergence analysis of OLAC is much more difficult because of the time-varying nature of $\boldsymbol{\beta}(t)$, and thus is left for future work.

OLAC2: OLAC2 achieves the $[O(\epsilon), O([\log(1/\epsilon)]^2)]$ utility-delay tradeoff for general stochastic optimization problems. In addition, it requires a convergence time of only $O(\epsilon^{-c} + \epsilon^{c/2-1}\log(1/\epsilon))$ with high probability. Therefore, by selecting $c = 2/3$ in OLAC2, we see that with very high probability, the system under OLAC2 will enter the near-optimal state in only $O(\epsilon^{-2/3}\log(1/\epsilon))$ time! This is in contrast to the Backpressure algorithm, whose convergence time is $\Theta(1/\epsilon)$. To the best of our knowledge, OLAC and OLAC2 are the first algorithms that simultaneously possess explicit near-optimal delay guarantee and sub-linear convergence time.

7. PERFORMANCE ANALYSIS

In this section, we first present some preliminaries needed for our analysis. Then, we present the detailed performance results for OLAC and OLAC2.

7.1 The augmented problem and preliminaries

Due to the introduction of $\boldsymbol{\beta}(t)$ in decision making, the performance of OLAC and OLAC2 cannot be obtained by directly applying the typical Lyapunov analysis. To overcome this obstacle, we introduce the following *augmented problem* and carry out our analysis based on it. Specifically, we define:

$$\min: F(\boldsymbol{x}) + \sum_j (\beta_j(t) - \theta_j) H_j(\boldsymbol{x}) \quad (17)$$
$$\text{s.t. } H_j(\boldsymbol{x}) \leq 0, \ \forall j,$$
$$x^{(s_i)} \in \mathcal{X}^{(s_i)} \quad \forall i = 1, 2, ..., M.$$

Let $\tilde{g}(\boldsymbol{\gamma})$ be the dual function of (17), i.e.,

$$\tilde{g}(\boldsymbol{\gamma}) = \inf_{x^{(s_i)} \in \mathcal{X}^{(s_i)}} \sum_{s_i} \pi_{s_i} \Big\{ Vf(s_i, x^{(s_i)}) \quad (18)$$

$$+\sum_j [\gamma_j + \beta_j(t) - \theta_j]\big[A_j(s_i, x^{(s_i)}) - \mu_j(s_i, x^{(s_i)})\big]\Big\}.$$

It is interesting to notice the similarity between (18) and (15) (note that $Q_j(t) = q_j(t) + \beta_j(t) - \theta_j$). Using the definition of $g(\boldsymbol{\gamma})$, we have:

$$\tilde{g}(\boldsymbol{\gamma}) = g(\boldsymbol{\gamma} + \boldsymbol{\beta}(t) - \boldsymbol{\theta}). \quad (19)$$

In the following, we state the assumptions we make throughout the paper. These assumptions are mild and can typically be satisfied in network optimization problems.

Assumption 1. *There exists a constant $\epsilon_s = \Theta(1) > 0$ such that for any valid state distribution $\boldsymbol{\pi}' = (\pi'_{s1}, ..., \pi'_{sM})$ with $\|\boldsymbol{\pi}' - \boldsymbol{\pi}\| \leq \epsilon_s$, there exists a set of actions $\{x_k^{(s_i)}\}_{i=1,...,M}^{k=1,2,...,\infty}$ with $x_k^{(s_i)} \in \mathcal{X}^{(s_i)}$ and some variables $\vartheta_k^{(s_i)} \geq 0$ for all s_i and k with $\sum_k \vartheta_k^{(s_i)} = 1$ for all s_i (possibly depending on $\boldsymbol{\pi}'$), such that:*

$$\sum_{s_i} \pi_{s_i} \Big\{ \sum_k \vartheta_k^{(s_i)} [A_j(s_i, x_k^{(s_i)}) - \mu_j(s_i, x_k^{(s_i)})] \Big\} \leq -\eta_0, \quad (20)$$

where $\eta_0 = \Theta(1) > 0$ is independent of $\boldsymbol{\pi}'$. ◇

Assumption 2. *There exists a set of actions $\{x_k^{(s_i)*}\}_{i=1,...,M}^{k=1,...,\infty}$ with $x_k^{(s_i)*} \in \mathcal{X}^{(s_i)}$ and some variables $\vartheta_k^{(s_i)*} \geq 0$ for all s_i and k with $\sum_k \vartheta_k^{(s_i)*} = 1$ for all s_i, such that:*

$$\sum_{s_i} \pi_{s_i} \sum_k \vartheta_k^{(s_i)*} f(s_i, x_k^{(s_i)*}) = f_{av}^*, \quad (21)$$

$$\sum_{s_i} \pi_{s_i} \Big\{ \sum_k \vartheta_k^{(s_i)*} [A_j(s_i, x_k^{(s_i)*}) - \mu_j(s_i, x_k^{(s_i)*})] \Big\} = 0. \quad \diamond$$

Assumption 3. *$\boldsymbol{\gamma}_0^*$ is the unique optimal solution of $g_0(\boldsymbol{\gamma})$ in $\mathbb{R}^r$.* ◇

Some remarks are in order. Notice that by having $\eta_0 > 0$ in Assumption 1, we assume that there exists at least one control policy under which the resulting system arrival rate vector is strictly smaller than the resulting service rate vector (or the arrival rate vector is strictly inside the capacity region if it is exogenous). This is known as the "slack" condition, and is commonly made in the literature with $\epsilon_s = 0$, e.g., [22], [23] (it is always necessary to have $\eta_0 \geq 0$ for system stability [1]). Here with $\epsilon_s > 0$, we assume in addition that when two systems are relatively "similar" to each other, they can both be stabilized by some randomized control policy (may be different) that results in the same slack. Assumption 2 is also commonly satisfied by most network optimization problems, especially when the cost $f(s_i, x^{(s_i)})$ increases with the increment of the services rate $\mu_j(s_i, x^{(s_i)})$. Finally, Assumption 3 holds for many network utility optimization problems, especially when the corresponding cost functions are strictly convex, e.g., [2] and [17].

Under these assumptions, our first lemma shows that the magnitude of $\boldsymbol{\beta}(t)$ quickly becomes bounded as time goes on.

Lemma 1. *There exists an $O(1)$ time $T_{\epsilon_s} < \infty$, such that with probability 1, for all $t \geq T_{\epsilon_s}$,*

$$\sum_j \beta_j(t) \leq \xi \triangleq \frac{V f_{\max}}{\eta_0}. \quad \diamond$$

PROOF. See Appendix A. □

With the above bound, we have the following corollary, which shows the convergence of $g(\boldsymbol{\beta}, t)$ to $g(\boldsymbol{\beta})$.

Corollary 1. *With probability 1, for all $t \geq T_{\epsilon_s}$ (here T_{ϵ_s} is defined in Lemma 1), the function $g(\boldsymbol{\beta}, t)$ satisfies:*

$$|g(\boldsymbol{\beta}(t), t) - g(\boldsymbol{\beta}(t))| \leq \max_{s_i} |\delta_{s_i}(t)| M (V f_{\max} + r\xi B).$$

Here $\xi = \frac{V f_{\max}}{\eta_0}$ is defined in Lemma 1, $\delta_{s_i}(t) \triangleq \pi_{s_i} - \pi_{s_i}(t)$ is the estimation error of the empirical distribution for state s_i, and M is the number of system states. ◇

PROOF. See Appendix B. □

With Lemma 1 and Corollary 1, we next show that $\boldsymbol{\beta}(t)$ converges to $\boldsymbol{\gamma}^*$ with probability 1.

Lemma 2. *$\lim_{t\to\infty} \boldsymbol{\beta}(t) = \boldsymbol{\gamma}^*$ w.p.1.* ◇

PROOF. Omitted due to space limitation. See [24] for details. □

Notice that while Assumption 3 assumes that there is a unique optimal for (4), it does not guarantee that $g(\boldsymbol{\beta}, t)$ will also only have a unique solution. Lemma 2 thus shows that although such a condition can appear, it is simply a transient phenomenon and $\boldsymbol{\beta}(t)$ will eventually converge to $\boldsymbol{\gamma}^*$. According to Assumption 3, (19) implies that the unique maximizer of $\tilde{g}(\boldsymbol{\gamma})$, denoted by $\tilde{\boldsymbol{\gamma}}^*(t)$, is given by $\tilde{\boldsymbol{\gamma}}^*(t) = \boldsymbol{\gamma}^* - \boldsymbol{\beta}(t) + \boldsymbol{\theta}$. Using Lemma 2, we also see that:

$$\lim_{t\to\infty} \tilde{\boldsymbol{\gamma}}^*(t) \to \boldsymbol{\theta}, \quad w.p.1. \quad (22)$$

In the following, we will carry out our analysis about the performance of OLAC and OLAC2 under a general system structure that commonly appears in practice. For our analysis, it is also useful to define $B \triangleq \frac{r}{2}\delta_{\max}^2$. It can be seen that $\|\boldsymbol{\mu}(t) - \boldsymbol{A}(t)\| \leq B$ at all time.

7.2 Performance of OLAC and OLAC2

We now carry out our analysis for OLAC and OLAC2 under a *polyhedral* system structure. Intuitively speaking, this structure appears in systems where the feasible control action sets are finite, in which case once an action becomes the minimizer of the dual function at $\boldsymbol{\gamma}$, it remains so at all $\boldsymbol{\gamma}'$ in some neighborhood of $\boldsymbol{\gamma}$, resulting in a constant service and arrival rate difference (which determines the slope of $g(\boldsymbol{\gamma})$). The formal definition of the polyhedral structure is as follows [17].

Definition 1. *A system is polyhedral with parameter $\rho > 0$ if the dual function $g_0(\boldsymbol{\gamma})$ satisfies:*

$$g_0(\boldsymbol{\gamma}_0^*) \geq g_0(\boldsymbol{\gamma}) + \rho\|\boldsymbol{\gamma}_0^* - \boldsymbol{\gamma}\|. \ \diamond \quad (23)$$

Using (23), we have:

$$V g_0(\boldsymbol{\gamma}_0^*) \geq V g_0(\boldsymbol{\gamma}/V) + V\rho\|\boldsymbol{\gamma}_0^* - \boldsymbol{\gamma}/V\|.$$

Together with (8) and the fact that $\boldsymbol{\gamma}^* = V\boldsymbol{\gamma}_0^*$, we see that the above implies:

$$g(\boldsymbol{\gamma}^*) \geq g(\boldsymbol{\gamma}) + \rho\|\boldsymbol{\gamma}^* - \boldsymbol{\gamma}\|, \quad (24)$$

i.e., the function $g(\boldsymbol{\gamma})$ also satisfies the polyhedral condition (23) with the same parameter ρ. Moreover, we have:

$$\begin{aligned} \tilde{g}(\tilde{\boldsymbol{\gamma}}^*(t)) &= g(\tilde{\boldsymbol{\gamma}}^*(t) + \boldsymbol{\beta}(t) - \boldsymbol{\theta}) \\ &\overset{(a)}{\geq} g(\boldsymbol{\gamma} + \boldsymbol{\beta}(t) - \boldsymbol{\theta}) + \rho\|\tilde{\boldsymbol{\gamma}}^*(t) - \boldsymbol{\gamma}\| \end{aligned}$$

$$= \tilde{g}(\boldsymbol{\gamma}) + \rho\|\tilde{\boldsymbol{\gamma}}^*(t) - \boldsymbol{\gamma}\|. \quad (25)$$

Here (a) is because $\boldsymbol{\gamma}^* = \tilde{\boldsymbol{\gamma}}^*(t) + \boldsymbol{\beta} - \boldsymbol{\theta}$. This shows that the function $\tilde{g}(\boldsymbol{\gamma})$ is also polyhedral. It turns out that this polyhedral condition has a special attraction property, under which the queue vector under OLAC and OLAC2 will be exponentially attracted towards $\tilde{\boldsymbol{\gamma}}^*(t)$. This is shown in the following important lemma:

Lemma 3. *Suppose (23) holds. Then, there exist a constant $D_p \triangleq \frac{B-\eta^2}{2(\rho-\eta)} = \Theta(1)$ with $\eta < \rho$, and a finite time $T_0 < \infty$, such that, with probability 1, for all $t \geq T_0$, if $\|\boldsymbol{q}(t) - \tilde{\boldsymbol{\gamma}}^*(t)\| \geq D$,*

$$\mathbb{E}\{\|\boldsymbol{q}(t+1) - \tilde{\boldsymbol{\gamma}}^*(t)\| \mid \boldsymbol{q}(t)\} \leq \|\boldsymbol{q}(t) - \tilde{\boldsymbol{\gamma}}^*(t)\| - \eta. \ \diamond \quad (26)$$

Proof. Omitted due to space limitation. See [24] for details. □

Lemma 3 states that, after some finite time T_0, if the queue vector $\boldsymbol{q}(t)$ is of distance $D = \Theta(1)$ away from $\tilde{\boldsymbol{\gamma}}^*(t)$, there will be an $\Theta(1)$ drift "pushing" the queue size towards $\tilde{\boldsymbol{\gamma}}^*(t)$. This intuitively explains why $\boldsymbol{q}(t)$ mostly stays close to a fixed point. Note that proof of Lemma 3 is based on the augmented problem (17). Below, we present the detailed performance results. Recall that all the results are obtained under Assumptions 1, 2, and 3.

7.2.1 Performance of OLAC

We now analyze the performance of the OLAC algorithm. It is important to note that $\tilde{\boldsymbol{\gamma}}^*(t)$ is a function of $\boldsymbol{\beta}(t)$. Under OLAC, however, the value of $\boldsymbol{\beta}(t)$ changes every time slot. Hence, analyzing the performance of OLAC is non-trivial. Fortunately, using (22), we know that $\tilde{\boldsymbol{\gamma}}^*(t)$ eventually converges to $\boldsymbol{\theta}$ with probability 1. This allows us to prove the following theorem, which states that the average queue size under OLAC is mainly determined by the vector $\boldsymbol{\theta}$.

Theorem 1. *Suppose (i) $g_0(\boldsymbol{\gamma})$ is polyhedral with $\rho = \Theta(1) > 0$, and (ii) $\boldsymbol{Q}(t)$ has a countable state space under* OLAC. *Then, under* OLAC, *we have w.p.1 that:*

$$\overline{q}_{av} = \sum_j \theta_j + O(1). \quad (27)$$

Proof. Omitted due to space limitation. See [24] for details. □

Theorem 1 shows that by using the decision making rule (15) with the effective backlog $\boldsymbol{Q}(t)$, one can guarantee that the average queue size is roughly $\sum_j \theta_j$. Hence, by choosing $\theta_j = \Theta([\log(V)]^2)$, we recover the delay performance achieved in [17] and [18].

It is tempting to choose $\theta_j = 0$, in which case one can indeed make the average queue size $\Theta(1)$. However, as discussed before, the choice of $\boldsymbol{\theta}$ also affects the utility performance of OLAC. Indeed, choosing a small $\boldsymbol{\theta}$ forces the system to run in an *over-provision* mode by always having an effectively backlog very close (or larger) to $\boldsymbol{\gamma}^*$. However, in order to achieve a near-optimal utility performance, the control algorithm must be able to timeshare the over-provision mode and under-provision actions [21]. Therefore, it is necessary to use a larger $\boldsymbol{\theta}$ value.

In the following theorem, we show that an $O(1/V)$ close-to-optimal utility can be achieved as long as we choose $\theta_j = \Theta([\log(V)]^2)$ for all $j = 1, ..., r$. Our analysis is different from the previous Lyapunov analysis and will be useful for analyzing similar problems (Recall that $\epsilon = 1/V$).

Theorem 2. *Suppose the conditions in Theorem 1 hold. Then, with a sufficiently large V and $\theta_j = [\log(V)]^2$ for all j, we have w.p.1 that:*

$$f_{av}^{\mathtt{OLAC}} = f_{av}^* + O(\frac{1}{V}). \quad (28)$$

Proof. See Appendix C. □

Theorems 1 and 2 together show that OLAC achieves the $[O(1/V), O([\log(V)]^2)]$ utility-delay tradeoff for general stochastic optimization problems. Compared to the algorithms developed in [17] [18], which also achieve the same tradeoff, OLAC preserves using the First-In-First-Out (FIFO) queueing discipline and does not require any pre-learning phase. Thus, it is more suitable for practical implementations.

7.2.2 Performance of OLAC2

We now present the performance results of OLAC2. Since OLAC2 is equivalent to LIFO-backpressure [18] except for the learning step and a finite backlog adjustment at time $t = T_l$, its performance is the same as LIFO-Backpressure. [3]

The following theorem from [18] summarizes the results.

Theorem 3. *Suppose (i) $g_0(\boldsymbol{\gamma})$ is polyhedral with $\rho = \Theta(1) > 0$, and (ii) $\boldsymbol{q}(t)$ has a countable state space under* OLAC2. *Then, with a sufficiently large V,*

1) *The utility under* OLAC2 *satisfies $f_{av}^{\mathtt{OLAC2}} = f_{av}^* + O(\frac{1}{V})$.*

2) *For any queue j with a time average input rate $\lambda_j > 0$, there are a subset of packets from the arrivals that eventually depart the queue and have an average rate $\tilde{\lambda}_j$ that satisfies:*

$$\lambda_j \geq \tilde{\lambda}_j \geq \left[\lambda_j - O(\frac{1}{V^{\log(V)}})\right]^+. \quad (29)$$

Moreover, the average delay of these packets is $O(\frac{[\log(V)]^2}{\tilde{\lambda}_j})$.

Proof. See [18]. □

Theorem 3 shows that if a queue $q_j(t)$ has an input rate $\lambda_j = \Theta(1)$, then, under OLAC2, almost all the packets going through $q_j(t)$ will experience only $O([\log(V)]^2)$ delay. Applying this argument to every queue in the network, we see that the average network delay is roughly $O(r[\log(V)]^2)$.

8. CONVERGENCE TIME ANALYSIS

In this section, we study another important performance metric of our techniques, the convergence time. Convergence time measures how fast an algorithm reaches its steady-state. Hence, it is an important indicator of the robustness of the technique. However, it turns out that due to the complex nature of the $\boldsymbol{\beta}(t)$ process and the structure of the systems, the convergence properties of the algorithms are hard to analyze. Therefore, we mainly focus on analyzing the convergence time of OLAC2. We now give the formal definition of the convergence time of an algorithm. In the definition, we use $\boldsymbol{\gamma}(t)$ to denote the estimated Lagrange multiplier under the control schemes, e.g., $\boldsymbol{q}(t)$ under Backpressure and OLAC2 and $\boldsymbol{\beta}(t) + \boldsymbol{\theta} + \boldsymbol{q}(t)$ under OLAC.

[3] Note that OLAC2 may need to discard packets in the backlog dropping step. However, such an event happens with very small probability, as can be seen in the proof of Theorem 5.

Definition 2. *Let $\zeta > 0$ be a given constant. The ζ-convergence time of the control algorithm, denoted by T_ζ, is the time it takes for the estimated Lagrange multiplier $\boldsymbol{\gamma}(t)$ to get to within ζ distance of $\boldsymbol{\gamma}^*$, i.e.,*

$$T_\zeta \triangleq \inf\{t \,|\, ||\boldsymbol{\gamma}(t) - \boldsymbol{\gamma}^*|| \leq \zeta\}. \ \diamond \tag{30}$$

Note that our definition is different from the definition in [25], where convergence time relates to how fast the time-average rates converge to the optimal values. In our case, the convergence time definition (30) is motivated by the fact that Backpressure, OLAC, and OLAC2 all use functions of the queue vector to estimate $\boldsymbol{\gamma}^*$, which is the key for determining the optimal control actions. Hence, the faster the algorithm learns $\boldsymbol{\gamma}^*$, the faster the system enters the optimal operating zone.

In the following, we present the convergence results of OLAC2. As a benchmark comparison, we first study the convergence time of the Backpressure algorithm. Since both Backpressure and OLAC2 use the actual queue size as the estimate of $\boldsymbol{\gamma}^*$, we will analyze the convergence time with $\boldsymbol{\gamma}(t) = \boldsymbol{q}(t)$.

8.1 Convergence time of Backpressure

We start by analyzing the convergence time of Backpressure. Our result is summarized in the following theorem.

Theorem 4. *Suppose that $g_0(\boldsymbol{\gamma})$ is polyhedral with parameter $\rho = \Theta(1) > 0$. Then,*

$$(||\boldsymbol{q}(0) - \boldsymbol{\gamma}^*|| - D_p)^+/B \leq \mathbb{E}\{T_{D_p}\} \leq ||\boldsymbol{q}(0) - \boldsymbol{\gamma}^*||/\eta. \tag{31}$$

Here $\eta \in [0, \rho) = \Theta(1)$ and $D_p = \frac{B-\eta^2}{2(\rho-\eta)} = \Theta(1)$. $\diamond$

Proof. See Appendix D. □

Since $\boldsymbol{\gamma}^* = \Theta(V)$, if $\boldsymbol{q}(0) = \Theta(1)$, e.g., $\boldsymbol{q}(0) = \boldsymbol{0}$, Theorem 4 states that the expected convergence time of Backpressure is $\Theta(V)$. This is consistent with the results that have been observed in previous works, e.g., [1] and [17].

8.2 Convergence time of OLAC2

We now study the convergence time of the OLAC2 scheme. Notice that under OLAC2 the convergence of $\boldsymbol{q}(t)$ to $\boldsymbol{\gamma}^*$ depends on both $\tilde{\boldsymbol{\beta}}$ and the dynamics of the queue vector $\boldsymbol{q}(t)$. The following theorem characterizes the convergence time of OLAC2.

Theorem 5. *Suppose (i) $g_0(\boldsymbol{\gamma})$ is polyhedral with $\rho = \Theta(1) > 0$, and (ii) $\boldsymbol{q}(t)$ has a countable state space under* OLAC2. *Then, with a sufficiently large V, we have with probability of at least $1 - \frac{M}{V^{4\log(V)}}$ that, under* OLAC2,

$$\mathbb{E}\{T_{D_p}\} = O(V^{1-c/2}\log(V) + V^c). \ \diamond \tag{32}$$

Proof. See Appendix E. □

Choosing $c = \frac{2}{3}$, we notice that with very high probability, the system under OLAC2 will enter the near-optimal state in only $O(V^{2/3}\log(V))$ time! This is in contrast to the Backpressure algorithm, whose convergence time is $\Theta(V)$ as shown in Theorem 4.

9. SIMULATION

In this section, we provide simulation results for OLAC and OLAC2 to demonstrate both the near-optimal performance and the the superior convergence rate. We consider a 2-queue system depicted in Fig. 2.

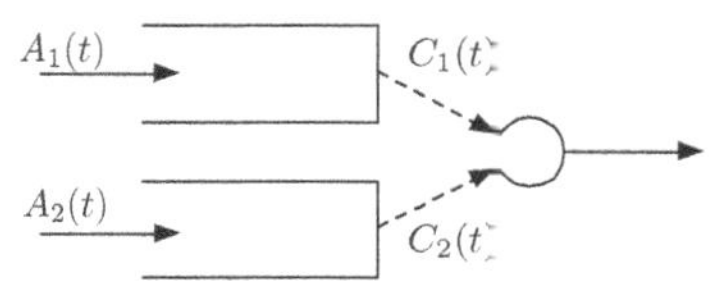

Figure 2: A 2-queue system. In this system, each queue receives random arrivals. The server can only serve one queue at a time.

Here $A_j(t)$ denotes the number of arriving packets to queue j at time t. We assume that $A_j(t)$ is i.i.d. with either 2 or 0 with probabilities p_j and $1-p_j$, where $p_1 = 0.3$ and $p_2 = 0.4$. In this case, we see that $\lambda_1 = 0.6$ and $\lambda_2 = 0.8$. We assume that each queue has a time-varying channel and denote its state by $C_j(t)$. $C_j(t)$ takes value in the set $\mathcal{C} = \{0, 2, 4, 6\}$. At each time, the server decides how much power to allocate to each queue. We denote $P_j(t)$ the power allocated to queue j at time t. Then, the instantaneous service rate a queue obtains is given by:

$$\mu_j(t) = \log(1 + C_j(t)P_j(t)). \tag{33}$$

The feasible power allocation set is given by $\mathcal{P} = \{0, 0.75, 1.5, 2.25, 3\}$. The objective is to stabilize the system with minimum average power. It is important to note that, even though this is a simple setting, it is actually quite representative and models many problems in different contexts, e.g., a downlink system in wireless network, workload scheduling in a power system, inventory control system, and traffic light control. Moreover, it can be verified that Assumptions 1, 2 and 3 all hold in this example.

We compare three algorithms, Backpressure, OLAC and OLAC2. We also consider two different channel distributions. In the first distribution, $C_j(t)$ takes each value in $\mathcal{C}$ with probability 0.25, whereas in the second distribution, $C_j(t)$ takes values 0 and 6 with probability 0.1 and takes values 2 and 4 with probability 0.4. This is to mimic the Gaussian distribution. Note that in each case, we have a total of 16 different channel state combinations.

Fig. 3 and 4 show that OLAC and OLAC2 significantly outperform the Backpressure in terms of delay. For example, in the uniform channel case, we can see from Fig. 3 that when $V = 100$, the average power performance is indistinguishable under the three algorithms. Backpressure results in an average delay of 210 slots while OLAC and OLAC2 only incur an average delay about 20 slots, which is 10 *times* smaller! Fig. 4 shows similar behavior of the algorithms under the unbalanced channel distribution.

Having seen the utility-delay tradeoff of the algorithms, we now look at the convergence rate of the algorithms. Fig. 1 shows the convergence behavior of the first queue under the three different algorithms under the uniform channel distribution with $V = 500$. As we can see, the virtual queue size under OLAC and the actual queue size under OLAC2 converge very quickly. Compared to Backpressure, the convergence time is reduced by about 2500 timeslots. The behavior of the other queue is similar and hence we do not present the results. It is important to notice here that since OLAC and OLAC2 converge very quickly, the early arrivals into the system will depart from the queue without much waiting time (see the queue process under OLAC), whereas in Backpres-

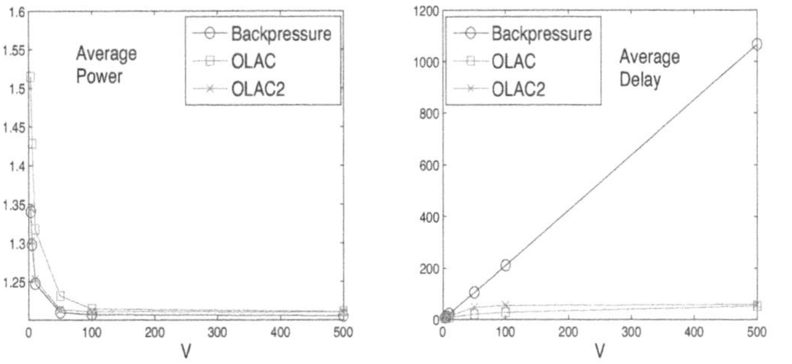

Figure 3: The power-delay performance of the algorithms under uniform channel distribution $[0.25, 0.25, 0.25, 0.25]$. We see that although all algorithms achieve similar near-minimum average power, OLAC and OLAC2 achieve this performance with much smaller delay.

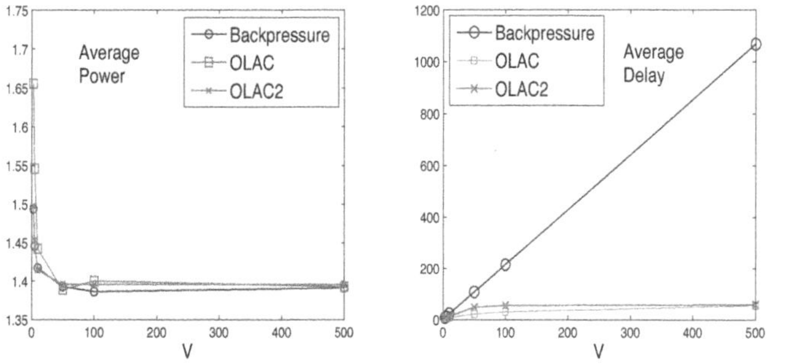

Figure 4: The power-delay performance of the algorithms under the unbalanced channel distribution $[0.1, 0.4, 0.4, 0.1]$. We see again that OLAC and OLAC2 significantly outperform Backpressure in delay.

sure, early arrivals must wait until the algorithm converge to get serve and suffer from a long delay. Fig. 5 also shows the "jump" behavior of the sizes of the queues under OLAC2 under the uniform channel distribution and $V = 500$. It can be seen that the convergence time is significantly reduced via such dual learning (by about 2500 timeslots).

10. CONCLUSION

In this paper, we take a first step to investigate the power of online learning in stochastic network optimization with unknown system statistics *a priori*. We propose two learning-aided control techniques OLAC and OLAC2 for controlling stochastic queueing systems. The design of OLAC and OLAC2 incorporates statistical learning into system control, and provides new ways for designing algorithms for achieving near-optimal system performance for general system utility maximization problems. Moreover, incorporating the learning step significantly improves the convergence speed of the control algorithms. Such insights are not only proven via novel analytical techniques, but also validated through numerical simulations. Our study demonstrates the promising power of online learning in stochastic network optimization. Much further investigation is desired. In particular, we would like to provide theoretical guarantees on the convergence speed on OLAC, and more importantly, understand the fundamental limit of convergence in the online-learning-aided stochastic network optimization. We would like to further investigate practical application scenarios of the proposed schemes and

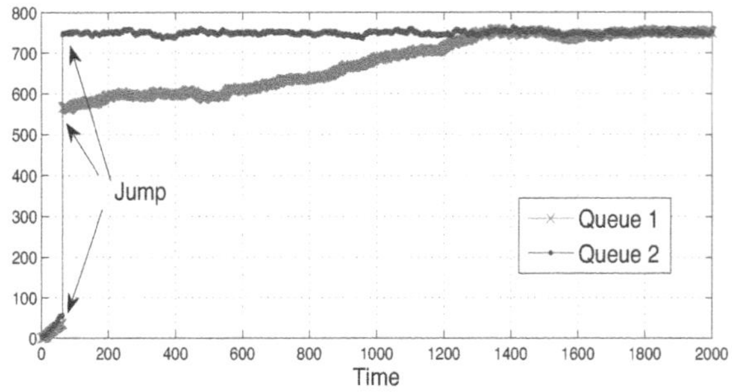

Figure 5: Convergence of the queues to the optimal Lagrange multiplier under OLAC2 with uniform channel distribution and $V = 500$. It can be seen that after only around 80 slots, dual learning already generates a very good estimation of γ^*. This significantly reduces the time for convergence.

address the corresponding challenges in real world applications.

11. ACKNOWLEDGEMENT

This work was supported in part by the National Basic Research Program of China Grant 2011CBA00300,2011CBA00301, the National Natural Science Foundation of China Grant 61033001, 61361136003, 041302007, the China youth 1000-talent grant 610502003, and the MSRA-Tsinghua joint lab grant 041902004.

12. REFERENCES

[1] L. Georgiadis, M. J. Neely, and L. Tassiulas. *Resource Allocation and Cross-Layer Control in Wireless Networks.* Foundations and Trends in Networking Vol. 1, no. 1, pp. 1-144, 2006.

[2] A. Eryilmaz and R. Srikant. Fair resource allocation in wireless networks using queue-length-based scheduling and congestion control. *IEEE/ACM Trans. Netw.*, 15(6):1333–1344, 2007.

[3] R. Urgaonkar and M. J. Neely. Opportunistic scheduling with reliability guarantees in cognitive radio networks. *IEEE Transactions on Mobile Computing*, 8(6):766–777, June 2009.

[4] L. Huang, J. Walrand, and K. Ramchandran. Optimal smart grid tariff. *Information Theory and Applications Workshop (ITA) (Invited), San Diego*, Feb 2012.

[5] M. J. Neely, A. S. Tehrani, and A. G. Dimakis. Effficient algorithms for renewable energy allocation to delay tolerant consumers. *Proceedings of IEEE SmartGridComm*, Oct 2010.

[6] M. J. Neely R. Urgaonkar, B. Urgaonkar and A. Sivasubramaniam. Optimal power cost management using stored energy in data centers. *Proceedings of ACM Sigmetrics*, June 2011.

[7] D. P. Bertsekas. *Dynamic Programming and Optimal Control, Vols. I and II.* Boston: Athena Scientific, 2005 and 2007.

[8] M. J. Neely and L. Huang. Dynamic product assembly and inventory control for maximum profit. *IEEE Conference on Decision and Control (CDC), Atlanta, Georgia*, Dec. 2010.

[9] J. G. Dai and W. Lin. Maximum pressure policies in stochastic processing networks. *Operations Research*, 53(2):197–218, March-April 2005.
[10] L. Jiang and J. Walrand. Stable and utility-maximizing scheduling for stochastic processing networks. *Allerton Conference on Communication, Control, and Computing*, 2009.
[11] P. Varaiya. *The Max-Pressure Controller for Arbitrary Networks of Signalized Intersections.* Advances in Dynamic Network Modeling in Complex 27 Transportation Systems, Complex Networks and Dynamic Systems 2, Springer Science+Business Media New York, 2013.
[12] T. Le, P. Kovacs, N. Walton, H. L. Vu, L. Andrew, and S. Hoogendoorn. Decentralized signal control for urban road networks. *ArXiv Technical Teport, arXiv:1310.0491v1*, Oct 2013.
[13] S. H. Low and D. E. Lapsley. Optimization flow control-I: Basic algorithm and convergence. *IEEE/ACM Transactions on Networking*, 7(6):861–875, Dec. 1999.
[14] M. Chiang, S. H. Low, A. R. Calderbank, and J. C. Doyle. Layering as optimization decomposition: A mathematical theory of network architectures. *Proceedings of the IEEE*, 95(1):255–312, January 2007.
[15] L. Huang and M. J. Neely. The optimality of two prices: Maximizing revenue in a stochastic network. *IEEE/ACM Transactions on Networking*, 18(2):406–419, April 2010.
[16] M. J. Neely. Super-fast delay tradeoffs for utility optimal fair scheduling in wireless networks. *IEEE Journal on Selected Areas in Communications (JSAC), Special Issue on Nonlinear Optimization of Communication Systems*, 24(8):1489–1501, Aug. 2006.
[17] L. Huang and M. J. Neely. Delay reduction via Lagrange multipliers in stochastic network optimization. *IEEE Trans. on Automatic Control*, 56(4):842–857, April 2011.
[18] L. Huang, S. Moeller, M. J. Neely, and B. Krishnamachari. LIFO-backpressure achieves near optimal utility-delay tradeoff. *IEEE/ACM Transactions on Networking*, 21(3):831–844, June 2013.
[19] D. P. Bertsekas, A. Nedic, and A. E. Ozdaglar. *Convex Analysis and Optimization.* Boston: Athena Scientific, 2003.
[20] Sean Meyn. *Control Techniques for Complex Networks.* Cambridge University Press, 2007.
[21] M. J. Neely. Optimal energy and delay tradeoffs for multi-user wireless downlinks. *IEEE Transactions on Information Theory*, 53(9):3095–3113, Sept. 2007.
[22] L. Ying, S. Shakkottai, and A. Reddy. On combining shortest-path and back-pressure routing over multihop wireless networks. *Proceedings of IEEE INFOCOM*, April 2009.
[23] L. Bui, R. Srikant, and A. Stolyar. Novel architectures and algorithms for delay reduction in back-pressure scheduling and routing. *Proceedings of IEEE INFOCOM Mini-Conference*, April 2009.
[24] L. Huang, X. Liu, and X. Hao. The power of online learning in stochastic network optimization. *arXiv Technical Report, arXiv:1404.1592*, 2014.
[25] B. Li, A. Eryilmaz, and R. Li. Wireless scheduling for utility maximization with optimal convergence speed. *Proceedings of IEEE INFOCOM, Turin, Italy*, April 2013.
[26] R. Durrett. *Probability: Theory and Examples.* Duxbury Press, 3rd edition, 2004.
[27] F. Chung and L. Lu. Concentration inequalities and martingale inequalities - a survey. *Internet Math.*, 3 (2006-2007), 79–127.

Appendix A – Proof of Lemma 1

We prove Lemma 1 here.

PROOF. (Lemma 1) First we see that $\pi_{s_i}(t)$ converges to π_{s_i} as t goes to infinity with probability 1 [26]. Thus, there exists a time $T_{\epsilon_s} < \infty$, such that $\|\boldsymbol{\pi}(t) - \boldsymbol{\pi}\| \leq \epsilon_s$ for all $t \geq T_{\epsilon_s}$ with probability 1. This implies that $\boldsymbol{\beta}(t) < \infty$ for all $t \geq T_{\epsilon_s}$ [19]. Indeed, under Assumption 1, we see that there exists an $\eta_0 > 0$ such that (20) holds. Since $-f(\cdot,\cdot)$, $A_j(\cdot,\cdot)$ and $\mu_j(\cdot,\cdot)$ are all concave, the slater condition is satisfied and strong duality holds [19]. Therefore, for any $t \geq T_{\epsilon_s}$, one can plug the variables that result in the slack in (20) into $g(\boldsymbol{\beta}, t)$ and obtain:

$$\begin{aligned} 0 &\leq F(\boldsymbol{x}, \boldsymbol{\pi}(t)) \\ &\overset{(a)}{=} g(\boldsymbol{\beta}(t), t) \\ &\overset{(b)}{\leq} \sum_{s_i} \pi_{s_i}(t)[Vf_{\max} - \eta_0 \sum_j \beta_j(t)]. \end{aligned}$$

Here (a) follows from strong duality, and (b) follows from the definition of $g(\boldsymbol{\beta}, t)$. This shows that $w.p.1$,

$$\sum_j \beta_j(t) \leq \xi \triangleq \frac{Vf_{\max}}{\eta_0}, \ \forall\, t \geq T_{\epsilon_s}. \tag{34}$$

This proves Lemma 1. □

Appendix B – Proof of Corollary 1

We carry out our proof for Corollary 1 here.

PROOF. (Corollary 1) From lemma 1, we see that $w.p.1$ after some T_{ϵ_s} time, $\|\boldsymbol{\beta}(t)\| \leq \xi$. This implies that, for all $t \geq T_{\epsilon_s}$ and all s_i, we have $w.p.1$ that:

$$g_{s_i}(\boldsymbol{\beta}(t)) \leq Vf_{\max} + r\xi B, \quad \forall s_i. \tag{35}$$

Now note that $g(\boldsymbol{\beta}(t), t)$ can be expressed as:

$$g(\boldsymbol{\beta}(t), t) = \sum_{s_i} [\pi_{s_i} + \delta_{s_i}(t)] g_{s_i}(\boldsymbol{\beta}(t)), \tag{36}$$

where $\delta_{s_i}(t) = \pi_{s_i}(t) - \pi_{s_i}$ denotes the error of the empirical distribution. Therefore,

$$\begin{aligned} |g(\boldsymbol{\beta}(t), t) - g(\boldsymbol{\beta}(t))| &\leq \max_{s_i} |\delta_{s_i}(t)| \sum_{s_i} |g_{s_i}(\boldsymbol{\beta}(t))| \qquad (37) \\ &\overset{(a)}{\leq} \max_{s_i} |\delta_{s_i}(t)| M(Vf_{\max} + r\xi B). \end{aligned}$$

The inequality (a) uses the fact that $g_{s_i}(\boldsymbol{\beta}(t)) \leq Vf_{\max} + r\xi B$ for all $t \geq T_{\epsilon_s}$. This implies that with probability 1, after some finite time T_{ϵ_s}, (37) holds for all points $\boldsymbol{\beta}(t)$ generated by solving (13). □

Appendix C – Proof of Theorem 2

To prove Theorem 2, we first have the following simple lemma, which will be used in the proof.

Lemma 4. *Suppose $g_0(\gamma)$ is polyhedral. Let $\overline{\mu}_j^{\texttt{OLAC}}$ and $\overline{A}_j^{\texttt{OLAC}}$ be the average service rate and average arrival rate to queue j under* OLAC. *Then, if $\theta_j > \tilde{D}_p + \delta_{\max}$, we have:*

$$\overline{\mu}_j^{\texttt{OLAC}} - \overline{A}_j^{\texttt{OLAC}} \leq \delta_{\max} c_p e^{-K_p(\theta_j - \tilde{D}_p - \delta_{\max})}, \ w.p.1. \ \diamond \quad (38)$$

PROOF. Omitted due to space limitation. See [24] for details. □

We are now ready to prove Theorem 2.

PROOF. (Theorem 2) We define a Lyapunov function $L(t) = \frac{1}{2}\sum_j q_j^2(t)$ and the one-slot conditional drift $\Delta(t) \triangleq \mathbb{E}\{L(t+1) - L(t) \mid \boldsymbol{q}(t)\}$. Using the queueing dynamic equations (1), we have:

$$\Delta(t) \leq B - \sum_j q_j(t)\mathbb{E}\{\mu_j(t) - A_j(t) \mid \boldsymbol{q}(t)\}. \quad (39)$$

By adding to both sides the term $V\mathbb{E}\{f(t) \mid \boldsymbol{q}(t)\} - \sum_j \mathbb{E}\{(\beta_j(t) - \theta_j)[\mu_j(t) - A_j(t)] \mid \boldsymbol{q}(t)\}$, we obtain:

$$\begin{aligned}
&\Delta(t) + V\mathbb{E}\{f(t) \mid \boldsymbol{q}(t)\} \quad (40)\\
&\quad - \sum_j \mathbb{E}\{(\beta_j(t) - \theta_j)[\mu_j(t) - A_j(t)] \mid \boldsymbol{q}(t)\}\\
&\leq B + V\mathbb{E}\{f(t) \mid \boldsymbol{q}(t)\}\\
&\quad - \sum_j \mathbb{E}\{(q_j(t) + \beta_j(t) - \theta_j)[\mu_j(t) - A_j(t)] \mid \boldsymbol{q}(t)\}.
\end{aligned}$$

Using Assumption 2 and plugging in (40) the optimal stationary and randomized policy $\{x_k^{(s_i)*}, \vartheta_k^{(s_i)*}\}_{s_i,k}$, we obtain:

$$\begin{aligned}
&\Delta(t) + V\mathbb{E}\{f^{\texttt{OLAC}}(t) \mid \boldsymbol{q}(t)\} \quad (41)\\
&\quad - \sum_j \mathbb{E}\{(\beta_j(t) - \theta_j)[\mu_j^{\texttt{OLAC}}(t) - A_j^{\texttt{OLAC}}(t)] \mid \boldsymbol{q}(t)\}\\
&\leq B + Vf_{\text{av}}^*.
\end{aligned}$$

Here $f^{\texttt{OLAC}}(t)$, $\mu_j^{\texttt{OLAC}}(t)$ and $A_j^{\texttt{OLAC}}(t)$ denote the cost, service rate and arrival rate under the OLAC algorithm. Rearranging the terms, we have:

$$\begin{aligned}
&\Delta(t) + V\mathbb{E}\{f^{\texttt{OLAC}}(t) \mid \boldsymbol{q}(t)\} \leq B + Vf_{\text{av}}^* \quad (42)\\
&\quad + \sum_j \mathbb{E}\{(\beta_j(t) - \theta_j)[\mu_j^{\texttt{OLAC}}(t) - A_j^{\texttt{OLAC}}(t)] \mid \boldsymbol{q}(t)\}.
\end{aligned}$$

Taking expectations on both sides of (42) over $\boldsymbol{q}(t)$, taking a telescoping sum over $t = 0, ..., T-1$, rearranging the terms, dividing both sides by TV, and taking a lim sup as $T \to \infty$, we have:

$$\begin{aligned}
&\limsup_{T\to\infty} \frac{1}{T}\sum_{t=0}^{T-1} \mathbb{E}\{f^{\texttt{OLAC}}(t)\} \leq \frac{B}{V} + f_{\text{av}}^* \quad (43)\\
&+ \limsup_{T\to\infty} \frac{1}{T}\sum_{t=0}^{T-1} \mathbb{E}\{\sum_j \frac{(\beta_j(t) - \theta_j)}{V}[\mu_j^{\texttt{OLAC}}(t) - A_j^{\texttt{OLAC}}(t)]\}.
\end{aligned}$$

It remains to show that the last term is $O(1/V)$. From Lemma 2 we know that $\beta_j(t) - \theta_j$ converges to $\gamma_j^* - \theta_j = \Theta(V)$ with probability 1. Thus, *w.p.*1, there exists a finite time T_ϵ, such that for all $t \geq T_\epsilon$,

$$|(\beta_j(t) - \theta_j) - (\gamma_j^* - \theta_j)| \leq \epsilon, \ \forall j. \quad (44)$$

Hence, we have:

$$\begin{aligned}
&\limsup_{T\to\infty} \frac{1}{T}\sum_{t=0}^{T-1} \mathbb{E}\{\frac{(\beta_j(t) - \theta_j)}{V}[\mu_j^{\texttt{OLAC}}(t) - A_j^{\texttt{OLAC}}(t)]\}\\
&\overset{(a)}{\leq} (\frac{\gamma_j^* - \theta_j + \epsilon}{V}) \limsup_{T\to\infty} \frac{1}{T}\sum_{t=0}^{T-1} \mathbb{E}\{\mu_j^{\texttt{OLAC}}(t)\}\\
&\quad - (\frac{\gamma_j^* - \theta_j - \epsilon}{V}) \limsup_{T\to\infty} \frac{1}{T}\sum_{t=0}^{T-1} \mathbb{E}\{A_j^{\texttt{OLAC}}(t)\}\\
&\leq \frac{\gamma_j^* - \theta_j}{V}(\overline{\mu}_j^{\texttt{OLAC}} - \overline{A}_j^{\texttt{OLAC}}) + \frac{2\epsilon\delta_{\max}}{V}. \quad (45)
\end{aligned}$$

Here (a) follows from the fact that $T_\epsilon < \infty$. Using Lemma 4 with $\theta_j = [\log(V)]^2$ and a sufficiently large V such that $K_p([\log(V)]^2 - \tilde{D}_p - \delta_{\max}) \geq 2\log(V)$, we have:

$$\overline{\mu}_j^{\texttt{OLAC}} - \overline{A}_j^{\texttt{OLAC}} \leq \frac{\delta_{\max} c_p e^{K_p(\tilde{D}_p + \delta_{\max})}}{e^{K_p[\log(V)]^2}} = O(\frac{1}{V^2}). \quad (46)$$

We first consider when $\gamma_{0j}^* > 0$. In this case, $\gamma_j^* = V\gamma_{0j}^* = \Theta(V)$. Thus, (46) implies that:

$$(\gamma_j^* - \theta_j)(\overline{\mu}_j^{\texttt{OLAC}} - \overline{A}_j^{\texttt{OLAC}}) = O(\frac{1}{V}). \quad (47)$$

Using (45) and (46), we conclude that, with probability 1,

$$\limsup_{T\to\infty} \frac{1}{T}\sum_{t=0}^{T-1} \mathbb{E}\{f^{\texttt{OLAC}}(t)\} \leq f_{\text{av}}^* + \frac{B}{V} + O(\frac{1}{V}). \quad (48)$$

In the case when $\gamma_j^* = 0$, we see that (47) still holds. Hence, (48) again follows from (47). This completes the proof of Theorem 2. □

Appendix D – Proof of Theorem 4

To prove the theorem, we make use of the following technical lemma from [19].

Lemma 5. *Let $\mathcal{F}_n$ be filtration, i.e., a sequence of increasing σ-algebras with $\mathcal{F}_n \subset \mathcal{F}_{n+1}$. Suppose the sequence of random variables $\{y_n\}_{n\geq 0}$ satisfy:*

$$\mathbb{E}\{||y_{n+1} - y^*|| \mid \mathcal{F}_n\} \leq \mathbb{E}\{||y_n - y^*|| \mid \mathcal{F}_n\} - u_n, \quad (49)$$

where u_n takes the following values:

$$u_n = \begin{cases} u & \text{if } ||y_n - y^*|| \geq D, \\ 0 & \text{else.} \end{cases} \quad (50)$$

Here $u > 0$ is a given constant. Then, by defining $N_D \triangleq \inf\{k \mid ||y_n - y^*|| \leq D\}$, we have:

$$\mathbb{E}\{N_D\} \leq ||y_0 - y^*||/u. \ \diamond \quad (51)$$

PROOF. See [19]. □

PROOF. (Theorem 4) From Lemma 3, we see that (26) holds for all t under Backpressure with $\eta < \rho$ and $D_p = \frac{B-\eta^2}{2(\rho-\eta)}$. Hence, using Lemma 5, we have:

$$\mathbb{E}\{T_{D_p}\} \leq ||\boldsymbol{q}(0) - \boldsymbol{\gamma}^*||/\eta.$$

On the other hand, since $\|\boldsymbol{q}(t+1) - \boldsymbol{q}(t)\| \leq B$, i.e., in every time the queue vector can change by at most B distance, we must have $\mathbb{E}\{T_{D_p}\} \geq (||\boldsymbol{q}(0) - \boldsymbol{\gamma}^*|| - D_p)^+/B$. □

Appendix E – Proof of Theorem 5

We prove Theorem 5 in this section. We first have the following lemma regarding the distance between $\boldsymbol{\beta}(t)$ and the distribution estimation accuracy.

Lemma 6. *With probability* 1, *there exists an* $\Theta(1)$ *time* T_{ϵ_s} *(defined in Lemma 1) such that, for all* $t \geq T_{\epsilon_s}$,

$$\|\boldsymbol{\beta}(t) - \boldsymbol{\gamma}^*\| \leq 2\max_{s_i} |\delta_{s_i}(t)| M(Vf_{\max} + r\xi B)/\rho. \quad (52)$$

PROOF. See Appendix F. □

Lemma 6 shows that under the polyhedral condition, the distance between the current estimate of the Lagrange multiplier value and the true value diminishes as the empirical distribution converges. This is an important result, as it allows us to focus mainly on the convergence of the distribution when studying the algorithm's convergence. To show our results, we also make use of the following theorem regarding distribution convergence [27].

Theorem 6. *Let* X_1, ..., X_n *be independent random variables with* $Pr\{X_i = 1\} = p_i$, *and* $Pr\{X_i = 0\} = 1 - p_i$. *Consider* $X = \sum_{i=1}^n X_i$ *with expectation* $\mathbb{E}\{X\} = \sum_{i=1}^n p_i$. *Then, we have:*

$$Pr\{X \leq \mathbb{E}\{X\} - m\} \leq e^{\frac{-m^2}{2\mathbb{E}\{X\}}}, \quad (53)$$

$$Pr\{X \geq \mathbb{E}\{X\} + m\} \leq e^{\frac{-m^2}{2(\mathbb{E}\{X\}+m/3)}}. \quad \diamond \quad (54)$$

We now state the proof of the convergence time for `OLAC2`.

PROOF. (Theorem 5) Choosing $n = T_l = V^c$ and $m = 4V^{c/2}\log(V)$ in Theorem 6, and let X_t be the indicator of state s_i at time t for $0 \leq t \leq n-1$. Then, we have $\mathbb{E}\{X\} = V^c\pi_{s_i}$. Thus, using the fact that $\pi_{s_i} \leq 1$, we see that at time $t = T_l$,

$$\Pr\{\pi_{s_i}(t) \leq \pi_{s_i} - \frac{4\log(V)}{V^{c/2}}\} \leq e^{-8[\log(V)]^2},$$

$$\Pr\{\pi_{s_i}(t) \geq \pi_{s_i} + \frac{4\log(V)}{V^{c/2}}\} \leq e^{-\frac{8[\log(V)]^2}{1+\frac{2}{3}\log(V)V^{-c/2}}}.$$

Using the union bound, we see that when V is large enough such that $\frac{2}{3}\log(V)V^{-c/2} \leq 1$,

$$\Pr\{\max_{s_i} |\pi_{s_i}(t) - \pi_{s_i}| \geq \frac{4\log(V)}{V^{c/2}}\} \leq Me^{-4[\log(V)]^2}. \quad (55)$$

Therefore, using Lemma 6, we see that with probability at least $1 - \frac{M}{V^{4\log(V)}}$, at time $t = T_l$,

$$\|\tilde{\boldsymbol{\beta}} - \boldsymbol{\gamma}^*\| \leq \frac{8\log(V)M(Vf_{\max} + r\xi B)}{\rho V^{c/2}} = \Theta(V^{1-c/2}\log(V)), \quad (56)$$

which implies that at time $t = T_l$,

$$\|\boldsymbol{q}(T_l) - \boldsymbol{\gamma}^*\| = \Theta(V^{1-c/2}\log(V)). \quad (57)$$

Now note that given the same backlog values, `OLAC2` always uses the same actions as LIFO-Backpressure. Using Lemma 3 with $T_{\epsilon_s} = 0$, we see that at any time $t \geq T_l$, if $\|\boldsymbol{q}(t) - \boldsymbol{\gamma}^*\| \geq D_p$, we have:

$$\mathbb{E}\{\|\boldsymbol{q}(t+1) - \boldsymbol{\gamma}^*\| \mid \boldsymbol{q}(t)\} \leq \|\boldsymbol{q}(t) - \boldsymbol{\gamma}^*\| - \eta. \quad (58)$$

Using Lemma 5, we conclude that with probability at least $1 - \frac{M}{V^{4\log(V)}}$:

$$\mathbb{E}\{T_{D_p}\} = O(V^{1-c/2}\log(V)) + T_l \quad (59)$$

$$= O(V^{1-c/2}\log(V) + V^c). \quad (60)$$

This completes the proof of Theorem 5. □

Appendix F – Proof of Lemma 6

Here we prove Lemma 6.

PROOF. (Lemma 6) As in Lemma 1, we have:

$$g(\boldsymbol{\beta}, t) = \sum_{s_i} [\pi_{s_i} + \delta_s(t)] g_{s_i}(\boldsymbol{\beta}). \quad (61)$$

Also, for any t, $g(\boldsymbol{\beta}(t), t) \geq g(\boldsymbol{\gamma}^*, t)$. By Lemma 1, we see that $w.p.1$, for all $t \geq T_{\epsilon_s}$,

$$|g(\boldsymbol{\beta}(t), t) - g(\boldsymbol{\beta}(t))| \leq \max_{s_i} |\delta_{s_i}(t)| M(Vf_{\max} + r\xi B).$$

This implies that:

$$g(\boldsymbol{\gamma}^*) - g(\boldsymbol{\beta}(t)) \leq 2\max_{s_i} |\delta_{s_i}(t)| M(Vf_{\max} + r\xi B). \quad (62)$$

This is so because if (62) does not hold, then:

$$\begin{aligned} & g(\boldsymbol{\beta}(t), t) - g(\boldsymbol{\gamma}^*, t) \\ \leq\ & g(\boldsymbol{\beta}(t)) + \max_{s_i} |\delta_{s_i}(t)| M(Vf_{\max} + r\xi B) \\ & -[g(\boldsymbol{\gamma}^*) - \max_{s_i} |\delta_{s_i}(t)| M(Vf_{\max} + r\xi B)] \\ <\ & 0, \end{aligned}$$

which contradicts with $g(\boldsymbol{\beta}(t), t) \geq g(\boldsymbol{\gamma}^*, t)$. Now with (62) and (23), i.e., $g(\boldsymbol{\gamma}^*) - g(\boldsymbol{\beta}) \geq \rho\|\boldsymbol{\gamma}^* - \boldsymbol{\beta}\|$, we see that $w.p.1$, for all $t \geq T_{\epsilon_s} = \Theta(1)$,

$$\|\boldsymbol{\beta}(t) - \boldsymbol{\gamma}^*\| \leq 2\max_{s_i} |\delta_{s_i}(t)| M(Vf_{\max} + r\xi B)/\rho. \quad (63)$$

This completes the proof of Lemma 6. □

Is Sharing with Retransmissions Causing Instabilities?

Predrag R. Jelenković Evangelia D. Skiani
Department of Electrical Engineering
Columbia University, New York, NY 10027
{predrag, valia}@ee.columbia.edu

ABSTRACT

Retransmissions represent a primary failure recovery mechanism on all layers of communication network architecture. Similarly, fair sharing, e.g. processor sharing (PS), is a widely accepted approach to resource allocation among multiple users. Recent work has shown that retransmissions in failure-prone, e.g. wireless ad hoc, networks can cause heavy tails and long delays. In this paper, we discover a new phenomenon showing that PS-based scheduling induces complete instability in the presence of retransmissions, regardless of how low the traffic load may be. This phenomenon occurs even when the job sizes are bounded/fragmented, e.g. deterministic. Our analytical results are further validated via simulation experiments. Moreover, our work demonstrates that scheduling one job at a time, such as first-come-first-serve, achieves stability and should be preferred in these systems.

Categories and Subject Descriptors

G.3 [**Probability And Statistics**]: Probabilistic algorithms; C.4 [**Performance of Systems**]: Performance Attributes; H.4 [**Information Systems Applications**]: Miscellaneous

General Terms

Theory, Performance

Keywords

Retransmissions; fair sharing; instabilities; failure-prone systems; Processor Sharing; Discriminatory Processor Sharing; FCFS; scheduling; M/G/1 queue

1. INTRODUCTION

High variability and frequent failures characterize the majority of large-scale systems, e.g. infrastructure-less wireless networks, cloud/parallel computing systems, etc. The nature of these systems imposes the employment of failure recovery mechanisms to guarantee their good performance. One of the most straightforward and widely used recovery mechanism is to simply restart all of the interrupted jobs from the beginning after a failure occurs. In communication systems, restart mechanisms lie at the core of the network architecture where retransmissions are used on all protocol layers to guarantee data delivery in the presence of channel failures e.g. Automatic Repeat reQuest (ARQ) protocol [3], contention based ALOHA type protocols in the medium access control (MAC) layer, end-to-end acknowledgements in the transport layer, HTTP downloading scheme in the application layer, and others.

Furthermore, sharing is a primary approach to fair scheduling and efficient management of the available resources. Fair allocation of the network resources among different users can be highly beneficial for increasing throughput and utilization. For instance, CDMA is a multiple access method used in communication networks where several users can transmit information simultaneously over a single channel via sharing the available bandwidth. Another example is Processor Sharing (PS) scheduling [19] where the capacity is equally shared between multiple classes of customers. In *Generalized* PS (GPS) [14, 15], service allocation is done according to some fixed weights. The related *Discriminatory* PS (DPS) [1, 5, 13] is used in computing to model the Weighted Round Robin (WRR) scheduling, while it is also used in communications, as a flow level model of heterogenous TCP connections. Similarly, fair queuing (FQ) is a scheduling algorithm where the link capacity is fairly shared among active network flows; in weighted fair queuing (WFQ), which is the discretized version of GPS, different scheduling priorities are assigned to each flow.

In general, PS-based scheduling disciplines have been widely used in modeling computer and communication networks. Early investigations of PS queues were motivated by applications in multiuser computer systems [4]. The M/G/1 PS queue has been studied extensively in the literature [18]. In the case of the M/M/1 PS system, the conditional Laplace transform of the waiting time was derived in [4]. The importance of scheduling in the presence of heavy tails was first recognized in [2], and later, in [7], the M/G/1 PS queue was studied assuming subexponential job sizes; see also [7] for additional references.

In [17], it was proven that, although there are policies known to optimize the sojourn time tail under a large class of heavy-tailed job sizes (e.g. PS and SRPT) and there

This work is supported by the National Science Foundation grant number 0915784.

SIGMETRICS'14, June 16–20, 2014, Austin, Texas, USA.

http://dx.doi.org/10.1145/2591971.2592001.

are policies known to optimize the sojourn time tail in the case of light-tailed job sizes, e.g. FCFS, no policies are known to optimize the sojourn time tail across both light and heavy-tailed job size distributions. Indeed, such policies must "learn" the job size distribution in order to optimize the sojourn time tail. In the heavy-tailed scenarios, any scheduling policy that assigns the server exclusively to a very large job, e.g. FCFS, may induce long delays, in which case, sharing guarantees better performance.

In this paper, we study the effects of sharing on the system performance when restarts are employed in the presence of failures. We revisit the well-studied M/G/1 queue with failures and restarts and focus on the PS scheduling policy. We use the following generic model, which was first introduced in [6] in the application context of computing. The system dynamics is described as a process $(A, \{A_n\}_{n\geqslant 1})$, where A_n correspond to the periods when the system is available. $(A, \{A_n\}_{n\geqslant 1})$ is a sequence of i.i.d random variables, independent of the job sizes. In each period of time that the system is available, say A_n, we attempt to execute a job of random size B. If $A_n > B$, we say that the job is successfully completed; otherwise, we restart the job from the beginning in the following period A_{n+1} when the channel is available.

With regard to retransmissions, it was first recognized in [6, 16] that restart mechanisms may result in heavy-tailed (power law) delays even if the job sizes and failure rates are light-tailed. In [11], it was shown that the power law delays arise whenever the hazard functions of the data and failure distributions are proportional. In the practically important case of bounded data units, a uniform characterization of the entire body of the retransmission distribution was derived in [10, 8], which allows for determining the optimal size of data units/fragments in order to alleviate the power law effect. Later, these results were extended to the case where the channel is highly correlated [9], i.e. switches between states with different characteristics, and was proved that the delays are insensitive to the channel correlations and are determined by the 'best' channel state.

In this paper, our main contributions are the following. First, we prove that the M/G/1 PS queue is always unstable, regardless of how light the load is and how small the job sizes may be, see Theorems 3.1 and 3.2 in Section 3. This is a new phenomenon, since, contrary to the conventional belief, sharing the service even between deterministic jobs can render the system completely unstable when retransmissions/restarts are employed. The intuition is the following. If a large number of jobs arrives in a short period of time, then under the elongated service time distribution induced by retransmissions, the queue will keep accumulating jobs that will equally share the capacity, which further exacerbates the problem. Every time a failure occurs, the system resets and the service requirement for each job elongates as the queue size increases. The expected delay until the system clears becomes increasingly long and, consequently, the queue will continue to grow leading to instability. This result also applies to the *Discriminatory* PS (DPS) queue, where the service is not shared equally but according to some fixed weights.

We would also like to emphasize that job fragmentation cannot stabilize the system regardless of how small the fragments are made, since Theorem 3.1 shows instability for any minimum job size $\beta > 0$. In our experimental results, we make an interesting observation on the system behavior before it saturates. There exists a transient period, during which the queue appears as if it were stable. Although it may occasionally accumulate a substantial number of jobs, it returns to zero and starts afresh. However, there exists a time when the queue reaches a critical size after which the service rate of the jobs reduces so much that neither of them can depart. Hence, as the queue continues to increase in size, the system becomes unstable.

Next, in order to gain further insight into the system, we focus on its transient behavior and study the properties of the completion time of a finite number of jobs with no future arrivals. Specifically, we compare two work-conserving policies: scheduling one job at a time, e.g. FCFS, and PS. Overall, we discover that serving one job at a time exhibits uniformly better performance than PS; compare Theorems 4.2 and 4.3, respectively. Furthermore, under more technical assumptions, and for light-tailed job/failure distributions, we show that PS performs distinctly worse compared to the heavy-tailed ones.

From an engineering perspective, our results indicate that traditional approaches in existing systems may be inadequate in the presence of failures. This new phenomenon demonstrates the need of revisiting existing techniques to large-scale failure-prone systems, where PS-based scheduling may perform poorly. For example, since PS is unstable even for deterministic jobs, packet fragmentation, which is widely used in communications, cannot alleviate instabilities. Indeed, fragmentation can only postpone the time when the instability occurs, but cannot eliminate the phenomenon; see Example 1 in Section 5. Therefore, serving one job at a time, e.g. FCFS, is highly advisable in such systems.

The paper is organized as follows. In Section 2, we introduce the model along with the necessary definitions and notation. Next, in Section 3, we present our main results on the M/G/1 queue. Later, in Section 4, we analyze a static system under two different scheduling policies, e.g. serving the jobs one at a time and PS. Last, Section 5 presents our simulation experiments that validate our main theoretical findings, while Section 6 concludes the paper.

2. DEFINITIONS AND NOTATION

First, we provide the necessary definitions and notation assuming that the jobs are served individually. Consider a generic job of random size B requesting service in a failure-prone system. Without loss of generality, we assume that the system is of unit capacity. Its dynamics is described as a process $(A, \{A_n\}_{n\geqslant 1})$ of availability periods, where at the end of each period A_n, the system experiences a failure, as shown in Figure 1.

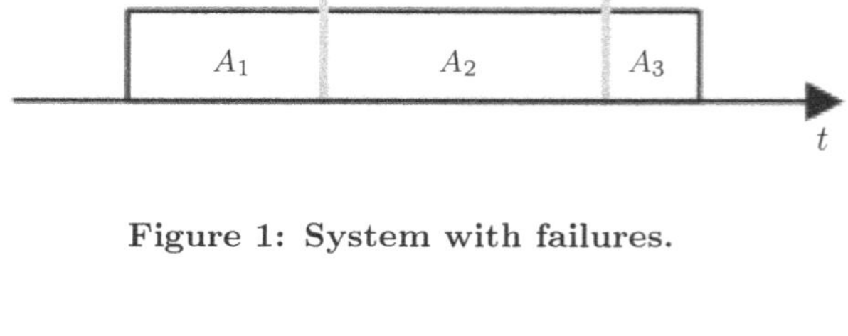

Figure 1: System with failures.

At each period of time that the system becomes available, say A_n, we attempt to process a generic job of size B. If $A_n > B$, we say that the job is completed successfully; otherwise, we wait until the next period A_{n+1} when the channel is available and restart the job. A sketch of the model depicting the system is drawn in Figure 2.

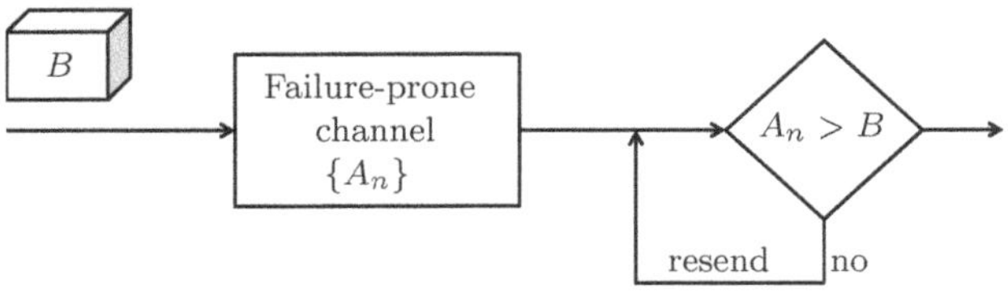

Figure 2: Jobs executed in system with failures.

Definition 2.1 *The number of restarts for a generic job of size B is defined as*

$$N \triangleq \inf\{n : A_n > B\}.$$

We are interested in computing the total service time S until B is successfully completed, which is formally defined as follows.

Definition 2.2 *The service time is the total time until a generic job of size B is successfully completed and is denoted as*

$$S \triangleq \sum_{i=1}^{N-1} A_i + B.$$

We denote the complementary cumulative distribution functions for A and B, respectively, as

$$\bar{G}(x) \triangleq \mathbb{P}(A > x) \qquad \text{and} \qquad \bar{F}(x) \triangleq \mathbb{P}(B > x).$$

Throughout the paper, we assume that the functions $\bar{G}(x)$ and $\bar{F}(x)$ are absolutely continuous for all $x \geqslant 0$. We also use the following standard notation. For any two real functions $f(x)$ and $g(x)$ and fixed $x_0 \in \mathbb{R} \cup \{\infty\}$, we say $f(x) \sim g(x)$ as $x \to x_0$, to denote $\lim_{x \to x_0} f(x)/g(x) = 1$.

3. M/G/1 QUEUE WITH RESTARTS

In this section, we discuss the stability of the M/G/1 queue under two scheduling disciplines: First Come First Serve (FCFS) and Processor Sharing (PS). In the following subsection, we derive the necessary and sufficient condition for the system to be stable when the jobs are processed one at a time and in the order they arrive in the system. Next, in subsection 3.2, we show in Theorems 3.1 and 3.2 that the M/G/1 PS queue is unstable.

3.1 First Come First Serve Queue

In the FCFS discipline, each job is processed one at a time and therefore the expected service time for a single job is given from Definition 2.2 as

$$\mathbb{E}[S] = \mathbb{E}\left[\sum_{i=1}^{N-1} A_i + B\right].$$

Note that $N \triangleq \inf\{n : A_n > B\}$ is a well defined stopping time for the process $(A, \{A_n\}_{n\geqslant 1})$, and thus the expected service time follows from Wald's identity as

$$\begin{aligned}\mathbb{E}[S] &= \mathbb{E}\left[\sum_{i=1}^{N} A_i - A_N + B\right] \\ &= \mathbb{E}[N]\mathbb{E}[A] - \mathbb{E}[A_N] + \mathbb{E}[B].\end{aligned}$$

Now, assuming that the availability periods A are exponentially distributed with rate μ (Poisson failures), the expected service time is given by

$$\begin{aligned}\mathbb{E}[S] &= \mathbb{E}[N]\mathbb{E}[A] - (\mathbb{E}[A] + \mathbb{E}[B]) + \mathbb{E}[B] \\ &= (\mathbb{E}[N] - 1)\mathbb{E}[A], \end{aligned} \tag{3.1}$$

since $\mathbb{E}[A_N] = \mathbb{E}[\mathbb{E}[A|A > B]] = \mathbb{E}[A+B] = \mathbb{E}[A]+\mathbb{E}[B]$, due to the memoryless property of the exponential distribution.

The necessary and sufficient condition for the stability of the M/G/1 FCFS queue is

$$\lambda\mathbb{E}[S] < 1.$$

Now, let the jobs be fixed and all equal to some positive constant $\beta > 0$. Since A is exponentially distributed with rate μ, then

$$\mathbb{P}[N > n] = \mathbb{P}(A \leqslant \beta)^n = G(\beta)^n,$$

and thus, the expected number of restarts is

$$\mathbb{E}[N] = \sum_{n=0}^{\infty} \mathbb{P}[N > n] = \sum_{n=0}^{\infty} G(\beta)^n = \bar{G}(\beta)^{-1} = e^{\mu\beta}. \tag{3.2}$$

Furthermore, for fixed jobs $B = \beta$, we can compute explicitly $\mathbb{E}[S]$ without the exponential assumption on A. To this end, note that

$$\begin{aligned}\mathbb{E}[S] &= \mathbb{E}\left[\sum_{i=1}^{N-1} A_i + \beta\right] = \mathbb{E}\left[\sum_{n=2}^{\infty} \mathbf{1}_{\{N=n\}} \sum_{i=1}^{n-1} A_i + \beta\right] \\ &= \mathbb{E}\left[\sum_{n=2}^{\infty} \mathbf{1}_{\{A_1<\beta, A_2<\beta, \dots, A_{n-1}<\beta, A_n \geqslant \beta\}} \sum_{i=1}^{n-1} A_i\right] + \beta \\ &= \sum_{n=2}^{\infty} \mathbb{E}\left(\sum_{i=1}^{n-1} A_i \mathbf{1}_{\{A_1<\beta, A_2<\beta, \dots, A_{n-1}<\beta, A_n\geqslant\beta\}}\right) + \beta,\end{aligned}$$

and since $(A, \{A_i\}_{i\geqslant 1})$ are i.i.d, we obtain

$$\begin{aligned}\mathbb{E}[S] &= \sum_{n=2}^{\infty} (n-1)\mathbb{E}\left[A\mathbf{1}_{\{A<\beta\}}\right] \mathbb{P}(A < \beta)^{n-2}\mathbb{P}(A \geqslant \beta) + \beta \\ &= \sum_{n=2}^{\infty} (n-1)\mathbb{E}\left[A\mathbf{1}_{\{A<\beta\}}\right] \mathbb{P}(N = n-1) + \beta,\end{aligned}$$

where we recall that $\mathbb{P}(N = n) = \mathbb{P}(A < \beta)^{n-1}\mathbb{P}(A \geqslant \beta)$, by definition, and thus,

$$\begin{aligned}\mathbb{E}[S] &= \mathbb{E}\left[A\mathbf{1}_{\{A<\beta\}}\right] \sum_{n=1}^{\infty} n\mathbb{P}(N = n) + \beta \\ &= \mathbb{E}\left[A\mathbf{1}_{\{A<\beta\}}\right] \mathbb{E}[N] + \beta. \end{aligned} \tag{3.3}$$

Hence, for exponential A, the preceding expression (or (3.1)) yields

$$\mathbb{E}[S] = (e^{\mu\beta} - 1)\mu^{-1},$$

and the stability region reduces to

$$\lambda\mathbb{E}[S] = \lambda\mu^{-1}(e^{\mu\beta} - 1) < 1. \qquad (3.4)$$

Note that $\mathbb{E}[S] \geqslant \mu^{-1}\mu\beta = \beta$, where $\lambda\beta < 1$ gives the stability region of the ordinary M/G/1 queue without failures. We observe that as the jobs grow in size, the stability region shrinks. In other words, the larger the β, the slower the arrival rate the queue can accommodate. For FCFS scheduling, if it is not possible to adjust the arrival rate, we could potentially decrease the job sizes, e.g. apply fragmentation techniques, in order to maintain a large stability region without generating too much overhead, resulting from dividing a single job into many smaller ones.

3.2 Instability of Processor Sharing Queue

Here, we show in Theorems 3.1 and 3.2 that the M/G/1 PS queue is unstable when jobs need to restart after failures. We prove that the queue size grows to infinity for general job size distributions, when the jobs have a minimum size. First, in Theorem 3.1, we assume that the job sizes are bounded from below by some positive constant β. This is a natural assumption for communication or computing applications where jobs, e.g. files, packets, threads, must have a header to contain the required information, such as destination address, thread id, etc. Hence, the job sizes, in practice, cannot be smaller than a positive constant. Finally, we drop this requirement and prove the instability result in general; see Theorem 3.2.

In this section, we will assume that A has finite first moment, e.g. $\mathbb{E}A < \infty$. Here, we can assume that the failure process is in stationarity, or more generally, that the first failure occurs at time $0 \leqslant A_0 < \infty$ a.s. and that the time between subsequent failures i and $i+1$, is A_i, where $\{A_i\}_{i\geqslant 1}$ are i.i.d., independent of A_0. If A_0 is the excess distribution of A_1, then the failure process is stationary. The following Theorem 3.1 shows that the queue is unstable, i.e. its size grows to infinity. Let Q_t be the queue size at time t.

Theorem 3.1 *If $\mathbb{E}A < \infty$ and $\mathbb{P}[B \geqslant \beta] = 1, \beta > 0$, then the M/G/1 PS queue is unstable, i.e., for any $Q_0 < \infty$, almost surely*

$$Q_t \to \infty \text{ as } t \to \infty.$$

Remark 1 Although in many applications job arrival times are well modeled by Poisson processes, our result can be generalized to more general arrivals at the expense of additional technical complications. Here, we avoid this analysis for simplicity reasons, but defer it to the extended version of the paper.

Remark 2 By carefully examining the proof, it can be seen that stronger statements about instability can be derived, i.e.

$$\lim_{t\to\infty} \mathbb{P}(\text{no job ever completes service after time } t) = 1.$$

This, along with other generalizations, will be developed in the journal version of the paper.

Proof: First, we begin with a preliminary result. We assume that there are at least k jobs in the queue and there is a failure at time $t = 0$, and provide a lower bound on the probability that any job departs the system. Specifically, we show that, given $Q_0 \geqslant k$,

$$\mathbb{P}(\text{no job ever completes service}) \geqslant 1 - H(\mathbb{E}A\mathbf{1}(A \geqslant \beta k) + e^{-\theta k}), \qquad (3.5)$$

for some $H, \theta > 0$ and all k large.

Let $T_1 = \sum_{i=1}^{ck} A_i$ be the cumulative time that includes the first ck failures; to simplify notation we write $\sum_x^y$ to denote $\sum_{\lceil x\rceil}^{\lfloor y\rfloor}$, where $\lceil x\rceil$ is the smallest integer $\geqslant x$ and $\lfloor y\rfloor$ is the largest integer $\leqslant y$. Now, define the event $\mathcal{A}_1 \equiv \mathcal{A}_1(k) \triangleq \{A_1 < \beta k, A_2 < \beta k, \ldots, A_{ck} < \beta k\}$. On this event, no job can leave the system since $Q_0 \geqslant k$ and all of them are at least of size β. Thus, if they were served in isolation, they could not have completed service in the first ck attempts.

Now, let E_1 denote the event that there is no departure in the first ck attempts and there are at least k arrivals in $(0, T_1]$; we use $Z_{(t_0,t_1]}$ to denote the number of Poisson arrivals in the interval $(t_0, t_1]$, whereas we simply write Z_t for intervals $(0, t]$. Formally,

$$E_1 \supset \underline{E}_1 \triangleq \{Z_{T_1} \geqslant k, \mathcal{A}_1\},$$

on the set $\{Q_0 \geqslant k\}$. Now, observe that

$$\begin{aligned}\mathbb{P}(\underline{E}_1) &\geqslant \mathbb{P}(Z_{T_1} \geqslant k, T_1 \geqslant 2k/\lambda, \mathcal{A}_1)\\ &\geqslant \mathbb{P}(Z_{2k/\lambda} \geqslant k, T_1 \geqslant 2k/\lambda, \mathcal{A}_1)\\ &\geqslant \mathbb{P}(Z_{2k/\lambda} \geqslant k)\mathbb{P}(T_1 \geqslant 2k/\lambda, \mathcal{A}_1),\end{aligned}$$

since Poisson arrivals are independent of the failure process. Thus,

$$\mathbb{P}(\underline{E}_1) \geqslant \mathbb{P}(Z_{2k/\lambda} \geqslant k)\left(\mathbb{P}(\mathcal{A}_1) - \mathbb{P}(T_1 < 2k/\lambda)\right).$$

First, note that

$$\begin{aligned}\mathbb{P}(Z_{2k/\lambda} \geqslant k) &= 1 - \mathbb{P}(Z_{2k/\lambda} < k) = 1 - \mathbb{P}(2k - Z_{2k/\lambda} > k)\\ &\geqslant 1 - e^{-\theta k}\mathbb{E}e^{\theta(2k - Z_{2k/\lambda})} = 1 - e^{\theta k}\mathbb{E}e^{-\theta Z_{2k/\lambda}},\end{aligned}$$

by Cramer's bound for $\theta > 0$. Next, observe that $Z_{2k/\lambda}$ is Poisson with rate $2k$ and thus

$$\mathbb{P}(Z_{2k/\lambda} \geqslant k) \geqslant 1 - e^{\theta k}e^{2(e^{-\theta}-1)k} = 1 - e^{-\theta_1 k},$$

where $\theta_1 = 2(1 - e^{-\theta}) - \theta > 0$, for θ small.

Second, observe that

$$\begin{aligned}\mathbb{P}(T_1 < 2k/\lambda) &= \mathbb{P}\left(\sum_{i=1}^{ck} A_i < 2k/\lambda\right)\\ &= \mathbb{P}\left(\sum_{i=1}^{ck}(A_i - \mathbb{E}A) < 2k/\lambda - ck\mathbb{E}A\right)\\ &\leqslant \mathbb{P}\left(\sum_{i=1}^{3k/\lambda\mathbb{E}A}(\mathbb{E}A - A_i) > k/\lambda\right),\end{aligned}$$

by picking $c \triangleq 3/(\lambda\mathbb{E}A)$. Now, let $X_i \triangleq \mathbb{E}A - A_i$, which are bounded from above since $X_i \leqslant \mathbb{E}A < \infty$, from our main assumption. Therefore, Cramer's large deviation bound implies that

$$\mathbb{P}(T_1 < 2k/\lambda) \leqslant \mathbb{P}\left(\sum_{i=1}^{3k/\lambda\mathbb{E}A} X_i > k/\lambda\right) \leqslant H_2 e^{-\theta_2 k},$$

for some $H_2, \theta_2 > 0$.

Therefore,

$$\begin{aligned}\mathbb{P}(\underline{E}_1) &\geqslant (1-e^{-\theta_1 k})\left(\mathbb{P}(\mathcal{A}_1) - H_2 e^{-\theta_2 k}\right)\\ &\geqslant \mathbb{P}(A<\beta k)^{ck} - (e^{-\theta_1 k} + H_2 e^{-\theta_2 k} - H_2 e^{-(\theta_1+\theta_2)k})\\ &\geqslant (1-\mathbb{P}(A\geqslant \beta k))^{ck} - He^{-\theta k},\end{aligned}$$

where $\theta = \min(\theta_1, \theta_2)$ and $H > 0$ such that $H < (1 + H_2)$. Next, using $1 - x \geqslant e^{-2x}$ for small x, we have for all $k \geqslant k_0$

$$\begin{aligned}\mathbb{P}(\underline{E}_1) &\geqslant e^{-2ck\mathbb{P}(A\geqslant\beta k)} - He^{-\theta k}\\ &\geqslant 1-2ck\mathbb{P}(A\geqslant\beta k) - He^{-\theta k}\\ &\geqslant e^{-4ck\mathbb{P}(A\geqslant\beta k)-2He^{-\theta k}}.\end{aligned}$$

Next, at time $\mathcal{T}_1 = T_1$, on event $\underline{E}_1$, the queue has at least $2k$ jobs, i.e. $Q_{\mathcal{T}_1} \geqslant 2k$, and no jobs have departed. Similarly as before, let $T_2 = \sum_{i=ck+1}^{3ck} A_i$ be the cumulative time that includes the next $2ck$ failures, and define $\mathcal{A}_2 \equiv \mathcal{A}_2(k) \triangleq \{A_{ck+1} < 2\beta k, A_{ck+2} < 2\beta k, \ldots, A_{3ck} < 2\beta k\}$. The probability that no job departs in $(0, \mathcal{T}_2]$, where $\mathcal{T}_2 = T_1 + T_2$, is lower bounded by

$$\begin{aligned}&\mathbb{P}(\text{no job departs in}(0,\mathcal{T}_2])\\ &\geqslant \mathbb{P}(Z_{T_1}\geqslant k, A_1, Q_{\mathcal{T}_1}\geqslant 2k, Z_{(\mathcal{T}_1,\mathcal{T}_2]}\geqslant 2k, A_2)\\ &\geqslant \mathbb{P}(Z_{T_1}\geqslant k, A_1, Z_{T_2}\geqslant 2k, A_2), \qquad (3.6)\end{aligned}$$

since $\{Q_{\mathcal{T}_1} \geqslant 2k\} \supseteq \{Z_{T_1} \geqslant k, A_1\}$ on the set $\{Q_0 \geqslant k\}$.

Now, if E_2 is the event that there is no departure in the next $2ck$ attempts and there are at least $2k$ arrivals in $(\mathcal{T}_1, \mathcal{T}_2]$, then $E_2 \supset \underline{E}_2 \triangleq \{Z_{T_2} \geqslant 2k, \mathcal{A}_2\}$; note that $\underline{E}_2$ is independent of $\underline{E}_1$. Via identical arguments as before, we obtain

$$\begin{aligned}\mathbb{P}(\underline{E}_2) &\geqslant \mathbb{P}(Z_{T_2}\geqslant 2k, T_2\geqslant 4k/\lambda, \mathcal{A}_2)\\ &\geqslant \mathbb{P}(Z_{4k/\lambda}\geqslant 2k)\left(\mathbb{P}(\mathcal{A}_2) - \mathbb{P}(T_2 < 4k/\lambda)\right)\\ &\geqslant e^{-8ck\mathbb{P}(A\geqslant 2\beta k)-2He^{-2\theta k}}.\end{aligned}$$

Therefore, at time $\mathcal{T}_2$, on event $\underline{E}_1 \cap \underline{E}_2$, there are at least $4k$ jobs.

In general, for any n, we can extend the reasoning from (3.6) to obtain

$$\begin{aligned}&\mathbb{P}(\text{no job departs in}(0,\mathcal{T}_n])\\ &\geqslant \mathbb{P}(Z_{T_1}\geqslant k, A_1, Z_{T_2}\geqslant 2k, A_2,\ldots, Z_{T_n}\geqslant 2^{n-1}k, A_n)\\ &= \mathbb{P}(\underline{E}_1\cap\underline{E}_2\cap\cdots\cap\underline{E}_n),\end{aligned}$$

where $\underline{E}_n = \{Z_{T_n} \geqslant 2^{n-1}k, A_n\}$ and $T_n = \sum_{i=(2^{n-1}-1)ck+1}^{(2^n-1)ck} A_i$. Similarly,

$$\mathbb{P}(\underline{E}_n) \geqslant e^{-2^{n+1}ck\mathbb{P}(A\geqslant 2^{n-1}\beta k)-2He^{-\theta 2^{n-1}k}}.$$

Hence, we obtain

$$\begin{aligned}\mathbb{P}(E_1\cap E_2\cap\cdots\cap E_n) &\geqslant \mathbb{P}(\underline{E}_1\cap\underline{E}_2\cap\cdots\cap\underline{E}_n)\\ &= \mathbb{P}(\underline{E}_1)\mathbb{P}(\underline{E}_2)\cdots\mathbb{P}(\underline{E}_n),\end{aligned}$$

since the events $\underline{E}_i$'s are independent. Thus,

$$\begin{aligned}&\mathbb{P}(E_1\cap E_2\cap\cdots\cap E_n)\\ &\geqslant \prod_{i=1}^{n} e^{-2^{i+1}ck\mathbb{P}(A\geqslant 2^{i-1}\beta k)-2He^{-2^{i-1}\theta k}}\\ &= e^{-4\sum_{i=0}^{n-1}2^i ck\mathbb{P}(A\geqslant 2^i\beta k)-2H\sum_{i=0}^{n-1}e^{-2^i\theta k}}\\ &\geqslant e^{-4\sum_{i=0}^{\infty}2^i ck\mathbb{P}(A\geqslant 2^i\beta k)-2He^{-\theta k}\sum_{i=0}^{\infty}e^{-(2^i-1)\theta k}}.\end{aligned}$$

Now, observe that $\sum_{i=0}^{\infty} e^{-(2^i-1)\theta k} < \infty$, and thus we can pick H such that

$$\mathbb{P}(E_1\cap E_2\cap\cdots\cap E_n) \geqslant e^{-4\sum_{i=0}^{\infty}2^i ck\mathbb{P}(A\geqslant 2^i\beta k)-He^{-\theta k}}.$$

Furthermore, we observe that

$$\begin{aligned}\sum_{i=0}^{\infty} 2^i ck\mathbb{P}(A\geqslant 2^i\beta k) &\leqslant \frac{c}{\beta}\sum_{i=0}^{\infty}\beta k\int_{2^i}^{2^{i+1}}\mathbb{P}(A\geqslant x\beta k)dx\\ &\leqslant \frac{c}{\beta}\beta k\int_1^{\infty}\mathbb{P}(A\geqslant x\beta k)dx\\ &= \frac{c}{\beta}\int_{\beta k}^{\infty}\mathbb{P}(A\geqslant y)dy = \frac{c}{\beta}\mathbb{E}A\mathbf{1}(A\geqslant\beta k).\end{aligned}$$

and thus

$$\begin{aligned}\mathbb{P}(E_1\cap E_2\cap\cdots\cap E_n) &\geqslant e^{-4c\beta^{-1}\mathbb{E}A\mathbf{1}(A\geqslant\beta k)-He^{-\theta k}}\\ &\geqslant 1-H(\mathbb{E}A\mathbf{1}(A\geqslant\beta k)+e^{-\theta k}),\end{aligned}$$

which further implies, by monotone convergence, that

$$\begin{aligned}\mathbb{P}(\cap_{i=1}^{\infty}E_i) &= \lim_{n\to\infty}\mathbb{P}(E_1\cap E_2\cap\cdots\cap E_n)\\ &\geqslant 1-H(\mathbb{E}A\mathbf{1}(A\geqslant\beta k)+e^{-\theta k}).\end{aligned}$$

Hence, (3.5) follows directly since by definition,

$$\mathbb{P}(\text{no job ever completes service}) \geqslant \mathbb{P}(\cap_{i=1}^{\infty}E_i).$$

Now, we are ready to finalize our proof. For any $k \geqslant 1$, let T_k be the first time that there are k jobs in the queue and a failure occurs. T_k is almost surely finite since it is upper bounded by the time $\bar{T}_k$ that there are at least k arrivals in an open interval of size β just before a failure. The probability of this event is $\mathbb{P}(Z_\beta \geqslant k) > 0$.

Next, for any fixed time t, we obtain

$$\begin{aligned}&\mathbb{P}(\text{no job leaves after time } t)\\ &\geqslant \mathbb{P}(T_k\leqslant t, \text{no job leaves after } T_k)\\ &= \mathbb{E}[\mathbb{P}(T_k\leqslant t|Q_{T_k},\mathcal{B})\mathbb{P}(\text{no job leaves after } T_k|Q_{T_k},\mathcal{B})]\\ &\geqslant \mathbb{P}(T_k\leqslant t)(1-\epsilon), \qquad (3.7)\end{aligned}$$

where $\mathcal{B} \triangleq \{B_1^{T_k}, \ldots, B_{Q_{T_k}}^{T_k}\}$ denotes the job sizes that are present in the queue at time T_k; the last inequality follows from (3.5) by letting $k \to \infty$ and observing that $\mathbb{E}A\mathbf{1}(A \geqslant \beta k) \to 0$; the equality follows from the fact the event {no job leaves after T_k} is independent of the past, i.e. $T_k \leqslant t$, given $Q_{T_k}, \mathcal{B}$. Next, recall that T_k is almost surely finite, i.e. $\lim_{t\to\infty}\mathbb{P}(T_k \leqslant t) = 1$, and thus taking the limit as $t \to \infty$ and letting $\epsilon \downarrow 0$ in (3.7) yields

$$\lim_{t\to\infty}\mathbb{P}(\text{no job leaves after time } t) = 1.$$

Last, note that the number of arrivals $Z_t \to \infty$ as $t \to \infty$ a.s. and, without loss of generality, we can assume that

$Z_t(\omega) \to \infty$ as $t \to \infty$ for every ω (by excluding the set of zero probability). Then, for any $v > 0$,

$$\{\text{no job ever leaves after time } v\} \subset \{Q_t \to \infty \text{ as } t \to \infty\}.$$

Now, since there are no departures, the rate of increase of Q_t is equal to the arrival rate, and thus $Q_t \to \infty$. Hence,

$$\mathbb{P}(Q_t \to \infty \text{ as } t \to \infty) \geqslant \mathbb{P}(\text{no job ever leaves after time } v)$$

and by passing $v \to \infty$, we obtain

$$\mathbb{P}(Q_t \to \infty \text{ as } t \to \infty) \geqslant \lim_{v\to\infty} \mathbb{P}(\text{no job ever leaves after } v) = 1.$$

□

Finally, we show instability, in general, without the condition $\mathbb{P}[B \geqslant \beta] = 1$.

Theorem 3.2 *In the M/G/1 PS queue, if* $\mathbb{E}A < \infty$ *and* $B > 0$ *a.s., we have as* $t \to \infty$,

$$Q_t \to \infty \quad a.s.$$

Remark 3 Note that $B > 0$ a.s. is just a non-triviality condition that excludes zero-sized jobs, i.e. non-existent ones.

Proof: First, by assumption, we can pick $\beta > 0$ such that $\mathbb{P}[B \geqslant \beta] > 0$. Then, for any time t, let Q_t^β be the number of jobs whose size is at least β, i.e. they satisfy $\mathbb{P}[B \geqslant \beta] = 1$, and q_t^β be the number of jobs that are smaller than β. Hence,

$$Q_t = Q_t^\beta + q_t^\beta \geqslant \underline{Q}_t^\beta,$$

where $\underline{Q}_t^\beta$ is the queue in a system with the same arrival process where jobs of size $B \geqslant \beta$ are served in isolation. By Theorem 3.1, $\underline{Q}_t^\beta \to \infty$ a.s., and, therefore, we obtain $Q_t \to \infty$ a.s. □

3.2.1 *Extension to DPS*

In modern system design, PS cannot capture the heterogeneity of users, which is associated with unequal sharing of resources. Hence, we discuss the *Discriminatory* Processor Sharing (DPS) queue which is a multi-class generalization of the PS queue: all jobs are served simultaneously at rates that are determined by a set of weights $w_i, i = 1, \ldots, K$. If there are n_j jobs in class j, each class-k job receives service at a rate $c_k = w_k / \sum_{j=1}^K w_j n_j$.

DPS has a broad range of applications. In computing, it is used to model Weighted-Round-Robin (WRR) scheduling. In communication networks, DPS is used for modeling heterogenous, e.g. with different round trip delays, TCP connections. Despite the fact that the PS queue is well understood, the analysis of DPS has proven to be very hard; yet, our previous result on PS is easily extended to DPS in the corollary below.

Corollary 3.1 *Under the conditions in Theorem 3.2, the Discriminatory Processor Sharing (DPS) queue is also always unstable.*

Proof: Without loss of generality, assume that the set of weights is ordered such that $w_1 \leqslant w_2 \ldots \leqslant w_K$. In the M/G/1 DPS queue, the service allocation at any given time t for a single customer in class k is given by

$$c_k(t) = \frac{w_k}{\sum_{i=1}^K w_i n_i(t)} \leqslant \frac{w_k}{w_1 \sum_{i=1}^K n_i(t)} \leqslant \frac{w_K}{w_1 Q_t}.$$

Note that $c(t) = w_K/(w_1 Q_t)$ is the service rate in a PS queue with capacity $c = w_K/w_1 \geqslant 1$. Therefore, each class-k job, $k = 1 \ldots K$, in the DPS queue is served at a lower rate than the rate c of the PS queue. Hence,

$$Q_t^{DPS} \geqslant Q_t^{PS(c)},$$

and since, under the conditions in Theorem 3.2, the PS queue is always unstable, it follows that the DPS queue is also unstable. □

4. TRANSIENT BEHAVIOR - SCHEDULING A FINITE NUMBER OF JOBS

In the previous section, we focused on the steady state behavior of the M/G/1 queue and proved that PS is always unstable for failure distributions with finite first moment. In this section, in order to gain further insight into this system, we study its transient behavior. In this regard, we consider a queue with a finite number of jobs and no future arrivals and compute the total time until all jobs are completed. In Subsections 4.1 and 4.2, we analyze the system performance when the jobs are served one at a time and when Processor Sharing (PS) is used, respectively. More precisely, for a finite number of jobs with sizes $B_i, 1 \leqslant i \leqslant m$, and assuming no future arrivals, we study the completion time Θ_m until all m jobs complete their service.

Note that in the case of traditional work conserving scheduling systems the completion time does not depend on the scheduling discipline and is always simply equal to $\sum_{i=1}^m B_i$. However, in channels with failures there can be a stark difference in the total completion time depending on the scheduling policy. This difference can be so large that in some systems the expected completion time can be infinite while in others finite, or even having many high moments.

Overall, we discover that, with respect to the distribution of the total completion time Θ_m, serving one job at a time exhibits uniformly better performance than PS; see Theorems 4.2 and 4.3. Furthermore, when the hazard functions of the job and failure distributions are proportional, i.e. $\log \bar{F}(x) \sim \alpha \log \bar{G}(x)$, we show that PS performs distinctly worse for the light-tailed job/failure distributions as opposed to the heavy-tailed ones, see parts (i) and (ii) of Theorem 4.3.

Before presenting our results, we restate the following theorem on the logarithmic asymptotics of the service time S (from Definition 2.2), which appears in [12].

Theorem 4.1 *If* $\log \bar{F}(x) \sim \alpha \log \bar{G}(x)$ *for all* $x \geqslant 0$ *and* $\alpha > 0$, *and* $\mathbb{E}[A^{1+\theta}] < \infty$ *for some* $\theta > 0$, *then*

$$\lim_{t\to\infty} \frac{\log \mathbb{P}[S > t]}{\log t} = -\alpha \qquad as\ t \to \infty. \tag{4.1}$$

Remark 4 By examining the proof of Theorem 4.1 in [12], it is easy to check that $\bar{S} = \sum_{i=1}^N A_i \geqslant S$, which includes the time from the job completion until the next failure, also satisfies (4.1).

4.1 Serving One Job at a Time

In this subsection, we consider the failure-prone system that was introduced in Section 2, with unit capacity. The jobs are served one at a time, e.g. First Come First Serve (FCFS). Herein, we analyze the performance of this system assuming that, initially, there are m jobs in the queue and there are no future arrivals. Specifically, we study the total completion time, which is defined below.

Definition 4.1 *The total completion time is defined as the total time until all the jobs are successfully completed and is denoted as*

$$\Theta_m \triangleq \sum_{i=1}^{m} S_i,$$

where m is the total number of jobs in the system and S_i is the service requirement for each job.

Next, we define the forward recurrence time, i.e. the elapsed time between some fixed t_0 until the time that the next failure occurs after t_0.

Definition 4.2 *Let L_t be the number of failures in the interval $(0,t)$, i.e. the number of regenerative points of the renewal process $(A, \{A_n\}_{n\geqslant 1})$. The forward recurrence time, which corresponds to the elapsed time until the next failure after time t, is defined as*

$$\tau_t := \sum_{n=1}^{L_t+1} A_n - t. \tag{4.2}$$

In the following theorem, we prove that the tail asymptotics of the total completion time, from Definition 4.1, under this policy is a power law of the same index as the service time of a single job.

Theorem 4.2 *If $\log \bar{F}(x) \sim \alpha \log \bar{G}(x)$ for all $x \geqslant 0$ and $\alpha > 0$, and $\mathbb{E}[A^{1+\theta}] < \infty$ for some $\theta > 0$, then*

$$\lim_{t\to\infty} \frac{\log \mathbb{P}[\Theta_m > t]}{\log t} = -\alpha.$$

Proof: Recall that the service requirement for a job B_i was previously defined as $S_i = \sum_{j=1}^{N_i-1} A_j + B_i$.

For the *lower* bound, we observe that

$$\mathbb{P}[\Theta_m > t] \geqslant \mathbb{P}[S_1 > t],$$

since the total completion time is at least equal to the service time of a single job. By taking the logarithm and using Theorem 4.1, we have

$$\frac{\log \mathbb{P}[\Theta_m > t]}{\log t} \geqslant -(1+\epsilon)\alpha. \tag{4.3}$$

For the *upper* bound, we compare Θ_m with the completion time in a system where the server is kept idle between the completion time of the previous job and the next failure. Clearly,

$$\Theta_m \leqslant \bar{\Theta}_m \triangleq \sum_{i=1}^{m} \bar{S}_i, \tag{4.4}$$

where $\bar{S}_i \triangleq \sum_{j=1}^{N_i} A_j$ are the service times that include the remaining availability period A_{N_i}. We prove this intuitive claim more formally by induction in the appendix.

Then, we argue that

$$\mathbb{P}[\Theta_m > t] \leqslant \mathbb{P}\left[\sum_{i=1}^{m} \bar{S}_i > t\right] \leqslant m\mathbb{P}\left[\bar{S}_1 > \frac{t}{m}\right],$$

which follows from the union bound. By taking the logarithm and using Theorem 4.1, we have

$$\frac{\log \mathbb{P}[\Theta_m > t]}{\log t} \leqslant -\alpha(1-\epsilon) + \frac{\log m}{\log t} \leqslant -(1-2\epsilon)\alpha, \tag{4.5}$$

where we pick t large enough such that $\log t \geqslant \log m/(\alpha\epsilon)$.

Letting $\epsilon \to 0$ in both (4.3) and (4.5) finishes the proof. □

4.2 Processor Sharing Discipline

In this subsection, we analyze the Processor Sharing discipline where m jobs share the (unit) capacity of a single server. We present our main theorem on the logarithmic scale, which shows that the tail asymptotics of the total completion time is determined by the shortest job in the queue. In particular, under our main assumptions, this time is a power law, but it exhibits a different exponent depending on the job size distribution.

- If the jobs are subexponential (heavy-tailed) or exponential, the total delay is simply determined by the time required for any single job to complete its service, as if it was the only one present in the queue.

- If the jobs are superexponential (light-tailed), the total delay is determined by the service time of the *shortest* job. This job generates the heaviest asymptotics among all the rest.

Our main result, stated in Theorem 4.3 below, shows that on the logarithmic scale the distribution of the total completion time Θ_m^{PS} is heavier by a factor $m^{\gamma-1}$ for superexponential jobs relative to the subexponential or exponential case. Therefore, in systems with failures and restarts, sharing the capacity among light-tailed jobs induces long delays, whereas, for heavy-tailed ones, PS appears to perform as good as serving the jobs one at a time. Interestingly enough, this deterioration in performance is determined by the time it takes to serve the shortest job in the system.

Note that in a PS queue with no future arrivals, the shortest job will depart first. Immediately after this, the server will continue serving the remaining $m-1$ jobs, and, similarly, the shortest job, i.e. the second shortest among the original m jobs, will depart before all the others. This pattern will continue until the departure of the largest job, which is served alone.

Theorem 4.3 *Assume that the hazard function $-\log \bar{F}(x)$ is regularly varying with index $\gamma \geqslant 0$. If $\log \bar{F}(x) \sim \alpha \log \bar{G}(x)$ for all $x \geqslant 0$ and $\alpha > 0$, and $\mathbb{E}[A^{1+\theta}] < \infty$ for some $\theta > 0$, then*

(i) if $\gamma \leqslant 1$, i.e. B is subexponential or exponential, then

$$\lim_{t\to\infty} \frac{-\log \mathbb{P}[\Theta_m^{PS} > t]}{\log t} = \alpha,$$

(ii) if $\gamma > 1$, i.e. B is superexponential, then

$$\lim_{t\to\infty} \frac{-\log \mathbb{P}[\Theta_m^{PS} > t]}{\log t} = \frac{\alpha}{m^{\gamma-1}} < \alpha.$$

Remark 5 When $\alpha > 1$, we easily verify that $\mathbb{E}[\Theta_m^{PS}] < \infty$ in case (i), and the system is stable; if the jobs are superexponential, e.g. case (ii), then $\mathbb{E}[\Theta_m^{PS}] = \infty$ if $\alpha < m^{\gamma-1}$.

Proof: Let $B^{(1)} \leqslant B^{(2)} \leqslant \ldots \leqslant B^{(m)}$ be the order statistics of the jobs $B_1, B_2, \ldots, B_m$.

The assumption that $-\log \bar{F}(x)$ is regularly varying with index γ implies that

$$\log \bar{F}(\lambda x) \sim \lambda^{\gamma} \log \bar{F}(x), \tag{4.6}$$

for any $\lambda > 0$.

We begin with the *lower* bound.

(i) Subexponential or exponential jobs ($\gamma \leqslant 1$).
The total completion time is lower bounded by the time required for a single job to depart when it is exclusively served, e.g. if the total capacity of the system is used. Hence, it follows that

$$\mathbb{P}[\Theta_m^{PS} > t] \geqslant \mathbb{P}[S_1 > t], \tag{4.7}$$

where S_1 is the service time of a single job of random size B_1, when there are no other jobs in the system. Now, recalling Theorem 4.1, it holds that

$$\lim_{t\to\infty} \frac{\log \mathbb{P}[S_1 > t]}{\log t} = -\alpha.$$

By taking the logarithm in (4.7), the lower bound follows immediately.

(ii) Superexponential jobs ($\gamma > 1$).
The total completion time is lower bounded by the delay experienced by the shortest job, and hence,

$$\mathbb{P}[\Theta_m^{PS} > t] \geqslant \mathbb{P}[S_1^{PS} > t], \tag{4.8}$$

where S_1^{PS} is the service time of the smallest job $B^{(1)}$. First, note that the distribution of $B^{(1)}$ is given by

$$\begin{aligned}\mathbb{P}(B^{(1)} > x) &= \mathbb{P}(B_1 > x, B_2 > x, \ldots, B_m > x)\\ &= \mathbb{P}(B_1 > x)\mathbb{P}(B_2 > x)\cdots\mathbb{P}(B_m > x)\\ &= \mathbb{P}(B_1 > x)^m = \bar{F}(x)^m, \end{aligned}\tag{4.9}$$

since $B_i, i = 1, \ldots, m$, are independent and identically distributed. Now, the service time S_1^{PS} is determined by the number of failures this job has experienced, i.e.

$$\mathbb{P}[N_1 > n] = \mathbb{E}\left[\mathbb{P}\left(B^{(1)} > \frac{A}{m}\right)\right]^n = \mathbb{E}\left(1 - \bar{G}(mB^{(1)})\right)^n,$$

and, using (4.9) and (4.6), together with our main assumption, we observe that

$$\begin{aligned}\log \mathbb{P}(mB^{(1)} > x) &= m \log \bar{F}\left(\frac{x}{m}\right)\\ &\sim m^{1-\gamma} \log \bar{F}(x) \sim \alpha m^{1-\gamma} \log \bar{G}(x).\end{aligned}$$

Then, Theorem 4.1 applies with $\alpha/m^{\gamma-1} \leqslant \alpha$, i.e.

$$\lim_{t\to\infty} \frac{\log \mathbb{P}[S_1^{PS} > t]}{\log t} = -\frac{\alpha}{m^{\gamma-1}}.$$

Next, we derive the *upper* bound. To this end, we consider a system where the server is kept idle after the completion of each job until the next failure occurs. At this time, all the remaining jobs are served under PS until the next shortest one departs. If there are more than one jobs of the same size, only one of these departs. Under this policy, it clearly holds that

$$\Theta_m^{PS} \leqslant \sum_{i=1}^{m} \bar{S}_i^{PS},$$

where $\bar{S}_i^{PS}$ corresponds to the service time of the ith smallest job and includes the time until the next failure.

Using the union bound, we obtain

$$\mathbb{P}[\Theta_m^{PS} > t] \leqslant \mathbb{P}\left[\sum_{i=1}^{m} \bar{S}_i^{PS} > t\right] \leqslant (1+\epsilon)\sum_{i=1}^{m} \mathbb{P}\left(\bar{S}_i^{PS} > \frac{t}{m}\right). \tag{4.10}$$

It is easy to see that the service time of the ith smallest job $B^{(i)}$ depends on the number of jobs that share the server, i.e. $m - i + 1$, since $m - i$ jobs have remained in the queue. Now, the distribution of the ith shortest job is derived as

$$\begin{aligned}\mathbb{P}(B^{(i)} > x) &= \sum_{k=0}^{i-1} \binom{m}{k} \mathbb{P}(B_1 \leqslant x)^k \mathbb{P}(B_1 > x)^{m-k}\\ &\sim \binom{m}{i-1} \mathbb{P}(B_1 > x)^{m-i+1} \sim \bar{F}(x)^{m-i+1}.\end{aligned}\tag{4.11}$$

The number of restarts for the ith smallest job, N_i, is computed as

$$\begin{aligned}\mathbb{P}[N_i > n] &= \mathbb{E}\left[\mathbb{P}\left(B^{(i)} > \frac{A}{m-i}\right)\right]^n\\ &= \mathbb{E}\left(1 - \bar{G}((m-i+1)B^{(i)})\right)^n.\end{aligned}$$

Next, starting from (4.11), it easily follows that

$$\begin{aligned}\log \mathbb{P}\left((m-i+1)B^{(i)} > x\right) &\sim \log \bar{F}\left(\frac{x}{m-i+1}\right)^{m-i+1}\\ &\sim (m-i+1)^{1-\gamma} \log \bar{F}(x)\\ &\sim \alpha(m-i+1)^{1-\gamma} \log \bar{G}(x),\end{aligned}$$

where we use (4.6) and our main assumption and define $\alpha_i \triangleq \alpha/(m-i)^{\gamma-1}$.

Now, recalling Theorem 4.1 and Remark 4 after it, we have

$$\frac{\log \mathbb{P}[\bar{S}_i^{PS} > t]}{\log t} \to \alpha_i \text{ as } t \to \infty,$$

and thus (4.10) yields

$$\frac{\log \mathbb{P}[\Theta_m^{PS} > t]}{\log t} \leqslant -(1-\epsilon) \min_{i=1\ldots m} \alpha_i,$$

for all $t \geqslant t_0$.

(i) Subexponential or exponential jobs ($\gamma \leqslant 1$).
Observe that $\min_{i=1\ldots m} \alpha_i = \alpha$, and thus

$$\frac{\log \mathbb{P}[\Theta_m^{PS} > t]}{\log t} \leqslant -(1-\epsilon)\alpha. \tag{4.12}$$

(ii) Superexponential jobs ($\gamma > 1$).
In this case, $\min_{i=1\ldots m} \alpha_i = \alpha/m^{\gamma-1}$, and thus

$$\frac{\log \mathbb{P}[\Theta_m^{PS} > t]}{\log t} \leqslant -(1-\epsilon)\frac{\alpha}{m^{\gamma-1}}. \quad (4.13)$$

Letting $\epsilon \to 0$ in (4.12) and (4.13), we obtain the upper bound. □

5. SIMULATION

In this section, we present our simulation experiments in order to demonstrate our theoretical findings. All the experiments result from $N = 10^8$ (or more) samples of each simulated scenario; this guarantees the existence of at least 100 occurrences in the lightest end of the tail that is presented in the figures. First, we illustrate the instability result from Theorem 3.1 of Section 3.

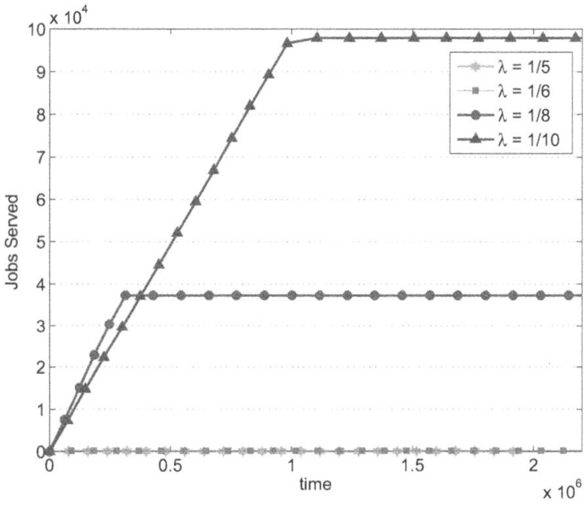

Figure 3: Example 1. Jobs served over time.

Example 1. *M/G/1 PS is unstable.* In this example, we show that the PS queue becomes unstable by simulating the M/G/1 PS queue for different arrival rates $\lambda > 0$, which all satisfy the stability condition for the M/G/1 FCFS queue, when jobs are served one at a time. In this regard, we assume constant job sizes $\beta = 1$ and Poisson failures of rate $\mu = 1/20$. Therefore, by evaluating (3.4), we obtain

$$\lambda \mathbb{E}[S] = \lambda \mu^{-1}(e^{\mu} - 1) = 20(e^{0.05} - 1)\lambda = 1.025\lambda < 1,$$

or equivalently the stability region for the FCFS queue is given by $\Lambda = \{\lambda \leqslant 0 : \lambda < 0.9752\}$. Hence, in this example, we use λ from the FCFS stability region, $\lambda \in \Lambda$.

In Fig. 3, we plot the number of jobs that have received service up to time t. We observe that the cumulative number of served jobs always converges to a fixed number and does not increase any further. This happens after some critical time when the queue starts to grow continuously until it becomes unable to drain. For larger values of λ, the system saturates faster meaning that the cumulative throughput at the saturated state is lower.

Furthermore, we observe from the simulation that the system behaves as if it were stable until some critical time or queue size after which it is unable to drain. From Fig. 3, we can see that the case $\lambda = 10^{-1}$ saturates at time $t = 10^6$ and the total number of served jobs reaches 10^5. Hence, the departure rate until saturation time is $10^5/10^6 = 10^{-1}$, which is exactly equal to the arrival rate $\lambda = 10^{-1}$, corresponding to the departure rate of a stable queue. This further emphasizes the importance of studying the stability of these systems since, at first glance, they may appear stable.

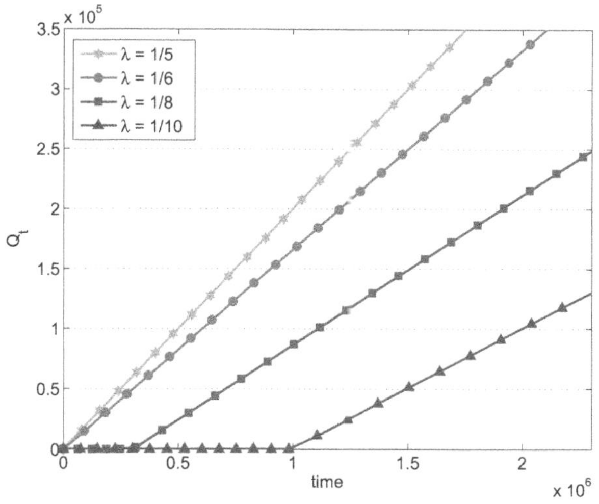

Figure 4: Example 1. Queue size over time.

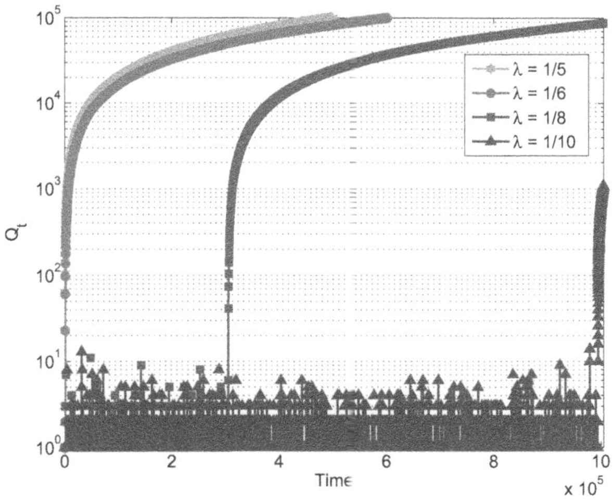

Figure 5: Example 1. Queue size for small t. It zooms in the time range $[0, 10^6]$ of Fig. 4; Q_t (y-axis) is shown on the logarithmic scale.

Fig. 4 demonstrates the queue size evolution over time. Similarly as in Fig. 3, we observe that for any arrival rate λ, there is a critical time after which the queue continues to grow and never empties. This time varies depending on the simulation experiment; yet, on average, we observe that the queue remains stable for longer time when λ is smaller. Now, we zoom in on the queue evolution on the logarithmic scale in Fig. 5. Again, we observe that the queue looks stable until some critical time/queue size.

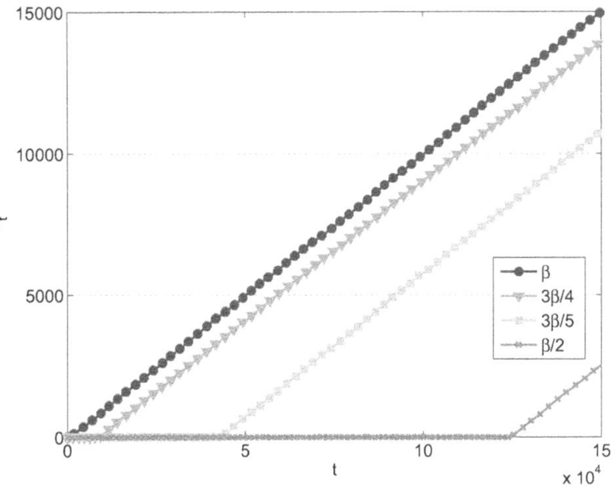

Figure 6: Example 1. Queue size over time parameterized by fragment length; $\beta = 2, \lambda = 0.1$.

Last, in Fig. 6, we plot the queue evolution for different job sizes, namely $\beta = 1, 1.2, 1.5$ and 2. We observe that larger job fragments cause instability much faster than the smaller units. For example, $\beta = 2$ leads to instability almost immediately, while $\beta = 1.5$ renders the queue unstable after 10^4 time units. Similarly, reducing the fragment size by 60% delays the process by an additional 3×10^4 units. Last, cutting the jobs in half causes instability after approximately 13×10^4 time units. This implies that one should apply fragmentation with caution in order to select the appropriate fragment size that will maintain good system performance for the longest time.

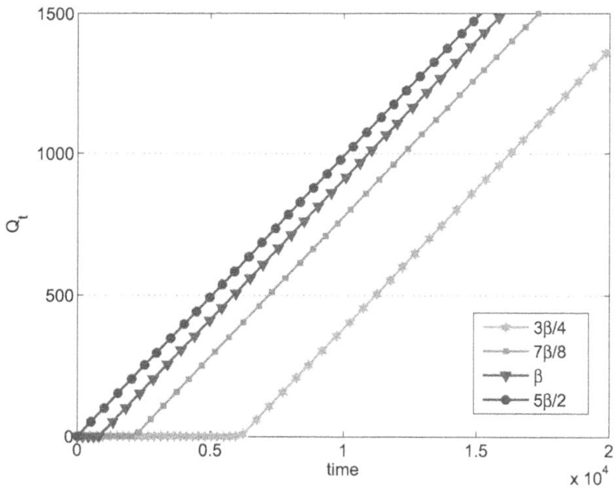

Figure 7: Example 2. Queue size over time parameterized by job size; $\beta = 4$.

Example 2. *General arrivals.* In this example, we consider non-Poisson arrivals. We assume that the failure distribution is exponential with mean $\mathbb{E}A = 10$ and that jobs interarrival times follow the Pareto distribution with $\alpha = 2$ and mean $\mathbb{E}A = 10.1$. Similarly as in the previous example, Fig. 7 shows the queue evolution with time for different job sizes β.

Next, we validate the results on the transient analysis from Section 4.

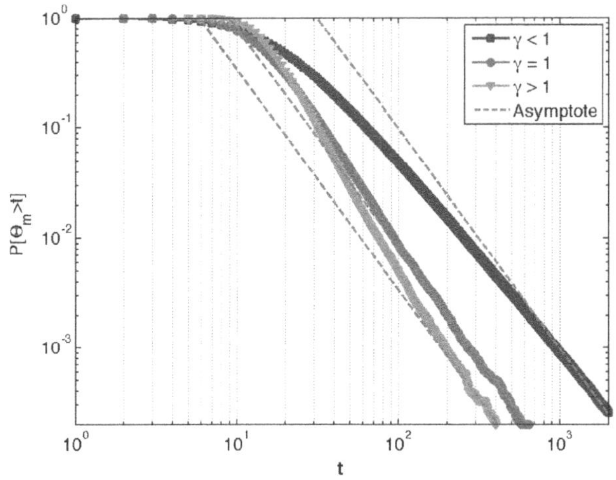

Figure 8: Example 3. FCFS: Logarithmic asymptotics when $\alpha = 2$ for exponential, superexponential ($\gamma > 1$) and subexponential ($\gamma < 1$) distributions.

Example 3. *Serving one job at a time/FCFS: Always the same index α.* In this example, we consider a queue of $m = 10$ jobs, which are served First Come First Serve (FCFS), i.e. one at a time. The logarithmic asymptotics from Theorem 4.1 implies that the tail is always a power law of index $\alpha = 2$.

In Fig. 8, we plot the distribution of the total completion time in a queue with 10 jobs that are processed one at a time. On the same graph, we plot the logarithmic asymptotics (dotted lines) that correspond to a power law of index $\alpha = 2$. We consider the following three scenarios:

1. Weibull distributions with $\gamma = 2$. The failures A are distributed according to $\bar{G}(x) = e^{-(x/\mu)^2}$ with mean $\mathbb{E}[A] = \mu\Gamma(1.5) = 1.5$, and jobs B also follow Weibull distributions with $\bar{F}(x) = e^{-(x/\lambda)^2}, \lambda = \mu/\sqrt{2}$. In this case, it is easy to check that the main assumption of Theorem 4.1 is satisfied, i.e.
$$\log \bar{F}(x) = -(x/\lambda)^2 = \alpha \log \bar{G}(x), \alpha = (\mu/\lambda)^2.$$
2. Exponential distributions. A's are exponential with $\mathbb{E}[A] = 2$, $\bar{G}(x) = e^{-x/2}$, and the jobs B are also exponential of unit mean, i.e. $\bar{F}(x) = e^{-x}$. Then, trivially,
$$\log \bar{F}(x) = 2 \log \bar{G}(x).$$
3. Weibull distributions with $\gamma = 0.5$. A's are Weibull with $\bar{G}(x) = e^{-\sqrt{x}/2}$, i.e $\mathbb{E}[A] = 8$. Also, we assume Weibull jobs B with $\bar{F}(x) = e^{-\sqrt{x}}$. Thus,
$$\log \bar{F}(x) = -\sqrt{x} = 2 \log \bar{G}(x).$$

In all three cases, we obtain $\alpha = 2$. Yet, we observe that the tail asymptotics is the same regardless of the distribution of the job sizes. For the subexponential jobs (case 3: Weibull with $\gamma < 1$), the power law tail appears later compared to the case of superexponential jobs. This is because the constant factor of the exact asymptotics is different for each case, and it depends on the mean size of A, $\mathbb{E}[A]$.

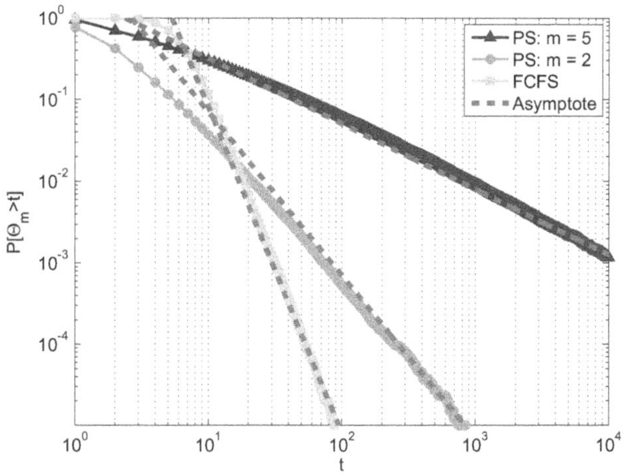

Figure 9: Example 4. Logarithmic asymptotics for different number of superexponential jobs when $\alpha = 4$ under PS and FCFS discipline.

Example 4. *PS: The effect of the number of jobs.* In this example, we consider a PS queue with $m = 5$ and $m = 2$ superexponential jobs, and compare it against a FCFS queue with $m = 5$ jobs. We assume superexponential job sizes B's and A's, namely Weibull with $\gamma = 2$; see case 1 of Example 3. Here α is taken equal to 4. The logarithmic asymptotics is given in Theorems 4.2 and 4.3.

In Fig. 9, we demonstrate the total completion time Θ_m^{PS}, for different number of jobs, when $\gamma = 2$. Theorem 4.2(ii) states that $\alpha(m) = \alpha/m^{\gamma-1}$ and, thus, for $\gamma = 2$ we have $\alpha(m) = \alpha/m$, e.g. we expect power law asymptotes with index α/m for the different values of m. On the same figure, we also plot the FCFS completion time Θ_m, which is always a power law of index $\alpha = 4$, as we previously observed in Example 3. It can be seen that PS generates heavier power laws, for superexponential jobs. In particular, PS with $m = 2$ results in power law asymptotics with $\alpha(2) = 2$, while PS with $m = 5$ jobs leads to system instability since $\alpha(5) = 4/5 < 1$.

Example 5. *PS: The effect of the distribution type.* In this example, for completeness, we evaluate the impact of the job distribution on the total completion time under both heavy and light-tailed job sizes. To this end, we consider the PS queue from Example 4, with $m = 5$ jobs, and compare it against FCFS. In Fig. 10, we re-plot the logarithmic asymptotics of the total completion time $\mathbb{P}(\Theta_m^{PS} > t)$, for different distribution types of the failures/jobs and index $\alpha = 4$, as before. In particular, we consider Weibull distributions as in Example 3 with $\gamma = 1/2 < 1$ and $\gamma = 2 > 1$ for the subexponential and superexponential cases, respectively.

On the same graph, we plot the distribution of the completion time Θ_m in FCFS, which is always a power law of the same index, as illustrated in Example 3. By fixing the number of jobs to be $m = 5$, Fig. 10 shows that when the jobs are superexponential, PS yields the heaviest asymptotics among all three scenarios; for subexponential jobs, PS generates asymptotics with the same power law index as in FCFS, albeit with a different constant factor.

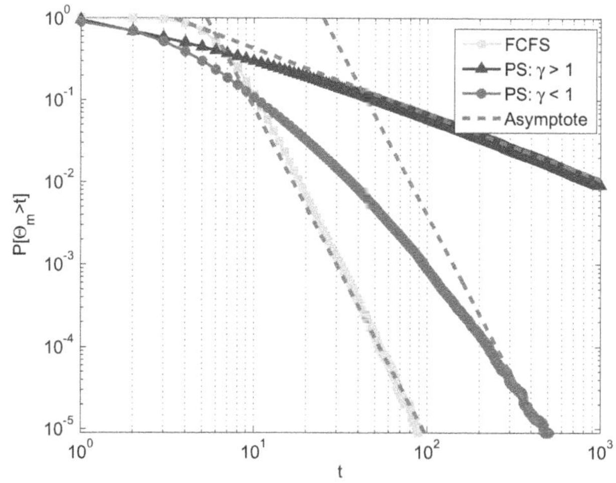

Figure 10: Example 5. Logarithmic asymptotics under FCFS, PS with subexponential and superexponential jobs.

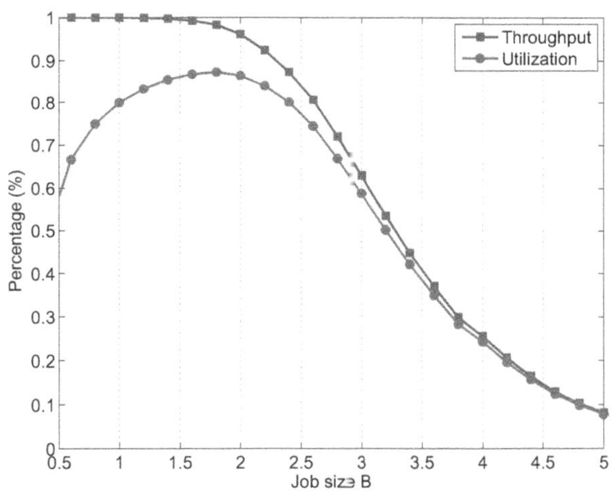

Figure 11: Example 6. Throughput vs. utilization tradeoff.

Example 6. *Limited queue: Throughput vs. overhead tradeoff.* In practice, job and buffer sizes are bounded and therefore the queue may never become unstable. However, our results indicate that the queue may lock itself in a 'nearly unstable' state, where it is at its maximum size and the throughput is very low. Here, we would like to emphasize that, unlike in the case of unlimited queue size, job fragmentation can be useful in increasing the throughput and the efficiency of the system. In this case, one has to be careful about the overhead cost of fragmentation. Basically, each fragment requires additional information, called the 'header' in the context of communications, which contains details on how it fits into the bigger job, e.g. destination/routing information in communication networks. Hence, if the fragments are too small, there will be a lot of overhead and waste of resources. In view of this fact, one would like to optimize the fragment sizes by striking a balance between throughput and utilization.

In this example, we demonstrate the tradeoff between throughput and generated overhead, assuming limited queue size $\tilde{Q}$. If the newly arriving job does not fit in the queue, i.e. the number of jobs currently in the queue is equal to $\tilde{Q}$, it is discarded. We define throughput as the percentage of the jobs that complete service among all jobs that arrive at the M/G/1 PS queue. It basically corresponds to the total work that is carried out in the system. On the other hand, we define utilization as the useful work that is served over the aggregated load in the system. Specifically, we consider jobs that require a minimum size β, where β represents the overhead, e.g. the packet header, thread id, etc. The remaining job size, $B - \beta$, represents the useful information.

We consider different job sizes B from 0.4 up to 5 bytes, with overhead $\beta = 0.2$. We simulate the M/G/1 PS queue with maximum queue size $\tilde{Q} = 10$ jobs for a fixed time $T = 10^8$ time units. The arrivals are Poisson with rate 1/10 and the failures are exponential of the same rate.

In Fig. 11, we observe that for small job sizes, the throughput is 100% and it deteriorates as the job size B increases. In particular, when the job size exceeds 1.5, the throughput drops exponentially. Utilization exhibits a different behavior; it is low when the job size is small, i.e. the useful job size is comparable to the overhead β, and reaches its peak at $B \approx 1.8$. After this, it starts decreasing following similar trend as the throughput. In this case, $B - \beta \approx 1.5$ appears to be the optimal size for the job fragments. This phenomenon of combining limited queue size with job fragmentation may require further investigation.

6. CONCLUDING REMARKS

Retransmissions/restarts represent a primary failure recovery mechanism in large-scale engineering systems, as it was argued in the introduction. In communication networks, retransmissions lie at the core of the network architecture, as they appear in all layers of the protocol stack. Similarly, PS/DPS based scheduling mechanisms, due to their inherent fairness, are commonly used in computing and communication systems. Such mechanisms allow for efficient and fair resource allocation, and thus they are preferred in engineering system design.

However, our results show that, under mild conditions, PS/DPS scheduling in systems with retransmissions is always unstable. Furthermore, this instability cannot be resolved by job fragmentation techniques. On the contrary, serving one job at a time, e.g. FCFS, can be stable and its performance can be further enhanced with fragmentation. Interestingly, systems where jobs are served one at a time can highly benefit from fragmentation and, in fact, their performance can approach closely the corresponding system without failures.

Overall, using PS in combination with retransmissions in the presence of failures deteriorates the system performance and induces instability. In addition, our findings suggest that further examination of existing techniques is necessary in the failure-prone environment with retransmission/restart failure recovery and sharing, e.g. see Example 6.

7. ACKNOWLEDGMENTS

The authors are grateful to the anonymous reviewers for their helpful comments.

APPENDIX

Proof: [of (4.4) in Theorem 4.2]
We formally prove that $\Theta_m \leqslant \bar{\Theta}_m = \sum_{i=1}^{m} \bar{S}_i$. The proof follows by induction.

n = 1. Let τ_{Θ_1} denote the time between Θ_1 until the first failure occurs after Θ_1, i.e. the time after the departure of the first job (see also Definition 4.2). Then the total service time for jobs B_1 and B_2 is

$$\Theta_2 = \begin{cases} \Theta_1 + \tau_{\Theta_1} + S_2, & \text{if } B_2 > \tau_{\Theta_1} \\ \Theta_1 + B_2, & \text{otherwise.} \end{cases}$$

If we idle the server after the successful completion of the first job until the next failure, the total completion time will be equal to $\bar{\Theta}_2 = \Theta_1 + \tau_{\Theta_1} + S_2$, since we discard the remaining interval τ_{Θ_1} and start service at $\Theta_1 + \tau_{\Theta_1}$. Therefore, $\Theta_2 \leqslant \bar{\Theta}_2$ (see Figure 12 for an illustration).

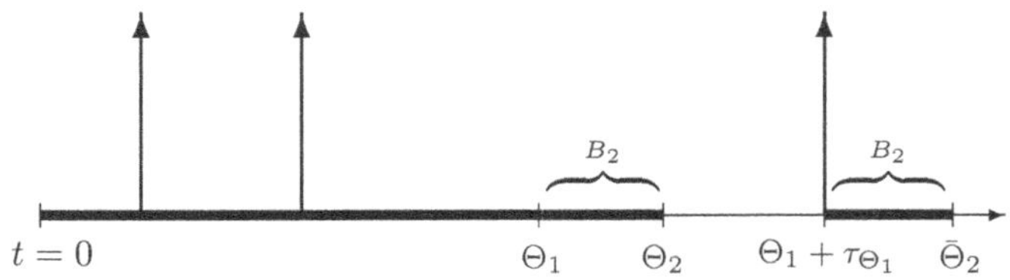

Figure 12: Completion time in a failure-prone system: Assume that there are two jobs B_1 and B_2 and the first succeeds at time Θ_1. In the original system, job B_2 starts service immediately and completes at time Θ_2, before the next failure occurs after τ_{Θ_1} time units. In the alternate system, B_2 will only start its service at time $\Theta_1 + \tau_{\Theta_1}$. If $B_2 < \tau_{\Theta_2}$, then $\bar{\Theta}_2 = \Theta_1 + \tau_{\Theta_1} + B_2$.

Induction step. Assume $\Theta_n \leqslant \bar{\Theta}_n$ for $n < m$. If Θ_n is the time when the nth job is completed, then τ_{Θ_n} is the time until the next failure after Θ_n. Now, for the following job B_{n+1}, we have

$$\Theta_{n+1} = \begin{cases} \Theta_n + \tau_{\Theta_n} + S_{n+1}, & \text{if } B_{n+1} > \tau_{\Theta_n} \\ \Theta_n + B_{n+1}, & \text{otherwise.} \end{cases}$$

If $\Theta_n = \bar{\Theta}_n$, then clearly $\bar{\Theta}_{n+1} = \Theta_n + \tau_{\Theta_n} + S_{n+1} \geqslant \Theta_{n+1}$.

If $\bar{\Theta}_n > \Theta_n$ then, by construction, job B_{n+1} can start its service after time $\Theta_n + \tau_{\Theta_n}$, i.e the time that the first failure occurs after Θ_n. This implies that $\bar{\Theta}_n \geqslant \Theta_n + \tau_{\Theta_n}$. Now, if B_{n+1} finishes before the failure occurs, then clearly $\bar{\Theta}_{n+1} \geqslant \Theta_{n+1}$. If not, it will either succeed during the period $(\Theta_n + \tau_{\Theta_n}, \bar{\Theta}_n)$ implying that $\Theta_{n+1} \leqslant \bar{\Theta}_{n+1}$, or it will synchronize with the other system and $\Theta_{n+1} = \bar{\Theta}_n + \tau_{\bar{\Theta}_n} + S_{n+1} \leqslant \bar{\Theta}_{n+1}$. □

A. REFERENCES

[1] E. Altman, K. Avrachenkov, and U. Ayesta. A survey on discriminatory processor sharing. *Queueing Systems*, 53(1-2):53–63, June 2006.

[2] V. Anantharam. Scheduling strategies and long-range dependence. *Queueing Systems*, 33(1/3):73–89, March 1999.

[3] D. P. Bertsekas and R. Gallager. *Data Networks*. Prentice Hall, 2nd edition, 1992.

[4] E. G. Coffman, Jr., R. R. Muntz, and H. Trotter. Waiting time distributions for processor-sharing systems. *Journal of the ACM*, 17(1):123–130, Jan. 1970.

[5] G. Fayolle, I. Mitrani, and R. Iasnogorodski. Sharing a processor among many job classes. *Journal of the ACM*, 27(3):519–532, July 1980.

[6] P. M. Fiorini, R. Sheahan, and L. Lipsky. On unreliable computing systems when heavy-tails appear as a result of the recovery procedure. *SIGMETRICS Performance Evaluation Review*, 33(2):15–17, December 2005.

[7] P. Jelenković and P. Momčilović. Large deviation analysis of subexponential waiting times in a processor sharing queue. *Mathematics of Operations Research*, 28(3):587–608, 2003.

[8] P. R. Jelenković and E. D. Skiani. Distribution of the number of retransmissions of bounded documents. *Advances in Applied Probability (submitted)*, New York, 2012, eprint arXiv:1210.8421v1.

[9] P. R. Jelenković and E. D. Skiani. Retransmissions over correlated channels. *SIGMETRICS Performance Evaluation Review*, 41(2):15–25, August 2013.

[10] P. R. Jelenković and E. D. Skiani. Uniform approximation of the distribution for the number of retransmissions of bounded documents. In *Proceedings of the 12th ACM SIGMETRICS/PERFORMANCE joint international conference on Measurement and Modeling of Computer Systems*, SIGMETRICS '12, pages 101–112, June 2012.

[11] P. R. Jelenković and J. Tan. Can retransmissions of superexponential documents cause subexponential delays? In *Proceedings of IEEE INFOCOM'07*, pages 892–900, May 2007.

[12] P. R. Jelenković and J. Tan. Characterizing heavy-tailed distributions induced by retransmissions. *Advances in Applied Probability*, 45(1): 106-138, 2013. (extended version) arXiv: 0709.1138v2.

[13] L. Kleinrock. Time-shared systems: A theoretical treatment. *Journal of the ACM*, 14(2):242–261, April 1967.

[14] A. K. Parekh and R. G. Gallager. A generalized processor sharing approach to flow control in integrated services networks: The single-node case. *IEEE/ACM Transactions on Networking*, 1(3):344–357, June 1993.

[15] A. K. Parekh and R. G. Gallagher. A generalized processor sharing approach to flow control in integrated services networks: The multiple node case. *IEEE/ACM Transactions on Networking*, 2(2):137–150, April 1994.

[16] R. Sheahan, L. Lipsky, P. M. Fiorini, and S. Asmussen. On the completion time distribution for tasks that must restart from the beginning if a failure occurs. *SIGMETRICS Performance Evaluation Review*, 34(3):24–26, December 2006.

[17] A. Wierman and B. Zwart. Is tail-optimal scheduling possible? *Operations Research*, 60(5):1249–1257, September 2012.

[18] S. Yashkov. Mathematical problems in the theory of shared-processor systems. *Journal of Soviet Mathematics*, 58(2):101–147, 1992.

[19] S. Yashkov and A. Yashkova. Processor sharing: A survey of the mathematical theory. *Automation and Remote Control*, 68(9):1662–1731, 2007.

Non-Work-Conserving Effects in MapReduce: Diffusion Limit and Criticality

Jian Tan, Yandong Wang, Weikuan Yu, Li Zhang
IBM T. J. Watson Research Center, NY 10598, USA
Auburn University, AL 36849, USA
tanji@us.ibm.com, {yzw0025,wkyu}@auburn.edu, zhangli@us.ibm.com

ABSTRACT

Sequentially arriving jobs share a MapReduce cluster, each desiring a fair allocation of computing resources to serve its associated map and reduce tasks. The model of such a system consists of a processor sharing queue for the MapTasks and a multi-server queue for the ReduceTasks. These two queues are dependent through a constraint that the input data of each ReduceTask are fetched from the intermediate data generated by the MapTasks belonging to the same job. A more generalized form of MapReduce queueing model can capture the essence of other distributed data processing systems that contain interdependent processor sharing queues and multi-server queues.

Through theoretical modeling and extensive experiments, we show that, this dependence, if not carefully dealt with, can cause non-work-conserving effects that negatively impact system performance and scalability. First, we characterize the heavy-traffic approximation. Depending on how tasks are scheduled, the number of jobs in the system can even exhibit jumps in diffusion limits, resulting in prolonged job execution times. This problem can be mitigated through carefully applying a tie-breaking rule for ReduceTasks, which as a theoretical finding has direct engineering implications. Second, we empirically validate a criticality phenomenon using experiments. MapReduce systems experience an undesirable performance degradation when they have reached certain critical points, another finding that offers fundamental guidance on managing MapReduce systems.

Categories and Subject Descriptors

G.3 [**Probability and Statistics**]: *Queuing Theory, Stochastic Processes*; D.2.8 [**Software Engineering**]: Metrics—*complexity measures, performance measures*

1. INTRODUCTION

A MapReduce cluster supports multiple users and processes a large number of jobs with distinctive service level objectives, such as job response time and throughput. To fulfill the service commitment, efficient scheduling is critical, as evidenced by the popularity of Hadoop Fair Scheduler [2] and Capacity Scheduler [1].

Each MapReduce job is composed of a certain number of map and reduce tasks. The MapReduce model for serving multiple jobs consists of a processor sharing queue for the MapTasks and a multi-server queue for the ReduceTasks [28]. The underlying rationale is based on the well-known pattern of map and reduce task execution durations. Usually MapTasks are short and ReduceTasks are long. For example, empirical studies show that MapTasks take 19 seconds and ReduceTasks take 231 seconds in median numbers [32]. The map queue model is attributed to the fact that round-robin task scheduling with a small time quantum at an appropriate scale can be well approximated by processor sharing. However, once the execution times become significant for long ReduceTasks, a different treatment at the same time scale, e.g., using a multi-server queue, can better capture the essence of the queueing behavior. Intriguingly, these two queues are dependent through a constraint that the intermediate data fetched by the ReduceTasks cannot exceed those already generated by the MapTasks at any time. Since data movement and processing can be conducted in a fine-grained unit (e.g., a few bytes) [22], this model is different from the traditional tandem queue model (e.g., [9]), for which a job in its entirety moves between several stations.

It is common for data to move through processing units governed by different scheduling disciplines. Thus, the previous MapReduce model can be generalized to capture the essential component of other distributed data processing systems that contain dependent processor sharing queues and multi-server queues. Some of the typical examples include graph computation framework [23], distributed dataflow computing [24], Dryad [16] (a computation framework structured as a directed graph), online streaming jobs [11], and distributed programs with partitioned tables [25].

As one of the dominant paradigms for processing large unstructured data sets in a massively parallel manner, MapReduce has attracted increasing interest in practice. However, there is still a lack of theoretical understanding on its fundamental performance trends at scale. Most of the previous studies seem to focus on either the execution of MapTasks or that of ReduceTasks, abiding by the distinct difference between them but ignoring the dependence therein [1, 2, 7, 17, 32]. This approach for analysis can provide reasonable approximations when the experienced workload is mild. However, under heavy traffic scenarios, the oblivion of this internal dependence misses some intriguing non-work-conserving

SIGMETRICS'14, June 16–20, 2014, Austin, Texas, USA.

http://dx.doi.org/10.1145/2591971.2592007 .

effects that, if not carefully dealt with, can greatly degrade system performance.

MapReduce background

MapReduce has a number of implementations. Hadoop [3] is a popular open source realization. Usually, a typical job includes both MapTasks and ReduceTasks. Each MapTask generates intermediate data in key-value pairs after taking a block of input data. Then, ReduceTasks fetch these intermediate data through the copy/shuffle phase according to keys, and proceed to the reduce phase after receiving all the intermediate results. The management of computing resources is through the allocation of task slots; each slot only permits a single task to be launched. As already mentioned, MapTasks are small and independent, executed in multiple parallel waves. Once a MapTask finishes, it immediately releases the occupied slot. Therefore, the available slots can be evenly allocated to multiple competing jobs in a fine-grained time scale. On the contrary, ReduceTasks tend to be long-running and are non-preemptive [17, 7, 32] in most of the MapReduce implementations. They lack the flexibility that MapTasks exhibit, and their execution times are usually on a much larger time scale than those of MapTasks [32].

Upon the completion of a small percentage (by default 5% for Hadoop [3]) of the MapTasks, ReduceTasks of the same job are launched greedily to a maximum that is determined by max-min fairness criteria constrained by the number of available slots. However, only using max-min fairness cannot fully describe the scheduling. A tie-breaking rule is needed when there are more competing jobs than the number of available slots. Interestingly, this tie-breaking rule, if not carefully chosen, can result in jumps to the number of jobs when the system is heavily loaded.

For many of the existing implementations [2, 16, 7, 17], ReduceTasks do not support preemptions; they only release the occupied slots after completion, once launched. That is also why their executions are modeled by a multi-server queue. Recently some implementations have introduced preemptions for ReduceTasks [29, 5, 27]. Though this mechanism is interesting, we do not study it in this paper, due to the following reasons. Apart from the fact that many existing MapReduce implementations do not support it yet, there are scenarios that data processing frameworks with components captured by the model studied in this paper are not preferable to execute preemptions due to possible heavy overhead.

Summary of contributions

We study two non-work-conserving effects for the scheduling model of MapReduce that are caused by the dependence constraint between map and reduce tasks. First, we use diffusion limit to describe the typical sample paths that happen with a high probability in a normalized time and space scale (heavy traffic regime). Second, we empirically characterize a criticality phenomenon for the impact on the tail of the job delay distribution, which occurs with a small probability (large deviation regime).

First, we investigate the diffusion approximation. In a heavy traffic regime, we derive the diffusion limits ($Q_m(t)$, $Q_r(t)$) for the number of jobs in the map queue and the reduce queue under a proper scaling. Specifically, the number of jobs in the system can even exhibit jumps in the diffusion limit. A similar result has been shown for servers with vacations [19]. In the case of MapReduce, the jumps are caused by the dependence constraint between the processor sharing queue and the multi-server queue. When the processor sharing queue of the MapTasks is heavily loaded, the intermediate data generating speed can be significantly lower than the fetching speed of the ReduceTasks. Because ReduceTasks are non-preemptive, the computing resources of the occupied slots will not be fully utilized while being taken by idle ReduceTasks. During these periods, the number of jobs in the system can built up quickly, which contributes to the jumps in the diffusion limit. Interestingly, this problem can be avoided through careful designing a tie-breaking rule. These underutilized periods can be minimized through choosing a job with the shortest remaining service time for its map phase. In some existing implementations, this tie-breaking rule is based on the arrival order. This rule can cause jumps in its diffusion limit if the map service time distribution has an increasing hazard function. However, if the distribution has a decreasing hazard function or a finite support, then it is almost as efficient as the one based on the shortest remaining service time for the map phase. This insight has direct engineering implications.

Second, we empirically validate a criticality phenomenon for MapReduce that was theoretically discovered in [28]. Specifically, this phenomenon is on configuring the number of ReduceTasks. It depicts an undesirable performance degradation when the system reaches certain critical points. The existing MapReduce systems often rely on users to specify the number of ReduceTasks. Most users apply large numbers of ReduceTasks to achieve high parallelism, expecting to accelerate the job execution without realizing the dynamics of the number of available reduce slots in a shared cluster. In general, a selfish optimal strategy taken by individuals does not necessarily lead to a globally optimal one. In this regard, an analytic result on how the number of ReduceTasks can impact the delay distribution is established in [28]. It reveals that when the number of ReduceTasks, configured by independent users, reaches a critical value that depends on all the jobs running in the cluster, then the job processing time distribution tail can even change by one order for typical heavy-tailed workload. It implies that, if not carefully managed, much longer job execution times can occur when multiple users configure their jobs independently in a shared cluster. This undesirable consequence is due to the non-work-conserving effect that some large jobs can occupy underutilized reduce slots beyond a critical number, even when they do not have enough work for their ReduceTasks to process. However, this phenomenon remains to be verified against real experiments. We empirically validate it with workloads that are similar to Facebook traffic [6].

Paper organization

Section 2 presents the MapReduce model, with a detailed description of the tie-breaking rules. In Section 3, we first prove a lower bound for the number of jobs in the system, independent of the tie-breaking rules. Then, we investigate conditions under which the previous lower bound is attainable. Specifically, we show that the diffusion limit can even exhibit jumps to the number of jobs in the system, depending on the tie-breaking rules. After that, we demonstrate in Section 4 the criticality phenomenon for typical MapReduce workloads using real experiments. Section 5 contains the details of the testbed and the conducted experiments, which is followed by the conclusion in Section 6.

2. MODEL DESCRIPTION

We use a schematic diagram in Fig. 1 to describe the MapReduce model with arriving jobs. The map phase is modeled as an $M/G/1$ processor sharing queue, and the reduce phase is modeled as a multi-server queue. This model was first proposed in [28].

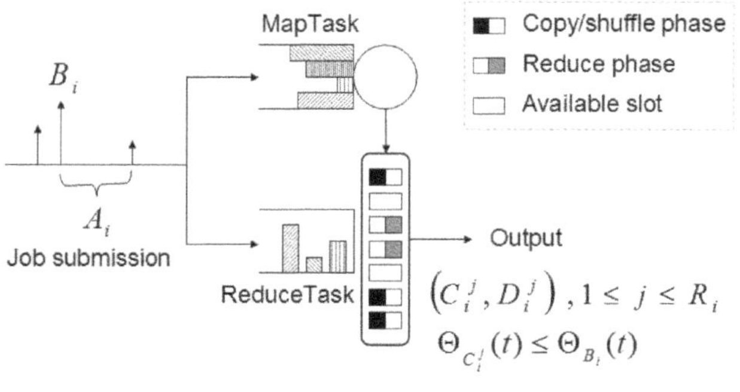

Figure 1: MapReduce model for job scheduling

Job arrivals are modeled by a Poisson random process with rate λ, with the inter-arrival times $\{A_i\}_{i>-}$. Let B_i be the total map service time of job i. The i.i.d. sequence $\{B_i\}_{i>-}$ is independent of other random variables with $B_i \overset{d}{=} B$ ("$\overset{d}{=}$" means equal in distribution).

The reduce phase is modeled as a multi-server queue. Let $r > 1$ be the total number of reduce slots (servers) in the cluster and R_i the number of ReduceTasks of Job i. ReduceTask scheduling follows the max-min fairness criteria. Denote by $R_i(t)$ the number of running ReduceTasks of job i at time t. When available reduce slots exist, all of them will be allocated to the maximum number of existing jobs such that the assignments $R_i(t)$ for all i in service are as close as possible, constrained by the condition that $R_i(t)$ cannot be larger than the number of unfinished ReduceTasks of job i. In addition, for any job i, the set of time points when at least one of its ReduceTasks are in service forms a time interval $[s_i, e_i]$. In other words, between the starting point s_i and the ending point e_i, there is always at least one ReduceTask running for job i. It means that intermittent services are avoided. We refer the previous scheduling rules as the *primary requirement*. Still, it is possible when multiple jobs compete for a single slot the primary requirement is not sufficient to fully describe the scheduling decisions. In this case, a tie-breaking rule is needed, which will be elaborated in the next section.

A reduce server permits a single ReduceTask to run, which needs to sequentially process the copy/shuffle phase and the reduce phase. We use a tuple (C_i^j, D_i^j) to characterize the jth reduce task of job i, which has a workload C_i^j for the copy/shuffle phase, and D_i^j for the reduce phase. The copy/shuffle phase of a job can overlap in time with its map phase but needs to wait for the map phase to generate the intermediate data. In order to capture this dependence constraint, we introduce function $\Theta_J(t)$, which is defined to be the finished percentage of the workload for job J at time t. For example, $\Theta_{C_i^j}(t)$ represents the attained fraction of service for copy/shuffle phase C_i^j, and $\Theta_{B_i}(t)$ the finished fraction of work for map phase B_i at time t. For MapReduce, we have $\Theta_{C_i^j}(t) \le \Theta_{B_i}(t)$ for all $t, i, 1 \le j \le R_i$, because intermediate data can be fetched by ReduceTasks only after MapTasks have generated them. We term it the *dependence constraint* for MapReduce. This dependence, seemingly simple, tremendously complicates the system and results in interesting analytical characterization.

For illustration purposes, we use measurements collected from a real experiment that is conducted using Fair Scheduler [2] on Hadoop [3]. We plot the number of map and reduce slots taken by each job at each time in the left part of Fig. 2, which are represented by different shaded areas. In addition, we also plot in the right part of Fig. 2 at each time the amount of intermediate data generated by the MapTasks for each job as well as for all of the jobs and the amount of data already fetched by the ReduceTasks.

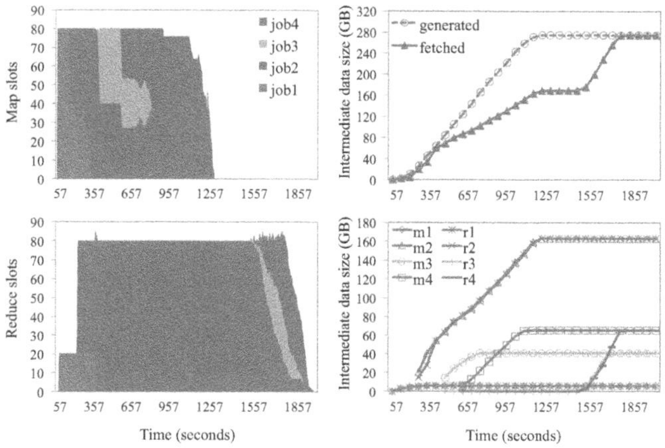

Figure 2: Runtime profile of slot allocation and intermediate data shuffling

As shown in the top-left of Fig. 2, when the second job arrives, the map slots are evenly shared between the first two jobs. However, as soon as the first job completes, all reduce slots are taken by job 2, as shown in the bottom-left of Fig. 2. When jobs 3 and 4 arrive, they can share the map slots evenly with job 2. But only until job 2 releases some reduce slots, can jobs 3 and 4 be able to share these available reduce slots. The curves on the *generated* and *fetched* intermediate data for all of the jobs demonstrate that the progress of copy/shuffle phase cannot exceed that of the map phase. In the bottom-right of Fig. 2, for $1 \le i \le 4$, m_i represents the generated data from the MapTasks of job i and r_i the fetched data by the ReduceTasks of job i.

ASSUMPTION 1. *The three mutually independent random sequences $\{C, C_i^j\}$, $\{D, D_i^j\}$ and $\{R, R_i\}$ are i.i.d. for each sequence. They are also independent of $\{A_i\}$.*

Because of the i.i.d. assumptions, we can simply represent the workload by (B, C, D, R) with arrival rate λ.

In this paper, we use the following notation. The function space $\mathcal{D}[0,1]$, endowed with the Skorohod metric, contains all right continuous functions on $[0,1]$ with left limits; many results in this space can be easily extended to $\mathcal{D}[0,\infty)$ [8]. A subspace of continuous functions is denoted by $\mathcal{C}[0,1]$; $W(t) \in \mathcal{C}[0,1]$ is the standard Brownian motion. Our analysis relies on the weak convergence of probability measures; see [8] for a complete treatment. If probability measures P_n and P satisfy $\lim_n \int_{\mathcal{D}} f dP_n = \int_{\mathcal{D}} f dP$ for every bounded, continuous and real-valued functions f on $\mathcal{D}$, then P_n is said to converge weakly to P as $n \to \infty$, denoted by $P_n \Rightarrow P$. Let $\rho(x, y) \triangleq \sup_{0 \le t \le 1} |x(t) - y(t)|$ be the uniform metric for $x, y \in \mathcal{D}$. When the limit has unmatched jumps, M_1 topology [19] is needed. Denote by $Y_n \xrightarrow{\mathcal{P}} Y$ that a sequence of random variables Y_n converges in distribution to Y. Recall that $a_n \to a$ represents a sequence of real numbers a_n converging to a. Let $\mathbf{1}_{\mathcal{S}}(t)$ be the indicator function of the set $\mathcal{S}$.

3. DIFFUSION LIMIT

Consider a sequence of MapReduce systems indexed by n. The workload $\left(B^{(n)}, C^{(n)}, D^{(n)}, R^{(n)}\right)$ is fed into the nth system with a Poisson arrival rate $\lambda^{(n)}$, $\lambda^{(n)} \to \lambda > 0$.

Let $Q_m^{(n)}(t)$ be the number of submitted jobs that still have not completed their map phases at time t. Regarding the total number of jobs in the reduce queue, we use a restricted definition as follows. Denote by $Q_r^{(n)}(t)$ the number of the jobs in the reduce queue at time t that either 1) have finished their map phases but still have not started any ReduceTasks before time t or 2) successfully occupy at least one reduce server at time t. In addition to the previous two kinds of jobs, the others are the jobs that are still running in the map queue but have not started any ReduceTasks yet. Here we intentionally exclude these jobs from being counted in the reduce queue, since this definition can ease the analysis and presentation. Denote by $Q^{(n)}(t)$ the total number of running jobs in the system at time t. Then, due to the r servers of the reduce queue, we have

$$Q_m^{(n)}(t) + Q_r^{(n)}(t) - r \le Q^{(n)}(t) \le Q_m^{(n)}(t) + Q_r^{(n)}(t). \quad (1)$$

In heavy traffic, we are interested in the scaled processes

$$\hat{Q}_m^{(n)}(t) = \frac{Q_m^{(n)}(nt)}{\sqrt{n}}, \hat{Q}_r^{(n)}(t) = \frac{Q_r^{(n)}(nt)}{\sqrt{n}}, \hat{Q}^{(n)}(t) = \frac{Q^{(n)}(nt)}{\sqrt{n}}.$$

Assume that the map queue is in stationarity at time 0. Thus, $Q_m^{(n)}(0)$ follows a geometric distribution with parameter $\lambda^{(n)}\mathbb{E}\left[B^{(n)}\right]$. Conditional on $Q_m^{(n)}(0) = n$, the first n job sizes are i.i.d. and follow the residual distribution of $B^{(n)}$. We make the following heavy traffic assumptions. For two positive constants η, ξ,

$$\sqrt{n}\left(1 - \lambda^{(n)}\mathbb{E}\left[B^{(n)}\right]\right) \to \eta, \quad (2)$$

$$\sqrt{n}\left(1 - \lambda^{(n)}\frac{1}{r}\mathbb{E}\left[\left(C^{(n)} + D^{(n)}\right)R^{(n)}\right]\right) \to \xi. \quad (3)$$

Under conditions (2) and (3), both the map queue and the reduce queue are in heavy traffic. Furthermore, we need the following technical assumption for the processor sharing queue [21], for $\theta > 0$, $\mu_b \triangleq \mathbb{E}[B] < \infty$ and $\sigma_b \triangleq (\mathbb{V}ar[B])^{1/2} < \infty$,

$$\left(\mathbb{E}\left[B^{(n)}\right], \mathbb{V}ar\left[B^{(n)}\right]\right) \to \left(\mu_b, \sigma_b^2\right). \quad (4)$$

For the reduce queue, assume that it is empty before time 0 ($Q_r^{(n)}(0-) = 0$). Let $Z_i^{(n)} \triangleq \sum_{j=1}^{R_i^{(n)}}\left(C_i^{(n),j} + D_i^{(n),j}\right)$ be an i.i.d. sequence with $Z_i^{(n)} \stackrel{d}{=} Z^{(n)}$. Specify $\nu_r^{(n)} \triangleq \mathbb{E}\left[R^{(n)}\right]$, $\mu_r^{(n)} \triangleq \mathbb{E}\left[Z^{(n)}\right] < \infty$, $\sigma_r^{(n)} \triangleq \left(\mathbb{V}ar\left[Z^{(n)}\right]\right)^{1/2} < \infty$. For $0 < \nu_r, \mu_r, \sigma_r < \infty$ and every $k > 0$,

$$\left(\nu_r^{(n)}, \mu_r^{(n)}, \sigma_r^{(n)}\right) \to \left(\nu_r, \mu_r, \sigma_r\right), \quad (5)$$

$$\lim_{n \to \infty} \int_{|y| > k\sqrt{n}} y^2 d\mathbb{P}\left[Z^{(n)} - \mu_r^{(n)} < y\right] < \infty. \quad (6)$$

Equation (6) is equivalent to the condition of Lindeberg [26]. This condition, by Theorem 3.1 in [26], ensures the weak convergence to a standard Brownian motion $W(t)$

$$\frac{\sum_{i=1}^{nt}\left(Z_i^{(n)} - \mu_r^{(n)}\right)}{\sigma_r^{(n)}\sqrt{n}} \Rightarrow W(t). \quad (7)$$

For $f \in D$, define a continuous mapping function $\Phi(f(t)) = f(t) - \inf_{0 \le s \le t} f(s)$.

Map queue: Under the aforementioned conditions, using Theorem 5.1 and Proposition 5.6 in [21] (see also Theorem 2.3 and Corollary 2.4 in [12]), we know, as $n \to \infty$,

$$\hat{Q}_m^{(n)}(t) \Rightarrow \Phi\left(\hat{Q}_m(0) + W_m(t)\right) \triangleq \hat{Q}_m(t), \quad (8)$$

where $W_m(t)$ is a Brownian motion with $W_m(0) = 0$, drift $-2\eta\mu_b/(\mu_b^2 + \sigma_b^2)$, variance $4(\mu_b/\lambda + \sigma_b^2)\mu_b/(\mu_b^2 + \sigma_b^2)^2$ and $\hat{Q}_m(0)$ independent of $W_m(t)$. The distribution of $\hat{Q}_m(0)$ follows from the stationarity assumption, for $x \ge 0$,

$$\mathbb{P}[\hat{Q}_m(0) > x] = \lim_{n \to \infty} \mathbb{P}\left[\frac{Q_m^{(n)}(0)}{\sqrt{n}} > x\right] = \lim_{n \to \infty}\left(1 - \frac{\eta}{\sqrt{n}}\right)^{\sqrt{n}x} = e^{-\eta x}.$$

The map queue, using processor sharing, is symmetric with Poisson arrivals. Thus, the departure process is also Poisson. Due to the reversibility (Theorem 3.11 of [20]), the departure process prior to t is independent of $Q_m^{(n)}(t)$.

Reduce queue: Because of the dependence constraint, the reduce queue can idle when the MapTasks do not generate enough intermediate data. We prove a lower bound to $\hat{Q}_r^{(n)}(t)$ in Section 3.2. Whether this lower bound is attainable depends on the tie-breaking rules described below.

In Section 2 we have specified the *primary requirement* for scheduling ReduceTasks. However, it is not sufficient to fully determine the scheduling. If there are more than r jobs running in the system, say k, then at least $k - r$ jobs are not in service in the reduce queue. In this case when a server becomes available, a tie-breaking rule is needed. In order to show that such a rule can greatly impact $\hat{Q}_r(t)$, we introduce three policies, all satisfying the *primary requirement.* When a tie-breaking decision is needed, we first consider jobs in the reduce queue that have already finished their map services. If there are multiple such jobs, an arbitrary rule that does not depend on the reduce service times (e.g., using the arrival order) can be used. Then, the remaining tie-breaking decision is according to one of the following policies.

- I: Jobs with smaller remaining map service times have higher priorities.
- II: Tie breaking is through uniform random selection.
- III: Jobs arrived earlier have higher priorities.

Interestingly, Policy I attains the lower bound. However, Policy II can incur jumps to the number of jobs in the reduce queue $\hat{Q}_r(t) \notin \mathcal{C}[0, \infty)$. Thus it cannot attain the lower bound, implying longer delays for the job executions. Policy III may or may not cause jumps, depending on the map service time distribution. These theoretical results have direct engineering implications.

3.1 Intuition

Before conducting the rigorous analysis, we first describe the underlying intuition on when the limit can exhibit jumps. In heavy traffic, $Q_m(t)$ can be approximated by a reflected Brownian motion with drift [12]. When heavily loaded, $Q_r(t)$ is larger than the number r of reduce slots most of the time. Because of the max-min fairness requirement for launching ReduceTasks, the reduce queue will be very close, but different, to a FIFO multi-server queue with a service time $\sum_{j=1}^{R_i}(C_j^i + D_j^i)$ for job i. In the following, we explain how the tie-breaking rules impact performance.

Policy I chooses the job with the smallest remaining map service. This job completes its map workload earlier than other jobs that are already in the system. The only problem is that the newly arrived jobs can have an even smaller map service. However, this event happens with a small probability. Thus, the arrival process of the reduce queue is close (yet not exactly due to $\Theta_{C_i^j}(t) \leq \Theta_{B_i}(t)$) to the departure process of the map queue. Since the map queue is symmetric, its departure process prior to t is independent of $Q_m(t)$. Because of this independence, $\hat{Q}_m^{(n)}(t)$ and $\hat{Q}_r^{(n)}(t)$ converge weakly to $\hat{Q}_m(t)$ and $\hat{Q}_r(t)$, two independent reflected Brownian motions with drifts.

Next, we explain the jumps in the diffusion limit under Policy II. Recall that time t is on the scale of n and the queue size on the scale of $\sqrt{n}$; let $Q_m(nt_0) = q_m\sqrt{n} + o(\sqrt{n})$ and later we will omit $o(\sqrt{n})$. Immediately when $Q_r(nt_0)$ is below r at time nt_0, a random job J from the $Q_m(nt_0)$ number of jobs running in the map queue will be selected to take the available reduce slot. Using the state space collapse result for processor sharing queue in heavy traffic (Theorem 4.7 in [12]), we know that approximately job J will have a remaining service time B^e that follows the residual distribution of B, with $\mathbb{P}[B^e > x] = \int_x \mathbb{P}[B > u]/\mathbb{E}[B]du, x \geq 0$. Let $B^e = b^e$. Job J shares the map queue equally with $q_m\sqrt{n}$ number of jobs. Therefore, job J will work on the reduce slot during the time interval $[nt_0, nt_0 + b^e q_m\sqrt{n}]$. However, during this period of time the reduce queue can only use at most $r-1$ slots to serve other ReduceTasks. Due to condition (3), the service rate of the reduce queue in this time interval is smaller than the input rate $\lambda\mu_r \approx r$ (μ_r is defined in (5)). By law of large numbers, when n is large, during $[nt_0, nt_0 + b^e q_m\sqrt{n}]$, there will be $\lambda b^e q_m\sqrt{n}$ number of jobs joining the reduce queue. Thus, job J will cause at least $\lambda b^e q_m\sqrt{n}/r$ number of jobs queueing in the reduce queue at time $nt_0 + b^e q_m\sqrt{n}$, i.e., $Q_r(nt_0 + b^e q_m\sqrt{n}) \gtrsim \lambda b^e q_m\sqrt{n}/r$. The time interval $[nt_0, nt_0 + b^e q_m\sqrt{n}]$ will degenerate to a single point t_0 since the time is on a scale of n. However, there will be a jump that is larger than $\lambda b^e q_m/r$ at time t_0, i.e., $\hat{Q}_r(t_0+) - \hat{Q}_r(t_0-) \geq \lambda b^e q_m/r$.

The analysis for Policy III is based on the arguments for Policy I and II. First, consider the case when B has an increasing hazard function. If a job has processed its map phase for a long time, then its remaining service time is expected to be also long. In this case, the chosen job will have a remaining service time that is stochastically larger than the one under Policy II (uniform random selection). Thus, it can incur jumps. The second case is when B has a decreasing hazard function or a finite support. The chosen job will likely have a short remaining service time. To better understand this point, consider a special case when $B \equiv c$ for a constant $c > 0$. In this case, Policy III is equivalent to Policy I. Thus, the diffusion limit does not have jumps.

3.2 Lower bound

We first prove a lower bound that holds independent of the tie-breaking policies. The proof relies on the construction of a work-conserving queue.

THEOREM 1. *There exists a sequence $\hat{Q}_r^{l,(n)}(t) \leq \hat{Q}_r^{(n)}(t)$ such that $\hat{Q}_r^{l,(n)}(t) \Rightarrow \Phi(W_r(t))$ where $W_r(t)$ is a Brownian motion with $W_r(0) = 0$, drift $-r\xi/\mu_r$, variance $\lambda + \sigma_r^2/\mu_r^3$ and independent of $W_m(t)$.*

Remark 1. When $\{C_i^{(n),j}, D_i^{(n),j}, R_i^{(n),j}\}$ is dependent of $\{B_i^{(n)}\}$, the two Brownian motions $W_r(t)$ and $W_m(t)$ can be also dependent, but we still have $\hat{Q}_r^{l,(n)}(t) \Rightarrow \Phi(W_r(t))$.

PROOF. The reduce queue is not work-conserving since $\Theta_{C_i^{(n),j}}(t) \leq \Theta_{B_i^{(n)}}(t)$. We construct a work-conserving reduce queue by coupling arguments. The new reduce queue has the same input as the original one.

In the new reduce queue, we specify the following three requirements. First, we abandon the constraint $\Theta_{C_i^{(n),j}}(t) \leq \Theta_{B_i^{(n)}}(t)$ so that a task can keep running until finish using the assigned server without being idle. Second, after a job arrives to the new queue it is always given at least an equal number of servers as the same job that is running in the original queue at any time unless it does not have any remaining workload in the new queue. Clearly, under these two requirements, a running job in the new queue completes no later than the same job running in the original queue. Third, only using the preceding two requirements, the new queue may idle even when there are enough workloads. In this case, it arbitrarily allocates the available servers to one of the jobs that are already in service by splitting the workload of its running ReduceTasks. Denote by $Q_r^{l,(n)}(t)$ the number of jobs and by $W_r^{l,(n)}(t)$ the total workload in the new reduce queue at time t. It is clear that $Q_r^{l,(n)}(t) \leq Q_r^{(n)}(t)$ for all t based on the construction. Furthermore, the new queue is work-conserving and can process at most r jobs simultaneously.

The only technical issue is that the arrival time points of the reduce queue are not equal to the departure points of the map queue; recall the definition of $Q_r^{(n)}(t)$ at the beginning of Section 3. There are two different cases for a departure from the map queue: 1) if this job still has not started any of its ReduceTasks, then this departure is immediately an arrival to the reduce queue; 2) if this job has taken at least one reduce slot earlier, then the departure does not correspond to an arrival of the reduce queue. The second case is illustrated in Fig. 3. When job i finishes its map phase at time t_i, it has already occupied at least one reduce slot before t_i. The arrival point of this job is the earliest time when a slot is taken, i.e., time ν_i in Fig. 3.

Denote by $L_r^{(n)}(t)$ the number of jobs that have arrived to the reduce queue and by $X^{(n)}(t)$ the number of departures from the map queue on $[0, t]$ for the nth system. It is easy to observe that, due to $\Theta_{C_i^{(n),j}}(t) \leq \Theta_{B_i^{(n)}}(t)$, r reduce slots,

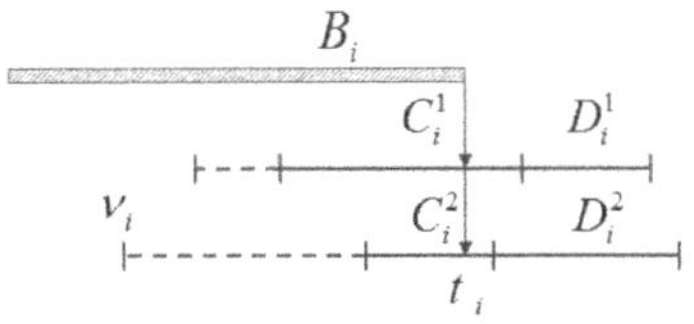

Figure 3: Arrivals of the reduce queue

and the fact that ReduceTasks are not preemptive,

$$X^{(n)}(t) \leq L_r^{(n)}(t) \leq X^{(n)}(t) + r, \tag{9}$$

which implies that

$$\rho\left(\frac{L_r^{(n)}(nt) - \lambda^{(n)}nt}{\sqrt{n}}, \frac{X^{(n)}(nt) - \lambda^{(n)}nt}{\sqrt{n}}\right) \leq \frac{r}{\sqrt{n}} \to 0. \tag{10}$$

Let $U_i^{(n)}$ be the inter-arrival time of the ith job into the reduce queue. Note that $U_i^{(n)}$ are not i.i.d. because some jobs arrive to the reduce queue before their map services finish; see Fig. 3. Therefore, we cannot directly apply Donsker's Theorem (pg.137 of [8]) to derive the diffusion limit. Instead, we use the relationship between the partial sum and the associated counting process.

Applying Theorem 3.1 in [26], we obtain $n^{-1/2}(X^{(n)}(nt) - \lambda^{(n)}nt) \Rightarrow \lambda^{1/2}W(t)$, which, by (10) and the Convergence Together Theorem (Theorem 4.1 in [8]), implies

$$\frac{\left(L_r^{(n)}(nt) - \lambda^{(n)}nt\right)}{\sqrt{n}} \Rightarrow \lambda^{1/2}W(t). \tag{11}$$

Then, using the connection between the counting process $L_r^{(n)}(nt)$ and the partial sums $\sum_{i=1}^{n}\left(U_i^{(n)} - 1/\lambda^{(n)}\right)$ (Theorem 1 of [15]), we obtain

$$\frac{\sum_{i=1}^{nt} U_i^{(n)} - nt/\lambda^{(n)}}{\sqrt{n}} \Rightarrow -\lambda^{-1}W(t). \tag{12}$$

Based on the construction, the workload $W_r^{l,(n)}(t)$ in the new queue is equal to the workload in a single server FIFO queue. Combining (7), (12) and (3) and using the well-known result on single server FIFO queues (e.g., see Section 6 in [9]) yield

$$\frac{W_r^{l,(n)}(nt)}{\sqrt{n}} \Rightarrow \mu_r\Phi\left(W_r(t)\right). \tag{13}$$

Because the new queue can only serve at most r jobs simultaneously and the remaining service of each job being served at time t is upper bounded by $\max_{1\leq k\leq L^{(n)}(t)} Z_k^{(n)}$, we obtain

$$\left|\sum_{i=L_r^{(n)}(t)-Q_r^{(n)}(t)}^{L_r^{(n)}(t)} Z_i^{(n)} - W_r^{l,(n)}(t)\right| \leq r \max_{1\leq k\leq L_r^{(n)}(t)} Z_k^{(n)}.$$

This result, using

$$\sum_{i=L_r^{(n)}(t)-Q_r^{(n)}(t)}^{L_r^{(n)}(t)} Z_i^{(n)} = Q_r^{(n)}(t)\mu_r^{(n)} + \left(\sum_{i=L_r^{(n)}(t)-Q_r^{(n)}(t)}^{L_r^{(n)}(t)} \left(Z_i^{(n)} - \mu_r^{(n)}\right)\right),$$

implies, for $t \in [0,1]$,

$$\rho\left(\frac{W_r^{l,(n)}(nt)}{\sqrt{n}}, \frac{\mu_r^{(n)}Q_r^{(n)}(nt)}{\sqrt{n}}\right) \leq \frac{r\max_{1\leq k\leq L_r^{(n)}(n)} Z_k^{(n)}}{\sqrt{n}} + \sup_{0\leq t\leq 1}\left|\sum_{i=L_r^{(n)}(nt)-Q_r^{(n)}(nt)}^{L_r^{(n)}(nt)} \left(Z_i^{(n)} - \mu_r^{(n)}\right)\right| \triangleq I_1^{(n)} + I_2^{(n)}. \tag{14}$$

Using $L_r^{(n)}(n)/n \to 1/\mu_r$, $\sigma_r^{(n)} \to \sigma_r < \infty$ and Lemma 3.3 in [13], we obtain $I_1^{(n)} \to 0$ almost surely. Observe that (7) validates the C-tightness (Lemma 3.2 in [13]) of the sequence $\left(\sum_{i=1}^{nt}\left(Z_i^{(n)} - \mu_r^{(n)}\right)\right)/\sqrt{n}$, we can repeat the same arguments in the proof of Lemma 5.1 (pg. 165) in [13] to show $I_2^{(n)} \xrightarrow{\mathcal{P}} 0$. These two facts yield

$$\rho\left(\frac{W_r^{l,(n)}(nt)}{\sqrt{n}}, \frac{\mu_r^{(n)}Q_r^{(n)}(nt)}{\sqrt{n}}\right) \xrightarrow{\mathcal{P}} 0, \tag{15}$$

which, by (13), the condition $\mu_r^{(n)} \to \mu_r$ and the Convergence Together Theorem (Theorem 4.1 in [8]), implies $\hat{Q}_r^{l,(n)}(t) \Rightarrow \Phi\left(W_r(t)\right)$ on $\mathcal{D}[0,1]$. This result can be easily extended to $\mathcal{D}[0,\infty)$. The reason why $W_r(t)$ is independent of $W_m(t)$ is from the fact that $\{X^{(n)}(s), s < t\}$ is independent of $Q_m^{(n)}(t)$ (Theorem 3.11 of [20]) and that $\{Z_i^{(n)}\}$ is also independent of $Q_m^{(n)}(t)$. □

3.3 Is the lower bound attainable?

Next, we investigate whether the previous lower bound is attainable or not. If the limit is continuous, we can use $\mathcal{D}([0,\infty), J_1)$ with the Skorohod J_1 topology [8]. If the limit has unmatched jumps, M_1 topology is needed [19]. Later our result shows that $Q_r^{(n)}(0) = 0$ but its limit can be equal to a nonzero jump size. Since the pointwise convergence must hold at 0 even using M_1 topology, we exclude the origin and use the space $\mathcal{D}((0,\infty), M_1)$. After excluding the origin, we do not have a problem; this approach to overcome this minor technical issue has been exploited in [19].

THEOREM 2. *1) Under Policy I, if* $\mathbb{P}[B_n \leq \kappa] = 1, \kappa > 0$, *then,*

$$\hat{Q}_r^{(n)}(t) \Rightarrow \Phi\left(W_r(t)\right), \tag{16}$$

and $\hat{Q}^{(n)}(t) \Rightarrow \hat{Q}_m(t) + \Phi\left(W_r(t)\right)$ *in* $\mathcal{D}([0,\infty), J_1)$.

2) Under Policy II, if $\mathbb{P}[B_n \leq \kappa] = 1, \kappa > 0$, *then,*

$$\hat{Q}_r^{(n)}(t) \Rightarrow \Phi^{\prime}\left(W_r(t)\right), \text{in } \mathcal{D}((0,\infty), \mathrm{M}_1), \tag{17}$$

where $\Phi^{\prime}\left(W_r(t)\right)$ *is modified from* $\Phi\left(W_r(t)\right)$ *by having jumps up of random size* J_k *when* $\Phi^{\prime}\left(W_r(t)\right)$ *hits zero at time* $\tau_k, k = 0,1,2,\cdots,\tau_0 = 0$, *with* $J_k \geq \lambda B_k^e \hat{Q}_m(\tau_k)/r$ *for i.i.d.* $B_k^e \stackrel{d}{=} B^e$. *In addition, we have* $\hat{Q}^{(n)}(t) \Rightarrow \hat{Q}_m(t) + \Phi^{\prime}\left(W_r(t)\right)$ *in* $\mathcal{D}((0,\infty), M_1)$.

3) Under Policy III, if B has an increasing hazard function, the result is the same as in (17) with $\Phi^{\prime}\left(W_r(t)\right)$ *having jumps. If B has a decreasing hazard function or a finite support, the result is the same as in (16).*

Remark 2. This result has a direct implication on throughput and delay. Even though these policies result in the same throughput when the system is stable, the experienced job delay will be different. By Little's law [20], the average delay is equal to the average number of jobs in the system divided by the throughput. These possible jumps increase the number of running jobs in the system, implying a prolonged average job execution time. It has been shown that servers with vacations can incur jumps to the number of jobs in heavy traffic [19]. Under Policy II and Policy III with some conditions, jumps also occur. This is an indication that the computing resources are not fully utilized, as if the servers took vacations from time to time. The result on Policy I shows that these jumps can be eliminated through careful scheduling.

Remark 3. The condition $\mathbb{P}[B_n \leq \kappa] = 1$ simplifies the proof, which can be relaxed. In addition, for Policy II, we can prove $J_k \leq \lambda \max\left\{B^e_{k,1}, B^e_{k,2}, \cdots, B^e_{k,r}\right\} \hat{Q}_m(\tau_k)$ for i.i.d. $B^e_{k,l} \overset{d}{=} B^e$. Note that $\{J_k\}$ are not i.i.d. since they depend on the map queue size observed at τ_k. It can be shown that $\{J_k\}$ is a Harris-recurrent Markov chain.

We first establish a lemma that shows the lower bound is indeed attainable if the MapReduce system does not have the dependence constraint between the map queue and the reduce queue. When the constraint $\Theta_{C_i^j}(t) \leq \Theta_{B_i}(t)$ is ignored, we term the model a *relaxed MapReduce*. Tie-breaking can use any rule that does not depend on the reduce service times. Though a relaxed MapReduce is not realistic, we will prove that under Policy I, typical sample paths in heavy traffic are close to the ones in the relaxed MapReduce. Therefore, even with the dependence constraint, the lower bound is still attainable with careful scheduling.

LEMMA 1. *For the relaxed MapReduce, as $n \to \infty$,*

$$\hat{Q}^{(n)}_r(t) \Rightarrow \Phi\left(W_r(t)\right).$$

PROOF. By Theorem 1, we only need to prove the upper bound. An upper bound for a multi-server queue in heavy traffic is provided in [13], relying the construction of a modified queuing system. The proof in [13] does not directly apply for the reduce queue, since a job have multiple ReduceTasks that can run simultaneously on several servers of the reduce queue. We take a different approach by first characterizing the number $\check{Q}^{(n)}_r(t)$ of ReduceTasks running in the reduce queue at time t. Then, we use the Convergence Together Theorem to connect $\check{Q}^{(n)}_r(t)$ and $Q^{(n)}_r(t)$.

Let $A^{(n)}(t)$ be the total number of ReduceTasks submitted to the reduce queue on $[0, t]$. Recall that $L^{(n)}_r(t)$ denote the number of jobs arriving in the reduce queue on $[0, t]$. Clearly, $A^{(n)}(t) = \sum_{i=1}^{L^{(n)}_r(t)} R^{(n)}_i$. Repeating the same arguments for showing $I^{(n)}_2 \overset{\mathcal{P}}{\to} 0$ in (14), we can prove that, on $\mathcal{D}[0, 1]$,

$$\rho\left(\frac{A^{(n)}(nt) - \lambda^{(n)}\mathbb{E}[R^{(n)}]nt}{\sqrt{n}}, \frac{\left(L^{(n)}_r(nt) - \lambda^{(n)}nt\right)\mathbb{E}[R^{(n)}]}{\sqrt{n}}\right)$$

$$\leq \sup_{1\ \ t\ \ 1} \frac{\sum_{i=1}^{L^{(n)}_r(nt)}\left(R^{(n)}_i - \mathbb{E}[R^{(n)}]\right)}{\sqrt{n}} \overset{\mathcal{P}}{\to} 0,$$

which, recalling $\mathbb{E}[R^{(n)}] \to \nu_r$ in (5), using (11) and applying Theorem 4.1 in [8], yields $\left(A^{(n)}(nt) - \lambda^{(n)}\mathbb{E}[R^{(n)}]nt\right)/\sqrt{n} \Rightarrow \lambda^{1/2}\nu_r W\ (t)$. The preceding result, in conjunction with (3) and using Theorem 1 in [14], implies

$$\frac{\check{Q}^{(n)}_r(nt)}{\sqrt{n}} \Rightarrow \nu_r \Phi\left(W_r(t)\right). \tag{18}$$

Next, we study $Q^{(n)}_r(t)$ using (13). Note that

$$\left|\sum_{i=L^{(n)}_r(t)\ \ Q^{(n)}_r(t)}^{L^{(n)}_r(t)} R^{(n)}_i - \check{Q}^{(n)}_r(t)\right| \leq r \max_{1\ \ k\ \ L^{(n)}_r(t)} R^{(n)}_k,$$

which, using the same argument for (14) and (15), implies that $Q^{(n)}_r(nt)/\sqrt{n} \Rightarrow \Phi\left(W_r(t)\right)$. ☐

In the next two subsections, we provide the proofs for Policy I and II. We skip the proof for Policy III, since the result is expected using the intuition explained in Section 3.1 and the proving methods for Policy I and II.

3.3.1 Proof for Policy I

Let $R^{(n)}(t)$ be the smallest remaining service time among all the jobs that are running in the processor sharing map queue at time t; if there are no tasks in the queue then $R^{(n)}(t) = 0$. In addition, let $M^{(n)}(t)$ be the maximum number of jobs in the map queue on the time interval $[0, t]$. Denote by $W^{(n)}_m(t)$ and $W^{(n)}_r(t)$ the total workload in the map queue and the reduce queue at time t, respectively. For $\epsilon_q, \epsilon_r > 0$, define

$$\mathcal{A}^{(n)}_{\epsilon_q,\epsilon_r} = \left\{R^{(n)}(t) < \epsilon_r, \forall t \in \left\{s : s \in [0, n], W^{(n)}_m(s) > \epsilon_q\sqrt{n}\right\}\right\}.$$

This event means that for each time $t \in [0, n]$ with $W^{(n)}_m(t) > \epsilon_q\sqrt{n}$, the processor sharing map queue always contains at least one task with a remaining service time less than ϵ_r.

LEMMA 2. *For any $\epsilon_q, \epsilon_r > 0$ and $0 < \eta < 1$, there exists n_0 such that $n > n_0$ implies*

$$\mathbb{P}\left[\mathcal{A}^{(n)}_{\epsilon_q,\epsilon_r}\right] \geq 1 - \eta. \tag{19}$$

PROOF. The proof relies on the state space collapse property of processor sharing queue in heavy traffic [12, 21]. The state descriptor $\{\mu^{(n)}_t : t \geq 0\}$ is such that for each $t \geq 0$, $\mu^{(n)}_t$ is a random measure on $[0, \infty)$ that has a unit of mass at the residual service time of each task in the nth processor sharing map queue. For $0 < \epsilon < \epsilon$ and a continuous function

$$g(x) = \mathbf{1}_{x\ \ [0,\epsilon]}(x) + \left(1 - \frac{\ \ - \epsilon}{\epsilon\ \ - \epsilon}\right)\mathbf{1}_{x\ \ (\epsilon,\epsilon^{\circ}]}(x),$$

define a random function

$$H(t) = \left|\int_0^{\epsilon^{\circ}} g(x)d\mu^{(n)}_t - W^{(n)}_m(t)\int_0^{\epsilon^{\circ}} g(x)\frac{\mathbb{P}[B^{(n)} > x]}{\mathbb{E}[B^{(n)}]}dx\right|.$$

The state space collapse is characterized by Theorem 4.7 in [12] for GI/GI/1 queue under the condition of a finite forth moment. For M/GI/1 queue it has been relaxed to a finite second moment condition [21]. It implies that, for any $0 < \eta < 1, \xi > 0$, there exists n_0 such that for all $n > n_0$,

$$\mathbb{P}\left[\sup_{t\ \ [0,n]} H(t) \leq \xi\sqrt{n}\right] \geq 1 - \eta. \tag{20}$$

Recall (4) with $\mathbb{E}[B^{(n)}] = \int_0 \mathbb{P}[B^{(n)} > x]dx \to \mu_b > 0$. Since $\mathbb{P}[B^{(n)} > 0-] = 1$ ($0-$ to avoid the mass at the origin) and $\mathbb{P}[B^{(n)} > x]$ is non-increasing in x, there exists $\zeta, \delta > 0$ and n_0 such that $\inf_{n>n_1} \mathbb{P}[B^{(n)} > \delta]/\mathbb{E}[B^{(n)}] > \zeta$.

The condition $W_m^{(n)}(t) > \epsilon_q\sqrt{n}$ implies, for $\epsilon \; < \delta$,

$$W_m^{(n)}(t) \int_0^{\epsilon^\circ} g(x) \frac{\mathbb{P}[B^{(n)} > x]}{\mathbb{E}[B^{(n)}]} dx \geq \epsilon\zeta\epsilon_q\sqrt{n}.$$

In addition, we have $\mu_t^{(n)}([0, \epsilon \;]) \geq \int_0^{\epsilon^\circ} g(x)d\mu_t$. Thus, for $0 < \epsilon < \epsilon \; < \delta$ and $0 < \xi < \epsilon\zeta\epsilon_q$, the event $H(t) \leq \xi\sqrt{n}$ implies that, if $W_m^{(n)}(t) > \epsilon_q\sqrt{n}$, then $\mu_t^{(n)}([0, \epsilon \;]) \geq (\epsilon\zeta\epsilon_q - \xi)\sqrt{n}$. Because $\epsilon\zeta\epsilon_q - \xi > 0$, choosing $\epsilon \; < \epsilon_r$, we know $R^{(n)}(t) < \epsilon_r$. Therefore, $\left\{\sup_{t \;\; [0,n]} H(t) \leq \xi\sqrt{n}\right\} \subseteq \mathcal{A}_{\epsilon_q,\epsilon_r}^{(n)}$, which finishes the proof. □

Lemma 3. *For any $0 < \eta < 1$, there exists m_η and n_0 such that $n > n_0$ implies*

$$\mathbb{P}[M^{(n)}(n) \leq m_\eta\sqrt{n}] \geq 1 - \eta. \tag{21}$$

Proof. This is a direct consequence of $\hat{Q}_m^{(n)}(t) \Rightarrow \hat{Q}_m(t)$ in $D([0,1], J_1)$, as shown in (8). Since taking the maximum of a function is a continuous mapping, we obtain $M^{(n)}(n)/\sqrt{n} \Rightarrow \sup_{t \;\; [0,1]} \hat{Q}_m(t) \triangleq M_Q$. By the well known result on the maximum of a reflected Brownian motion with negative drift on $[0, 1]$, M_Q is almost sure finite, which proves the lemma. □

For $\epsilon_q, \epsilon_m > 0$, define

$$\mathcal{B}_{\epsilon_q,\epsilon_m}^{(n)} = \left\{ \sup_{0 \;\; s,t \;\; n, \; s \;\; t < \epsilon_m n} |W_m^{(n)}(s) - W_m^{(n)}(t)| < \epsilon_q\sqrt{n} \right\}.$$

It characterizes the continuity of $W_m^{(n)}(t)$ on $[0, n]$. Using Lemma 3.2 of [13], we obtain the following lemma.

Lemma 4. *For ϵ_q, η, there exists $0 < \epsilon_m < 1$ and n_0 such that $n > n_0$ implies*

$$\mathbb{P}\left[\mathcal{B}_{\epsilon_q,\epsilon_m}^{(n)}\right] \geq 1 - \eta. \tag{22}$$

Since there are r servers in the reduce queue, at any time t we denote by $\mathcal{T}_t$ the set that contains the running reduce tasks on these servers. If no such task exists at time t, then $\mathcal{T}_t = \emptyset$. Each element in $\mathcal{T}_t$, if not empty, can be denoted by r_i^j, meaning the jth reduce task of job i. For a reduce task r_i^j, denote by $V_m^{(n)}(r_i^j, t)$ the remaining map workload of job i observed at time t (with $V_m^{(n)}(\emptyset, t) \equiv 0$), and by $V_r^{(n)}(r_i^j, t)$ the remaining workload of task r_i^j at time t.

Proof for Policy I. We only need to prove the result on $D([0, 1], J_1)$, since it can be extended to $D([0, \infty), J_1)$ [30]. The proof is based on constructing a new work-conserving reduce queue. It has a larger workload than the original non-work-conserving reduce queue. Then, we compare the workloads in the new queue and the relaxed MapReduce (defined before Lemma 1), and show that the difference of the normalized queue sizes vanishes.

For any $\epsilon_q, \epsilon_r > 0$ and $0 < \eta < 1$, due to Lemmas 2, 3 and 4, the subset $\mathcal{E}^{(n)} \triangleq \{M^{(n)}(n) \leq m_\eta\sqrt{n}\} \cap \mathcal{A}_{\epsilon_q,\epsilon_r}^{(n)} \cap \mathcal{B}_{\epsilon_q,\epsilon_m}^{(n)}$ satisfies $\mathbb{P}[\mathcal{E}^{(n)}] > 1 - 3\eta$ for $n > n_0$. In the following discussion, we only work on the sample paths within $\mathcal{E}^{(n)}$, since we can pass $\eta \to 0$.

Let t_y^x be the time when ReduceTask r_y^x is first assigned to a reduce server. If $V_m^{(n)}(r_y^x, t_y^x) = 0$ then task r_y^x always satisfies the dependence constraint. Therefore, we only need to take care of the case $V_m^{(n)}(r_y^x, t_y^x) > 0$. Consider the map queue workload $W_m^{(n)}(t)$ observed at time t_y^x with $V_m^{(n)}(r_y^x, t_y^x) > 0$. For $\epsilon_q > 0$, there are two different cases: 1) $W_m^{(n)}(t_y^x) \leq \epsilon_q\sqrt{n}$ and 2) $W_m^{(n)}(t_y^x) > \epsilon_q\sqrt{n}$.

For the first case, within $\mathcal{B}_{\epsilon_q,\epsilon_m}^{(n)}$, the event $W_m^{(n)}(t_y^x) \leq \epsilon_q\sqrt{n}$ implies $W_m^{(n)}(t_y^x + \epsilon_m n) \leq 2\epsilon_q\sqrt{n}$. Define $\mathcal{C}_{\epsilon_q}^{(n)} = \left\{Q_m^{(n)}(t) \leq K\epsilon_q\sqrt{n}, \forall t \in \left\{s : W_m^{(n)}(s) \leq 2\epsilon_q\sqrt{n}, s \in [0, n]\right\}\right\}$. The state space collapse property [12, 21] shows $\mathbb{P}\left[\mathcal{C}_{\epsilon_q}^{(n)}\right] > 1 - \eta$, for n large enough and some $K > 0$ that does not depend on ϵ_q. Therefore, within $\mathcal{B}_{\epsilon_q,\epsilon_m}^{(n)} \cap \mathcal{C}_{\epsilon_q}^{(n)}$, task r_y^x share with at most $K\epsilon_q\sqrt{n}$ number of jobs in the processor sharing map queue during $[t_y^x, t_y^x + \epsilon_m n]$. Since $\mathbb{P}[B_n \leq \kappa] = 1$, choosing $n > (K\kappa\epsilon_q/\epsilon_m)^2$, we know that task r_y^x can finish before time $t_y^x + \epsilon_m n$. Furthermore, it can only idle for at most $K\kappa\epsilon_q\sqrt{n}$ time when waiting for its map phase to finish. Thus, we can upper bound the remaining processing time of r_y^x by $K\kappa\epsilon_q\sqrt{n} + V_r^{(n)}(r_y^x, t_y^x)$. For the second case, task r_y^x has the smallest remaining map service time among all the jobs in the system at time t_y^x under Policy I. By Lemma 2, we know $V_r^{(n)}(r_y^x, t_y^x) < \epsilon_r$ within $\mathcal{E}^{(n)}$. In addition, $M^{(n)}(n) \leq m_\eta\sqrt{n}$ within $\mathcal{E}^{(n)}$, at most $m_\eta\sqrt{n}$ number of jobs share the map queue. Thus, task r_i^j can idle for at most $\epsilon_r m_\eta\sqrt{n}$ time. For $\epsilon_r = \epsilon_q$ and $\bar{K} = \max\{K\kappa, m_\eta\}$, we obtain an upper bound $\bar{K}\epsilon_q\sqrt{n} + V_r^{(n)}(r_y^x, t_y^x)$ to the remaining processing time of task r_y^x for both cases.

Now, we construct a new work-conserving reduce queue, with $W_{new}^{(n)}(t)$ being its workload at time t. The new queue is constructed by replacing the remaining workload of a ReduceTask r_y^x by $\bar{K}\epsilon_q\sqrt{n} + V_r^{(n)}(r_y^x, t_y^x)$ if $V_m^{(n)}(r_y^x, t_y^x) > 0$ and ignoring the dependence constraint $\Theta_{C_i^j}(t) \leq \Theta_{B_i}(t)$ for all i, j. With this construction, conditional on $\mathcal{E}^{(n)} \cap \mathcal{C}_{\epsilon_q}^{(n)}$, the execution time of each job is no smaller in the new queue than in the original queue. In addition, the new queue is work-conserving with $W_{new}^{(n)}(t) \geq W_r^{(n)}(t)$ for $t \in [0, n]$. Note that outside of the set $\mathcal{E}^{(n)} \cap \mathcal{C}_{\epsilon_q}^{(n)}$, these results may not hold.

We operate the new reduce queue and the relaxed MapReduce under Policy I using the same input and the same order to serve ReduceTasks. Let the workload of the reduce queue in the relaxed MapReduce be $W_{relax}^{(n)}(t)$. Denote by $Q_{new}^{(n)}(t)$ and $Q_{relax}^{(n)}(t)$ the number of ReduceTasks in the reduce queue for the new system and the relaxed MapReduce, respectively. It is clear that $W_{new}^{(n)}(t) \geq W_{relax}^{(n)}(t)$ and $Q_{new}^{(n)}(t) \geq Q_{relax}^{(n)}(t)$. Note that a ReduceTask r_y^x can only increase its workload by $\bar{K}\epsilon_q\sqrt{n}$ when $Q_{new}^{(n)}(t_y^x) \leq r$ for the new system. Thus, when $Q_{new}^{(n)}(t) \leq r$, we have $W_{new}^{(n)}(t) - W_{relax}^{(n)}(t) \leq r\bar{K}\epsilon_q\sqrt{n}$ since there are r servers. On the other hand, when $Q_{new}^{(n)}(t) > r$, the workloads $W_{new}^{(n)}(t)$ and $W_{relax}^{(n)}(t)$ always change by the same value. Therefore, uniformly for both cases, we obtain, within $\mathcal{E}^{(n)} \cap \mathcal{C}_{\epsilon_q}^{(n)}$,

$$W_{new}^{(n)}(t) - W_{relax}^{(n)}(t) \leq r\bar{K}\epsilon_q\sqrt{n}, \text{ for all t} \in [0, \text{n}]. \tag{23}$$

Repeating the same arguments as for (15), we can connect the workloads and the number of jobs between the new queue and the relaxed MapReduce. Therefore, by (23), there exist n_0 and a constant $d > 0$ such that for all $n > n_0$ and $s \in [0, 1]$,

$$\mathbb{P}\left[\rho\left(\frac{Q^{(n)}_{new}(sn)}{\sqrt{n}} - \frac{Q^{(n)}_{relax}(sn)}{\sqrt{n}}\right) \le d\epsilon_q, \mathcal{E}^{(n)} \cap \mathcal{C}^{(n)}\right]$$
$$> 1 - 5\eta. \qquad (24)$$

Recalling Lemma 1, we obtain

$$\frac{Q^{(n)}_{relax}(sn)}{\sqrt{n}} \Rightarrow \Phi(W_r(s)). \qquad (25)$$

Passing $\epsilon_q \to 0, \eta \to 0, m_\eta \to \infty$ and using (25), (24) with Convergence Together Theorem, we finish the proof of (16). The proof of the result on $\hat{Q}^{(n)}(t)$ is a direct consequence of (16) and Theorem 1, in view of (1). □

3.3.2 *Proof for Policy II*

We can define two modes for the reduce queue at each time t. Mode A is when at least one reduce task r^x_y running on a server (i.e., $r^x_y \in \mathcal{T}_t$) has unfinished map phase $V_m(r^x_y, t) > 0$. Mode B is when $V^{(n)}_m(r^x_y, t) = 0$ for every $r^x_y \in \mathcal{T}_t$; recall $V^{(n)}_m(\emptyset, t) = 0$. Let $\mathcal{X}_r(t)$ denote the mode of the reduce queue at time t. It is clearly that the reduce queue can be either in mode A or mode B, i.e., $\mathcal{X}_r(t) \in \{A, B\}$.

Now, we can inductively define successive cycles. Recall that the reduce queue is empty at time 0− and new reduce tasks join at 0 ($\mathcal{X}_r(0) = A$). Let $T^{(n)}_1 = 0$ and $T^{(n)}_{A,1} = \inf\{t : \mathcal{X}_r(t) = B, t > 0\}$. Denote by $T^{(n)}_2$ the first time after $T^{(n)}_{A,1}$ when the reduce queue turns from mode B to mode A, i.e., $T^{(n)}_2 = \inf\left\{t : \mathcal{X}_r(t) = A, t > T^{(n)}_{A,1}\right\}$. Inductively, let $T^{(n)}_{A,k} = \inf\left\{t : \mathcal{X}_r(t) = B, t > T^{(n)}_k\right\}$ and $T^{(n)}_{(k+1)} = \inf\left\{t : \mathcal{X}_r(t) = A, t > T^{(n)}_{A,k}\right\}$. Let $L^{(n)}_k$ be the length of the kth cycle in the system indexed by n, i.e., $L^{(n)}_k = T^{(n)}_{k+1} - T^{(n)}_k$. Note that $\{T^{(n)}_k, k = 1, 2, \cdots\}$ are not regenerative.

Proof for Policy II. 2) We break the queueing process of the reduce queue over the successive cycles along the time sequence $T^{(n)}_k, k = 1, 2, \cdots$. Consider the process during the kth cycle, $Q^{(n),k}_r(nt) \triangleq Q^{(n)}_r(t)\mathbf{1}_{[T^{(n)}_k, T^{(n)}_{k+1})}(nt)$ for $t \ge 0$. Thus, $T^{(n)}_k = \sum^{k-1}_{i=1} L^{(n)}_i, k \ge 2$ and

$$\hat{Q}^{(n)}_r(t) = \sum_{k=1} Q^{(n),k}_r(nt)/\sqrt{n}. \qquad (26)$$

The proof follows a similar approach in [19]. However, the difference is that in our case $T^{(n)}_k, k = 1, 2, \cdots$ are not regenerative points. The issue is that at the beginning of the kth cycle $T^{(n)}_k, k \ge 2$, some of the ReduceTasks in the system can have remaining service times that depend on the queueing dynamics of cycle $k - 1$. Let $R^{(n)}_{max}(k)$ be the maximum of the remaining service times for all the ReduceTasks that are still in the system observed immediately before $T^{(n)}_k$.

If we can show that, for each k,

$$\frac{1}{\sqrt{n}}\left(Q^{(n),1}_r(nt), Q^{(n),2}_r(nt), \cdots, Q^{(n),k}_r(nt), L^{(n)}_1, L^{(n)}_2, \cdots, L^{(n)}_k\right)$$
$$\Rightarrow \left(\hat{Q}^1_r(t), \hat{Q}^2_r(t), \cdots, \hat{Q}^k_r(t), L_1, L_2, \cdots, L_k\right) \qquad (27)$$

and $\mathbb{P}[L_k > 0] = 1$ with $T_k \triangleq L_1 + L_1 + \cdots + L_k \xrightarrow{\mathcal{P}} \infty$ as $k \to \infty$, then, we obtain, as $n \to \infty$,

$$\hat{Q}^{(n)}_r(t) \Rightarrow \sum_{k=1} \hat{Q}^k_r(t). \qquad (28)$$

We use mathematical induction on the cycle indexed by k, as illustrated in Fig. 4. Assuming it is true for the first

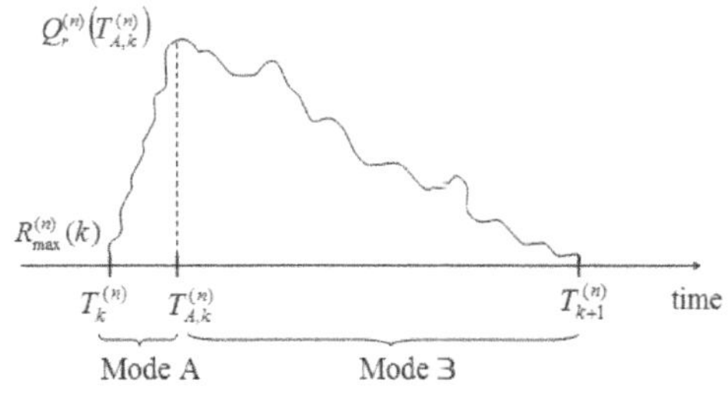

Figure 4: Illustration of the kth cycle

$k - 1$ cycles, we prove five results for the kth cycle. (a) $R^{(n)}_{max}(k)/\sqrt{n} \xrightarrow{\mathcal{P}} 0$ (the remaining workload left from cycle $k - 1$ vanishes on the scale $\sqrt{n}$) and $\left(T^{(n)}_{A,k} - T^{(n)}_k\right)/n \xrightarrow{\mathcal{P}} 0$ (the time spent in mode A within a cycle vanishes on the scale n). (b) The normalized number of jobs in the reduce queue $Q^{(n)}_r(t)/\sqrt{n}$ observed at $T^{(n)}_{A,k}$ converges in probability to J_k, which has a lower bound $\lambda B^e_k \hat{Q}_m(T_k)/r$. (c) For any $0 < \eta < 1$, there exists $l^\eta_k > 1$ such that $\mathbb{P}\left[T^{(n)}_{k+1} < (l^\eta_k - 1)n\right] > 1 - \eta$ for n large enough. Because of this result, we only need to focus on $t \in [0, l^\eta_k n]$ for studying the first k cycles. On $[0, l^\eta_k n]$, we can use Lemmas 3 and 4, which hold for any fixed $l^\eta_k > 0$. (d) The queueing process $\hat{Q}^{(n)}(t)$ after $T^{(n)}_{A,k}$ converges weakly to a Brownian motion $BM(t)$ starting at J_k with drift $-r\xi/\mu_r$ and variance $\lambda + \sigma^2_r/\mu^3_r$. (e) $T^{(n)}_{k+1}$ converges weakly to the first-passage time to 0 of $BM(t)$. Comparing the proof of Theorem 2.1 in [19] with ours, we only need to prove (a), (b) and (c).

The assumption $\mathbb{P}[B^{(n)} < \kappa]$ makes $R^{(n)}_{max}(k)/\sqrt{n} \to 0$ trivial. Actually, it can be shown that (a) holds even when $B^{(n)}$ has an infinite support. For the first $k - 1$ cycles, we distinguish two cases A) $Q^{(n)}_m\left(T^{(n)}_k\right) \le \epsilon_q\sqrt{n}$ and B) $Q^{(n)}_m\left(T^{(n)}_k\right) > \epsilon_q\sqrt{n}$. For case A), using a similar approach to case 1) in the proof of Policy I and the state space collapse property, we can prove that $Q^{(n)}_r\left(T^{(n)}_{A,k}\right) \le K\epsilon_q\sqrt{n}$ for some $K > 0$. Passing $\epsilon_q \to 0$ takes care of this case.

Therefore, we only need to focus on case B). Recall that the tie-breaking rule is uniform random selection. At time $T^{(n)}_k$, the chosen task J has a remaining service time $X^{(n)}_k$ with CDF $\nu^{(n)}_k(x), x \ge 0$. Note that $\mathbb{P}[B^{(e)} \le x]$ is a continuous function. We can construct a sequence of simple CDF functions $F_m(x) = \sum^{k_m}_{i=1} f^m_i \mathbf{1}_{[b^m_{i-1}, b^m_i)}(x), b^m_i > 0, 1 \le i \le k_m$ for $m = 1, 2, \cdots$, with $\rho\left(F_m(x), \mathbb{P}[B^{(e)} \le x]\right) < \epsilon/2$ for m large enough. By the state space collapse property of processor sharing [12], we know $\rho\left(\nu^{(n)}_k(x), \mathbb{P}[B^{(e)} \le x]\right) < \epsilon/2$ for n large enough, which implies $\rho\left(\nu^{(n)}_k(x), F_m(x)\right) < \epsilon$. Thus, we can first assume $X^{(n)}_k \in \{b^m_i, 1 \le i \le k_m\}$ for a fixed m that is large enough.

Define $\mathcal{D}_q^{(n)} = \left\{Q_m^{(n)}\left(T_k^{(n)}\right)/\sqrt{n} > q\right\}$ for $q \geq \epsilon_q$. Denote by Y_k the length of the time interval when task J occupies a server. Using Lemma 4 and the state space collapse property, we can repeat the similar arguments in proving case 1) for Policy I to show, for $1 > \epsilon > 0$ and n large enough,

$$\mathbb{P}\left[Y_k \geq (1-\epsilon)b_i^m q\sqrt{n}|X_k^{(n)} = b_i^m, \mathcal{D}_q^{(n)}\right] > 1-\eta. \quad (29)$$

Let

$$\mathcal{W}_k^{(n)} = \left\{Q_r^{(n)}\left(T_k^{(n)} + Y_k\right) > (1-\epsilon)\lambda \min\{b_i^m\}\epsilon_q\sqrt{n}/r\right\}.$$

Due to Poisson departures from the map queue and the law of large numbers, using (29) with $q = \epsilon_q$ on $Y_k \geq (1-\epsilon)\min\{b_i^m\}\epsilon_q\sqrt{n}$, we obtain $\mathbb{P}\left[\mathcal{W}_k^{(n)}|\mathcal{D}_{\epsilon_q}^{(n)}\right] > 1-2\eta$, for n large enough. For $\mathcal{E}^{(n)} = \left\{M^{(n)}(l_{k\;1}^{\eta}n) \leq m_\eta\sqrt{n}\right\}$, with $M^{(n)}(l_{k\;1}^{\eta}n)$ being the maximum of $W_m^{(n)}(t)$ on the interval $[0, l_{k\;1}^{\eta}n]$ (noting that $\mathbb{P}[T_{k\;1}^{(n)} < (l_{k\;1}^{\eta} - 1)n] > 1-\eta$), we have, by Lemma 2, for any $0 < \eta < 1$, there exist m_η and n_0 such that $\mathbb{P}\left[\mathcal{E}^{(n)}\right] \geq 1-\eta$ for all $n > n_0$. We can prove

$$\mathbb{P}\left[\left\{T_{A,k}^{(n)} - T_k^{(n)} < r\kappa m_\eta\sqrt{n}\right\} \cap \mathcal{E}^{(n)} \cap \mathcal{W}_k^{(n)}|\mathcal{D}_{\epsilon_q}^{(n)}\right] > 1-3\eta$$

for n large enough, which, in combination with the upper bound for case A), proves (a). The previous arguments, by (29), at the same time also provide a better lower bound

$$\mathbb{P}\left[Q_r^{(n)}\left(T_k^{(n)} + Y_k\right) > (1-\epsilon)\lambda b_i^m q\sqrt{n}/r|\mathcal{G}^{(n)}\right] > 1-2\eta,$$

where $\mathcal{G}^{(n)} = \mathcal{D}_q^{(n)} \cap \{X_k^{(n)} = b_i^m\}$ with n large enough. It can be used to prove (b). We skip the lengthy technical details and the proof of (c) here. Putting all together and using the M_1 topology, by the arguments in the proof of Theorem 2.1 in [19], we finish the proof. □

4. CRITICALITY PHENOMENON

The criticality phenomenon was first characterized through analysis by the logarithmic asymptotics derived in Theorem 4 of [28]. It assumes that B follows a power law distribution, which represents typical MapReduce workloads [6, 10, 18]. Essentially, it says that if $R = \sup\{n : \mathbb{P}[R = n] > 0\}$ is smaller than a critical value $\lambda\mathbb{E}[R]\mathbb{E}[C + D]$ then $\log\mathbb{P}[T > x]/\log x \approx -\alpha + 1$; if $R > \lambda\mathbb{E}[R]\mathbb{E}[C + D]$ then $\log\mathbb{P}[T > x]/\log x \approx -\alpha$. It reveals that when the number of ReduceTasks, configured by independent users, reaches a critical value that depends on the statistic characteristics of the jobs running in the system, then the job processing time distribution tail can even change by one order. This can result in much longer job execution times when multiple users configure the number of ReduceTasks for their jobs independently in a shared cluster.

We empirically validate this criticality phenomenon for representative workloads that are similar to Facebook traffic [6]. The details of the testbed are described in Section 5. We can find the best configuration for the number of ReduceTasks that optimizes each job's processing time in a stand-alone environment. However, using these configurations in a shared run-time, we demonstrate that the job execution distribution exhibits much worse performance than using a different configuration, under which every job runs slower in a stand-alone environment. This result provides guidance on configuring the number of ReduceTasks for MapReduce.

To validate the criticality phenomenon, we test a flow consisting of 506 jobs that represent the Facebook traffic as described in [6]. This workload captures two critical features in real traffic [6, 10]. First, the input job sizes exhibit a power law distribution with an exponent equal to 1.6, as measured in [6]. Second, it contains a diverse set of jobs that stress different resource bottlenecks (e.g., CPU, I/O, network) in the cluster. Some jobs such as Wordcount and Termvector consume a large amount of CPU computation while generating little intermediate data. Other jobs such as Sequencecount and Terasort impose heavy pressure on both network and storage systems, straining the copy/shuffle phase.

The job composition of the flow is shown in Table 1. In the table, we sort all the jobs according to their input data sizes and the number of ReduceTasks specified by a given job. All of these jobs are categorized into 9 different groups in increasing order.

Table 1: Composition of 506 jobs that are similar to the Facebook workload [6]

Group	Benchmark	Input Size	Job (#)	ReduceTasks (#)	
				Test-1	Test-2
1	Wordcount	64MB	330	1	1
2	Termvector	128MB	109	4	4
3	Invertedindex	256MB	36	8	18
4	Termvector	512MB	16	12	24
5	Invertedindex	1GB	5	12	32
6	Terasort	2GB	4	16	46
7	Adjancylist	4GB	3	16	46
8	Sequencecount	8GB	2	20	46
9	Sequencecount	16GB	1	20	46

We conduct two sets of tests: all configurations for Test 1 and Test 2 are identical except that the number of ReduceTasks are different, as shown in the column on ReduceTasks for Test 1 and Test 2 in Table 1. In both tests, job submission time points follow the same Poisson process with an average interval of 8 seconds. Test 1 configures each job with a small/medium number of ReduceTasks; none of them takes the full reduce slots. On the contrary, Test 2 sets a large number of ReduceTasks to jobs in Group 6-9. In practice, users optimize their individual jobs in a selfish manner, applying large numbers of ReduceTasks to achieve high parallelism and accelerate job executions. We indeed observe that, with the configuration in Table 1, every job running in a stand-alone environment takes longer time under Test 1 than under Test 2.

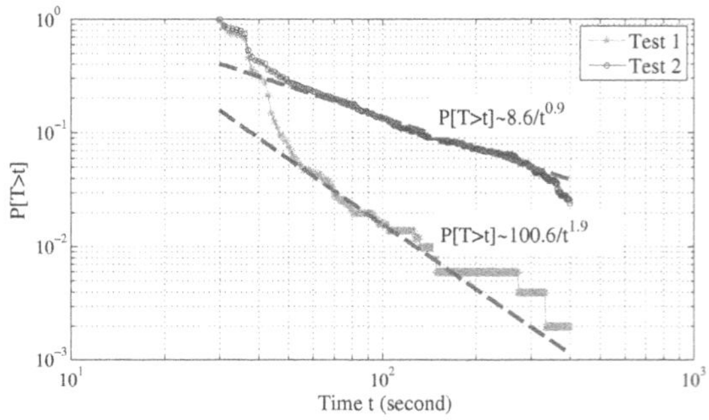

Figure 5: Criticality phenomenon exhibited by workloads similar to Facebook traffic [6]

However, running in a shared environment, as shown in Fig. 5, the job processing time under Test 2 is much worse than under Test 1, in the sense that they even have one order magnitude of difference for the empirical distribution tail (i.e., 1.9 for Test 1 and 0.9 for Test 2). The average execution time for Test 1 is 42.6 seconds, contrasting to the prolonged average execution time 70.66 seconds under Test 2. In Test 1, we do not observe job starvation, which is defined to be the phenomenon that a job cannot successfully take a reduce slot even after its map phase completes [31]. Nevertheless, in Test 2, though each job runs faster in a stand-alone environment, we observe dramatically increased job delays to many small jobs that are submitted after large ones, since these large jobs can monopolize the availalbe slots. The one order difference of the empirical distributions for the job processing times under the two tests sufficiently validates the criticality phenomenon in Theorem 4 of [28]. The criticality phenomenon shows that that selfish optimization for individual jobs can deviate significantly from a global optimum for configuring MapReduce.

5. EXPERIMENTS

This section describes the test bed and the experiment that illustrates the performance in heavy-traffic.

5.1 Environment

Test-bed Setup: All experiments are conducted on a cluster with 24 nodes using Linux 22.6.18-194.17.4.el5 kernel. Each node is equipped with four 2.67GHz hex-core Intel Xeon X5650 CPUs with Hyper-threading capability, 24GB memory, and two 500GB Western Digital SATA hard drivers. All nodes are connected to the same Top-of-Rack 1Gigabit Ethernet switch.

Hadoop Configuration: One master node is dedicated as the NameNode of the Hadoop Distributed File System and JobTracker of the Hadoop MapReduce. Each of the other slave nodes has 4 map slots and 2 reduce slots, totaling 92 map slots and 46 reduce slots in the cluster. We assign 8GB heap memory to the JobTracker and 1GB heap memory to each map and reduce task, respectively. HDFS block size is 128MB. Given that Hadoop contains hundreds of configuration parameters, we follow the default setting for most of them, such as 3 seconds heartbeat interval, 3 data block replicas, 5% slowstart, etc.

Benchmarks: We employ Tarazu benchmark suite designed in [4] to compose the workloads. It is designed to represent typical workload, including Wordcount, Terasort, Termvector, Invertedindex, Sequencecount and Adjancylist. This benchmark is used to empirically validate the criticality phenomenon in Section 4.

5.2 Detailed desciption

ReduceTasks are launched once a small percentage of MapTasks of a job complete so that the copy/shuffle phase of ReduceTasks can overlap with the map phase. Ideally, as soon as the map phase of a job finishes, ReduceTasks should quickly step into the reduce phase to execute reduce functions without further waiting for intermediate data transfer. However, when the system is heavily loaded, we observe that MapTasks and ReduceTasks cannot overlap in time. To demonstrate this issue, we submit 180 Terasort jobs according to a Poisson process with average arrival interval 18 seconds. The stand-alone execution time of each Terasort job is 120 seconds.

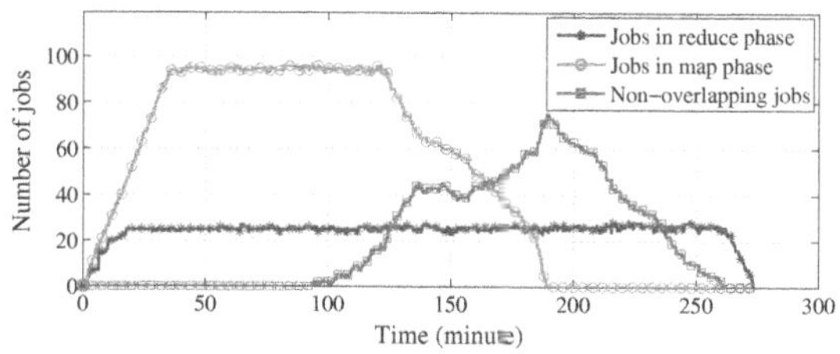

Figure 6: Non-overlap for map and reduce tasks in heavy traffic

In Fig. 6, we profile the number of running jobs that are in the map phase and the reduce phase. In addition, we also monitor the number of non-overlapping jobs, of which all ReduceTasks are launched after all MapTasks of the same job complete. Since a majority of the jobs have not finished their map phases before 100 minutes, these jobs are not non-overlapping jobs. After 100 minutes, we observe a quick increase in the number of non-overlapping jobs in the system. As more and more jobs finish their map phases, a large fraction of them find their copy/shuffle phases severely delayed. The number of non-overlapping jobs reaches 73 (40.5% of total jobs) at around 200 minutes. After 200 minutes, the number of non-overlapping jobs gradually declines due to job departures. This experiment demonstrates that the map phase and the reduce phase of the same job cannot effectively overlap in heavy traffic.

6. CONCLUSION

A MapReduce system serving multiple jobs can be modeled by a processor sharing queue coupled with a multi-server queue. Theoretically understanding its scaling performance can provide guidance in managing the system and configuring job parameters. Through modeling analysis and real experiments, we show that this system, if not carefully dealt with, can cause interesting non-work-conserving effects. First, we derive the diffusion limit when the system is in heavy traffic. We show that, some seemingly innocuous design choices for a tie-breaking rule can result in undesirable performance. Depending on how tasks are scheduled, the diffusion limit can even exhibit spiking behaviors, implying longer job execution times. Second, we empirically validate a criticality phenomenon by real experiments. The results offer insights on configuring MapReduce systems and user job parameters.

References

[1] Capacity scheduler. `http://hadoop.apache.org/mapreduce/docs/r1.2.1/capacity_scheduler.html`.

[2] Fair scheduler. `http://hadoop.apache.org/mapreduce/docs/r1.2.1/fair_scheduler.html`.

[3] Hadoop. http://hadoop.apache.org.

[4] F. Ahmad, S. T. Chakradhar, A. Raghunathan, and T. N. Vijaykumar. Tarazu: optimizing mapreduce on heterogeneous clusters. In *Proceedings of the seventeenth international conference on Architectural Support for Programming Languages and Operating Systems*, ASPLOS '12, pages 61–74, London, England, UK, 2012. ACM.

[5] G. Ananthanarayanan, C. Douglas, R. Ramakrishnan, S. Rao, and I. Stoica. True elasticity in multi-tenant data-intensive compute clusters. In *Proceedings of the*

Third ACM Symposium on Cloud Computing, SoCC '12, pages 24:1–24:7, San Jose, California, 2012. ACM.

[6] G. Ananthanarayanan, A. Ghodsi, A. Wang, D. Borthakur, S. Kandula, S. Shenker, and I. Stoica. PACMan: coordinated memory caching for parallel jobs. In *Proceedings of the 9th USENIX conference on Networked Systems Design and Implementation*, NSDI'12, San Jose, California, 2012. USENIX Association.

[7] G. Ananthanarayanan, S. Kandula, A. Greenberg, I. Stoica, Y. Lu, B. Saha, and E. Harris. Reining in the outliers in map-reduce clusters using Mantri. In *Proceedings of the 9th USENIX Conference on Operating Systems Design and Implementation (OSDI'10)*, pages 1–16, Vancouver, BC, Canada, 2010. USENIX Association.

[8] P. Billingsley. *Convergence of probability measures*. John Wiley & Sons, New York, 1968.

[9] H. Chen and D. D. Yao. *Fundamentals of Queueing Networks*. Springer, 1 edition, 2001.

[10] Y. Chen, A. Ganapathi, R. Griffith, and R. H. Katz. The case for evaluating MapReduce performance using workload suites. In *Proceedings of the 19th IEEE International Symposium on Modeling, Analysis and Simulation of Computer and Telecommunication Systems (MASCOTS)*, Singapore, July 2011.

[11] T. Condie, N. Conway, P. Alvaro, J. M. Hellerstein, K. Elmeleegy, and R. Sears. MapReduce online. In *Proceedings of the 7th USENIX Conference on Networked Systems Design and Implementation*, NSDI'10, San Jose, California, 2010. USENIX Association.

[12] H. C. Gromoll. Diffusion approximation for a processor sharing queue in heavy traffic. *Annals of Applied Probability*, 14:555–611, 2004.

[13] D. L. Iglehart and W. Whitt. Multiple channel queues in heavy traffic. I. *Advances in Applied Probability*, 2(1):pp. 150–177, 1970.

[14] D. L. Iglehart and W. Whitt. Multiple channel queues in heavy traffic. II: Sequences, networks, and batches. *Advances in Applied Probability*, 2(2):pp. 355–369, 1970.

[15] D. L. Iglehart and W. Whitt. The equivalence of functional central limit theorems for counting processes and associated partial sums. *The Annals of Mathematical Statistics*, 42(4):1372–1378, 1971.

[16] M. Isard, M. Budiu, Y. Yu, A. Birrell, and D. Fetterly. Dryad: Distributed data-parallel programs from sequential building blocks. In *Proceedings of the 2Nd ACM SIGOPS/EuroSys European Conference on Computer Systems 2007*, EuroSys '07, pages 59–72, Lisbon, Portugal, 2007. ACM.

[17] M. Isard, V. Prabhakaran, J. Currey, U. Wieder, K. Talwar, and A. Goldberg. Quincy: fair scheduling for distributed computing clusters. In *Proceedings of the ACM SIGOPS 22nd symposium on Operating systems principles*, SOSP '09, pages 261–276, Big Sky, Montana, USA, 2009. ACM.

[18] S. Kavulya, J. Tan, R. Gandhi, and P. Narasimhan. An analysis of traces from a production MapReduce cluster. In *Proceedings of the 2010 10th IEEE/ACM International Conference on Cluster, Cloud and Grid Computing*, CCGRID '10, pages 94–103, Washington, DC, USA, 2010. IEEE Computer Society.

[19] O. Kella and W. Whitt. Diffusion approximations for queues with server vacations. *Advances in Applied Probability*, 22(3):706–729, 1990.

[20] F. P. Kelly. *Reversibility and Stochastic Networks*. John Wiley & Sons, 1979.

[21] A. Lambert, F. Simatos, and B. Zwart. Scaling limits via excursion theory: Interplay between Crump-Mode-Jagers branching processes and processor-sharing queues. *The Annals of Applied Probability*, 23:2161–2603, 2013.

[22] M. Lin, L. Zhang, A. Wierman, and J. Tan. Joint optimization of overlapping phases in MapReduce. *Performance Evaluation*, 70(10):720–735, 2013.

[23] G. Malewicz, M. H. Austern, A. J. Bik, J. C. Dehnert, I. Horn, N. Leiser, and G. Czajkowski. Pregel: A system for large-scale graph processing. In *Proceedings of the 2010 ACM SIGMOD International Conference on Management of Data*, SIGMOD '10, pages 135–146, Indianapolis, Indiana, USA, 2010. ACM.

[24] D. G. Murray, M. Schwarzkopf, C. Smowton, S. Smith, A. Madhavapeddy, and S. Hand. CIEL: A universal execution engine for distributed data-flow computing. In *Proceedings of the 8th USENIX Conference on Networked Systems Design and Implementation*, NSDI'11, Boston, MA, 2011. USENIX Association.

[25] R. Power and J. Li. Piccolo: Building fast, distributed programs with partitioned tables. In *Proceedings of the 9th USENIX Conference on Operating Systems Design and Implementation*, OSDI'10, pages 1–14, Vancouver, BC, Canada, 2010. USENIX Association.

[26] Y. Prokhorov. Convergence of random processes and limit theorems in probability theory. *Theory of Probability & Its Applications*, 1(2):157–214, 1956.

[27] J. Tan, A. Chin, Z. Z. Hu, Y. Hu, S. Meng, X. Meng, and L. Zhang. DynMR: Dynamic MapReduce with ReduceTask interleaving and MapTask backfilling. In *Proceedings of the 9th ACM European Conference on Computer Systems*, EuroSys '14, Amsterdam, The Netherlands, 2014. ACM.

[28] J. Tan, X. Meng, and L. Zhang. Delay tails in MapReduce scheduling. In *Proceedings of the 12th ACM SIGMETRICS/PERFORMANCE joint international conference on Measurement and Modeling of Computer Systems*, SIGMETRICS '12, pages 5–16, London, England, UK, 2012. ACM.

[29] Y. Wang, J. Tan, W. Yu, L. Zhang, and X. Meng. Preemptive ReduceTask scheduling for fair and fast job completion. In *Proceedings of the USENIX International Conference on Autonomic Computing*, 2013.

[30] W. Whitt. *Stochastic-Process Limits: An Introduction to Stochastic-Process Limits and Their Application to Queues*. Springer, February 1, 2002.

[31] M. Zaharia, D. Borthakur, J. S. Sarma, K. Elmeleegy, S. Shenker, and I. Stoica. Job scheduling for multi-user mapreduce clusters. Technical Report UCB/EECS-2009-55, EECS Department, University of California, Berkeley, April 2009.

[32] M. Zaharia, D. Borthakur, J. Sen Sarma, K. Elmeleegy, S. Shenker, and I. Stoica. Delay scheduling: a simple technique for achieving locality and fairness in cluster scheduling. In *Proceedings of the 5th European conference on computer systems*, EuroSys '10, pages 265–278, Paris, France, 2010. ACM.

Conquering Big Data with Spark and BDAS

Prof. Ion Stoica
UC Berkeley, Databricks and Conviva, California, USA

Abstract

Today, big and small organizations alike collect huge amounts of data, and they do so with one goal in mind: extract "value" through sophisticated exploratory analysis, and use it as the basis to make decisions as varied as personalized treatment and ad targeting. Unfortunately, existing data analytics tools are slow in answering queries, as they typically require to sift through huge amounts of data stored on disk, and are even less suitable for complex computations, such as machine learning algorithms. These limitations leave the potential of extracting value of big data unfulfilled.

To address this challenge, we are developing Berkeley Data Analytics Stack (BDAS), an open source data analytics stack that provides interactive response times for complex computations on massive data. To achieve this goal, BDAS supports efficient, large-scale in-memory data processing, and allows users and applications to trade between query accuracy, time, and cost. In this talk, I'll present the architecture, challenges, results, and our experience with developing BDAS, with a focus on Apache Spark, an in-memory cluster computing engine that provides support for a variety of workloads, including batch, streaming, and iterative computations. In a relatively short time, Spark has become the most active big data project in the open source community, and is already being used by over one hundred of companies and research institutions.

Categories and Subject Descriptors: C.2.4 Distributed systems; C.4 Fault tolerance; D.1.3 Parallel Programming

Keywords: big data; cluster computing; distributed algorithms

Short Bio

Ion Stoica is a Professor in the EECS Department at University of California at Berkeley. He received his PhD from Carnegie Mellon University in 2000. He does research on cloud computing and networked computer systems. Past work includes the Dynamic Packet State (DPS), Chord DHT, Internet Indirection Infrastructure (i3), declarative networks, replay-debugging, and multi-layer tracing in distributed systems. His current research focuses on resource management and scheduling for data centers, cluster computing frameworks, and network architectures. He is an ACM Fellow and has received numerous awards, including the SIGCOMM Test of Time Award (2011), and the ACM doctoral dissertation award (2001). In 2006, he co-founded Conviva, a startup to commercialize technologies for large scale video distribution, and in 2013, he co-founded Databricks as startup to commercialize technologies for Big Data processing.

SIGMETRICS'14, June 16–20, 2014, Austin, Texas, USA.
ACM 978-1-4503-2789-3/14/06.
http://dx.doi.org/10.1145/2591971.2611389

Hershel: Single-Packet OS Fingerprinting

Zain Shamsi, Ankur Nandwani, Derek Leonard and Dmitri Loguinov*
Department of Computer Science and Engineering
Texas A&M University, College Station, TX 77843 USA
{zain, abn9457, dleonard, dmitri}@cse.tamu.edu

ABSTRACT

Traditional TCP/IP fingerprinting tools (e.g., nmap) are poorly suited for Internet-wide use due to the large amount of traffic and intrusive nature of the probes. This can be overcome by approaches that rely on a single SYN packet to elicit a vector of features from the remote server; however, these methods face difficult classification problems due to the high volatility of the features and severely limited amounts of information contained therein. Since these techniques have not been studied before, we first pioneer stochastic theory of single-packet OS fingerprinting, build a database of 116 OSes, design a classifier based on our models, evaluate its accuracy in simulations, and then perform OS classification of 37.8M hosts from an Internet-wide scan.

Categories and Subject Descriptors

C.4 [**Performance of Systems**]: Measurement Techniques

General Terms

Design, Measurement, Algorithms, Theory, Security

Keywords

OS Fingerprinting; OS Classification; Internet Measurement

1. INTRODUCTION

With the explosive growth and distributed nature of computer networks, it has become progressively more difficult to manage, secure, and identify Internet devices. One of the approaches that greatly helps in understanding the composition of internal and external networks is *OS fingerprinting*, which is a process that determines the operating system of remote hosts based on peculiarities of their network-level behavior. This differentiation is possible due to certain freedom in selection of default stack parameters, ambiguities in IETF RFCs [7], [32], [33], non-compliant TCP/IP implementations, and lacking standardization for responses to malformed requests.

Over the last 20 years, these observations have led to a variety of methods [2], [3], [4], [6], [8], [16], [22], [25], [41], [42], [43], [45], [46], [50], [52], [53], [54] that perform classification using application-layer traffic, TCP/IP/UDP headers, ICMP packets, or some combination thereof. These algorithms are useful not only in network security (i.e., detection of outdated/unpatched hosts), but also market analysis [28] and Internet characterization [17], [23], [29], [31], [45]. However, their usage, scalability, and accuracy at very large scale (i.e., millions of destinations) have not been explored before. We aim to address this issue below.

1.1 Methodology and Objectives

The Internet has been the target of numerous measurement studies, with the trend recently shifting from covering a small subset of destinations [31], [36] to scanning the entire IP space [11], [17], [23], [37]. This allows researchers to enumerate live hosts, detect vulnerabilities, and shed light on deployment of new protocols. Over the years, network scanning has become progressively faster – from 4 months [37] down to 30 days [17], then one day [23], and now 45 minutes [13]. In conjunction with these studies, low-overhead OS fingerprinting can allow significantly better understanding of the systems researchers interact with and improve our general knowledge about the Internet.

OS fingerprinting consists of two approaches – *passive* and *active*. The former [21], [54] monitors ongoing communication (inbound and/or outbound) with remote hosts, but does not generate traffic of its own. Unless each studied device voluntarily connects to the measurement server, this technique is difficult to use for classifying each IP on the Internet. The latter approach, which is the topic of this paper, actively sends packets to targets and infers their operating system from the collected responses.

One important aspect that differentiates between the active methods is the potential maliciousness of probing traffic, where certain nonsensical combinations of TCP flags (e.g., SYN-FIN-RST-ACK) or intrusive actions (e.g., trying to delete the root directory in HTTP fingerprinting [42]) may harm or crash the target. Additionally, these packets are easily detected and dropped by IDS [44], which leads to complaints against research institutions using these methods and possibly reduced accuracy of the results.

The second aspect is the amount of outbound traffic required by the classifier, which ranges from a single SYN probe [3], [50] to lengthy multi-packet exchanges [25], [29],

*Supported by NSF grants CNS-1017766 and CNS-1319984.

SIGMETRICS'14, June 16–20, 2014, Austin, Texas, USA.
Copyright 2014 ACM 978-1-4503-2789-3/14/06 ...$15.00.
http://dx.doi.org/10.1145/2591971.2591972.

[42], [46], [52]. Ideally, fingerprinting should be performed with no extra overhead to scan traffic, which rules out techniques [29], [52] that expect to reach the target on multiple open ports, using different protocols (e.g., ICMP, TCP, UDP), and elicit responses on closed ports. While LAN environments can tolerate high traffic rates and may allow multi-protocol access to each host, these conditions are generally difficult to satisfy when scanning the entire Internet.

The third aspect is the ability of the underlying estimator to correctly identify the target OS under realistic network conditions and without using retransmission. Since prior single-packet techniques [3], [50] were mainly developed for local use, they are not well provisioned to overcome high amounts of fluctuation and loss in temporal features. They also lack resilience to OS tuning, which can be applied by end-users in hopes of optimizing network performance or obfuscating the default parameters of the stack. Either way, the modified OS features may exhibit little correlation to those originally present at the host, which cripples estimation accuracy of existing tools.

1.2 Contributions

Given the many open issues in wide-scale fingerprinting and lacking performance analysis in the literature, our first goal is to formalize the estimation problem in single-packet OS classification and study the pitfalls of existing techniques. We then develop a low-overhead framework we call *Hershel*[1] for overcoming the various randomization effects (i.e., queuing delays, packet loss, manual tuning) and apply it as proof-of-concept in a measurement study that classifies every visible webserver on the Internet.

2. RELATED WORK

OS fingerprinting has roots in *banner grabbing*, which relies on application-layer protocols (e.g., HTTP, SSH, SMTP, FTP, telnet) to provide a textual description of the OS as part of the communication sequence. While this worked well 20 years ago, banner grabbing today faces many impediments, including high overhead, administrator ban on OS-identifying strings in responses, generic software (e.g., Apache) that can run on multiple platforms without exposing the underlying OS, and purposefully incorrect banners that aim to mislead the various fingerprinting tools.

2.1 Multiple Packets

The second wave of OS classification started in 1997 with the release of nmap [29], which pioneered TCP/IP tricks that would elicit different responses from different implementations. By default, it sends 1032 probes to the target, including a vertical port scan and certain malformed packets that trigger popular IDS such as Snort [39]. Nmap ideally expects the target to accept a TCP connection, send ICMP port unreachable on a closed UDP port, and respond to a ping. Under bandwidth-optimized settings for OS classification, nmap requires no fewer than 38 different types of probes; however, due to mandatory retransmission, this in practice corresponds to well over 100 packets per host.

Due to its popularity, nmap has received a great deal of attention in the literature, which includes usage of neural networks to differentiate between versions of a same OS [41],

[1]William J. Hershel is known for inventing forensic usage of fingerprints in 1858.

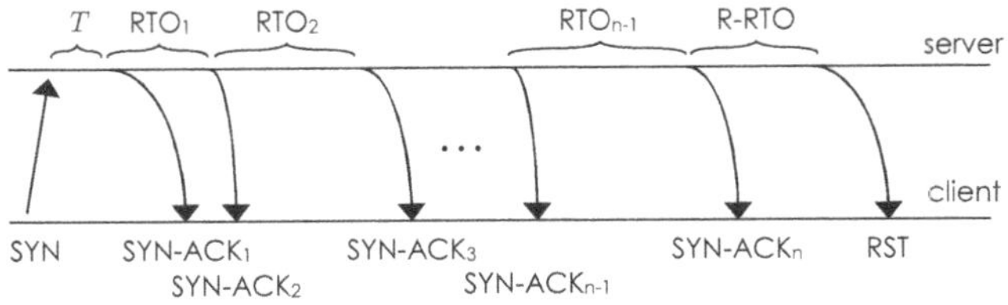

Figure 1: Retransmission timeouts (RTOs) between SYN-ACK packets.

detection of unknown devices [24], and techniques for reducing the number of sent probes [15]. Additional work includes fuzzy matching [52], automatic generation of OS features that aid fingerprinting [8], [38], application of formal testing methods to the detection problem [16], and classification using lengthy observations (up to 100K packets) of Initial Sequence Numbers (ISNs) from the TCP header [25].

2.2 Single Packet

RING [50] and Snacktime [3] are the only tools that perform classification using a single outbound probe. As shown in Figure 1, each measurement consists of a SYN packet, server processing delay T needed to accept the connection, and a stream of n SYN-ACK responses from the target OS, followed by an optional TCP reset (RST) with its own RTO. RING uses the $n-1$ values in the RTO vector and presence of the final RST packet in classification. Snacktime ignores the RST feature, but instead uses the default TCP window size and TTL carried in the SYN-ACKs, which allows it to differentiate between 25 operating systems [3]. We analyze its classification process in more detail later in the paper. A simplified version of Snacktime and extension to 98 signatures was offered in [19], [23]; however, no accuracy analysis, modeling, or verified improvement was provided.

Another tool with a related capability is p0f [54]. In addition to passive fingerprinting, it can actively generate SYN packets and profile remote network stacks based on a set of fixed features from the SYN-ACKs (i.e., window size, TTL, IP flags, and TCP options); however, it does not leverage the RTOs and by default is quite verbose (i.e., sends eight copies of the same SYN per target). The current version can differentiate between 18 operating systems.

2.3 Common Defenses

There exist many approaches to thwart remote OS fingerprinting. The most basic tools tweak Windows registry [10] or implement plugins [4], [5], [40] for the Unix packet-mangling module Netfilter [27]. Their objective is to modify the fixed features of departing packets to no longer resemble those of the underlying host. A similar direction is to deploy network honeypots [35], [49] or standalone systems [51] that spoof arbitrary operating systems and their services. Placing obfuscation into the network gives rise to intermediate devices known as *fingerprint scrubbers* [34], [43].

While these techniques can effectively deal with static header fields, they are not well suited for distorting the temporal features of departing packets, which requires expensive buffering of packets and per-flow state. Additionally, lack of technical support and possibility for various side-effects (e.g., disabling SACK in TCP may lead to significantly lower throughput) raise questions about deployment of these tools in production systems and/or at large-scale.

3. STOCHASTIC MODEL

We assume a single-packet scanner similar to Snacktime in Figure 1. While this approach has minimal intrusiveness, lowest transmission overhead, and non-malicious operation, it also exhibits several fundamental challenges. These arise due to the complex ways in which the RTOs can be modified by packet traversal across wide-area networks, scarcity of information about the target host contained in the samples, and user tuning of features, all of which has a strong influence on one's ability to detect the underlying OS.

It should be noted that straightforward application of machine-learning methods [47] to our problem is difficult. Experimentation with support vector machines, neural networks, and decision trees has led to the realization that they perform poorly when the measured samples contain missing data (i.e., the RTO vector is corrupted by packet loss). Statistical imputation [14] is a common technique for dealing with these problems; however, it requires knowing *which* features are missing and ability to accurately reconstruct the *remaining* (non-missing) features. In our case, lost packets go completely unnoticed and additionally modify the following RTOs to produce feature vectors that have little resemblance to the original (see below).

Our contribution in this section is to formalize single-packet OS fingerprinting, set forth clear goals for the classifier, study the impact of network delay and loss on the measured samples, analyze the existing methods, and outline the assumptions under which the classification problem is tractable.

3.1 Objectives

Assume a database $\mathcal{D} = (1, 2, \ldots, M)$ of $M \geq 1$ known operating systems, where each OS j has some vector-valued fingerprint y_j collected during a-priori measurement of the OS. The fingerprint consists of multiple features, which we partition into those modified only by the network (e.g., RTOs) and those only by the user (e.g., TCP window size). Suppose the former are described by some vector δ_j and the latter by another vector u_j. While the length of δ_j normally depends on j, that of u_j is constant across all operating systems.

As both vectors undergo random modification before being observed by the scanner, the response of OS j to probe traffic is some random variable that is a function of y_j. Given an observation $x = (\delta; u)$ from an Internet host, a typical estimation problem is to find the most likely OS $s(x)$ that could have produced that vector:

$$s(x) := \operatorname*{argmax}_{j \in \mathcal{D}} p(y_j|x) = \operatorname*{argmax}_{j \in \mathcal{D}} \frac{p(x|y_j)p(y_j)}{p(x)} = \operatorname*{argmax}_{j \in \mathcal{D}} p(x|y_j)p(y_j), \quad (1)$$

where notation $p(x|y)$ refers to the probability (or conditional density, if more convenient) of x given y. Observe that the probability $p(x)$ that some OS in $\mathcal{D}$ has produced x is constant for a given observation and can be omitted from the optimization. If the fraction of Internet hosts $p(y_j)$ running OS j is unknown, it is common to set each value to $1/M$, which removes this term from the optimization as well.

The more interesting component of (1) is the probability $p(x|y_j)$ that OS j has produced the observation, or equivalently that y_j has become distorted into x. Before investigating this metric further, observe that network and user modifications to the OS features can be treated as independent, from which it follows that:

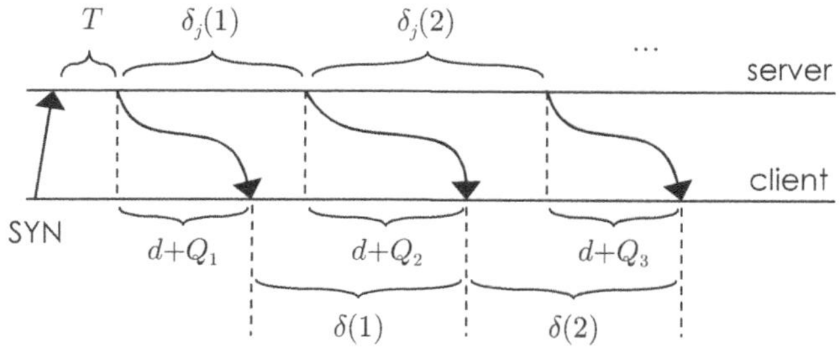

Figure 2: Effect of jitter on observed RTOs.

$$p(x|y_j) = p(\delta|\delta_j)p(u|u_j). \quad (2)$$

This means that the two terms can be dealt with separately, which we do in the rest of the section.

3.2 Network Features: Jitter

For single-packet techniques [3], [50] in Figure 1, the vector of temporal features δ_j consists of individual RTOs generated by network stack j. Classification based on δ_j is possible not only because some devices deviate from TCP algorithms (e.g., exponential timer backoff), but also because RFCs that govern TCP retransmission [7], [32], [33] do not specify the initial RTO or how many SYN-ACKs must be generated. As a result, a wide variety of unique RTO patterns exists.

For the time being, assume loss-free conditions. During the measurement of sample x, suppose d is the sum of propagation and transmission delays along the path from the server back to the scanner. Note that d is a constant due to the fixed size of SYN-ACKs. Now define Q_m to be a random queuing delay of the m-th packet in the return path. As shown in Figure 2, the RTO vector δ_j undergoes distortion that is independent of the forward path, server think time T, and propagation delay d:

$$\delta(m) = \delta_j(m) + Q_{m+1} - Q_m, \quad m = 1, 2, \ldots, |\delta_j| \quad (3)$$

Defining OWD (one-way delay) jitter $J_m = Q_{m+1} - Q_m$ and considering that the gap between subsequent SYN-ACKs is sufficiently large (i.e., at least several seconds), it follows that back-to-back packets arriving from the server are not likely to encounter the same busy period of the queues they traverse. In that case, sequence $Q_1, Q_2, \ldots$ consists of independent and identically distributed (iid) random variables. Furthermore, since the number of hops and congestion of the path is not affected by j, the distribution of each Q_m does not depend on the OS being profiled. This leads to:

$$p(\delta|\delta_j) = \begin{cases} \prod_{m=1}^{|\delta|} f(\delta(m) - \delta_j(m)) & |\delta| = |\delta_j| \\ 0 & \text{otherwise} \end{cases}, \quad (4)$$

where $f(.)$ is the PDF (probability density function) or PMF (probability mass function) of OWD jitter, depending on whether J_m is treated as continuous or discrete. It should also be noted that $Var[J_m] = 2Var[Q_m]$, while $f(.)$ is zero-mean and symmetric. For certain models of OWD, jitter can be obtained in closed-form. For example, exponential Q_m produces the Laplace distribution with the same parameter λ and Gaussian $N(\mu, \sigma^2)$ becomes $N(0, 2\sigma^2)$.

	RTO₁ (sec)	Y_{j1}	RTO₂ (sec)	Y_{j2}	W_j
Observation δ	3.0		24.0		
Fingerprint δ_1	3.0	6	12.0	0	6
Fingerprint δ_2	2.9	1	23.9	1	2

Table 1: Snacktime example.

We next contrast (4) with the RTO classifier in Snacktime [3], which is a tool that is the closest to our objectives and most advanced in single-packet OS fingerprinting. For each RTO, this method first computes the number of matching digits (limited to 6 decimal places of precision) between the sample and all known fingerprints j:

$$Y_{jm} = \max(\lceil -\log_{10}(\max(|\delta(m) - \delta_j(m)|, 10^{-6}))\rceil, 0). \quad (5)$$

It then assigns score W_j to OS j using the sum of these weights across all available RTOs:

$$W_j = \sum_{m=1}^{|\delta|} Y_{jm}. \quad (6)$$

For the example in Table 1, which exemplifies the common pitfalls of Snacktime, (6) scores six for the first OS and two for the second OS, indicating that jitter combination $(0, 12)$ is more likely than $(0.1, 0.1)$. Taking the log of (4), our model can also be reduced to optimizing a summation:

$$\log p(\delta|\delta_j) = \sum_{m=1}^{|\delta|} \log f(\delta(m) - \delta_j(m)); \quad (7)$$

however, it differs from (6) in two important ways. First, the log is applied to the distribution function $f(.)$ rather than the jitter itself. Second, there is no loss of precision due to rounding to the nearest integer or capping the jitter at 10^{-6}. Nevertheless, while (4) is a good starting point, it does not work in real networks due to the lacking robustness against packet loss. This is our next topic.

3.3 Network Features: Loss

The main problem with (4) is that loss-free conditions are impossible to satisfy during Internet scans. Besides congestion, routing loops, and various checksum violations, the RTOs may be altered by the target server crashing or shutting down during the measurement, which affects the tail of the RTO vector and appears similar to packet loss. Since single-packet fingerprinting *by definition* cannot retransmit SYN probes, OS detection must be performed using only the features available in observation x, which calls for more sophistication in the model.

To exacerbate the situation, packet loss creates more dramatic changes to the RTO vector than delay jitter. For example, consider a scenario with $\delta_j = (3, 6, 12)$, where all delays are given in seconds. Even with a relatively large $E[Q_m] = 100$ ms, delay jitter remains small compared to each RTO. On the other hand, the loss of a single packet produces one of four dissimilar combinations – $(3, 6)$, $(3, 18)$, $(6, 12)$, or $(9, 12)$ – while that of two packets leads to six additional options – (3), (6), (9), (12), (18), or (21). The RTO swing in these cases is significantly higher, which makes mapping x to the correct OS more challenging.

We now examine how to model the combined probability that loss and jitter transform δ_j into observation δ. This will allow us to solve such dilemmas as whether $\delta = (3, 18)$ is a more likely match to $(3, 6, 12)$ with one lost packet or to some other signature $(2.6, 17.9)$ without any loss. To deal with these cases, we propose to generalize the concept of RTO. First, let τ_j be a vector of $|\delta_j| + 1$ packet-transmission timestamps from OS j:

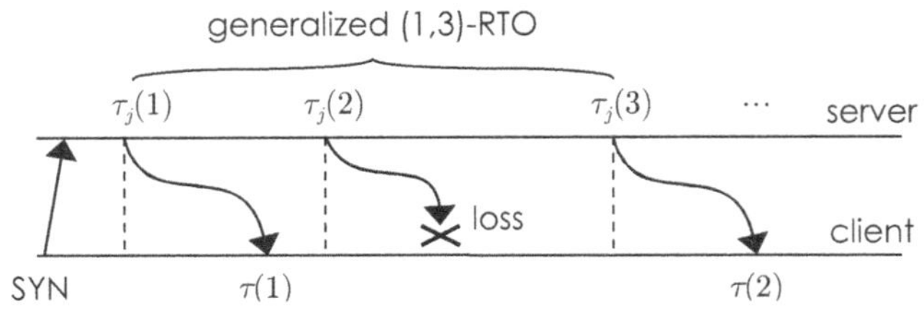

Figure 3: Generalized RTOs under packet loss.

$$\tau_j(m) = \begin{cases} 0 & m = 1 \\ \tau_j(m-1) + \delta_j(m-1) & m \geq 2 \end{cases} \quad (8)$$

and τ be the corresponding random vector observed in x after the packets have traversed the network. Then, a generalized $(m, m+k)$-RTO is the distance $\tau_j(m+k) - \tau_j(m)$, which is illustrated in Figure 3 for $m = 1$ and $k = 2$. Note that $k = 1$ produces the usual RTO and that all timestamps are given using local clocks (i.e., τ_j at the server and τ at the client).

Now suppose set $\Gamma(\tau, \tau_j)$ contains all subsets of size $|\tau|$ of integer sequence $(1, 2, \ldots, |\tau_j|)$. We can view each $\gamma \in \Gamma(\tau, \tau_j)$ as a mapping of received packets in τ to their position in the original vector τ_j, i.e., $\gamma(m) = k$ means that the m-th received SYN-ACK was initially in position k. For the example in Figure 3, we have $\gamma(1) = 1$ and $\gamma(2) = 3$. Assuming no reordering of SYN-ACKs, which is reasonable given at least several seconds between them, each γ is a vector of strictly increasing integers.

Armed with these definitions, we get:

$$p(\tau|\tau_j) = \begin{cases} \sum_{\gamma \in \Gamma(\tau, \tau_j)} p(\gamma) p(\tau|\tau_j, \gamma) & |\tau| \leq |\tau_j| \\ 0 & \text{otherwise} \end{cases}, \quad (9)$$

where the number of summation terms equals the number of ways to select $|\tau|$ objects from $|\tau_j|$ available options and (9) is non-zero only if the number of received packets does not exceed that in the fingerprint. This is in contrast to (4), where the two vectors had to have equal length.

Again leveraging the large spacing between server responses, we can treat congestion events affecting SYN-ACKs as independent, which allows one to approximate packet loss as an iid Bernoulli process with some probability q. Since each loss combination is equally likely, we trivially get:

$$p(\gamma) = q^{|\tau_j| - |\tau|}(1 - q)^{|\tau|}, \quad (10)$$

which can be moved outside the summation in (9). To deal with $p(\tau|\tau_j, \gamma)$, which is the probability to observe τ from OS j under loss pattern γ, notice that the gap between each adjacent pair of received packets is determined by the generalized RTO:

$$\tau(m) - \tau(m-1) = \tau_j(\gamma(m)) - \tau_j(\gamma(m-1)) + J'_m, \quad (11)$$

where $m \geq 2$ and generalized jitter J'_m is given by:

$$J'_m = Q_{\gamma(m)} - Q_{\gamma(m-1)}. \quad (12)$$

Rearranging the terms in (11), define the m-th jitter sample under pattern γ as:

$$R_{jm}^{\gamma} = \tau(m) - \tau(m-1) - \tau_j(\gamma(m)) + \tau_j(\gamma(m-1)). \quad (13)$$

Noticing that J'_m has the same distribution as J_m yields:

$$p(\tau|\tau_j, \gamma) = \prod_{m=2}^{|\tau|} f(R_{jm}^{\gamma}). \quad (14)$$

We thus get for $|\tau| \leq |\tau_j|$:

$$p(\tau|\tau_j) = q^{|\tau_j|-|\tau|}(1-q)^{|\tau|} \sum_{\gamma \in \Gamma(\tau,\tau_j)} \prod_{m=2}^{|\tau|} f(R_{jm}^{\gamma}), \quad (15)$$

which replaces $p(\delta|\delta_j)$ in (2).

We finish this subsection by noting that Snacktime only considers operating systems with the same number of RTOs as the measured sample x, which automatically results in a mismatch for observations that have sustained loss.

3.4 User Features

OS tuning is common practice in the current Internet, with numerous online guides recommending optimizations to network settings [30], [48] and automated software offering tuning capabilities to the TCP/IP stack to achieve better performance [12]. A number of fixed header parameters in general-purpose kernels (e.g., Unix, Windows) can be changed through registry or using command-line tools. Unlike jitter-induced noise, where small distortions are generally more likely that large ones, the main difference with OS tuning is that *there may be no correlation between the manually selected values of the user and those installed in the OS by default.* For example, TCP window size may be more likely to jump from 8192 to 65535 than to 8193.

While accurate modeling of manual modification and human psychology is difficult, it makes sense for the analysis to at least take into account whether a given feature under user control has been changed. Suppose that π_m is the probability of such modification in feature m and assume that user tuning is applied independently to each available parameter. Defining $I_{jm} = \mathbf{1}_{\{u(m)=u_j(m)\}}$ to be an indicator of the event that the m-th measured feature matches the original of OS j, we get:

$$p(u|u_j) = \prod_{m=1}^{|u|} \Big[(1-\pi_m)I_{jm} + \pi_m(1-I_{jm})\Big]. \quad (16)$$

Besides user interference, vector u_j may be modified by intermediate devices along the path (e.g., NAT, IDS, fingerprint scrubbers [10], [34], [40], [43], [51]), whose actions can be clumped under the same umbrella of (16). Since buffering packets for periods of time comparable to RTO (i.e., 3 – 6 seconds) and per-flow state are expensive, it is often safe to assume that these devices do not alter the RTO pattern in significant ways and thus leave enough features by which the OS can still be identified. This underscores the importance of having a robust RTO estimator.

The Snacktime algorithm for scoring user-modified features can be generalized as a sum of weights assigned to each match:

$$W'_j = \sum_{m=1}^{|u|} w_m I_{jm} = \sum_{I_{jm}=1} w_m, \quad (17)$$

which is added to the RTO score W_j in (6) for a final result. One open issue, however, is selection of proper weights, which need to be somehow correlated with feature volatility. Our model is much simpler since π_m directly provides this probability. To better understand the difference between (16) and (17), assume that $\pi_m > 0$ for all m and write:

$$\log p(u|u_j) = \sum_{I_{jm}=1} \log(1-\pi_m) + \sum_{I_{jm}=0} \log \pi_m. \quad (18)$$

For $\pi_m \approx 1$, we get $\log \pi_m \approx 0$, the second term of (18) disappears, and our model reduces to Snacktime with weights $w_m = \log(1-\pi_m)$. However, in more realistic cases of $\pi_m \ll 1$, the second term of (18) becomes non-negligible and serves the role of balancing non-matching features against those that do match. Snacktime has no such mechanism.

3.5 Final Result

We now consolidate the various models into one formula. Combining (15) and (16) in (2) and (1), dropping terms that do not depend on j, and performing straightforward manipulations, we get:

$$s(x) = \underset{j \in \mathcal{D}:|\tau| \leq |\tau_j|}{\operatorname{argmax}} \Big\{ p(y_j) q^{|\tau_j|-|\cdot|} \sum_{\gamma \in \Gamma(\tau,\tau_j)} \prod_{m=2}^{|\tau|} f(R_{jm}^{\gamma}) \times \prod_{I_{jm}=1} (1-\pi_m) \prod_{I_{jm}=0} \pi_m \Big\}. \quad (19)$$

Although (19) maximizes the OS-detection probability under the assumptions stated throughout this section, its performance with a-priori-unknown q π_m, $f(.)$, and $p(y_j)$ is an open question that needs to be examined. We perform this later in the paper. In the meantime, we outline the various remaining issues.

3.6 Limitations

First, the SYN packet may be lost and never reach the target. Since there is no way to verify this, the host will automatically be considered non-responsive and will be excluded from fingerprinting. Not much can be done to overcome this problem unless SYN retransmission is allowed. If we relax the single-packet assumption, the estimator will face the problem of determining which of the SYNs triggered which SYN-ACK response, without which the RTOs cannot be computed correctly. This problem can be solved in the future by encoding the retransmission attempt into the source port of the SYN.

Second, our model allows only the *network* to modify the RTOs; however, this may not hold if users manage to alter SYN-ACK spacing during OS tuning. This is not of wide-spread concern as few optimization guides target the RTO pattern. With enough effort, scrubbers and obfuscation tools can disrupt inter-SYN-ACK delays; however, we do not consider development of end-to-end methods to combat such approaches a fruitful objective. A related problem arises with middleboxes and caches that accept the connection on behalf of the server [18], in which case any fingerprinting tool is bound to classify only the visible side of the TCP stream (i.e., the OS of the middlebox).

Third, Hershel's accuracy may deteriorate if the network jitter process J_m becomes non-iid or deviates from the predicted bounds, e.g., due to significant kernel scheduling la-

Operating system	Win	TTL	DF	Reset				MSS	OPT	SA-RTO	R-RTO
				RST	RA	RN	RW				
Windows 7	8192	128	1	1	0	1	0	1460	MNWST	3, 6	12
Linux 2.6	5792	64	1	0	–	–	–	1460	MSTNW	3.8, 5.9, 12.1, 24, 48.2	–
Linux 2.0	32736	64	0	0	–	–	–	1414	M	3, 6, 12, 24, 48, 96	–
Mac OS 10.3	33304	64	1	1	1	1	32768	1460	MNWNNT	2.92, 6, 12, 24	30
NetBSD 4.0.1	32768	64	1	0	–	–	–	1460	MNWNNTSNN	2.92, 6, 12, 24	–
VxWorks 5.4.2	8192	64	0	1	1	1	8192	512	MNW	5.58, 24	45
Juniper Netscreen	8192	64	0	1	0	0	8192	1380	M	1.67, 2, 2, 2, 2, 2, 2, 2	2

Table 2: Sample signatures (M = MSS, N = NOP, W = window scale, S = SACK, T = timestamp).

Operating system	All enabled	Drop S	Drop T	Drop W	Drop ST	Drop SW	Drop WT	Drop all
Linux 2.6	MSTNW	MNNTNW	MNNSNW	MST	MNW	MNNT	MNNS	M
Windows XP/2003	MNWNNTNNS	MNWNNT	MNWNNS	MNNTNNS	MNW	MNNT	MNNS	MNW
Windows 7/2008	MNWST	–	–	MST	–	–	–	–
FreeBSD 8.2	MNWST	MNWNNT	–	–	–	–	MSE	M
Solaris 10	NNTMNWNNS	NNTMNW	–	–	–	–	–	–

Table 3: Examples of transformations applied by the OS to TCP options (dashes indicate impossible cases).

tency during CPU overload. Similar issues may surface if network loss depends on j, users modify different operating systems with different probability, or there is correlation in loss events within a single stream of SYN-ACKs. Solving these problems requires a per-OS set of parameters $(q_j, f_j(.), \pi_{jm})$ and multi-dimensional covariance matrices for joint distributions of RTOs and individual features modified by tuning, all sampled under realistic load conditions. Needless to say, these are difficult to come by, but we may consider this direction in future work.

4. CLASSIFIER

Our next contribution is to enhance Snacktime's feature vector, describe a working classifier based on the theory developed in the previous section, bring awareness to RTO randomization performed by certain OSes, and explain how to collect signature databases under these conditions.

4.1 Features

Snacktime uses only two non-RTO features – TCP advertised window size and TTL; however, additional parameters are readily available from the SYN-ACKs. Following Table 2, these include the Do Not Fragment (DF) flag in the IP header, four different fields from the RST packet (more on this below), the Maximum Segment Size (MSS) declared by TCP, the order in which the OS assembles the option fields (OPT), SYN-ACK RTOs (SA-RTO), and the RST RTO (R-RTO). Some of these features are self-explanatory, but others require additional elaboration.

First, it should be noted that the initial TTL cannot be reconstructed exactly at the receiver. We use the common technique of rounding this value up to the nearest "likely" boundary, which includes four values used by the OSes in our database $\mathcal{D}$ – 32, 64, 128, and 255. Second, the reset features are quite rich. In Table 2, the binary flag RST is 1 for the fingerprints that contain a reset packet, RA indicates whether the RST has the ACK bit set, RN is 1 if the ACK sequence is non-zero, and RW records the window of the reset packet. RST features represent peculiarities of internal stack operation and cannot be modified via OS tuning. However, fingerprint scrubbers, NAT/IDS, and kernel recompilation can still change them.

Third, as seen in the table, support for TCP options differs between the operating systems since no specific subset is required to be implemented [20]. More importantly, users have the freedom to disable them as needed. As certain options are considered security risks (e.g., timestamps), they may be disabled by default, although users can still re-enable them. Certain devices (e.g., printers) do not allow OPT tweaking at all, while newer versions of popular operating systems tend to support fewer choices. For example, even though Windows 7/2008 provides registry keys to disable TCP timestamps, the modification does not work. Similarly, SACK can be disabled only if the entire TCP stack is offloaded to the NIC [26].

What makes OPT a good feature is not the specific string, but rather *the order in which non-padding options appear.* This is illustrated in Table 3, where we progressively disable various combinations of options and observe the resulting SYN-ACK packets. For example, Windows XP supports four options MWTS. Turning off W produces MTS interspersed by NOPs as padding. Simplicity of implementation and lacking reasons to reorder the options suggests that this phenomenon likely exists in other stacks.

As a result, OPT requires a more advanced classification logic than straight comparison. Specifically, a match is registered if the observed sample x contains a *feasible* string, which we examine by taking an intersection of non-NOP options between x and each fingerprint, followed by verification that the order of the resulting letters is the same. For example, MTW is a match to Linux, VxWorks, and Juniper in Table 2, but not the other OSes.

Fourth, the reset RTO (R-RTO) helps in resolving additional ambiguities, such as between Mac OS 10.3 and NetBSD 4.0.1 in Table 2, which otherwise have identical SA-RTO patterns. Additionally, we expand Snacktime's default measurement time limit from 65 seconds to 120, the latter of which is the MSL (Maximum Segment Lifetime) of TCP [33]. For instance without considering the 96-second RTO of Linux 2.0 in Table 2, it might be hard to differentiate it from Linux 2.6.

Table 4 summarizes the features used in our classification and compares them to those in nmap, p0f, and Xprobe [29], [46], [50], [52], [54]. We have four novel features and one match type (subset) never used in fingerprinting before.

Feature	Description	Appeared In
Win	Receiver window	[3], [29], [46], [52], [54]
TTL	Time-to-live field	[3], [29], [46], [52], [54]
DF	Do Not Fragment	[29] [46] [52], [54]
SA-RTO	RTO sequence	[3], [46], [50]
RST	True if RST packet	[50]
MSS	Max segment size	[29], [46], [54]
OPT	TCP options (exact)	[29], [54]
RA	ACK bit in RST	New
RN	ACK seq $\neq 0$ in RST	New
RW	Window in RST	New
OPT	TCP options (subset)	New
R-RTO	RTO of RST packet	New

Table 4: Enhanced feature vector.

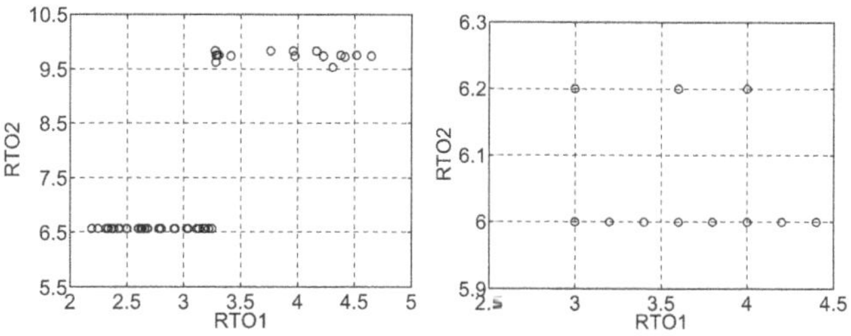

(a) Windows Server 2003 (b) Linux 2.6

Figure 4: RTO randomness in TCP/IP scheduler.

4.2 Stochastic Timers

Table 2 shows SA-RTOs from a single captured sample of the OS; however, it turns out that many kernels naturally exhibit significant RTO variation, sometimes by as much as 50%. Two examples are shown in Figure 4 using a 2D scatter plot of the first two SA-RTOs. For Server 2003 in subfigure (a), there are two distinct patterns – the lower left corner, with RTO_1 distributed in $[2.2, 3.3]$ and RTO_2 frozen at 6.56, and the upper section, with RTO_1 scattered in $[3.3, 4.6]$ and RTO_2 in $[9.5, 9.8]$. Furthermore, the two scenarios are not equally likely as the bottom one occurs 68% of the time. This shows that the temporal model must take into account not just the possible RTO regions, but also their likelihoods.

A similar picture emerges for Linux 2.6 in subfigure (b). The mass of the RTO is now concentrated on 11 distinct points, where RTO_1 ranges from 3 to 4.4 seconds and RTO_2 from 6 to 6.2. Again, the popularity of individual points is non-uniform, swinging from 2% to 16%. Note that both cases in Figure 4 have been collected from idle hosts over a single-hop network consisting of one switch, *which makes this behavior part of the fingerprint itself rather than an artifact of the sampling environment.*

Possible reasons for this fluctuation are the absence of per-connection RTO timers during the SYN-ACK phase and discretization of retransmission delays. What these examples show is that internal OS operation is a complex stochastic system that requires measuring the RTO *distribution* (rather than a single snapshot) during creation of the signature database. This is necessary because such large variations are not taken into account by the jitter model, which normally assumes OWDs on the order of tens or hundreds of milliseconds, with similarly sized jitter.

Our approach is to treat RTOs as random variables, unlike prior work that has always considered them deterministic. Specifically, suppose OS j has w_j unique types of behavior, each occurring with probability β_{jr}, where $r = 1, 2, \ldots, w_j$. We call each of these types a *subOS* and assign it a separate RTO vector τ_{jr}, which updates (14) to:

$$p(\tau|\tau_j, \gamma) = \sum_{r=1}^{w_j} \beta_{jr} p(\tau|\tau_{jr}, \gamma). \qquad (20)$$

A simpler technique is to measure each host w times and let each obtained RTO vector τ_{jr} be a subOS with $\beta_{jr} = 1/w$. In that case, (20) becomes:

$$p(\tau|\tau_j, \gamma) = \frac{1}{w} \sum_{r=1}^{w} \prod_{m=2}^{|\tau|} f(R^{\gamma}_{jrm}), \qquad (21)$$

where R^{γ}_{jrm} is the generalized jitter of the m-th RTO under subOS r of OS j and loss-pattern γ. Note that summations involving $\Gamma(\tau, \tau_j)$ remain the same since all subOSes within a given OS send a fixed number of SYN-ACKs. They also exhibit deterministic user features, which keeps (16) unchanged.

4.3 Fingerprint Database

In order to produce an accurate fingerprint τ_j, the OS must be measured in some isolated testbed with low end-to-end delays and idle conditions at the server. To avoid loss-related bias, each host must be sampled multiple times to determine the longest vector of RTOs it produces, which should then be used to collect w loss-free samples for the database. Following these guidelines, we installed a variety of commodity operating systems in our lab, determined the proper size of their RTO vectors, and collected $w = 50$ clean fingerprints from each. We also captured a number of embedded devices found in our department LAN.

The final step was to perform a scan of the university network for additional signatures not already in the database. Once found, these devices were fingerprinted in a similar fashion, producing w clean samples per OS. When the owner of the device could not be contacted and the server's webpage did not provide enough detail we used nmap to identify the device. While Snacktime ships with 25 signatures and [23] uses 98, our database contains 116 network stacks. We can distinguish not only between different operating systems (e.g., Windows, Linux, FreeBSD), but also sometimes identify their versions and patches (e.g., Windows Server 2003 with and without SP1, MacOS 10.3 vs MacOS 10.4).

4.4 Hershel

Our classification method, which we call *Hershel*, builds upon (19) and (21), where we treat all $w = 50$ subOSes as deterministic. Common sense suggests that users, scrubbers, and network devices are not likely to directly tweak individual RST features RA, RN, and RW; instead, these fields (if modified at all) will be simultaneously replaced with another set that comes from a different OS. We thus combine all four RST values in Table 2 into one atomic feature for classification purposes. This makes vector u_j consist of six fields – Win, TTL, DF, aggregated RST, MSS, and OPT.

RTO vectors τ and τ_j includes timestamps of all SYN-ACKs and the first RST (if present). To account for resets that might be injected by firewalls/IDS after they time out the connection, (9) and (16) require a revision. Specifically, if the measured vector τ contains a reset, but $|\tau_j|$ does not, the RST is removed from τ prior to computing (9). To

OWD	μ	Snacktime		Hershel $\lambda = 2, q = 0.038$						Hershel	Hershel
		RTO	+Win/TTL	RTO	+Win/TTL	+DF	+OPT	+MSS	+RST	$\lambda = 10$	$q = 0.1$
$q_{real} = 0, \pi_{real} = 0$ ($\chi = 100\%$)											
Pareto	0.5	12.6	58.3	22.1	86.2	88.5	96.2	99.72	99.72	94.62	99.69
Exp	0.5	12.8	58.3	21.9	86.9	89.4	96.5	99.92	99.94	96.21	99.82
Uniform	0.5	13.0	58.4	21.7	87.4	89.8	96.8	99.99	99.99	98.50	99.99
Pareto	0.1	16.3	62.9	33.1	94.9	96.7	99.0	99.99	99.99	99.69	99.99
$q_{real} = 3.8\%, \pi_{real} = 0$ ($\chi = 84\%$)											
Pareto	0.5	10.0	49.0	21.4	85.1	87.7	96.1	99.69	99.69	94.68	99.66
Exp	0.5	10.1	49.0	21.5	85.6	88.1	96.3	99.76	99.82	96.21	99.80
Uniform	0.5	10.3	49.0	21.7	86.4	89.0	96.7	99.96	99.96	98.50	99.96
Pareto	0.1	13.1	53.2	31.6	93.6	95.6	98.8	99.96	99.96	99.66	99.97
$q_{real} = 3.8\%, \pi_{real} = 10\%$ ($\chi = 49\%$)											
Pareto	0.5	10.0	44.4	21.4	77.7	78.6	91.4	94.93	95.37	90.13	95.25
Exp	0.5	10.1	44.4	21.5	78.3	79.1	91.6	95.02	95.55	91.78	95.34
Uniform	0.5	10.3	44.4	21.7	78.9	79.7	91.9	95.20	95.63	93.97	95.57
Pareto	0.1	13.1	48.5	31.6	87.3	87.7	95.0	96.54	96.92	96.67	96.87
$q_{real} = 10\%, \pi_{real} = 10\%$ ($\chi = 34\%$)											
Pareto	0.5	6.9	33.4	20.1	76.2	77.1	91.2	94.84	95.22	90.01	95.14
Exp	0.5	7.0	33.4	20.1	76.8	77.7	91.5	94.98	95.43	91.76	95.20
Uniform	0.5	7.2	33.4	20.1	77.4	78.3	91.7	95.13	95.51	93.82	95.46
Pareto	0.1	9.3	36.8	29.4	85.3	85.7	94.5	96.38	96.71	96.46	96.67
$q_{real} = 50\%, \pi_{real} = 50\%$ ($\chi = 0.13\%$)											
Pareto	0.5	0.82	2.49	10.4	28.1	35.6	53.7	56.65	59.95	58.95	60.23
Exp	0.5	0.83	2.49	10.5	28.4	35.9	53.8	56.74	60.12	60.40	60.31
Uniform	0.5	0.84	2.49	10.6	28.6	36.5	54.0	56.89	60.25	60.79	60.46
Pareto	0.1	1.11	2.95	14.4	32.0	40.5	56.8	59.45	62.68	64.84	63.06

Table 5: Classification accuracy (percent) in simulations of 2^{18} samples.

account for the mismatch in the RST feature, (16) gets multiplied by π_4. In the opposite case, i.e., $|\tau_j|$ contains a RST, but $|\tau|$ does not, it is important to avoid mistaking packet loss for changes in the RST feature and improperly penalizing $p(u|u_j)$ with π_4. Next, if both vectors contain a reset packet, (16) gets hit with either π_4 or $1 - \pi_4$ depending on the match in (RA, RN, RW). Finally, if neither vector has a RST, then (16) enjoys multiplication by $1 - \pi_4$.

5. SIMULATIONS

Our contribution in this section is to explain how to select the parameters of the model, and examine Hershel's accuracy in simulations in comparison to Snacktime.

5.1 Parameters

For lack of a better assumption, we suppose that all OSes are equally likely to appear in the trace and set $p(y_j) = 1/M$ to be a uniform PMF. While it is possible to consider multiple iterations and refine this value after each pass, the resulting system sometimes exhibits instability and divergence into inferior states. We thus leave stability analysis for future work and only perform a single iteration in our evaluation below.

We use $\pi_m = 0.01$ for RST and OPT, while keeping $\pi_m = 0.1$ for the other features. The rationale is that RST behavior and option ordering can be changed only through kernel source-code modifications and usage of aggressive intermediate devices, neither of which we believe is that common in today's Internet compared to stack tuning. For queuing delay, we use a simple exponential distribution with CDF $1-e^{-\lambda x}$ whose mean is set to 0.5 seconds (rate $\lambda = 2$). This produces Laplace jitter density:

$$f(z) = \frac{\lambda}{2} e^{-\lambda|z|}. \tag{22}$$

Note that usage of $\lambda = 2$ is fairly pessimistic, with the majority of paths likely exhibiting significantly smaller delays. For example, this model assumes 82% of the paths produce over 100 ms queuing delays, 37% over 500 ms, and 14% over 1 second. For packet loss, we use Google's study [9] to set $q = 3.8\%$, which was their highest rate of SYN-ACK loss.

5.2 Results

Our next goal is to examine Hershel's robustness in the presence of OWD jitter, packet loss, and random feature modification by the user. We also aim to assess the sensitivity of results to our choices of default parameters above. We simulate a FIFO queue between the server and the client with a given delay distribution. Each packet is dropped by the router with some probability q_{real} and each feature is independently modified with another probability π_{real}. Since these are per-packet and per-feature metrics, it also makes sense to examine the fraction $\chi = E[(1-q_{real})^{|\tau_j|}](1-\pi_{real})^6$ of all generated samples that do not have any loss or feature modification, where the expectation is taken over all j.

The distribution of popularity $p_{real}(y_j) \sim j^{-\alpha}$ is set to Zipf with shape parameter $\alpha = 1.2$, which approximates the fact that some OSes are much more popular than others. We do not attempt to make our assignment of index j to each physical OS such that its $p_{real}(y_j)$ closely follows that in the Internet (which is unknown anyway); instead, the simulation simply verifies performance of the proposed estimator when the OS frequency is highly non-uniform. For that purpose, random ordering of OSes in the database is sufficient.

Table 5 shows classification accuracy for several scenarios of interest. We examine three types of OWD with mean μ in the first column – Pareto $1-(1+x/\beta)^{-\alpha}$ with $\alpha = 3$ and $\beta = \mu(\alpha - 1)$, exponential with rate $1/\mu$, and uniform in $[0, 2\mu]$. We use the original Snacktime since the simplified version from [19] performs worse. Using just the RTOs, Snacktime in the table starts at 13%, but then deteriorates below 1%

RTOs	Hosts	Sigs	Group
3	9,639,810	27	all
2	9,070,991	16	windows, embedded
5	7,834,027	23	linux, embedded, other
4	5,066,940	16	unix, embedded
1	2,669,222	1	Dell printer
0	1,992,196	0	–
6	540,042	9	linux, embedded, other
19	202,733	2	embedded
18	162,442	0	–
17	110,335	0	–

Table 6: Top RTO counts (99% of total).

Window	Hosts	Sigs	Group
5,792	10,143,772	4	linux
16,384	7,051,858	6	windows, embedded, other
8,192	4,266,370	17	windows, embedded
65,535	3,551,640	9	windows, other
5,760	2,643,274	0	–
5,840	981,136	3	embedded
16,000	781,225	5	embedded
4,096	775,473	5	embedded
1,024	758,230	4	embedded
2,800	677,211	1	TP-Link router

Table 7: Top window sizes (87% of total).

near the bottom. This amounts to essentially guessing across the 116 available options (i.e., $1/116 = 0.86\%$). Augmented with Win/TTL, Snacktime begins at a more healthy 58%, but then quickly reduces to single digits.

The next six columns show Hershel with its default $\lambda = 2$. Classifying just based on the RTO vector, Hershel doubles Snacktime's accuracy in the first three scenarios (i.e., the first 12 rows of the table), triples it in the next one, and improves by an order of magnitude in the last one. As additional features are added, Hershel becomes even better, with significant gains seen at the Win/TTL and OPT boundaries. This shows that unlike DF, option strings form an orthogonal dimension to Win/TTL. The MSS improves the result further by 3% and the RST packet by an additional 0.5–3%, with the impact mostly limited to high-loss cases.

Staying with $\lambda = 2$, observe that Hershel is quite insensitive to selection of $f(z)$. Specifically, classification accuracy improves *not* when λ equals $1/\mu$ or the PDF of real delay matches (22), but *as μ gets smaller or the tail of the delay gets lighter*. This can be seen by contrasting the two Pareto cases ($\mu = 0.1$ and $\mu = 0.5$) and comparing Pareto, exponential, and uniform cases (all with $\mu = 0.5$). As the difference between the last three scenarios is quite small, we conclude that the distribution of network jitter, as opposed to its mean, generally has a minor effect on accuracy. Therefore, keeping the Laplace model (22) for the experiments in the next section appears reasonable.

To shed additional light on selection of parameters, the next column of the table re-runs Hershel with all available features and $\lambda = 10$. While this slightly improves the $\mu = 0.1$ case, this happens only under 50% packet loss and at the expense of significant reduction in accuracy in other rows, which suggests that $1/\lambda$ should *overestimate*, rather than *underestimate*, the real network delay. To this end, our previous conservative choice $\lambda = 2$ seems quite appropriate. The last column of the table reverts to $\lambda = 2$ and demonstrates that the model is insensitive to selection of q. We thus keep $q = 3.8\%$ for the Internet classification below.

6. EXPERIMENTS

Our contribution in this section is to apply Hershel to a wide-scale Internet scan and provide an assessment of the obtained classification.

6.1 Dataset Properties

We use Internet scan data from [19], which is based on a 2010 survey of webservers in [23]. These IPs were discovered by sending port-80 SYN packets to every address in BGP. The experiment garnered 37.8M samples x that contained at least one SYN-ACK, which we later feed into Hershel.

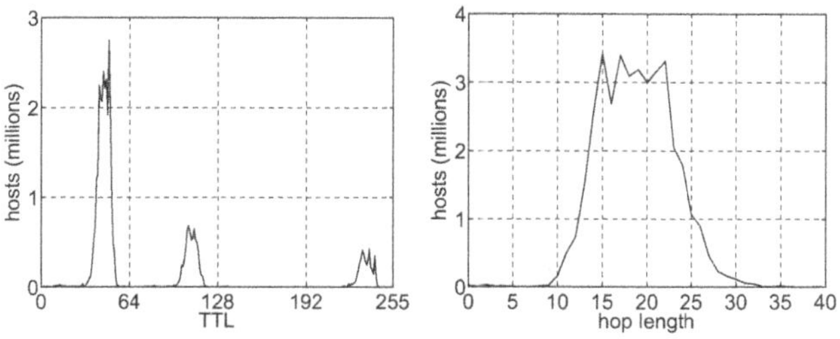

(a) received TTL (b) reverse distance

Figure 5: Received TTL and reverse path length.

We start by examining occurrence of various features in the dataset and their mapping to signatures in $\mathcal{D}$. We qualitatively group them into four types – linux, windows, embedded (routers, modems, cameras, hardware gadgets), and other (BSD, Mac, AIX, NetApp, Big-IP, SunOS).

To first step is to ensure that packet loss has not produced totally unworkable temporal features in the dataset. Table 6 shows the number of available RTOs per destination. It is encouraging to see that the top four spots retain enough information for a meaningful match and the most difficult case (i.e., single SYN-ACK) follows in distant sixth place. We next analyze sanity of the remaining features and build intuition for what to expected from Hershel classification.

The scan contains a staggering 3,815 unique window sizes, while our fingerprint collection $\mathcal{D}$ has only 51. The good news is that the distribution of window size is heavily skewed towards mostly well-known values, as seen in Table 7. The most common window is unique to Linux variants, while the most ambiguous is split across 17 operating systems. Interestingly, window size 5760 in position #5, which we later discovered belongs to Ubuntu, is also not present in other fingerprinting databases (p0f, xprobe). We come back to these hosts later in the section and examine how Hershel classifies them. Ideally, unknown devices should be mapped to the same OS family (i.e., Linux in this case).

The TTL values of received packets are plotted in Figure 5(a), covering 251 unique points out of the 255 possible. A vast majority of the hosts are clustered on the values just before the initial TTL defaults 64, 128, and 255. Figure 5(b) shows the distribution of reverse hop length for each host back to the scanner, calculated by subtracting the received TTL from the nearest well-known initial value. This distribution appears reasonable, with less than 0.4% of the mass below 10 or above 30 hops. This suggests the number of non-standard initial TTLs (if any) is small. Table 8 shows the

TTL	Hosts	Sigs	Group
64	26,275,301	70	linux, embedded, other
128	7,129,667	17	windows, embedded, other
255	4,214,927	22	linux, embedded, other
32	190,697	7	embedded

Table 8: Initial TTL distribution.

Feature	Hosts	Sigs	Group
RA= 1, RN= 1	4,368,098	35	embedded, other
RA= 0, RN= 1	1,167,761	11	windows, embedded
RA= 0, RN= 0	367,915	10	embedded
RA= 1, RN= 0	37,113	0	-

Table 9: Breakdown of 5.9M hosts with RSTs.

distribution seen by Hershel and the corresponding number of signatures in $\mathcal{D}$.

A good number of hosts (69%) set the DF flag, indicating they intend to perform path-MTU discovery, which matches 45% of the signatures. Out of 37.8M responsive targets, 5.9M (16%) send at least one reset packet (in addition to the SYN-ACKs), which is consistent with 56 OSes. The reset window (RW) deviates from that in the SYN-ACK for 20.8% of the IPs and 8 fingerprints in $\mathcal{D}$.

Table 9 examines the interplay between RA and RN in reset packets. In the most common scenario, hosts indicate that the ACK sequence is valid and correctly acknowledge values one larger than transmitted by the scanner in the SYN packet (which encodes the destination IP); however, there are also 37K hosts (last row) with broken implementations that indicate a valid ACK, but set the field to zero. None of our signatures exhibit this behavior.

We have 21 unique combinations of options in $\mathcal{D}$; however, the dataset shows 264 different strings, with the top 10 provided in Table 10. Similar to Table 7, a few popular cases account for the majority of IPs and Linux variants hold a clear lead, but now the most ambiguous combination splits across 41 embedded devices. While Akamai currently reports 137K servers [1], it seems reasonable that multiple NICs and IP aliasing can produce 339K samples in last row.

Practically every host (99.5%) supports the MSS option, with Table 11 showing the top 10 cases out of the 1,021 observed in the dataset. The most common MSS 1460 does not provide much information about the OS, but the other values appear useful at partitioning the dataset into small groups. On the downside, general-purpose OSes often set the MSS as a function of the underlying data-link layer (i.e., MSS = MTU − 40), which creates some interesting dilemmas. For example, MSS 1452 in third place can be classified as one of two embedded devices or as home computers with

Options	Hosts	Sigs	Group
MSTNW	13,156,171	8	linux
MNWNNT	6,214,837	18	embedded, other
MNWNNTNNS	5,579,866	12	windows, other
M	5,431,682	41	embedded
MNW	2,656,342	5	linux, embedded, other
MNWST	1,107,935	2	windows, unix
MNWNNTSEE	762,593	4	other
MNNSWNNNT	412,602	0	-
MST	370,699	1	Windows Vista/7
MNNSNW	339,215	1	Akamai linux

Table 10: Top options strings (95% of total).

MSS	Hosts	Sigs	Group
1460	21,969,799	70	all
512	3,523,272	9	embedded
1452	3,512,626	2	embedded
1380	1,633,852	3	windows, embedded
1440	1,472,969	2	linux, embedded
1400	1,074,502	2	embedded
536	620,013	7	embedded
1448	562,961	0	-
1420	431,720	1	Avocent KVM switch
768	419,326	2	embedded

Table 11: Top MSS values (93% of total).

Feature	Fraction	RST possibilities	Fraction
Win	70.3%	Neither has RST	80.9%
TTL	95.2%	Both have RST, match	10.4%
DF	96.2%	Missing RST	4.2%
MSS	70.6%	Both have RST, non-match	3.5%
OPT	99.4%	Bogus extra RST	1.0%

Table 12: Hershel's feature match rate.

1492-byte MTUs commonly seen over PPP links such as DSL. This emphasizes importance of Hershel's probabilistic matching (16) and explains the significantly smaller number of unique MSS values in $\mathcal{D}$ (i.e., only 20).

6.2 Classification

We run Hershel on the scan dataset and obtain a non-zero classification probability for 37.4M devices. Before showing these results, we perform additional sanity checks by examining how often individual features of each IP matched those in the most-likely OS suggested by Hershel.

Starting with the first two columns of Table 12, observe that window size is quite volatile, with 30% of the decisions going to signatures with a different window. This was expected given the willingness of end-users to experiment with this field and the large amount of unique values seen earlier. Additionally, these 30% cover unknown devices whose RTOs and other features may match some OS in $\mathcal{D}$, but not the window size. Hershel remains robust in these cases and simply identifies the closest signature based on the available information. For example, 98.4% of Ubuntu cases with the unknown window 5760 are classified to Linux 2.4/2.6. These 2.6M hosts account for 1/4 of all window mismatch.

TTL and DF both exhibit match rates over 95%, while MSS comes in much lower at 71%. This is not surprising in light of its dependency on the MTU. The OPT string proves extremely reliable, where 77.4% of the cases match exactly and 22% are feasible subsets/supersets of the original. The five possible cases with RST packets are shown in the other two columns of Table 12. Combining the first two rows, we can conclude that 91% of the hosts have a matching RST feature. The next row with missing RSTs allows us to ballpark network packet loss at q_{real} = 4.2%, not too far from the model's 3.8%. The majority of non-matching combinations (RA, RN, RW), responsible for 3.5% in the table, are caused by RW. Some of this behavior was also expected since user tweaking of window size causes some OSes to alter RW as well. Finally, we see 1.0% of the cases with an extra RST packet, which we suspect are injected by firewalls, NAT boxes, and other devices as indication that they have expired the per-flow state.

OS	Count
Linux 2.6 / 2.4	9,610,732
VxWorks embedded systems	4,179,583
Windows Server 2003 SP1 SP2	2,316,590
VxWorks 5.4.2 / Xerox embedded	1,890,585
Linux 2.6 / Debian / CentOS / SonicWall	1,196,143
Embedded Linux / Mikrotik routers	1,190,102
Windows Server 2008 SP1 SP2 R2 / Vista / 7	1,146,609
TP-Link / Iball / Huawei home routers	1,046,985
Windows Server 2003 / 2000 / XP SP1	1,001,343
Cisco / Scientific Atlanta cable modems	827,285

Table 13: Top individual signatures.

Having verified the general soundness of Hershel's output, we show it in Table 13. Linux attracts the most classification decisions, accounting for nearly a quarter of the webservers. This signature is quite unique, which makes accidental lumping of unknown devices or misclassified hosts into this category highly unlikely. In second and fourth place is VxWorks, which is an embedded OS extensively used in routers, modems, cameras, and printers. Interestingly, Windows 2003 is third, well above Server 2008 in seventh position. More Linux, home routers/modems, and Server 2003/XP make up the remaining OSes.

Table 14 groups fingerprints by type. Linux not just takes the first spot, but it dominates all other types of unix combined by a factor of 6. Embedded systems continue in second place, while windows is firmly in third. Interestingly, these results differ quite a bit from those in prior application of Snacktime to this dataset [23], with the most noticeable difference being 9M hosts moving from windows to embedded. This is not surprising as Snacktime's ability to overcome noise, packet loss, and feature corruption is quite weak. Further, as shown above, Microsoft OSes often share the window size and TTL with embedded devices, making this distinction even more difficult for Snacktime.

To shed additional light on this issue, we carry out comparison between the two methods using manual analysis of 1000 random targets. Table 15 shows the result. The first category in the table breaks down 429 hosts on which both methods produce the same exact OS. Out of these, 424 are correct matches, 3 incorrect, and 2 indeterminate. The last option occurs for devices inadequately represented in the database (i.e., no resemblance to any signature) or when multiple OSes appear to be probable. Among 571 disputed hosts, Hershel delivers 476 correct results and Snacktime 9.

Out of the 918 cases for which we can make a decision, Hershel's accuracy is 98% and Snacktime's is 47%. The 9 cases where Hershel is wrong, but Snacktime is right, are caused by bogus RSTs, which Snacktime ignores, but Hershel takes into account. Overall, we find that when the two methods disagree, Hershel is overwhelmingly more accurate.

7. CONCLUSION

We modeled the problem of single-packet OS fingerprinting and developed novel approaches for tackling delay jitter, packet loss, and user modification to SYN-ACK features. Based on this theory, we developed a classification method that significantly increased the accuracy of existing techniques, both in simulation and the real Internet.

Future work involves multi-pass extraction of the jitter distribution, packet loss probability, and OS popularity from the observed samples, which should improve estimation accuracy even further. We also plan to develop better result-verification techniques for wide-scale use.

Group	Count
Linux	13,882,999
Embedded	13,590,803
Windows	7,561,839
Other	2,396,455

Table 14: Common families of operating systems.

Category	Result	Count	Total
	Both correct	424	
Consensus	Neither correct	3	
	Indeterminate	2	429
	Hershel correct	476	
Disagreement	Snacktime correct	9	
	Neither correct	6	
	Indeterminate	80	571

Table 15: Manual verification.

8. REFERENCES

[1] Akamai. [Online]. Available: http://www.akamai.com/html/about/facts_figures.html.

[2] P. Auffret, "SinFP, Unification of Active and Passive Operating System Fingerprinting," *Journal in Computer Virology*, vol. 6, no. 3, pp. 197–205, Nov. 2010.

[3] T. Beardsley, "Snacktime: A Perl Solution for Remote OS Fingerprinting," Jun. 2003. [Online]. Available: http://www.planb-security.net/wp/snacktime.html.

[4] R. Beck, "Passive-Aggressive Resistance: OS Fingerprint Evasion," *Linux Journal*, vol. 2001, no. 89, Aug. 2001.

[5] D. B. Berrueta, "A Practical Approach for Defeating Nmap OS-Fingerprinting," 2003. [Online]. Available: http://nmap.org/misc/defeat-nmap-osdetect.html.

[6] R. Beverly, "A Robust Classifier for Passive TCP/IP Fingerprinting," in *Proc. PAM*, Apr. 2004, p. 158.

[7] R. Braden, "Requirements for Internet Hosts – Communication Layers," *IETF RFC 1122*, Oct. 1989.

[8] J. Caballero, S. Venkataraman, P. Poosankam, M. G. Kang, D. Song, and A. Blum, "FiG: Automatic Fingerprint Generation," in *Proc. NDSS*, Feb. 2007, pp. 27–42.

[9] H. K. J. Chu, "Tuning TCP Parameters for the 21st Century," Jul. 2009. [Online]. Available: http://www.ietf.org/proceedings/75/slides/tcpm-1.pdf.

[10] A. Crenshaw, "OSfuscate," 2008. [Online]. Available: http://www.irongeek.com/i.php?page=security/code.

[11] D. Dagon, N. Provos, C. P. Lee, and W. Lee, "Corrupted DNS Resolution Paths: The Rise of a Malicious Resolution Authority," in *Proc. NDSS*, Feb. 2008.

[12] T. Dunigan, M. Mathis, and B. Tierney, "A TCP Tuning Daemon," in *Proc. ACM/IEEE Supercomputing*, Nov. 2002, pp. 1–16.

[13] Z. Durumeric, E. Wustrow, and J. Halderman, "ZMap: Fast Internet-wide scanning and its security applications," in *Proc. USENIX Security*, Aug. 2013, pp. 605–620.

[14] P. Garcia-Laencina, J.-L. Sancho-Gomez, and A. Figueiras-Vidal, "Pattern Classification with Missing Data: A Review," *Neural Computing and Applications*, vol. 19, no. 2, pp. 263–282, Mar. 2010.

[15] L. G. Greenwald and T. J. Thomas, "Toward undetected operating system fingerprinting," in *Proc. USENIX WOOT*, Aug. 2007, pp. 1–10.

[16] S. Guoqiang and D. Lee, "Network Protocol System Fingerprinting: A Formal Approach," in *Proc. IEEE INFOCOM*, Apr. 2006, pp. 1–12.

[17] J. Heidemann, Y. Pradkin, R. Govindan, C. Papadopoulos, G. Bartlett, and J. Bannister, "Census and Survey of the Visible Internet," in *Proc. ACM IMC*, Oct. 2008, pp. 169–182.

[18] M. Honda, Y. Nishida, C. Raiciu, A. Greenhalgh, M. Handley, and H. Tokuda, "Is It Still Possible to Extend TCP?" in *Proc. ACM IMC*, Nov. 2011, pp. 181–194.

[19] IRL Fingerprinting Dataset. [Online]. Available: http://irl.cs.tamu.edu/projects/sampling/.

[20] V. Jacobson, R. Braden, and D. Borman, "TCP Extensions for High Performance," *IETF RFC 1323*, May 1992.

[21] T. Kohno, A. Broido, and K. C. Claffy, "Remote physical device fingerprinting," *IEEE Transactions on Dependable and Secure Computing*, vol. 2, no. 2, pp. 93–108, May 2005.

[22] E. Kollmann, "Chatter on the Wire: A Look at DHCP Traffic." [Online]. Available: http://myweb.cableone.net/xnih/download/chatter-dhcp.pdf.

[23] D. Leonard and D. Loguinov, "Demystifying Service Discovery: Implementing an Internet-Wide Scanner," in *Proc. ACM IMC*, Nov. 2010, pp. 109–122.

[24] J. Medeiros, A. Brito, and P. Pires, "A Data Mining Based Analysis of Nmap Operating System Fingerprint Database," in *Proc. IEEE CISIS*, Sep. 2009, pp. 1–8.

[25] J. Medeiros, A. Brito, and P. Pires, "An Effective TCP/IP Fingerprinting Technique Based on Strange Attractors Classification," in *Proc. DPM/SETOP*, Sep. 2009, pp. 208–221.

[26] Microsoft Support. [Online]. Available: http://support.microsoft.com/kb/2525390.

[27] D. Napier, "IPTables/NetFilter – Linux's Next Generation Stateful Packet Filter," *SysAdmin Magazine*, vol. 10, pp. 8–16, Nov. 2001.

[28] Netcraft Web Server Survey. [Online]. Available: http://news.netcraft.com/.

[29] Nmap. [Online]. Available: http://nmap.org/.

[30] Oracle, "Operating System Tuning." [Online]. Available: http://docs.oracle.com/cd/E12839_01/web.1111/e13814/os_tuning.htm.

[31] J. Padhye and S. Floyd, "On Inferring TCP Behavior," in *Proc. ACM SIGCOMM*, Aug. 2001, pp. 287–298.

[32] V. Paxson, M. Allman, J. Chu, and M. Sargent, "Computing TCP's Retransmission Timer," *IETF RFC 6298*, Jun. 2011.

[33] J. Postel, "Transmission Control Protocol," *IETF RFC 793*, Sep. 1981.

[34] G. Prigent, F. Vichot, and F. Harrouet, "IpMorph: fingerprinting spoofing unification," *Journal in Computer Virology*, vol. 6, no. 4, pp. 329–342, Nov. 2010.

[35] N. Provos, "A Virtual Honeypot Framework," in *Proc. USENIX Security*, Aug. 2004, pp. 1–14.

[36] N. Provos and P. Honeyman, "ScanSSH - Scanning the Internet for SSH Servers," in *Proc. USENIX LISA*, Dec. 2001, pp. 25–30.

[37] Y. Pryadkin, R. Lindell, J. Bannister, and R. Govindan, "An Empirical Evaluation of IP Address Space Occupancy," USC/ISI, Tech. Rep. ISI-TR-2004-598, Nov. 2004.

[38] D. Richardson, S. Gribble, and T. Kohno, "The Limits of Automatic OS Fingerprint Generation," in *Proc. ACM AISec*, Oct 2010, pp. 24–34.

[39] M. Roesch, "Snort – Lightweight Intrusion Detection for Networks," in *Proc. USENIX LISA*, Nov. 1999, pp. 229–238.

[40] G. Roualland and J.-M. Saffroy, "IP Personality." [Online]. Available: http://ippersonality.sourceforge.net/.

[41] C. Sarraute and J. Burroni, "Using Neural Networks to Improve Classical Operating System Fingerprinting Techniques," *Electronic Journal of SADIO*, vol. 8, no. 1, Mar. 2008.

[42] S. Shah, "An Introduction to HTTP Fingerprinting," May 2004. [Online]. Available: http://net-square.com/httprint_paper.html.

[43] M. Smart, G. R. Malan, and F. Jahanian, "Defeating TCP/IP Stack Fingerprinting," in *Proc. USENIX Security*, Jun. 2000, pp. 229–240.

[44] Snort IDS. [Online]. Available: http://www.snort.org.

[45] G. Taleck, "Ambiguity Resolution via Passive OS Fingerprinting," in *Proc. RAID*, Sep. 2003, pp. 192–206.

[46] G. Taleck, "SYNSCAN: Towards Complete TCP/IP Fingerprinting," *CanSecWest*, Apr. 2004.

[47] S. Theodoridis and K. Koutroumbas, *Pattern Recognition*, 4th ed. Academic Press, 2009.

[48] B. Tierney, "TCP Tuning Guide for Distributed Applications on Wide Area Networks," *USENIX & SAGE Login*, vol. 26, no. 1, pp. 33–39, Feb. 2001.

[49] C. Valli, "Honeyd – A OS Fingerprinting Artifice," in *Proc. Australian Computer, Network and Information Forensics Conference*, Nov. 2003.

[50] F. Veysset, O. Courtay, O. Heen, and I. R. Team, "New Tool and Technique for Remote Operating System Fingerprinting," Apr. 2002. [Online]. Available: http://www.ouah.org/ring-full-paper.pdf.

[51] K. Wang, "Frustrating OS Fingerprinting with Morph," 2004. [Online]. Available: http://hackerpoetry.com/images/defcon-12/dc-12-presentations/Wang/dc-12-wang.pdf.

[52] F. V. Yarochkin, O. Arkin, M. Kydyraliev, S.-Y. Dai, Y. Huang, and S.-Y. Kuo, "Xprobe2++: Low Volume Remote Network Information Gathering Tool," in *Proc. IEEE/IFIP DSN*, Jun. 2009, pp. 205–210.

[53] M. Zalewski, "Strange Attractors and TCP/IP Sequence Number Analysis," Apr. 2001. [Online]. Available: http://lcamtuf.coredump.cx/newtcp/.

[54] M. Zalewski, "p0f v3: Passive Fingerprinter," 2012. [Online]. Available: http://lcamtuf.coredump.cx/p0f3.

Noise Can Help: Accurate and Efficient Per-flow Latency Measurement without Packet Probing and Time Stamping

Muhammad Shahzad and Alex X. Liu
Department of Computer Science and Engineering
Michigan State University
East Lansing, Michigan, USA
{shahzadm, alexliu}@cse.msu.edu

ABSTRACT

With the growth in number and significance of the emerging applications that require extremely low latencies, network operators are facing increasing need to perform latency measurement on per-flow basis for network monitoring and troubleshooting. In this paper, we propose COLATE, the first per-flow latency measurement scheme that requires no probe packets and time stamping. Given a set of observation points, COLATE records packet timing information at each point so that later for any two points, it can accurately estimate the average and standard deviation of the latencies experienced by the packets of any flow in passing the two points. The key idea is that when recording packet timing information, COLATE purposely allows noise to be introduced for minimizing storage space, and when querying the latency of a target flow, COLATE uses statistical techniques to denoise and obtain an accurate latency estimate. COLATE is designed to be efficiently implementable on network middleboxes. In terms of processing overhead, COLATE performs only one hash and one memory update per packet. In terms of storage space, COLATE uses less than 0.1 bit per packet, which means that, on a backbone link with about half a million packets per second, using a 256GB drive, COLATE can accumulate time stamps of packets traversing the link for over 1.5 years. We evaluated COLATE using three real traffic traces that include a backbone traffic trace, an enterprise network traffic trace, and a data center traffic trace. Results show that COLATE always achieves the required reliability for any given confidence interval.

Categories and Subject Descriptors

C.2.3 [**Computer-Communication Networks**]: Network Operations – *Network management*; C.4 [**Performance of Systems**]: Measurement Techniques

Keywords

Latency Measurement; Passive Measurement; Flows

SIGMETRICS'14, June 16–20, 2014, Austin, TX, USA.

http://dx.doi.org/10.1145/2591971.2591988.

1. INTRODUCTION

1.1 Motivation

Although traditionally throughput has been the primary focus of network engineers, nowadays latency has seen growing importance because a wide variety of emerging applications and architectures require extremely low (in microseconds) and stable (low jitter) latencies. First, many emerging applications, such as financial trading applications [28], storage applications utilizing Fiber Channel over Ethernet [5], and high performance computing applications in data center networks [13], demand low latency. A small increase in latency may cause violations of service level agreements and result in significant revenue losses. For example, a one-millisecond advantage in financial trading applications can be worth $100 million a year for major brokerage firms [28]. Second, many emerging architectures, such as content delivery networks (CDNs) and mission-critical data center networks, demand low latency. CDN providers are mostly evaluated and ranked by content publishers based on latency. Companies such as Cedexis [3] and Turbobytes [10] constantly evaluate and rank CDN providers mostly based on latency. A one-millisecond disadvantage could put one CDN provider behind others and result in loss of business with content publishers. Similarly, the transit providers are primarily evaluated and ranked by CDN providers based on latency. For data centers running mission-critical applications, latency guarantee is a key requirement for the underlying networks. Low latency data center networks have become the primary focus of many data center network solution providers such as Sidera [7].

In managing networks with stringent latency demands, operators often need to measure the latency between two observation points for a particular flow. An *observation point* is either a port in a middlebox (such as a router or a switch) or a network card in an end host. Per-flow latency measurement can be used reactively by network operators to perform tasks such as detecting and localizing delay spikes in a network, isolating offending flows that are responsible for causing delay bursts, and rerouting them through other paths. It can also be used proactively by network operators to continuously monitor latencies between observation points for locating bottleneck links and replace them with higher capacity links.

Existing routers and switches provide little help for latency measurement and monitoring. SNMP counters measure the number of packets passing through a port. NetFlow measures basic statistics, such as the numbers of packets and bytes, of a flow. Both provide no measurement on latency. Network operators often rely on injecting probe packets to measure end-to-end delays and then use tomographic techniques to infer link and hop properties [16, 17]. However, to achieve latency measurement with extremely high accuracy, the required number of probe packets will be extremely large; consequently, the probe packets will consume too much bandwidth and the measured latency does not reflect the real latency without probe packets. Although some specialized latency monitoring devices are commercially available, they are too costly to be widely deployed. For example, London, Singapore, and Tokyo stock exchanges use latency monitoring devices manufactured by Corvil [8, 9, 11] costing around USD 180,000 for a 2×10Gbps box [4].

1.2 Problem Statement

This paper addresses the fundamental problem of *per-flow latency measurement*: for any flow that passed through any two observation points, measure (or say estimate) the average and standard deviation of the latencies experienced by the packets of that flow in passing through the two observation points. Formally, *given a confidence interval* $\beta \in (0, 1]$ *and a required reliability* $\alpha \in [0, 1)$, *for any flow* f *that passed through any two observation points* S *and* R, *obtain estimates* $\tilde{\mu}_f$ *of the average* μ_f *and* $\tilde{\sigma}_f$ *of the standard deviation* σ_f *of the latencies experienced by the packets of* f *in passing through* S *and* R *so that* $P\{|\tilde{\mu}_f - \mu_f| \leq \beta\mu_f\} \geq \alpha$ *and* $P\{|\tilde{\sigma}_f - \sigma_f| \leq \beta\sigma_f\} \geq \alpha$.

An accurate per-flow latency measurement scheme should further satisfy the following two requirements. (1) *No packet probing*: As probe packets may use up a significant portion of network bandwidth, the latency measured with the insertion of probe packets may significantly deviate from the real latency. Thus, the estimates obtained with probe packets may not suffice for microsecond level accuracy. (2) *No time stamping*: First, IP headers do not have a time stamp field and the TCP time stamp option is meant for measuring end-to-end latencies. Embedding time stamps at observation points requires modifications to packet header formats, which further requires modifications to the data forwarding paths of existing routers and middleboxes. Furthermore, the added packet header fields may consume a significant portion of network bandwidth. Second, the process of attaching time stamps to each packet takes a non-negligible amount of time at observation points. Thus, the latency measured with time stamping may significantly deviate from the real latency.

1.3 Limitations of Prior Art

To the best of our knowledge, there are only two per-flow latency measurement schemes, namely RLI [23] and MAPLE [24]. However, neither of them satisfies both requirements because RLI uses packet probing and MAPLE attaches time stamps to every packet. Other than RLI and MAPLE, the closest work is LDA [21], which performs *aggregate latency measurement, i.e., given any two observation points, measure (or say estimate) the average and standard deviation of the latencies experienced by all the packets that passed through the two observation points, regardless of the flow that each packet belongs to.* Aggregate latency measurement is useful; however, it does not provide fine grained per-flow latency information. Here is an important fact: for all flows that passed through two arbitrary observation points S and R, the latencies experienced by the packets of different flows in passing through S and R can be quite different. First, there may be multiple paths from S to R and different flows may be routed via different paths. Second, at each intermediate middlebox along a path from S to R, packets of different flows may take different amount of processing time due to mechanisms such as QoS. As aggregate latency measurement does not reflect the latency of every flow, it falls short in engineering latency sensitive networks. On one hand, when the aggregate latency between two observation points appears normal, the latency experienced by an individual flow may be wildly abnormal. On the other hand, when the aggregate latency between two observation points appears abnormal, aggregate latency measurement does not provide operators the per-flow latency information needed to identify the flows being hurt.

1.4 Proposed Approach

In this paper, we propose COLATE, a Counter based Per-flow Latency Estimation scheme. The key idea of COLATE is that it records timing information of packets at each observation point and purposely allows noise to be introduced in the recorded timing information for minimizing storage space. When querying the latency of a target flow, COLATE statistically denoises the recorded information to obtain an accurate latency estimate. COLATE has two phases: recording phase and querying phase. Next, we give an overview of these two phases.

Recording Phase: In this phase, at each observation point, COLATE records the timing information of each packet arriving at or departing from that point using a vector of counters in RAM, which we call *counter vector*. For each flow with a unique ID, COLATE maps it to a unique subset of these counters, which we call *counter subvector*. The ID of a flow can be any flow identifier such as the standard five tuple (*i.e.*, source IP, destination IP, source port, destination port, and protocol type). To make the mapping unique and memoryless (*i.e.*, using no memory to keep track of the mapping), COLATE maps each flow to a random subvector such that the probability of two different flows being mapped to the same subvector is practically zero. A counter may belong to multiple counter subvectors. Figure 1 shows an example counter vector and its three counter subvectors, from which we see that counters 5 and 8 belong to multiple counter subvectors. For each arriving or departing packet at the observation point, COLATE executes two simple steps: (1) randomly maps the packet to a counter in the counter subvector of the flow that the packet belongs to; (2) adds the current time to that counter. Before any counter overflows, COLATE dumps the counter vector to a permanent storage (such as a solid state drive (SSD)) and resets counters to zero. We call a dumped counter vector a *counter epoch*, which has two attributes: the time stamp of the first recorded packet and the time stamp of the last recorded packet. The recording module can be implemented in hardware to keep up with wire speed. For the hashing function, we can use hardware hash implementations such as those proposed in [20, 31]. For each counter, we can store its less significant bits as a counter in SRAM and the more significant bits as a counter in DRAM – when the counter in SRAM overflows, we increment the corresponding counter in DRAM.

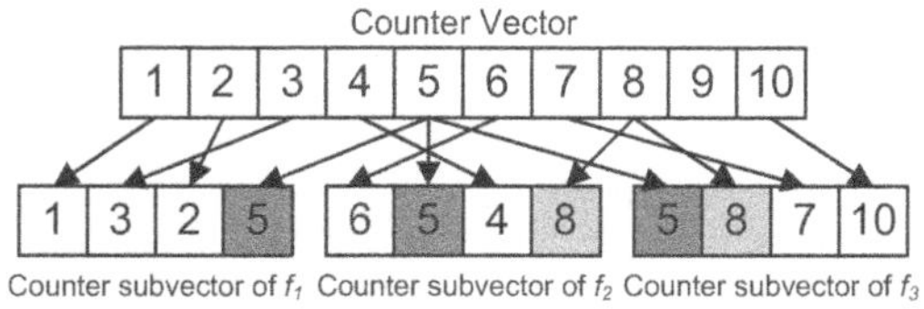

Figure 1: Counter vector and counter subvectors

Querying Phase: In this phase, given a latency measurement query of a flow f, which contains the flow ID, the starting and ending time of the flow, and two observation points that the flow passed through within the time frame, COLATE first finds all the counter epochs whose time frame overlaps with the starting and ending time of the flow f at each of the two given observation points. Second, for each counter epoch, COLATE applies statistical techniques to estimate the sum of time stamps contributed only by flow f from each counter in the counter subvector of f. COLATE uses these extracted values to estimate the average and standard deviation of the latencies experienced by the packets of flow f in passing through the two observation points. COLATE requires the clocks of different observation points to be accurately synchronized; otherwise, the measured latencies will contain a constant offset. This synchronization can be simply achieved by the standard time synchronization protocol IEEE 1588, which provides microsecond level time synchronization [6].

Key Intuition: The intuition behind mapping a flow to multiple counters (in a counter subvector), instead of a single counter, is to mitigate counter overflow for elephant flows. The motivation behind sharing counters among multiple flows, instead of allocating unique counters for each individual flow, is to save memory. Due to the sharing of counters among multiple flows, the counter subvector of a flow f contains not only the timing information of the packets in f but also that of the packets in other flows. The intuition behind allowing this "mixing" is that later in the querying phase, we can extract the timing information of only the packets in the flow f using statistical techniques by treating the mixed-in timing information of the packets from other flows as noise.

Deployability: COLATE is designed to be efficiently implementable on network middleboxes (such as routers and switches) from both processing overhead and storage space perspectives. In terms of processing overhead, COLATE performs only one hash and one memory update per packet. On traditional memory architecture, one memory update requires two memory accesses (*i.e.*, one read and one write); however, in modern memory architecture used in high speed routers (such as the smart memory architecture developed by Huawei [27] and the bandwidth engine developed by MoSys [29]), where each memory location has built-in circuitry for handling updates on site, one memory update (such as incrementing by up to a 64-bit number) requires only one memory access. In terms of storage space, COLATE uses less than 0.1 bit per packet. To get an idea of the length of time for which COLATE can accumulate time stamps using commodity permanent storage devices, consider the 10GigE backbone link in San Jose monitored by CAIDA. At the time of writing this paper, an interactive tool at CAIDA's website reported that on average approximately 0.484 million packets traversed this link per second between Nov. 01 and Nov. 29, 2013 [1]. With 0.1 bits per packet, on a commodity 256GB SSD, COLATE can accumulate time stamps of packets traversing this link for about 1.5 years, which means that a network operator can measure average and standard deviation of up to 1.5 years old flows. This gives not only enough time to identify and debug any problems, but also enough information to study other aspects related to packet delays such as diurnal patterns in flow latencies. On a 12TB SSD, as recently showcased by OCZ at CES-2012 [12], COLATE can accumulate time stamps of packets traversing this link for more than 69 years.

Packet Losses: COLATE, as described above, assumes no packet losses. However, to handle packet losses in COLATE, we can easily adapt the strategy proposed in [21] for handling packet losses in the aggregate latency measurement scheme LDA. According to this strategy, instead of maintaining a single counter vector, COLATE can maintain a set of counter vectors at each observation point, where each counter vector has a sampling probability and a packet counter associated with it. The sum of the sampling probabilities of all counter vectors is 1. The sampling probability of a counter vector is the fraction of packets whose time stamps COLATE will add to this counter vector. The packet counter of a counter vector keeps track of the number of packets whose time stamps have been added to this counter vector. In the recording phase, when a packet arrives at or departs from an observation point, COLATE first uses a hash function to map the packet to a counter vector such that in the long run, the fraction of packets that it maps to any counter vector is equal to its sampling probability. Then, COLATE adds the time stamp of the packet to this vector as described earlier. Note that all observation points use the same hash function to guarantee that the same packet is mapped to the same counter vector at all observation points. In the querying phase, for a target flow between two observation points, COLATE compares the packet counter of each counter vector at one observation point with that of the corresponding counter vector at the other observation point. Then, COLATE selects those two counter vectors at the two observation points that have the highest sampling probability associated with them and equal values of packet counters. After this, COLATE follows the procedure of the querying phase described earlier. For simplicity, in the rest of this paper in describing COLATE, we assume no packet losses.

1.5 Technical Challenges and Solutions

The first challenge is to denoise the recorded information to extract the sum of the time stamps of the packets in the target flow from the counter subvector of the flow. To address this challenge, we first show that for each counter in the counter subvector of the target flow, the value contributed by the time stamps from the packets in the target flow and that from the packets in other flows can both be modeled with binomial distributions. We then derive an expression to calculate the expected value of each counter in the counter subvector of the target flow. From this expression, we estimate the sum of the time stamps of all the packets of the target flow. Using this estimate in conjunction with maximum likelihood estimation, we extract the sum of the time stamps of the packets in the target flow from each counter in the counter subvector.

The second challenge is to calculate the sum of the squares of the latencies of each packet in a target flow, which is needed for calculating the standard deviation of packet latencies. To address this challenge, we first use the time stamp sum extracted from counter subvectors to construct a virtual deviation vector and then use this vector to estimate this sum of the squares of the latencies.

1.6 Advantages of COLATE over Prior Art

COLATE brings forward the state-of-the-art in per-flow latency measurement on the following fronts: reliability, passiveness, scalability, memory, efficiency, and flexibility. For reliability, COLATE takes the required reliability and confidence interval specified by network operators as input whereas existing schemes do not. For passiveness, COLATE neither sends probe packets nor attaches time stamps to packets. For scalability, COLATE maintains only one counter vector at each observation point regardless of how many other observation points are sending and receiving packets from it; in contrast, LDA and RLI have to maintain separate vectors of counters for each pair of sender and receiver. For memory, COLATE uses less than 0.1 bit of storage space per packet, which is over 128 *times* improvement compared to 12.8 bits of storage space per packet used by MAPLE. Due to this, on a commodity 256GB SSD, where COLATE can accumulate time stamps of packets traversing the San Jose backbone link for about one and a half year, MAPLE can accumulate the time stamps for only 4.1 days. For efficiency, COLATE performs only 1 hash and 1 memory update per packet whereas MAPLE uses 9 hashes and 12 memory accesses per packet. For flexibility, COLATE allows different observation points to allocate different amount of RAM based on their available resources whereas LDA requires both the sender and receiver to allocate the same amount of RAM.

2. RELATED WORK

To the best of our knowledge, there are only two per-flow latency measurement schemes, namely MAPLE [24] and RLI [23]. In MAPLE, for any packet passing through two observation points S and R, S attaches a time stamp to the packet and R calculates the latency of the packet from S to R by subtracting the time stamp from its current time. To reduce space for storing latency values of all packets, MAPLE maps the calculated latency of each packet to the closest value in a set of predetermined latency values. Thus, instead of storing the latency of every packet, MAPLE only stores these predetermined latency values and for each predetermined latency value MAPLE uses a Bloom filter to store all packets mapped to it. To query the latency of a given packet, MAPLE first finds the predetermined latency value that the packet was mapped to by querying Bloom filters and uses that value as the estimated latency of the packet. Compared with COLATE, MAPLE falls short from a few perspectives. First, MAPLE is based on a strong assumption that packet latencies between two observation points are tightly clustered around a set of predetermined latency values. We have not found any theoretical or empirical validation of this assumption in prior literature. Second, MAPLE requires attaching time stamps to packets and thus has the limitations we pointed out in Section 1.2 for time stamping based latency measurement schemes. Furthermore, time stamping individual packets can consume up to 10% of the available bandwidth [21]. Third, MAPLE has large memory overhead (12.8 bits/packet at each observation point) and large processing overhead (9 hash computations and 12 memory accesses per packet: 9 for hash functions, 2 for updating counters, and 1 for determining the cluster a packet's latency belongs to), whereas COLATE uses 0.1 bits/packet and performs 1 hash and 1 memory update per packet.

In RLI, for a flow passing through two observation points S and R, S inserts probe packets with time stamps into the flow and R calculates the latency of each probe packet similarly to MAPLE. To calculate the latency of the regular packets between two probe packets whose latency has been calculated as l_1 and l_2, R simply uses the straight line equation to calculate the latency of these regular packets based on their arrival time and the latency of the two probe packets. Compared with COLATE, RLI has the following limitations. First, RLI is based on the strong assumption that packet latency between S and R increases or decreases linearly in the time interval between receiving any two probe packets at R. When the time interval between two probe packets is extremely small, this assumption may practically hold but the extremely small time interval implies that the number of probe packets is extremely large. For example, to achieve an accuracy of only 81%, RLI inserts, on average, 1 probe packet every 4.78 regular packets. Furthermore, as we mentioned in Section 1.2, latency measured with a large number of probe packets may significantly deviate from the real latency when there are no probe packets. When the time interval between two probe packets is large, this assumption does not make intuitive sense and may not hold in practice. Similarly, we have not found any theoretical or empirical validation of this assumption in prior literature.

The other latency measurement schemes are LDA [21] and FineComb [25], which provide aggregate, not per-flow, latency measurement between a sender and a receiver. In LDA, both the sender and the receiver maintain several counter vectors where each element is a pair of counters: time stamp counter for accumulating packet time stamps and packet counter for counting the number of arriving/departing packets. Each vector has a sampling probability and a sampling function. For each arriving or departing packet, LDA first maps the packet to a counter vector such that in the long run, the fraction of packets that LDA maps to any counter vector is equal to its sampling probability. It then randomly maps the packet to a counter pair in this counter vector and adds the time stamp of the packet to the time stamp counter and increments the packet counter by one. To obtain the aggregate latency estimate between the sender and receiver, for each counter pair in each vector, LDA checks whether they have the same packet counter value and selects all counter pairs that have the same packet counter value for both the sender and receiver. Then, LDA can easily calculate the total number of successfully delivered packets and the sum of their time stamps at both sides. Finally, to obtain the aggregate average latency between the sender and receiver, it subtracts the sum of time stamps at the sender side from that at the receiver side and divides it with the total number of successfully delivered packets.

3. COLATE – RECORDING PHASE

In this section, we present the recording phase and the statistical modeling of COLATE. Table 1 summarizes the symbols used throughout this paper.

Table 1: Symbols used in the paper

Symbol	Description
X, S, R	observation points
α	overall required reliability
β	overall required confidence interval
A	individual required reliability
B	individual required confidence interval
$f, \overline{f}$	different flows
μ_f	average latency of packets in flow f
$\tilde{\mu}_f$	estimated value of μ_f
$g\{.\}$	expected value function of C
σ_f	standard deviation of latency of packets in f
$\tilde{\sigma}_f$	estimated value of σ_f
$h\{.\}$	standard deviation function of C
$\mathbf{C}_X$	vector of all counters at X
$\mathbf{S}_X^f$	counter subvector of flow f at X
n	# of counters in vector $\mathbf{C}_X$
m	# of counters in $\mathbf{S}_X^f$
b	size of each counter in bits
H	hash function with output following $\sim U(1, n)$
C_f	random variable for sum of time stamps of f in $\mathbf{S}_X^f[j]$
C_r	random variable for sum of time stamps contributed by all flows, other than f, in $\mathbf{S}_X^f[j]$
C	random variable for value of counter $\mathbf{S}_X^f[j]$
$\tilde{C}$	observed average value of C from m counters
z	an arbitrary packet of flow f
$u_{f,X}[z]$	actual time stamp of packet z of f at X
$w_{f,X}[j]$	sum of time stamps contributed by f to $\mathbf{S}_X^f[j]$
$\tilde{w}_{f,X}[j]$	maximum likelihood estimate of $w_{f,X}[j]$
$v_{f,X}[l]$	a value of the deviation vector
$t_{f,X}$	sum of all time stamps of f at X
$\tilde{t}_{f,X}$	estimated value of $t_{f,X}$
$t_{f,X}^{max}$	maximum value of $t_{f,X}$ at X
$t_{f,X}^{min}$	minimum value of $t_{f,X}$ at X
t_X	sum of all time stamps in a counter epoch at X
T	maximum value that t_X can take on
$\mathcal{T}_f$	random variable for time stamp values of flow f
Q	random array of all m values in the range $[1, m]$
$\mathcal{Y}_{lX}$	set of all time stamps contributed by f to $\mathbf{S}_X^f[Q[2l]]$ and $\mathbf{S}_X^f[Q[2l-1]]$
p_f	# of packets in flow f
$P_{f,j}$	random variable for # of packets of f that contributed time stamps to $\mathbf{S}_X^f[j]$
D_f	random variable for latency of any packet in f
G_z	random variable with values $+1$ and -1
g_z	value that G_z takes on
ξ	$\mathbf{S}_X^f[j] - w_{f,X}[j]$
τ	$t_X - t_{f,X}$
γ	# of virtual repetitions
Z	standard normal random variable
M	amount of RAM allocated to COLATE

3.1 Noisy Accumulation of Time Stamps

At each observation point X, COLATE maintains a vector $\mathbf{C}_X$ of n counters where each counter $\mathbf{C}_X[i]$ $(1 \le i \le n)$ has b bits with initial value 0. When a packet arrives at or departs from an observation point X, COLATE extracts its flow ID f, chooses a random number j from a uniform distribution in the range $[1, m]$ where $m << n$, calculates the hash function $H(f, j)$ whose output is uniformly distributed in range $[1, n]$, and adds the time stamp of this packet (*i.e.*, the current time at observation point X) to the counter $\mathbf{C}_X[H(f, j)]$. Thus, the time stamp of all packets in flow f will be uniformly distributed to m counters: $\mathbf{C}_X[H(f,1)], \mathbf{C}_X[H(f,2)], \cdots, \mathbf{C}_X[H(f,m)]$. These m counters constitute the counter subvector of flow f, which is denoted by $\mathbf{S}_X^f$ where $\mathbf{S}_X^f[j] = \mathbf{C}_X[H(f,j)]$ for $j \in [1, m]$. In this recording phase, for each packet, COLATE performs one memory update to update the value of $\mathbf{C}_X[H(f,j)]$. For different flows, the probability that COLATE maps them to the same counter subvector is $\frac{m!}{n^m}$ ($=2.4 \times 10^{-62}$ for $n = 10000$ and $m = 20$, for example), which is practically zero. Note that an observation point is a port of a middlebox, not a middlebox itself, because the arriving and departing time of a packet at a middlebox are different due to the non-negligible packet processing time within the middlebox.

3.2 Analysis of Noisy Accumulation

First, by Lemma 1, we show that in any counter epoch, on average, a flow contributes the same amount to each counter in its counter subvector. We further show that the amount contributed by a flow to each counter in its counter subvector can be modeled by a binomial distribution. Second, we derive expressions for the expected value and variance of a counter in counter vector in Theorem 1. In Section 4, we use the expression of expected value to estimate the average and standard deviation of packet latencies for any given flow. In Section 5, we use the expression of variance to determine the parameter values that can ensure that the actual reliability achieved by COLATE is no less than the required reliability.

LEMMA 1. *Let C_f be the random variable representing the sum of time stamps contributed by flow f to a counter $\mathbf{S}_X^f[j]$, $1 \le j \le m$, in its counter subvector of length m at observation point X. Let p_f be the number of packets in flow f that contributed time stamps to the current counter epoch $\mathbf{C}_X$. Let $\mathcal{T}_f$ be an independent random variable representing the time stamp contributed by each packet of flow f to $\mathbf{C}_X$. Then, we have $E[C_f] = \frac{p_f \times E[\mathcal{T}_f]}{m}$.*

PROOF. Let $P_{f,j}$ be a random variable representing the number of packets in flow f that contributed time stamps to counter $\mathbf{S}_X^f[j]$. Therefore, $E[C_f] = E\left[\sum_{P_{f,j}} \mathcal{T}_f\right]$. Applying Wald's Lemma, we get $E[C_f] = E[P_{f,j}] \times E[\mathcal{T}_f]$. As the output of hash function H is uniformly distributed in range $[1, n]$, its output is also uniformly distributed in $[1, m]$ for the packets in flow f. Thus, the probability that COLATE adds the time stamp of a packet of the flow f to counter $\mathbf{S}_X^f[j]$ is $1/m$. The random variable $P_{f,j}$ follows the binomial distribution *i.e.*, $P_{f,j} \sim \text{Binom}(p_f, 1/m)$. Therefore, $E[C_f] = \frac{p_f}{m} \times E[\mathcal{T}_f]$. □

Figure 2 plots the CDF of the ratio of the observed values of C_f from simulations of our ICSI traffic trace to the $E[C_f]$ from Lemma 1. We observe from this figure that there is a steep rise in the CDF when the value of this ratio is around 1. We also observe from the simulations that the mean and median of the ratio are both equal to 1. This empirically establishes the result in Lemma 1.

Lemma 1 shows that the sum of time stamps of all packets of flow f is equally divided among all counters in its counter subvector, which conforms to binomial distribution. Thus, we approximate the distribution of C_f with a binomial distribution as $C_f \sim \text{Binom}(t_{f,X}, 1/m)$, where $t_{f,X}$ represents sum of all times-stamps contributed by flow f to the counters in its counter subvector at observation point X. Let C_r be the random variable representing the sum of time stamps

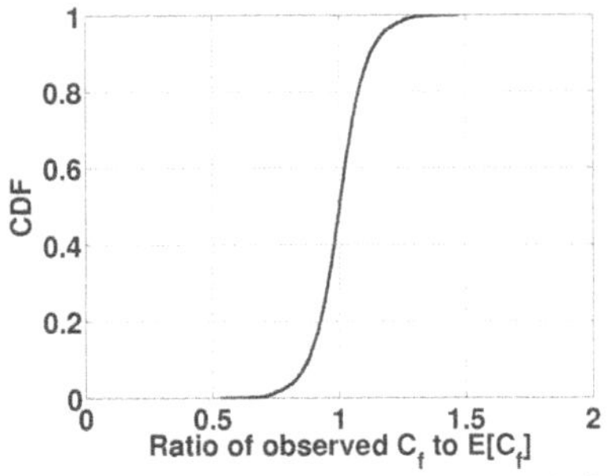

Figure 2: CDF of *observed* $C_f/E[C_f]$

contributed by packets of all flows other than f to counter $\mathbf{S}_X^f[j]$. Using similar reasoning as for C_f, we approximate the distribution of C_r with a binomial distribution. The probability that a packet of a flow $\bar{f} \neq f$ contributes a time stamp to counter $\mathbf{S}_X^f[j]$ is the product of the probability that H maps the packet to $\mathbf{S}_X^f[j]$ given that $\mathbf{S}_X^f[j] \in \mathbf{S}_X^{\bar{f}}$, which is $1/m$, and the probability that counter $\mathbf{S}_X^f[j]$ is in the counter subvector of $\bar{f}$, which is denoted by $P\{\mathbf{S}_X^f[j] \in \mathbf{S}_X^{\bar{f}}\}$ and calculated as

$$P\{\mathbf{S}_X^f[j] \in \mathbf{S}_X^{\bar{f}}\} = 1 - \left\{\binom{m}{0}\left(\frac{1}{n}\right)^0\left(1-\frac{1}{n}\right)^m\right\}$$
$$= 1 - \left\{1 - \frac{m}{n} + \frac{(m)(m-1)}{n^2 \times 2!} - \dots\right\}$$
$$\approx \frac{m}{n} \qquad \because m << n$$

Thus, the probability that a packet of a flow $\bar{f} \neq f$ contributes a time stamp to counter $\mathbf{S}_X^f[j]$ is $\frac{1}{m} \times \frac{m}{n} = \frac{1}{n}$. Thus, $C_r \sim \text{Binom}(t_X - t_{f,X}, 1/n)$.

THEOREM 1. *Let C be the random variable representing the value of a counter $\mathbf{S}_X^f[j]$, $1 \leq j \leq m$, in the counter subvector of a flow f. Let $t_{f,X}$ be the sum of all time stamps contributed by packets of flow f to all counters in its counter subvector and t_X be the sum of all time stamps contributed by packets of all flows in the counter epoch at observation point X. Let $C_f \sim Binom(t_{f,X}, 1/m)$ represent the sum of time stamps contributed by packets of flow f to $\mathbf{S}_X^f[j]$ and let $C_r \sim Binom(t_X - t_{f,X}, 1/n)$ represent the sum of time stamps contributed by packets of all flows other than f to counter $\mathbf{S}_X^f[j]$. Let C_f and C_r be independent of each other. The expected value and variance of C are calculated as follows*

$$E[C] = \frac{t_{f,X}}{m} + \frac{t_X - t_{f,X}}{n} \tag{1}$$

$$\text{Var}(C) = \left(\frac{t_{f,X}}{m}\right)\left(1 - \frac{1}{m}\right) + \left(\frac{t_X - t_{f,X}}{n}\right)\left(1 - \frac{1}{n}\right) \tag{2}$$

PROOF. As $C = C_f + C_r$, we get, $E[C] = E[C_f] + E[C_r] = \frac{t_{f,X}}{m} + \frac{t_X - t_{f,X}}{n}$. As C_f and C_r are assumed to be independent, $\text{Var}(C) = \text{Var}(C_f) + \text{Var}(C_r)$. As variance of $Binom(v, w)$ is $vw(1-w)$, we get $\text{Var}(C_f) = (\frac{t_{f,X}}{m})(1 - \frac{1}{m})$ and $\text{Var}(C_r) = (\frac{t_X - t_{f,X}}{n})(1 - \frac{1}{n})$. ☐

In Theorem 1, we assumed C_f and C_r to be independent of each other, which is true whenever $t_{f,X} << t_X$. In practice $t_{f,X}$ indeed is much smaller than t_X because $t_{f,X}$ is the sum of the time stamps added by a single flow in the counter epoch while t_X is the sum of the time stamps added by all flows (in the order of tens and hundreds of thousands). Furthermore, in Theorem 1, we approximate the distributions of C_f and C_r with binomial distributions because when there are a large number of packets that contribute time stamps to the counters in the counter vector, we can approximate each time stamp to be smeared over the counters. This approximation makes the formal development of variance of C and its subsequent use in calculating parameters for COLATE tractable. If the exact equation for variance of C is desired, it can be obtained as follows. Consider any packet with time stamp t_p not belonging to a flow f. This packet has a probability $\frac{1}{n}$ of being mapped to a counter in the counter subvector of the flow f. Thus, the time stamp for each such packet will contribute a variance of $t_p^2(\frac{1}{n})(1 - \frac{1}{n})$ to the overall variance of C. In Theorem 1, $t_{f,X}/m$ models the average sum of the time stamps contributed by flow f, and $(t_X - t_{f,X})/m$ models the average *noise* contributed by all other flows to counter $\mathbf{S}_X^f[j]$.

4. COLATE - QUERYING PHASE

In this section, we present the methods that COLATE uses to estimate the average and standard deviation of the latencies of the packets of a flow in passing any two observation points.

4.1 Estimating Latency Average

For a flow f passing through observation point S and then observation point R, we want to calculate $\tilde{\mu}_f$, the estimate of average latency μ_f of flow f. For a packet z in flow f, let $u_{f,S}[z]$ be its time stamp at observation point S and $u_{f,R}[z]$ be its time stamp at observation point R. The delay experienced by this packet in traveling from S to R is thus $u_{f,R}[z] - u_{f,S}[z]$. Let $t_{f,S}$ and $t_{f,R}$ be the sums of all time stamps of the packets in flow f at S and R, respectively. Recall that p_f denotes the number of packets in f. Thus,

$$\mu_f = \frac{1}{p_f}\sum_{\forall z}(u_{f,R}[z] - u_{f,S}[z])$$
$$= \frac{1}{p_f}\Big(\sum_{\forall z} u_{f,R}[z] - \sum_{\forall z} u_{f,S}[z]\Big) = \frac{1}{p_f}(t_{f,R} - t_{f,S})$$

Note that the value of p_f can be measured by tools such as NetFlow available on Cisco routers or by schemes proposed in [22, 26]. Thus, to estimate the value of μ_f, we need to obtain the estimated values $\tilde{t}_{f,S}$ and $\tilde{t}_{f,R}$ for $t_{f,S}$ and $t_{f,R}$, respectively. Then, we can calculate

$$\tilde{\mu_f} = \frac{1}{p_f}(\tilde{t}_{f,R} - \tilde{t}_{f,S}) \tag{3}$$

Theorem 2 shows how to obtain $\tilde{t}_{f,X}$ at X.

THEOREM 2. *Given a counter epoch $\mathbf{C}_X$ of length n at observation point X where each counter subvector is of length m, let t_X denote the sum of all counters in $\mathbf{C}_X$, the estimate $\tilde{t}_{f,X}$ of the sum of all time stamps of the packets in flow f is calculated as follows*

$$\tilde{t}_{f,X} = \frac{1}{n-m}\left\{n\sum_{j=1}^{m}\mathbf{S}_X^f[j] - mt_X\right\} \tag{4}$$

PROOF. Given $\mathbf{C}_X$ and flow f, we can easily obtain the values of every counter in the counter subvector $\mathbf{S}_X^f$ of f. Thus, we can calculate $E[C]$ as $E[C] = \frac{1}{m}\sum_{j=1}^{m}\mathbf{S}_X^f[j]$. Substituting $E[C]$ in Equation (1) by $\frac{1}{m}\sum_{j=1}^{m}\mathbf{S}_X^f[j]$, replacing $t_{f,X}$ by $\tilde{t}_{f,X}$, and solving for $\tilde{t}_{f,X}$, gives Equation (4). ☐

4.2 Estimating Latency Standard Deviation

Let D_f be the random variable representing the latency experienced by a packet in flow f. The standard deviation of D_f can be calculated by $\tilde{\sigma}_f = \sqrt{\text{Var}(D_f)}$, where $\text{Var}(D_f)$ can be calculated as follows:

$$\text{Var}(D_f) = E[D_f^2] - E^2[D_f]$$
$$= \left\{\frac{1}{p_f}\sum_{\forall z}(u_{f,R}[z]-u_{f,S}[z])^2\right\} - \left\{\frac{1}{p_f}\sum_{\forall z}(u_{f,R}[z]-u_{f,S}[z])\right\}^2$$
$$= \left\{\frac{1}{p_f}\sum_{\forall z}(u_{f,R}[z]-u_{f,S}[z])^2\right\} - \left\{\frac{1}{p_f}(t_{f,R}-t_{f,S})\right\}^2 \qquad (5)$$

We can calculate the second term $\{\frac{1}{p_f}(t_{f,R} - t_{f,S})\}^2$ in Equation (5) based on Theorem 2. Now the key challenge is to calculate the first term $\{\frac{1}{p_f}\sum_{\forall z}(u_{f,R}[z] - u_{f,S}[z])^2\}$ in Equation (5). Our solution to this challenge is based on the statistical technique proposed by Alon *et al.* in [14]. The main idea is to introduce a random variable G_z where the value g_z that this random variable takes on is either $+1$ or -1 with equal probability. Before adding the time stamp of a packet z to a counter, if we randomly multiply the time stamp with g_z and then add it to the counter, then we will get Equation (6).

$$E\left[\left\{\sum_{\forall z}(g_z u_{f,R}[z] - g_z u_{f,S}[z])\right\}^2\right] = \sum_{\forall z}(u_{f,R}[z]-u_{f,S}[z])^2 \qquad (6)$$

This can be proven as follows:

$$E\left[\left\{\sum_{\forall z} g_z(u_{f,R}[z]-u_{f,S}[z])\right\}^2\right] = E\left[\sum_{\forall z} g_z^2(u_{f,R}[z]-u_{f,S}[z])^2 + \sum_{\forall z\neq\overline{z}} g_z g_{\overline{z}}(u_{f,R}[z]-u_{f,S}[z])(u_{f,R}[\overline{z}]-u_{f,S}[\overline{z}])\right]$$

Using the well known result that expectation of sum of random variables is the sum of their individual expectations and that $g_z^2 = 1$, we get:

$$= \sum_{\forall z}(u_{f,R}[z]-u_{f,S}[z])^2 + \sum_{\forall z\neq\overline{z}}(u_{f,R}[z]-u_{f,S}[z])(u_{f,R}[z]-u_{f,S}[z]) \times E[G_z G_{\overline{z}}]$$

Note that $\{G_1, G_2, G_3, \dots\}$ is a set of independent and identically distributed random variables. So, $E[G_z G_{\overline{z}}] = E[G_z] \times E[G_{\overline{z}}]$. As $E[G_z] = 0$ for all values of z, this implies $E[G_z G_{\overline{z}}] = 0$. Thus, the second term in the equation above is 0, which proves Equation (6).

We now present our method for calculating the first term in Equation (5). First, for each counter in the counter subvector of f, whose value is contributed by the time stamps of the packets in flow f and those of the packets in other flows, we use Theorem 3 to extract an estimate of the value that is contributed by only the time stamps of the packets in f. In other words, we eliminate the noise introduced by the packets of flows other than f from the counter subvector of f. Second, we statistically simulate the process of multiplying the time stamp of a packet in f with the random variable G_z and then adding the multiplication result to the corresponding counter in the counter subvector of f. By repeating this process a statistically sufficient number of times, we obtain an accurate estimate of $\sum_{\forall z}(u_{f,R}[z] - u_{f,S}[z])^2$ based on Theorem 4. Note that this simulation does not require any changes to the recording phase. Next, we present our denoising solution and statistical simulation process.

4.2.1 Denoising Counter Subvectors

Our denoising solution is based on Theorem 3. The numerical solution of Equation (7) gives us the estimate of the value that is contributed by only the time stamps of the packets in f for each counter in f's subvector.

THEOREM 3. *Let $w_{f,X}[j]$ $(1 \leq j \leq m)$ be the sum of the time stamps of flow f's packets that are mapped to counter $\mathbf{S}_X^f[j]$ at observation point X. Let $\tilde{t}_{f,X}$ be the estimate of sum of all time stamps contributed by packets of flow f to all counters in f's counter subvector and t_X be the sum of all time stamps contributed by packets of all flows in the counter epoch at observation point X. The maximum likelihood estimate $\tilde{w}_{f,X}[j]$ of $w_{f,X}[j]$ satisfies the following equation:*

$$\ln\{n-1\} = \psi^{(0)}\{t_X - \tilde{t}_{f,X} - \mathbf{S}_X^f[j] + \tilde{w}_{f,X}[j] + 1\} - \psi^{(0)}\{\mathbf{S}_X^f[j] - \tilde{w}_{f,X}[j] + 1\} \qquad (7)$$

where $\psi^{(0)}\{.\}$ is the 0th order polygamma function.

PROOF. The maximum likelihood estimate of $w_{f,X}[j]$ is the value of $w_{f,X}[j]$ that maximizes the probability that the counter $\mathbf{S}_X^f[j]$ takes the observed value.

$$\arg\max_{w_{f,X}[j]} P\{C = \mathbf{S}_X^f[j] | w_{f,X}[j]\}$$

This value of $w_{f,X}[j]$ can be obtained by differentiating $P\{C = \mathbf{S}_X^f[j] | w_{f,X}[j]\}$ w.r.t $w_{f,X}[j]$ and equating to 0.

$$\frac{d}{d(w_{f,X}[j])}P\{C = \mathbf{S}_X^f[j] | w_{f,X}[j]\} = 0$$

As $C = C_f + C_r$ and $C_f = w_{f,X}[j]$, the L.H.S. becomes

$$\frac{d}{d(w_{f,X}[j])}P\{C_r = \mathbf{S}_X^f[j] - w_{f,X}[j]\}$$

For simplicity, let $\xi = \mathbf{S}_X^f[j] - w_{f,X}[j]$ and $\tau = t_X - t_{f,X}$. As C_r is a binomial random variable, this derivative further becomes

$$\frac{d}{d(w_{f,X}[j])}\binom{\tau}{\xi}\left(\frac{1}{n}\right)^{\xi}\left(1-\frac{1}{n}\right)^{\tau-\xi} = \left\{\binom{\tau}{\xi}\left(\frac{1}{n}\right)^{\xi}\left(1-\frac{1}{n}\right)^{\tau-\xi}\right\}$$
$$\times\left\{\psi^{(0)}\{\xi+1\} - \psi^{(0)}\{\tau-\xi+1\} + \ln\left\{1-\frac{1}{n}\right\} - \ln\left\{\frac{1}{n}\right\}\right\} \qquad (8)$$

Due to space limitations, we have skipped the intermediate derivation steps, which use the following identity:

$$\frac{d}{dw}\binom{v}{w} = \binom{v}{w}\left(\psi^{(0)}\{v-w+1\} - \psi^{(0)}\{w+1\}\right)$$

By replacing $t_{f,X}$ with $\tilde{t}_{f,X}$, which is calculated using Theorem 2, in $\tau = t_X - t_{f,X}$ and further in the R.H.S of Equation (8) and equating it to zero, we obtain the maximum likelihood estimate $\tilde{w}_{f,X}[j]$ of $w_{f,X}[j]$ As $\binom{\tau}{\xi}\left(\frac{1}{n}\right)^{\xi}\left(1-\frac{1}{n}\right)^{\tau-\xi}$ is $P\{C_f = \mathbf{S}_X^f[j] | w_{f,X}[j]\}$, which is not equal to zero, we have

$$\left\{\psi^{(0)}\{\xi+1\} - \psi^{(0)}\{\tau-\xi+1\} + \ln\left\{1-\frac{1}{n}\right\} - \ln\left\{\frac{1}{n}\right\}\right\} = 0$$

Simplifying the $\ln\{.\}$ terms results in Equation (7). □

4.2.2 Statistical Simulations

We have obtained the m values extracted using Theorem 3 from f's counter subvector at observation point X. For flow f that passes observation point X, each unique permutation of the m distinct integers from 1 to m, denoted by vector Q, defines a unique *deviation vector* $v_{f,X}$ of size $m/2$ as follows. To ensure that $m/2$ is an integer, we choose m to be an even number.

$$v_{f,X}[l] = \tilde{w}_{f,X}\left[Q[2l]\right] - \tilde{w}_{f,X}\left[Q[2l-1]\right] \quad 1 \le l \le m/2 \quad (9)$$

Each unique permutation of the m distinct integers from 1 to m is essentially a unique simulation of the aforementioned statistical process of multiplying half the time stamps with $G_z = +1$ and the other half with $G_z = -1$. Theorem 4 gives us the way to estimate $\sum_{\forall z}(u_{f,R}[z] - u_{f,S}[z])^2$, which is needed for calculating $\text{Var}(D_f)$ based on Equation (5).

THEOREM 4. *Given any two observation points S and R, for any permutation Q of the m distinct integers from 1 to m, let $v_{f,S}$ and $v_{f,R}$ be the corresponding deviation vectors of flow f at observation points S and R, respectively. The following equation holds:*

$$\sum_{\forall z}\left(u_{f,R}[z] - u_{f,S}[z]\right)^2 = E\left[\sum_{l=1}^{\frac{m}{2}}(v_{f,R}[l] - v_{f,S}[l])^2\right] \quad (10)$$

PROOF. Let $\mathcal{Y}_{lS}$ be the set of all the time stamps contributed by the packets of flow f to counters $\boldsymbol{S}_S^f[Q[2l]]$ and $\boldsymbol{S}_S^f[Q[2l-1]]$. Similarly, let $\mathcal{Y}_{lR}$ be the set of all the time stamps contributed by the packets of flow f to counters $\boldsymbol{S}_R^f[Q[2l]]$ and $\boldsymbol{S}_R^f[Q[2l-1]]$. Let $y_{lS}[i]$ be the i-th element of $\mathcal{Y}_{lS}$, where $1 \le i \le |\mathcal{Y}_{lS}|$. Similarly, let $y_{lR}[i]$ be the i-th element of $\mathcal{Y}_{lR}$, where $1 \le i \le |\mathcal{Y}_{lR}|$. Starting from the R.H.S of Equation (10), we have:

$$= \sum_{l=1}^{\frac{m}{2}} E\left[(v_{f,R}[l] - v_{f,S}[l])^2\right]$$

$$= \sum_{l=1}^{\frac{m}{2}} E\left[\left\{\sum_{i=1}^{|\mathcal{Y}_{lR}|} g_i.y_{lR}[i] - \sum_{i=1}^{|\mathcal{Y}_{lS}|} g_i.y_{lS}[i]\right\}^2\right]$$

$$= \sum_{l=1}^{\frac{m}{2}} E\left[\left\{\sum_{i=1}^{|\mathcal{Y}_{lR}|} (g_i.y_{lR}[i] - g_i.y_{lS}[i])\right\}^2\right] \because |\mathcal{Y}_{lR}| = |\mathcal{Y}_{lS}|$$

$$= \sum_{l=1}^{\frac{m}{2}} \sum_{i=1}^{|\mathcal{Y}_{lR}|} (y_{lR}[i] - y_{lS}[i])^2, \text{ using Equation (6)}$$

$$= \sum_{\forall z}(u_{f,R}[z] - u_{f,S}[z])^2$$

The last equality follows from the fact that each $y_{lX}[i]$ is actually the value of some time stamp $u_{f,X}[z]$ at observation point X. □

For any permutation Q of the m distinct integers from 1 to m, we calculate $v_{f,R}[l]$ and $v_{f,S}[l]$ for each $1 \le l \le m/2$ based on Equation (9), and then calculate $\sum_{l=1}^{\frac{m}{2}}(v_{f,R}[l] - v_{f,S}[l])^2$, which is one estimate of $\sum_{\forall z}\left(u_{f,R}[z] - u_{f,S}[z]\right)^2$ according to Theorem 4. As $\sum_{l=1}^{\frac{m}{2}}(v_{f,R}[l] - v_{f,S}[l])^2$ is a random variable, its variance can be reduced by γ times if we repeat the above process γ times using a different random permutation Q each time and use the average of the γ values of $\sum_{l=1}^{\frac{m}{2}}(v_{f,R}[l] - v_{f,S}[l])^2$ as the estimate of $\sum_{\forall z}\left(u_{f,R}[z] - u_{f,S}[z]\right)^2$. As the R.H.S. of Equation (10) is an expected value, to get an accurate estimate of $\sum_{\forall z}\left(u_{f,R}[z] - u_{f,S}[z]\right)^2$, we need to calculate $\sum_{l=1}^{\frac{m}{2}}(v_{f,R}[l] - v_{f,S}[l])^2$ for a statistically sufficient number of unique permutations of the m distinct integers from 1 to m. The process of calculating $\sum_{l=1}^{\frac{m}{2}}(v_{f,R}[l] - v_{f,S}[l])^2$ for different permutations of Q is essentially simulating the aforementioned *random* statistical process of multiplying the time stamp of each packet with random variable G_z that takes the value of $+1$ and -1 with equal probability *without having to perform this process in the recording phase.* We name this process of calculating $\sum_{l=1}^{\frac{m}{2}}(v_{f,R}[l] - v_{f,S}[l])^2$ using different permutations of Q as *virtual repetitions*. The number of distinct ways in which we can repeat this process is $\prod_{i=1}^{\frac{m}{2}}\binom{m-2(i-1)}{2}$, which is large enough for us to obtain any required reliability α for estimating the standard deviation. For example, when $m = 20$, $\prod_{i=1}^{\frac{m}{2}}\binom{m-2(i-1)}{2} = 2.38 \times 10^{15}$.

4.2.3 Steps of Estimating Standard Deviation

To summarize, COLATE performs the following six steps to estimate the standard deviation of the latencies that the packets in flow f experienced in traversing from observation points S to R. (1) Obtain the number of packets in flow f, denoted by p_f, using NetFlow or the schemes proposed in [22, 26]. (2) Obtain the estimates of $t_{f,S}$ and $t_{f,R}$, which are the sum of the time stamps of all packets in flow f at observation points S and R respectively, using Theorem 2. (3) Extract the values of $w_{f,S}[j]$ and $w_{f,R}[j]$, which are the sum of the time stamps of flow f's packets that are mapped to counter $\boldsymbol{S}_S^f[j]$ at observation point S and to counter $\boldsymbol{S}_R^f[j]$ at observation point R, respectively, for all $1 \le j \le m$, using Theorem 3. (4) Randomly choose γ permutations of the m distinct integers from 1 to m. For each permutation Q, first calculate $v_{f,R}[l]$ and $v_{f,S}[l]$ for all $1 \le l \le m/2$ using Equation (9) and then calculate $\sum_{l=1}^{\frac{m}{2}}(v_{f,R}[l] - v_{f,S}[l])^2$. (5) Calculate the average of the γ values of $\sum_{l=1}^{\frac{m}{2}}(v_{f,R}[l] - v_{f,S}[l])^2$, which is the estimated value of $\sum_{\forall z}\left(u_{f,R}[z] - u_{f,S}[z]\right)^2$ (6) Estimate of the standard deviation using Equation (5).

5. COLATE - RELIABILITY

COLATE has four parameters: (1) the total number of counters denoted by n, (2) the number of counters in each counter subvector denoted by m, (3) the number of bits in each counter denoted by b, and (4) the vector threshold denoted by T. Note that when the sum of all n counters in a counter vector reaches T, COLATE dumps the counter vector into permanent storage as a counter epoch and then resets all counter values to be zero. In this section, we present solutions to find the values for these parameters so that our estimated average latency achieves the required reliability $\alpha \in [0, 1)$ for the given confidence interval $\beta \in (0, 1]$. Note that for standard deviation, we have already presented a method in Section 4 that can achieve arbitrarily high required reliability. Recall $\tilde{\mu}_f = \frac{1}{p_f}(\tilde{t}_{f,R} - \tilde{t}_{f,S})$ (in Equation (3)), which shows that the estimate $\tilde{\mu}_f$ depends on two other estimates $\tilde{t}_{f,S}$ and $\tilde{t}_{f,R}$. Next, we find the confidence interval B and required reliability A that the estimate $\tilde{t}_{f,X}$ for $t_{f,X}$ at each observation point X must satisfy so that the estimate $\tilde{\mu}_f$ for μ_f satisfies the confidence interval β and required reliability α. That is, we want to find the values of B and A so that if for every observation point X we have $P\left\{|\tilde{t}_{f,X} - t_{f,X}| \le Bt_{f,X}\right\} \ge A$, then we will have $P\left\{|\tilde{\mu}_f - \mu_f| \le \beta\mu_f\right\} \ge \alpha$. After we find the values for B and A, we present a solution to calculate the optimal values of the four parameters n, m, b, and T.

5.1 Individual Reliability Requirements

Individual Required Reliability: The maximum fraction of estimated values $\tilde{\mu}_f$ that can violate the requirement of $|\tilde{\mu}_f - \mu_f| \leq \beta\mu_f$, while the overall estimate still satisfies the required reliability α, is $1-\alpha$. Thus, the maximum fraction of estimates $\tilde{t}_{f,X}$ at either observation points of S and R that can violate the requirement $|\tilde{t}_{f,X} - t_{f,X}| \leq Bt_{f,X}$ must be no greater than $(1-\alpha)/2$. Thus,

$$A = 1 - (1-\alpha)/2 = (1+\alpha)/2 \tag{11}$$

Individual Confidence Interval: The estimate $\tilde{\mu}_f$ obtained by COLATE needs to satisfy the requirement of $|\tilde{\mu}_f - \mu_f| \leq \beta\mu_f$ with probability of at least α. As $\tilde{\mu}_f = \frac{1}{p_f}(\tilde{t}_{f,R} - \tilde{t}_{f,S})$ and $\mu_f = \frac{1}{p_f}(t_{f,R} - t_{f,S})$, the confidence interval requirement $|\tilde{\mu}_f - \mu_f| \leq \beta\mu_f$ becomes:

$$\begin{aligned}&\left|(\tilde{t}_{f,R} - t_{f,R}) - (\tilde{t}_{f,S} - t_{f,S})\right| \\ =& \left|(\tilde{t}_{f,R} - \tilde{t}_{f,S}) - (t_{f,R} - t_{f,S})\right| \leq \beta(t_{f,R} - t_{f,S})\end{aligned}$$

The largest value of $\left|(\tilde{t}_{f,R} - t_{f,R}) - (\tilde{t}_{f,S} - t_{f,S})\right|$ is $Bt_{f,R} + Bt_{f,S}$, which must be no greater than $\beta(t_{f,R} - t_{f,S})$.

$$Bt_{f,R} + Bt_{f,S} \leq \beta(t_{f,R} - t_{f,S})$$

Thus, we get

$$B \leq \beta\left(\frac{t_{f,R} - t_{f,S}}{t_{f,R} + t_{f,S}}\right) \tag{12}$$

To determine B for a given network, we conduct measurement of $(t_{f,R} - t_{f,S})/(t_{f,R} + t_{f,S})$ on the network to find the appropriate value so that Equation (12) statistically holds.

5.2 Reliability Centered Parameter Selection

As we have four unknown parameters (*i.e.*, n, m, b, and T), we need at least four equations so that we can calculate the values of these parameters by solving the four equations. Next we develop these four equations.

Equation 1: Let M be the total number of bits of the RAM that an observation point can allocate for storing the counter vector, which requires $n \times b$ bits. Thus,

$$n \times b = M \tag{13}$$

Equation 2: Based on Lemma 1, the sum of all the time stamps of all packets of all flows is equally divided among all n counters on average. Thus, the value of each counter on average can go up to T/n. Thus, the number of bits in each counter, which is b, needs to satisfy the following equation.

$$b = \log_2\left\{\frac{T}{n}\right\} + 1 \tag{14}$$

Note that we add 1 in the R.H.S of this equation to double the capacity of each counter to avoid overflows.

Equation 3: As the expected value of a counter in a counter subvector, which is specified in Equation (1), should never exceed the maximum capacity of the counter, we have

$$\frac{t_{f,X}}{m} + \frac{T - t_{f,X}}{n} \leq 2^b - 1$$

Let $t_{f,X}^{max}$ be the maximum value of $t_{f,X}$ for all flows on a network. Thus, the value of b should satisfy the following equation:

$$\frac{t_{f,X}^{max}}{m} + \frac{T - t_{f,X}^{max}}{n} = 2^b - 1 \tag{15}$$

Here $t_{f,X}^{max}$ can be obtained by some measurement on the sum of the time stamps of all packets on a per-flow basis on the given network.

Equation 4: To achieve the required reliability, $P\left\{|\tilde{t}_{f,X} - t_{f,X}| \leq Bt_{f,X}\right\}$ should at least be equal to its lower bound A, *i.e.*,

$$P\left\{(1-B)t_{f,X} \leq \tilde{t}_{f,X} \leq (1+B)t_{f,X}\right\} = A \tag{16}$$

Based on Equation (1), we can represent $E[C]$ as a function of $t_{f,X}$; denoting this function by g, we have $E[C] = g\{t_{f,X}\}$. Thus, $t_{f,X} = g^{-1}\{E[C]\}$. Let $\tilde{C}$ be the observed value of $E[C]$. Then, we have $\tilde{t}_{f,X} = g^{-1}\{\tilde{C}\}$. Equation (16) becomes

$$\begin{aligned}A &= P\left\{(1-B)t_{f,X} \leq g^{-1}\{\tilde{C}\} \leq (1+B)t_{f,X}\right\} \\ &= P\left\{g\{(1-B)t_{f,X}\} \leq \tilde{C} \leq g\{(1+B)t_{f,X}\}\right\} \end{aligned} \tag{17}$$

Similarly, based on Equation (2), we can represent standard deviation of C as a function of $t_{f,X}$; denoting this function by h, we have $\text{Var}(C) = h^2\{t_{f,X}\}$. Based on the fact that the variance of a random variable reduces by m times if the random event is repeated m times, by observing the values of C from m counters, the variance of C becomes $\frac{h^2\{t_{f,X}\}}{m}$ and the standard deviation of C becomes $\frac{h\{t_{f,X}\}}{\sqrt{m}}$. Let Z denote $\frac{\tilde{C} - g\{t_{f,X}\}}{h\{t_{f,X}\}/\sqrt{m}}$. Thus, Equation (17) becomes

$$P\left\{\frac{g\{(1-B)t_{f,X}\} - g\{t_{f,X}\}}{h\{t_{f,X}\}/\sqrt{m}} \leq Z \leq \frac{g\{(1+B)t_{f,X}\} - g\{t_{f,X}\}}{h\{t_{f,X}\}/\sqrt{m}}\right\} = A \tag{18}$$

By the central limit theorem, Z approximates a standard normal random variable. The area under the standard normal curve gives the success probability, which is the required reliability in our context. As our confidence interval requirement is symmetric on both the upper and lower sides of $t_{f,X}$, we can represent the required reliability A in terms of a constant k as follows:

$$P\{-k \leq Z \leq k\} = A \tag{19}$$

Let Φ be the cumulative distribution function (CDF) of a standard normal distribution and erf$\{.\}$ be the standard error function, we get

$$P\{-k \leq Z \leq k\} = \Phi(k) - \Phi(-k) = \text{erf}\left\{\frac{k}{\sqrt{2}}\right\} \tag{20}$$

From Equations (19) and (20), we get

$$k = \sqrt{2}\,\text{erf}^{-1}\{A\}$$

We observe that the absolute values of the upper and lower bounds of Z in Equation (18) are the same. Thus, equating the lower bound with $-k$ or the upper bound with k results in the following equation:

$$B^2 t_{f,X}^2 = \frac{k^2 n^2 m}{n-m}\left\{\left(\frac{t_{f,X}}{m}\right)\left(1 - \frac{1}{m}\right) + \left(\frac{T - t_{f,X}}{n}\right)\left(1 - \frac{1}{n}\right)\right\} \tag{21}$$

By rearranging Equation (21), we get.

$$\begin{aligned}B^2 =& \frac{1}{t_{f,X}}\left[\frac{k^2n^2m}{n-m}\left\{\left(\frac{1}{m}\right)\left(1-\frac{1}{m}\right) - \left(\frac{1}{n}\right)\left(1-\frac{1}{n}\right)\right\}\right] \\ &+ \frac{1}{t_{f,X}^2}\left[\frac{k^2n^2m}{n-m}\left(\frac{1}{n}\right)\left(1-\frac{1}{n}\right)T\right]\end{aligned}$$

This equation shows that B is inversely proportional to $t_{f,X}$ when other parameters are fixed. This makes intuitive sense because the more packets in flow f in passing observation point X (*i.e.*, the larger $t_{f,X}$ is), the more timing information we can obtain from the packets, and the smaller confidence interval can be achieved. Thus, we should use the statistically minimum observable value of $t_{f,X}$, denoted $t_{f,X}^{min}$, for the given network, in Equation (21). Here $t_{f,X}^{min}$ can be obtained by some measurement on the sum of the time stamps of all packets on a per-flow basis on the given network. The parameter values obtained using $t_{f,X}^{min}$ in Equation (21) will ensure that the estimates for all flows whose sum of time stamps are $\geq t_{f,X}^{min}$ satisfy $P\left\{|\tilde{t}_{f,X} - t_{f,X}| \leq Bt_{f,X}\right\} \geq A$. By replacing $t_{f,X}$ by $t_{f,X}^{min}$ in Equation (21), we get

$$B^2 t_{f,X}^{min\,2} = \frac{k^2n^2m}{n-m}\left\{\left(\frac{t_{f,X}^{min}}{m}\right)\left(1-\frac{1}{m}\right) + \left(\frac{T - t_{f,X}^{min}}{n}\right)\left(1-\frac{1}{n}\right)\right\} \quad (22)$$

Solving Equations: COLATE takes M, α, β, $t_{f,X}^{min}$, and $t_{f,X}^{max}$ as input. The values of required reliability α and confidence interval β are provided by network operators. The value of RAM space M depends on the amount of RAM available at an observation point. For $t_{f,X}^{min}$ and $t_{f,X}^{max}$, network operators can obtain them by measurements on targeted flows in the given network. With the values of M, α, β, $t_{f,X}^{min}$, and $t_{f,X}^{max}$, COLATE simultaneously solves the four equations (*i.e.*, (13), (14), (15), and (22)) to obtain the appropriate values of the four parameters n, m, b, and T. To simultaneously solve these equations, we express m, b, and T in terms of n using Equations (13), (14), and (15) and replace them in Equation (22). This results in an expression with only one unknown parameter n. We numerically solve this expression to obtain n and then the other three unknown parameters.

RAM Space vs. Storage Space: From the simultaneous solution of these four equations, we have an interesting observation that COLATE requires smaller amount of permanent storage space for storing counter epochs when it is allocated with more RAM for storing counter vectors. Figure 3 plots an example graph of the permanent storage size vs. RAM size for COLATE.

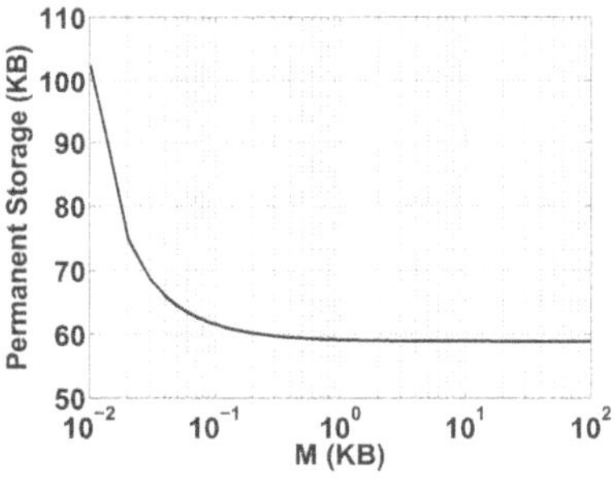

Figure 3: Permanent storage vs. RAM size

While this observation seems surprising, it makes intuitive sense because the sum of the two maximum values of two b-bit numbers is $2 \times 2^b = 2^{b+1}$ whereas the maximum value of a $2b$-bit number is $2^{2b} >> 2^{b+1}$. As we increase the total number of bits in a counter vector, *i.e.*, M, the counter value threshold T increases as shown in Figure 4. This implies that the frequency of writing the counter vector into permanent storage is reduced, and although each counter epoch takes more space, the overall required storage space is reduced as shown in Figure 3. The M value at the knee of the curve in Figure 3 represents the best tradeoff point between RAM space and permanent storage space.

5.3 Flexibility in Parameter Selection

If we only measure average per-flow latency, each observation point can choose its own values for the parameters of n, m, b, and T based on its available resources and traffic condition without global coordination among observation points.

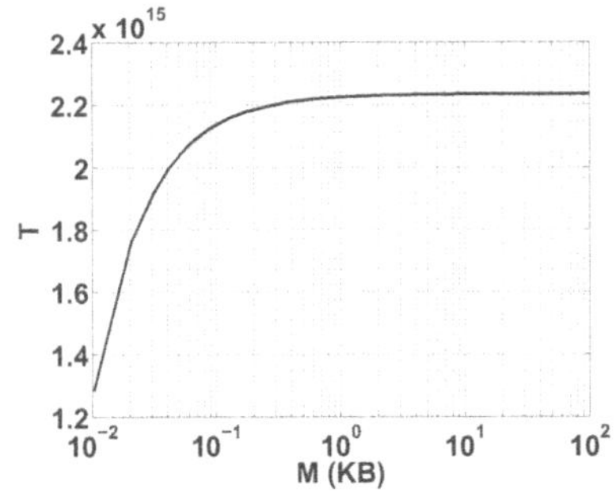

Figure 4: Threshold T vs. RAM size

If we also need to measure standard deviation, then all observation points need to use the same value of m because Theorem 4 requires that the two sets $\mathcal{Y}_{lS}$ and $\mathcal{Y}_{lR}$ contain the time stamps from the same set of packets at the two observation points, which is possible only when the value of m is the same at both observation points. The remaining three parameters can still be chosen independently at each observation point.

6. PERFORMANCE EVALUATION

We implemented COLATE in Matlab. We also implemented RLI [23] in Matlab for comparison purposes. We did not implement LDA [21] and MAPLE [24] because LDA can not provide per-flow latency measurement and MAPLE requires attaching time stamps to every packet *i.e.*, MAPLE is not a latency estimation scheme but a storage scheme. In this section, we present our evaluation results of COLATE in comparison with RLI. We first give details of the three network traces that we used. Second, we evaluate the accuracy of COLATE as well as the impact of RAM space on permanent storage space used by COLATE. Last, we compare COLATE with RLI and with Count-Min (CM) sketch [19], a summarizing data structure for queries on data streams.

6.1 Network Traces

To evaluate COLATE, we need real packet traces with high-resolution time stamps collected simultaneously from at least two observation points. Unfortunately, no such traces are publicly available. Thus, we resort to three real network traces where each is collected at a single observation point at a time. These traces include CHIC [2], ICSI [30], and DC [15]. CHIC is a backbone header trace, published by CAIDA, which includes the arrival times of packets at a 10GigE link interface. We used traces generated from 5 minutes of packet capture. Note that the authors of RLI and MAPLE also evaluated their schemes on the header trace of this backbone link collected by CAIDA. ICSI is an enterprise network traffic trace, collected at a medium-sized site, which includes the arrival times of packets on an ethernet link for a duration of over 41.1 hours. ICSI is available in the form of 41 trace files collected at 17 different ports in an enterprise network. DC is a data center traffic trace, collected at a university data center, which includes the arrival times of packets on an ethernet link for a duration of a little more than an hour. DC is available in the form of 20 trace files collected at the same port. Figure 5 shows the CDFs of sizes of flows in each trace. We observe that the traces contain both mice flows as well as elephant flows. Table 2 reports the total duration, number of packets, number of flows, and average data rate of each trace.

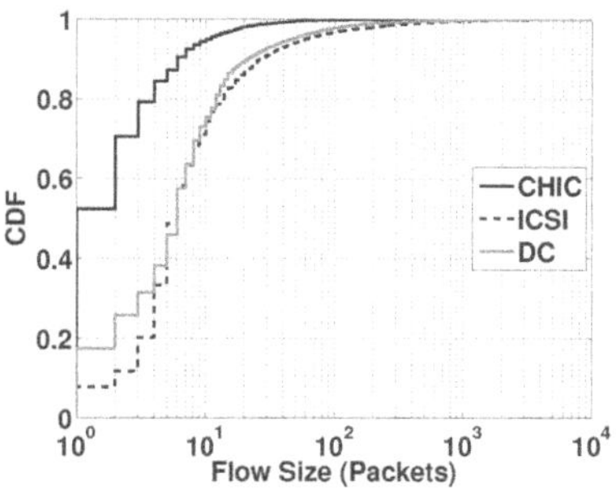

Figure 5: CDFs of flow sizes

As these network traces contain only the arrival time stamps of packets, we adopt the simulation strategy used by RLI and MAPLE, which simulates the traversal of packets in each trace through a queue to get a departure time stamp for each packet and uses random early detection (RED) [18] as the queue management strategy because RED is most popular. As modern routers typically use a queue size that can hold 0.5 seconds of traffic at their maximum line rates, we also use the same queue size. For the remaining parameters of RED queue management strategy, we use $\min_{th} = 0.475 \times$queue size, $\max_{th} = 0.95\times$queue size, $w_q = 0.002$, and $\max_p = \frac{1}{50}$ as per the guidelines in [18].

Table 2: Summary of network traces

Trace	Duration	# pkts	# flows	Mbps
CHIC	5 mins	37.3M	3.01M	411
ICSI	41.1 hours	46.9M	0.387M	1.31
DC	1.08 hours	19.9M	0.439M	49.6

6.2 COLATE Accuracy

Now we evaluate the accuracy of the average and standard deviation of the flows in the three network traces estimated by COLATE.

6.2.1 Average Latency

We evaluated COLATE for both the scenario of only two observation points (where one sender sends and one receiver receives) and that of more than two observation points (where multiple senders send and multiple receivers receive). For the scenario with more than two observation points, we choose three observation points forming a triangle topology where everyone sends to and receives from everyone else. We choose three observation points and the triangle topology for the sake of simplicity as the number of senders and receivers does not affect the accuracy of COLATE. For a triangle topology, there are 6 unidirectional links. We used the largest 6 of the 41 trace files from ICSI data set, each trace file representing the traffic on one of the 6 links. This choice is arbitrary.

We performed our evaluation for three different accuracy requirements: low ($\alpha = 0.90$, $\beta = 0.10$), medium ($\alpha = 0.95$, $\beta = 0.05$), and high ($\alpha = 0.99$, $\beta = 0.01$). For each of these three accuracy requirements, we evaluated COLATE using three values of available RAM: small (M = 1MB), medium (M = 10MB), and large (M = 100MB). We obtained the values of $t_{f,X}^{min}$ and $t_{f,X}^{max}$ from simple measurement of the network traces. We calculated the values of the parameters b, m, n, and T using the method described in Section 5. For example, for M = 1MB, $\alpha = 0.95$, and $\beta = 0.05$, typical values of these parameters are $b = 19$, $m = 20$, $n = 455334$, and $T = 8 \times 10^{10}$.

Our results show that COLATE always achieves the required reliability. Figures 6(a), 6(b), and 6(c) show the CDFs of the observed values of β *i.e.*, $|\tilde{\mu}_f - \mu_f|/\mu_f$, for the average latency estimated by COLATE for the three traces under the scenario of one sender and one receiver using the low, medium, and high accuracy requirements, respectively. Figures 8(a), 8(b), and 8(c) show the CDFs of the observed values of β *i.e.*, $|\tilde{\mu}_f - \mu_f|/\mu_f$, for the average latency estimated by COLATE for the six links under the scenario of multiple senders and receivers using the low, medium, and high accuracy requirements, respectively. The horizontal line in each of these figures shows the required reliability. We see that every plot of CDF always crosses the horizontal line for an observed value of β that is smaller than the required confidence interval. This shows that COLATE always achieves the required reliability. Due to lack of space, we only show plots for M = 10MB. Observations from M = 1MB and M = 100MB are the same.

6.2.2 Standard Deviation

Our results show that the relative error in the standard deviation estimates of over 91% *flows is less than* 0.05 *with only 1000 virtual repetitions.* Relative error is defined as (`actual value` − `estimated value`)/`actual value`. Figure 7 plots the CDFs of the relative errors in standard deviation estimated by COLATE for each of the three traces.

Our results also show that the percentage of flows, for which the relative error is less than 0.05, *increases with the increase in the number of virtual repetitions.* Figure 9 plots this percentage versus the number of virtual repetitions for the three traces. With 10^5 iterations, this percentage reaches 98%. Although 10^5 iterations may take some time depending on the available computing power, it is not an issue as the estimation of standard deviation is an offline process and does not have to keep up with high line rates.

6.3 RAM and Storage Size

Our results show that COLATE uses less than 0.1 bit of permanent storage per packet. Figure 10 shows the bar graph of the number of bits per packet used by each of the three traces for all three values of M, when $\alpha = 0.99$ and $\beta = 0.01$. This small size of storage required per packet results in a very low frequency of transferring the counter vectors from RAM to permanent storage. For example, for ICSI network trace, COLATE transfers a counter vector to SSD every 24.6 hours when M = 1MB, $\alpha = 0.95$, and $\beta = 0.05$. Transferring 1MB of content from RAM to SSD once a day is trivial for modern devices. The number of bits per packet in permanent storage decreases with the increase in RAM size M, which confirms our analysis based on Figures 3 and 4. However, this decrease is hard to observe from Figure 10 because the difference is small. Nevertheless, this difference becomes significant for longer time durations (on the order of say days and weeks).

6.4 Comparison with RLI

Our results show that COLATE always achieves higher accuracy than RLI. RLI requires two inputs, namely the lower and upper limits of the Probe packet Injection Rate (PIR). The authors of RLI used the lower limit as 1 probe packet per 300 regular packets and the upper limit as 1 probe packet per 10 regular packets in [23]. We first evaluated RLI using this pair of PIR values. Because the accuracy of RLI increases as

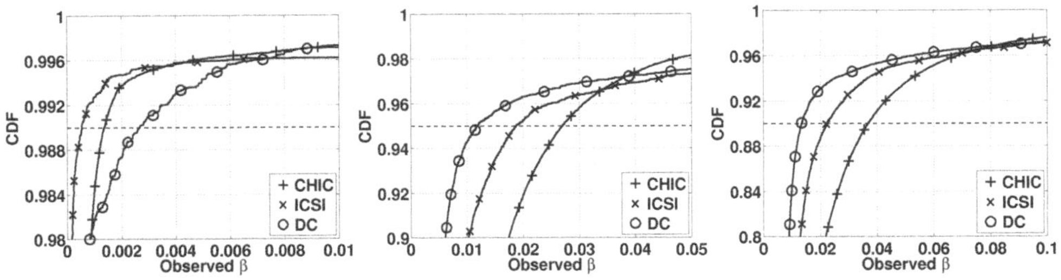

(a) $\alpha = 0.99, \beta = 0.01$ (b) $\alpha = 0.95, \beta = 0.05$ (c) $\alpha = 0.9, \beta = 0.1$

Figure 6: CDF of observed β in average estimate (one sender & one receiver)

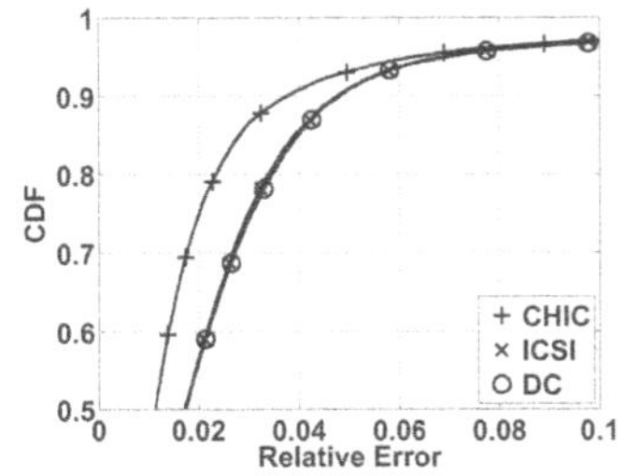

Figure 7: CDFs of relative errors in STD

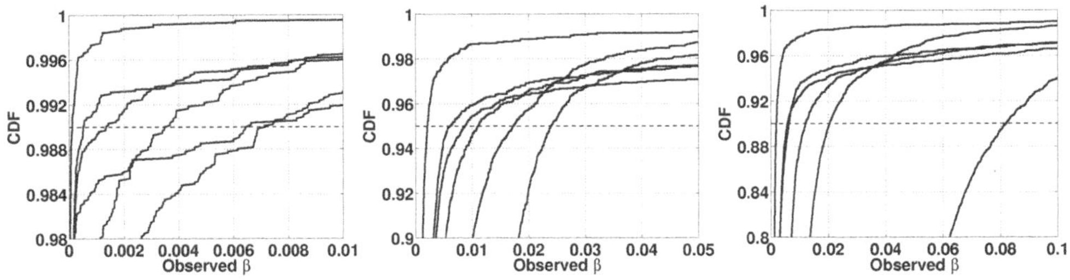

(a) $\alpha = 0.99, \beta = 0.01$ (b) $\alpha = 0.95, \beta = 0.05$ (c) $\alpha = 0.9, \beta = 0.1$

Figure 8: CDF of observed β in average estimate (multiple senders & receivers)

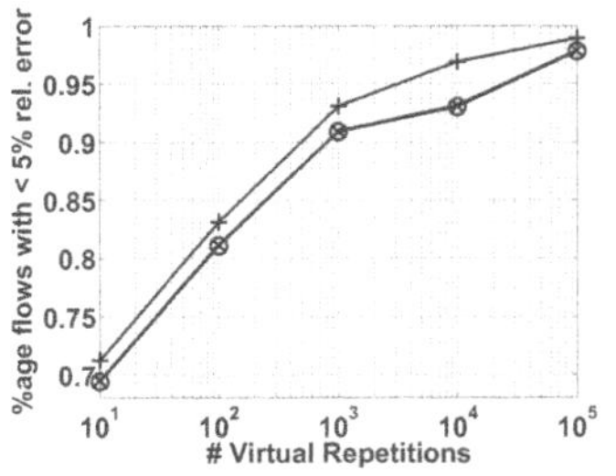

Figure 9: Relative error in STD vs. #repetitions

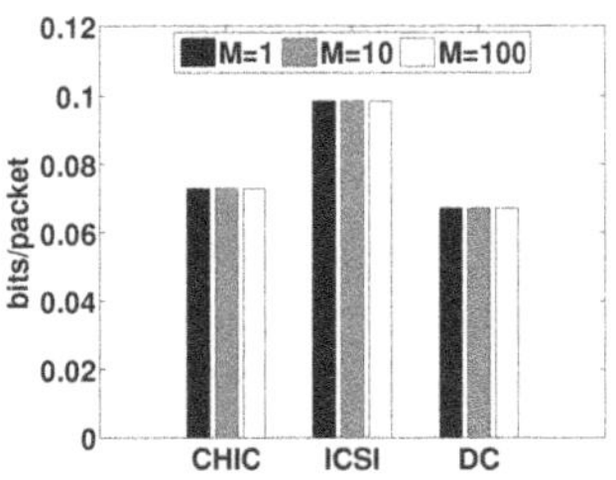

Figure 10: Storage bits per packet

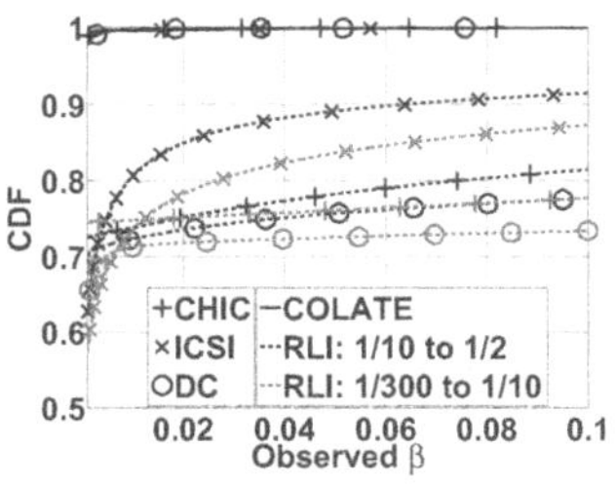

Figure 11: Comparison of delay estimates

PIR increases, to improve the estimation accuracy of RLI, although at the cost of larger bandwidth usage, we also evaluated RLI using much higher PIRs – 1 probe packet per 10 regular packets as the lower limit and 1 probe packet per 2 regular packets as the upper limit. Figure 11 plots the CDFs of the observed value of β in the average latency estimated by RLI in the three traces for these two configurations of PIRs. For comparison, we also plot the CDF of the observed value of β in the estimates obtained using COLATE for high accuracy requirement ($\alpha = 0.99, \beta = 0.01$). Note that the observed value of β is essentially the relative error in the estimated values of average latency. Figure 11 shows that the relative error of COLATE is much smaller than that of RLI. This relative error can be made arbitrarily small by specifying smaller values of β and larger values of α. This figure further shows that the relative error of RLI is smaller when PIR is larger. With the PIR proposed by the authors, on average, only 77% flows have relative error less than 5%. At this rate, on average, RLI inserts one probe packet after 21.66 regular packets. With our high PIR configuration, on average, only 81% flows have a relative error less than 5%, but at this rate, on average, RLI inserts one probe packet every 4.78 regular packets in the three traces. Table 3 shows the average number of regular packets after which RLI inserts a probe packet for each of the three traces. In contrast, COLATE does not insert any probe packet at the cost of a small amount of memory at observation points.

Table 3: Average number of regular packets after which RLI inserts a probe packet

Trace	# reg. pkts 1:300 to 1:10	# reg. pkts 1:10 to 1:2
CHIC	18.66	10.0
ICSI	17.19	2.97
DC	245.7	9.06

6.5 Comparison with Count-Min Sketch

Count-Min (CM) sketches can theoretically be used for latency measurement but practically, there is a fundamental limitation. Let t_{f_i} represent the sum of time stamps of all packets in flow f_i and let there be j flows in total whose time stamps need to be stored for latency measurements. We can use a CM-sketch to store time stamps of multiple flows and obtain the estimate $\tilde{t}_{f_i}$ of the sum of time stamps of any flow f_i as per the method described in [19]. The estimate $\tilde{t}_{f_i}$ obtained through CM-sketch can satisfy the condition $\tilde{t}_{f_i} \leq t_{f_i} + B \times \sum_{\forall j} t_{f_j}$ with probability α. This is problematic because we require the estimate to satisfy the condition $\tilde{t}_{f_i} \leq t_{f_i} + B \times t_{f_i}$ with probability α. Therefore, to achieve the required reliability using CM-sketch, we need to ensure that $\sum_{\forall j} t_{f_j} \leq t_{f_i}$, which is possible if and only if we do not add time stamps of any flow other than f_i to the CM-sketch. Consequently we need to maintain a CM-sketch for each flow, which results in large memory requirements. For example, for $\alpha = 0.95$ and $\beta = 0.05$, CM-sketch requires 165 counters per flow and 3 hash functions and 3 memory accesses per packet. Assuming the same counter size of 19 bits as for COLATE in this scenario, CM-sketch requires $165 \times 19 = 3135$ bits per flow. In comparison, COLATE requires 0.1 bit per packet. The memory requirement of CM-sketch matches that of COLATE only if each flow has at least 31350 packets, which is impractical as seen in Figure 5. The number of memory accesses and the number of hash functions per packet for CM-sktech are always greater than those for COLATE.

7. CONCLUSION

The key contribution of this paper is in proposing an accurate and efficient per-flow latency measurement scheme without packet probing and time stamping. The key novelty of this paper is that we purposely allow noise to be introduced in recording packet timing information for minimizing storage space and use statistical techniques to denoise the recorded information to obtain accurate latency estimates when latency of a target flow is queried. The key technical depth of this paper is in the mathematical development of the estimation theory that our scheme is based upon. Our theoretical analysis and experimental results show that our scheme always achieves the required reliability. Our scheme has a much smaller processing overhead in terms of number of hash computations and memory updates compared to existing schemes, which further require sending probe packets or attaching time stamps to every packet. Our scheme is scalable in that the amount of memory required at each observation point is only dependent on the number of packets and not on the number of sending and receiving observation points. The memory requirement is so low that a commodity storage device can store time stamps of several years worth of flows.

8. REFERENCES

[1] CAIDA passive network monitors. http://www.caida.org/data/realtime/passive/.

[2] The CAIDA UCSD anonymized 2011 internet traces. http://www.caida.org/data/passive/passive_2011_dataset.xml.

[3] Cedexis. http://www.cedexis.com/.

[4] Corvil claims to minimize network latency. http://www.pcworld.idg.com.au/article/196828/corvil_claims_minimize_network_latency/.

[5] *Fibre Channel Backbone - 5 (FC-BB-5) REV 2.*

[6] IEEE 1588 standard for a precision clock synchronization protocol for networked measurement and control systems.

[7] Sidera. http://www.sidera.net/.

[8] Singapore exchange (sgx) selects corvil for latency management. http://www.corvil.com/News/Press-Releases/Singapore-Exchange-(SGX)-Selects-Corvil-For-Latenc.aspx.

[9] Tokyo stock exchange select corvil. http://www.corvil.com/News/Press-Releases/Tokyo-Stock-Exchange-Select-Corvil.aspx.

[10] Turbobytes. http://www.turbobytes.com/.

[11] While london stock exchange selects corvil for low latency network monitoring and analysis solution. http://low-latency.com/article/\%E2\%80\%A6-while-london-stock-exchange-selects-corvil-low-latency-network-monitoring-and-analysis-sol.

[12] Z-Drive R4 and R5 PCIe SSD. http://lensfire.in/2012/01/ocz-launches-new-z-drive-r4-and-r5-pcie-ssd-ces-2012-2012/.

[13] HP expands high-performance computing offering with infiniband solutions from cisco. http://www.hp.com/hpinfo/newsroom/press/2007/070524xa.html, May 2007.

[14] N. Alon, Y. Matias, and M. Szegedy. The space complexity of approximating the frequency moments. In *Proc. ACM SoTC*, pages 20–29, 1996.

[15] T. Benson, A. Akella, and D. A. Maltz. Network traffic characteristics of data centers in the wild. In *Proc. ACM IMC*, pages 267–280, 2010.

[16] Y. Chen, D. Bindel, H. Song, and R. H. Katz. An algebraic approach to practical and scalable overlay network monitoring. In *Proc. ACM SIGCOMM*, pages 55–66, 2004.

[17] N. Duffield. Simple network performance tomography. In *Proc. ACM IMC*, pages 210–215, 2003.

[18] S. Floyd and V. Jacobson. Random early detection gateways for congestion avoidance. *IEEE/ACM Transactions on Networking*, 1(4):397–413, 1993.

[19] G. Cormode and S. Muthukrishnan. An improved data stream summary: the count-min sketch and its applications. *Journal of Algorithms*, 55(1):58–75, 2005.

[20] N. Hua, E. Norige, S. Kumar and B. Lynch. Non-crypto hardware hash functions for high performance networking ASICs. In *Proc. ACM/IEEE Symposium on Architectures for Networking and Communications Systems*, pages 156–166, 2011.

[21] R. R. Kompella, K. Levchenko, A. C. Snoeren, and G. Varghese. Every microsecond counts: tracking fine-grain latencies with a lossy difference aggregator. In *Proc. ACM SIGCOMM*, pages 255–266, 2009.

[22] A. Kumar, J. J. Xu, J. Wang, O. Spatschekt, and L. E. Lit. Space-code bloom filter for efficient per-flow traffic measurement. In *Proc. IEEE INFOCOM*, pages 1762–1773, 2004.

[23] M. Lee, N. Duffield, and R. R. Kompella. Not all microseconds are equal: fine-grained per-flow measurements with reference latency interpolation. In *Proc. ACM SIGCOMM*, pages 27–38, 2010.

[24] M. Lee, N. Duffield, and R. R. Kompella. A scalable architecture for maintaining packet latency measurements. In *Proc. ACM IMC*, pages 101–114, 2012.

[25] M. Lee, S. Goldberg, R. R. Kompella, and G. Varghese. Fine-grained latency and loss measurements in the presence of reordering. In *Proc. ACM SIGMETRICS*, pages 329–340, 2011.

[26] Y. Lu, A. Montanari, B. Prabhakar, S. Dharmapurikar, and A. Kabbani. Counter braids: a novel counter architecture for per-flow measurement. In *Proc. ACM SIGMETRICS*, pages 121–132, 2008.

[27] B. Lynch and S. Kumar. Smart memory for high performance network packet forwarding. In *Proc. Hot Chips Symposium*, 2010.

[28] R. Martin. Wall street's quest to process data at the speed of light. *Information Week*, 4(21), 2007.

[29] M. J. Miller. Bandwidth engine serial memory chip breaks 2 billion accesses/sec. In *Proc. Hot Chips Symposium*, 2011.

[30] R. Pang, M. Allman, M. Bennett, J. Lee, V. Paxson, and B. Tierney. A first look at modern enterprise traffic. In *Proc. ACM IMC*, pages 15–28, 2005.

[31] M. Ramakrishna, E. Fu, and E. Bahcekapili. Efficient hardware hashing functions for high performance computers. *IEEE Transactions on Computers*, 46(12):1378–1381, 1997.

A Measurement Study of Google Play

Nicolas Viennot
Computer Science Department
Columbia University
New York, NY, USA
nviennot@cs.columbia.edu

Edward Garcia
Computer Science Department
Columbia University
New York, NY, USA
ewg2115@columbia.edu

Jason Nieh
Computer Science Department
Columbia University
New York, NY, USA
nieh@cs.columbia.edu

ABSTRACT

Although millions of users download and use third-party Android applications from the Google Play store, little information is known on an aggregated level about these applications. We have built PLAYDRONE, the first scalable Google Play store crawler, and used it to index and analyze over 1,100,000 applications in the Google Play store on a daily basis, the largest such index of Android applications. PLAYDRONE leverages various hacking techniques to circumvent Google's roadblocks for indexing Google Play store content, and makes proprietary application sources available, including source code for over 880,000 free applications. We demonstrate the usefulness of PLAYDRONE in decompiling and analyzing application content by exploring four previously unaddressed issues: the characterization of Google Play application content at large scale and its evolution over time, library usage in applications and its impact on application portability, duplicative application content in Google Play, and the ineffectiveness of OAuth and related service authentication mechanisms resulting in malicious users being able to easily gain unauthorized access to user data and resources on Amazon Web Services and Facebook.

Categories and Subject Descriptors

C.2.4 [**Computer-Communication Networks**]: Distributed Systems; C.4 [**Performance of Systems**]: Measurement techniques; C.5.3 [**Computer System Implementation**]: Microcomputers–Portable devices; H.3.3 [**Information Storage and Retrieval**]: Information Search and Retrieval–Information filtering; J.7 [**Computers in Other Systems**]: Consumer products; K.6.2 [**Management of Computing and Information Systems**]: Installation Management–Performance and usage measurement; K.6.5 [**Management of Computing and Information Systems**]: Security and Protection–Authentication

SIGMETRICS'14, June 16–20, 2014, Austin, Texas, USA.

ACM 978-1-4503-2789-3/14/06 ...$15.00.
http://dx.doi.org/10.1145/2591971.2592003.

Keywords

Android; Authentication; Clone Detection; Decompilation; Google Play; Mobile Computing; OAuth; Security;

1. INTRODUCTION

The Google Play store allows users to download and use a vast amount of third-party applications. Millions of users register personal information both with Google and third-party services to download and use these applications on their personal Android phones and tablets. Hundreds of thousands of developers upload content to the Google Play store and millions of users download the content despite the fact that the content is largely unchecked.

However, little is known at an aggregate level about the hundreds of thousands of applications available in the Google Play store. This is due in large part to the lack of scalable tools available for discovering and analyzing Android applications in the Google Play store. Application source code is also only available to the respective third-party developers. Not even Google has access to the source code, as applications are submitted directly as compressed binary packages by application developers to Google Play. Furthermore, Google imposes various mechanisms to prevent others from crawling and indexing Google Play store content. For example, discovery of applications in the Google Play store is limited as only the first 500 applications belonging to any category or matching any search term can be found by browsing the store's web interface. Some applications also require specific hardware features or other existing applications and libraries to be available on the end-user device. Such applications are only available if the Google Play interface is accessed with an account registered on a device with the prerequisites available.

To explore Google Play content, we have created PLAYDRONE, the first scalable Google Play store crawler and application analysis framework. PLAYDRONE uses four key techniques. First, PLAYDRONE leverages common hacking techniques to easily circumvent security measures that Google uses to prevent indexing Google Play store content. These techniques include simple dictionary-based attacks for discovering applications, and decompiling and rebuilding the Google Play Android client to use insecure communication protocols to communicate with the Google Play servers to capture, understand, and reproduce the necessary protocols. Second, PLAYDRONE leverages higher-level languages and frameworks to provide highly concurrent, distributed processing with modest implementation effort. PLAYDRONE is written in Ruby and uses the Sidekiq [31] asynchronous processing framework and the Redis [33] key-value store. Its performance scales easily by simply adding servers to the cluster, enabling PLAYDRONE to efficiently crawl the Google Play store on a daily basis even as its content continues to grow. Third, PLAYDRONE stores each application's metadata and decompiled sources in a Git repository. This provides a simple versioning system for PLAYDRONE to track and manage multiple versions of each application and analyze how Google Play store content evolves over time. Finally, PLAYDRONE leverages the Elasticsearch [19] distributed real-time search and analytics engine using an indexing schema based on the Google Play store API to make it easy to analyze and explore the Google Play store metadata and content.

We have used PLAYDRONE to crawl the Google Play store and analyze over 1,100,000 Android applications, including decompiling the source code for over 880,000 free Android applications and analyzing over 100 billion lines of decompiled code. We demonstrate the usefulness of PLAYDRONE for analyzing application content by exploring four previously unaddressed issues in understanding Android applications. First, we provide a characterization of Google Play application content at scale. We discuss the relationship between application ratings and download frequency, discuss how applications are categorized in Google Play and how the choice of self-categorization can affect application visibility. We show how Google Play store content evolves over time, providing a measure of how often applications are released, updated, and removed. We also show that a small percentage of free applications account for almost all downloads.

Second, we perform the first large-scale source code analysis of library usage in Android applications. We show how library usage differs between popular and unpopular applications, including that native libraries are heavily used among the most popular applications. As a result, Android systems which only support Java-based applications are inadequate to support the most widely-used Android applications [12, 40]. We show that over half of the free Android applications use advertising libraries and discuss the size of the different advertising networks. We also show that cross-platform frameworks and application generators make up a very small fraction of the overall Google Play application content.

Third, we describe a new simple approach for efficiently detecting similar Android applications in the Google Play store. We use the structure of Android applications to analyze similarity by considering application assets and resources rather than requiring detailed source code analysis. This provides a more scalable approach than code analysis approaches with comparable results. Our results show that roughly 25% of Google Play store application content is duplicative, including various types of spam, application rebranding, and application cloning.

Finally, we present the first study of secret authentication key usage and its problems in Android applications. We show that developers often store secret authentication keys in their Android applications without realizing their credentials are easily compromised through decompilation. These secrets are publicly available in Google Play. We show these keys can be used by malicious users to steal server resources or user data available through services such as Amazon Web Services (AWS) or Facebook. Unlike compromised applications that only affect users who download and run them, these server vulnerabilities affect users without even running the applications. Our results demonstrate developer confusion may subvert the effectiveness of the widely used OAuth open source standard for authentication. We notified and worked with service providers to prevent these attacks, including providing Google with code to help them scan for secret keys in applications as part of the Google Play application publication process to protect users and developers.

This rest of this paper is organized as follows. Section 2 describes how PLAYDRONE intefaces with the Google Play API. Section 3 describes the PLAYDRONE crawler architecture. and Section 4 measures its scalable performance. Section 5 characterizes Android applications in Google Play. Section 6 discusses library usage in Android applications. Section 7 describes our approach for efficiently detecting similar Android applications and our measurements of similarity among applications in Google Play. Section 8 presents a study of secret authentication key usage and its problems in Android applications. Section 9 discusses related work. Finally, we present some concluding remarks.

2. INTERFACING WITH GOOGLE PLAY

To crawl the Google Play store, PLAYDRONE needs to communicate with the Google Play store, which requires use of a Google account for all the necessary functionality. Using only a few Google accounts to crawl the entire store might risk having the accounts disabled by Google, so we decided to harvest a large number of Google accounts. To do this quickly and efficiently, we had to address two problems. First, registering for a Google account requires solving CAPTCHAs. Second, registering for a Google account requires phone verification when the same IP attempts to register more than five accounts on a given day.

We addressed both issues by using a crowdsourcing Internet marketplace service to cheaply use other human users to register for Google accounts from a diverse set of IPs. Any such service could be used, including dedicated CAPTCHA solver services such as Death by Captcha [15]. We used Amazon's Mechanical Turk [1] for this purpose and deployed a website, `http://playdrone.io`, for users to submit the registered Google account information back to us. Mechanical Turk is a service where registered users are paid small dollar amounts to carry out trivial manual jobs. We posted a task description on Mechanical Turk with the following simple instructions: (1) Start your browser in incognito/guest mode. (2) Go on `https://accounts.google.com/SignUp`. (3) Fill out the requested information except "Mobile phone" and "Current email address" as they are not necessary. (4) Go to `http://playdrone.io/accounts/new` and enter the email and password of the account you created. (5) Answer with the returned confirmation code. The return confirmation code allows the user to be paid for the work. Before the code is given, `playdrone.io` validates the submitted Google account information to ensure that it is not duplicative and can authenticate with Google services. Mechanical Turk prevents users from carrying out the same task twice, so four copies of the task were created to benefit from dedicated users. We paid 10 cents per account, resulting in the creation of more than 500 Google accounts in just a few hours for a little more than $50. Note that Google accounts can be found on the black market for a similar price.

Google exposes an internal, non-documented API to its Android Play clients to access the store and download applications over the air. PLAYDRONE replicates the behavior of legitimate Android Play clients, each using a previously harvested Google account associated with Galaxy Nexus device profiles. PlayDrone interacts with Google Play servers through four different APIs. The first one is the *checkin* API to associate a Google account with an Android device, necessary to access the three other Google Play APIs. Based on the device used, Google Play may make available a different set of applications for the device. For example, some applications may only be available to devices in certain geographic locations. The *search*, *details*, and *purchase* APIs are used to discover applications, fetch application details, and retrieve binary download links, respectively. We were fortunately able to leverage additional information from non-Google sources [34, 24] to implement most of the APIs.

However, because of the lack of documentation and source code for the checkin API and our desire to make use of multiple Google accounts efficiently, we had to reverse engineer that API ourselves. Google makes it difficult to derive the checkin API by ensuring that communications between the Google Play client and servers are over SSL, preventing the capture of the wire protocol. However, since the Google Play client and related service applications are compiled to Dalvik bytecode, they were straightforward to disassemble with baksmali [26]. We changed all `https` strings to `http` ones and recompiled the client to send and receive unencrypted communications via an SSL proxy to the Google Play servers. This man-in-the-middle attack allowed the capture of a real device registration over the wire and the ability to reproduce it to reverse engineer the checkin API. Based on this API, we created a tool to register a fake Android device given an email password pair corresponding to a Google account. During the registration process, device capabilities and metadata need to be sent to the Google servers, including more than 50 data fields such as the mobile network provider, an IMEI number, the WiFi MAC address, and OpenGL capabilities. We extracted this information from a legitimate T-Mobile Galaxy Nexus device; all of our search results are therefore restricted to what would be accessible on such a device. The tool then uses this information, but randomly generates valid IMEI and MAC addresses to prevent device blacklisting by Google. A similar approach could be used for reverse engineering the other APIs if needed.

3. CRAWLER ARCHITECTURE

Given a set of Google accounts and the APIs for communicating with the Google Play servers, the PlayDrone crawler discovers and downloads Android applications with their metadata. Figure 1 shows the six components of the PlayDrone crawler architecture: a Sidekiq job scheduler for distributing work to multiple machines, a Redis key-value store to store the jobs, an Amazon EC2 proxy, Git version control repositories, an Elasticsearch distributed search and analytics engine, and an Nginx web server frontend. These components work together to provide four key benefits. First, since crawling and analyzing the evolution of Google Play on a daily basis requires a fair amount of CPU power and storage space, PlayDrone is designed using a higher-level language that makes it simple to build a powerful distributed system that scales out by just adding more servers. PlayDrone is written in Ruby, which provides an excellent higher-level language ecosystem that is simple to

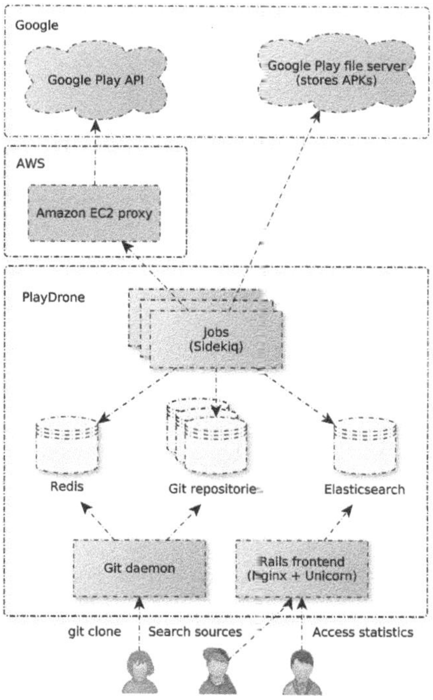

Figure 1: PlayDrone crawler architecture.

use and allows PlayDrone to leverage existing, well-tested mechanisms such as Sidekiq, Redis, and Elasticsearch to further simplify its implementation. Second, to circumvent attempts by Google to limit crawling of the Google Play store, PlayDrone uses various techniques to hide its activities, including using multiple Google accounts, rate limiting the number of requests for each account, and proxying requests through a third-party service provider. Third, to analyze the behavior of the Google Play store and its applications over time, PlayDrone leverages Git to store and track multiple versions of each Android application and metadata to allow the system to analyze how applications evolve as they are updated from one version to another. Finally, PlayDrone is designed with an easy-to-use web interface supported by Nginx and Elasticsearch to make it simple to search and perform various forms of analysis on the Android applications and their metadata. For example, Figure 2 shows the use of PlayDrone to identify how the Gmail application code has been updated.

PlayDrone uses the Redis key-value store [33] and the Sidekiq background processing framework [31] to efficiently implement master-slave distributed computing. Sidekiq assigns jobs to different slave machines. PlayDrone uses two Sidekiq job queues, one for discovering Android applications in Google Play, and the other for downloading and processing applications. Redis runs on a master machine to store the job queues and track the use of Google accounts, which applications need to be processed, and what machines have been assigned to process which applications. Although only a single master machine is used, PlayDrone leverages Redis very efficiently so that the architecture can scale out to support hundreds of slave worker machines.

Discovering applications in Google Play is not straightforward because Google does not provide any public list of all the available applications in Google Play and limits

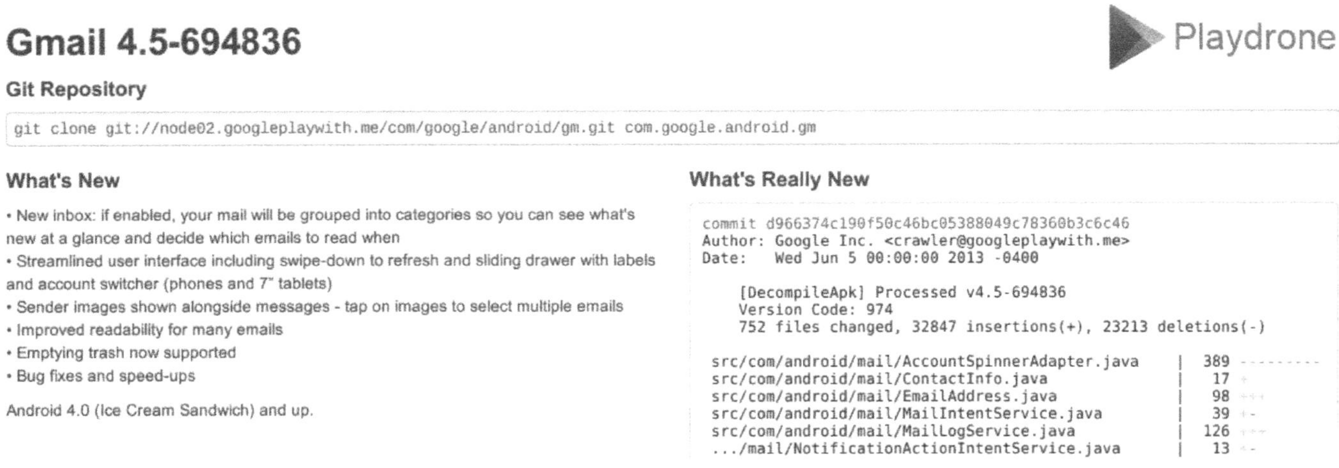

Figure 2: PLAYDRONE's web interface showing the Gmail application and its Git diff.

the search results returned from querying Google Play to no more than 500 applications. To overcome these problems, PLAYDRONE uses a dictionary attack method involving roughly a million words as search terms to search Google Play to find applications. To cover a broad range, words are used from multiple languages, including English, German, French, Spanish, Swahili, Japanese, Italian, Danish and Swedish. A Sidekiq job is created for each search term, making the discovery queue roughly a million jobs in length. For each search job, PLAYDRONE sends a search request to Google Play through its proxy. Because each search request is a separate job, requests that need to be retried are isolated in the event of a network issue or other problem. It is interesting to note that the Google Play API does not return any search results when hit directly from the PLAYDRONE servers in Canada, but proxying the connection through an Amazon EC2 public IP in North Virginia causes the API to successfully return results. We do not know if the IPs we are using are banned, or if the filtering is based on IP geolocation, but this anecdotal evidence demonstrates the benefit of our proxy approach. For each search request, Google Play returns a list of applications in batches of 20 applications, with a link to the next page if there are more results to be fetched; the pagination stops at 500 results. Each application in the list includes a link to a details page for the application, which provides a description of the application. When PLAYDRONE finds an application that it has not seen before, it stores the application unique identifier in Redis, and adds the application to the Sidekiq processing queue to be downloaded.

When a new application identifier is discovered, PLAYDRONE downloads and processes the application. PLAYDRONE uses Redis to atomically assign the application to a machine for processing and instantiates a Git repository for the application on the assigned machine. PLAYDRONE fetches the application's details page, from which it extracts all of the application's metadata and downloads and stores the application binary package (APK) into its Git repository. Application metadata includes a list of related applications, which PLAYDRONE uses to discover applications not identified via the dictionary-based method. Only free application APKs are downloaded to avoid the costly expense of downloading all paid applications. Future processing of the application is done on the machine where its Git repository resides. This simple distribution mechanism takes better advantage of file locality as opposed to relying on a distributed file system, which would result in much worse file system performance using Git and would add unnecessary complexity to the system.

PLAYDRONE provides a plugin architecture to allow a user of the system to write plugin middleware to perform various forms of processing and analysis on applications once they have been downloaded. For example, we wrote a plugin for decompiling APKs into readable Java sources to enable easier comprehension of application behavior. The decompile plugin uses apktool [35] to deflate the XML files and dex2jar [17] with a command-line version of JD-Core [37] for Java decompilation. The resulting Java sources are quite readable and complete, though not directly suitable to recompile back into an APK. As another example, we wrote a plugin for parsing the `./res/values/public.xml` file to extract resource names and compute the MD5 hashes of asset and resource files in the application to facilitate detection of similar applications as discussed in Section 7.

PLAYDRONE stores the raw application metadata and decompiled sources from crawling the Google Play store in its respective Git repositories, with each commit tagged with the crawl date or the application version when applicable. PLAYDRONE stores source code and application metadata in Elasticsearch, a distributed search and analytics engine [19]. Elasticsearch has a simple web interface, allowing fast searching of the data and various forms of simple analysis before writing a middleware plugin to perform more complete analysis of the data. A different index is used for each day of metadata from the Google Play store, making it possible to visualize the evolution of the Google Play store. For space reasons, only the most recent decompiled sources are indexed in Elasticsearch; older versions are stored in the respective Git repositories. Users can reindex data in Elasticsearch from the Git repositories as they store all the raw data collected from Google Play.

4. CRAWLER PERFORMANCE

Because of the use of the Ruby ecosystem, the effort to build and deploy PLAYDRONE was fairly low. The entire application was less than 2000 lines of Ruby and HTML. As a (unfair) comparison, GNU `cat` is 550 lines of code. PLAYDRONE deployment is also quite simple and the sys-

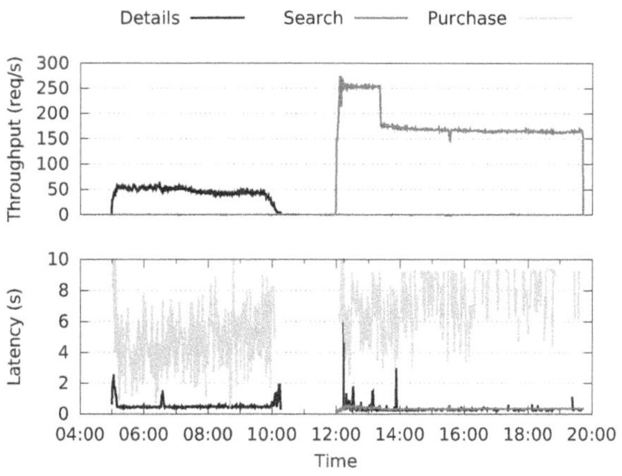

Figure 3: A typical daily crawl from May 21, 2013 showing the throughput and latency of the Google Play API.

tem setup is entirely automated with Chef [10] and Capistrano [9], which are tools written in Ruby. The amount of code we had to write to manage the entire system was less than 550 lines of code, including configuration file templates (e.g. upstart). PLAYDRONE is simple enough to be understood and used by others, and yet can provide powerful insights into Google Play. We have made PLAYDRONE source code available on GitHub [38] for others to use.

We deployed PLAYDRONE on ten servers on April 24, 2013, each with Intel Xeon E3 turbo boosted at 3.8Ghz, 32GB of RAM, and 2x2TB drives. The initial crawling took around two days, limited by CPU due to the source decompilation. Once the initial crawling was complete on April 26, 2013, the total size occupied by the Git repositories was 3.9TB with 790,000 applications, an average of about 5MB per application. Subsequently, crawling Google Play for new applications and application updates as well as identifying deleted applications took only several hours, enabling PLAYDRONE to crawl the entire Google Play store on a daily basis. Note that subsequent crawls after the initial crawl operate in exactly the same manner as the initial crawl, but PLAYDRONE does not need to download and decompile APKs for applications that have not changed. After two months of crawling, the total size of the compacted Git repositories reached 5.3TB with roughly 960,000 applications, among which 70,000 applications were removed from the Google Play store but archived by PLAYDRONE. We decommissioned the crawler on June 22, 2013 to save resources. In November 2013, we redeployed the crawler to validate that our crawling method was still valid and analyze the evolution of the Google Play store five months later.

Figure 3 shows the throughput and latency of the Google API during a daily crawl using PLAYDRONE. A daily crawl updates all the metadata of each known application, and discovers and downloads new applications. From 05:00 to 10:00, PLAYDRONE updates the metadata of all known applications in the system. The *Details* API endpoint is called once for each application. The response from Google servers includes various metadata including the current number of downloads, the current version of the application, and a list of related applications. Because all application metadata is stored in Git, PLAYDRONE bottlenecks at 50 requests per second (req/s) due to disk I/O. Later in the afternoon from 12:00 to 20:00, PLAYDRONE performs a dictionary search to

Number of applications

	June 22, 2013	**November 30, 2013**
Free apps	691,517	884,217 (+28%)
Paid apps	195,703	223,259 (+14%)
All apps	887,220	1,107,476 (+25%)

Cumulative download counts (min-max)

	June 22, 2013	**November 30, 2013**
Free apps	22G-85G	31G-116G (+37%)
Paid apps	111M-428M	126M-488M (+14%)
All apps	23G-85G	31G-117G (+37%)

Table 1: Number of applications and cumulative download counts on June 22, 2013 and November 30, 2013.

discover additional applications. During the first 90 minutes, the *Search* API is called at full capacity, artificially rate limited to 250 req/s to avoid getting our Google accounts flagged; we empirically measured the rate limit enforced by Google at 1000 req/min per account. The throughput reaches maximum capacity because many words do not generate any results and the average API response is small to parse. After 90 minutes, the response size gets larger and PLAYDRONE bottlenecks on CPU, parsing these lengthy responses. When the *Details* API returns with a new version of the application that PLAYDRONE has not previously downloaded, the *Purchase* API endpoint is called to retrieve the download link, and proceed to downloading the APK.

Table 1 shows the number of applications PLAYDRONE discovered and downloaded from Google Play. By June 22, 2013, we indexed 887,220 applications. By November 30, 2013, we indexed 1,107,476 applications, which is to the best of our knowledge the most extensive coverage of the Google Play store. Table 1 also shows cumulative download counts based on the download count ranges reported by Google Play. From June to November, The Google Play store grew by 25% in the number of applications, and 37% in download counts. Based on the last official report from Google indicating Google Play having 1 million applications as of July 24, 2013 [39] and the rate of growth of Google Play content shown in Figure 4, we estimate that our method covers over 90% of the Google Play applications with a Galaxy Nexus on T-Mobile profile. To increase coverage, we could check in other types of Android devices to fetch, for example, applications that are restricted to tablets, or applications reserved for a specific mobile carrier. Unless otherwise indicated, the analysis of Google Play in the remainder of this paper focuses on the June 22, 2013 data collection.

5. GOOGLE PLAY CHARACTERISTICS

Using PLAYDRONE, we present aggregated characteristics of Android applications based on a comprehensive index of Google Play application sources and metadata. Table 2 shows the list of 887,220 applications available in the Google Play store indexed by PLAYDRONE, separated into their respective categories and whether they are free or paid. Game applications are listed and categorized separately since they are shown in a separate top-level directory in Google Play. Categories are listed from most to least number of applications, and each application can only belong to one category in Google Play. Overall, there are more than 3.5 times as many free applications as paid applications. The aggregate download counts of paid applications accounts for only 0.05% of total downloads from the store as shown in Table 1.

Applications			
Category	**Free apps**	**Paid apps**	**Total apps**
Personalization	59,477	33,682	93,159
Entertainment	72,685	16,772	89,457
Education	41,115	16,985	58,100
Lifestyle	48,763	11,269	60,032
Tools	47,608	12,092	59,700
Books & Reference	34,990	22,703	57,693
Business	41,701	2,675	44,376
Travel & Local	28,473	13,379	41,852
Music & Audio	33,221	4,550	37,771
Sports	19,906	4,889	24,795
Productivity	18,575	5,557	24,132
Health & Fitness	18,078	5,707	23,785
News & Magazines	21,919	1,260	23,179
Social	17,548	1,858	19,406
Finance	16,731	2,191	18,922
Communication	14,725	2,999	17,724
Media & Video	15,014	2,438	17,452
Shopping	11,547	678	12,225
Photography	8,407	2,331	10,738
Medical	7,137	3,405	10,542
Transportation	8,099	1,340	9,439
Comics	3,798	1,721	5,519
Libraries & Demo	3,760	256	4,016
Weather	2,810	563	3,373
Total	596,087	171,300	767,387
Games			
Category	**Free apps**	**Paid apps**	**Total apps**
Brain	36,533	8,938	45,471
Casual	24,370	5,901	30,271
Arcade	22,517	6,309	28,826
Cards	5,589	1,619	7,208
Sports Games	3,821	1,167	4,988
Racing	2,600	469	3,069
Total	95,430	24,403	119,833
Grand Total	691,517	195,703	887,220

Table 2: Applications in Google Play as of June 22, 2013.

We also measured that the top 10% of most downloaded applications accounts for over 96% of the total downloads, and the top 1% of most downloaded applications accounts for over 78% of the total downloads as of June 22, 2013. As of November 30, 2013, the top 1% of most downloaded applications accounts for over 81% of the total downloads. This suggests that a decreasing number of applications accounts for almost all application usage in Google Play, indicating the increasing difficulty of releasing a popular application.

Other than games, personalization, a somewhat vague category name, represents the largest category of applications, with over 90,000 applications. To find out more about this category, we ranked the most recurring terms in the titles and descriptions of applications, discarding common nondescriptive words such as not, the, can, it, or, etc. The top three words among personalization applications were *wallpaper*, *please*, and *like*, accounting for 64,341 (69%), 35,953 (39%), and 26,563 (29%) applications, respectively. To compare with other categories, the proportions of applications that contain these words across the rest of Google Play were 4%, 12% and 12%, respectively. This suggests that the personalization category may be infected with many useless applications that users would consider as spam. This result also suggests that wallpapers deserve their own category.

The problems with the personalization category are just one of the problems with the application categorization used by Google Play. Category names are confusing and overlapping. Since an application can only belong to one category, the social and photography categories are mutually exclusive, so a user browsing the latter category will find no sign of Instagram, arguably the most popular photo sharing application. Similarly, business and productivity applications are categorized separately, health and fitness applications cannot correspond to lifestyle ones, and music and audio applications must be categorized separately from media and video applications. Given the large differences in the number of applications in each category and the already confusing category names, Table 2 may be useful to developers in deciding which category to use for applications to increase their visibility by using a less populated category.

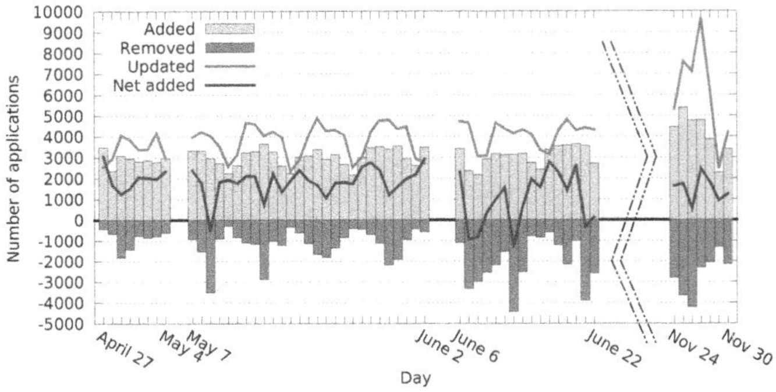

Figure 4: Evolution of Google Play from April 26, 2013 to November 30, 2013. Missing bars represents lack of crawling.

Figure 4 shows how the content of Google Play evolves over time in terms of how often applications are released, updated, and removed from Google Play. Google removes applications that do not comply with their terms and conditions. On most days, more applications are added than removed, and more applications are updated than added. During the May-June 2013 period, roughly 3000 new applications arrived daily on Google Play. This is far more than the Top New listing in Google Play, which is limited to 500 applications and provides an incomplete picture of new application content in Google Play. The November 2013 crawl shows a 30% increase in application release and update rate. The Google Play store is growing even faster than earlier in the year, motivating the need for automated auditing and quality control solutions.

Figure 5 shows a distribution of the average rating versus download count for applications in Google Play. Download counts are shown in bucketed ranges provided by Google Play; exact download counts are not available. Free and paid applications are shown separately. There are no paid applications with more than 5 million downloads. Users can rate an application with stars from 1 to 5, 5 being the highest possible rating, and these ratings are aggregated by Google Play per application to compute an overall average rating for each application. For example, Figure 5 shows that for applications with less than 500 downloads, there are applications with an overall rating as low as 1, applications with an overall rating as high as 5, and on average, paid applications have an overall rating of 4 with free applications having an overall rating of greater than 4. One might expect that applications with higher ratings would have higher download counts, but in fact the average of the overall ratings across all applications in any bucket of download counts was between 4 and 4.5. What did change was that as the download

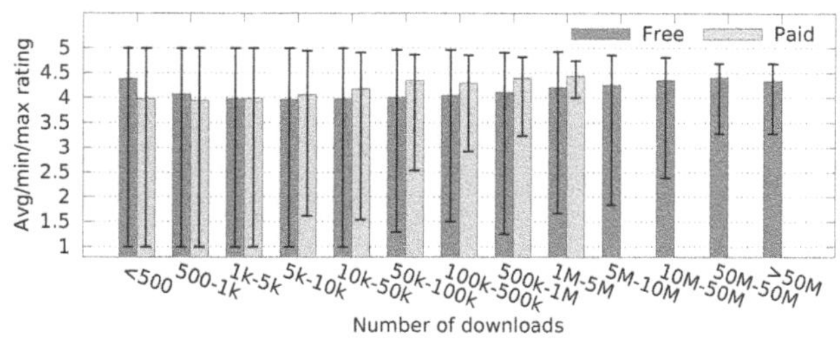

Figure 5: Ratings vs download counts for free/paid applications on June 22, 2013.

counts increased, the rating for the lowest rated application in a given download count bucket generally increased. For example, there are free applications with only 1 star overall ratings with less than 50 thousand downloads, but there are no applications with less than a 2.5 star overall rating with 10 million or more downloads. This increase in the minimum overall rating as the download count increases is even more pronounced for paid applications. Surprisingly though, there are still quite a few applications with very low ratings despite their high download counts.

Table 3 shows the top ten applications with the worse and best ratings which have at least a million downloads. The ten worst rated list shows three applications that come preinstalled, namely the T-Mobile one, the Motorola fitness watch application, and the HRS hotel application preinstalled on some HTC phones. Another interesting case is the Outlook.com application that advertises in its description to be the official Microsoft application for outlook.com. The developer, "Microsoft + SEVEN", has only one application released under his account, while the official Microsoft account, "Microsoft Corporation", has 18 applications. We were surprised that Microsoft hired SEVEN to develop their outlook.com application and did not release it under the official Microsoft account as releasing official applications under other accounts trains users to be more vulnerable to phishing attacks. The worst rated application with at least one million downloads is DroidScale, which gives the users the ability to turn their phones into a scale, enabling them to weight regular household objects. We decompiled the sources, to find that the weight is simply measured with `Random.nextDouble()`, a randomly generated number. An ad-free version of the application is even offered for $0.99 that has 1000-5000 downloads.

The top ten best rated list shows half of the applications on the list being related to the Holy Quran. Such high ratings can be explained by the target audience that prefers to rate the content rather than the application. For example, reading comments in the TvQuran application reveals unhappy users having sound issues or readability issues while still giving 5 stars. User comments and ratings are publicly available through Google+, so certain users may not be comfortable putting a bad rating on a Holy Quran application. We also observe that some applications such as Slots Deluxe or Cool Wallpapers have 10 times more ratings count than other applications in the same download counts bucket. While there might be some aggressive incentive from the application telling the user to rate the application, it is hard to draw any conclusions as Google does not give exact download counts.

Application	Downloads	# Ratings	Rating
TvQuran	1M-5M	13,675	4.93
Билеты ПДД 2013 РФ	1M-5M	15,738	4.92
Holy Quran Maher Moagely	1M-5M	6,341	4.91
Slots Deluxe - Slot Machines	1M-5M	108,431	4.90
[illegible]	1M-5M	19,567	4.89
Alchemy Classic HD	1M-5M	37,706	4.89
Zombies...OMG!	1M-5M	46,236	4.89
Quran - [illegible]	1M-5M	17,666	4.89
My Prayer - [illegible]	1M-5M	33,893	4.88
Cool Wallpapers HD	1M-5M	210,320	4.87
GoToMeeting	1M-5M	4,696	2.41
Outlook.com	10M-50M	78,049	2.39
TAMAGO hd	1M-5M	5,706	2.31
MOTOACTV	1M-5M	4,191	2.30
Screen Capture - No Rooting	1M-5M	2,963	2.28
Wet Lesbian	1M-5M	2,865	2.23
Ameba	1M-5M	35,933	2.21
HRS App	1M-5M	5,778	1.99
T-Mobile More For Me	5M-10M	1,763	1.84
DroidScale	1M-5M	5,450	1.67

Table 3: Top 10 of the best and worse rated applications with at least 1 million downloads on June 22, 2013.

6. APPLICATION LIBRARY USAGE

Using PLAYDRONE to decompile applications, we present the first large-scale source code analysis of library usage in Android applications. One important question regarding library usage is how often native libraries are used in the context of Android's Java applications to improve their user experience. A native library contains code compiled directly for ARM and is invoked from the Java part of the application to improve performance or access low-level system calls. Figure 6 shows the number and percentage of Android applications that use native libraries versus download counts. For non-popular applications, those with less than 50,000 downloads, 14% of them on average have at least one native library. However, for popular applications, native library usage increases significantly such that among applications with more than 50 million downloads, the vast majority of them, 70% of them on average, have at least one native library. For example, Instagram uses seven different native libraries to optimize image processing and encoding performance, and Facebook uses nine different native libraries to access low-level system functionality, such as getting and setting the file descriptors limit of the current process.

As an application rises in popularity, developers are perhaps more willing to spend time and money to use native libraries to optimize the user experience of the application. Although there are efforts to run Android on non-ARM platforms for offloading and other reasons [12, 40], these systems rely on Java bytecode portability and do not support native library execution. Our results suggest that such approaches are problematic in that they will be unable to run the most popular Android applications. Despite Java's portability, these results indicate that the wide use of native libraries in popular Android applications may increasingly tie Android to ARM-based systems.

Table 4 shows the breakdown of the most popular Java libraries used among free applications, separated into non-popular (<50k downloads) and popular applications (≥50k downloads). Applications may use more than one library, so the sum of the percentages may exceed 100%. The breakdown shows that ad libraries are most widely used, with al-

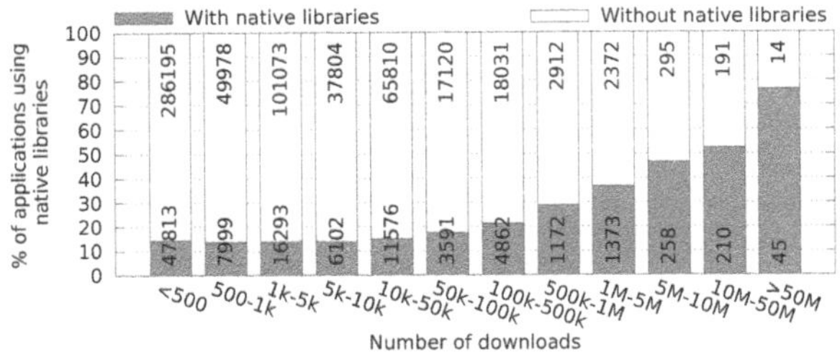

Figure 6: Native libraries usage compared to application popularity on June 22, 2013.

most half of the non-popular applications using ad libraries while almost two-thirds of the popular applications use ad libraries. Ad libraries are most likely more common in popular free applications because there is a greater focus on monetization for successful applications than many non-popular free applications. Google is the most popular advertising platform, with almost half of the popular applications using Google Ads. Among applications that use ad libraries, Google dominates with roughly 75% market share. This general trend of increased monetization of popular applications and Google's dominant role is also seen for billing libraries used for in-app purchases. Other than advertising, social libraries are the next most popular with almost 15% of free applications using those libraries. The official Facebook SDK is the most widely used, followed by Twitter4J, an unofficial Twitter library.

Table 4 also shows the percentage of free applications built using cross-platform frameworks or application generators. Almost 15% of non-popular applications are built using these frameworks and generators, but only about 3% of popular applications use these frameworks and generators. Beginning developers may find it useful to use application generators to simplifying development, or use cross-platform frameworks to be able to deploy an application on both Android and iOS platforms. However, the measurements suggest that these generators and frameworks most likely lack the necessary functionality and degree of control for building more sophisticated applications with richer user experiences that are more likely to become popular and widely used.

7. SIMILAR APPLICATIONS

Leveraging PLAYDRONE, we introduce a simple approach to identify similar applications in Google Play for the purposes of detecting duplicative content and application clones. Similar applications are those that appear to share the same source code origin, share common design and layout patterns, and offer comparable application level experiences to the end user. Previous studies have shown Android application clones to be vectors in spreading malware [43] as well as instruments to divert users and advertising revenues from legitimate applications [23]. While prior research has focused on code analysis to identify similar applications, this can be problematic for obfuscated code or applications where the core logic is written in multiple programming languages, such as in PhoneGap and Adobe Air applications. Additionally, code analysis methods are often too computationally expensive to scale to analyze all of Google Play.

Our scalable approach comes from a simple observation: humans can typically just look at the screenshots of applications to determine if applications are similar. Humans recognize patterns by looking at the UI layouts or the similarity of images. Android applications are structured such that these visual aspects are embodied in resources and assets, such as images, sounds, UI layouts, or application settings.

Advertising platform

Name	Non-popular apps	Popular apps
Google Ads	225,344 (35.73%)	25,946 (49.47%)
Google Analytics	64,799 (10.28%)	7,522 (14.34%)
Flurry	34,040 (5.40%)	6,477 (12.35%)
Millennial Media Ads	23,120 (3.67%)	3,480 (6.64%)
MobFox	19,709 (3.13%)	1,219 (2.32%)
InMobi	17,432 (2.76%)	3,128 (5.96%)
RevMob	18,064 (2.86%)	1,018 (1.94%)
Urban Airship Push	14,657 (2.32%)	525 (1.00%)
Mobclix	12,315 (1.95%)	1,866 (3.56%)
Smaato	12,290 (1.95%)	241 (0.46%)
AirPush	10,773 (1.71%)	657 (1.25%)
SendDroid	9,907 (1.57%)	742 (1.41%)
Adfonic	9,170 (1.45%)	435 (0.83%)
Jumptap	8,968 (1.42%)	570 (1.09%)
HuntMads	7,275 (1.15%)	135 (0.26%)
TapIt	7,131 (1.13%)	259 (0.49%)
Umeng	5,742 (0.91%)	805 (1.53%)
TapJoy	3,358 (0.53%)	2,645 (5.04%)
AppLovin	5,124 (0.81%)	824 (1.57%)
MoPub	4,187 (0.66%)	1,167 (2.23%)
LeadBolt	3,517 (0.56%)	475 (0.91%)
Total	302,611 (47.98%)	34,348 (65.49%)

Social

Name	Non-popular apps	Popular apps
Facebook SDK	77,489 (12.29%)	6,206 (11.83%)
Twitter4J	41,606 (6.60%)	2,057 (3.92%)
Total	92,495 (14.67%)	6,990 (13.33%)

Cross-platform framework

Name	Non-popular apps	Popular apps
PhoneGap	36,915 (5.85%)	606 (1.16%)
Adobe Air	12,761 (2.02%)	619 (1.18%)
Titanium	8,316 (1.32%)	138 (0.26%)
Total	57,991 (9.20%)	1,363 (2.60%)

Application generator

Name	Non-popular apps	Popular apps
Bizness Apps	10,011 (1.59%)	3 (0.01%)
App Inventor	9,560 (1.52%)	152 (0.29%)
Andromo	6,294 (1.00%)	156 (0.30%)
iBuildApp	4,149 (0.66%)	25 (0.05%)
Mobile by Conduit	3,989 (0.63%)	21 (0.04%)
Total	34,003 (5.39%)	357 (0.68%)

Bug tracking

Name	Non-popular apps	Popular apps
BugSense	59,550 (9.44%)	4,251 (8.11%)
Acra	25,658 (4.07%)	1,450 (2.76%)
Total	84,896 (13.46%)	5,663 (10.80%)

Billing

Name	Non-popular apps	Popular apps
Google Billing	27,846 (4.42%)	6,312 (12.04%)
Paypal	16,943 (2.69%)	374 (0.71%)
Authorize.net	8,464 (1.34%)	1 (0.00%)
Amazon Purchasing	3,356 (0.53%)	1,044 (1.99%)
Total	44,798 (7.10%)	6,686 (12.75%)

Audio/graphics engine

Name	Non-popular apps	Popular apps
FMOD	8,199 (1.30%)	1,705 (3.25%)
Unity3D	8,158 (1.29%)	1,601 (3.05%)
AndEngine	7,098 (1.13%)	1,080 (2.06%)
libGDX	6,311 (1.00%)	1,395 (2.66%)
Corona SDK	3,750 (0.59%)	396 (0.76%)
Total	23,774 (3.77%)	4,222 (8.05%)

Table 4: Application libraries usage on June 22, 2013.

Resources and assets are two different ways to embed visual elements in Android applications, the former having a locale-aware naming hierarchy through the 'R' Java class while the latter provides raw access to files. Based on this observation, we leverage the structure of Android applications to use a feature set of resource names and asset signatures, the latter generated by taking the MD5 hash of each asset of an application excluding its icon and XML files. This feature set is easy to identify and compute even for obfuscated application code, making it fast enough to use with daily crawls of Google Play.

Using PLAYDRONE to study 610,000 free applications downloaded and decompiled on May 5, 2013, we found roughly 58 million unique resource names and 45 million unique asset signatures. Because the most common resource names and asset signatures occur in widely-used application libraries, their frequency is high and they are poor indicators of application similarity. To address this issue, we use a simple blacklist approach with a cutoff parameter C that ignores resource names and asset signatures appearing in more than C applications. With a cutoff of 300, 45,000 resource names and 14,000 asset signatures are ignored, which represent 0.08% of the unique resource names and 0.03% of the unique asset signatures considered.

To determine whether two applications App_A and App_B with respective feature sets A and B are similar, we use the Jaccard index $J(A, B) = \frac{|A \cap B|}{|A \cup B|}$. The resulting score is a real number $[0, 1]$. If the Jaccard index is above a certain threshold T, the two applications compared are considered similar. We compute the Jaccard index separately for resource names and asset signatures, ignoring the blacklisted ones. Similar applications are grouped into clusters. For simplicity, we assume that applications typically derive from one other application, so that each application should only be included in at most one cluster. We therefore merge clusters whenever an application has multiple matches belonging to different clusters. Each cluster is assigned a victim application, which is the application with the most downloads, under the assumption that it is also the one most likely to have been the duplicated. We then merge the clusters based on resource names with those based on asset signatures. All of this is accomplished by first indexing all resource names and asset signatures in Elasticsearch, then querying Elasticsearch to match applications. The former is done once per APK and takes a couple of hours while the latter takes around 20 minutes on our cluster of ten machines. The number of similar applications is the sum of the size of each detected cluster, excluding their victim application.

Figure 7 shows the number of similar applications detected when varying the score threshold T ranging from 0.6 to 1.0. A value of 1.0 represents an exact match of resources and assets, while 0.8 allows similar applications to have some differences. We compare the effectiveness of using both resource names and asset signatures versus only using one or the other. Asset signatures alone detect fewer similar applications because many applications have no assets at all. Figure 8 shows the distribution of clusters by sizes. The distribution shows that clusters with sizes larger than 300 are infrequent, suggesting 300 as a suitable cutoff to exclude common application libraries. We base the rest of our discussion on using $C = 300$ and $T = 0.8$. Using these parameters, there were 158,204 free duplicative applications in Google Play, roughly 25% of the free application content.

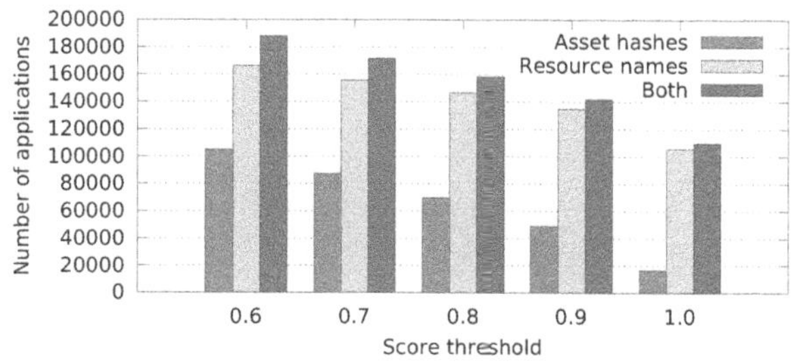

Figure 7: Similar apps vs score threshold (cutoff = 300).

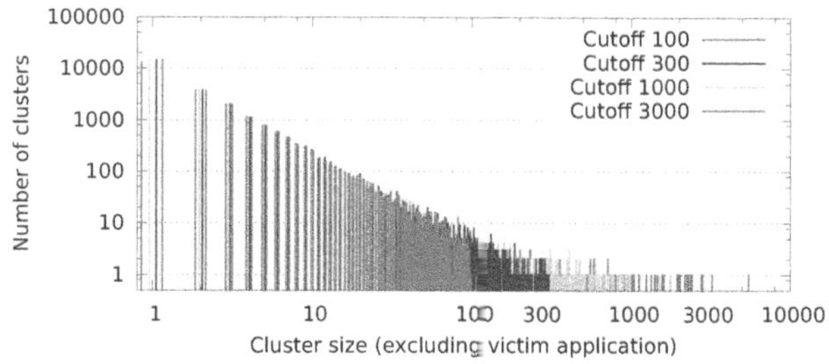

Figure 8: Number of clusters of similar apps vs cluster size (threshold = 0.8).

We then divided the similar applications taking into account developer information. Each application uploaded to Google Play is signed by a developer using a private key. We compared the ownership of each similar application by examining both the developer name associated with the application account and the certificate included in the application package. If either of these attributes match, applications are labeled as rebranded. If neither author attributes match, applications are labeled as clones. Out of 158,204 similar free applications, 115,896 were rebranded and 42,308 were clones. Sources of rebranding included changing the languages displayed in the user interface and reusing code from one application as a template for a new application, especially for wallpaper, trivia, and travel information applications. Sources of cloning included use of automated tools and wizard services, copying open source applications, contracting the same third party to develop applications for a range of clients in a specific industry, and plagiarism, though the latter is difficult to detect without knowing the relationships among developers. For a developer of an original application who therefore does know these relationships, PLAYDRONE can be useful to detect application cloning in various ways, from identifying plagiarized applications to monitoring statistics over all clones to gauge the health and popularity of an open-source project.

To evaluate the accuracy of our approach, we took a random sample of 400 applications flagged as similar and manually compared them to their corresponding victim application. Out of 400 applications identified as similar, manual inspection indicated that 5% were false positives that included similar resources and assets but actually differed on account of visible design and functionality differences. We also compared PLAYDRONE's method of similarity detection to a code analysis tool we built based on extracting a feature set of Android SDK methods from the DEX bytecode of an application [41]. Running the same 400 applications through the code analysis tool, only 79% of the manually verified applications were correctly identified.

PlayDrone's better performance can be explained by classifying code cloning techniques [32]. While most code analysis methods are able to identify similar applications with variations in identifiers, literals, types, whitespace, layout and comments (Type-1 and Type-2), they are less reliable in detecting similar applications with changed, added, or removed statements (Type-3) and ineffective at detecting similar applications implemented through different syntatic variants (Type-4). Because PlayDrone's detection technique is agnostic to the complexity of the code transformations used for cloning, it is the first system that can identify similar Android applications across all four clone types, including Type-3 and Type-4 clones. This makes PlayDrone not only fast and efficient, but also a more robust system for detecting application similarity in Google Play.

8. AUTHENTICATION TOKENS

The rise of the Web 2.0 architecture has seen a proliferation of cloud service APIs. Service to service communication is usually authenticated with secret tokens that are known only by the involved parties. When implemented as intended, secret tokens are never shared and are stored on trusted servers where they can be properly safeguarded. However, as these service to service protocols have been adapted to mobile applications, we have discovered using PlayDrone that developers are now embedding secret tokens directly into applications. While developers may believe their application sources are well guarded, the ease of decompilation and the widespread availability of mobile applications makes recovering secret tokens relatively simple. We discuss how we used PlayDrone to discover secret tokens used with Amazon Web Services (AWS) and several OAuth providers and demonstrate the potential for abuse of these tokens by malicious actors.

8.1 Discovering Tokens

We used PlayDrone's search engine to quickly probe application source code by searching words such as "secret" and found a large number of insecure tokens used for various services because developers often use constant names with the substring "secret" to identify their secret tokens. Our search results show that services often use tokens with service-specific formats. For example, the AWS API is accessed with an `AccessKeyId` which starts with the substring "AKIA". Figure 9 shows a source search for all strings starting with "AKIA" revealing many AWS tokens. To extract authentication tokens, we created a flexible framework that searches for secret tokens in the decompiled Java source files of applications using regular expressions. Tokens usually come in pairs, typically a client ID and its corresponding secret key functioning similar to a username and password. For example, in the case of AWS, requests are signed using a 40 character string `SecretAccessKey`. To discover AWS credentials, we configured PlayDrone to find pairs of strings matching `AKIA[0-9A-Z]{16}` and `[0-9a-zA-Z/+]{40}` that are at most 5 lines apart.

Table 5 summarizes various authentication tokens for widely-used services that we found using PlayDrone. *Total Candidates* denotes the number of tokens found across the entire Google play store from the June 22, 2013 snapshot. *Unique Candidates* denotes the number of different tokens. The difference between total candidates and unique candidates can be explained by developer keys reuse, and various libraries directly embedding tokens in their SDKs. *Unique % Valid* denotes how many of the unique tokens from the June 22, 2013 snapshot were still valid on November 11, 2013. To test the validity of tokens, we sent authentication requests to their respective providers. Note that these results represent a conservative measure of the number of tokens in applications in Google Play as the simple search method does not detect tokens in obfuscated code because of its reliance on regular expression pattern matching.

8.2 Amazon Web Services

AWS provides various cloud computing resources that can be purchased by developers using AWS accounts and accessed by the developers' applications using AWS tokens associated with the respective AWS accounts. As shown in Table 5, we found 308 unique AWS tokens from the June 22, 2013 snapshot. Five month later, we tested the validity of these tokens by sending an AWS API request to count the number of storage buckets in the AWS Simple Storage Service (S3). We found 94% of the tokens were still valid five months later. These read-only API calls were carefully chosen to preclude any impact to AWS customer's data or resources. Amazon provides documentation describing best practices and a variety of ways to configure AWS tokens with different levels of privilege [2]. Despite this documented flexibility, we were surprised to find that even though some developers only intended their applications to use AWS tokens to access AWS Simple Database or Flexible Payment Services, the tokens embedded in the applications were root-level credentials providing access to all the other AWS services, including creating and shutting down Elastic Compute Cloud (EC2) instances or freely accessing S3 data.

Exposure of the AWS tokens can provide access to existing AWS resources, potentially leading to a range of confidentiality, integrity, and availability attacks, as well as the capability to allocate new resources at the owner's expense. With 288 valid tokens, an attacker could potentially setup a botnet of AWS EC2 instances. While AWS has a number of mechanisms to thwart such activities [30], usage patterns on AWS are elastic and inherently unpredictable, which may make it hard to detect stolen resources. Unless billing alerts are manually configured, billing statements will not reflect usage until the end of the billing cycle. Amazon recognizes the risks of embedding secret keys in Android applications and actively advises developers against this practice in their Android SDK documentation [5]. Additionally, AWS provides mechanisms for Android developers to securely leverage AWS from their application, such as AWS Token Vending Machine [4] and AWS Web Identity Framework [3]. The problem is that developers often find it simpler to embed tokens in their applications without being aware of best practices and understanding the resulting security risks.

Because of the potential for malicious use of the AWS tokens in Google Play, we reached out to Amazon to warn them of this security risk. Amazon responded quickly by identifying their affected customers based on the list of tokens we provided, and reaching out and working with their customers to resolve the security issues, though some mistakenly assumed that Amazon itself was scanning for secret keys in Android applications [8, 11, 28]. We also reached out to Google to ask them to scan for AWS and other tokens in applications as part of the Google Play application publication process to help protect users and developers. Google

	Amazon	Facebook	Twitter	Bitly	Flickr	Foursquare	Google	LinkedIn	Titanium
Total candidates	1,241	1,477	28,235	3,132	159	326	414	1,434	1,914
Unique candidates	308	460	6,228	616	89	177	225	181	1,783
Unique % valid	93.5%	71.7%	95.2%	88.8%	100%	97.7%	96.0%	97.2%	99.8%

Table 5: Credentials statistics from June 22, 2013 and validated on November 11, 2013. A credential may consist of an ID token and secret authentication token.

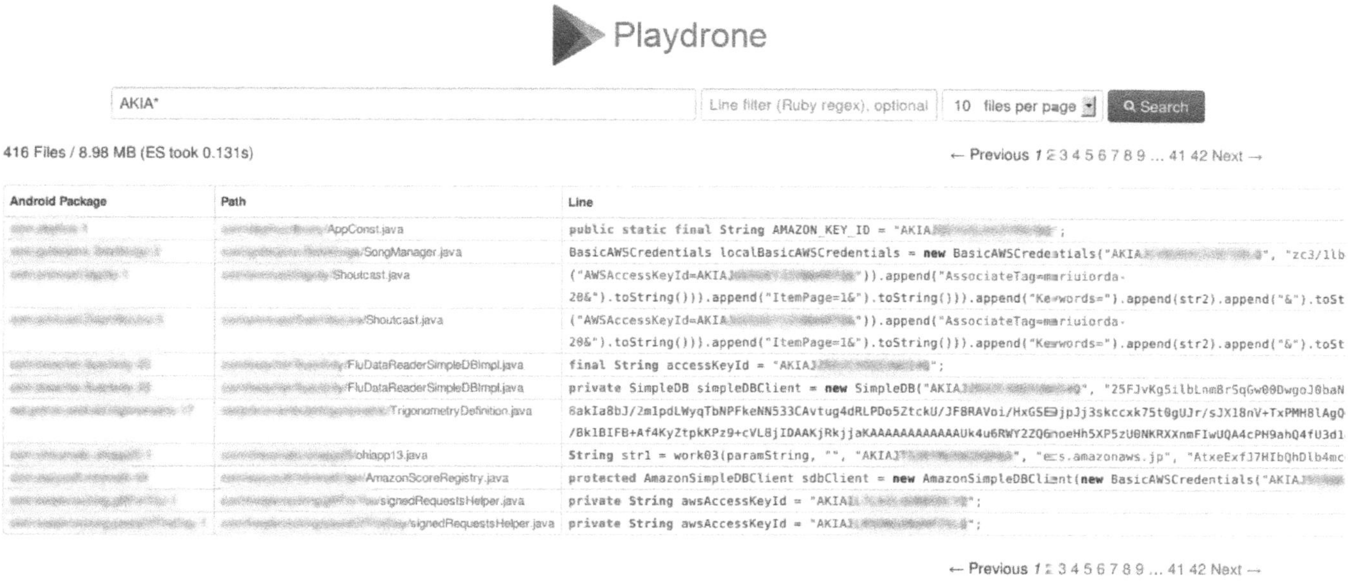

Figure 9: PLAYDRONE's web interface to search decompiled sources showing Amazon Web Service tokens found in 130 ms.

automatically scans for some vulnerabilities, but plans to add checks and automated notices to developers for these specific issues as part of the Google Play application publication process. At Google's request, we provided some of our tools to help them develop these checks.

8.3 OAuth Tokens

Applications often request access to users' data to perform actions on their behalf. The standard protocol used by service providers to give access to users' data is OAuth. A third-party can register his application with an OAuth provider to receive OAuth client credentials consisting of a (`client_id`, `client_secret`) key pair. OAuth credentials are typically used in two ways. One way is to issue requests to the OAuth provider on behalf of the application, for example to ban a specific user or consume a rate-limited API (e.g. search). Another way is to request a user-specific `access_token` to perform actions on the user's behalf. For example, to acquire an access token, the third-party provides a link such as "Login with Facebook" on his website that would initiate the OAuth authentication process, including asking a user to grant permissions requested by the third-party application. Upon user acceptance, the third-party client receives an access token that can be used to read the user's Facebook friend list or post on his public feed.

When implemented correctly, the OAuth authentication protocol never reveals the tokens associated with a client's OAuth credentials. The tokens are stored on the third-party's server where it can be properly safeguarded. Requests can then be proxied through the third-party's server where the tokens reside. Unfortunately, developers often adapt this protocol to mobile applications by embedding OAuth tokens directly into their mobile applications without realizing their credentials are easily compromised through decompilation. Once an attacker acquires a secret OAuth token, a wide range of attacks can be performed as the targeted third-party application is open to impersonation. For example, an attacker can perform denial of service attacks on rate limited services, access and modify application settings, expose private user information, and launch phishing attacks in an attempt to get users' access tokens. Table 5 shows the total number of OAuth credentials we found in Android applications on Google Play for Facebook, Twitter, Bitly, Flickr, Foursquare, LinkedIn, Google+, and Appcelerator's Titanium cloud services. After five months, over 90% of most of the OAuth credentials were still valid.

Focusing on Facebook and Twitter, we discovered 1,477 Facebook credentials and 28,235 Twitter credentials among all the free applications in Google Play. Finding 20 times as many Twitter tokens than Facebook tokens is surprising as Table 4 shows that the Facebook SDK is used twice as much as the Twitter4J library. One possible explanation is that until recently, Twitter encouraged developers to embed their secret tokens directly in client applications and even provided an official tutorial detailing this practice for Android using Twitter4J [36]. In contrast, as shown on the Facebook developer page [21], Facebook stresses the importance of never storing OAuth secret tokens in client applications: *Note that [this OAuth request] must never be made in client-side code or in an app binary that could be decompiled. It is important that your app secret is never shared with anyone. Therefore, this API call should only be made using server-side code.* To avoid the need of storing secret tokens on a mobile device, Facebook leverages the presence of the official Facebook Android application on Android devices. The Facebook SDK allows third-party applications to use Android intents to proxy requests for user access tokens through Facebook's Android application, where the user is already authenticated. To retrieve a user's access token with the Facebook SDK, the Android application identifier of a third-party application must be registered on its Facebook application settings page. This allows Facebook's Android application to respond to the third-party application's access token request by verifying the application identifier in the intent to the one officially registered online. Only the application identifier is needed and no secret key is compromised since it is retrieved at runtime. This technique relies on the robustness of Android since the source of the Android intent is assumed not to be spoofable.

Despite all the measures Facebook takes to make writing secure application easy, Table 5 shows that numerous developers still embed OAuth tokens in their applications and even seasoned developers have trouble following Facebook's simple security guidelines. For example, the popular Airbnb application still contained their Facebook, Google, LinkedIn, Microsoft, and Yahoo secret tokens from June 22, 2013 until well past November 11, 2013. Airbnb is the leader in peer-to-peer apartment rentals with more than 10 million users who are required to register on Facebook or Google+ to verify their identity. This is problematic in the case of Facebook because its API is too flexible by default, permitting user context queries to be performed in an application context. The default application settings allow an application to perform actions on behalf of a user at any later time once the user has authenticated the application. Even if an application does not subsequently retrieve a user access token, it still retains whatever permissions the user granted the first time the OAuth authentication process was run for the application. For example, we were able to access the email and friends list of Airbnb users using the URL: `https://graph.facebook.com/<user_id>?fields=email&access_token=<oauth_client_id>|<oauth_secret_key>`. Fortunately, the Airbnb application did not have permission to post on users' walls, otherwise we could write arbitrary content on millions of Facebook walls.

We notified Facebook of this problem and they immediately revoked the Airbnb OAuth credentials on Facebook. In a matter of hours, Airbnb published a new version of their application in Google Play, properly using the Facebook SDK for authentication and removing all secret tokens from the application. We also provided Facebook with a list of other Facebook tokens that we identified and Facebook promptly disabled Facebook access for those applications as well to protect Facebook users from potential unauthorized access. The affected applications would have to be updated using secure methods to regain functionality, resulting in service disruption for many users until updated applications are published in Google Play and users download the updated applications. Our results show that developers often ignore best practices, so it is important for OAuth providers to provide protection mechanisms such as limiting the service scope of tokens to help mitigate this security problem.

9. RELATED WORK

Besides Google, several companies maintain and publicize regular statistics about Google Play applications. AndroLib [6], AppBrain [7], and MixRank [29] offer services to help discover new applications and regularly publish statistics about the applications they have collected. d'Heureuse et al. [18] provide a temporal study of application statistics for Apple, Google, Microsoft and BlackBerry markets based on metadata collected from web scraping. Unlike previous studies and services, PLAYDRONE provides a scalable tool to crawl Google Play on a daily basis and a framework to analyze Google Play content at scale, including analysis based on Android application source code.

Some previous work has considered aspects of some of the issues we have studied. A number of approaches have explored how to detect similar Android applications, though not at the scale of the entire Google Play store. These approaches are computationally complex as they are based on application code analysis, either using pairwise comparisons [16, 13, 27, 42] or comparing applications to a subset of their closest neighbors [14, 41]. In contrast, PLAYDRONE indexes application resource signatures with Elasticsearch to efficiently match applications with common features.

Much work has focused on the security of Android applications and the presence of malware in Google Play, but this work has focused on possible compromises of user data and privacy on the Android devices themselves [20, 22, 25, 44]. While PLAYDRONE can be used as a tool to enable similar studies, we show how PLAYDRONE can be used to analyze a completely different type of security threat. By simply analyzing Android application content, we show that malicious attackers can go beyond Android devices to compromise server resources without even having users execute vulnerable Android applications. We present the first study to investigate these type of server-side vulnerabilities from mobile client code, showing evidence of how mobile developers leak secret tokens used in OAuth authorization and the Amazon Web Services API.

10. CONCLUSIONS

We have built PLAYDRONE, a system that uses various hacking techniques to circumvent Google security to successfully crawl Google Play. PLAYDRONE scales by simply adding more servers and is fast enough to crawl Google Play on a daily basis, downloading over 1.1 million Android applications and decompiling over 880,000 free applications. We use PLAYDRONE to perform a large-scale characterization of Android applications in Google Play and demonstrate how application content evolves over time, how even highly downloaded applications can be poorly rated, and that despite the large number of applications in Google Play, only a small percentage of free applications account for almost all downloads. We further show that (1) native libraries are heavily used by popular Android applications, limiting the benefits of Java portability and the ability of Android server offloading systems to run these applications, (2) 25% of Google Play is duplicative application content, and (3) Android applications contain thousands of leaked secret authentication keys which can be used by malicious users to gain unauthorized access to server resources through Amazon Web Services and compromise user accounts on Facebook. We worked with service providers, including Amazon, Facebook, and Google, to identify and notify customers at risk, and make the Google Play store a safer place. These results demonstrate that PLAYDRONE can serve as a useful tool to better understand Android applications and improve the quality of application content in Google Play.

11. ACKNOWLEDGMENTS

Don Bailey, Eric Davis, and Larry Rudolph provided helpful comments on earlier drafts of this paper. This work was supported in part by NSF grants CNS-1162447, CNS-1018355, CNS-0905246, and CCF-1162021.

12. REFERENCES

[1] Amazon Mechanical Turk. https://www.mturk.com.

[2] Amazon Web Services. IAM Best Practices, May 2010. http://docs.aws.amazon.com/IAM/latest/UserGuide/IAMBestPractices.html.

[3] Amazon Web Services. Creating Temporary Security Credentials for Mobile Apps Using Identity Providers. AWS Security Token Service, June 2011. http://docs.aws.amazon.com/STS/latest/UsingSTS/CreatingWIF.html.

[4] Amazon Web Services. Authenticating Users of AWS Mobile Applications with a Token Vending Machine. AWS Identity and Access Management, July 2013. http://aws.amazon.com/articles/4611615499399490.

[5] Amazon Web Services. Getting Started with the AWS SDK for Android. AWS SDK for Android, Sept. 2013. http://docs.aws.amazon.com/mobile/sdkforandroid/gsg/Welcome.html.

[6] AndroLib. http://www.androlib.com.

[7] AppBrain. http://www.appbrain.com.

[8] R. Bala. Amazon Is Downloading Apps From Google Play and Inspecting Them. Y Combinator Hacker News, Mar. 2014. https://news.ycombinator.com/item?id=7491272.

[9] Capistrano. http://capistranorb.com.

[10] Chef. http://www.getchef.com.

[11] R. Chirgwin. Amazon Is Decompiling Our Apps in Security Gaff Hunt, Says Dev. The Register, Mar. 2014. http://www.theregister.co.uk/2014/03/31/dev_lashes_out_at_amazon_for_decompiling_his_app.

[12] B.-G. Chun, S. Ihm, P. Maniatis, M. Naik, and A. Patti. CloneCloud: Elastic Execution Between Mobile Device and Cloud. In *Proceedings of the 6th European Conference on Computer systems (EuroSys 2011)*, Apr. 2011.

[13] J. Crussell, C. Gibler, and H. Chen. Attack of the Clones: Detecting Cloned Applications on Android Markets. In *Proceedings of 17th European Symposium on Research in Computer Security (ESORICS 2012)*, Sept. 2012.

[14] J. Crussell, C. Gibler, and H. Chen. AnDarwin: Scalable Detection of Semantically Similar Android Applications. In *Proceedings of 18th European Symposium on Research in Computer Security (ESORICS 2013)*, Sept. 2013.

[15] Death by Captcha. http://www.deathbycaptcha.com.

[16] A. Desnos. Androguard. https://code.google.com/p/androguard.

[17] dex2jar. http://code.google.com/p/dex2jar.

[18] N. d'Heureuse, F. Huici, M. Arumaithurai, M. Ahmed, K. Papagiannaki, and S. Niccolini. What's App?: A Wide-Scale Measurement Study of Smart Phone Markets. *Mobile Computing and Communications Review*, 16(2):16–27, Apr. 2012.

[19] Elasticsearch. http://www.elasticsearch.org.

[20] W. Enck, D. Octeau, P. McDaniel, and S. Chaudhuri. A Study of Android Application Security. In *Proceedings of the 20th USENIX Security Symposium*, Aug. 2011.

[21] Facebook. Login Security. https://developers.facebook.com/docs/facebook-login/security.

[22] A. P. Felt, M. Finifter, E. Chin, S. Hanna, and D. Wagner. A Survey of Mobile Malware in the Wild. In *Proceedings of the 1st ACM Workshop on Security and Privacy in Smartphones and Mobile Devices (SPSM 2011)*, July 2011.

[23] C. Gibler, R. Stevens, J. Crussell, H. Chen, H. Zang, and H. Choi. AdRob: Examining the Landscape and Impact of Android Application Plagiarism. In *Proceedings of the 11th International Conference on Mobile Systems, Applications, and Services (MobiSys 2013)*, June 2013.

[24] E. Girault. Google Play Unofficial Python API. https://github.com/egirault/googleplay-api.

[25] M. Grace, Y. Zhou, Q. Zhang, S. Zou, and X. Jiang. RiskRanker: Scalable and Accurate Zero-day Android Malware Detection. In *Proceedings of the 10th International Conference on Mobile Systems, Applications, and Services (MobiSys 2012)*, June 2012.

[26] B. Gruver. smali/baksmali assembler/disassembler. https://code.google.com/p/smali.

[27] S. Hanna, L. Huang, E. X. Wu, S. Li, C. Chen, and D. Song. Juxtapp: A Scalable System for Detecting Code Reuse Among Android Applications. In *Proceedings of the 9th International Conference on Detection of Intrusions and Malware, and Vulnerability Assessment (DIMVA 2012)*, July 2012.

[28] M. Kotadia. AWS Admits Scanning Android App in Secret Key Hunt. iTnews, Apr. 2014. http://www.itnews.com.au/News/381432,aws-admits-scanning-android-app-in-secret-key-hunt.aspx.

[29] MixRank. http://www.mixrank.com.

[30] R. Mogull. My $500 Cloud Security Screwup-UPDATED. Securosis Blog, Jan. 2014. https://securosis.com/blog/my-500-cloud-security-screwup.

[31] M. Perham. Sidekiq. http://sidekiq.org.

[32] C. K. Roy, J. R. Cordy, and R. Koschke. Comparison and Evaluation of Code Clone Detection Techniques and Tools: A Qualitative Approach. *Sci. Comput. Program.*, 74(7):470–495, May 2009.

[33] S. Sanfilippo. Redis. http://redis.io.

[34] A. Thiel. Android-market-api. https://code.google.com/p/android-market-api.

[35] C. Tumbleson. Android-apktool http://code.google.com/p/android-apktool.

[36] Twitter. Implementing the Twitter OAuth flow in Android. https://dev.twitter.com/docs/implementing-twitter-oauth-flow-android.

[37] N. Viennot. Java Library for JD-Core. https://github.com/nviennot/jd-core-java.

[38] N. Viennot. PLAYDRONE sources. https://github.com/nviennot/google-play-crawler.

[39] C. Warren. Google Play Hits 1 Million Apps. Mashable, July 2013. http://mashable.com/2013/07/24/google-play-1-million.

[40] Y. Zhang, G. Huang, X. Liu, W. Zhang, H. Mei, and S. Yang. Refactoring Android Java Code for On-Demand Computation Offloading. In *Proceedings of the 27th Annual ACM SIGPLAN Conference on Object-Oriented Programming, Systems, Languages, and Applications (OOPSLA 2012)*, Oct. 2012.

[41] W. Zhou, Y. Zhou, M. C. Grace, X. Jiang, and S. Zou. Fast, Scalable Detection of "Piggybacked" Mobile Applications. In *Proceedings of the 3rd ACM Conference on Data and Application Security and Privacy (CODASPY 2013)*, Feb. 2013.

[42] W. Zhou, Y. Zhou, X. Jiang, and P. Ning. Detecting Repackaged Smartphone Applications in Third-party Android Marketplaces. In *Proceedings of the 2nd ACM Conference on Data and Application Security and Privacy (CODASPY 2012)*, Feb. 2012.

[43] Y. Zhou and X. Jiang. Dissecting Android Malware: Characterization and Evolution. In *Proceedings of the 2012 IEEE Symposium on Security and Privacy (SP 12)*, May 2012.

[44] Y. Zhou, Z. Wang, W. Zhou, and X. Jiang. Hey, You, Get Off of My Market: Detecting Malicious Apps in Official and Alternative Android Markets. In *Proceedings of the 19th Annual Symposium on Network and Distributed System Security (NDSS 2012)*, Feb. 2012.

IntroPerf: Transparent Context-Sensitive Multi-Layer Performance Inference using System Stack Traces

Chung Hwan Kim[†], Junghwan Rhee[‡], Hui Zhang[‡], Nipun Arora[‡],
Guofei Jiang[‡], Xiangyu Zhang[†], Dongyan Xu[†]
[†]Purdue University and CERIAS, [‡]NEC Laboratories America
[†]{chungkim,xyzhang,dxu}@cs.purdue.edu, [‡]{rhee,huizhang,nipun,gfj}@nec-labs.com

ABSTRACT

Performance bugs are frequently observed in commodity software. While profilers or source code-based tools can be used at development stage where a program is diagnosed in a well-defined environment, many performance bugs survive such a stage and affect production runs. OS kernel-level tracers are commonly used in post-development diagnosis due to their independence from programs and libraries; however, they lack detailed program-specific metrics to reason about performance problems such as function latencies and program contexts. In this paper, we propose a novel performance inference system, called IntroPerf, that generates fine-grained performance information – like that from application profiling tools – transparently by leveraging OS tracers that are widely available in most commodity operating systems. With system stack traces as input, IntroPerf enables transparent context-sensitive performance inference, and diagnoses application performance in a multi-layered scope ranging from user functions to the kernel. Evaluated with various performance bugs in multiple open source software projects, IntroPerf automatically ranks potential internal and external root causes of performance bugs with high accuracy without any prior knowledge about or instrumentation on the subject software. Our results show IntroPerf's effectiveness as a lightweight performance introspection tool for post-development diagnosis.

Categories and Subject Descriptors

C.4 [**Performance of Systems**]: Measurement techniques

Keywords

Performance inference; stack trace analysis; context-sensitive performance analysis

Work done during an internship at NEC Laboratories America, Princeton.

SIGMETRICS 14, June 16–20, 2014, Austin, Texas, USA.

ACM 978-1-4503-2789-3/14/06 ...$15.00.
http://dx.doi.org/10.1145/2591971.2592008 .

1. INTRODUCTION

Performance diagnosis and optimization are essential to software development life cycle for quality assurance. Existing performance tools such as profilers [3, 6, 7, 19] and compiler-driven systems [17, 22, 34, 33] are extensively used in application development and testing stages to identify inefficient code and diagnose performance problems at fine granularity. Despite these efforts, performance bugs may still escape the development stage, and incur costs and frustration to software users [21].

In a post-development setting, software users investigating performance issues are usually not the developers, who have source code and can debug line by line. Therefore, it is desirable for those users to have a diagnosis tool that will work transparently at the binary level, look into all components in the vertical software layers with a system-wide scope, and pinpoint the component(s) responsible for a performance issue. Furthermore, detailed and context-rich diagnosis reports are always helpful to such users so that they can provide meaningful feedback to the developers hence speeding up the resolution of performance issues.

Commodity software is commonly built on top of many other software components. For instance, the Apache HTTP server in Ubuntu has recursive dependencies on over two hundred packages for execution and over 8,000 packages to build. Unfortunately, the maintenance of such diverse, inter-dependent components is usually not well coordinated. Various components of different versions are distributed via multiple vendors, and they are integrated and updated by individual users. Such complexity in the maintenance of software components makes the localization of performance anomaly challenging due to the increased chances of unexpected behavior.

OS tracers [1, 2, 15, 27] are commonly used as "Swiss Army Knives" in modern operating systems to diagnose application performance problems. These tools enable deep performance inspection across multiple system layers and allow users to spot the "root cause" software component. Given diverse applications and their complex dependencies on libraries and lower layer components, compatibility with all layers is an important requirement. OS tracers are very effective in this aspect because they are free from the dependencies by operating in the OS kernel – below any application software or library.

On the other hand, the tracers' location in the OS kernel makes them lose track of details of program internals such as function latencies and program contexts, which are very

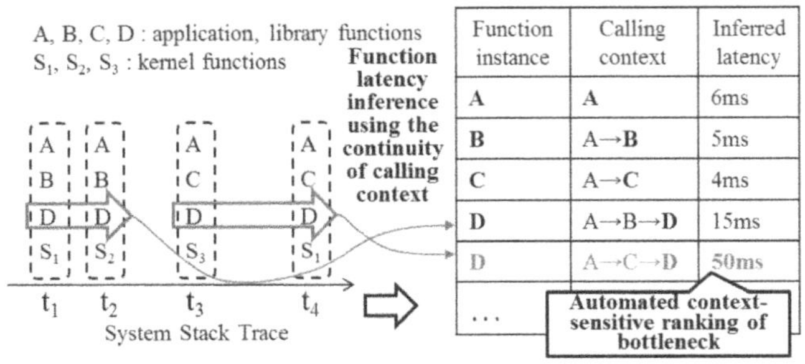

Figure 1: Main idea of IntroPerf: context-sensitive performance diagnosis using inferred latency from system stack traces.

useful to localize root cause functions. These tools collect information on coarse-grained kernel-level events; they do not precisely capture the calls and returns of application functions, the tracing of which is often performed by application profilers or dynamic analysis engines.

Recently, OS tracers provide stack traces generated on OS kernel events [1, 15, 27] to improve the visibility into programs. They cover all system layers from applications to the kernel as shown on the left of Figure 1; therefore, we call the traces *system stack traces*. While they provide improved software performance views, their usage is mostly within event-based performance analysis. For example, Windows Performance Analyzer provides a summary of system performance computed with the weights of program functions' appearances in the system stack traces. An important performance feature missing for performance analysis is *the measurement of application-level function latencies*. Since the system stack events are generated not on the boundaries of function calls but on OS kernel events (e.g., system calls), the timestamps of the events do not accurately reflect how long each function executes.

We propose a novel performance inference system, called IntroPerf, that offers fine-grained performance diagnosis data like those from application profiling tools. IntroPerf works transparently by leveraging the OS tracers widely available in most operating systems. Figure 1 illustrates the main idea. With system stack traces as input, IntroPerf transparently infers context-sensitive performance data of the traced software by measuring the *continuity of calling context*[1] – the continuous period of a function in a stack with the same calling context. The usage of stack traces commonly available from production OS tracers [1] allows IntroPerf to avoid the requirement of source code or modification to application programs while it analyzes detailed performance data of the traced application across all layers. Furthermore, it provides context-driven performance analysis for automating the diagnosis process.

Contributions: The contributions of this paper are summarized as follows.

Transparent inference of function latency in multiple layers based on stack traces: We propose a novel performance inference technique to estimate the latency of program function instances with system stack traces [1] based on the continuity of calling context. This technique essentially converts system stack traces from OS tracers to latencies of function instances to enable fine-grained localization of performance anomalies.

Automated localization of internal and external performance bottlenecks via context-sensitive performance analysis across multiple system layers: IntroPerf localizes performance bottlenecks in a context-sensitive manner by organizing and analyzing the estimated function latencies in a *calling context tree*. IntroPerf's ranking mechanism on performance-annotated call paths automatically highlights potential performance bottlenecks, regardless of whether they are internal or external to the subject programs.

Section 2 presents related work. The design of IntroPerf is presented in Section 3. The implementation of IntroPerf is described in Section 4. Section 5 presents evaluation results. Discussion and future work are presented in Section 6. Section 7 concludes this paper.

2. RELATED WORK

Root cause localization in distributed systems: There is a large body of research work on performance analysis and root cause localization in distributed systems [9, 11, 16, 18, 24, 29, 31, 28]. They typically focus on end-to-end tracing of service transactions and performance analysis on transaction paths across distributed nodes. These nodes are connected through *interactions* such as network connections, remote procedure calls, or interprocess procedure calls. While there is a similarity in the goal of localizing performance anomaly, the performance symptoms in our study do not necessarily involve interactions; instead, they require a finer-grained analysis because the localization target could be any possibly small code. For instance, if a performance anomaly is caused by an unexpectedly extended loop count or a costly sequence of function calls, the related approaches will not be able to localize it because all program execution is seen as a single node without differentiating internal code structures. Therefore, the related approaches are not directly applicable to our performance debugging problem due to their coarse granularity.

Profilers: Profilers [3, 6, 19] are tools for debugging application performance symptoms. Many tools such as `gprof` require source code to embed profiling code into programs. However, in a post-development stage these tools are often not applicable because the subject software may be in binary-only form. Also, user-space profilers may not be able to detect the slowdown of lower layer functions such as system calls due to their limited tracing scope.

Oprofile [6] provides whole system profiling via support from recent Linux kernels. Oprofile samples the program counter during execution using a system timer or hardware performance counters. Oprofile's output is based on a call graph, which is not context-sensitive. In addition, relatively infrequent appearance of lower layer code in the execution may lead to a less accurate capture of program behaviors. In contrast, system stack traces recorded by the OS kernel reliably capture all code layers in a context-sensitive way.

Dynamic binary translators: Dynamic binary translators [23, 26] are commonly used in the research community

[1]Calling context is a sequence of active function invocations as observed in a stack. We interchangeably use *calling context*, *call path*, and *stack trace event* in this paper because we obtain calling contexts from the stack traces.

and some of production profiling tools (e.g., Intel vTune is based on Pin) for binary program analysis. These tools can transparently insert profiling code without requiring source code. However, the significantly high performance overhead makes them suitable mainly for the development stage.

Performance bug analysis: Performance analysis has been an active area in debugging and optimization of application performance. Jin et al. [21] analyzed the characteristics of performance bugs found from bug repositories, and reported new bugs by analyzing similar code patterns across software. This method requires source code that is often not available in a post-development stage. StackMine [20] and DeltaInfer [32] are closely related to IntroPerf in the aspect of using run-time information to detect performance bugs. StackMine focuses on enabling performance debugging by clustering similar call stacks in a large number of reports. StackMine relies on PerfTrack for detecting performance bugs. PerfTrack works by inserting `assert`-like statements in Microsoft's software products for possible performance degradation of functions of interest. This is a very efficient and effective approach for generating warnings when the monitored functions experience a slowdown. However, it requires manual insertion of performance checks in certain locations of the source code that may become a bottleneck.

DeltaInfer analyzes context-sensitive performance bugs [32]. It focuses on workload-dependent performance bottlenecks (WDPB) which are usually caused in loops which incur extended delay depending on workload. IntroPerf is different from DeltaInfer in several aspects. First, it is less intrusive since it avoids source code modification required by DeltaInfer, and thus is suitable for a post-development stage. Second, in code coverage, DeltaInfer mostly focuses on characteristics of the main binary similar to profilers. IntroPerf, however, is able to cover all layers in the localization of root causes; this is due to its input, system-wide stack traces, which include information regarding the main binary, libraries, plug-ins, and the kernel.

Diagnosis with OS tracers: Production OS tracers are commonly used in modern OSes. DTrace [15] is the de facto analysis tool in Solaris and Mac OS X. Linux has a variety of tracing solutions such as LTTng [5], Ftrace [2], Dprobe [25], and SystemTap [27]. Event Tracing for Windows (ETW) is the tracing mechanism in Windows supported by Microsoft [1]. These tools are widely used for diagnosis of system problems. For instance, ETW is used not only by the performance utilities of Windows (e.g., Performance Monitor) but also as an underlying mechanism of other diagnosis tools (e.g., Google Chrome Developer Mode). Stack walking [8] is an advanced feature to collect stack traces on specified OS events. This feature is included in ETW from Windows Vista. Other OS tracers such as DTrace and SystemTap also have similar features. The prototype of IntroPerf is built on top of ETW stack walking, but its mechanism is generic and is applicable to other platforms.

Calling context analysis: Calling context has been used in program optimization and debugging [10, 35]. IntroPerf uses dynamic calling context from stack traces to differentiate function latencies in different contexts and enable context-sensitive performance analysis. Several approaches [12, 13, 30] have been proposed to efficiently encode calling context for various debugging purposes. If combined with OS tracers, these approaches will benefit IntroPerf by simplifying the context indexing process.

3. DESIGN OF INTROPERF

In this section, we present the design rationale of IntroPerf for transparent performance inference across multiple software layers.

Effective diagnosis of performance bugs in post-development stage poses several requirements:

> **RQ1**: Collection of traces using a widely deployed common tracing framework.
>
> **RQ2**: Application performance analysis at the fine-grained function level with calling context information.
>
> **RQ3**: Reasonable coverage of program execution captured by system stack traces for performance debugging.

In general, profilers and source code level debugging tools provide high precision and accuracy in analysis at the cost of stronger usage prerequisites such as availability of source code. In a post-development stage, such requirements may not be easily satisfied. Instead, IntroPerf uses system stack traces from OS tracers which are widely deployed for software performance analysis. These tracers operate at the kernel layer without strong dependency on programs or libraries; therefore, IntroPerf can be easily applied as an add-on feature on top of existing tracers without causing extra efforts in instrumenting or recompiling a program.

The metrics of runtime program behavior such as function latency and dynamic calling context have been used to analyze program performance issues [3, 7, 19]. This information is typically collected using instrumentation that captures function calls and returns in profilers and in source code-based approaches. In IntroPerf we aim to obtain fine-grained performance monitoring information without program instrumentation. Instead, such information is inferred using stack traces generated on OS kernel events, which occur in coarser granularity compared to program function calls, leading to lower overhead.

The last requirement in the design of IntroPerf is reasonable coverage of program execution by system stack traces. Our observation is that, even though there are inherent inference errors in the performance analysis results due to the coarse granularity of OS level input events, the accuracy is reasonable for our purpose – performance debugging. This is because performance bottleneck functions with stretched execution time have higher likelihood to appear in call stack samples compared to other functions with short execution time. The inferred results of IntroPerf of such functions hence give high accuracy to analyze the root causes of performance problems. This observation is intuitive and should apply to any sampling-based approach. Our evaluation results (Section 5) support this claim.

3.1 Architecture

The architecture of IntroPerf is shown in Figure 2. The input is system stack traces which are stack traces collected by OS tracers. As briefly described in Section 1, these events do not directly indicate function latency – a useful metric for bottleneck analysis – because the timestamps of the events are for OS events.

To address this challenge, IntroPerf provides transparent inference of application performance, which is the second block from the left in Figure 2. The key idea of our inference

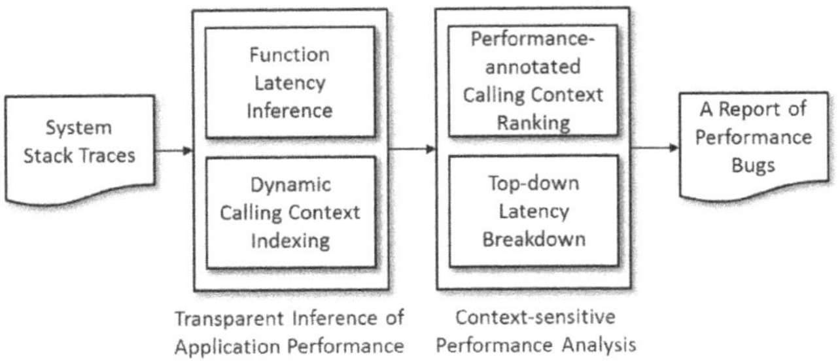

Figure 2: Architecture of IntroPerf

mechanism from stack traces is the *continuity of a function context in the stack*: measuring how long a function's context continues without a change in the stack. Essentially IntroPerf converts system stack traces to a set of function latencies (Section 3.3) along with their calling context information. This context shows a specific sequence of function calls from the "main" function; therefore, it is useful to detect any correlation between performance anomaly and how a function is executed. This context-sensitive performance analysis requires recording and retrieving calling context frequently and efficiently; to do that, IntroPerf has a component for dynamic calling context indexing (Section 3.2).

The third component in Figure 2, context-sensitive performance analysis, determines which functions are performance bottlenecks and in which calling contexts they exist. Our mechanism infers function latency from all layers of the stack in the traces. This leads to potential overlaps of function latencies. The true contributing latency is extracted using the hierarchy of function calls (Section 3.4.1). Our algorithm then ranks the performance of each dynamic calling context and lists the top latency calling context and the top latency functions within each context (Section 3.4.2), which are the list of performance bug candidates generated as the output of IntroPerf.

Next, we will present the underlying functions to support context-sensitive performance analysis and then present our main idea for the inference of function latency.

3.2 Calling Context Tree Construction and Dynamic Calling Context Indexing

Calling context has been widely used in program optimization and debugging [10, 12, 35, 30]. At runtime there are numerous instances of function calls with diverse contexts, forming a distinct order of a function call sequence starting from the "main" function. To reason about the relevance between performance symptoms and calling contexts, it is necessary to associate each function call with its indexed dynamic calling context.

There are several approaches proposed to represent calling context in a unique and concise way [13, 30]. Such approaches require maintaining the context at runtime, and therefore, demand mechanisms to instrument the code and compute the context on the fly. As an offline analysis, we adopt a simple method to represent a dynamic calling context concisely. We use a variant of the calling context tree (CCT) data structure [10]. By assigning a unique number to the pointer going to the end of each path, we index each path with a unique integer ID. Here we define several notations to represent the information.

Algorithm 1 Dynamic Calling Context Indexing

```
s_i = f_1, ..., f_k : a call stack        ▷ order: bottom to top
function PathToID(s_i, CCT_w)
    Node *v = &root of CCT_w
    for f in s_i do
        v = getNode(v, f)
    if v.pid == −1 then
        v.pid = path_counter++
        map_path[v.pid] = v
    return v.pid
function getNode(Node* v, function f)
    if  v′ f == v′.f and v′  v.children  then
        return v′
    else
        v′ = new Node(); v′.parent = v; v′.f = f
        v.children = v.children  v′
        v′.id = node_counter++
        map_node[v′.id] = v′
        return v′
function IDToPath(i, CCT_w)
    Node *v = map_path[i]
    s =
    while *v != root of CCT_w do
        s = v.f  s
        v = v.parent
    return s
```

Let a calling context tree be a tree denoted by F, V, E : $F = f_1, \dots, f_m$ is a set of functions at multiple layers in a program's execution. $V = v_1, \dots, v_n$ is a set of nodes representing functions in different contexts. Note there could be multiple nodes for a function as the function may occur in distinct contexts. $E = e_1, \dots, e_o \quad V \quad V$ is a set of function call edges. An edge e is represented as v_1, v_2 where $v_1, v_2 \quad V$. A calling context (i.e., a call path) $p_k = v_1, \dots, v_k$ in the CCT is a sequence of function nodes from the root node v_1 to a leaf node v_k. We use the ending function node to uniquely identify a call path.

The input to IntroPerf is a system stack trace $T = (t_1, s_1), \dots, (t_u, s_u)$ which is a sequence of OS events with stack traces. Each trace event is represented as a pair: (1) a dynamic calling context $s_i = f_1, \dots f_k$ and (2) the timestamp t_i of an OS kernel event (e.g., a system call) which triggers the generation of s_i. `PathToID` in Algorithm 1 presents how to generate the nodes and edges of a dynamic calling context tree for s_i and index it with a unique ID. Each node has several properties: $v.f \quad F$ indicates the function that v represents; *v.children* is a set of edges connecting v and its child nodes; *v.id* is the node ID number; *v.pid* is the path ID in case v is a leaf node.

Once a path is created in the CCT, any path having the same context will share the same ID by traversing the same path of the tree. The pair of the unique path ID and the pointer to the leaf is stored in a hash map, `map_path`, for quick retrieval of a path as shown in the `IDToPath` function.

Our context-sensitive performance analysis uses this indexing scheme and the enhanced CCT as the underlying mechanism and data structure to store and efficiently retrieve intermediate analysis results.

3.3 Inference of Function Latencies

In this section, we describe how we infer the latency of function instances using system stack traces which include

Table 1: Inference of function instances of the example shown in Figure 3. I: `isNew`, A: `AllNew`, L: `LastStack`, T: `ThisStack[0]`, R: `Register[0-2]`.

Time	t_1					t_2					t_3					t_4				
Depth	I	A	L	T	R	I	A	L	T	R	I	A	L	T	R	I	A	L	T	R
0	1	1	-	A	(t_1,t_1,A)	0	0	A	A	(t_1,t_2,A)	0	0	A	A	(t_1,t_3,A)	0	0	A	A	(t_1,t_4,A)
1	1	1	-	B	(t_1,t_1,B)	0	0	B	B	(t_1,t_2,B)	1	1	B	C	(t_3,t_3,C)	0	0	C	C	(t_3,t_4,C)
2	1	1	-	D	(t_1,t_1,D)	0	0	D	D	(t_1,t_2,D)	1	1	D	D	(t_3,t_3,D)	-	-	D	-	-

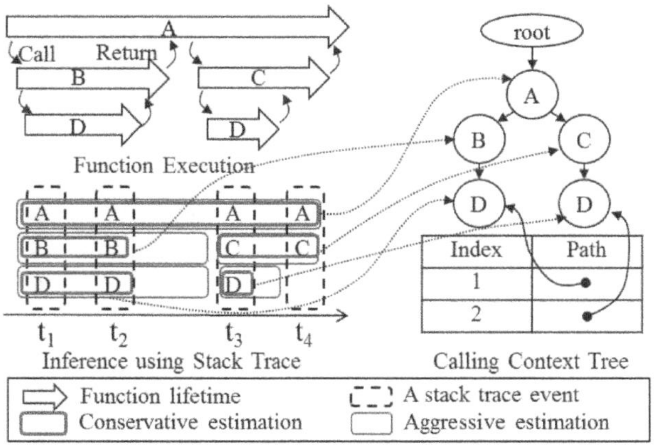

Figure 3: Inference of function latencies across multiple layers using stack trace events.

the function information across the application, intermediate libraries, and the kernel (e.g., system calls).

Figure 3 presents the high-level idea of the inference algorithm 2. The sub-figure at top left shows an example of the latencies between the calls and returns of five function instances: A, B, C, D, and D' (the notation on the second D' indicates its distinct context). Capturing these function call boundaries precisely would require code instrumentation for profilers. Instead, the input to our algorithm is a set of system stack traces which are illustrated as four dotted rectangles at times t_1, t_2, t_3, and t_4.

The algorithm infers the latency of function calls based on the *continuity of a function context*. In Figure 3, we can see that function `A` continues from time t_1 to t_4 without any disruption in its calling context; thus, the algorithm considers this whole period as its latency. On the other hand, function `D` experiences a change in its context. During t_1 and t_2, it was called in the context of `A->B->D`. However, at t_3 its context changes to `A->C->D` leading to discontinuity of its context even though function `D` stays at the same stack depth. Note that this discontinuity propagates towards the top of the stack. If there are any further calls from `D` in this case, their context will be disrupted all together. The algorithm scans the stack trace events in the temporal order and tracks the continuity of each function in the stack frame along with its context.

Our approach infers function latencies in two modes, conservative estimation and aggressive estimation, as illustrated in Figure 3. The conservative mode estimates the end of a function with the last event of the context while the aggressive mode estimates it with the start event of a distinct context. In our analysis, we mainly use the conservative mode. However, we also observe that these two modes are complementary when context change is frequent.

Algorithm 2 Function Call Latency Inference

```
    T : a system stack trace, s_i: a call stack at time t_i
 1: function InferFunctionInstances(Trace T, CCT_w)
 2:     for (t_k, s_k) in T do
 3:         newStackEvent(t_k, s_k, CCT_w)
 4:     for d in (0, ..., Register ) do
 5:         closeRegister(t_last, d)
 6: function NewStackEvent(t_k, s_k, CCT_w)
 7:     initialize ThisStack, LastStack, Register
 8:     AllNew = 0, d = 0
 9:     pid = PathToID(s_k, CCT_w)
10:     for f in s_k do
11:         isNew = (f == LastStack[d])
12:         if AllNew==1 then
13:             isNew = 1            ▷ Context change propagates.
14:         if isNew==1 then
15:             AllNew = 1           ▷ Context change triggered.
16:         ThisStack[d++] = (f, d, isNew)
17:     if LastStack > ThisStack then
18:         i = LastStack[ LastStack - 1]
19:         while i >= ThisStack do
20:             closeRegister(t_k, i)
21:             remove LastStack[i - - ]
22:     reverse ThisStack
23:     for (f, d, isNew) in ThisStack do
24:         if isNew == 1 then
25:             closeRegister(t_k, d)
26:             nid = getNodeIDfromCCT(pid, d, s_k , CCT_w)
27:             Register[d] = [t_k, t_k, f, nid, pid]
28:         else
29:             Register[d][1] = t_k      ▷ The end time stamp
30:         LastStack[d] = f
31:     t_last = t_k
32: function closeRegister(t_k, d)
33:     (t_s, t_e, f, nid, pid) = Register[d]
34:     t_a = t_k - t_s; t_c = t_e - t_s
35:     newFunctionInstance(f, pid, nid, t_a, t_c)
36:     remove Register[d]
```

Now we present how Algorithm 2 processes the illustrated example in detail step by step. The states of variables in each step of the algorithm are illustrated in Table 1. Function **`inferFunctionInstances`** calls **`newStackEvent`** for each stack event. This function tracks the continuity of a function context by putting each frame of the stack in a register as far as the context continues. **`isNew`** is a boolean value showing whether a function newly appears or not (Line 11). Table 1 shows that **`isNew`** (shown as I) is set to 1 for all stack levels at time t_1 due to their initial appearance. Then at time t_2 the values become 0 due to the identical stack status. The duration of the context continuity of the currently active functions in the stack are tracked using the **`Register`** array (shown as R in the Table). On a new function, its registration is performed in Line 27. As the function's context continues over time, its duration in **`Register`** is updated accordingly (Line 29). For instance, three function instances are registered at time t_1 as shown in the R column (6th column in Table 1). At time t_2 the duration of all three functions are updated from t_1 to t_2 (11th column).

If discontinuity of a function context is detected, the contexts of the functions in the higher level of the stack should all be discontinued because they are from a different context. This mechanism is performed by enforcing `isNew`'s status (Line 12-15). Function D appears twice (at times t_2 and t_3) at the same stack depth. But they have different contexts and hence are considered distinct instances.

Function returns are inferred using the moments when the context changes or at the end of the trace. When that happens, the registered functions are closed by calling `closeRegister` (Lines 5, 20, 25). Inside this function the new function instance is created as `newFunctionInstance`.

The inferred function latencies are associated with their contexts by recording the corresponding function node in the calling context tree. When a function is registered, the corresponding CCT node ID (*nid*) is obtained using the current context (*pid*) and the depth (d) of the given function in the context (Line 26-27). Later when this function is removed from `Register` and stored as an inferred function instance (Line 32-36), the CCT node ID (*nid*) is recorded along with the latency.

The inferred latency of a program L is a set of function latency instances (l L) where $l =$ f, pid, nid, t_a, t_c . t_a and t_c are aggressive and conservative estimations of a function latency, respectively. *nid* is a function node ID in CCT (when the node is v V, $v.id = nid$). *pid* is the ID of the call path that this node belongs to. f F is the function ID that this node represents.

We manage the extracted function latency instances in two ways. First, we keep the inferred latencies in a list to enable the examination of individual cases in a timeline for the developers. Second, we aggregate the instances in the CCT so as to have an aggregated view of function latencies accumulated in each context. This is performed using the *nid* field which can directly point to the corresponding node in the CCT using data structure `map_node` in Algorithm 1. A function node v is extended to have three additional fields: $v.C$ is the number of function counts accumulated in each node; $v.\mu_a$ and $v.\mu_c$ are the average function latencies in the aggressive and conservative modes respectively. Let L' be a subset of L where its estimated function instances belong to a function node, v_j, whose node ID is j, $L' =$ l l L, $l.nid = j$. v_j's average function latency is computed as follows.

$$v_j.\mu = \frac{1}{v_j.C} \sum_{l \in L'} l.t,$$

The operations on function latency are applied to both estimation modes, and we will use one expression in the following description for brevity.

We call this extended CCT with the accumulated function latency a *performance-annotated calling context tree (PA-CCT)*. We will use it in the next stage to localize performance bugs.

3.4 Context-Sensitive Analysis of Inferred Performance

IntroPerf provides a holistic and contextual view regarding the performance of all layers of a program by associating the inferred function latencies and the calling contexts available in the stack traces. We use such information to localize the root causes of performance bugs at the function level along with its specific calling context, which is valuable information to understand the bugs and generate patches. In this section we present how to automatically localize a potential performance bottleneck in a PA-CCT that we construct in the previous stage.

Algorithm 3 Top-Down Latency Normalization and Differential Context Ranking

function LatencyNormalization(Node *v)
    $\mu_{children} = 0;$
    for v_i $v.children$ **do**
        $LatencyNormalization(v_i)$
        $\mu_{childen}$ += $v_i.t_a$
    $v.\mu_{own} = v.\mu$ $\mu_{children}$
function GetPathSet(CCT_w)
    return $getPath$(the root of CCT_w, [], 0)
function GetPath(Node *v, p)
    $P =$
    if $v.children =$ **then**
        $P = P$ p v
    else
        for v_i $v.children$ **do**
            $P = P$ $getPath(v_i,$ p $v)$
    return P
function DiffRankPaths(N, CCT_{base}, CCT_{buggy})
    $P_{base} = getPathSet(CCT_{base})$
    $P_{buggy} = getPathSet(CCT_{buggy})$
    for p' P_{buggy} **do**
        if p P_{base} p' p **then**
            $c = \Sigma$ diff μ of equivalent nodes in p' and p
        else
            $c = \Sigma$ μ in each node in p'
        ΔP.append(c, p')
    for (c, p') ΔP **do**
        Sort all function nodes in p' with regard to $v.\mu$
        Annotate the rank of each node v in p' in $v.rank$
    Sort all paths in ΔP with regard to c
    return top N paths of ΔP

To determine the likely root causes of performance symptoms in terms of latency and context, we perform several steps of processing of the inferred function latencies. First, we normalize the function latencies at multiple layers to remove overlaps across call stack layers and extract true contributing latencies in a top down manner. Second, we present a calling context-based ranking mechanism which localizes potential root cause contexts and the bottleneck functions within the contexts automatically.

3.4.1 Top-Down Latency Normalization

IntroPerf estimates the latency of all function instances (i.e., duration between their invocations and returns) in the call stack. While this estimation strictly follows the definition of function latency, raw latencies could be misleading for identifying inefficient functions because there are overlaps in the execution time across multiple stack layers as illustrated in Figure 4. With raw latencies, function `A` would be determined as the slowest function because its duration is the longest. Without properly offsetting the latency of child functions, such top level functions (e.g., "main") that stay at the bottom of the call stack would always be considered as expensive functions. Note that this challenge does not oc-

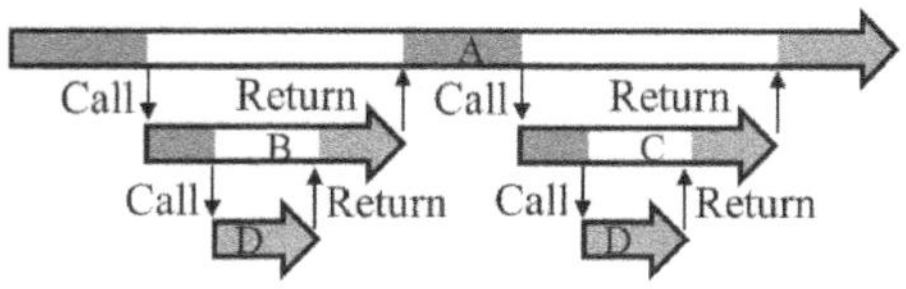

Figure 4: Top-down latency normalization. Non-overlapped latency is shown in shade.

cur in profilers because their approaches are bottom-up by sampling the program counters and always accounting for latency at the low shaded levels in Figure 4.

To remedy this problem, we use the association between callers and callees in the CCT. As shown in Figure 4, the latencies of callees always overlap with the latency of their caller. This relationship can be expressed as the following formula. Let $V' = \;\; v_i \;\; v_j, v_i \;\; v_j.children$, and the non-overlapped latency of v be $v.\mu_{own}$:

$$v_j.\mu = v_j.\mu_{own} + \sum_{v_i \in V'} v_i.\mu$$

Based on this observation, we address the above issue by recursively subtracting the latency of callee functions from the caller functions in a PA-CCT. Given the root node of a PA-CCT, function `LatencyNormalization` (Line 1-6 in Algorithm 3) recursively traverses the entire tree and subtracts the sum of the child node latencies from its parent's, leaving the latency truly contributing to the execution of that function.

3.4.2 Performance-Annotated Calling Context Ranking

In this section, we present how INTROPERF automatically localizes the likely cause of performance problems. We use the runtime cost of executed code estimated by the inferred latency from system stack traces to localize the root cause. While this approach is able to localize hot spot symptoms, there is an additional challenge in finding out which code region should be fixed because program semantics need to be considered. For instance, the root cause of high latency could be due to a bug triggered inside a function. On the other hand, it is also possible that the root cause is in other related functions such as a caller of a hot spot function because it introduces the symptom due to its invocation parameters. Our validation case in the evaluation section 5.1 indeed shows that in some applications the final patched functions could be away from the hot spots by a couple of frames in the call stack.

Our approach *ranks hot calling contexts*, which expose closely related functions in the call stack such as callers and callees in addition to the hot function particularly in the context when a high latency is triggered. The invocation relationship in calling contexts allows developers to inspect neighboring functions in the call stack that may have impact on the hot spot function and to find the most suitable code region to patch especially when complex code semantics are involved.

In order to locate the hot spot calling contexts, we generate a set of call paths by traversing a CCT and rank them. Let P_s be a set of paths observed in an execution s. Function `getPathSet` in Algorithm 3 recursively traverses the CCT and generates P_s. As the algorithm moves from a node to its child node, the path is updated by concatenating the function node ($p \;\; v$). When the algorithm reaches a leaf node which does not have any children, it stores the path from the root to the current node in the path set (P_s).

One challenge in hot spot ranking to investigate performance bugs is that some code is inherently CPU intensive and ranked high regardless of workload changes (e.g., crypto, compression functions). While such code region needs careful inspection for optimization, its behavior is not unusual in the developers' perspective because it reflects the characteristics of the program. Performance bugs reported in the community typically describe unexpected symptoms that are triggered in a particular input or workload (e.g., a large input file). In that sense, such originally costly code is less important for our purpose to determine the root cause of a performance bug symptom.

To address this problem and improve the quality of ranking output, we employ a systematic *differential method* in the ranking of calling contexts. The method uses two sets of CCTs produced from the workload samples under two different inputs: a *base* input that a program was tested and confirmed to work as expected with, and another *buggy* input that a user discovered and reported to have a performance bug symptom (e.g., a moderate sized input and a large input). By subtracting the inferred execution summary based on a base input from that based on a buggy input, we prioritize the hot spots sensitive to the buggy input in a higher rank and reduce the significance of the commonly observed hot spots. To apply this technique, we first need to define the equivalence of paths in multiple workloads.

Let there exist two paths which respectively belong to P_1 and P_2 ($p_k = \;\; v_1, \ldots, v_k \;\; , \; p_k \;\; P_1, \; p'_k = \;\; v'_1, \ldots, v'_k \;\; , \; p'_k \;\; P_2$). We define that two paths are equivalent ($p_k \;\; p'_k$) if the represented functions of two paths are identical in the same order. The differential cost of the paths is calculated as follows: P_1 and P_2 are for a base input and a buggy input, respectively. In comparison between the two sets of paths in dynamic calling contexts, a new context may appear due to the buggy input. In such a case, we consider the latency of the base workload as zero and use only the context of the buggy input.

$$\begin{array}{ll} \sum_{x=1}^{k} (v'_x.\mu - v_x.\mu) & : \; p_k, \;\; p'_k, \; p_k \;\; p'_k \\ \sum_{x=1}^{k} v'_x.\mu & : Otherwise \end{array}$$

The paths are ranked using the above cost formula and the top N ranked functions are listed for evaluation (function `DiffRankPaths` in Algorithm 3). The number of dynamic calling contexts can go up to tens of thousands even though a partial workload is sampled depending on the complexity of workload. Such context ranking significantly reduces analysis efforts by limiting the scope to a small set of *hot calling contexts*. Furthermore, for each hot calling context we provide the ranking of function nodes illustrating *hot functions* inside the path.

Later in Section 5 (Figure 7), we will present a few cases of real world performance bugs with the top-N% hot calling contexts and hot functions in the ranked order in the heat-map (i.e., a color-mapped table with rows for distinct contexts, columns for the functions within a path, and colors for function latencies). It provides a concise and intuitive view on context-sensitive hot spots and assists developers by automatically narrowing down their focus from massive amount of dynamic calling contexts to a few highly ranked code contexts.

4. IMPLEMENTATION

IntroPerf is built on top of a production tracer, Event Tracing Framework for Windows (ETW) [1] – a tracing facility available on Windows (introduced in Windows 2000) and is used by management tools such as `Resource Monitor`. We use ETW to generate system stack traces, which are the stack dumps generated when kernel events happen, thus including a range of function information from user functions to kernel functions. Stack traces are generated on a selection of kernel events specified as input to the framework as the stack walking mode. We use two configurations: (1) system call events, and (2) system call + context switch events. In addition, we include several miscellaneous events in tracing (e.g., process, thread, and image loading events) without stack walking. These events are included as a common practice to disclose execution status during tracing such as the loaded program images and the memory address of the kernel necessary to understand the trace.

The front-end of IntroPerf parses the ETL (Event Tracing Log, the output of ETW) files and extracts both kernel and user space function information which are sliced for each process and thread. The back-end consists of several stages of programs performing the construction of the calling context tree, inference of function latencies, and ranking of the performance annotated-CCT. The entire framework including both the front-end and back-end has a total of 42K lines of Windows code written in Visual C++. All experiments are done on a machine with Intel Core i5 3.40 GHz CPU, 8GB RAM, and Windows Server 2008 R2.

In the presentation of our evaluation, we use the debugging information in the program database (PDB) format for convenience of illustration and validation of data. However, it is not a requirement for our mechanism because our framework, instead, can represent instructions (e.g., function entries) by their offsets within the binary. As an example usage scenario, IntroPerf can generate detailed bug localization reports on problematic performance symptoms only based on the binary packages on users' sites. If the user determines that a root cause belongs to a software component, he/she can report it to the vendor. The developers on the vendor side should have the debugging information which is stripped in the release. They can interpret the details of IntroPerf's report with function names using symbolic information.

The Visual Studio compiler produces PDB files for both executable files (e.g., `*.exe`) and libraries (e.g., `*.dll`) regardless whether it uses the debug or release mode. Most Microsoft software products (e.g., Internet Explore, Windows kernel, and low level Windows subsystems) provide such information which can be automatically retrieved from the central server with a configuration. Therefore interpreting the software layers of Windows including the kernel and GUI system is straightforward even though Windows is a proprietary OS. Most open source projects make their symbol files available in addition to the binary packages to assist debugging. If not, this information can be easily generated by compiling the code.

Currently ETW does not support the stacks of virtual machines (e.g., Java) or interpreters due to limited parsing capability of non-native stacks. Supplemental stack interpretation layers such as in `jstack` [4] will resolve this problem.

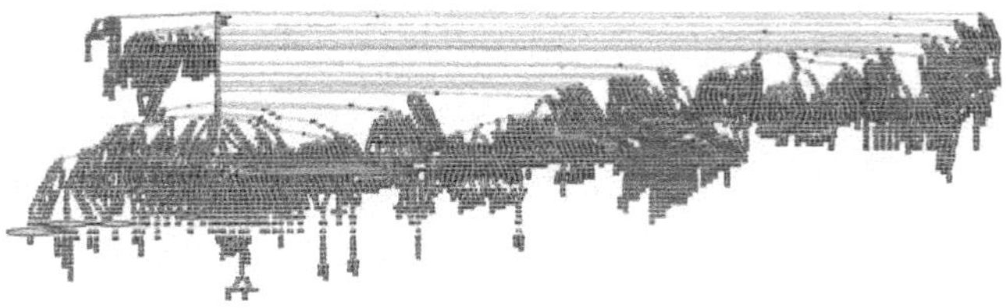

Figure 5: Dynamic calling contexts of the Apache 45464 case showing hundreds of distinct call paths.

5. EVALUATION

In this section, we evaluate several aspects of IntroPerf experimentally. Here are the key questions in the evaluation:

How effective is IntroPerf at diagnosing performance bugs?

What is the coverage of program execution captured by system stack traces?

What is the runtime overhead of IntroPerf?

5.1 Localizing Root Causes of Performance Bugs

IntroPerf enables transparent performance introspection of multiple software layers which includes relative performance cost of individual functions in each specific context. This information is valuable for developers to understand "where" and "how" (in terms of function call sequences) performance bugs occur and eventually to determine the most suitable code regions to be fixed. In this section, we evaluate the effectiveness of IntroPerf in localizing the root causes of performance bugs in a set of open source projects which are actively developed and used.

Evaluation setup: We selected open source projects with various characteristics such as server programs (Apache HTTP server: web server, MySQL: database server), desktop applications (7zip: file compressor/decompressor), and a low-level system utility (ProcessHacker: an advanced version of Task Manager) to highlight generic applicability of IntroPerf. The life span of these projects range from five to eighteen years as of 2014 with continuous development and improvement of code due to popularity and user bases.

Input to experiments: As the input cases to be analyzed, we use the performance bug symptoms that are reported by users. We checked the forums of the projects where users post their complaints on performance issues, and collected cases which include instructions to trigger the performance issues. In addition to the workload described to trigger symptoms, we created another workload with a similar input on a smaller scale as a base input to offset costly code which is not closely relevant to the symptom.

IntroPerf analyzes bug symptoms without any prior knowledge; thus it is capable of identifying the root causes of new bugs. Such a process, however, typically requires non-trivial turn-around time for evaluation by developers and patch generation. While our long-term evaluation plan includes finding un-patched bugs, in this paper, for validation purposes we use the cases whose patches are available to

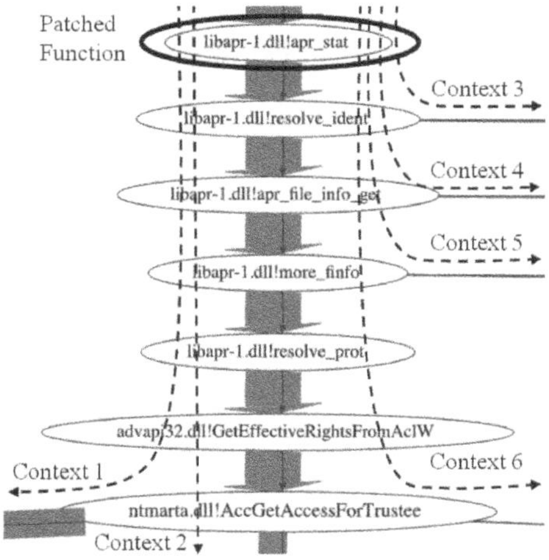

Figure 6: A zoomed-in view of the PA-CCTs of the Apache 45464 case.

compare with INTROPERF's output derived with zero knowledge and evaluate its efficacy.

Performance-annotated calling context tree (PA-CCT): A calling context tree provides a very informative view to developers to understand the root cause by distinguishing the overhead along with distinct call paths. INTROPERF creates this view on all layers by overlaying the estimated function latencies from system stack traces. Figure 5 illustrates this holistic view of a dynamic calling context for the Apache 45464 case with hundreds of distinct call paths. Due to its complexity, we show a zoom-in view in Figure 6 around a costly function call path of Figure 5. Each node represents a function and an edge shows a function call. We use two workloads in a combined view showing the edges from two PA-CCTs. The workloads of a large input and a small input are respectively illustrated as thick red arrows and thin blue arrows. The thickness of the arrows represents the inferred latency showing a clear contrast of the performance of the two workloads. Note that a PA-CCT shows a more informative view than a program CCT due to the distinct calling context in all software component layers.

The details of the PA-CCTs in the evaluated cases are presented in Table 2. Columns 3, 4, 5, and 6 show the runtime program characteristics captured in stack traces: the number of loaded program binaries and libraries (I), the number of distinct dynamic calling contexts (P), the total number of functions present in the stack (F), and the average length of paths (l).

Costly calling contexts and functions: While human inspection of a PA-CCT is useful for analysis on a small scale, for a PA-CCT with non-trivial size, as shown in Figure 5, the amount of details would be overwhelming for a manual approach. Hence INTROPERF provides an automated ranking of costly (i.e., hot) calling contexts. Algorithm 3 ranks call paths using their runtime cost, which is the sum of the function's aggregated inferred latencies.

In this evaluation, we use two metrics: hot calling contexts (i.e., paths) and hot functions within the paths. To validate how effective INTROPERF is, we compare INTROPERF's results with the patch (considered as the ground truth) and present how closely INTROPERF's metrics match the ground truth using two distance metrics. A path distance, p_{min}, represents the similarity between the bottleneck path and the root cause path in the ground truth using the top (minimum) rank of the path that includes a patched function. A function distance, f_{min}, shows the effectiveness of INTROPERF in a finer function level using the minimum number of edges between the most costly function node and a patched function node *within a path.*

The comparison result is presented in columns 7-10 in Table 2. As in-depth information, top ranked costly calling contexts are further illustrated as heat-maps in Figure 7, where each row represents the cost of one path and the top row is the call path (context) with the highest estimated latency. The latency of an individual function is represented in colors (log10 scale) showing the bottlenecks in red and the patched functions (ground truth) are illustrated as circled "P" marks. To ease the identification of a bottleneck within a path, the function with the highest latency is marked as 0 and the adjacent functions are marked with the distance from it.

In all cases, we can confirm that the bottleneck contexts ranked by INTROPERF effectively cover the patched functions from the data shown in Table 2 and illustrated in Figure 7 while such data vary depending on the characteristics of the program and the performance symptoms. For instance, the patch can be placed in a hot function if the bottleneck is in the function. On the other hand, a patch could be placed in its caller if its parameter is anomalous. Note that in both cases INTROPERF offers *an opportunity to correlate the bottleneck and the patch* using calling context performance ranking. It enables developers to easily check the adjacent functions around the bottleneck function in the context and to reason about the suitable program points for patches.

5.2 External Root Causes of Performance Bugs

So far we have presented the cases that the root causes of performance bug symptoms are present *inside* the program. In a post-development stage, software components are installed, integrated, and updated in an un-coordinated manner. If any of the multiple layers has a problem, it will impact the overall performance of the software. Note that this problem is beyond a typical scope of traditional debugging or testing techniques because the analysis requires the capability to inspect multiple software layers that are separately built.

Since INTROPERF uses system stack traces that include information at multiple system layers, INTROPERF is not limited to the analysis of software's internal code but is able to address performance problems external to the program binary as well. In this section, we evaluate potential cases that a dependent but *external* software component, such as a plug-in or an external library, causes performance issues. It shows the unique advantage of INTROPERF: *introspecting all vertical layers and identifying the source of performance impact* automatically without requiring source code.

This type of performance bugs are in general not well studied because the root causes may depend on the integration and deployment of external components including the system environment. This type of performance anomaly tends to be quite common in the field. However, because of currently limited documentation of real cases and time constraints, we choose one of the components on which the target software depends, and manually inject a time lag into

Table 2: **Evaluation of IntroPerf on the root cause contexts of real world and injected performance bugs.**

Program Name	Bug ID	Program Characteristics				IntroPerf Evaluation				Internal/ External	Ground Truth
		I	P	F	l	p_{min}	f_{min}	Root Cause Binary	Root Cause Function		
Apache	45464	29	319	712	40.96	1	36	`libapr-1.dll`, Internal Library	`apr_stat`	Internal	Patch
MySQL	15811	36	1051	1275	31.22	1	0	`mysql.exe`, Main Binary	`strlen`	Internal	Patch
MySQL	49491	13	144	368	33.71	3	5	`mysqld.exe`, Main Binary	`Item_func_sha::val_str`	Internal	Patch
ProcessHacker	3744	23	2704	1172	49.34	1	0	`ProcessHacker.exe`, Main Binary	`PhSearchMemoryString`	Internal	Patch
7zip	S1	28	1160	1182	72.21	11	16	`7zFM.exe`, Main Binary	`CPanel::RefreshListCtrl`	Internal	Patch
7zip	S2	33	1793	1496	59.61	3	16	`7zFM.exe`, Main Binary	`CPanel::RefreshListCtrl`	Internal	Patch
7zip	S3	22	656	819	58.78	1	15	`7zFM.exe`, Main Binary	`CPanel::Post_Refresh_StatusBar`	Internal	Patch
7zip	S4	30	1002	1274	55.95	2	16	`7zFM.exe`, Main Binary	`CPanel::RefreshListCtrl`	Internal	Patch
ProcessHacker	5424	25	1488	978	40.60	1	54	`ToolStatus.dll`, Plug-in	`MainWndSubclassProc`	External	Patch
ProcessHacker	-	26	1241	906	41.56	1	0	`ToolStatus.dll`, Plug-in	`NcAreaWndSubclassProc`	External	Inject
Internet Explorer	-	92	18716	6168	71.64	1	0	`MotleyFool.dll`, Toolbar Plug-in	`CMFToolbar::GetQuote`	External	Inject
Miranda	-	42	1032	1245	52.40	1	0	`Yahoo.dll`, Plug-in	`upload_file`	External	Inject
Apache	-	14	77	302	26.12	3	0	`mod_log_config.so`, Plug-in	`ap_default_log_writer`	External	Inject
Apache	-	18	96	331	25.89	2	0	`mod_deflate.so`, Plug-in	`deflate_out_filter`	External	Inject
VirtualBox	-	39	1288	1031	39.36	1	0	`QtCore4.dll`, External Library	`QEventDispatcherWin32::processEvents`	External	Inject

it. Injection of the code enables the validation by knowing the ground truth of the fault. In the long term, we expect to study real cases in future work.

Evaluation setup: For evaluation, we selected the cases where the source of the bottleneck is separate from the main software binary. Such external modules are integrated on the deployment site or optionally activated such as independent libraries which the main software is relying on or plug-ins implemented as dynamic libraries. In addition to one real case of ProcessHacker, we have six delay-injection cases: `ToolStatus` is a plug-in for ProcessHacker. `MotleyFool` is a toolbar for Internet Explorer. Miranda is a multi-protocol instant messenger and we selected the file transfer module of the Yahoo messenger plug-in. VirtualBox relies on several libraries for graphics and multimedia. We injected a bottleneck in the Qt library. Also we injected bottlenecks in the `mod_log_config` and `mod_deflate` modules of Apache HTTP server which log and compress user requests respectively.

Ranked costly contexts: The bottom 7 rows of Table 2 show the results of IntroPerf's capability of localizing the external root causes of performance bottlenecks. In all cases, IntroPerf successfully identified the root cause of the injected bottleneck with high accuracy.

5.3 Coverage of System Call Stack Traces

The system stack trace is a collection of snapshots of the program stack sampled on OS kernel events. Therefore, the sampled calling context and function instances will be limited to the frequency of the kernel events (e.g., system calls, context switch). However, we found that this coarse granularity suffices for diagnosis of performance anomalies based on a critical observation that *the quality of this sampled view improves as the latency of a function increases*. This property leads to a larger number of appearances of function contexts and instances in the stack traces and higher accuracy in the inference accordingly. In this section, we will experimentally confirm this hypothesis.

Evaluation method: The necessary information for this experiment is the fine-grained function call instances and the kernel events which trigger the generation of system stack traces. We used a dynamic translator, Pin [23], to capture function calls and returns. System stack traces are generated by taking the snapshots of the stack on kernel events. System calls are captured by Pin because they are triggered by the program. However, context switches are driven by the kernel; hence, they are hard to capture in user mode experiments on Pin. Therefore, such events are simulated by taking stack snapshots for every time quantum in the offline trace analysis.

We evaluate three configurations regarding the kernel events to generate system stack traces: (1) system calls, (2) system calls and low rate context switches, and (3) system calls and high rate context switches. The context switch quantum in Windows systems vary from 20 ms to 120 ms depending on scheduling policies and the configuration of the system [14]. We use 120 ms as the low rate of context switch in the second configuration as a conservative measure. We also evaluate the higher context switch rate (20 ms interval) in the third configuration. These three configurations present the views of stack traces in three sampling rates. Note that the dynamic translation framework is slower than the native execution having an effect similar to executing on a slow machine. Thus we mainly focus on the relative comparison of the three configurations.

We evaluate the coverage of stack traces in two criteria. First, the dynamics of calling context are analyzed to evaluate the diversity of call paths shown in the stack traces. The second criterion is regarding the function call instances that are captured by the stack traces.

Coverage of dynamic calling context: Figures 8 (a)-(c) illustrate the coverage of dynamic calling context based on the three configurations described above. The X-axis shows the order of dynamic calling contexts in percentage sorted by the latency in the ascending order. The graph shows the coverage of dynamic calling contexts for all calling contexts whose ranks are the same or higher than the order shown in the X-axis, and the Y-axis shows the coverage of dynamic calling contexts in percentage. For example, if x is 0%, the corresponding y value shows the coverage of all dynamic calling contexts. If x is 99%, y shows the coverage of calling contexts with the top 1% high latencies.

Each figure shows multiple lines due to MySQL's usage of multiple processes/threads. In the experiment using Pin on Windows, we observed that some threads only execute OS functions in their entire lifetime. We used the processes and threads that include the application code (e.g., "main") in the execution since OS-only behavior could be dependent on platforms (e.g., program runtime setup) and may not be representative application characteristics.

In the overall scope ($x = 0$), the stack traces cover under 20% of dynamic calling contexts. However, the results are improved on high latency contexts which are the focus of IntroPerf for performance diagnosis. The right sides of

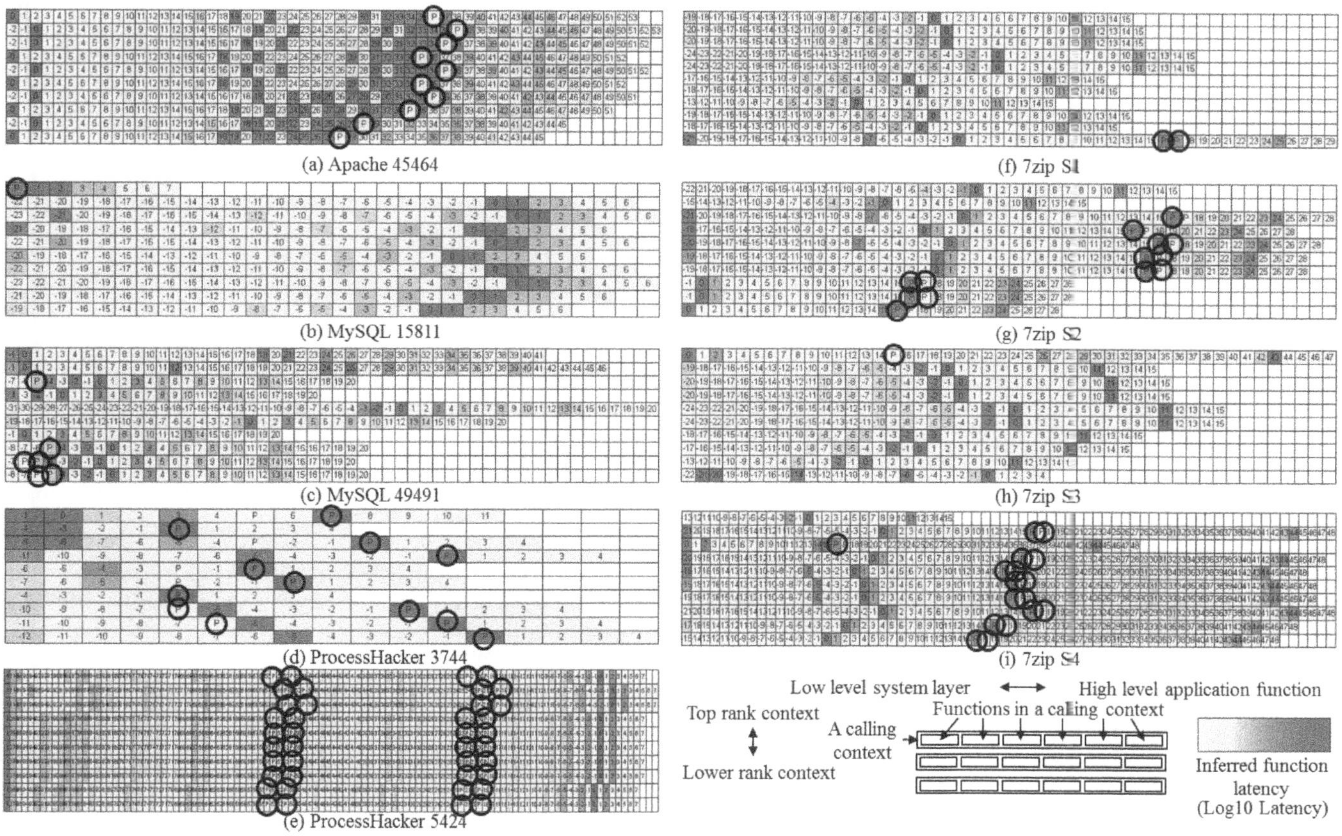

Figure 7: Top ranked contexts of performance bug symptoms. Each row represents a calling context. Columns represent the functions within contexts. The root causes in the ground truth are highlighted with circles.

Figures 8 (a)-(c) show that the coverage increases for top ranked contexts. For the top 1 % slowest functions shown at the right end of the X-axis ($x = 99$), the coverage increases to 34.7%-100% depending on processes/threads.

Coverage of function call instances: Figures 8 (d)-(f) show the coverage of individual function call instances in the stack traces. In all the executions, most threads covered 1.2%-8.05% of the instances. However, for the top 1% high latency functions the coverage increases to 29.1%-100%.

Table 3 summarizes the coverage analysis of dynamic calling contexts and function call instances on three programs: Apache HTTP server, MySQL server, and 7zip. Apache and MySQL are the examples of web and database server programs with I/O oriented workload. 7zip is a data compression/decompression program which would be an example of a desktop application with intensive CPU workload. The table shows different characteristics of these programs. The second column shows the percentage of system calls compared to regular function calls.

Although there are variations in the behavior of the three programs due to their characteristics as shown in columns, the general observation applies in the same way in the comparison between the coverage of the entire scope (columns "Cov. of Context: All," "Cov. of Instances: All") and the coverage of top 1% slowest contexts and latencies (columns "Cov. of Context: Top 1%," "Cov. of Instances: Top 1%"): the coverage of contexts and function instances is significantly higher for high latency functions. In other words, for slow functions experiencing performance bug symptoms, INTROPERF generates higher quality views compared to shorter (time-wise) functions. This is the core reason for INTROPERF's effectiveness in performance bug diagnosis despite the relatively coarse granularity of stack traces.

5.4 Performance

INTROPERF can work with any system stack trace from production event tracers [1, 15, 27], which are already deployed and being used in production systems. INTROPERF is an offline trace analysis engine. The tracing efficiency is entirely determined by the design and implementation of OS kernel tracers. Even though studying the performance of the tracing sessions is not the focus of this work and cannot be generalized due to the differences and evolution of tracing mechanisms, we present the tracing performance that we measured for ETW [1] to provide some insight into the potential overhead of current production tracers.

We present the overhead for the tracing sessions of three benchmarks: the Apache benchmarking tool (`ab`), MySQL benchmark suite (`sql-bench --small-test`), and 7zip benchmark (`7z.exe b`). `Ab` measures the time that an Apache HTTP server takes to handle 10k requests. `Sql-bench` provides a set of sub-benchmarks that measure the wall-clock times of database operations such as SELECT, INSERT, UPDATE, etc. The Apache and MySQL benchmarks are performed in a local network. 7zip has a built-in benchmark that operates with the `b` option which measures the compression and decompression performance with internal data.

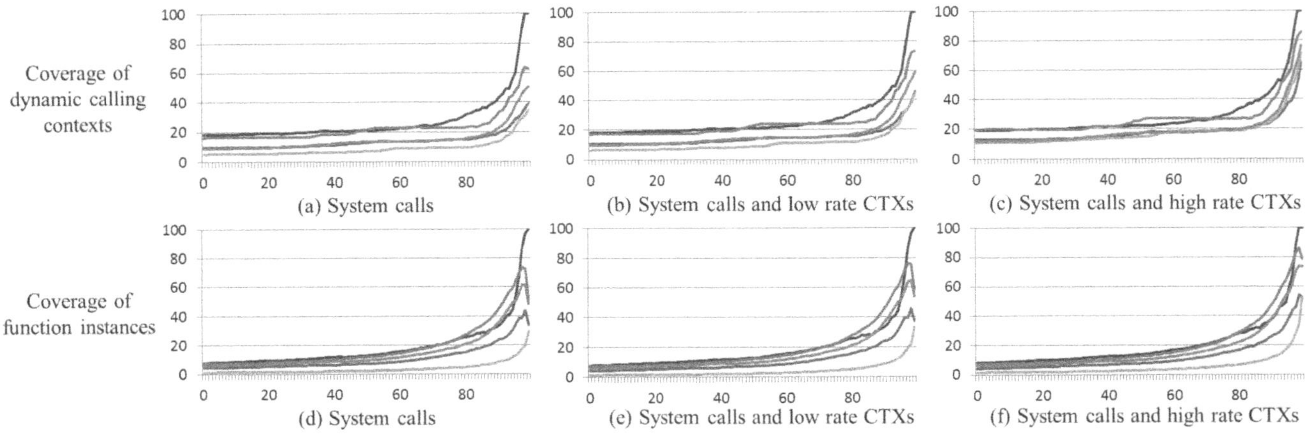

Figure 8: Coverage of dynamic calling contexts (a)-(c) and function instances (d)-(f) of MySQL database.

Table 3: Coverage of dynamic calling context and function instances in multiple sampling schemes of system stack traces in percentage. Ranges are used due to the data of multiple threads. Sys: system calls, LCTX: system calls and low rate context switch events, HCTX: system calls and high rate context switch events.

Program Name	Syscall Rate	Cov. of Context: All			Cov. of Context: Top 1 %			Cov. of Instances: All			Cov. of Instances: Top 1 %		
		Sys	LCTX	HCTX	Sys	LCTX	HCTX	Sys	LCTX	HCTX	Sys	LCTX	HCTX
Apache	0.33-2.79	18.7-19.3	19.3-20	22.3-24.5	58.6-84.6	61.8-92.3	75.3-100	1.5-20.1	1.5-20.3	1.8-21.6	27-86.7	30.1-93.3	42.6-100
MySQL	0.21-1.48	5.3-18.2	6.4-18.2	10.8-19.2	34.7-100	44.2-100	64.7-100	1.2-7.48	1.3-7.48	1.7-8.05	29.1-100	33.3-100	52.3-100
7zip	0.11-5.03	13.6-47.5	14.5-49.4	17.5-47.5	38.5-100	41-100	50.1-100	0.6-30.2	0.6-30.2	0.8-31.2	16.6-100	18.6-100	26.5-100

Our configuration of ETW flushes the trace records to the disk when the 512 MB kernel buffer is full. The goal of this experiment is to measure the runtime impact due to the generation of stack traces. To minimize the impact due to the flush to disk, we stored the trace on RAM disk. ETW provides another option, on-the-fly trace processing, instead of flushing events to disk. If a custom tracer can be built, it can further lower the overhead.

Figure 9 shows the overhead for tracing OS kernel events along with system stack traces. When system calls and miscellaneous events, which are required to comprehend events described in Section 4, are recorded, the overhead is 1.38%-8.2%. If context switch events are additionally collected, the overhead increases to 2.4%-9.11%. Note that IntroPerf is not required to be active for the entire execution of a program because OS tracers can dynamically start and stop a tracing session without interfering applications. A reasonable scenario would be to sample the abnormal period when the program begins to show it. Moreover, with the efficiency of OS tracers being improved, IntroPerf will be able to perform faster offline analyses.

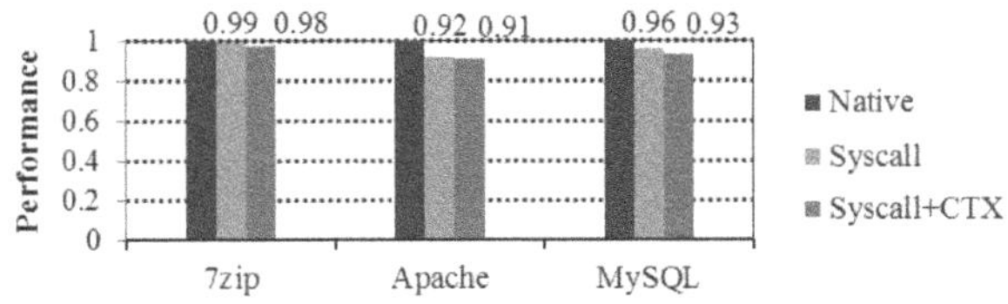

Figure 9: Overhead of ETW stack trace collection.

6. DISCUSSION AND FUTURE WORK

Our evaluation in Section 5 is based on a simple and conservative scheme (i.e., conservative estimation shown in Figure 3) to estimate the latencies of functions. A more relaxed latency estimation scheme (e.g., aggressive estimation or variants) may have either increased or decreased accuracy depending on which scheme closely matches the actural timing of function calls and returns. Improving the estimation accuracy with advanced schemes would be an interesting direction for future work.

Applications heavily relying on system functions may cause high frequency of kernel events. Since the overhead of the OS tracer is likely proportional to the frequency of the events recorded, it would be important to lower the number of recorded events for efficiency as far as the coverage is not significantly affected. Sampling could be leveraged to mitigate the problem. Existing sampling schemes such as those employed by traditional profilers could be similarly effective.

7. CONCLUSION

We present IntroPerf, a performance inference technique that transparently introspects the latency of multiple layers of software in a fine-grained and context-sensitive manner. We tested it on a set of widely used open source software, and both internal and external root causes of real performance bugs and delay-injected cases were automatically localized and confirmed. The results showed the effectiveness and practicality of IntroPerf as a lightweight application performance introspection tool in a post-development stage.

Acknowledgments

We thank Brendan Saltaformaggio and anonymous reviewers who provided valuable feedback for the improvement of this paper.

8. REFERENCES

[1] Event Tracing for Windows (ETW). `http://msdn.microsoft.com/en-us/library/windows/desktop/aa363668(v=vs.85).aspx`.

[2] Ftrace: Function Tracer. `https://www.kernel.org/doc/Documentation/trace/ftrace.txt`.

[3] gperftools: Fast, multi-threaded malloc() and nifty performance analysis tools. `https://code.google.com/p/gperftools/`.

[4] jstack - Stack Trace. `http://docs.oracle.com/javase/7/docs/technotes/tools/share/jstack.html`.

[5] LTTng: Linux Tracing Toolkit - next generation. `http://lttng.org`.

[6] Oprofile: a system-wide profiler for linux systems. `http://oprofile.sourceforge.net/`.

[7] perf: Linux profiling with performance counters. `https://perf.wiki.kernel.org/`.

[8] Stack Walking (Windows Driver). `http://msdn.microsoft.com/en-us/library/windows/desktop/ff191014(v=vs.85).aspx/`.

[9] M. K. Aguilera, J. C. Mogul, J. L. Wiener, P. Reynolds, and A. Muthitacharoen. Performance debugging for distributed systems of black boxes. In *SOSP'03*.

[10] G. Ammons, T. Ball, and J. R. Larus. Exploiting hardware performance counters with flow and context sensitive profiling. In *PLDI'97*.

[11] P. Barham, A. Donnelly, R. Isaacs, and R. Mortier. Using magpie for request extraction and workload modelling. In *OSDI'04*.

[12] M. D. Bond, G. Z. Baker, and S. Z. Guyer. Breadcrumbs: efficient context sensitivity for dynamic bug detection analyses. In *PLDI'10*.

[13] M. D. Bond and K. S. McKinley. Probabilistic calling context. In *OOPSLA '07*.

[14] M. Buchanan and A. A. Chien. Coordinated thread scheduling for workstation clusters under windows nt. In *Proceedings of the USENIX Windows NT Workshop 1997*.

[15] B. M. Cantrill, M. W. Shapiro, and A. H. Leventhal. Dynamic instrumentation of production systems. In *USENIX'04*.

[16] M. Y. Chen, E. Kiciman, E. Fratkin, A. Fox, and E. Brewer. Pinpoint: Problem determination in large, dynamic internet services. In *DSN'02*.

[17] T. Chilimbi, B. Liblit, K. Mehra, A. Nori, and K. Vaswani. Holmes: Effective statistical debugging via efficient path profiling. In *ICSE'09*.

[18] U. Erlingsson, M. Peinado, S. Peter, and M. Budiu. Fay: extensible distributed tracing from kernels to clusters. In *SOSP '11*.

[19] S. L. Graham, P. B. Kessler, and M. K. McKusick. gprof: a call graph execution profiler. *SIGPLAN Not.*, 39(4):49–57, Apr. 2004.

[20] S. Han, Y. Dang, S. Ge, D. Zhang, and T. Xie. Performance debugging in the large via mining millions of stack traces. In *ICSE'12*.

[21] G. Jin, L. Song, X. Shi, J. Scherpelz, and S. Lu. Understanding and detecting real-world performance bugs. In *PLDI'12*.

[22] B. Liblit, M. Naik, A. X. Zheng, A. Aiken, and M. I. Jordan. Scalable statistical bug isolation. In *PLDI'05*.

[23] C.-K. Luk, R. Cohn, R. Muth, H. Patil, A. Klauser, G. Lowney, S. Wallace, V. J. Reddi, and K. Hazelwood. Pin: building customized program analysis tools with dynamic instrumentation. In *PLDI '05*.

[24] M. L. Massie, B. N. Chun, and D. E. Culler. The ganglia distributed monitoring system: Design, implementation and experience. In *Parallel Computing*, 2004.

[25] R. J. Moore. A universal dynamic trace for linux and other operating systems. In *Proceedings of the FREENIX Track: 2001 USENIX Annual Technical Conference*, 2001.

[26] N. Nethercote and J. Seward. Valgrind: a framework for heavyweight dynamic binary instrumentation. In *PLDI '07*.

[27] V. Prasad, W. Cohen, F. C. Eigler, M. Hunt, J. Keniston, and B. Chen. Locating system problems using dynamic instrumentation. In *Proceedings of the 2005 Ottawa Linux Symposium (OLS)*, 2005.

[28] P. Reynolds, C. Killian, J. L. Wiener, J. C. Mogul, M. A. Shah, and A. Vahdat. Pip: detecting the unexpected in distributed systems. In *NSDI'06*.

[29] B. H. Sigelman, L. A. Barroso, M. Burrows, P. Stephenson, M. Plakal, D. Beaver, S. Jaspan, and C. Shanbhag. Dapper, a large-scale distributed systems tracing infrastructure. Technical report, Google, Inc., 2010.

[30] W. Sumner, Y. Zheng, D. Weeratunge, and X. Zhang. Precise calling context encoding. *Software Engineering, IEEE Transactions on*, 38(5), 2012.

[31] B. C. Tak, C. Tang, C. Zhang, S. Govindan, B. Urgaonkar, and R. N. Chang. vpath: precise discovery of request processing paths from black-box observations of thread and network activities. In *USENIX '09*.

[32] X. Xiao, S. Han, D. Zhang, and T. Xie. Context-sensitive delta inference for identifying workload-dependent performance bottlenecks. In *ISSTA'13*.

[33] D. Yuan, H. Mai, W. Xiong, L. Tan, Y. Zhou, and S. Pasupathy. Sherlog: Error diagnosis by connecting clues from run-time logs. In *ASPLOS'10*.

[34] D. Yuan, J. Zheng, S. Park, Y. Zhou, and S. Savage. Improving software diagnosability via log enhancement. In *ASPLOS'11*.

[35] X. Zhuang, M. J. Serrano, H. W. Cain, and J.-D. Choi. Accurate, efficient, and adaptive calling context profiling. In *PLDI'06*.

Non-intrusive, Out-of-band and Out-of-the-box Systems Monitoring in the Cloud

Sahil Suneja
University of Toronto
sahil@cs.toronto.edu

Canturk Isci
IBM T.J. Watson Research
canturk@us.ibm.com

Vasanth Bala
IBM T.J. Watson Research
vbala@us.ibm.com

Eyal de Lara
University of Toronto
delara@cs.toronto.edu

Todd Mummert
IBM T.J. Watson Research
mummert@us.ibm.com

ABSTRACT

The dramatic proliferation of virtual machines (VMs) in datacenters and the highly-dynamic and transient nature of VM provisioning has revolutionized datacenter operations. However, the management of these environments is still carried out using re-purposed versions of traditional agents, originally developed for managing physical systems, or most recently via newer virtualization-aware alternatives that require guest cooperation and accessibility. We show that these existing approaches are a poor match for monitoring and managing (virtual) systems in the cloud due to their dependence on guest cooperation and operational health, and their growing lifecycle management overheads in the cloud.

In this work, we first present *Near Field Monitoring* (NFM), our non-intrusive, out-of-band cloud monitoring and analytics approach that is designed based on cloud operation principles and to address the limitations of existing techniques. NFM decouples system execution from monitoring and analytics functions by pushing monitoring out of the targets systems' scope. By leveraging and extending VM introspection techniques, our framework provides simple, standard interfaces to monitor running systems in the cloud that require no guest cooperation or modification, and have minimal effect on guest execution. By decoupling monitoring and analytics from target system context, NFM provides "always-on" monitoring, even when the target system is unresponsive. NFM also works "out-of-the-box" for any cloud instance as it eliminates any need for installing and maintaining agents or hooks in the monitored systems. We describe the end-to-end implementation of our framework with two real-system prototypes based on two virtualization platforms. We discuss the new cloud analytics opportunities enabled by our decoupled execution, monitoring and analytics architecture. We present four applications that are built on top of our framework and show their use for across-time and across-system analytics.

SIGMETRICS'14, June 16–20, 2014, Austin, Texas, USA.

http://dx.doi.org/10.1145/2591971.2592009 .

Categories and Subject Descriptors

K.6.4 [**Management of Computing and Information Systems**]: System Management—*Centralization/ decentralization*; D.4.7 [**Operating Systems**]: Organization and Design—*Distributed systems*; C.5.0 [**Computer System Implementation**]: General; C.4 [**Performance of Systems**]: Design studies

Keywords

Virtualization; Virtual Machine; Cloud; Data Center; Monitoring; Analytics; Agentless; VMI

1. INTRODUCTION

Cloud computing and virtualization technologies are dramatically changing how IT systems operate. What used to be a relatively static environment, with fixed physical nodes, has quickly transformed into a highly-dynamic environment, where (clusters of) virtual machines (VMs) are programmatically provisioned, started, replicated, stopped and deprovisioned with cloud APIs. VMs have become the processes of the cloud OS, with short lifetimes and a rapid proliferation trend [24].

While the nature of data center operations has changed, the management methodology of these (virtual) machines has not adapted appropriately. Tasks, such as performance monitoring, compliance and security scans, and product discovery amongst others are carried out using re-purposed versions of tools originally developed for managing physical systems or via newer virtualization-aware alternatives that require guest cooperation and accessibility. These approaches require a communication channel, i.e., a *hook*, into the running system, or the introduction of a software component, i.e., an *agent*, within the system runtime. There are two key problems with the existing approaches:

First, proliferation of VMs and their ephemeral, short-lived nature, makes the cost of provisioning and maintaining hooks and agents a major pain point. Moreover, the monitoring extensions "pollute" the end-user system, intervene with guest execution, and potentially open up new points of vulnerability. A recent observation from Amazon Web Services [3] highlights how agent operation and maintenance issues can impact managed systems. In this case, an incomplete maintenance update for DNS configuration in some of the agents, coupled with a memory leak issue led to a performance degradation for part of Amazon storage services.

This observation drives the first research question we address in our work: *How can we perform IT operations (monitoring, compliance, etc.) without relying on guest cooperation or in-VM hooks?*

Second, existing techniques work only so long as the monitored systems function properly, and they fail once a system becomes unresponsive—exactly when such monitoring information is the most valuable. A recent Google outage [12] presents a prime example to the effect of this limitation, where a significant portion of Google's production systems became unresponsive due to a dynamic loader misconfiguration. As a result of this, none of the in-system agents could publish data outside, neither was it possible to log in to the impacted systems for manual diagnosis. Thus,it was extremely difficult to get system information when it was most crucial. This observation drives our second research question: *How can we monitor and manage systems even when they become unresponsive or are compromised?*

To address these research challenges, this paper introduces *Near Field Monitoring* (NFM), a new approach for system monitoring that leverages virtualization technology to decouple system monitoring from system context. NFM extends VM introspection (VMI) techniques, and combines these with a backend cloud analytics platform to perform monitoring and management functions without requiring access into, or cooperation of the target systems. NFM *crawls* VM memory and disk state in an *out-of-band* manner from outside the guest's context, to collect system state which is then fed to the analytics backend. The monitoring functions simply query this systems data, instead of accessing and intruding each running system. In stark contrast with existing techniques, NFM seamlessly works even when a system becomes unresponsive (*always-on* monitoring), and does not require the installation and configuration of any hooks or agents in the target system (it works *out-of-the-box*). Unlike the in-VM solutions that run within the guest context and compete for resources allocated to the guest VMs, NFM is *non-intrusive* and does not steal guests' cycles or interfere with their actual operation. We believe our approach lays the foundation for the right way of systems monitoring in the cloud; very much like how we monitor processes in an OS today. NFM is better suited for responding to the ephemeral nature of VMs and further opens up new opportunities for cloud analytics by decoupling VM execution and monitoring.

There are three primary contributions of our work. First, we present our novel non-intrusive, out-of-band cloud monitoring and analytics framework, which we fully implement on real systems. It provides a service to query live as well as historical information about the cloud, with cloud monitoring and analytics applications acting as clients of this service. Our work presents how we can treat systems as documents and leverage familiar paradigms from the data analytics domain such as document differencing and semantic annotations to analyze systems. We also develop methods for low-latency, live access to VM's memory with optional consistency support, as well as optimizations that enable subsecond monitoring of systems. Second, we build several applications on top of our NFM framework based on actual enterprise use cases. These include (i) a cloud topology discovery and evolution tracker application, (ii) a cloud-wide realtime resource monitor providing a more accurate and holistic view of guests' resource utilization, (iii) an out-of-VM console-like interface enabling administrators to query system state without having to log into guest systems, as well as a handy "time travel" capability for forensic analysis of systems, and (iv) a hypervisor-paging aware out-VM virus scanner that demonstrates how across-stack knowledge of system state can dramatically improve the operational efficiency of common management applications like virus scan. Finally, we present a quantitative evaluation showcasing NFM's high accuracy, monitoring frequency, reliability and efficiency, as well as low impact on monitored systems.

The rest of the paper is organized as follows. Section 2 summarizes the techniques employed today for enterprise virtual systems monitoring. Section 3 gives a high level view of our solution architecture and discusses its benefits over existing alternatives. Section 4 gives the implementation details. Section 5 describes the applications we have built to demonstrate NFM's capability. Section 6 evaluates NFM's performance. Section 7 presents related work and Section 8 offers our conclusions.

2. EXISTING TECHNIQUES

System monitoring has been a major part of enterprise IT operations. We categorize the various techniques employed today as follows:

1. Application-specific in-VM agents for monitoring guest systems.
2. Application specific hooks for remotely accessing and monitoring systems.
3. Limited black-box metrics collected by the virtualization layer without guest cooperation.
4. General purpose agents or hooks that provide generic in-VM information through the virtualization layer.

Existing cloud monitoring and management solutions employ one or more of the above methods to deliver their services. For example, Amazon's CloudWatch [2] service falls under the third category in its base operation, while it can be extended by the end users with in-VM data providers (as in the first category) to provide deeper VM-level information. Other solutions such as Dell Quest/VKernel Foglight [14] is a combination of all three - guest remote access, in-VM agents, and hypervisor level metrics exported by VM management consoles like VMware vCenter and Red Hat Enterprise Management. To mitigate the limitations, and in particular, intrusiveness of custom in-VM techniques, an emerging approach has been the use of general purpose agents or *backdoors* inside the VMs that supply in-VM state information to the virtualization layer (fourth category). Various virtualization extensions such as VMware tools [48], VMSafe API [50], VMCI driver [47] and vShield endpoint [49] follow this approach. Other solutions also employ similar techniques and are summarized in Section 7.

There are important caveats with either of these options. First, in-VM solutions are only as good as the monitored system's operational health. This poses an interesting conundrum, where the system information becomes unavailable exactly when it is most critical—when the VM hangs, is unresponsive or subverted. Second, in-VM solutions face an uphill battle against the emerging cloud operation principles—ephemeral, short-lived VMs—and increasing VM proliferation. Their maintenance and lifecycle management has become a major pain point in enterprises. Furthermore,

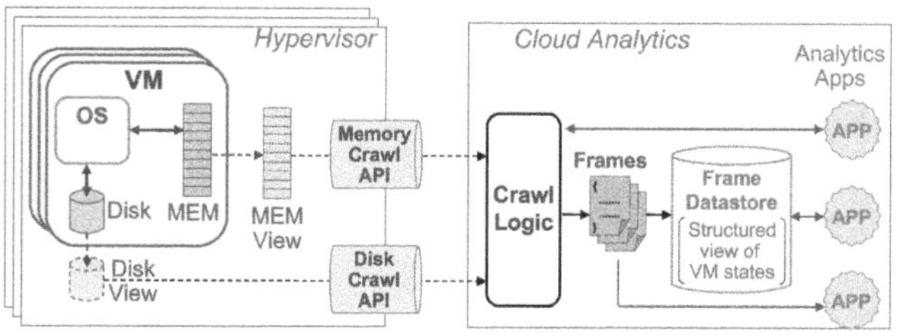

Figure 1: Introspection and analytics architecture

both agents and hooks modify the target systems, interfere with their operation, consume end-user cycles and are prime candidates for security vulnerabilities due to their external-facing nature. Third, even with generic-agent-based approaches, the problems of guest cooperation and intrusion do not completely disappear—although mitigated to some extent. However, these create a new challenge that goes against one of the key aspects of cloud computing: portability. Generic agents/hooks require specialization of VMs for the virtualization layer providing the monitoring APIs, which leads to vendor locking. Additionally, custom solutions need to be designed to work with each such agent provider.

3. NFM'S DESIGN

NFM's key differentiating value is its ability to provide monitoring and management capabilities without requiring guest system cooperation and without interfering with the guest's runtime environment. Architecturally, our overall framework, depicted in Figure 1, can be viewed as an introspection frontend and an analytics backend, which enables the VM execution - monitoring decoupling. The frontend provides an out-of-band view into the running systems, while the backend extracts and maintains their runtime state. The analogy is that of a Google like service running atop the cloud, enabling a query interface to seek live, as well as historical information about the cloud. Cloud monitoring and analytics applications then simply act as the clients of this service. We develop introspection techniques that build upon and extend traditional VMI approaches [20, 30], to gain an out-of-band view of VM runtime state. The analytics backend triggers VM introspection and accesses exposed VM state via *Crawl APIs*. Through these APIs, our *Crawl Logic* accesses raw VM disk and memory structures. VM disk state is accessed only once, before crawling a VM for the first time, to extract a small amount of information on the VM's OS configuration. *Crawl Logic* uses this information to access and parse raw VM memory to create a structured, logical view of the live VM state. We refer to this crawl output as a *frame*, representing a point-in-time view of the VM state. All frames of all VMs are stored in a *Frame Datastore* that the cloud monitoring and management applications run against, to perform their core functions, as well as to run more complex, cloud-level analytics across time or across VMs. By decoupling monitoring and management from the VM runtime, we enable these tasks to proceed without interfering with VM execution. The VMs being monitored are never modified in our approach, nor is the hypervisor or the VMM.

NFM is designed to alleviate most of the issues with existing solutions (Section 2). We follow three key principles to achieve this in a form that is tailored to the cloud operation principles:

1. **Decoupled Execution and Monitoring:** By decoupling target system execution from our monitoring and analytics tasks, we eliminate any implicit dependency between the two. NFM operates completely out of band, and can continue tracking system state even when a system is hung, unresponsive or compromised.
2. **No Guest Interference or Enforced Cooperation:** Guest context and cycles are precious and belong to the end user. Unlike most agent- or hook-based techniques that are explicitly disruptive to system operation, our design is completely non-intrusive. NFM does not interfere with guest system operation at all, nor does it require any guest cooperation or access to the monitored systems.
3. **Vendor-agnostic Design:** Our design is based on a generic introspection frontend, which provides standard crawl APIs. Our contract with the virtualization layer is only for base VMI functions—commonly available across hypervisors—exposing VM state in its rawest form (disk blocks and memory bytes). We do not require any custom APIs or backdoors between the VM and the virtualization layer in our design. All the data interpretation and custom intelligence are performed at the analytics backend, which also means simplified manageability as opposed to maintaining in-VM agents or hooks across several VMs.

In addition to alleviating some of the limitations of existing solutions, our design further opens up **new opportunities for cloud monitoring and analytics**. First, the decoupling of VM execution and monitoring inherently achieves *computation offloading*, where the monitoring / analysis computation is carried out outside the VM. This enables us to run some heavy-handed, *complex analytics*, such as full compliance scans with no impact on the actual systems. Second, many existing solutions actually track similar system features. By providing a singular data provider (backend datastore) for all analytics applications, we *eliminate redundancy* in information collection. Third, by shifting the scope of collected systems data from individual VMs to multiple cloud instances at the backend, we enable *across-VM analytics*, such as VM patterns, topology analysis, with simple analytics applications running against the datastore. Fourth, alongwith VM-level metrics, NFM is also exposed to host-level resource accounting measures, enabling it to derive a *holistic and true view* of VMs' resource utilization and demand characteristics.

NFM supports arbitrarily complex monitoring and analytics functions on cloud VMs with no VM interference and no setup requisites for the users. Our framework is designed to serve as the cornerstone of an *analytics as a service* (AaaS) cloud offering, where the users can seamlessly subscribe and unsubscribe to various out-of-the-box monitoring and analytics services, with no impact on their execution environments. These services span a wide range, from simple resource and security monitoring to across-the-cloud (anonymous) comparative systems analysis. Users would have the choice to opt into this service, paying for the cycles the hypervisor and the monitoring/analytics subsystem spends on behalf of them. One consideration for such a service is privacy for end users, however the guests already relinquish the same level of control to the existing agents running inside their systems, we only argue in favour of the same level of trust without the downside of having a potentially insecure foreign entity installed inside their runtime environment.

One limitation of NFM is a by-product of its reliance on VMI to crawl VM memory state, which involves interpreting kernel data structures in memory. These data structures may vary across OS versions and not be publicly documented for proprietary OSes. We discuss the tractability of this in our implementation discussion (Section 4.2). Also, as NFM focuses on the OS-level system view, application-level (e.g., a MapReduce worker's health) or architectural (e.g., hardware counters) state are not immediately observable via NFM unless exposed by the guest OS. Although, the hypervisor might allow measuring certain architectural states (e.g., perf counters) for a guest from outside.

4. IMPLEMENTATION

We implement NFM on two real-system prototypes based on two virtualization platforms, Xen and KVM. Currently we only support Linux guests, support for other OSes is discussed at the end of Section 4.2. Our overall implementation can be broken into four parts: (i) exposing VM runtime state, i.e., accessing VM memory and disk state and making them available over the crawl APIs; (ii) exploiting VM runtime state, i.e., interpreting the memory and disk images with the Crawl Logic to reconstruct the guest's runtime information; (iii) persisting this VM state information in the Frame Datastore for the subscribed applications; and (iv) developing high level applications to build on top of the extracted VM runtime state.

4.1 Exposing VM State

Most hypervisors provide different methods to obtain a view of guest VM memory. VMWare provides VMSafe APIs [50] to access guest memory. Xen [7] provides userspace routine (`xc_map_foreign_range`) via its Xen Control library (`libxc`) to re-map a guest VM's memory into a privileged VM. We use this technique to obtain a live read-only handle on the VM's memory. KVM [26] does not have default support for live memory handles. Although other techniques [8, 22] are able to provide guest memory access by modifying QEMU, our goal is to use stock hypervisors for generality. For KVM, options exist to dump VM memory to a file, via QEMU's `pmemsave` memory snapshotting, or `migrate`-to-file, or `libvirt`'s `dump`. While the VM's memory can be exposed in this manner, the overheads associated are non-trivial, as the guest gets paused during the dump duration. Therefore, for KVM, we develop an alternative solution to acquire a live handle on VM memory, while inducing negligible overhead on the running VM. As KVM is part of a standard Linux environment, we leverage Linux memory management primitives and access VM memory via QEMU process' `/proc/<pid>/mem` pseudo-file, indexed by the virtual address space backing the VM's memory from `/proc/<pid>/maps`.

We develop equivalent techniques for exposing VM disk state. We crawl VM disk state only once to collect required persistent system information that we use to interpret raw memory data structures (Section 4.2). We use standard filesystem methods to access and expose VM disks, which are represented as regular files on the host system.

In both prototypes, the obtained external view of raw VM memory and disk is wrapped and exposed as network-attached devices (FUSE over iSCSI) to the backend's *Crawl Logic* over common *Memory* and *Disk Crawl APIs*. Thus, the actual crawling and analytics components are completely decoupled from VM execution, and the upstream logic is transparent to the underlying virtualization technology.

Enhancements. (i) While our methods for exposing VM state generally have negligible latencies for most cloud monitoring and analytics applications, we build further optimizations to our techniques to curb down their latencies. Among these, one notable optimization is *selective memory extraction* for applications that rely on near-realtime information. The key insight behind this is that most applications actually require access to a tiny fraction of VM memory space, and therefore we can trade off completeness for speed. After an initial full crawl, we identify VM memory regions that hold the relevant information, and in subsequent iterations we opportunistically crawl only those sections. For dump-based handles, we batch relevant distributed memory regions together, to optimize the dump size and minimize dump cycles. Since some data structures like `task` lists, dynamically grow, we add additional buffering and resizing heuristics to accommodate these. Also, several distributed memory regions contained the relevant kernel data structure into small number of larger sized chunks. Overall, with such optimizations, we further reduce our overall latency impact by an order of magnitude. For example, for one of our realtime applications, *CTop*, this approach enables subsecond granularity realtime system monitoring even with heavyweight, dump-based methods, reducing overall latencies from few seconds to milliseconds.

(ii) We do not expect the guest OS to be in some steady state while extracting its live runtime state from outside the guest context. Since we avoid making any monitoring specific changes to the guest and not enforce any guest co-operation, lack of synchronization with the guest OS can potentially lead to inconsistency of views between the actual runtime state that exists inside the VM and what gets reconstructed from the view exposed outside, eg. a process terminating inside the guest while its memory mappings (`mm_struct`) are being traversed outside. To tackle this, we build additional routines for (optional) consistency support for KVM guest memory access via `ptrace()`- attach/detach on the QEMU container process. This trades off minor VM stuns for increased consistency. Our experiments show that even with a heavy (10 times/s) fork and kill workload consuming significant CPU, memory and network resources inside a VM, inconsistency of extracted state occurs not very often—in about 2% of crawler iterations, while extracting *full* system runtime state (Section 6.1).

4.2 Exploiting VM State

The backend attaches to the VM view exposed by the frontend, and implements the Crawl Logic that performs the logical interpretation of this raw state consisting of the disk block device and the memory byte array. Interpretation of the disk state is relatively well defined by leveraging standard filesystem drivers. The key challenge, however, is bridging the inherent semantic gap between the exposed raw VM memory state and the logical OS-level VM-internal view. The traditional in-VM approaches simply leverage guest OS context to extract system information, such as the `/proc` tree for process information. Our Crawl Logic achieves the same function by translating the byte-level memory view into structured runtime VM state. VM runtime information is distributed into several in-memory kernel data structures for processes (`task_struct`), memory mapping (`mm_ struct`), open files (`files_struct`), and network information (`net_devices`) among others. We overlay these `struct` templates over the exposed memory, and traverse them to read the various structure fields holding the relevant information [30]. To correctly map these data structures, we extract three important pieces of information from the VM disk image and/or a kernel repository:

1. **Version, Architecture and Map Parameters:** From the VM kernel log, we extract the running kernel version and the target VM architecture (32 vs. 64bit) for correctly sizing the data structures. Also read is the BIOS RAM map for determining the amount of VM memory to map and the size and layout of the VM memory regions.
2. **Starting Addresses for *structs*:** To identify the starting addresses for various kernel structures, such as initial task (`init_task`), module list (`modules`), and kernel page table (`init_level4_pgt`), we read the *System.map* file for the guest kernel, which includes the kernel exported addresses for these structures.
3. **Field Offsets:** After identifying entry points for kernel structures, we calculate the offsets to the relevant fields in these structures. We use the kernel source (or *vmlinux* build image) and the build configuration to determine offsets of desired fields.

Given a live VM memory handle and the above-mentioned pieces of information, the Crawl Logic's overall memory crawl process can be summarized as:

1. Reading a kernel exported address (X), such as the initial process' address (symbol `init_task`).
2. Mapping the associated data structure template (`struct task_struct`) to the memory region at address X.
3. Reading the relevant structure member fields after adding their relative offsets to the starting address X.
4. Continuing with the next object by reading its address via linked list traversal (`prev`, `next` member fields, together with offset arithmetic).

In addition to kernel structure traversal, we also traverse per-process page tables inside the extracted memory view, to translate a virtual addresses in a guest process' address space. We extract the process' page directory from its `mm_ struct`, and traverse its page tables. Our Crawl Logic can currently crawl all X86, X86_PAE, and x86_64 architectures, and also supports huge pages.

After introspecting all the relevant data structures, the Crawl Logic creates a single structured document (frame) for the crawled VM. This crawl document captures a rich set of information on VM state that the cloud monitoring and analytics applications can build upon. Our current frame format covers various VM features, including system, cpu, memory and process information, modules, address mappings, open files, network information and runtime resource use. This VM frame, with its corresponding timestamp and VM ID, is then loaded into the frame datastore described in the next section.

Discussion. (i) While we focus our backend implementation on Linux, NFM's applicability is not limited to a particular OS. Structure-offset extraction and VMI have been shown to work for Mac and Windows as well [5, 8, 34, 44]. Also, their versions are few as compared to Linux, and change slowly. (ii) The tractability of kernel data structure (DS) traversal based introspection solution is corroborated by prior studies reporting modest DS modifications across major Linux versions [37]. Indeed, our parsers for kernel versions 3.2 and 3.4.4 differ only in their network-device related DS among all of our tracked DS. Furthermore, the standardization trends in enterprise clouds also work in favor of this approach, limiting the OS-version variability. Even Amazon EC2 has a small number of base VM image types (5 different Linux OS versions). (iii) To portray NFM's generality, we have implemented our memory crawler to operate across a diverse configuration set- multi architecture (x86 / x86_64), multi core, variably (RAM) sized VMs running Linux kernels far apart in the version chain and from different vendors — RHEL6 / Linux2.6.32, Fedora14 / 2.6.35, Ubuntu12.04 / 3.2.0, Fedora16 / 3.4.4. (iv) In our experience, to generate structure-field information manually it takes a one-time effort of roughly an hour for a new OS version. This process can be automated by using crash [13] or gdb on debugging information enabled *vmlinux* kernel images. There also exist alternate OS-version independent memory introspection techniques (Section 7).

4.3 The Frame Datastore

The frame datastore is a repository of historical as well as live VM runtime states of all of the guest VMs, sent to it as structured frame documents by the "crawler" VM running the Crawl Logic. Although intended to be an actual database system for a full cloud deployment, in most cases we simply use the crawler VM file system as our current frame datastore. To ensure scalability with respect to the space overhead for maintaining VM state history (frames) for cloud-scale deployment, we control this by keeping incremental *delta frames* across successive crawls of a VM over time. Depending upon whether the delta is obtained over the base crawl or the most recent crawl, there are tradeoffs with regards to the ease of delta insertion/deletion vs. delta sizes, the former being trivial with base crawl deltas, while the latter being more manageable with latest crawl deltas. Section 6.7 evaluates this space overhead for maintaining system states across time.

4.4 Application Architecture

In our framework, the Cloud monitoring applications act as clients of the Frame Datastore, building on top of the rich system state it maintains throughout the VMs' lifetimes, to perform cloud analytics across time (past vs present system states) and space (across systems). Some of our target applications bypass the frame datastore for realtime operations (e.g. *CTop* resource monitoring), or for interfacing directly against the raw VM memory view (e.g. *PaVScan* virus scanning).

A benefit of visualizing system information as data documents (aka frames) is that it enables leveraging familiar paradigms from the data analytics domain such as diff-ing systems just like diff-ing documents and tagging systems with semantic annotations. This makes it easier to tackle modern day cloud management concerns arising from aggressive cloud expansion such as tackling system-drift— tracking how a deployed system with an initial desired state deviates over time— and performing problem diagnosis—drilling down into individual VM's to diagnose what caused the drift. Tagging point-in-time system states as being 'healthy' and

	TopoLog	CTop	RConsole	PavScan
Across-system analytics	•	•		
Across-time analytics	•		•	
Monitoring unresponsive or compromised systems		•	•	
Deep, across the stack system knowledge		•		•

Table 1: Key capabilities of our prototype applications

diff-ing them against faulty states, makes it easier and efficient to potentially troubleshoot system issues.

5. PROTOTYPE APPLICATIONS

Here we describe four concrete applications that we have built over our cloud analytics framework. These applications highlight NFM's capabilities and target some interesting use cases. Our fundamental principles for system analytics in the cloud are preserved amongst all applications: they all operate out-of-band with VM execution, are completely non-intrusive, and operate without requiring any guest cooperation.

Table 1 shows our four applications, *TopoLog*, *CTop*, *RConsole* and *PaVScan* and the key capabilities they highlight. *TopoLog* is a cloud topology discovery application that focuses on across-system analytics. It discovers VM and application connectivity by analyzing and correlating frames of cloud instances. It can also provide across-time analytics by tracing the evolution of cloud topology over frame history. *CTop* is a cloud-wide, realtime resource monitor that can monitor even unresponsive systems. CTop also showcases how deep, across-the-stack system information can provide more accurate and reliable system information. *RConsole* is an out-of-VM, console-like interface that is mainly designed with cloud operators in mind. Its pseudo-console interface enables administrators to query system state without having to log into guest systems, and even when the system is compromised. It also enables a handy "time travel" capability for forensic analysis of systems. *PaVScan* is a hypervisor-paging aware virus scanner, and is a prime example of how across-stack knowledge of system state, combining the in-VM view with the out-of-VM view, can dramatically improve the operational efficiency of common management applications like virus scan.

5.1 TopoLog

TopoLog is a network and application topology analyzer for cloud instances. It discovers (i) the interconnectivity across VMs, (ii) communicating processes inside each VM, (iii) connectivity patterns across high level applications, and (iv) (topology-permitting) per VM network flow statistics, without installing any hooks inside the VMs. TopoLog facilitates continuous validation in the cloud by ensuring that a desired topology for a distributed application (deployed as a pattern/set of VMs, e.g. via a Chef recipe [36]) is maintained. It detects unauthorized connections, bottleneck nodes and network resource use patterns. TopoLog offers other potential use cases, such as (i) optimizing inter- and intra-rack network use by identifying and bringing closer highly-communicating VMs, and (ii) simultaneous patching of interconnected VMs for minimal service downtime at the application level.

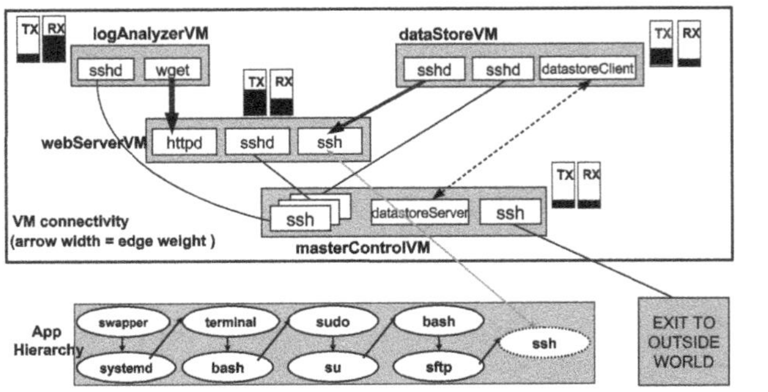

Figure 2: VM and app connectivity discovered by Topology Analyzer for 4 VMs

For each VM, topology analyzer extracts the per-process network information from the latest frame in the Frame Datastore. The extracted information (containing the socket type and state, associated source and destination IP addresses, and the process owning the socket) is correlated across all or a specified subset of cloud instances to generate a connectivity graph. We discover higher-level application information for the communicating processes by traversing the process tree within each VM frame. These steps are sufficient to generate the cloud network and application topology. In addition to these, TopoLog further discovers network traffic statistics for each VM by extracting and comparing counts for received, transmitted and dropped packets/bytes across two different timestamped frames.

Depending upon application knowledge and a particular topology, we can go one step further and estimate the weight of the connection edges in the topology graph. Since Linux does not maintain per process data transfer statistics, we estimate these by converting the connectivity graph to a linear system of equations. For a VM-to-VM connectivity graph of N VMs, we have at most $N^2 - N$ potential unknowns (graph edges) and $2 * N$ equations (per-VM system-wide received and transmitted bytes). If the number of equations are sufficient to solve for the actual number of edges, we can determine the weight of each connection. To bring down the number of unknowns, we also use domain knowledge such as information about connections with negligible or known constant weights.

Figure 2 shows one such connectivity graph generated automatically by the topology analyzer for an application pattern composed of 4 VMs. This application includes (i) a *MasterControl VM*, which monitors each application component and serves data to a DataStore VM; (ii) a *WebServer VM*, which serves client-side requests over http; (iii) a *DataStore VM*, which warehouses application data and receives updates from the MasterControl VM; and (iv) a *LogAnalyzer VM*, which downloads and analyzes the logs from the WebServer VM. As can be seen, the topology analyzer was able to discover all cluster connections such as the *masterControlVM* having long lived hooks into all other VMs over `ssh`, and feeding the *dataStoreVM* with data files. Also found was a connection that does not belong to the cluster, labeled as "exit to outside world". Also note that although the connection between *dataStoreVM* and *httpWebServerVM* is detected as an `ssh` connection, by traversing the process tree inside the latter's frame, we can get the higher level picture of this actually being a secure file transfer. A packet sniffing based topology discovery would not be able to detect intra-host connections for colocated VMs, or

	L-VM	W-VM	D-VM	M-VM	Ext
LogAnalyticsVM	0.00	109.08	0.00	0.00	0.00
WebServerVM	0.56	0.00	42.67	0.00	0.00
DataStoreVM	0.00	0.86	0.00	0.22	0.00
MasterCtlVM	0.00	0.00	0.14	0.00	0.00
External	0.00	0.00	0.00	0.00	0.00

Figure 3: VM Connectivity Matrix [Mbps].

capture application-level information for the communicating systems.

Figure 3 further shows a snapshot of the derived network traffic statistics, as a *VM connectivity matrix* depicted as an intensity plot, for the same application pattern. An entry $M(r, c)$ in the matrix represents the rate of data transferred from VM_c to VM_r in Mbps. The row and column labels are identical (column labels are abbreviated in the plot). The connectivity matrix highlights the strongly-connected application components, which are the $\{WebServerVM \rightarrow LogAnalyzerVM\}$ and $\{DataStoreVM \rightarrow WebServerVM\}$ tuples in our case. This information is useful for both network-aware optimization of application resources and for continuous validation—by identifying unauthorized or abnormal application communication patterns.

5.2 CTop

CTop is a cloud-wide, realtime consolidated resource monitoring application. CTop is of equivalent fidelity and time granularity as the standard, in-band Linux `top` utility, with two enhancements for cloud-centric monitoring rather than traditional, system-centric techniques. First, modern cloud applications typically span across multiple VMs and hosts, requiring a distributed application-level view of resource use across system boundaries. CTop provides a single unified view of resource utilization across all applications and VMs distributed onto various physical machines within a cloud. Allowing for host and VM normalization (scaling), CTop dissolves VM and host boundaries to view individual processes as belonging to a single global cloud computer, with additional drill-down capabilities for restricting the view within hosts or VMs. Second, since CTop operates outside the VM scope, it is aware of both VM-level and hypervisor-level resource usage. Thus, it can provide a more accurate and holistic view of utilization than what the guest sees in its virtualized world. It appropriately normalizes a process' resource usage inside a VM to its corresponding usage on the host, or in terms of what the user paid for, for direct comparison of the overall application's processes across VMs. Equation 1 shows this normalization, where the actual CPU usage of a VM V's process P on host H is calculated in terms of the CPU usage of P inside the VM (CPU_V^P), overall CPU utilization of V (CPU_V^*), and the CPU usage of the VM on host H (CPU_H^V).

$$CPU_H^P = \frac{CPU_V^P}{CPU_V^*} \times CPU_H^V \qquad (1)$$

To achieve realtime monitoring, CTop directly uses the crawler to emit a custom frame on demand at the desired

```
top - 11:58:42 up 1 day, 22:19,  1 user, load average: 0.90, 0.22, 0.11
Tasks: 57 total,  3 running,   54 sleeping,   stopped,    0 zombie
Cpu(s): 99.0%us, 0.0%sy, 0.0%ni, 0.0%id, 0.0%wa, 0.7%hi, 0.0%si, 0.3%st
Mem:  2052104k total, 1976340k used,   75764k free,    3996k buffers
Swap: 6160380k total,  304068k used, 5856312k free,    1868k cached

 PID  USER  PR  NI   VIRT   RES  SHR S %CPU %MEM   TIME+   COMMAND
1942  root  20   0  1028m  1.0g  188 R 49 9 51.0  0:08.98 malloc
1940  root  20   0  1028m  780m  136 R 49 5 38.9  0:11:91 malloc
   1  root  20   0  56220  1164  408 S  0 0  0.1  0:00.71 systemd
   2  root  20   0      0     0    0 S  0 0  0.0  0:00.00 kthreadd
```

```
Every 0.5s: ./topUpdate.sh

CPU up time: 4461430125 jiffies

 PID        VIRT         RES  %CPU  %MEM    TIME+    COMMAND
1942   1052704KB   1047368KB  45.8  51.0  0:08:33    malloc
1940   1052704KB    798816KB  45.8  38.9  0:11.92    malloc
   1     56220KB      1164KB   0.0   0.1  0:00.70    systemd
   2           0           0   0.0   0.0  0:00.00    kthreadd
   :
```

Figure 4: Above: in-VM *top*; Below: *CTop*

monitoring frequency, bypassing the Frame Datastore. Fields of the frame include per-process PID, PPID, command, virtual and physical memory usage, scheduling statistics and CPU runtime. CTop analyzes frames from successive monitoring iterations to generate a *top*-like per-process resource usage monitor. Figure 4 compares the output of CTop with the standard in-VM *top* for a single VM. In this case, in VM measures and CTop measures match, as there is no host-level contention.

CTop's unified application-level resource utilization view allows for straightforward comparison of different instances of the same application across different VMs. This provides a simple form of problem diagnosis in the cloud, by tracking unexpected resource use variability among instances of an application. As we show in Section 6.3, CTop's holistic view of the operating environment helps explain performance and capacity conflicts that are hard to reason when monitoring is bound to the VM scope. We also evaluate CTop's latency and accuracy in Sections 6.1 and 6.2.

5.3 RConsole

RConsole is an out-of-band "console-like" interface for VMs being monitored by NFM. It is a read-only interface, with no side effects on the running instances. RConsole supports basic system functions such as `ls` `lsmod`, `ps`, `netstat` and `ifconfig`. It is designed for cloud operators, to provide visibility into running instances without requiring access into the systems. RConsole runs against the system state captured in the frames indexed into the Frame Datastore. It implements a `sync` API call to crawl the current live state of a VM and retrieve its most up-to-date state, and a `seed` API to retrieve a prior stored state of a VM, which enables traveling back in time to observe past system state.

With RConsole, we perform simple security, compliance and configuration monitoring in an out-of-band fashion, without disrupting or accessing into the running systems. As RConsole operates by interpreting raw VM memory structures rather than relying on in-VM OS functions, it is also more robust against certain security attacks that may compromise a guest OS. We demonstrate this by infecting our VMs with the *AverageCoder* rootkit [18] that covertly starts and hides malicious processes, unauthorized users and open network connections from the guest OS. Figure 5 shows an example to this for network connections. Here the top box shows the (simplified) output of the standard in-VM **netstat** command, while the bottom box shows the output from

In-VM Console:

```
Active Internet connections (servers and established)
Proto Local Address       Foreign Address     State
tcp   127.0.0.1:25        0.0.0.0:*           LISTEN
tcp   9.XX.XXX.110:52019  9.XX.XXX.109:22     ESTABLISHED
:
tcp   9.XX.XXX.110:22     9.XX.XXX.15:49845   ESTABLISHED
```

RConsole:

```
Active Internet connections
Proto  Local Address      Foreign Address    State              PID Process
tcp    127.0.0.1:25       0.0.0.0:0          SS_UNCONNECTED     741 [sendmail]
tcp    9.XX.XXX.110:52019 9.XX.XXX.109:22    SS_CONNECTED      6177 [ssh]
:
tcp    9.XX.XXX.110:22    9.XX.XXX.15:49845  SS_CONNECTED     14894 [sshd]
tcp    0.0.0.0:2476       0.0.0.0:0          SS_UNCONNECTED   23304 [datacpy]
```

Figure 5: RConsole captures datacpy's hidden listener connection

RConsole's **netstat**. Both outputs remain mostly similar, except for one additional entry in RConsole: a malicious **datacpy** process with a listening connection on **port 2476**. In-VM **netstat** fails to discover this as it relies on compromised guest OS exported functions, while RConsole can easily capture it from crawled VM state. More sophisticated attacks and VM introspection based counter-measures are well-established in prior studies [6, 20, 51].

RConsole is also greatly useful in troubleshooting system issues owing to its ability to travel back and forth in time. Once an anomaly is detected, it can trace back system state to detect the root cause, and compare across systems to identify similar good and bad system configurations. RConsole is even able to inspect a VM that we made completely dysfunctional by forcing a kernel panic; the entire runtime state still exists in the VM's memory, which RConsole is able to retrieve to pinpoint the culprit process and module. This ability to analyze unresponsive systems also plays a critical role in dramatically improving time to resolution in certain problems, as in the Google outage example of Section 1. A similar example to this has also been recently observed in one of our cloud deployments, where a network misconfiguration in one of the systems caused a serious routing problem in VM network traffic, rendering most of the VMs inaccessible. In both cases, RConsole's ability to perform simple troubleshooting operations (such as tracking network configurations via **ifconfig**) across time and across systems plays a critical role to pinpoint the offending systems and configurations in a simple and more efficient way.

5.4 PaVScan

PaVScan is a hypervisor paging [52] aware virus scanner that operates outside a VM's context, working directly on the raw VM memory state. We built PaVScan over the popular open source anti-virus project, ClamAV [11] and used its publicly available virus signature database. PaVScan searches for signatures of known viruses inside the VM's memory using the Aho-Corasick algorithm for pattern matching, and works by building and traversing a finite state machine from the signature database. Our use of the PaVScan application bypasses the Frame Datastore and interfaces with the memory crawler directly to get the live handle on the target VM's memory. Once VM memory is exposed, the virus signatures are directly scanned over the raw memory.

While one obvious main advantage of PaVScan is its ability to perform out-of-band virus scanning, this is not unique to this work [25]. The key differentiating aspect of our application is that it tracks hypervisor-paging—guest-agnostic reclaim of VM memory by the hypervisor. Using the crawler's interface to the hypervisor, PaVScan identifies which VM page frames are actually mapped on the physical RAM and which are paged out on disk. It then scans only the RAM-backed VM memory, while scanning the rest of the pages when they originally get paged out. This prevents unnecessary and costly page-ins from disk and ensures that the VM's working set does not get "thrashed" by the virus scan operation.

PaVScan presents a prime example of how deep, across-the-stack knowledge of system state can crucially impact across-system performance in the cloud. Traditional in-VM scanning techniques—for viruses or otherwise—are limited by their guest-only scope. Their actions, oblivious to the broader operating environment view, can be severely detrimental to both the system itself that they are monitoring and other instances sharing the cloud. In our case of virus scanning, a typical in-VM scanner(or even a paging-unaware out-of-VM solution) will indiscriminately scan all memory pages, as neither the guest nor the scanner are aware of any guest pages that have been paged out. Every such page access will cause a page-in from swap and potentially a page-out of a currently-loaded page (so long as the hypervisor doesn't give this VM more memory), severely impacting the performance of other applications on the VM. Depending on overall resource allocation and resource scheduler actions, this paging behavior can further impact other instances sharing the same memory and I/O resources in the cloud. In contrast, PaVScan's paging-aware, out-of-VM scanning approach operates with negligible impact on the monitored systems, while providing the same level of system integrity. We compare PaVScan with an in-VM scanner in Section 6.4.

6. EVALUATION

To evaluate NFM's performance, we use our cloud analytics applications to answer the following questions:

1. How frequently can we extract runtime VM information?
2. How accurate is our out-of-band VM monitoring?
3. Can we perform better than existing in-VM techniques with our holistic view of cloud operating environment?
4. How does out-of-VM monitoring improve operational efficiency in the cloud?
5. What is the overhead imposed on the VMs being monitored?
6. What is the impact of out-of-band monitoring on co-located VMs?
7. What is the space overhead of storing across-time (forensic) frame data in the datastore for each cloud instance?

Our experimental setup consists of physical systems with Intel Core-i5 processors, 4-64GB of memory and VT-x hardware virtualization support. These serve as the hypervisor hosts of our cloud environment, where our VM instances are deployed. The hosts run Linux 3.7.9, Xen 4.2.1 and QEMU-KVM 1.4. Our VMs run a variety of Fedora, RedHat and Ubuntu distributions (both 32 and 64 bit) in our experiments to ensure our crawlers work with a range of OS versions. Our analytics backend is run as a specialized VM with baked-in datastore and API components. The benchmarks used in our experiments are: **bonnie++** v1.96 [42], **x264** v1.7.0 [35], and **httperf** v0.9.0 [33]

6.1 Latency and Frequency of Monitoring

The amount of time it takes for our crawlers to extract runtime VM information varies with the richness of the de-

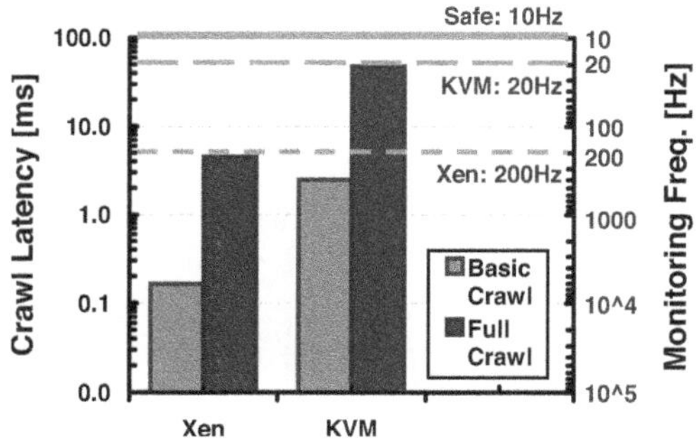

Figure 6: Measured crawling latencies and achievable monitoring frequencies (log scale).

sired information. Here we compare time required to extract *basic* process level resource use information for our `CTop` application, as well for deeper, *full* system information including all of system configuration, OS, module, process, file, CPU, memory, network connection data. All times are averaged over several runs while varying configured VM memory and CPUs, and the in-VM workloads emulating heavy process fork/kill behaviour and stressing the CPU, memory, disk and network (500 runs for each configuration).

For Xen, there is a one-time only operation for getting an initial handle on a target VM's memory (Section 4.1). This takes on average 0.37s per GB of VM memory. After this one-time operation, the crawler takes on an average 0.165 ms to extract the *basic* state and 4.5 ms for *full* state. For KVM, there is no separate memory handle acquisition step. The time taken to extract *basic* and *full* VM state information is 2.5 ms and 47.4 ms respectively. Figure 6 summarizes these results and highlights the corresponding achievable monitoring frequencies. As shown in the figure, full system crawls can be performed over 20 times/s (`Hz`) for KVM and 200 times/s for Xen (dashed horizontal lines). These times do not include the frame indexing time into the datastore, as this is off the critical path and is bypassed by the realtime monitoring applications, where latency matters. In either case, our results show that NFM can safely operate at a 10Hz monitoring frequency (solid horizontal line), which more than meets the practical requirements of most cloud applications.

The crawler has a negligible memory footprint and its CPU usage is proportional to the desired monitoring frequency and the number of VMs being monitored. In our KVM setup, for example, the crawler utilizing a full CPU core can monitor 1 VM at 20Hz or 20 VMs at 1Hz. Thus, there also exists a tradeoff between time granularity of monitoring and number of VMs that can be monitored in parallel.

Summary: Our crawlers extract full system state in less than 50ms, and our live out-of-VM monitoring can easily operate at a 10Hz frequency.

6.2 Monitoring Accuracy

We use our `CTop` application here to validate NFM's accuracy. We run a custom workload that dynamically varies its CPU and memory demand based on a configurable sinusoidal pattern. Figure 7 shows how well our remote monitor tracks the CPU resource use for a VM process with respect to *top*. The memory results are similar and omitted for brevity. The slight variation in measurements is due to the inevitable misalignment of the update cycles / sampling time points, as the two solutions operate asynchronously. Overall, our out-of-VM CTop monitoring is very accurate and reliable. The average sample variation between in-VM *top* and `CTop` metrics is very low, ranging between 4% and 1% at different time scales.

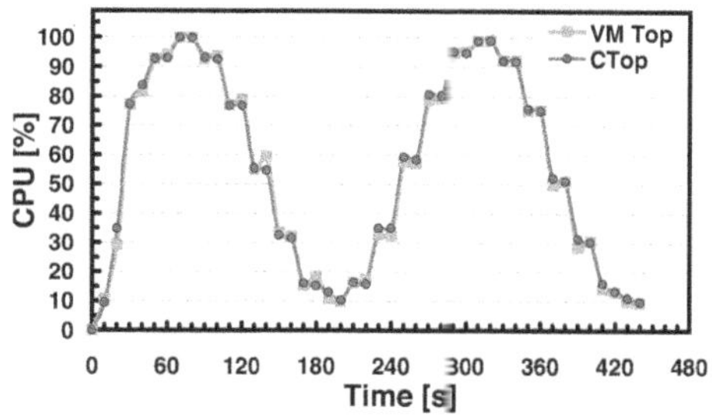

Figure 7: CPU utilization: in-VM `top` vs. `CTop`.

Summary: Our out-of-VM monitors accurately track VM process and resource usage information, providing the same level of fidelity and time granularity as in-VM techniques.

6.3 Benefits of Holistic Knowledge

As we previously discussed, NFM is privy to both in-VM and out-of-VM resource use measures. This unified, holistic view of systems enables significantly-better resource management in the cloud. We demonstrate the quantitative elements of this capability here with a webserver application, distributed across 3 identical instances, each running a LAMP stack. The VMs are facing high incoming HTTP load causing them to run at full utilization, the load originating from three separate `httperf` clients (one per server VM) generating identical request streams for 2MB files. While the VMs' configurations are identical, their current allocation of resources is not. Due to varying contention and priorities with respect to other colocated instances, the three VMs receive a 100%, 70% and 30% share of the CPU respectively. We demonstrate the holistic view of application performance characteristics with `CTop` and contrast this with the VM-only view of in-VM `top` in Figure 8.

Figure 8 shows the `httperf` statistics observed for each of the three VMs (top chart), the CPU utilization of the Apache, PHP and MySql processes inside each of these VMs as measured by *top* (middle chart) and as derived by `CTop` (bottom chart). As seen, *top*'s CPU utilization statistics look the same for all three VMs and thus cannot be used to reason for the different `httperf` sustained request rate, observed bandwidth and response times across the three VMs.

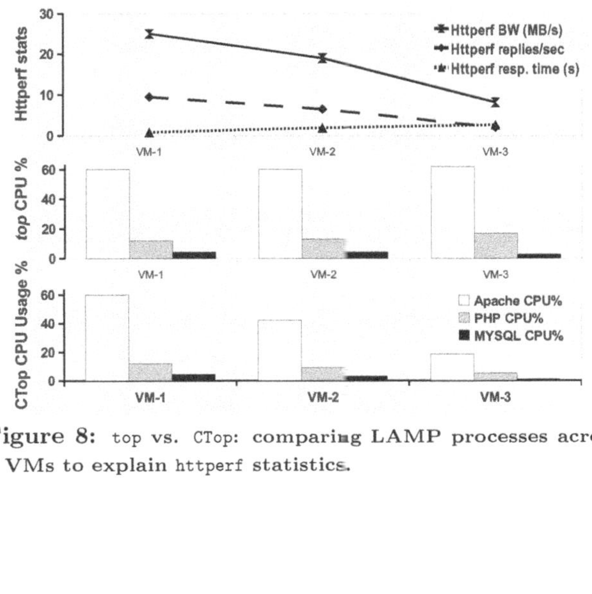

Figure 8: `top` vs. `CTop`: comparing LAMP processes across 3 VMs to explain `httperf` statistics.

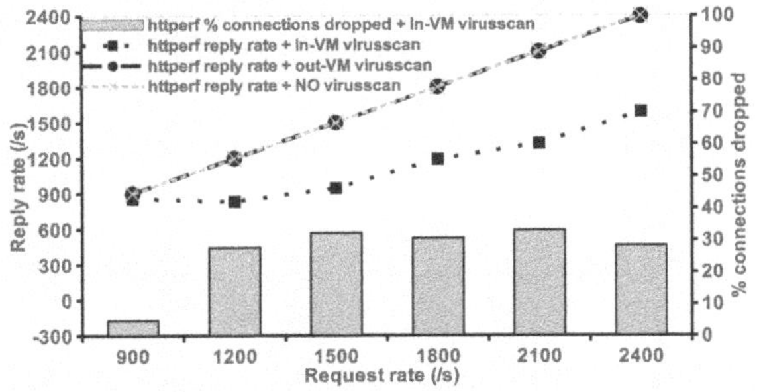

Figure 9: Httperf replyrate, connection drops vs Virusscan

However, by using `CTop`'s CPU utilization metrics (Section 5.2) that dissolve VM boundaries and normalize utilization of all of the LAMP processes across the application's instances at the host level, a clear CPU utilization difference can be spotted across the LAMP processes in different VMs. Thus, although the CPU utilization of the LAMP processes looks very similar when viewed inside the VMs in isolation, the true picture is in fact very different as captured by `CTop`. This clearly explains the application-level performance variability in `httperf` statistics comparing the true resource utilization across the application's distributed instances.

Summary: The unified, holistic view of the cloud environment enables accurate monitoring and interpretation of distributed application performance.

6.4 Operational Efficiency Improvements

We quantify the efficiency improvements achievable with NFM by evaluating virus scanning—representative of common scanning/inspection operations in the cloud—in our experimental framework. We use PaVScan as our out-of-VM scanner and install an identical in-VM scanner in the test VM, and compare their impact on the test VM's primary workload. We configure the VM with two VCPUs, where a web server is run as the primary application on one CPU and the in-VM virusscan application is run on a separate CPUs to avoid introducing any CPU contention. Hypervisor paging is enabled on the host via Xenpaging reclaiming 256MB from the VM's configured 1GB memory. A medium workload `httperf` server is setup on the VM with a working set of 256MB, from which it serves 2KB random content files to 3 different `httperf` clients running on 3 separate machines. The file size is chosen to be 2KB so that server is not network bound, and the working set size is chosen to be 256MB so that no guest level swapping is introduced. The average base-case runtime for the virus scanner was 17.5s to scan the entire VM memory. All `httperf` server statistics that follow are averaged over 5 runs.

Figure 9 shows the kind of reply rates that can be sustained by the webserver VM in this setup. Specifically, with the virusscanner turned off, the webserver VM is able to match an incoming request rate of upto 2400 requests/s without dropping any connections. PaVScan matches this reply rate very closely, reaching 2395 replies/sec with only 0.27% connection drops. On the other hand, `httperf` experiences a major performance hit with the in-VM scanner, where around 30% of connections are dropped with requests rates higher than 900 requests/s. Even with 900 requests/s, a drop rate of 5% is observed meaning that the actual sustainable rate is even below that. Effectively there is a decrease in performance by more than 63% (from 2400 to 900 serviced requests/s with in-VM scanning.). Additionally, response times degrade by an order of magnitude. The virusscanner's running time itself degrades to around 59s from 17.5s.

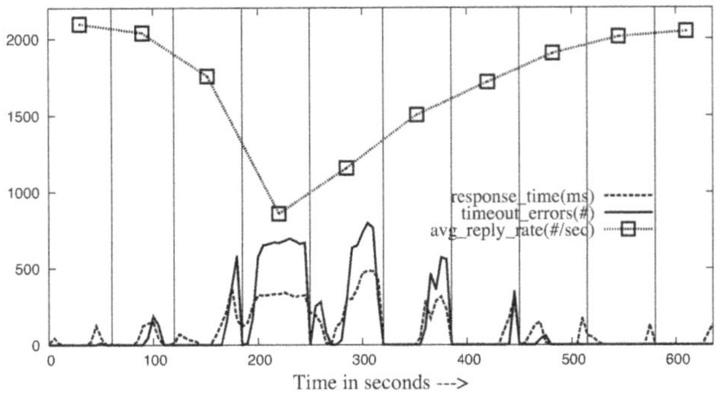

Figure 10: Httperf over 10 rounds (each bounded between successive vertical lines); Virusscan starts between round 2-3

Furthermore, the performance impact of the in-VM virus scanner lasts much longer than just the scan duration. Figure 10 shows that it takes a much longer time for `httperf` to recover after the in-VM virusscanner destroys `httperf`'s file cache due to swapped page-ins. Shown are 10 `httperf` rounds (bounded by vertical lines in the figure) of servicing 256MB worth file requests each, fired at a rate of 2100 requests/s. The in-VM virusscanner starts around between rounds 2-3 and completes by round 5. As can be seen it takes about 7 rounds (460 seconds) for `httperf` to re-establish its file cache for sustaining the incoming request rate. For the entire 10 rounds, there is an 18.6% performance degradation in terms of serviced requests per second and 12.5% connection drops. Thus, in this hypervisor paging scenario, the in-VM scanner's impact is felt even long after it exits. In contrast the out-of-VM scanner shows only negligible impact on the guest during and after its execution.

Summary: The ability to push common cloud operations out of the VMs' scope can lead to dramatic improvements in system performance compared to their in-VM counterparts.

6.5 Impact on VM's Performance

We measure NFM's overhead on a target system's workload with three experiments. We expose the live VM state to (i) monitor the VM with `CTop`, (ii) hash the VM's memory, and (iii) scan the VM's memory with `PaVScan`. All experiments are repeated 5 times. The target VM and workload setup are similar to those in Section 6.4 (except hypervisor paging turned off). We use two workload configurations for the webserver VM: (i) A 256 MB working set to avoid guest swapping, serving all requests from memory without accessing the disk, and (ii) a 512 MB working set that involves the standard *kswapd* swap daemon. The `httperf` server is pushed to CPU saturation in both cases. The host system is never overloaded in the experiments. Figure 11 shows the performance impact on the VM for both workload configurations, when the three described out-of-VM monitoring applications are run for the same VM.

Realtime Monitoring: We measure the impact of monitoring the webserver VM at a 10Hz frequency, while extracting the *full* system state (Section 6.1) in addition to `CTop`'s per process state, at each monitoring iteration. No drop is recorded in the VM's serviced request rate, but the response time degrades by about 2%, only for 256 MB working set.

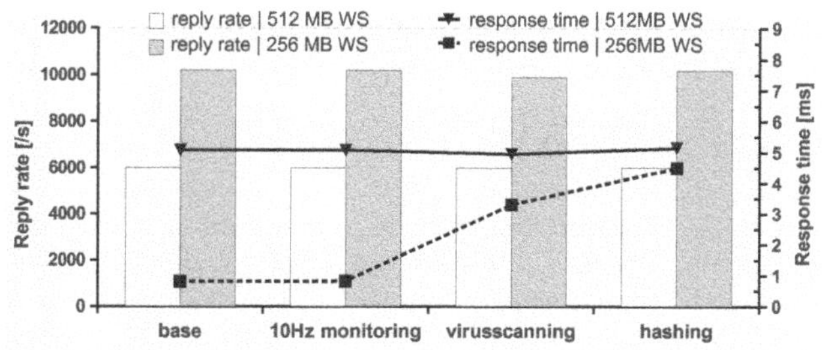

Figure 11: Impact on webserver VM with parallel out-of-band monitoring and management

Hashing VM's Memory: As a stress-test benchmark for memory crawling, we hash all of the VM's memory pages with *Mhash* library's MD5 hashing [31]. Even this benchmark has no visible impact on the VM's `httperf` server capacity as it continues to sustain the original request rate. However, the average response time degrades from 0.8 ms/ request to 4.5 ms/request for the 256 MB working set scenario, while remaining within the timeout threshold. For the 512 MB working set, the overhead is merely 1.5%.

VM Memory Scanning: Our virus scanner prototype, which is close to a worst-case application, introduces a 2.9% degradation on the `httperf` sustainable request rate with an average response time of 3.3ms for the 256 MB working set. In this case, the VM runs at its absolute limit, continuously serving requests directly from memory. Interestingly, the higher `httperf` working set size of 512MB (involving *kswapd*) records no impact on the `httperf` server capacity with PaVScan running simultaneously, as the application occasionally requires new page-ins, which is the common case for most practical applications.

Summary: The target VMs are not heavily impacted in the common operating case of realtime monitoring. The negative impact observed with heavy handed operations needs further analysis.

6.6 Impact on Co-located VMs

Here, we measure the performance overhead introduced on a VM (X) while other co-located VM's on the same host are being monitored. Since the VM X itself is not being monitored, any impact on its performance can be attributed as a side effect of monitoring the other colocated VMs. We use Xen for a clean administrative domain-guest domain separation for this experiment. We run the memory crawler inside `Dom0` itself, and monitor VMs at 10Hz, extracting the *full* system state from the VM at each iteration. Alongside `Dom0`, three other VMs run on their separate cores on a quad-core host. We measure the impact on each VM separately, while monitoring the other two VMs. The 3 VMs are put under stress, each running a different workload: (i) CPU-bound `x264` video encoding benchmark, (ii) disk-bound `bonnie++` disk benchmark, and (ii) a full-system stress workload simulated by an `httperf` webserver configured exactly as described in Section 6.5. By virtue of Xen's frontend/backend driver model, `Dom0` becomes responsible for arbitrating VMs' access to network and disk. Disk caching at hypervisor is disabled so that true disk throughputs can be measured. The host system (including `Dom0`) itself is never overloaded for repeatable and consistent measurements.

While monitoring the remaining 2 VMs at a 10Hz frequency, and repeating each experiment 5 times, neither the `bonnie++` VM nor the `x264` VM see any impact on their read/write throughputs and framerate respectively, but the `httperf` server VM's maximum sustainable request rate drops by 2.2%. For the latter, as in Section 6.5, relaxing the artificial "no guest swapping" constraint and thus increasing the working set size from 256MB to 512MB, also results in no impact on VM performance. An important point to further note is that a 10Hz frequency is actually high for most cloud monitoring and analytics operations, and the crawler's impact can be further minimized by operating at lower but still largely practical frequencies at 1Hz or less. Moreover, our execution - monitoring decoupled design favours these operations to be handed off to other lightly loaded or dedicated hosts, further minimizing crawler impact.

Summary: NFM is lightweight and does not have a heavy monitoring side-effect on the host's colocated VMs.

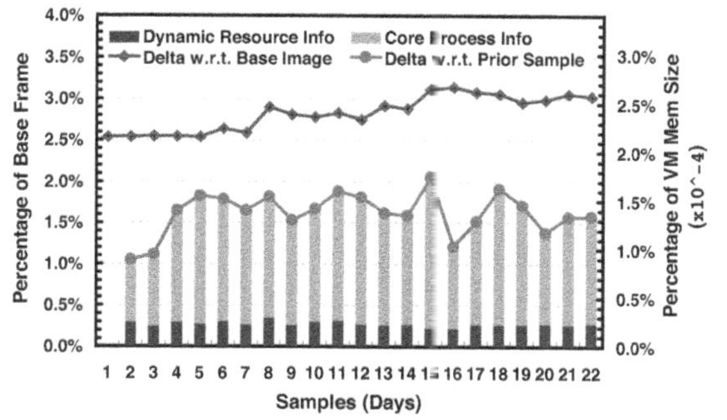

Figure 12: State management overhead with delta frames.

6.7 Space Overhead

Here we evaluate the storage requirements for maintaining VM state history in our frame datastore to enable across-time system analytics. We use the two delta frame extraction approaches described in Section 4.3. Shown in Figure 12 are the delta frame sizes relative to the base frame and relative to the previous frame, for a daily crawl of a VM over a 3-week period, while running various routine tasks and additional end-user applications. When computing deltas over the base fame (top curve) the frame sizes grow from 2.5% to 3% of the base frame size. However, when deltas are computed over the most-recent crawled state, the frame sizes do not grow over time (lower curve), averaging around 1.5% of the full frame size. Also, as can be seen, the amount of information that we need to keep for each VM for across-time analysis is minuscule compared to the actual VM sizes (delta frame sizes are only 0.00015% of the VM's 4GB memory size). In our experiments, the full frame sizes vary around 300KB-400KB and the delta frames are about 3KB-8KB.

If we scale these numbers out for a hypothetical cloud deployment with 10,000 VMs, the overall space overhead for our datastore with daily system snapshots and a year-long time horizon amounts to 14GB to 33GB, which is quite manageable even without any potential across-VM optimizations.

Summary: The overall space overhead of maintaining VM state across all instances and across time is manageable and is potentially scalable to large-scale cloud deployments.

7. RELATED WORK

Memory Introspection Techniques. Previous studies explored various methods for exposing VM memory state for introspection. Some of these employ hardware methods, such as direct memory access [1, 32] or PCI hooks [9]. While others rely on software techniques, including in-VM kernel modules (Volatilux [17]), in-VM memory mapping (i.e., via `/dev/mem`), VMM-level memory mapping / snapshotting, and remapping of guest address space inside a trusted VM (XenAccess [38], and LibVMI [8]). Prior work on interpreting the memory data structures describe different approaches with different requisites and degrees of inference. IDetect [30] interprets memory by accessing OS-specific, predetermined offsets to extract specified system information. Other techniques for automatically detecting the offsets also exist, which rely on pattern matching, function disassembly heuristics, guest support or additional kernel debug information [17, 27, 4, 10, 28, 13]. Recent work has also proposed automated introspection solutions that do not require detailed knowledge of OS kernel internals. Virtuoso [15] collects in-VM training code traces to create out-of-VM introspection code. VM Space Traveler [19] uses instruction monitoring at VMM layer to identify and redirect introspection related data to guest OS memory. Our framework leverages VMM memory mapping or snapshotting capabilities for our two prototypes, and our crawling approach shares some aspects of IDetect. We use this introspection framework, however, for fundamentally different applications- non-intrusive, out-of-band cloud monitoring.

Memory Introspection Applications. Most previous VM introspection work focuses on security, digital forensics, malware and intrusion detection applications [21, 43, 50]. Garfinkel and Rosenblum [20] use memory introspection for intrusion detection, with detectors for tracking program integrity, virus signatures and network sockets. Other work employs introspection techniques for detecting rootkits, identifying hidden drivers and anti-malware solutions [16, 19, 25]. Outside the security domain, IBMon [40] comes closest to our approach, using memory introspection to estimate bandwidth resource use for VMM-bypass network devices.

Other Cloud Monitoring Techniques. In addition to the ones already discussed, other existing VM monitoring techniques can also be viewed as falling into one or more categories described in section 2. PHD Virtual's [39] basic VM-as-blackbox metrics use only hypervisor level information, while in depth VM level metrics requires running scripts / installing 'intelligent agents' inside the VMs. Reflex vWatch monitoring [41] uses information from VMware vCenter. VMware vCenter Operations Management Suite [45] is also a combination of hypervisor level metrics, together with in-guest agent (vFabric Hyperic). VMware VIX API [46] uses VMware Tools to track VM information and actuate actions through this interface. Several security solutions such as McAfee MOVE, TrendMicro DeepSecurity, Reflex vTrust, SADE, CloudSec use VMSafe / vShield single agent approach.

Some exceptions include: (i) Hypertection [23], that also calls its security solution agentless, it can access memory of Hyper-V VMs only but their approach is unknown, and (ii) Litty and Lie's out-of-VM patch auditing [29] that uses architectural/ hardware introspection to be guest OS-agnostic. They monitor virtual hardware information (page bits, cpu registers) that exists at the hypervisor level to detect execution of unpatched binaries and non-binary files, given a database of known binaries and patches. A departure from the usual memory introspection way of inferring VM's runtime state, it is limited in the kind of information that can be recovered while operating at the virtual hardware level and relies on a functional VM environment.

8. CONCLUSION

In this paper we propose *Near Field Monitoring*, a fundamentally different approach to systems monitoring and analytics in the cloud. We show that traditional in-VM techniques or newer virtualization-aware alternatives are not a good fit for modern data centers, and address their limitations with our non-intrusive, out-of-band cloud monitoring and analytics framework. NFM decouples system execution from monitoring and analytics functions, and pushes these functions out of the systems' scope. The NFM framework provides "always-on" monitoring, even when the monitored systems are unresponsive or compromised, and works "out-of-the-box" by eliminating any need for guest cooperation or modification. We describe the implementation of NFM across two virtualization platforms, and present four prototype applications that we built on top of our framework to highlight its capabilities for across-systems and across-time analytics. Our evaluations show that we can accurately and reliably monitor cloud instances, in realtime, with minimal impact on both the monitored systems and the cloud infrastructure. Our ongoing work with NFM involves deploying our framework in a real production data center to evaluate its scalability characteristics, to explore new potential applications, and to discover emerging patterns across large-scale system data.

We believe our work lays the foundation for the right way of systems monitoring and analytics in the cloud. With its ability to support non-intrusive, fine-grain monitoring and complex analytics, NFM serves as the the cornerstone of an "analytics as a service (AaaS)" cloud offering, where the end users of the cloud can seamlessly subscribe to various out-of-the-box monitoring and analytics services, with no impact or setup requisites on their execution environments.

9. ACKNOWLEDGEMENTS

We would like to thank our anonymous reviewers and our shepherd Thu Nguyen for their helpful suggestions on improving this paper. This work is supported by an IBM Open Collaboration Research award.

10. REFERENCES

[1] Adam Boileau. Hit by a Bus: Physical Access Attacks with Firewire. *RuxCon* 2006. http://www.security-assessment.com/files/presentations/ab_firewire_rux2k6-final.pdf.

[2] Amazon. CloudWatch. http://aws.amazon.com/cloudwatch/.

[3] Amazon. Summary of the October 22,2012 AWS Service Event in the US-East Region. https://aws.amazon.com/message/680342/.

[4] Anthony Desnos. Draugr - Live memory forensics on Linux. http://code.google.com/p/draugr/.

[5] M. Auty, A. Case, M. Cohen, B. Dolan-Gavitt, M. H. Ligh, J. Levy, and A. Walters. Volatility - An advanced memory forensics framework. http://code.google.com/p/volatility.

[6] S. Bahram, X. Jiang, Z. Wang, M. Grace, J. Li, D. Srinivasan, J. Rhee, and D. Xu. DKSM: Subverting Virtual Machine Introspection for Fun and Profit. In *SRDS*, pages 82 -91, 2010.

[7] P. Barham, B. Dragovic, K. Fraser, S. Hand, T. Harris, A. Ho, R. Neugebauer, I. Pratt, and A. Warfield. Xen and the art of virtualization. In *SOSP*, pages 164–177, 2003.

[8] Bryan Payne. Vmitools - An introduction to LibVMI. http://code.google.com/p/vmitools/wiki/LibVMIIntroduction.

[9] B. D. Carrier and J. Grand. A hardware-based memory acquisition procedure for digital investigations. *Digital Investigation*, 1(1):50–60, 2004.

[10] A. Case, L. Marziale, and G. G. RichardIII. Dynamic recreation of kernel data structures for live forensics. *Digital Investigation*, 7, Supplement(0):S32 – S40, 2010.

[11] ClamAV. Clam AntiVirus. `http://www.clamav.net`.

[12] C. Colohan. The Scariest Outage Ever. CMU SDI/ISTC Seminar Series, 2012.

[13] David Anderson. White Paper: Red Hat Crash Utility. `http://people.redhat.com/anderson/crash_whitepaper/`.

[14] Dell Quest/VKernel. Foglight for Virtualization. `http://www.quest.com/foglight-for-virtualization-enterprise-edition/`.

[15] B. Dolan-Gavitt, T. Leek, M. Zhivich, J. Giffin, and W. Lee. Virtuoso: Narrowing the Semantic Gap in Virtual Machine Introspection. In *IEEE Security and Privacy '11*, pages 297–312.

[16] B. Dolan-Gavitt, B. Payne, and W. Lee. Leveraging forensic tools for virtual machine introspection. Technical Report GT-CS-11-05, Georgia Institute of Technology, 2011.

[17] Emilien Girault. Volatilitux- Memory forensics framework to help analyzing Linux physical memory dumps. `http://code.google.com/p/volatilitux/`.

[18] M. F. Linux Rootkit Implementation. `http://average-coder.blogspot.com/2011/12/linux-rootkit.html`, 2011.

[19] Y. Fu and Z. Lin. Space Traveling across VM: Automatically Bridging the Semantic Gap in Virtual Machine Introspection via Online Kernel Data Redirection. In *IEEE Security&Privacy'12*.

[20] T. Garfinkel and M. Rosenblum. A Virtual Machine Introspection Based Architecture for Intrusion Detection. In *NDSS*, pages 191–206, 2003.

[21] B. Hay and K. Nance. Forensics examination of volatile system data using virtual introspection. *SIGOPS Oper. Syst. Rev.*, 42(3):74–82, 2008.

[22] O. S. Hofmann, A. M. Dunn, S. Kim, I. Roy, and E. Witchel. Ensuring operating system kernel integrity with OSck. In *ASPLOS*, pages 279–290, 2011.

[23] Hypertection. Hypervisor-Based Antivirus. `hypertection.com`.

[24] Jack of all Clouds. Recounting EC2 One Year Later. `www.jackofallclouds.com/2010/12/recounting-ec2/`.

[25] X. Jiang, X. Wang, and D. Xu. Stealthy malware detection through VMM-based out-of-the-box semantic view reconstruction. In *CCS '07*, pages 128–138.

[26] A. Kivity, Y. Kamay, D. Laor, U. Lublin, and A. Liguori. KVM: the Linux Virtual Machine Monitor. In *OLS '07: The 2007 Ottawa Linux Symposium*, pages 225–230, 2007.

[27] I. Kollar. Forensic RAM dump image analyser. Master's Thesis, Charles University in Prague, 2010. `hysteria.sk/~niekt0/fmem/doc/foriana.pdf`.

[28] Z. Lin, J. Rhee, X. Zhang, D. Xu, and X. Jiang. SigGraph: Brute Force Scanning of Kernel Data Structure Instances Using Graph-based Signatures. In *NDSS*, 2011.

[29] L. Litty and D. Lie. Patch auditing in infrastructure as a service clouds. In *VEE '11*.

[30] Mariusz Burdach. Digital forensics of the physical memory. 2005. `http://forensic.seccure.net/pdf/mburdach_digital_forensics_of_physical_memory.pdf`.

[31] N. Mavroyanopoulos and S. Schumann. Mhash. `http://mhash.sourceforge.net`.

[32] Maximillian Dornseif. 0wned by an iPod. *PacSec Applied Security Conference* 2004. `http://md.hudora.de/presentations/firewire/PacSec2004.pdf`.

[33] D. Mosberger and T. Jin. httperf - a tool for measuring web server performance. *SIGMETRICS Perform. Eval. Rev.*, 26(3):31–37, 1998.

[34] Nirsoft. Windows Vista Kernel Structures. `http://www.nirsoft.net/kernel_struct/vista/`.

[35] OpenBenchmarking/Phoronix. x264 Test Profile. `http://openbenchmarking.org/test/pts/x264-1.7.0`.

[36] Opscode. Chef. `http://www.opscode.com/chef/`.

[37] Y. Padioleau, J. L. Lawall, and G. Muller. Understanding collateral evolution in linux device drivers. In *EuroSys'06*.

[38] B. Payne, M. de Carbone, and W. Lee. Secure and Flexible Monitoring of Virtual Machines. In *Twenty-Third Annual Computer Security Applications Conference*, pages 385 –397, 2007.

[39] PHD Virtual. Virtual Monitoring. `http://www.phdvirtual.com/`.

[40] A. Ranadive, A. Gavrilovska, and K. Schwan. Ibmon: monitoring vmm-bypass capable infiniband devices using memory introspection. In *HPCVirt*, pages 25–32, 2009.

[41] Reflex. vWatch Monitoring. `http://www.reflexsystems.com/Products/vWatch`.

[42] Russell Coker. Bonnie++. `http://www.coker.com.au/bonnie++/`.

[43] A. Srivastava and J. Giffin. Tamper-Resistant, Application-Aware Blocking of Malicious Network Connections. In *RAID*, pages 39–58, 2008.

[44] S. Thomas, K. Sherly, and S. Dija. Extraction of memory forensic artifacts from windows 7 ram image. In *IEEE ICT '13*, pages 937–942, April 2013.

[45] VMware. vCenter Operations Management Suite. `http://www.vmware.com/products/vcenter-operations-management/`.

[46] VMware. VIX API Documentation. `http://www.vmware.com/support/developer/vix-api/`.

[47] VMware. VMCI Overview. `http://pubs.vmware.com/vmci-sdk/`.

[48] VMware. VMWare Tools. `http://kb.vmware.com/kb/340`.

[49] VMware. vShield Endpoint. `http://www.vmware.com/products/vsphere/features-endpoint`.

[50] VMWare Inc. VMWare VMSafe security technology. `http://www.vmware.com/company/news/releases/vmsafe_vmworld.html`.

[51] S. Vogl. A bottom-up Approach to VMI-based Kernel-level Rootkit Detection. PhD Thesis, Technische Unversitat Munchen., 2010.

[52] C. A. Waldspurger. Memory resource management in VMware ESX server. *SIGOPS Oper. Syst. Rev.*, 36(SI):181–194, 2002.

The Behavior of Epidemics under Bounded Susceptibility

Subhashini Krishnasamy
Department of ECE
UT Austin
subhashini.kb@utexas.edu

Siddhartha Banerjee
Department of MS&E
Stanford University
sidb@stanford.edu

Sanjay Shakkottai
Department of ECE
UT Austin
shakkott@austin.utexas.edu

ABSTRACT

We investigate the sensitivity of epidemic behavior to a *bounded susceptibility* constraint – susceptible nodes are infected by their neighbors via the regular SI/SIS dynamics, but subject to a *cap on the infection rate*. Such a constraint is motivated by modern social networks, wherein messages are broadcast to all neighbors, but attention spans are limited. Bounded susceptibility also arises in distributed computing applications with download bandwidth constraints, and in human epidemics under quarantine policies.

Network epidemics have been extensively studied in literature; prior work characterizes the graph structures required to ensure fast spreading under the SI dynamics, and long lifetime under the SIS dynamics. In particular, these conditions turn out to be meaningful for two classes of networks of practical relevance – dense, uniform (i.e., *clique-like*) graphs, and sparse, structured (i.e., *star-like*) graphs. We show that bounded susceptibility has a surprising impact on epidemic behavior in these graph families. For the SI dynamics, bounded susceptibility has no effect on star-like networks, but dramatically alters the spreading time in clique-like networks. In contrast, for the SIS dynamics, clique-like networks are unaffected, but star-like networks exhibit a sharp change in extinction times under bounded susceptibility.

Our findings are useful for the design of disease-resistant networks and infrastructure networks. More generally, they show that results for existing epidemic models are sensitive to modeling assumptions in non-intuitive ways, and suggest caution in directly using these as guidelines for real systems.

Categories and Subject Descriptors

H.4 [**Information Systems Applications**]: Miscellaneous

Keywords

Network Epidemics; SI/SIS Dynamics; Non-linear Dynamics; Bounded Susceptibility

SIGMETRICS'14, June 16–20, 2014, Austin, Texas, USA.

ACM 978-1-4503-2789-3/14/06 ...$15.00.
http://dx.doi.org/10.1145/2591971.2591977.

1. INTRODUCTION

Epidemic processes – stochastic models for spreading in graphs – play an important role in a variety of domains ranging from social networks (opinion spread), epidemiology (disease spread) and distributed computing (information spread). Though there are several models in literature for such processes, a characteristic feature of these is the spread of the process from 'infected' to 'non-infected' nodes along the edges of the network. In this work, we investigate the behavior of such processes under the assumption that *the maximum susceptibility of a node to infection from its neighbors is bounded.* This constraint seems natural (and we present several settings where it is so) – however we show that imposing it brings to light some surprising behavior of epidemic processes in different networks.

In this paper, we focus on two major classes of epidemic processes: the SI process where nodes never recover from infection, and the SIS process where nodes recover, but can get reinfected. The SI or 'Susceptible-Infected' dynamics [1, 2, 3, 4] is the most common model for one-way dissemination. Nodes exist in 2 states – 'susceptible' (S) and 'infected' (I). Infected nodes never recover, and try to infect each neighboring susceptible node at a rate β (after a random delay, drawn from an i.i.d. *Exponential*(β) distribution). We refer to β as the *virulence* of the infection process. The SI dynamics terminate when all nodes are infected, and the corresponding time interval is called the *spreading time*. In particular, we are interested in networks with small spreading time (ideally $O(1)$ in the number of nodes).

A small modification of this model gives the popular SIS or 'Susceptible-Infected-Susceptible' dynamics [5, 6, 7, 8, 9, 10, 11] for epidemic processes. This is identical to the SI dynamics, except that now an infected node can revert to being susceptible at a (normalised) rate of '1'. The absorbing state for the SIS epidemic is when all nodes become susceptible; the time taken to reach this state is called the *extinction time*. We are interested in networks where this extinction time is exponentially large (i.e., $\Omega(e^{poly(n)})$, where n is the number of nodes in the network).

A key assumption in both models is that *the infection rate for a susceptible node scales linearly in the size of the infected neighborhood*; formally, a susceptible node j transitions to being infected at a rate $\beta|I_j|$, where I_j is the set of infected neighbors of j. This assumption makes the models conceptually simple and tractable. However, it also means that in these models, high-degree nodes may get infected at unrealistically high rates. In several real-life settings, this is unreasonable; for example, in social networks, users broadcast content to all their neighbors, but attention-span constraints limit consumption of content to only a few neighbors. Similarly, in sensor networks using epidemic protocols, nodes can broadcast easily, but have download bandwidth constraints, and so can listen to only some of their neighbors. Refer to Section 1.2 for more examples.

To modify epidemic dynamics to fit such settings, we need to assume that nodes have *bounded susceptibility*, i.e., a maximum rate at which they can get infected, *which is independent of network size.* We can capture this via the notion of an *infection-profile*: a susceptible node j, we assume, is infected at a rate $\Phi(\beta|I_j|)$, where $\Phi(\cdot)$ is a *bounded* function. Now, in order to use epidemic models to understand real-life processes, one hopes that the behavior of these epidemics is somewhat insensitive to the infection-profile Φ. This motivates the central question we address in this paper:

How robust is SI/SIS epidemic behavior under an additional bounded susceptibility constraint?

The answer turns out to depend on the dynamics and network structure in a surprisingly subtle way. In particular, bounded susceptibility exposes a sharp dichotomy between two classes of networks of practical relevance:

- *Star-like networks,* i.e., sparse, structured graphs, with a small number of edges, mostly concentrated among a dense core, with all other nodes at a short distance from the core. These are good models for *engineered networks*, which are designed to be highly connected while using only a small number of edges.
- *Clique-like networks,* i.e., dense, uniform graphs, with edges spread evenly among nodes. A good example is the connected-regime Erdös-Rényi graph (i.e., $G(n,p)$ with $p = \Omega(\log n/n)$). These are good models for *organically-formed networks.*

In prior work, the distinction between the two classes is suggested, but not explicitly made; we formalize this classification in Section 2.1. It turns out that this is crucial to our study of bounded susceptibility, as follows:

For a fixed virulence β, the spreading time in the SI dynamics on star-like networks is small ($O(\log n)$, under fairly weak conditions on the non-core subgraph); in clique-like networks, the spreading time is $O(1)$[1]. In case of the SIS epidemic, both clique-like networks and star-like networks experience exponential extinction times [8]. Thus, in a sense, *both star-like and clique-like networks are well suited for epidemic processes* – this behavior, however, *no longer holds under bounded susceptibility.*

1.1 An Overview of our Results

We refer to our modified epidemic models, incorporating bounded susceptibility, as the SI_{bs} and SIS_{bs} dynamics. As mentioned, we assume that in both models, a susceptible node j gets infected at a rate $\Phi(\beta|I_j|)$, where I_j are the infected neighbors of j; in the SI_{bs} model, infected nodes remain so forever, while in the SIS_{bs} model, they recover to become susceptible at a rate 1. We assume that $\Phi(0) = 0$, and $\Phi(\cdot)$ is concave, non-decreasing, and bounded above by some $\Phi_{\max} = \Theta(1)$.

SI_{bs} **Dynamics:** In the SI_{bs} model, we are interested in finding the (expected) spreading time, under the assumption that both β and $\Phi_{\max}$ are $\Theta(1)$. In this context, we show:

- For clique-like networks, the spreading time switches from $O(1)$ under SI dynamics to $\Omega(\log n)$ under the SI_{bs} dynamics. In particular, for a $G(n,p)$ graph in the connected regime (i.e., $p \sim \omega\,(\log n/n)$), the spreading time switches from $o(1)$ to $\Omega(\log n)$ under the SI_{bs} dynamics.
- For star-like networks, the spreading time is $\Theta(\log n)$ under both SI and SI_{bs} dynamics (under some assumptions on the network structure). Thus, imposing bounded susceptibility does not significantly alter the epidemic behavior.

Thus, the SI model is highly sensitive to bounded susceptibility in clique-like networks – note that the spreading time has switched from vanishing with network size to actually scaling with network size. On the other hand, it is insensitive in star-like networks.

A moment's thought suggests that this behavior is indeed reasonable – we have greatly reduced the (potential) susceptibility of high-degree nodes, which should hinder the spread of the epidemic. Furthermore, since high-degree nodes are more affected, it seems natural that bounded susceptibility should adversely affect dense graphs much more than sparse graphs. Surprisingly, the latter intuition is completely reversed in case of the SIS_{bs} model.

SIS_{bs} **Dynamics:** Recall that in the SIS_{bs} model, we want to find the (expected) extinction time under $\beta, \Phi_{\max} = \Theta(1)$ and recovery rate 1. In this context, we show the following:

- For clique-like networks, the extinction time is exponential (i.e., $\exp(\Omega(poly(n)))$) both with and without the bounded susceptibility assumption. In fact, this robustness property holds *for any network which contains a polynomial-sized subgraph which resembles a random $G(n,p)$ graph in the connected regime* (i.e., with $p \sim \omega\,(\log n/n)$).
- However for star-like networks, we now observe a sharp transition in extinction time. While star-like networks experience epidemics with exponential lifetimes under the SIS process [8, 9], we prove that this is not true in the case of SIS_{bs} infections. In particular, for any network which can be decomposed into a small *core*, plus an outer sparse subgraph, *the SIS_{bs} epidemic lifetime is sub-exponential for any virulence $\beta = \Theta(1)$.*

This reversal of results may seem paradoxical – there is however an intuitive explanation for this. Note that the absorbing states in the SI and SIS epidemics are exactly the opposite (all-infected vs. all-susceptible). Moreover, in the SI model, we want the epidemic to move rapidly towards the all-infected state, while in the SIS, we want to deter it from reaching the all-susceptible state. Rapid transition to the all-infected state in the SI dynamics is aided by having many high-degree nodes – this is hampered by imposing bounded susceptibility. On the other hand in the SIS dynamics, high degree nodes impede transition to the all-susceptible state – having many such nodes helps distribute this effect, but too few high-degree nodes means that these are now critical bottlenecks. Under bounded susceptibility, these bottleneck nodes are the most affected, resulting in a sharp transition in the epidemic behavior.

To make this intuition more transparent, in Section 2.2 we demonstrate the effect of the various dynamics in the clique and star networks, which are in a sense the extreme-case scenarios. Our main contribution in this work is to show how these phenomena extend to large classes of networks,

[1]Special cases of this result can be found in [2, 4]

occupying the space between these two extremes. In the process, we develop some structural lemmas relating the dynamics of epidemics to network properties, which may be of independent interest.

Technical Contributions. Most of our arguments involve standard Markov chain machinery, along with careful use of measure concentration. Some of the ideas we use are of fairly recent origin, in particular, the sharp expressions for extinction time in SIS models via embedding in an ergodic Markov chain (Lemma 1, which we adapt from Lemma 8 in [10]), and characterization of the SI spreading time in clique-like graphs, which is similar to results for first-passage percolation in random graphs [4]. However, unlike [4], our results (Theorems 1,3, 4 and 6) do not focus on a particular graph or generative model, but rather, relate the epidemic behavior to structural properties of the network. We believe these lemmas could be useful in studying other related settings. Finally, our results follow from elementary arguments, and hold for finite networks, with explicit error bounds in terms of network size.

We note that our classification of networks into clique-like and star-like does not cover all networks. In particular, there are networks which are a mix of the two, and where our results may not be tight; sharper techniques could perhaps be used to bridge this gap. Furthermore, our techniques do not immediately extend to other epidemic models, in particular, the SIR dynamics (see [12, 13] for details) – this is an interesting avenue for future exploration.

1.2 Bounded Susceptibility: Applications in Real-World Settings

Before we formally state our results, we first discuss three important real-life settings which exhibit bounded susceptibility, and point out applications of our results therein.

Social and Economic Networks. Perhaps the most compelling example of bounded susceptibility in network epidemics comes from online social networks. Sites such as Twitter and Facebook are built on a broadcast model – users upload content to the website, intending it to be broadcast to all neighbors. However, users are known to consume content from only a small set of neighbors – this is due to a combination of limited attention-spans and content filtering algorithms, and has been observed empirically in Twitter data [14, 15]. Epidemic models have been used to understand why content 'goes viral' on such media, however existing works do not account for bounded susceptibility.

Non-linear propagation models are also used in economics to model network externalities in the spread of opinions, technologies, etc. For example, the adoption of a new technology on a network is often subject to diminishing returns due to wearing out of novelty with increasing number of recommendations [16] – this naturally suggests a concave infection-profile, and further, bounded susceptibility.

Human-Disease Epidemiology. Network epidemic models are widely used to study human epidemics, and also computer viruses. Here again, bounded susceptibility is often a key feature of real epidemics, due to spread of awareness and adoption of preventive measures. Non-linear infection models have been used to capture the effect of risk perception in the spread of epidemics [17, 18], by combining the effect of infection spread and the protection measures taken by the susceptible individual. However these works focus on approximate and mean-field treatments for the problem.

Our work provides both intuition and technical tools for studying the effects of bounded susceptibility on epidemics. One important application of our findings is in the design of vaccination and quarantining policies on networks – such policies help reduce the susceptibility of nodes to infection, but usually nodes retain some susceptibility. A closely related design question is of distributing antidotes in a network [11] – there, the epidemic is controlled by increasing the recovery rate of a node, whereas our control is via limiting the susceptibility of a node.

Distributed Computing on Networks. A third application of epidemic processes is as a primitive for designing low-complexity distributed algorithms. The SI dynamics is the basis of the *flooding algorithm* which is used for broadcast messaging in networks, distributed database synchronization, etc [19]. The SIS dynamics is sometimes used to ensure persistent storage in distributed storage/sensing applications with disk failures [20]. Existing work focuses on using the standard SI/SIS dynamics, or modifies them to impose *bounded influence*, i.e., a bound on the upload bandwidth of a node.

However many of the above settings, in reality, exhibit bounded susceptibility. Modern distributed/P2P systems are based on a virtual network architecture, where nodes upload content to a central location, from where it is downloaded by its neighbors. Thus, broadcasting is easy, but downloading is bandwidth constrained. This is also true for sensor networks – a node needs to broadcast a message once, but it is limited in how many neighbors it can listen to, due to a fixed download bandwidth. Thus, bounded susceptibility is natural in these settings. We discuss all these applications in Section 2.4, after presenting our results.

1.3 Related Work

Epidemic processes on networks have been studied across many disciplines; readers interested in more details regarding epidemics are referred to several excellent books on the subject [1, 12, 21, 22]. Specifically, there is a vast literature to characterize spreading time in various contexts for SI processes [1, 2, 3, 4], and phase transitions/extinction time for SIS processes [6, 7, 8, 9, 10, 11]. Phase transitions for SIR processes are available in [13].

Non-linear epidemic models have been explored in the past in various contexts. A large body of work is devoted to settings with *bounded influence*, where the total rate at which a node infects its neighbors is bounded [23, 24], but the infection-profile $\Phi(\cdot)$ is still linear. One popular model with non-linear $\Phi(\cdot)$ is the Bootstrap Percolation, and related variants [25, 26]. Several authors have also studied non-linear infection models at the population level using mean field approximations [17, 18] – these works show the existence of epidemic thresholds under different non-linear models. However, to the best of our knowledge, ours is the first work that explicitly characterizes epidemic behavior under bounded susceptibility.

2. MAIN RESULTS AND DISCUSSION

We now present and discuss our main results. Our general theorems are presented in Section 2.3, followed by a discussion of their application in Section 2.4; before that, in Section 2.2, we specialize our results for the clique and star networks, and give an outline of the proofs for these cases. The complete proofs are somewhat technical – we outline the main proof ideas after each theorem, deferring complete proofs to Section 3.

2.1 System Model

The SI/SIS Dynamics

The SI, SIS dynamics models we use are standard in literature [8, 10]. We consider a graph $G(V, E)$ with n nodes (vertices). The various processes ($SI, SI_{bs}, SIS, SIS_{bs}$) evolve on this graph in continuous time. Associated with each node $i \in \{1, 2, \ldots, n\}$ is a random process $X_i(t) \in \{0, 1\}$. Here, '0' corresponds to the susceptible state and '1' corresponds to the infected state (the entire state vector is denoted by $\mathbf{X}(t)$). For the SI and SIS models, nodes in state '1' (infected nodes) attempt to infect a neighbor *independently* at a rate β, i.e., after a i.i.d random interval drawn from an *Exponential*(β) distribution. In the SI dynamics, an infected node never recovers. In contrast in the SIS dynamics, an infected node returns back to the susceptible state at rate 1 (i.e., after an *Exponential*(1) time).

We assume that the infection starts off at a single node, arbitrarily chosen. This is natural for the SI epidemic since we want to study spreading-time. For the SIS epidemic, our results generalize for any constant-sized initial infected set. For the SI dynamics, the only absorbing state is the *all-infected* state (i.e., $X_i = 1\ \forall i$), and the spreading-time is defined as $\tau_s \triangleq \inf_t\{X_i(t) = 1\ \forall i\}$. In contrast, for the SIS dynamics, the only absorbing state is the *all-susceptible* state (i.e., $X_i = 0\ \forall i$), and the extinction-time is defined as $\tau_e \triangleq \inf_t\{X_i(t) = 0\ \forall i\}$. We also assume throughout that β is a constant, independent of n; however, our analysis extends for settings where β is a function of n.

Infection-Profiles and Bounded Susceptibility

A critical assumption in both SI and SIS models is that the infection rate for a susceptible node scales in proportion to the number of infected neighbors. In order to study the effect of non-linearity in the infection-rate, we introduce the notion of an infection-profile: we assume that a susceptible node j is infected at a rate $\Phi(\beta|I_j|)$, where I_j is the number of infected neighbors of node j (at some time t; we suppress the dependence on t for ease of notation). Thus, in both the SI_{bs} and the SIS_{bs} dynamics, we have:

$$X_i : 0 \to 1 \quad \text{at rate } \Phi\left(\beta \sum_{(i,j)\in E} X_j\right),$$

and in the SIS_{bs}, we additionally have $X_i : 1 \to 0$ at rate 1.

$\Phi : \mathbb{R}_+ \to \mathbb{R}_+$ represents the overall effect that the infected neighbors together have on a susceptible node. We assume that $\Phi(0) = 0$, and that $\Phi(\cdot)$ is non-decreasing, concave and bounded. Note that these assumptions imply that $\Phi_{max} := \sup_{x\in\mathbb{R}} \Phi(x)$ exists, and $\Phi(\beta) > 0\, \forall\, \beta > 0$.

Clique-Like and Star-Like Networks

We now formalize the two classes of networks, which we introduced in Section 1. Intuitively, clique-like networks are those which are dense (i.e., where $|E| = \omega(n)$) and have edges evenly distributed across the cuts of the network. One way to formalize this is via the expansion properties of the underlying graph. There are different ways to quantify the expansion of a graph. For example, the *edge expansion* of a graph is characterized by the *generalized isoperimetric constant*:

$$\eta^e_m(G) := \inf_{S\subset V, |S|\le m} \frac{|\delta(S)|}{|S|}, \quad 0 < m \le \lfloor n/2 \rfloor,$$

where, for any set $A \subseteq V$, $\delta(A) = \{(i,j) \in E \text{ s.t. } i \in A, j \notin A\}$ are the edges in the cut defined by A. The case of $m = n/2$ is referred to as the *isoperimetric/Cheeger constant*:

$$\eta(G) := \inf_{S\subset V, |S|\le n/2} \frac{|\delta(S)|}{|S|}.$$

We can also define an alternate notion of isoperimetry based on *vertex expansion*, as follows:

$$\eta^v_m(G) := \inf_{S\subset V, |S|\le m} \frac{|\Gamma(S)|}{|S|}, \quad 0 < m \le \lfloor n/2 \rfloor,$$

where $\Gamma(S)$ is the *neighborhood* of S, i.e., the set of nodes in S^C with at least one neighbor in S. It is easy to check that for any fixed m, we have $\eta^e_m(G) \ge \eta^v_m(G)$.

The isoperimetric constants characterize bottleneck sets, i.e., those containing the smallest fraction of the potential edges in the cut. For a clique, it is easy to check that $\eta(G) = \Theta(n)$, which is the highest possible. To show that epidemic properties hold over a large class of graphs, we want to admit graphs with smaller isoperimetric constants. This motivates the following characterizations for clique-like networks:

Definition 1 (Clique-like Networks). *We define a graph G to be clique-like if it satisfies one of the following:*
(A) If $\eta(G) = \Omega(\log n)$.
(B) If for some $m = n^\alpha$, $\alpha \in (0, 1)$, we have $\eta^v_m(G) = \omega(1)$.

The two definitions arise from analyzing the two epidemic dynamics on graphs. Although not equivalent, they both characterize networks with good expansion properties. To demonstrate their wide applicability, we show that random (*Erdös-Rényi*) graphs in the connected regime (i.e., $G(n,p)$ with $p \sim \Omega(\log n/n)$) are clique-like under both definitions.

On the other hand, star-like networks intuitively are those which can be partitioned into a *dense core* and a *sparse periphery*. Here, the natural notions of density turn out to be the average degree $d_{avg}(G)$, and the spectral radius $\rho(G)$, i.e., the largest eigenvalue of the adjacency matrix, which is closely related to the node degrees (in particular, $d_{avg}(G) \le \rho(G) \le d_{\max}(G)$. Formally, we write $V = V_c \cup V_p$, where V_c denotes the core and V_p the periphery. As for clique-like networks, we have two characterizations:

Definition 2 (Star-like Networks). *We define a graph G to be star-like if it satisfies one of the following:*
(A) If $|V_p| = \Omega(n)$ and the average degree of nodes in the periphery is $O(1)$. In addition, the diameter of the graph is $O(\log n)$.
(B) If $|V_c| = O(poly \log n)$ and the subgraph $G(V_p)$ induced by the periphery has spectral radius $\rho(G(V_p)) = o(1)$.

Again, the class of graphs that are star-like by the two definitions above are not equivalent but broadly include networks which have a sparse periphery and a small (possibly dense) core. We derive our results for SI dynamics based on definition (A) of clique-like and star-like networks, while the results for SIS dynamics are based on definition (B) for both the networks.

2.2 Two Examples: The Clique and the Star

Before presenting our full results, we first illustrate them by considering our two representative graphs – the clique and the star. This comparison brings out the dichotomy between the two network classes. Further, it allows us to build intuition for our main results, since these special cases admit simple proofs. In all these results, we use standard notation (O, Θ, Ω, o and ω) to characterize the scaling behavior with the graph size, n. We also use the notation $[n] \triangleq \{1, 2, \ldots, n\}$, and $\mathcal{H}_n = \sum_{i=1}^{n} \frac{1}{i}$.

$SI - SI_{bs}$ Dynamics

Consider first the SI/SI_{bs} epidemic on K_n, the clique on n nodes. We now show that the spreading-time is *vanishingly small* under the SI dynamics, while it *scales with* n under the SI_{bs} dynamics.

PROPOSITION 1. *For the SI/SI_{bs} epidemic on K_n starting at an arbitrary node,*
1. *Under the SI dynamics,* $\mathbb{E}[\tau_s] = \Theta(\frac{\log n}{n})$.
2. *Under the SI_{bs} dynamics* $\mathbb{E}[\tau_s] = \Theta(\log n)$.

PROOF. The first part is known from previous results [4] and follows from standard Markov-chain arguments. By denoting $N(t)$ to be the number of infected nodes at time t, and analyzing the steady-state of the resulting (one-dimensional) CTMC, we immediately get the result.

Next, for the bounded-susceptibility spreading process, SI_{bs}, we again consider the process $\{N(t)\}$, i.e., the total number of infected nodes. $\{N(t)\}$ has transition rates as follows:

$$z \to z+1 \quad \text{at rate } \Phi(\beta z)(n-z) \quad \forall 1 \le z \le n-1,$$

and hence the expected spreading-time is given by:

$$\mathbb{E}[\tau_s] = \sum_{k=1}^{n-1} \frac{1}{\Phi(\beta k)(n-k)} \ge \sum_{k=1}^{n-1} \frac{1}{(n-k)\Phi_{max}} = \frac{\mathcal{H}_{n-1}}{\Phi_{max}},$$

where the inequality follows since $\Phi(\beta k) \le \Phi_{max}$. From the same equation, we also have:

$$\mathbb{E}[\tau_s] = \sum_{k=1}^{n-1} \frac{1}{\Phi(\beta k)(n-k)} \le \frac{\mathcal{H}_{n-1}}{\Phi(\beta)},$$

since Φ is a non-decreasing function. Finally, since both $\Phi(\beta)$ and $\Phi_{\max}$ are $\Theta(1)$, and using $\ln(n+1) \le \mathcal{H}_n \le \ln(n) + 1$, we get the second assertion. □

Thus there is a sharp change in the spreading-time between the SI and SI_{bs} epidemic processes in cliques. This is clearly visible in Figure 1, where we simulate and plot the spreading-time under the SI and SI_{bs} dynamics on a clique, as a function of network size n. Further, in Section 3.1, we derive concentration bounds showing that the above result holds with high probability.

On the other hand, the same behavior is not seen in a star network, as we show via our next result:

PROPOSITION 2. *In a star network with a single hub and $n-1$ leaves, under both the SI and SI_{bs} epidemics, we have:*

$$\mathbb{E}[\tau_s] = \Theta(\log n)$$

PROOF. Consider first the SI process on a star network. We denote the hub as node 1 and define:

$$\tau_1 = \inf_{t>0}\{\text{Node 1 is infected}\},$$

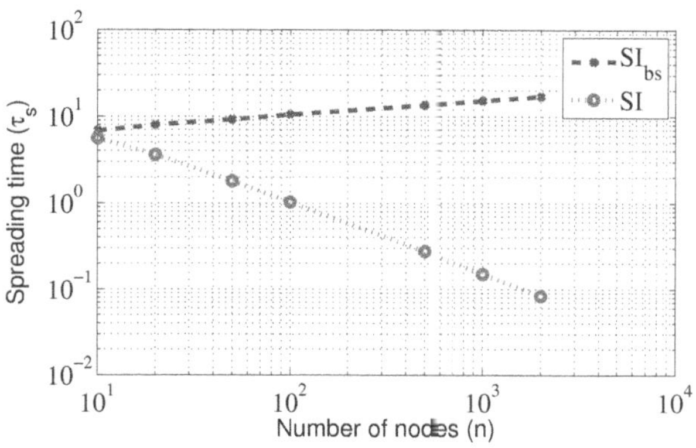

Figure 1: Simulated epidemic spreading-time in a clique under SI and SI_{bs}, averaged over 500 runs for $\beta = 0.1$ and $\Phi_{max} = 0.5$. Note that $\mathbb{E}[\tau_s]$ switches from $o(1)$ under the SI dynamics, to $\Omega(\log n)$ under SI_{bs} (decreasing to increasing on log – log plot).

i.e., the first time that the hub gets infected. Since the epidemic starts at a single (arbitrary) node, we can split the spreading-time as: $\tau_s = \tau_1 + (\tau_s - \tau_1)$. Next, we have that $\mathbb{E}[\tau_1] = O(1)$ and $\tau_s - \tau_1$ corresponds to the maximum of $m \in \{n-2, n-1\}$ i.i.d random variables, each drawn from a *Exponential*(β) distribution; thus $\mathbb{E}[\tau_s - \tau_1] = \frac{\mathcal{H}_m}{\beta} \sim \Theta(\log n)$. Finally, note that no susceptible node ever has more than 1 infected neighbor – hence the SI_{bs} model is identical to the SI model with $\beta' = \Phi(\beta) = \Theta(1)$. Therefore, the result also holds for SI_{bs} epidemics. □

$SIS - SIS_{bs}$ Dynamics

Next, we consider the SIS/SIS_{bs} epidemic. Here, it is known [8] that the expected extinction-time is exponential in cliques – we will prove that it is exponential even for the SIS_{bs} dynamics.

We first state and prove a lemma that gives a closed-form expression for expected time to absorption in a birth-death Markov chain. The lemma is adapted from [10, Lemma 8] – it re-obtains the result for SIS epidemic on cliques, and also extends to our new result for the SIS_{bs} epidemic.

Consider a birth-death CTMC $\{U(t)\}$ on $\{0, 1, \ldots, n\}$, with the following transition rates:

$$i \to i+1 \quad \text{at rate } q_{i,i+1} \quad \forall 1 \le i \le n-1,$$
$$i \to i-1 \quad \text{at rate } q_{i,i-1} \quad \forall 1 \le i \le n.$$

Note that 0 is the only absorbing state for the above process. Let $T(i,j) := inf\{t : U(t) = j || U(0) = i\}$. Then we have:

LEMMA 1 (LEMMA 8 FROM [10]).

$$\mathbb{E}[T(1,0)] = \frac{1}{q_{1,0}} \left(1 + \sum_{k=2}^{n} \prod_{i=1}^{k-1} \frac{q_{i,i+1}}{q_{i+1,i}}\right).$$

We now use this to get lower bounds on the expected extinction-time in cliques.

PROPOSITION 3. *For the SIS/SIS_{bs} epidemic on clique K_n starting at an arbitrary node under both the SIS and SIS_{bs} dynamics,* $\log(\mathbb{E}[\tau_e]) = \Omega(n)$.

PROOF. We prove the statement for the SIS_{bs} dynamics; the claim for the SIS dynamics follows similarly (and is also known from previous work [8]). As in Proposition 1, it is sufficient to consider the total number of infected nodes $N(t)$ at time t. $\{N(t)\}$ has transition rates as follows:

$$z \to z+1 \quad \text{at rate } \Phi(\beta z)(n-z) \quad \forall 1 \le z \le n-1,$$
$$z \to z-1 \quad \text{at rate } z \quad \forall 1 \le z \le n.$$

Let $k_0 = \inf\{k \in \mathbb{N} : \Phi(\beta k) \ge \Phi_{max}/2\}$. Since Φ is concave and $\Phi(0) = 0$, we have $\Phi(\beta k) \ge \frac{k}{k_0}\Phi(\beta k_0) \ge \frac{k}{k_0}\frac{\Phi_{max}}{2} \quad \forall k \le k_0$. Note that $k_0 = \Theta(1)$. Now, from Lemma 1, we have:

$$\begin{aligned}
\mathbb{E}[\tau_e] &= 1 + \sum_{k=2}^{n} \prod_{i=1}^{k-1} \frac{\Phi(\beta i)(n-i)}{i+1} \\
&\ge 1 + \sum_{k=2}^{k_0} \prod_{i=1}^{k-1} \frac{\Phi_{max}}{2k_0} \frac{i(n-i)}{i+1} \\
&\quad + \sum_{k=k_0+1}^{n} \prod_{i=1}^{k_0-1} \frac{\Phi_{max}}{2k_0} \frac{i(n-i)}{i+1} \prod_{j=k_0}^{k-1} \frac{\Phi_{max}}{2} \frac{(n-j)}{j+1} \\
&\ge \frac{2k_0!}{n\Phi_{max} k_0^{k_0}} \sum_{k=1}^{n} \binom{n}{k} \left(\frac{\Phi_{max}}{2}\right)^k \\
&= \frac{2k_0!}{n\Phi_{max} k_0^{k_0}} \left(\left(1 + \frac{\Phi_{max}}{2}\right)^n - 1 \right).
\end{aligned}$$

Since Φ_{max}, k_0 are $\Theta(1)$, $\log(\mathbb{E}[\tau_e]) = \Omega(n)$. □

The more interesting phenomenon in the SIS model occurs in the star network. As in the clique,it is known [8, 9] that the expected extinction-time in star networks is exponential. However, under the SIS_{bs} dynamics, we show that it is sub-exponential. More precisely, we show that the epidemic survives in a star network for a time that is *at most polynomial in n*.

PROPOSITION 4. *For an SIS_{bs} epidemic originating at any node in a star graph, $\mathbb{E}[\tau_e] = O(n^{\Phi_{max}+1})$.*

This change from exponential to polynomial infection time is clearly seen in simulation results shown in Figure 2. The proof of this proposition is somewhat technical, so we provide only a proof sketch here. The high-level proof structure is similar to existing analysis of the SIS epidemic on a star [8, 9] – the novelty lies in showing that bounded susceptibility causes a sharp transition in the epidemic lifetime.

PROOF OUTLINE. We consider cycles of the epidemic evolution – each cyclical epoch starts off with the hub infected, then recovering to become susceptible, and finally getting reinfected, thereby starting the next cycle. The time from the start of an epoch to when the hub first becomes susceptible is an i.i.d *Exponential*(1) variable – at this time, some subset of leaf nodes are infected. Subsequently, either the hub is re-infected (i.e., a new epoch starts), or all these leaf nodes recover before the hub is re-infected -(i.e., the epidemic becomes extinct). *The crux of the proof lies in estimating the probability that, under the SIS_{bs} model, the leaf nodes recover before the hub is reinfected.* Given this, we then show that the total number of such epochs is stochastically dominated by a geometric random variable, whose mean is polynomial in n – this gives the above result. □

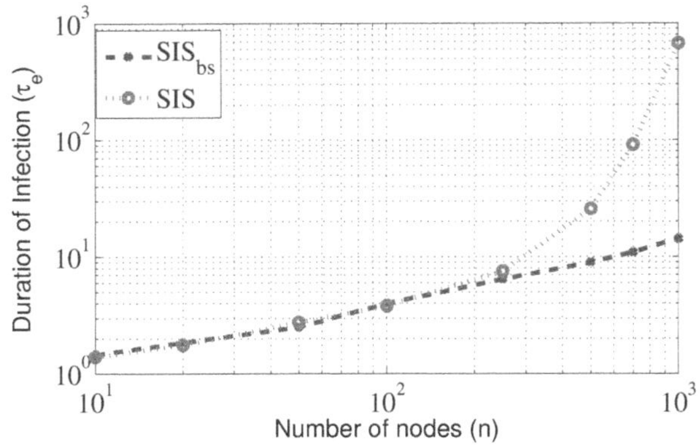

Figure 2: Simulated epidemic extinction-time in a star under SIS and SIS_{bs}, averaged over 500 simulation runs for $\beta = 0.1$ and $\Phi_{max} = 0.5$. Note that$\mathbb{E}[\tau_e]$ switches from exponential under SIS to polynomial under SIS_{bs} (polynomial to linear on $\log - \log$ plot).

In Section 2.3, we state a much more general version (Theorem 6) of this result, extending it to star-like networks. The complete proof of both results are given in Section 3.

2.3 Main Results

We now state our main results, which generalize results from the previous section to clique-like and star-like graphs.

2.3.1 $SI - SI_{bs}$ Dynamics

Recall that, for a graph G, the Cheeger constant is given by $\eta(G) = \inf_{S \subset V, |S| \le n/2} \frac{|\delta(S)|}{|S|}$. We now have the following theorem, which allows us to bound the spreading-time of the SI epidemic in clique-like graphs:

THEOREM 1. *Given underlying graph G with Cheeger constant $\eta(G)$, the spreading-time for an SI epidemic with virulence β originating at a single arbitrary node, obeys:*

$$\mathbb{E}[\tau_s] \le \frac{(2 + o(1))\log(n)}{\beta\eta(G)}.$$

The proof of this theorem, presented in Section 3, is similar to that of Proposition 1. Note that for the clique, we have $\eta(G) = n/2$. Plugging this into the above bound immediately gives back Proposition 1. However the theorem captures in finer detail the impact of expansion (as captured by $\eta(G)$) on spreading-time. As a corollary to the theorem, we have the following result for clique-like networks:

COROLLARY 1. *In a network that is clique-like as per Defintion 1(A) (i.e., $\eta(G) = \Omega(\log n)$), the expected spreading time of an SI epidemic is $O(1)$.*

We note also that although Theorem 1 bounds the *expected* spreading-time, we can extend it in Section 3.1 to get a concentration bound for the spreading-time. To see how the result can be used to characterize the spreading-time in a variety of clique-like graphs, we present the following corollary for the case of dense random graphs, i.e., Erdös-Rényi graphs in the connected regime:

COROLLARY 2. *Let G be an Erdös-Rényi graph $G(n,p)$, with $p > \frac{32 \log n}{n}$. Then with probability at least $1 - \frac{1}{n^2}$, we* *have* $\eta(G) \geq \frac{np}{4}$. *Therefore, for an SI epidemic,*

$$\mathbb{E}[\tau_s] \leq \frac{(8+o(1))\log n}{\beta np}$$

with probability at least $1 - \frac{1}{n^2}$.

Note that by the Borel-Cantelli Lemma, the above bound on the expected spreading-time holds almost surely as $n \to \infty$. The proof is provided in Section 3.

Putting the pieces together, we can now compare the SI and SI_{bs} processes in dense random graphs:

THEOREM 2. *Let* G *be an Erdös-Rényi graph* $G(n,p)$, *with* $p > \frac{32 \log n}{n}$. *For the* SI/SI_{bs} *epidemic on* G, *starting at an arbitrary node, we have:*

1. *Under the SI dynamics,* $\mathbb{E}[\tau_s] = O\left(\frac{\log n}{np}\right)$ *with probability at least* $1 - \frac{1}{n^2}$.
2. *Under the* SI_{bs} *dynamics* $\mathbb{E}[\tau_s] = \Omega(\log n)$.

PROOF. The first claim follows from Corollary 2 and Theorem 1. For the second, note that given any graph G, and G' obtained by adding edges to G, $\tau_s(G') \leq_{st} \tau_s(G)$ – this can be shown via a standard coupling argument. Thus, for any graph G, we can always lower bound the spreading-time under the SI_{bs} dynamics by that on the clique K_n. The second claim thus follows from Proposition 1. □

Next we turn to the case of star-like graphs. To characterize SI epidemics on such networks, we first state a lemma that gives a lower bound on $\mathbb{E}[\tau_s]$ in terms of average degree:

LEMMA 2. *Consider a graph* G *with* $|V| = n$, *and an SI epidemic on* G, *starting at some node* v_1. *Let* $A \subseteq V$ *be a subset of nodes containing* v_1, *and let* $\widehat{d}_{A^c}$ *be the average degree of the nodes in* $V \setminus A$, *i.e.,* $\widehat{d}_{A^c} = \frac{\sum_{v \notin A} d(v)}{n-|A|}$. *Then:*

$$\mathbb{E}[\tau_s] \geq \frac{\log(n-|A|)}{\beta \widehat{d}_{A^c}}$$

For example, for the star graph with v_1 chosen to be the hub, we have $\widehat{d}_{\{v_1\}^c} = 1$, and so we get back the lower bound in Proposition 2. We now use the above lemma to show that imposing bounded susceptibility does not significantly change the spreading-time in star-like networks:

THEOREM 3. *Consider a network* G *of diameter* $O(\log n)$ *that is star-like by Definition 2(A). In other words, there exists a partition of the nodes into a core* V_c *and periphery* V_p, *parametrized by:*

- Core size: $|V_c| = m$ *is at most a constant fraction of nodes (i.e.* $m \leq cn$ *for some* $c < 1$*). In other words,* $|V_p| = \Omega(n)$.
- Sparse periphery: $\widehat{d}_p = O(1)$, *i.e., the average degree of nodes in the periphery is constant (or lesser).*

Then both under the SI and SI_{bs} *dynamics,* $\mathbb{E}[\tau_s] = \Theta(\log n)$.

Note that the sparsity constraint is on the average degree of nodes in V_p, not in the subgraph induced by V_p, i.e., it also accounts for the edges in the cut $\delta(V_p)$.

PROOF. First consider the SI dynamics, starting at some arbitrary node v_1. We want to derive a lower bound on the spreading-time using Lemma 2 – to do so, we choose $A = V_c \cup \{v_1\}$, and hence $A^c = V_p \setminus \{v_1\}$. Now using Lemma 2 and the fact that $|V_p| \sim poly(n)$. and that both β and $\widehat{d}_p$ are $\Theta(1)$ we have that $\mathbb{E}[\tau_s] = \Omega(\log n)$.

To obtain an upper bound on the spreading-time, we underdominate the spread by considering epidemic spread on the shortest-path spanning tree of the network rooted at the initial infected node. The resulting depth is at most the diameter of the tree. Thus, the spreading-time is stochastically upper bounded by the maximum of n i.i.d random variables distributed as sum of $diam(G)$ number of exponential random variables with rate β. Finally, using standard concentration results for the sum of exponentials (refer [3]), we have that $\mathbb{E}[\tau_s] = O(\log n)$.

For SI_{bs} epidemic, we can first over-dominate the epidemic spread by converting the network into a clique – we have from Proposition 1 that the time taken to infect all nodes is $\Omega(\log n)$. On the other hand, we can again underdominate the spread by considering an SI_{bs} process on the minimum spanning tree which is equivalent to an SI process of rate $\Phi(\beta)$. Consequently, $\mathbb{E}[\tau_s] = \Theta(\log n)$. □

2.3.2 $SIS - SIS_{bs}$ Dynamics

Next we look at the $SIS - SIS_{bs}$ dynamics on clique-like and star-like graphs. Recall that in this case, we are interested in the extinction-time τ_e. In particular, we are interested in characterizing networks in which the epidemic is *persistent*, i.e. the extinction-time is exponential in n (i.e., $\mathbb{E}[\tau_e] \sim \Omega(e^{poly(n)})$).

Existing works [8, 9, 10] demonstrate that the virulence thresholds for short-lived ($\mathbb{E}[\tau_e] \sim O(\log n)$) SIS epidemics depend on the spectral radius, $\rho(G)$, while thresholds for persistent epidemics are related to the generalized isoperimetric constants. Though the results for the SIS epidemic depend on edge-expansion isoperimetric constant $\eta^e_m(G)$, the vertex-expansion isoperimetric constant $\eta^v_m(G)$ turns out to be the appropriate notion for the SIS_{bs} epidemic, as follows:

THEOREM 4. *Consider an* SIS_{bs} *epidemic on graph* G, *with virulence* β *and infection-profile* $\Phi(\cdot)$. *Suppose for* $m = n^\alpha$ *for some* $0 < \alpha < 1$, *we have that:*

$$\Phi(\beta)\eta^v_m(G) > 1,$$

then $\mathbb{E}[\tau_e] = e^{\Omega(n^\alpha)}$, *i.e., the* SIS_{bs} *epidemic is persistent .*

PROOF OUTLINE. The proof is similar to that of Proposition 3. In particular, we construct an under-dominating CTMC for the number of infected nodes under SIS_{bs}. Next, we use Lemma 1 to get an expression for the extinction-time, and show that the bound is indeed exponential in n if $\Phi(\beta)\eta^v_m(G) > 1$. For complete proof, see Section 3. □

An immediate consequence of this result is the following corollary for clique-like networks.

COROLLARY 3. *An* SIS_{bs} *epidemic is persistent in any network belonging to the class of clique-like networks as per Definition 1(B).*

Returning to the SIS epidemic, the strongest known condition for a persistent SIS epidemic is $\beta\eta^e_m(G) > 1$ [8]. Now since $\eta^e_m(G) > \eta^v_m(G)$, this implies that $\beta\eta^v_m(G) > 1$ *is also sufficient for a persistent SIS epidemic*, i.e., without bounded susceptibility. Theorem 4 shows that the condition for a persistent SIS_{bs} epidemic is closely related. Furthermore, as we show subsequently, the vertex-expansion condition is strong enough to recover all the results from [8], in particular for the $G(n,p)$ and power-law graphs.

We now use Theorem 4 to demonstrate that both SIS and SIS_{bs} epidemics have exponential extinction-times in dense random graphs:

THEOREM 5. *For both the SIS and SIS_{bs} epidemics on a $G(n,p)$ graph with $p > \frac{16 \log n}{n}$. For a large enough n, with probability at least $1 - \frac{1}{n^2}$ we have,*

$$\log(\mathbb{E}[\tau_e]) = \Omega(n).$$

PROOF OUTLINE. We show under the conditions of the theorem that $\Phi(\beta)\eta_m^v(G) > 1$ with probability $\geq 1 - \frac{1}{n^2}$ if $m = n^\alpha$ for any constant $\alpha \in (0,1)$. The result then follows using Theorem 4. Complete proof is given in Section 3. □

Note also that any graph that contains a large clique-like subgraph is prone to an exponentially long lasting infection, even under bounded susceptibility, if the initial infected node belongs to the subgraph. Clearly a clique, or a realization of an Erdös-Rényi graph in the connected regime experiences long lasting infection – however such dense random subgraphs appear in other graph families including 'power-law' or scale-free networks. We discuss this further in Section 2.4 (in particular, Corollary 5).

More generally, these results show that large dense networks experience persistent epidemics even under bounded susceptibility *due to the presence of large clique-like subgraphs.* This is in sharp contrast to existing work (for example, [9]) which suggests that persistent epidemics in such networks arise due to the presence of high-degree nodes ('hubs').

In fact, it turns out that the presence of such 'hubs' do not help – we took a step towards showing this in Proposition 4, where we showed that a star graph does not experience persistent SIS_{bs} epidemics. We now show that this is true for a much larger class of star-like graphs. As before, the node-set V is decomposed into core V_c and periphery V_p. We characterize the sparsity of the periphery via the *spectral radius* $\rho(G(V_p))$ of the periphery subgraph – recall that $d_{avg}(G(V_p)) \leq \rho(G(V_p)) \leq d_{\max}(G(V_p))$. Now we have:

THEOREM 6. *Consider a network G, with the nodes partitioned into a core V_c and periphery V_p characterized by:*

- Core size: $|V_c| = m$.
- Periphery sparsity: *Parametrized by* $\rho(G(V_p))$.

Suppose $G(V_p)$ satisfies $\Phi(\beta)\rho(G(V_p)) = 1 - \epsilon$, for some $\epsilon > 0$. Then for an SIS_{bs} epidemic on G,:

$$\log(\mathbb{E}[\tau_e]) = O(m \log n).$$

PROOF OUTLINE. The high-level proof structure is similar to the outline we gave for Proposition 2. We again consider cyclic epochs. An epoch starts with some node in the core infected, transitioning to all core nodes becoming susceptible, and finally ends when some node in the core gets reinfected beginning the next epoch. Next, we bound under the SIS_{bs} model the probability that, in any epoch, the epidemic dies out in all nodes of the periphery before any node in the core is reinfected. Finally, via stochastic domination by a geometric random variable, we get the above result. The complete proof is given in Section 3. □

Though we state the above theorem for a general core size, it is most significant in settings the core is small. For example, if the core is of constant size, then $\mathbb{E}[\tau_e]$ *scales only polynomially with n* – note that this includes the star network (where $\rho(G(V_p)) = 0$, as the periphery is fully disconnected if we remove the hub) that we characterized in Proposition 4. More generally, the following result for star-like networks holds as a result of Theorem 6.

COROLLARY 4. *The extinction time of an SIS_{bs} epidemic is sub-exponential in any network that is star-like as per Definition 2(B).*

In Section 3.1, we derive concentration results, showing that the bound holds with high probability.

2.4 Discussion

We now show how our results apply to the settings we discuss in Section 1.2.

Social and Economic Networks. Epidemic models have been widely used to model the viral spread of content in social networks. In particular, the SIS model can be used to study the spread of 'memes', i.e., related pieces of content that re-appear cyclically. Furthermore, the exponential extinction-time of an epidemic is in a sense connected to long-lasting nature of popular memes.

However, the existence of popular memes is often regarded to be as a result of highly influential nodes, i.e., those with high degree. Such high-degree nodes are a distinctive feature of power-law graphs, which are often used to model such networks. Our results however suggest that persistent epidemics arise due to large random subgraphs rather than high-degree nodes. We now formalize this notion by applying Theorem 5 to power-law graphs.

We consider the case of power law graphs with exponent $2 < \gamma < 3$. For random power law graphs generated under the Chung-Lu model [27] with exponent $2 < \gamma < 3$, it is known that they contain a n^{ϵ_1} connected random graph [8], and further, that they contain an n^{ϵ_2} clique [28] for some $\epsilon_1, \epsilon_2 > 0$. The SIS epidemic is known to have exponential lifetime in such graphs [8]; using Theorem 5, we recover this behavior under bounded susceptibility:

COROLLARY 5. *For networks generated via the Chung-Lu model [27], if the power-law exponent $\gamma \in (2,3)$ and $\Phi_{max} > 1 + v$ for some $v > 0$, the SIS_{bs} epidemic has exponentially long lifetime.*

Thus scale-free networks do experience persistent epidemics *even under bounded susceptibility,* due to the presence of large clique-like subgraphs. *This questions the belief that highly-connected nodes are most responsible for viral content.*

Epidemiology. Epidemic models help understand the dynamics of infectious diseases amongst human/animal populations, and the spread of computer viruses and worms. These models also help in the design of defense mechanisms against such epidemics – for example, policies for spreading *antidotes,* which increase the recovery rate in the SIS epidemic [11]. In this regard, our work helps in developing a theory for *partial quarantine policies,* wherein adopting preventative measures helps reduce (and bound) the susceptibility of a node. We make a distinction here between partial and *perfect* quarantine policies, wherein a node can be completely disconnected from the network. Achieving a perfect quarantine is often unfeasible and there is always some residual susceptibility.

In this regard, our results paint a somewhat bleak picture – *enforcing quarantine policies in dense networks has an insignificant effect on the epidemic lifetime.* More specifically, as long as there is some $\Theta(1)$ residual susceptibility, the epidemic lifetime remains exponential in clique-like networks. Note also that a similar effect is seen in [11] (under linear susceptibility), where an effective policy needs to give an amount of antidote to a node which is proportional to its degree – this is clearly more difficult in dense graphs.

The story is somewhat more positive in star-like networks, where Theorem 6 shows that in a network with a small core and a sparse outer network, partial quarantining affects a large change in the extinction-time, reducing it to $poly(n)$. Star-like networks are relevant for studying the spread of an infectious disease through human transportation networks, which comprise a core of long distance air-links, overlaid on a slower road network. In case of an epidemic, a natural policy is to focus on safeguarding the core cities (via quarantining). For this, we have the following corollary:

COROLLARY 6. *Consider a network which can be decomposed into:*

- *A dense core of size $O(1)$, which can be fully connected.*
- *A sparse periphery, with $\rho(G(V_p)) = O(1)$ (no restriction on edges between periphery and core).*

Now suppose only core nodes have bounded susceptibility *(via quarantining), and the unprotected periphery satisfies $\beta\rho(G(V_p)) \leq 1-\epsilon$ for some $\epsilon > 0$. Then the epidemic is not persistent, i.e., $\mathbb{E}[\tau_e] = O(poly(n))$.*

Note that given $\Omega(n)$ edges between the hub and the periphery, the SIS epidemic has an exponential lifetime. Thus, safeguarding hub cities does help reduce the epidemic lifetime dramatically. However, *distributing antidotes may be a much more effective policy than quarantining as it can effect much faster (upto $O(\log n)$) extinction-times.*

Distributed Computing Applications. Another important application of SI epidemics is as a primitive for algorithms like *flooding* [19], i.e., forwarding a message to all network nodes. In order to minimize the flooding time, one approach would be to make the underlying network clique-like – however our results indicate that under bounded susceptibility, the flooding time is $\Omega(\log n)$, which is identical to that in a star-like network (for example, a hierarchical network, with a constant-sized core and all other nodes connected to the core). On the other hand, our results also show that star-like networks are much easier to protect from viruses which spread like an SIS process. Considering the tradeoff between performance and robustness to infection, *star-like architectures appear more appropriate than clique-like architectures for distributed computing applications.*

In case of networks using SIS epidemics to ensure persistent data storage [20], the story is strikingly different from the above. Here, the presence of bounded susceptibility results in a sharp difference between epidemic lifetime in star-like and clique-like networks. However, our results also indicate that it is not necessary to have very high edge densities, or very well-designed networks in order to achieve long lifetimes – on the contrary, *as long as there exists a large-enough connected random subgraph, the epidemic lifetime is exponential even under bounded susceptibility.*

3. PROOFS

We now give detailed proofs for all our results. We use the standard stochastic dominance notation $\{\leq_{st}, \geq_{st}\}$ for relations between random variables. Specifically, $(X \leq_{st} Y) \implies \forall z, \mathbb{P}[X > z] \leq \mathbb{P}[Y > z]$.

Proofs from Section 2.3.1.

PROOF OF THEOREM 1. Let $N(t)$ be the number of infected nodes at time t and T_k be the first time at least k nodes are infected, i.e., $T_k = \inf\{t : N(t) = k\}$. Also, $\forall\, k \in [n]$, let $\mathcal{V}_k$ denote the set of all subsets of V of size k, and let $S_k \in \mathcal{V}_k$ be the set of infected nodes at T_k.

Since $T_1 = 0$ and $T_n = \tau_s$, we can telescope and write $\tau_s = \sum_{k=1}^{n-1}(T_{k+1} - T_k)$. Recall that in case of the clique in Proposition 1, we had that $\mathbb{E}[T_{k+1} - T_k] = \frac{1}{\beta k(n-k)}$. This is no longer true, but we can upper bound the time in terms of the isoperimetric constant $\eta(G)$ as follows.

$$\mathbb{E}[T_{k+1} - T_k] = \sum_{s_k \in \mathcal{V}_k} \mathbb{E}[T_{k+1} - T_k | S_k = s_k]\mathbb{P}[S_k = s_k]$$
$$= \mathbb{E}\left[\frac{1}{\beta|\delta(S_k)|}\right].$$

By the definition of $\eta(G)$,

$$|\delta(S_k)| \geq \begin{cases} \eta(G)k & \text{if } k < n/2 \\ \eta(G)(n-k) & \text{if } k \geq n/2. \end{cases}$$

Therefore, we have

$$\mathbb{E}[\tau_s] \leq 2\sum_{k=1}^{\lfloor n/2 \rfloor} \frac{1}{\beta\eta(G)k} \leq \frac{(2+o(1))\log(n/2)}{\beta\eta(G)}.$$

This completes the proof. □

Next we show that a $G(n,p)$ in the connected regime has a large isoperimetric constant with high probability.

PROOF OF COROLLARY 2. Let graph G be a realization of a $G(n,p)$ random graph with $p > \frac{32\log n}{n}$. We claim that

$$\mathbb{P}\left[\eta(G) < np/4\right] \leq \frac{1}{n^2}.$$

In other words, for all but a vanishing fraction of graphs (of measure $\leq 1/n^2$), we have the required bound on $\eta(G)$. To show this, we write

$$\mathbb{P}\left[\eta(G) < np/4\right] = \mathbb{P}\left[\bigcup_{k \leq \lfloor n/2 \rfloor} \bigcup_{s_k \in \mathcal{V}_k} |\delta(s_k)| < nkp/4\right]$$
$$\leq \sum_{k \leq \lfloor n/2 \rfloor} \sum_{s_k \in \mathcal{V}_k} \mathbb{P}\left[|\delta(s_k)| < k(n-k)p/2\right].$$

We can now use the following Chernoff bound – for any r.v. B taking values in $[0,1]$, we have

$$\mathbb{P}\left[B < (1-\delta)\mathbb{E}[B]\right] \leq \exp\left(\frac{-\mathbb{E}[B]\delta^2}{2}\right).$$

Since $|\delta(s_k)| \sim Binom(k(n-k), p)$,

$$\mathbb{P}\left[\eta(G) < np/4\right] \leq \sum_{k=1}^{\lfloor n/2 \rfloor} \binom{n}{k} \exp\left(\frac{-1}{8}k(n-k)p\right)$$
$$\leq n\binom{n}{1} \exp\left(\frac{-1}{8}(n-1)p\right).$$

Using the condition $p > \frac{32\log n}{n}$, we get our result. □

Next, we turn to Lemma 2, wherein we derive a lower bound on the spreading-time in terms of the average degree of a graph. First, we need the following lemma:

LEMMA 3. *Let $\{X_i\}_{i=1}^m$ be independent exponential random variables with rate a_i (i.e., Exponential(a_i)) such that $\sum_{i=1}^m a_i = A$, and let $\{Y_i\}_{i=1}^m$ be i.i.d exponential random variables with rate A/m. If $X_{\max} = \max\{X_1, X_2, \ldots, X_m\}$ and $Y_{\max} = \max\{Y_1, Y_2, \ldots, Y_m\}$, then $X_{\max} \geq_{st} Y_{\max}$.*

PROOF. For stochastic dominance, we want to show that $\mathbb{P}[X_{\max} \leq x] \leq \mathbb{P}[Y_{\max} \leq x] \; \forall x > 0$. For any $x > 0$, define $Q_x(\mathbf{a}) = \prod_{i=1}^m (1 - \exp(-a_i x))$. We now show that $\mathbf{a}^* = (A/m, A/m, \ldots, A/m)$ maximizes Q_x over the set $\mathcal{A} = \{\mathbf{a} : \sum_{i=1}^m a_i = A\}$. For $m = 2$, one can check that $\mathbf{a}^* = (A/2, A/2)$ is the unique maximum. Thus, $Q_x(\mathbf{a}^*) > Q_x(\mathbf{a})$ for any $\mathbf{a} \neq \mathbf{a}^*$. If $m > 2$, suppose that $\tilde{\mathbf{a}} \in \mathcal{A}$ and $\tilde{\mathbf{a}} \neq \mathbf{a}^*$, maximizes Q_x over $\mathcal{A}$. Then $\exists i, j$ such that $\tilde{a}_i \neq \tilde{a}_j$. Then, for $\hat{\mathbf{a}}$ equal to $\tilde{\mathbf{a}}$ except with the i, j elements replaced with $(\tilde{a}_i + \tilde{a}_j)/2$, we have $Q_x(\hat{\mathbf{a}}) > Q_x(\tilde{\mathbf{a}})$, which is a contradiction. Therefore, $\mathbf{a}^* = (A/m, A/m, \ldots, A/m)$ maximizes Q_x over the set $\mathcal{A}$, and $\mathbb{P}[Y_{\max} \leq x] = Q_x(\mathbf{a}^*) \geq Q_x(\mathbf{a}) = \mathbb{P}[X_{\max} \leq x]$ for any $x > 0$. □

Using this, we now prove Lemma 2.

PROOF OF LEMMA 2. Let the nodes be numbered from 1 to n such that $A = \{1, 2, \ldots, |A|\}$ and let $\mathbf{d} = (d_1, d_2, \ldots, d_n)$ be the degree sequence of G. At any time, the rate at which a susceptible node i is infected is upper bounded by βd_i. Therefore, $\tau_s \geq_{st} \max\{X_{|A|+1}, \ldots, X_n\}$ where $\{X_i\}$ are independent exponential random variables with mean $1/\beta d_i$. By Lemma 3, $\tau_s \geq_{st} Y$, where Y is the maximum of $n - |A|$ i.i.d. exponential random variables with mean $\frac{n-|A|}{\sum_{i=|A|+1}^n \beta d_i} = \frac{1}{\beta \hat{d}_{A^c}}$.

$$\mathbb{E}[\tau_s] \geq \mathbb{E}[Y] = \frac{\mathcal{H}_{n-|A|}}{\beta \widehat{d}_{A^c}} > \frac{\log(n - |A|)}{\beta \widehat{d}_{A^c}}.$$

This completes the proof. □

Proofs from Section 2.3.2.

PROOF OF THEOREM 4. We analyze a CTMC $Z(t)$ that is stochastically dominated by the total number of infected nodes $N(t)$ in the SIS_{bs} epidemic. This being true, we have that the expected time to absorption for $Z(t)$ is less than that of $N(t)$. We note that this proof structure is similar to that of Theorem 4.1 from [8]; however it is much simplified via the ergodic embedding technique of [10].

Note that for any set of nodes $A \subseteq V$ of size $|A| \leq m$ (for some $m = n^\alpha$), we have that the neighborhood of A has size at least $\eta_m^v(G)|A|$. Now suppose the set of infected nodes I satisfies $|I| \leq m$. Under bounded susceptibility, each node in $\Gamma(I)$ is infected at a rate which is $\geq \Phi(\beta)$. Using this observation, we define $Z(t)$ to have transition rates given by

$$\begin{aligned} z \to z+1 & \quad \text{at rate } \eta_m^v(G)\Phi(\beta) z \quad \forall 1 \leq z \leq m-1, \\ z \to z-1 & \quad \text{at rate } z \quad \forall 1 \leq z \leq m, \end{aligned}$$

and all other transitions equal to 0. Note that $Z(t)$ is a finite state space CTMC on state space $\{0, 1, \ldots, m\}$ – standard coupling arguments (for example, see [12]) show that it is dominated by $N(t)$. Now using Lemma 1, we have

$$\mathbb{E}[\tau_e] \geq \mathbb{E}[\inf\{t : Z(t) = 0\}] = \sum_{k=0}^{m-1} (\eta_m^v(G)\Phi(\beta))^k.$$

So, if $\Phi(\beta)\eta_m^v(G) > 1$, we have $\log(\mathbb{E}[\tau_e]) = \Omega(n^\alpha)$. □

Now we show that for the Erdös-Rényi graph in the connected regime, the condition for persistent SIS_{bs} epidemics is satisfied with high probability. Note that this proof also immediately gives persistence for the SIS epidemic.

PROOF OF THEOREM 5. Let G be a realization of a $G(n, p)$ graph. Fix $\alpha \in (0, 1), m = n^\alpha$, and choosing some $\gamma > 1$, we define $b = \gamma/\Phi(\beta)$. We now prove that $\mathbb{P}[\eta_m^v(G) < b] \leq 1/n^2$ for $p = \frac{16 \log n}{n}$. Then by stochastic dominance, the statement is true for any $p > \frac{16 \log n}{n}$. First we have

$$\mathbb{P}[\eta_m^v(G) < b] \leq \sum_{i=1}^m \sum_{S:|S|=i} \mathbb{P}[|\Gamma(S)| < bi].$$

Defining $B(n, p, i) \sim Binomial(n - i, 1 - (1-p)^i)$, we can write

$$\mathbb{P}[\eta_m^v(G) < b] \leq \sum_{i=1}^m \binom{n}{i} \mathbb{P}[B(n, p, i) < bi].$$

Note that $(1-p)^i \leq 1 - ip + i^2p^2/2 \, \forall i$. This implies that

$$\mathbb{E}[B] \geq (n-i)ip(1 - ip/2).$$

Defining $\delta = \left(1 - \frac{bi}{(n-i)ip(1-ip/2)}\right)$ and using Chernoff bound,

$$\begin{aligned} \mathbb{P}[B(n,p,i) < bi] &\leq \mathbb{P}[B(n,p,i) < (1-\delta)\mathbb{E}[B(n,p,i)]] \\ &\leq \exp\left(\frac{-\mathbb{E}[B(n,p,i)]\delta^2}{2}\right) \\ &\leq \exp\left(\frac{-(n-i)ip(1-ip/2)\delta^2}{2}\right). \end{aligned}$$

Note that $\frac{(n-i)}{n}(1 - ip/2)\delta^2 \to 1$ as $n \to \infty$. So for n large enough, $(n-i)(1-ip/2)\delta^2 > n/2$ which implies

$$\begin{aligned} \mathbb{P}[\eta_m^v(G) < b] &\leq \sum_{i=1}^m \binom{n}{i} \exp\left(-\frac{1}{2}(n-i)ip(1-ip/2)\delta^2\right) \\ &= \sum_{i=1}^m \frac{1}{i!} \exp(-i(np/4 - \log n)) < \frac{1}{n^2}. \end{aligned}$$

□

Next we turn to Theorem 6. The high-level proof structure is similar to existing analysis for the SIS epidemics on stars [8, 9]. However, to study the effect of bounded susceptibility, we need to carefully characterize various inter-epoch events, which require controlling the size of the core and the sparsity of the periphery.

We need two crucial lemmas for the proof. The first lemma is a crude but general upper bound for SIS_{bs} extinction-time in *all graphs*,

LEMMA 4. *For any network of size n, and for any arbitrary initial set of infected nodes, the expected extinction-time for SIS_{bs} dynamics has an upper bound given by*

$$\mathbb{E}[\tau_e] \leq \frac{(1 + \Phi_{max})^n}{n\Phi_{max}}.$$

PROOF. We use the expression for $\mathbb{E}[\tau_e]$ from Lemma 1. For any susceptible node with an infected neighbor, we have that the infection rate is bounded by Φ_{max}. Further, at any time when the number of infected nodes $|I| \geq 1$, we can stochastically upper bound the infection by assuming that *all susceptible nodes* have an infected neighbor. Thus

$$\mathbb{E}[\tau_e] \le 1 + \sum_{k=2}^{n} \prod_{i=1}^{k-1} \frac{\Phi_{max}(n-i)}{i+1}$$
$$= \frac{1}{n\Phi_{max}} \sum_{k=1}^{n} \binom{n}{k} \Phi_{max}^k \le \frac{(1+\Phi_{max})^n}{n\Phi_{max}}.$$

□

We use Lemma 4 to control extinction-time in dense subgraphs. In case of sparse subgraphs, we can use a result from [8], which gives conditions for fast extinction of the SIS epidemic (and hence SIS_{bs} epidemic) in terms of $\rho(G)$.

LEMMA 5. *[8, Theorem 3.1] Let $\rho(A)$ be the spectral radius of the adjacency matrix A. If $\beta < 1/\rho(A)$, then the probability that the epidemic has not died out by time t, given the initial condition $X(0)$, admits the following upper bound.*

$$\mathbb{P}[X(t) \neq 0] \le \sqrt{n}\|X(0)\|_1 e^{-(1-\beta\rho(A))t},$$

where $\|X(0)\|_1 = \sum_{i=1}^n X_i(0)$.

With these two ingredients, we can now prove Theorem 6.

PROOF OF THEOREM 6. We define cyclical epochs, starting with some (arbitrary) set of nodes in the core V_c infected, transitioning to all nodes in V_c becoming susceptible, and then finally at least one node in V_c getting reinfected. This technique is similar those used in [8, 9] – however instead of a star, we now have to deal with *core and periphery subgraphs* and also *bounded susceptibility*.

Consider epoch j (for any $j \in \mathbb{N}$) starting at time $T_{0,j}$. We define $T_{1,j} := \inf\{t > T_{0,j} : \sum_{i \in V_c} X_i(t) = 0\}$, i.e., all nodes in V_c become uninfected. From Lemma 4, we have

$$\mathbb{E}[T_{1,j} - T_{0,j}] \le \frac{(1+\Phi_{max})^m}{m\Phi_{max}}, \tag{1}$$

where $m = |V_c|$. Note that, under bounded susceptibility, this *only depends on m and not on core/periphery topologies.*

Next, we define $T_{0,j+1}$ to be the first time after $T_{1,j}$ when either some node in V_c gets re-infected or all the nodes in V_p recover – in case of the former, the next epoch starts, while in case of the latter, the infection dies out (i.e., $T_{0,j+1} = \tau_e$).

It is clear that the random variable $T_{0,j+1} - T_{1,j}$ is stochastically dominated by ζ_1, the time taken by all the nodes in V_p to completely recover if the periphery was isolated from the core at $T_{1,j}$. Now given that the infection profile Φ is concave, and $\Phi(0) = 0$, we have $\Phi(\beta x) \le \Phi(\beta)x \quad \forall x \ge 1$ and so the number of infected nodes under the SIS_{bs} dynamics is stochastically dominated by that in an SIS infection process with rate $\Phi(\beta)$. Now given that $\Phi(\beta)\rho(G(V_p)) = 1 - \epsilon$ for some $\epsilon > 0$, where $\rho(G(V_p))$ is the spectral radius of the periphery subgraph, we have from Lemma 5 that $\mathbb{P}(\zeta_1 > t) \le \min\left\{ne^{-(1-\Phi(\beta)\rho(G(V_p)))t}, 1\right\}$. Thus

$$\mathbb{E}[T_{0,j+1} - T_{1,j}] \le \mathbb{E}[\zeta_1] = \int_0^\infty \mathbb{P}(\zeta_1 > t)dt$$
$$\le \int_0^\infty ne^{-(1-\Phi(\beta)\rho(G(V_p)))t}dt$$
$$= \frac{n}{1-\Phi(\beta)\rho(G(V_p))}. \tag{2}$$

We now derive a lower bound for the probability q that the infection dies in the periphery $G(V_p)$ before any node in the core gets reinfected. Since each node in the core V_c is infected at a rate at most Φ_{max}, the time after $T_{1,j}$ for the core to get infected can be bounded from below by ζ_2, an $Exponential(m\Phi_{max})$ random variable, where $m = |V_c|$. Defining $t_0 = \frac{\log n}{1-\Phi(\beta)\rho(G(V_p))}$, we have

$$\mathbb{P}[\zeta_1 > \zeta_2] = m\Phi_{max} \int_0^\infty \mathbb{P}(\zeta_1 > t)e^{-m\Phi_{max}t}dt$$
$$\le m\Phi_{max} \int_0^{t_0} e^{-m\Phi_{max}t}dt \ldots$$
$$+ m\Phi_{max} \int_{t_0}^\infty ne^{-(1-\Phi(\beta)\rho(G(V_p))+m\Phi_{max})t}dt$$
$$= 1 - \frac{\epsilon}{\epsilon + m\Phi_{max}} n^{\frac{-m\Phi_{max}}{\epsilon}}.$$

The probability q that the infection dies before any node in the core gets infected can thus be bounded from below.

$$q \ge \mathbb{P}[\zeta_1 \le \zeta_2] \ge \left(Cn^{\frac{m\Phi_{max}}{\epsilon}}\right)^{-1}, \tag{3}$$

where $C = 1 + m\Phi_{max}/\epsilon > 1$.

Finally, the extinction-time τ_e can now be bounded as

$$\tau_e \le_{st} \sum_{i=1}^{V+1} U_i,$$

where V is a geometric random variable with mean $\frac{1}{q}$ and U_i are i.i.d. random variables independent of V with mean equal to the sum of upper bounds (R.H.S) in Equations 1 and 2. Thus, using Equations 3,1, 2, we have

$$\mathbb{E}[\tau_e] \le \frac{1}{q}\mathbb{E}[U_1]$$
$$\le Cn^{\frac{m\Phi_{max}}{\epsilon}} \left(\frac{(1+\Phi_{max})^m}{m\Phi_{max}} + \frac{n}{1-\Phi(\beta)\rho(G(V_p))}\right).$$

Simplifying we get that $\log \mathbb{E}[\tau_e] = O(m \log n)$. □

3.1 Concentration Bounds

SI: Upper Bound in Clique-like Networks

THEOREM 7. *Under the conditions of Theorem 1, the spreading-time $\tau_s \le \frac{(4+o(1))(\log n)^2}{\beta\eta(G)}$ with probability at least $1 - \frac{1}{n}$.*

PROOF. Define $\Delta(k) = \frac{2\log n}{\beta\eta(G)\min(k,n-k)}$. Then we have:

$$\mathbb{P}[T_{k+1} - T_k > \Delta(k)]$$
$$= \sum_{s_k \in \mathcal{V}_k} \mathbb{P}[T_{k+1} - T_k > \Delta(k) \; S_k = s_k]\mathbb{P}[S_k = s_k]$$
$$= \mathbb{E}\left[\exp\left(-\frac{2\beta|\delta(S_k)|\log n}{\beta\eta(G)\min(k,n-k)}\right)\right] \le \exp(-2\log n).$$

By telescoping, we have $\tau_s = \sum_{k=1}^{n-1} T_{k+1} - T_k$. Further:

$$\sum_{k=1}^{n-1} \Delta(k) = \sum_{k=1}^{n-1} \frac{2\log n}{\beta\eta(G)\min(k,n-k)} \le \frac{4(\log n)^2}{\beta\eta(G)},$$

Putting all the above together, we get:

$$\mathbb{P}\left[\tau_s > \frac{4(\log n)^2}{\beta\eta(G)}\right] \leq \mathbb{P}\left[\sum_{k=1}^{n-1} T_{k+1} - T_k > \sum_{k=1}^{n-1} \Delta(k)\right]$$
$$\leq \sum_{k=1}^{n-1} \mathbb{P}\left[T_{k+1} - T_k > \Delta(k)\right] \leq \frac{1}{n}.$$

This completes the proof. □

Therefore, in clique-like networks with $\eta(G) = \omega\left((\log n)^2\right)$, the spread time under the SI model is vanishingly small with high probability. Again, as in Proposition 1, we show that this is not the case with the SI_{bs} epidemic.

SI_{bs}: Lower Bound

THEOREM 8. *For any graph under SI_{bs} dynamics, $\tau_s > \frac{\log n}{2\Phi_{max}}$ w.p. at least $1 - \frac{1}{\sqrt{n}}$.*

PROOF. As in Theorem 3, we can dominate spreading on any graph G via spreading on the clique K_n. Now, since any susceptible node is infected by rate at most Φ_{max}, $T_{k+1} - T_k \geq_{st} Z_k$, where Z_k has *Exponential*$((n-k)\Phi_{max})$ distribution. Using the Chernoff bound, we have:

$$\mathbb{P}\left[\sum_{k=1}^{n-1} Z_k \leq t\right] \leq e^{\Phi_{max}t} \prod_{k=1}^{n-1} \mathbb{E}[e^{-\Phi_{max}Z_k}]$$
$$= e^{\Phi_{max}t} \prod_{k=1}^{n-1} \frac{k}{k+1} = \frac{e^{\Phi_{max}t}}{n}.$$

Therefore,

$$\mathbb{P}\left[\tau_s \leq \frac{\log n}{2\Phi_{max}}\right] \leq \mathbb{P}\left[\sum_{k=1}^{n-1} Z_k \leq \frac{\log n}{2\Phi_{max}}\right] \leq \frac{1}{\sqrt{n}}.$$

This completes the proof. □

SIS_{bs}: Lower Bound in Star-like Networks

LEMMA 6. *In a clique K_n, with an arbitrary initial-infected node, the second moment of extinction time under the SIS_{bs} dynamics can be bounded as:*

$$\mathbb{E}[\tau_e^2] \leq \frac{2(1+\max(1,\Phi_{max}))^{2n}}{n\Phi_{max}^2}.$$

PROOF. We again consider the evolution of the total number of infected nodes with transition rates $q_{i,i+1} \leq (n-i)\Phi_{max}$ and $q_{i+1,i} = i+1$. The second moment for the first passage time to 0 starting from state 1 for a general birth and death process is derived in [29] and is given by:

$$\mathbb{E}[\tau_e^2] = \frac{2}{q_{1,0}\pi_0} \sum_{i=1}^{n} \frac{1}{q_{i-1,i}\pi_{i-1}} (\sum_{k=i}^{n} \pi_k)^2$$
$$= \frac{2}{q_{1,0}\pi_0} \sum_{i=1}^{n} \frac{\pi_i}{q_{i,i-1}} \left(1 + \sum_{k=i}^{n-1} \prod_{l=i}^{k} \frac{q_{l,l+1}}{q_{l+1,l}}\right)^2.$$

Using this equation, and $q_{i,i+1} \leq (n-i)\Phi_{max}$ and $q_{i+1,i} = i+1$, we have

$$\mathbb{E}[\tau_e^2] \leq \frac{2}{n\Phi_{max}\pi_0} \sum_{i=1}^{n} \frac{\pi_0 \Phi_{max}^i \binom{n}{i}}{i} \left(\frac{\sum_{k=i}^{n} \Phi_{max}^k \binom{n}{k}}{\Phi_{max}^i \binom{n}{i}}\right)^2$$
$$\leq \begin{cases} \frac{2}{n\Phi_{max}} \frac{(1+\Phi_{max})^{2n}}{\Phi_{max}} & \text{if } \Phi_{max} > 1 \\ \frac{2}{n\Phi_{max}} 2^{2n} & \text{if } \Phi_{max} \leq 1 \end{cases}$$

□

Using the above lemma, we have the following concentration result:

THEOREM 9. *Under the conditions of Theorem 6, $\log \tau_e = O(m \log n)$ with probability at least $1 - 2n^{-1} - n^{\frac{-m\Phi_{max}}{2\epsilon}}$, for n large enough.*

PROOF. As in the proof of Theorem 6, we consider cycles of epidemic evolution. We first bound the total number of cycles and then give a bound for the duration of each cycle. As shown in Theorem 6, the total number of cycles is stochastically dominated by V, a geometric random variable with mean $\frac{1}{q}$. Let $K = Cn^{\frac{m}{\epsilon}\Phi_{max}} \log n$. Therefore, from Equation 3:

$$\mathbb{P}[V > K] = (1-q)^K \leq \exp(-qK) \leq \frac{1}{n} \tag{4}$$

We next bound the duration of the first epoch in the cycle – the duration of the cycle in which at least one node in the core is infected. Since this time is stochastically dominated by the duration of infection in a clique of size m (size of the core), we have:

$$\mathbb{E}[(T_{1,j} - T_{0,j})^2] \leq \frac{2(1+\Phi_{max})^{2m}}{m\Phi_{max}^2}.$$

Using Markov's inequality, we get:

$$\mathbb{P}[T_{1,j} - T_{0,j} > 2n^{\frac{m}{\epsilon}\Phi_{max}}] \leq \frac{\mathbb{E}[(T_{1,j} - T_{0,j})^2]}{4n^{\frac{2m}{\epsilon}\Phi_{max}}}$$
$$\leq \frac{(1+\Phi_{max})^{2m}}{2m\Phi_{max}^2 n^{\frac{2m}{\epsilon}\Phi_{max}}}.$$

Now from the union bound, the total duration of these first epochs in K cycles can bounded as follows:

$$\mathbb{P}[\sum_{j=1}^{K} T_{1,j} - T_{0,j} > 2Kn^{\frac{m}{\epsilon}\Phi_{max}}] \leq K\frac{(1+\Phi_{max})^{2m}}{2m\Phi_{max}^2 n^{\frac{2m}{\epsilon}\Phi_{max}}}$$
$$\leq n^{\frac{-m}{2\epsilon}\Phi_{max}}, \tag{5}$$

for n large enough. Similarly, we upper bound the duration of the second epoch which is stochastically dominated by ζ_1 defined in Section 3. We have:

$$\mathbb{P}[T_{0,j+1} - T_{1,j} > \frac{2C}{\epsilon} \log n] \leq ne^{-2C \log n}.$$

Thus, the duration of the second epochs in K cycles obeys:

$$\mathbb{P}[\sum_{j=1}^{K} T_{0,j+1} - T_{1,j} > \frac{2KC}{\epsilon} \log n]$$
$$\leq Kne^{-2C \log n} = \frac{C \log n}{n^C} < \frac{1}{n} \tag{6}$$

for large enough n. Since $\tau_e = \sum_{j=1}^{V} T_{0,j+1} - T_{0,j}$, which can be decomposed as $\sum_{j=1}^{V}(T_{0,j+1} - T_{1,j}) + (T_{1,j} - T_{0,j})$, using union bound we have:

$$\begin{aligned}&\mathbb{P}[\tau_e > 2K(n^{\frac{m}{\epsilon}\Phi_{max}} + C\log n)] \\ \leq &\mathbb{P}[V > K] + \mathbb{P}[\sum_{j=1}^{K} T_{1,j} - T_{0,j} > 2Kn^{\frac{m}{\epsilon}\Phi_{max}}] \\ &+ \mathbb{P}[\sum_{j=1}^{K} T_{0,j+1} - T_{1,j} > \frac{2KC}{\epsilon}\log n].\end{aligned}$$

Finally, using Equations 4, 5, 6, we have for n large enough,

$$\mathbb{P}[\tau_e > 2K(n^{\frac{m}{\epsilon}\Phi_{max}} + \frac{C}{\epsilon}\log n)] \leq 2n^{-1} + n^{\frac{-m\Phi_{max}}{2\epsilon}}.$$

Since $\log(K(n^{\frac{m}{\epsilon}\Phi_{max}} + \frac{C}{\epsilon}\log n)) = O(m\log n)$, we have our result. □

4. CONCLUSION

We have studied the effect of bounded susceptibility on the *SI* and *SIS* epidemics. In particular, we showed that imposing this constraint brings out a sharp dichotomy between star-like and clique-like networks. Our results are applicable in several real-life settings which exhibit bounded susceptibility – social networks, human-disease networks, infrastructure networks, etc. Along the way, we also develop a suite of lemmas relating graph structure and epidemic behavior – some extend/simplify existing results while others are novel. We hope these will prove useful in other settings.

Acknowledgements

This work was supported by NSF grants IIS-1017525, CNS-1320175 and ARO grant W911NF-11-1-0265. We thank the reviewers for their suggestions which helped in greatly improving the clarity of this paper.

5. REFERENCES

[1] H. Kesten, "First-passage percolation," in *From classical to modern probability*. Springer, 2003.

[2] I. Benjamini and Y. Peres, "Tree-indexed random walks on groups and first passage percolation," *Probability Theory and Related Fields*, 1994.

[3] S. Banerjee, A. Gopalan, A. K. Das, and S. Shakkottai, "Epidemic spreading with external agents," *IEEE Trans. Information Theory*, 2014.

[4] S. Bhamidi, R. Van der Hofstad, and G. Hooghiemstra, "First passage percolation on the erds-renyi random graph," *Combinatorics, Probability & Computing*, 2011.

[5] T. M. Liggett, *Stochastic interacting systems: contact, voter and exclusion processes*. Springer, 1999.

[6] J. O. Kephart and S. R. White, "Directed-graph epidemiological models of computer viruses," in *IEEE Symposium on Security and Privacy*, 1991.

[7] R. Pastor-Satorras and A. Vespignani, "Epidemic Dynamics in Finite Size Scale-Free Networks," *Phys. Rev. E*, 2002.

[8] A. J. Ganesh, L. Massoulié, and D. F. Towsley, "The effect of network topology on the spread of epidemics," in *IEEE INFOCOM*, 2005.

[9] N. Berger, C. Borgs, J. T. Chayes, and A. Saberi, "On the spread of viruses on the internet," in *ACM-SIAM SODA*, 2005.

[10] S. Banerjee, A. Chatterjee, and S. Shakkottai, "Epidemic thresholds with external agents," in *IEEE INFOCOM*, 2014.

[11] C. Borgs, J. Chayes, A. Ganesh, and A. Saberi, "How to distribute antidote to control epidemics," *Random Structures & Algorithms*, 2010.

[12] M. Draief and L. Massoulié, *Epidemics and rumours in complex networks, volume 369 of London Mathematical Society Lecture Notes*. Cambridge University Press, Cambridge, 2010.

[13] M. Draief, A. Ganesh, and L. Massoulie, "Thresholds for virus spread on networks," *The Annals of Appl. Prob.*, vol. 18, pp. 359–378, 2008.

[14] N. O. Hodas and K. Lerman, "How visibility and divided attention constrain social contagion," in *IEEE Privacy, Security, Risk and Trust*, 2012.

[15] L. Weng, A. Flammini, A. Vespignani, and F. Menczer, "Competition among memes in a world with limited attention," *Scientific Reports*, 2012.

[16] J. Leskovec, L. A. Adamic, and B. A. Huberman, "The dynamics of viral marketing," *ACM Transactions on the Web (TWEB)*, 2007.

[17] S. Funk, E. Gilad, C. Watkins, and V. A. A. Jansen, "The spread of awareness and its impact on epidemic outbreaks," *PNAS*, 2009.

[18] Q. Wu, X. Fu, M. Small, and X.-J. Xu, "The impact of awareness on epidemic spreading in networks," *Chaos: Interdisciplinary Journal of Nonlinear Science*, 2012.

[19] P. T. Eugster, R. Guerraoui, A.-M. Kermarrec, and L. Massoulié, "From epidemics to distributed computing," *IEEE Computer*, vol. 37, 2004.

[20] D. Chakrabarti, J. Leskovec, C. Faloutsos, S. Madden, C. Guestrin, and M. Faloutsos, "Information survival threshold in sensor and p2p networks," in *IEEE INFOCOM*, 2007.

[21] R. M. Anderson and R. M. May, *Infectious Diseases of Humans Dynamics and Control*. OUP, 1992.

[22] R. Durrett, *Random graph dynamics*. Cambridge university press, 2007.

[23] D. Shah, "Gossip algorithms," *Foundations and Trends in Networking*, 2009.

[24] S. Sanghavi, B. Hajek, and L. Massoulié, "Gossiping with multiple messages," in *IEEE INFOCOM*, 2007.

[25] S. Janson, T. Łuczak, T. Turova, and T. Vallier, "Bootstrap percolation on the random graph $g\_\{n,p\}$," *The Annals of Applied Probability*, 2012.

[26] M. Lelarge, "Efficient control of epidemics over random networks," in *Proceedings of the eleventh international joint conference on Measurement and modeling of computer systems*, 2009.

[27] F. Chung, L. Lu, and V. Vu, "Eigenvalues of random power law graphs," *Annals of Combinatorics*, 2003.

[28] S. Janson, T. Łuczak, and I. Norros, "Large cliques in a power-law random graph," *Journal of Applied Probability*, 2010.

[29] O. Jouini and Y. Dallery, "Moments of first passage times in general birth–death processes," *Mathematical Methods of Operations Research*, 2008.

Studying Social Networks at Scale: Macroscopic Anatomy of the Twitter Social Graph

Maksym Gabielkov
Inria
Sophia Antipolis, France
maksym.gabielkov@inria.fr

Ashwin Rao
Inria
Sophia Antipolis, France
ashwin.rao@inria.fr

Arnaud Legout
Inria
Sophia Antipolis, France
arnaud.legout@inria.fr

ABSTRACT

Twitter is one of the largest social networks using exclusively directed links among accounts. This makes the Twitter social graph much closer to the social graph supporting real life communications than, for instance, Facebook. Therefore, understanding the structure of the Twitter social graph is interesting not only for computer scientists, but also for researchers in other fields, such as sociologists. However, little is known about how the information propagation in Twitter is constrained by its inner structure.

In this paper, we present an in-depth study of the macroscopic structure of the Twitter social graph unveiling the highways on which tweets propagate, the specific user activity associated with each component of this macroscopic structure, and the evolution of this macroscopic structure with time for the past 6 years. For this study, we crawled Twitter to retrieve all accounts and all social relationships (follow links) among accounts; the crawl completed in July 2012 with 505 million accounts interconnected by 23 billion links. Then, we present a methodology to unveil the macroscopic structure of the Twitter social graph. This macroscopic structure consists of 8 components defined by their connectivity characteristics. Each component group users with a specific usage of Twitter. For instance, we identified components gathering together spammers, or celebrities. Finally, we present a method to approximate the macroscopic structure of the Twitter social graph in the past, validate this method using old datasets, and discuss the evolution of the macroscopic structure of the Twitter social graph during the past 6 years.

Categories and Subject Descriptors

H.3.5 [**On-line Information Services**]: Web-based services

Keywords

Twitter; social networks; data mining; graph structure.

SIGMETRICS'14, June 16–20, 2014, Austin, Texas, USA.

ACM 978-1-4503-2789-3/14/06 ...$15.00.
http://dx.doi.org/10.1145/2591971.2591985.

1. INTRODUCTION

Twitter is one of the largest social networks with more than 500 million registered accounts. However, it differs from other large social networks such as Facebook and Google+, because it uses exclusively arcs among accounts[1]. Therefore, the way information propagates on Twitter is close to how information propagates in real life. Indeed, real life communications are characterized by a high asymmetry between information producers (such as media, celebrities, etc.) and content consumers. Consequently, understanding how information propagates on Twitter has implications beyond computer science.

However, studying information propagation on a large social network is a complex task. Indeed, information propagation is a combination of two phenomena. First, the content of the messages sent on the social network will determine its chance to be relayed. Second, the structure of the social graph will constrain the propagation of messages. In this paper, we specifically focus on how the structure of the Twitter social graph constrains the propagation of information. This problem is important because its answer will unveil the highways used by the flows of information. To achieve this goal, we need to overcome two challenges. First, we need an up-to-date and complete social graph. The most recent publicly available Twitter datasets are from 2009 [16, 9], at that time Twitter was 10 times smaller than in July 2012. Moreover, these datasets are not exhaustive, thus some subtle properties may not be visible. Second, we need a methodology revealing the underlying social relationships among users, a methodology that scales for hundreds of millions of accounts and tens of billions of arcs. Standard aggregate graph metrics such as degree distribution are of no help because we need to identify the highways of the graph followed by messages. Therefore, we need a methodology to both reduce the social graph and keep its main structure.

In this paper, we overcome these challenges and make the following specific contributions.

1. We collected the entire Twitter social graph, representing 505 million accounts connected with 23 billion arcs. To the best of our knowledge, this is the largest *complete* social graph ever collected.

2. We unveil a macroscopic structure in the Twitter social graph that preserves the highways of information propagation. Our method extends the one of Broder

[1] Arcs—that are directed edges—represent the follow relationship in Twitter. If A follows B, A receives tweets from B, but B will not receive tweets from A, unless B follows A.

et al. [7] and can be applied to any kind of directed social graph.

3. We show that not only the macroscopic structure of the Twitter social graph constrains information propagation, but that each component of the macrostructure corresponds to group of users with a specific usage of Twitter. In particular, we show that regular, abandoned, and malicious accounts are not uniformly spread on the components of the macroscopic structure of the Twitter social graph. This result is important to understand how Twitter is used, where users with a specific usage are, and how to sample Twitter without a significant bias.

4. We present a simple methodology to explore the evolution of the macroscopic structure of Twitter with time, we validate this methodology, and show that old datasets from 2009 do not represent the current structure of the Twitter social graph. We explore this time evolution to understand the changes in the usage of Twitter since its creation.

The remainder of this paper is structured as follows. In Section 2, we present our methodology to crawl Twitter and discuss the dataset we collected. We present and discuss, in Section 3, the notion of macroscopic structure, then we describe a methodology to unveil this macroscopic structure. We present the result of applying this methodology to our dataset in Section 4. In Section 5, we propose a simple approach to estimate the evolution of the macroscopic structure of the graph with time, validate this approach, and discuss the evolution of the Twitter social graph from 2007 to 2012. Finally, we present the related work in Section 6, and conclude in Section 7.

2. MEASURING TWITTER AT SCALE

In this section, we describe the methodology used to crawl the Twitter social graph, some high level characteristics of the dataset, the limitations of our crawl, and the ethical issues.

2.1 Crawling Methodology

In order to collect our dataset, we used the Twitter REST API version 1.0 [3] to crawl the information about user accounts and arcs between users. The main challenge of the crawl is that API requests are rate-limited; an unauthenticated host could make at most 150 requests per hour with that API. However this limit could be overcome by using a whitelisted machine. Twitter used to whitelist the servers of research teams and data-intensive services upon request, this service has been discontinued since February 2011, but existing whitelisted machines could still be used. We used four whitelisted machines to perform our crawl, two machines with a rate limit of 20,000 requests per hour and two with 100,000 requests per hour.

We also implemented and deployed a distributed crawler on 550 machines of PlanetLab [2], doubling the crawling rate compared to whitelisted machines only.

We crawled Twitter by user ID, such numeric IDs are assigned for new accounts sequentially, but with gaps [14]. Therefore, we first determined using a random polling that the largest assigned ID is lower than 800 million, then we divided the range from 1 to 800 million into chunks of 10,000

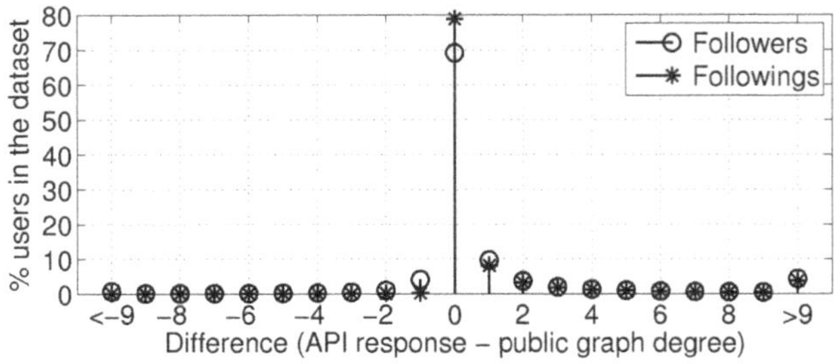

Figure 1: The difference in number of followers and followings between the data from user accounts and the public social graph reconstructed from our dataset.

IDs. We selected an upper bound (800 million) much larger than the largest observed ID to be sure to do not miss any account.

We performed our crawl from March 20, 2012 to July 24, 2012. We implemented a crawler that assigns chunks of 10,000 IDs to each crawling machine. Then, for a given chunk, each crawling machine performs two steps. First, the machine makes 100 requests for 100 IDs, the maximum number of IDs the lookup method of the API accepts, using an API call [20]. When an ID corresponds to a valid account, we retrieve public numerical, boolean and date information[2]. Second, the machine collects the list of followings for all non-protected and valid accounts with at least one following.

We now define the notions of following, followers, and protected accounts that we use in this paper. Each Twitter account can have *followings* and *followers*. An account receives all published tweets from its *followings*, and all its *followers* receive its tweets. Tweets, and list of followers and followings, are by default visible to everyone. However, users can make their account *protected* which makes this information visible only to its followers. Furthermore, following a *protected* account requires manual approval from its owner [5].

2.2 Limitations of the crawl

There are some accounts that we could not crawl, representing 6.33% of the entire Twitter social graph. We explain in the following the reasons why some accounts are not present in our dataset.

1. 32,112,668 accounts (5.97% of the accounts in our dataset) are protected, so we cannot get their list of followings. The degrees of nodes in the graph we analyzed do not take into account arcs to and from protected accounts.

2. 1,855,945 accounts were referenced in the list of followings of other accounts, but the API lookup did not return any profile information for these referenced accounts. Then we tried to perform further API lookups for these referenced accounts, and we obtained profile information for only 137,899 (7.43%) of them. For the rest, the API lookups did not return any profile information. We guess that these accounts were either

[2]The public information returned by the API call we make is described in this URL `https://dev.twitter.com/docs/platform-objects/users`. We note that the history of the published tweets is not part of it.

deactivated [6] during the crawl or suspended by Twitter because these accounts violated Twitter's terms of use. Users can reactivate their account at any time during 30 days after deactivation, so we guess that the observed 7.43% have reactivated their accounts.

3. For 5,938 accounts, we did not crawl the list of followings because the API consistently returned an error code. We counted the number of followings for such accounts as 0.

4. 1,180 user accounts were lost because our archives with data were partially corrupted due to a system bug on two crawling machines.

The number of followings and followers for each account can be obtained in two ways. Either we get these values from an API call, or we compute them based only on the list of followings for each account. We use the latter to build our social graph, so we cross-validated the number of following and followers using the latter method with the former one. We see in Figure 1 that there is no difference between the numbers of followers (resp. followings) returned by the API and the number of followers (resp. followings) in the social graph we computed for 69.14% (resp. 78.79%) of the collected accounts. The difference observed for the other accounts is due to three different reasons. First, our graph does not include protected accounts and their incoming and outgoing arcs, so the number of following and followers in the computed graph is smaller than from the API, which explains that we observe a higher number of positive differences in Figure 1. Second, there is a delay between the time the account information was crawled and the time the list of followings was crawled because of the implementation of the crawler described in Section 2.1. This delay of 9 hours on average (9.5 minutes median) causes a difference in the number of followings reported by the API and the number of followings obtained by computing the social graph, because some arcs might be added or removed during this delay. Third, we crawled all accounts during a four months period. So a given account crawled at time T might be followed (resp. unfollowed) by accounts after time T, accounts that we crawled after they added (resp. removed) the follow links. Thus, there is a larger (resp. smaller) number of followers for this given account in the computed social graph than returned by the API.

2.3 Measured Twitter Social Graph

We collected all Twitter accounts, consisting of 537 million accounts at the end date of our crawl in July 2012, and accounts' public information (including account creation date, number of published tweets, number of followings and followers, etc.) We remind that there are 5.97% of all accounts (32 million) that are protected, which means one needs their approval to get the lists of their followings. So we collected the list of all followings for non-protected accounts only, resulting in a social graph with 505 million nodes and 23 billion arcs. The average node in-degree of this graph is 45.6, the median is 1, and the 90th percentile is 33.

Our dataset is, to the best of our knowledge, the largest and most complete dataset of a social network available today. We also believe that it will be harder in the future to collect such a large and complete dataset. Indeed, companies are taking measures to prevent large crawls of their

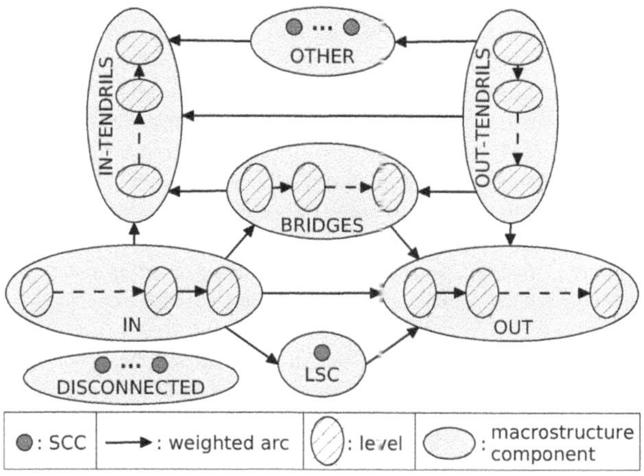

Figure 2: Macrostructure of any directed graph.

social networks. For instance, Twitter is no more whitelisting machines. Moreover it has discontinued on June 11, 2013 the API 1.0 that supported anonymous requests and use of already whitelisted machines. The new API 1.1 requires user authentication for each request making crawls harder and longer to perform. For these reasons, we acknowledge that our dataset has value to communities interested in social graphs, and we release it for academic use only (with precautions described in Section 2 4) [1].

2.4 Ethical Issues

There are two main ethical issues with large scale measurement studies. First, we need to take care of users privacy. All data collected in this study are publicly available through the Twitter API, the Twitter applications, and the Twitter Web site. In particular, we did not collect any data that is not publicly available, or did not work around any protection mechanisms.

Second, we need to respect Twitter terms of use. We used the regular Twitter API to perform our crawl. We made half of our crawl using machines whitelisted by Twitter, and half of the crawl using a distributed crawler which used the regular Twitter API and conformed to its rate constraint. On average, we generated from the distributed crawler around 20 requests per second to the API, a rate of requests we believe to be negligible for the Twitter infrastructure.

We release our dataset [1] that consists of the Twitter social graph in the format of an adjacency list. In the released dataset each account ID is anonymized.

3. GRAPH ANALYSIS METHODOLOGY

We start discussing the motivation and insights behind the analysis of the macroscopic structure—henceforth called the macrostructure—of the Twitter social graph. There is a fundamental difference between directed social graphs such as Twitter and other directed graphs such as the Web. In a directed social graph, not only the links among accounts show the influence of accounts, but they also constrain the propagation of information. Therefore, unveiling the macrostructure of a social graph sheds light on the highways of information propagation.

However, it is a challenge to extract a macrostructure on a social graph of the size of Twitter. The intuition behind our macrostructure analysis is the following. We want to understand how the Twitter graph constrains the flow of information. Therefore, we start by identifying all the strongly connected components (SCCs) that are components with a directed path between any two nodes. In such components, the information can freely circulate, so we abstract each of these components by a single node. After this stage, we obtain a directed acyclic graph (DAG) that is half of the size of the original graph (in terms of number of nodes), still too large to be analyzed. Consequently, the next stage is to group nodes in this DAG based on their connectivity to the largest SCC. As discussed in the following, the largest SCC represents roughly half of the nodes. This is large and there is undoubtedly an interesting analysis to make on this component, but we keep this analysis for future work and focus in this paper on the macrostructure. After this stage, we have 8 components representing a tractable graph. We now describe the details of this process.

We compute the macrostructure of the Twitter social graph in two stages. In the first stage, we use the Tarjan algorithm [23] to compute the SCCs of the Twitter social graph. Then, we replace each SCC with a single vertex, and the multiple arcs between any two vertices with a weighted arc of weight equal to the number of arcs it replaces. As a result, we obtain a directed acyclic graph.

In the second stage, to uncover the macrostructure of the directed acyclic graph shown in Figure 2, we use the following procedure. We first identify the Largest Strongly Connected (LSC) component, the component with the largest number of original nodes. From this LSC component, we run a breadth first search (BFS). We define the set of vertices we find to be the OUT component, that is the set of nodes with a directed path from the LSC component. Inside the OUT component we distinguish *levels* (shown as hatched ellipses on Figure 2). Each level is a bin of SCCs that have the same distance from the LSC component. Then we run a reverse BFS from the LSC component and define the set of vertices we find to be the IN component which is a set of nodes with a directed path to the LSC component. Similarly to OUT we distinguish levels inside the IN component based on the distance to the LSC component. Next, we perform a BFS starting from the IN component and a reverse BFS from the OUT component, reachable nodes that were not yet in the LSC, IN or OUT components were identified as IN-TENDRILS and OUT-TENDRILS respectively. Inside the tendrils we can also identify levels depending on the distance to the components these tendrils are growing from. We separated nodes that were identified as both IN-TENDRILS and OUT-TENDRILS into the BRIDGES category that consist of accounts connecting the IN and OUT bypassing the LSC component, we can also distinguish levels based on the distance to OUT and distance to IN. After that we put the nodes that were not categorized on previous steps into the OTHER category when there is an undirected path from them to categorized nodes or to DISCONNECTED category otherwise. All the possible arcs between the components of the macrostructure are shown on Figure 2.

The methodology we describe and the macrostructure representation is inspired from the work of Broder *et al.* [7] in the context of the Web for 203 million Web pages. However, our methodology is significantly different from the one presented by Broder *et al.* Indeed, unlike our methodology that is exhaustive, they used a small random sample of 570 nodes from the LSC component to find other components. This difference in methodology has two important consequences. First, we perform a complete and accurate classification of all accounts, which is not possible with the methodology of Broder *et al.*, a methodology only intended to show the macrostructure, but not to accurately classify accounts. Second, the macrostructure we describe is more detailed and accurate. In particular, unlike Broder *et al.*, we identified a new component called OTHER, the structure of levels within components, links between components, and the exact number of such links.

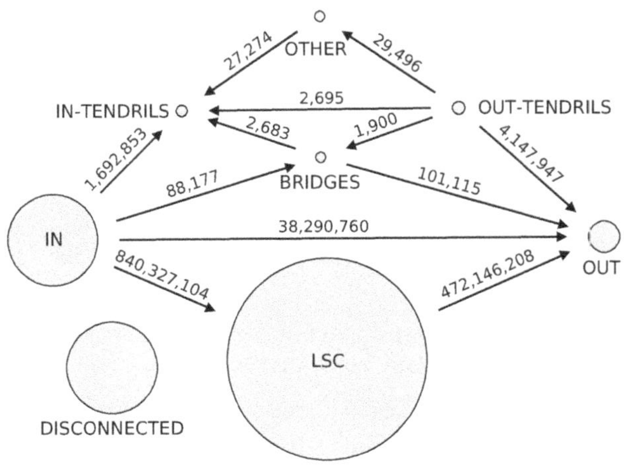

Figure 3: Macrostructure of Twitter in July 2012. *The size of the circles is proportional to the number of accounts in components. The labels on arrows give the number of arcs between components.*

In addition, insight we can get from unveiling the macrostructure of the Web is very different from the insight we can get from unveiling the one of a directed social graph such as Twitter. Indeed, the Web forms a directed graph and the arcs among Web pages are hypertext links. Therefore, the directed graph of the Web represents the paths to access Web pages, but no information propagates along the arcs of the graph. On the contrary, the directed graph of Twitter consists of the follow relationship among accounts. Each tweet published can only propagate along the paths of this graph. Therefore, whereas the notion of content propagation is irrelevant in the context of the Web graph, it is central in the context of the Twitter graph.

In summary, we present a method to compute the macrostructure of any directed graph. Figure 2 is not specific to Twitter and can be applied to any directed graph, and in particular to social graphs, where the components group together accounts with different roles in the social graph. This representation is, to the best of our knowledge, the first attempt to extract *exhaustively* a macrostructure of a large social graph, such as the one of Twitter, taking into account the connectivity of accounts in this graph. In Section 4, we will discuss the role of the Twitter accounts, depending on the component they belong too.

4. THE MACROSTRUCTURE OF TWITTER IN JULY 2012

Exploring the macrostructure of the Twitter social graph is interesting because it sheds light on how information prop-

Component	Top followed (%)	Top following (%)	Top tweeting (%)	Experts (%)	Verified (%)	Suspended (%)
LSC	96.95	100	88.66	94.28	97.01	1.17
OUT	3.05	0	10.79	1.33	2.99	0.43
IN	0	0	0.07	0.01	0	1.77
DISC.	0	0	0.47	0.01	0	5.11
OUT-T.	0	0	0	0	0	0.18
IN-T.	0	0	0	0	0	0.49
BRID.	0	0	0	0	0	0
OTHER	0	0	0.01	0	0	1.25

Table 1: Distribution of noteworthy accounts among components. *The first three columns represent the 10,000 accounts with the largest number of followers, followings, and tweets for the entire Twitter social graph. The fourth column represents the 2.91 million experts identified by Sharma et al. [22] as influential users in their field (the sum of this column is not 100% because 4.37% of the experts are not present in our dataset, most likely because they closed their account, or have been suspended). The fifth column represents the accounts verified by Twitter. The last column represents the percentage of suspended accounts.*

	Arcs (%)		Tweets (%)	Accounts (%)
	followers	followings		
LSC	98.01	96.13	98.05	50.71
OUT	1.96	0.02	1.49	5.30
IN	0.02	3.83	0.25	21.36
DISC.	<0.01	<0.01	0.21	21.60
Others	<0.01	0.02	<0.01	1.03
Total	23×10^9		127×10^9	505×10^6

Table 2: Distribution of the arcs, tweets and accounts per component. *At the scale of the entire Twitter social graph, there is the same number of followings and followers, because they represent the same notion of arc. But, for each component, the number of followings and followers might be different due to the ingress and egress arcs, so we make a distinction between followings and followers for each component.*

Component	No follower (%)	No following (%)	No tweet (%)
LSC	0	0	23.87
OUT	0	92.97	61.82
IN	96.13	0	60.10
DISCONNECTED	99.63	99.63	79.31
OUT-TENDRILS	99.13	0	73.20
IN-TENDRILS	0	98.78	70.40
BRIDGES	0	0	67.34
OTHER	51.39	46.67	67.56

Table 3: Percentage of accounts with no follower, no following or no tweet per component.

agation is constrained. However, this macrostructure would be even more interesting if we can map specific usages of Twitter to components in this macrostructure. Unraveling a correlation between accounts usages and the macrostructure will improve the understanding of how Twitter is used.

In this section, we dissect the macrostructure of the Twitter social graph, focusing on regular, abandoned, and suspicious accounts. i) **Regular accounts** are by definition accounts that are neither abandoned or suspended. Such accounts show the regular activity on Twitter. ii) **Abandoned accounts** are accounts with few followers and followings, and no recent tweet activity. Such accounts are important to understand Twitter adoption and to accurately quantify the bias when analyzing Twitter, bias due to these accounts that do not take part in any social activity. iii) **Suspicious accounts** are often suspended by Twitter because they infringed its terms of use. We checked that most suspended accounts show evident signs of malicious activity (bunch of sequentially generated accounts, accounts' user name generated with automatic patterns, etc.). There is no ground truth for the malicious activity, but the notion of suspended accounts is a reasonable metric to detect (in retrospect) malicious accounts [24]. For the purposes of our study we have recrawled a set of 1 million random users from our dataset on May 6, 2013 to check if they are still active. In the rest of the paper, we refer to the number of suspended accounts as the number of accounts for which Twitter returned the 'suspended' status during this recrawl.

Figure 3 shows the macrostructure of Twitter computed with the methodology presented in Section 3. We identify 8 components in this graph, with 4 of them (LSC, OUT, IN, DISCONNECTED) representing 98.96% of all Twitter accounts; so we focus on them.

The LSC (Largest Strongly Connected) component is the core of the regular Twitter activity. Indeed, according to Table 1, the LSC component contains 96.95% of the 10,000 most followed accounts, 100% of the 10,000 accounts that follow the most, 88.66% of the 10,000 accounts that tweet the most, 94.28% of the 2.91 million experts identified by Sharma *et al.* [22] as influential accounts in their field, and 97.01% of the verified accounts [4] that are accounts of highly sought users (in music, acting, politics, etc.) that Twitter verified to be authentic. In addition, Table 2 shows that more than 96% of the following and follower links, and 98.05% of the tweets are for accounts in the LSC.

However, it is wrong to believe that the LSC component is the only one that matters when studying Twitter, other components contain a lot of accounts with specific roles in the Twitter ecosystem. We see in Table 2 that the LSC contains only 50.71% of all accounts. This is surprising because it is easy to be part of the LSC component, an account only needs one following and one follower already in the LSC component. Also, we observe that a large fraction of the suspicious activity in Twitter is outside of the LSC component, as we see in Table 1 (last column). Finally, when looking at the percentage of accounts with no follower, no following, or no tweet, we see in Table 3 that each of the four main components has fundamentally different characteristics. Indeed 92.97% of the accounts in the OUT component have no following, 96.13% of the accounts in the IN component have no follower, and almost all accounts in the DISCONNECTED

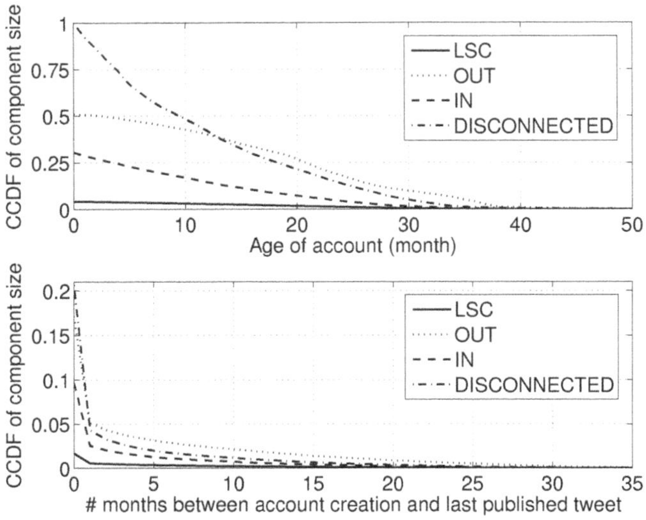

Figure 4: Characterization of abandoned accounts. *(top) Identification of old abandoned accounts. CCDF of accounts with at most one follower and one following in a component according to the account creation date. (bottom) Characterization of accounts who published at least one tweet. CCDF of the duration between the creation date of an account and the date of its last published tweet for accounts with at most one follower and one following.*

component have no following and no follower. Moreover, at least 60% of the accounts in these three components never sent any tweet, whereas it is only 23.87% for the LSC.

In summary, we see that even if most of the regular Twitter activity is in the LSC component, other components contain half of the Twitter accounts and present characteristics worth studying. In the following, we dig into each component to discuss its main characteristics.

4.1 LSC Component

We have seen that most of the regular Twitter activity is in the LSC component. However, due to the simplicity to belong to the LSC component, many abandoned and suspicious accounts also belong to it.

4.1.1 Abandoned Accounts

Most accounts with one following and one follower in the LSC are abandoned accounts. We see in Figure 4 (top, solid line) that there are 4.18% of accounts in the LSC component with one following and one follower. In addition, out of the accounts with one following and one follower in the LSC component, 86.34% are more than 6 months old and 59.57% never sent any tweet.

In summary, a large fraction of accounts in the LSC component with one following and one follower did not have any change in their number of followings and followers for months and did not send tweets recently. Considering that it is unlikely that such accounts will actively follow a single other account for month (so no serious follow activity) without tweeting anything (so no publishing activity), it is reasonable to believe that these accounts are abandoned.

Component	Top followed (%)	Top following (%)	Top tweeting (%)	Top following with ≤ 1 follower (%)	Top tweet with ≤ 1 follower (%)
LSC	0.33	1.15	1.99	97.83	3.02
OUT	1.15	10.30	5.20	0.45	5.26
IN	2.78	96.87	3.87	96.87	3.89
DISC.	1.38	1.33	7.43	2.84	7.48

Table 4: Percentage of suspended accounts (on the 6th of May 2013) per component for 5 outlier categories. *The first three columns represent the 10,000 accounts with the largest number of followers, followings, and tweets for the entire Twitter social graph. The fourth column is for the 10,000 accounts with the largest number of followings and at most one follower. The last column is for the 10,000 accounts with the largest number of tweets and at most one follower.*

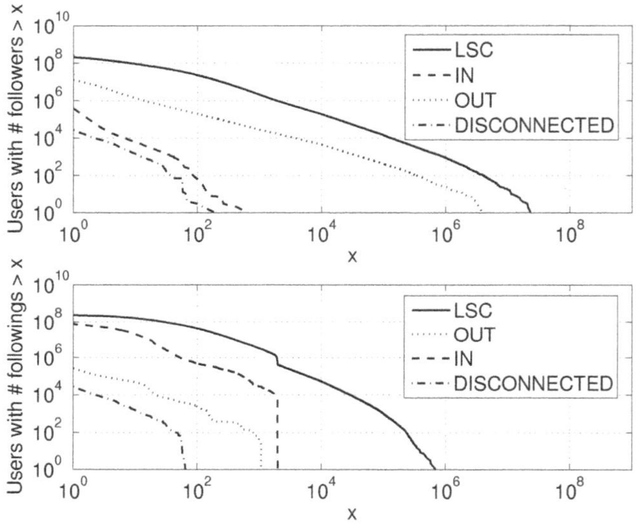

Figure 5: Distribution of followers (top) and followings (bottom) by category. *Accounts with no follower (top) and no following (bottom) are filtered out (see Table 3)*

4.1.2 Suspicious Accounts

The LSC component also contains suspicious accounts. We present in Table 4 the percentage of suspended accounts per component for five outlier categories. An *outlier* account is followed, following, or tweeting much more than a regular account, thus it is a good candidate for suspicious activity. The first three columns represent accounts with the largest number of followers, largest number of followings, and largest number of tweets. The fourth and fifth columns are for the accounts with the largest number of followings and tweets, but with at most one follower. We consider this notion of outliers because following a lot of accounts is a known technique used by spammers [24]. To reduce the impact of spammers, we remind that Twitter imposes a limit of 2,000 followings for accounts with no follower, and then a

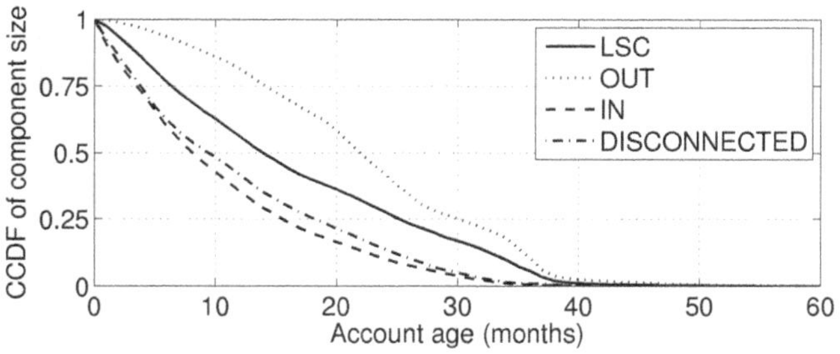

Figure 6: Age of accounts in each component. *CCDF of accounts in a component according to the account creation date.*

linear increase with the number of followers. Accounts close to this limit and with at most one follower are more likely to be spammers. The last column is for accounts that send the largest number of tweets, but with at most one follower. This is also a suspicious behavior, because it is strange to send a lot of tweets if nobody (or a single other account) follows them. Spammers can send a lot of tweets to interfere with trending topics or the Twitter search functionality, and to direct messages to a specific user using *@mentions* [24].

Considering the huge number of suspicious accounts, we cannot afford to manually inspect all of them. Therefore, we consider a suspicious account to be malicious if it was suspended by Twitter, see Table 4.

As expected, the top followed accounts in the LSC component are regular, only 0.33% have been suspended. Indeed, it is complex to manipulate the number of followers, because it requires to either manipulate other accounts in order to incite them to follow, or to create fake accounts whose only one goal is to follow. More surprising, the top following accounts are also regular for Twitter, only 1.15% have been suspended. We expect accounts that follow a lot of other accounts to be spammers, but, according to Figure 5 (bottom), the LSC component is the only one to have accounts that break the limit of 2,000 followings. So the top following in the LSC component also have a lot of followers, thus the low number of suspended accounts.

Then we observe in Table 4 two important behaviors that characterize well the outlier activity in the LSC component. First, 97.83% of the top following with at most 1 follower have been suspended. This means that most of the accounts in the LSC component close to the limit of 2,000 followings are malicious. Second, only 3.02% of the top tweeting accounts, but with at most a single follower have been suspended. The rest looks like regular for Twitter. By manually inspecting these accounts that looks regular for Twitter, we found bots used as an interface to job forums, news site, Yahoo!Answers, YouTube published videos, etc. So, it seems that Twitter is used by developers to generate a stream of data collected from third party Web sites. As these accounts have only one follower, we guess that they are either used for tests only, or that the developers are using a Twitter widget to embed their account timeline into a Web site.

4.2 OUT Component

The OUT component represents all Twitter accounts with a directed path from the LSC component. In addition, these accounts can also have directed paths from other components, but no account in OUT can have a directed path to any other component (directed paths among OUT accounts are possible, so if an OUT account has following links, they necessarily come to other OUT accounts).

4.2.1 *Regular Accounts*

A specificity of the OUT component is that a small set of accounts (belonging to celebrities) attract most of the follower links for this component. These are regular OUT accounts. We see in Figure 3 that more than 500 million links between components are directed to OUT, 37.93% of all inter-components links, whereas the OUT component represents only 5.30% of all accounts. Also, we see in Table 2 that accounts in OUT presents 1.96% of all follower links, which make it the second component with the largest number of follower links (we sum all follower links for all accounts in a given component). Among the 100 accounts that have the largest number of followers, we found that there are 35 verified accounts representing 12% of the arcs from the LSC to OUT. These accounts are owned by celebrities that belong to the OUT component because they do not follow any other account.

We observe another interesting specificity of the OUT component in Figures 4 (top) and Figures 6. The OUT component is the only one to show an inflection point for both curves around 20 months, meaning that the proportion of recent accounts in the component is lower than for other components. To explain this inflection point, we need to characterize the kind of accounts that stay in the OUT component. According to Table 3, 92,97% of the OUT accounts have no followings, but they all have at least one follower because they belong to the OUT component. These accounts are what we call selfish (they are not interested in tweets from other accounts), a decreasing trend in Twitter in the past two years. We will discuss further this trend in Section 5.3.

4.2.2 *Abandoned Accounts*

As we discussed in Section 4.1, most accounts with at most one following and one follower are also abandoned accounts for the OUT component. We see in Figure 4 (top) that 50.94% of the accounts have at most one following and one follower, and 40.11% are more than 1 year old. We see in Figure 4 (bottom) that 82.89% of the accounts with at most one following and one follower never sent a tweet, and that only 5.13% of the accounts with at least one following and one follower sent a tweet more that 1 month after their creation date. This is a consequence of the *Find friends* feature available in Twitter that allows users to search their entire contact lists for Twitter accounts. By default, once the search is done, all accounts are checked to be followed. As a consequence, we observe many accounts in the LSC component that followed abandoned accounts in the DISCONNECTED component, making these abandoned accounts move to the OUT component.

4.2.3 *Suspicious Accounts*

There are fewer malicious accounts in the OUT component than for other components. We see in Table 4 that the percentage of suspended accounts for outlier accounts is low for the OUT component. We explain the low number of suspended accounts for the top followings because no account reaches the limit of 2,000 followings, and that few accounts have more than a hundred followings, see Figure 5

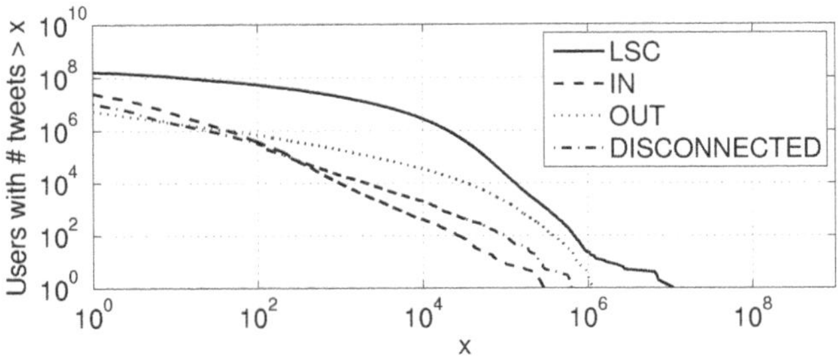

Figure 7: The distribution of number of tweets by component. *Accounts with no tweets are filtered out (see Table 3).*

(bottom). As long as an account in OUT follows an account in the LSC, it belongs to the LSC, so spammers using following links to spam are likely to escape in the LSC component. We explain the low number of suspended accounts for the top tweeting with at most one follower because (as for the LSC component) most of these accounts are operated by bots. Finally, we see in Table 1 that out of the 4 main components, OUT is the component with the smallest number of malicious accounts.

4.3 IN Component

The IN component is much different from the two previous ones because accounts in this component have few followers (see Figure 5, top) and the distribution of the number of tweets is very different (see Figure 7) from the ones of the LSC and OUT components. The IN component contains the second largest fraction of abandoned and suspicious accounts, after the DISCONNECTED component.

4.3.1 Regular Accounts

The regular users for the IN component are passive followers, that are accounts who follow accounts in the LSC, but never publish tweets and are not followed. Indeed, in Tables 2 and 3 we see that the IN component contains 21.36% of all Twitter accounts, but 96.13% of them have no follower, and 60.10% of them published no tweet (we remind that accounts with followers in IN are followed by other accounts in IN only). This component consists of accounts who follow accounts in the LSC (99.6%) or an account in IN (0.4%). We will see in Section 5.3 that the trend of accounts to be passive followers on Twitter (that is, belong to IN component) has been growing since 2009.

Many accounts belonging to the IN component move to the LSC component. We see in Figure 4 (top) that 30.56% of the accounts in the IN component have at most one following and one follower, but that only 14.61% are more than one year old. So even if few of them have been tweeting close to the creation date of their accounts (see Figure 4, bottom), it is likely that they moved to the LSC component and tweeted from it. Indeed, we see in Table 1 that only 1.77% of the accounts in the IN component have been suspended, but that accounts are much younger in the IN component than in the LSC and OUT components, see Figure 6.

4.3.2 Abandoned Accounts

Whereas 96.13% of the accounts in the IN component never published any tweet (see Table 3), the fraction of abandoned accounts is much lower in this component than in the OUT and DISCONNECTED components. Indeed, we see in Figure 4 (top) that only 30.56% of the accounts in the IN component have at most one following and one follower, and 20.88% have at most one following, one follower, and never published any tweet. Moreover, according to Figure 5 (bottom), 23.04% of the accounts follow at least 10 other accounts, thus a passive follower activity.

4.3.3 Suspicious Accounts

The IN component contains many malicious accounts among the outliers. We see in Table 4 that 96.87% of the accounts with the largest number of followings are suspended. We note that all top followings have at most 1 follower in this component. There is also 3.87% of the accounts that tweeted the most that were suspended. For the rest, after manual inspection, we also found, as for the two previous components, that they are used by bots.

Finally, the IN component has a very interesting property for people looking for a reliable metric to assess influencers. Cha *et al.* [9] show that the number of followers is not a reliable metric, because users perform link farming [10] to increase their number of followers. However, this is a rare problem in the IN component. Indeed, accounts in the IN are clearly not interested in increasing their number of followers (see Figure 5, top) thus the accounts they follow will not be biased by this problem. Evaluating the benefit of considering accounts in the IN to assess influencers is an interesting problem for future work.

4.4 DISCONNECTED Component

Accounts in the DISCONNECTED component, like in the IN one, have few followers (see Figure 5, top) and the distribution of their number of tweets is very different (see Figure 7) from the ones of the LSC and OUT. The DISCONNECTED component contains the largest fraction of abandoned and suspicious accounts. There are almost no regular users in this component.

4.4.1 Abandoned Accounts

A specificity of the DISCONNECTED component is that is contains a lot of abandoned accounts. In spite of being the second largest component with 21.6% of all accounts (see Table 2), 78.94% of accounts in the DISCONNECTED component have no followers and no followings, and never published any tweet. Furthermore, 72.44% of accounts in DISCONNECTED component are older than one month. Therefore, we can conclude that the DISCONNECTED component has, by far, the largest number of abandoned accounts. We see in Fig. 4 (top) that 99.97% of its accounts have at most one following and one follower, but only 41.93% of them are older than 12 months. Like for the IN component, many account in the DISCONNECTED component are recent (see Figure 6), thus some accounts in this component have moved to another component.

4.4.2 Suspicious Accounts

Finally, we see in Table 1 that the DISCONNECTED component contains the largest fraction of malicious accounts, but we don't observe in Table 4 an outlier category grouping them. Indeed, most accounts have no followings, no followers and no tweets, so the number of outliers is much smaller than our sample size.

In summary, the DISCONNECTED component hosts a

lot of abandoned accounts and a large fraction of the malicious activity on Twitter, it is also a transitional place for new accounts before they migrate to another component.

4.5 Other Components

The smallest components, IN-TENDRILS, OUT-TENDRILS, BRIDGES, and OTHER represent 1.03% of all accounts. Most accounts in these components are either accounts created for test, or new accounts that will migrate to another component after some time. We do not discuss deeper these components as their impact on the Twitter social graph is small compared to the 4 main components.

4.6 Discussion

We can draw several important lessons from the results discussed in this section.

First, the macrostructure of the Twitter social graph significantly constrains the propagation of information. Therefore, models of information propagation in social networks might lead to wrong results when abstracting the underlying social graph. This work sheds light on how to correctly abstract the social graph, and because the macrostructure is reasonably simple, with 3 main components with active accounts, we believe it is possible to model the underlying graph constraint.

Second, we identify a correlation between components in the macrostructure and the usage of accounts in these components. This result challenges the sampling techniques that follow arcs (such as random walks or bi-directional breadth first search) because the statistical validity of the sample might be low. For instance, all sampling techniques following arcs that start from well connected (or active) accounts will miss all of the malicious activity located in the DISCONNECTED component.

Last, the identification of the role of accounts in each components is important to understand who are the influencers in Twitter. For instance, as discussed in Section 4.3.3, users try to increase their popularity in Twitter by either offering reciprocation to the users that accept to follow them, or by buying follower links on the black market. Therefore, we can identify real influencers by focusing exclusively on the followers in the IN component, removing suspicious accounts by filtering out all accounts younger than, e.g., six months.

5. EVOLUTION OF THE MACROSTRUCTURE OF THE TWITTER SOCIAL GRAPH WITH TIME

In this section, we discuss the evolution of the macrostructure of the Twitter social graph with time from January 2007 to July 2012. To present this evolution, we first describe the estimation technique we use to estimate the Twitter social graph in the past. Then we validate our technique using two public datasets collected in 2009 [16, 9]. We discuss the evolution of the macrostructure of the Twitter social graph with time and explain how new accounts led to the time evolution we observed, shedding light on the evolution of the usage of Twitter in the past 6 years.

5.1 Methodology to Estimate the Macrostructure

The evolution with time of the macrostructure of the Twitter social graph is interesting, because it shows the evolution of the Twitter usage. We have seen in Section 4 that components represent specific categories of usage. However, the Twitter API does not give access to the past social graph of Twitter.

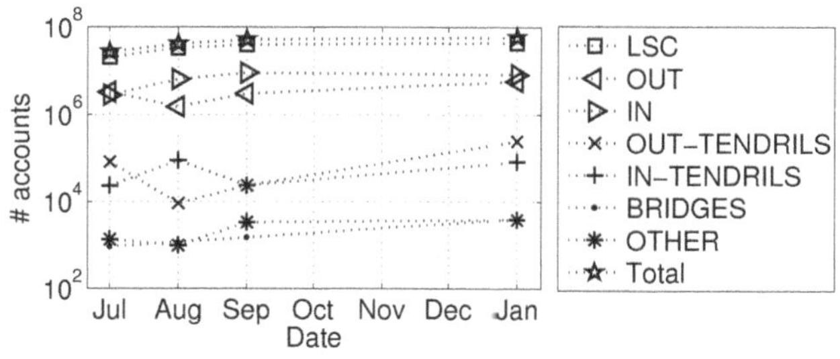

Figure 8: Comparison of our estimated graphs of 2009 (labeled Jul and Jan) with two existing Twitter datasets made in August [16] and September [9] 2009. *Our simple methodology gives an approximation of the macrostructure of the Twitter social graph that is consistent with existing datasets.*

We propose a simple approach to approximate the macrostructure of the Twitter social graph. The dataset we describe in Section 2.3 covers all Twitter accounts in July 2012 (with the limitation described in Section 2.2), and for each account we have the creation date. To approximate the macrostructure of the Twitter social graph at date D, we remove from our dataset all accounts created after this date, and all arcs to and from these accounts. Then, we use the methodology described in Section 3 to compute the macrostructure of the resulting graph at date D.

This simple methodology has two important limitations. First, we do not have any suspended and deactivated accounts in our dataset. Accounts are suspended by Twitter because they infringed the terms of use, most of the time they are spammers. Deactivated accounts have been closed by users themselves. We believe such accounts, when they were still active, had a small impact of the Twitter social graph. Second, the Twitter API does not give access to the arc creation date[3]. Therefore, we assume that all arcs between any two accounts in July 2012 existed at date D as long as the two accounts existed at this date; equivalently we assume that if there is an arc between two accounts, it is created close to the creation date of the youngest account. We are aware that, as reported by Kwak *et al.*, the creation of arcs among accounts is more complex than our simple approximation [15]. However, our goal is to understand the evolution of the macrostructure of the Twitter social graph with time, not the fine grain evolution of arcs between accounts. For this reason, we believe that our approximation is reasonable.

Moreover, to validate this approximation on creation dates of arcs, we compare our approximation with two datasets collected in 2009 [16, 9]. Kwak *et al.* [16] and Cha *et al.* [9] independently collected two Twitter datasets in August 2009 and September 2009 respectively and used different methodology. Kwak *et al.* used a technique close to

[3]For a given account, Meeder *et al.* observed that the 1.0 Twitter API returned the arcs in an order that was the reverse order of creation of the arcs for this account [19]. Our recent experiments with the Twitter API have shown that it is no more possible to rely on this ordering property.

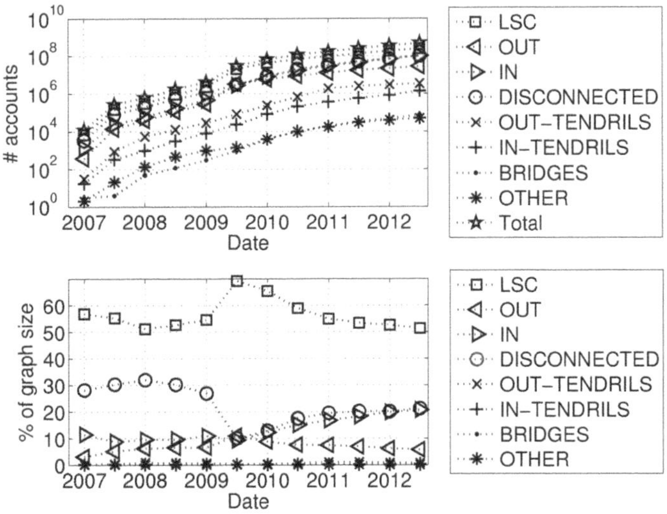

Figure 9: The estimated evolution of the macrostructure of Twitter with time. *(top) Sizes of components in log scale. (bottom) Sizes of the same components as a percentage of the size of the graph.*

a BFS and reverse BFS from a popular account and also collected accounts referring to trending topics (so active accounts only), and Cha *et al.* used a crawl by account ID (as we did). For each of the two datasets we computed the Twitter macrostructure according to the methodology described in Section 3, and we approximated the macrostructure of Twitter using our dataset in July 2009 and January 2010. We show in Figure 8 the result of this validation: the order of the size of each components is consistent between the two validation datasets and our dataset. In addition, we have compared the dataset by Kwak *et al.* with our closest estimation (July 2009). We found that 88.25% of the users common to both datasets belong to the same components in both datasets. We cannot make such a validation for the second dataset because Cha *et al.* have anonymized it. In summary, the dynamics of the creation and deletion of arcs is complex [15], but we have shown that our simple approximation is reliable enough for the purpose of our macrostructure study.

There is no DISCONNECTED component in Figure 8, because this component is missing in the two validation datasets. Either the methodology did not permit to crawl accounts in this component [16], or these accounts were filtered out in the published dataset [9]. We observe in Figure 8 some small variations for the OUT, IN-TENDRILS, and OUT-TENDRILS components between the two validation datasets and our dataset. These variations can be explained by a major change in the Twitter macrostructure that happened in 2009. We discuss further this change in the next section.

5.2 Evolution of the Macrostructure

To observe the evolution of the Twitter social graph with time, we approximate its macrostructure using the simple methodology discussed in Section 5.1 every six months from January 1, 2007 to July 1, 2012. The first account on Twitter was created on March 21, 2006, but due to the small number of accounts created between March and July 2006, we decided to skip the macrostructure of the Twitter social graph in July 2006 and start our analysis in January 2007.

We see in Figure 9 (top) the evolution of the size of each component with time, confirming that the LSC, OUT, IN, and DISCONNECTED have always been the largest components in Twitter. However, by looking at the size of each component normalized with the graph size in Figure 9 (bottom), we observe an interesting change in proportion of macrostructure components in 2009.

Before 2009, the proportion of the DISCONNECTED component was around 30%, the IN component was stable in size, and the size of the OUT component was increasing. The real public adoption of Twitter started in 2009 where the total number of accounts went from 4.265 million in January 2009 to 67.487 million in January 2010. Several events contributed to attract new users on Twitter during that period: the terrorist attacks in Mumbai was one of the first event followed on Twitter in November 2008, attracting the attention of other news media such as CNN; some influential celebrities started to use Twitter such as Oprah Winfrey, and, for the first time, some accounts reached one million followers.

We see in Figure 9 (bottom) that the large adoption of Twitter in 2009 led to changes in the macrostructure of its social graph. The proportion of the DISCONNECTED component dropped to 10% while the LSC jumped to 70%. We have seen in Section 4 that the DISCONNECTED component corresponds to abandoned accounts, so during such a large adoption phase, the proportion of abandoned accounts is much lower. However, this proportion increased in 2010 and 2011 to reach a stable value, with the DISCONNECTED component representing around 20% of all accounts.

We also observe in Figure 9 (bottom) that the proportion of the OUT component has been decreasing since 2009. The reason is that a large fraction of celebrities joined Twitter in 2009 and 2010. Some of these celebrities created an account to increase their visibility, but never intended to follow other accounts, thus they joined the OUT component. The fraction of such celebrities is decreasing compared to regular accounts, and also joining Twitter without following anyone in the LSC component is a decreasing trend. Indeed, the proportion of the IN component has been increasing since 2009, showing that it is an increasing trend to follow accounts in the LSC component without tweeting and being followed.

It is worth noticing that the two most popular Twitter datasets [16, 9] have been collected in 2009. We have seen that the Twitter social graph macrostructure has significantly changed during the period 2009/2010, calling for a newer dataset such as the one we collected, which is more representative of the actual Twitter social graph. We also note that the two datasets of 2009 do not contain accounts belonging to the DISCONNECTED component, unlike our dataset, which is an issue for researchers focusing on malicious activities and abandoned accounts on Twitter.

5.3 Distribution of New Accounts in Components

In this section, we evaluate to which component the new accounts created during each 6 months period belong to. To find this distribution, we use the approximations of the Twitter social graph macrostructure described in Sec-

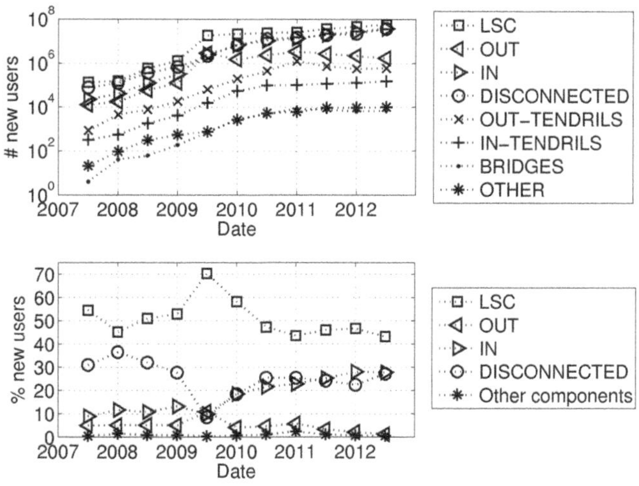

Figure 10: Distribution of new accounts per components with time. *(top) Number of new accounts per component. (bottom) Fraction of the total number of new accounts per component.*

tion 5.2. Then, for each pair of contiguous approximations in time (e.g., July 2008 and January 2009), we remove all accounts already present in the oldest one to the newest one. This way, we obtain the evolution with time of the distribution of the new accounts in components, see Figure 10.

We observe in Figure 10 (top) that the total number of new accounts increases with time for the LSC, IN, and DISCONNECTED components, but not for OUT. This decrease confirms our discussion in Section 4.2 on the OUT component, explaining that new selfish accounts are decreasing in Twitter.

Figure 10 (bottom) shows the fraction of the total number of new accounts per component. We observe that new accounts join most the LSC component, but this is a decreasing trend at the benefit of the IN and DISCONNECTED components. We explain this trend by two changes in the usage of Twitter initiated in 2009. First, passive followers are taking an increasing role in Twitter; passive followers are accounts that follow other accounts, but that are not followed and never publish tweets, as described in Section 4.3. This increasing role of passive followers shows that Twitter is more and more used as a regular information media in which people receive information, but do not produce any. However, more than 40% of new accounts are still joining the LSC component, making Twitter the largest and most participative information media. Second, as Twitter is very popular, it is attracting a large fraction of users that are just creating a Twitter account out of curiosity, but never effectively use it. Most of these accounts end up in the DISCONNECTED component.

6. RELATED WORK

Twitter has been widely studied for years. A large fraction of the literature is on the identification of malicious behavior on Twitter [24, 27, 10], on the study of tweets propagation [21, 26], and on privacy [12, 18]. All these studies are not directly related to our work as they do not crawl the Twitter social graph and do not explore its properties.

Closer to our work, several studies focused on the Twitter social graph. Some of them crawled partially the graph before 2009 [13, 14, 11], so before the wide adoption of Twitter. Two studies made a large crawl of the Twitter social graph. Kwak *et al.* used a technique close to a BFS and reverse BFS from a popular account and also collected accounts referring to trending topics. This crawling methodology cannot capture some users that are not connected to the LSC component, and that do not tweet about trending topic, thus a partial view of the Twitter social graph. Cha *et al.* [9] used a crawl by account ID, that is close to what we did. Both of these studies made their dataset publicly available and others built on it [17, 25, 8, 22], but the datasets were collected in 2009 during the main change in the Twitter social graph we discussed in Section 5.2.

To the best of our knowledge, the dataset we present is the most up-to-date and the most complete description of the Twitter social graph. Moreover, none of these studies explores the macrostructure of the Twitter social graph, a new way to represent directed social graphs. Broder *et al.* [7] introduced first the notion of macrostructure for a directed graph in the context of the Web, but we significantly improved it, and we are the first ones to apply it to Twitter. Unlike what Broder *et al.* proposed, we present a methodology to compute the exhaustive macrostructure of any large directed social graph, along with the categorization of each account in the identified component, which is a significant methodological step.

7. CONCLUSION

In this paper, we present the largest, most complete, and most up-to-date crawl of the Twitter social graph. This graph contains 505 million accounts connected with 23 billion arcs. In addition, we present a methodology to practically compute the macrostructure of any directed social graph and to exhaustively classify each account to one of the identified components. We applied this methodology to the Twitter social graph and found that only 50.71% of the accounts belong to the LSC component, and that 21.60% of the accounts (in the DISCONNECTED component) have no path to the other accounts.

We show that the main components of the macrostructure of the Twitter social graph correspond to specific usages. For instance, the LSC component hold most of the regular Twitter activity, and the IN component holds passive followers. Finally, we present a simple methodology to explore the evolution of the macrostructure of Twitter with time, we validate this methodology, and we show that the public datasets crawled in 2009 do not represent the current macrostructure of the Twitter social graph.

We believe that our collected dataset is a gold mine for any researcher working on social graphs and that the macrostructure analysis sheds a new light on the Twitter social graph that will be useful for both theoreticians and experimenters.

8. ACKNOWLEDGEMENTS

The authors thank Krishna P. Gummadi (MPI-SWS) for insights on the analysis of the dataset we collected and valuable feedback from the early stages of this work. We also thank him for sharing the list of influential Twitter users identified by Sharma *et al.* [22].

9. REFERENCES

[1] soTweet: Studying Twitter at Scale. `http://www-sop.inria.fr/members/Arnaud.Legout/Projects/sotweet.html`

[2] PlanetLab. `https://www.planet-lab.org/`

[3] Twitter REST API 1.0. `https://dev.twitter.com/docs/api/1`

[4] FAQs about verified accounts. `https://support.twitter.com/groups/31-twitter-basics/topics/111-features/articles/119135-about-verified-accounts`

[5] About public and protected Tweets. `https://support.twitter.com/entries/14016`

[6] How to deactivate your account. `https://support.twitter.com/articles/15358-how-to-deactivate-your-account`

[7] A. Broder, R. Kumar, F. Maghoul, P. Raghavan, S. Rajagopalan, R. Stata, A. Tomkins, and J. Wiener. Graph structure in the Web. In *Proc. of WWW'00*, Amsterdam, The Netherlands, April 2000.

[8] M. Cha, F. Benevenuto, H. Haddadi, and K. P. Gummadi. The world of connections and information flow in Twitter. *Systems, Man and Cybernetics, Part A: Systems and Humans, IEEE Transactions*, 42(4):991–998, 2012.

[9] M. Cha, H. Haddadi, F. Benevenuto, and K. P. Gummadi. Measuring user influence in Twitter: The million follower fallacy. In *Proc. of AAAI ICWSM'10*, Washington DC, USA, May 2010.

[10] S. Ghosh, B. Viswanath, F. Kooti, N. K. Sharma, G. Korlam, F. Benevenuto, N. Ganguly, and K. P. Gummadi. Understanding and combating link farming in the Twitter social network. In *Proc. of WWW'12*, Lyon, France, April 2012.

[11] B. Huberman, D. Romero, and F. Wu. Social networks that matter: Twitter under the microscope. *First Monday*, 14(1), 2008.

[12] L. Humphreys, P. Gill, and B. Krishnamurthy. How much is too much? Privacy issues on Twitter. In *Proc. of the Conference of International Communication Association*, Singapore, June 2010.

[13] A. Java, X. Song, T. Finin, and B. Tseng. Why we Twitter: understanding microblogging usage and communities. In *Proc. of WebKDD/SNA-KDD'07*, San Jose, California, August 2007.

[14] B. Krishnamurthy, P. Gill, and M. Arlitt. A few chirps about Twitter. In *Proc. of WOSN'08*, Seattle, WA, USA, August 2008.

[15] H. Kwak, H. Chun, and S. Moon. Fragile online relationship: a first look at unfollow dynamics in Twitter. In *Proc. of ACM CHI'11*, Vancouver, BC, Canada, 2011.

[16] H. Kwak, C. Lee, H. Park, and S. Moon. What is Twitter, a social network or a news media? In *Proc. of WWW'10*, Raleigh, NC, USA, May 2010.

[17] J. G. Lee, P. Antoniadis, and K. Salamatian. Faving reciprocity in content sharing communities: A comparative analysis of Flickr and Twitter. In *Proc. of ASONAM'10*, Odense, Denmark, August 2010.

[18] H. Mao, X. Shuai, and A. Kapadia. Loose tweets: an analysis of privacy leaks on Twitter. In *Proc. of WPES'11*, Chicago, IL, USA, October 2011.

[19] B. Meeder, B. Karrer, A. Sayedi, R. Ravi, C. Borgs, and J. Chayes. We know who you followed last summer: inferring social link creation times in twitter. In *Proc. of WWW'11*, Hyderabad, India, March 2011.

[20] M. Russell. *21 Recipes for Mining Twitter*. Real Time Bks. O'Reilly Media, Inc., 2011.

[21] E. Sadikov and M. M. M. Martinez. Information propagation on Twitter. CS322 project report, Stanford University, 2009.

[22] N. K. Sharma, S. Ghosh, F. Benevenuto, N. Ganguly, and K. P. Gummadi. Inferring who-is-who in the Twitter social network. In *Proc. of ACM WOSN'12*, Helsinki, Finland, August 2012.

[23] R. Tarjan. Depth-first search and linear graph algorithms. In *Proc. of 12th Annual Symposium on Switching and Automata Theory*, 1971.

[24] K. Thomas, C. Grier, D. Song, and V. Paxson. Suspended accounts in retrospect: an analysis of Twitter spam. In *Proc. of ACM SIGCOMM IMC'11*, Berlin, Germany, November 2011.

[25] S. Wu, J. M. Hofman, W. A. Mason, and D. J. Watts. Who says what to whom on Twitter. In *Proc. of WWW'11*, Hyderabad, India, March 2011.

[26] S. Ye and S. F. Wu. Measuring message propagation and social influence on Twitter.com. In *Proc. of SocInfo'10*, Laxenburg, Austria, October 2010.

[27] C. M. Zhang and V. Paxson. Detecting and analyzing automated activity on Twitter. In *Proc. of PAM'11*, Atlanta, GA, USA, March 2011.

Stochastic Bandits with Side Observations on Networks

Swapna Buccapatnam, Atilla Eryilmaz
Department of ECE
The Ohio State University
Columbus, OH - 43210
buccapat@ece.osu.edu,
eryilmaz.2@osu.edu

Ness B. Shroff
Departments of ECE and CSE
The Ohio State University
Columbus, OH - 43210
shroff.11@osu.edu

ABSTRACT

We study the stochastic multi-armed bandit (MAB) problem in the presence of side-observations across actions. In our model, choosing an action provides additional side observations for a subset of the remaining actions. One example of this model occurs in the problem of targeting users in online social networks where users respond to their friends's activity, thus providing information about each other's preferences. Our contributions are as follows: 1) We derive an asymptotic (with respect to time) lower bound (as a function of the network structure) on the regret (loss) of any *uniformly good policy* that achieves the maximum long term average reward. 2) We propose two policies - a randomized policy and a policy based on the well-known upper confidence bound (UCB) policies, both of which explore each action at a rate that is a function of its network position. We show that these policies achieve the asymptotic lower bound on the regret up to a multiplicative factor independent of network structure. The upper bound guarantees on the regret of these policies are better than those of existing policies. Finally, we use numerical examples on a real-world social network to demonstrate the significant benefits obtained by our policies against other existing policies.

Categories and Subject Descriptors

H.1 [**Models and Principles**]: Miscellaneous; I.2 [**Artificial Intelligence**]: Miscellaneous

Keywords

Multiarmed bandits; Side observations; Social networks

1. INTRODUCTION

Multi-armed bandit (MAB) problems have received renewed interest over the past decade because of the emergence of content recommendation, online advertising, and social networks. In the classical MAB setting, at each time, a policy must choose an action from a set of K actions with unknown probability distributions Choosing an action i at time t gives a random reward $X_i(t)$ drawn from the distribution of action i. The regret of any policy is defined as the difference between the total reward obtained from the action with the highest average reward and the given policy's total reward. The goal is to find policies that minimize the expected regret over a given time horizon.

In our work, we consider an important MAB setting, similar to that of [12] and [6], where choosing an action i not only generates a reward from action i, but also reveals observations for a subset of the remaining actions. An example of such a scenario is as follows: a decision maker must choose one user at each time in an online social network (FaceBook, etc.) to offer a promotion [6]. Each time the decision maker offers a promotion to a user, he also has an opportunity to survey[1] the user's neighbors in the network regarding their potential interest in a similar offer (see Figure 1). Users are found to be more responsive to such surveys using social network information compared to generic surveys [3] and this effect can be leveraged to construct side-observations. In this example, choosing an action in the multi-armed bandit problem corresponds to choosing a user in the network and side-observations across actions are captured by the links in the social network. Another example is when the actions in the MAB problem are advertisements [12] - the decision maker constructs a graph of different vacation places (Hawaii, Caribbean, Paris, etc.), where links capture similarities between different places. When a customer shows interest in one of the places, he is also asked to provide his opinion about the neighboring places in the graph.

For the setting of side-observations, the authors in [12] consider adversarial bandits, while [6] considers stochastic bandits as in our current work. In [6], the authors propose modified upper-confidence bound (UCB) based policies and show that the regret of these policies is at most $O(\bar{\chi}(G)\log(t))$, where $\bar{\chi}(G)$ is the clique partition number (see Definition 1) of the side-observation network $G(\mathcal{K})$. However, it is possible to achieve a lower regret. For example, in the star network with one central action linked to all other actions, exploring the central action yields sufficient exploration for the rest of the network. In this case, the optimal regret is at most $O(\log(t))$, while $\bar{\chi}(G)$ scales as $O(K)$ for the star network.

[1]This is possible when the online network has an additional survey feature that generates side observations. For example, when user i is offered a promotion, her neighbors may be queried as follows: "User i was recently offered a promotion. Would you also be interested in the offer?"

SIGMETRICS'14, June 16–20, 2014, Austin, Texas, USA.

http://dx.doi.org/10.1145/2591971.2591989.

Motivated by this observation, in our work, we aim to characterize the asymptotic lower bound on the regret for a general stochastic multi-armed bandit problem in the presence of side-observations and investigate policies that achieve this lower bound by taking the network structure into account. Our main contributions are as follows:

- We model the MAB problem in the presence of side-observations and derive an asymptotic (with respect to time) lower bound (as a function of the network structure) on the regret of any uniformly good policy which achieves the maximum long term average reward. This lower bound is presented in terms of the optimal value of a linear program (LP), namely, P_1.
- Motivated by LP P_1, we propose and investigate the performance of a randomized policy, we call ϵ_t-greedy-LP policy, as well as an upper confidence bound based policy, we call UCB-LP policy. Both of these policies *explore each action at a rate that is a function of its network position.* We show that these policies are optimal in the sense that they achieve the asymptotic lower bound on the regret up to a multiplicative constant independent of the network structure under mild assumptions.
- We also show that the upper bound on the regret of our policies scales as $O(\gamma(G)\log(t))$, where $\gamma(G)$ is the size of the minimum dominating set of the network of actions. We show that the regret performance of our policies can be strictly better than those proposed in [6] for some important network structures. Finally, we use numerical results on a social network dataset obtained from Flixster[2] to empirically compare the performance of our policies against those in [6].

The model considered in our work can be viewed as a first step in the direction of more general models of interdependence across actions. For this model, we show that as the number of actions becomes large, significant benefits can be obtained from policies that explicitly take network structure into account. While ϵ_t-greedy-LP policy explores actions at a rate proportional to their network position, its exploration is oblivious to the average rewards of the suboptimal actions. On the other hand, UCB-LP policy takes into account both the upper confidence bounds on the mean rewards as well as network position of different actions at each time. The rest of the paper is organized as follows. In Section 2, we briefly discuss the related existing literature. We introduce the model in Section 3 and we present our main results in Sections 4, 5, 6. Finally, we present some numerical results in Section 7 and the proofs of our theoretical results are given in Section 8. We conclude our work in Section 9.

2. RELATED WORK

The seminal work of [10] shows that the asymptotic lower bound on the regret of any uniformly good policy scales logarithmically with time with a multiplicative constant which is a function of the distributions of actions. Further, the authors of [10] provide constructive policies called Upper Confidence Bound (UCB) policies based on the concept of optimism in the face of uncertainty that asymptotically achieve the lower bound. More recently, the authors in [1] consider the case of bounded rewards and propose simpler sample-mean based UCB policies and decreasing-ϵ_t-greedy policy that achieve logarithmic regret uniformly over time, rather than only asymptotically as in the previous works. The UCB index of any action i at time t introduced in [1] is given below:

$$\bar{x}_i(t) + \sqrt{\frac{2\log(t)}{s_i(t)}}, \quad (1)$$

where $\bar{x}_i(t)$ is the average reward and $s_i(t)$ is the total number of observations available for action i at time t.

The traditional multi-armed bandit policies incur a regret that is linear in the number of suboptimal arms. This makes them unsuitable in settings such as content recommendation, advertising, etc, where the action space is typically very large. To overcome this difficulty, richer models specifying additional information across reward distributions of different actions have been studied, such as dependent bandits [13], $\mathcal{X}$-armed bandits [5], linear bandits [14], contextual side information in bandit problems [11], etc..

More recently, [12] and [6] propose to handle the large number of actions by assuming that choosing an action reveals observations for a larger set of actions. The policies proposed in [12] achieve the best possible regret in the adversarial setting (see [4] for a survey of adversarial MABs) with side-observations and the regret bounds of these policies are in terms of the independence number of the network.

For the setting of stochastic bandits with side-observations, it can be easily shown that, except in the trivial case where all actions have a neighboring action which is optimal, the regret due to any uniformly good policy is lower bounded by $\Omega(\log(t))$. A formal proof is given in [6]. Further, the authors in [6] propose two modified UCB policies, namely, UCB-N and UCB-MaxN, and show that the regret of these policies is at most $O(\bar{\chi}(G)\log(t))$, where $\bar{\chi}(G)$ is the clique partition number (see Definition 1).

In our work, we consider the stochastic MAB problem with side-observations similar to [6] and characterize the asymptotic lower bound on the regret as a function of the network structure for the stochastic MAB problem in the presence of side-observations. Further, we propose two policies: 1) ϵ_t-greedy-LP policy, 2) UCB-LP policy, which achieve the asymptotic regret lower bound up to a multiplicative constant independent of the network structure. Further, the regret of our policies is at most $O(\gamma(G)\log(t))$, where $\gamma(G)$ is the size of the minimum dominating set of the network of actions. Since, $\gamma(G) \leq \bar{\chi}(G)$ for any network G, the regret obtained by our policies can be better than that of UCB-N and UCB-MaxN proposed in [6].

3. MODEL

In this section, we formally define the K-armed bandit problem in the presence of side observations across actions. Let $\mathcal{K} = \{1, \ldots, K\}$ denote the set of actions. A decision maker must choose an action $i \in \mathcal{K}$ at each time t. Let $X_i(t)$ denote the reward obtained by the decision maker on choosing action i at time t. The random variable $X_i(t)$ has an unknown probability distribution F_i. Let μ_i be the mean

[2]Flixster is a movie recommendation network with a social graph. Datasets from this network are made publicly available by authors of [9] at `http://www.cs.ubc.ca/~jamalim/datasets/`.

of the random variable $X_i(t)$. We assume that $\{X_i(t), t \geq 0\}$ are *i.i.d* for each i and $\{X_i(t), \forall i \in \mathcal{K}\}$ are independent for each time t. We further assume that the distribution, F_i has a bounded support in $[0, b]$ for each i. We let $b = 1$ for simplicity of exposition in our work.

Side-observation model : The actions $\mathcal{K}$ form nodes in a network $G(\mathcal{K})$, represented by the adjacency matrix $G = [g(i,j)]_{i,j\in\mathcal{K}}$, where $g(i,j) \in \{0,1\}$ and $g(i,i) = 1$ for all i. Let $\mathcal{K}_i$ be the set of neighbors of action i (including i), i.e, $g(j,i) = 1, \forall j \in \mathcal{K}_i$. While all the results in our work can be easily extended to directed networks, we assume that $G(\mathcal{K})$ is undirected for simplicity of notation.

We assume that when the decision maker chooses an action i at time t, he receives a reward $X_i(t)$ and also receives observations $X_j(t)$, for all $j \in \mathcal{K}_i$ such that $\mathbb{E}[X_j(t)] = \mu_j$. In general, not all neighboring actions are equally responsive in providing side-observations. This scenario can be modeled by assuming that each action i has a known probability p_i of providing side-observations when any of its neighbors are actually chosen. We let $p_i = 1$ for all i for the sake of clarity. Our results can be easily extended to the setting of imperfect side-observations with $p_i \leq 1$. We will discuss this extension in Remark 5 in Section 6.

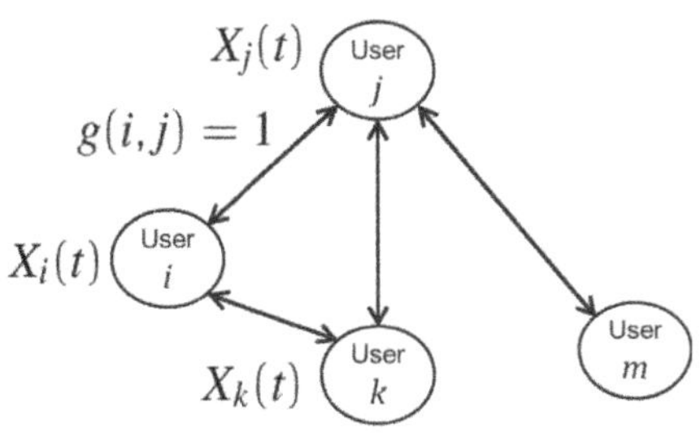

Figure 1: At time t, suppose the decision maker chooses user i to offer a promotion. He then receives a response $X_i(t)$ from user i. Using the social interconnections, he also observes responses $X_j(t)$ and $X_k(t)$ of i's neighbors j and k.

Figure 1 illustrates the side-observation model for the example of targeting users in an online social network. Such side observations are made possible in settings of online social networks like Facebook by surveying or tracking a user's neighbors reactions (likes, dislikes, no opinion, etc.) to the user's activity. This is possible when the online social network has a survey or a like/dislike indicator that generates side observations. For example, when user i is offered a promotion, her neighbors may be queried as follows: "User i was recently offered a promotion. Would you also be interested in the offer?[3]"

Objective: An allocation strategy or policy ϕ chooses the action to be played at each time. Formally, ϕ is a sequence of random variables $\{\phi(t), t \geq 0\}$, where $\phi(t) \in \mathcal{K}$ is the action chosen by policy ϕ at time t. Let $\mathbf{X}^\phi(t)$ be the reward and side-observations obtained by the policy ϕ at time t. Then, the event $\{\phi_i(t) = i\}$ belongs to the σ-field generated by $\{\phi(m), \mathbf{X}^\phi(m), m \leq t-1\}$.

[3]Since, the neighbors do not have any information on whether the user i accepted the promotion, they act independently according to their own preferences in answering this survey. The network itself provides a better way for surveying and obtaining side observations.

Let $T_i^\phi(t)$ be the total number of times action i is chosen up to time t by policy ϕ. For each action, rewards are only obtained when the action is chosen by the policy (side-observations do not contribute to the total reward). Then, the regret of policy ϕ at time t for a fixed $\boldsymbol{\mu} = (\mu_1, \ldots, \mu_K)$ is defined by

$$R_{\boldsymbol{\mu}}^\phi(t) = \mu^* t - \sum_{i=1}^{K} \mu_i \mathbb{E}[T_i^\phi(t)] = \sum_{i=1}^{K} \Delta_i \mathbb{E}[T_i^\phi(t)],$$

where $\Delta_i \triangleq \mu^* - \mu_i$ and $\mu^* \triangleq \max_{i\in\mathcal{K}} \mu_i$. Henceforth, we drop the superscript ϕ unless it is required. The objective is to find policies that minimize the rate at which the regret grows as a function of time for every fixed network $G(\mathcal{K})$. We focus our investigation on the class of uniformly good policies [10] defined below:

Uniformly good policies: An allocation rule ϕ is said to be uniformly good if for every fixed $\boldsymbol{\mu}$, the following condition is satisfied as $t \to \infty$:

$$R_{\boldsymbol{\mu}}(t) = o(t^b), \text{ for every } b > 0.$$

The above condition implies that uniformly good policies achieve the optimal long term average reward of μ^*. Next, we define two structures that will be useful later to bound the performance of allocation strategies in terms of the network structure $G(\mathcal{K})$.

Definition 1. A *clique covering* $\mathcal{C}$ of a network $G(\mathcal{K})$ is a partition of all its nodes into sets $C \in \mathcal{C}$ such that the sub-network formed by each C is a clique. Let $\bar{\chi}(G)$ be the smallest number of cliques into which the nodes of the network $G(\mathcal{K})$ can be partitioned, also called the clique partition number.

Definition 2. A *dominating set* $\mathcal{D}$ of a network $G(\mathcal{K})$ is such that every node in the network is either in $\mathcal{D}$ or has at least one neighbor in $\mathcal{D}$. Let $\gamma(G)$ denote the size of the minimum dominating set of network $G(\mathcal{K})$, also called the domination number. Note that $\gamma(G) \leq \bar{\chi}(G)$ for any network $G(\mathcal{K})$.

In the next section, we obtain an asymptotic lower bound on the regret of uniformly good policies for the setting of MABs with side-observations. This lower bound is expressed as the optimal value of a linear program (LP), where the constraints of the LP capture the connectivity of each action in the network.

4. REGRET LOWER BOUND

In order to derive a lower bound on the regret, we need some mild regularity assumptions (Assumptions 1, 2, and 3) on the distributions F_i that are similar to the ones in [10]. Let the probability distribution F_i have a univariate density function $f(x;\theta_i)$ with unknown parameters θ_i. Let $D(\theta||\sigma)$ denote the Kullback Leibler (KL) distance between distributions with density functions $f(x;\theta)$ and $f(x;\sigma)$ and with means $\mu(\theta)$ and $\mu(\sigma)$ respectively.

ASSUMPTION 1. *(Finiteness) We assume that $f(\cdot;\cdot)$ is such that $0 < D(\theta||\sigma) < \infty$ whenever $\mu(\sigma) > \mu(\theta)$.*

ASSUMPTION 2. *(Continuity) For any $\epsilon > 0$ and θ, σ such that $\mu(\sigma) > \mu(\theta)$, there exists $\eta > 0$ for which $|D(\theta||\sigma) - D(\theta||\rho)| < \epsilon$ whenever $\mu(\sigma) < \mu(\rho) < \mu(\sigma) + \eta$.*

ASSUMPTION 3. *(Denseness) For each $i \in \mathcal{K}$, $\theta_i \in \Theta$ where the set Θ satisfies: for all $\theta \in \Theta$ and for all $\eta > 0$, there exists $\theta' \in \Theta$ such that $\mu(\theta) < \mu(\theta') < \mu(\theta) + \eta$.*

The following proposition is obtained using Theorem 2 in [10]. It provides an asymptotic lower bound on the regret of any uniformly good policy under the model described in Section 3:

PROPOSITION 1. *Suppose Assumptions 1, 2, and 3 hold. Let $\mathcal{U} = \{i : \mu_i < \mu^*\}$ be the set of suboptimal actions. Also, let $\Delta_i = \mu^* - \mu_i$. Recall that $\mathcal{K}_i$ is the set of neighbors of i, including i, in the network $G(\mathcal{K})$. Then, under any uniformly good policy ϕ, the expected regret is asymptotically bounded below as follows:*

$$\liminf_{t\to\infty} \frac{R_{\boldsymbol{\mu}}(t)}{\log(t)} \geq c_{\boldsymbol{\mu}}, \tag{2}$$

where $c_{\boldsymbol{\mu}}$ is the optimal value of the following linear program (LP) P_1:

$$P_1 : \min \sum_{i\in\mathcal{U}} \Delta_i w_i,$$

$$\textit{subject to: } \sum_{j\in\mathcal{K}_i} w_j \geq \frac{1}{D(\theta_i||\theta^*)}, \ \forall i \in \mathcal{U},$$

$$w_i \geq 0, \ \forall i \in \mathcal{K}.$$

PROOF. *(Sketch)* Let $S_i(t)$ be the total number of observations corresponding to action i available at time t. Then, by modifying the proof of Theorem 2 of [10], we have that, for $i \in \mathcal{U}$,

$$\liminf_{t\to\infty} \frac{\mathbb{E}[S_i(t)]}{\log(t)} \geq \frac{1}{D(\theta_i||\theta^*)}.$$

An observation is received for action i whenever any action in $\mathcal{K}_i$ is chosen. Hence, $S_i(t) = \sum_{j\in\mathcal{K}_i} T_j(t)$. These two facts give us the constraints in LP P_1. See Section 8 for the full proof. □

The linear program given in P_1 contains the graphical information that governs the lower bound. However, it requires the knowledge of θ_i and θ^*, which are unknown. This motivates the construction of the following linear program, LP P_2, which preserves the graphical structure while eliminating the distributional dependence on θ_i and θ^*.

$$P_2 : \min \sum_{i\in\mathcal{K}} z_i$$

$$\text{subject to: } \sum_{j\in\mathcal{K}_i} z_j \geq 1, \ \forall i \in \mathcal{K},$$

$$\text{and } z_i \geq 0, \ \forall i \in \mathcal{K}.$$

Let $\mathbf{z}^* = (z_i^*)_{i\in\mathcal{K}}$ be the optimal solution of LP P_2. In Sections 5 and 6, we use the above LP P_2 to modify the ϵ-greedy policy in [1] and UCB policy in [2] for the setting of side-observations. We provide regret guarantees of these modified policies in terms of the optimal value $\sum_{i\in\mathcal{K}} z_i^*$ of LP P_2. We note that the linear program P_2 is, in fact, the LP relaxation of the minimum dominating set problem on network $G(\mathcal{K})$. Since, any dominating set of network $G(\mathcal{K})$ is a feasible solution to the LP P_2, we have that the optimal value of the LP $\sum_{i\in\mathcal{K}} z_i^* \leq \gamma(G) \leq \bar{\chi}(G)$. As we will see in Remark 2, for a rich network structure, it is possible to have $\gamma(G) << \bar{\chi}(G)$.

In the next proposition, we provide a lower bound on $c_{\boldsymbol{\mu}}$ in Equation (2) using the optimal solution $\mathbf{z}^* = (z_i^*)_{i\in\mathcal{K}}$ of LP P_2.

PROPOSITION 2. *Let $\mathcal{U} = \{i : \mu_i < \mu_i^*\}$ be the set of suboptimal actions. Let $\mathcal{O} = \{i : \mu_i = \mu^*\}$ be the set of optimal actions. Then,*

$$\frac{\max_{i\in\mathcal{U}} D(\theta_i||\theta^*)}{\min_{i\in\mathcal{U}} \Delta_i} c_{\boldsymbol{\mu}} + |\mathcal{O}| \geq \sum_{i\in\mathcal{K}} z_i^* \geq \frac{\min_{i\in\mathcal{U}} D(\theta_i||\theta^*)}{\max_{i\in\mathcal{U}} \Delta_i} c_{\boldsymbol{\mu}}. \tag{3}$$

PROOF. *(Sketch)* Let $\mathcal{I} = \{i \in \mathcal{U} : \mathcal{K}_i \cap \mathcal{O} \neq \emptyset\}$ be the set of suboptimal actions with neighbors in $\mathcal{O}$. Using the optimal solution of LP P_1, we construct a feasible solution satisfying constraints in LP P_2 for actions in $\mathcal{U} \setminus \mathcal{I}$. In order to satisfy the constraints for actions in $\mathcal{I} \cup \mathcal{O}$, we use $z_i = 1$ for all i in $\mathcal{O}$. The feasible solution constructed in this way gives an upper bound on the optimal value of LP P_2 in terms of the optimal value of LP P_1. For the lower bound, any feasible solution of P_2, in particular $\mathbf{z}^*$, can be used to construct a feasible solution of P_1. See Section 8 for the full proof. □

$\sum_{i\in\mathcal{K}} z_i^* = \Theta(c_{\boldsymbol{\mu}})$ completely captures the time dependence of regret on network structure under the following assumption:

ASSUMPTION 4. *The quantities $|\mathcal{O}|$, $\min_{i\in\mathcal{U}} \Delta_i$, and $\min_{i\in\mathcal{U}} D(\theta_i||\theta^*)$ are constants that are independent of network size K.*

Note that the constants in the above assumption are unknown to the decision maker. In the next section, we propose the ϵ_t-greedy-LP policy which achieves the regret lower bound of $c_{\boldsymbol{\mu}} \log(t)$ up to a multiplicative constant factor that is independent of the network structure and time.

5. EPSILON-GREEDY-LP POLICY

Motivated by the LPs P_1 and P_2, we propose a *network-aware* randomized policy called the ϵ_t-greedy-LP policy. We provide an upper bound on the regret of this policy and show that it achieves the asymptotic lower bound up to a constant multiplier, independent of network structure. Let $\bar{x}_i(t)$ be the empirical average of observations (rewards and side-observations combined) available for action i up to time t. The ϵ_t-greedy-LP policy is described in Algorithm 1. The policy consists of two phases - exploitation and exploration, where the exploration probability decreases as $1/t$, similar to the ϵ_t-greedy policy proposed in [1]. However, in our policy, we choose the exploration probability for action i to be proportional to z_i^*/t, where $\mathbf{z}^*$ is the optimal solution of LP P_2, while in the original policy in [1], the exploration probability is uniform over all actions.

The following proposition provides performance guarantees on the ϵ_t-greedy-LP policy:

PROPOSITION 3. *For $0 < d < \min_{i\in\mathcal{U}} \Delta_i$, any $c > 0$, and $\alpha > 1$, the probability with which a suboptimal action i is selected by the ϵ_t-greedy-LP policy, described in Algorithm 1,*

Algorithm 1 : ϵ_t-greedy-LP

Input: $c > 0$, $0 < d < 1$, optimal solution $\mathbf{z}^*$ of LP P_2.
for each time t **do**

Let $\epsilon(t) = \min\left(1, \frac{c\sum_{i\in\mathcal{K}} z_i^*}{d^2 t}\right)$ and $a^* = \arg\max_{i\in\mathcal{K}} \bar{x}_i(t)$.

With probability $1-\epsilon(t)$, pick action $\phi(t) = a^*$

With probability $\epsilon(t)$, pick action $\phi(t) = i$ with probability $\frac{z_i^*}{\sum_{i\in\mathcal{K}} z_i^*}$ for all $i \in \mathcal{K}$.

end for

Update average rewards $\bar{x}_v(t+1), \forall v \in \mathcal{K}_{\phi(t)}$.

for all $t > t' = \frac{c\sum_{i\in\mathcal{K}} z_i^*}{d^2}$ *is at most*

$$\left(\frac{c}{d^2 t} z_i^*\right) + \frac{4}{d^2}\left(\frac{et'}{t}\right)^{c/2\alpha} + \frac{2\delta c}{\alpha d^2}\left(\frac{et'}{t}\right)^{cr/\alpha d^2} \log\left(\frac{e^2 t}{t'}\right), \tag{4}$$

where $r = \frac{3(\alpha-1)^2}{8\alpha-2}$, *and* δ *is the maximum degree in the network.*

Proof. *(Sketch)* Since $\mathbf{z}^*$ satisfies the constraints in LP P_2, there is sufficient exploration within each suboptimal action's neighborhood. The proof is then a combination of this fact and the proof of Theorem 3 in [1]. See Section 8 for the full proof. □

In the above proposition, for large enough c, we see that second and third terms are $O(1/t^{1+\epsilon})$ for some $\epsilon > 0$ [1]. Using this fact, the following corollary bounds the expected regret of the ϵ_t-greedy-LP policy:

Corollary 1. *Choose parameters c and d such that,*

$$0 < d < \min_{i\in\mathcal{U}} \Delta_i, \quad \text{and} \quad c > \max(2\alpha d^2/r, 2\alpha),$$

for any $\alpha > 1$. *Then, the expected regret at time t of the* ϵ_t*-greedy-LP policy described in Algorithm 1 is at most*

$$\left(\frac{c}{d^2}\sum_{i\in\mathcal{U}} \Delta_i z_i^*\right)\log(t) + O(K), \tag{5}$$

where the $O(K)$ *term captures constants independent of time but dependent on the network structure.*

Remark 1. Under Assumption 4, we can see from Proposition 2 and Corollary 1 that, ϵ_t-greedy-LP algorithm is *order optimal* achieving the lower bound $O\left(\sum_{i\in\mathcal{U}} z_i^* \log(t)\right) = O\left(c_\mu \log(t)\right)$ as the network and time scale.

While ϵ_t-greedy-LP policy is network aware, its exploration is oblivious to the average rewards of the sub-optimal actions. Further, its performance guarantees depend on the knowledge of $\min_{i\in\mathcal{U}} \Delta_i$, which is the difference between the best and the second best optimal actions. On the other hand, the UCB-LP policy proposed in the next section is network-aware taking into account the average rewards of suboptimal actions. This could lead to better performance compared to ϵ_t-greedy-LP policy in certain situations, for example, when the highly connected action is also highly suboptimal.

6. UCB-LP POLICY

In this section we propose the UCB-LP policy defined in Algorithm 2 and obtain upper bounds on its regret. The UCB-LP policy is based on the improved UCB policy proposed in [2], which can be summarized as follows: the policy estimates the values of Δ_i in each round by a value $\tilde{\Delta}_m$ which is initialized to 1 and halved in each round m. By each round m, the policy draws $n(m)$ observations for each action in the set of actions not eliminated by round m, where $n(m)$ is determined by $\tilde{\Delta}_m$. Then, it eliminates those actions whose UCB indices perform poorly. Our policy differs from the one in [2] by accounting for the presence of side-observations - this is achieved by choosing each action according to the optimal solution of LP P_2, while ensuring that $n(m)$ observations are available for each action not eliminated by round m.

Algorithm 2 : UCB-LP policy

Input: Set of actions $\mathcal{K}$, time horizon T, and optimal solution $\mathbf{z}^*$ of LP P_2.

Initialization: Let $\tilde{\Delta}_0 := 1$, $S_0 := \mathcal{K}$, and $B_0 := \mathcal{K}$
for round $m = 0, 1, 2, \ldots, \lfloor \frac{1}{2}\log_2 \frac{T}{e} \rfloor$ **do**

Action Selection: Let $n(m) := \left\lceil \frac{2\log(T\tilde{\Delta}_m^2)}{\tilde{\Delta}_m^2} \right\rceil$

If $|B_m| == 1$: choose the single action in B_m until time T.

Else If $\sum_{i\in S_m} z_i^* \le 2|B_m|\tilde{\Delta}_m$: For each action i in S_m, choose it $z_i^*\,[n(m) - n(m-1)]$ times.

Else For each action i in B_m, choose it $[n(m) - n(m-1)]$ times.

Update the average rewards of all actions in B_m.

Action Elimination:
To get B_{m+1}, delete all actions i in B_m for which

$$\bar{x}_i(m) + \sqrt{\frac{\log(T\tilde{\Delta}_m^2)}{2s_i(m)}} \le \max_{a\in B_m}\left\{\bar{x}_a(m) - \sqrt{\frac{\log(T\tilde{\Delta}_m^2)}{2s_a(m)}}\right\},$$

where $\bar{x}_i(m)$ is the empirical average reward of action i, and $s_i(m)$ is the total number of observations for action i up to round m.

Reset:
The set S_{m+1} of actions with neighbors in B_{m+1} is given as $S_{m+1} = \{i : \mathcal{K}_i \cap B_{m+1} \neq \emptyset\}$. Note that $B_{m+1} \subseteq S_{m+1}$.
Let $\tilde{\Delta}_{m+1} = \frac{\tilde{\Delta}_m}{2}$.

end for

The following proposition provides performance guarantees on the expected regret due to UCB-LP policy:

Proposition 4. *For action i, define round* m_i *as follows:*

$$m_i := \min\left\{m : \tilde{\Delta}_m < \frac{\Delta_i}{2}\right\}.$$

Define $\bar{m} = \min\left\{m : \sum_{i\in\mathcal{K}} z_i^* > \sum_{i:m_i>m} 2^{-m+1}\right\}$ *and the set* $B = \{i \in \mathcal{U} : m_i > \bar{m}\}$.

Then, the expected regret due to the UCB-LP policy described in Algorithm 2 is at most

$$\sum_{i\in\mathcal{U}\setminus B} \Delta_i z_i^* \frac{32\log(T\hat{\Delta}_i^2)}{\hat{\Delta}_i^2} + \sum_{i\in B} \frac{32\log(T\Delta_i^2)}{\Delta_i} + O(K\delta), \quad (6)$$

where $\hat{\Delta}_i = \max\{2^{-\bar{m}+2}, \min_{\mathcal{K}_i}\{\Delta_j\}\}$ *and* (z_i^*) *is the solution of LP* P_2. δ *is the maximum degree in the network. The* $O(K\delta)$ *term captures constants independent of time. Further, under Assumption 4, the regret is also at most*

$$O\left(\sum_{i\in\mathcal{K}} z_i^* \log(T)\right) + O(K\delta), \quad (7)$$

where (z_i^*) *entirely captures the time dependence on network structure.*

PROOF. *(Sketch)* The $\log(T)$ term in the regret follows from the fact that, with high probability, each suboptimal action i is eliminated (from the set B_m) on or before the first round m such that $\tilde{\Delta}_m < \Delta_i/2$. See Section 8 for the full proof. □

Next, we briefly describe the policies UCB-N and UCB-MaxN proposed in [6]. In UCB-N policy, at each time, the action with the highest UCB index (see (1)) is chosen similar to UCB1 policy in [1]. In UCB-MaxN policy, at each time t, the action i with the highest UCB index (1) is identified and its neighboring action $j \in \mathcal{K}_i$ with the highest empirical average reward at time t is chosen.

Remark 2. The regret upper bound of UCB-N policy is

$$\inf_{\mathcal{C}} \sum_{C\in\mathcal{C}} \frac{8\max_{i\in C}\Delta_i}{\min_{i\in C}\Delta_i^2}\log(T) + O(K),$$

where $\mathcal{C}$ is a clique covering of the sub-network of suboptimal actions. The regret upper bound for UCB-MaxN is the same as that for UCB-N with an $O(|\mathcal{C}|)$ term instead of the time-invariant $O(K)$ term. We show a better regret performance for UCB-LP policy and ϵ_t-greedy-LP policies with respect to the $\log(T)$ term because $\sum_{i\in\mathcal{K}} z_i^* \le \gamma(G) \le \bar{\chi}(G)$. However, the time-invariant term in our policies is $O(K)$ and $O(K\delta)$, which can be worse than the time-invariant term $O(|\mathcal{C}|)$ in UCB-MaxN.

To see the possible gap between $\gamma(G)$ and $\bar{\chi}(G)$, consider an Erdos-Renyi random graph $G(K,p)$. As noted in [12], as $K \to \infty$, for any fixed $p > 0$, $\gamma(G)$ is at most $O(\log(K))$ while $\bar{\chi}(G)$ is at least $O(K/\log(K))$. On the other hand, it has been shown [7] that for power law graphs, both $\gamma(G)$ and $\bar{\chi}(G)$ scale linearly with N, although $\gamma(G)$ has a lower slope. We note that the social network of interest may or may not display a power law behavior. We find that the subgraphs of the Flixster network have a degree distribution that is a straight line on a log-log plot indicating a power law distribution display while the authors in [15] show that the degree distribution of the global Facebook network is not a straight line on log-log plot. Our numerical results in Section 7 show that our policies outperform existing policies even for the Flixster network.

Remark 3. All uniformly good policies that ignore side-observations incur a regret that is at least $\Omega(|\mathcal{U}|\log(t))$ [10], where $|\mathcal{U}|$ is the number of suboptimal actions. This could be significantly higher than the guarantees on the regret of both ϵ_t-greedy-LP policy and UCB-LP policy for a rich network structure as discussed in Remark 2.

Remark 4. While ϵ_t-greedy-LP does not require knowledge of the time horizon T, UCB-LP policy requires the knowledge of T. UCB-LP policy can be extended to the case of an unknown time horizon similar to the suggestion in [2]. Start with $T_0 = 2$ and at end of each T_l, set $T_{l+1} = T_l^2$. The regret bound for this case is expected to be similar to the one in Proposition 4.

Remark 5. In our work, we assumed that the side observations are always available. However, in reality, side observations may only be obtained sporadically. Suppose that when action i is chosen, side-observations are obtained for each neighboring action j with a known probability p_j. In this case, Proposition 1 holds with the replacement of LP P_1 with LP P_1' as follows:

$$P_1' : \min \sum_{i\in\mathcal{U}} \Delta_i w_i,$$

$$\text{subject to: } w_i + p_i \sum_{j\in\mathcal{K}_i\setminus\{i\}} w_j \ge \frac{1}{D(\theta_i||\theta^*)}, \ \forall i \in \mathcal{U},$$

$$w_i \ge 0, \ \forall i \in \mathcal{K}.$$

Both of our policies work for this setting by changing the LP P_2 to P_2' as follows:

$$P_2' : \min \sum_{i\in\mathcal{K}} z_i$$

$$\text{subject to: } z_i + p_i \sum_{j\in\mathcal{K}_i\setminus\{i\}} z_j \ge 1, \ \forall i \in \mathcal{K},$$

$$\text{and } z_i \ge 0, \ \forall i \in \mathcal{K}.$$

The regret bounds of our policies will now depend on the optimal solution of LP P_2'.

7. NUMERICAL RESULTS

We consider the Flixster network dataset for the numerical evaluation of our algorithms. The authors in [9] collected this social network data, which contains about 1 million users and 14 million links. We use graph clustering [8] to identify two strongly clustered sub-networks of sizes 1000 and 2000 nodes. Both these sub-networks have a degree distribution that is a straight line on a log-log plot indicating a power law distribution commonly observed in social networks.

Our empirical setup is as follows. Each user in the network is offered a promotion at each time, and accepts the promotion with probability $\mu_i \in [0.3, 0.9]$. The decision maker receives a random reward of 1 if a user accepts the promotion or 0 reward otherwise. μ_i is chosen uniformly at random from $[0.3, 0.8]$ and there are 50 randomly chosen users with optimal $\mu_i = 0.9$. Figures 2 and 3 show the regret performance as a function of time for the two sub-networks of sizes 1000 and 2000 respectively. For the ϵ_t-greedy-LP policy, we let $c = 5$ and $d = 0.2$. For both networks, we see that our policies outperform the UCB-N and UCB-MaxN policies.

We also observe that the improvement obtained by UCB-N policy over the baseline UCB1 policy is marginal.

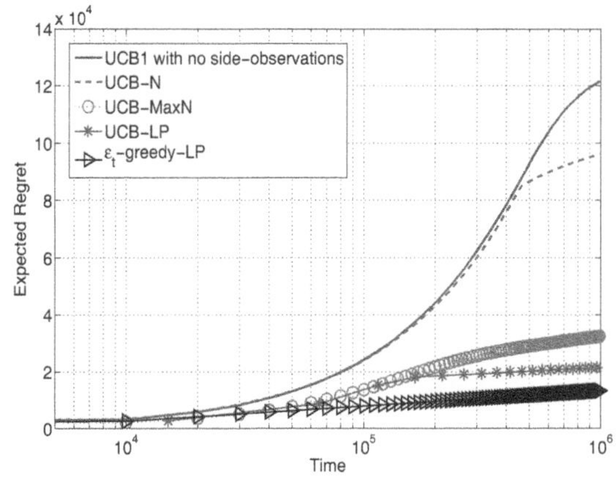

Figure 2: Regret of all the policies for a network of size 1000.

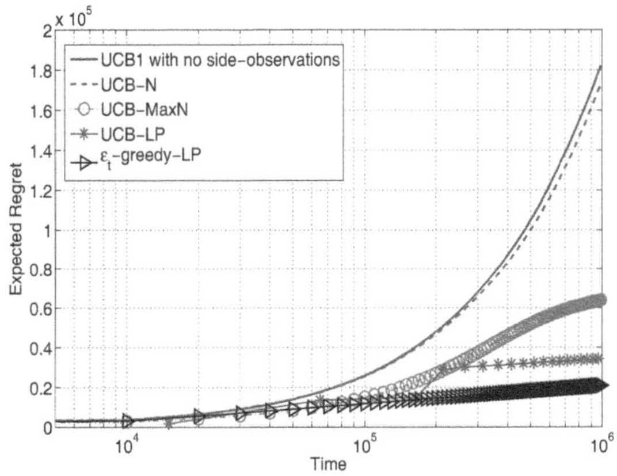

Figure 3: Regret of all the policies for a network of size 2000.

8. PROOFS

In what follows, we give the proofs of all propositions stated in the earlier sections. These proofs make use of Lemmas 1, 2, and 3, and Proposition 5 given in the Appendix.

Proof of Proposition 1

Let $\mathcal{U} = \{i : \mu_i < \mu^*\}$ be the set of suboptimal actions. Also, let $\Delta_i = \mu^* - \mu_i$. Recall that $\mathcal{K}_i$ is the set of neighbors of i, including i, in the network $G(\mathcal{K})$. Also, $T_i(t)$ is the total number of times action i is chosen up to time t by policy ϕ. Let $S_i(t)$ be the total number of observations corresponding to action i available at time t. From Proposition 5 given in the Appendix, we have,

$$\liminf_{t\to\infty} \frac{\mathbb{E}[S_i(t)]}{\log(t)} \geq \frac{1}{D(\theta_i||\theta^*)}, \ \forall i \in \mathcal{U}. \tag{8}$$

An observation is received for action i whenever any action in $\mathcal{K}_i$ is chosen. Hence,

$$S_i(t) = \sum_{j\in\mathcal{K}_i} T_j(t). \tag{9}$$

Now, from Equations (8) and (9), for each $i \in \mathcal{U}$,

$$\liminf_{t\to\infty} \frac{\sum_{j\in\mathcal{K}_i}\mathbb{E}[T_j(t)]}{\log(t)} \geq \frac{1}{D(\theta_i||\theta^*)}. \tag{10}$$

Using (10), we get the constraints of LP P_1. Further, we have from definition of regret that,

$$\liminf_{t\to\infty} \frac{R_\mu(t)}{\log(t)} = \liminf_{t\to\infty} \sum_{i\in\mathcal{U}} \Delta_i \frac{\mathbb{E}[T_i(t)]}{\log(t)}.$$

The above equation along with the constraints of the LP P_1 obtained from (10) gives us the required lower bound on regret.

Proof of Proposition 2

Let $\mathcal{I} = \{i \in \mathcal{U} : \mathcal{K}_i \cap \mathcal{O} \neq \emptyset\}$ be the set of suboptimal actions with neighbors in $\mathcal{O}$. Let $(z_i^*)_{i\in\mathcal{K}}$ be the optimal solution of LP P_2.

We will first prove the upper bound in Equation 3. Using the optimal solution $(w_i^*)_{i\in\mathcal{K}}$ of LP P_1, we construct a feasible solution satisfying constraints in LP P_2 in the following way: For actions $i \in \mathcal{U}$, let $z_i = \left(\max_{i\in\mathcal{U}} D(\theta_i||\theta^*)\right) w_i^*$. Then $(z_i)_{i\in\mathcal{U}}$ satisfy constraints for all actions $i \in \mathcal{U}\setminus\mathcal{I}$ because w_i^* satisfy constraints of LP P_1.

In order to satisfy the constraints for actions in $\mathcal{I}\cup\mathcal{O}$, we use $z_i = 1$ for all i in $\mathcal{O}$. The feasible solution constructed in this way gives an upper bound on the optimal value of LP P_2. Hence,

$$\begin{aligned}\sum_{i\in\mathcal{K}} z_i^* &\leq \sum_{i\in\mathcal{U}} z_i + |\mathcal{O}| \\ &\leq \sum_{i\in\mathcal{U}} \left(\max_{i\in\mathcal{U}} D(\theta_i||\theta^*)\right) w_i^* + |\mathcal{O}| \\ &\leq \frac{\max_{i\in\mathcal{U}} D(\theta_i||\theta^*)}{\min_{i\in\mathcal{U}}\Delta_i} \sum_{i\in\mathcal{U}} \Delta_i w_i^* + |\mathcal{O}| \\ &\leq \frac{\max_{i\in\mathcal{U}} D(\theta_i||\theta^*)}{\min_{i\in\mathcal{U}}\Delta_i} c_\mu + |\mathcal{O}|\end{aligned}$$

For the lower bound, any feasible solution of P_2, in particular $\mathbf{z}^*$, can be used to construct a feasible solution of P_1. For actions $i \in \mathcal{K}$, let $w_i = \frac{z_i^*}{\min_{i\in\mathcal{U}} D(\theta_i||\theta^*)}$. Then $(w_i)_{i\in\mathcal{K}}$ satisfies the constraints of LP P_1 and hence gives an upper bound on its optimal value. Therefore, we have

$$\begin{aligned} c_\mu &= \sum_{i\in\mathcal{U}} \Delta_i w_i^*, \\ &\leq \sum_{i\in\mathcal{K}} \frac{\Delta_i z_i^*}{\min_{i\in\mathcal{U}} D(\theta_i||\theta^*)} \\ &\leq \sum_{i\in\mathcal{K}} \frac{\max_{i\in\mathcal{U}}\Delta_i z_i^*}{\min_{i\in\mathcal{U}} D(\theta_i||\theta^*)}\end{aligned}$$

which gives us the required lower bound.

Proof of Proposition 3

Since $\mathbf{z}^*$ satisfies the constraints in LP P_2, there is sufficient exploration within each suboptimal action's neighborhood. The proof is then a combination of this fact and the proof of Theorem 3 in [1]. Let $\bar{X}_i(t)$ be the random variable denoting the sample mean of all observations available for action i at time t. Let $\bar{X}^*(t)$ be the random variable denoting the sample mean of all observations available for an optimal action at time t. Let $X_{i,m}$ denote the sample mean of m random variables drawn from the distribution F_i. Fix a suboptimal action i. For some $\alpha > 1$, define m_i as follows,

$$m_i = \frac{1}{\alpha}\frac{\sum_{j\in\mathcal{K}_i} z_j^*}{\sum_{j\in\mathcal{K}} z_i^*}\sum_{m=1}^{t}\epsilon(m)$$

Let $\phi(t)$ be the action chosen by ϵ_t-greedy-LP policy at time t. Then,

$$\mathbb{P}[\phi(t) = i] \leq \frac{\epsilon(t)z_i^*}{\sum_{i\in\mathcal{K}} z_i^*} + (1-\epsilon(t))\mathbb{P}[\bar{X}_i(t) \geq \bar{X}^*(t)]$$

We also have that,

$$\mathbb{P}[\bar{X}_i(t) \geq \bar{X}^*(t)] \leq \mathbb{P}\left[\bar{X}_i(t) \geq \mu_i + \frac{\Delta_i}{2}\right] + \mathbb{P}\left[\bar{X}^*(t) \leq \mu^* - \frac{\Delta_i}{2}\right].$$

The analysis of both the terms in the right hand side of the above expression is similar. Let $S_i^{(R)}(t)$ be the total number of observations available for action i from the exploration phase of the policy up to time t. Let $S_i(t)$ be the total number of observations available for action i up to time t. Hence, we have,

$$\begin{aligned}
\mathbb{P}\left[\bar{X}_i(t) \geq \mu_i + \frac{\Delta_i}{2}\right] &= \sum_{m=1}^{t}\mathbb{P}\left[S_i(t) = m; \bar{X}_i(t) \geq \mu_i + \frac{\Delta_i}{2}\right] \\
&= \sum_{m=1}^{t}\mathbb{P}\left[S_i(t) = m | \bar{X}_{i,m} \geq \mu_i + \frac{\Delta_i}{2}\right]\mathbb{P}\left[\bar{X}_{i,m} \geq \mu_i + \frac{\Delta_i}{2}\right] \\
&\leq \sum_{m=1}^{\lfloor t\rfloor}\mathbb{P}\left[S_i(t) = m | \bar{X}_{i,m} \geq \mu_i + \frac{\Delta_i}{2}\right] e^{\frac{-\Delta_i^2 m}{2}}
\end{aligned}$$

(follows from Chernoff-Hoeffding bound in Lemma 1)

$$\leq \sum_{m=1}^{\lfloor m_i\rfloor}\mathbb{P}\left[S_i(t) = m | \bar{X}_{i,m} \geq \mu_i + \frac{\Delta_i}{2}\right] + \frac{2}{\Delta_i^2}e^{\frac{-\Delta_i^2 m_i}{2}}$$

$$\left(\text{since } \sum_{m+1}^{\infty} e^{-ku} = \frac{1}{k}e^{-km}\right)$$

$$\leq \sum_{m=1}^{\lfloor m_i\rfloor}\mathbb{P}\left[S_i^{(R)}(t) \leq m | \bar{X}_{i,m} \geq \mu_i + \frac{\Delta_i}{2}\right] + \frac{2}{\Delta_i^2}e^{\frac{-\Delta_i^2 m_i}{2}}$$

$$\leq m_i \mathbb{P}\left[S_i^{(R)}(t) \leq m_i\right] + \frac{2}{d^2}e^{\frac{-d^2 m_i}{2}}$$

In the above, the last equation follows from the fact that $S_i^{(R)}(t)$, which is the total number of observations for action i available from the exploration phase of the policy up to time t, is independent of the sample means of all actions. Now,

$$\begin{aligned}
\mathbb{E}\left[S_i^{(R)}(t)\right] &= \sum_{m=1}^{t}\epsilon(m)\sum_{j\in\mathcal{K}_i}\frac{z_j^*}{\sum_{j\in\mathcal{K}} z_i^*} \\
&= \frac{\sum_{j\in\mathcal{K}_i} z_j^*}{\sum_{j\in\mathcal{K}} z_i^*}\sum_{m=1}^{t}\epsilon(m) = \alpha m_i
\end{aligned}$$

$$\begin{aligned}
var\left[S_i^{(R)}(t)\right] &= \sum_{m=1}^{t}\left[\epsilon(m)\sum_{j\in\mathcal{K}_i}\frac{z_j^*}{\sum_{j\in\mathcal{K}} z_i^*} - \left(\epsilon(m)\sum_{j\in\mathcal{K}_i}\frac{z_j^*}{\sum_{j\in\mathcal{K}} z_i^*}\right)^2\right] \\
&\leq \sum_{m=1}^{t}\epsilon(m)\sum_{j\in\mathcal{K}_i}\frac{z_j^*}{\sum_{j\in\mathcal{K}} z_i^*} = \mathbb{E}\left[S_i^{(R)}(t)\right]
\end{aligned}$$

Now, using Bernstein's inequality given in Lemma 2, we have

$$\begin{aligned}
\mathbb{P}\left[S_i^{(R)}(t) \leq m_i\right] &= \mathbb{P}\left[S_i^{(R)}(t) \leq \mathbb{E}\left[S_i^{(R)}(t)\right] - (\alpha-1)m_i\right] \\
&\leq \exp(-rm_i),
\end{aligned}$$

where $r = \frac{3(\alpha-1)^2}{8\alpha-2}$. Now, we will obtain upper and lower bounds on m_i. For the upper bound, for any $t > t' = \frac{c\sum_{i\in\mathcal{K}} z_i^*}{d^2}$,

$$\begin{aligned}
m_i &= \frac{1}{\alpha}\frac{\sum_{j\in\mathcal{K}_i} z_j^*}{\sum_{j\in\mathcal{K}} z_i^*}\sum_{m=1}^{t}\epsilon(m) \\
&= \frac{1}{\alpha}\frac{\sum_{j\in\mathcal{K}_i} z_j^*}{\sum_{j\in\mathcal{K}} z_i^*}t' + \frac{1}{\alpha}\frac{\sum_{j\in\mathcal{K}_i} z_j^*}{\sum_{j\in\mathcal{K}} z_i^*}\sum_{m=t'+1}^{t}\frac{c\sum_{j\in\mathcal{K}} z_j^*}{d^2 t} \\
&\leq \frac{1}{\alpha}\frac{\sum_{j\in\mathcal{K}_i} z_j^*}{\sum_{j\in\mathcal{K}} z_i^*}\frac{c\sum_{i\in\mathcal{K}} z_i^*}{d^2} + \frac{\delta c}{\alpha d^2}\sum_{m=t'+1}^{t}\frac{1}{t} \\
&\leq \frac{\delta c}{\alpha d^2}\log\left(\frac{e^2 t}{t'}\right),
\end{aligned}$$

where δ is the maximum degree in the network. In the above, $\sum_{i\in\mathcal{K}_i} z_i^* \leq \delta$ because $z_i^* \leq 1$, which is due to the fact that $(z_i^*)_{i\in\mathcal{K}}$ is the optimal solution of LP P_2. Next, for the lower bound, we use the fact that $\sum_{j\in\mathcal{K}_i} z_i^* \geq 1$ for all i because $(z_i^*)_{i\in\mathcal{K}}$ satisfies the constraints of LP P_2. Thus

$$\begin{aligned}
m_i &= \frac{1}{\alpha}\frac{\sum_{j\in\mathcal{K}_i} z_j^*}{\sum_{j\in\mathcal{K}} z_i^*}\sum_{m=1}^{t}\epsilon(m) \\
&\geq \frac{1}{\alpha}\frac{\sum_{j\in\mathcal{K}_i} z_j^*}{\sum_{j\in\mathcal{K}} z_i^*}\sum_{m=t'+1}^{t}\frac{c\sum_{j\in\mathcal{K}} z_j^*}{d^2 t} \\
&\geq \frac{c}{\alpha d^2}\sum_{m=t'+1}^{t}\frac{1}{t} \geq \frac{c}{\alpha d^2}\log\left(\frac{t}{et'}\right).
\end{aligned}$$

Hence, combining the inequalities above,

$$\begin{aligned}
\mathbb{P}\left[\bar{X}_i(t) \geq \mu_i + \frac{\Delta_i}{2}\right] &\leq m_i\mathbb{P}\left[S_i^{(R)}(t) \leq m_i\right] + \frac{2}{d^2}e^{\frac{-d^2 m_i}{2}} \\
&\leq m_i\exp(-rm_i) + \frac{2}{d^2}e^{\frac{-d^2 m_i}{2}} \\
&\leq \frac{\delta c}{\alpha d^2}\left(\frac{et'}{t}\right)^{cr/\alpha d^2}\log\left(\frac{e^2 t}{t'}\right) + \frac{2}{d^2}\left(\frac{et'}{t}\right)^{c/2\alpha}.
\end{aligned}$$

Now, similarly for the optimal action, we have, for all $t > t'$

$$\mathbb{P}\left[\bar{X}^*(t) \leq \mu^* - \frac{\Delta_i}{2}\right] \leq \frac{\delta c}{\alpha d^2}\left(\frac{et'}{t}\right)^{cr/\alpha d^2}\log\left(\frac{e^2 t}{t'}\right) + \frac{2}{d^2}\left(\frac{et'}{t}\right)^{c/2\alpha}.$$

Combining everything, we have for any suboptimal action i, for all $t > t'$

$$\mathbb{P}[\phi(t) = i] \le \left(\frac{c}{d^2 t} z_i^*\right) + \frac{4}{d^2}\left(\frac{et'}{t}\right)^{c/2\alpha} + \frac{2\delta c}{\alpha d^2}\left(\frac{et'}{t}\right)^{cr/\alpha d^2} \log\left(\frac{e^2 t}{t'}\right).$$

Proof of Proposition 4

The proof technique in similar to that in [2]. We will analyze the regret by conditioning on two disjoint events. The first event is that each suboptimal action a is eliminated by an optimal action on or before the first round m such that $\tilde{\Delta}_m < \Delta_a/2$. This happens with high probability and leads to logarithmic regret. The compliment of the first event yields linear regret in time but occurs with probability proportional to $1/T$. The main difference from the proof in [2] is that on the first event, the number of times we choose each action is proportional to $z_i^* \log(T)$ in the exploration phase of the policy. This gives us the required upper bound in terms of optimal solution $\mathbf{z}^*$ of LP P_2.

Let $*$ denote any optimal action. Let m^* denote the round in which the last optimal action $*$ is eliminated. For each suboptimal action, define round $m_i := \min\{m : \tilde{\Delta}_m < \frac{\Delta_i}{2}\}$. For an optimal action i, $m_i = \infty$ by convention. Then, by the definition of m_i, for all rounds $m < m_i$, $\Delta_i \le 2\tilde{\Delta}_m$, and

$$\frac{2}{\Delta_i} < 2^{m_i} = \frac{1}{\tilde{\Delta}_{m_i}} \le \frac{4}{\Delta_i} < \frac{1}{\Delta_{m_i+1}} = 2^{m_i+1}. \qquad (11)$$

From Lemma 3 in the Appendix, the probability that action i is not eliminated in round m_i by $*$ is at most $\frac{2}{T\tilde{\Delta}_{m_i}^2}$.

Let $\mathcal{U}_i = \mathcal{K}_i \cap \mathcal{U}$ be the set of suboptimal neighbors of action i. Let $I(t)$ be the action chosen at time t by the UCB-LP policy.

Let E_{m^*} be the event that all suboptimal actions with $m_i \le m^*$ are eliminated by $*$ on or before their respective m_i. Then, the complement of E_{m^*}, denoted as $E_{m^*}^c$, is the event that there exists some suboptimal action i with $m_i \le m^*$, which is not eliminated in round m_i. Let E_i^c be the event that action i is not eliminated by round m_i by $*$. Let $m_f = \lfloor \frac{1}{2}\log_2 \frac{T}{e} \rfloor$ and $I(t)$ denote the action chosen at time t by the policy. Recall that regret is denoted by $R_{\boldsymbol{\mu}}(T)$. Let $\mathbb{P}[m^* = m]$ be denoted by p_m. Hence, $\sum_{m=0}^{m_f} p_m = 1$.

$$\begin{aligned}
\mathbb{E}[R_{\boldsymbol{\mu}}(T)] &= \sum_{m=0}^{m_f} \mathbb{E}[R_{\boldsymbol{\mu}}(T)|\{m^* = m\}]\,\mathbb{P}[m^* = m] \\
&= \sum_{m=0}^{m_f}\sum_{t=1}^{T}\sum_{j\in\mathcal{U}} \Delta_j \mathbb{P}[I(t) = j|\{m^* = m\}]\, p_m \\
&= \sum_{m=0}^{m_f}\sum_{t=1}^{T}\sum_{j\in\mathcal{U}} \Delta_j \mathbb{P}[\{I(t) = j\} \cap E_{m^*}|\{m^* = m\}]\, p_m \\
&+ \sum_{m=0}^{m_f}\sum_{t=1}^{T}\sum_{j\in\mathcal{U}} \Delta_j \mathbb{P}[\{I(t) = j\} \cap E_{m^*}^c|\{m^* = m\}]\, p_m \\
&= (i) + (ii)
\end{aligned}$$

Next we will show that term (i) leads to logarithmic regret while term (ii) leads to a constant regret with time.

First, consider the term (ii) of the regret expression. Recall that $\mathcal{U}_j = \mathcal{K}_j \cap \mathcal{U}$ is the set of suboptimal neighbors of j. For each $j \in \mathcal{U}$, we have,

$$\begin{aligned}
&\sum_{m=0}^{m_f}\sum_{t=1}^{T} \mathbb{P}[\{I(t) = j\} \cap E_{m^*}^c|\{m^* = m\}]\,\mathbb{P}[m^* = m] \\
&\le \sum_{m=0}^{m_f}\sum_{t=1}^{T} \mathbb{P}[\{I(t) = j\} \cap (\cup_{i\in\mathcal{U}:m_i\le m^*} E_i^c)\,|\{m^* = m\}]\, p_m \\
&= \sum_{m=0}^{m_f}\sum_{t=1}^{T} \mathbb{P}\left[\{I(t) = j\} \cap \left(\cup_{i\in\mathcal{U}_j:m_i\le m^*} E_i^c\right)|\{m^* = m\}\right] p_m \\
&\quad \text{(because } \{I((t) = j\} \text{ depends only on neighbors of } j.) \\
&\le \sum_{m=0}^{m_f}\sum_{t=1}^{T} \Big(\mathbb{P}\left[\{I(t) = j\}|\left(\cup_{i\in\mathcal{U}_j:m_i\le m^*} E_i^c\right), \{m^* = m\}\right] \\
&\qquad \mathbb{P}\left[\cup_{i\in\mathcal{U}_j:m_i\le m^*} E_i^c|\{m^* = m\}\right] p_m\Big) \\
&\le T\mathbb{P}\left[\cup_{i\in\mathcal{U}_j} E_i^c|\{m^* = m_f\}\right] \sum_{m=0}^{m_f} p_m \\
&\le T \sum_{i\in\mathcal{U}_j} \frac{2}{T\tilde{\Delta}_{m_i}^2}, \\
&\left(\text{using Lemma 3, } P\left[E_i^c|\{m^* = m_f\}\right] \le \frac{2}{T\tilde{\Delta}_{m_i}^2}\right) \\
&\le \sum_{i\in\mathcal{U}_j} \frac{32}{\Delta_i^2},
\end{aligned}$$

where the last inequality follows from Equation (11). Hence, the term (ii) of regret is

$$\begin{aligned}
&\sum_{m=0}^{m_f}\sum_{t=1}^{T}\sum_{j\in\mathcal{U}} \Delta_j \mathbb{P}[\{I(t) = j\} \cap E_{m^*}^c|\{m^* = m\}]\, p_m \\
&\le \sum_{j\in\mathcal{U}} \Delta_j \sum_{i\in\mathcal{U}_j} \frac{32}{\Delta_i^2} = O(K\delta), \qquad (12)
\end{aligned}$$

where δ is the maximum degree in the network.

Next, we consider the term (i). Recall that, in this term, we consider the case that all suboptimal actions i with $m_i \le m^*$ are eliminated by $*$ on or before m_i.

$$\begin{aligned}
(i) &= \sum_{m=0}^{m_f}\sum_{t=1}^{T}\sum_{j\in\mathcal{U}} \Delta_j \mathbb{P}[\{I(t) = j\} \cap E_{m^*}|\{m^* = m\}]\, p_m \\
&= \sum_{m=0}^{m_f} \mathbb{E}[R_{\boldsymbol{\mu}}(T)|\{m^* = m\}, E_{m^*}]\,\mathbb{P}[E_{m^*}|\{m^* = m\}] p_m \\
&\le \sum_{m=0}^{m_f} \Big(\mathbb{E}[\text{Regret from } \{i : m_i \le m^*\}|\{m^* = m\}, E_{m^*}] \\
&\quad + \mathbb{E}[\text{Regret from } \{i : m_i > m^*\}|\{m^* = m\}, E_{m^*}]\Big) p_m \\
&\le \sum_{m=0}^{m_f} \Big(\mathbb{E}\left[\text{Regret from } \{i : m_i \le m_f\}|\{m^* = m_f\}, E_{m_f}\right] \\
&\quad + \mathbb{E}[\text{Regret from } \{i : m_i > m^*\}|\{m^* = m\}, E_{m^*}]\Big) p_m
\end{aligned}$$

$$\leq \mathbb{E}\left[R_{\mu}(T)|\{m^* = m_f\}, E_{m_f}\right] \sum_{m=0}^{m_f} p_m$$
$$+ \sum_{m=0}^{m_f} \mathbb{E}\left[\text{Regret from } \{i : m_i > m^*\}|\{m^* = m\}, E_{m^*}\right] p_m$$
$$= (ia) + (ib)$$

Once again, we will consider the above two terms separately. For the term (ia), under the event E_{m_f}, each suboptimal action i is eliminated by $*$ by round m_i. Define round $\bar{m}$ and the set B as follows:

$$\bar{m} = \min\{m : \sum_{i \in \mathcal{K}} z_i^* > \sum_{i:m_i > m} 2^{-m+1}\},$$
$$B = \{i \in \mathcal{U} : m_i > \bar{m}\}.$$

After round $\bar{m}$, Algorithm 2 chooses only those actions with $m_i > \bar{m}$. Also, by the definition of the **Reset** phase of Algorithm 2, we have that any suboptimal action $i \notin B$ is chosen (i.e. appears in the set S_m at round m) only until all actions in its neighborhood are eliminated or until $\bar{m}$, whichever happens first. Define $n_i = \min\{\bar{m}, \max_{\mathcal{K}_i}\{m_j\}\}$ for each suboptimal action i. Then any suboptimal action $i \notin B$ is chosen for at most n_i rounds.

$$(ia) = \mathbb{E}\left[R_{\mu}(T)|\{m^* = m_f\}, E_{m_f}\right]$$
$$\leq \sum_{i \in \mathcal{U} \setminus B} \Delta_i z_i^* \frac{2\log(T\tilde{\Delta}_{n_i}^2)}{\tilde{\Delta}_{n_i}^2} + \sum_{i \in B} \Delta_i \frac{2\log(T\tilde{\Delta}_{m_i}^2)}{\tilde{\Delta}_{m_i}^2}$$
$$\leq \sum_{i \in \mathcal{U} \setminus B} \Delta_i z_i^* \frac{32\log(T\hat{\Delta}_i^2)}{\hat{\Delta}_i^2} + \sum_{i \in B} \Delta_i \frac{32\log(T\Delta_i^2)}{\Delta_i^2}, \quad (13)$$

where $\hat{\Delta}_i = \max\{2^{-\bar{m}+2}, \min_{\mathcal{K}_i}\{\Delta_j\}\}$ and (z_i^*) is the solution of LP P_2.

Finally, we consider the term (ib). An optimal action $*$ is not eliminated in round m^* if (16) holds for $m = m^*$. Hence, using (17) and (18), the probability p_m that $*$ is eliminated by a suboptimal action in any round m^* is at most $\frac{2}{T\tilde{\Delta}_{m^*}^2}$. Hence, term (ib) is given as:

$$\sum_{m=0}^{m_f} \mathbb{E}\left[\text{Regret from } \{i : m_i > m^*\}|\{m^* = m\}, E_{m^*}\right] p_m$$
$$\leq \sum_{m=0}^{m_f} \sum_{i \in \mathcal{U}: m_i \geq m} \frac{2}{T\tilde{\Delta}_m^2}.T \max_{\mathcal{U}} \Delta_j$$
$$\leq \max_{\mathcal{U}} \Delta_j \sum_{m=0}^{m_f} \sum_{i \in \mathcal{U}: m_i \geq m} \frac{2}{\tilde{\Delta}_m^2}.$$
$$\leq \sum_{i \in \mathcal{U}} \sum_{m=0}^{m_i} \frac{2}{\tilde{\Delta}_m^2}$$
$$= \sum_{i \in \mathcal{U}} 2.2^{2m_i+2} \leq \sum_{i \in \mathcal{U}} \frac{32}{\Delta_i^2} = O(K). \quad (14)$$

Now we get the result (6) by combining the bounds in (12), (13), and (14).

Further, the definition of set B ensures that we have

$$\sum_{i \in B} \Delta_i \leq \sum_{i \in \mathcal{K}} z_i^*.$$

Also, using the Assumption 4, $\frac{32\Delta_i \log(T\hat{\Delta}_i^2)}{\hat{\Delta}_i^2}$, $\frac{32\log(T\Delta_i^2)}{\Delta_i^2}$ are bounded by $C\log(T)$, where C is a constant independent of network structure. Hence, (13) can be bounded as:

$$\sum_{i \in \mathcal{U} \setminus B} \Delta_i z_i^* \frac{32\log(T\hat{\Delta}_i^2)}{\hat{\Delta}_i^2} + \sum_{i \in B} \Delta_i \frac{32\log(T\Delta_i^2)}{\Delta_i^2}$$
$$\leq \sum_{i \in \mathcal{U} \setminus B} z_i^* C\log(T) + \sum_{i \in B} \Delta_i C\log(T)$$
$$\leq \sum_{i \in \mathcal{U} \setminus B} z_i^* C\log(T) + \sum_{i \in B} 2^{-\bar{m}+1} C\log(T)$$
$$\leq 2\sum_{i \in \mathcal{K}} z_i^* C\log(T). \quad (15)$$

Hence, we get (7) from (15), (12), and (14).

9. CONCLUSION

In this work, we studied the stochastic multi-armed bandit problem in the presence of side-observations across actions that are embedded in a network. We obtained an asymptotic (with respect to time) lower bound as a function of the network structure on the regret of any uniformly good policy. Further, we proposed two policies: 1) the ϵ_t-greedy-LP policy, and 2) the UCB-LP policy, both of which are optimal in the sense that they achieve the asymptotic lower bound on the regret, up to a multiplicative constant that is independent of the network structure. These policies can have a better regret performance than existing policies for some important network structures. The ϵ_t-greedy-LP policy is a network-aware any-time policy, but its exploration is oblivious to the average rewards of the suboptimal actions. On the other hand, UCB-LP considers both the network structure and the average rewards of actions. Finally, using numerical examples on the Flixster network dataset, we confirmed the significant benefits obtained by our policies against other existing policies.

Acknowledgments

This work is supported by the NSF grants: CAREER-CNS-0953515, CCF-0916664, CNS-1012700, CNS-1065136, and by grants from the Army Research Office: W911NF-08-1-0238 and W911NF-12-1-0385. Also, the work of A. Eryilmaz was supported in part by the QNRF grant number NPRP 09-1168-2-455.

10. REFERENCES

[1] P. Auer, N. Cesa-Bianchi, and P. Fischer. Finite-time analysis of the multiarmed bandit problem. *Machine Learning*, 47(2-3):235–256, May 2002.

[2] P. Auer and R. Ortner. UCB revisited: Improved regret bounds for the stochastic multi-armed bandit problem. *Periodica Mathematica Hungarica*, 61(1-2):55–65, 2010.

[3] R. M. Bond, C. J. Fariss, J. J. Jones, A. D. I. Kramer, C. Marlow, J. E. Settle, and J. H. Fowler. A 61-million-person experiment in social influence and political mobilization. *Nature*, 489:295–298, 2012.

[4] S. Bubeck and N. Cesa-Bianchi. Regret analysis of stochastic and nonstochastic multi-armed bandit problems. *Foundations and Trends in Machine Learning*, 5(1):1–122, 2012.

[5] S. Bubeck, R. Munos, G. Stoltz, and C. Szepesvári. X-armed bandits. *Journal of Machine Learning Research*, 12:1655–1695, 2011.
[6] S. Caron, B. Kveton, M. Lelarge, and S. Bhagat. Leveraging side observations in stochastic bandits. In *UAI*, pages 142–151. AUAI Press, 2012.
[7] C. Cooper, R. Klasing, and M. Zito. Lower bounds and algorithms for dominating sets in web graphs. *Internet Mathematics*, 2:275–300, 2005.
[8] I. S. Dhillon, Y. Guan, and B. Kulis. Weighted graph cuts without eigenvectors: A multilevel approach. *IEEE Transactions on Pattern Analysis and Machine Intelligence*, 29(11):1944–1957, 2007.
[9] M. Jamali and M. Ester. A matrix factorization technique with trust propagation for recommendation in social networks. In *Proceedings of the fourth ACM conference on Recommender systems*, RecSys '10, pages 135–142. ACM, 2010.
[10] T. L. Lai and H. Robbins. Asymptotically efficient adaptive allocation rules. *Advances in Applied Mathematics*, 6(1):4–22, 1985.
[11] L. Li, W. Chu, J. Langford, and R. E. Schapire. A contextual-bandit approach to personalized news article recommendation. In *Proceedings of the 19th International Conference on World Wide Web*, WWW '10, pages 661–670. ACM, 2010.
[12] S. Mannor and O. Shamir. From bandits to experts: On the value of side-observations. In *NIPS*, pages 684–692, 2011.
[13] S. Pandey, D. Chakrabarti, and D. Agarwal. Multi-armed bandit problems with dependent arms. In *Proceedings of the 24th International Conference on Machine Learning*, ICML '07, pages 721–728, New York, NY, USA, 2007. ACM.
[14] P. Rusmevichientong and J. N. Tsitsiklis. Linearly parameterized bandits. *Math. Oper. Res.*, 35(2):395–411, 2010.
[15] J. Ugander, B. Karrer, L. Backstrom, and C. Marlow. The anatomy of the facebook social graph. *CoRR*, abs/1111.4503, 2011.

APPENDIX

Notation: $S_n = \frac{1}{n}\sum_{j=1}^{n} X_j$ is called the sample mean of the random variables $X_1, \ldots, X_n$. The first two lemmas below state the Chernoff-Hoeffding inequality and Bernstein's inequality.

LEMMA 1. *Let $X_1, \ldots, X_n$ be a sequence of random variables with support $[0,1]$ and $\mathbb{E}[X_t] = \mu$ for all $t \le n$. Let $S_n = \frac{1}{n}\sum_{j=1}^{n} X_j$. Then, for all $\epsilon > 0$, we have,*

$$\mathbb{P}[S_n \ge \mu + \epsilon] \le e^{-2n\epsilon^2}$$
$$\mathbb{P}[S_n \le \mu - \epsilon] \le e^{-2n\epsilon^2}.$$

LEMMA 2. *Let $X_1, \ldots, X_n$ be a sequence of random variables with support $[0,1]$ and $\sum_{k=1}^{t} var[X_k|X_1, \ldots, X_{k-1}] \le \sigma^2$ for all $t \le n$. Let $S_n = \sum_{j=1}^{n} X_j$. Then, for all $\epsilon > 0$, we have,*

$$\mathbb{P}[S_n \ge \mathbb{E}[S_n] + \epsilon] \le \exp\left\{-\frac{\epsilon^2}{2\sigma^2 + \frac{2}{3}\epsilon}\right\}$$

$$\mathbb{P}[S_n \le \mathbb{E}[S_n] - \epsilon] \le \exp\left\{-\frac{\epsilon^2}{2\sigma^2 + \frac{2}{3}\epsilon}\right\}.$$

The next lemma is used in the proof of Proposition 4.

LEMMA 3. *The probability that action i is not eliminated in round m_i by $*$ is at most $\frac{2}{T\tilde{\Delta}^2_{m_i}}$.*

PROOF. Let $\bar{X}_i(m)$ be the sample mean of all observations for action i available in round m. Let $\bar{X}^*(m)$ be the sample mean of the optimal action. The constraints of LP P_2 ensure that at the end of each round m, for all actions in B_m, we have $n(m) := \left\lceil \frac{2\log(T\tilde{\Delta}^2_m)}{\tilde{\Delta}^2_m} \right\rceil$ observations. Now, for $m = m_i$, if we have,

$$\bar{X}_i(m) \le \mu_i + \sqrt{\frac{\log(T\tilde{\Delta}^2_m)}{2n(m)}} \text{ and } \bar{X}^*(m) \ge \mu^* - \sqrt{\frac{\log(T\tilde{\Delta}^2_m)}{2n(m)}}, \tag{16}$$

then, action i is eliminated by $*$ in round m_i. In fact, in round m_i, we have

$$\sqrt{\frac{\log(T\tilde{\Delta}^2_{m_i})}{2n(m_i)}} \le \frac{\tilde{\Delta}_{m_i}}{2} < \frac{\Delta_i}{4}.$$

Hence, in the elimination phase of the UCB-LP policy, if (16) holds for action i in round m_i, we have,

$$\begin{aligned}\bar{X}_i(m_i) + \sqrt{\frac{\log(T\tilde{\Delta}^2_{m_i})}{2n(m_i)}} &\le \mu_i - 2\sqrt{\frac{\log(T\tilde{\Delta}^2_{m_i})}{2n(m_i)}} \\ &< \mu_i - \Delta_i - 2\sqrt{\frac{\log(T\tilde{\Delta}^2_{m_i})}{2n(m_i)}} \\ &= \mu^* - 2\sqrt{\frac{\log(T\tilde{\Delta}^2_{m_i})}{2n(m_i)}} \\ &\le \bar{X}^*(m_i) - \sqrt{\frac{\log(T\tilde{\Delta}^2_{m_i})}{2n(m_i)}},\end{aligned}$$

and action i is eliminated. Hence, the probability that action i is not eliminated in round m_i is the probability that either one of the inequalities in (16) do not hold. Using Chernoff-Hoeffding bound (Lemma 1), we can bound this as follows,

$$\mathbb{P}\left[\bar{X}_i(m) > \mu_i + \sqrt{\frac{\log(T\tilde{\Delta}^2_m)}{2n(m)}}\right] \le \frac{1}{T\tilde{\Delta}^2_m} \tag{17}$$

$$\mathbb{P}\left[\bar{X}^*(m) < \mu^* - \sqrt{\frac{\log(T\tilde{\Delta}^2_m)}{2n(m)}}\right] \le \frac{1}{T\tilde{\Delta}^2_m}. \tag{18}$$

Summing the above two inequalities for $m = m_i$ gives us that the probability that action i is not eliminated in round m_i by $*$ is at most $\frac{2}{T\tilde{\Delta}^2_{m_i}}$. □

The next proposition is a modified version of Theorem 2 in [10]. We use it to obtain the regret lower bound in Proposition 1.

PROPOSITION 5. *Suppose Assumptions 1, 2, and 3 hold. Then, under any uniformly good policy ϕ, we have that, for each action i with $\mu_i < \mu^*$,*

$$\liminf_{t\to\infty} \frac{\mathbb{E}[S_i(t)]}{\log(t)} \ge \frac{1}{D(\theta_i||\theta^*)}. \tag{19}$$

PROOF. This proof follows from the proof of Theorem 2 in [10]. To fix ideas, suppose $i = 1$ is a suboptimal action and suppose action 2 is optimal. Let the parameters of the reward distributions be $\boldsymbol{\theta} = (\theta_1, \ldots, \theta_K)$ and the associated means be $\boldsymbol{\mu} = (\mu_1, \ldots, \mu_K)$. Then, for any $0 < \delta < 1$, due to Assumptions 1, 2, 3, we have that there exists a parameter λ and mean μ_λ associated with the density function $f(\cdot, \lambda)$ such that

$$\mu_\lambda > \mu_2 \text{ and } |D(\theta_1||\theta_2) - D(\theta_1||\lambda)| \leq \delta D(\theta_1||\theta_2). \quad (20)$$

Now, consider the new sets of parameters $\boldsymbol{\eta} = (\lambda, \ldots, \theta_K)$, where the mean rewards are changed to $(\mu_\lambda, \mu_2, \ldots, \mu_K)$. For this set of parameters, action 1 is the unique optimal. Then, for any uniformly good policy, for $0 < b < \delta$,

$$\mathbb{E}_{\boldsymbol{\eta}}[t - T_1(t)] = o(t^b)$$

and therefore,

$$\mathbb{P}_{\boldsymbol{\eta}}\left[T_1(t) < (1-\delta)\log(t)/D(\theta_1||\lambda)\right] = o(t^{b-1}),$$

similar to the asymptotic lower bound proof in [10]. Now, using the fact that $S_1(t) \geq T_1(t)$, we have

$$\mathbb{P}_{\boldsymbol{\eta}}\left[S_1(t) < (1-\delta)\log(t)/D(\theta_{11}||\lambda)\right] = o(t^{b-1}).$$

Now the rest of the proof of Theorem 2 in [10] applies directly to $S_1(t)$. We will repeat it below for completeness. Let $(Y_i(k))_{k\geq 1}$ be the observations drawn from distribution F_i and define

$$L_m = \sum_{k=1}^{m} \log\left(\frac{f(Y_1(k);\theta_1)}{f(Y_1(k);\lambda)}\right).$$

Now, we have that $\mathbb{P}_{\boldsymbol{\eta}}[C_t] = o(t^{b-1})$ where $C_t = \{S_1(t) < (1-\delta)\log(t)/D(\theta_1||\lambda)$ and $L_{S_1(t)} \leq (1-b)\log(t)\}$.

Now,

$$\begin{aligned}
&\mathbb{P}_{\boldsymbol{\eta}}[T_1(t) = t_1, \ldots, T_K(t) = t_K, L_{s_1} \leq (1-b)\log(t)] \\
&= \mathbb{E}_{\boldsymbol{\eta}}\big[\mathbb{P}_{\boldsymbol{\eta}}\left[T_1(t) = t_1, \ldots, T_K(t) = t_K,\right. \\
&\qquad \left. L_{s_1} \leq (1-b)\log(t) | (Y_i(k))_{\{i\in\mathcal{K}, k=1,\ldots,t\}}\right]\big] \\
&= \mathbb{E}_{\boldsymbol{\theta}}\Big[\prod_{k=1}^{s_1} \frac{f(Y_1(k);\lambda)}{f(Y_1(k);\theta_1)} \\
&\qquad \mathbb{P}_{\boldsymbol{\theta}}\left[T_1(t) = t_1, \ldots, T_K(t) = t_K,\right. \\
&\qquad \left. L_{s_1} \leq (1-b)\log(t) | (Y_i(k))_{\{i\in\mathcal{K}, k=1,\ldots,s_i\}}\right]\Big] \\
&\geq \exp(-(1-b)\log(t))\mathbb{P}_{\boldsymbol{\theta}}\left[T_1(t) = t_1, \ldots,\right. \\
&\qquad \left. T_K(t) = t_K, L_{s_1} \leq (1-b)\log(t)\right], \quad (21)
\end{aligned}$$

In the above, we used the definition $s_1 = \sum_{j\in\mathcal{K}_1} t_j$.
Also, C_t is a disjoint union of events of the form $\{T_1(t) = t_1, \ldots, T_K(t) = t_K, L_{s_1} \leq (1-b)\log(t)\}$ with $t_1 + \ldots + t_M = t$ and $s_1 \leq (1-\delta)\log(t)/D(\theta_1||\lambda)$. Hence using (21),

$$P_{\boldsymbol{\theta}}[C_t] \leq t^{(1-b)} P_{\boldsymbol{\eta}}[C_t] \to 0. \quad (22)$$

By strong law of large numbers $L_m/m \to D(\theta_1||\lambda)$ as $m \to \infty$ and $\max_{k\leq m} L_k/m \to D(\theta_1||\lambda)$ almost surely. Now, since $1-b > 1-\delta$, it follows that as $t \to \infty$,

$$\begin{aligned}
&\mathbb{P}_{\boldsymbol{\theta}}\left[L_k \geq (1-b)\log(t) \text{ for some}\right. \\
&\qquad \left. k < (1-\delta)\log(t)/D(\theta_1||\lambda)\right] \to 0. \quad (23)
\end{aligned}$$

Hence, from (22) and (23),

$$\mathbb{P}_{\boldsymbol{\theta}}\left[S_1(t) < (1-\delta)\log(t)/D(\theta_1||\lambda)\right] = 0.$$

Now using the above equation with (20) gives us the asymptotic lower bound in (19). □

On Maximizing Diffusion Speed in Social Networks: Impact of Random Seeding and Clustering *

Jungseul Ok, Youngmi Jin, Jinwoo Shin, and Yung Yi
Department of Electrical Engineering, KAIST
Daejeon, Republic of Korea
{ockjs, youngmi_jin, jinwoos, yiyung}@kaist.ac.kr

ABSTRACT

A variety of models have been proposed and analyzed to understand how a new innovation (e.g., a technology, a product, or even a behavior) diffuses over a social network, broadly classified into either of epidemic-based or game-based ones. In this paper, we consider a game-based model, where each individual makes a selfish, rational choice in terms of its payoff in adopting the new innovation, but with some noise. We study how diffusion effect can be maximized by seeding a subset of individuals (within a given budget), i.e., convincing them to pre-adopt a new innovation. In particular, we aim at finding 'good' seeds for minimizing the time to infect all others, i.e., *diffusion speed maximization*. To this end, we design polynomial-time approximation algorithms for three representative classes, Erdős-Rényi, planted partition and geometrically structured graph models, which correspond to globally well-connected, locally well-connected with large clusters and locally well-connected with small clusters, respectively, provide their performance guarantee in terms of approximation and complexity. First, for the dense Erdős-Rényi and planted partition graphs, we show that an arbitrary seeding and a simple seeding proportional to the size of clusters are almost optimal with high probability. Second, for geometrically structured sparse graphs, including planar and d-dimensional graphs, our algorithm that (a) constructs clusters, (b) seeds the border individuals among clusters, and (c) greedily seeds inside each cluster always outputs an almost optimal solution. We validate our theoretical findings with extensive simulations under a real social graph. We believe that our results provide new practical insights on how to seed over a social network depending on its connection structure, where individuals rationally adopt a new innovation. To our best knowledge, we are the first to study such diffusion speed maximization on the game-based diffusion, while the extensive research efforts have been made in epidemic-based models, often referred to as *influence maximization*.

*This work was supported by the National Research Foundation of Korea (NRF) grant funded by the Korea government (MSIP) (NRF-2013R1A2A2A01067633, NRF-2013R1A1A3A04007104)

SIGMETRICS'14, June 16–20, 2014, Austin, Texas, USA.

http://dx.doi.org/10.1145/2591971.2591991.

Categories and Subject Descriptors

F.2.2 [**Analysis of Algorithms and Problem Complexity**]: Nonnumerical Algorithms and Problems

General Terms

Algorithms, Theory, Performance

Keywords

Influence Maximization, Clustering, Random Seeding

1. INTRODUCTION

People are actively using social networks to get new information, exchange new ideas or behaviors, and adopt new innovations. Clearly, it is of significant importance to understand how such information diffuses over time, where diffusion by local interaction is the most prominent feature. Various fields including computer science, economics, and sociology have expressed their interests in understanding diffusion, e.g., [10, 40, 42]. People have first started to propose diffusion models in social network with close relevance to studies with long history on raging epidemic, e.g., SIRS model [26] or interacting particle system, e.g., Ising model [20]. Examples of such epidemic-based diffusion model also include [15] and [6], often referred to as independent cascade or linear threshold models [24].

Different from epidemic-based models, people often make strategic choices, i.e., an individual adopts a new technology only if the new technology provides sufficient utility, which increases with the number of neighbors who adopt the same technology (i.e., coordination effect) [14, 19, 33, 35]. This is called game-based diffusion model, which is the main focus of this paper. A recent work by Montanari and Saberi [33] addressed the question of the equilibrium behavior as well as the impact of topological properties on convergence speed. Under the assumption that individuals behave with bounded rationality (i.e., noisy best response dynamic), it has been proved that the number of innovation adopters increases and the innovation finally becomes widespread. However, the diffusion time can be significantly long so that in practice the innovation often diffuses within only a small number of individuals or even become extinct in practice. One of the approaches to reduce the convergence time is to *seed* some individuals, i.e., convince a subset of individuals to pre-adopt the new innovation, e.g., by providing some incentives to those users.

The problem of maximizing the "degree of diffusion" by properly selecting seeds has been popularly studied in epidemic-based models, often referred to as *influence maximization*, whose major goal is to maximize the number of infected individuals. However, in game-based models, as in e.g., [33], the problem becomes completely different mainly because diffusion is widespread at the equilibrium. Thus, we study how to choose a constrained set of individuals to accelerate the speed of diffusion, which we call *diffusion speed maximization*.

1.1 Contribution

We first formulate a diffusion speed maximization problem, say ***P1***, as minimizing the notion of typical hitting time which measures the time when every individual adopts the innovation. We discuss its computational challenges mainly stemming from (i) MCMC (Markov Chain Monte Carlo) based estimation and (ii) probabilistic feature of a typical hitting time, which is neither algebraic nor combinatorial (see Section 2.3). Therefore, we transform the original problem ***P1*** into a combinatorial optimization, say ***P2***, using the theory of meta-stability of Markov chains [39], which, however, turns out to be computationally intractable as well as difficult to be reduced to a classical NP-hard problem amenable to approximation. For example, the influence maximization in epidemic-based models becomes the submodular maximization in most cases, whose greedy algorithm guarantees constant approximation [24]. However, we found that the optimization ***P2*** is not a submodular problem (see our discussion in Section 2.3).

Despite this hardness of ***P2***, we propose polynomial-time approximation algorithms for three graph classes, Erdős-Rényi, planted partition and geometrically structured graphs, and their provable performance guarantees in terms of approximation ratio as well as complexity. Our contribution lies in providing new insights on how to seed individuals depending on the connection structure of underlying graph topologies.

- ***Erdős-Rényi and planted partition graphs.*** We show that an arbitrary seeding and a simple seeding proportional to the size of clusters are close to an optimal one with high probability for the dense Erdős-Rényi and planted partition graphs, respectively (see Theorems 3.1 and 3.2). The main technical ingredient for this result is on our concentration inequalities on the so-called 'energy function' (see Lemma 4.1), which provides the exact approximation qualities of the random seeding via a solution of certain quartic equations. Then it is provably almost optimal via obtaining its approximate close-form solution.
- ***Geometrically structured graphs.*** For this graph class, including planar and d-dimensional graphs, we design an algorithmic framework, called PaS (Partitioning and Seeding), and provide a condition, which, if met, provably guarantees good approximation with polynomial complexity (see Theorem 3.3). PaS consists of two phases: (i) partitioning the graph into multiple clusters, and (ii) seeding within each cluster. The proposed PaS framework relies on our finding that the diffusion process in a graph is dominated by the slowest diffusion process among the underlying clusters. Thus, in the partitioning phase, a given graph should be smartly partitioned into the clusters in which a seeding problem becomes tractable (via seeding the "border individuals" among clusters). Then, to minimize the diffusion time, our focus simply becomes a good seed budget allocation to each cluster that minimizes the overall diffusion time. A greedy algorithm is run to achieve the desired budget allocation in the seeding phase.

The practical implications from our theoretical findings are summarized in what follows: Erdős-Rényi, planted partition and geometrically structured graphs represent *(a)* globally well-connected, *(b)* locally well-connected with big clusters, and *(c)* locally well-connected with small clusters, respectively. First, for globally well-connected graphs like Erdős-Rényi graphs, careful seeding is not highly required, because the underlying topological structure such as high symmetry and connectivity does not change significantly even after seeding with a small budget. However, for locally well-connected graphs, it is necessary to intelligently exploit their clustering characteristics, where the network-wide diffusion time is governed by both intra-cluster diffusion and inter-cluster correlation. As is in sharp contrast to epidemic-based models, in game-based ones, it turns out that in *(b)* intra-cluster diffusion becomes the dominant factor, as opposed to in *(c)* where inter-cluster correlation dominantly determines the network-wide diffusion speed. Thus, as described in Sections 3.2 and 3.3, for planted partition graphs, we focus only on how to distribute the seed budget to each (big) cluster, while for geometrically structured graphs, the seeds are mainly selected from the border individuals to remove inter-cluster correlation.

1.2 Related Work

As discussed earlier, diffusion models in literature can be broadly classified into: (i) epidemic-based [2–4,13,17,24,26] and (ii) game-based [5, 14, 23, 43], depending on how diffusion occurs, i.e., just like a contagious disease or individuals' strategic choices. In particular, game-based diffusion models [5, 14, 23, 43] adopt a networked coordination game where the payoff matrix appropriately models the value of accepting new technology for the neighbors' selections, and studied the equilibrium and the dynamics. Especially, Kandori et al. [23] proved that the noisy best response dynamic converges to the equilibrium that the innovation becomes widespread. Recently, significant attention has been paid to the study of convergence time. In [33], it was shown that in highly connected graph, the convergence becomes slower as opposed to in epidemic models. In [21], the authors showed that the external information such as advertisement on a new technology may slow down diffusion, again on the contrary to in epidemic models [4]. In practice, a small set of influential nodes, called *seeds*, can be convinced to pre-adopt a new technology, which can increase the effect of diffusion. See [12] for motivation in viral marketing, [37] in graph detection, and [27] in computer virus vaccine dissemination. The problem of how to maximize the diffusion effect for both diffusion models are summarized next, where depending on the adopted diffusion model, different problems can be formulated.

Epidemic-based model. In [24, 25], the authors addressed the so-called influence maximization problem in linear threshold (LT) and independent cascade (IC) models. In both LT and IC models, each individual has only one chance to infect its neighbors right after its infection. Thus, a main goal is to maximize the influence spread, i.e., maximize the number of infected individuals. In [24,25], it was first discussed that the problem is computationally intractable because of #P-completeness in measuring influence spread for a given seed set and NP-completeness in finding the optimal seed set that maximizes influence spread. Using the technique on the submodular set function maximization in [36], they showed that a greedy algorithm achieves at least $(1 - 1/e - \varepsilon)$ of the optimal influence spread where ε represents the inaccuracy of Monte Carlo simulation for measuring the influence spread. Since the Monte-Carlo based measurement does not tend to scale with the network size, the authors in [9] proposed a scalable method called MIA using a tree structure. In [18], a clustering concept is proposed to reduce the computational complexity in measuring the influence spread. In [8], Chen et al. proposed modified LT and IC models by adding contact process, which delays infection chance of the infected individual from its infection. Using the modified models, the authors formulated an influence maximization with time deadline and proposed a greedy algorithm motivated by [24,25]. In [16], Goyal et al. generalized the influence maximization problem in LT and IC models as an optimization problem with three dimensions: influence spread, seed budget, and time deadline.

Game-based model. In [11,23,28,35], the authors considered only the best-response dynamics and studied the conditions (of network topology and the payoff difference between old and new technologies) on the existence of a small seed set, referred as the so-called "contagion set," under which all individuals adopt new technology. In [29], a noisy best response was considered with objective of maximizing the influence spread by choosing a seed set assuming that there exists a set of "negative individuals," and a greedy algorithm was proposed with simulation-based evaluations. As discussed in [33], without negative seeding, it is guaranteed to converge to a state where all individuals adopt the new technology. This paper studies a problem of minimizing the convergence time to such an equilibrium under a noisy best response dynamic. To the best of our knowledge, this paper is the first to study this diffusion speed maximization in a game-based diffusion model.

2. MODEL AND FORMULATION

2.1 Network Model and Coordination Game

Network model. We consider a social network as an undirected graph $G = (V, E)$, where V is the set of n nodes and E is the set of edges. Each node represents an individual (or a user) and each edge represents a social relationship between two individuals. We let $N(i)$ be the set of node i's neighbors, i.e., $N(i) = \{j \in V \mid (i,j) \in E\}$. We simply use +1 and -1 to refer to new and old technologies, respectively. We are interested in how a new technology diffuses over the network.

Networked coordination game. We first consider the famous two-person coordination game whose payoff matrix is given by Table 1, where an individual can choose one of new or old technologies, +1 and -1. We make the following practical assumptions on the payoffs. First, there always exists coordination gain, i.e., $a > d$ and $b > c$. Second, coordination gain becomes larger for the new technology, i.e., $a - d > b - c$.

Table 1: Two-person coordination game

P	$+1$	-1
$+1$	(a,a)	(c,d)
-1	(d,c)	(b,b)

The two-person coordination game is extended to an n-person game over G. We let $\boldsymbol{x} = (x_j \in \{-1,+1\} : j \in V)$, and $\boldsymbol{x}_{-i} = (x_j : j \in V \setminus \{i\})$ be the states (i.e., a strategy vector chosen by the entire nodes) of all and those except for i, respectively. Then, in n-person game over G, node i's payoff $P_i(x_i, \boldsymbol{x}_{-i})$ for the state $\boldsymbol{x}$ is modeled to be the aggregate payoff against all of i's neighbors, i.e.,

$$P_i(x_i, \boldsymbol{x}_{-i}) \quad = \quad \sum_{j \in N(i)} P(x_i, x_j), \tag{1}$$

where $P(x_i, x_j)$ is the payoff from the two-person coordination game, as in Table 1. For notational convenience, let $\mathbf{-1}$ = (resp. $\mathbf{+1}$) denote the state where every user adopts -1 (resp. $+1$).

2.2 Diffusion Dynamics

Seed set. We consider a continuous time model, where each node updates its strategy whenever its own independent Poisson clock with unit rate ticks. Let $\boldsymbol{x}(t) = (x_i(t) : i \in V) \in \{+1,-1\}^V$ be the network state at time t, representing the strategies of all nodes at time t. We introduce the notion of *seed set* $C \subset V$, where each node in C is initialized by $+1$ and does not change its strategy over all time, i.e., for any $i \in C$, $x_i(t) = +1$ for all $t \geq 0$. Next, we describe how each non-seed individual updates its strategy.

Best response. As is well-known in game theory, in the best response dynamics, each (non-seed) individual selects a strategy that maximizes its own payoff: a node i chooses $+1$, if

$$(a-d)|N^+(i)| \quad \geq \quad (b-c)|N^-(i)| \tag{2}$$

where $N^+(i)$ and $N^-(i)$ denote the sets of node i's neighbors adopting $+1$ and -1, respectively. Noting that for a given state $\boldsymbol{x}$ $P_i(+1, \boldsymbol{x}_{-i}) - P_i(-1, \boldsymbol{x}_{-i})$ represents the payoff difference between when node i chooses +1 and -1, the best response of node i is sign$(P_i(+1, \boldsymbol{x}_{-i}) - P_i(-1, \boldsymbol{x}_{-i}))$, simply expressed as:

$$\text{sign}\left(h_i + \sum_{j \in N(i)} x_j\right), \tag{3}$$

where $h_i = h|N(i)|$ and $h = \frac{a-d-b-c}{a-d+b-c}$

Noisy best response: Logit dynamics. In practice, individuals do not always make the "best" decision. We model such behavior by introducing small mutation probability that non-optimal strategy is chosen, often called noisy best response. A version of the noisy best response we focus on in this paper is *logit dynamics* [5,31,32,34] that individuals adopt a strategy according to a distribution of the logit form which allocates larger probability to those strategies delivering larger payoffs. More formally, for the given state $\boldsymbol{x}$, non-seeded node i chooses the strategy $y_i \in \{-1,+1\}$ with the following probability:

$$\mathbb{P}_\beta(y_i|\boldsymbol{x}) = \frac{\exp(\beta y_i K_i(\boldsymbol{x}))}{\exp(\beta K_i(\boldsymbol{x})) + \exp(-\beta K_i(\boldsymbol{x}))}. \tag{4}$$

where

$$K_i(\boldsymbol{x}) = \frac{1}{2}\left(h_i + \sum_{j \in N(i)} x_j\right).$$

Note that $(a-d+b-c)y_i K_i(\boldsymbol{x})$ is the payoff gain for the strategy y_i instead of $-y_i$ from (3) and $(a-d+b-c)$ is removed just for convenient handling of other quantities later. Here, the parameter β represents the degree of user rationality, where $\beta = \infty$ corresponds to the best response and $\beta = 0$ lets users update their strategies uniformly at random. When the state changes according to the probability (4) and nodes' independent Poisson clock ticks, the system can be viewed as a continuous Markov chain with the state space $\mathcal{S}_C = \{\boldsymbol{z} \in \{-1,+1\}^V \mid z_i = 1 \text{ if } i \in C\}$, recall C is a given seed set. The dynamics here is also called the Glauber dynamics in the "truncated" Ising model [38], where the truncation occurs due to the existence of hard-coded nodes (i.e., the nodes in the seed set C). Then, it is not hard to see that this chain is time-reversible with the following stationary distribution μ_β:

$$\mu_\beta(\boldsymbol{x}) \propto \exp(-\beta H(\boldsymbol{x})),$$

where

$$H(\boldsymbol{x}) = -\frac{1}{2}\left\{\sum_{(i,j)\in E} x_i x_j + \sum_{i \in V} h_i x_i\right\} + (1+2h)|E|. \tag{5}$$

In the above, the constant term $(1+2h)|E|$ is not necessarily needed to characterize the stationary distribution, but we add due to notational convenience in our proofs. We note that $-H$ is often referred to as a *potential* function of the n-person game described in Section 2.1 and H is called the *energy* function in literature.

2.3 Problem Formulation

Our objective is to find a seed set C (within some budget constraint) which maximizes the speed of diffusion. To this end, we define a couple of related concepts.

First, a random variable called the hitting time (to the state where all users adopt $+1$) of our system with a seed set C starting from the initial state $\boldsymbol{y} \in \mathcal{S}_C$ defined by:

$$T_+(C, \boldsymbol{y}) = \inf\{t \geq 0 \mid \boldsymbol{x}(t) = +\mathbf{1},\ \boldsymbol{x}(0) = \boldsymbol{y}\}.$$

Using this, we next define the *typical hitting time* to be:

$$\tau_+(C) = \sup_{\boldsymbol{y} \in \mathcal{S}_C} \inf\Big\{t \geq 0 \mid \mathbb{P}_\beta\{T_+(C, \boldsymbol{y}) \geq t\} \leq e^{-1}\Big\}.$$

This means that with probability $1 - 1/e$ ($> 1/2$), every node adopts the innovation $+1$ within time $\tau_+(C)$. This typical hitting time has also been used to measure the diffusion speed for a similar model via close relation between hitting and mixing of the Markov chain, e.g., see [33]. Our goal is to solve the following optimization problem:

$$\textbf{\textit{P1.}} \qquad \min_{C \subset V} \ \tau_+(C) \qquad \text{subject to } |C| \leq k,$$

where k is the given seed budget.

Computational challenges of P1. First, given a seed set C, the computation of the typical hitting time $\tau_+(C)$ is a highly nontrivial task, primarily because the hitting time $T_+(C, \cdot)$ is a random variable decided by the Markov chain of the logit dynamics whose underlying space is exponentially large, i.e., $|\mathcal{S}_C|$. One can use the Markov Chain Monte Carlo (MCMC) method for estimating $\tau_+(C)$, which, however, takes at least the mixing time of the Markov chain of the logit dynamic that is typically exponentially large [33]. Even worse, a naive exhaustive search for the optimization ***P1*** requires computing the typical hitting time $2^{\Omega(n)}$ times for $k = \Omega(n)$. Second, the hardness of the optimization ***P1*** also comes from the probabilistic definition of the minimizing objective $\tau_+(C)$, which is neither algebraic nor combinatorial. Due to these reasons, at a first glance, the optimization ***P1*** is a highly challenging computational task, similarly to other influence maximization problems in epidemic-based diffusion models, e.g., see [24]. It is not even clear whether the decision version of the optimization ***P1*** is in the computational class NP.

Problem formulation via a combinatorial optimization. To overcome such difficulties, we use the known combinatorial characterization of the typical hitting time $\tau_+(C)$ from the theory of metastability [33, 39], where it was proved that for a given seed set $C \subset V$,

$$\tau_+(C) = \exp(\beta\Gamma^*(C) + o(\beta)), \qquad \text{as } \beta \to \infty., \qquad (6)$$

where we refer to $\Gamma^*(C)$ as the *diffusion exponent* with respect to the seed set C. In the above, $\Gamma^*(C)$ is defined as

$$\Gamma^*(C) = \max_{w_0 \in \mathcal{S}_C} \ \min_{\underline{w}: w_0 \to +\mathbf{1}} \ \max_{t < |\underline{w}|} [H(w_t) - H(w_0)]. \qquad (7)$$

where the minimization is taken over every possible path $\underline{w} = (w_0, w_1, \cdots, w_T = +\mathbf{1})$ such that for each t, w_t and w_{t+1} are same except for one coordinate. This implies that Γ^* dominates the exponent of diffusion time $\tau_+(C)$ for large β. Also, Γ^* can be interpreted as the "energy barrier" along the most probable path to $+\mathbf{1}$. Two maximums in (7) choose the largest energy difference along a path toward $+\mathbf{1}$. Then the (middle) minimum in (7) finds a path that has the smallest energy barrier to the ground state $+\mathbf{1}$ so that it is the most probable. In [33], it is known that the minimization of (7) is achieved just at a *monotone* path $w_0 \prec w_2 \cdots \prec w_T$, i.e., a user is not allowed to take back from $+1$ to -1.

The formula (6) provides a tractable approach for bounding $\tau_+(C)$ through $\Gamma^*(C)$ and motivated by this, we will focus on the following optimization instead of ***P1***:

$$\textbf{\textit{P2.}} \qquad \min_{C \subset V} \ \Gamma^*(C) \qquad \text{subject to } |C| \leq k,$$

where it becomes identical to ***P1*** as $\beta \to \infty$ from (6).

Further challenges of P2. Note that it is still challenging to compute $\Gamma^*(C)$ for a given seed set C for the following two reasons.

- First, there exist exponentially many monotone paths to consider for the minimization in (7). Characterizations of $\Gamma^*(C)$ using 'tilted cut' and 'tilted cut-width' are known, but they are also computationally intractable, e.g., see Section 4.2 of [33]. Nevertheless, $\Gamma^*(C)$ is defined as a form of combinatorial optimization and potentially more amenable to theoretical analysis than $\tau_+(C)$.
- Second, in epidemic-based diffusion models, the influence maximization problem [24], which maximizes the number of infected individuals, could enjoy an algorithmic convenience because of the key feature the objective function turns out to be submodular. Similar convenient features may also be applied to our case, which, if so, would facilitate our analysis significantly. However, unfortunately our objective function $\Gamma^*(\cdot)$ is neither supermodular nor submodular, as proved by a counter-example in Appendix A, which motivates our study of a different kind of approximation techniques.

3. MAIN RESULT

In this section, we describe our polynomial-time approximation algorithms for the seeding problem ***P2***. Each algorithm provides the guideline on which nodes should be seeded for fast diffusion over a game-based diffusion model for each of three graph classes, which is classified by the criterion on how globally and locally well-connected nodes are. To this end, we first introduce the following notion of "approximate solution".

DEFINITION 3.1. *A seed set $C \subset V$ with $|C| \leq k$ is called a (γ, δ)-approximate solution of the seeding problem **P2** if*

$$\Gamma^*(C) \leq \gamma \cdot \min_{C' : |C'| \leq \delta k} \Gamma^*(C'),$$

where $\gamma \geq 1$ and $\delta \leq 1$.

The parameters γ and δ measure the quality of an approximation solution, quantifying the degrees of suboptimality in *objective value* and *budget*, respectively. One can observe that the solution with $(\gamma, \delta) = (1, 1)$ corresponds to an optimal solution. In what follows, we present the characteristics of approximate solutions in three graph classes which have different topological structures in terms of connectivity and the degree of clustering.

3.1 Erdős-Rényi Graphs

We first consider the popular *Erdős-Rényi (ER) graph,* denoted by $G_{\text{ER}}(n, p)$, which is a random graph on n nodes such that every node pair has an edge with probability p. Let $\lambda = np$, roughly corresponding to the average number of neighbors per node, where our focus is when $\lambda = \Omega(1)$. For ER graphs, we obtain the following result, whose proof is presented in Section 4.1.

where

$$\xi = \min_{\{\boldsymbol{\nu} \in [0,1]^m : |\boldsymbol{\nu}|_1 \le \kappa\}} \max_{1 \le l \le m} \left(\frac{1-h}{2} \omega_l - \nu_l \right).$$

In particular, for the homogeneous cluster size, i.e., $\boldsymbol{\omega} = (\frac{1}{m}, ..., \frac{1}{m})$,

$$\xi = \frac{1}{m} \left(\frac{1-h}{2} - \kappa \right).$$

Theorem 3.2 provides a guideline on how to allocate seeds, coming from solving a "simple" min-max optimization (8) whose computational complexity is $O(1)$ (m is a given constant and only cardinality of $C' \cap V_l$ is necessary in computing the min-max solution). Intuitively the resulting seed set C in (8) allocates seeds proportionally to the size of each cluster, and intra-cluster seeding does not have to be carefully chosen. More formally, any seed set C with such an allocation is an almost optimal solution, regardless of how to seed inside each cluster if the graph is locally well-connected with big clusters whose sizes scales with respect to n and number of inter-cluster edges is ignorable comparing to intra-cluster ones, i.e., $|V_l| = O(n)$ and $p/q = \omega(1)$. Similarly to the ER graphs, we remark that in this case, a seed budget larger than $\frac{1-h}{2} n$ is required in order to have an order-wise reduction in Γ^*. We also analyze quality of the simple seeding when the inter-cluster edges are relatively substantial, i.e., $p/q = \Theta(1)$. Performance of the seeding gets closer to optimality as the ratio of intra-cluster edges to inter-cluster edges increases, i.e., higher p/q.

For locally well-connected graphs with clusters, it is necessary to intelligently exploit their clustering characteristics, where the network-wide diffusion time is governed by both *(a)* intra-cluster diffusion and *(b)* inter-cluster correlation. In locally well-connected with *big* clusters such as $G_{\text{PP}}(n, p, q, \boldsymbol{\omega})$, the intra-cluster diffusion Γ^* in each V_l dominates the inter-cluster correlation between V_l and $V_{l'}$ with $l \neq l'$. Hence it suffices to focus on how much seed budget is distributed to each (big) cluster depending on its size.

3.3 Geometrically Structured Graphs

Third, we consider locally well-connected graphs with *small* clusters. Those graphs include geometrically structured graphs such as planar and d-dimensional graphs. In these graphs, the *inter-cluster correlation* dominantly determines the network-wide diffusion speed, and hence seeds should be selected with goal of removing the correlation. Different from the earlier two types of graphs, we here take an approach that rather than studying a particular type of graph, we first propose an algorithm and then study a sufficient condition that ensures good diffusion performance and is satisfied in the well-known geometrically structured graphs such as planar and d-dimensional graphs.

One of achieving the goal of removing inter-cluster correlation would be to seed the *border nodes* among small clusters. Motivated by this, we design a generic algorithm, called PaS (Partitioning and Seeding) (see **Algorithm 1** for a formal description) for finding good seeds. As the name implies, PaS has two phases: (i) partitioning and (ii) seeding, as elaborated in what follows.

(i) Partitioning phase: In this phase, PaS finds a partitioning with, a finite number of node clusters, where the number of clusters are chosen appropriately, depending on the underlying graph topologies. Except for a special cluster, say V_0, which will be used as the initial seed set, PaS will find the seeds contained in each cluster by the seeding phase.

(ii) Seeding phase: In this phase, PaS runs in multiple rounds, where it starts from the initial seed set V_0 (step **2-1**) and the seed set C increases by one in each round, until the entire seed set size becomes the target budget k. Let G_l and C_l be the subgraph induced

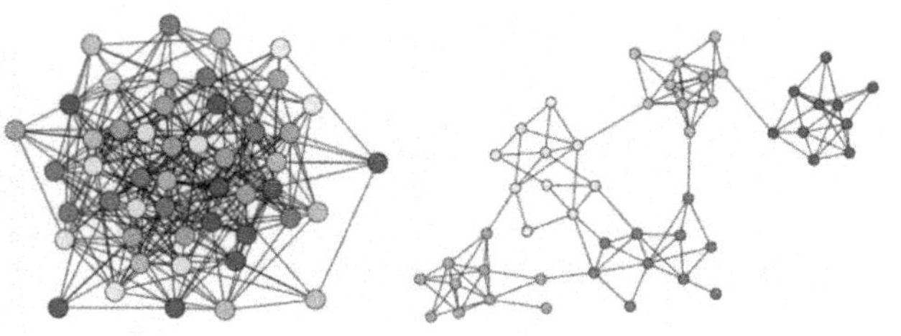

Figure 1: An instance of ER-graph (left) and planted partition graph (right). Source: Lecture note of the network analysis and modeling course in Santa Fe Institute [1].

THEOREM 3.1. *For a ER graph* $G_{\text{ER}}(n, p)$ *and the seed budget* $k = \kappa n$ *with* $\kappa < \left(\frac{1-h}{2} - \frac{h}{\sqrt{\lambda}}\right)$, *every* $C \subset V$ *with* $|C| = k$ *is almost surely a* (γ, δ)*-approximate solution as* $n \to \infty$, *where*

$$\delta = 1 \quad \text{and} \quad \gamma = \begin{cases} 1 + \varepsilon & \text{for any given } \varepsilon > 0 \quad \text{if} \quad \lambda = \omega(1), \\ 1 + \frac{2}{\frac{\sqrt{\lambda}}{2(1-h^2)}\left(\kappa - \frac{1-h}{2}\right)^2 - 1} & \text{if} \quad \lambda = \Theta(1). \end{cases}$$

Theorem 3.1 implies that for the relatively dense and (globally) well-connected ER graph, formally for the case $\lambda = \omega(1)$, an *arbitrary* seed set C is, somewhat surprisingly, an almost optimal solution, i.e., $(\gamma, \delta) \to (1, 1)$. Furthermore, we remark that in this case, the diffusion exponent Γ^* is $\lambda n \left[\kappa - \frac{1-h}{2}\right]_+^2 + o(\lambda n)$ with high probability.[1] Thus, one needs a seed budget larger than $\frac{1-h}{2} n$ in order to have an order-wise reduction in Γ^*. The near optimality of an arbitrary seeding in the dense ER graphs mainly comes from globally symmetric connectivities of nodes which makes the influencing effect by each node indistinguishable. Therefore no careful seeding mechanism is necessary for this globally well-connected graph.

3.2 Planted Partition Graphs

Second, we consider a generalized version of ER graphs and study the so-called *planted partition graph* [2], which we denote by $G_{\text{PP}}(n, p, q, \boldsymbol{\omega})$. It is a popular model, e.g., [7], for social networks with big communities (also called clusters); Given a disjoint partition of the clusters $\{V_1, ..., V_m\}$, with $\bigcup_{l=1}^m V_l = V$, let the fraction of nodes in the graph that belongs to a cluster l be $\omega_l = |V_l|/n$ where $\boldsymbol{\omega} = (\omega_1, ..., \omega_m) \in (0, 1)^m$. For a pair of $i, j \in V$, an edge (i, j) exists between them with probability $p = \Theta(1)$ for the nodes i and j if i, j belong to a same cluster, and with probability $q < p$, otherwise. We obtain the following result, whose proof is presented in Section 4.2.

THEOREM 3.2. *For a planted partition graph* $G_{\text{PP}}(n, p, q, \boldsymbol{\omega})$ *and the seed budget* $k = \kappa n$ *with* $\kappa < \frac{1-h}{2}$, *every* $C \subset V$ *such that*

$$C \in \arg \min_{\{C' : |C'| \le k\}} \max_{1 \le l \le m} \left(\frac{1-h}{2} |V_l| - |C' \cap V_l| \right) \quad (8)$$

is almost surely a (γ, δ)*-approximate solution as* $n \to \infty$, *where for any given* $\varepsilon > 0$,

$$\delta = 1, \quad \text{and} \quad \gamma = \begin{cases} 1 + \varepsilon & \text{if} \quad p/q = \omega(1), \\ 1 + \frac{2}{p\xi^2/(q+\varepsilon) - 3} & \text{if} \quad p/q = \Theta(1), \end{cases}$$

[1] Here $[x]_+$ is x if $x > 0$ and 0 otherwise.

[2] This is often referred to as the stochastic block model.

and the seed contained, by l-th cluster V_l, respectively. The seeding phase consists of two sub-phases (a) partition selection and (b) seed selection. In (a), PaS finds the partition $l^\star$ that has the slowest diffusion time with the current seed set C_l (step **2-1**). In (b), for the chosen partition $l^\star$, we replace the existing seeds $C_{l^\star}$ by completely new set of seeds whose size increases by one. The new seed set is chosen such that the diffusion time in cluster $l^\star$ is minimized (step **2-2**). Finally, the temporary seed C is updated by a new seed set in cluster $l^\star$, which is repeated until $|C| = k$ (steps **2-3** and **2-4**). The choices of partition $\{V_0, V_1 \dots, V_m\}$ in step **1** determines the performance and complexity of the PaS algorithm, where we will consider different choices for different social networks for rigorous analysis.

Now, we are ready to present the performance guarantees of the PaS algorithm. To that end, we introduce a notation: E_l is the edge set of the subgraph induced by $V_l \cup V_0$, where V_l is the l-th cluster resulting from the partitioning phase.

THEOREM 3.3. *For given graph $G = (V, E)$ and seeding budget $k = \kappa n$ with $\kappa \in (0, 1)$, suppose that $\{V_l : l = 0, 1, \dots, m\}$ in the partitioning phase of the PaS algorithm has the following condition:*

For some $\varepsilon \in (0, 1)$,

$$|V_0| \le \varepsilon n \quad \text{and} \quad |V_l| = O(1), \quad \text{for all } l = 1, ..., m. \tag{9}$$

Then, the PaS algorithm outputs a $(1, 1 - \frac{\varepsilon}{\kappa})$-approximation solution and its seeding phase takes $O(n^2)$ time.

The proof of Theorem 3.3 is presented in Section 4.3. Theorem 3.3 implies that if there exists an algorithm finding a 'good' partition (i.e., $|V_0|/n \le \varepsilon$ for some small $\varepsilon > 0$) with small clusters (i.e., $V_l = O(1)$), as specified in the condition (9), the PaS algorithm outputs an almost optimal solution. Note that V_0 corresponds to the set of border nodes among clusters. This condition (9) does not always hold. However, for the following classes of social networks, polynomial-time algorithms are known for computing such a partition satisfying the condition for *any* $\varepsilon = \Omega(1)$ [22].[3]

- ***d-dimensional Graph.*** A graph is called called a d-dimensional graph, denoted by $G_{\mathrm{dD}}(n, d, D, R)$, if each node i can be embedded to a position π_i in $\mathbb{R}^d$ such that $(i, j) \in E$ implies that the Euclidean distance between π_i and π_j is less than R and any cube of volume of B contains at most $D \cdot B$ nodes, where $d, D, R = O(1)$.
- ***Planar Graph.*** A planar graph, denoted by $G_{\mathrm{PL}}(n, \Delta)$, can be drawn on the plane without intersection of edges except nodes which is endpoints of edges and its maximum degree $\Delta = O(1)$.

Therefore, we can state the following corollary of Theorem 3.3.

COROLLARY 3.1. *For a d-dimensional graph $G_{\mathrm{dD}}(n, d, D, R)$ or planar graph $G_{\mathrm{PL}}(n, \Delta)$ and seeding budget $k = \kappa n$ with $\kappa \in (0, 1)$, there exists a polynomial-time[4] algorithm such that it outputs a $(1, 1 - \varepsilon)$-approximation solution for any $\varepsilon \in (0, 1)$.*

In Section 6, we will show that PaS algorithm shows indeed a good performance for a real social graph, showing its practicability.

[3]In fact, the author [22] considers polynomially-growing graphs and minor-excluded graphs, where d-dimensional graphs and planar graphs are their special cases, respectively.

[4]It is a polynomial with respect to n, but may be exponential with respect to $1/\varepsilon$.

Input: Graph $G = (V, E)$ and seed budget k

Output: Seed set C^{PaS}

---

1. Partitioning phase.

Construct a partition $\{V_l : l = 0, 1, \dots, m\}$, where there exists no edge between V_l and $V_{l'}$ for all $l \ne l' \ge 1$,

$$\bigcup_{l=0}^{m} V_l = V \quad \text{and} \quad V_l \cap V_{l'} = \emptyset, \quad \text{for all } l \ne l' \ge 0.$$

We call V_0 "separator cluster" and each component V_l becomes a cluster, i.e., $m + 1$ is the number of clusters found in this phase.

2. Seeding phase.

2-1. Seed V_0, i.e., $C \leftarrow V_0$.

2-2. Cluster selection.
Find a cluster $1 \le l^* \le m$ such that

$$l^* \in \arg \max_{1 \le l \le m : |C_l| < |V_l|} \Gamma^*(G_l, C_l \cup V_0),$$

where G_l is the subgraph induced by $V_l \cup V_0$ and C_l is the set of seeds in V_l, i.e., $C_l = C \cap V_l$.

2-3. Seed selection in the selected cluster.
Find a new seed set D in V_{l^*} such that

$$D \in \arg \min_{D' \subset V_{l^*} : |D'| = |C_{l^*}| + 1} \Gamma^* \left(G_{l^*}, D' \cup V_0\right).$$

2-4. Update $C \leftarrow (C \setminus C_{l^*}) \cup D$, and repeat the steps **2-2**, **2.3**, and **2-4** whenever $|C| < k$.

3. Terminate. Output C.

Algorithm 1: PaS (Partitioning and Seeding) Algorithm

4. PROOFS OF THEOREMS

This section provides the proofs of Theorems 3.1, 3.2 and 3.3.

4.1 Proof of Theorem 3.1

We first present the proof of Theorem 3.1 in this section. Consider Erdős-Rényi graph $G_{\mathrm{ER}}(n, p)$ and seed budget $k = \kappa n$. We will show that for $\kappa < \left(\frac{1-h}{2} - \frac{h}{\sqrt{\lambda}}\right)$, the following event occurs almost surely as $n \to \infty$:

$$\mathcal{L} \le \frac{\Gamma^*(C)}{\lambda n} \le \mathcal{U}, \quad \text{for all } C \text{ with } |C| = k, \tag{10}$$

where

$$\mathcal{L} = \left(\kappa - \frac{1-h}{2}\right)^2 - \frac{2(1-h^2)}{\sqrt{\lambda}},$$

$$\mathcal{U} = \left(\kappa - \frac{1-h}{2}\right)^2 + \frac{2(1-h^2)}{\sqrt{\lambda}}.$$

The above inequality (10) implies that $\Gamma^*(C)$ is highly concentrated on the interval $[\mathcal{L}, \mathcal{U}]$ for any arbitrary seed set C such that $|C| = k$. Then, we should have $\gamma = \mathcal{U}/\mathcal{L}$ from Definition 3.1. Theorem 3.1 is a direct implication of (10), because when $\lambda = \lambda_n = \omega(1)$ for any given $\varepsilon > 0$, we can find sufficiently large n such that $\mathcal{U}/\mathcal{L} = 1 + \varepsilon$, and when $\lambda = \omega(1)$ we can re-express

$\mathcal{U}/\mathcal{L}$ as in Theorem 3.1. In the rest of this section, we focus on the proof of (10).

To begin with, recall the energy function $H(\boldsymbol{x})$ in (7). For convenience, we abuse the terminology and define the energy function $H(S)$ for a set $S \subset V$ (not for a state $\boldsymbol{x}$ as in (7)) as:

$$H(S) \quad = \quad \text{cut}(S, V \backslash S) - \sum_{i \in S} h|N(i)|$$

where cut(A, B) is the cardinality of the set $\{(i,j) \in E \mid i \in A, j \in B\}$ for two disjoint subsets $A, B \subset V$. Note that the above definition coincides with the original definition (5) by setting $x_i = 1$ if and only if $i \in S$. Using this energy function, one can express the function $\Gamma^*(C)$ in (7) by:

$$\Gamma^*(C) = \max_{C \subset S_0 \subset V} \min_{\underline{S}: S_0 \to V} \max_{t < |\underline{S}|} \left[H(S_t) - H(S_0)\right], \tag{11}$$

where for $A \subset V$, $\underline{S} : A \to V$ is a monotone sequence of sets, $A = S_0, S_1, ..., S_{|\underline{S}|} = V$ such that $S_{t-1} \subset S_t$ and $S_t \backslash S_{t-1}$ is a vertex in $V \backslash A$ for $1 \le t \le |\underline{S}|$.

To show the concentration of Γ^*, we first show the concentration of the energy function H, as stated in the next lemma whose proof is presented in Section 5.1.

LEMMA 4.1. *Consider Erdős-Rényi graph $G_{\text{ER}}(n,p)$ with $\lambda = np = \Omega(1)$. The following events occurs almost surely as $n \to \infty$:*

$$|H(S) - a(|S|)| \le \eta(|S|),$$

where

$$a(s) = (1-h)s(n-s)p - hs(s-1)p,$$
$$\eta(s) = (1-h)\sqrt{2\lambda s(n-s)} + 2h\sqrt{\lambda s(s-1)}.$$

In Lemma 4.1, $H(S)$ is bounded by $a(|S|) \pm \eta(|S|)$ which depends only cardinality of $|S|$. Thus, the paths, which are taken in min of Γ^*, have same bounds if they have same start S_0. Hence we have following:

$$\frac{\Gamma^*(C)}{\lambda n} = \frac{1}{\lambda n} \max_{C \subset S_0 \subset V} \min_{\underline{S}: S_0 \to V} \max_{t < |\underline{S}|} \left[H(S_t) - H(S_0)\right]$$
$$\le \frac{1}{\lambda n} \max_{|C| \le s_1 \le s_2} a(s_2) + \eta(s_2) - a(s_1) + \eta(s_1) \tag{12}$$
$$= O\left(\frac{1}{n}\right) + \max_{\kappa \le \sigma_1 \le \sigma_2} \widehat{a}(\sigma_2) + \widehat{\eta}(\sigma_2) - \widehat{a}(\sigma_1) + \widehat{\eta}(\sigma_1), \tag{13}$$

where

$$\widehat{a}(\sigma) = (1-h)\sigma(1-\sigma) - h\sigma^2,$$
$$\widehat{\eta}(\sigma) = \frac{1-h}{\sqrt{\lambda}} + \frac{2h}{\sqrt{\lambda}}\sigma.$$

In (12), we have max over $|C| \le s_1 \le s_2$ since $C \subset S_0 \subset S_t$ for $t < |\underline{S}|$. Also, in (13), the $O(\frac{1}{n})$ term is from $O\left(\frac{1}{n} + \frac{1}{\lambda n}\right)$ since we have $\lambda = \Omega(1)$.

We bound a, η by $\widehat{a}, \widehat{\eta}$ for achieving an upper bound of a succinct close-form for $\frac{\Gamma^*(C)}{\lambda n}$. However, we note that one can directly consider (12) and obtain a tighter (but of a complicated form) upper bound for $\frac{\Gamma^*(C)}{\lambda n}$. Now it is not hard to check the maximum in (13) is

$$\left(\kappa - \left(\frac{1-h}{2} - \frac{h}{\sqrt{\lambda}}\right)\right)^2 + \frac{2(1-h^2)}{\sqrt{\lambda}}$$

at $\sigma_1 = \kappa$ and $\sigma_2 = \left(\frac{1-h}{2} + \frac{h}{\sqrt{\lambda}}\right)$ if $\kappa \le \left(\frac{1-h}{2} - \frac{h}{\sqrt{\lambda}}\right)$. This implies that $\frac{\Gamma^*(C)}{\lambda n} \le \mathcal{U}$. The proof of the lower bound $\frac{\Gamma^*(C)}{\lambda n} \ge \mathcal{L}$ can be obtained similarly. This completes the proof of (10) and hence that of Theorem 3.1.

4.2 Proof of Theorem 3.2

In this section, we present the proof of Theorem 3.2. Consider a planted partition graph $G_{\text{PP}}(n, p, q, \boldsymbol{\omega})$, and a seed set C' with budget $k < \frac{1-h}{2}n$ satisfying the conditions in Theorem 3.2. Then, to show Theorem 3.2, it suffices to show that the following events occur almost surely as $n \to \infty$:

$$\frac{\Gamma^*(C') - \Gamma^*(C^*)}{\Gamma^*(C^*)} \le \frac{2}{\frac{p}{(c+n^{-0.4})}\xi^2 - 3} \tag{14}$$

where

$$\xi = \min_{\{\nu \in [0,1]^m : |\nu|_1 \le \kappa\}} \max_{1 \le l \le m} \left(\frac{1-h}{2}\omega_l - \nu_l\right),$$

and C^* is an optimal seed set, i.e., $C^* \in \arg\min_{C:|C| \le k = \kappa n} \Gamma^*(C)$. This is because when $p/q = \omega(1)$, i.e., $q = o(1)$, we have $n^{-0.4}$ becomes arbitrarily small as $n \to \infty$, thus the result follows.

We first let G_l be the subgraph induced by each l-th cluster V_l, and E_l be the edges of G_l. We also let $E_0 = E \setminus \cup_{l=1}^m E_l$, which corresponds to the set of inter-cluster edges. Consider the "split graph" $G' = (V, E' = E \setminus E_0)$, i.e., G' is a graph removing the inter-cluster edges from G.

It is easy to have the following, which states that the difference of Γ^* between G and G' is bounded by the number of inter-cluster edges: For every $C \subset V$,

$$|\Gamma^*(G, C) - \Gamma^*(G', C)| \quad \le \quad 2|E_0|. \tag{15}$$

To check the above, for A, B such that $A \subset B \subset V$, we calculate $H(B) - H(A)$ as below:

$$\begin{aligned} &H(B) - H(A) \\ &= (1-h) \cdot \text{cut}(B \setminus A, V \setminus B) - (1-3h) \cdot \text{cut}(A, B \setminus A) \\ &\quad + 2h \cdot \text{edge}(B \setminus A) \end{aligned} \tag{16}$$

where edge(S) is number of edges among nodes in S, i.e., edge(S) $= |\{(i,j) \in E | i,j \in S\}|$. Note that in (16), three edge sets counted by cut and edge are disjoint. Thus, from removing an edge, change in value of (16) is at most $\max(1-h, |1-3h|, 2h) \le 2$ because of $0 < h < 1$. Also, we have $S_0 \subset S_t$ in the expression of Γ^* in (11). Hence we have (15) since G' is the graph where E_0 is removed from G.

Since the number of inter-cluster edges are stochastically dominated by a random variable with the binomial distribution $B\left(\frac{n(n-1)}{2}, q\right)$, we have:

$$\mathbb{P}\left[\frac{|E_0|}{n^2} \le \frac{q}{2} + \frac{1}{4}n^{-0.4}\right] \to 1 \quad \text{as } n \to \infty, \tag{17}$$

where note that $\mathbb{E}[|E_0|] = q\frac{n(n-1)}{2}$.

We now present a key lemma for the proof of Theorem 3.2, stating that where $\Gamma^*(G', C')$ and $\min_C \Gamma^*(G', C)$ is located.

LEMMA 4.2. *For every C' satisfying the conditions in Theorem 3.2, the following holds almost surely as $n \to \infty$,*

$$\begin{aligned} \left|\frac{\Gamma^*(G', C')}{n^2} - \xi^2 p\right| &\le \frac{1}{2}n^{-0.4} \\ \left|\min_{C:|C| \le k} \frac{\Gamma^*(G', C)}{n^2} - \xi^2 p\right| &\le \frac{1}{2}n^{-0.4}. \end{aligned} \tag{18}$$

Now, combining (15), (17), and Lemma 4.2, leads to:

$$\left|\frac{\Gamma^*(C')}{n^2} - \xi^2 p\right| \le (q + n^{-0.4}) \tag{19}$$

Furthermore, the following occurs almost surely as $n \to \infty$:

$$\frac{\Gamma^*(G,C)-\Gamma^*(G,C^*)}{n^2} \overset{(a)}{\le} \frac{\Gamma^*(G,C')-\Gamma^*(G',C^*)}{n^2} + \frac{2|E_0|}{n^2}$$
$$\overset{(b)}{\le} \frac{\Gamma^*(G',C')}{n^2} - \min_{C:|C|\le k} \frac{\Gamma^*(G',C)}{n^2} + \frac{4|E_0|}{n^2}$$
$$\overset{(c)}{\le} n^{-0.4} + \frac{4|E_0|}{n^2} \overset{(d)}{\le} 2(q+n^{-0.4}), \quad (20)$$

where (a) is from (15), (b) is from (15) and the inequality: $\min_C \Gamma^*(G',C) \le \Gamma^*(G',C^*)$, (c) is from Lemma 4.2, and finally (d) is from (17).

Then, (14) is a direct implication of (19) and (20), noting the the bound $\frac{\Gamma^*(C')}{\Gamma^*(C^*)} \le \frac{\xi^2 p - 2(q+n^{-0.4})}{\xi^2 p - 3(q+n^{-0.4})}$. This completes the proof.

4.3 Proof of Theorem 3.3

This section provides the proof of Theorem 3.3. It is not hard to check the complexity of the seeding phase is $O(n^2)$ for the following reason: In the seeding phase, we have total $k = O(n)$ iterations. In each iteration, the number of clusters in the partition satisfying **P1** is $O(n)(= m)$. Further, the subphases of partition selection take $O(m)$ and $O(1)$ times, respectively, because using $|V_l| = O(1), l = 1, \dots, m$, we can compute the value Γ^* in each subgraph G_l in $O(1)$ time (note that the nodes in V_0 are already seeded).

We henceforth focus on the approximation quality of the output from the PaS algorithm. To this end, one can observe that the output C^{PaS} of the PaS algorithm minimizes Γ^* in each subgraph G_l for the budget allocation $v_l^{\text{PaS}} = |C^{\text{PaS}} \cap V_l|$, i.e.,

$$C_l^{\text{PaS}} \in \arg \min_{\{C_l \subset V_l : |C_l| \le |C_l^{\text{PaS}}|\}} \Gamma^*(G_l, C_l \cup V_0), \quad (21)$$

where $C_l^{\text{PaS}} = C^{\text{PaS}} \cap V_l$. Recall that G_l is the subgraph induced by $V_l \cup V_0$. In addition, we use the following lemma whose proof is given in Section 5.3.

LEMMA 4.3. *For every seed set C such that $V_0 \subset C \subset V$,*

$$\Gamma^*(C) = \max_{l=1,\dots,m} \Gamma^*(G_l, C_l \cup V_0),$$

where $C_l = C \cap V_l$.

From Lemma 4.3 and (21), we have that

$$\Gamma^*(C^{\text{PaS}}) = \max_{1\le l\le m} \min_{\{C_l \subset V_l : |C_l| \le |C_l^{\text{PaS}}|\}} \Gamma^*(G_l, C_l \cup V_0). \quad (22)$$

Now we state the following key lemma, where its proof uses the above characterization of $\Gamma^*(G, C^{\text{PaS}})$ and is presented in Section 5.4.

LEMMA 4.4. *Given graph $G = (V,E)$ and budget k, the output C^{PaS} of the PaS algorithm satisfies that*

$$C^{\text{PaS}} \in \arg \min_{C:|C|\le k, V_0 \subset C} \Gamma^*(C).$$

From Lemma 4.4, it follows that C^{PaS} is a $(1, 1-\frac{\varepsilon}{\kappa})$-approximation solution, since

$$\Gamma^*(C^{\text{PaS}}) = \min_{C:|C|\le k, V_0\subset C} \Gamma^*(C) \le \min_{C:|C|\le k-|V_0|} \Gamma^*(C) \le \min_{C:|C|\le k(1-\frac{\varepsilon}{\kappa})} \Gamma^*(C),$$

where we use $|V_0| \le \varepsilon n$, $k = \kappa n$ and the monotone property of Γ^*, i.e., for all A, B such that $A \subset B \subset V$, $\Gamma^*(B) \le \Gamma^*(A)$. This completes the proof of Theorem 3.3.

5. PROOF OF LEMMAS

This section provides the proofs of Lemmas 4.1, 4.2, 4.3 and 4.4.

5.1 Proof of Lemma 4.1

Consider a subset $S \subset V$, where let $s = |S|$. For $i \in S$, we can split $N(i)$ into two disjoint sets as $N(i) = \big(N(i)\setminus S\big) \cup \big(N(i) \cap S\big)$. Using this separation, $H(S)$ in (11) can be written as:

$$H(S) = (1-h)\text{cut}(S, V\setminus S) - h\sum_{i\in S} |N(i)\cap S|. \quad (23)$$

In the ER graph, note that cut$(S, V\setminus S)$ and $\frac{1}{2}\sum_{i\in S}|N(i)\cap S|$ follows the binomial distributions $B(s(n-s),p)$ and $B(s(s-1)/2,p)$, respectively. Then, from the Chernoff's bound, we have

$$\mathbb{P}\Big[\big|\text{cut}(S,V\setminus S) - ps(n-s)\big| \ge \sqrt{2\lambda s(n-s)}\Big] \le 2\exp(-n), \quad (24)$$

$$\mathbb{P}\Big[\big|\frac{1}{2}\sum_{i\in S}|N(i)\cap S| - ps(s-1)/2\big| \ge \sqrt{\lambda s(s-1)}\Big] \le 2\exp(-n). \quad (25)$$

Thus, by applying the union bound to (24) and (25) and using (23), it follows that

$$\mathbb{P}\Big[\big|H(S) - a(s)\big| \ge \eta(s)\Big] \le 4\exp(-n), \quad (26)$$

where $a(s)$ and $\eta(s)$ are defined in Lemma 4.1. Finally, we complete the proof using the above inequality:

$$\mathbb{P}\Big[\bigcap_{S\subset V} \big[|H(S) - a(|S|)| \le \eta(|S|)\big]\Big] \ge 1 - 4\exp(-n)\cdot 2^n \to 1 \quad \text{as } n \to \infty,$$

where we use the union bound and (26) for the first inequality.

5.2 Proof of Lemma 4.2

We first note that each subgraph G_l is an ER graph $G_{\text{ER}}(\omega_l n, p)$ where its $\Gamma^*(G_l, \cdot)$ was already studied in Section 4.1. Hence, from (13) with $p = \Theta(1)$, we have $\widehat{\eta}(\sigma) = O(n^{-0.5}) = o(n^{-0.4})$.[5] Thus, for any $C_l \subset V_l$ we have almost surely as $n \to \infty$:

$$\frac{\Gamma^*(G_{\text{ER}}(\omega_l n, p), C_l)}{n^2} = \begin{cases} \left(\frac{1-h}{2}\omega_l - \nu_l\right)^2 p + \frac{1}{2}n^{-0.4} & \text{if } \nu_l \le \frac{1-h}{2} \\ \frac{1}{2}n^{-0.4} & \text{otherwise,} \end{cases}$$

where $\nu_l = \frac{|C_l|}{n}$. Also, we note that $|V_l| = \omega_l n = \Omega(n)$. Using the above, we have that almost surely as $n \to \infty$, for every $C_l \subset V_l$,

$$\frac{\Gamma^*(G_l, C_l)}{n^2} = \left(\max\left(\frac{1-h}{2}\omega_l - \nu_l, 0\right)\right)^2 p + \frac{1}{2}n^{-0.4}. \quad (27)$$

Since G' consists of disconnected subgraphs $G_1, \dots, G_m$, we provide the following which implies that the value Γ^* in the entire graph is decided by the maximum of the corresponding values in subgraphs: for every seed set $C \subset V$,

$$\Gamma^*(G', C) = \max_{l=1,\dots,m} \Gamma^*(G_l, C_l). \quad (28)$$

[5]Here we have $\lambda = np = \Theta(n)$.

The proof of (28) is almost identical to that of Lemma 4.3, and we omit it for brevity.

Now observe that for every $C \subset V$ with $\frac{|C|}{n} \le \kappa \le \frac{1-h}{2}$, there exists l such that $\frac{|C_l|}{n} = \nu_l \le \frac{1-h}{2}\omega_l$. Thus, from (27) and (28), it follows that for every $C \subset V$ such that $|C| \le k \le \frac{1-h}{2}n$,

$$\frac{\Gamma^*(G', C)}{n^2} = \left(\max_{1\le l\le m}\left(\frac{1-h}{2}\omega_l - \nu_l\right)\right)^2 p + \frac{1}{2}n^{-0.4}, \quad (29)$$

where $\nu_l = \frac{|C_l|}{n}$.

Therefore, it suffices to show the following:

$$\left|\max_{1\le l\le m}\left(\frac{1-h}{2}\omega_l - \nu_l'\right) - \xi\right| \le \frac{1}{2}n^{-0.4} \quad (30)$$

where $\nu_l' = \frac{|C_l'|}{n}$.

Since we consider C' satisfying (8), $\max_{1\le l\le m}\left(\frac{1-h}{2}\omega_l - \nu_l'\right)$ and ξ are the same except that the min is taken over $\boldsymbol{\nu}$ consisting of continuous v_l in ξ but we have the discreteness of $\nu_l' = \frac{|C'\cap V_l|}{n}$. Due to this discreteness, ξ and $\max_{l=1,\ldots,m} \frac{f(G_l, C_l')}{n}$ have at most $\frac{1}{n}$ difference which is less than $n^{-0.4}$ as $n \to \infty$. This completes the proof.

5.3 Proof of Lemma 4.3

We use proof by induction with respect to the number of clusters, i.e. m. The following claim states formally the base case $m = 2$, where its proof is presented in Appendix B.

PROPOSITION 5.1. *For given $G = (V, E)$, consider a partition $\{V_l : l = 0, 1, 2\}$, where there exists no edge between V_1 and V_2,*

$$\bigcup_{l\in\{0,1,2\}} V_l = V \quad \text{and} \quad V_l \cap V_{l'} = \emptyset, \quad \text{for all } l \ne l' \ge 0.$$

Then, it follows that for any seed set C such that $V_0 \subset C \subset V$,

$$\Gamma^*(C) = \max_{l=1,2} \Gamma^*(G_l, C_l \cup V_0),$$

where $G_l = (V_l \cup V_0, E_l)$ is the induced subgraph by $V_l \cup V_0$ and $C_l = C \cap V_l$.

We now consider two subgraphs $G_1 = (V_1 \cup V_0, E_1)$ and $G_{\text{-}1} = (V_{\text{-}1} \cup V_0, E_{\text{-}1})$ where

$$V_{\text{-}1} = \cup_{l=2}^m V_l \text{ and } E_{\text{-}1} = \cup_{l=2}^m E_l.$$

Note that the separator V_0 also partitions G into G_1 and $G_{\text{-}1}$ which are the subgraphs induced by V_1 and $V_{\text{-}1}$, respectively. Then, from the construction of $G_{\text{-}1}$ and Proposition 5.1, for any seed set C such that $V_0 \subset C \subset V$, we have

$$\Gamma^*(C) = \max\left\{\Gamma^*(G_1, C_1 \cup V_0), \Gamma^*(G_{\text{-}1}, C_{\text{-}1} \cup V_0)\right\},$$

where $C_{\text{-}1} = C \cap V_{\text{-}1}$.

Observe that V_0 also partitions $G_{\text{-}1} = (V_{\text{-}1} \cup V_0, E_{\text{-}1})$ into two subgraphs $G_2 = (V_2 \cup V_0, E_2), G_{\text{-}2} = (V_{\text{-}2} \cup V_0, E_{\text{-}2})$ where $V_{\text{-}2} = \cup_{l=3}^m V_l$ and $E_{\text{-}2} = \cup_{l=3}^m E_l$. Then, one can also apply Proposition 5.1 to $G_{\text{-}1}$ again: for any seed set C such that $V_0 \subset C \subset V_{\text{-}1}$,

$$\Gamma^*(G_{\text{-}1}, C_{\text{-}1} \cup V_0) = \max\left\{\Gamma^*(G_2, C_2 \cup V_0), \Gamma^*(G_{\text{-}2}, C_{\text{-}2} \cup V_0)\right\},$$

where $C_{\text{-}2} = C \cap V_{\text{-}2}$. Thus, we have, for any seed set C such that $V_0 \subset C \subset V$,

$$\Gamma^*(C) = \max\left\{\Gamma^*(G_{\text{-}2}, C_{\text{-}2} \cup V_0), \max_{l=1,2} \Gamma^*(G_l, C_l \cup V_0)\right\}.$$

This provides the proof of Lemma 4.3 for the case $m = 3$. One can repeat this procedure to complete the proof of Lemma 4.3.

5.4 Proof of Lemma 4.4

We use proof by contradiction. To this end, suppose that there exists $C^* \ne C^{\text{PaS}}$ such that, $|C^*| = k$ $V_0 \subset C^* \subset V$ and

$$\Gamma^*(C^{\text{PaS}}) > \Gamma^*(C^*). \quad (31)$$

Let $C_l^{\text{PaS}} = C^{\text{PaS}} \cap V_l$ and $C_l^* = C^* \cap V_l$. Then, from $C^* \ne C^{\text{PaS}}$, there must exist l' such that

$$|C_{l'}^{\text{PaS}}| > |C_{l'}^*|. \quad (32)$$

The above inequality implies that the PaS algorithm selects the cluster l' (in step **2-3**) more than $|C_{l'}^*|$ times, where we say that it does for the $|C_{l'}^*| + 1$ time at the *t-th* iteration of the seeding phase. This means that at the end of the $(t-1)$-*th* iteration, the set of seeds in the cluster l' has cardinality $|C_{l'}^*|$ and the largest Γ^* among clusters, i.e., $|C_{l'}^{\text{PaS}}(t-1)| = C_{l'}^*|$, and

$$\begin{aligned}\Gamma^*(C^{\text{PaS}}(t-1)) &= \Gamma^*(G_{l'}, C_{l'}^{\text{PaS}}(t-1)) \\ &= \min_{C_{l'} \subset V_{l'} : |C_{l'}| \le |C_{l'}^{\text{PaS}}(t-1)|} \Gamma^*(G_{l'}, C_{l'} \cup V_0) \\ &= \min_{C_{l'} \subset V_{l'} : |C_{l'}| \le |C_{l'}^*|} \Gamma^*(G_{l'}, C_{l'} \cup V_0) \quad (33)\end{aligned}$$

where $C^{\text{PaS}}(t-1)$ denotes the intermediate seed set at the end of the $(t-1)$-*th* iteration of the seeding phase. Therefore, it follows that

$$\begin{aligned}\Gamma^*(C^{\text{PaS}}) &\overset{(a)}{\le} \Gamma^*(C^{\text{PaS}}(t'-1)) \\ &\overset{(b)}{=} \min_{C_{l'} \subset V_{l'} : |C_{l'}| \le |C_{l'}^*|} \Gamma^*(G_{l'}, C_{l'} \cup V_0) \\ &\le \Gamma^*(G_{l'}, C_{l'}^* \cup V_0) \\ &\le \max_{1\le l\le m} \Gamma^*(G_l, C_l^* \cup V_0) \\ &\overset{(c)}{=} \Gamma^*(C^*),\end{aligned}$$

where (a) is from the fact that the PaS algorithm keeps reducing Γ^* at every iteration, (b) is due to (33), and (c) uses Lemma 4.3. This conflicts to (31), and completes the proof of Lemma 4.4.

6. SIMULATION RESULTS

In this section, we perform simulations using a real social network graph and show how our theoretical findings can be applied to the diffusion speed maximization in practice. Guided by the implications drawn from the analytic results based on three graph classes, we propose a practical, heuristic seeding algorithm and show how it performs, compared to other seeding algorithms.

6.1 Setup

A real-world social network. We use a topology data set of the social network extracted from 10 ego networks among Facebook users originally used in [30]. The network is an undirected graph consisting of 4039 nodes and 88234 edges where each node corresponds to a Facebook account and an edge corresponds to a social relationship (called "FriendList") in Facebook. Figure 2(a) depicts a blueprint of the network, where we observe that there exist about 10 giant clusters, corresponding to 10 ego networks. Figure 2(b) presents the adjacency matrix of the graph with partitioning, showing 90 clusters that is obtained from the partitioning scheme in [41] (we use this for our seeding algorithm, as will be described shortly). We use $\beta = 10$ for the degree of rationality and vary h from 0 to 1 to investigate the impact of the difference between new and old technologies. We are interested in the regime of users are sufficiently rational and hence we tested various values of β larger than

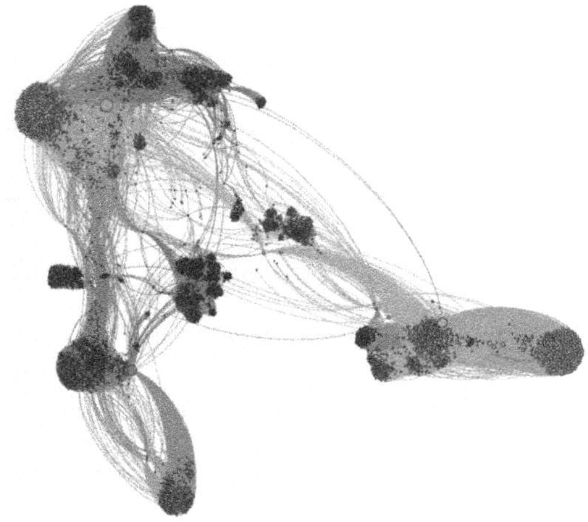

(a) A blueprint of the Facebook ego networks consisting of 4039 users and 88234 edges.

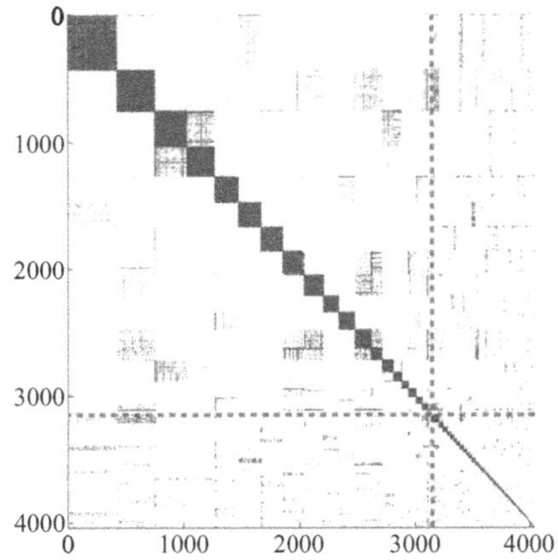

(b) The adjacency matrix of the Facebook ego networks

Figure 2: The Facebook ego networks used for our simulation.

10. They resulted in a similar trend and thus we just report the case of $\beta = 10$ in this paper due to space limitation.

Tested seeding algorithms. We compare the performance of the following four algorithms for comparison, each of which is described in what follows.

- ◦ **Degree.** This choose k nodes in the order of their degrees.
- ◦ **GreedyCut.** This runs k iterations where at each iteration a node with the maximum number of edges is selected, and then removed from the seed candidates.
- ◦ **Random.** This selects k nodes uniformly at random.
- ◦ **PrPaS.** This first identifies the partition, say $\{V_1, ..., V_m\}$, from the given graph using the random-walk based approach [41], and then generates a seed set C whose per-cluster portion is kept equal, i.e., $|C \cap V_l|/|V_l| = k/n$ for $l = 1, ..., m$. In each cluster, seeds are selected uniformly at random.

PrPaS (Practical PaS) is the algorithm that is motivated by our theoretical findings. According to our analysis, we prefer a "good" partition consisting of locally well-connected clusters. We employ the random walk based partitioning scheme, borrowed from [41]. Then, with the resulting partition, we just balance the fraction of seeds in each cluster, so that the entire seed budget is allocated in proportion to the cluster size. This can be regarded as a practical version of **PaS** in Section 3.3 in the sense that (i) it works without explicit knowledge of h, which may be hard to be quantified in practice, and (ii) partitioning based on simple random walks is scalable and applicable to large-scale social networks. We assume the case when h is unknown, thus exact computation of $\Gamma^\star$ inside each cluster is infeasible, which is reason why we use per-cluster random seeding.

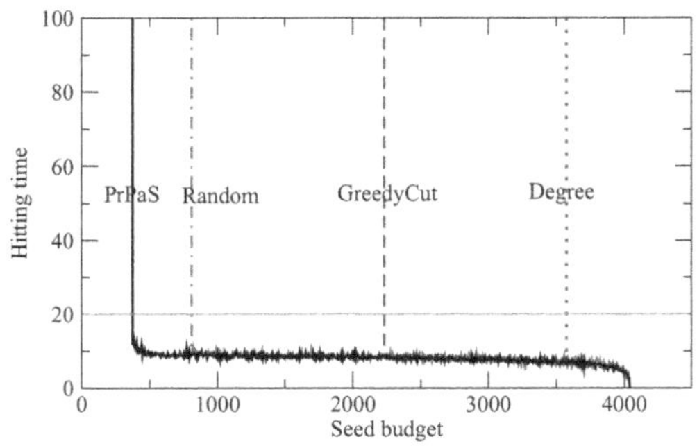

(a) Hitting times with varying seed budgets. $h = 0.5$

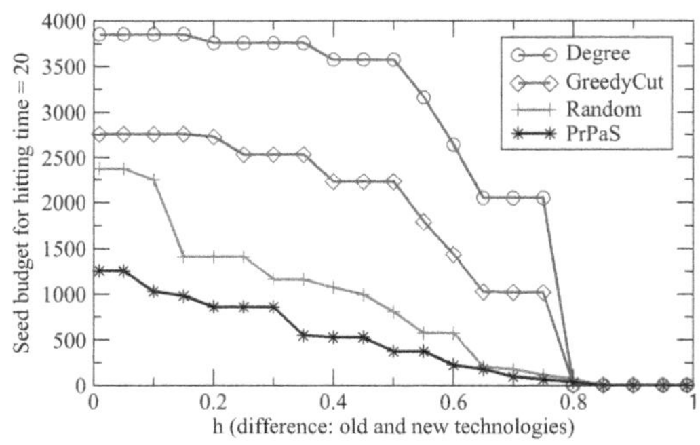

(b) Threshold (20) with varying h for different algorithms.

Figure 3: Simulation results for the Facebook ego networks.

6.2 Results

We compare the algorithms by the minimum seed budget with which the system hits the state $+\mathbf{1}$ in a reasonable time. For convenience, we call this minimum seed budget for a given hitting time x, *threshold* (x).

We first understand how hitting time changes with varying seed budgets. As shown in Figure 3(a), we observe that there exists a phase transition that the hitting time blows up after some seed budget, which differs across the algorithms. Due to space limitations we omit the results for other h values, where we observe a similar behavior with different seed budget leading to the hitting time blow-up. This phase transition is due to the existence of "bottleneck clusters", without which diffusion would become fast. Hence, the seeding quality can be evaluated by how efficiently such bottleneck clusters are removed by the seeding. In our setting, we see that time 20 (a horizontal line in Figure 3(a)) can be a reasonable required hitting time to differentiate the tested algorithms. Hitting time 20 may or may not be the required time by seeders, because the absolute time should be computed by the duration of unit time and unit time can be different how actively individuals interact with each other over the given social network.

To investigate how the tested algorithms perform, we choose the time 20 as a given hitting time, and compare *threshold (20)* for all tested algorithms with varying h, whose results are shown in Figure 3(b). We first observe that across all ranges of h, **PrPaS** has the lowest threshold budget, performing significantly better than others by more than 100% difference. It is natural that for significantly high h (e.g., larger than 0.7) the performance difference is marginal because diffusion should occur very fast irrespective of the quality of seeding . **Degree** and **GreedyCut** do not perform well. Those algorithms are known to generate good seeds in epidemic-based diffusion models. This is because in epidemic-based diffusion just a contact is an efficient way of infecting neighbors, whereas in game-based models local interaction becomes much more complicated due to individuals' rational decisions. Similar phenomenon was also studied in [33] which proves that the hitting time becomes slower as individuals are connected better. **Random** significantly outperforms **Degree** and **GreedyCut**, because uniformly random seed selection allocates more seeds in larger clusters in the *average* sense. **PrPaS** performs much better than **Random** because **PrPaS** performs further optimization by considering the clustering and connectivity structure of the underlying graph.

7. CONCLUSION

In this paper, we have studied the question on how the diffusion speed of a new innovation can be maximized under a noisy game-based model, by seeding a subset of individuals (within a give budget), i.e., convincing them to pre-adopt a new innovation. By analyzing three representative graph classes, i.e., Erdős-Rényi, planted partition and geometrically structured graphs, we obtain new topological insights for the question, which does not exists in the literature for popular epidemic-based models. Our results first implies that for globally well-connected graphs, a careful seeding is not necessary. On the other hand, for locally well-connected graphs, their clustering characteristics should be understood for good seeding, where seeding inside and cross clusters are important for such graphs having big and small clusters, respectively. We believe that these new insights will provide useful tools to understand and control the sociological evolution of innovations spread over large-scale social networks.

8. REFERENCES

[1] http://tuvalu.santafe.edu/~aaronc/courses/5352/.

[2] R. M. Anderson and R. M. May. *Infectious Diseases of Humans*. Oxford University Press, 1991.

[3] N. T. J. Bailey. *The Mathematical Theory of Infectious Diseases and Its Applications*. Hafner Press, 1975.

[4] S. Banerjee, A. Gopalan, A. K. Das, and S. Shakkottai. Epidemic spreading with external agents. *arXiv preprint arXiv:1206.3599*, 2012.

[5] L. E. Blume. The statistical mechanics of strategic interaction. *Games and Economic Behavior*, 5(3):387–424, 1993.

[6] D. Chakrabarti, Y. Wang, C. Wang, J. Leskovec, and C. Faloutsos. Epidemic thresholds in real networks. *ACM Transactions on Infroamtion and System Security*, 10(4):13:1–13:25, 2005.

[7] K. Chaudhuri, F. C. Graham, and A. Tsiatas. Spectral clustering of graphs with general degrees in the extended planted partition model. *Journal of Machine Learning Research-Proceedings Track*, 23 35–1, 2012.

[8] W. Chen, W. Lu, and N. Zhang. Time-critical influence maximization in social networks with time-delayed diffusion process. In *Proc. of AAAI*, 2012.

[9] W. Chen, C. Wang, and Y. Wang. Scalable influence maximization for prevalent viral marketing in large-scale social networks. In *Proc. of ACM SIGKDD*, 2010.

[10] J. S. Coleman, E. Katz, H. Menzel, et al. *Medical innovation: A diffusion study*. Bobbs-Merrill Company New York, NY, 1966.

[11] E. Coupechoux and M. Lelarge. Impact of clustering on diffusions and contagions in random networks. In *Proc. of IEEE NetGCooP*, 2011.

[12] P. Domingos and M. Richardson. Mining the network value of customers. In *Proc. of ACM SIGKDD*, 2001.

[13] M. Draief and A. Ganesh. A random walk model for infection on graphs: spread of epidemics rumours with mobile agents. *Discrete Event Dynamic Systems*, 21(1):41–61, Mar. 2011.

[14] G. Ellison. Learning, local action, and coordination. *Econometrica*, 61(5):1047–107[illegible], Sep. 1993.

[15] A. Ganesh, L. Massouli, and D. Towsley. The effect of network topology on the spread of epidemics. In *Proc. of IEEE Infocom*, 2003.

[16] A. Goyal, F. Bonchi, L. V. S. Lakshmanan, and S. Venkatasubramanian. On minimizing budget and time in influence propagation over social networks. *Social Network Analysis and Mining*, pages 1–14, 2013.

[17] H. W. Hethcote. The mathematics of infectious diseases. *SIAM review*, 42(4):599–653, 2000.

[18] J. Hu, K. Meng, X. Chen, C. Lin, and J. Huang. Analysis of influence maximization in large-scale social networks. In *Proc. of ACM SIGMETRICS*, 2013.

[19] N. Immorlica, J. Kleinberg, M. Mahidian, and T. Wexler. The role of compatibility in the diffusion of technologies through social networks. In *Proc. of ACM EC*, 2007.

[20] E. Ising. Beitrag zur theorie des ferromagnetismus. *Zeitschrift für Physik A Hadrons and Nuclei*, 31(1):253–258, 1925.

[21] Y. Jin, J. Ok, Y. Yi, and J. Shin On the impact of global information on diffusion of innovations over social networks. In *Proc. of IEEE Infocom NetSci*, 2013.

[22] K. Jung. *Approximate inference: decomposition methods with applications to networks*. PhD thesis, Massachusetts Institute of Technology, 2009.

[23] M. Kandori, G. J. Mailath, and R. Rob. Learning, mutation, and long run equilibria in games. *Econometrica*, 61(1):29–56, Jan. 1993.

[24] D. Kempe, J. Kleinberg, and E. Tardos. Maximizing the spread of influence through a social network. In *Proc. of ACM SIGKDD*, 2003.

[25] D. Kempe, J. Kleinberg, and E. Tardos. Influential nodes in a diffusion model for social networks. In *Proc. of Intl. Colloq. on Automata, Languages and Programming*, pages 1127–1138. Springer, 2005.

[26] W. O. Kermack and A. G. McKendrick. Contributions to the mathematical theory of epidemics. ii. the problem of endemicity. In *Proc. of the Royal society of London. Series A*, 1932.

[27] M. Lelarge. Coordination in network security games. In *Proc. of INFOCOM*, 2012.

[28] M. Lelarge. Diffusion and cascading behavior in random networks. *Games and Economic Behavior*, 75(2):752–775, 2012.

[29] S. Liu, L. Ying, and S. Shakkottai. Influence maximization in social networks: An ising-model-based approach. In *Proc. of IEEE Allerton*, 2010.

[30] J. McAuley and J. Leskovec. Learning to discover social circles in ego networks. In *Proc. of NIPS*, 2012.

[31] D. McFadden. *Chapter 4: Conditional logit analysis of qualitative choice behavior in Frontiers in Econometrics.* Academic Press, New York, 1973.

[32] R. D. McKelvey and T. R. Palfrey. Quantal response equilibria for normal form games. *Games and Economic Behavior*, 10(1):6–38, 1995.

[33] A. Montanari and A. Saberi. Convergence to equilibrium in local interaction games. In *Proc. of IEEE FOCS*, 2009.

[34] D. Mookherjee and B. Sopher. Learning behavior in an experimental matching pennies game. *Games and Economic Behavior*, 7(1):62–91, 1994.

[35] S. Morris. Contagion. *The Review of Economic Studies*, 67(1):57–78, 2000.

[36] G. L. Nemhauser, L. A. Wolsey, and M. L. Fisher. An analysis of approximations for maximizing submodular set functionsâĂŤi. *Mathematical Programming*, 14(1):265–294, 1978.

[37] P. Netrapalli and S. Sanghavi. Learning the graph of epidemic cascades. In *Proc. of ACM SIGMETRICS*, 2012.

[38] E. J. Neves and R. H. Schonmann. Behavior of droplets for a class of glauber dynamics at very low temperature. *Probability theory and related fields*, 91(3-4):331–354, 1992.

[39] E. Olivieri and M. E. Vares. *Large Deviations and Metastability.* Cambridge University Press, 2005.

[40] E. M. Rogers. *Diffusion of innovations.* Free Press, 1962.

[41] M. Rosvall and C. T. Bergstrom. Maps of random walks on complex networks reveal community structure. *PNAS*, 105(4):1118–1123, 2008.

[42] D. Strang and S. A. Soule. Diffusion in organizations and social movements: From hybrid corn to poison pills. *Annual review of sociology*, 24:265–290, 1998.

[43] H. P. Young. *Individual strategy and social structure: An evolutionary theory of institutions.* Princeton University Press, 1998.

APPENDIX

A. EXAMPLE IN SECTION 2.3

Consider a graph G consisting of two disconnected complete graphs G_1 and G_2, both of which has n nodes. Then, it is easy to show that for any seed set C in G_1, $\Gamma^\star(G_1, C) = 0$ (we explicitly express the parameter G_1 if needed, but omit it for the graph G for notational simplicity), when $|C| \geq \frac{1-h}{2}n$, similarly applied to G_2, also. Note that $\Gamma^\star(G_1, \emptyset) = \Gamma^\star(G_2, \emptyset)$, which corresponds to the diffusion exponent without any seeding. First, observe that $\Gamma^\star(\emptyset) = \Gamma^\star(G_1, \emptyset) = \Gamma^\star(G_2, \emptyset)$ due to symmetry and disconnectedness of G_1 and G_2. We now consider a seed set C_1 and C_2 in G_1, G_2, respectively, where $|C_1| = |C_2| = \frac{1-h}{2}n + 1$ (thus the diffusion exponent of both subgraphs is 0). Then, we have:

$$\Gamma^*(C_2) - \Gamma^*(\emptyset) > \Gamma^*(C_1 \cup C_2) - \Gamma^*(C_1),$$

since in LHS $\Gamma^\star(C_2) = \Gamma^\star(\emptyset) = \Gamma^\star(G_1, \emptyset)$, and in RHS $\Gamma^\star(C_1 \cup C_2) = 0$ and $\Gamma^\star(C_1) = \Gamma^\star(G_2, \emptyset) > 0$. This disproves supermodularity of $\Gamma^\star(\cdot)$. Also, to disprove submodularity of $\Gamma^\star(\cdot)$, we additionally consider two seed sets C'_1, C'_2 in G_1, G_2, respectively, such that $C_l \cap C'_l = \emptyset$ with $|C_l| = |C'_l|$ for $l = 1, 2$ (note that we can do this for sufficiently large n since $\frac{1-h}{2} < \frac{1}{2}$). Then, we have:

$$\Gamma^*(C'_1 \cup C'_2) - \Gamma^*(\emptyset) < \Gamma^*(C'_1 \cup C'_2 \cup C_1 \cup C_2) - \Gamma^*(C_1 \cup C_2),$$

since, in the above, every term except $\Gamma^*(\emptyset)$ (which is positive) is 0. This also disproves submodularity of $\Gamma^*(\cdot)$.

B. PROOF OF PROPOSITION 5.1

For notational convenience, we will use the following definitions: for subset $S_0 \subset V$ and monotone sequence of set $\underline{S} \in S_0 \to V$, we define

$$\Gamma(G, \underline{S}) = \max_{t \leq |\underline{S}|} [H(G, S_t) - H(G, S_0)] \quad (34)$$

$$\tilde{\Gamma}(G, S_0) = \min_{\underline{S}: S_0 \to V} \Gamma(G, \underline{S}).$$

Then, from the definition of Γ^*, we can write

$$\Gamma^*(G, C) = \max_{C \subset S_0 \subset V} \tilde{\Gamma}(G, S_0) \quad = \max_{C \subset S_0 \subset V} \min_{\underline{S}: S_0 \to V} \Gamma(G, \underline{S}).$$

With the given partition, the following simple equality can be derived using (23) for any subset S such that $V_0 \subset S$,

$$H(S) = H(G_1, S \cap W_1) + H(G_2, S \cap W_2). \quad (35)$$

where we let $W_1 = V_1 \cup V_0$ and $W_2 = V_2 \cup V_0$.

Let C denote a seed set such that $V_0 \subset C \subset V$. Also, let $C_1 = C \cap V_1$ and $C_2 = C \cap V_2$. To complete the proof of this proposition, we will show that the followings hold:

$$\max_{l=1,2} \Gamma^*(G_l, C_l \cup V_0) \leq \Gamma^*(C), \quad (36)$$

$$\Gamma^*(C) \leq \max_{l=1,2} \Gamma^*(G_l, C_l \cup V_0). \quad (37)$$

Proof of (36). For a subset $X \subset V$ such that $C \subset X$, define

$$\mathcal{P}_l(X) = \{\underline{S}' : X \cap W_l \to W_l\},$$
$$\mathcal{Q}_l(X) = \{\underline{S} : X \cup W_l \to V\}.$$

Then, we have

$$\begin{aligned}
&\tilde{\Gamma}(X \cup W_2) \\
&= \min_{\underline{S} \in \mathcal{Q}_2(X)} \max_{t \leq |\underline{S}|} [(H(S_t) - H(S_0))] \\
&= \min_{\underline{S} \in \mathcal{Q}_2(X)} \max_{t \leq |\underline{S}|} [(H(G_1, S_t \cap W_1) + H(G_2, S_t \cap W_2))] \\
&\quad - [H(G_1, S_0 \cap W_1) + H(G_2, S_0 \cap W_2))] \qquad (\because (35)) \\
&\overset{(a)}{=} \min_{\underline{S} \in \mathcal{Q}_2(X)} \max_{t \leq |\underline{S}|} [H(G_1, S_t \cap W_1) - H(G_1, S_0 \cap W_1)] \\
&\overset{(b)}{=} \min_{\underline{S}' \in \mathcal{P}_1(X)} \max_{t \leq |\underline{S}'|} [H(G_1, S'_t) - H(G_1, S'_0)] \\
&= \tilde{\Gamma}(G_1, X \cap W_1) \qquad (38)
\end{aligned}$$

In the above, (a) holds since $H(G_2, S_t \cap W_2) = H(G_2, W_2)$ for all t, which comes from the fact that $V_2 \cup V_0 \subset S_t$. (b) holds since there is a one-to-one correspondence between $\mathcal{P}_1(X)$ and $\mathcal{Q}_2(X)$; i.e., $\underline{S}'$ can be induced from $\underline{S}$ by $\underline{S}' = (S_0 - V_2, .., S_t - V_2, ..., V - V_2(= W_1))$ and vice versa. Similarly, one can show that

$$\tilde{\Gamma}(X \cup W_1) = \tilde{\Gamma}(G_2, X \cap W_2). \quad (39)$$

Since $C \subset X \subset V$, it follows that

$$\begin{aligned}\Gamma^*(C) &= \max_{C \subset S_0 \subset V} \tilde{\Gamma}(S_0) \\ &\geq \max_{l=1,2} \tilde{\Gamma}(X \cup W_l) \;=\; \max_{l=1,2} \tilde{\Gamma}(G_l, X \cap W_l)\end{aligned}$$

where the last equality holds from (38) and (39).

Now by taking the maximum of $\max_{l=1,2} \tilde{\Gamma}(G_l, X \cap W_l)$ over all X such that $C \subset X \subset V$, we conclude that

$$\begin{aligned}\Gamma^*(C) &\geq \max_{C \subset X \subset V} \max_{l=1,2} \tilde{\Gamma}(G_l, X \cap W_l) \\ &= \max_{l=1,2} \max_{C \subset X \subset V} \tilde{\Gamma}(G_l, X \cap W_l) \\ &= \max_{l=1,2} \Gamma^*(G_l, C_l \cup V_0).\end{aligned}$$

This completes the proof of (36).

Proof of (37). Let S_0^* and $\underline{S}^*$ be an optimal subset of V and an optimal monotone sequence of sets for G, i.e., $C \subset S_0^* \subset V$, $\underline{S}^* : S_0^* \to V$, and

$$\Gamma^*(C) = \tilde{\Gamma}(S_0^*) = \Gamma(\underline{S}^*).$$

In addition, let $\underline{S}^1 : S_0^* \cap W_1 \to W_1$ and $\underline{S}^2 : S_0^* \cap W_2 \to W_2$ be an optimal monotone sequences of sets for G_1, G_2, respectively. Then we have

$$\begin{aligned}\Gamma^*(G_1, C_1) &= \tilde{\Gamma}(G_1, S_0^* \cap W_1) &= \Gamma(G_1, \underline{S}^1), \\ \Gamma^*(G_2, C_2) &= \tilde{\Gamma}(G_2, S_0^* \cap W_2) &= \Gamma(G_2, \underline{S}^2).\end{aligned}$$

Now, construct $\underline{S}^1 \cup S_0^* : S_0^* \to S_0^* \cup V_1$ and $\underline{S}^1 \cup S_0^* : S_0^* \cup V_1 \to V$ such that

$$\begin{aligned}\underline{S}^1 \cup S_0^* &= (S_0^1 \cup S_0^* ..., S_t^1 \cup S_0^*, ...S_{|\underline{S}^1|}^1 \cup S_0^*), \\ \underline{S}^2 \cup V_1 &= (S_0^2 \cup V_1 ..., S_t^2 \cup V_1, ...S_{|\underline{S}^2|}^2 \cup V_1).\end{aligned}$$

Since the end of $\underline{S}^1 \cup S_0^*$ and the start of $\underline{S}^1 \cup S_0^*$ are the same (note that $S_0^1 \cup S_0^* = S_0^*$, $S_{|\underline{S}^1|}^1 \cup S_0^* = S_0^* \cup V_1 = S_0^2 \cup V_1$ and $S_{|\underline{S}^2|}^2 \cup V_1 = W_2 \cup V_1 = V$.). and $V_0 \subset S_0^*$, we can construct a new monotone sequence of sets $\underline{T} : S_0^* \to V$ by concatenating $\underline{S}^1 \cup S_0^*$ and $\underline{S}^2 \cup V_1$:

$$\begin{aligned}\underline{T} = (S_0^*, &S_1^1 \cup S_0^*, S_2^1 \cup S_0^*, ..., S_{|\underline{S}^1|}^1 \cup S_0^*, \\ &S_1^2 \cup V_1, S_2^2 \cup V_1, ..., S_{|\underline{S}^2|-1}^2 \cup V_1, V).\end{aligned}$$

Thus, we have

$$\Gamma(\underline{T}) = \max\left(\max_{t \leq |\underline{S}^1|} H(S_t^1 \cup S_0^*), \max_{t \leq |\underline{S}^2|} H(S_t^2 \cup V_1)\right) - H(S_0^*).$$

Using the construction of $\underline{T}$ with (34) and (35), it is not hard to check that

$$\max_{t \leq |\underline{S}^1|} H(S_t^1 \cup S_0^*) = \Gamma(G_1, \underline{S}^1) + H(S_0^*) \quad (40)$$

$$\max_{t \leq |\underline{S}^2|} H(S_t^2 \cup V_1) = \Gamma(G_2, \underline{S}^2) + H(G_1, W_1) + H(G_2, S_0^* \cap W_2). \quad (41)$$

Furthermore, using (40), (41) and (35), we have

$$\max_{t \leq |\underline{S}^1|} H(S_t^1 \cup S_0^*) - H(S_0^*) = \Gamma(G_1, \underline{S}_1^1) \quad (42)$$

$$\begin{aligned}&\max_{t \leq |\underline{S}^2|} H(S_t^2 \cup V_1) - H(S_0^*) \\ &= \Gamma(G_2, \underline{S}^2) + H(G_1, W_1) - H(G_1, S_0^* \cap W_1). \quad (43)\end{aligned}$$

Recall that the state that all players choose $+1$ has the minimum of $H(\cdot)$. Hence on the subgraph G_1, $H(G_1, \cdot)$ has the minimum at W_1, i.e., $H(G_1, W_1) = \min_{S \subset W_1} H(G_1, S)$. Thus, we have

$$H(G_1, W_1) - H(G_1, S_0^* \cap W_1) \; < \; 0.$$

Combining (42) and (43) leads us to:

$$\begin{aligned}\Gamma(\underline{T}) &\leq \max(\Gamma(G_1, \underline{S}^1), \Gamma(G_2, \underline{S}^2)) \\ &= \max(\tilde{\Gamma}(G_1, S_0^* \cap W_1), \tilde{\Gamma}(G_2, S_0^* \cap W_2)) \\ &\leq \max(\Gamma^*(G_1, C_1 \cup V_0), \Gamma^*(G_2, C_2 \cup V_0)),\end{aligned}$$

where the last inequality is due to $C \subset S_0^*$. Since $\underline{T}$ and $\underline{S}^*$ are monotone sequences of sets from $S_0^* \to V$, we have

$$\Gamma(\underline{S}^*) \leq \Gamma(\underline{T}) \leq \max_{l=1,2} \Gamma^*(G_l, C_l \cup V_0),$$

where the first equality holds by the definition of $\underline{S}^*$. This completes the proof of (37) and hence completes the proof of Proposition 5.1.

Tunable Survivable Spanning Trees

Jose Yallouz, Ori Rottenstreich and Ariel Orda
Department of Electrical Engineering
Technion, Israel Institute of Technology
{jose@tx, or@tx, ariel@ee}.technion.ac.il

ABSTRACT

Coping with network failures has become a major networking challenge. The concept of tunable survivability provides a quantitative measure for specifying any desired level (0%-100%) of survivability, thus offering flexibility in the routing choice. Previous works focused on implementing this concept on unicast transmissions. However, vital network information is often broadcasted via spanning trees. Accordingly, in this study, we investigate the application of tunable survivability for efficient maintenance of spanning trees under the presence of failures. We establish efficient algorithmic schemes for optimizing the level of survivability under various QoS requirements. In addition, we derive theoretical bounds on the number of required trees for maximum survivability. Finally, through extensive simulations, we demonstrate the effectiveness of the tunable survivability concept in the construction of spanning trees. Most notably, we show that, typically, *negligible* reduction in the level of survivability results in *major* improvement in the QoS performance of the resulting spanning trees.

Categories and Subject Descriptors

C.4 [**Performance of Systems**]: Reliability, availability, and serviceability; Fault tolerance; G.2.2 [**Discrete Mathematics**]: Graph Theory—*Graph algorithms; Network problems; Trees*

Keywords

Survivability; Reliability; Fault-Tolerance; Spanning-Tree

1. INTRODUCTION

Network infrastructures have been progressing very rapidly. While about a few decades ago the $56Kbps$ dial-up modem, was a widely deployed device, nowadays technologies, such as Ethernet and InfiniBand operate at rates of $100Gbps$ and beyond [1]. With this extreme increase in transmission rates, any failure in the network infrastructure may lead to a vast amount of data loss. Hence, failures in the network should be recovered promptly. Accordingly, common standards, e.g. [2] [3], introduce requirements for recovery from a single failure within $50ms$. Several studies have focused on survivability methods for coping with network failures, e.g. [4] [5] [6] [7] [8]. However, most of these studies focus on the protection of *unicast* transmission between a pair of nodes.

A widely employed transmission method is to *broadcast* a message to all recipients simultaneously. Indeed, several protocols at various layers utilize broadcast functionality, e.g. ARP [9], DHCP [10]. While the straightforward broadcast technique of flooding the data over every network link ensures maximum protection from failures, this approach incurs a heavy, at times prohibitive, toll in terms of communication overhead. Furthermore, in order to prevent undesirable effects such as a "broadcast storm" [11], the flooding approach requires the implementation of a complex control mechanism for terminating the transmission process.

A *spanning tree*, i.e. a tree composed of all network nodes, offers an alternative approach for broadcasting messages with minimal communication overhead precluding network loops. Indeed, spanning trees are often employed for broadcasting in various networking environments, such as the Ethernet local area network [12], in which the Spanning Tree Protocol (STP) ensures a single transmission path between any two Ethernet local network nodes. However, the basic implementation of this protocol suffers from lengthy recovery period of about $30 - 50$ seconds. Accordingly, the Multiple Spanning Tree Protocol [13] has been proposed as an extension for the STP protocol; it enables the establishment of different spanning trees in a local network to accelerate STP recovery period [14].

Spanning trees are not limited to the Ethernet framework, and are also employed in the context of wireless and optical networks. In sensor [15] [16] and ad-hoc [17] networks, spanning trees are utilized to enable efficient energy consumption. In optical networks [18], shared backup trees can be employed to protect a group of working light paths towards the same destination in multi-protocol lambda switching networks. This paper presents *a novel generic approach for network failure protection when employing spanning trees.*

We adopt the widely used single-link failure model that has been the focus of most of the studies on survivability, e.g. [19] [20] [21]. This model is selected for its simplicity and the fact that it addresses the common requirement in various standards of protecting against a single failure, e.g. [2] [3]. According to this model, reliable broadcasting can

SIGMETRICS'14, June 16–20, 2014, Austin, Texas, USA.

http://dx.doi.org/10.1145/2591971.2591997.

be accomplished by transmitting the data through a pair of link-disjoint spanning trees. Algorithmic solutions for finding such trees have been studied in [22] and [23]. Moreover, some interesting properties related to the number of disjoint spanning trees were presented in [24] and [25]. The employment of disjoint spanning trees has been considered also in the context of specific network architectures, e.g. in [26], where it was proposed to improve both aggregate throughput and fault-tolerance in metropolitan area Ethernet networks.

However, the requirement of full link-disjointedness is often too restrictive and, in practice, demands excessive redundancy. Link-disjoint spanning trees of sufficient quality may not exist, occasionally making the requirement unfeasible. Therefore, a milder and more flexible survivability concept is called for, which would relax the rigid requirement of disjointedness by also considering trees that do contain common links.

Previous studies [19] [27] introduced the concept of *tunable survivability*, which provides a quantitative measure for specifying the desired level of survivability. This concept allows any degree of survivability in the range of 0% to 100%, thus transforming survivability into a quantifiable Quality of Service (QoS) metric. Consequently, these studies showed how to combine this new survivability metric with other QoS guarantees, such as bottleneck QoS metrics [19] and additive QoS metrics [27]. However, these studies focused solely on the survivability between a source-destination pair, i.e. a unicast connection. The goal of this work is to employ the novel concept of tunable survivability within the framework of broadcasting through spanning trees while considering additional QoS requirements.

Specifically, tunable survivability within this framework enables the establishment of spanning trees that can survive network failures with any desired probability. Given a connection that consists of several spanning trees under the single failure model, only a failure on a link that is common to *all* trees can disrupt the connection. Accordingly, we characterize the survivability level of a connection as the probability to have all common links operational during the connection's lifetime. Moreover, we aim to guarantee a certain level of bandwidth requirement for this connection. The bandwidth of a connection is a bottleneck metric, given by the worst-case (minimal) bandwidth in any of the links of the spanning trees in the connection.

The following example demonstrates the concept of tunable survivability within the framework of spanning trees, while also considering bandwidth requirements. Consider the network example depicted in Fig. 1, where each link is associated with a failure probability p_e and a bandwidth b_e. Assume that we need to broadcast a reliable message to all nodes in the network through a spanning tree. The network contains several possible spanning trees, namely $T_1 = \{(a,b),(a,c),(a,d),(d,e)\}$, $T_2 = \{(a,e),(b,c),(c,d),(b,e)\}$, $T_3 = \{(a,b),(b,c),(c,d),(b,e)\}$ and $T_4 = \{(a,c),(b,c),(c,d),(d,e)\}$, illustrated by the four sub-figures bellow the network example, respectively. Clearly, the pair of link-disjoint spanning trees T_1 and T_2 guarantees full protection against a single link failure. Indeed, even if a single link fails, at least one of the trees does not contain any faulty links. Yet, this pair sustains just a single unit of bandwidth, since this is the minimal bandwidth over the links of both trees. However, if we are

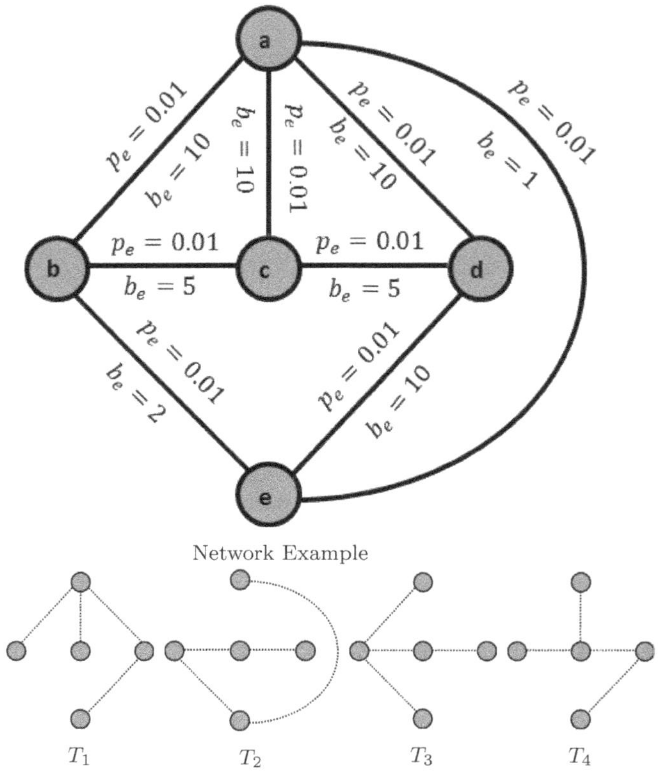

Figure 1: Example of tunable survivable spanning trees

satisfied with a survivability level of 0.99 against single network failures, then the pair of spanning trees T_1 and T_3 is a valid solution, since the only (single) failure that can concurrently damage both trees is in the common link (a,b). As this link fails with a probability of 0.01, the survivability level is 0.99 and the sustained bandwidth grows to 2. Now, suppose that we are satisfied with a survivability level of 0.99^2. Clearly, the spanning trees T_1 and T_4 also constitute a valid solution, for which the sustained bandwidth grows to 5. Finally, assume that we are satisfied with a survivability level of 0.99^4. Now, the single spanning tree T_1 also becomes a valid solution, thus increasing the sustained bandwidth to 10. We can see that there is a clear tradeoff between the survivability level and the bandwidth of the connection. We note that the above cases focused on pairs of spanning trees, while in general we can construct more than a pair. For example, by employing the triplet of spanning trees that consists of the links $T_1 = \{(a,b),(a,c),(a,d),(d,e)\}$, $T_3 = \{(a,b),(b,c),(c,d),(b,e)\}$ and $T_4 = \{(a,c),(b,c),(c,d),(d,e)\}$, we provide a full protection against a single link failure sustaining a bandwidth of 2. Therefore, this scheme improves the survivability level of 0.99 of connection supplied by the pair of spanning trees T_1 and T_3. In general, employing more spanning trees increases the survivability level but it also imposes higher management overhead.

Motivated by [19] and [27], we investigate how to implement the tunable survivability concept in the spanning tree framework. To that end, in Section 2, we formulate an optimization problem that considers two requirements, namely the level of survivability and some bottleneck QoS guarantee. Consequently, in Section 3, we establish some fundamental properties of the problem by investigating bounds on the number of trees that is needed to obtain a maximum level of survivability. Then, in Section 4, we design and validate an efficient algorithmic scheme for solving the considered optimization problem. Specifically, we present a novel polynomial-time algorithm for providing an optimal set of any number k of spanning trees that maximizes its survivability level while guaranteeing a required bandwidth. Additionally, in Section 5, we study an alternative optimization problem that considers additive, rather than bottleneck, QoS requirements. Although this is a much more complex class of problems, we present an algorithmic solution that is efficient for a case of practical interest. While the upper bound of Section 3 can be theoretically as large as the number of nodes in the network, in Section 6, through comprehensive simulations, we demonstrate that, in practice, this number is usually much smaller (in the range of $2-4$ trees). Furthermore, we show that, typically, a modest relaxation (of less than a percent) in the survivability level is enough to provide a dramatic improvement in terms of the sustained QoS. In Section 7, we provide some observations in order to extend our model for coping with double failures. Finally, Section 8 summarizes our results and discusses directions for future research.

2. PROBLEM FORMULATION

A *network* is represented by an undirected graph $G(V, E)$, where V is the set of nodes and E is the set of links. Each link $e \in E$ is assigned with a failure probability value $p_e \in (0,1)$[1]. Specifically, p_e represents the probability for a permanent fault in a specific link; we note that these probabilities are often estimated out of the available failure statistics of each network component [28] [29] [30] [31]. We assume that each link $e \in E$ fails independently. Each link $e \in E$ is also associated with a value b_e, which corresponds to some bottleneck QoS metric, e.g. the available bandwidth in the link.

A *tree* is an undirected graph in which any two vertices are connected by exactly one simple path. Given a network $G(V, E)$, a *spanning tree* $T(\tilde{V}, \tilde{E})$ of $G(V, E)$ is a tree composed of all network nodes V and some of the links in E, i.e., $\tilde{V} = V$ and $\tilde{E} \subseteq E$. Furthermore, we will also use the abbreviation T for specifying the spanning tree $T(\tilde{V}, \tilde{E})$ as well as its link set $\tilde{E}$.

As mentioned, we adopt the *single link failure model*, which considers handling at most one link failure in the network. A link is classified as either *faulty* or *operational*: it becomes faulty upon a failure and remains to be such until it is repaired, otherwise it is operational. Likewise, we say that a spanning tree T is *operational* if it has no faulty links, i.e. for each $e \in T$, link e is operational; otherwise, the spanning tree is faulty.

We proceed to formulate the concept of survivable spanning trees, through the following definitions.

DEFINITION 2.1. *Given a network $G(V, E)$ and an integer $k > 0$, a* k-survivable spanning connection *is a tuple of k spanning trees $(T_1, T_2, ..., T_k)$ of $G(V, E)$.*[2]

[1]For simplicity, we assume $p_e \neq 0, 1$, however, the extension for considering these values is trivial.

[2]The spanning trees are not necessarily disjoint.

Survivability is defined as the capability of the network to maintain service continuity in the presence of failures. Accordingly, we say that a k-survivable spanning connection $(T_1, T_2, ..., T_k)$ is operational if one of its k spanning trees are operational. Note that the spanning trees of a k-survivable spanning connection are not necessarily disjoint and might contain common links. Under the single link failure model, a k-survivable spanning connection $(T_1, T_2, ..., T_k)$ is operational iff the links that are common to *all* k spanning trees are operational. Consequently, as the failure probabilities are independent, we quantify the level of survivability of survivable connections as follows.

DEFINITION 2.2. *Given a k-survivable spanning connection $(T_1, ..., T_k)$, its* survivability level *$S((T_1, ..., T_k))$ is defined as the probability that at least one of the spanning trees in the connection is operational, i.e. all links that are common to all spanning trees are operational, namely $S((T_1, ..., T_k)) = \prod_{e \in \bigcap_{i=1}^{k} T_i} (1 - p_e)$.*

The above definition formalizes the notion of tunable survivability for the single link failure model. In case that there are no links that appear in all spanning trees $T_1, ..., T_k$, i.e. $\bigcap_{i=1}^{k} T_i = \emptyset$, there is no single failure that can make $(T_1, ..., T_k)$ fail; for this case, $S((T_1, ..., T_k))$ is defined to be 1.

We proceed to quantify the bandwidth of a survivable spanning connection.

DEFINITION 2.3. *Given a network $G(V, E)$ and a spanning tree T, its* bandwidth *$B(T)$ is defined as the bandwidth of its bottleneck link, i.e. $B(T) = \min_{e \in T}\{b_e\}$.*

DEFINITION 2.4. *Given a network $G(V, E)$ and a k-survivable spanning connection $(T_1, ..., T_k)$, its* bandwidth *$B((T_1, ..., T_k))$ is defined as the bandwidth of the bottleneck spanning tree, i.e. $B((T_1, ..., T_k)) = \min\{B(T_1), ..., B(T_k)\} = \min_{e \in \bigcup_{i=1}^{k} T_i}\{b_e\}$.*

As mentioned earlier, k spanning trees that do not share common links might not necessarily exist. Accordingly, the survivability level that can be obtained by any k spanning trees might be smaller than 1. For a given network $G(V, E)$, there might be several survivable spanning connections, among them we would be interested in those that have the best "quality", giving rise to the following optimization problems.

DEFINITION 2.5. **Constrained Bandwidth Max-Survivability (CBMS) Problem**: *Given are a network $G(V, E)$, a specified integer $k > 0$ of allowable spanning trees and a bandwidth constraint $B_0 > 0$. Find a k-survivable spanning connection $(T_1, ..., T_k)$ such that:*

$$\max S((T_1, .., T_k))$$

$$s.t.\ B((T_1, ..., T_k)) \geq B_0.$$

DEFINITION 2.6. **Constrained Survivability Max-Bandwidth (CSMB) Problem**: *Given are a network $G(V, E)$, a specified integer $k > 0$ of allowable spanning trees and a lower bound on the survivability level $S_0 \in [0, 1]$. Find a k-survivable spanning connection $(T_1, ..., T_k)$ such that:*

$$\max B((T_1, ..., T_k))$$

$$s.t.\ S((T_1, ..., T_k)) \geq S_0.$$

In the following sections, we will study the above problems and establish efficient algorithmic solutions for them. We begin by investigating the effect of the number k of allowable spanning trees on the quality of the solution.

3. HOW MANY SPANNING TREES?

While, in general, employing more spanning trees increases the survivability level, it also imposes higher management overhead. Moreover, it is clear that, beyond a certain number, the utilization of additional spanning trees would not further improve the obtained survivability level. Thus, an interesting question is how many trees are needed in order to obtain the maximum level of survivability. Accordingly, in this section we establish bounds on this number.

We proceed to demonstrate, through a simple example, the potential effect of the number of employed spanning trees, k, on the survivability level. Fig. 2 depicts a network where the link failure probability p_e is shown next to each link. The pairs of lines next to the network in Fig. 2a represent the three possible spanning trees of this specific network, namely $T_1 = \{(a,c),(b,c)\}$, $T_2 = \{(a,c),(a,b)\}$ and $T_3 = \{(a,b),(b,c)\}$. In case $k=1$, the highest survivability level is $S((T_1)) = 0.99 \cdot 0.98$ accomplished by the 1-survivable spanning connection (T_1). In case $k=2$, since this network instance does not contain two fully-disjoint spanning trees, the survivability level of any pair of spanning trees is lower than 1. Specifically, the 2-survivable spanning connection (T_1, T_2) provides the highest survivability level of $S((T_1,T_2)) = 0.99$. However, for $k=3$, the three illustrated spanning trees, i.e. the 3-survivable spanning connection (T_1,T_2,T_3), provide a survivability level of $S((T_1,T_2,T_3)) = 1$, since upon the failure of any single link, at least one of these trees remains operational. This is because there is not any link that is common to the three trees, i.e. $\bigcap_{i=1}^{k} T_i = \emptyset$.

We note that a given bandwidth constraint B_0 can be translated to a transformed $\tilde{G}(\tilde{V},\tilde{E})$ containing only the links that accomplish the requirement B_0, i.e $\tilde{E} = \{e | b_e > B_0\}$. Accordingly, the bandwidth consideration is omitted from the following discussion. We continue with several definitions.

Definition 3.1. *Given a network $G(V,E)$ and an integer $k > 0$, the* k-optimum survivability level $OPT^k(G)$ *is the maximum value of the survivability level that can be obtained by any k-survivable spanning connection $(T_1,...,T_k)$, i.e. $OPT^k(G) = \max_{(T_1,...,T_k)} S((T_1,...,T_k))$.*

Clearly, the value of the *k-optimum survivability level*, $OPT^k(G)$, depends on the number of spanning trees, k. Specifically, $OPT^k(G)$ is a non-decreasing function of k. The minimum value of this function is accomplished by $k=1$, namely $OPT^1(G)$, and its maximum value is considered by the following definition.

Definition 3.2. *Given a network $G(V,E)$, the* maximum level of survivability *$OPT(G)$ is the maximal survivability level that can be obtained by a spanning connection with any number k of spanning trees, where* $k \in [1, \binom{|E|}{|V|-1}]$, [3] *i.e., $OPT(G) = \max_k (OPT^k(G)) = \max_k \left(\max_{(T_1,...,T_k)} S((T_1,...,T_k))\right)$.*

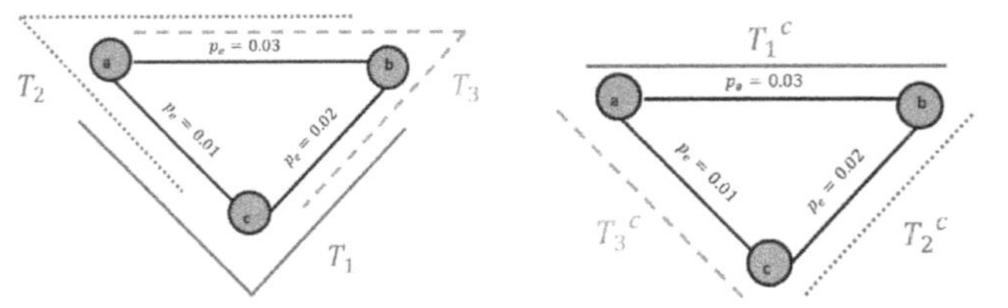

(a) Three possible spanning trees in a cycle of three nodes (b) The complementary sets of links for the three spanning trees

Figure 2: Three nodes cycle example

Definition 3.3. *Given an undirected network $G(V,E)$, its* number of sufficient spanning trees *$\phi(G)$ is the minimum number of spanning trees required to obtain the maximum level of survivability $OPT(G)$, i.e. $\phi(G) = \min(\{k | OPT^k(G) = OPT(G)\})$.*

Based on Def. 2.2, in order to maximize the survivability level of a k-survivable spanning connection, we aim to find k spanning trees such that the probability of a failure in at least one of the links that appears in all spanning trees is minimized. Equivalently, we can also consider the set of complementary links, i.e., for a set of links $\tilde{E}$, we have $(\tilde{E}^c) = E \setminus \tilde{E}$. For a spanning connection $(T_1,...,T_k)$ in a network $G(V,E)$, its survivability level is represented by $S((T_1,...,T_k)) = \prod_{e \in \bigcap_{i=1}^{k} T_i}(1-p_e) = \prod_{e \in (\bigcup_{i=1}^{k}(T_i^c))^c}(1-p_e)$, considering De-Morgan's Law [33]. Informally, given a spanning tree T, its complementary set T^c represents the links that are protected by T. Therefore, we would like to have more links in $(\bigcup_{i=1}^{k}(T_i^c))$, and, specifically, by satisfying the property that each link appears in at least one complement set, i.e. $\bigcup_{i=1}^{k}(T_i^c) = E$, a survivability level of 1 is guaranteed.

Fig. 2b presents the complementary sets of links for the three spanning trees from Fig. 2a. Since $T_1^c = \{(a,b)\}$, $T_2^c = \{(c,b)\}$ and $T_3^c = \{(a,c)\}$ then $\bigcup_{i=1}^{k}(T_i^c) = \{(a,b),(a,c),(c,b)\} = E$ and the survivability level of (T_1,T_2,T_3) satisfies $S((T_1,T_2,T_3)) = 1$.

In some graphs, one or more of the links must be a part of any spanning tree. We call such a link *a bridge*. If a graph contains a bridge, assuming that $p_e > 0$, a survivability level of 1 cannot be achieved.

Definition 3.4. *Given an undirected network $G(V,E)$,* a bridge *is a link e whose deletion increases the number of connected components. Accordingly, we define $Bridge(G)$ as the set of all bridges in the network.*

By the last definition, a bridge is a link that must be a part of any spanning tree while for any other link there exists at least one spanning tree that does not include it. The following theorem shows the dependency of the maximal survivability level of G on the failure probabilities of the set of bridges $Bridge(G)$.

[3] A trivial upper bound for the number of different spanning trees is $\binom{|E|}{|V|-1}$. An exact number is given by Kirchhoff's matrix tree theorem [32].

THEOREM 3.1. *The maximum level of survivability of $G(V,E)$ satisfies $OPT(G) = \prod_{e \in Bridge(G)}(1 - p_e)$.*

PROOF. Let k be the number of all possible spanning trees and let $(T_1, ..., T_k)$ be a spanning connection with these k spanning trees. By Def. 3.4, we have that $Bridge(G) = \bigcap_{i=1}^{k} T_i$. Since $OPT^k(G)$ is a non-decreasing function of k then $OPT(G)$ is obtained by this specific spanning connection, i.e. $OPT(G) = S((T_1, ..., T_k))$. Then, by Def. 2.2 we have $OPT(G) = S((T_1, ..., T_k)) = \prod_{e \in \bigcap_{i=1}^{k} T_i}(1 - p_e) = \prod_{e \in Bridge(G)}(1 - p_e)$. If $Bridge(G) = \emptyset$, a survivability level of 1 is obtained. □

The next theorem provides, for a network G, a simple upper bound on the number of sufficient spanning trees $\phi(G)$ required to obtain $OPT(G)$.

THEOREM 3.2. *For a network $G(V,E)$, the number of sufficient spanning trees satisfies $\phi(G) \leq |V|$.*

PROOF. For a network $G(V,E)$, consider a spanning connection $(T_1, ..., T_k)$ with the minimal possible number of spanning trees $k = \phi(G)$ required to obtain $OPT(G)$. Its survivability level is $S((T_1, ..., T_k)) = \prod_{e \in \bigcap_{i=1}^{k} T_i}(1 - p_e) = \prod_{e \in (\bigcup_{i=1}^{k}(T_i^c))^c}(1 - p_e)$. Consider the first spanning tree T_1. Clearly, $|T_1| = |E \setminus T_1^c| = |V| - 1$ and $|T_1^c| = |E| - |V| + 1$. Each of the $(k-1)$ additional spanning trees $(T_2, ..., T_k)$ must contribute at least one link to the union $(\bigcup_{i=1}^{k}(T_i^c)) \subseteq E$. Otherwise, spanning trees can be eliminated from the spanning connection, contradicting its minimality. We then have $(k - 1) \leq |E \setminus T_1^c| = |V| - 1$ and $\phi(G) = k \leq |V|$. □

Based on the above observations, we proceed to bound the number of sufficient spanning trees, $\phi(G)$, also from below.

THEOREM 3.3. *Given a network $G(V,E)$, let $\tilde{E} \subseteq E$ be the set of links $\tilde{E} = E \setminus Bridge(G)$. Then, the number of sufficient spanning trees of G satisfies $\phi(G) \geq \left\lceil \frac{|\tilde{E}|}{|E|-|V|+1} \right\rceil$.*

PROOF. Consider a spanning connection $(T_1, ..., T_k)$ with $k = \phi(G)$ spanning trees that satisfies $S((T_1, ..., T_k)) = OPT(G)$. We showed earlier that $S((T_1, ..., T_k)) = \prod_{e \in (\bigcup_{i=1}^{k}(T_i^c))^c}(1 - p_e)$ and by Theorem 3.1 we have $OPT(G) = \prod_{e \in Bridge(G)}(1 - p_e)$. Then necessarily $\tilde{E} \subseteq \bigcup_{i=1}^{k}(T_i^c)$, i.e. any non-bridge link must be a member of one of the set complements $T_1^c, ..., T_k^c$. The number of links in each spanning tree is fixed and for $i \in [1,k]$ $|T_i| = (|V| - 1)$, $|T_i^c| = |E| - |V| + 1$. Then, $|\tilde{E}| \leq |\bigcup_{i=1}^{k}(T_i^c)| \leq \sum_{i=1}^{k}(|T_i^c|) = k \cdot (|E| - |V| + 1) = \phi(G) \cdot (|E| - |V| + 1)$. In addition, by definition $\phi(G)$ is an integer. The result then follows. □

We proceed to demonstrate the tightness of both previous presented bounds through two network examples. First, we provide a tight upper bound example considering the special case of a *cycle*, i.e. an undirected connected network $G(V,E)$ where every node has exactly two links incident with it.

THEOREM 3.4. *Let $G(V,E)$ be a cycle of $|V|$ nodes. Then:*

1. *Its maximum level of survivability satisfies $OPT(G) = 1$.*

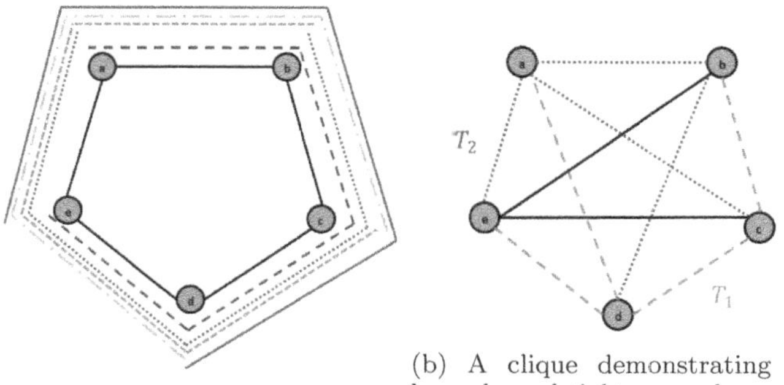

(a) A cycle demonstrating an upper bound tight example

(b) A clique demonstrating a lower bound tight example

Figure 3: Tightness examples

2. *Its number of sufficient spanning trees satisfies $\phi(G) = |V|$.*

PROOF. Clearly, for a cycle $G(V,E)$, we have $|E| = |V|$ and $Bridge(G) = \emptyset$. Then, by Theorem 3.1, we have $OPT(G) = \prod_{e \in Bridge(G)}(1 - p_e) = 1$. In addition, by Theorem 3.2. $\phi(G) \leq |V|$. Likewise, by Theorem 3.3, for $\tilde{E} = E \setminus Bridge(G) = E$, we have $\phi(G) \geq \frac{|\tilde{E}|}{|E|-|V|+1} = |E| = |V|$ and the result follows. □

Next, we demonstrate the tightness of the presented lower bound of Theorem 3.3 on the number of sufficient spanning trees by considering a *clique* with $|V| \geq 4$ nodes, i.e. an undirected connected network $G(V,E)$ where every two nodes are connected by a link.

THEOREM 3.5. *Let $G(V,E)$ be a clique of $|V| \geq 4$ nodes. Then:*

1. *Its maximum level of survivability satisfies $OPT(G) = 1$.*
2. *The value of the lower bound is $\left\lceil \frac{|\tilde{E}|}{|E|-|V|+1} \right\rceil = 2$.*
3. *Its number of sufficient spanning trees satisfies $\phi(G) = 2 = \left\lceil \frac{|\tilde{E}|}{|E|-|V|+1} \right\rceil$.*

PROOF. We start by showing that $\frac{|\tilde{E}|}{|E|-|V|+1} > 1$ and that $\frac{|\tilde{E}|}{|E|-|V|+1} \leq 2$. For a clique G with $|V| \geq 4$ nodes, there are no bridges and $Bridge(G) = \emptyset$, $\tilde{E} = E$ and by Theorem 3.1 $OPT(G) = 1$. Likewise, $|E| = \frac{1}{2} \cdot |V|(|V| - 1)$. For $|V| \geq 4$, we have $|V| > 1$ and $|E| > |E| - |V| + 1 > 0$ so the lower bound follows. For $|V| \geq 4$, we also have $2 \cdot (|V| - 1) \leq \frac{1}{2} \cdot |V|(|V| - 1) = |E|$. Thus $|E| \leq 2 \cdot (|E| - |V| + 1)$ and the upper bound follows as well and $\left\lceil \frac{|\tilde{E}|}{|E|-|V|+1} \right\rceil = 2$.

We would now like to show that in such a clique with $|V| \geq 4$ nodes, the number of sufficient spanning trees is indeed $\phi(G) = 2$. We show that by presenting two link-disjoint spanning trees. Consider four distinct arbitrary nodes a, b, c, d. We define the trees $T_1 = \{(a,x)|x \in V \setminus \{a,d\}\} \bigcup \{(b,d)\}$ and $T_2 = \{(d,x)|x \in V \setminus \{b,d\}\} \bigcup \{(b,c)\}$. Both spanning trees are obtained by replacing one link by another in the simple spanning trees that include only all the links connected to the nodes a and d, respectively. These spanning trees have no links in common. □

Fig. 3 demonstrates a particular instance of the networks presented in Theorems 3.4 and 3.5. Specifically, Fig. 3a depicts a tight upper bound consisting of a cycle of 5 nodes, where its maximum level of survivability of $OPT(G) = 1$ is achieved by the 5 dashed lined spanning trees. Contrarily, the clique of 5 nodes illustrated in Fig. 3b represents a tight lower bound, where its maximum level of survivability of $OPT(G) = 1$ is accomplished by the 2 dashed lined spanning trees.

According to theorem 3.2, for a network $G(V, E)$ we might need to employ up to $|V|$ spanning trees in order to obtain a maximum survivability level. In practice, due to the overhead incurred by managing a large number of trees, one typically seeks solutions with a much smaller number of spanning trees. Fortunately, as shall be demonstrated at Section 6, the number of required trees for achieving the maximum survivability level is, in practice, much smaller than the bound $|V|$, namely, it is typically 2 and rarely above 3.

4. ESTABLISHING SURVIVABLE SPANNING CONNECTIONS

In this section, we show how to construct a k-survivable spanning connection that solves the CBMS and CSMB optimization problems that have been defined in section 2.

4.1 Establishing k-survivable spanning connections for the CBMS Problem

We proceed to present an efficient polynomial algorithmic scheme, termed the CBMS Algorithm, for solving the CBMS Problem. The algorithm applies, as a building block, the Minimum-Cost Edge Disjoint Spanning Tree Algorithm (EDSTA) [22] [23], which finds k link disjoint spanning trees in a graph with minimum real cost, on a constructed auxiliary graph. Indeed, EDSTA algorithm is based on the well-known matroid theory [34] [35]. Specifically, the links of a network $G(V, E)$ form a matroid by defining a set of edges $F \subset E$ to be independent iff F can be partitioned into k forests. Thus, the matroid greedy algorithm can be employed to solve the problem in polynomial time. The CBMS Algorithm, specified in Fig. 5, consists of four stages.

The first stage comprises of the construction of an auxiliary network $\tilde{G}(\tilde{V}, \tilde{E})$, such that $\tilde{V} = \{\tilde{u} | u \in V\}, \tilde{E} = \{\tilde{e}_1, \ldots, \tilde{e}_k | e \in E, b_e \geq B_0\}$. That is, each link in the original network that accommodates the bandwidth requirement B_0 is duplicated k times, constituting a set defined as follows.

DEFINITION 4.1. *Given a link $e \in E$ of a network $G(V, E)$, a* k-Duplicate Link set *is the set of k-duplicated links at $\tilde{G}(\tilde{V}, \tilde{E})$ representing a single link $e \in E$. Accordingly, we denote the k-Duplicate Link set of link $e \in E$ as DL_e^k.*

The weight of one link in the k-Duplicate Link set is determined to be $w_{\tilde{e}_1} = -ln(1 - p_e)$, thus transforming the multiplicative (survivability) metric into an additive one. Note that $p_e \neq 0, 1$ by definition of Section 2, therefore $w_{\tilde{e}_1} \in (0, \infty)$. However, this trivial case can be treated at the same manner for $p_e = 0$ and by discarding the links e that $p_e = 1$. Additionally, the weights of the other $(k - 1)$ links are set to be $w_{\tilde{e}_2} = \cdots = w_{\tilde{e}_k} = 0$. Consequently, each k-Duplicate Link set contains exactly one link with a positive weight, i.e. $w_{\tilde{e}_1} > 0$. This transformation is depicted in Fig. 4.

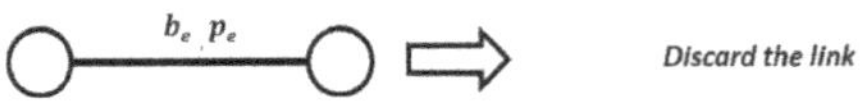

(a) For each link with a bandwidth $b_e < B_0$

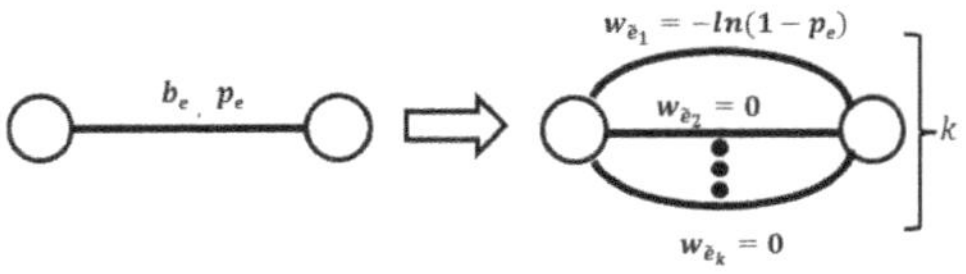

(b) For each link with a bandwidth $b_e \geq B_0$

Figure 4: CBMS Algorithm Link Transformation

Input:
$G(V, E)$-network, p_e-link failure probability, B_0-bandwidth constraint, k-the number of allowable spanning trees.
Variables:
$\tilde{G}(\tilde{V}, \tilde{E})$-transformed network, DL_e^k-a k-Duplicate Link set of link e, $w_{\tilde{e}_1}, \ldots, w_{\tilde{e}_k}$-success cost, $(\tilde{T}_1, ..., \tilde{T}_k)$-auxiliary network solution, $(T_1, ..., T_k)$-the survivable spanning connection solution.
Stage *1- Transformed network $\tilde{G}(\tilde{V}, \tilde{E})$ construction.*
- $\tilde{V} \leftarrow \{\tilde{u} | u \in V\}$.
foreach $e : (u, v) \in E$ **do**
  if $b_e \geq B_0$ **then**
    - Construct k links $\tilde{e}_1, ..., \tilde{e}_k$ between $\tilde{u}$ and $\tilde{v}$
    - Assign $w_{\tilde{e}_1}$ to be $-ln(1 - p_e)$
    - Assign $w_{\tilde{e}_2}, ..., w_{\tilde{e}_k}$ to be 0
    - $DL_e^k = (\tilde{e}_1, ..., \tilde{e}_k)$
  end
end
Stage *2- Connectivity Test.*
if *$\tilde{G}(\tilde{V}, \tilde{E})$ is not connected* **then**
  return Fail
end
Stage *3- Minimum Edge Disjoint Spanning Tree Calculation.*
- Execute the Minimum-Cost Edge Disjoint Spanning Tree Algorithm [22] for the instance $< \tilde{G}(\tilde{V}, \tilde{E}), w_{\tilde{e}}, k >$.
- Let $(\tilde{T}_1, ..., \tilde{T}_k)$ represent the solution of the Algorithm.
Stage *4- Survivable Spanning Connection Construction.*
for $i = 1$ *to* k **do**
  $T_i = \{e | (\exists \tilde{l} \in \tilde{T}_i) \wedge \tilde{l} \in DL_e^k\}$
end
return $(T_1, ..., T_k)$

Figure 5: CBMS Algorithm

In the second stage, the algorithm executes a connectivity test on the auxiliary network $\tilde{G}(\tilde{V}, \tilde{E})$, using some standard connectivity test procedure, e.g. Depth First Search (DFS) [34]. If $\tilde{G}(\tilde{V}, \tilde{E})$ is found to be disconnected, the algorithm stops with a failure indication.

Otherwise, the third stage finds out k link disjoint spanning trees of minimum cost in the auxiliary network $\tilde{G}(\tilde{V}, \tilde{E})$ by applying the EDSTA algorithm from [22] or [23]. We note that the auxiliary network $\tilde{G}(\tilde{V}, \tilde{E})$ necessarily contains k link disjoint spanning trees (see Lemma 4.1). Moreover, since the EDSTA algorithm aims to find minimum cost spanning trees, the positive weighted link at each k-Duplicate Link set will be chosen only if all the other alternative (zero-weight) links are selected.

Accordingly, in the fourth stage, we construct the sought k-survivable spanning connection according to the k link-disjoint spanning trees solution identified above. Specifically, each tree T_i in the k-survivable spanning connection in $G(V, E)$ is deduced from a tree $\tilde{T}_i$ out of k link-disjoint spanning trees solution in $\tilde{G}(\tilde{V}, \tilde{E})$ by choosing the links $e \in E$ associated with the k-Duplicate Link set DL_e^k containing the links $\{\tilde{e}_1, \ldots, \tilde{e}_k\}$ in $\tilde{T}_i$. Then, the algorithm outputs them as the optimal spanning connection solution $(T_1, ..., T_k)$.

We proceed to prove the correctness of the CBMS Algorithm (Fig. 5).

LEMMA 4.1. *If the auxiliary network $\tilde{G}(\tilde{V}, \tilde{E})$ is connected then there are k link-disjoint spanning trees.*

PROOF. We will prove the lemma by construction. Since $\tilde{G}(\tilde{V}, \tilde{E})$ is connected, there is necessarily a tree spanning the network, denoted as $\tilde{T}$. Let us construct another $k-1$ spanning trees, each containing a different link of the k-Duplicated Links sets containing the links of $\tilde{T}$. We thus have k disjoint spanning trees. □

The following theorem establishes the correctness of the CBMS Algorithm.

THEOREM 4.1. *Given are a network $G(V, E)$, a requirement $k > 0$ on the number of the spanning trees and a bandwidth requirement $B_0 > 0$. If there exists a k-survivable spanning connection $(T_1, ..., T_k)$ with a bandwidth of at least B_0, then the CBMS Algorithm returns a k-survivable spanning connection that is a solution to the CBMS Problem (Def. 2.5); otherwise, the algorithm fails.*

PROOF. The auxiliary network $\tilde{G}(\tilde{V}, \tilde{E})$ constructed at Stage 1 excludes all links with a bandwidth smaller than B_0, thus guaranteeing that the bandwidth of the k-survivable spanning connection $(T_1, ..., T_k)$ would be at least B_0. Lemma 4.1 establishes that the algorithm fails if and only if the auxiliary network $\tilde{G}(\tilde{V}, \tilde{E})$ is not connected (Stage 2). Therefore, at Stage 3, the EDSTA algorithm [22] outputs a feasible solution $(\tilde{T}_1, ..., \tilde{T}_k)$. We note that at each k-Duplicate Link set exactly one link has a positive weight $w_{\tilde{e}_1} > 0$ and the rest are of zero weight $w_{\tilde{e}_2} = \cdots = w_{\tilde{e}_k} = 0$. Therefore, since the EDSTA algorithm aims to find minimum cost spanning trees, only the k-Duplicate Link sets that are fully selected by all spanning trees $\tilde{T}_1, ..., \tilde{T}_k$ affect the weight of the optimal solution $(\tilde{T}_1, ..., \tilde{T}_k)$. By applying the indicator function $I(\cdot)$, which takes the value of 1 if the condition that it receives as a parameter is satisfied, and 0 otherwise, the weight of the optimal solution $(\tilde{T}_1, ..., \tilde{T}_k)$ minimizes $\sum_{\tilde{T}_i \in (\tilde{T}_1, ..., \tilde{T}_k)} \sum_{\tilde{e}_j \in \tilde{T}_i} w_{\tilde{e}_j} =$

$$\sum_{e \in E} \sum_{\tilde{T}_i \in (\tilde{T}_1, ..., \tilde{T}_k)} \sum_{j \in [1,k]} I(\tilde{e}_j \in \tilde{T}_i) \cdot w_{\tilde{e}_j} =$$

$$\sum_{e \in E} -\ln(1-p_e) \cdot I((\forall i \in [1,k])(\exists j \in [1,k])\tilde{e}_j \in \tilde{T}_i) =$$

$$\sum_{e \in E} -\ln(1-p_e) \cdot I((\forall i \in [1,k])e \in T_i) = -\ln \prod_{e \in \bigcap_{i=1}^{k} T_i} (1-p_e).$$

Equivalently, it maximizes $\prod_{e \in \bigcap_{i=1}^{k} T_i}(1-p_e)$, which is the optimal solution value of the CBMS Problem. Accordingly, the fourth stage outputs the optimal solution. □

Input: $G(V, E)$-network, p_e-link failure probability, S_0-survivability level constraint, k-the number of allowable spanning trees.
Variables: Q-set of available bandwidth values, $(T_1, ..., T_k)$-the survivable spanning connection solution.
- Create a sorted set $Q = \{b_e | e \in E\}$.
- Perform a Binary Search over the set Q in order to find the largest $B_0 \in Q$ by executing the CBMS Algorithm with bandwidth constraint of B_0, as follows.
  - Denote $(T_1, ..., T_k)$ the solution of CBMS Algorithm.
  if $S((T_1, ..., T_k)) \geq S_0$ **then**
    increase the value of B_0 according to the binary search.
  end
  else
    reduce the value of B_0 according to the binary search.
  end
return $(T_1, ..., T_k)$

Figure 6: CSMB Algorithm

We proceed to analyze the running time of the CBMS Algorithm.

THEOREM 4.2. *The time complexity of the CBMS Algorithm is $O(k \cdot |E| \cdot \log(k \cdot |E|) + k^2 \cdot |V|^2)$.*

PROOF. We note that, at Stage 1, the construction of the transformed network $\tilde{G}(\tilde{V}, \tilde{E})$ contains at most $k \cdot |E|$ links. Moreover, the connectivity test performed at Stage 2 can be performed in $O(k \cdot |E| + |V|)$ [34]. According to [22] and considering the number of links in the new transformed network, the Minimum-Cost Edge Disjoint Spanning Tree Algorithm executed at Stage 3 incurs $O(k \cdot |E| \cdot \log(k \cdot |E|) + k^2 \cdot |V|^2)$. Clearly, the time complexity of the CBMS Algorithm is solely affected by the running time of Stage 3. □

4.2 Establishing k-survivable spanning connections for the CSMB Problem

We proceed to establish an efficient algorithmic scheme for the second optimization problem, namely the CSMB Problem (as defined in Def. 2.6). This is achieved by employing the previously presented CBMS Algorithm (Fig. 5), as follows. Given are a network $G(V, E)$, a specified number k of allowable spanning trees and a survivability level constraint S_0. Accordingly, we aim to find the largest value of B_0 such that the survivability level of the most survivable k-survivable spanning connection with a bandwidth of at least B_0, which is a solution to the CBMS Problem, is at least S_0. Clearly, the efficiency of this strategy depends on the number of times that the CBMS Algorithm needs to be executed. We proceed to show that it is sufficient to consider just $O(\log |E|)$ such executions.

First, we observe that the bandwidth of a k-survivable spanning connection $B((T_1, ..., T_k))$, per Def. 2.4, is a bottleneck metric. Therefore, for every given network $G(V, E)$

of $|E|$ links, the maximum bandwidth of a k-survivable spanning connection belongs to a set of at most $|E|$ values, i.e. $Q = \{b_e | e \in E\}$. According to Lemma 4.2, it is enough to perform a *binary search* over the set Q executing the CBMS Algorithm. Each time the CBMS Algorithm provides a solution that accomplishes the survivability constraint S_O, the bandwidth constraint B_O that serves as input to the CBMS Algorithm is increased. Otherwise, the B_O input is reduced. Accordingly, Fig. 6 depicts a formal specification of this algorithmic scheme, namely the *CSMB Algorithm*.

We proceed to prove the correctness of the CSMB Algorithm. Denote the survivability level value of the solution of the CBMS Problem 2.5 with a constraint of B_O as $CBMS_{MAX}(B_O)$.

LEMMA 4.2. *The function $CBMS_{MAX}(B_O)$ is a non-increasing monotonic function in the parameter $B_O \in Q = \{b_e | e \in E\}$, i.e for each $B_{O_1}, B_{O_2} \in Q$ such that $B_{O_1} < B_{O_2}$ then $CBMS_{MAX}(B_{O_1}) \geq CBMS_{MAX}(B_{O_2})$.*

PROOF. Given are $B_{O_1}, B_{O_2} \in Q$ such that $B_{O_1} < B_{O_2}$ and the associated solutions T_{O_1}, T_{O_2} to the CBMS Problem, respectively. Clearly, T_{O_2} is also a feasible solution for the CBMS problem with a bandwidth constraint of B_{O_1}, since $B(T_{O_2}) \geq B_{O_2} > B_{O_1}$. Therefore, $CBMS_{MAX}(B_{O_1}) \geq CBMS_{MAX}(B_{O_2})$, otherwise it contradicts its maximality. □

The following theorem establishes the correctness of the CSMB Algorithm.

THEOREM 4.3. *Given are a network $G(V, E)$, a requirement $k > 0$ on the number of the spanning trees and a survivability level constraint $S_O \in [0, 1]$. If there exists a k-survivable spanning connection $(T_1, ..., T_k)$ with a survivability level of at least S_O, then the CSMB Algorithm returns a k-survivable spanning connection that is a solution to a CSMB Problem 2.5; otherwise, the algorithm fails.*

PROOF. Lemma 4.2 establishes that the execution of the CBMS Algorithm for incrementing values of B_O results in solutions with non-increasing survivability levels. Moreover, the set $Q = \{b_e | e \in E\}$ of available bandwidth values contains at most $|E|$ values. Therefore, in order to solve the CSMB Problem, it is enough to perform a binary search over the solution of the CBMS Algorithm for different values of $B_O \in Q$. □

We consider now the complexity incurred by the CSMB Algorithm. To that end, we denote by $T(k, |V|, |E|)$ the running time of the CBMS Algorithm. Since the CSMB Algorithm consists of a binary search over a set of size $|E|$, performing the CBMS Algorithm at each step, its time complexity is $O(T(k, |V|, |E|) \cdot \log |E|)$.

5. ADDITIVE METRICS

We proceed to consider a variant of the model presented in Section 2, which addresses an additive QoS metric instead of the bandwidth (bottleneck) metric. Accordingly, each link $e \in E$ is associated with an additive metric value w_e, which corresponds to an additive QoS target, such as delay or cost. We proceed to quantify the weight of a survivable spanning connection.

DEFINITION 5.1. *Given a network $G(V, E)$ and a spanning tree T, its* weight $W(T)$ *is defined as the sum of the weights of its links, namely $\sum_{e \in T} w_e$. Likewise, for a k-survivable spanning connection $(T_1, ..., T_k)$, its* weight $W((T_1, ..., T_k))$ *is defined as the sum of the weights of its k trees, namely $W((T_1, ..., T_k)) = \sum_{i=1}^{k} W(T_i) = \sum_{i=1}^{k} \sum_{e \in T_i} w_e$.*

We note that the problem of finding a spanning tree in a graph with two additive costs, namely minimizing one cost under a restriction on the other cost, is NP-Hard [36]. Ac-

(a) For each common link

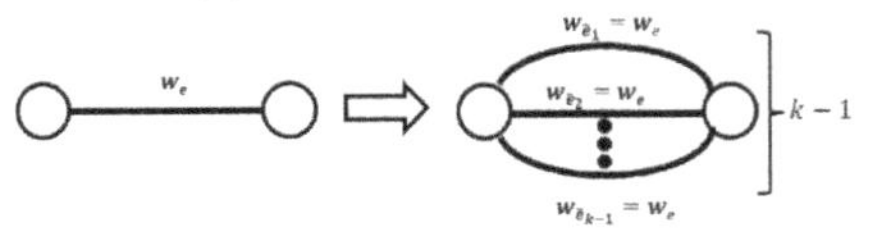

(b) For the rest of the links

Figure 7: MSSC Algorithm Link Transformation

Input:
$G(V, E)$-network, w_e-link weights, l-maximal number of common links.
Variables:
$\tilde{G}(\tilde{V}, \tilde{E})$-auxiliary network, E_{sub}-a subset of E, $DL_e^{(k-1)}$-a $(k-1)$-Duplicate Link set of link e, $\mathcal{P}_{\leq l}(E)$-the power set of E with cardinality of at most l, $(T_1, ..., T_k)$-the survivable spanning connection solution, W_{min}-weight of the survivable spanning connection solution (initialized to ∞), $(\tilde{T}_1, ..., \tilde{T}_k)$-auxiliary network solution, $\tilde{W}_{min}$-weight of the candidate solution.

foreach $E_{sub} \in \mathcal{P}_{\leq l}(E)$ **do**
- Construct $\tilde{G}(\tilde{V}, \tilde{E})$ as follows:
  - $\tilde{V} \leftarrow \{\tilde{u} | u \in V\}$.

  foreach $e : (u, v) \in E_{sub}$ **do**
    - Concatenate the nodes $\tilde{u}, \tilde{v}$ to a single node in $\tilde{V}$.

  end

  foreach $e : (u, v) \in E \backslash E_{sub}$ **do**
    - Construct $(k-1)$ links $\tilde{e}_1, ..., \tilde{e}_{k-1}$ between $\tilde{u}$ and $\tilde{v}$.
    - Assign $w_{\tilde{e}_1}, ..., w_{\tilde{e}_{k-1}}$ to be w_e.
    - $DL_e^{(k-1)} = (\tilde{e}_1, ..., \tilde{e}_{k-1})$.

  end
- Execute the Minimum-Cost Edge Disjoint Spanning Tree Algorithm [22] for the instance $< \tilde{G}(\tilde{V}, \tilde{E}), w_{\tilde{e}}, k >$.
- Let $(\tilde{T}_1, ..., \tilde{T}_k)$ represent the solution of the Algorithm and $\tilde{W}_{min}$ its weight.

if $W_{min} > \tilde{W}_{min} + k \cdot \Sigma_{e \in E_{sub}} w_e$ **then**
  - $W_{min} = \tilde{W}_{min} + k \cdot \Sigma_{e \in E_{sub}} w_e$
  - $\forall i = 1, ..., k,$
    $T_i = \{e | (\exists \tilde{l} \in \tilde{T}_i) \wedge \tilde{l} \in DL_e^{(k-1)}\} \cup E_{sub}$

end

end
- return $(T_1, ..., T_k)$

Figure 8: MSSC Algorithm

---

cordingly, we consider the following simpler version of the optimization problem. We assume that all links have the same failure probability. In this case, by Def. 2.2 a lower bound on the survivability level is translated into an upper bound on the number of common links. We denote this number by l.

DEFINITION 5.2. **Minimal Survivable Spanning Connection (MSSC) Problem**: *Given are a network $G(V, E)$, a requirement $k > 0$ on the number of the spanning trees and a restriction l on the maximal number of common links. Find a k-survivable spanning connection $(T_1, ..., T_k)$ with at most l common links and of minimum weight.*

The MSSC Algorithm, specified in Fig. 8, solves the MSSC optimization problem 5.2. As will be shown, its time complexity is exponential in the allowable number of common links, l. However, in many practical instances, the required level of survivability is high, and hence, the number of overlapped links needs to be small (thus inducing a small value of l), which in turn makes the algorithm computationally permissible. The algorithm considers all possible combinations of at most l common links out of the set E. Specifically, we construct an auxiliary network $\tilde{G}(\tilde{V}, \tilde{E})$ for each set of common links E_{sub} in the power set of E with cardinality of at most l, i.e. the set of all subsets of E whose size is at most l. The auxiliary network $\tilde{G}(\tilde{V}, \tilde{E})$ consists of a link transformation, depicted in Fig. 7. Initially, each link $(u, v) \in E_{sub}$ is excluded by concatenating the nodes u and v to a single node. Moreover, the rest of the links are duplicated $k - 1$ times and their weights are set to be w_e. Consequently, given the new constructed network $\tilde{G}(\tilde{V}, \tilde{E})$, the algorithm identifies a k link-disjoint spanning tree with minimum cost, by employing the Minimum-Cost Edge Disjoint Spanning Tree Algorithm (EDSTA) [22] [23]. Then, we construct the sought survivable spanning connection out of the links in the link-disjoint spanning tree solution. Finally, the optimal survivable spanning connection solution $(T_1, ..., T_k)$ is the smallest survivable spanning connection discovered out of all constructed auxiliary networks (one for each possible combination of at most l common links).

The following theorem establishes the correctness of the MSSC Algorithm.

THEOREM 5.1. *Given are a network $G(V, E)$, a requirement $k > 0$ on the number of the spanning trees and a restriction l on the number of common links. If there exists a k-survivable spanning connection $(T_1, ..., T_k)$ with at most l common links, then the MSSC Algorithm returns a k-survivable spanning connection that is a solution to a MSSC Problem 5.2; otherwise, the algorithm fails.*

PROOF. We will prove that at each iteration of the first "foreach" loop, the MSSC Algorithm finds a minimum weight solution which its common links are E_{sub}. Since this loop examines all possible cases (over the $\mathcal{P}_{\leq l}(E)$), the algorithm outputs the optimal solution.

In order to prove the above, we will show that at the auxiliary network $\tilde{G}(\tilde{V}, \tilde{E})$ a minimum cost k-edge disjoint spanning tree $(\tilde{T}_1, ..., \tilde{T}_k)$ with a weight $\tilde{W}_{min}$ has an equivalent minimal k-survivable spanning connection solution $(T_1, ..., T_k)$ in $G(V, E)$ whose weight is $\tilde{W}_{min} + k \cdot \Sigma_{e \in E_{sub}} w_e$ and $T_i = \{e | (\exists \tilde{l} \in \tilde{T}_i) \wedge \tilde{l} \in DL_e^{(k-1)}\} \cup E_{sub}$. By applying the indicator function $I(\cdot)$, which takes the value of 1 if the condition that it receives as a parameter is satisfied, and 0 otherwise, the weight of the optimal solution $(\tilde{T}_1, ..., \tilde{T}_k)$ minimizes $\sum_{\tilde{T}_i \in (\tilde{T}_1,...,\tilde{T}_k)} \sum_{\tilde{e}_j \in \tilde{T}_i} w_{\tilde{e}_j} + k \cdot \Sigma_{e \in E_{sub}} w_e =$

$$\sum_{e \in E} \sum_{\tilde{T}_i \in (\tilde{T}_1,...,\tilde{T}_k)} \sum_{j \in [1,k-1]} I(\tilde{e}_j \in \tilde{T}_i) \cdot w_e + k \cdot \Sigma_{e \in E_{sub}} w_e =$$

$$\sum_{e \in E} \sum_{i \in [1,k]} I(e \in T_i) \cdot w_e = \sum_{i=1}^{k} \sum_{e \in T_i} w_e = W((T_1, ..., T_k))$$

Accordingly, the spanning connection obtained from the solution of the Minimum-Cost Edge Disjoint Spanning Tree Algorithm at the auxiliary network $\tilde{G}(\tilde{V}, \tilde{E})$ minimizes the weight of a k-survivable spanning connection solution $(T_1, ..., T_k)$ in $G(V, E)$ where its common links are the set E_{sub}. Therefore, the algorithm outputs the optimal solution. □

The MSSC Algorithm time complexity is $O(\sum_{i=1}^{l} \binom{|E|}{i} \cdot ((k \cdot |E|) \cdot \log(k \cdot |E|) + k^2 \cdot |V|^2))$, i.e., exponential in l but polynomial in all other values. As noted, the value of l would be typically small, in which case the algorithm offers a time-efficient optimal solution.

6. SIMULATION STUDY

In this section, we demonstrate the advantages of employing *tunable* survivable spanning connections over the traditional full protection schemes on common network topologies. First, we examine the effect of the number of different spanning trees k in a survivable spanning connection on the accomplished survivability level. Specifically, we demonstrate that the number of required spanning trees is much smaller than the theoretical upper bound described in Theorem 3.2 and, in practice, two spanning trees are sufficient for getting extremely (namely, in the order of four-nines[4]) close to the maximum survivability level. Motivated by this finding, we focus on $k = 2$ and compare between the performance (in terms of bandwidth and feasibility) of an optimal 2-survivable spanning connection with a survivability level of at least S_0, where $S_0 \in [0.95, 1]$, and the performance of a pair of fully disjoint spanning trees (i.e., $S_0 = 1$). Most notably, we show that, by slightly relaxing the traditional requirement of 100% protection, major improvements in terms of bandwidth and feasibility are accomplished.

6.1 Setup

We generated two classes of well-known random network topologies, namely Power-Law topology [37] and Waxman topology [38]. First, we consider the Power-Law topology, which is widely employed for modeling typical network interconnections, in particular in the context of the Internet [37]. We then extend our findings to other classes of network topologies by analyzing the Waxman topology.

For both classes, we generated 10,000 random networks, each containing 200 nodes. In all simulation instances, we assumed a uniform distribution of the link bandwidth, in the range of [5, 150] MB/s. Additionally, the failure probability of each link was distributed normally with a mean of 0.01 and a standard deviation of 0.003 assuming a non-negative value.

For each of the above generated random networks, we employed the CBMS Algorithm (Fig. 5) with several band-

[4] i.e. 0.9999.

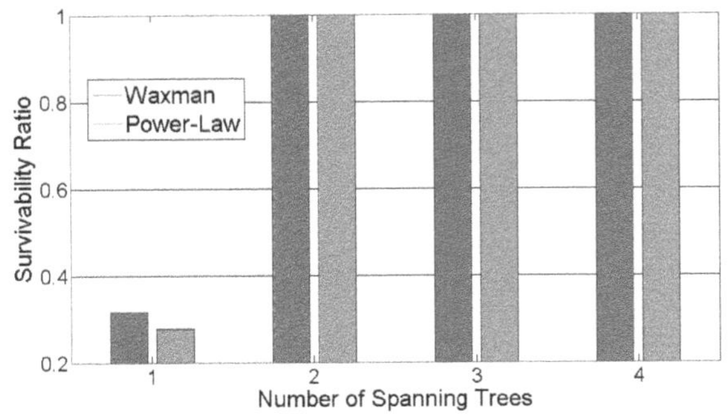

(a) Maximum survivability level ratio $OPT^k(G)/OPT(G)$ versus the number of spanning trees k

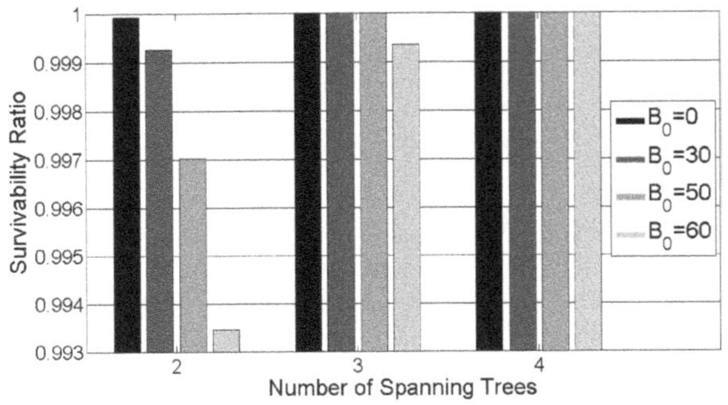

(b) Maximum survivability level ratio $OPT^k_{B_0}(G)/OPT_{B_0}(G)$ versus the number of spanning trees k for different bandwidth requirements B_0 in Waxman Topology

Figure 9: Maximum survivability as a function of the number of spanning trees

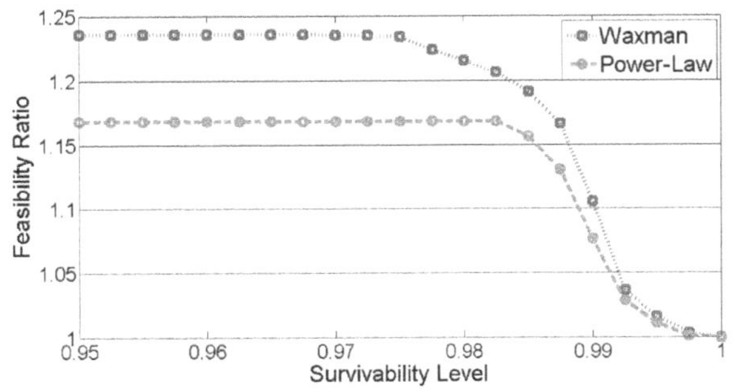

(a) Feasibility ratio $N(S_0)/N(1)$ versus the survivability level requirement S_0

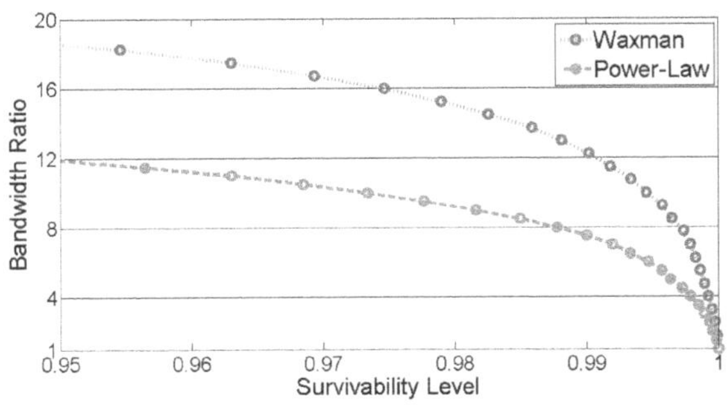

(b) Bandwidth ratio $B(S_0)/B(1)$ versus the survivability level requirement S_0

Figure 10: Performance as a function of the survivability level requirement

width constraint values, namely $B_0 = 0, 30, 50, 60$, and with various values of the number of allowable spanning trees, namely $k = 1, 2, 3, 4$. For each bandwidth constraint B_0, we measured the network's maximum level of survivability denoted as $OPT_{B_0}(G)$ and the maximum survivability of the k-survivable spanning connection $OPT^k_{B_0}(G)$. Then, we derived the *survivability ratio*, defined as $\sigma_{B_0}(k) \triangleq \frac{OPT^k_{B_0}(G)}{OPT_{B_0}(G)}$ and, accordingly, calculated the average value over the simulated networks, denoted as $\overline{\sigma_{B_0}(k)}$.

Next, we consider the case of 2-survivable spanning connection through the following simulations. For each generated network and survivability level constraint S_0 in the range of $[0.95, 1]$, we employed the CSMB Algorithm (Fig. 6) and conducted the following measurements. First, we measured the number of networks that admit a 2-survivable spanning connection with a survivability level of at least S_0 (without any bandwidth requirement) among the 10,000 random networks, denoted as $N(S_0)$. Note that $N(1)$ represents the number of networks that admit fully disjoint spanning trees since $p_e > 0$. Accordingly, we derived the *feasibility ratio* defined as $\rho(S_0) \triangleq \frac{N(S_0)}{N(1)}$. Then, for each of the $N(1)$, we measured the maximum bandwidth of a 2-survivable spanning connection with a survivability level of at least S_0, denoted as $B(S_0)$. Note that $B(1)$ is the maximum bandwidth of a fully disjoint spanning connection. Thus, we derived the *bandwidth ratio*, defined as $\beta(S_0) \triangleq \frac{B(S_0)}{B(1)}$ and, accordingly, calculated the average value over the corresponding $N(1)$ networks, denoted as $\overline{\beta(S_0)}$.

We proceed to further specify the generation of the random topologies. For Power-Law topologies, following [37], we randomly assigned a certain number of out-degree credits to each node, using the Power-Law distribution $\beta \cdot x^{-\alpha}$, where x is a random number out of the number of network nodes, $\alpha = 0.61$ and $\beta = 100$. We connected the nodes so that every node obtained the assigned out-degree. Specifically, we randomly picked pairs of nodes u and v, such that u still had some remaining out-degree credits, and then assigned a link (u, v) between them in case that such a link had not been assigned yet. Upon assigning such a new link, we decreased the out-degree credit of node u. Each simulated Power-Law networks consists of 200 nodes, and, in average, 900 links.

We turn to specify the generation of the Waxman topologies, following [38]. Initially, we located the source and the destination at the diagonally opposite corners of a square of unit dimension. Then, we randomly spread 198 additional nodes over the square. Finally, for each pair of nodes u, v we introduced a link (u, v) with the following probability, where $\delta(u, v)$ is the distance between the nodes: $prob(u, v) = \alpha \cdot \exp \frac{-\delta(u,v)}{\beta \cdot \sqrt{2}}$ considering $\alpha = 1$ and $\beta = 0.058$. Each simulated Waxman network consists of 200 nodes, and, in average, 1200 links.

6.2 Results

The simulation results are illustrated in Fig. 9 and Fig. 10. First, the graph depicted in Fig. 9a presents the average survivability ratio $\overline{\sigma_{B_0}(k)}$ without a bandwidth restriction, i.e. $B_0 = 0$, as a function of the allowable different spanning trees $k \in [1,4]$, for each of the two network topology classes, i.e. Power-Law and Waxman. For both classes, we observe a substantial improvement (resulting in a survivability level of almost $OPT(G)$) by utilizing two spanning trees rather than one. Furthermore, the employment of $k > 2$ spanning trees has a very marginal effect on the survivability level. Accordingly, Fig. 9b exhibits a zoomed view of the above Waxman-class results for a range of values close to the optimal solution, i.e. $\overline{\sigma_{B_0}(k)} \in [0.993, 1]$, and, additionally, considers other bandwidth restrictions, namely $B_0 = 0, 30, 50, 60$. The graph shows that, for all bandwidth restrictions, 4 spanning trees are sufficient for the maximum level of survivability and 3 spanning trees achieves a survivability ratio of 1 for the three softer bandwidth restrictions $B_0 = 0, 30, 50$. However, a 2-survivable spanning connection provides a solution that is just one percentile away from optimum. Furthermore, by alleviating the restriction B_0 on the bandwidth, there is an improvement in the efficiency of a 2-survivable spanning connection. Specifically, while for $B_0 = 60$ its survivability ratio is $\overline{\sigma_{60}(2)} = 0.9935$, for a non-restricted network $B_0 = 0$, a 2-survivable spanning connection's survivability level is in the order of four-nines from the optimum. Thus, we can conclude that, in practice, two spanning trees are enough for providing a close-to-optimal survivability level.

The graphs depicted in Fig. 10 demonstrate the advantages of employing a 2-survivable spanning connection, with not-necessarily-disjoint trees, over the traditional approach of employing fully disjoint spanning trees. Specifically, the graph depicted in Fig. 10a presents the feasibility ratio $\rho(S_0)$ as a function of the survivability level requirement $S_0 \in [0.95, 1]$, for Power-Law and Waxman classes. We observe that, with a relaxation of just 1% in the survivability level, the feasibility ratio increases by a factor of 24% for Waxman networks and 17% for Power-Law networks. Next, the graph illustrated in Fig. 10b presents the average bandwidth ratio $\overline{\beta(S_0)}$ as a function of the survivability level requirement $S_0 \in [0.95, 1]$ out of the networks that admit the establishment of a pair of fully disjoint spanning trees, i.e. accomplish a survivability level of $S_0 = 1$. We note that the number of such networks was in the range of 8,000 to 9,000 (out of 10,000), hence the samples were always significant. Overall, we observe that a minor relaxation, of a few percentiles, in the survivability level, is enough to provide dramatic improvement in terms of the sustained bandwidth. Specifically, a relaxation of about 0.5% in the survivability level provides an improvement of a factor of 12 for Waxman networks and a factor of 8 for Power-Law networks.

7. TWO FAILURES PROTECTION

We proceed to briefly discuss a generalization of the model in order to handle failures in up to two links. As in the single link failure model, we again define the survivability level of a spanning connection as the probability that at least one of the spanning trees in the connection is operational, i.e. at least one of the spanning trees does not contain any faulty links.

In order to have a survivability level of 1, we need to guarantee that we have a spanning tree that does not include any of the (up to two) faulty links. To do so, we require that, for any pair of links, there is at least one spanning tree that does not include both of the links in the faulty pair. Consider a network $G(V,E)$ with a spanning connection $(T_1, ..., T_k)$. As in the single link failure model, the spanning tree $T_i(V,E_i)$ guarantees the existence of an operational spanning tree in any single failure in one of the links $T_i^c = E \setminus E_i$. Furthermore, this spanning tree remains operational if both links in a pair of links in $T_i^c \times T_i^c$ fail. Accordingly, if the spanning connection satisfies the property $\bigcup_{i=1}^{k}(T_i^c \times T_i^c) = E \times E$, a survivability level of 1 is guaranteed.

We saw that, in the single link failure model, a spanning connection with two link-disjoint spanning trees results in a survivability level of 1. The next theorem shows that this is not the case in the generalized model.

THEOREM 7.1. *Let $G = (V,E)$ be a network for which the link failure probabilities satisfy $\forall e \in E, p_e > 0$. In the two links failure model,* any *spanning connection with $k = 2$ spanning trees $(T_1(V,E_1), T_2(V,E_2))$ has a survivability level smaller than* 1.

PROOF. Consider a pair of links $(e_1, e_2) \in E_1 \times E_2$. Since $p_{e_1}, p_{e_2} > 0$, there is a positive probability that both links would fail. In this case, both spanning trees are faulty and there is not any operational spanning tree. □

On the other hand, it is easy to see that a spanning connection with three link-disjoint spanning trees results in a survivability level of 1.

THEOREM 7.2. *In the two links failure model, a spanning connection with $k = 3$ link-disjoint spanning trees $(T_1(V,E_1), T_2(V,E_2), T_3(V,E_3))$ has a survivability level of* 1.

PROOF. Consider the worst-case in which there are two faulty links e_1, e_2. Since $E_1 \bigcap E_2 = E_1 \bigcap E_3 = E_2 \bigcap E_3 = \emptyset$, we must have each of the faulty links e_1, e_2 appear in at most one of the three spanning trees. Thus, one of the three spanning trees does not include any faulty links and is operational. □

8. CONCLUSIONS

Tunable survivability is a novel quantitative approach for coping with network failures, which can be tuned to accommodate any desired level (0%-100%) of survivability, yet till now it has been studied only in the context of unicast connections [19] [27]. This study extended the tunable survivability concept for handling broadcast through spanning trees. Specifically, we established a novel polynomial-time algorithm for providing an optimal set of (any) k spanning trees that maximizes its survivability level while ensuring a guaranteed bandwidth. Additionally, we provided tight bounds on the number of spanning trees that may be needed in order to achieve a maximum level of survivability. Finally, through comprehensive simulations, we showed that the maximum level of survivability can be well-approximated (namely, within order of four-nines) by establishing just two spanning trees. Moreover, the simulations clearly demonstrated the advantages of tunable survivability over traditional survivability schemes.

Motivated by [39], we are currently investigating the practical aspects of our findings by implementing tunable survivability schemes in Ethernet architectures, through an extension to the Multiple Spanning Tree Protocol [13] (as has been proposed in [26] for the link-disjoint case). Moreover, similarly to [40] and [41], we consider the extension of our model beyond the traditional single failure in order to cope with multiple failures extending the preliminary results presented in Section 7.

While there is still much to be done towards the actual deployment of the tunable survivability approach, we believe that this study provides evidence for the benefits of employing this concept in the scope of spanning trees and broadcast connections. Furthermore, it establishes a substantial milestone towards the construction of a comprehensive methodology.

9. ACKNOWLEDGMENTS

This research was supported by the Israel Science Foundation (grant no. 1129/10), by the Israeli Ministry of Science and Technology, and by the United States - Israel Binational Science Foundation (grant no. 2010414).

10. REFERENCES

[1] Christopher R. Cole. 100-Gb/s and beyond transceiver technologies. *Optical Fiber Technology*, 17(5):472 – 479, 2011.

[2] ITU-T. G.8032: Ethernet ring protection switching, 2008.

[3] Nurit Sprecher and Adrian Farrel. MPLS Transport Profile (MPLS-TP) Survivability Framework. RFC 6372, 2011.

[4] Greg Kuperman and Eytan Modiano. Network protection with guaranteed recovery times using recovery domains. In *IEEE Infocom*, 2013.

[5] Abdelhamid E. Eshoul and Hussein T. Mouftah. Survivability approaches using p-cycles in wdm mesh networks under static traffic. *IEEE/ACM Trans. Networking*, 17(2):671–683, 2009.

[6] Jianping Wang, Chunming Qiao, and Hongfang Yu. On progressive network recovery after a major disruption. In *IEEE Infocom*, 2011.

[7] Daniel Sadoc Menasché, Alberto Avritzer, Sindhu Suresh, Rosa M Leão, Edmundo Souza e Silva, Morganna Diniz, Kishor Trivedi, Lucia Happe, and Anne Koziolek. Assessing survivability of smart grid distribution network designs accounting for multiple failures. *Concurrency and Computation: Practice and Experience*, 2014.

[8] Martin Suchara, Dahai Xu, Robert Doverspike, David Johnson, and Jennifer Rexford. Network architecture for joint failure recovery and traffic engineering. In *ACM SIGMETRICS*, 2011.

[9] David Plummer. Ethernet Address Resolution Protocol. RFC 826, 1982.

[10] Ralph Droms. Dynamic Host Configuration Protocol. RFC 2131, 1997.

[11] Yu-Chee Tseng, Sze-Yao Ni, Yuh-Shyan Chen, and Jang-Ping Sheu. The broadcast storm problem in a mobile ad hoc network. *Wireless networks*, 8(2-3):153–167, 2002.

[12] IEEE. 802.1d: Standard for local and metropolitan area networks: Media access control (mac) bridges, 1990.

[13] IEEE. 802.1s: Standard for local and metropolitan area networks: Multiple spanning trees, 2001.

[14] Jian Qiu, Mohan Gurusamy, Kee Chaing Chua, and Yong Liu. Local restoration with multiple spanning trees in metro ethernet networks. *IEEE/ACM Trans. on Networking*, 19(2):602–614, 2011.

[15] Bart Braem, Benoit Latre, Ingrid Moerman, Chris Blondia, and Piet Demeester. The wireless autonomous spanning tree protocol for multihop wireless body area networks. In *Mobile and Ubiquitous Systems*. IEEE, 2006.

[16] Junbin Liang, Jianxin Wang, Jiannong Cao, Jianer Chen, and Mingming Lu. An efficient algorithm for constructing maximum lifetime tree for data gathering without aggregation in wireless sensor networks. In *IEEE Infocom*, 2010.

[17] Hichem Baala, Olivier Flauzac, Jaafar Gaber, Marc Bui, and Tarek El-Ghazawi. A self-stabilizing distributed algorithm for spanning tree construction in wireless ad hoc networks. *Journal of Parallel and Distributed Computing*, 63(1):97–104, 2003.

[18] Adelbert Groebbens, Didier Colle, Sophie De Maesschalck, Ilse Lievens, Mario Pickavet, Piet Demeester, Lan Tran, Kris Steenhaut, and Ann Nowé. Efficient protection in mpλs networks using backup trees. *Photonic Network Communications*, 6(3):191–206, 2003.

[19] Ron Banner and Ariel Orda. The power of tuning: A novel approach for the efficient design of survivable networks. *IEEE/ACM Trans. Networking*, 15(4):737 –749, 2007.

[20] Poul E. Heegaard and Kishor S. Trivedi. Network survivability modeling. *Computer Networks*, 53(8):1215–1234, 2009.

[21] János Tapolcai, Bin Wu, and Pin-Han Ho. On monitoring and failure localization in mesh all-optical networks. In *IEEE Infocom*, 2009.

[22] James Roskind and Robert E Tarjan. A note on finding minimum-cost edge-disjoint spanning trees. *Mathematics of Operations Research*, 10(4):701–708, 1985.

[23] Jens Clausen and Lone Aalekjær Hansen. Finding k edge-disjoint spanning trees of minimum total weight in a network: an application of matroid theory. *Combinatorial Optimization II*, pages 88–101, 1980.

[24] Crispin St. John Alvah Nash-Williams. Edge-disjoint spanning trees of finite graphs. *J. of the London Mathematical Society*, 1(1):445–450, 1961.

[25] William T. Tutte. On the problem of decomposing a graph into n connected factors. *J. of the London Mathematical Society*, 1(1):221–230, 1961.

[26] Srikant Sharma, Kartik Gopalan, Susanta Nanda, and Tzi-cker Chiueh. Viking: A multi-spanning-tree ethernet architecture for metropolitan area and cluster networks. In *IEEE Infocom*, 2004.

[27] Jose Yallouz and Ariel Orda. Tunable QoS-aware network survivability. In *IEEE Infocom*, 2013.

[28] Andrea Fumagalli and Marco Tacca. Optimal design of differentiated reliability (dir) optical ring networks. In *Int. Workshop on QoS in Multiservice IP Net.*, 2001.

[29] Alec Woo, Terence Tong, and David Culler. Taming the underlying challenges of reliable multihop routing in sensor networks. In *ACM Embedded networked sensor systems*, 2003.

[30] Weidong Cui, Ion Stoica, and Randy H. Katz. Backup path allocation based on a correlated link failure probability model in overlay networks. In *IEEE ICNMP*, 2002.

[31] Abhishek Chandra, Rohini Prinja, Sourabh Jain, and ZhiLi Zhang. Co-designing the failure analysis and monitoring of large-scale systems. *ACM SIGMETRICS*, 2008.

[32] Seth Chaiken and Daniel J. Kleitman. Matrix tree theorems. *Journal of combinatorial theory, Series A*, 24(3):377–381, 1978.

[33] Augustus De Morgan. *On the syllogism: and other logical writings.* Yale University Press, 1966.

[34] Thomas H. Cormen, Charles E. Leiserson, Ronald L. Rivest, and Clifford Stein. *Introduction to Algorithms, Third Edition.* MIT Press, 3rd edition, 2009.

[35] Eugene L. Lawler. *Combinatorial optimization: networks and matroids.* DoverPublications. com, 2001.

[36] Ram Ravi and Michel X. Goemans. The constrained minimum spanning tree problem. In *Algorithm Theory*, pages 66–75. Springer, 1996.

[37] Michalis Faloutsos, Petros Faloutsos, and Christos Faloutsos. On power-law relationships of the internet topology. In *ACM SIGCOMM*, 1999.

[38] Bernard M. Waxman. Routing of multipoint connections. *IEEE JSAC*, 6(9):1617–1622, 1988.

[39] David Applegate, Lee Breslau, and Edith Cohen. Coping with network failures: Routing strategies for optimal demand oblivious restoration. In *ACM SIGMETRICS*, 2004.

[40] Matthew Johnston, Hyang-Won Lee, and Eytan Modiano. A robust optimization approach to backup network design with random failures. In *IEEE Infocom*, 2011.

[41] Kayi Lee, Hyang-Won Lee, and Eytan Modiano. Reliability in layered networks with random link failures. In *IEEE Infocom*, 2010.

Balanced Resource Allocations Across Multiple Dynamic MapReduce Clusters

Bogdan Ghiț[§], Nezih Yigitbasi[†], Alexandru Iosup[§], Dick Epema[§$]
[§]Delft University of Technology, the Netherlands
[$]Eindhoven University of Technology, the Netherlands
[†]Intel Labs, USA
b.i.ghit@tudelft.nl, nezih.yigitbasi@intel.com
{a.iosup,d.h.j.epema}@tudelft.nl

ABSTRACT

Running multiple instances of the MapReduce framework concurrently in a multicluster system or datacenter enables data, failure, and version isolation, which is attractive for many organizations. It may also provide some form of performance isolation, but in order to achieve this in the face of time-varying workloads submitted to the MapReduce instances, a mechanism for dynamic resource (re-)allocations to those instances is required. In this paper, we present such a mechanism called FAWKES that attempts to balance the allocations to MapReduce instances so that they experience similar service levels. FAWKES proposes a new abstraction for deploying MapReduce instances on physical resources, the MR-cluster, which represents a set of resources that can grow and shrink, and that has a core on which MapReduce is installed with the usual data locality assumptions but that relaxes those assumptions for nodes outside the core. FAWKES dynamically grows and shrinks the active MR-clusters based on a family of weighting policies with weights derived from monitoring their operation.

We empirically evaluate FAWKES on a multicluster system and show that it can deliver good performance and balanced resource allocations, even when the workloads of the MR-clusters are very uneven and bursty, with workloads composed from both synthetic and real-world benchmarks.

Categories and Subject Descriptors

C.2.4 [**Distributed Systems**]: Distributed Applications; D.2.8 [**Metrics**]: Performance measures

General Terms

Experimentation, Measurement, Performance

Keywords

MapReduce clusters; Scheduling; Dynamic provisioning; Performance; Fairness; Datacenters; Multicluster systems.

SIGMETRICS'14, June 16–20, 2014, Austin, Texas, USA.

http://dx.doi.org/10.1145/2591971.2591998.

1. INTRODUCTION

MapReduce and similar computing frameworks are now widely used by institutes and commercial companies (e.g., Google [9], Facebook [33], Yahoo! [7]) because of their ability to efficiently use large sets of computing resources and to analyze large data volumes. MapReduce workloads may be very heterogeneous in terms of their data size and their resource requirements [18], and mixing them within a single instance of a computing framework may lead to conflicting optimization goals. Therefore, *isolating* MapReduce workloads and their data while dynamically *balancing* the resources across them is very attractive for many organizations. In this paper, we present the design and analysis of FAWKES[1], a scheduling system for *dynamic* resource provisioning of multiple MapReduce instances in single large-scale infrastructures.

Running multiple MapReduce frameworks concurrently within the same physical infrastructure enables *four types of isolation.* First, different (groups of) users each working with their own data set may prefer to have their own MapReduce framework to avoid interference, or for privacy and security reasons, thus requiring *data isolation.* A second type of isolation is *failure isolation*, which hides the failures of one MapReduce framework from the applications running in other concurrent MapReduce frameworks. Third, with the multiple MapReduce frameworks approach, *version isolation*, with different versions of the MapReduce framework running simultaneously, may be achieved as well. Finally, it can enable *performance isolation* between streams of jobs with different characteristics, for instance, by having separate MapReduce frameworks for large and small jobs, or for production and experimental jobs.

Whereas the first three forms of isolation are easily enforced by a resource manager that can deploy multiple instances of the MapReduce framework along with their corresponding filesystems on disjoint sets of nodes, performance isolation is more difficult to achieve (and define)—as the workloads of the instances may vary considerably over their lifetimes, deploying them on static partitions of the system may lead to an imbalance in the levels of service they receive. To dynamically provision multiple framework instances at runtime, FAWKES defines a new abstraction of the MapReduce framework called the *MR-cluster.* An MR-cluster is initially deployed (along with its filesystem) on a system

[1]FAWKES is a phoenix bird which in Greek mythology is reborn from its own ashes just like our MapReduce clusters grow and shrink.

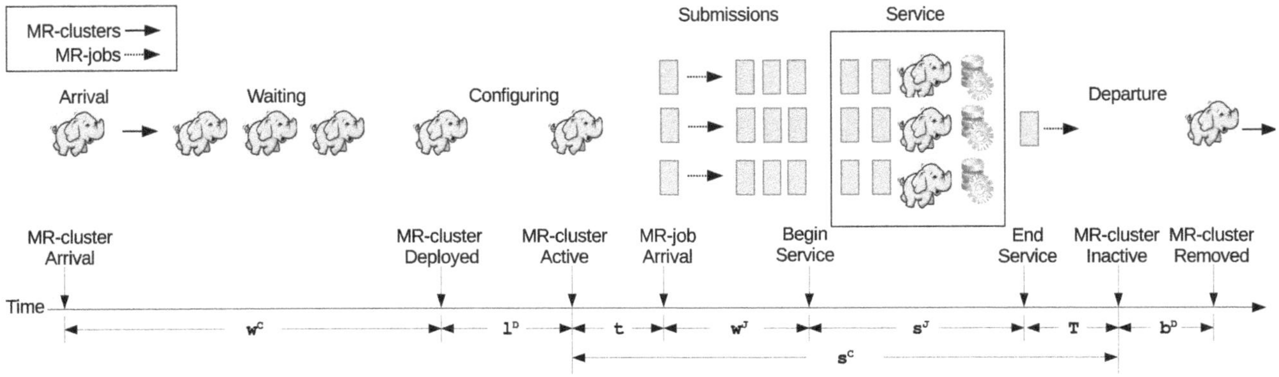

Figure 1: An overview of the queuing system of FAWKES. The system handles requests for deploying MapReduce frameworks (MR-clusters) with a global queue, and each active MR-cluster manages an internal queue of MapReduce jobs (MR-jobs). The Hadoop logo is taken from [2].

partition of a certain minimum size consisting of *core* nodes when its first job is submitted, and it will remain active as long as it receives additional jobs. The allocation of an MR-cluster can grow (and later shrink) by adding (removing) *transient* or *transient-core* nodes that don't store any data or only output data, respectively, thus breaking the standard MapReduce data locality assumption but allowing fast reconfiguration. FAWKES implements three types of policies for setting and periodically adjusting the *weights* of the active MR-clusters that indicate the shares of the resources they are entitled to, and to resize their allocations accordingly. These policies try to assess the load conditions of the MR-clusters by considering their queue lengths, their resource utilizations, or their performance (in terms of, e.g., job slowdown) when setting the weights. The most important performance metric we use to assess the actual performance of the MR-clusters is the average job slowdown.

Another possible solution for provisioning multiple MapReduce instances is to share the distributed file system across all frameworks and to employ two-level scheduling by delegating the scheduling control to the frameworks, as is done in Mesos [19]. There, a high-level resource manager initiates resource offers to the frameworks, which need specific policies to decide whether to accept or reject these offers. Mesos achieves near-optimal data locality when resources are frequently released by the frameworks. Instead, our solution targets performance isolation for time-varying workloads, but breaks the data locality assumptions to enable fast framework reconfigurations. Whereas Mesos has an offer-based scheduling system, FAWKES employs a feedback mechanism and balances the allocations of multiple frameworks by monitoring their operation.

The contributions of this paper are as follows:

1. We define the abstraction of the MR-cluster which is a set of resources that can grow and shrink, that has MapReduce installed on its core in the usual way, but that relaxes the MapReduce data locality assumptions for nodes outside its core (Section 3).

2. We provide a comprehensive taxonomy of policies for provisioning multiple MR-clusters that take into account their dynamic load conditions as perceived from their queue lengths, the utilizations of the resources allocated to them, or the performance they deliver (Section 4).

3. With a set of micro-experiments in a real multicluster system, we analyze, among other aspects of FAWKES, the benefit of trading data locality for dynamicity (Section 6). We find that the performance penalty induced by a relaxed data locality model in MapReduce is not prohibitive.

4. With a set of macro-experiments in the multicluster system, we evaluate the weighting policies of FAWKES for balancing the allocations of multiple MR-clusters. We show that our system delivers good results even for unfavorable workloads (Section 7).

2. BACKGROUND

MapReduce [9] is a programming model that exploits the parallelism in applications processing large, regular data sets. With the open-source implementation of MapReduce Hadoop [2], a new software stack emerged for big data processing on inexpensive hardware. Hadoop provides a distributed file system (HDFS), which accommodates very large files, divided into chunks or data blocks of 64 or 128 MB in size. Data blocks are replicated at different compute nodes (DataNodes) and their locations are provided by a master node (NameNode).

The flow of a MapReduce computation can be split into three phases. First, each data block of the input data set is assigned to a *map task*, which generates key-value pairs as specified by a user-defined map function. Secondly, during the *shuffle phase*, the key-value pairs are sorted by key and divided among a number of *reduce tasks*. Finally, the reduce tasks, after receiving all key-value pairs with the same key, execute a user-defined reduce function.

To execute a MapReduce computation, a master node (JobTracker) assigns tasks based on the location of their input data blocks to different compute nodes (TaskTrackers). Despite the simplicity of the MapReduce programming model, today it is also common to create MapReduce programs from SQL-like higher-level programming languages (Pig Latin [25]). Although MapReduce can be employed for large jobs processing terabytes of data, most of the jobs in production clusters are short (minutes) SQL-like queries, with small input sizes (GBs) [7], [28].

3. SYSTEM MODEL

In this section, we propose a scheduling and provisioning structure for deploying multiple concurrent MapReduce frameworks, which can be resized dynamically at runtime.

3.1 Scheduling and Provisioning Structure

The system architecture assumed by MapReduce has resources where processors and storage are co-located. We assume these resources to be organized in multiple physical clusters that operate as a single distributed computing system managed by the resource manager FAWKES, which decides how resources are to be balanced across multiple MapReduce frameworks.

In Figure 1 we show the queuing system managed by FAWKES. FAWKES receives two types of requests, one for activating new MR-clusters, and one for executing MapReduce jobs (MR-jobs) that identify the MR-cluster in which they have to be executed. These requests are serviced in multiple queues, all using the FIFO scheduling discipline. The system queues requests for new MR-clusters in a global queue managed by FAWKES. The time required to activate a new MR-cluster consists of the time the MR-cluster has to wait to be deployed on physical resources (w^C) and the time required to load the input data set from an external persistent storage (l^D). Each active MR-cluster maintains an internal queue of MR-job requests targeted at it. The response time of an MR-job is equal to the sum of its waiting time in the MR-cluster's queue (w^J) and its execution time (s^J). If the weight of an MR-cluster in the FAWKES mechanism is equal to 0 indicating no task execution for at least a certain duration T (see Section 4.2), FAWKES marks it as inactive, deallocates its resources, and removes it from the system. Prior to the removal of an MR-cluster, its (output) data is saved on the persistent storage in the time interval of length b^D.

3.2 Dynamic MR-Clusters

In order to balance resources across the active MR-clusters, FAWKES has to be able to resize them by growing and shrinking the number of resources allocated to them at runtime. In the traditional static deployment of the MapReduce frameworks, the data of the HDFS are replicated and distributed uniformly across the nodes. Then, techniques like delay scheduling [33] can maximize the number of tasks that achieve data locality. FAWKES has the ability of changing the allocations, and has a relaxed data locality model, through a new abstraction of the MapReduce framework that we call *dynamic MR-cluster*, which comprises three types of nodes.

The most important requirement for FAWKES is to provide reliable data management so that when nodes are removed from an MR-cluster and the number of replicas is small, no data are lost. However, creating numerous replicas is not desired because of the increased usage of storage space. Thus, when removing nodes from an active MR-cluster, FAWKES needs to replicate the data they store. As data-intensive applications are processing large volumes of data, its replication makes the resizing of the MR-cluster slow. To enable fast reconfigurations, the removed nodes of the MR-cluster should store relatively small amounts of data.

Similar to the static deployment of MapReduce, FAWKES permanently allocates to an MR-cluster an initial set of *core nodes* used for both executing jobs and storing (input and output) data. During the time an MR-cluster is active, FAWKES may temporarily increase its capacity by provisioning *transient* or *transient-core* nodes, which break the traditional model for data locality. The former are instantiated without local storage such that the jobs they execute read and write input/output data from/to core nodes. The latter are different from the core nodes only by the lack of input data, thus the jobs they execute also need to transfer input data from core nodes, but they can use the local storage to write output data. As a consequence, FAWKES can grow the size of an MR-cluster fast as no data movement will be involved at all. Shrinking the size of an MR-cluster by removing transient-core nodes does require saving the output data stored on them, the amounts of which is usually very small in comparison to the input data set distributed on the core nodes. Nevertheless, large fractions of these nodes may saturate the network (both) or increase the contention on the physical disks of the core nodes (especially the transient nodes). When to resize an MR-cluster, and whether then to use transient or transient-core nodes, is explained in Section 4. Different from our dynamic MR-cluster approach, Amazon Elastic MapReduce [1] does not support data redistribution when shrinking the size of the cluster.

4. BALANCED SERVICE LEVELS

In this section, we derive a fairness metric to determine the imbalance between concurrent MR-clusters (Section 4.1). Our scheduling system, FAWKES, targets weighted fair allocations, such that different MR-clusters converge to fractions of the system resources proportional to their weights (Section 4.2). FAWKES dynamically updates the weights based on different metrics exposed by the MR-clusters at runtime. We design three classes of weighting policies which consider the input to the MR-clusters (*demand*), the operation of the MR-clusters (*usage*), and the output of the MR-clusters (*runtime performance*) (Section 4.3).

4.1 Fairness

Fairness is a major issue in resource provisioning and job scheduling, and is an optimization target that may conflict with performance metrics such as response time [21], [33]. Although there exists a large volume of literature that analyzes the notion of fairness in communication systems [16], there is no generally agreed upon measure of the fairness between jobs. The fairness of a queuing system has been defined either as a measure of the time spent waiting [5], possibly with respect to job size [31]. A fairness metric which accounts for both job arrival times and sizes is proposed in [26]. We adapt the latter for evaluating the fairness of a provisioning policy.

The key element is the assumption that, at any moment of time t, the MR-clusters may be entitled to shares of the total data center capacity C, proportionally to their given weights. For an MR-cluster i, the difference between the fraction $c_i(t)$ of resources it currently has and the share of resources it should have based on its weight $w_i(t)$ (see Section 4.2.2) at moment t is defined as its *temporal discrimination*

$$d_i(t) = c_i(t) - w_i(t). \quad (1)$$

We define the *discrimination* of MR-cluster i during a time interval $[t_1, t_2]$ by

$$D_i(t_1, t_2) = \int_{t_1}^{t_2} (c_i(t) - w_i(t))dt. \quad (2)$$

Setting $t_1 = d_i$ and $t_2 = r_i$ with d_i and r_i the moments of the request for the deployment and the removal of the MR-cluster, respectively, we obtain the *overall discrimination* of the MR-cluster.

When all the resources of the datacenter are occupied all the time, every positive discrimination is balanced with negative discrimination, and so $\sum_i D_i(t_1, t_2) = 0$ for any time interval $[t_1, t_2]$, which makes the expected mean value of the discrimination $E[D] = 0$. The fairness (or balance) of the system is given by the variance of the discrimination, which we call the *global discrimination factor*:

$$Var(D) = E[D^2] - E[D]^2 = E[D^2] \quad (3)$$

We consider the allocations of the MR-clusters to be *imbalanced* or *unfair*, when the global discrimination factor is larger than a predefined parameter τ.

4.2 The FAWKES Mechanism

We want to provision resources to multiple MR-clusters in a single datacenter or multicluster system to give MR-clusters similar levels of service. To achieve this, we want to assign each MR-cluster a dynamically changing weight that indicates the share of the resources it is entitled to.

4.2.1 Admission Policy

For each MR-cluster i FAWKES assumes that there is a minimum number of core nodes m_i (and a corresponding minimum share), which may be set by a system administrator or computed based on the amount of data the cluster has to process. The system guarantees the minimum share of an MR-cluster as long as it has running jobs, even if according to its current weight it is only entitled to a smaller share.

If on the arrival of a new MR-cluster, the sum of its minimum share and of the minimum shares of the active MR-clusters exceeds 1, the new MR-cluster is queued (in FIFO order). Otherwise, the system gives it its minimum share of the resources within a time interval T from its arrival, by shrinking the active MR-clusters which are above their minimum shares proportionally to their current weights (but not going below their minimum shares). When later an active MR-cluster finishes its workload and releases the resources it holds, FAWKES checks to see if the MR-cluster at the head of the queue fits. After a new MR-cluster receives its minimum share, the system monitors its state along with the states of the other active MR-clusters. The weights of the active MR-clusters are periodically updated after every interval of length T.

4.2.2 Changing Shares

To ensure that MR-clusters with different workloads experience similar service levels (e.g, job slowdown), we propose three complementary mechanisms, employed by FAWKES, which target either a subset or the entire set of the active MR-clusters, and operate at different timescales.

The MR-clusters collect periodically samples of different aspects of system operation, such as demand $d(t)$, resource utilization $r(t)$, or actual performance $p(t)$. FAWKES *monitors* a specific metric related to these aspects and sets the weight (*weighting mechanism*) $w_i(t)$ of MR-cluster i at time t to the average value of the samples y_i collected during the last time interval T:

$$w_i(t) = \frac{y_i(t)}{\sum_{k=1}^{n} y_k(t)}, \quad (4)$$

where n is the number of active clusters at time t.

After updating the weights, the temporal discriminations of the MR-cluster are determined as well. When the MR-clusters are imbalanced that is, the global discrimination factor exceeds the predefined threshold τ, FAWKES changes their shares proportionally to their dynamic weights. To resize an MR-cluster, FAWKES employs the *grow and shrink mechanisms* based on provisioning temporary nodes, which can be either transient or transient-core (see Section 3).

The shrinking mechanism guarantees that the MR-clusters with positive discrimination reach their fair shares by releasing the surplus of resources they hold. Based on the type of nodes which are removed, we distinguish two possible ways of shrinking an active MR-cluster, *instant preemption* (IP) or *delayed preemption* (DP). The former is suitable for transient nodes and simply kills the currently running tasks, which are later re-scheduled by the MR-cluster. The latter applies to transient-core nodes, which besides removing their running tasks also require the replication of their local data. FAWKES removes transient-cores nodes in non-decreasing order of the amount of data they locally store.

The growing mechanism ensures that MR-clusters with negative discrimination achieve their fair shares by extending their current shares. To do so, the MR-cluster is grown either with transient (TR) or with transient-core (TC) nodes. The former have good performance only for compute intensive workloads, which generate small amounts of data. The local storage of the latter type of nodes significantly improves the performance of highly disk intensive workloads (Section 6). The type of growing employed by FAWKES is a predefined system parameter.

4.3 Weighting Policies

To balance the allocations of multiple MR-clusters, we investigate a comprehensive design space, which covers the input to the system, the state of the system, and the output (runtime performance) of the system. We focus, respectively, on the demand of the workloads submitted to MR-clusters, on the usage of resources allocated to them, and on the runtime performance. For each of these, we propose three exemplary policies.

For all policies we investigate in this work, the weights of the MR-clusters and the global discrimination are recomputed after every interval of length T. Only when the global discrimination exceeds a threshold τ are the allocations of the MR-clusters actually changed according to the new weights.

4.3.1 Demand-based Weighting

Demand-based weighting policies take into account the input to the system (the demand). They establish the fair shares of the MR-clusters as proportional to the sizes of the workloads submitted to their queues. As we do not assume any prior knowledge about the workloads, we identify three ways of defining the size of a workload at time t, viz. with respect to the number of waiting jobs, the size of the input data of the jobs, and the number of waiting tasks:

1. **Job Demand (JD).** The JD policy sets the demand of the MR-cluster to the total *number of jobs* waiting in the queue.
2. **Data Demand (DD).** The DD policy sets the weight of the MR-cluster to the total *input data volume* of the jobs waiting in the queue.
3. **Task Demand (TD).** The TD policy gives an estimate of the MR-cluster demand at finer granularity than JD, by taking into account the total *number of tasks* waiting in the queue.

Although each of these policies is inherently inaccurate, for example JD because the duration of jobs ranges from minutes to hours, we expect demand-based weighting policies to lead to better system performance than no policy.

4.3.2 Usage-based Weighting

Usage-based policies monitor the state of the system; here, we propose policies that monitor the utilization of the physical resources currently allocated to MR-clusters. We identify two main resources to monitor, processor usage and disk usage, and derive three policies:

1. **Processor Usage (PU).** The PU policy sets the usage at time t to the fraction of *utilized processing units* (cores or slots) from the total configured capacity of the MR-cluster.
2. **Disk Usage (DU).** The DU policy sets the usage at time t to the ratio between the total *output data* generated by the MR-cluster and its current storage capacity.
3. **Resource Usage (RU).** The MU policy combines the previous two policies by accounting for *both compute and storage resources*, processor and disk, as follows:

$$u_i(t) = \psi \cdot u_i^P + (1 - \psi) \cdot u_i^D, \tag{5}$$

where u_i^P and u_i^D are the (normalized) resource usages as computed by the PU and DU policies, respectively, and the parameter $\psi \in (0, 1)$ reflects the relative importance of the two resources.

4.3.3 Performance-based Weighting

The performance-based policies assign the fair shares of the MR-clusters based on the performance of the system at runtime, so that MR-clusters with poor performance receive larger fractions of resources and, thus, improve their performance. We use in this work two performance metrics, slowdown (low values are ideal) and throughput (high values are ideal) to calculate the weights of the MR-clusters as follows:

1. **Job Slowdown (JS).** The JS policy calculates the slowdown of each running job at time t as the ratio between the elapsed time since the job started and the job execution time on a reference static MR-cluster (only for this policy, assumed known at the start of the job in the MR-cluster). We consider the weights of the MR-clusters to be all equal and positive at time $t = 0$. The weight of the MR-cluster i at time $t > 0$ is set to the *average job slowdown* of all jobs s_i which are waiting in the queue.
2. **Job Throughput (JT).** The JT policy considers the performance of MR-cluster i at time t to be the ratio q_i between the number of *jobs* completed and the total number of jobs waiting in the queue. The weight is, then:

$$p_i(t) = a^{-q_i(t)} \tag{6}$$

where $a > 1$ is a constant (we set $a = 2$). The share of an MR-cluster i is entitled to increases inversely proportional with the measured throughput from C/a ($q_i \to 1$) to C ($q_i \to 0$).
3. **Task Throughput (TT).** The TT policy is similar to the JT policy. The TT policy uses a throughput computed as the ratio between the number of *tasks* completed and the total number of tasks waiting in the queue. Eq. (6) still holds, with the ratio q_i now referring to tasks instead of jobs.

We compare our policies with two *baselines*, **No policy (None)** and **Equal Shares (EQ)**. The former makes the MR-clusters run permanently on their minimum shares. For the latter, the available resources are always equally divided between the active MR-clusters.

5. EXPERIMENTAL SETUP

In this section, we present the experimental setup for assessing the performance of several aspects of system operation (Section 6) and of the full FAWKES mechanism for balancing resources across MR-clusters (Section 7). The main differences between our and previous experimental setup are the use of a comprehensive set of representative MapReduce applications (including a real, complex workflow), the design of five workloads (including several unfavorable cases), and the use of a multicluster testbed (only in one experiment). The total time used for experimentation exceeded 3 real months and over 60,000 hours system time.

5.1 Clusters

We run experiments on the Dutch six-cluster wide-area computer system DAS-4 [3]. The system has in total roughly 200 dual-quad-core compute nodes with 24 GB memory per node and 150 TB total storage, connected within the clusters through 1 Gigabit Ethernet (GbE) and 20 Gbps QDR InfiniBand (IB) networks. The compute nodes from different clusters communicate over dedicated 10 Gbps light paths provided by SURFnet. The largest cluster in terms of the number of nodes, situated at the VU Amsterdam, has roughly 70 nodes divided into 4 racks. The GbE interconnect is based on two 48-ports 1 GbE switches (symmetric, backplane cabled). The IB network is enabled by six 36-ports InfiniBand switches, organized in a fat tree, with 4 access switches, 2 at root. This architecture, which is useful for both data processing and high-performance computing, currently services about 300 scientists.

In our experiments, we restrict ourselves to well-connected datacenters and we use a standard setup of Hadoop-1.0.0 over InfiniBand. We configure the HDFS on a virtual disk device (with RAID0 software) that runs over 2 physical devices with 2 TB storage in total per node. The data are stored in the HDFS in blocks of 128 MB with a default replication factor of 3. With 8 cores per node enabled (no hyperthreading), we configure the TaskTrackers with 6 map slots and 2 reduce slots.

Job	Type	Data	Input	Output
WC	compute	Random	200 GB	5.5 MB
ST	disk	Random	200 GB	200 GB
PR	compute	Random	50 GB	1.5 MB
KM	compute,disk	Random	70 GB	72 GB
TT	compute	BitTorrent	100 GB	3.9 MB
AH	disk,compute	BitTorrent	100 GB	90 KB

Table 1: A summary of the MapReduce applications used in our experiments.

Real-world experimentation was greatly facilitated by the DAS-4 system. However, as the system is shared between many users, we also encountered practical restrictions. We have completed the set of micro-experiments presented in Section 6 reserving 20 up to 30 nodes for a week. As we explore a large design space experimentally, we summarize for the large experiments in Section 7 only results from single executions. It took more than 2 months to complete the macro-experiments we have designed in this paper.

5.2 MapReduce Applications

The choice of MapReduce applications is crucial for a meaningful experimental evaluation. We use both simple, synthetic *applications* from a popular MapReduce benchmark, HiBench [20] and a complex, real MapReduce-based *logical workflow*, BTWorld [17], [32]. Table 1 gives a high-level summary of these MapReduce applications, which we extend with a detailed description in this section.

5.2.1 The HiBench Benchmark

HiBench includes a suite of simple synthetic benchmarks for data transformation, web search, and machine learning, along with automatic tools for data generation:

1. **Wordcount (WC)** counts the number of occurrences of each word in a given set of input files. The map tasks simply emit key-value pairs with the partial counts of each word, and the reduce tasks aggregate these counts into the final sum. Wordcount is mostly compute intensive and shuffles a small number of bytes from map to reduce tasks.

2. **Sort (ST)** is a disk-intensive application in which the identity function stands as both map and reduce functions and the actual sorting is executed while the data is shuffled from map to reduce tasks.

3. **PageRank (PR)** is a link analysis algorithm widely used in web search engines to calculate the ranks of the web pages based on the number of reference links. The MapReduce implementation of the workload consists of three compute-intensive jobs which iteratively compute the ranking scores of all pages.

4. **K-Means (KM)** is a data mining clustering algorithm for multi-dimensional numerical samples. The workload employs two MapReduce jobs which resemble the characteristics of Wordcount and Sort. The former is mostly compute-intensive and iteratively computes the centroid of each cluster, thus swallowing a large fraction of the input. The latter is disk-intensive and reorders the data by assigning each sample to a cluster.

5.2.2 The BTWorld Workflow

BTWorld is a complex, real-world MapReduce-based logical workflow for processing the data collected periodically over many years from the global-scale peer-to-peer system BitTorrent [32]. The data set contains per tracker statistics (*scrapes*) stored in a multi-column layout which includes the identifier for the BitTorrent content (*hash*), the URL of the BitTorrent tracker (*tracker*), the time when the status information was logged (*timestamp*), the number of users having the full and part of the content (*seeders* and *leechers*), and the number of downloads at the moment of sampling (*downloads*).

A MapReduce-based workflow which currently consists of 14 high-level queries expressed in Pig Latin processes data and leads to understand the evolution over time of the global BitTorrent system. The queries expressed in this MapReduce workflow cover a broad range of SQL-like operators (e.g., join, aggregation, filtering, projection), break down into more than 20 MapReduce jobs, and exhibit three levels of data dependency: inter-query (when the input of the query needs to be generated by another query), inter-job (when a query is divided into several MapReduce jobs), and intra-job (between map and reduce tasks). The workflow combines both compute and disk intensive jobs with small (10^{-6}) and high (10^{2}) job selectivities, where job selectivity is defined as the ratio between the output and input sizes. Thus, this real workflow is very challenging for MapReduce-based data processing.

In our experiments, we use not only the complete workflow, but also two single queries individually:

1. **TrackerOverTime (TT)** groups the input data set by tracker, sorts it by timestamp field, and applies different aggregation functions (e.g., count, avg, sum) on the remaining fields of the records. The query translates into a single, compute-intensive *map-heavy* job, and its output is 5 orders of magnitude smaller than the data set size.

2. **ActiveHashes (AH)** determines the number of active hashes in the system at every moment of time. The query is split in two MapReduce jobs, one disk-intensive with high (1) selectivity, and the other compute-intensive with very small (10^{-6}) selectivity. The first job emits all distinct hash and timestamp pairs to a second job, which further counts the number of unique hashes at every moment of time.

5.3 MapReduce Workloads

We consider workloads that cover many aspects (e.g., job types, data sizes, submission patterns) identified in synthetic benchmarks, production clusters, and BTWorld [20], [7]. To this end, we design 3 categories of workloads, based on which we generate 19 different workloads which we use in our micro- and macro-experiments:

1. **Single job - Single size (SS).** The SS workloads contain a number of identical synthetic or real-world jobs presented in Table 1. We use 6 such workloads of size one (one job) with fixed input data sizes (see Table 1) in Section 6. In Sections 7.1 and 7.2 we use SS workloads with 50 and 100 jobs, respectively, in which we employ the same submission pattern with all jobs submitted at once (*batch*), which is also used in many synthetic benchmarks.

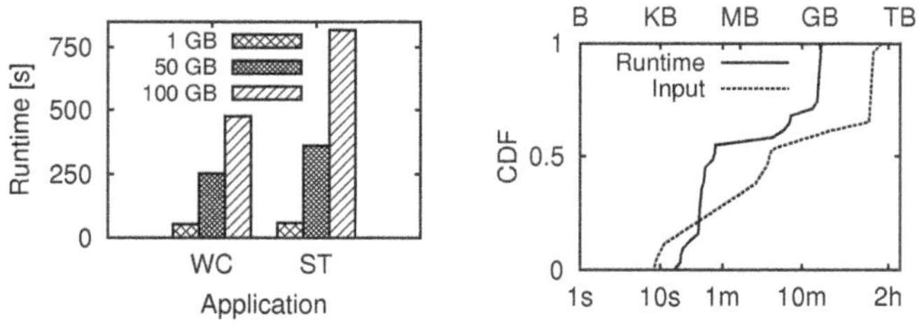

(a) HiBench jobs

(b) BTWorld jobs

Figure 2: The runtime performance of the jobs in HiBench and BTWorld on a 10-node static MR-cluster used as reference for the job slowdowns.

2. **Multiple jobs - Single size (MS).** The MS workloads combine several types of jobs (e.g., WC and ST) with the following input data sizes: 1 GB (small), 50 GB (medium), and 100 GB (large). We generate 3 workloads of this type based on WC and ST (Section 7.3, where we also describe the job arrival process) which have hundreds of small jobs.

3. **Multiple jobs - Multiple sizes (MM).** The MM workloads combine several job types with different input data sizes which are summarized in Figure 2. The jobs in HiBench (e.g., WC and ST) have the same input sizes as in the MS workloads. BTWorld employs 26 jobs with 13 distinct input sizes. We use 3 instances of this type of workloads in which small jobs prevail (Section 7.3, including the arrival process).

Given the high imbalance between the workloads we use, the discrimination threshold does not have a significant impact, thus we set τ to a small value (10 in our experiments). In our workloads, most of the jobs take between 1 and 4 minutes to complete (Figure 2) and a couple of them arrive every minute. Thus, we set the weight update interval T to a value in the order of a few minutes (1 or 2 minutes in our experiments).

We design the evaluation of FAWKES in two steps. First, we design four *micro-experiments* using SS workloads to assess different aspects of system operation (see Section 6). Then we design five *macro-experiments* using instances of all types of workloads to assess the performance of FAWKES. Towards this end, we combine highly imbalanced workloads to create extreme conditions of variable load across distinct MR-clusters (Section 7).

6. MICRO-EXPERIMENTS

In this section, we present the results of four experiments that each address a separate aspect of the performance of single MR-clusters. We investigate the performance of several MapReduce applications in single MR-clusters with different configurations with respect to the types of nodes (Section 6.1) and whether a single or multiple physical clusters are used (Section 6.2), and we assess the performance of growing (Section 6.3) and shrinking (Section 6.4) single MR-clusters at runtime. We measure the overhead of these configurations relative to a static MR-cluster with only core nodes. For all jobs in the micro-experiments we use the input data set sizes defined in Table 1.

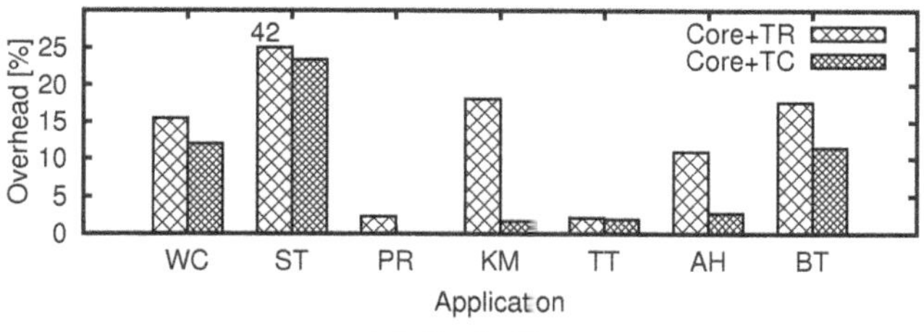

(a) Node Types

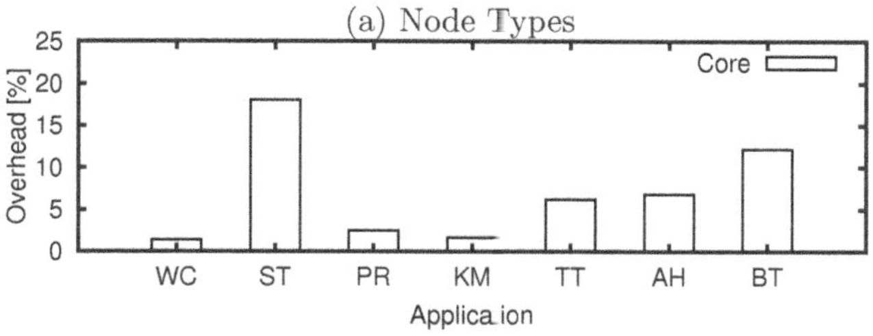

(b) Multicluster Deployment

Figure 3: The overhead of running a single MR-job on 20-node MR-clusters with equal fractions of core and transient, and of core and transient-core nodes (a), and with resources evenly co-allocated from two physical clusters (b).

6.1 Node Types

We assess the impact on the runtimes of jobs of using the three types of MR-cluster nodes presented in our system model in Section 3. In our previous work [12], we have found that the execution time of disk-intensive jobs increases with the ratio between transient and core nodes, while the performance of compute-intensive jobs is independent of the types of nodes.

Using transient-core nodes instead of transient nodes reduces the overhead for disk-intensive jobs considerably (Figure 3a). We set up static 20-node MR-clusters with only core nodes and with equal numbers of core and transient/transient-core nodes. In the former configuration, the input data set is distributed across all nodes of the MR-cluster, while in the latter two configurations, the input data set is distributed on 50% of the MR-cluster nodes. Figure 3a shows that with transient-core nodes instead of transient nodes, the overhead for disk-intensive jobs relative to the job execution on only core nodes is much smaller. In particular, Sort shows a significant improvement, decreasing the overhead from 40% with transient nodes to 23% with transient-core nodes, as do KMeans and ActiveHashes.

In our model, dynamically provisioning MR-clusters by means of a grow-shrink mechanism at runtime comes at the expense of poor data locality, as the tasks executed on transient or transient-core nodes need to transfer their input across the network. Nevertheless, we have shown here, at least in a cluster with a high-bandwidth network, that the impact of running non-local tasks can be limited by using transient-core nodes.

6.2 Multicluster Deployment

We assess the impact on job execution time of deploying single MR-clusters by co-allocating resources from different physical clusters in our multicluster system with high-speed wide-area connections. Previous work [10] has shown that co-allocation of parallel applications in multicluster systems is beneficial because of reduced job wait times if the overhead due to the slower wide-area communication is less than 25%.

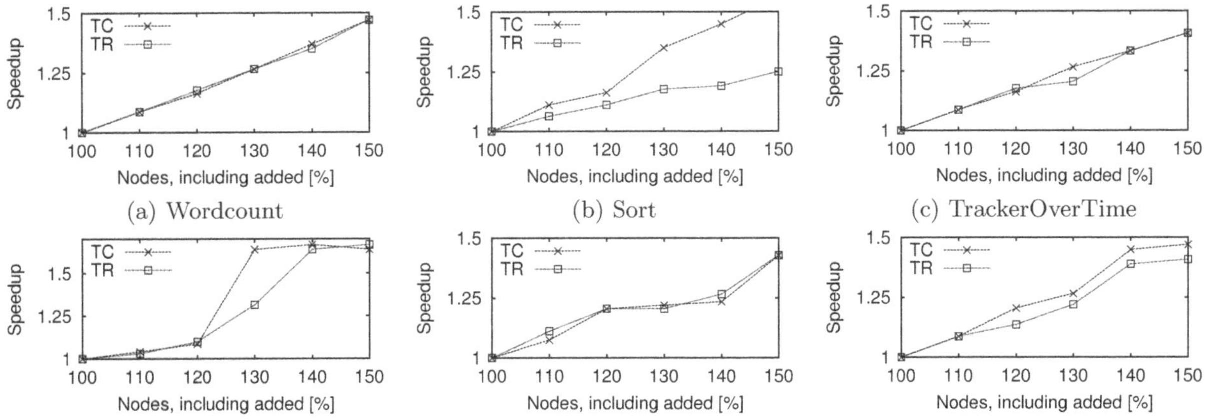

(a) Wordcount (b) Sort (c) TrackerOverTime

(d) PageRank (e) KMeans (f) ActiveHashes

Figure 4: The job speedup relative to the execution time measured on a static 20-node MR-cluster, when growing the MR-cluster with different fractions of transient (TR) or transient-core (TC) nodes.

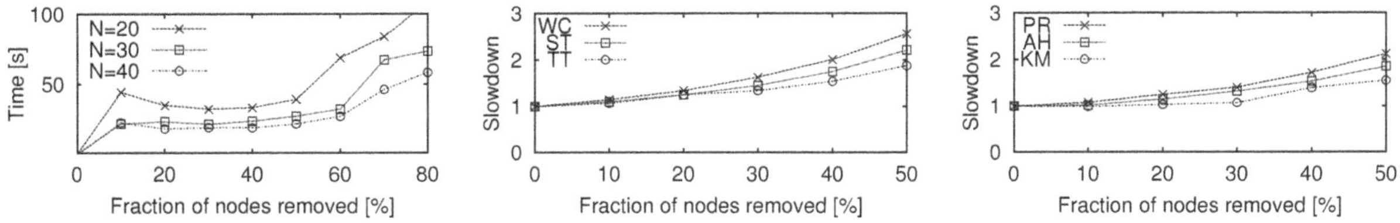

(a) Data replication (b) Single jobs (c) Multiple jobs

Figure 5: The average per-node shrinking time of MR-clusters with N nodes in total (a). The job slowdown relative to the execution time measured on a static 20-node MR-cluster, when shrinking a 20-node MR-cluster (b),(c).

MapReduce jobs can run with low to moderate overhead in co-allocated MR-clusters over a high-speed interconnect (Figure 3b). We set up 20-node static MR-clusters, with nodes co-allocated evenly from two physical clusters located at two universities in Amsterdam. Figure 3b shows that most of the applications exhibit low overhead when they run on co-allocated MR-clusters. For the complete BTWorld workflow and Sort, which are mostly composed by disk-intensive jobs, a co-allocated MR-cluster increases their execution times by less than 20% relative to the single physical cluster deployment.

Although we have shown here that MR-clusters may be provisioned with co-allocated resources, we design the remaining experiments within a single physical cluster.

6.3 Growing MR-clusters

We measure the speedup of single jobs when the MR-cluster grows with different fractions of transient-core or transient nodes before the job starts. The conveniently parallel layout of MapReduce applications [9] with only a single predetermined synchronization point between the map and reduce phases, in principle makes them malleable applications [11] that can benefit from dynamic resource provisioning at runtime [8].

The execution time of MapReduce jobs can be improved with a growing mechanism at runtime by relaxing the data locality constraints. We set up dynamic MR-clusters with 20 core nodes which we extend at runtime with different fractions of transient or transient-core nodes.

Despite the lack of data locality, transient (TR) nodes show good performance with one exception. For Sort, which is a highly disk intensive job, large fractions of TR nodes increase the contention on the physical disks of the core nodes (Figure 4b), thus limiting the speedup. With the relaxed data locality model of the transient-core (TC) nodes, jobs may write the data they generate on their local storage. This explains the linear increase of the applications speedups with the number of transient-core nodes (Figure 4). The supra-linear speedup of PageRank is an anomaly due to the non-deterministic convergence of the iterative MapReduce jobs.

We can improve the performance of a broad range of MapReduce applications by relaxing the data locality model. Moreover, even in more extreme cases of no locality, transient nodes show good performance for applications which generate small amounts of data.

6.4 Shrinking MR-clusters

In this section, we investigate the overhead of reorganizing the data within HDFS (Figure 5a) and the job slowdown when different fractions of transient-core nodes are removed from the MR-cluster at the moment the job starts running (Figure 5b, 5c). Although in practice the transient-core nodes store less data than the core nodes, we assume in this micro-experiment a *worst-case scenario* in which both types of nodes store the same amounts of data.

When resizing an MR-cluster to 50% of its size, the time overhead of reorganizing the data in HDFS increases linearly with the number of nodes removed. We set up MR-clusters with different numbers of core and

					Job Types			Job Arrivals		
Sec.	Workload	Nodes	Weight	Apps.	c-1	c-2	c-3	c-1	c-2	c-3
7.1	WKLD-A	TR	JD	WC	50 x small			batch		
7.2	WKLD-B	all	TD	WC	90 x small	5 x medium	5 x large	batch		
	WKLD-C	all	TD	ST	90 x small	5 x medium	5 x large	batch		
7.3	WKLD-D	TC	all	WC,ST	165 x small	188 x all	555 x small	average	bursty	average
	WKLD-E	TC	TD	WC,ST,BT	359 x all	26 x all	559 x small	average	sequential	average

Table 2: The design space coverage of the macro-experiments presented in Section 7. For each experiment, the table summarizes the provisioning policy (node type and weighting policy) employed by the resource manager, and the workload instances (application type and job types, sizes, and arrival pattern) submitted to three concurrent MR-clusters.

transient-core nodes. The former represent 20% of the cluster size and each node of the cluster stores 10 GB of data. There are no running jobs while the MR-clusters are resized.

We find the average per-node removing time is constant when the MR-cluster is shrunk with up to 50% of its total size, and increases exponentially for larger fractions of transient-core nodes removed, as more data are replicated on fewer nodes (Figure 5a).

When shrinking an MR-cluster at runtime, the job runtime is determined by the total size of the replicated data. We set up 20-node MR-clusters with 10 core nodes which we shrink at runtime by different fractions of transient-core nodes. Figures 5b and 5c show that shrinking MapReduce applications at runtime increases the job slowdown linearly with the number of transient-core nodes removed. However, we observe that less compute-intensive jobs (e.g., ST and WC), which run on 200 GB, have higher slowdown than more computational intensive jobs (e.g., TT, PR), which run on less than 100 GB.

As MapReduce is usually employed for data-intensive applications, it is important to reduce the overhead of data replication by limiting the frequency of MR-cluster reconfigurations and by removing nodes with smaller data volumes.

7. MACRO-EXPERIMENTS

In this section, we evaluate FAWKES's resource provisioning and balancing mechanisms. Towards this end, we design a comprehensive set of scenarios, summarized in Table 2 w.r.t. to both system operation (e.g., nodes and weights) and experiment instrumentation (e.g., applications and workloads). We show how FAWKES effectively provisions newly arriving MR-clusters (Section 7.1) and achieves good balancing when the workloads are imbalanced (Section 7.2). Moreover, even under extreme imbalance and unfavorable conditions, we show evidence of up to 25% improvement of average job slowdown (Section 7.3).

7.1 Arriving MR-clusters

In this section, we show how FAWKES balances idle resources across the active MR-clusters and gracefully shrinks them to make space for new MR-cluster deployments.

FAWKES **effectively uses its grow and shrink mechanisms to dynamically provision multiple arriving MR-clusters.** Given 60 resources, FAWKES receives requests for 3 MR-clusters, at intervals of 100 s. All MR-clusters store 50 GB of data on their minimum shares of 10 core nodes. FAWKES uses transient (TR) nodes and employs the JD weighting policy (see Section 4.2). The weights are updated every $T = 60$ s. We combine 3 instances of the SS workload (see Section 5.3) into WKLD-A (see Table 2).

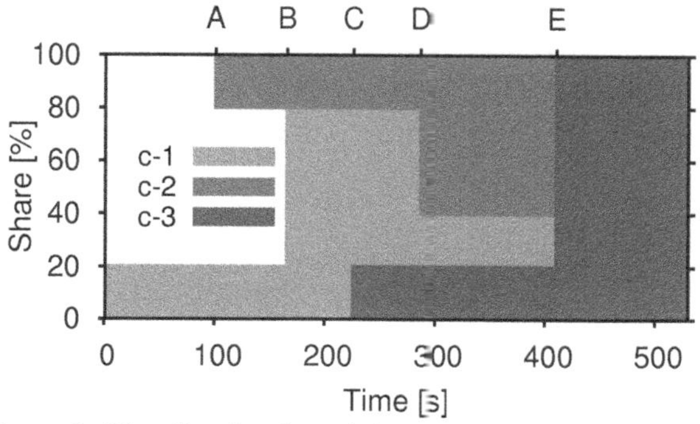

Figure 6: The distribution of the resources across three MR-clusters (c-1, c-2, c-3) arriving at different moments in time. (Points A-E explained in Section 7.1.)

In Figure 6, FAWKES initially provisions 10 core nodes to c-1. While c-1 loads its data c-2 arrives and receives 10 core nodes from remaining 50 idle resources (A). MR-cluster c-1 starts running jobs when c-2 is still loading the data. Thus, all 40 remaining resources are allocated to c-1 (B). Later MR-cluster c-1 is successively shrunk to make space for c-3 (C) and to allow the share of c-2 to grow (D). When both c-1 and c-2 finish their workloads, c-3 grows to the full capacity of the system (E).

With a static partitioning approach, when the system is fully utilized, requests for new MR-clusters need to wait for active MR-clusters to complete their workloads and release the resources. Dynamic provisioning allows new MR-clusters to be deployed even when the active MR-clusters use the entire system capacity.

7.2 Growing and Shrinking MR-clusters

In this section, we show the impact of the type of nodes (transient or transient-core) and the type of workload on FAWKES's balancing mechanism.

FAWKES **is able to balance the allocations for disk intensive workloads with TC growing and DP shrinking, but fails to do so when using TR growing and IP shrinking (all defined in Section 4.2).** We consider 60 resources in total, which FAWKES uses to deploy simultaneously 3 concurrent MR-clusters with 10 core nodes to which we submit workloads WKLD-B and WKLD-C which differ by the growing (TC or TR) and the application (WC or ST) type (see Table 2). The weights are updated every $T = 60$ s. In Figure 7, we show the queue sizes of the three MR-clusters over time for None EQ and TD policies (all defined in Section 4.3).

Apparently, neither the queue size nor the makespan of MR-cluster c-1 with small jobs is affected by growing or shrinking. Whereas FAWKES balances the medium and large

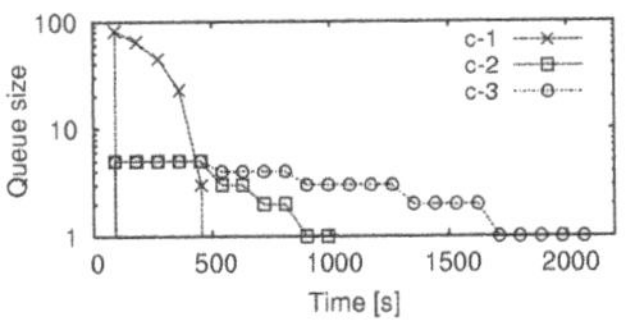

(a) WKLD-B None.

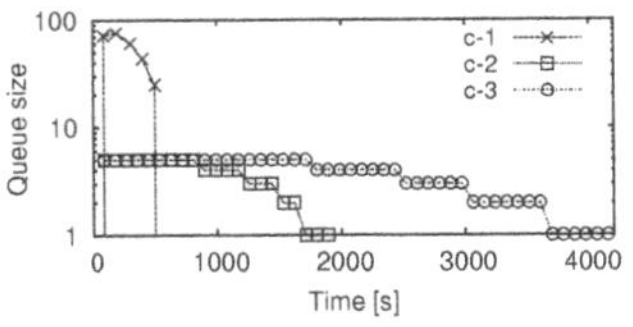

(b) WKLD-C None.

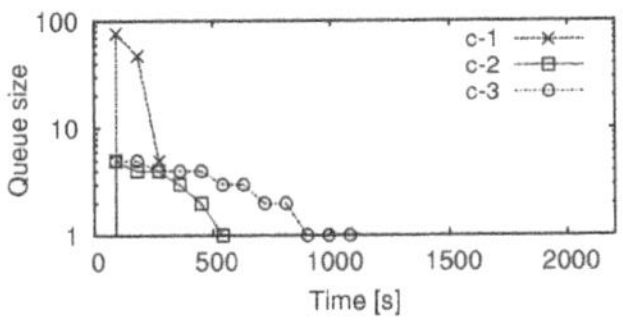

(c) WKLD-B TR-EQ.

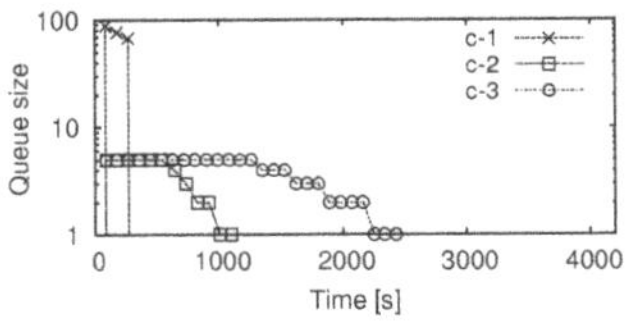

(d) WKLD-C TC-EQ.

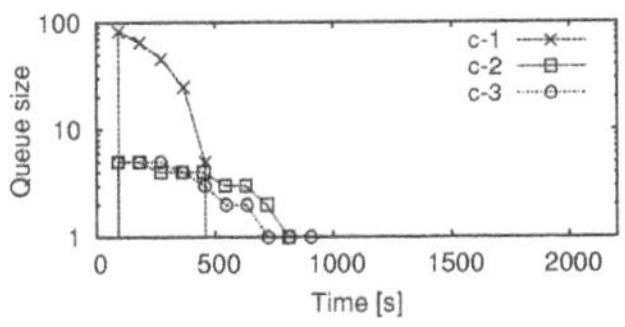

(e) WKLD-B TR-TD.

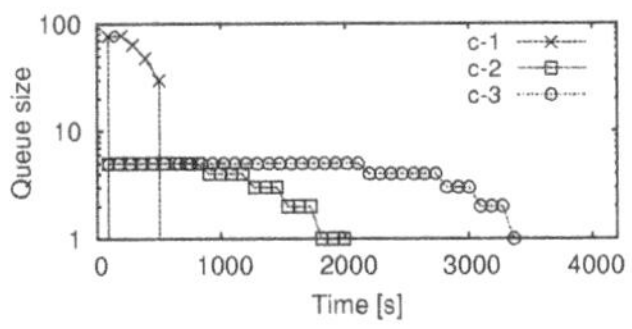

(f) WKLD-C TR-TD.

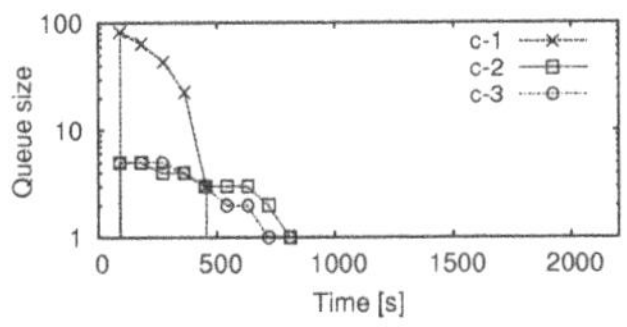

(g) WKLD-B TC-TD.

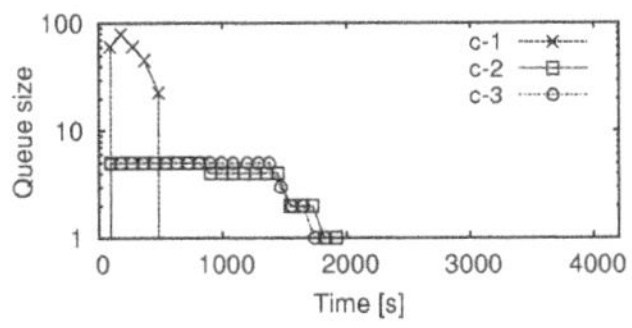

(h) WKLD-C TC-TD.

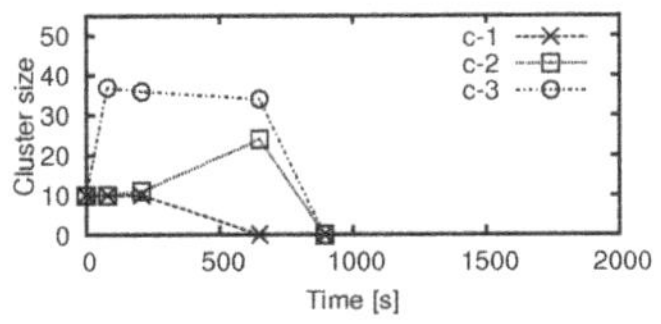

(i) WKLD-B TC-TD.

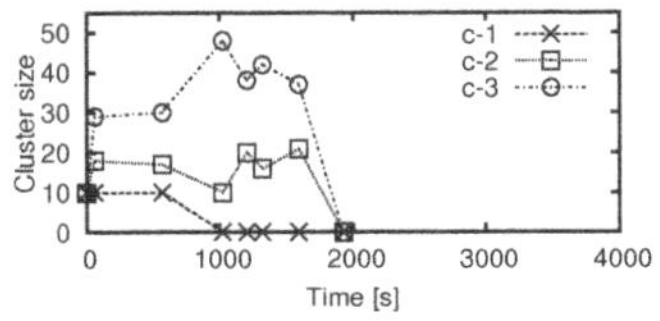

(j) WKLD-C TC-TD.

Figure 7: The queue and cluster sizes of three MR-clusters running workloads WKLD-B and WKLD-C (Table 2) for different growing and weighting types.

WC workloads with both TR and TC nodes (MR-clusters c-2 and c-3 in Figures 7e and 7g), the mechanism is not effective for ST-based workloads with TR nodes (MR-cluster c-3 in Figure 7f). For the latter scenario, the data volumes shuffled by the large ST jobs (MR-cluster c-3) increase the execution overhead as we have shown in Section 6. With TC growing, FAWKES balances the allocations even for highly disk intensive workloads (MR-clusters c-2 and c-3 in Figure 7h).

Without the dynamic growing and shrinking, the resources released once an MR-cluster executes its workload remain idle. Instead, FAWKES allocates the unused capacity to provision the active MR-clusters according to their weights, thus reducing the imbalance and the makespan.

7.3 Weighting MR-clusters

In this section, we assess the balancing properties of FAWKES in two scenarios with three MR-clusters running extremely imbalanced workloads.

FAWKES **balances the allocations to workloads even in very unfavorable situations.** In both scenarios, we reserve 48 resources to deploy simultaneously three MR-clusters with 10 core nodes and 200 GB of data each. FAWKES

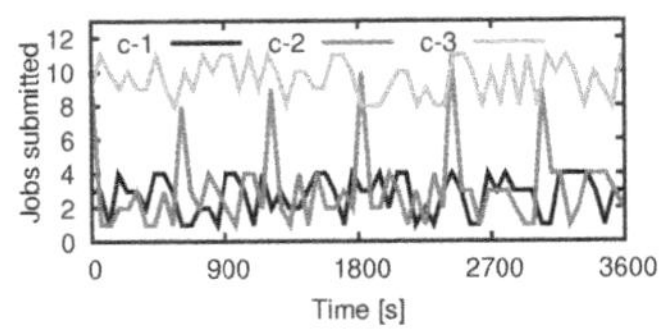

(a) WKLD-D.

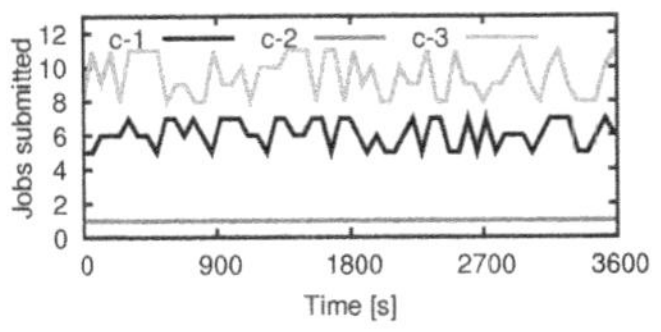

(b) WKLD-E.

Figure 8: Arrival processes (numbers of submissions per 2-minute intervals) for the two highly imbalanced workloads WKLD-D and WKLD-E (see Table 2).

updates the weights of the MR-clusters every $T = 120$ s and provisions them with TC nodes. The two scenarios we analyze use workloads WKLD-D and WKLD-E (Table 2) with the arrival processes depicted in Figures 8a and 8b. WKLD-D mixes WC and ST jobs in two MS instances submitted to c-1 and c-3 and one MM instance submitted to c-2 and has bursts with large jobs in cluster c-2. WKLD-E submits the complete BTWorld workflow to c-2 as an MM instance and mixes WC and ST jobs submitted to c-1 and c-3 as MM and MS instances, respectively, with c-3 permanently having a much higher load than c-1 and c-2. Both workloads are imbalanced, with the ratio between the average number of tasks executed in the clusters with the highest and lowest loads being 3 and 8, respectively.

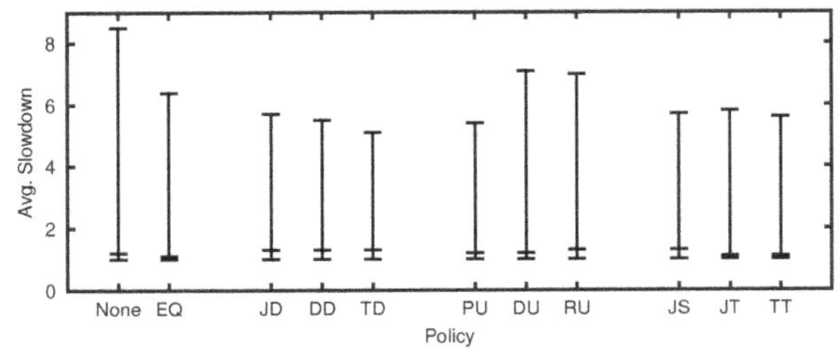

Figure 9: The minimum, the maximum, and the median of the average job slowdowns of three MR-clusters with workload WKLD-D for all weighting policies.

In Figure 9 we compare in the first scenario the weighting policies w.r.t. the average job slowdown measured for each MR-cluster running WKLD-D. For the demand-based policies (JD, DD, TD), the finer the granularity of calculating the queue sizes (number of tasks with TD) is, the more balanced the workloads of the MR-clusters are (25% improvement of job slowdown compared to None). FAWKES achieves the best improvement of the average job slowdown of 25% with the TD policy. Furthermore, we observe that FAWKES reduces the average job slowdown in the most loaded cluster (c-2) without significant impact on the performance of the low demand clusters (c-1 and c-3). From the usage-based policies (PU, DU, RU), only PU performs reasonably well. RU ($\psi = 0.5$) and its derivative DU ($\psi = 0$) are not effective because of some small jobs which generate large amounts of data, yet are completed relatively fast (see ST in Figure 2a). Counterintuitively, the performance-based policies (JS, JT, TT) do not outperform the demand-based policies. The reason is that in WKLD-D, small WC and ST jobs, which have the same runtimes (see Figure 2), prevail. Therefore, the weights assigned with the performance-based policies are similar and do not reflect the actual imbalance between the workloads.

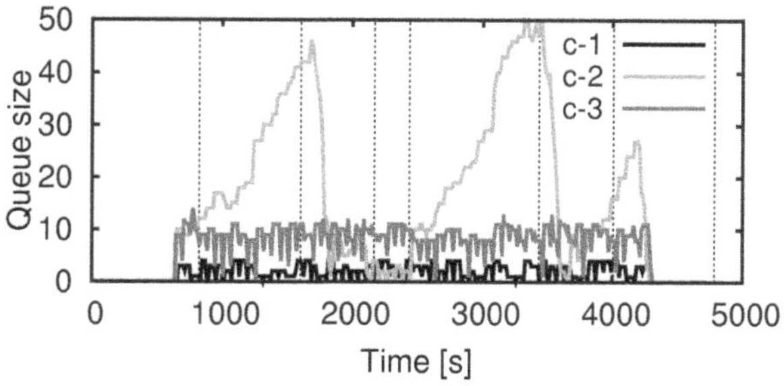

(a) WKLD-D EQ weighting.

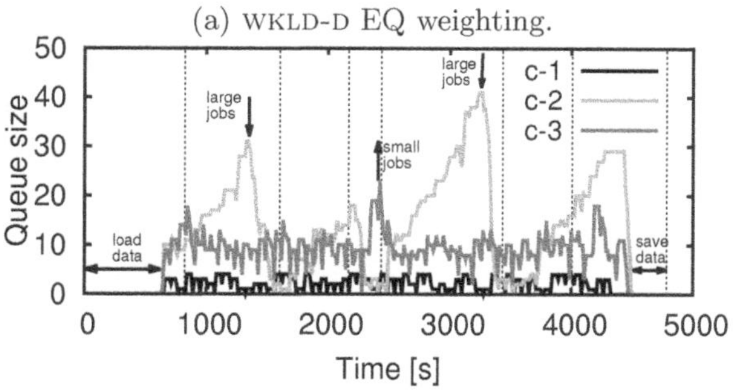

(b) WKLD-D TD weighting.

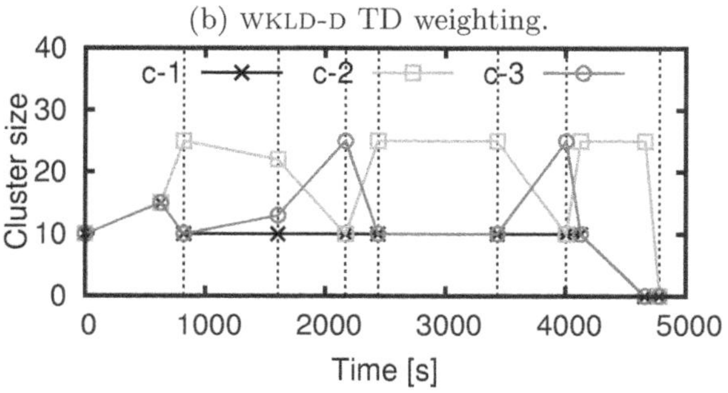

(c) WKLD-D TD weighting.

Figure 10: The performance of TD weighting for WKLD-D.

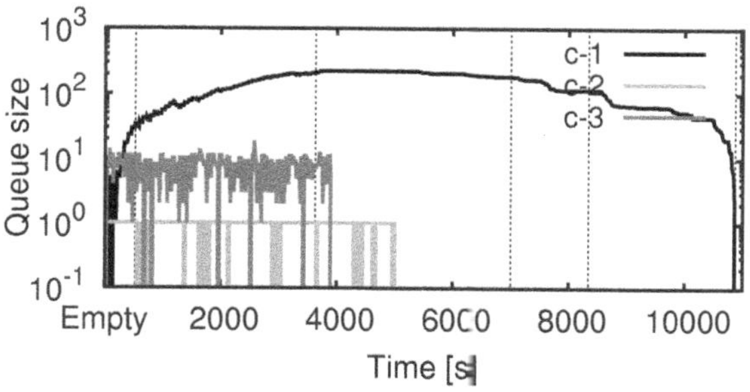

(a) WKLD-E EQ weighting (logscale).

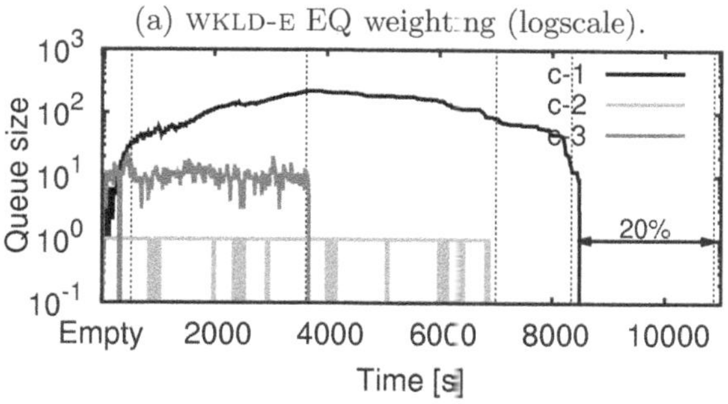

(b) WKLD-E TD weighting (logscale).

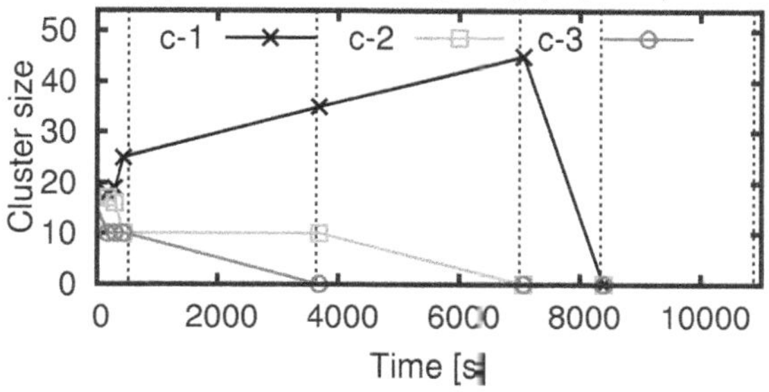

(c) WKLD-E TD weighting.

Figure 11: The performance of TD weighting for WKLD-E.

Figures 10 and 11 show the queue and cluster sizes with the weighting policy that performs best in the first scenario, TD, and the EQ baseline, for scenario 1 and 2, respectively. FAWKES makes 16 and 5 reconfigurations (excluding MR-cluster deployments and deallocations) in the two scenarios, see Figure 10c and 11c. For WKLD-D we notice that MR-clusters are reconfigured when bursts of large jobs arrive at c-2 or many small jobs are submitted to c-3. For WKLD-E, the most loaded MR-cluster (c-1) acquires most of the system resources, thus reducing the overall makespan of the experiment. In both cases, FAWKES is as effective as it can be because it moves (almost) all resources that it can move to the cluster with the highest load (c-2 in scenario 1 and c-1 in scenario 2), almost always leaving the other clusters at their minimum shares.

8. RELATED WORK

In this section, we summarize the related work from four aspects: resource sharing mechanisms for multicluster environments, malleability of parallel applications, cluster sizing problems, and fair-sharing provisioning policies.

Resource Sharing. To simplify cluster programming, a diverse array of specific frameworks for big data processing has been developed. Having multiple such frameworks within the same cluster or datacenter infrastructure requires a high-level resource management layer. Closest to our work are Yarn [29], Mesos [19], and Koala [23], all having the same design goal of sharing resources between multiple cluster computing frameworks. Yarn considers the resource requests received from the applications, the resource availability, and the internal scheduling policies to dynamically allocate resources to different frameworks. Heavy users or large jobs are prevented from monopolizing the cluster through system partitioning which can be employed with the Capacity [4] and Fair schedulers [33]. Mesos takes a different approach to resource allocation by delegating the scheduling decisions to the frameworks, rather than to individual applications. To reduce the overhead of the distributed scheduling, Mesos allows frameworks to specify through filters which are the resources they will never accept. Koala is a resource manager which co-allocates processors, possibly from multiple clusters, to various HPC applications and to isolated MapReduce [12] frameworks. When resources are available, each framework may receive additional resources from Koala, but it is their decision to accept or reject them.

FAWKES is fundamentally different from Yarn and Mesos. While the latter target near-optimal data locality, FAWKES achieves performance isolation and balanced resource allocations by relaxing the strict data locality assumptions through a fast and reliable grow and shrink mechanism. Furthermore, instead of the request and offer-based approaches, FAWKES controls the scheduling by observing the jobs submitted within each framework. Although FAWKES mechanism can be incorporated into Koala, we are currently maintaining and using it as a standalone research prototype.

Malleable Applications. To improve resource utilization, jobs which can be executed on a variable number of processors have emerged. When the number of processors assigned to a job can be increased or decreased by the scheduler at runtime, the job is called malleable [6], [11]. There are two ways to enable job malleability in parallel applications, either by creating a large number of threads equal to the cluster capacity, coupled with a multiplexing mechanism, or by inserting application specific code at synchronization points to repartition the data when the allocation changes. The poor performance of the former approach and the additional coding effort of the latter have limited the popularity of exploiting the job malleability for (tightly coupled) parallel applications. However, certain parallel applications based on the master-slave programming model, in which processors are required to execute relatively small and independent units of computations from a central scheduler (e.g., MapReduce [9]), can use malleability relatively easy. Moreover, MapReduce applications can be accelerated by using Amazon's spot instances, despite their variable and unknown lifetime [8].

Novel in this paper, instead of dynamically changing the allocations of single jobs [6], we exploit malleability of sets of MapReduce jobs, by growing and shrinking the framework itself. To do so, we propose a data-oriented mechanism in order to gracefully remove nodes from MapReduce frameworks at runtime. Towards this goal, we relax the traditional data locality constraints and we provision the MapReduce frameworks with temporary nodes that retrieve their input data for the tasks they run from core nodes.

Cluster Sizing. Cluster sizing problems are notoriously difficult because of the large parameter space related to the number of resources, the type of resources, and the job configuration. GreenHadoop [15] is mainly powered by solar energy source and uses the electrical grid only as backup. The scheduler minimizes the consumption of electrical energy by allowing MapReduce jobs to use more resources when green energy is available and less resources during peaks of electrical energy costs. Elastizer [18] provides an offline automated technique to solve cluster sizing problems using job profiles and simulations to search through the parameter space. Datacenters may benefit from a dynamic right-sizing mechanism that limits the number of active servers during periods of low load. Towards this end, optimization-based models and corresponding online algorithms for capacity provisioning in power proportional datacenters have been proposed and analyzed [22], [30].

Although we do not optimize for energy consumption, we investigate a similar problem of dynamic right-sizing a MapReduce cluster, but in a different setting. FAWKES attempts to find the fair share of each MapReduce cluster relative to the service levels of other concurrent clusters.

Fair Allocations. Fair-sharing algorithms have been explored in networking and operating systems domains for decades (see [33] and references therein). Datacenter schedulers like Fair [33] and Quincy [21] provide fairness for a single resource type by maximizing the minimum allocation (*max-min fairness*) received by each user in the system. To provide fairness in more general settings in which jobs may have heterogeneous requirements and hard placement constraints, the max-min fairness model has been extended to support multiple resource types [13] and to satisfy users constraints [14]. Pisces [27] is a datacenter scheduler that isolates the performance of multiple users of a shared key-value storage and provides max-min fairness. Pisces employs weighted fair-sharing and combines complementary mechanisms (partition placement, weight allocations, replica selection, and weighted fair queuing) which operate on per-application requests. A general framework that enables weighted proportional allocations for user differentiation is analyzed from a theoretical perspective in [24].

Unlike the former schedulers, FAWKES operates at the framework level, maintains a global view of the system by observing the jobs during their lifetime, and assigns to each framework a dynamically changing weight. In this paper, we propose three elements to differentiate MapReduce frameworks at runtime, viz. based on demand, on usage, and on performance.

9. CONCLUSION

Isolating the performance of multiple time-varying MapReduce workloads is an attractive yet challenging target for many organizations with large-scale data processing infrastructures. Towards this end, we have presented FAWKES, a mechanism for balancing the allocations of multiple MapReduce instances such that they experience similar service levels. FAWKES is based on the MR-cluster, a new abstraction for deploying MapReduce instances on physical resources which assumes the usual data locality constraints for a set of core nodes, but relaxes these constraints for nodes outside the core. For the fair-sharing problem, FAWKES employs weighted proportional allocations. The specific provisioning policies assign dynamic weights to different MR-clusters that take into account their dynamic load conditions.

In this paper, we take an experimental approach to provisioning multiple MR-clusters in a datacenter or multicluster system. With our micro-experiments we find that a relaxed data locality model has a limited impact on the application performance. Furthermore, our macro-experiments show that FAWKES delivers good performance and balanced resource allocations, even in unfavorable conditions of highly imbalanced workloads.

10. ACKNOWLEDGMENT

We thank Kees Verstoep of VU Amsterdam for his help with configuring and fixing software issues in the DAS-4 system. This research was supported by the Dutch national program COMMIT and STW/NWO Veni grant 11881.

11. REFERENCES

[1] Amazon Elastic MapReduce. http://aws.amazon.com/elasticmapreduce.
[2] Apache Hadoop. http://hadoop.apache.org.
[3] The Distributed ASCI Supercomputer 4. http://www.cs.vu.nl/das4.
[4] Hadoop Capacity Scheduler. http://hadoop.apache.org/docs/r2.3.0/hadoop-yarn/hadoop-yarn-site/CapacityScheduler.html.
[5] B. Avi-Itzhak and H. Levy. On Measuring Fairness in Queues. *Advances in Applied Probability*, 36(3), 2004.

[6] J. Buisson, O. Sonmez, H. Mohamed, W. Lammers, and D. Epema. Scheduling Malleable Applications in Multicluster Systems. *IEEE Cluster*, 2007.

[7] Y. Chen, S. Alspaugh, and R. Katz. Interactive Analytical Processing in Big Data Systems: A Cross-Industry Study of MapReduce Workloads. *VLDB*, 2012.

[8] N. Chohan, C. Castillo, M. Spreitzer, M. Steinder, A. Tantawi, and C. Krintz. See Spot Run: Using Spot Instances for MapReduce Workflows. *HotCloud*, 2010.

[9] J. Dean and S. Ghemawat. Mapreduce: Simplified Data Processing on Large Clusters. *Comm. of the ACM*, 51(1), 2008.

[10] C. Ernemann, V. Hamscher, U. Schwiegelshohn, R. Yahyapour, and A. Streit. On Advantages of Grid Computing for Parallel Job Scheduling. *CCGrid*, 2002.

[11] D. Feitelson, L. Rudolph, U. Schwiegelshohn, K. Sevcik, and P. Wong. Theory and Practice in Parallel Job Scheduling. *JSSPP*, 1997.

[12] B. Ghit, N. Yigitbasi, and D. Epema. Resource Management for Dynamic MapReduce Clusters in Multicluster Systems. *MTAGS*, 2012.

[13] A. Ghodsi, M. Zaharia, B. Hindman, A. Konwinski, S. Shenker, and I. Stoica. Dominant Resource Fairness: Fair Allocation of Multiple Resource Types. *NSDI*, 2011.

[14] A. Ghodsi, M. Zaharia, S. Shenker, and I. Stoica. Choosy: Max-Min Fair Sharing for Datacenter Jobs with Constraints. *Eurosys*, 2013.

[15] Í. Goiri, K. Le, T. D. Nguyen, J. Guitart, J. Torres, and R. Bianchini. GreenHadoop: Leveraging Green Energy in Data-Processing Frameworks. *EuroSys*, 2012.

[16] A. G. Greenberg and N. Madras. How Fair Is Fair Queuing. *JACM*, 39(3), 1992.

[17] T. Hegeman, B. Ghit, M. Capota, J. Hidders, D. Epema, and A. Iosup. The BTWorld Use Case for Big Data Analytics: Description, MapReduce Logical Workflow, and Empirical Evaluation. *IEEE Big Data*, 2013.

[18] H. Herodotou, F. Dong, and S. Babu. No One (Cluster) Size Fits All: Automatic Cluster Sizing for Data-Intensive Analytics. *SOCC*, 2011.

[19] B. Hindman, A. Konwinski, M. Zaharia, A. Ghodsi, A. Joseph, R. Katz, S. Shenker, and I. Stoica. Mesos: A Platform for Fine-grained Resource Sharing in the Data Center. *NSDI*, 2011.

[20] S. Huang, J. Huang, J. Dai, T. Xie, and B. Huang. The Hibench Benchmark Suite: Characterization of the MapReduce-based Data Analysis. *ICDEW*, 2010.

[21] M. Isard, V. Prabhakaran, J. Currey, U. Wieder, K. Talwar, and A. Goldberg. Quincy: Fair Scheduling for Distributed Computing Clusters. *SIGOPS*, 2009.

[22] M. Lin, A. Wierman, L. Andrew, and E. Thereska. Dynamic Right-Sizing for Power-Proportional Data Centers. *INFOCOM*, 2011.

[23] H. Mohamed and D. Epema. Koala: A Co-allocating Grid Scheduler. *Concurrency and Computation: Practice and Experience*, 20(16), 2008.

[24] T. Nguyen and M. Vojnovic. Weighted Proportional Allocation. *SIGMETRICS*, 2011.

[25] C. Olston, B. Reed, U. Srivastava, R. Kumar, and A. Tomkins. Pig Latin: A Not-So-Foreign Language for Data Processing. *SIGMOD*, 2008.

[26] D. Raz, H. Levy, and B. Avi-Itzhak. A Resource-Allocation Queueing Fairness Measure. *SIGMETRICS/PERFORMANCE*, 2004.

[27] D. Shue, M. J. Freedman, and A. Shaikh. Performance Isolation and Fairness for Multi-Tenant Cloud Storage. *OSDI*, 2012.

[28] J. Tan, X. Meng, and L. Zhang. Delay Tails in MapReduce Scheduling. *SIGMETRICS*, 2012.

[29] V. K. Vavilapalli, A. C. Murthy, C. Douglas, S. Agarwal, M. Konar, R. Evans, T. Graves, J. Lowe, H. Shah, S. Seth, et al. Apache Hadoop Yarn: Yet Another Resource Negotiator. *SOCC*, 2013.

[30] K. Wang, M. Lin, F. Ciucu, A. Wierman, and C. Lin. Characterizing the Impact of the Workload on the Value of Dynamic Resizing in Data Centers. *SIGMETRICS*, 2012.

[31] A. Wierman and M. Harchol-Balter. Classifying Scheduling Policies with Respect to Unfairness in an M/GI/1. *SIGMETRICS*, 2003.

[32] M. Wojciechowski, M. Capotă, J. Pouwelse, and A. Iosup. BTWorld: Towards Observing the Global BitTorrent File-Sharing Network. *HPDC*, 2010.

[33] M. Zaharia, D. Borthakur, J. Sarma, K. Elmeleegy, S. Shenker, and I. Stoica. Delay Scheduling: A Simple Technique for Achieving Locality and Fairness in Cluster Scheduling. *EuroSys*, 2010.

On the Relevance of Adversarial Queueing Theory in Practice

Daniel S. Berger
Distributed Computer Systems (DISCO) Lab
University of Kaiserslautern
Germany
berger@cs.uni-kl.de

Martin Karsten
David R. Cheriton School of Computer Science
University of Waterloo
Canada
mkarsten@uwaterloo.ca

Jens Schmitt
Distributed Computer Systems (DISCO) Lab
University of Kaiserslautern
Germany
jschmitt@cs.uni-kl.de

ABSTRACT

Adversarial Queueing Theory (AQT) has shown that seemingly innocent traffic injection rates might lead to unbounded queues in packet-switched networks - depending on scheduling strategies as well as topological characteristics. Little attention has been given to quantifying these effects in realistic network configurations. In particular, the existing AQT literature makes two unrealistic assumptions: infinite buffers and perfect synchrony. Because finite buffers inherently limit queue sizes, adversarial effects ultimately lead to packet loss which we address in this work. In addition, we study the effect of imperfect network synchronization under the packet loss metric. Our results, using analysis and simulation, indicate that classical AQT examples appear harmless under realistic assumptions but for a novel class of adversaries considerably higher loss can be observed. We introduce this class by giving examples of two new AQT concepts to construct loss-efficient network adversaries. Our analysis proves the robustness of these new adversaries against randomized de-synchronization effects in terms of variable link delays and nodal processing.

Categories and Subject Descriptors

C.2.1 [**Network Architecture and Design**]: Network topology; C.4 [**Performance of Systems**]: Modeling techniques

Keywords

Adversarial Queueing Theory; network stability; finite buffers

1. INTRODUCTION

Adversarial Queueing Theory (AQT) [7] has been introduced to analyze the inherent stability characteristics of network topologies assuming certain scheduling policies. In particular, it has been shown for FIFO scheduling that seemingly innocent continuous packet injection strategies, where the aggregated arrival rate of requests for each link does not exceed the link capacity, can lead to unbounded queue lengths and thus, unbounded delay. Such a network configuration is termed *unstable*.

In reality, such patterns can be caused by misconfiguration, or unfortunate circumstances and have also been considered as a possible security threat [13]. In fact, descriptions of network adversaries read like a cookbook for stealthy low-rate denial-of-service (DoS) attacks inducing arbitrary long queues in a target network, which in turn cause high delays and loss.

After a period of very high activity in AQT research in the late 1990s and early 2000s, recently there has been only little work on analytical aspects of adversarial queueing theory. This might be due to the fact that fundamental results about the stability of network systems have been obtained. Unfortunately, these fundamental results are mainly concerned with the notion of *universal stability*[1], which has only been shown for networks that are restricted in topology or employ unrealistic scheduling policies (see Section 2 for details). In contrast, the actual threat potential of adversarial queueing effects in systems that are not universally stable has not been systematically studied. This paper is a first attempt to complement existing AQT research by studying adversarial effects for more realistic network configurations.

Although topological considerations suggest that adversarial instability may be possible in realistic network topologies [20], it is not immediately obvious whether instability effects really pose a practical threat. The most striking theoretical and "analytically convenient" assumptions of AQT are infinite buffers and a synchronized network model. The central question of AQT about the existence of upper bounds on queue lengths (→ stability) only poses itself under the assumption of unbounded queues. However, device buffers are always finite in length and thus not subject to infinite growth. This paper approaches AQT from a completely different angle than existing literature and investigates the *quantitative* effects of adversarial queueing in finite buffer networks (→ loss) with some asynchrony due to random effects in nodal processing and link delays. We consider timing variations for adversarial injections and various degrees of randomization for the network model.

This leads to two interesting questions. The first is whether classical AQT examples result in excessive packet loss. We show that this is not the case, but instead, finite buffers

[1] Universal stability refers to stable behavior of a scheduling policy, or a topology – under any adversary (cf. [3,7])

SIGMETRICS'14, June 16–20, 2014, Austin, Texas, USA.

http://dx.doi.org/10.1145/2591971.2592006.

stabilize the system enough to limit the overall loss rate effectively. This could lead to the conjecture that AQT is a somewhat theoretical artifact with little practical relevance. Thus, the second question is about the existence of more efficient adversaries. This is positively confirmed by presenting new adversarial configurations that do suffer from considerably higher loss rates than previous scenarios and prove robust against randomization effects. In particular, these adversarial scenarios introduce two novel approaches: *interlocking* of adversaries and *reactive* adversaries. These approaches are used to construct *loss-efficient* adversaries. Here, efficiency is seen from the perspective of the network adversary and denotes its ability to effectuate a high loss rate at a low injection rate of adversarial traffic. We quantify the loss behavior of both, the classical and the newly constructed adversaries, using analytical methods and simulation. The new adversarial constructions are more complex than existing AQT scenarios and are not amenable to a straightforward analytical evaluation of their worst-case loss. Therefore, *deterministic simulation* is used to observe their behavior. In addition, simulation is also used to assess the impact of reduced event synchronization by randomizing certain parts of the network model. To this end, we have extended an open-source simulation framework with a (randomized) network model and corresponding adversary implementations which we release as an open-source contribution[2].

Following our goal of assessing AQT in a practical context, this work is focused on FIFO scheduling. While other scheduling schemes have been found to be universally stable in the AQT literature [3], FIFO is essentially the only relevant scheduling discipline in practice among those typically studied.

The rest of the paper is organized as follows. Section 2 surveys the existing literature. Section 3 briefly recapitulates AQT essentials, while Section 4 gives a modified model of adversarial effects in finite buffer settings. Section 5 presents the loss rate analysis for classical AQT scenarios and Section 6 introduces the novel scenarios. In Section 7 we present simulation results on the robustness against randomization and the paper is wrapped up with a brief conclusion in Section 8.

2. RELATED WORK

Previous work investigating the adversarial queueing model is focused on the conditions for network stability. A network is called stable if there exists an upper bound on the number of packets in this network for any arbitrary long time interval [3]. The time evolution is studied as a distributed game between the network system (topology and scheduling) and a hypothetical adversary. The network system is shown to be either stable or unstable, i.e., possessing an upper bound on packet delay or not.

Previous results have explored the boundaries of stability conditions, in particular with respect to the scheduling policy [3], the longest path in the network [17], graph minors [2, 3, 12, 20], and injection rate [3, 5, 10, 14, 17]. Most notably, Bhattacharjee and Goel [5] prove that networks with FIFO scheduling can be unstable at arbitrary small injection rates. Furthermore, the family of stable topologies with FIFO scheduling is restricted to a super-class of directed acyclic graphs, the so-called *decorated cycles* as shown by Weinard [20]. Yet, the class of decorated cycles does not encompass many realistic network topologies, thus indicating a potential threat for the stability of real-world networks.

Simulation has been employed to study adversarial scenarios before, most notably in [9], [11], and recently in [4], which all study unbounded queues. In contrast, our work is focused on quantifying loss in a finite buffer setting. Chroni *et al.* [9] use a simulation model to determine the stability of compositions of different schedulers in a network. They do not assess FIFO and do not report quantitative results, but use simulation to determine whether a network appears to be stable or not. Cespedes *et al.* [11] do not focus on particular adversarial scenarios, but instead choose packet destinations distributed uniformly over the network and investigate the effects of clock asynchrony on timing-based scheduling algorithms.

A related issue to the randomized AQT model are randomized scheduling decisions and their effects on network stability as considered by Lorion and Weinard [16]. Similarly, the asynchronous timers of Cespedes *et al.* [11] only affect algorithms which base scheduling decisions on timers. This is different from the randomization assessed in our work as we focus on deterministic FIFO scheduling and randomness in the *timing of packet injections* and *variability in link delays*.

A finite buffer AQT model is also studied by Aiello *et al.* [1] using a competitive analysis, but they do not consider a network system's total number of dropped packets as a performance metric, but instead use throughput as a metric since no scheduling policy admits a competitive ratio for the number of dropped packets. In the present paper, we propose to use network loss (i.e. the ratio of dropped to successfully delivered packets) as a performance metric and show that previously proposed adversaries appear harmless under this metric.

To the best of our knowledge, no previous work has reported results on network loss in a finite-buffer AQT setting and no results are known under the condition of a network model that is not assumed to proceed in synchronous uniform steps. We appear to be the first to quantify these effects and to propose dedicated network adversaries tailored to this setting.

We remark that a possible perspective on adversarial queueing effects is their interpretation as low-rate DoS attacks [13]. These attacks often rely on synchronizing flows so that packets arrive as correlated bursts as first reported by Kuzmanovic and Knightly [15]. In fact, the temporal evolution of these burst arrivals (shown in Figure 1) appears similar to what can be observed in AQT simulations (shown in Figure 2): an attacker induces periodic waves of packet arrivals which quickly fill up queues. Although the effect is related, our work is concerned with more fundamental aspects of this problem and the analysis is carried out starting from the original theoretical AQT settings where, e.g., no congestion control algorithms exist.

3. BACKGROUND

The network in an adversarial scenario is represented as a directed graph $\mathcal{G} = (V, E)$ with network nodes as vertices V and links as edges E. Time is divided into discrete time steps and each node processes one unit packet per one unit time step. Each edge in the graph is associated with a queue where packets wait if they arrive at an already busy edge

[2]All source code is available on our project page
`http://disco.cs.uni-kl.de/content/Aqtmodel`

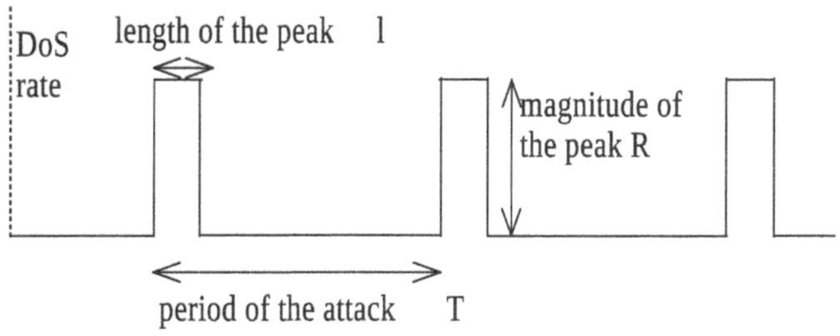

Figure 1: Example of a low-rate DoS (due to Kuzmanovic *et al.* [15], Copyright 2003 ACM).

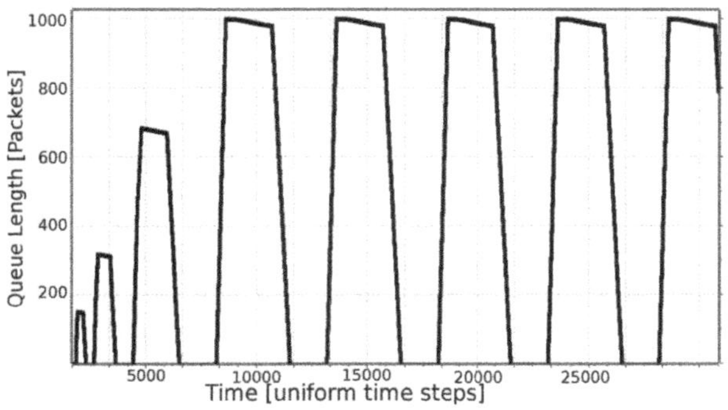

Figure 2: Periodic Bursts in AQT Simulation Trace.

(output queue buffering). If more than one packet is available to be processed at some edge, then the next packet is chosen according to FIFO scheduling. Each time step consists of the following sub-steps: 1) injection of new requests by the adversary, 2) edge traversals of packets already in the system, 3) absorption of packets, if they reach their destination.

The adversary can inject packets with chosen loop-free paths into the network, i.e., each path contains each edge at most once. In order to not trivially overload the system, the adversary's requests are subject to a local load condition. Previous work has introduced different models to express this condition – see [8] for a comparison. We adopt an adversary definition that is less bursty than the original definition [7] but still sufficient to fulfill the requirements of the first result about FIFO instability [3] and all subsequently published instability examples. The *injection rate* $0 < r < 1$ is bounded for every path at any time: for any time interval $[s, t)$, the adversary's injections requiring any particular edge in the graph must not exceed $r(t - s)$ packets. Additionally to this, adversaries are allowed to require an initial configuration of packets in queues in the network. This is allowed only once at the start of time and can be considered as a warm-start assumption. The number of packets required for a warm start is considered to be very small in particular when being compared to the lengths of queues over time. Previous work has introduced transformations of adversaries, so that this requirement can always be satisfied [3,6]. Additionally, simulation results on the minimal size of initial configurations required for classical adversaries support the claim that already a small number of packets suffices [4].

An adversarial scenario is defined as a specific combination of a topology $\mathcal{G}$ and an adversarial strategy $\mathcal{A}$ that describes a traffic flow pattern. AQT studies the time evolution of the tuple $(\mathcal{G}, \mathcal{A})$ as specific worst-case flow patterns $\mathcal{A}$ repeatedly emerge in $\mathcal{G}$. As such, AQT studies pessimistic effects over

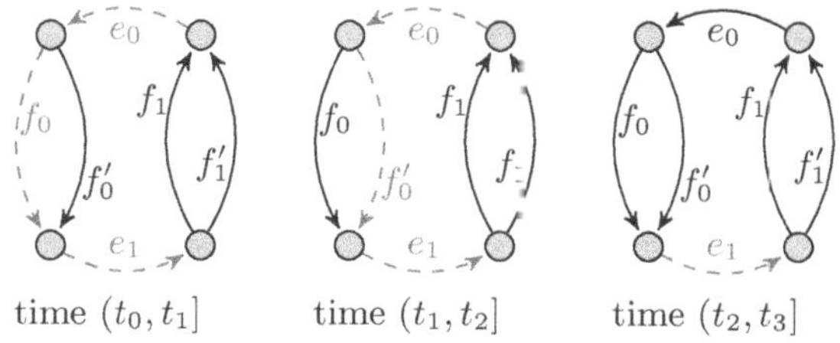

Figure 3: A network called the *Baseball graph* with the corresponding adversarial strategy indicated by dashed edges and in tabular form below.

ADVERSARY 1. *Baseball Adversary* $(\mathcal{A}_1)$

time interval	*set*	*at*	*with path*	*size*
at t_0	S_n	e_0	(e_0)	s_n
$(t_0, t_1 = t_0 + s_n]$	X_n	e_0	(e_0, f_0, e_1)	$r\, s_n$
$(t_1, t_2 = t_1 + r s_n]$	Y_n	e_0	(e_0, f_0', e_1)	$r^2\, s_n$
$(t_1, t_1 + \frac{s_n r}{1+r}]$	C_n	f_0	(f_0)	$\frac{s_n r^2}{1+r}$
$(t_2, t_3 = t_2 + r^2 s_n]$	Z_n	e_1	(e_1)	$r^3\, s_n$

The induction hypothesis (at t_0) indicates an initial set.

long time scales. The evolution of the scenario is given in the form of an induction over time intervals $n \in \mathbb{N}$ which are called *phases*. The induction hypothesis is based on the state of the network at the beginning of a phase n when some queues already hold packets. These queues are called *initial sets* and for the induction base they are satisfied by the initial configuration. In the induction step, traffic flows are generated by injections of the adversary such that for the next phase $n + 1$ the hypothesis of initial sets is satisfied again and thus the same injection pattern can be performed again.

3.1 Example

An important example is the Baseball topology which is due to [3] and called Baseball graph (BB). The topology and the adversary are illustrated in Figure 3 and Adversary 1, respectively. As induction hypothesis in phase n, assume that s_n packets are queued in e_0 at time t_0; this set of packets forms the initial set in this example. One phase corresponds to injections in intervals $(t_0, t_3]$ where we omit the reference to n, the current phase, in order not to clutter notation. At the end of phase n (at time t_3) and for $r \geq 0.85$, s_{n+1} packets with $s_{n+1} > s_n$ are queued in e_1 which can be used to execute the same pattern in the symmetric part of the network in phase $n + 1$.

The adversary's goal is for the two sets X_n and Y_n to arrive simultaneously at e_1. This is achieved by X_n's advance being blocked first by S_n and then by C_n packets while Y_n is injected. For this reason, the size of consecutive injections depends on the size of S_n. Because X_n, Y_n, and Z_n form the eventual queue in e_1 these are called *bottleneck* packets and we call C_n *confinement* packets, as packets of this type confine other approaching packet flows. Over time, the repeated adversarial traffic pattern causes packets to aggregate in the network and the bottleneck buffers e_0 and e_1 face periodic, increasing bursts.

4. FINITE BUFFERS

We now depart from existing adversarial queueing models by assuming that queues are of finite length; for the ease of presentation, we assume a uniform buffer size of b packets throughout the network.

4.1 The Notion of Steady State

For infinite buffers, unstable systems experience ever growing delays; yet, in a model with finite buffers (and thus for any real-world network) this clearly does not hold. At some point, the packet burst s_{m+1} of some phase m does not fit into the queue buffer b any more, and the excess of $s_{m+1} - b$ leaves the system as loss. If the traffic flows continue unchanged, the system enters a *steady state* where any set $s_n, n > m$ is always bounded by the finite buffer size b.

An intuitive example for steady-state behavior can be observed in Figure 2. By means of a queue length plot of a bottleneck queue, the figure shows the transition of the Baseball scenario from a transient state of growing periodic bursts to a steady state of fixed-sized periodic bursts. We capture this intuition by the following definition.

Definition 1 (Steady State). *A network system representing an adversarial scenario $(\mathcal{G}, \mathcal{A})$ with uniform buffer size b is in steady state when all initial sets are of size b from some phase onward.*

For the network adversaries defined in [3, 5, 10, 14, 20] being unstable under the infinite buffer assumption implies to reach such a steady-state in a finite queue setting. For the given examples, instability arises for configurations with r greater than some lower bound r_0 (see, e.g., Section 3.1). In turn, the corresponding finite-queue system with the same configuration reaches steady state.

The fundamental adversarial mechanism underlying the known adversarial queueing scenarios is an incremental build-up of packet bursts relying on the congestion caused by the initial sets in each phase. Because of this incremental build-up, the worst-case behavior of such scenarios can be obtained by setting the cardinality of all initial sets to their maximal value, i.e., to b. For the scenarios analyzed in Sections 5 and 6, the long-term behavior of the system converges asymptotically to this worst case.

4.2 Loss as the New Threat Measure

To assess the severity of adversarial effects quantitatively, we propose to measure loss, which is a common indicator of congestion in a network. Instead of computing the loss for individual network segments though, the number of lost packets is compared to the total number of packets injected by the adversary:

$$(network)\ loss = \frac{\#\ packets\ lost}{\#\ packets\ injected}$$

On a network-system level this ratio can be considered as the loss rate over time or as the probability to lose any injected packet independent from its path. Other threat measures could easily exaggerate the severity of adversarial effects. For example the maximum burst size or the length of a single congestion event can grow arbitrarily large, if no topological parameters are considered. However, in such cases the total relative loss usually remains small, because the adversary has to inject a large number of packets in order to create these bursts; while, many of these packets are unaffected by congestion (see Section 5.2).

Besides indicating inherent global risk, the total relative loss also helps to quantitatively estimate the feasibility of adversarial network attacks. Attackers may inject packets into the network to artificially create adversarial effects, which would cause denial of service in the target network. It is desirable to obtain a lower bound on the effort needed to launch attacks of this type, assuming that an attacker attempts to use available resources as efficiently and stealthily as possible.

For the loss analysis, assume a system $(\mathcal{G}, \mathcal{A})$ that is unstable for $r \geq r_0$ (assuming an infinite amount of buffer). The analysis is limited to injection rates greater than r_0, since the system will endure loss only in this parameter range. As the adversarial queueing scenarios analyzed in the next section reach their respective steady states for $r \geq r_0$ (proofs omitted), their analysis proceeds by setting the cardinality of all initial sets to b.

5. LOSS IN CLASSICAL AQT EXAMPLES

This section presents an analytical study of the loss for two well-known examples of adversarial scenarios given in [3] and [5]. To estimate network loss for a system $(\mathcal{G}, \mathcal{A})$ the number of packets lost and the number of packets injected need to be determined. Loss depends on the injection scheme of the adversary $\mathcal{A}$, the cardinality of initial sets, and on $\mathcal{G}$. The total number of injections can be derived from the description of $\mathcal{A}$.

5.1 Loss in the Baseball Graph

The first example is the system $(\mathcal{G}_{BB}, \mathcal{A}_1)$ shown in Figure 3. We assume the system to be in some phase n and that the initial set has the cardinality s_n $(= b)$. $\mathcal{A}_1$ induces a queue of $s_{n+1} = r^3 s_n + r^2 s_n/(r+1)$ packets in the bottleneck at the end of the phase, as stated in [3]. To get the total number of injections, it is necessary to find the exact cardinality of the confinement set C_n (see Section 3.1), because this cardinality is not stated in the original description of $\mathcal{A}_1$ [3]. For efficiency reasons, the cardinality of C_n must be such that throughout $(t_1, t_2]$ packets compete with X to traverse f_0, but after t_2 no packets of C_n may remain in the queue of f_0. In other words, $|C_n| = \frac{s_n r^2}{1+r}$. As all cardinalities stated here ignore static offsets, this leads to an upper bound as follows:

$$\begin{aligned} loss &\leq \frac{s_{n+1} - s_n}{|X_n \cup Y_n \cup Z_n \cup C_n|} \\ &= \frac{s_n(r^3 + \frac{r^2}{1+r} - 1)}{s_n(r + r^2 + r^3 + \frac{r^2}{1+r})} \\ &= \frac{r^4 + r^3 + r^2 - r - 1}{r^4 + 2r^3 + 3r^2 + r} \end{aligned}$$

It is interesting to note that the loss scales independently of the buffer size b. This is due to the length of individual phases being directly dependent on the initial set's cardinality s_n and our worst-case assumption of steady-state loss, i.e., that $s_n = b$. For $r < 0.85$ the system $(\mathcal{G}_{BB}, \mathcal{A}_1)$ does not necessarily reach a steady state and insignificant loss occurs (see also simulation results in Section 6.4). With growing injection rate r, the loss increases approximately linear to $\frac{1}{7} \approx 14.23\%$ for $r = 1.0$.

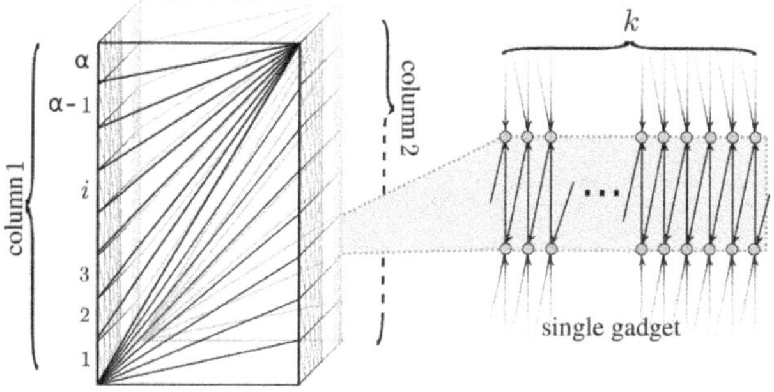

Figure 4: FIFO-unstable topology at arbitrary small injection rates.

Another observation that can be drawn from this example is that the small in-degree of e_0 and e_1 inherently limits the arrival rate and thus the numerator of the loss equations. If there were another incoming edge, the numerator could comprise additional terms (besides r^3 and $\frac{r^2}{1+r}$). However, greater in-degrees amplify the role of another factor that can limit packet loss as shown in the next example.

5.2 Loss at Extremely Small Injection Rates

Following the initial baseball graph instability example, further work on FIFO instability has sought to decrease the bound at which instability occurs (see also the comprehensive survey in [8]). The ultimate goal has been reached in [5] where Bhattacharjee and Goel present a system which is unstable at arbitrary small injection rates, i.e., $r = 0 + \epsilon$ for infinitesimal $\epsilon > 0$. The corresponding graph is constructed in a parameterized way from basic building blocks and can therefore compensate low injection rates by increasing graph size.

We use the following notation, which is slightly adapted from the original one used by Bhattacharjee and Goel. The network consists of two columns of α concatenated gadgets of width k (Figure 4); label the gadgets $i \in 1, \ldots, \alpha$. Additionally each gadget i in column one is connected to the first gadget of column two by an additional chain of gadgets, a so-called connector; the same holds vice versa. The parameters α and k are actually functions of r, for details we refer to [5].

In each phase n an initial set S_n travels through one column. Every time it traverses a gadget i, its advance is blocked by k single-edge injections. The resulting queue S_n^i at each gadget i is then used to inject bottleneck packets into the connectors towards the symmetric column's first gadget.

As a rough bound on the number of lost packets we assume that all injected packets arrive at the bottleneck at the same time (which is not the case and largely overrates the adversary's efficiency). Furthermore, we rely on the bound on $s_n^i = |S_n^i|$ from Lemma 5.1 in [5]: $s_n/2 < s_n^i < s_n$, where $s_n = |S_n|$. In each sub-phase i a set X_n^i of cardinality $x_n^i \leq s_n^i\, r/k$ packets is injected into each path towards the bottleneck. As each gadget has k paths, and there are α such sub-phases, it holds that:

$$s_{n+1} \leq \sum k\, x_n^i \leq \sum_{n=1}^{\alpha} s_n^i\, r < \alpha\, s_n\, r. \tag{1}$$

For a rough upper bound on the loss, it is sufficient to bound additional injections used to hold back each X_n^i's packets until all of them are injected. This is achieved by k additional single-edge injections into each gadget chain of each X_n^i; after it is is injected, it needs to be held back for another $\alpha - i$ sub-phases. Now, each X_n^i needs at least $s_n^i > \frac{s_n}{2}$ time steps for injection, and hence one sub-phase produces at least $(rs_n^i)\, r\, k$ confinement packets. Thus, the total number of packets injected is at least:

$$\sum_{i=1}^{\alpha} (rs_n^i)\, r\, k\, (\alpha - i) > \sum_{i=1}^{\alpha-1} r^2 \frac{s_n}{2}\, k\, i = \alpha\, s_n\, r \left(\frac{1}{4} rk(\alpha - 1)\right)$$

Finally, we use the upper bound from (1) $\alpha s_n r$ on the number of bottleneck packets and obtain $loss < \frac{1}{\frac{1}{4}rk(\alpha-1)}$.

For the limit $r \to 1$ and the best choice of parameters, the loss of this system stays below 0.3%. The reason why this rough estimation gives such an expressive bound is that the number of confinement packets – injected by the adversary to delay packet flows in order for them to arrive at the bottleneck link at the same time – is excessively large. We conclude that loss can be safely ignored for this system.

5.3 Conclusion for Loss in Classical Examples

We have studied several additional adversarial scenarios from the literature and found that the baseball graph actually has the worst loss characteristics, despite its simplicity. Accordingly, we argue that classical AQT examples do not show excessive loss. However, these examples were not targeted at a finite buffer model and cannot necessarily be expected to deliver worst-case results for loss. Therefore, we reformulate the goal of the adversary to *maximize loss*, that is, be as *effective* (induce instability) and *efficient* (use the least number of packets) in terms of injections as possible. We propose two appropriate adversarial scenarios that are described in the next section.

6. NEW ADVERSARIAL SCENARIOS

The analysis presented in the previous section shows that for small topologies like the baseball graph, small in-degrees limit the arrival rate at bottleneck buffers and as such the loss. For larger graphs, on the other hand, the number of confinement packets (defined in Section 3.1) required by classic adversaries is so high that it always keeps the global loss rate low.

We propose a new adversarial concept called *interlocking* which alleviates the need for large numbers of confinement packets: several adversarial components are interweaved, such that the bottleneck packets of one component act as confinement packets for the others and vice versa. This idea turns previously unused confinement packets into bottleneck packets enabling highly loss-efficient adversaries. For readability we introduce the concept via two examples (as is typical for AQT results, e.g., [3, 5, 10, 14, 17]) but point out that many adversarial components can be reused within this concept.

6.1 Interlocked Baseballs

As the first example, the interlocking concept is applied to two baseball networks denoted as *Outer Adversary* and *Inner Adversary* (see Figure 5). These adversaries are synchronized, so that the injections of the Outer Adversary are held back by packets of the Inner Adversary, and vice versa. In such a scenario, significantly fewer dedicated confinement packets are needed, which results in higher network loss. To see the

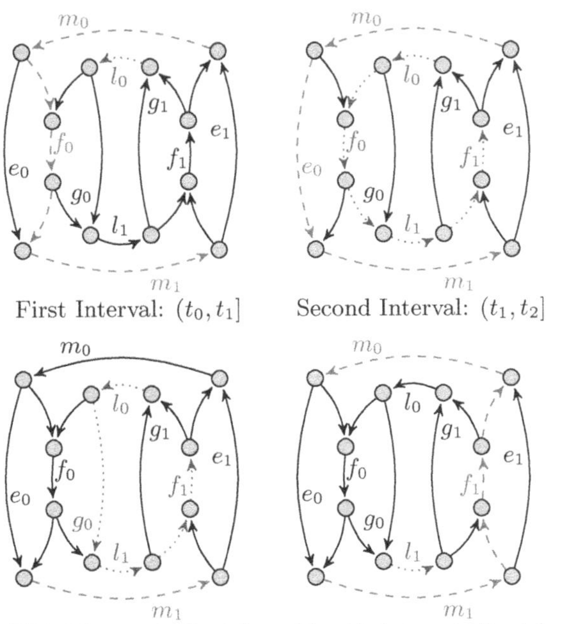

First Interval: $(t_0, t_1]$ Second Interval: $(t_1, t_2]$

Third Interval: $(t_2, t_3]$ Fourth Interval: $(t_3, t_4]$

Figure 5: The Interlocked Baseballs (IB) scenario comprises two baseball graphs. Corresponding injection patterns are shifted by one interval and are indicated by dashed and dotted edges. The phase overlap due to each sub-adversary being completed in three intervals can be observed in $(t_0, t_1]$ and in $(t_3, t_4]$. Only the subset of edges needed for uniqueness of path description is labeled.

analogy of the Outer Adversary with the original Baseball graph, compare m_0, e_0, f_0, m_1, e_1, and f_1 in Figure 5 with e_0, f_0, f_0', e_1, f_1', and f_1 in Figure 3. A respective analogy exists between the Inner Adversary and the original Baseball graph. This mapping is illustrated in Figure 6.

Both Baseball-type components in this adversarial scenario execute in lockstep during alternating phases. Therefore, the adversary is described with two induction hypotheses: an initial set O_n in m_0 for the Outer Adversary and I_n in l_0 for the Inner Adversary. In terms of the overall scenario, numbered phases are divided into even and odd phases; each phase n is subdivided into intervals of length o_n, where $o_n = |O_n|$. We describe roughly what happens to the injections, which are detailed in Adversary 2. As before, we omit the description for the symmetric part of the network because the adversary uses the same strategy for odd phases $n+1, n+3, n+5, \ldots$.

In the first interval, the initial set O_n starts traversing m_0 at $t_0 + 1$ and by doing so, it blocks the path of O_n^1 until $t_1 + 1$. Next, O_n^1 competes with X_n to traverse the edge f_0. This competition is the basic mechanism connecting the two interlocked adversaries with each other. At the same time, O_n^2 is injected and its packets are queued up behind O_n^1. After $r\,o_n + 1$ time steps, O_n^1 will have left the queue of m_0 and O_n^2 starts traversing m_0. Simultaneously, I_n^1 is injected into l_0. Its long path (and the path of I_n^2) is necessary to form X_{n+1} for the next phase. The packets in I_n^1 are buffered behind the initial set I_n at l_0 and start traversing l_0 at time step $t_1 + i_n$. In the third interval, O_n^1 and O_n^2 arrive

ADVERSARY 2. *Interlocked Baseballs Adversary*

time interval	*set*	*at*	*with path*	*size*
at t_0 (ind. hypothesis)	O_n	m_0	(m_0)	o_n
$(t_0, t_1 = t_0 + o_n]$	O_n^1	m_0	(m_0, f_0, m_1)	$o_n\,r$
at t_1 (ind. hypothesis)	I_n	l_0	(l_0)	i_n
at t_1 (ind. hypothesis)	X_n	l_0	(l_0, f_0)	x_n
$(t_1, t_2 = t_1 + o_n]$	O_n^2	m_0	(m_0, e_0, m_1)	$r\,o_n$
(t_1, t_2)	I_n^1	l_0	(l_0, f_0, l_1, f_1)	$r\,o_n$
$(t_2, t_3 = t_2 + o_n]$	O_n^3	m_1	(m_1)	$r\,o_n$
(t_2, t_3)	I_n^2	m_0	(l_0, g_0, l_1, f_1)	$r\,o_n$
$(t_3, t_4 = t_3 + o_n]$	I_n^3	(l_1)	(l_1)	$r\,o_n$

The induction hypothesis (ind. hypothesis) indicates an initial set. Note that X_n is a subset of I_n – both are initial sets that reside in the same queue, but differ in that the packets in I_n require to traverse the path (l_0, f_0).

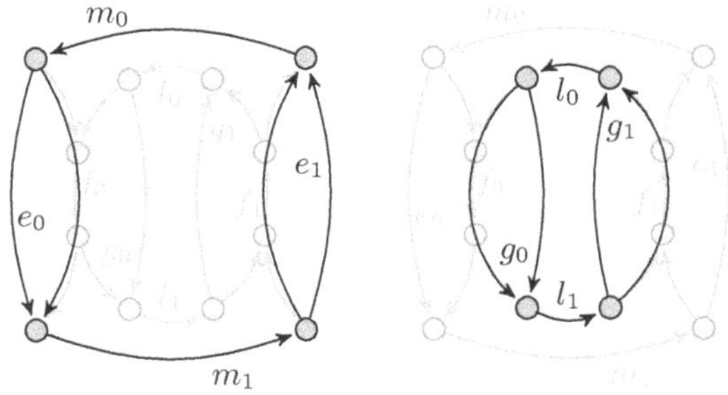

Figure 6: Mapping the Interlocked Baseballs (IB) scenario to its two baseball graphs. Left: the Outer Adversary, right: the Inner Adversary.

at m_1, while O_n^3 gets directly injected into the same edge. These arrivals fill the queue of m_1 rapidly and form O_{n+1}, which becomes the initial set of the next phase. Still in the same time interval, another set I_n^2 is injected by the inner adversary while I_n^1 is still queued behind O_n^1. Finally, in the fourth time interval, I_n^1 and I_n^2 arrive at l_1 together with an additional injection I_n^3. Note that the phases n and $n+1$ overlap. While the arrivals at l_0 form I_{n+1} in (t_3, t_4), the next phase of the outer adversary has already started. In other words, $(t_0, t_1]$ of phase $n+1$ is already active.

6.2 Loss in the Interlocked Baseballs Scenario

In the analysis, we ignore constant offsets towards lower bounds. For example, Set O_n^1 competes to traverse f_0 at $t_1 + 3$ with Set X_n but we count as if it arrived at t_1. Also, some expressions of set cardinalities may become negative, but we omit the $[\ldots]^+$ operator, because set sizes cannot become negative.

LEMMA 1.

$$o_{n+1} = \frac{(4\,o_n\,r - 2\,o_n)\,x_n + 3\,o_n\,i_n\,r - 2\,o_n\,i_n}{x_n + i_n} \tag{2}$$

$$i_{n+1} = o_n(4\,r - 3) + x_n \tag{3}$$

$$x_{n+1} \geq o_n\,(4\,r - 3) + x_n - \frac{2\,o_n\,r}{r+2} \tag{4}$$

PROOF. In $(t_1, t_2]$, X_n competes with O_n^1 to traverse f_0. X_n arrives on average at rate x_n/i_n and O_n^1-packets arrive at rate 1. Thus, X_n traverses f_0 at rate $\frac{x_n/i_n}{x_n/i_n+1}$, and O_n^1 at rate $\frac{1}{x_n/i_n+1}$. Overall, $\frac{o_n\,(x_n/i_n)}{x_n/i_n+1}$ X_n-packets, and $\frac{o_n}{x_n/i_n+1}$ O_n^1-packets traverse f_0 as this interval is o_n time steps long.

At t_2, $r\,o_n + x_n - o_n$ packets from O_n^1 and X_n are left in queue f_0 to block the advancing packets of I_n^1. Thus, until t_3, another $o_n - (r\,o_n + x_n - o_n) = 2o_n - r\,o_n - x_n$ packets will traverse f_0 and therefore, I_n^1 will decrease by that number of packets.

While O_n^2 gets injected into m_0 in $(t_1, t_2]$, the queue of m_0 holds only $r\,o_n$ packets of O_n^1. Therefore, $o_n(1-r)$ packets from O_n^2 traverse m_0 before the set is fully injected. These packets arrive at m_1 with rate 1. Concurrently, packets from O_n^1 arrive at m_1 with rate $\frac{1}{x_n/i_n+1}$, while traversals at m_1 occur at rate 1, so that in $(t_2 + ro_n, t_3]$, these arrivals will form an additional set E_n at m_1. This set grows at rate $\frac{1}{x_n/i_n+1}$.

Similarly to O_n^2, I_n^2 diminishes by $i_n(1-r)$ packets at l_0 in $(t_2, t_3]$. Also, by the same mechanism as E_n, a set F_n builds up in $(t_3 + ro_n, t_4]$ in the queue of l_1, as early traversals of the sets I_n^1 and I_n^2 arrive at edge l_1 with an arrival rate of 2 while traversals occur at rate 1.

At t_4 the queue of m_1 consists of the remaining packets of new injections (denoted by *rem*), the additional set E_n and traversals in $t_4 - t_3 = o_n$:

$$\begin{aligned} o_{n+1} =& rem(O_n^1) + rem(O_n^2) + O_n^3 + E_n - o_n \\ =& r\,o_n - \frac{o_n}{x_n/i_n + 1} + r\,o_n - (1-r)o_n + r\,o_n \\ &+ (1-r)o_n\left(\frac{1}{\frac{x_n}{i_n}+1}\right) - o_n \\ =& \frac{(4\,o_n\,r - 2\,o_n)\,x_n + 3\,o_n\,i_n\,r - 2\,o_n\,i_n}{x_n + i_n} \end{aligned}$$

Analogously, the queue length of l_1 at time t_5 can be derived from the remaining arrivals and traversals:

$$\begin{aligned} i_{n+1} =& rem(I_n^1) + rem(I_n^2) + I_n^3 + F_n - o_n \\ =& r\,o_n - (2o_n - r\,o_n - x_n) + r\,o_n - (1-r)o_n \\ &+ r\,o_n + (1-r)o_n - o_n \\ =& x_n + 4\,o_n\,r - 3\,o_n \end{aligned}$$

Finally, we estimate a lower bound on X_{n+1} – the initial packets at l_0 which include f_0 (resp. at l_1 and f_1). This set is only composed of packets from I_n^1 and I_n^2. Both sets' path includes f_1 whereas I_n^3's path does not. Because of this, only a fraction of the traversals at l_1 diminishes X_{n+1}. This fraction can be upper-bounded by considering the corresponding rates of arrivals.

In $[t_4, t_5]$, I_n^1 and I_n^2 each arrive at rate 1 at l_0 while I_n^3 is injected at rate r. Packets from the former two sets traverse at most with rate $\frac{2}{2+r}$. The set F_n only decreases the number of traversals but does not directly count towards X_{n+1}:

$$\begin{aligned} x_{n+1} \geq& rem(I_n^1) + rem(I_n^2) - \left(\frac{2}{2+r}\right)(o_n - F_n) \\ =& o_n\,(4\,r - 3) + x_n - \frac{2\,o_n\,r}{r+2} \end{aligned}$$

because F_n-packets appear first in the queue l_1. □

The ratio x_n/i_n plays a central role to assess instability and loss, but its recursive nature prevents a straightforward evaluation. The following lemma addresses this issue via an auxiliary function, which captures the variety of dependencies from Eqs. 2-4 with a single fixed-point iterator.

We restrict the analysis to $r \geq 0.9$ for ease of presentation.

LEMMA 2. *Assume $r \in [0.9, 1]$, $i_0 \geq o_0$, and $x_0 \geq i_0/3$. Then $i_n \geq o_n$ and $x_n \geq i_n/3$. Furthermore, it holds that $\lim_{n\to\infty} x_n/i_n = (1191/500)\,r - (361/200)$.*

PROOF. The proof is by induction on n. From Lemma 1, i_n/o_n is monotonic in r. Assume $i_{n-1} \geq o_{n-1}$ and $x_{n-1} \geq i_{n-1}/3$. Then, for $r = 0.9$ the ratio i_n/o_n evaluates to a value greater than 1.009. For $r = 1.0$ the ratio is greater than 16/15. This shows the first claim $i_n \geq o_n$ for step n.

It remains to be shown that $x_n \geq i_n/3$ is satisfied. This is done by showing that for the fixed-point of x_n/i_n the ratio is always greater than 1/3 for $r \in [0.9, 1]$. In particular, the fixed-point equation is monotonic and the claim follows by induction.

Even if x_{n-1} and i_{n-1} are known from previous computation steps, computing the ratio of x_n/i_n is not trivial and approximations are used. Assume $R(k-1)$ is the ratio produced by the fixed-point iterator in iteration $k-1$ and $k \leq n$. Then, for the k-th step, we estimate $R(k) = x_k/i_k$ by using $x_{k-1}' = R(k-1)\,o_{k-1}$. Observe that $x_{k-1}' \leq x_{k-1}$ because $k \leq n$, $R(k-1)\,i_{k-1} = x_{k-1}$, and because we can prove that $i_n \geq o_n$ for the current induction step n (first paragraph in this proof). This approximation leads to the following algebraic simplification:

$$R(n) \geq \frac{(r+2)\,R(n-1) + 4\,r^2 + 3\,r - 6}{(r+2)\,R(n-1) + 4\,r^2 + 5\,r - 6}$$

Using $R(n-1) \geq \frac{1}{3}$ and then evaluating for $r \in [0.9, 1]$ shows that $x_k \geq i_k/3$, which completes the induction proof.

The injection rate r remains as a parameter of $R(n)$. It can be used to obtain a better lower bound on $R(n)$ by expressing it as a linear lower bound below the fixed-point iteration curve for $r \in [0.9, 1.0]$. This is possible by interpolating at the limit values, 0.9 and 1, due to the fixed-point curve being monotonically increasing in r. The result from this interpolation is the limit given in the second part of the lemma. □

The base case, $i_0 \geq o_0$ can be assumed without loss of generality, because it is a constant offset and i_0 and o_0 are small compared to i_n and o_n. The same holds for $x_0 \geq i_0/3$.

PROPOSITION 1. *Under infinite buffers, the Interlocked Baseballs scenario is unstable for $r > 0.916$.*

PROOF. From Lemma 1 we know an equation for o_{n+1}. We use $i_n \geq o_n$ and the bound on x_n to simplify this equation as follows:

$$\begin{aligned} o_{n+1} =& \frac{(4\,o_n\,r - 2\,o_n)\,x_n + 3\,o_n\,i_n\,r - 2\,o_n\,i_n}{x_n + i_n} \\ \geq& \frac{9528\,r^2 - 8984\,r + 1610}{(2382\,r - 805)}o_n \end{aligned}$$

This proves that o_n grows without bound for $r \geq 0.916$. Because $i_n \geq o_n$ from Lemma 2 this also applies to i_{n+1}, so that the number of packets in the Inner Adversary's grows without bound, too. □

The Interlocked Baseball adversary's initial sets will thus reach the buffer size b. We additionally claim that the Interlocked Baseballs scenario reaches steady state. This can be

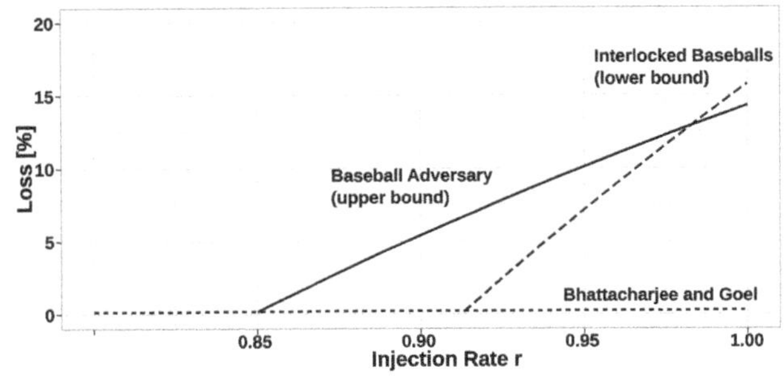

Figure 7: Analytical loss bounds of two classical scenarios in comparison to the Interlocked Baseballs scenario show that there exist new scenarios that can exceed the loss of classical scenarios. Note that the actual difference is more pronounced as we here compare upper to lower bounds (cf. Figure 11).

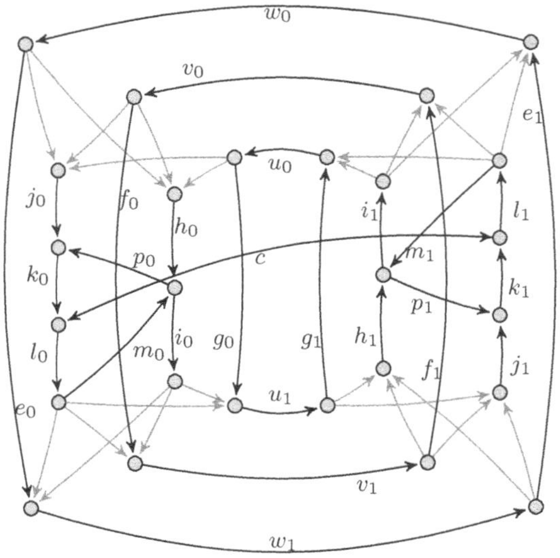

Figure 8: An extension to the Interlocked Baseballs topology with maximum in-degree three which allows for more than three sets to be injected per adversary. The edges m_0, p_0, m_1, p_1, and c are exploited by the Reactive Adversary to create additional confinement by the sets I_n^1 and Z_n.

seen by reconsidering the proof of Lemma 1 under the condition that initial sets of phase n are of cardinality b. Observe that all flows retain their timing (and cardinality) because intermediate buffers (e.g., f_0) do not overrun. Therefore, the expressions from the Lemma hold also in the finite buffer system and can be used in the following proposition.

PROPOSITION 2. *For $r > 0.916$, the lower bound on the loss for the Interlocked Baseballs scenario is*

$$\frac{8243308\,r^2 - 10110340\,r + 2362675}{4764000\,r^2 - 1610000\,r} \tag{5}$$

PROOF. From the description of Adversary 2 we obtain that overall $6\,o_n\,r$ packets are injected in one phase. The loss for one phase can be derived from Lemma 1 and 2 similarly to the proof of Proposition 1:

$$loss = \frac{[\widetilde{o}_{n+1} - b]^+ + [\widetilde{i}_{n+1} - b]^+}{6\,o_n\,r}$$

Here, $\widetilde{o}_{n+1}, \widetilde{i}_{n+1}$ denote the cardinality of the initial sets in the (hypothetical) infinite buffer system. These can be expanded using Lemma 1 and using Lemma 2's fixed point estimate for x_n. Under the assumption of steady state, where $o_n = b$ and $i_n = b$, the closed form of the loss can be derived. □

This analytical result shows that the classical examples can be "outperformed" in terms of loss. As an illustration, Figure 7 shows that the loss bound of the classical Baseball adversary (BB) is eventually surpassed by the lower bound of the Interlock Baseballs adversary (IB). While the difference in this case remains small, note that we are comparing upper to lower bounds where both are not tight (cf. Figures 9 and 10). A more powerful reactive adversary is introduced in the next section and evaluated using simulation in Section 6.4.

6.3 The Reactive Adversary

A refinement of the interlocking concept is possible with three BB-adversaries. Conceptually, interlocking greater numbers of adversaries is a straightforward task. However, to preserve the precise timing of packet flows the construction requires caution, because the different adversaries find different network conditions at the start of each phase.

Previously published adversaries fix an injection pattern which remains the same for each phase; the number of injected packets depends linearly on the cardinality of an initial set. We introduce the notion of a *reactive adversary* which is allowed to adjust more parameters of its strategy based on the network state at the start of a phase. This creates more powerful adversaries, but nevertheless still complies with all previous restrictions on the adversary's power.

We present a simple reactive adversary based on the topology in Figure 8. The adversarial strategy in Adversary 3 utilizes edge c to synchronize packet flows across phases. In particular, if the set Z_n is injected, it affects phase $n+1$ where it creates additional confinement in the path of M_{n+1}^1 and M_{n+1}^2. The essential idea is to conditionally inject Z_n, only if needed, in order to hold the denominator in its loss equation small (cf. the insight from Section 5.2). An efficient condition is to check whether the RA is *not* in steady state, i.e., the threshold in the definition of Adversary 3 is set to $T := b - 1$.

To exploit the graph's maximum in-degree of three, the adversary interlocks three sub-adversaries denoted by *Inner*, *Middle*, and *Outer Adversary* and each adversary injects four (instead of three for the IB) sets (e.g., $O_n^1 - O_n^4$). The first three sets travel along the three paths that connect each two bottleneck links (w_0/w_1, v_0/v_1, u_0/u_1), and the fourth set is a direct injection into the bottleneck link. This extends the duration of each phase n from $4\,o_n$ (for the IB) to $6\,o_n$ time steps (for the RA).

The mutual interdependence of various packet flows makes analytical treatment of this case hard. However, we argue that this construction is very interesting; firstly to study a generalization to the class of interlocked scenarios, and secondly because the network loss of this scenario exceeds all others, as shown by simulations in the next section.

Adversary 3. *Reactive Adversary (RA)*

time interval	*set*	*at*	*with path*	*size*
at t_0 *(ih)*	O_n	w_0	w_0	o_n
$(t_0, t_1 = t_0 + o_n]$	O_n^1	w_0	w_0, j_0, k_0, l_0, w_1	$o_n\ r$
at t_1 *(ih)*	M_n	v_0	v_0	m_n
at t_1 *(ih)*	X_n	v_0	v_0, j_0	x_n
$(t_1, t_2 = t_1 + o_n]$	O_n^2	w_0	w_0, h_0, i_0, w_1	$r\ o_n$
$(t_1, t_2]$	M_n^1	v_0	$v_0, j_0, k_0, l_0, v_1, j_1$	$r\ o_n$
at t_2 *(ih)*	I_n	u_0	u_0	i_n
at t_2 *(ih)*	Y_n	u_0	u_0, h_0, p_0, k_0	y_n
$(t_2, t_3 = t_2 + o_n]$	O_n^3	w_0	w_0, e_0, w_1	$r\ o_n$
$(t_2, t_3]$	M_n^2	v_0	v_0, h_0, i_0, v_1	$r\ o_n$
$(t_2, t_3]$	I_n^1	u_0	$u_0, j_0, k_0, l_0, u_1, h_1, p_1, k_1$	$r\ o_n$
$(t_3, t_4 = t_3 + o_n]$	O_n^4	w_1	w_1	$r\ o_n$
$(t_3, t_4]$	M_n^3	v_0	v_0, f_0, v_1	$r\ o_n$
$(t_3, t_4]$	I_n^2	u_0	u_0, h_0, i_0, u_1	$r\ o_n$
$(t_4, t_5 = t_4 + o_n]$	M_n^4	v_1	v_1	$r\ o_n$
$(t_4, t_5]$	I_n^3	u_0	u_0, g_0, u_1	$r\ o_n$
$(t_4, t_5]$ *(cond.)*	Z_n	j_0	$j_0, k_0, c, l_1, m_1, i_1$	$r\ o_n$
$(t_5, t_6 = t_5 + o_n]$	I_n^4	u_1	u_1	$r\ o_n$

The abbreviation (denoted as 'ih') indicates the inductive assumption of an initial set. The injection denoted by *(cond.)* takes place as long as $o_n = |O_n|$ is less than some threshold T depending on the buffer size b.
Note that X_n is a subset of M_n – both are initial sets that reside in the same queue, but differ in that the packets in M_n require to traverse the path (v_0, j_0). Analogously, $Y_n \subset I_n$ has a remaining path (u_0, h_0, p_0, k_0).

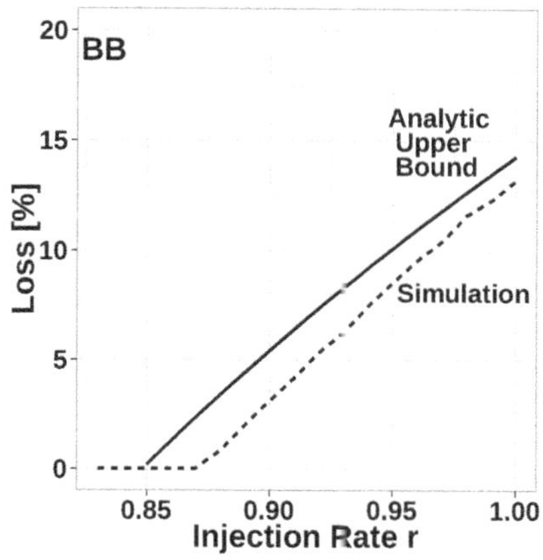

Figure 9: Simulation of Baseball scenario (BB)

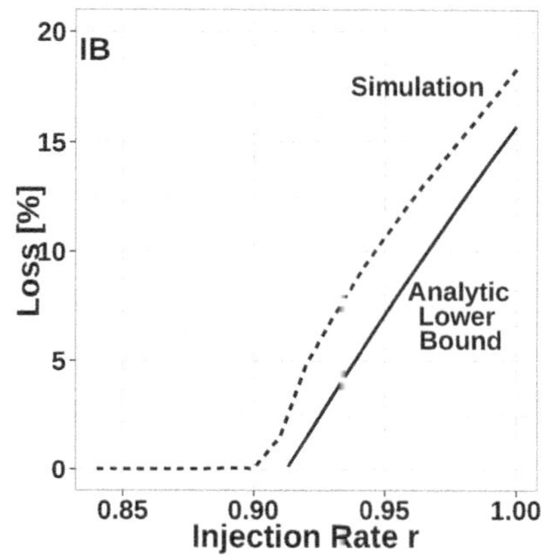

Figure 10: Simulation of Interlocked Baseballs scenario (IB)

6.4 Simulation Results

We implemented the deterministic simulation framework for AQT in OMNeT++ [19]. While previous work in adversarial queueing models relies on pencil and paper evaluation, our new tool allows efficient exploration of the parameter space of various graphs and adversaries. In particular, the simulations are used to obtain quantitative results on the loss in the reactive adversary scenario. Besides analyzing the reactive adversary, the analytical results and the correctness of the simulations are mutually validated by comparing the results in Figures 9 and 10.

For the Baseball scenario, it can be observed that the upper bound is correct (with some overestimation) and the simulation is reasonably close to the upper bound. For the Interlocked Baseball scenario, the lower bound also appears to be correct. In fact, loss has been underestimated by 2-3% using the bound from Proposition 2.

In Figure 11, the loss of several scenarios is compared against each other. In particular, the results for the novel proposals (Interlocked Baseball (IB) and Reactive Adversary (RA)) are shown, but also for the Baseball (BB) from [3] and another scenario termed Gadget Chain [17] (see Figure 12), which also exhibits an interesting behavior. It introduces a very distinct idea from other previous work and utilized the first example of a parametric topology. However, the Gadget Chain scenario oscillates under finite queue conditions, because the timing of adversarial packet flows is interrupted due to lost packets. With a minimal change, however, this adversary can cause some loss, as shown in Figure 11.

The results demonstrate that the new scenarios incur significantly higher loss than the classical AQT scenarios. In particular, the Reactive Adversary rises relatively steep up to 27% loss in the deterministic simulations starting from $r = 0.85$. Also the difference between the Interlocked Baseballs and the Baseball scenarios becomes more pronounced. Further, the behavior of the Gadget Chain scenario [17] is quite different from the others: while loss occurs at low injection rates, the loss curve flattens out and never exceeds 6%. Nevertheless, this gives rise to speculation about the feasibility of loss-maximizing adversaries to threaten a network at low injection rates.

7. EVENT RANDOMIZATION

Adversarial effects reported in the literature are closely coupled to the tight synchronization of packet-level events. As such, considering them as blueprints for problematic configurations or malicious attacks appears somewhat paranoid. Therefore, the impact of randomization effects on loss is

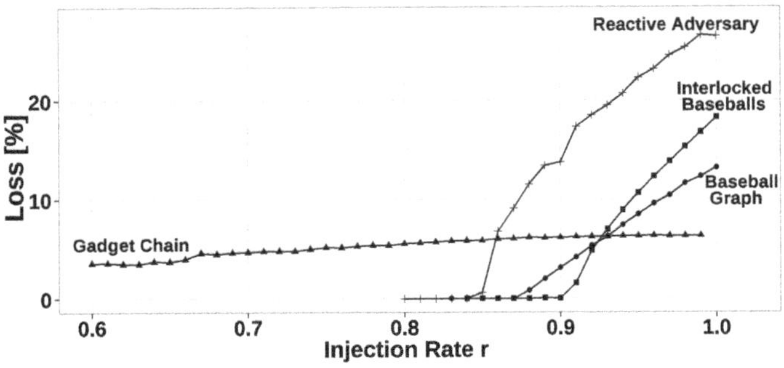

Figure 11: Loss results from deterministic simulation for different scenarios. The new adversarial scenarios yield significantly higher loss than classical adversaries. Note also the low-rate behavior of the Gadget Chain (due to [17]): although flat in shape, the scenario results in about four to six percent loss even for low injection rates.

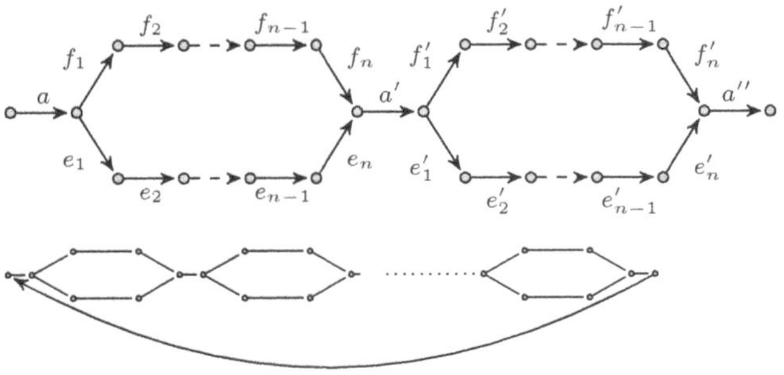

Figure 12: Topology of another adversarial scenario: the Gadget Chain from [17] is constructed by connecting gadgets one after another (top). Each "gadget" $F(i)$ (bottom) composes two lines which join at either end into a common input and output edge.

studied here to better assess the real-world implications of AQT from that perspective as well.

7.1 Imperfect Adversary Synchronization

We model differences in clock time or processing variability that affect the timing of adversarial injections. The time at which the adversary schedules any specific injection is now a random variable. In the classical model, the injection time is deterministic and controlled by the adversary. In the randomized model, realistic differences in clock time or processing variability are expressed as a variance affecting the time at which each injected packet arrives at its target edge. We have chosen a normal distribution because of the distribution's simplicity and symmetry properties. The random variable is truncated at time zero and the impact of varying standard deviations is studied. The empirical CDFs for such randomized injections are shown in Figure 13.

Figure 14 shows that for an example of the classical adversarial scenarios (the Baseball scenario [3]) large values of standard deviation indeed break the inner synchronization of the adversary resulting in smaller network loss. We have found similar behavior for other classical scenarios, but omit the detailed results for brevity. On the other hand, the newly proposed adversaries prove more robust as the effect

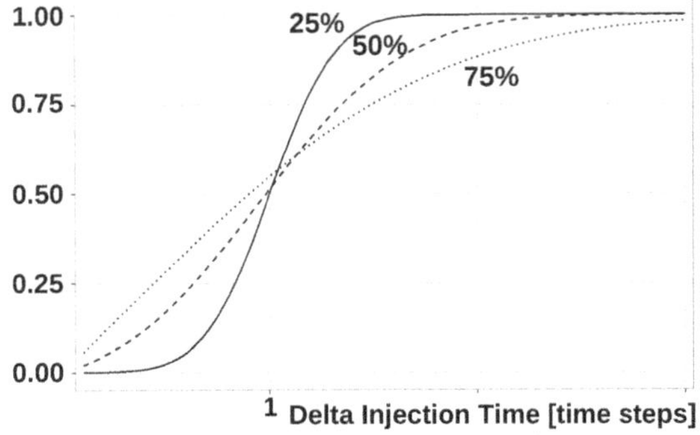

Figure 13: Empirical CDF of the inter-injection time. The inter-injection time follows a truncated normal distribution.

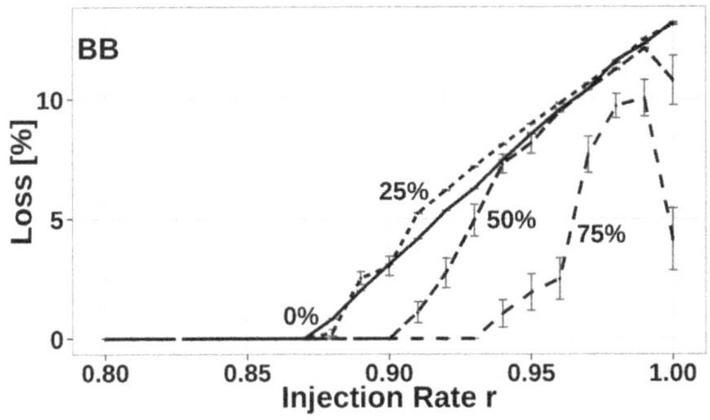

Figure 14: Randomized Injections (BB)

of this form of desynchronization remains small. In fact, the measured loss remains almost unchanged, as depicted in Figures 15 and 16.

7.2 Randomized Network Model

Instead of assuming a deterministic network model with uniform and synchronized network links, each channel's delay (the corresponding server delay for processing a single packet) is now modeled as a Weibull distributed random variable with mean one. Again, the effect of different standard deviations is investigated; we chose up to 300% of the mean as the largest deviation. For comparison, 200% roughly corresponds to the real-world measurements reported in [18]. This delay variability may be due to various effects such as processing variability or volatile cross-flows. Clearly, this only approximates reality since the impact of volatile cross-flows is only represented implicitly because actual cross-flows do not exist in our model. A Weibull model has been shown to be realistic [18] and allows using the standard deviation as parameter in this case (compared to a truncated normal distribution). The empirical CDF for a randomized channel delay is shown in Figure 17.

The results are shown in Figures 18-20. The Baseball scenario (Figure 18) is a typical representative of classical adversaries and its loss diminishes to irrelevant values unless the network utilization closely approaches 1. The Interlocked Baseballs scenario (Figure 19) is similarly affected but appears slightly more robust. Finally, the Reactive Adversary scenario (Figure 20) can yield loss rates of about 10% even for large values of the standard deviation. This adversary's

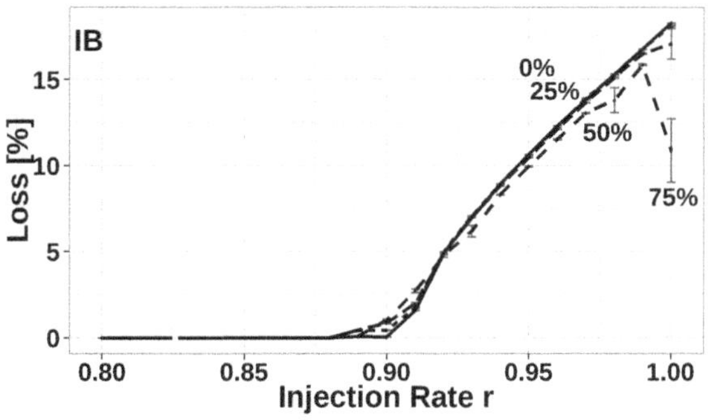

Figure 15: Randomized Injections (IB)

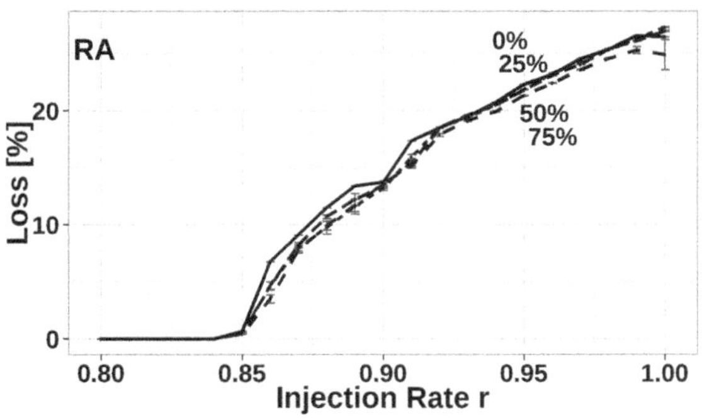

Figure 16: Randomized Injections (RA)

self-stabilizing property seems to retain its general behavior and thus also the loss curve's shape.

We conjecture that for both the Baseball and the Interlocked Baseballs scenario the adversarial effect does not play a major role any more under channel delay randomization exhibiting no significant deviation, but the losses are rather due to the typical hyperbolic growth known from classical queueing theory when the average arrival rate approaches the server capacity.

7.3 Discussion of Results

It is interesting to see that all three scenarios appear more robust against changes in the timing of injections than to variability in link delay. We have observed that this is due to packet flows being repeatedly aggregated in queues so that the exact timing of their arrivals in the network has only limited impact. For example, all bottleneck packets are first stored in a queue before they start traversing their first edge. Then, the variability of injection timings are averaged to close to the mean (smoothing effect). Their subsequent travels through the network then depends mostly on the server delay experienced at each edge. This is also why changes in the channel delay have a more pronounced effect on the loss behavior (e.g., compare the results for 50% deviation of Figure 15 to the results in Figure 19).

Both novel scenarios, the Interlocked Baseballs and the Reactive Adversary, prove to be more efficient and more stable than previous examples. Analyzing packet trajectories by simulation shows that indeed the two concepts, interlocking and reaction, are instrumental to achieve this robustness. Firstly, the Interlocked Baseballs adversary is the first scenario not requiring active confinement, i.e., packets which are only injected to slow down another packet flow. Instead, all

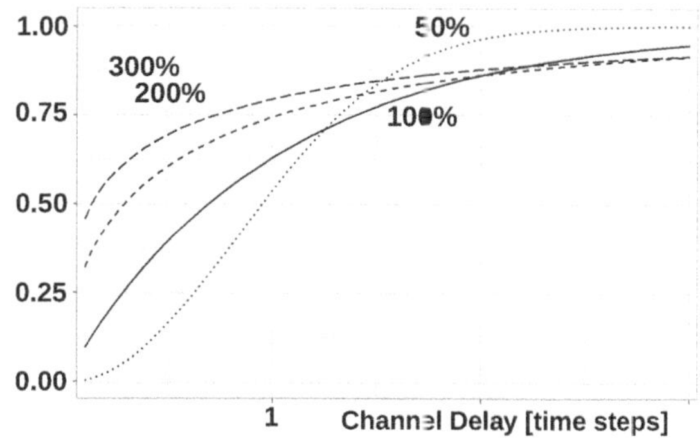

Figure 17: Empirical CDF of the channel delay. The channel delay follows a Weibull distribution.

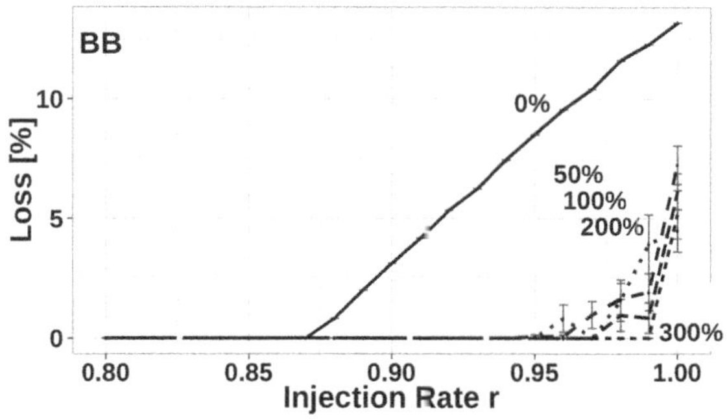

Figure 18: Channel Delay Variation (BB)

packet injections are targeted at some bottleneck queue. This strategy improves robustness against randomization due to the queue-aggregation effect described above. Secondly, the new concept of reactive injections, which is used for the set Z_n in the Reactive Adversary, protects the adversary's injections against randomization effects. For previously published adversaries, we have observed that under randomization the initial queue lengths often drop below a certain threshold not allowing further adversarial activity. The Z_n injections prevent these situations by "boosting" the cardinality of initial sets in such situations.

8. CONCLUSION

Adversarial queueing theory has introduced the notion of network instability. However, it is also important to understand and quantify the robustness of adversarial scenarios when assessing them from a practical network engineering perspective. In this paper, we report an investigation of the threat potential of adversarial effects under the realistic assumptions of finite buffers and imperfect synchrony. The hypothesis that classical instability scenarios do not translate into excessive loss under these assumptions is corroborated. However, a novel class of adversarial scenarios is introduced; these exhibit considerably more loss and prove to be more robust under realistic conditions. The results are derived analytically and, untypical for AQT work, through simulations.

Further work is needed to conclusively determine whether there are conditions under which adversarial queueing effects constitute a real-world threat. For example, we conjecture that more efficient loss-maximizing adversarial scenarios can

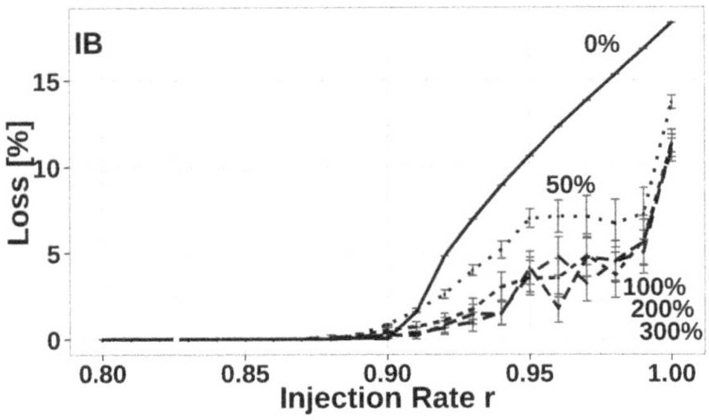

Figure 19: Channel Delay Variation (IB)

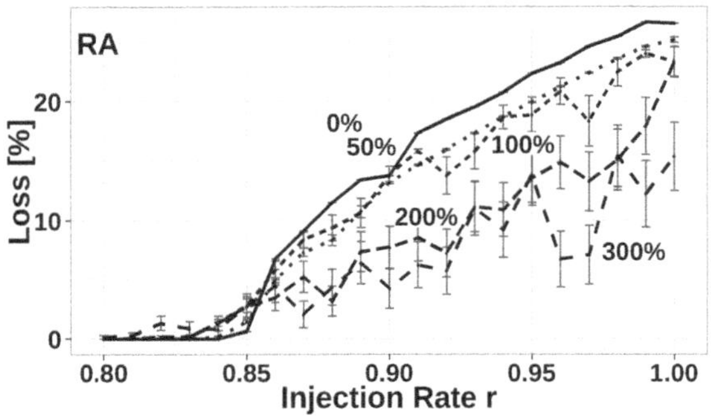

Figure 20: Channel Delay Variation (RA)

be conceived, possibly at lower injection rates. On the other hand, the complexity of such adversarial scenarios probably makes them an unlikely blueprint for actual attacks. As well, the chance of such patterns occurring naturally as a result of misconfiguration or unfortunate circumstances is probably small. This paper is the first to systematically address these fundamental questions and presents first steps towards their answering.

9. ACKNOWLEDGEMENTS

This research was supported by the German Research Foundation (DFG) and the Natural Sciences and Engineering Research Council of Canada (NSERC).

10. REFERENCES

[1] W. Aiello, R. Ostrovsky, E. Kushilevitz, and A. Rosén. Dynamic routing on networks with fixed-size buffers. In *Proceedings of the Fourteenth Annual ACM-SIAM Symposium on Discrete Algorithms*, pages 771–780. Society for Industrial and Applied Mathematics, 2003.

[2] C. Alvarez, M. Blesa, and M. Serna. A characterization of universal stability in the adversarial queuing model. *SIAM Journal on Computing*, 34(1):41, 2004.

[3] M. Andrews, B. Awerbuch, A. Fernández, T. Leighton, Z. Liu, and J. Kleinberg. Universal-stability results and performance bounds for greedy contention-resolution protocols. *Journal of the ACM*, 48(1):39–69, Jan. 2001.

[4] D. Berger, M. Karsten, and J. Schmitt. Simulation of adversarial scenarios in OMNeT++: Putting adversarial queueing theory from its head to feet. In *Proceedings of the 6th ICST Conference on Simulation Tools and Techniques*, pages 291–298, 2013.

[5] R. Bhattacharjee and A. Goel. Instability of FIFO at Arbitrarily Low Rates in the Adversarial Queueing Model. *SIAM Journal on Computing*, 34(2):318, 2005.

[6] M. J. Blesa. *Stability in communication networks under adversarial models*. PhD thesis, Universitat Politècnica de Catalunya, 2005.

[7] A. Borodin, J. Kleinberg, P. Raghavan, M. Sudan, and D. P. Williamson. Adversarial queuing theory. *Journal of the ACM*, 48(1):13–38, Jan. 2001.

[8] V. Cholvi and J. Echague. Stability of FIFO networks under adversarial models: State of the art. *Computer Networks*, 51(15):4460–4474, Oct. 2007.

[9] M. Chroni, D. Koukopoulos, and S. D. Nikolopoulos. An experimental study of stability in heterogeneous networks. In *Experimental Algorithms*, volume 4525 of *Lecture Notes in Computer Science*, pages 189–202. Springer-Verlag, 2007.

[10] J. Diaz, D. Koukopoulos, S. Nikoletseas, M. Serna, P. Spirakis, and D. M. Thilikos. Stability and non-stability of the FIFO protocol. In *Proceedings of the Thirteenth Annual ACM Symposium on Parallel Algorithms and Architectures*, pages 48–52, 2001.

[11] A. Fernandez Anta, J. L. Lopez-Presa, M. A. Lorenzo, P. Manzano, J. Martinez-Romo, A. Mozo, and C. Thraves. Performance of scheduling policies in adversarial networks with non synchronized clocks. *Theory of Computing Systems*, 48(1):1–22, Jan. 2011.

[12] A. Goel. Stability of networks and protocols in the adversarial queueing model for packet routing. *Networks*, 37(4):219–224, July 2001.

[13] D. Koukopoulos. The impact of dynamic adversarial attacks on the stability of heterogeneous multimedia networks. *Computer Communications*, 33(14):1695–1706, Sept. 2010.

[14] D. Koukopoulos, M. Mavronicolas, S. E. Nikoletseas, and P. G. Spirakis. On the stability of compositions of universally stable, greedy contention-resolution protocols. In *Proceedings of the 16th International Conference on Distributed Computing*, pages 88–102, 2002.

[15] A. Kuzmanovic and E. W. Knightly. Low-rate TCP-targeted denial of service attacks: the shrew vs. the mice and elephants. In *Proceedings of ACM SIGCOMM*, pages 75–86, 2003.

[16] Y. Lorion and M. Weinard. The effects of local randomness in the adversarial queueing model. In *Algorithms - ESA 2008*, volume 5193 of *Lecture Notes in Computer Science*, pages 672 – 683. Springer-Verlag, 2008.

[17] Z. Lotker, B. Patt-Shamir, and A. Rosen. New stability results for adversarial queuing. *SIAM Journal on Computing*, 33(2):286, 2004.

[18] K. Papagiannaki, S. Moon, C. Fraleigh, P. Thiran, and C. Diot. Measurement and analysis of single-hop delay on an IP backbone network. *IEEE Journal on Selected Areas in Communications*, 21(6):908–921, Aug. 2003.

[19] A. Varga. The OMNeT++ discrete event simulation system. In *Proceedings of the 15th European Simulation Multiconference*, 2001.

[20] M. Weinard. Deciding the FIFO stability of networks in polynomial time. *Algorithms and Complexity*, (3):81–92, 2006.

GemDroid: A Framework to Evaluate Mobile Platforms

Nachiappan Chidambaram Nachiappan† Praveen Yedlapalli† Niranjan Soundararajan§
Mahmut T. Kandemir† Anand Sivasubramaniam† Chita R. Das†
†The Pennsylvania State University §Intel Corp.
{nachi, praveen, kandemir, anand, das}@cse.psu.edu {niranjan.k.soundararajan@intel.com}

ABSTRACT

As the demand for feature-rich mobile systems such as smartphones and tablets has outpaced other computing systems and is expected to continue at a faster rate, it is projected that SoCs with tens of cores and hundreds of IPs (or accelerator) will be designed to provide unprecedented level of features and functionality in future. Design of such mobile systems with required QoS and power budgets along with other design constraints will be a daunting task for computer architects since any ad hoc, piece-meal solution is unlikely to result in an optimal design. This requires early exploration of the complete design space to understand the system-level design trade-offs. To the best of our knowledge, there is no such publicly available tool to conduct a holistic evaluation of mobile platforms consisting of cores, IPs and system software.

This paper presents GemDroid, a comprehensive simulation infrastructure to address these concerns. GemDroid has been designed by integrating the Android open-source emulator for facilitating execution of mobile applications, the GEM5 core simulator for analyzing the CPU and memory centric designs, and models for several IPs to collectively study their impact on system-level performance and power. Analyzing a spectrum of applications with GemDroid, we observed that the memory subsystem is a vital cog in the mobile platform because, it needs to handle both core and IP traffic, which have very different characteristics. Consequently, we present a heterogeneous memory controller (HMC) design, where we divide the memory physically into two address regions, where the first region with one memory controller (MC) handles core-specific application data and the second region with another MC handles all IP related data. The proposed modifications to the memory controller design results in an average 25% reduction in execution time for CPU bound applications, up to 11% reduction in frame drops, and on average 17% reduction in CPU busy time for on-screen (IP bound) applications.

SIGMETRICS'14, June 16–20, 2014, Austin, Texas, USA.

http://dx.doi.org/10.1145/2591971.2591973.

Categories and Subject Descriptors

C.1.4 [**Processor Architectures**] Parallel Architectures—*Mobile Processors*; I.6.5 [**Computing Methodologies**]: Simulation and Modeling—*Model Development*

General Terms

Measurement, Performance

Keywords

Memory Optimization; Simulation; SoC Modeling; Metrics;

1. INTRODUCTION

There is an exploding demand for mobile systems, which include smartphones, tablets, and wearable devices. Gartner research projects that 2 billion of these units will be sold in 2013 [15] and there will be over 10 billion mobile devices by the end of 2017 [8]. Moreover, it is projected that global mobile data will increase 13-fold between 2012 and 2017 reaching 11 Exabytes per month and two-thirds of this data is projected to be video data [8]. These numbers clearly indicate the importance of designing feature-rich mobile devices to cope up with the market demand. The ITRS roadmap for designing System-on-Chip architectures (SoCs) over the next decade projects that a mobile device could have up to 50 processing cores with about 300 TFLOPS computing capability and more than 400 IP blocks for enabling such feature-rich mobile platforms [14]. Thus, major companies like AMD, ARM, Apple, Intel, NVidia, Qualcomm, and Samsung have already ventured into this growing market targeting devices ranging from wearable wrist watches, glasses, to hand-held smartphones, phablets and tablets. Design and analysis of these devices with required QoS provisioning, power budgets and evolving technology artifacts is a daunting task that computer architects have to deal with in the coming years.

Mobile systems are based on the SoC design philosophy, having the core(s) (CPUs) and multiple accelerators on die or as part of the complete platform. These accelerators, or IPs [1] as they are commonly called, are customized to implement specific functionalities very efficiently, and hence

The authors would like to confirm that this work is an academic exploration and does not reflect any effort within Intel.

[1] We use the term accelerator or IP interchangeably throughout this paper.

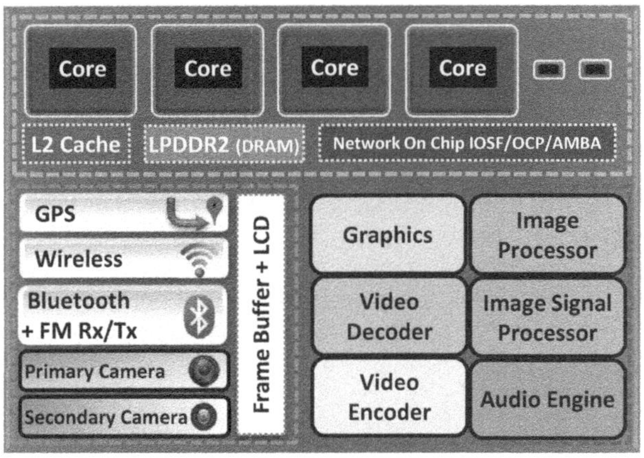

Figure 1: A sample SoC Platform with a high-level view of different functional blocks.

off-load the work from the core. As the IPs are task specific hardware components, they provide high performance delivering superior performance-per-watt compared to running the same task on cores. The set of IPs employed by a typical mobile platform includes the graphics, video encoder, video decoder, imaging, modem, communications (e.g., Wi-Fi, bluetooth) and others as shown in Figure 1.

Given the growing need for these mobile devices that have become an essential part of our daily life, it is essential that we understand the underlying platform issues better to develop more efficient designs from the performance and power standpoints. Also, the growing number of use-cases which get integrated into these devices and the associated software complexity can often lead to conflicting performance and power requirements all of which need to be analyzed carefully for optimal design decisions. The important research questions relevant to emerging mobile platforms include: (i) topology exploration that determines the ideal number and types of cores, and types of IPs to best match the demands of the target workloads; (ii) design of scalable on-chip networks to cater to the divergent needs of IPs and cores; (iii) design of memory schedulers and scheduling algorithms that can handle both IP and core requests; and (iv) workload mapping and scheduling algorithms to maximize performance and minimize energy consumption. Clearly, answering these types of questions requires access to a simulation framework, capable of *capturing such issues and enabling exploration of design alternatives/tradeoffs at the complete platform level.*

While there are existing individual IP [9,42] and core simulators [5], to the best of our knowledge, there is *no* open source integrated simulation platform to conduct holistic studies of a complete mobile platform that can (i) capture activities across multiple IPs and cores, (ii) run an operating system (like Android [16]), (iii) execute real-world applications to capture and analyze realistic events, (iv) simulate architectural features such as core, caches, network and memory, in detail to understand the application-architecture interactions, and (v) provide various application level and IP-specific metrics in addition to global (chip-wide) performance metrics.

In this work, we intend to fill this critical void by making the following contributions:

• We propose a comprehensive simulation infrastructure, called **GemDroid**, which incorporates the GEM5 architecture simulator [5], Attila graphics simulator [9] and internal models for the other IPs, and, is capable of running the Android mobile OS [16] for facilitating mobile platform design and optimization research. GemDroid is comprised of two primary layers. The first layer provides emulation of Android OS by the Google Android Emulator [17] and allows us to capture system-level interaction between multiple IPs and I/O devices, including OS activities. What the emulator cannot provide is the timing information of different IP activities and therefore, as our second layer, we integrate/build the timing piece using existing simulation platforms or model them analytically as needed for different IPs. The framework is flexible for integrating models of varying complexities for the cores and IPs.

• Using several smartphone/tablet applications such as games, video-playback, video-recording, as well as core-centric workloads that run on Android, we demonstrate that it is possible to simultaneously capture the activities of the cores and IPs for conducting a multitude of design and optimization studies, and focus on analyzing the memory system performance in this work.

• We demonstrate through extensive workload analysis, that the shared memory subsystem is a critical bottleneck because of the combined memory requests from the core and IPs with different characteristics. For example, memory access patterns of IPs exhibit high levels of regularity (e.g., sequential data accesses by frame-buffers), as opposed to the memory access patterns of, say, well-known SPEC benchmarks [21]. Similarly, the memory bandwidth demanded by cores and IP when running a video on YouTube are very different from each other as depicted in Figure 2. Specifically, while the core's bandwidth demand is more or less constant (requiring $<$ 0.2GBPS for the studied workloads), display IP's needs are very bursty in nature (needing around 0.8GBPS), and the total bandwidth demand for a video recorder can be much higher than that of the memory system. Moreover, these requests not only differ in terms on bandwidth demands, but also their latency demands are also very different from each other. While IPs have strict latency deadlines that *need* to be met, cores do not have deadlines. On the other hand, IPs have time window before which they can be served without affecting the user-experience, but, each cores memory request directly affects the performance of the system.

• Based on the insights obtained from the characterization of memory requests, we propose a novel heterogeneous memory controller (HMC) design for SoCs, where one MC is dedicated for latency critical core requests and the second MC is optimized to enhance the bank-level parallelism of the memory requests it serves. The two memory controllers are still responsible for two distinct (non-intersecting) address ranges. Our evaluation of this new MC design results in better performance and user experience; specifically, it results in average 25% reduction in execution time for CPU bound applications, up to 11% reduction in frame drops, and on average 17% reduction in CPU busy time for on-screen applications.

2. SYSTEM OVERVIEW

Mobile platforms are system-on-chip (SoC) devices with at least one processor core and specialized accelerators/IPs to which computations get offloaded by the operating system for performance and/or power efficiency. Based on the application characteristics, the work gets split between the

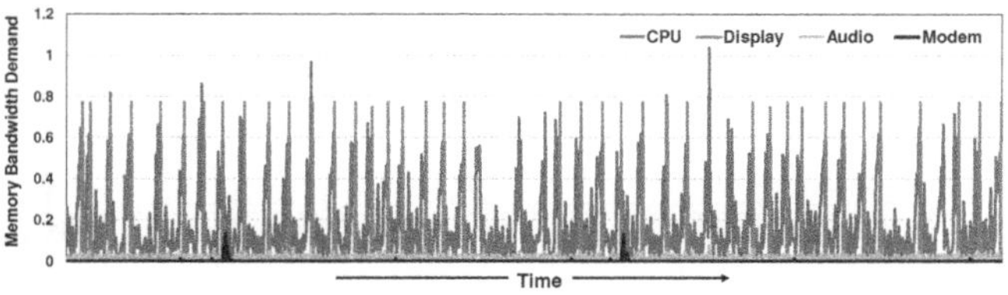

Figure 2: Memory bandwidth demand of cores and IPs when YouTube is played.

core and multiple IPs. Data transfers between the cores and the IPs take place through the main memory. Figure 3 provides an overview of video playback on YouTube highlighting the tasks that are run on the core and those that are run on individual IPs (audio and video HW). The interactions between core, IPs and OS are described next.

2.1 OS-IP Interaction

The phone and tablet operating systems such as Android and iOS include different software drivers to interact with the respective IPs. The device maker optimizes these drivers according to their requirements. Note that a driver acts as the link between the different applications running on the OS and the underlying hardware. Besides the functionality, the drivers also control the power states of the IPs. Android also includes an additional framework layer, which provides an interface for applications to interact with the drivers and the underlying libraries which control the IPs. Further discussion of Android OS can be found elsewhere [16], but it is important to note that the software complexity and features have greatly increased with the newer devices and contribute to an important portion of the overall power, performance and user experience with the device. Together, these play an important role in determining the battery life of the device, which is critical in the mobile ecosystem.

2.2 Core-IP Interactions

One of the main difficulties in analyzing SoCs is that the individual IPs are owned by third party vendors. These are licensed by the phone and tablet makers to build their products. The intricate details of the architecture and the working details of the IPs are not released to the public to maintain the competitive edge. In this part, we briefly explain how an IP works without getting into intricacies about each IP specifically.

Each IP gets a region of memory allocated for it, where its input and output data get stored. The software (OS and IP-driver) stores the data that is supposed to be sent to an IP at the region allocated, and the corresponding address is set in IP registers. The IP independently accesses the data through DMA (direct memory access).

It is important to emphasize that IPs do not directly communicate with the cores. They work based on scheduling triggered from their driver. Different modes of interaction exist – some of the IPs like the display panel operate at a constant rate, where they read their frame buffer at 60 FPS irrespective of when the updates to the frames happen by a core, while others, such as the graphics and imaging IPs, are asynchronously triggered when required.

To get better clarity about the interaction and the consequent impact on overall performance, let us consider Figure 3 that involves video streaming to display.

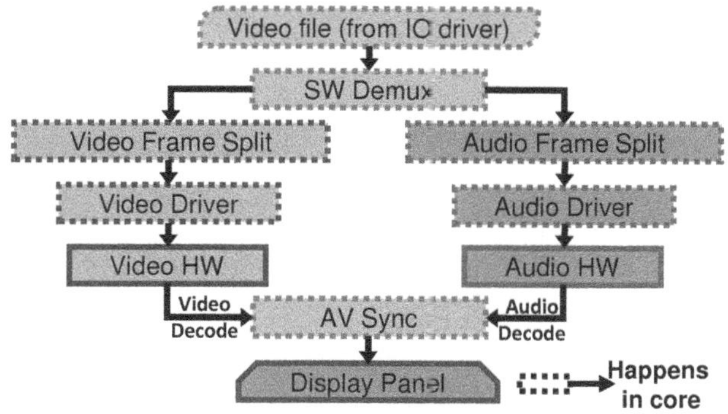

Figure 3: Simplified work-flow diagram of video streaming use case highlighting the core-IPs interaction.

2.2.1 *Core-Video/Audio Interaction*

Incoming video file gets demultiplexed by the core and the individual frames are marked. The video and audio drivers then direct their respective IPs to pick the frames and decode them at a specific rate. These IPs wait for the core to complete the first step of splitting the audio and video data before starting their specific activities. The performance of the core determines the overall processing rate since it handles these critical portions of the overall use-case.

2.2.2 *Video Decoder-Display Interaction*

The display panel operates independently of the other IPs since it refreshes the screen continuously. There are three possible scenarios of relative speeds. In the first scenario, where both video decoder (after completing the AV sync) and display work at the same rate, a two-entry frame buffer (FB0 and FB1) is sufficient. When display reads from FB0, video decoder can write to FB1. In the next time frame, display reads from FB1 and video decoder writes to FB0, and this process repeats in a cyclic fashion. In the second scenario, where the video decoder (producing 60 frames per second (FPS)) is working much faster than the display panel (30 FPS), the frame buffer needs to have a larger number of entries to be consumed by the slower display panel. Note that, in the steady state, n/2 frames from the video decoder are read by the display and the other n/2 frames are dropped (50% frame drops). Finally, in the third scenario, where the video decoder is working at a slower pace than the display IP, the system performance is bottlenecked by the video decoder performance. In this case, while computed frames need not be dropped, many frames are skipped from being computed to maintain the sync between audio/video with real-time. Further, the display panel does unnecessary refreshes as the frames are not updated, which is clearly non-optimal from an overall platform power perspective. While the first scenario is the most preferable one, the third scenario is often encountered in most SoC devices.

2.3 Application Requirements

Table 1 lists a set of our target applications and specifies the IPs they employ at some point during their executions. Note that an application can access multiple IPs at different portions of its execution, or send requests to different IPs at the same time. As user requirements increase, the application complexity correspondingly is scaled to cater to their needs for different platforms to provide competing solutions.

Table 1: Shows 9 IPs and two classes of applications (CPU-bound and On-screen applications) evaluated using GemDroid. The table shows IP usage across applications. High/Low indicates a particular IP's dominance in IP utilization compared to others.

	OnScreen-bound								CPU-bound								
Apps / IPs	Game 1	Ar-Game 2	Browser	Video Rec.	Soundplay	Youtube	Video Player	Gallery	Antutu-RAM	RG Bandwidth	Linpack	RLBench	CFBench	Caffein Mark	And-EBench	Antutu-Core	Antutu-GFX
Core/MEM	Low	Low	High	Low	Low	High	Low	Low	High	High	High	High	High	High	High	High	Low
Display-Out	High	High	-	High	-	High	High	Low	-	-	-	-	-	-	-	-	-
Touch-In	Low	Low	-	-	-	-	-	Low	-	-	-	-	-	-	-	-	-
NW-Out	-	-	Low	-	-	Low	-	-	Low	-	Low	-	-	-	-	Low	Low
NW-In	-	-	Low	-	-	High	-	-	Low	-	Low	-	-	-	-	Low	Low
Cam-In	-	High	-	High	-	-	-	-	-	-	-	-	-	-	-	-	-
Aud-Out	Low	Low	-	-	High	-	-	-	-	-	-	-	-	-	-	-	-
GPU	High	High	-	-	-	-	-	-	-	-	-	-	-	-	-	-	High
Vid/Img-Dec	-	-	-	-	-	High	High	High	-	-	-	-	-	-	-	-	-
Aud-Dec	Low	Low	-	-	High	-	-	-	-	-	-	-	-	-	-	-	-

An example is, emerging applications in the augmented reality space [31], where the devices and applications attempt to enhance the surroundings with additional details to help the user with their specific needs. These applications place heavy requirements on core, graphics, network, memory and other IPs on the platform. Further, slowdown in any portion of the platform or any specific IP will affect the overall experience. Hence, it is critical to analyze the entire SoC platform as a whole when optimizing features, which in turn, makes a case for a complete simulation infrastructure that can enable this.

3. A COMPREHENSIVE EVALUATION PLATFORM

Given the diversity in the types of phones and tablets that get built and used, the goal of the proposed framework is to provide flexibility for evaluating these designs with multiple cores and IPs. The framework is agnostic to the details in the IP model, which can be a simple analytical model or a complex cycle-accurate model of the IP's micro-architecture.

3.1 GemDroid - Simulation Infrastructure

Currently very limited infrastructure exists for enabling platform level studies across multiple IPs running realistic and/or relevant workloads. GEM5 framework is the closest, that the authors are aware of, which can simulate an ARM or x86 cycle-accurate core with Android/Linux Kernel running on top of it [5, 19]. Currently, GEM5 can simulate only a limited set of IPs (core and only display panel). This limited support and drastic simulation slow down severely restricts the number of apps that can be run. Further, it is not possible to do IP-centric evaluations. While incorporating GEM5 in its infrastructure, GemDroid expands on the number of IPs modeled to get close to a complete device (see Figure 4). Further, GemDroid makes it flexible in terms of the modeling technique adopted for the IPs for which cycle-accurate models are hard to build mainly due to unavailable public information (see Figure 4).

GemDroid relies heavily on the Google Android's open-source emulator and it has been enhanced for our needs. Android emulator meets two of our essential goals – booting an operating system and running commonly used applications on top. The emulator runs the latest version of Android compiled for ARMv7 ISA with Neon instructions. The core of the emulator, based on the Qemu tool [17], translates each ARM instruction to a set of native machine instructions and executes them on the host. During this translation, instruction level traces are captured. The framework also emulates other IPs such as the imaging (handles the images captured using the camera), display, network, audio and there are hooks available to emulate sensors such as accelerometer, gyrometer, etc.

However, the emulator misses out on the crucial part needed for performance studies: it does not incorporate the simulation time for any of the IPs. The emulator's goal is to enable application development for Android and hence has a different set of goals than ours. GemDroid integrates existing performance models - GEM5 for the core and memory subsystem, Attila for graphics [9] - and analytical models for the other IPs missing a model (like Video, Network and others). We *do not* claim to have developed performance/power models for all IPs, but our proposed framework is extensible, and will allow for other users in the community to incorporate their models as needed. We are looking to make our framework open for others in the community to contribute and do their studies on this platform.

3.2 Trace-based simulation

Unlike server workloads or widely available benchmarks like SPEC, PARSEC [4], etc., mobile applications are more user interactive. Providing user inputs and studying the system is not an easy task due to the associated non-determinism; for that, one possible method is to capture user inputs that are sent to the OS, replay it exactly while evaluating the system [33,40]. In our infrastructure, we use Android emulator as the front end, where one can install almost all applications available on Google Play and provide inputs like the way it is done on SoCs. The emulator has been instrumented to capture the ARM instructions and IP calls along with their interactions with the memory in a trace file. Using such a trace, provides determinism in evaluating such applications with user inputs.

3.3 Model characteristics

While a cycle-accurate full system simulation meets the accuracy goals for micro-architectural and system level studies, they cannot simulate considerable durations of our target mobile workloads due to complexity associated with handling multiple IPs. On the other hand, while development boards can meet the speed requirements they fail to provide control for exploring the system by changing the underlying parameters. As described in [5], GEM5 can cycle-accurately simulate 200K instructions per second, potentially leading to 800X slowdown for a processor-core based system. If the simulator is augmented with accurate models of GPU, audio/video encoder/decoder, and imaging IPs, the simulation times would become unreasonable. Hence GemDroid looks to keep the infrastructure flexible for integrating models with differing levels of complexity and allowing them to interact. Depending on the IP of interest, users can inte-

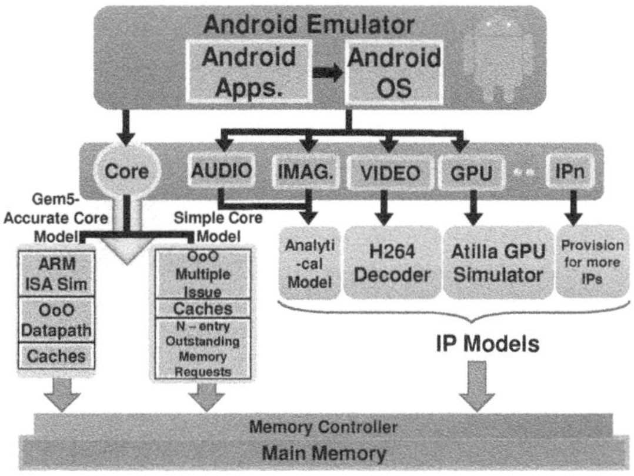

Figure 4: Detailed Infrastructure Diagram.

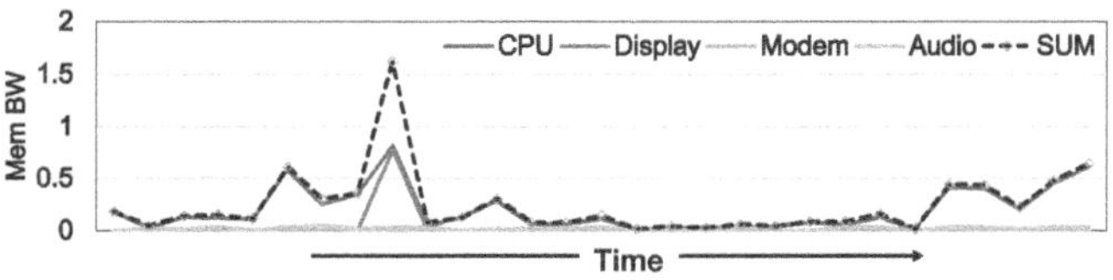

Figure 5: Execution where display IP reads a frame from memory at the same time core is writing a new frame.

grate accurate models for specific IPs and integrate *less accurate models* for the rest of the system. The less accuracy is with respective to not modeling the micro-architecture details of IPs, but having enough information to capture timing associated with different activities. In our work, for studying system-level memory characteristics across IPs, we developed an alternate simplified core model in our infrastructure which assumes a 1-IPC model. This does not affect the timing accuracy of the execution significantly as many frequently used ARM ISA instructions are single-cycle instructions [2]. Such a system had only a 180X slowdown compared to real hardware. Users though have the flexibility to switch between the highly accurate GEM5 core model or our simplified core model based on their requirements. Note that when the system is extended with cycle-accurate core model, significant slowdowns were observed resulting in only a short duration of execution time being simulated. Such a simulation is unsuitable for IP based system studies as not many IP calls are seen in such short duration.

For the graphics IP, we used the Attila graphics simulator [9], which handles the openGL calls issued by applications. These OpenGL calls that are used for rendering different images to the screen, are captured in the trace. For video IP, we used the open-source H264 RTL model [42] to capture the timing associated with decoding. For audio, and imaging (applications that use camera for capturing pictures or recording video), we use the emulator to capture the calls to audio and imaging IP. These calls provide us with the sizes of the frames, and the arrival rate of the frame requests (based on the number of instructions between frames). Reasonable amount of application time was simulated by capturing the system level metrics with at least 2 billion core instructions.

3.4 Capabilities of GemDroid

Our infrastructure can be used to conduct multiple types of studies starting from the core, memory and individual

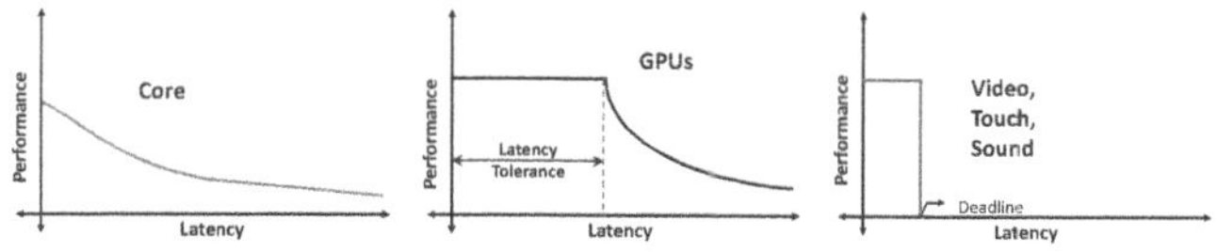

(a) Cores *(b)* GPUs *(c)* IPs(display, sound)

Figure 6: Effects of varying memory latency on performance for (a)cores, (b) GPUs, and (c) other IPs.

IPs to system-level performance/power analyses. The first insight we can get from using GemDroid is the usage pattern of IPs for different applications. Currently, we have incorporated 9 IP models in GemDroid and have analyzed the behavior of a wide spectrum of applications such as games, video recording and video playback. Table 1 already shows the application-specific usage of IPs.

In addition to understand IP usage, the platform can help in studying contention for shared resources. Consider the example shown in Figure 5. The figure illustrates a scenario when YouTube video playback traces were simulated on the system and different IP's memory accesses were analyzed. We note that there are instants when two IPs perform memory access at the same time. Further, multi-core studies are also possible once we collect application-level traces for multiple applications. We leave this as a future work. Instead, in this paper, we analyze the memory system of current SoCs to quantify its impact on application performance, and explain how a heterogeneous memory controller design can help mitigate some of the problems the memory system brings.

4. EVALUATION METRICS

Performance evaluation of SoCs is more challenging than the conventional CPU-centric platforms because of the emergence of new IPs and use-cases with their different characteristics and requirements. In particular, having one global performance metric does not provide a right picture on how the platform is behaving or to identify the bottlenecks in the system. In this section, we classify target applications into following classes, and define appropriate metrics for each application class.

CPU/GPU-bound Applications – IPC/CPI: CPUs are the traditional processing cores, where each load or store instruction that goes to memory critically stalls the core, because out-of-order processing capability is very limited in these cores due to power constraints. Figure 6a depicts how the performance of such a core degrades as the load/store delays increase. Typically these cores do not operate under any deadlines. For our core-bound benchmarks like Linpack and Antutu-CPU, since job execution time is a standard performance metric, we can use IPC (Instructions Per Cycle) or CPI (Cycles per Instruction) for gauging their performance.

GPU workloads (that are not display refresh limited) also involve throughput-oriented computation; but, they slightly differ from CPU cores. Specifically, they have some inherent latency tolerance because of the high thread level parallelism (TLP) [24]. GPUs can hide memory access latency up to a point (marked with dotted lines in Figure 6b), beyond which their performance starts to drop, following the pattern of the CPU cores. Typically, GPUs do not have any deadline when they are used for compute purposes. However, while they are used for graphics/rendering purposes, they act like the other IPs with well-defined QoS targets. Thus, both IPC/CPI can serve the purpose for evaluating GPUs.

Onscreen Applications – Frame Drops: For on-screen applications which have a visual aspect to them, such as video/audio playback or graphics oriented applications, job turnaround time may not be an effective metric. For example, when a game is being played, the smoothness of the transitions and game playback are commonly defined performance metrics. These applications are limited by the rate at which the display panel refreshes the screen (at say 60 FPS). Even if the components compute faster, it does not change the user perception but will have an impact on overall power. Similarly, when playing a video or audio file, execution time is dependent only on the clip's duration, and execution should be controlled such that execution time is equal to the clip's duration. For example, a 1-minute video has to be played for exactly 1-minute. Any deviation from this may result in distortion in quality or lags become visible. In these situations, one of the ways of quantifying performance is to check whether the system is capable of playing X frames per second (FPS) consistently, if the video file had been encoded in X-FPS (24 FPS is the most commonly encoded video frame rate, though 30 and 60 FPS videos and games are also becoming increasingly popular).

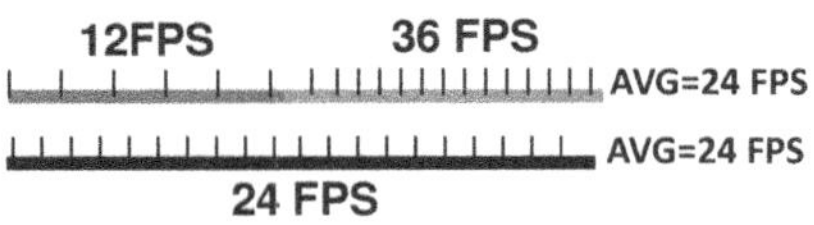

Figure 7: Two different scenarios with different FPS rates over time.

Consider the scenario shown in Figure 7, where in case (1) the system manages to play a 1-minute video file at two different FPS rates, 12 FPS for the first half (30 seconds), and 36 FPS for the second half. The average FPS for the video file being played would be 24 frames per second. In case (2) on the other hand, the system manages to play the file at a constant 24 FPS. Although both the videos are played at 24 FPS on the average, certainly the user would not be satisfied with a choppy frame rate experience delivered by the first scenario. From this, it is clear that FPS may not be the right metric. That is, the average FPS value does not capture the overall behavior of the system.

Instead of FPS, if *frame drops per second* (FDPS) is used as a metric, one can distinguish between the two cases depicted in Figure 7. More specifically, if the required frame rate is 24 FPS, case (i) would leave us 6 FDPS, whereas case (ii) would have 0 FDPS. This clearly shows that case (ii) is preferable over case (i).

Real-time Applications – Response Time: Several IPs in the SoC are responsible for meeting the immediate deadlines like touch, accelerometer (and other sensors) and interrupt-handling to user pressing different buttons. These are different from the CPU and GPU cores as they are response time oriented in order to meet certain deadlines. Their performance is captured by monitoring if they meet their strict deadlines or not. For an input request, their performance is determined through a yes or no question: *if the IP met the deadline set for the request.* Figure 6c shows this. The width of the bar shown corresponds to the available latency before which the deadline expires. However, GemDroid does not model these IPs at this point. This metric is provided only for the sake of completeness.

Core-Utilization: In addition to the above metrics, we also measure core-utilization (percentage of busy-cycles), which measures the total amount of time for which the core is working. By lowering core-utilization without affecting performance, one can make the system more energy efficient.

5. IMPACT OF MEMORY SUBSYSTEM IN MOBILE PLATFORMS

As depicted in Figure 4, memory is a shared resource between the cores and IPs and any performance issues in its path is more likely to manifest as a system bottleneck, as has been the case for traditional computing systems. Design of high performance memory systems including memory controllers (MCs) has been an active area of research for the uniprocessor and CMP (chip multi-processor) domain [26, 43]. However, memory access patterns of our target mobile applications are different from scientific workloads like SPEC, Parsec [4] or server workloads, as we will illustrate shortly. To our knowledge, no other work has investigated the memory system design for such multiple IP SoC systems. This section describes our analysis of these memory systems.

5.1 Memory Access Patterns

To show how SoC applications differ in their memory behavior, we plot in Figure 8 the memory access patterns of a SPEC applications (*h264.ref*) and a video recording application running on our SoC platform plotted over time. The Y-axis shows a sample address range, and only a portion of the full execution has been shown for clarity. We see similar trends for many other SPEC benchmarks. One can make two important observations from these plots:

First, while SPEC applications have quite irregular memory address patterns over time, the video recording and the browser applications use a specific set of data over and over again, indicating good data locality. We observed similar patterns for many other display-bound applications. We investigated the address regions and found that, this reuse pattern was caused by two reasons: (i) for the display bound applications, frames were written into the same physical address region repeatedly almost every 1/60th of a second; and (ii) the source devices (like cores/ GPUs/ video decoder) write into the same address region, from where the sink devices (display, audio output) read data.

Second, at some time instants, we see two regions of address being used concurrently. This happens when the core is accessing two different regions, or when a core and an IP

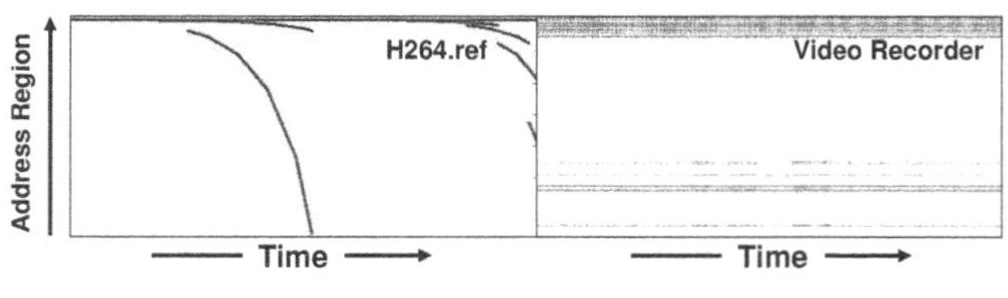

Figure 8: Comparing the memory access patterns of SPEC application (h264.ref) with video recorder mobile application from our experimental suite.

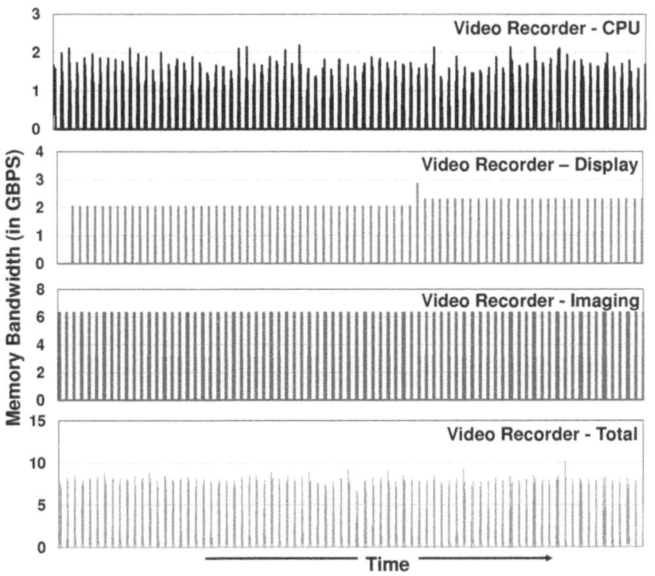

(a) Bandwidth demand of VideoRecorder.

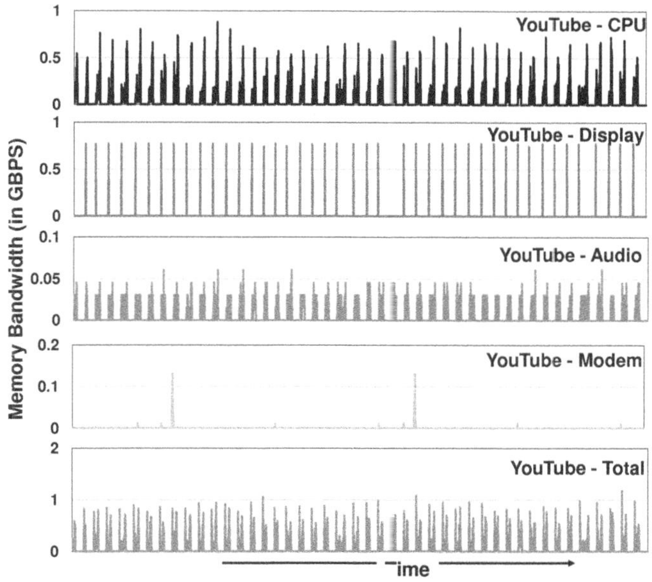

(b) Bandwidth demand of video playback on YouTube.

Figure 9: Variations in the bandwidth demand of applications over time.

are accessing the memory concurrently. Such a scenario increases the bandwidth demand placed by the application on the memory system. We observed that the number of concurrent accesses to memory can increase depending on how many IPs are used by an application. Thus, the peak memory pressure could change significantly across applications, making the memory system design complex. This is because, unlike SPEC, PARSEC and many other applications, which typically do not have hard deadlines, most of the mobile applications and hence IPs have real-time constraints. Thus, provisioning only for the average memory bandwidth may not be adequate to meet the real-time constraints.

Analyzing Memory Access Characteristics of IPs: We analyzed the memory access characteristics of IPs requests belonging to our applications, and noted some interesting characteristics. While modem, audio, display and camera IPs primarily sent and received fixed size packets for an application, across applications their sizes varied. For example, an application involving HD video capture or photo capturing applications had different sizes of frames being sent compared to a 720p video capturing. One interesting feature that we observed was, when the Android Emulator writes data into the frame buffer region for the display to read, it does not write "framesize-amount" of data for every frame. Instead, it only overwrites parts of the frame that need to be changed. For applications like browsers, if only parts of the screen are changed due to animation, then data only for that part is overwritten in memory. For a YouTube video running on a browser, we plotted the distribution of frame sizes in Figure11a. Typically, the distribution shows that 3 sizes of frames were transmitted. Whenever full sized frames were transferred, we observed 0.73 MB of data per frame being written by the CPU. If most of the frame, except the borders/system panel changed, then 0.6 MB data per frame was transmitted. Otherwise, negligible amount was transferred (this includes writing and reading from memory-mapped registers of the display IPs, or some small part like clock display being changed on the screen). In Figure 11b, we plotted the inter-arrival time of the display frames software-rendered by the CPU (the frames are sorted in ascending order based on their inter-arrival times). Ideally, CPU is expected to produce the frame exactly every 1/30th of a second (in this experiment, the required FPS limit was set as 30 FPS). But, we can observe that the delays vary. This variation is attributed to many reasons like the complexity of the frame needed to be rendered, interference at shared resources at that instant, etc. One crucial point to be noted is that, while most of the frames arrive before the deadline time ($1/30 = 3.33 \times 10^7 ns$), some arrive very late (towards the right most side of the graph). Frames that arrive later than this point forces the following frame to be dropped. When we curve-fit this plot, we observe the distribution follows an exponential distribution, with an R^2 value of 0.943 for this application.

Similar characterizations are possible for other applications as well. These results are interesting because one can use these inter-arrival time distributions along with frame rates and packet size distributions to simulate a YouTube workload on the GemDroid simulator.

5.2 Memory Demand of Applications

Figure 9 shows the memory bandwidth demand of two applications over time. Only a part of the full timeline is shown for clarity. Most of the other applications are similar to at least one of these two applications as far as their bandwidth demand is concerned. In this figure, we separately plot the memory demand of each IP during the execution of an application, and then show the total demand. For example, in Figure 9b, we see that the YouTube videoplayback application uses CPU, display, audio device and the GSM network for data, and their corresponding bandwidth demand is shown in the top four sub-graphs. The last graph of Figure 9b shows the total bandwidth demand placed on the memory. We observe that, at some instants, the bandwidth demand is much higher than the average. These peaks are primarily observed when the data request bursts from different IPs overlap with each other. In applications like video recording, we notice that the peak demand requested

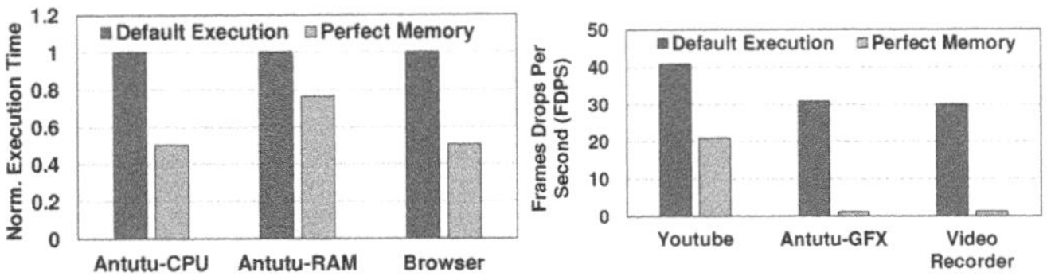

(a) Execution time difference of CPU-bound applications in a system with a *perfect memory.* *(b)* Difference in FPS of Display-bound applications in a system with a *perfect memory.*

Figure 10: Impact of a *perfect memory* on applications.

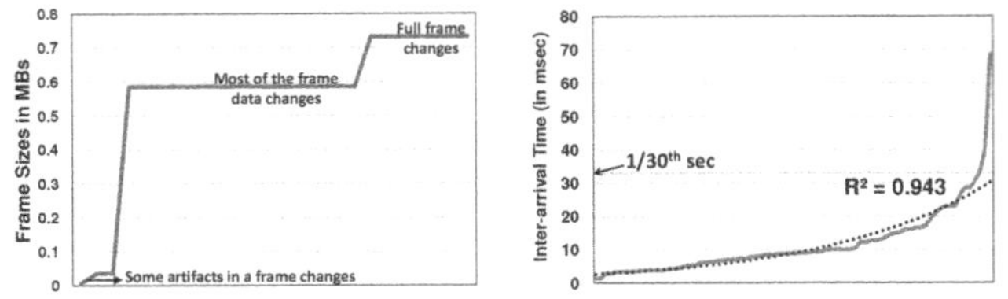

(a) Shows the distribution of the frame sizes when a sample YouTube video is played. *(b)* Shows distribution of inter-arrival times between two frames when a sample YouTube video is played.

Figure 11: Characteristics of frames in YouTube application.

is much higher than the peak bandwidth (3.2 GBPS) provided by the memory system (LPDDR2-400). These are the instants when a frame can possibly get dropped. Note that, in the video recording application, all frames demand more than 3.2 GBPS, but not all get dropped. This is because, the required frame rate is 60 FPS, each frame gets 1/60th of a second to be processed. If the frame currently being processed is not served within that limit, the next frame that arrives is dropped.

Investigating core-bound benchmarks like Linpack and AntutuCPU, we observed that the impact on memory is substantially lesser than display bound applications[2]. We also noted that such applications have higher instruction throughput than the rest, due to fewer memory stall cycles.

5.3 Impact of Memory on Applications

To understand how memory contributes towards application's stalls, we analyzed how much improvement a *perfect* memory can provide. We define a *perfect* memory to have 0 cycles turn-around time for requests. We found that, for core-bound applications (Figure 10a), the execution time decreases substantially for many workloads, and moderately for some. For display bound applications on the other hand, we noted that the system improved its frames-per-second and lesser number of frames were dropped with the perfect memory (see Figure 10b). This is primarily attributed to two reasons – (1) the core that produces the data for the frame, produces it earlier, thus, avoiding frame drops; and (2) the IPs (producers/consumers) are able to write/read the data much faster, not exceeding the deadline imposed. Note that the display bound applications are limited to 60 FPS. Once the required 60 FPS is reached, applications are throttled to remain at that rate. If the FPS drops, throttling is stopped.

Consider the scenario, where the base case has 60 FPS. Then, no performance improvements can be observed. Here, we use the number of busy cycles in core and IP devices to quantify the impact of perfect memory. The lower the number of busy cycles, the better would be the power savings. Similarly, the improvements seen with applications reaching 60 FPS are not the true maximum. For these, benefits should be seen through the reduced number of busy cycles as well.

[2]We noted that for some CPU bound benchmarks, there was noticeable network activity during every run of the benchmark. They were found to be the addresses that were rendered during the execution, or when the application's communicated the results back to a server towards the end of the execution.

5.4 Summary of Observations:

Specifically, we observe the following primary differences between the traffic from cores and the IPs:

1 - IPs have more or less regular request inter-arrival times, with their requests coming in bursts. CPUs have irregular arrival rates, and are typically not bursty.

2 - IPs requests have substantial memory latency tolerance compared to CPU cores. Thus, they can be stalled for sometime without any effect on performance or user-experience.

3 - Arrival rates of memory requests from CPU and IP are very different. While CPUs requests are fewer in number, IP requests come in bursts of tens or hundreds or even thousands. Their inter-arrival time distributions can be used to simulate any specific IP.

4 - IPs demand bandwidth. The higher the bandwidth, the faster they read/write data; achieving two purposes: (1) they move to low power states sooner, allowing for some power savings, (2) it lets the next component (core or another IP) that needs to feed on what was provided by this IP to start its work sooner, therefore reducing frame drops, and improving response time.

Based on the core and IP request properties described above, we present in the next section a Heterogeneous Memory Controller (HMC) design that has been tailored for SoC systems.

6. A CASE FOR A HETEROGENEOUS MEMORY CONTROLLER

In this section, we provide a brief overview of the baseline memory design, explain the proposed heterogeneous memory controller (HMC) design, and finally evaluate our proposal.

6.1 Locality-Parallelism Tradeoff in Memory Design

Baseline Memory System: Figure 12 (A) shows the memory design of our baseline system. It consists of 2 memory controllers (MCs) controlling two distinct regions of memory. As shown, the cores and IPs *share* this memory subsystem. Traditionally, these MCs are the gateway to access data in memory, which is logically organized as DRAM banks. Each bank has cells (memory elements) laid out in arrays of rows and columns. The data can be striped across banks at various granularity, for example, at *page-level* or at *cache-line-level.* In *page-level,* the distribution of data across banks is at a granularity of a OS page, which is a chunk of multiple consecutive cache lines. For example, if page size is 4KB (used in our paper), the first 4KB of consecutive data is mapped to the first bank, and the next 4KB to the next bank, and so on. In our baseline system, we use this page-level striping for both the memory controllers, as shown in Figure 12 (A). In *cache-line-level* striping, the distribution of data across banks is at a much finer granularity – at cache-line granularity. In this case, every other cache line is mapped to a different bank.

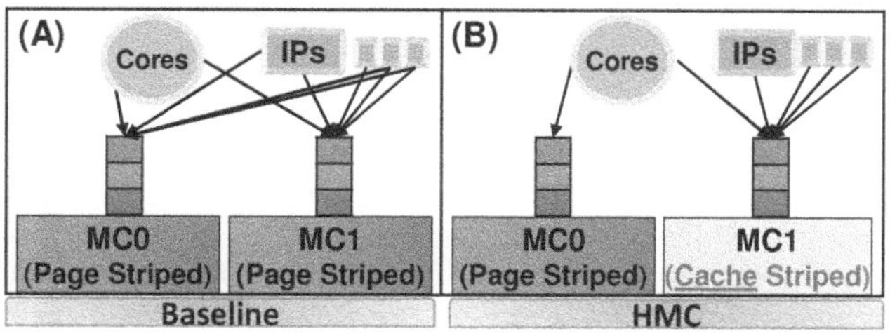

Figure 12: Schematic of (A) Baseline memory design and (B) Proposed HMC memory design.

Locality vs. Parallelism: When accessing a cache line from memory, the row that contains the cache line is brought to a buffer called *row buffer*, which is associated with every DRAM bank. Once the contents are placed in the *row buffer*, subsequent memory requests to the same row are served from the row buffer (row-buffer hits), instead of fetching them again from the memory array. This reduces access latency, improves performance, and saves the energy-expensive job of reading the row from memory array. Instead, if a different row from the one in the row buffer is requested, the current row is closed, and the new row gets placed in the buffer. This incurs high memory latency and is a high energy consuming task. Therefore, it is optimal to receive and serve requests from the row buffer. For this very reason, the most popular form of data distribution in CMPs is page-level striping, where up to 4KB of consecutive data can be mapped to a bank, and if requests are scheduled timely, all the data can be fetched from the row-buffer, thereby improving DRAM locality and energy efficiency. On the other hand, page-level striping restricts parallelism, as not many DRAM banks can be utilized in parallel. This is because if the requests possessing good locality are scheduled roughly at the same time, only a limited set of the banks will be accessed and the other DRAM banks will be idle. This limitation can be addressed by cache-line striping, where the same 4KB of data is striped across banks, and hence the same requests will access multiple banks. Such striping, although increases parallelism, it reduces locality. It is apparent that both techniques of data-distribution have pros and cons.

Auxiliary Metrics: In this context, we define two auxiliary metrics, which will be used to understand this trade-off. First, Bank Level Parallelism (BLP), which is defined as the average number of memory banks that are busy when there is at least one request being served at this memory controller [27]. Improving BLP enables better utilization of DRAM bandwidth. Second, Row-Buffer Locality (RBL), which is defined as the average row-buffer hit rate across all memory banks [27]. Improving RBL decreases average latency for memory requests, and increases the memory service rate.

6.2 Overview of the Proposed Design

As discussed in Section 5, the IPs have significantly higher memory bandwidth requirements compared to cores. This is shown in Figure 9a, where imaging IP demands more bandwidth compared to CPUs (note that the y-axis scales are different). This manifests into two primary problems: (1) the IP requests arrive in bursts thereby causing large queuing delays for CPU requests reducing the core performance, and (2) the IP memory requests interfere with core requests, thereby impacting the row-buffer locality of all the requests. Due to these two issues, the DRAM bandwidth utilization is severely affected leading to degradation of system performance. To address this, we propose having separate memory regions for mobile systems.

6.2.1 Memory Region Separation

In this design, we divide the address space into two regions: first region – associated with a dedicated memory controller (MC1) for CPU data which is accessed only by the CPUs, and the second region – associated with MC2 for IP data, which can be accessed by both cores and IPs. Note that, we cannot have completely dedicated memory controllers for IP and CPU requests, because the data produced by IPs need to be used by cores (or vice versa).

The goal of this design is to offer dedicated memory controller for core requests, as these requests are more latency critical. On the other hand, requests for the IP region are bandwidth intensive, as they arrive in bursts and access large chunks of data. Now, with separate memory regions, the bursts of requests coming to IP regions access consecutive cache lines. Due to this, these requests have very good row buffer locality. But, the downside of such an access pattern is that the bank-level-parallelism is very low.

6.2.2 Heterogeneity in Data Striping

To address the above problem, we enhance the design of memory with appropriate data striping. We adopt two different data striping techniques for MCs: MC0 uses page-level striping, and MC1 uses cache-line striping as shown in Figure 12(B). The motive of having two different striping techniques is to increase the BLP for IP memory region, while retaining the row-locality at CPU memory region. Note that, in general, cache-line striping reduces row-buffer locality. However, in this scenario (especially for IPs), typically the row-buffer locality is not affected, because these regions receive requests to large chunks of contiguous data. Consider the example where the system has cache-line striped n memory banks, and the display IP is accessing a large frame region. In such a system, consecutive cache lines are mapped to different banks in a cyclic manner, such that every n^{th} cache line is mapped to the same bank. Because the IPs typically access consecutive cache lines, the requests that are mapped to the same bank are likely to hit in the row buffer, leading to high row-buffer locality. Also, as the IP requests are sent to different banks, they take advantage of BLP. Note that in the proposed design, there are no extra overheads in terms of data copies or data duplication. All IP-associated data are written to DRAM through a separate memory controller(MC1) by cores or other IPs. While MC0 can be accessed by the cores, MC1 can be accessed by the cores and the IPs.

6.3 Evaluation of HMC Design

We compare our HMC design to an iso-resource baseline system with 2 memory controllers which are page-striped. In the baseline system, the memory controllers are not aware

(a) Reduction in execution time for CPU-bound applications.

(b) Reduction in CPU busy cycles with HMC.

(c) Improvement in average FDPS for Onscreen applications

Figure 13: Performance improvements of HMC with respect to baseline system. *Lower is better.*

of the characteristics of IPs' and cores' requests. We do not consider cache-line striped memory controllers as they increase the memory latency for all core's memory operations, thus reducing system performance and energy efficiency. In the proposed design, *Heterogeneous Memory Controller* (HMC), we isolate the requests targeted to IP and CPU memory regions.

Figure 13a shows the performance comparison of HMC with the baseline system for representative CPU bound and Onscreen applications. We report their respective evaluation metrics (execution times for CPU bound applications, and CPU-busy cycles and FDPS for Onscreen applications). From Figure 13a, we observe that, on average, the execution time of CPU-bound applications is reduced by 25% (up to 56% in cfbench). This improvement is primarily attributed to two reasons. First is the reduced interference from IP accesses on the CPU requests at MC0, because of memory region separation (discussed in Section 6.2.1). Second is the reduction in latency at MC1 because of increased RBL and BLP as discussed in Section 6.2.2.

The variance in reduction in execution times are attributed to the impact of IP accesses on the CPU accesses. If an application has relatively more number of IP accesses, it is likely to perform better with our HMC design. Note that for core bound applications, which do not have *any IP calls* (antutu-ram and antutu-cpu), will mostly not take advantage of HMC's optimizations. In fact, in some cases, they might lose performance due to reduced memory channel parallelism for CPU requests. In our studies, we find that the execution time of Antutu-CPU application increases by less than 1%.

The graph in Figure 13b shows the CPU activity under different memory system designs. In on-screen applications, CPU has to process data before an IP can consume it or vice versa. By employing our HMC design, the CPU processes the data quicker leaving it idle for more cycles. This can be seen in the second set of bars in the graph. This reduction in busy cycles directly translates to power savings.[3] Figure 13c shows the metric Frames Dropped Per Second (FDPS) under different memory system designs. HMC design makes the memory subsystem faster for both CPU and IP memory requests leading to fewer frame drops per second.

To understand the impact of our HMC design, we analyze some auxiliary metrics below. First, we look at how the locality at the memory controllers is affected due to HMC in Figure 14. Sub-graph (a) shows that the locality (row-buffer hit rates) at MC0 which is receiving only CPU requests in the HMC case did not change much, while (b) shows the row-buffer hit rates increase to almost 100%. This is mainly because, when the address regions are partitioned, only requests to IP memory space arrive at MC1. These requests typically access consecutive cache lines, contributing to high number of row-buffer hits.

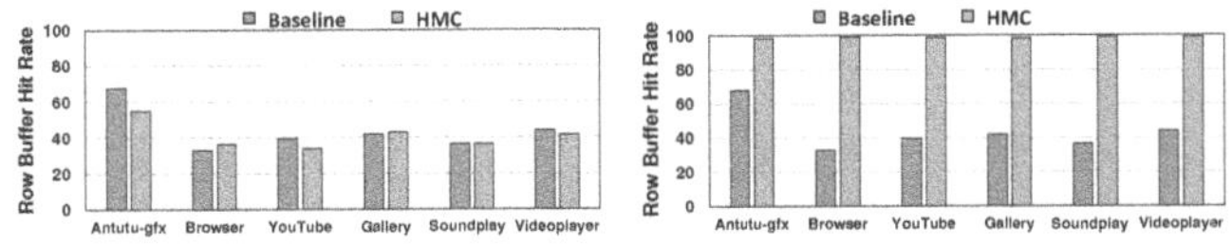

(a) Effect on locality in CPU-region addresses.

(b) Effect on locality in IP-region addresses.

Figure 14: Impact of HMC on locality. Baseline has both MCs serving both CPU and IP requests without distinguishing between them. *Higher is better.*

In HMC, though there is significant locality, because consecutive accesses go to the different banks due to cache-line striping, the bank level parallelism is also observed to be substantially higher than the base case. Particularly, this can be seen in Figure 15 (b), where the BLP for base-case averages around 1.25 banks only, whereas for HMC averages around 5.8 banks across all applications. In this IP memory region, as the requests that arrive typically go to consecutive banks in cyclic fashion, BLP tends to remain so high. Thus, Figures 14 and 15 together clearly show that our design did not lose locality when striping cache lines across banks. It is also clear from these graphs that with intelligent data mapping in memory, like in HMC, we can get the benefits of both, locality and parallelism.

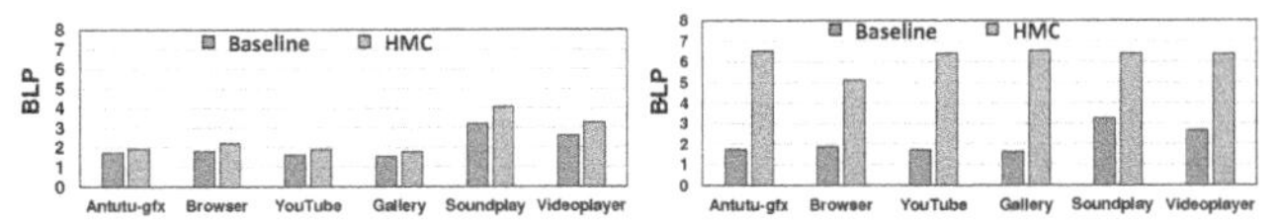

(a) Effect on bank-level parallelism in CPU-region addresses.

(b) Effect on bank-level parallelism in IP-region addresses.

Figure 15: Impact of HMC on Bandwidth. Baseline has both MCs with default page-striped addresses. *Higher is better.*

We observe that locality and parallelism in this system have significant impact on the latency of memory requests. Figure 16 shows the average latency of requests arriving at the memory controllers. We observe that, with HMC, in MC0, average latency improves because the core's requests are isolated from IP's requests. Thus, the latency critical core requests are served much faster, leading to performance improvements. In IP-region memory controller, the latencies were not affected significantly even though the requests are coming in bursts.

Finally, in Figure 17, we plot the cumulative distribution function of latencies of memory requests that arrived at the IP-region memory controller for YouTube and Browser application. The x-axis in this plot is the memory latency in

[3]In this work, we focus on performance and do not have a comprehensive power model for the system components.

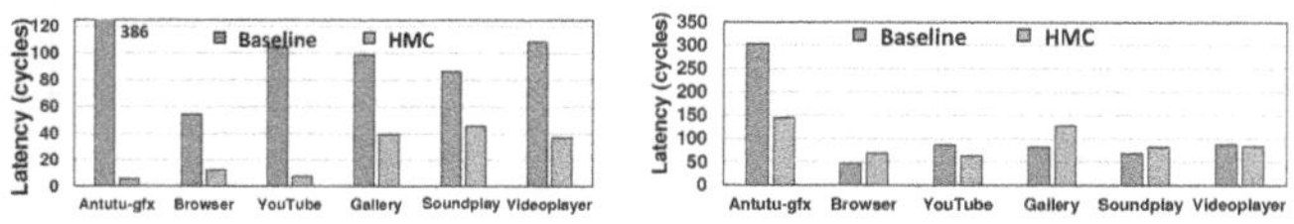

(a) Effect on latency in CPU-region addresses.

(b) Effect on latency in IP-region addresses.

Figure 16: Impact of HMC on Latency. Baseline has both MCs serving both CPU and IP requests without distinguishing between them. *Lower is better.*

cycles. We can observe that, with HMC, 99 % of the requests have latencies less than 300 cycles, while in baseline system, only 82% (youtube) and 95% (browser) of the requests have this latency. This clearly shows the benefits of HMC in reducing the memory latencies.

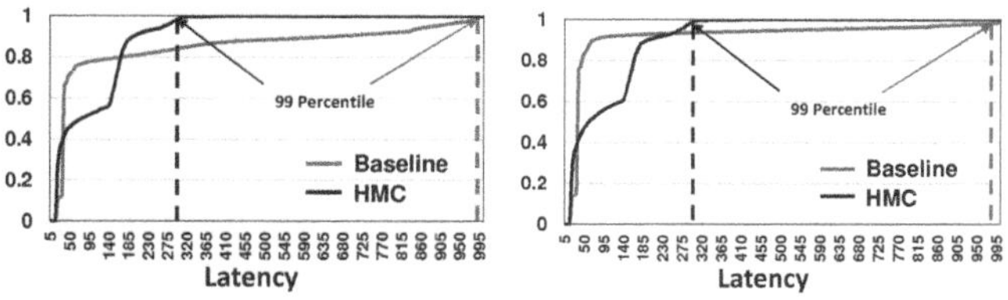

(a) CDF of latencies of memory accesses sent to IP address region in YouTube application.

(b) CDF of latencies of memory accesses sent to IP address region when using Browser application.

Figure 17: Impact of HMC showing how increase in bank-level parallelism reduces latency of requests in IP-address region.

7. RELATED WORK

Simulation Infrastructure and Application Characterization: A closely related work to ours by Gutierrez et al. [19] analyse the micro-architectural characteristics of smartphone applications without focusing on IP behavior. Another recent work by Sunwoo et al. [40] proposes an infrastructure to simulate smartphone cores, by integrating the architectural simulator GEM5 and OS, to study emerging smartphone workloads. Again this study is only core centric and lacks IP analyses. In this paper, we develop an infrastructure that can simulate multiple IPs as well as cores with OS, and can be easily extended to include more IP models. Also, we characterize the memory accesses generated by CPUs and IPs, and design a memory scheduling mechanism based on this characterization. Several works have investigated the power consumption of different applications [35], and different IPs [6] in smartphones, and proposed simulation infrastructure to simulate mobile networks [7,18]. These works neither characterize the memory sub-system, nor look at commonly used mobile applications.

IP Design and Optimizations: Ozer et al. [32] describe the steps involved in the design and verification of ARM IPs. Saleh et. al [37] discuss reusability, integrity, and scalability of IPs used in SoCs. Along with IP design and analysis, several works have proposed IP-specific optimizations [13, 20, 25, 34, 38, 39]. Our work does not consider specific IP design or optimizations, instead focuses on characterizing the interaction of different IPs and cores, and intelligently schedules their memory requests to improve overall system performance. A large body of work on power in smartphones include propose a system-call-based power model [36], power consumption of network devices and protocols in smartphones [3], a network-based power reduction technique for smartphones [12], and the power consumption of various IPs and applications in smartphones [22, 41, 44].

Memory Controller Design and QoS: Several works have investigated memory scheduling techniques in the context of smartphones. Lee and Change [28] describe the essential issues in memory system design for SoCs. Lee et al. [29] propose a memory scheduling mechanism that provides latency and bandwidth guarantees for memory accesses. Akesson et al. [1] propose a memory scheduling technique that provides a guaranteed minimum bandwidth and maximum latency bound to IPs. Lin et al. [30] employ a hierarchical memory scheduler that improves system throughput. Jeong et al. [23] provide QoS guarantees to frames by balancing memory requests at the memory controller. In the context of CMPs and uni-processor systems, several works have proposed low-power memory designs [10, 11] that can be applied in smartphones for better energy efficiency. In this paper, we propose a MC design specifically tailored for both CPUs and IPs.

8. CONCLUSIONS

In this paper, we present a comprehensive simulation framework for exploring the SoC design space, targeted specifically for mobile systems. The proposed GemDroid platform primarily consists of the Android emulator that enables collecting core traces and IP calls for mobile applications and the GEM5 core simulator that enables in-depth analysis of the core and memory subsystems. In addition, we have included several IP models for characterizing the execution profile of IPs, invoked by different applications.

To demonstrate the capabilities of the infrastructure, in this paper we focused on the memory system analysis of SoCs since it is a known performance bottleneck for both latency critical core executions and bandwidth critical IP executions. Thus, we present a heterogeneous MC design, where one MC is optimized for core requests and the other MC is dedicated to enhance bank-level parallelism of IP requests. The proposed modifications to the MC design results in improving both core and IP performance.

The proposed GemDroid simulator is expected to fill a void in the mobile system design space by facilitating a holistic performance and power analyses of evolving SoC designs. The novelty of the framework is that it is flexible where users can add more IPs, different simulation and analytical models for IPs either to make detailed or faster evaluation, simulate multiple cores, on-chip interconnect design and emerging memory technologies for system-wide performance and power optimization. We are currently looking into some of these issues for making GemDroid a more powerful tool. We propose to make the entire GemDroid framework available in the public domain, together with modular capabilities to allow the broader academic community to undertake numerous studies.

Acknowledgments

We thank the anonymous reviewers, Ashutosh Pattnaik, Adwait Jog, Onur Kayiran, Prashanth Thinakaran and other HPCL members for their feedback on this paper. This research is supported in part by the following NSF grants – #1302557, #0963839, #1205618, #1213052, #1320478, #1317560, #1302225, #1017882, and grants from Intel.

9. REFERENCES

[1] B. Akesson, K. Goossens, and M. Ringhofer. Predator: A predictable sdram memory controller. In *CODES+ISSS*, 2007.

[2] ARM. ARMv7-A Technical Reference Manual. 2011.

[3] N. Balasubramanian, A. Balasubramanian, and A. Venkataramani. Energy consumption in mobile phones: A measurement study and implications for network applications. In *IMC*, 2009.

[4] C. Bienia. *Benchmarking Modern Multiprocessors*. PhD thesis, Princeton University, January 2011.

[5] N. Binkert, B. Beckmann, G. Black, S. K. Reinhardt, A. Saidi, A. Basu, J. Hestness, D. R. Hower, T. Krishna, S. Sardashti, R. Sen, K. Sewell, M. Shoaib, N. Vaish, M. D. Hill, and D. A. Wood. The gem5 simulator. *SIGARCH Comput. Archit. News*, 2011.

[6] A. Carroll and G. Heiser. An analysis of power consumption in a smartphone. In *USENIXATC*, 2010.

[7] L. Chen, W. Chen, B. Wang, X. Zhang, H. Chen, and D. Yang. System-level simulation methodology and platform for mobile cellular systems. *Communications Magazine, IEEE*, 2011.

[8] Cisco. Cisco Visual Networking Index: Forecast and Methodology, 2012:2017. 2013.

[9] V. del Barrio, C. Gonzalez, J. Roca, A. Fernandez, and R. Espasa. Attila: a cycle-level execution-driven simulator for modern gpu architectures. In *Performance Analysis of Systems and Software, 2006 IEEE International Symposium on*, 2006.

[10] Q. Deng, D. Meisner, L. Ramos, T. F. Wenisch, and R. Bianchini. Memscale: Active low-power modes for main memory. In *ASPLOS*, 2011.

[11] B. Diniz, D. O. G. Neto, W. M. Jr., and R. Bianchini. Limiting the power consumption of main memory. In *ISCA*, 2007.

[12] H. Falaki, D. Lymberopoulos, R. Mahajan, S. Kandula, and D. Estrin. A first look at traffic on smartphones. In *IMC*, 2010.

[13] S. Fenney. Texture compression using low-frequency signal modulation. In *HWWS*, 2003.

[14] T. I. T. R. for Semiconductors. 2008 update, 2008.

[15] Gartner. Worldwide PC, Tablet and Mobile Phone Combined Shipments to Reach 2.4 Billion Units in 2013.

[16] Google. Android Developers, 2013.

[17] Google. Android SDK - Emulator, 2013.

[18] P. Guo. Simulation and testing of mobile computing platforms using fujaba.

[19] A. Gutierrez, R. Dreslinski, T. Wenisch, T. Mudge, A. Saidi, C. Emmons, and N. Paver. Full-system analysis and characterization of interactive smartphone applications. In *IISWC*, 2011.

[20] K. Han, A. Min, N. Jeganathan, and P. Diefenbaugh. A hybrid display frame buffer architecture for energy efficient display subsystems. In *ISPLED*, 2013.

[21] J. L. Henning. Spec cpu2006 benchmark descriptions. *SIGARCH Comput. Archit. News*, 34(4), Sept. 2006.

[22] V. Janapa Reddi, B. C. Lee, T. Chilimbi, and K. Vaid. Web search using mobile cores: Quantifying and mitigating the price of efficiency. In *ISCA*, 2010.

[23] M. K. Jeong, M. Erez, C. Sudanthi, and N. Paver. A qos-aware memory controller for dynamically balancing gpu and cpu bandwidth use in an mpsoc. In *DAC*, 2012.

[24] A. Jog, O. Kayiran, N. C. Nachiappan, A. K. Mishra, M. T. Kandemir, O. Mutlu, R. Iyer, and C. R. Das. OWL: Cooperative Thread Array Aware Scheduling Techniques for Improving GPGPU Performance. In *ASPLOS*, 2013.

[25] H. b. T. Khan and M. K. Anwar. Quality-aware Frame Skipping for MPEG-2 Video Based on Inter-frame Similarity. Technical report, Malardalen University.

[26] Y. Kim, D. Han, O. Mutlu, and M. Harchol-Balter. ATLAS: A Scalable and High-performance Scheduling Algorithm for Multiple Memory Controllers. In *HPCA*, 2010.

[27] Y. Kim, M. Papamichael, O. Mutlu, and M. Harchol-Balter. Thread Cluster Memory Scheduling: Exploiting Differences in Memory Access Behavior. In *MICRO*, 2010.

[28] K.-B. Lee and T.-S. Chang. *Essential Issues in SoC Design Designing - Complex Systems-on-Chip*, chapter SoC Memory System Design. Springer, 2006.

[29] K.-B. Lee, T.-C. Lin, and C.-W. Jen. An efficient quality-aware memory controller for multimedia platform soc. *Circuits and Systems for Video Technology, IEEE Transactions on*, 2005.

[30] Y.-J. Lin, C.-L. Yang, T.-J. Lin, J.-W. Huang, and N. Chang. Hierarchical memory scheduling for multimedia mpsocs. In *ICCAD*, 2010.

[31] T. Olsson and M. Salo. Online user survey on current mobile augmented reality applications. In *ISMAR*, 2011.

[32] E. Ozer, N. Chong, and K. Flautner. *Processor and System-on-Chip Simulation*, chapter IP Modeling and Verification. Springer, 2010.

[33] D. Pandiyan, S.-Y. Lee, and C.-J. Wu. Performance, energy characterizations and architectural implications of an emerging mobile platform benchmark suite : Mobilebench. In *Workload Characterization (IISWC), 2013 IEEE International Symposium on*, 2013.

[34] K. Patel, E. Macii, and M. Poncino. Frame buffer energy optimization by pixel prediction. In *ICCD*, 2005.

[35] A. Pathak, Y. C. Hu, and M. Zhang. Where is the energy spent inside my app?: Fine grained energy accounting on smartphones with eprof. In *EuroSys*, 2012.

[36] A. Pathak, Y. C. Hu, M. Zhang, P. Bahl, and Y.-M. Wang. Fine-grained power modeling for smartphones using system call tracing. In *EuroSys*, 2011.

[37] R. Saleh, S. Wilton, S. Mirabbasi, A. Hu, M. Greenstreet, G. Lemieux, P. Pande, C. Grecu, and A. Ivanov. System-on-chip: Reuse and integration. *Proceedings of the IEEE*, 2006.

[38] H. Shim, N. Chang, and M. Pedram. A compressed frame buffer to reduce display power consumption in mobile systems. In *ASP-DAC*, 2004.

[39] H. M. Siqueira, I. S. Silva, M. E. Kreutz, and E. F. Correa. Ddr sdram memory controller for digital tv decoders. In *SBESC*, 2011.

[40] D. Sunwoo, W. Wang, M. Ghosh, C. Sudanthi, G. Blake, C. D. Emmons, and N. Paver. A structured approach to the simulation, analysis and characterization of smartphone applications. In *IISWC*, 2013.

[41] Y. Xiao, R. S. Kalyanaraman, and A. Yla-Jaaski. Energy consumption of mobile youtube: Quantitative measurement and analysis. In *NGMAST*, 2008.

[42] K. Xu. Nova : H.264/avc baseline decoder. OpenCores, Apr 2008. RTL verified.

[43] P. Yedlapalli, J. Kotra, E. Kultursay, M. T. Kandemir, C. R. Das, and A. Sivasubramaniam. Meeting midway: Improving cmp performance with memory-side prefetching. In *PACT*, 2013.

[44] Y. Zhu and V. J. Reddi. High-performance and energy-efficient mobile web browsing on big/little systems. In *HPCA*, 2013.

Understanding the Impact of Network Dynamics on Mobile Video User Engagement

M. Zubair Shafiq†, Jeffrey Erman‡, Lusheng Ji‡, Alex X. Liu†, Jeffrey Pang‡, Jia Wang‡
†Department of Computer Science and Engineering, Michigan State University, East Lansing, MI, USA
‡AT&T Labs – Research, Bedminster, NJ, USA
{shafiqmu,alexliu}@cse.msu.edu, {erman,lji,jeffpang,jiawang}@research.att.com

ABSTRACT

Mobile network operators have a significant interest in the performance of streaming video on their networks because network dynamics directly influence the Quality of Experience (QoE). However, unlike video service providers, network operators are not privy to the client- or server-side logs typically used to measure key video performance metrics, such as user engagement. To address this limitation, this paper presents the first large-scale study characterizing the impact of cellular network performance on mobile video user engagement from the perspective of a network operator. Our study on a month-long anonymized data set from a major cellular network makes two main contributions. First, we quantify the effect that 31 different network factors have on user behavior in mobile video. Our results provide network operators direct guidance on how to improve user engagement — for example, improving mean signal-to-interference ratio by 1 dB reduces the likelihood of video abandonment by 2%. Second, we model the complex relationships between these factors and video abandonment, enabling operators to monitor mobile video user engagement in real-time. Our model can predict whether a user completely downloads a video with more than 87% accuracy by observing only the initial 10 seconds of video streaming sessions. Moreover, our model achieves significantly better accuracy than prior models that require client- or server-side logs, yet we only use standard radio network statistics and/or TCP/IP headers available to network operators.

Categories and Subject Descriptors

C.2.3 [**Computer System Organization**]: computer communication networks—*network operations*; C.4 [**Performance of Systems**]: measurement techniques, performance attributes

Keywords

Cellular Network; Performance; Quality of Experience (QoE); Video Streaming

SIGMETRICS'14, June 16–20, 2014, Austin, Texas, USA.

http://dx.doi.org/10.1145/2591971.2591975.

1. INTRODUCTION

Online video services such as YouTube, Netflix, and Hulu are very popular on mobile networks. It has been estimated that video currently makes up more than half of all mobile data traffic and will grow by a factor of 16 by 2017 [5]. Therefore, it is crucial for mobile network operators to monitor the user experience, or Quality of Experience (QoE), of video streaming and understand how network characteristics and performance influence it.

Unfortunately, prior approaches for monitoring and understanding the user experience of video streaming are insufficient for mobile network operators. Recent seminal work [7–9, 15] investigated how video streaming quality influences important user engagement metrics, such as video abandonment rate. However, these studies rely on client-side instrumentation to measure video quality metrics such as buffering, startup delay, and bitrate. This instrumentation is not available to network operators, so the ability to measure user engagement using only network-side measurements is crucial from their perspective. Other work used network traffic analysis to study video streaming volume and abandonment rates in wired [12, 14] and wireless networks [10]. However, these techniques use deep-packet-inspection to extract information beyond TCP/IP headers, which requires significant computational resources to employ at the scale of network carriers and can pose privacy problems in practice. Moreover, these studies did not provide insight into how network characteristics and performance influence abandonment rates.

To redress these limitations, this paper presents the first large-scale study to characterize video streaming performance in cellular networks and its impact on user engagement. Our study is based on month-long anonymized data sets collected from the core network and radio access network of a tier-1 cellular network in the United States. We analyze 27 terabytes of video streaming traffic from nearly half a million users in this data set. Our analysis makes two main contributions.

First, to the best of our knowledge, our analysis is the first to quantify the impact that network characteristics have on mobile video user engagement in the wild. We quantify the effect that 31 different cellular network factors have on video abandonment rate and video skip (*e.g.*, fast forward) rate. In particular, we quantify user engagement by labeling video streaming sessions in our data set as `completed/abandoned` and `skipped/non-skipped`, and then evaluate the extent to which core network and radio network factors correlate with abandonment rate and skip rate. These factors include

TCP flow throughput, flow duration, handover rate, signal strength, and the physical location's land cover type. Our results provide network operators insights and direct guidance on how to improve user engagement. For example, improving mean signal-to-interference ratio by 1 dB reduces the likelihood of video abandonment by 2%. Moreover, reducing the load in a cell sector by 10 active users reduces the likelihood of video abandonment by 7%. Through these insights, network operators can identify and prioritize network factors that have the most impact on user engagement.

Second, we are the first to show how a network operator can monitor mobile video user engagement using only standard radio network statistics and/or TCP/IP flow records, a necessity for continuous monitoring at scale and for mitigating privacy concerns. Moreover, we show that our approach can predict video abandonment very early in a video session, which can help future networks decide which users to optimize performance for (*e.g.*, using LTE self-organizing networks [1]). Specifically, we model the complex relationships between network factors and video abandonment. We find that the C4.5/M5P algorithm with bootstrap aggregation can build decision/regression tree models that accurately predict video abandonment. Our results show that it can predict whether a video streaming session is `abandoned` or `skipped` with more than 87% accuracy by observing only the initial 10 seconds. Our model achieves significantly better accuracy than prior models that require video service provider logs [7,8], while only using standard radio network statistics and/or TCP/IP headers readily available to network operators.

Paper Organization: The rest of this paper is organized as follows. In Section 2, we present a brief background and details of the data collection process. Section 3 presents the characterization of video mobile video streaming performance and its impact on user engagement. We develop a machine learning model for user engagement and present the results in Section 4. Section 5 reviews related work and the paper is concluded in Section 6 with an outlook to our future work.

2. DATA

To study mobile video streaming performance, we collected anonymized flow-level logs from a tier-1 cellular network in the United States. Next, we first provide a brief background of video streaming in cellular networks, description of our data collection methodology, and some high-level statistics of the collected data set.

2.1 Cellular Network Background

A typical UMTS cellular network, shown in Figure 1, can be visualized as consisting of two major components: Radio Access Network (RAN) and Core Network (CN). RAN consists of NodeBs and Radio Network Controllers (RNCs). Each NodeB has multiple antennas, where each antenna corresponds to a different cell sector. A user via user equipment (UE) connects to an *active set* of one or more cell sectors in the RAN. The UE periodically selects a primary or serving cell among the active set based on their signal strength information. From the active set, only the primary cell actually transmits downlink data to the UE. The traffic generated by a UE is sent to the corresponding NodeB by cell sectors. Each RNC controls and exchanges traffic with multiple NodeBs, each of which serves many users in its coverage area. RNCs manage control signaling such as Radio Access Bearer (RAB) assignments, transmission scheduling, and handovers. Each UE negotiates allocation of radio resources with the RAN based on a wide range of factors, such as available radio resources and signal strength [6].

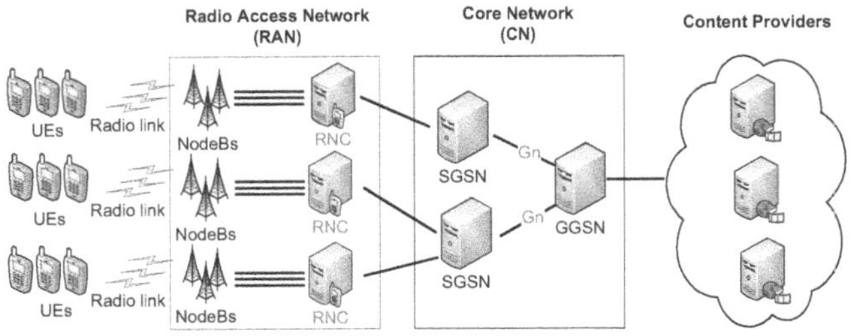

Figure 1: Cellular network architecture

CN consists of Serving GPRS Support Nodes (SGSNs) facing the user and Gateway GPRS Support Nodes (GGSNs) facing the Internet and other external networks. RNCs send traffic from NodeBs to SGSNs, which then send it to GGSNs. GGSNs eventually send traffic to external networks, such as the Internet. For data connections, the IP layer of a UE is peered with the IP layer of GGSNs in the form of tunnels known as Packet Data Protocol (PDP) contexts. These tunnels, implemented as GPRS Tunneling Protocol (GTP) tunnels, carry IP packets between the UEs and their peering GGSNs. From the perspective of an external network such as the Internet, a GGSN connecting CN to the Internet appears just like an IP router and the UEs that connect through the GGSN appear as IP hosts behind the router.

2.2 Data Collection and Pre-processing

For our study, we simultaneously collected two anonymized data sets from the RAN and CN of a tier-1 cellular network in the United States. Our data collection covers a major metropolitan area in the Western United States over the duration of one month in 2012. The RAN data set is collected at the RNCs and contains event-driven signaling information such as current active set, RAB state, handovers, bitrate, signal strength, and RRC requests from users and corresponding responses from the network. The CN data set is collected from the Gn interfaces between SGSNs and GGSNs, and contains flow-level information of video streaming traffic such as server IP and port, client IP and port, flow duration, TCP flags, anonymized user identifier (IMSI), and anonymized device identifier (IMEI). These fields require only TCP/IP or GTP level information, which is efficiently collected [22].

In order to determine the ground-truth of video abandonment, we also collected the following HTTP-level information: URL, host, user agent, content type, content length, and byte-range request from clients and response from servers. Large scale monitoring tools often do not collect HTTP information because it requires processing hundreds of bytes of text beyond the 40-byte TCP/IP header. Thus, it is important that day-to-day monitoring does not require its collection at scale. All device and user identifiers (*e.g.*, IMSI, IMEI) in our data sets are anonymized to protect privacy without affecting the usefulness of our analysis.

The data sets do not permit the reversal of the anonymization or re-identification of users.

To minimize the confounding factors that different content providers (live vs. video-on-demand), connectivity (cellular vs. cable), and device type (mobile vs. desktop) could have on our network-centric analysis, we chose to focus on the most popular video service provider in our cellular network data set. This provider (anonymized for business confidentiality) serves user generated content on demand, and according to a recent study [10], it serves over 37% of all video objects. This provider streams videos using progressive download with byte-range requests, which is the most common protocol currently in use. We believe the conclusions we draw in this paper apply to 9 of the 14 most popular mobile video content providers as they use the same protocol [10]. Previous work found the top providers that use this protocol behave similarly in wired networks [19].

Since our collected data contains traffic records for all types of content, we first need to separate video streaming traffic from the rest. Towards this end, we use the HTTP host and content-type headers to separate the video streaming traffic from other TCP/IP traffic. We can also separate video traffic based only on the server IP and port, since all video streaming traffic is served by a known block of CDN cache servers.

A video is progressively downloaded in one or multiple HTTP byte-range requests, which represent different portions of the video [10]. Figure 2 illustrates a video streaming session that involves multiple HTTP byte-range server response flows. The x-axis represents time, which starts with the first HTTP byte-range server response flow. The y-axis represents byte-range of the video file with maximum value same as the video file size, which is highlighted by the horizontal broken line. Consequently, each gray rectangle represents a distinct HTTP byte-range server response flow. Note that flows may have different byte-range lengths and durations, they may be overlapping, and there may be time gaps between consecutive flows.

For the purpose of our analysis, we group HTTP flows into video sessions based on a unique ID that is the same in the URLs of each video session. In practice, we found that we can group flows into sessions without any HTTP information. In particular, by looking for a change in the server IP to determine when a new video session for a user starts, we can detect session starts correctly with 98% accuracy. This is because videos are served from a CDN and different videos are likely served from different cache servers. Even if all videos were served from a single server, we found that we can still detect session starts with 97% accuracy using a simple decision tree classifier trained on the size of and inter-arrival time gap between HTTP flows. (We omit details due to space constraints.) Thus, we conclude that TCP/IP information would be sufficient to detect and group HTTP flows into video sessions.

2.3 Video Traffic Statistics

Next we present some details of our collected data set such as aggregate statistics, container types, encoding bitrates, and video player types. Overall, our data set consists of more than 27 terabytes worth of video streaming traffic, from more than 37 million flows, from almost half a million users over the course of one month.

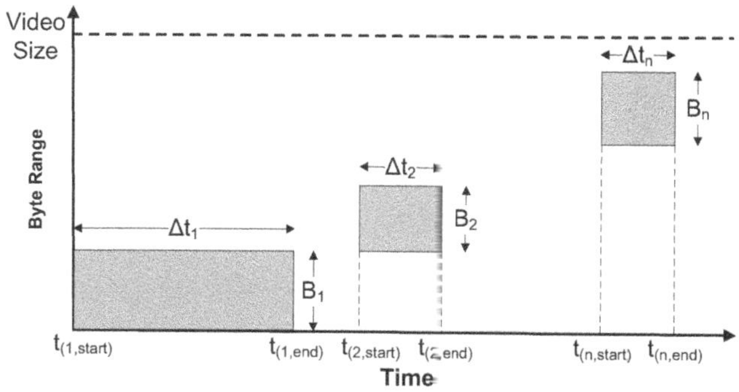

Figure 2: Illustration of a video streaming session. Gray rectangles represent distinct flows in a session.

Our data set mostly contains standard definition video streaming streaming traffic. Figure 3(a) shows the distribution of video streaming traffic with respect to container types. The most common container types [3] are: (1) 3GP (3GPP file format), (2) MPEG-4, (3) FLV (Flash), (4) WebM, and (5) MP2T (MPEG transport stream). We observe that a vast majority, almost 70%, of video streaming traffic uses the 3GPP container type – followed by MPEG-4 and Flash container types as distant 2nd and 3rd most popular, respectively. Only a small fraction, less than 2%, of the video streaming traffic belongs to containers types used for live content. We exclude these from our analysis since our focus is on video-on-demand streaming. Further analysis of video encoding bitrate showed that a majority of video streaming traffic belongs to lower bitrates, which correspond to 144/240p video resolution. 240p is the most commonly used video resolution. Only a small fraction of video streaming traffic belongs to higher video resolutions. For example, less than 5% video streaming traffic belongs to high definition (HD) 720p content.

Short duration videos account for most of the streaming traffic in our data set. In Figure 3(b), we plot the cumulative distribution function (CDF) of video duration. We observe that more than 70% videos are less than 5 minutes long and only 10% videos are longer than 15 minutes. This type of skewed distribution is expected for content providers that serve user generated content [10].

Users employ only a few distinct video players to play video content in our data set. We plot the CDF of users across video player types (reverse-sorted with respect to fraction of users) in Figure 3(c). We identify video player types using the available user agent information [23, 24], which enables us to differentiate among video players on different hardware models, operating system versions, and web browsers. Our data set contains several dozen distinct video player types whose distribution is highly skewed, *i.e.*, a small fraction of video player types account for most users in our data set. Specifically, top-5 player types account for approximately 80% users in our data set and they represent both iOS- and Android-based devices.

2.4 Quantifying User Engagement

As a first step towards analyzing user engagement, we discuss two ways to quantify it: discrete and continuous.

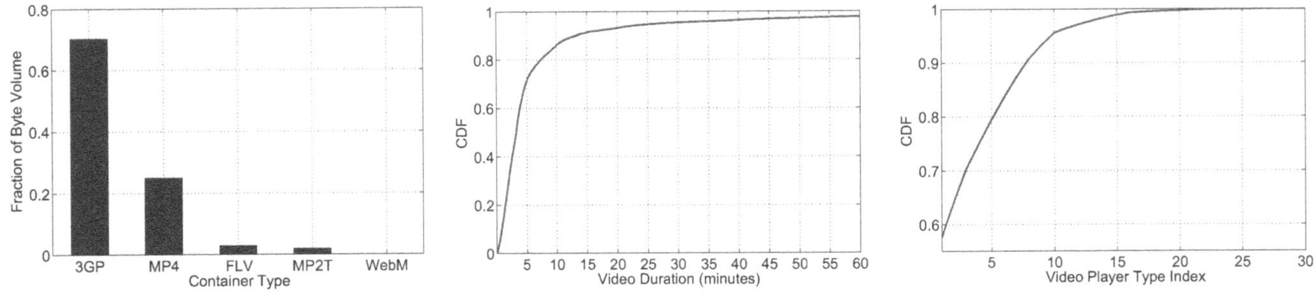

(a) Container type (b) Video duration (c) Video player type

Figure 3: Distributions of container type, video duration, and video player type

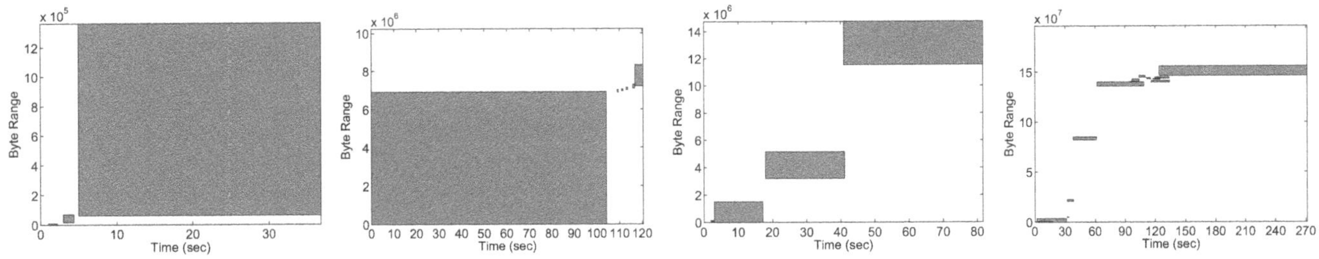

(a) `completed, non-skipped` (b) `abandoned, non-skipped` (c) `completed, skipped` (d) `abandoned, skipped`

Figure 4: Examples of video streaming session classes. Y-axis limits are set to the video sizes.

Discrete quantification of user engagement. For discrete quantification, we first use a nominal variable that represents the following classes: `completed` and `abandoned`. The `completed` class represents video streaming sessions in which the download process reaches the end-point. The `abandoned` class represents video streaming sessions in which the download process is abandoned before reaching the end-point. In our data set, 21.2% sessions belong to the `completed` class and 78.8% sessions belong to the `abandoned` class. Since users tend to skip videos when streaming gets stuck, we also use a nominal variable that represents the following classes: `skipped` and `non-skipped`. The `skipped` class represents video streaming sessions in which the download process includes at least one seek-forward between the start-point and the last byte downloaded. The `non-skipped` class represents video streaming sessions in which the download process does not include seek-forward between the start-point and the last byte downloaded. In our data set, 33.9% sessions belong to the `skipped` class and 66.1% sessions belong to the `non-skipped` class. Combining the aforementioned user engagement classification schemes, we can define the following four non-overlapping classes: (1) `completed, non-skipped`, (2) `abandoned, non-skipped`, (3) `completed, skipped`, and (4) `abandoned, skipped`. In our data set, 17.6% sessions belong to the `completed, non-skipped` class, 48.5% sessions belong to the `abandoned, non-skipped` class, 3.6% sessions belong to the `completed, skipped` class, and 30.3% sessions belong to the `abandoned, skipped` class. Figure 4 illustrates examples of video streaming sessions for the four user engagement classes. As mentioned earlier and observable in Figure 4, sessions generally consist of more than one flow. On average, a video streaming session in our data set consists of 11 flows, where earlier flows tend to be larger than the following flows. This trend is because video players tend to aggressively download larger chunks to fill up the available buffer during the initial buffering phase of a video streaming session [19]. The download rate in this initial phase is limited by the end-to-end available bandwidth. Afterwards in the steady state phase, the remaining video is generally downloaded in multiple smaller flows. The download rate in this phase depends on the video encoding rate and the playback progress.

Continuous quantification of user engagement. For continuous quantification, we use a continuous variable ($\in [0,1]$) representing the fraction of video download completion. Figure 5 shows the CDF of video download completion. Comparing videos of different durations, as expected we observe that shorter videos achieve higher download completion than longer videos [16]. For aggregate distribution, almost 15% of video streaming sessions are abandoned with less than 5% download completion. However, after the 5% completion mark, the distribution is fairly uniform until the 80% completion mark. The initial modality in the distribution indicates abandonment that is likely either because users tend to sample videos [7] or due to longer join times [9]. The later modality in the distribution (excluding the 100% completion mark) indicates abandonment that is likely either because users lose interest in the content (*e.g.*, due to video closing credits) or because shorter videos achieve higher download completion due to aggressive initial buffering.

We note that our definitions of user engagement detect abandonment and skips only during the download phase of a video. We cannot detect a video abandonment or skip if these events occur after a video has downloaded completely (*e.g.*, due to lack of user interest). However, network operators are typically not interested in those events because they are unlikely to be influenced by network factors.

Table 1: CN (top) and RAN (bottom) features. i denotes the flow index of a session with N flows.

Feature	Description
Flow volume	(B_i) The number of bytes transferred during the ith flow. (Summary stats)
Flow duration	(t_i) The duration (in seconds) from the SYN packet to the last packet in the ith flow. (Summary stats)
Flow TCP throughput	(T_i) The ratio of flow volume to flow duration in the ith flow, in KB/s. (Summary stats)
Flow inter-arrival time	(I_i) Time (in seconds) between the end of the ith flow and the start of the $i+1^{\text{th}}$ flow. (Summary stats)
Flow flags	FIN_i and RST_i respectively denote the number of packets with TCP-Finish (no more data from sender indicating completion) and TCP-Reset (reset the connection indicating some unexpected error) flags set in the ith flow. Based on the direction of packet transfer, we distinguish between client-to-server (c→s) and server-to-client (s→c) flags. (Summary stats)
Largest flow volume	(B_j) The largest flow volume among all flow volumes, where j denotes the index of this flow.
Largest flow duration	(t_j) The duration of the jth flow.
Largest flow TCP throughput	(T_j) The throughput of the jth flow.
Largest flow flags	FIN_j and RST_j respectively denote the number of packets with TCP-Finish and TCP-Reset flags set in the jth flow. We distinguish between c→s and s→c flags.
Number of flows	(N) The total number of flows in a session.
Session volume	(**B**) The sum of all flow volumes in a session.
Session duration	(**t**) The sum of all flow durations in a session. $\mathbf{t} = \sum_{i=1}^{N} t_i$.
Session TCP throughput	(**T**) The average throughput of a session. $\mathbf{T} = \sum_{i=1}^{N} B_i \;/\; \sum_{i=1}^{N} t_i$.
Session inter-arrival time	(**I**) The sum of all flow inter-arrival times (in seconds) in a session
Session flags	(**FIN** and **RST**) respectively denote the number of packets with TCP-Finish and TCP-Reset flags set in a session. We distinguish between c→s and s→c flags.
# soft handovers	(H_S) This handover occurs when a cell is added or removed from the active set [25]. (Session- and cell-level)
# inter-frequency handovers	(H_{IF}) This type of handover occurs when a UE switches to cell sector of the same or different NodeB with different operating frequency [25]. (Session- and cell-level)
# IRAT handovers	(H_{RAT}) This type of handover occurs when a UE switches between different radio access technologies (*e.g.*, UMTS and GPRS) [25]. (Session- and cell-level)
# RRC failure events	A RRC failure event is logged when a request by a user to allocate more radio resources is denied by the respective RNC due to network overload or other issues [21]. (Session- and cell-level)
# admission control failures	These events occur when a user cannot finish the admission control procedure often due to lack of available capacity. (Session- and cell-level)
Received signal code power	RSCP is the RF energy of the downlink signal obtained after the correlation and descrambling process [25]. It is usually measured in dBm. (Summary stats)
Signal energy to interference	This ratio (E_c/I_o) denotes the ratio of the received energy to the interference level of the downlink common pilot channel [25]. It is usually measured in dB. (Summary stats)
Received signal strength	RSSI takes into account both RSCP and E_c/I_o [25]. It is usually measured in dBm. It is defined as: RSSI = RSCP - E_c/I_o. (Summary stats)
Size of active set	(S_{AS}) The number of unique cell sectors in the active set. (Summary stats)
Radio access bearer state	Our measurement apparatus distinguishes among 84 different RAB states. RAB state encodes encodes information about RRC state (*e.g.*, FACH shared channel vs. DCH dedicated channel), RAB type (*e.g.*, interactive vs. streaming), and maximum data rate. Since a session may have multiple RAB states over time, we use the most common state for session-level and top-3 most common states for cell-level features.
Uplink RLC throughput	(T_U) The uplink data rate for UE in the DCH state (in kbps). (Session- and cell-level summary stats)
Downlink RLC throughput	(T_D) The downlink data rate for UE in the DCH state (in kbps). (Session- and cell-level summary stats)
# Users in DCH state	(U_{DCH}) Users served by the representative cell over a window of 1 hour.
Frequency	The operating frequency of the representative cell.
Landcover	A nominal variable that defines the geographical terrain of a cell. 2006 National Land Cover Database contains the 16-class geographical terrain categorization of the United States at a spatial resolution of 30 meters [2, 13]. The categories include developed-open space, developed-high intensity, perennial ice/snow, deciduous forest, open water, *etc.* We extract the top-3 most common landcover categories in terms of spatial area within 1 km of the representative cell.
Elevation	Elevation of a cell is extracted from the National Elevation Dataset (NED) at a spatial resolution of 30 meters [4]. We use average elevation of the representative cell as a feature.

3. ANALYSIS OF NETWORK FACTORS

Our main goal is to understand the influence of network factors on user engagement. Towards this end, this section presents an in-depth analysis of the relationships between network factors and video abandonment.

We first itemize a wide range of factors that can potentially impact or be influenced by mobile video user engagement. We compile a comprehensive list of features from the information available in both CN and RAN data sets. It is noteworthy that while features extracted from the RAN data set are only applicable for cellular networks, features extracted from the CN data set are applicable for other kinds of wired and wireless networks as well. Table 1 summarizes the features.

Core Network (CN) features. For each video streaming session, we can extract CN features for individual flows and the whole session (labeled as *Flow* and *Session* features in

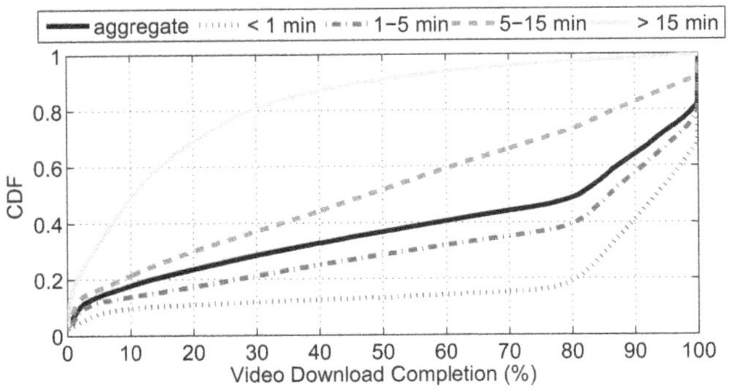

Figure 5: Distribution of video download completion

the top half of Table 1, respectively). Since sessions may have different number of flows, we compute the following statistical measures to summarize the flow-level features for whole sessions: mean, standard deviation, minimum, maximum, 25th percentile, median (50th percentile), and 75th percentile. Hence each flow-level feature listed in Table 1 (labeled with "Summary stats") represents 7 summary values. We also extract these features for the largest flow (in terms of byte volume) of a video streaming session, as a single flow typically dominates each video session.

Radio Access Network (RAN) features. For each video streaming session, we also extract RAN features for the user and the cell sectors that service the user during the session. The RAN features are described in the bottom half of Table 1. For session-level features, the RAN data set records belonging to a user can be identified using the combination of IMSI and session start and end timestamp information. For cell-level features, however, the selection criterion of the representative cell for a session is not obvious because the active set and the primary cell may change between the start and end of a session. Towards this end, we select the most common cell sector (in terms of number of records) to be the representative cell for a session. For each session, cell-level features are computed for all users served by the representative cell in the time window at the session start. Features in Table 1 labeled with "Session- and cell-level" indicate features that we compute both a session-level value and cell-level value, as defined above. For example, for # soft handovers, we compute one feature as the number of soft handovers for the user during the session, and another as the number of soft handovers for all users in the representative cell of that session. For features that can hold multiple values during a session (*e.g.*, RSSI), we compute the same 7 summary statistic values listed above for flow features. These features are labeled with "Summary stats" in Table 1.

To better understand the relationship between features and user engagement, we plot the abandonment rate distributions of prominent features in Figure 6. The abandonment rate is defined as the fraction of sessions in the data set that are abandoned. The shaded areas represent the 95% confidence interval [26]. The horizontal line in each plot denotes the average abandonment rate. Figure 6 suggests the following implications:

Abandoned sessions are shorter. Although this result is expected, we find that each measure of session length provides unique information. Figure 6(a) shows sessions shorter than 15 seconds are significantly more likely to be abandoned. The sharp inflection point may be due to automated failure of sessions that do not complete the initial buffering phase. Similarly, Figure 6(b) shows a sharp drop in abandonment rate for sessions with average flow duration longer than 1-3 seconds. Figures 6(c) and 6(d), both measures of flow count, show that sessions with more flows are less likely to be abandoned. Thus, each of these features provides information useful for detecting abandonment.

Network load increases the abandonment rate. Despite the low bitrate of video streams relative to the capacity of a cell (~500 kbps vs. 3-14 Mbps), we find there is a nearly linear relationship between various measures of RAN load and abandonment rate. For example, Figure 6(e) shows that the abandonment rate goes up by roughly 7% for each 10 active users in a sector, even though these resources are scheduled in a proportional fair manner every 2 ms [6]. This load relationship can also be seen in Figure 6(f), which shows that abandonment rate is highest during the peak load hours of the day and much lower during the off-peak hours. This effect can be explained by Figure 6(g), which shows that the abandonment rate begins to grow when aggregate cell uplink throughput is just 50 kbps, significantly less than the cell capacity. This is likely because even small amounts of uplink traffic can cause interference, and Figure 6(h) shows that abandonment rate decreases by 2% for each dB increase in the signal-to-interference ratio (E_c/I_o). Furthermore, Figures 6(i) and 6(j) show that the abandonment rate increases as RSSI and RSCP increase, contrary to the general belief that higher received power means a better user experience. These E_c/I_o, RSSI, and RSCP results strongly suggest that users with higher received power also experience more interference. Hence, user engagement in our data set is more limited by interference rather than poor coverage. In summary, these results suggest that measures a cellular operator takes to reduce per-sector load and interference will improve user engagement in a roughly linear manner.

Handovers increase the abandonment rate. Another important question for operators is whether cell handovers disrupt the user experience. Our results suggest that all handover types are correlated with a decrease in user engagement. Figure 6(k) shows that cells with soft handovers, which are "make-before-break" handovers, have significantly higher abandonment rates. This result is supported by Figure 6(l), which shows increase abandonment rates for non-integral mean active set values (i.e., sessions that incurred active set additions or deletions during soft handovers). These effects may be partially due to the RRC signalling required for handover. Figure 6(m) shows that when RRC signalling errors occur, abandonment rate increases as well.

Higher throughput does not always mean lower abandonment. Although measured throughput is often used as a proxy for network quality (*e.g.*, [14]), our results suggest higher average throughput does not always indicate lower abandonment. Figures 6(n) and 6(o) show that abandonment rate decreases as average TCP and RLC throughput increases up to a point. However, the abandonment rate is lowest at TCP throughput equal to the steady state streaming rate, and it grows for higher throughput values. This

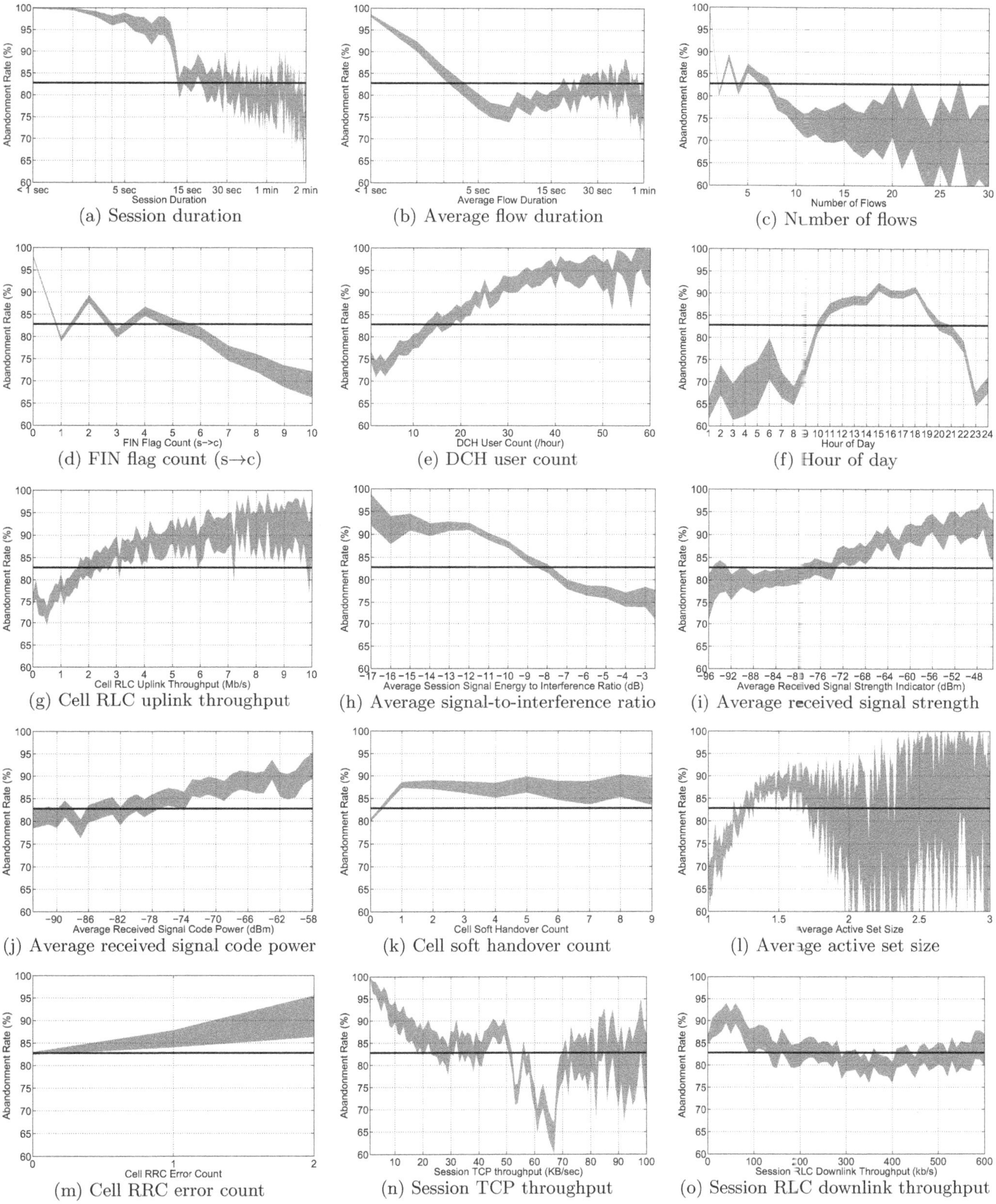

(a) Session duration (b) Average flow duration (c) Number of flows

(d) FIN flag count (s→c) (e) DCH user count (f) Hour of day

(g) Cell RLC uplink throughput (h) Average signal-to-interference ratio (i) Average received signal strength

(j) Average received signal code power (k) Cell soft handover count (l) Average active set size

(m) Cell RRC error count (n) Session TCP throughput (o) Session RLC downlink throughput

Figure 6: Abandonment rate distributions. Shaded areas represent the 95% confidence interval.

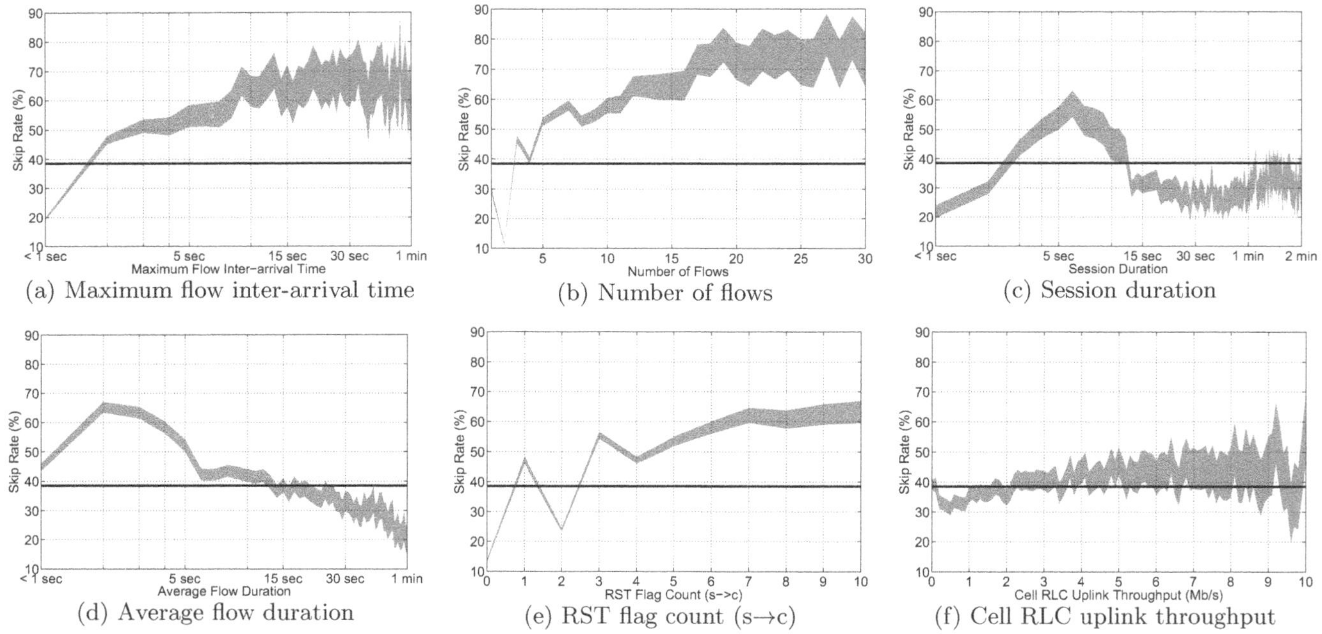

(a) Maximum flow inter-arrival time (b) Number of flows (c) Session duration (d) Average flow duration (e) RST flag count (s→c) (f) Cell RLC uplink throughput

Figure 7: Skip rate distributions. Shaded areas represent the 95% confidence interval.

pattern is because early abandonment, while the video is still in the non-rate-limited buffering phase, actually results in higher average throughput than watching a video through the rate-limited steady state phase.

In Figure 7, we plot the skip rate distributions of prominent features. The skip rate is defined as the fraction of sessions in the data set that are skipped. Due to space constraints, we only plot the skip rate curves for features that have different trends than the respective abandonment rate curves. The shaded areas represent the 95% confidence interval [26]. The horizontal line in these plots denotes the average skip rate.

We note that skip rate has a direct relationship with maximum flow inter-arrival time (Figure 7(a)) and number of flows (Figure 7(b)). This is likely because skips result in more flows and larger gaps between them. Skip rate peaks at session and flow durations of just a few seconds (Figures 7(c) and 7(d)), suggesting that users chose to skip early in a session, either due to network issues or lack of interest. Figure 7(e) shows larger RST flag count correlated with higher skip rate likely because skips cause connection resets. These contrasting patterns imply that it is more challenging to measure both skips and abandonment than a single engagement metric.

4. MODELING USER ENGAGEMENT

In this section, we develop models to accurately predict user engagement using only standard radio network statistics and/or TCP/IP header information.

4.1 Background and Problem Statement

Network operators would like to predict user engagement for three main applications. First, directly estimating these metrics from network traffic requires cost-prohibitive collection of sensitive data (requiring deep-packet-inspection) beyond TCP/IP headers. Thus, cost and privacy concerns would be alleviated with a model that accurately predicts these engagement metrics using only standard radio network statistics and/or TCP/IP header information that is already collected. A simple and efficient model would be able to monitor video engagement metrics over an entire network in real-time to facilitate trending and alarming applications. Second, self-organizing networks [1] (SON) enable mobile networks to adapt resource allocation dynamically. Thus, the ability to accurately predict video abandonment early in a video session can help guide SONs to provide more resources to the most vulnerable sessions. Third, an interpretable model that relates network factors to user engagement metrics can help network operators in prioritizing infrastructure upgrades by identifying the combination of factors that need to be adjusted for improving engagement.

Our goal is to jointly use the available features to accurately model both nominal and continuous measures of user engagement (defined in Section 2). Moreover, we want our models to make the prediction decisions as early as possible in a video session. Therefore, we define the modeling problem as follows: *given the feature set computed over the initial τ seconds ($\tau \leq \mathbf{t}$) of a video session, predict the user engagement metric.*

4.2 Proposed Approach

As we observed in Section 3, many network features are not independent of each other and the relationships among them can be non-linear. Therefore, modeling user engagement given all available features is a non-trivial prediction task. Furthermore, our modeling approach should answer pertinent questions such as: Which features are more useful for prediction? How many features do we need to reap a substantial accuracy gain?

To address these challenges, we use a machine learning approach for modeling the complex relationships between network features and user engagement metrics. The choice of learning algorithm is crucial to successfully modeling feature interdependence and non-linearity. After some pilot experiments, we found that decision tree algorithms with bootstrap aggregation (or bagging) [27] work well for both nominal (classification) and continuous (regression) user engagement metrics. Other commonly used Bayes and linear regression algorithms were outperformed by the decision tree algorithms in our pilot experiments. Decision trees do not require feature independence assumption and can handle non-linearities by employing multiple splits/breaks for each feature. Furthermore, decision tree models comprise of simple if-then-else branches, which can process data efficiently. For our experiments, we used C4.5 decision tree algorithm [17] and M5P regression tree algorithm [18].

4.3 Experimental Setup

We evaluate the effectiveness of classification models in terms of the following standard Receiver Operating Characteristic (ROC) metrics [11]: (1) True Positives (TP), (2) True Negatives (TN), (3) False Positives (FP), and (4) False Negatives (FN). We summarize the classification results in terms of the following ROC metrics: True positive rate $= \frac{|TP|}{|TP|+|FN|}$, False positive rate $= \frac{|FP|}{|FP|+|TN|}$, and Accuracy $= \frac{|TP|+|TN|}{|TP|+|TN|+|FP|+|FN|}$. We also plot the standard ROC threshold curves in our evaluation. An ideal ROC threshold curve approaches the top-left corner corresponding to 100% true positive rate and 0% false alarm rate. The Area Under Curve (AUC $\in [0,1]$) metric summarizes the classification effectiveness of an ROC threshold curve, where the AUC values approaching 1 indicate better accuracy. Besides, we evaluate the effectiveness of regression models in terms of the standard root-mean-square error (RMSE $\in [0,1]$) metric.

To avoid class imbalance and over-fitting during model training, we use k-fold cross-validation with class resampling [27]. In our pilot experiments, different values of k yielded very similar results. All experimental results reported in this paper are presented for $k = 10$. Furthermore, we evaluate the feature sets on varying initial time window sizes: $\tau = \mathbf{t}$ (*i.e.*, use all available data), $\tau \leq 60$ seconds, and $\tau \leq 10$ seconds. We expect the classification accuracy to degrade for smaller initial time windows.

We separately evaluate the core network feature set (abbreviated as **CN**), the radio network feature set (abbreviated as **RAN**), and the combined feature set (abbreviated as **All**). The radio network and core network features are separately grouped because they require different types of instrumentation. Recall from Section 2, measuring radio network features requires instrumentation at RNCs and measuring core network features requires instrumentation at Gn interfaces in a cellular network.

4.4 Evaluation

Our experimental results demonstrate that the proposed machine learning model can predict both video abandonment and skips with high accuracy using only the initial 10 seconds of a session, while meeting the constraints of network operators. We find that although some features are more useful than the rest for prediction, using all available features results in significant accuracy gain as compared to using only a few top features. Moreover, our decision and regression tree models are interpretable; they inform us about the relative usefulness of features by ordering them at different tree levels and we can understand the specific set of network conditions that impact user engagement by following each path in the tree. Many of these conditions can be influenced by a network operator, and thus provide guidance on how to improve user engagement in different situations.

Table 2: Accuracy of 4-way classification

Feature Set	`completed non-ski.` (%)	`abandoned non-ski.` (%)	`completed skipped` (%)	`abandoned skipped` (%)	Avg. (%)
$\tau = \mathbf{t}$					
CN	72.0	78.4	76.2	73.4	75.0
RAN	64.1	53.7	73.2	55.7	61.7
All	73.1	77.8	77.4	74.4	**75.7**
$\tau \leq 60$ seconds					
CN	69.5	62.7	63.8	64.6	65.2
RAN	62.6	47.8	58.5	57.0	56.5
All	70.4	63.7	65.7	65.4	**66.3**
$\tau \leq 10$ seconds					
CN	69.5	59.6	63.3	65.3	64.4
RAN	60.5	46.6	59.0	57.4	55.9
All	69.6	60.7	64.9	65.5	**65.2**

Next we present detailed results for both classification and regression. For classification, we build decision tree models to predict both individual classes and their combinations. For individual classes, we train the decision tree algorithm for 4-way classification. By combining classes, we change the granularity at which the model predicts user engagement. We use the following two class pairs: `completed` vs. `abandoned` and `completed, non-skipped` vs. `rest`. For combined classes, we train the decision tree algorithm for 2-way classification. Naturally, we expect better accuracy for 2-way classification than 4-way classification because the model is trained at a coarser granularity.

For 4-way classification, we observe that the core network feature set outperforms the radio network feature set. Combining the core and radio network feature sets improves the average accuracy. In Table 2, we observe the best average accuracy of 75.7% for the combined feature set at $\tau = \mathbf{t}$ seconds. In practice, improvement in accuracy means that fewer sessions need to be measured before the network operator can be confident that a real change in user engagement has occurred and an alarm can be raised. For a cell sector serving only a handful of users simultaneously, this can mean a significant reduction in time to detection of issues since video sessions may not be frequent. For the combined feature set, ROC threshold curves are plotted in Figure 8(a). The ordering of ROC curves conforms with the class-wise accuracy results in Table 2. The best operating accuracy of 77.8% is observed for `abandoned, non-skipped` class, which corresponds to 95.5% AUC. As expected, in Table 2 we observe that the average accuracy degrades for smaller values of τ. We observe the best average accuracy of 65.2% for the combined feature set at $\tau \leq 10$ seconds, representing more than 10% accuracy reduction as compared to $\tau = \mathbf{t}$ seconds.

Since operators may only be interested in predicting video abandonment, it is also important to build models to accurately predict `completed` vs. `abandoned` and `completed, non-skipped` vs. `rest` class pairs (instead of all four classes). These class pairs compare the scenarios when users either abandon or skip the video streaming session. Table 3 presents the classification results for these two class pairs. As expected, we observe significant improvement in accuracy for both class pairs as compared to 4-way classification due to reduced number of classes. Moreover, we observe that the average accuracy suffers only minor degradation (less than 5%) as τ is reduced. For `completed` vs. `abandoned` class pair, we observe the best average accuracy of

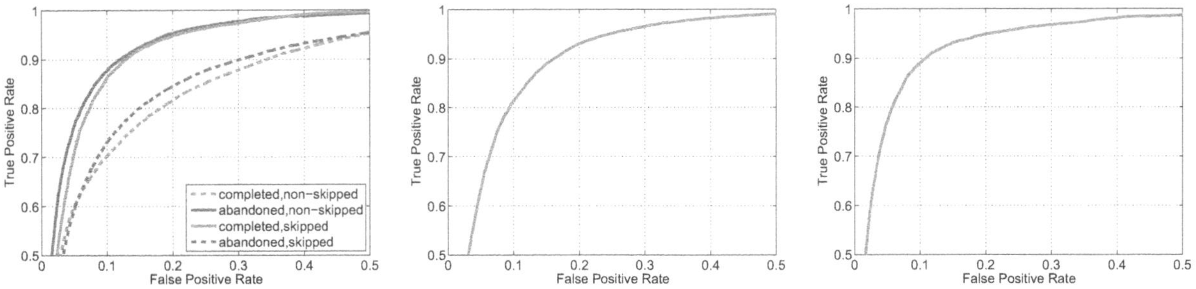

(a) 4-way (b) `completed` vs. `abandoned` (c) `completed, non-skip.` vs. `rest`

Figure 8: ROC threshold plots for various class pairs

Table 3: Accuracy of `completed` vs. `abandoned` and `completed, non-skipped` vs. `rest` classification

Feature Set	comp. (%)	abandoned (%)	Avg. (%)	completed, non-ski. (%)	rest (%)	Avg. (%)
$\tau = \mathbf{t}$						
CN	80.5	85.9	83.2	77.2	92.3	**88.5**
RAN	73.9	77.9	75.9	71.9	88.8	84.5
All	80.5	86.5	**83.5**	76.9	92.4	**88.5**
$\tau \leq 60$ seconds						
CN	79.5	82.1	**80.8**	78.0	91.5	**88.1**
RAN	74.1	78.4	76.3	72.7	88.4	84.4
All	78.8	82.6	80.7	77.6	91.4	88.0
$\tau \leq 10$ seconds						
CN	79.6	80.7	**80.1**	77.1	90.7	**87.3**
RAN	74.2	78.9	76.5	73.2	89.2	85.1
All	77.8	82.1	79.9	76.6	90.7	87.2

83.5% for the combined feature set at $\tau = \mathbf{t}$ seconds. For the combined feature set, the ROC threshold curve is plotted in Figure 8(b), which corresponds to 93.4% AUC. For `completed, non-skipped` vs. `rest` class pair, we observe the best average accuracy of 88.5% for the combined feature set at $\tau = \mathbf{t}$ seconds. For the combined feature set, the ROC threshold curve is plotted in Figure 8(c), which corresponds to 95.1% AUC.

For regression, we build regression tree models to predict video download completion. Overall, we observe similar patterns across feature sets and varying initial window sizes for regression results as observed for classification results earlier. Table 4 presents the results of M5P regression tree algorithm and a simple linear regression algorithm. We note that M5P regression tree algorithm consistently outperforms the simple linear regression algorithm, indicating that M5P can successfully capture the non-linear dependencies between features and video download completion that are not modeled by the simple linear regression algorithm. RMSE is lower for larger τ values, and **All** feature set has the lowest RMSE as compared to individual **CN** and **RAN** feature sets. We observe the best RMSE of 0.14 for $\tau = \mathbf{t}$ and **All** feature set.

4.5 Discussion

How many features to use? Our evaluation highlighted that using all features together results in better classification/regression accuracy than using their subsets. To systematically analyze the utility of adding features to the classification/regression model, we plot accuracy versus feature set size for `completed` vs. `abandoned` classification in Figure 9. Towards this end, we iteratively rank the feature set using the following greedy approach: for k^{th} iteration, we evaluate the accuracy gain of the model by separately adding candidate features and selecting the $k+1^{th}$ feature which provides the best accuracy. The top features are related to session size and TCP throughput which we believe are correlated with user engagement, as sufficient throughput is required for video streaming and abandonment results in low volume sessions. The plot shows that a few top features provide most of the accuracy gain. However, the gains in accuracy we achieve from including 5% to 100% of features are not diminishing. Thus, it makes sense to use all available features because the computational overheads of feature extraction and testing for additional features is low (in order of milliseconds).

Actionable insights. The decision/regression tree models also provide actionable insights. The pruned versions of the

Table 4: Root-mean-square error of regression

Feature Set	Linear Regression	M5P Regression Tree
$\tau = \mathbf{t}$		
CN	0.25	0.15
RAN	0.30	0.27
All	0.23	**0.14**
$\tau \leq 60$ seconds		
CN	0.27	0.18
RAN	0.36	0.34
All	0.24	**0.17**
$\tau \leq 10$ seconds		
CN	0.29	0.22
RAN	0.37	0.34
All	0.28	**0.21**

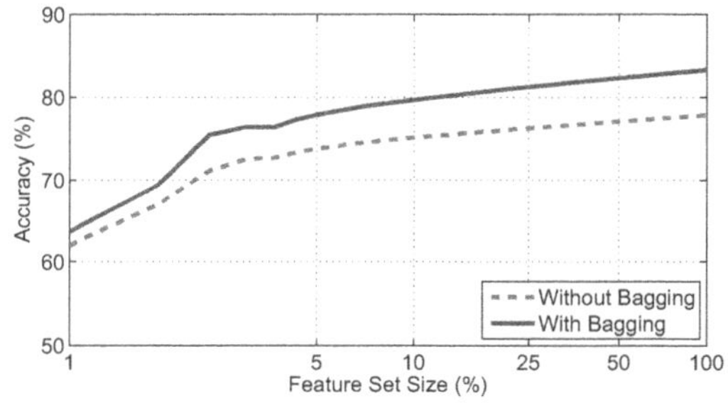

Figure 9: Accuracy vs. feature set size for `completed` vs. `abandoned` classification

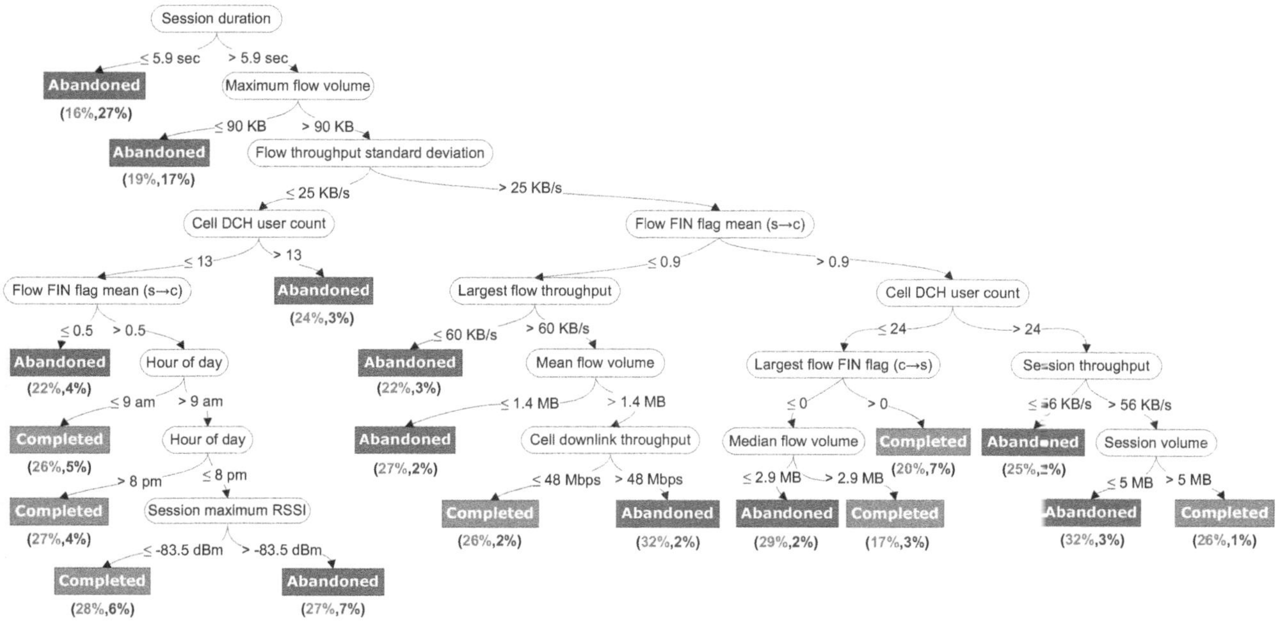

(a) C4.5 decision tree model for `completed` vs. `abandoned` class pair

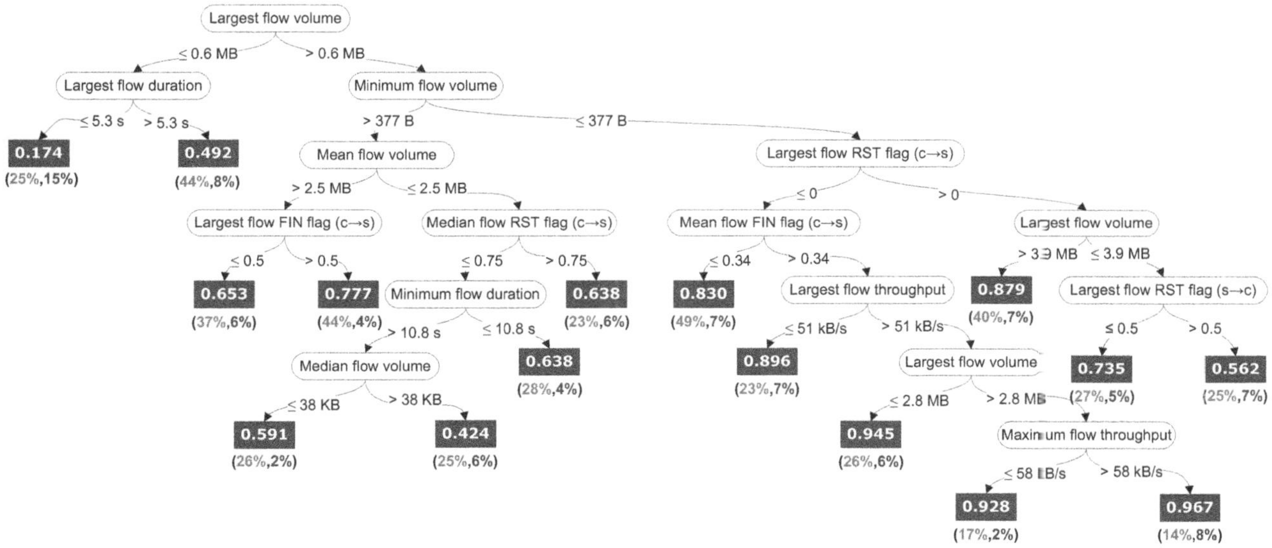

(b) M5P regression tree model for video download completion

Figure 10: Pruned decision and regression tree models for $\tau \leq 10$ seconds using All feature set. The tuples below leaf nodes represent (error%,population size%).

decision tree model for `completed` vs. `abandoned` class pair and the regression tree model for video download completion are plotted in Figures 10(a) and (b), respectively. The tuples below the rectangular leaf nodes represent their error and population size. Due to space constraints, we only plot the tree models for $\tau \leq 10$ seconds which are useful for network operators to predict user engagement by observing only the initial 10 seconds of video streaming sessions.

From the model, network operators can identify network factors that may have the most impact on user engagement and make decisions to prioritize certain infrastructure upgrades. The features at the higher levels of a tree tend to have more distinguishing power and account for more population size than lower level features. The root node is session duration for Figure 10(a) and largest flow volume in Figure 10(b). However, it is noteworthy that the ordering of network factors in Figure 10 does not strictly determine their importance. First, trees shown in Figure 10 represent one of many candidate tree models generated during bagging – other candidate trees have different feature ordering. Second, these features are not independent – session duration and maximum flow volume (top two features in Figure 10(a)) jointly account for session throughput and largest flow throughput to some extent.

The paths from the root node to leaves represent the equivalent rule sets, which inform network operators of the interdependence among multiple features. For the regression tree in Figure 10(b), if largest flow volume is ≤ 0.6 MB and largest flow duration is ≤ 5.3 seconds then video download completion prediction is 17.4%. In contrast, if largest flow volume is ≤ 0.6 MB and largest flow duration is > 5.3 seconds then video download completion prediction is increased to 49.2%. Moreover, for the decision tree in Figure 10(a), if session duration > 5.9 seconds and maximum flow volume is ≤ 90 KB after the first 10 seconds then our model predicts that the video session will be abandoned with 19% error probability.

A network operator can influence many network factors to improve user engagement. The feature splits in Figure 10 provide network operators actionable insights for this purpose. For example, the decision tree predicts a session to be abandoned if cell DCH user count is larger than a threshold under certain conditions. Most cellular network users are covered by multiple cell sectors, and handover algorithms use signal quality and sector load to determine which sector each user should receive data from. The thresholds used for handover are typically fixed at a single global value. However, the feature splits in Figure 10(a) suggest that the network operator can tolerate a higher cell sector load threshold for sessions with higher throughput variance than sessions with lower throughput variance (24 vs. 13 users occupying DCH channels).

Limitations. Below, we discuss the limitations of our analysis and results. First, our results are based on traces from a single video service provider that uses progressive download with byte-range requests. Therefore, our findings may not be representative of video service providers that use other streaming methods. Second, our user engagement model cannot differentiate between video abandonment due to network-related issues and due to lack of user interest. Distinguishing between these two cases requires either client- or server-side information, which is not available to network operators.

5. RELATED WORK

Prior related studies can be categorized based on whether they use network-side or user-side instrumentation.

5.1 Network-side Instrumentation

Our study builds upon previous work by Gill *et al.* [14], Finamore *et al.* [12], and Erman *et al.* [10]. Each of these studies characterized the abandonment rate of video streaming sessions by collecting passive network traces at a campus edge network, 5 different wired edge locations, and a cellular network, respectively. To estimate video quality, these studies use deep-packet-inspection techniques (*e.g.*, [20]) to understand the video provider protocol. Our finding that 77% of video sessions are not completely streamed is closest to Finamore's result (80%), whereas Gill and Erman found lower abandonment rates (50% and 60%, respectively). All these results indicate that abandonment rates are high. Based on the ratio of download rate to encoding bitrate of video, Gill *et al.* concluded that approximately 20% of the video streaming sessions were interrupted due to poor performance. However, we find that average throughput is not always a good indicator of abandonment rate.

Our work makes two significant contributions on top of these studies. First, in order to measure abandonment, previous studies relied on deep-packet-inspection to extract information beyond TCP/IP headers, which requires prohibitive computational resources to employ at the scale of network carriers and can pose privacy problems in practice. Our work demonstrates that we can accurately measure abandonment without such information. Second, these studies did not provide insight into how network characteristics and performance impact abandonment rates. Our study is the first to examine the relationship between mobile network factors and user engagement and the first to provide guidance on how operators can reduce video abandonment.

5.2 Client-side Instrumentation

In [19], Rao *et al.* conducted an active measurement study of video streaming traffic from YouTube and Netflix. They proposed models to express various properties of completed and interrupted video streaming traffic as a function of the video parameters. However, the authors did not study user engagement because this work is based on active measurement data.

Dobrian *et al.* conducted a large scale, passive, user-side study to understand the impact of video streaming quality on user engagement [9]. They used video player instrumentation to quantify video streaming quality metrics such as join time, buffering ratio, average bitrate, rendering quality, and rate of buffering. Their analysis showed that buffering ratio has the largest impact on user engagement for non-live content and average bitrate significantly impacts user engagement for live content. Krishnan and Sitaraman also conducted a large scale, passive, user-side study to understand the impact of video streaming quality on user engagement [15]. They quantified the impact of video streaming quality metrics on user engagement using quasi-experimental designs. In [7,8], Balachandran *et al.* developed a QoE model using various user-side video quality metrics. Specifically, they developed a decision tree based machine learning model to predict the extent of the video watched by users. For the two-class problem (completed vs. interrupted/abandoned), their trained model achieved up to 70% accuracy which progressively decreases as the number of classes is increased.

While these studies analyzed user engagement using data collected via video player instrumentation, our work focuses on characterizing and modeling user engagement using network-side measurements. Modeling user engagement using network-side data is particularly important for network operators because they do not have access to video player instrumentation data. Interestingly, our model based on network-side data can predict whether a user completely downloads a video with more than 87% accuracy, which is significantly better than the client-side model developed by Balachandran *et al.* Furthermore, since our model does not require client-side instrumentation, it can be used by any network operator, not just the video content provider.

6. CONCLUSIONS

This paper represents the first characterization of mobile video streaming performance and models its impact on user engagement from the perspective of network operators. We observed that many network features exhibit strong correlation with abandonment rate and skip rate. Our proposed model achieved more than 87% accuracy by observing only the initial 10 seconds of video streaming sessions. Overall, we conclude that the proposed model based on standard radio network statistics and/or TCP/IP header information can be successfully used by network operators to predict video abandonment. Our model is useful for network operators to continuously monitor at scale to proactively mitigate the factors that can adversely impact user engagement.

In future, we plan to evaluate our proposed model on other types of networks (*e.g.*, DSL, WiFi). Recall from our evaluations that the core network feature set alone can provide most of the accuracy gain. Towards this end, we can reuse the core network feature set, which is not specific to cellular network infrastructure.

Acknowledgements

We thank our shepherd, Ranveer Chandra, and the anonymous reviewers for their useful feedback on this paper.

7. REFERENCES

[1] 3GPP Self-Organizing Networks. http://www.3gpp.org/SON.

[2] Multi-Resolution Land Characterization (MRLC) consortium, National Land Cover Database 2006 (NLCD 2006). `http://www.mrlc.gov/nlcd2006.php`.

[3] RFC 2046, Multipurpose Internet Mail Extensions (MIME) Part Two: Media Types. `http://tools.ietf.org/html/rfc2046`.

[4] U.S. Geological Survey, National Elevation Dataset. `http://ned.usgs.gov/`.

[5] Cisco Visual Networking Index: Global Mobile Data Traffic Forecast Update 2012–2017. Technical report, Cisco, 2013.

[6] V. Aggarwal, R. Jana, K. Ramakrishnan, J. Pang, and N. Shankaranarayanan. Characterizing fairness for 3G wireless networks. In *IEEE LANMAN*, 2011.

[7] A. Balachandran, V. Sekar, A. Akella, S. Seshan, I. Stoica, and H. Zhang. A quest for an internet video quality-of-experience metric. In *11th ACM Workshop on Hot Topics in Networks (HotNets-IX)*, 2012.

[8] A. Balachandran, V. Sekar, A. Akella, S. Seshan, I. Stoica, and H. Zhang. Developing a predictive model of quality of experience for internet video. In *ACM SIGCOMM*, 2013.

[9] F. Dobrian, V. Sekar, A. Awan, I. Stoica, D. Joseph, A. Ganjam, J. Zhan, and H. Zhang. Understanding the impact of video quality on user engagement. In *ACM SIGCOMM*, 2011.

[10] J. Erman, A. Gerber, K. Ramakrishnan, S. Sen, and O. Spatscheck. Over the top video: The gorilla in cellular networks. In *ACM IMC*, 2011.

[11] T. Fawcett. ROC Graphs: Notes and Practical Considerations for Researchers. Technical report, HP Laboratories, 2004.

[12] A. Finamore, M. Mellia, M. Munafo, R. Torres, and S. R. Rao. YouTube Everywhere: Impact of Device and Infrastructure Synergies on User Experience. In *ACM IMC*, 2011.

[13] J. Fry, G. Xian, S. Jin, J. Dewitz, C. Homer, L. Yang, C. Barnes, N. Herold, and J. Wickham. Completion of the 2006 National Land Cover Database for the Conterminous United States. *Photogrammetric Engineering & Remote Sensing (PE&RS)*, 77(9):858–864, 2011.

[14] P. Gill, M. Arlitt, Z. Li, and A. Mahanti. YouTube Traffic Characterization: A View From the Edge. In *ACM IMC*, 2007.

[15] S. S. Krishnan and R. K. Sitaraman. Video stream quality impacts viewer behavior: Inferring causality using quasi-experimental designs. In *ACM IMC*, 2012.

[16] Z. Li, J. Lin, M.-I. Akodjenou, G. Xie, M. A. Kaafar, Y. Jin, and G. Peng. Watching videos from everywhere: a study of the PPTV mobile VoD system. In *ACM IMC*, 2012.

[17] J. R. Quinlan. *C4.5: programs for machine learning.* Morgan Kaufmann, 1993.

[18] R. J. Quinlan. Learning with continuous classes. In *5th Australian Joint Conference on Artificial Intelligence*, 1992.

[19] A. Rao, Y. sup Lim, C. Barakat, A. Legout, D. Towsley, and W. Dabbous. Network characteristics of video streaming traffic. In *ACM CoNEXT*, 2011.

[20] R. Schatz, T. Hobfeld, and P. Casas. Passive YouTube QoE Monitoring for ISPs. In *Sixth International Conference on Innovative Mobile and Internet Services in Ubiquitous Computing (IMIS)*, 2012.

[21] M. Z. Shafiq, L. Ji, A. X. Liu, J. Pang, S. Venkataraman, and J. Wang. A first look at cellular network performance during crowded events. In *ACM SIGMETRICS*, 2013.

[22] M. Z. Shafiq, L. Ji, A. X. Liu, J. Pang, and J. Wang. Characterizing geospatial dynamics of application usage in a 3G cellular data network. In *IEEE INFOCOM*, 2012.

[23] M. Z. Shafiq, L. Ji, A. X. Liu, J. Pang, and J. Wang. A first look at cellular machine-to-machine traffic - large scale measurement and characterization. In *ACM SIGMETRICS/Performance*, 2012.

[24] M. Z. Shafiq, L. Ji, A. X. Liu and J. Wang. Characterizing and modeling Internet traffic dynamics of cellular devices. In *ACM SIGMETRICS*, 2011.

[25] L. Song and J. Shen, editors. *Evolved Cellular Network Planning and Optimization for UMTS and LTE.* CRC Press, 2010.

[26] E. B. Wilson. Probable inference, the law of succession, and statistical inference. *Journal of the American Statistical Association*, 22(158):209–212, 1927.

[27] I. H. Witten, E. Frank, and M. A. Hall. *Data Mining: Practical Machine Learning Tools and Techniques.* Morgan Kaufmann, 2011.

Error Estimating Codes for Insertion and Deletion Channels

Jiwei Huang
Department of Computer Science and Technology
Tsinghua University
Beijing, China
huangjw05@gmail.com

Sen Yang
School of Electrical and Computer Engineering
Georgia Institute of Technology
Atlanta, GA, USA
sen.yang@gatech.edu

Ashwin Lall
Department of Math and Computer Science
Denison University
Granville, OH, USA
lalla@denison.edu

Justin Romberg
School of Electrical and Computer Engineering
Georgia Institute of Technology
Atlanta, GA, USA
jrom@ece.gatech.edu

Jun (Jim) Xu
School of Computer Science
Georgia Institute of Technology
Atlanta, GA, USA
jx@cc.gatech.edu

Chuang Lin
Department of Computer Science and Technology
Tsinghua University
Beijing, China
chlin@tsinghua.edu.cn

ABSTRACT

Error estimating codes (EEC) have recently been proposed for measuring the bit error rate (BER) in packets transmitted over wireless links. They however can provide such measurements only when there are no insertion and deletion errors, which could occur in various wireless network environments. In this work, we propose "idEEC", the first technique that can do so even in the presence of insertion and deletion errors. We show that idEEC is provable robust under most bit insertion and deletion scenarios, provided insertion/deletion errors occur with much lower probability than bit flipping errors. Our idEEC design can build upon any existing EEC scheme. The basic idea of the idEEC encoding is to divide the packet into a number of segments, each of which is encoded using the underlying EEC scheme. The basic idea of the idEEC decoding is to divide the packet into a few slices in a randomized manner – each of which may contain several segments – and then try to identify a slice that has no insertion and deletion errors in it (called a "clean slice"). Once such a clean slice is found, it is removed from the packet for later processing, and this "randomized divide and search" procedure will be iteratively performed on the rest of the packet until no more clean slices can be found. The BER will then be estimated from all the clean slices discovered through all the iterations. A careful analysis of the accuracy guarantees of the idEEC decoding is provided, and the efficacy of idEEC is further validated by simulation experiments.

SIGMETRICS'14, June 16–20, 2014, Austin, Texas, USA.
Copyright 2014 ACM 978-1-4503-2789-3/14/06 ...$15.00.
http://dx.doi.org/10.1145/2591971.2591976.

Categories and Subject Descriptors

E.4 [**Coding and Information Theory**]: Error control codes; C.2.1 [**Computer-Communication Networks**]: Network Architecture and Design - Wireless communication

General Terms

Algorithms, Theory

Keywords

Error Estimating Coding, Insertion Channel, Deletion Channel

1. INTRODUCTION

Recently, there has been a series of works on designing error estimating codes, that is, estimating the bit error rate (BER) in packets transmitted over wireless networks [2, 5, 6]. The basic idea of such codes is to have the transmitter send a small error estimating codeword of $O(\log(n))$ bits along with a packet n bits long, which allows the receiver to decode the information and estimate the number of bits in the packet flipped during the transmission (i.e., the BER). Such codes are in general stronger – and a bit more expensive – than error detection codes, which inform whether or not there are bit errors, but weaker – and much less expensive – than the error correction codes.

The aforementioned techniques, however, can provide such estimations only when there are no insertion and deletion errors. None of them will work even if a single bit is inserted or deleted for the following reason. In all existing error estimating coding (EEC) schemes, a sub-codeword is computed as a function of a subset of bits sampled from the packet as identified by their indices, i.e., their positions in the packet relative to the beginning of the packet. If there are one or more insertion and deletion errors, a very different set of bits will be sampled and hence a very different sub-codeword computed from them. In wireless network applications EEC schemes are designed for, however, insertion and deletion error may occur due to factors such as imperfect synchronization between a transmitter and a receiver, or uneven propagation delays to successive bits in a packet (e.g., due to the movement of a transmitter or receiver). Therefore, for existing EEC schemes to be widely applicable in various wireless network environments, it is important that they are enhanced to work over insertion/deletion channels. However, this appears an extremely difficult task, and readers will appreciate this difficulty when we describe in Sec. 2.

In this work, we make an attempt at filling this gap and propose error estimating codes for the insertion and deletion channels, called "idEEC". More specifically, our idEEC scheme allows for the estimation of the number of bit flipping errors in a packet despite the existence of bit insertions and deletions. Our idEEC scheme can build upon any existing EEC scheme, and its encoding efficiency (i.e., code density) is proportional to that of the underlying EEC scheme. For the purpose of describing how idEEC works – which is the main thrust of this paper – however, we pick the plain vanilla tug-of-war sketch [1] as the underlying EEC, even though its encoding efficiency is worse than the two most recent EEC schemes, namely EToW and gEEC [5, 6], for two reasons. First, the encoding efficiency of Tug-of-War (ToW) is worse than that of EToW and gEEC by only a constant factor, and is still asymptotically optimal. Second, the encoding and decoding algorithms of ToW, which idEEC must "interface" with, are much simpler than that of EToW and gEEC. Building idEEC upon ToW allows us to focus on describing the encoding and decoding algorithms (for withstanding insertion/deletion errors) of idEEC and their mathematical analyses, without being entangled into additional mathematical and algorithmic details involved in "interfacing" with more efficient but mathematically sophisticated EEC schemes such as EToW and gEEC, and risking diluting the main thrust of this paper.

We describe here the basic idea behind idEEC encoding (at the transmitter) and decoding (at the receiver) algorithms, deferring readers to Sec. 3 for details. We assume that, during the transmission, no more than a total of ϕ insertion and deletion errors may occur to the packet. This ϕ is usually a small number (say no more than 10) in the aforementioned wireless applications. The encoding algorithm is very simple. A packet is first divided into a number of segments, and an EEC codeword for each segment is computed. The number of segments needed for accurate BER estimation is in general no more than an order of magnitude larger than ϕ. The idEEC codeword is simply these EEC codewords pieced together, and will be further protected by error detection or correction codes against one or two insertion/deletion errors and a small number of bit flipping errors that may occur to the EEC codeword [4]. Since adding this protection will only increase the size of an idEEC codeword by a small constant factor, it will not affect the asymptotic space complexity of the idEEC.

The decoding algorithm – for inferring the number of flipping errors from the packet and its idEEC codeword – at the receiver's end is more involved. Suppose the actual number of insertion and deletion errors are ϕ. The basic idea of the algorithm is to uniformly randomly insert or delete ϕ or (slightly) more "phantom" bits along the segment boundaries in the packet. These phantom insertions and deletions are intended to partially "cancel out" the actual insertions and deletions that occur to the packet during the transmission, and the uniform randomization is needed for this partial cancellation to be provably robust under all bit insertion and deletion scenarios, with high probability. The "bit-stuffed" packet will then be divided into at least $\phi+1$ slices by the positions (at least ϕ of them as explained earlier) at which the phantom insertions or deletions occur. Each slice may contain one to several segments. It can be proved that no insertion or deletion happens to at least one out of these slices, which we call a "clean slice". In other words, in a clean slice, the index of every bit, relative to beginning of the "bit-stuffed" packet, is equal to a constant (could be 0) plus that relative to the beginning of the original packet.

Our decoding algorithm then searches for and removes such a clean slice from the packet. A clean slice can be found by shifting the "bit-stuffed" packet around, computing the EEC codewords for the shifted slice, and comparing them with the EEC codeword for the slice in the original packet (equal to the sum of EEC codewords for the segments that the slice consists of). Once a clean slice is found, it is removed from the "bit-stuffed" packet, and this "randomized slicing and shift-and-compare" procedure will be performed on the rest iteratively to identify more clean slices, until these ϕ insertion and deletions errors are localized to within roughly ϕ "dirty slices", each of which ideally contains only a single "dirty segment". The number of bit errors in the original packet can then be estimated from the bit errors that occur in all the clean slices discovered through the above iterative procedure, under a very mild assumption on the fluctuations of bit flipping error rates across the original packet. Note the randomizations performed in these iterations are mutually independent, allowing us to establish accuracy guarantees of our estimation procedure as rigorously as possible.

For a packet n bits long, the encoding overhead of the idEEC is $O(\phi \log(n))$, where $O(\log(n))$ is the encoding overhead of the underlying EEC (ToW in our case). Therefore, asymptotically we are paying only a multiplicative factor of ϕ for making idEEC robust against insertion and deletion errors. We are able to make this encoding overhead so small because an idEEC codeword needs to help us localize an insertion and deletion error only to the segment rather than to the very bit position where it occurs, as in the error correction codes for the insertion and deletion channels [4, 9, 11]. The computational complexity of idEEC decoding is $O(\phi^2\Lambda)$, where Λ is computational complexity of decoding the underlying EEC codewords. This multiplicative factor of ϕ^2 is tolerable when ϕ is quite small (< 10) as in the aforementioned communication applications. Furthermore, when there are only insertions or only deletions, this computational complexity decreases to $O(\phi\Lambda)$, for a clean slice can be found without shifting the "bit-stuffed" packet around in such a situation, as we will show in Sec. 3.

Note that even if the transmitted and the received packets (i.e., bit strings) were placed side-by-side, it is not possible to say with certainty how many insertion, deletion, and substitution errors occur respectively that results in the difference between the two strings. For one thing, it could be impossible to distinguish a substitution error from that caused by a pair of insertion and deletion. However, under mild assumptions such as that insertions and deletions happen with very low probabilities, it can be proven that the "simplest" explanation for this difference – as implied by the calculation of the edit distance between the two strings [8] – is also the most likely and with high probability equal to the ground truth. Therefore, by comparing the estimates of substitution/flipping errors with that implied by the edit distance between the two strings in our evaluations of idEEC, we are not distorting the ground truth in any significant way.

The remainder of this paper is organized as follows. In Sec. 2 we discuss the background and related work most pertinent to this paper. In Sec. 3, we propose the EEC scheme for insertion and deletion channels under homogeneous bit flipping model, and provide detailed corresponding analysis and estimator design. In Sec. 4, we generalize the scheme to heterogeneous bit error models. We evaluate the performance of the schemes experimentally in Sec. 5. Finally, we conclude the paper in Sec. 6.

2. BACKGROUND AND RELATED WORK

In this section, we introduce some background on insertion and deletion channels, and briefly survey the existing error correction codes for such channels. We describe prior approaches for solving bit error rate (BER) estimation problems, and demonstrate the difficulty of doing so in insertion and deletion channels.

2.1 Error Correcting Codes for Insertion and Deletion Channels

Channels that allow insertions and deletions as well as substitution (i.e., bit flipping) errors enjoy a long and rich history, and are remarkably challenging. Insertion and deletion errors do occur in various wireless network environments. For example, poor time synchronization between a sender and a receiver may lead to some bits (of a packet) being deleted, or some non-existing random bits being inserted [10]. While much progress on error correction codes for such insertion/deletion channels has been made in the past decade, a coding scheme with provably asymptotically optimal coding efficiency remains elusive thus far [10].

In most of the literatures on insertion and deletion channels, error correcting coding has been playing a key role. Some researchers started with the additional properties of the channels, and proposed 1-deletion / 1-insertion correcting codes. In [9], it has been assumed that there is a minimal gap between insertions and deletions, as many synchronization errors are due to small drifts in clock synchronization and a minimal amount of time is needed before the timing mismatch results in another bit error. They made a segmentation assumption that there is at most one insertion or deletion per segment (a contiguous chunk of a packet), which appears natural for many practical settings. In [4], Reed-Muller RM $(1, m)$ codes were studied and used for correcting substitution errors over channels in which a bit sampling error could cause a synchronization error (similar but not identical to an insertion/deletion error). This scheme can correct multiple substitution errors in the presence of one synchronization error. In [11], codes for correcting synchronization errors were designed, which were capable of correcting a certain number of synchronization errors, in the presence of one substitution error.

2.2 Error Estimating for Channels Without Insertion and Deletion Errors

While there has been much work on error correction codes, error estimating coding began to be studied only recently in the seminal work of Chen et al. [2]. The basic idea of this work [2] is for the transmitter to send along with a packet a set of parity-check bits, each of which is the exclusive-or of a group of bits randomly sampled from the packet. These parity equations are designed in such a way that, by counting how many of them are violated after the packet transmission, the receiver can estimate, with low relative error, this BER.

Hua et al. made further studies on error estimation coding in [5] and [6]. In [5], they used tug-of-war (ToW) sketch, which is a sketch data structure to estimate the L_2 norm of a data stream, for Hamming distance estimation. The ToW sketch of a bit array (packet) $\vec{b}$ consists of a set of sub-sketches, each of which is set to the inner product of $\vec{b}$ with a pre-defined pseudorandom vector $\vec{s}$. Upon the receipt of the transmitted bit array $\vec{b}'$ and the sketch, the receiver computes the inner product of $\vec{b}' \cdot \vec{s}$, takes the difference between it and that contained in the corresponding sub-sketches, and squares the result. Furthermore, they proved that even when approximation and randomization are allowed, the cost of BER estimation to achieve an (ϵ, δ)-approximation is $\Omega(\log(n))$, and EEC in [2] is therefore asymptotically optimal. They also showed however that EEC had not achieve the optimal tradeoff down to the constant factor, and proposed the *Enhanced Tug-of War* (EToW) sketch that attains a better constant factor. In [6], they present an information-theoretic study of EEC, stemming from the question whether EEC achieves the best tradeoff between the space and estimation accuracy, through the lens of Fisher information analysis. This analysis led to a new and better EEC scheme, called "gEEC", which could hold $25 - 35\%$ more information – and hence deliver better estimation accuracy – with the same coding overhead.

Though these approaches can all estimate the BER with good accuracies, they cannot handle insertion and deletion channels. This is because, when an insertion or deletion error occurs, certain parts of the packet will be shifted, and about half of these shifted – but correct – bits will be counted as substitution errors by existing EEC techniques. Our idEEC scheme, to be described next, is designed to fill this gap.

3. DESIGN AND ANALYSIS OF IDEEC UNDER HOMOGENEOUS BIT FLIPPING MODEL

This section describes the encoding and decoding algorithms of idEEC. Our goal is to estimate the number of bit flipping errors as accurately as possible, despite the presence of insertion and deletion errors. Here the estimator used in the decoding algorithm assumes that the flipping error happens to each bit independently and with an identical – but unknown – small probability $p << 1$. This model will be much relaxed later in Sec. 4. We further assume that the probability with which an insertion or deletion error occurs, referred to as p_e, is much smaller than the flipping error probability p. This is clearly a reasonable assumption since it would otherwise be impossible to distinguish between insertion/deletion errors and flipping errors. In the following, we will first give an overview of idEEC in Sec. 3.1, then describe the key routine of identifying a clean slice in Sec. 3.2, and finally present the detailed analysis of the accuracy of our estimations in Sec. 3.3.

3.1 Overview

Like in the Code Division Multiple Access (CDMA) literature, we view a '0' bit as symbol '-1', and a '1' bit as symbol '+1'. Then a packet $\vec{b}$ is modeled as a symbol vector of length n, with each symbol takes value in $\{-1, +1\}$. In idEEC encoding, the packet is first divided into m segments of equal lengths, say $\vec{b} = [\vec{b}_1, \vec{b}_2, \ldots, \vec{b}_m]$. For idEEC to be robust against insertion and deletion errors, m should be at least several times larger than the actual number of insertion and deletion errors, which is typically quite small, as explained before. For each segment $\vec{b}_i$, we generate its EEC codeword. Our idEEC codeword is simply these EEC codewords pieced together. Since this idEEC codeword itself may be subject to insertion/deletion and bit flipping errors during transmission, it needs to be protected by error detection or correction codes against such errors. Since the length of such error detection or correction codes will only be a fraction of that of the idEEC codeword, this extra protection will not increase the asymptotic coding overhead of the idEEC scheme. The details of our encoding scheme are given in Algorithm 2.

The procedures for encoding and decoding of a bit array $\vec{b}$ using plain vanilla tug-of-war sketch are illuminated in Algorithm 1. The ToW sketch consists of a constant number c of counters, each of which is generated by the inner product of $\vec{b}$ with a pre-defined pseudorandom vector $\vec{s}_j \in \{+1, -1\}^{|\vec{b}|}$. At the time of decoding, the receiver computes the inner products of the transmitted bit array

Algorithm 1 The tug-of-war sketch for EEC [5].

SKETCH–CREATION($\vec{b}$)

Input $\vec{b}$: original data bits vector.
Output $\vec{q}$: the sketch encoding $\vec{b}$.
pre-compute random vectors $\vec{s}_{j,1\le j\le c} : [|\vec{b}|] \rightarrow \{-1,1\}$
for $j = 1$ to c **do**
    $\vec{q}_j := (\vec{b} \cdot \vec{s}_j)/2$
return $\vec{q} = \langle \vec{q}_1, \ldots, \vec{q}_c \rangle$

DISTANCE–ESTIMATION($\vec{b}'$, $\vec{q}$)

Input $\vec{b}'$: received data bits vector, $\vec{q}$: received sketch.
Output $\hat{d}$: the estimated number of flipping error.
pre-compute random vectors $\vec{s}_{j,1\le j\le c} : [|\vec{b}|] \rightarrow \{-1,1\}$
for $j = 1$ to c **do**
    $X_j := (\vec{q}_j - \vec{b'} \cdot \vec{s}_j/2)^2$
return $\hat{d}$=average($X_1, \ldots, X_c$)

Algorithm 2 Encoding of idEEC.

Input: $\vec{b} = [\vec{b}_1, \vec{b}_2, \ldots, \vec{b}_m]$: original data bits vector.
Output: $\vec{z}$: the sketches encoding $\vec{b}$.
for $i = 1$ to m **do**
    $\vec{q}_i :=$ EEC.SKETCH-CREATION($\vec{b}_i$)
return $\vec{z} = \langle \vec{q}_1, \ldots, \vec{q}_m \rangle$

$\vec{b}'$ with $\vec{s}_j$, $j = 1, 2, ..., c$, takes the differences between the c inner products and the c counters respectively, and infer the hamming distance $\hat{d}$ between $\vec{b}$ and $\vec{b}'$ from these differences.

Upon the receipt of a packet $\vec{b}'$, the original (before any insertion/deletion) length of the packet l (sent along with the packet and could also be protected by the error correction or detection codes that protect the idEEC codeword), and the sketch $\vec{z}$, the receiver uses a iterative algorithm EST to estimate the BER during the transmission. The EST algorithm returns two values, namely $\hat{d}'$ and l', where $\hat{d}'$ denotes the estimated number of flipping errors in all the clean slices in which the idEEC decoder believes no insertion or deletion errors occur, and l' is the total length of these clean slices. Therefore, the number of flipping errors can be estimated by $\hat{d} = \hat{d}' \cdot \frac{l}{l'}$, and one can further obtain the BER estimation by $\hat{p} = \hat{d}/l$. The accuracy of this estimator will later be analyzed in Sec. 3.3. However, our algorithm may return "Failed" meaning that it is not able to provide an accurate estimate. There are two possible ways for this to happen. First, our algorithm may find that the number of insertions and deletions is larger than the pre-determined upper bound. Second, our algorithm may find that the number of flipping errors exceeds a pre-determined upper bound. In both situations, the idEEC decoder will inform us which situation causes it to "fail". The aforementioned decoding procedure of our idEEC scheme is shown in Algorithm 3. The detailed design and analysis of the iterative algorithm EST will be presented in the following sections.

The receiver views a packet as a "manifold", identifying the first bit of a packet with the bit immediately following the last bit. When cutting up packets into slices for decoding, the receiver will randomly choose a starting position. As will be explained shortly, such randomization is needed for the decoder to be robust against insertions and deletions that happen to the beginning and/or the end of the original packet. Furthermore, the aforementioned shifting-

Algorithm 3 Decoding of idEEC.

Input: $\vec{b}'$: received data bits vector, $\vec{z}$: received sketch, l: length of original packet $\vec{b}$.
Output: $\hat{d}$: the estimated number of flipping errors.
/ l' is the length of selected part of packet in which there is no insertion or deletion. $\hat{d}'$ is the estimator for the number of flipping errors in this selected part. */*
$\langle \hat{d}', l' \rangle =$ EST $(\vec{b}', \vec{z}, l)$
if $l' \neq 0$ **and** $\hat{d}' \cdot \frac{l}{l'} \le D$ **then**
    return $\hat{d} = \hat{d}' \cdot \frac{l}{l'}$
else
    return Failed

and-compare procedure needed for identifying clean slices will also benefit from this "manifoldization".

3.1.1 Case with Only Insertions or Only Deletions

In this section, we study the simpler case where either insertion errors or deletion errors – but not both – occur during the transmission, in addition to flipping errors. We believe this is the more common case, since insertion and deletion errors are often caused by clock speed mismatch between the sender and the receiver, and this mismatch should not change direction often.

We propose a divide and conquer algorithm called EST($\vec{x}, \vec{z}, h$) that given a packet or a packet residue $\vec{x}$ – which is the received packet at the first iteration but later becomes the "residue" of the packet with more and more clean slices removed during the iterations – and its idEEC codeword $\vec{z}$, tries to identify all clean slices within $\vec{x}$, and returns (a) the total number of bit errors in them and (b) the total length of all these clean slices. Here h represents the length of what remains of the packet after zero or more clean slices had been removed from the packet during the recursive execution of the "Est" routine up until this point. The description of the algorithm can be found in Algorithm 4.

In describing algorithm EST, we assume there are only insertions. In cases where there are only deletions, we need only replace the phantom deletions by phantom insertions in Step 6 of the algorithm. One may infer the number of insertions $\hat{\phi}$ from the difference between the lengths of the received packet and the original one. In each iteration of the algorithm, it randomly deletes $\hat{\phi}$ (phantom) bits uniformly along the segment boundaries in the packet, to "cancel out" the actual insertions in the transmitted packet. By the $\hat{\phi}$ positions at which bits are deleted, the packet is divided into $\hat{\phi}+1$ slices. From the pigeonhole principle, there should be at least one slice that has no insertions in it, which we call a "clean slice". Furthermore, with Lemma 1 which will be proven in Sec. 3.2, one should be able to find a clean slice that not only has no insertion errors in it, but also has the same starting bit index, relative to the beginning of the "bit-destuffed" packet, as that relative to the beginning of the original packet. We call such a clean slice a "perfect match". We will show in Theorem 1 that, our scheme benefits from the existence of such a perfect match to reduce the computational overhead by a factor of ϕ.

This algorithm first performs a hypothesis testing to confirm the suspected number of insertions $\hat{\phi}$, by trying to find such a perfect match, after these $\hat{\phi}$ phantom deletions are made. Intuitively, when we try to estimate the number of bit errors in a dirty slice (in which insertion and deletions errors are localized) from its EEC codeword, this number is going to be quite large, with high probability, because a single insertion may lead to many bits being shifted and

Algorithm 4 The iterative algorithm for EEC with insertions only.

$\text{EST}(\vec{x}, \vec{z}, h)$

Input: $\vec{x}$: received data bits; $\vec{z}$: received sketches corresponding to $\vec{x}$; h: length of the original data bits.

Output: $\langle \hat{d}, \hat{h} \rangle$: $\hat{d}$ is the estimated number of flipping errors in all clean slices, $\hat{d}$ is the total length of clean slices.

$\hat{\phi} = |\vec{x}| - h$

/* *Test the stopping criterion.* */
if $\hat{\phi} \geq \frac{hm}{l}$ **or** $\hat{\phi} > \phi_{max}$ **then**
  return $\langle 0, 0 \rangle$

/* *Phantom deletions.* */
Delete $\hat{\phi}$ phantom bits at random positions, and divide $\vec{x}$ into $\hat{\phi} + 1$ slices $\langle \vec{x}_1, \ldots, \vec{x}_{\hat{\phi}+1} \rangle$ with corresponding sketches $\langle \vec{z}_1, \ldots, \vec{z}_{\hat{\phi}+1} \rangle$

/* *Hypothesis test if* $\hat{\phi} = \phi$ */
for $j = 1$ **to** $\hat{\phi} + 1$ **do**
  $\hat{d}_j = \text{EEC.DISTANCE-ESTIMATION}(\vec{x}_j, \vec{z}_j)$
if $\hat{d}_t = \min_j\{\hat{d}_j\} < threshold$ **then**
  /* *Find a clean slice and iteratively perform the algorithm on the others.* */
  $\vec{x}' \Leftarrow$ remove $\vec{x}_t$ from $\vec{x}$;
  $\vec{z}' \Leftarrow$ remove $\vec{z}_t$ from $\vec{z}$;
  $h_t = |\vec{x}_t|$, $h' = h - h_t$
  $\langle \hat{d}'_t, h'_t \rangle = \text{EST}(\vec{x}', \vec{z}', h')$
  return $\langle \hat{d}_t + \hat{d}'_t, h_t + h'_t \rangle$
else
  /* *Unable to find a clean slice, then test the hypothesis whether there are both insertions and deletions.* */
  return $\text{GEST}(\vec{x}, \vec{z}, h, 1)$

hence a totally different EEC codeword computed. Therefore, a clean slice can be identified through the following threshold-based approach. The threshold is given by $\beta \frac{Dh}{(\phi+1)l}$, where $\beta > 1$ is a small constant, D is the upper bound of the flipping errors in a packet, and thus $\frac{Dh}{(\phi+1)l}$ is the average number of flipping errors in each slice. If the estimated number of bit errors in a slice is above the threshold, it is considered dirty. Otherwise, it is considered clean. If there appears more than one clean slices, our algorithm will only save the cleanest slice (i.e., with fewest estimated flipping errors in it). It then removes this slice from the packet (residue), and repeats the procedure iteratively on the rest, until a stopping criterion is met (described shortly). If our scheme fails to identify such a clean slice in this iteration, it has reason to suspect that both insertions and deletions have occurred. In this case, we call a more sophisticated algorithm GEST, which will be explained in Sec. 3.1.2.

Fig. 1 shows an example indicating how this algorithm works when 3 insertion errors occurred during the transmission. The algorithm randomly divides the packet into 4 slices and deletes 3 phantom bits. The Hamming distance between each slice in the received packet and that in the original packet is estimated using the corresponding tug-of-war counters. Based on these estimated Hamming distances, we are able to identify the third slice as a perfect match, with high probability. The Hamming distance estimation for the third – and perfectly matched – slice is then used to estimate the bit error rate of the transmission. Note that although there is no insertion or deletion error in the second slice, this slice

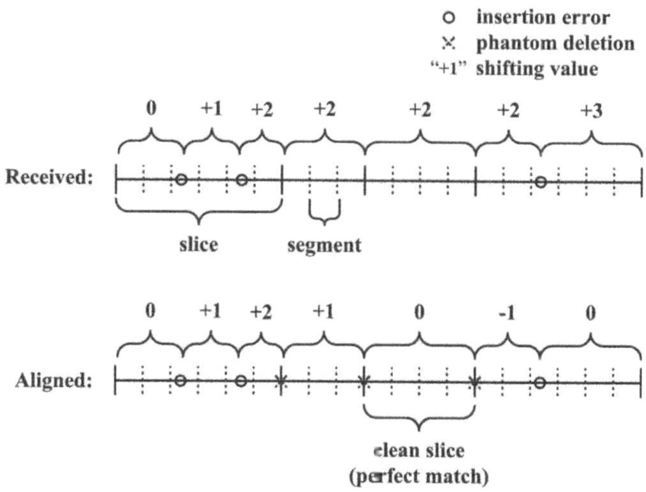

Figure 1: One of the iterations when there are 3 insertions in the received packet.

does not align with the original part, as all the bits are right shifted by one.

The computational complexity of the iterative algorithm when there are only insertions or only deletions is given by the following theorem.

THEOREM 1. *Let Λ denote the total number of operations involved in Hamming distance estimations for all slices in the original packet, using the underlying EEC. If there are only insertions or only deletions in the received packet, the computational complexity of our algorithm is $O(\phi\Lambda)$.*

PROOF. Let s_0 and h_0 denote the total number of operations and number of iterations, respectively. When there are only insertions or deletions, with high probability, the algorithm will keep operating on the packet (residue) iteratively, which shrinks by approximately a multiplicative factor of $\frac{\phi}{\phi+1}$ in length after each iteration instead of calling GEST. Therefore, the number of operations in the j-th iteration is $\left(\frac{\phi}{\phi+1}\right)^{j-1}\Lambda$, and the total complexity is

$$\begin{aligned}\mathbf{E}[s_0] &= \sum_{j=1}^{h_0} \left(\frac{\phi}{\phi+1}\right)^{j-1} \Lambda \\ &= (\phi+1)\left[1 - \left(\frac{\phi}{\phi+1}\right)^{h_0}\right]\Lambda \\ &\leq (\phi+1)\Lambda \\ &= O(\phi\Lambda)\end{aligned}$$

□

Therefore, we are paying only a multiplicative factor of ϕ on the computational overhead of underlying EEC scheme for making idEEC robust against up to ϕ insertion or deletion errors.

3.1.2 Case with Both Insertions and Deletions

Cases where there are both insertions and deletions are more complicated. For one thing, even if we have made a correct hypothesis on the number of insertions and deletions, it is still possible that we cannot find a perfect match using the above algorithm without shifting the packet around. Fig. 2 shows such an example. In case 1, the third slice is a perfect match, because there is one insertion

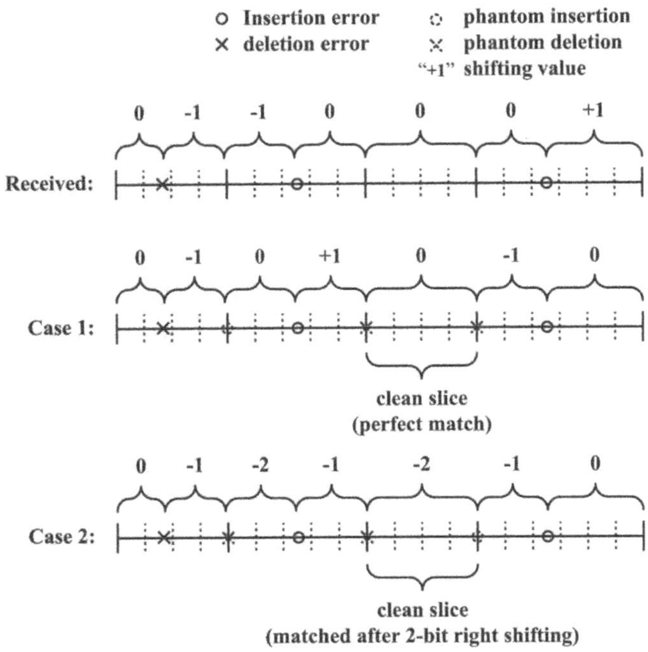

Figure 2: One of the iterations when there are 2 insertions and 1 deletion in the received packet.

and one deletion in the first two slices respectively, and we happen to insert 1 bit and delete 1 bit in these two slices respectively, resulting in no shift to the bit indices of the third (clean) slice. However, in case 2, the third slice is shifted to the left by 2 bits because of the mismatch between the phantom insertions and deletions we make and the actual insertion/deletion errors that occur during transmission. In this case, the algorithm has to shift these slices around in trying to identify a clean slice.

Algorithm 5 shows the details of the generalized estimation of number of flipping errors over both insertion and deletion channels. At level k, we make a hypothesis on the number of insertions n_i and the number of deletions n_d according to the length of the received packet $|\vec{x}|$ and that of the original one h. If we observe that the received packet is longer than the original one ($|\vec{x}| > h$), the hypothesis is that there are $\hat{n}_i = |\vec{x}| - h + k$ insertions and $\hat{n}_d = k$ deletions. Otherwise, $\hat{n}_i = k$, and $\hat{n}_d = h - |\vec{x}| + k$. Then we randomly insert $\hat{n}_d$ and delete $\hat{n}_i$ phantom bits in the packet and divide the packet into $\hat{\phi} + 1$ slices from the $\hat{\phi} = \hat{n}_i + \hat{n}_d$ insertion or deletion positions. The algorithm then attempts to find the clean slices by shifting the packet around to align it with the original one. When a clean slice is identified, the algorithm will remove such a slice from the packet and perform the search (for clean slices) on the rest iterative at the same level k until every single clean slice is located. If not a single clean slice can be identified at this level, which means that the current hypothesis testing has failed, the algorithm will proceed to the next (i.e, the $(k+1)$-th) level, testing the hypothesis that there is one more insertion error and deletion error each in the packet.

The aforementioned threshold-based approach is again taken here to identify a clean slice. However, as insertions and deletions may cancel each other out, it might be difficult to distinguish the flipping errors from the misaligned bits caused by insertions and deletions since the latter could even be smaller than the former, if such insertions or deletions happen very close to the boundary of a slice. Therefore, in order to bound the estimator's error to within a

Algorithm 5 The iterative algorithm for EEC with both insertions and deletions.

GEST($\vec{x}, \vec{z}, h, k$)

Input: $\vec{x}$: received data bits; $\vec{z}$: received sketches corresponding to $\vec{x}$; h: length of the original data bits; k: level of recursion.

Output: $\langle \hat{d}, \hat{h} \rangle$: $\hat{d}$ is the estimated number of flipping errors in all clean slices, $\hat{d}$ is the total length of clean slices.

/* *Estimate the number of insertions and deletions.* */
if $|\vec{x}| > h$ **then**
  $\hat{n}_i = |\vec{x}| - h + k, \hat{n}_d = k, \hat{\phi} = \hat{n}_i + \hat{n}_d$
else
  $\hat{n}_d = h - |\vec{x}| + k, \hat{n}_i = k, \hat{\phi} = \hat{n}_i + \hat{n}_d$

/* *Test the stopping criterion.* */
if $\hat{\phi} \geq \frac{hm}{l}$ **or** $\hat{\phi} > \phi_{max}$ **then**
  return $\langle 0, 0 \rangle$

/* *Phantom insertions and deletions.* */
Delete $\hat{n}_i$ and insert $\hat{n}_d$ phantom bits at random positions.

/* *Hypothesis test if* $\hat{\phi} = \phi$ * /
for all $\sigma \in \{0, \pm 1, \pm 2, \ldots, \pm \hat{\phi}\}$ **do**
  /* *Test all the shifting to find a clean slice.* */
  $\vec{x}_\sigma \Leftarrow$ Right shift $\vec{x}$ σ bits (Left shift if $\sigma < 0$).
  Divide $\vec{x}_\sigma$ into $\hat{\phi} + 1$ slices $\langle \vec{x}_{\sigma,1}, \ldots, \vec{x}_{\sigma,\hat{\phi}+1} \rangle$ by the positions of phantom insertions and deletions, with corresponding sketches $\langle \vec{z}_1, \ldots, \vec{z}_{\hat{\phi}+1} \rangle$
  for $j = 1$ **to** $\hat{\phi} + 1$ **do**
    $\hat{d}_{\sigma,j} =$ EEC.DISTANCE-ESTIMATION($\vec{x}_{\sigma,j}, \vec{z}_j$)
if $d_{s,t} = \min_{\sigma,j}\{\hat{d}_{\sigma,j}\} < threshold$ **then**
  $\vec{x}' \Leftarrow$ remove $\vec{x}_{s,t}$ from $\vec{x}$;
  $\vec{z}' \Leftarrow$ remove $\vec{z}_t$ from $\vec{z}$;
  $h_t = |\vec{x}_{s,t}|, h' = h - h_t$
  $\langle \hat{d}'_t, l'_t \rangle =$ GEST ($\vec{x}', \vec{z}', h', k$)
  return $\langle \hat{d}_t + \hat{d}'_t, h_t + h'_t \rangle$
else
  return GEST($\vec{x}, \vec{z}, h, k+1$)

reasonable range, it is assumed that there is a minimal gap between the location of an insertion and that of a deletion. This assumption is in fact quite weak: We need only assume a minimal gap between an insertion and a deletion, and need not make any assumption concerning the distance between insertions or that between deletions like in [9].

The computational overhead of our algorithm in this case can be given by the follow theorem.

THEOREM 2. *Again let Λ denote the total number of operations involved in Hamming distance estimations for all slices in the original packet, using the underlying EEC. If there are both insertions and deletions, the computational complexity is $O(\phi^2\Lambda)$.*

PROOF. Similar to the proof of Theorem 1, we let s_k and h_k denote the total number of operations and number of iterations in the k-th level, respectively. When there are both insertions and deletions, the algorithm first has to make $O(\phi)$ hypothesis testings to find out the actual number of insertions and deletions in the packet, each of which has a computational complexity $O(\phi\Lambda)$. Hence this "exploratory" phase aimed at finding the very first perfect match has complexity $O(\phi^2\Lambda)$.

Once the first perfect match is found, the gEST routine then operates on the "residue" of the packet iteratively to find more perfect matches. The complexity of each iteration here can be as large as $\left(\frac{\phi}{\phi+1}\right)^{j-1}\phi\Lambda$ – which is ϕ times of that in EST – because the packet residue may need to be shifted around up to ϕ times in order for a perfect match to emerge. The total computational complexity of this second phase is

$$\begin{aligned}\mathbf{E}[s_k] &= \sum_{j=1}^{h_k}\left(\frac{\phi}{\phi+1}\right)^{j-1}\phi\Lambda \\ &= \phi(\phi+1)\left[1-\left(\frac{\phi}{\phi+1}\right)^{h_k}\right]\Lambda \\ &\le \phi(\phi+1)\Lambda \\ &= O(\phi^2\Lambda)\end{aligned}$$

Therefore the total computational complexity of both phases is $O(\phi^2\Lambda) + O(\phi^2\Lambda) = O(\phi^2\Lambda)$. □

The number of insertion and deletion errors in a packet is usually very small. In such cases, the decoding computational complexity of our algorithm is larger than that of the underlying EEC (for channel that are free of insertion/deletion errors) by only a small multiplicative factor.

3.2 Identifying "Clean Slices"

Recall that our iterative algorithm randomly deletes n_i phantom bits and inserts n_d phantom bits, and divides the packet $\vec{x}$ into $\hat{\phi}+1$ slices. The goal is to find a clean slice – which must exist if the "$n_i + n_d$" hypothesis is correct – by shifting the slices around. Furthermore, in cases where there are only insertions or only deletions, there must exist a perfect match (a slice where the index of every bit relative to the beginning of the received packet is equal to that relative to the beginning of the original packet) in each iteration, provided the corresponding hypothesis is correct. This property is proven in the following lemma.

LEMMA 1. *If there are only insertions (or deletions), there is at least one slice which is a "perfect match".*

PROOF. We prove this lemma constructively. We first define two pointers a and b, which are initialized as $a = b = 1$. Denote the number of insertions (or deletions) in the j-th slice by ϕ_j. If $\sum_{j=a}^{b}\phi_j = 0$, the b-th slice is a perfect match. Otherwise, update a to b and b to $b + \sum_{j=a}^{b}\phi_j$ and repeat these steps. Since there are $\sum_{j=1}^{\phi+1}\phi_j = \phi$ insertions (or deletions), we always have $b < \phi+1$. Thus we can finally find a perfect match in the $(\phi+1)$ slices. □

As an intuitive explanation of the proof, one can imagine this as a race between the actual insertions (or deletions) and the phantom deletions (or insertions). Since they are equal in number, they should "meet" each other at some point by the finishing line, which indicates that there should be at least one perfect match throughout the packet. Therefore, when there are only insertions (or deletions), it is unnecessary to shift the packet around to find a "clean slice". This, in addition to the fact that there is no need to test all "$n_i + n_d$" hypothesis, reduces the computational complexity of the general algorithm (for handling the presence of both insertion and deletion errors) by a multiplicative factor of ϕ.

For more complex cases where there are both insertions and deletions, even when the "$n_i + n_d$" hypothesis is correct, there might still be no perfect match, as we have shown earlier. However, we can prove similarly that a clean slice, albeit shifted, must exist, when the "$n_i + n_d$" hypothesis is correct. This slice can then be found by the aforementioned shift-and-compare steps in Algorithm 5. In the following section, we will analyze the threshold-based approach to determining whether a (shifted) slice is clean.

3.3 Mean Square Error Analysis

Once the algorithm has identified the segments that are likely to contain insertion and deletion errors, it uses the remaining "clean" segments to estimate the number of flipping errors. The accuracy of the BER estimation thus depends on how reliably we can identify which slices are *clean* (do not have any insertions or deletions within them) at each iteration. As described before, the decoding algorithm tries to identify clean slices by comparing the decoded Hamming distances against a pre-determined threshold.

There are two ways we can make an error in identifying clean slices: a *false alarm* (FA) when we tag slice as dirty even though it is clean, and a *miss* (M) when we do not tag a dirty slice. False alarms and misses have different effects on the BER estimation. When the algorithm terminates, the segments which have been labeled as "clean" will be used to estimate the number of flipping errors in the entire packet. When a miss occurs, this estimation can include segments which have an insertion/deletion error, which will typically have a higher error rate, which in turn biases our estimate upwards. However, as a miss happens only when the estimator is smaller than the threshold, this bias is negligible.

False alarms affect the estimator in a different way. When a false alarm occurs, the corresponding slice is simply dropped in the current iteration, but it will still be involved in the next iteration. If a false alarm occurs in all of the clean slices, the algorithm will directly go to the next level and re-slice the packet. The overall effect of the false alarm is a slight increase in the total amount of dropped segments, up to $O(\phi + m\delta_{FA})$ on average, where δ_{FA} is an upper bound on the false alarm rate.

Let $\hat{d}$ denote the our estimator for the number of flipping errors in the received packet. We measure the performance of our estimator using the standard Mean Square Error (MSE) metric, which is defined as

$$MSE(\hat{d}) = \mathbf{E}[(\hat{d}-d)^2] = \mathbf{Var}(\hat{d}) + \mathbf{E}[Bias(\hat{d})^2]$$

where $Bias(\hat{d}) = \mathbf{E}[\hat{d}] - d$.

Theorem 3 below shows how we can incorporate uniform (over all slices visited) bounds on the false alarm and miss probabilities into the accuracy of the flipping error estimator.

THEOREM 3. *Let E_s be the event that a certain slice s contains an insertion or deletion, and let E_s' be the event that our algorithm labels it as such. Let δ_{FA} be an upper bound on the probability of false alarm,*

$$Pr(E_s', \overline{E}_s) = Pr\left(E_s'|\overline{E}_s\right)Pr(\overline{E}_s) \le \delta_{FA} \quad \textit{for all slices } s,$$

and δ_M be an upper bound on the probability of a miss,

$$Pr(\overline{E}_s', E_s) = Pr\left(\overline{E}_s'|E_s\right)Pr(E_s) \le \delta_M \quad \textit{for all slices } s.$$

Then the mean square error of our estimator on the number of flipping errors, $\hat{d}$, is bounded by

$$MSE(\hat{d}) = O\left(\frac{d^2}{c} + \delta_M D^2 - \frac{d(\frac{\phi}{m}+\delta_{FA})}{1-(\frac{\phi}{m}+\delta_{FA})}\right). \quad (1)$$

PROOF. Since $MSE(\hat{d}) = \mathbf{Var}(\hat{d}) + \mathbf{E}[Bias(\hat{d})^2]$, we will calculate the variance and bias of $\hat{d}$ respectively in the follows.

We first define some notations that will be used in our proof. Let $\vec{x}$ and $\vec{x}'$ denote the received packet and the selected part of it.

Let $\hat{d}$ and $\hat{d}'$ denote the estimator for the number of flipping errors in $\vec{x}$ and $\vec{x'}$ respectively. Let d and d' denote the actual number of flipping errors in $\vec{x}$ and $\vec{x'}$. Let B and B' denote the bias of $\hat{d}$ and $\hat{d}'$. Let $0 < \theta < 1$ denote the proportion of the dropped part of the packet. Define $D' = (1-\theta)D$. Generally we have $\mathbf{E}[B] = O(\delta_M D)$ and $\mathbf{E}[B'] = O(\delta_M D')$. The variance of $\hat{d}'$ is given by

$$\mathbf{Var}(\hat{d}'|d') = \mathbf{E}_{B'}[\mathbf{Var}(\hat{d}'|B', d')] + \mathbf{Var}_{B'}(\mathbf{E}[\hat{d}'|B', d'])$$

Recall the variance of tug-of-war sketch based EEC given in [5], we have

$$\begin{aligned}\mathbf{E}_{B'}\left[\mathbf{Var}(\hat{d}'|B', d')\right] &= \mathbf{E}\left[\frac{1}{c}\left(2(d'+B')^2 - 2(d'+B')\right)|d'\right] \\ &\le \frac{1}{c}\mathbf{E}\left[2(d'+B')^2|d'\right] \\ &= \frac{1}{c}\mathbf{E}\left[2(d'^2 + 2d'B' + B'^2)|d'\right] \\ &= O\left(\frac{2}{c}(d'^2 + 2d'\delta_M D' + \delta_M D'^2)\right) \\ &= O\left(\frac{2}{c}(d' + \sqrt{\delta_M}D')^2\right)\end{aligned}$$

and

$$\begin{aligned}\mathbf{Var}_{B'}(\mathbf{E}[\hat{d}'|B', d']) &= \mathbf{Var}_{B'}(d' + B'|d') \\ &= \mathbf{Var}(B') \\ &= \mathbf{E}\left[(B' - \mathbf{E}[B'])^2\right] \\ &= \mathbf{E}\left[(B')^2\right] - \mathbf{E}\left[B'\right]^2 \\ &= \mathbf{E}\left[\left(\frac{B'}{D'}\right)^2\right](D')^2 - \mathbf{E}[B']^2 \\ &\le \mathbf{E}\left[\frac{B'}{D'}\right](D')^2 - \mathbf{E}[B']^2 \\ &= \mathbf{E}[B']D' - \mathbf{E}[B']^2 \\ &= O\left(\delta_M D'^2 - \delta_M^2 D'^2\right) \\ &= O\left(\delta_M D'^2\right)\end{aligned}$$

In the first inequality, $(\frac{B'}{D'})^2 \le \frac{B'}{D'}$ because $\frac{B'}{D'} \le 1$. Since part of the segments are dropped at the end of the algorithm and the overall flipping error of the received packets is estimated just from the selected ones, sampling errors may introduced to our estimator. Since $\hat{d} = \frac{1}{1-\theta}\hat{d}'$, according to the proof of Theorem 2 in [12], we have

$$\begin{aligned}\mathbf{Var}(\hat{d}) &\approx \frac{1}{(1-\theta)^2}\mathbf{Var}(\hat{d}'|d' = (1-\theta)d) + \frac{d\theta}{1-\theta} \\ &= \frac{1}{(1-\theta)^2}\cdot O\left(\frac{2}{c}\left((1-\theta)d + \sqrt{\delta_M}D'\right)^2 + \delta_M D'^2\right) \\ &\qquad + \frac{d\theta}{1-\theta} \\ &= O\left(\frac{d^2}{c} + \delta_M D^2 + \frac{d\theta}{1-\theta}\right)\end{aligned}$$

As to the bias of $\hat{d}$, we have

$$\mathbf{E}[B^2] = O\left(\delta_M D^2\right)$$

Generally, we have $\theta = O\left(\frac{\phi}{m} + \delta_{FA}\right)$. Thus

$$\begin{aligned}MSE(\hat{d}) &= \mathbf{Var}(\hat{d}) + \mathbf{E}[B^2] \\ &= O\left(\frac{d^2}{c} + \delta_M D^2 + \frac{d\theta}{1-\theta}\right) \\ &= O\left(\frac{d^2}{c} + \delta_M D^2 + \frac{d(\frac{\phi}{m} + \delta_{FA})}{1 - (\frac{\phi}{m} + \delta_{FA})}\right)\end{aligned}$$

□

Here we offer an intuitive explanation of Theorem 3. The first term in the expression for the MSE, $O(\frac{d^2}{c})$, is the same as that of a standard EEC using tug-of-war sketches when there are no insertion/deletion errors. The additional error terms result from the need to deal with insertions and deletions errors. The second term corresponds to the aforementioned bias introduced by a miss. D is a parameter determined by the channel conditions, which is not tunable in our algorithm. It characterizes to what extent potential fluctuations of the BER across the packet can negatively impact the accuracy of the estimator. The third term is the "sampling error" since we estimate the BER only from up to $m - \phi$ clean slices "sampled" out of a total of up to m slices. Even with this sampling error term alone, it is clear that our algorithm requires the number of segments to be proportional to the number of insertions and deletions. This suggests that the coding overhead of our scheme is $O(m \log n) = O(\phi \log n)$. Therefore, we are paying only a multiplicative factor of ϕ for making idEEC robust against insertion and deletion errors. As an extreme case, when $\phi = 0$, we have $MSE(\hat{d}) = O\left(\frac{d^2}{c} + \frac{d\delta_{FA}}{1-\delta_{FA}}\right)$. The second term, $O\left(\frac{d\delta_{FA}}{1-\delta_{FA}}\right)$, comes from the fact that even if there is no insertion/deletion it is still possible for the estimator to exceed the threshold due to the rare event that the underlying ToW sketch grossly overestimates the Hamming distance. Although $\delta_{FA} \neq 0$ when $\phi = 0$, in Lemma 2 below we'll show that this cost is very small since it decreases exponentially when the number of codeword c increases.

It remains to determine a uniform bound on the false alarm and miss probabilities for our algorithm. Lemmas 2, 3, and 4 below bound these probabilities when the slice s is chosen independently of the sketches and bit errors. These conditions hold strictly for the first iteration of the algorithm; in latter iterations, however, a weak dependence develops between the actual bit errors and which slice is the "cleanest" in what remains of the packet (i.e., the "packet residue"). Our analysis ignores this weak dependence and therefore is an approximation from this point on. In the i-th iteration of our algorithm, the threshold for determining whether or not a slice is clean is given by $\alpha_i = \beta\frac{D}{S}\cdot\frac{l_i}{l}$, where $\beta > 1$ is a constant, D is the upper bound on the total number of flipping errors for the entire packet, $S = \hat{\phi} + 1$ is the number of slices at the current iteration, l is the length of the entire packet and l_i is the length of the part of the packet that remains at the i-th iteration.

Let c denote the number of sketches (codewords) for each segment and d denote the actual number of flipping errors in the received packet. The upper bound of the false alarm probability is given by Lemma 2. Its proof is provided in Appendix A.

LEMMA 2. *Consider a slice s chosen independently of the bit errors and sketches. Let E_s be the event that this slice contains an insertion or a deletion, and let E'_s be the event that our algorithm labels it as such. Then if $\phi = 0$, we can bound the probability of* *false alarm with*

$$Pr(E_s', \overline{E}_s) < e^{-\frac{1}{4}\left(-\sqrt{c}+\sqrt{(2\beta-1)c}\right)^2}.$$

For $\phi \neq 0$, we have

$$Pr(E_s', \overline{E}_s) < 1 - \left(1 - e^{-\frac{1}{4}\left(-\sqrt{c}+\sqrt{\frac{(2-\tau_1)c}{\tau_1}}\right)^2}\right) \cdot \left(1 - A_1 e^{-A_2 \cdot \tau_1 \beta \frac{D}{S}}\right)$$

where $0 < \tau_1 < 1$, $A_1 > 0$ and $A_2 > 0$ are constants.

Remark: In the proof of Lemma 2, we have proposed a tighter probability tail bound on the variance of the tug-of-war instance used in our scheme. In particular, our technique improved the bound from vanishing quadratically fast to vanishing exponentially fast. However, this improvement is restricted to the case when the vectors at issue are binary and does not apply to the tug-of-war sketch in general.

For the miss probability, if $\phi = 0$, each slice in the packet is a clean slice, meaning $Pr(E_s) = 0$, and so $Pr(\overline{E}_s', E_s) = 0$ as well.

When $\phi \neq 0$, and if there are only insertions or only deletions in the received packet, the probability of a miss is bounded by Lemma 3 below, whose proof is given in Appendix B.

LEMMA 3. *Consider a slice s chosen as in Lemma 2, and suppose that there are only ϕ insertions or only ϕ deletions in the received packet. If $\phi \neq 0$, for any $0 < \tau_1 < 1$, $\tau_2 \geq 2$ and $\epsilon > 1$, we have the following bound on the miss probability*

$$Pr(\overline{E}_s', E_s) < 1 - \left(1 - e^{-\frac{1}{4}\left(-\sqrt{c}+\sqrt{\frac{(2-\tau_1)c}{\tau_1}}\right)^2}\right)\left(1 - e^{-\left(\frac{\tau_2-2}{2\tau_2}\right)^2 c}\right) \cdot \left(1 - f_1(d,S)e^{-f_2(d,S)\cdot\tau_1\epsilon\frac{d}{S}}\right)\left(1 - 2\tau_2\epsilon \cdot \frac{\phi d}{l}\right)$$

where $f_1(d,S)$ and $f_2(d,S)$ are functions of d and S.

If there are both insertions and deletions in the received packet, it is more difficult to distinguish the flipping errors from the mismatched bits caused by insertions and deletions, as an insertion and an deletion that are close together may cancel each other out. In [9], it is assumed that there is a minimal gap between two insertion or deletion errors, as synchronization errors that cause such insertions or deletions often result from a slow drift in clock synchronization and in this case it takes some time for this drift to build up to cause another synchronization error. Here we make a weaker assumption that there is a minimum gap between an insertion and a deletion (but two insertions or two deletions could occur to bits very close to each other). With this weaker assumption, the miss probability is given by Lemma 4. Its proof can be found in Appendix C.

LEMMA 4. *Suppose there are both insertions and deletions in the received packet, $\phi \neq 0$, and let Δ denote the minimal gap between insertions and deletions. Consider a slice s chosen as in Lemmas 2 and 3. If $\Delta > \max\{\tau_2\beta\frac{D}{S}, \tau_2\epsilon\frac{D}{S}\}$, then we have the following bound on the miss probability*

$$Pr(\overline{E}_s', E_s) < \begin{cases} \max\{\delta_1, \delta_2\} & \text{if } S < \phi + 1 \\ \delta_2 & \text{otherwise} \end{cases}$$

δ_1 and δ_2 are defined as

$$\delta_1 = 1 - \left(1 - e^{-\left(\frac{\tau_2-2}{2\tau_2}\right)^2 c}\right)\left(1 - 2\tau_2\beta \cdot \frac{\phi D}{l}\right)$$

$$\delta_2 = 1 - \left(1 - e^{-\frac{1}{4}\left(-\sqrt{c}+\sqrt{\frac{(2-\tau_1)c}{\tau_1}}\right)^2}\right)\left(1 - e^{-\left(\frac{\tau_2-2}{2\tau_2}\right)^2 c}\right) \cdot \left(1 - f_1(d,S)e^{-f_2(d,S)\cdot\tau_1\epsilon\frac{d}{S}}\right)\left(1 - 2\tau_2\epsilon \cdot \frac{\phi d}{l}\right)$$

where $f_1(d,S)$ and $f_2(d,S)$ are functions of d and S. $0 < \tau_1 < 1$, $\tau_2 \geq 2$ and $\epsilon > 0$ are constants.

Remark: $f_1(d,S)$ and $f_2(d,S)$ in Lemma 3 and Lemma 4 are factors from Chernoff bound and can be calculated by numerical methods. When $d \to 0$, we have $f_1(d,S) \to 1$ and $f_1(d,S) \to \infty$. τ_1, τ_2 and ϵ in Lemma 2, Lemma 3 and Lemma 4 are constants used to balance the terms in the bounds. One may adjust these factors to make the bound tight enough in different scenarios. As an extreme case, in Lemma 3 when $d \to 0$, we could have the miss probability $Pr(\overline{E}_s', E_s) \to 0$ by making $\tau_1 \to 0$, $\tau_2 \to \infty$ and $\epsilon \to \infty$.

4. EEC UNDER HETEROGENEOUS BIT FLIPPING MODEL

The proposed scheme for accounting for insertion and deletion errors can be extended to the more general case where the bit-flip probability is different in different portions of the packet. The mitigation strategy discussed above depends only on finding gross differences in the mismatch between (re)encoding of the received slices and the code; it is relatively insensitive to subtle variations in the bit error rate.

Throughout the procedure, an estimate of the bit error rate in each of the m segments, $P = [p_i]_{1 \leq i \leq m}$ is maintained. In Step 14 of Algorithm 4 and Step 21 of Algorithm 5, the algorithm not only returns the number of flipping errors $\hat{d}_t$ in the clean slice $\vec{x}_t$, but also stores the estimated BER $p_i = \frac{m\hat{d}_i}{l}$ of each segment $\vec{b}_i$ in the slice, where $\hat{d}_i$ is the estimated Hamming distance between the transmitted segment and the original one. On finishing all the iterations of the algorithm, we can treat this set of estimates as a discrete set of data points tells us about the BER in different regions of the packet. With the segments containing insertion/deletion errors removed, the proportion of bits left in the packet we can use to estimate the BER is at least $\Theta\left((m-\varphi)/m\right)$.

The type of information we have about the channel might affect how we combine these estimates in each segment. For example, if we are confident that the bit error rate is changing very little throughout the time it takes to transmit the packet, we might simply average the estimates in each segment. Otherwise, if we have some type of statistical model for how the error rate is changing in time, we might weigh this against our estimates in a Bayesian framework. In particular, if we believe the channel is being affected by "deep fades" which are very localized in time (within one packet), we can imagine detecting and segmenting these fades.

5. EVALUATION

In this section, we evaluate the accuracy of the BER estimation made by idEEC using simulation experiments with various parameter settings. We simulate unreliable communication channels where insertion, deletion and substitution errors may occur during transmission. In order for "enough" insertion and deletion errors to occur despite their low occurence probability, the length of the packet

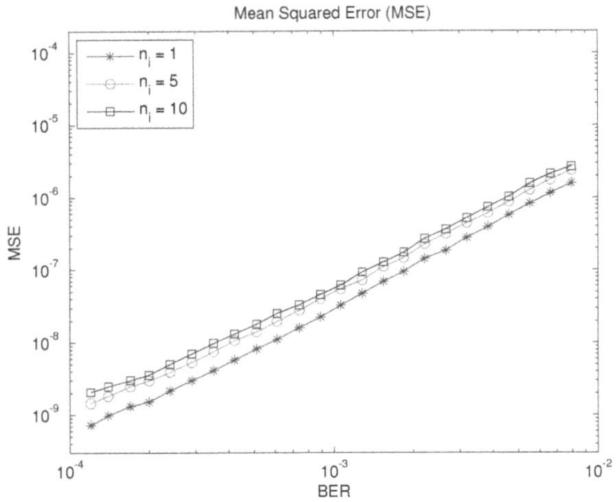

Figure 3: Empirical Results of Estimators for Insertion-Only Channels.

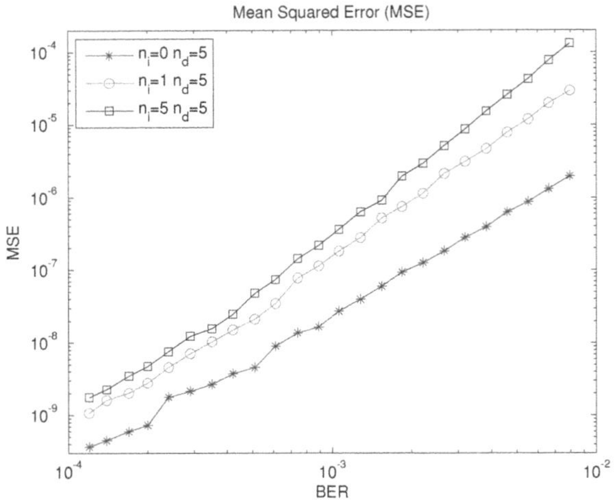

Figure 4: Empirical Results of Estimators for Insertion and Deletion Channels.

is set to $l = 10^5$ bits. For the results to converge properly, each value in each result in this study is obtained by averaging 1,000 simulation runs for it to converge properly. In all experiments, the packet is divided into $m = 50$ segments, each of which is coded by $c = 5$ tug-of-war codewords.

In our experiments, we vary the actual BER and compare it with the estimated number of flipping errors $\hat{p}$, the estimated number of flipping errors $\hat{d}$ divided by the packet length l. In this way, we obtain the empirical MSE's of the estimator under various parameter settings, which be plotted in the following two figures.

We start with the cases where there are only insertions or only deletions. Here we only present the insertions-only cases, since the deletions-only cases have identical performance characteristics. Fig. 3 shows the accuracy of the idEEC scheme under a set of different BER's and three different numbers of insertion errors ($n_i = 1, 5, 10$) in a log-log plot. We observe that the MSE of the estimation grows roughly quadratically with the actual BER in all three cases, as predicted by our analytical BER formula in Theorem 3. In other words, the average relative estimation error remains roughly a constant when the actual BER increases.

Next, we present the cases where there are both insertions and deletions. We fix the number of deletions n_d to 5 and let the number of insertion n_i vary across three different values $0, 1, 5$. The experimental results are shown in Fig. 4. We observe that the lowest line (corresponding to $n_i = 0, n_d = 5$) is almost identical to the middle line (corresponding to $n_i = 5, n_d = 0$) in Fig. 3 as expected. We observe also that we pay a steep price in terms of the MSE increment – as reflected by the wide gap between the lowest line and the middle line – for having just one insertion (i.e., $n_i = 1$). In comparison, this price becomes much smaller thereafter, as reflected by the much narrower gap between the highest line ($n_i = 5$) and the middle line, even though four more insertions are introduced. This behavior is expected since when there are both insertions and deletions, the decoding process becomes more complicated and error-prone. It is also consistent with that predicted by the analytical BER formula. We observe also that when there are one or more insertions, the MSE grows more than quadratically with the actual BER, which implies that the average relative estimation error grows larger with the actual BER.

6. CONCLUSION

Error estimating coding is a novel technique for measuring the bit error rate, with applications towards improving performance of wireless network where recent emerging systems can leverage partially correct packets [2]. However, the existing approaches [2, 5, 6] meet challenges in insertion or deletion channels. In this paper, we designed idEEC scheme that allows for the estimation of the number of flipping errors in a packet despite the existence of bit insertions and deletions during the transmission. Our idEEC scheme can build on any existing EEC scheme, with encoding efficiency proportional to that of the underlying EEC scheme. Taking the plain vanilla tug-of-war sketch as the underlying EEC for example, our design provides provable estimation quality with rather low overhead. The efficacy of our approach has been demonstrated both theoretically and experimentally. To our knowledge, this work represents the first study of building EEC for insertion and deletion channels.

7. ACKNOWLEDGEMENTS

This work has been supported in part by the collaborative NSF project that includes awards CNS 1218092 and CNS 1217758, and by the NSF award CNS 0910592.

8. REFERENCES

[1] ALON, N., GIBBONS, P. B., MATIAS, Y., AND SZEGEDY, M. Tracking join and self-join sizes in limited storage. *Journal of Computer and System Sciences 64*, 3 (2002), 719–747.

[2] CHEN, B., ZHOU, Z., ZHAO, Y., AND YU, H. Efficient error estimating coding: feasibility and applications. In *Proceedings of ACM SIGCOMM* (2010), pp. 3–14.

[3] DAVID, H. A., AND NAGARAJA, H. N. *Order statistics*. John Wiley & Sons, Inc., 1970.

[4] DOLECEK, L., AND ANANTHARAM, V. Using Reed-Muller RM $(1, m)$ codes over channels with synchronization and substitution errors. *IEEE Transactions on Information Theory 53*, 4 (2007), 1430–1443.

[5] HUA, N., LALL, A., LI, B., AND XU, J. A simpler and better design of error estimating coding. In *Proceedings of IEEE INFOCOM* (2012), pp. 235–243.

[6] HUA, N., LALL, A., LI, B., AND XU, J. Towards optimal error-estimating codes through the lens of fisher information analysis. In *Proceedings of ACM SIGMETRICS* (2012), pp. 125–136.

[7] LAURENT, B., AND MASSART, P. Adaptive estimation of a quadratic functional by model selection. *Annals of Statistics 28*, 5 (2000), 1302–1338.

[8] LEVENSHTEIN, V. Binary codes capable of correcting spurious insertions and deletions of ones. *Problems of Information Transmission 1*, 1 (1965), 8–17.

[9] LIU, Z., AND MITZENMACHER, M. Codes for deletion and insertion channels with segmented errors. *IEEE Transactions on Information Theory 56*, 1 (2010), 224–232.

[10] MITZENMACHER, M. A survey of results for deletion channels and related synchronization channels. *Probability Surveys 6* (2009), 1–33.

[11] WANG, H., AND LIN, B. Designing efficient codes for synchronization error channels. In *Proceedings of IEEE IWQoS* (2011), pp. 1–9.

[12] ZHAO, Q., KUMAR, A., WANG, J., AND XU, J. Data streaming algorithms for accurate and efficient measurement of traffic and flow matrices. In *Proceedings of ACM SIGMETRICS* (2005), pp. 350–361.

APPENDIX

A. PROOF OF LEMMA 2

PROOF. Let ξ_i denote the estimator for the number of bit flipping errors that occur to the i-th slice T_i in the received packet. Recall that this estimator is simply the mean of the c estimations given in Algorithm 1.

$$X_j = Y_j^2 = \left(\sum_{\substack{k \in T_i \\ b_k \neq b'_k}} b_k s_j[k] \right)^2 \quad j = 1, 2, \ldots, c$$

each of which is obtained from taking the difference between the j-th counter value $\sum_{k \in T_i} b_k s_j[k]$ encoding the slice in the tug-of-war sketch that was sent along with the packet, and $\sum_{k \in T_i} b'_k s_j[k]$, the j-th counter value computed from the slice in the received packet, and then squaring the difference up.

$$\xi_i = \frac{1}{c} \sum_{j=1}^{c} X_j = \frac{1}{c} \sum_{j=1}^{c} Y_j^2$$

We will show that, if the slice T_i is indeed clean, this estimator is sharp in the sense, with high probability, the estimated value are very close to the real value. By the Central Limit Theorem, Y_j is approximately a Gaussian distributed random variable, thus ξ_i is approximately a chi-square random variable with c degrees of freedom. Recall the tail bounds for chi-square distributed variables given in [7], for a standard chi-square random variable $X \sim \chi_c^2$, we have

$$P(X - c > 2\sqrt{cx} + 2x) \leq e^{-x} \tag{2}$$

$$P(c - X > 2\sqrt{cx}) \leq e^{-x} \tag{3}$$

As shown in Step 7 to 12 of Algorithm 4 and Step 11 to 19 of Algorithm 5, in each iteration, after attempting all kinds of shift of the packet, the algorithm chooses the slice with the minimal estimated Hamming distance to the original packet, and test if this slice is a "clean one". If the selected slice in this iteration contains no insertion/deletion but fails the test, a false alarm happens and the slice is declared as a "dirty one". In such a case, the estimator for the number of flipping errors in this slice is $\xi = \min_i \xi_i$.

Here, we only derive the false alarm probability for the first iteration. As the threshold changes proportional to the remaining part of the packet, it's easy to generalize this result to other iterations. Let d_i denote the number of flipping errors in the i-th slice. Define random variables $x_{i,j}$ as

$$x_{i,j} = \begin{cases} 1 & \text{if the } j\text{-th bit in the } i\text{-th slice is flipped} \\ 0 & \text{otherwise} \end{cases}$$

Apparently $x_{i,j} \sim Bernoulli(p)$ and $d_i = \sum_{i=1}^{\eta_i} x_{i,j}$, where η_i is the length of the i-th slice.

When $\phi \neq 0$, we have $S \geq 2$. By the theory of order statistics [3], η_i, $i = 1, 2, \ldots, S$, is approximately a Beta distributed random variable[1] with shape parameters 1 and $S - 1$, i.e. $\eta_i \sim l \cdot Beta(1, S-1)$. According to Chernoff bound, for any $t > 0$ we have

$$Pr(d_i \geq \tau_1 \alpha_1) \leq e^{-\tau_1 \alpha_1 t} \mathbf{E}[e^{d_i t}] \tag{4}$$

where $0 < \tau_1 < 1$ and

$$\begin{aligned}
\mathbf{E}\left[e^{d_i t}\right] &= \mathbf{E}\left[e^{\sum_{j=1}^{\eta_i} x_{i,j} t}\right] &(5)\\
&= \mathbf{E}_{\eta_i}\left[\mathbf{E}\left[e^{\sum_{j=1}^{\eta_i} x_{i,j} t} \,\middle|\, \eta_i\right]\right] &(6)\\
&= \mathbf{E}_{\eta_i}\left[(pe^t + (1-p))^{\eta_i}\right] &(7)\\
&\leq \mathbf{E}_{\eta_i}\left[e^{(e^t - 1)\eta_i p}\right] &(8)\\
&\approx \int_0^1 (S-1)(1-\omega)^{S-2} e^{(e^t-1)l\omega p} d\omega &(9)\\
&\leq \int_0^1 (S-1)(1-\omega)^{S-2} e^{(e^t-1)\omega D} d\omega &(10)\\
&= \frac{e^{(e^t-1)D}}{((e^t-1)D)^{S-1}} \left(\Gamma(S-1) - \Gamma\left(S-1, (e^t-1)D\right)\right)
\end{aligned}$$

where $\Gamma(S-1)$ is the gamma function and $\Gamma\left(S-1, (e^t-1)D\right)$ is the upper incomplete gamma function.[2] The inequality (8) holds since $1 + x < e^x$ for any $x > 0$.

Minimize the right-hand side of Equation (4) over $t > 0$, we have

$$\min_{t>0} e^{-\tau_1 \alpha_1 t} \mathbf{E}[e^{d_i t}] = A_1 e^{-A_2 \tau_1 \alpha_1}$$

where $A_1 > 0$ and $A_2 > 0$ are deterministic constants.

[1] A random variable $0 \leq X \leq 1$ that is Beta-distributed with shape parameters α and β is denoted as $X \sim Beta(\alpha, \beta)$. The PDF of $Beta(\alpha, \beta)$ is $f(x; \alpha, \beta) = \frac{\Gamma(\alpha+\beta)}{\Gamma(\alpha)\Gamma(\beta)} x^{\alpha-1}(1-x)^{\beta-1}$.

[2] The gamma function is defined as $\Gamma(s) = \int_0^\infty t^{s-1}e^{-t}dt$. The upper incomplete gamma function is defined as $\Gamma(s, x) = \int_x^\infty t^{s-1}e^{-t}dt$

Since $\xi = \min_i \xi_i$, we have

$$\begin{aligned}
&Pr(\overline{E'_s}|\overline{E}_s) \\
&= Pr(\xi < \alpha_1|\overline{E}_s) \\
&\geq Pr(\xi_i < \alpha_1|\overline{E}_s) \\
&\geq Pr\left(\xi_i < d_i + (1-\tau_1)\alpha_1, d_i < \tau_1\alpha_1 \middle| \overline{E}_s\right) \\
&= Pr\left(\xi_i < d_i + (1-\tau_1)\alpha_1 \middle| d_i < \tau_1\alpha_1, \overline{E}_s\right) \\
&\qquad \cdot Pr\left(d_i < \tau_1\alpha_1 \middle| \overline{E}_s\right) \\
&\geq Pr\left(\xi_i < d_i + (1-\tau_1)\alpha_1 \middle| d_i < \tau_1\alpha_1, \overline{E}_s\right) \quad (11) \\
&\qquad \cdot Pr\left(d_i < \tau_1\alpha_1\right) \\
&\geq Pr\left(\frac{\xi_i c}{d_i} < c + c(1-\tau_1)\frac{\alpha_1}{d_i} \middle| d_i < \tau_1\alpha_1, \overline{E}_s\right) \\
&\qquad \cdot Pr\left(d_i < \tau_1\alpha_1\right) \\
&\geq Pr\left(\chi_c^2 < c + \frac{1-\tau_1}{\tau_1}c\right)\left(1 - A_1 e^{-A_2\tau_1\alpha_1}\right) \quad (12) \\
&\geq \left(1 - e^{-\frac{1}{4}\left(-\sqrt{c}+\sqrt{\frac{(2-\tau_1)c}{\tau_1}}\right)^2}\right)\left(1 - A_1 e^{-A_2\tau_1\cdot\beta\frac{D}{S}}\right)
\end{aligned}$$

In the inequality (11), $Pr\left(d_i < \tau_1\alpha_1 \middle| \overline{E}_s\right) > Pr\left(d_i < \tau_1\alpha_1\right)$ because the smaller the slice is, the less possible it is corrupted, and vice versa. Also, the inequality (12) holds since $\frac{\xi_i c}{d_i} \sim \chi_c^2$ and $d_i/\alpha_1 > \tau_1$. And finally, the last inequality follows from Inequation (2), in which $x = -\frac{1}{4}\left(-\sqrt{c}+\sqrt{\frac{(2-\tau_1)c}{\tau_1}}\right)^2$.

Thus, when $\phi \neq 0$ the probability of false alarm is

$$\begin{aligned}
&Pr(E'_s, \overline{E}_s) \\
&= Pr(E'_s|\overline{E}_s)P(\overline{E}_s) \\
&\leq Pr(E'_s|\overline{E}_s) \quad (13) \\
&= 1 - Pr(\overline{E'_s}|\overline{E}_s) \\
&< 1 - \left(1 - e^{-\frac{1}{4}\left(-\sqrt{c}+\sqrt{\frac{(2-\tau_1)c}{\tau_1}}\right)^2}\right)\left(1 - A_1 e^{-A_2\cdot\tau_1\beta\frac{D}{S}}\right)
\end{aligned}$$

When $\phi = 0$, we have $S = 1$. Let $\tau_1 = \frac{1}{\beta}$ in Equation (4), we have

$$Pr(d_i \geq \tau_1\alpha_1) = Pr(d_i \geq D) \approx 0$$

Similarly, we can prove

$$\begin{aligned}
Pr(E'_s, \overline{E}_s) &\leq Pr(E'_s|\overline{E}_s) \\
&= 1 - Pr(\overline{E'_s}|\overline{E}_s) \\
&< 1 - \left(1 - e^{-\frac{1}{4}\left(-\sqrt{c}+\sqrt{(2\beta-1)c}\right)^2}\right) \\
&= e^{-\frac{1}{4}\left(-\sqrt{c}+\sqrt{(2\beta-1)c}\right)^2}
\end{aligned}$$

□

B. PROOF OF LEMMA 3

PROOF. If there are only insertions or only deletions in the received packet, there is at least one clean slice in each iteration. Similar to Lemma 2, we only derive the miss probability for the first iteration as the derivation can be generalized, in a straightforward manner, for other iterations. In the first iteration, let ξ_i denote the estimator for the i-th "clean slice". Let ξ'_i denote the estimator for the i-th "dirty slice". Define $\xi = \min_i \xi_i$ and $\xi' = \min_i \xi'_i$.

Let $t = \arg\min_i \xi'_i$. Slice $\vec{x}_t$ is the dirty slice with minimal estimated Hamming distance. Let λ'_t denote the length of its mismatched part. Let $z_{j,k}$ denote the distance between the j-th insertion (or deletion) and the k-th phantom deletion (or insertion). As shown in Step 6 of Algorithm 4 and Step 10 of Algorithm 5, the phantom deletions (or insertions) are uniformly distributed. Thus,

$$Pr\left(z_{j,k} < \tau_2\epsilon\frac{d}{S}\right) = 2\cdot\tau_2\epsilon\frac{d}{S}\cdot\frac{1}{l}$$

where $\tau_2 \geq 2$, $\epsilon > 1$ are constants. Since $\lambda'_t \geq \min_{j,k}\{z_{j,k}\}$, we have

$$\begin{aligned}
Pr\left(\lambda'_t < \tau_2\epsilon\frac{d}{S}\right) &\leq Pr\left(\min_{\substack{1\leq j\leq\phi \\ 1\leq k\leq S}}\{z_{j,k}\} < \tau_2\epsilon\frac{d}{S}\right) \\
&\leq \phi S\cdot Pr\left(z_{j,k} < \tau_2\epsilon\frac{d}{S}\right) \\
&= \phi S\cdot 2\tau_2\epsilon\frac{d}{Sl} \\
&= 2\tau_2\epsilon\cdot\frac{\phi d}{l}
\end{aligned}$$

When λ'_t is given, we have $\mathbf{E}[\xi'] \geq \frac{\lambda'_t}{2}$. Thus

$$\begin{aligned}
Pr\left(\xi' > \epsilon\frac{d}{S}\right) &\geq Pr\left(\xi' > \epsilon\frac{d}{S}, \lambda'_t > \tau_2\epsilon\frac{d}{S}\right) \\
&= Pr\left(\xi' > \epsilon\frac{d}{S} \middle| \lambda'_t > \tau_2\epsilon\frac{d}{S}\right) Pr\left(\lambda'_t > \tau_2\epsilon\frac{d}{S}\right) \\
&= Pr\left(\frac{c\xi'}{\lambda'_t/2} > \frac{2c\epsilon d}{S\lambda'_t} \middle| \lambda'_t > \tau_2\epsilon\frac{d}{S}\right) \\
&\quad \cdot Pr\left(\lambda'_t > \tau_2\epsilon\frac{d}{S}\right) \\
&\geq Pr\left(\chi_c^2 > \frac{2c}{\tau_2}\right)\left(1 - 2\tau_2\epsilon\cdot\frac{\phi d}{l}\right) \quad (14) \\
&\geq \left(1 - e^{-\left(\frac{\tau_2-2}{2\tau_2}\right)^2 c}\right)\left(1 - 2\tau_2\epsilon\cdot\frac{\phi d}{l}\right)
\end{aligned}$$

The inequality (14) holds since $\frac{c\xi'}{\mathbf{E}[\xi']} \sim \chi_c^2$, $\mathbf{E}[\xi'] \geq \frac{\lambda'_t}{2}$ and $\frac{S\lambda'_t}{\epsilon d} > \tau_2$. The last inequality follows from Inequation (3), in which $x = -(\frac{\tau_2-2}{2\tau_2})^2 c$. Similar to Lemma 2, we can prove

$$\begin{aligned}
&Pr(\xi < \epsilon\frac{d}{S}) \\
&\geq \left(1 - e^{-\frac{1}{4}\left(-\sqrt{c}+\sqrt{\frac{(2-\tau_1)c}{\tau_1}}\right)^2}\right)\left(1 - f_1(d,S)e^{-f_2(d,S)\cdot\tau_1\epsilon\frac{d}{S}}\right)
\end{aligned}$$

where $f_1(d, S)$ and $f_2(d, S)$ are functions of d and S.

Furthermore, we have

$$\begin{aligned}
Pr(\overline{E}_s) &\geq Pr(\xi < \xi') \\
&\geq Pr\left(\xi < \epsilon\frac{d}{S}, \xi' > \epsilon\frac{d}{S}\right) \\
&= Pr\left(\xi < \epsilon\frac{d}{S} \middle| \xi' > \epsilon\frac{d}{S}\right) Pr\left(\xi' > \epsilon\frac{d}{S}\right) \\
&\geq Pr\left(\xi < \epsilon\frac{d}{S}\right) Pr\left(\xi' > \epsilon\frac{d}{S}\right)
\end{aligned}$$

Thus

$$\begin{aligned}
&Pr(\overline{E'_s}, E_s) \\
&= Pr(E'_s|E_s)Pr(E_s) \\
&\leq Pr(E_s) \\
&= 1 - Pr(\overline{E_s}) \\
&\leq 1 - Pr\left(\xi < \epsilon\frac{d}{S}\right) Pr\left(\xi' > \epsilon\frac{d}{S}\right) \\
&< 1 - \left(1 - e^{-\frac{1}{4}\left(-\sqrt{c}+\sqrt{\frac{(2-\tau_1)c}{\tau_1}}\right)^2}\right)\left(1 - e^{-\left(\frac{\tau_2-2}{2\tau_2}\right)^2 c}\right) \\
&\quad \cdot \left(1 - f_1(d,S)e^{-f_2(d,S)\cdot\tau_1\epsilon\frac{d}{S}}\right)\left(1 - 2\tau_2\epsilon\cdot\frac{\phi d}{l}\right)
\end{aligned}$$

□

C. PROOF OF LEMMA 4

PROOF. (Notations used in this proof is identical with that used in the proof of Lemma 3.) If there are both insertions and deletions in the packet, when $S < \phi + 1$ it is possible that there is no clean slice in some iterations. If this happens, we have

$$Pr(E_s) = 1$$

and

$$\begin{aligned}
Pr(\overline{E'_s}, E_s) &= Pr(\overline{E'_s}|E_s)P(E_s) \\
&= Pr(\overline{E'_s}|E_s) \\
&= Pr(\xi' < \alpha_1) \qquad (15)\\
&= 1 - Pr(\xi' > \alpha_1) \\
&< \delta_1
\end{aligned}$$

The proof of the above upper bound for $Pr(\xi' > \alpha_1)$ is quite similar to the proof of $Pr\left(\xi' > \epsilon\frac{d}{S}\right)$ in Lemma 3. The only difference is the lower bound of $\mathbf{E}[\xi']$. Specifically, we want to prove

$$Pr(\mathbf{E}[\xi'] > \frac{1}{2}\tau_2\alpha_1) > 1 - 2\tau_2\beta\cdot\frac{\phi D}{l} \qquad (16)$$

Note that $\lambda'_t \geq \min_{j,k}\{z_{j,k}\}$ if there are only insertions or only deletions in the selected slice. Otherwise, there are at least one insertion W_{ins} and one deletion W_{del} in the slice. Without of loss of generality, assume W_{del} is located on the right of W_{ins}, and there's no other deletions between W_{ins} and the left end of the slice. Let $\vec{x}_{t,1}$ denote the part of slice between W_{ins} and W_{del}. Let $\vec{x}_{t,2}$ denote the part between W_{ins} and the left end of the slice. Then, either $\vec{x}_{t,1}$ is mismatched or $\vec{x}_{t,2}$ is mismatched. Since the length of $\vec{x}_{t,1}$ is larger than Δ and the length of $\vec{x}_{t,2}$ is larger than $\min_{j,k}\{z_{j,k}\}$, we have $\lambda'_t \geq \min\{\min_{j,k}\{z_{j,k}\}, \Delta\}$. Hence,

$$\begin{aligned}
\mathbf{E}[\xi_i] &\geq \frac{1}{2}\lambda'_t \\
&\geq \frac{1}{2}\min\left\{\min_{j,k} z_{j,k}, \Delta\right\} \qquad (17)
\end{aligned}$$

Furthermore, we have

$$\begin{aligned}
&Pr\left(\min\left\{\min_{j,k} z_{j,k}, \Delta\right\} < \tau_2\alpha_1\right) \\
&= Pr\left(\min_{j,k} z_{j,k} < \tau_2\alpha_1\right) \qquad (18)\\
&< 2\tau_2\beta\cdot\frac{\phi D}{l}
\end{aligned}$$

Thus, Inequation (16) can be obtained by combining Inequation (17) and (18).

When $S \geq \phi+1$, there must exist at least one clean slice. Similar to that in Lemma 3, we can prove

$$Pr(\overline{E'_s}, E_s) \leq Pr(E_s) < \delta_2 \qquad (19)$$

Thus the lemma follows by combining Equation (15) and Equation (19). □

Data Dissemination Performance in Large-Scale Sensor Networks

Thomas M.M. Meyfroyt, Sem C. Borst, Onno J. Boxma
Eindhoven University of Technology
P.O. Box 513, 5600 MB Eindhoven, The Netherlands
{t.m.m.meyfroyt, s.c.borst, o.j.boxma}@tue.nl

Dee Denteneer
Philips Research
HTC 34, 5656 AE Eindhoven, The Netherlands
dee.denteneer@philips.com

ABSTRACT

As the use of wireless sensor networks increases, the need for (energy-)efficient and reliable broadcasting algorithms grows. Ideally, a broadcasting algorithm should have the ability to quickly disseminate data, while keeping the number of transmissions low. In this paper we develop a model describing the message count in large-scale wireless sensor networks. We focus our attention on the popular Trickle algorithm, which has been proposed as a suitable communication protocol for code maintenance and propagation in wireless sensor networks. Besides providing a mathematical analysis of the algorithm, we propose a generalized version of Trickle, with an additional parameter defining the length of a listen-only period. This generalization proves to be useful for optimizing the design and usage of the algorithm. For single-cell networks we show how the message count increases with the size of the network and how this depends on the Trickle parameters. Furthermore, we derive distributions of inter-broadcasting times and investigate their asymptotic behavior. Our results prove conjectures made in the literature concerning the effect of a listen-only period. Additionally, we develop an approximation for the expected number of transmissions in multi-cell networks. All results are validated by simulations.

Categories and Subject Descriptors

C.2.1 [**Computer-Communication Networks**]: Network Architecture and Design—*Wireless Communication*

General Terms

ALGORITHMS, DESIGN, PERFORMANCE

Keywords

Analytical model, gossip protocol, message count, message overhead, Trickle algorithm, wireless sensor networks

SIGMETRICS'14, June 16–20, 2014, Austin, Texas, USA.

http://dx.doi.org/10.1145/2591971.2591981.

1. INTRODUCTION

Wireless sensor networks (WSNs) have become more and more popular in the last few years and have many applications [1]. These networks consist of compact, inexpensive sensor units that can communicate with each other by wireless transmissions. They require efficient and reliable communication protocols that can quickly propagate new information, while keeping the number of transmissions low, in order to conserve energy and maximize the lifetime of the network. Several data dissemination protocols have been proposed in recent years for this purpose [3, 5, 13, 18, 20].

In [13] the Trickle algorithm has been proposed in order to effectively and efficiently distribute and maintain code in wireless sensor networks. Trickle relies on a "polite gossip" policy to quickly propagate updates across a network of nodes. It uses a counter method to reduce the number of redundant transmissions in a network and to prevent a broadcast storm [15]. This makes Trickle also a very energy-efficient and popular method of maintaining a sensor network. The algorithm has been standardized by the IETF as the mechanism that regulates the transmission of the control messages used to create the network graph in the IPv6 Routing Protocol for Low power and Lossy Networks (RPL) [19]. Additionally, it is used in the Multicast Protocol for Low power and Lossy Networks (MPL), which provides IPv6 multicast forwarding in constrained networks and is currently being standardized [8]. Since the algorithm has such a broad applicability, the definition of Trickle has been documented in its own IETF RFC 6206 [12].

Because of the popularity of the algorithm, it is crucial to gain insight in how the various Trickle parameters influence network performance measures, such as energy consumption, available bandwidth and latency. It is clear that such insights are crucial for optimizing the performance of wireless sensor networks. However, there are only a few results in that regard, most of them obtained via simulation studies [11, 13].

Some analytical results are obtained in [2, 10, 11]. First, in [11] qualitative results are provided for the scalability of the Trickle algorithm, but a complete analysis is not given. More specifically, the authors of [11] state that in a lossless single-cell network without a listen-only period the expected number of messages per time interval scales as $\mathcal{O}(\sqrt{n})$. Here n is the number of nodes in the network and single-cell means that all the nodes in the network are within communication range from each other. Supposedly, introducing a listen-only period bounds the expected number of transmissions by a constant. The analysis in our paper confirms these claims and provides more explicit results. Secondly, in [10] a model is developed for estimating the message count of the Trickle algorithm in a multi-cell network, assuming a uniformly random spatial distribution of the nodes in the network. However, the influence of specific Trickle parameters on the message count is not explicitly addressed. Lastly, in [2] an analytical model is developed for the time it takes the Trickle algorithm to update a network, through the use of Laplace transforms. To the best of the authors' knowledge, no other analytical models for the performance of the Trickle algorithm have been published yet.

The goal of this paper is to develop and analyze stochastic models describing the Trickle algorithm and gain insight in how the Trickle parameters influence inter-transmission times and the message count. These insights could help optimize the energy-efficiency of the algorithm and consequently the lifetime of wireless sensor networks. Furthermore, knowing how the inter-transmission times depend on the various parameters, could help prevent hidden-node problems in a network and optimize the capacity of wireless sensor networks. Additionally, our models are relevant for the analysis of other communication protocols that build upon Trickle, such as CTP [7], Deluge [9] and Melete [20], and could give insight in their performance.

As key contributions of this paper, we first propose a generalized version of the Trickle algorithm by introducing a new parameter η, defining the length of a listen-only period. This addition proves to be useful for optimizing the design and usage of the algorithm. Furthermore, we derive the distribution of an inter-transmission time and the joint distribution of consecutive inter-transmission times for large-scale single-cell networks. We show how they depend on the Trickle parameters and investigate their asymptotic behavior. Additionally, we show that in a single-cell network without a listen-only period the expected number of transmissions per time interval is unbounded and grows as $\sqrt{2n}\Gamma\left[\frac{k+1}{2}\right]/\Gamma\left[\frac{k}{2}\right]$, where k is called the redundancy constant and n the number of nodes as before. When a listen-only period of $\eta > 0$ is introduced, the message count is bounded by k/η from above. We then use the results from the single-cell analysis to develop an approximation for the transmission count in multi-cell networks. All our results are compared and validated with simulation results and prove to be accurate, even for networks consisting of relatively few nodes.

1.1 Organization of the Paper

The remainder of this paper is organized as follows. In Section 2 we give a detailed description of the Trickle algorithm. Furthermore, we introduce a new parameter defining the length of a listen-only period and discuss its relevance. In Section 3 we develop a mathematical model describing the behavior of the Trickle algorithm in large-scale single-cell networks. We first briefly list the main results, before presenting the details of the model and its analysis. This is followed by a brief discussion of our results and finally we validate our findings with simulations. In Section 4, we use the results from Section 3 to approximate the message count in multi-cell networks and again compare our approximations with simulation results. In Section 5 we make some concluding remarks.

2. THE TRICKLE ALGORITHM

The Trickle algorithm has two main goals. First, whenever a new update enters the network, it must be propagated quickly throughout the network. Secondly, when there is no new update in the network, communication overhead has to be kept to a minimum.

The Trickle algorithm achieves this by using a "polite gossip" policy. Nodes divide time into intervals of varying length. During each interval a node will broadcast its current information, if it has heard fewer than, say, k other nodes transmit the same information during that interval, in order to check if its information is up to date. If it has recently heard at least k other nodes transmit the same information it currently has, it will stay quiet, assuming there is no new information to be received. Additionally, it will increase the length of its intervals, decreasing its broadcasting rate. Whenever a node receives an update or hears outdated information, it will reduce the length of its intervals, increasing its broadcasting rate, in order to quickly update nodes that have outdated information. This way inconsistencies are detected and resolved quickly, while keeping the number of transmissions low.

2.1 Algorithm Description

We now describe the Trickle algorithm in its most general form (see also [13]). The algorithm has four parameters:

- A threshold value k, called the redundancy constant.
- The maximum interval length τ_h.
- The minimum interval length τ_l.
- The listen-only parameter η, defining the length of a listen-only period.

Furthermore, each node in the network has its own timer and keeps track of three variables:

- The current interval length τ.
- A counter c, counting the number of messages heard during an interval.
- A broadcasting time θ during the current interval.

The behavior of each node is described by the following set of rules:

1. At the start of a new interval a node resets its timer and counter c and sets θ to a value in $[\eta\tau, \tau]$ uniformly at random.
2. When a node hears a message that is consistent with the information it has, it increments c by 1.
3. When a node's timer hits time θ, the node broadcasts its message if $c < k$.
4. When a node's timer hits time τ, it doubles its interval length τ up to τ_h and starts a new interval.
5. When a node hears a message that is inconsistent with its own information, then if $\tau > \tau_l$ it sets τ to τ_l and starts a new interval, otherwise it does nothing.

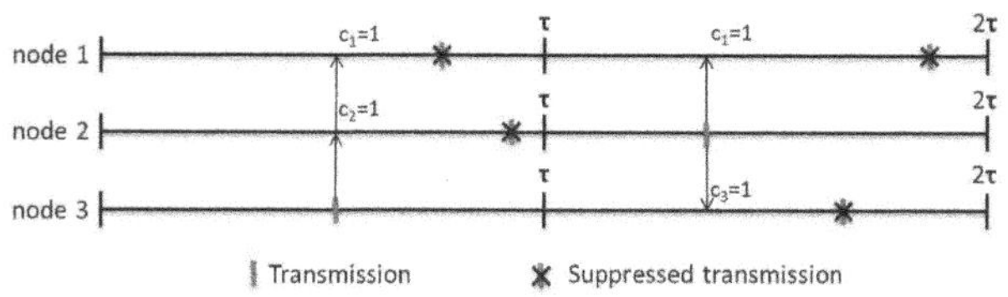

Figure 1: Example of three synchronized nodes using the Trickle algorithm.

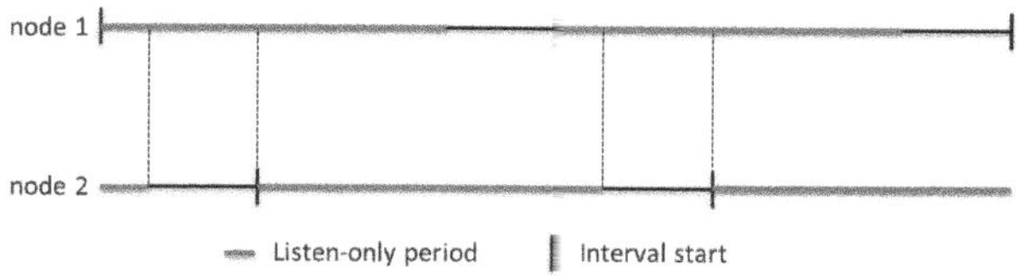

Figure 2: One node carries the complete transmission load of the network.

In Figure 1 an example is depicted of a network consisting of three nodes using the Trickle algorithm with $k = 1$ and $\tau = \tau_h$ for all nodes. During the first interval, node 3 is the first node that attempts to broadcast and consequently it is successful. The broadcasts of nodes 1 and 2 during that interval are then suppressed. During the second interval the broadcast of node 2 suppresses the other broadcasts.

Note that in the example in Figure 1, the intervals of the three nodes are synchronized. However, in general, the times at which nodes start their intervals need not be synchronized. In a synchronized network, all the nodes start their intervals at the same time, while in an unsynchronized network this is not necessarily the case. In practice, networks will generally not be synchronized, since synchronization requires additional communication and consequently imposes energy overhead. Furthermore, as nodes get updated and start new intervals, they automatically lose synchronicity.

2.2 The Listen-Only Parameter η

Note that the parameter η is not introduced in the description of the Trickle algorithm in [12] and [13]. We have added this parameter ourselves, so we can analyze a more general version of the Trickle algorithm. The authors of [13] propose to always use a listen-only period of half an interval, i.e., $\eta = \frac{1}{2}$, because of the so-called short-listen problem, which is discussed in the same paper. When no listen-only period is used, i.e., $\eta = 0$, sometimes nodes will broadcast soon after the beginning of their interval, listening for only a short time, before anyone else has a chance to speak up. If we have a perfectly synchronized network this does not give a problem, because the first k transmissions will simply suppress all the other broadcasts during that interval. However in an unsynchronized network, if a node has a short listening period, it might broadcast just before another node starts its interval and that node possibly also has a short listening period. This possibly leads to a lot of redundant messages and is referred to as the short-listen problem.

In [13] it is claimed that not having a listen-only period and $k = 1$ makes the number of messages per time interval scale as $\mathcal{O}(\sqrt{n})$, due to the short-listen problem. When a listen-only period of $\tau/2$ is used, the expected number of messages per interval is supposedly bounded by 2, resolving the short-listen problem and improving scalability.

However, introducing a listen-only period also has its disadvantages. Firstly, when a listen-only period of $\tau/2$ is used, newly updated nodes will always have to wait for a period of at least $\tau_l/2$, before attempting to propagate the received update. Consequently, in an m-hop network, the end-to-end delay is at least $m\frac{\tau_l}{2}$. Hence, a listen-only period greatly affects the speed at which the Trickle algorithm can propagate updates. Secondly, introducing a listen-only period has a negative effect on the load distribution. This is illustrated by Figure 2, where node 2's broadcasting intervals completely overlap with node 1's listen-only periods and vice versa. Consequently, one node will always transmit and suppress the other node's transmissions, depending on which node first starts broadcasting. The probability of having an uneven load distribution increases as η increases.

For these reasons one might want to consider using a shorter listen-only period, which raises the question what length is optimal. Therefore we have added the parameter η, which allows us to investigate the effect of using a listen-only period of general length on the message count.

3. SINGLE-CELL NETWORK

In this section we will develop a mathematical model for the message count in single-cell networks. We consider a steady-state regime, where all nodes are up to date and their interval lengths have settled to $\tau = \tau_h$. Since in this state all communication is essentially redundant, energy-consumption is the critical performance measure. We denote by $N^{(k,n)}$ the number of transmissions during an interval of length τ_h for a given threshold value k in a single-cell network consisting of n nodes. Without loss of generality, we will assume that $\tau_h = 1$. We are interested in determining the behavior of $\mathbb{E}[N^{(k,n)}]$ as n grows large. Additionally, let us denote an inter-transmission time for a given value of k and cell-size n by $T^{(k,n)}$. We will determine the distribution of $T^{(k,n)}$ as n grows large. Whenever we write $a(n) \sim b(n) + c$, where c is a constant, this means $a(n) - c$ is approximately equal to $b(n)$ as n grows large and more formally

$$a(n) \sim b(n) + c \text{ denotes } \lim_{n\to\infty} (a(n) - c)/b(n) = 1.$$

We first give a brief overview of our main results, before presenting the analytical model and its analysis. We then discuss our results and show through simulations, that our asymptotic results also provide good estimates for networks consisting of relatively few nodes.

3.1 Main Results

First we look at the case $k = 1$. We show that the cumulative distribution function of $T^{(1,n)}$ for large n behaves as

$$F^{(1,n)}(t) = \begin{cases} 0, & t < \eta, \\ 1 - e^{-\frac{n}{2}\frac{(t-\eta)^2}{1-\eta}}, & t \geq \eta. \end{cases} \tag{1}$$

This lets us deduce that

$$\mathbb{E}\left[T^{(1,n)}\right] \sim \eta + \sqrt{\frac{\pi(1-\eta)}{2n}}. \tag{2}$$

We conclude that $\mathbb{E}[N^{(1,n)}] \sim \sqrt{\frac{2n}{\pi}}$, when $\eta = 0$. This proves the claim from [13], that when no listen-only period is used, $\mathbb{E}[N^{(1,n)}] = \mathcal{O}(\sqrt{n})$, and shows that the pre-factor is $\sqrt{\frac{2}{\pi}}$. Furthermore, when $\eta > 0$, $\mathbb{E}[N^{(1,n)}] \uparrow \frac{1}{\eta}$, with a convergence rate of $\sqrt{n}$, proving another claim from [13].

For the case $k \geq 2$, we first derive the density function for the distribution of $k-1$ consecutive inter-broadcasting times. We then use this result to deduce that the density function of the distribution of $T^{(k,n)}$ for large n behaves as

$$f^{(k,n)}(t) = \frac{C_{(k,n)}}{(k-2)!}\int_0^\infty \lambda(t \mid \nu)\nu^{k-2}\exp\left[-\frac{n(t+\nu-\eta)^2}{2(1-\eta)}\right]\mathrm{d}\nu. \quad (3)$$

Here

$$\lambda(t \mid \nu) = \begin{cases} 0, & t+\nu < \eta, \\ \frac{n}{1-\eta}(t+\nu-\eta), & t+\nu \geq \eta, \end{cases} \quad (4)$$

and

$$C_{(k,n)} = \left(\frac{\eta^{k-1}}{(k-1)!} + \int_\eta^\infty \frac{t^{k-2}}{(k-2)!}\exp\left[-\frac{n(t-\eta)^2}{2(1-\eta)}\right]\mathrm{d}t\right)^{-1}. \quad (5)$$

Additionally we find for the jth moment of $T^{(k,n)}$:

$$\mathbb{E}\left[\left(T^{(k,n)}\right)^j\right] \sim j!\frac{C_{(k,n)}}{C_{(k+j,n)}}. \quad (6)$$

Hence, for $\eta = 0$, $\mathbb{E}[N^{(k,n)}] \sim \sqrt{2n}\Gamma\left[\frac{k+1}{2}\right]/\Gamma\left[\frac{k}{2}\right]$, which is again $\mathcal{O}(\sqrt{n})$. Moreover, when $\eta > 0$, $\mathbb{E}[N^{(k,n)}] \uparrow \frac{k}{\eta}$, as $n \to \infty$, with a convergence rate of $\sqrt{n}$.

We then use these results to derive the asymptotic distributions of inter-broadcasting times. When $\eta > 0$ and $k \geq 2$, we show that

$$\frac{1}{\eta}T^{(k,n)} \xrightarrow{d} \mathrm{Beta}(1, k-1), \text{ as } n \to \infty, \quad (7)$$

and

$$\frac{k}{\eta}T^{(k,n)} \xrightarrow{d} \mathrm{Exp}(1), \text{ as } n \to \infty \text{ and } k \to \infty. \quad (8)$$

For the case $\eta = 0$ we show that the density function $f^{(k)}(t)$ of the limiting distribution of $\sqrt{\frac{n}{2}}T^{(k,n)}$ as $n \to \infty$, satisfies

$$f^{(k)}(t) = \frac{k-2}{k-3}f^{(k-2)}(t) - \frac{\Gamma\left[\frac{k}{2}\right]}{\Gamma\left[\frac{k-1}{2}\right]}\frac{2t}{k-3}f^{(k-1)}(t), \quad (9)$$

where

$$f^{(2)}(t) = \frac{2}{\sqrt{\pi}}e^{-t^2},$$
$$f^{(3)}(t) = \sqrt{\pi}\mathrm{erfc}(t).$$

Lastly we show that

$$\sqrt{nk}T^{(k,n)} \xrightarrow{d} \mathrm{Exp}(1), \text{ as } n \to \infty \text{ and } k \to \infty. \quad (10)$$

3.2 Analytical Model

Suppose we have a single-cell network consisting of n nodes which are all perfect receivers and transmitters. Furthermore, we assume that all nodes are up to date and $\tau = \tau_h = 1$ for all nodes. Lastly, we assume that the interval skew of the nodes is uniformly distributed, meaning each node has one interval starting at some time in the interval $[0, 1)$ uniformly at random.

An important first observation we can make under these assumptions, is that the properly scaled process of nodes attempting to broadcast behaves as a Poisson process with rate 1 as n grows large.

LEMMA 1. *Let N_n be the point process of times that nodes attempt to broadcast in a single cell consisting of n nodes with $\eta \in [0, 1]$. Then if we dilate the timescale by a factor n, the process N_n converges weakly to a Poisson process with rate 1 as n grows large.*

PROOF. See Appendix A. □

We now use Lemma 1 to analyze the message count. In light of Lemma 1, we treat the process of nodes attempting to broadcast as a Poisson process with rate n. We will determine the PDF and CDF of an inter-transmission time $T_P^{(k,n)}$ for this process, which we denote by $f^{(k,n)}(t)$ and $F^{(k,n)}(t)$ respectively. Recall, that by $T^{(k,n)}$ we denote an inter-transmission time for a given value of k and cell-size n, for the original broadcasting process, which is not Poisson. We will use the fact that the distribution functions of $T_P^{(k,n)}$ and $T^{(k,n)}$ will behave the same for large n (because of Lemma 1), to investigate the behavior of $T^{(k,n)}$. It is important to keep in mind that we are analyzing the Poisson broadcasting process, and all results for $T^{(k,n)}$ (and $N^{(k,n)}$) are only true asymptotically, for $n \to \infty$.

3.2.1 $k = 1$

We first consider the case $k = 1$. Suppose at time 0 a broadcast occurs. Now assume at time t a node ends its listening period and attempts to broadcast. In order for the node's transmission to not be suppressed, it must have started its listening period after time 0. If it started listening before this time, it would have heard the transmission at time 0 and its broadcast would have been suppressed. This means that the node's broadcast will be successful if its corresponding timer was smaller than t. Since broadcasting times are picked uniformly in $[\eta, 1]$, this probability is 0 if $t < \eta$ and $\frac{t-\eta}{1-\eta}$ otherwise. Hence, if we define $\lambda(t)$ to be the instantaneous rate at which successful broadcasts occur, we can write

$$\lambda(t) = \begin{cases} 0, & t < \eta, \\ \frac{n}{1-\eta}(t-\eta), & t \geq \eta. \end{cases}$$

It is well known that the hazard rate $\lambda(t) = \frac{f^{(1,n)}(t)}{1-F^{(1,n)}(t)}$ uniquely determines $F^{(1,n)}(t) = \mathbb{P}[T_P^{(1,n)} \leq t]$ (see [6], Theorem 2.1):

$$F^{(1,n)}(t) = 1 - e^{-\int_0^t \lambda(u)\,du} = \begin{cases} 0, & t < \eta, \\ 1 - e^{-\frac{n}{2}\frac{(t-\eta)^2}{1-\eta}}, & t \geq \eta. \end{cases} \quad (11)$$

Hence, $\sqrt{\frac{n}{1-\eta}}(T_P^{(1,n)} - \eta)$ is a Rayleigh distributed random variable with scale parameter $\sigma = 1$. Therefore,

$$\mathbb{E}\left[T^{(1,n)}\right] \sim \mathbb{E}\left[T_P^{(1,n)}\right] = \eta + \sqrt{\frac{\pi(1-\eta)}{2n}}.$$

We conclude

$$\mathbb{E}\left[N^{(1,n)}\right] = \left(\mathbb{E}\left[T^{(1,n)}\right]\right)^{-1} \sim \left(\sqrt{\frac{\pi(1-\eta)}{2n}} + \eta\right)^{-1}. \quad (12)$$

Hence, for the case $\eta = 0$ we find $\mathbb{E}[N^{(1,n)}] \sim \sqrt{\frac{2n}{\pi}}$. This proves the claim from [13], that $\mathbb{E}[N^{(1,n)}] = \mathcal{O}(\sqrt{n})$ when no listen-only period is used. For $\eta > 0$ we get from (12) that

$$\mathbb{E}\left[N^{(1,n)}\right] \sim \frac{1}{\eta} - \frac{1}{\eta^2}\sqrt{\frac{\pi(1-\eta)}{2n}} + \mathcal{O}(n^{-1}).$$

This implies $\mathbb{E}[N^{(1,n)}] \uparrow \frac{1}{\eta}$ from below, proving the claim that introducing a listen-only period bounds the number of transmissions per interval by a constant.

3.2.2 $k = 2$

Let us now look at the case $k = 2$. We can apply a similar reasoning. Suppose again that at time 0 a broadcast occurs and let $-T_{-1}$ be the time of the last broadcast before time 0. Now similarly as before, a broadcasting attempt at time t will be successful, if the corresponding node started its listening interval after time $-T_{-1}$. Hence, the instantaneous rate at which successful broadcasts occur conditioned on $T_{-1} = \nu$ is given by

$$\lambda(t \mid \nu) = \begin{cases} 0, & t+\nu < \eta, \\ \frac{n}{1-\eta}(t+\nu-\eta), & t+\nu \geq \eta. \end{cases} \quad (13)$$

Hence,

$$\mathbb{P}\left[T_P^{(2,n)} \leq t \mid T_{-1} = \nu\right] = 1 - \exp\left[-\int_0^t \lambda(u \mid \nu)\mathrm{d}u\right]$$

$$= \begin{cases} 0, & t+\nu < \eta, \\ 1-\exp\left[-\frac{n(t+\nu-\eta)^2}{2(1-\eta)}\right], & \nu < \eta \wedge t+\nu \geq \eta, \\ 1-\exp\left[-\frac{n(t^2/2+t(\nu-\eta))}{1-\eta}\right], & \nu \geq \eta. \end{cases} \quad (14)$$

This tells us that for $k = 2$ the sequence of consecutive inter-transmission times $\boldsymbol{T_P^{(2,n)}} = \{T_{P,i}^{(2,n)}\}_{i=0}^{\infty}$ forms a Markov chain with transition probabilities as in (14). Clearly the chain is ϕ-irreducible, that is every set $A \subset \mathbb{R}^+$ with Lebesgue measure $\mu_L(A) > 0$ will eventually be reached, since we can reach any state within two steps. Furthermore, the chain is Harris recurrent since every set $A \subset \mathbb{R}^+$ with $\mu_L(A) > 0$ will eventually be reached. Then, since the chain is also aperiodic, the following theorem applies (see [14], Theorem 13.0.1):

THEOREM 1. *Suppose $\boldsymbol{X}$ is a Markov chain. Suppose it is ϕ-irreducible, Harris recurrent and aperiodic and it admits a finite invariant probability measure $f(t)$, then this measure is unique.*

Hence, if our chain $\boldsymbol{T_P^{(2,n)}}$ admits an invariant distribution $f^{(2,n)}(t)$, it is the unique stationary distribution and it should satisfy

$$F^{(2,n)}(t) = \int_0^{\infty} \mathbb{P}\left[T_P^{(2,n)} \leq t \mid T_{-1} = \nu\right] \mathrm{d}F^{(2,n)}(\nu). \quad (15)$$

Substituting Equation (14) into (15) and differentiating with respect to t gives an integral equation for $f^{(2,n)}(t)$:

$$f^{(2,n)}(t) = \int_0^{\infty} f^{(2,n)}(\nu)\lambda(t \mid \nu)\exp\left[-\int_0^t \lambda(u \mid \nu)\mathrm{d}u\right]\mathrm{d}\nu. \quad (16)$$

By substituting Equation (13) we can write the right-hand side of Equation (16) for $t < \eta$ as

$$\begin{aligned} &\int_{\eta-t}^{\eta} f^{(2,n)}(\nu)\frac{n(t+\nu-\eta)}{1-\eta}\exp\left[-\frac{n(t+\nu-\eta)^2}{2(1-\eta)}\right]\mathrm{d}\nu \\ &+ \int_{\eta}^{\infty} f^{(2,n)}(\nu)\frac{n(t+\nu-\eta)}{1-\eta}\exp\left[-\frac{n(t^2/2+t(\nu-\eta))}{1-\eta}\right]\mathrm{d}\nu, \end{aligned} \quad (17)$$

and for $t \geq \eta$ we get

$$\begin{aligned} &\int_0^{\eta} f^{(2,n)}(\nu)\frac{n(t+\nu-\eta)}{1-\eta}\exp\left[-\frac{n(t+\nu-\eta)^2}{2(1-\eta)}\right]\mathrm{d}\nu \\ &+ \int_{\eta}^{\infty} f^{(2,n)}(\nu)\frac{n(t+\nu-\eta)}{1-\eta}\exp\left[-\frac{n(t^2/2+t(\nu-\eta))}{1-\eta}\right]\mathrm{d}\nu. \end{aligned} \quad (18)$$

We show that the solution to this equation is given by

$$f^{(2,n)}(t) = \begin{cases} C_{(2,n)}, & t < \eta, \\ C_{(2,n)}\exp\left[-\frac{n(t-\eta)^2}{2(1-\eta)}\right], & t \geq \eta, \end{cases} \quad (19)$$

where $C_{(2,n)} = \left(\eta + \sqrt{\frac{(1-\eta)\pi}{2n}}\right)^{-1}$ is a normalization constant. Substitution of (19) reduces (17) for $t < \eta$ to

$$C_{(2,n)}\int_{\eta-t}^{\infty} \frac{n(t+\nu-\eta)}{1-\eta}\exp\left[-\frac{n(t+\nu-\eta)^2}{2(1-\eta)}\right]\mathrm{d}\nu$$
$$= C_{(2,n)}\int_0^{\infty} z\exp\left[-\frac{z^2}{2}\right]\mathrm{d}z = C_{(2,n)}.$$

Similarly, for $t \geq \eta$ substitution of (19) reduces Equation (18) to

$$C_{(2,n)}\int_0^{\infty} \frac{n(t+\nu-\eta)}{1-\eta}\exp\left[-\frac{n(t+\nu-\eta)^2}{2(1-\eta)}\right]\mathrm{d}\nu$$
$$= C_{(2,n)}\int_{\frac{\sqrt{n}(t-\eta)}{\sqrt{1-\eta}}}^{\infty} z\exp\left[-\frac{z^2}{2}\right]\mathrm{d}z = C_{(2,n)}\exp\left[-\frac{n(t-\eta)^2}{2(1-\eta)}\right].$$

Thus, we have shown that $f^{(2,n)}(t)$ as given in Equation (19) is the unique solution to (16). Calculating the expectation of $T_P^{(2,n)}$ we conclude

$$\mathbb{E}\left[T^{(2,n)}\right] \sim \mathbb{E}\left[T_P^{(2,n)}\right] = \frac{\left(\frac{\eta^2}{2} + \eta\sqrt{\frac{\pi(1-\eta)}{2n}} + \frac{1-\eta}{n}\right)}{\left(\eta + \sqrt{\frac{\pi(1-\eta)}{2n}}\right)}. \quad (20)$$

For $\eta = 0$ this gives $\mathbb{E}[N^{(2,n)}] \sim \sqrt{\frac{\pi n}{2}}$, which is again $\mathcal{O}(\sqrt{n})$. If a listen-only period is used, i.e., $\eta > 0$, then from (20) we get

$$\mathbb{E}\left[N^{(2,n)}\right] \sim \frac{2}{\eta} - \frac{1}{\eta^2}\sqrt{\frac{2\pi(1-\eta)}{n}} + \mathcal{O}(n^{-1}),$$

implying $\mathbb{E}[N^{(2,n)}] \uparrow \frac{2}{\eta}$ from below as n grows large.

3.2.3 General $k \geq 2$

We move on to the more general case $k \geq 2$. Again suppose that at time 0 a broadcast occurs and let $-T_{-(k-1)}$ be the time of the $(k-1)$th broadcast before time 0. Now similarly as before, a broadcasting attempt at time t will be successful, if the corresponding node started its listening interval after time $-T_{-(k-1)}$. Hence, the instantaneous rate at which broadcasts occur conditioned on $T_{-(k-1)} = \nu$ is again given by Equation (13). Thus, the sequence $\boldsymbol{T_P^{(k,n)}} = \left\{\left(T_{P,i}^{(k,n)}, \ldots, T_{P,i+k-2}^{(k,n)}\right)\right\}_{i=0}^{\infty}$ forms a Markov chain. Since this chain is able to move from any state to any other state within k steps, it is easily seen that again Theorem 1 applies. Consequently, if it admits an invariant probability measure, it is unique. Let us denote the steady-state joint probability density function of $k-1$ consecutive inter-transmission times by $\tilde{f}^{(k,n)}(t_1, ..., t_{k-1})$. Similar to (16), $\tilde{f}^{(k,n)}(t_1, ..., t_{k-1})$ can then be written as

$$\tilde{f}^{(k,n)}(t_1, ..., t_{k-1}) = \int_0^\infty \tilde{f}^{(k,n)}(t_2, ..., t_k)\lambda\left(t_1 \mid \sum_{i=2}^{k} t_i\right) \cdot \exp\left[-\int_0^{t_1} \lambda\left(u \mid \sum_{i=2}^{k} t_i\right) du\right] dt_k. \quad (21)$$

Consequently, $\tilde{f}^{(k,n)}(t_1, ..., t_{k-1})$ has the same form as the solution in (19) and is given by

$$\tilde{f}^{(k,n)}(t_1, ..., t_{k-1}) = \begin{cases} C_{(k,n)}, & \sum_{i=1}^{k-1} t_i < \eta, \\ C_{(k,n)} \exp\left[-\frac{n}{2(1-\eta)}\left(\sum_{i=1}^{k-1} t_i - \eta\right)^2\right], & \sum_{i=1}^{k-1} t_i \geq \eta. \end{cases} \quad (22)$$

Here the normalization constant $C_{(k,n)}$ satisfies

$$C_{(k,n)} = \left(\frac{\eta^{k-1}}{(k-1)!} + \int_\eta^\infty \frac{t^{k-2}}{(k-2)!} \exp\left[-\frac{n(t-\eta)^2}{2(1-\eta)}\right] dt\right)^{-1}, \quad (23)$$

where we have used the following lemma:

LEMMA 2. *Let $k \in \mathbb{N}$ and $F(x)$ be a positive real-valued integrable function. Assume that $\int_0^\infty x^k F(x)dx < \infty$, then*

$$\int_0^\infty \cdots \int_0^\infty F\left(\sum_{i=1}^{k+1} x_i\right) dx_1 \cdots dx_{k+1} = \int_0^\infty \frac{x^k}{k!} F(x) dx.$$

PROOF. By writing $x = \sum_{i=1}^{k+1} x_i$ and a change of variables, we can write

$$\int_0^\infty \cdots \int_0^\infty F\left(\sum_{i=1}^{k+1} x_i\right) dx_1 \cdots dx_{k+1} = \int_0^\infty F(x) \underset{\substack{x_1+\cdots+x_k \leq x \\ x_i \geq 0 \text{ for } 1 \leq i \leq k}}{\int \cdots \int} dx_1 \cdots dx_k \, dx.$$

The inner k-tuple integral is equal to the volume of the k-dimensional simplex $\{(x_1, \cdots, x_k) \mid \sum_{i=1}^k x_i \leq x \text{ and } x_i \geq 0 \text{ for } 1 \leq i \leq k\}$, which is known to be $x^k/k!$ [16]. Applying this result completes the proof. □

Alternatively, by a change of variables and splitting the integral, we can write (23) in terms of a finite sum as

$$C_{(k,n)} = \left(\frac{\eta^{k-1}}{(k-1)!} + \frac{1}{2(k-2)!}\sum_{i=0}^{k-2}\binom{k-2}{i}\eta^{k-i-2}\left(\frac{2(1-\eta)}{n}\right)^{\frac{i+1}{2}}\Gamma\left[\frac{i+1}{2}\right]\right)^{-1},$$

which more clearly reveals the role of some of the parameters.

There are two important observations we can make regarding the normalization constant $C_{(k,n)}$. First, for $\eta = 0$ (23) reduces to $C_{(k,n)} = \pi^{-\frac{1}{2}}(2n)^{\frac{k-1}{2}}\Gamma[k/2]$. Secondly, for $\eta > 0$ we have that $C_{(k,n)} \downarrow \frac{(k-1)!}{\eta^{k-1}}$ as n grows large.

Let us look at the sequence $\mathbf{\Sigma}^{(k,n)} = \{\sum_{j=0}^{k-2} T_{P,i+j}^{(k,n)}\}_{i=0}^\infty$, i.e., the sequence of the sum of $k-1$ consecutive intertransmissions times. Integrating Equation (22) and applying Lemma 2, we can easily determine its steady-state probability density function:

$$f_\Sigma^{(k,n)}(s) = \begin{cases} \frac{C_{(k,n)}}{(k-2)!} s^{k-2}, & s < \eta, \\ \frac{C_{(k,n)}}{(k-2)!} s^{k-2} \exp\left[-\frac{n(s-\eta)^2}{2(1-\eta)}\right], & s \geq \eta. \end{cases} \quad (24)$$

This lets us deduce that for large n:

$$\mathbb{E}\left[T^{(k,n)}\right] \sim \frac{1}{k-1}\int_0^\infty s f_\Sigma^{(k,n)}(s) ds = \frac{C_{(k,n)}}{C_{(k+1,n)}}. \quad (25)$$

For the case $\eta = 0$ this implies

$$\mathbb{E}\left[N^{(k,n)}\right] = \left(\mathbb{E}\left[T^{(k,n)}\right]\right)^{-1} \sim \sqrt{2n}\frac{\Gamma\left[\frac{k+1}{2}\right]}{\Gamma\left[\frac{k}{2}\right]}, \quad (26)$$

which is again $\mathcal{O}(\sqrt{n})$. When a listen-only period is used, i.e., $\eta > 0$,

$$\mathbb{E}\left[N^{(k,n)}\right] \sim \frac{k}{\eta} - \frac{k}{\eta^2}\sqrt{\frac{\pi(1-\eta)}{2n}} + \mathcal{O}(n^{-1}), \quad (27)$$

implying that $\mathbb{E}[N^{(k,n)}] \uparrow \frac{k}{\eta}$ from below as $n \to \infty$.

Moreover, the function $f_\Sigma^{(k,n)}(s)$ allows us to determine the steady-state probability density function $f^{(k,n)}(t)$. Analogously to Equation (15), we can write

$$\begin{aligned} F^{(k,n)}(t) &= \int_0^\infty \mathbb{P}\left[T_P^{(k,n)} \leq t \mid T_{-(k-1)} = \nu\right] d\mathbb{P}[T_{-(k-1)} \leq \nu] \\ &= \int_0^\infty \left(1 - \exp\left[-\int_0^t \lambda(u \mid \nu)\, du\right]\right) f_\Sigma^{(k,n)}(\nu)\, d\nu. \end{aligned} \quad (28)$$

Differentiating (28) with respect to t and substituting Equation (24) gives

$$f^{(k,n)}(t) = \frac{C_{(k,n)}}{(k-2)!}\int_0^\infty \lambda(t \mid \nu)\nu^{k-2} \exp\left[-\frac{n(t+\nu-\eta)^2}{2(1-\eta)}\right] d\nu. \quad (29)$$

Substitution of Equation (13) reduces the right-hand side of (29) for $t < \eta$ to

$$\frac{n}{1-\eta}\frac{C_{(k,n)}}{(k-2)!}\int_{\eta-t}^\infty (t+\nu-\eta)\nu^{k-2} \exp\left[-\frac{n(t+\nu-\eta)^2}{2(1-\eta)}\right] d\nu, \quad (30)$$

and for $t \geq \eta$ the right-hand side reduces to

$$\frac{n}{1-\eta}\frac{C_{(k,n)}}{(k-2)!}\int_0^\infty (t+\nu-\eta)\nu^{k-2} \exp\left[-\frac{n(t+\nu-\eta)^2}{2(1-\eta)}\right] d\nu. \quad (31)$$

Lastly, Equation (28) in combination with Equations (13) and (24) allows to calculate the moments of $T_P^{(k,n)}$ as follows:

$$\begin{aligned} \mathbb{E}\left[\left(T_P^{(k,n)}\right)^j\right] &= j\int_0^\infty t^{j-1}(1 - F^{(k,n)}(t))\, dt = \\ &\frac{jC_{(k,n)}}{(k-2)!}\int_0^\infty \int_0^\infty t^{j-1}v^{k-2} \exp\left[-\frac{n \max[(t+v-\eta), 0]^2}{2(1-\eta)}\right] dt d\nu. \end{aligned} \quad (32)$$

Here we have used the max function, so we do not have to split the integral for the separate cases $t + \nu < \eta$ and $t + \nu \geq \eta$. In this form, Equation (32) can be rewritten with the use of the following lemma:

LEMMA 3. *Let $k \in \mathbb{N}$ and $F(x)$ be a positive real-valued integrable function. Assume that $\int_0^\infty x^{k+j+1}F(x)dx < \infty$, then*

$$\int_0^\infty \int_0^\infty x^j y^k F(x+y)\, dx dy = \frac{k!j!}{(k+j+1)!}\int_0^\infty z^{k+j+1}F(z)\, dz.$$

PROOF. Write $z = x + y$, then

$$\int_0^\infty \int_0^\infty x^j y^k F(x+y)\,\mathrm{d}x\,\mathrm{d}y$$
$$= \int_0^\infty \int_y^\infty (z-y)^j y^k F(z)\,\mathrm{d}z\,\mathrm{d}y$$
$$= \sum_{i=0}^{j} (-1)^i \binom{j}{i} \int_0^\infty \int_y^\infty z^{j-i} y^{k+i} F(z)\,\mathrm{d}z\,\mathrm{d}y$$
$$= \sum_{i=0}^{j} (-1)^i \binom{j}{i} \int_0^\infty z^{j-i} F(z) \int_0^z y^{k+i}\,\mathrm{d}y\,\mathrm{d}z$$
$$= \left(\sum_{i=0}^{j} (-1)^i \binom{j}{i} \frac{1}{1+i+k} \right) \int_0^\infty z^{1+k+j} F(z)\,\mathrm{d}z$$
$$= \frac{k!j!}{(k+j+1)!} \int_0^\infty z^{k+j+1} F(z)\,\mathrm{d}z.$$

The last equality follows from a known identity involving the reciprocal of binomial coefficients (see [17], Corollary 2.2). □

Applying Lemma 3 to Equation (32) gives

$$\frac{j!C_{(k,n)}}{(k+j-1)!} \int_0^\infty z^{k+j-1} \exp\left[-\frac{n \max[(z-\eta),0]^2}{2(1-\eta)} \right] \mathrm{d}z$$
$$= j!C_{(k,n)} \left(\frac{\eta^{k+j-1}}{(k+j-1)!} + \int_\eta^\infty \frac{z^{k+j-2}}{(k+j-2)!} \exp\left[-\frac{n(z-\eta)^2}{2(1-\eta)} \right] \mathrm{d}z \right).$$

Finally, using (23), we obtain the following insightful expression for the jth moment of an inter-transmission time

$$\mathbb{E}\left[\left(T^{(k,n)} \right)^j \right] \sim \mathbb{E}\left[\left(T_P^{(k,n)} \right)^j \right] = j! \frac{C_{(k,n)}}{C_{(k+j,n)}}. \quad (33)$$

For the special case $\eta = 0$ this reduces to

$$\mathbb{E}\left[\left(T^{(k,n)} \right)^j \right] \sim \frac{j!}{(2n)^{\frac{j}{2}}} \frac{\Gamma\left[\frac{k}{2}\right]}{\Gamma\left[\frac{k+j}{2}\right]}. \quad (34)$$

For the case $\eta > 0$ we deduce

$$\mathbb{E}\left[\left(T^{(k,n)} \right)^j \right] \to \frac{(k-1)!j!}{(k+j-1)!} \eta^j, \text{ as } n \to \infty. \quad (35)$$

3.2.4 Limiting Distributions

The previous analysis allows us to determine the limiting distributions of $T^{(k,n)}$ as n and k grow large. We distinguish between two cases.

Case 1: $\eta > 0$.

First, Equation (35) implies that for $\eta > 0$ and $k \geq 2$

$$\frac{1}{\eta} T^{(k,n)} \xrightarrow{d} \text{Beta}(1, k-1), \text{ as } n \to \infty, \quad (36)$$

since all moments converge to the moments of the Beta distribution. For the density function of $T_P^{(k,n)}$ (and hence also that of $T^{(k,n)}$) this implies that as $n \to \infty$,

$$f^{(k,n)}(t) \to \begin{cases} \frac{(k-1)}{\eta} \left(1 - \frac{t}{\eta}\right)^{k-2}, & 0 \leq t \leq \eta, \\ 0, & \text{otherwise.} \end{cases} \quad (37)$$

Furthermore, since $k\text{Beta}(1,k) \xrightarrow{d} \text{Exp}(1)$ for $k \to \infty$,

$$\frac{k}{\eta} T^{(k,n)} \xrightarrow{d} \text{Exp}(1), \text{ as } n \to \infty \text{ and } k \to \infty. \quad (38)$$

We can relate this result to Equation (22). We know that the sum of k consecutive inter-transmission times converges to η as $n \to \infty$. Equation (22) then tells us that if we look at an interval of length η, $k-1$ broadcasting times are distributed uniformly in this interval, when $n \to \infty$. Therefore, if we scale time by a factor k we will see a Poisson process with intensity 1, as $k \to \infty$, and expect to see exponential inter-broadcasting times, which is in agreement with (38).

Case 2: $\eta = 0$.

For the case $\eta = 0$, we can write the density function $f^{(k)}(t)$ of the limiting distribution of $\sqrt{\frac{n}{2}} T^{(k,n)}$ for $k \geq 2$ after scaling Equation (31) as

$$f^{(k)}(t) = \frac{4}{\Gamma\left[\frac{k-1}{2}\right]} \int_0^\infty (t+\nu)\nu^{k-2} \exp\left[-(t+\nu)^2\right] \mathrm{d}\nu$$
$$= \frac{4}{\Gamma\left[\frac{k-1}{2}\right]} t \int_0^\infty \nu^{k-2} \exp\left[-(t+\nu)^2\right] \mathrm{d}\nu \quad (39)$$
$$- \frac{4}{\Gamma\left[\frac{k-1}{2}\right]} \int_0^\infty \nu^{k-1} \exp\left[-(t+\nu)^2\right] \mathrm{d}\nu.$$

Alternatively, performing integration by parts gives

$$f^{(k)}(t) = \frac{2(k-1)}{\Gamma\left[\frac{k-1}{2}\right]} \int_0^\infty \nu^{k-3} \exp\left[-(t+\nu)^2\right] \mathrm{d}\nu. \quad (40)$$

Combining (39) and (40), we find after some rewriting

$$f^{(k)}(t) = \frac{k-2}{k-3} f^{(k-2)}(t) - \frac{\Gamma\left[\frac{k}{2}\right]}{\Gamma\left[\frac{k-1}{2}\right]} \frac{2t}{k-3} f^{(k-1)}(t). \quad (41)$$

Direct computation gives

$$f^{(2)}(t) = \frac{2}{\sqrt{\pi}} e^{-t^2},$$

and

$$f^{(3)}(t) = \sqrt{\pi}\,\text{erfc}(t).$$

All other distribution functions then follow from Equation (41). Additionally, from Equation (34) we have

$$\mathbb{E}\left[\left(\sqrt{n} T^{(k,n)} \right)^j \right] \to \frac{j!}{2^{\frac{j}{2}}} \frac{\Gamma\left[\frac{k}{2}\right]}{\Gamma\left[\frac{k+j}{2}\right]}, \text{ as } n \to \infty. \quad (42)$$

Using the fact that

$$\lim_{k \to \infty} \frac{\Gamma\left[\frac{k}{2}\right] \left(\frac{k}{2}\right)^{\frac{j}{2}}}{\Gamma\left[\frac{k+j}{2}\right]} = 1,$$

we find

$$\mathbb{E}\left[\left(\sqrt{nk} T^{(k,n)} \right)^j \right] \to j!, \text{ as } n \to \infty \text{ and } k \to \infty. \quad (43)$$

This finally implies that

$$\sqrt{nk} T^{(k,n)} \xrightarrow{d} \text{Exp}(1), \text{ as } n \to \infty \text{ and } k \to \infty, \quad (44)$$

since all moments converge to the moments of the exponential distribution.

The last result can be related to Lemma 1. If we look at the special case $k = n$, we know all broadcasting attempts will be successful. Hence, the process of nodes broadcasting will be the same as the process of nodes attempting to broadcast, from which we know it converges to a Poisson process with rate 1, as $n \to \infty$, if we scale time by a factor

n, because of Lemma 1. Furthermore, (44) also tells us that for this case, if we scale time by a factor n, we expect to see exponential inter-transmission times with rate 1. So these results are in good agreement with each other.

3.3 Discussion of Results

We briefly discuss the implications of our results. First, Equation (26) gives us insight in the effects of the short-listen problem. We found that without a listen-only period the number of transmissions per time unit scales as $\mathcal{O}(\sqrt{n})$, due to the short-listen problem. However, by introducing a listen-only period, the expected number of transmissions per interval is bounded by k/η, see (27). Hence, having $\eta = \frac{1}{2}$ as suggested in [13] reduces the number of redundant transmissions and resolves the short-listen problem.

However, one could also consider using lower values of η. For example, one could consider setting $\eta = \frac{1}{4}$. We know this roughly doubles the expected number of redundant transmissions, but it could also double the propagation speed. Indeed, whenever a node gets updated, it only has to wait for a period of at least $\tau_l/4$ before propagating the update, as opposed to a period of $\tau_l/2$. Hence, the choice of η involves a trade-off. Lowering η increases the propagation speed, but also the number of transmissions. In order to get a full understanding of this trade-off, more knowledge is needed on the propagation speed of the algorithm. Combined with results from this paper, this knowledge could provide guidelines for how to optimally set the Trickle parameters and the length of the listen-only period.

Second, Equations (11), (29), (37), (38), (41) and (44) provide insight in the distributions of inter-transmission times. In our derivations, we have assumed that transmissions are instantaneous. However, in reality transmissions take some time, although this time is generally short compared to the interval length τ_h. Using the inter-transmission time distributions, one can estimate the probability that transmissions would overlap in time and hence interfere. Potentially, one can use this knowledge to optimize the medium access protocol and the capacity of the wireless network.

3.4 Simulations

The model we have developed assumes that the process of nodes attempting to broadcast is Poisson with rate n. Lemma 1 shows that this is true as n grows large. We now investigate how well this assumption holds in networks with only a few nodes. In order to do so, we compare our analytic results for the message count and the distribution of inter-transmissions times with simulations done in Mathematica. We simulate a lossless single-cell network using the Trickle algorithm, where transmissions occur instantaneously. In Figure 3, we compare simulation results for the case $\eta = 0$ with the analytic results from Equation (26). For each combination of k and n, we simulate a network consisting of n nodes using the Trickle algorithm and average over 10^3 runs of 100 virtual time units. Each run, we use a different interval skew chosen uniformly at random for each of the nodes. We see that the simulation results and the analytic results coincide very well, even for small cell-sizes, and that the analytic results provide a conservative estimate for the mean number of transmissions per interval.

In Figure 4, we compare simulation results for the case $\eta = 0$, $k = 1$ and $n = 50$ with the analytic results from Equation (11). We show a histogram of the observed inter-

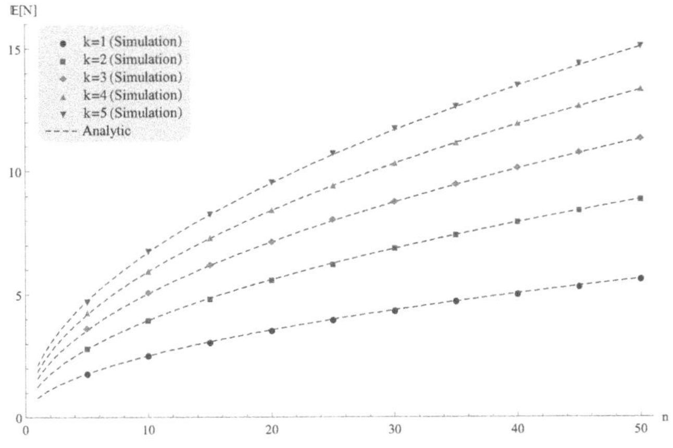

Figure 3: Mean number of transmissions per interval for $\eta = 0$: analysis vs simulation.

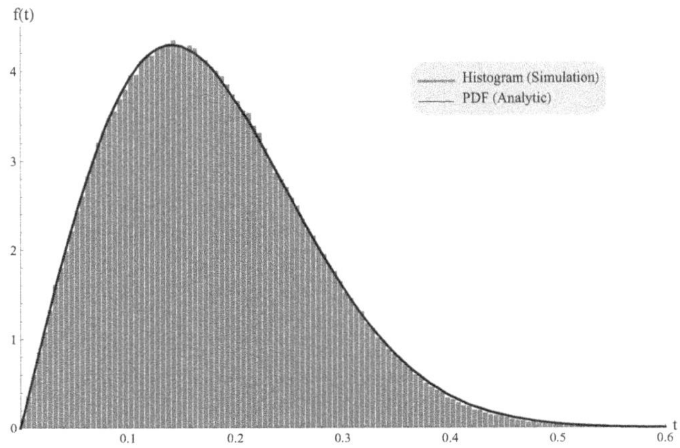

Figure 4: Density plot of inter-transmission times for $\eta = 0$, $k = 1$ and $n = 50$: analysis vs simulation.

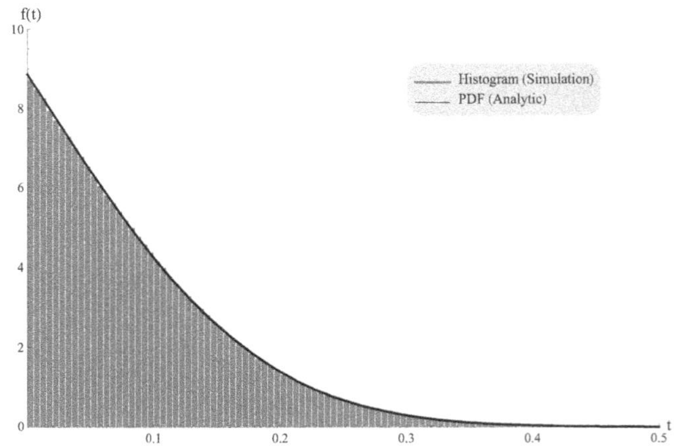

Figure 5: Density plot of inter-transmission times for $\eta = 0$, $k = 3$ and $n = 50$: analysis vs simulation.

transmission times obtained from 10^3 runs of 100 virtual time units and the probability density function from (11). We see a very good match between the analytic result and simulations, even though we consider a network consisting of only 50 nodes.

In Figure 5, we compare (29) with simulations for the case $\eta = 0$, $k = 3$ and $n = 50$. Again, both results are in good agreement with each other, despite the relatively small size of the network. Note, also, that the asymptotically exponential behavior from (44) can already be seen in the density plot.

In Figure 6 we compare simulation results for the case $\eta = \frac{1}{2}$ with analytic results from Equation (27). Here, also, we find that the analysis gives an accurate estimate for the mean number of transmissions in small networks. From our analysis we also know that $\mathbb{E}[N^{(k,n)}]$ should converge to $2k$ as n grows large. From the graph we see that this convergence is quite slow.

In Figures 7 and 8 we compare simulation results for $k = 1$ and $k = 3$ respectively with the analytic results from Equations (11) and (29), where $\eta = \frac{1}{2}$ and $n = 50$. Like before, we see a very good match between the analytic results and simulations. Note, that the asymptotic behavior from (36) can already be recognized in the density plot of Figure 8.

Additionally, we have simulated more realistic network settings in the OMNeT++ simulation tool. As mentioned in Section 3.3, in reality, transmissions do not occur instantaneously but take some time M, hence collisions can occur. To investigate the effect of not having instantaneous and possibly colliding transmissions, we have simulated the same scenarios as we did with Mathematica and compared the results. The simulator incorporates IEEE standard 802.15.4.

We find that the OMNeT++ and Mathematica simulations produce nearly indistinguishable results, which is not surprising. Since τ_h tends to be very large compared to a transmission length M, the probability of nodes trying to broadcast simultaneously tends to be very small. Furthermore, since we are dealing with a single-cell network, the CSMA/CA protocol prevents all collisions in the OMNeT++ simulations. Therefore, both simulators provide nearly the same results. Since the Mathematica simulations are computationally less demanding and much more easily reproducible, we have omitted the OMNeT++ simulation data.

4. MULTI-CELL NETWORK

Suppose now that we have a network consisting of n^2 nodes placed on a square grid, where not all nodes are able to directly communicate with each other. Instead, each node has a fixed transmission range R, which means that when a node sends a message, only nodes within a distance R of the broadcaster receive the message. While a full-fledged analysis of multi-cell networks is beyond the scope of the present paper, we now briefly examine how the results for the single-cell scenario obtained in Subsection 3.2 can be leveraged to derive a useful approximation. We denote by $N_{MC}^{(k,n,R)}$ the number of transmissions during an interval of length τ_h for a given threshold value k in a cell consisting of $n \times n$ nodes with broadcasting range R. Hence, we are interested in determining the behavior of $\mathbb{E}\left[N_{MC}^{(k,n,R)}\right]$.

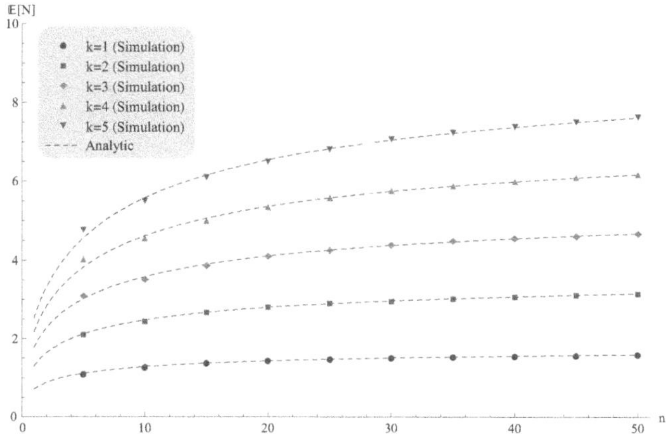

Figure 6: Mean number of transmissions per interval for $\eta = \frac{1}{2}$: analysis vs simulation.

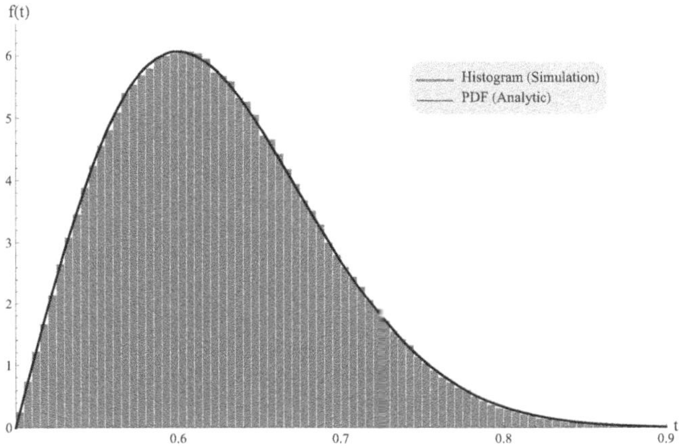

Figure 7: Density plot of inter-transmission times for $\eta = \frac{1}{2}$, $k = 1$ and $n = 50$: analysis vs simulation.

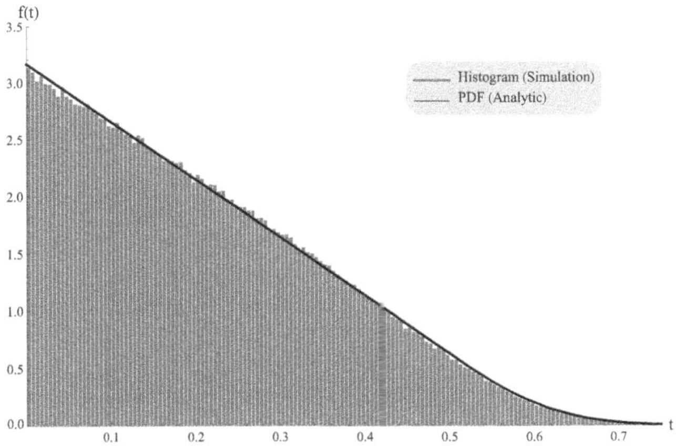

Figure 8: Density plot of inter-transmission times for $\eta = \frac{1}{2}$, $k = 3$ and $n = 50$: analysis vs simulation.

4.1 Approximation

We will use the analytical results from Section 3 to develop an approximation for the expected number of transmissions per interval in multi-cell networks. Let us denote by $S(R)$ the number of nodes a single broadcasting node having a broadcasting range of R can reach, i.e., the size of a single broadcasting-cell. Heuristically, we can reason as follows. We have an $n \times n$ grid consisting of approximately $n^2/S(R)$ distinct non-overlapping broadcasting-cells. Assuming each cell behaves independently of the others we can approximate the expected number of transmissions per interval in the multi-cell case as follows:

$$\mathbb{E}\left[N_{MC}^{(k,n,R)}\right] \approx \frac{n^2}{S(R)}\mathbb{E}\left[N^{(k,S(R))}\right] \approx \frac{n^2}{S(R)}\frac{C_{(k+1,S(R))}}{C_{(k,S(R))}}. \quad (45)$$

Using the fact that $S(R) \sim \pi R^2$ and Equations (26) and (27), we can get more insight in the behavior of our approximation. For $\eta = 0$ we have that as R grows large:

$$\frac{n^2}{S(R)}\mathbb{E}\left[N^{(k,S(R))}\right] \approx \sqrt{\frac{2}{\pi}}\frac{n^2}{R}\frac{\Gamma\left[\frac{k+1}{2}\right]}{\Gamma\left[\frac{k}{2}\right]}.$$

Similarly, when a listen-only period is used, i.e., $\eta > 0$, we have that as R grows large:

$$\frac{n^2}{S(R)}\mathbb{E}\left[N^{(k,S(R))}\right] \approx \frac{n^2}{R^2}\frac{k}{\pi\eta}.$$

Consequently, we see how the short-listen problem potentially plays a role in multi-cell networks.

4.2 Simulations

We compare the approximation with simulations in order to evaluate its accuracy. We do so by plotting the ratio

$$\theta(k,n,R) = \mathbb{E}\left[N_{MC}^{(k,n,R)}\right] / \left(\frac{n^2}{S(R)}\frac{C_{(k+1,S(R))}}{C_{(k,S(R))}}\right). \quad (46)$$

In Mathematica we simulate a network consisting of 50×50 nodes placed on a grid for several values of k and R. For each combination of k and R, we simulate a lossless multi-cell network for 100 virtual time units. Each run, we use a different randomly chosen interval skew for the nodes. We use toroidal distance in order to cope with edge effects.

In Figure 9 we show a plot of (46) for the case $\eta = 0$. We see that the estimate given in Equation (45) tends to slightly underestimate the number of transmissions per interval. However, the approximation is accurate within a factor 1.2. Furthermore, as k increases, the approximation becomes more accurate. We also note that for fixed k the accuracy remains fairly constant as R grows.

Finally, let us consider the effect of a listen-only period. In Figure 10 we show a plot of (46) for the case $\eta = \frac{1}{2}$. We see again that the estimate given in Equation (45) tends to underestimate the number of transmissions per interval, more than for the case $\eta = 0$. The error slowly increases with the transmission range R. However, as k increases, the approximation becomes more accurate.

Note that in [10] a method is presented for estimating the message count in synchronized networks. It is shown that this method also gives an accurate approximation for unsynchronized networks with $\eta = \frac{1}{2}$. However, the method is not suitable for smaller values of η and assumes a uniformly random spatial distribution of the nodes. Hence, if one is interested in listen-only periods of different length or regular network topologies, our approximation is preferable.

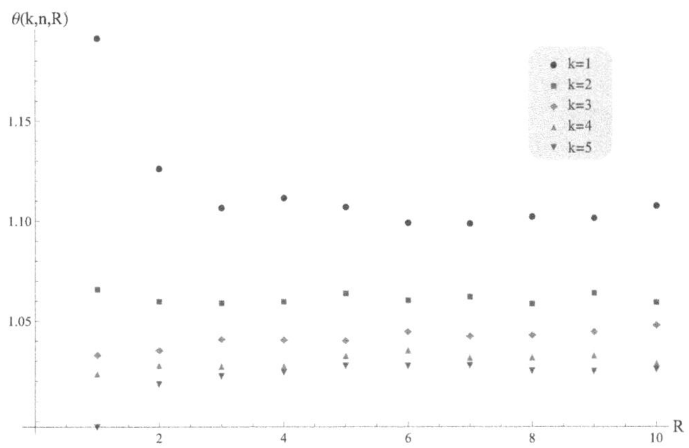

Figure 9: Ratio of simulated transmission count and approximation for $\eta = 0$.

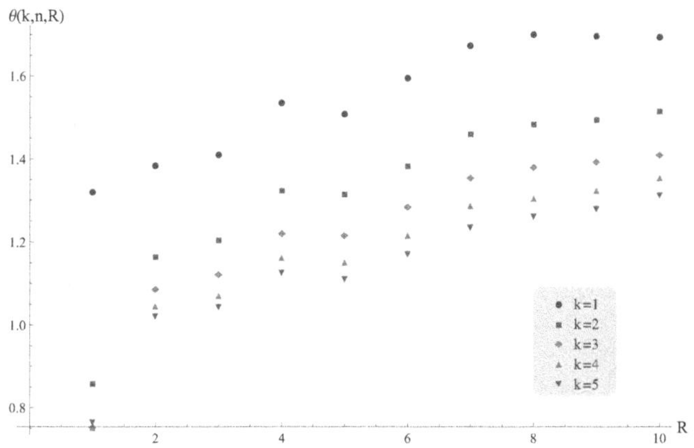

Figure 10: Ratio of simulated transmission count and approximation for $\eta = \frac{1}{2}$.

5. CONCLUSION

In this paper, we presented a generalized version of the Trickle algorithm with a new parameter η, which allows us to set the length of a listen-only period. This parameter can greatly increase the speed at which the algorithm can propagate updates, while still controlling the number of transmissions. Furthermore, we have shown that this parameter influences how the transmission load is distributed among nodes in a network. We then presented a mathematical model describing how the message count and inter-transmission times of the Trickle algorithm depend on its various parameters. We were particularly interested in the effect of a listen-only period on the message count and on the inter-transmission time distributions.

For single-cell networks we derived the distribution of inter-transmission times and the joint distribution of consecutive inter-transmission times. We showed how they depend on the redundancy constant k, the network-size n and the length of a listen-only period η. We also investigated their asymptotic behavior as n and k go to infinity. These distributions give insight in the energy-efficiency of the algorithm and the probability that nodes try to broadcast simultaneously. These insights contribute to optimizing the design and usage of the Trickle algorithm in WSNs.

Specifically, we showed that in a network without a listen-only period the expected number of transmissions grows as $\mathcal{O}(\sqrt{n})$, proving a conjecture from [13], and we identified that the pre-factor is $\sqrt{2}\Gamma\left[\frac{k+1}{2}\right]/\Gamma\left[\frac{k}{2}\right]$. Additionally, we showed that, when a listen-only period is used, the number of transmissions per interval is bounded from above by $\frac{k}{\eta}$, proving a second conjecture from [13].

We have also performed a simulation study in Mathematica and the OMNeT++ simulation tool. We compared our analytic results, which hold for very large networks with instantaneous transmissions, with simulation results of small and more realistic wireless networks. We found a very good match between the analytic results and the simulations.

Additionally, we used the results from the single-cell analysis to get an approximation for the message count in multi-cell networks. These results were also compared to simulation results from Mathematica and the OMNeT++ simulation tool. The approximation proved to be fairly accurate, in particular for small values of η. A more comprehensive investigation of multi-cell networks would be an interesting topic for further research.

Finally, we note that the speed at which the Trickle algorithm can disseminate updates in WSNs is a topic of ongoing research for the authors. Combined with results from this paper, this could provide insight in how to optimally set the Trickle parameters and the length of the listen-only period.

6. ACKNOWLEDGMENTS

The authors would like to thank Guido Janssen for useful discussions regarding the integral equations presented in this paper. Additionally, they are grateful to Marc Aoun for his contributions to the performed OMNeT++ simulations. The research of the third author was done in the framework of the IAP BESTCOM program, funded by the Belgian government.

7. REFERENCES

[1] I. F. Akyildiz, W. Su, Y. Sankarasubramaniam, and E. Cayirci. Wireless sensor networks: a survey. *Computer Networks*, 38(4):393–422, March 2002.

[2] M. Becker, K. Kuladinithi, and C. Görg. Modelling and simulating the Trickle algorithm. In *Proceedings of MONAMI*, pages 135–144. Springer, 2011.

[3] Y. Busnel, M. Bertier, E. Fleury, and A.-M. Kermarrec. GCP: gossip-based code propagation for large-scale mobile wireless sensor networks. In *Proceedings of the 1st International Conference on Autonomic computing and Communication Systems*, Autonomics '07, pages 11:1–11:5, 2007.

[4] D. J. Daley and D. Vere-Jones. *An Introduction to the Theory of Point Processes. Vol. II.* Probability and its Applications. Springer, New York, 2008.

[5] W. Dong, Y. Liu, X. Wu, L. Gu, and C. Chen. Elon: enabling efficient and long-term reprogramming for wireless sensor networks. In *Proceedings of the ACM SIGMETRICS International Conference on Measurement and Modeling of Computer Systems*, SIGMETRICS '10, pages 49–60, 2010.

[6] M. Finkelstein. *Failure Rate Modelling for Reliability and Risk.* Reliability Engineering. Springer, London, 2008.

[7] O. Gnawali, R. Fonseca, K. Jamieson, M. Kazandjieva, D. Moss, and P. Levis. CTP: An efficient, robust, and reliable collection tree protocol for wireless sensor networks *ACM Transactions on Sensor Networks (TOSN)*, 10(3), 2013.

[8] J. Hui and R. Kelsey. Multicast Protocol for Low power and Lossy Networks (MPL). *IETF, Internet-Draft draft-ietf-roll-trickle-mcast-07.txt*, February 2014.

[9] J. W. Hui and D. Culler. The dynamic behavior of a data dissemination protocol for network programming at scale. In *Proceedings of the 2nd International Conference on Embedded Networked Sensor Systems*, SenSys '04, pages 81–94, 2004.

[10] H. Kermajani, C. Gomez, and M. H. Arshad. Modeling the message count of the Trickle algorithm in a steady-state, static wireless sensor network. *Communications Letters, IEEE*, 16(12):1960–1963, December 2012.

[11] P. Levis, E. Brewer, D. Culler, D. Gay, S. Madden, N. Patel, J. Polastre, S. Shenker, R. Szewczyk, and A. Woo. The emergence of a networking primitive in wireless sensor networks. *Communications of the ACM*, 51(7):99–106, July 2008.

[12] P. Levis, T. Clausen, J. Hui O. Gnawali, and J. Ko. The Trickle algorithm. *Internet RFC 6206*, March 2011.

[13] P. Levis, N. Patel, D. Culler, and S. Shenker. Trickle: A self-regulating algorithm for code propagation and maintenance in wireless sensor networks. In *Proceedings of the First USENIX/ACM Symposium on Networked Systems Design and Implementation*, pages 15–28, 2004.

[14] S. P. Meyn and R. L. Tweedie. *Markov Chains and Stochastic Stability.* Communications and Control Engineering. Springer, London, 1993.

[15] S.-Y. Ni, Y.-C. Tseng, Y.-S. Chen, and J.-P. Sheu. The broadcast storm problem in a mobile ad hoc network. In *Proceedings of the 5th annual ACM/IEEE International Conference on Mobile Computing and Networking*, MobiCom '99, pages 151–162, 1999.

[16] P. Stein. A note on the volume of a simplex. *The American Mathematical Monthly*, 73(3):299–301, March 1966.

[17] B. Sury, T. Wang, and F.-Z. Zhao. Identities involving reciprocals of binomial coefficients. *Journal of Integer Sequences*, 7(2), July 2004.

[18] C.-Y. Wan, A. T. Campbell, and L. Krishnamurthy. Pump-slowly, fetch-quickly (PSFG): A reliable transport protocol for sensor networks. *IEEE Journal on Selected Areas in Communications*, 23(4):862–872, April 2005.

[19] T. Winter, P. Thubert, A. Brandt, J. Hui, R. Kelsey, P. Levis, K. Pister, R. Struik, J. Vasseur, and R. Alexander. RPL: IPv6 routing protocol for low-power and lossy networks. *Internet RFC 6550*, March 2012.

[20] Y. Yu, L. J. Rittle, V. Bhandari, and J. B. Lebrun. Supporting concurrent applications in wireless sensor networks. In *Proceedings of the 4th International Conference on Embedded Networked Sensor Systems*, pages 139–152, 2006.

APPENDIX

A. PROOF OF LEMMA 1

In order to prove Lemma 1 we will use the following theorem (see [4], Proposition 11.2.VI).

THEOREM 2. *Let M be a simple stationary point process on $X = \mathbb{R}$ with finite intensity λ, and let M_n denote the point process obtained by superposing n independent replicates of M and dilating the scale of X by a factor n. Then as $n \to \infty$, M_n converges weakly to a Poisson process with parameter measure $\lambda\mu_L(\cdot)$, where $\mu_L(\cdot)$ denotes the Lebesgue measure on $\mathbb{R}$.*

Let N be the process of an arbitrary node's broadcasting moments. Then evidently the superposition of n of these processes N_n gives us the process of broadcasting attempts by all the nodes in our cell. Hence if we show that N is a simple stationary point process with finite intensity $\lambda = 1$, we can apply Theorem 2, resulting in Lemma 1.

Let $\{B_i\}$ with $i \in \mathbb{Z}$ be the sequence of broadcasting times for an arbitrary node defining our process N. Then if we denote by S the interval skew and assume it is uniform, i.e., $S \sim U[0,1]$, we can write

$$B_i \sim (S + i) + T_i,\ i \in \mathbb{Z}.$$

Here T_i represents the timer of the corresponding node in the ith interval, thus $T_i \sim U[\eta, 1]$. It is easy to see that N is a simple point process with intensity $\lambda = 1$.

It remains to show stationarity. Let N^s be the point process resulting from applying a shift operator to the process N. That is, if $\{B_i^s\}$ with $i \in \mathbb{Z}$ is the sequence of events for the shifted process N^s we have

$$B_i^s \sim (S + i) + T_i + s,\ i \in \mathbb{Z}.$$

We show that $\{B_i\}$ and $\{B_i^s\}$ with $i \in \mathbb{Z}$ have the same distribution, which means that the processes N and N^s coincide in distribution, implying stationarity. We first write

$$\{B_i^s\}_{i\in\mathbb{Z}} = \{(S + i) + T_i + s\}_{i\in\mathbb{Z}}$$

$$= \{(S + s - \lfloor S + s \rfloor) + (i + \lfloor S + s \rfloor + T_i)\}_{i\in\mathbb{Z}}$$

Now note that $(S + s - \lfloor S + s \rfloor) \sim U[0,1] \sim S$. Furthermore, $(i + \lfloor S + s \rfloor + T_i) \sim \left(i + \lfloor S + s \rfloor + T_{i+\lfloor S+s \rfloor}\right)$, since the T_i are independent and identically distributed. Moreover, $\left\{i + \lfloor S + s \rfloor + T_{i+\lfloor S+s \rfloor}\right\}_{i\in\mathbb{Z}} \sim \{i + T_i\}_{i\in\mathbb{Z}}$. This allows us to conclude

$$\{B_i^s\}_{i\in\mathbb{Z}} \sim \{B_i\}_{i\in\mathbb{Z}}.$$

Consequently Theorem 2 applies and Lemma 1 follows.

Movers and Shakers: Kinetic Energy Harvesting for the Internet of Things

Maria Gorlatova, John Sarik, Guy Grebla, Mina Cong, Ioannis Kymissis, Gil Zussman
Department of Electrical Engineering
Columbia University
New York, NY, 10027, USA
{mag2206@, jcs2160@, guy@ee., mc3415@, johnkym@ee., gil@ee.}columbia.edu

ABSTRACT

Numerous energy harvesting wireless devices that will serve as building blocks for the Internet of Things (IoT) are currently under development. However, there is still only limited understanding of the properties of various energy sources and their impact on energy harvesting adaptive algorithms. Hence, we focus on *characterizing the kinetic (motion) energy that can be harvested by a wireless node with an IoT form factor* and on *developing energy allocation algorithms* for such nodes. In this paper, we describe methods for estimating harvested energy from acceleration traces. To characterize the energy availability associated with specific human activities (e.g., relaxing, walking, cycling), we analyze a motion dataset with over 40 participants. Based on acceleration measurements that we collected for over 200 hours, we study energy generation processes associated with day-long human routines. We also briefly summarize our experiments with moving objects. We develop energy allocation algorithms that *take into account practical IoT node design considerations*, and evaluate the algorithms using the collected measurements. Our observations provide insights into the design of motion energy harvesters, IoT nodes, and energy harvesting adaptive algorithms.

Categories and Subject Descriptors: C.2.1 [Computer-Communication Networks]: Network Architecture and Design—Network communications, Wireless communication

General Terms: Measurement; Algorithms

Keywords: Energy harvesting; motion energy; measurements; low-power networking; Algorithms; Internet of Things

1. INTRODUCTION

Advances in the areas of solar, kinetic, and thermal energy harvesting as well as in low-power wireless communications will soon enable the realization of *self-sustainable wireless devices* [16, 23, 36, 44]. These devices can compose networks of rechargeable sensors [23, 44], active tags [16], or computational RFIDs [20]. Such networks will serve as building blocks for emerging Internet-of-Things (IoT) applications (e.g., supply chain management and wearable computing).

Two promising energy sources for IoT nodes are *light and motion.*[1] Accordingly, extensive effort has been dedicated to the design of solar cells and kinetic energy harvesters (e.g., [1,26,27,31]). Moreover, the design of energy harvesting-adaptive communication and networking algorithms recently gained extensive attention [11, 19, 23, 28, 40]. To complement these efforts, [19, 44, 45] collected traces and studied the impact of the energy source properties on higher layer algorithms. However, there is still only limited understanding of motion energy availability and its impact on the design of both hardware (energy harvesters, energy storage components) and algorithms. Hence, we focus on *characterizing the kinetic (motion) energy that can be harvested by an IoT node and on the impact of the energy characteristics on harvesting adaptive algorithms.* Self-sustainable IoT nodes powered by motion will be implemented in ultra-low-power architectures. Thus, we additionally focus on *developing algorithms that take practical IoT node design considerations into account.*

Everyday activities such as walking can generate substantial power [37]. Therefore, many harvesters are under development, including shoe inserts that harvest energy from footfalls [26] and mobile phone chargers integrated in backpacks [1] or phones [27]. While there are several ways of harvesting motion energy, we focus on inertial energy harvesters, since their form factor fits IoT applications. An inertial harvester suitable for a small wireless device (e.g., under 5cm x 5cm, and weighing less than 2 grams) can generate 100–200 μW from walking [21, 38], which is sufficient for many applications.[2] However, the harvesting level changes dynamically as illustrated in Fig. 3 that shows the power harvesting level corresponding to a device carried by a walking person.

In inertial harvesters, the output power is maximized when the harvester resonant frequency is "matched" to the motion frequency [31] (see Section 4 for details). Human motion is a combination of low frequency vibrations (<10 Hz) that vary from activity to activity and from person to person. Therefore, characterizing the properties of the harvested power requires an in-depth study of human motion (e.g., the fre-

SIGMETRICS'14, June 16–20, 2014, Austin, Texas, USA.

ACM 978-1-4503-2789-3/14/06 ...$15.00.
http://dx.doi.org/10.1145/2591971.2591986.

[1]The power available from *RF harvesting* is *100 times less than the power available from indoor light [39]. Thermal gradients* can provide substantial power in industrial applications, but are currently impractical for non-industrial IoT applications.

[2]This is comparable to the power a solar cell of similar size can harvest from indoor light [19, 44].

quencies associated with different motions) and human mobility patterns. Namely, characterizing kinetic energy harvesting is substantially more complex than characterizing light energy harvesting (e.g., [19]).

We first describe methods for collecting motion acceleration traces and the methods of [31, 38, 45] for estimating harvested power from the traces. Our study is based on traces that we collected using SparkFun ADXL345 boards[3] and traces collected in [41] using similar devices. While the traces in [41] were collected to examine activity recognition, we use them to estimate the amount of energy that could be harvested.

We examine the energy availability associated with specific human motions, such as walking, running, and cycling. Unlike previous studies that obtained estimates based on small numbers of participants [10, 21, 38], we use a motion dataset *with over 40 participants* [41], obtaining extensive and general kinetic energy characterization for common human motions. The study demonstrates the range of motion frequencies and harvested powers for different participants and activities, and *uniquely demonstrates the importance of human physical parameters for energy harvesting.* For example, the taller half of the participants can harvest on average 20% more power than the shorter half.

The short duration traces in [41] are for specific motions. In order to study the energy generation processes associated with *day-scale human routines* (as opposed to specific motions), we conducted a measurement campaign with 5 participants over a total of 25 days. We collected traces with over 200 hours of acceleration information for normal human routines. The traces provide important input for IoT node design (e.g., for determining the battery capacity and harvester size necessary for self-sustainable operation) and for algorithm design (as will be discussed below). Hence, *we share the collected dataset in [8] and via CRAWDAD [12].*[4] We analyze the traces and show that the power availability from normal routines and from indoor lights are comparable. We also demonstrate that the power generation process associated with human motion is highly variable. We compare this process with i.i.d. and Markov processes, demonstrating the importance of evaluating algorithms with real world traces.

We note that the primary goal of collecting and analyzing traces is to set a reasonable upper bound on the available energy and to study the energy availability dynamics. Commercially available kinetic energy harvesters [4,6,7] are optimized for harvesting energy from machine vibrations above 40Hz. Therefore, these harvesters would generate essentially no energy when subjected to human motion. In general, measuring acceleration is preferable to measuring the energy harvested by a particular harvester, since the traces can be used to calculate how much energy any past, present, or future harvester would generate. While our results are based on the assumption that a harvester is modeled as a mass-spring system, the acceleration traces can be applied to any such future kinetic energy harvester (e.g., conductive droplet sliding on electret film [43], reverse electrowetting [25]).

[3] Although smartphones include accelerometers, we use dedicated sensing units, since the phones' accelerometers have a limited range, restricted sampling rate control, and high energy consumption (that hinders day-scale trace collection).

[4] To the best of our knowledge, this is the first publicly available long-term human motion acceleration dataset.

As the IoT will incorporate many objects, we additionally briefly present results regarding measurements with a variety of *moving objects.* For example, we measured the power that can be harvested from everyday activities such as writing with a pencil and opening a door. We also collected measurements for objects in transit. We shipped a FedEx box with a measurement unit across the U.S., placed a unit in a checked-in luggage during a 3 hour flight, and carried units on cars and trains. We confirm that, as expected based on inertial harvesters' filter properties (see Section 3.1), the energy availability is low for many common non-periodic motions. We additionally demonstrate that the energy availability is low for many high-amplitude periodic object motions. For example, we show that inertial harvesters can harvest little energy from opening and closing a door, opening cabinet drawers, and spinning a swivel chair.

Next, we develop *energy allocation algorithms* for wireless IoT nodes. Due to the high variability of energy obtained from motion, IoT nodes that harvest this energy will implement algorithms that control the node's energy spending rates [11, 13, 19, 23, 28, 32]. The spending rates will provide inputs for determining node transmission power, duty cycle, sensing rate, or communication rate. We formulate an optimization problem of a node whose objective is to *maximize the utility of its energy allocations*, and develop algorithms for solving it. The problem formulation and the algorithms take into account *realistic properties of an ultra-low-power IoT node.*

In particular, IoT nodes that are powered by the motion energy will likely to be implemented in *ultra-low-power architectures.* As such, they will support only a limited number of possible energy spending rates, and their energy use patterns may call for considering various possible utility functions. Moreover, these nodes will likely to use *capacitors* [19, 20, 47], rather than *batteries*, as their energy storage components. This is due to the fact that capacitors can be charged and discharged many more times than batteries, which is an important feature for nodes powered by the widely varying motion energy. Additionally, capacitors are more environmentally friendly than batteries [20], and are therefore more suitable for human-facing IoT applications such as wearable computing. To the best of our knowledge, these aspects of IoT node modeling have not been jointly considered before.

For solving the energy allocation problem, we develop an optimal offline algorithm, an efficient approximation scheme, and an online algorithm which is optimal in certain cases. We evaluate the algorithms using the collected measurement traces. The evaluation results demonstrate that the approximation and online algorithms perform well and highlight the importance of designing algorithms that take into account the energy storage properties of the IoT nodes.

To summarize, the main contributions of this paper are: (i) insights into energy availability from human motion, based on a dataset with a large number of participants, (ii) collection of a dataset of long-term human motion and a study of the corresponding energy generation processes, and (iii) energy allocation algorithms that take practical IoT node design considerations into account. The collected motion traces are already available online [8]. The paper contributes to the understanding of motion energy harvesting availability and properties, and provides insights that are important for the design of motion energy harvesters, IoT nodes, and energy harvesting adaptive algorithms.

The paper is organized as follows. Section 2 summarizes the related work and Section 3 describes the harvester model, the measurements, the procedures for determining the harvester parameters, and the wireless node model. Section 4 focuses on common human motions and Section 5 focuses on our measurement campaign and day-scale human motion measurements. Section 6 provides brief comments regarding motion of objects. Section 7 describes our algorithms and provides the results of algorithm evaluations with the collected measurements. Section 8 concludes the paper. Due to space constraints, the proofs are omitted and appear in [18].

2. RELATED WORK

To the best of our knowledge, our experiments with long-term activities (Section 5.1) and with object motion (Section 6) are unique. Below we briefly summarize the related work for our other contributions.

Previous studies that examined energy of *particular human motions* had a small number of participants (10 in [21] and 8 in [38,45]). Additionally, with the exception of [45], they examined short intervals of walking and running on a treadmill at a constant pace. We examine a dataset [41] with over 40 participants performing a set of several unrestricted motions[5] and *labeled with human physical parameters*. To the best of our knowledge, this is the first publicly available acceleration dataset collected for a large number of participants. It *was not previously used for an energy study*.

Day-scale human motion acceleration traces were previously collected for 8 participants over 3 days and examined in [45], which established energy budgets for wearable nodes using assumptions suitable for larger electronic devices. The data collected in [45] is not publicly available. We collect day-scale data that in some cases has more information per participant, examine the traces under assumptions suitable for small IoT nodes, and characterize energy harvesting process variability and properties that *have not been considered before*.

Many energy harvesting adaptive communication and networking algorithms have been recently developed (e.g., [11, 13, 23, 28, 30, 32, 34, 35, 40, 42]). We consider a wireless node model and develop algorithms that capture several practical IoT node design aspects: (i) *discrete*, rather than continuous [11, 13, 19, 28, 40], energy spending rates; (ii) *general*, rather than concave [11, 13, 19, 28, 40] or linear [23], utility functions; and (iii) use of a *capacitor* [19, 47], rather than a battery [11, 13, 28, 40], as an energy storage component. These aspects have not been jointly considered before. Existing algorithms are typically evaluated with light [11, 23, 47] or wind [11] energy traces. We evaluate the algorithms with the collected day-scale human motion energy measurements.

3. MODELS & MEASUREMENT SETUP

Our motion energy study is based on recorded *acceleration* traces which are processed, following the methods developed in [31, 38, 45], to determine the energy generated by an inertial harvester. Our algorithms are developed based on a model that extends existing models [11, 13, 19, 23, 28] to capture important IoT node design considerations. In this section, we describe the kinetic energy harvester model, the collection of acceleration measurements, the procedures for determining the harvester parameters, and the wireless node model. The notation is summarized in Table 1.

[5]The properties of restricted and unrestricted human motions are known to differ [33].

Table 1: Nomenclature

m	Harvester proof mass [kg]
Z_L	Harvester proof mass displacement limit [m]
k	Harvester spring constant [kg·s^2]
b	Harvester damping factor [kg/s]
f_r	Harvester resonant frequency [Hz]
f_m	Dominant motion frequency [Hz]
$a(t)$	Acceleration [m/s^2]
D	Absolute deviation of acceleration [m/s^2]
$P(t)$, $z(t)$	Power [W] and proof mass displacement [m]
i, K	Time slot index and a number of time slots
$s(i)$	Energy spending rate [J/slot]
$\mathcal{S}$	Set of feasible $s(i)$ values
$r(i)$, $U(s(i))$	Data rate [Kb/s] and utility function
$B(i)$	Energy storage level [J]
$e(i)$	Environmental energy level [J]
$Q(e(i), B(i))$	Energy harvesting rate [J/slot]
$L(i, B(i))$	Energy loss (leakage) rate [J/slot]
$\eta(i, B(i))$	Energy conversion efficiency [dimensionless]
C	Energy storage capacity [J]

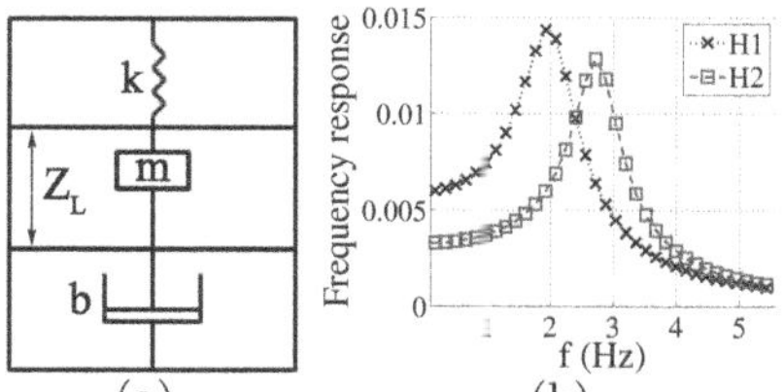

(a) (b)

Figure 1: (a) A *second-order mass-spring system model* of a harvester with proof mass m, proof mass displacement limit Z_L, spring constant k, and damping factor b, and (b) the frequency response magnitude for harvesters $H1$ and $H2$.

3.1 Inertial Harvester Model

An inertial harvester can be modeled as a second-order mass-spring system with a harvester proof mass m, proof mass displacement limit Z_L, spring constant k, and spring damping factor b [31, 38]. Fig. 1(a) demonstrates such a harvester model.

Two important *harvester design parameters* are m and Z_L. The harvester output power, P, increases linearly with m [9], and is non-decreasing (but generally non-linear) in Z_L. Yet, m and Z_L are limited by the harvester weight and size considerations, which ultimately depend on the application. We use the following values that are consistent with the IoT restrictions on the size and weight of a node, and correspond to one of the configurations examined in [38]: (i) $m = 1 \cdot 10^{-3}$ kg and (ii) $Z_L = 10$ mm.

The other two model parameters, k and b, are tuned to optimize the energy harvested for given motion properties. The parameter k determines the *harvester resonant frequency*, $f_r = 2\pi\sqrt{k/m}$. To maximize power output, *the resonant frequency, f_r, should match, reasonably closely, the dominant frequency of motion, f_m.*

Jointly, k and b determine the *harvester quality factor*, $Q = \sqrt{km}/b$, which determines the spectral width of the harvester. A harvester with a small Q harvests a wide range of frequencies with a low peak value, while a harvester with a large Q is finely tuned to its resonant frequency f_r. The

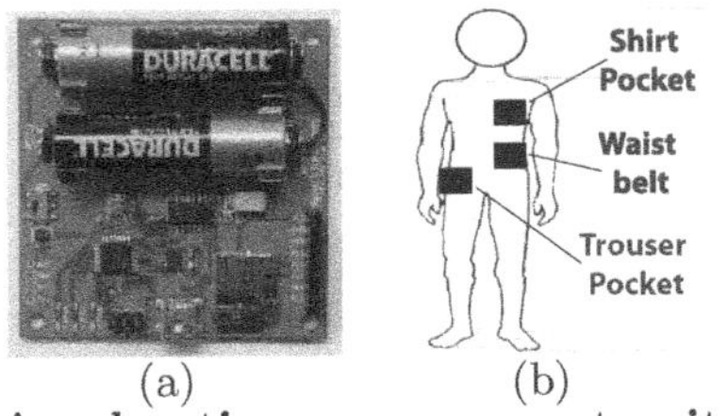

Figure 2: Acceleration measurement unit and placements: (a) our sensing unit based on a SparkFun ADXL345 board, and (b) the sensing unit placements in a multi-participant human motion characterization study [41].

role of f_r and Q can be observed in Fig. 1(b), which shows the magnitude of the frequency response of two different harvesters, denoted by $H1$ and $H2$. For $H1$, $f_r = 2.06$ Hz (which corresponds to a typical frequency of human walking) and $Q = 2.35$ ($k = 0.17$, $b = 0.0055$). For $H2$, $f_r = 2.77$ Hz (which corresponds to a typical frequency of human running) and $Q = 3.87$ ($k = 0.30$, $b = 0.0045$).

3.2 Collecting Motion Information

In Sections 4-6, we examine measurements that we collected and measurements provided in a triaxial acceleration dataset of common human motions [41]. Our measurements were obtained with sensing units based on SparkFun ADXL345 evaluation boards (see Fig. 2(a)). Each unit includes an ADXL345 tri-axis accelerometer, an Atmega328P microcontroller, and a microSD card for data logging. The sensing units record acceleration along the x, y, and z axes, $a_x(t)$, $a_y(t)$, $a_z(t)$, with a 100 Hz sampling frequency. We conducted multiple experiments with multiple sensing unit placements, as described in Sections 5 and 6.

The dataset of [41] was obtained using an ADXL330 tri-axis accelerometers with a 100 Hz sampling frequency. The measurements of [41] were conducted with sensing unit placements corresponding to a shirt pocket, waist belt, and trouser pocket, as shown in Fig. 2(b). In all the measurements, the orientation of the sensing unit is not controlled. We examine $a(t) = \sqrt{a_x(t)^2 + a_y(t)^2 + a_z(t)^2}$, the overall magnitude of the acceleration. Due to the earth gravity of 9.8 m/s^2 ("1g"), the measured acceleration includes a constant component that we filter out (similarly to [38, 45], we use a 3rd order Butterworth high-pass filter with a 0.1 Hz cutoff frequency).

We examine two motion properties of the measurements: the *average absolute deviation of the acceleration*, D, and the dominant frequency of motion, f_m. D quantifies the variability in the $a(t)$ value and is a measure of the "amount of motion". It is calculated as $D = \frac{1}{T}\sum_T(a(t) - \overline{a}(t))$, where $\overline{a}(t)$ denotes the average of $a(t)$ over time interval T. We obtain f_m by determining the maximum spectral component of the Fourier Transform of $a(t)$.

3.3 Harvesting Rates and Data Rates

We calculate the power generated by a harvester, $P(t)$, subjected to acceleration $a(t)$, using the following procedure based on the methods developed in [45]. We first convert $a(t)$ to proof mass displacement, $z(t)$, using the Laplace-domain transfer function

$$z(t) = \mathcal{L}^{-1}\{z(s)\} = \frac{a(s)}{s^2 + (2\pi f_r/Q)s + (2\pi f_r)^2}.$$

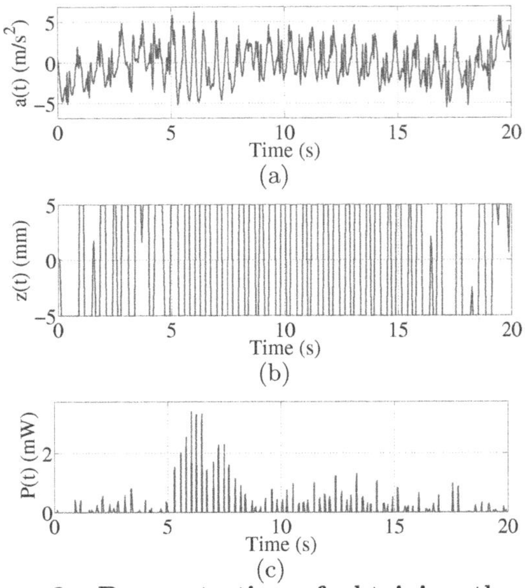

Figure 3: Demonstration of obtaining the power generated by a harvester, $P(t)$, from the recorded acceleration, $a(t)$: (a) $a(t)$ recorded by a person walking, (b) the corresponding harvester proof mass displacement, $z(t)$, and (c) the resulting $P(t)$ for harvester $H1$ ($k = 0.17$, $b = 0.0055$).

Next, to account for Z_L, we limit $z(t)$ using a Simulink limiter block. The power $P(t)$ generated by the harvester is then determined as $P(t) = b(dz(t)/dt)^2$. The average of $P(t)$ is denoted by $\overline{P}$.

We implemented this procedure in MATLAB and Simulink. Fig. 3 shows an example of obtaining $P(t)$ for a particular $a(t)$. The $a(t)$ values were recorded by a sensing unit carried by a walking person (Fig. 3(a)), and the $z(t)$ and $P(t)$ values were obtained using the procedure described above for the harvester $H1$.

To characterize the performance of wireless IoT nodes, we calculate the data rates, $\overline{r}$, that a node would be able to maintain when harvesting the generated $\overline{P}$. The harvester energy conversion efficiency, η_h, depends on various factors [6] (e.g., selected regulated output and temperature). While perfectly optimized energy harvesting systems obtain energy conversion efficiency values between 30% and 90% [3], we use $\eta_h = 20\%$ which is more realistic for practical systems where the harvester cannot be continuously aligned with the axis that generates the maximum output throughout the day. Similar to [19], we assume that the communication cost is $c_{\text{tx}} = 1$ nJ/bit for ultra-low-power transceivers appropriate for IoT nodes. Hence, $\overline{r} = \eta_h \overline{P}/c_{\text{tx}} = 2 \cdot 10^5\ \overline{P}$ (Kb/s).

3.4 Optimizing the Harvester Parameters

Finding the optimal harvester parameters k and b is difficult because it requires optimizing over a multi-dimensional surface of unknown geometry [38]. For example, Fig. 4 shows the average power ($\overline{P}$) values calculated from a set of $a(t)$ measurements (corresponding to a person running) for different f_r and b combinations. To determine the optimal harvester parameters for short $a(t)$ samples, we implemented an *exhaustive search* algorithm. The algorithm considers a large number of k and b combinations, obtains the corresponding $\overline{P}$ (using the procedure described in Section 3.3), and chooses the k and b combination that maximizes $\overline{P}$.

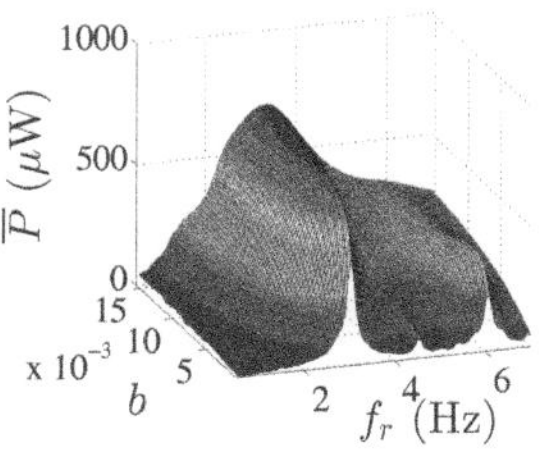

Figure 4: The average power generated by a harvester, $\overline{P}$, from the same motion (human running) for different combinations of harvester resonant frequencies, f_r, and damping factors, b.

The exhaustive search algorithm is time-consuming even for relatively short $a(t)$ samples. For longer $a(t)$ samples, we implemented a simplified procedure developed in [45]. The procedure first determines the k value that matches the harvester's f_r to the dominant frequency in the $a(t)$ sample, f_m. Specifically, the procedure selects k such that $k = mf_r^2/(2\pi)^2 = (mf_m^2)/(2\pi)^2$. It then considers a relatively large number of b values and selects the b that maximizes $\overline{P}$.

3.5 Wireless Node Model

We model an ultra-low-power IoT node that harvests energy, stores it in an energy storage device, and uses it to communicate wirelessly (e.g., a wearable node may be communicating with a human-carried mobile phone). We assume that the time is slotted and denote the slot index by i and the number of slots by K. We will develop algorithms that control the node energy spending rates, $s(i)$, which can provide inputs for determining node transmission power, duty cycle, sensing rate, or communication rate. An IoT node is likely to support only a restricted number of modes of operation (i.e., sleep, idle), transmission power levels[6], and transmission rates, thereby supporting only a finite set $\mathcal{S}$ of $s(i)$ values. We thus *restrict* $s(i)$ *as* $s(i) \in \mathcal{S} \cup \{0\}$ (note that $s(i)$ is typically modeled as a continuous variable [13,19,46]). This complicates the energy allocation problems, as we will demonstrate in Section 7.1.

We formulate an optimization problem for a single node which maximizes *the sum of the utilities of its per-time-slot energy allocations*. This problem is important, for example, in networks where nodes transmit mostly ID information [17] to a common gateway[7]. We consider a utility function $U(s(i))$ that corresponds to the *data rate* $r(i)$ *obtained when the energy spending rate is* $s(i)$[8]. The node may achieve different $r(i)$ in a slot i by transmitting different number of packets, changing the transmission power, or changing the packet size. Thus the utility function, U, may be *concave* (when the node changes its transmission power [13,40,46]), *linear* (when it transmits different number of packets), *convex* (when it changes the packet size under certain settings [14]), or *not concave and not convex* (when it changes a combination of the parameters). Correspondingly, *we place no restrictions on* $U(s(i))$ *except that it can be computed efficiently.*

An IoT node may use a *battery* or a *capacitor* as its energy storage device. For a slot i, $B(i)$ is the node energy storage level, $e(i)$ is the environmental energy available to the node, and $L(i, B(i))$ is the energy loss (leakage) from the storage. $Q(e(i), B(i))$ is the energy harvested by the node; its dependency on $B(i)$ is characteristic of capacitor-based nodes [19,29]. $\eta(i, B(i))$ is the *energy conversion efficiency* and C is the storage capacity. Between time slots, the energy storage evolves as

$$B(i) = \min\{B(i-1) + Q(e(i-1), B(i-1)) - L(i-1, B(i-1)) - s(i-1)/\eta(i-1, B(i-1)), C\}.$$

$\eta(i, B(i))$ depends on the difference between the energy storage voltage, $V_{\text{out}}(i)$, and the node's operating voltage, V_{op}. Within a *battery*'s operating region, $V_{\text{out}}(i)$ is nearly constant. For a *capacitor*, $V_{\text{out}}(i)$ depends on $B(i)$ [19,29]. We define two node models: for a *battery model*, $\eta(i, B(i)) = 1$, while for a *capacitor model*, $\eta(i, B(i))$ is a non-linear function. The $\eta(i, B(i))$ that we use in the performance evaluations is described in Section 7.3.

4. HUMAN MOTION

We now examine a dataset with over 40 participants performing 7 common motions in unconstrained environments. We emphasize that this dataset, previously used to examine techniques for activity recognition [41], *has not been used for energy characterization.* We first introduce the study. Then, we characterize the energy availability for different motions, the variability in motion properties among sensing unit placements and participants, and the dependence of energy availability on the participant's physical parameters.

4.1 Study Summary

The dataset we examine [41] contains motion samples for 7 common human activities – relaxing, walking, fast walking, running, cycling, going upstairs, and going downstairs, – performed by *over 40 participants* and recorded from the 3 sensing unit placements, shown in Fig. 2(b). For each 20-second motion sample, we use the acceleration, $a(t)$, trace to calculate D, f_m, $\overline{P}$, and r. To obtain $\overline{P}$, we use the exhaustive search harvester optimization algorithm from Section 3.4. By determining the best harvester for each motion, we can offer important insights into the harvester design.

To validate the data from [41], we replicated the measurements using our sensing units. The results of our measurements were consistent with the provided data. Namely, both the D and f_m values in our experiments were well within range of the data in [41]. We note that the f_m values calculated for the different motions in the dataset are consistent with the physiology of human motion. For example, the range of the calculated f_m values for running motion samples in the dataset corresponds to the typical foot strike cadence for running (180 foot strikes per minute, i.e., $f_m = 3$Hz, is considered an optimal running cadence [15]).

The statistics of the calculated D, f_m, and $\overline{P}$ are summarized in the boxplots in Fig. 5. For each of the 7 motions the leftmost (black), middle (red), and rightmost (blue) boxes

[6]For example, the ultra-low-power Chipcon CC1000, Chipcon CC2420, and Nordic NRF24L01 RF transceivers support, correspondingly, only 32, 8, and 4 transmission power levels.

[7]Single node energy allocation problems were studied in [13, 19, 40] under simpler models. In Section 7.1 we show that even for a single node, the considered optimization problem is NP-hard. The extension to the case of multiple nodes is a subject for future research.

[8]The model allows $U(s(i))$ to account for other considerations as well (e.g., the number of activations of nodes' sensors when the energy spending rate is $s(i)$).

Table 2: **Energy budgets and data rates based on measurements of common human activities.**

Activity	Sensing unit placement	# subjects	Median f_m (Hz)	$\overline{P}$ (μW) 25th percentile	Median	75th percentile	Median r (Kb/s)
Relaxing	Trouser pocket	42	N/A	1.0	3.1	4.8	0.6
	Waist belt	42	N/A	0.3	2.4	4.8	0.5
	Trouser pocket	42	N/A	0.2	1.4	5.9	0.3
Walking	Shirt pocket	42	1.9	128.6	155.2	186.0	31.0
	Waist belt	42	2.0	151.8	180.3	200.3	36.0
	Trouser pocket	42	2.0	163.4	202.4	274.5	40.4
Running	Shirt pocket	42	2.8	724.2	813.3	910.0	162.6
	Waist belt	41	2.8	623.5	678.3	752.8	135.6
	Trouser pocket	42	2.8	542.3	612.7	727.4	122.5
Cycling	Shirt pocket	30	3.5	37.4	52.0	72.3	10.4
	Waist belt	29	3.8	36.3	45.4	59.2	9.1
	Trouser pocket	30	1.1	35.6	41.3	59.5	8.3

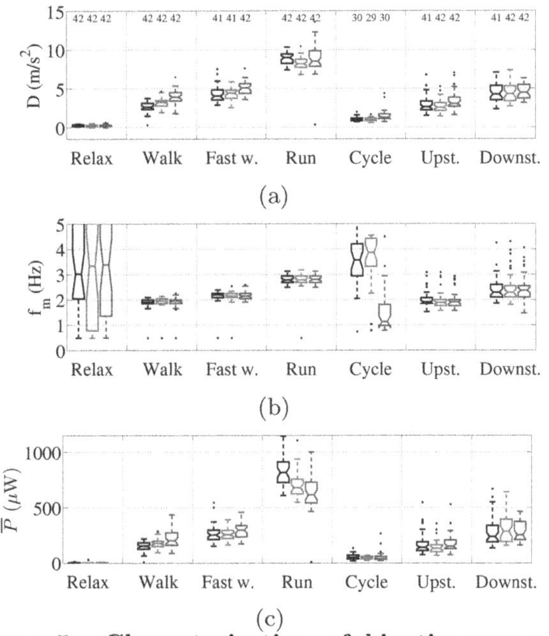

Figure 5: Characterization of kinetic energy for common human activities, based on a 40-participant study: (a) average absolute deviation of acceleration, D, (b) dominant motion frequency, f_m, and (c) power harvested by an optimized harvester, $\overline{P}$.

correspond to the *shirt pocket*, *waist belt*, and *trouser pocket* sensing unit placements, respectively. For each motion and sensing unit placement, the number of participants that had $a(t)$ samples appears on the top of Fig. 5(a). At each box, the central mark is the median, the edges are the 25th and 75th percentiles, the "whiskers" cover 2.7σ of the data, and the outliers are plotted individually. In Table 2 we separately summarize the results for 4 important motions.

4.2 Energy for Different Activities

Relaxing: As expected, almost no energy can be harvested when a person is not moving ($\overline{P} < 5$ μW).

Walking and fast walking: Walking is the predominant periodic motion in normal human lives and thus particularly important for motion energy harvesting. For walking, the median $\overline{P}$ is 155 μW for shirt pocket sensing unit placement, 180 μW for waist belt placement, and 202 μW for trouser pocket placement. These $\overline{P}$ values are in agreement with previous studies of energy harvesting for human walking [21,38]. In comparison, *indoor light energy* availability is on the order of 50–100 μW/cm^2. Considering harvester energy conversion efficiency estimates [19,45], *a similarly sized harvester would harvest more energy from walking than from indoor light.* Fast walking (identified as "fast" by the participants themselves) has higher D and f_m than walking at a normal pace (Fig. 5) and generates up to twice as much $\overline{P}$.

Running: Running, an intense repetitive activity, is associated with high D and f_m (Fig. 5(a,b)), and hence results in $612 \leq \overline{P} \leq 813$ μW.

Cycling: For the examined unit placements, cycling generates relatively little energy – the median $\overline{P}$ values are 41–52 μW, 3.7–3.9 times less than the $\overline{P}$ for walking. While the high cadence of cycling motion results in relatively high f_m (Fig. 5(b)), a harvester not on the legs will be subject to only small displacements, resulting in small values of D (Fig. 5(a)) and $\overline{P}$ (Fig. 5(c)). For cycling-specific IoT applications, *harvester placements on the lower legs should be considered.*

Walking upstairs and downstairs: Comparing the $\overline{P}$ values for relaxing, walking, and running, one may conclude that higher exertion (perceived effort and energy expenditure) corresponds to higher energy harvesting rates. Our examination of walking upstairs and downstairs demonstrates that this is not the case. While people exert themselves more going upstairs, the $\overline{P}$ for going downstairs is *substantially higher than for going upstairs*, with the median $\overline{P}$ values differing by 1.65–2.1 times depending on the sensing unit placement. Although counterintuitive, going downstairs is associated with higher magnitudes of motion and higher motion frequencies (Fig. 5(a,b)), which leads to the higher $\overline{P}$. We observed the disconnect between perceived effort and energy harvesting rates in other measurements as well. For example, in our measurements highly strenuous push-ups and sit-ups resulted in lower $\overline{P}$ than non-strenuous walking at a normal pace.

4.3 Consistency of Dominant Motion Frequency

To maximize power output, the resonant frequency of a harvester, f_r, should "match" the dominant frequency of motion, f_m. In this section, we comment on the variability in f_m and provide important observations for harvester design. Due to space constraints, we leave the study of harvester sensitivity to different design parameters to future work.

Consistency among sensing unit placements: The same motion will result in a different f_m depending on the sensing unit's placement on the human body [21,45]. We observed this in measurements that we conducted, especially for sensing units attached to the lower legs and lower arms. However, for the sensing unit placements examined in this section (shirt, waist, and trousers), the same motion resulted in similar f_m values, as can be seen in Fig. 5(b). These placements are on or near the torso, and are subjected to similar stresses. Cycling is an exception; the f_m for the trouser placement is different from the other placements. Because the body is in a sitting position, the stresses experienced by the legs and the torso are different and f_m differs for the different placements.

The uniformity of f_m offers valuable hints for energy harvesting node designers. People are likely to keep many objects that will become IoT nodes (keys, wallets, and cell phones) in pockets located in places that correspond to the placements we examine. This suggests that *a harvester tuned to a particular f_m will perform well regardless of where a person chooses to carry such an object.*

Inter-participant consistency: For common periodic motions, such as walking and running, the f_m values are relatively consistent among the different participants. The 25th and 75th percentiles of the participants' f_m values are separated by only 0.15 Hz for walking and by only 0.3 Hz for running. For less commonly practiced motions (cycling, going upstairs, going downstairs), the values of f_m are less consistent, but are still somewhat similar. This consistency indicates that *an all-purpose harvester designed for human walking or running will work reasonably well for a large number of different people.* The next section examines whether harvesters can be tuned to particular human parameters.

4.4 Dependency on Human Height and Weight

We examine the dependency of energy availability on human physiological parameters. We correlate D, f_m, and $\overline{P}$ obtained for different motions and different participants with their height and weight data from [41].[9] The participants' heights range was 155–182 cm, and their weights range was 44–65 kg. We verified that, in agreement with general human physiology studies, the participants' height and weight are strongly positively correlated ($\rho = 0.7$, $p < 0.001$).

As indicated in the previous subsection, for many activities f_m is consistent among different participants. Yet, we additionally observed f_m dependencies on human physiology. For many of the activities we examined, we determined *negative correlations of f_m with the participants' height and weight.* When walking, running, and going upstairs and downstairs, heavier and taller people took fewer steps per time interval than lighter and shorter people.

For example, for going upstairs with waist unit placement, f_m and the participant's height are correlated as $\rho = -0.34$ ($p = 0.03$, $n = 39$). When going upstairs, the taller half of the participants made, on average, 9 fewer steps per minute (0.15 Hz) than the shorter half ($f_m = 1.85$ and 2.05 Hz, correspondingly). For running, with trouser placement, f_m and the participant's weight are correlated as $\rho = -0.46$ ($p < 0.01$, $n = 39$). When running, the heavier half of the participants made, on average, 18 fewer steps per minute (0.3 Hz) than the lighter half. This suggests that future harvester designs may benefit from *targeting harvesters with different f_r values for human groups with different physiological parameters.* For example, *different harvesters may be integrated in clothing of different sizes.*

Generally, motion energy availability increases as f_m increases [31]. However, in human motion, other dependencies may additionally come into play. In our study, for running with trouser unit placement, we determined a positive correlation between D and participants' height ($\rho = 0.35$, $p = 0.03$, $n = 38$) and a positive correlation between $\overline{P}$ and participants' height ($\rho = 0.38$, $p = 0.01, n = 38$). *For the taller half of the participants, the average $\overline{P}$ is 20% higher than for the shorter half* (704 and 582 μW, respectively). Studies with larger number of participants, wider participant demographics, and wider range of participant parameters will most likely identify many additional dependencies. This will allow harvester designers to *develop harvesters for different demographics*, as well as to provide guarantees on the performance of different harvesters based on different human parameters.

[9]The dataset [41] is also annotated with participants' age and gender. However, the age range (20 to 23 years) and the number of females (10 participants) are insufficient for obtaining statistically significant correlations.

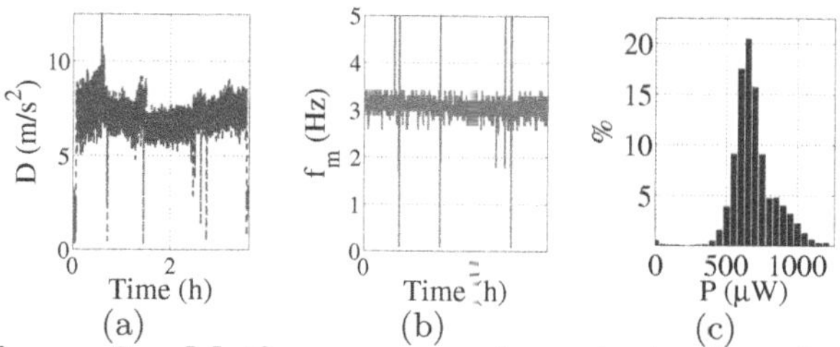

Figure 6: Motion energy characterization for a 3 hour run: (a) the absolute deviation of acceleration, D, and (b) dominant motion frequency, f_m, as functions of time, and (c) the distribution of the corresponding power harvested, $P(t)$.

5. LONG-TERM HUMAN MOBILITY

The results presented in the previous section are based on short motion samples from an activity recognition dataset. In this section, we present results of our own, *longer-term, motion measurements.* We describe our set of day-long human mobility measurements and discuss energy budgets and generation process properties.

5.1 Prolonged Activities

To study motion energy properties over time, we collected a set of measurements of longer activity durations (over 20 minutes). We considered long walks, bike rides, runs, and other activities, performed in normal environments (i.e., not on a treadmill or a stationary bike). To the best of our knowledge, the properties of motion of longer samples have not been analyzed before.

The measurements demonstrate that for prolonged activities, D, f_m, and $P(t)$ vary substantially over time. This variability is related to physiological parameters, such as changes in cadence or posture over time due to fatigue, and changes in the surrounding environment, such as traffic lights, terrain changes, or pedestrian traffic. For example, Fig. 6 shows D, f_m, and P corresponding to a 3 hour run, calculated for 1-second $a(t)$ intervals. In this trace, the average D changes subtly over time (Fig. 6(a)), and f_m varies continuously in the 2.6–3.4 Hz range (Fig. 6(b)). Correspondingly, while the mean $P(t)$ is 550 μW, the 10th–90th percentiles of the $P(t)$ span the range of 459–710 μW (Fig. 6(c)).

The variability of $P(t)$ throughout an activity suggests that node energy management policies are essential even for specifically targeted IoT applications, such as nodes for fitness runners or cyclists. In the following section we demon-

Table 3: Energy budgets, variability, and data rates based on collected traces for daily human routines.

Participant	Occupation and commute	# days	Total dur. (h)	Optimized harvester		r_d, avg (Kb/s)	$\overline{P}^{H4}$ (μW), min/avg/max	% ON, min/avg/max
				$\overline{P}$ (μW), min/avg/max	$\overline{P_d}$ (μW), min/avg/max			
$M1$	Undergraduate student, male, living on campus, always goes to the lab	5	60.4	6.9 / 13.8 / 17.3	4.8 / 6.5 / 8.1	1.3	5.0 / 8.5 / 10.9	5.4 / 9.9 / 12.2
$M2$	Undergraduate student, male, commuting to campus, always goes to the lab	3	27.7	23.3 / 29.0 / 38.2	8.4 / 11.5 / 17.7	2.3	17.1 / 19.6 / 24.5	13.6 / 16.1 / 18.4
$M3$	Undergraduate student, female, living on campus, sometimes works from home	9	62.0	2.4 / 7.16 / 13.4	0.6 / 2.02 / 3.6	0.4	2.0 / 5.8 / 12.2	3.6 / 6.0 /9.95
$M4$	Graduate student, female, commuting to campus, sometimes works from home	7	80.1	1.4 / 11.98 / 25.3	0.6 / 5.6 / 10.7	1.1	1.4 / 11.98 / 25.3	2.8 / 12.7 / 18.1
$M5$	Software developer, male, commuting to office, always goes to the office	1	11.0	16.3	7.5	1.5	15.9	11.5

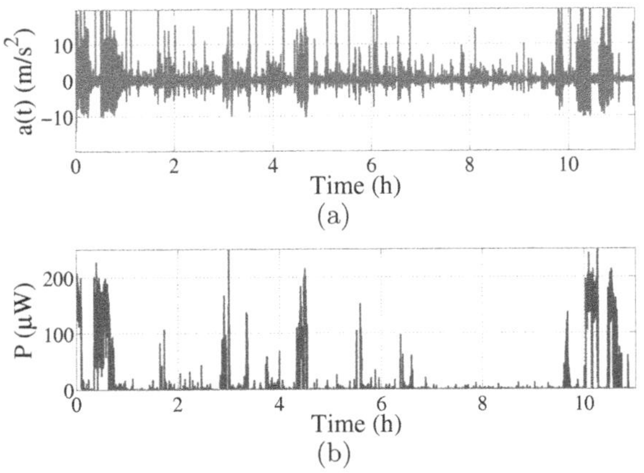

Figure 7: Kinetic energy for normal daily human routine: (a) acceleration, $a(t)$, recorded over 11 hours for participant $M5$, and (b) the power harvested, $P(t)$.

strate even more variability in $P(t)$ for the regular everyday human mobility patterns.

5.2 Day-Long Human Mobility

To determine the daily energy available to an IoT node with an inertial harvester, we collected acceleration traces from different participants during their normal daily routines. We obtained over 200 hours of acceleration information for 5 participants for a total of 25 days. The participants (see Table 3) were instructed to carry a sensing unit in any convenient way. Thus, the measurements correspond to the motion that a participant's keys, mobile phone, or wallet would experience. Typical daily activities of the participants included commuting to office or lab (by train, bus, or subway), working on the computer or on an electronics bench, attending meetings, and walking outside for lunch and coffee breaks.

Fig. 7 shows the $a(t)$ for a day-long trace of participant $M5$, and the corresponding $P(t)$. For all the collected traces, the dominant motion frequency, f_m, range is 1.92–2.8 Hz, corresponding to human walking.

The calculated energy budgets are summarized in Table 3. We calculated $\overline{P}$, the average power a harvester would generate over the length of the trace, as well as $\overline{P_d}$, the average power a harvester would generate over a 24-hour interval. To calculate $\overline{P_d}$ we assumed that when the sensing unit did not record data (e.g., before the participants got dressed for school or work), it was stationary and that a harvester would not generate energy during these intervals. Specifically, for a T hour-long measurement trace, $\overline{P_d} = \overline{P} \cdot T/24$. For each of the participants, Table 3 summarizes the minimum, average, and maximum $\overline{P}$ and $\overline{P_d}$ over the different measurement days, and the data rate r_d that a node would be able to maintain continuously throughout a day when powered by the harvested $\overline{P}_d$. For completeness, for all participants we additionally calculate $\overline{P}^{H4}$, the average power a particular harvester, same for all participants (in this case, the harvester calculated based on the traces for participant $M4$), would harvest. An extensive examination of the sensitivity of power harvested to different harvester design parameters is subject of ongoing work.

5.2.1 Power Budgets

For most participants, an inertial harvester can provide sufficient power to continuously maintain a data rate of at least 1 Kb/s (i.e., $\overline{P_d} > 5$ μW). This is comparable with the data rates estimated in [19] for nodes with a similarly sized *light* harvester in indoor environments (not exposed to outdoor light).

The majority of inter-participant and inter-day differences seem to relate to the *participants' amount of walking*. For example, participant $M2$, whose $\overline{P}$ and $\overline{P_d}$ values are higher than the others, has a relatively long walk to the office, and walks frequently between two different offices in the same building. Other factors (unit placement, amount of daily activity as perceived by the participants) appear to be only of secondary importance. We note that the majority of traces that correspond to $\overline{P_d} < 5$ μW (and thus r_d <1 Kb/s) correspond to participants *working from home*[10]. Overall, daily routines that involve a lot of walking correspond to relatively high levels of energy availability.

5.2.2 Harvesting Process Variability & Properties

The amount of energy that can be harvested varies widely throughout the day. As shown in Section 4, walking generates substantial amounts of energy, while being stationary generates little. Physiological studies (e.g., [33]) have shown that people are at rest the majority of the time. Correspondingly, in our measurements, $P(t)$ is low for most of the day and over 95% of the total energy is collected during

[10] As indicated by the minimum value of $\overline{P_d}$ in Table 3, several individual traces with $\overline{P_d} < 5$ μW were considered for participants M1, M3, and M4.

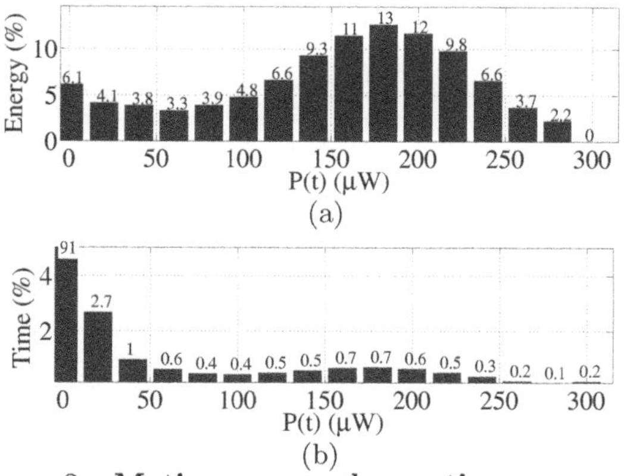

Figure 8: Motion energy harvesting process variability for participant $M1$: (a) the percentage of the total energy harvested at different power levels $P(t)$, and (b) the *percentage of time* the power is harvested at the different $P(t)$ (notice that for $0 \leq P(t) \leq 15$, the value is 91%).

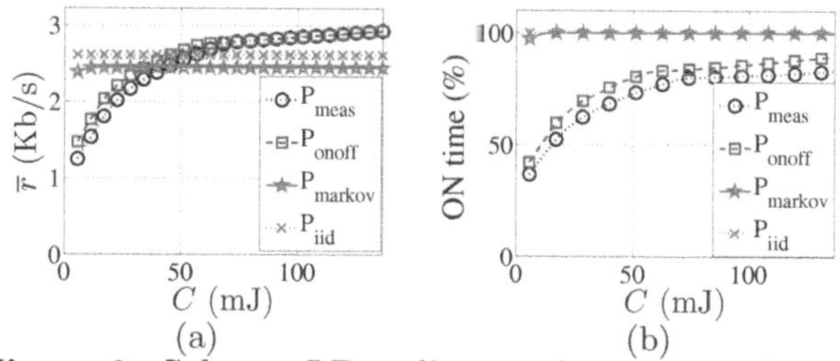

Figure 9: Scheme-LB policy performance using energy traces (P_{meas}) for participant $M1$ and using the corresponding ON/OFF (P_{onoff}), Markov (P_{markov}), and i.i.d. (P_{iid}) processes: (a) average data rates, $\bar{r}$, and (b) node ON times.

only 4–7% of a day. For example, Fig. 8 shows, for participant $M1$, the percentage of the total energy that would be harvested over different ranges of $P(t)$ and the *percentage of the time* that the harvester would generate these $P(t)$ values. For this participant, the harvester would generate $P(t) < 15$ μW 91% of the time, and only 6.1% of the total energy would be harvested during this time.

Consider an *ON/OFF representation* of the energy harvesting process, $P_{\text{onoff}}(t)$, where $P_{\text{onoff}}(t) \leftarrow ON$ if $P(t) > \gamma$, and $P_{\text{onoff}}(t) \leftarrow OFF$ otherwise. For the analysis below, we empirically set $\gamma = 10$ μW; the results are similar for $10 \leq \gamma \leq 40$ μW. For all participants, P_{onoff} is ON for less than 20% of the time (Table 3). The participants do not lead sedentary lifestyles; their activity patterns are in line with general health guidelines. However, the generally recommended 30 minutes of physical activity per day correspond to only 9% of an 11-hour trace. Additionally, the typical *duration* of ON intervals is short – *on the order of seconds.* While some of the ON intervals are long (over 200 seconds), the vast majority of the ON intervals (78.5–89.0%) are shorter than 30 seconds; the *median ON intervals are 5–9.5 seconds.* The longer ON intervals correspond to commuting (e.g., walking from a public transit station to a campus building), and represent only 1–3% of the ON intervals. These results are consistent with the overall results for *walking intervals* examined in a physiological study of human mobility [33].

In summary, $P(t)$ is low for the majority of the time, and when it does become high, it stays high for only a brief period of time. This emphasizes the need for energy harvesting-adaptive algorithms.

5.2.3 Harvesting Process vs. I.i.d. and Markov Processes

Several energy harvesting adaptive algorithms were developed under the assumption that the energy harvesting process is Markov, or has independent identically distributed (i.i.d.) per-slot energy inputs [19,22,40]. However, such assumptions, realistic in certain scenarios [19], *do not hold for our motion energy traces.* We use a slotted representation of the energy harvesting processes, P_{meas}, setting the time slot length $T_{\text{int}} = 1$ second, and determining the $P_{\text{meas}}(i)$ by computing the average value of the $P(t)$ for each T_{int}.

For all day-long traces, P_{meas} is *clearly not i.i.d. or Markovian.* For example, for the P_{meas} for participant $M1$ for $\gamma = 20$ μW, $p(P_{\text{meas}}(i) > \gamma | P_{\text{meas}}(i-1) > \gamma) = 0.84$, while $p(P_{\text{meas}}(i) > \gamma | P_{\text{meas}}(i-1) > \gamma, P_{\text{meas}}(i-2) < \gamma) = 0.45$.

To demonstrate the differences between the traces and i.i.d. and Markov processes, we examine the performance of the Scheme-LB policies [11] with the different processes. In the Scheme-LB policies [11], $s(i) \leftarrow (1-\epsilon)\hat{Q}(i)$ if $B(i) + Q(i) \geq (1-\epsilon)\hat{Q}(i)$, and $s(i) \leftarrow B(i) + Q(i)$ otherwise, where $\hat{Q}(i)$ is the running average of $Q(i)$ ($\hat{Q}(i) \leftarrow \sum_{j=0}^{i-1} Q(j)/i$), and ϵ is a small constant (we use $\epsilon = 0.01$). For a process P_{meas}, we generate a corresponding i.i.d. process, P_{iid}, by randomly permuting the values of P_{meas} (we use the Wald-Wolfowitz runs test to verify the independence of the P_{iid} values). To generate a Markov process, P_{markov}, we calculate the empirical state transition probabilities of the P_{onoff} process (defined in Section 5.2.2) and generate a Markov process with states {ON,OFF} and the calculated transition probabilities. We set the P_{markov} values for ON and OFF states to the average values of $P_{\text{meas}}(i)$ for which $P_{\text{onoff}}(i) = ON$, and for which $P_{\text{onoff}}(i) = OFF$, respectively. This ensures that *the processes have the same first-order statistics.*[11]

The policy performance observed using i.i.d. and Markov processes differs dramatically from the policy performance observed using the traces. For example, Fig. 9 shows the $\bar{r}$ and the ON times obtained under the Scheme-LB policy for the different processes based on a trace of participant $M1$. Using the process P_{onoff}, the performance is similar to the performance obtained using P_{meas} – the $\bar{r}$ values differ by at most 17% (0.23 Kb/s), and the ON times differ by at most 7%. However, the performance observed using P_{iid} and P_{markov} differs greatly from the performance observed using P_{meas}. The differences in $\bar{r}$ values reach over 105% (1.35 Kb/s), and the differences in ON times reach 63%.

Moreover, using i.i.d. and Markov processes results in *different performance trends.* Using P_{meas}, the performance strongly depends on C, with $\bar{r}$ for the different values of C differing by over 2.3 times, and with the ON percentages differing by over 45%. However, using P_{iid} and P_{markov}, both $\bar{r}$ and ON times are nearly independent of C. Additionally, evaluating policy performance using P_{meas} shows that the ON times are an important metric because they can be low for small values of C (Fig. 9(b)). However, when evaluating using P_{iid} and P_{markov}, the ON times are nearly 100% for all

[11] For each of the processes, we calculate $Q(i)$ as $Q(i) \leftarrow \eta_h \cdot T_{\text{int}} \cdot P(i)$, where $\eta_h = 20\%$ [45]. We rely on a *battery* node model and set $B_0 = 0.5C$. We calculate the data rate as $r(i) \leftarrow s(i)/c_{\text{tx}}$.

Table 4: Object motion measurements.

Scenario	$\overline{P}$
Taking a book off a shelf	<10 μW
Putting on reading glasses	<10 μW
Reading a book	<10 μW
Writing with a pencil	10–15 μW
Opening a drawer	10–30 μW
Spinning in a swivel chair	<10 μW
Opening a building door	<1 μW
Shaking an object	>3,000 μW

values of C, including values as low as 15 mJ (i.e., less than 15% of the average energy harvested per day). This *emphasizes the need to evaluate energy harvesting-adaptive policies for wireless nodes equipped with an inertial harvester using real traces.*

6. OBJECT MOTION ENERGY

While Sections 4 and 5 focus on *human motion*, in this section we also provide some brief observations regarding the energy availability associated with the *motion of objects*. We conducted extensive experiments, recording $a(t)$ and calculating $\overline{P}$ for a wide range of motions. Our experiments included performing everyday activities with a variety of everyday objects (see Table 4), shipping a FedEx box with a sensing unit in it from Houston, TX to New York, NY, transporting sensing units in carry-on and checked airport luggage, and taking sensing units on cars, subways, and trains. Below, we present observations based on our measurements. To put the $\overline{P}$ values in perspective, we note that, as we demonstrated in Section 4, *human walking* typically corresponds to $120 \leq \overline{P} \leq 280$ μW.

Expectedly, for the vast majority of common object motion the energy availability is low. Due to the filter properties of inertial harvesters (see Section 3.1), a motion needs to be *periodic* to be "harvestable". The vast majority of common object motion is not periodic, and hence the corresponding energy availability is low. For example, we attached a sensing unit to a book and observed that when the book is being taken off the shelf, read, or put back on the shelf, $\overline{P} < 10$ μW. For a sensing unit attached to a pencil used by a student to write homework, $10 \leq \overline{P} \leq 15$ μW. Even high-acceleration non-periodic motions, such as a plane landing and taking off, and an accelerating or decelerating car, correspond to only limited energy availability ($\overline{P} < 5$ μW). For example, when a unit was placed in a bag checked in on a 3:13 hour flight the recorded $a(t)$ showed that the luggage was subjected to varying high-acceleration motions, but the $\overline{P}$ did not exceed 5 μW even during the most turbulent intervals of the flight. Furthermore, substantially more energy could be harvested from a human walking around the airport with the luggage (i.e., periodic motion of a human walk) than from the motion associated with the entire flight.

Our study additionally demonstrated low levels of energy availability for many *high-amplitude and high-periodicity* motions. The motion of many objects in our environment is *damped* for human comfort (e.g., by door dampers, cabinet drawer dampers, and springs in swirling chairs). In such cases, most of the motion energy is absorbed in the dampers and only small amounts can be harvested (e.g., by sticker form factor harvesters [16]). Opening and closing a drawer, spinning a swivel chair, and opening and closing a building door corresponded to $10 \leq \overline{P} \leq 30$ μW, $1 \leq \overline{P} \leq 6.5$ μW, and $\overline{P} < 1$ μW, respectively. This suggest that IoT nodes embedded in objects such as doors and drawers should *integrate motion energy harvesters with the mechanical dampers.*

Finally, our study confirmed that purposeful object motion can be extremely energy rich. Periodic shaking of objects can generate a relatively large amount of energy in a short time (as demonstrated by "shake" flashlights). In our experiments, purposeful shaking corresponded to $\overline{P}$ of up to 3,500 μW, that is, *12–29 times more than the power for walking.* In IoT applications with mobile nodes, this can be useful for quickly recharging battery-depleted nodes.

7. ENERGY-AWARE ALGORITHMS

We now formulate an optimization problem of energy allocation for ultra-low-power energy harvesting IoT node and prove it to be NP-hard. As mentioned in Section 3.5, the formulation captures realistic constraints that have not been jointly considered before: (i) *discrete*, rather than continuous, energy spending rates; (ii) *general*, rather than concave or linear, utility functions; and (iii) use of a *capacitor*, rather than a battery, as an energy storage component.

In Section 5.2.3 we demonstrated that the environmental energy available to the node in each slot i, $e(i)$, cannot be represented by a Markov or an i.i.d. process. Therefore, there is need to develop algorithms that do not make an assumption on the distribution of $e(i)$. Since the energy allocation problem is NP-hard, solving it is difficult even if $e(i)\ \forall i$ is known in advance. We distinguish between two types of energy allocation algorithms: (i) *offline*, where $e(i)\ \forall i$ is part of the input; an offline algorithm can be used as a benchmark since it provides an upper bound on the utility a node can achieve in practice, and (ii) *online*, where a decision in slot i is made based only on $e(i')\ \forall i' < i$; an online algorithm can be used by a real node to determine spending rate $s(i)$ in each slot. We develop optimal and approximate offline algorithms. We then develop an online algorithm and prove it to be optimal for some cases. We also evaluate the performance of the algorithms with the collected motion energy traces. Due to space constraints, the proofs are omitted and appear in [18].

7.1 Energy Allocation Problem

We start by formulating the energy allocation problem for a wireless IoT node:

Energy Allocation (EA) Problem:

$$\max_{s(i)} \left\{ \sum_{i=0}^{K-1} U(s(i)) \right\} \text{ s.t.:}$$

$$\frac{s(i)}{\eta(i, B(i))} \leq B(i),\ s(i) \in \mathcal{S} \cup \{0\}\ \forall\ i \quad (1)$$

$$B(i) \leq B(i-1) + Q(e(i-1), B(i-1)) - L(i-1, B(i-1)) - \frac{s(i-1)}{\eta(i-1, B(i-1))}\ \forall\ i \geq 1 \quad (2)$$

$$0 \leq B(i) \leq C\ \forall\ i;\ B(0) = B_0; B(K) \geq B_K \quad (3)$$

This is an integer optimization problem, namely, all the coefficients and function values are integers. Constraint (1) ensures that a node does not spend more energy than it has stored and that the spending rate, $s(i)$, is from a fixed set, (2) represents the energy storage evolution dynamics, and (3) imposes the storage component capacity constraints and sets the initial and final energy levels to B_0 and B_K. To simplify the notation, we omit the dependency of $\eta(i, B(i))$, $Q(e(i), B(i))$, and $L(i, B(i))$, on $B(i)$ in the rest of the section. However, unless mentioned otherwise, *the proofs and the algorithms are also valid when the dependency on $B(i)$ is considered.*

The proof of the following theorem demonstrates the NP-hardness of the EA Problem even for "simple" cases (e.g., $B_0 = B_K = 0$ and linear $U(s(i))$).

THEOREM 1. *The EA Problem is NP-hard.*

7.2 Energy Allocation Algorithms

For solving the EA Problem, we present a dynamic programming-based pseudopolynomial algorithm[12], a Fully Polynomial Time Approximation Scheme (FPTAS)[13], and a greedy online algorithm which is optimal in particular scenarios.

We first present an optimal offline dynamic programming algorithm for solving the EA Problem. Thus, the algorithm jointly considers realistic constraints that have not been jointly considered before and uses similar ideas to the dynamic programming algorithm from [19]. However, compared to [19], the dynamic programming procedure's parameters and return value switch places. This difference is used to develop the FPTAS we present later in this section.

Dynamic programming algorithm: We determine $M(i, U)$ which is the maximum battery level when obtaining utility U in the beginning of slot i. We set $M(0,0) = B_0$ and $M(0,U) = -\infty \ \forall\ U > 0$. For $i > 0$, $M(i,U)$ is calculated as $M(i,U) = \max_{s(i-1)\in \mathcal{S}\cup\{0\}}\{M(i-1, U-U(s(i-1)))+Q(i-1) - s(i-1)/\eta(i-1) - L(i-1)\}$. Let the optimal solution utility be U^*, and let $U^H \geq U^*$ be an upper bound. We calculate $M(i,U)$ for $1 \leq i \leq K$ and $0 \leq U \leq U^H$. Then, $U^* = \arg\max\{M(K,U) \text{ s.t. } M(K,U) \geq B_K\}$. The optimal energy spending values $s^*(i)$ are found by maintaining an array $A(i,U)$ that stores the $s(i-1)$ values chosen when calculating $M(i,U)$. Then, $s^*(K-1) = A(K,U^*)$. We can obtain $s(K-2)$ using $A(K-1, U^* - U(s^*(K-1)))$. This process is repeated to find $s^*(i)$ for $0 \leq i \leq K-1$.

The space complexity of the algorithm is $O(K \cdot U^H)$ for storing $A(i,U)$. Since in every calculation of $M(i,U)$ we go over $\mathcal{S}$, the time complexity is $O(K\cdot|\mathcal{S}|\cdot U^H)$. Let $s_{\max}$ be the maximum item in $\mathcal{S}$, clearly $U^H = K \cdot U(s_{\max})$ is an upper bound, for which we obtain space and time complexities of $O(K^2 \cdot U(s_{\max}))$ and $O(K^2 \cdot U(s_{\max}) \cdot |\mathcal{S}|)$, respectively.

FPTAS: For large values of $U(s_{\max})$, the time and space complexities render the dynamic programming algorithm impractical. Therefore, we develop an approximation scheme. It relies on a lower bound $U^L = U(s_{\max})$, which is a lower bound, since if spending only $s_{\max}$ energy at some slot is always infeasible, $s_{\max}$ can be removed from $\mathcal{S}$. We define a scaling factor $\mu = \epsilon \cdot U(s_{\max})/K$ and a new utility function $\tilde{U}(s) = \lfloor U(s)/\mu \rfloor$. Next, we invoke the dynamic programming algorithm for $\tilde{U}()$ to compute $M(i, \tilde{U})$ for $0 \leq i \leq K$ and $0 \leq \tilde{U} \leq U^H/\mu$. The algorithm returns the energy spending rates $\tilde{s}(i)$ found by the dynamic programming algorithm. Below we show that the algorithm is an FPTAS.

THEOREM 2. *The above algorithm runs in times poly($1/\epsilon$, K), and the solution $\tilde{s}(i)$ is a $(1-\epsilon)$-approximation.*

Greedy online algorithm: In every time slot, the algorithm tries to maximize the utility while not letting the energy storage level go below B_K. Namely, in each slot i the algorithm spends $s(i) = \max\{U(s) \mid s \in \mathcal{S}\cup\{0\} \wedge (B(i) - s/\eta) \geq B_K\}$.

We first focus on the *battery* node model and on a scenario where (i) for x, y, $U(x+y) = U(x)+U(y)$, and (ii) the set $\mathcal{S}$ is $\{j\cdot s\ , j = 1, \ldots, |\mathcal{S}|\}$ and $s > 0$. Such conditions hold, for example, when a node uses a fixed power level and changes its transmission rate by transmitting a different number of equal-sized packets.

THEOREM 3. *For battery energy storage model, for $B_K = 0$, if conditions (i) and (ii) hold, the greedy algorithm is optimal.*

In Section 7.3 we evaluate the performance of the greedy online algorithm under the capacitor model and for cases where $B_K > 0$.

We additionally demonstrate a set of cases where no performance is guaranteed for any online algorithm. Since we showed in Section 5.2.3 that $e(i)$ cannot be represented by a Markov or an i.i.d process, for these cases any online algorithm may perform arbitrary worse and it should be evaluated with collected traces in order to assess its performance.

THEOREM 4. *For $B_K > 0$, the performance of any online algorithm that guarantees a feasible solution can be arbitrarily worse for $K \geq 2$.*

7.3 Trace-based Performance Evaluation

In this section, we evaluate the algorithms using the motion energy traces we collected, for both *battery* and *capacitor* node models defined in Section 3.5. We refer to the algorithm and model combinations as follows:

Algorithms invoked for the battery model:

- **ALG-OB:** The optimal dynamic programming algorithm.
- **ALG-FB:** The FPTAS.
- **ALG-GB:** The greedy online algorithm.

Algorithms invoked for the capacitor model:

- **ALG-OC:** The optimal dynamic programming algorithm.
- **ALG-FC:** The FPTAS.
- **ALG-GC:** The greedy online algorithm.

We consider an IoT node that changes its data rate $r(i)$ by changing the number of packets it sends in a time slot (where the length of a time slot is $T_{\text{int}} = 1$ second). The maximal $r(i)$ is 250 Kb/s, the packet size is 127 bytes[14], and $c_{\text{tx}} = 1$ nJ/bit (i.e., it takes 1,016 nJ to transmit 1 packet). Thus, $\mathcal{S} = \{1016 \cdot j, j = 1, \ldots, 246\}$, and $s_{\min} = \min\{s \in \mathcal{S}\} = 1016$. We set $L(i, B(i)) = 0$. We use the day-long motion energy traces (see Table 3)[15]. We evaluated the algorithms for traces of different users and for different

[12]A *pseudopolynomial algorithm* is an algorithm whose running time is polynomial if the input is encoded in unary format.

[13]An *FPTAS* is an algorithm which takes an instance of an optimization problem and a parameter $\epsilon > 0$ and, in polynomial time in both the problem size and $1/\epsilon$, produces a solution that is within a $1-\epsilon$ factor of the optimal solution.

[14]These parameters correspond to IEEE 802.15.4/Zigbee nodes [5].

[15]From the traces, we calculate $Q(i)$ as $Q(i) \leftarrow \eta_h \cdot T_{\text{int}} \cdot P_{\text{meas}}(i)$, where $\eta_h = 20\%$. To evaluate ALG-GB, ALG-FC, and ALG-GC, we compare their performance with the optimal algorithms ALG-OC and ALG-OB.

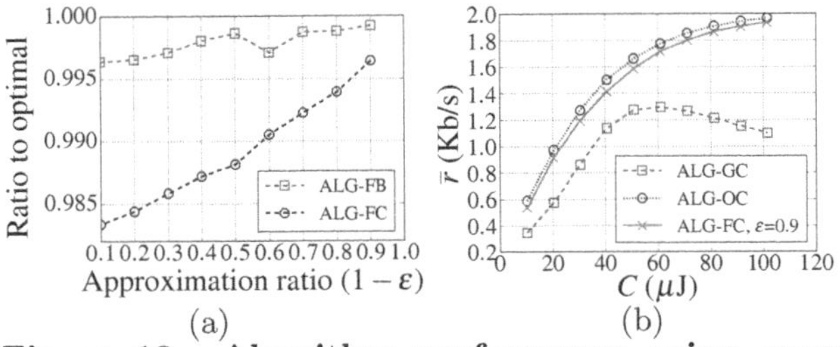

Figure 10: Algorithm performance using energy traces for participant $M1$, for: (a) battery and capacitor models, performance ratio between ALG-FC (ALG-FB) and ALG-OC (ALG-OB), and (b) the capacitor model, average data rate, $\bar{r}$, achieved by different algorithms.

days. We observed that the performance trends of the algorithms are very similar for all the considered day-long traces. Therefore, only the graphs corresponding to a day-long trace of participant $M1$ are shown. Since for the day-long traces K is very large, to draw a single point in the graphs we run the algorithms over 66 consecutive 10-minute intervals of $Q(i)$ and average the results. Unless specified otherwise, the evaluation results are shown for $B_0 = B_K = 0$ and for $10 \cdot s_{\min} \leq C \leq 100 \cdot s_{\min}$.

We first explain in detail how to compute the conversion efficiency $\eta()$. Recall that $\eta()$ depends on the node's fixed operating voltage $V_{\rm op}$ and energy storage voltage $V_{\rm out}(i)$ (see Section 3.5). For the *battery* model, we assume $V_{\rm out}(i) = V_{\rm op}$ and set $\eta = 1$. For the *capacitor* model, approximating voltage converter properties [2], we compute:

$$\eta(i, B(i)) = \begin{cases} \frac{V_{\rm out}(i)}{V_{\rm op}}, & V_{\min} \leq V_{\rm out}(i) \leq V_{\rm op} \\ 1 - \frac{V_{\rm out}(i) - V_{\rm op}}{2 \cdot (V_{\max} - V_{\rm op})}, & V_{\rm op} < V_{\rm out}(i) \leq V_{\max} \\ 0 & \text{otherwise,} \end{cases}$$

where $V_{\max} = 2.8$ V is the maximum voltage of the capacitor, $V_{\rm out}(i)$ is node's voltage in a time slot i ($V_{\rm out}(i) = \sqrt{B(i)/C} \cdot V_{\max}$), $V_{\rm op} = 2.5$ V, and $V_{\min} = 0.7$ V.

For the evaluations, we implemented an improved iterative version of the dynamic programming algorithm using the following definition:

DEFINITION 1. *An entry $M(i, U)$ dominates an entry $M(i, U')$ if $U \geq U'$ and $M(i, U) > M(i, U')$.*

A dominated entry will never be considered for the optimal solution and can be removed during the calculation [24].

We first examine the performance of ALG-FC and ALG-FB as a function of their approximation ratio, $1 - \epsilon$ (see Theorem 2). Fig. 10(a) shows the ratio of the ALG-FC and ALG-FB performance to the optimal (ALG-OC and ALG-OB) for $C = 100 \cdot s_{\min}$. Even for small $1-\epsilon$, the ALG-FC and ALG-FB performance is close to the optimal (much closer than the theoretical bound).

Next, we examine the performance of the ALG-GC, ALG-OC, and ALG-FC for the capacitor mode. Fig. 10(b) shows the average data rates $\bar{r}$ obtained by the algorithms. The performance of ALG-FC is close to that of ALG-OC. The performance of ALG-GC gets worse compared to ALG-OC for larger C because it obtains lower $V_{\rm out}(i)$ (recall that $V_{\rm out}(i) = \sqrt{B(i)/C} \cdot V_{\max}$), resulting in lower $\eta()$. Furthermore, for $C > 60$ μJ, its obtained $\bar{r}$ *decreases* as C increases.

We also examine the performance of the ALG-GB and ALG-OB algorithms for the battery model. Since for $B_K = 0$ ALG-GB is optimal (see Theorem 3), we consider $B_K = B_0 = 10 \cdot s_{\min}$. Fig. 11(a) shows the $\bar{r}$ values obtained by ALG-GB and ALG-OB. Since ALG-GB cannot take advantage of the initial energy (because $B_0 = B_K$), for a particular C value the capacity available to ALG-GB is $C - B_0$. Correspondingly, since consecutive plotted points differ by B_0 in their C value, the plotted points (C, $\bar{r}$) for ALG-OB and ($C+B_0$, $\bar{r}$) for ALG-GB appear in the figure.

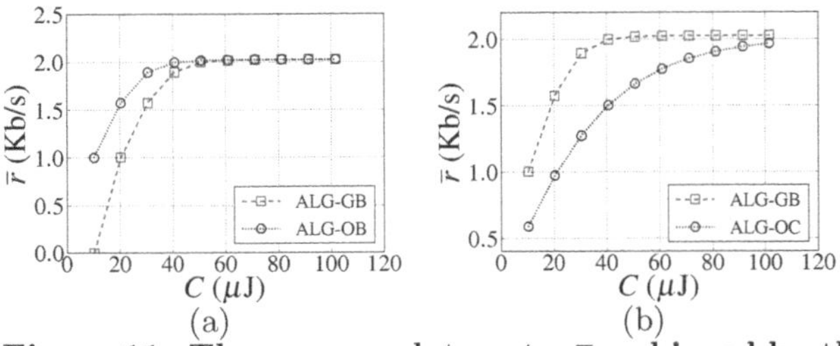

Figure 11: The average data rate, $\bar{r}$, achieved by the algorithms using energy traces for participant $M1$, for (a) the battery model, for $B_K = B_0 = 10 \cdot s_{\min}$, and (b) the battery and capacitor models.

To compare the performance for the battery and the capacitor models, Fig. 11(b) shows the data rates obtained by ALG-GB and ALG-OC. For ALG-OC, for larger C there is a wider range of charge level for which $\eta()$ is close to 1. Correspondingly, ALG-OC can keep $\eta()$ close to 1, thus its performance approaches that of ALG-GB.

In summary, the evaluations demonstrate that the algorithms perform well and showcase that for the *capacitor* node model, having a larger energy storage may worsen the overall performance.

8. CONCLUSIONS

This paper considers motion (kinetic) energy availability for Internet of Things (IoT) applications. We thoroughly study *human motion* and provide observations regarding *object motion*. For human motion, we use the results of our measurement campaign that include 200 hours of acceleration traces from day-long human activities. Moreover, we use a dataset of 7 common human motions performed by over 40 participants [41]. We consider a wireless energy harvesting node model that captures several practical IoT node design considerations. We design optimal, approximation, and online *energy allocation algorithms* and evaluate their performance using the collected motion energy traces.

In future work we will expand our measurement study to include additional motions and additional human participants. We will jointly measure light and motion energy (available to the same device) to obtain insight into the use of multipurpose harvesters. We will evaluate the performance and energy consumption of the energy allocation algorithms in real devices under various utility functions. Finally, we will develop algorithms for more complex networking scenarios (e.g., multihop networks of IoT nodes) and evaluate their performance using the traces.

Acknowledgments

This work was supported in part by Vodafone Americas Foundation Wireless Innovation Project and NSF grants CCF-09-64497 and CNS-10-54856. We thank Sonal Shetkar for her contributions to the development of the measurement setup and study methodology, and Craig Gutterman for his contributions to preliminary data analysis. We additionally thank Chang Sun and Kanghwan Kim for their contributions. We also thank our shepherd Ranveer Chandra for valuable feedback.

9. REFERENCES

[1] nPower Personal Energy Generator. http://www.npowerpeg.com.

[2] Linear technology. LTM4607 $36V_{IN}$, $24V_{OUT}$ high efficiency buck-boost DC/DC μmodule regulator. 2008. http://cds.linear.com/docs/en/datasheet/4607fb.pdf.

[3] Linear technology. LTC3588 piezoelectric energy harvesting power supply datasheet. 2010. http://cds.linear.com/docs/en/datasheet/35881fa.pdf.

[4] Piezo systems. piezo energy harvester datasheet. 2011. http://www.piezo.com/catalog8.pdf%20files/Cat8.20&21.pdf.

[5] Chipcon. CC2420 2.4gGHz IEEE802.15.4/ZigBee-ready RF transceiver datasheet. Nov. 2013. http://www.ti.com/lit/ds/symlink/cc2420.pdf.

[6] Mide. volture piezoelectric energy harvesters datasheet. Jan. 2013. http://www.mide.com/pdfs/Volture_Datasheet_001.pdf.

[7] Smart material. macro fiber composite - mfc datasheet. 2013. http://www.smart-material.com/media/Datasheet/MFC-V2.1-2013-web.pdf.

[8] EnHANTs kinetic energy measurements. Mar. 2014. http://enhants.ee.columbia.edu/kinetic-datasets.

[9] S. Beeby, M. Tudor, and N. White. Energy harvesting vibration sources for microsystems applications. *Measurement science and technology*, 17(12):R175, 2006.

[10] T. Buren, P. Lukowicz, and G. Troster. Kinetic energy powered computing: experimental feasibility study. In *Proc. IEEE ISWC'03*, Feb. 2003.

[11] S. Chen, P. Sinha, N. Shroff, and C. Joo. A simple asymptotically optimal energy allocation and routing scheme in rechargeable sensor networks. In *Proc. IEEE INFOCOM'12*, Mar. 2012.

[12] M. Cong, K. Kim, M. Gorlatova, J. Sarik, I. Kymissis, and G. Zussman. CRAWDAD data set columbia/kinetic. http://crawdad.cs.dartmouth.edu/columbia/kinetic, Apr. 2014.

[13] B. Devillers and D. Gunduz. A general framework for the optimization of energy harvesting communication systems with battery imperfections. *IEEE J. Commun. Netw.*, 14(2):130–139, 2012.

[14] M. C. Domingo. Packet size optimization for improving the energy efficiency in body sensor networks. *ETRI Journal*, 33(3):299–309, June 2011.

[15] J. Galloway. Pick up the beat. In *Runners World*, July 2007. http://www.runnersworld.com/running-tips/pick-beat.

[16] M. Gorlatova, P. Kinget, I. Kymissis, D. Rubenstein, X. Wang, and G. Zussman. Energy-harvesting active networked tags (EnHANTs) for ubiquitous object networking. *IEEE Wireless Commun.*, 17(6), Dec. 2010.

[17] M. Gorlatova, R. Margolies, J. Sarik, G. Stanje, J. Zhu, B. Vigraham, M. Szczodrak, L. Carloni, P. Kinget, I. Kymissis, and G. Zussman. Prototyping energy harvesting active networked tags (EnHANTs). In *Proc. IEEE INFOCOM'13 mini-conference*, Apr. 2013.

[18] M. Gorlatova, J. Sarik, G. Grebla, M. Cong, I. Kymissis, and G. Zussman. Movers and shakers: Kinetic energy harvesting for the internet of things, Columbia University Electrical Engineering Technical Report 2014-03-27. http://enhants.ee.columbia.edu/images/papers/MoversShakers_Technical_Report_03272014.pdf, 2014.

[19] M. Gorlatova, A. Wallwater, and G. Zussman. Networking low-power energy harvesting devices: Measurements and algorithms. *IEEE Trans. Mobile Comput.*, 13(9):1853–1865, Sept. 2013.

[20] J. Gummeson, S. S. Clark, K. Fu, and D. Ganesan. On the limits of effective micro-energy harvesting on mobile CRFID sensors. In *Proc. ACM MobiSys'10*, June 2010.

[21] H. Huang, G. Merrett, and N. White. Human-powered inertial energy harvesters: the effect of orientation, location and activity on obtainable power. In *Proc. Eurosensors'11*, Sept. 2011.

[22] L. Huang and M. Neely. Utility optimal scheduling in energy harvesting networks. *IEEE/ACM Trans. Netw.*, 21(4):1117–1130, Aug. 2013.

[23] A. Kansal, J. Hsu, S. Zahedi, and M. B. Srivastava. Power management in energy harvesting sensor networks. *ACM Trans. Embedded Comput. Syst*, 6(4):32:1–32:38, 2007.

[24] H. Kellerer, U. Pferschy, and D. Pisinger. *Knapsack Problems*. Springer, 2004.

[25] T. Krupenkin and J. A. Taylor. Reverse electrowetting as a new approach to high-power energy harvesting. *Nature Communications*, 2:448, 2011.

[26] J. Kymissis, C. Kendall, J. Paradiso, and N. Gershenfeld. Parasitic power harvesting in shoes. In *Proc. IEEE ISWC'98*, Oct. 1998.

[27] G. Lin, P. Rahul, M. Rosenblatt, T. Nakajima, B. Germansderfer, and S. Dasgupta. Harnessing power through electromagnetic induction utilizing printed coils. United States Patent Application #20120235510, Sept. 2012.

[28] R.-S. Liu, P. Sinha, and C. E. Koksal. Joint energy management and resource allocation in rechargeable sensor networks. In *Proc. IEEE INFOCOM'10*, Mar. 2010.

[29] G. V. Merrett, A. S. Weddell, A. P. Lewis, N. R. Harris, B. M. Al-Hashimi, and N. M. White. An empirical energy model for supercapacitor powered wireless sensor nodes. In *Proc. IEEE ICCCN'08*, Aug. 2008.

[30] N. Michelusi, K. Stamatiou, and M. Zorzi. Transmission policies for energy harvesting sensors with time-correlated energy supply. *IEEE Trans. Commun.*, 61(7):2988–3001, July 2013.

[31] P. Mitcheson, E. Yeatman, G. Rao, A. Holmes, and T. Green. Energy harvesting from human and machine motion for wireless electronic devices. *Proc. of the IEEE*, 96(9):1457 –1486, Sept. 2008.

[32] D. Noh and T. Abdelzaher. Efficient flow-control algorithm cooperating with energy allocation scheme for solar-powered WSNs. *Wireless Comm. and Mobile Comput.*, 2010.

[33] M. Orendurff, J. Schoen, G. Bernatz, A. Segal, and G. Klute. How humans walk: bout duration, steps per bout, and rest duration. *J. Rehabil. Res. Dev.*, 45(7):1077–89, 2008.

[34] O. Orhan, D. Gunduz, and E. Erkip. Optimal packet scheduling for an energy harvesting transmitter with processing cost. In *Proc. IEEE ICC'13*, June 2013.

[35] O. Ozel, K. Tutuncuoglu, J. Yang, S. Ulukus, and A. Yener. Transmission with energy harvesting nodes in fading wireless channels: Optimal policies. *IEEE J. Sel. Areas Commun.*, 29(8):1732–1743, Sept. 2011.

[36] J. Paradiso and T. Starner. Energy scavenging for mobile and wireless electronics. *IEEE Perv. Comput.*, 4(1):18–27, 2005.

[37] T. Starner. Human-powered wearable computing. *IBM systems J.*, 35(3.4):618–629, 1996.

[38] T. Von Buren, P. Mitcheson, T. Green, E. Yeatman, A. Holmes, and G. Troster. Optimization of inertial micropower generators for human walking motion. *IEEE Sensors J.*, 6(1):28–38, 2006.

[39] R. Vullers, R. van Schaijk, I. Doms, C. Van Hoof, and R. Mertens. Micropower energy harvesting. *Solid-State Electron.*, 53(7):684 – 693, Apr. 2009.

[40] Q. Wang and M. Liu. When simplicity meets optimality: Efficient transmission power control with stochastic energy harvesting. In *Proc. IEEE INFOCOM'13*, Apr. 2013.

[41] Y. Xue and L. Jin. A naturalistic 3D acceleration-based activity dataset and benchmark evaluations. In *Proc. IEEE SMC'10*, Oct. 2010.

[42] J. Yang and S. Ulukus. Optimal packet scheduling in an energy harvesting communication system. *IEEE Trans. Commun.*, 60(1):220–230, Jan. 2012.

[43] Z. Yang, E. Halvorsen, and T. Dong. Power generation from conductive droplet sliding on electret film. *Appl. Phys. Lett.*, 100(21):213905, 2012.

[44] L. Yerva, B. Campbell, A. Bansal, T. Schmid, and P. Dutta. Grafting energy-harvesting leaves onto the sensornet tree. In *Proc. IEEE IPSN'12*, Apr. 2012.

[45] J. Yun, S. Patel, M. Reynolds, and G. Abowd. Design and performance of an optimal inertial power harvester for human-powered devices. *IEEE Trans. Mobile Comput.*, 10(5):669 –683, May 2011.

[46] M. Zafer and E. Modiano. A calculus approach to energy-efficient data transmission with quality-of-service constraints. *IEEE/ACM Trans. Netw.*, 17(3):898–911, 2009.

[47] T. Zhu, Z. Zhong, Y. Gu, T. He, and Z.-L. Zhang. Leakage-aware energy synchronization for wireless sensor networks. In *Proc. ACM MobiSys'09*, June 2009.

Pricing Link by Time

Chengdi Lai*
Department of Electrical and Electronic Engineering
The University of Hong Kong
Pokfulam Road, Hong Kong
laichengdi@eee.hku.hk

Steven H. Low
CMS & EE
California Institute of Technology
Pasadena, 91125 CA, U.S.A.
slow@cms.caltech.edu

Ka-Cheong Leung
Department of Electrical and Electronic Engineering
The University of Hong Kong
Pokfulam Road, Hong Kong
kcleung@eee.hku.hk

Victor O.K. Li
Department of Electrical and Electronic Engineering
The University of Hong Kong
Pokfulam Road, Hong Kong
vli@eee.hku.hk

ABSTRACT

The combination of loss-based TCP and drop-tail routers often results in full buffers, creating large queueing delays. The challenge with parameter tuning and the drastic consequence of improper tuning have discouraged network administrators from enabling AQM even when routers support it. To address this problem, we propose a novel design principle for AQM, called the pricing-link-by-time (PLT) principle. PLT increases the link price as the backlog stays above a threshold β, and resets the price once the backlog goes below β. We prove that such a system exhibits cyclic behavior that is robust against changes in network environment and protocol parameters. While β approximately controls the level of backlog, the backlog dynamics are invariant for β across a wide range of values. Therefore, β can be chosen to reduce delay without undermining system performance. We validate these analytical results using packet-level simulation.

Categories and Subject Descriptors

C.2.1 [**Computer-Communication Networks**]: Network Architecture and Design—*Distributed networks*

Keywords

active queue management; congestion control; hybrid dynamical system.

*The work was performed in part during visit to the Rigorous Systems Research Group, California Institute of Technology.

SIGMETRICS'14, June 16–20, 2014, Austin, Texas, USA.

http://dx.doi.org/10.1145/2591971.2591974 .

1. INTRODUCTION

1.1 Motivation

Congestion control is a distributed feedback mechanism to share network resources among competing flows. It consists of a source algorithm that adapts the sending rate of a flow to the congestion level, measured by "congestion prices," in its path and a router algorithm that updates its congestion prices, implicitly or explicitly, based on the local aggregate flow rate. On the Internet, the source algorithm is implemented in the transmission control protocol (TCP) of a host and is *loss-based*, where the congestion price takes the form of packet loss probability. The default router algorithm is implicit and called *drop-tail* where packets are dropped when, and only when, they arrive at a full buffer. The combination of loss-based TCP and drop-tail routers results in buffers constantly being filled, creating large queueing delays. The installation of large buffers in the network and the proliferation of applications with stringent delay requirements (e.g., IP telephony and video conferencing) have made this problem, recently termed "bufferbloat" [3, 14], a pressing issue.

In order to avoid persistent and high queueing delay, provide more timely congestion feedback, and desynchronize flow responses, active queue management (AQM) algorithms have been proposed where packets are probabilistically dropped before a buffer overflows. The most popular AQM is Random Early Detection (RED) proposed in 1993 [12]. Numerous variants have since been proposed, such as [5, 10, 11, 16, 20]. However, none of these AQM algorithms are widely deployed [9].[1]

This is because the performance of these algorithms are usually very sensitive to parameter tuning. See Section 5.1 for an example with RED. These algorithms all compute a packet dropping probability based on some *parameterized* function of the backlog. For desirable performance, the parameters must incorporate network information such as capacity, delay, and the number of TCP flows sharing the link. Not only is it difficult for network administrators

[1]Even though most routers implement RED, apparently most do not turn it on.

to determine the right parameter value if they know this information, more importantly, some of this information is constantly changing, rendering these AQM algorithms ineffective when the parameters are statically set. Adapting AQM parameters dynamically has proved to be very difficult due to the challenge in real-time estimation of network information. Besides, such adaptation process gives rise to an outer loop of feedback control and thus extra stability issue. Despite two decades of intense effort by the research and engineering communities, the challenge with parameter tuning and the drastic consequence of improper tuning continue to prevent network administrators from enabling AQM even when routers support it.

In this paper, we propose a method to address this problem through a core property of AQM design, we call the pricing-link-by-time (PLT) principle, for loss-based congestion control. We will show that an AQM algorithm that satisfies the PLT principle is:

- *Robust:* its performance does not degrade drastically even when its parameters are not well tuned.
- *Simple:* the average queueing delay is adjustable via a simple parameter tuning without side effects.

1.2 Our Contribution: PLT Principle

Recall that each link that implements an AQM algorithm computes a "link price." For loss-based congestion control, the price corresponds to packet dropping (or marking) probability at the link. We say that *an AQM algorithm satisfies the PLT principle* if it has the following simple properties:

1. There is a preselected threshold β (in unit of packets or transmission time).
2. The link price monotonically increases with the duration of time for which the backlog $b(t)$ stays above β.
3. The link price is reset to a fixed value (e.g., zero) when the backlog $b(t)$ drops below β.

The PLT principle is defined mathematically in Section 2 by (3)–(4). It is illustrated and compared with RED in Fig. 1. PLT is *insensitive* to the magnitude of the backlog; only whether (and how long) it exceeds β matters. This stands in sharp contrast to existing AQM algorithms like RED, under which the link price depends critically on the *exact magnitude* of the backlog.

For the rest of the paper, we explore the implications of the PLT principle. Specifically, we make the following contributions:

- We present an analytical model of a congestion control system consisting of a TCP variant and an AQM algorithm that satisfies the PLT principle with a threshold β (Section 2).
- We *characterize completely* the behavior of the system when there is a single bottleneck link (Section 3). In particular, we prove that such a system has no equilibrium point. Instead, the backlog will go above and below β infinitely often. Surprisingly, starting from $b(t) = \beta$, the recurrent time for $b(t)$ to return to β is independent of the parameter β. Hence, β approximately controls the average level of backlog.

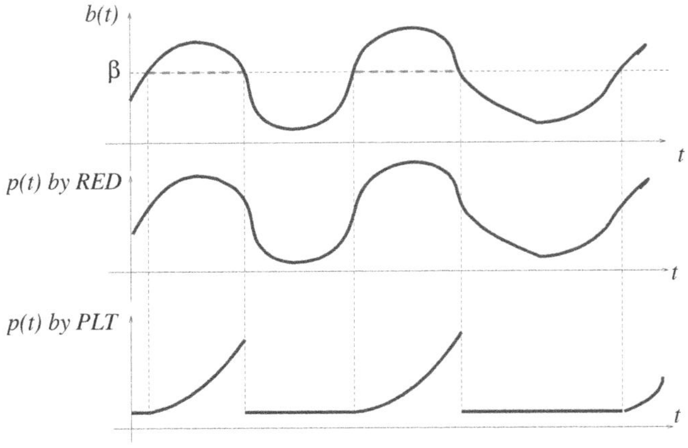

Figure 1: The PLT principle. The upper panel shows a backlog trajectory $b(t)$ and the threshold β. The middle panel shows the price $p(t)$ under RED that increases as $b(t)$ increases. The lower panel shows that price $p(t)$ under PLT that increases as the duration for which $b(t) > \beta$ increases.

The system possesses a family of cycles and we provide a sufficient condition for these limit cycles to be stable limit cycles. We prove a striking invariance property of these cycles with respect to β: the backlog trajectory $b(t)$ remains identical, except for a constant shift by $\tilde{\beta} - \beta$, if the threshold is changed from β to $\tilde{\beta}$.

- We explain why the recently proposed CoDel [25] and Data Center TCP (DCTCP) [1, 2] are AQM examples that satisfy the PLT principle (Section 4). CoDel has been experimentally shown to work well across various network settings with a single set of parameters. Our analysis explains the underlying reason for this robustness. The cyclic behavior of DCTCP has been reported in [2]. Our results provide additional insights on its behavior.
- We illustrate the PLT principle through ns-2 simulation of CoDel and DCTCP and compare their behavior with RED [12] and PI [16] that do not satisfy the PLT principle (Section 5). The simulation results confirm the robust cyclic behavior and verify the invariance of cycles against β.

Finally, we discuss related work in Section 6 and conclude in Section 7.

In summary, we have proposed the PLT principle and demonstrated both analytically and through simulation its effectiveness in solving the bufferbloat problem. Unlike traditional AQM algorithms that strive to attain a static equilibrium point, a PLT-based AQM algorithm has no equilibrium point but a family of cycles. *Nonetheless, these cycles are much more robust against changes in network environments and protocol parameters than the static equilibrium of traditional AQM algorithms. The threshold parameter β controls the level of delay without affecting other aspects of the system performance.*

On the technical aspect, our method is novel in applying the control-theoretic vehicle of cycles and a construct similar to Poincaré maps to study the congestion control system. This differs significantly from the popular stability analysis

Table 1: Notations

notation	meaning
$b(t)$	queue size at Time t
$b^{\mathcal{A}}$ / $b^{\mathcal{B}}$	queue size under Mode $\mathcal{A}$ / Mode $\mathcal{B}$
c	link capacity
$\mathbf{F}^{\mathcal{A}}/\mathbf{F}^{\mathcal{B}}$	mapping of flow rates from the start of Mode $\mathcal{A}$ / Mode $\mathcal{B}$ to the end of Mode $\mathcal{A}$ / Mode $\mathcal{B}$; see (11) / (16)
$\mathbf{F}$	$\mathbf{F}^{\mathcal{A}} \circ \mathbf{F}^{\mathcal{B}}$
$H^{\mathcal{A}}$ / $H^{\mathcal{B}}$	hitting time under Mode $\mathcal{A}$ / Mode $\mathcal{B}$
I_β	time elapsed since the queue size exceed β; see (3)
$p(t)$	link price at Time t
U_f	utility function of Flow f
$x_f(t)$	flow rate of Flow f at Time t
$\mathbf{x}$	$(x_f(t) : f \in \mathcal{F})$
$\mathbf{x}^{\mathcal{A}}$ / $\mathbf{x}^{\mathcal{B}}$	set of flow rates under Mode $\mathcal{A}$ / Mode $\mathcal{B}$
$y^{\mathcal{A}}$ / $y^{\mathcal{B}}$	aggregate flow rate under Mode $\mathcal{A}$ / Mode $\mathcal{B}$

approach [18, 22, 28] that assumes the existence of equilibrium, and is necessitated by the absence of equilibrium in our interested system.

2. MODEL OF PLT PRINCIPLE

We use bold fonts to denote vectors and matrices. Unless otherwise specified, $\|\cdot\|$ denotes the 1-norm of a vector, i.e., $\|\mathbf{v}\| = \sum_i |v_i|$. We use $\mathbb{R}$, $\mathbb{R}_+$, and $\mathbb{R}_{++}$ to denote the sets of real numbers, nonnegative real numbers, and positive real numbers, respectively. A summary of frequently used notations is shown in Table 1.

We begin by considering a network with a single bottleneck link shared by a set $\mathcal{F}$ of TCP flows.

Flow f adapts its rate according to:

$$\dot{x}_f(t) = \kappa_f \left(1 - \frac{p(t)}{U_f'(x_f(t))}\right) \quad (1)$$

where κ_f is a scaling constant, U_f is the utility function of Flow f, and $p(t)$ is the price of the bottleneck link. We assume $U_f : (0, \infty) \to \mathbb{R}$ to be strictly increasing, convex, and twice differentiable, with $\lim_{x_f \to 0} U_f'(x_f) = +\infty$. Thus, the utility U_f increases as the flow rate increases, but the marginal utility U_f' decreases. The flow dynamics aims to match the marginal utility to the link price.

This description of flow dynamics is customary in the literature and satisfied by most TCP variants. For example, TCP Reno exhibits such dynamics with $\kappa_f = \frac{1}{d_f^2}$ and $U_f(x_f) = -\frac{1}{d_f^2 x_f}$, where d_f is the round-trip time [21, 23].

At the bottleneck link, the backlog evolves according to the fluid model:

$$\dot{b}(t) = \sum_{f \in \mathcal{F}} x_f(t) - c \quad (2)$$

In reality, the backlog cannot be negative. Thus, a complete model should in addition enforce $\dot{b}(t) = 0$ when $b(t) = 0$ and $\sum_{f \in \mathcal{F}} x_f(t) - c < 0$. However, this will unnecessarily complicate our following analysis. We thus proceed with the simple model of (2). We postpone the discussion on the consequence of making such simplification to the performance validation section (Section 5.3).

Now, we are going to model the PLT principle. The time elapsed since the backlog exceeds β can be formally expressed as:

$$I_\beta(t) \quad = \quad \sup\{d \geq 0 : b(t - \delta) > \beta \; \forall \; \delta \in [0, d]\} \quad (3)$$

The link price is determined via:

$$p(t) = h(I_\beta(t)) \quad (4)$$

where h maps $I_\beta(t)$ to the link price.

$p(t)$ and $b(t)$ are thus related as follows in consistency with the PLT principle:

1. Once $b(t)$ exceeds β, the increase in $p(t)$ is determined by $h(\cdot)$ and *independent of the magnitude of* $b(t)$. In other words, $b(t)$ only determines when $p(t)$ will increase, but not how $p(t)$ increases.

2. When $b(t)$ goes below β, $I_\beta(t)$ becomes zero. It follows that $p(t)$ will be automatically reset as $h(0)$, regardless of its previous value.

We make the following mild assumption on $h(\cdot)$ to eliminate degenerate situations.

Assumption 1. *$h(\cdot)$ is continuous and non-decreasing over $[0, \infty)$. Moreover,*

$$\frac{\sum_{f \in \mathcal{F}} \kappa_f}{\max_{\|\mathbf{x}\|=c, \mathbf{x} \succeq 0} \sum_{f \in \mathcal{F}} \frac{\kappa_f}{U'(x_f)}} > h(0) \quad (5)$$

$$\frac{\sum_{f \in \mathcal{F}} \kappa_f}{\min_{\|\mathbf{x}\|=c, \mathbf{x} \succeq 0} \sum_{f \in \mathcal{F}} \frac{\kappa_f}{U'(x_f)}} < h(\infty) \quad (6)$$

(5) provides an upper bound for the link price when the backlog is under β. It ensures that the aggregate flow rate will increase with time when the backlog is below β. (6) provides a lower bound for the asymptotic link price when the backlog stays above β. It ensures that the aggregate data rate will eventually decrease with time when the backlog is above β.

Definition 1. *The system specified in (1)-(6) is referred to as the* PLT(β) system.

Furthermore, we introduce the following concepts from the theory of dynamical systems [19].

Definition 2. *(Trajectory, cycle, and stable limit cycle) $\{(\mathbf{x}(t), b(t)) : t \geq 0\}$ is the* trajectory *of the PLT(β) system. When there exists $T > 0$ such that $(\mathbf{x}(t), b(t)) = (\mathbf{x}(t+T), b(t+T))$ for all $t \geq 0$, the trajectory is said to be a cycle. The minimum T satisfying this condition is the* period *of the cycle. A cycle is a* stable limit cycle *if all nearby trajectories asymptotically converge to it.*

3. ANALYSIS OF PLT PRINCIPLE

In this section, we analyze the PLT principle rigorously by studying the PLT(β) system. Our main result is summarized by the following main theorem on the PLT(β) system:

Theorem 1. *The PLT(β) system has no equilibrium but a family of cycles, which are stable limit cycles under numerically checkable conditions. Consider $\beta \neq \tilde{\beta}$. A cycle of the PLT(β) system becomes a cycle of PLT($\tilde{\beta}$) after shifting $b(t)$ by $(\tilde{\beta} - \beta)$.*

The cyclic behavior can be viewed as dynamic equilibrium. As a major consequence of the theorem, the behavior of a PLT(β) system is very robust against changes in parameters and the network environment. Such robustness is maintained across combinations of different network environments (U_f, c) and detailed protocol specifications and parameters (h, β). Moreover, the cycles are invariant across different values of β except for a shift of the backlog size. Therefore, the average backlog can be directly controlled via setting β, without affecting other aspects of the system performance.

We prove Theorem 1 in the rest of the section. Our analysis follows from the following initial observation:

PROPOSITION 1. *(Recurrent return) For any $t_0 \geq 0$, there exists $t > t_0$ such that $b(t) = \beta$.*

The proposition essentially says that the backlog $b(t)$ will recurrently return to β. The instances when $b(t) = \beta$ divide the time horizon into intervals of finite length. By capturing the dynamics over each such interval, we will have the full characterization of the system dynamics.

During these intervals, the PLT(β) system operates in either one of the two possible modes. When $b(t) > \beta$, $I_\beta(t)$ increases with time and so does the price. When $b(t) \leq \beta$, $I_\beta(t)$ becomes zero and the price will be fixed as $p(t) = h(0)$. We refer to these as Modes $\mathcal{A}$(bove) and $\mathcal{B}$(elow), respectively.

We study two continuous dynamical systems, namely, PLT-$\mathcal{A}$ and PLT-$\mathcal{B}$ systems, in Sections 3.1 and 3.2, respectively. With proper initialization, these two systems emulate the behavior of the PLT(β) system when it is in Mode $\mathcal{A}$ and Mode $\mathcal{B}$, respectively. On this basis, we establish our main results on the PLT(β) system in Section 3.3.

3.1 PLT-$\mathcal{A}$ System

We now consider the PLT-$\mathcal{A}$ system that emulates the behavior of the PLT(β) system at Mode $\mathcal{A}$. The PLT(β) system starts operating at Mode $\mathcal{A}$ when the backlog crosses β from below. Therefore, let $\mathbf{R} \in \mathbb{R}_+^{|\mathcal{F}|}$ be the set of flow rates at that instant, we initialize the PLT-$\mathcal{A}$ system as:

$$(\mathbf{x}(0), b(0)) = (\mathbf{R}, \beta) \tag{7}$$

It is easy to establish that $\|\mathbf{R}\| \geq c$, which is a necessary condition for the backlog to cross β from below.

Let $\tau \geq 0$ track the time elapsed since the system initialization. The dynamics of the PLT-$\mathcal{A}$ system are specified by:

$$\dot{b}(\tau) = \sum_{f \in \mathcal{F}} x_f(\tau) - c \tag{8}$$

$$\dot{x}_f(\tau) = \kappa_f \left(1 - \frac{h(\tau)}{U_f'(x_f(\tau))}\right) \; \forall f \in \mathcal{F} \tag{9}$$

These are almost identical to the dynamics of the PLT(β) system except that the link price becomes $h(\tau)$. This eliminates the discrete component in the dynamics of the PLT(β) system, making the analysis of the PLT-$\mathcal{A}$ system easier. On the other hand, with the initialization in (7), (8)-(9) will exactly emulate the dynamics of the PLT(β) system at Mode $\mathcal{A}$ up to when $b(\tau)$ goes below β.

We denote the solution to (7)-(9) by $(\mathbf{x}^{\mathcal{A}}(\mathbf{R}, \tau), b^{\mathcal{A}}(\mathbf{R}, \beta, \tau))$. We do not include β in the argument list of $\mathbf{x}^{\mathcal{A}}$ as the flow rates are obviously independent of β from (9).

To characterize the time instant after which $b^{\mathcal{A}}(\mathbf{R}, \beta, \tau)$ goes below β, we consider the following candidate, $H^{\mathcal{A}} : \{\mathbf{R} \in \mathbb{R}_+^{|\mathcal{F}|} : \|\mathbf{R}\| \geq c\} \to [0, \infty]$, which is defined as:

$$H^{\mathcal{A}}(\mathbf{R}) \triangleq \inf\{\tau > 0 : b^{\mathcal{A}}(\mathbf{R}, \beta, \tau) = \beta\} \tag{10}$$

where we adopt the convention that $H^{\mathcal{A}}(\mathbf{R}) = \infty$ if the set on R.H.S. is empty.

The next result says that $H^{\mathcal{A}}(\mathbf{R})$ is the first time that the backlog returns to its initial level β.

PROPOSITION 2. *For $\mathbf{R} \in \mathbb{R}_+^{|\mathcal{F}|}$ with $\|\mathbf{R}\| \geq c$:*

1. *$H^{\mathcal{A}}(\mathbf{R})$ is independent of β.*
2. *$H^{\mathcal{A}}(\mathbf{R}) \in (0, \infty)$.*
3. *$b^{\mathcal{A}}(\mathbf{R}, \beta, \tau) > \beta$ for all $\tau \in (0, H^{\mathcal{A}}(\mathbf{R}))$.*
4. *$b^{\mathcal{A}}(\mathbf{R}, \beta, H^{\mathcal{A}}(\mathbf{R})) = \beta$.*

REMARK 1. *Part 1 of Proposition 2 justifies our convention of excluding β from the argument list of $H^{\mathcal{A}}$. Combining with the rest of the proposition, it actually implies remarkably that the time taken for $b^{\mathcal{A}}(\mathbf{R}, \beta, \tau)$ to return to β is invariant across β.*

Now, we show that $H^{\mathcal{A}}(\mathbf{R})$ is actually the time instant after which $b^{\mathcal{A}}(\mathbf{R}, \beta, \tau)$ goes below β if we eliminate some degenerate cases.

When the backlog returns to β, the set of flow data rates $\mathbf{x}(\tau)$ will be mapped from the initial level to a new level. Formally, we define such a mapping as $\mathbf{F}^{\mathcal{A}} : \{\mathbf{R} \in \mathbb{R}_+^{|\mathcal{F}|} : \|\mathbf{R}\| \geq c\} \to \{\mathbf{r} \in \mathbb{R}_+^{|\mathcal{F}|} : \|\mathbf{r}\| \leq c\}$:

$$\mathbf{F}^{\mathcal{A}}(\mathbf{R}) \triangleq \mathbf{x}^{\mathcal{A}}(\mathbf{R}, H^{\mathcal{A}}(\mathbf{R})) \tag{11}$$

PROPOSITION 3. *For $\mathbf{R} \in \mathbb{R}_+^{|\mathcal{F}|}$ with $\|\mathbf{R}\| \geq c$:*

1. *$\|\mathbf{F}^{\mathcal{A}}(\mathbf{R})\| \leq c$.*
2. *If $\|\mathbf{F}^{\mathcal{A}}(\mathbf{R})\| < c$, $H^{\mathcal{A}}$ and $\mathbf{F}^{\mathcal{A}}$ are differentiable at $\mathbf{R}$.*

REMARK 2. *For readers familiar with the dynamical systems, a remark on the subtle difference between the Poincaré map and $\mathbf{F}^{\mathcal{A}}$ is in order. In defining a Poincaré map $\tilde{\mathbf{F}}$, a hyperplane Σ tangential to a cycle of the system is selected as the Poincaré section. In (10), the constraint $b^{\mathcal{A}}(\mathbf{R}, \beta, \tau) = \beta$ determines such a Poincaré section. Let $\mathbf{R}$ be the intersection of the cycle with the Poincaré section. $\tilde{\mathbf{F}}(\mathbf{R})$ is defined as the next intersection, which is exactly $\mathbf{F}^{\mathcal{A}}(\mathbf{R})$. However, the definition of $\tilde{\mathbf{F}}(\widetilde{\mathbf{R}})$ for $\widetilde{\mathbf{R}}$ near $\mathbf{R}$ is then different. By the implicit function theorem, one can show that there exists a continuous mapping $\tilde{H}$ such that $\mathbf{x}^{\mathcal{A}}(\widetilde{\mathbf{R}}, \tilde{H}(\widetilde{\mathbf{R}})) \in \Sigma$, with $\tilde{H}(\mathbf{R}) = H^{\mathcal{A}}(\mathbf{R})$. For $\widetilde{\mathbf{R}}$ near $\mathbf{R}$, the Poincaré section is then defined as $\tilde{\mathbf{F}}(\widetilde{\mathbf{R}}) \triangleq \mathbf{x}^{\mathcal{A}}(\widetilde{\mathbf{R}}, \tilde{H}(\widetilde{\mathbf{R}}))$. However, when $\widetilde{\mathbf{R}} \neq \mathbf{R}$, there is no guarantee that the system trajectory starting from $\widetilde{\mathbf{R}}$ will not intersect Σ during $(0, \tilde{H}(\widetilde{\mathbf{R}}))$. When such intersection does happen, the Poincaré map $\tilde{H}(\widetilde{\mathbf{R}})$ fails to capture the time for the first return.*

Now, the time derivative of the backlog at Time $H^{\mathcal{A}}(\mathbf{R})$ is $\|\mathbf{F}^{\mathcal{A}}(\mathbf{R})\| - c$. Following Proposition 3, this derivative is either negative or zero. In the former case, the backlog will go below β immediately after Time $H^{\mathcal{A}}(\mathbf{R})$. The latter case is actually a degenerate case that the aggregate flow rate coincides with the link capacity upon the return of the backlog to β. We eliminate this degenerate case by making the following assumption in our subsequent discussion.

ASSUMPTION 2. $\|\mathbf{F}^{\mathcal{A}}(\mathbf{R})\| < c, \forall \|\mathbf{R}\| \geq c$.

REMARK 3. *The assumption actually imposes a constraint on $U_f(\cdot)$ and/or $h(\cdot)$. For example, it is satisfied when κ_f is invariant across all flows $f \in \mathcal{F}$ and $U_f(\cdot) = \log(\cdot)$. We also conjecture that it is satisfied when $h(t)$ increases fast enough in t.*

3.2 PLT-$\mathcal{B}$ System

We now consider the PLT-$\mathcal{B}$ system that emulates the behavior of the PLT(β) system at Mode $\mathcal{B}$. The PLT(β) system starts operating at Mode $\mathcal{B}$ when the backlog crosses β from above. Therefore, let $\mathbf{r} \in \mathbb{R}_+^{|\mathcal{F}|}$ be the set of flow rates at that instant (note that we actually have $\|\mathbf{r}\| \leq c$). We initialize the PLT-$\mathcal{B}$ system as:

$$(\mathbf{x}(0), b(0)) = (\mathbf{r}, \beta) \tag{12}$$

Let $\tau \geq 0$ track the time elapsed since the system initialization. The dynamics of the PLT-$\mathcal{B}$ system are specified by:

$$\dot{b}(\tau) = \sum_{f \in \mathcal{F}} x_f(\tau) - c \tag{13}$$

$$\dot{x}_f(\tau) = \kappa_f \left(1 - \frac{h(0)}{U_f'(x_f(\tau))}\right) \quad \forall f \in \mathcal{F} \tag{14}$$

(12)-(14) will exactly emulate the dynamics of the PLT(β) system at Mode $\mathcal{B}$ up to when $b(\tau)$ goes above β. We denote the solution to (12)-(14) by $(\mathbf{x}^{\mathcal{B}}(\mathbf{r}, \tau), b^{\mathcal{B}}(\mathbf{r}, \beta, \tau))$.

In general, the dynamics of the PLT-$\mathcal{B}$ system are simpler than that of the PLT-$\mathcal{A}$ system, since the link price is fixed as $h(0)$. We establish the following results in parallel to their counterparts for the PLT-$\mathcal{A}$ system. Their interpretations are similar and will not be repeated.

The time taken for $b^{\mathcal{B}}(\mathbf{r}, \beta, \tau)$ to return to β is $H^{\mathcal{B}} : \{\mathbf{r} \in \mathbb{R}_+^{|\mathcal{F}|} : \|\mathbf{r}\| \leq c\} \rightarrow \mathbb{R}$:

$$H^{\mathcal{B}}(\mathbf{r}) \triangleq \begin{cases} \inf\{\tau > 0 : b^{\mathcal{B}}(\mathbf{R}, \beta, \tau) = \beta\} & \|\mathbf{r}\| < c \\ 0 & \|\mathbf{r}\| = c \end{cases} \tag{15}$$

Again, this is due to the following proposition.

PROPOSITION 4. Consider $\mathbf{r} \in \mathbb{R}_+^{|\mathcal{F}|}$. If $\|\mathbf{r}\| < c$, then:

1. $H^{\mathcal{B}}(\mathbf{r})$ is independent of β.
2. $H^{\mathcal{B}}(\mathbf{r}) \in (0, \infty)$.
3. $b^{\mathcal{B}}(\mathbf{r}, \beta, \tau) < \beta$ for all $t \in (0, H^{\mathcal{B}}(\mathbf{r}))$.
4. $b^{\mathcal{B}}(\mathbf{r}, \beta, H^{\mathcal{B}}(\mathbf{r})) = \beta$.

The mapping of data rates from when $\tau = 0$ to when $b^{\mathcal{B}}(\mathbf{r}, \beta, \tau)$ returns to β is defined as $\mathbf{F}^{\mathcal{B}} : \{\mathbf{r} \in \mathbb{R}_+^{|\mathcal{F}|} : \|\mathbf{R}\| \leq c\} \rightarrow \{\mathbf{R} \in \mathbb{R}_+^{|\mathcal{F}|} : \|\mathbf{R}\| \geq c\}$:

$$\mathbf{F}^{\mathcal{B}}(\mathbf{r}) \triangleq \mathbf{x}^{\mathcal{B}}(\mathbf{r}, H^{\mathcal{B}}(\mathbf{r})) \tag{16}$$

PROPOSITION 5. *For $\mathbf{r} \in \mathbb{R}_+^{|\mathcal{F}|}$ with $\|\mathbf{r}\| \leq c$:*

1. $\|\mathbf{F}^{\mathcal{B}}(\mathbf{r})\| > c$.
2. *$H^{\mathcal{B}}$ and $\mathbf{F}^{\mathcal{B}}$ are continuous at $\mathbf{r}$. If $\|\mathbf{r}\| < c$, they are differentiable at $\mathbf{r}$.*

3.3 Complete PLT(β) System

We now come back to the PLT(β) system. We first look at the system trajectory (Proposition 6). On this basis, we study the cycles (Propositions 7-8). These lead to the establishment of the main result, Theorem 1.

The next result says that the trajectory is periodic in which the behavior of the backlog alternates between Modes $\mathcal{A}$ and $\mathcal{B}$ deterministically. The time it stays in Mode $\mathcal{X}$ is given by $H^{\mathcal{X}}$ ($\mathcal{X} = \mathcal{A}, \mathcal{B}$). Within Mode $\mathcal{X}$, the system state is determined by $(\mathbf{x}^{\mathcal{X}}, b^{\mathcal{X}})$. The set of flow rates when the system enters Mode $\mathcal{X}$ is mapped to the set of flow rates when the system exits Mode $\mathcal{X}$ via $\mathbf{F}^{\mathcal{X}}$.

PROPOSITION 6. *(Trajectory) Let $s[1]$ be the first time instant when $b(t) = \beta$ with $\|\mathbf{x}(t)\| < c$. Denote the instant when $b(t)$ returns to β for the $(k-1)$th time after $s[1]$ as $s[k]$. Let $\mathcal{M}[k] \in \{\mathcal{A}, \mathcal{B}\}$ be the mode of the PLT(β) system during $(s[k], s[k+1])$.*

1. *The mode of the PLT(β) system is:*

$$\mathcal{M}[k] = \begin{cases} \mathcal{A} & k \text{ is even} \\ \mathcal{B} & k \text{ is odd} \end{cases} \tag{17}$$

2. *The duration of the kth interval is:*

$$s[k+1] - s[k] = H^{\mathcal{M}[k]}(\mathbf{x}(s[k])) \tag{18}$$

3. *For $t \in (s[k], s[k+1])$,*

$$\mathbf{x}(t) = \mathbf{x}^{\mathcal{M}[k]}(\mathbf{x}(s[k]), t - s[k]) \tag{19}$$

$$b(t) = b^{\mathcal{M}[k]}(\mathbf{x}(s[k]), \beta, t - s[k]) \tag{20}$$

4. *$x(s[k+1]) = \mathbf{F}^{\mathcal{M}[k]}(x(s[k]))$. Moreover, $x(s[k]) > c$ if k is odd, and $x(s[k]) < c$ if k is even.*

PROOF. We prove it by induction.

We first establish the case for $k = 1$ and 2. During $(s[1], s[2])$, we start with $\|\mathbf{x}(s[1])\| < c$. Thus, $b(t)$ has a negative derivative at $t = s[1]$, and will drop below β. Therefore, the system will operate in Mode $\mathcal{B}$ and behaves as the PLT-$\mathcal{B}$ system before $b(t)$ returns to β at $t = s[2]$. (18)-(20) then follow with $\mathcal{M}[1] = \mathcal{B}$. Moreover,

$$\mathbf{x}(s[2]) = \mathbf{F}^{\mathcal{B}}(\mathbf{x}(s[1])) \tag{21}$$

By Proposition 5, we have $\mathbf{x}(s[2]) > c$.

Thus, $b(t)$ has a positive derivative at $t = s[2]$, and will exceed β. Thus, during $(s[2], s[3])$, the system will operate in Mode $\mathcal{A}$ and behaves as the PLT-$\mathcal{A}$ system before $b(t)$ returns to β at $t = s[3]$. (18)-(20) then follow with $\mathcal{M}[2] = \mathcal{A}$. Moreover, by Assumption 2, we have $\|\mathbf{x}(s[3])\| < c$.

Now, suppose that the result holds for all $k \leq K-1$. If K is odd, then $K-1$ is even. It follows from the supposition that $\mathcal{M}[K-1] = \mathcal{B}$, $\|\mathbf{x}(s[K-1])\| < c$. Thus, $x(s[K]) = \mathbf{F}^{\mathcal{A}}(\mathbf{x}(s[K-1])$ and, by Proportion 5, $\|\mathbf{x}(s[K])\| > c$. Thus, during $(s[K], s[K+1])$, $b(t)$ will go above β and the PLT(β) system operate in Mode $\mathcal{A}$. (18)-(20) then follow with $\mathcal{M}[K] = \mathcal{A}$. Moreover,

$$\mathbf{x}(s[K+1]) = \mathbf{F}^{\mathcal{A}}(\mathbf{x}(s[K])) \tag{22}$$

Thus, all the results hold for $k = K$.

Similar arguments apply to the case when K is even. □

Therefore, the system constantly switches between the two modes of operations, implying the *non-existence* of equilibrium for the system.

COROLLARY 1. *The PLT(β) system has no equilibrium.*

Now, let $\mathbf{F} \triangleq \mathbf{F}^{\mathcal{A}} \circ \mathbf{F}^{\mathcal{B}}$, and $\mathbf{F}^n$ denote the nth composites of $\mathbf{F}$. If $\mathbf{x}(t)$ starts off at a fixed point of $\mathbf{F}^n$, the system state $(\mathbf{x}(t), b(t))$ will have identical states at $t = s[1]$ and $t = s[2n+1]$, thereby exhibiting the cyclic behavior. It turns out that all cycles of the PLT(β) system can be identified via the fixed points of $\mathbf{F}^n$.

A few definitions are in order.

DEFINITION 3. *Let*

$$\mathbb{I} \triangleq \{\mathbf{r} \in \mathbb{R}_+^{|\mathcal{F}|} : \|\mathbf{r}\| \le c \text{ and } \mathbf{F}^n(\mathbf{r}) = \mathbf{r} \text{ for some } n\} \tag{23}$$

and, for $\mathbf{r} \in \mathbb{I}$,

$$\gamma(\mathbf{r}) \triangleq \min\{n : \mathbf{F}^n(\mathbf{r}) = \mathbf{r}\} \tag{24}$$

For $\mathbf{r}, \tilde{\mathbf{r}} \in \mathbb{I}$, $\mathbf{r}$ *is said to be equivalent to* $\tilde{\mathbf{r}}$, *written as* $\mathbf{r} \sim \tilde{\mathbf{r}}$, *if* $\gamma(\mathbf{r}) = \gamma(\tilde{\mathbf{r}})$ *and* $\tilde{\mathbf{r}} = \mathbf{F}^m(\mathbf{r})$ *for some* m. *The equivalent class of* $\mathbf{r}$, *written as* $[\mathbf{r}]$, *is a subset of* $\mathbb{I}$ *that contains all elements equivalent to* $\mathbf{r}$.[2]

PROPOSITION 7. *(Cycles and stable limit cycles)*

1. *$\mathbb{I}$ is non-empty.*
2. *There is one-to-one correspondence between the equivalent classes of $\mathbb{I}$ and cycles of the PLT(β) system.*
3. *A cycle corresponding to $[\mathbf{r}]$ is a stable limit cycle if the radius of the Jacobian matrix $D\mathbf{F}^{\gamma(\mathbf{r})}(\mathbf{r})$ is less than one.*

PROOF. *1)* Observe that $\mathbf{F}$ is a continuous mapping over a convex compact subset of $\mathbb{R}^{|\mathcal{F}|}$. By the Brouwer fixed point theorem, $\mathbf{F}$ has a fixed point. Thus, $\mathbb{I}$ has at least a fixed point of $\mathbf{F}$.

2) Denote the set of all equivalent classes in $\mathbb{I}$ by $\mathbb{I}/\!\sim$ and the set of cycles of the PLT(β) system by $\mathbb{C}$. We now construct a bijective mapping $\varphi : \mathbb{I}/\!\sim \rightarrow \mathbb{C}$.

Let $\varphi([\mathbf{r}])$ be the trajectory of the PLT(β) system when $\mathbf{x}(0) = \mathbf{r}$ and $b(0) = \beta$. By Part 2 of Proposition 6, $\mathbf{x}(t)$ will return to $\mathbf{x}(0)$ when $b(t)$ returns to β for the $2\gamma(\mathbf{r})$th time. Thus, $\varphi([\mathbf{r}])$ is a cycle.

Claim 1: φ is well defined. In other words, if $\mathbf{r} \sim \tilde{\mathbf{r}}$, $\varphi([\mathbf{r}]) = \varphi([\tilde{\mathbf{r}}])$.

By definition, $\tilde{\mathbf{r}} = \mathbf{F}^m(\mathbf{r})$ for some $m < \gamma(\mathbf{r})$. Thus, when the system starts with $\mathbf{x}(0) = \mathbf{r}$ and $b(0) = \beta$, $\mathbf{x}(t)$ will reach $\tilde{\mathbf{r}}$ when $b(t)$ returns to β for the $(2m)$th time (say, at time T').

Now, suppose $(\overline{\mathbf{x}}, \overline{b}) \in \varphi([\tilde{\mathbf{r}}])$. When the system starts with $\mathbf{x}(0) = \tilde{\mathbf{r}}$ and $b(0) = \beta$, we have $(\mathbf{x}(t_0), b(t_0)) = (\overline{\mathbf{x}}, \overline{b})$ for some $t_0 > 0$. It follows that, when the system starts with $\mathbf{x}(0) = \mathbf{r}$ and $b(0) = \beta$, $(\mathbf{x}(t_0+T'), b(t_0+T')) = (\overline{\mathbf{x}}, \overline{b})$. This implies $(\overline{\mathbf{x}}, \overline{b}) \in \varphi([\mathbf{r}])$, and hence $\varphi([\tilde{\mathbf{r}}]) \subset \varphi([\mathbf{r}])$.

By the symmetry of equivalence relation, we can similarly establish $\varphi([\tilde{\mathbf{r}}]) \supset \varphi([\mathbf{r}])$. Thus, $\varphi([\tilde{\mathbf{r}}]) = \varphi([\mathbf{r}])$.

Claim 2: φ is injective. In other words, $\varphi([\mathbf{r}]) = \varphi([\tilde{\mathbf{r}}])$ implies $[\mathbf{r}] = [\tilde{\mathbf{r}}]$, or $\mathbf{r} \sim \tilde{\mathbf{r}}$.

Since $(\tilde{\mathbf{r}}, \beta) \in \varphi([\tilde{\mathbf{r}}])$, we have $(\tilde{\mathbf{r}}, \beta) \in \varphi([\mathbf{r}])$. Therefore, when starting with $(\mathbf{x}(0), b(0)) = (\mathbf{r}, \beta)$, $\mathbf{x}(t)$ reaches $\tilde{\mathbf{r}}$ when $b(t)$ returns to β for the kth time, for some k. Moreover, since $\|\tilde{\mathbf{r}}\| < c$, by Proposition 6, k is even and $\tilde{\mathbf{r}} = \mathbf{F}^{\frac{k}{2}}(\mathbf{r})$. Thus, $\mathbf{r} \sim \tilde{\mathbf{r}}$.

Claim 3: φ is surjective. In other words, any cycle of the system can be constructed from some $\mathbf{r} \in \mathbb{I}$ via the prescribed mapping.

Let $\Gamma = \{(\tilde{x}(t), \tilde{b}(t)) : t \ge 0\}$ be a cycle of the system with trajectory T. Pick an instant t_0 when $\|\mathbf{x}(t_0)\| < c$ and $b(t_0) = \beta$. The existence of such an instance is guaranteed by Propositions 1 and 5.

We now show that $\varphi(\mathbf{x}(t_0)) = \Gamma$.

For $t < t_0$, there exists a positive integer n such that $t + nT > t_0$. We have by periodicity of cycles of the system:

$$(\tilde{x}(t), b(t)) = (\tilde{x}(t+nT), b(t+nT)) \tag{25}$$

It follows that:

$$\{(\tilde{x}(t), \tilde{b}(t)) : 0 \le t < t_0\} \subset \{(\tilde{x}(t), \tilde{b}(t)) : t \ge t_0\} \tag{26}$$

Therefore,

$$\begin{aligned}\Gamma &= \{(\tilde{x}(t), \tilde{b}(t)) : t \ge 0\} \\ &= \{(\tilde{x}(t), \tilde{b}(t)) : 0 \le t < t_0\} \cup \{(\tilde{x}(t), \tilde{b}(t)) : t \ge t_0\} \\ &= \{(\tilde{x}(t), \tilde{b}(t)) : t \ge t_0\}\end{aligned} \tag{27}$$

By definition and time-invariance of the system, we have:

$$\varphi(\mathbf{r}) = \{(\tilde{x}(t), \tilde{b}(t)) : t \ge t_0\} \tag{28}$$

Thus, $\Gamma = \varphi(\mathbf{r})$ and the claim follows.

Combining Claims 1-3, we establish Part 2 of the theorem.

3) The condition implies that the mapping $\mathbf{F}^{\gamma(\mathbf{r})}$ is locally asymptotically stable, which in turn implies that the cycle is locally asymptotically stable, or a stable limit cycle. □

REMARK 4. *$D\mathbf{F}^{\gamma(\mathbf{r})}(\mathbf{r})$ can be expanded as:*

$$D\mathbf{F}(\hat{\mathbf{x}}[\gamma(\mathbf{r})])D\mathbf{F}(\hat{\mathbf{x}}[\gamma(\mathbf{r})-1]) \cdots D\mathbf{F}(\hat{\mathbf{x}}[1]) \tag{29}$$

where $\hat{\mathbf{x}}[1] = \mathbf{r}$ *and* $\hat{\mathbf{x}}[k+1] = \mathbf{F}(\hat{\mathbf{x}}[k])$ *for* $k \ge 1$. $D\mathbf{F}(\hat{\mathbf{x}}[k])$ *can in turn be written as:*

$$D\mathbf{F}^{\mathcal{A}}(\mathbf{F}^{\mathcal{B}}(\hat{\mathbf{x}}[k]))D\mathbf{F}^{\mathcal{B}}(\hat{\mathbf{x}}[k]) \tag{30}$$

All the matrices involved in (30) can be computed numerically by applying standard techniques for continuous *dynamical systems. Interested readers can refer to Chapter 3 of [27] for details.*

PROPOSITION 8. *(Invariance property) Consider $\beta > 0$ and $\tilde{\beta} > 0$. A cycle of PLT(β) becomes a cycle of PLT($\tilde{\beta}$) after shifting $b(t)$ by $(\tilde{\beta} - \beta)$. Both cycles correspond to the same equivalent class in $\mathbb{I}$.*

PROOF. Let Γ be a cycle of PLT(β) corresponding to the equivalence class $[\mathbf{r}]$. Similar to the proof of Proposition 7, Γ is in fact the trajectory of the PLT(β) system starting from $\mathbf{x}(0) = \mathbf{r}$ and $b(0) = \beta$. Thus, by Proposition 6, we have:

$$\Gamma = \cup_{k=1}^{\infty} \Gamma[k] \tag{31}$$

$$\Gamma[k] \triangleq \{(\mathbf{x}^{\mathcal{M}[k]}(\hat{\mathbf{x}}[k], \tau), b^{\mathcal{M}[k]}(\hat{\mathbf{x}}([k]), \beta, \tau)) : \tau \in [0, H^{\mathcal{M}[k]}(\hat{\mathbf{x}}[k]]\} \tag{32}$$

where $\hat{\mathbf{x}}[k] \triangleq \mathbf{x}(s[k])$. Since $\hat{\mathbf{x}}[k]$ returns to $\hat{\mathbf{x}}[1]$ when $k = \gamma(\mathbf{r}) + 1$, we have $\Gamma[k] = \Gamma[k + \gamma(\mathbf{r})]$. It follows that:

$$\Gamma = \cup_{k=1}^{\gamma(\mathbf{r})} \Gamma[k] \tag{33}$$

[2]It is straightforward to verify that this is a well-defined equivalence relation. In other words, it satisfies reflexivity ($\mathbf{r} \sim \mathbf{r}$), symmetry ($\mathbf{r} \sim \tilde{\mathbf{r}} \Rightarrow \tilde{\mathbf{r}} \sim \mathbf{r}$), and transitivity ($\mathbf{r} \sim \tilde{\mathbf{r}} \wedge \tilde{\mathbf{r}} \sim \hat{\mathbf{r}} \Rightarrow \mathbf{r} \sim \hat{\mathbf{r}}$).

Let $\widetilde{\Gamma}$ be a cycle of PLT($\tilde{\beta}$) corresponding to the equivalence class [**r**]. Similarly, we have:

$$\widetilde{\Gamma} = \cup_{k=1}^{\gamma(\mathbf{r})}\widetilde{\Gamma}[k] \tag{34}$$

$$\begin{aligned}\widetilde{\Gamma}[k] &\triangleq \{(\mathbf{x}^{\mathcal{M}[k]}(\hat{\mathbf{x}}[k],\tau), b^{\mathcal{M}[k]}(\hat{\mathbf{x}}([k]),\tilde{\beta},\tau)) : \\ &\quad \tau \in [0, H^{\mathcal{M}[k]}(\hat{\mathbf{x}}[k]]\}\end{aligned} \tag{35}$$

Now, noting that, for either $\mathcal{X} = \mathcal{A}$ or $\mathcal{X} = \mathcal{B}$,

$$\begin{aligned}&b^{\mathcal{X}}(\mathbf{R},\tilde{\beta},\tau) \\ &= \tilde{\beta} + \int_0^{\tau}(\|\mathbf{x}^{\mathcal{X}}(\mathbf{R},\tilde{\tau})\| - c)d\tilde{\tau} \\ &= (\tilde{\beta}-\beta) + \overbrace{(\beta + \int_0^{\tau}(\|\mathbf{x}^{\mathcal{X}}(\mathbf{R},\tilde{\tau})\| - c)d\tilde{\tau})}^{b^{\mathcal{X}}(\mathbf{R},\beta,\tau)}\end{aligned} \tag{36}$$

It follows that:

$$\widetilde{\Gamma}[k] = \Gamma[k] + (\mathbf{0}, \tilde{\beta} - \beta) \tag{37}$$

where $\mathbf{0}$ denotes the zero vector of dimension $|\mathcal{F}|$. Hence,

$$\begin{aligned}\widetilde{\Gamma} &= \cup_{k=1}^{\gamma(\mathbf{r})}\widetilde{\Gamma}[k] \\ &= \cup_{k=1}^{\gamma(\mathbf{r})}\Gamma[k] + (\mathbf{0}, \tilde{\beta} - \beta) \\ &= \Gamma + (\mathbf{0}, \tilde{\beta} - \beta)\end{aligned} \tag{38}$$

□

Theorem 1 follows directly from Propositions 6-8.

4. EXAMPLE AQM ALGORITHMS

In this section, we describe CoDel and DCTCP and show that their models are special cases of the PLT(β) system. This demonstrates analytically that CoDel and DCTCP implement the PLT principle.

4.1 CoDel

CoDel [25] has been devised on the principle of differentiating between "good queues" and "bad queues" of packets at router buffers. Good queues are queues built up due to the arrival of bursty traffic. Such queues are in general transient. Bad queues refer to persistent queues due to the aggressive transmission behavior of TCP.

To differentiate, CoDel selects a target level, *target*, and monitors the queueing delay experienced by packets. When the queueing delay exceeds *target* for a time period *interval*, CoDel concludes that a bad queue is present and activates a control law for dropping packets. CoDel first drops a packet to induce a TCP backoff. If the queueing delay is persistently above *target*, the time period for the next packet drop is inversely proportional to the square root of the number of drops since entering the dropping period.

Let $\beta = c\cdot target$ and $I_0 = interval$. $I_\beta(t)$ then corresponds to the duration of time elapsed since the queueing delay exceeds target at Time t. Suppose that n packet drops have occurred over this time period $I_\beta(t)$, we have:

$$I_0 + \sum_{j=1}^{n-1}\frac{I_0}{\sqrt{j}} \approx I_\beta(t) \tag{39}$$

which gives $n \approx \rho(\frac{I_\beta(t)}{I_0})$ for some increasing function ρ. For simplicity, we may take fractional values for n and assume that ρ is continuous. Since no drops occur when the backlog is below β (i.e. $I_\beta(t) = 0$), we can set $\rho(0) = 0$.

The time elapsed between the $(n-1)$th drop and the nth drop is $\frac{I_0}{\sqrt{n}}$. During this interval, there are approximately $c\frac{I_0}{\sqrt{n}}$ arriving packets, one of which will be dropped. Therefore, the dropping rate (as the link price) at Time t is approximately:

$$p(t) = \frac{1}{c\frac{I_0}{\sqrt{n}}} \approx \frac{1}{cI_0}\sqrt{\rho(\frac{I_\beta(t)}{I_0})} \tag{40}$$

Therefore, the model of CoDel amounts to a special case of the PLT(β) system with $h(\cdot) = \frac{1}{cI_0}\sqrt{\rho(\frac{\cdot}{I_0})}$.

4.2 DCTCP

Data center TCP (DCTCP) [1] adapts congestion control to the needs of data centers in keeping end-to-end delay minimal. It involves modifications to both TCP and AQM. Congestion notifications are conveyed from AQM to TCP by marking packets instead of actually dropping packets. Therefore, link price corresponds to the packet marking rate. When the number of packets buffered is K, every arrived packet will be marked. Otherwise, they are not marked. At the end of each round-trip time (RTT) round, a DCTCP source computes the fraction of packets marked (say α), and reduces the window by a factor of $(1-\frac{\alpha}{2})$.

A model for DCTCP has been developed in [2]. With some simplifying assumptions, we present an equivalent form in the framework of the PLT(β) system. Let S be the average packet size and $\beta = K\cdot S$. For a DCTCP flow f, let the RTT be d_f and the congestion window size be $w_f(t)$. It follows that $x_f(t) = \frac{w_f(t)}{d_f}$. In each round-trip time, $w_f(t)$ is increased by S. If the fraction of marked packets is $\alpha(t)$, $w_f(t)$ is reduced by a factor of $\frac{\alpha(t)}{2}$. Thus, the net change of $w_f(t)$ on every d_f is:

$$S - \frac{\alpha(t)w_f(t)}{2} \tag{41}$$

It follows that:

$$\begin{aligned}\dot{x_f}(t) &= \frac{\dot{w_f}(t)}{d_f} \\ &\approx \frac{1}{d_f^2}(S - \frac{\alpha(t)w_f(t)}{2})\end{aligned} \tag{42}$$

If $I_\beta(t) > d_f$, the number of packets at the router buffer is above K for the whole RTT. All packets will be marked and thus $\alpha(t) = 1$. Otherwise, around a proportion $\frac{I_\beta(t)}{d_f}$ of the packets will be marked and $\alpha(t) \approx \frac{I_\beta(t)}{d_f}$. Therefore,

$$\alpha(t) \approx \sigma(\frac{I_\beta(t)}{d_f}) \tag{43}$$

where

$$\sigma(x) \triangleq \begin{cases} x & 0 \le x \le 1 \\ 1 & x > 1 \end{cases} \tag{44}$$

We can approximate σ with an arbitrarily small error by a non-decreasing, smooth function, say, $\tilde{\sigma}$. It follows that:

$$\alpha(t) \approx \tilde{\sigma}(\frac{I_\beta(t)}{d_f}) \tag{45}$$

Therefore, the model of DCTCP amounts to a special case of the PLT(β) system with $U_f(\cdot) = \frac{2}{d_f}\log(\cdot)$, $\kappa_f = \frac{1}{d_f^2}$, and $h(\cdot) = \tilde{\sigma}(\frac{\cdot}{d_f})$.

5. PERFORMANCE VALIDATION

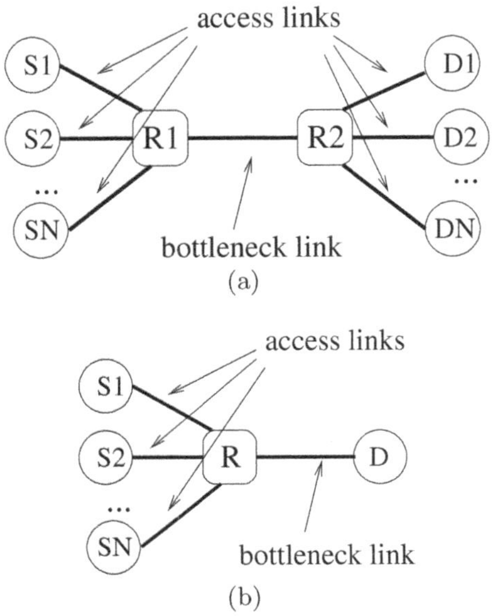

Figure 2: Simulation topologies.

In this section, we present our simulation results. Recall that, in Section 3, our analysis predicts that 1) congestion control systems implementing the PLT principle will exhibit the cyclic behavior, and 2) the cycles are independent of β except for a shift in the backlog level. In this section, we conduct our simulation using Network Simulator (ns) Version 2.35 to validate these results in realistic network settings, complementing the theoretical study in the following manners:

1. The PLT(β) system approximates the network dynamics at the flow level by modeling the data traffic as a continuous stream of data with time-varying rates. Our simulation has been conducted at the finer packet level.

2. In congestion control systems, the source observes time-lagged link price and transmits data on the link with further time lag. Such delays are pertinent to the system stability but hard to be incorporated with nonlinear analysis that involves the cycles. ns-2 automatically simulates such delays as an event-driven simulator.

3. We include some classical AQM algorithms in the literature for comparison. This helps identify the unique features of the PLT principle.

Rather than specifying a particular AQM algorithm, the PLT principle gives rise to a family of congestion control algorithms. While the analysis of the PLT(β) system studies the general PLT principle, a simulation-based study necessarily focuses on its special realizations. Therefore, our simulations examine CoDel and DCTCP that have been shown in Section 4 to be two realizations of the PLT principle.

The classical AQM algorithms compared are RED [7] and the proportional-integral controller (PI) [16]. RED is the first AQM algorithm and by far the most popular one. It maintains a running average of the backlog size, *b_aver*, and compares it to two threshold parameters, namely, *minThresh* and *maxThresh*. The packet dropping rate is then set as:

$$\begin{cases} 0 & b\_aver \le minThresh \\ 1 & b\_aver \ge maxThresh \\ \frac{p\_max(b\_aver - minThresh)}{maxThresh - minThresh} & \text{otherwise} \end{cases}$$

where the parameter *p_max* is the maximum packet dropping rate when *b_aver* falls between *minThresh* and *maxThresh*, the intended operational region of RED. Obviously, it is a challenge for setting *p_max* properly as there is a trade off between exerting prompt response to congestion and avoiding over-control.[3]

PI is another popular AQM algorithm. Along with REM [5], PI is representative of a class of AQM algorithms that track the backlog to a preselected threshold value. This is done by adjusting the packet dropping rate based on the deviation of the backlog from the threshold value. Such scheme bears some resemblance to the PLT principle. However, PLT essentially interprets the deviation in a discrete manner by only looking at whether the deviation is positive or negative. In contrast, PI and similar AQM algorithms take into account the actual magnitude of the deviation. This makes their performance highly sensitive to parameters relating the magnitude of backlog deviation to the packet dropping rate.

Specifically, PI records the backlog size in the previous and current time steps, say, as *q_old* and *q_new*, respectively. In each time step, it *adds to* the packet dropping rate:

$$a(q\_new - q\_ref) + b(q\_new - q\_old) \tag{46}$$

where a and b are weighting parameters, and *q_ref* is the preselected threshold value. For PI to function properly, a and b need to be carefully selected based on the network settings [16].

Two simulation topologies are investigated, as shown in Fig. 2. In Fig. 2(a), the sources and destinations of N TCP connections are connected to $R1$ and $R2$, routers at two ends of a bottleneck link, via access links, respectively. In Fig. 2(b), the sources of N TCP connections are connected to a router at one end of a bottleneck link via access links. These connections share a common destination at the other end of the bottleneck link. The configuration settings are summarized in Table 2. C_b, d_b, C_a, and d_a denote the bandwidth and delay of the bottleneck link, and the bandwidth and the delay of an access link, respectively. The final column of the table corresponds to *target* for CoDel, K for DCTCP, and *q_ref* for PI. Recall that, for CoDel, the parameter *target* is essentially β divided by the bottleneck bandwidth C_b (Section 4.1). For DCTCP, the parameter K is essentially β normalized by the packet size (Section 4.2). Therefore, changes in *target* and K induce proportional changes in the effective value of β for CoDel and DCTCP, respectively.

Section 5.1 examines the cyclic behavior of CoDel and compares it with RED and PI. Section 5.2 examines the invariance of cycles of CoDel and DCTCP. While the simulation results validate most of our analytic results, we do identify one major discrepancy due to modeling simplifications, which we examine in Section 5.3.

[3]We have also tried adaptive RED (ARED) [11], an RED variant that dynamically adapts the parameters, but it behaves similarly as RED.

Table 2: **Network configurations**

Figure	TCP:AQM	Topology	N	C_a	d_a	C_b	d_b	*target / K / q_ref*
Fig. 3(a)	Reno:CoDel	Fig. 2(a)	60	150 Mbps	40 ms	15 Mbps	20 ms	50 ms
Fig. 3(b)	Reno:RED	Fig. 2(a)	60	150 Mbps	40 ms	15 Mbps	20 ms	-
Fig. 3(c)	Reno:CoDel	Fig. 2(a)	30	750 Mbps	40 ms	75 Mbps	20 ms	50 ms
Fig. 3(d)	Reno:RED	Fig. 2(a)	30	750 Mbps	40 ms	75 Mbps	20 ms	-
Fig. 4(a)	Reno:CoDel	Fig. 2(a)	60	150 Mbps	40 ms	15 Mbps	20 ms	50 ms
Fig. 4(b)	Reno:PI	Fig. 2(a)	60	150 Mbps	40 ms	15 Mbps	20 ms	93.75 Kbytes
Fig. 4(c)	Reno:CoDel	Fig. 2(a)	60	750 Mbps	40 ms	75 Mbps	20 ms	50 ms
Fig. 4(d)	Reno:PI	Fig. 2(a)	60	750 Mbps	40 ms	75 Mbps	20 ms	468.75 Kbytes
Fig. 5(a)	Reno:CoDel	Fig. 2(a)	15	1 Gbps	20 ms	100 Mbps	10 ms	{20 ms, 30 ms, 40 ms}
Fig. 5(b)	Reno:CoDel	Fig. 2(a)	15	1 Gbps	20 ms	100 Mbps	10 ms	{20 ms, 30 ms, 40 ms}
Fig. 6(a)	Reno:CoDel	Fig. 2(a)	30	1 Gbps	20 ms	100 Mbps	10 ms	{20 ms, 30 ms, 40 ms}
Fig. 6(b)	Reno:CoDel	Fig. 2(a)	15	1 Gbps	20 ms	50 Mbps	10 ms	{20 ms, 30 ms, 40 ms}
Fig. 6(c)	Reno:CoDel	Fig. 2(a)	15	1 Gbps	10 ms	100 Mbps	5 ms	{20 ms, 30 ms, 40 ms}
Fig. 7(a)	DCTCP	Fig. 2(b)	8	11 Gbps	0.025 ms	10 Gbps	0.025 ms	{45, 65, 85}
Fig. 7(b)	DCTCP	Fig. 2(b)	8	11 Gbps	0.05 ms	10 Gbps	0.05 ms	{45, 65, 85}

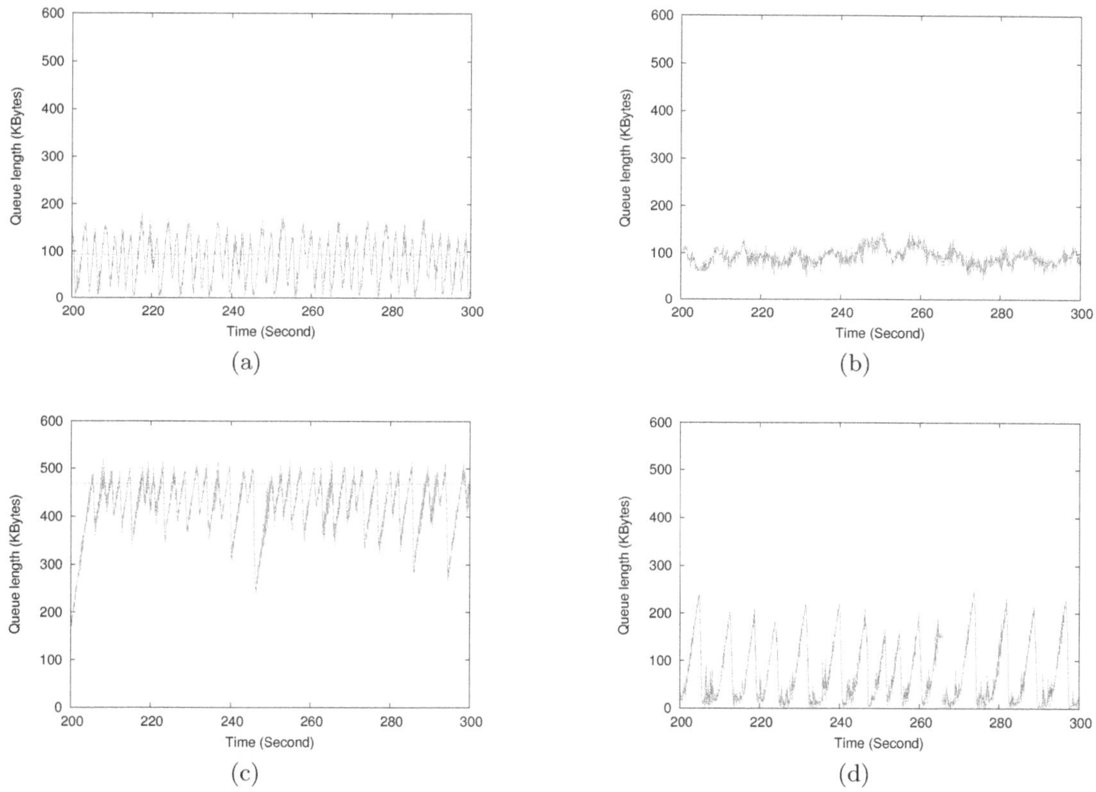

Figure 3: Comparison between CoDel and RED.

5.1 Cyclic Behavior

Fig. 3(a)-(b) compare the queue dynamics of CoDel and RED. The effective value of β for CoDel is plotted horizontally in Fig. 3(a) as well. The network configuration and the parameters of RED follow those in [16]. Cyclic pattern can be clearly identified in the backlog with CoDel (Fig. 3(a)) as predicted.[4] On the other hand, no cyclic pattern can be identified in the backlog with RED (Fig. 3(b)). In this case, RED essentially keeps the backlog fluctuation small by computing the link price as a well-tuned function of the *magnitude* of the backlog.

[4]Indeed, this pattern is approximate but not exact. In loss-based congestion control, a TCP connection backs off when a packet loss occurs. On the other hand, the flow rate adaptation process of the PLT(β) system in (1) adopts the well-established fluid model [23], which eliminates the randomness by looking at the *expected* flow rate. The queueing dynamics, which are determined by the aggregate flow rates, in turn inherit similar modeling errors.

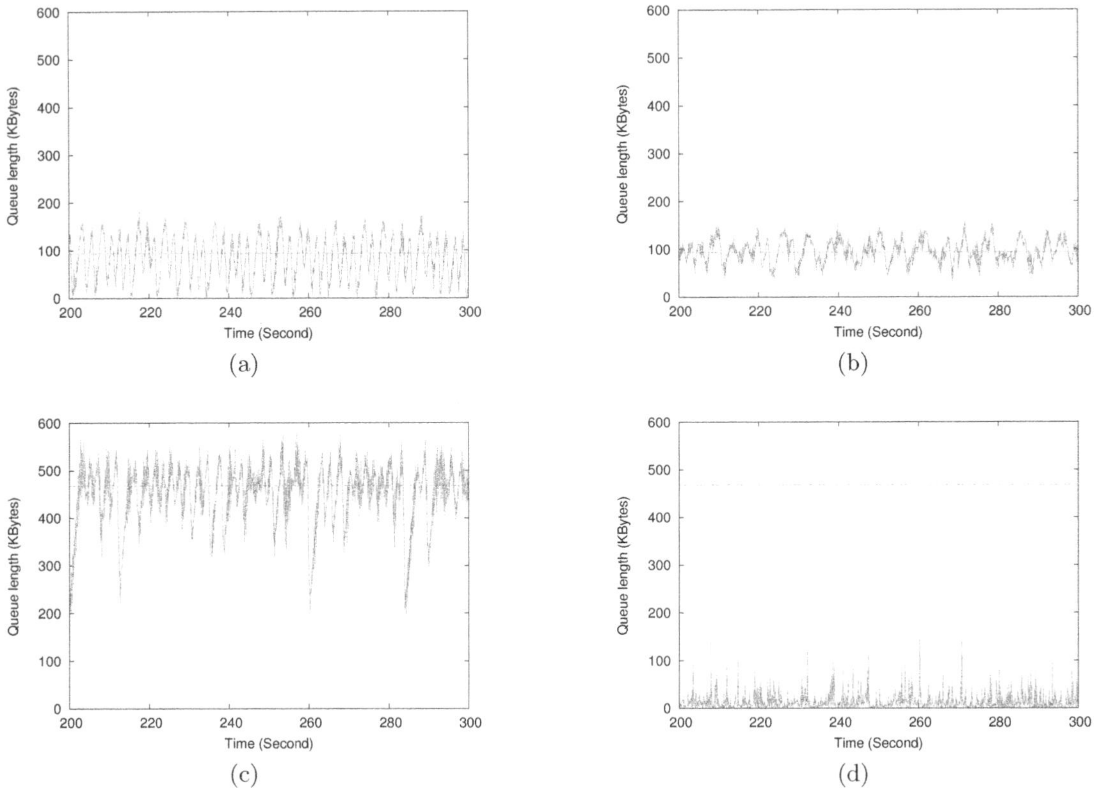

Figure 4: Comparison between CoDel and PI.

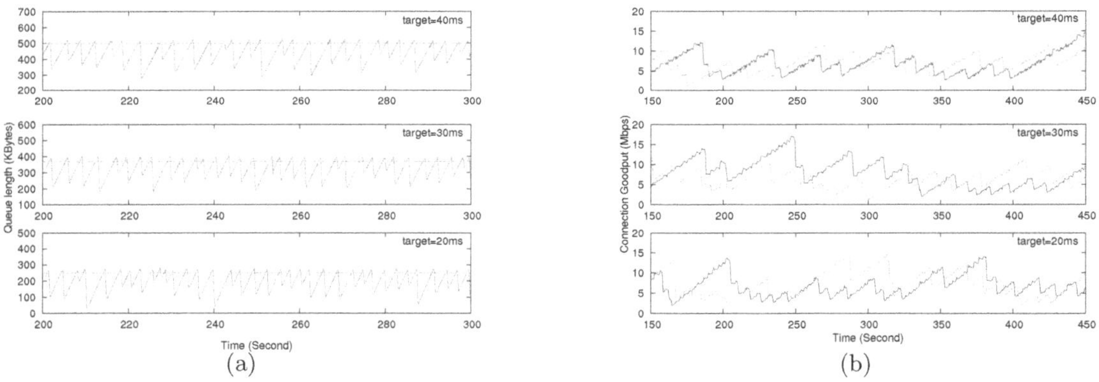

Figure 5: Invariance of cycles with CoDel: base case.

Fig. 3(c)-(d) plot the queue dynamics of CoDel and RED, respectively, when the bandwidth of the bottleneck link is increased by five-fold and the number of connections is reduced by half with the parameters of CoDel and RED unchanged. The backlog with CoDel continues to exhibit the regular cyclic pattern. Moreover, the backlog is non-empty, keeping the bottleneck link fully utilized. On the other hand, without parameters well tuned to the new network environment, RED fails to maintain its intended operational behavior. Rather, the backlog is often driven to become empty due to excessive packet dropping when the link is backlogged. This severely undermines the link utilization.

Fig. 4(a)-(b) compare the queue dynamics of CoDel and PI. In addition, the effective value of β for CoDel and the value of *q_ref* for PI are plotted horizontally in Fig. 4(a)-(b), respectively. The network configuration and the parameter of PI follow those in [16]. We set *target* of CoDel such that the resulting β is equal to *q_ref* of PI for better comparison. Again, the cyclic pattern can be clearly identified in the backlog with CoDel (Fig. 4(a)) but not in the backlog with PI (Fig. 4(b)). PI demonstrates a smaller magnitude of the backlog deviation. This is because PI explicitly counteract the deviation by taking its magnitude and derivative into account when deciding the packet dropping rate. It is intended for the backlog to closely track *q_ref*.

Fig. 4(c)-(d) plot the queue dynamics of CoDel and PI, respectively, when the bandwidth of the bottleneck link is increased by five-fold with the parameters of CoDel and PI unchanged. CoDel continues to exhibit the regular cyclic behavior in keeping the backlog non-empty and evolve following the cyclic pattern. On the other hand, without parameters well tuned to the new network environment, PI fails to maintain its intended operational behavior. Rather, the backlog is almost always empty.

Therefore, the cyclic behavior of CoDel is in general robust across different network environments *without* careful tuning of parameters. While the fluctuation in the backlog with CoDel is more severe than those with carefully tuned conventional AQM algorithms, CoDel is nevertheless able to maintain a low buffer occupancy in the long run. In practice, this gives network administrators incentives to simply "turn it on" rather than leaving the buffers unmanaged. In general, the AQM and congestion control algorithms implementing the PLT principle are expected to exhibit such robust cyclic behavior. For example, such similar cyclic behavior has been reported in the case of DCTCP in [2].

5.2 Invariance of Cycles

We now examine the invariance of the cycles against the threshold β.

Fig. 5(a) plots the queue dynamics of CoDel under three different values of *target*, which results in three different values of β as plotted horizontally. Fig. 6(b) plots the corresponding dynamics in goodput of two TCP connections. In Fig. 5(a), the dynamic deviation of the queue dynamics from their respective levels of β are remarkably similar across different levels of β. In Fig. 5(b), the goodput dynamics are also similar across different values of β, although the cyclic pattern is not clear in these dynamics due to the randomness in the backoffs of a single connection. Thus, we have clearly observed the invariance property, that the cycles of PLT(β) system is invariant across different values of β, except for a shift in the backlog size.

Fig. 6(a)-(c) plot the queue dynamics of CoDel when the network is changed by doubling the number of TCP flows, halving the bottleneck link capacity, and halving the delays of all links, respectively. It can be seen that, in each resulting network scenario, similar inferences to those from Fig. 5(a) can be made. Moreover, the dynamics in these figures are obviously different from those of Fig. 5(a). Hence, the queue dynamics around β are determined by the network characteristics and invariant across different values of β.

Fig. 7 plots the queue dynamics of DCTCP under different levels of K, which result in three different values of β horizontally plotted. All other configurations follow that in [1]. We observe that the queue dynamics across different values of β are similar except for the shift. In comparison with CoDel, the cycling period is much shorter and the magnitude deviation is much smaller. This is due to the high-speed, low-latency links in the simulated data center environment, which makes the round-trip time minimal.

Therefore, the invariance properties of CoDel and DCTCP are verified. This property greatly simplifies their parameter tuning. When configuring β, one only needs to worry about the desirable level of delay, and avoid overly small β that leads to idle links.

5.3 Discussion: Lower Bound for β

In addition to the plotted results, we have explored various levels of β. It is found that there is a lower bound on β,

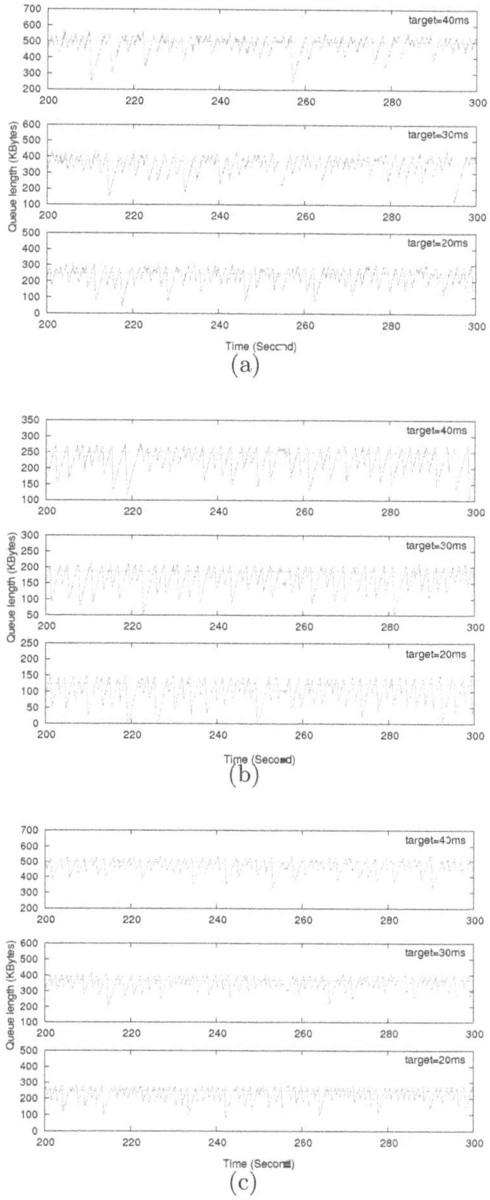

Figure 6: Invariance of cycles with CoDel: extended cases.

below which the predicted invariance property breaks down. This is because our model assumes that the bottleneck link is always backlogged. When β is small, it is possible that backoffs in TCP connections will leave the link idle for some time. The smaller the value of β is, the more frequent a link will become idle.

In obtaining a lower bound for practical settings of β, we propose to leverage existing results on the right size for a router buffer, such as [4]. Under the assumption that the buffer is managed by the passive drop-tail algorithm, these results generally establish that the buffer size can be made much smaller than the bandwidth delay product without undermining the bandwidth utilization. While the PLT principle guides the design of AQM, it is similar to the drop-tail algorithm in that no packet is dropped when the backlog is below a threshold value (which is β in the case of PLT,

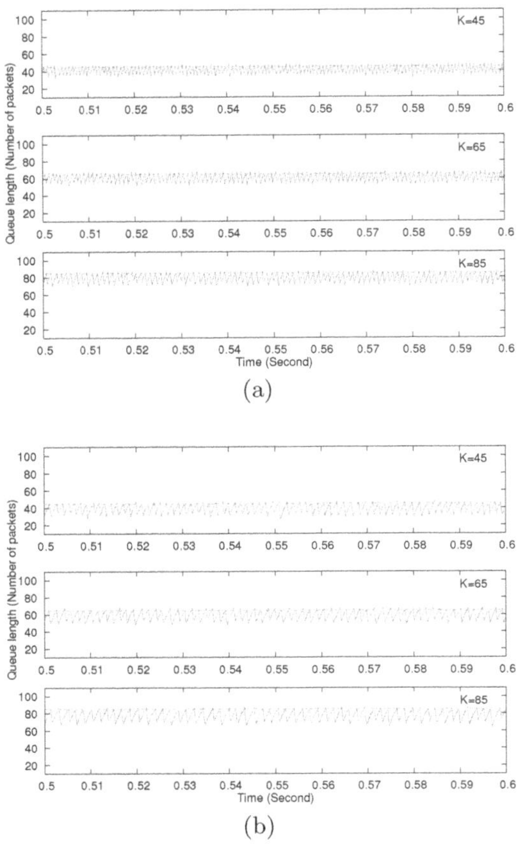

Figure 7: Invariance of cycles with DCTCP.

and the buffer size in the case of drop-tail).[5] On the other hand, drop-tail exerts more abrupt control than PLT when the backlog exceeds its respective threshold value. Therefore, the lower bound for β should be lower than the derived buffer size. We leave a complete examination of this issue as part of future work.

6. RELATED WORK

Solutions for the bufferbloat problem can be network-based or end-to-end. The network-based solutions aim to enhance the robustness of AQM against protocol parameters. Inheriting the idea of adaptive RED [11], [26] proposes that AQM should automatically estimate global information and adapt parameters to the estimation. [13] proposes only updating packet drop rate at the end of fixed time intervals instead of at every packet arrival. In general, it remains to conduct comprehensive evaluation of these novel AQM proposals. Most notably, the period at which the packet dropping rate/protocol parameter is updated form a new parameter itself, and should be carefully selected. This is out of the scope of the present paper and left as our future work.

The end-to-end solutions propose to improve the responsiveness TCP to incipient network congestion, so that buffer occupancy level can be reduced at routers. Several TCP variants, such as [8, 30, 31], suggest that TCP could incorporate delay information in inferring network loading condition to attain congestion avoidance at a finer granularity, and in particular attain more prompt congestion response. Alternatively, [17] suggests that TCP receiver could exert extra control by adapting the size of advertised window *awnd* based on the estimated queueing delay. However, a TCP connection with these enhancements in general tends to yield its fair share of bandwidth to the prevalent loss-based TCP due to earlier backoff [24]. Moreover, the resulting system may have multiple equilibrium [29]. These side effects hinder the incremental deployment of the end-to-end solutions in the heterogeneous Internet.

As a link pricing scheme, the PLT(β) system guides the update of packet dropping rate in AQM and thus mostly belongs to network-based solutions. Nevertheless, it can also be (partly) implemented end-to-end, as in the case of DCTCP.

Exhibiting both discrete and continuous dynamics, the PLT(β) system belongs to the general class of the hybrid dynamical systems [15]. Existing studies of such systems, however, mostly consider systems that possesses equilibrium. They cannot apply to the PLT(β) system, which possess no equilibrium but limit cycles. In [2], the limit cycle behavior of DCTCP is reported. The stability of the limit cycle is studied via checking stability of the Poincaré maps. Our work considers the more general PLT(β) system, and shows that any congestion control system implementing the PLT principle will exhibit the limit cycle behavior. Moreover, we formally establish the invariance property, and experimentally validate it in the cases of CoDel and DCTCP.

7. CONCLUSION

In this paper, we have presented the pricing-link-by-time (PLT) principle. We have developed a model of a congestion control system designed under the PLT principle, the PLT(β) system. We have shown that the PLT(β) system exhibits a family of cycles instead of equilibrium, and have provided numerically checkable conditions under which such cycles become stable limit cycles. We further establish the invariance property, that the cycles are invariant across different values of β except for a shift of the backlog trajectory. Our simulation results show that CoDel and DCTCP, two realizations of the PLT principle, exhibit the cyclic behavior and their cycles are invariant across different values of β. Thus, when tuning β for an AQM algorithm implementing the PLT principle, one needs only focus on the desirable level of queueing delay. This makes the parameter tuning for AQM an optional and simple process, and provides an integral solution to combatting bufferbloat.

There are several possible extensions to our work, including analyzing PLT in networks with multiple bottleneck links and comparing various specific forms of the pricing function h.

8. ACKNOWLEDGMENTS

We would like to thank the anonymous reviewers for their useful comments. This research is supported in part by the Research Grants Council of the Hong Kong Special Administrative Region, China, under Grant No. HKU 714510E, ARO MURI grant W911NF-08-1-0233, NSF NetSE grant CNS 0911041, and Bell Labs, Lucent-Alcatel.

[5]Arguably, this simple structure leads to the common robustness of drop-tail and PLT.

9. REFERENCES

[1] M. Alizadeh, A. Greenberg, D.A. Maltz, J. Padhye, P. Patel, B. Prabhakar, S. Sengupta, and M. Sridharan. Data Center TCP (DCTCP). *ACM SIGCOMM Computer Communication Review*, Vol. 40, No. 4, pp. 63-74, October 2010.

[2] M. Alizadeh, A. Javanmard, and B. Prabhakar. Analysis of DCTCP: Stability, Convergence, and Fairness. *ACM SIGMETRICS Performance Evaluation Review*, Vol. 39, No. 1, pp. 73-84, June 2011.

[3] M. Allman. Comments on Bufferbloat. *ACM SIGCOMM Computer Communication Review*, Vol. 43, No. 1, pp. 31-37, January 2013.

[4] G. Appenzeller, I. Keslassy, and N. McKeown. Sizing Router Buffers. *ACM SIGCOMM Computer Communication Review*, Vol. 34, No. 4, pp. 281-292, October 2004.

[5] S. Athuraliya, V.H. Li, S.H. Low, and Q. Yin. REM: Active Queue Management. *IEEE Network*, Vol. 15, No. 3, pp. 48-53, May 2001.

[6] C. Berge. Topological Spaces. *Oliver & Boyd*, 1963.

[7] B. Braden, D. Clark, J. Crowcroft, B. Davie, S. Deering, D. Estrin, S. Floyd, V. Jacobson, G. Minshall, C. Partridge, L. Peterson, K. Ramakrishnan, S. Shenker, J. Wroclawski, and L. Zhang. Recommendations on Queue Management and Congestion Avoidance in the Internet. *IETF RFC 2309*, April 1998.

[8] L.S. Brakmo and L.L. Peterson. TCP Vegas: End to End Congestion Avoidance on a Global Internet. *IEEE Journal on Selected Areas in Communications*, Vol. 13, No. 8, pp. 1465-1480, October 1995.

[9] M. Dischinger, A. Haeberlen, K.P. Gummadi, and S. Saroiu. Characterizing Residential Broadband Networks. *Proc. of ACM SIGCOMM IMC*, pp. 43-56, October 2007.

[10] W.-C. Feng, K.G. Shin, D.D. Kandlur, and D. Saha. The BLUE Active Queue Management Algorithms. *IEEE/ACM Transactions on Networking*, Vol. 10, No. 4, pp. 513-528, August 2002.

[11] S. Floyd, R. Gummadi, and S. Shenker. Adaptive RED: An Algorithm for Increasing the Robustness of RED's Active Queue Management. *Technical Report, ACIRI*, August 2001.

[12] S. Floyd and V. Jacobson. Random Early Detection Gateways for Congestion Avoidance. *IEEE/ACM Transactions on Networking*, Vol. 1, No. 4, pp. 397-413, August 1993.

[13] A. Francini. Periodic Early Detection for Improved TCP Performance and Energy Efficiency. *Computer Networks*, Vol. 56, No. 13, pp. 3076-3086, September 2012.

[14] J. Gettys and K. Nichols. Bufferbloat: Dark Buffers in the Internet. *Communications of the ACM*, Vol. 55, No. 1, pp. 57-65, January 2012.

[15] R. Goebel and R.G. Sanfelice, and A.R. Teel. Hybrid Dynamical Systems. *IEEE Control Systems*, Vol. 29, No. 2, pp. 28-93, April 2009.

[16] C.V. Hollot, V. Misra, D. Towsley, and W. Gong. Analysis and Design of Controllers for AQM Routers Supporting TCP Flows. *IEEE Transactions on Automatic Control*, Vol. 47, No. 6, pp. 945-959, June 2002.

[17] H. Jiang, Y. Wang, K. Lee, and I. Rhee. Tackling Bufferbloat in 3G/4G Networks. *Proc. of ACM IMC*, pp. 329-342, November 2012.

[18] F. Kelly, A. Maulloo, and D. Tan. Rate Control in Communication Networks: Shadow Prices, Proportional Fairness and Stability. *Journal of the Operational Research Society*, Vol. 49, No. 3, pp. 237-252, March 1998.

[19] H.K. Khalil. Nonlinear Systems. *Upper Saddle River, Prentice-Hall*, 2002.

[20] S. Kunniyur and R. Srikant Analysis and Design of an Adaptive Virtual Queue (AVQ) Algorithm for Active Queue Management. *ACM SIGCOMM Computer Communication Review*, Vol. 31, No. 4, pp. 123-134, August 2001.

[21] S.H. Low. A Duality Model of TCP and Queue Management Algorithms. *IEEE/ACM Transactions on Networking*, Vol. 11, No. 4, pp. 525-536, August 2003.

[22] S.H. Low, F. Paganini, and J.C. Doyle. Internet Congestion Control. *IEEE Control Systems Magazine*, Vol. 22, No. 1, pp. 28-43, February 2002.

[23] V. Misra, W.-B. Gong, and D. Towsley. Fluid-based Analysis of a Network of AQM Routers Supporting TCP Flows with An Application to RED. *SIGCOMM Computer Communication Review*, Vol. 30, No. 4, pp. 151-160, August 2000.

[24] J. Mo, R.J. La, V. Anantharam, and J. Walrand. Analysis and Comparison of TCP Reno and Vegas. *Proc. of IEEE INFOCOM'99*, Vol. 3, pp. 1556-1563, March 1999.

[25] K. Nichols and V. Jacobson Controlling Queue Delay. *ACM Queue*, Vol. 10, No. 5, pp. 1-15, May 2012.

[26] R. Pan, P. Natarajan, C. Piglione, M.S. Prabhu, V. Subramanian, F. Baker, and B.V. Steeg. PIE: A Lightweight Control Scheme to Address the Bufferbloat Problem. *Proc. of IEEE HPSR*, pp. 148-155, July 2013.

[27] T.S. Parker and L.O. Chua. Practical Numerical Algorithms for Chaotic Systems. *Springer-Verlag*, 1989.

[28] R. Srikant. *The Mathematics of Internet Congestion Control.* Cambridge, MA:Birkhauser, 2004.

[29] A. Tang, J. Wang, S.H. Low, and M. Chiang. Equilibrium of Heterogeneous Congestion Control: Existence and Uniqueness. *IEEE/ACM Transactions on Networking*, Vol. 15, No. 4, pp. 824-837, October 2007.

[30] D.X. Wei, J. Cheng, S.H. Low, and S. Hegde. FAST TCP: Motivation, Architecture, Algorithms, Performance. *IEEE/ACM Transactions on Networking*, Vol. 14, No. 6, pp. 1246-1259, December 2006.

[31] K. Winstein and H. Balakrishnan. TCP ex Machina: Computer-Generated Congestion Control. *ACM SIGCOMM Computer Communication Review*, Vol. 43, No. 4, pp. 123-134, Oct. 2013.

Serving Content with Unknown Demand: the High-Dimensional Regime

Sharayu Moharir
Department of ECE
University of Texas at Austin
Austin, TX 78712
sharayu.moharir@gmail.com

Javad Ghaderi
Department of ECE
University of Texas at Austin
Austin, TX 78712
jghaderi@ee.columbia.edu

Sujay Sanghavi
Department of ECE
University of Texas at Austin
Austin, TX 78712
sanghavi@mail.utexas.edu

Sanjay Shakkottai
Department of ECE
University of Texas at Austin
Austin, TX 78712
shakkott@austin.utexas.edu

ABSTRACT

In this paper we look at content placement in the high-dimensional regime: there are n servers, and $O(n)$ distinct types of content. Each server can store and serve $O(1)$ types at any given time. Demands for these content types arrive, and have to be served in an online fashion; over time, there are a total of $O(n)$ of these demands. We consider the algorithmic task of content placement: determining which types of content should be on which server at any given time, in the setting where the demand statistics (i.e. the relative popularity of each type of content) are not known a-priori, but have to be inferred from the very demands we are trying to satisfy. This is the high-dimensional regime because this scaling (everything being $O(n)$) prevents consistent estimation of demand statistics; it models many modern settings where large numbers of users, servers and videos/webpages interact in this way.

We characterize the performance of *any* scheme that separates learning and placement (i.e. which use a portion of the demands to gain some estimate of the demand statistics, and then uses the same for the remaining demands), showing it is order-wise strictly suboptimal. We then study a simple adaptive scheme - which myopically attempts to store the most recently requested content on idle servers - and show it outperforms schemes that separate learning and placement. Our results also generalize to the setting where the demand statistics change with time. Overall, our results demonstrate that separating the estimation of demand, and the subsequent use of the same, is strictly suboptimal.

SIGMETRICS'14, June 16–20, 2014, Austin, Texas, USA.

http://dx.doi.org/10.1145/2591971.2591978.

Categories and Subject Descriptors

C.2.4 [**Computer-Communication Networks**]: Distributed Systems

Keywords

Content Delivery Systems; Large Scale Systems; Content Replication Strategies

1. INTRODUCTION

Ever increasing volumes of multimedia content is now requested and delivered over the Internet. Content delivery systems (e.g., YouTube [23]), consisting of a large collection of servers (each with limited storage/service capability), process and service these requests. Naturally, the storage and content replication strategy (i.e., what content should be stored on each of these servers) forms an important part of the service and storage architecture.

Two trends have emerged in such settings of large-scale distributed content delivery systems. First, there has been a sharp rise in not just the volume of data, but indeed in *the number of content-types* (e.g., number of distinct YouTube videos) that are delivered to users [23]. Second, the popularity and demand for most of this content is *uneven and ephemeral*; in many cases, a particular content-type (e.g., a specific video clip) becomes popular for a small interval of time after which the demand disappears; further a large fraction of the content-types languish in the shadows with almost no demand [1,5].

To understand the effect of these trends, we study a stylized model for the content placement and delivery in large-scale distributed content delivery systems. The system consists of n servers, each with constant storage and service capacities, and αn content-types (α is some constant number). We consider the scaling where the system size n tends to infinity. The requests for the content-types arrive dynamically over time and need to be served in an online manner by the free servers storing the corresponding contents. The requests that are "deferred" (i.e., cannot be immediately served by a free server with requested content-type) incur a high cost. To ensure reliability, we assume that there are alternate server resources (e.g., a central server with large enough backup storage and service capacity, or additional servers that can be freed up on-demand) that can serve such deferred requests.

The performance of any content placement strategy crucially depends on the popularity distribution of the content. Empirical studies in many services such as YouTube, Peer-to-Peer (P2P) VoD systems, various large video streaming systems, and web caching, [2,5,7,17,24] have shown that access for different content-types is very inhomogeneous and typically matches well with power-law (Zipf-like) distributions, i.e., the request rate for the i-th most popular content-type is proportional to $i^{-\beta}$, for some parameter $\beta > 0$. For the performance analysis, we assume that the content-types have a popularity that is governed by some power-law distribution with unknown β and further this distribution changes over time.

Our objective is to provide efficient content placement strategies that minimize the number of requests deferred. It is natural to expect that content placement strategies in which more popular content-types are replicated more will have a good performance. However, there is still a lot of flexibility in designing such strategies and the extent of replication of each content-type has to be determined. Moreover, the requests arrive dynamically over time and popularities of different content-types might vary significantly over time; thus the content placement strategy needs to be online and robust.

The fact that the number of contents is very large and their popularities are time-varying creates two new challenges that are not present in traditional queueing systems. First, it is imperative to *measure the performance of content replication strategies over the time scale in which changes in popularities occur.* In particular, the steady-state metrics typically used in queueing systems are not a right measure of performance in this context. Second, the number of content-types is enormous and *learning the popularities of all content-types over the time scale of interest is infeasible.* This is in contrast with traditional multi-class multi-server systems where the number of demand classes does not scale with the number of servers (low-dimensional setting) and thus learning the demand rates can be done in a time duration that does not scale with the system size.

1.1 Contributions

The main contributions of our work can be summarized as follows.

High dimensional vs. low dimensional: We consider the high dimensional regime where the number of servers, the number of content-types, and the number of requests to be served over any time interval all scale as $O(n)$; further the demand statistics are not known a-priori. This scaling means that consistent estimation of demand statistics is not possible. We show that a "*learn-and-optimize*" approach, namely, learning the demand statistics based on requests and then locally caching content on servers according to this empirical statistics, is strictly sub-optimal (even when using high-dimensional estimators such as the Good-Turing estimator [13]). This is in contrast to the conventional low-dimensional setting (finite number of content-types) where the "learn-and-optimize" approach is asymptotically optimal.

Adaptive vs. learn-and-optimize: We study an adaptive content replication strategy which myopically attempts to cache the most recently requested content-types on idle servers. Our key result is that even this simple adaptive strategy strictly outperforms *any* content placement strategy based on the "learn-and-optimize" approach. Our results also generalize to the setting where the demand statistics change with time.

Overall, our results demonstrate that separating the estimation of demands and the subsequent use of the estimations to design optimal content placement policies is deprecated in the high-dimensional setting.

1.2 Organization and Basic Notations

The rest of this paper is organized as follows. We describe our system model and setting in Section 2. The main results are presented in Section 3. Our simulation results are discussed in Section 4. Section 5 contains the proofs of some of our key results. Section 7 gives an overview of related works. We finally end the paper with conclusions. The rest of the proofs can be found in the Appendix.

Some of the basic notations are as follows. Given two functions f and g, we write $f = O(g)$ if $\limsup_{n\to\infty} |f(n)/g(n)| < \infty$. $f = \Omega(g)$ if $g = O(f)$. If both $f = O(g)$ and $f = \Omega(g)$, then $f = \Theta(g)$. Similarly, $f = o(g)$ if $\limsup_{n\to\infty} |f(n)/g(n)| = 0$, and $f = \omega(g)$ if $g = o(f)$. The term *w.h.p.* means with high probability as $n \to \infty$.

2. SETTING AND MODEL

In this section, we consider a stylized model for large scale distributed content systems that captures two emerging trends, namely, a large number of content types, and uneven and time-varying demands.

2.1 Server and Storage Model

The system consists of n front-end servers, each with constant storage and service capacity, and a back-end server that contains a catalog of m content-types (one copy of each content-type, e.g., a copy of each YouTube video). The contents can be copied from the back-end server and placed on the front-end servers. Each front-end server can store at most d content pieces (d is a constant) and serve at most d requests at each time, under the constraint that no two requests can read the same content piece simultaneously on a server[1]. The system is essentially equivalent to a system of nd servers, each with 1 content piece storage. Since we are interested in the scaling performance, as $n, m \to \infty$, for clarity we assume that there are n servers and each server can store 1 content and can serve 1 request at any time.

2.2 Service Model

When a request for a content arrives, it is routed to an idle (front-end) server which has the corresponding content-type stored on it, if possible. We assume that the service time of each request is exponentially distributed with mean 1. The requests have to be served in an online manner; further service is non-preemptive, i.e., once a request is assigned to

[1]Even without the constraint "no two requests can read the same content piece simultaneously on a server", the performance can be bounded from above by the performance of a system with dn servers with a storage of 1 each, and from below by that of another system with n servers with a storage of 1 each. Thus asymptotically in a scaling-sense, the system is still equivalent to a system of n servers where each server can store 1 content and can serve 1 content request at any time.

a server, its service cannot be interrupted and also cannot be re-routed to another server. Requests that cannot be served (no free server with requested content-type) incur a high cost (e.g., need to be served by the back-end server, or content needs to be fetched from the back-end server and loaded on to a new server). As discussed before, we refer to such requests as deferred requests. The goal is to design content placement policies such that the number of requests deferred is minimized.

2.3 Content Request Model

There are m content-types (e.g., m distinct YouTube videos). We consider the setting where the number of content-types m is very large and scales linearly with the system size n, i.e., $m = \alpha n$ for some constant $\alpha > 1$. We assume that requests for each content arrive according to a Poisson process and request rates (popularities) follow a Zipf distribution. Formally, we make the following assumptions on the arrival process.

ASSUMPTION 1. *(Arrival and Content Request Process)*

- *The arrival process for each content-type i is a Poisson process with rate λ_i.*
- *The load on the system at any time is $\bar{\lambda} < 1$, where $\bar{\lambda} = \frac{\sum_{i=1}^{m} \lambda_i}{n}$.*
- *Without loss of generality, content-types are indexed in the order of popularity. The request rate for content-type i is $\lambda_i = n\bar{\lambda}p_i$ where $p_i \propto i^{-\beta}$ for some $\beta > 0$. This is the Zipf distribution with parameter β.*

We have used the Zipf distribution to model the popularity distribution of various contents because empirical studies in many content delivery systems have shown that the distribution of popularities matches well with such distributions, see e.g., [5], [2], [24], [7], [17].

2.4 Time Scales of Change in Arrival Process

A key trend discussed earlier is the time-varying nature of popularities in content delivery systems [1,5]. For example, the empirical study in [5] (based on 25 millions transactions on YouTube) shows that daily top 100 list of videos changes frequently. To understand the effect of this trend on the performance of content placement strategies, we consider the following two change models.

Block Change Model: In this model, we assume that the popularity of various content-types remains constant for some duration of time $T(n)$, and then changes to some other arbitrarily chosen distribution that satisfies Assumption 1. Thus $T(n)$ reflects the time-scale over which changes in popularities occur. Under this model, we characterize the performance of content placement strategies over such a time-scale $T(n)$.

Continuous Change Model: Under this model, we assume that each content-type has a Poisson clock at some constant rate $\nu > 0$. Whenever the clock of content-type i ticks, content-type i exchanges its popularity with some other content-type j, chosen uniformly at random. Note that if $T(n) = \theta(1)$, the average time over which the popularity distribution "completely" changes is comparable to that of the Block Change Model; however, here the change occurs incrementally and continuously. Note that this model ensures that the content-type popularity always has the Zipf distribution. Under this model, we characterize the performance of content placement strategies over constant intervals of time.

3. MAIN RESULTS AND DISCUSSION

In this section, we state and discuss our main results. The proofs are provided in Section 5.

3.1 Separating Learning from Content Placement

In this section, we analyze the performance of storage policies which separate the task of learning and that of content placement as follows. Consider time intervals of length $T(n)$. The operation of the policy in each time interval is divided into two phases:

Phase 1. Learning: Over this interval of time, use the demands from the arrivals (see Figure 1) to estimate the content-type popularity statistics.

Phase 2. Storage: Using the estimated popularity of various content-types, determine which content-types are to be replicated and stored on each server. The storage is fixed for the remaining time interval. The content-types not requested even once in the learning phase are treated equally in the storage phase. In other words, the popularity of all *unseen* content-types in the learning phase is assumed to be the same.

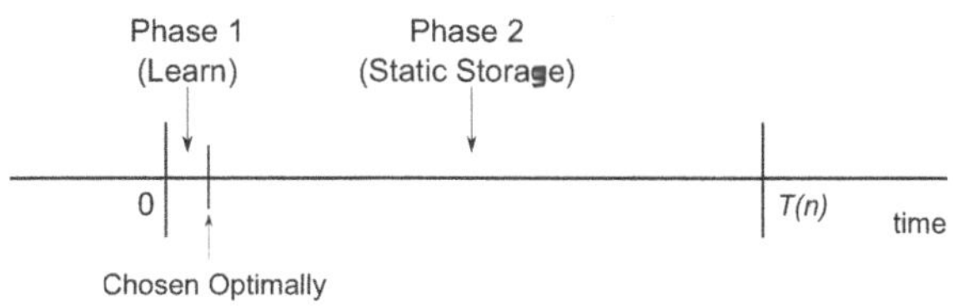

Figure 1: Learning-Based Static Storage Policies – *The interval $T(n)$ is split into the Learning and Storage phases. The length of time spent in the Learning phase can be chosen optimally using the knowledge of the value of $T(n)$ and the Zipf parameter β.*

Further, we allow the interval of time for the Learning phase potentially to be chosen optimally using knowledge of $T(n)$ (the interval over which statistics remain stationary) and β (the Zipf parameter for content-types popularity).

This is a natural class of policies to consider because it is obvious that popular content-types should be stored on more servers than the less popular content-types. Therefore, knowing the arrival rates can help in the design of better storage policies. Moreover, for the content-types which are not seen in the learning phase, the storage policy has no information about their relative popularity. It is therefore natural to treat them as if they are equally popular.

The replication and storage in Phase 2 (Storage) can be performed by *any* static policy that relies on the knowledge (estimate) of arrival rates, e.g., the proportional placement policy [10] where the number of copies of each content-type is proportional to its arrival rate, or the storage policy of [11] which was shown to be approximately optimal in the steady state.

We now analyze the performance of learning-based static storage policies under the Block Change Model defined in Section 2.4 where the statistics remain invariant over the time intervals of length $T(n)$. The performance metric of interest is the number of requests deferred by any policy belonging to class of learning-based static storage policies in the interval of interest. We assume that at the beginning of this interval, the storage policy has no information about the relative popularity of various content-types. Therefore, we start with an initial loading where each content-type is placed on exactly one server. This loading is not changed during Phase 1 (the learning phase) at the end of which, the content-type on idle servers is changed as per the new storage policy. As mentioned before, this storage is not changed for the remaining duration in the interval of interest.

The following theorem provides a lower bound on the number of requests deferred by any learning-based static storage policy.

THEOREM 1. *Under Assumption 1 and the Block Change Model defined in Section 2.4, for $\beta > 2$, if $T(n) = \Omega(1)$, the expected number of requests deferred by any learning-based static storage policy is $\Omega(n^{0.5})$.*

We therefore conclude that even if the division of the interval of interest into Phase 1 (Learning) and Phase 2 (Storage) is done in the optimal manner, no learning-based static storage policy can defer fewer than $\Omega(n^{0.5})$ jobs in the interval of interest. Therefore, Theorem 1 provides a fundamental lower bound on the number of jobs deferred by any policy which separates learning and storage. It is worth pointing out that this result holds even when the time-scale of change in statistics is quite slow. Thus, even when $T(n)$, the time-scale over which statistics remains invariant, goes to infinity and the time duration of the two phases (Learning, Storage) is chosen optimally based on $\beta, T(n)$, $\Omega(n^{0.5})$ requests are still deferred.

Next, we explore *adaptive storage policies* which perform the task of learning and storage simultaneously.

3.2 Myopic Joint Learning and Placement

We next study a natural adaptive storage policy called MYOPIC. In an adaptive storage policy, depending on the requests that arrive and depart, the content-type stored on a server can be changed when the server is idle while other servers of the system might be busy serving requests. Therefore, adaptive policies perform the tasks of learning and placement jointly. Many variants of such adaptive policies have been studied for decades in the context of cache management (e.g. LRU, LRU-MIN [21]).

Let C_i refer to the ith content-type, $1 \leq i \leq m$. The MYOPIC policy works as follows: When a request for content-type C_i arrives, it is assigned to a server if possible, or deferred otherwise. Recall that a deferred request is a request for which on arrival, no currently idle server can serve it and thus its service invokes a backup mechanism such as a back-end server which can serve it at a high cost. After the assigment/defer decision is made, if there are no currently idle servers with content-type C_i, MYOPIC replaces the content-type of one of the idle servers with C_i. This idle server is chosen as follows:

- If there is a content-type C_j stored on more than one currently idle servers, the content-type of one of those servers is replaced with C_i,
- Else, place C_i on that currently idle server whose content-type has been requested least recently among the content-types on the currently idle servers.

For a formal definition of MYOPIC, refer to Figure 2.

```
On arrival (request for C_i) do,
Allocate request to an idle server if possible.
if no other idle server has a copy of C_i, then
   if ∃j: C_j stored on > 1 idle servers, then
      replace C_j with C_i on any one of them.
   else
      find C_j: least recently requested on idle servers,
      replace C_j with C_i.
   end if
end if
```

Figure 2: MYOPIC – *An adaptive storage policy which changes the content stored on idle servers in a greedy manner to ensure that recently requested content pieces are available on idle servers.*

REMARK 1. *Some key properties of MYOPIC are:*

1. *The content-types on servers can be potentially changed only when there is an arrival.*
2. *The content-type of at most one idle server is changed after each arrival. However, for many popular content-types, it is likely that there is already an idle server with the content-type, in which case there is no content-type change.*
3. *To implement MYOPIC, the system needs to maintain a list of content types ordered according to the time at which recent most request of each content-type was made.*

The following theorem provides an upper bound on the number of requests deferred by MYOPIC for the Block Change Model defined in Section 2.4.

THEOREM 2. *Under Assumption 1 and the Block Change Model defined in Section 2.4, over any time interval $T(n)$ such that $T(n) = o(n^{\beta-1})$, the number of requests deferred by MYOPIC is $O((nT(n))^{1/\beta})$ w.h.p.*

We now compare this upper bound with the lower bound on the number of requests deferred by any learning-based static storage policy obtained in Theorem 1.

COROLLARY 1. *Under Assumption 1, the Block Change Model defined in Section 2.4, and for $\beta > 2$, over any time interval $T(n)$ such that $T(n) = \Omega(1)$ and $T(n) = o(n^{\frac{\beta}{2}-1})$, the expected number of requests deferred by any learning-based static storage policy is $\Omega(n^{0.5})$ and the number of requests deferred by the MYOPIC policy is $o(n^{0.5})$ w.h.p.*

From Corollary 1, we conclude that MYOPIC outperforms all learning-based static storage policies. Note that:

i. Corollary 1 holds even when the interval of interest $T(n)$ grows to infinity (scaling polynomially in n), or correspondingly, even when the content-type popularity changes very slowly with time.

ii. Even if the partitioning of the $(T(n))$ into a Learning phase and a Static Storage phase is done in an optimal manner with the help of some side information $(\beta, T(n))$, the MYOPIC algorithm outperforms any learning-based static storage policy.

iii. Since we consider the high-dimensional setting, the learning problem at hand is a large-alphabet learning problem. It is well known that standard estimation techniques like using the empirical values as estimates of the true statistics is suboptimal in this setting. Many learning algorithm like the classical Good-Turing estimator [13] and other linear estimators [16] have been proposed, and shown to have good performance for the problem of large-alphabet learning. From Corollary 1, we conclude that, even if the learning-based storage policy uses the best possible large-alphabet estimator, it cannot match the performance of the MYOPIC policy.

Therefore, in the high-dimensional setting we consider, separating the task of estimation of the demand statistics, and the subsequent use of the same to design a static storage policy, is strictly suboptimal. This is the key message of this paper.

Theorem 2 characterizes the performance of MYOPIC under the Block Change Model, where the statistics of the arrival process do not change in interval of interest. To gain further insight into robustness of MYOPIC against changes in the arrival process, we now analyze the performance of MYOPIC when the arrival process can change in the interval of interest according to the Continuous Change Model defined in Section 2.4.

Recall that under the Continuous Change Model, on average, we expect $\Theta(n)$ shuffles in the popularity of various content-types in an interval of constant duration. For the Block Change Model, if $T(n) = \Theta(1)$, the entire popularity distribution can change at the end of the block, which is equivalent to n shuffles. Therefore, for both the change models, the expected number of changes to the popularity distribution in an interval of constant duration is of the same order. However, these changes occur constantly but slowly in the Continuous Change Model as opposed to a one-shot change in the Block Change Model.

THEOREM 3. *Under Assumption 1, and the Continuous Change Model defined in Section 2.4, the number of requests deferred by the MYOPIC storage policy in any interval of constant duration is* $O(n^{1/\beta})$ *w.h.p.*

In view of Theorem 2, if the arrival rates do not vary in an interval of constant duration, under the MYOPIC storage policy, the number of requests deferred in that interval is $O(n^{1/\beta})$ w.h.p. Theorem 3 implies that the number of requests deferred in a constant duration interval is of the same order even if the arrival rates change according to the Continuous Change Model. This shows that the performance of the MYOPIC policy is robust to changes in the popularity statistics.

3.3 Genie-Aided Optimal Storage Policy

In this section, our objective is to study the setting where the content-type statistics is available "for free". We consider the setting where the popularity statistics are known, and show that a simple adaptive policy is optimal in the class of all policies which know popularity statistics of various content-types. We denote the class of such policies as $\mathbb{A}$ and refer to the optimal policy as the GENIE policy.
Let the content-types be indexed from $i = 1$ to m and let C_i be the ith content-type. Without loss of generality, we assume that the content-types are indexed in the order of popularity, i.e, $\lambda_i \geq \lambda_{i+1}$ for all $i \geq 1$. Let $k(t)$ denote the number of idle servers at time t.

The key idea of the GENIE storage policy is to ensure that at any time t, if the number of idle servers is $k(t)$, the $k(t)$ most popular content-types are stored on exactly one idle server each. The GENIE storage policy can be implemented as follows. Recall C_i is the ith most popular content-type. At time t,

- If there is a request for content-type C_i with $i < k(t^-)$, then allocate the request to the corresponding idle server. Further, replace the content-type on server storing $C_{k(t^-)}$ with content-type C_i.

- If there is a request for content-type C_i with $i > k(t^-)$, defer this request. There is no storage update.

- If there is a request for content-type C_i with $i = k(t^-)$, then allocate the request to the corresponding idle server. There is no storage update.

- If a server becomes idle (due to a departure), replace its content-type with $C_{k(t^- +1}$.

For a formal definition, please refer to Figure 3.

```
Initialize: Number of idle-servers := k = n.
while true do
    if new request (for C_i) routed to a server, then
        if i ≠ k, then
            replace content-type of idle server storing C_k with
            C_i
        end if
        k ← k − 1
    end if
    if departure, then
        replace content-type of new idle server with C_{k+1}
        k ← k + 1
    end if
end while
```

Figure 3: GENIE – *An adaptive storage policy which has content popularity statistics available for "free". At time t, if the number of idle servers is $k(t)$, the $k(t)$ most popular content-types are stored on exactly one idle server each.*

REMARK 2. *Some key properties of GENIE are:*

1. *The implementation of GENIE requires replacing the content-type of at most one server on each arrival and departure.*

2. *The GENIE storage policy only requires the knowledge of the relative popularity of various content types.*

To characterize the performance of GENIE, we assume that the system starts from the empty state (all servers are idle) at time $t = 0$. The performance metric for any policy $\mathcal{A}$ is $D^{(\mathcal{A})}(t)$, defined as the number of requests deferred by time t under the adaptive storage policy $\mathcal{A}$. We say that an adaptive storage policy $\mathcal{O}$ is optimal if

$$D^{(\mathcal{O})}(t) \leq_{st} D^{(\mathcal{A})}(t), \tag{1}$$

for any storage policy $\mathcal{A} \in \mathbb{A}$ and any time $t \geq 0$. Where Equation 1 implies that,

$$\mathbb{P}(D^{(\mathcal{O})}(t) > x) \leq \mathbb{P}(D^{(\mathcal{A})}(t) > x),$$

for all $x \geq 0$ and $t \geq 0$.

THEOREM 4. *If the arrival process to the content-type delivery system is Poisson and the service times are exponential random variables with mean 1, for the Block Change Model defined in Section 2.4, let $D^{(\mathcal{A})}(t)$ be the number of requests deferred by time t under the adaptive storage policy $\mathcal{A} \in \mathbb{A}$. Then, we have that,*

$$D^{(GENIE)}(t) \leq_{st} D^{(\mathcal{A})}(t),$$

for any storage policy $\mathcal{A} \in \mathbb{A}$ and any time $t \geq 0$.

Note that this theorem holds even if the λ_is are not distributed according to the Zipf distribution. We thus conclude that GENIE is the optimal storage policy in the class of all storage policies which at time t, have no additional knowledge of the future arrivals except the values of λ_i for all content-types and the arrivals and departures in $[0, t)$. Next, we compute a lower bound on the performance of GENIE.

THEOREM 5. *Under Assumption 1, for $\beta > 2$, the Block Change Model defined in Section 2.4 and if the interval of interest is of constant length, the expected number of requests deferred by GENIE is $\Omega(n^{2-\beta})$.*

From Theorems 2 and 5 we see that there is a gap in the performance of the MYOPIC policy and the GENIE policy (which has additional knowledge of the content-type popularity statistics). Since for the GENIE policy, learning the statistics of the arrival process comes for "free", this gap provides an upper bound on the cost of serving content-type with *unknown* demands. We compare the performance of the all the policies considered so far in the next section via simulations.

4. SIMULATION RESULTS

We compare the performance of the MYOPIC policy with the performance of the GENIE policy and the following two learning-based static storage policies:

- The *"Empirical + Static Storage"* policy uses the empirical popularity statistics of content types in the learning phase as estimates of the the true popularity statistics. At the end of the learning phase, the number of servers on which a content is stored is proportional to its estimated popularity.
- The *"Good Turing + Static Storage"* policy uses the Good-Turing estimator [13] to compute an estimate of the missing mass at the end of the learning phase. The missing mass is defined as total probability mass of the content types that were not requested in the learning phase. Recall that we assume that learning-based static storage policies treat all the missing content-types equally, i.e., all missing content-types are estimated to be equally popular.

  Let M_0 be the total probability mass of the content types that were not requested in the learning phase and S_1 be the set of content types which were requested exactly once in the learning phase. The Good-Turing estimator of the missing mass ($\widehat{M_0}$) is given by

  $$\widehat{M_0} = \frac{|S_1|}{\text{number of samples}}.$$

  See [13] for details.

  Let N_i be the number of times content i was requested in the learning phase and $\mathcal{C}_{\text{missing}}$ be the set of content-types not requested in the learning phase. The "Good Turing + Static Storage" policy computes an estimate of the content-popularity as follows:

  i: If $N_i = 0$, $p_i = \dfrac{\widehat{M_0}}{|\mathcal{C}_{\text{missing}}|}$.

  ii: If $N_i > 0$, $p_i = (1 - \widehat{M_0})\dfrac{N_i}{\text{number of samples}}$.

  At the end of the learning phase, the number of servers on which a content is stored is proportional to its estimated popularity.

We simulate the content distribution system for arrival and service process which satisfy Assumption 1 to compare the performance of the four policies mentioned above and also understand how their performance depends on various parameters like system size (n), load ($\bar{\lambda}$) and Zipf parameter (β). In Tables 1, 2 and 3, we report the mean and variance of the fraction of jobs served by the policies over a duration of 5 s ($T(n) = 5$) for $\alpha = 1$.

For each set of system parameters, we repeat the simulations between 1000 to 10000 times for each policy in order to ensure that the standard deviation of the quantity of interest (fraction of jobs served) is small and comparable. For the two adaptive policies (GENIE and MYOPIC), the results are averaged over 1000 iterations and for the learning-based policies ("Empirical + Static Storage" and "Good-Turing + Static Storage"), the results are averaged over 10000 iterations. In addition, the results for the learning-based policies are reported for empirically optimized values for the fraction of time spent by the policy in learning the distribution.

In Table 1, we compare the performance of the policies for different values of system size (n). For the results reported in Table 1, the "Empirical + Static Storage" policy learns for 0.1 s and the "Good Turing + Static Storage" policy learns for 0.7 s. The performance of all four policies improves as the system size increases and the adaptive policies significantly outperform the two learning-based static storage policies. Figure 4 is a plot of the mean values reported in Table 1.

In Table 2, we compare the performance of the policies for different values of Zipf parameter β. For the results reported in Table 2, the duration of the learning phase for

Policy	n	Mean	σ
GENIE	200	0.9577	0.0081
	400	0.9698	0.0045
	600	0.9752	0.0034
	800	0.9788	0.0030
	1000	0.9814	0.0025
MYOPIC	200	0.8995	0.0258
	400	0.9260	0.0167
	600	0.9380	0.0132
	800	0.9481	0.0101
	1000	0.9532	0.0080
Empirical + Static Storage	200	0.6292	0.0662
	400	0.6918	0.0443
	600	0.7246	0.0353
	800	0.7464	0.0304
	1000	0.7622	0.0268
Good Turing + Static Storage	200	0.6875	0.0274
	400	0.7249	0.0180
	600	0.7443	0.0140
	800	0.7566	0.0118
	1000	0.7651	0.0104

Table 1: *The performance of the four policies as a function of the system size (n) for fixed values of load $\bar{\lambda} = 0.8$ and $\beta = 1.5$. The values reported are the mean and standard deviation (σ) of the fraction of jobs served. Both adaptive policies (GENIE and MYOPIC) significantly outperform the two learning-based static storage policies.*

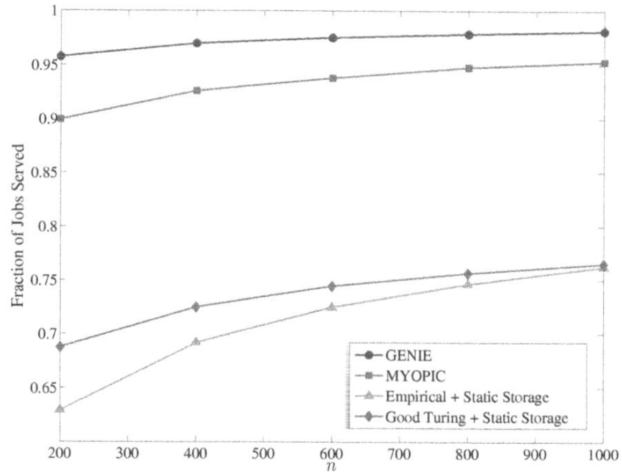

Figure 4: *Plot of the mean values reported in Table 1 – performance of the storage policies as a function of system size (n) for $\bar{\lambda} = 0.8$ and $\beta = 1.5$.*

Policy	β	Mean	σ
GENIE	2.0	0.9940	0.0025
	3.5	0.9998	0.0013
	5.0	0.9997	0.0017
MYOPIC	2.0	0.9774	0.0063
	3.5	0.9981	0.0024
	5.0	0.9990	0.0014
Empirical + Static Storage	2.0	0.8592	0.0206
	3.5	0.9328	0.0138
	5.0	0.9458	0.0092
Good Turing + Static Storage	2.0	0.8448	0.0231
	3.5	0.9314	0.0139
	5.0	0.9457	0.0091

Table 2: *The performance of the four policies as a function of the Zipf parameter (β) for fixed values of system size $n = 500$ and load $\bar{\lambda} = 0.9$. The values reported are the mean and standard deviation (σ) of the fraction of jobs served. The MYOPIC policy outperforms the two learning-based static storage policies for all values of β considered.*

both learning based policies is fixed such that the expected number of arrivals in that duration is 100. The performance of all four policies improves as the value of the Zipf parameter β increases, however, the MYOPIC policy outperforms both learning-based static storage policies for all values of β considered.

In Table 3, we compare the performance of the policies for different values of load $\bar{\lambda}$. For the results reported in Table 3, the duration of the learning phase for both learning based policies is fixed such that the expected number of arrivals in that duration is 100. The performance of all four policies deteriorates as the load increases, however, for all loads considered, the MYOPIC policies outperforms the two learning-based static storage policies.

5. PROOFS OF MAIN RESULTS

In this section, we provide the proofs of our main results.

5.1 Proof of Theorem 1

We first present an outline of the proof of Theorem 1. We consider two cases. We first focus on the case when the learning-based storage policies use fewer than n arrivals to learn the distribution.

1. If the learning phase lasts for the first n^γ arrivals for some $0 < \gamma \leq 1$, we show that under Assumption 1, w.h.p., in the learning phase, there are no arrivals for content-types $k, k+1, ..m = \alpha n$ for $k = (n^\gamma \log n)^{\frac{1}{\beta-1}} + 1$ (Lemma 1).

2. Next, we show that w.h.p., among the first n^γ arrivals, i.e., during the learning phase, $\Omega(n^\gamma)$ requests are deferred (Lemma 3).

3. Using Lemma 1, we compute a lower bound on the number of requests deferred in Phase 2 (after the learning phase) by any learning-based static storage policy (Lemma 4).

4. Using Steps 2 and 3, we lower bound the number of requests deferred in the interval of interest.

In the case when the learning phase lasts for more than n arrivals, we show that the number of requests deferred in the learning phase alone is $\Omega(n)$, thus proving the theorem for this case.

LEMMA 1. *Let E_1 be the event that in the first n^γ arrivals for $0 < \gamma \leq 1$, there are no arrivals of types $k, k+1, ...m = \alpha n$ where $k = (n^\gamma \log n)^{\frac{1}{\beta-1}} + 1$. Then,*

$$\mathbb{P}(E_1) \geq \exp\left(-\frac{1}{2\log n}\right), \quad (2)$$

for n large enough.

Policy	λ	Mean	σ
GENIE	0.500	0.9892	0.0025
	0.725	0.9788	0.0013
	0.950	0.9531	0.0017
MYOPIC	0.500	0.9605	0.0113
	0.725	0.9484	0.0105
	0.950	0.8973	0.0221
Empirical + Static Storage	0.500	0.7756	0.0222
	0.725	0.7705	0.0238
	0.950	0.7352	0.0235
Good Turing + Static Storage	0.500	0.7849	0.0230
	0.725	0.7589	0.0249
	0.950	0.6869	0.0348

Table 3: *The performance of the four policies as a function of the load ($\bar{\lambda}$) for fixed values of system size $n = 500$ and $\beta = 1.2$. The values reported are the mean and standard deviation (σ) of the fraction of jobs served. The MYOPIC policy significantly outperforms the two learning-based static storage policies for all loads considered.*

PROOF. Recall $\lambda_i = \bar{\lambda} n p_i$ where $p_i = \frac{i^{-\beta}}{Z(\beta)}$ for $Z(\beta) = \sum_{i=1}^{m} i^{-\beta}$.

$$Z(\beta) = \sum_{i=1}^{\alpha n} i^{-\beta} \geq \int_1^{\alpha n+1} i^{-\beta} di \geq \frac{0.9}{\beta - 1}$$

for n large enough. Therefore, for all i,

$$p_i \leq \frac{\beta - 1}{0.9} i^{-\beta}.$$

The total mass of all content types $i = k, ..m = \alpha n$ is

$$\sum_{i=k}^{\alpha n} p_i \leq \sum_{i=k}^{\alpha n} \frac{\beta - 1}{0.9} i^{-\beta} \leq \int_{k-1}^{\alpha n} \frac{\beta - 1}{0.9} i^{-\beta} di \leq \frac{1}{0.9} \frac{1}{(k-1)^{\beta - 1}}.$$

For $k = (n^\gamma \log n)^{\frac{1}{\beta - 1}} + 1$, we have that,

$$\mathbb{P}(E_1) \geq \left(1 - \frac{1}{0.9} \frac{1}{(k-1)^{\beta-1}}\right)^{n^\gamma} \geq \exp\left(-\frac{1}{2 \log n}\right),$$

for n large enough. □

We use the following concentration result for Exponential random variables.

LEMMA 2. *Let X_k for $0 \leq k \leq v$, be i.i.d. exponential random variables with mean 1, then,*

$$\mathbb{P}\left(\sum_{k=1}^{v} X_i \leq a\right) \leq \exp(v - a) \left(\frac{a}{v}\right)^v. \quad (3)$$

The proof of Lemma 2 follows from elementary calculations.

LEMMA 3. *Suppose the system starts with each content piece stored on exactly one server. Let E_2 be the event that in the first n^γ arrivals for γ such that $0 < \gamma \leq 1$, at most $((n^\gamma \log n)^{\frac{1}{\beta-1}} + 1)(\log n + 1)$ are served (not deferred). Then, for $\beta > 2$,*

$$\mathbb{P}(E_2) \geq 1 - \frac{1}{2 \log n}. \quad (4)$$

PROOF. This proof is conditioned on the event E_1 defined in Lemma 1. Conditioned on E_1, in the first n^γ arrivals, at most $(n^\gamma \log n)^{\frac{1}{\beta-1}} + 1$ different content types are requested. Therefore, at most $(n^\gamma \log n)^{\frac{1}{\beta-1}} + 1$ servers can serve requests during the first n^γ arrivals.

Let E_3 be the event that the time taken for the first n^γ arrivals is less than $\frac{2n^\gamma}{\bar{\lambda} n}$. Since the expected time for the first n^γ arrivals is $\frac{n^\gamma}{\bar{\lambda} n}$, by the Chernoff bound, $\mathbb{P}(E_3) \geq 1 - o(1/n)$. The rest of this proof is conditioned on the event E_3.

If the system serves (does not defer) more than

$$((n^\gamma \log n)^{\frac{1}{\beta-1}} + 1)(\log n + 1)$$

requests in this interval, at least one server needs to serve more than $\log n$ requests. By substituting $a = cn^{-1+\gamma}$ and $v = \log n$ in Lemma 2, we have that,

$$\mathbb{P}\left(\sum_{k=1}^{\log n} X_k \leq cn^{-1+\gamma}\right) \leq \exp(\log n - cn^{-1+\gamma}) \times \left(\frac{cn^{-1+\gamma}}{\log n}\right)^{\log n} = o\left(\frac{1}{n}\right).$$

Therefore, the probability that a server serves more than $\log n$ requests in an interval of $\frac{2n^\gamma}{\bar{\lambda} n}$ time is $o(\frac{1}{n})$. Therefore, using the union bound, the probability that none of these $(n^\gamma \log n)^{\frac{1}{\beta-1}} + 1$ servers serve more than $\log n$ requests each in $\frac{2n^\gamma}{\bar{\lambda} n}$ time is greater than $1 - ((n^\gamma \log n)^{\frac{1}{\beta-1}} + 1) o(\frac{1}{n})$. Therefore, we have that,

$$\mathbb{P}(E_2^c) \leq ((n^\gamma \log n)^{\frac{1}{\beta-1}} + 1) o\left(\frac{1}{n}\right) + P(E_1^c) + P(E_3^c) \leq \frac{1}{2 \log n}$$

for n large enough. □

LEMMA 4. *Let the interval of interest be $T(n)$ such that $T(n) = \Omega(1)$. If the learning phase of the storage policy lasts for the first n^γ arrivals, $0 < \gamma \leq 1$, the expected number of requests deferred in Phase 2 is $\Omega\left(\frac{T(n) n^{1-\gamma}}{\log n}\right)$.*

PROOF. Let N_2 be the number of arrivals in Phase 2, then we have that, $E[N_2] = T(n) \bar{\lambda} n - n^\gamma$.

Let E_4 be the event that $N_2 > E[N_2]/2$. Using the Chernoff bound, it can be shown that $P(E_4^c) = o(1/n)$.

The rest of this proof is conditioned on E_1 defined in Lemma 1 and E_4 defined above. We consider the following two cases depending on the number of servers allocated to content types not seen in Phase 1.

Case I: The number of servers allocated to content types not seen in Phase 1 is less than ϵn for some $\epsilon \leq 1 - \frac{\bar{\lambda}}{1000}$. For $\beta > 2$,

$$Z(\beta) = \sum_{i=1}^{\alpha n} i^{-\beta} \leq \sum_{i=1}^{\alpha n} i^{-2} \leq \sum_{i=1}^{\infty} i^{-2} = \frac{\pi^2}{6}.$$

Therefore, for all i, $p_i \geq \frac{6}{\pi^2} i^{-\beta}$. The total mass of all content types $k, k+1, ..\alpha n$ is

$$\sum_{i=k}^{\alpha n} p_i \geq \sum_{i=k}^{\alpha n} \frac{6}{\pi^2} i^{-\beta} \geq \int_k^{\alpha n+1} \frac{6}{\pi^2} i^{-\beta} di = \frac{0.54}{\pi^2(\beta - 1)} \frac{1}{k^{\beta-1}},$$

for n large enough. Therefore, the expected number of arrivals of types $k, k+1, ..m = \alpha n$, where $k = (n^\gamma \log n)^{\frac{1}{\beta-1}} + 1$ in Phase 2 is at least $(\frac{T(n)\bar{\lambda}n - n^\gamma}{2})\frac{0.54}{\pi^2(\beta-1)}\frac{1}{n^\gamma \log n}$.

Let E_5 be the event that in Phase 2, there are at least $(\frac{T(n)\bar{\lambda}n-n^\gamma}{2})\frac{0.54}{2\pi^2(\beta-1)}\frac{1}{n^\gamma \log n}$ arrivals of type $k, k+1, ..m = \alpha n$, where $k = (n^\gamma \log n)^{\frac{1}{\beta-1}} + 1$. Using the Chernoff bound, $\mathbb{P}(E_5^c) = o(1/n)$.

Conditioned on E_1, all content types $k, k+1, ..m = \alpha n$, where $k = (n^\gamma \log n)^{\frac{1}{\beta-1}} + 1$, are not requested in Phase 1. Recall that all learning-based policies treat all these content types equally and that the total number of servers allocated to store the content types not seen in Phase 1 is less than ϵn. Let η be the probability that C_k for $k \geq (n^\gamma \log n)^{\frac{1}{\beta-1}} + 1$ is not stored by the storage policy under consideration. Then,

$$\eta \geq 1 - \frac{\epsilon n}{n - (n^\gamma \log n)^{\frac{1}{\beta-1}} - 1} \geq 1 - \frac{\epsilon}{2},$$

for n large enough.

Let $E_6 = E_1 \cap E_3 \cap E_4 \cap E_5$ and D_2 be the number of requests deferred in Phase 2.

$$\begin{aligned} E[D_2|E_6] &\geq \eta\left(\left(\frac{T(n)\bar{\lambda}n - n^\gamma}{2}\right)\frac{0.54}{2\pi^2(\beta-1)}\frac{1}{n^\gamma \log n}\right) \\ &\geq \left(1-\frac{\epsilon}{2}\right)\left(\frac{T(n)\bar{\lambda}n - n^\gamma}{2}\right)\frac{0.54}{2\pi^2(\beta-1)}\frac{1}{n^\gamma \log n} \\ &= \Omega\left(\frac{T(n)n^{1-\gamma}}{\log n}\right). \end{aligned}$$

Therefore,

$$\begin{aligned} E[D_2] &\geq E[D_2|E_6]\mathbb{P}(E_6) \\ &\geq E[D_2|E_6]\left(1 - \frac{1}{\log n} - \frac{3}{n}\right) = \Omega\left(\frac{T(n)n^{1-\gamma}}{\log n}\right). \end{aligned}$$

Case II: The number of servers allocated to content types not seen in Phase 1 is more than ϵn for some $\epsilon > 1 - \frac{\bar{\lambda}}{1000}$.

Let $f(n)$ be the number of servers allocated to store all content types that are requested in Phase 1. By our assumption, $f(n) \leq \frac{\bar{\lambda}}{1000}n$.

Let $\mathbf{C}_1$ be the set of content types requested in Phase 1. Let $p = \sum_{c \in \mathbf{C}_1} p_c$ be the total mass of all content types $c \in \mathbf{C}_1$. Let $\hat{p}_c$ be the fraction of requests for content-type c in Phase 1. By the definition of $\mathbf{C}_1$, the total empirical mass of all content types $c \in \mathbf{C}_1$ is obviously $\hat{p} = \sum_{c \in \mathbf{C}_1} \hat{p}_c = 1$.

Recall that there are n^γ arrivals in Phase 1. Let $r = n^\gamma$. We now use the Chernoff bound to compute a lower bound on the true mass p, using a technique similar to that used in [13] (Lemma 4). By the Chernoff bound, we know that,

$$\mathbb{P}(\hat{p} > (1+\kappa)p) \leq \exp\left(-\frac{pr\kappa^2}{3}\right).$$

Let $\delta = \exp\left(-\frac{pr\kappa^2}{3}\right)$, then, we have that, with probability greater than $1 - \delta$,

$$\hat{p} - p > \sqrt{\frac{-3p\log\delta}{r}}.$$

Solving for p, we get that, with probability greater than $1 - \delta$, $p > 1 - \frac{3\log(1/\delta)}{2r}$, for n large enough. Let $\delta = 1/n$, then we have that, with probability greater than $1 - 1/n$, $p > 1 - \frac{3\log n}{2n^\gamma}$. Conditioned on the event E_4, there are at least $\frac{T(n)\bar{\lambda}n - n^\gamma}{2}$ arrivals in Phase 2. The remainder of this proof is conditioned on E_4. Let A_2 be the number of arrivals of types $c \in \mathbf{C}_1$ in phase 2. Let E_7 be the event that

$$A_2 > \frac{T(n)\bar{\lambda}n - n^\gamma}{2}\left(1 - \frac{3\log n}{2n^\gamma}\right).$$

Since the expected number of arrivals of content types $c \in \mathbf{C}_1$ in Phase 2 is at least

$$(T(n)\bar{\lambda}n - n^\gamma)\left(1 - \frac{3\log n}{2n^\gamma}\right),$$

using the Chernoff bound, we can show that $\mathbb{P}(E_7^c) = o(1/n)$. The rest of this proof is conditioned on E_7. By our assumption, the number of servers which can serve arrivals of types $c \in \mathbf{C}_1$ in Phase 2 is $f(n)$. Therefore, if at least $A_2/2$ requests are to be served in Phase 2, the sum of the service times of these $A_2/2$ requests should be less than $T(n)f(n)$ (since the number of servers which can serve these requests is $f(n)$). Let E_8 be the event that the sum of $A_2/2$ independent Exponential random variables with mean 1 is less than $T(n)f(n)$. By substituting $v = A_2/2$ and $a = T(n)f(n)$ in Lemma 2, we have that,

$$\begin{aligned} \mathbb{P}(E_8) &\leq \exp\left(\frac{A_2}{2} - T(n)\right)\left(\frac{2T(n)f(n)}{A_2}\right)^{\frac{A_2}{2}} \\ &\leq \exp\left(\frac{A_2}{2}\right)\left(\frac{2T(n)f(n)}{A_2}\right)^{\frac{A_2}{2}} = o\left(\frac{1}{n}\right) \end{aligned}$$

for n large enough. Hence,

$$\begin{aligned} \mathbb{P}\left(D_2 \geq \frac{A_2}{2}\right) &\geq 1 - \mathbb{P}(E_1^c) - o\left(\frac{1}{n}\right) \\ \Rightarrow E[D_2] &= \Omega\left(\frac{T(n)n^{1-\gamma}}{\log n}\right). \end{aligned}$$

□

PROOF. (of Theorem 1)
We consider two cases:
Case I: The learning phase lasts for the first n^γ arrivals where $0 \leq \gamma \leq 1$.
Let D_1 be the number of requests deferred in Phase 1 and D be total number of requests deferred in the interval of interest. Then, we have that,

$$E[D] = E[D_1] + E[D_2].$$

By Lemmas 3 and 4 and since $T(n) = \Omega(1)$, we have that,

$$\begin{aligned} E[D] &\geq n^\gamma - (n^\gamma \log n)^{\frac{1}{\beta-1}} \log n + E[D_2] \\ &= \Omega(n^{0.5}). \end{aligned}$$

Case II: The learning phase lasts for longer than the time taken for the first n arrivals.
By Lemma 3, the number of requests deferred in the first n arrivals is at least $n - (n \log n)^{\frac{1}{\beta-1}} \log n$ with probability greater than $1 - 1/\log n$. Therefore, we have that,

$$E[D] \geq \left(n - (n\log n)^{\frac{1}{\beta-1}} \log n\right)\left(1 - \frac{1}{\log n}\right) = \Omega(n^{0.5}).$$

□

5.2 Proof of Theorem 2

We first present an outline the proof of Theorem 2.

1. We first show that under Assumption 1, on every arrival in the interval of interest ($T(n)$), there are $\Theta(n)$ idle servers w.h.p. (Lemma 6).
2. Next, we show that w.h.p., in the interval of interest of length $T(n)$, only $O((nT(n))^{\frac{1}{\beta}})$ unique content types are requested (Lemma 7).
3. Conditioned on Steps 1 and 2, we show that, the MYOPIC policy ensures that in the interval of interest, once a content type is requested for the first time, there is always at least one idle server which can serve an incoming request for that content.
4. Using Step 3, we conclude that, in the interval of interest, only the first request for a particular content type will be deferred. The proof of Theorem 2 then follows from Step 2.

LEMMA 5. *Let the cumulative arrival process to the content delivery system be a Poisson process with rate $\bar{\lambda}n$. At time t, let $\chi(t)$ be the number of occupied servers under the MYOPIC storage policy. Then, we have that, $\chi(t) \leq_{st} S(t)$, where $S(t)$ is a poisson random variable with rate $\bar{\lambda}n(1-e^{-t})$.*

PROOF. Consider an $M/M/\infty$ queue where the arrival process is Poisson($\bar{\lambda}n$). Let $S(t)$ be the number of occupied servers at time t in this system. It is well known that $S(t)$ is a Poisson random variable with rate $\bar{\lambda}n(1-e^{-t})$.

Here we provide a proof of this result for completeness. Consider a request r^* which arrived into the system at time $t_0 < t$. If the request is still being served by a server, we have that, $t_0 + \mu(r^*) > t$, where $\mu(r^*)$ is the service time of request r^*. Since $\mu(r^*) \sim \text{Exp}(1)$, we have that, $\mathbb{P}(\mu(r^*) > t - t_0 | t_0) = e^{-(t-t_0)}$. Therefore, $\mathbb{P}(r^*$ in the system at time $t) \leq \int_0^t \frac{1}{t} e^{-(t-t_0)} dt_0$.

To show $\chi(t) \leq_{st} S(t)$, we use a coupled construction similar to Figure 5. The intuition behind the proof is the following: the rate of arrivals to the content delivery system and the $M/M/\infty$ system (where each server can serve all types of requests) is the same. The content delivery system serves fewer requests than the $M/M/\infty$ system because some requests are deferred even when the servers are idle. Hence, the number of busy servers is the content delivery system is stochastically dominated by the number of busy servers in the $M/M/\infty$ queueing system. □

LEMMA 6. *Let the interval of interest be $[t_0, t_0 + T(n)]$ where $T(n) = o(n^{\beta-1})$ and $\varepsilon \leq \frac{1-\bar{\lambda}}{2}$. Let F_1 be the event that at the instant of each arrival in the interval of interest, the number of idle servers in the system is at least $(1-\bar{\lambda}-\varepsilon)n$. Then, $\mathbb{P}(F_1^c) = o(\frac{1}{n})$.*

PROOF. Let F_2 be the event that the number of arrivals in $[t_0, t_0 + T(n)] \leq nT(n)(\bar{\lambda}+\varepsilon)$. Using the Chernoff bound for the Poisson process, we have that,

$$\mathbb{P}(F_2^c) = o\left(\frac{1}{n}\right).$$

Consider any $t \in [t_0, t_0 + T(n)]$. By Lemma 5, $\chi(t) \leq_{st} S(t)$, where $S(t) \sim \text{Poisson}(\bar{\lambda}n(1-e^{-t}))$. Therefore,

$$\mathbb{P}(\chi(t) > (\bar{\lambda}+\varepsilon)n) \leq \mathbb{P}(S(t) > (\bar{\lambda}+\varepsilon)n).$$

Moreover, $S(t) \leq_{st} W(t)$ where $W(t) = \text{Poisson}(\bar{\lambda}n)$. Therefore, using the Chernoff bound for $W(t)$, we have that,

$$\mathbb{P}(S(t) > (\bar{\lambda}+\varepsilon)n) \leq \mathbb{P}(W(t) > (\bar{\lambda}+\varepsilon)n) = e^{-c_1 n},$$

for some constant $c_1 > 0$. Therefore,

$$\begin{aligned}\mathbb{P}(F_1^c) &\leq \mathbb{P}(F_2^c) + (\bar{\lambda}+\varepsilon)nT(n)\mathbb{P}(\chi(t) > (\bar{\lambda}+\varepsilon)n) \\ &= o\left(\frac{1}{n}\right).\end{aligned}$$

□

LEMMA 7. *Let F_3 be the event that in the interval of interest of duration $T(n)$ such that $T(n) = o(n^{\beta-1})$, no more than $O((nT(n))^{1/\beta})$ different types of contents are requested. Then, $\mathbb{P}(F_3^c) = o(\frac{1}{n})$.*

PROOF. Recall from the proof of Lemma 1 that the total mass of all content types $k, ..m = \alpha n$ is

$$\sum_{i=k}^{\alpha n} p_i \leq \frac{1}{0.9} \frac{1}{(k-1)^{\beta-1}}.$$

Now, for $k = (nT(n))^{1/\beta} + 1$, we have that,

$$\sum_{i=k}^{\alpha n} p_i \leq \frac{1}{0.9} (nT(n))^{-\frac{\beta-1}{\beta}}.$$

Conditioned on the event F_2 defined in Lemma 6, the expected number of requests for content types $k, k+1, ..\alpha n$ is less than $\frac{1}{0.9}(\bar{\lambda}+\varepsilon)(nT(n))^{1/\beta}$. Using the Chernoff bound, the probability that there are more than $\frac{2}{0.9}(\bar{\lambda}+\varepsilon)(nT(n))^{1/\beta}$ requests for content types $k, k+1, ..\alpha n$ in the interval of interest is less than $\frac{1}{n^2}$ for n large enough.

Therefore, with probability greater than $1 - 1/n^2 - \mathbb{P}(F_2^c)$, the number different types of contents requests for in the interval of interest is less than $(nT(n))^{1/\beta} + \frac{2}{0.9}(\bar{\lambda}+\varepsilon)(nT(n))^{1/\beta}$. Hence the result follows. □

PROOF. (of Theorem 2)
Let F_4 be the event that, in the interval of interest, every request for a particular content type except the first request is not deferred. The rest of this proof is conditioned on F_1 and F_3. Let $U(t)$ be the number of unique contents which have been requested in the interval of interest before time t for $t \in [t_0, t_0 + T(n)]$. Conditioned on F_3, as defined in Lemma 7, $U(t) \leq k_1(nT(n))^{1/\beta}$ for some constant $k_1 > 0$ and n large enough. Conditioned on F_1, there are always $(1-\bar{\lambda}-\varepsilon)n$ idle servers in the interval of interest.

CLAIM: For every i and n large enough, once a content C_i is requested for the first time in the interval of interest, the MYOPIC policy ensures that there is always at least 1 idle server which can serve a request for C_i.

Note that since $T(n) = o(n^{\beta-1})$, $(nT(n))^{1/\beta} = o(n)$. Let n be large enough such that $k_1(nT(n))^{1/\beta} < (1-\bar{\lambda}-\varepsilon)n$, i.e., at any time $t \in [t_0, t_0 + T(n)]$, the number of idle servers is greater than $U(t)$. We prove the claim by induction. Let the claim hold for time t^- and let there be a request at time t for content C_i. If this is not the first request for C_i in $[t_0, t_0 + T(n)]$, by the claim, at $t = t^-$, there is at least one idle server which can serve this request. In addition, if there is exactly one server which can serve C_i at t^-, then the MYOPIC policy replaces the content of some other idle server with C_i. Since there are more than $k_1(nT(n))^{1/\beta}$ idle servers and $U(t) < k_1(nT(n))^{1/\beta}$, at t^+, each content type requested in the interval of interest so far, is stored on at least one currently idle server. Therefore, conditioned on F_1 and F_3, every request for a particular content type except the first request, is not deferred.

Hence, putting everything together,

$$\mathbb{P}(F_4) \geq 1 - \mathbb{P}(F_1^c) - \mathbb{P}(F_3^c),$$

thus $\mathbb{P}(F_4) \to 1$ as $n \to \infty$ and the result follows. □

PROOF. (of Corollary 1)
From Theorem 2 we have that, w.h.p., the number of requests deferred by the MYOPIC storage policy is $O(nT(n))^{1/\beta} = o(n^{0.5})$ and by Theorem 1, we know that, the expected number of requests deferred by any learning-based storage policy is $\Omega(n^{0.5})$. □

5.3 Proof of Theorem 3

In this section, we first present an outline of the proof of Theorem 3 followed by the proof details.

1. Since we are studying the performance of the MYOPIC policy for the Continuous Change Model, the relative order of popularity of contents keeps changing in the interval of interest. We show that w.h.p., the number of content types which are in the $n^{1/\beta}$ most popular content types at least once in the interval of interest is $O(n^{1/\beta})$ (Lemma 8).

2. Next, we show that w.h.p., in the interval of interest of length b, only $O(n^{1/\beta})$ content types are requested (Lemma 9).

3. By Lemma 6 and the proof of Theorem 2, we know that, conditioned on Step 3, the MYOPIC storage policy ensures that in the interval of interest, once a content type is requested for the first time, there is always at least one idle server which can serve an incoming request for that content. Using this, we conclude that, in the interval of interest, only the first request for a particular content type will be deferred. The proof of Theorem 3 then follows from Step 2.

LEMMA 8. *Let G_1 be the event that, in the interval of interest of length b, the number of times that a content among the current top $n^{1/\beta}$ most popular contents changes its position in the popularity ranking is at most $\frac{4b}{\alpha}n^{1/\beta}\nu$. Then, $P(G_1) \geq 1 - o(\frac{1}{n})$.*

PROOF. The expected number of clock ticks in b time-units is $bn\nu$. The probability that a change in arrival process involves at least one of the current $n^{1/\beta}$ most popular contents is $\frac{n^{1/\beta}}{\alpha n}$. Therefore, the expected number of changes in arrival process which involve at least one of the current $n^{1/\beta}$ most popular contents is $\frac{2b\nu}{\alpha}n^{1/\beta}$. By the Chernoff bound, we have that $P(G_1) \geq 1 - o(\frac{1}{n})$. □

LEMMA 9. *Let G_2 be the event that in the interval of interest, no more than $O(n^{1/\beta})$ different types of contents are requested. Then, $\mathbb{P}(G_2^c) = o(\frac{1}{n})$.*

PROOF. Conditioned on the event G_1 defined in Lemma 8, we have that in the interval of interest, at most $(\frac{2b}{\alpha}\nu + 1)n^{1/\beta}$ different contents are among the top $n^{1/\beta}$ most popular contents. Given this, the proof follows the same lines of arguments as in the proof of Lemma 7. □

PROOF. (of Theorem 3) The proof of the theorem 3 follows from Lemma 9 and uses the same line of arguments as in the proof of Theorem 2. □

5.4 Proof of Theorem 4

To show that GENIE is the optimal policy, we consider the process $X(t)$ which is the number of occupied servers at time t when the storage policy is GENIE. Let $Y(t)$ be the number of occupied servers at time t for some other storage policy $\mathcal{A} \in \mathbb{A}$. We construct a coupled process $(X^*(t), Y^*(t))$ such that the marginal rates of change in $X^*(t)$ and $Y^*(t)$ is the same as that of $X(t)$ and $Y(t)$ respectively.

Recall $\bar{\lambda} = \frac{\sum_{i=1}^{m} \lambda_i}{n}$. At time t, let $\mathbf{C}^{\mathbf{GENIE}}(t)$ and $\mathbf{C}^{\mathcal{A}}(t)$ be the sets of contents stored on idle servers by GENIE and $\mathcal{A}$ respectively. The construction of the coupled process $(X^*(t), Y^*(t))$ is described in Figure 5. We assume that the system starts at time $t = 0$ and $X^*(0) = Y^*(0) = 0$. In this construction, we maintain two counters Z_{X^*} and Z_{Y^*} which keep track of the number of departures from the system. Let $Z_{X^*}(0) = Z_{Y^*}(0) = 0$. Let Exp$(\mu)$ be an Exponential random variable with mean $\frac{1}{\mu}$ and Ber(p) be a Bernoulli random variable which is 1 with probability (w.p.) p.

LEMMA 10. *$X^*(t)$ and $Y^*(t)$ have the same marginal rates of transition as $X(t)$ and $Y(t)$ respectively.*

PROOF. This follows from the properties of the coupled process described in Figure 5 using standard arguments. □

LEMMA 11. *Let $D^{(GENIE)}(t)$ be the number of jobs deferred by time t by the GENIE adaptive storage policy and $D^{(\mathcal{A})}(t)$ to be the number of jobs deferred by time t by a policy $\mathcal{A} \in \mathbb{A}$. In the coupled construction, let $W^*(t)$ be the number of arrivals by time t. Let, $D^{X^*}(t) = W^*(t) - Z_{(X^*)}(t) - X^*(t)$ and $D^{Y^*}(t) = W^*(t) - Z_{(Y^*)}(t) - Y^*(t)$. Then, $D^{X^*}(t)$ and $D^{Y^*}(t)$ have the same marginal rates of transition as $D^{(GENIE)}(t)$ and $D^{(\mathcal{A})}(t)$ respectively.*

PROOF. This follows from Lemma 10 due to the fact that $X(t)$ have the same distribution as $X^*(t)$ and the marginal rate of increase of $D^{X^*}(t)$ given $X^*(t)$ is the same as the rate of increase of $D^{(GENIE)}(t)$ given $X(t)$. The result for $D^{Y^*}(t)$ follows by the same argument. □

LEMMA 12. *$X^* \geq Y^*$ for all t on every sample path.*

PROOF. The proof follows by induction. $X^*(0) = Y^*(0)$ by construction. Let $X^*(t_0^-) \geq Y^*(t_0^-)$ and let there be an arrival or departure at time t_0. There are 4 possible cases:

i: If ARR<DEP and $X^*(t_0^-) = Y^*(t_0^-)$, $Y^*(t_0) = Y^*(t_0^-)+1$ only if $X^*(t_0) = X^*(t_0^-) + 1$. Therefore, $X^*(t_0) \geq Y^*(t_0)$.

ii: If ARR<DEP and $X^*(t_0^-) > Y^*(t_0^-)$, $Y^*(t_0) \leq Y^*(t_0^-)+1 \leq X^*(t_0^-) \leq X^*(t_0)$. Therefore, $X^*(t_0) \geq Y^*(t_0)$.

iii: If DEP<ARR and $X^*(t_0^-) = Y^*(t_0^-)$, $X^*(t_0) = Y^*(t_0)$.

iv: If DEP<ARR and $X^*(t_0^-) > Y^*(t_0^-)$, $X^*(t_0) = X^*(t_0^-) - 1 \geq Y^*(t_0^-) \geq Y^*(t_0)$. Therefore, $X^*(t_0) \geq Y^*(t_0)$.

Generate: ARR $\sim \text{Exp}(n\bar{\lambda})$, DEP $\sim \text{Exp}(\max\{X^*, Y^*\})$
$t = t + \min\{\text{ARR}, \text{DEP}\}$
if ARR<DEP, **then**
  if $(X^* = Y^*)$ **then**
    Generate $u_1 \sim \text{Ber}\left(\frac{\sum_{i \in \mathbf{C}^{\text{GENIE}}(t)} \lambda_i}{n\bar{\lambda}}\right)$
    if $(u_1 = 1)$ **then**
      $X^* \leftarrow X^* + 1$
      Generate $u_2 \sim \text{Ber}\left(\frac{\sum_{i \in \mathbf{C}^{\mathcal{A}}(t)} \lambda_i}{\sum_{i \in \mathbf{C}^{\text{GENIE}}(t)} \lambda_i}\right)$
      if $(u_2 = 1)$ **then** $Y^* \leftarrow Y^* + 1$
    end if
  else
    Generate $u_1 \sim \text{Ber}\left(\frac{\sum_{i \in \mathbf{C}^{\text{GENIE}}(t)} \lambda_i}{n\bar{\lambda}}\right)$
    if$(u_1 = 1)$ **then** $X^* \leftarrow X^* + 1$
    Generate $u_2 \sim \text{Ber}\left(\frac{\sum_{i \in \mathbf{C}^{\mathcal{A}}(t)} \lambda_i}{\sum_{i \in \mathbf{C}^{\text{GENIE}}(t)} \lambda_i}\right)$
    if$(u_2 = 1)$ **then** $Y^* \leftarrow Y^* + 1$
  end if
else
  if $(X^* \geq Y^*)$ **then**
    $X^* \leftarrow X^* - 1$, $Z_{X^*} \leftarrow Z_{X^*} + 1$
    Generate $u_3 \sim \text{Ber}\left(\frac{Y^*}{X^*}\right)$
    if $(u_3 = 1)$ **then** $Y^* \leftarrow Y^* - 1$, $Z_{Y^*} \leftarrow Z_{Y^*} + 1$
  else
    $Y^* \leftarrow Y^* - 1$, $Z_{Y^*} \leftarrow Z_{Y^*} + 1$
    Generate $u_4 \sim \text{Ber}\left(\frac{X^*}{Y^*}\right)$
    if $(u_4 = 1)$ **then** $X^* \leftarrow X^* - 1$, $Z_{X^*} \leftarrow Z_{X^*} + 1$
  end if
end if
Goto 1

Figure 5: Coupled Process

□

LEMMA 13. *$Z_{X^*} \geq Z_{Y^*}$ for all t on every sample path.*

PROOF. The proof follows by induction. Since the system starts at time $t = 0$, $Z_{X^*}(0) = Z_{Y^*}(0)$. Let $Z_{X^*}(t_0^-) \geq Z_{Y^*}(t_0^-)$ and let there be a departure at time t_0. By Lemma 12, we know that, $X^*(t_0^-) \geq Y^*(t_0^-)$. Therefore, $Z_{X^*}(t_0) \geq Z_{Y^*}(t_0)$ by the coupling construction. □

PROOF. (of Theorem 4)
By Lemmas 12 and 13, for any sample path,

$$X^*(t) + Z_{X^*}(t) \geq Y^*(t) + Z_{Y^*}(t).$$

Therefore, for every sample path, the number of requests already served (not deferred) or being served by the servers by a content delivery system implementing the GENIE policy is more than that by any other storage policy. This implies that for each sample path, the number of requests deferred by GENIE is less than that of any other storage policy. Sample path dominance in the coupled system implies stochastic dominance of the original process. Using this and Lemma 11, we have that,

$$D^{(GENIE)}(t) \leq_{st} D^{(\mathcal{A})}(t).$$

□

6. PROOF OF THEOREM 5

PROOF. (of Theorem 5) The key idea of the GENIE policy is to ensure that at any time t, if the number of idle servers is $k(t)$, the $k(t)$ most popular contents are stored on exactly one idle server each. Since the total number of servers is n, and the number of content-types is $m = \alpha n$ for some constant $\alpha > 1$, all content-types C_i for $i > n$ are never stored on idle servers by the GENIE policy. This means that under the GENIE policy, all arrivals for content types C_i for $i > n$ are deferred. For $\beta > 2$, for all i, $p_i \geq \frac{6}{\pi^2} i^{-\beta}$. The cumulative mass of all content types $i = n+1, ..\alpha n$ is

$$\sum_{i=n+1}^{\alpha n} p_i \;\geq\; \sum_{i=k}^{\alpha n} \frac{6}{\pi^2} i^{-\beta} \geq \int_{n+1}^{\alpha n+1} \frac{6}{\pi^2} i^{-\beta} di$$
$$\geq\; \frac{0.54}{\pi^2(\beta-1)} \frac{1}{(n+1)^{\beta-1}},$$

for n large enough.

Let the length of the interval of interest be b. The expected number of arrivals of types $n+1, n+2, ..\alpha n$, in the interval of interest is at least $\frac{0.54 b\bar{\lambda} n}{\pi^2(\beta-1)} \frac{1}{(n+1)^{\beta-1}}$. Therefore, the expected number of jobs deferred by the GENIE policy in an interval of length b is $\Omega(n^{2-\beta})$. □

7. RELATED WORK

Our model of content delivery systems shares several features with recent models and analyses for content placement and request scheduling in multi-server queueing systems [10, 11, 15, 18]. All these works either assume known demand statistics, or a low-dimensional regime (thus permiting "easy" learning). Our study is different in its focus on unknown, high-dimensional and time-varying demand statistics, thus making it difficult to consistently estimate statistics. Our setting also shares some aspects of estimating large alphabet distributions with only limited samples, with early contributions from Good and Turing [6], to recent variants of such estimators [13, 16].

Our work is also related to the rich body of work on the content replication strategies in peer-to-peer networks, e.g., [3, 4, 8, 9, 12, 14, 22, 25, 26]. Replication is used in various contexts: [14] utilizes it in a setting with large storage limits, [9, 12] use it to decrease the time taken to locate specific content, [3, 25, 26] use it to increase bandwidth in the setting of video streaming, and [4] uses it to minimize the number of hosts that need to be probed to resolve a query for a file in unstructured peer-to-peer networks.

However, the common assumption is that the number of content-types does not scale with the number of peers, and that a request can be served in parallel by multiple servers (and with increased network bandwidth as the number of peers with a specific content-type increases) which is fundamentally different from our setting.

Finally, our work is also related to the vast literature on content replacement algorithms in server/web cache management. As discussed in [19], parameters of the content (e.g., how large is the content, when was it last requested) are used to derive a cost, which in-turn, is used to replace content. Examples of algorithms that have a cost-based interpretation include the Least Recently Used (LRU) policy, the Least Frequently Used (LFU) policy, and the Max-Size policy [20]. We refer to [19] for a survey of web caching schemes. There is a huge amount of work on the performance of replication strategies in single-cache systems; however the analysis of adaptive caching schemes in distributed cache systems under stochastic models of arrivals and departures is very limited.

8. ACKNOWLEDGEMENTS

We acknowledge the support of NSF Grant CNS-0964391, ARO Grant W911NF-11-1-0265 and DTRA Grant HDTRA1-13-1-0024.

9. CONCLUSIONS

In this paper, we considered the high dimensional setting where the number of servers, the number of content-types, and the number of requests to be served over any time interval all scale as $O(n)$; further the demand statistics are not known a-priori. This setting is motivated by the enormity of the contents and their time-varying popularity which prevent the consistent estimation of demands.

The main message of this paper is that in such settings, separating the estimation of demands and the subsequent use of the estimations to design optimal content placement policies ("learn-and-optimize" approach) is order-wise suboptimal. This is in contrast to the low dimensional setting, where the existence of a constant bound on the number of content-types allows asymptotic optimality of a learn-and-optimize approach.

10. REFERENCES

[1] M. Ahmed, S. Traverso, M. Garetto, P. Giaccone, E. Leonardi, and S. Niccolini. Temporal locality in today's content caching: why it matters and how to model it. *ACM SIGCOMM Computer Communication Review*, 43(5):5–12, October 2013.

[2] L. Breslau, P. Cao, L. Fan, G. Phillips, and S. Shenker. Web caching and Zipf-like distributions: Evidence and implications. In *IEEE INFOCOM'99*, pages 126–134, 1999.

[3] D. Ciullo, V. Martina, M. Garetto, E. Leonardi, and G. Torrisi. Stochastic analysis of self-sustainability in peer-assisted VoD systems. In *IEEE INFOCOM*, pages 1539–1547, 2012.

[4] E. Cohen and S. Shenker. Replication strategies in unstructured peer-to-peer networks. In *ACM SIGCOMM Computer Communication Review*, volume 32, pages 177–190. ACM, 2002.

[5] P. Gill, M. Arlitt, Z. Li, and A. Mahanti. YouTube traffic characterization: A view from the edge. In *7th ACM SIGCOMM Conference on Internet Measurement*, pages 15–28, 2007.

[6] I. J. Good. The population frequencies of species and the estimation of population parameters. *Biometrika*, 40(3-4):237–264, 1953.

[7] A. Iamnitchi, M. Ripeanu, and I. Foster. Small-world file-sharing communities. In *IEEE INFOCOM*, March 2004.

[8] J. Kangasharju, K. Ross, and D. Turner. Optimizing file availability in peer-to-peer content distribution. In *INFOCOM*, 2007.

[9] J. Kangasharjua, J. Roberts, and K. Ross. Object replication strategies in content distribution networks. *Computer Communications* 25:376–383, 2002.

[10] M. Leconte, M. Lelarge, and L. Massoulie. Bipartite graph structures for efficient balancing of heterogeneous loads. In *the 12th ACM SIGMETRICS Conference*, pages 41–52, 2012.

[11] M. Leconte, M. Lelarge, and L. Massoulie. Adaptive replication in distributed content delivery networks. *Preprint*, 2013.

[12] Q. Lv, P. Cao, E. Cohen, K Li, and S. Shenker. Search and replication in unstructured peer-to-peer networks. In *16th international conference on Supercomputing*, 2002.

[13] A. McAllester and R. Schapire. On the convergence rate of Good-Turing estimators. In *COLT Conference*, pages 1 – 6, 2000.

[14] B. Tan and L. Massoulie. Optimal content placement for peer-to-peer video-on-demand systems. *IEEE/ACM Trans. Networking*, 21:566–579, 2013.

[15] J. Tsitsiklis and K. Xu. Queueing system topologies with limited flexibility. In *SIGMETRICS '13*, 2013.

[16] G. Valiant and P. Valiant. Estimating the unseen: An n/log (n)-sample estimator for entropy and support size, shown optimal via new clts. In *Proceedings of the 43rd annual ACM Symposium on Theory of Computing*, pages 685–694, 2011.

[17] E. Veloso, V. Almeida, W. Meira, A. Bestavros, and S. Jin. A hierarchical characterization of a live streaming media workload. In *Proceedings of the 2nd ACM SIGCOMM Workshop on Internet measurment*, pages 117–130, 2002.

[18] R. B. Wallace and W. Whitt. A staffing algorithm for call centers with skill-based routing. *Manufacturing and Service Operations Management*, 7:276–294, 2007.

[19] J. Wang. A survey of web caching schemes for the Internet. *ACM SIGCOMM Computer Communication Review*, 29:36–46, 1999.

[20] S. Williams, M. Abrams, C. Standridge, G. Abdulla, and E. Fox. Removal policies in network caches for world-wide web documents. In *SIGCOMM'96*, 1996.

[21] S. Williams, M. Abrams, C. Standridge, G. Abdulla, and E. Fox. Caching proxies: limitations and potentials. In *the 4th International WWW Conference*, December 1995.

[22] W. Wu and J. Lui. Exploring the optimal replication strategy in P2P-VoD systems: Characterization and evaluation. *IEEE Transactions on Parallel and Distributed Systems*, 23, August 2012.

[23] www.youtube.com/yt/press/statistics.html.

[24] H. Yu, D. Zheng, B. Zhao, and W. Zheng. Understanding user behavior in large scale video-on-demand systems. In *EuroSys*, April 2006.

[25] X. Zhou and C. Xu. Optimal video replication and placement on a cluster of video-on-demand servers. In *International Conference on Parallel Processing*, pages 547–555, 2002.

[26] Y. Zhou, T. Fu, and D. Chiu On replication algorithm in P2P-VoD. *IEEE/ACM Transactions on Networking*, pages 233 – 243, 2013.

Network-Design Sensitivity Analysis

Paul Tune and Matthew Roughan
School of Mathematical Sciences
The University of Adelaide, Australia
{paul.tune,matthew.roughan}@adelaide.edu.au

ABSTRACT

Traffic matrices are used in many network engineering tasks, for instance optimal network design. Unfortunately, measurements of these matrices are error-prone, a problem that is exacerbated when they are extrapolated to provide the predictions used in planning. Practical network design and management should consider sensitivity to such errors, but although robust optimisation techniques exist, it seems they are rarely used, at least in part because of the difficulty in generating an ensemble of admissible traffic matrices with a controllable error level. We address this problem in our paper by presenting a fast and flexible technique of generating synthetic traffic matrices. We demonstrate the utility of the method by presenting a methodology for robust network design based on adaptation of the *mean-risk analysis* concept from finance.

Categories and Subject Descriptors

C.2.1 [**Computer Communications**]: Network architecture and design; C.4 [**Performance of Systems**]: Modeling Techniques

Keywords

Mean-risk analysis; network design; network planning; sensitivity analysis; traffic matrix synthesis

1. INTRODUCTION

Network planning is a crucial task for maintaining the operational status quo of an existing network, as well as integration of future link expansions and technology into the network. Examples of some planning tasks include optimising the capacity of links and assigning an optimal routing plan based on the network topology and link capacities. All these tasks require a key input: the *traffic matrix*.

Unfortunately, the traffic matrix is not easy to measure accurately [26]. Inferring the traffic matrix from indirect measurements is an ill-conditioned, underconstrained problem, resulting in errors. Direct measurement methods are rarely economically viable, and sampling introduces errors. Moreover, planning must be performed using predicted traffic matrices, and *planning horizons* may be as long as a year in advance. Prediction errors may therefore be substantial, even when good data is available. In green-fields planning [19], predictions may be highly inaccurate.

As a result, an alternative set of ideas have been proposed: oblivious routing [1], and Valiant network design [31], which seek to design a network and its routing so as to work well with any traffic matrix. These network designs are *oblivious* to the traffic matrix, *i.e.*, the network performance is guaranteed for any matrix. The penalty is a loss of efficiency, as the network must be over-engineered by as much as a factor of two.

In reality, there is some information about the network beforehand, and this is useful in constraining the set of likely traffic matrices. The information allows operators to make informed guesses even in green-fields planning. The information may be coarser than needed and certainly contains errors, so we need an approach that finds the middle ground between complete ignorance and omniscience.

The other issue for oblivious approaches is that different operators may have different degrees of *risk aversion*. There is a continuous tradeoff between over-engineering to allow for potential unknowns, and the risk of congestion and its resultant performance degradation. Some operators may be sanguine about congestion, allowing it on occasion in order to provide a cheaper service, whereas others may wish to provide a "gold-class" service, with guaranteed SLAs, and are prepared to pay the extra cost required.

We start with the simple idea that operators should at least understand the sensitivity of their designs to prediction errors, and take these into account as part of planning. Arguably, the simplest approach requires a method to generate an ensemble of traffic matrices that model the errors in the predicted matrix. Such matrices must be:

- *admissible*, *i.e.*, that satisfy some set of constraints (*e.g.*, non-negativity);
- *centred*, *i.e.*, their average centres on the predicted matrix; and
- *controlled*, *i.e.*, their variance around the predicted matrix can be controlled, ideally through a simple, linear parameter.

The canonical example of such an ensemble in many practical situations is IID (Independent Identically Distributed)

SIGMETRICS'14, June 16–20, 2014, Austin, Texas, USA.

ACM 978-1-4503-2789-3/14/06 ...$15.00.
http://dx.doi.org/10.1145/2591971.2591979.

Gaussian additive noise. However, in our problem, simple additive noise fails the first two criteria. We present here a method satisfying these criteria.

In addition, we wish the ensemble to be as realistic as possible, though this is intrinsically hard to test given the fact that we can't (by the nature of the problem) obtain a complete ensemble of such data against which to compare the synthetic matrices. Instead, here we test the *usefulness* of our model[1] in the network capacity planning problem.

We do not aim to provide novel optimisation algorithms, but simply to demonstrate the importance and utility of an ensemble of "error" matrices. We do so through a proposed framework to optimise traffic engineering metrics of a network in a systematic way. Our framework is based on *mean-risk analysis* ideas, commonly used in finance for portfolio management. The key idea here is to develop both a *utility function* and simple model of *risk averseness* of a network operator with regard to chosen traffic engineering metrics against which we can optimise.

To summarise, our main contributions are:

- a fast, flexible and simple algorithm to generate an ensemble of synthetic traffic matrices around a predicted traffic matrix possessing desirable criteria such as admissibility, centredness and controlled by a single linear parameter,
- theoretical results on the performance of the algorithm, which are empirically validated on real traffic,
- evaluation of the sensitivity of important network designs with respect to edge capacity prediction errors via the use of our synthetic traffic matrices, and
- a simple framework for network design optimisation incorporating robustness into the design using our synthetic traffic matrices.

We validated our results using real traffic from the Abilene network [15].

2. BACKGROUND

2.1 Traffic Matrices

A traffic matrix describes the volume of traffic (typically in bytes) from one point in a network to another during some time interval. Its natural representation is a three dimensional array $\mathbf{T}(\tau)$ with elements $t_{i,j}(\tau)$ that represent the traffic volume from source i to destination j during the time interval $[\tau, \tau + \Delta\tau)$. Time intervals depend on the time resolution of measurements, and the aim is to be able to observe a stationary sequence of measurements. Typical intervals are of the order of minutes to hours (5, 15, and 60 minutes are very common). In our applications, the locations i and j will either be routers or, more typically Points-of-Presence (PoPs), and we only consider Ingress/Egress (IE) traffic matrices here (not underlying Origin/Destination (OD) matrices as these are usually unobservable). We will denote the number of ingress and egress points by N. Throughout the paper, we concentrate on a single snapshot of the traffic matrix at time τ, so we will omit the time index for convenience. For a much more complete description of all of the issues involved in such a matrix please see [26].

[1] We remind the reader of the quote "Essentially, all models are wrong, but some are useful." [2, p. 424]

The best current practice for measuring a network's traffic matrix is to use sampled flow-level measurements (*e.g.*, [7]). These measurements provide traffic matrices on a time granularity on the order of minutes, but these matrices will contain errors. Such errors arise from sampling and from lack of synchronisation in time intervals used in measurements. Control and calibration of the size of these errors, as far as we are aware, is not currently implemented. However, one might hope they were fairly small, say at the level of a few percent, in a well-engineered measurement system.

Alternative approaches to direct (sampled) collection include a body of research [13, 28–30] devoted to developing traffic matrix inference methods from more easily collected link-load measurements. These methods, however, are limited by the underconstrained nature of the problem, so average errors on the order of 10–20% are possible. Despite these errors, [22] showed that traffic engineering tasks, such as routing, can certainly benefit from an inferred traffic matrix as compared to having no knowledge whatsoever.

More importantly, one of the underlying themes of that research is that it is much easier to measure the traffic volumes on links than it is to determine where that traffic is going (and hence the traffic matrix). As a result, it is quite easy to measure values such as the row sums of the traffic matrices $r_i = \sum_j t_{i,j}$ (which tell us the total traffic coming into a PoP) and the column sums $c_j = \sum_i t_{i,j}$ (which tell us the total traffic leaving through a PoP).

Network planning requires forecasting future traffic matrices to the date relevant for the plans, the time in advance often called the *planning horizon*. The prediction process may vary, but it will inevitably introduce prediction errors. Common sources of error are

- *Statistical inference errors:* due to stochastic variability within the model, *i.e.*, the model for the data is a good approximation, but the particular realisation we observed varies from that predicted.
- *Large, short-term fluctuations from the prediction:* *e.g.*, routing changes (either caused by internal link failures, or external routing policy changes), can alter the egress points of traffic, altering the IE traffic matrix (even if the underlying OD matrix remains unchanged) [25]; or flash-crowds can cause large, short-term changes to traffic. Some of these changes might be considered simple stochastic variation (as above), but some are larger, and more sudden than can be accounted for by normal variation, and their causes can often be identified as singular events.
- *Modelling errors:* resulting from use of a prediction technique whose underlying model is inaccurate over the prediction period. For instance, growth in traffic may appear to be exponential over some period, but actually be logistic (appearing exponential early on, but slowing as demand becomes saturated).

Modelling errors should be preventable by careful analysis of sufficient periods of historical data. The other two fluctuations are intrinsically hard to prevent, and it is these that we primarily focus on here.

The level of aggregation of traffic is often a large factor in the size of these stochastic prediction errors. Large aggregates of traffic are more predictable because they statistically aggregate the behaviour of many more sources. It is natural then to expect errors to have some dependence on the size of traffic matrix element. Traffic matrix elements have a somewhat skewed distribution (with many small values, and few large) though not formally heavy-tailed [17, 18, 24], implying that we have a large group of smaller, more inaccurate predictions, and a smaller group of large, but comparatively accurate predictions. The Norros model [16], empirically tested in [20] and somewhat based on equivalent assumptions to the independent flow model [6] proposed for traffic matrices, proposes that variance should be proportional to the mean of the traffic. Moreover, the model has consistent variances for aggregated traffic. We need an error model satisfying this property, which we call *proportional error variance aggregation*, or PEVA.

We might also reasonably assume that prediction errors for aggregates such as the $2N$ row and column sums of a traffic matrix will be smaller than for the N^2 elements. Moreover, prediction of PoP (in/out) volumes can take advantage of demographic, marketing, business and financial predictions much more easily than can the $t_{i,j}$.

The point we are making is that traffic matrix (and related data) contains considerable value, but it must be assumed that it contains errors. However, these errors are not completely arbitrary. Larger matrix elements have smaller relative errors, and aggregates (such as row and column sums) often have much smaller errors than those in the traffic matrix elements themselves.

2.2 Mean-Risk Analysis

The literature on network planning (and related optimisation problems) is vast (for instance see [3]), and we do not aim to survey it here. However, relatively few network operators seem to use formal optimisation as part of their design process, and none that we are aware of use robust optimisation (where robust is used here to mean that the solutions are not sensitive to uncertainty in the inputs).

The approach we adopt here extends the ideas of mean-risk analysis – one approach for the analysis of the potential volatility in financial portfolio returns.

Generally, operators are interested in maximising the utilisation of the network, but at the same time, providing enough capacity to meet network policies and quality of service (QoS) constraints for the customers' applications. A common approach to allow for uncertainty (say, because of prediction errors) is to include some engineering *overhead*, or *over-dimensioning*. That is, instead of designing a network to carry the predicted traffic, the network is designed to carry this traffic, multiplied by some *safety* factor.

A simple tradeoff arises here: if the network is over-engineered with a high factor, there is much lower risk in the sense that it is able to cope with unexpected traffic, but at a higher cost. Different operators use different factors, based on experience and their degree of risk aversion. Yet, few if any operators formally calculate risk, and specify precisely what their degree of risk aversion is. Our approach – mean-risk analysis – makes this tradeoff explicit through the calculation of an appropriate measure of risk for networks.

To the best of our knowledge, a direct application of mean-risk analysis to network design has not been developed. One paper introducing a measure of risk in the context of routing, called the *bit risk mile*, is [5]. Risk here is directly related to the geographic distance and the expected outage between a source and a destination PoP on a particular path. Although a concept of *risk* was used, their definition is not the same as ours, as they study routing, whereas here we study the network design, which requires the traffic matrix.

The closest work to introduce some of these ideas, in the context of maximising bandwidth revenue of a network, is [14]. The paper discussed how a network operator can balance between wholesale and retail bandwidth revenue against his risk averseness by formulating an optimisation problem and studying the properties of the solution. However, it was assumed the underlying distribution of the revenue (a truncated Gaussian distribution) is known, and the network operator is thus able to compute the mean and standard deviation. Such an assumption is common in finance problems.

However, the multi-dimensional nature of traffic matrices, and the constraints on these matrices prevent us from providing a closed-form for the distribution of these matrices. Instead, we use our synthetic model to calculate risk, and it is this we describe next.

3. TRAFFIC MATRIX SYNTHESIS

Our main goal is to generate an ensemble of traffic matrices to test a network design. Not every matrix, however, can be a traffic matrix. As noted in the introduction such a traffic matrix must be *admissible*, which means that it satisfies some set of constraints. There are multiple possible constraints, but for illustration purposes in this paper we will focus on 4 simple, intuitive, and yet reasonably powerful constraints. For a matrix $\mathbf{T} = [t_{i,j}]$, we have

(i) *Non-negativity*: $t_{i,j} \geq 0, \forall i \ j = 1, 2, \cdots, N$,

(ii) *Row sums*: $\sum_j t_{i,j} = r_i, \forall i$

(iii) *Column sums*: $\sum_i t_{i,j} = c_j \ \ \forall j$, and

(iv) *Total traffic*: $\sum_{i,j} t_{i,j} = \sum_i r_i = \sum_j c_j = T$,

where row and column sums are summarised in vectors $\mathbf{r}$ and $\mathbf{c}$ respectively. The last constraint is actually redundant given the previous constraints, but we include it for its explanatory value.

The constraints above are motivated by the fact that the row and column sums represent the total ingress and egress traffic of a network, which are relatively easy to obtain from SNMP information [26]. We aim to preserve the row, column and total traffic constraints because these will allow us to make fair comparisons between different network designs (see case studies in Sections 4 and 5). In general we might replace the row, column and total traffic constraints with any set of linear (or more generally, convex) constraints on the matrix, but we use the single constraints above for illustration because of their clear meanings in context.

Previous work [17, 18] focussed on generating such matrices, with the additional aim of matching some statistical properties of empirically measured matrices. The main difference between those papers, and ours is that we also aim to generate matrices which are *centred* [2] around a predicted matrix, with *controlled* variation around that matrix.

[2] It is perhaps more common to refer to "centring" as lack of bias, but we prefer the term here as we shall use it to mean lack of bias with respect to particular functions of expectation, not simple expectation.

For instance, the most commonly used noise models are additive, or multiplicative white noise, *i.e.*, we generate a matrix $\mathbf{Y}$ from prediction $\mathbf{T}$ by either

$$\begin{aligned} \textbf{Additive}: \quad & y_{i,j} = t_{i,j} + \sigma z_{i,j}, \\ \textbf{Multiplicative}: \quad & y_{i,j} = t_{i,j}(1 + \sigma z_{i,j}), \end{aligned}$$

where the $z_{i,j}$ are IID random variables forming the *error* or *noise* matrix $\mathbf{Z}$. In many cases, the $z_{i,j}$ would be Gaussian distributed with mean zero, and variance 1, *i.e.*, $z_{i,j} \sim \mathcal{N}(0,1)$, thus the parameter σ *controls* the variance of the errors, and both are centred (with respect to the average, or the average of the log, respectively).

However, simple generation methods are subtly difficult. We immediately see that with $z_{i,j} \sim \mathcal{N}(0,1)$ the two models above may generate inadmissible matrices, because they may violate non-negativity. Naturally, we truncate the distribution to prevent this, but that results in a significant number of "zero" elements of the resulting matrix, and this *uncentres* the matrix. Moreover, the resulting matrices no longer satisfy the row, column or total traffic constraints.

So the question remains: how can we generate a randomised traffic matrix satisfying the set of constraints? There are many possible noise models, and procedures for fitting constraints, however, we shall aim here to provide an approach which is intuitively well-matched to traffic matrix generation, as well as simple and fast (speed is important, as traffic matrices inhabit a high-dimensional space, so sensitivity analysis may require generation of a large number of these matrices to explore this space adequately).

3.1 Error Model and Non-Negativity

The goal of our approach is to guarantee the admissibility constraints are (at least in part) automatically satisfied by any matrix we generate. To do so we divide the constraints into *particular* constraints (the summation constraints, which are dependent on the particular network), and *universal* constraints (non-negativity), which all traffic matrices should satisfy.

Given the non-negativity, it is possible to write any traffic matrix $\mathbf{T} = [t_{i,j}]$ in the form

$$\mathbf{T} = \left[a_{i,j}^2\right],$$

where $a_{i,j} = \sqrt{t_{i,j}}$. The modification seems trivial, but given real values $a_{i,j}$, the matrix is now inherently non-negative. Moreover, the total traffic matrix constraint becomes

$$\sum_{i,j} a_{i,j}^2 = T,$$

so we can see the $a_{i,j}$s as lying on the N^2-dimensional hypersphere with radius $\sqrt{T}$.

Our approach, therefore, is to perturb the matrix by finding a new point on this hypersphere via an approximately additive model. This allows us to add noise in a controlled and centred manner, while preserving the universal constraint.

Our *Spherically Additive Noise Model* (SANM) is

$$y_{i,j} = (a_{i,j} + \beta z_{i,j})^2, \text{ for all } i, j, \tag{1}$$

where $z_{i,j} \sim \mathcal{N}(0,1)$, and $\beta \in [0, \infty)$ is a parameter we can use to tune the strength of the noise. We chose a simple IID noise process, as we have no *a priori* reason to assume correlations in the noise.

Although we allow the possibility of large β, as we shall see, there is a restricted range of reasonable values of β in practice. However, large β is not a detriment, as the model saturates to the gravity model as $\beta \to \infty$, see [27]. We will discuss this in-depth below.

The beauty of the simplicity of this model is that it guarantees non-negativity without truncation, and so not only does it not introduce zeros into the matrix, it is also simple to analyse. Since $z_{i,j} \sim \mathcal{N}(0,1)$, independent of $a_{i,j}$, we get

$$\begin{aligned} \mathbb{E}[y_{i,j}] &= \mathbb{E}\left[(a_{i,j} + \beta z_{i,j})^2\right] \\ &= \mathbb{E}\left[a_{i,j}^2 + 2\beta a_{i,j} z_{i,j} + \beta^2 z_{i,j}^2\right] \\ &= t_{i,j} + 2\beta \mathbb{E}[a_{i,j} z_{i,j}] + \beta^2 \mathbb{E}\left[z_{i,j}^2\right] \\ &= t_{i,j} + 2\beta a_{i,j} \mathbb{E}[z_{i,j}] + \beta^2 \\ &= t_{i,j} + \beta^2. \end{aligned}$$

This is not ideal (yet), because the resulting matrix clearly doesn't satisfy the centring condition, so a procedure is needed to force the matrix to satisfy the additional constraints.

3.2 Iterative Proportional Fitting (IPF)

The matrix $\mathbf{Y}$ no longer sits on the hypersphere defined by the total traffic constraints (or the manifolds defined by the other constraints). Intuitively, what we need is a procedure to *project* the perturbed solution onto the space defined by the set of constraints. We use the Iterative Proportional Fitting (IPF). Algorithm 1 and 2 outline our method. The algorithm is very simple indeed, with the only complication occurring in the implementation of IPF, which we detail below.

Input: $\mathbf{T}$, the predicted traffic matrix
Input: β, noise variance
Input: $\mathbf{r}$, $\mathbf{c}$, row and column sum constraints
Input: ϵ, tolerance for IPF
Output: $\mathbf{S}$, the synthetic traffic matrix
1 Generate $\mathbf{Z}$, with $z_{i,j} \sim \mathcal{N}(0,1)$
2 Generate $\mathbf{Y}$, where $y_{i,j} = (t_{i,j}^{1/2} + \beta z_{i,j})^2$
3 $\mathbf{S} = \text{IPF}(\mathbf{Y}, \mathbf{r}, \mathbf{c}, \epsilon)$ `/* See Algorithm 2 */`

Algorithm 1: Traffic Matrix Perturbation

IPF was originally developed to adjust contingency tables in statistics such that their marginals, given by the row and column sums, satisfy known constraints [4]. This is almost exactly what we aim to do, the only difference being terminology, where we apply IPF to traffic matrices instead. More recently, IPF has been adapted to work with an arbitrary set of measurement constraints (provided the constraints lie in a convex set) [11]. This implies that many types of constraints in network design can be incorporated into IPF. Here, we restrict our attention to only row and column sum constraints which naturally map to our current problem.

IPF consists of iteratively scaling the rows and columns of the matrix until the scaled row and column sums match the objective row and column sums (see Algorithm 2). Here, $*$ denotes a wildcard to specify the rows or columns of the matrix at once. The typical test for convergence is to compare the row and column sums of the iterate $\mathbf{S}^{(k)}$ to $\mathbf{r}$ and $\mathbf{c}$ at the end of each iteration k. Once the total difference falls below some required tolerance ϵ, the algorithm has converged.

Input: $\mathbf{Y}$, the raw perturbed traffic matrix
Input: $\mathbf{r}$, $\mathbf{c}$, row and column sum constraints
Input: ϵ, tolerance for IPF
Output: $\mathbf{S}$, the synthetic traffic matrix

$\mathbf{S}^{(0)} \leftarrow \mathbf{Y}$
$k \leftarrow 1$
while *(not converged)* **do**
    `/* Scale the rows */`
    for $i \leftarrow 1$ **to** N **do**
        $\mathbf{S}_{i,*}^{(k-1/2)} \leftarrow \mathbf{S}_{i,*}^{(k-1)} r_i / \sum_i \mathbf{S}_{i,*}^{(k-1)}$
    end
    `/* Scale the columns */`
    for $j \leftarrow 1$ **to** N **do**
        $\mathbf{S}_{*,j}^{(k)} \leftarrow \mathbf{S}_{*,j}^{(k-1/2)} c_j / \sum_i \mathbf{S}_{*,j}^{(k-1/2)}$
    end
    $k \leftarrow k+1$
end

Algorithm 2: Iterative Proportional Fitting (IPF)

IPF has a strong connection to the generalised Kullback-Leibler (GKL) divergence used in non-negative matrix decomposition [10]. IPF is an iterative, fixed-point solution to the problem of minimising the GKL divergence between the input to the final solution, subject to constraints (see proof in [27]). More complex algorithms can be used to solve this problem, but IPF's simplicity and fast convergence are ideal here.

An additional property of IPF worth mentioning is that it is guaranteed to converge to a solution satisfying the row and column constraints only if the initial input matrix is non-negative [4]. Our error model is guaranteed to be non-negative, so convergence is assured.

Moreover, IPF preserves zeros [4, 23]. Thus problematic zeros introduced by truncation (if a simplistic error model was used) would be retained by this step. This is undesirable, as real traffic matrices generally do not have many zero elements. Our model is unlikely to have zero elements for $\beta > 0$. Such an event occurs only if $t_{i,j}^{1/2} = -\beta z_{i,j}$, but since $z_{i,j}$ is a continuous random variable, this would occur with probability 0. So our noise model creates elements that are almost-surely positive (simulations confirm this, the results of which we omit here in the interest of space). Therefore, IPF's outputs are also positive.

IPF isn't novel, even in the context of traffic matrices, where it has been used to enforce row and column constraints before [29]. However, in the cases we are aware of, the method was being used as part of an inference technique, whereas here it is being used for synthesis.

3.3 Discussion

In this synthesis problem, we are essentially finding a set of random matrices $\mathbf{S} = \mathbf{T} + \mathbf{W}$ that satisfy a set of constraints

$$\mathcal{A}(\mathbf{S}) = \mathbf{b}.$$

The operator $\mathcal{A}$ might represent a set of measurement operations, where $\mathbf{b}$ are observed measurements, or in the preceding section we considered $\mathcal{A}$ to take row and column sums and $\mathbf{b}$ to be the specified values of those sums.

In general, however, we consider linear operators $\mathcal{A}$, and hence we are requiring that $\mathcal{A}(\mathbf{T}) = \mathcal{A}(\mathbf{S}) = \mathcal{A}(\mathbf{T} + \mathbf{W}) = \mathcal{A}(\mathbf{T}) + \mathcal{A}(\mathbf{W}) = \mathbf{b}$, or

$$\mathcal{A}(\mathbf{W}) = \mathbf{0},$$

i.e., the noise $\mathbf{W}$ must lie in the null space of $\mathcal{A}$, though with the additional complication of requiring non-negativity.

One method of finding such matrices is by defining a manifold on which all valid traffic matrices reside and forming the above additive model on this manifold. However, that requires (i) defining invertible maps between the manifold and the generated traffic matrices and (ii) search algorithms on manifolds (which are much slower than IPF). For instance, see [8] for an example of a manifold and its relationship to IPF. So the approach we propose is solving a more general problem, but in a fast, easy to implement manner.

Although some measurements are more accurate, they are not perfect. For example, the row and column sums may contain errors, albeit small. The row and column sums themselves may be subject to variations in traffic over time. Either way, regularisation methods may be used to handle variations of these measurements, but a simpler way we adopt in the paper is to add a small amount of noise to the constraint values $\mathbf{b}$ prior to traffic matrix generation. For a valid traffic matrix, the constraints must be self-consistent, for instance, the total of the row and column sums must be equal to the total traffic traversing the network, but this is easy to ensure. So the SANM allows controllable errors in the constraints as well as the generated traffic matrices themselves. We test SANM on variations of the row and column sums in a case study in Section 4.2.

It is worth noting that our method does not constraint the individual elements of the traffic matrix directly. One motivation for direct constraints occurs between the different customers of an ISP, as each may have different SLAs, and are therefore each sensitive to different variations in traffic. To capture these variations, ideally, one would have to define a distribution to specify the traffic variations. It is possible to do so in our model, however, this would (i) require additional work in specifying the type of noise used in SANM, as the noise may no longer be IID, and (ii) define new constraints in IPF.

3.4 Properties

Two criteria for this model were that it be centred and controllable. The SANM is nonlinear, and hence somewhat hard to analyse, but intuitively, IPF is finding the *closest* point on the appropriate manifold to project the perturbed solution to, so we might hope for these properties.

Analytically, we consider the simplest case where the row and column constraints are ignored, and only the total traffic constraint is included (for more complex row and column problems we quantify the effect in the following section). In the simple case, IPF will scale the values so that the total is correct, *i.e.*,

$$\mathbb{E}[s_{i,j}] = c\mathbb{E}[y_{i,j}] = c\left(t_{i,j} + \beta^2\right).$$

The scaling constant c will be chosen so that $\sum_{i,j} s_{i,j} = T$, so we know that

$$\mathbb{E}\left[\sum_{i,j} s_{i,j}\right] = c\mathbb{E}\left[\sum_{i,j} t_{i,j} + \beta^2\right] = c\left(T + N^2\beta^2\right) = T,$$

and so

$$c = \frac{1}{1 + N^2\beta^2/T}.$$

Take the average matrix element to be $\bar{t} = T/N^2$ and we get

$$\mathbb{E}[s_{i,j}] = \frac{t_{i,j} + \beta^2}{1 + \beta^2/\bar{t}} = t_{i,j} + \beta^2\left(1 - \frac{t_{i,j}}{\bar{t}}\right) + O(\beta^4).$$

So, in expectation, larger elements of the matrix become smaller, and smaller elements become larger, but the effect is $O(\beta^2)$, and so for small values of β the non-linearity is negligible. We therefore have approximate centring of the synthetic matrices.

In addition, we can consider the variance of the synthetic matrix about the predicted matrix by looking at the variance of $s_{i,j}$ and noting that, at least approximately this is the same as the variation around $t_{i,j}$:

$$\mathrm{Var}[s_{i,j}] = \mathbb{E}\left[s_{i,j}^2\right] - \mathbb{E}[s_{i,j}]^2 \simeq \mathbb{E}\left[s_{i,j}^2\right] - t_{i,j}^2 = \mathbb{E}\left[(s_{i,j} - t_{i,j})^2\right],$$

and

$$\begin{aligned}\mathbb{E}\left[s_{i,j}^2\right] &= c^2\mathbb{E}\left[y_{i,j}^2\right] = \frac{\mathbb{E}\left[(a_{i,j} + \beta z_{i,j})^4\right]}{(1 + \beta^2/\bar{t})^2} \\ &= t_{i,j}^2 + \beta^2 t_{i,j}\left(6 - 2\frac{t_{i,j}}{\bar{t}}\right) + O(\beta^4), \qquad (2)\end{aligned}$$

so the standard deviation of the variability around the predicted matrix is approximately linear in β, for small β. Averaging over the whole matrix to obtain a relative measure of standard deviation around matrix elements we get

$$\sqrt{\frac{1}{N^2}\sum_{i,j}\frac{\mathbb{E}\left[s_{i,j}^2\right] - t_{i,j}^2}{t_{i,j}^2}} \simeq \beta\sqrt{\frac{1}{N^2}\sum_{i,j}\frac{6}{t_{i,j}} - \frac{2}{\bar{t}}}. \qquad (3)$$

We will examine the range of linearity of this approximation empirically for the more general case including row and column constraints in the following section. We find the approximation to be very good in the range $0 \leq \beta \leq 0.2$, and reasonable for β up to 0.4.

Finally, as the noise level increases, *i.e.*, $\beta \to \infty$, and the errors are very large, **Y** becomes less informative as a prior, as useful information from **T** is overwhelmed by noise, resulting in a saturated response of each $s_{i,j}$. We prove that this response approaches the response of the gravity model $\mathbf{rc}^{\mathrm{T}}/T$ in [27].

This well-behaved asymptotic behaviour is another advantage of our model over the additive and multiplicative models. As the noise strength increases for the latter models, the generated traffic matrices depart significantly from realistic traffic matrices, due to the presence of a large number of zeros (the effect of truncation). In contrast, with our model, even with high noise, the generated traffic matrices can be used to study network designs under high uncertainty, *i.e.*, when predictions are way off the mark.

3.5 Validation

In the following results, the predicted traffic matrix **T** is a single snapshot from the Abilene [15] data, the average traffic over time 0200 to 0205 hours, 1st March 2004.

We first test the approximation (2). In Figure 1, we set $\beta = 0.2$ and plot approximation (2) against empirical measurements of $\mathbb{E}\left[s_{i,j}^2\right]$ (which also includes the row and column sum constraints), averaged over 1000 trials. The middle solid line denotes the equality between elements, *i.e.*, if the approximation equals $\mathbb{E}\left[s_{i,j}^2\right]$. We find that the fit is very good indeed, as the data points lie close to the solid line, despite the fact the approximation did not try to account for the row and column sum constraints. We have tested this with various predicted traffic matrices with similar results. The approximation is fair up to $\beta = 0.4$, beyond which the approximation quality degrades. This is not surprising since with small noise, there is less distortion to the row and column sums of **Y**, so the total traffic and non-negativity constraints have a bigger effect on the final output of IPF.

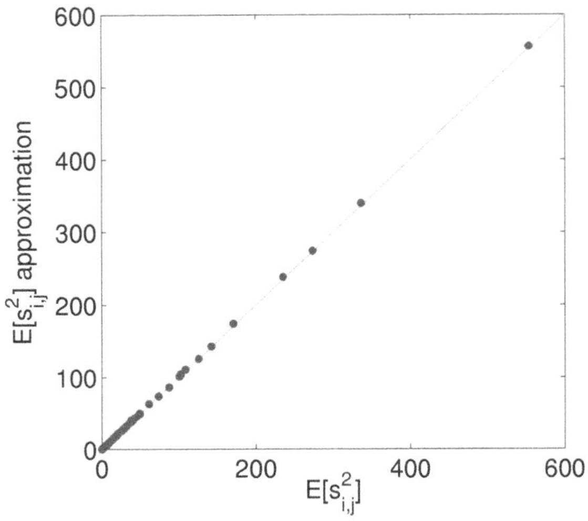

Figure 1: Testing the approximation (2) against IPF's output $\mathbb{E}\left[s_{i,j}^2\right]$ on a single snapshot from the Abilene [15] data, the average traffic over time 0200 to 0205 hours, 1st March 2004, with $\beta = 0.2$.

Our model also coincides with the intuition about the modelling of aggregated flows per the Norros model [21]. In real traffic, as flows are combined, the aggregated flow has a higher variance, and this variation is modelled to be proportional to the size of the aggregated traffic flow in the Norros model. These larger flows would naturally have larger measurement error. From approximation (2), we find the errors scale in proportion to $t_{i,j}$, aligning with the intuition of the Norros model. In the SANM, the error would therefore scale proportional to the size of the predicted traffic matrix's elements. We call this the *proportional error variance aggregation* (PEVA) property.

Another consideration is how far the generated traffic matrices are from the original input. Since the SANM is nonlinear, will there be significant distortions of the matrices?

We measure the distortion using the Mean Relative Square Error (MRSE) of the generated traffic matrices to the input **T**, defined by

$$\mathrm{MRSE}(\beta) = \sqrt{\frac{1}{N^2}\sum_{i,j}\frac{(s_{i,j}(\beta) - t_{i,j})^2}{t_{i,j}^2}}.$$

The metric quantifies the effect of the perturbation of IPF's solution to the predicted traffic matrix. Ideally, we would like a linear relationship between β and the MRSE, implying that $s_{i,j}$ is proportional to $t_{i,j}$, and this is predicted for small β by (3), but without row and column sum constraints. Here, we include those constraints and test the MRSE response.

We examine the MRSE response of IPF in Figure 2. The solid curve is the average response of the generated traffic matrices. The curve was generated from 200 data points,

Model	Parameter	Mean % zeros	Admissible	Centred	Controlled	PEVA
Additive	$\sigma = \bar{t}$	≈ 50.0	✓	✗	✓	✗
Multiplicative	$\sigma = 1$	13.6	✓	✗	✓	✗
SANM	$\beta = 0.2$	0.0	✓	✓	✓	✓

Table 1: Comparing the (truncated) additive, multiplicative and SANM over several important criteria. PEVA implies that the error of the generated matrix elements scale in proportion to the size of the predicted traffic matrix element as noise increases. Model parameters were chosen so that their MRSEs are roughly 1.

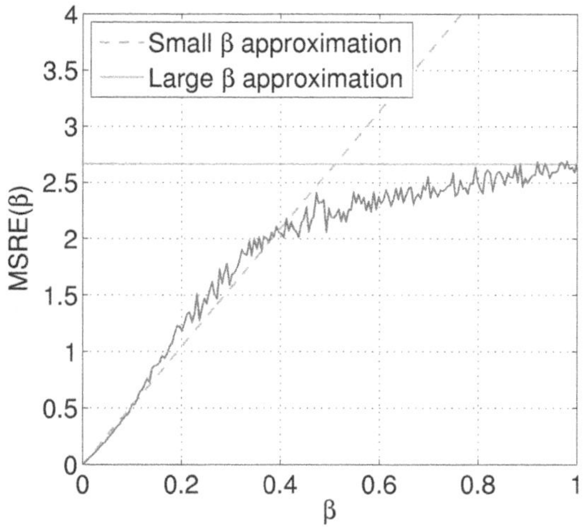

Figure 2: MRSE as a function of β. The solid curve is the average response of IPF's output over 1000 trials per data point. The predicted traffic matrix T is from Abilene data, the average traffic over time 0200 to 0205 hours, 1st March 2004. The dashed and flat lines show the approximation for small β (see approximation (3)) and large β (see details in [27]).

each data point an average of 1000 trials. The sloped dashed line is the response of the approximation (3) for the small β regime, while the flat line is the response of the gravity model for the large β regime.

In Figure 2, the response of the MRSE to β is almost linear up to about $\beta = 0.4$ before starting to saturate to the response of the gravity model (see [27]).

Table 1 compares the SANM against the (truncated) additive and multiplicative models across several important criteria. Their parameters were chosen so that their MRSEs are roughly 1. The SANM satisfies all the required criteria. Also, because the other models produce a high number of zeros, convergence of IPF based on their inputs is not guaranteed. In contrast, our model has both theoretical and empirical convergence guarantees.

In practice, the saturation is not a handicap in any way. Since we are mostly interested in variations around **T** in the MRSE range $(0, 1]$, so β does not have to exceed 0.2 in most cases. If there are large errors present in traffic measurements, then the measurements essentially convey no information in the first place. Our model handles large errors gracefully, since it produces a positive matrix almost surely, so IPF is guaranteed to converge to a solution, and that solution is the gravity model which is a reasonable choice in the absence of other information.

4. CASE STUDY 1: DESIGN COMPARISON

It is intrinsically difficult to determine whether our test matrices are "accurate". We are generating an ensemble of synthetic traffic matrices to model variability WRT a single real traffic matrix, so we don't have anything to compare against. Instead, we opt to demonstrate that they are *useful* via two simple case studies.

In our first study, we consider the question of whether oblivious design is wasteful given some, potentially flawed, information about the traffic matrix. Our approach is to test five design strategies:

Abilene: We will perform our test using the Abilene network data (from 2004), and so our baseline design will be the actual Abilene network, but rather than use the actual link capacities, we choose link capacities that are the minimum required to carry **T**, the predicted TM. Note that although these are not the real network capacities, this choice is made so that we can perform a fair comparison across all designs.

Robust Abilene: The previous network design assumed that we knew the traffic matrix **T** accurately, and chose capacities accordingly. Now we use the same set of links, but choose capacities to allow for errors in the traffic predictions. This is common practice in network design: first optimise the network according to an objective, then over-engineer to allow a margin of safety. In practice, the over-engineering may appear in the form of a constant factor determined empirically. Here, we shall explicitly use our synthesis methodology to determine how much over-engineered capacity is required. We generate a set of 100 synthetic matrices and set the link capacities so that we can carry any of these. This *robust* design then allows for errors in the traffic matrix inputs, but with some extra "overhead" capacity, which we will assess below as a function of β. Note that when $\beta = 0$, this design will be the same as the Abilene design.

Star: Also known as a "hub-and-spoke" design, it consists of a single central node with all other nodes connected to it. The central node has the highest access capacity as it needs to handle all incoming traffic from the other nodes. All traffic flows on this network travel at most two hops. The star design, with clever link capacity choices and load balancing, is the design with the minimum capacity required to serve *any* admissible traffic matrix with prescribed edge capacities, *i.e.*, row and column sums. It is therefore the optimal oblivious network. Although a common design amongst enterprise level networks, backbone networks do not use the star design as failure of the central node leads to catastrophic failure of the entire network.

Valiant (oblivious) design: The key idea here is a design of a network that can carry, without congestion, any admissible traffic matrix [31] with some failure resilience. This may sound impossible, but it does so by using the clever idea of indirect routing from switching. The network design is a clique (with links between all pairs of routers), and each packet is routed along two hops, rather than traversing a direct route. The first hop is spread amongst all of the available routers and the second is to the destination router. In [31], the authors show that this type of network design and load balancing combination can guarantee that any possible traffic matrix (given access link capacities) can be carried as long as sufficient capacity is allocated to the links. Moreover, they presented an algorithm for selecting the proportions of traffic which go to each intermediate node (oblivious of the actual traffic matrix) and for designing the correct network capacities. We apply this technique to derive a set of link capacities in a network, using the row and column sums of the traffic matrix to derive lower bounds on the access link capacity. We use the row and column sums of the predicted traffic matrix in our capacity planning rather than an arbitrary access link capacity because this will produce a tighter network design, and allow for a fairer comparison against other capacity planning techniques. The capacity of link connecting i to j is calculated according to [31]

$$x_{i,j} = \left(\sum_{k=1}^{N} \frac{w_k}{T - 2w_k} \right)^{-1} \left(\frac{w_i w_j}{T - 2w_j} + \frac{w_i w_j}{T - 2w_i} \right), \quad (4)$$

where $w_i := \max(r_i, c_i)$. The total capacity of the Valiant design is at most twice that of the star design.

Robust clique: If one seeks to minimise the bandwidth-distance product on a network, the optimal network design is a clique, where traffic only ever has to traverse a single hop. Although this is an obvious simplification of real costs, it provides a simple comparison against the Valiant design, which also uses a clique. The minimal link capacities are given by the corresponding traffic matrix element. However, as noted, we will not use the capacities determined by one traffic matrix, but rather, choose capacities that can carry any of our synthetic traffic matrices.

4.1 Experiment 1: Fixed c and r

We test the five designs with traffic matrices from Abilene [15]. The 2004 network had $N = 12$ PoPs. We draw one week of Abilene traffic matrices, starting from the first week of April 2004, aggregated into 168 one-hour traffic matrices, and we use these matrices as if they were the predicted traffic matrices $\mathbf{T}$. For each predicted matrix, we generate $M = 100$ synthetic matrices (using the procedure described above, assuming the $\mathbf{c}$ and $\mathbf{r}$ given by the matrix are correct), and calculate the total bandwidth $\times$ distance product for the network.

According to the simple optimisation used here, an efficient network would have a low bandwidth $\times$ distance product. When the errors in the prediction are zero (*i.e.*, $\beta = 0$) the clique will produce the optimal design, and so we use the bandwidth-capacity product of this network as a baseline, and measure all other networks as a factor of this capacity, hence the minimum possible value is 1. Thus we see the degree of "over-build" required by each strategy, as a function of the size of the prediction errors.

Figure 3(a) plots the total bandwidth miles (bandwidth $\times$ distance) for the different network designs.

Observe that the Valiant, star and Abilene network designs are constant WRT to β. The overbuild of the Valiant network is slightly over two because our choice of the baseline is not the star design. However, it is within a factor of two compared to the star design (about 1.3), confirming the results in [31]. These designs are two extremes: the first two assume no knowledge, and the second takes no account of errors, so neither changes WRT to β. Obviously, the Abilene strategy needs a much smaller overbuild, at the cost of being sensitive to errors in the inputs.

The second curve to note is the robust clique, whose performance stretches from optimal for $\beta = 0$ (as expected, though it might be surprising that the Abilene design does almost as well), to being quite poor for large β. This type of result is the key motivation for approaches such as Valiant design, which achieves much better performance when there is no information about traffic.

The big surprise is that the robust Abilene design is even more efficient than both of the alternative robust designs when there are significant prediction errors. What is happening here is that the shared nature of many of the main paths through the Abilene network allows errors in the traffic matrix to balance out (a fact that we shall make further use of below). In any case, we can see that for this relatively simple network, the designers did a pretty good job. More to the point, the completely oblivious approach is wasteful, given even moderately accurate data about traffic.

4.2 Experiment 2: Row/column variations

In the Valiant and star designs, the total access capacity at each PoP is assumed known. However, networks do evolve over time, say, as customers upgrade links or depart the network, so the total access capacity will change. Thus, there can be errors in predictions of the edge capacities. As with other designs, both the Valiant and star designs could accommodate such errors by over-engineering, and so in this section we compare robustness of the different designs allowing both variations in the traffic matrix, and variations in the row and column sums.

We chose a simple model for the errors in the predictions of the edge capacities by simply adding IID Gaussian noise to the row and column sums in our constraints. We scale these errors by $\beta/\sqrt{N}$, intentionally simulating that predictions for total incoming and outgoing traffic of a PoP are likely to be more accurate in comparison to predictions of individual traffic matrix elements.

Figure 3(b) plots the %–change WRT to the results in Figure 3(a). Most designs behave almost as before. The prediction errors in rows and columns are small compared to those in the traffic matrices, and so have little effect.

The robust clique has the highest variation, which is expected, because there is greater variation in generated traffic matrices due to the row and column sum variations.

The Valiant and star designs must account for these explicitly to remain oblivious, and hence their overall capacity requirement increase as the errors in the edge capacities increase. Although the star design maintains a total capacity less than twice that of the Valiant, its confidence intervals are larger. Due to prediction errors, the "optimal" central node chosen according to predictions may not be the optimal central node based on the true traffic matrix. One mistake would disrupt the carefully planned traffic load balance.

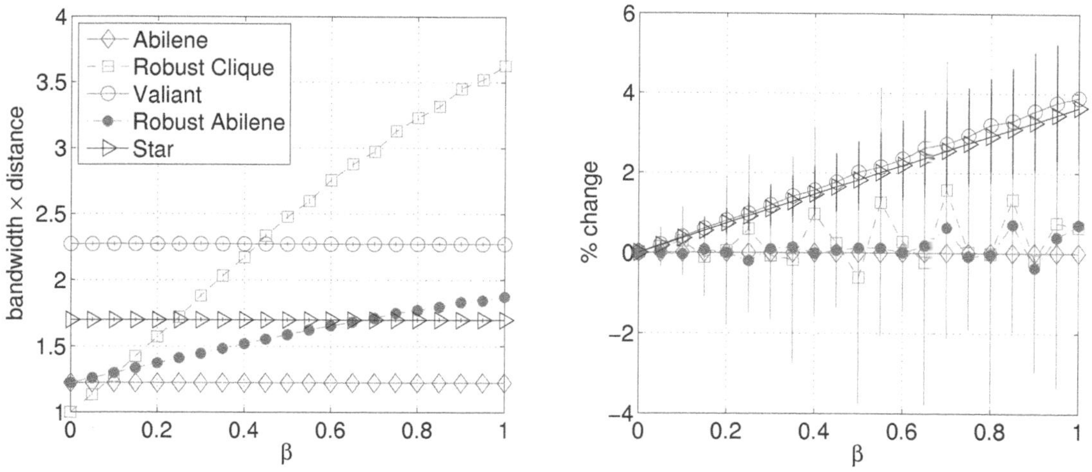

(a) Fixed row and column sums

(b) Variable row and column sums

Figure 3: Network design tests based on an average of performance over 168 Abilene traffic matrices relative to the optimal design. 95th percentile confidence intervals are given for the data. In (a), in most cases are so small as to be almost unobservable. In (b), the %-change over the fixed case is plotted, with little statistical variation except for the Valiant and star designs.

Both designs demonstrate a near linear relationship with β. These designs allocate capacities proportional to the total T. The assigned capacities would scale linearly with β, since we assign capacities by choosing the design with the maximum total capacity, which is a Gaussian distributed random variable with a standard deviation of $O(\beta)$, due to the prediction errors.

The example illustrates an interesting principle of robustness. Both designs attempt to carefully optimise the network, not against a particular traffic matrix, but all matrices given the edge capacities. They have strong protection against errors in individual elements of the traffic matrix, provided the measurement of edge capacities are accurate. When this assumption is violated, the performance of these designs degrade.

We point out that there are a number of simplifications here in our cost model and system constraints (typical link capacities are symmetric and constrained to take a fixed set of values). However, we have shown how the choice of network design algorithm can be influenced by the nature of the data we have available, and that illustrates very simply the value of being able to generate an ensemble of potential matrices to use in planning.

However, for all these approaches, there is no ability to tradeoff risk and value. Network operators would have to design the network to allow for any possible traffic generated by the model. In reality, operators have different degrees of risk aversion, and we consider network design in that context in the following section.

Moreover, our design approaches are only robustified versions of existing designs, *i.e.*, we choose the link capacities, but don't assess where the links should be. In the next case study we will allow for a full design process.

5. CASE STUDY 2: RISK TRADEOFFS

5.1 Mean-Risk Analysis and Network Design

The fundamental ideas of portfolio analysis trace back to Markowitz's famous work [12]. The objective was to construct a portfolio of financial assets yielding a better overall return compared to the individual assets at lower overall risk by selecting assets whose risk and return profiles are uncorrelated to balanced the total risk of the portfolio. In network design, we might consider multiplexing multiple traffic matrix elements on the same links to reduce the relative variance of the link flows to achieve a similar effect.

Mean-risk analysis is a simple, but useful approach within the (much larger) field of portfolio design. The goal (as suggested by the name) is to optimise the portfolio with respect to the average risk and utility. The assumption is that risk is bad, and so portfolio managers are *risk averse*, but to different degrees, so we aim solve the problem

$$\max_{\mathbf{x}} \quad \mathbb{E}_{\mathbf{y}}[U(\mathbf{x},\mathbf{y})] - \delta\, \mathbb{E}_{\mathbf{y}}[R(\mathbf{x},\mathbf{y})],$$

where $\mathbf{x}$ is a set of decision variables, and $\mathbf{y}$ are the potential outcomes (expectations are across the space of outcomes), and the optimisation may also contain some constraints. The parameter $\delta > 0$ allows the portfolio manager to tune their tradeoff between utility U and risk R. In the context of portfolios, utility is a given function of return (sometimes simply just the return itself), and there are various notions of risk, depending on context, often based on the variance or the standard deviation of the utility function.

It is worth noting, though, that choice of risk metric is non-trivial, and there is a considerable body of work on this factor alone in finance. Here, we propose a rudimentary mean-risk analysis for network design and management. A network operator wants to maximise a certain objective, say, the utilisation of the entire network, given a predicted traffic demand. In this case, the decision variables are the link capacities (which we will denote by $\mathbf{x}$, noting that $x_\ell > 0$ indicates that a link ℓ is present), the outcomes are the L

link traffics $\mathbf{y}$, and the utility function is the *total utilisation* of the network

$$U(\mathbf{x}, \mathbf{y}) = \sum_{x_\ell > 0} y_\ell / x_\ell.$$

Note that high utilisation of the network is important because high utilisation lowers the network cost per unit bit, and increases profits for given transit charges.

However, total utilisation is not the only metric that can be incorporated into the framework. Depending on the operator's objective, other metrics such as total link delay can certainly be included.

Risk is slightly harder to define. Simplistically, the risk here is that the bandwidth will be insufficient to accommodate traffic, resulting in congestion. The cost of congestion is that performance will suffer, and so SLAs may not be satisfied, or disappointed customers will leave the network, but quantification of these risks is difficult, so we aim to simply provide a measure of congestion. In finance, several decades of research has not yielded a perfect risk metric and this suggests there is potential for much further research on network risk metrics. We chose two simple alternatives for this case study, without claiming that either is the perfect choice. The two are:

- *Hard threshold*: $R(\mathbf{x}, \mathbf{y}) = \sum_{x_\ell > 0} [y_\ell / x_\ell - \gamma]^+$, where $[z]^+ = \max(z, 0)$. This measure enforces a hard threshold, with a tuneable *translation* parameter $\gamma > 0$ determining the placement of the threshold.
- *Soft threshold*: $R(\mathbf{x}, \mathbf{y}) = \sum_{x_\ell > 0} y_\ell / (x_\ell - y_\ell)$, though we improve performance by using the piece-wise linear approximation of $R(\mathbf{x}, \mathbf{y})$ developed for optimising OSPF weights [9], a relaxed version of the former. This measure provides more incentive to avoid heavily over-utilised links, and thus balance overall traffic more evenly across the network.

Note that these risk measures deal with correlation in traffic variations in very different ways, and the resulting network design would be reflective of the chosen risk measure. One could imagine all admissible traffic matrices as *stocks* in a portfolio, with link capacities as the *allocation proportion* for the entire network to form a joint portfolio. The hard threshold risk measure caps variations at each link to achieve overall lower utlisation, but the soft threshold allows some links with lower capacity to be sacrificed, *i.e.*, allowing more variations for a small number of links, while ensuring a low global utlisation. The former risk measure is similar to uniformly limiting the volatility of aggregates of stocks, while the latter is akin to proportionally allocating more to the best stocks in a portfolio. This will be clearer in our case study below.

Our optimisation problem is

$$\begin{array}{ll} \max\limits_{\mathbf{x}} & \mathbb{E}_{\mathbf{y}}[U(\mathbf{x}, \mathbf{y})] - \delta\, \mathbb{E}_{\mathbf{y}}[R(\mathbf{x}, \mathbf{y})] \\ \text{s.t.} & \mathbf{x} \geq \mathbf{0}, \text{ and } \mathbf{y} = \mathcal{A}_{\mathbf{x}}(\mathbf{S}),\ \mathbf{S} \in \mathcal{S}_{TM}, \end{array} \tag{5}$$

where $\mathcal{S}_{TM}$ is the set of admissible traffic matrices, and $\mathcal{A}_{\mathbf{x}}(\mathbf{S})$ represents the link loads resulting from routing the traffic matrix $\mathbf{S}$ across the network with capacities $\mathbf{x}$ ($\mathbf{x} \geq \mathbf{0}$ denotes element-wise non-negativity).

The optimisation is, in theory, performed on the expectation of our metrics over all admissible traffic matrices. Unfortunately, this is impractical as we don't know their true distribution, and even if we did the optimisation would likely be computationally intractable. Instead, our approach is to use our synthesis algorithm to generate an ensemble of traffic matrices, over which the solution to both problems can be approximated. This has a two-fold effect: first, performance of the most likely variations around the predicted traffic matrix can be assessed, and second, the time required to obtain a solution can be controlled by the number of generated traffic matrices.

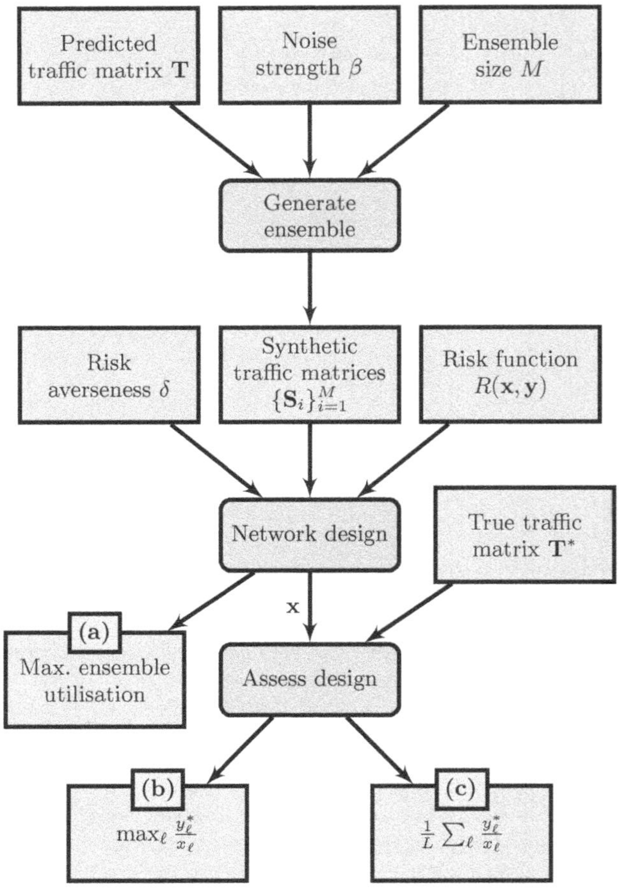

Figure 4: Flow chart of the design methodology with mean and risk tradeoffs. The rectangles denote the inputs and outputs at each stage, while the rounded rectangles are the stages in the methodology. Here, y_ℓ^* denotes the load on link ℓ with the true matrix $\mathbf{T}^*$. Labels on outputs match to Figures 5 and 6.

5.2 Experiments

We test the idea presented above as shown in Figure 4, though the reader should note that this is not intended to be a full exposition on network optimisation, but rather an example of how to use the synthetic matrices.

We start by using a predicted traffic matrix $\mathbf{T}$ to generate an ensemble of traffic matrices $\{\mathbf{S}_i\}_{i=1}^M$ with noise strength β. In order to make the scenario somewhat realistic, we will once again use the traffic matrix data from Abilene [15] (from 0000 to 0005 hours on the 1st March 2004), but this time the network designers do not have access to the true traffic matrix. They are only given a forecast on the incoming and outgoing traffic of the network, and they form a predicted matrix $\mathbf{T}^*$ using the gravity model [29]. This is the natural estimate given no other information [30], though it certainly does contain errors [29]. The tests below are over a range of 40 values of $\beta \in (0, 0.4]$, each with $M = 100$ matrices.

The real errors between $\mathbf{T}$ and $\mathbf{T}^*$ are known to us and we can calibrate the meaning of the results. The real MRSE is 1.33, which corresponds to $\beta_{err} \simeq 0.17$, well within the approximate linearity range, *i.e.*, $\beta \leq 0.2$. Note $\mathbf{T}^*$ here is not the same as that in Figure 2 and β_{err} was computed using approximation (3).

Once we have an ensemble of possible matrices, we perform the network design. We do so for the two risk functions described above (with $\gamma = 1$ in the hard threshold), and a range of risk averse parameters δ. Optimisation was performed by using the Matlab function `fmincon`. Despite the non-convex nature of the optimisation problem, the time taken to generate the 100 synthetic matrices and compute the optimal capacity design was approximately 2 minutes on a machine with a 3.06 GHz processor and 4 GB of RAM.

As the optimisation problem is non-convex, there is the possibility that the optimisation performs badly, so our first set of figures tests the quality of the optimisation. Although we optimise against total utilisation and risk, we assess performance here against maximum utilisation. We do so for two reasons: (i) the maximum provides a worst case measure of how badly the overall design can fail, and (ii) we wish to avoid the circularity of testing against exactly the same criteria against which we optimise. Figures 5(a) and 6(a) show the maximum utilisation across the whole ensemble. One immediately notes that for all δ, this increases almost linearly with β. This is entirely reasonable – as the variety in the ensemble increases (approximately linearly with β), the optimisation finds it harder to both ensure high average utilisation, and low maximum utilisation, and the maximum utilisation increases.

Importantly, however, the maximum utilisation decreases as we become more risk averse, and it is precisely this effect we are trying to achieve by tuning the parameter δ.

The performance of the network designs on the true traffic matrix is more important than the performance across the artificial ensemble. Figures 5 and 6 plots (b) and (c) show two performance metrics: the maximum and average utilisations for the network design, given the true Abilene traffic matrix $\mathbf{T}^*$. The maximum is a worst case measure of the risk (lower is better), and the average utilisation is a measure of the utility achieved (higher is better).

The maximum utilisation (for the true matrix) generally decreases with increasing risk aversion, though surprisingly there is little difference for the hard threshold between $\delta = 5$ and 10. As δ increases, we see that the average utilisations decrease. This is simply because as we become more risk averse, we provide more excess capacity to provide for inaccuracies, and so overall utilisation decreases.

Moreover, the maximum utilisation roughly decreases as β increases. Increasing β indicates that we have less confidence in our estimate, and so again we need to allow more *headroom* to allow for errors in predictions. Consequently we see that as β increases the average utilisation decreases.

However, note that we aren't just providing extra capacity to account for errors. As the parameters δ and β change, the actual network designs change. When we are more risk averse, or less sure about the accuracy of predictions, it makes sense to multiplex larger streams of traffic onto fewer links to reduce the relative variance of the link loads. We can see this in the non-smooth, non-linear nature of these functions. We can also see this in the fact that for the hard threshold, and moderate degrees of risk aversion, *e.g.*, $\delta = 5$, the average network utilisation is relatively insensitive to β, even as the maximum utilisation decreases. This is highly desirable, as we might only be able to estimate the prediction errors approximately.

The choice of risk metric obviously has a large effect on the results, though neither is universally *better*.

The Fortz-Thorup risk penalises heavy over-utilisation, but this depends on the load of the link. For links with small loads, a compromise is accepted where these links are allowed to be congested, as long as the overall network has a favourable average utilisation. Links with large loads matter more under this risk measure, so their utilisation is kept below 1. This can be seen in Figure 6(b) when β is small with $\delta = 1$, where the maximum utilisation with $\mathbf{T}^*$ only stabilises after $\beta = 0.1$, as the traffic matrix has a proportion of small elements. Once β increases, elements of the synthetic ensemble get larger, so the subsequent designs are over-provisioned as there are less links with small loads that can be "sacrificed". Thus, designs using this risk metric maintain average utilisation below 1, but may sacrifice some links in an effort to do so.

In contrast, the hard threshold penalises all overloads linearly, without normalising according to load size. Designs using the hard threshold would attempt to keep maximum utilisation near 1 for all links. So we see a more uniform response of the maximum and average utilisation across β when tested on $\mathbf{T}^*$.

Overall, for most given network designs the Fortz-Thorup risk is therefore larger, forcing both the maximum and average utilisations lower for a given δ. It also shows more sensitivity to the parameter β for maximum utilisation, and less for average, due to its sensitivity to the more extreme utilisations resulting from the traffic matrix ensemble.

Although increasing β and δ have somewhat similar effects (to decrease the risk, and to compensate, the overall utilisation also decreases), the parameters have different meanings. The parameter β is a technical measure of the accuracy of our predictions, while the parameter δ is a business parameter expressing the degree of our concern about congestion.

Finally, the main point of this given the actual prediction errors for Abilene, $\beta_{err} \simeq 0.17$, is that we could use the above to start to choose between designs. Given δ we can examine for the given risk metrics the designs based on a prediction, and use these to build a network robust against prediction errors, while still as efficient as possible.

6. CONCLUSION AND FUTURE WORK

In this paper, we examined the generation of synthetic traffic matrices for sensitivity analysis of network design algorithms. The main point we aim to get across is that all measurements contain errors and likewise with predictions. To further compound the problem, there are no "valid" traffic matrices and obtaining a ground truth to evaluate a network design with is nearly impossible. Thus, we advocate using fast, simple traffic matrix synthesis models so as to allow testing of network designs under variations around the predicted traffic matrix.

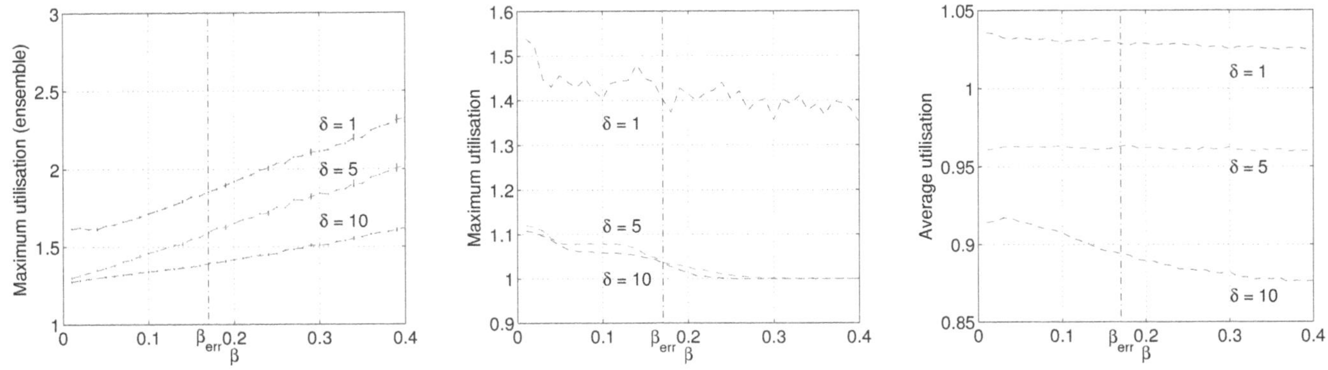

(a) Maximum utilisation over ensemble (b) Maximum utilisation (c) Average utilisation

Figure 5: Evaluating the network design with risk averseness $\delta = \{1, 5, 10\}$ using the hard threshold risk, with $\gamma = 1$, in the network optimisation for (a) the maximum utilisation over an ensemble of $M = 100$ synthetic matrices per data point, (b) the maximum utilisation and (c) average utilisation, when the true traffic matrix, a single snapshot taken from Abilene in 2004, is used in the network. $\beta_{err} = 0.17$ denotes the required noise strength to match the MRSE with respect to the true matrix $\mathbf{T}^*$.

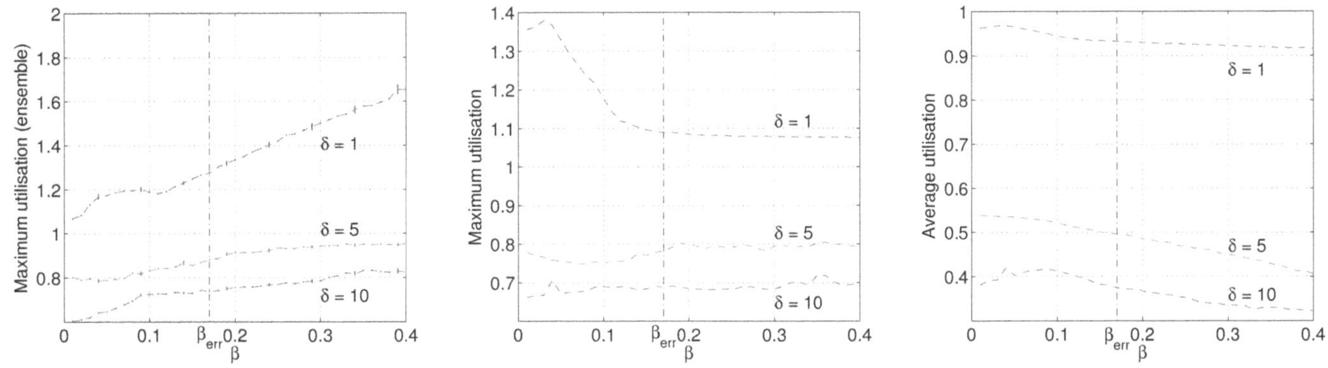

(a) Maximum utilisation over ensemble (b) Maximum utilisation (c) Average utilisation

Figure 6: Evaluating the network design with risk averseness $\delta = \{1, 5, 10\}$ using the Fortz–Thorup risk in the network optimisation for (a) the maximum utilisation over an ensemble of $M = 100$ synthetic matrices per data point, (b) the maximum utilisation and (c) average utilisation, when the true traffic matrix, a single snapshot taken from Abilene in 2004, is used in the network. $\beta_{err} = 0.17$ denotes the required noise strength to match the MRSE with respect to the true matrix $\mathbf{T}^*$.

The results in our paper demonstrate the usefulness of our approach. We can use our synthetic traffic matrices to understand network designs better, such as Valiant's lack of sensitivity to variations in incoming and outgoing traffic. Moreover, we can design networks with a degree of robustness to input errors. We have shown how robust versions of existing network designs can often be more resilient when faced with significant changes in the traffic matrix.

We further advanced a mean-risk analysis framework for network design. The rationale is that different network operators have different risk averseness. We used simple utility and risk functions, coupled with our traffic matrix synthesis algorithm to assign capacities to links of a network. These ideas were tested on real data and simulations. Future work will further extend and validate the framework with more traffic snapshots, and study other risk measures.

Sensitivity of network design algorithms to errors is important but is often ignored. If sensitivity and robustness to error receive more care, network optimisations might receive more attention from the operator community.

7. ACKNOWLEDGEMENTS

The authors wish to thank the anonymous reviewers for their useful feedback. This work was supported by the Australian Research Council Centre of Excellence for Mathematical and Statistical Frontiers (ACEMS).

8. REFERENCES

[1] D. Applegate and E. Cohen. Making intra-domain routing robust to changing and uncertain traffic demands: Understanding fundamental tradeoffs. In *ACM SIGCOMM*, pages 313–324, August 2003.

[2] G. E. P. Box and N. R. Draper. *Empirical Model-Building and Response Surfaces.* Wiley, 1987.

[3] R. S. Cahn. *Wide Area Network Design.* Morgan Kaufman, 1998.

[4] W. E. Deming and F. F. Stephan. On a least squares adjustment of a sampled frequency table when the expected marginal totals are known. *Ann. Math. Stat*, 11(4):427–444, 1940.

[5] B. Eriksson, R. Durairajan, and P. Barford. RiskRoute: A framework for mitigating network outage threats. In *CoNEXT '13*, pages 405–416, December 2013.

[6] V. Erramilli, M. Crovella, and N. Taft. An independent-connection model for traffic matrices. In *ACM IMC 2006*, pages 251–256, October 2006.

[7] A. Feldmann, A. Greenberg, C. Lund, N. Reingold, J. Rexford, and F. True. Deriving demands for operational IP networks: Methodology and experience. *IEEE/ACM Trans. Networking*, 9:265–280, June 2001.

[8] S. E. Fienberg. An iterative procedure for estimation in contingency tables. *Ann. Math. Stat.*, 41(3):907–917, 1970.

[9] B. Fortz and M. Thorup. Optimizing OSPF/IS–IS weights in a changing world. *IEEE J. Selected Areas in Communications*, 20(4):756–767, May 2002.

[10] D. D. Lee and H. S. Seung. Algorithms for non-negative matrix factorization. In *NIPS*, pages 556–562, 2000.

[11] G. Liang, B. Yu, and N. Taft. A fast lightweight approach to origin-destination IP traffic estimation using partial measurements. *IEEE/ACM Trans. Networking*, 14:2634–2648, June 2006.

[12] H. Markowitz. Portfolio selection. *The Journal of Finance*, 7(1):77–91, March 1952.

[13] A. Medina, N. Taft, K. Salmatian, S. Bhattacharyya, and C. Diot. Traffic matrix estimation: Existing techniques and new directions. In *ACM SIGCOMM*, 2002.

[14] D. Mitra and Q. Wang. Stochastic traffic engineering for demand uncertainty and risk-aware network revenue management. *IEEE/ACM Trans. Networking*, 13(2):221–233, April 2005.

[15] NLANR. Abilene Trace Data. `http://pma.nlanr.net/Special/ipls3.html`.

[16] I. Norros. On the use of fractional Brownian motion in the theory of connectionless networks. *IEEE Journal on Selected Areas in Communications*, 13(6):953–961, 1995.

[17] A. Nucci, A. Sridharan, and N. Taft. The problem of synthetically generating IP traffic matrices: Initial recommendations. *SIGCOMM Comput. Commun. Rev.*, 35:19–32, July 2005.

[18] M. Roughan. Simplifying the synthesis of Internet traffic matrices. *SIGCOMM Comput. Commun. Rev.*, 35(5):93–96, 2005.

[19] M. Roughan. Robust network planning. In C. R. Kalmanek, S. Misra, and R. Yang, editors, *The Guide to Reliable Internet Services and Applications*, chapter 5, pages 137–177. Springer, 2010.

[20] M. Roughan and J. Gottlieb. Large-scale measurement and modeling of backbone Internet traffic. In *SPIE ITCom*, Boston, 2002.

[21] M. Roughan, A. Greenberg, C. Kalmanek, M. Rumsewicz, J. Yates, and Y. Zhang. Experience in measuring backbone traffic variability: Models, metrics, measurements and meaning. In *ACM IMW*, 2002.

[22] M. Roughan, M. Thorup, and Y. Zhang. Traffic engineering with estimated traffic matrices. In *ACM IMC 2003*, pages 248–258, October 2003.

[23] R. Sinkhorn and P. Knopp. Concerning nonnegative matrices and doubly stochastic matrices. *Pacific Journal of Mathematics*, 21(2), 1967.

[24] A. Soule, A. Nucci, R. Cruz, E. Leonardi, and N. Taft. How to identify and estimate the largest traffic matrix elements in a dynamic environment. *SIGMETRICS Perform. Eval. Rev.*, 32(1):73–84, June 2004.

[25] R. Teixera, N. Duffield, J. Rexford, and M. Roughan. Traffic matrix reloaded: Impact of routing changes. In *Workshop on Passive and Active Measurements*, 2005.

[26] P. Tune and M. Roughan. Internet traffic matrices: A primer. In H. Haddadi and O. Bonaventure, editors, *Recent Advances in Networking, Vol. 1*. ACM SIGCOMM, August 2013.

[27] P. Tune and M. Roughan. Network-design sensitivity analysis. Technical report, School of Mathematical Sciences, University of Adelaide, January 2014.

[28] Y. Vardi. Network Tomography: Estimating source-destination traffic intensities from link data. *J. Am. Statist. Assoc.*, 91:365–377, 1996.

[29] Y. Zhang, M. Roughan, N. Duffield, and A. Greenberg. Fast accurate computation of large-scale IP traffic matrices from link loads. In *ACM SIGMETRICS 2003*, pages 206–217, 2003.

[30] Y. Zhang, M. Roughan, C. Lund, and D. Donoho. Estimating Point-to-Point and Point-to-Multipoint traffic matrices: An information-theoretic approach. *IEEE/ACM Trans. Networking*, 13(5):947–960, October 2005.

[31] R. Zhang-Shen and M. McKeown. Designing a predictable Internet backbone with Valiant load-balancing. In *Proceedings of the 13th International Conference on Quality of Service (IWQoS)*, pages 178–192, 2005.

The Multi-shop Ski Rental Problem

Lingqing Ai
IIIS, Tsinghua University
ailingqing@126.com

Xian Wu
IIIS, Tsinghua University
wuxian12@mails.tsinghua.edu.cn

Lingxiao Huang
IIIS, Tsinghua University
huanglingxiao1990@126.com

Longbo Huang
IIIS, Tsinghua University
longbohuang@tsinghua.edu.cn

Pingzhong Tang
IIIS, Tsinghua University
kenshin@tsinghua.edu.cn

Jian Li
IIIS, Tsinghua University
lijian83@tsinghua.edu.cn

ABSTRACT

We consider the *multi-shop ski rental* problem. This problem generalizes the classic ski rental problem to a multi-shop setting, in which each shop has different prices for renting and purchasing a pair of skis, and a *consumer* has to make decisions on when and where to buy. We are interested in the *optimal online (competitive-ratio minimizing) mixed strategy* from the consumer's perspective. For our problem in its basic form, we obtain exciting closed-form solutions and a linear time algorithm for computing them. We further demonstrate the generality of our approach by investigating three extensions of our basic problem, namely ones that consider costs incurred by entering a shop or switching to another shop. Our solutions to these problems suggest that the consumer must assign positive probability in *exactly one* shop at any buying time. Our results apply to many real-world applications, ranging from cost management in IaaS cloud to scheduling in distributed computing.

Categories and Subject Descriptors

G.3 [**Probability and Statistics**]: Distribution functions; F.2 [**Analysis of Algorithms and Problem of Complexity**]: Miscellaneous

General Terms

Algorithms, Performance, Theory

Keywords

multi-shop ski rental, ski rental, optimal strategy, Nash equilibrium, online algorithm

1. INTRODUCTION

The ski rental problem (SR) is a dilemma faced by a consumer, who is uncertain about how many days she will ski and has to trade off between buying and renting skis: once she buys the skis, she will enjoy the remaining days rent-free, but before that she must pay the daily renting cost. The literature is interested in investigating the *online optimal strategy* of the consumer. That is, a strategy that yields the lowest competitive ratio *without having any information of the future* (as is standard in the literature, competitive ratio is defined as the the ratio between the cost yielded by the consumer's strategy and the cost yielded by the optimal strategy of a prophet, who foresees how many days the trip will last and design the optimal strategy accordingly). The ski rental problem and its variants constitute an important part of the online algorithm design literature from both theoretical and applied perspectives [9, 12, 16, 17, 18, 22].

In this paper, we consider the *multi-shop ski rental problem*(MSR), in which the consumer faces multiple shops that offer different renting and buying prices. She must choose one shop immediately after she arrives at the ski field and must rent or buy the skis *in that particular shop* since then. In other words, once she has chosen a shop, the only decision variable is when to buy the skis. Beyond the basic setting, we also propose three important extensions of MSR as below:

- MSR *with switching cost* (MSR-S): The consumer is allowed to switch from one shop to another and each switching costs her some constant amount of money.
- MSR *with entry fee* (MSR-E): Each shop requires some entry fee and the consumer *cannot* switch shops.
- MSR *with entry fee and switching* (MSR-ES): The consumer is able to switch from one shop to another, and she pays the entry fee as long as she enters any shop[1].

In all the settings above, the consumer's objective is to minimize the competitive ratio. In MSR and MSR-E, she has to consider two questions *at the very beginning*: (1) where should she rent or buy the skis (place), and (2) when should she buy the skis (timing)? While MSR-S and MSR-ES allow the consumer to switch shops and are thus more fine-grained than the previous two, in the sense that she is able to decide where to rent or buy the skis *at any time*. For example, it is among her options to rent in shop 1 on day 1, switch to shop 2 from day 2, and finally switch to shop 3 and then buys the skis.

[1]For example, if she switches from shop 1 to shop 2, and then switches back to shop 1, she pays the entry fee of shop 1 twice and the entry fee of shop 2 once.

SIGMETRICS'14, June 16–20, 2014, Austin, Texas, USA.
Copyright 2014 ACM 978-1-4503-2789-3/14/06 ...$15.00.
http://dx.doi.org/10.1145/2591971.2591984.

The multi-shop ski rental problem naturally extends the ski rental problem and allows heterogeneity in consumer's options, a desirable feature that makes the ski rental problem a more general modeling framework for online algorithm design. Below, we present a few real world scenarios that can be modeled with the multi-shop ski rental problem.

1. Scheduling in distributed computing: A file is replicated and stored in different machines in the cluster. Some node undertaking some computing job needs data in the file during the execution. The node can either request the corresponding data block of the file from some selected machine whenever it needs to, which incurs some delay, or it can simply ask that machine to transmit the whole file beforehand, at the sacrifice of a longer delay at the beginning without any further waiting. When selecting the replicating machine, the scheduling node needs to consider the current bandwidth, read latency, etc. In this application, each replicating machine is considered as a shop, and renting corresponds to requesting for the data block on-demand while buying means to fetch the whole file beforehand.

2. Cost management in IaaS cloud: Multiple `IaaS` cloud vendors, such as Amazon EC2 [1], ElasticHosts [4] and Microsoft Windows Azure [6], offer different price options, which can be classified into two commitment levels: users pay for *on-demand* server instances at an hourly rate or make a one-time, upfront payment to host each instances for some duration (e.g., monthly or annually), during which users either use the instances for free [4], or enjoy a discount on renting the instance [1].

Consider an example in Table 1. Table 1 lists the pricing options for the instances with identical configurations offered by Amazon EC2 and ElasticHosts. Each pricing option can be considered as a shop in the multi-shop ski rental problem, where in the 1(3) year(s) term contract in Amazon EC2, the entry fee is the upfront payment and the hourly price is the renting price.

Vendor	Option	Upfront($)	Hourly($)
Amazon	On-Demand	0	0.145
	1 yr Term	161	0.09
	3 yr Term	243	0.079
ElasticHosts	1 mo Term	97.60	0
	1 yr Term	976.04	0

Table 1: Pricing Options of the 'same' instance in Amazon EC2 (c1.medium) and ElasticHosts (2400MHz cpu, 1792MHz memory, 350Gb storage and no data transfer).

3. Purchase decisions: A company offering high-resolution aerial or satellite map service chooses between Astrium [2] and DigitalGlobe [3]. It can either subscribe imagery from one company or exclusively occupy the service by 'purchasing' one satellite like what Google has done [19]. Similar applications include some person purchasing a SIM card from different telecommunication companies.

1.1 Related Work

The ski rental problem is first considered by Karlin *et al.* [14], and then studied by Karlin's seminal paper [13] which proposes a randomized algorithm and gives a $\frac{e}{e-1}$ competitive ratio. Later researchers propose a few variants, including the Bahncard problem [9] and the TCP acknowledgment problem [12]. A more recent work [15] analyzes the case in which the first or the second moment of the skiing days are known and gives an optimal online solution. However, all the aforementioned works deal with the case where a single consumer rents or buys the skis in one single shop. In their problems, the consumer only needs to decide when to buy. While in the multi-shop ski rental problem, the consumer has to make a two-fold decision (time and place). Closest to our work is the work by Lotker *et al.* [17], which considers the case where the consumer has multiple options in one shop, i.e., the multi-slop problem and their problem can be regarded as a special case of our problem by setting all the buying prices sufficiently large.

Research on "multiple consumers in one single shop" have been conducted from applied perspectives [16, 18, 22]. Lin *et al.* [16] investigate a dynamical 'right-sizing' strategy by turning off servers during periods of low load. Their model and lazy capacity provisioning algorithms closely tie to the ski rental problem. Lu *et al.* [18] derive the "dynamic provisioning techniques" to turn on or off the servers to minimize the energy consumption. They dispatch the servers so that each individual server is reduced to a standard ski rental problem. Wei *et al.* [22] propose an online algorithm to serve the time-varying demands at the minimum cost in `IaaS` cloud given one price option, in which the 'consumers' (servers) may be related to each other.

Another line of work [7, 11] focusing on minimizing the cost in data centers or other cloud services assumes that the long-term workloads are stationary and thus can be predicted, and Guenter *et al.* [10] consider the cases of short predictions. However, for many real-world applications, future workloads can exhibit non-stationarity [20]. Other researchers [16, 18, 21, 22] that require *no priori* knowledge of the future workload minimize the cost *given one option is selected.* Our paper is orthogonal to theirs since we focus on how to select a price option.

1.2 Our Contributions

In this paper, we consider the multi-shop ski-rental problem and its extensions, in which there are multiple shops and the consumer must make two-fold decisions (time and place) to minimize the competitive ratio. We model each problem using a zero-sum game played by the consumer and nature. We simplify the strategy space of the consumer via *removal of strictly dominated strategies* and derive the form of the optimal mixed strategy of the consumer. We summarize the key contributions as follows:

1. For each of the problems, we prove that under the optimal mixed strategy of the consumer, the consumer only assigns positive buying probability to *exactly one* shop at any time. As the buying time increases, she follows the shop order in which the ratio between buying price and renting price is increasing. This order also holds in `MSR-E` and `MSR-ES`, where entry fee is involved.

2. We derive a novel, easy-to-implement *linear time* algorithm for computing the optimal strategy of the consumer, which drastically reduces the complexity of computing the solution to `MSR`.

3. For `MSR-S`, we prove that under the optimal mixed strategy, the consumer only needs to consider switching to another shop at the buying time, i.e., she will

never switch to another shop and continue renting. Moreover, we show that MSR-S can be reduced to an equivalent MSR problem with modified buying prices.

4. For MSR-ES, we prove that under the optimal mixed strategy, the consumer may switch to another shop either during the renting period or at the buying time, but she only follows some particular order of switching. Moreover, the number of times of switching is no more n where n is the number of shops.

5. We characterize any action of the consumer in MSR-ES by proving that the action can be decoupled into a sequence of operations. We further show that each operation can be viewed as a virtual shop in MSR-E and in total, we create $O(n^2)$ 'virtual' shops of MSR-E. Therefore, MSR-ES can be reduced to MSR-E with minor modifications.

Due to limited space, most of the proofs are omitted and the readers can find them in our technical report [5].

2. BASIC PROBLEM

In the *multi-shop ski rental problem* (also MSR), a person goes skiing for an anbiguous time period. There are multiple shops providing skies either for rental or for buying. The person must choose one shop *as soon as* she arrives at the ski field, and she can decide whether or not to buy the skis in that particular shop at any time[2]. Note that she cannot change the shop once she chooses one. The objective is to minimize the worst-case ratio between the amount she actually pays and the money she would have paid if she knew the duration of skiing in advance. We assume that there are n shops in total, denoted by $[n] \triangleq \{1, 2, 3, \cdots, n\}$. Each shop j offers skis at a renting price of r_j dollars per unit time and at a buying price of b_j dollars. This problem is a natural extension of the classic ski rental problem (SR) and it is exactly SR when $n = 1$.

In MSR, it is clear that if there is a shop of which the rental and buying prices are both larger than those of another shop, it is always suboptimal to choose this shop. We assume that

$$0 < r_1 < r_2 < \cdots < r_n$$
$$b_1 > b_2 > \cdots > b_n > 0$$

We apply a game-theoretic approach for solving our problem. For the case of expressing the formulation, we assume that how long the consumer skis is determined by a player called *nature*. Therefore, there are two parties in the problem, and we focus on the optimal strategy of the consumer.

In the remainder of this section, we first formulate our problem as a zero-sum game, and simplify the strategy space in Lemma 1. Then, we combine Lemma 2-5, and fully characterize the optimal strategy of the consumer in Theorem 1. We show that optimally the consumer assigns positive buying probability to *exactly one* shop at any time. Moreover, the possible times the consumer buys the skis in a shop constitute a continuous interval. Thus, we can partition the optimal strategy of the consumer into different sub-intervals which relate to different shops, and the problem is reduced to how to find the optimal breakpoints. Based on Lemma 7 and 8, we develop a linear time algorithm for computing the optimal breakpoints and prove its correctness in Theorem 2.

[2] In this paper, we focus on the continuous time model.

2.1 Formulation

We first analyze the action set for both players in the game. For the consumer, we denote by j the index of the shop in which she rents or buys the skis. Let x be the time when she chooses to buy the skis, i.e., the consumer will rent the skis before x and buy at x if nature has not yet stopped her. The action of the consumer is thus represented by a pair (j, x). Denote by Ψ_c the action set of the consumer:

$$\Psi_c \triangleq \{(j,x) : j \in [n], x \in [0, +\infty) \cup \{+\infty\}\}$$

where $x = +\infty$ means that the consumer always rents and never buys. Next, let y denote the time when nature stops the consumer from skiing. Thus, the action set of nature is

$$\Psi_n \triangleq \{y : y \in (0, +\infty) \cup \{+\infty\}\}$$

where $y = +\infty$ means that nature always allows the consumer to keep skiing. If $y = x$, we regard it as the case that right after the consumer buys the skis, nature stops her. Given the strategy profile $\langle (j,x), y \rangle$, let $c_j(x,y) \geq 0$ denote the cost paid by the consumer:

$$c_j(x,y) \triangleq \begin{cases} r_j y, & y < x \\ r_j x + b_j, & y \geq x \end{cases}$$

Now we define the strategy space for the consumer and nature. Let $\mathbf{p} \triangleq (p_1, \cdots, p_n)$ be a mixed strategy represented by a vector of probability density functions. $p_j(x)$ is the density assigned to the strategy (j, x) for any $j = 1, \cdots, n$ and $x \in [0, +\infty) \cup \{+\infty\}$. In this paper, we assume that for each point, either probability density function exists or it is probability mass.[3] If $p_j(x)$ is probability mass, we regard $p_j(x)$ as $+\infty$ and define $p_{j,x} \triangleq \int_{x-}^{x} p_j(t)dt$ satisfying $p_{j,x} \in (0, 1]$. The strategy space $\mathcal{P}$ of the consumer is as follows: [4]

$$\mathcal{P} = \left\{ \mathbf{p} : \quad \sum_{j=1}^{n} \int_0^{\infty} p_j(x)\mathrm{d}x = 1, \right.$$
$$\left. p_j(x) \geq 0, \forall x \in [0, +\infty) \cup \{+\infty\}, \forall j \in [n] \right\}$$

Similarly, define $q(y)$ to be the probability density of nature choosing y and the strategy space $\mathcal{Q}$ of nature is given by

$$\mathcal{Q} = \left\{ \mathbf{q} : \int_0^{\infty} q(y)\mathrm{d}y = 1, q(y) \geq 0, \forall y \in (0, +\infty) \cup \{+\infty\} \right\}$$

When the consumer chooses the mixed strategy $\mathbf{p}$ and nature chooses the stopping time y, the expected cost to the consumer is:

$$C(\mathbf{p}, y) \triangleq \sum_{j=1}^{n} C_j(p_j, y)$$

[3] In fact, our results can be extended to the case where in the strategy space the cumulative distribution function is not absolutely continuous and thus no probability density function exists.

[4] For convenience, we denote by $\int_a^b f(x)dx$ $(a < b)$ the integral over $(a, b]$, except that when $a = 0$, the integral is over $[0, b]$.

in which

$$
\begin{aligned}
C_j(p_j, y) &\triangleq \int_0^{\infty} c_j(x, y) p_j(x) \mathrm{d}x \\
&= \int_0^{y} (r_j x + b_j) p_j(x) \mathrm{d}x + \int_y^{\infty} y r_j p_j(x) \mathrm{d}x
\end{aligned}
$$

is the expected payment to shop j for all $j \in [n]$. Given the strategy profile $\langle \mathbf{p}, \mathbf{q} \rangle$, the competitive ratio is defined as:

$$
R(\mathbf{p}, \mathbf{q}) \triangleq \int_0^{\infty} \frac{C(\mathbf{p}, y)}{\mathrm{OPT}(y)} q(y) \mathrm{d}y \tag{1}
$$

Here $\mathrm{OPT}(y)$ is the optimal offline cost and can be seen to have the following form:

$$
\mathrm{OPT}(y) = \begin{cases} r_1 y, & y \in (0, B] \\ b_n, & y > B \end{cases} \tag{2}
$$

where B is defined as $B \triangleq \frac{b_n}{r_1}$.

Note that B is the dividing line between the minimum buying cost and the minimum renting cost. When $y < B$, the offline optimal is always to rent at the first shop, and when $y > B$, the offline optimal is to buy the skis at the last shop. We will show that B determines the effective action sets of the consumer and nature in section 2.1.1 .

The objective of the consumer is to minimize the worst-case competitive ratio, i.e., to choose a strategy $\mathbf{p} \in \mathcal{P}$ that solves the problem

$$
\begin{aligned}
\text{minimize} \quad & \max_{y>0} \left\{ \frac{C(\mathbf{p}, y)}{\mathrm{OPT}(y)} \right\} \\
\text{subject to} \quad & \mathbf{p} \in \mathcal{P}
\end{aligned}
$$

which is equivalent to the following:

$$
\begin{aligned}
\text{minimize} \quad & \lambda \\
\text{subject to} \quad & \frac{C(\mathbf{p}, y)}{r_1 y} \le \lambda \\
& \sum_{j=1}^{n} \int_0^{\infty} p_j(x) \mathrm{d}x = 1 \\
& p_j(x) \ge 0 \ \ \forall x \in [0, +\infty) \cup \{+\infty\} \\
& \forall y \in (0, +\infty) \cup \{+\infty\}, \forall j \in [n]
\end{aligned} \tag{3}
$$

2.1.1 Simplifying the Zero-sum Game

In this section, we show that the game can be greatly simplified and the action set for both the consumer and nature can be reduced. Specifically, nature prefers the strategy $y = +\infty$ to any other strategy $y' > B$. For the consumer, for any $j \in [n]$, she prefers the strategy (j, B) to any other strategy (j, x') where $x' > B$.

LEMMA 1. *For nature, any strategy $y \in [B, +\infty)$ is dominated. While for the consumer, any strategy (j, x) is dominated, in which $x \in (B, +\infty) \cup \{+\infty\}, \forall j \in [n]$.*

PROOF. Recall the cost $c_j(x, y)$ is defined as follows:

$$
c_j(x, y) = \begin{cases} r_j y, & y < x \\ r_j x + b_j, & y \ge x \end{cases}
$$

Thus for any fixed (j, x), $c_j(x, y)$ is a non-decreasing function of y. Further, from (2), we can see that the offline optimal cost is unchanged when $y \ge B$. Thus, for any $y \ge B$ it holds that

$$
\frac{c_j(x, y)}{b_n} \le \lim_{y \to +\infty} \frac{c_j(x, y)}{b_n} = \frac{r_j x + b_j}{b_n}
$$

Therefore, any strategy of nature that includes $y \ge B$ is dominated by the strategy of never stopping the consumer.

Now for the consumer, for any shop $j \in \{1, \cdots, n\}$, and any $x' \in (B, +\infty) \cup \{+\infty\}$, it holds that

$$
c_j(B, y) - c_j(x', y) \le 0, \quad \forall y \in (0, B) \cup \{+\infty\}
$$

Therefore, any strategy of the consumer that includes buying at time x' in any shop is dominated by the strategy of buying at B in the same shop. □

From this lemma, the consumer's buying time is restricted in $[0, B]$. Note that for any (j, x) in which $x \in [0, B]$, it holds that

$$
\frac{c_j(x, B)}{\mathrm{OPT}(B)} = \frac{c_j(x, +\infty)}{\mathrm{OPT}(+\infty)}
$$

Therefore, the action set of nature Ψ_n can be reduced to $\Psi_n = \{y \in (0, B]\}$.

Similarly, in the strategy space of the consumer $\mathcal{P}$, nature $\mathcal{Q}$, the expected cost $C(\mathbf{p}, y)$ and the competitive ratio $R(\mathbf{p}, \mathbf{q})$, we can replace $+\infty$ by B.

Comments on B: recall that the boundary B is defined as $\frac{\min\{b_i\}}{\min\{r_i\}} = \frac{b_n}{r_1}$ in MSR, while this value is $\frac{b_j}{r_j}$ if shop j is the only shop in SR. For instance, if only shop n appears in SR, then the consumer will never consider to buy at any time $x > \frac{b_n}{r_n}$. However, in MSR, the consumer may want to put some positive possibility to the strategy of buying at time $x > \frac{b_n}{r_n}$ in shop n (since $r_1 < r_n$). The difference between these two cases is due to the fact that in MSR, the consumer has the global information of all the shops and the offline optimal is always to rent at shop 1 at the cost of r_1 per unit time until the total cost reaches the minimum buying price b_n, whereas in SR, the consumer always rents at the cost of $r_n \ge r_1$ per unit time until b_n.

With the above results, problem (3) can now be reduced to the following:

$$
\begin{aligned}
\text{minimize} \quad & \lambda && (4) \\
\text{subject to} \quad & \frac{C(\mathbf{p}, y)}{r_1 y} \le \lambda && (4a) \\
& \sum_{j=1}^{n} \int_0^{B} p_j(x) \mathrm{d}x = 1 && (4b) \\
& p_j(x) \ge 0 && (4c) \\
& \forall x \in [0, B], \forall y \in (0, B], \forall j \in [n] && (4d)
\end{aligned}
$$

We will show that the optimal strategy of the consumer results in exact equality in (4a) in the next subsection.

2.2 Optimal Strategy of the Consumer

In this subsection, we look into the optimal solution $\mathbf{p}^*$ for (4). In short, $\mathbf{p}^*$ yields the same expected utility for nature whenever nature chooses to stop. In other words, given $\mathbf{p}^*$, any pure strategy of nature yields the same utility for both the consumer and nature. Moreover, at any time x, the consumer assigns positive buying probability to exactly one of the shops, say shop j, and j is decreasing as x increases. Finally, we can see that for any shop j and the time interval in which the consumer chooses to buy at shop j, the density function $p_j(x)$ is $\alpha_j e^{r_j/b_j x}$ where α_j is some constant to be specified later.

We now state our first theorem that summarizes the structure of the optimal strategy.

THEOREM 1. *The optimal solution* $\mathbf{p}^*$ *satisfies the following properties:*

(a) There exists a constant λ, *such that* $\forall y \in (0, B]$,

$$\frac{C(\mathbf{p}^*, y)}{r_1 y} = \lambda$$

(b) There exist $n+1$ *breakpoints:* $d_1, d_2, \cdots, d_{n+1}$, *such that* $B = d_1 \geq d_2 \geq \cdots \geq d_n \geq d_{n+1} = 0$, *and* $\forall j \in [n]$, *we have*

$$p_j^*(x) = \begin{cases} \alpha_j e^{r_j x/b_j}, & x \in (d_{j+1}, d_j) \\ 0, & \textit{otherwise} \end{cases}$$

in which α_j *satisfies that*

$$\alpha_j b_j e^{r_j d_j/b_j} = \alpha_{j-1} b_{j-1} e^{r_{j-1} d_j/b_{j-1}} \quad \forall j = 2, \cdots, n$$

In the following, We will prove property (a) by Lemma 2, property (b) by Lemma 3-5. All proof details can be found in our technical report [5].

LEMMA 2. $\forall y \in (0, B]$, $\exists$ *a constant* λ, *such that* $\mathbf{p}^*$ *satisfies that*

$$\frac{C(\mathbf{p}^*, y)}{r_1 y} = \lambda \tag{5}$$

PROOF. (sketch) By reductio ad absurdum, we assume that $\frac{C(\mathbf{p}^*, y)}{r_1 y}$, which can be considered as a function with respect to y, is not a constant. Then we can find a valley in the graph of this function and there are 3 cases depending on the positions of the maximum points of the function:

- Maximum points only appear on the left side of the valley;
- Maximum points only appear on the right side of the valley;
- Maximum points appear on the both side of the valley.

Then we prove that there is a better strategy in each case which makes contradiction. □

From the above lemma, the problem (4) is thus equivalent to the following:

$$\begin{aligned} &\text{minimize} \quad \lambda \\ &\text{subject to} \quad (5), (4b), (4c), (4d) \end{aligned} \tag{6}$$

Here are some intuitions of `MSR`: In the extreme case where the buying time x is sufficiently small, the consumer will prefer shop n than any other shops since b_n is the minimum buying price. As x increases, the renting cost weights more and the skier gradually chooses the shop with lower rent yet higher buying price. In the other extreme case when the skier decides to buy at time x close to B, shop 1 may be the best place since it has the lowest rent. Thus,in the optimal strategy, the interval $[0, B]$ may be partitioned into several sub-intervals. In each interval, the consumer only chooses to buy at one and only one shop. The following two lemmas formally show that the above intuitions are indeed the case.

LEMMA 3. $\forall j \in [n]$, *we have* $p_j^*(0) < +\infty$, *and* $\forall x \in (0, B]$, $p_j^*(x) < \frac{2b_1 r_1}{b_n^2}$.

LEMMA 4. *In the optimal strategy* $\mathbf{p}^*$, *there exists* $n+1$ *breakpoints* $B = d_1 \geq d_2 \geq \cdots \geq d_{n+1} = 0$, *which partition* $[0, B]$ *into* n *sub-intervals, such that* $\forall j = 1, \cdots, n$, $\forall x \in (d_{j+1}, d_j)$, $p_j^*(x) > 0$ *and* $p_i^*(x) = 0$ *for any* $i \neq j$.

PROOF. (sketch) It suffices to show that $\forall x \in (0, B)$, $\forall \epsilon > 0$, if there exists some j such that $\int_{x-\epsilon}^{x} p_j^*(t)\mathrm{d}t > 0$, then $\forall j' > j, x' \geq x$, we must have $\int_{x'}^{B} p_{j'}^*(t)\mathrm{d}t = 0$. We use reductio ad absurdum to prove this proposition.

We first show that if there exists some $j' > j, x' > x, \epsilon > 0$ such that $\int_{x-\epsilon}^{x} p_j^*(t)\mathrm{d}t > 0$, $\int_{x'}^{x'+\epsilon} p_{j'}^*(t)\mathrm{d}t > 0$, then there exist 2 intervals $(x_1, x_1+\theta) \subseteq (x-\epsilon, x)$ and $(x_2, x_2+\theta) \subseteq (x', x'+\epsilon)$, such that

$$\int_0^{\epsilon_0} \min\{p_j^*(x_1+\theta), p_{j'}^*(x_2+\theta)\}\mathrm{d}\theta > 0$$

We next move some suitable buying probabilities of $p_{j'}^*$ from $(x_2, x_2+\theta)$ to $(x_1, x_1+\theta)$ for shop j', and correspondingly move some purchase probabilities of p_j^* from $(x_1, x_1+\theta)$ to $(x_2, x_2+\theta)$ for shop j. Then we obtain a new strategy $\mathbf{p^1}$. We show that $\forall y \in (0, B]$, $\mathbf{p^1}$ is no worse than $\mathbf{p}^*$, and $\forall y \in (x_1, B]$, $\mathbf{p^1}$ is strictly better than $\mathbf{p}^*$, which makes a contradiction. □

The lemma explicitly specifies the order of the shops in the optimal strategy: as x increases, the index of the shop where the consumer assigns positive density decreases. Based on this lemma, for any $j \in [n], x \in (d_{j+1}, d_j)$, multiplying both sides of (5) by $r_1 y$, and taking twice derivatives, we have

$$b_i \frac{\mathrm{d}p_j^*(x)}{dx} = r_j p_j^*(x) \quad \forall x \in (d_{j+1}, d_j) \tag{7}$$

Solving this differentiable equation, we obtain the optimal solutions as follows[5]:

$$p_j^*(x) = \begin{cases} \alpha_j e^{r_j x/b_j}, & x \in (d_{j+1}, d_j) \\ 0, & \textit{otherwise} \end{cases} \tag{8}$$

where α_j is some constant. The relationship between α_j and α_{j-1} is described in the following lemma:

LEMMA 5.

$$\alpha_j b_j e^{r_j d_j/b_j} = \alpha_{j-1} b_{j-1} e^{r_{j-1} d_j/b_{j-1}} \quad \forall j = 2, \cdots, n \tag{9}$$

2.3 Computing the Optimal Strategy

In this section we propose a linear time algorithm to compute the optimal strategy for the consumer. First we show the relationship between the competitive ratio λ and α_1 by the following lemma:

LEMMA 6. *For any strategy* $\mathbf{p}$ *which satisfies property (b) in Theorem 1, it holds that*

$$\frac{C(\mathbf{p}, y)}{r_1 y} = \alpha_1 \frac{b_1}{r_1} e^{\frac{r_1}{b_1} B}, \quad \forall y \in (0, B]$$

From the above lemma, we know that minimizing λ is equivalent to minimizing α_1. Therefore, problem (6) is now equivalent to the following:

$$\text{minimize} \quad \alpha_1 \tag{10}$$

[5]Because $p_j(x)$ is finite, we say $p_j(d_i) = 0$ for all $i, j \in N$, which does not affect the expected cost at all.

$$\text{subject to} \quad \sum_{j=1}^{n} \alpha_j \frac{b_j}{r_j} \left(e^{\frac{r_j}{b_j} d_{j-1}} - e^{\frac{r_j}{b_j} d_j} \right) = 1 \tag{11}$$

$$\alpha_j e^{r_j d_j / b_j} = \alpha_{j-1} e^{r_{j-1} d_j / b_{j-1}}, \forall j = 2, \cdots, n$$

$$\alpha_j > 0, \quad \forall j \in [n]$$

$$B = d_1 \geq d_2 \geq \cdots \geq d_n \geq d_{n+1} = 0$$

where (11) is computed directly from (4b).

In Theorem 1, if we know $(d_1, d_2, \cdots, d_{n+1})$, then we can see that α_j is proportional to α_1. Therefore, we can get a constant Ω_j such that $\Omega_j \alpha_1 = \int_{d_{j+1}}^{d_j} p_j(x)dx$ since the breakpoints are known. Finally we can get a constant $\Omega = \sum_{j=1}^{n} \Omega_j$ such that $\Omega \alpha_1 = \sum_{j=1}^{n} (\int_0^B p_j(x)dx)$. Using the fact that $\sum_{j=1}^{n} (\int_0^B p_j(x)dx) = 1$, we can easily solve α_1, all the α_j and the whole problem.

Therefore, the computation of $\mathbf{p}$ reduces to computing $\{d_1, d_2, \cdots, d_{n+1}\}$. Notice that $d_1 \equiv B, d_{n+1} \equiv 0$.

In this case, we treat this problem from another prospective. We first fix α_1 to be 1. After that, without considering the constraint (11), we compute the optimal breakpoints $(d_1, d_2, \cdots, d_{n+1})$ to maximize $\sum_{j=1}^{n} (\int_0^B p_j(x)dx)$. Denote the optimal value of this problem as Ω. We then normalize all the probability functions, i.e., reset all the α_j to be α_j / Ω. By Lemma 5, we know the ratio λ is proportional to α_1, which is fixed at first and normalized at last. Hence, maximizing Ω is equivalent to minimizing λ. Notice that all the probability functions in the remainder of section 2.3 is unnormalized when $\alpha_1 = 1$.

In the following 2 sections 2.3.1 and 2.3.2, we show some intuitions and ideas of our algorithm about how to compute the breakpoints. In Section 2.3.3, we formally propose our algorithm and prove the optimality and complexity of our algorithm.

2.3.1 *Computing* d_n

To facilitate further calculations, we denote P_j to be the probability sum of shop j to shop n, i.e.,

$$P_j \triangleq \sum_{\tau=j}^{n} (\int_0^B p_\tau(x)\mathrm{d}x) = \sum_{\tau=j}^{n} (\int_0^{d_j} p_\tau(x)\mathrm{d}x)$$

Now we just need to maximize P_1 since by definition $P_1 = \Omega$. To compute some breakpoint d_j, we assume that all the breakpoints $\{d_i : i \neq j\}$ are fixed. Since breakpoints $d_1, d_2, \cdots, d_{j-1}$ are fixed, parameters $\alpha_1, \alpha_2, \cdots, \alpha_{j-1}$ are constants. Therefore, $\sum_{\tau=1}^{j-2} (\int_0^B p_\tau(x)dx)$, part of the probability sum, is a constant and we just need to maximize the rest of the sum which is P_{j-1}.

First we consider how to compute $\arg\max_{d_n} P_{n-1}(d_n)$ when given $d_1, \cdots, d_{n-1}$, where

$$P_{n-1}(d_n) = \alpha_n \int_0^{d_n} e^{\frac{r_n x}{b_n}} dx + \alpha_{n-1} \int_{d_n}^{d_{n-1}} e^{\frac{r_{n-1} x}{b_{n-1}}} dx$$

Notice that α_{n-1} is a constant but α_n depends on d_n. From Lemma 5 we know that:

$$\alpha_n = \alpha_{n-1} b_{n-1} e^{(r_{n-1}/b_{n-1} - r_n/b_n) d_n} / b_n$$

The following lemma shows the concavity of $P_{n-1}(d_n)$:

LEMMA 7. *$P_{n-1}(d_n)$ is a strictly concave function.*

Notice that $P'_{n-1}(d_n) > 0$ when $d_n = 0$. This implies that: if $d_n < d_{n-1}$, we must have $P'_{n-1}(d_n) = 0$ since it is concave. Otherwise, $d_{n-1} = d_n$ which means $\forall x, p_{n-1}(x) = 0$, i.e., shop $n-1$ does not exist. Thus we can delete shop $n-1$ and view shop $n-2$ as shop $n-1$. Similarly, if $d_n < d_{n-2}$, $P'_{n-2}(d_n) = 0$; otherwise delete shop $n-2$ and treat shop $n-3$ as shop $n-1$. Repeat this procedure until we find some shop k, such that $d_n = d_{n-1} = \cdots = d_{k+1} < d_k$. Then d_n should be the maximal point because of the concavity derived by Lemma 7, i.e.,

$$d_n = \frac{b_n}{r_n} \ln(\frac{b_k r_n - b_n r_k}{b_n(r_n - r_k)})$$

Notice that d_n is always positive.

2.3.2 *Computing* d_j

Notice that d_n is unrelated to d_{n-1} if $d_n < d_{n-1}$. Therefore, we can work out all the breakpoints d_j in descending order of the subscript of d. Here we show how to obtain d_j after $d_n, d_{n-1}, \cdots, d_{j+1}$.

If $j = n$, we just temporarily take

$$d_n = \frac{b_n}{r_n} \ln(\frac{b_{n-1} r_n - b_n r_{n-1}}{b_n(r_n - r_{n-1})})$$

If $j \neq n$, our target becomes $\arg\max_{d_j} P_{j-1}(d_j)$. According to the definition, we have

$$P_{j-1}(d_j) = \alpha_j (D_j + \int_0^{d_j} e^{\frac{r_j x}{b_j}} dx) + \alpha_{j-1} \int_{d_j}^{d_{j-1}} e^{\frac{r_{j-1} x}{b_{j-1}}} dx$$

where

$$D_j \triangleq -\int_0^{d_{j+1}} e^{r_j x / b_j} dx + \sum_{\tau=j+1}^{n} \frac{\alpha_\tau}{\alpha_j} \int_{d_{\tau+1}}^{d_\tau} e^{r_\tau x / b_\tau} dx \geq 0$$

Notice that the breakpoints $d_n, d_{n-1}, \cdots, d_{j+1}$ are fixed and we can compute α_τ / α_j by the following equations which is derived from Lemma 5:

$$\alpha_\tau = \alpha_{\tau-1} b_{\tau-1} e^{(r_{\tau-1}/b_{\tau-1} - r_\tau/b_\tau) d_\tau} / b_\tau, \forall \tau \in [n] \backslash [j]$$

Therefore, D_j is a constant.

It can be seen that we can compute D_j recursively, i.e.,

$$D_j = \frac{\alpha_{j+1}}{\alpha_j} (D_{j+1} + \int_0^{d_{j+1}} e^{\frac{r_{j+1}}{b_{j+1}} x} \mathrm{d}x - \int_0^{d_{j+1}} e^{\frac{r_j}{b_j} x} \mathrm{d}x)$$

Also note that α_{j-1} is a constant but α_j depends on d_j:

$$\alpha_j = \alpha_{j-1} b_{j-1} e^{(r_{j-1}/b_{j-1} - r_j/b_j) d_j} / b_j$$

The following lemma shows that $P_{j-1}(d_j)$ is a quasi-concave function:

LEMMA 8. *If $D_j r_j / b_j \geq 1$, we always have $P'_{j-1}(d_j) < 0$; if $D_j r_j / b_j < 1$, $P''_{j-1}(d_j) < 0$, i.e., $P_{j-1}(d_j)$ is strictly concave.*

Similarly with the computation of d_n, if $D_j r_j / b_j > 1$, then we always have $P'_{j-1}(d_j) < 0$ and the optimal d_j is d_{j+1}. Hence we delete shop j and treat shop $j-1$ as shop j. Then we need to recompute d_{j+1} and let $d_j = d_{j+1}$; otherwise it is concave and we temporarily get the maximal point:

$$d_j = \frac{b_j}{r_j} \ln(\frac{(b_{j-1} r_j - b_j r_{j-1})(1 - D_j r_j / b_j)}{b_j (r_j - r_{j-1})})$$

Here if the temporary d_j is no larger than d_{j+1}, it means that the optimal solution is d_{j+1} because of the constraints

$d_{j+1} \le d_j \le d_{j-1}$. So we have $d_j = d_{j+1}$ which means that $\forall x, p_j(x) = 0$. Therefore, we delete shop j and treat shop $j-1$ as shop j. Then recompute d_{j+1} and temporarily skip d_j. At last we set $d_j = d_{j+1}$.

2.3.3 A Linear Time Algorithm

Now we are ready to show our algorithm for computing the optimal strategy of the consumer.

THEOREM 2. *There is an algorithm for computing the unique optimal strategy of the consumer. The time and space complexity of the algorithm are linear.*

We first show how to construct our algorithm, and analyze the correctness and the complexity of our algorithm later.

Since delete operations may be executed frequently in the algorithm, we use a linked list to store the shop info. Each shop is an element in this linked list and the shop index decreases when we traverse from the head to the tail. So the head is shop n and the tail is shop 1. Considering that the shops appear in the form of linked list in the algorithm, we rewrite some equations we may use in the algorithm:

$$\begin{aligned} D_j &= \frac{\alpha_{prev[j]}}{\alpha_j}(D_{prev[j]} + \int_0^{d_{prev[j]}} \exp(\frac{r_{prev[j]}x}{b_{prev[j]}})dx) \\ &\quad - \int_0^{d_{prev[j]}} \exp(\frac{r_j x}{b_j})dx \\ &= \frac{\alpha_{prev[j]}}{\alpha_j} D_{prev[j]} - \frac{b_j}{r_j}(\exp(\frac{r_j d_{prev[j]}}{b_j}) - 1) \\ &\quad + \frac{\alpha_{prev[j]} b_{prev[j]}}{\alpha_j r_{prev[j]}}(\exp(\frac{r_{prev[j]} d_{prev[j]}}{b_{prev[j]}}) - 1) \end{aligned} \tag{12}$$

Here $\frac{\alpha_{prev[j]}}{\alpha_j}$ is represented as follow:

$$\frac{\alpha_{prev[j]}}{\alpha_j} = \frac{b_j}{b_{prev[j]}} e^{(\frac{r_j}{b_j} - \frac{r_{prev[j]}}{b_{prev[j]}})d_{prev[j]}}$$

$$d_j = \frac{b_j}{r_j} \ln(\frac{(b_{next[j]} r_j - b_j r_{next[j]})(1 - D_j r_j / b_j)}{b_j (r_j - r_{next[j]})}) \tag{13}$$

Here is the pseudocode of our algorithm.:

Algorithm 1 MSR Algorithm

```
D_n ← 0;
for j ← 1 to n do
    next[j] ← j − 1;
    prev[j] ← j + 1;
end for
for j ← n to 2 do
    ComputingBP(j);
end for
for j ← n to 2 do
    if d_j ≠"decide later" then
        if d_j > B then
            d_j ← B;
        end if
    else
        d_j ← d_{j+1};
    end if
end for
```

Though we may revise those breakpoints for many times when running the algorithm, it will still lead to the exact optimal solution at the end. Since the feasible solution of $(d_2, d_3, \cdots, d_n)$ is convex and functions $P_{j-1}(\cdot)$ are always concave, we have the following properties for the optimal solution:

If $d_{j-1} > d_j$, $P'_{j-1}(d_j) \le 0$; if $d_{j+1} < d_j$, $P'_{j-1}(d_j) \ge 0$.

So in our computation method, we delete a shop when and only when the shop should be deleted in the optimal solution. Notice that Line $5, 6, 7$ and Line $15, 16, 17$ are what we actually do when we say we delete shop j. We say a shop is *alive* if it has not been deleted. Based on the following lemma, we rigorously prove the correctness and complexity of this algorithm.

Algorithm 2 Function *ComputingBP(j)*

```
1: if j ≠ n then
2:     Update D_j according to (12);
3: end if
4: if D_j ≥ b_j/r_j then
5:     d_j ←"decide later";
6:     next[prev[j]] ← next[j];
7:     prev[next[j]] ← prev[j];
8:     ComputingBP(prev[j]);
9: else
10:    Compute d_j according to (13);
11:    if d_j ≤ d_{j+1} then
12:        d_j ←"decide later";
13:        next[prev[j]] ← next[j];
14:        prev[next[j]] ← prev[j];
15:        ComputingBP(prev[j]);
16:    end if
17: end if
```

LEMMA 9. *After an invocation of ComputingBP(j) is completed, the temporary breakpoints, whose indexes are less than or equal to j,* $\mathbf{td} = (td_n, td_{n-1}, \cdots, td_j)$ *are identical with the optimal solution* $\mathbf{d}^* = (d^*_n, d^*_{n-1}, \cdots, d^*_j)$ *if* $d^*_j < d^*_{next[j]}$. *And all the deletions are correct, i.e., once a shop j is deleted in the algorithm,* d^*_j *must be equal to* d^*_{j+1}.

PROOF. (sketch) This lemma is proved by inductions(an outer induction and an inner induction). In the outer induction, we prove the lemma for the invocation of *ComputingBP(j)* under the 2 assumptions:

- all the deletions in the past is correct;
- $\forall \tau > j$, the lemma holds for *ComputingBP*(τ)

In each step of the outer induction, we consider 2 cases:

1 one or more shops are deleted during this invocation;

2 no shop is deleted during this invocation.

For Case 1, we construct a sequence of vectors and prove the correctness of Case 1 based on its monotonicity. The monotonicity of the sequence is also proved by induction (the inner induction). And Case 2 is proved based on Case 1. □

Here $\mathbf{td} = (td_n, td_{n-1}, \cdots, td_j)$ are the temporary values of $d_n, d_{n-1}, \cdots, d_j$ just after this invocation, $d^*_n, d^*_{n-1}, \cdots, d^*_2$ are the optimal breakpoints, and $next[\cdot]$ and $prev[\cdot]$ denote the current state of the linked list not the eventual result.

PROOF. (Theorem 2) We first show the correctness of the algorithm. According to Lemma 9, we know that all the deletions are correct. Also, we know that $\forall j_1, j_2$ such that $1 < j_1 < j_2$, and that shop j_1 and shop j_2 are alive, $td_{j_1} > td_{j_2}$ when the algorithm terminates. There are 2 cases:

Case 1: $B = d_1^* > d_{prev[1]}^*$, the final solution is the unique optimal solution by Lemma 9.

Case 2: $B = d_1^* = d_{prev[1]}^*$. Similar to the proof of Case 1 in Lemma 9, the solution of the alive breakpoints $\mathbf{td}^* = (td_n^*, td_{next[n]}^*, \cdots, td_{prev[1]}^*, d_1^*)$, satisfying that $\forall \tau \in [n], td_\tau^* = \min\{td_\tau, d_1^*\}$, is the unique optimal solution.

Next, we analyze the complexity of the algorithm. Obviously, the space complexity is $O(n)$. For the time complexity, we just need to prove that this algorithm invokes the function *ComputingBP* for $O(n)$ times. The main function invokes *ComputingBP* for $O(n)$ times. And notice that a shop is deleted once *ComputingBP* is invoked recursively by *ComputingBP*. The algorithm can delete $O(n)$ shops at most, therefore the total number of the invocations is $O(n)$. □

2.4 Optimal Strategy of Nature

Now we briefly show the optimal strategy $\mathbf{q}^*$ of nature in the following theorem:

THEOREM 3. *Suppose that the probability for nature of choosing $y = B$ (actually $y = +\infty$) is q_B^*. The optimal strategy q^* of nature satisfies the following properties:*

(a) $\forall j > 1$, we have $\int_{d_j^*-}^{d_j^*+} q^*(y)dy = 0$.

(b) $q^*(y) = \beta_j y e^{-\frac{r_j}{b_j}y}, \qquad y \in (d_{j+1}^*, d_j^*)$.

(c) $\beta_1 = (q_B r_1/Bb_1)e^{\frac{r_1}{b_1}B}$.

(d) $\frac{b_j}{r_j}\beta_j e^{-\frac{r_j}{b_j}d_j^*} = \frac{b_{j-1}}{r_{j-1}}\beta_{j-1}e^{-\frac{r_{j-1}}{b_{j-1}}d_j^*}, \qquad j = 2, 3, \ldots, n$.

PROOF. (sketch) When the consumer chooses a pure strategy (j, x) and nature chooses $\mathbf{q}^*$, the competitive ratio is as follows:

$$R_j(x, \mathbf{q}^*) \triangleq \int_0^x \frac{r_j}{r_1}q^*(y)dy + \int_x^B \frac{r_j x + b_j}{r_1 y}q^*(y)dy$$

We know that $\mathbf{p}^*$ and $\mathbf{q}^*$ reach a Nash equilibrium with a competitive ratio λ and that $p_j^*(x) > 0$ when $x \in (d_{j+1}^*, d_j^*)$. Therefore, $R_j(x, \mathbf{q}^*) = \lambda$ when $x \in (d_{j+1}^*, d_j^*)$ and the 4 properties of $\mathbf{q}^*$ can be easily derived from it. □

Recall that $\mathbf{d}^*$ is computed by Algorithm 1. Thus $\forall j \in [n]$, we can compute β_j/q_B and we can obtain $1/q_B$ by computing the sum $\sum_{\tau=1}^n \int_{d_\tau}^{d_{\tau+1}} q(y)/q_B dy$. Since the sum of probability is 1, i.e., $\int_0^B q(y)dy = 1$, it is not hard to work out $\mathbf{q}^*$ after normalization.

2.5 Including Switching Cost

In this subsection, we consider an extension, the *multi-shop ski rental with switching cost problem*(also MSR-S), in which we allow the consumer switches from one shop to another, but with some extra fee to be paid. At any time, suppose the consumer chooses to switch from shop i to shop j, she has to pay for an extra switching cost $c_{ij} \geq 0$. If there exists some $i \neq j$, such that $c_{ij} = +\infty$, then the consumer cannot *directly* switch from shop i to shop j. Consider the following 2 cases:

- If the consumer is allowed to switch from shop to shop freely, i.e. the switching cost is always 0, she will optimally rent at the shop with the lowest renting price and buy at the shop with the lowest buying price. All that she concerns is when to buy the skies. Thus, this problem (MSR-S) is reduced to the basic ski rental problem (SR).

- If the switching cost is always $+\infty$, she will never switch to another shop and the MSR-S becomes MSR.

We will prove that the consumer never switches between shops even in MSR-S later.

The settings of MSR-S can be viewed as a directed graph $G = (V, A)$, where $V = \{1, \cdots, n\}$, and $A = \{(i, j) : c_{ij} < +\infty\}$. Each arc $(i, j) \in A$ has a cost c_{ij}. We define a path $\mathbf{p} \subseteq G$ as a sequence of arcs. Define the cost of $\mathbf{p}$ as the summation of the costs of all arcs on $\mathbf{p}$. Note that if the consumer is allowed to switch from shop i to shop j $(i \neq j)$, there must be a path $\mathbf{p}$ which starts at i and ends at j.

It is clear that if the consumer decides to switch from shop i to shop j $((i, j) \in A)$ at any time, she will choose the shortest path from i to j in the graph G. Denote the cost of the shortest path from i to j by c_{ij}^*. We obtain that $c_{ij}^* \leq c_{ij}$, for any $(i, j) \in A$. Moreover, for any different $i, j, k \in V$ such that $(i, j), (j, k), (i, k) \in A$, we have:

$$c_{ik}^* \leq c_{ij}^* + c_{jk}^* \qquad (14)$$

Comparing to MSR, MSR-S has a much richer action set for the consumer, where the consumer is able to choose where to rent and for how long to rent at that shop.

Although we allow the consumer to switch from shop to shop as many times as she wants, the following lemma shows that the consumer will never choose to switch to another shop and continue renting, i.e. the only moment that the consumer will switch is exactly when she buys the skis.

LEMMA 10. *Any strategy which includes switching from one shop to another shop and continuely renting the skis is dominated.*

PROOF. Given an action ψ, we assume that the buying time in ψ is x and there exists a switching operation strictly before x. Now we need to prove that ψ is dominated.

We assume that the first switching operation in ψ is from shop i to shop j at time x_0 $(0 \leq x_0 < x)$. If there are more than one switching operations at time x_0, they can be considered as a big switching operation. But the switching cost is the sum of all the switching cost at time x_0. We assume that the last switching operation at x_0 is from some shop to shop k. If the switching cost at x_0 is larger than c_{ik}^*, then obviously it is dominated. But if not, then there will be 2 cases.

Case 1 : when $r_i < r_k$,

Denote by x_1 the switching time just after x_0. But if switching only happens at time x_0 in ψ, we let x_1 to be x. It can be seen that $x_0 < x_1$. Since $r_i \leq r_k$, in action ψ it is better for the consumer to move the switching operation(s) from time x_0 to time x_1. It can be verified that the cost remains the same when $y < x_0$ and decreases when $y \geq x_0$. Thus, ψ is dominated.

Case 2 : when $r_i \geq r_k$,

Consider another action ψ^1: the consumer enters shop k at the very beginning and does not execute any switching operation at time x_0, but she acts the same as ψ after time

x_0. It can be verified that the cost does not increase when $y < x_0$ and decreases when $y \geq x_0$. Thus, it is dominated by ψ^1. □

This lemma significantly reduces the action set of the consumer to the same one as MSR. Thus, if the consumer considers to switch, she must switch to another shop at the buying time. Further, she chooses a shop such that the sum of the buying cost and the switching cost (if any) is minimized. Once the consumer decides to switch for buying, she will switch at most once, since the buying cost only increases otherwise. Therefore, for any strategy, suppose s is the shop in which the consumer rents the skis right before the buying time, we define the buying price of s as follows:

$$b'_s = \min\{b_s, b_j + c_{sj}, \forall j \neq s\}$$

Observe that once s is settled, b'_s is settled. As a result, MSR-S is reduced to MSR, in which for any shop j, the rent is still r_j per unit time while the buying price b'_j is $\min\{b_j, \min_{i\neq j}\{b_i + c_{ji}\}\}$.

3. SKI RENTAL WITH ENTRY FEE

In this section, we discuss another extension of MSR, the *multi-shop ski rental with entry fee included problem* (MSR-E). In this problem, all the settings are the same to those of MSR, except that each shop has an entry fee. Once the consumer enters a shop, she pays for the entry fee of this shop and cannot switch to another shop. Our goal is to minimize the worst case competitive ratio. Notice that MSR can be viewed as a special case of MSR-E in which the entry fee of each shop is zero.

We introduce this problem not only as an extension of MSR, but more importantly, as a necessary step to solve a more general extension, the (MSR-ES) problem in next section. We will show that MSR-ES can be converted into MSR-E with minor modifications.

3.1 Single Shop Ski Rental with Entry Fee

We start by briefly introducing the special case of MSR-E when $n = 1$. The entry fee, renting price and buying price are supposed to be $a \geq 0$, $r > 0$ and $b > 0$. Without loss of generality, we assume that $r = 1$.

It can be verified that

(i) Using dominance, the buying time of the consumer $x \in [0, b]$, and the stopping time chosen by nature $y \in (0, b]$.

(ii) For all $y \in (0, b]$, the ratio is a constant if the consumer chooses the optimal mixed strategy.

(iii) No probability mass appears in $(0, b]$.

By calculation, we obtain the following optimal mixed strategy:

- The probability that the consumer buys at time $x = 0$ is $p_0 = a/((a+b)e - b)$.
- The probability density function that the consumer buys at time $x \in (0, b]$ is $p(x) = \frac{\exp(x/b)}{b(e - \frac{b}{a+b})}$.
- The competitive ratio is $\frac{e}{e - \frac{b}{a+b}}$.

Note that the biggest difference from MSR is that p_0 may be probability mass, which means that the consumer may have non-zero probability to buy at the initial time.

3.2 Analysis of MSR-E

In this problem, assume that there are n shops in total. For any shop $j \in [n]$, the entry fee, renting price and buying price of shop j are $a_j \geq 0$, $r_j > 0$ and $b_j > 0$, respectively. Similar to the procedures in MSR, we use a tuple (j, x) in which $j \in [n], x \in [0, +\infty) \cup \{+\infty\}$ to denote an action for the consumer and a number $y \in (0, +\infty) \cup \{+\infty\}$ for nature.

Without loss of generality, in this problem, we assume that

- $r_1 \leq r_2 \leq \cdots \leq r_n$;
- $\forall i, j,\ a_i < a_j + b_j$;
- $\forall i < j,\ a_i > a_j$ or $a_i + b_i > a_j + b_j$.

The second condition is because that shop i is dominated by shop j if $a_i \geq a_j + b_j$. For the third condition, we know $r_i \leq r_j$ since $i < j$. So shop j is dominated by shop i if we also have $a_i \leq a_j$ and $a_i + b_i \leq a_j + b_j$.

Denote B as follows:

$$\begin{aligned} \text{minmize} \quad & B \\ \text{subject to} \quad & \forall i,\ a_i + Br_i \geq \min_j (a_j + b_j) \end{aligned}$$

Similar to Lemma 1 in MSR, we reduce the action sets for both players by the following lemma:

LEMMA 11. *For nature, any action $y \in [B, +\infty)$ is dominated. For the consumer, any action (j, x) is dominated, in which $x \in (B, +\infty) \cup \{+\infty\}, j \in [n]$.*

Similar to MSR, the consumer's action set is reduced to buying time $x \in [0, B]$, and nature's action set is reduced to $\{y \in (0, B]\}$.

The strategy spaces for both the consumer and the nature are identical to those in MSR. Similarly, we use $\mathbf{p}$ to denote a mixed strategy of the consumer and $\mathbf{p}^*$ to denote the optimal mixed strategy. If the consumer chooses mixed strategy $\mathbf{p}$ and nature chooses y, we denote the cost function as follows:

$$\begin{aligned} C(\mathbf{p}, y) \quad = \quad & \sum_{j\in[n]} \left(\int_0^y (a_j + r_j x + b_j) p_j(x) \mathrm{d}x \right. \\ & \left. + \int_y^B (a_j + r_j y) p_j(x) \mathrm{d}x \right) \end{aligned} \tag{15}$$

We define $\mathrm{OPT}(y)$ as the offline optimal strategy when nature chooses the action y, i.e.

$$\mathrm{OPT}(y) = \min_j \{a_j + r_j y\}, \quad y \in (0, B]$$

By [8], we can compute the function $\mathrm{OPT}(y)$ in linear time. The objective of the consumer is $\min_{\mathbf{p}} \max_y \frac{C(\mathbf{p}, y)}{\mathrm{OPT}(y)}$.

Similar to MSR, we give the following lemmas:

LEMMA 12. *For the optimal strategy p^* of the consumer, $\frac{C(\mathbf{p}^*, y)}{\mathrm{OPT}(y)}$ is a constant for any $y \in (0, B]$,.*

LEMMA 13. $\forall x \in (0, B], p_j^*(x) < +\infty$.

The problem is formalized as follows:

$$\begin{aligned} \text{minimize} \quad & \lambda & (16) \\ \text{subject to} \quad & \frac{C(\mathbf{p}, y)}{\mathrm{OPT}(y)} = \lambda, \quad \forall y \in (0, B] & (16a) \end{aligned}$$

$$\sum_{j=1}^{n} \int_0^B p_j(x)\mathrm{d}x = 1 \quad (16b)$$

$$p_j(x) \geq 0, \quad \forall x \in [0, B] \quad (16c)$$

Note that there may be probability mass at $x = 0$. For Problem 16, we find that the optimal mixed strategy $\mathbf{p}^*$ of the consumer is also segmented.

LEMMA 14. *In the optimal mixed strategy* $\mathbf{p}^*$, *there exists* $n+1$ *breakpoints* $B = d_1 \geq d_2 \geq \cdots \geq d_{n+1} = 0$, *which partition* $[0, B]$ *into* n *sub-intervals, such that* $\forall j = 1, \cdots, n$, $\forall x \in (d_{j+1}, d_j)$, $p_j^*(x) > 0$ *and* $p_i^*(x) = 0$ *for any* $i \neq j$.

Remark: Though we prove the form of the optimal solution to MSR-E, computing the analytical solution is very challenging. The point mass at $x = 0$ makes this problem much more difficult than MSR, because one needs to guarantee the nonnegativity of this probability mass. Moreover, the non differentiable points of $\mathrm{OPT}(y)$, which we call the offline breakpoints, complicate the probability density function form in each segment (d_{j+1}, d_j). In fact, we can obtain the exact analytic optimal solution when $n = 2$.

4. SKI RENTAL WITH ENTRY FEE AND SWITCHING

Now we introduce the last extension of MSR, the *entry fee included, switching allowed problem* (MSR-ES). All the settings are identical to those of MSR-E, except that the consumer is allowed to switch at any time. When a consumer enters or switches to a shop, she pays the entry fee of the shop. For instance, if a consumer enters shop 1 at first, then switches from shop 1 to shop 2 and returns to shop 1 at last, she pays the entry fee of shop 1 twice and the entry fee of shop 2 once.

Similar to MSR-E, there exist n shops. The entry fee, renting price, buying price of shop j are denoted by $a_j \geq 0, r_j > 0, b_j > 0$, respectively. Without loss of generality, we assume that

- $r_1 \leq r_2 \leq \cdots \leq r_n$;
- $\forall i, j,\ a_i < a_j + b_j$;
- $\forall i < j,\ a_i > a_j$ or $a_i + b_i > a_j + b_j$.

As in the MSR-S case, if there exists $i, j \in [n]$ such that $b_i > a_j + b_j$, then instead of buying in shop i, the consumer will switch from shop i to shop j to buy skis [6]. This is equivalent to setting b_i to be $\min_{j \neq i}\{a_j + b_j\}$. Therefore, without loss of generality, we assume that

- $\forall i, j,\ b_i \leq a_j + b_j$.

In the remainder of this section, we first define the action set and formulate our problem. Then, we show that the strategy space can be reduced by Lemma 15, 16 and 17. In Lemma 18, we show that for each switching operation, the operations of the consumer before or after the switching is not important. The only things we care about are when the switching happens, and which shops the switching operation relates to. Thus, we can construct a virtual shop for each switching operation, and (nearly) reduce this MSR-ES problem to MSR-E. Finally, we show that MSR-ES has the similar nice properties as MSR-E which we have known in Lemma 13 and 14.

[6] This phenomenon is called "switching for buying".

4.1 Notations and Analysis of MSR-ES

4.1.1 Reduced Strategy Space

The action set for nature is $\{y > 0\}$, defined as before. To represent the action set formally, we firstly introduce the operation tuple $\sigma = (i, j, x)$ to denote the switching operation of switching from shop i to shop j at time x. For special cases, $(0, j, 0)$ denotes the entering operation that the consumer enters shop j at the very beginning; $(i, 0, x)$ denotes the buying operation that the consumer buys at shop i at time x. An operation tuple can also be represented as (j, x) for short, denoting the switching operation to shop j at time x if $j > 0$, the entering operation if $x = 0$, and the buying operation at time x if $j = 0$.

Then, an action ψ is expressed as a sequence (may be infinite) of the operation tuples:

$$\psi = \{(j_0, x_0), (j_1, x_1), (j_2, x_2), \cdots\}$$

satisfying that

- $0 = x_0 \leq x_1 \leq x_2 \leq \cdots$;
- if there exists $x \geq 0$ such that $(0, x) \in \psi$, it is the last element in ψ.

or the full form with the same constraints:

$$\psi = \{(0, j_0, x_0), (j_0, j_1, x_1), (j_1, j_2, x_2), \cdots\}$$

Similar to other extensions, we reduce the action set. In this model, the definition of B is the same as those of MSR-E:

$$\begin{aligned} &\text{minimize} && B \\ &\text{subject to} && \forall i,\ a_i + Br_i \geq \min_j(a_j + b_j) \end{aligned}$$

and we give the following lemma:

LEMMA 15. *From the perspective of nature, any strategy* $y \in [B, +\infty)$ *is dominated. While for the consumer, any strategy in which the buying time* $x \in (B, +\infty) \cup \{+\infty\}$ *is dominated.*

Similar to MSR, we reduce the consumer's buying time to the interval $[0, B]$, and nature's action set to $\{y \in (0, B]\}$.

The following lemma shows that a consumer may switch from shop i to shop j for renting, only when $r_i > r_j$ and $a_i < a_j$.

LEMMA 16. *If a strategy of the consumer:*

$$\psi = \{(0, j_0, x_0), (j_0, j_1, x_1), \cdots, (j_{|\psi|-2}, 0, x_{|\psi|-1})\}$$

satisfies any of the following conditions, then it is dominated.

- $\exists 0 < \tau < |\psi| - 1$ *such that* $x_{\tau-1} = x_\tau$;
- $\exists (i, j, x) \in \psi$ *such that* $r_i \leq r_j$ *and* $(j, 0, x) \notin \psi$;
- $\exists (i, j, x) \in \psi$ *such that* $a_i \geq a_j$ *and* $(j, 0, x) \notin \psi$.

Here we give some intuitions. In these three cases, we can construct a new action ψ' by deleting one specified operation from ψ, and show that ψ is dominated by ψ'.

This lemma rules out a huge amount of dominated strategies from our action set and allows us to define the operation set:

$$\Sigma \triangleq \Big\{\sigma = (i, j, x) : i, j \in [n],\ r_i > r_j,\ a_i < a_j,$$

$$x \in (0, B]\Big\} \bigcup \Big\{(0, j, 0) : j \in [n]\Big\}$$
$$\bigcup \Big\{(j, 0, x) : j \in [n], x \in [0, B]\Big\}$$

Thus, we only need to consider such an action set:

$$\Psi_c \triangleq \Big\{\psi = \{(0, j_0, x_0), (j_0, j_1, x_1), \cdots, (j_{|\psi|-2}, 0, x_{|\psi|-1})\} : 0 = x_0 < x_1 < \cdots < x_{|\psi|-2} \leq x_{|\psi|-1} \leq B, r_{j_0} > r_{j_1} > \cdots > r_{j_{|\psi|-2}}, a_{j_0} < a_{j_1} < \cdots < a_{j_{|\psi|-2}}\Big\}$$

Since $r_{j_0} > r_{j_1} > \cdots > r_{j_k}$, we get $j_0 > j_1 > \cdots > j_k$ and $2 \leq |\psi| \leq n + 1$.

4.1.2 Mathematical Expression of the Cost, Ratio and the optimization problem

For nature's action $y \in (0, B]$ and the consumer's action $\psi = \{(j_0, x_0), \cdots, (0, x_{|\psi|-1})\} \in \Psi_c$, we define the cost $c(\psi, y)$ as follows:

$$c(\psi, y) \triangleq \begin{cases} \sum_{\tau=0}^{k-1}[a_{j_\tau} + r_{j_\tau}(x_{\tau+1} - x_\tau)] + r_{j_k}(y - x_k), \\ \quad \text{if } \exists 0 < k < |\psi|, x_{k-1} \leq y < x_k; \\ \sum_{\tau=0}^{|\psi|-2}(a_{j_\tau} + r_{j_\tau}(x_{\tau+1} - x_\tau)) + b_{j_{|\psi|-2}}, \\ \quad \text{if } y \geq x_{|\psi|-1}. \end{cases}$$

For any action $\psi = \{(j_0, x_0), \cdots, (0, x_{|\psi|-1})\}$, we use $\mathbf{s}(\psi)$ to denote the order of the operations:

$$\mathbf{s}(\psi) \triangleq \{(0, j_0), (j_0, j_1), \cdots, (j_{|\psi|-2}, 0)\}$$

or the short form:

$$\mathbf{s}(\psi) \triangleq \{j_0, j_1, \cdots, j_{|\psi|-2}, 0\}$$

Further, we define $\mathcal{S}$ as the collection $\mathbf{s}(\Psi_c)$ as follows:

$$\mathcal{S} \triangleq \{\mathbf{s} = \{j_0, j_1, \cdots, j_k, 0\} : k \geq 0, r_{j_0} > r_{j_1} > \cdots > r_{j_k}, a_{j_0} < a_{j_1} < \cdots < a_{j_k}\}$$

Note that $j_0, j_1, \cdots, j_k \in [n]$ and $\{0\} \notin \mathcal{S}$, so the amount of elements in $\mathcal{S}$ is upper bounded by $|\mathcal{S}| \leq 2^n - 1$.
We group all the actions in Ψ_c whose $\mathbf{s}(\psi)$ are identical. Thus, we partition Ψ_c into $|\mathcal{S}|$ subsets.
For any action ψ, let $\mathbf{x}(\psi)$ denote the sequence of the operation time, defined as follows:

$$\mathbf{x}(\psi) \triangleq (x_1, \cdots, x_{|\psi|-1})$$

For each operation order $\mathbf{s} \in \mathcal{S}$, we define $\mathcal{X}_\mathbf{s}$ as the collection $\{\mathbf{x}(\psi) : \mathbf{s}(\psi) = \mathbf{s}\}$, i.e.,

$$\mathcal{X}_\mathbf{s} \triangleq \{\mathbf{x} = (x_1, x_2, \cdots, x_{|\mathbf{s}|-1}) : 0 < x_1 < \cdots < x_{|\mathbf{s}|-1} \leq B\}$$

We observe that any $\mathbf{s} \in \mathcal{S}$ and $\mathbf{x} \in \mathcal{X}_\mathbf{s}$ can be combined to a unique action $\psi(\mathbf{s}, \mathbf{x})$. Further, we can use $c_\mathbf{s}(\mathbf{x}, y)$ and $c(\psi(\mathbf{s}, \mathbf{x}), y)$ interchangeably.
For each $\mathbf{s} \in \mathcal{S}$, we define the probability density function $f_\mathbf{s} : \mathcal{X}_\mathbf{s} \to [0, +\infty) \cup \{+\infty\}$ [7], which satisfies

$$\sum_{\mathbf{s}\in\mathcal{S}} \int \cdots \int_{\mathbf{x}\in\mathcal{X}_\mathbf{s}} f_\mathbf{s}(\mathbf{x})d\mathbf{x} = 1$$

[7] $f_\mathbf{s}(\mathbf{x}) = +\infty$ represents probability mass on $\mathbf{x}$.

Let $\mathbf{f} = \{f_\mathbf{s} : \mathbf{s} \in \mathcal{S}\}$ denote a mixed strategy for the consumer. Given a mixed strategy $\mathbf{f}$ of the consumer and nature's choice y, the expected competitive ratio is defined as follows:

$$R(\mathbf{f}, y) \triangleq \frac{C(\mathbf{f}, y)}{\mathrm{OPT}(y)} \tag{17}$$

where $\mathrm{OPT}(y) = \min_{j\in[n]}\{a_j + r_j y\}$, and

$$C(\mathbf{f}, y) \triangleq \sum_{\mathbf{s}\in\mathcal{S}} \int \cdots \int_{\mathbf{x}\in\mathcal{X}_\mathbf{s}} c_\mathbf{s}(\mathbf{x}, y) f_\mathbf{s}(\mathbf{x})d\mathbf{x} \tag{18}$$

The objective of the consumer is $\min_\mathbf{f} \max_y R(\mathbf{f}, y)$. The following lemma proves that $\forall y \in (0, B]$, $R(\mathbf{f}^*, y)$ is a constant in which $\mathbf{f}^*$ is an optimal mixed strategy.

LEMMA 17. *If $\mathbf{f}^*$ is an optimal solution of the problem $\arg\min_\mathbf{f} \max_y R(\mathbf{f}, y)$, then there exists a constant λ such that $\forall y \in (0, B]$, $R(\mathbf{f}^*, y) = \lambda$.*

The formalized optimization problem is as follows:

$$\text{minimize } \lambda \tag{19}$$
$$\text{subject to } \frac{C(\mathbf{f}, y)}{\mathrm{OPT}(y)} = \lambda, \forall y \in (0, B] \tag{19a}$$
$$\sum_{\mathbf{s}\in\mathcal{S}} \int \cdots \int_{\mathbf{x}\in\mathcal{X}_\mathbf{s}} f_\mathbf{s}(\mathbf{x})d\mathbf{x} = 1 \tag{19b}$$
$$f_\mathbf{s}(\mathbf{x}) \geq 0, \forall \mathbf{s} \in \mathcal{S} \tag{19c}$$

4.2 Reduction to MSR-E

For a mixed strategy $\mathbf{f}$, we define the probability density function of an operation $\sigma = (i, j\ x)$ as follows:

$$\mathbf{p}^{(\mathbf{f})}(\sigma) \triangleq \sum_{\mathbf{s}\in\mathcal{S}:(i,j)\in\mathbf{s}} \int \cdots \int_{\mathbf{x}_{-\{x\}}:\sigma\in\psi(\mathbf{s},\mathbf{x})} f_\mathbf{s}(\mathbf{x})d(\mathbf{x}_{-\{x\}}) \tag{20}$$

where $\mathbf{x}_{-\{x\}}$ is the vector $\mathbf{x}$ in which the element corresponding to x is eliminated. Here $p^{(\mathbf{f})}_{(i,j)}(x)$ can also be viewed as a marginal probability density function. Also the p.d.f of an operation can be expressed in another form:

$$p^{(\mathbf{f})}_{(i,j)}(x) \triangleq \mathbf{p}^{(\mathbf{f})}((i, j, x))$$

Then we give the following lemma:

LEMMA 18. *For any 2 mixed strategies $\mathbf{f_1}, \mathbf{f_2}$ for the consumer, we have $C(\mathbf{f_1}, y) = C(\mathbf{f_2}, y)$ for all $y \in (0, B]$ if $\mathbf{p}^{(\mathbf{f_1})}(\sigma) = \mathbf{p}^{(\mathbf{f_2})}(\sigma)$ for all $\sigma \in \Sigma$, i.e., for a mixed strategy $\mathbf{f}$, we only care about its marginal $\mathbf{p}^{(\mathbf{f})}(\sigma)$.*

Therefore, the target of the problem converts from the optimal $\mathbf{f}$ to the optimal $\mathbf{p}$. Note that for the switching operation from shop i to shop j, we do not care about which action ψ it belongs to. Instead, the only thing that matters is when this switching operation happens. This is similar to the one shop case, in which we only care about when the consumer decides to buy. Thus, for each switching pair (i, j), we consider it as a virtual shop. Among these $O(n^2)$ virtual shops, no switching will appear. Thus, we show that the `MSR-ES` problem is almost the same as `MSR-E`.

Now we show our settings for virtual shops. For all $i, j \in [n]$ such that $a_i < a_j, r_i > r_j$, we define the virtual shop (i, j) with entry fee $a_{(i,j)} = a_i - a_j$, renting price $r_{(i,j)} = r_i - r_j$ and buying price $b_{(i,j)} = a_j$. We regard the switching time from

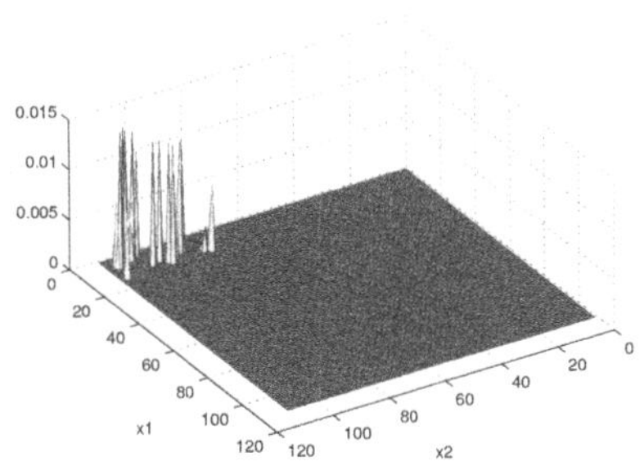

Figure 2: PDF of the strategies with switching actions, i.e., function $f_{\mathbf{s}}^*(x)$ when $\mathbf{s} = \{2,1,0\}$. x_1 is the switching time and x_2 is the buying time.

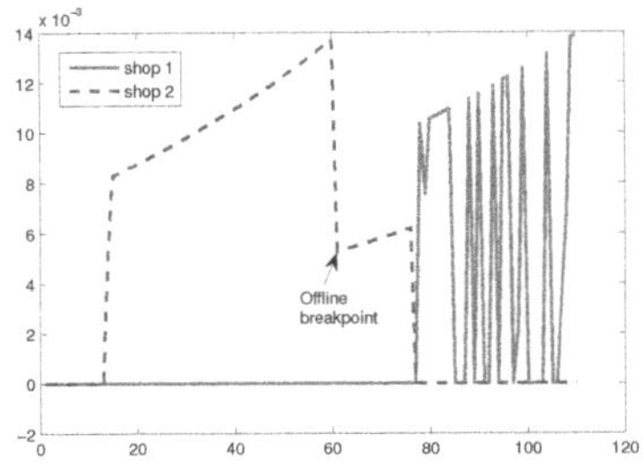

Figure 3: PDF of the strategies without switching actions, i.e., function $f_{\mathbf{s}}^*(x)$ when $|s| = 2$. Blue: $f_{\mathbf{s}}^*(x)$ when $\mathbf{s} = \{2,0\}$; Red: $f_{\mathbf{s}}^*(x)$ when $\mathbf{s} = \{1,0\}$.

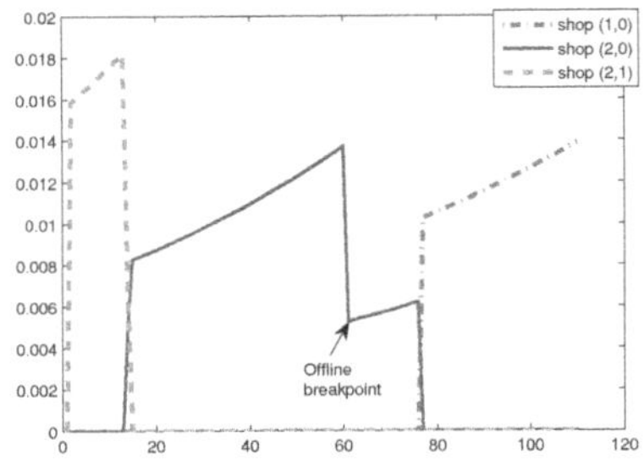

Figure 4: PDF of the virtual shops, i.e., function $p_{(i,j)}^{(\mathbf{f})}(x)$ when (i,j) is a virtual shop. Green: $p_{(2,1)}^*(x)$; Blue: $p_{(2,0)}^*(x)$; Red: $p_{(1,0)}^*(x)$.

i to j as the buying time in virtual shop (i,j). For special case, the prices of virtual shop $(j,0)$ is the same as the real shop j. Through this setting, it is not hard to verify that for any action ψ and any $0 \le y \le B$, the cost function $c(\psi, y)$ is exactly the summation of the cost in the corresponding virtual shops. Similar to a real shop, we define the cost for each virtual shop (i,j):

$$C_{(i,j)}(\mathbf{p}^{(\mathbf{f})}, y) \triangleq \int_0^y (a_{(i,j)} + r_{(i,j)}x + b_{(i,j)})p_{(i,j)}^{(\mathbf{f})}(x)\mathrm{d}x + \int_y^B (a_{(i,j)} + r_{(i,j)}y)p_{(i,j)}^{(\mathbf{f})}(x)\mathrm{d}x$$

Now we are ready to formalize MSR-ES by the following theorem:

THEOREM 4. *The optimization problem for the consumer can be formalized as follows:*

$$\text{minimize } \lambda \tag{21}$$

$$\text{subject to } \frac{C(\mathbf{f}, y)}{\mathrm{OPT}(y)} = \lambda \tag{21a}$$

$$C(\mathbf{f}, y) = \sum_{(i,j)\in[n]^2 : a_i < a_j, r_i > r_j} C_{(i,j)}(\mathbf{p}^{(\mathbf{f})}, y) + \sum_{j\in[n]} C_{(j,0)}(\mathbf{p}^{(\mathbf{f})}, y), \quad \forall y \in [0, B] \tag{21b}$$

$$\sum_{j\in[n]} \int_0^B p_{(j,0)}^{(\mathbf{f})}(x)\mathrm{d}x = 1 \tag{21c}$$

$$\sum_{j\in[n]: a_j < a_i, r_j > r_i} \int_y^B p_{(j,i)}^{(\mathbf{f})}(x)\mathrm{d}x \le \int_y^B p_{(i,0)}^{(\mathbf{f})}(x)\mathrm{d}x + \sum_{j\in[n]: a_i > a_j, r_i < r_j} \int_y^B p_{(i,j)}^{(\mathbf{f})}(x)\mathrm{d}x, \quad \forall i \in [n], y \in (0, B] \tag{21d}$$

Thus, MSR-ES can be regarded as MSR-E with $O(n^2)$ shops. The difference is that the summation of the buying probabilities in each virtual shop may be larger than 1. Fortunately, those nice properties of MSR-E still hold for MSR-ES.

LEMMA 19. *Lemma 13 and 14 still hold for the virtual shops in the MSR-ES problem.*

As in other extensions before, the probability density function of the virtual shops is segmented and each segment is an exponential function. The consumer only assigns positive buying probability in exactly one virtual shop at any time. As the buying time increases, she follows the virtual shop order in which the ratio between buying price and renting price is increasing.

In the 3 figures above, we give a simple example when $n = 2$ in order to make Lemma 19 easier to understand. We approach the optimal strategy through the discrete model and the figures show the p.d.f. functions in the optimal strategy. It can be seen that Lemma 19 is verified. Since there is a proof for Lemma 19, we do not give more complicated examples. The parameters for the 2 shops are as follows: $a_1 = 80, r_1 = 1, b_1 = 110, a_2 = 20, r_2 = 2, b_2 = 180$.

5. CONCLUSIONS

In this paper, we consider the multi-shop ski rental problem (MSR) and its extensions (MSR-S, MSR-E, and MSR-ES), in which there are multiple shops and the consumer wants to minimize the competitive ratio.

For each problem, we prove that in the optimal mixed strategy of the consumer, she only assigns positive buying probability to *exactly one* shop at any time. The shop order strongly relates to the ratio between buying price and renting price, even in which entry fee is involved. Further, in the basic problem (MSR), we derive a linear time algorithm for computing the optimal strategy of the consumer. For MSR-S, we prove that under the optimal mixed strategy, the consumer only switches to another shop at the buying time.

In problems MSR-E and MSR-ES, we show that the optimal strategy can be solved if the breakpoints are known. Similar to the basic problem (MSR), we conjecture that the quasi-concave property also holds for these two variants. Further, we conjecture that there exists an iteration algorithm using gradient decent technique, which might converge to the optimal solution.

6. ACKNOWLEDGEMENT

This work was supported in part by the National Basic Research Program of China Grant 2011CBA00300,2011CBA00301, the National Natural Science Foundation of China Grant 61033001, 61361136003, 041302007, the China youth 1000-talent grant 610502003, and the MSRA-Tsinghua joint lab grant 041902004.

7. REFERENCES

[1] Amazon EC2, `http://aws.amazon.com/ec2/`.

[2] Astrium, `http://www.astrium-geo.com/`.

[3] Digitalglobe, `http://www.digitalglobe.com/`.

[4] Elastichosts, `http://www.elastichosts.com/`.

[5] The multi-shop ski rental problem, `http://sites.google.com/site/multishopskirental/MSRtech.pdf`.

[6] Microsoft Windows Azure, `http://www.gogrid.com/`.

[7] C. Bodenstein, M. Hedwig, and D. Neumann. Strategic decision support for smart-leasing infrastructure-as-a-service. 2011.

[8] M. de Berg, M. van Kreveld, M. Overmars, O. Schwarzkopf, and M. Overmars. Computational geometry: algorithms and applications. 2000. *New York, New York.*

[9] R. Fleischer. On the bahncard problem. *Theoretical Computer Science*, 268(1):161–174, 2001.

[10] B. Guenter, N. Jain, and C. Williams. Managing cost, performance, and reliability tradeoffs for energy-aware server provisioning. In *INFOCOM, 2011 Proceedings IEEE*, pages 1332–1340. IEEE, 2011.

[11] Y.-J. Hong, J. Xue, and M. Thottethodi. Dynamic server provisioning to minimize cost in an iaas cloud. In *Proceedings of the ACM SIGMETRICS joint international conference on Measurement and modeling of computer systems*, pages 147–148. ACM, 2011.

[12] A. R. Karlin, C. Kenyon, and D. Randall. Dynamic tcp acknowledgement and other stories about e/(e-1). In *Proceedings of the thirty-third annual ACM symposium on Theory of computing*, pages 502–509. ACM, 2001.

[13] A. R. Karlin, M. S. Manasse, L. A. McGeoch, and S. Owicki. Competitive randomized algorithms for nonuniform problems. *Algorithmica*, 11(6):542–571, 1994.

[14] A. R. Karlin, M. S. Manasse, L. Rudolph, and D. D. Sleator. Competitive snoopy caching. *Algorithmica*, 3(1-4):79–119, 1988.

[15] A. Khanafer, M. Kodialam, and K. P. Puttaswamy. The constrained ski-rental problem and its application to online cloud cost optimization. In *Proc. IEEE INFOCOM*, 2013.

[16] M. Lin, A. Wierman, L. L. Andrew, and E. Thereska. Dynamic right-sizing for power-proportional data centers. In *INFOCOM, 2011 Proceedings IEEE*, pages 1098–1106. IEEE, 2011.

[17] Z. Lotker, B. Patt-Shamir, D. Rawitz, S. Albers, and P. Weil. Rent, lease or buy: Randomized algorithms for multislope ski rental. In *25th International Symposium on Theoretical Aspects of Computer Science (STACS 2008)*, volume 1, pages 503–514. Schloss Dagstuhl–Leibniz-Zentrum fuer Informatik, 2008.

[18] T. Lu and M. Chen. Simple and effective dynamic provisioning for power-proportional data centers. In *Information Sciences and Systems (CISS), 2012 46th Annual Conference on*, pages 1–6. IEEE, 2012.

[19] S. Shankland. Google to buy GeoEye satellite imagery, `http://news.cnet.com/8301-1023_3-10028842-93.html`.

[20] R. Singh, U. Sharma, E. Cecchet, and P. Shenoy. Autonomic mix-aware provisioning for non-stationary data center workloads. In *Proceedings of the 7th international conference on Autonomic computing*, pages 21–30. ACM, 2010.

[21] C. Wang, B. Urgaonkar, Q. Wang, G. Kesidis, and A. Sivasubramaniam. Data center cost optimization via workload modulation under real-world electricity pricing. *arXiv preprint arXiv:1308.0585*, 2013.

[22] W. Wang, B. Li, and B. Liang. To reserve or not to reserve: Optimal online multi-instance acquisition in iaas clouds. *arXiv preprint arXiv:1305.5608*, 2013.

CApRI: CAche-conscious data Reordering for Irregular codes

Wei Ding
Department of Computer Science and Engineering
The Pennsylvania State University
University Park, Pennsylvania, USA
wzd109@cse.psu.edu

Mahmut Taylan Kandemir
Department of Computer Science and Engineering
The Pennsylvania State University
University Park, Pennsylvania, USA
kandemir@cse.psu.edu

ABSTRACT

Caches play a critical role in today's computer systems and optimizing their performance has been a critical objective in the last couple of decades. Unfortunately, compared to a plethora of work in software and hardware directed code/data optimizations, much less effort has been spent in understanding the fundamental characteristics of data access patterns exhibited by application programs and their interaction with the underlying cache hardware. Therefore, in general it is hard to reason about cache behavior of a program running on a target system. Motivated by this observation, we first set up a "locality model" that can help us determine the theoretical bounds of the cache misses caused by irregular data accesses. We then explain how this locality model can be used for different data locality optimization purposes. After that, based on our model, we propose a data reordering (data layout reorganization) scheme that can be applied after any existing data reordering schemes for irregular applications to improve cache performance by further reducing the cache misses. We evaluate the effectiveness of our scheme using a set of 8 programs with irregular data accesses, and show that it brings significant improvements over the state-of-the-art on two commercial multicore machines.

Categories and Subject Descriptors

D.3.4 [**Programming Languages**]: Processors—*Compilers, Optimization*

Keywords

Data locality; compiler; irregular application; cache

1. INTRODUCTION

Many modern computing systems employ *caches* as a means of improving program performance and reduce power consumption. While the exact parameters of a cache (e.g., the number of layers in the cache hierarchy, capacity and associativity at each layer, interconnect topology) may change from one system to another, it is well-known that optimizing *data locality*[1] is critical for improving the cache performance of an application. This observation motivated intense research in the last couple of decades across the compiler and architecture communities, resulting in numerous publications. It is clear from an architecture viewpoint that tuning cache parameters carefully and engineering them better can provide magnitudes of improvements in cache access latencies and power consumption. It is also accepted that compiler-directed as well as run-time based data locality optimizations[2] can play a complementary role in bridging the gap between program data access patterns and target cache parameters.

Loop nest is one of the main targets for data locality optimizations since it is the most time-consuming structure in most data-intensive applications, e.g., those from scientific computing and embedded image/video processing. The references in a loop nest can be *regular* or *irregular*. Computations with irregular data access patterns are typically used to solve very complex problems, and therefore they are becoming increasingly important in different application domains. In computational fluid dynamics (CFD) for example, irregular data accesses are involved in simulating the interaction of liquids and gases with surfaces defined by boundary conditions. In n-body solvers, e.g., those employed in molecular dynamics, the simulation of physical movements of atoms and molecules makes the data accesses inherently irregular. Similarly, many applications that implement machine learning, computational geometry, SAT solving and data mining have irregular data access patterns. In these applications, the ability to exploit data locality by ensuring that most of the data requests are satisfied from caches can be a major factor affecting performance.

The prior compiler-based work on data locality optimization for irregular applications can be roughly categorized into two main groups: *computation reordering* and *data reordering*. While the former deals with rearranging data accesses at a program code level to ensure that consecutive accesses touch nearby data elements [15, 10], the latter

[1]Data locality can be defined as the reuse of data in a cache block before the block gets displaced from the cache. Therefore, in general, better data locality means fewer cache misses and higher performance.

[2]In compiler and architecture literature, the word "optimization" usually means "improvement" or "enhancement".

SIGMETRICS'14, June 16–20, 2014, Austin, Texas, USA.

http://dx.doi.org/10.1145/2591971.2591992 .

determines a data element-to-memory location mapping to achieve the same goal [15, 10]. However, most of these data locality oriented efforts are "heuristic approaches" since the locality optimization is a very hard problem in its general form [27]. In addition, much less effort has been spent in understanding the fundamental characteristics of data access patterns [34] exhibited by application programs and their interaction with underlying cache hardware [27].

Motivated by this, our *goals* in this paper include (i) understanding the characteristics of irregular data access patterns, (ii) investigating – in a formal setting – how these characteristics can be exploited for reordering data layout in irregular applications to improve their cache performance, and (iii) presenting a practical data reordering scheme that has both compile-time and run-time components. Specifically, this paper makes the following main *contributions*:

- We set up a *locality model* that can help us determine the theoretical bounds of the cache misses caused by irregular data accesses.
- We explain how this model can be used for different locality oriented optimizations.
- Based on our locality model, we propose a *data reordering* scheme, called *CApRI*, which can be used after any existing (data reordering) scheme to reduce the number of cache misses further. Our proposed scheme is performed at run time, and consequently, it can be used for most irregular applications without any profile data.
- We present experimental results obtained by applying CApRI to a set of 8 irregular applications. Our experimental evaluation on two commercial multicore systems reveals that the proposed strategy brings further execution time improvements over two previously-proposed state-of-the-art data reordering schemes.

Overall, this paper shows that, by employing a more formal view of data locality, one can improve over any given data layout optimization strategy.

The remainder of this paper is structured as follows. The next section revisits the basics of cache and irregular applications. Section 3 discusses the cache-conscious data reordering problem in optimizing irregular applications. Section 4 introduces our block distance-based locality model. Section 5 explains how this model can be used for data reordering. Section 6 discusses the detail of our implementation. Section 7 shows our experimental results on eight representative irregular applications. Section 8 discusses related work, and the paper is concluded in Section 9.

2. BACKGROUND

2.1 Cache Organization and Memory Layout

Multiple levels of on-chip caches are common today in both single-core and multi-core machines. Most on-chip caches are organized as a collection of *cache blocks (lines)*. A cache block is the unit of data transfer to/from an underlying layer in the memory hierarchy (DRAM or a lower level cache memory). Typical block sizes in commercial systems can vary between 32 bytes and 256 bytes. The mapping between memory blocks (a contiguous memory space of cache block size) and cache blocks is an important design issue. In a k-way *set-associative* cache, a memory block can be mapped to any of k different cache blocks. Figure 1 shows the different possible cache blocks that can hold given main memory blocks, depending on the associativity. The set (within the ways) is determined by the index in the address (which is divided into tag, index, block-offset and byte-offset bits). The number of sets in a way is $2^{\#ofindexbits}$. The tag is then compared to the tag field in the cache. If there is no index field (i.e., after block and byte offset, all the remaining bits are tag), the cache is *fully associative*. If there is only one way, the cache is *direct mapped*.

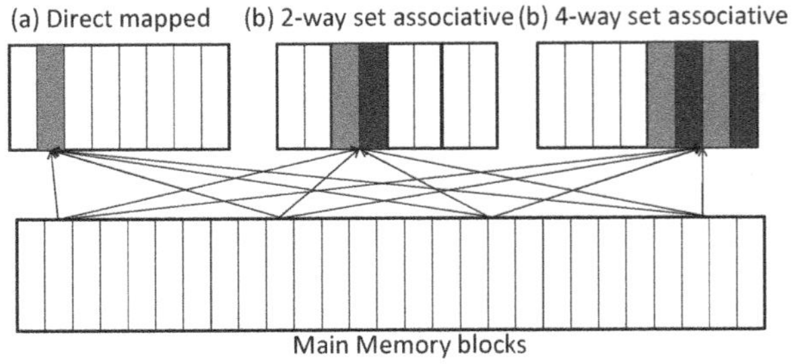

Figure 1: Comparing different cache organizations: showing different possible locations (shaded) in a cache to which a main memory block can be mapped, as the associativity of the cache varies.

Besides the set associativity, a cache also has a *replacement policy*. It tells which block to replace when the cache is full. The state-of-the-art on-chip caches employ various policies such as Random Replacement [16], LRU (Least Recently Used) [16], SLRU [20], Round-robin [2], and PLRU [1]. Each of these policies has its own advantages and disadvantages. Further, except Random Replacement, these policies determine the cache block/line to be replaced by looking at the past references history. LRU is the most commonly used policy where the next cache block to be evicted is the one that has been least recently used. It requires several bits to track when each cache block is accessed. The number of these bits increases as the set-associativity increases. However, the LRU is too extreme in terms of implementation cost and performance. This is the reason why the various heuristics mentioned earlier, e.g., PLRU and SLRU, have been proposed to reduce the hardware cost by approximating the LRU mechanism. In this work, we focus on the on-chip caches that employ the LRU-like cache replacement policies.

A memory (data) layout indicates the memory blocks of a set of data elements stored in the memory. Data reordering changes the memory layout, which in turn can have a significant impact on the cache behavior, e.g., whether an access incurs a cache miss or not. If the memory layout and data access pattern are in synch, then the limited capacity of the cache and associativity can be better utilized. As an example, let us assume that we have a direct-mapped cache and two scalar variables (x and y) are being accessed by a program in the order "x, y, x, y, $\cdots$". If these two variables are laid out in memory such that they belong to two different memory blocks that map to two different cache blocks, then this access pattern leads to only two misses. On the other hand, if the memory layout is such that x and y map

```
/* Moldyn*/
do t= 1, time
   do i =1, num_interactions
      force = f(x[left [i]], x[right[i]])
      y[left[i]] + = force
      y[right[i]] + = - force
   end do
end do
```

(a) Kernel of Moldyn [15].

```
/* NBF*/
do t= 1, time
   do i =1, num_atoms
      do j = start[i], start[i+1] -1
         force = f(x[i], x[partners[j]])
         y[i] + = force
         y[partners[j]] + = - force
   end do
end do
```

(b) Kernel of NBF [15].

Figure 2: Kernel computations of Moldyn and NBF.

to two memory blocks that in turn get mapped to the same cache block, the same access pattern with the same cache organization may lead to all accesses being misses (resulting in a cache miss rate of 100%).

2.2 Irregular Applications

One distinguishing characteristic of many array-based irregular applications is that their data accesses are made through *index arrays* [10]. Specifically, an array reference in an irregular application usually has the form of $A[f(i)]$, where the value of $f(i)$ is typically *not* known at compile-time. Here, f is an index array. A typical irregular program can be thought of having two parts. The first part starts at the beginning of the application code and ends where the index arrays are assigned. The second part on the other hand starts with the index array assignment and is where main data arrays are manipulated (through index arrays). We want to emphasize that, many important large scale applications fit in this irregular computation template. Examples include iterative partial differential equation (PDE) codes used in computational fluid dynamic (CFD) and quantum mechanics, molecular dynamic applications, global climate modeling codes, and thermodynamic applications [12].

Figure 2 shows the computation kernels of two irregular applications: Moldyn [15] and NBF [15]. Most of the prior work [15, 24, 10] that targets at optimizing these types of application programs insert some transformation code between these two parts (the detailed implementation of this will be discussed in Section 6). For example, Moldyn is a program used for simulating the particle movements caused by corss-interactions. The program maintains an interaction list, which is represented by the index arrays $left[]$ and $right[]$ in Figure 2(a), to record the particles that are close by. Each entry of the list, e.g., $left[i]$ and $right[i]$, is a pair of particles that are close enough to have interactions. Note that the code contains a time-step loop. In each iteration, the program first checks if it is time to update the interaction list; if so, it traverses the interaction list, and computes the force that a particle receives from its neighbors (represented by array y in Figure 2(a)). After that, it updates the location of each particle based on the newly computed forces (represented by the array x in Figure 2(a)). As can be observed from this code fragment, the accesses to arrays x and y are irregular, and the index array determines the data elements to which x and y refer at each iteration. Each time the index array gets updated, the patterns of accessing these two arrays change accordingly.

Compared to the regular computations, irregular computations have characteristics that make it very difficult to utilize caches efficiently. For example, in a regular application that has an array reference of the form $A[i]$, the accesses to array A are to consecutive memory locations. This regular access pattern allows the application to reuse each cache line (block) multiple times before it gets flushed from the cache. More importantly, regular codes can benefit from compiler optimizations, because compilers can analyze their data access patterns and improve their locality using estimates of cache performance to guide data transformations [22]. On the other hand, for the irregular accesses to arrays x and y in the Moldyn example, it is not trivial to exploit any data locality that may exist, since there is relatively little information available at compile time to extract data access patterns.

Recent works have shown that the cache performance of irregular programs can be improved by both data reordering and computation reordering [10, 15], which can be applied separately. Data reordering focuses on how to place the elements in an array to improve data locality. To the best of our knowledge, in most of the existing works, the basic strategy is to *reorder (reorganize) the data elements in memory space such that the elements that tend to be accessed in close proximity in time become spatially-close in the memory space.* Data reordering is usually followed by a computation ordering in which the compiler inserts calls to runtime routines to reorder the computations based on accessing order of the iterations. In the Moldyn example, the i loop, which encloses the irregular references, is reordered. In this paper, we only focus on data reordering.

3. PROBLEM DEFINITION

Since determining an optimal memory layout is an NP-hard problem in its general form [27], researchers have proposed various "heuristics" that reposition elements in an array to improve data locality. These algorithms include consecutive packing (CPACK) [10], Reverse Cuthill-McKee (RCM) [23], space filling curves (SFC) [24], recursive coordinate bisection (RCB) [5], multilevel graph partitioning (METIS) [19], and hierarchical clustering algorithm (GPART) [15]. For example, in consecutive packing (CPACK) [10], data is moved into adjacent locations in the order they are first accessed by the computation. Implementing this "first touch" policy requires a single pass over the data access sequence. In the Moldyn example, this data access sequence can be obtained by traversing the index array based on the i loop. In this way, data locality is likely to be improved as compared to the original storage order. CPACK has very low overhead since only one pass through the index array is required to mark the order at which data is accessed. It needs to be noted however that, this algorithm does not consider the impact of data affinity (on data locality), i.e., how frequently two data elements are accessed together (one after another). For example, given a data access sequence (pattern) "x y w x z u x z", where the memory block size is 2 (in terms of the number of data elements), CPACK will simply place x and y into the same memory block since they are first accessed together. However, it is easy to see that placing x and z into the same memory block should be a better choice since this would improve the data locality for the two accesses to z, compared to the original placement, which can only improve the data locality for the access to y.

Another layout optimization framework, GPART [15], operates on a graph (constructed by traversing the index array) where each data location is a node. There is an edge between two nodes whenever the corresponding data are accessed by the same loop iteration. GPART first sorts the nodes in a descending order based on their degrees, i.e, the number of incident edges. It then visits the nodes one-by-one in this order, and arbitrarily chooses one node from among the neighboring nodes of the currently-visited node to group them together. In the data access sequence "$x\ y\ w\ x\ z\ u\ x\ z$", for example, sorting the nodes increases the likelihood to place x and z into the same memory block. However, similar to the problem with CPACK, since (once the graph is built) GPART arbitrarily chooses the neighboring nodes to be grouped together, it can easily miss a better placement for some data elements.

These heuristic algorithms are based on a vague but well practiced rule: "placing data elements that are accessed together in a short period of time into nearby locations in memory increases the likelihood that cache lines will be reused multiple times before they get flushed from the cache." However, as discussed above, there could exist a better memory layout that can exhibit better data locality than the one obtained by these existing solutions. Based on this observation, we are motivated to consider the data reordering problem from a different angle. Specifically, the problem we address in this paper can be defined as follows:

> **After obtaining an optimized memory layout by applying any of the existing data reordering algorithms, is there a way to *improve* this layout through additional data reordering, so that the overall last level cache misses can be further reduced?**

That is, we want to quantify how much the performance of a well-optimized irregular code can be further improved. In the rest of this paper, we introduce a "locality model" that can be used to answer this question, and discuss how this model can be exploited for data layout optimization.

4. BLOCK DISTANCE-BASED LOCALITY MODEL

In this section, we explain the locality model employed in CApRI. To help abstract this problem, we introduce the following notation. We use T to represent the data access sequence in the irregular application, which can be obtained by traversing the index array based on the innermost loop(s), and a_x to represent the *access* to a particular data element x in T. Since the data elements are accessed sequentially in T, each access a_x can be assigned a "logical time stamp", which is denoted using $t(a_x)$. In addition, since each data element is placed into a memory block, each access to a data element in T corresponds to an access to the memory block that contains that data element. We use b_x to denote the memory block where x resides and $a_{\bar{x}}$ to represent the "most recent access" to b_x before a_x, and $C(b_x)$ to denote the set of cache blocks to which b_x is mapped in a k-way set-associative cache.

4.1 Block Distance

We now give the first of the two important definitions employed in our locality model.

DEFINITION 4.1. ***Block Distance.*** *The* block distance *between two accesses a_x and a_y, where $t(a_y) < t(a_x)$, is the number of "distinct" memory blocks that are mapped to the same set of cache blocks as x and accessed during time period $[t(a_y), t(a_x)]$.*

Note that, in this definition, only the memory blocks that are mapped to the same set of cache blocks are considered in the computation of this distance. In particular, when $t(a_y) = t(a_{\bar{x}})$, $dis(a_y, a_x)$ is referred to as the *block reuse distance* of a_x. If a_x is the first access (or a_y is the last access) to the memory block b_x in T, we define $dis(a_y, a_x)$ as ∞.

It is to be noted that the block reuse distance can be used to explain the concept of *data locality*: Given a k-way set associative cache and two accesses a_x and a_y where a_y is the most recent access to b_x before a_x, if $dis(a_y, a_x) \leq k$, then a_y ensures that b_x is in the target cache at time $t(a_x)$, and consequently, a_x will incur a "hit". In this case, we say that a_y exhibits *locality* due to a_x, and denote this relationship using $a_y \rightarrow a_x$. Also, we say that x and y have a *locality relationship*, denoted using $x \leftrightarrow y$, if there exist a_x and a_y in T such that $a_y \rightarrow a_x$ or $a_x \rightarrow a_y$. Note that, this also implies that the relative position of a data element within the memory block (with respect to other elements in the same block) may not affect whether the access to this data element will incur a hit or a miss in the target cache. Therefore, when performing data reordering to reduce the cache misses, we only need to focus on which "memory block" that the data elements should be moved to.

4.2 Locality Group

Moving a data element from one memory block to another will affect the block reuse distance of the accesses to other data elements. Therefore, reordering data elements in this way can be very costly. Next, we introduce a novel concept called *locality group*, which is a subset of the data elements that reside in the same memory block and have explicit or implicit locality relationship with each other. As will be shown shortly, performing data reordering *among locality groups* tends to incur lower overhead compared to the former case.

DEFINITION 4.2. ***Locality Group.*** *Given a data access sequence T, a set of data elements, denoted by G, forms a* locality group, *if and only if:*

1. *$\forall\ x,\ y \in G \wedge x \neq y$, x and y satisfy either of the following two conditions:*
   (a) $x \leftrightarrow y$.
   (b) there exist $x_1, x_2, \cdots, x_n \in G$, such that $x \leftrightarrow x_1$, $x_1 \leftrightarrow x_2, \cdots, x_n \leftrightarrow y$.
2. *there does not exist $x \notin G$ and $y \in G$, such that $x \leftrightarrow y$.*

Let us now consider the data access sequence "$u\ v \cdots z\ y \cdots x\ z$", where x, y, z, u, v are the only data elements placed into the memory block B. Since u and v are successively accessed, the block reuse distance of a_v is 1, which indicates that, no matter what value k takes, this distance is definitely less than or equal to k. Therefore, we have $a_u \rightarrow a_v$. Clearly, we have $u \leftrightarrow v$, and $\{u, v\}$ satisfies Condition 1 in Definition 4.2. Similarly, $x \leftrightarrow z$ and $z \leftrightarrow y$ and $\{x, y, z\}$ also satisfy Condition 1 in Definition 4.2 (note that, x and y satisfy Condition 1(b)). Assuming further that, in this data access sequence, there is no other access to $\{x, y, z, u, v\}$ and $v \leftrightarrow z$ does not hold, then a data element in $\{x, y, z\}$ cannot have the locality relationship ($\leftrightarrow$) with any data element in $\{u, v\}$ (Condition 2 in Definition 4.2). As a result, $\{x, y, z\}$ and $\{u, v\}$ are two different locality groups.

The block distance and locality group concepts are the foundation of our locality model. Informally speaking, block distance is a result of inherent interaction among data access sequence, memory layout and cache performance for the caches that employ LRU-like replacement policy. In fact, using the block distance and cache parameters (e.g., associativity), one can compute the number of cache misses (i.e., block distances larger than the set associativity of the target cache indicate misses). On the other hand, the locality group provides an insight of how to use the block distance for locality oriented optimizations. In other words, while block distance captures current cache performance, locality group captures potential improvement of cache performance. When performing data reordering at a locality group granularity, we have the following two conclusions:

LEMMA 4.3. ***Non-increased Cache Misses:*** *Moving G from b_x to b_y will not increase the total number of cache misses in T if $C(b_y) = C(b_x)$.*

PROOF. Let a_i denote an arbitrary access in T that originally incurs a cache hit, i.e., $dis(a_i^-, a_i) \leq k$. Clearly, if $C(b_i) \neq C(b_x)$, then performing the above movement will not change $dis(a_i^-, a_i)$. If $C(b_i) = C(b_x)$, then after moving G from b_x to b_y, none of the distinct memory blocks in $C(b_x)$ that are accessed during time period $[t(a_i^-), t(a_i)]$ would change except that b_x will be replaced by b_y. Therefore, in this case, $dis(a_i^-, a_i)$ will not be increased, neither. As a result, for any access in T that originally incurs a cache hit, the stated move operation will not change its block reuse distance, i.e., it will still incur a cache hit after this movement. □

LEMMA 4.4. ***Decreased Cache Misses:*** *Let $C(b_x) = C(b_y) = C(b_z)$, $x \in G_1$ and $y \in G_2$. If $dis(a_x^-, a_x) > k$ and $dis(a_y, a_x) \leq k$, then moving G_1 and G_2 to b_z will reduce the total number of cache misses by 1. Here we assume that the total number of data elements in G_1 and G_2 is no greater than the cache/memory block size.*

PROOF. First, according to Lemma 4.3, after moving G_1 and G_2 to b_z, all the accesses that originally incur cache hits will remain as hits. In addition, except for b_x, which is replaced by b_y, none of the distinct memory blocks in $C(b_x)$ that are accessed during time period $[t(a_y), t(a_x)]$ would be changed. Therefore, we would still have $dis(a_y, a_x) \leq k$. However, since both x and y now reside in b_z, a_x will incur a hit in the target cache. Therefore, the total number of cache misses will be reduced by 1. □

4.3 Potential Uses of Our Locality Model

We envision at least three potential uses of our locality model. The first is data/memory layout optimization to improve the overall cache performance, which is the main topic of this paper and discussed in the next section in detail. The second is the row-buffer optimization for improving memory performance. A row-buffer is a small buffer employed in modern memory chips that allows quick and easy access to multiple data words (usually the page size) located on a common physical row in the memory. Normally, accessing a data in the row buffer (which incurs a *row buffer hit*) will be much faster than accessing a data not in the row buffer (which incurs a *row buffer miss*). The row buffer locality refers to the reuse of the same row while it is buffered (i.e., a sequence of requests on the same pages goes to the same row buffer). Since both the memory performance and cache performance are important as far as application performance is concerned, a practical problem is how to improve both of them by taking both the row buffer locality and cache locality into account. Since an application optimized for cache locality may not exhibit good row buffer locality, and vice versa, how to isolate the cache performance from the memory performance becomes very critical. This is where our locality model comes into the picture. More specifically, Lemma 4.3 provides several constraints to manipulate the memory layout such that cache miss rate will not be increased. If there exists a row buffer locality optimization scheme that can satisfy these constraints, then the row buffer locality can be improved and, at the same time, the cache performance will not be affected. Further, note that Lemma 4.4 gives the constraints that needs to be satisfied for reducing the cache miss rate. If the proposed row buffer locality optimization scheme can satisfy these constraints, then both row buffer locality and cache locality can be improved. The third potential use of our locality model is data prefetching. If the data access pattern is known, then the "block distance" can be used to evaluate the effectiveness of a given data prefetching scheme. For example, assuming that a proposed prefetching scheme tries to prefetch x in order to make the future access to y hit in the cache (x and y reside in the same memory block), then in order to measure whether this can be realized or not (or whether this scheme is good or not), one can simply check the block reuse distance of the future access to y. We postpone an evaluation of our locality model when targeting row buffers and prefetching to a future study.

Algorithm 1 Cache-conscious data reordering.

/* Step 1: Determining the Locality Groups */
for every access a_x in T **do**
  if $list_{C(b_x)}$ is not full or ($\forall a_y \in list_{C(b_x)} : b_x \neq b_y$) **then**
    place a_x into $list_{C(b_x)}$
  else if $\exists a_y \in list_{C(b_x)} : b_x = b_y$ **then**
    replace a_y with a_x in $list_{C(b_x)}$
    place x and y into the same locality group
  end if
end for
/* Step 2: Constructing the Affinity Graph*/
for every access a_x in T **do**
  update the affinity between the locality group of x and any other locality group in $list_{C(b_x)}$
end for
/* Step 3: Merging the Locality Groups*/
sort the edges in the affinity graph in descending order
for each edge e in sorted order **do**
  if the total size of the two nodes connected through e is no larger than the memory block size **then**
    merge these nodes into one node
    redirect the edges via these nodes to the new node
    update the affinities on the these edges accordingly
  end if
end for

5. DATA REORDERING

5.1 Algorithm

Given a k-way set-associative last level cache,[3] a memory layout, and a data access sequence, we now discuss how CApRI finds an improved memory layout based on our proposed locality model (specifically, Lemmas 4.3 and 4.4). The idea behind our approach is that, if the accesses to the data elements in two locality groups (in different cache lines) always appear together with a very high frequency, then we try to place these two groups into the same cache line so that the total number of cache misses is reduced.

Step 1: Determining the Locality Groups. We determine all the locality groups by scanning the data access sequence (indicated by the index array). Specifically, if there exists an access before a_x (denoted as a_y) that satisfies $dis(a_y, a_x) \leq k$, then we place x and y into the same locality group. Thus, after one scanning of the index array, all the locality groups are determined. The pseudo-code for this step is given in lines 1–9 of Algorithm 1. The key here is to maintain a list for each cache set, e.g, $list_{C(b_x)}$, which stores the most recent accesses to k different memory blocks that are mapped to $C(b_x)$. An advantage of this list is that the block distance between the current access a_x and any other access in the list is always less than or equal to k ($dis(a_y, a_x) \leq k$). Therefore, if there exists an access a_y in the pool such that $b_y = b_x$, then x and y should be placed into the *same* locality group.

Step 2: Constructing the Affinity Graph. After determining the locality groups, we next construct an *affinity graph* (an example of which is shown in Figure 3), where each node represents a locality group, and the weight attached to an edge between two locality groups that are mapped to the same cache set indicates their *affinity* (defined below).

DEFINITION 5.1. ***Affinity.*** *Given two locality groups G_1 and G_2, the number of pairs $\langle a_x, a_y \rangle$ that satisfy $x \in G_1$, $y \in G_2$, $C(b_x) = C(b_y)$ and $dis(a_y, a_x) \leq k$ is referred to as the "affinity" between G_1 and G_2.*

The pseudo-code of this step is captured in lines 10–13 of Algorithm 1. Note that, for each a_x, similar to the first step, we make one pass over the pool. Therefore, we can combine the process of constructing the affinity graph with the process of determining the locality groups in a single pass over this list. During this pass, we can determine the locality group of x (the first step), and if necessary, also update the affinity between the locality groups of the data elements whose accesses are stored in the list accordingly.

Step 3: Merging the Locality Groups. We first sort the edges in the affinity graph in a non-increasing order based their weights. This is because, larger the weight of an edge that connects two nodes, more cache misses can be eliminated by merging these two nodes. Next, we merge the nodes that are connected by the edge with the largest weight. Once two nodes are merged into a node, all the edges from other nodes to these two nodes are redirected to the new node. We also update the weight after the merge. Specifically, if there exists another node G_3 connected to both G_1 and G_2, with the weights w_1 and w_2, respectively, then after merging G_1 and G_2 into a single node G, the weight between

[3]It should be noted that, although we only target last level cache, our scheme can also be extended to multi-level caches.

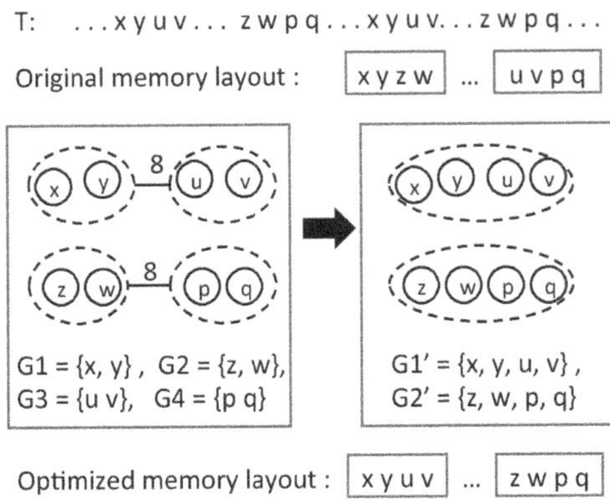

Figure 3: Data reordering example. In the original layout, x, y, z and w reside in the same memory block, u, v, p and q reside in another memory block, and both of these memory blocks are mapped to the same cache sets. After CApRI reorders the layouts, x, y, u and v are placed into the same memory block and z, w, p and q are placed into another memory block. As a result, the 4 misses incurred by the accesses to u and p n the original layout are turned into cache hits, and the total number of cache misses is reduced by 4.

G and G_3 will be assigned as $w_1 + w_2$. Note that one locality group can be merged with multiple locality groups. We then continue merging the nodes connected by the edge with the second largest weight, and so on. This step is repeated until no further nodes could be merged. The pseudo-code of this step is given in lines 14–22 in Algorithm 1. Figure 3 shows the improved memory layout generated by our data reordering scheme.

In conclusion, the data reordering scheme described above first determines all the locality groups; then, it evaluates how frequently the data elements in two groups are always accessed together (based on the concept of affinity defined above); if they have very high affinity, it tries to place all the data elements in these groups into the same memory block. The foundation behind this algorithm is captured in Lemmas 4.3 and 4.4. Specifically, in Step 3, since the memory block that two locality groups are moved to and their original memory blocks are mapped to the same cache sets, Lemma 4.3 ensures that this step will *not* increase the total number of cache misses. In addition, due to the high run-time overhead, it is hard to merge the locality groups by checking each condition listed in Lemma 4.4. However, based on Lemma 4.4, we note that, if there exist a_x and a_y such that $dis(a_y, a_x) \leq k$, then it is possible to eliminate one cache miss by moving the locality groups of x and y to the *same* memory block. *This is where the concept of affinity comes into the picture.* The affinity between two groups can be used to indicate the maximum number of cache misses that could possibly be eliminated. Therefore, when merging the locality groups with high affinity, there will be a good chance that more cache misses are eliminated.

5.2 Complexity Analysis

We now discuss the algorithmic complexities of CApRI, CPACK [10], GPART [15] RCB [5] and METIS [19]. We assume that the number of data elements in the data access sequence is N, the length of the index array is E, and the

```
/* Executor*/
do t= 1, time
   /*If it is time to update the
      interaction list */
   x', y' = Trans(x, y);
   do i =1, num_interactions
      force = f(x'[left [i]], x'[right[i]])
      y'[left[i]] + = force
      y'[right[i]] + = - force
   end do
end do
```

```
/* Inspector*/
Trans(x, y)
  do i =1, num_interactions
    /*data reordering
       algorithms*/
  end do
return (x' y')
```

Figure 4: Using the inspector module for data reordering in Moldyn.

Table 1: Benchmark codes used in our evaluation.

Benchmark	Description	Input Size	L2 Miss Rate
NBF	Force field of molecular dynamics simulation [15]	16.6MB	27.3%
IRREG	Kernel of an iterative partial differential equation solver [15]	12.9MB	16.8%
MOLDYN	Molecular dynamics simulation [15]	27.3MB	28.4%
MESH	Unstructured mesh simulation [33]	41.8MB	31.6%
CDF	Unstructured grid finite volume solver [33]	23.9MB	34.3%
SNNET	Discrete event simulation of large scale networks	54.1MB	46.2%
TR5	Large scale ocean simulation	27.8MB	19.7%
MIGEND	Content similarity search engine	34.7MB	24.9%

cache size is C. The consecutive packing (CPACK) has a cost of $O(E)$, since it rearranges the data elements based on their "first-touch" order and requires one pass through the index array. *GPART* has a cost of $O(E * g(C))$, where $g(C)$ is a constant function greater than 1, RCB has the complexity of $O(N(log_2 N)^2)$, and METIS has the cost $O(2N log_2 N) + O(E)$. As can be seen, GPART is a little more expensive than CPACK, and comparing to CPACK and GPART, RCB and METIS have higher complexity. In comparison, assuming that the size of $list_{C(b_x)}$ (defined in Step 1 of our algorithm) is p ($p << N$) and the number of edges in the affinity graph is E', then the complexity of our scheme is $O(p * N) + O(E')$. Since our affinity graph is constructed at a coarser granularity than CPART and GPART, we usually have $O(E') < O(E) << O(N)$. Therefore, the complexity of CApRI is higher than CPACK and GPART but lower than RCB and METIS.

6. IMPLEMENTATION DETAILS

The inspector-executor technique [9, 14, 10, 15] is a design methodology widely used in compiler optimizations for irregular applications (i.e., data reordering and computation reordering). The inspector is used to preprocess memory access patterns, e.g., identify non-local data needed by each processor; and the executor simply performs the optimization based on the imformation obtained by the inspector. There also exist several works on automically generating inspectors and executors [14, 15]. In our implementation, we developed a simplified/customized version of inspector/executor for our proposed data reordering scheme. Specifically, CApRI generates run-time library calls to the *inspector module* to process memory access patterns at runtime and identify non-local data needed by each processor. These locality inspectors are typically inserted by a compiler into the code and modify the data order at run-time.[4] Figure 4 shows the structure of the inspector module used to implement the data reordering in Moldyn (one of the benchmarks we used), where $Trans(x, y)$ is the inspector inserted after each update of the interaction list. It should be noted that, for different data reordering algorithms, the differences are mainly in $Trans(x, y)$.

As a result, we implement the proposed data reordering strategy in $Trans(x, y)$. It should be noted that this scheme can be embedded into most existing data reordering algorithms. This is because our scheme tries to obtain a "better" memory layout from a *given memory layout*, instead of trying to determine an optimized layout from scratch. That is, when the given layout is the one optimized by other techniques, we can still apply our scheme to improve cache performance further. We also want to emphasize that, while the way in which our data reordering scheme is used for irregular applications is similar to the previously-proposed techniques (i.e., inserting – at compile-time – a piece of code to be executed at runtime), our data reordering algorithm itself (which is based on the concept of locality group) is entirely different from any prior work we are aware of.

Another problem that needs to be addressed in our implementation is how to obtain the data access sequence. In a single-threaded (serial) irregular application, this sequence is *exactly* the one obtained through the index array. However, in case of a multi-threaded irregular application, due to the unpredictable interferences among the threads, the data access sequence obtained in this way may not be the actual sequence of data accessed during the execution. This creates a difficulty in applying our data reordering scheme to multi-threaded applications. There exist several approaches to accurately predict the data access sequence of a multi-threaded application [6, 28]. However, in our current implementation, we simply use the sequence obtained through the index array for the multithreaded application as well. This is because the locality group and the affinity between two locality groups are determined by the most-recent k accesses before each access. Therefore, they have certain tolerance to the mismatch between the assumed and actual data access sequences. In other words, it is still possible to apply our approach to multi-threaded applications, expecting that the mentioned mismatch would be tolerated. For example, when determine whether x and y belong to the same locality group or not, we only need to consider whether a_y appears in the most-recent k accesses before a_x or vice versa, and do not need to consider the exact position of a_y in the actual data access sequence. As a result, the locality groups as well as the affinity graph determined by the assumed data access sequence can be considered as a reasonable approximation of the actual data access sequence at run-time.

[4]The runtime overhead caused by this can be reduced by the approaches proposed in [10].

Table 2: Intel Harpertown configuration.

Core Count	8 (2 sockets)
Clock Frequency	3.2GHz
L1	32KB/core; 8-way; 64-byte line, 3 cycle latency
L2	6MB, 24-way, 64-byte line, 15 cycle latency
Off-Chip Memory	~ 100ns

Table 3: Important statistics.

Benchmark	Number of Locality Groups	Number of Merges	Code Size Increase	Compiler Time Increase
NBF	126	51	19%	47%
IRREG	109	44	18%	55%
MOLDYN	187	111	22%	41%
MESH	468	196	9%	59%
CDF	674	193	12%	53%
SNNET	1814	488	6%	66%
TR5	854	287	9%	62%
MIGEND	1016	321	7%	68%

7. EXPERIMENTAL EVALUATION

7.1 Setup and Workloads

We implemented CApRI using SUIF [3]. which is a public compiler infrastructure. It includes a series of extensible compiler passes (phases) built on the top of a kernel. Its scalable interface enables quick implementation of data locality and parallelism optimizations. We inserted a new pass in SUIF to perform the locality group analysis (and therefore generate/identify the locality groups). We also manually inserted the directives in the program to be optimized to let the compiler know where to start this pass. The compiler can identify and parallelize irregular reductions. Therefore, the inspectors are inserted based on when the memory access patterns are changed. For our experimental evaluations, we used eight application programs listed in Table 1. The first five of these applications programs are collected from different sources, and the remaining three are maintained by us locally. A common characteristic of these applications is that they are highly *irregular*, i.e., most of the data accesses they make are through index arrays. For the outside applications, we used the largest input size we have access to. The third column of Table 1 gives the input data set sizes in MBs. These benchmarks also represent a mix as far as code size is concerned; excluding comment lines, the total number of program lines range between 147 (NBF) and 6,133 (SNNET). Most of our experiments are performed on an Intel Harpertown machine. Table 2 gives important characteristics of this machine, and the last column of Table 1 shows the L2 miss rates on Harpertown when using the original applications (*without* any data reordering scheme being applied). Unless otherwise stated, the results are presented for a *single core*; later, we also give scalability results when using multiple cores. Each experiment reported below has been repeated ten times to capture runtime variations, and the result shown represents the average value after excluding the minimum and maximum values observed during the experiments.

Before discussing the results from our experimental evaluation, we first present some statistics resulting from our

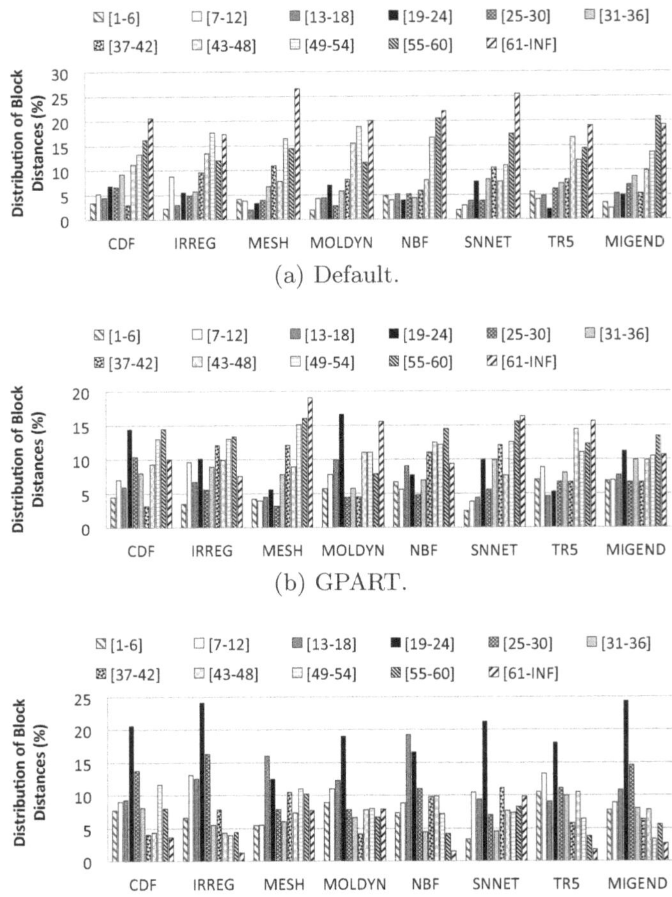

(a) Default.

(b) GPART.

(c) GPART+.

Figure 5: Distribution of block sizes for (a) Default, (b) GPART and (c) GPART+.

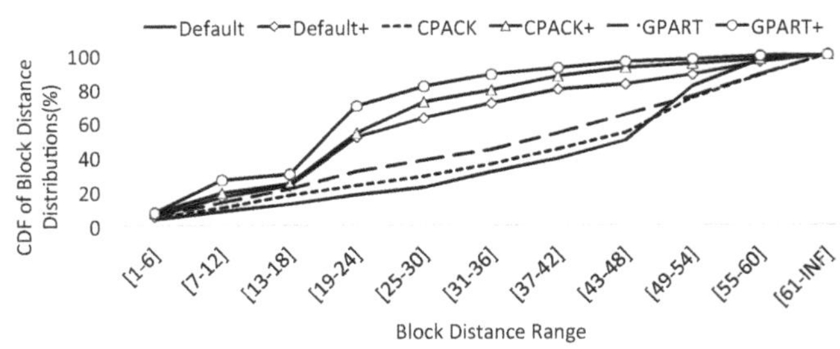

Figure 6: The CDF of block distances, where the curve for each version (Default, Default+, CPACK, CPACK+, GPART, and GPART+) represents average values across all applications.

compiler optimization. Table 3 gives, for each benchmark code we compiled, the total number of locality groups detected (second column), the number of merge operations performed on locality groups (third column), the increase in the original code size (fourth column), and the increase in the compilation time (last column). We see that the average increase in code size (GPART+ over GPART, as will be described shortly) is around 12.7%, and the average increase in compilation time (GPART+ over GPART) is around 56.4%.

For each application program in our suite, we performed experiments with six different versions:

- *Default.* This represents the original application code without any data reordering scheme applied.
- *CPACK.* This is the code obtained using the CPACK approach presented in [10].
- *GPART.* This is the code obtained using the GPART approach presented in [15].
- *Default+, CPACK+, GPART+.* These versions correspond to *Default*, *CPACK* and *GPART*, respectively, followed by CApRI.

We also want to point out that, other algorithms such METIS [19] and RCB [5], mentioned in Section 5.2, have significantly higher runtime overheads than GPART and CPACK, and they are quite expensive when used for cache optimizations [15]. Therefore, in a scenario like ours where the layout should be modified during execution (at runtime), there is a motivation to adopt reordering-based techniques instead of graph partitioning based techniques. In addition, GPART performs better than METIS for most cases [15]. And, since our preliminary experiments also indicated the same, we chose GPART for comparison (instead of METIS). However, METIS and similar graph partitioning tools have a very important role in sparse/irregular HPC codes. For example, in a cluster based environment, the target-graph can be partitioned using METIS to minimize inter-node communication, and then the local-portion of each node can be laid out in memory using our approach. In that case, METIS and our approach each address different aspects of locality: one across nodes(minimizing communication in distributed-memory space), and the other across cores in a node (shared cache locality).

7.2 Results

We present our main results in a bottom up fashion, starting with the lowest metric and moving towards the highest metric. More specifically, we first give results that demonstrate the effectiveness of our layout optimization strategy in reducing the block distances. Next, we show how these reductions in block distances reflect on last level cache misses. Then, we show how these improved miss rates translate to reductions in average data access latency. Finally, we discuss what the improved data access latencies mean as far as the overall application performance (execution latency) is concerned.

Block Distance Results. Figure 5 gives, in (a), (b) and (c), respectively, the distribution of block sizes for Default, GPART and GPART+. Each bar in these bar-charts represents a different block distance range and the y-axis gives the frequency of occurrence of these ranges. The general trend that can be observed in these plots is the reduction in block distances as we go from Default to GPART, and also from GPART to GPART+. In particular, in the case of Default, the fraction of block distances that fall in the [1-24] range (recall that the last level cache in Harpertown is 24-way set-associative) is 17%, whereas the corresponding numbers in the cases of GPART and GPART+ are 28.4% and 49.1% in that order. We would like to emphasize that GPART represents a highly-optimized memory layout and our strategy (GPART+) is able to achieve significant additional reductions in block distances over GPART (as a result, most block distances fall into smaller block distances after CApRI is used). Figure 6 gives the CDF of block distances, where the curve for each version (Default, Default+, CPACK, CPACK+, GPART, and GPART+) represents average value across all applications (for each block distance range). We note that, when our approach is applied to Default, the fraction of the block distances in the range of [1-24] is increased by 33.4%. Further, when it is applied to CPACK (resp. GPART), the fraction of the block distances in the range of [1-24] is increased by 30.2% (resp 38.3%).

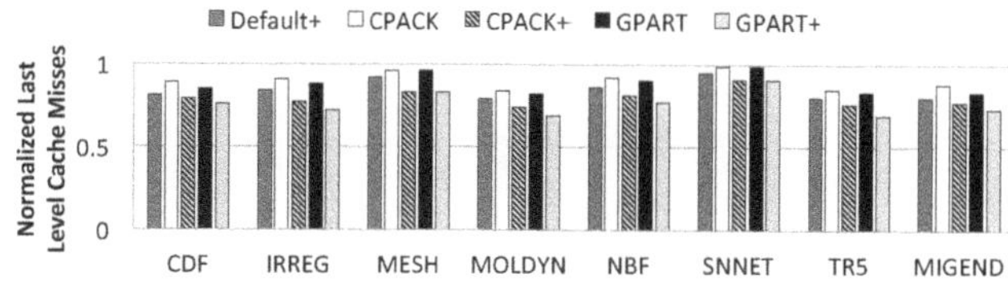

Figure 7: Normalized L2 misses on Intel Harpertown.

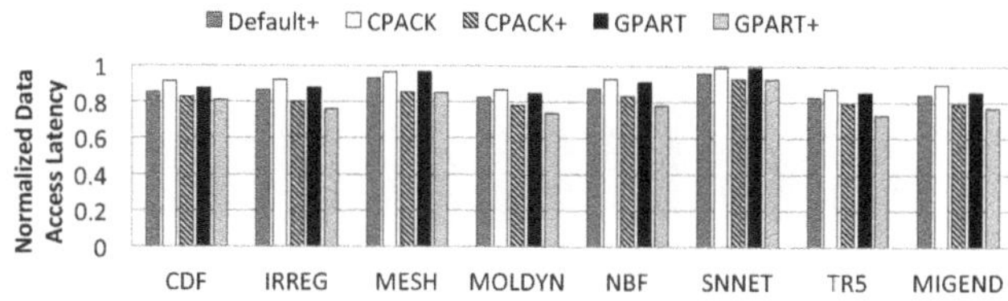

Figure 8: The normalized average data access latency values for our benchmark programs under different schemes.

Cache Miss Results. We now discuss how these improvements on block distances translate to cache performance improvements. We present the L2 misses (of Harpertown) in Figure 7, *normalized* with respect to the *Default* version.[5] One can make two critical observations from these results. First, both GPART and CPACK reduce cache misses compared to *Default*. Second, our proposed data reordering scheme is able to bring additional improvements in all benchmarks tested when applied following *Default*, *CPACK*, or *GPART*. Specifically, the average cache miss reductions brought *GPART+* over *GPART* is 13.6%, and that brought by *CPACK+* over *CPACK* is 11.9%.

Data Access Latency Results. The average data access latency is a metric that can be used to measure the effectiveness of data locality optimizations, and include the impact of cache hits and misses as well as delays in buses and memory controllers. Figure 8 gives the normalized average data access latency values for our benchmark programs under different schemes. We see that Default+, CPACK+ and GPART+ improve over Default, CPACK and GPART by 8.7%, 9.4% and 10.2% in that order.

Execution Time Results. While these reductions in cache misses and average data access latencies are important, the ultimate metric for measuring the effectiveness of any data locality optimization is the execution time. In particular, our approach applies data reordering at runtime, and this leads to additional overheads during execution. Fur-

[5]L1 behaviors of different versions were very similar; so, we mainly focus on L2 behavior, which is more critical from the perspective of miss latency.

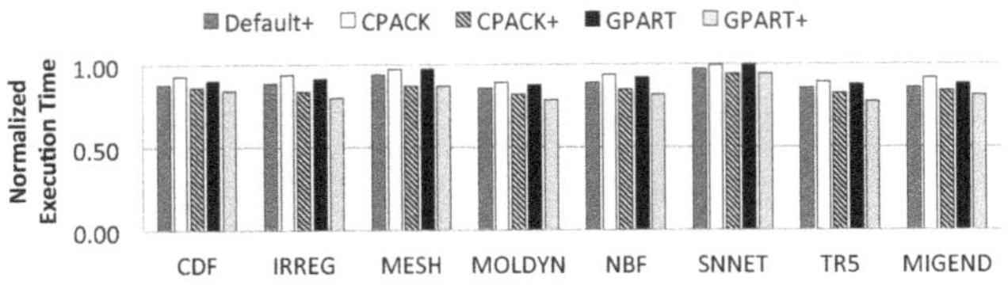

Figure 9: Normalized execution times on Intel Harpertown.

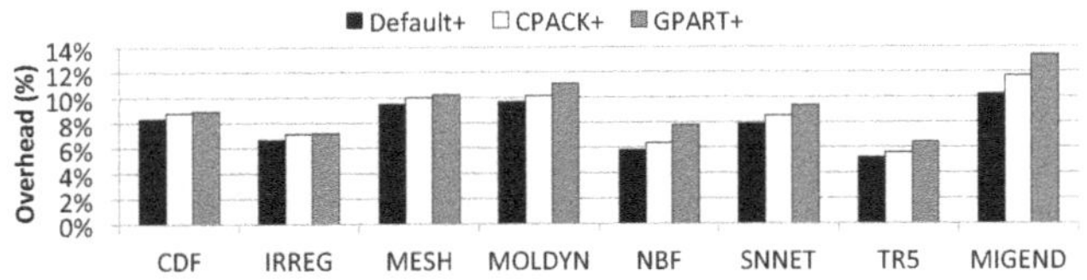

Figure 10: Runtime overheads as a fraction of the total execution time.

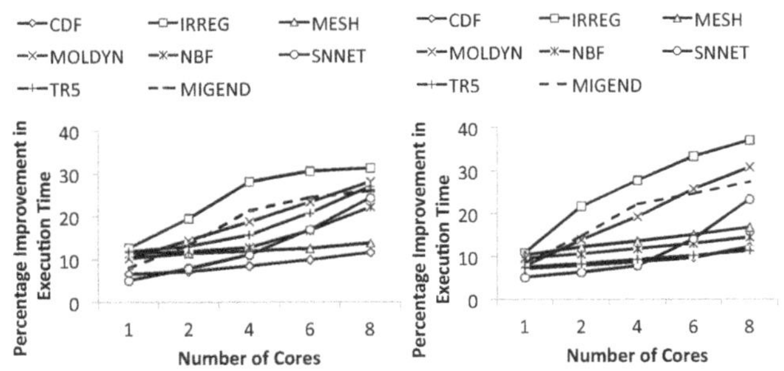

(a) GPART+ over GPART. (b) CPACK+ over CPACK.

Figure 11: Scalability results on Intel Harpertown.

thermore, data accesses is only one component of execution; execution of other types of instructions, on-chip resource conflicts, pipeline effects, and branches are among the other factors that can impact the total number of execution cycles. Figure 9 gives the execution times of the application programs when our approach is used. Each bar in this plot is *normalized* with respect to *Default*, and the execution times given for *Default+*, *CPACK+*, and *GPART+* include *all* runtime overheads incurred by our data reordering scheme. While, as expected, our execution time savings are in general lower than the improvements in L2 miss rates and data access latencies, we notice that our data reordering scheme is able to reduce execution cycles no matter what the input layout is. Specifically, the execution time improvements brought by *Default+* over *Default*, *CPACK+* over *CPACK*, and *GPART+* over *GPART* are 11%, 8.3% and 9.6%, respectively, on average. Overall, the results given in Figures 7, 8 and 9 clearly demonstrate that our approach is able to improve over state-of-the-art schemes (CPACK and GPART).

Recall that the results for *Default+*, *CPACK+*, and *GPART+* in Figure 9 already include the runtime overheads caused by our scheme. Figure 10 quantifies these overheads explicitly as *a fraction of the total execution time*. We observe that these runtime overheads average on 8.6% when all eight application programs are considered.

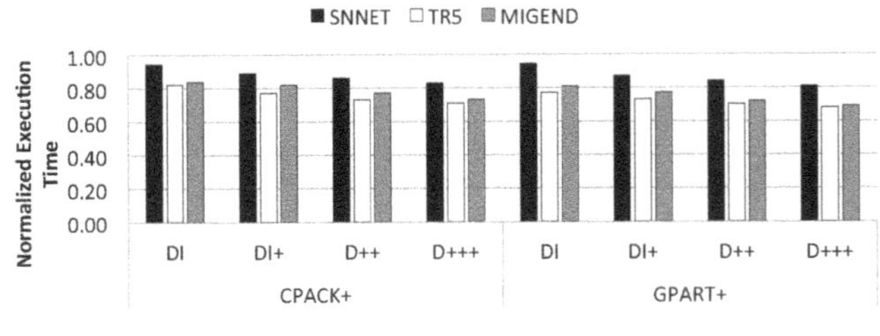

Figure 12: Impact of changing the input size.

Multicore Results. Our next set of results gives the improvements brought by our strategy under different core counts. Specifically, Figure 11(a) and Figure 11(b) show, respectively, the percentage execution time improvements brought by *GPART+* over *GPART* and by *CPACK+* over *CPACK*, under different core counts. We see that *the effectiveness of our approach increases as we increase the core counts.* This is mainly because as the number of cores used to execute an application increases, the access patterns exhibited by individual cores become sparser, making the importance of optimized-layout even more pronounced. Consequently, our approach becomes more successful with increased core counts. It should be noted however that our current approach (presented in this paper) does not do anything specific to multithreaded execution (in fact, such an extension is in our future research agenda). The increase in savings observed here with increased core counts are solely due to the access pattern exhibited by multicore/multithreaded execution being significantly worse (much less cache friendly) than that of single-core execution in *GPART* and *CPACK*.

As noted earlier in Section 6, in the case of multithreaded execution, the trace predicted by our approach may not exactly match the actual trace. To quantify how much this affects our results, we also made an additional set of experiments using the actual traces (collected through a separate run), and measured the difference. Our results showed that, when averaged over all application programs we have, the resulting performance difference between our predicted trace and the actual trace was less than 3%.

Sentivity to Input Size and Data Prefetching. For three of our applications (SNNET, TR5 and MIGEND), we have control in input size and changed it to investigate the impact of doing so on our savings. In the x-axis of Figure 12, DI corresponds to the default input size for each benchmark, as given in Table 1. On the other hand, DI+, DI++, and DI+++ correspond to the results with larger inputs. More specifically, in benchmark SNNET, DI+, DI++, and DI+++ represent input sizes of 62.4MB, 71MB, and 86.4MB; in benchmark TR5, 32.6MB, 41.1MB, and 44.8MB; and in benchmark MIGEND, 30.9MB, 37.3MB and 41.2MB, in the same order. The y-axis of the graph gives the *normalized* execution cycles. A key observation from these results is that the effectiveness of our approach improves as the input size increases. For example, with the largest input sizes tested for each benchmark (DI+++), the average improvements brought by CPACK+ and GPART+ over the Default version are 24.3% and 27.3%, respectively, which are much higher than the corresponding improvement values with the default input (DI) – 13.2% and 15.9%. This result is important since data-intensive applications witness a continuous

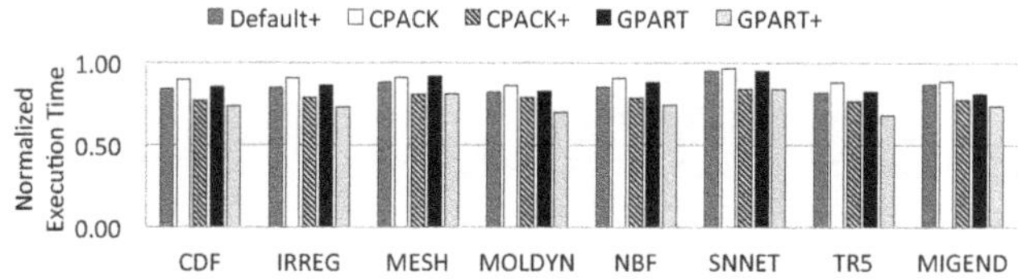

Figure 13: Normalized execution times on a 48-node multicore system.

Table 4: 48-core system.

Number of Cores	48 cores (4 sockets)
Clock Frequency	2.20GHz
L1	64KB, full, 64-byte line size
L2	512KB, 4-way, 64-byte line size
L3	12MB, 16-way, 64-byte line size
TLB Size	1024 4K pages
Address Sizes	48 bits physical, 48 bits virtual

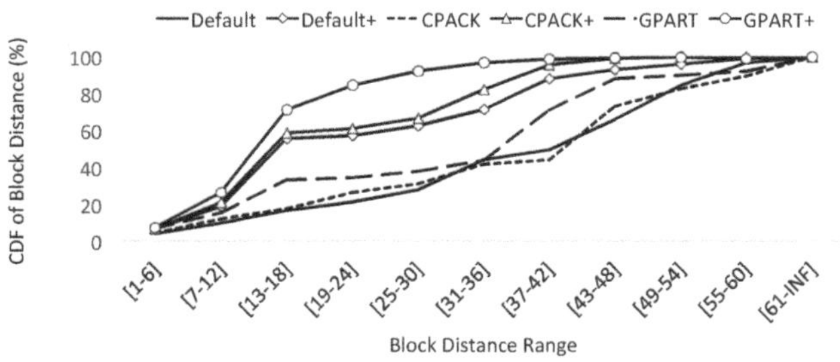

Figure 14: The CDF of block distances averaged over all 8 applications.

increase in their data set sizes [12], and we can expect our approach to be even more successful in the future. It is to be emphasized that while this paper mainly targets at codes where index arrays are assigned once during execution, our approach can also be applied to irregular codes where index arrays are updated multiple times. In such cases, each time index array is updated, we need to apply our proposed transformation, leading to an increase in overhead. For example, we applied our approach to such a code, FEM [11], which evaluates a 3D blast wave using a Discrete Galerkin finite element method for system of nonlinear conservation laws. The results show that, with this code, our approach improves over CPACK by 9.6%, and over GPART by 14.3%.

Note also that, in our experiments, we did not turn on hardware-prefetching as it does not bring much benefit in irregular-applications. The experiments with our approach with hardware prefetching turned-on did not change our savings much(it reduced the (execution time) benefits brought by our approach by less than 1%). We would like to point out that, if the prefetching-algorithm is exposed to our approach, we can adapt our approach by tuning the block-distance-calculation.

Results with a Larger Multicore Based System. Finally, to evaluate the effectiveness of our approach in a larger system, we also experimented with a 48-core AMD machine with 4 sockets (Figure 14), whose important parameters are listed in Table 4. The corresponding performance results are given in Figure 13 which plots *normalized execution cycles* when each application is executed on all 48 cores (note that this system has an L3 as the last level cache). Specifically, the average additional improvement brought by *Default+* over *Default*, *CPACK+* over *CPACK*, and *GPART+* over *GPART* are 14%, 12.2% and 13.8%, respectively, on average. These results clearly show that our proposed approach is successful in larger systems as well.

Figure 14 plots the CDF of block distances averaged over all 8 applications we have (recall that CApRI takes, as input, the number of ways in the target cache and changes the block distances of the accesses that incur last level cache misses into smaller ones). The reduction in block distances when our approach is employed can be easily observed from this graph. In particular, when we move from Default to Default+, the fraction of block distances in the range of [1-16] is increased by 38.9%. Similarly, when we move from CAPCK (resp. GPART), we observe an increase of 41% (resp 38%), in the block distances that fall in the range of [1-16].

8. RELATED WORK

Data/memory layout optimization has been extensively studied to improve the data locality for array-based regular applications. O'Boyle and Knijnenburg [26] propose a nonsingular layout transformation scheme by employing the data transformation matrix. Leung and Zahorjan [22] propose a memory consumption reduction scheme by a layout transformation. Anderson et al [4] propose a transformation technique that accesses contiguous data elements. Henretty et al [17] propose a novel data layout transformation that avoids the stream alignment conflicts, along with a static analysis technique for determining where this transformation is applicable. Zhange et al [35] explore data layout optimizations to improve the locality of data accesses in a NUCA-based system. Sung et al [31] present automatic data layout transformation as an effective compiler performance optimization for memory-bound structured grid applications. So et al [29] describe a generalized approach to deriving a custom data layout in multiple memory banks for array-based computations.

Data reordering (layout optimization) has also been studied to improve the cache locality for irregular applications [14, 10, 15, 24, 25, 30]. Mellor-Crummey et al [24] use the inspector-executor paradigm to achieve good data locality in irregular and dynamic applications. Ding and Kennedy [10] propose the *consecutive packing* (CPACK) whereby the data are reordered based on the sequence they are first accessed. Since this approach only requires one pass over the loop, it has very low overhead; however, it does not take into account the underlying data structure. Han and Tseng [15] develop a hierarchical graph clustering algorithm for memory layout optimization that improve the data locality with low overhead. As shown through our experiments, our scheme outperforms CPACK. Mitchell et al [25] present a technique to localize non-affine array references. Their algorithm combines elements of tiling, data-centric tiling, data remapping and inspector-executor parallelization together to achieve better application performance. Strout et al [30] propose a compile-time framework that explicit combines run-time data and iteration-reordering transformations to improve data locality. In a recent study, Kulkarni et al [21] explore potential parallelism in irregular computations. Thabit [32] shows that determine an optimal layout for a given block size using pairwise access frequency is NP-hard.

Petrank and Rawitz [27] investigate the complexity of finding the optimal data/code placement in memory and prove that, if $P \neq NP$, no efficient approximation of the optimal solution could be achieved. They also show that, if we only keep pairwise information (e.g., the number of misses caused by placing two data elements in the same memory block), even an algorithm that has no execution time bound cannot come close to the optimal solution. Hirzel [18] presents a novel framework for evaluating the goodness of a data layout in object-oriented programs running under JVM.

There exist several studies related to our block-distance based locality model. Gloy and Smith [13] use reuse distance to estimate the affinity relations for code placement in the program trace. Zhang et al [36] define the "inter core" used and demonstrate that exploiting all available intercore reuse could boost overall application performance. Zhong et al [37] propose a hierarchical affinity model that considers the distance between data accesses, and present a statistical clustering strategy to identify affinity groups. Zhong et al [37] also employ a heuristic k-distance analysis in structure splitting and array regrouping according to this hierarchical model. Our locality group is different from the concept of "affinity group" proposed in [37, 34]. Zhang et al [34] analyze the affinity model in detail and give the algorithmic complexity of finding reference affinity in the program trace. As opposed to [27], they target a common data access pattern rather than all patterns of data access. While affinity group is used to measure how close a group of data are accessed together in an execution using the LRU stack distance, our locality group is used to capture the set of data elements that exhibit data locality in the target cache. Second, to our knowledge, there is no any prior data reordering strategy based on the concept of affinity groups. In comparison, we present a data reordering scheme, CApRI, to obtain an improved memory layout that tries to reduce the cache misses. In order to improve the cache behavior of data structures larger than a cache block, Chilimbi et al [8] exploit pair-wise affinity through techniques such as *structure splitting* and *field reordering*. In a later work, Chilimbi [7] describes an efficient data reference representation and an exploitable locality abstraction (called hot data streams).

9. CONCLUDING REMARKS

Targeting data-intensive irregular applications, where main data structures are accessed through index arrays, this paper makes three main contributions. First, it presents a new concept – locality group – and studies its properties. Second, it discusses how the concept of locality group can be used for data reordering. Third, it evaluates the proposed data reordering strategy, CApRI, with eight array-based irregular applications. Our experimental evaluation using two multi-core systems reveals that CApRI brings further execution time improvements over two previously-proposed data reordering schemes. Our future work includes testing its effectiveness on emerging petaflops machines, and retargeting our locality model to memory related optimizations.

Acknowledgment

This research is supported in part by NSF grants #0963839, #1302557, #1213052, #1017882, and #1205618, a grant from INTEL an a grant from MICROSOFT.

10. REFERENCES

[1] Intel pentium 4 and intel xeon processor optimization, reference manual. *http://developer.intel.com.*

[2] Intel Xscale core, developer's manual. *http://developer.intel.com.*

[3] SUIF2. *http://suif.stanford.edu.*

[4] J. Anderson, S. P. Amarasinghe, and M. S. Lam. Data and computation transformations for multiprocessors. *In Proceedings of the ACM SIGPLAN Symposium on Principles and Practice of Parallel Programming*, 1995.

[5] M. Berger and S. Bokhari. A partitioning strategy for non-uniform problems on multiprocessors. *IEEE Trans. Computers*, 1987.

[6] P. Boonserm, B. Wang, S. See, and T. Achalakul. Improving data processing time with access sequence prediction. In *Proceedings of the International Conference on Parallel and Distributed Systems*, 2012.

[7] T. M. Chilimbi. Efficient representations and abstractions for quantifying and exploiting data reference locality. *In Proceedings of the Conference on Programming Language Design and Implementation*, 2001.

[8] T. M. Chilimbi, B. Davidson, and J. R. Larus. Cache-conscious structure definition. *In Proceedings of the Conference on Programming Language Design and Implementation*, 1999.

[9] R. Das, M. Uysal, J. Saltz, and Y. shin Hwang. Communication optimizations for irregular scientific computations on distributed memory architectures. *Journal of Parallel and Distributed Computing*, 1993.

[10] C. Ding and K. Kennedy. Improving cache performance in dynamic applications through data and computation reorganization at run time. *In Proceedings of the Conference on Programming Language Design and Implementation*, 1999.

[11] M. Erez, J. H. Ahn, J. Gummaraju, M. Rosenblum, and W. J. Dally. Executing irregular scientific applications on stream architectures. *In Proceedings of the International Conference on Supercomputing*, 2007.

[12] I. Foster and C. Kesselman. *The Grid 2: Blueprint for a New Computing Infrastructure.* Morgan Kaufmann Publishers Inc., San Francisco, CA, USA, 2003.

[13] N. Gloy and M. D. Smith. Procedure placement using temporal-ordering information. *ACM Trans. Program. Lang. Syst.*, 1999.

[14] H. Han and C.-W. Tseng. A comparison of locality transformations for irregular codes. *LCR 2000*, pages 70–84, 2000.

[15] H. Han and C.-W. Tseng. Exploiting locality for irregular scientific codes. *IEEE Trans. Parallel Distrib. Syst.*, 2006.

[16] J. L. Hennessy and D. Patterson. *Computer Architecture: A Quantitative Approach.* Morgan Kaufmann, 2003.

[17] T. Henretty, K. Stock, L.-N. Pouchet, F. Franchetti, J. Ramanujam, and P. Sadayappan. Data layout transformation for stencil computations on short-vector simd architectures. *In Proceedings of the International Conference on Compiler Construction*, 2011.

[18] M. Hirzel. Data layouts for object-oriented programs. *In Proceedings of SIGMETRICS*, 2007.

[19] G. Karypis and V. Kumar. A fast and high quality multilevel scheme for partitioning irregular graphs. *SIAM Journal on Scientific Computing*, 1998.

[20] D. Kroft. Lockup-free instruction fetch/prefetch cache organization. *Computer Architecture*, 1981.

[21] M. Kulkarni, M. Burtscher, R. Inkulu, K. Pingali, and C. Casçaval. How much parallelism is there in irregular applications? *In Proceedings of the ACM SIGPLAN symposium on Principles and practice of parallel programming*, pages 3–14, 2009.

[22] S.-T. Leung and J. Zahorjan. Optimizing data locality by array restructuring. *Technical Report, Dept. of Computer Science and Eng., Univ. of Washington*, 1995.

[23] W. Liu and A. Sherman. Comparative analysis of the cuthill-mckee and the reverse cuthill-mckee ordering algorithms for sparse matrices. *SIAM Journal on Numerical Analysis*, 1976.

[24] J. Mellor-Crummey, D. Whalley, and K. Kennedy. Improving memory hierarchy performance for irregular applications. *In Proceedings of the International Conference on Supercomputing*, 1999.

[25] N. Mitchell, L. Carter, and J. Ferrante. Localizing non-affine array references. *In Proceedings of the International Conference on Parallel Architectures and Compilation Techniques*, 1999.

[26] M. O'Boyle and P. Knijnenburg. Non-singular data transformations: definition, validity and applications. *In Proceedings of the International Conference on Supercomputing*, 1997.

[27] E. Petrank and D. Rawitz. The hardness of cache conscious data placement. *In Proceedings of the Conference on Principles of Programming Languages*, 2002.

[28] M. F. Sakr, S. P. Levitan, D. M. Chiarulli, B. G. Horne, and C. L. Giles. Predicting multiprocessor memory access patterns with learning models. *In Proceedings of the International Conference on Machine Learning*, 1997.

[29] B. So, M. W. Hall, and H. E. Ziegler. Custom data layout for memory parallelism. *In Proceedings of the International Symposium on Code Generation and Optimization*, 2004.

[30] M. M. Strout, L. Carter, and J. Ferrante. Compile-time composition of run-time data and iteration reorderings. *In Proceedings of the Conference on Programming Language Design and Implementation*, 2003.

[31] I.-J. Sung, J. A. Stratton, and W.-M. W. Hwu. Data layout transformation exploiting memory-level parallelism in structured grid many-core applications. *In Proceedings of the International Conference on Parallel Architectures and Compilation Techniques*, 2010.

[32] K. Thabit. *Cache Management by the Compiler*. PhD thesis, Rice University, Houston, TX, USA, 1982.

[33] B. Wu, E. Z. Zhang, and X. Shen. Enhancing data locality for dynamic simulations through asynchronous data transformations and adaptive control. *In Proceedings of the International Conference on Parallel Architectures and Compilation Techniques*, 2011.

[34] C. Zhang, C. Ding, M. Ogihara, Y. Zhong, and Y. Wu. A hierarchical model of data locality. *In Proceedings of the Conference on Principles of Programming Languages*, 2006.

[35] Y. Zhang, W. Ding, M. Kandemir, J. Liu, and O. Jang. A data layout optimization framework for nuca-based multicores. *In Proceedings of the International Symposium on Microarchitecture*, 2011.

[36] Y. Zhang, M. Kandemir, and T. Yemliha. Studying inter-core data reuse in multicores. *In Proceedings of SIGMETRICS*, 2011.

[37] Y. Zhong, M. Orlovich, X. Shen, and C. Ding. Array regrouping and structure splitting using whole-program reference affinity. *In Proceedings of the Conference on Programming Language Design and Implementation*, 2004.

Neighbor-Cell Assisted Error Correction for MLC NAND Flash Memories

Yu Cai[1], Gulay Yalcin[2], Onur Mutlu[1], Erich F. Haratsch[4],
Osman Unsal[2], Adrian Cristal[2,3], and Ken Mai[1]
[1]Electrical and Computer Engineering Department, Carnegie Mellon University
[2]Barcelona Supercomputing Center, Spain [3]IIIA – CSIC – Spain National Research Council [4]LSI Corporation
yucaicai@gmail.com, {omutlu, kenmai}@ece.cmu.edu, {gulay.yalcin, adrian.cristal, osman.unsal}@bsc.es

ABSTRACT

Continued scaling of NAND flash memory to smaller process technology nodes decreases its reliability, necessitating more sophisticated mechanisms to correctly read stored data values. To distinguish between different potential stored values, conventional techniques to read data from flash memory employ a single set of reference voltage values, which are determined based on the overall threshold voltage distribution of flash cells. Unfortunately, the phenomenon of program interference, in which a cell's threshold voltage unintentionally changes when a neighboring cell is programmed, makes this conventional approach increasingly inaccurate in determining the values of cells.

This paper makes the new empirical observation that identifying the value stored in the immediate-neighbor cell makes it easier to determine the data value stored in the cell that is being read. We provide a detailed statistical and experimental characterization of threshold voltage distribution of flash memory cells *conditional upon* the immediate-neighbor cell values, and show that such conditional distributions can be used to determine a set of read reference voltages that lead to error rates much lower than when a single set of reference voltage values based on the overall distribution are used. Based on our analyses, we propose a new method for correcting errors in a flash memory page, neighbor-cell assisted correction (NAC). The key idea is to re-read a flash memory page that fails error correction codes (ECC) with the set of read reference voltage values corresponding to the conditional threshold voltage distribution assuming a neighbor cell value and use the re-read values to correct the cells that have neighbors with that value. Our simulations show that NAC effectively improves flash memory lifetime by 33% while having no (at nominal lifetime) or very modest (less than 5% at extended lifetime) performance overhead.

Categories and Subject Descriptors

B.3.4 [**Memory Structure**]: Reliability, Testing, and Fault-Tolerance, C.4 [**Performance of Systems**]: Modeling techniques; Reliability

General Terms

Algorithms, Measurement, Performance, Design, Reliability.

Keywords

NAND flash memory, Program Interference, Threshold Voltage Distribution, Error Correction, ECC, Fault Tolerance.

SIGMETRICS'14, June 16–20, 2014, Austin, TX, USA.

1. INTRODUCTION

NAND flash memory is widely used in diverse applications, ranging from mobile electronics to enterprise servers. Such a wide application range is mainly driven by the ever-increasing, low-cost, non-volatile storage capacity provided by NAND flash memory due to aggressive transistor scaling. Unfortunately, as flash cells scale down to smaller technology nodes, they become increasingly vulnerable to circuit level noise, reducing the probability that stored data will be read correctly (even if it were stored correctly at the time it was written) even with the use of aggressive error-correcting codes (ECC) [1][2][3]. As a result, more accurate and sophisticated mechanisms to accurately read and correct the data values stored in flash cells become increasingly necessary. This paper introduces such a new mechanism based on a rigorous experimental analysis of real Multi-Level Cell (MLC) NAND flash memory chips and new findings on how the threshold voltage distribution of flash memory cells can be classified for more accurate identification of the logical data values stored in cells

In MLC NAND flash memory, the logical value stored in a memory cell is determined by the threshold voltage range (or, window) into which the cell's actual threshold voltage falls [3][4]. As cell size is scaled down and more bits per cell are stored, the threshold voltage range used to represent each logical value becomes smaller, leading to increased error rates in determining a cell's logical value. This is because process variations become more prevalent when the amount of charge stored in a flash cell reduces with feature size, causing the threshold voltages of different cells storing the same value to become significantly different. Hence, deciding what logical value a cell's threshold voltage actually corresponds to is increasingly difficult.

The distribution of threshold voltages across different cells in flash memory is called the "threshold voltage (probability) distribution" [4]. A flash controller uses this distribution across all cells (in a flash memory chip) to determine the "reference threshold voltage values" to distinguish between cells that store different logical values upon reading an address in flash memory. For example, distinguishing between 11, 10, 00, and 01 in a 2-bit flash cell requires three read reference voltages, each one used to distinguish between the adjacent two logical values in terms of threshold voltage ranges. Traditionally, the read reference voltage used to distinguish between two adjacent logical values is a single reference voltage, and this voltage is determined by the manufacturer to minimize the probability that a cell's programmed logical value is misread as another, incorrect value.

Unfortunately, using a single read reference voltage to determine a cell's logical value becomes increasingly difficult due to the phenomenon of program interference [3]. Program interference is the phenomenon where the threshold voltage of a flash cell, called the victim cell, unintentionally changes (that is, gets disturbed) while another, neighboring, cell's value is being programmed

[1][2][3][5][6]. If the change in threshold voltage due to program interference causes the victim cell's voltage to shift to a different threshold voltage range (based on a single read reference voltage), then the victim cell's logical value becomes incorrect, leading to an error when the cell is read. As previous works have shown [3], program interference is responsible for a large fraction of difficult-to-correct errors in flash memory and therefore is a key challenge against scaling flash memory to higher densities.

In this paper, we make the new observation that knowing (or, more broadly, distinguishing) the value programmed in the immediate-neighbor cell makes it easier to determine the value stored in the flash cell that is being read. In other words, one can classify the threshold voltage distribution of flash memory cells into *multiple* threshold voltage distributions based on the logical value of the immediate-neighbor flash cell and use the appropriate *"classified" (or, conditional) voltage distribution* (and the corresponding read reference voltage values associated with it, called the "local optimum read reference voltages") to more accurately determine the value of the cell that is being read. Doing so leads to a more accurate identification of the logical value of the flash cell being read because the classified voltage distributions of the flash cells based on neighbor cell values have smaller overlap between threshold voltage ranges of different logical values than a single overall threshold voltage distribution for all cells. We show both experimentally and analytically this is the case.

Based upon this new observation, we introduce a new error correction method, called neighbor-cell assisted error correction (NAC). With this method, a flash memory page is first read using the regular read reference voltages (and the read logical values are buffered). If there are no errors uncorrectable by ECC, nothing else is done. However, if there are errors uncorrectable by ECC, the flash page is re-read with the read reference voltages corresponding to the voltage distribution assuming a particular immediate-neighbor value. The buffered values of the cells with that particular immediate-neighbor cell value are replaced using this reading, and ECC is applied again. If ECC is successful this time, the buffered page is deemed to be corrected and is supplied to the system. If ECC fails again, the process is repeated with another set of read reference voltages corresponding to the voltage distribution assuming another particular immediate-neighbor value until either ECC passes or all different potential immediate-neighbor values are exhausted. We evaluate NAC and show that it can significantly improve flash memory lifetime with very modest performance loss during the extended lifetime and no performance loss during the nominal lifetime.

To our knowledge, this is the first paper that classifies threshold voltage probability distributions of flash memory cells based on neighboring cell values, analyzes these distributions both statistically and experimentally, and makes use of these classified threshold voltage distributions to improve error correction capability for MLC NAND flash memory. Our major contributions in this paper are as follows:

1. We provide a detailed statistical and experimental characterization of threshold voltage distributions of flash memory cells conditional upon the immediate-neighbor cell values, and show that such conditional distributions can be used to determine read reference voltages that can minimize raw bit error rate (RBER) when the cells are read. We show that RBER can be reduced by using information from neighbor cell values. (Sections 4 and 5)
2. Based on our analyses, we propose a new method for correcting errors in flash memory, *neighbor-cell assisted correction (NAC)*, which complements ECC (Section 6). The key idea is to re-read a flash memory page that initially failed ECC with a set of read reference voltages corresponding to the conditional threshold voltage distribution assuming a neighbor cell value and use the re-read values to correct the cells that have neighbors with that value. We show that the error correction capability of particular neighbor cell values is higher than that of others because the threshold voltage changes interference caused by some neighbor cell values are more likely to lead to errors in the cells they interfere with. Based on this, we propose the idea of *prioritized NAC,* which prioritizes reading assuming such neighbor cell values (Section 6.2). We also show that even if the reading of the neighbor cells fails ECC, the read raw data from the neighbors is accurate enough to provide better correction capability than ECC alone (Section 6.3).
3. We evaluate all our techniques using real I/O workload traces and a high-fidelity simulation infrastructure that is driven by measured data from real flash chips. Our evaluations show that NAC increases flash memory lifetime by 33% without any performance loss within the nominal lifetime and with less than 5% performance loss during the extended lifetime (Section 7).

2. BACKGROUND

We briefly provide background on relevant aspects of NAND flash memory necessary to understand the rest of the paper. For more detailed background on flash memory operation and characteristics, please refer to Cai et al. [1][3][4][7][8].

2.1 Basics of NAND Flash Memory

As mentioned, the logical value stored in a flash memory cell is determined by the threshold voltage range into which the cell's actual threshold voltage falls. The threshold voltage of a flash cell can be modulated by the amount of electrons programmed on the floating gates. For n-bit MLC NAND flash memory, the threshold voltage of a cell is logically divided into 2^n separate regions and each region represents a unique n-bit value. For the specific case of 2-bit MLC NAND flash memory, the bits stored in a cell can be classified into the most significant bit (MSB) and the least significant bit (LSB), depending on the location of the bit inside the flash bit-string [1][3].

NAND flash memory generally contains thousands of blocks. A block consists of a 2-D array of flash cells. Each row of the array forms one wordline and each column forms one bitline. A block has *N* wordlines and the address of the wordline increases one by one from the bottom to the top inside a block. Thus, a cell location can be uniquely determined by its wordline and bitline address inside a block. In this paper, we define *C(x,y)* to be the flash cell that is on the *x-th* wordline and *y-th* bitline. For *All-Bit-Line* NAND flash memory, the MSBs of *all the cells on the same wordline* are programmed and read simultaneously: these set of MSBs on the same wordline are referred to as an *MSB page*. Similarly, the LSBs of all the cells on a wordline form one *LSB page*. Each page has its unique physical address inside a block. Fig. 1(a) shows an example of the page address mapping inside a flash block. We can see that the LSB page number on wordline *n* is *2n-1,* and the MSB page number on wordline *n* is *2n+2* for all-bit-line flash memory. The exceptions are the bottom wordline (i.e., wordline 0) and top wordline (i.e., wordline *N*) of a block.

2.2 NAND Flash Operations

Program Operation: Programming the threshold voltage of flash cells to the target threshold voltage region requires two steps for 2-bit MLC flash memory. These two steps are shown in Fig. 1(b): 1) LSB programming, which programs the threshold voltage of the cell into either the erased state region (ER) or a temporary state region (Temp) based on the value of LSB; and 2) MSB programming, which programs the threshold voltage of the cell into one of the four regions (ER, P1, P2, P3) determined by both the LSB and MSB bit values.

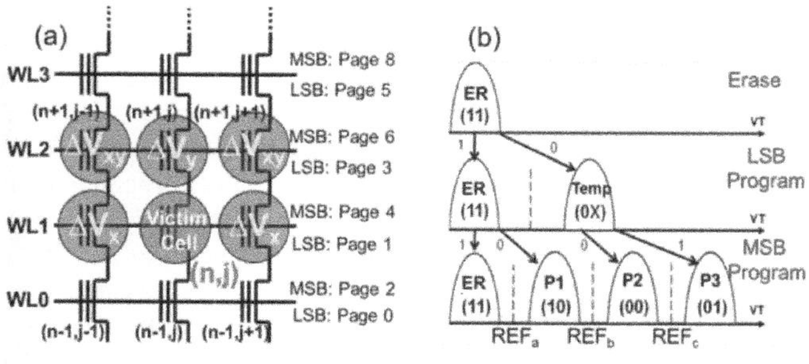

Fig. 1 (a) All-bit-line flash block architecture with the victim cell circled in red and aggressor cells circled in grey; (b) Two-bit MLC flash programming scheme. Cell states are encoded in format (LSB, MSB)

Read Operation: The read operation determines the logical value of a flash cell by determining the region its threshold voltage falls in. To read the LSB of 2-bit MLC flash memory, a reference voltage (REF_b in Fig. 1(b)) is selected to compare with the threshold voltage of the flash cell. If the threshold voltage of the flash cell is larger than REF_b, the LSB is read as 0, otherwise it is read as 1. To read the MSB, the threshold voltage of a cell is compared to two reference voltages (REF_a and REF_c in Fig. 1(b)). If the cell's threshold voltage is within the range of [REF_a, REF_c], the MSB is read as 0, otherwise it is read as 1. Each of the reference voltages is called a *read reference voltage*.

If the set of read reference voltages is set to a set of values that are not optimal, a cell's logical value may be incorrectly read (i.e., the cell may be attributed to belong to a threshold voltage window that is different from the window corresponding to the logical value it was programmed with). This leads to errors in read operation. There are at least two issues that complicate the optimal determination of read reference voltage values: 1) the threshold voltage distribution of flash cells gets distorted as the cells wear out (i.e., as the number of P/E cycles increases) [4], 2) the threshold voltages of cells get disturbed as neighboring cells are programmed [3].

Recent flash memory devices [9] allow the read reference voltages to be configurable online, which allows the flash controller to try different reference voltages in order to find one that leads to a lower error rate. This functionality is called ***read-retry***. Previous works [3][4] leverage the *read-retry* feature to identify the exact threshold voltage of each flash cell and experimentally characterize the threshold voltage distributions.

2.3 Cell-to-cell Program Interference

Due to coupling capacitance between flash cells, the threshold voltage of a flash cell can change when its neighbor cells are being programmed [3][5]. The former cell is called the *victim cell*, while the latter are called *aggressor cells*, as shown in Fig. 1(a). Generally, the pages inside a block are programmed in page number order to reduce program interference [3]. The flash cells on lower wordlines will finish programming before the MSB page programming of the upper wordlines. Thus, the cells on a lower wordline will not be the aggressor cells for those on an upper wordline. For all-bit-line flash memory, the cells on the same wordline are programmed simultaneously and finish programming at the same time [3][5]. Therefore, program interference from neighbor cells on the same wordline is negligible, as demonstrated in [3][5]. The program interference on a victim flash cell $C(n,j)$ due to the aggressor cells on the wordline that is immediately above the victim wordline and can be modeled as [3]:

$$\Delta V_{victim}(n,j) = \sum_{y=j-K}^{j+K} \sum_{x=n+1}^{n+M} \alpha(x,y)\Delta V_{neighbor}(x,y) + \alpha_0 V_{victim}^{before}(n,j) \quad (1)$$

Here V_{victim}^{before} is the threshold voltage of the victim cell before aggressor cells are programmed and $\Delta V_{neighbor}(x, y)$ is the threshold voltage change of the aggressor cell $C(x,y)$. $\alpha(x,y)$ is a positive coefficient, which represents the ratio of the coupling capacitance between the aggressor cell $C(x,y)$ and the victim cell $C(n,j)$ over the total capacitance of the victim cell $C(n,j)$. α_0 is a negative coefficient, which models the fact that the victim cell with more electrons programmed tends to suffer less from program interference. The coupling coefficients decrease exponentially with the distance between neighbor cells [3] and the dominant interference to a victim cell in all-bit-line NAND flash comes from the aggressor cell that is directly above the victim [3], i.e. the *direct or immediate neighbor* (e.g., aggressor $C(n+1, j)$ to victim $C(n, j)$). Thus, equation (1) can be simplified to:

$$\Delta V_{victim}(n,j) \approx k \times \Delta V_{neighbor}(n+1,j) \quad (2)$$

3. OUR GOALS AND RELATED WORK

Our goal in this work is threefold. First, we would like to empirically and statistically analyze the threshold voltage distributions of flash cells *conditionally upon the values of immediately neighboring cells*. Second, we would like to find better sets of read reference voltages that can minimize read error rates *by using information from neighboring cell values*. Third, we aim to devise new error correction mechanisms that can *take advantage of the values of neighboring cells* to reduce error rates after the application of conventional ECC.

To our knowledge, no previous work explored the effect of neighboring cell values on flash memory threshold voltage distributions and provided ways of taking advantage of neighboring cell *values* to minimize flash memory error rates. We briefly discuss the most relevant works below.

Cai et al. [4] was the first to characterize and propose an empirical model for threshold voltage distributions in MLC NAND flash memory. Cai et al. [3] also characterized the effect of programming of neighboring cells (program interference) on threshold voltage distributions of cells. Building upon the empirical measurements in [3], they proposed a mechanism that can predict and use a set of read reference voltages to minimize bit error rate, taking into account the changes in the *overall threshold voltage distribution* of cells due to program interference. However, [3] did not characterize or take advantage of the fact that the changes in threshold voltage distribution are dependent on the *values* programmed in the neighboring aggressor cells. This paper builds upon [3] and shows that knowing the values stored in neighboring cells can lead to the determination of a better set of read reference voltages that can further reduce bit error rate and improve lifetime compared to the neighbor-cell-value-unaware read reference voltage prediction mechanism of [3] (Section 7.1).

Two other works [10][11] proposed signal processing techniques to overcome program interference effects in flash memory. However, these works face multiple implementation challenges and are based on hypothesized (as opposed to experimentally measured and validated) models for program interference, which we briefly summarize. First, these works rely on accurate measurement of 1) the threshold voltage changes of neighbor aggressor cells and 2) threshold voltages of the victim cells. This means that an n-bit representation (e.g. 4~6 bits to represent the threshold voltage for 2-bit MLC flash) needs $2x2^n$ read operations to sense the threshold voltage of neighbor aggressor cells (LSB and MSB pages) and 2^n read operations for the victim cell to be read. This will cause severe performance and energy overheads during a read operation. Second, these works need to record the threshold voltage *changes* of all the aggressor cells, which cannot be accurately obtained as at the time of reading: only the *current* threshold voltage of neighboring aggressor cells can be measured while their *past* threshold voltages before they were fully programmed are difficult to obtain. To circumvent this problem, [11] uses the mean threshold voltage value of the erased (ER) state to estimate the threshold voltages of *all* aggressor cells before they are programmed, which is inaccurate (see Cai et al. [4], which shows that the cells in the same state can have greatly different threshold voltages) and difficult to implement (it is difficult to apply negative read voltage on the control gate to measure threshold voltages of cells in the erased state). In contrast to these works, the mechanisms proposed in this paper to improve bit error rates do not need to measure, record or estimate the voltage of aggressor cells *before* they were fully programmed.

To our knowledge, this is the first work that uses information stored in neighbor cells to correct errors in a victim cell with low-overhead mechanisms that can be implemented practically. We propose to still use conventional ECC, such as BCH codes [12], to correct most of the errors (including those due to program interference) upon reading a flash cell, but leverage information of neighbor cells *only when* conventional ECC fails and minimize the number of read operations on the neighbor cells by taking advantage of our experimental observations from real flash chips.

4. Flash Voltage Distribution Measurement

We first describe our methodology to measure cell threshold voltage distributions using real flash memory chips. As shown in previous work [4], the threshold voltages of different flash cells are different even when the cells are programmed with the same value. This is due to manufacturing process variations within a flash chip. The threshold voltage of flash cells can be represented by a random variable x. The probability density function (PDF) of x, $p(x)$, is generally called the *(threshold) voltage distribution*. The value programmed on a cell's direct-neighbor aggressor cell is a discrete bit value, which can be denoted as z. For n-bit MLC NAND flash memory, z can take up to 2^n values and can be treated as a discrete random variable. As such, the voltage distribution of flash cells can be expressed as:

$$p(x) = \sum_{m=1}^{2^n} p(z = m)p(x \mid z = m) \tag{3}$$

where $p(z=m)$ is the probability that the direct-neighbor aggressor cell is programmed with the logical data value m. $p(x|z=m)$ is the conditional probability that the threshold voltage of a (victim) cell equals x given that value m is programmed to its direct-neighbor aggressor cell z. Equation (3) can be reformulated as:

$$p(x) = \sum_{m=1}^{2^n} p(x, z = m) \tag{4}$$

where $p(x, z=m)$ is the joint probability density function of random variable x (threshold voltage of the victim cell) and z (value programmed in the direct-neighbor aggressor cell). For the rest of this paper, we refer to $p(x, z=m)$ as the *conditional distribution* and $p(x)$ as the *overall distribution* of threshold voltages for all flash memory cells.

Experimental Measurement Methodology: To measure the threshold voltage distributions, we use an FPGA-based testing platform [4][13] that can issue commands to raw flash chips. We tested 2-bit MLC NAND flash memory devices manufactured in 2Y-nm technology. There are four conditional distributions $p(x, z=11)$, $p(x, z=10)$, $p(x, z=00)$ and $p(x, z=01)$. Recall that $p(x, z=m)$ is equal to $p(z=m)p(x|z=m)$. $p(z=m)$ is measured by dividing the number of direct-neighbor aggressor cells with value $z=m$ by the total number of direct-neighbor aggressor cells. Since random (or pseudo-random) data is generally programmed into raw flash chips due to data encryption and randomization techniques employed before programming [14][15], we measure the threshold voltage of cells with random data values programmed in all cells. As a result, $p(z=m)$ is approximately 25% for each possible value of m. Each *conditional distribution* $p(x|z=m)$ is measured via the following steps: 1) program flash memory with random data; 2) select all the cells whose direct neighbor aggressor cell is programmed with value $z=m$ and measure the threshold voltage of these selected cells; 3) count the number of cells with threshold voltage equal to x; 4) divide the count found in step 3 by the total number of cells selected in step 2. The *overall distribution* $p(x)$ can be measured by dividing the number of cells whose threshold voltage equals x over the total number of flash cells.

Example Distribution and Initial Observations: Fig. 2 shows the overall distribution (dotted line) and all four conditional distributions (solid line) for a flash memory chip tested after 35k P/E cycles (More details on threshold voltage distribution measurement methodology can be found in our past works [3][4].). We make several observations, which we will formally back up in Section 5 with statistical analyses. We will also use some of these observations to develop new error correction methods in Section 6. First, and most importantly, *two neighboring states in each conditional distribution are farther apart from each other than they are in the overall distribution*, as shown by the "large margin" and "small margin" arrows in the figure between states P1 and P2. This indicates that accurately distinguishing between the neighboring states (i.e., identifying the logical values of flash cells) can be easier if the conditional threshold voltage distribution is used instead of the overall distribution, which in turn suggests that knowing the value of the immediate-neighbor cell can enable more accurate identification of the logical value of a cell when it is read. Second, for a given state, each of the conditional distributions has a smaller variance (informally, spread of the threshold voltage values belonging to that state) than the overall distribution. Third, the overall distribution is the sum of all the conditional distributions (as expected). Fourth, the conditional distributions for direct-neighbor cell values 10 and 01 are similar to each other and have the highest average threshold voltage values for each state, whereas the conditional distribution for the direct-neighbor cell value 11 (corresponding to the Erased state in the neighbor cell) has the lowest average threshold voltage values for each state. This latter observation is expected because programming a direct-neighbor cell to 11 (the erased state) leads to the smallest amount of injected charge into that cell (causing the smallest amount of program interference to the victim cell) and programming a direct-neighbor cell to 10 or 01 leads to the largest amount of injected charge as can be seen in Fig. 1(b) (causing the largest amount of program interference to the victim cell).

5. Flash Voltage Distribution Analysis

In this section, we first statistically analyze the threshold voltage distribution characteristics of flash memory from a formal standpoint and develop a model for both overall and conditional threshold voltage distributions (Sections 5.1-5.3). We then provide empirical measurement results that validate the statistical

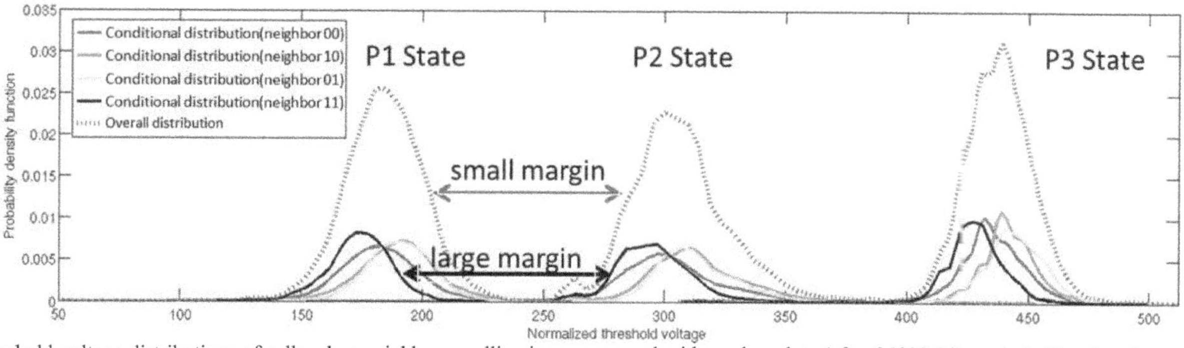

Fig. 2 Threshold voltage distributions of cells when neighbor wordline is programmed with random data (after 35000 P/E cycles). The dotted curve shows the overall distribution of all cells. Solid curves show the four conditional distributions corresponding to four possible direct-neighbor cell values.

model (Sections 5.4-5.5). In particular, our statistical analyses are to show that: 1) there exists an optimum read reference voltage between two neighboring logical states that minimizes the raw bit error rate (Section 5.1), 2) raw bit error rate can be minimized by either increasing the distance between the average threshold voltage values of neighboring states or reducing the variance of threshold voltage distributions of each logical state (Section 5.2), and 3) the conditional distributions for each logical state have smaller variances and larger signal-to-noise ratios than the overall distribution and therefore using the conditional distribution to determine the value of a cell that is being read leads to a smaller bit error rate than using the overall distribution (Section 5.3).

5.1 Optimizing the Read Reference Voltage

We first show that there exists an optimum read reference voltage to distinguish between two logical states in a threshold voltage distribution. Fig 3(a) shows an illustration of the threshold voltage distributions of two neighboring states of NAND flash memory. Assume that the probability density functions (PDFs) of cells programmed into state P_i and state P_{i+1} are *f(x)* and *g(x)* respectively. When voltage V_{ref} is selected as the read reference voltage to differentiate between these two neighboring states during a read operation, the fraction of cells that are actually programmed into the P_i state but misread as belonging to the P_{i+1} state is shown in the blue area in Fig. 3(a). We call this fraction as the *error rate due to P_i misread as P_{i+1}* and formulate it as:

$$ErrRate^{P_i->P_{i+1}} = \int_{v}^{+\infty} f(x)dx \tag{5}$$

Similarly, the fraction of cells that are actually programmed into the P_{i+1} state but misread as belonging to the P_i state is shown in the red area in Fig. 3(a) and can be formulated as:

$$ErrRate^{P_{i+1}->P_i} = \int_{-\infty}^{v} g(x)dx \tag{6}$$

Assume that the probability of a cell to be programmed into the P_i state is P_0 and the probability of a cell to be programmed into the P_{i+1} state is P_1. Then, the total error rate is the sum of equations (5) and (6) weighted by these probabilities:

$$ErrRate^{total} = P_0 \times \int_{v}^{+\infty} f(x)dx + P_1 \times \int_{-\infty}^{v} g(x)dx \tag{7}$$

The optimum read reference voltage, V_{opt}, which minimizes the total error rate between these two states, is obtained by setting $\partial ErrRate^{total} / \partial v$ to zero. V_{opt} satisfies the following equation:

$$P_0 \times f(V_{opt}) = P_1 \times g(V_{opt}) \tag{8}$$

If the probabilities of programming a cell into the P_i state and P_{i+1} state are equal (i.e., P_0 equals to P_1), the optimum read reference voltage V_{opt} satisfies the criteria $f(V_{opt})=g(V_{opt})$ and V_{opt} is at the cross-point of neighboring distributions, as shown in [3].

Previous works [4][16] have shown that the threshold voltage distributions of each state approximately follow the Gaussian distribution. Due to the characteristics of the Gaussian distribution, the distribution PDF can be completely defined by the statistics of the mean and variance pair (e.g., (μ_1, σ_1) for the P_i state and (μ_2, σ_2) for the P_{i+1} state, as illustrated in Fig. 3(a)). We replace the *f(.)* and *g(.)* functions in Equation (8) with Gaussian PDFs. Thus, the optimum read reference voltage V_{opt} between two neighboring states should satisfy:

$$P_0 \times \frac{1}{\sqrt{2\pi}\sigma_1} \exp(-\frac{(v_{opt}-\mu_1)^2}{2\sigma_1^2}) = P_1 \times \frac{1}{\sqrt{2\pi}\sigma_2} \exp(-\frac{(v_{opt}-\mu_2)^2}{2\sigma_2^2}) \tag{9}$$

By applying logarithmic operation to both sides of Equation (9) and solving the quadratic equation, we can get the optimum read reference voltage as $V_{opt} = (-B \pm \sqrt{B^2 - 4C})/2$. Here, B is $(\mu_2\sigma_1^2 - \mu_1\sigma_2^2)/\sigma_1^2\sigma_2^2(\sigma_2^2 - \sigma_1^2)$ and C is $\frac{\mu_1^2\sigma_2^2 - \mu_2^2\sigma_1^2}{2\sigma_1^2\sigma^2(\sigma_2^2-\sigma_1^2)} - (\log\frac{P0}{P1} + \log\frac{\sigma_2}{\sigma 1})$. When the variances of the two neighboring states are approximately equal (σ_1 and σ_2 equal to value σ), the optimum read reference voltage that achieves the minimum raw BER can be simplified as:

$$V_{opt} = \frac{\mu_1 + \mu_2}{2} + \frac{\sigma^2}{\mu_2 - \mu_1} \log\frac{P0}{P1} \tag{10}$$

If the probabilities of programming a cell into the P_i state and P_{i+1} state are equal (i.e., P_0 equals to P_1), which is the case for data values that are random or pseudo-random (which was shown for real flash memory chips due to the heavy use of data encryption and randomization techniques employed before programming [14][15]), the optimum read reference voltage is the average of the mean threshold voltages of the neighboring states:

$$v_{opt} = (\mu_1 + \mu_2)/2 \tag{11}$$

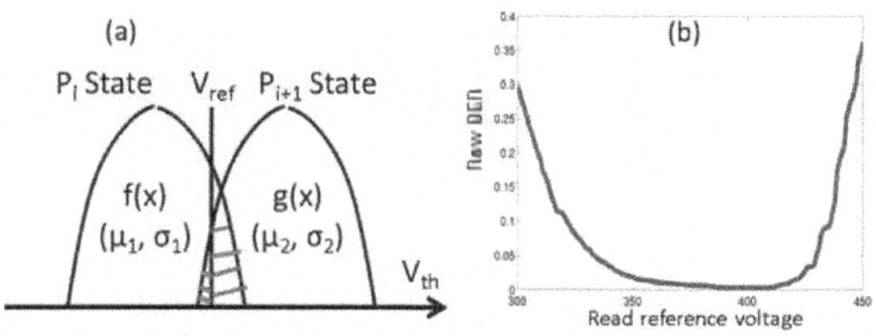

Fig. 3 (a) Read reference voltage V_{ref} between neighboring states. The area marked by blue lines correspond to Equation 5 and red lines correspond to Equation 6; (b) Measured raw BER vs. read reference voltage between P2 and P3 states at 35k P/E cycle endurance.

Measurement: To experimentally demonstrate how raw BER changes with read reference voltage, we sweep the read reference voltage between neighboring states and calculate the corresponding raw BER on our testing platform. Fig. 3(b) shows raw BER vs. read reference voltage when sweeping the latter from the center of the P2 state to the center of the P3 state for flash memory at 35k P/E cycles. We can see that raw BER first decreases as read reference voltage increases but increases after a certain point. There exists a point that can achieve minimum raw BER, as these empirical results demonstrate.

5.2 Minimizing Raw Bit Error Rate

The minimum raw bit error rate can be obtained by setting the variable v in Equation (7) to be the optimum read reference voltage. To get a simple closed-form expression, we assume that the threshold voltage distributions follow Gaussian distributions with equal variance, as shown as an approximation in [3][16]. The mean values of the neighboring states are μ_1 and μ_2 respectively. We also assume that the probabilities for each state are equal since random data are programmed to cells [14][15] and thus the optimum read reference voltage is $(\mu_1+\mu_2)/2$ according to Equation (11). Thus, the minimum raw BER can be expressed as:

$$\frac{1}{2}\times\frac{1}{\sqrt{2\pi}\sigma}\left(\int_{(\mu1+\mu2)/2}^{+\infty}\exp\left(-\frac{(x-\mu_1)^2}{2\sigma^2}\right)dx+\int_{-\infty}^{(\mu1+\mu2)/2}\exp\left(-\frac{(x-\mu_2)^2}{2\sigma^2}\right)\right)dx \qquad (12)$$

After a series of algebraic manipulation, this can be simplified to:

$$\frac{1}{\sqrt{2\pi}}\int_{(\mu2-\mu1)/2\sigma}^{+\infty}\exp(-x^2/2)dx \qquad (13)$$

To simplify the notation, we define the function $Q(x)$ as:

$$Q(x)=\frac{1}{\sqrt{2\pi}}\int_{x}^{+\infty}\exp(-x^2/2)dx \qquad (14)$$

By setting x to be $(\mu_2-\mu_1)/2\sigma$ in $Q(x)$, we can obtain the minimum raw BER. Fig. 4 plots the function $Q(x)$. We can see that $Q(x)$ monotonically decreases as x increases. Thus, in order to decrease the minimum raw BER, it is desirable to have distributions that have a higher value of $(\mu_2-\mu_1)/2\sigma$. This is possible in two ways:

1. Have a larger threshold voltage distance $(\mu_2-\mu_1)$ between neighboring distributions. The farther apart from each other the neighbor distributions, the larger the value of $(\mu_2-\mu_1)/2\sigma$.
2. Have a smaller variance σ^2 for the threshold voltage distributions. The narrower the distributions (i.e., their standard deviation σ), the larger the value of $(\mu_2-\mu_1)/2\sigma$.

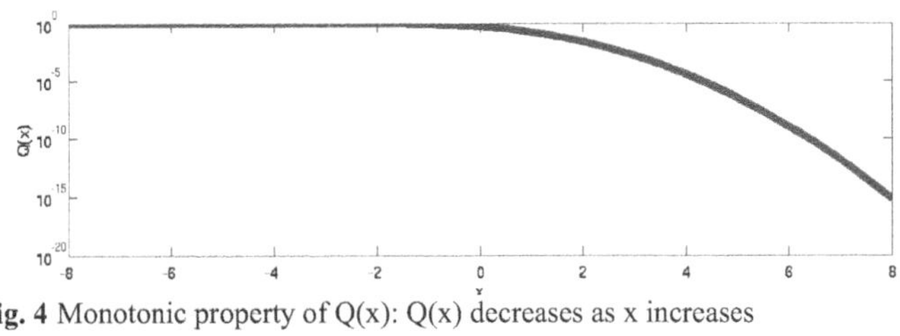

Fig. 4 Monotonic property of Q(x): Q(x) decreases as x increases

Signal to Noise Ratio (SNR): The half distance $(\mu_2-\mu_1)/2$ between neighboring states can be thought of as the signal and the standard deviation σ of the threshold voltage distribution can be thought of as noise. The ratio $(\mu_2-\mu_1)/2\sigma$ can therefore be defined as signal-to-noise ratio (SNR) when reading flash memory. The larger the SNR ($(\mu_2-\mu_1)/2\sigma$), the smaller the minimum raw BER, which is equal to Q(SNR).

The next section shows that conditional distributions of flash memory cells that distinguish between the values of the direct-neighbor cell (as opposed to the overall distribution that does not) lead to a larger SNR: two neighboring states in each conditional distribution have a similar threshold voltage distance $(\mu_2-\mu_1)$ *as* the same two neighboring states in the overall distribution but they have a significantly smaller variance σ^2. As such, using conditional distributions to determine the value of cells improves SNR, thereby reducing the minimum raw BER.

5.3 SNR and Minimum Raw BER Analysis of Conditional and Overall Distributions

Since a cell's direct-neighbor aggressor cell can take up to $N=2^n$ possible values for n-bit MLC flash memory, the threshold voltage X of a cell can be one of the N conditional random variables x_m as $X\in\{x_0,x_1,x_2,x_3,\ldots,x_{N-1}\}$. Here, x_m represents the threshold voltage of a cell with direct neighbor aggressor cell programmed to value m. *The PDF of X is the overall threshold voltage distribution. The PDF of x_m is the conditional distribution.* We now statistically analyze the distance of neighboring distributions, the variance of distributions, and their resulting SNR and BER comparatively between the overall distribution and conditional distributions. Our key finding is that the threshold voltage distance between neighboring states is similar for both the overall distribution and the conditional distributions, while the variance of the overall distribution is much larger than those of the conditional distributions, and thus using the conditional distributions to determine the optimum set of read reference voltages leads to larger SNR and smaller BER.

Distance of Neighboring Distributions: The mean of the overall distribution is the average of the means of all the conditional distributions (i.e., $E(X)=\sum E(x_m)/N$). Therefore, the distance of neighboring states in the overall distribution is equal to:

$$\begin{aligned}&E(X^{P(i+1)})-E(X^{P(i)})\\&=\frac{1}{N}\sum E(x_m^{P(i+1)})-\frac{1}{N}\sum E(x_m^{P(i)})=\frac{1}{N}\sum(E(x_m^{P(i+1)})-E(x_m^{P(i)}))\end{aligned} \qquad (15)$$

where $E(X^{P(i+1)})$ and $E(X^{P(i)})$ are the mean values of the threshold voltage distributions of all the cells in state P_{i+1} and state P_i respectively. $E(x_m^{P(i+1)})$ and $E(x_m^{P(i)})$ are the means of the *conditional* distributions for cells in state P_{i+1} and P_i respectively with direct aggressor cell programmed to value m. $E(x_m^{P(i+1)})-E(x_m^{P(i)})$ is the distance between neighboring states in the same conditional distribution. We can see from Equation (15) that the distance of two neighboring states in the overall distribution is the average of the distances of the same two neighboring states in all of the conditional distributions.

Variance of Distributions: The variance of the threshold voltage of all the cells in a state is equal to $Var(X)=E(X^2)-(E(X))^2$. By applying $E(X^2)=\Sigma E(x_m^2)/N$ and $E(X)=\Sigma E(x_m)/N$, we can get the variance of the threshold voltage distribution after algebraic manipulation:

$$Var(X)=\frac{1}{N}\sum Var(x_m)+\frac{1}{N^2}\sum\sum(E(x_m)-E(x_n))^2 \qquad (16)$$

From Equation (16), we can see that the variance of the overall distribution consists of two parts: 1) the average of the variances of all of its conditional distributions, $\sum Var(x_m)/N$ and 2) the average of the square of the differences between the mean values of every pair of conditional distributions, $\sum\sum(E(x_m)-E(x_n))^2/N^2$. Since the latter is non-negative, the variance of the overall distribution is no less than the average of the variance of all of its conditional distributions. We can consider two hypothetical extreme cases:

1. The conditional distributions completely overlap with each other. As a result, the variance of the overall distribution would simply be the average of the variances of all of its conditional distributions since $E(x_m)$-$E(x_n)$ is zero for (m,n) pairs (i.e., the second sum part of Equation (16) is zero).

2. The conditional distributions are completely separate (i.e., far away) from each other. As a result, the variance of the overall distribution would be much larger than the average variance of all of its conditional distributions and would be dominated by the second sum part of equation (16).

We next analyze the mean values of conditional distributions to show that the latter hypothetical case is closer to empirical reality and, as a result, the variance of the overall distribution is much larger than the average variance of the conditional distributions.

Analysis of the Mean Values of Conditional Distributions: Assume the threshold voltage of a cell before program interference is a random variable Y, and the voltage change caused by the program interference is ΔV. Then the threshold voltage after program interference will be X=Y+ΔV. As in equation (2), ΔV is mainly determined by the threshold voltage change of the direct-neighbor aggressor cell [3]. Assuming the threshold voltages of the direct-neighbor aggressor cell before and after programming value *m* are $V_{before}^{Nb(m)}$ and $V_{after}^{Nb(m)}$ respectively, then ΔV approximately equals $k\times(V_{after}^{Nb(m)}-V_{before}^{Nb(m)})$ according to Equation (2), where *k* is the coefficient denoting the coupling capacitance over the total capacitance of the victim cell. Then, the mean value of the conditional distribution x_m is

$$E(x_m)\approx E(Y)+E(k)\times(E(V_{after}^{Nb(m)})-E(V_{before}^{Nb(m)})) \tag{17}$$

As the LSB page number of an upper wordline is always smaller than the MSB page number of a lower wordline in the same block (see Fig. 1(a)) and the pages inside a block are programmed in sequential page number order to minimize program interference [3], only MSB page programming of the aggressor cell affects the threshold voltage of the victim cell. For 2-bit MLC flash memory (as in Fig. 1(b)), the starting state before MSB page programming is either the ER state or the Temp state, and the ending state could be the ER, P1, P2 or P3 state. When either P3 (value 01) or P1 (value 10) is programmed to the aggressor cell, the threshold voltage of the aggressor cell changes either from TEMP to P3 or from ER state to P2, respectively. Either of these cases leads to a larger threshold voltage change $E(V_{after}^{Nb(m)})-E(V_{before}^{Nb(m)})$, as illustrated in Fig. 1(b) [3], compared to when ER (value 11) or P2 (value 00) is programmed to the aggressor cell. Thus, the mean values of conditional distributions of x_{01} and x_{10} are larger than the mean values of the conditional distributions of x_{11} and x_{00}. When value 11 is programmed on aggressor cell, the starting and ending states are the same, i.e., the ER state, which corresponds to the smallest threshold voltage change. Therefore, the mean of the conditional distribution of x_{11} is the smallest [3]. Through similar reasoning, the mean of the conditional distribution of x_{00} sits in-between the mean of the conditional distribution of x_{11} and the mean of the conditional distributions of x_{01} and x_{10}. In summary, the means of conditional distributions for 2-bit MLC satisfy the following property:

$$E(x_{11})<E(x_{00})<E(x_{01})\approx E(x_{10}) \tag{18}$$

Fig. 2 shows that this property empirically holds for different conditional distributions; in Fig. 2, it is clear that the mean threshold voltage value of the conditional distributions with direct neighbor values 01 and 10 are similar and the highest for all states, whereas the mean value of the conditional distribution with direct neighbor value 11 is the smallest.

The result in Equation (18), empirically supported by Fig. 2, shows that the second sum part of Equation (16) is clearly greater than zero as the mean values of conditional distributions do not completely overlap. As a result, the variance of the overall distribution is larger than the average variance of the conditional distributions.

Analysis of Variance of Conditional Distributions: The variance of the conditional distribution x_i can be expressed as:

$$\text{var}(x_m)\approx \text{var}(Y)+k^2\times(\text{var}(V_{after}^{Nb(m)})+\text{var}(V_{before}^{Nb(m)})) \tag{19}$$

Due to the accurate control of the distribution width of each programmed state through incremental step pulse programming (ISPP), the variances of threshold voltage distributions of aggressor cells before and after programming are approximately close for different programming values [4][16]. For example, $var(V_{after}^{Nb(m)})$ is close to $var(V_{after}^{Nb(n)})$, even when the programmed value m and n are not the same. Also, the model coefficient *k* is around 0.06 [3] and the small value of k^2 can further reduce the value-dependent differences of variances of different conditional distributions in Equation (19). Therefore, the variances of conditional distributions of victim cells are close when different values are programmed to their direct-neighbor aggressor cells (e.g., $var(x_m)$ is close to $var(x_n)$ even if *m* is not equal to *n*) and thus are approximately equal to the average variance of all conditional distributions. Since the variance of the overall distribution is larger than the average of the variances of conditional distributions (as we have shown based on Equation (18)), the variance of the overall distribution is larger than the variance of each of the conditional distributions.

Analysis of the Distance of Distributions between Neighboring States: Assume the threshold voltages of cells that are interfered with by a direct-neighbor with value *m* in the P_i and P_{i+1} states are respectively x_m^{Pi} and x_m^{Pi+1}. The threshold voltages before neighbor interference are respectively Y^{Pi} and Y^{Pi+1}, which are independent of the value *m* programmed into the direct-neighbor cells. The amounts of interference the victim cells receive are respectively Δ_m^{Pi} and Δ_m^{Pi+1}. Thus, the distance of the conditional distributions between the two neighboring states is $E(x_m^{Pi+1})$-$E(x_m^{Pi})$, which is equal to $E(Y^{Pi+1}+\Delta_m^{Pi+1})$-$E(Y^{Pi}+\Delta_m^{Pi})$. Since program interference is mainly determined by the threshold voltage changes on the direct-neighbor aggressor cells, $E(\Delta_m^{Pi+1})$ and $E(\Delta_m^{Pi})$ are close as the neighbors are programmed to the same value *m*. Thus, $E(x_m^{Pi+1})$-$E(x_m^{Pi})$ is similar to $E(Y^{Pi+1})$-$E(Y^{Pi})$, which is equal to the distance of the neighboring distributions before neighbor cells are programmed and is independent of the exact values programmed to the direct-neighbor aggressor cells. Thus, the distance of the different conditional distributions in neighboring states are equal (or close). Therefore, the distance of the overall distributions between neighboring states is also equal to or close to the distance of any of the conditional distributions between neighboring states.

Final SNR and BER Analysis: So far, we have shown that: 1) the variance of each of the conditional distributions is smaller than the variance of the overall distribution, 2) the distance of the conditional distributions of two neighboring states is similar to the distance of the overall distributions of the same two neighboring states. As a result, the signal-to-noise ratio (SNR), $(\mu_2$-$\mu_1)/2\sigma$, of the overall distribution is smaller than that of the conditional distribution, as σ of the overall distribution is larger. Therefore, the minimum raw BER, i.e., *Q(SNR)* (see Equations (13) and (14)), obtained with the set of read reference voltages,determined based on the overall distribution would be larger than the minimum raw BER obtained with the set of read reference voltages determined based on the conditional distributions. We will make use of this statistically-demonstrated conclusion to devise our error correction mechanisms in Section 6.

5.4 Experimental Measurement Results

We now show experimental results that empirically validate the major conclusions of the statistical model we have developed so far in Sections 5.1-5.3. We program random data into 2Y-nm 2-bit MLC NAND flash devices after 10K P/E cycles and leverage the methodology discussed in Section 4 to measure the overall and the conditional distributions. Table 1 shows the results: the average distance of different distributions between neighboring states (signal), along with the average variance (noise), the signal-to-noise ratio (SNR) and the resulting minimum raw BER of the overall distribution and all four conditional distributions. The empirical data supports the main conclusions we have drawn from statistical analyses: 1) average distance between neighboring states is similar regardless of whether we use the overall distribution or any of the conditional distributions, 2) the variance, the SNR, and the resulting BER of each of the conditional distributions is smaller than those of the overall distribution. As such, experimental data also favors using conditional distributions to maximize SNR and therefore minimize BER. Section 5.5 explains the BER evaluations in more detail.

Table 1. Measurement Results of Different Distributions

	Overall	x_{11} (ER)	x_{10} (P1)	x_{00} (P2)	X_{01} (P3)
Distance	65.4	65.4	64.7	66.4	65.8
Variance	385.9	286.2	256.7	242.8	252.1
SNR	3.4	3.8	3.9	4.2	4.1
BER	$3\text{x}10^{-4}$	$7\text{x}10^{-5}$	$5\text{x}10^{-5}$	$2\text{x}10^{-5}$	$3\text{x}10^{-5}$

5.5 Minimizing BER using Conditional Distributions – Mechanism and Measurements

To measure the minimum BER of reading with the overall distribution, we set the read reference voltage between two neighboring states to $REFx=(\mu^{P(i)}+\mu^{P(i+1)})/2$, which is the average of the mean values of the overall distribution in neighboring states P_i and P_{i+1}. We define this set of read reference voltages as the *global optimum read reference voltage*. The read data is compared with the originally programmed data to count the number of errors. The BER is measured by dividing the error count with the total number of bits read.

To measure the minimum BER of reading with each conditional distribution (e.g., x_{10}), we first set the read reference voltage between states P_i and P_{i+1} to be $\text{REF}_{x10}=(\mu_{x10}^{P(i)}+\mu_{x10}^{P(i+1)})/2$. Here, $\mu_{x10}^{P(i)}$ and $\mu_{x10}^{P(i+1)}$ are the mean values of the conditional distribution of x_{10} in the P_i state and the P_{i+1} state respectively. Then, we read flash memory using this read reference voltage. We only compare the data read out from the cells that have direct-neighbor aggressors with value 10 to the data originally programmed to those cells to get the raw BER of reading with the conditional distribution of x_{10}. We repeat the same procedure three more times by setting the read reference voltages between two neighboring states to $\text{REF}_{x11}=(\mu_{x11}^{P(i)}+\mu_{x11}^{P(i+1)})/2$, $\text{REF}_{x00}=(\mu_{x00}^{P(i)}+\mu_{x00}^{P(i+1)})/2$ and $\text{REF}_{x01}=(\mu_{x01}^{P(i)}+\mu_{x01}^{P(i+1)})/2$ to get the raw BER of reading with conditional distributions of x_{11}, x_{00} and x_{01} respectively. The final raw BER of reading with conditional distributions is the equally weighted sum of the raw BER obtained after reading with each of the conditional distributions (with a weight of 0.25 for each BER as direct-neighbor cells have equal probabilities of being programmed to 00, 01, 10, 11). We define these four sets of read reference voltages as the *local optimum read reference voltages*. Based on Equation (18) and our empirical measurements, the read reference voltages obey the following property:

$$REFx_{11} < REFx_{00} < REFx < REFx_{01} \approx REFx_{10} \quad (20)$$

The threshold voltage distributions before and after random data are programmed in neighbor cells are illustrated in Figure 5(a) and 5(b) respectively. The relative location of the global and local optimum read reference voltages are illustrated in Fig. 5(b). N11, N00, N01 and N10 illustrate the conditional distributions of those cells with direct-neighbor aggressor cell programed to 11, 00, 01 and 10 respectively. The optimum BERs of reading with the overall distribution and the conditional distributions are shown on the fourth row of Table 1. Reading the flash memory cells using the set of the local optimum read reference voltages for each conditional distribution leads to a raw BER of $4.25\text{x}10^{-5}$ (equal to 0.25 times the sum of the raw BER values for each state in Table 1) whereas reading the same cells with the global optimum set of read reference voltages based on only the overall distribution leads to a raw BER of $3\text{x}10^{-4}$. As such, using the conditional distributions to determine read reference voltages to read flash memory leads to an 86% reduction in minimum raw bit error rate.

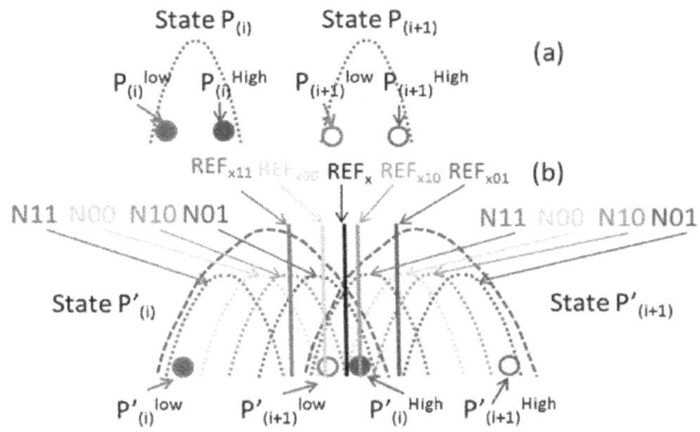

Fig. 5 (a) Threshold voltage distributions of two neighboring states *before* direct-neighbor cells are programmed; (b) Overall and conditional threshold voltage distributions, the global optimum read reference voltage of the overall distribution (REFx*)*, and local optimum read reference voltage of each conditional distribution (REF_{x11}, REF_{x00}, REF_{x10}, REF_{x01}) *after* neighbor pages are fully programmed.

5.6 Summary

Our experimental results (Sec. 5.4-5.5) validate our statistical analyses (Sec. 5.1-5.3) in that: 1) there exists an optimum read reference that can achieve the minimum raw BER; 2) the minimum raw BER decreases as signal-to-noise ratio increases; 3) the distance (signal) of the overall distribution between neighboring states is close to that of each of the conditional distributions; 4) the variance (noise) of each conditional distribution is smaller than that of the overall distribution; 5) the variances of different conditional distributions are close; 6) the signal-to-noise ratio of the conditional distribution is larger than that of the overall distribution; 7) the minimum raw BER obtained after reading with the conditional distribution is much smaller than that obtained after reading with the overall distribution.

6. Neighbor-cell Assisted Error Correction

In Section 5, we have established that the bit error rate obtained by reading flash memory with the set of *local optimum read reference voltages* for each conditional threshold voltage distribution dependent on the direct-neighbor cell value is significantly lower than the bit error rate obtained by reading flash memory with the conventional set of *global optimum read reference voltages* determined based on the overall threshold voltage distribution of *all* flash cells. In this section, we build upon this observation to introduce two mechanisms that both aim to minimize bit error rate: ***Neighbor-cell Assisted Reading (NAR)*** and ***Neighbor-cell Assisted Error Correction (NAC)***.

We have actually already described the key idea of ***Neighbor-cell Assisted Reading (NAR)*** in Sec. 5.5. **NAR** classifies the cells to be read in a wordline into N types based on the values stored in the corresponding direct-neighbor aggressor cells (N is equal to 4 in 2-bit MLC flash because the direct-neighbor can take 4 possible values). To read the cells of each type, a different set of local optimum read reference voltages (that minimizes the bit error rate) is used (i.e., REF_{x11}, REF_{x00}, REF_{x10}, REF_{x01} in Sec. 5.5). Thus, determining the values of cells in an entire flash page is an iterative operation that takes N reading steps: in every step, the values of those cells with the same common direct-neighbor value are determined, which corresponds to approximately 1/N-th of the entire page's contents. For example, first the page is read to determine the values of cells that have direct neighbor values 11 using the set of local optimum read reference voltages corresponding to the conditional distribution assuming neighbor values of 11. Afterwards, the step is repeated for cells with neighbor values 00, 10, 01, respectively. At the end of all steps, the cell values determined in each step are combined to get the complete page. This reduces the bit error rate because each type of cell is read more accurately using its corresponding local optimum read reference voltage.

Unfortunately, NAR significantly degrades read latency because determining the contents of a page requires N+2 read operations (whereas using the global optimum read reference voltage requires only one read operation): NAR first needs to read the LSB page and the MSB page of the direct-neighbor cells to determine the contents of direct-neighbors, which requires two read operations. After that, NAR needs to read the selected page N times to determine the contents of the cells classified into N types based on direct-neighbor cell values. The increase in the number of read operations from 1 to N+2 (i.e., 6 in the case of 2-bit MLC flash memory) degrades read latency to by N+2 times and thus can severely degrade system performance.

To mitigate such performance degradation with NAR, we propose ***Neighbor-cell Assisted Error Correction (NAC)***. The idea is to first read the page with the global optimum read reference voltage (which requires only one read operation) and trigger NAR only if ECC fails to correct the page data. Doing so requires a total of $(1+P_{fail} \times (N+2))$ read operations, where P_{fail} is ECC failure rate when reading with the global optimum reference voltage. If the ECC failure rate is low, average read latency would still be low. Extending this reasoning, we further optimize NAC by checking whether or not ECC can correct the current set of data after each step that reads 1/N-th of the page. After a set of local optimum read reference voltages is used to read 1/N-th of the page more accurately, ECC is applied to the entire page. If ECC can correct the entire page, then there is no need to go to the next step, i.e., apply the next set of local optimum read reference voltages to correct the next 1/N-th of the page. The next step is triggered only if ECC fails in the previous step. Thus, number of read operations is further reduced.

6.1 NAC Flow and System Operation

We briefly describe how NAC fits into the flash-based SSD controller architecture (shown in Fig. 6). The SSD controller usually contains an internal buffer to store requests and the data to be programmed and recently read. To correct raw bit errors in flash media, binary BCH codes [12], which can correct multiple bit errors, are widely deployed. The data is encoded before programming and decoded after reading. To increase error correction capability, we add two NAC-specific blocks to the controller: 1) the engine that performs NAC, 2) we reserve a small portion of the controller's internal buffer as the *NAC-buffer*, which stores the current page and neighbor pages (Fig. 6).

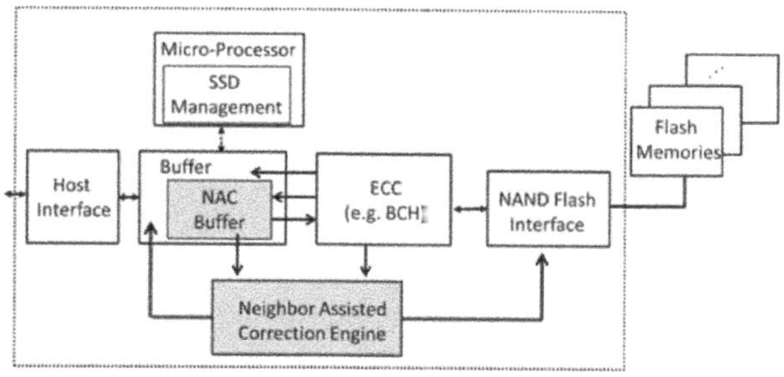

Fig. 6 Flash controller with Neighbor Assisted Error Correction.

Fig. 7 shows the flow of a page read request with NAC. When the controller starts a read operation, it first checks whether the requested page is already in the NAC-buffer (or in the internal flash buffer, as done in a state-of-the-art controller) before requesting the page from the flash memory. If so and if error-free, the page is returned to the requestor (e.g., the host machine). If not, the NAND flash interface fetches the requested page from flash memory and sends it to the ECC engine. If ECC successfully corrects all errors, flash controller sends the corrected page to the requestor, and also stores it in the NAC-buffer. If ECC fails, NAC is triggered for further correction. When NAC is triggered, it requires the direct-neighbor LSB and MSB pages above the requested page in order to classify the cells of the requested page. If these direct-neighbor pages are not in the NAC-buffer, the flash controller reads the neighbor pages out from flash memory. After ECC attempts to correct these neighbor pages, they are saved into the NAC-buffer, either error-free or erroneously (which is indicated by a bit for each page). When both neighbor pages are in the NAC-buffer, NAC is ready to correct the requested page. NAC iteratively applies a set of local optimum read reference voltages to correct 1/N-th of the requested page. ECC attempts to correct the page after every step and when ECC passes, NAC iterations stop and the requested page data is sent to the requestor. If ECC fails after all NAC iterations, the page cannot be corrected even with NAC and an exception is raised.

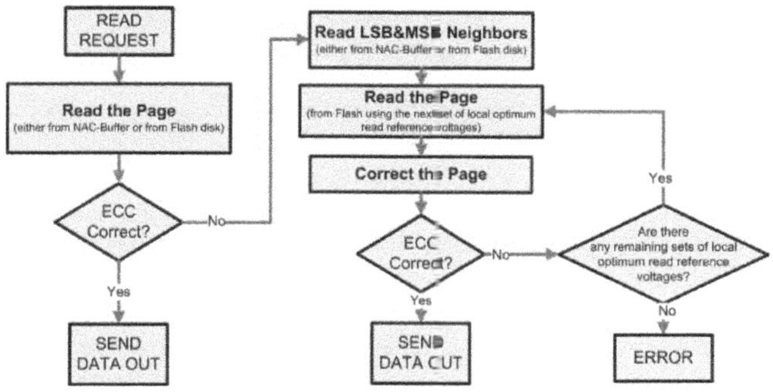

Fig. 7 Flow of the Neighbor Assisted Error Correction (NAC) mechanism

The size of the NAC-buffer is an important parameter. In order to determine the optimum size, we assume the worst-case scenario in which every read page requires NAC correction. It is common that pages are read from the flash memory in page number order due to common sequential access patterns and access to large data chunks. For instance, as in Fig. 1(a), when Page 3 fails and needs to be corrected by NAC, Pages 5 and 8 are saved to NAC-buffer. Pages 5 and 8 are also the neighbors of Page 6, hence, we prefer buffering those pages in anticipation that Page 6 will also be read due to sequential access. However, when Page 5 is read between Pages 3 and 6, two more neighbor pages are added to the NAC-buffer (i.e., Pages 7 and 10). Therefore, we set the size of the NAC-buffer to 5 pages to be able to buffer Pages 5, 6, 7, 8, 10 at the same time. When the buffer is full and a new page needs to be added, we evict the one with the lowest page number. We have investigated performance sensitivity to NAC buffer size, management policies, and prefetching mechanisms; space limits prevent us from presenting these detailed evaluations. Our empirical results (not shown in this paper) indicate that a NAC-buffer size of 5 pages leads to minimal read latency.

6.2 Prioritized NAC

In this section, we make several observations that improve the effectiveness of NAC by allowing us to apply the N sets of local optimum read reference voltages in an order that minimizes the latency overhead of NAC. In other words, we observe that some sets of local optimum read reference voltages provide better error correction capability (as they are associated with neighbor cell values that are more likely to lead to errors) and we prioritize their use when NAC is triggered such that we can reduce the number of steps in NAC correction. We call this ***Prioritized NAC.***

Error Type Analysis: When a page is read with a single global optimum read reference voltage, REFx (see Fig. 5), the resulting errors can be classified into *eight* types. The errors for cells programmed to a lower-voltage state (P_i state) with direct-neighbor cell value 11, 10, 00 and 01, but misread as belonging to a higher-voltage state (P_{i+1} state) are denoted as $P_i(11) \rightarrow P_{i+1}$, $P_i(10) \rightarrow P_{i+1}$, $P_i(00) \rightarrow P_{i+1}$, $P_i(01) \rightarrow P_{i+1}$. The errors for cells programmed to a higher-voltage state (P_{i+1} state) with direct-neighbor cell value 11, 10, 00 and 01, but misread as belonging to a lower-voltage state (P_i state) are denoted as $P_{i+1}(11) \rightarrow P_i$, $P_{i+1}(10) \rightarrow P_i$, $P_{i+1}(00) \rightarrow P_i$ and $P_{i+1}(01) \rightarrow P_i$. The relative percentages of all eight types of errors are shown in Fig. 8 for 2Y-nm flash under various P/E cycles. We can see that $P_{i+1}(11) \rightarrow P_i$, $P_i(10) \rightarrow P_{i+1}$ and $P_i(01) \rightarrow P_{i+1}$ are the three dominant errors.

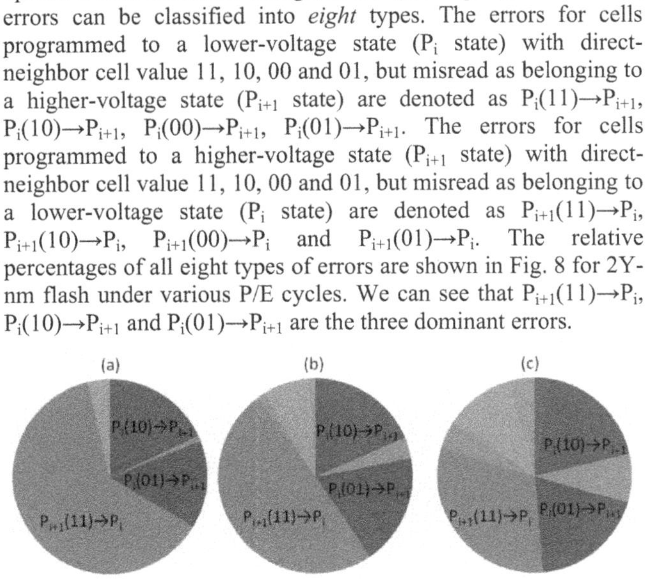

Fig. 8 Error type percentage for all eight types of read errors at (a) 3k (b) 10k and (c) 30k P/E cycles for 2Y-nm flash.

Some types of errors are more dominant because cells with threshold voltage near the border of the neighboring state's threshold voltage distribution tend to have errors as they are the most likely ones to be misclassified using a single reference voltage. To understand this, let us examine Fig. 5(a) and 5(b) that respectively plot threshold voltage distributions of victim cells before and after neighbor cells are programmed. Let us focus on two cells, each of which has an initial threshold voltage that is close to the border of the neighbor state's threshold voltage distribution: $P_{(i+1)}^{low}$ and $P_{(i)}^{high}$ in Fig. 5(a). If $P_{(i+1)}^{low}$'s direct-neighbor cell is programmed to 11, the resulting threshold voltage for this cell, $P'_{(i+1)}{}^{low}$, will be at the bottom end of the conditional distribution N11 for state $P_{(i+1)}$ (see Fig. 5(b)) because programming the neighbor cell with 11 (ER state) leads to the smallest amount of program interference. Unfortunately, using REFx as the read reference voltage might cause the value of this cell to be misread as belonging to state P_i, leading to the $P_{i+1}(11) \rightarrow P_i$ error type, the most common error type according to Fig. 8. Similarly, if $P_{(i)}^{high}$'s direct-neighbor cell is programmed to 01, the resulting threshold voltage for this cell, will be at the highest end of the conditional distribution N01 for state $P_{(i)}$ (see Fig. 5(b)) because programming the neighbor cell with 01 leads to the highest amount of program interference. Unfortunately, using REFx as the read reference voltage might cause the value of this cell to be misread as belonging to state P_{i+1}, leading to the $P_i(01) \rightarrow P_{i+1}$ error type, second most common error type according to Fig. 8. This example shows that two types of cells are more vulnerable to errors: 1) those that are at the bottom of the distribution of a higher-voltage state and receive the least amount of interference from their direct-neighbor, 2) those that are at the top of the distribution of a lower-voltage state and receive the highest amount of interference from their direct-neighbor. This leads to the dominance of corresponding error types.

Note that the $P_{i+1}(11) \rightarrow P_i$ type error is the most dominant one. This is because the program interference of aggressor cells with values 10 and 01 are close (N01 and N10 almost overlap in Fig. 5(b)). Thus, more cells are located at the top region of the overall distribution of each state. The global optimum read reference voltage therefore deviates toward the higher-voltage state. As a result, more cells of N11 in the higher-voltage state tend to be misread as belonging to the lower-voltage state.

Prioritized NAC: We take advantage of the above analysis to prioritize the selection of the set of local optimum read reference voltages during NAC. After a page that is read using the set of global optimum read reference voltages fails ECC, we select REF_{x11} as the first set of local optimum read reference voltages to read the failed page to fix the dominant $P_{i+1}(11) \rightarrow P_i$ errors. At this step of NAC, the read data of the cells with direct-neighbor values 11 will be replaced with the new reading performed with REF_{x11}. This leads to three cases: 1) The read data of a cell remains unchanged upon the NAC reading. This is the case for cells of type-N11 with threshold voltage larger than REFx or smaller than $REFx_{11}$. 2) The new data read using $REFx_{11}$ is correct and the old data read using REFx was incorrect. This is the case for cells of type-N11 in P_{i+1} state with threshold voltage in the window [$REFx_{11}$, REFx]. 3) The new data read using $REFx_{11}$ is incorrect and the old data read using REFx was correct. This is the case for cells of type-N11 in the P_i state with threshold voltage in the window [$REFx_{11}$, REFx]. Since $REFx_{11}$ is the optimum read reference voltage for cells of type-N11, the number of corrected cells (case 2) is larger than that of mis-corrected cells (case 3). Fig. 9 demonstrates this empirically: the net number of corrected cells (number of corrected minus the number of mis-corrected cells) of type-N11 can reduce the total errors by 58%, 44% and 22% for flash memory at 3k, 10k and 30k P/E cycles respectively. Since the read data of types N00, N01, and N10 are unchanged, the total number of errors is significantly reduced after applying NAC with $REFx_{11}$. ECC may be able to correct the remaining errors without requiring another NAC step. In such a case, system performance is improved due to Prioritized NAC. If ECC still fails after applying $REFx_{11}$, our mechanism tries $REFx_{10}$ next, and if ECC still fails again it applies $REFx_{01}$ as the error correction capability of these are the second and third highest, as Fig. 9 also demonstrates empirically.

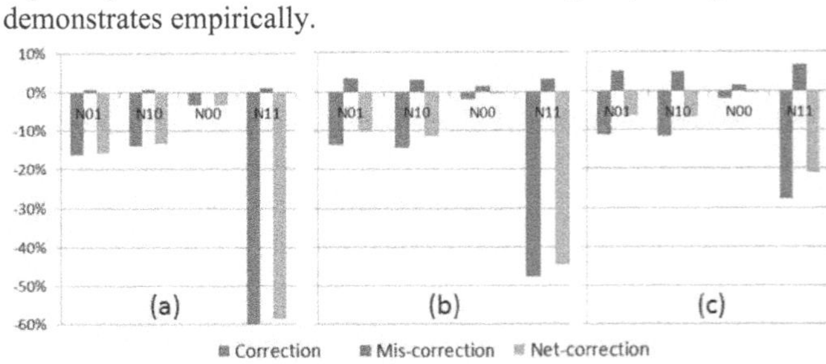

Fig. 9 Percentage of corrected errors, mis-corrected errors and net-corrected errors over total errors for flash memory when local optimum read reference voltages corresponding to N01, N10, N00 and N11 distributions are used at (a) 3k (b) 10k (c) 30k P/E cycles.

6.3 Policy When Neighbor Cells Have Errors

So far, we assumed that the neighbor cell values can be obtained correctly for NAC. However, the neighbor page may fail ECC and may not be correctly read. If the neighbor page fails ECC, we propose to use the uncorrected raw data from the neighbor page to classify cells for NAC. This section analyzes the effect of neighbor failure on the error correction capability of NAC.

Neighbor Page Failure Analysis: First, the neighbor page failure rate is low. Assume P_{fail} is the ECC failure rate. The probability of one of the two neighbor pages failing when the victim page fails is approximately $2(P_{fail})^2$, which is much smaller than P_{fail}. Even when neighbor pages fail ECC, most of the raw values read from neighbor pages are still correct because the raw BER is less than a few percent even at very high P/E cycles [1][2]. As a result, most cells in the page can be correctly classified using correct neighbor values, enabling NAC to correct errors in the victim page. For the neighbor cells that are misread, NAC may still be able fix the errors on the corresponding victim cells although it could also inject additional errors. We demonstrate this with an example. Consider a victim cell of type-N11 with its direct-neighbor cell programmed as 11 but misread as 10. The threshold voltage of this victim cell will be compared to the wrongly-selected local read reference voltage $REFx_{10}$ instead of $REFx_{11}$ during NAC. If the threshold voltage of this victim cell is less than $REFx_{11}$ or larger than $REFx_{10}$, the read value using the wrong reference voltage $REFx_{10}$ is the same as the value if read with the correct reference voltage $REFx_{11}$. Thus, there is no additional error introduced. Only when the threshold voltage of the victim cell is smaller than $REFx_{10}$ or larger than $REFx_{11}$, the read value could be different. For a cell like this, there are still two cases:

1. Cell is actually in state P_i: The correct local read reference voltage $REFx_{11}$ would have misread the cell as belonging to state P_{i+1} while the wrongly-selected $REFx_{10}$ correctly reads it as belonging to state P_i. Hence, the error in the neighbor cell eliminates a potential error when reading the victim cell.
2. Cell is actually in state P_{i+1}: The correct local read reference voltage $REFx_{11}$ would have correctly read the cell as belonging to state P_{i+1}. However, $REFx_{10}$ misreads it as belonging to state Pi. Hence, the error in the neighbor cell introduces a new error when reading the victim cell.

Since the threshold voltages of flash cells in different locations are independent of each other [4], the event that a neighbor cell has an error is independent from the event that its victim cell's threshold voltage falls in the range of [$REFx_{11}$, $REFx_{10}$]. Thus, the additional error rate caused by neighbor failure is equal to:

$$P^{11\text{->}10}_{neighbor} \times \left(\int_{REFx11}^{REFx10} f_{11}^{Pi+1}(x)dx - \int_{REFx11}^{REFx10} f_{11}^{Pi}(x)dx\right) \quad (21)$$

$P^{11\text{->}10}_{neighbor}$ is the probability that the cell on the neighbor wordline was programmed as 11 but misread as 10. $f_{11}^{Pi}(x)$ and $f_{11}^{Pi+1}(x)$ are the PDF functions of the threshold voltages of type-N11 cells programmed in states P_i and P_{i+1} respectively. $P^{11\text{->}10}_{neighbor}$ is less than a few percent at high P/E cycles. $\int_{REFx11}^{REFx10} f_{11}^{Pi+1}(x)dx - \int_{REFx11}^{REFx10} f_{11}^{Pi}(x)dx$ is much smaller than 1 since the region of [$REFx_{11}$, $REFx_{10}$] is far away from the center of the distribution $f_{11}^{Pi+1}(x)$ and $f_{11}^{Pi}(x)$ (see Fig. 5(b)). Similarly to the case of neighbor 11 being misread as 10, the additionally injected errors caused by the other types of neighbor cell failures are also very small.

Measurement of Effect on NAC Error Correction Rate: Fig. 10 plots the fraction of additional errors caused by neighbor failure over the errors that are corrected by NAC under various P/E cycles as measured for 2Y-nm flash devices. We can see that the number of errors corrected by NAC is much larger than the additionally injected errors caused by neighbor failure. The fraction of injected errors due to neighbor failure increases with P/E cycles because the raw error rate of neighbor pages increases with P/E cycles and therefore the probability of errors due to misclassification of victim cells increases. However, we can see that even at 35k P/E cycles, the number of additional errors due to neighbor failures is less than 10% of the errors that are corrected by NAC. We conclude that neighbor cell errors do not significantly reduce the error correction capability of NAC.

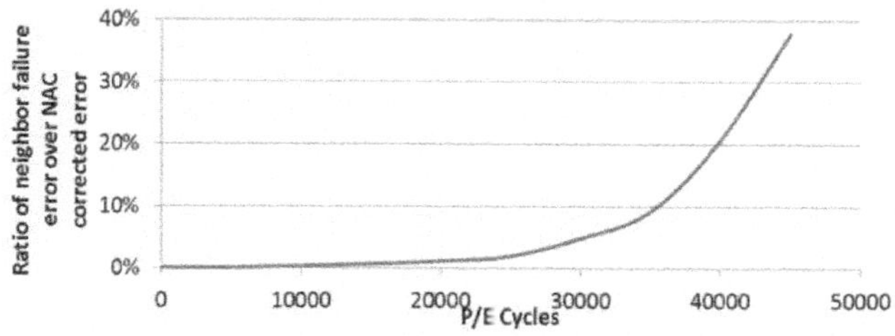

Fig. 10 The fraction of errors due to neighbor cell read failure over total errors that are corrected by NAC.

6.4 Implementation of NAC

Optimum Read Reference Voltage Learning: NAC needs to read the page multiple times using the global optimum and up to N local optimum read reference voltages. The optimum reference voltage is the average of the mean values of the threshold voltage distributions of neighboring states. To learn the mean values of state voltage distributions, we propose to periodically (e.g., every 100 P/E cycles) measure the overall and conditional threshold voltage distribution statistics for a set of sampled wordlines. The details of this periodic sampling based learning mechanism are straightforward and omitted for brevity. The learning overhead is kept low: even for write-intensive applications (e.g., 10 full disk writes per day) [7], 100 P/E cycles will be consumed after at least 10 days. The learning task runs in background with low priority so that it does not interfere with normal operation.

NAC Microarchitecture: Fig. 11 shows the microarchitecture of NAC. It contains four buffers, one comparator (Comp) vector and one pass circuit vector. The neighbor LSB page buffer and MSB page buffer store the neighbor LSB/MSB page data of the current failed page respectively. The *Page-to-be-Corrected* buffer initially contains the data of the page that was read with the global optimum read reference voltage and failed ECC. The *Local-Optimum-Read* buffer is loaded with the page data that is read using the local optimum read reference voltage at each step of NAC. Two bits, Bit1/Bit2, indicate which of the four local optimum read reference voltages (corresponding to four possible values in the neighbor cells) is used to read the current data in the Local-Optimum-Read buffer. In each step of NAC, after the page is read using the local optimum read reference voltage, each comparator circuit compares Bit1/Bit2 to the corresponding MSB/LSB neighbor bits. If there is a match (indicating that the neighbor cell value is the same as the value for which the local optimum read reference voltage is selected), the corresponding pass circuit is enabled, which causes the corresponding data in the *Local-Optimum-Read* buffer to overwrite the corresponding cell in the *Page-to-be-Corrected* buffer, thereby enabling the NAC correction of the cell that has a neighbor value that matches Bit1/Bit2. All other circuitry supporting the NAC flow in Fig. 7 is not shown.

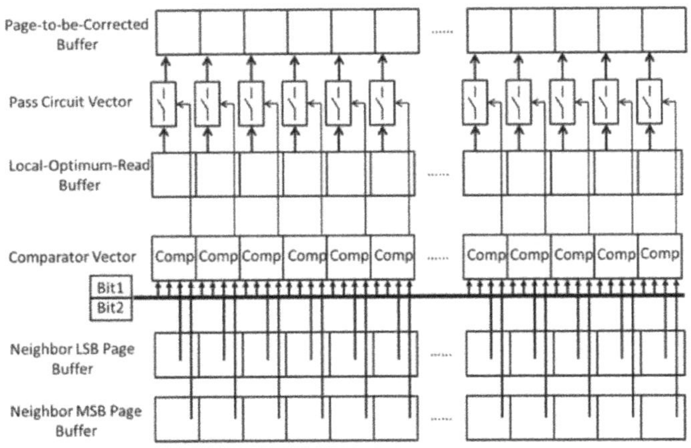

Fig. 11 Microarchitecture of Neighbor Assisted Error Correction.

7. EVALUATION RESULTS

7.1 P/E Cycle Lifetime Evaluation

Since ECCs that can correct 40 bit errors per 1k-Byte data are recommended for 20nm MLC flash memory [17], we chose such ECC as baseline in our evaluations. Following the methodology of [2], the probability of ECC failure can be calculated as:

$$P_{CW} = \sum_{n=E+1}^{N} \binom{N}{n} RBER^n \times (1 - RBER)^{N-n} \quad (22)$$

Here, N is the number of bits protected by ECC and E is the maximum number of errors that can be corrected. RBER is the raw bit error rate before error correction. Raw BER and ECC failure rate are listed in Table 2. When RBER is larger than $10^{-2.64}$, ECC almost always fails. Also, to guarantee ECC failure rate to be below 10^{-15}, the acceptable RBER should be less than 10^{-3}.

Table 2. Correlation of raw BER and ECC failure

Raw BER	10^{-3}	$10^{-2.9}$	$10^{-2.8}$	$10^{-2.7}$	$10^{-2.65}$	$10^{-2.64}$
ECC FER	10^{-15}	10^{-10}	10^{-6}	10^{-2}	0.07	100%

P/E Cycle Lifetime Evaluation: We program random data into 2Y-nm 2-bit MLC flash memory for up to 50k P/E cycles. Assuming that retention errors can be fixed by using flash refresh techniques [6][7], the programmed data are read out after one-week retention at room temperature. The raw BER values resulting from reading with the global optimum read reference voltage without NAC and reading with different strengths of NAC using respectively one, two, three or four potential sets of local optimum read reference voltages are shown in Fig. 12 over different P/E cycles. To guarantee system reliability, the raw BER must be less than the acceptable raw BER (i.e., 10^{-3}) of the baseline ECC. Thus, the maximum P/E cycle lifetime of the baseline flash memory without NAC is only 18k P/E cycles, as shown in Fig. 12. NAC increases the P/E cycle lifetime by 22% (22k P/E cycles), 33% (24k P/E cycles) and 39% (25k P/E cycles) respectively for different strengths. Since the fourth set of local optimum read reference voltages mainly corrects errors for the conditional distribution that is in the middle of the overall distribution where there are fewer errors (see Fig. 8), its raw BER curve almost overlaps with that of using three sets of local optimum read reference voltages. We conclude that NAC is effective in improving flash memory lifetime and as NAC strength is increased lifetime improvement increases.

NAC Frequency Analysis: As Fig. 12 shows, the extended lifetime due to NAC is divided into three regions based on NAC strength: stage 1, stage 2, and stage 3. At the beginning of the extended lifetime, the raw BER is about 10^{-3} and the ECC failure rate before NAC is 10^{-14}. NAC is seldom triggered. As P/E cycles increase, the raw BER after reading with global optimum read reference voltage increases. Raw BERs without NAC at the end of stage-1, stage-2 and stage-3 are $1.6\text{x}10^{-3}$, $2\text{x}10^{-3}$ and $2.2\text{x}10^{-3}$ respectively. These cause the ECC failure rates without NAC to be 10^{-5}, 10^{-2} and 33% respectively. This means that ECC does not *always* fail during the extended lifetime and hence NAC is not triggered for all requested pages. We use the ECC failure rate without NAC at the end of each stage to estimate the worst-case NAC trigger frequency in that stage. Note that the ECC failure rate within a stage is generally lower than this worst-case value as it increases with P/E cycles. In stage-1, NAC trigger frequency is very low (<10^{-5}). However, the ECC failure rate would not satisfy modern storage systems' requirement (less than 10^{-15} failure rate) without NAC protection. In stage-2, NAC is triggered at a rate <1%. Only in the third region, NAC is triggered often (<33%). However, if NAC is applied, the raw BER of all these stages can be reduced to lower than 10^{-3}. Hence, using NAC guarantees the uncorrectable failure rate to be below 10^{-15}, which is the error rate requirement for storage.

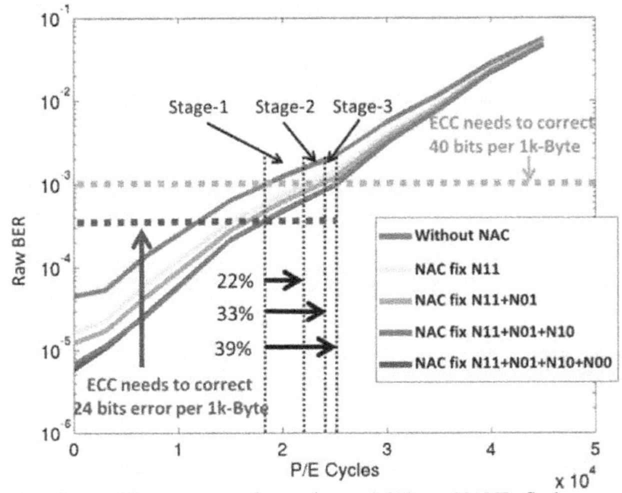

Fig. 12 Raw bit error rate of experimental 2Y-nm NAND flash memory with and without NAC of varying levels of strength.

Reducing the Cost of ECC using NAC: If P/E-cycle lifetime that is desired is the same as that of the baseline without NAC, the employed ECC mechanism can be simplified in the presence of NAC. We explore how much NAC can help reduce ECC cost to achieve the same P/E-cycle lifetime as the baseline ECC mechanism. The maximum P/E cycle lifetime of the employed baseline ECC is 18K P/E cycles, as seen in Fig. 12 (at this lifetime, the raw BER of the baseline reaches 10^{-3}, which is the maximum acceptable raw BER that leads to an ECC failure rate of 10^{-15}, as shown in Table 2). At 18K P/E cycles, using NAC reduces the acceptable raw BER for ECC by 65% from 10^{-3} to $3.5\text{x}10^{-4}$. To satisfy this raw BER, simpler ECC that can correct only 24 bit errors (as opposed to 40 in the baseline) for 1k-Byte data can be used. Since ECC complexity increases linearly with the number of errors that ECC can correct [12], the ECC design cost can be reduced by approximately 40% when NAC is employed. This can lead to significant power and area savings in the system.

P/E Cycle Analysis: NAC provides diminishing returns on raw BER rate as the number of P/E cycles increases. The raw BER reduction with NAC can be more than 90% at the beginning of flash lifetime. However, at high P/E cycles (e.g., 35k P/E cycles), NAC reduces raw BER by only 30%. This is mainly due to two reasons. First, at low P/E cycles program interference related errors, which are the errors that can be fixed by NAC, constitute a higher fraction of all flash errors, whereas at higher P/E cycles they constitute a smaller fraction [3] and other errors, e.g., those due to P/E cycling noise, which cannot be fixed by NAC, become dominant [1][4]. Note that this is because program interference is due to cell-to-cell coupling and is mainly determined by the geometry of flash cells (e.g., the distance between neighboring flash cells) instead of P/E cycles whereas many other flash error types increase with P/E cycles [3]. Second, the ECC failure rate of, and correspondingly the number of, erroneously read cells on the neighbor pages, which are needed by NAC for error correction, increases over P/E cycles. Neighbor page ECC failure causes misclassification of cells and can partly counteract the errors corrected by NAC (Sec. 5.3). When flash memory scales to smaller geometries and program interference becomes more dominant, we would expect NAC to have even higher benefits in error reduction and relative lifetime improvement.

7.2 Performance Evaluation

We evaluate the performance of NAC by using Disksim [18][19] with SSD extensions [19]. We use I/O traces from various workloads: cello99 [20], postmark [21], MS-Cambridge [22], Financial OLTP [23] and Web Search Engine [23]. Details of these traces can be found in [7]. We configure the simulated flash based SSD with four channels. Each channel has eight flash chips. Each flash chip has 8096 blocks containing 256 pages per block. Each page is 8KB unless specified otherwise.

7.2.1 Workload NAC-Buffer Locality Analysis

To help explain the performance impact of NAC in Sec. 7.2.2, we first analyze the locality behavior of read operations in the workloads in the NAC-buffer. NAC presents time overhead for reading the neighbor LSB and MSB pages of a requested page (called the victim page) that fails ECC. NAC keeps these pages in a 5-entry NAC-buffer, as described in Sec. 6.1. If the victim and neighbor pages are needed while they are in the NAC-buffer, these requests are served from the NAC-buffer instead of flash memory.

We first explore hit rates in a 5-entry NAC-buffer. We study a system that always keeps the 5 last accessed pages in the NAC-buffer (but the system is error-free for the purposes of this study). In Fig. 13, we show the hit rate of different types of pages in the NAC-buffer. The victim page hit rate shows the caching effect of the NAC-buffer: this is the fraction of all flash requests that hit in the 5-entry NAC-buffer. The higher this fraction, the more effective the NAC-buffer as a latency reduction mechanism for *all* requests in the system. The LSB/MSB neighbor page hit rate specifies the fraction of all flash requests for which the LSB/MSB neighbor is also in the NAC buffer when the request is received. The higher this fraction, the less the overhead of a potential NAC correction as there is no need to fetch the LSB/MSB neighbor from flash memory to perform NAC correction when these neighbors are already in the NAC-buffer. For workloads with heavily sequential access patterns, we expect the hit rates of the neighbor pages to be higher since the program may have already fetched neighbor pages before it requests a (victim) page.

We make several observations from Fig. 13. First, the NAC-buffer hit rate is in general low (i.e., less than 5%), which indicates that only a small fraction of pages are accessed repeatedly from the small NAC buffer. This is because, in order to reduce disk accesses, the operating system keeps the recently used pages in main memory and it is unlikely that a page that is recently accessed will be evicted from main memory to be accessed again soon after. However, *Financial* has a remarkably high hit rate in the small NAC-buffer, which affects its performance positively with NAC (see Sec. 7.2.2). Second, we find that the LSB/MSB Neighbor Page hit rates are high for *Cello*, *MS-Cambridge* and *Web-Search* workloads, as these have more than 30% of their read operations as sequential requests. In contrast, *Financial* and *Postmark* workloads have relatively small request sizes; therefore, they feature less sequential read requests, leading to lower hit rates. We expect the overhead of NAC correction to be low for the former type of (sequential-access) workloads. Third, the hit rate of the LSB neighbors is higher than that of the MSB neighbors. This is because the number of pages between the victim page and its MSB neighbor is higher than the number of pages between the victim page and its LSB neighbor As a result, workloads that only have higher levels of spatial locality, of which there are fewer, can take advantage of the MSB neighbors.

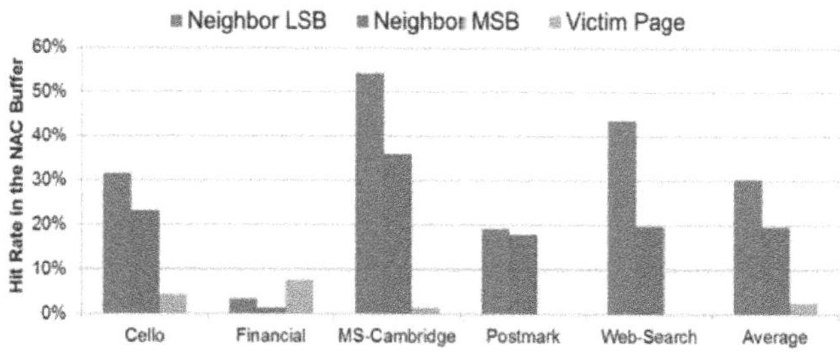

Fig. 13 The hit rate of different page types in the NAC-Buffer during error-free Execution (i.e., when ECC fail rate is zero). Victim Page indicates the overall hit rate of the NAC-buffer for all flash accesses.

7.2.2 NAC Performance Overhead Analysis

Fig. 14 shows the increase in read latency due to NAC at distinct P/E cycles. We activate the NAC mechanism when the first ECC failure is experienced in flash memory. After that, each requested page is first searched in the NAC-buffer before accessing the flash disk. Note that the time spent for this search operation is around 1% of the latency of flash disk access latency. We make three major observations.

First, NAC does not present any performance impact when the flash memory is within the same lifetime as the baseline (<18K P/E cycles).

Second, at relatively low P/E cycles after the extended lifetime, NAC presents either only negligible performance degradation or slight performance improvement. This is because, for especially the workloads with good locality, the 5-entry NAC-buffer behaves as an effective small cache in front of the flash memory, as indicated by the hit ratio of different types of pages in Fig. 13. Even when NAC incurs overhead by fetching the neighbor pages upon an ECC failure from flash, the later requests to these pages made by the workload can hit in the NAC-buffer, thereby potentially hiding the NAC overhead for these neighbor pages.

Third, NAC incurs less than 5% performance degradation while providing a 33% lifetime improvement (i.e., from 18k to 24k P/E cycles). Moreover, this performance degradation is only introduced for the higher P/E cycles during which a normal flash memory without NAC is considered to be non-functional.

Finally, there is a sharp increase in read latency overhead between 24k P/E cycles and 25k P/E cycles. The main reason of this increase is the drastic increase in ECC failure rate from 10^{-2} to 33% between these two points. At 25k P/E cycles, one out of every 3 read operations requires NAC correction with its associated overhead. However, using NAC still enables a high lifetime of 25K P/E cycles, which cannot be achieved by the baseline ECC.

We conclude that NAC is effective at improving flash memory lifetime beyond ECC without significantly degrading system performance (up until the point where ECC failure rate increases drastically).

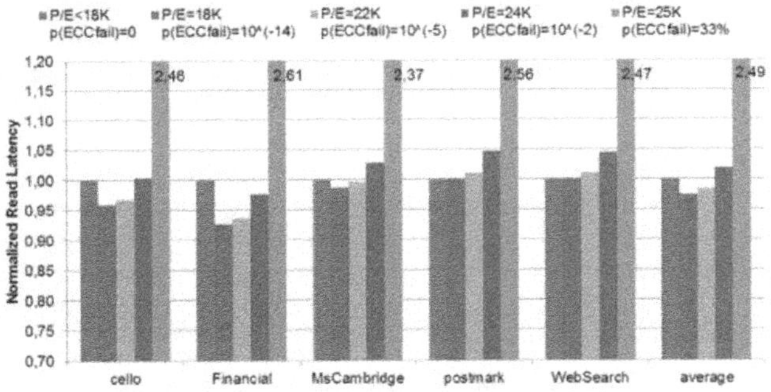

Fig. 14 The read latency overhead of NAC at different P/E cycles with different ECC failure rates in each P/E cycle.

Effect on a System with Prefetching: Fig. 15 shows the read latency overhead of NAC on a system that prefetches 2 or 4 consecutive pages for every read request. We increase the bandwidth between the flash controller and the flash disk so that the prefetched pages can be read to the flash controller in parallel with the requested pages. When the number of pages prefetched is increased, NAC presents less performance degradation at high ECC failure rate, i.e., when p(ECCfail)=33%. This is because a more aggressive prefetcher increases the probability of finding the neighbor pages in the NAC-buffer when NAC needs them. However, at low ECC failure rate, NAC presents more performance degradation when number of pages prefetched is higher. This is because prefetching aggressively consumes NAC-buffer entries and reduces the overall hit rate of the victim pages. We conclude that NAC has even less performance overhead in a state-of-the-art system that employs aggressive prefetching.

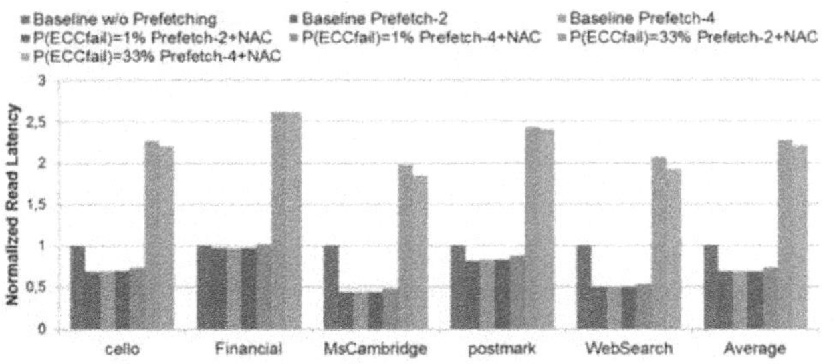

Fig. 15 The performance overhead of NAC in a system with prefetching. Each bar is normalized to the baseline, error-free system that does not employ prefetching.

8. CONCLUSION

We comprehensively analyzed threshold voltage distributions in state-of-the-art 2Y-nm MLC NAND flash memory and both statistically and experimentally demonstrated that bit error rate when reading flash memory can be decreased by classifying flash cells based on their immediately-neighboring cells' values. Building on these analyses, we introduced the first low-overhead and high-accuracy neighbor-cell assisted error correction methods that leverage information from neighbor cells to correct errors in cells that are being read from flash memory. Our experimental evaluations using I/O traces from real workloads and error data obtained from real flash memory chips show that our new error correction methods can significantly reduce the raw bit error rate and improve flash memory lifetime at zero or very modest performance overheads. As flash memory scales down to smaller technology nodes and cell-to-cell interference therefore becomes an even more dominant cause of errors, we expect that the error correction techniques proposed in this paper will become even more important for reliable operation. We also hope that the statistical and experimental analyses provided in this paper can enable the development of even more sophisticated and effective error tolerance mechanisms.

ACKNOWLEDGMENTS

We thank the anonymous reviewers for helpful feedback. This work was partially supported by the Intel Science and Technology Center for Cloud Computing, Data Storage Systems Center (DSSC) at Carnegie Mellon University, NSF Award CCF 12122962, the FP7 ParaDIME Project, grant agreement no. 318693 and by the Ministry of Science and Technology of Spain and the European Union (FEDER funds) under contracts TIN2008-02055-E and TIN2012-34557.

REFERENCES

[1] Y. Cai et al., "Error Patterns in MLC NAND Flash Memory: Measurement, Characterization and Analysis", DATE 2012.

[2] N. Mielke et al., "Bit Error Rate in NAND Flash Memories", IRPS 2008.

[3] Y. Cai et al., "Program Interference in MLC NAND Flash Memory: Characterization, Modeling, and Mitigation", ICCD 2013.

[4] Y. Cai et al. "Threshold Voltage Distribution in MLC NAND Flash Memory: Characterization, Analysis, and Modeling", DATE 2013.

[5] K. Park et al., "A Zeroing Cell-to-cell Interference Page Architecture with Temporary LSB Storing and Parallel MSB Program Scheme for MLC NAND Flash Memories", JSSC 2008.

[6] R. Liu et al., "Optimizing NAND Flash-Based SSDs via Retention Relaxation", FAST 2012.

[7] Y. Cai et al. "Flash Correct-and-Refresh: Retention-Aware Error Management for Increased Flash Memory Lifetime", ICCD 2012.

[8] Y. Cai et al., "Error Analysis and Retention-Aware Error Management for NAND flash memory," Intel Technology Journal 2013.

[9] H. Shim et al., "Highly Reliable 26nm 64Gb MLC E2NAND Flash Memory with MSP Controller", VLSIT, 2011.

[10] T. Kim et al., "Cell-to-cell Interference Compensation Schemes Using Reduced Symbol Pattern of Interfering Cells for MLC NAND Flash Memory", IEEE Transactions on Magnetics 2013.

[11] G. Dong et al., "Using Data Postcompensation and Predistortion to Tolerate Cell-to-cell Interference in MLC NAND Flash Memory", IEEE Transactions on Circuits and Systems I, 2010.

[12] S. Lin et al., "Error Control Coding (2nd Edition)", Prentice Hall 2004.

[13] Y. Cai et al. "FPGA-Based Solid-State Drive Prototyping Platform", FCCM 2011.

[14] J. Cha et al., "Data Randomization Scheme for Endurance Enhancement and Interference Mitigation of Multilevel Flash Memory Devices", ETRI Journal, 2013.

[15] C. Kim et al., "A 21 nm High Performance 64 Gb MLC NAND Flash Memory with 400 MB/s Asynchronous Toggle DDR Interface", JSSC 2012.

[16] D. Lee et al., "Estimation of NAND Flash Memory Threshold Voltage Distribution for Optimum Soft-Decision Error Correction", IEEE Transactions on Signal Processing 2013.

[17] S. Yasarapu, "Architectural Requirements for MLC based SSDs", FMS 2011.

[18] J. Bucy et al., "The DiskSim Simulation Environment Version 4.0 Reference Manual", Technical Report 2008.

[19] N. Agrawal et al., "Design Tradeoffs for SSD Performance", USENIX 2008.

[20] Open Source at HP Labs, http://tesla.hpl.hp.com/opensource

[21] J. Katcher, "Postmark: a New File System Benchmark", Technical Report, 1997.

[22] SNIA: IOTTA Repository, http://iotta.snia.org/tracetypes/3.

[23] UMass Trace: http://traces.cs.umass.edu/index.php/Storage/Storage

ANATOMY: An Analytical Model of Memory System Performance

Nagendra Gulur,
Mahesh Mehendale
Texas Instruments
Bangalore, India
nagendra@ti.com,
m-mehendale@ti.com

Raman Manikantan,
Ramaswamy Govindarajan
Indian Institute of Science
Bangalore, India
r.manikantan@gmail.com,
govind@serc.iisc.ernet.in

ABSTRACT

Memory system design is increasingly influencing modern multi-core architectures from both performance and power perspectives. However predicting the performance of memory systems is complex, compounded by the myriad design choices and parameters along multiple dimensions, namely (i) technology, (ii) design and (iii) architectural choices. In this work, we construct an analytical model of the memory system to comprehend this diverse space and to study the impact of memory system parameters from latency and bandwidth perspectives. Our model, called ANATOMY, consists of two key components that are coupled with each other, to model the memory system accurately. The first component is a queuing model of memory which models in detail various design choices and captures the impact of technological choices in memory systems. The second component is an analytical model to summarize key workload characteristics, namely row buffer hit rate (RBH), bank-level parallelism (BLP), and request spread (*S*) which are used as inputs to the queuing model to estimate memory performance. We validate the model across a wide variety of memory configurations on 4, 8 and 16 cores using a total of 44 workloads. ANATOMY is able to predict memory latency with an average error of 8.1%, 4.1% and 9.7% over 4, 8 and 16 core configurations. We demonstrate the extensibility and applicability of our model by exploring a variety of memory design choices such as the impact of clock speed, benefit of multiple memory controllers, the role of banks and channel width, and so on. We also demonstrate ANATOMY's ability to capture architectural elements such as scheduling mechanisms (using FR_FCFS and PAR_BS) and impact of DRAM refresh cycles. In all of these studies, ANATOMY provides insight into sources of memory performance bottlenecks and is able to quantitatively predict the benefit of redressing them.

Categories and Subject Descriptors

B.3.1 [**MEMORY STRUCTURES**]: Semiconductor Memories; C.4 [**PERFORMANCE OF SYSTEMS**]: [Modeling techniques]; D.4.8 [**PERFORMANCE OF SYSTEMS**]: Performance—*Modeling and prediction*; I.6.4 [**SIMULATION AND MODELING**]: Model Validation and Analysis

Keywords

DRAM, Memory System Performance, Analytical Model

SIGMETRICS'14, June 16–20, 2014, Austin, Texas, USA.
Copyright 2014 ACM 978-1-4503-2789-3/14/06 ...$15.00.
http://dx.doi.org/10.1145/2591971.2591995.

1. INTRODUCTION

The emergence of multi-cores, and the widening of the processor-memory gap have emphasized the significance of *memory wall* [33] and *bandwidth wall* [27] problems, making off-chip memory to be one of the key performance bottlenecks. Hence designing an efficient off-chip memory hierarchy is one of the biggest challenges faced by system designers. The problem is compounded by the myriad design choices and parameters along multiple dimensions that need to be considered and evaluated to arrive at a decision.

1.1 Challenges in Off-chip Memory Design

At a high level, off-chip memory design choices/alternatives can be viewed along three dimensions: (1) Technology, (2) Design and (3) Architectural choices. It is to be noted that these three dimensions are not independent of each other and choices made along one dimension can have significant impact on the design decisions made/alternatives available along other dimensions.

Technological Alternatives:

DDR3 DRAM [11] is the prevailing off-chip memory technology of choice. The technological alternatives arise not only in the form of new protocol specifications like DDR4 [1], but more importantly in the form of emerging technologies, like PCM [32]. Most of these emerging technologies, are close to fruition and in the near future can be expected to challenge/co-exist with DDR* technologies [15, 25]. The emerging memory technologies not just differ fundamentally from DRAM but also have differing strengths and weaknesses in comparison to DRAM and also with respect to each other. From a performance point of view, the timing details of the individual operations varies across the technologies. For example, in PCMs, writes take longer than reads. The different technologies and hence devices built using them also exhibit significant differences in their energy requirements. Thus there are a number of factors that need to be considered while making a decision along the technology dimension. And more importantly while technology is only the first step, the real impact of the technological alternative can be seen only when considered together with the design and architectural dimensions.

Design Choices:

From a design perspective, there are a plethora of alternatives. In a memory system design, the key factors of interest when it comes to memory performance are the number of memory controllers, their placement and the number of channels supported by each controller [2, 4, 11, 13]. From a memory device organization perspective, a multitude of choices exists. For instance off-chip memories associated with each memory channel are organized hierarchically in terms of ranks, banks, rows and columns [11]. And a related design dimension to the overall layout of the device is the size of the row buffer (also known as memory page) [11, 30]. Hence there are myriad ways to organize off-chip memory of any given capacity. The choices made have a direct impact on performance since they affect locality, parallelism and other latency/bandwidth related parameters. An orthogonal dimension/factor that has an impact on the design choices is the nature and demands of the workloads. An effective memory design, to a certain extent, is also workload specific and hence a knowledge of the target domain/applications plays a role in the design of the memory hierarchy.

Architectural Enhancements:

Architectural solutions to improve the performance and energy efficiency of DRAM and emerging memory technologies have received much research focus. One key direction, that falls under architectural enhancements is memory access command scheduling [13,26]. The proposed solutions range from improving the row-buffer hit rate [10,13,16,26,30], exploiting the parallelism available in memory accesses [21] to application aware scheduling [14]. In the case of emerging technologies like PCM, the proposed enhancements include using a DRAM cache [25], scheduling techniques to mitigate impact of long-latency writes [24] and provisioning multiple row-buffers [15]. The architectural enhancements extend all the way to data/page placement in the presence of multiple memory controllers [4] and memory channel partitioning [20]. From an energy perspective, recent solutions [7, 8] advocate monitoring mechanisms to employ DVFS at main memory. These solutions are not just restricted to the memory controller, but need to interact closely with the rest of the system and more importantly are application/workload aware.

Thus, efficient design of off-chip memory systems depends on evaluating a number of interlinked alternatives along multiple design dimensions, factoring workload characteristics adequately.

1.2 ANATOMY: Key Features

To address the above problem, we develop an analytical performance model for the memory system. A well developed and validated analytical model can evaluate a large number of design alternatives quickly and in an inexpensive fashion. Also an analytical model helps in capturing/understanding the interactions between various critical parameters. ANATOMY developed with these goals in mind, can evaluate the relative performance of various design alternatives quickly, narrow the design space to a limited number of alternatives on which detailed simulation can be run to estimate their performance more accurately. While we demonstrate that ANATOMY can predict memory performance (average latency and bandwidth), our intent is to use ANATOMY more to predict the *relative* performance of different design points.

ANATOMY is an analytical tool consisting of two key components. The first component captures the workload behavior in terms of the locality and parallelism it exhibits in its memory accesses using a simple analytical model. This helps us to succinctly summarize the workload characteristic in a technology independent fashion. In the second component, these workload characteristics are fed into a simple queuing model of the off-chip memory to predict performance (in terms of latency and bandwidth). The queuing model takes into account the parameters from the technology and design dimensions. More importantly, our network-of-queues formulation has a simple closed form solution. Hence once the workload characteristics are captured, its performance across a variety of design points can be evaluated quickly.

To summarize the key contributions of this paper are:

- We develop an analytical model for memory systems that helps to analyze/understand the interplay between myriad memory parameters and workload characteristics and its effect on memory system performance.
- ANATOMY is able to predict various memory system performance parameters like row buffer hit rate, bank level parallelism, and average memory latency with a reasonable accuracy (average error of 3.9%, 4.2% and 4.0% respectively, as compared to detailed simulations) across a wide variety of memory configurations for 4, 8 and 16 core workloads. Also ANATOMY allows us to estimate the peak bandwidth achievable at various design points.
- We demonstrate the extensibility and applicability of our model to alternative memory technologies such as PCM. We also demonstrate ANATOMY's ability to capture impact of sophisticated scheduling mechanisms such as FR-FCFS [26] and PAR-BS [21].

2. BACKGROUND AND MOTIVATION

We motivate our work in the context of JEDEC-style DRAMs [11]. But the problems faced are common/applicable to other memory technologies too.

2.1 Background

DRAM devices are packaged as Dual In-line Memory Modules (*DIMMs*) which are interfaced typically to an on-chip memory controller. DIMMs contain one or more *ranks*. A rank is a collection of DRAM devices that operate in parallel. Each DRAM device typically serves up a few bits at the specified (row, column) location. Operating together, the devices in a rank match the data bus width. For example, an $x16$ device supplies 16 bits of data and 4 such devices making up a rank can supply data needed to match the 64-bit interface of the memory controller. Each device in a rank is organized into a number (4, 8 or 16) of logically independent banks. Each bank consists of multiple *rows* (also called *pages*) of data. Banks can operate in parallel and this provides for some degree of parallelism in accessing memory.

For any read request, a row of data is read into the row-buffer associated with the bank and the data is supplied from the row-buffers. If an access is not to a currently open row, then the memory controller should (1) write back the currently open row in the row-buffer (precharge); (2) bring the new row's data into the row-buffer (activate); and (3) read the required columns of data from the row-buffer (column access). In case the access is to a currently open row, commonly referred to as a *row-buffer hit*, then only column access operation is required. Hence, intuitively, the fraction of accesses that hit in the row buffer, referred to as row-buffer hit rate (RBH), has a significant impact on the overall latency. Also if the requests are spread out over the banks, then the bank level parallelism (BLP) and the resulting temporal overlap helps amortize the memory access latency. It is widely accepted that RBH and BLP are two critical factors that have a significant impact on overall memory system performance.

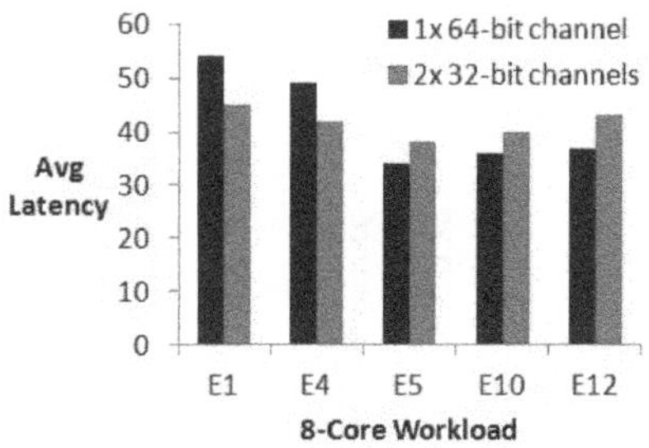

Figure 2: Latency variation across workloads for two different channel configurations

2.2 Motivation

In this section, we demonstrate that even in the case of the very well studied and understood DDR3 DRAM it is very hard to reason about/predict the impact of simple design changes carried out in a controlled fashion. As most of the recent research emphasizes on improving RBH and/or BLP to improve the memory performance (in terms of average memory latency), we first study to what extent the memory latency can be predicted by studying the variations in RBH and BLP.

In the first experiment, we consider the scenario of increasing the number of banks in a 4GB DRAM, keeping the DRAM page size fixed at 4KB. Intuitively, we may predict that increasing the number of banks improves BLP by spreading out the requests across more banks. Likewise, the increased number of banks allows more pages to be kept open, improving the RBH. However, it is hard to quantify its impact on RBH. Figure 1 summarizes the performance impact[1] of increasing the bank count on a representative subset of the quad-core workloads.

As Figure 1(a) shows, increasing the bank count has a different extent of impact on RBH across different workloads. And this directly translates to a reduction in the average latency (Figure 1(b)). However, the surprising fact is that the increased number of banks has negligible impact on BLP, especially in workloads Q7, Q14 and Q18.

In the second experiment, we investigate the joint impact of data channel width, frequency and number of banks. We compare two memory system configurations each with a total of 8GB DRAM organized; the first configuration is organized as one memory controller interfaced to a single 64-bit data channel operating at 1GHz, provisioned with 16 banks, while the second one consists of two controllers, each interfaced to a 32-bit data channel operating at 1GHz, provisioned with 16 banks (a total of 32 banks across both the controllers). Figure 2 shows that the two configurations exhibit widely differing behavior across 8-core workloads, with E1, and E4 benefiting from the provision of multiple smaller channels, while workloads E5, E10, E12 benefit from the single faster, wider channel.

To summarize,

- It is hard to predict the performance impact of even a controlled and simple design exploration.
- The overall performance is dictated by subtle and non-trivial interactions between a variety of performance critical factors (like RBH and BLP) and workload characteristics.

[1]Obtained from a modified GEM5 simulation (details given in Section 4).

3. ANATOMY - AN ANALYTICAL PERFORMANCE MODEL OF MEMORY

In this section, we develop ANATOMY, an analytical model of memory performance, that can be used to evaluate the performance of various design points in a rapid and accurate fashion.

ANATOMY has two key components that work together:

- A queuing model of memory that models in detail the key technological characteristics and design choices. The queuing model is decoupled from the workload aspects.
- A trace based analytical model that estimates key workload characteristics, namely arrival rate, row-buffer hit rate (RBH), bank-level parallelism (BLP) and request spread (S), that are used as inputs to the queuing model to estimate memory performance.

3.1 Queuing Model of the Memory System

The queuing model of ANATOMY considers a memory system $\mathcal{M}$ with M memory controllers. Each controller has a single channel and manages a memory system consisting of D DIMMs, each consisting of R ranks, and each rank having B banks. In this work, we do not model the rank parameters in detail [2] and treat that there is a total of $N = D \times R \times B$ banks. Each channel has a command bus and data bus.

We summarize the actions from the time a request reaches the memory controller to the time the required data is sent back. For ease of understanding, we consider DRAM memory in the rest of this section. But the concepts that we model are generic enough and are applicable, in fact they are the same, even for memories built using other technologies (see Section 6.3).

A request can either result in a row-buffer hit or a miss. While a row-buffer hit requires only a column access command to the DRAM bank, a row-buffer miss requires a precharge, activate and finally a column-access command to be sent to the corresponding bank. Note that these operations required are common to various technologies [3]. A command can be sent only when the command bus is free and the corresponding DRAM bank is not busy. Also in the case of column access, it can be scheduled/sent only if the data bus will be available at the time the DRAM bank writes data on the data bus. The memory controller schedules commands using a scheduling policy while ensuring that all timing and protocol-specific constraints are met. First, we present a model of the memory system that accounts for the memory-side performance observed by a single memory controller. In section 3.1.3, we extend this to multiple memory controllers. Section 3.7 discusses modeling scheduling policies.

3.1.1 *3-stage Network of Queues Model*

The memory system is modeled as a collection of 3-stage queuing networks with each network representing a single memory controller and its associated channel, DIMMs, ranks and banks. Each 3-stage network model of a single memory controller, as shown in Figure 3, consists of a command bus server, N bank servers and a data bus server.

Stage 1: Command Bus

The command bus server captures issuing of necessary commands to the memory banks. We assume that the inter-arrival times of

[2]We observe that the rank parameters, such as the rank-to-rank switching delay do not significantly affect the memory performance.

[3]Some memory technologies such as PCM do not require a precharge and/or refresh operation.

(a) Row-Buffer Hit Rate (RBH) (b) Average Latency (c) Bank Level Parallelism (BLP)

Figure 1: Impact of Increasing Number of Banks in DRAM

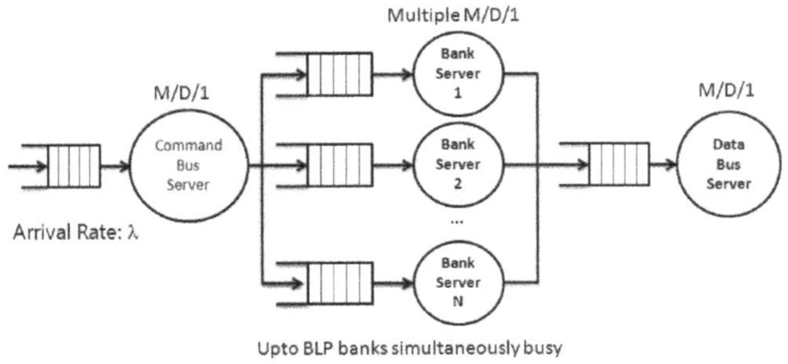

Figure 3: Queuing Model of Memory Controller as a 3-Stage Network of Queues

memory requests are exponentially distributed with a mean $\frac{1}{\lambda}$. The arrival rate λ is a characteristic of application/workload and we discuss techniques to estimate it in Section 3.2. We validate the assumption of exponential distribution in Section 5.1. As explained earlier, based on whether an access turns into a row-buffer hit or a miss, the command bus issues either one (column access) or three (precharge, activate and column access) commands respectively to the corresponding DRAM bank. The time required to send any one command is fixed, and equal to one cycle of memory clock(T_{clk}). Hence the average service time at the command bus can be approximated as a function of Row-buffer Hit rate (RBH), the fraction of requests that experience a row-buffer hit. RBH is primarily a workload characteristic with some design parameters like page size affecting it. Estimating RBH is discussed in Section 3.2. For a given RBH value of R (see Table 1), the average service time required by the command bus is $(R \times 1 + (1 - R) \times 3) \times T_{clk}$. Since RBH is a workload specific constant, the average service time required can be treated as fixed. As we consider multi-programmed workloads (details in Section 4), considering the interleaved nature of memory requests from the various programs, we treat that the arrival process is Markovian, with an arrival rate λ which is a characteristic of the workload. We validate this in Section 5.1. Hence we model the command bus as an $M/D/1$ queue.

Stage 2: Memory Banks

The second stage comprises a set of bank servers to model the actual servicing of any request by the memory. This stage takes into account the key memory technology-specific timing parameters as well as the inherent parallelism present in a multi-bank memory. Although these delays are incurred waiting in the memory controller, we associated them with the memory banks in our model.

In real memory systems, the number of banks that operate in parallel depends to a great extent on the amount of parallelism found in the memory accesses made by the workload. This workload characteristic is commonly referred to as Bank Level Parallelism (BLP) [4]. Note that in real memory, the requests are queued at memory controller in bank-specific queues until the bank becomes available. Also the memory controller uses per-bank queues [26] and as the functioning of each bank is completely independent of other banks[5], we treat this stage as a collection of M/D/1 queues operating in parallel (rather than as a single $M/D/N$ queue). Modeling the banks as multiple $M/D/1$ models the behavior that multiple requests could either be in service or held in bank-specific queues in real controllers.

As the service time of stage 1, the command bus server, is really small, we make the simplifying assumption that the input process at the second stage is also Markovian [22], with the same mean λ. Assuming a BLP of b, the per-bank arrival rate is: $\frac{\lambda}{b}$. It is well known that such an operation still retains the Markovian nature of the arrivals at each bank [28].

Next, we consider the average service time of a request in one of the banks. The service time depends on whether the actual request turns into a row-buffer hit or miss. In the case of a row-buffer hit, the time required is the column access latency (T_{CL}). If the access turns into a row-buffer miss, then the time required is a sum of the time required to complete precharge (T_{PRE}), activate (T_{RCD}) and column access (T_{CL}). Hence with the application locality being characterized by a RBH of R, the average service time for a request is $(T_{CL} \times R + (T_{PRE} + T_{RCD} + T_{CL}) \times (1 - R))$. As the latencies (for hit and miss) are fixed values (which in reality allows memory scheduler to schedule commands appropriately), we treat the average service time as fixed, resulting in each bank being modeled as an $M/D/1$ queue.

The important thing to note regarding the service time computations is that the values for T_{CL}, T_{PRE} and T_{RCD} are technology specific. Hence choice with respect to technology (like PCM or STRAM) can be captured here by choosing appropriate latencies for the various actions. We describe later (in Section 6.3) as to how special cases like writes taking longer in PCM [32] and non-volatile memory technologies can be captured under this generic queuing model with minor modification to it.

[4]Some of the memory design choices also have an impact on BLP.
[5]Except for peak-power limiting timing constraints such as T_{FAW}, the banks operate pretty much independently.

Stage 3: Data Bus

Finally, the last stage is the data bus server which captures the actual data transfer on the channel. In real world, once the data is available at the end of a column access operation, the data bus controller transfers the data in BL bursts. This operation takes a fixed time of $BL \times T_{clk}$. Again, we make the simplifying assumption that the input to this server, which is a combination of the outputs from the N parallel Bank servers, is Markovian[6] (with the same arrival rate of λ). As the service time is a constant, we model the data bus as a $M/D/1$ queue.

To summarize, we model each memory controller by a 3-stage open queuing network. Note that the memory controller itself is not explicitly modeled. However, the queuing delays in the command bus, bank, and data bus essentially model the queuing delay experienced at the memory controller. In Section 3.1.4, we address the important question of modeling processor performance.

Limitations of the Model

In order to keep the model simple, we have ignored a few parameters encountered in any DRAM specification, e.g., the rank-to-rank switching delay (T_{RTRS}) and the four-activation window constraint (T_{FAW}, the minimum rolling window of time in which at most 4 banks can be activated). For simplicity, we have also made the assumption of an open queueing system although a closed system would model the impact of memory performance on future memory requests. However, the validation results in Section 5 show that, despite these limitations, ANATOMY is able to predict memory performance with reasonable accuracy.

3.1.2 Latency and Bandwidth Estimates

Using the proposed model, we can derive the average latency for a memory request to be the sum of the queuing delays and service times at the command bus, memory bank and the data bus. Total queuing delay QD is

$$QD = QD_{Cmd\_Bus} + QD_{Bank} + QD_{Data\_Bus} \quad (1)$$

Using the queuing theory result for the $M/D/1$ queue [22], the queue delays for the command and data bus are given by:

$$QD_{Cmd\_Bus} = \frac{1}{2\mu_{cmd}} \frac{\rho_{cmd}}{(1-\rho_{cmd})} \quad (2)$$

where $\mu_{cmd} = \frac{1}{(R \times 1 + (1-R) \times 3) \times T_{clk}}$ and $\rho_{cmd} = \frac{\lambda}{\mu_{cmd}}$. Similarly,

$$QD_{Data\_Bus} = \frac{1}{2\mu_{data}} \frac{\rho_{data}}{(1-\rho_{data})} \quad (3)$$

where μ_{data} is $\frac{1}{(BL * \times T_{clk})}$ and $\rho_{data} = \frac{\lambda}{\mu_{data}}$

Computation of the average queuing delay at the banks needs to take into account two possibilities: (i) A new request goes to an idle bank (ii) A new request goes to an already busy bank.

A request going to an idle bank sees no queuing delay while a request to a busy bank sees an average delay given by:

$$QD_{Bank} = \frac{1}{2\mu_{bank}} \frac{\rho_{bank}}{(1-\rho_{bank})} \quad (4)$$

where μ_{bank} is $\frac{1}{(T_{CL} * r + (T_{RCD} + T_{PRE} + T_{CL}) * (1-r))}$ and $\rho_{bank} = \frac{\lambda_{busy\_bank}}{\mu_{bank}}$, where λ_{busy_bank} is the per-busy-bank arrival rate. We observe that while the BLP is typically a small fraction of the total available banks in the system, the workload generates addresses that exercise all of the banks over time, and thus the actual collection of b banks is a rolling set. We refer to this as *Request Spread* (denoted by S), the fraction of requests that go to idle banks, and estimate it from the application trace (see Section 3.6).

Thus, a fraction S of requests incur no queuing delay at the banks. The rest of the requests (fraction $(1-S)$) are assumed to be distributed uniformly amongst the b busy banks yielding a per-busy-bank arrival rate of $\lambda_{busy\_bank} = \frac{(1-S)\lambda}{b}$ and we estimate

$$QD_{Bank} = \frac{1}{2\mu_{bank}} \frac{\rho_{bank}}{(1-\rho_{bank})} \quad (5)$$

Now the total latency of the memory system may be computed as:

$$Lat_{Avg} = QD + \frac{1}{\mu_{cmd}} + \frac{1}{\mu_{bank}} + \frac{1}{\mu_{data}} \quad (6)$$

Note that our formulation has yielded an explicit break-up of the queuing delays associated with each key resource in the system, thereby allowing us to study their impact separately or together. The delays and service times are in terms of the row-buffer hit rate R the bank-level parallelism b and request spread S. We observe that the latency is affected by the queuing delay at the bank, which in turn is controlled by the achieved BLP. Thus, unlike traditional results that view BLP as only governing delivered bandwidth, we demonstrate that it plays a significant role in achieved latency.

Peak and Achieved Bandwidth

The peak bandwidth achieved (measured in number of requests per second) is nothing but the maximum possible arrival rate λ_{max} that the system can sustain. This is in turn limited by the slowest of the 3 servers, and can be expressed as:

$$Peak\_BW = \lambda_{max} = min\,(\mu_{cmd}, N\mu_{bank}, \mu_{data}) \quad (7)$$

where N is the number of banks. With an observed arrival rate λ, the bandwidth utilization achieved by the workload may thus be written:

$$Bandwidth\_Utilization = \frac{\lambda}{Peak\_BW} \quad (8)$$

In Section 6.4, we demonstrate this effect and the impact of adding additional data channels.

3.1.3 Extension to Multiple Memory Controllers

With multiple memory controllers, we simply associate a 3-stage queue with each controller and estimate each controller's observed latency and bandwidth. With M controllers each having an arrival rate λ_i for $1 \leq i \leq M$, we compute the average latency seen by each controller and compute a system-wide average using:

$$Lat_{Avg} = \sum_{i=1}^{M} \frac{\lambda_i}{\sum_{j=1}^{M} \lambda_j} * Lat_{Avg}(i) \quad (9)$$

Note that we can estimate λ_i from the input memory reference trace using a suitable address mapping scheme that maps addresses to memory controllers. Peak bandwidth by the system of controllers is simply the sum of bandwidths delivered by each controller.

3.1.4 Processor Performance Model

We characterize impact on processor performance by use of the CPI (Cycles-Per-Instruction) additive formula [12]:

$$CPI_i \approx CPI_i^{ideal\_MEM} + Penalty_i$$

where CPI_i is the CPI for the ith core, $CPI_i^{ideal\_MEM}$ is its CPI with an ideal memory which has 0-cycle latency and $Penalty_i$

[6] see [19] for a more detailed discussion.

is the per-instruction average miss penalty in CPU cycles. If F_i is the processor clock rate and M_i its LLC misses per instruction (MPI), then we can rewrite:

$$CPI_i = CPI_i^{ideal\_MEM} + Lat_{avg} * F_i * M_i \quad (10)$$

where Lat_{avg} is ANATOMY's estimate of average memory latency from Equation 6.

Note that the above is only an approximation as the observed CPI is a result of complex interactions of several factors affecting performance including the program's ability to tolerate LLC misses, and the extent of overlap amongst memory requests (MLP).

3.2 Analytically Estimating Workload Characteristics

There are four parameters of interest, used by the queueing model, that are highly specific to individual workloads. They are: (i) The arrival rate λ, (ii) The row-buffer hit rate (RBH) R, (iii) The bank level parallelism (BLP) b, and, (iv) The request spread S. To estimate these parameters analytically for any memory configuration, we use a trace of off-chip memory accesses (misses at the last level cache) made by the workload for *a given memory configuration*. We use simulation (details in Section 4) to obtain the trace. Note that ANATOMY does not model on-chip hierarchy (e.g., L1, L2, L3 caches) and the trace for the memory system is obtained for a specific L1/L2/L3 cache configuration using the simulator.

3.3 Arrival Rate

Arrival rate (λ), is primarily the misses at the last level cache and reflects the memory intensity of the workload. As will be shown in Section 5.1, the design choices at the memory level are likely to have only a minor impact on the arrival rate. Hence in this work, we ignore any feedback effect that memory performance can have on the arrival rate and estimate it as a value determined entirely by the workload. We use Misses Per Kilo Instructions at the last level cache and the cycle time of the processor to estimate λ. This requires us to process the trace (of each workload) only once for the entire design space exploration.

3.4 Row-Buffer Hit Rate

Row-buffer hit rate (RBH) is primarily determined by the locality exhibited by the workload in its memory accesses. Key memory related parameters that influence RBH are the size of the row-buffer, and the number of banks. In the following discussion, a page refers to the page in memory which is brought into the row-buffer upon a row-activation. To summarize the locality characteristics of the workload, we use the well known measure of *reuse distance*. Reuse distance is defined as the number of unique addresses referred between two successive references to the same address. In this case, we consider addresses at the granularity of pages. Let RD_k represent the fraction of accesses with a reuse distance of k. Intuitively, for an access with reuse distance of k to experience a row-buffer hit in any bank, none of the intervening k unique pages should map to that particular bank.

For simplicity, we assume that the intervening requests are independent and are equally likely to map to any of the N banks[7]. Thus, the probability that all the k unique pages referred to by the intervening accesses [8] not getting mapped to the current bank is $((N-1)/N)^k$.

[7] In practice, we observe that this assumption holds in the simulation as long as the address mapping scheme does not place the bank-select bits as the most significant bits.

[8] The number of intermediate references $\geq k$.

From this, we can estimate the RBH experienced by a workload in a memory with N banks as:

$$RBH(N) = R = \sum_{k=0}^{k=\infty} RD_k \times \left(\frac{N-1}{N}\right)^k \quad (11)$$

The above equation, as will be shown in Section 5, estimates RBH with a very high accuracy for FCFS scheduling policy. Note that RBH values for different page sizes are estimated from the same trace. Extensions to other scheduling policies are discussed in Section 3.7. From a computational effort point of view, estimating reuse distance in an offline fashion and for multiple page sizes is a well studied problem with highly efficient solutions being available.

3.5 Bank Level Parallelism

We define Bank Level Parallelism (BLP) as the average number of banks that are active when at least one bank is active. Intuitively, it can be seen that BLP depends on (i) the average time taken to service a request, (ii) the number of arrivals during that time and, (iii) the number of banks over which these arrivals are spread out. The last two factors mentioned above are primarily determined by the workload.

With an inter-arrival time $t_{arr} = \frac{1}{\lambda}$ and per-bank service time $t_b = \frac{1}{\mu_{bank}}$, the number of new requests that arrive during the time that a bank is busy is given by: $n_{req} = \frac{t_b}{t_{arr}}$. These n_{req} requests distribute over the available N banks and largely determine the resulting BLP. Requests that go to already busy banks increase the duration that those banks stay busy, and thus provide a bigger window of time for additional requests to come in and distribute to other banks. This causes an increase in BLP. A wider distribution of requests on the otherhand reduces queuing delays per bank. This in turn shortens the available window of time for new requests to come in while some banks stay busy. Thus we implement an iterative procedure that iterates over BLP values until convergence.

While the actual distribution of requests to banks is application-specific, at each iteration we simply estimate BLP as a combinatorial solution of counting the number of ways that n_{req} objects can be distributed into N available slots where b of them are busy[9].

Assuming that at least one bank is busy, we compute BLP as:

$$BLP(n_{req}) \approx 1 + \sum_{k=1}^{MIN(n_{req},N-1)} k * Pr(N-1, n_{req}, k) \quad (12)$$

where $Pr(N, M, k)$ denotes the probability that M requests distribute to exactly k out of N available banks.

Last, as n_{req} may not always be an integer, we discretize the problem using $\lfloor n_{req} \rfloor$ and $\lceil n_{req} \rceil$ and then obtain the final BLP as a weighted sum.

$$\begin{aligned} BLP &\approx (\lceil n_{req} \rceil - n_{req}) * BLP(\lfloor n_{req} \rfloor) \\ &+ (n_{req} - \lfloor n_{req} \rfloor) * BLP(\lceil n_{req} \rceil) \end{aligned}$$

3.6 Spread

While BLP is a measure of how many banks are simultaneously busy, the actual set of busy banks is a rolling set of some b banks from among the available N banks. It is important to estimate this spread S - the fraction of requests that go to idle banks - since such

[9] Alternately, one could process the memory trace keeping track of busy and idle banks as each request arrives, and obtain an estimate of BLP.

requests will have no queuing delay at the bank servers, while the other requests that go to already busy banks encounter a delay. We estimate the spread from the application memory trace by keeping track of busy and idle banks over sliding time windows. The window is set to a duration of time equal to the average service time of a bank, namely $t_b = \frac{1}{\mu_{bank}}$.

3.7 Modeling Impact of Scheduling Policies

While the above discussion of the queueing model assumes an $FCFS$ priority scheme, in reality, memory controllers employ sophisticated scheduling policies to ensure higher performance or fairness or other objectives. ANATOMY enables modeling of arbitrary scheduling policies by simulating the chosen scheduling algorithm over the application trace and suitably re-ordering the accesses in the trace. For instance, in the FR_FCFS scheme [26], the scheduler prioritizes row-buffer hits over misses. To model this, the FR_FCFS scheduler is run on the memory trace, and RBH, $Spread$ re-estimated from the reordered memory trace. In section 6.5, we demonstrate the validity of this approach on 2 schedulers, namely FR_FCFS [26] and PAR_BS [21].

3.8 Modeling of DRAM Refresh Operations

Refresh operations in DRAM are required to recharge capacitors that store data. Depending on the technology and operating temperature, capacitors will need to be recharged periodically. Since refresh is expected to occupy an increasingly large fraction of available bank time in future process technologies [18, 29], it is important to model refresh in ANATOMY. In the *auto-refresh* mode, every T_{REFI} period (the refresh interval), all banks are refreshed taking a time of T_{RFC}. Every T_{REFI}, we incur this un-availability of banks for a duration T_{RFC}. This mode is preferred if the refresh overhead is low. We model this refresh mode in ANATOMY simply as the fraction of time that banks are not available by dilating the bank service time by the factor: $\frac{(T_{REFI}+T_{RFC})}{T_{REFI}}$

In the *RAS-only* refresh mode, essentially a refresh operation is performed at the granularity of a specific row in a specific DRAM bank. By performing a refresh operation, the bank precharges the specified row and leaves the bank in an idle state. Thus in the *RAS-only* mode, the refresh operation has two impacts on memory system performance: (i) it reduces RBH since it closes open pages and, (ii) it makes banks unavailable for normal memory accesses during refresh operations.

We model both these effects by inserting refresh requests into the application trace. The refresh requests are inserted either following a simple periodic refresh scheme or one of the smarter algorithms [9, 29]. For simplicity, a refresh request is treated as if it were a normal read request to a row. After inserting these requests, we re-estimate λ', RBH', BLP' and S' as before. Note, however, that unlike real read operations, refresh operations do not consume data bus cycles. Thus, we use the original arrival rate λ for the data bus server.

Table 1 shows a list of key terms used in this paper and how they are obtained/used in our work.

Term	Description and How it is obtained
F_i	Frequency of ith core - Input to ANATOMY
M_i	LLC Misses per Instruction from the ith core - Input to ANATOMY
T_{CL}, T_{PRE}, T_{RCD}	Key DDR3 Timing Parameters - Input to ANATOMY
λ	Arrival Rate - Estimated from time-annotated LLC miss trace ($8KB \times 32$) once; re-used across all configurations explored.
RBH^{mdl}(R)	Row-Buffer Hit Rate - Estimated from LLC miss trace once for each page size.
BLP^{mdl} (b)	Bank Level Parallelism - Estimate from ANATOMY once for each bank count N
Spread (S)	Request Spread - Estimated from LLC miss trace once for each bank count N
QD_{Cmd_Bus}	Queue Delay due to Command Bus - Estimate from ANATOMY
QD_{Data_Bus}	Queue Delay due to Data Bus - Estimate from ANATOMY for each memory configuration
QD_{Bank}	Queue Delay due to Banks - Estimate from ANATOMY for each memory configuration
QD	Total Queue Delay - Estimate from ANATOMY for each memory configuration
$Lat_{Avg}, Lat^{mdl}_{Avg}$	Average Latency - Estimate from ANATOMY for each memory configuration
CPI^{mdl}_i	Cycles Per Instruction for i^{th} core - Estimate from ANATOMY for each memory configuration
RBH^{sim}	Row-Buffer Hit Rate - Measured from Simulation
BLP^{sim}	Bank Level Parallelism - Measured from Simulation
Lat^{sim}_{Avg}	Average Latency - Measured from Simulation
CPI^{sim}_i	Cycles Per Instruction for i^{th} core - Measured from Simulation

Table 1: Glossary of Terms

4. EXPERIMENTAL METHODOLOGY

We validate our model by comparing its results against results obtained using the M5 [5] simulator integrated with a detailed in-house DRAM simulator. The DRAM simulator *faithfully* models both the memory controller and the DRAM with accurate timing, including hierarchical DIMM organization, channel width, frequency, timing parameters such as T_{FAW}, T_{RTRS}, T_{WTR}, and refresh operations. Each program in the workload is executed in fast-forward mode for 9 billion instructions, then in in detailed cycle-accurate mode for 500 million instructions. Multi-core simulations are run until all the programs complete 500 million instructions. As is the standard practice, programs that finish early continue to execute but the performance of only the first 500 million instructions is considered for each core.

The baseline machine configuration used in our studies is shown in Table 2. L2 is the last level cache and is shared across all the cores. While the quad-core has one memory controller, the eight and sixteen cores have two and four memory controllers respectively.

We use multi-programmed workloads comprising programs from SPEC2000 and SPEC2006 suites to evaluate our proposal. The workloads are typically a mix of programs with varying levels of memory intensity (based on their L2 MPKI). We evaluated our model using 23 quad-core, 15 eight-core and 6 sixteen-core workloads. The workload details are listed in Table 3. The table specifies the SPEC 2000/2006 benchmark number (e.g: 462 denotes 462.libquantum in the SPEC 2006 suite) used in each workload. The position of the benchmark number in each array denotes which core the benchmark was run on (e.g: In the quad-core workload mix

Processor	3.2 GHz OOO Alpha ISA
L1I Cache	32kB private, 64B blocks, Direct-mapped, 3 cycle hit latency
L1D Cache	32kB private, 64B blocks, 2-way set-associative, 3 cycle hit latency
L2 Cache	For 4/8/16 cores: 4MB/8MB/16MB, 8-way/16-way/32-way, 128/256/512 MSHRs, 64-byte blocks, 15 cycle hit latency
Controller	On-chip; 64-bit interface to DRAM, 256-entry command queue FCFS scheduling [26], open-page policy Address-interleaving: row-rank-bank-mc-column
DRAM	DDR3-1600H, BL (cycles)=4, CL-nRCD-nRP=9-9-9 a rank comprises 4 1GB x16 devices, each device has 8 banks, each bank has 65536 rows, 1024 columns Refresh related: T_{REFI} of 7.8us and T_{RFC} of 280nCK

Table 2: CMP configuration

Quad-Core Workloads
Q1:(462,459,470,433), Q2:(429,183,462,459), Q3:(429,462,471,464), Q4:(470,437,187,300), Q5:(462,470,473,300), Q6:(459,464,183,433), Q7:(410,464,445,433), Q8:(462,459,445,410), Q9:(429,456,450,459), Q10:(181,186,300,177),Q11:(168,401,435,464),Q12:(434,435,437,171), Q13:(444,445,459,462),Q14:(401,410,178,177), Q15:(300,254,255,470), Q16:(171,181,464,465),Q17:(464,450,465,473),Q18:(453,433,458,410), Q19:(462,471,254,186),Q20:(462,191,433,437), Q21:(401,473,435,177), Q22:(416,429,454,175),Q23:(254,172,178,188)
Eight Core Workloads
E1:(462,459,433,456,464,473,450,445), E2:(300,456,470,179,464,473,450,445), E3:(187,172,173,410,470,433,444,177), E4:(434,435,450,453,462,471,164,186), E5:(416,473,401,172,177,178,179,435), E6:(437,459,445,454,456,465,171,197), E7:(183,179,433,454,464,435,444,458), E8:(183,462,450,471,473,433,254,168), E9:(300,173,178,187,188,191,410,171), E10:(470,177,168,434,410,172,464,171), E11:(459,473,444,453,450,197,175,164), E12:(471,462,186,254,465,445,410,179), E13:(187,470,401,416,433,437,456,454), E14:(300,458,462,470,433,172,191,471), E15:(183,473,401,435,188,434,164,427)
Sixteen Core Workloads
S1:(462,459,433,456,464,473,450,445,453,179,183,168,416,434,444,191), S2:(435,465,471,164,186,434,416,256,172,177,178,437,454,171,197,458), S3:(462,473,254,168,183,453,300,173,187,178,188,410,171,434,470,191), S4:(470,177,464,171,172,168,434,410,175,164,444,450,254,465,179,471), S5:(410,433,189,187,177,173,300,255,254,471,458,456,454,437,444,434), S6:(191,189,177,183,179,168,470,164,470,464,459,450,435,256,416,445)

Table 3: Workloads

Q1, 462.libquantum was run on core-0, 459.GemsFDTD on core-1, 470.lbm on core-2 and 433.milc on core-3.).

To estimate memory performance from ANATOMY we obtain a memory access trace of all the workloads (using simulation) at one particular design point, DDR3 with 8KB pages and 32 banks. The trace records all the memory accesses made during detailed simulation along with their time stamps. From the trace, we estimate the arrival rate (λ), the RBH value (R) (for each page size), BLP (b) and Request Spread (S) (for each memory configuration). These values are then used by our analytical model to estimate the queuing delay, average memory access time and peak bandwidth. We compare these values with those obtained from detailed simulations.

5. VALIDATION OF ANATOMY

In this section, we validate ANATOMY and then demonstrate in Section 6 its ability to capture the impact of design choices, technological alternatives and architectural enhancements. We also study the ability of the queuing model to identify performance bottlenecks. The evaluation of ANATOMY will be primarily carried out in the context of DDR3 DRAM. The primary output of interest is the average latency per access (referred to as Lat_{avg} in the rest of this section). We are also interested in the RBH and BLP predicted by the analytical model. We use Lat^{sim}_{avg} to indicate that the latency is obtained using simulation and Lat^{mdl}_{avg} to indicate that it is predicted by ANATOMY. A similar convention is used with RBH and BLP to indicate its origin. ANATOMY, just like any other analytical model, can either under-predict or over estimate any metric of interest. Hence we compute average errors by considering only the magnitude of the errors, to ensure that positive and negative errors do not cancel out each other. To emphasize this, we use the term "average of absolute error".

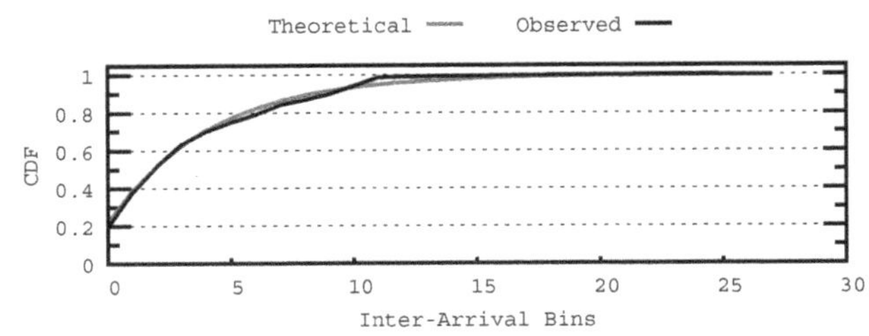

Figure 4: Plot of the actual and theoretical inter-arrival time distributions for 8-core workload E5

5.1 Validation of Model Assumptions - Exponential Inter-Arrival Times

We compare the actual inter-arrival time distributions for each 4, 8 and 16-core workload against exponential distributions with corresponding average arrival rates and using the $Chi\text{-}square$ goodness-of-fit test [23] with 30 degrees of freedom. The p-values[10] averaged over 4, 8 and 16-core workloads are 0.11, 0.04 and 0.016 respectively, denoting reasonably high confidence of match between the actual and theoretical distributions. It may also be observed that the confidence improves (i.e., p-value decreases) with core count. As an example, Figure 4 shows the actual and theoretical cumulative distributions for the 8-core workload E5.

5.2 Queuing Model Validation

The first step is to ensure that the simple queuing model of memory captures all the performance critical factors. Before evaluating and validating the complete analytical model, we first estimate the errors introduced due to RBH and BLP prediction, by determining Lat_{avg} using Equation 6, but with RBH^{sim}, BLP^{sim} and Spread S^{sim} which are values obtained from detailed simulation. Note that RBH^{sim}, BLP^{sim} and S^{sim} are used **only** in this experiment. Figure 5 shows the average error in Lat_{avg} predicted by ANATOMY at various design points (given as $PageSize \times \#Banks$) for the quad-core workloads. At each design point, we report the average (arithmetic mean across all workloads) error (only magnitude is considered as mentioned above) in Lat_{avg}. The model is able to predict performance with average error of 6.0% across the design points. In the case of 8-core, the average error in Lat_{avg} across various design points ranges from 3.2% – 7.4%.

5.3 End-To-End Validation

In this section, we are interested in validating ANATOMY end-to-end. In particular we are interested in the errors in RBH^{mdl} and

[10] p-value is a statistical measure of deviation of the actual distribution from the hypothesis.

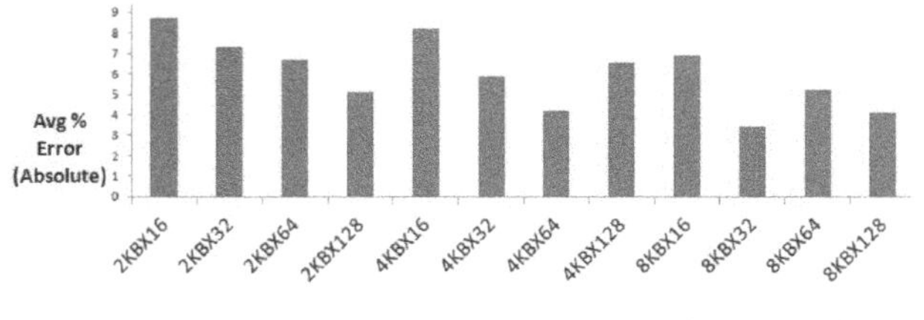

Figure 5: Error in predicting Lat_{avg} with RBH^{sim}, BLP^{sim} and S^{sim} values in Quad-Core

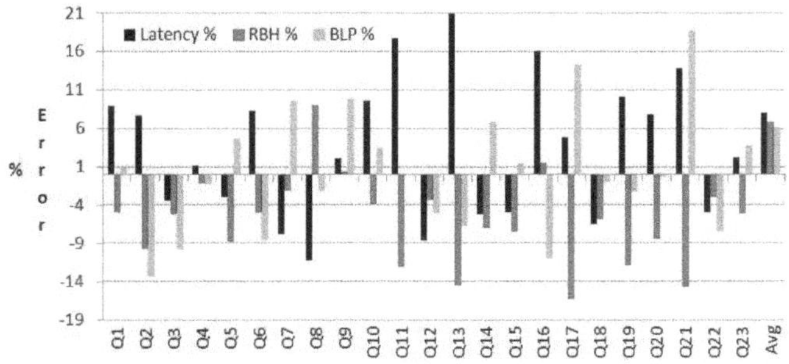

Figure 6: Error in predicting Lat_{avg}, RBH and BLP in Quad-Core Workloads

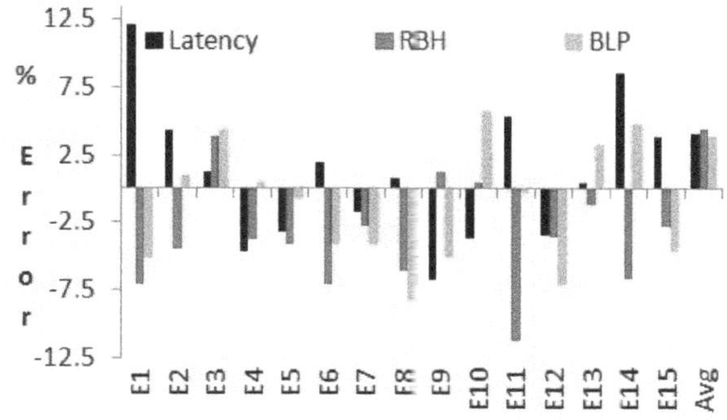

Figure 7: Error in predicting Lat_{avg} RBH and BLP in Eight-Core

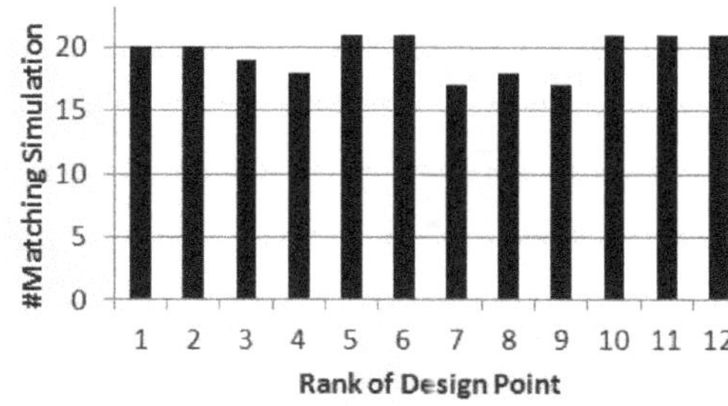

Figure 8: Identifying Best Design Point for Quad-core Workloads

BLP^{mdl} and their cumulative impact on Lat^{mdl}_{avg}. Figures 6 and 7 show the error in RBH, BLP and Lat_{avg} predicted by ANATOMY at one representative design point ($4KB \times 32$) for quad and eight core workloads respectively. A negative value for error indicates over-estimation by ANATOMYIt can be seen that, even though the trace was obtained at a different ($8KB \times 32$) configuration, the error in Lat_{avg} is $\leq 10\%$ in 19 out of the 23 quad-core workloads and all but one of the eight core workloads. The average of absolute errors (shown in the last set of bars in Figures 6,& 7) for Lat^{mdl}_{avg} is 8.1% for quad core workloads and 4.1% in the case of eight core. In the case of 16-cores, the average error in Lat^{mdl}_{avg} is 9.7%. Note that in all cases, the memory configuration for which the validation is done is different from the design point used for trace generation ($8KB \times 32$). Thus, the average absolute errors, observed across workloads for 4,8, and 16-core are low, indicating a reasonable accuracy of our model. Further such low errors are seen despite many simplifying assumptions in our model. This shows that ANATOMY captures the performance critical aspects of memory reasonably well.

In workloads like Q2, where RBH and BLP are over-estimated, as can be expected, we underestimate Lat_{avg}. In workloads like Q5, Q8 where one of RBH or BLP is over-estimated and the other is under-estimated, Lat_{avg} is over/under estimated depending on the relative errors and the impact of RBH/BLP on Lat_{avg} in the individual workload.

5.4 Using ANATOMY for Predicting Trends

We study the ability of ANATOMY to predict better performing (in terms of average memory latency) design alternatives across configurations with different page (row-buffer) sizes, and number of banks. For quad-core workloads, we consider the 12 design choices using page sizes of 2KB, 4KB, 8KB and varying the number of banks from 16 – 128. For each workload, the 12 design alternatives are ranked based on average latency, with Rank1 being the smallest latency to Rank12 being the largest. Figure 8 shows the number of times ANATOMY based ranking of design alternatives matches the results obtained using simulation for the quad-core workloads. It can be seen that, despite relying on traces obtained from one particular memory configuration ($8K \times 32$), ANATOMY predicts latency trends across the design points with reasonable accuracy. In 20 out of 23 workloads, ANATOMY identifies the best design point (as identified by the M5 simulation) accurately. In the other 3, ANATOMY identifies it as the predicted second-best. ANATOMY also identifies the worst design alternatives (last 3 ranks) with a high accuracy (in 21 out of the 23 workloads). Identifying poor design points (lower ranked ones) helps to eliminate these design choices early and quickly using the analytical model. We also found that ANATOMY *ranked every design point within* ± 1 *of the simulation-assigned rank.*

For eight-core, we consider 4 design points – 4KB or 8KB pages with 32 or 64 banks. In all the 15 workloads, the best performing design point (Rank1) identified by ANATOMY is the same as that identified using simulation. In all but one of the workloads, ANATOMY also identifies the second best performing design point (Rank2) accurately. Further, the worst design point (Rank4) matched simulation in all 15 workloads. We thus note that while ANATOMY may over-estimate or under-estimate latency compared to simulation across workloads, it shows consistent rankings across design points *for the same workload.*

5.5 CPI Estimation

ANATOMY predicts the magnitude of variation in CPI fairly accurately as shown in Figure 9 which plots normalized CPI values (i.e., CPI^{mdl}/CPI^{sim}) for each core in several quad-core workloads (both CPI^{mdl} and CPI^{sim} reported on the $8KB \times 16$ configuration). Despite the simplifying assumptions made in the CPI computation, the predicted CPI values are a good indicator of processor performance in nearly all cases, with only workloads $Q3$ and $Q15$ showing deviation $> 20\%$. Further, note that in almost all cases (notable exception being $Q2$), $CPI^{mdl} > CPI^{sim}$ which is to be expected since our approximation does not account for any memory level parallelism and penalizes CPI additively

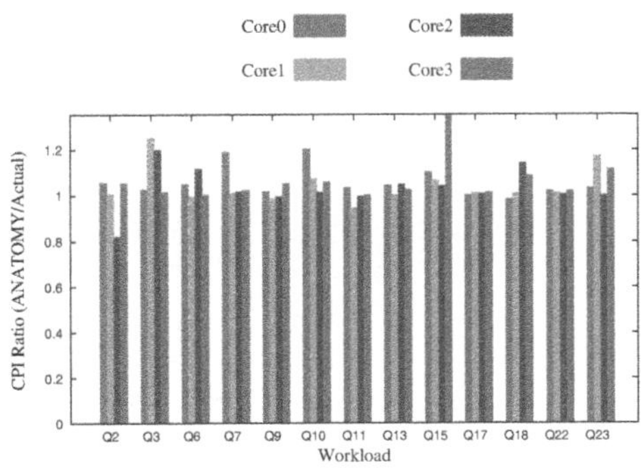

Figure 9: Accuracy in CPI estimation

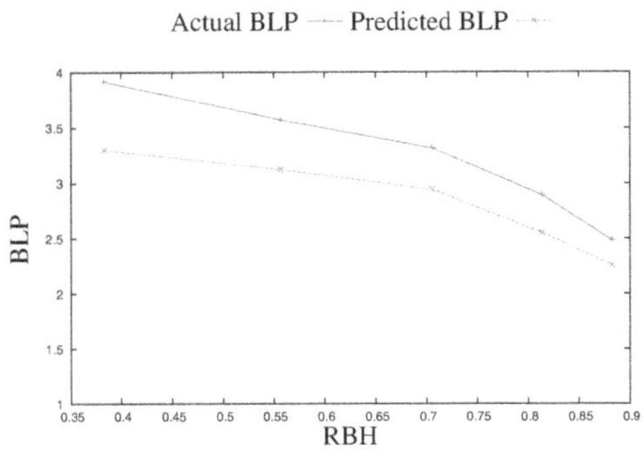

Figure 10: BLP^{sim} and BLP^{mdl} versus RBH^{sim} in workload $Q1$

with the average memory latency. A better approximation would need to take into account the extent of such memory level parallelism for each core's requests and suitably weigh this parallelism into the additive term. We leave this for future work.

In Section 6.3, we demonstrate that ANATOMY is able to correctly predict performance trends for PCM technology using traces obtained from DDR3-based simulations.

6. INSIGHTS FROM ANATOMY

In this section, we demonstrate that ANATOMY allows us to arrive at non-trivial insights and validate them with a lot less effort compared to simulation. In several results, we show that ANATOMY is able to capture workload-specific trends accurately across a variety of explored alternatives allowing designers to study these behaviors quickly and focus on interesting configurations.

6.1 Impact of RBH, and BLP on Latency

As discussed in Section 3.2, BLP is largely determined by how many requests arrive in the time that a bank is busy. In other words, BLP is generally determined by $\frac{\lambda}{\mu_{bank}}$. Since $\frac{1}{\mu_{bank}} = R * T_{CL} + (1 - R) * (T_{PRE} + T_{RCD} + T_{CL})$, as R increases, the bank service time reduces thereby reducing the opportunity for parallelism bringing BLP down. In Figure 10 we have plotted the actual and predicted BLP values against RBH^{sim} values at several bank counts ($16 - 256$) for the $Q1$ workload. The figure clearly demonstrates this inverse relationship between BLP and RBH (all workloads show similar trends). This study is perhaps the first to suggest that BLP and RBH be viewed jointly due to this dependence rather than as independently varying/tunable memory performance parameters.

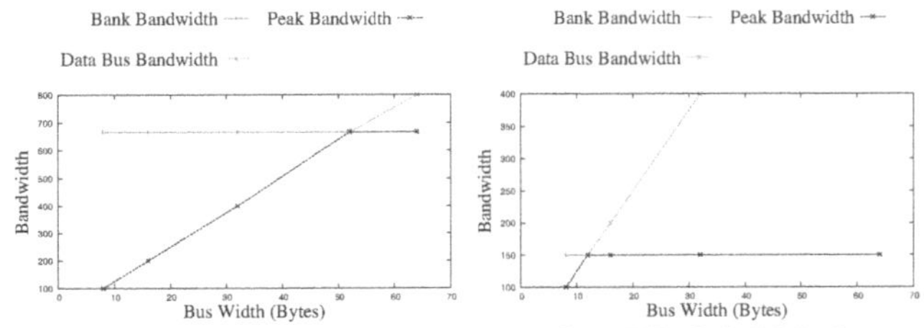

(a) RBH=0.75, BLP=10 (b) RBH=0.5, BLP=3

Figure 11: Peak Bandwidth Estimation using ANATOMY

6.2 Impact of Data Bus Throughput

Our second finding concerns the relative importance of improving the bank throughput versus the data bus throughput. We demonstrate below that the data bus throughput can quickly become a bottleneck as BLP improves. Figure11 plots the bank and data bus bandwidths (in millions of requests per second) achieved versus data bus width at two different settings of BLP. For both settings, the amount of data transfer per request is set to 128 bytes and IO clock rate set to 800MHz. In the left figure, BLP is set to 10.0 (typically seen in systems with higher core to memory controller ratios), and the plots show that the delivered bandwidth is limited by the data bus width at widths $<= 50$ bytes, and subsequently limited by the bank bandwidth. On the right, BLP is set to 3, and the delivered bandwidth is limited by the data bus width at widths $<= 12$ bytes. Thus, for the configuration on the left, a very wide bus is preferred to match its high BLP and provide for high bandwidth transfers.

This suggests that we can classify workloads based on what they are bandwidth-limited by: insufficient BLP or insufficient data bus service rate. From equation 7, we may write this as:

BLP Limited: $b\mu_{bank} < \mu_{data}$

Data Bus Limited: $b\mu_{bank} >= \mu_{data}$

This characterization is revealing in the sense that it helps system designers identify what type of architectural enhancement has the most benefit on a workload. For workloads that are data bus limited, improving clock-rate or having a wider bus width can increase the peak memory bandwidth; whereas these are unlikely to give any benefit in BLP-limited workloads.

Since burst length, bus clock frequency and bus width are all inherently controlling how much data is delivered in what time, ANATOMY is useful for scenarios where the designer needs to explore different choices of bus widths or clock settings as shown in the next section.

Doubling the Bus Clock

Using equation 6, we can predict the benefit of doubling the IO bus clock rate on Lat_{avg}. Doubling the bus clock doubles μ_{data} and reduces QD_{data} by slightly more than half. However, the bank service time and its queue delay are unaffected by this improvement. Thus doubling the clock rate has benefit that depends on the relative magnitudes of the bank and data bus components in Lat_{avg}. Figure 12 plots the normalized latencies of several quad-core workloads at 4 different clock rate settings. First of all, this shows that even doubling the bus clock results in a relatively lower ($< 20\%$) improvement in overall latency. Second, the improvement is workload-specific, with workload $Q1$ experiencing only a 7% latency reduction, while $Q13$ sees 14% reduction (going from 600MHz to 1200MHz).

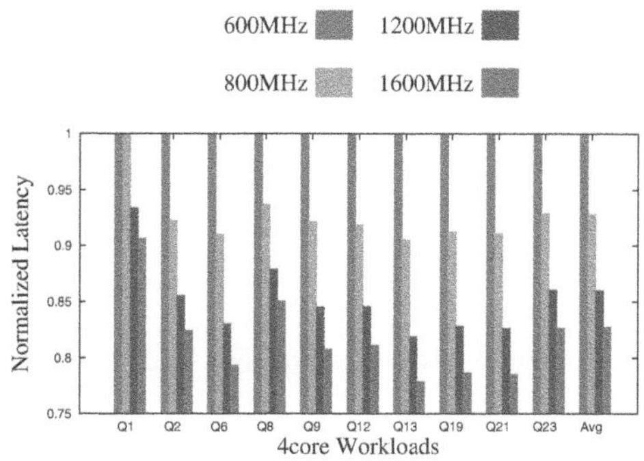

Figure 12: Effect of Doubling the IO Clock Speed

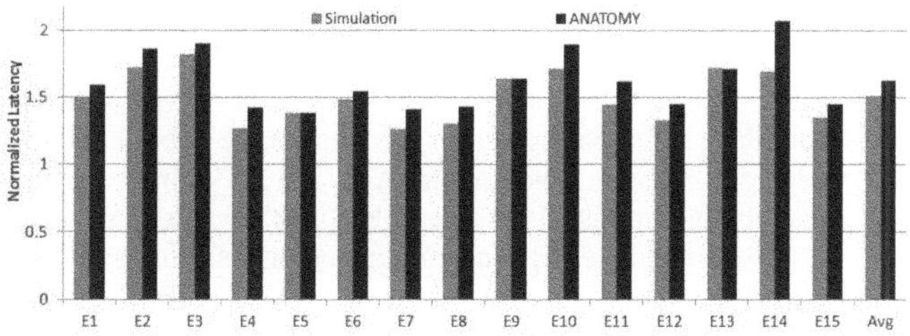

Figure 13: Lat_{avg}^{sim} and Lat_{avg}^{mdl} of PCM normalized to DDR3

6.3 Technological Alternatives - PCM

Next, we demonstrate the extensibility of ANATOMY to support emerging memory technologies such as PCM.

Phase Change Memory (PCM) [32] is becoming an attractive alternative to DRAMs due to their reduced energy requirements. While the PCM technology is very different from DRAM, the underlying phenomena governing latency and bandwidth remain the same. PCM is also organized in terms of channels, ranks and banks with row-buffers. PCM chips are characterized by having different read versus write timings (due to the fact that writes need to modify bit cell resistance and this requires a heating and cooling cycle). Also PCM does not require a precharge. However only minor changes are required in ANATOMY to model PCM memory. More specifically, the average service time at the bank server is expressed as:

$$(f_r * (T_{CL} * h_r + (T_{RD} + T_{CL}) * (1 - h_r)))+ \\ ((1 - f_r)(T_{CL} * h_w + (T_{WR} + T_{CL}) * (1 - h_w))),$$

where T_{RD} and T_{WR} denote the average read and write timing associated with the device respectively[11]. The terms h_r and h_w are the row-buffer hit-rates for reads and writes, while f_r denotes the fraction of requests that were reads. We evaluate an eight core machine using a PCM memory with 64 banks and 4KB row-buffer.

We are interested in capturing the relative performance trends i.e. which technology provides better latencies. Hence we show Lat_{avg}^{sim} and Lat_{avg}^{mdl} for the emerging technology normalized to that of their corresponding values in the case of DDR3. Ideally, ANATOMY should show similar trends (above 1 or below 1) when we consider the normalized Lat_{avg}^{sim} and Lat_{avg}^{mdl} in each individual workload. Figure 13 shows the normalized (to DDR3) Lat_{avg}^{sim} and Lat_{avg}^{mdl} for the individual 8-core workloads. It can be seen that

[11] A more detailed model could take into account the differences in timing of Set, Reset and Bit-Alterable writes.

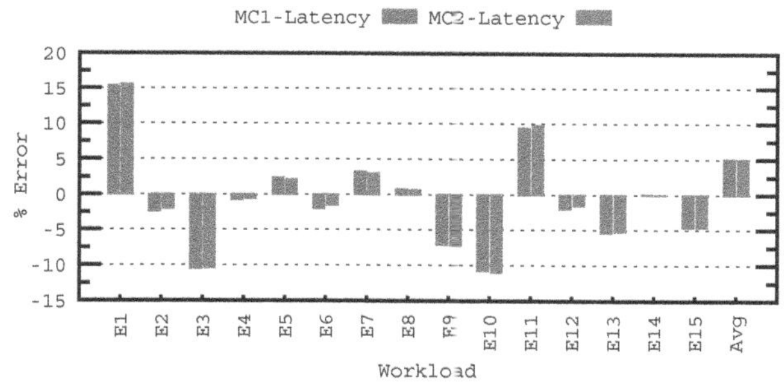

Figure 14: ANATOMY in Eight Core Machine with 2 Memory Controllers

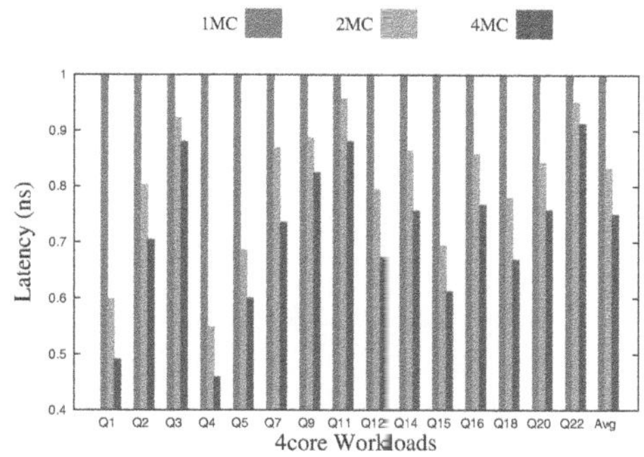

Figure 15: Latency Reduction with More Controllers

simulation results reveal that for all the workloads, PCM exhibits a higher Lat_{avg} compared to DDR3. Not only does ANATOMY predict the same trend as simulation, but it also captures the relative increase in the Lat_avg for PCM over DDR3 with a reasonable accuracy (average error of 9.5

6.4 Impact of Multiple Memory Controllers

An interesting design point to explore/study is the impact of increasing the number of memory controllers. In Section 3.1, we claimed that ANATOMY can model such a configuration with a collection of independent 3-stage queuing networks, one per controller. Figure 14 shows the error in Lat_{avg}^{mdl} experienced in a 8-core configuration with two memory controllers. The page size is 4KB and there are 32 banks. The error in Lat_{avg} is $\leq 10\%$ in all but one of the workloads.

With a single trace obtained with one configuration, ANATOMY allows us to study how Lat_{avg} varies with varying number of memory controllers. Figure 15 shows ANATOMY's prediction of Lat_{avg} (obtained from eqn 9) for several 4-core workloads at 1, 2 and 4 controllers (each controller is interfaced to a $4KB \times 16$ memory configuration and each has its own data channel). Workloads exhibit very different benefits going from one controller to four. While workload $Q4$ has its average latency reduced by more than $2\times$, $Q22$ shows only a 10% reduction in latency. ANATOMY is thus a useful tool for exploring these dimensions on a variety of workloads to identify what design points provide the best benefit for what workloads.

6.5 Evaluating Scheduler Impact

Scheduling policies typically aim to improve RBH and/or BLP by re-ordering requests present in the memory controller. For instance, FR_FCFS [26] scheduler re-orders memory requests to pri-

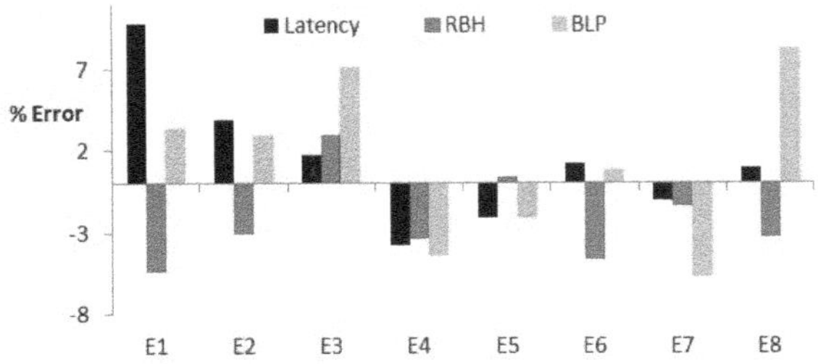

Figure 16: Eight core workload errors with FR_FCFS

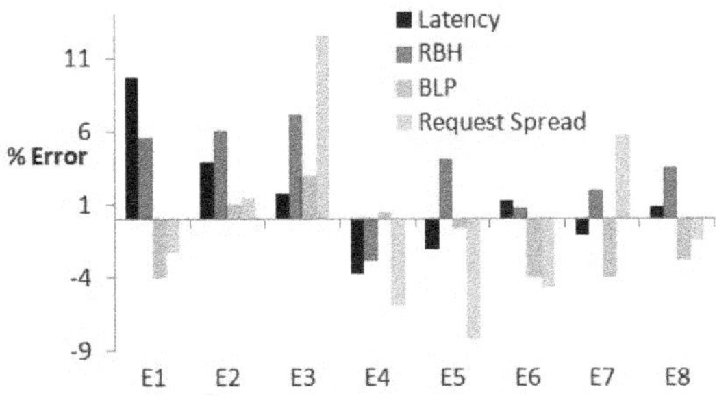

Figure 17: Eight core workload errors with PAR_BS

oritize those that go to already open rows thereby improving RBH. As discussed in Section 3.7, we model the impact of scheduling policies by simulating the scheduling algorithm over the memory trace to re-oder its entries as per the order in which the scheduler would issue requests to the memory. We demonstrate the effectiveness of this approach with two scheduling algorithms - FR_FCFS [26] and PAR_BS [21]. FR_FCFS prioritizes and schedules row-buffer hits over misses. Figure 16 shows ANATOMY errors in RBH, BLP, and Latency for several 8-core workloads. The re-ordering from FR_FCFS results in average latency error of just 3.4%. It may also be observed that the FR_FCFS re-ordering has led to highly accurate estimation of RBH in each workload.

PAR_BS scheduler batches up requests and schedules requests in a batch ahead of requests in subsequent batches to ensure progress, and it also assigns ranks to threads in a batch to help prioritize threads with fewer requests as well as to improve bank-level parallelism in the batch. Note that this scheduler is application-aware as it uses knowledge of issuing threads. Hence, in our experiments, thread-ids were also gathered along with the memory access trace. By simulating the algorithm over the trace, crucially we obtain an accurate estimate of the request spread *S* (as well as RBH and BLP). Figure 17 shows ANATOMY errors in Latency, RBH, BLP, and Request Spread for several 8-core workloads using the PAR_BS re-ordered traces. Note that the re-ordered trace has led to highly accurate BLP estimates. With the PAR_BS re-ordered trace, ANATOMY incurs an average latency estimation error of 5.9%. This result indicates that ANATOMY can be used to model the effects of sophisticated memory access schedulers.

6.6 Evaluating Impact of Auto-Refresh

One can easily estimate the overhead of auto-refresh mode by setting the right values of T_{REFI} and T_{RFC} parameters in ANATOMY. T_{RFC} is expected to increase roughly linearly with DRAM density and T_{REFI} decreases with increasing temperature. While a typical 8Gb device has T_{REFI} = 7.8us and T_{RFC} = 350ns (from [1]) (resulting in bank service time extended by a factor of 1.04), a future 32Gb device (refer [18]) operating at higher temperature is expected to have T_{REFI} = 3.9us and T_{RFC} = 800ns with resulting bank service time stretched by a factor of 1.2X – a 20% increase! Figure 18 shows the overall latency impact (normalized to a configuration with no refresh) under 2 configurations as predicted by ANATOMY: (i) Refresh overhead factor of 1.04X on bank service time (ii) Refresh overhead factor of 1.2X on bank service time. It shows that the 32Gb configuration has an average overall latency overhead of 17% over a memory with no refresh overhead while for some configurations (E6, E8, and E10), the overhead goes up above 20% owing to the large increase in queing delay at the banks. Similar studies could be carried out on the impact of the *RAS-only* refresh mode in conjunction with use of smart refresh algorithms.

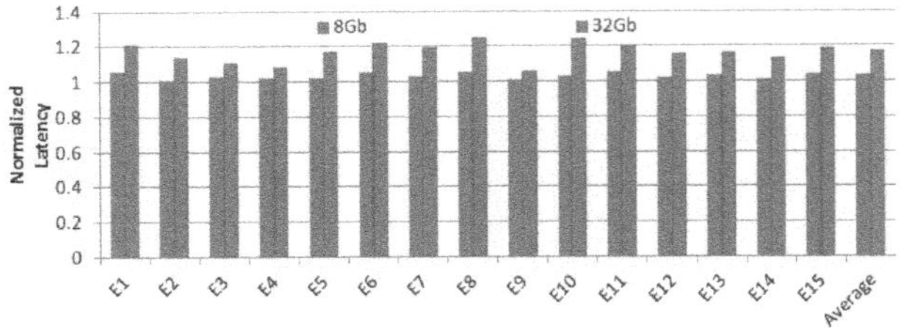

Figure 18: Refresh overhead in eight-core workloads

7. RELATED WORK AND CONCLUSIONS

Related Work: While analytical models for memory systems exist [3, 6, 7, 11, 17, 31, 34, 35], to the best of our knowledge, no existing approach combines key workload aspects (RBH and BLP) coupled with memory system design and technology parameters to predict performance across a wide range of design points. Typically, existing approaches have either sought to model DRAM systems accurately [6, 11, 34], or aimed at obtaining coarse estimates of latency and bandwidth to fulfill a different system performance or energy modeling objective [7, 17, 31]. In [31], a bandwidth-centric analysis is presented with respect to the cache hierarchy, but the model does not address external memory, and is not capable of providing latency oriented analysis. Liu et al [17] consider the question of off-chip memory bandwidth partitioning for optimal performance. The model in [35] is based on [17] and incorporates the effect of write bandwidth which is an important consideration in emerging technologies such as PCM that have large write latencies. These models are aimed at obtaining gross bandwidth estimates and as such abstract out the details of memory operations.

In the works of Hyojin et al [6] and Yuan et al [34], hybrid analytical models which use detailed address traces to estimate DRAM efficiency are constructed. While these models account for detailed timing aspects of DRAM systems, they do not address the complex interactions between application characteristics, memory system parameters and the resulting latency & bandwidth. ANATOMY is closest to these works but focuses more on the problem of predicting performance of several different memory configurations using a single input trace, rather than on a highly accurate model of performance for any given workload/memory access stream. The work in [6] characterizes DRAM performance by estimating the bank busy time as a linear combination of DRAM timing parameters with workload-specific weights. The model is able to predict impact of various DRAM timing parameters accurately for any given workload/memory access stream, but can not predict performance at different memory configurations that require changes to the workload-specific weights. Further, it does not take into account the crucial effect of queuing delay in the memory controller. In [34], a hybrid model is developed, wherein memory access traces are re-played through a simplified DRAM model keeping track of row buffer hits, bank busy periods and other relevant parameters to compute DRAM efficiency. While our work on modeling scheduler impact discussed in Section 3.7 is somewhat similar, ANATOMY is able to provide analytical insight by formulating the problem as a network-of-queues coupled with workload characterization. Thus, ANATOMY is able to quickly provide results for questions such as the impact of doubling clock speed, or adding more memory controllers without requiring changes to the trace simulation.

In [7], the authors propose a DRAM performance model with a view to estimating allowed slack for energy savings. Their approach is a hybrid of using real performance counter readings as input to a timing model and as such can not be used to assess behavior of the system under different parameters. Ahn et al [3] provide a design-space exploration of DRAM systems and study the impact of various knobs in the system. However, their analytical model is limited to a few access patterns and is demonstrated on only two micro-benchmarks.

8. CONCLUSIONS

In this paper we have presented ANATOMY, a simple two- component analytical model of memory that captures the impact of design choices, technological parameters and application specific characteristics. ANATOMY is able to estimate latency and bandwidth on a variety of 4-, 8- and 16-core workloads across a wide range of memory configurations with high accuracy permitting fast design space exploration across memory configurations, schedulers, refresh algorithms, and even alternate memory technologies.

9. REFERENCES

[1] "DDR3, DDR4," 2013. [Online]. Available: http://www.jedec.org/category/technology-focus-area/main-memory-ddr3-ddr4-sdram

[2] D. Abts et al, "Achieving predictable performance through better memory controller placement in many-core CMPs," in *ISCA-36*, 2009.

[3] J. H. Ahn, M. Erez, and W. J. Dally, "The design space of data-parallel memory systems," in *SC*, 2006.

[4] M. Awasthi et al, "Handling the problems and opportunities posed by multiple on-chip memory controllers," in *PACT-19*, 2010.

[5] N. Binkert et al, "The GEM5 simulator," *SIGARCH Comput. Archit. News*, 2011.

[6] H. Choi, J. Lee, and W. Sung, "Memory access pattern-aware DRAM performance model for multi-core systems," in *ISPASS*, 2011.

[7] Q. Deng et al, "Memscale: active low-power modes for main memory," in *ASPLOS-16*, 2011.

[8] ——, "Multiscale: memory system dvfs with multiple memory controllers," in *ISLPED '12*, 2012.

[9] M. Ghosh et al, "Smart refresh: An enhanced memory controller design for reducing energy in conventional and 3d die-stacked drams," in *MICRO 40*, 2007.

[10] E. Ipek et al, "Self-optimizing memory controllers: A reinforcement learning approach," in *Proceedings of the 35th Annual International Symposium on Computer Architecture*, ser. ISCA '08, 2008.

[11] B. Jacob, S. Ng, and D. Wang, *Memory Systems: Cache, DRAM, Disk*. Morgan Kaufmann Publishers Inc., 2007.

[12] T. S. Karkhanis and J. E. Smith, "A first-order superscalar processor model," *SIGARCH Comput. Archit. News*, 2004.

[13] Y. Kim et al, "Atlas: A scalable and high-performance scheduling algorithm for multiple memory controllers," in *HPCA-16*, 2010.

[14] ——, "Thread cluster memory scheduling: Exploiting differences in memory access behavior," in *MICRO-43*, 2010.

[15] B. C. Lee et al, "Architecting phase change memory as a scalable DRAM alternative," in *ISCA-36*, 2009.

[16] C. J. Lee et al, "Prefetch-aware DRAM controllers," in *MICRO-41*, 2008.

[17] F. Liu et al, "Understanding how off-chip memory bandwidth partitioning in chip multiprocessors affects system performance," in *HPCA-16*, 2010.

[18] J. Liu et al, "Raidr: Retention-aware intelligent dram refresh," in *ISCA 12*, 2012.

[19] E. Modiano et al, "An approach for the analysis of packet delay in an integrated mobile radio network," in *Proc. of the Twenty-Seventh Annual Conference on Information Sciences and Systems*, 1993.

[20] S. P. Muralidhara et al, "Reducing memory interference in multicore systems via application-aware memory channel partitioning," in *MICRO-44*, 2011.

[21] O. Mutlu et al, "Parallelism-aware batch scheduling: Enhancing both performance and fairness of shared DRAM systems," in *ISCA-35*, 2008.

[22] C. D. Pack, "The output of an m/d/1 queue," *Operations Research , Vol. 23, No. 4*, 1975.

[23] R. L. Plackett, "Karl pearson and the chi-squared test," *International Statistical Review (ISI) 51(1):59-72*, 1983.

[24] M. K. Qureshi et al, "Preset: improving performance of phase change memories by exploiting asymmetry in write times," *SIGARCH Comput. Archit. News*, 2012.

[25] ——, "Scalable high performance main memory system using phase-change memory technology," in *ISCA-36*, 2009.

[26] S. Rixner et al, "Memory access scheduling," in *ISCA-27*, 2000.

[27] B. M. Rogers et al, "Scaling the bandwidth wall: challenges in and avenues for CMP scaling," in *ISCA-36*, 2009.

[28] S. M. Ross, "Stochastic processes," *Wiley Series in Probability and Statistics*, 1995.

[29] J. Stuecheli et al, "Elastic refresh: Techniques to mitigate refresh penalties in high density memory," in *MICRO 43*, 2010.

[30] K. Sudan et al, "Micro-pages: increasing DRAM efficiency with locality-aware data placement," in *ASPLOS-15*, 2010.

[31] G. Sun et al, "Moguls: a model to explore the memory hierarchy for bandwidth improvements," in *ISCA-38*, 2011.

[32] H. Wong et al, "Phase change memory," *Proc. of the IEEE*, 2010.

[33] W. A. Wulf and S. A. McKee, "Hitting the memory wall: implications of the obvious," *SIGARCH Comput. Archit. News*, 1995.

[34] G. L. Yuan et al, "A hybrid analytical DRAM performance model," 2009.

[35] M. Zhou, Y. Du, B. R. Childers, R. Melhem, and D. Mosse, "Writeback-aware bandwidth partitioning for multi-core systems with pcm," in *PACT*, 2013.

The Efficacy of Error Mitigation Techniques for DRAM Retention Failures: A Comparative Experimental Study

Samira Khan[†*] samirakhan@cmu.edu
Donghyuk Lee[†] donghyuk1@cmu.edu
Yoongu Kim[†] yoongukim@cmu.edu
Alaa R. Alameldeen[*] alaa.r.alameldeen@intel.com
Chris Wilkerson[*] chris.wilkerson@intel.com
Onur Mutlu[†] onur@cmu.edu
[†]Carnegie Mellon University [*]Intel Labs

ABSTRACT

As DRAM cells continue to shrink, they become more susceptible to retention failures. DRAM cells that permanently exhibit short retention times are fairly easy to identify and repair through the use of memory tests and row and column redundancy. However, the retention time of many cells may vary over time due to a property called *Variable Retention Time (VRT)*. Since these cells intermittently transition between failing and non-failing states, they are particularly difficult to identify through memory tests alone. In addition, the high temperature packaging process may aggravate this problem as the susceptibility of cells to VRT increases after the assembly of DRAM chips. A promising alternative to manufacture-time testing is to detect and mitigate retention failures after the system has become operational. Such a system would require mechanisms to detect and mitigate retention failures in the field, but would be responsive to retention failures introduced after system assembly and could dramatically reduce the cost of testing, enabling much longer tests than are practical with manufacturer testing equipment.

In this paper, we analyze the efficacy of three common error mitigation techniques (memory tests, guardbands, and error correcting codes (ECC)) in real DRAM chips exhibiting both intermittent and permanent retention failures. Our analysis allows us to quantify the efficacy of recent system-level error mitigation mechanisms that build upon these techniques. We revisit prior works in the context of the experimental data we present, showing that our measured results significantly impact these works' conclusions. We find that mitigation techniques that rely on run-time testing alone [38, 27, 50, 26] are unable to ensure reliable operation even after many months of testing. Techniques that incorporate ECC [4, 52], however, can ensure reliable DRAM operation after only a few hours of testing. For example, VS-ECC [4], which couples testing with variable strength codes to allocate the strongest codes to the most error-prone memory regions, can ensure reliable operation for 10 years after only 19 minutes of testing. We conclude that the viability of these mitigation techniques depend on efficient online profiling of DRAM performed without disrupting system operation.

SIGMETRICS'14, June 16–20, 2014, Austin, Texas, USA.

http://dx.doi.org/10.1145/2591971.2592000.

Categories and Subject Descriptors

B.3.1 [**Memory Structure**]: Semiconductor Memories—*Dynamic memory (DRAM)*; B.3.4 [**Memory Structure**]: Reliability, Testing, and Fault-Tolerance

Keywords

DRAM, retention failures, system-level detection and mitigation, error correction, ECC, fault tolerance, memory scaling

1. INTRODUCTION

The increasing number of cores and extensive use of data-intensive applications demand high capacity main memories. Scaling of DRAM to smaller technology nodes enabled higher capacity in the same die area for the past few decades. However, as DRAM cells scale down in size, they become significantly less reliable. Ensuring reliability with technology scaling is a key challenge for DRAM [36, 31, 18, 34].

A DRAM cell cannot retain its data permanently as the capacitor used to store the data leaks its charge gradually over time. The time a cell can retain its data is called the *retention time* of the cell. In order to maintain correct data in DRAM, cells are periodically refreshed every 64 ms. A cell that cannot retain its data for 64 ms results in a failure, referred to as *retention failure*.[1] In order to avoid retention failures, the worst-case retention time of cells must be no less than 64 ms. However, several technology trends make this requirement increasingly difficult to efficiently satisfy. On the one hand, as cell dimensions shrink, cells become more susceptible to retention failures (or, reducing retention times) [10, 13, 11, 54], motivating higher refresh rates. On the other hand, increasing DRAM chip capacity makes even the current nominal refresh rate untenable in future technology DRAMs. For example, one study showed that a 32 Gb DRAM chip will spend 35% of the memory power and 25% of the available DRAM chip bandwidth on refreshes [27]. Another study showed that the performance penalty of refresh in a system with 32 Gb DRAM chips can be 20% [6]. A higher refresh rate will result in a significant throughput loss, power overhead, and performance loss [27, 6, 37].

Currently, DRAM vendors guarantee worst-case retention time of 64 ms by detecting and mitigating cells having retention time less than 64 ms during manufacturing time. However, detection of retention failures is extremely challenging as the same cell can fail or operate correctly at different times. These retention failures are defined as *intermittent retention failures* in DRAM cells.

[1] We assume each failure can potentially cause an error and use failure and error interchangeably in the rest of the paper.

There are two sources of intermittent retention failures in DRAM: 1) *Data pattern sensitivity*: A DRAM cell can fail depending on the data stored in the neighboring cells [23, 28], and 2) *Variable retention time (VRT)*: A cell can transition among different retention times at different points in time and can fail when it moves to a retention time less than the current refresh interval [41, 55, 33, 28]. Due to these intermittent retention failures, manufacturers perform exhaustive testing to detect and mitigate these failures. A recent work showed that it can take days to test a chip to identify all intermittent retention failures [28]. In fact, one of the major DRAM vendors confirmed that detection of such failures leads to some of the most expensive tests during manufacturing time. As retention failures become more prominent with technology scaling [10, 13, 11, 54, 28], the manufacturing-time retention failure tests will become longer, making it more difficult and more costly for the DRAM manufacturers to scale the density of DRAM chips as aggressively as was done in the past. More importantly, some of the DRAM cells start exhibiting VRT characteristics as they are exposed to high temperature during the packaging of the DRAM chips [44, 21, 28], so pre-packaging tests cannot always screen all VRT failures.

Instead of DRAM manufacturers providing retention-error-free DRAM chips after exhaustive and expensive manufacturing-time tests, an alternative approach is detecting and mitigating retention failures of DRAM cells in the field, during the operation of DRAM in the system. We refer to system-level error detection as *online profiling*. In this case, the memory controller would be responsible for detecting and mitigating the retention failures while the system is running. An online profiling mechanism has three significant advantages over traditional manufacturing time testing. First, such a system can reduce manufacturing cost and increase yield by enabling the manufacturers to ship DRAM chips without fully ensuring that all cells operate correctly at a minimum specified retention time. Second, online testing is capable of tolerating the new intermittent failures induced by the high temperature packaging process. Third, an online profiling system is more suitable compared to manufacturing tests to detect the intermittent retention failures that takes hours/days of testing, as it can amortize the cost of profiling by performing online tests in the background spread across a very large time interval (days/months).

System-level detection and mitigation of intermittent retention failures seems to be a promising direction into the future. However, there is no prior work that assesses the efficacy of different mitigation techniques in the presence of intermittent failures. Some recent works proposed error mitigation techniques that rely on system-level testing, but assume there are no intermittent failures. These mechanisms perform a simple test at system boot-up to detect the failing cells and cannot tolerate any new failures after the initial testing [38, 27, 50, 26]. If error mitigation techniques do not consider intermittent failures, data loss can occur due to potentially inaccurate identification of failing cells.

Our goal is to analyze the efficacy of existing error mitigation techniques in the system in the presence of intermittent retention failures to enable the development of more efficient and effective detection and mitigation techniques. We use an FPGA-based DRAM testing infrastructure to test 96 DRAM chips from three different manufacturers to analyze the effectiveness of system-level testing, guardbanding, and ECC for intermittent retention failures. We use our analysis to quantify the effectiveness of recently proposed architectural error mitigation techniques [38, 27, 50, 4, 52, 26] in the presence of intermittent failures.

To our knowledge, this paper presents the first work that quantifies system-level detection and mitigation techniques in the presence of intermittent failures. Our major contributions are:

- We analyze the effectiveness of testing in discovering retention failures. We show that only a small amount of testing can discover the majority of failing cells. We quantify testing using the metric *rounds*, where a round consists of writing the entire module, waiting for some specific time to make sure all the cells have been idle for the refresh interval and reading back the data again to locate the failing cells. From our experiments, we show that only 5 rounds of tests can discover most of the intermittent failures and reduce the probability of discovering a new failure by 100 times. However, even after thousands of rounds of testing, we find that a very small number of cells exhibit new failures not discovered before, which indicates that testing is not enough by itself to mitigate all retention failures.
- We present the efficacy of using a guardband to avoid intermittent retention failures. Adding a guardband X on the refresh interval of 64 ms means that all DRAM chips that are detected to have cell failures at X times 64 ms (i.e., $64X$ ms) refresh interval are discarded by the manufacturer [51, 2]. If VRT cells exhibit retention times less than the applied guardband, these cells will fail and get detected at $64X$ ms, making the guardband 100% effective. We show that a small amount of guardband (e.g., $2X$) can avoid 85-95% of the intermittently failing cells and reduce the probability of a new retention failure by 10 times. However, even a large guardband (e.g., $5X$) is not effective for the remaining VRT cells, indicating that using a guardband alone is not effective to mitigate all failures.
- We show the efficacy of error correction codes (ECC) in the presence of other error mitigation techniques. We find that a combination of error mitigation techniques is much more effective in tolerating a high number of retention errors than using only ECC. An uncorrectable retention error in the presence of ECC results in a failure. Using only single error correction codes can reduce the probability of retention failure by only 100 times, but using single error correction codes together with testing and guardbanding can reduce the probability of failure by as much as 10^{12} times.
- We revisit prior works [38, 27, 50, 4, 52, 26] in the context of the experimental data and analysis, showing that our measured results significantly impact these works' conclusions. We show that bit repair mechanisms that rely on testing cannot provide strong reliability guarantees even after performing system-level testing for months. However, ECC-based mitigation techniques can be effective at ensuring reliable DRAM operation with online testing in the presence of intermittent failures after just a few hours of testing. We conclude that the viability of these techniques depend on efficient continuous online profiling performed periodically at a longer interval without disrupting system operation.

Based on our experimental evaluation, we discuss a possible online profiling system to detect and mitigate intermittent retention failures. We hope that our findings will be useful in developing new low-cost architectural techniques to mitigate DRAM retention failures, thereby enabling better scaling of DRAM into future technology generations.

2. BACKGROUND AND RELATED WORK

In this section, we briefly provide background information necessary to understand our technical contributions. Interested readers can find more details on DRAM in [22, 20].

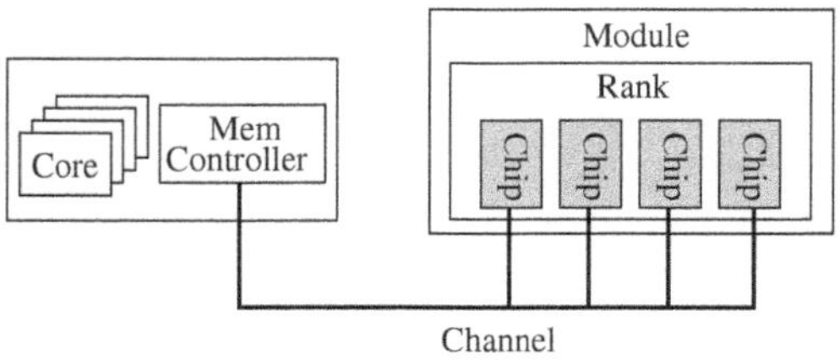

Figure 1: DRAM Organization

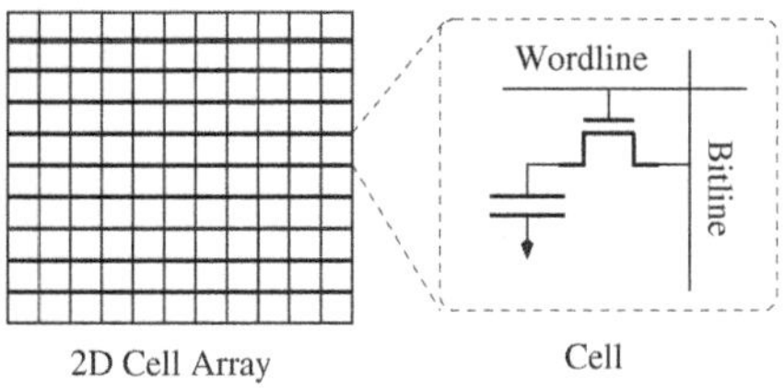

Figure 2: DRAM Cells in a Bank

2.1 DRAM Basics

Figure 1 shows the high level DRAM organization. DRAM is hierarchically organized as channels, modules, ranks, and chips. Each channel consists of multiple modules. On every module there can be more than one rank that consists of multiple DRAM chips. For example, a typical 2 GB module with 64-wide data bus can have one rank with 8 chips. Each chip can have 2 Gb capacity with an 8-bit bus. All chips in a rank respond to the same DRAM command. With this configuration, 8 chips can transfer 64 bits of data in parallel. DRAM cells are organized as 2D arrays called banks. Figure 2 shows the structure of a bank and a cell within the bank. A cell consists of a capacitor and a transistor. The cells in a row are connected through a wire (wordline) and the cells in a column are connected to another wire (bitline). In order to access the data stored in a cell, a high voltage is applied to the wordline of the row containing the cell, which turns on the access transistor and connects the capacitor to the bitline. When the access transistor is on, charge can flow to/from the capacitor through the bitline and data can be accessed.

Charge stored in the capacitor leaks over time. The time a cell can retain its data is called the retention time of the cell. To retain the data in the cell, DRAM cells have to be periodically refreshed. The DDR3 specification guarantees the lowest retention time of 64 ms [15], which means that each row in DRAM is refreshed every 64 ms to maintain the data in the cells.

2.2 Retention Failures

DRAM cells that cannot hold data for 64 ms cause retention failures. Retention time is a key constraint to enabling high density DRAM. As the cell size shrinks with technology scaling, the manufacturers are facing increasing challenges to fabricate a low leakage cell with adequate capacitance to retain the data for 64 ms [31, 18, 34]. DRAM yield is limited by a small fraction of leaky cells whose retention time is significantly lower than other cells [19, 11]. Detecting retention failures (i.e., cells that cannot maintain data as long as the minimum specified retention time) requires exhaustive testing as these failures can occur intermittently. Next, we provide two prevalent characteristics of the retention failures.

2.2.1 *Data Pattern Sensitivity*

The retention time of a cell is strongly dependent on the charge stored in that cell, as well as in the neighboring cells, a phenomenon referred to as *data pattern sensitivity* [23, 28]. A data pattern sensitive retention failure is hard to detect as each cell in the DRAM chip has to be exhaustively tested with different kinds of patterns stored in the cell itself as well as the neighboring cells.

2.2.2 *Variable Retention Time*

The retention time of a cell also depends on the current state of the cell. Some DRAM cells can randomly transition between different retention states. These cells are said to demonstrate *variable retention time* (VRT) [41, 55, 33, 28] and are called VRT cells. Depending on the current retention time, a cell may or may not fail at that particular time. In order to guarantee that all cells have retention time greater than 64 ms, every VRT cell with a potential retention time less than 64 ms must get discovered during testing. Manufacturing tests can detect VRT cells if they are actually in the failing retention state during the tests. Unfortunately, the existence of VRT cells cause two major challenges in deploying retention-failure-free DRAM chips in the field. First, discovering whether or not VRT cells have a failing retention state may require prohibitively long tests, as some of the cells can spend a long time in the high retention state before moving to a low retention state [28, 17, 55]. Second, thermal stress during packaging of DRAM chips induces new VRT cells [44, 21]. As such, tests done by DRAM manufacturers before packaging cannot discover these failures.

2.3 Mitigating Retention Failures

2.3.1 *Testing*

Conventional DRAM retention tests verify that all cells retain their charge for the specified refresh interval (64 ms). The phenomena of data pattern sensitivity and variable retention states make retention testing a challenging problem. Several test algorithms with different patterns need to be applied to achieve a reasonable fault coverage for pattern sensitivity. On the other hand, VRT cells are hard to detect even with very long tests. Previous works have described the effectiveness of different test patterns and algorithms for manufacturing-time testing [49, 28, 3]. However, no previous work shows the efficacy of testing for retention failures at the system level in the presence of both pattern sensitivity and VRT cells.

2.3.2 *Guardbanding*

A guardband on the refresh interval is defined as adding an extra margin (X) on the refresh interval of 64 ms such that all cells have a retention time greater than X times 64 ms (i.e., $64Xms$) [51, 2]. The process of *guardbanding* (adding a guardband X) consists of three steps. First, a screening test is run at a higher refresh interval ($64X$ ms) to detect all the cells with retention time less than $64X$ ms. This includes VRT cells with retention times less than the added guardband. Second, either all the failing bits that are found during the screening test get repaired through some repair mechanism, such as row and column sparing, or the chip exhibiting the bit failures gets discarded, making sure that the chips passing the tests will operate correctly at 64 ms. Finally the original refresh interval of 64 ms is reintroduced. Ideally, with a large enough guardband, one would hope that all causes of potential intermittent retention failures can be avoided at manufacturing time. However, there are two disadvantages of using a large guardband. First, a large number of chips would get discarded since the number of retention failures increases exponentially as refresh interval increases [28, 11, 14], resulting in a significant yield loss. Second, a guardband applied during manufacturing time may not be enough to avoid the new VRT failures induced during the packaging process. To our knowledge, no prior work shows the effectiveness of guardbanding for retention failures in the presence of VRT cells.

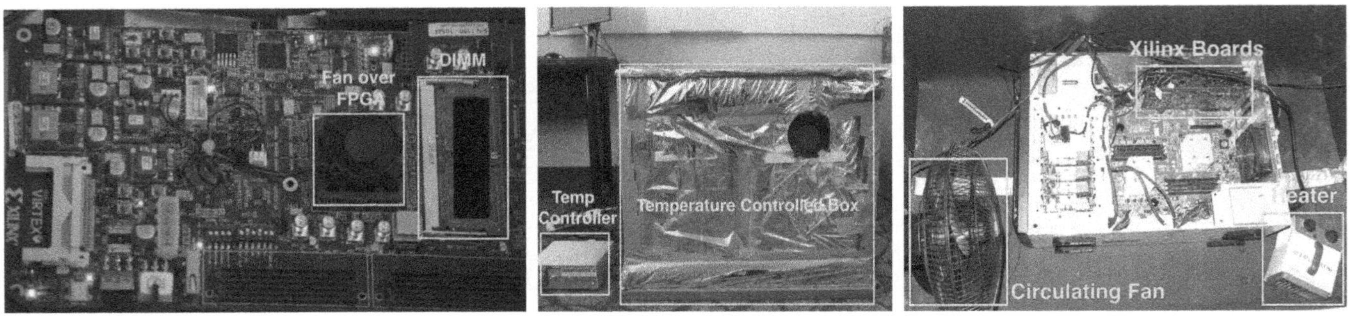

(a) (b) (c)

Figure 3: Testing Infrastructure: (a) ML605 Board (b) Temperature Controller and Heat Chamber, and (c) Inside of the Heat Chamber

2.3.3 Error Correction Codes

Error correction codes and parity are used to repair faulty bits using redundant information. Prior works proposed to use ECC to tolerate retention errors [8, 52]. There are some studies on the bit error rate (number of bit errors divided by the total number of bits during a specific time interval) of industrial DIMMs in the field [43, 24, 46, 45]. However, no prior work provided an experimental study and analysis of the retention error rate reduction with ECC in presence of other error mitigation techniques for intermittent retention failures.

2.3.4 Recent Error Mitigation Techniques

Recent system-level error detection and mitigation techniques can be divided into two categories:

1. Bit Repair Mechanisms: These mechanisms rely on tests at system boot time to locate failing bits and then use different repair mechanisms to repair those faulty bits. For example, ArchShield [38] remaps the faulty bits in a specified region of memory. RAIDR [27] uses higher refresh rates for rows containing weak cells to avoid retention failures. RAPID [50] uses software remapping to disable pages with potential retention failures. SECRET [26] applies error correcting pointers [42] only to the faulty bits found during the initial testing. However, all these works assume that a simple initial test can detect all the failures and do not consider the intermittent failures caused by data pattern sensitivity and VRT.

2. ECC-Based Mitigation Techniques: These mechanisms rely on strong ECC and apply such codes in ways to minimize the overall cost of ECC. We discuss two examples. VS-ECC [4] is an ECC-based mitigation mechanism that uses online testing to determine the needed ECC strength for different cache lines. Any cache line with one or more potential errors is protected by a strong ECC, a 4-bit correcting, 5-bit detecting code (4EC5ED). All other lines are protected using simple single error correcting, double error detecting (SECDED) codes, which reduces the overall cost of ECC by applying strong codes to only those lines that need strong codes. However, VS-ECC does not consider intermittent failures and as a result can fail in the presence of a 2-bit failure in lines protected only by SECDED code. Hi-ECC [52] proposes to amortize the cost of strong ECC by protecting data at a coarse granularity (1KB instead of 64B). This mechanism can potentially tolerate intermittent failures with the strong ECC code applied uniformly. However, it has a significant bandwidth and performance overhead, as the memory controller reads the entire 1KB data chunk (as opposed to the much smaller 64B cache line) upon each access to verify ECC.

2.4 Our Goal and Scope

Our goal in this work is to analyze the system-level efficacy of existing mitigation techniques for retention failures using experimental data from commodity DRAM chips. We evaluate recently proposed mitigation techniques in the context of intermittent retention failures. We do not take into consideration the effect of other functional failure mechanisms (e.g., stuck-at faults, decoder faults, etc. [48, 1, 39]) as these mechanisms lead to consistent and repeatable failures which can be detected relatively easily during manufacturing tests. We also do not consider alpha particle or cosmic ray induced soft failures [40, 32] as previous works have already provided strong analyses for these [5, 12, 47, 35], which can be used in conjunction with the findings of our paper.

3. TESTING INFRASTRUCTURE

To study the efficacy of system-level detection and mitigation techniques for intermittent retention failures, we would like to experimentally analyze how retention time of cells change at different times with different data patterns. To do these studies, we have devised an FPGA-based experimental infrastructure that consists of Xilinx ML605 boards (Figure 3a) [53]. An ML605 board has a slot for a *small outline dual in-line memory module* (SO-DIMM) and integrates a DDR3 interface. The host PC communicates with the boards through a PCI Express bus. We have customized the memory interface such that the refresh interval can be changed from the specific software in the host PC. DRAM manufacturers ensure that there are no failures at the nominal refresh interval of 64 ms by discarding or repairing chips with failures during manufacturing tests. As a result, DRAM chips in the field do not exhibit any retention failures at the refresh interval of 64 ms. In order to expose the retention failures in commodity DRAM chips, we increase the refresh interval in our experiments. A higher refresh interval results in a higher number of retention failures in the system. This allows us to emulate future generation DIMMs with chips not fully tested for retention failures where many cells can actually fail at the nominal refresh interval. We analyze the efficacy of detection and mitigation techniques for retention failures at different refresh intervals, and show that our experimental observations on the intermittent failures hold, irrespective of the refresh interval.

Prior works have demonstrated that the retention time of DRAM cells decreases exponentially as temperature increases [11, 28]. In order to isolate the effect of temperature on retention failures, we perform temperature controlled experiments in a heat chamber (Figure 3b and 3c). Manufacturing-time retention tests are usually performed at a temperature of 85 °C. However, any system-level detection and mitigation technique will be deployed at run-time,

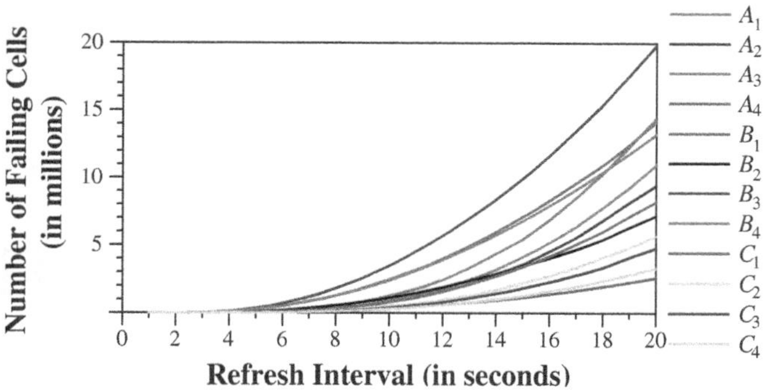

Figure 4: Number of Failures at Different Refresh Intervals

where the operating conditions would not reach such high temperatures most of the time (e.g., the system might stop being operational at around 60 °C as hard-disks, for example, can have a thermal rating less than 60 °C). Our experiments are done at 45 °C to analyze the retention behavior in a typical system operating in the field.

Our results can be compared to prior work on retention time distribution at 85 °C, by scaling the refresh intervals used in our experiments to account for the change in temperature. Prior works showed that a 10 °C increase in temperature approximately halves the refresh interval [11, 28]. Based on experiments in our infrastructure, increasing the temperature by 10 °C reduces the refresh interval by 46.5% (Refer to the Appendix for details) [28]. We analyze retention failures with refresh intervals 1 second to 20 seconds at 45 °C, which correspond to 82 ms to 1640 ms at 85 °C.

We have tested twelve modules containing 96 chips from three major DRAM manufacturers. The capacity of each module is 2 GB. All the modules have a single rank and eight 2 Gb chips in the rank. The assembly dates of the modules are listed in Table 1.

Manufacturer	Module Name	Assembly Date (Year-Week)	Number of Chips
$\mathcal{A}$	A_1	2013-18	8
$\mathcal{A}$	A_2	2012-26	8
$\mathcal{A}$	A_3	2013-18	8
$\mathcal{A}$	A_4	2014-08	8
$\mathcal{B}$	B_1	2012-37	8
$\mathcal{B}$	B_2	2012-37	8
$\mathcal{B}$	B_3	2012-41	8
$\mathcal{B}$	B_4	2012-20	8
$\mathcal{C}$	C_1	2012-29	8
$\mathcal{C}$	C_2	2012-29	8
$\mathcal{C}$	C_3	2013-22	8
$\mathcal{C}$	C_4	2012-29	8

Table 1: Tested DRAM Modules

We perform a simple test to validate our infrastructure. Figure 4 shows the number of failing cells in each module at various refresh intervals of 1 to 20 seconds with an increment of 1 second at 45 °C (which corresponds to various refresh intervals between 82 ms to 1640 ms with 82 ms increment at 85 °C). At each interval, we write all ones to the entire module and then change the refresh interval. We wait for some specific amount of time to make sure that all the rows in the DIMM have been refreshed according to the new interval. Then we read out the entire DIMM and determine the number of cells that do not contain the original value written to them (i.e., failing cells). Then we repeat the experiment with all

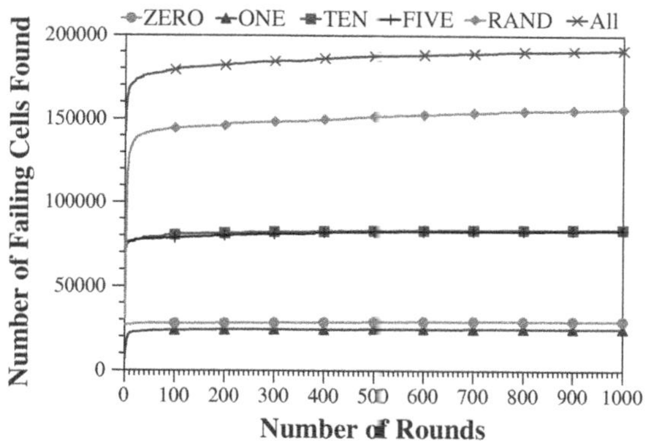

Figure 5: Number of Failures with Testing in *Module* A_1

zeros to get the total number of failing cells at that refresh interval. Figure 4 presents the number of failing cells for all the modules. The number of retention failures increases exponentially with the refresh interval, as reported in the prior works [28, 11, 14]. We also performed other tests validating the failure rate with different data patterns in modules manufactured by different vendors and found that the results are consistent with previous works [28, 14, 45]. As our results are consistent with prior works, we conclude that our apparatus and methodology are sound.

4. EFFICACY OF TESTING

In this section, we analyze the adequacy of testing in detecting retention failures. We perform experiments to answer these questions: 1) How many rounds of testing are required for detecting the VRT failures? 2) How does the probability of finding a new failure reduce with rounds of testing? 3) How long does a VRT cell stay in different retention states?

4.1 Detecting Retention Failures with Testing

4.1.1 Description of the Experiment

In this experiment, we test the modules at a refresh interval of 5 s for 1000 rounds at 45 °C (410 ms at 85 °C). The intent of the experiment is to study the effectiveness of testing in the context of a high number of retention failures to emulate future modules with chips not fully tested for retention failures, where many cells can actually fail at the nominal refresh rate. We found that a refresh interval of 5 seconds yields a retention failure rate of 10^{-6}, which provides insights into the behavior of intermittent failures with a relatively higher failure rate. We also provide results at other refresh intervals to show that the observations hold irrespective of the refresh interval deployed in the system.

We run experiments with different data patterns (zeroes (0b0000), ones (0b1111), tens (0b1010), fives (0b0101), and random) written to the entire DRAM for 1000 rounds. In the experiment with the random patterns, we write a randomly generated data pattern at each round. Thus, in tests with random data patterns, the pattern changes in each round. For all other tests, the data pattern (ones, zeroes, tens, and fives) remains the same across rounds. We also perform an experiment where all patterns are tested in each round (denoted as "All" in graphs). We count the number of failing cells discovered so far in each round. Our methodology of testing with rounds is similar to that described in [28].

Figure 5 shows the number of failing cells found versus number of rounds used for testing for the module A_1. We plot the number of failing cells for each of the patterns tested (ZERO, ONE,

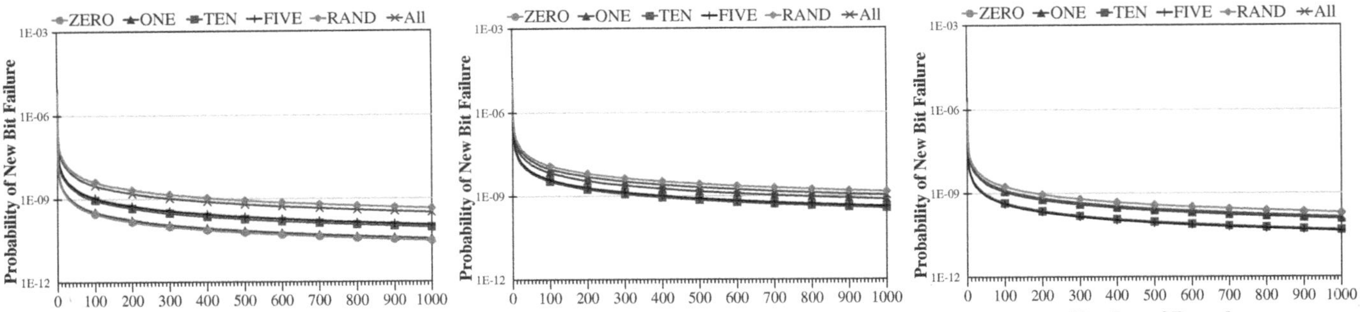

(a) *Module A_1*

(b) *Module B_1*

(c) *Module C_1*

Figure 6: Probability of Discovering New Errors with Testing

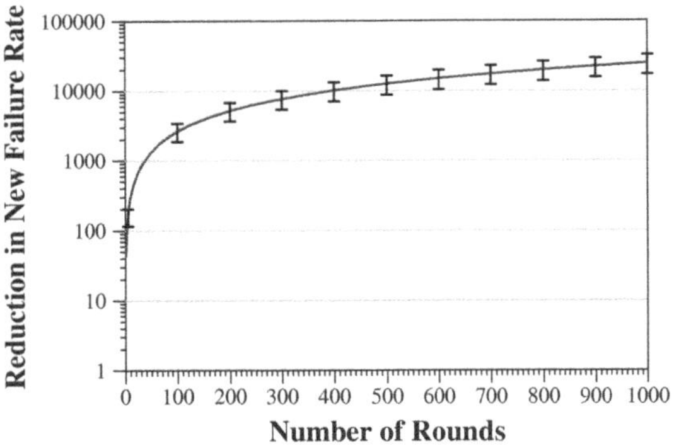

Figure 7: Reduction in Failure Rate in All Tested Modules

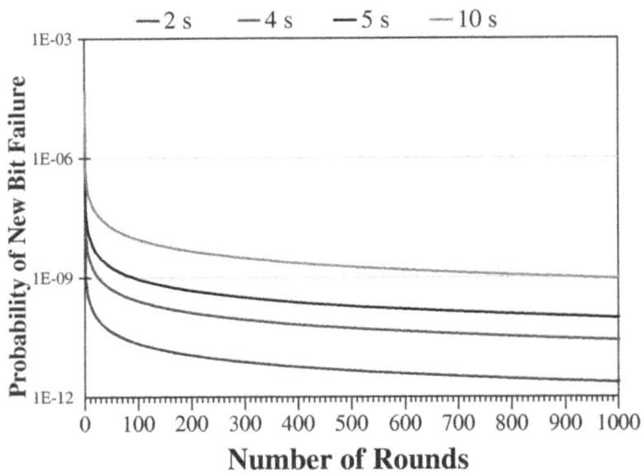

Figure 8: Probability of Retention Failure at Different Refresh Intervals in *Module A_1*

TEN, FIVE, RAND, All). We observe that there is a common trend among all the patterns: There is a sharp increase in the number of new failing cells within the first few rounds, but then the curves become relatively flat. This implies that the first few rounds of tests discover most of the intermittent failures and not too many new cells are found to fail after the first few rounds. However, a small number of new cells fail even after a considerable number of rounds. We observe that other modules demonstrate very similar behavior. Due to space constraints, we do not present all the results for each of the modules, but present results for one module from each vendor and a summary of the results over all the tested modules. However, detailed figures for all modules and data sets can be found online at the SAFARI Research Group website [16].

Observation: *Only a few rounds of tests can discover most of the retention failures. However, even after thousands of rounds of testing, a very small number of new cells are discovered to be failing.*

Implication: *Significant retention failure rate reduction is possible with only a few rounds of tests, but testing alone cannot detect all possible retention failures.*

4.1.2 *Reducing Retention Failure Rate with Testing*

We have empirically observed that only a few rounds of tests can detect most of the retention failures. This observation implies that the probability of detecting a new failure reduces significantly after only a few rounds of testing. We use the number of new failures detected at each round from Figure 5 and calculate the probability of discovering a new failure per round (using Equation (1) in Appendix). Figure 6 presents the reduction in failure rate with rounds of testing for one module from each vendor. This reduction in failure rate with testing can enable the estimation of number of required rounds of online testing to achieve a target reliability guarantee. A system-level profiling mechanism can observe the number of failures incurred at run-time and can determine the number of testing rounds required to reduce the probability of discovering a new failure to an acceptable limit. For example, Figure 5 shows there are more than 170000 retention failures in *module A_1* with all tested patterns (retention failure rate of 10^{-6}). The system-level profiling mechanism can be configured to perform 300 rounds of testing (at which point there are around 18 new bit failures occurring every round, as can be calculated from Figure 5), reducing the retention failure rate to 10^{-9}. The number of required rounds is obtained by observing the point at which the curve for the probability of a new failure with all the tested patterns crosses 10^{-9} in Figure 6a.

Figure 7 shows the average reduction in the probability of a new failure versus the number of testing rounds for all the tested modules. Standard deviation of the reduction in failure rate is also plotted (as error bars on data points). This figure shows that only 5 rounds of tests can reduce the new failure rate by more than 100 times, but the reduction in failure rate becomes greatly diminished as the number of testing rounds increases beyond 100: each additional round finds a small number of retention failures. We also present the probability of a new failure with testing at different refresh intervals in Figure 8. This figure shows that the probability of discovering a new failure with testing reduces at a similar rate irrespective of the refresh interval.

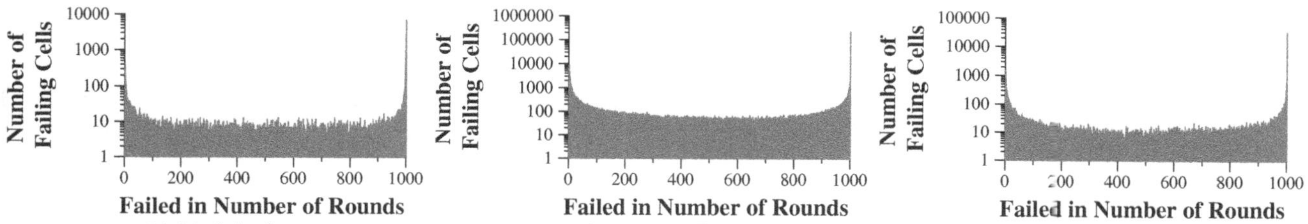

(a) *Module* A_1 (b) *Module* B_1 (c) *Module* C_1

Figure 9: Number of Cells Failing in Different Number of Rounds

Based on our experiments, we conclude that 1) although the absolute number of retention failures varies across modules and refresh intervals, only a few rounds of tests can reduce the probability of a new failure significantly, 2) however, even after 1000 rounds of testing there is a small number of new failures discovered every round, and 3) the probability of discovering a new failure decreases slowly after the initial rounds of testing. These results imply that testing by itself, is not enough to detect and mitigate all the retention failures.

4.1.3 Retention Failure Coverage with Testing Rounds

The efficacy of testing depends on the consistency of a particular cell failing in different rounds of tests. We discuss three cases to demonstrate how consistency of failure can affect the efficacy of testing for a cell: 1) if a cell consistently fails in *all* rounds of tests, it is likely a very weak cell, perhaps with a permanent retention failure; these can be effectively discovered with testing, 2) if a cell fails in a majority of rounds of tests, it is again likely that testing will effectively discover it, 3) if a cell fails in only a few rounds of tests, then it is less likely to be discovered with testing (at least within a reasonable amount of time). We present the total number of rounds a particular cell fails in our experiments to determine how effective testing could be across all cells. Instead of showing each unique cell, we group all cells that fail in the same number of rounds. Figure 9 plots the number of cells that fail in a total of N rounds, where N varies from 1 to 1000. The peak at 1000 rounds suggests that the majority of the failing cells are very weak cells that fail in every round. All the other cells are VRT cells that fail only intermittently. The second highest peak around round 1 shows that a significant number of cells fail only in one round, indicating that it will likely be difficult to discover a significant portion of intermittent failures through system-level testing. Figure 10 shows the average, minimum and maximum number of cells failing in one to 1000 rounds across all tested modules. Based on the similarity of the curves, and the consistent existence of a large fraction of cells that fail in only a small number of testing rounds, we conclude that testing alone is likely ineffective at efficiently discovering a large fraction of the intermittently failing cells.

4.2 Undetected Retention Failures

The previous experiment showed that a large fraction of intermittently failing cells can remain undetected by testing as there are some VRT cells that operate correctly (pass) for a long time and then fail for a short period of time. Next, we analyze the time a VRT cell spends in its different retention (time) states. The intent of the experiment is to determine the percentage of VRT cells that fail after spending a long time in the non-failing retention state, and that are therefore are hard to detect through testing.

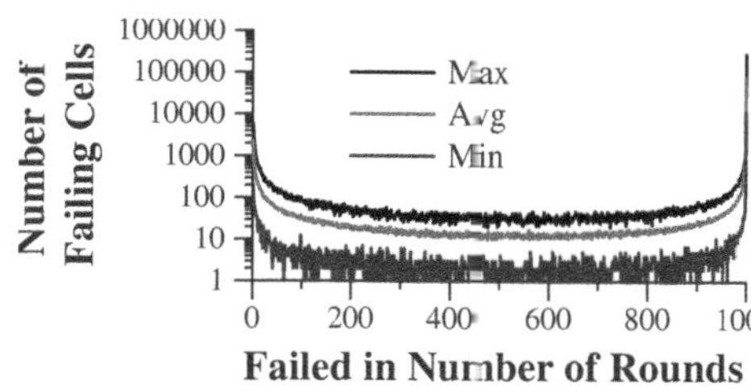

Figure 10: Average, Minimum and Maximum Number of Cells Failing in Different Number of Rounds

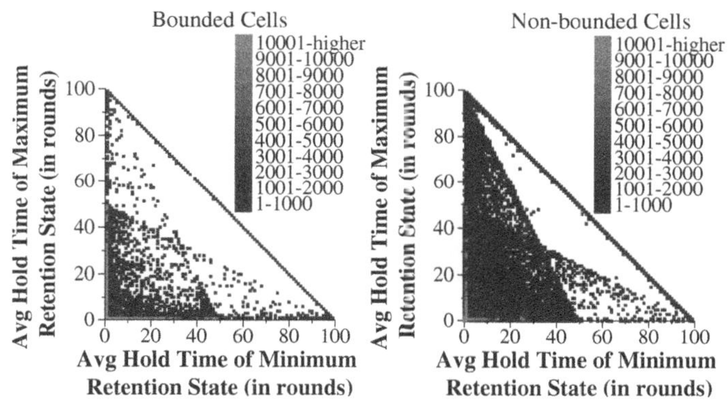

Figure 11: Average Hold Time of Cells in *Module* A_1

4.2.1 Description of the Experiment

In this experiment, we measure the average amount of time a cell spends in its different retention states. We have tested the modules at a refresh interval of 1 to 20 seconds with a 1-second increment for 100 rounds at 45 °C (corresponding to 82 ms to 1640 ms with an 82 ms increment at 85 °C). We monitor the number of rounds a cell spends at a specific retention state before it moves to some other retention state, referred to as *hold time*. After 100 rounds, we calculate the average hold time a cell spends in its minimum and maximum retention state.

We divide the cells into two different categories: cells with bound-ed and unbounded maximum retention times. The first category, called the bounded cells, consists of the cells that always have retention states lower than 20 s. These cells always fail at potentially different refresh intervals within our tested refresh interval of 20 s. The other category, called the non-bounded cells, consists of cells that fail within the 20 s of refresh interval in some rounds, but do not fail at all in at least one round. Since they do not fail in a round, we cannot accurately determine (hence, bound) the maximum retention time of these cells. Figure 11 plots the average hold times of the maximum and minimum retention states of bounded

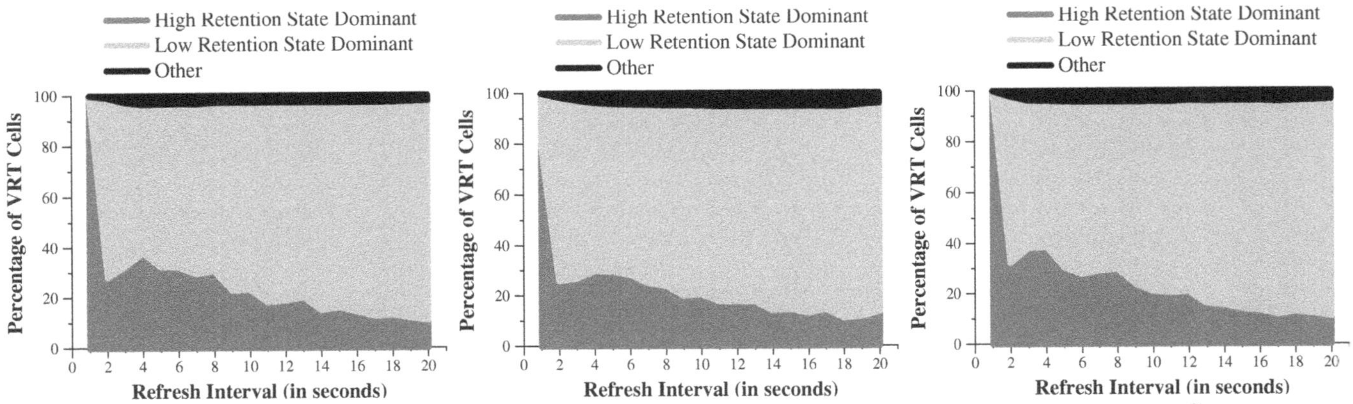

(a) *Module A_1* (b) *Module B_1* (c) *Module C_1*

Figure 12: Percentage of VRT Cells with High or Low Retention States Dominant

and non-bounded cells in module A_1. Instead of representing each cell, we group the failing cells that have the same hold times. Each point (x, y) in the figure represents a group of cells that spends on average x rounds in the minimum retention state and y rounds in the maximum retention state. We use color intensity to represent the number of cells at each point. The more cells belonging to a specific bin, the brighter the color of that bin.

We observe from the figure that most of the cells appear in the bins that are very close to either the x axis or the y axis. The cells near the y axis spend a very short time (1-2 rounds) in the low retention state. Similarly, the cells near the x axis spend a very short time in the high retention state. This characteristic is similar for bounded and non-bounded cells in all the tested modules. This trend implies that most cells have dominant states. We call those cells that spend more than 98 (out of 100) rounds in either the low or high retention states as dominant-state cells. Cells with a dominant low retention state frequently fail in tests and can be discovered easily. However, cells with a dominant high retention state mostly spend their time in the high retention state. Therefore, these cells tend to not fail in most of the testing rounds. As a result, these cells are hard to discover through testing.

Observation: *Most VRT cells have dominant retention time states: they spend most of the time either at a low or high retention state.*

Implication: *VRT cells with a dominant high retention state are hard to discover through testing.*

4.2.2 Number of Undiscovered Retention Failures

Based on our data, we present the percentage of cells that spend a long time in the high retention state among all the VRT cells. Figure 12 shows the percentage of dominant-state cells at each refresh interval for one module from three manufacturers. Figure 13 shows the percentage of dominant-state cells averaged over all the tested modules, along with the standard deviation. Based on the figures, we make three conclusions on the behavior of VRT cells. First, on average around 90% of the cells are either low-state-dominant or high-state-dominant cells. Second, a significant portion of the VRT cells (around 40-20%) are high-state-dominant cells irrespective of the refresh interval. These cells would be hard to discover. Third, the percentage of high-state-dominant cells decreases with refresh interval. The reason is high refresh interval increases the chance that a cell is more likely to have a lower retention state.

Based on these experimental observations, we conclude that there will likely be a significant portion of VRT cells that remain

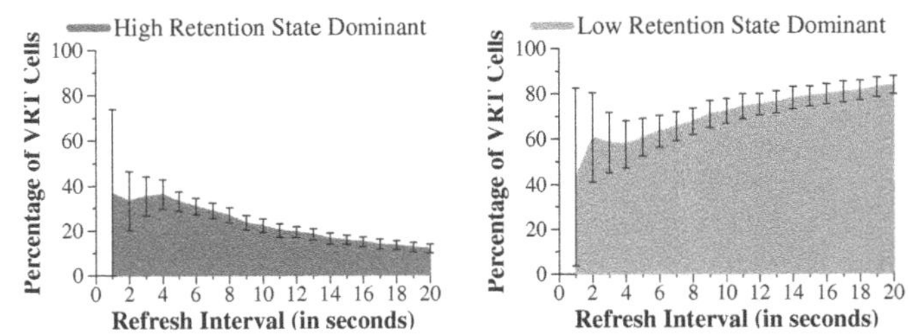

(a) High State Dominant (b) Low State Dominant

Figure 13: Percentage High and Low Retention State Dominant Cells in All Tested Modules

undetected by testing at any refresh interval deployed in the system. This reinforces our previous observation (in Section 4.1) that testing alone is likely not enough to discover all retention failures.

5. EFFICACY OF GUARDBANDING

The effectiveness of the guardband depends on the differences in retention states of a VRT cell. A small guardband would be effective if the retention time difference between the retention states of a cell is small. We want to answer these questions: 1) How much difference is present in the retention time states of VRT cells? 2) How effective is adding a guardband at the system-level, in the presence of a large number of intermittent VRT failures?

5.1 Description of the Experiment

In this experiment, similar to Section 4.2, we have tested the modules at a refresh interval of 1 to 20 seconds with a 1-second increment for 100 rounds at 45 °C (corresponding to 82 ms to 1640 ms with an 82 ms increment at 85 °C). However, this time, we monitor the retention state of the cells in each round. VRT cells exhibit more than one retention time state in different rounds. We categorize the cells into two-state and multi-state cells. The two-state cells are the cells that move back and forth between only two retention states. The multi-state cells exhibit more than two states. Similar to the prior experiment, we further categorize these cells as bounded and non-bounded cells (Section 4.2 provides the definition of these). Recall that a bounded cell always has retention states lower than 20 s, the maximum tested retention time, whereas a non-bounded cell does not fail the retention test in at least one

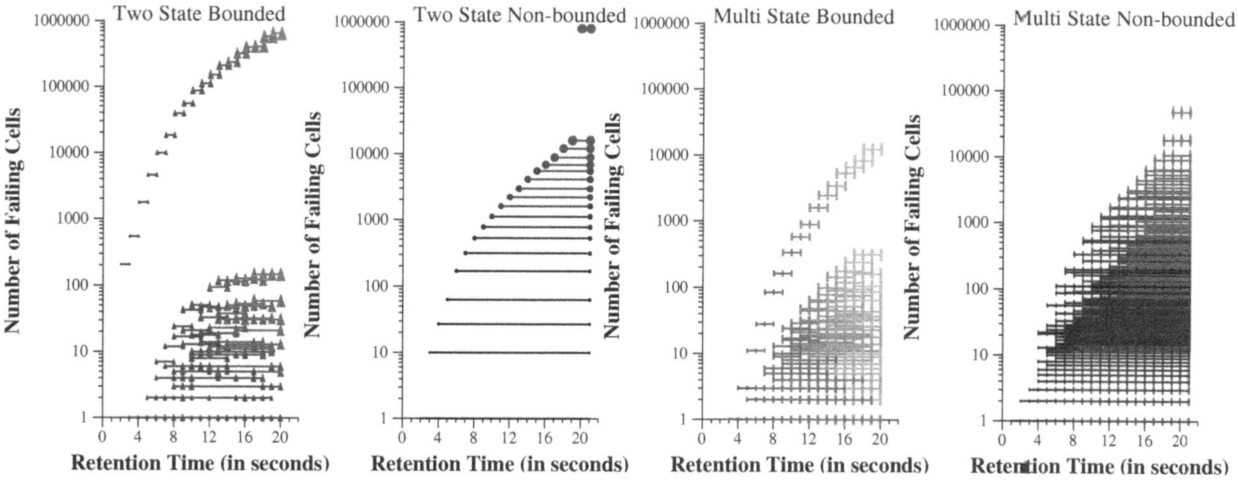

Figure 14: Retention States in *Module* A_1

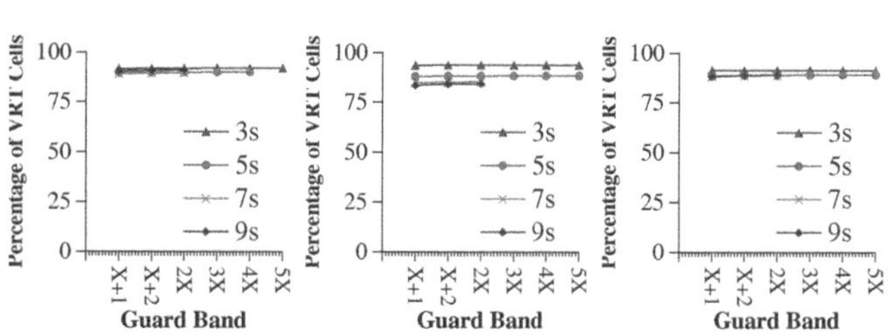

(a) *Module* A_1 (b) *Module* B_1 (c) *Module* C_1

Figure 15: Coverage of Guardbanding in Module A_1, B_1, and C_1

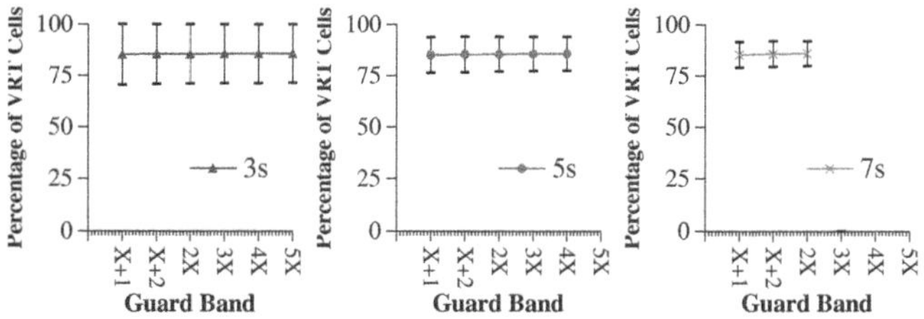

Figure 16: Coverage of Guardbanding in All Modules

round, which means that its maximum retention time cannot be determined with our experiments. Figure 14 presents the retention states of all the VRT cells found in this experiment for *module* A_1. Due to space constraints, we place the results from other modules online [16]. The behavior remains similar across the tested modules and we summarize the results for one module from each vendor in Figure 15.

Figure 14 shows the retention states of two-state (bounded and non-bounded) cells and multi-state (bounded and non-bounded) cells in different plots. Instead of plotting every cell, we group the cells having the same retention states. Each line in the plots represents a group of cells with the same retention states. The markers in the line represent the retention states of that group of cells. For example, a line at (x_1, y) to (x_2, y) represents that there are y cells that have retention states x_1 and x_2. The overlapping lines indicate that there are some groups of cells with different retention states but the same number of cells in the group. To distinguish among these groups, we use different marker sizes for different groups. a larger marker size represents a higher retention state. We plot the non-bounded retention time state as 21 s in the plots.

The first plot shows the retention states of the two-state bounded cells. We observe that most of the cells have very close retention states (notice the log scale in the y axis). There are only a few cells that have non-consecutive retention states. The next plot shows the retention states of the two-state non-bounded cells. We observe that the number of cells that exhibit non-bounded behavior is almost 10X lower than the bounded cells. For example, for module A_1, 110 cells have retention states of 3 s and 4 s, but only 10 cells move between the retention state of 3 s and the non-bounded state. This implies that a small guardband can be effective for a large fraction of the cells for tolerating intermittent retention time changes. We see a similar trend with the multi-state cells: most of the cells have close-by retention states and only a small number of cells shows a large difference among the multiple states. For cells where there is a large difference in the different retention time states, even a large amount of guardband may not be effective at tolerating intermittent retention time changes.

Observation: *Most of the intermittently failing cells have very close retention states in terms of retention time. However, there also exists VRT cells with large differences in retention states.*

Implication: *Even a small guardband is likely effective for most of the VRT cells. However, even a large guardband is likely ineffective for the remaining VRT cells with large differences in retention time states.*

5.2 Coverage of Guardbanding

We determine the fraction of failing cells that different amounts of guardbanding can effectively mitigate (i.e., avoid failures for). To determine the coverage of each guardband, we perform three steps as described in Section 2.3.2. For example, at a refresh interval of 3 s the steps to determine the coverage of a $2X$ guardband are: 1) We identify the failing bits at a refresh interval of 6 seconds ($2X$). 2) These faulty bits are assumed to be repaired using different mitigation techniques and do not cause any further failures in the original refresh interval of 3 s. 3) Then, we determine the coverage of the guardband at 3 s by determining the fraction of VRT cells observed in our experiment that now operate correctly with the guardband but otherwise would have failed.

The guardbands considered are $X + 1s$, $X + 2s$, $2X$, $3X$, $4X$, and $5X$ at refresh intervals of 3, 5, 7, and 9 seconds. We show the

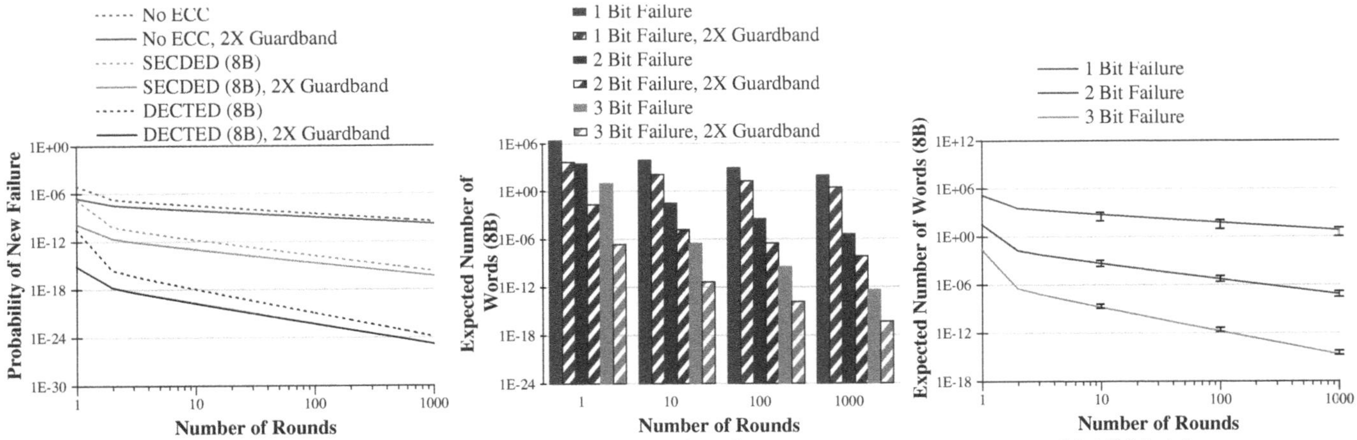

(a) *Module A_1* (b) *Module A_1* (c) All Modules

Figure 17: Effectiveness of ECC with Testing and Guardbanding

coverage of failing VRT cells with each guardband in Figure 15 for one module from each vendor. We also present the coverage averaged over all tested modules at each refresh interval, along with the standard deviation of coverage across all tested modules in Figure 16. Based on the figures, we make three observations. First, even a small guardband can achieve $85-95\%$ coverage. The reason is that most of the cells exhibit very close retention states and get repaired by the guardband. Second, the coverage does not change significantly even if we increase the amount of guardband to $5X$. This characteristic can be explained by our experimental observation that only a very small fraction of cells have large differences in retention time states. Third, coverage does not depend on the refresh interval and remains mostly the same.

We conclude that a small guardband (e.g., $2X$) can avoid most of the failing cells. However, even a large guardband (e.g., $5X$) is not effective for the remaining VRT cells, indicating that using a guardband alone is not effective to mitigate all intermittent retention failures.

6. EFFICACY OF ECC

In this section, we present the effectiveness of ECC when used with other mitigation techniques. We focus on two aspects of ECC, 1) reduction in the probability of a new failure and 2) expected number of multi-bit failures when the system can perform online testing and guardbanding.

When a system is capable of online testing, it can detect retention failures and repair those bits. Repairing the bits reduces the probability of a new bit failure and thus the system can adjust the amount of ECC required to correct the random VRT failures that occur after the system-level testing. The dotted lines in Figure 17a show the number of rounds required to reduce the probability of a new retention failure in the presence of single error correcting, double error detecting (SECDED) code and double error correcting, triple error detecting (DECTED) code versus the number of rounds rounds of tests employed. The solid lines also represent the probability of retention failure with SECDED and DECTED, but with an added guardband ($2X$). The retention failure rate with all the patterns (All) from Figure 6 is used to calculate the probability of failure in the presence of ECC at 8B granularity (derived from the Equations (2), (3), and (4) in Appendix). We make two observations from this figure. First, we can achieve a much higher reduction in the probability of a new failure, when the system employs testing and guardbanding *along with* ECC. Only a few rounds of testing can reduce the retention failure rate by $10^7/10^{12}$ times, when used in conjunction with SECDED/DECTED and a $2X$ guardband. Contrast this with the much smaller $100/10^5$ times reduction in retention failure rate when only SECDED/DECTED is used. Second, a higher number of rounds of tests *along with* ECC can further reduce the retention failure rate. The probability of a new failure can be reduced by as much as $10^{12}/10^{18}$ times after 1000 rounds of testing when testing is used in conjunction with SECDED/DECTED.

These observations imply that ECC, when used with other mitigation techniques, can effectively tolerate a high error rate.

Observation: *Testing and guardbanding along with ECC protection can significantly reduce the retention failure rate.*

Implication: *A combination of error mitigation techniques is more effective at tolerating a high error rate than each technique alone.*

The strength of the required ECC depends on the probability of the multi-bit failures in a module. We present the expected number of words with 1, 2 and 3 bit failures when the system employs other mitigation techniques in Figures 17b and 17c (refer to Equation (5) in Appendix). These figures clearly show that the number of multi-bit failures reduces with rounds of testing. We make two observations. First, the expected number of single-bit failures reduces with testing, but does not reach to zero. Second, with 1000 rounds of testing, the expected number of 2-bit and 3-bit failures become negligible (10^{-6}). We conclude that a system-level online profiling mechanism can tolerate a higher failure rate when used in conjunction with other mitigation techniques.

7. EFFICACY OF SOPHISTICATED MITIGATION TECHNIQUES

In light of the efficacy of testing, guardbanding, and ECC observed and quantified in our experiments, we evaluate the adequacy of some recently proposed error mitigation techniques.

7.1 Bit Repair Techniques

System-level bit repair techniques perform online testing and repair the detected faulty bits using different mechanisms (remapping, higher refresh rate for the faulty rows, disabling faulty pages, error correcting pointers, etc) [38, 27, 50, 26]. These mechanisms assume that all bit failures can be detected by testing after the initial

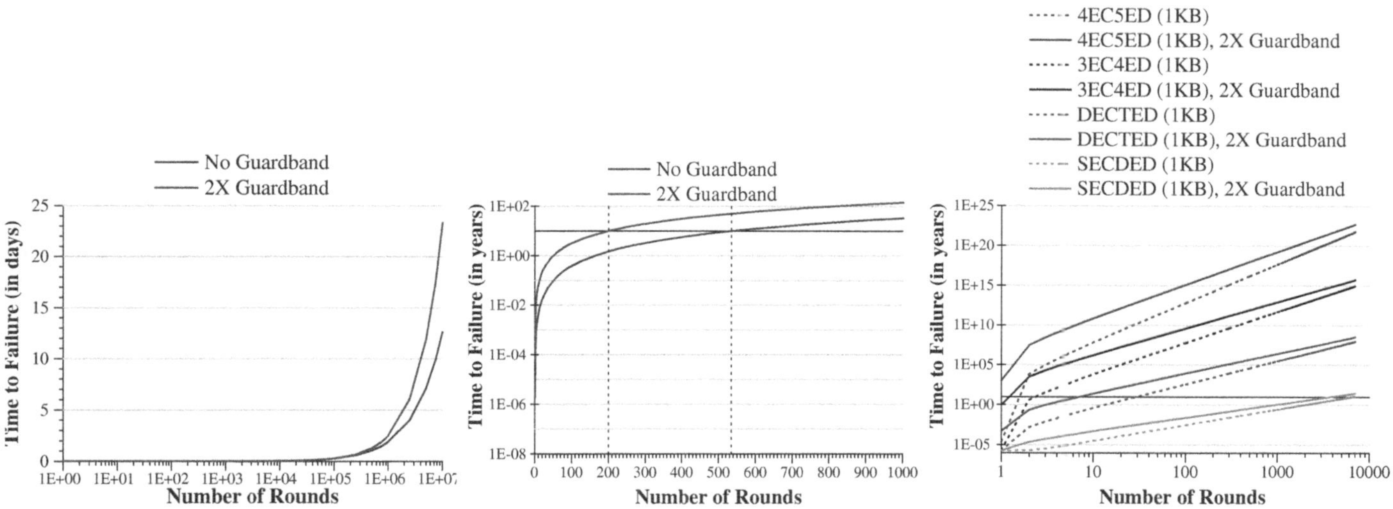

(a) Bit Repair [38, 27, 50] (b) VS-ECC [4] (c) Hi-ECC [52]

Figure 18: Effectiveness of Recent Error Mitigation Techniques with Testing and Guardbanding

system boot-up and no new errors occur in DRAM after repairing the failing bits detected by the initial test. In our experiments, we observe that even after thousands rounds of testing, new bits keep failing at a very low rate. This implies that all these mechanisms will fail even after very long (initial) tests. Figure 18a presents the expected time to failure of these mechanisms when the system can run a million rounds of tests. The time to failure of the system is calculated using the probability of a new failure from Figure 6 (refer to Equation (6) in Appendix). With each round of testing, the detected faulty bits get repaired and the probability of a new failure keeps decreasing. However, in these mechanisms, the system will fail even if a single bit failure occurs during runtime after the initial testing. Figure 18a shows that the system will fail within hours after 10 thousand rounds of tests. Even after 10 million rounds of initial testing, the system will fail in 13 days. We also present the expected time to failure with an added guardband. Even though adding a guardband improves time to failure, the system still fails within 23 days after more than 10 million rounds of initial testing. In a real system, each round of test consists of writing one specific data pattern in the entire module, waiting for 64 ms to keep the cells idle so that the retention failures can manifest and then reading the entire module to detect the failing cells. It will take 413.96 ms to test a 2 GB module for a round with just one data pattern (refer to Equation (8) in Appendix for details). 10 million rounds of initial testing with all our tested patterns would take more than 7.9 months. Even so, the system would fail within a month after the initial test. Our analysis, thus shows that bit-repair mechanisms that perform only initial tests (as they were proposed) are not feasible to deploy in a practical system in the presence of intermittent retention failures.

7.2 Variable Strength ECC (VS-ECC)

VS-ECC uses variable strength ECC to protect different lines in memory [4]. The system performs an initial test to detect lines with one or more errors and protect them using 4EC5ED code, but uses SECDED for rest of the memory. VS-ECC will fail if there are two or more errors in the lines protected by SECDED. We calculate the probability of failure for VS-ECC and determine the expected time to failure using the probability of failure from Figure 6 (refer to Equation (7) in Appendix). After each round of testing, the new failing words found are protected by stronger ECC. Figure 18b shows the expected time to failure with number of rounds of testing. Within 550 rounds of testing (which takes around 19 minutes) the system achieves a time-to-failure of 10 years. This figure also shows that adding a guardband can reduce the number of rounds of testing required to achieve the same guarantee. With a $2X$ guardband, the system needs only 200 rounds of testing (which takes around 7 minutes). Our analysis illustrates that a system has to run the initial test for several minutes to achieve a reasonable reliability guarantee even with a 2 Gb chip. The length of the initial test could be longer in future high density chips. Blocking entire memory for a significant amount of time may result in throughput loss and thus such a mechanism would be difficult to deploy in a practical system. This implies that a practical and efficient online profiling system should be designed to make VS-ECC effective. In such a mechanism, testing would be spread across a large interval and be performed in isolated parts of the memory such that other programs can still use the remaining parts of the memory.

7.3 Higher Strength ECC (Hi-ECC)

Hi-ECC is an ECC based mechanism that uses very strong ECC (5EC6ED) to tolerate a high error rate [52]. It amortizes the cost of ECC by protecting a larger chunk of data (1KB). We show that testing and guardbanding can be very effective at providing the same reliability guarantee but using weaker ECC. In Figure 18c, we present the expected time to failure of a system that can use online testing and guardbanding. This figure shows that with only one round of test (which takes 2.06 s), the system can effectively reduce ECC strength to 3-bit correcting, 4-bit detecting (3EC4ED) code and can still provide a 10-year time-to-failure guarantee. After 100 rounds of tests (which takes around 3.5 minutes), ECC strength can be reduced to DECTED. To decrease the strength to SECDED, the system will need to perform around 7000 rounds of tests (taking almost 4 hours), reducing the overhead of ECC by 80%. This figure also shows that with an added guardband, this system can start with 4EC5ED and can reduce ECC strength to DECTED within 10 rounds of testing (20.6 s). However, the system will still need to go through 7000 rounds of tests (taking almost 4 hours) to apply SECDED. Though blocking memory for 4 hours is not acceptable, if these 7000 rounds of tests are spread over time for only some rows in memory (such that testing can be efficient), we can still provide 10-years of time to failure guarantee using only SECDED.

This observation implies an interesting characteristic of online mitigation techniques. We show that we can enable many different optimizations if an effective online profiling mechanism can be designed to run continuous tests in the background without disrupting other programs. A system can start with a strong ECC code at the beginning (same as Hi-ECC), but instead of paying the latency, area, and power penalty for strong ECC at every access, an effective online profiling mechanism can use SECDED after profiling for errors for some time. Based on our observations and analysis, we sketch a high-level architectural design for an efficient system-level online profiling mechanism in the next section.

8. ENABLING A SYSTEM-LEVEL ONLINE PROFILING MECHANISM

An online profiling technique for DRAM would test the module while the system is running and the memory is in use. The memory controller would be responsible for locating and repairing the faulty cells to mitigate the errors and ensure reliable DRAM operation. Such a system would not only improve DRAM reliability, but would also increase DRAM yield even in the presence of high error rates, by identifying and repairing bit errors rather than discarding chips with errors. An effective online profiling mechanism can address DRAM scaling challenges and play a critical role in enabling high-density, low-cost DRAM in the future.

8.1 Designing an Online Profiling Mechanism

An online profiler needs to be non-intrusive, operating in the background to allow continual testing without disrupting the use of the system. Long tests are undesirable as they would prevent user programs from accessing memory, resulting in a significant performance overhead. In light of our observations, we suggest that an online profiling mechanism can be designed by using a combination of testing, guardbanding, and ECC. The goal of an effective online profiling mechanism is to detect most of the errors with short tests performed at regular intervals. Here, we sketch the steps involved in a preliminary online profiling mechanism. The evaluation of such a mechanism is outside the scope of this work.

Initial Reliability Guarantee using ECC: Initially, before any profiling, the chips are protected by ECC to guarantee reliable DRAM operation. The memory controller is responsible for correcting erroneous data through a mechanism like virtualized ECC [56] whose error correction strength can be varied dynamically. Without any testing and guardbanding, the cost of ECC would likely be high.

Discovering Errors with Short Tests: Next, the memory controller runs tests to discover and repair the faulty bits. Adding a guardband can reduce the error rate by ten times(Section 5). The test for adding a guardband involves testing the chips at a high refresh interval and can be done just after the system starts. The guardband test can be done within a short period as it does not require rounds of tests. Later, during the regular use of the memory, the memory controller can run short rounds of tests to discover the intermittently failing cells. In order to prevent major performance overheads, a round of test is run after some regular interval. Thus, in order to reduce the overhead of testing, we propose that future online profilers test small regions of memory at regular intervals.

Adjusting the ECC strength: After some number of testing rounds, most of the failing bits get discovered and effectively get repaired. When the rate of retention failures reduces by an acceptable amount, the strength of the employed ECC can be correspondingly adjusted to reduce the ECC overhead.

8.2 Challenges and Opportunities of an Online Profiling Mechanism

We briefly describe some of the challenges and potential opportunities of designing an online profiler.

Reducing Performance Overhead: In a real system, the overhead of running even one round of test in a specific region of memory can have noticeable performance overhead. A round of test consists of writing some data pattern in the region under test, waiting for a certain amount of time to make sure cells are idle for the entire refresh interval and then reading out that region to locate the failures. This test would make the region under test unavailable to programs for hundreds of milliseconds. We argue that future online profiling works must address the challenges of reducing this performance overhead by designing intelligent mechanisms. We sketch some potential directions that can be used to mitigate the performance overhead: 1) One mechanism can be pinning the specific memory region into the cache while that region is being tested. Memory requests to the region under test would be satisfied by the cache and would not block the programs. However, there is a trade-off between the size of the region that can be temporally stored in the cache without evicting a large portion of the working set vs. the number of individual tests that would be required to profile the whole module. 2) Keeping a pool of unallocated pages and testing them extensively before they are allocated to a program can improve performance at the cost of some effective memory capacity loss. This hardware-software collaborative mechanism would need an interface to the system software to prevent allocating pages under test. 3) Many applications have periodic compute and memory phases. A memory controller can be designed to predict phases where a portion of memory remains idle and run online tests during those periods to reduce the performance overhead.

Reducing Mitigation Overhead: The ultimate goal of detecting failures through online profiling is to mitigate those failures and provide reliable operation. Recent mechanisms proposed efficient techniques to reduce the overhead of mitigation mechanisms. For example, ArchShield, which mitigates failures by remapping faulty words in a region of memory, uses a fault map to efficiently determine the location of remapping [38]. Using a higher refresh rate for rows with failures is another mitigation technique. RAIDR uses Bloom filters to efficiently store the location of the rows that are required to be refreshed more frequently [27]. However, as we have shown in Section 7, these mechanisms as proposed, do not consider intermittent failures and lead to potential data loss. We envision these techniques would be extended with online profiling mechanisms to dynamically determine the current set of failures and optimize the overheads depending on the current failure rate.

Enabling Failure-aware Optimizations: An online profiling mechanism enables optimization techniques to take advantage of the inherent resiliency of some applications at run-time. Many of the previously proposed resiliency techniques that allocate error-prone regions to data that can tolerate errors [29, 7, 30, 25, 9] would directly benefit from an efficient online profiling mechanism, by being able to determine the error-prone locations at run-time.

9. CONCLUSION

We have studied and analyzed the effectiveness of different system-level error mitigation techniques for retention failures in commodity DRAM, with the goal of enabling efficient and effective reliability techniques for future DRAM. We make several observations on the error mitigation techniques based on the experimental data collected from 96 DRAM chips manufactured by three different vendors, using an FPGA-based DRAM testing infrastructure. First, we show that only a small amount of testing can discover the majority of cells with intermittent retention failures. From our experiments, only 5 rounds of tests can discover most of the intermittent failures and reduce the probability of retention failure by 100 times. However, even after thousands of rounds of testing, a very small number of cells exhibit new failures not discovered before. Second, we show that even a small guardband (e.g., $2X$) can avoid 85-95% of the intermittently failing cells and reduce the probability of retention failure by ten times. At the same time, even a large guardband (e.g., $5X$) is not effective for the remaining intermittently failing cells. Third, we show that using only single error correction codes can reduce the retention error rate by only 100 times, but using single error correction codes together with testing and guardbanding can reduce the error rate by as much as 10^{12} times. Fourth, based on our data, we quantify recently proposed system-level error mitigation techniques that do not consider intermittent failures, showing that our measured results significantly impact these works' conclusions. We show that bit repair mechanisms that rely on testing [38, 27, 50, 26] cannot provide strong reliability guarantees even after months of testing. On the other hand, ECC-based mitigation techniques [4, 52] can ensure reliable DRAM operation when employed in conjunction with online testing in a relatively short amount of time. We conclude that the viability of these techniques depend on the development of an efficient online profiling mechanism that does not significantly disrupt the operation of the programs running on the system.

We hope that the empirical study and analysis of retention error mitigation techniques, driven by experimental measurements from real DRAM chips, presented in this paper can enable new, effective, and efficient mechanisms in the future that will lead to more reliable design and operation of future DRAM systems. In particular, we believe the development of efficient online retention time profiling techniques for DRAM is a promising area of immediate future work that can benefit from our characterizations and analyses.

ACKNOWLEDGEMENTS

We are grateful to Uksong Kang from Samsung for his helpful comments. We thank the anonymous reviewers for their helpful feedback, and gratefully acknowledge the SAFARI Research Group members for providing useful feedback. We acknowledge the support of the Intel Science and Technology Center on Cloud Computing. We thank our industrial partners for their support: IBM, Intel, Qualcomm, and Samsung. This research was also partially supported by grants from NSF (CAREER Award CCF 0953246, CCF 1212962, and CNS 1065112).

REFERENCES

[1] R. D. Adams. *High performance memory testing: Design principles, fault modeling and self-test.* Springer, 2003.

[2] J.-H. Ahn et al. Adaptive self refresh scheme for battery operated high-density mobile DRAM applications. ASSCC, 2006.

[3] Z. Al-Ars et al. DRAM-specific space of memory tests. ITC, 2006.

[4] A. R. Alameldeen et al. Energy-efficient cache design using variable-strength error-correcting codes. ISCA, 2011.

[5] R. Baumann. The impact of technology scaling on soft error rate performance and limits to the efficacy of error correction. IEDM, 2002.

[6] K. Chang et al. Improving DRAM performance by parallelizing refreshes with accesses. HPCA, 2014.

[7] M. de Kruijf et al. Relax: An architectural framework for software recovery of hardware faults. ISCA, 2010.

[8] P. G. Emma et al. Rethinking refresh: Increasing availability and reducing power in DRAM for cache applications. *IEEE Micro*, 28(6), Nov. 2008.

[9] H. Esmaeilzadeh et al. Neural acceleration for general-purpose approximate programs. MICRO, 2012.

[10] D. Frank et al. Device scaling limits of Si MOSFETs and their application dependencies. *Proceedings of the IEEE*, 89(3), 2001.

[11] T. Hamamoto et al. On the retention time distribution of Dynamic Random Access Memory (DRAM). 1998.

[12] P. Hazucha and C. Svensson. Impact of CMOS technology scaling on the atmospheric neutron soft error rate. *TNS*, 47(6), 2000.

[13] A. Hiraiwa et al. Local-field-enhancement model of DRAM retention failure. IEDM, 1998.

[14] C.-S. Hou et al. An FPGA-based test platform for analyzing data retention time distribution of DRAMs. VLSI-DAT, 2013.

[15] JEDEC. *Standard No. 79-3F. DDR3 SDRAM Specification*, July 2012.

[16] S. Khan et al. The efficacy of error mitigation techniques for DRAM retention failures: A comparative experimental study – Full data sets. http://www.ece.cmu.edu/~safari/tools/dram-sigmetrics2014-fulldata.html.

[17] H. Kim et al. Characterization of the variable retention time in dynamic random access memory. *IEEE Trans. Electron Dev.*, 58(9), 2011.

[18] K. Kim. Technology for sub-50nm DRAM and NAND flash manufacturing. IEDM, 2005.

[19] K. Kim and J. Lee. A new investigation of data retention time in truly nanoscaled DRAMs. *IEEE Electron Device Letters*, 30(8), 2009.

[20] Y. Kim et al. A case for exploiting subarray-level parallelism (SALP) in DRAM. ISCA, 2012.

[21] Y. I. Kim et al. Thermal degradation of DRAM retention time: Characterization and improving techniques. IRPS, 2004.

[22] D. Lee et al. Tiered-latency DRAM: A low latency and low cost DRAM architecture. HPCA, 2013.

[23] M. J. Lee and K. W. Park. A mechanism for dependence of refresh time on data pattern in DRAM. *Electron Device Letters*, 31(2), 2010.

[24] X. Li et al. A realistic evaluation of memory hardware errors and software system susceptibility. ATC, 2010.

[25] X. Li and D. Yeung. Application-level correctness and its impact on fault tolerance. HPCA, 2007.

[26] C.-H. Lin et al. SECRET: Selective error correction for refresh energy reduction in DRAMs. ICCD, 2012.

[27] J. Liu et al. RAIDR: Retention-aware intelligent DRAM refresh. ISCA, 2012.

[28] J. Liu et al. An experimental study of data retention behavior in modern DRAM devices: Implications for retention time profiling mechanisms. ISCA, 2013.

[29] S. Liu et al. Flikker: Saving DRAM refresh-power through critical data partitioning. ASPLOS, 2011.

[30] Y. Luo. Characterizing application memory error vulnerability to optimize data center cost. DSN, 2014.

[31] J. A. Mandelman et al. Challenges and future directions for the scaling of dynamic random-access memory (DRAM). *IBM J. of Res. and Dev.*, 2002.

[32] T. C. May et al. Alpha-particle-induced soft errors in dynamic memories. *IEEE Trans. Electron Dev.*, 1979.

[33] Y. Mori et al. The origin of variable retention time in DRAM. IEDM, 2005.

[34] W. Mueller et al. Challenges for the DRAM cell scaling to 40nm. IEDM, 2005.

[35] S. S. Mukherjee et al. The soft error problem: An architectural perspective. HPCA, 2005.

[36] O. Mutlu. Memory scaling: A systems architecture perspective. *IMW*, 2013.

[37] P. Nair et al. A case for refresh pausing in DRAM memory systems. HPCA, 2012.

[38] P. J. Nair et al. ArchShield: Architectural framework for assisting DRAM scaling by tolerating high error rates. ISCA, 2013.

[39] H.-D. Oberle et al. Enhanced fault modeling for DRAM test and analysis. VTS, 1991.

[40] T. J. O'Gorman. The effect of cosmic rays on the soft error rate of a DRAM at ground level. *IEEE Trans. Electron Dev.*, 41(4), 1994.

[41] P. J. Restle, J. W. Park, and B. F. Lloyd. DRAM variable retention time. IEDM, 1992.

[42] S. E. Schechter, G. H. Loh, et al. Use ECP, not ECC, for hard failures in resistive memories. ISCA, 2010.

[43] B. Schroeder et al. DRAM errors in the wild: A large-scale field study. SIGMETRICS, 2009.

[44] H. W. Seo et al. Charge trapping induced DRAM data retention time degradation under wafer-level burn-in stress. IRPS, 2002.

[45] V. Sridharan et al. Feng Shui of supercomputer memory: Positional effects in DRAM and SRAM faults. SC, 2013.

[46] V. Sridharan and D. Liberty. A study of DRAM failures in the field. SC, 2012.

[47] G. R. Srinivasan et al. Accurate, predictive modeling of soft error rate due to cosmic rays and chip alpha radiation. IRPS, 1994.

[48] A. J. van de Goor et al. An overview of deterministic functional RAM chip testing. *ACM Computing Surveys*, 1990.

[49] A. J. van de Goor and A. Paalvast. Industrial evaluation of DRAM SIMM tests. ITC, 2000.

[50] R. K. Venkatesan et al. Retention-aware placement in DRAM (RAPID): Software methods for quasi-non-volatile DRAM. HPCA, 2006.

[51] M.-J. Wang et al. Guardband determination for the detection of off-state and junction leakages in DRAM testing. ATS, 2001.

[52] C. Wilkerson et al. Reducing cache power with low-cost, multi-bit error-correcting codes. ISCA, 2010.

[53] Xilinx. *ML605 Hardware User Guide*, Oct. 2012.

[54] K. Yamaguchi. Theoretical study of deep-trap-assisted anomalous currents in worst-bit cells of dynamic random-access memories (DRAM's). *IEEE Trans. Electron Dev.*, 47(4), 2000.

[55] D. Yaney et al. A meta-stable leakage phenomenon in DRAM charge storage - Variable hold time. IEDM, 1987.

[56] D. H. Yoon and M. Erez. Virtualized and flexible ECC for main memory. ASPLOS, 2010.

APPENDIX

- **Effect of Temperature:** In our experiments, the curve for normalized retention time at different temperature corresponds to $e^{-0.0625T}$, where T is the temperature. A $10\,^{\circ}\mathrm{C}$ increase in temperature results in a reduction of $1 - e^{-0.0625*10} = 46.5\%$.

- **Probability of a New Failure with Rounds:** The probability of finding a new error with r rounds of tests is calculated as,
  probability of a new bit failure at round r
  $= \frac{\text{number of new cells failing at round } r}{\text{total number of cells}} \ldots(1)$

- **Probability of Failure with ECC:** Error correction codes are associated with blocks of data. All our results assume that ECC protects 8B of data. We calculate the probability of failure in n bits from the bit error rate, where $n = 64$ bits. If p is the probability of bit failure, probability of failure in n bits, p_n
  $=$ probability of any of the n bits failing
  $= 1 -$ probability of all of the n bits not failing
  $= 1 - (1-p)^n \ldots(2)$
  The probability of failure with *single error correction, double error detection* (SECDED) in n bits is calculated as, $p_{nSECDED}$
  $=$ probability of more than one bit in n bits failing
  $= 1 -$ (probability of all of the n bits not failing $+$
  probability of $n-1$ of the n bits not failing)
  $= 1 - ((1-p)^n + \binom{n}{1}p(1-p)^{(n-1)}) \ldots(3)$
  Similarly, the probability of failure with *double error correction, triple error detection* (DECTED) in n bits is calculated as, $p_{nDECTED}$
  $=$ probability of more than two bits in n bits failing
  $= 1 -$ (probability of all of the n bits not failing $+$
  probability of $n-1$ of the n bits not failing $+$
  probability of $n-2$ of the n bits not failing)
  $= 1-((1-p)^n + \binom{n}{1}p(1-p)^{(n-1)} + \binom{n}{2}p^2(1-p)^{(n-2)}) \ldots(4)$

- **Expected Number of Multi-Bit Failures:** The expected number of faulty bits per word is $p*n$. If $p*n \ll 1$, then the probability (P_k) that the word has k errors $(k \geq 1)$ can be approximated by $P_k = (pn)^k/k! \ldots(5)$

- **Time to Failure with Bit-Repair:** Let the probability of a bit failing be p and the probability of the system failing be p_{system}. If there are n bits in the module, then, p_{system}
  $= 1 -$ probability of no error in the entire module
  $= 1 - (1-p)^n$
  The expected number of trials to fail the system, $t = 1/p_{system}$. In our infrastructure, there are np bit failures at every minute. Therefore, Time to Failure in hours$= t/60 \ldots(6)$

- **Time to Failure with ECC:** Let the system can correct $k-1$ bits per word, the probability of k or more bit failure is p_k and the probability of the system failing is p_{system}. if there are n words in the module, then, p_{system}
  $= 1 -$ probability of no k or more bit error in n words
  $= 1 - (1-p_k)^n$
  The expected number of trials to fail the system, $t = 1/p_{system}$. In our infrastructure, we test for error every minute. Therefore, Mean Time to Failure in hours$= t/60 \ldots(7)$

- **Time to Test a Module:** To test a module, we need to write a data pattern in the entire module, wait for 64 ms and read the module to detect the failures. In order to read/write a row, we need to read the data from the cells in the row buffer (t_{RCD}), transfer the row to the memory controller, and close the row (t_{RP}). According to DDR3-1600 timing, time to read/write an $8KB$ row, $t_r = t_{RCD} + t_{CCD} * (8KB/64B) + t_{RP} = 13.75 + 5*128 + 13.75 = 667.5$ ns. In a 2GB module, there are 262144 rows, so reading/writing the entire module would take $t_r * 262144$ ns = 174.98 ms. So, to test a module for a pattern it would take $174.98 + 64 + 174.98$ ms = 413.96 ms. We test the modules with five data patterns, so each round with all data patterns takes 2.06 s. $\ldots(8)$

GDM: Device Memory Management for GPGPU Computing

Kaibo Wang
The Ohio State University
wangka@cse.ohio-state.edu

Xiaoning Ding
New Jersey Institute of Technology
xiaoning.ding@njit.edu

Rubao Lee
The Ohio State University
liru@cse.ohio-state.edu

Shinpei Kato
Nagoya University
shinpei@is.nagoya-u.ac.jp

Xiaodong Zhang
The Ohio State University
zhang@cse.ohio-state.edu

ABSTRACT

GPGPUs are evolving from dedicated accelerators towards mainstream commodity computing resources. During the transition, the lack of system management of device memory space on GPGPUs has become a major hurdle. In existing GPGPU systems, device memory space is still managed explicitly by individual applications, which not only increases the burden of programmers but can also cause application crashes, hangs, or low performance.

In this paper, we present the design and implementation of GDM, a fully functional GPGPU device memory manager to address the above problems and unleash the computing power of GPGPUs in general-purpose environments. To effectively coordinate the device memory usage of different applications, GDM takes control over device memory allocations and data transfers to and from device memory, leveraging a buffer allocated in each application's virtual memory. GDM utilizes the unique features of GPGPU systems and relies on several effective optimization techniques to guarantee the efficient usage of device memory space and to achieve high performance.

We have evaluated GDM and compared it against state-of-the-art GPGPU system software on a range of workloads. The results show that GDM can prevent applications from crashes, including those induced by device memory leaks, and improve system performance by up to 43%.

Categories and Subject Descriptors

C.3 [**Computer Systems Organization**]: Special-Purpose and Application-Based Systems; D.4.8 [**Operating Systems**]: Performance—*Memory management*

Keywords

GPU; Memory Management; Operating System

SIGMETRICS'14, June 16–20, 2014, Austin, Texas, USA.
Copyright 2014 ACM 978-1-4503-2789-3/14/06 ...$15.00.
http://dx.doi.org/10.1145/2591971.2592002.

1. INTRODUCTION

General-purpose GPUs (Graphics Processing Units), a.k.a. GPGPUs[1], are quickly evolving from conventional, dedicated accelerators towards mainstream commodity computing devices, which is driven by the demands for cost-effective high performance from new application domains and supported by GPU hardware and system software advancement [35, 37, 39, 16]. During the transition, system software plays an increasingly important role on managing GPUs. System software relieves application developers from explicit resource management in their programs. It must also coordinate the utilization of GPU resources, ensuring that applications can make continuous progress and no application can be deprived of resource usage indefinitely [22, 23].

Recent research and improvements on GPGPU resource management have mainly focused on supporting GPU abstractions [41], GPU file system [42], and the management of GPU computing units [30, 26, 31]. These system enhancements improve the usability and performance of GPGPU computing. However, despite these improvements, with state-of-the-art GPGPU system software an application still can easily crash, hang, or lose performance (§2.3). The major reason behind this problem is the lack of GPU device memory management at the operating system (OS) level, which has become a major hurdle of GPGPUs as truly general-purpose mainstream computing facilities. This paper identifies these problems and systematically studies the essentiality and design of GPGPU device memory management.

1.1 Problems with Application-Level Device Memory Management

Device memory is the primary onboard DRAM storage for the computation performed on GPU. Unlike system memory where the OS controls space allocation and reclamation, GPU device memory is still directly controlled by individual applications in current systems, which complicates GPGPU application design. In large applications, managing the usage of device memory space is a heavy burden for programmers. There have been numerous reports on application and system crashes [1, 2, 3, 4, 5, 6] caused by application's failure to manage device memory correctly.

Managing device memory space at application level becomes even more difficult when there are multiple applica-

[1]We use GPU and GPGPU interchangeably, with the latter emphasizing more on general-purpose computing.

tions or application components (e.g., multiple worker threads in a server) with conflicting demands for device memory. Due to the lack of an arbitrator to coordinate the conflicts, applications can crash or hang on unexpected shortage of device memory space. Even if an application may manage to survive by using smaller device memory space or shifting computation back to the CPU, its performance can suffer dramatically.

For instance, in Matlab, each worker thread can offload its computation tasks to GPUs for acceleration. However, if their working sets cannot totally fit into the device memory, some workers can easily fail or encounter severe performance degradation [1]. Device memory conflicts will become increasingly common, when GPGPUs are more prevalently adopted in large-scale applications (e.g., Matlab, AutoCAD, relational databases, etc.), or in the cloud where resources are shared by virtual machines [26].

We will discuss the problems with existing GPU system design in more details in §2.3 and illustrate their consequences in §6.

1.2 GDM: OS Device Memory Management

As a critical system resource, device memory space must be managed by the OS to effectively coordinate conflicting demands and to guarantee efficiency. In this paper, we present the design and implementation of GDM(**G**PGPU **D**evice-memory **M**anager) in the OS. With experiments, we show that such a device memory management component in the OS is indispensable for unleashing the high computing power of GPUs in general-purpose systems.

Without requiring modifications to existing APIs, GDM transparently takes control over device memory allocations and data transfers to and from device memory. Instead of letting applications directly allocate device memory space and exchange data with GPUs, GDM sits between applications and GPU devices, acting as an agent and coordinator for carrying out these operations, leveraging a *staging area* created in each application's virtual memory space. It monitors the utilization of device memory space allocated to each application, and dynamically reclaims under-utilized space by swapping out the content to staging areas. In this way, GDM controls and coordinates the actual device memory consumption of different applications, or different phases of a single application, so as to achieve system-wide benefits of performance and service quality. With support of GDM, even multiple applications with conflicting memory requirements can efficiently share the same GPU and make progress concurrently. As we will demonstrate in §6, GDM also enhances the capability of GPGPU systems to tolerate device memory leaks and defend against malicious device memory usage.

The above benefits, however, do not come without any overhead, which is mainly from the extra data movements incurred by GDM management. Several unique characteristics of the GPGPU system make it especially challenging to reduce the overhead. Firstly, GPGPU applications are usually data-intensive. Thus, GDM must handle large sets of data that potentially incur high cost. Secondly, the data-driven nature of GPGPU computing involves synchronizations at various stages, which hinder the overlapping between data transfer and the computation over the data. This makes the performance of GPGPU applications sensitive to the delay caused by data movement. Finally, GPU devices may lack necessary hardware support for efficiently minimizing the overhead, which makes the solution even more challenging. To address these challenges, we have developed a series of optimization techniques in GDM, such as object-level access pattern inference, hashing-based dirty block detection, and cost-aware data replacement policy. These techniques can effectively reduce unnecessary data movement to achieve high performance.

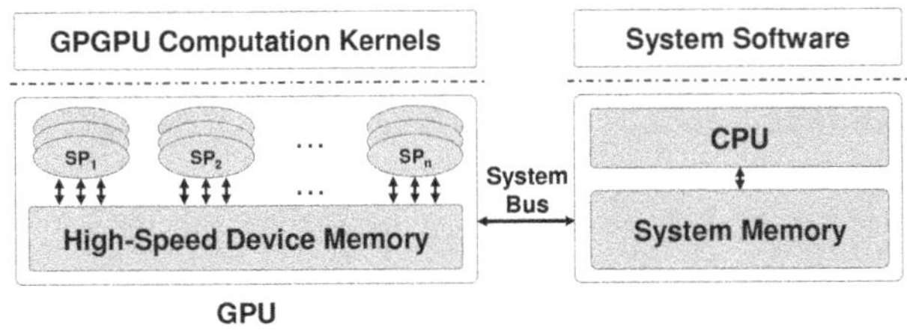

Figure 1: GPGPU system organization.

1.3 Contributions

This paper systematically studies the essentiality and design of GPGPU device memory management. It makes the following main contributions: (1) We have identified and analyzed the serious problems caused by the lack of OS management of device memory space on existing GPGPU systems. (2) We have explored the design space of managing device memory at system level. (3) We have implemented a prototype of GDM in an open-source GPGPU driver and on commonly used hardware to best utilize device memory resource for general-purpose systems, including a set of optimization techniques and principles that are crucial to the performance of device memory management for GPUs. (4) We have conducted extensive performance evaluation on GPU systems with insights. The experiments show that GDM can effectively prevent applications from crashing or stalling due to unexpected shortage of free device memory space. The experiments also show that the optimization techniques can increase system throughput by up to 46%.

2. DEMAND FOR SYSTEM-LEVEL DEVICE MEMORY MANAGEMENT

To deliver high performance, GPGPU computing not only relies on vectorized GPU processors to process data in parallel but also requires high-speed memory to guarantee fast data accesses. Thus, a common practice is to integrate GPU processors with device memory on the same GPU board, which is connected with the system bus to accept data-parallel tasks. This section introduces the system organization, which this paper mainly focuses on, and validates the indispensability of efficient device memory management.

2.1 GPGPU Computing Architecture

GPUs are suitable for performing data-parallel computation. They are often used together with the CPUs to form a hybrid computing system, as shown in Figure 1.

For high performance, a GPU usually has tens of hundreds of stream processors (SPs). Each SP is a many-lane SIMD (Single Instruction Multiple Data) engine. To satisfy data accesses from such a large number of SPs, a wide and fast memory interface must be employed. The device memory designed for GPUs is therefore optimized for high bandwidth and integrated close to the SPs.

Generally, the bandwidth of GPU device memory is several times higher than the bandwidth of system memory accessed by CPUs, which emphasizes more on low latency. For example, a server-class NVIDIA Tesla K10 GPU provides over 300 GB/s device memory access. In contrast, the maximum memory bandwidth of a similar-level Intel Xeon E5-4650 CPU can only reach about 50 GB/s. Compared with system memory, the capacity of device memory, however, is much more limited, due to the pincount and power constraints suffered by the memory technology (e.g. GDDR) used for GPUs [33]. For example, a high-end GPU card is usually equipped with only a few gigabytes of device memory, while tens of gigabytes of system memory has been common on a modern server for years.

GPUs are connected to the system bus to accept data-parallel tasks, which are often called GPGPU kernels (or *kernels* for brevity), and the data to be processed. GPGPU system software is responsible for task scheduling, initiating data transfers, and handling task exceptions. The operations performed by system software are mostly control-intensive, and thus can only be executed efficiently on CPUs.

In the paper, we mainly target the mainstream GPGPU computing architecture described above, in which dedicated device memory modules are used by GPUs to maximize throughput. Another GPGPU architecture, represented by AMD's APU [7], fuses graphics units and CPU cores on the same die and lets them share system memory. It cannot provide the same high computing power as a GPU with dedicated device memory does. Processors with the fused architecture are mostly used in mobile and low-end desktop systems to handle graphics workload at a low cost. The performance is bottlenecked by the number of graphics units that can be integrated on the same CPU chip and by the narrow system memory bandwidth contended by both CPU and graphics cores. To alleviate memory bandwidth bottleneck, there are proposals to integrate fast memory modules (e.g. stacked memory [18] or eDRAM [40]) into this architecture. These memory modules will play an important role to improve the performance of computation on the graphics cores. The principles and techniques developed in this paper can be adapted to manage these memory modules and other accelerators (e.g., DSP) with similar memory structures as well.

2.2 Device Memory: A Critical Resource

Device memory provides a high-speed data storage for GPGPU computing, and must be well managed in order to achieve high performance. Despite its limited capacity, applications have high demands for device memory space. On one hand, as applications become increasingly data-intensive, the data sets handled by a GPGPU task also grows rapidly, requiring larger device memory space. On the other hand, GPGPU applications tend to keep their working sets on the device memory for future reuses to minimize data transfers.

As an example, when GPUs are used to process database queries in data warehousing applications, main accelerator structures such as hash tables have to be loaded into device memory [45]. These data structures can be very large, especially for big-data problems [19]. Meanwhile, these data structures are usually used by different queries repeatedly. Keeping them in the device memory helps improving application performance. The small capacity and the high demands from applications make GPU device memory a critical but limited system resource.

2.3 Issues with Existing System Designs

Despite the cruciality of device memory it has not been well managed by the system. In a general-purpose computing environment, applications are still forced to manually manage device memory on their own. Before a task can be offloaded to GPU, the application must ensure that enough space has been reserved on the device memory and the working set of the task has been transferred to the reserved space. After the task finishes, it also has to decide whether the data sets should continue staying on the device memory in case of reuses by other tasks, or can be transferred back to the system memory to make room for other data to be processed.

The above design used to be more or less acceptable in the early era of GPGPU computing when GPUs were dedicated to applications with clear, static demands for device memory space. However, as both the scale and scope of GPGPU applications expand, it has become an increasingly heavy burden, or impossible, for programmers to correctly keep track of the demands for device memory space and manage the consumption accordingly.

For example, some applications consist of GPU-accelerated modules developed by different groups of developers, or third-party GPGPU libraries and runtimes (e.g., CULA [15], PyCUDA [8], and Theano [17]). It is difficult to monitor and coordinate the device memory space consumption of different components. Applications such as Matlab, Boinc, and GPU databases may also launch multiple workers, whose activities and demands for device memory space depend on user requests and are affected by the OS scheduling. It is laborious and inefficient to deal with such dynamics at the programming stage. When GPGPUs are shared by multiple applications (e.g. in the cloud), managing device memory space inside each individual application also leads to uncoordinated contention for the space.

Due to the complexity of managing device memory, applications may frequently experience shortage of free device memory space. For example one worker thread may not be able to obtain enough device memory space if other worker threads have occupied too much of it. The application may crash or hang if it cannot handle the situation correctly. There have been an increasing number of device memory-related crash reports in both open-source and commercial GPGPU software such as Matlab [1], Boinc [2], and Theano [5]. An application may survive by reducing the granularity of GPGPU tasks or shifting computation back to the CPU dynamically. But either method can significantly reduce application performance. Please note that the shortage of free device memory may happen even when the allocated device memory space is not being actively used, which leads to resource underutilization.

The absence of system management of device memory also causes other system issues. For instance, device memory leaks are a common type of software bugs that exist in many real-world GPGPU systems, including key computation libraries [9, 3], popular language runtimes [5, 6], and widely-deployed applications [10, 11]. Without system management, the leaked memory space cannot be reclaimed until the leaking application crashes or is terminated. This shrinks the device memory space available to applications and significantly degrades system performance. Even worse, without system management, a malicious program can reserve most device memory space without releasing it, causing the whole GPGPU system unusable.

2.4 Demand for System Management

The above issues cannot be effectively addressed at application level due to the lack of system-wide information and the authority required for managing a shared resource. For example, a library that implements device memory management functionalities can relieve the burden of application programmers. However, a library can only provide local management within each individual application or application component adopting the library. The conflicting demands between applications or application components still cannot be addressed.

To address the above issues, GPGPU system software must be enhanced to control device memory management. This will not only relieve application developers from this tedious obligation, but also present an arbitrator to coordinate the contention for device memory space. With the new improvements of GPU hardware and firmware, especially those to support multitasking [38, 25], the application domains and environments of GPGPU computing will continue expanding. The demand for system management of device memory space is also becoming more imperative.

The demand for system management of device memory is analogous to that for the OS to manage the physical space of system memory [21]. Before virtual memory was introduced, the large efforts spent by programmers to incorporate memory overlaying procedures into their programs proved inefficient and unrealistic as applications became increasingly complex. Nowadays, in almost all modern systems, the physical space of system memory is managed by the OS; applications just need to allocate and deallocate objects in their virtual spaces to use system memory.

However, unlike system memory management, because of the special characteristics of GPGPU systems and applications, the management of device memory must address a set of unique challenges to achieve high performance. We will introduce these challenges and the design of GDM in the next two sections.

3. GDM OVERVIEW

The objective of GDM is to take over the control of device memory space from applications without changing current APIs for device memory operations. For this purpose, GDM creates a ***Staging Area*** in each GPGPU application's virtual memory space. This staging area effectively serves as the device memory extensions for the GPU kernels launched in the application. Thus, device memory operations from the application can be redirected to the corresponding staging area, while the actual control of device memory space is released to GDM.

Figure 2 illustrates the positions of GDM and GDM staging areas in the system and how GDM interacts with other system components. GDM is built as part of the GPGPU driver in the OS. It intercepts and handles device memory related operations from GPGPU applications. GDM handles an allocation operation (e.g., *cuMemAlloc* in CUDA [39]) by allocating the required space in the staging area. Data to be transferred to device memory is first copied to the staging area, and is later transferred to the device memory when the kernel accessing the data is launched. This is shown

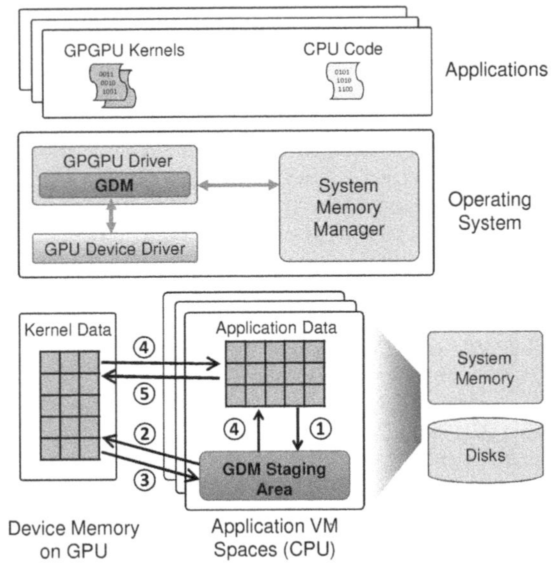

Figure 2: Overall Architecture of GDM.

with the arrows ① and ② respectively. After the kernel finishes, the data may stay in the device memory. When the device memory is short of free space, GDM transfers some data back to the corresponding staging area and reclaims the space, as shown by arrow ③. When an application calls the function to copy some data (e.g. computation results) from the device memory, GDM locates the latest version of the data (either in the staging area or in the device memory) and copies the data to the user buffer designated by the application. The arrows marked by ④ show the data transfers. To handle a deallocation operation (e.g. *cuMemFree* in CUDA), GDM frees and reclaims the corresponding space in both the staging area and the device memory.

3.1 Minimizing Overhead: A Major Challenge

GDM relieves applications from the burden of directly managing device memory space. While it avoids the problems due to uncoordinated usage of device memory space, the benefit does not come without cost. The main overhead of GDM is from the extra data copying (to and from staging areas) and data transferring (to and from device memory).

Some unique features of the GPU hardware and GPGPU application execution model make minimizing the overhead particularly challenging. Firstly, kernels running on GPU devices are usually data-intensive. Transferring large data sets over system bus may incur high overhead[2]. As shown from previous studies [41, 24] and our own measurement (§6.1), data transfers already account for a considerable portion of GPU operation time for many applications. If the amount of data movement incurred by GDM cannot be effectively controlled, the benefits of device memory management can be easily out-weighted by the potential high cost, diminishing the usefulness of the whole system.

Secondly, the performance of GPGPU applications is sensitive to the delays caused by bulky data transfers. The data-driven nature of GPGPU computing requires synchronizations at various stages. For example, a kernel cannot be launched before the transfer of its input data to the device memory finishes. These synchronization barriers reduce

[2]Data transfer rate via system bus is about one order of magnitude lower than device memory bandwidth.

the opportunities of overlapping operations before and after the synchronization points, making application performance sensitive to the delays on these operations. Among these operations, most are related to data transfers between the CPU and the device. Thus, the extra data transfers incurred by GDM management may degrade application performance if not handled properly. Meanwhile, system bus transactions are usually non-preemptive. A data transfer through PCIe, for example, cannot be interrupted once the DMA command is sent to the GPU copy engine. This exacerbates the problem caused by GDM-initiated data movement.

Finally, some hardware facilities for minimizing the cost have not been or cannot be efficiently implemented on GPUs. For example, in current GPU designs, there is no support for page reference bits to track fine-grained data access patterns. This poses great challenges to identifying inactive device memory areas. Hardware setting page dirty bits, a convenient feature for detecting data modifications, is also missing. On GPUs, page faults usually incur prohibitive costs [36]. On some GPGPU systems, page faults even cause application crashes. As far as we know, in the foreseeable future, there have not been clear plans on improving these facilities in GPU hardware.

To address these challenges, GDM minimizes the cost following two directions. One is to minimize data movements. This is achieved mainly through lazy copying, exploiting data locality, and careful classification of the data. The other direction is to reduce the latency incurred by data movements. GDM reduces the latency in two ways. Without compromising the correctness of program executions, GDM implicitly makes the handling of some heavy synchronous operations asynchronous to user programs, allowing programs to proceed while the operation is delegated to GDM for processing. GDM also internally breaks some bulky synchronous operations into several smaller pieces so that the processing of one piece can be overlapped with another to reduce costs. This also practically makes a long, bulky operation interruptible.

3.2 Guidelines for GDM Design

There are a few guidelines that have greatly influenced the design of GDM. One important guideline regards the choice between ***demand loading and anticipatory loading.*** In the paper, we classify the methods of loading data to memory into two categories, namely *demand loading* and *anticipatory loading*. Demand loading refers to the method in which data loading is triggered by data accesses. It is usually achieved by hardware-supported exception mechanisms. For example, in demand paging, page fault handler is triggered automatically by hardware when a page being accessed is not present in the memory. The page fault handler loads the missing page from the disk and may prefetch a few more pages that it predicts to be accessed soon.

Anticipatory loading refers to the method in which the working set of a task is loaded into memory before the task is scheduled to run. It is the mechanism used in current GPGPU computing systems. An application reserves device memory space and transfers the working set of a GPU kernel to the device memory before it launches the kernel.

Demand loading is motivated by the high cost of loading data into memory. It pays the cost of handling page faults to load only the data that is demanded by the application and minimize the cost incurred by loading extra data. Anticipatory loading is more advantageous when the data sets handled by an application can be accurately determined before its execution. Though there are proposals to provide hardware support for demand paging on GPUs [36, 32], we argue that anticipatory loading will continue playing an important role in device memory management on future GPU devices. This is based on the following two observations.

In contrast with the data sets handled by CPUs, the data sets handled by GPUs are usually more predictable before the kernel starts execution. For example, some data sets to be referenced can be inferred from the data transfer APIs (e.g. *cuMemcpyHtoD* in CUDA) before launching a kernel; some are specified in the parameters of the GPU kernel. This makes anticipatory loading a viable approach in practice.

Handling page faults on a GPU incurs much higher overhead than doing so on a CPU, because it stalls a *faster* processor for a *longer* time. A GPU kernel is usually executed by hundreds of thousands of threads on a GPU, with the running state of each thread maintained in large register files, shared memory, and hardware caches which are often virtually addressed [34]. Saving the state of a GPU kernel on page faults, flushing caches, and restoring kernel state to resume execution thus take much longer time than that on the CPU. As the numbers of GPU cores and threads launched by GPU kernels keep increasing on future GPUs, the cost of handling page faults will also escalate significantly. Moreover, handling GPU page faults requires the involvement of system software running on the CPU (e.g., to carry out the corresponding memory management and re-scheduling operations). The extra delays and operations on the critical path of page fault handling further prolongs GPU stall time. The large overhead associated with page fault handling on a GPU thus may not be justified.

In GDM design, we use anticipatory loading for the data sets that are predicted to be accessed. To minimize the overhead incurred by handling page faults, demand loading is only used to handle unexpected data accesses if the GPU device supports page faults.

The second guideline regards the ***the granularities of device memory management*** to match the data-parallel nature of GPGPU computing. The granularities determine the units in which data in the staging areas and device memory space should be managed. In system memory management, memory page of a few kilobytes is a commonly used granularity by the OS. But this granularity is too small for GPGPU computing. The data-parallel feature of GPGPU computing determines that the data sets handled in GPGPU programs are usually very large (even the register file sizes on GPUs are at least hundreds of kilobytes). Using small granularities increases the overhead of managing metadata. More importantly, data transfers to and from the device memory in small units cannot amortize the start-up latency of memory controller, incurring prohibitive costs.

Memory regions have been used in several studies. A device memory region is allocated by the user program through the memory reservation API call, and can be as large as hundreds of megabytes or even gigabytes. Thus, data transfers in units of regions can cause high synchronization and data movement overhead. Moreover, managing data at the region level is incapable of capturing the distinct access patterns of user data structures created within a single region, which are important information for the management of device memory space.

Ideal granularities are those that can balance the latency and throughput of data movement and can preserve program-level data structure information to minimize overhead. GDM manages device memory space with both *block* and *object*-level information. We will introduce these concepts and how GDM utilizes them for management in the next section.

The third guideline regards the ***generality*** of GDM design. We realize that GPU hardware design is still evolving towards mature, general-purpose computing device. Thus, in our design, we do not exclude possible new features in future GPU hardware that may help with device memory management. At the same time, we try to keep the GDM design as general as possible. We explore the techniques that can minimize its reliance on the uncertainties of future GPU hardware features. This also helps it be adopted, starting with current GPU hardware.

4. GDM DESIGN

This section presents the details of GDM, focusing on the design tradeoffs and optimization techniques for minimizing the overhead of device memory management.

4.1 Staging Areas

GDM creates a staging area for each GPGPU application in its virtual memory space. Instead of using a large chunk of space with continuous virtual addresses, a staging area consists of a set of virtual memory areas. These areas are dynamically allocated when GDM handles the requests from applications for device memory reservations. Because these areas are located in the application's virtual memory space, physical memory is not allocated until they are populated.

Staging areas first serve as a temporary storage for the data to be transferred onto device memory. With staging areas, data transfers to the device memory can be fulfilled asynchronously. Specifically, when an application calls the API function to transfer some data from a user source buffer to the device memory, this function returns after GDM marks the source buffer copy-on-write. The data is transferred to the device memory later from the source buffer if it has not been changed (arrow ⑤ in Figure 2). Otherwise, the data is copied to the staging area when it is about to be changed in the source buffer, and is later transferred to the device memory from the staging area. In many GPGPU applications, a source buffer is often not modified before the data transferred from it is used in a kernel. Thus, copy-on-write can effectively reduce the memory consumption of staging areas and the cost incurred by data copying.

Staging areas also serve as the swap space for the data that can no longer stay on the device memory due to space contentions. When an application needs more free device memory space to launch kernels, GDM evicts some data from device memory to the staging area and reclaims the space for its own data sets. The data swapped to the staging area may later be loaded back to the device memory when the kernel referencing the data is to be issued.

Creating staging areas inside the virtual address spaces of applications provides a few benefits. The low-level management of staging areas, from space allocation/deallocation to data swapping between system memory and disks when the system memory is under pressure, relies on the existing virtual memory manager in the operating system. This, on one hand, simplifies the design of GDM. On the other hand, it puts the system memory space occupied by staging areas under the unified management with other system components and applications. This helps the operating system balance system memory usage for the overall benefit of system performance.

```
cuMemAlloc(&region1, 800MB);
dest_buf_1 = region1;
cuMemcpyHtoD(dest_buf_1, src_buf_1, 400MB);
dest_buf_2 = dest_buf_1 + 400MB;
cuMemcpyHtoD(dest_buf_2, src_buf_2, 200MB);
dest_buf_3 = dest_buf_2 + 200MB;
cuMemcpyHtoD(dest_buf_3, src_buf_3, 10KB);
```

Figure 3: Device memory region and object.

4.2 Device Memory Regions, Objects, Blocks

A fundamental design decision to make is the granularity at which the device memory space should be managed. One natural choice is device memory region. A device memory ***region*** is allocated/deallocated by the user program through the device memory reservation/release API calls. Applications may reserve different regions for different data sets to be handled by GPU kernels. In these cases, data in the same memory region may show good access uniformity; managing data based on regions can thus be an efficient choice. Regions have been used as the units of device memory management in some existing studies [31, 29].

However, in some important GPGPU applications [28, 44], we do see cases in which a memory region includes multiple data sets with distinct access patterns (e.g. data structures with different read/write properties or being referenced by different kernels). Data sets can also be shared among different GPU contexts easily with a single IPC call, which makes the program structure much clearer to maintain. For these applications, managing data with regions fails to classify fine-grained data access characteristics and increases both space and data movement overhead.

GDM identifies this demand and adds an object-based memory management layer below regions to differentiate data sets with different access patterns in each memory region. In GDM, an ***object*** is a data set handled by a data transfer operation. This is based on the observation that programs usually invoke separate data transfer API calls to pack multiple data sets into the same device memory region. The region area modified by each data transfer API call corresponds to an object in GDM. For efficiency, GDM merges small objects with their neighboring objects in the same device memory region. As an example, based on the pseudo code snippet in Figure 3, GDM creates one region (i.e. *region1*) and three objects, one for *dest_buf_1*, one for *dest_buf_2* , and one for the rest part of the region.

Objects can still be very large and cumbersome to manage. Meanwhile, object sizes usually vary widely in GPGPU programs, which introduces unnecessary complexity and overhead in memory management. For example, transferring large objects leads to high synchronization cost; evicting a whole object lowers the utilization of device memory if the required space is smaller than the object size. To address these problems, GDM further breaks objects into fixed-size ***blocks***. Then, it allocates/reclaims device memory space and transfers data in units of blocks. The block size is selected to effectively amortize the start-up latency of data transfers.

As will be explained in the following subsections, this hierarchical layout of regions, objects, and blocks makes the management of device memory space especially efficient.

4.3 Loading Data to Device Memory

For the correct and efficient execution of a kernel, GDM must load the working set of the kernel onto device memory. Basically, two key questions must be addressed: which data sets should be loaded, and when should they be loaded.

To address the first question, GDM uses different techniques for different types of GPU devices. If page faults are correctly supported on the GPU device, GDM monitors and analyzes the parameters used to launch a GPU kernel and the data transfer API calls made before the kernel launch. It extracts the objects involved in the parameters and API calls. Usually these objects are the data sets to be handled by the kernel. For these objects, GDM transfers the data block by block into the device memory before the kernel is issued (i.e. anticipatory loading). Other data sets, if accessed, will be loaded on demand on page faults.

If page faults are not supported, GDM by default loads the whole context to the device memory. To reduce data transferring, GDM provides interfaces for programs to specify objects needed by a kernel, with which advanced programmers can direct GDM to only load the specified objects.

For anticipatory loading, another key question is what is the good time to transfer the data sets to device memory. If a data set is transferred to the device memory too early, it may be evicted prematurely before the kernel referencing it is issued. This incurs extra data transfers. If a data set is transferred to the device memory too late, the execution of the kernel will be delayed.

In a busy system, where kernels queue up waiting to be issued, the system throughput depends on how quickly these kernels can be issued. Thus, the most efficient way is to transfer the data sets used by the kernels according to the order of the kernels in the queue. When GDM finishes transferring the data sets used by a kernel, it can start to transfer the data sets used by the next kernel in the queue. In this way, GDM can overlap data transfers with GPU computation to a great extent and minimize the time that kernels must wait for their working sets.

When all the launched kernels have been issued, if the device memory still has free space and the GPU copy engine is idle, GDM will trace back recent application requests of data transfers to the device memory for unfulfilled requests. As explained in Section 4.1, with staging areas, GDM handles data transfer requests to the device memory asynchronously. Thus, there may be some data sets in staging areas that have not been transferred to the device memory even the applications have requested to do so (e.g. by calling *cuMemcpyHtoD*). GDM takes the opportunity and loads these data sets onto device memory because they are more likely to be accessed in kernels soon. To prevent performance loss, GDM stops loading the data when the device memory is filled. GDM also stops loading the data when a kernel is launched, so that the GPU copy engine can be quickly released to transfer the data sets of the newly launched kernel.

4.4 Management of Device Memory Space

GDM makes every effort to satisfy the device memory demand of the kernel to be issued. If the device memory is short of free space, GDM must evict some data of finished kernels and reclaim the space. Thus, a core issue with the management of device memory space is data replacement, i.e. the policy that determines which data sets should be evicted when the free device memory space is insufficient.

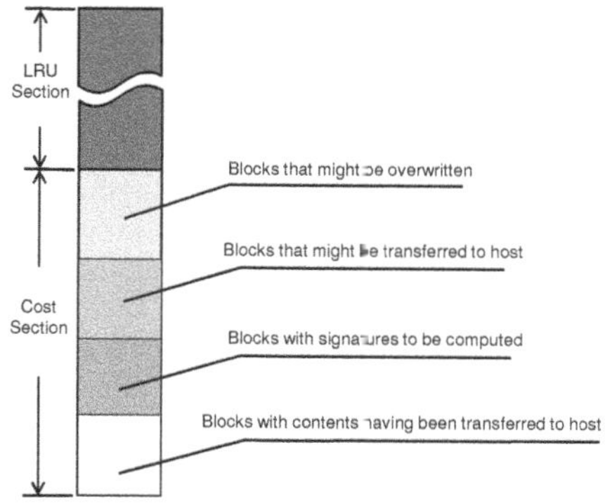

Figure 4: An LRU stack is structured for the LRU-COST replacement policy.

A large number of replacement policies have been proposed in previous studies of system memory and buffer management. The goal of these policies is mainly to maximize hit ratios, i.e. reuses of data in the memory. Every time when a replacement decision has to be made, these policies try to select an item that is least possible to be reused in the future.

However, conventional replacement policies are usually designed for systems where small amounts of data (e.g. pages or blocks) are loaded on demand. Directly adopting them will lead to sub-optimal performance in GPGPU systems, where usually a large amount of data (e.g. that can fill two thirds of device memory capacity) must be loaded before the corresponding kernel can start execution. Therefore, in GDM, other than maximizing hit ratios, the design of a replacement policy must achieve an additional goal — minimizing the time to spare the space for loading the data sets of the incoming kernel. The latency of readying the required space has direct impact on application performance.

GDM enhances the LRU replacement policy to maximize data reuses in the device memory and to minimize the latency of data eviction. The replacement policy with the enhancement is named *LRU-COST* [3]. LRU-COST uses a stack to manage the data sets loaded into the device memory. When a kernel is issued, all the data sets it will operate are put on the top of the LRU stack, pushing existing data sets in the stack down towards the bottom. As shown in Figure 4, LRU-COST partitions the stack into two sections. The part on the top is named *LRU section*, and the part at the bottom is named *COST section*. The size of COST section is from 0 to $selection\_factor \times len\_stack$, where $selection\_factor$ is an adjustable parameter with a default value of 0.2 and len_stack is the size of the whole stack. Data sets in the COST section are classified and sorted to minimize the eviction cost, as we will explain later. The data sets with the lowest costs are put at the bottom. When more free space is needed, LRU-COST selects the data sets at the bottom of COST section to evict. When COST section is depleted, it is refilled with the data sets in the LRU section that belong to the working sets of finished kernels. It preferentially selects the data sets at the bottom of the LRU section until it reaches its maximum size.

The cost of evicting a data set is determined by its status. Evicting a *clean* data set incurs lower cost than evicting a

[3]While other replacement policies can also be enhanced with similar approach, we select LRU because it is widely used and easy to implement.

dirty one. A data set is clean if it has not been changed since it is loaded to the device memory. Otherwise, the data set is dirty. The cost of evicting a clean data set is minimal, because there is a copy of the data set in the virtual memory space of the application, either in the staging area or in the corresponding source buffer. To evict a dirty data set, some cost has to be paid to transfer the data back to the staging area to preserve the changes.

In real-world applications, usually a considerable portion of GPU data is read-only during kernel executions. For example, based on our analysis of 16 benchmarks in the Rodinia benchmark suite [20], on average, 61% of all the GPU data referenced during kernel executions are not modified. Thus, there is a good potential to improve performance by preferentially evicting clean data sets.

In the future, the clean/dirty status of data sets may be traced by hardware automatically. However, as mentioned earlier, existing GPU hardware does not provide such support. Thus, after a kernel finishes execution, GDM has no immediate information to determine whether a data set has been modified. If GDM cannot find a way to differentiate clean data from dirty data, it must write back the data sets being evicted indiscriminately to the corresponding staging areas. This may significantly increase wasteful system bus traffic and cause delay of kernel execution.

To address this problem, GDM computes a signature for each data block in the COST section, which is a set of MD5 hash values of the data in the block (please refer to §5.2 for details). When the COST section is refilled, GDM immediately issues a maintenance kernel to compute the new signatures for the data blocks in the section from bottom to top. If the new signature of a block is different from its previous signature or if its previous signature does not exist, the block is marked dirty. For a 4MB block, its signature can be kept with only 4KB and is transferred along with the block. Computing the signature of a data block on a GPU can be made over an order of magnitude faster than transferring the data back to the staging area.

Although computing signatures can significantly reduce the data traffic on system bus, it increases the workload of GPU processors. When there are other application kernels that have been issued on the device, the maintenance kernel and the application kernels may compete for GPU processors. This reduces system throughput (because the execution of application kernels is delayed) and/or increase the latency incurred by data eviction (because computing signatures is delayed). To address the above problem, GDM uses three heuristics to reduce the amount of computation.

Uniformity Heuristic: In the same object, if the first data block, the data block in the middle of the object, and the last data block are dirty blocks, GDM assumes that other blocks are also dirty blocks. This is based on the observation that kernels usually carry out similar operations on the data in the same object, because of the data-parallel nature of GPGPU computing. This is to reduce signature computation for write-mostly data.

Overwrite Elimination: A data block in the device memory is invalidated and its space can be reclaimed when the application overwrites its content via a data transfer API call. This usually takes place when an application performs computation on a data set larger than device memory capacity. In a loop, the application repeatedly updates its data in the device memory and launches a kernel to process each partition of the data set. Thus, if GDM expects a block may be invalidated based on its overwriting history, it gives a low priority to computing its signature by putting it on the top of the COST section (see Figure 4). This heuristic can be used to reduce signature computation for both read-mostly and write-mostly data.

Double-Transfer Avoidance: A data block becomes a clean block if the application calls an API to copy its content out from the device memory. Thus, if GDM expects that a data block may be transferred to system memory upon application requests, it gives a low priority to computing its signature by putting it far away from the bottom of the COST section (refer to Figure 4). When the content has been transferred and the block is still in the COST section, GDM moves the block to the bottom of the stack.

To apply the last two heuristics, GDM keeps track of the blocks that changed status to "clean" or were overwritten, and use the information as hints to predict whether the behaviors will repeat.

5. IMPLEMENTATION

We have implemented a prototype of GDM in the GPGPU driver, Gdev [31], on Linux. We choose Gdev because it is open-source and has been shown in previous research [31] to perform comparably with the proprietary commercial CUDA system. Our prototype system targets discrete GPU cards, which are usually connected to the host CPU system through PCIe bus. In this section, we highlight some of the implementation details that deserve articulation.

5.1 Regions, Blocks, and Objects

When an application reserves a device memory region, GDM allocates two virtual memory areas for it: one from the CPU program's virtual memory space, which is used as the region's staging area; the other from the GPU context's virtual device address space, which is used by the GPU kernels to access data in the region. The starting address of the virtual device memory area is returned to the application as the identifier of the data region allocated. We set block size to 4MB in our prototype system, which is small enough compared with common object sizes in GPGPU programs and meanwhile preserves over 98% of PCIe efficiency. Nouveau [12], the GPU device driver Gdev relies on, currently does not allow users to allocate/deallocate virtual and physical device memory areas separately, nor does it support dynamic mapping/unmapping between them. We have thus modified the source code of Nouveau (less than 400 lines of changes) to expose such functionalities to GDM.

Objects are maintained by GDM to infer user data structures and improve data replacement efficiency. Initially, every data region is a single object. A host-to-device data transfer, if larger than block size, can split an object into two or three smaller objects and/or merge several objects into a larger one. In our implementation, objects are aligned at the block boundary.

5.2 Signature Computing

By definition, computing the MD5 hash value of a given data block is inherently sequential. A block has to be logically broken into 64-byte chunks. For each chunk, a 16-byte hash value is computed based on the data in this chunk and the hash value computed from the previous chunk. The hash value computed for the last chunk is used as the MD5 hash

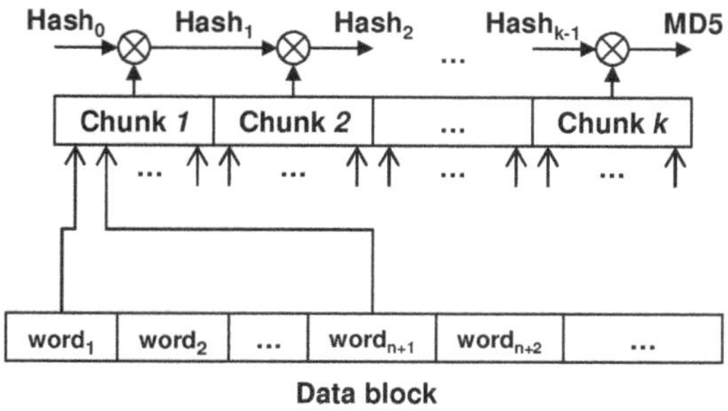

Figure 5: The Computation of data signatures.

value of the whole data block. To enable efficient parallelization on GPUs, GDM computes an array of MD5 hash values, instead of a single one, for a data block, and uses them together as the signature of the block.

This is illustrated in Figure 5. The data in a block are equally partitioned among GPU threads; each thread computes a MD5 hash value for the data assigned to it. Consecutive 4-byte words are allocated to different threads, so that device memory accesses can be coalesced for maximal kernel efficiency. Figure 5 shows how a data block is partitioned and the MD5 computed by one thread in an n-thread kernel. The signature of the data block comprises the MD5 values computed by all GPU threads. Optimal number of threads for computing the signature of a data block is determined by the block size and GPU hardware parameters. In our implementation, we set the number of threads per 4MB data block to 256, which achieves very good performance. To maximize GPU core utilization, GDM computes the signatures of multiple blocks in one kernel, which further improves performance.

6. EVALUATION

This section evaluates GDM under various workloads. Before presenting the results, we first introduce the setup and methodology of our experiments.

6.1 Experiment Setup and Methodology

The experiments were carried out on a machine equipped with a 2.80GHz Intel Core i7-860 CPU, 8GB system memory, and an NVIDIA GTX 480 GPU card[4]. The operating system is Red Hat Enterprise Linux 6 running 3.3 kernel. The GPU device driver is Nouveau patched with our code to enable separate allocation of virtual and physical device memory areas and dynamic mapping between them. The GPGPU drivers are Gdev (i.e. the stock Gdev) and GDM (i.e. Gdev with GDM enhancement). The CUDA compiler is NVIDIA nvcc 4.0. Excluding the space reserved by Gdev and Nouveau, there is about 1400MB of device memory space available to user applications.

The benchmarks used in our experiments, as listed below, represent a variety of typical GPGPU applications and systems, including scientific computing, databases, machine learning, and image processing. Among them, four benchmarks, *backprop*, *hotspot*, *nn*, and *srad*, were selected from the Rodinia benchmark suite. Other benchmarks were extracted from real-world applications or existing open-source projects.

[4]We choose a GPU with NVIDIA GF100 architecture because Gdev supports it most reliably. Other GPUs (e.g. Kepler) are fundamentally the same with respect to memory management.

Name	Size (MB)	Name	Size (MB)
backprop	668	mpe	658
hj	2114	nn	1138
hotspot	1316	srad	619
kmeans	120	theano	4253

Table 1: Total size of device memory space allocated in each benchmark.

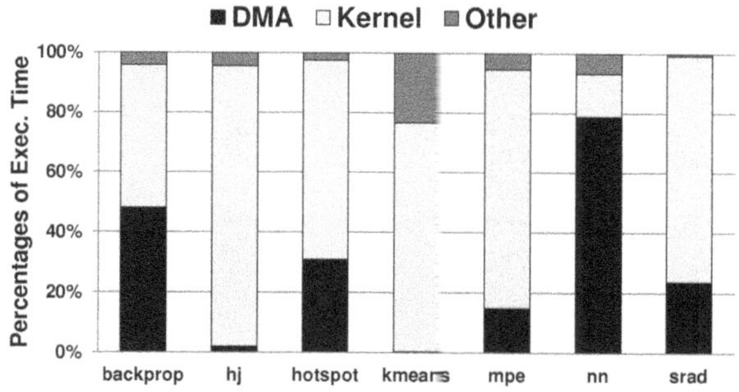

Figure 6: Decompositions of benchmark execution times.

- **backprop** is an implementation of the backpropagation machine learning algorithm.
- **hj** performs a hash join operation over two database table columns. The data types of the two columns are both four-byte integers.
- **hotspot** solves a differential function extracted from a popular thermal modeling tool called HotSpot.
- **kmeans** implements the k-means clustering algorithm that partitions an array of multidimensional data elements into several clusters [13].
- **mpe** evaluates the value of expression $A \times B + C \times D$, in which A, B, C, D are four large matrices.
- **nn** computes the k-nearest neighbors of a given target within a large cloud of data points.
- **srad** is a diffusion method used mainly in ultrasonic and radar imaging applications to remove speckles.
- **theano** reproduces a real-world device memory leak bug in the Theano scientific Python library (the first commit in [5]). This bug is caused by incorrect increment of the reference counting value for a device memory region.

These benchmarks are highly optimized to maximize the utilization of GPU cores and have different demands for device memory space. The total size of device memory regions allocated in each benchmark is listed in Table 1. Figure 6 shows the percentages of execution time spent on DMA transfers, GPU kernels, and other operations (e.g., CPU computations and disk accesses) when each benchmark executes alone with stock Gdev. *theano* is DMA-bound and is not drawn because it crashes due to device memory leak and cannot finish execution with stock Gdev. As shown in Figure 6, all the benchmarks are GPGPU-intensive. At the same time, they incur different amount of data movement between the host and GPU device. Thus, the benchmarks can stress the design of GDM and test its components to minimize data movement overhead.

We evaluated GDM under two types of workloads: solo runs and combo runs. In a solo run, a benchmark executes alone. In a combo run, two benchmarks co-run with each other, and the benchmarks run multiple times to ensure the full overlap of their executions. Since our imple-

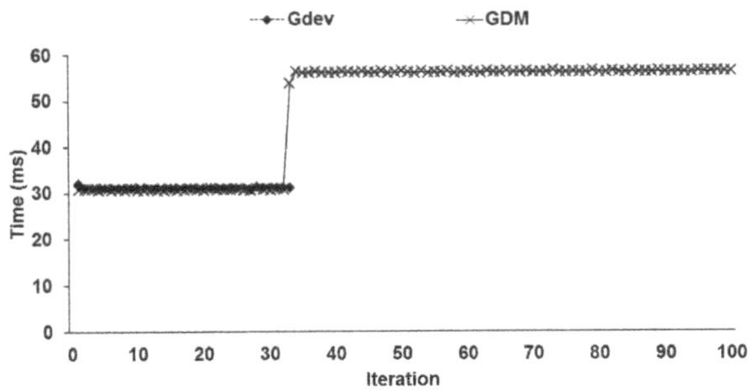

(a) Performance of theano over time.

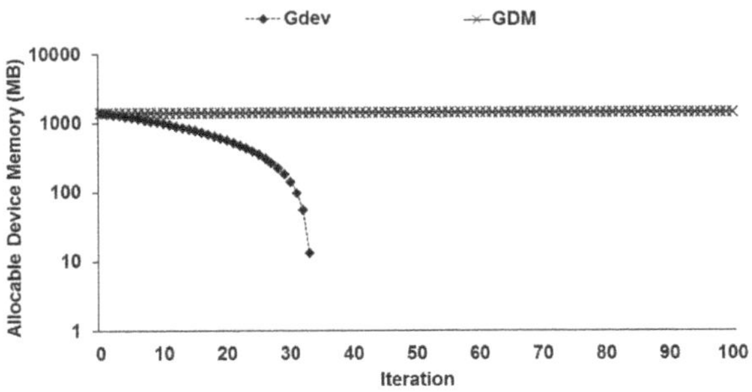

(b) Size of allocable device memory over time.

Figure 7: The impact of device memory leaks with and without GDM management.

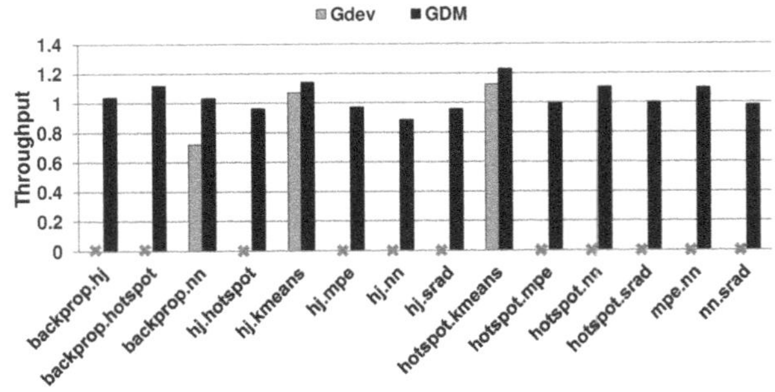

(a) Throughput of workloads with device memory contentions (A 'X' mark means the corresponding combo run crashed and the throughput could not be measured).

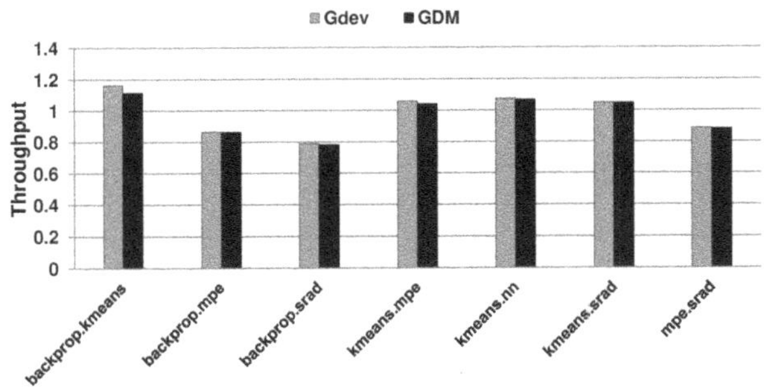

(b) Throughput of workloads without device memory contentions.

Figure 8: Performance of multitasking workloads with and without GDM management.

mentation of GDM is built into Gdev, we use the performance with the stock Gdev as baseline. The metrics we use to compare the performance are execution time for solo runs and weighted speedup for combo-runs. The weighted speedup of a combo run is the sum of the speedups of the participating benchmarks over their solo executions, i.e., $\sum_{i=1}^{n}(solo\_time_i/combo\_time_i)$ [43]. For brevity, we call the weighted speedup of a combo run its throughput.

6.2 Tolerating Device Memory Leaks

Leveraging host memory and, subsequently, disks as swap space, GDM identifies and removes inactive blocks from the device memory. This greatly postpones device memory exhaustion and increases the capability of the system to tolerate device memory leaks.

We use *theano* as a real-world example to demonstrate this advantage. *theano* is a Python script written using the Theano library. It invokes an in-place add operation for 100 times in a loop. In each iteration, the underlying Theano runtime creates an array on the device memory and launches a GPU kernel to update the elements in the array with an incremental value. However, there is a bug in Theano and the array is not released by Theano when the iteration finishes, adding a memory leak delta of about 40MB.

Figure 7(a) shows the per-iteration execution times of *theano*. Figure 7(b) illustrates the amount of allocable device memory (in logarithmic scale) after each iteration. Without GDM support, the leak quickly drains the device memory and causes *theano* to crash before one third of the iterations can be finished. Gdev cannot deal with device memory leaks in this case because data swapping is not fully supported.

In the experiment, we use the stock Gdev as a representative of exiting GPGPU systems without fully functional device memory management. However, the problem demonstrated with it is not limited to Gdev, but exists in similar systems too. For example, we have also run *theano* with the commercial NVIDIA driver; it crashes after 36 iterations.

With GDM support, though the device memory may be filled, the space occupied by leaked regions can be reclaimed and is considered to be allocable. This allows *theano* to continue launching kernels and making progress continuously. Thus, *theano* is able to complete execution correctly. Since the leaked regions are modified during kernel executions, GDM incurs a constant overhead on data swapping after iteration 33. But, before GDM starts to swap out leaked regions, it does not slow down *theano*, as shown in Figure 7(a).

6.3 Multitasking Performance

In this subsection, we study the performance of GDM under multitasking workloads. We select all the possible combo runs consisting of two of the benchmarks excluding *theano*. We classify them into two groups based on their device memory demands. The first group have 14 combo runs with high demands. In each combo run, the total demand exceeds the device memory capacity, and the benchmarks contend for device memory space during the execution. The second group consists of the rest 7 combo runs. They have low demands for device memory space, and the benchmarks can share the device memory without contention. Before starting the combo-run experiments, we first measured the solo execution times of each benchmark with the stock Gdev and GDM respectively. Due to management activities, GDM performs slightly slower than the stock Gdev, but the difference is less than 2% on average.

Figure 8(a) shows the throughput of the combo runs in the first group with Gdev and GDM. With GDM, all the combo runs can finish their executions correctly. However, with Gdev, only 3 combo runs can finish without failures.

Eleven combo runs suffer program crashes, which happen to either one or both participating benchmarks. We have also performed the same experiment with commercial NVIDIA driver; all combo runs in the first group failed due to program crashes.

Most combo runs fail without GDM support because state-of-the-art approaches either do not support (e.g. CUDA) or use only primitive memory management policies (e.g. Gdev). For example, Gdev implements a simple data swapping mechanism based on its shared device memory support. With Gdev, when a region A in application P is to be loaded into the device memory short of free space, only a *single* region whose size is *larger* than A can be selected under the strict conditions that (1) it is not in application P, and (2) it has never replaced or been replaced by any other regions than A in P. If a region cannot be found to meet these constraints, the program may be blocked or crash due to insufficient device memory space for it to launch kernels. Unlike Gdev, GDM provides fully functional device memory management that allows the device memory space to be flexibly shared by any regions. This guarantees the successful executions of GPGPU applications on multitasking systems.

Figure 8(a) also shows that GDM can handle device memory contentions more efficiently than the stock Gdev. With Gdev, even though a few combo runs successfully finish their executions, they suffer substantial performance losses. For example, for the combo run of *backprop* and *nn*, the throughput achieved with the stock Gdev is only 70% of that with GDM. Due to the lack of necessary mechanisms and policies to reduce data movement, Gdev cannot support data swapping with low overhead. The optimization techniques in GDM can effectively minimize the overhead. Thus, GDM can improve the performance of these workloads by 20% on average (up to 43%).

Figure 8(b) compares the performance of GDM and the stock Gdev under the workloads in the second group. For all the workloads except the co-running of *backprop* and *kmeans*, the performance difference between GDM and Gdev is barely observable. When *backprop* co-runs with *kmeans*, the throughput with GDM is slightly lower (by 4%) than that with Gdev. This shows the low overhead of GDM for multitasking workloads without device memory contentions.

6.4 Validation of Design Optimizations

Throughout the design of GDM, optimization techniques are adopted to minimize data transfers and the associated cost. In this subsection, we validate the effectiveness of these optimization techniques through experiments. We compare the performance of the full-fledged GDM with a simplified version of GDM, named GDM-Base, which only provides basic management over device memory to guarantee the correct executions of the combo-run workloads.

Specifically, GDM-Base handles host-to-device data transfer eagerly. It carries out data transfers immediately upon application's requests (e.g. *cuMemcpyHtoD*). When the device memory is short of free space, traditional LRU algorithm is used to select a victim data set to replace. The victim data set is transferred back to the corresponding staging area. When a kernel is to be launched, GDM-Base examines the data sets in the context, and loads the data sets that are not resident in the device memory.

Since the overhead of device memory management is mainly incurred when device memory space is under pressure, we

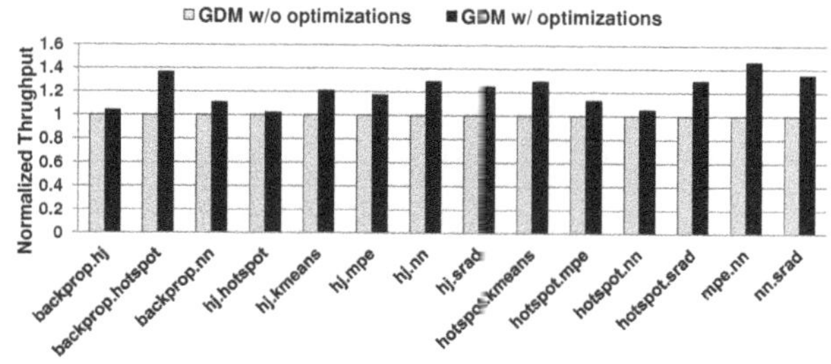

(a) Normalized throughput with and without GDM optimizations.

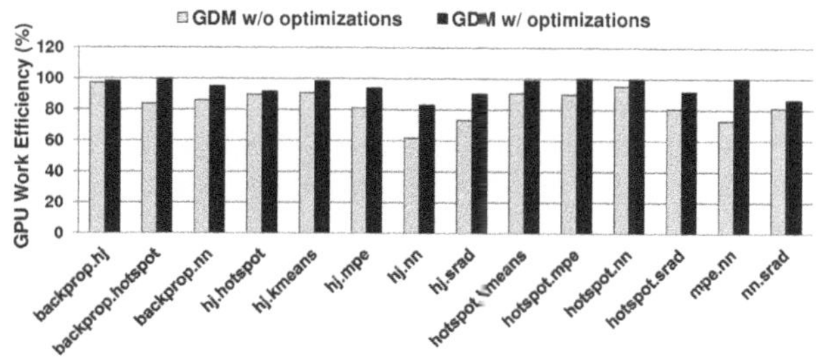

(b) GPU work efficiency with and without GDM optimizations.

Figure 9: Effectiveness of GDM optimizations.

select the combo runs in the first group and compare the performance of GDM and GDM-Base under these workloads. As shown in Figure 9(a), with optimizations, GDM is able to consistently improve the throughput of the workloads by 21% on average and up to 46% (relative to GDM-Base).

To further understand how the optimization techniques improve performance, we have collected the *work efficiency* of GPU, which is defined as the percentage of total GPU time spent on kernel executions and *effective* data movement. A data movement is effective if it is carried out when the benchmark runs alone. For example, in a combo-run workload of program A and program B, x repetitions of program A fully overlap with y repetitions of program B. During the co-running of the programs, the total time spent by the GPU to execute kernels and move data is c. If the time used for kernel execution and data movement is a for program A and b for program B when each of program A and B executes alone, the GPU work efficiency for this combo run is $(ax + by)/c$. Work efficiency reflects the amount of overhead incurred by device memory management, with high efficiency indicating low overhead. Though the overhead is mainly from extra data transfers incurred by device memory management, kernel execution time is included in work efficiency measurement because we want to correlate overhead reduction with throughput increase.

Figure 9(b) shows that the optimization techniques improve GPU work efficiency by 14% on average and up to 37%. This explains the throughput improvement observed in Figure 9(a). Meanwhile, it also explains the varying degrees of performance enhancement for different combo runs. For example, the throughput of the co-running of *backprop* and *hj* only rises by 4%. This is because the GPU has already been working at almost full efficiency before and after optimizations are applied (97% vs 98%), as shown by the first two bars in Figure 9(b).

For most workloads, with the optimization techniques in GDM, the GPU work efficiency is close to 100%. This shows that the optimization techniques work effectively on controlling the overhead. However, we notice that there are a few workloads with GPU work efficiency below 90%. This indicates that there is still potential to further improve the performance of GDM in future work.

6.5 Defending against DoS Attacks

GDM makes the system capable of thwarting denial-of-service (DoS) attacks that deplete the device memory space available to GPGPU applications. To demonstrate this capability of GDM, we have designed a malicious program which reserves a device memory region with the same size as the usable device memory capacity. The program repeatedly issues a GPU kernel that updates the data content in the reserved region so as to cause the largest performance degradation to GDM management.

We co-run each of the benchmarks (except *theano*) with the malicious program, and measure its execution time[5]. With GDM, all benchmarks successfully finish executions in spite of the presence of the malicious program. The performance of the benchmarks is lowered by the malicious program compared to their solo executions, but kept at an acceptable level (69% on average). The highest slowdown happens with *srad* (284%) because it launches kernels frequently and each kernel accesses a moderately large working set, causing more data evictions than other benchmarks. The lowest slowdown is observed with *kmeans* (9%) because it has the least demand on device memory space.

7. RELATED WORK

We are not the first to realize the problems caused by having GPU programmers directly and explicitly manage the device memory. Gdev [31] provides a data sharing mechanism for inter-process communication (IPC) and shows that this mechanism can be used to support device memory swapping. However, because it is based on an IPC mechanism and lacks generality, this proof-of-concept workaround barely works in practice and suffers serious performance issues as have been shown with our experiments. RSVM [29] provides an application-level device memory manager in a library. It relieves programmers from explicitly managing device memory, but programs must call the functions it provides to gain the benefits. Meanwhile, it suffers from the problems with application-level management. For example, it cannot address the contention between applications and does not allow an application to use other libraries that call CUDA APIs to allocate device memory or transfer data. Compared with these studies, GDM identifies the critical issues of device memory management at system level and provides a general and non-intrusive solution.

System management of GPGPU resources other than device memory has received attention in several recent studies. Pegasus [26] is a computation scheduling facility for virtualized, accelerator-based multiprocessor systems. It makes GPU a schedulable entity in the hypervisor and supports both high-throughput and low-latency scheduling among multiple guest OSes. TimeGraph [30] is a GPU command scheduler to support fair sharing of GPU computing resource for real-time, multitasking GPU applications. PTask [41] provides an OS abstraction for GPU computing resource and data transfer management. It presents a dataflow programming model that exposes information for OS kernel to provide performance isolation and to coordinate data movement between collaborative processes. GPUfs [42] proposes file system support for GPGPUs to allow a GPU program to access host files directly.

Some research projects in architecture and compiler areas improve the usability of GPUs as main-stream computing devices. iGPU [36] is a GPGPU architecture to support exceptions and speculative executions with compiler support. ADSM [24] is a data-centric programming model for heterogeneous computing that maintains an asymmetric shared memory space to achieve low cost. CGCM [27] is an automatic management and optimization system to reduce programmer's efforts for CPU-GPU data transfer. There are plans to provide unified and shared virtual spaces for CPU and GPU to access [14]. They do not provide or have not provided a solution to manage the physical space in the device memory. Instead, they pose a higher demand for operating system managing the device memory space, which is targeted by the research in this paper.

8. CONCLUSION AND FUTURE WORK

This paper identifies a crucial problem with existing GPGPU system software design. Namely, the lack of sophisticated device memory management causes application crashes, hangs, and inefficient utilization of GPGPU resources. This problem can seriously hinder the adoption of GPGPUs as mainstream computing devices in general-purpose systems.

The paper presents GDM, a fully functional device memory manager, to effectively address the problem. The design fully considers the unique features of GPGPU computing and GPGPU devices from the perspectives of both challenging problems and optimization opportunities. GDM manages device memory with both block and object-level information, and employs various optimization techniques to ensure system performance. Experiments verify the capabilities of GDM to tolerate device memory leaks, prevent program crashes, defend against malicious programs, and achieve high performance.

As future work, we plan to improve the management over GPU device memory following two directions. First, it is possible to further reduce the overhead by leveraging the information from compilers or applications. Through static analysis of kernel source code, the compiler can infer some information that may otherwise need to be obtained with extra cost. In many applications such as databases and in-memory big data engines, similar information can also be easily inferred from application-level semantics. Second, we also plan to investigate the collaboration between device memory manager and GPU kernel scheduler for more optimization opportunities. For example, when there is not enough free space in the device memory for the execution of a selected kernel, the system should balance the benefit of launching the kernel and the potential overhead. It may also decide whether to schedule another kernel with a smaller working set, or to wait for an issued kernel to finish execution and free up the space.

[5]On existing systems, a malicious program can also attack the system by issuing a non-terminating kernel (e.g. an infinite loop) or a large number of kernels. Thus, a thorough solution requires enhancements on GPU kernel scheduling, which is beyond the scope of the paper. This paper only focuses on the attacks through device memory space, and lets the system schedule GPU kernels in a round-robin manner in the experiment.

9. ACKNOWLEDGMENTS

We thank Yihong (Eric) Zhao from Yahoo! Inc. and the anonymous reviewers for their help and feedback. This work was partially supported by the National Science Foundation under grants CCF-0913050, OCI-1147522, and CNS-1162165.

10. REFERENCES

[1] http://mathworks.com/matlabcentral/newsreader/view_thread/324086.

[2] http://milkyway.cs.rpi.edu/milkyway/forum_thread.php?id=2780.

[3] http://culatools.com/blog/2012/03/12/3099.

[4] http://blenderartists.org/forum/showthread.php?269777.

[5] https://github.com/Theano/Theano (commit#: 5a755867f21b9a61, fe69a5a5b3a44695, 410016f9d6025064, 9bdeda96639e77af).

[6] http://mail-archive.com/pycuda@tiker.net/msg02432.html.

[7] http://amd.com/en-us/innovations/software-technologies/apu.

[8] http://documen.tician.de/pycuda/.

[9] https://devtalk.nvidia.com/default/topic/513370/cublas-problem.

[10] http://setiweb.ssl.berkeley.edu/beta/forum_thread.php?id=1441.

[11] http://mathworks.com/matlabcentral/answers/85601-unavoidable-memory-leaks-in-mex.

[12] http://nouveau.freedesktop.org.

[13] https://github.com/serban/kmeans.

[14] http://www.hsafoundation.com/.

[15] CULA linear algebra libraries. culatools.com.

[16] AMD. AMD accelerated parallel processing OpenCL programming guide, 2013.

[17] J. Bergstra, O. Breuleux, F. Bastien, P. Lamblin, R. Pascanu, G. Desjardins, J. Turian, D. Warde-Farley, and Y. Bengio. Theano: a CPU and GPU math expression compiler. In *SciPy*, 2010.

[18] B. Black, M. Annavaram, N. Brekelbaum, J. DeVale, L. Jiang, G. H. Loh, D. McCaule, P. Morrow, D. W. Nelson, D. Pantuso, P. Reed, J. Rupley, S. Shankar, J. Shen, and C. Webb. Die stacking (3d) microarchitecture. In *MICRO*, 2006.

[19] R. Chaiken, B. Jenkins, P.-A. Larson, B. Ramsey, D. Shakib, S. Weaver, and J. Zhou. Scope: easy and efficient parallel processing of massive data sets. *Proc. VLDB Endow.*, 1(2):1265–1276, 2008.

[20] S. Che, M. Boyer, J. Meng, D. Tarjan, J. W. Sheaffer, S.-H. Lee, and K. Skadron. Rodinia: A benchmark suite for heterogeneous computing. In *IISWC*, 2009.

[21] P. J. Denning. Virtual memory. *ACM Comput. Surv.*, 2(3):153–189, 1970.

[22] P. J. Denning. Third generation computer systems. *ACM Comput. Surv.*, 3(4):175–216, Dec. 1971.

[23] D. R. Engler and M. F. Kaashoek. Exterminate all operating system abstractions. In *HOTOS*, 1995.

[24] I. Gelado, J. E. Stone, J. Cabezas, S. Patel, N. Navarro, and W.-m. W. Hwu. An asymmetric distributed shared memory model for heterogeneous parallel systems. In *ASPLOS*, 2010.

[25] K. O. W. Group. The OpenCL specification 1.2, 2013.

[26] V. Gupta, K. Schwan, N. Tolia, V. Talwar, and P. Ranganathan. Pegasus: coordinated scheduling for virtualized accelerator-based systems. In *USENIX ATC*, 2011.

[27] T. B. Jablin, P. Prabhu, J. A. Jablin, N. P. Johnson, S. R. Beard, and D. I. August. Automatic CPU-GPU communication management and optimization. In *PLDI*, 2011.

[28] K. Jang, S. Han, S. Han, S. Moon, and K. Park. SSLShader: cheap SSL acceleration with commodity processors. In *NSDI*, 2011.

[29] F. Ji, H. Lin, and X. Ma. RSVM: a region-based software virtual memory for GPU. In *PACT*, 2013.

[30] S. Kato, K. Lakshmanan, R. Rajkumar, and Y. Ishikawa. TimeGraph: GPU scheduling for real-time multi-tasking environments. In *USENIX ATC*, 2011.

[31] S. Kato, M. McThrow, C. Maltzahn, and S. Brandt. Gdev: first-class GPU resource management in the operating system. In *USENIX ATC*, 2012.

[32] H. Kim. Supporting virtual memory in GPGPU without supporting precise exceptions. In *MSPC*, 2012.

[33] V. W. Lee, C. Kim, J. Chhugani, M. Deisher, D. Kim, A. D. Nguyen, N. Satish, M. Smelyanskiy, S. Chennupaty, P. Hammarlund, R. Singhal, and P. Dubey. Debunking the 100x GPU vs. CPU myth: an evaluation of throughput computing on CPU and GPU. In *ISCA*, 2010.

[34] E. Lindholm, J. Nickolls, S. Oberman, and J. Montrym. NVIDIA Tesla: A unified graphics and computing architecture. *IEEE Micro*, 28(2), 2008.

[35] M. Macedonia. The GPU enters computing's mainstream. *Computer*, 36(10):106–108, 2003.

[36] J. Menon, M. De Kruijf, and K. Sankaralingam. iGPU: exception support and speculative execution on GPUs. In *ISCA*, 2012.

[37] T. Ni. Direct Compute: Bring GPU computing to the mainstream. In *GTC*, 2009.

[38] NVIDIA. NVIDIA's next generation CUDA compute architecture: Kepler GK110, 2012.

[39] NVIDIA. NVIDIA CUDA C programming guide, 2013.

[40] J. Poulton. An embedded DRAM for CMOS ASICs. In *ARVLSI*, 1997.

[41] C. J. Rossbach, J. Currey, M. Silberstein, B. Ray, and E. Witchel. PTask: operating system abstractions to manage GPUs as compute devices. In *SOSP*, 2011.

[42] M. Silberstein, B. Ford, I. Keidar, and E. Witchel. GPUfs: integrating a file system with GPUs. In *ASPLOS*, 2013.

[43] A. Snavely and D. M. Tullsen. Symbiotic jobscheduling for a simultaneous multithreaded processor. In *ASPLOS*, 2000.

[44] K. Wang, Y. Huai, R. Lee, F. Wang, X. Zhang, and J. H. Saltz. Accelerating pathology image data cross-comparison on CPU-GPU hybrid systems. *Proc. VLDB Endow.*, 5(11), 2012.

[45] Y. Yuan, R. Lee, and X. Zhang. The yin and yang of processing data warehousing queries on GPU devices. *Proc. VLDB Endow.*, 6(10):817–828, 2013.

On the Energy and Performance of Commodity Hardware Transactional Memory

Nuno Diegues
INESC-ID / Instituto Superior Técnico, Univ. of Lisbon
nmld@tecnico.ulisboa.pt

Paolo Romano
INESC-ID / Instituto Superior Técnico, Univ. of Lisbon
romano@inesc-id.pt

Luís Rodrigues
INESC-ID / Instituto Superior Técnico, Univ. of Lisbon
ler@tecnico.ulisboa.pt

ABSTRACT

The advent of multi-core architectures has brought concurrent programming to the forefront of software development. In this context, Transactional Memory (TM) has gained increasing popularity as a simpler, attractive alternative to traditional lock-based synchronization. The recent integration of Hardware TM (HTM) in the last generation of Intel commodity processors turned TM into a mainstream technology, raising a number of questions on its future and that of concurrent programming.

To evaluate the potential impact of Intel's HTM, we conducted the largest study on TM to date, comparing different locking techniques, hardware and software TMs, as well as different combinations of these mechanisms, from the dual perspective of performance and power consumption. As a result we perform a workload characterization, to help programmers better exploit the currently available TM facilities, and identify important research directions.

Categories and Subject Descriptors

D.1.3 [**Software**]: Programming Techniques - Concurrent Programming

Keywords

Transactional Memory; Performance Evaluation; Energy

1. INTRODUCTION

For many years, locking has represented the *de-facto* standard approach to synchronization in concurrent applications. However, its inherent complexity and error-proneness motivated the research for alternatives. Transactional Memory (TM) is an appealing alternative in which programmers are required only to identify which code blocks should run atomically, and not how concurrent accesses to shared state should be synchronized to enforce isolation (as with locks). The TM is then responsible for guaranteeing correctness, by aborting transactions that would generate unsafe histories.

SIGMETRICS'14, June 16–20, 2014, Austin, Texas, USA.
ACM 978-1-4503-2789-3/14/06.
http://dx.doi.org/10.1145/2591971.2592030 .

Over the last decade a large body of TM research focused on software-based implementations (STM) due to their ease of prototyping [1]. Unlike hardware-based implementations, however, STM needs to instrument reads and writes, to trace conflicts at run-time between concurrent transactions. These instrumentation costs can, in certain scenarios, introduce large overheads and hinder performance. HTM support, which has recently been commercialized in commodity processors [3], avoids that problem by relying on the cache coherence protocol of the processor. On the downside, commodity HTMs have architectural restrictions that may limit their practical ability to efficiently deal with some workloads.

The advent of commodity HTM raises a number of questions concerning the future of TM and concurrent programming: how competitive are available HTMs when compared with state of the art STMs? Will the achievable performance be sufficiently alluring to make TM mainstream? What role will STM play now that HTMs are widely available? How limiting are the architectural restrictions of existing HTMs?

2. COMPARATIVE STUDY

In this work we contribute to answer the previous questions by conducting the largest study to date on TM-based synchronization. We compare, from the twofold perspective of performance and energy-efficiency, a range of synchronization mechanisms: 6 lock approaches with different granularities; 4 STMs; HTM (using Intel TSX); and 2 Hybrid TMs (HyTM) that use STM and HTM mechanisms in synergy. In the following we summarize some of our results; details can be found in an extended version of the paper [2].

Pros and Cons for HTM: We found that in STAMP, a standard benchmark suite for TM we tested 560 different scenarios and identified three categories of applications in which HTM exhibits different performance (Table 1). Performance of HTM is highly dependent on the memory access patterns on the L1 cache, and long running transactions can lead to frequent cache capacity exceptions and spurious aborts. As such, HTM is the best approach only in Kmeans and SSCA2, which have short transactions interleaved with large non-transactional code blocks. When transaction-intensity is medium, HTM is only the best choice for a limited degree of parallelism, and it is generally better on the energy side than on the performance side. The impact of its hardware limitations is highlighted by several STAMP benchmarks that generate long transactions, in which HTM is outperformed by both locking and STM solutions. By also considering the synchronization of a concurrent Hash-Map and a RedBlack-Tree, HTM clearly unveiled its effectiveness

Table 1: Summary of results according to workload characterization in the STAMP suite, showing the strategies that achieve highest performance, and least energy consumption (note that t = number of threads). Transaction intensity, split in three categories, also shows the percentage of time spent in transactional mode in the application.

	TxIntensity (%)	Speedup	Least Energy
kmeans	low (7)	HTM	HTM
ssca2	low (17)	HTM	HTM
intruder	medium (33)	HTM $\leq 4t$ STM $\geq 5t$	HTM $\leq 5t$ STM $\geq 6t$
vacation	medium (89)	HTM $\leq 2t$ STM $\geq 3t$	HTM $\leq 4t$ STM $\geq 5t$
genome	high (97)	STM	STM
yada	high (99)	STM	STM
labyrinth	high (100)	STM	STM

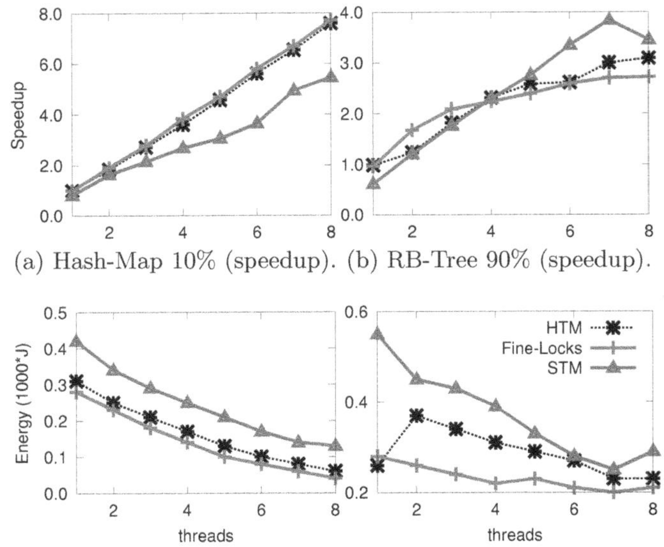

(a) Hash-Map 10% (speedup). (b) RB-Tree 90% (speedup).

(c) Hash-Map 10% (energy). (d) RB-Tree 90% (energy).

Figure 1: Concurrent collections with varying % of updates.

in scenarios with small transactions, in which it is competitive with fine-grained locking (see Fig. 1 for a sample of the workloads). Tests with Memcached (a popular in-memory caching system) confirmed that HTM performed as good as fine locks (4% less performance).

STM is still competitive: Our experiments also show that STM is a robust all-around solution. Among the 4 STMs, there was always one performing best than HTM in 5 out of the 7 STAMP benchmarks. In concurrent data-structures STM is competitive, or even the best, in workloads with many updates (see Fig. 1 for an example). On the other hand, STM has a larger energy consumption. Although STM was initially proposed as a prototyping alternative to actual hardware implementations of TM, its evolution throughout a decade of intense research has resulted in several highly-optimized mechanisms, achieving performance comparable to that of fine-grained locking. This does not mean that STMs embody a perfect solution; instead, these results highlight the current limitations of HTM support, which make STM still a very competitive solution.

3. RESEARCH DIRECTIONS

The results of our study unveil a number of critical issues related with HTM performance and allow for identifying several research problems, whose timely solution could significantly enhance the chances for HTM to turn into a mainstream paradigm for parallel programming:

HyTMs: still a mismatch? The results for HyTM do not live up to the expectation of obtaining the best out of both STMs and HTM. Across our 10 benchmarks and various workloads, HyTMs were never the best solution, and were only competitive in 2 benchmarks. The problem is the mechanisms currently employed for allowing the coexistence of HTM and STM induce overheads in terms of additional spurious aborts. This motivates research in the design of support for non-transactional memory accesses from transactions to allow more efficient synergies of HTM and STM.

Complexity of HTM tuning. HTM performance can be significantly affected by the settings of several parameters and mechanisms. Without proper tuning, Intel TSX yields an average throughput loss of 72% and of 89% in energy consumption. Also, the optimal configuration of these parameters can significantly vary depending on the characteristics of the application's workload. These findings urge for novel approaches capable of removing from programmers the burden of manually tuning HTM parameters, and instead delegating this task to middleware or compiler based solutions.

Relevance of selective instrumentation. Both TSX, as well as current GCC's library for STM, basically trace every memory access performed within a transaction. This causes significant increases of the transaction footprint's size, amplifying the instrumentation overheads in STM, and the chances of incurring in capacity exceptions in HTM. These results motivate research on cross-layer mechanisms, both at compiler and hardware level, to achieve selective instrumentation in a way that is both convenient for the programmer and efficiently implementable in hardware.

4. ACKNOWLEDGMENTS

This work was supported by PEst-OE/EEI/LA0021/2013 from Fundação para a Ciência e Tecnologia, and by the GreenTM project (EXPL/EEI-ESS/0361/2013).

5. REFERENCES

[1] N. Diegues and P. Romano. Time-warp: Lightweight abort minimization in transactional memory. In *Proceedings of the 19th ACM SIGPLAN Symposium on Principles and Practice of Parallel Programming*, PPoPP '14, pages 167–178, 2014.

[2] N. Diegues, P. Romano, and L. Rodrigues. The moment of truth: virtues and limitations of commodity Hardware Transactional Memory. Technical Report RT/29/2013, INESC-ID Lisboa, December 2013.

[3] R. M. Yoo, C. J. Hughes, K. Lai, and R. Rajwar. Performance evaluation of intel transactional synchronization extensions for high-performance computing. In *Proceedings of International Conference for High Performance Computing, Networking, Storage and Analysis*, SC '13, pages 1–19, 2013.

Impact of Correlated Mobility and Cluster Scalability on Connectivity of Wireless Networks

Qi Wang[†], Liang Liu[†], Jinbei Zhang[†], Xinyu Wang[†], Xinbing Wang[†], Songwu Lu[§]
[†] Dept. of Electronic Engineering, Shanghai Jiao Tong University, China
[§] Dept. of Computer Science, University of California, Los Angeles
{wq911206, liuliang582, abelchina, maiamibangqiu, xwang8}@sjtu.edu.cn,
slu@cs.ucla.edu

ABSTRACT

We propose the *correlated mobile k-hop clustered networks model* to implement correlated node movements and scalable clusters. We divide network states into three categories, i.e., *cluster-sparse state*, *cluster-dense state* and *cluster-inferior dense state*, and achieve the critical transmission range for the last two states. Furthermore, we find that correlated mobility and cluster scalability are closely related with each other and the impact of these two properties on connectivity is mainly through influencing network state transition.

Categories and Subject Descriptors

C.2.1 [**Computer-Communication Networks**]: Network Architecture and Design—*Wireless Communications*

Keywords

Network Connectivity, Correlated Mobility, Cluster Scalability, Critical Transmission Range.

1. INTRODUCTION

Since the seminal work [2] done by Gupta *et al.*, there has been a great interest in the scaling analysis of network performance and many follow-up works have explored the *asymptotic connectivity* of wireless networks. But most of these works focus on stationary and flat networks, where nodes are independently and uniformly distributed in the whole network. Since mobility and clustering property have been found to improve various aspects of network performance, it is interesting to explore the impact of correlated mobility and cluster scalability on network connectivity. Although correlated mobility and cluster scalability are ubiquitous in reality, combining them into one network model is difficult. In [3], Wang *et al.* studied the critical transmission range for various networks under different mobility models, but it doesn't achieve real clustering effect. Nevertheless, it provides the major motivation for our work.

SIGMETRICS'14, June 16–20, 2014, Austin, Texas, USA.
ACM 978-1-4503-2789-3/14/06.
http://http://dx.doi.org/10.1145/2591971.2592012.

In order to understand the nature of correlated node movements and node spatial heterogeneity, and explore their mutual interactions, implications and impact on the asymptotic connectivity, we propose the *correlated mobile k-hop clustered networks model* to take into consideration both the *correlated mobility* and *cluster scalability*. We adopt the correlated mobility model in [1] to implement the group mobility, and suppose that there are $n^\alpha (0 < \alpha \le 1)$ cluster heads and $n^\gamma (0 < \gamma \le 1)$ clusters, each with a radius of $R = \Theta(n^\beta)(\beta \le 0)$ in the whole network $\mathcal{O}$, which is assumed to be a unit torus. The cluster radius can scale with the number of nodes n, and with different values of β we can implement cluster scalability.

To investigate the impact of correlated mobility and cluster scalability on connectivity in correlated mobile k-hop clustered networks when the number of nodes $n \to \infty$ and study the influence that α, β and γ has on network performance, we divide the network states into three categories according to the value of these three parameters, the *cluster-sparse state* ($\alpha + 2\beta < 0$), *cluster-dense state* ($\alpha + 2\beta \ge \frac{1-\gamma}{k}$) and *cluster-inferior dense state* ($0 \le \alpha + 2\beta < \frac{1-\gamma}{k}$). We prove the critical transmission range to be $\sqrt{\frac{\log n}{k\pi n^\alpha}}$ for cluster-dense state and $\sqrt{\frac{[k(\alpha+2\beta)+\gamma]\log n}{k\pi n^\alpha}}$ for cluster-inferior dense state.

2. NETWORK MODEL

2.1 Network Deployment

In this part, we illustrate the initial network architecture deployment before cluster members begin to move. We suppose there are n cluster-member nodes and n^α cluster-head nodes in a unit square $\mathcal{O}$, where the *cluster head exponent* $0 < \alpha \le 1$. The cluster-head nodes are *uniformly and independently distributed* in $\mathcal{O}$, which is assumed to be a torus in $\mathbb{R}^2$ to avoid border effects. Different from the network model in [3], cluster-member nodes are grouped into m clusters where $m = n^\gamma$ and the *cluster exponent* $0 < \gamma \le 1$. Each cluster region is centered around a logical center (*home point*) and has a circular shape with radius R as $R = \Theta(n^\beta)$, where the *cluster radius exponent* $\beta \le 0$. The home points are *uniformly and independently distributed* in $\mathcal{O}$ and the cluster-member nodes are *uniformly and independently distributed* in their belonging cluster regions, each of which has a circular area of πR^2. We assume that each cluster is comprised of $\varpi = \frac{n}{m} = n^{1-\gamma}$ cluster members. We also assume n^α and n^γ to be integers for convenience.

2.2 Correlated Mobility

After deploying the initial network architecture, the cluster heads will remain stationary while the cluster members will move. We illustrate our *Correlated Mobility Model* as follows:

Correlated Mobility Model: After the network deployment, home points and cluster members will move. Time is slotted into k time slots. At the beginning of each time slot, each home point will *uniformly and independently* choose a position within the unit torus $\mathcal{O}$ and then each cluster member will *uniformly and independently* choose its location in its corresponding cluster region. In the rest of each time slot, the home points and cluster members will remain stationary.

2.3 Cluster Scalability

After introducing the system model, we will present the unique characteristic of our network, ***cluster scalability***. As we can see, the cluster radius scales with n by assuming $R = \Theta(n^{\beta})$ where $\beta \leq 0$. Hence, when β is small (with large absolute value), the cluster size will be small and clusters are sparsely distributed in $\mathcal{O}$. While the cluster region will become relatively large when β is large (with small absolute value), which leads to densely distributed clusters.

This is the qualitative illustration of cluster scalability and we should also provide a quantitative definition. We compare the average coverage of cluster heads, $\frac{1}{n^{\alpha}}$, with the cluster region $\pi R^2 = \Theta(n^{2\beta})$ and give the following three cases:

(C1). *Cluster-sparse state* (member-dense state).

When $\pi R^2 = o(\frac{1}{n^{\alpha}})$, we have $\alpha + 2\beta < 0$. The cluster size is sufficiently small compared with the average coverage of each cluster head and clusters are sparsely distributed in the whole network $\mathcal{O}$. Besides, the member density of each cluster $d = \frac{\varpi}{\pi R^2} = \Theta(n^{1-2\beta-\gamma})$ is large. Thus, this is also the member-dense state and the clustering property is fairly dominant. Each cluster can be regarded as an entirety because cluster members stay so close and move so consistently.

(C2). *Cluster-dense state* (member sparse state).

In contrast to the previous case, we have $\alpha + 2\beta \geq \frac{1-\gamma}{k}$ in this state and can further have $\pi R^2 = \omega(\frac{1}{n^{\alpha}})$. The cluster size is relatively large, clusters are densely distributed in $\mathcal{O}$ and they might intersect with each other. The member density d is relatively small, and hence this is the member-sparse state and there is almost no substantial clustering. In this case, every cluster member performs more like an independent node.

(C3). *Cluster-inferior dense state* (member-inferior sparse state).

In this case, we have $0 \leq \alpha + 2\beta < \frac{1-\gamma}{k}$ and still have $\pi R^2 = \omega(\frac{1}{n^{\alpha}})$. It is the transitional state between the cluster-sparse state and cluster-dense state. In this case, we can neither regard members in the same cluster as a whole nor treat them as totally independent nodes. Instead, we group the nodes into sub-clusters.

3. MAIN RESULTS AND INTUITIONS

We summarize our main results as follows.

(C2). *Cluster-dense state* ($\alpha + 2\beta \geq \frac{1-\gamma}{k}$).

We have $r_c = \sqrt{\frac{\log n}{k\pi n^{\alpha}}}$, where $0 < \alpha \leq 1, 0 < \gamma \leq 1$.

(C3). *Cluster-inferior dense state* ($0 \leq \alpha + 2\beta < \frac{1-\gamma}{k}$).

We have $r_c = \sqrt{\frac{[k(\alpha+2\beta)+\gamma]\log n}{k\pi n^{\alpha}}}$, where $0 < \alpha \leq 1, 0 < \gamma \leq 1$.

4. CONCLUSION

We illustrate our results in Figure 4.1. Although the three parameters all have an influence on network state transition, thus affecting network connectivity, their separate functions are different. α can serve as a centralized network coordinator because this parameter can adjust r_c from the perspective of the whole network. In contrast, β controls network in a distributed manner, since it influences cluster radius R and node density ϖ on the cluster level. γ can control the number of clusters as well as node density, so it regulates the network both in centralized and distributed manner.

With *correlated mobility* and *cluster scalability*, we can achieve network connectivity with a smaller critical transmission range than that in an i.i.d. mobility network. **Thus, we can save transmission power by bringing *correlated mobility* and *cluster scalability* into the networks.**

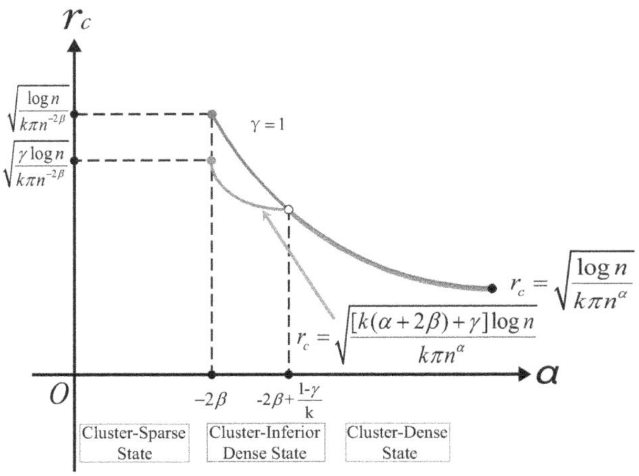

Figure 4.1: Impact of α, β and γ on Network State Transition. ***Network state transition is jointly affected by α, β and γ. Among the three factors, α is the most influential, and r_c monotonically decreases with α. While γ can on some level shape the curve, the impact of β on r_c is mainly through determining the transition points.***

5. REFERENCES

[1] D. Ciullo, V. Martina, M. Garetto, and E. Leonardi. Impact of correlated mobility on delay-throughput performance in mobile ad hoc networks. *IEEE/ACM Trans. Networking*, 19(6):1745–1758, Dec. 2011.

[2] P. Gupta and P. R. Kumar. The capacity of wireless networks. *IEEE Trans. Information Theory*, 46(2):388–404, Mar. 2000.

[3] Q. Wang, X. Wang, and X. Lin. Mobility increases the connectivity of k-hop clustered wireless networks. In *Proc. ACM MobiCom*, pages 121–132, Sept. 2009.

Unleashing the Potentials of Dynamism for Page Allocation Strategies in SSDs

Arash Tavakkol†, Mohammad Arjomand†, and Hamid Sarbazi-Azad†‡
†HPCAN Lab, Computer Engineering Department, Sharif University of Technology, Tehran, Iran
‡School of Computer Science, Institute for Research in Fundamental Sciences (IPM), Tehran, Iran
{tavakkol,arjomand}@ce.sharif.edu, azad@{sharif.edu,ipm.ir}

ABSTRACT

In Solid-State Drives (SSDs) with tens of flash chips and highly parallel architecture, we can speed up I/O operations by well-utilizing resources during page allocation. Proposals already exist for using static page allocation which does not balance the IO load and its efficiency depends on access address patterns. To our best knowledge, there have been no research thus far to show what happens if one or more internal resources can be freely allocated regardless of the request address. This paper explores the possibility of using different degrees of dynamism in page allocation and identifies key design opportunities that they present to improve SSD's characteristics.

Categories and Subject Descriptors

D.4.2 [**Operating Systems**]: Storage Management—*Secondary Storage*

Keywords

Solid State Drive, Page Allocation, Dynamism.

1. INTRODUCTION

The main feature of modern SSDs is that they employ a large set of various resources, including flash packages and communication channels that are organized to achieve high level of internal parallelism. Besides, the architecture of flash packages provides increased number of planes and dies to boost parallelism. Each of these parallelism levels has its own limitations and opportunities that causes SSD's performance to be highly dependent to the strategy used for conducting flash operations in parallel. This is known as *allocation strategy* and determines how to efficiently exploit resource parallelism and avoid their inherent limitations. The main focus of past studies was on allocation schemes where the target of a flash operation is statically determined using a predefined priority order of parallelism levels [1, 3]. The efficiency of these approaches highly depends on the address patterns of I/O requests and may lead to conflicts on shared resources. To address this issue, one can relax deterministic resource assignment in one or more levels of parallelism, and use dynamism instead. Accordingly, we introduce new allocation schemes with various degree of freedom of one, two, three or four, and analyze their performance issues with respect to static allocation. While a number of prior work adopted fully-dynamic allocation (with a freedom degree of 4) as the extreme design point [1], our evaluations confirm that it cannot efficiently utilize all parallelism opportunities. Especially, allocations with freedom degrees of 2 and 3 can better exploit intra-flash parallelism.

SIGMETRICS'14, June 16–20, 2014, Austin, Texas, USA.
ACM 978-1-4503-2789-3/14/06.
http://dx.doi.org/10.1145/2591971.2592013.

2. DYNAMIC ALLOCATION STRATEGIES

The page allocation (*PLAlloc*) determines the target Channel ID (CID), Way ID (WID), Die ID (DID), and Plane ID (PID) of a page-sized transaction following a specific priority order of the parallelism levels. Unfortunately, making an appropriate decision for *PLAlloc* prioritization strategy is not a trivial task since each choice acts in favor of some parallelism levels and diminishes the chance of utilizing others. Worse, some of the parallelisms, such as plane-level, are inherently restricted [1] and require extra design considerations to achieve reasonable performance [2]. In static strategies, CID, WID, DID and PID are calculated by successive divisions of the LPA. This approach makes their performance to be highly dependent to the LPA access patterns. As an alternative approach, we suggest to relax deterministic assignment of resource ID(s) in one or more dimensions of parallelism and use dynamic assignment instead. For a certain level of parallelism, dynamism may be provided by *round-robin* or *load-aware* resource allocations. Our choice is busy-aware round-robin which immediately tries to assign next resource, if current candidate is busy. This results in a better address striping and resource utilization especially when resources are limited. Based on this definition, 41 dynamic *PLAlloc* strategies are possible which are classified into four categories by considering their degree of freedom:

Degree one. Just one resource ID is determined dynamically and others are assigned in the static approach:

$$L_1L_2L_3, \forall i, L_i \in \{C, W, D, P\} \quad for \quad L_i \neq L_j, \quad i \neq j.$$

Degree two. Two resource IDs are determined dynamically and the others are extracted statically:

$$L_1L_2, \forall i, L_i \in \{C, W, D, P\} \quad for \quad L_1 \neq L_2$$

Degree three. One resource ID is statically calculated:

$$L_1, L_1 \in \{C, W, D, P\}$$

Degree four. There is one *PLAlloc* strategy, namely F, to which all resource IDs are dynamically assigned. Various implementations of this strategy were previously presented [1, 6] as the only choice of dynamic allocation.

Figure 1 presents the steps of translation within CP dynamic allocation. As can be seen, CID and PID are deterministically calculated from the LPA, and the two remaining resource IDs are allocated using busy-aware round-robin algorithm. Note that when more than one level of parallelism is dynamically assigned, *PLAlloc* calculates them in order of channel, way, die, and plane for better striping.

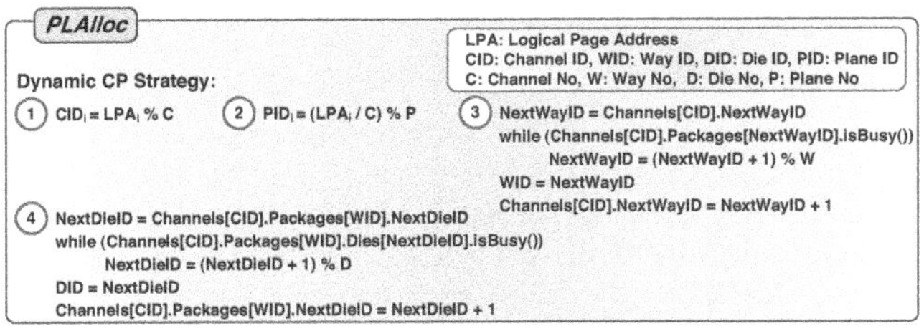

Figure 1: The steps of translation for dynamic CP *PLAlloc*.

3. EVALUATION

We perform discrete-event simulations using SSDSim [1]. We model two SSD configurations, SSD-ENT and SSD-CLN, representing the enterprise and client class SSDs, respectively. SSD-ENT uses 64 SLC NAND flash chips [5] organized in 8 channels while SSD-CLN has 16 MLC NAND flash chips [4] connected through 4 communication channels. We conducted a set of micro-benchmark simulations with varying I/O request sizes and read/write ratios. The evaluations are performed on *PLAllocs* that present best performance based on our observations. Figure 2a depicts the results of IOPS and RT for SSD-ENT. As expected, dynamism greatly enhances the IOPS of small and medium size requests and F, PD, and DP always show the outstanding results among all possible choices. Besides, increasing the request size weakens the superiority of dynamic schemes since the probability of unresolvable resource contentions grows. As the final point, the RT results prove that the amount of resources within SSD-ENT are enough to equally decrease the contentions probability for both static and dynamic schemes. Regarding this metric, the C, CP, and CWDP schemes show the best results while F and PD are ranked second. As can be seen in Figure 2b, the micro-benchmark results for SSD-CLN show the impressive performance impact of dynamic schemes, especially when using D strategy. In fact, the IOPS results of D are considerably higher than static *PLAlloc*s and it even shows better values with respect to other dynamic schemes. Regarding RT results, D shows minor increase for medium size requests but achieves noticeable improvement for larger sizes. Our observations show that the superior performance of D is due to higher chance of exploiting multi-plane and multi-die parallelism in this scheme. We deduce that either of F and PD are the best *PLAlloc*s for SSD-ENT and D is the proper solution for SSD-CLN.

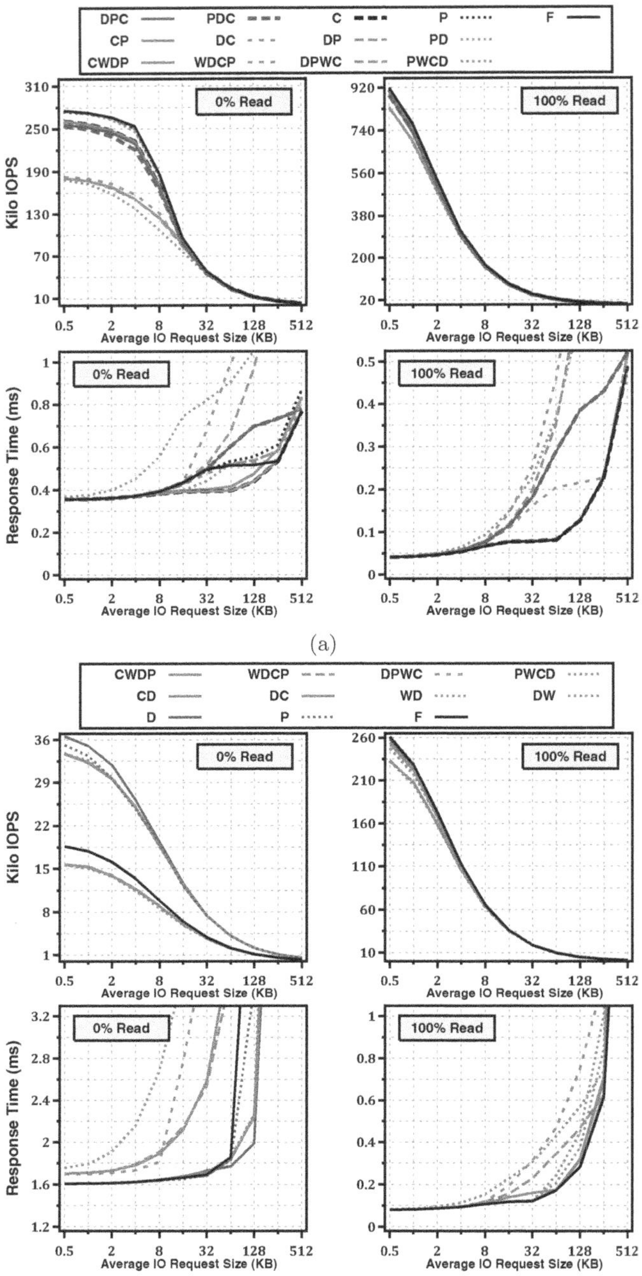

(a)

(b)

Figure 2: Performance analysis of sample *PLAlloc* strategies for (a) SSD-ENT and (b) SSD-CLN.

4. REFERENCES

[1] Y. Hu et al. Performance impact and interplay of ssd parallelism through advanced commands, allocation strategy and data granularity. In *ICS '11*.

[2] M. Jung et al. Physically addressed queueing (PAQ): improving parallelism in solid state disks. In *ISCA'12*.

[3] M. Jung and M. Kandemir. An evaluation of different page allocation strategies on high-speed ssds. In *HotStorage'12*.

[4] Micron Technology, Inc. MT29E256G08CMCAB NAND flash memory, 2010.

[5] Micron Technology, Inc. MT29F128G08AMCABJ2 NAND flash memory, 2010.

[6] C. Park et al. Exploiting internal parallelism of flash-based ssds. *Computer Architecture Letters*, 9(1):9–12, 2010.

Traffic Congestion: Models, Costs and Optimal Transport

Chinmoy V. Mandayam
Department of Electrical Engineering
Stanford University
chinmoy@stanford.edu

Balaji Prabhakar
Departments of Electrical Engineering and
Computer Science
Stanford University
balaji@stanford.edu

ABSTRACT

We develop two models of highway traffic: (i) a deterministic fluid model based on conservation laws building on previous work and (ii) a mean-field model of a series of infinite server queues, where each stage in the tandem models a segment of highway. The models define the "highway-map"—a transformation of time-varying arrival rate functions according to which vehicles arrive at the highway to the corresponding departure rate functions of vehicles exiting the highway. The two models are shown to be equivalent in that they obtain the same highway-map. The cost of congestion for vehicles traversing the highway is the total extra time they spend on the highway due to congestion. This cost is shown to be equal to the "d-bar" distance between the input and the output rate measures of the highway-map. This fact is used to formulate a convex optimization problem for determining the optimal way to shift users from peak to off-peak hours using incentives so that congestion costs are lowered.

Categories and Subject Descriptors

G.3 [**Mathematics of Computing**]: Probability and Statistics—*queueing theory*

Keywords

Highway traffic; Congestion; Optimal transport; Fluid models

1. INTRODUCTION

Urbanization–the tendency for the world's population to move to cities–is placing serious demands on transportation networks, both road and public transport. Traffic snarls on roads are expensive: measured in terms of the *extra* time and fuel consumed by drivers and vehicles, the cost of congestion in the U.S. in 2012 was $120 billion [8]. When faced with this, transport network operators face two choices: increase peak supply or shift peak demand. Increasing supply can be prohibitively expensive or simply impossible—there may be no space to expand roads or add trains. Shifting peak demand by levying extra charges for peak time travel, called congestion charging, requires peak prices to be set high enough to shift the load.

In this work we explore a complementary approach to peak shifting by monetarily incentivizing commuters to travel during off-peak hours, extending work by Mandayam and Prabhakar[5]. We wish to understand several key issues in this setting and, to simplify, consider the cost of congestion purely in terms of time. Thus, the cost of congestion merely equals the extra time vehicles spend in traffic, and the cost of shifting some load to off-peak time equals the time by which the load is shifted. Viewed this way, we ask: Is the cost of load shifting plus the cost of congestion for the resulting shifted load less than the cost of congestion for the original unshifted load? If yes, what is the optimal way to shift the load?

2. MODEL DESCRIPTION

In order to answer the above questions, we develop two models of highway systems subject to *time-varying loads.* The first is a fluid model, following work initiated by Lighthill and Whitham [4] and Richards [7] The second is a relaxation of the K-exclusion process [3].

Fluid flow models of highway traffic, commonly called LWR models (after Lighthill, Whitham and Richards) assume that the local velocity and the local density of traffic are related by the so-called *fundamental diagram.* In general, velocity is a decreasing function of density. We study a model[1], where there is a rapid transition from a free-flow speed v_f to a slower congested speed $v_c \geq 0$, at some threshold density θ.The maximum flow-rate or *flux* achievable at free-flow speed is $C = v_f\theta$

We model traffic on a uni-directional highway segment of length X. For $x \in [0, X]$, $\rho(x,t)$ and $v(x,t)$ are the traffic density and velocity respectively at location x at time $t \geq 0$. Vehicles enter the initially empty highway at $x = 0$, with arrival rate $\lambda(t)$. Let $\Lambda(t)$ be the cumulative arrivals in $[0, t]$.

The law of conservation of mass is used to obtain $\rho(x, t)$ and $v(x, t)$ at all locations $x \in (0, X]$ and for all times $t > 0$. The flux at the exit of the highway $\rho(X, t)v(X, t)$ then determines the rate $\lambda_d^X(t)$ at which fluid or vehicles exit the highway segment at time t. The cumulative departure process is denoted by $\Lambda_d^X(\cdot)$. The "highway-map", H_X is

[1]Here we do not limit the maximum possible density, which can be achieved by considering a variant of the current model where the speed drops to zero for very high densities. We shall address this variant in future work.

SIGMETRICS'14, June 16–20, 2014, Austin, Texas, USA.
ACM 978-1-4503-2789-3/14/06.
http://dx.doi.org/10.1145/2591971.2592014.

a transformation on the space of positive measures with a total mass of $\Lambda(T)$, such that $\Lambda_d^X(\cdot) = H_X(\Lambda(\cdot))$.

Consider the set of all arrival rate functions $\lambda(\cdot)$ supported in $[0,T]$ and bounded above by L. The following theorem determines H, the highway-map for a long highway.

THEOREM 1. *For each $t \geq 0$, there exist $X(L,T)$ and $\Lambda_d(t)$, such that $\Lambda_d(t) = \Lambda_d^X(t)$ for all $X \geq X(L,T)$. Denoting $H_{X(L,T)}$ by H, we have that H is equivalent to a fluid queue with a maximum processing capacity of C vehicles per unit time.*

The second model builds on the totally asymmetric simple exclusion process (or TASEP). The K-TASEP [3] is a generalization in which each site can hold up to K particles. We consider the following relaxation of K-TASEP. A series of infinite server queues with independent and exponentially distributed service times is used to model consecutive segments of the highway. The rate at which vehicles at stage i are served depends on the density of vehicles at stage $i+1$; the dependence is an appropriately scaled version of that defined in the fundamental diagram discussed previously. We use a mean-field approach [2] to analyze this model and find that, in the law-of-large-numbers limit, it closely approximates the fluid model. We verify this proximity using simulations.

3. COST OF CONGESTION AND INCENTIVES.

The cost of congestion is defined as the sum of the "waiting times" of vehicles passing through the highway. This is the extra time the vehicles take to traverse the highway when there is congestion. For simplicity, we consider the map H obtained from the long-highway limit. Let $W(\Lambda)$ denote the sum of the waiting times for the given arrival distribution $\Lambda(\cdot)$. For the equivalent fluid queue whose capacity is $C = \theta v_f$, the queue-size under any work-conserving service discipline is given by

$$q(t) = \Lambda(t) - \Lambda_d(t).$$

Let $Q(\Lambda) = \int_0^\infty q(t)dt$ and let $\bar{d}(\Lambda, \Lambda_d)$ be the "d-bar" distance [1] (also called the "Wasserstein distance" in optimal transport theory [6]) between Λ and Λ_d. We then have the following theorems:

THEOREM 2. $W(\Lambda) = Q(\Lambda) = \bar{d}(\Lambda, \Lambda_d)$.

THEOREM 3. *For the fluid queue with capacity C and arrival measure Λ, $W(\Lambda)$ is convex in Λ.*

3.1 Optimal shift

A given arrival measure Λ may have a peak load that is too high. Seeking to shift some of this load, say a fraction p of the load, to the off-peak hours, we define the set of all possible shifts as follows:

$$\mathcal{S} = \{\hat{\Lambda} : \hat{\Lambda}(\infty) = \Lambda(\infty)\ ,\ \hat{\lambda}(t) \geq (1-p)\lambda(t)\ \forall t\}$$

We can add other constraints as well. For instance, we can restrict any changes in the arrival rate to a particular set of intervals. This is particularly useful if we seek to set up simple incentive schemes to motivate commuters to shift their arrival times[2].

[2]An example of such a rule is "Receive \$5 if you travel before 8:00 AM."

We define the cost of shifting as follows – given two measures Λ and $\hat{\Lambda}$, the *cost of shifting* Λ to $\hat{\Lambda}$, $S(\Lambda, \hat{\Lambda})$, is defined as the d-bar distance between the two measures. Similar to $W(\Lambda)$ being convex in Λ, $S(\Lambda, \hat{\Lambda})$ is convex in $\hat{\Lambda}$. Furthermore, the set of possible shifts is convex. Therefore, we can efficiently find the optimal arrival distribution.

We use this optimization procedure on a simple example and found that shifting 10% of the peak traffic to a 15 minute interval slightly before the peak hour reduces the cost of congestion (including the cost of the shift) by more than 19%.

4. CONCLUSIONS

Urban transportation networks face increasing challenges due to limited capacity. Peak hour congestion can by mitigated be shifting some of the load to a less congested time. Using two models of traffic flow over a highway, we showed that the cost of congestion, measured as the total *extra* time spent by vehicles in traversing the highway, is equal to the d-bar distance between arrival and departure measures. This allowed us to formulate a convex optimization problem for determining the optimal way to shift the peak load using incentives so as to reduce congestion costs. An example showed that the benefit can be significant. Modeling highways with multiple entries and exits as well as the effect of random fluctuations in the arrival rate are interesting future directions.

5. ACKNOWLEDGEMENTS

We would like to thank Prof. Peter Glynn and the anonymous reviewers for their helpful suggestions. This work is supported by the Stanford Center for Societal Networks. Chinmoy Mandayam is supported by the Sequoia Capital Stanford Graduate Fellowship.

6. REFERENCES

[1] R. M. Gray. *Probability, random processes, and ergodic properties.* Springer, 1988.

[2] T. G. Kurtz. *Approximation of population processes.* Number 36-40. SIAM, 1981.

[3] T. M. Liggett. *Interacting particle systems.* Springer, 2005.

[4] M. J. Lighthill and G. B. Whitham. On kinematic waves. II. A theory of traffic flow on long crowded roads. *Proceedings of the Royal Society of London. Series A. Mathematical and Physical Sciences,* 229(1178):317–345, 1955.

[5] C. V. Mandayam and B. Prabhakar. Road traffic networks: Optimal transport and incentives. In *Communication, Control, and Computing (Allerton), 2013 51st Annual Allerton Conference on,* pages 1090–1097, 2013.

[6] S. T. Rachev. The Monge-Kantorovich mass transference problem and its stochastic applications. *Theory of Probability & Its Applications,* 29(4):647–676, 1985.

[7] P. I. Richards. Shock waves on the highway. *Operations research,* 4(1):42–51, 1956.

[8] D. Schrank, B. Eisele, and T. Lomax. TTI's 2012 Urban Mobility Report. *Texas A&M Transportation Institute. The Texas A&M University System,* 2012.

Randomized Routing Schemes for Large Processor Sharing Systems with Multiple Service Rates

Arpan Mukhopadhyay
Department of Electrical and Computer Engineering
University of Waterloo
Waterloo, ON N2L 3G9, Canada
arpan.mukhopadhyay@uwaterloo.ca

Ravi R. Mazumdar
Department of Electrical and Computer Engineering
University of Waterloo
Waterloo, ON N2L 3G9, Canada
mazum@ece.uwaterloo.ca

ABSTRACT

We consider randomized job routing techniques for a system consisting of a large number of parallel processor sharing servers with heterogeneous server speeds. In particular, a scheme, that routes an incoming job request to the server providing the highest instantaneous processing rate per job among two servers, chosen uniformly at random, is proposed. We show that, unlike the homogeneous case, in the heterogeneous case, such randomized dynamic schemes need not always perform better than the optimal static scheme (in which jobs are assigned to servers with fixed probabilities independent of server states) in terms of reducing the mean response time of jobs. Specifically, we show that the stability region under the proposed scheme is a subset of that under the optimal static routing scheme. We also obtain the stationary tail distribution of server occupancies for the proposed scheme in the limit as the system size grows to infinity. This distribution has been shown to be insensitive to job length distribution and decay super-exponentially.

Categories and Subject Descriptors

G.3 [**Probability and Statistics**]: Queueing Theory

Keywords

Load Balancing; mean-field analysis; power-of-two; asymptotic independence; insensitivity

1. INTRODUCTION

Randomized dynamic job routing techniques are known to be good alternatives to the join-the-shortest-queue (JSQ) scheme for data centres which typically run thousands of servers, since such schemes require the state information of only small random subset of servers at each job arrival instant and yet result in reasonably small mean response time of jobs. A randomized dynamic scheme known as the power-of-two scheme or SQ(2) scheme [1, 2] assigns an incoming job to the server having the least instantaneous number of unfinished jobs among two servers chosen uniformly at random from the set of all servers. In the literature, the performance of the SQ(2) scheme has been analyzed for large systems of identical servers. It has been shown that the SQ(2) scheme results in an exponential reduction in the mean sojourn time of jobs as compared to the static (state independent) scheme which assigns jobs to servers with fixed probabilities independent of server states.

However, the performance analysis of randomized dynamic routing schemes has thus far been limited to only homogeneous systems having identical servers. In this paper, we consider a system of N parallel processor sharing (PS) servers where the server speeds can be different. We assume that a server can have one of the M possible values of server speed from the set $\mathcal{C} = \{C_1, C_2, \ldots, C_M\}$. We define $\mathcal{J} = \{1, 2, \ldots, M\}$. We further denote by γ_j, $j \in \mathcal{J}$, the proportion of servers having speed C_j. Jobs are assumed to arrive according to a Poisson process with rate $N\lambda$ and job lengths are assumed to be independent and identically distributed with mean $\frac{1}{\mu}$.

We propose the following modification of the SQ(2) scheme for the heterogeneous system described above: Upon arrival of a job request, two servers are chosen uniformly at random from the set of N servers and the job is routed to the server that provides the highest instantaneous processing rate per job among the two selected servers. For PS servers the processing rate per job at a server is defined as the ratio of server speed to the instantaneous number of unfinished jobs at the server. Ties are broken randomly by tossing a fair coin. We refer to this scheme as the HR(2) scheme. Clearly, unlike the SQ(2) scheme, the HR(2) scheme considers both server speed and the number of unfinished jobs at a server into the criterion for server selection.

2. ANALYTICAL RESULTS

We first characterize the stability region of the system described above under the proposed HR(2) scheme. We keep the proportions γ_j, $j \in \mathcal{J}$, fixed and increase N as $N = kN^*$ for $k \in \mathbb{N}$, where N^* denotes the minimum value of N for which $N\gamma_j \in \mathbb{N}$ for all $j \in \mathcal{J}$. We denote the stability region corresponding to $N = kN^*$ as Λ_k. Further, if Λ denotes the stability region under the static routing scheme, then from [3] we know that $\Lambda = \left\{0 \leq \lambda < \mu \sum_{j=1}^{M} \gamma_j C_j\right\}$. We show that $\Lambda \supseteq \Lambda_1 \supseteq \Lambda_2 \supseteq \ldots$. Furthermore, if $\Lambda_\infty = \cap_{k=1}^{\infty} \Lambda_k$ denotes the stability

SIGMETRICS'14, June 16–20, 2014, Austin, Texas, USA.
ACM 978-1-4503-2789-3/14/06.
http://dx.doi.org/10.1145/2591971.2592015.

region of the system as $N \to \infty$, then Λ_∞ is given by $\Lambda_\infty = \left\{0 \le \lambda < \mu \min_{\mathcal{I} \subseteq \mathcal{J}} \left\{ \frac{(\sum_{j\in\mathcal{I}} \gamma_j C_j)}{(\sum_{j\in\mathcal{I}} \gamma_j)^2} \right\}\right\}$. Hence, it is clear that the stability region under the HR(2) scheme is a subset of that under the static routing scheme. The stability region Λ can be recovered by using a combination of the static routing scheme and the SQ(2) scheme, which will appear elsewhere.

We now obtain the stationary distribution of server occupancies under the HR(2) scheme in the limit as $N \to \infty$. Using the mean-field approach we show that for exponential job length distribution, the underlying Markov process defined as $\mathbf{x}_N(t) = \left\{x_n^{(j)}(t), 1 \le j \le M, n \in \mathbb{Z}_+\right\}$, where $x_n^{(j)}(t)$ denotes the fraction of servers having capacity C_j with at least n unfinished jobs, weakly converges to the deterministic process $\mathbf{u}(t) = \left\{u_n^{(j)}(t), n \in \mathbb{Z}_+, 1 \le j \le M\right\}$ which satisfies the following system of differential equations:

$$\mathbf{u}(0) = \mathbf{g}, \tag{1}$$
$$\dot{\mathbf{u}}(t) = \mathbf{h}(\mathbf{u}(t)), \tag{2}$$

where $\mathbf{g}$ is some initial state and for $j \in \mathcal{J}$,

$$h_0^{(j)}(\mathbf{u}) = 0, \tag{3}$$
$$h_n^{(j)}(\mathbf{u}) = \lambda \left(u_{n-1}^{(j)} - u_n^{(j)}\right) \sum_{i=1}^{M} \gamma_i \left(u^{(i)}_{\langle (n-1)C_i/C_j \rangle} + u^{(i)}_{\lfloor (n-1)C_i/C_j \rfloor + 1}\right) - \mu C_j \left(u_n^{(j)} - u_{n+1}^{(j)}\right) \tag{4}$$

for all $n \ge 1$. In the above equations, $\lfloor w \rfloor$ denotes the greatest integer not exceeding w and $\langle w \rangle = \lfloor w \rfloor + 1$ if $w \notin \mathbb{Z}_+$ and $\langle w \rangle = w$, otherwise. We show that the above system has a unique solution in the M-fold product of the space of tail probability distributions on $\mathbb{Z}_+$ and under condition $\lambda \in \Lambda_\infty$ there exists a unique equilibrium point $\mathbf{P}$ satisfying $\mathbf{h}(\mathbf{P}) = 0$ such that $\sum_{k=0}^{\infty} P_k^{(j)} < \infty$ for all $j \in \mathcal{J}$. Further, we show that for any initial state $\mathbf{g}$, the solution $\mathbf{u}(t, \mathbf{g})$ of the system (1)-(4) converges to the point $\mathbf{P}$ as $t \to \infty$ under suitable metric.

Combining these facts together we conclude the following $\lim_{t\to\infty} \lim_{N\to\infty} \mathbf{x}_N(t) = \lim_{N\to\infty} \lim_{t\to\infty} \mathbf{x}_N(t) = \mathbf{P}$ holds in the sense of weak convergence. Therefore, the stationary tail probabilities of server occupancies for a server of speed C_j, $j \in \mathcal{J}$, in the limiting system is given by $\left\{P_k^{(j)}, k \in \mathbb{Z}_+\right\}$. We further show that for each $j \in \mathcal{J}$, the sequence $\left\{P_k^{(j)}, k \in \mathbb{Z}_+\right\}$ decreases to 0 super-exponentially.

Moreover, assuming that any finite subset of servers in the limiting system ($N \to \infty$) becomes independent under the stationary distribution, we show that the mean-field limit $\mathbf{P}$ is insensitive to the job length distribution so long as its mean remains unchanged. Therefore, the system is *asymptotically insensitive* to job length distributions.

3. NUMERICAL RESULTS

In Figure 1, we plot the mean sojourn time of jobs in the heterogeneous system as a function of the normalized arrival rate λ for the HR(2) scheme, SQ(2) scheme and the optimal static scheme assuming the following parameter setting: $C_1 = 1/3$, $C_2 = 5/3$, $\gamma_1 = \gamma_2 = 1/2$, $\mu = 1$, and $N = 200$. In this setting, we have $\Lambda = \{0 \le \lambda < 1\}$ and $\Lambda_\infty = \{0 \le \lambda < 2/3\}$. It is clear from the figure that the optimal static scheme results in lower mean sojourn time of jobs than the SQ(2) and HR(2) schemes. We also observe a good match between the analysis and simulation results for the HR(2) scheme. This implies that the asymptotic analysis accurately captures the performance of the HR(2) scheme for a large but finite system of servers.

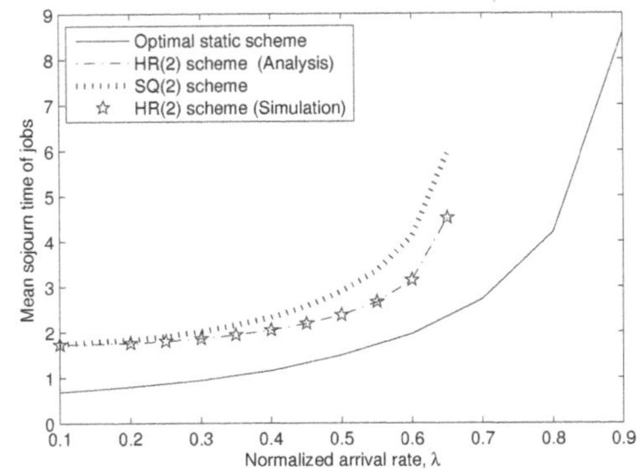

Figure 1: Mean sojourn time jobs as a function of λ for $C_1 = 1/3$, $C_2 = 5/3$, and $\gamma_1 = \gamma_2 = 1/2$

To investigate the asymptotic insensitivity, we consider two job length distributions: i) constant, with mean 1, ii) power law, with distribution satisfying $F(x) = 1 - 1/4x^2$ for $x \ge \frac{1}{2}$ and $F(x) = 0$, otherwise. In Table 1, we show the mean sojourn time of jobs for the following parameter setting: $C_1 = 4/3$, $C_2 = 2/3$, $N = 200$ and $\gamma_1 = \gamma_2 = \frac{1}{2}$. As expected we observe very little deviation of the simulation results from the theoretical values. This validates the asymptotic independence assumption.

Table 1: Insensitivity of Scheme 2

λ	Mean sojourn time T Theoretical	Constant Simulation	Power Law Simulation
0.2	1.1479	1.1475	1.1481
0.3	1.1956	1.1957	1.1960
0.5	1.3801	1.3800	1.3798
0.7	1.7735	1.7743	1.7745
0.8	2.1641	2.1628	2.1650
0.9	2.9604	2.9704	2.9710

4. REFERENCES

[1] N. D. Vvedenskaya, R. L. Dobrushin, and F. I. Karpelevich. Queueing system with selection of the shortest of two queues: an asymptotic approach. *Problems of Information Transmission*, 32(1):20–34, 1996.

[2] M. Bramson, Y. Lu, and B. Prabhakar. Randomized load balancing with general service time distributions. In *Proceedings of ACM SIGMETRICS*, pages 275–286, 2010.

[3] E. Altman, U. Ayesta, and B. J. Prabhu. Load balancing in processor sharing systems. *Telecommunication Systems*, 47(1-2):35–48, 2008.

Automated Analysis of Multithreaded Programs for Performance Modeling

Alexander Tarvo
Brown University
Providence, RI, USA
alexta@cs.brown.edu

Steven P. Reiss
Brown University
Providence, RI, USA
spr@cs.brown.edu

ABSTRACT

We present an approach for building performance models of multithreaded programs automatically. We use a combination of static and a dynamic analyses of a single representative run of the program to build its model. The model can predict performance of the program under a variety of configurations. This paper outlines how we construct the model and demonstrates how the resultant models accurately predict the performance of complex multithreaded programs.

Categories and Subject Descriptors

C.4 [**Computer Systems Organization**]: Performance of systems—*Modeling techniques*; F.3.2 [**General**]: Logics and Meaning of Programs—*Program analysis*

General Terms

Performance

Keywords

Performance, modeling, program analysis

1. INTRODUCTION AND BACKGROUND

Multithreaded applications, such as servers, multimedia programs, and scientific computing applications, access hardware resources simultaneously and perform a variety of synchronization operations. This results in a complex non-linear dependency between the configuration and performance of such programs. Configurations may reflect variations in the workload, program options such as the number of threads, and characteristics of the hardware.

To help understanding the dependency between the configuration and performance of a program a *performance prediction model* is used. Such model predicts performance of a program in different configurations. Performance models are essential for a variety of applications, including automatic deploying of programs [3], answering "what-if" questions [5], and detecting performance anomalies.

SIGMETRICS'14, June 16–20, 2014, Austin, Texas, USA.
ACM 978-1-4503-2789-3/14/06.
http://dx.doi.org/10.1145/2591971.2592016 .

Multithreaded programs can be large and complex, and modeling them manually is time consuming and error prone. To be practical, analyzing these programs and building their models should be automated. However, existing approaches to automatic performance modeling require either running the program in many different configurations [4], or are concentrated on building models of message-passing programs and distributed systems [7],[2]. Applying these techniques to complex muiltithreaded programs, where multiple threads perform locking and engage in concurrent I/O operations, may result in significant decrease of accuracy [7].

Previously we developed a three-tier discrete-event model that accurately predicts performance of multithreaded programs [6]. The high-tier model simulates the flow of data through the program. It is a queuing network, whose nodes correspond to the program's threads. The mid-tier model simulates program's threads using probabilistic call graphs (PCGs). PCG vertices S corresponds to pieces of the thread's code – *code fragments (CF)*. PCG edges represent a possible transition of control flow between the CFs and are labeled with their probabilities $\delta : S \rightarrow P(S)$. The lower-tier model include models of the shared resources: the CPU and the thread scheduler, the disk I/O subsystem, and synchronization constructs (*locks*) presented in the program.

Executing each CF $s_i \in S$ results in delay τ_i. The contention of shared resources can cause τ_i to vary across different configurations. Instead of explicitly defining τ_i we describe each CF s_i with its class c_i and parameters Π_i. The *class* $c_i \in C$ represents a nature of computations performed by a CF, where $C = \{c_{cpu}, c_{io}, c_{sync}, c_{in}, c_{out}\}$ correspond to CPU-intense computations, I/O operations, synchronization, and reading and writing to the program's queues. Parameters Π of c_{cpu} and c_{io} CFs represent demand for corresponding resources. Parameters of c_{sync}, c_{in}, and c_{out} CFs include the ID of the lock or queue accessed and, possibly, the timeout. When the mid-tier model has to compute τ_i for the s_i, it calls the lower-tier model and passes it parameters Π_i. The lower-tier model calculates τ_i and notifies the mid-tier model once the delay is complete.

2. AUTOMATIC MODEL CONSTRUCTION

Building performance models requires massive amount of information. Constructing the high-tier model requires knowledge of queues and threads in the program, and their interaction. It also requires knowledge of thread pools, since their sizes are major factors affecting performance. Constructing mid-tier models requires knowledge of code fragments (CFs) S in the program, their types and parameters Π, and the structure δ of the probabilistic call graph (PCG). Constructing the low-tier model requires knowing all the locks present in the program, their types (e.g. if the particular lock a mutex, a semaphore, or a barrier), and parameters.

Out of all the aspects of the program's analysis, discovering semantics of thread interaction is the most challenging problem. There are numerous ways to implement locks and queues, and to expose their functionality to threads. In general, retrieving this information automatically requires very complex and potentially inaccurate program analysis. However, we discovered that the analysis of a program could be greatly simplified if that program relies on well-defined implementation of high-level locks and queues.

Based on this finding we developed a methodology for automatic construction of performance models using a combination of static and dynamic analysis. First, our framework executes the program.As the program runs, the framework periodically takes "snapshots" of the call stack. The results of the stack sampling are the set of thread pools in the program and the set of functions that belong to the program's libraries.

Second, our framework performs the static analysis of the program. The analyzer scans the program's code and detects calls to locks, queues, and I/O routines. These calls are considered as c_{sync}, c_{in}/c_{out}, and c_{io} CFs correspondingly. The analyzer also detects construction of queues and locks in the program and determines their types.

Third, the framework performs the dynamic analysis. It instruments the program by inserting probes at the boundaries of detected CFs and runs the program in the same configuration as during the stack sampling run. Each probe reports its ID, the ID of the thread, and the timestamp. The sequence of probe hits constitute the *trace* for the program's threads. Every pair of adjacent probe hits in the trace represents the execution of a single CF.

The trace is used to generate PCGs for the program's threads. Some additional post-processing is required to generate a useful model. First, to ensure that the model is compact and robust we remove CFs with negligent impact on the performance. Second, the presence of CFs from the program's libraries may result in incorrect behavior of the model. Thus we split library CFs into the multiple nodes in the call graph, depending on their calling contexts.

Parameters Π are also obtained from the trace. Parameters of c_{sync}, c_{in}, c_{out} are the ID of the lock or a queue and operation timeout, which are reported by instrumentation. Parameters of locks and queues themselves (e.g. the number of permits for a semaphore or a maximum capacity of the queue) are obtained by instrumenting their constructors. Parameters of c_{cpu} CFs are execution times obtained from timestamps of these CFs. Parameters of c_{io} CFs are the sequence of low-level disk I/O operations initiated by the corresponding CF. These are obtained by matching the kernel-mode log of I/O operations to the program trace.

Finally, the framework translates the discovered information into the three-tier model, which can be executed using the OMNET++ discrete event simulation framework [1].

3. EXPERIMENTAL EVALUATION

We evaluate performance models by their prediction accuracy. We build the model of a multithreaded program using a single configuration. Then we predict performance of that program in a set of other configurations, and compare our predictions with the actual performance measured in the same configurations. The mean relative error ε between measured and predicted performance serves as a metric of prediction accuracy.

Table 1: Information on programs and their models

	Tomcat (web server)	Tomcat+iText (servlet container)	Sunflow
Program size (LOC)	182810	283143	21987
No. of probes	3178	3926	380
No. of PCG nodes	82	49	42
Mean relative error	0.269 (R) 0.027 (T)	0.122 (R) 0.099 (T)	0.032

To verify our approach we modeled a number of programs, including scientific computing programs, financial and multimedia applications, and servers. In this paper we concentrate on modeling two large applications: the Sunflow 3D renderer and the Apache Tomcat servlet container.

Configuration parameters of Sunflow are the the number of working threads used for computations (1 to 8) and the number of active CPU cores (1 to 4). Its performance is measured as the time required to render the image. Configuration of Tomcat includes the number of working threads to serve HTTP requests (1 to 10) and the rate of incoming HTTP requests. Its performance metrics are response time R and throughput T. We modeled Tomcat in two different setups. In the first setup Tomcat was serving requests for static web pages. In the second setup it was hosting a servlet that used iText library to create PDF documents. Results of our experiments are provided in the Table 1.

The main contribution of our work is the approach for automatic modeling of multithreaded programs and framework for building these models. Our experiments demonstrated the possibility to build accurate performance models of complex multithreaded programs.

4. REFERENCES

[1] http://www.omnetpp.org/.

[2] S. Becker, H. Koziolek, and R. Reussner. Model-based performance prediction with the palladio component model. In *International Workshop on Software and Performance*, pages 54–65. ACM, 2007.

[3] M. Bennani and D. Menasce. Resource allocation for autonomic data centers using analytic performance models. In *International Conference on Automatic Computing*, pages 229–240. IEEE, 2005.

[4] B. C. Lee, D. M. Brooks, B. R. de Supinski, M. Schulz, K. Singh, and S. A. McKee. Methods of inference and learning for performance modeling of parallel applications. In *Symposium on Principles and Practice of Parallel Programming*, pages 249–258. ACM, 2007.

[5] D. Narayanan, E. Thereska, and A. Ailamaki. Continuous resource monitoring for self-predicting dbms. In *MASCOTS*, pages 239–248. IEEE, 2005.

[6] A. Tarvo and S. P. Reiss. Using computer simulation to predict the performance of multithreaded programs. In *International Conference on Performance Engineering*, ICPE '12, pages 217–228. ACM, 2012.

[7] Q. Xu and J. Subhlok. Construction and evaluation of coordinated performance skeletons. In *International Conference on High performance computing*, pages 73–86. Springer-Verlag, 2008.

A Comparison of Core Power Gating Strategies Implemented in Modern Hardware

Manish Arora
AMD Research & UC San Diego

Srilatha Manne
AMD Research

Yasuko Eckert
AMD Research

Indrani Paul
AMD Research & Georgia Tech

Nuwan Jayasena
AMD Research

Dean Tullsen
UC San Diego

ABSTRACT

Idle power is a significant contributor to overall energy consumption in modern multi-core processors. Cores can enter a full-sleep state, also known as C6, to reduce idle power; however, entering C6 incurs performance and power overheads. Since power gating can result in negative savings, hardware vendors implement various algorithms to manage C6 entry. In this paper, we examine state-of-the-art C6 entry algorithms and present a comparative analysis in the context of consumer and CPU-GPU benchmarks.

Categories and Subject Descriptors: C.4 [**Performance of Systems**][Design Studies]
General Terms: Power, Performance, Algorithms
Keywords: Power Gating, Consumer, CPU-GPU

1. INTRODUCTION

Leakage power minimization is a first-order goal of modern processor design. While leakage power scales with supply voltage, the only way to eliminate it completely is by power gating (C6 entry). What makes exploiting core idle time difficult is that it is not simply a matter of power gating the core when it is idle for long periods (not running any jobs). Rather, many important computing applications, especially in the consumer space, have significant idle time during which power gating may be invoked while the application is "running". This can happen for many reasons, including the interactive or I/O-intensive nature of the applications, insufficient work in the CPU, or insufficient parallelism [4]. Even in traditional compute intensive application domains, CPU cores that were previously active are now being rendered idle during application execution because of the inclusion of general purpose programmable GPUs [6] and hardware accelerators [1].

Exploiting C6 entry faces 2 challenges. First, transitioning to and from active to C6 sleep state requires time and power to save architectural state and cold-miss penalties of lost micro-architectural state. Second, much of the idle time in modern client applications is composed of short duration idle events.

SIGMETRICS'14, June 16–20, 2014, Austin, Texas, USA.
ACM 978-1-4503-2789-3/14/06.

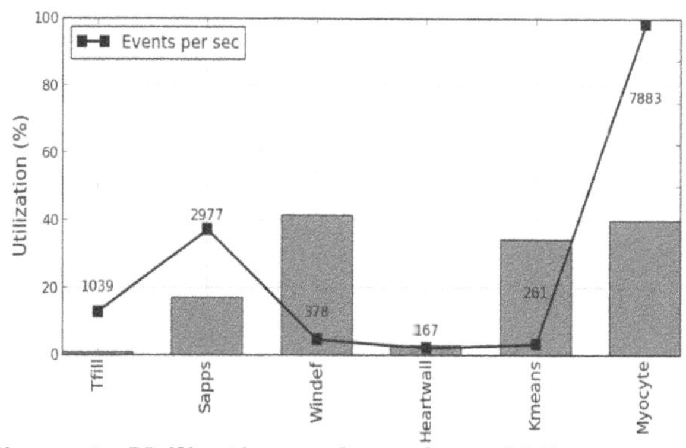

Figure 1: Utilization and number of idle events.

Figure 1 shows the average utilization and the average number of idle events per second across a subset of client applications from the consumer [2] and CPU-GPU space [5]. The y-axis shows utilization (the percent of time the application is active). The line shows the idle events per second for each benchmark. For optimal power savings, the idle time of the application should be characterized by very few long idle events. Unfortunately, most applications, regardless of their utilization, have a high frequency of idle events, ranging from an average of 6ms (*Heartwall*) to 125 usec between idle events (*Myocyte*), making it difficult to predict when to enter the C6 state.

2. C6 DESIGN SPACE EVALUATION

Whenever a core idles there is an option to either stay in clock gated state or choose to initiate entry into C6. We examine two specific C6 entry algorithms, *fixed preflush filtering* and *autodemotion* that represent the state of the art in commercially available hardware today.

Fixed Preflush Filtering (FPF). The FPF algorithm delays C6 entry for a fixed amount of time, referred to as the PreFlush latency, in order to filter out the high frequency, low duration idle events that can be detrimental to performance and energy. This scheme is used in production in the AMD 15h Trinity processor systems [3].

Autodemotion Autodemotion assumes that short duration idle events are clustered and come in *interrupt storms*. Hence Autodemotion either enables or disables C6 entry based on the frequency of idle events. If the number is

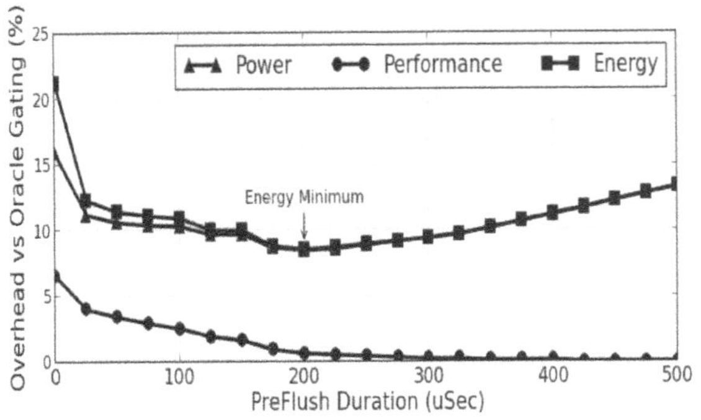

(a)

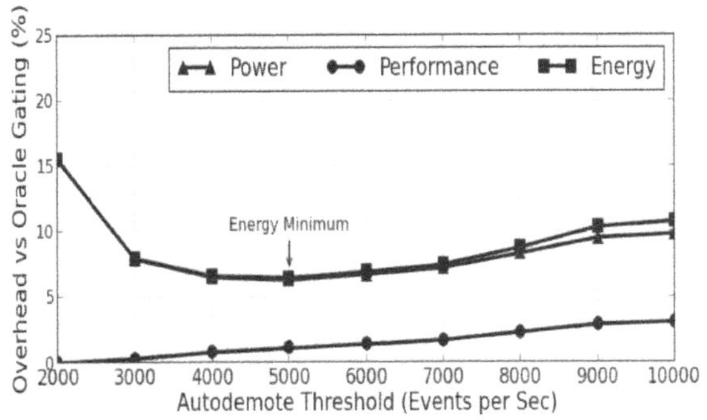

(b)

Figure 2: (a) Fixed preflush filtering design space. (b) Autodemotion design space.

greater than or equal to a threshold of events/sec for the current time interval, C6 is disabled for the next time interval. Otherwise, C6 is enabled and the system immediately enters C6. The Autodemotion scheme is implemented in the Intel SandyBridge family of processors [7].

Both the FPF and Autodemotion algorithms rely heavily on a threshold – FPF on the preflush latency and Autodemotion on the number of events that constitute a storm. We used a trace driven simulator to collect idleness and activeness traces together with a power modeling framework to perform a design space evaluation of both the schemes.

Using our modeling framework, we evaluate the FPF design space, varying the PreFlush latency from 0-500 usec. Similarly, we varied the Autodemotion threshold from 2000-10,000 events per second. We assume a 1 msec sampling interval for the Autodemotion scheme; hence a decision to enter C6 is made for the current 1 msec based on the number of events received in the last 1 msec interval. Figure 2 shows the results of our evaluation. We show the average power, performance, and energy across twenty seven consumer and CPU-GPU benchmarks. All numbers are provided as overheads relative to Oracle gating. Oracle gating is the best possible power gating scheme – it uses precise information on the length of the idle event to power gate (immediately) only when it saves power.

As shown, there is a severe power and performance penalty when the PreFlush latency is low because of the overheads of power gating. Increasing PreFlush latency always improves the performance, as power gating is never a performance win. A high PreFlush latency sacrifices power and energy because we spend more time in the PreFlush state instead

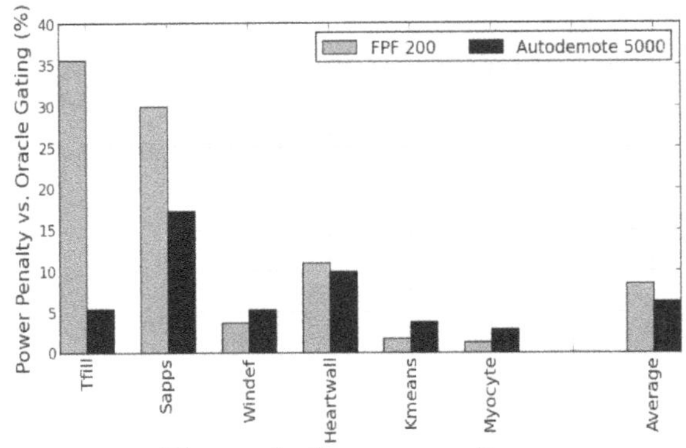

Figure 3: Power results.

of entering C6. The energy minimum for the FPF scheme is at 200 usec.

Figure 2 (b) shows the results for the Autodemotion scheme. The threshold of 2000 events per second turns off power gating if two events occur during the last 1 msec interval. This most conservative value preserves the most performance, but suffers a large power penalty as nearly all power gating opportunities are missed. As the threshold increases, the scheme is more aggressive, resulting in performance loss and energy gains. Beyond the energy minimum of 5000 events per second, this scheme begins to allow too many small events to occur, resulting in lost performance and increased energy.

The results of the design space evaluation indicate that on average the best operating points for FPF and Autodemotion schemes are still short of Oracle gating by 8% and 6.2% on average. Figure 3 compares the power of the FPF and Autodemotion best operating points with Oracle gating. As seen in the figure, FPF can be worse than Oracle gating by as much as 35%. However, no one algorithm completely dominates the other. In 3 of the 6 benchmarks FPF is better than Autodemotion and on an average Autodemotion is only slightly better than FPF. Both the algorithms have large opportunities of improvement for benchmarks such as *Sapps* and *Heartwall*.

3. CONCLUSION

We present a comparative analysis of existing state-of-the-art power gating entry algorithms on modern consumer and CPU-GPU benchmarks. Idleness is common in these important benchmarks and dominated by short idle events that may occur thousands of times a second. Existing algorithms used in hardware still leave significant room for improvement and power gating strategies need to be further investigated as GPUs and other hardware accelerators get integrated in systems leading to increased CPU idleness.

4. REFERENCES

[1] http://www.hsafoundation.com.
[2] Pcmark 7 pc performance testing white paper, 2011.
[3] Bkdg for amd family 15h model processors, 2012.
[4] G. Blake et al. Evolution of thread-level parallelism in desktop applications. ISCA 2010.
[5] S. Che et al. Rodinia: A benchmark suite for heterogeneous computing. IISWC 2009.
[6] D. Foley et al. Amd llano fusion apu. HotChips 2011.
[7] H. Jiang. Intel next generation microarchitecture code named sandybridge. Intel Developer Forum, 2010.

Topic Modeling from Network Spread

Avik Ray
University of Texas at Austin
Austin, Texas, USA
avik@utexas.edu

Sujay Sanghavi
University of Texas at Austin
Austin, Texas, USA
sanghavi@mail.utexas.edu

Sanjay Shakkottai
University of Texas at Austin
Austin, Texas, USA
shakkott@austin.utexas.edu

ABSTRACT

Topic modeling refers to the task of inferring, only from data, the abstract "topics" that occur in a collection of content. In this paper we look at latent topic modeling in a setting where unlike traditional topic modeling (a) there are no/few features (like words in documents) that are directly indicative of content topics (e.g. un-annotated videos and images, URLs etc.), but (b) users share and view content over a social network. We provide a new algorithm for inferring both the topics in which every user is interested, and thus also the topics in each content piece. We study its theoretical performance and demonstrate its empirical effectiveness over standard topic modeling algorithms.

1. INTRODUCTION

Topic modeling [1–3] refers to the task, classically arising in text document analysis, of assigning / recovering the abstract "topics" that characterize a corpus of several text documents. For example, the topics for news stories could be politics, sports, business, etc., while those for academic articles in networking could be wireless, BGP, 802.11, tomography etc. Importantly, what the topics are is *not pre-assigned*, but has to be learnt from the data. In particular, given documents, a topic model algorithm will *automatically* come up with a number K of abstract topics; each document is then associated with some subset of labels from the overall set $\{1,\ldots,K\}$. What these topics mean is not pre-specified; it is just learnt from the data, and may be interpreted ex post facto.

In this paper we are interested in doing topic modeling for settings in which the content to be modeled is such that it may be hard to find features that are directly relevant to its topic; for example, videos and pictures with little associated text, memes shared over social networks, etc. Such informative features are crucially needed in all existing approaches to topic modeling. The **main insight** we leverage: if we also have data on which people/users have interacted with / "liked" the content, we can *treat the users as informative features.* In particular, each user is likely interested in a small set of topics, and similarly each piece of content is a mix of a small set of topics; the more these sets are in alignment, the more likely it is for that user to react with that piece of content. Standard topic modeling algorithms [1–3] can be directly applied here treating users as words. However they do not perform well since the graph fundamentally governs the statistics which the existing algorithms fail to leverage. We propose a new probabilistic latent topic model that captures the dynamics of content spread in this setting and develop new algorithms that can efficiently learn both *(a)* set of topics each user is interested in, and *(b)* set of topics in each content (which has been shared by many users). We provide theoretical guarantees for our algorithms and empirical results showing their practical applicability.

SIGMETRICS'14, June 16–20, 2014, Austin, Texas, USA.
ACM 978-1-4503-2789-3/14/06.
http://http://dx.doi.org/10.1145/2591971.2592018.

2. SETTING AND ALGORITHM

We consider the following setting. There are n nodes, each corresponding to an user, connected by a graph $G = (V, E)$. There are also content pieces (videos, images etc.), which the users view and share. In particular, a user can *view* a piece of content if and only if it has been shared by one of its neighbors; it can subsequently *share* it further; it does so probabilistically according to a process we describe below. Thus, each piece of content is a *cascade* on the graph.

The **latent topic model** is what governs the probability of whether a user node, that has viewed a piece of content, decides to share it further. Consider a setting where there is a set $\mathcal{K}$ of K latent topics. Each user i has a set $C_i \subseteq \mathcal{K}$ of topics it is interested in. Similarly, each content piece t also has an associated topic set $C^t \subseteq \mathcal{K}$. The **content spread model** is as follows. At first a randomly chosen user (called the *seed*) first shares a content t. The spread of the content in the graph G then follows a discrete time SIR cascade process similar to [5]. On viewing the content for the first time an user i, shares it further with probability $\overline{p}$ if and only if their topic sets have a non-zero intersection, i.e. $C^t \cap C_i \neq \emptyset$. On the other hand, if the intersection is zero, i.e. $C^t \cap C_i = \emptyset$ then user i shares with probability $\underline{p}$; also, clearly, $\underline{p} < \overline{p}$. Represent each cascade S_t as an n length $0-1$ column vector whose i^{th} row is 1 if node i shares the tth content and zero otherwise for every t, this is what is recorded. The **algorithmic task** we are interested in is: given only the cascades $S_1, S_2, \ldots$ for content pieces, infer the latent topic set C_i for each user i, and C^t for content pieces t.

We now describe our main algorithm, called $LatentInterest$, that finds the interest set C_i for each user $i \in V$. Define *in-*

terest group V_k as $V_k := \{i \in V : k \in C_i\}$. Then finding all the sets $\{C_i\}_{i=1}^n$ is equivalent to finding all the groups $V_1, \ldots, V_K$. The *LatentInterest* algorithm takes as input the set of cascades $\mathcal{S} = \{S_1, \ldots, S_m\}$, the graph G, and two threshold parameters θ_1 and θ_2. It outputs the estimated interest groups $\widehat{V}_1, \ldots, \widehat{V}_K$ (pseudo-code in Algorithm 1).

Algorithm 1 *LatentInterest*$(\mathcal{S}, G, \theta_1, \theta_2)$

```
P ← AnchorNodeDetect(S, θ1, θ2)
V̂1, ..., V̂K ← InterestGroup(G, S, P, θ1)
```

Algorithm 2 *AnchorNodeDetect*$(\mathcal{S}, \theta_1, \theta_2)$

```
for i = 1 to |V| do
    R_i ← {j : (1/m) Σ_{t=1}^{m} 1[i, j ∈ S_t] ≥ θ1}
end for
Starting from the node with smallest co-infection set R_i
    find a set P of K nodes with smallest and most dissimilar
    co-infection sets; where R_i is called similar to R_j if the
    Jaccard distance d_J(R_i, R_j) ≤ θ2.
Output anchor node set P.
```

Algorithm 3 *InterestGroup*$(G, \mathcal{S}, \mathcal{P}, \theta_1)$

```
S ← [S_1, ..., S_m]; P ← (1/m) S S^T
for k = 1 to K do
    Remove a node i* from P; V̂_k ← i*
    Pick a neighbor l ∈ N(V̂_k). Add it to V̂_k if P_{i*,l} ≥ θ1.
    Stop when no such node l can be found.
end for
Output interest groups V̂1, ..., V̂K.
```

The algorithm has two main steps which are as follows. An *anchor node* i is a node which has interest in only a few topic (i.e. a node i for which $|C_i|$ is small). The analogous notion in topic modeling has been previously introduced in [2] with the name of *anchor word*. In the *first step* the algorithm finds a set $\mathcal{P}$ containing K such anchor nodes, whose interests are dissimilar from each other. These anchor nodes are in a way representative nodes for each interest group. This task is performed by calling the *AnchorNodeDetect* subroutine (pseudo-code in Algorithm 2). In the *second step* the *InterestGroup* subroutine (pseudo-code in Algorithm 3) uses the anchor node set $\mathcal{P}$ and the graph G to find the interest group estimates $\widehat{V}_1, \ldots, \widehat{V}_K$. Finding content topics C^t is now straightforward. We say $k \in C^t$ if a large fraction of users in V_k share content t.

3. PERFORMANCE

In this section we state our main theorem that guarantees that under certain mild assumptions the *LatentInterest* algorithm correctly recovers all interest groups. We briefly state our assumptions. 1. Each topic is equally likely to appear in a content independent of other topics and the expected number of topics in the content is constant. 2. The graph G is a union of $K+1$ random graphs [4], one connected graph for each interest group V_k and an overall Erdos-Renyi noise graph $\mathcal{G}_{n,q}$. 3. For each k there exists at least one pure anchor node $i \in V_k$, such that $|C_i| = 1$. 4. $\exists \beta > 0$ such that for any two interest groups V_{k_1}, V_{k_2}, $|V_{k_1} \cap V_{k_2}^c| \geq \beta n$. 5. If the smallest and largest interest group have αn and $\alpha' n$ nodes respectively then, $\alpha' < \alpha + \beta$. 6. Let $g_k(x)$ be the generating polynomial of degree distribution for the random graph on V_k, then $\overline{p} > \max_{k \in \mathcal{K}} \frac{g_k'(1)}{g_k''(1)}$ and $\underline{p} < \min_{k \in \mathcal{K}} \frac{g_k'(1)}{g_k''(1)}$. Define function η as follows. $\eta = 1 - \beta$ if $qn = \Omega(\log n)$, and $\eta = \alpha$ otherwise.

THEOREM 1. *Let the maximum fraction of topics in any user topic set* C_i *be* $\gamma = O(\beta\eta/\alpha)$, *and the minimum probability of a node sharing a content be* $\underline{p} = O\left(\frac{\beta\eta}{K}\right)$. *For any* $\delta \in (0,1)$, *under above conditions* $1-6$, *with* $\theta_1 = \Omega(\frac{\alpha}{K})$, $\theta_2 = \Theta(\frac{\beta}{\alpha})$, *the LatentInterest algorithm can recover the interest groups* $V_1, \ldots V_K$ *with probability greater than* $1 - \delta$ *when the number of cascades* $m = \Omega\left(\frac{K^2}{\eta^2\beta^2}\log\frac{n}{\delta}\right)$.

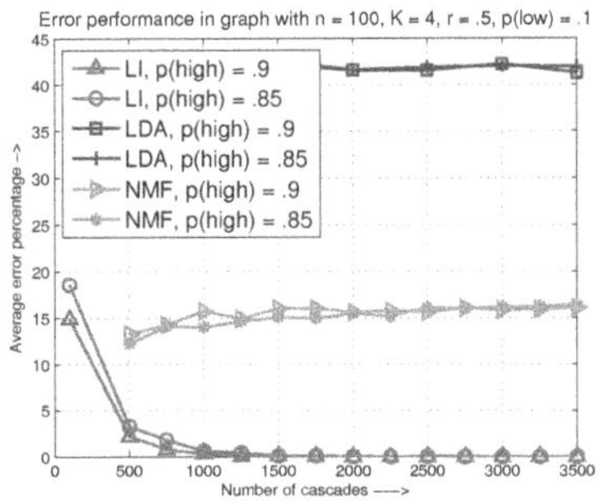

Figure 1: Figure showing the average error performance of ***LatentInterest*** **(LI), LDA [3] and NMF [2] algorithms. The average error of our algorithm LI goes to zero with increasing samples and it exactly recovers all the interest groups, however for LDA and NMF algorithms average error always remain high. The experiment parameters were:** $n = 100, K = 4$, **average number of topics per content** $= 2$, $\underline{p}$ **or** $p(\text{low}) = .1$ **and two different values of** $\overline{p}$ **(or** $p(\text{high})$**). Average error percentage is calculated as** $e = \frac{100}{nK}\sum_{k=1}^{K}|(\widehat{V}_k \backslash V_k) \cup (V_k \backslash \widehat{V}_k)|$.

4. ACKNOWLEDGMENTS

This work was supported by NSF grants IIS-1017525, CNS-1320175, ARO grant W911NF-11-1-0265 and DTRA grant number HDTRA1-13-1-0024.

5. REFERENCES

[1] A. Anandkumar, D. P. Foster, D. Hsu, S. M. Kakade, and Y. K. Liu. A spectral algorithm for latent dirichlet allocation, 2012. `http://arxiv.org/abs/1204.6703`.

[2] S. Arora, Y. Halpern, D. Mimno, A. Moitra, D. Sontag, Y. Wu, and M. Zhu. A practical algorithm for topic modeling with provable guarantees. In *Proc. of ICML*, 2013.

[3] D. M. Blei, A. Y. Ng, and M. I. Jordan. Latent dirichlet allocation. *the Journal of machine Learning research*, 3:993–1022, 2003.

[4] F. Chung and L. Lu. *Complex graphs and networks*. American Mathematical Soc., 2006.

[5] P. Netrapalli and S. Sanghavi. Learning the graph of epidemic cascades. In *ACM SIGMETRICS*, 2012.

BATS: Budget-Constrained Autoscaling for Cloud Performance Optimization

A. Hasan Mahmud
Florida International University

Yuxiong He
Microsoft Research

Shaolei Ren
Florida International University

1. INTRODUCTION

In recent years, cloud computing has experienced an exponential growth, providing a wide range of services such as scientific computing and web hosting. Cloud service users desire two major benefits: good performance and low operational costs. Autoscaling is a key property of the cloud systems that aims to achieve this goal. Using autoscaling, users can dynamically request more resources (e.g., virtual machines, or VMs) and pay more when their demand increases, and vice versa. In this paper, we propose to optimize cloud application performance by leveraging autoscaling while satisfying a long-term budget constraint (e.g., monthly or yearly budget). Such budget constraints are commonly applied to businesses, universities and governments, which typically allocate annual IT operational budgets at the beginning of each fiscal year [6]. We focus on delay-sensitive cloud applications (e.g., web services) where application performance is measured by the delay of responses. While optimizing delay performance under a budget constraint is important for cloud users, it is practically challenging. Requesting more VMs at the current time will reduce the available budget for future uses and hence, optimally scaling VM acquisitions requires the complete offline information (e.g., future workload demand) over the entire budgeting period, which is very difficult, if not impossible, to obtain in advance, especially considering highly dynamic workloads and possible traffic spikes due to breaking events.

The default autoscaling mechanisms offered by major cloud service providers, such as Amazon EC2 and Windows Azure, typically scale VM instances based on resource utilization indicators such as CPU and memory usage: e.g., adding a new VM instance or switching to a bigger VM instance that has more virtual CPU cores when the current CPU utilization exceeds a certain user-specified threshold [1, 3]. However, when considering the budget constraint, it is difficult to decide the optimal resource usage threshold *a priori*, because the threshold value depends on the user budget and the workloads during the entire budgeting period (e.g., setting a low threshold increases performance but may violate budget constraint, and vice versa). Recent efforts on autoscaling for optimizing the performance under long-term budget constraints have primarily focused on evenly distributing budgets across time or predicting the long-term future workloads, neither of which applies to highly-dynamic delay-sensitive workloads in practice [4, 5].

In this paper, in view of the practical difficulty in accurately predicting long-term future workloads, we develop an online autoscaling system, called BATS (Budget-constrained AuToScaling), that dynamically scales VM instances to optimize the delay performance while satisfying user budget constraint in the long run. The core of BATS is an online autoscaling algorithm, which only requires the past and instantaneous workload information to make effective scaling decisions. The key idea of our algorithm is to keep track of the budget deficit online and incorporate it into the online autoscaling decision: if the actual VM expenses exceed the expected cost thus far, BATS will request fewer and/or smaller VM instances subject to the minimum delay performance requirement, such that the budget deficit can be decreased. Thus, the budget deficit tracked online serves as a feedback mechanism to guide BATS towards satisfying the long-term budget constraint.

The contribution of our work is that we provide a full-fledged autoscaling solution to optimize delay performance while meeting users' long-term budget constraints that widely exist in practice. In particular, we offer a provably-efficient autoscaling algorithm, a user-friendly automated system implemented on Windows Azure, and comprehensive performance evaluation showing advantages of the proposed solution compared with state of the art using both system implementation and simulation.

2. SYSTEM IMPLEMENTATION

We describe the software architecture of BATS autoscaler. It has three main modules: (1)***Monitor***: gathering different performance metrics or resource utilization indicators of the hosted cloud application, such as number of web server connections, (2) ***Scheduler***: deciding the optimal number of VMs for the cloud application based on BATS algorithm with a goal of minimizing delay while meeting the budget constraint, and (3) ***Scaler***: executing the scheduler decision and submits the scaling request to Windows Azure. The *Scheduler* has two submodules that uses the output from the *Monitor*: a *Predictor* that predicts the workload arrival using an auto-regressive model and a *Performance Watcher* that detects the current workload status. *Performance Watcher* ensures that autoscaler meets the delay per-

SIGMETRICS'14, June 16–20, 2014, Austin, Texas, USA.
ACM 978-1-4503-2789-3/14/06.
http://dx.doi.org/10.1145/2591971.2592019.

formance goal in case of workload prediction error or sudden workload spike. While we use Windows Azure as an example, the modular design of our autoscaler is also applicable for other cloud platforms such as Amazone EC2 by modifying the *Scaler* and *Monitor* modules.

3. EXPERIMENTAL RESULT

First, we discuss our experimental setup. We consider a time slotted model and generate workload arrivals based on the MSR (Microsoft Research) workload trace to drive our experiment. To limit lengthy experiment, the budgeting period in our study consists of 48 time slots and the duration of each time slot is 1 hour. The default budget for our experiment is \$8.5 while the cost for one VM instance per hour is \$0.02. We deploy the RUBiS [2] benchmarking application into the web role of Azure Cloud Service and scale the underlying resources by varying the number of VM instances. We use extra-small VM instances. The performance goal is to achieve an average delay of 520ms while the maximum tolerable average delay is 1500ms. To make the optimal scaling decision (i.e., number of VM instances) at each time slot, BATS needs to determine the resulting delay for the incoming workload under various scaling configuration (i.e., number of VM instances). We model delay of RUBiS workload using a delay lookup table. Specifically, we vary the number of clients from the workload generator and obtain average delay for each different scaling configuration. Thus, we build the delay lookup table for various combinations of workload arrival rates and numbers of VM instances.

We now describe three benchmarks to compare BATS: (1) **EqualSC:** evenly dividing the available budget across all the time slots and obtains the number of VM instances that can be reserved for the entire budgeting period based on discounted pricing (20% for reserved instances [3]), (2) **ReactSC:** widely adopted autoscaler [1, 3] that constantly monitors the average workload arrival rates measured over the last 5 minutes and uses the delay lookup table to determine the minimum number of VM instances such that the resulting delay is less than a specified threshold (520ms), and (3) **OptOffline:** optimally dividing the whole budget among time slots with perfect workload arrival information over the entire budgeting period.

Next, we compare the performance of BATS with benchmark algorithms and show cumulative average delay and cumulative cost in Fig. 1(a) and Fig. 1(b), respectively. The cumulative average value for a time slot t is the corresponding average value of time slot 0 to t. We show the average delay performance and cost comparisons for each individual time slot in Fig. 1(c) and Fig. 1(d), respectively. As shown in Fig. 1(a), BATS reduces delay by 34% compared to EqualSC while achieving the same budget constraint, even though EqualSC receives discounted pricing. This is mainly because EqualSC evenly divides the budget across each time slot and reserves 11 VM instances without considering the workload variation. As a result, when there is a workload spike (e.g., in the 4th time slot), the delay becomes very large, as shown in Fig. 1(c). The average delay reduction of BATS is 10% compared to ReactSC. The degrading performance of ReactSC comes from the long *lagging* time: it takes up to 5 minutes to detect the system status change (e.g., workload variation) and even after detection, it takes up to 10 minutes to acquire a new VM instance. During the lagging time, all the incoming workloads experience longer

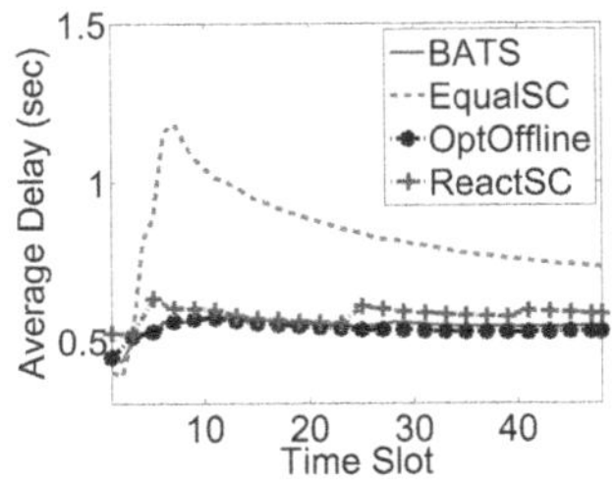

(a) Average delay.

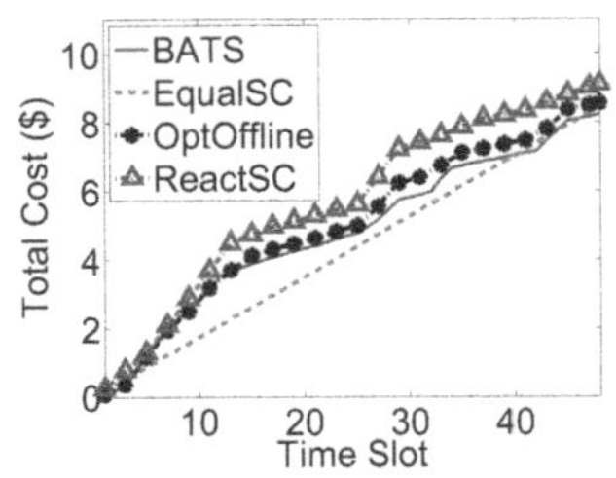

(b) Total Cost.

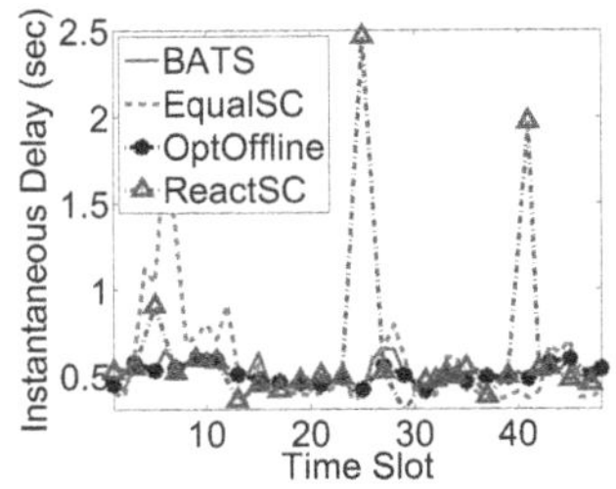

(c) Instantaneous delay.

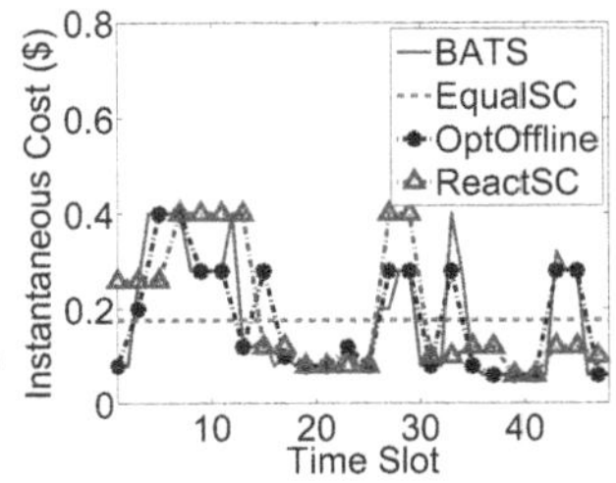

(d) Instantaneous Cost.

Figure 1: Comparing BATS with other algorithms.

average delays. This demonstrates the importance of proactively predicting the near-future (e.g., hour-ahead) workloads as used by BATS, thereby highlighting the limitations of reactive autoscaling rules. Moreover, Fig. 1(b) shows that the cost saving of BATS is 10% compared to ReactSC. It is mainly because ReactSC ignores the budget constraint and always makes scaling decisions such that resulting average delay equals 520ms. ReactSC also violates \$8.5 budget constraint. We also observe that the average delay of BATS is very close to OptOffline (with a difference less than 4%), while Fig. 1(b) shows that the cost is almost the same. Thus, the results demonstrate the effectiveness of BATS.

Finally, we summarize the simulation study that demonstrates the benefits and robustness of BATS on a wide range of scenarios. Even with high workload prediction errors, the performance of BATS is still robust: e.g., for 20% prediction error, the resulting average delay only increases by 1.4%. Moreover, by leveraging both horizontal and vertical scaling, BATS can further improve delay performance while satisfying the budget constraint. BATS can also incorporate reserved instances in its operation to lower operational cost and improve delay performance. The simulation study for other workload traces also demonstrates that BATS performs better even under fairly smooth workloads.

4. REFERENCES

[1] Amazon ec2. `http://aws.amazon.com/autoscaling/`.

[2] Rubis. `http://rubis.ow2.org/`.

[3] Windows azure. `http://www.windowsazure.com/`.

[4] M. Malawski, G. Juve, E. Deelman, and J. Nabrzyski. Cost-and deadline-constrained provisioning for scientific workflow ensembles in iaas clouds. In *SC*, 2012.

[5] M. Mao, J. Li, and M. Humphrey. Cloud auto-scaling with deadline and budget constraints. In *GRID*, 2010.

[6] S. VanRoekel. The FY14 President's IT budget: Innovate, deliver, protect, `https://cio.gov/the-fy14-presidents-it-budget-innovate-deliver-protect/`.

What's Your Choice? Learning the Mixed Multi-nomial Logit Model

Ammar Ammar
ammar@mit.edu

Sewoong Oh
swoh@illinois.edu

Devavrat Shah
devavrat@mit.edu

Luis Filipe Voloch
voloch@mit.edu

ABSTRACT

Computing a ranking over choices using consumer data gathered from a heterogenous population has become an indispensable module for any modern consumer information system, e.g. Yelp, Netflix, Amazon and app-stores like Google play. In such applications, a ranking or recommendation algorithm needs to extract meaningful information from noisy data *accurately* and in a *scalable* manner. A principled approach to resolve this challenge requires a *model* that connects observations to recommendation decisions and a tractable inference algorithm utilizing this model. To that end, we abstract the preference data generated by consumers as noisy, partial realizations of their innate preferences, i.e. orderings or permutations over choices. Inspired by the seminal works of Samuelson (cf. *axiom of revealed preferences*) and that of McFadden (cf. discrete choice models for transportation), we model the population's innate preferences as a mixture of the so called Multi-nomial Logit (MMNL) model. Under this model, the recommendation problem boils down to (a) learning the MMNL model from population data, (b) finding am MNL component within the mixture that closely represents the revealed preferences of the consumer at hand, and (c) recommending other choices to her/him that are ranked high according to thus found component. In this work, we address the problem of learning MMNL model from partial preferences. We identify fundamental limitations of *any* algorithm to learn such a model as well as provide conditions under which, a simple, data-driven (non-parametric) algorithm learns the model effectively. The proposed algorithm has a pleasant similarity to the standard *collaborative filtering* for scalar (or star) ratings, but in the domain of permutations. This work advances the state-of-art in the domain of learning distribution over permutations (cf. [2]) as well as in the context of learning mixture distributions (cf. [4]).

Model and Problem Statement:

This section explains the problem of learning the mixed Multi-nomial Logit (MMNL) model. In particular, it provides a definition of the model, a procedure for generating the data from this model, and a lower-bound that reflects the difficulty in learning the model.

SIGMETRICS'14, June 16–20, 2014, Austin, Texas, USA.
ACM 978-1-4503-2789-3/14/06.
http://dx.doi.org/10.1145/2591971.2592020.

The MNL Model: the Multi-nomial Logit (MNL) model is a probability distribution over permutations. For a set of n items, this model is specified by a set of weight parameters $w_1, \ldots, w_n$. Given a set of items, C, the probability of choosing an item $i \in C$ is

$$\mathbb{P}_C(i; w) = \frac{w_i}{\sum_{j \in C} w_j} . \qquad (1)$$

and the probability of a permutation σ has the form

$$\mathbb{P}(\sigma; w) = \prod_{j=1}^{n} \frac{w_{\sigma^{-1}(j)}}{w_{\sigma^{-1}(j)} + w_{\sigma^{-1}(j+1)} + \cdots + w_{\sigma^{-1}(n)}} . \qquad (2)$$

This expression suggests the following (sequential) sampling procedure for generating σ: choose the first item, $\sigma^{-1}(1)$, from the set of all n items, then choose the second item, $\sigma^{-1}(2)$, from the remaining $n-1$ items, and so on, for n steps. Furthermore, to sample a partial permutation of length l items, terminate this procedure after l steps.

The MMNL Model: the mixed MNL (MMNL) model is a probability mixture of several MNL models. The probability assigned to a permutation σ under this model takes the form

$$\mathbb{P}(\sigma) = \sum_{k=1}^{K} \alpha_k \cdot \mathbb{P}(\sigma; w^k) , \qquad (3)$$

where K denotes the number of components in the mixture, $\{\alpha_k\}$ the prior of the mixture (i.e., $\alpha_k \geq 0$ and $\sum_{k=1}^{K} \alpha_k = 1$), and $w^k \in \mathbb{R}^n$ the parameter vector of the k-th MNL component. To sample a full, or partial, permutation from this model, one can start by sampling an integer $k \in \{1, \ldots, K\}$ using the prior $\{\alpha_k\}$. The desired sample can then be obtained from the corresponding MNL, $\mathbb{P}(\cdot; w^k)$, as outlined previously.

Problem Statement: given a MMNL model over n items, with K mixing components, and data generated from this model, the problem of interest is that of learning the parameters α_k and w^k for all the components. The data available for this purpose consists of N IID samples in the form of partial permutations of length l, where $l < n$.

Drawing on previous work (e.g. [5][3][1]), the learning problem can be decoupled into two stages. First, identify the label of the MNL component that generated each sample. Once the labels have been identified, the samples associated with a given label can be used to estimate the parameters, α_k and w^k. That said, note $\{\alpha_k\}$ can be estimated in a straight-forward fashion from the label assignment. Given one such assignment, one only needs to estimate the parameter vectors w^k. To that end, several algorithms have been proposed (e.g. [3] and [5]). With that in mind, the problem of learning the MMNL model reduces to that of computing a 'correct' label assignment for the data. We consider this problem in the next section.

Main Results

Intuitively, to solve the label assignment problem one has to be able to distinguish between samples coming from different MNL components, if at all possible. To this end, we provides two concrete results: one negative, in the form of a lower bound, and one positive in the form of a set of sufficient conditions under which we are able to learn the MMNL model.

A Lower Bound: the richness of the MMNL family presents us with some difficulties. One such difficulty is demonstrated by the following result; it establishes the impossibility of distinguishing members of a certain family of 'limiting' MMNL models using samples of length l for certain values of l.

Theorem 1. *For any non-negative integer i, there exist pairs of 'limiting' MMNL models with $n = 2^{i+1}$ items and $k = 2^i$ mixing components, and identical mixing distributions, where the datasets generated by both models using samples of length $l = 2i + 1$ are identical in distribution (i.e., data cannot be used to distinguish between the two mixtures).*

With this in mind, we present an algorithm for computing a label assignment for the available data points. Roughly, the algorithm partitions the data set into subsets, where the data points in each subset originate from the same MNL component. The proposed algorithm consists of two steps: a preprocessing step and a clustering step. The preprocessing step produces a *sample graph* where the nodes correspond to the data samples, and the presence (absence) of an edge reflects whether a pair of data samples share a common (or different) MNL origin. The clustering step takes this graph as an input and produces the desired partition. Finally, we provide a set of sufficient conditions, under which the computed partition is guaranteed to be consistent with the underlying MMNL model.

The Sample Graph: given a set of partial permutations $\{\sigma^1, \dots, \sigma^N\}$ (of length l), our algorithm constructs a graph on N, with adjacency matrix $W = [W_{ij}]$ given by:

$$W_{ij} = \begin{cases} 0, & \text{if overlap}(\sigma^i, \sigma^j) < 1/2 \text{ OR affinity}(\sigma^i, \sigma^j) < 1/2 \\ 1, & \text{otherwise,} \end{cases}$$

where overlap(σ^i, σ^j) denotes the fraction of items shared among the l items of σ^i and σ^j. As for affinity(σ^i, σ^j), it is defined as

$$\text{affinity}(\sigma^i, \sigma^j) = \sum_{k,l \in S, k \neq l} \sigma^i_{kl} \cdot \sigma^j_{kl} \Big/ \binom{|S|}{2}$$

where S is the set of items where σ^i and σ^j overlap, and σ_{kl} is a $+1/-1$ indicator that item k is preferred to item l.

Clustering: given the *sample graph* produced in the preprocessing step, we present the following algorithm to compute a partition of the nodes:

Algorithm 1 Common Neighbors

Input: Symmetric adjacency matrix $W \in \{0,1\}^{N \times N}$

Initialize clustering $C = \{\{\sigma_i\}\}$.
for $(u, v) \in A$ **do**
  if $|N(u) \cap N(v)| > \frac{1}{2} \min\{|N(u)|, |N(v)|\}$ **then**
    perform operation $UNION(u, v)$
  end if
end for

The algorithm uses the Union-find data structure for partitions. We begin with each node in its set, and use the union operation whenever their neighbors overlap by more than half. Upon termination, the algorithm creates a clustering of the samples.

Sufficient Conditions We would like to provide the guarantee that with high probability nodes will be clustered together if and only if they come from the same component in the mixture distribution. Theorem 2, provides one such guarantee in the form of sufficient conditions on the underlying MMNL model and the length, l, of the partial permutation. In order to state these conditions, we use the following definitions.

Definition 1. *(Geometric MNL Model)*
Let $\mathbb{P}(.; w)$ be an MNL model over n items, and let the permutation π be the ordering of the the parameters $w_{\pi_1}, w_{\pi_2}, \dots, w_{\pi_n}$. We call this MNL model geometric if

$$\frac{w_{\pi_i}}{w_{\pi_{i+1}}} \geq a$$

for some constant $a > 1$ and for each $i < n$. Further, we use $\mathbb{P}(\sigma; \pi, a)$ to shorthand notation for this kinds of models.

Definition 2. *(Uniform Geometric MNL Model with K components)*
Let $\mathbb{P}(.; w^1, \dots, w^K, \{\alpha_k\})$ denote an MMNL model over n items, with K mixing components, $\mathbb{P}(.; w^k)$ with $k \in \{1, \dots, K\}$, and mixing distribution $\{\alpha^k\}$. We call this model a uniform geometric MMNL model if

(i) Each component $\mathbb{P}(.; w^k) = \mathbb{P}(.; \pi^k, a^k)$ is a geometric MNL (as per definition 1).

(ii) Each permutation π^k is drawn uniformly at random from the set of all permutations of length n items.

(iii) The mixing distribution $\{\alpha_k\}$ is a discrete uniform distribution (i.e., $\alpha_k = 1/K \quad \forall k$).

We can now state a guarantee for the Algorithm 1 with the following theorem.

Theorem 2. *Given a* uniform geometric MMNL *model over n items with K (fixed) components, and N samples, of length l drawn, from this distribution. For $l = \Theta(\log n)$, and $N = \Theta(\text{poly} \log n)$, algorithm 1 produces a correct partition with probability at least $1 - O(\frac{\text{poly} \log n}{n})$.*

Note that this theorem requires a fixed number of components K, whereas theorem 1 relies on K growing on the order of $\Theta(n)$, with $l = \Theta(\log n)$ in both cases.

References

[1] A. P. Dempster, N. M. Laird, D. B. Rubin, et al. Maximum likelihood from incomplete data via the em algorithm. *Journal of the Royal statistical Society*, 39(1):1–38, 1977.

[2] V. F. Farias, S. Jagabathula, and D. Shah. A nonparametric approach to modeling choice with limited data. *Management Science*, 59(2):305–322, 2013.

[3] D. McFadden. Conditional logit analysis of qualitative choice behavior. 1973.

[4] A. Moitra and G. Valiant. Settling the polynomial learnability of mixtures of gaussians. In *Foundations of Computer Science (FOCS), 2010 51st Annual IEEE Symposium on*, pages 93–102. IEEE, 2010.

[5] S. Negahban, S. Oh, and D. Shah. Iterative ranking from pair-wise comparisons. In *NIPS*, pages 2483–2491, 2012.

Revisiting Caching in Content Delivery Networks

M. Zubair Shafiq†, Alex X. Liu†, Amir R. Khakpour‡
†Department of Computer Science and Engineering, Michigan State University, East Lansing, MI, USA
‡Verizon/EdgeCast, Santa Monica, CA, USA
{shafiqmu,alexliu}@cse.msu.edu, amir@edgecast.com

ABSTRACT

Content Delivery Networks (CDNs) differ from other caching systems in terms of both workload characteristics and performance metrics. However, there has been little prior work on large-scale measurement and characterization of content requests and caching performance in CDNs. For workload characteristics, CDNs deal with extremely large content volume, high content diversity, and strong temporal dynamics. For performance metrics, other than hit ratio, CDNs also need to minimize the disk operations and the volume of traffic from origin servers. In this paper, we conduct a large-scale measurement study to characterize the content request patterns using real-world data from a commercial CDN provider.

Categories and Subject Descriptors

C.2.3 [**Computer System Organization**]: Computer Communication Networks—*Network Operations*

Keywords

Caching; Content Delivery Network (CDN)

1. INTRODUCTION

Most major content publishers such as Netflix, Hulu, Facebook, Pinterest, and CNN use Content Delivery Networks (CDNs), often run by third parties, to bring content closer to their end users. More than 70% of all Internet traffic nowadays is carried by CDNs [6]. A CDN provider typically owns or rents spaces from multiple data centers, called Points of Presence (PoPs), which are geographically distributed around the world. When a content publisher contracts a CDN to host their content, a user request to their content (such as a web page, an image, or a video file) is redirected to the closest PoP via DNS redirection, HTTP redirection, URL rewriting, or anycast [7]. If that PoP does not have the content, then the PoP fetches it from the origin server of the content publisher, sends it to the user, and also caches the content in storage such as Solid State Drives (SSDs) or Hard Disk Drives (HDDs). Thus, for later requests to the same content, the PoP directly sends its cached copy to the users if the Time-To-Live (TTL) value has not expired. CDNs provide many benefits such as faster content delivery to end users, higher service availability, better user experience, less traffic to content publisher servers, and better protection of content publishers from Denial of Service (DoS) due to their larger capacity of handling legitimate flash crowds and malicious attack traffic.

There has been little prior work on characterization of content requests and caching performance in CDNs. This is partially because CDNs have emerged only for about ten years and have became prevalent only recently as video, image, and other User Generated Content (UGC) has become dominant sources of traffic on the Internet and way passed the capacity that content publishers can handle by themselves. In particular, no caching schemes have been designed particularly for CDNs in prior literature, to the best of our knowledge. CDN providers still commonly use the standard cache replacement algorithms such as Least Recently Used (LRU), Least Frequently Used (LFU), and their minor variants. However, CDNs deserve specialized caching schemes because they differ from other caching systems in terms of both *workload characteristics* and *performance metrics*.

The first step towards designing effective caching schemes tailored for CDNs is to understand the characteristics of content requests because their dynamics strongly impact CDN caching performance. However, little prior work has been done towards this end. Some passive measurement studies on CDNs have been done [3, 10]; however, they are limited to analyzing traffic from CoralCDN, a free and open CDN based on the PlanetLab testbed, whose load is orders of magnitude smaller than that of large commercial CDNs. Some active measurement studies on CDNs have been done [1,2,4,5,8,9]; however, they are small-scale studies due to the active nature and they do not provide a characterization of content requests other than those they injected. To the best of our knowledge, a large-scale measurement and characterization of content requests is missing in prior literature.

In this paper, we conduct a comprehensive measurement study to characterize the content requests in large CDNs using real-world data from one of the world's largest commercial CDN providers. Our data set contains detailed traffic logs from multiple PoPs of the CDN provider over the duration of one week in 2012 consisting of more than 600 million requests. All personally identifiable information in our data

SIGMETRICS'14, June 16–20, 2014, Austin, Texas, USA.
ACM 978-1-4503-2789-3/14/06.
http://dx.doi.org/10.1145/2591971.2592021.

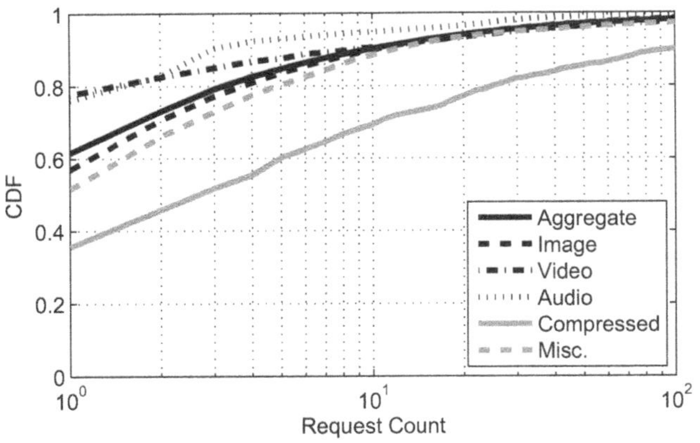

Figure 1: Request count distributions

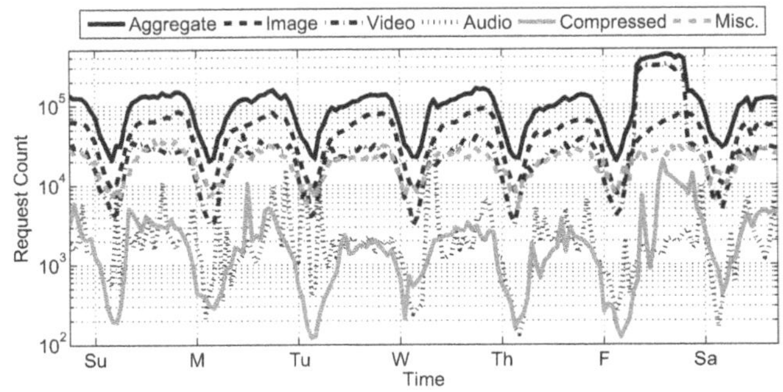

Figure 2: Timeseries of object request volume

set (*e.g.*, IP addresses) has been anonymized to protect the privacy of end users without affecting the usefulness of our results. Each record in our logs contains the content publisher's identifier, hashed URL, object file type, object size in bytes, and the timestamp when the request was received. We analyze content requests from the perspective of their popularity and temporal dynamics.

2. RESULTS

2.1 Object Popularity

We investigate individual object popularity, which is quantified in terms of request count. Figure 1 plots the CDFs of request count for different content types. We observe the expected long-tail distributions for different content types. The distributions highlight that a small fraction of objects appear in most requests and most objects are requested very infrequently. Object popularity distributions have long tails. For example, more than 60% objects are requested only once. We also observe significant variations across different content types.

2.2 Temporal Dynamics

To understand how content requests change over time, we first analyze the timeseries of request counts. Figure 2 shows the timeseries of request counts for different content types. We observe that all timeseries exhibit diurnal variations, with minor variations across different content types. Overall, the request volume peaks from morning till late evening and bottoms out after mid-night. The timeseries of `audio` and `compressed` content are spiky because of their lower volumes. The request volume of `video` and `compressed` content substantially increases on Friday, while other content types exhibit regular diurnal patterns.

3. CONCLUSION

Our measurements characterizing CDN content request patterns highlight the following key findings.

- First, *the distribution of object popularity is highly skewed*; that is, only a small fraction of objects seen by the CDN are requested very frequently while the majority of objects are requested very infrequently. This implies that CDNs can avoid caching infrequently requested objects so that frequently requested objects can be better served.
- Seconds, *object popularity distribution and temporal dynamics vary significantly for different content types.* This implies that we can partition the total CDN cache space into sub-caches of different sizes where we use different sub-caches to cache objects of different types and this partition dynamically evolves over time.

We plan to investigate these ideas and their implication on content caching in our future work.

4. REFERENCES

[1] V. K. Adhikari, Y. Guo, F. Hao, V. Hilt, and Z.-L. Zhang. A tale of 3 CDNs: An active measurement study of Hulu and its CDNs. In *IEEE Global Internet Symposium*, 2012.

[2] V. K. Adhikari, Y. Guo, F. Hao, M. Varvello, M. Steiner, V. Hilt, and Z.-L. Zhang. Unreeling Netflix: Understanding and improving multi-CDN movie delivery. In *IEEE INFOCOM*, 2012.

[3] M. J. Freedman. Experiences with CoralCDN: A five-year operational view. In *USENIX/ACM NSDI*, 2010.

[4] C. Huang, A. Wang, J. Li, and K. W. Ross. Measuring and evaluating large-scale CDNs: (paper withdrawn at Mirosoft's request). In *ACM IMC*, 2008.

[5] B. Krishnamurthy, C. Wills, and Y. Zhang. On the use and performance of content distribution networks. In *ACM SIGCOMM Workshop on Internet Measurement*, 2001.

[6] C. Labovitz. First Data on Changing Netflix and CDN Market Share, June 2012. http://www.deepfield.net/2012/06/first-data-on-changing-netflix-and-cdn-market-share/.

[7] M. Pathan and R. Buyya. *Content Delivery Networks, Chapter 2: A Taxonomy of CDNs.* Springer, 2008.

[8] A.-J. Su and A. Kuzmanovic. Thinning Akamai. In *ACM IMC*, 2008.

[9] S. Triukose, Z. Wen, and M. Rabinovich. Measuring a commercial content delivery network. In *ACM WWW*, 2011.

[10] P. Wendell and M. J. Freedman. Going viral: Flash crowds in an open CDN. In *ACM IMC*, 2011.

FLOWR: A Self-Learning System for Classifying Mobile Application Traffic

Qiang Xu#, Thomas Andrews#, Yong Liao*, Stanislav Miskovic*, Z. Morley Mao#
Mario Baldi*, Antonio Nucci*
#University of Michigan, *Narus Inc.

Categories and Subject Descriptors

C.2.3 [**Computer-Communication Networks**]: network monitoring, wireless communication; C.4 [**Performance of Systems**]: measurement techniques

General Terms

Experimentation, Measurement, Performance

Keywords

Mobile Application Identification, Traffic Classification

1. INTRODUCTION

We aim to devise a method that can identify mobile apps related to each individual traffic flow in the wild. Mobile apps are becoming preferred means of Internet access for a growing user population. Such departure from browser based Internet poses a unique challenge to traffic management tools, still largely incapable of handling mobile apps. Consequently, enterprises and service providers become hindered by being unable to deploy effective mobile policies and security solutions.

Traditionally, desktop applications and networking protocols were identified by signatures derived from transport-layer ports, ip addresses, or domain names [2, 5]. It is not suitable for mobile apps any more. The main reason is that most mobile apps communicate via generic HTTP/HTTPS traffic, thus being a priori indistinguishable from Internet browsing. State-of-the-art solutions attempted to develop signatures via user studies or app emulations [6, 4, 1]. Neither of the two approaches scales due to a number of key challenges:

- **Similarity.** Besides using similar protocols (HTTP/HTTPS), mobiles apps communicate with largely similar IP-/domain-level destinations, Content Delivery Networks (CDNs), and cloud services, which makes them difficult to distinguish.
- **Scalability.** With hundreds of thousands of apps, the identification has to devise very efficient matching algorithms at line speeds. Moreover, the references for matching have to be obtained efficiently. One cannot assume running all existing apps to get the references, or keeping a large state as means of identification.
- **Ground truth.** Being infeasible to exhaustively establish references for app characterization, one loses strong ground truth. Generally, such ground truth would be attainable via app-identifying and a priori unknown features such as developer tags in traffic, proprietary app-identifying URL parameters, hostnames, etc.
- **Coverage.** The issue of coverage is closely related to app matching efficacy: Ideally, one should know all communication states and patterns of each app to perfectly characterize each traffic flow, similarly to a sophisticated app signature generation scheme described in [3]. However, such thorough identification of all apps' flows would require exhaustive and unattainable offline training.

In this paper, we develop a flow recognition system called FLOWR, which identifies in real time the app origins of individual flows in traffic. The system is based on discovering and learning a priori uncertain hints that may exist in the traffic and point to particular apps. Over time, FLOWR automatically learns an increasing number of such hints and evaluates the confidence in their app-identifying capabilities. To optimize our identification capabilities to line speeds, we only look into HTTP header metadata.

We believe there are many reasons for the existence of app-identifying features in the traffic. For example, developers generally like to track adoption of their apps, so they put some reporting capabilities in the apps' communications, e.g., using specific user agent tags. Moreover, we know that ads and analytic services (such as `doubleclick.net` and `flurry.com`) embed explicit app identifiers in HTTP headers for accounting purposes. Nevertheless, our preliminary experiments showed that the percentage of such explicitly identifiable flows is extremely small, while our goal is to enable large flow-identification coverage.

Our methodology consists of three key components: (1) KV tokenization, which parses HTTP traffic and extracts all key-value (KV) pairs that may become app-identifying features, (2) knowledge base, which contains all previously known KV pairs and a confidence measure of their app-identifying capabilities, and (3) flow regression, which measures co-occurrence of flows (and their embedded KV pairs) as a confidence indication of the flows (and their KV pairs) originating from the same apps. To the best of our knowledge, this constitutes the first system to identify apps at flow level in real time and at a scale suitable to large operational networks, such as nationwide mobile networks or large enterprises.

SIGMETRICS'14, June 16–20, 2014, Austin, Texas, USA.
ACM 978-1-4503-2789-3/14/06..

2. CLASSIFICATION TECHNIQUES

Here, we describe the three key components of the FLOWR system.

2.1 Extracting Flow Signatures

We extract KV pairs from HTTP URIs. We only focus on HTTP requests because our preliminary experiments showed that HTTP responses contribute only marginally to app-identification. HTTP URIs have the following well-formatted syntax: `http://host_name/path?query#fragment`. The `query` consists of a sequence of KVs formatted as `k1=v1&k2=v2&...&kN=vN`. For example, KV pairs can be `adkapid=67526`, `age=45`, and `zipcode=90210`.

2.2 Seeding the Knowledge Base

We identified three general types of KV pairs based on their app-identifying capabilities: irrelevant KVs (e.g., `age=45`), KVs explicitly referring to app identities (e.g., `packageName=zz.rings.rww2`), and other KVs whose app identifying capabilities are initially ambiguous (e.g., `sdkapid=67526`) and which need to be evaluated further by our algorithm. Ad and analytic services, such as `doubleclick.net`, are particularly rich of explicit KV pairs. Hence, FLOWR relies on them to provide seeds for our knowledge base. Then, by means of flow regression, we spread these knowledge seeds to other observed KV pairs.

2.3 Flow Regression - Inferring KV Identities

We devised flow regression as a technique to eliminate irrelevant KVs and infer app identities via scoring ambiguous KVs. Intuitively, if two flows repeatedly co-occur, they are likely to come from the same app. To be confident in flow co-occurrence properties, we observe flows over various users and various disjoint time intervals. As a result, flow regression scores observed flow co-occurrence likelihoods, as well as ties the ambiguous KVs in these flows to app identities of readily app-identifying KVs also found in the flow set.

FLOWR digests co-occurrence likelihoods as follows. In the background, if a KV appears frequently close to some flow related to an app X, i.e., $P[A = X|KV] \approx 1$, FLOWR adds KV to its signature set that uniquely identifies the app in the knowledge base of app identities. Instead of $P[A = X|KV] \approx 1$, we found that a more common case is that KV co-occurs with X with a certain likelihood of less than 1, i.e., $0 \ll P[KV|A = X] < 1$, which indicates that KV may be generated by apps other than X as well. Then, as best effort, FLOWR puts KV into a signature set that narrows down the set of the flow's candidate apps.

Next, FLOWR generally extracts multiple KV pairs per flow and based on the KV scores the algorithm needs to determine app identity. In our implementation, the best KV determines the identity, i.e., the KV pair with most frequent and most unique co-occurrence with an app ties the entire flow to that app's identity.

3. EVALUATION

FLOWR is evaluated using an anonymized traffic trace captured on a major 3G cellular network in the US. Our evaluation demonstrates that FLOWR is able to learn new KVs from a minimal seeding app identification knowledge base. The learned new KVs are consumed by FLOWR to classify an order of magnitude more HTTP flows, whose originating apps could not be identified via the seeding knowledge.

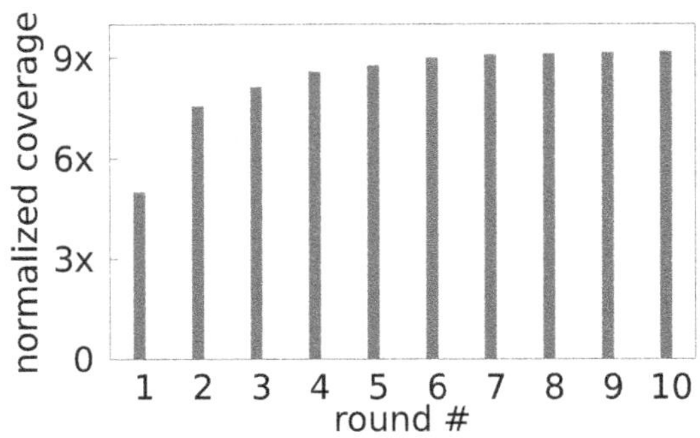

Figure 1: Flow coverage.

Our experiment is seeded with only one piece of manually created knowledge. FLOWR is instructed as to which KV in an HTTP message sent to `doubleclick.net`, a popular ad service used by both Android and iOS apps, indicates mobile app identities. We run FLOWR's flow regression on the traffic trace iteratively. In each round, FLOWR considers a new KV as identifying an app only when the estimated false positive rate of using that KV is lower than 1%. FLOWR estimates the false positive rate via a set of carefully tuned and tested heuristics, whose details are omitted here due to space limit. Additional KVs selected in earlier execution rounds are used in later rounds as seeding knowledge. Figure 1 shows the coverage, i.e., the number of classified flows, normalized to the one obtained with the initial seeding knowledge. Note that almost 9× more flows can be classified with only $3 \sim 4$ rounds of flow regression.

4. CONCLUSION

In this study, we developed the FLOWR system for determining the app identities of network flows in mobile networks in real time with minimal supervised learning. FLOWR adopts three creative techniques: KV tokenization, ad and analytic services based training, and flow regression. Without consuming exhaustive training effort, flow regression can determine the app identities for the flow signatures produced by KV tokenization through monitoring the co-occurrence events between flow signatures. We believe that FLOWR enables mobile network operators to extract valuable insight from mobile network traffic.

5. REFERENCES

[1] Netsense. http://netsense.nd.edu.

[2] Cui, W., Kannan, J., and Wang, H. Discoverer: Automatic Protocol Reverse Engineering from Network Traces. In *Proc. USENIX Security* (2007).

[3] Dai, S., Tongaonkar, A., Wang, X., Nucci, A., and Song, D. NetworkProfiler: Towards Automatic Fingerprinting of Android Apps. In *Proc. IEEE INFOCOM* (2013).

[4] Qian, F., Wang, Z., Gerber, A., Mao, Z., Sen, S., and Spatscheck, O. Profiling Resource Usage for Mobile Applications: A Cross-Layer Approach. In *Proc. ACM MobiSys* (2011).

[5] Sen, S., Spatscheck, O., and Wang, D. Accurate, Scalable In-Network Identification of P2P Traffic Using Application Signatures. In *Proc. ACM WWW* (2004).

[6] Wei, X., Gomez, L., Neamtiu, I., and Faloutsos, M. ProfileDroid: Multi-Layer Profiling of Android Applications. In *Proc. ACM MOBICOM* (2012).

Accurate and Robust Time Reconstruction for Deployed Sensor Networks

Wei Dong†, Xuefeng Zhang†, Jiliang Wang‡, Yi Gao†, Chun Chen† and Jiajun Bu†
†College of Computer Science, Zhejiang University
‡School of Software and TNLIST, Tsinghua University
{dongw,zhangxf,gaoy}@emnets.org, jiliang@greenorbs.com, {chenc,bjj}@zju.edu.cn

ABSTRACT

The notion of global time is of great importance for many sensor network applications. To achieve microsecond accuracy, MAC-level timestamping is required for recording packet transmission and reception times. The MAC-level timestamps, however, are known to be error-prone, especially with low power listening techniques. In this paper, we propose ART, an accurate and robust time reconstruction approach to detecting invalid timestamps and recovering the needed information. We evaluate our approach in both testbed and a real-world deployment. Results show ART is accurate and robust for deployed sensor networks.

Categories and Subject Descriptors

C.2.1 [**Computer Communication Networks**]: Network Architecture and Design—*Distributed networks*

Keywords

Sensor networks, time reconstruction, reference clock

1. INTRODUCTION

The notion of global time is of great importance for many sensor network applications. Time reconstruction methods aim to reconstruct the global time with respect to a reference clock [1, 2]. To achieve microsecond accuracy, MAC-level timestamping is required for recording packet transmission and reception times [3]. The MAC-level timestamps, however, are known to be error-prone, especially with low power listening techniques.

In this paper, we propose ART, an accurate and robust time reconstruction approach to detecting invalid timestamps and recovering the needed information. Our approach tries to find out the properties valid packets (i.e., packets with valid timestamps) have and utilize these properties for identifying valid packets. The basic idea of our approach is based on the fact that valid packets from the same source node are conforming to each other considering the constraint on the relative clock drift. Random errors in invalid packets will break such a constraint with high probability, i.e., an invalid packet will be non-conforming to a valid or an invalid packet with a high probability. The valid packet identification problem can thus be reduced to the maximum clique problem which is NP-hard in a general graph. To solve this problem, we employ a strict conformance relation, transforming the original problem to a problem which can be solved in polynomial time. After we have identified the valid packets, we are able to utilize them for error recovery.

SIGMETRICS'14, June 16–20, 2014, Austin, Texas, USA.
ACM 978-1-4503-2789-3/14/06.
http://dx.doi.org/10.1145/2591971.2592023.

2. DESIGN

There are three steps. First, a packet timestamping component is installed on each sensor node for estimating the network sojourn time. Second, ART employs a graph theoretical approach for detecting valid/invalid timestamps in the received packets. Third, ART utilizes the valid timestamps for time reconstruction for packets with invalid timestamps.

We assume a data collection sensor network in which all (or a subset of) nodes collect sensing data and forward the data to the sink via multihop wireless. We do not assume a specific data generation model. Data packets can follow different paths to the sink from a specific sender.

1) Packet Timestamping. We would like to reconstruct the packet generation time with respect to the sink's clock. We instrument the data packet to achieve this goal. In each data packet, there are two 4-byte fields. (i) Local packet generation time (denoted as s) which is the packet generation time with respect to the local clock of the source node. (ii) MAC-level timestamp which is accumulated hop by hop and is used to convert the *local* packet generation time to the *global* packet generation time with respect to the sink's clock.

A received packet at the sink node can be described as a tuple $(s,k,\hat{sk})$ where s is the packet generation time measured at the source node (in ms), k is the packet reception time measured at the sink node (in ms), and $\hat{sk}$ is the estimated packet generation time with respect to the sink's clock. We would like to get an accurate estimate of sk.

The measurement of sk uses MAC-level timestamping [4] which can yield accurate measurement results since the sojourn time at each node on the routing path essentially captures the non-deterministic delays at local nodes including software routines and MAC backoffs. On the other hand, MAC-level timestamps are prone to measurement errors [5]. This is because the radio stack records the actual transmission or reception times in the SFD interrupt before the packet is fully transmitted or received. The timestamps are thus likely to be invalid when the packet transmission or reception fail. In such cases, the estimated value of $\hat{sk}$ cannot be trusted.

2) Error Detection. A simple threshold-based approach is to setup a maximum delay threshold d_m to cutoff invalid packets. Valid packets are those with $\hat{sk} : 0 < \hat{d} = k - \hat{sk} \leq d_m$. The selection of d_m is, however, non-trivial considering varying transmission delays with dynamic routing protocols.

We avoid the selection of d_m by employing another approach. Two valid packets from the same source node satisfy a certain constraint. Conceptually, the difference of s and the difference of $\hat{sk}$ should be very close considering a sufficiently small clock drift, i.e., $s_2 - s_1 \approx \hat{sk}_2 - \hat{sk}_1$. Concretely, the following theorem describes this constraint exactly.

THEOREM 1. *For two valid packets $p_1 = (s_1, k_1, \hat{sk}_1)$ and $p_2 = (s_2, k_2, \hat{sk}_2)$ from source node S ($s_1 < s_2$), they satisfy the following constraint:*

$$\frac{\Delta s}{1+\rho_m} - \frac{\rho_m}{1-\rho_m} \cdot \Sigma\hat{d} \leq \Delta\hat{sk} \leq \frac{\Delta s}{1-\rho_m} + \frac{\rho_m}{1-\rho_m} \cdot \Sigma\hat{d} \quad (1)$$

where $\Delta s = s_2 - s_1$, $\Delta\hat{sk} = \hat{sk}_2 - \hat{sk}_1$, $\Sigma\hat{d} = \hat{d}_1 + \hat{d}_2$, ρ_m is the maximum clock drift.

DEFINITION 1. *Two packets p_1 and p_2 from source node S are conforming (denoted as $p_1 \simeq p_2$) iff Eq. 1 is satisfied.*

We see that packet conformance is a necessary condition for packet correctness. Consider an ideal condition in which all the packets from a source node are valid and they form the set P. According to Theorem 1, any two packets in P are conforming, i.e., $\forall p_i, p_j \in P, p_i \simeq p_j$. With a graph representation $G = (V, E)$ where V represents the set of received packets from a source node (we will use packets and vertices interchangeably), and $e = (p_i, p_j) \in E$ iff $p_i \simeq p_j$. If all packets are valid, G is a clique.

Assume a random error occurs, then the probability that an invalid packet conform to a valid packet is low. The two packets will no longer conform to each other. It means that G is no longer a clique. *It is reasonable to consider that the valid packets will form the maximum clique in G.*

Based on the above idea, a straightforward method to identify valid packets is to find the maximum clique in G. However, it is NP-hard to find the maximum clique in a general graph [6].

We try to solve the valid packets detection problem (i.e., maximum clique problem) by redefining a graph G having good properties. In particular, we redefine the edges in $G(V, E)$: instead of using the conformance relation $\simeq$ defined in Def. 1, we use a more "strict" conformance relation $\sim$ defined in Def. 2, i.e., $e = (p_i, p_j) \in E$ iff $p_i \sim p_j$.

DEFINITION 2. *Two packets p_1 and p_2 from source node S are strictly conforming (denoted as $p_1 \sim p_2$) iff*

$$\frac{\Delta s}{1+\rho_m} \leq \Delta\hat{sk} \leq \frac{\Delta s}{1-\rho_m}. \quad (2)$$

In theory, using Eq. 2 for identifying valid packets, it is probable that there will be false negatives (i.e., valid packets misidentified as invalid) since there is probability that two valid packets conform but do not strictly conform. Such probabilities are very small under certain conditions. We find that more than 99.99% conforming packet pairs are strictly conforming for our deployed sensor network, CitySee.

The benefits of using the strict conformance relation in defining the edges in G is that it will make an equivalent directed acyclic graph *transitive*. It is known that the maximum clique problem in a transitive graph has polynomial time algorithms [7].

3) Error Recovery. After we have detected the set of valid packets, we are able to recover the global packet generation time sk for the invalid packets. The basic idea is simple: for each invalid packet, we find the nearest two valid packets right before and after it. Then we use a linear clock model to get an estimate of sk.

Table 1: Detection results

	Testbed	CitySee
Unfiltered packet trace		
Correct pkts (i.e. total pkts)	3,629	764,541
Drift violations	2,180(60.1%)	542,824(71.0%)
Threshold-based approach		
Correct pkts	2,401(66.2%)	334,104(43.7%)
Drift violations	579(24.1%)	85,864 (25.7%)
Our approach		
Correct pkts	2,020(55.7%)	257,650(33.7%)
Drift violations	0(0%)	0(0%)

3. EVALUATION

We apply ART in CitySee, a large-scale deployed sensor network in urban areas. We evaluate the time reconstruction performance for 764,541 packets collected from one subnet with more than 280 nodes from July 19, 2011 to July 25, 2011. In addition, we also use a small testbed with 24 TelosB nodes to reveal more system insights.

Table 1 shows our detection results. In the simple threshold-based approach, we use $d_m = 5,000$ ms for the testbed and $d_m = 10,000$ ms for CitySee, considering the duty cycle of 500ms and a maximum hop counts of 10 and 20, respectively. We believe that most valid packets have delays falling in this range.

We use a metric called drift violations to compare the detection quality of different approaches. The number of drift violations is computed as follows. For a sequence of received packets from a single source node, we count the number of times that two successive packets are not conforming. Then we sum up all the numbers for all nodes. Clearly, if all packets are valid, the number of violations must be 0. On the other hand, if there exist many errors, the number of violations will be large. Hence, we can use this metric for comparing the quality of detection result. It is obvious to see that our approach yields the highest detection quality.

Acknowledgments. This work is supported by the National Science Foundation of China Grant No. 61202402, the Research Fund for the Doctoral Program of Higher Education of China (20120101120179), and the Fundamental Research Funds for the Central Universities.

4. REFERENCES

[1] M. Keller, L. Thiele, and J. Beutel, "Reconstruction of the correct temporal order of sensor network data," in *Proc. of IPSN*, 2011.

[2] M. Keller, J. Beutel, and L. Thiele, "How Was Your Journey? Uncovering Routing Dynamics in Deployed Sensor Networks with Multi-hop Network Tomography," in *Proc. of ACM SenSys*, 2012.

[3] J. Wang, W. Dong, Z. Cao, and Y. Liu, "On the delay performance analysis in a large scale wireless sensor network," in *Proc. of IEEE RTSS*, 2012.

[4] B. Kusy, P. Dutta, P. Levis, M. Maróti, Á. Lédeczi, and D. E. Culler, "Elapsed time on arrival: a simple and versatile primitive for canonical time synchronisation services," *Int'l Journal of Ad Hoc and Ubiquitous Computing*, vol. 1, no. 4, pp. 239–251, 2006.

[5] Tinyos-help mailing list: CC2420 and microsecond precision timestamps. [Online]. Available: https://www.millennium.berkeley.edu/pipermail/tinyos-help/2010-August/047507.html

[6] M. R. Garey and D. S. Johnson, *Computers and Intractability: A Guide to the Theory of NP-Completeness*. 1979 Bell Telephone Laboratories, Incorporated, 1979.

[7] S. Even, A. Pnueli, and A. Lempel, "Permutation graphs and transitive graphs," *J. ACM*, vol. 19, no. 3, pp. 400–410, Jul. 1972.

Effect of Proactive Serving on User Delay Reduction in Service Systems

Shaoquan Zhang
The Chinese University of Hong Kong

Longbo Huang
Tsinghua University

Minghua Chen
The Chinese University of Hong Kong

Xin Liu
Microsoft Research Asia

ABSTRACT

In online service systems, delay experienced by a user from the service request to the service completion is one of the most critical performance metrics. To improve user delay experience, in this paper, we investigate a novel aspect of system design: *proactive serving*, where the system can predict future user request arrivals and allocate its capacity to serve these upcoming requests proactively. In particular, we investigate the average user delay under proactive serving from a queuing theory perspective. We show that proactive serving reduces the average user delay *exponentially* (as a function of the prediction window size) under M/M/1 queueing models. Our simulation results show that, for G/G/1 queueing models, the average user delay also decreases significantly under proactive serving.

Categories and Subject Descriptors

C.4 [**Computer Systems Organization**]: Performance of Systems

Keywords

Proactive serving, user delay, service system, queueing

1. INTRODUCTION

Consider a service system as shown in Fig. 1. In the system, the single backend server provides service to incoming user requests that arrive at the system according to a Poisson process $\{A(t)\}_t$ with rate λ. When a user request arrives and the server is idle, the request will be served. Otherwise, the request waits in the queue $Q(t)$ for service. The queueing discipline is FCFS. After being served, the request leaves the system. We assume that service times of requests are i.i.d. exponential random variables with mean $\frac{1}{\mu}$. Such system can be modeled as a standard M/M/1 queue. We define user delay as the time from when the user request arrives at the system till it leaves the system.

Now suppose that the service system has proactive serving capability. As shown in Fig. 2, we assume that the system can perfectly predict user request arrivals ω time ahead.

SIGMETRICS'14, June 16–20, 2014, Austin, Texas, USA.
ACM 978-1-4503-2789-3/14/06.
http://dx.doi.org/10.1145/2591971.2592024.

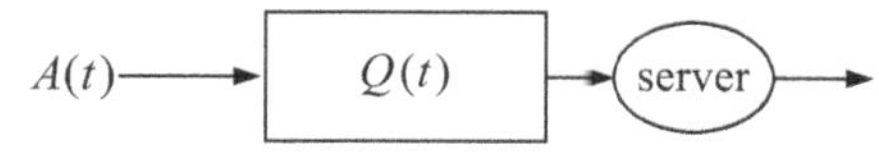

Figure 1: A Single queue service system.

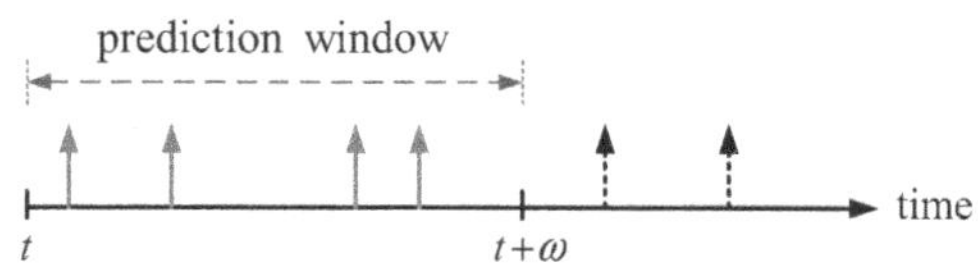

Figure 2: Prediction model.

That is, at time t, the system knows exactly in $(t, t+\omega)$ the request arrival epochs (red solid arrows) and the corresponding users who generate the requests. Meanwhile, we do not assume the knowledge of the workload of each user request.

Based on the arrival prediction, the system can allocate its service capacity to serve future requests proactively. Specifically, the servers can provide service to the users who are predicted to generate requests. The user requests that get pre-served will not enter the system. Such a proactive serving model captures service systems that can perform cache pre-loading or command pre-fetching. As a practical example of cache pre-loading, the web browser in Amazon's Kindle Fire can predict web page requests and pre-load desired web pages to users' tablets beforehand. When the user clicks on the predicted content, it gets the content immediately.

We depict the service system which can proactively serve future requests based on perfect prediction in Fig. 3. Let $Q_0(t)$ represent the queue of the requests that have arrived at the system and are waiting for service at time t, and $W_\omega(t)$ be the prediction window of size ω.

Each user request first goes through the prediction window $W_\omega(t)$ and then enters the queue $Q_0(t)$. The servers can serve the requests in both $Q_0(t)$ and $W_\omega(t)$. We remark that each request entering $W_\omega(t)$ will transit to $Q_0(t)$ after exactly ω amount of time, if it has not been pre-served before that. The requests will not queue up in $W_\omega(t)$. Thus $W_\omega(t)$ should be viewed as a pipe. User delay corresponds to the time that the request spends in $Q_0(t)$ and with the server, and it does not include the time spent in $W_\omega(t)$.

Previous work either focus on request scheduling algorithm design based on future prediction but without proactive serving capacity [1], [2], [3] or investigate how proactive serving reduces the probability of server outage [4]. Different from previous work, in this paper, we are interested in the following fundamental question: How much user delay reduction can we obtain by proactive serving?

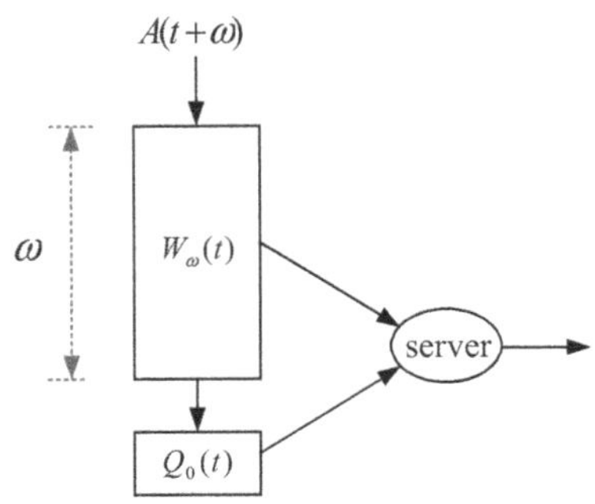

Figure 3: Service system with perfect prediction.

2. AVERAGE USER DELAY

In this section, we characterize the average user delay of the system shown in Fig. 3. Let D^ω denote the user delay when the system can predict ω time ahead.

When $\omega = 0$, *i.e.*, without proactive serving, the system reduces to the classical M/M/1 queue. It's well known that the average user delay is given by

$$E\left[D^0\right] = \frac{1}{\mu - \lambda}. \quad (1)$$

The probability density function of D^0 is also known as

$$f_{D^0}(t) = (\mu - \lambda)e^{-(\mu-\lambda)t}, t \geq 0. \quad (2)$$

To characterize the user delay, we first observe an interesting result that $Q^{sum}(t) \triangleq Q_0(t) + W_\omega(t)$ evolves the same as an M/M/1 system with a properly initialized queue. Based on this observation, the distribution of user delay under proactive serving, *i.e.*, D^ω, turns out to be a "shifted" version of that of user delay without proactive serving as shown in (2). Once we know the distribution of D^ω, we can compute the average user delay $E\left[D^\omega\right]$ as shown in the following theorem. Detailed proof can be found in [5].

Theorem 1. *Assume $\mu > \lambda$. The average user delay is given by*

$$E[D^\omega] = \frac{1}{\mu - \lambda}e^{-(\mu-\lambda)\omega}. \quad (3)$$

Theorem 1 reveals that the average user delay decays exponentially in the prediction window size ω. This result suggests that proactive serving is very powerful in reducing user delay.

From Theorem 1, in the heavy-load regime where the arrival rate λ is close to the service rate μ, (3) can be approximated by $\frac{1}{\mu-\lambda} - \omega$ when ω is small, which is linear in ω. As contrast, when the system is in the light-load regime, (3) decreases exponentially in ω. This indicates that proactive serving is less effective in reducing delay in the heavy-load regime than in the light-load regime. The reason is as follows. In the light-load regime, the number of requests that enter $Q_0(t)$ for service is small and thus most of the serve capacity can be spared to serve future requests. In contrast, in the heavy-load regime, the server is busy with serving requests in $Q_0(t)$ most of time. As a result, the chance that a request gets served proactively by the server is small when going through a small prediction window. Therefore, proactive serving has limited effect on the delay reduction. When the system is in the heavy-load regime, to achieve small user delay, the system needs to guarantee a sufficient large prediction window so that the probability that a request gets served proactively is high.

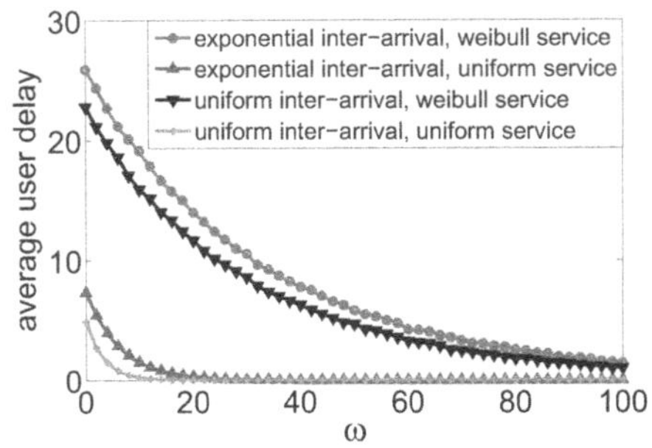

Figure 4: The average request delay vs how far we predict the future under perfect prediction under different inter-arrival time distributions and service time distributions.

3. SIMULATION RESULTS

We carry out simulations to show the impact of proactive serving on reducing the average user delay under different arrival processes and service time distributions. We consider four different pairs of request inter-arrival time distribution and service time distribution: (Exponential, Uniform), (Uniform, Uniform), (Exponential, Weibull), (Uniform, Weibull). The mean arrival rate is $\lambda = 0.4$ and the mean service rate is $\mu = 0.5$. For the Uniform distribution, boundaries are 0 and double mean. For the Weibull distribution, the scale parameter is equal to 1. There is a single server in the system under four settings. The server adopts FCFS as its service policy.

The results are shown in Fig. 4. As seen, proactive serving reduces the average user delay significantly under all settings.

4. ACKNOWLEDGMENTS

This work described in this paper was partially supported by the National Basic Research Program of China Grant Project No. 2011CBA00300, 2011CBA00301, 2012CB315904, 2013CB336700, the National Natural Science Foundation of China Grant Project No. 61033001, 61361136003, 041302007, the China youth 1000-talent grant Project No. 610502003, the MSRA-Tsinghua joint lab grant Project No. 041902004, and several grants from the University Grants Committee of the Hong Kong Special Administrative Region, China (Area of Excellence Grant Project No. AoE/E-02/08, Theme-based Research Scheme Project No. T23-407/13-N, and General Research Fund Project No. 411011).

5. REFERENCES

[1] B. Coleman. Quality vs. performance in lookahead scheduling. In *JCIS*, 2006.

[2] M. Mandelbaum and D. Shabtay. Scheduling unit length jobs on parallel machines with lookahead information. *Journal of Scheduling*, 2011.

[3] J. Spencer, M. Sudan, and K. Xu. Queueing with future information. *arXiv:1211.0618*, 2012.

[4] J. Tadrous, A. Eryilmaz, and H. El Gamal. Proactive resource allocation: harnessing the diversity and multicast gains. *IEEE Trans. Information Theory*, 2013.

[5] S. Zhang, L. Huang, M. Chen, and X. Liu. Effect of proactive serving on user delay reduction in service systems. Technical report. `https://sites.google.com/site/proactivetechreport/paper.pdf`.

Optimal Energy Source Selection and Capacity Planning for Green Datacenters *

Fanxin Kong
School of Computer Science
McGill University, Canada
fanxin.kong@mail.mcgill.ca

Xue Liu
School of Computer Science
McGill University, Canada
xueliu@cs.mcgill.ca

Lei Rao
Silicon Valley Office, General
Motors US Research Lab
lei.rao@gm.com

ABSTRACT

To reduce cost and emission, modern datacenter operators are beginning to incorporate green energy sources into datacenters' power supply. To improve service availability, they also back up datacenters using traditional (usually brown) energy sources. However, challenge arises due to distinct characteristics of energy sources used for different goals. How to select optimal energy sources and plan their capacity for datacenters to meet cost, emission and service availability requirement remains an open research problem. In this extended abstract, we briefly describe recent work in [4], which provides a holistic solution to address this problem. In [4], we present GreenPlanning, a framework to strike a judicious balance among multiple energy sources, the electrical grid and energy storage devices for a datacenter in terms of cost, emission, and service availability. GreenPlanning explores different features and operations of both green and traditional energy sources available to datacenters. The framework minimizes the lifetime total cost including both capital and operational cost for a datacenter. We conduct extensive experiments to evaluate GreenPlanning with real-life computational workload and meteorological data traces. Results demonstrate that GreenPlanning can reduce the lifetime total cost and emission by more than 50% compared to traditional configurations without integration of green energy, while still meeting service availability requirement.

Categories and Subject Descriptors

C.0 [**Computer Systems Organization**]: General

Keywords

datacenter, renewable energy, carbon emission, service availability, capacity planning

*This work was supported in part by the NSERC Discovery Grant 341823 and McGill Tomlinson Scientist Award.

SIGMETRICS'14, June 16–20, 2014, Austin, Texas, USA.
ACM 978-1-4503-2789-3/14/06.
http://dx.doi.org/10.1145/2591971.2592025.

1. INTRODUCTION

The computing capacity and scale of datacenters are increasing to meet the soaring demand for IT applications and services. Each datacenter consumes megawatts of electricity and causes a growing concern over carbon emission. Modern datacenters such as Apple [2] have been integrating green energy sources (e.g., wind or solar power) into their power supply to cut their cost and emission. Moreover, requirement for high service availability forces them to use traditional energy sources (e.g., diesel generators) as backup supply. In this extended abstract, we study an important open problem of how to select optimal energy sources and plan their capacity for a datacenter to meet cost, emission and service availability requirement.

Renewable energy sources and brown energy sources have different characteristics in terms of cost, emission and reliability. First, constructing renewable power generation facilities (wind or solar farms) is usually very expensive but there is little expense thereafter. In contrast, building brown power generation facilities (diesel or natural gas generators) is relatively cheaper but there is high fuel cost over the lifetime. Second, renewable energy is much more compatible with sustainable development than are diesel and natural gas, in regard to both resource limitations and environmental impacts. Third, the intermittent nature of wind and solar power makes them not as reliable as brown energy resources. For example, wind and solar power are closely tied to weather conditions and thus fluctuate significantly at power output. By contrast, brown energy generators produce reliable power output.

For companies that rely on datacenters to deliver business-critical services, downtime has been always a key concern. For example, recent service interruption of Amazon website costs the company 5 million dollars [1]. Excessively pursuing cost and emission reduction will overshadow the importance of service availability in the datacenter power management. Hence, we propose GreenPlanning in [4], a framework that judiciously balances multiple energy sources, the electrical grid and energy storage devices for a datacenter in terms of cost, emission, and service availability. The novelty of GreenPlanning is threefold. (i) **Loosening dependence on the electrical grid.** GreenPlanning decouples the dependence of datacenter service availability on the electrical grid. Coordinating energy storage, reliable energy sources, and datacenter power demand guarantees service availability no matter when the electrical grid is during normal operation or under outage. (ii) **Exploring and analyzing energy sources in depth.** The framework integrates a

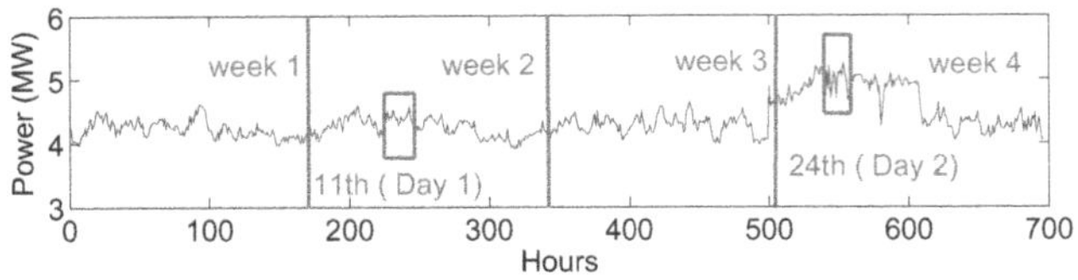

Figure 1: Datacenter power load using Google trace [3].

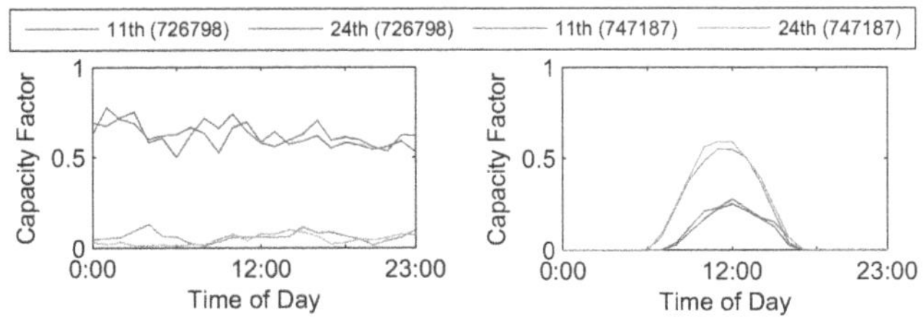

(a) Wind power (b) Solar power

Figure 2: Wind and solar power capacity factor traces for site 726798 and site 747187 in January.

wind spectrum of energy sources, provides in-depth analysis of the operation of energy sources, and develops more accurate way for estimating their power output using large amount of real-life data. (iii) **Planning based on a long term optimization.** The framework models four different time scales together, including a lifetime of power generation facilities and datacenters, seasonal pattern of solar and wind power, monthly peak charge and hourly price of the electrical grid, and hourly datacenter workload. GreenPlanning provides a solution for minimizing lifetime total cost across two different phases: capital and operational cost.

2. OVERVIEW OF RESULTS

In this extended abstract, we briefly discuss the main results of our work [4]. We evaluate GreenPlanning using real-world data: Google computational workload trace [3] (as shown in Figure 1) and NSRDB meteorological data [5] (as shown in Figure 2), product datasheets, official predictions. Our evaluations provide interesting observations and insights with answers to the following questions. (i) How datacenter service availability affects the lifetime total cost and emission? Can a datacenter be independent of the electrical grid? Do diesel generators or energy storage really help on reducing the lifetime total cost or emission? (ii) What is the optimal portfolio of energy sources? What is key determinant for the selection and capacity of each energy source? (iii) What is the effect of lifetime planning on the selection of different energy sources?

An example of these results is shown in Figure 3, where we compare the lifetime total costs and emissions between *Trad*, *Nrgbuff*, *Avg* and *GreenPlanning* under different electricity price. The first solution is powering up a datacenter with the electrical grid and using a diesel generator only as backup power. The energy storage are equipped only as the bridge from the electrical grid to the diesel generator when outage occurs. This solution corresponds to the *traditional* views on diesel generators and energy storage for datacenters. We call it *Trad*. The second solution is the same as Trad except that energy storage can be also employed as *energy buffer* and a diesel generator can be also used as a dispatchable energy source during normal operation. We call it *Nrgbuff*. The third solution is planning energy sources based on our

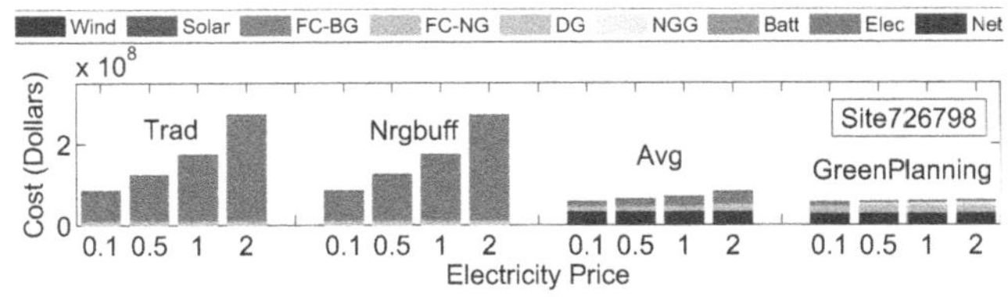

(a) Lifetime total cost comparison

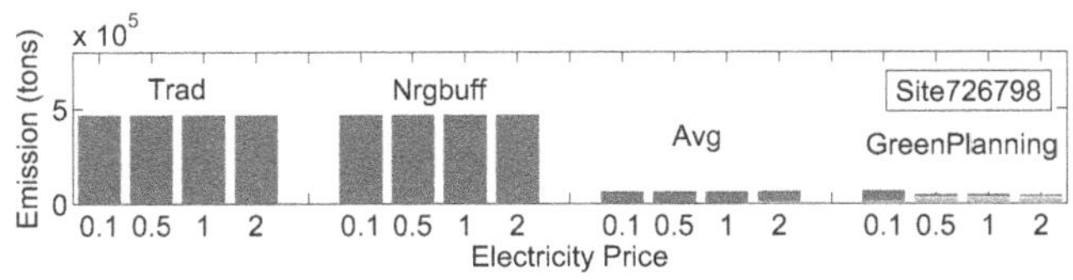

(b) Lifetime total emission comparison

Figure 3: Lifetime total cost and emission comparison between Trad, Nrgbuff, Avg and GreenPlanning under different electricity price, using data from Day1. X-axis: $x = \{0.1, 0.5, 1, 2\}$ **means** x **times the default price.**

optimization model using an *average* capacity factor of wind (solar) power over the twenty years. We call it *Avg*.

First, compared to Trad and Nrgbuff, GreenPlanning dramatically reduces lifetime total cost (Figure 3(a)) and emission (Figure 3(b)). For the default electricity price, the cost reduction is more than 70% for site726798; while the emission reduction is up to 90% for site726798. Even for 10% of the default price, GreenPlanning saves more than 30% cost and cuts more than 25% emission. The main reason is that GreenPlanning incorporates much wind power and fuel cell power which significantly reduce emission and its cost. Second, compared to Avg, GreenPlanning also reduce much lifetime total cost and emission for datacenters sourcing from renewable energy sources. For site726798, GreenPlanning reduces the cost by 16.6% and cuts the emission by 27.7% when using the default electricity price. The saving increases as electricity price rises. Avg ignores fluctuations of wind or solar power, which results in sub-optimal planning for their capacity. Third, Trad and Nrgbuff have nearly the same performance on the lifetime total cost and emission. The prime cost is caused by the electrical grid instead of DG or energy storage.

Please refer to [4] for the full version.

3. REFERENCES

[1] Amazon website goes down for 40 minutes, costing the company $5 million. *http://venturebeat.com/2013/08/19/amazon-website-down/*.

[2] Apple. Apple and the environment. *http://www.apple.com/environment/renewable-energy/*.

[3] Google. ClusterData2011_1. *https://code.google.com/p/googleclusterdata/wiki/ClusterData2011_1*.

[4] F. Kong, X. Liu, and L. Rao. Greenplanning: Optimal energy source selection and capacity planning for green datacenters. Technical report, SOCS, McGill University, 2014.

[5] NCDC. Solar & filled meteorological fields. *http://rredc.nrel.gov/solar/old_data/nsrdb/1991-2010/NCDCStationData/*.

Scheduling using Interactive Oracles: Connection between Iterative Optimization and Low-complexity Scheduling

Jinwoo Shin
Department of Electrical Engineering
Korea Advanced Institute of Science and Technology
Daejeon 305-701, Korea
jinwoos@kaist.ac.kr

Tonghoon Suk *
H. Milton Stewart School of Industrial & Systems Engineering
Georgia Institute of Technology
Atlanta, GA 30332, USA
tonghoons@gatech.edu

ABSTRACT

Since Tassiulas and Ephremides proposed the maximum weight scheduling algorithm of throughput-optimality for constrained queueing networks in 1992, extensive research efforts have been made for resolving its high complexity issue under various directions. In this paper, we resolve this issue by developing a generic framework for designing throughput-optimal and low-complexity scheduling algorithms. Under the framework, an algorithm updates current schedules via an interaction with a given oracle system that generates a solution of a certain discrete optimization problem in a finite number of interactive queries. The complexity of the resulting algorithm is decided by the number of operations required for an oracle processing a single query, which is typically very small. Somewhat surprisingly, we prove that an algorithm using any such oracle is throughput-optimal for general constrained queueing network models that arise in the context of emerging large-scale communication networks.To our best knowledge, our result is the first that establishes a rigorous connection between iterative optimization methods and low-complexity scheduling algorithms, which we believe provides various future directions and new insights in both areas.

Categories and Subject Descriptors

G.3 [**Probability and Statistics**]: Markov processes,Queueing theory,Stochastic processes; C.2.1 [**Network Architecture and Design**]: Distributed networks,wireless communication

General Terms

Algorithms, Performance, Design

*Author names appear in the alphabetical order of their last names.

SIGMETRICS'14, June 16–20, 2014, Austin, Texas, USA.
ACM 978-1-4503-2789-3/14/06.
http://dx.doi.org/10.1145/2591971.2592026.

Keywords

Network scheduling, Markov chain

1. INTRODUCTION

The problem of dynamic resource allocation in constrained queueing networks is fundamental to modern communication networks. This has long been the subject of significant research, where the seminar work [1] of Tassiulas and Ephremides proposed the MW (maximum weight) scheduling algorithm of throughput-optimality. It has been also a powerful paradigm in cross-layer control and resource allocation [2]. However, the algorithm cannot be implemented in practice due to its high algorithmic complexity.

Recently, there have been exciting progresses for the topic that even fully distributed random access algorithms based on CSMA (Carrier Sense Multiple Access) can achieve the desired high performance, i.e., throughput-optimality, in wireless interference network models, e.g., see [3, 4, 5]. The main intuition underlying these results is that nodes in a network can adjust their CSMA parameters dynamically using local information such as queue-length so that they can simulate the MW algorithm asymptotically for throughput-optimality. However, it is known that the queue-based CSMA algorithms suffer from very poor delay performance and the throughput-optimality proof in [3, 5] is very sensitive to the underlying wireless network model. Namely, it is not an easy task to design similar CSMA-like throughput-optimal algorithms in other network models since one has to reproduce painful, long and routine proof-arguments for throughput-optimality in each different model.

In this paper, we resolve these issues of the recent queue-based CSMA algorithms by developing a general framework that can produce a variety of throughput-optimal and low-complexity scheduling algorithms, yet is not sensitive to the underlying network models. In Section 2, we describe the network model of our interest, and our proposed scheduling algorithms and their performance guarantees are presented in Section 3.

2. NETWORK MODEL

We consider a stochastic network of n queues represented by V with $|V| = n$, and time is discrete indexed by $t \in \mathbb{Z}_+ := \{0, 1, \dots\}$. External packets (or jobs) arrive at each queue as per an exogenous stochastic process, where we let $A_i(t)$ denote the number of packets arriving at queue i during the time interval $[t, t+1)$. We assume that $\{A_i(t) \in \{0, 1\}$:

$t \in \mathbb{Z}_+$, $i \in V\}$ are independent Bernoulli random variables with mean $\lambda_i \in [0,1]$, called the *arrival rate* for queue i.

Packets in queues are served at unit rate subject to scheduling constraints. Formally, a schedule is denoted by $\boldsymbol{\sigma} = [\sigma_i : i \in V] \in \{0,1\}^n$, where $\sigma_i = 1$ means queue i is transmitting (or active) and $\sigma_i = 0$ otherwise. We let $S \subset \{0,1\}^n$ be a set of all available schedules and let $\boldsymbol{\sigma}(t) \in S$ be the schedule during $[t, t+1)$ for $t \in \mathbb{Z}_+$.

To describe the dynamics in the network, we let $Q_i(t) \in \mathbb{Z}_+$ denote the number of packets in i-th queue at time t (i.e., *length of i-th queue*). Then the queueing dynamics for i-th queue can be described as

$$Q_i(t+1) = Q_i(t) + A_i(t) - \sigma_i(t) I_{\{Q_i(t)>0\}},$$

where $t \in \mathbb{Z}_+$ and $I_{\{x\}} = \begin{cases} 1 & \text{if } x \text{ is 'true'} \\ 0 & \text{otherwise} \end{cases}$.

For given V and S, our goal is to develop low-complexity and high-performance scheduling algorithms which determine $\boldsymbol{\sigma}(t)$ for each time instance $t \in \mathbb{Z}_+$.

3. MAIN RESULT

We describe the generic concept of our scheduling algorithms utilizing certain oracle systems for a network model with set of queues V with $|V| = n$ and available schedules $S \subset \{0,1\}^n$. The oracle systems are motivated by (randomized or deterministic) iterative algorithms which find an approximate optimal solution to the following optimization problem:

$$\max_{\boldsymbol{\rho} \in S} \boldsymbol{\rho} \cdot \boldsymbol{W}. \tag{1}$$

The oracle system we are interested in has an advice space $\mathbb{A}$ with the following input and output:

- It takes inputs $\boldsymbol{a} \in \mathbb{A}$ and $\boldsymbol{W} = [W_i \in \mathbb{Z}_+ : i \in V]$,
- It outputs (or returns) $\boldsymbol{\sigma} \in S$ and $\widehat{\boldsymbol{a}} \in \mathbb{A}$,

where $\boldsymbol{W}$, $\boldsymbol{a}$, and $\widehat{\boldsymbol{a}}$ are called 'weights' on queues, 'advice', and 'updated advice', respectively. Formally, let the outputs $\boldsymbol{\sigma} = \boldsymbol{\sigma}_{\text{oracle}}(\boldsymbol{a}) = \boldsymbol{\sigma}_{\text{oracle}}(\boldsymbol{W}, \boldsymbol{a})$ and $\widehat{\boldsymbol{a}} = \boldsymbol{a}_{\text{oracle}}(\boldsymbol{a}) = \boldsymbol{a}_{\text{oracle}}(\boldsymbol{W}, \boldsymbol{a})$, where the oracle can generate random outputs in general. We assume that the oracle system satisfies the following properties:

A1. For any $\eta, \delta \in (0,1)$, if $W_{\max} := \max_{i \in V} W_i$ is large enough, then there exists $h = h(W_{\max}, \eta, \delta)$ such that for any $t \geq h$ and advice $\boldsymbol{a} \in \mathbb{A}$,

$$\left(\boldsymbol{\sigma}_{\text{oracle}}(\boldsymbol{a}^{(t)}_{\text{oracle}}(\boldsymbol{a}))\right) \cdot \boldsymbol{W} \;\geq\; (1-\eta) \max_{\boldsymbol{\rho} \in S} \boldsymbol{\rho} \cdot \boldsymbol{W},$$

with probability $\geq 1 - \delta$

where $\boldsymbol{a}^{(t)}_{\text{oracle}}$ is the function composing $\boldsymbol{a}_{\text{oracle}}$ 't times', i.e., $\boldsymbol{a}^{(t)}_{\text{oracle}} = \boldsymbol{a}^{(t-1)}_{\text{oracle}} \circ \boldsymbol{a}_{\text{oracle}}$.

A2. For any $\boldsymbol{W}$, $\left|\mathbb{A}(\boldsymbol{W}) := \bigcup_{\boldsymbol{a} \in \mathbb{A}} \boldsymbol{a}_{\text{oracle}}(\boldsymbol{W}, \boldsymbol{a})\right| < \infty$.

The first assumption **A1** implies that the schedule $\boldsymbol{\sigma}$ generated by the oracle system after h interactions is an approximate solution to the optimization problem (1).

Now, we introduce our scheduling algorithm given an oracle system. To this end, we let $f, g : \mathbb{R}_+ \to \mathbb{R}_+$ be positive-real-valued functions and let

$$U_i(t) := \max\{f(Q_i(t)), g(Q_{\max}(t))\},$$

where $Q_{\max}(t) = \max_{i \in V} Q_i(t)$. The algorithm maintains parameters $\boldsymbol{W}(t) \in \mathbb{Z}_+^n$ and $\boldsymbol{a}(t) \in \mathbb{A}$. It outputs the schedule $\boldsymbol{\sigma}(t)$ and updates parameters $\boldsymbol{W}(t), \boldsymbol{a}(t)$ under an interaction with the oracle system as follows:

- $\boldsymbol{\sigma}(t+1) = \boldsymbol{\sigma}_{\text{oracle}}(\boldsymbol{W}(t), \boldsymbol{a}(t))$,
- $\boldsymbol{a}(t+1) = \boldsymbol{a}_{\text{oracle}}(\boldsymbol{W}(t), \boldsymbol{a}(t))$,
- $W_i(t+1)$ is the closest integer to $U_i(t+1)$ if

  $$|W_i(t) - U_i(t+1)| \geq 2,$$

  and $W_i(t+1) = W_i(t)$ otherwise.

We established the following sufficient conditions on functions f and g so that the proposed scheduling algorithm is throughput-optimal.

THEOREM 1. *The above scheduling algorithm is throughput-optimal if functions f, g, h satisfy the assumptions* **A1-A2** *and the following conditions:*

C1. *f and g are increasing, differentiable and concave.*

C2. $\lim_{x\to\infty} \frac{g(x)}{f(x)} = 0$ *and* $\lim_{x\to\infty} g(x) = \infty$.

C3. $f(0) = 0$.

C4. $\lim_{x\to\infty} f'(x) = \lim_{n\to\infty} g'(x) = 0$.

C5. *For any fixed $\eta, \delta > 0$,* $\lim_{x\to\infty} \frac{h(f(x),\eta,\delta)}{x} = 0$.

C6. *There exists $c \in (0,1)$ such that, for any fixed $\eta, \delta > 0$,*

$$\lim_{x\to\infty} f'\left(f^{-1}\left(g\left((1-c)x\right)\right)\right) h\left(f((1+c)x), \eta, \delta\right) = 0.$$

One can design a variety of scheduling algorithm under this framework by choosing different oracles, e.g., the exhaustive search (ES), the markov chain monte carlo (MCMC), and the belief propagation (BP), where recent queue-based CSMA [3] can be understood as such algorithms using MCMC. At a high level, we use the interactive oracle concept to provide a 'black-box' tool for designing scheduling algorithms of high performance and low-complexity. This establishes a rigorous connection between iterative optimization methods and low-complexity scheduling algorithms, which provides various future directions and new insights in both areas.

4. REFERENCES

[1] L. Tassiulas and A. Ephremides. Stability properties of constrained queueing systems and scheduling policies for maximum throughput in multihop radio networks. *IEEE Transactions on Automatic Control*, 37:1936-1948, 1992.

[2] L. Georgiadis, M. J. Neely, and L. Tassiulas. Resource allocation and cross-layer control in wireless networks. *Foundations and Trends in Networking*, 1:1-144, 2006.

[3] S. Rajagopalan, D. Shah, and J. Shin. Network adiabatic theorem: An efficient randomized protocol for contention resolution. *ACM SIGMETRICS*, 2009.

[4] L. Jiang, D. Shah, J. Shin, and J. Walrand. Distributed random access algorithm: Scheduling and congestion control. *IEEE Transactions on Information Theory*, 56(12):6182-6207, 2010.

[5] D. Shah and J. Shin. Randomized scheduling algorithm for queueing networks. *Annals of Applied Probability*, 22:128-171, 2012.

Unified Localization Framework Using Trajectory Signatures

Swati Rallapalli Wei Dong Lili Qiu Yin Zhang
The University of Texas at Austin
{swati,wdong86,lili,yzhang}@cs.utexas.edu

ABSTRACT

We develop a novel trajectory-based localization scheme which (i) identifies a user's current trajectory based on the measurements collected while the user is moving, by finding the best match among the training traces (trajectory matching) and then (ii) localizes the user on the trajectory (localization). The core requirement of both the steps is an accurate and robust algorithm to match two time-series that may contain significant noise and perturbation due to differences in mobility, devices, and environments. To achieve this, we develop an enhanced Dynamic Time Warping (DTW) alignment, and apply it to RSS, channel state information, or magnetic field measurements collected from a trajectory. We use indoor and outdoor experiments to demonstrate its effectiveness.

Categories and Subject Descriptors

C.2.3 [**Network Operations**]: Network monitoring

General Terms

Measurement, Performance

Keywords

Localization, Magnetic Field, WiFi, Dynamic Time Warping (DTW)

1. INTRODUCTION

Motivation: Localization has been extensively studied due to its important role in many applications. Limited availability and high energy consumption of the Global Positioning System (GPS) have motivated researchers to develop alternative localization schemes. Despite much research on localization, significant challenges remain. First, most existing works use Wi-Fi for localization, but Wi-Fi may not always be available. Even when it is available, its density may not be high enough to allow accurate localization. Second, while it is natural to localize based on measurements collected from an individual point, such point-based localization schemes yield limited accuracy due to significant aliasing (*i.e.*, more than one location has similar RSS or channel state information (CSI)).

Approach: We first seek an alternative to Wi-Fi signatures for localization. We find that universally available magnetic field can serve as a useful signature indoors and outdoors. However, the magnetic field readings from different locations can be similar. Unlike Wi-Fi, in which we can reduce aliasing by deploying more APs, aliases in the magnetic field are hard to remove. Interestingly, we show that magnetic field readings over a trajectory are distinguishable enough to be used as a signature. So we let a mobile device collect magnetic field readings while moving with its user, and use the measurement time-series as a signature for localization. Localization is performed by (i) collecting training traces which associate measured magnetic field with locations (*e.g.*, GPS coordinates), (ii) matching a new measurement trace without location information with one of the training traces (*i.e.*, trajectory matching), and (iii) narrowing down to the exact location based on the matched point on the training trace (*i.e.*, localization).

Our trajectory-based localization is general and can be applied to measurements other than magnetic field, such as RSS and CSI. When applied to RSS and CSI, it out-performs existing point-based localization because (i) measurements collected over a trajectory offer more information and trajectory matching is likely to be more accurate than point matching, (ii) localizing a point on a trajectory is much easier than localizing a point in an area. Therefore, by leveraging more information and decomposing the problem into the two easier tasks, we improve accuracy. While it is evident that trajectory based localization requires more information than point based localization, it is not more expensive to collect such data since people walk and drive in a few common trajectories (*e.g.*, corridors in a building, aisles in grocery stores, and lanes on roads).

The core requirement of both steps is an accurate and robust algorithm to match two time-series that may be noisy and subject to various perturbations arising from different speeds, similar but not identical trajectories, different devices, and environmental changes. To find an alignment between the two time-series, we apply well known Dynamic Time Warping (DTW) [1], which is widely used in signal processing, speech recognition, and signature recognition [3]. To improve robustness against different speeds and noise, we develop a few enhancements and apply our enhanced DTW approaches to measurements collected from trajectories. Our results show that this approach significantly improves accuracy and power efficiency over the existing localization schemes.

2. OUR APPROACH

Problem formulation: The problem consists of (i) trajectory matching and (ii) localization. In (i), given measurements from a set of trajectories, we identify the trajectory whose measurement best matches our current measurement. In (ii), we localize a point on the testing trace to the matched point on the identified training trace.

We apply dynamic time warping (DTW) [1] for both steps. It stretches or compresses portions of the input sequence to improve

SIGMETRICS'14, June 16–20, 2014, Austin, Texas, USA.
ACM 978-1-4503-2789-3/14/06.
http://dx.doi.org/10.1145/2591971.2592027.

the alignment and minimize the total distance. This is useful when we try to match traces collected at different speeds. Specifically, given two sequences: $X = (x_1, x_2, ..., x_N), Y = (y_1, y_2, ..., y_M)$ and distance between any two points $d(x_i, y_j)$, DTW applies dynamic programming to find the best alignment of points on X to points on Y based on the recursion: $DTW(i, j) = d(x[i], y[j]) + min(DTW(i-1, j), DTW(i-1, j-1), DTW(i, j-1))$.

Trajectory matching & Localization: We use DTW subsequence [1], which tries to find the subsequence of Y such that it best matches with the complete sequence of X. DTW subsequence is more useful than DTW complete sequence in our context because we need to localize a user while she is in the middle of a trajectory and the input sequence is not complete. In this case, DTW subsequence not only allows us to find a match, but also outputs the alignment which gives the current location of the user. We enhance the DTW algorithm as follows:

- To handle different speeds, we perform multi-level wavelet decomposition on the measurement data and search for the wavelet level that minimizes the normalized DTW distance (*i.e.*, DTW distance normalized by the length of the warping path to avoid bias towards shorter paths, where warping path refers to the set of matrix elements that define the mapping between X and Y).
- We address the singularity problems in DTW by (i) pre-processing the data via smoothing using Savitzky–Golay filter [2] and removing the mean before alignment, (ii) using different local weights in DTW [1], and (iii) constraining the window when looking for a match where the window size is determined based on the maximum speed ratio.
- We use spectral clustering to cluster training traces from the same trajectory to capture possibly different patterns. We then use the minimum DTW distance between the testing trace and the training traces across all clusters as the final DTW distance.
- We speed up the computation by incrementally computing DTW.

Full path localization: We further develop full path localization by calling DTW subsequence at every intersection to identify the new segment. Afterwards, we periodically localize the user on the segment using incremental DTW subsequence. Then we detect the end point of the current segment, and repeat the steps.

3. EVALUATION

We measure the magnetic field outdoors while driving in Austin and Seattle. We measure the magnetic field and Wi-Fi RSS indoors while walking in a regular office building. We report the magnetic field results here, and the Wi-Fi results are comparable.

Matching & Localization: Figure 1(a) compares the trajectory matching accuracy. DTW, LEVEL2, and LEVEL4 are DTW based on the original trace, approximate wavelet coefficients at level 2 and level 4, respectively. These three DTW-based approaches consistently out-perform longest common subsequence (LCS) and matching based on average of the traces (AVG). Using wavelet coefficients performs similarly to using the original traces. Moreover, spectral clustering is 10% better than natural clustering (*i.e.*, clustering based on measurement settings), which outperforms random clustering by 23%. Spectral clustering is better than natural clustering because the traces collected in the same way may not exhibit the same pattern. Figure 1(b) compares the localization error, where CP localizes a point on the testing trace to the point on the training trace whose signal is most similar. The three DTW based schemes significantly out-perform LCS and CP.

Figure 2 evaluates different speed ratios between testing and training traces outdoors. Our MULTI LEVEL, which searches for the

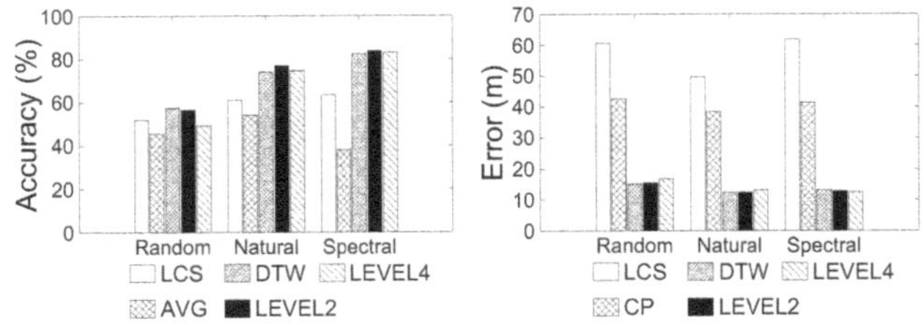

(a) Trajectory Matching (b) Localization Median Error

Figure 1: Outdoors: schemes across different clustering.

wavelet level that minimizes DTW distance, is robust to such speed variation, and outperforms LEVEL2-W2, which uses fixed window size assuming the maximum speed ratio between the test and training traces is 2 and LEVEL2-W-INC, which adjusts the window based on the actual speed ratio (not available in practice).

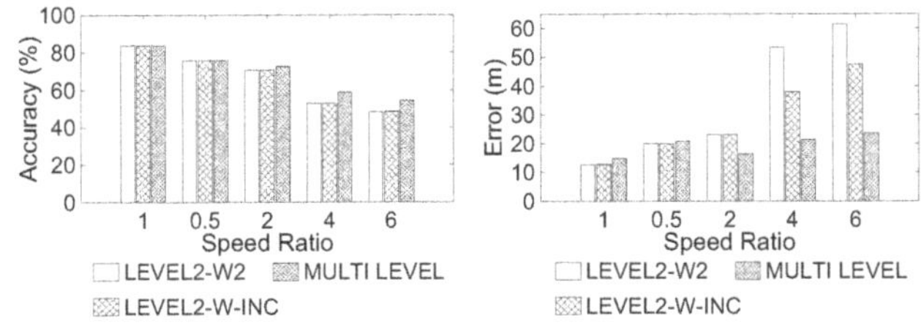

(a) Trajectory Matching (b) Localization Error

Figure 2: Outdoors: Accuracy with varying speeds.

As shown in Figure 3, the trend indoors is similar to outdoors, but the accuracy is much higher indoors (matching accuracy as high as 96% and localization error as low as 0.28m even at speed ratio 6) due to lower speeds and more stable measurements.

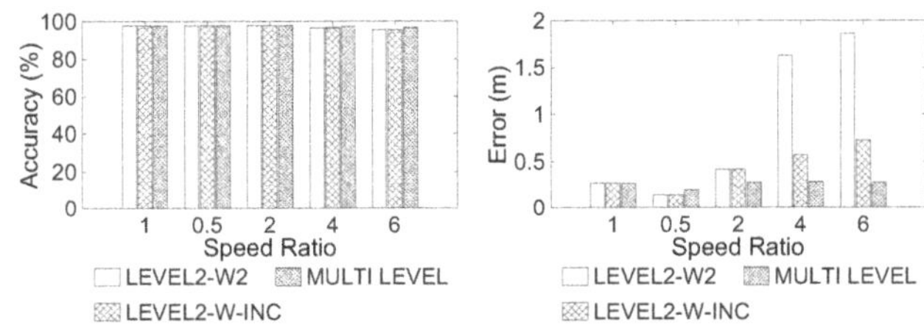

(a) Trajectory Matching (b) Localization Error

Figure 3: Indoors: Accuracy with varying speeds.

Full Path Localization: Figure 4 compares full path localization indoors. It considers cumulative errors (*i.e.*, incorrect matching in one segment will lead to incorrect matching in subsequent segments). Even after 4 segments, the matching accuracy is still as high as 96% and the localization error is only 0.3m.

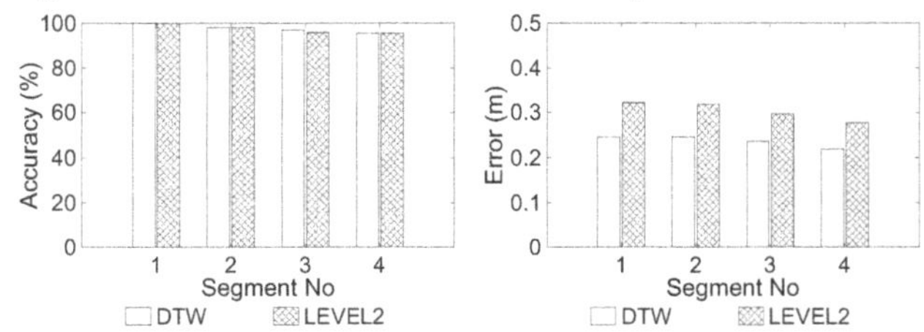

(a) Trajectory Matching (b) Localization Error

Figure 4: Indoors: Accuracy across intersections.

4. REFERENCES

[1] M. Müller. *Information retrieval for music and motion*. Springer, 2007.
[2] S. J. Orfanidis. *Introduction to Signal Processing*. Prentice Hall, 1996.
[3] H. Sakoe and S. Chiba. Dynamic programming algorithm optimization for spoken word recognition. *IEEE Transactions on Acoustics, Speech, and Signal Processing*, 26(1), Feb. 1978.

TS-CLOCK: Temporal and Spatial Locality Aware Buffer Replacement Algorithm for NAND Flash Storages *

Dong Hyun Kang
Sungkyunkwan University
Suwon, Korea
kkangsu@skku.edu

Changwoo Min
Sungkyunkwan University
Suwon, Korea
multics69@skku.edu

Young Ik Eom
Sungkyunkwan University
Suwon, Korea
yieom@skku.edu

ABSTRACT

NAND flash storage is widely adopted in all classes of computing devices. However, random write performance and lifetime issues remain to be addressed. In this paper, we propose a novel buffer replacement algorithm called TS-CLOCK that effectively resolves the remaining problems. Our experimental results show that TS-CLOCK outperforms state-of-the-art algorithms in terms of performance and lifetime.

Categories and Subject Descriptors

D.4.2 [**Software**]: Operating Systems—*Storage Management*

Keywords

NAND flash storage, buffer replacement, locality

1. INTRODUCTION

In recent years, flash-aware buffer replacement algorithm has been actively studied because traditional algorithms, such as LRU, CLOCK, and Linux2Q, are not suitable for NAND flash storages. Most previous research focused on two performance characteristics of NAND flash storages. One is *asymmetric read/write cost* that the write operation is slower than the read operation [6], and the other is *performance variability in write patterns* that sequential writes are significantly faster than random writes [3, 1, 4, 5].

CFLRU [6] is a representative flash-aware buffer replacement algorithm that evicts clean pages over dirty pages to reduce the number of expensive write operations. However, CFLRU generates a large number of hidden writes inside NAND flash storage since it does not consider the write patterns of the evicted pages. In contrast, FAB [3], LB-CLOCK [1], and Sp.Clock [4] focuses on write patterns to reduce hidden writes. FAB and LB-CLOCK perform eviction at the granularity of a block rather than a page to generate sequential write patterns. However, they negatively impact cache hit ratio and performance due to the *early eviction problem* [7]. Among the existing flash-aware buffer replacement algorithms, Sp.Clock is most efficient. It manages page frames in order of logical sector number rather than recency order, for the sorted eviction scheme. However, Sp.Clock suffers from high garbage collection (GC) cost with wide I/O ranges such as server workloads, since the evicted patterns become random. The major drawback of existing algorithms is that they ignore lifetime of NAND flash storage. However, it is important to extend the lifetime because increasing flash capacity by storing additional bits per cell reduces the flash chip's lifetime by orders of magnitude [2].

*This work was supported by the IT R&D program of MKE/KEIT. [10041244, SmartTV 2.0 Software Platform]

SIGMETRICS'14, June 16–20, 2014, Austin, Texas, USA.
ACM 978-1-4503-2789-3/14/06.
http://dx.doi.org/10.1145/2591971.2592028.

2. TS-CLOCK ALGORITHM

We propose *Temporal and Spatial locality aware CLOCK* (TS-CLOCK) replacement algorithm. The goal of our algorithm is to improve the performance and lifetime of NAND flash storage. To achieve it, TS-CLOCK extends traditional CLOCK algorithm for temporal locality, and exploits spatial locality by using the reference count and two hands.

Algorithm 1: Victim selection algorithm

```
Input: head of circular list t-hand, head of sorted list
       s-hand, new page np
while true do
  if t-hand.ref_count is zero then
    if t-hand.status is clean then
      evict t-hand;
    else
      if s-hand is null then
        s-hand = the first page in the sorted list of
        t-hand.block;
      while s-hand.ref_count is not zero do
        if s-hand is the last of the block then
          s-hand = the first page in the sorted list
          of t-hand.block;
        else
          s-hand = the next page in the sorted list
          of the block;
      evict s-hand;
    insert np into the position of t-hand;
    if np.status is dirty then
      insert np into the sorted list of np.block;
    break;
  else
    t-hand.ref_count = t-hand.ref_count - 1;
    t-hand = the next page of in the circular list;
```

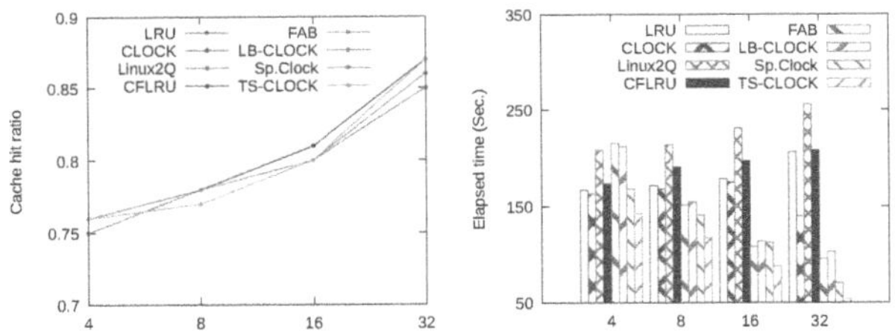

(a) Cache hit ratio (b) Elapsed time

Figure 1: Cache hit ratio and elapsed time for mobile workload on the Patriot microSD card

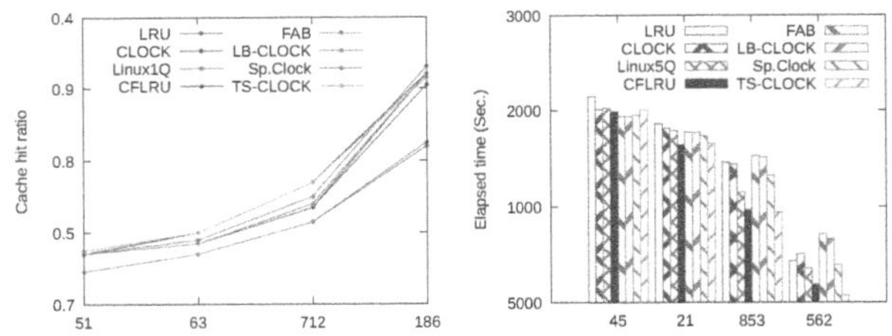

(a) Cache hit ratio (b) Elapsed time

Figure 2: Cache hit ratio and elapsed time for server workload on the Samsung SSD

Reference count. TS-CLOCK maintains a reference count per page to evict clean pages preferentially. A reference count of every clean page is always set to 1 when the page is accessed. On the other hand, that of every dirty page is differently set depending on *update likelihood* of the block that it belongs to. The update likelihood of a block is calculated as the ratio of dirty pages (i.e., the number of pages whose reference count is not 0 in a block / the number of pages per block). In our scheme, we set the reference count to 1, 2, 3, and 4 for 0-25%, 25-50%, 50-75%, and 75-100% update likelihoods, respectively.

Two hands. TS-CLOCK manages *t-hand* and *s-hand* to shape evicted dirty pages into flash-friendly sequential pattern. Similarly to CLOCK, *t-hand* scans pages in the circular list and decrements its reference count by 1 for selecting a victim page. If a selected page whose reference count is 0 is clean, it is immediately evicted. Otherwise, *s-hand* scans dirty pages, which belong to the block, by their sector numbers until a page with reference count of 0 is found. Even though *s-hand* does not decrement the reference count of each page during scanning, it guarantees to find a victim page. This is because *s-hand* is set to the first page of the block, which includes the page pointed by *t-hand*, when *s-hand* reaches the last page in a block. If *s-hand* finds a page with reference count of 0 in a block, it is evicted. After evicting the page, TS-CLOCK inserts a new page into the position of the *t-hand* to grant at least one full life to the page. In this way, TS-CLOCK minimizes hidden writes by generating flash-friendly sequential write patterns. Algorithm 1 shows our victim selection algorithm.

3. EVALUATION

We evaluated TS-CLOCK and compared it with well-known replacement algorithms by trace-driven simulation and real NAND flash storage based experimentation. We also used two workloads: a mobile workload, which is a mixed application from Sp.Clock [4], and a server workload which is acquired from Dbench benchmark.

Experiment on the microSD card. We first compared the performance of eight replacement algorithms on the microSD card. Figure 1 shows the hit ratio and elapsed time of each algorithm while varying buffer cache size from 4MB to 32MB. As shown in Figure 1, TS-CLOCK significantly outperforms the other algorithms by up to 90%. The main reason is that TS-CLOCK reduces the hidden writes by exploiting spatial locality.

Experiment on the SSD. Figure 2 presents our experimental results on the triple-level cell (TLC) based SSD in terms of cache hit ratio and performance. We set cache

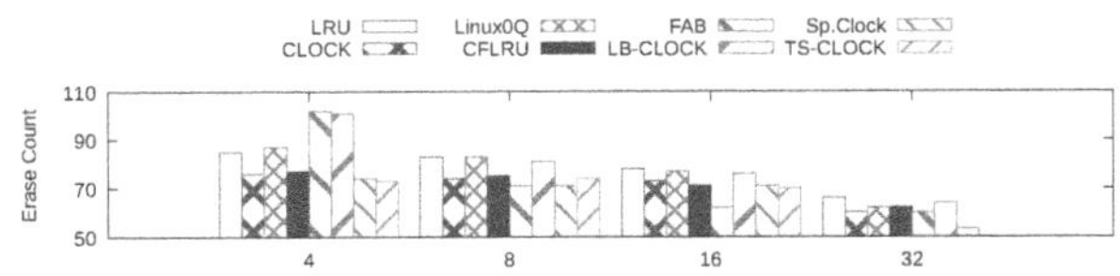

(a) FAST FTL with mobile workload

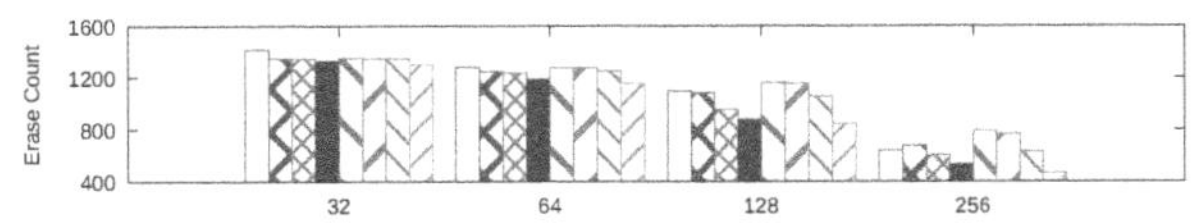

(b) page-level FTL with server workload

Figure 3: Comparison of erase count

sizes from 32MB to 256MB, which are more realistic ranges for high performance SSD. Figure 2 clearly shows that TS-CLOCK significantly outperforms the state-of-the-art algorithm, Sp.Clock, by up to 22.7%. To understand the results, we analyzed the amount of evicted I/O requests. As a result, we found that TS-CLOCK generates the smallest write requests due to clean-first eviction. Furthermore, TS-CLOCK minimizes the number of hidden writes by generating flash-friendly patterns.

Effect on Lifetime. We also measured the lifetime of NAND flash storage by implementing a trace-driven flash translation layer (FTL) simulator, which supports FAST FTL and page-level FTL. Figure 3 clearly shows that TS-CLOCK extends the lifetime by up to 29% compared to CFLRU using FAST FTL and by up to 40% compared to FAB using page-level FTL.

4. REFERENCES

[1] B. Debnath, S. Subramanya, D. Du, and D. J. Lilja. Large Block CLOCK (LB-CLOCK): A write caching algorithm for solid state disks. In *Proc. IEEE MASCOTS*, 2009.

[2] L. M. Grupp, J. D. Davis, and S. Swanson. The bleak future of NAND flash memory. In *Proc. USENIX FAST*, 2012.

[3] H. Jo, J.-U. Kang, S.-Y. Park, J.-S. Kim, and J. Lee. FAB: flash-aware buffer management policy for portable media players. *IEEE Trans. Consum. Electron.*, 52(2):485–493, May 2006.

[4] H. Kim, M. Ryu, and U. Ramachandran. What is a good buffer cache replacement scheme for mobile flash storage? In *Proc. ACM SIGMETRICS*, 2012.

[5] C. Min, K. Kim, H. Cho, S.-W. Lee, and Y. I. Eom. SFS: Random write considered harmful in solid state drives. In *Proc. USENIX FAST*, 2012.

[6] S.-Y. Park, D. Jung, J.-U. Kang, J.-S. Kim, and J. Lee. CFLRU: A replacement algorithm for flash memory. In *Proc. ACM CASES*, 2006.

[7] G. Wu, X. He, and B. Eckart. An adaptive write buffer management scheme for flash-based SSDs. *ACM Trans. Storage*, 8(1):1, Feb. 2012.

Multi-source Multipath HTTP (mHTTP): A Proposal

Juhoon Kim† Yung-Chih Chen‡
Ramin Khalili† Don Towsley‡ Anja Feldmann†

†TU Berlin/T-Labs, Germany
{jkim,ramin,anja}@net.t-labs.tu-berlin.de
‡UMass Amherst, USA
{yungchih,towsley}@cs.umass.edu

ABSTRACT

Today, most devices have multiple network interfaces. Coupled with wide-spread replication of popular content at multiple locations, this provides substantial path diversity in the Internet. We propose Multi-source Multipath HTTP, mHTTP, which takes advantage of all existing types of path diversity in the Internet. mHTTP needs only client-side but not server-side or network modifications as it is a receiver-oriented mechanism. Moreover, the modifications are restricted to the socket interface. Thus, no changes are needed to the applications or to the kernel.

Categories and Subject Descriptors

C.2.2 [**Computer Systems Organization**]: COMPUTER-COMMUNICATION NETWORKS—*Network Protocols*

Keywords

multi-source;multipath;content delivery improvement

1. INTRODUCTION

In today's Internet, one of the main detriments in user experience is completion times of data transfers that for large objects is limited by network capacity. However, recent developments have opened new opportunities for reducing end-to-end latencies. First, most end-user devices have multiple network interfaces (e.g., 3G/LTE and WiFi interfaces for smart-phones). Second, popular contents are often available at multiple locations in the network. When combined, these provide substantial path diversity within the Internet that can be used by users to improve their quality of experience.

Previous work has taken partial advantage of this path diversity in the Internet. Multipath TCP (MPTCP) uses the path diversity available between a single server and a single client [3]. Content Distribution Networks (CDNs) provide replication of content and smart matching of users to appropriate CDN server, e.g., via PaDIS [6] or ALTO [7] services, which takes advantage of this replication. Bittorrent is another sophisticated application which takes advantage of content replication among its users [2]. The drawback of each of the above approaches is that they do not utilize all of different types of path diversity in the Internet or if they do, they are application specific.

SIGMETRICS'14, June 16–20, 2014, Austin, Texas, USA.
ACM 978-1-4503-2789-3/14/06.
http://dx.doi.org/10.1145/2591971.2592029.

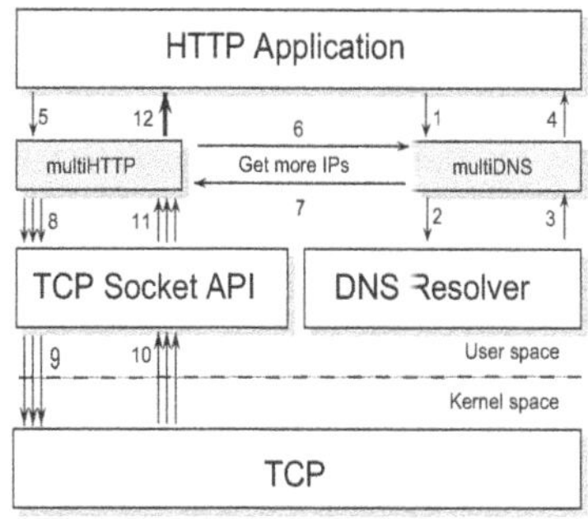

Figure 1: mHTTP architecture at a client.

We propose Multi-source Multipath HTTP, mHTTP, which enables users to establish simultaneous connections with multiple servers to fetch a single content. mHTTP is designed to combine the advantage obtained from distributed network infrastructures provided by CDNs with the advantage of multiple interfaces at end-users. Key features of the proposed technique are: a) mHTTP is a purely receiver-oriented mechanism that requires no modification either at the server or at the network, b) the modifications are restricted to the socket interface; hence, no changes are needed to the applications or to the kernel, and c) it takes advantage of all existing types of path diversity in the Internet.

2. Multi-source Multipath HTTP

The key idea of mHTTP is to use the HTTP range request feature to fetch different content chunks from different servers. We define a chunk as a block of content delivered within one HTTP response message. mHTTP includes two components, *multiHTTP* and *multiDNS* as shown in Figure 1. These components extend the functionality of HTTP and the DNS resolver. The main purpose of multiHTTP is to handle chunked data delivery between the application and multiple servers; and that of multiDNS is to collect IP addresses of available content sources.

2.1 multiDNS

When an application needs to obtain an IP address from a human-readable URL, it invokes name resolvers such as *gethostbyname()* or *getaddrinfo()*. The resolver, then, creates a request message and sends it to the local DNS server usually provided by the local ISP. Depending on the content sources, if content is only available at a single server, the DNS returns the IP address of that particular server so that the request can be routed to the server. However, if

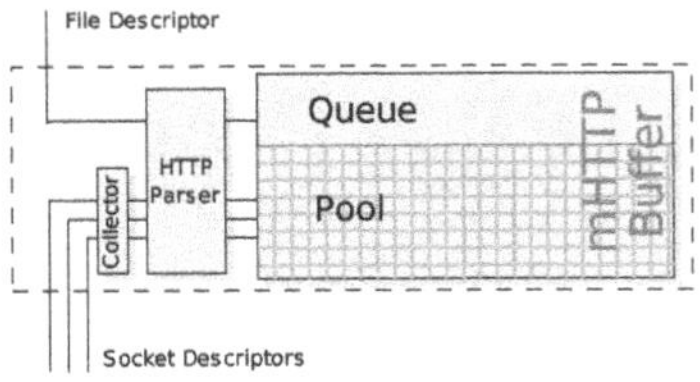

Figure 2: multiHTTP design: a) *mHTTP buffer* temporarily stores fragmented data b) *HTTP parser* examines and modifies HTTP headers c) *collector* gathers data from individual TCP connection buffers.

content is available at multiple places (e.g., a server farm or CDNs), DNS returns a list of IP addresses. In the case of multiple IP addresses, a typical behavior of an application is to choose the first IP address in order to establish the connection and to discard the rest. multiDNS, however, keeps the rest of the IP addresses for later use. For each interface, multiDNS receives a list of IP addresses from each access network, and chooses desired number of IP addresses from every list.

2.2 multiHTTP

The main task of multiHTTP is to interpret mHTTP for regular HTTP speakers such as web servers and client-side applications.

RFC2616 specifies the use of a *byte range request* which enables the partial delivery of content. A client initiates such a request by adding a *range* field within the header of an HTTP request message including offsets of the first byte and the last byte of the partial content. If the server supports this operation, it replies with 206 as the status code (on acceptance of the request message) followed by sequences of bytes. Otherwise, the server replies with a different status code (e.g., 200 OK on success). Our tests on well-known web servers during the development of mHTTP show that almost all web servers accept *range* requests.

multiHTTP initializes *mHTTP buffer* and creates a file descriptor associated with the buffer when *socket()* is called by the application. The buffer consists of a *queue* and a *pool* of content blocks (chunks). The queue is a large memory block that is continuously read by the application. Thus, the file descriptor plays the role of a communication channel between the application and the mHTTP buffer (Figure 2). The pool maintains multiple content blocks in which chunked data collected from individual TCP buffers is stored. A content block can be indexed by the combination of the socket descriptor and the starting byte of the chunk. Data within content blocks is moved to the queue as soon as it is continuous from the last byte that is stored in the queue.

Once the connection is identified as an HTTP connection, multiHTTP enables an HTTP parser, which examines HTTP messages and modify the header during the content delivery period. Upon confirmation of the complete delivery of the initial response message, multiHTTP establishes additional TCP connections using different IP addresses provided by multiDNS. multiHTTP operates *collector*, a background process that collects data from individual TCP connection buffers. Each new connection must be attached to the *collector* as soon as it is successfully established. Likewise, a connection can be detached from the *collector*.

3. EVALUATION

We conduct performance measurements of mHTTP on an existing CDN infrastructure. We choose a 16MB file from a well-known site on *Alexa.com*'s top-50 list, where the content is hosted in a CDN. multiDNS queries Google's DNS over each interface separately, and uses the set of IP addresses returned for each interface. The client device is equipped with two wireless interfaces (WiFi and LTE) that respectively connect to a WiFi network and a cellular network. We depict the download times of the file using single-path or mHTTP with different chunk sizes in Figure 3. Note that for single-path TCP, each interface by default queries its local DNS resolver. The results are presented for different mHTTP chunk sizes. We observe that (1) the connection over LTE has a much better performance than the one over WIFI; (2) mHTTP greatly benefits from the existing diversity in the network, it reduces download times by up to 50% when compared to the single-path case; and (3) it performs very well across a wide range of chunk sizes.

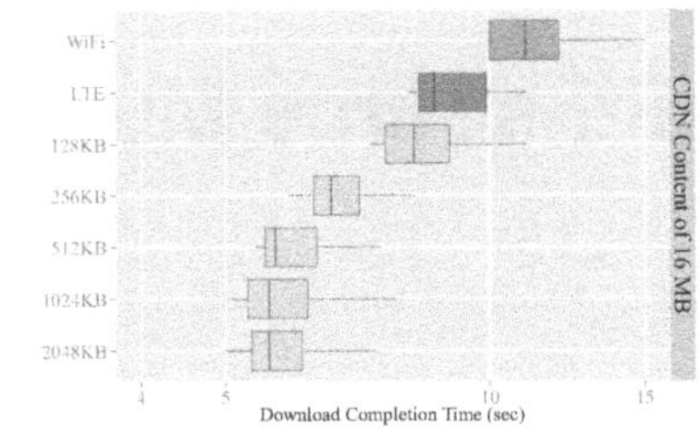

Figure 3: Measurement on a CDN infrastructure. We depict download completion time of regular HTTP vs. mHTTP for different chunk sizes. We observe that mHTTP can efficiently take advantage of the diversity exists in the network.

4. SUMMARY

Advantages of simultaneously utilizing multiple paths over a network communication are widely evaluated and understood [1, 3]. mHTTP's key contribution is to bring significant benefits to the end-to-end content delivery by utilizing path diversity and data source diversity in the Internet without any changes on existing applications and the server-side network stack.

Our result showed that mHTTP's download completion time of large objects is remarkably short as compared to that of a regular HTTP. Given the fact that HTTP accounts for more than 60 % [5] of today's Internet traffic and that the major fraction of the total web servers are operated on content distribution infrastructures [4], this performance gain is rather significant.

5. REFERENCES

[1] CHEN, Y.-C., LIM, Y.-S., GIBBENS, R. J., NAHUM, E. M., KHALILI, R., AND TOWSLEY, D. A measurement-based study of multipath tcp performance over wireless networks. In *ACM IMC 2013*.

[2] COHEN, B. Incentives build robustness in bittorrent. In *Workshop on Economics of Peer-to-Peer systems 2003*.

[3] FORD, A., RAICIU, C., HANDLEY, M., BARRE, S., AND IYENGAR, J. Architectural guidelines for multipath tcp development. In *RFC 6182*.

[4] HUANG, C., WANG, A., LI, J., AND ROSS, K. W. Measuring and evaluating large-scale cdns. In *ACM IMC 2008*.

[5] MAIER, G., FELDMANN, A., PAXSON, V., AND ALLMAN, M. On dominant characteristics of residential broadband internet traffic. In *ACM IMC 2009*.

[6] POESE, I., FRANK, B., AGER, B., SMARAGDAKIS, G., AND FELDMANN, A. Improving content delivery using provider-aided distance information. In *ACM IMC 2010*.

[7] SEEDORF, J., AND BURGER, E. Application-layer traffic optimization (alto) problem statement. In *RFC 5693*.

Performance Analysis of MAC for Power-Line Communications

Christina Vlachou
EPFL, Switzerland
christina.vlachou@epfl.ch

Albert Banchs
Universidad Carlos III de Madrid, Spain
banchs@it.uc3m.es

Julien Herzen
EPFL, Switzerland
julien.herzen@epfl.ch

Patrick Thiran
EPFL, Switzerland
patrick.thiran@epfl.ch

ABSTRACT

We investigate the IEEE 1901 MAC protocol, the dominant protocol for high data rate power-line communications. 1901 employs a CSMA/CA mechanism similar to – but much more complex than – the backoff mechanism of 802.11. Because of this extra complexity, and although this mechanism is the only widely used MAC layer for power-line networks, there are few analytical results on its performance. We propose a model for the 1901 MAC that comes in the form of a single fixed-point equation for the collision probability. We prove that this equation admits a unique solution, and we evaluate the accuracy of our model by using simulations.

Categories and Subject Descriptors

C.4 [**Performance of Systems**]: Modeling techniques

Keywords

Power-line communications; CSMA/CA; analysis.

1. BACKGROUND

Due to the shared nature of power lines, the vast majority of devices employ a multiple-access scheme based on CSMA/CA, which is specified by the IEEE 1901 standard [1]. We first present the relevant aspects of this protocol. The CSMA/CA process of 1901 uses two counters: the backoff counter (BC) and the deferral counter (DC). In addition, there are four *backoff stages*. Upon the arrival of a new packet, a transmitting station starts at backoff stage 0. It then draws the backoff counter BC uniformly at random in $\{0, \ldots, CW_0 - 1\}$, where CW_0 refers to the contention window used at backoff stage 0. Similarly to 802.11, BC is decreased by 1 at each time slot if the station senses the medium to be idle (i.e., below the carrier-sensing threshold), and BC is frozen when the medium is sensed busy, in which case BC will be also decreased by 1 once the medium is sensed idle again. When BC reaches 0, the station attempts to transmit the packet. Also similarly to 802.11, the station jumps to the next backoff stage if the transmission fails (unless it is already at the last backoff stage, in which case it re-enters this backoff stage). When entering backoff stage i, a station draws BC uniformly at random in $\{0, \ldots, CW_i - 1\}$, where CW_i is the contention window at backoff stage i, and the process is repeated. The default CW_i values are $CW_i \in \{8, 16, 32, 64\}$ for 1901.

Now, the main difference between 1901 and 802.11 is that a 1901 station might enter the next backoff stage even if it did not attempt a transmission. The mechanism for deciding when this occurs uses the deferral counter DC, and works as follows. When entering backoff stage i, DC is set at an *an initial DC value* d_i (the defaults being $\{0, 1, 3, 15\}$ [1]). After having sensed the medium busy, a station decreases DC by 1 (in addition to BC). If the medium is sensed busy and $DC = 0$, then the station jumps to the next backoff stage (or re-enters the last backoff stage, if it is already at this stage), and it re-draws BC *without attempting a transmission.*

The deferral counter significantly increases the complexity of the 1901 backoff procedure. To the best of our knowledge, the only work that analyzes this procedure is [2], and uses a Markov chain. To compute the collision probability γ, a costly system of more than a thousand non-linear equations needs to be solved [2]. Moreover, the authors do not study whether this system of equations has a unique solution. We introduce here a simplification of [2] and prove that our model admits a unique solution. Our model can be later employed to investigate enhancements of the 1901 MAC.

2. ANALYSIS

We investigate the 1901 CSMA/CA protocol under the following assumptions. First, there are N stations in a single contention domain. Second, there is no packet loss or error due to the physical layer. Third, the stations have an infinite retry limit.

Our modeling assumptions are similar to the ones in [3] and are referred to as the *decoupling assumption*. We assume that the backoff process of a station is independent of the aggregate attempt process of the other $N - 1$ stations and that transmission attempts experience a fixed collision probability γ. In addition, γ refers to the probability that the medium is busy at any time slot. Finally, the stations

SIGMETRICS'14, June 16–20, 2014, Austin, Texas, USA.
ACM 978-1-4503-2789-3/14/06.
http://dx.doi.org/10.1145/2591971.2592033.

attempt a transmission in each time slot, with a constant transmission probability equal to the average attempt rate τ.

A 1901 station with DC initially equal to d_i can change its backoff stage either (i) after attempting a transmission or (ii) due to sensing the medium busy $d_i + 1$ times. We need to compute the probabilities of the events (i) and (ii). To this end, we introduce x_k, the probability that a station at backoff stage i jumps to the next backoff stage $i+1$ in k or fewer time slots due to (ii). The event that (ii) happens during the first k slots follows the binomial distribution $\text{Bin}(k, \gamma)$, whence $x_k = \sum_{j=d_i+1}^{k} \binom{k}{j} \gamma^j (1-\gamma)^{k-j}$.

Let us write bc_i for the expected number of time slots spent by a station at backoff stage i. Now, recall that when entering stage i, the stations draw a backoff counter BC uniformly at random in $\{0, \ldots, CW_i - 1\}$. Let k denote this initial value of BC, and d_i be the value of DC when the station enters stage i. If $k > d_i$, then event (i) occurs with probability $(1-x_k)$, in which case the station spends $(k+1)$ slots in stage i (the $(k+1)th$ slot being used for transmission), whence event (ii) occurs at slot j, with $d_i + 1 \le j \le k$, with probability $(x_j - x_{j-1})$, in which case the station spends j slots in stage i. Finally, if $k \le d_i$, then (ii) cannot happen and (i) always takes place. It follows that bc_i is given by

$$bc_i = \frac{1}{CW_i} \sum_{k=d_i+1}^{CW_i-1} \left[(k+1)(1-x_k) + \sum_{j=d_i+1}^{k} j(x_j - x_{j-1}) \right] + \frac{(d_i+1)(d_i+2)}{2CW_i}. \tag{1}$$

Let R be a random variable describing the number of transmission attempts experienced by a successfully transmitted packet and let X be a random variable describing the total number of slots spent in backoff for a successfully transmitted packet. Then by using the renewal-reward theorem as in [3], the average attempt rate can be computed as

$$\tau = \mathbb{E}[R]/\mathbb{E}[X]. \tag{2}$$

We now compute separately $\mathbb{E}[R]$ and $\mathbb{E}[X]$. Let t_i be the probability that a station at backoff stage i ends this backoff stage by attempting a transmission. Using a similar reasoning as for (1), t_i is given by

$$t_i = \frac{d_i+1}{CW_i} + \sum_{k=d_i+1}^{CW_i-1} \frac{1}{CW_i}(1-x_k). \tag{3}$$

Let $s_i = (1-\gamma)t_i$ be the probability that a station at backoff stage i ends this stage due to a successful transmission and let m be the total number of backoff stages. We express $\mathbb{E}[R]$ and $\mathbb{E}[X]$ as a function of all bc_i, t_i, s_i. The expected number of backoff slots per successfully transmitted packet is

$$\mathbb{E}[X] = \sum_{i=0}^{m-2} bc_i \prod_{j=0}^{i-1}(1-s_j) + \prod_{i=0}^{m-2}(1-s_i)\frac{bc_{m-1}}{s_{m-1}}.$$

Finally, the expected number of transmission attempts per successfully transmitted packet is

$$\mathbb{E}[R] = \sum_{i=0}^{m-2} t_i \prod_{j=0}^{i-1}(1-s_j) + \prod_{i=0}^{m-2}(1-s_i)\frac{t_{m-1}}{s_{m-1}} = \frac{1}{1-\gamma}.$$

Let $G(\gamma) = \mathbb{E}[R]/\mathbb{E}[X]$. Now, γ is the probability that at least one other station transmits and it can be expressed as a function of τ: $\gamma = \Gamma(\tau) = 1 - (1-\tau)^{N-1}$. The composition of the two functions above yields the fixed-point equation for the collision probability: $\gamma = \Gamma(G(\gamma))$. Theorem 1 below establishes the uniqueness of the solution of $\gamma = \Gamma(G(\gamma))$.

THEOREM 1. *The fixed-point equation $\gamma = \Gamma(G(\gamma))$ has a unique solution if $CW_{i+1} > 2CW_i - d_i - 1$, $0 \le i \le m-1$.*

3. PERFORMANCE EVALUATION

We use simulations to evaluate the 1901 performance. We wrote a custom simulator in Matlab, which implements the full CSMA/CA mechanism of 1901.

Figure 1 presents the collision probability and the normalized throughput of the network obtained by simulations and our model. We observe that the accuracy of the model improves as N increases. We attribute the reduced accuracy when N is small to the decoupling assumption: For small N, the stations are coupled in 1901 because they change their state when some other station transmits. We leave the investigation of the validity of the decoupling assumption for future work.

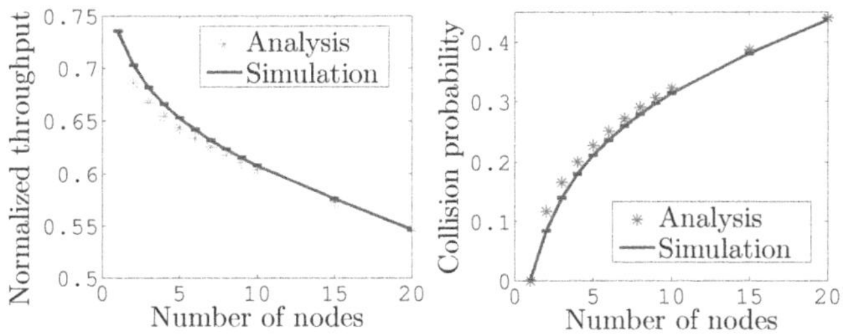

Figure 1: Performance metrics obtained by simulation and our model for the 1901 CSMA/CA method.

4. CONCLUSION

We have proposed a model for analyzing the performance of IEEE 1901 CSMA/CA method, which is the dominant protocol for power-line networks. Our model is equivalent to the Markov chain in [2], but its simplicity allows us to prove the uniqueness of the solution for the collision probability.

Our future research directions include enhancements of 1901 based on the model presented in this paper. Furthermore, we plan to investigate the validity of the decoupling assumption for 1901, as we observed that the accuracy of the model suffers when there are few stations in the network.

Acknowledgments

This work is financially supported by a grant of the SmartWorld project of the Hasler Foundation, Bern, Switzerland.

5. REFERENCES

[1] IEEE Standard for Broadband over Power Line Networks: Medium Access Control and Physical Layer Specifications. *IEEE Std 1901-2010*, pages 1–1586, 2010.

[2] M. Chung, M. Jung, T. Lee, and Y. Lee. Performance analysis of HomePlug 1.0 MAC with CSMA/CA. *Selected Areas in Communications, IEEE Journal on*, 24(7):1411–1420, 2006.

[3] A. Kumar, E. Altman, D. Miorandi, and M. Goyal. New Insights From a Fixed-Point Analysis of Single Cell IEEE 802.11 WLANs. *Networking, IEEE/ACM Transactions on*, 15(3):588–601, june 2007.

Impact of DHCP Churn on Network Characterization

Long Vu, Deepak S. Turaga, Srinivasan Parthasarathy
IBM Watson Research Center
P.O. Box 218, Yorktown Heights, NY 10598
{lhvu,turaga,spartha}@us.ibm.com

ABSTRACT

We investigate the DHCP churn impact on network characterization by analyzing 18 months of DHCP, DNS, Firewall Alert, and Netflow data collected from an enterprise network of 30,000 clients. We find that DHCP churn has clear impact on network metrics.

1. INTRODUCTION

Dynamic Host Configuration Protocol (DHCP) [6] allows networks to assign Internet Protocol addresses (IP) automatically to clients. DHCP has been used extensively to reduce client configuration when allocating IP addresses, especially when networks have a limited IP address space but includes many occasionally connected clients. One fundamental characteristic of DHCP is that *DHCP churn* exists in the network. That is, the DHCP server may assign the same IP address to different clients, and one single client may receive distinct IP addresses at different times. Essentially, DHCP churn creates a many-to-many mapping between clients and IP addresses, which results in ambiguity in distinguishing network clients.

Past research on DHCP focused on how to improve IP address allocation, how to configure the lease duration [6], or how to detect abnormal IP addresses from DHCP logs [3]. However, there is no study on how DHCP churn changes network metrics. In this paper, we study the impact of DHCP churn removal on network metrics derived from DNS, Firewall Alert, and Netflow data. Our findings show that DHCP churn changes these metrics considerably.

2. SETTINGS

We collected data from an enterprise network of 30,000 clients, stretching from Jan 2012 to Jun 2013. About 8,000 of these 30,000 clients are dynamic clients, which receive dynamic IP address from DHCP servers. Dynamic clients include laptops, cellular phones, and other portable devices. Traffic from inside of our network to the Internet goes through a main router, through a main firewall, and then to the Internet. Traffic from the Internet to a client inside our network traverses in the opposite direction. We collected DHCP from the DHCP server, Domain Name Service (DNS) data from DNS server, Netflow from the main router, and Firewall Alert data from the main firewall.

For DHCP data set, each record has a lease period, the IP, and the MAC of the host that is given the IP for the lease period. For DNS, Netflow, and Firewall Alert data sets, each record has a timestamp and the IP address of the host. To perform DHCP churn removal, we replace the IP in records of DNS, Netflow, and Firewall Alert data sets with the MAC in records of DHCP data set if the timestamp of a record in DNS, Netflow, Firewall Alerts belongs to the lease period of a record in DHCP data set.

To measure impact of DHCP churn, we use histogram. For example, we have two data sets S and S' from DNS data, one is for before and one is for after DHCP churn removal. Each set has 18 months or 12000 hours of DNS data. For each hour, we create a histogram h_a (and h_b) of number of DNS requests per host from S (and S'). The number of bin of the histogram is set to a large number (i.e., $|h_a| = |h_b| = 10000$) to avoid bias comparison. Since h_a and h_b essentially are two vectors, we use Cosine similarity distance to measure the difference between h_a and h_b, and denote it $\gamma(h_a, h_b)$. This methodology is also used to measure DHCP churn impact on Netflow and Firewall Alerts.

3. DHCP CHURN IMPACT

3.1 DNS-based Metrics

DNS data has been utilized extensively in previous projects to study the anomalies in operation of DNS servers and DNS clients [1]. As presented above, we have two data sets S and S' for before and after DHCP churn removal. In this section, we study "number of DNS requests per host per hour" since it has been widely used to evaluate whether a DNS client performs an abnormal activity.

Figure 1(a) shows that $\gamma(h_a, h_b)$ of the "number of DNS requests per host per hour" metric varies in the range of [0,0.1]. This means DHCP churn removal changes the DNS-based metrics noticeably and thus previous studies [1] may have obtained different outcomes if DHCP churn is removed from their input DNS data.

3.2 Firewall Alert-based Metrics

Firewall Alert is a crucial piece of information for network monitoring and network administration since it provides most direct indication of network usage violations.

SIGMETRICS'14, June 16–20, 2014, Austin, Texas, USA.
ACM 978-1-4503-2789-3/14/06.
http://dx.doi.org/10.1145/2591971.2592034.

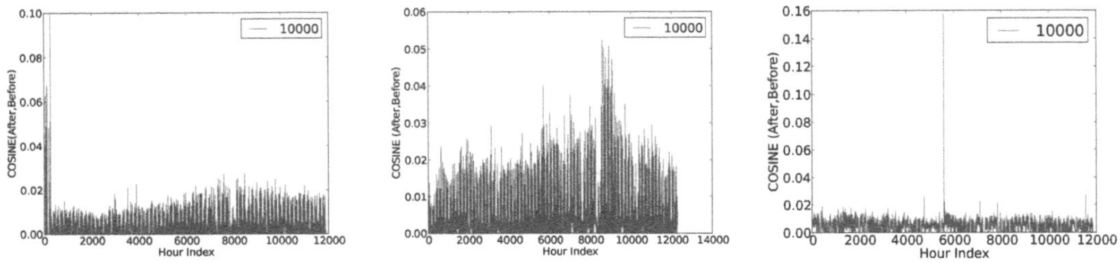

(a) DNS Request (b) Firewall Alert (c) Netflow Byte

Figure 1: DHCP churn removal incurs considerable changes in network metrics

Due to its importance in network adminstration, Firewall Alerts are usually handled with special care to avoid both false positives and false negatives, which may lead to unwanted subsequent issues. Here, we study the "number of total Firewall Alerts per host per hour" metric. Figure 1(b) shows that $\gamma(h_a, h_b)$ is in the range of [0,0.054]. This clearly indicates that DHCP churn removal changes the "number of total Firewall Alerts per host per hour" metric considerably.

Without DHCP churn removal from Firewall Alerts, non-malicious clients would be justified as malicious, and vice versa. This leads to both false positive and false negative results, as well as wrong decision in network adminstration. Higher Cosine similarity values in Figure 1(b) than those in Figure 1(a) implies that DHCP churn changes "number of total Firewall Alerts per host per hour" metric more than "number of DNS requests per host per hour" metric.

3.3 Netflow-based Metrics

Netflow data has been widely studied in network measurement and network anomaly detection literature [2]. Here, we study the "number of Netflow flows per host per hour" metric. Figure 1(c) shows that $\gamma(h_a, h_b)$ values of the "number of Netflow flows per source per hour" metric typically lie in the range of [0,0.02]. Moreover, one peak value of 0.16 exists at the 6000th hour, which implies a remarkable difference between h_a and h_b. Previous research projects used "number of Netflow flows per host" as a fundamental input feature of their algorithms [4], DHCP churn removal thus must be done for an accurate Netflow-based analysis.

3.4 Entropy-based Network Anomaly Detection

Entropy-based anomaly detection has been one of the most popular methods to quickly detect anomalies in computer networks since it is computationally efficient and can be used to find anomalies that cannot be detected by traffic volume-based approach. Previous projects showed that changes in distributions of fundamental traffic features (i.e., IP addresses and ports), when summarized by entropy, can be used to detect a broad spectrum of anomalies [5]. In this section, we measure the change of entropy when DHCP churn is removed from Netflow data in percentage as follows: $\Delta H(X) = 100 \times \frac{H(X)-H(X')}{H(X)}$. Here, X and X' represent the traffic feature (e.g., "SrcIP" or "DstIP") obtained from before and after DHCP churn removal from Netflow data, respectively, and $H(X) = -\sum_{x_i \in X} p(x_i) \times log\ p(x_i)$. Figure 2 shows that $\Delta H(SrcIP)$ varies in the range of [-2.3%,0.5%]. Meanwhile, Figure 3 shows that $\Delta H(DstIP)$ varies in the range of [-2.1%,0.5%].

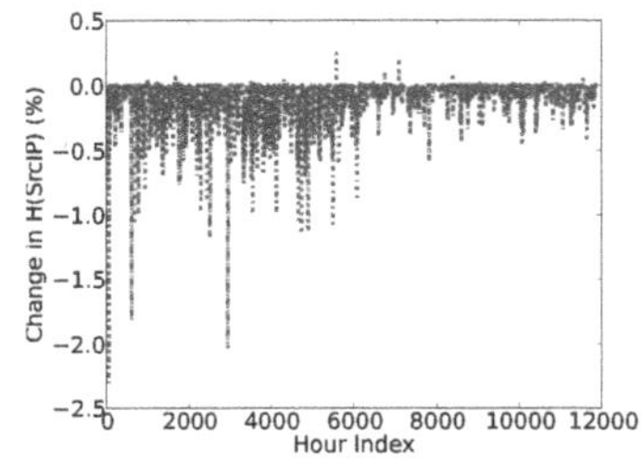

Figure 2: $\Delta H(SrcIP)$

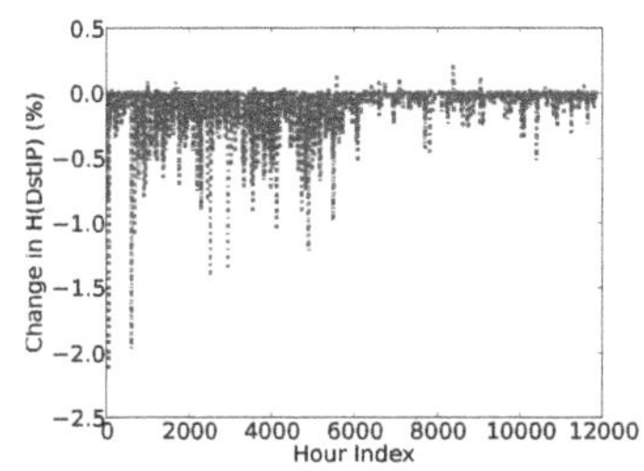

Figure 3: $\Delta H(DstIP)$

4. CONCLUSION

Our results show that DHCP churn changes network metrics considerably. Therefore, we believe DHCP churn must be addressed for relevant and accurate scientific results in the future research of computer networking domain.

5. REFERENCES

[1] L. Bilge, E. Kirda, C. Kruegel, and M. Balduzzi. EXPOSURE: Finding Malicious Domains Using Passive DNS Analysis. In *Proceedings of NDSS*, 2011.

[2] D. Brauckhoff, B. Tellenbach, A. Wagner, M. May, and A. Lakhina. Impact of packet sampling on anomaly detection metrics. In *Proceedings of IMC*, 2006.

[3] J.-W. Dai and L.-F. Chiang. A new method to detect abnormal ip address on dhcp. *Journal of Networks*, 4, 2009.

[4] A. Kind, M. P. Stoecklin, and X. Dimitropoulos. Histogram-based traffic anomaly detection. *IEEE Transactions on Network and Service Management*, 6, June 2009.

[5] A. Lakhina, M. Crovella, and C. Diot. Mining anomalies using traffic feature distributions. In *Proceedings of ACM SIGCOMM*, 2005.

[6] I. Papapanagiotou, E. Nahum, and V. Pappas. Configuring dhcp leases in the smartphone era. In *Proceedings of IMC*, 2012.

Online Algorithms for Joint Application-VM-Physical-Machine Auto-Scaling in a Cloud

Yang Guo
Bell Labs, Alcatel-Lucent
Holmdel, NJ 07733
yang.guo@alcatel-lucent.com

Alexander L. Stolyar
Bell Labs, Alcatel-Lucent
Murray Hill, NJ 07974
stolyar@research.bell-labs.com

Anwar Walid
Bell Labs, Alcatel-Lucent
Murray Hill, NJ 07974
anwar@research.bell-labs.com

ABSTRACT

We develop *shadow routing* based online algorithms for the joint problem of application-to-VM and VM-to-PM assignments in a cloud environment. The asymptotic optimality of the shadow algorithm is proved and the performance is evaluated by simulations.

Categories and Subject Descriptors

G.1.6 [**NUMERICAL ANALYSIS**]: Optimization—*Convex programming, Linear programming*; G.3 [**PROBABILITY AND STATISTICS**]: Probabilistic algorithms, Queueing theory

Keywords

Cloud, VM choice and placement, Shadow routing

1. INTRODUCTION

A Cloud data-center typically consists of a large number of physical machines (PMs). Virtualization technology enables cloud service providers to offer customers virtual machines (VMs) to run their applications. VMs can be configured and allocated dynamically to meet demand variations. The cloud service providers may further wish to "pack" the allocated VMs into a smaller number of PMs so as to minimize operational costs and save energy. The design of efficient algorithms for the application-to-VM and VM-to-PM assignments is a challenging research problem.

Considerable prior works exist on cloud resource management with the focus on either the application-to-VM assignments or VM-to-PM assignments, e.g., [1,2,4]. In this paper, we consider the *joint* assignment of applications to VMs and VMs to PMs. In our framework, we explicitly consider (i) the time-varying demand load for applications; (ii) the VM type(s) an application may require; and (iii) the physical machines and their resource configurations.

We employ the *shadow routing* approach, adopting a specially constructed virtual queueing system, which in essence dynamically produces and maintains a solution to the underlying optimization problem that guides the actual assignment algorithm. The advantage of shadow routing approach is that it is simple and adaptive: no need to know a priori, or explicitly measure, the application request arrival rates; if the arrival rates change, the algorithm adapt automatically. Yet, as we show, the algorithm is asymptotically optimal. All these features are confirmed by our simulation experiments.

SIGMETRICS'14, June 16–20, 2014, Austin, Texas, USA.
ACM 978-1-4503-2789-3/14/06.
http://dx.doi.org/10.1145/2591971.2592035.

2. MODEL AND PROBLEM STATEMENT

There are several applications, indexed by $i \in \mathcal{I} = \{1, \dots, I\}$, and several classes of VMs, indexed by $j \in \mathcal{J} = \{1, \dots, J\}$. At any given time, each application i employs a group of VMs, denoted by a vector $m_i = (m_{ij}, j = 1, \dots, J)$ to provide the service, where m_{ij} is the number of VMs of class j assigned to application i. User service requests for application i arrive at the rate λ_i. A service request for application i is assigned to one of the VMs of application i and is serviced by that VM. The average service time of an application i request is $1/\mu_i$. A VM of class j can service an interger number $w_{ij} \geq 0$ of concurrent application i requests.

Each class j VM needs several computing resources of different types when it is served; namely, the amount $a_{jk} > 0$ of resources $k = 1, \dots, K$. The DC contains $\beta > 0$ physical machines (PM), each of which has the amount $A_k > 0$ of resource $k \in \mathcal{K}_\ell$. If a class j VM is instantialized in the DC, it is placed into one of the PMs, where the amounts a_{jk} of resources are allocated (if they are still available at that specific PM). This means, in particular, that a PM in the DC can simultaneously serve the numbers of different VM class types given by a vector $s = (s_j,\ j = 1, \dots, J)$ if

$$\sum_i s_j a_{jk} \leq A_k, \ \ \forall k \in \mathcal{K}_\ell. \tag{1}$$

Vectors s (with non-negative integer components) satisfying this condition we call *(feasible) configurations* of a PM in the DC. The set of configurations which are not dominated by convex combinations of other configurations is denoted by S.

Denote by $\phi_s \geq 0$ the fraction of PMs in the DC that are used in the configuration $s \in S$. We want an algorithm that allocates fractions ϕ_s, and numbers of VMs, m_{ij}, such that ideally they are close to the optimal solution of the following linear program:

$$\min_{\{m_{ij}\},\{\phi_s\},\rho} \rho, \tag{2}$$

subject to

$$m_{ij} \geq 0,\ \forall (i,j), \quad \phi_s \geq 0,\ \forall s, \tag{3}$$

$$\lambda_i/\mu_i \leq \sum_j w_{ij} \cdot m_{ij},\ \ \forall i, \tag{4}$$

$$\sum_i m_{ij} \leq \sum_{s \in S} s_j \phi_s \beta,\ \ \forall j, \tag{5}$$

$$\sum_{s \in S} \phi_s = \rho. \tag{6}$$

Note that in this LP the variables ϕ_s and m_{ij} are non-negative *real* numbers; they have the meaning of *average* values (of the corresponding "true" variables), such that the *average* system workload can be handled. The LHS of (4) is the aggregate (average) workload for application i, while the RHS of (4) is the aggregate (average) service capacity allocated this application. In the constraint (5) $\phi_s \beta$ is the (average) number of PMs used in configuration s and, therefore, the RHS is the (average) number of j-VMs that can be served by PMs in all configurations. The meaning of ρ is the average fraction of the utilized PMs. (The LP makes sense even if the optimal ρ is greater than 1 – if this is the case, the DC is overloaded.)

3. SHADOW ROUTING BASED SCHEME

Shadow algorithm: The algorithm maintains the virtual queues Q_i and V_j, and uses positive parameters c_1, c_2, satisfying

$$c_1 > \max_i 1/\mu_i, \quad c_2 > c_1/\beta. \tag{7}$$

There are additional (small) parameters $\eta > 0$ and $\theta > 0$, and parameter $\alpha > 0$.

Upon each new service request arrival, say of type i to be specific, the algorithm does the following (in sequence):

1. $Q_i(t) := Q_i(t) + 1/\mu_i$.
2. Set $b_{\ell j} := 0$ for all (ℓj). Compute

$$j* \in \arg\max_j [\alpha w_{ij} Q_i - (1/\beta) V_j], \tag{8}$$

and if

$$\alpha w_{ij*} Q_i - (1/\beta) V_{j*} \geq 0 \tag{9}$$

do

$$Q_i := \max\{Q_i - c_1 w_{ij*}, 0\}, \quad V_{j*} := V_{j*} + c_1/\beta, \quad b_{ij*} := 1.$$

3. Set $b_s = 0$ for all $s \in S$. Find configuration vector σ such that

$$\sigma \in \arg\max_{s \in S} \sum_{j \in \mathcal{J}} s_j V_j. \tag{10}$$

If condition

$$\eta \sum_j \sigma_j V_j \geq 1 \tag{11}$$

holds, set $b_\sigma := 1$. Update virtual queues $V_j(t)$ as follows:

$$V_j := \max\{V_j - \sum_{s \in S} s_j b_s, 0\},\ \ \forall j \in \mathcal{J}.$$

4. Update variables $\bar{p}_{\ell j}$ and $\bar{\phi}_s$.

$$\bar{p}_{\ell j} := (1-\theta)\bar{p}_{\ell j} + \theta b_{\ell j},\ \ \forall (\ell, j),$$

$$\bar{\phi}_s := (1-\theta)\bar{\phi}_s + \theta b_s,\ \ \forall s.$$

End of Algorithm

The Shadow algorithm is an instance of *Greedy Primal-Dual* (GPD) algorithm [5], applied to a specially constructed two-stage virtual queueing system [3].

PROPOSITION 1. *Suppose all system parameters and all Shadow algorithm parameters, except maybe η, are fixed rational numbers. Assume that condition (7) holds. Suppose the input flows are Poisson, with fixed rates λ_i. Consider a sequence of systems with parameter $\eta \to 0$. Then, for any η, the virtual queueing process is a positive recurrent countable discrete-time Markov chain. Moreover, stationary distributions of the processes are such that the following holds. Denote by $\bar{\phi}_s^{(\eta)}$ the steady-state probability that configuration s is chosen in (10) and condition (11) holds for it. Similarly, let $\bar{p}_{ij}^{(\eta)}$ be the steady-state probability that the arriving request is of type i, index j is chosen in (8) and condition (9) holds. Then, as $\eta \to 0$, the sequence of vectors $(\{\bar{\phi}_s^{(\eta)}\}, \{\bar{p}_{ij}^{(\eta)}\})$ is such that its any limiting point $(\{\bar{\phi}_s\}, \{\bar{p}_{ij}\})$ satisfies (using notation $\lambda = \sum_i \lambda_i$)*

$$\lambda c_1 \bar{p}_{ij} = m_{ij},\ \ \forall (i,j),$$

$$\lambda c_2 \bar{\phi}_s = \phi_s,\ \ \forall\ s \in S,$$

where vector $(\{\phi_s\}, \{m_{ij}\})$ is an optimal solution of LP (2)-(6).

Proposition 1 shows that the values of $\bar{\phi}_s$ and $\bar{p}_{ij}$ dynamically "maintained" by the Shadow algorithm are proportional to the optimal values ϕ_s and m_{ij}, respectively. This allows us to devise very simple dynamic algorithms [3] for assignining an arriving applications to VM types, and assigning VMs to PMs; both algorithms have access to the current values of $\bar{\phi}_s$ and $\bar{p}_{ij}$.

The evaluation of Shadow algorithm in realistic scenarios is presented in [3]. (There we also show how to set the algorithm parameters.) The evaluations show very good accuracy of the algorithm as well as its great robustness and adaptability.

4. REFERENCES

[1] Auto Scaling - Amazon Web Services, *http://aws.amazon.com/documentation/autoscaling/*

[2] Y. Guo, A. L. Stolyar, A. Walid. Shadow-routing based dynamic algorithms for Virtual Machine placement in a network cloud. *INFOCOM-2013.*

[3] Y. Guo, A. L. Stolyar, A. Walid. Online Algorithms for Joint Application-VM-Physical-Machine Auto-Scaling in a Cloud. Bell Labs Technical Memo, 2014. http://ect.bell-labs.com/who/stolyar/publications/gsw-sigm-14-full.pdf

[4] T. Lorido-Botran, J. Miguel-Alonso and J. Lozano. Auto-scaling Techniques for Elastic Applications in Cloud Environments. Technical Report EHU-KAT-IK-09-12, University of the Basque Country, 2012.

[5] A. L. Stolyar. Maximizing Queueing Network Utility subject to Stability: Greedy Primal-Dual Algorithm. *Queueing Systems*, Vol. 50, pp. 401-457 (2005).

Distributed Optimal Load Shedding for Disaster Recovery in Smart Electric Power Grids: A Second-Order Approach

Jia Liu[†] Cathy H. Xia[‡] Ness B. Shroff[†*] Hanif D. Sherali[*]
[†]Dept. of Electrical and Computer Engineering, The Ohio State University
[‡]Dept. of Integrated Systems Engineering, The Ohio State University
[*]Dept. of Industrial and Systems Engineering, Virginia Tech
[†]{liu.1736, xia.52, shroff.11}@osu.edu, [*]hanifs@vt.edu

ABSTRACT

In this paper, we consider the problem of distributed load shedding optimization for disaster recovery in smart grids. We develop distributed second-order interior-point based load shedding algorithms that enjoy a fast quadratic convergence rate. Our main contributions are two-fold: (i) We propose a rooted spanning tree based reformulation that enables our distributed algorithm design; (ii) Based on the spanning tree reformulation, we design distributed computation schemes for our proposed second-order interior-point based load shedding. Collectively, these results serve as an important first step in load shedding and disaster recovery that uses second-order distributed techniques.

1. PROBLEM FORMULATION

Consider a power (sub)network that remains connected upon removal of the failed portion of the system after a disaster strikes. However, we do *not* assume the availability of *any* centralized controller in this sub-network. We represent this subnetwork by a directed graph $\mathcal{G} = \{\mathcal{N}, \mathcal{L}\}$, where $\mathcal{N}$ and $\mathcal{L}$ are the sets of buses and transmission lines, with number of elements $|\mathcal{N}| = N$ and $|\mathcal{L}| = L$, respectively. We use an incidence matrix $\mathbf{A} \in \mathbb{R}^{N\times L}$ to represent the network topology, where the entry $(\mathbf{A})_{nl} = 1$ if edge l is coming out of node n, -1 if edge l is going into node n, and 0 otherwise [1]. We let b_l denote the admittance of line l and let $\mathbf{B} \triangleq \text{Diag}\{b_1, \ldots, b_L\}$ be a diagonal matrix that contains all admittances. Suppose that there are G generator buses in this subnetwork and they are labeled $1, \ldots, G$. The remaining $N - G$ buses are load buses and are labeled $G+1, \ldots, N$. We let $\mathcal{K}$ denote the set of generators, with $|\mathcal{K}| = G$. We use $z_n \geq 0$, $n \notin \mathcal{K}$, to represent the amount of potential power shed at a load bus. At each generator bus $n \in \mathcal{K}$, we let $z_n \geq 0$ denote the power generation to meet the demands. We use $\mathbf{z} \triangleq [z_1, \ldots, z_N]^\top$ to group all z-variables. Following conventions, we let $p_n < 0$ denote the power demand at a load bus $n \notin \mathcal{K}$. For convenience, we let $\mathbf{p} \triangleq [0, \ldots, 0, p_{G+1}, \ldots, p_N]^\top$ denote the expanded power demand vector of all buses. We let $f_l \in \mathbb{R}$ represent the power flow on line l, where f_l could be negative in the sense that f_l's direction is against the direction of line l (recall that $\mathcal{G}$ is a directed graph). We use $\mathbf{f} \triangleq [f_1, \ldots, f_L]^\top$ to group all line flow variables. We let $\boldsymbol{\theta} \triangleq [\theta_1, \ldots, \theta_N]^\top$ group the phase angle variables of all buses. Then, the load shedding problem under the DC power flow model can be formulated as follows:

$$\min_{\mathbf{z},\boldsymbol{\theta}} \left\{ \sum_{n\notin\mathcal{K}} C_n(z_n) \,\middle|\, \begin{array}{l} \mathbf{f} = \mathbf{B}\mathbf{A}^\top\boldsymbol{\theta},\ \mathbf{A}\mathbf{f} - \mathbf{z} = \mathbf{p}, \\ |f_l| \leq f_{\max}, \forall l,\ 0 \leq z_n \leq K_n, \forall n. \end{array} \right\}. \quad (1)$$

In (1), $C_n(z_n)$ is a convex and twice-differentiable function that evaluates the cost incurred by shedding z_n units of load (a standard cost model in power systems analysis [2]); $\mathbf{f} = \mathbf{B}\mathbf{A}^\top\boldsymbol{\theta}$ corresponds to the DC power flow model (assuming fixed bus voltages and thus $\boldsymbol{\theta}$ can fully describe power constraints [2]); $\mathbf{A}\mathbf{f} - \mathbf{z} = \mathbf{p}$ represents the power flow conservation law (i.e., incoming plus generated power equals outgoing and consumed power at all buses); and $|f_l| \leq f_{\max}$ corresponds to line flow security constraints. In (1), the constraint $0 \leq z_n \leq K_n$ models the fact that we cannot shed more load than the actual demand and cannot produce more power than the limit of each generator bus, where $K_n \triangleq -p_n$ for $n \notin \mathcal{K}$ and $K_n \triangleq B_n^{\max}$ for $n \in \mathcal{K}$, and where $B_n^{\max} > 0$ denotes the capacity of generator n.

2. A DISTRIBUTED INTERIOR-POINT SECOND-ORDER ALGORITHM

In this paper, we solve Problem (1) by developing an *interior-point second-order distributed* approach. The fundamental rationale behind our approach is that the operating point of the system enforced by the interior-point framework is guaranteed to be feasible throughout *all* iterations of the algorithm. In contrast, most existing first-order gradient based schemes in the literature (see, e.g., [3] and references therein) do not have such feasibility guarantee and would produce iterates that constantly violate the feasibility constraints. This is particular problematic for ensuring the grid's security if the algorithm needs to be terminated in a predefined finite number iterations. In what follows, we outline the key design steps and refer readers to our online technical report [4] for further details.

Step 1) Rooted Spanning Tree-Based Reformulation: Suppose that we have a *rooted spanning tree* (RST) rooted at a generator bus. Without loss of generality, we let this generator bus be labeled "0". We attach an artificial root arc l_0 to the root with arbitrary admittance b_0 and an artificial line

SIGMETRICS'14, June 16–20, 2014, Austin, Texas, USA.
ACM 978-1-4503-2789-3/14/06.
http://dx.doi.org/10.1145/2591971.2592036 .

flow f_0.Let $\mathcal{T} = \{\mathcal{N}, \mathcal{L}'_0\}$ denote this RST, where the link set $\mathcal{L}'_0 \triangleq \mathcal{L}' \cup \{l_0\}$ with $\mathcal{L}' \subseteq \mathcal{L}$ and $|\mathcal{L}'| = N - 1$. Let $\widetilde{\mathbf{A}}$ be the incidence matrix of $\mathcal{T}$. Let vector $\widetilde{\mathbf{f}} \triangleq [f_l : l \in \mathcal{L}'_0]^\top \in \mathbb{R}^N$ group all the line flows in $\mathcal{T}$. Let $\widetilde{\mathbf{B}} \triangleq \mathrm{Diag}\{b_l : l \in \mathcal{L}'_0\} \in \mathbb{R}^{N\times N}$ be the diagonal line admittance matrix with respect to $\mathcal{T}$. Then, it can be shown that Problem (1) can be equivalently reformulated based on the RST as follows [4]:

$$\min_{\mathbf{z},\boldsymbol{\theta}} \left\{ \sum_{n\notin\mathcal{K}} C_n(z_n) \middle| \begin{array}{l} (\widetilde{\mathbf{A}}\widetilde{\mathbf{B}}\widetilde{\mathbf{A}}^\top)\boldsymbol{\theta} - \mathbf{z} = \mathbf{p},\ \mathbf{1}^\top(\mathbf{p}+\mathbf{z}) = 0, \\ |\theta_{\mathrm{Tx}(l)} - \theta_{\mathrm{Rx}(l)}| \le \beta_l,\ 0 \le z_n \le K_n. \end{array} \right\}, \quad (2)$$

where $\beta_l \triangleq f_l^{\max}/b_l$, $\mathbf{1} \in \mathbb{R}^N$ is an all-one vector, and $\mathrm{Tx}(l)$ and $\mathrm{Rx}(l)$ represent the transmitting and receiving ends of line l, respectively. Note that the generation-load balance constraint $\mathbf{1}^\top(\mathbf{p}+\mathbf{z}) = 0$ ensures that $f_0 \equiv 0$, implying that Problem (1) is equivalent to Problem (2) [4].

Step 2) An Interior-Point Algorithmic Framework Coupled with Newton's Method: Utilizing an interior-point approach [5], we can rewrite Problem (2) as follows:

$$\begin{array}{ll} \text{Minimize} & g_\mu(\mathbf{y}) \\ \text{subject to} & \mathbf{M}\mathbf{y} = \mathbf{d}, \end{array} \quad (3)$$

where $\mathbf{y} \triangleq [z_1 \cdots z_N, \theta_1 \cdots \theta_N]^\top$ groups all variables; $g_\mu(\mathbf{y}) \triangleq \mu \sum_{n\notin\mathcal{K}} C_n(z_n) - \sum_{n=1}^N (\log(z_n) + \log(K_n - z_n)) - \sum_{l=1}^L (\log(\beta_l - \theta_{\mathrm{Tx}(l)} + \theta_{\mathrm{Rx}(l)}) + \log(\beta_l + \theta_{\mathrm{Tx}(l)} - \theta_{\mathrm{Rx}(l)}))$ is an augmented objective function, where we apply a logarithmic barrier function to all inequality constraints in Problem (2) and then accommodate them into the objective function; and matrix $\mathbf{M}$ and vector $\mathbf{d}$ groups all network topology and demand information, respectively (see [4] for details). In (3), $\mu > 0$ is the barrier parameter such that as μ gets large, the solution of Problem (3) will approach the original solution of Problem (2). The equality-constrained formulation in (3) allows us to employ Newton's method to solve the Karash-Kuhn-Tucker (KKT) system of (3). Starting from some initial feasible solution $\mathbf{y}^0$, the (centralized) Newton's method is the following iterative scheme: $\mathbf{y}^{k+1} = \mathbf{y}^k + s^k \Delta\mathbf{y}^k$, where $s^k > 0$ is the step-size in the kth iteration and $\Delta\mathbf{y}^k$ denotes the primal Newton direction, which can be computed as:

$$\Delta\mathbf{y}^k = -\mathbf{H}_k^{-1}(\nabla g_\mu(\mathbf{y}^k) + \mathbf{M}^T\mathbf{w}^k), \quad (4)$$

$$\mathbf{w}^k = (\mathbf{M}\mathbf{H}_k^{-1}\mathbf{M}^T)^{-1}(-\mathbf{M}\mathbf{H}_k^{-1}\nabla g_\mu(\mathbf{y}^k)). \quad (5)$$

where $\nabla g_\mu(\mathbf{y}^k)$ and $\mathbf{H}_k$ denote the gradient vector and Hessian matrix of $g_\mu(\cdot)$ evaluated at $\mathbf{y}^k$, respectively; $\mathbf{w}^k$ contains dual variables associated with $\mathbf{M}\mathbf{y} = \mathbf{d}$ in the kth iteration. Note that the scheme in (4)–(5) is a *second-order* algorithmic framework since it exploits not only the first-order gradient information $\nabla g_\mu(\mathbf{y}^k)$, but also the second-order Hessian information $\mathbf{H}_k$. Hence, it enjoys a powerful quadratic rate of convergence performance [6]. That is, given a desired control precision ϵ, the distributed algorithmic framework outlined in (4)–(5) converges in at most $\log_2 \log_2(\Phi/\epsilon)$ iterations, where Φ is some constant that depends on the network topology and the objective function.

Step 3) RST-Based Decentralization: Lastly, the decentralization of the scheme in (4)–(5) boils down to the distributed computations of $\mathbf{H}_k^{-1}$ and $(\mathbf{M}\mathbf{H}_k^{-1}\mathbf{M}^\top)^{-1}$, which are challenging due to their *non-separable* structure. Fortunately, by exploiting the nice *upper triangular* structure of the RST incidence matrix $\widetilde{\mathbf{A}}$, we are able to develop a *double Sherman-Morrison-Woodbury* (dSWM) distributed scheme for $\mathbf{H}_k^{-1}$ and $(\mathbf{M}\mathbf{H}_k^{-1}\mathbf{M}^\top)^{-1}$, which leads to the following result on distributed computations [4]:

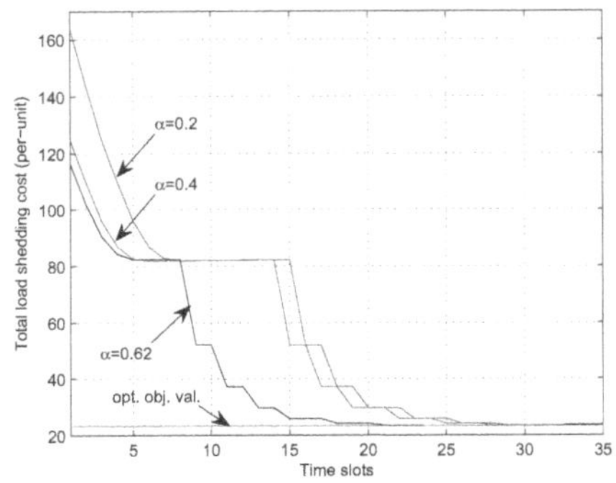

Figure 1: The convergence process of the proposed distributed second-order load shedding algorithm with different choices of initial scaling factors.

THEOREM 1. *The second-order scheme in (4)–(5) can be decentralized by using the RST structure: the Newton direction of load shed variables z_n can be distributedly computed at bus n with local information; the Newton direction of phase angle variables θ_n can be distributedly computed following any link-ordering on the RST in exactly N steps.*

To identify a starting point, we let $\widehat{\boldsymbol{\theta}}$ be the phase angles before load shedding. Our proposed initialization is to shrink all $\widehat{\theta}$-variables by the same scaling factor $0 < \alpha < 1$, i.e., $\mathbf{f} = \mathbf{B}\mathbf{A}^T(\alpha\widehat{\boldsymbol{\theta}})$. Clearly, there always exists a small enough α such that $\mathbf{f}$ will not exceed any line capacity (i.e., in the interior of the new feasible domain).

To illustrate the convergence speed of our algorithm, we use the IEEE 30-bus benchmark system [7] as an example. For this 30-bus benchmark system, the convergence processes of our proposed distributed second-order load shedding algorithm with different choices of initial scaling factors α are illustrated in Figure 1. We can see that, in all cases, our distributed second-order method converges in less than 35 iterations, which demonstrates the powerful second-order convergence speed.

3. REFERENCES

[1] M. S. Bazaraa, J. J. Jarvis, and H. D. Sherali, *Linear Programming and Network Flows*, 4th ed. New York: John Wiley & Sons Inc., 2010.

[2] J. J. Grainger and W. D. Stevenson, *Power System Analysis*. New York: McGraw-Hill Inc., 1994.

[3] D. Bienstock, "Optimal control of cascading power grid failures," in *Proc. IEEE CDC*, Orlando, FL, Dec. 12-15, 2011, pp. 2166–2173.

[4] J. Liu, C. H. Xia, N. B. Shroff, and H. D. Sherali, "Distributed optimal load shedding for disaster recovery in smart electric power grids: A second-order approach," *Technical Report, Dept. of ECE, The Ohio State University*, 2014. [Online]. Available: http://www2.ece.ohio-state.edu/~liu/publications/

[5] Y. Nesterov and A. Nemirovskii, *Interior-Point Polynomial Algorithms in Convex Programming*, 3rd ed. Philadelphia, PA: SIAM, 2001.

[6] M. S. Bazaraa, H. D. Sherali, and C. M. Shetty, *Nonlinear Programming: Theory and Algorithms*, 3rd ed. New York, NY: John Wiley & Sons Inc., 2006.

[7] "Power systems test case archive." [Online]. Available: http://www.ee.washington.edu/research/pstca/

TARDIS: Stably Shifting Traffic in Space and Time

Richard G. Clegg, Dept of Elec. Eng. University College London richard@richardclegg.org

Raul Landa, Dept of Elec. Eng. University College London raul.landa@ucl.ac.uk

João Taveira Araújo, Dept of Elec. Eng. University College London j.araujo@ucl.ac.uk

Eleni Mykoniati, Dept of Elec. Eng. University College London e.mykoniati@ucl.ac.uk

David Griffin, Dept of Elec. Eng. University College London dgriffin@ee.ucl.ac.uk

Miguel Rio, Dept of Elec. Eng. University College London miguel.rio@ucl.ac.uk

ABSTRACT

This paper describes TARDIS (Traffic Assignment and Retiming Dynamics with Inherent Stability) which is an algorithmic procedure designed to reallocate traffic within Internet Service Provider (ISP) networks. Recent work has investigated the idea of shifting traffic in time (from peak to off-peak) or in space (by using different links). This work gives a unified scheme for both time and space shifting to reduce costs. Particular attention is given to the commonly used 95th percentile pricing scheme.

The work has three main innovations: firstly, introducing the Shapley Gradient, a way of comparing traffic pricing between different links at different times of day; secondly, a unified way of reallocating traffic in time and/or in space; thirdly, a continuous approximation to this system is proved to be stable. A trace-driven investigation using data from two service providers shows that the algorithm can create large savings in transit costs even when only small proportions of the traffic can be shifted.

1. INTRODUCTION

This paper considers opportunities for Internet Service Providers (ISPs) to move traffic in order to reduce transit bills. Recent research has considered how ISPs might route traffic via different links (or download from different locations) [8, 2] or (with user permission) shift traffic to different times of day [4, 3].

This paper combines the spatial shifting and the time shifting into a single framework. The contributions of the paper are threefold. Firstly, the Shapley gradient is introduced, a means to compare the costs associated with traffic flows from different sources at different times and subject to different pricing schemes (in particular the 95th percentile scheme). Secondly, a unified mathematical framework is presented for reallocating traffic across both time and space. Thirdly this reallocation strategy is shown to be stable. The strategy is tested by analysis of its responses to real user data given behavioural assumptions. An expanded version of this paper is available online [1].

The system described is known as TARDIS (Traffic Assignment and Retiming Dynamics with Inherent Stability). Given pricing policies, traffic flows and their possible reassignments TARDIS returns a strategy for allocating those flows in time and space. The combination of shifting in space and time is done by formalising the notion of a "slot" which is a combination of a particular link (space) and a particular time.

SIGMETRICS'14, June 16–20, 2014, Austin, Texas, USA.
ACM 978-1-4503-2789-3/14/06.
http://dx.doi.org/10.1145/2591971.2592037.

2. SHAPLEY GRADIENT PRICING

The pricing problem in this work arises from the fact that the bulk of transit traffic is priced using the 95th percentile mechanism. This means that there is not a one-to-one mapping between the amount of traffic and the price charged. In its simplest form, a transit provider sets the 95th percentile rate to some fixed value e.g. r dollars per Gbps. The ISP's traffic over some time period (usually a month) is measured and split into smaller time periods (say fifteen minutes). The 5% of time periods with the most traffic are discarded and the next highest level is used (the 95th percentile level). The mean traffic rate over this time period is multiplied by r to calculate the bill. The problem with this scheme is that the traffic profile in time across links is not necessarily even. So if link 1 is charged at rate r_1 and link 2 is charged at rate r_2 it can make sense to move traffic from link 1 to link 2 even if $r_2 > r_1$. It can also save costs to delay traffic for several hours (from peak to off-peak). The question remains what strategy to use to move traffic. One solution is provided in [6] which uses the game theoretic notion of the Shapley value but the procedure is computationally intensive and does not answer the main question which is important for this work "What *would* the increase in cost be moving a unit of traffic into this slot?"

The pricing problem is solved by introducing the notion of the Shapley gradient for a slot. This is the derivative of the Shapley value for the slot with respect to the amount of traffic moved into the slot. It can be thought of as the predicted rate of increase in cost caused by adding traffic to that slot. It can be shown that for this problem, unlike the Shapley value, the Shapley gradient need only be calculated for a single user greatly reducing the computational cost. The full proof of this is found in [1] section 3.

3. TARDIS AS A DYNAMICAL SYSTEM

Having assigned a price p_i to each slot i, it is still necessary to create a mechanism to assign traffic to slots especially as not every piece of traffic can be assigned to every slot. (In fact the usual assumption is that most traffic cannot be reassigned at all, some traffic can be reassigned only spatially and some only temporally). The problem is solved by creating a dynamical system based on refining splitting rates for each possible choice of slots. A continuous time approximation of the system is shown to be stable with a proof inspired by the work of Smith [5]. Full details of the proof are given in [1] section 4 and only a sketch is presented here.

The aim is to bring the system to a user equilibrium of the type defined in road traffic analysis as a Wardrop equilibrium of the first type [7]. In the current case the definition of Wardrop equilibrium becomes: if any traffic is using slot j then that slot is the lowest priced slot that the traffic can choose (this may be a single slot or a number of slots with equal cost).

Define a choice set $\mathcal{C}$ as a set of slots to which a particular flow could be assigned (depending on details of which links and times it can be assigned to). If $\mathcal{C}$ consists of more than one slot traffic can be reassigned. Note $\mathcal{C}$ will always contain at least the slot that the traffic was originally assigned (the option to not move the traffic). Let s_{ij} be the proportion of traffic which could be assigned to exactly those slots within choice set $\mathcal{C}_i$ which should be assigned to slot j. The TARDIS system then works with these "splitting rates" so when flow arrives which can choose in slot $\mathcal{C}_i$ then that flow can be assigned probabilistically according to these proportions (obviously while keeping individual TCP flows on the same path to avoid out-of-order problems). The key insight required is how to move splitting rates as a result of calculated slot prices. The TARDIS system moves splitting rates from a higher priced slot and into a lower priced slot at a rate proportional to how much traffic is already on the higher slot and proportional to the difference in price between them. Using a proof inspired by the methods in [5] it can be shown (given certain natural assumptions) that this adjustment procedure converges to a unique, Lyapunov stable Wardrop equilibrium, or, to put it more simply, all traffic will be assigned to lowest cost paths.

4. DATA DRIVEN MODELLING

The TARDIS system is tested on two real traffic data sets, one from an EU based ISP and one from a Japanese academic network. Because pricing information and the proportion of traffic which could be swapped in time and space is not known various scenarios are tried. In particular the proportion of traffic which can swap in time is varied from 0% to 20% and the proportion of traffic which can swap in space is varied from 0% to 60%. Full details of the assumptions behind the analysis are given in [1] sections 5 and 6.

Figure 1 shows the base case modelling results for the EU data. The figure should be interpreted as follows: The main figure is the mean proportion of saving in cost over the case where no traffic moves (averaged over fifty simulated days). The error bars are two standard deviations either side (an approximate 95% confidence interval for normal data) within those simulated days. The number in brackets represents the maximum possible saving if all shifted traffic shifts to a slot where its cost is zero. As can be seen the system is achieving a considerable proportion of the maximum possible saving. The results for the Japanese data are very similar and can be seen in [1] section 6.

5. CONCLUSIONS

This paper introduced TARDIS (Traffic Assignment and Retiming Dynamics with Inherent Stability) an algorithm for determining how to reassign traffic in time and space to reduce ISP transit costs. A method was given to assign a cost to a given link at a

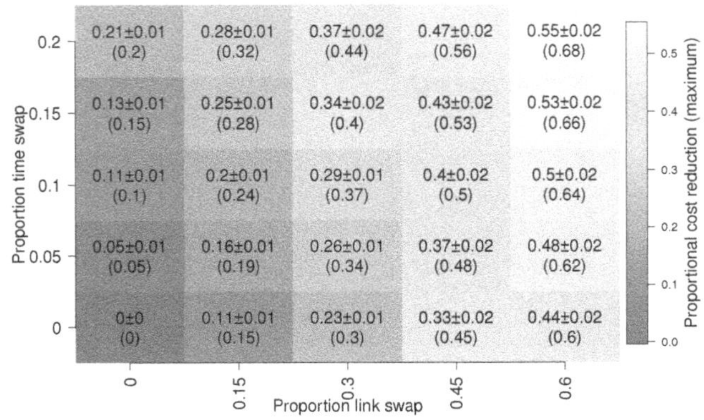

Figure 1: Base case model for EU data.

given time of day according to any of a number of widely used pricing schemes. This time of day cost was used as an input to a reassignment scheme for traffic. By modelling the scheme as a dynamical system it was shown that a continuous approximation to the scheme was provably stable and it moved traffic assignment to an equilibrium.

The scheme was tested in a realistic context by analysis of real life data sets. This analysis tested several different assumptions about pricing levels and about proportions of traffic space and time shifting. In the majority of cases a large financial saving was found to be possible. Time shifting alone appears to create a considerable saving in most situations. Space shifting creates a saving in all situations except those where all links are equally priced and traffic is split equally across all links.

This research has received funding from the Seventh Framework Programme (FP7/2007-2013) of the European Union, through the FUSION project (grant agreement 318205).

6. REFERENCES

[1] R. Clegg, R. Landa, J. Araujo, E. Mykoniati, D. Griffin, and M. Rio. TARDIS: Stably shifting traffic in space and time (extended version). http://arxiv.org/abs/1404.2325, 2014.

[2] B. Frank, I. Poese, G. Smaragdakis, S. Uhlig, and A. Feldmann. Content-aware Traffic Engineering. In *Proceedings of ACM SIGMETRICS/Performance 2012*, London, UK, June 2012.

[3] C. Joe-Wong, S. Ha, and M. Chiang. Time-dependent broadband pricing: Feasibility and benefits. In *Proc. of IEEE ICDCS*, 2011.

[4] N. Laoutaris and P. Rodriguez. Good things come to those who (can) wait: or how to handle Delay Tolerant traffic and make peace on the internet. In *Proc. of ACM HotNets*, 2008.

[5] M. J. Smith. The stability of a dynamic model of traffic assignment – an application of a method of Lyapunov. *Transp. Science*, 18(3):245–252, 1984.

[6] R. Stanojevic, N. Laoutaris, and P. Rodriguez. On economic heavy hitters: Shapley value analysis of 95th percentile pricing. In *Proc. of ACM/SIGCOMM IMC*, 2010.

[7] J. G. Wardrop. Some theoretical aspects of road traffic research. *Proc. of the Inst. of Civil Engineers II*, 1:325–378, 1952.

[8] H. Xie, Y. R. Yang, A. Krishnamurthy, Y. Liu, and A. Silverschatz. P4P: Provider portal for applications. In *Proc. of ACM SIGCOMM*, 2008.

Exact Analysis of TTL Cache Networks –

The Case of Caching Policies Driven by Stopping Times

Daniel S. Berger
Distributed Computer Systems (DISCO) Lab
University of Kaiserslautern
berger@cs.uni-kl.de

Philipp Gland
Institute for Mathematics
Technical University Berlin
gland@mailbox.tu-berlin.de

Sahil Singla
School of Computer Science
Carnegie Mellon University
ssingla@cmu.edu

Florin Ciucu
Computer Science Department
University of Warwick
f.ciucu@warwick.ac.uk

ABSTRACT

TTL caching models have recently regained significant research interest, largely due to their ability to fit popular caching policies such as LRU. In this extended abstract we briefly describe our recent work on two *exact* methods to analyze TTL cache networks. The first method generalizes existing results for line networks under renewal requests to the broad class of caching policies whereby evictions are driven by stopping times. The obtained results are further generalized, using the second method, to feedforward networks with Markov arrival processes (MAP) requests. MAPs are particularly suitable for non-line networks because they are closed not only under superposition and splitting, as known, but also under input-output caching operations as proven herein for phase-type TTL distributions. The crucial benefit of the two closure properties is that they jointly enable the first exact analysis of feedforward networks of TTL caches in great generality.

Categories and Subject Descriptors

C.4 [**Performance of Systems**]: Modeling techniques

Keywords

Cache networks, Analytical model, cache performance

1. INTRODUCTION

Time-to-Live (TTL) caches decouple the eviction mechanisms amongst objects by associating each object with a timer. When a timer expires, the corresponding object is evicted from the cache. This seemingly simple scheme has been widely deployed in DNS, web caching, and flow tables of software-defined networking switches. What has recently additionally popularized TTL analytical models is a subtle mapping between *capacity-driven* (e.g., Least-Recently-Used (LRU)) and *TTL-based* caching policies. This mapping was firstly established through a remarkably accurate approximation by Che *et al.* [3] for the popular LRU policy, and has received theoretical justifications and extensions to a variety of cache policies [4, 6]. While the analysis of TTL caches is arguably simpler and more general than the analysis of capacity-driven policies, the exact analysis of TTL networks in general has remained an open problem.

When considering a network of caches, the analysis has to address two inherent network operations. Given a caching node and some object, the first operation relates the request point process (the *input*) to the corresponding miss process (the *output*), which is a sample of the request process at those points when the object is absent from the cache. The *superposition* operation occurs when merging miss processes from upstream caches into a new input process. The exact characterization of these processes is challenging; for instance, the input-output relation does not retain the memorylessness property of request processes and renewals are not closed under the superposition operation.

In this extended abstract we summarize our recent results [2] on the first exact analysis of caching networks. We address lines of caches under renewal request processes and a general TTL distribution, and feedforward caching networks under Markov arrival processes (MAPs) and a TTL phase-type (PH) renewal process. In our abstract model for TTL caching policies, cache evictions are driven by stopping times, which capture three popular policies (amongst others). The '$\mathcal{R}$' policy regenerates the TTLs at every object's request and maps to the LRU policy. The 'Σ' policy regenerates the TTLs only at those requests resulting in cache misses and maps to FIFO and RND policies. Besides unifying the analysis of the '$\mathcal{R}$' and 'Σ', which have already been studied (see, e.g., an overview in [2]), our stopping time model covers an emerging new policy, called '$\min(\Sigma,\mathcal{R})$', which combines the key features of Σ and $\mathcal{R}$, i.e., weak consistency guarantee and efficient utilization of cache space. In '$\min(\Sigma,\mathcal{R})$' caches, two TTLs run in parallel and an object is evicted upon the expiration of *either* of them. This policy has been recently implemented in both SDN switches (e.g., in the OpenFlow Switch Specification 1.4.0) and Amazon web services.

SIGMETRICS'14, June 16–20, 2014, Austin, Texas, USA.

http://dx.doi.org/10.1145/2591971.2592038.

2. OUR RESULTS

We formally define the relation of the input (request) process and the output (miss) process as a stopped sum. We state the definition in the renewal case as the corresponding definition for the non-renewal case can be stated similarly.

DEFINITION 1 (MISS/OUTPUT PROCESS). *Let a caching node with inter-request times and TTL's be given by two independent renewal processes: $\{X_t\}_{t\geq 1}$ and $\{T_t\}_{t\geq 1}$. The corresponding miss process is also a renewal process with the same distribution as the stopped sum*

$$S_\tau := X_1 + \cdots + X_\tau \ , \quad (1)$$

where τ is a stopping time[1] *defined separately for each caching (TTL) policy:*

$$\text{Policy } \mathcal{R}: \quad \tau := \min\{t : X_t > T_t\} \quad (2)$$

$$\text{Policy } \Sigma: \quad \tau := \min\{t : \sum_{s=1}^{t} X_s > T_1\} \quad (3)$$

$$\text{Policy } \min(\Sigma,\mathcal{R}): \quad \tau := \min\{\min\{t : \sum_{s=1}^{t} X_s > T_1^{\Sigma}\}, \min\{t : X_t > T_t^{\mathcal{R}}\}\} \ . \quad (4)$$

For $\min(\Sigma,\mathcal{R})$, T_1^{Σ} and $T_t^{\mathcal{R}}$ are independent renewal processes.

2.1 Lines of Caches

The key problem to obtain caching metrics at the downstream nodes in a line of cache is to recursively characterize the inter-miss time S_τ. We aim to derive explicit solution for the Laplace transform of the stopped sum, i.e., $\mathcal{L}_\omega(S_\tau)$. One may remark that, due to the intrinsic dependencies amongst X_t's, T_t's, and the stopping time τ, the analysis of the stopped sum is conceivably quite involved. Even for stopping times, which depend only on the X_t's, higher moments are typically only known in terms of bounds (cf. Gut [5]).

Our approach is motivated by martingale theory, in which stopping times preserve certain martingale results, e.g., if L_t is a martingale and τ is a bounded stopping time then $E[L_\tau] = E[L_1]$. In particular, we can adopt the general change of measure theory based on martingales [1] to our stopping time τ and the Wald's martingale $L_t := e^{-\omega S_t}/\mathcal{L}_\omega(X)^t$. This allows to properly define a new probability measure $\tilde{\mathbb{P}}_t(F) := E[L_t 1_F]$, which incorporates the dependencies of S_τ into the measure, and allows to derive an explicit solution.

THEOREM 1 (PROOF IN [2]). *For an (a.s.) finite stopping time τ, the Laplace transform of the stopped sum S_τ from Eq. (1) is given by*

$$\mathcal{L}_\omega(S_\tau) = \tilde{E}\left[\mathcal{L}_\omega(X)^\tau\right] \ . \quad (5)$$

This result fundamentally simplifies the analysis because $\tilde{E}\left[\mathcal{L}_\omega(X)^\tau\right]$ only requires to derive the pmf $\tilde{\mathbb{P}}(\tau = k)$, which is straightforward to obtain in the new space (cf. [2]).

2.2 Feedforward Cache Networks

We use the canonical definition of a MAP as a tuple of matrices $(\mathbf{D}_0, \mathbf{D}_1)$, where $\mathbf{D}_0$ contains the rates of the so-called *hidden transitions*, and $\mathbf{D}_1$ contains the (positive) rates of the so-called *active transitions*. We further assume that TTLs follow a PH distribution, which is defined by the tuple $(\mathbf{S}, \pi)$, where $\mathbf{S}$ is a $m \times m$ subintensity, $\mathbf{S}_0 := -\mathbf{S1}$, and π a stochastic m-vector. We use the less standard notation of a PH generator of the form $\mathbf{P} := \begin{pmatrix} 0 & \mathbf{0} \\ \mathbf{S}_0 & \mathbf{S} \end{pmatrix}$, because this choice permits convenient expressions for the caching operation.

Using this notation, the output of any $\mathcal{R}$, Σ, and $\min(\Sigma,\mathcal{R})$ cache can be explicitly stated using the Kronecker product $\otimes$ and sum $\oplus$. We give an example for the Σ cache.

THEOREM 2 (PROOF IN [2]). *Consider a Σ-cache under requests given by $(\mathbf{D}_0, \mathbf{D}_1)$ and TTLs given by $(\mathbf{S}, \pi)$ with generator $\mathbf{P}$. Then the miss process is a MAP $(\mathbf{D}'_0, \mathbf{D}'_1)$ given by*

$$\mathbf{D}'_0 = (\mathbf{P} \oplus \mathbf{D}_0) + \mathbf{1}' \otimes D_1 \quad \text{and} \quad \mathbf{D}'_1 = \begin{pmatrix} \mathbf{0}_{n\times n} & \pi\mathbf{D}_1 \\ \mathbf{0}_{m\times n} & \mathbf{0}_{n\times m} \end{pmatrix} ,$$

where $\mathbf{1}'$ is a modified $n(m+1) \times n(m+1)$ identity matrix with $\mathbf{1}'_{1,1} = 0$, if M has n states and T has m transient and one absorbing states, and the $\mathbf{0}_{x\times y}$ are $x \times y$ zero matrices.

Together with corresponding theorems for $\mathcal{R}$ and $\min(\Sigma,\mathcal{R})$ caches and the known superposition property of MAPs, this method allows the characterization of miss processes at each node in a feedforward cache network. The key drawback of using MAPs is, however, that the state-spaces of the involved MAPs increase multiplicatively in the number of caches and the number of states of the TTLs' PH distribution. Nevertheless, because the underlying MAPs' matrices are sparse, the numerical complexity can be significantly reduced by using appropriate numerical methods or by formulating lower and upper bound stochastic models.

3. CONCLUSION

Our two methods jointly enable the exact analysis of caching networks and offer an interesting tradeoff: the first method is computationally fast but restricted to line networks, whereas the second has a much wider applicability but suffers from a high computational complexity.

4. REFERENCES

[1] S. Asmussen. *Applied probability and queues*, volume 2. Springer, 2003.

[2] D. S. Berger, P. Gland, S. Singla, and F. Ciucu. Exact analysis of TTL cache networks: The case of caching policies driven by stopping times. *CoRR*, abs/1402.5987, 2014.

[3] H. Che, Y. Tung, and Z. Wang. Hierarchical web caching systems: Modeling, design and experimental results. *IEEE Journal on Selected Areas in Communications*, 20(7):1305–1314, 2002.

[4] C. Fricker, P. Robert, and J. Roberts. A versatile and accurate approximation for LRU cache performance. In *Proceedings of ITC*, pages 1–8, 2012.

[5] A. Gut. *Stopped Random Walks: Limit Theorems and Applications*. Springer, 2009.

[6] V. Martina, M. Garetto, and E. Leonardi. A unified approach to the performance analysis of caching systems. In *Proceedings of IEEE INFOCOM (preprint)*, 2014. http://arxiv.org/abs/1307.6702.

[1] We here consider the filtration generated by $\sigma((X_1, T_1), \ldots, (X_t, T_t))$ for the $\mathcal{R}$ model; results for Σ and $\min(\Sigma,\mathcal{R})$ follow analogously.

Measuring Throughput of Data Center Network Topologies

Sangeetha Abdu Jyothi, Ankit Singla, P. Brighten Godfrey, Alexandra Kolla
University of Illinois at Urbana–Champaign

ABSTRACT

High throughput is a fundamental goal of network design. While myriad network topologies have been proposed to meet this goal, particularly in data center and HPC networking, a consistent and accurate method of evaluating a design's throughput performance and comparing it to past proposals is conspicuously absent. In this work, we develop a framework to benchmark the throughput of network topologies and apply this methodology to reveal insights about network structure. We show that despite being commonly used, cut-based metrics such as bisection bandwidth are the wrong metrics: they yield incorrect conclusions about the throughput performance of networks. We therefore measure flow-based throughput directly and show how to evaluate topologies with nearly-worst-case traffic matrices. We use the flow-based throughput metric to compare the throughput performance of a variety of computer networks. We have made our evaluation framework freely available to facilitate future work on design and evaluation of networks.

Categories and Subject Descriptors

C.2.1 [**Computer-Communication networks**]: Network Architecture and Design—*network topology*

Keywords

throughput; topology comparison; network design

1. INTRODUCTION

A fundamental property of a network is its carrying capacity – how much data can be transported between the desired end-points per unit time? In settings varying from transport networks to communication networks, high capacity has been a core goal of network design. A large number of topologies have been proposed in the past few years in the communication networks domain, particularly in the areas of data centers [1, 2, 7] and high performance computing (HPC), to achieve high capacity at low cost.

SIGMETRICS'14, June 16–20, 2014, Austin, Texas, USA.
ACM 978-1-4503-2789-3/14/06.
http://dx.doi.org/10.1145/2591971.2592040.

However, there exists no framework that allows comparison of throughput performance of networks. Hence, network operators face an increasingly complex problem of choosing their network topology. The absence of a well specified benchmark also complicates research on network design, making it difficult to evaluate a new design against the numerous past proposals.

In fact, not only are we lacking throughput comparisons across a spectrum of topologies, we argue that the situation is worse: the community has been using the wrong metrics for measuring throughput. Cut-based metrics, in particular bisection bandwidth, are commonly used to estimate throughput, because minimum cuts are assumed to measure worst-case throughput [4]. However, while this is true for the case where the network carries only one flow, it does not hold for general traffic matrices. In the latter case, the cut is only an upper bound on throughput. The resulting gap between the cut-metric and the throughput leaves open the possibility that in a comparison of two topologies, the cut-metric could be larger in one topology, while the throughput could be greater in the other. An example scenario with precisely such an anomaly can be found in our technical report [5].

The goals of this work are precisely to overcome the above described problems: (a) allowing a fair, consistent, and accurate evaluation of network throughput to facilitate future network design efforts; (b) benchmarking existing network design proposals to inform the choice of topologies for applications; (c) examining the relationship of throughput with other graph metrics across several natural topologies such as biological networks and social networks to understand what gives a topology high throughput.

2. EVALUATION OF TOPOLOGIES

A **network topology** is a graph $G = (V, E)$ with capacities $c(u, v)$ for every edge $(u, v) \in E_G$. Among the nodes V are **servers**, which send and receive traffic flows, connected through non-terminal nodes called **switches**. Each server is connected to one switch, and each switch is connected to zero or more servers, and other switches. For switch-to-switch edges (u, v), we set $c(u, v) = 1$, while server-to-switch links have infinite capacity. This allows us to stress-test the topology. A **traffic matrix (TM)** T defines the traffic demand: for any two servers v and w, $T(v, w)$ is an amount of requested flow from v to w.

The **throughput** of a network G with TM T is defined as the maximum value t for which $T \cdot t$ is feasible in G. That is, we seek the maximum t for which there exists a feasible multicommodity flow that routes flow $T(v, w) \cdot t$ through the

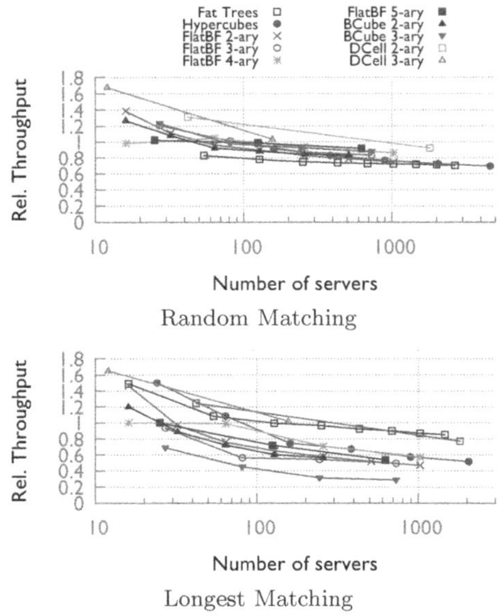

Figure 1: Relative throughput of computer networks under different traffic matrices

network from each v to each w, subject to the link capacity and the usual flow conservation constraints. This can be formulated in a standard way as a linear program (which we omit for brevity) and is thus computable in polynomial time. If the nonzero traffic demands $T(v, w)$ have equal weight, as they will throughout this paper, this is equivalent to maximizing the minimum throughput of any of the requested end-to-end flows. This maximization is a standard problem called *maximum concurrent flow* [6]. Furthermore, this objective function captures the notion of fairness among flows. We use the Gurobi [3] solver to compute throughput by solving this linear program.

We use this framework to evaluate the performance of different classes of computer networks. Our evaluation addresses the following questions: (a) How do we fairly compare networks with different sizes and degree distributions? (b) Which networks achieve highest throughput?

Our high-level approach to evaluating a network is to: (i) compute the network's throughput for a certain TM; (ii) build a random graph with precisely the same degree distribution and compute its throughput under the same traffic model; (iii) normalize the network's throughput with the random graph's throughput to obtain the relative throughput for comparison against other networks. For example, a fat-tree network may have a relative throughput of around 0.75, indicating that it has 25% lower throughput than a random network built with the same equipment.

For ensuring high network performance across different applications (TMs), it is necessary to benchmark networks using worst-case throughput, *i.e.,* to evaluate networks with TMs for which it is hard to achieve high throughput. While finding the worst-case TM is NP-Hard, in our technical report [5], we prove that an all-to-all TM is within a factor of two of the worst-case TM. Further, we experiment with other traffic patterns that are (empirically) even harder than an all-to-all TM. We include here results for two such nearly worst-case traffic matrices – (a) random permutation (each server sends traffic to and receives traffic from exactly one other randomly chosen server in the network) and (b) longest matching (each server sends traffic to and receives traffic from a server located farthest from it). Figure 1 shows that as size increases, relative throughput drops below 1 for all networks we tested, indicating that random graphs achieve higher throughput than the others. Further, the longest matching TM widens the throughput gap between different networks, with some (such as BCube) taking a large performance hit. Among structured networks, DCell and flattened butterflies achieve highest throughput for random matching, but for longest matching, the fat-tree achieves highest throughput at the largest scale. The worst degradation was observed in BCube under longest matching TM.

Our technical report [5] includes additional results addressing the following questions:

- What are the shortcomings of existing cut-based throughput metrics such as bisection bandwidth and sparsest-cut? Why is a flow-based metric more accurate than a cut-based metric?
- What traffic matrices should we use to test the performance of a network?
- What throughput characteristics do naturally occurring networks exhibit?
- How well do other graph metrics such as clustering or path length correlate with throughput? Can we use such correlations (if any) to improve network design?
- Do models of natural networks faithfully reproduce their throughput?

3. CONCLUSION

In this work, we present a framework that allows fair comparison of network topologies by direct, flow-based measurement of throughput. Using this benchmark, we analyzed the throughput performance of a variety of networks and demonstrated that carefully structured computer networks perform poorly compared to random graphs. Our evaluation should be useful to network operators and researchers alike. Our tool is freely available [8]. More comparisons can be found in the technical report [5].

4. REFERENCES

[1] M. Al-Fares, A. Loukissas, and A. Vahdat. A scalable, commodity data center network architecture. In *SIGCOMM*, 2008.

[2] C. Guo, H. Wu, K. Tan, L. Shi, Y. Zhang, and S. Lu. Dcell: A scalable and fault-tolerant network structure for data centers. In *SIGCOMM*, 2008.

[3] Gurobi Optimization Inc. Gurobi optimizer reference manual. `http://www.gurobi.com`, 2013.

[4] D. Padua. *Encyclopedia of Parallel Computing*. Number v. 4 in Springer reference. Springer, 2011.

[5] A. J. Sangeetha, A. Singla, B. Godfrey, and A. Kolla. Measuring and understanding throughput of network topologies. *CoRR*, abs/1402.2531, 2014.

[6] F. Shahrokhi and D. Matula. The maximum concurrent flow problem. *Journal of the ACM*, 37(2):318–334, 1990.

[7] A. Singla, C.-Y. Hong, L. Popa, and P. B. Godfrey. Jellyfish: Network data centers randomly. In *NSDI*, 2012.

[8] A. Singla, C.-Y. Hong, A. J. Sangeetha, B. Godfrey, and L. Popa. Our topology evaluation framework. `https://github.com/ankitsingla/topobench`.

Efficient Task Replication for Fast Response Times in Parallel Computation

Da Wang
EECS Dept., MIT
Cambridge, MA, 02139, USA
dawang@mit.edu

Gauri Joshi
EECS Dept., MIT
Cambridge, MA, 02139, USA
gauri@mit.edu

Gregory Wornell
EECS Dept., MIT
Cambridge, MA 02139, USA
gww@mit.edu

ABSTRACT

Large-scale distributed computing systems divide a job into many independent tasks and run them in parallel on different machines. A challenge in such parallel computing is that the time taken by a machine to execute a task is inherently variable, and thus the slowest machine becomes the bottleneck in the completion of the job. One way to combat the variability in machine response is to replicate tasks on multiple machines and waiting for the machine that finishes first. While task replication reduces response time, it generally increases resource usage. In this work, we propose a theoretical framework to analyze the trade-off between response time and resource usage. Given an execution time distribution for machines, our analysis gives insights on when and how replication helps. We also propose efficient scheduling algorithms for large-scale distributed computing systems.

1. INTRODUCTION

One of the typical scenarios in cloud computing is large scale computation in a data centers with a large number of computers, which is pioneered by companies like Google with the support from distributed computing frameworks such as MapReduce [5]. An important category of large scale computation in data center is called "embarrassingly parallel" computation, where the computation can be easily separated into a number of parallel tasks, that are executed on separate machines.

For an embarrassingly parallel job, the completion time is determined by the slowest computing node, as one needs to wait for all parallel tasks to finish. However, machine response time in data centers are inherently variable due to factors such as co-hosting, virtualization, network congestion, etc. As the computing scale increases, waiting for the slowest machine to finish its assigned task delays the job completion significantly. For example, [4, Table 1] shows that while the 99%-percentile finishing time for each task is 10ms, the 99%-percentile finishing time for the slowest task in a large computation job could take up to 140ms.

SIGMETRICS'14, June 16–20, 2014, Austin, Texas, USA.
ACM 978-1-4503-2789-3/14/06.
http://dx.doi.org/10.1145/2591971.2592042 .

One of the techniques used by system designers to combat variability in machine response time is *task replication*, i.e., sending the same task to multiple machines and taking the result from whichever finishes first. The idea of replicating tasks was recognized by system designers for parallel commutating [3, 6], and first adopted in cloud computing via the "backup tasks" in MapReduce [5]. A line of system work [1, 2, 10, 12] further develop this idea to handle various performance variability issues in data centers.

While this approach of replicating tasks reduces task completion time, it may cause additional resource usage in terms of machine running time. In this paper, we introduce a stylized yet realistic system model to analyze this trade-off between completion time and resource usage. Our analysis reveals when and how task replication works, and provides insights into the design of scheduling algorithms in practical distributed computing systems.

To the best of our knowledge, this is the first theoretical analysis of task replication in distributed computing. A few theoretical works [7–9] have investigated the use of replication or redundancy to reduce latency, but in the context of content download from distributed storage.

2. SYSTEM MODEL

We consider the problem of executing a set of n *embarrassingly parallel tasks* in a data center. Due to randomness in execution time, replicating a task at multiple machines can significantly improve its completion time.

A *scheduling policy* π assigns the starting times of each task at different machines,

$$\pi \triangleq \left[(t_{i,j}), i \in \{1, 2, \ldots, n\}, t_{i,j} \in \mathbb{R}_+, j \in \mathbb{Z}^+ \right],$$

where i is the task of interest, and $t_{i,j}$ is the start time for the j-th replica of task i.

We consider that the scheduler receives an instantaneous notification when any machine finishes its assigned task. When the earliest replica of task i finishes, the scheduler terminates all the replicas of task i. We assume that the scheduler cannot preferentially terminate some replicas while keeping others running. Further, we consider only static policies, where all the starting times $t_{i,j}$ are chosen at time 0 and not changed afterwards. Although there is loss of generality in static launching, it may be of interest in practice because it allows more time for resource provisioning.

Let $X_{i,j}$ be the running time of the j-th replica of task i. We assume $X_{i,j}$ are i.i.d. discrete random variables, with probability mass function (PMF),

$$\text{or, } P_X(\alpha_i) = \Pr(X = \alpha_i) = p_i, \quad 1 \le i \le l, \qquad (1)$$

where $p_i \in [0,1]$ and $\sum_{i=1}^{l} p_i = 1$.

We can use log files or traces to estimate the execution time distribution, for example, by finding a histogram of the execution times with certain bin size (e.g., 10 seconds).

2.1 Performance metrics

We evaluate the performance of a scheduling policy π by the following two performance metrics:

- completion time $T(\pi)$: the time when at least one replica of each of the tasks finishes;

$$T(\pi) \triangleq \max_i \min_j (t_{i,j} + X_{i,j}) \qquad (2)$$

- machine time $C(\pi)$: sum of the running times for all machines, normalized by the number of tasks n;

$$C(\pi) \triangleq \frac{1}{n} \sum_{i=1}^{n} \sum_{j} |T_i(\pi) - t_{i,j}|^+, \qquad (3)$$

where $|x|^+ = \max\{0, x\}$.

The machine time $C(\pi)$ can be viewed as the cost of using a cloud service, such as Amazon Web Service (AWS), which charges user per hour of machine usage. Intuitively, task replication reduces T, but may increase C.

We investigate the trade-off between $T(\pi)$ and $C(\pi)$ using the cost function

$$J_\lambda(\pi) = \lambda \mathbb{E}[T(\pi)] + (1-\lambda)\mathbb{E}[C(\pi)], \qquad (4)$$

where $0 \le \lambda \le 1$ reflects the relative importance of reducing $\mathbb{E}[T(\pi)]$. Given λ, the *optimal* scheduling policy π^* is

$$\pi^* = \arg\min_\pi J_\lambda(\pi).$$

3. OUR CONTRIBUTIONS

Our analysis shows that:

1. While in general there is a trade-off between expected completion time $\mathbb{E}[T(\pi)]$ and expected machine time $\mathbb{E}[C(\pi)]$, there exist scenarios where task replication simultaneously reduces $\mathbb{E}[T(\pi)]$ and $\mathbb{E}[C(\pi)]$.

2. Given the execution time distribution P_X, the optimal scheduling policy that minimizes the cost function J_λ has starting times $t_{i,j}$ that are integer combinations of $\alpha_1, \alpha_2, \dots \alpha_l$, the possible values of the execution time. Thus we reduce the search space for the optimal policy to a discrete and finite set of policies.

3. When the machine execution time follows a bimodal distribution, we find the optimal single-task scheduling policy for the special case of two machines. In the optimal policy we start the task at one machine at time 0. The other machine is started at time α_1, or not started at all, depending on λ in (4), and the system parameters.

4. We propose a heuristic algorithm to choose the scheduling policy for both single-task and multi-task cases. The algorithm adds new machines one-by-one by looking ahead at the next k possible starting times, and chooses from among them the starting time that minimizes the cost function J_λ.

5. When scheduling multiple tasks, it is useful to take the interaction of completion times among different tasks into account, i.e., scheduling each task independently can be strictly suboptimal.

The detailed analysis and results are in [11], the extended version of this paper. A future research direction is to develop a strategy that can learn the execution time distribution while simultaneously scheduling jobs. It would also be useful to consider how queueing of requests impacts system performance.

Acknowledgement

We thank Devavrat Shah for helpful discussions.

4. REFERENCES

[1] Ananthanarayanan, G., Ghodsi, A., Shenker, S., and Stoica, I. Effective straggler mitigation: Attack of the clones. NSDI'13, USENIX, pp. 185–198.

[2] Ananthanarayanan, G., Kandula, S., Greenberg, A., Stoica, I., Lu, Y., Saha, B., and Harris, E. Reining in the outliers in map-reduce clusters using mantri. OSDI'10, USENIX, pp. 1–16.

[3] Cirne, W., Brasileiro, F., Paranhos, D., Luís Fabrício W. Góes, and Voorsluys, W. On the efficacy, efficiency and emergent behavior of task replication in large distributed systems. *Parallel Computing 33*, 3 (2007), 213–234.

[4] Dean, J., and Barroso, L. A. The tail at scale. *Commun. ACM 56*, 2 (2013), 74–80.

[5] Dean, J., and Ghemawat, S. MapReduce: simplified data processing on large clusters. *Commun. ACM 51*, 1 (2008), 107–113.

[6] Ghare, G. D., and Leutenegger, S. T. Improving speedup and response times by replicating parallel programs on a SNOW. In *Job Scheduling Strategies for Parallel Processing*. Springer Berlin Heidelberg, Jan. 2005, pp. 264–287.

[7] Joshi, G., Liu, Y., and Soljanin, E. Coding for fast content download. In *Proc. Annu. Allerton Conf. on Commu. Control. & Comput.* (Oct. 2012), pp. 326–333.

[8] Joshi, G., Liu, Y., and Soljanin, E. On the Delay-Storage trade-off in content download from coded distributed storage systems. *arXiv:1305.3945 [cs, math]* (May 2013).

[9] Shah, N. B., Lee, K., and Ramachandran, K. When do redundant requests reduce latency? *arXiv:1311.2851 [cs]* (Nov. 2013).

[10] Vulimiri, A., Godfrey, P. B., Mittal, R., Sherry, J., Ratnasamy, S., and Shenker, S. Low latency via redundancy. *arXiv:1306.3707 [cs]* (June 2013).

[11] Wang, D., Joshi, G., and Wornell, G. Efficient job replication for fast response times in parallel computation. *arXiv:1404.1328 [cs.DC]* (Apr. 2014).

[12] Zaharia, M., Konwinski, A., Joseph, A. D., Katz, R., and Stoica, I. Improving MapReduce performance in heterogeneous environments. OSDI'08, USENIX, pp. 29–42.

Author Index

www.ingramcontent.com/pod-product-compliance
Ingram Content Group UK Ltd.
Pitfield, Milton Keynes, MK11 3LW, UK
UKHW051417290926
15471UKWH00009B/1651

9 781450 33088